CHASE'S

CALENDAR OF EVENTS

1998

CB
CONTEMPORARY BOOKS

☆ Chase's 1998 Calendar of Events ☆

NTC/CONTEMPORARY PUBLISHING COMPANY
A TRIBUNE EDUCATION COMPANY
4255 WEST TOUHY AVENUE
LINCOLNWOOD, ILLINOIS 60646-1975
FAX: (847) 679-6388
PHONE: (847) 679-5500

Printed in USA

— NOTICE —

Events listed herein are not necessarily endorsed by the editors or publisher. Every effort has been made to assure the correctness of all entries, but neither the authors nor the publisher can warrant their accuracy. IT IS IMPERATIVE, IF FINANCIAL PLANS ARE TO BE MADE IN CONNECTION WITH DATES OR EVENTS LISTED HEREIN, THAT PRINCIPALS BE CONSULTED FOR FINAL INFORMATION.

ILLUSTRATIONS

Woodcuts at the beginning of each month are from *The Shepheards Calendar,* by Edmund Spenser, London, 1579. The woodcuts of people at various types of work are from a collection of drawings by Swiss painter and print maker Jost Amman, that was published in Leipzig in the 16th century. Many are from *The Book of Days*, by R. Chambers, London, 1864. Other engravings used in this book have been selected to represent almanac, advertising and book illustrations of the 15th–19th and early 20th centuries. Some interior art courtesy of Dover Publications Inc.

Chase's 1998 calendar of events,
Chicago, NTC/Contemporary Publishing Company (c. 1997)

736 p., ill.
Includes index and tables.
Published annually since 1958.
Previous title: (1992–1994): Chase's Annual Events: The Day-by-Day Directory
(1984–1991): Chase's Annual Events
(1958–1983): Chases' Calendar of Annual Events
1. Calendars, 2. Almanacs, 3. Holidays, 4. Festivals, 5. Chronology, 6. Anniversaries, 7. Manners and customs, 8. Year-books. I. Title.

D11.5C48 ISBN: 0-8092-3017-8
LC 57-14540 529.3 (calendars)
ISSN: 0740-5286 394.26 (holidays)

☆ Chase's 1998 Calendar of Events ☆

TABLE OF CONTENTS

★ in text indicates Presidential Proclamations

WELCOME TO *CHASE'S 1998*—THE 41st EDITION

What's New at* Chase's *This Year?

We've restored the list of anniversaries and gifts that you told us you missed last year. We've also added a list of the twelve symbols for the Chinese years and a list of the members of the Broadcasting Hall of Fame. This 1998 edition contains a list of the winners of the Peabody Awards and the Daytime Emmys. There is information on the 1998 Winter Olympics, plus hundreds of new historical events, birthdays, fairs and festivals.

This year you'll find a CD-ROM in a pocket at the back of the book. While we have always provided a detailed index in *Chase's*, if we were to index every significant word the index would be as big as the book. Now, using the CD-ROM, you can search on every word in the database. You can search for events in specific cities, historical events that happened in a specific year or entries that contain words such as "Emmy" or "Supreme Court." Advertising agencies and PR firms can use the CD-ROM to generate custom lists of events for clients and librarians can use it to search for that elusive fact they can't find in the index.

We are working on a Web site where we can post events for which 1998 dates were set too late to be included in this book/CD-ROM. After the first of the year, visit our site at http://www.chases.com.

Process for Declaring Special Observances

How do special days, weeks and months get created? The President has the authority to declare any commemorative event by proclamation, but this is done infrequently. In 1996, for example, the President issued about 100 proclamations. For a good number of these, such as Mother's Day and Bill of Rights Week, there was legislation giving continuing authority for a proclamation to be issued each year. The White House Clerk's Office initiates the issuing of these proclamations each year, since they are mandated by authorizing legislation.

Until January 1995, Congress had been active in seeing that special observances were commemorated. Members of the Senate and House could introduce legislation for a special observance to commemorate people, events and other activities they thought worthy of national recognition. Because these bills took up a disproportionate amount of time on the part of senators and representatives and their staffs, when Congress met in January 1995 to review and reform its rules and procedures, it was decided to discontinue this process. Some state legislatures and governors still proclaim special days, as do mayors of cities.

How do organizations promote awareness about a person, group, event or concern that they feel deserves recognition by the public? They can send their information to us for free listing in THE standard reference book for event and observance information—***Chase's Calendar of Events***.

***Types of Events in* Chase's**

PRESIDENTIAL PROCLAMATIONS: In addition to the complete list of proclamations issued Jan 1, 1996–June 15, 1997, we have included in the day-by-day directory proclamations that have continuing authority and a clear formula for calculating dates of observance.

NATIONAL DAYS AND STATE DAYS: Public holidays of other nations are gleaned from United Nations documents and from information we obtain from consulates and tourism agencies. For state days and statutory observances we consult governors' offices or other official state agencies.

SPONSORED EVENTS: Events for which there is individual or organizational sponsorship are listed with the name of the event, inclusive dates and place of observance, brief description, approximate attendance and the sponsor's name, address and phone number. We obtain information for these events directly from the sponsors.

ASTRONOMICAL PHENOMENA: Information about eclipses, equinoxes and solstices, moon phases and other astronomical information is calculated largely from data prepared by the US Naval Observatory's Nautical Almanac Office and Her Majesty's Nautical Almanac Office (Royal Greenwich Observatory).

HISTORIC ANNIVERSARIES, FOLKLORIC EVENTS AND BIRTHDAYS: Compiled from a wide variety of materials covering events in virtually every part of the world, these entries are supported whenever possible by two independent sources. Usually, living persons are listed under "Birthdays Today."

RELIGIOUS OBSERVANCES: Principal observances of the Christian, Jewish, Hindu and Baha'i faiths are presented with background information from their respective calendars. Where known, religious and secular events of China and Japan are also listed. We include anticipated dates for Muslim holidays based on information supplied to us by the American Muslim Council.

Omissions/Errors

The omission of an event usually means that information was not available in time for inclusion. Errors in dates are most often the result of tentative information that was later changed by the sponsoring organization.

We welcome the submission of new entries. Instructions for this are on page 736. Final selection and format of information included in *Chase's* is, of course, the decision of the editors.

Acknowledgments

Thanks to the many people who helped in the process of compiling this 1998 edition: the reference staffs at the Evanston, Lincolnwood and Skokie public libraries and the Northwestern University Library (especially the government documents staff), the White House Clerk's Office, Buck Trawicky, Steve Gietschier of *The Sporting News* and those who provided us with the various awards lists.

Special thanks to my colleagues at NTC/Contemporary Publishing: Richard Spears, Susan Schwartz, Martha Best, John Reyes, Milton Juarez, Gigi Grajdura, Kim Bartko and Terry Stone and his crew. Now *Chase's* Assistant Editor Kim Summers and I invite you to join us in the celebration of the coming year.

July 1997 Sandy Whiteley, Editor

Spotlight *Banner 1998 Events*

The following section focuses on milestone anniversaries in 1998. In Spotlight on the Past we highlight five different years, from 150 years ago to 25 years ago, and provide a sample of what people were reading and singing that year, the events in politics and science that affected them and the sporting contests they enjoyed. In Spotlight on the World and Spotlight on America, we give more detailed information on some landmark events that are being commemorated in 1998. If observances are planned, addresses are provided for further information. In Spotlight on Education, we provide brief histories of some colleges and universities that are celebrating centennials, sesquicentennials, or more in 1998. Spotlight on People concentrates on noted persons from the past with milestone birth or death anniversaries in 1998. Spotlight on 1998 Events contains the schedule for the 1998 Winter Games and information about Expo '98 in Lisbon. And we hope Spotlight on the Calendar clears up the millennium debate—is it 2000 or 2001?

Spotlight *Contents*

Spotlight on the Past *milestone anniversary years*

1848 *150 years ago*

Culture

Publications

- Translations of *Communist Manifesto*, by Karl Marx and Friedrich Engels (published previous year), sold briskly, spreading socialist principles throughout Europe
- *Wage, Labour and Capital*, pamphlet by Karl Marx
- *Principles of Political Economy*, by John Stuart Mill
- *History of England*, by Lord Macaulay
- *The Romance of Yachting*, in which J. C. Hart questions whether Shakespeare or Bacon wrote the works attributed to Shakespeare
- *La Dame aux Camélias*, by Alexandre Dumas (fils)
- *Mary Barton*, by Elizabeth Gaskell
- *The Biglow Papers*, First Series, poetry by James Russell Lowell
- *Pepita Jimenez*, by Juan Valera
- *The Oak Openings*, by James Fenimore Cooper
- *Dealings with the Firm of Dombey and Son, Wholesale, Retail and for Exportation*, by Charles Dickens
- *The Tenant of Wildfell Hall*, by Anne Brontë
- *Alphabetical Index to Subjects Treated in . . . Periodicals*, by librarian William Frederick Poole, which later evolved into *Reader's Guide to Periodical Literature*
- *Vanity Fair*, by William Makepeace Thackeray
- *Eureka: A Prose Poem*, by Edgar Allan Poe

Entertainment

Feb 15 *A Glance at New York*, musical play by Benjamin A. Baker.

Dec 16 New York's historic 50-year-old Park Theater burned down.

Dec 25 *Monte Cristo*, play by Alexandre Dumas (père), American premiere.

- *The Merry Wives of Windsor*, opera by Carl Nicolai.
- "Radetzky March," by Johann Strauss the elder.
- Polka craze in the US as symbol of support for freedom seekers in the revolutions sweeping Europe.

Popular Songs

Feb 25 "Oh! Susanna!" (written the year before by Stephen Foster) performed by G.N. Christy of the Christy Minstrels became a major hit, swept across the country by the developing California gold rush

- "Ben Bolt, or Oh! Don't You Remember," music by Nelson Kneass, lyrics by Thomas Dunn English
- "Old Uncle Ned"
- "Twas Off the Blue Canaries, or, My Last Cigar"

Landmark Events

Jan 3 Girard College for fatherless boys opened at Philadelphia.

April Seville Fair in Spain originated as a cattle market, now a six-day extravaganza considered the greatest fair in Europe.

May 29 Wisconsin became 30th state.

July 4 Cornerstone laid for Washington Monument (completed in 1884).

Sept 20 American Association for the Advancement of Science founded at Philadelphia.

Nov 7 First uniform national election day under the Elections Act of 1845.

- Jacob B. Martin appointed first US representative to the Vatican.
- Pennsylvania passed first state child labor law; minimum age set at 12.
- Free-Soil Party originated at Buffalo, NY.
- University of Mississippi opened its doors.
- University of Wisconsin founded at Madison.
- Astor Library founded at New York with funds left by John Jacob Astor. Later to become part of New York Public Library.
- Oneida Community established by John Humphrey Noyes and followers at Oneida, NY.
- First chewing gum manufactured for commercial sale by John B. Curtis at Bangor, ME.
- New York High Bridge built for aqueduct into Manhattan.
- Waterloo Station opened at London.
- The Associated Press, the oldest press association in the US, was formed by six New York dailies to share the cost of gathering national news. Eventually, it became a worldwide news service.

Spotlight on the Past *milestone anniversary years*

Firsts for Women

April New York State passed Married Women's Property Act, granting New York women limited ownership rights in the event of divorce.

May 1 Queen's College chartered at London, the first English women's college; most of the funding came from The Governesses' Benevolent Institution and from a maid of honour to Queen Victoria.

July 19 First convention on the rights of women held at Seneca Falls, NY.

Nov 1 Boston Female Medical School, first medical school for women, opened to teach midwifery; it later merged with Boston University School of Medicine.

People in the News

Feb 23 Former president John Quincy Adams died at age 80.

Mar 29 Richest man in America, fur trade and real estate mogul John Jacob Astor died at age 84, leaving $20 million.

Dec 19 English novelist Emily Brontë died at age 30.

- Poor 13-year-old Scottish immigrant Andrew Carnegie got a job as a cotton mill "bobbin boy" in Allegheny, PA.

Sports

- New solid rubber "gutta-percha" golf ball introduced; previously balls were made of leather stuffed with feathers.

Modesty Before Malady

US physician Charles Meigs in his 1848 publication *Females and Their Diseases* stated that he is ***proud*** ". . . that there are women who prefer to suffer the extremity of danger and pain rather than waive those scruples of delicacy which prevent their maladies from being fully explored." In other words, he felt women should suffer and die rather than remove their clothes for a careful medical examination. Dr Meigs trained physicians at the Jefferson Medical School at Philadelphia.

- Baseball rules changed so runner was out at first base if the fielder with ball beat him to the bag.

US Events

Jan 24 Gold discovered on California estate of John Sutter, who tried to keep it secret.

Feb 2 Mexican-American War ended with signing of Treaty of Gaudalupe Hidalgo, recognizing US control of Texas and 500,000 square miles of other territory in the southwest that would become California, Nevada, Utah, most of New Mexico and Arizona and parts of Colorado and Wyoming. Mexico got $15 million.

June 3 Right of way across Isthmus of Panama secured by treaty with New Granada (now Colombia), a crucial aid to US businesses.

Aug 19 California gold discovery published in *New York Herald* and word began to spread, some 6,000 men arriving in California by the end of the year.

Oct 25 First steam locomotive, the *Pioneer* of the Galena & Chicago line, departed Chicago.

Nov 7 Whig candidate Zachary Taylor elected US president over Democrat Lewis Cass and Barnburner party candidate Martin Van Buren.

Dec 5 Lame duck president James Polk gave news of California gold discovery to Congress, thereby informing the whole country and igniting the gold rush of 1849.

Science

June 27 Broadway Theatre at New York City announced installation of what was probably the first air conditioning, designed by a Mr. J.E. Coffee.

- First cast-iron building constructed in New York City, designed by architect James Bogardus.
- Power loom for weaving heavy carpets and tapestries invented by Erastus B. Bigelow.
- In Scotland William Thomson Kelvin devised his absolute scale of temperature.
- Operation of a telegraph line strung between New York and Chicago began.

Spotlight on the Past *milestone anniversary years*

1898 *100 years ago*

Culture

Publications

- *Reflections and Memoirs*, by Otto von Bismarck
- *Songs from the Ghetto*, by Morris Rosenfeld, immigrant from Russian Poland
- *Mr. Dooley in Peace and in War* and *Mr. Dooley in the Hearts of His Countrymen*, both by humorist Finley Peter Dunne
- *When Knighthood Was in Flower*, by Charles Major
- "The Turn of the Screw," novella by Henry James
- *The Open Boat and Other Stories*, by Stephen Crane
- *The War of the Worlds*, by H.G. Wells
- *David Harum, A Story of American Life*, by Edward N. Westcott
- "The Ballad of Reading Gaol," poetry by Oscar Wilde
- *New York Times* circulation tripled when price was cut from 3¢ to 1¢.
- *Sunset* magazine, published by Southern Pacific Railroad to attract people to the West.

Operatic Debuts

June 3 Croatian soprano Milka Ternina, Covent Garden debut as Wagner's Isolde

Nov 7 Austrian-American contralto Ernestine Schumann-Heink, American debut in Chicago

- German Fritzi Scheff, Met debut as Beethoven's Marcelline

Stage and Screen

Feb 7 *Way Down East*, a popular play by Lottie Blair Parker premiered.

Sept 26 *The Fortune Teller*, musical by composer Victor Herbert and playwright-lyricist Harry B. Smith, premiered on Broadway.

October *Cyrano de Bergerac*, by Edmond Rostand, premiered in America, an immediate success.

December Chekhov's play *The Seagull* produced by the Moscow Arts Theatre, which was cofounded by Konstantin Stanislavski, who began developing his "psychological realism" technique in directing the production.

The European Revolutions of 1848

Most of the revolutions that swept through Europe in 1848 failed in the short term, but they succeeded in exposing weaknesses inherent in the monarchist structure of Europe. The fact that many of these revolts were initiated by the emerging middle class and declining nobility is significant for it demonstrates the final breakdown of the old order that had dominated Europe for centuries. The rise of the Industrial Revolution combined with Karl Marx's ideas to highlight the great dislocations that the new capitalism was causing for the lower and middle classes alike. There was also a strong nationalist element to many of these revolutions in areas that were to become Germany, Italy, Austria and Hungary.

The first uprising was in Sicily and it sparked rebellions throughout the rest of Europe. The revolution in France was the only one that succeeded in ousting the old order. King Louis Philippe was replaced by the Second Republic, based on universal sufferage and more liberal laws. This new republic was itself beset by revolt in June 1848, and the subsequent brutal repression lead to the presidency of Napoleon I's nephew, Louis Napoleon III.

In the territory that is now Germany, Austria and Hungary there were a series of mostly urban revolts that were nationalist in character, driven by a desire to form a unified German state. These revolutionaries formed the Frankfort Congress to discuss the possibility of unification and even invited Prussia's Frederich Wilhelm IV to be its head of state. His refusal set back the unification of Germany for two decades.

Although most of these rebellions failed, in all these countries the revolutions led to eventual social and political reform and later to nationalist aims. The Revolutions of 1848 were the beginning of the end for the old order, sowing the seeds of modern Europe as we know it today.

- Early French filmmaker Léon Gaumont established an office in London.
- Early English filmmaker Cecil Hepworth built a small studio in his yard.
- Early American filmmaker J. Stuart Blackton filmed a dramatic showstopper depicting a Spanish flag being torn down and replaced by an American flag.

Popular Songs

- "Gypsy Love Song," from *The Fortune Teller*
- "The Rosary," music by Ethelbert Nevin, lyrics by Robert Cameron Rogers
- "When You Were Sweet Sixteen," by English-American songwriter James Thornton
- "I Guess I'll Have to Telegraph My Baby"
- "Gold Will Buy Most Anything but a True Girl's Heart"

Art

- *The Triumph of the Republic,* sculpture by Jules Dalou
- *The Kiss,* sculpture by Auguste Rodin

Landmark Events

Institutions and Organizations

- Biltmore Forest School, first forestry school in the US, opened at Biltmore, NC, by Dr Carl Schenck.
- The Boxers, an antiforeign society, founded in China to fight Westernization and combat the spread of Christianity.
- Central Hindu College founded at Benares, India.
- Cornell University Medical College founded at New York City.
- Gideons International formed at Boscobel, WI, by traveling salesmen John H. Nicholson and Sam Hill as an association of Christian business and professional men to raise money to "put the Word of God into the hands of the unconverted" by placing Bibles in hotel rooms.
- Mackintosh School of Art founded at Glasgow, Scotland.
- American Institute of Arts and Letters founded by the American Social Science Association.
- Northeastern University founded at Boston, MA.
- Canadian-American Daniel David Palmer established the Palmer School of Chiropractic at Davenport, IA, for practice and teaching of his system of manual manipulation of joints and spine.
- Paris Métro System inaugurated.

Products and Businesses

- Joseph Campbell Preserve Co began selling condensed soup in a can with a red and white label.
- Alfred Cartier and his sons opened their jewelry shop at Paris.
- Claridge's Hotel opened at London on site of an earlier hotel of the same name.
- Goodyear Tire and Rubber founded at Akron, OH.
- Kellogg brothers' first cornflakes flopped when introduced by their Sanitas Nut Food Co.
- National Biscuit Co formed by merger. Uneeda Biscuits, named to establish brand identification in cracker sales, introduced by National Biscuit Co.
- Paris Ritz opened.
- Pepsi-Cola introduced by pharmacist Caleb Bradham at New Bren, NC.
- Republic Steel established by merger.
- Union Carbide founded.
- Farbenfabriken vorm. Friedrich Bayer, German chemical company, introduced a new brand of cough medicine named "Heroin" that was derived from opium.
- Indian motorcycle developed by new Hendee Manufacturing Co, Springfield, MO.
- Opel motorcar invented by bicycle maker Adam Opel at Rüsselsheim, Germany.

Female Firsts

- New Zealand granted women equal voting rights, the first country in the world to do so.
- Women in Ireland were given the right to serve on district councils.
- US Army got its first female assistant surgeon, Anita Newcombe McGee.

1898 *continued*

Places

June 13 Canada created the Yukon Territory.

Aug 12 The Hawaiian Islands became a territory of the US per Joint Resolution passed by the US House and Senate, signed by the president on July 7.

- Nome, AK, was founded.

People in the News

Jan 18 Paris newspaper *L'Aurore* headlined the words of novelist Emile Zola, "J'accuse!" over the text of an open letter Zola had written. He was enraged over the false conviction of Alfred Dreyfus; the attention generated by his words forced a new trial and Dreyfus was exonerated.

Sept 6 Wilhelmina Helena Pauline Maria crowned queen of the Netherlands, having reached the age of 18.

Sept 10 Sixty-year-old Austrian empress Elizabeth was attacked by a knife-wielding Italian anarchist and died within a few hours.

Sports Winners

- Stanley Cup: Montreal Victorias
- Kentucky Derby: Plaudit
- Belmont Stakes: Bowling Brook
- Preakness: Sly Fox
- US lawn tennis singles: Malcolm D. Whitman; Juliette P. Atkinson
- USGA Amateur: Findlay S. Douglas; Open: Fred Herd
- National League baseball pennant: Boston
- College football national champion: Harvard

National Events

Domestic

Jan 1 Greater New York officially created, uniting the five boroughs: Kings County (Brooklyn), Richmond County (Staten Island), Bronx County, Queens County and New York County (Manhattan).

Mar 7 Supreme Court established the doctrine of judicial review in deciding a case regarding railroad rates.

June 13 War Revenue Act imposed federal taxes on inheritance, as well as on tea, tobacco, liquor and amusements.

Oct 12 Striking UMW mine workers rioted at Virden, IL, when scabs were brought in; 13 people killed and 25 injured.

Nov 8 Teddy Roosevelt elected governor of New York.

- Louisiana adopted new constitution including "grandfather" clause, a ploy to restrict black voting.

World Events

Apr 25 Russia and Japan signed Nishi-Rosen protocol pledging not to interfere with Korea.

June 11–Sept 21 Hundred Days' Reform: convinced of need to end corruption of Manchu dynasty, enlightened young Chinese emperor Guangxu (Kuang Hsü) initiated reform program to create constitutional monarchy and modernize economy and educational system. After 100 days, his aunt, Dowager Empress Cixi (Tz'u Hsi), who as regent for her son and for him had ruled China for 28 years, sided with the entrenched Manchu officials and with the help of the military imprisoned Guangxu and crushed the reform movement.

Sept 2 Using Maxim machine guns, British army under General Kitchener defeated Sudanese forces in the Battle of Omdurman (killing 11,000, wounding 16,000 and taking 4,000 prisoners, while suffering only 48 casualties). Kitchener went on to take Khartoum and force France out of Fashoda (now Kodok) to solidify a partnership with Egypt in control of northern Africa.

Science

- "Plum-pudding" theory of atomic structure proposed by British physicist Joseph Thomson.
- The radioactive element radium isolated by French physicist Marie Curie and her husband, Pierre Curie.
- The element neon discovered by William Ramsay.

- The Telegraphone, the first magnetic wire recording device, invented by Danish engineer Valdemar Paulsen.
- The Graflex camera, first high-speed, multiple-split focal plane camera patented by US inventor William F. Folmer.

1923 *75 years ago*

Culture

Publications

Fiction

- *The Able McLaughlins*, by Margaret Wilson (Pulitzer)
- *Babbitt*, by Sinclair Lewis
- *Cane*, by Jean Toomer
- *The Dim Lantern*, by Temple Bailey
- *Kangaroo*, by D.H. Lawrence
- *A Lost Lady*, by Willa Cather
- *Flaming Youth*, by Warner Fabian
- *The Hi-Jackers*, by Robert Chambers
- *Streets of Night*, by John Dos Passos
- *Three Stories and Ten Poems*, by Ernest Hemingway
- *The Wanderer of the Wasteland*, by Zane Grey

Nonfiction

- *Absentee Ownership and Business Enterprise in Recent Times*, by Thorstein Veblen
- *The American Revolution*, by Charles H. McIlwain (Pulitzer)
- *The Dance of Life*, by Havelock Ellis
- *The Ego and the Id*, by Sigmund Freud
- *From Immigrant to Inventor*, by Michael Pupin (Pulitzer)
- *I and Thou*, by Martin Buber
- *Indiscretions*, by Ezra Pound
- *The Mind in the Making*, by James Harvey Robinson
- *My Life and Loves*, by Frank Harris
- *The Outline of History*, by H. G. Wells
- *Psychological Types*, by Carl Jung
- *Science and Life*, by Robert Millikan
- *Skepticism and Animal Faith*, by George Santayana
- *The Story of the Bible*, by Hendrik Willem van Loon
- *The Structure of the Atom*, by E. N. da C. Andrade
- *Woman Suffrage and Politics: The Inner Study of the Suffrage Movement*, by Carrie Chapman Catt
- *His Religion and Hers: A Study of the Faith of Our Fathers and the Work of Our Mothers*, by Charlotte Perkins Gilman

Poetry

- *Body of This Death*, by Louise Bogan
- *Collected Poems*, by Vachel Lindsay (included "In Praise of Johnny Appleseed")
- *The Harp-Weaver and Other Poems*, by Edna St. Vincent Millay
- *Harmonium*, by Wallace Stevens
- *Marriage*, by Marianne Moore
- *New Hampshire: A Poem with Notes and Grace Notes*, by Robert Frost (Pulitzer)
- *The Prophet*, by Kahlil Gibran
- *Red Candle*, by Wen I-tuo (Chinese poet)
- *Sonnets to Orpheus*, by Rainer Maria Rilke
- *Spring and All*, by William Carlos Williams
- *Tulips and Chimneys*, by e.e. cummings

Landmark Events

- Dorothy Sayers introduced Lord Peter Wimsey, gentleman detective, in *Whose Body?*.
- "Skippy" comic strip by Percy Crosby.
- "Moon Mullins" comic strip by Frank Willard.
- *Time* magazine founded at New York.
- *The Adelphi* first published.
- Frank Gannett acquired four upstate New York papers and founded the Gannett Co.
- July issue of British medical journal *The Practitioner* carried article about contraception for the first time.

Theater Premieres

Feb 1 *The Young Idea*, by Nöel Coward, at Savoy, London

Feb 10 *Icebound*, by Owen Davis, starring Boots Wooster at Sam Harris Theater, New York (Pulitzer)

Mar 9 *The Adding Machine*, by Elmer Rice, at Garrick, New York

Apr 9 *The Shadow of a Gunman*, by Sean O'Casey, at Abbey, Dublin; about the 1916 Easter Rising

June 18 *George White's Scandals*, musical by George Gershwin, E. Ray Goetz, B.G. DeSylva and Ballard MacDonald at Globe, New York

Aug 20 *Artists and Models*,

1923 *continued*

musical by Jean Schwartz and Harold Atteridge, at Shubert, New York; featured seminude showgirls, creating censorship controversy

Sept 3 *Poppy*, musical by Dorothy Donelly, Stephen Jones and Arthur Samuels, at Apollo, New York, with W.C. Fields

Oct 29 *Runnin' Wild*, black revue at Colonial, New York; included "Charleston" by Cecil Mack (Richard McPherson) and Jimmy Johnson

Nov 5 *White Cargo*, by Leon Gordon, at Greenwich Village, New York

Dec 28 *Saint Joan*, by George Bernard Shaw, at Garrick, New York (Nobel)

Dec 31 *The Song and Dance Man*, by George M. Cohan, at the George M. Cohan, New York

- ***Vaudeville note:*** George Burns teamed up with Gracie Allen

Dance

June 14 *Les Noches (The Wedding)*, ballet with music by Igor Stravinsky, choreography by Bronislava Nijinska, at Gaîté-Lyrique, Paris

- *Greenwich Village Follies*, featuring dance company formed by former ballet dancer Mikhail Mordkin, inspiring Martha Graham to join.
- "Charleston" became *the* hot song and dance (introduced in *Runnin' Wild*).
- Dance marathon craze swept US.

Radio Premieres

- "Eveready Hour" variety show
- "The Happiness Boys," featuring Billy Jones and Ernie Hare in the first comedy series
- "Roxy and His Gang"
- "Dr. Walter Damrosch"
- "Joseph M. White, 'The Silver-Masked Tenor'"
- "A & P Gypsies" with Harry Orlich Orchestra
- "The Laughing Lady," featuring Ethel Barrymore in the first radio drama

Dec 31 Pittsburgh station KDKA transmitted program to England by shortwave

Film

Premieres

- *Anna Christie*, starring Blanche Sweet in Eugene O'Neill story directed by John Griffith Wray
- *The Hunchback of Notre Dame*, starring Lon Chaney and directed by Wallace Worsley
- *Our Hospitality*, starring Buster Keaton
- *The Pilgrim*, starring and directed by Charles Chaplin
- *Rosita*, starring Mary Pickford, directed by Ernst Lubitsch
- *Safety Last*, starring Harold Lloyd and Mildred Davis
- *The Ten Commandments*, starring Richard Dix, Rod La Rocque, Estelle Taylor, Nita Naldi and 1,000 or so others, directed by Cecil B. DeMille
- *White Sister*, starring Lillian Gish and Ronald Colman
- *A Woman of Paris*, directed by Charles Chaplin

Film Notes

- Rin Tin Tin, who was rescued from World War I by an American GI, became hot new star.
- Famous 50′ letters were installed on hill, initially spelling HOLLYWOODLAND.
- Edith Head, only 18, became chief designer at Paramount.

Mar 13 Inventor Lee De Forest stunned the film industry with his Phonofilm process for making movies with sound.

Classical Music

Premieres

Feb 19 *Symphony No. 6*, by Jean Sibelius, Helsinki

May 30 *Nordic Symphony*, by Howard Hanson, Rome

June 23 *The Black Maskers*, by Roger Sessions, Smith College, Northampton, MA

Nov 19 *Dance Suite*, by Béla Bartòk, Budapest

- *Hyperprism*, by Edgard Varèse, New York
- *Scarecrow Sketches*, by Frank S. Converse, Boston

New Compositions

- *As It Fell Upon a Day*, by Aaron Copland
- *A Victory Ball*, by Ernest Schelling

Opera

- *Master Pédros*, by Manuel de Falla
- *The Perfect Fool*, by Gustav Holst
- Richard Strauss's *Salomé* banned in Boston

Spotlight on the Past *milestone anniversary years*

Popular Music

Hit Records

- "Barney Google," Jones and Hare
- "Down-Hearted Blues," Bessie Smith
- "I Won't Say I Will, but I Won't Say I Won't" Irene Bordoni
- "Linger Awhile," Paul Whiteman
- "Somebody Stole My Gal," Ted Williams
- "Three O"Clock in the Morning," Paul Whiteman
- "Twelve O'Clock at Night," Sophie Tucker

Other Popular Songs

- "Charleston," by Cecil Mack and Jimmy Johnson
- "I Cried for You," by Gus Arnheim, Abe Lyman and Arthur Freed
- "It Ain't Gonna Rain No Mo'," by Wendell Woods Hall from the old folk song
- "Mexicali Rose," by Jack B. Tenny and Helen Stone
- "Nobody Knows You When You're Down and Out," by Jimmy Cox
- "Who's Sorry Now?" by Ted Snyder and Bert Kalmar
- "Yes, We Have No Bananas," by Frank Silver and Irving Cohn
- "You Were Meant for Me," by Eubie Blake and Noble Sissle
- "You Gotta See Mamma Ev'ry Night, or You Can't See Mamma at All," by Con Conran and Billy Rose

New Jazz Bands

- Leon Bismarck "Bix" Beiderbecke's Wolverine Orchestra
- Jelly Roll Morton's Red Hot Peppers
- Jabbo Smith's Rhythm Aces
- Reuben Reeves River Boys

Art

- *Circles in the Circle*, painting by Vassily Kandinsky
- *Emma and Her Children*, painting by George Bellows
- *Entering the Mine, Freeing of the Peon, The First of May* and other murals by Diego Rivera
- *Ivry Town Hall*, painting by Maurice Utrillo
- *Love Idyll*, painting by Marc Chagall
- *Mask from the Fountain of Time*, sculpture by Lorado Taft
- *The Pipes of Pan, The Lovers, Seated Woman* and *Melancholy*, paintings by Pablo Picasso
- *Revolutionary Trinity*, mural by José Orozco
- *Ship, Sea and Sky Forms* and *Impression*, watercolors by John Marin
- *Still Life with Violin*, painting by Suzanne Valadon
- *The Trapeze*, painting by Max Beckman
- *The Workman Sacrificed*, mural by David Siqueiros

ASCAP Wins Pay to Play

In 1923 a court decision in favor of the American Society of Composers, Authors, and Publishers (ASCAP) required broadcasters to pay royalties whenever copyrighted music is played on the air. ASCAP is a membership association of more than 68,000 composers, songwriters, lyricists and music publishers. ASCAP's function is to protect the rights of its members by licensing for royalties the public performances of their copyrighted works.

For information:
ASCAP–Los Angeles
7920 Sunset Blvd
Ste 300
Los Angeles, CA 90046
Phone: (213) 883-1000
Fax: (213) 883-1049
Web: http://www.ascap.com

1923 *continued*

Landmark Events

Institutions and Organizations

Jan 1 Angelus Temple opened in Los Angeles by evangelist Aimee Semple McPherson.

Dec 6 Calvin Coolidge's message to Congress became the first presidential radio broadcast.

- Canadian National Railway created by mergers and takeovers to preserve an effective rail system across Canada.
- Bethune-Cookman College founded at Daytona, FL, by merger of Mary McLeod Bethune's Daytona Normal and Industrial Institute for Negro Girls with the Cookman Institute for Men.
- League of Composers founded at New York to promote performance of contemporary music.
- President Calvin Coolidge held the first White House Christmas tree lighting ceremony.
- Sanger Research Clinic opened at New York by American Birth Control League.
- Chicago Tribune building completed.

New Products and Businesses

- Birdseye Seafoods
- Maiden Form Brassiere Co, founded by Ida and William Rosenthal
- Butterfinger candy bar, introduced by Curtiss Candy Co of Chicago and promoted by dropping bars from airplanes over major US cities
- US Chinchilla fur industry begun with 11 imported chinchillas
- Libby's tomato soup
- Milky Way candy bar, created by Frank C. Mars
- Neon advertising sign
- Pet Milk Company
- Sanka
- Welch's grape jelly
- Aeroflot, Russian airline
- Pan American World Airways, founded at New York City by Juan Trippe and John Hambleton
- Messerschmitt aircraft manufacturing company
- Sabena, Belgian airline
- Hertz Drive-Ur-Self System, founded at Chicago by John D. Hertz, head of Yellow Cab Co
- Zenith Radio, founded by Eugene F. McDonald, Jr
- Planned obsolescence began in auto manufacturing when major US automakers began to change car styles every year
- A.C. Nielsen Co, market research

People in the News

Apr 23 England's Duke of York, Prince Albert, married Elizabeth Bowes-Lyon, becoming first prince to marry a commoner since 1660 and first king's son to wed in Westminster Abbey since 1382.

Aug 2 President Warren G. Harding died at San Francisco after trip to Alaska; VP Calvin Coolidge sworn in the following day.

- Robert Millikan became first American physicist to receive Nobel Prize, awarded for his work in isolating the electron at the University of Chicago.
- *Chicago Tribune* featured exchange of views on evolution and fundamentalist religion by Clarence Darrow and William Jennings Bryan.
- Homer Morehouse, 27, danced to death competing in record-setting marathon.

Obits

Jan 9 New Zealand–born British short-story writer, Katherine Mansfield, died of tuberculosis, near Fontainebleau, France, age 34.

Feb 10 German physicist who discovered x-rays and was awarded first Nobel Prize in physics, Wilhelm von Roentgen, died at Munich.

Mar 26 "The divine Sarah," widely acclaimed and beloved French actress Sarah Bernhardt, died at Paris, aged 78.

June 10 French naval officer and novelist, Pierre Loti (pen name of Louis Marie Julien Viaud), died at Hendaye, Basses-Pyrénées, France.

June 20 Mexican revolutionary Francisco "Pancho" Villa assassinated at his ranch at Parral, Chihuahua.

Aug 24 American writer of children's books (including *Rebecca of Sunnybrook Farm*) and leader of the movement for kindergarten education in the US, Kate Douglas Wiggin, died at Harrow, England.

Dec 27 Alexandre Gustave Eiffel, French structural engineer who built the Eiffel Tower, died at Paris.

Sports Winners

- Rose Bowl: Southern California
- Wimbledon Singles: William Johnston, Suzanne Lenglen
- US Tennis Open singles: Bill Tilden, Helen N. Wills
- Davis Cup: US
- USGA Amateur: Max R. Marston
- USGA Open: Bobby Jones
- PGA: Gene Sarazen
- Kentucky Derby: Zev
- Preakness: Vigil
- Belmont Stakes: Zev
- World Series: New York Yankees over Giants, 4–2
- College football: Illinois
- College basketball: Kansas
- NFL: Canton Bulldogs
- Stanley Cup: Ottawa Senators
- Indy 500: Tommy Milton
- Boxing: Jack Dempsey over Luis Firpo

Sports Notes

Apr 19 Yankee Stadium, "the house that Ruth built," opened at New York City.

Oct 6 Lt Al Williams won the Pulitzer Trophy air race at St. Louis, MO, averaging 243.76 mph, a new air speed record.

- Football legend Red Grange, the Galloping Ghost, began his college football career at the University of Illinois.
- Red Grange of Illinois and Cal Hubbard of Harvard named College All-Americans.
- Johnny Weismuller set new record of 1:59.2 in 200-yard free-style swimming.

National Events

Jan 10 President Harding ordered return of US troops still occupying Germany.

Mar 3 Proposal to join International Court of Justice voted down in Senate.

Mar 5 First old-age pension grants passed by Montana and Nevada.

Apr 9 Supreme Court struck down 1918 Washington, DC women's minimum wage law.

May 4 Perhaps turning the tide on prohibition, New York State Assembly voted to repeal the NY State Prohibition Enforcement Act.

May 9 US District Court ruled prohibition did not limit doctors' prescriptions for whiskey.

Aug 3 Calvin Coolidge sworn in as president the day after death of President Warren G. Harding.

Sept 1 US Post Office issued commemorative 2¢ black stamp in honor of President Harding.

Sept 3 US gave recognition to new Mexican government.

Sept 15 Oklahoma governor John C. Walton declared martial law to combat Ku Klux Klan terrorism.

Oct 25 Senate began investigation of Teapot Dome scandal.

Dec 8 US and Germany signed treaty of friendship and commerce.

- National Woman's Party endorsed "Lucretia Mott" Equal Rights Amendment drafted by Alice Paul.
- Montana devastated by swarm of locusts 300 miles × 100 miles × 1/2 mile high.

World Events

Jan 11 Ruhr occupied by French and Belgian forces due to Germany's failure to pay war reparations.

Apr 20 New constitution adopted by Egypt, which was granted independence with strings by the British in 1922.

May 26 British protectorate Transjordania became autonomous.

July 10 All Italian nonfascist

Hitler's Beer Hall Putsch • Nov 8

Adolf Hitler and 600 of his National Socialist storm troopers marched on a Munich beer hall and captured Bavarian chief official Gustav von Kahr, who was making a public address there, and his associates. Supported by General Erich Ludendorff, Hitler declared a new national government in von Kahr's name and the captives were released. The next day von Kahr sent the police after the rebels, who put up a brief fight and then fled. Hitler was later arrested and wound up with a five-year prison term, during which he dictated his master plan, *Mein Kampf*, to Rudolf Hess.

(opposition) political parties abolished by Mussolini.

July 18 British women granted equal rights in divorce suits with Parliament's passage of Matrimonial Causes Act.

July 24 Treaty of Lausanne signed, setting out distribution of territory of eastern Mediterranean area after World War I.

Sept 1 Tokyo and Yokahama destroyed by earthquake and fire; 100,000 killed, 752,000 injured, 83,000 homes destroyed, 380,000 damaged.

Sept 10 Irish Free State admitted to League of Nations.

Oct 13 Ankara (Angora) became the new Turkish capital in place of the ancient Ottoman and Byzantine capital city, Istanbul (Constantinople).

Oct 29 Turkish Republic proclaimed.

Nov 14 Mussolini rammed election law through Italian parliament that was de facto guarantee of Fascist party's election victory, cementing his hold on power.

Nov 29 Committees appointed by War Reparations Commission to investigate economic upheaval in Germany.

Dec 17 Military coup in Greece

- First Soviet forced-labor camp established by Lenin.
- In the course of the year German mark fell from 7,260 marks to the US dollar on Jan 2 to 4.2 trillion marks to the dollar by end of November, accompanied by escalating economic chaos.

Science

Nov 6 Colonel Jacob Schick issued a patent for Schick dry shaver, world's first practical electric shaver.

- Mathematical explanation for ionization of electrolytes developed by Dutch-American physicist Peter Debye.
- Tetanus toxoid developed by French bacteriologist Gaston Ramon.
- In a step toward the helicopter, Spanish aeronaut Juan de la Cierva invented autogyro powered by large horizontal rotor.
- Chemical element hafnium isolated by Dutch physicists Georg von Hevesy and Dirk Coster.
- The iconoscope television camera tube invented by Vladimir Zworykin.
- US Navy commissioned the *Shenandoah*, originally known as the ZR1, the first zeppelin-type airship of entirely American construction and the first filled with helium gas.

1948 *50 years ago*

Culture

Publications

Fiction

- *The Big Fisherman*, by Lloyd C. Douglas
- *The City and the Pillar*, by Gore Vidal
- *City of Corpses*, by Yoko Ota, Hiroshima survivor
- *Cry, the Beloved Country*, by Alan Paton
- *Guard of Honor*, by James Gould Cozzens (Pulitzer)
- *The Ides of March*, by Thornton Wilder
- *Intruder in the Dust*, by William Faulkner
- *The Naked and the Dead*, by Norman Mailer
- *Other Voices, Other Rooms*, by Truman Capote
- *Pilgrim's Inn*, by Elizabeth Goudge
- *Raintree County*, by Ross Lockridge, Jr
- *Tomorrow Will Be Better*, by Betty Smith
- *The Young Lions*, by Irwin Shaw

Nonfiction

- *Crusade in Europe*, by Dwight D. Eisenhower
- *The Disruption of American Democracy*, by Roy F. Nichols (Pulitzer, US History)
- *The Early Tales of the Atomic Age*, by Daniel Lang
- *The Gathering Storm*, by Winston Churchill
- *A Guide to Confident Living*, by Norman Vincent Peale

- *How to Stop Worrying and Start Living*, by Dale Carnegie
- *The Life and Times of the Shmoo*, by Al Capp
- *Our Plundered Planet*, by Fairfield Osborn, on dangers of DDT
- *The Plague and I*, by Betty MacDonald
- *The Protestant Era*, by Paul Tillich
- *Roosevelt and Hopkins*, by Robert E. Sherwood (Pulitzer)
- *The Seven Storey Mountain*, by Thomas Merton
- *Sexual Behavior in the Human Male*, by A. C. Kinsey

Poetry

- *The Double Axe*, by Robinson Jeffers
- *Losses*, by Randall Jarrell
- *The Lost Sun*, by Theodore Roethke
- *Paterson*, Book Two, by William Carlos Williams
- *The Pisan Cantos* (72–84), by Ezra Pound
- *Terror and Decorum*, by Peter Viereck (Pulitzer)

Notes

- T.S. Eliot awarded Nobel Prize.
- Comic books containing violence or sex banned by 50 cities.
- Edmund Wilson lost appeal to Supreme Court over banning of his book, *Memoirs of Hecate County*, for obscenity.
- *US News and World Report* formed by merger.
- Comic book/strip debuts: *Little Audrey*, *Pogo* and in Canada *Jasper the Bear*.

Theater Premieres

Jan 19 *Look, Ma, I'm Dancin'*, Hugh Martin musical starring Nancy Walker and Harold Lang

Feb 18 *Mister Roberts*, by Thomas Heggen and Joshua Logan, starring Henry Fonda; Tony for best play

Mar 11 *The Lady's Not for Burning*, Christopher Fry play at London

Oct 6 *Summer and Smoke*, Tennessee Williams steamer with Anne Jackson

Oct 11 *Where's Charley?* musical by Frank Loesser, starring Ray Bolger

Oct 27 *State of Siege*, by Albert Camus, Paris

Dec 8 *Anne of the Thousand Days*, Rex Harrison and Joyce Redman in Maxwell Anderson play

Dec 16 *Lend an Ear*, Carol Channing and William Eythe in Charles Gaynor musical

Dec 30 *Kiss Me, Kate*, Cole Porter musical based on Shakespeare's *Taming of the Shrew*

- Margaret Webster Shakespeare Company founded; it toured the US for years, getting the bard's works out into the communities.

Radio Premieres

- "Life with Luigi," J. Carrol Naish
- "My Favorite Husband," Lucille Ball, Gale Gordon
- "Our Miss Brooks," Eve Arden
- "Stop the Music," Bert Parks
- "This Is Your Life," Ralph Edwards

Film Premieres

- *Abbott and Costello Meet Frankenstein*, with Lon Chaney and Bela Lugosi
- *Easter Parade*, starring Fred Astaire, Ann Miller, Judy Garland
- *Hamlet*, starring and directed by Laurence Olivier; Oscars for best picture and best actor
- *Johnny Belinda*, with Jane Wyman (best actress Oscar) and Lew Ayres, directed by Jean Negulesco
- *Key Largo*, John Huston directed Bogart, Bacall and Edward G. Robinson
- *The Paleface*, with Bob Hope and Jane Russell
- *The Pirate*, with Judy Garland and Gene Kelly
- *Red River*, with John Wayne, Montgomery Clift, Joanne Dru
- *The Red Shoes*, starring Moira Shearer
- *The Snake Pit*, with Olivia de Havilland
- *Sorry, Wrong Number*, with Barbara Stanwyck and Burt Lancaster
- *State of the Union*, starring Tracy and Hepburn, Frank Capra directing
- *The Treasure of Sierra Madre*, John Huston (best director Oscar); with Humphrey Bogart and Walter Huston

May 11 Howard Hughes bought RKO

- Lee "Method Acting" Strasberg became director of the Actor's Studio

1948 *continued*

TV Premieres

Jan 18 "The Original Amateur Hour," Ted Mack
Mar 20 First live TV broadcasts of orchestra concerts: Philadelphia Symphony under Ormandy and the NBC Symphony under Toscanini
June 8 "Texaco Star Theater," starring "Mr. Television," Milton Berle
June 20 "The Toast of the Town," Ed Sullivan's variety show
June 24 Republican convention, first convention televised
July 26 15-minute show featured first black TV host, pianist Bob Howard
Aug 10 "Candid Camera," Allen Funt
Oct 3 "The NFL"
Oct 22 "Break the Bank," Bert Parks
Nov 7 "Studio One"
Nov 29 "Kukla, Fran & Ollie," Fran Allison
Nov 29 New York Met's *Othello*, first live opera televised
Dec 6 "Arthur Godfrey's Talent Scouts"
Dec 24 "The Chesterfield Supper Club," Perry Como in sweaters

Notes

- Channel 1 reserved for military.

Classical Music

Premieres

Jan 9 *Symphony No. 4*, by Piston, Boston
Jan 23 *Mandu-Carara*, by Villa-Lobos, New York
Feb 12 *Fantasy for Trombone and Orchestra*, by Creston, Los Angeles
Feb 24 *The Seine at Night*, by Thomson, Kansas City
Apr 19 *Knoxville: Summer of 1915*, by Samuel Barber, James Agee
May 24 *The Beggar's Opera*, opera by Britten, London
July 28 *Magdalena*, opera by Villa-Lobos, Los Angeles
Oct 27 *Mass*, by Stravinsky, Milan
Nov 4 *Suvivor from Warsaw*, by Schoenberg, Albuquerque
Dec 31 *Piano Concerto No. 1*, by Hanson, Boston

- *Symphony in D Minor*, by Rachmaninoff, Philadelphia
- *The Old Maid and the Thief*, opera by Menotti, New York

Music Notes

Feb 11 In the USSR the music of Aram Kachaturian, Sergei Prokofiev and Dimitri Shostakovich was criticized by the Central Committee: ". . . strongly smells of the spirit of current modernistic bourgeois music of Europe and America."

- First season of Benjamin Britten's Aldeburgh Festival in England

Ballet Premieres

Apr 22 *Fall River Legend*, Agnes de Mille, choreographer, and Martin Gould, composer
Apr 28 *Orpheus*, New York City Ballet, music by Igor Stravinsky
Dec 27 *Cinderella*, choreographer Frederick Ashton, composer Serge Prokofiev, at London

- New York City Ballet formed when two-year-old Ballet Society moved to New York City Center; company included ballerina Maria Tallchief and choreographer George Balanchine

Popular Music

Hit Songs

- "All I Want for Christmas Is My Two Front Teeth," Spike Jones & His City Slickers
- "Because," Perry Como
- "Buttons and Bows," Doris Day
- "Confess," Patti Page
- "Early Autumn," Stan Getz
- "Enjoy Yourself–It's Later Than You Think"
- "The Fat Man," Fats Domino
- "If I Had a Hammer"
- "I'll Be Home for Christmas"
- "I'm Looking Over a Four-Leaf Clover," Art Mooney & His Orchestra
- "It's a Most Unusual Day," Jane Powell
- "It's Magic," Doris Day
- "It's Too Soon to Know," Dinah Washington
- "Lazy River," Mills Brothers
- "Mañana," Peggy Lee
- "My Happiness," Ella Fitzgerald
- "Nature Boy," Nat "King" Cole
- "Now Is the Hour," Bing Crosby
- "Sleigh Ride"
- "Smoke, Smoke, Smoke That Cigarette," Tex Williams
- "A Tree in a Meadow," Margaret Whiting

Spotlight on the Past *milestone anniversary years*

Notes

June 21 The 12-inch, 33⅓-rpm LP record invented by Peter Goldmark of CBS.

December RCA Victor brought out the seven-inch, 45-rpm record.

Dec 14 Year-long musicians' strike against recording ended with the American Federation of Musicians getting an agreement for royalties on each record sold to finance a union welfare fund.

- Californian Clarence Leo Fender created the first electric guitar.

Art

- *Aspen, Snow Flurry*, sculpture, Alexander Calder
- *Christina's World*, painting by Andrew Wyeth
- *Composition No. 1*, painting by Jackson Pollock
- *Family Group*, sculpture, Henry Moore
- *Miners' Wives*, Ben Shahn
- *Seven* A.M., painting by Edward Hopper
- *Teilhard de Chardin*, bust, Melvina Hoffman
- *Woman*, painting by Willem de Kooning

Notes

- Des Moines Art Center built, designed by Eero Saarinen.
- Eero Saarinen and his team awarded $40,000 first prize for Gateway Arch design for Jefferson National Expansion Memorial at St. Louis, which wasn't built until 1967.

Landmark Events

Jan 12 American Red Cross, which had collected blood for soldiers during WWII, began a civilian blood program.

Mar 15 Overseas air parcel service begun by US Post Office.

Apr 28 First nonstop Paris–New York commercial flight by Air France.

Apr 30 Liberty Walking replaced by Franklin on half-dollar.

June 16 At Hong Kong 26 died in first airplane hijacking attempt.

July 1 New York's Idlewild International Airport dedicated, later to be renamed after John F. Kennedy.

Aug 22 World Council of Churches, an organization of more than 320 Protestant, Anglican, and Orthodox churches, inaugurated at Amsterdam.

Sept 13 Margaret Chase Smith (Maryland) elected US Senator, first female to win regular full term.

- Missionaries of Charity founded by Mother Teresa.
- Brandeis University founded, Waltham, MA.
- Congress of Democrats, white wing of African National Congress, founded in South Africa by socialite Helen Joseph and others.
- Indian Cooperative Union founded by Kamaldevi Chattopadhyay to aid people displaced by the partitioning of India and Pakistan.
- International Planned Parenthood Federation founded by Margaret Sanger.

Products and Businesses

- Auto air conditioner
- Baskin-Robbins formed by merger
- Bikini bathing suit
- Dial, first deodorant soap, by Armour
- Garbage disposal
- Honda Motor Co founded, began making Honda motorcycles
- Land Rover
- McDonald brothers' fast-food business, starting out as a California hamburger stand and later bought by Ray Kroc, who would build the McDonald's empire
- Michelin unveiled first radial tires
- Nestlé's Quik
- Nikon 35mm camera
- Polaroid Land camera
- Porsche sports car
- Scandinavian Airlines formed by merger of Danish, Norwegian and Swedish aviation companies
- Scrabble copyrighted
- Textron, first business conglomerate, formed when textile business Royal Little acquired Cleveland Pneumatic Tool
- V-8 juice from Campbell

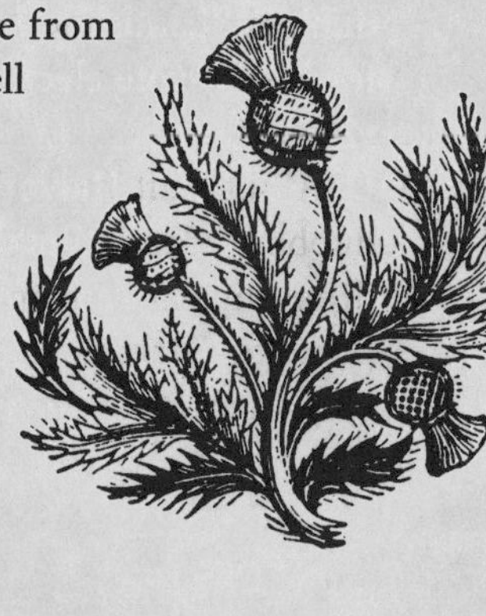

1948 *continued*

People in the News

Apr 20 UAW president Walter Reuther shot through his kitchen window, seriously wounded.

Apr 21 Canada's William L. Mackenzie King became longest-serving prime minister of British Commonwealth.

July 26 Babe Ruth made last public appearance at New York premiere of *The Babe Ruth Story*.

Sept 4 The Netherlands' Queen Wilhelmina, age 68, abdicated in favor of daughter Juliana.

Nov 14 At Buckingham Palace, Princess Elizabeth gave birth to Charles Philip Arthur George, heir to the British throne.

Dec 27 Cardinal Jozsef Mindszenty arrested over refusal of Hungarian Catholics to meet government demands

- Jack Benny nicked by the IRS at 75% personal income tax rate rather than 25% capital gains rate when he sold his radio show to NBC for about $2.5 million.
- New senator Lyndon Johnson dubbed "Landslide Johnson" for his 87-vote election victory.
- USAF Lt Gail Halvorson dubbed "Candy Bomber" for dropping candy from his plane to German children to help them overcome fear of planes.

Obits

Jan 30 Orville Wright, hero of Kitty Hawk, first man of flight

Feb 11 Sergey Eisenstein, Soviet film innovator and director, *Potemkin*

Mar 6 Ross Lockridge, author of *Raintree County*, suicide, age 33

June 6 Louis Lumière, developed first camera-projector with his brother Auguste

June 6 Charles W. Nash, founder of Nash Motors

July 14 Harry Brearley, Englishman who brought stainless steel to cutlery

July 23 D.W. Griffith, film pioneer, developed full-length silent film, *The Birth of a Nation*

Aug 16 George Herman "Babe" Ruth, baseball legend, "Sultan of Swat," age 53

Aug 27 Charles Evans Hughes, associate justice of the Supreme Court 1910–16, chief justice 1930–41

Sept 3 Edward Benes, Czechoslovakian nationalist and ally.

Sept 13 John Pershing, American general, led the American Expeditionary Force in Europe during World War I

Sept 17 Ruth Benedict, anthropologist, author of *Patterns of Culture*

Sept 30 Edith Roosevelt, widow of Teddy Roosevelt, first lady 1901–09

Nov 24 Anna Jarvis, founder of Mother's Day

Dec 5 Frederick Mills, composer of "Meet Me in St. Louis, Louis"

Gandhi Assassinated Jan 30, 1948 50 Years

Mohandas Karamchand Gandhi led the Indian people in an independence movement of nonviolent resistance that generated a moral force the British finally could not deny. India was divided, however, by longstanding conflict between its Hindu, Sikh and Muslim populations and unable to unite all factions into one government. Thus, under the Indian Independence Act, the country was partitioned into majority-Hindu India and majority-Muslim Pakistan. The 78-year-old Gandhi fasted in sorrow over the religious division and in hopes of subduing the ensuing violence among militants of the various factions. After five days the violence subsided, the fast successful. But 12 days later, as Gandhi walked to his daily prayer meeting, he was assassinated by Nathuram Godse, a Hindu fanatic. Both new nations mourned as millions crammed the streets of Delhi for the funeral procession and cremation.

Dec 28 Nokrashy Pasha, premier of Egypt, assassinated
- Susan Glaspell, playwright, winner of Pulitzer Prize for *Alison's House*
- Manuel Ponce, Mexican composer, *Estrellita*

Satchel Paige Plays in the Majors

Pitching for the Cleveland Indians in his major-league debut on Aug 13, 1948, Negro Leagues legend Satchel Paige shut out the White Sox 5–0, then hurled another shutout in his second start. Paige's arm was a major factor in the Indians' taking the American League pennant and going on to defeat Boston 4–2 in the World Series.

When reporters suggested Paige might be named Rookie of the Year, Satchel answered, "Twenty-two years is a long time to be a rookie."

Born Leroy Robert Paige at Mobile, AL, he acquired his nickname working as a baggage handler as a boy. He pitched in the Negro Leagues for 20 years, played in Canada and many other countries and barnstormed throughout the US. Well known for his amusing words of wisdom, Paige often quipped, "Don't look back. Something might be gaining on you." He was elected to the Baseball Hall of Fame in 1971; died 1982.

Sports Winners

- Rose Bowl: Michigan
- NCAA basketball: Kentucky
- Wimbledon: Robert Faulkenburg, Louise Brough
- US Lawn Tennis Open singles: Pancho Gonzalez, Margaret du Pont
- Davis Cup: US
- USGA Amateur: Willie Turnesa
- USGA Open: Ben Hogan
- PGA: Ben Hogan
- Eddie Arcaro rode Citation to Triple Crown
- World Series: Cleveland over Boston
- NFL: Philadelphia Eagles
- Boxing: Joe Louis over "Jersey Joe" Walcott
- Chess: Soviet Mikhail Botvinnik

Sports Notes

Feb 20 Boxer Sam Baroudi's death 10 hours after being knocked down by heavyweight contender Ezzard Charles prompted National Boxing Association to add rule that a boxer must take an eight-second count after a knockdown.

Mar 11 Reginald Weir became first black to play in a US national tennis tournament.

Sept 21 French challenger Marcel Cerdan beat Tony Zale, becoming first non-American middleweight champ.

Oct 4 Cleveland beat Boston in first American League playoff.

Nov 30 Negro National League dissolved as top black players hired by the majors.
- Winter Olympics held at St. Moritz, Switzerland.
- Summer Olympics held at London.
- NBA formed from BAA and four teams from NBL.

National Events

Jan 27 Voice of America made permanent agency.

Mar 8 Voting 8–1 in the case of *McCollum v. Board of Education*, the Supreme Court ruled teaching religion in public schools unconstitutional.

Mar 30 Established during the war, rent control extended another year.

Apr 3 Congress passed Foreign Assistance Act (the "Marshall Plan") to provide aid in rebuilding Europe.

Apr 30 Organization of American States created, but US Congress took three years to ratify it.

May 3 Landmark Supreme Court decision rules restrictive racial covenants unconstitutional.

June 24 President Truman signed Selective Service Act, instituting peacetime draft.

June 25 Passage of the Displaced Persons Act permitted immigration of 205,000 European refugees (labeled "DPs").

July 26 Truman issued two executive orders calling for the gradual desegregation of US military and proposing institution of a fair employment policy.

Sept 10 American-born Mildred Gillars indicted for treason for her role as "Axis Sally," broad-

1948 *continued*

casting Nazi propaganda to US troops.

Nov 2 *Chicago Tribune* headline gave Dewey the win, but final tallies proved Harry S. Truman the presidential victor.

Dec 15 Alger Hiss indicted for perjury.

- US conducted three atomic tests at Eniwetok in the Marshall Islands.
- Prostitution legalized in Nevada.
- GM instituted an automatic cost-of-living increase for a quarter million hourly employees.
- NAACP decided to focus on integration instead of on equalizing the so-called separate-but-equal black facilities.
- Toxic smog from US Steel mill at Donora, PA, killed 22.

World Events

Jan 1 Original GATT, General Agreement on Tariffs and Trade, signed by 23 nations to reduce artificial trade barriers.

Feb 21 Communists took control of Czechoslovakia.

Mar 17 Brussels Pact for mutual military and economic aid signed by Britain, France, Belgium, Netherlands and Luxembourg to deter Soviet aggression.

Apr 7 World Health Organization (WHO) established by UN.

Apr 30 Organization of American States, a regional alliance of the nations of the Americas, founded. The Pan American Union is its General Secretariat.

May 14 Israel declared its independence, and Arab neighbors attacked.

May 26 National Party with apartheid platform won control in South African election.

July 5 National Health Insurance Program, providing free medical treatment, went into effect in Britain.

July 30 All Commonwealth citizens became British citizens under British Citizenship Act.

Aug 15 Republic of Korea proclaimed by President Syngman Rhee.

Sept 9 In North Korea Soviets declared Korean People's Democratic Republic under Kim Il-Sung.

November Republic of Ireland Bill passed by Dáil of Eire.

Nov 29 Custom of "untouchability" abolished in India.

Nov 30: Arab-Israeli cease-fire signed at Jerusalem, Arabs having failed to destroy the new Israeli state.

Dec 10 UN adopted the Universal Declaration of Human Rights.

Dec 23 Hedeki Tojo and six other convicted Japanese war criminals hanged.

Dec 31 Almost 700,000 POWs released since Jan 1.

- Bering Strait border closed by Soviets.

Berlin Airlift

June 18 Britain, France and US declared plan to unify their occupation zones into a single federal state; USSR barred surface traffic in response.

June 23 Soviets stopped rail service and cut off electrial power.

June 28 US and Britain began Berlin Airlift, landing a plane with supplies every three minutes, delivering 4,000 tons of supplies per day by September and continuing for another year.

Science

February Fifth moon of Uranus discovered by astronomer Gerald Kuiper.

June 3 The 200-inch Hale telescope dedicated at Mount Palomar Observatory, San Diego. Twice as large as any existing telescope and 20 years in the making at a cost of $6.55 million, it was named for astronomer George Hale, who convinced the Rockefellers to finance the construction.

June 30 Bell Telephone hosted demonstration of the transistor, a revolutionary achievement by company physicists John Bardeen,

Origin of *Cold War*

Speaking to the Senate War Investigating Committee on Oct 24 in reference to Soviet aggression, Bernard Baruch asserted, "Although the war is over, we are in the midst of a cold war which is getting warmer."

Walter Brattain and William Shockley; in 1956 the three were awarded the Nobel Prize for their work.

Oct 22: Optical Society annual meeting featured demonstration of the duplicating process Chester F. Carlson devised 10 years earlier and named *xerography* from the Greek for "dry writing."

Dec 1 Du Pont announced development of Orlon.

- In his book *Cybernetics,* mathematician Norbert Wiener summarized his theories about automatic computing and feedback in machines and in the human brain and nervous system.
- New quantum theory of electrodynamics devised by US physicists Richard Feynman and Julian Schwinger.
- Vitamin B-12 isolated by Karl Folkers and found to cure pernicious anemia.
- New antibiotics aureomycin and chloromycetin developed.
- Cortisone synthesized by Mayo biochemist Philip Hench.
- Dramamine developed by Johns Hopkins physicians.

1973 *25 Years Ago*

Culture

Publications

Fiction

- *The Optimist's Daughter*, by Eudora Welty (Pulitzer)
- *Gravity's Rainbow*, by Thomas Pynchon
- *Fear of Flying*, by Erica Jong
- *Ninety-Two in the Shade*, by Thomas McGuane
- *Breakfast of Champions*, by Kurt Vonnegut
- *The Taking of Pelham One Two Three*, by John Godey, a thriller about the hijacking of a NY subway train
- *The Onion Field*, by Joseph Wambaugh, a police novel
- *Serpico*, by Peter Maas, another police novel
- *Going Home*, by Danielle Steel, her first novel
- *The Gulag Archipelago*, by Aleksander Solzhenitsyn. Its publication in Paris led to his exile to the West in 1974.
- *Burr*, by Gore Vidal
- *The Hot L Baltimore*, by Lanford Wilson, a play
- *That Championship Season*, by Jason Miller (Pulitzer for drama)

Poetry

- *Diving into the Wreck*, by Adrienne Rich
- *The Fall of America*, by Allen Ginsberg
- *Sleepers Joining Hands*, by Robert Bly

Nonfiction

- *Our Bodies, Our Selves: A Course by and for Women*, by the Boston Women's Health Collective
- *Pentimento: A Book of Portraits*, by Lillian Hellman, autobiographical essays
- *The Coming of Post-Industrial Society*, by Daniel Bell
- *Portrait of a Marriage*, by Nigel Nicholson
- *The Imperial Presidency*, by Arthur M. Schlesinger, Jr
- *Luce and His Empire*, by W.A. Swanberg (Pulitzer)
- *Fire in the Lake: The Vietnamese and Americans in Vietnam*, by Frances FitzGerald (Pulitzer)
- *Children of Crisis* (v. 2 and 3), by Robert Coles (Pulitzer)
- *People of Paradox: An Inquiry Concerning the Origin of American Civilization*, by Michael Kammen (Pulitzer)
- Nobel prize for Literature: Patrick White of Australia

TV Premieres

- "Barnaby Jones," starring Buddy Ebsen as a mild-mannered private eye who comes out of retirement after his son's murder.
- "Kojak," starring Telly Savalas as a New York City police detective.
- "The Six Million Dollar Man," starring Lee Majors as astronaut Steve Austin who was "rebuilt" with bionic parts. "The Bionic Woman," starring Lindsay Wagner, was spun off from this show.

1973 *continued*

- "Upstairs, Downstairs" debuted on Masterpiece Theatre on PBS.
- "The Young and the Restless," a daytime serial that is still on the air, debuted. It has won numerous Emmys. The program's large and changing cast has included the now famous actors David Hasselhoff, Tom Selleck and Deidre Hall.
- "Police Story," a drama anthology.

Film Premieres

- *American Graffiti*, directed by George Lucas, starring Richard Dreyfuss, Ron Howard, Harrison Ford and several other young actors who were later to become well known; inspired the TV show "Happy Days"
- *The Sting*, directed by George Roy Hill, starring Robert Redford and Paul Newman; featured Scott Joplin's music
- *The Way We Were*, directed by Sydney Pollack, starring Robert Redford and Barbra Streisand
- *Paper Moon*, directed by Peter Bogdanovich, starring Ryan and Tatum O'Neal
- *The Exorcist*, directed by William Friedkin, starring Ellen Burstyn, Max von Sydow and Linda Blair
- *Bang the Drum Slowly*, directed by John Hancock, starring Robert DeNiro
- *The Last Detail*, directed by Hal Ashby, starring Jack Nicholson, Randy Quaid
- *Mean Streets*, directed by Martin Scorsese, starring Robert DeNiro, Harvey Keitel
- *Serpico*, directed by Sidney Lumet, starring Al Pacino, Tony Roberts
- *Sleeper*, directed by Woody Allen, starring Diane Keaton and Woody Allen
- *Live and Let Die*, starring Roger Moore as the fourth James Bond
- *Last Tango in Paris*, starring Marlon Brando

Academy Award winners for 1973 (awarded in 1974)

- Best Picture: *The Sting*
- Best Director: George Roy Hill for *The Sting*
- Best Actor: Jack Lemmon in *Save the Tiger*
- Best Actress: Glenda Jackson in *A Touch of Class*

Theater Premieres

- "A Little Night Music," a musical by Stephen Sondheim, with the song "Send in the Clowns."
- "The Changing Room," by David Storey.
- "Raisin," a musical adaptation of the Lorraine Hansberry play, "A Raisin in the Sun."
- "Godspell," a musical.

Popular songs

- "Tie a Yellow Ribbon Round the Old Oak Tree," Tony Orlando and Dawn
- "I Shot the Sheriff," written and recorded by Bob Marley
- "Killing Me Softly with His Song," Roberta Flack
- "You Are the Sunshine of My Life," written and recorded by Stevie Wonder
- "Crocodile Rock," Elton John
- "Half-Breed," Cher
- "Midnight Train to Georgia," Gladys Knight & the Pips
- "You're So Vain," written and recorded by Carly Simon
- "Bad, Bad Leroy Brown," Jim Croce, who was killed in a plane crash this year
- "Sing," The Carpenters
- "Could It Be I'm Falling in Love," The Spinners
- "Delta Dawn," Helen Reddy
- "Love Train," The O'Jays
- "My Love," Paul McCartney and Wings
- "The Night the Lights Went Out in Georgia," Vicki Lawrence

Albums

- "Greetings from Asbury Park, NJ," Bruce Springsteen album, was not initially successful
- "Anticipation," Carly Simon
- "I Am Woman," Helen Reddy
- "The Dark Side of the Moon," Pink Floyd
- "We're an American Band," Grand Funk Railroad
- "Goat's Head Soup," The Rolling Stones
- Nineteen million "Sound of Music" albums sold this year

Watergate Heats Up

Conflict over Watergate consumed the nation. In response to the June 1972 break-in at the Watergate offices of the Democratic National Committee and the subsequent conviction of the perpetrators, in Feb 1973 the Senate established an investigative committee headed by Senator Sam Ervin to look into the growing scandal. Hearings were televised live during the summer. The existence of tape recordings made in the Oval Office by the president became known in June along with the existence of the White House "enemies list." On Oct 20, 1973, the "Saturday Night Massacre" occurred as Attorney General Elliot Richardson resigned rather than firing special prosecutor Archibald Cox, who had been insisting that Nixon turn over the tapes. Solicitor General Robert Bork, next in command, then fired Cox, heightening suspicion that Nixon had something to hide. Leon Jaworski, who replaced Cox as special prosecutor, continued to press for the release of the tapes. The White House finally released them, although there were gaps in crucial conversations and some subpoenaed tapes were declared to be nonexistent. Their disclosures led to Nixon's resignation in Aug 1974 and Gerald Ford's swearing in as the 39th US president.

Landmark Events

Jan 22 Roe v. Wade Supreme Court rules that abortion should be a decision between a woman and her physician.

Feb 27 At Wounded Knee, SD, militant members of the American Indian Movement occupied the unincorporated community to dramatize their demands for free elections of tribal leaders, investigation of the Bureau of Indian Affairs and a review of all US-Indian treaties. They surrendered on May 8 after officials promised to investigate their complaints.

May 3 The 110-story Sears Tower in Chicago was topped out at 1450 feet, making it the world's tallest building.

May 14 The Supreme Court ruled that spouses of women in the armed forces were eligible for the same benefits as those given to the spouses of men.

Oct 6 The October War or Yom Kippur War, a surprise attack by Egypt and Syria, pushed Israeli forces several miles behind the 1967 cease-fire lines. Israel was caught off guard, partly because the attack came on the holiest Jewish religious day. After 18 days of fighting, hostilities were halted by the UN. Although it recovered from the initial setback, Israel failed to regain all the land lost in the fighting.

Oct 10 Spiro Agnew resigned as vice-president in a scandal unrelated to Watergate. Rep Gerald Ford of Michigan was nominated by President Nixon on Oct 12 to take Agnew's place. On Dec 6 Ford was sworn in as vice-president, under a provision of the 25th Amendment to the Constitution. This was the first time these procedures were used.

Oct 16 The Nobel Peace Prize was awarded jointly to Secretary of State Henry Kissinger and Le Duc Tho for their efforts in ending the Vietnam War.

Oct 17 Arab oil embargo in retaliation for US support of Israel in October Arab-Israeli War resulted in long lines at the fuel pumps. Organization of Petroleum Exporting Countries raised prices dramatically. Resulting efforts for energy self-sufficiency in the US included the 55 mph speed limit and extension of Daylight Savings Time.

Dec 15 The American Psychiatric Association announced that homosexuality is not a mental illness, overturning its 100-year old position on the subject.

Politics and Government

- After 300 years of British rule, the Bahamas were granted independence.
- Salvador Allende Gossens, president of Chile since 1970, was overthrown in a bloody military coup and reportedly commited suicide.
- Great Britain, Ireland and Denmark formally joined the Common Market.

1973 *continued*

- Screening of airline passengers to prevent highjacking began.

Sports

JAN 11 The American League adds a 10th player to the roster, a designated hitter who will step up to bat in place of the pitcher.

JAN 14 Super Bowl VII was won by the Miami Dolphins who defeated the Washington Redskins 14 to 7.

MAR 1 Robyn Smith became the first woman jockey to win a stakes race with her victory in the Paumonok Handicap at Aqueduct.

MAR 26 The NCAA basketball championship was won for the seventh consecutive year by UCLA, who defeated Memphis state 87 to 66.

MAY 10 The New York Knicks won the NBA basketball championship, defeating the Los Angeles Lakers four games to one.

MAY 12 The ABA basketball championship was won by the Indiana Pacers, defeating the Kentucky Colonels four games to three.

JUNE 17 The US Open golf tournament was won by Johnny Miller.

JULY 7 Billie Jean King won women's singles at Wimbledon for the second year in a row. Men's singles were won by Jan Kodes of Czechoslovakia.

AUG 12 Jack Nicklaus won the PGA golf tournament.

SEPT 20 In what promoters dubbed the "Battle of the Sexes," Billie Jean King easily defeated Bobby Riggs.

OCT 21 The Oakland Athletics won the World Series for the second year in a row, beating the New York Mets four games to three.

DEC 2 The Davis Cup tennis championship was won by Australia, beating the US team in five straight matches.

- Secretariat wins horse racing's Triple Crown: the Kentucky Derby, the Preakness Stakes and the Belmont Stakes.
- O. J. Simpson rushed for a record 2,003 yards.

Science and Technology

NOV 3 Mariner 10, the first US probe of the planet Mercury, was launched. It was to fly by Venus on its way to Mercury.

APR 5 Pioneer 11 was launched for a December rendevous with the planet Jupiter.

MAY 25 Skylab, the first US space station, was launched on a 28-day mission.

JULY 29 Skylab was launched again on a 59-day mission.

NOV 16 The third Skylab mission lasted 84 days.

- A committee formed in 1970 by US grocers and food manufacturers issues a recommendation for a Universal Product Code (i.e., bar codes) for supermarket items that will permit electronic scanning of prices.
- The Sydney, Australia Opera House opened, following 16 years of design and construction.
- The first Endangered and Threatened Species List was issued by the US Fish and Wildlife Bureau.
- The World Trade Center towers were completed, the second tallest buildings in the world, after the Sears Tower, which was also completed this year.
- BART, San Francisco's Bay Area Rapid Transit System, was opened.
- MRI, or Magnetic Resonance Imaging, was first used for medical diagnosis.
- A computerized brain scanner (CAT) was first marketed.

- The World Health Organization declared the Western Hemisphere free of smallpox.
- The first color photocopier released by Xerox.

Vietnam War Winds Down

1973 was a year of negotiations. US troop strength had been greatly reduced the preceding year and heavy bombing of the North led the North Vietnamese to the table. On Jan 27, the Paris Accords were signed, the major terms of which were maintenance of the 17th parallel as a temporary demarcation line between the North and South, US withdrawal from Vietnam and return of American POWs. Nothing else was settled; political issues were left for the two Vietnamese governments to negotiate. A multi-nation commission was to supervise the cease-fire. The last POWs returned to the US in March and the last troops in April. However, the US continued to bomb Cambodia. In the spring, Watergate weakened Nixon's position and Congress passed an amendment requiring cessation of military operations in and over Indochina by Aug 15. In November, Congress passed the War Deployment Act, virtually guaranteeing the end of US involvement in Indochina. However, fighting between North and South Vietnamese forces didn't cease until the fall of Saigon, Apr 30, 1975.

Obits

Jan 22 Lyndon Baines Johnson, 36th President of the US.

Mar 6 Pearl Buck, author (*The Good Earth*) and humanitarian.

Mar 14 Murat "Chic" Young, creator of the comic stip *Blondie*.

Mar 26 Noel Coward, actor, playwright, composer and writer.

Apr 8 Pablo Picasso, artist.

May 18 Jeannette Rankin, the first woman elected to Congress (from Montana).

July 2 Betty Grable, actress.

July 23 Eddie Rickenbaker, WWI flying ace and airline executive.

Aug 31 John Ford, film director.

Sept 2 J.R.R. Tolkien, British novelist (*The Hobbit* and *The Lord of the Ring*).

Sept 28 W.H. Auden, British-American poet.

Oct 18 Walt Kelly, creator of the comic strip *Pogo*.

Oct 22 Pablo Casals, world-renowned cellist.

Dec 1 David Ben-Gurion, former Israeli prime minister.

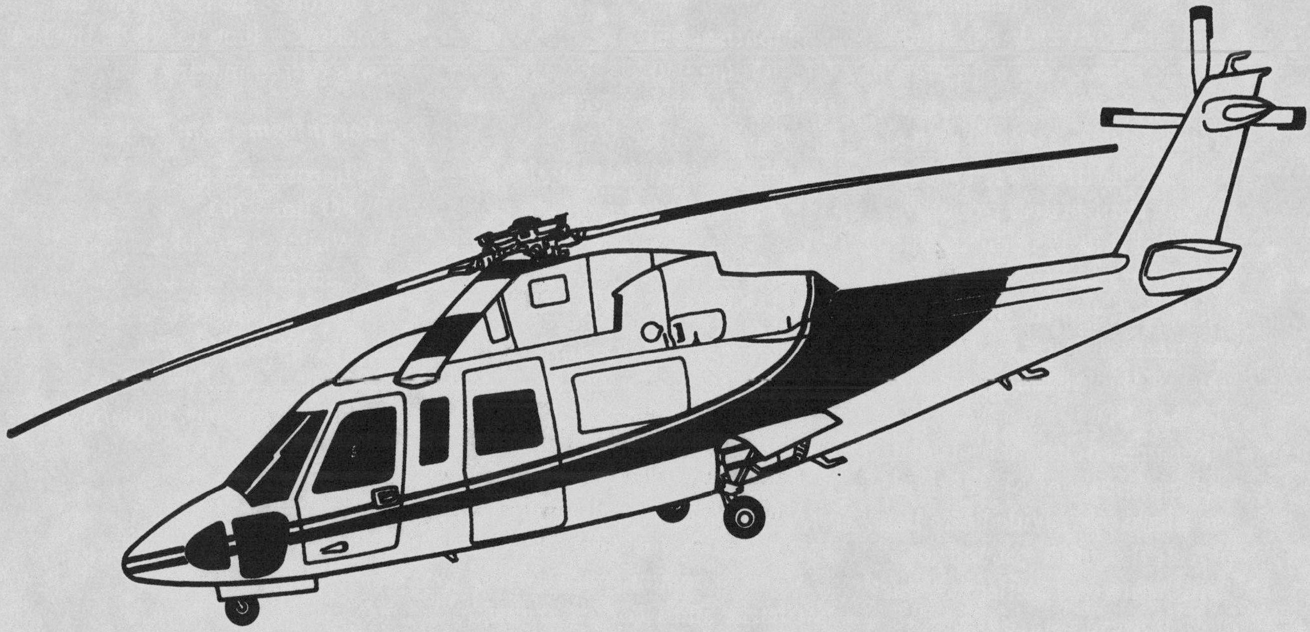

Spotlight on the World *milestone anniversary years*

Prince Edward Island

July 1, 1873 • 125 years

Prince Edward Island became part of the Canadian Confederation on July 1, 1873. One of Canada's three Maritime provinces, it is bounded on the north, east and west by the Gulf of Saint Lawrence and on the south by Northumberland Strait, which separates it from Nova Scotia and New Brunswick. It is Canada's smallest province.

The first Europeans to visit the island were the French explorers Jacques Cartier in 1534 and Samuel de Champlain in 1603, who claimed it for France and named it Ile-St-Jean. It was located just off the French colony Acadia (Nova Scotia) and considered part of that province, but it remained an insignificant part of French colonial holdings until Britain took possession of mainland Acadia in 1713 and the island became a haven for both French refugees from Acadia and new French settlers. Control shifted back and forth between the two powers until British troops occupied it in 1758 during the French and Indian War. It was finally ceded to the British by the Treaty of Paris in 1763, and most of the French were ejected.

Renamed Saint John's Island and made part of Nova Scotia, the island was divided into large parcels that were granted to British citizens. Settlement was slow, however, since the prospect of tenant farming for an absentee landlord on an isolated island colony was not particularly attractive. In 1769 the island was again broken off from Nova Scotia and administered separately. Thirty years later it received its final name change, this time in honor of King George's son Edward, who was commander in chief of British forces in North America.

When the Confederation of Canada was formed in 1867, Prince Edward Island chose to remain independent. Six years later, bankrupt after trying to build a railroad, the colony negotiated a deal with the confederation: the Canadian federal government would assume the railroad and operate ferries, install telegraph lines and pay off the recipients of the original land grants, permitting the tenants to buy the land. In exchange, Prince Edward Island became a province.

For information:

Tourism PEI
PO Box 940
Charlottetown, PEI
Canada C1A 7M5
Phone: (800) 463-4PEI
Web: http://www.gov.pe.ca

Yukon Territory

June 13, 1898 • 100 years

The Yukon was a vast expanse in the northwestern corner of Canada peopled mainly by a few Hudson's Bay Company trading posts along the Yukon River when Skookum Jim, Dawson Charlie and George Carmack discovered gold on Aug 16, 1896. In the greatest gold rush of all time, thousands of treasure seekers hazarded the treacherous journey to the hastily constructed remote Dawson City. Almost overnight the stampeders made Dawson City the largest settlement west of Winnipeg and north of San Francisco, its population hitting 40,000 within two years.

Along with the prospectors came all the people necessary to supply their needs, take their money and collect their taxes. For some, the most coveted resource in the Yukon was the tax on liquor. Since the Yukon belonged to the Northwest Territories at the time, those tax dollars went to the territorial government until the revenue from the stampeders came to the attention of the Canadian federal government. Those officials quickly decided to make the Yukon a separate territory, subject to the administrative control of the federal government. On June 13, 1898, the law was passed making it so.

For information:

Tourism Yukon
PO Box 2703
Whitehorse, Yukon
Canada Y1A 2C6
Phone: (403) 667-5340
Fax: (403) 667-3546
Web:
http://www.parallel.ca/yukon

Republic of Turkey

Oct 29, 1923 • 75 years

Marking the end of the Ottoman Empire and the beginning of modern Turkey, charismatic leader Mustafa Kemal Atatürk declared Turkey a republic on Oct 29, 1923. Bounded on the west by the Aegean Sea and Greece, on the north by Bulgaria and the Black Sea, on the east by Georgia, Armenia and Iran and on the south by Iraq, Syria and the Mediterrean Sea, the area that is Turkey has long been the natural passageway between the East and West.

The city of Constantinople (Istanbul) was the center of the Byzantine Empire. In the 11th through 14th centuries Turkic tribes invaded and occupied parts of the area called Anatolia, established the Ottoman dynasty and gradually took control of much of the Byzantine territory. Eventually the Muslim Ottoman Empire ruled most of the Balkans and parts of Hungary as well as the bulk of the Middle East and northern Africa. The empire declined in the late 1600s and by the 19th century had lost control of most of the territory it had conquered.

When World War I began, the Turkish ruling triumvirate formed an alliance with the Central Powers. One important battle of the war was fought at Gallipoli, with Turkish troops led by Mustafa Kemal (later to take the name Atatürk). After the Central Powers lost the war, parts of the country were occupied by Allied forces. This incursion ignited Turkish nationalists, who began the War of Independence and under the leadership of Atatürk resisted the planned settlement, drove out the occupation forces and achieved a new settlement (embodied in the Treaty of Lausanne), which left eastern Thrace and Anatolia as the Turkish Republic.

For information:

Republic of Turkey
Tourism Information Bureau
1717 Massachusetts Ave NW, Ste 306
Washington, DC 20036
Phone: (202) 429-9844
Fax: (202) 429-5649
Email: tourismdc@aol.com
Web: http://www.turkey.org/tourism

Israel

May 14, 1948 • 50 years

April 30, 1998, is the Western calendar date of the 50th anniversary of Israel's statehood, which takes place on Jewish calendar date Iyar 5, 5758. (Dates in the Hebrew calendar vary from their Gregorian equivalents from year to year.) It celebrates the culmination of a truly remarkable series of events.

Although the area that is now Israel is regarded as the homeland of the Jewish people, the Jews of the Bible were displaced by the Romans and dispersed around the world. For almost 2,000 years they had only their strong sense of culture and religion to bind them together into a coherent community in the diaspora.

It was not until 1897 that Theodor Herzl started the Zionist movement at Basel, Switzerland, for the purpose of creating "for the Jewish people a home in Palestine secured by public law." The difficulties involved would be comparable to the Seminole Indians wanting to return to their "homeland" in Florida, now heavily populated by others.

Though the number of Jews in Palestine was small in the early 20th century, it increased as the Zionist movement gained strength. Palestine was under British control, and by 1916 the British were trying to gain support from the Jewish world community for the war with Germany. On Nov 2, 1917, the Balfour Declaration expressed Britain's support in principle for the creation of an independent Jewish state in Palestine. This declaration was validated by the League of Nations and Britain was charged with administering the area.

The resulting situation proved unstable as the Jewish population increased and bought more land for settlements, friction with the Arab Palestinians increased, and the British became hated by both. World War II brought this animosity to a head as Nazi atrocities caused more Jews to flee to Palestine for safety, followed after the war by tens of thousands of displaced Jewish concentration camp survivors in search of new homes. The Zionists needed to expand settlements rapidly to accommodate the new waves of immigrants. The British felt forced to oppose this development because of their obligation as governors of both Jewish and Arab residents, the latter of whom were incensed at seeing more land taken over by the Jews. By the end of the war, the Jewish Yishuv (community) was in open revolt against the British. Exhausted after seven years of one war, Britain did not want to fight another with the Yishuv and decided to pass the problem on to the new United Nations and withdrew from the area.

On Nov 29, 1947, the UN voted to partition Palestine, creating separate Jewish and Arab states. The Palestinian Arabs, refusing to recognize UN authority, began civil warfare and turned to their Arab neighbors for help. The British were determined not to intervene. The Jews officially declared the creation of the state of Israel on May 14, 1948, and on May 15 the combined armies of Egypt, Transjordan, Syria, Lebanon and Iraq joined with the Palestinians to destroy the new Jewish state. The Israelis fought back tenaciously, the combined Arab forces failed and the fighting ended with the new state firmly established and recognized worldwide. Though its borders would change over the years due to further battles with its Arab neighbors, the Israeli state has given a displaced people a homeland, an unprecedented feat.

For information:

Israel Government Tourist Office
800 Second Ave, 16th Floor
New York, NY 10117
Phone: (212) 499-5600
Fax: (212) 499-5695
Email: icenter@imot.org
Web: http://www.infotour.co.il

Bahamas

July 10, 1973 • 25 years

The Bahamas are a group of some 700 islands and 2,000 cays, an archipelago spread out for about 750 miles from southeast of Florida to east of Cuba. Christopher Columbus's first stop in the New World was in the Bahamas, probably on San Salvador, where he encountered friendly Arawak natives, whom he called Indians. The Spanish did not establish any settlements in the islands, having discovered the riches in South America, but they did wipe out the Arawaks, capturing them for slavery.

The British arrived in the 17th century and claimed the islands, but their early settlements were not prosperous and became a haven for pirates. Colonists brought African slaves to the islands to work cotton plantations but prosperity was short lived as the soil gave out and slavery was abolished.

Although the Bahamas are now an independent nation, having been granted independence in 1973 in a peaceful transfer of power, they remain in the British Commonwealth. Bahamians are English-speaking and of British and African descent. The islands' subtropical climate, beautiful beaches and unique culture have attracted a large tourist trade, which is the main revenue source.

For information:

Bahamas Ministry of Tourism
50 E 52nd St
28th Floor North
New York, NY 10022
Phone: (212) 758-2777
Fax: (212) 753-6531

Boston Tea Party

Dec 16, 1773 • 225 years

The famous Boston Tea party was not so much about tea as it was about trade. To the British the colonies were an investment from which profits should be made. To the colonists they were an opportunity to make their own personal fortunes. Conflict was inevitable.

The Townshend Act imposed duties on goods imported into the colonies. It was repealed in 1770, but the tax on tea was retained. Enterprising colonists smuggled tea and sold it at a good profit. In 1773 the East India Company was nearly bankrupt, so Parliament reduced the tax on tea exported to America and for the first time let the company ship tea directly to the colonies. The East India Company appointed certain colonists as their agents. The enterprising American smugglers were outraged, for now these agents could beat their prices and monopolize colonial tea sales. Politicians talked about taxation without representation, getting the general public excited about the issue. In Boston on Dec 16, 1773, a group of American patriots disguised themselves as Indians, boarded the East India ships and dumped tea into the harbor.

In commemoration, the Tea Party Ship docked in Boston is planning an anniversary celebration.

For information:

Tea Party Ship
Congress Street Bridge
Boston, MA 02210
Phone (617) 338-1773
Fax: (617) 338-1974

The Monroe Doctrine

Dec 2, 1823 • 175 years

A change in US foreign policy was expressed by President James Monroe in his annual message to Congress in 1823. He declared that the Old World and the New World had different spheres of interest. What became known as the Monroe Doctrine had four points: The US would not interfere in conflicts between European powers; the US recognized and would not interfere with existing European colonies in the Western Hemisphere; the Western Hemisphere was closed to further colonization; and any attempt to control a nation in the Western Hemisphere would be seen as a hostile act by the US.

The Monroe Doctrine arose out of a concern that Spain would try to recolonize parts of Latin America. The US was not in a position militarily to enforce this policy and did nothing when, for example, Great Britain seized the Falkland Islands in 1833. But after the Civil War, as the US became a world power, the interpretation of the Monroe Doctrine became increasingly broad. From the Spanish American War to the present, the US has frequently intervened in Latin America, especially in the Caribbean in such places as Cuba and Grenada.

Wisconsin Statehood

May 29, 1848 • 150 years

The first European to set foot on Wisconsin soil was a French explorer, Jean Nicolet, in 1634. Later in the 17th century French Jesuits established missions and fur traders set up trading posts. In 1689 the Upper Mississippi Valley, including what was to become Wisconsin, was claimed for France.

At the close of the French and Indian War in 1763, the French possessions east of the Mississippi were ceded to Great Britain. In 1787 Wisconsin became part of the Northwest Territory of the independent United States; thereafter it was a part of the Indiana Territory in 1800, a part of the Illinois Territory in 1809 and the Michigan Territory in 1818.

Large-scale immigration into the territory didn't begin until 1820. After the Black Hawk War of 1832, settlers flocked to the region. Wisconsin was made a separate territory in 1836 and included the present states of Iowa and Minnesota and parts of the Dakotas. By 1848 all Indian land titles in Wisconsin had been relinquished. On May 29, 1848, Wisconsin, with its present boundaries, was admitted to the Union as the 30th state.

Wisconsin will be celebrating its sesquicentennial with a series of special events. Wisconsin Public Television will air a series of Wisconsin history programs, Wisconsin Public Radio will develop special broadcasts, there will be special exhibitions at the Wisconsin Historical Society and other museums, the Military Road Sesquicentennial Wagon Train will travel 300 miles along the route of the original Military Road from Prairie du Chien to Green Bay, and there will be many other special performances and educational events.

For information:

Wisconsin Sesquicentennial Commission
8 S. Carroll St
Madison, WI 53701-1848
Phone: (608) 264-2990
Fax: (608) 264-7994
Web:
http://www.150years.state.wi.us

Spanish-American War

April 21, 1898 • 100 years

The Spanish-American War was sparked by Cuban nationalists' struggle for their independence from Spain. This concerned the US because the fighting caused extensive damage to US business interests in Cuba and prevented trade there. Popular support for action against the Spanish was generated by inflammatory reports in newspapers owned by Joseph Pulitzer and William Randolph Hearst, reports that implied the Spanish were a direct threat to the US itself, creating a war hysteria that pressured reluctant politicians into hasty action.

The incident that triggered the war was the sinking of the US battleship *Maine* by an explosion that killed 260, an event the Spanish claimed was due to a defective boiler while the US claimed it was an act of sabotage by the Spanish. "Remember the *Maine*!" became the rallying cry used to generate support for a war against Spain. President McKinley and Congress were pressured by an indignant public to demand Spain's withdrawal from Cuba. McKinley ordered a naval blockade and Spain declared war on the US after one of its ships was boarded.

Although the US declared that it was not interested in establishing an empire of its own, the net result of the war was US ownership of Puerto Rico, Guam and the Philippines, and almost total domination of the newly independent Cuba. Mark Twain was one of the most vocal opponents of this war, particularly condemning the actions the US took in subjugating the independence-seeking Filipinos.

Jan 25 US battleship *Maine* arrived at Havana, Cuba, on a secret assignment to protect American life and property while Cuban rebels fought for independence from Spain.

Feb 15 *Maine* exploded and sank in harbor at Havana, killing 260 and becoming a cause célèbre as Americans accuse the Spanish of sabotage.

Apr 19 Joint resolution of Congress demanded Spain withdraw from Cuba and authorized use of military force; Spain severed diplomatic relations with US.

Apr 22 US President McKinley ordered blockade of Cuban ports and the USS *Nashville* seized a Spanish ship later that day.

Apr 24 Spain declared war on US.

Apr 25 Congress declared war on Spain, retroactive to Apr 21.

May 1 The US six-ship Asiatic fleet under Commodore George Dewey surprised the larger Spanish fleet in the Battle of Manila Bay, destroying or capturing every ship and losing no American lives.

May 25–June 14 US forces embarked: 2,500 sailed for the Philippines while the rest headed to Cuba–600 marines to Guantánamo and 17,000 army troops under General William R. Shafter to Santiago.

June 21 When the USS *Charleston* under Captain Henry Glass fired on Guam, the Spanish commander surrendered quickly, not knowing there was a war and not having any ammunition on the island.

June 24 On Cuba, US troops under Major General Joseph Wheeler and Colonel Leonard Wood, along with Colonel Theodore Roosevelt and his

Rough Riders, beat the Spanish at the Battle of Las Guasimas.

July 1–2 US and Spanish troops met again at El Caney and in the famous Battle of San Juan Hill. The US won the day, but both sides suffered heavy casualties.

July 3 US ships destroyed the Spanish fleet at Cuba as it tried to leave Santiago.

July 8: Dewey's forces occupied Isla Grande in Subic Bay, despite interference from a German gunboat.

July 25–28 US troops under General Nelson Miles invaded Puerto Rico, landing successfully at Guanica and accepting the surrender three days later of Ponce, Puerto Rico's second largest city.

Aug 12 The fighting ended with Spain granting independence to Cuba, giving Puerto Rico and Guam to the US and agreeing to negotiate later over the Philippines.

Aug 13: Unaware of the cease fire, forces under Dewey and General Wesley Merritt captured Manila.

Dec 10 After Spain agreed to cede the Philippines to the US for $20 million, the Spanish-American War ended with the formal signing of a treaty at Paris.

College and University Founding Anniversaries

There are more than 3,000 colleges and universities across the US, ranging from private to state-supported, single-sex to coeducational, small to large, liberal arts-based to technically or vocationally oriented. While all share some characteristics and perspectives, each has its unique history. The following is a selection of colleges and universities celebrating a founding anniversary in 1998.

Dickinson College

1773 • 225 years

Dickinson was founded in 1773 as a grammar school by the citizens of Carlisle, PA, on land donated by Thomas and John Penn. With the support of Pennsylvania governor John Dickinson it was chartered as a college of liberal arts for men on Sept 9, 1783, one of the 15 "colonial colleges." It was named in honor of Dickinson, the drafter of the Articles of Confederation and a signer of the US Constitution. In 1884 the college began to admit women.

For Information:

Office of College Relations
Dickinson College
PO Box 1773
Carlisle, PA 17013-2896
Phone: (717) 245-1289
Fax: (717) 245-1457
E-mail: colrel@dickinson.edu
Web: http://www.dickinson.edu/

University of Louisville

1798 • 200 years

One of the oldest public universities in the US, the University of Louisville celebrates Apr 3, 1798 as its founding date, when eight prominent Louisville citizens contributed funds to support higher education and challenged their young community to pitch in. Originally called the Jefferson Seminary, through a merger with the Louisville Medical Institute and the Louisville Collegiate Institute in 1846 it became the University of Louisville. In 1970 it joined the state system of higher education; it is Kentucky's second-largest university.

For information:

Bicentennial Celebration
Event Coordinator
University of Louisville
Louisville, KY 40292
Phone: (502) 852-7681
Fax: (502) 852-7590
Web: http://www.louisville.edu

Trinity College

1823 • 175 years

In May of 1823, this liberal arts college was founded under the name Washington College in an Episcopal church in Hartford, CT, as an alternative to the Congregationalist-controlled Yale. The name was changed to Trinity in 1845. One of the nation's 60 oldest institutions of higher education, it is now an independent, non-sectarian college. In 1969 it began to admit women.

For information:

Trinity College
300 Summit St
Hartford, CT 06106-3100
Web: http://www.trincoll.edu

Boston University School of Medicine

1848 • 150 years

Boston University's School of Medicine traces its roots to the founding of the Boston Female Medical School, the first medical school for women in the US, which opened its doors with 12 students on Nov 1, 1848. It became the New England Female Medical College in 1851, then merged with Boston University in 1874 to become the Boston University School of Medicine, one of the first coed medical schools in the world.

For information:

Public Relations
Boston University School of Medicine
80 E Concord St
Boston, MA 02118-2394
Phone: (617) 638-8000
E-mail: cl@bu.edu
Web: http://med-amsa.bu.edu/Main.html

Muhlenberg College

1848 • 150 years

Founded in 1848 to provide a liberal arts education in the Christian humanistic tradition, Muhlenberg is an independent liberal arts college affiliated with the Evangelical Lutheran Church of America. It was named in honor of Henry Melchior Muhlenberg, the patriarch of the Lutheran Church in America. The college is also celebrating the 40th anniversary of its first admission of women.

For information:

Sesquicentennial Coordinator
Public Relations Office
Muhlenberg College
2400 W Chew St
Allentown, PA 18104-5586
Phone: (610) 821-3233
Fax: (610) 821-3477
E-mail: webmaster@www.muhlberg.edu
Web: http://hal.muhlberg.edu

Rhodes College

1848 • 150 years

On Feb 4, 1848, the trustees of a small preparatory school in Clarksville, TN, signed that property over to the Masonic Order of Tennessee with the stipulation that they establish a first-rate college. The resulting Masonic University of Tennessee was bought by the Presbyterians seven years later and has been named Montgomery Masonic College, Stewart College and Southwestern Presbyterian University. It was moved to Memphis in 1925 as Southwestern, changed its name to Southwestern at Memphis in 1945, then to its current name, Rhodes College, in 1984, in honor of Peyton Nalle Rhodes, president of the college 1949–65. This liberal arts college has been coed since 1916.

For information:

Exec Dir, Media Relations
Rhodes College
2000 N Parkway
Memphis, TN 38112-1690
Phone: (901) 843-3873
E-mail: hayes@rhodes.edu
Web: http://www.rhodes.edu

University of Mississippi

1844–48 • 150 years

Ole Miss's sesquicentennial activities began on Feb 24, 1994, and will end Nov 6, 1998, celebrating from the date the Mississippi Legislature chartered the university as the foundation for public higher education in the state on Feb 24, 1844, through the date it opened its doors on Nov 6, 1848. The university began to admit women in 1882, one of the first in the South to do so, and to admit blacks in 1962. It's a comprehensive university with an enrollment of more than 12,000.

For information:

Public Relations/Marketing
University of Mississippi
University, MS 38677
Phone: (601) 232-7236
E-mail: idea@olemiss.edu
Web: http://www.olemiss.edu

University of Wisconsin

1848 • 150 years

On Sept 10–12, 1998, as part of the Wisconsin State Sesquicentennial Celebration the UW system will commemorate the signing of the charter legislation on July 26, 1848, that established this public land-grant institution. The UW system today has more than 120,000 students attending its 12 universities, 13 two-year colleges, continuing education and outreach programs. The University of Wisconsin–Madison is the original and largest UW campus, beginning classes Feb 5, 1849, and will have its own sesquicentennial celebration throughout 1999.

For information:

Sesquicentennial Coord
University of Wisconsin
Office of the Chancellor
96 Bascom Hall
500 Lincoln Dr
Madison, WI 53706
Phone: (608) 265-3044
Fax: (608) 265-8011
E-mail: plsmith@mail.bascom.wisc.edu
Web: http://www.wisc.edu

North Georgia College & State University

1873 • 125 years

NGCSU is a publicly supported, liberal arts college and a senior unit of the university system of Georgia. It was established Jan 6, 1873, as a coed land-grant school of agriculture and mechanical arts named North Georgia Agricultural College. It soon added military training, which became an official Army ROTC unit when ROTC was legislated in 1916. When the school's mission changed from agriculture to arts and sciences in 1932, it was renamed North Georgia College. With the addition of graduate schools, the school was granted university status and acquired its present name.

For information:

North Georgia College & State University
Office of Public Information
College Circle
Dahlonega, GA 30597
Phone: (706) 864-1949
Fax: (706) 864-1859
E-mail: mclark@nugget.ngc.peachnet.edu
Web: http://www.ngc.peachnet.edu

Southeast Missouri State University

1873 • 125 years

Southeast was established at Cape Girardeau as the Third District Normal School for teacher training and evolved into Southeast Missouri State Teachers' College in 1919, Southeast Missouri State College in 1945 and finally, in recognition of its role as a comprehensive institution, into Southeast Missouri State University. It has twice been given the prestigious Christa McAuliffe Showcase for Excellence award.

For information:

University Relations
Southeast Missouri State University
1 University Plaza
Cape Girardeau, MO 63701
Phone: (573) 651-2000
E-mail: f333rec@semovm.semo.edu
Web: http://www.semo.edu

Texas Christian University

1873 • 125 years

TCU was founded as AddRan Male and Female College in 1873 at Thorp Spring, TX by preacher-teachers Addison and Randolph Clark. In 1889 the school became affiliated with the Christian Churches of Texas and was renamed AddRan Christian College. It moved to Waco in 1895 and some years later became Texas Christian University, but after a fire in 1910, it relocated to Fort Worth. Today TCU is a major private university, affiliated with the Disciples of Christ but welcoming students of all backgrounds.

For information:

Office of Communications
Texas Christian University
Fort Worth, TX 76129
Phone: (817) 921-7810
Fax: (817) 921-7272
Web: http://www.tcu.edu

DePaul University

1898 • 100 years

A private, coed urban university, DePaul was founded by the Vincentian Fathers in 1898 to educate the children of immigrants. Named for St. Vincent de Paul, the school is now the second largest Catholic university in the US. Its mission is to foster a deep respect for the God-given dignity of all people and to instill in its students a dedication to the service of others.

For information:

University Relations
DePaul University
1 E Jackson Blvd
Chicago, IL 60604-2287
Phone: (312) 362-8000
Fax: (312) 362-6639
Web: http://www.depaul.edu

Frostburg State University

1898 • 100 years

FSU was chartered in 1898 and opened in 1902 as State Normal School No 2, a two-year coed teacher-training program. In 1934 it became a four-year college, the State Teachers College at Frostburg. It underwent additional name changes as it developed and diversified, in 1963 becoming Frostburg State College and in 1987 being renamed Frostburg State University. In 1988 FSU was made part of the University of Maryland System.

For information:

Office of University Advancement
Frostburg State University
Midlothian Rd
Frostburg, MD 21532
Phone: (301) 687-4161
Fax: (301) 687-4069
E-mail: d2pcmum@fraoi.fsu.umd.edu
Web: http://www.fsu.umd.edu

Northeastern University

1898 • 100 years

On Oct 3, 1898, the Department of Law of the Boston YMCA's Evening Institute offered the first program at what was to become Northeastern University. In 1909 Northeastern opened the Cooperative Engineering School, one of the earliest cooperative education experiments in the US, and by 1935 had severed its ties to the YMCA and had six separate colleges. Cooperative education remains a hallmark of the University's unique approach. The centennial celebration runs from Oct 15, 1997, through Oct 3, 1998.

For information:

Centennial Office
Northeastern University
360 Huntington Ave
Boston, MA 02115-5096
Phone: (617) 373-5447
Fax: (617) 373-5430
Web: http://www.neu.edu

Entertainment

Enrico Caruso

Birth • Feb 25, 1873 • 125 years

Italian operatic tenor, born at Naples, Caruso became the most popular and highest paid opera singer in the world—the opera superstar of his day. His powerful voice was one of the first recorded on gramophone. With a repertoire of more than 40 operas, he created roles in Cilea's *Adriana Lecouvreur* and in Puccini's *The Girl of the Golden West*; and was acclaimed for the roles of Canio in Leoncavallo's *Pagliacci* and the Duke of Mantua in Verdi's *Rigoletto*. Died Aug 2, 1921, at Naples.

Sir Gerald du Maurier

Birth • Mar 26, 1873 • 125 years

A British actor, theater manager and early filmmaker, born at Hampstead, was the son of writer and artist George du Maurier and father of writer Dame Daphne du Maurier, also an early filmmaker. Among noted works: actor, *The Admirable Crichton, Peter Pan, Raffles*; producer, *A Kiss for Cinderella, Dear Brutus, Bulldog Drummond*. Died Apr 11, 1934, at London.

Feodor Ivanovich Chaliapin

Birth • Feb 15, 1873 • 125 years

Russian operatic bass, born in Kazan, Chaliapin brought superb acting ability as well as outstanding vocal tone to his operatic performances and was known worldwide for his roles in the operas of Russian composers. He immigrated to France after the Russian Revolution. Among noted works: roles in Mussorgsky's *Boris Godunov*, Glinka's *A Life for the Czar*, Borodin's *Prince Igor* and Rimski-Korsakov's *Sadko*. Died Apr 12, 1938, at Paris.

William Macready

Death • Apr 27, 1873 • 125 years

English actor, born at London, remembered most for his rivalry with American actor Edwin Forrest which caused the 1849 Astor Place Theatre riot in which 22 people were killed. Among noted works: various Shakespearean tragedies; title role in Knowles's *Virginius*. Born Mar 3, 1793. Died at Cheltenham.

Max Reinhardt

Birth • Sept 9, 1873 • 125 years

Austrian-American director who established directing as a distinct profession rather than a side job left to a play's leading actor. Originally named Max Goldmann, born at Baden, he became a US citizen in 1940. Innovative and highly imaginative, he is known for the religious pageant *The Miracle*; for founding the music and drama festival at Salzburg; for von Hofmannsthal's *Everyman*; and for a film version of *Midsummer Night's Dream*. Died Oct 31, 1943, at New York City.

Sergey Eisenstein

Birth • Jan 23, 1898 • 100 years

A Russian stage and film director born at Riga, Latvia, Eisenstein is remembered for his unconventional approach to staging and directing. He used contrasting images in unique ways to elicit strong emotional reactions from the audience, a technique he employed in his film work as well. Among noted works: films *Potemkin, Ten Days That Shook the World, Ivan the Terrible, Part I* and *Part II*; books on film *Film Sense* and *Film Essays*. Died Feb 11, 1949, at Moscow.

Paul Robeson

Birth • Apr 9, 1898 • 100 years

Black All-American football player turned lawyer, born at Princeton, NJ, was a star of both stage and film in both musical and dramatic roles. His political activities in later life led to his being blacklisted in the 1950s when he refused to sign an affidavit as to whether he had ever been a member of the Communist Party. He then pursued his career abroad, where he was extremely popular. Among noted works: dramatic stage roles in O'Neill's *Emperor Jones* (film also) and Shakespeare's *Othello* (which became the longest-running Shakespearean play in Broadway history); musical stage roles in *Showboat* (in which his singing of "Ol' Man River" was a show stopper) and *Porgy and Bess*; film roles in *King Solomon's Mines* and *Song of Freedom*. Died Jan 23, 1976, at Philadelphia.

Spotlight on People *milestone anniversary years*

Dame Judith Anderson

Birth • Feb 10, 1898 • 100 years

Australian-American actor, born at Adelaide, Anderson immigrated to the US in 1918, where she became a leading Broadway star and also appeared in many films and television productions. She played the title role in *Medea* and *Mourning Becomes Electra* and the role of Gertrude opposite Sir John Gielgud in *Hamlet.* Made a Dame Commander of the Order of the British Empire in 1960. Died Jan 3, 1992, at Santa Barbara, CA.

René Clair

Birth • Nov 11, 1898 • 100 years

French film director born René Chomette at Paris, Clair was an early innovator in the use of sound in film. He also wrote and produced, making films in both French and English, silent and sound. Among noted works: in French *Un chapeau de paille d'Italie (The Italian Straw Hat)* and *Le million*; in English *I Married a Witch* and *It Happened Tomorrow.* Died Mar 15, 1981, at Neuilly, France.

Emmet Kelly

Birth • Dec 9, 1898 • 100 years

American circus clown, born at Sedan, KS, Kelly was known as Willie, the tramp with the sad face, a character he had created in his early days as a cartoonist. Kelly also appeared in film and on television. Among noted works outside of the circus: DeMille's *The Greatest Show on Earth* (in which he played his clown character) and *Wind Across the Everglades*; his autobiography *Clown: My Life in Tatters and Smiles.* Died Mar 28, 1979.

Gertrude Lawrence

Birth • July 4, 1898 • 100 years

English actor, born at London, Lawrence became a star of musical revue and light comedy in London and later on Broadway. She was featured in many of the plays of Noel Coward and also appeared in film and television roles. Among noted stage works: *Private Lives, Pygmalion, Lady in the Dark* and *The King and I.* Died Sept 6, 1952, at New York City.

Literature

Tirso de Molina

Death • 1648 • 350 years

Born Gabriel Tellez around 1571 at Madrid, Spanish playwright Tirso de Molina was the first to bring the legendary Don Juan out of folklore and into formal literature. He also is remembered for his understanding of human nature, which he brought to hundreds of plays, combining comedy and tragedy. Among noted works: *The Trickster of Seville and His Guest of Stone*, noted for the Don Juan debut; historical play *La prudencia en la mujer (Prudence in Woman).*

Pietro Metastasio

Birth • 1698 • 300 years

Metastasio, born at Rome, was known as *the* librettist of 18th-century opera and was also a poet. He wrote 27 librettos in the heroic tradition, stressing the conflict between reason and emotion. Some of the greatest composers of his era (Mozart, Gluck, J. C. Bach, Handel and others) used his librettos more than 800 times in composing operas. Among noted works: *Artaserse, La clemenza di Tito (The Clemency of Titus).* Died 1782.

Chesterfield, Philip Dormer Stanhope

Death • Mar 24, 1773 • 225 years

The fourth Earl of Chesterfield, born Sept 22, 1694, at London, was a brilliant politician and orator, instrumental in getting the Gregorian calendar adopted in place of the Julian calendar in Britain. He is remembered best, however, for the series of letters he wrote to his illegitimate son Philip and to his godson and distant cousin Philip, whom he later adopted and made his heir, in which he gave counsel on manners, morals and the ways of the world. Died at London.

Auguste Comte

Birth • Jan 19, 1798 • 200 years

French philosopher Comte, born at Montpellier, is considered the founder of positivism and originator of the term *sociology.* Among noted works: *Cours de philosophie positive,* his six-volume masterwork, and his rather strange *Système de politique positive, ou Traité de sociologie instituant la religion de l'humanité,* a four-volume work generally dismissed because of his mental illness. Died Sept 5, 1857, at Paris.

Giacomo Leopardi

Birth • June 29, 1798 • 200 years

Considered one of the finest lyric poets of the romantic era, this Italian writer, born at Recanati, is known for his poetry collection *Canti (Songs)*, poem "La ginestra" ("The Broom Flower"); essay collection *Operette morali (Short Moral Works)* and *Pensieri (Thoughts)*. Died June 14, 1837, at Naples.

Ann Radcliffe

Death • Feb 7, 1823 • 175 years

English gothic novelist, born July 9, 1764, at London, Radcliffe is famous for her skillful intertwining of terror, suspense and romance. Among noted works: *The Romance of the Forest*, *The Mysteries of Udolpho* and *The Italian*. Died at London.

Mary Boykin Miller Chesnut

Birth • Mar 31, 1823 • 175 years

Chesnut, an American Confederate military wife born at Pleasant Hill, SC, is remembered for the journal she kept of her experiences during the Civil War. Published posthumously as *A Diary from Dixie*, this valuable work gave a perceptive portrait of Confederate military and political leaders and an insightful view of Southern life during the war. Died Nov 22, 1886, at Camden, SC.

Steen Steensen Blicher

Death • 1848 • 150 years

A Danish poet and novelist born in 1782 at Vium, Jutland, Blicher recorded the legends and folktales of his native land with skill and grace. Among noted works: *The Knitting Room* and 33 other volumes of poems and stories.

Joel Chandler Harris

Birth • Dec 9, 1848 • 150 years

This American writer and journalist, born at Eatonton, GA, is best known as the creator of the beloved "Uncle Remus" tales, some of the first recorded black folk tales. Among noted works: the Remus stories *Uncle Remus, His Songs and His Sayings*; *Nights with Uncle Remus*; and *Uncle Remus and Brer Rabbit*; other works, *Mingo, and Other Sketches in Black and White* and *Gabriel Tolliver*. Died July 3, 1908, at Atlanta.

Willa Cather

Birth • Dec 7, 1873 • 125 years

Born at Winchester, VA, Cather is known for her novels about early-20th-century American life, especially on the frontier, which often explored enduring values and condemned a changing world. Among noted works: *O Pioneers!*, *One of Ours* (Pulitzer Prize 1922), *Death Comes to the Archbishop*. Died Apr 24, 1947, at New York City.

Ford Madox Ford

Birth • Dec 17, 1873 • 125 years

Born Ford Hermann Hueffer at Merton, Surrey, Ford founded the *English Review* in 1908, which published the top writers of his day, including D.H. Lawrence, Ezra Pound and Wyndham Lewis. The novelist and critic also collaborated on several books with his friend Joseph Conrad. Among noted works: *The Good Soldier*, considered his best work, and his *Parade's End* series. Died June 26, 1939, at Deauville, France.

Alfred Jarry

Birth • Sept 8, 1873 • 125 years

French playwright and poet Jarry, born at Laval, is known for his outrageous humor and bizarre lifestyle. His most famous work, the savage farce *Ubu roi* (which caused a riot when it opened), is considered the seminal work of the theater of the absurd. Among other noted works: surrealistic novel *The Supermale*. Died Nov 1, 1907, at Paris.

Lewis Carroll

Death • Jan 14, 1898 • 100 years

Born Charles Lutwidge Dodgson, Jan 27, 1832, at Daresbury, Cheshire, Carroll is best known for his creation of the "Alice" stories for children. Also a mathematician, he taught at Oxford and was an amateur photographer. Among noted works: fiction *Alice's Adventures in Wonderland*, *Through the Looking-Glass and What Alice Found There* and *The Hunting of the Snark*; letters to children *The Letters of Lewis Carroll*; mathematical treatise *Euclid and His Modern Rivals*. Died at Guildford, Surrey.

Spotlight on People *milestone anniversary years*

Berthold Brecht

Birth • Feb 10, 1898 • 100 years

Born at Augsburg, Germany, this playwright and poet was founder of the Berliner Ensemble, a famous theater company. Some of his plays, such as *The Threepenny Opera*, were written with composer Kurt Weill. Other plays include *Galileo, Mother Courage and her Children, The Good Woman of Setzuan,* and *The Caucasian Chalk Circle.* Though a Marxist, Brecht's works often did not fit the Communist aesthetic of Social Realism, so he was a figure of controversy in Eastern Europe as well as the West. He died at East Berlin, Aug 14, 1956.

Edward Bellamy

Death • May 22, 1898 • 100 years

One of the earliest American socialists, this writer and journalist, born Mar 26, 1850, at Chicopee Falls, MA, wrote for the *Springfield Union* and the *New York Evening Post* and published his own magazines, *The Nationalist* and *The New Nation*, all of which he used as vehicles for promoting his social agenda. Among noted works: *Looking Backward, 2,000–1887, Equality* and *Edward Bellamy Speaks Again!*. Died at Chicopee Falls.

Federico García Lorca

Birth • June 5, 1898 • 100 years

Spanish poet and playwright, born at Fuente Vaqueros, García Lorca is considered the greatest and most widely known poet in the Spanish-speaking world. He organized festivals and traveling theater and was instrumental in popularizing Andalusian Gypsy song, a strong influence in his own work. Among noted works: poetry collections *Primer romancero gitano (First Book of Gypsy Ballads), Poet in New York and Other Poems* and *Lament for the Death of a Bullfighter and Other Poems*; plays *Blood Wedding, Yerma, La casa de Bernarda Alba (The House of Bernard Alba), Doña Rosita la soltera (Doña Rosita the Spinster)*. Killed by Franco's troops during the Spanish Civil War on the night of Aug 19–20, 1936.

Stephen Vincent Benét

Birth • July 22, 1898 • 100 years

An influential writer of the early 20th century, Benét, born at Bethlehem, PA, is known for the narrative Civil War poem "John Brown's Body," the novel *The Red Badge of Courage* and the short story "The Devil and Daniel Webster," among other works. Died Mar 13, 1943, at New York City.

Stéphane Mallarmé

Death • Sept 9,1898 • 100 years

Born Mar 18, 1842, at Paris, French poet Mallarmé is credited as one of the greatest influences on 20th-century poetry and remembered as the center of the "Tuesdays of the rue de Rome" group of writers and artists. His most well-known poem, *L'Après-midi d'un faune*, considered one of the most skillful of French poems, inspired *Prélude à l'après-midi d'un faune*, which Debussy composed as an overture to the recital of the poem. Also known for translating into French the poetry of Edgar Allan Poe. Died at Valvins, near Fontainebleau.

Music

William Byrd

Death • July 4, 1623 • 375 years

Born in the middle of the Elizabethan era, around 1543, Byrd is considered the premier English composer of the age. Organist at the Chapel Royal, he composed for both the Anglican and Roman Catholic Churches. Among noted works: three Latin masses, 140 harpsichord pieces and various secular vocal music. Died at Stondon, Essex.

(Victor Antoine) Édouard Lalo

Birth • Jan 27, 1823 • 175 years

Sophisticated orchestration and memorable melodies distinguish the music of this French composer born at Lille who also played violin and viola. Among noted works: *Violin Concerto in F Major, Symphonie Espagnole* for violin and orchestra, *Symphony in G Minor* and the opera *Le Roi d'Ys*. Died Apr 22, 1892, at Paris.

Gaetano Donizetti

Death • Apr 8, 1848 • 150 years

An enormously successful Italian composer born at Bergamo on Nov 29, 1797, Donizetti produced operas in both Italian and French. His body of work includes 65 operas and operettas, two masses and other church music, cantatas, string quartets and various orchestral works. Among noted works: *L'Elisir d'Amore (The Elixir of Love)*, *Lucia di Lammermoor* and his comic masterpiece *Don Pasquale*. Died at Bergamo at age 50.

W. C. Handy

Birth • Nov 16, 1873 • 125 years

African-American composer born at Florence, AL, William Christopher Handy integrated ragtime music with the traditional blues sound during the early jazz years. Because of the racial taboos of his day, Handy started his own publishing house to publish not only his own music but also anthologies of spirituals and blues and studies of black musicians. He also composed marches and symphonic pieces. Among noted works: "Memphis Blues," "St. Louis Blues," "Beale Street Blues" and "Careless Love." Died Mar 28, 1958, at New York City.

Sergey Vasilyevich Rachmaninoff

Birth • Apr 1, 1873 • 125 years

Considered the last of the great romantic composers as well as a brilliant concert pianist and a leading conductor, Rachmaninoff was born at Onege, Novgorod. Following the Russian Revolution in 1917, he relocated to the US, but it never became his home and he composed little after that, putting most of his energy into concertizing and conducting. Among noted works: his four piano concertos and 15 *Études-Tableaux*, *Rhapsody on a Theme of Paganini*,*Symphony No 3 in A Minor*, choral symphony *The Bells* and the symphonic tone poem *The Isle of the Dead*. Died Mar 28, 1943, at Beverly Hills, CA.

George Gershwin

Birth • Sept 26, 1898 • 100 years

Brooklyn-born Gershwin was one of the first composers to incorporate jazz rhythms into his music, from popular songs to musicals and concert works. Lyrics for most of his music were written by his brother, Ira Gershwin. Among noted works: songs "Swanee," "The Man I Love," "I Got Rhythm," "Strike Up the Band" and "Someone to Watch Over Me;" musicals *Lady Be Good*, *Funny Face*; tone poem *An American in Paris*; concerto *Rhapsody in Blue* and his masterpiece, the opera *Porgy and Bess*. Died July 11, 1937, at Beverly Hills, CA.

Roy Harris

Birth • Feb 12, 1898 • 100 years

Credited with bringing a distinct American flavor to his music, Harris, born at Lincoln County, OK, drew on all facets of American culture in his compositions. Among them: *Folk-Song Symphony* in which he included American folk tunes; *Sixth Symphony*, which references Lincoln's Gettysburg Address; and *Ninth Symphony*, based on poetry of Walt Whitman. Died Oct 1, 1979, at Santa Monica, CA.

Vincent Youmans

Birth • Sept 27, 1898 • 100 years

American pop music composer, born at New York City, is noted particularly for producing musical entertainment for servicemen during World War I. He composed music for Broadway, as well as many hit songs. Noted works include musicals *Two Little Girls in Blue*, *No, No, Nanette* and *Hit the Deck*; film score for Fred Astaire's first film pairing with Ginger Rogers, *Flying Down to Rio*; songs "Sometimes I'm Happy," "Without a Song" and "Time on My Hands." Died Apr 5, 1946, at Denver.

Art

Hans Burgkmair the Elder

Birth • 1473 • 525 years

This German Renaissance painter and woodcut artist was a pioneer in the use of the color woodcut. His 700 woodcuts helped spread the Renaissance style throughout Germany. Also known for his religious works. Died 1531 at Augsburg.

Perugino

Death • 1523 • 475 years

An early Italian Renaissance painter born at Città della Pieve, Umbria, in about 1445, Perugino is noted for his religious paintings and frescoes and also as a teacher of Raphael. Among noted works: *Madonna with Saints and Angels*, *The Pietà* (Pitti Palace at Florence) and a fresco in the Sistine Chapel,

Christ Giving the Keys to Saint Peter.

Gerard David

Death • 1523 • 475 years

Netherlandish painter born at Oudewater in about 1460, David is remembered for his stark but rich and subtly colored altarpieces and panels. Influenced by such early Flemish painters as Jan van Eyck and Hans Memling, he brought a fine sense of spatial organization to his art. Among noted works: the two panels named *Judgment of Cambyses* and *Virgin and Child with Angels and Saints.* Died Aug 13, 1523, at Bruges.

Francisco de Zurbarán

Birth • Nov 7, 1598 • 400 years

This Spanish painter of religious subjects, born at Fuente de Cantos, Badajoz, combined mysticism and realism in his works, achieving a uniquely Spanish flavor. Among noted works: *Crucifixion* and *The Apotheosis of St. Thomas Aquinas.* Died Aug 27, 1664, at Madrid.

Gian Lorenzo Bernini

Birth • Dec 7, 1598 • 400 years

Born at Naples, the enormously prolific Bernini was the most significant artistic talent of the Italian baroque, the range of his talents and interests paralleling the greatest of the Renaissance artists. Largely remembered for his sculpture (portrait busts, fountain and tomb design), he was also gifted as a painter, architect, draftsman, stage set designer–almost anything he set his hand to, even fireworks displays. He was one of the architects for St. Peter's in Rome. Among noted works: sculptures *The Abduction of Proserpina* and his masterpiece *Ecstasy of Saint Teresa*; architectural designs for the palaces Palazzo Ludovisi (Montecitorio) and Palazzo Chigi and for the church at Castelgandolfo and the magnificent Sant' Andrea al Quirinale in Rome. Bernini continued working actively until his death on Nov 28, 1680, a week before his 82nd birthday.

Grinling Gibbons

Birth • Apr 4, 1648 • 350 years

The decorative woodwork carvings of this English sculptor, ranging from mantels to wall panels, graced such places as Windsor Castle, Hampton Court and Trinity College at Oxford. Gibbon's style became a model for English interior decoration during the Baroque period. Died Aug 3, 1721, at London.

Salvator Rosa

Death • 1673 • 325 years

Rosa, Italian baroque painter and etcher born in 1615, earned acclaim for his dramatic landscapes featuring rocky crags and blasted trees, often illuminated by lightning flashes and populated by bandits and mythical beings. Rosa prefigured the romantic movement in Europe and England by 150 years, and his work was greatly admired by the romantic painters. Also well known in his time as a satirical poet, musician and actor. Died Mar 15, 1673, at Rome.

Sir Joshua Reynolds

Birth • July 16, 1723 • 275 years

Born at Plympton, Devonshire the son of a cleric, Reynolds became *the* English portrait painter of his time, painting more than 2,000 portraits. Much of his work was done in the grand manner (huge paintings of important people); he was knighted in 1768 and appointed painter to the king in 1784. Among noted works: *The Tragic Muse* (portrait of actress Sarah Siddons) and *Lady Sarah Bunbury.* Died Feb 23, 1792, at London.

Jacques-Louis David

Birth • Aug 30, 1748 • 250 years

A French painter born at Paris, David developed the neoclassical style that combined classical forms with contemporary subject matter, capturing events of the French Revolution and later the exploits of Napoleon I. Also a prolific portraitist, painting in a more intimate style. Among noted works: the enormous *Coronation of Napoleon and Josephine* and the portrait *Madame Récamier.* Died Dec 29, 1825, at Brussels.

Eugène Delacroix

Birth • Apr 26, 1798 • 200 years

Born at Charenton–Saint Maurice, French painter (Ferdinand-Victor) Eugène Delacroix trained in the French neoclassic style of David but gravitated to the looser painting of Rubens and the spirit of his contemporary, early romantic Theodore Gericault, whose depictions of brutal action appealed to him. Much of Delacroix's work expressed the romantic notion of the struggle of the human spirit toward freedom. His paintings are characterized by violent, colorful subjects engaged in dramatic action. Among noted works: *Death of Sardanapalus*, and the famous *Liberty Leading the People*. Died Aug 13, 1863, at Paris.

Mathew B. Brady

Birth • 1823 • 175 years

Famous particularly for his portraits of Abraham Lincoln, American photography pioneer Brady was born at Warren County, NY, and later became the official photographer of the American Civil War. In addition to more than 3,500 war photographs–an incredible feat considering all the heavy equipment he had to haul with him and the long exposure times that made people look so stiff in early photography–his work included portraits of most of the important people of the time. Died Jan 15, 1896, at New York City.

Louis Comfort Tiffany

Birth • Feb 18, 1848 • 150 years

An American craftsman, decorator and designer born at New York City, Tiffany originally trained as a painter but became intrigued by stained glass. At his Tiffany Glass and Decorating Company he developed unique kinds of glass and pioneered the art nouveau style of design. Among noted works: design for the chapel for the World's Columbian Exposition at Chicago, an enormous glass curtain for the Palacio de Bellas Artes at Mexico City and a vast array of pieces in his Favrile glass. Established the Louis Comfort Tiffany Foundation for art students at his estate. Died Jan 17, 1933, at New York City.

Paul Gauguin

Birth • June 7, 1848 • 150 years

Paris-born (Eugène-Henri-) Paul Gauguin was a married businessman and weekend painter when at about age 35 he left his family and his job to devote himself to painting. Seeking emotional release through painting, he rejected impressionism in favor of his own style, marked by brilliant color and strong, simple forms, ultimately becoming one of the most famous postimpressionists. Among noted works: *The Vision After the Sermon–Jacob Wrestling with the Angel* and *Manao Tupapau–The Spirit of the Dead Watching*, one of his many famous paintings done in Tahiti. Died May 8, 1903, at age 54, at Atuana, Marquesas Islands.

Thomas Cole

Death • Feb 11, 1848 • 150 years

Born at Bolton, Lancashire, England, Feb 1, 1801, Cole immigrated to the US in 1819 and became the first significant American landscape painter. He and his emulators became known as the Hudson River school. Among noted works: *The Oxbow* and *In the Catskills*. He died at Catskill, NY.

Frank Duveneck

Birth • Oct 9, 1848 • 150 years

American painter and etcher born at Covington, KY, is known primarily for his portraits done in the Munich style. Among noted works: *The Whistling Boy*. Died Jan 3, 1919, at Cincinnati, OH.

Spotlight on People *milestone anniversary years*

Augustus Saint-Gaudens

Birth • Mar 1, 1848 • 150 years

Dublin-born but raised in New York City, this American sculptor is noted for his many public monuments, among them the statue of Admiral David Farragut at Madison Square in New York City, of Abraham Lincoln at Chicago, of General William Tecumseh Sherman on horseback in New York's Central Park and the *Adams Memorial* in Rock Creek Cemetery, Washington, DC. Died Aug 3, 1907, at Cornish, NH.

J.E.H. MacDonald

Birth • May 12, 1873 • 125 years

English-Canadian landscape painter known for his use of bright color and stylization, a member of the Group of Seven. Died Nov 22, 1932, at Toronto.

Aubrey Beardsley

Death • Mar 16, 1898 • 100 years

Known for his black and white art nouveau illustrations for books and magazines, Beardsley was born Aug 21, 1872, at Brighton, England. Among noted works: many of Oscar Wilde's books, Malory's *Le Morte Darthur*, *The Savoy* magazine illustrations. Died of consumption at age 25 at Menton, France.

Gustave Moreau

Death • Apr 18, 1898 • 100 years

Religious and mythological subjects were the focus of French painter Moreau, born Apr 6, 1826, at Paris. Moving away from his neoclassical training, Moreau adopted a somewhat stylized method that emphasized sensuality and color. Among noted works: *Apparition* and *Oedipus and the Sphinx*. He was also an influential teacher. Died at Paris.

Alexander Calder

Birth • July 22, 1898 • 100 years

An American sculptor born at Philadelphia, PA, the son and grandson of sculptors. Calder spent time in Europe, where he was influenced by painters such as Miró and Mondrian, which led to his development of the mobile and stabile forms. Calder's work includes giant stabiles and mobiles created for public buildings and spaces all over the world, the most famous being the enormous red and black mobile hung in the National Gallery of Art at Washington, DC. Died Nov 11, 1976, at New York City.

Henry Moore

Birth • July 30, 1898 • 100 years

British sculptor Moore, born at Castleford, Yorkshire, created large human figures, both abstract and realistic. Many of these wood and stone sculptures were rounded pieces pierced by numerous holes to create positive and negative spaces. Among noted works: *Reclining Figure* and *Internal and External Forms*, as well as a series of drawings made during the London Blitz, called shelter drawings. Died Aug 31, 1986, at Much Hadham.

Berenice Abbott

Birth • July 17, 1898 • 100 years

Abbott, an American photographer born at Springfield, OH, is known for her photographic recording of New York City and for her photographic exploration in the field of physics. Among noted works: *Changing New York*. Died Dec 9, 1991, at Abbot Village, ME.

René François Ghislain Magritte

Birth • Nov 21, 1898 • 100 years

This Belgian surrealist painter, born at Lessines, is considered the primary exponent of *magic realism*. Among his surrealist versions of famous paintings: *Madame Récamier de David*. Died Aug 15, 1967, at Brussels.

Ben Shahn

Birth • Sept 12, 1898 • 100 years

Born at Kovno, Lithuania, painter and lithographer Shahn immigrated to the US in 1906. He is noted for his use of strong line and clear flat colors and for the social consciousness or "social realism" he expressed in his sympathetic portrayals of the less fortunate and his negative portraits of the powerful. Among noted works: *The Passion of Sacco and Vanzetti*. Died Mar 14, 1969, at New York City.

Architecture

Sir Christopher Wren

Death • Feb 25, 1723 • 275 years

English architect, designer and astronomer, Wren was born Oct 20, 1632, at East Knoyle, Wiltshire, and is remembered chiefly for the rebuilding of St. Paul's Cathedral and many other public buildings after the devastation of the Great London Fire of 1666. Knighted in 1673, he also executed private commissions such as the new library for Trinity College at Cambridge and many projects for the crown, including additions to Kensington Palace and Hampton Court. Died at Hampton Court and was buried in St. Paul's.

Eliel Saarinen

Birth • Aug 20, 1873 • 125 years

Finnish architect (Gottlieb) Eliel Saarinen was born at Rantasalmi and moved to the US in 1923 after placing second in the Chicago Tribune Building design competition. Influenced modern architecture through his use of clean lines and basic materials and through the noted school of design and architecture he designed and directed, Cranbrook Academy of Art in Michigan. Died July 1, 1950, at Cranbrook.

(Hugo) Alvar Henrik Aalto

Birth • Feb 3, 1898 • 100 years

The work of Finnish architect and designer Aalto, born at Kuortane, featured both elegance and utility. Among noted works: the Paimio Tuberculosis Sanatorium, the Finnish Pavilion for the 1937 Paris Exposition, the Finlandia House cultural center in Helsinki and the Baker House dormitory at MIT. Many of his furniture designs are still being produced today. Died May 11, 1976, at Helsinki.

(Jean Louis) Charles Garnier

Death • Aug 3, 1898 • 100 years

This French architect of the beaux arts school was born Nov 6, 1825, at Paris. He was known for his eclecticism, which is evident in the opulent Paris Opéra, considered as a masterwork of his century. Died at Paris.

History

Jules Michelet

Birth • Aug 21, 1798 • 200 years

French historian and moralist Michelet, born at Paris, devoted his life to forming a synthesis between the history of the French people and their religious destiny. A firm supporter of the French republican movement, he suffered under the rule of Napoleon II as the dictator attempted to reconstitute the former glories of the empire. With the return of the French republic, he resumed his work as the nation's historian. His histories are noted for their dramatic narrative style. Among noted works: histories *History of France, The People, History of the French Revolution*; moral and religious works *Love* and *The Bible of Humanity*. Died Feb 9, 1874, at Hyères.

Francis Parkman

Birth • Sept 16, 1823 • 175 years

Parkman is remembered best as the author of *The Oregon Trail: Sketches of a Prairie and Rocky-Mountain Life*, an account of his experiences on his journey of exploration to the American West. The American historian, born at Jamaica Plain, MA, was also an authority on English and French influence in North America. Among other noted works: his monumental eight-volume history *England and France in North America*. Died Nov 8, 1893, at Jamaica Plain. Elected to the Hall of Fame of Great Americans in 1915.

Brooks Adams

Birth • June 24, 1848 • 100 years

American historian, born at Quincy, MA, originally trained as a lawyer, is known for his approach to historical analysis based on economics. Among noted works: histories *The Law of Civilization and Decay, America's Economic Supremacy, The New Empire*; political science *The Theory of Social Revolution*, an examination of American democracy. Died Feb 13, 1927, at Quincy.

Spotlight on People *milestone anniversary years*

Exploration

Jedediah Strong Smith

Birth • June 24, 1798 • 200 years

Starting out as a fur trapper, Smith went in search of trade routes and ended up a noted explorer and trail blazer of the American West. He began at the Great Salt Lake and set out west, becoming probably the first white man to arrive in California from the east. He then journeyed northeast, becoming the first American to cross the Sierra Nevada, and continued across present-day Nevada to became the first American to cross the Great Salt Lake Desert. He finally ended up at Fort Vancouver (now Vancouver, WA). Born at Bainbridge, NY, died May 27, 1831 at age 33, killed by Comanches on the Santa Fe Trail.

David Livingstone

Death • 1873 • 125 years

Livingstone left his native Scotland for Africa as a physician, missionary and explorer. Born Mar 19, 1813, at Blantyre, he ultimately was hailed as one of the most important explorers of the interior regions of the continent. His work contributed to the mapping of great portions of Africa, a fact recognized by the British Royal Geographical Society. It was in 1866 that he embarked on his last missionary trip, during which he also planned to chart the central Africa watershed and search for the source of the Nile. When he dropped from sight, worldwide concern moved the enterprising newsman Henry Morton Stanley to lead a search expedition, culminating in the immortal greeting, "Dr. Livingstone, I presume." Remaining in Africa to continue his explorations, Livingstone died about Apr 30, 1873, at Chitambo (in present-day Zambia). His heart was buried in his beloved Africa, while his body was shipped to England and interred in Westminster Abbey.

American Politics

William Henry Harrison

Birth • Feb 9, 1773 • 225 years

The ninth president of the US, born at Berkeley County, VA, had the shortest presidential term in history–he died 32 days after his inauguration in March 1841, having caught pneumonia during the festivities. Harrison is often remembered for his campaign nickname "General Mum," bestowed by his opponents because he took his party leaders' advice and kept his mouth shut on the issues, and for his campaign slogan "Tippecanoe and Tyler too" (his running mate was John Tyler), which alluded to his having put down the Shawnee uprising at Tippecanoe incited by his policies as governor of the Indiana Territory. During his time as governor he negotiated many treaties with Native Americans to gain control of enormous areas of tribal lands for the US. Died Apr 4, 1841, at Washington, DC.

Mirabeau Buonaparte Lamar

Birth • Aug 16, 1798 • 200 years

American soldier and Texas hero Lamar, born at Warren County, GA, is remembered chiefly as the commander at the Battle of San Jacinto and as second president of the republic of Texas. He also laid the groundwork for the Texas public school system and the University of Texas. Died Dec 19, 1859, at Richmond, TX.

Schuyler Colfax

Birth • Mar 23, 1823 • 175 years

Born at New York City, Colfax moved with his family to Indiana at age 13. He later became a journalist and politician, a three-term speaker of the House of Representatives and vice president of the US during the first term of U.S. Grant. He was forced out of politics by scandal. Died Jan 13, 1885, at Mankato, MN.

William Marcy "Boss" Tweed

Birth • Apr 3, 1823 • 175 years

Having risen from lowly bookkeeper to political boss, Tweed used his power as leader of the Tweed ring to plunder the city in which he was born during New York's infamous Tammany Hall days. Estimates of the amount of money pocketed by Tweed and his underlings range from \$30 million–\$200 million. Following exposure of the corruption by the *New York Times*, Tweed went to prison for embezzlement for a year, then, sent back on other charges, escaped and fled to Spain, where he was caught and returned to prison. Died Apr 12, 1878, at New York City.

John Sherman

Birth • May 10, 1823 • 175 years

Ohio congressman and US cabinet member, born at Lancaster, OH, Sherman is noted as author of the Sherman Silver Purchase Act and the Sherman Antitrust Act. He was appointed secretary of the treasury by Rutherford Hayes and of state by William McKinley. Died Oct 22, 1900, at Washington, DC.

John Quincy Adams

Death • Feb 23, 1848 •150 years

The sixth president of the US, Adams was the only president to be the son of a president. Born July 11, 1767, at Braintree (later renamed Quincy), MA, he served as president 1825–29, then was elected to eight terms as a US congressman. He was known particularly for his skills in foreign policy and diplomacy, representing the new United States in many foreign countries and serving as secretary of state under James Monroe before becoming president. Died at Washington, DC, two days after suffering a stroke on the floor of the House of Representatives.

Alfred E. Smith

Birth • Dec 30, 1873 • 125 years

Born at New York City, Smith became a four-term, reform-minded governor of New York but staged two unsuccessful Democratic campaigns for US president. His Roman Catholic faith was a big issue in the campaigns. In later life Smith was instrumental in having the Empire State Building constructed. Died Oct 4, 1944, at New York City.

Justin Smith Morrill

Death • Dec 28, 1898 • 100 years

Vermont politician Morrill, born Apr 14, 1810, at Strafford, VT, represented his state in the US Congress for more than four decades. While there, he sponsored the Morrill Act, which established the land-grant college system that was the basis for the development of many state universities. Died at Washington, DC.

Founding Fathers

Early American Patriots

1998 is a milestone anniversary year for a number of the men involved in the events leading to the establishment of the United States of America as a nation and/or of the drafting and adoption of the US Constitution.

- **John Witherspoon** was born 275 years ago on Feb 15, 1723, at Gifford, East Lothian, Scotland, and immigrated to America in 1768 to serve as president of the College of New Jersey (now Princeton University). Head of the Somerset County Committee of Correspondence; member of the Continental Congress; the only clergyman to sign the Declaration of Independence; delegate to the NJ convention for ratification of the US Constitution. Died Nov 15, 1794, at Tusculum, NJ.
- **William Livingston**, was born 275 years ago in Nov 1723, at Albany, NY. Later he moved to New Jersey, where he was governor 1776–1790; NJ delegate to the Constitutional Convention and a signer of that document. Died July 25, 1790, at Elizabethtown, NJ.
- **George Read**, born 225 years ago on Sept 18, 1773, in Maryland, grew up in Delaware and became a member of the Continental Congress, signer of the Declaration of Independence, delegate to the Constitutional Convention and a signer of that document and one of the first US senators from Delaware. Died 200 years ago on Sept 21, 1798, at New Castle, DE.
- **James Wilson**, born on Sept 14, 1742, near St. Andrews, Scotland, immigrated to America in 1765, settling in Philadelphia. He became a member of the Continental Congress, signer of the Declaration of Independence, a delegate to the Constitutional Convention and one of the first US Supreme Court justices. Died 200 years ago on Aug 21, 1798, at Edenton, NC.
- **Lewis Morris**, born Apr 8, 1726, at Morrisania, NY, became a member of the Continental Congress and signer of the Declaration of Independence, a brigadier general of the NY militia in the Revolutionary War and a delegate to NY state convention for ratification of the US

Constitution. Died 200 years ago on Jan 22, 1798.

- **George Cabot**, born on Dec 3, 1751, at Salem, MA, became a delegate to MA state convention for ratification of the US Constitution and an early US senator from Massachusetts. Died 175 years ago on Apr 18, 1823, at Boston, MA.

World Politics

Marie de Médicis

Birth • Apr 26, 1573 • 425 years

Born at Florence, daughter of the duke of Tuscany, the Italian noblewoman became queen of France as second wife of King Henry IV and regent during the minority of Louix XIII. Known for political intrigue that got her tossed out of the palace by her son for five years, she was eventually sent into permanent exile. Immortalized by Rubens in a series of 21 paintings. Died July 3, 1642, at Cologne.

Arthur James Balfour

Birth • July 25, 1848 • 150 years

The British prime minister, Conservative party leader and first Earl of Balfour, born at Whittingehame, Scotland, is known for his work in foreign relations during World War I and for the Balfour Declaration of Great Britain's support for the creation of a Jewish homeland in Palestine. Balfour was a delegate to the Versailles peace conference, to the League of Nations and to the Washington Conference. Died Mar 19, 1930, at Woking, England.

William Melbourne

Death • Nov 24, 1848 • 150 years

English statesman, born Mar 15, 1779, at Brockett Hall, Hertfordshire, Melbourne left his imprint on history by shaping Queen Victoria's early world view with his moderate Whig politics. As prime minister, he educated the young queen in the arts of politics and diplomacy. Died at Brockett Hall.

Zhou Enlai (Chou En-lai)

Birth • 1898 • 100 years

Chinese political leader, born at Huaian, Jiangsu Province, Zhou was one of the founders of the Chinese Communist party and the leader with Mao Zedong (Mao Tse-tung) of the legendary Long March. A keen politician, he became the first premier of the People's Republic of China and was instrumental in holding the country together during the infamous Cultural Revolution. In 1972 he signed the Shanghai Communiqué with US president Richard Nixon, the first step in normalizing relations between the two powers. Died Jan 8, 1976, at Beijing.

Golda Meir

Birth • May 3, 1898 • 100 years

A founder of the state of Israel and one of its prime ministers. Born Goldie Mabovitz in Kyyiv, Russia, Meir immigrated to the US in 1906 with her family, where she grew up in Milwaukee, WI. An ardent Zionist, she moved with her husband to Palestine in 1921 and was a prime mover throughout the fight for an independent Jewish homeland, and then was prominent in Israeli government and politics for more than 35 years. Meir was prime minister at the time of the Yom Kippur War, which led her to resign in the face of charges of military unpreparedness. She is also fondly remembered for her question to Egyptian prime minister Anwar Sadat when he made his historic trip to Israel: "What took you so long?" Died Dec 8, 1978, at Jerusalem.

Bismarck

Death • July 30, 1898 • 100 years

Prusso-German statesman Prince Otto Edward Leopold von Bismarck, born Apr 1, 1815, at Schönhausen, is considered the designer of the modern German state and served as its first chancellor. He was a clever, ruthless politician who let nothing deter him from his objectives, as expressed in his famous statement, "The great questions of the day will not be settled by speeches and majority decision . . . but by blood and iron." Died at his estate, Friedrichsruh, near Hamburg.

William Gladstone

Death • May 19, 1898 • 100 years

The British politician, born Dec 29, 1809, at Liverpool, is known as *the* liberal prime minister of England, champion of labor and civil service and supporter of Irish Home Rule. Gladstone and Benjamin Disraeli were celebrated verbal sparring partners in Parliament. Died at Hawarden, Wales and buried in Westminster Abbey.

Economics

Adam Smith

Birth • June 5, 1723 • 275 years

Scottish social philosopher and political economist, born at Kirkcaldy, Fife, considered one of the founders of the science of economics. Smith's basic concept of the marketplace as driven by "the invisible hand of competition" based on individual self-interest is still used today. Among noted works: the famous *An Inquiry into the Nature and Causes of the Wealth of Nations*; *The Theory of Moral Sentiments*, an expression of his moral philosophy. Died July 17, 1790, at Edinburgh.

John Stuart Mill

Death • May 8, 1873 • 125 years

Born May 20, 1806, at London, he was the son of Scottish economist, historian and philosopher James Mill, and is viewed historically as a giant in his field. Mill was the transitional link between 18th- and 19th-century economic and philosophical thought and was part of the movement that championed the idea of individual liberty and human reason. Among noted works: his celebrated essay "On Liberty;" *Utilitarianism*; *Principles of Political Economy*; *On the Subjection of Women* (he supported equality and suffrage for women); *Autobiography*. Died at Avignon, France.

Law

Sir William Blackstone

Birth • July 10, 1723 • 275 years

The understandable style and logical presentation of his four-volume *Commentaries on the Laws of England* helped establish Blackstone's seminal work as the cornerstone for the study of law in the UK and the US. Among other noted works of the British jurist and legal scholar, born at London: *An Analysis of the Laws of England*. Died Feb 14, 1780, at London.

Thomas Erskine

Death • Nov 17, 1823 • 175 years

British legal advocate and statesman Erskine, born Jan 10, 1750, at Edinburgh, Scotland, is remembered as an opponent of oppressive laws and a champion of the rights of the accused. Considered England's premier advocate, he defended the principles of freedom of the press, trial by jury and the right to counsel. Among noted clients: American Thomas Paine, whom he defended on the charge of sedition following publication of Paine's *Rights of Man*; James Hadfield, who attempted to kill King George III and on whose behalf Erskine mounted the first insanity defense. Died at West Lothian, Scotland.

Salmon Portland Chase

Death • May 7, 1873 • 125 years

An American statesman and chief justice of the US Supreme Court, born Jan 13, 1808, at Cornish, NH, Chase is remembered as an important foe of slavery and founder of both the Free-Soil and Republican parties. He served as a US senator, governor of Ohio, and secretary of the treasury under Lincoln, who later appointed him to the Supreme Court as chief justice. He presided over the impeachment trial of Andrew Johnson and wrote the minority opinion in the famous Slaughterhouse cases. Died at New York City.

William O. Douglas

Birth • Oct 16, 1898 • 100 years

Douglas was an American jurist and an associate justice of the US Supreme Court, born at Maine, MN, and known as the leader of the liberal wing of the famous Warren Court. Among noted controversial opinions during his record 36-year court tenure: a ban on prayers in public schools; the right of privacy as implied in the US Constitution, the right to abortion in *Roe v. Wade*; dissents against making draft-card-burning a crime and in the exemption of church property from local real estate taxes. Among noted works: *The Bible and the Schools*, *Towards a Global Federalism*. Died Jan 19, 1980, at Washington, DC.

Spotlight on People *milestone anniversary years*

Military

Maarten Tromp

Birth • Apr 23, 1598 • 400 years

Dutch naval officer Tromp, born at Brielle, is credited with destroying a large Spanish fleet in February 1639 and defeating combined Spanish and Portuguese fleets in September of that year. He is particularly celebrated for his routing of an English fleet on Nov 30, 1652, (during the First Anglo-Dutch War), after which legend says he sailed up the English Channel with a broom attached to his ship's masthead to symbolize his having swept the enemy from the seas. Died in battle at sea Aug 10, 1653.

Charles Wilkes

Birth • Apr 3, 1798 • 200 years

Born at New York City, American naval officer and explorer Wilkes is most remembered for the *Trent* affair: interrupting a British ship during the Civil War to take into custody the Confederacy's commissioners to England and France almost caused the British to declare war on the Union. He was later court-martialed because of this and other misguided actions. He also served as the first head of the Depot of Charts and Instruments, the forerunner of the Naval Observatory, and as head of a government expedition that explored the northwest coast and part of Antarctica (named Wilkes Land after him). He is known for having charted some 300 Pacific islands and circled the globe. Died Feb 8, 1877.

Thomas Higginson

Birth • Dec 22, 1823 • 175 years

Higginson was an abolitionist who enlisted at the beginning of the Civil War and became commander of the first black regiment of the US Army, an experience he recounted in *Army Life in a Black Regiment.* An American Unitarian minister and soldier, born at Cambridge, MA, he is also noted as a friend of poet Emily Dickinson and as posthumous editor of her two-volume work *Poems.* Died May 9, 1911, at Cambridge.

Stephen Kearny

Death • 1848 • 150 years

American Army officer, born in 1794, at Newark, NJ, Kearny is remembered for his distinguished service in the Battle of Queenston Heights during the War of 1812 and for helping to capture New Mexico and California territories in the Mexican War.

Religion and Philosophy

Girolamo Savonarola

Death • May 23, 1498 • 500 years

Italian priest Savonarola, born Sept 21, 1452, at Ferrara, was martyred for his deep desire to reform the Roman Catholic Church. Unlike Calvin and Luther, who broke away from the Roman Church, Savonarola tried to address the corruption from within. He was also a supporter of the republican form of government, a position that further ensured his doom. After being convicted in three separate trials for which the "evidence" was secured by torturing him, Savonarola was publicly hanged and burned. Died at Florence.

Philippe de Mornay

Death • Nov 11, 1623 • 375 years

Born Nov 5, 1549, at Buhy, Normandy, Mornay was a leader of the French Protestant movement (the Huguenots) during the turbulent period of French history referred to as the "wars of religion." Died at La-Forêt-sur-Sèvre.

Robert Barclay

Birth • Dec 23, 1648 • 350 years

Born at Gordonstown, Moray County, Scottish Quaker Barclay walked the streets of Aberdeen wearing sackcloth and ashes. Along with William Penn and others, he was later granted land in "East Jersey," a province of the American colonies. Barclay was named governor, but he never went to America. Among noted works: *Treatise on Universal Love* and *An Apology for the True Christian Divinity, as the Same Is Held Forth and Preached by the People Called in Scorn Quakers.* Died Oct 3, 1690, near Aberdeen.

Madame Guyon

Birth • Apr 13, 1648 • 350 years

The French mystic born Jeanne Marie Bouvier de la Motte Guyon at Montargis is known for having developed the doctrine of quietism, a philosophy that centered on religious contemplation. In and out of trouble with the Roman Church, she was imprisoned on two occasions, then banished from Paris. Among noted works: *The Song of Solomon Interpreted According to Its Mystical Sense.* Died June 9, 1717, at Blois.

William Tennent

Birth • 1673 • 325 years

The Presbyterian minister and educator, born in Ireland, immigrated to America about 1718, where he established a school that came to be called the Log College, which is said to have eventually evolved into Princeton University. Many of its graduates founded other schools as the country pushed westward. Died May 6, 1746, at Neshaminy, Pennsylvania Colony.

Increase Mather

Death • Aug 23, 1723 • 275 years

Born June 21, 1639, at Dorchester, MA, pastor of the famous North Church in Boston, 1664–1723; he also served as president of Harvard College 1685–1701 and was responsible for the restoration of the Massachusetts Charter after it was revoked by King Charles II. Mather opposed the witch hunt mentality of the time, writing that it was better to let ten witches go than condemn one innocent person. Died at Boston.

Jeremy Bentham

Birth • Feb 15, 1748 • 250 years

The British philosopher, economist and jurist, born at London, is known as the founder of the doctrine of utilitarianism (what's right is whatever produces the greatest happiness for the greatest number of people); as a jurist who reformed the English legal system based on a general theory of law and morality; as a leader of the Philosophical Radicals, a group that included John Stuart Mill; and as the man who asked for his body to be dissected in front of his friends–it was and is kept in a glass case at University College. Among noted works: *Introduction to the Principles of Morals and Legislation.* Died June 6, 1832, at London.

Elias Hicks

Birth • Mar 19, 1748 • 250 years

American Quaker minister and abolitionist Hicks, born at Hempstead, NY, caused the split into Orthodox and Liberal (called Hicksite) sects in the American Society of Friends. Died Feb 27, 1830, at Jericho, NY.

Isaac Watts

Death • 1748 • 250 years

English theologian Watts, born in 1674 at Southampton, is known for his religious poems and hymn lyrics. His well-known hymns include "When I Survey the Wondrous Cross" and "O God, Our Help in Ages Past." Died at London.

Pius VII

Death • July 20, 1823 • 175 years

Born Luigi Barnaba Chiaramonti, Apr 14, 1742, at Emilia, Italy, Pius VII became pope in 1800. Fighting to maintain the authority of the Roman Catholic Church as Napoleon I sought to control the church in France, he was twice imprisoned by Napoleon. Also known for reviving the Inquisition. Died at Vatican City.

Randall Davidson

Birth • Apr 7, 1748 • 250 years

This British Anglican archbishop of Canterbury, born at Edinburgh, strengthened the Church of England through his moderating influence in various religious controversies and his strong leadership during World War I. He also promoted the ecumenical movement and worked for the League of Nations. Died May 25, 1930, at London.

Bernard Bosanquet

Birth • June 14, 1748 • 250 years

English philosopher Bosanquet, born at Rock Hall, Northumberland, is noted for his work in logic, metaphysics and aesthetics and as a leader of English absolute idealism, based on the idea that a thing can be understood only if considered in its full context. Died Feb 8, 1923, at London.

Spotlight on People *milestone anniversary years*

Saint Theresa of Lisieux

Birth • Jan 2, 1873 • 125 years

Known as "The Little Flower of Jesus" for her humility and goodness, the French Carmelite nun born Thérèse Martin at Alençon was canonized in 1925. She is a patron saint of France (along with Joan of Arc), and also of missionaries and aviators; her feast day is Oct 3. Died Sept 30, 1898, at Lisieux, France.

Norman Vincent Peale

Birth • May 31, 1898 • 100 years

This American clergyman and writer, born at Bowersville, OH, is famous for his inspirational sermons broadcast on radio promoting the value of a positive attitude and for his bestselling book *The Power of Positive Thinking*. Initially ordained in the Methodist Episcopal Church, he later became a pastor of the Reformed Church in America. Died Dec 24, 1993 at Pawling, NY.

Science

Nicolaus Copernicus

Birth • Feb 19, 1473 • 525 years

Polish astronomer and priest Copernicus, born at Torun, is celebrated for having revolutionized scientific thought by identifying the sun instead of the earth as the center of our planetary system, religious blasphemy at the time. His discovery was so controversial that he did not permit his work to be published until shortly before his death. Given the limited scientific tools of the time, Copernicus's calculations were truly astounding. Died May 24, 1543, in East Prussia.

Gabriel Fallopius

Birth • 1523 • 475 years

Born Gabriele Falloppio at Modena, Italian scientist Fallopius is credited as one of the founders of human anatomy. He achieved his extensive knowledge through dissection of human bodies (a practice the Church opposed) including adults, children, newborns and fetuses. His discoveries involving the female reproductive system resulted in the Fallopian tubes being named for him. Died Oct 3, 1562, at Padua.

Blaise Pascal

Birth • June 19, 1623 • 375 years

Considered one of the greatest minds of the 17th century, French mathematician, physicist and religious philosopher Pascal, born at Clermont-Ferrand, is credited as the founder of the modern theory of probabilities. Other accomplishments include his discoveries about pressure, including what is known as Pascal's Principle and the resulting invention of the hydraulic press and the syringe as well as perfection of the barometer and invention of the first digital calculator. At age 16 he formulated Pascal's theorem in projective geometry. Pascal embraced Jansenism in 1646, and after experiencing a mystical vision on Nov 23, 1654, he went to live at the Jansenist Port-Royal convent, giving up his research in favor of religious and philosophical studies, and ultimately becoming known for his mystical writings. Died Aug 19, 1662, at Paris.

Antoni van Leeuwenhoek

Death • Aug 26, 1723 • 275 years

Dutch naturalist, born Oct 24, 1632, at Delft, von Leeuwenhoek invented a double-convex lens microscope with a 300x magnification that allowed him to make groundbreaking discoveries about microorganisms, nutrient transport in plants and animals and sexual reproduction. As a result he refuted the popular belief in spontaneous generation. Died at Delft.

Nathaniel Bowditch

Birth • Mar 26, 1773 • 225 years

Born at Salem, MA, American mathematician and astronomer Bowditch introduced celestial navigation via *The New American Practical Navigator*, a book deemed the best guide to navigation of the time. Adopted by the US Navy, it went through more than 60 editions and has been revised and kept up to date by the US Hydrographic Office under the title *The American Practical Navigator*. His study of the swinging of pendulums produced his discovery of Bowditch curves. Died Mar 16, 1838, at Boston.

Robert Brown

Birth • Dec 21, 1773 • 225 years

Scottish botanist Brown, born at Montrose, developed the botanical department at the British Museum into an internationally acclaimed center for the study of phytotaxonomy. In the process he made several valuable discoveries: the erratic motion of microscopic particles in solution which came to be called Brownian Motion, the plant cell nucleus and the difference between angiosperms and gymnosperms. Died June 10, 1858, at London.

Sir George Cayley

Birth • Dec 27, 1773 • 225 years

This English inventor and aviation pioneer, born at Scarborough, Yorkshire, is considered the "father of aerodynamics" and credited with conducting the first successful manned glider flight. Cayley also invented the caterpillar tractor. Died Dec 15, 1857, at Scarborough.

Luigi Galvani

Death • Dec 4, 1798 • 200 years

Italian physiologist Galvani, born Sept 9, 1737, at Bologna, discovered that a frog's leg reacted to an electrical charge and that muscular contractions could be attributed to an electrical stimulus. His work led to the invention of an early type of battery. The terms "galvanism" and "galvanization" are derived from his name. Died at Bologna.

Alfred Wallace

Birth • Jan 8, 1823 • 175 years

Although it is not widely known, British naturalist Wallace, born at Usk, Monmouthshire, Wales, independently developed a theory of natural selection at the same time as Darwin, and their findings were published jointly in 1858. Wallace is also noted for his discovery of fundamental differences between animal species of Asia and of Australia and for pinpointing the zoological dividing line later known as Wallace's Line. Died Nov 7, 1913, at Broadstone, Dorset.

Edward Jenner

Death • Jan 26, 1823 • 175 years

Born May 17, 1749, at Berkeley, Gloucestershire, English physician Jenner is credited with launching the study of immunology and virology. He developed a vaccine for smallpox that has since saved millions of lives worldwide, and he originated the term *virus.* Pasteur built on Jenner's work some 75 years later. Died at Berkeley.

Edmund Cartwright

Death • Oct 30, 1823 • 175 years

Born Apr 24, 1743, at Marnham, Nottinghamshire, British inventor Cartwright gave the world the first wool-combing machine, the first power loom, a rope-making machine and a steam engine that ran on alcohol. Died at Hastings, Sussex.

Caroline Herschel

Death • Jan 8, 1848 • 150 years

Born Mar 16, 1750, at Hannover, Germany, Herschel is considered the first significant female astronomer. She moved to England in 1772 to live with her brother, astronomer Sir William Herschel, giving up her own musical career to organize his notes, do the tedious routine calculations and prepare his papers for publication. He encouraged her to do her own research as well, which resulted in her discovering eight comets and three nebulas. She revised, corrected and updated the standard star catalog of the day (Flamsteed's), a project for which the Royal Astronomical Society awarded her its gold medal. Died at Hannover.

Jöns Jakob Berzelius

Death • Aug 1, 1848 • 150 years

Swedish chemist, born Aug 20, 1779, at Väversunda, Östergötland, Berzelius is credited as one of the founders of modern chemistry. A giant in the field, he developed the system of chemical notation. He defined the method of measuring atomic weights and published a revised table of them; the table also included the chemical composition of close to 2,000 compounds. He defined the concept of catalysis and originated the term "catalyst." He wrote a chemistry textbook that was the most authoritative of its time. He formulated an electrochemical theory that indicated the presence of negatively and positively charged components in chemical compounds and laid the groundwork for the theory of radicals. For most of his work, Berzelius had to devise his own apparatus and analytical methods. Died at Stockholm.

Gottlob Frege

Birth • Nov 8, 1848 • 150 years

Considered the founder of modern mathematical logic, German mathematician and philosopher Frege was born at Wismar. He devised a system of symbolic notation to express the principles of arithmetic in logical format. Died July 26, 1925, at Bad Kleinen.

Baron Justus von Liebig

Death • Apr 18, 1873 • 125 years

The German chemist was born May 12, 1803, at Darmstadt and died at Munich. This pioneer in organic chemistry and biochemistry is noted for his work in applying chemistry to medicine and agriculture.

Alexis Carrel

Birth • June 28, 1873 • 125 years

The French surgeon and medical researcher, born at Lyon, is known as an early pioneer in organ transplant research, such as inventing (in collaboration with aviator Charles Lindbergh) a mechanical heart that could pump vital fluids through organs after removal from the body. He also won a Nobel prize for a suturing technique he developed. Died Nov 5, 1944, at Paris.

Lee De Forest

Birth • Aug 26, 1873 • 125 years

The self-proclaimed "father of radio," American inventor De Forest, born at Council Bluffs, IA, deserved the title: he transmitted the first music broadcast (Enrico Caruso at the Met) and the first radio news broadcast. He invented many devices for radio communication, including transmitters, various antennas and the Audion/triode vacuum tube, which became the foundation for the electronics industry. Later he turned his attention to talking pictures and television. Died July 22, 1961, at Hollywood.

Ejnar Hertzsprung

Birth • Oct 8, 1873 • 125 years

This Danish astrophysicist, born at Frederiksberg, broke ground in the study of the formation and evolution of stars. The Hertzsprung-Russell diagram, named for him and his collaborator, astronomer Henry Norris Russell, is still the foundation of all research related to the birth and death of stars. Died Oct 21, 1967, at Roskilde.

Louis Agassiz

Death • Dec 14, 1873 • 125 years

American naturalist, geologist and educator, Agassiz is known both for his discoveries and his contributions to natural science teaching techniques. Born May 28, 1807, at Môtier-en-Vuly, Switzerland, he immigrated to the US in 1848, and became known as the founder of paleichthyology for his research on fish fossils and for designating the Ice Age as a geological period through his research on glaciers. Agassiz championed learning through contact with the natural world. By advocating the collection of natural artifacts for study, he furthered the establishment of many museums and popularized science through his public lectures. Died at Cambridge, MA.

Leo Szilard

Birth • Feb 11, 1898 • 100 years

American nuclear physicist Szilard, born at Budapest, Hungary, who immigrated to the US in 1938, is considered one of the most creative thinkers of this century. A prime mover in getting US President Roosevelt to commit to atomic research, he and Enrico Fermi achieved the first controlled, self-sustaining nuclear reaction at the University of Chicago in 1942. Although he contributed to the development of the atomic bomb, after its use in Japan he was very active in the movement to ban the use of nuclear energy in weapons. Died May 30, 1964, at La Jolla, CA.

Sir Henry Bessemer

Death • Mar 15, 1898 • 100 years

This English inventor, engineer and industrialist, born Jan 19, 1813, at Charlton, Hertfordshire, is best known for his invention in 1856 of the Bessemer converter process, the breakthrough technology for the inexpensive mass production of steel. Among his other inventions were a solar furnace, an astronomical telescope and diamond-polishing machines. Died at London.

Ferdinand Cohn

Death • June 25, 1898 • 100 years

Born Jan 24, 1828, at Breslau (now Wroclaw, Poland), German botanist and bacteriologist Cohn is known as one of the founders of the science of bacteriology, for proving that bacteria are plants and identifying similarities in certain plant and animal cells–an important step toward the later discovery that all life is made from the same basic stuff. Died at Breslau.

Isidor Isaac Rabi

Birth • July 29, 1898 • 100 years

Born at Rymanow, Austria (now in Poland), Rabi's family immigrated to the US in 1899. This American nuclear physicist is known as one of the scientists who developed the atomic bomb and as the developer of magnetic resonance imaging (MRI). His research on the magnetic properties of atomic nuclei made possible the invention of the laser and the atomic clock. He was awarded the 1944 Nobel prize in physics. Died Jan 11, 1988, at New York City.

Howard Florey

Birth • Sept 24, 1898 • 100 years

This British pathologist, born at Adelaide, Australia, is credited as codiscoverer of penicillin. (The mold itself was discovered in 1928 by Sir Alexander Fleming.) Florey and his colleague Ernst Chain isolated and purified it, ascertained its bacterial-fighting capability and developed production methods. Florey, Chain and Fleming were awarded the 1945 Nobel Prize for physiology or medicine. Died Feb 22, 1968, at Oxford.

Archaeology

Giovanni Battista Belzoni

Death • Dec 3, 1823 • 175 years

An Italian archaeologist, born Nov 5, 1778, at Padua, Belzoni trained in hydraulic engineering, then went to England and performed in the circus for a dozen years before being hired to collect Egyptiana for the British Museum. Among noted accomplishments: moving the bust of Ramses II (*The Young Memnon*) from Thebes to London; digging out the entrance to the temple at Abu Simbel; discovering the tomb of King Seti I in the Valley of the Kings. He was the first person to enter the pyramid of Khafre at Giza since it was sealed and he identified the ruins of Berenice on the Red Sea. He described his experiences in *Narrative of the Operations and Recent Discoveries Within the Pyramids, Temples, Tombs, and Excavations, in Egypt and Nubia.* Died at Nigeria.

Howard Carter

Birth • May 9, 1873 • 125 years

London-born archaeologist and Egyptologist, Carter is famous for having discovered with fellow Egyptologist George Herbert the treasure-filled tomb of Tutankhamen in the Valley of Kings at Luxor in 1922. Carter also discovered the tombs of Thutmose IV and Queen Hatshepsut and served as inspector in chief of the antiquities department of the Egyptian government. Died Mar 2, 1939 at London.

Georg Moritz Ebers

Death • Aug 7, 1898 • 100 years

German Egyptologist and novelist, born Mar 1, 1837, at Berlin, is known for finding an Egyptian hieratic medical papyrus. In addition to books in his field, Ebers wrote historical fiction to promote interest in Egyptology. Among noted written works: Egypt and the Books of Moses and the three-volume novel *An Egyptian Princess*. Died at Tutzing, Bavaria.

Sports

John Joseph McGraw

Birth • Apr 7, 1873 • 125 years

American pro baseball player and manager, born at Truxton, NY, McGraw is also noted for taking baseball to Europe and eastern Asia. He played third base for Baltimore (lifetime batting average .334) and became its manager in 1899. He then managed the New York Giants 1902–1932. With 10 National League and 3 world championships, he had one of the best managerial records ever seen in baseball. Elected to the Baseball Hall of Fame in 1937. Died Feb 25, 1934, at New Rochelle, NY.

Spotlight on People *milestone anniversary years*

Gene Tunney

Birth • May 25, 1898 • 100 years

Heavyweight boxing champion, business executive, New York City–born Tunney is remembered particularly for the famous "long count" in the 7th round of the Jack Dempsey–Gene Tunney world championship fight on Sept 22, 1927, in Soldier Field at Chicago, IL. Died Nov 7, 1978, at Greenwich, CT.

Frankie Frisch

Birth • Sept 9, 1898 • 100 years

American baseball player Frisch was born at New York City and became a member of the 1934 world champion Gashouse Gang. From his rookie days at second base for the New York Giants to his last season on the field for the St. Louis Cardinals 20 years later, the "Fordham Flash" racked up more than 2,800 hits in 2,300 games, for a lifetime batting average of .316. Frisch rounded out his career as manager for the Pittsburgh Pirates and the Chicago Cubs and did a stint as a radio broadcaster for the Giants. Inducted into the Baseball Hall of Fame in 1947. Died Mar 12, 1973, at Wilmington, DE.

Miscellaneous

Wyatt Earp

Birth • Mar 19, 1848 • 150 years

An American lawman, Earp, born at Monmouth, IL, made his name as a deputy US marshall and is remembered particularly for the famous gunfight at O.K. Corral at Tombstone in the Arizona Territory. Considered an Old West hero of law and order, Earp also worked at various times as a railroad hand, saloonkeeper, gambler, gunslinger, miner and real estate investor. His life has since taken on legendary proportions and he has been immortalized in books, films and a television series. Died Jan 13, 1929, at Los Angeles.

William McGuffey

Death • May 4, 1873 • 125 years

McGuffey, an American educator, born Sept 28, 1800, at Washington County, PA, is known chiefly for the series of elementary school textbooks he compiled and edited, *Eclectic Readers*, commonly called McGuffey's Readers. Initially published between 1836 and 1841, the readers were highly influential both for their pedagogical value and for their moral and ethical content. More than 120 million copies of the six readers were sold. Died at Charlottesville, VA.

Frances Willard

Death • Feb 18, 1898 • 100 years

This American educator and reformer, born Sept 28, 1839, at Churchville, NY, founded the World's Women's Christian Temperance Union in 1883, becoming its president eight years later. Willard was also very active in the women's suffrage movement and in promoting women's education and workplace safety and helped to organize the Prohibition party. Among noted works: *Woman and Temperance* and *Glimpses of Fifty Years*. Died at New York City.

Amelia Earhart

Birth • July 24, 1898 • 100 years

American aviator Earhart, who disappeared during her legendary attempt to become the first woman to fly around the world, is still celebrated as the first woman to cross the Atlantic solo and for greatly enhancing the image of women in aviation. Born at Atchison, KS, Earhart accomplished many other firsts and set many records. Among her written works: *20 Hrs. 40 Min.*, *The Fun of It* and *Last Flight*, which is the account of the fatal flight that she had been transmitting, published posthumously by her husband. Died sometime after her last transmission over the South Pacific in early July, 1937.

Feb 7–Feb 22, 1998

- The ancient Olympic Games are thought to have started in Greece in the city of Olympia in 776 BC. For more than 50 years the only event was the 200-yard dash. Various competitions were added over the years, until AD 394 when the Games were abolished by Roman Emperor Theodosius.
- The modern Olympics began in 1896 when the Games were revived and made international; the first summer Games were held in Athens, Greece that year. The first Winter Olympics were held in 1924.
- The purpose of the Olympic Games is to foster peace and fellowship among countries and to promote the ideal of a sound mind and body.
- The Games are held every four years. Since 1992 the Winter and Summer Games no longer take place in the same year; instead there is a two-year interval between them. The 2000 Summer Olympics will be held in Sydney, Australia; the 2002 Winter Olympics will take place in Salt Lake City, UT.
- The 1998 Winter Olympics will be held at Nagano, Japan, a city of 347,000 people about 100 miles northwest of Tokyo. The last time the Winter Olympics were held in Japan was 1972, when the Games were held at Sapporo, on Hokkaido, the northernmost island of Japan.

The 1998 Olympic Program

The dates given here are those on which events are taking place in Japan. Because of the 14-hour time difference, some events will be occurring a day earlier in the US. For example, the Opening Ceremony, which takes place at 11 AM on Feb 7 in Nagano, will be at 9 PM on Feb 6 EST. Most events probably won't be broadcast live in the US because they will be happening in the middle of the night in North America.

• Opening Ceremony	Feb 7
• Alpine Skiing	Feb 8-10; Feb 13-15; Feb 17-20; Feb 22
• Biathlon	Feb 9; Feb 11; Feb 15; Feb 17; Feb 19; Feb 21
• Bobsled	Feb 14-15; Feb 20-21
• Cross Country Skiing	Feb 8-9; Feb 12; Feb 16; Feb 18; Feb 20; Feb 22
• Curling	Feb 9-15
• Figure Skating	Feb 8; Feb 10; Feb 12-16; Feb 18; Feb 20-21
• Freestyle Skiing	Feb 8; Feb 11; Feb 16; Feb 18
• Ice Hockey	Feb 7-18; Feb 20-22
• Luge	Feb 8-11; Feb 13
• Nordic Combined	Feb 13-14; Feb 19-20
• Ski Jumping	Feb 11; Feb 15; Feb 17
• Snowboarding	Feb 8-9; Feb 12
• Speed Skating	Feb 8-21
• Closing Ceremony	Feb 22

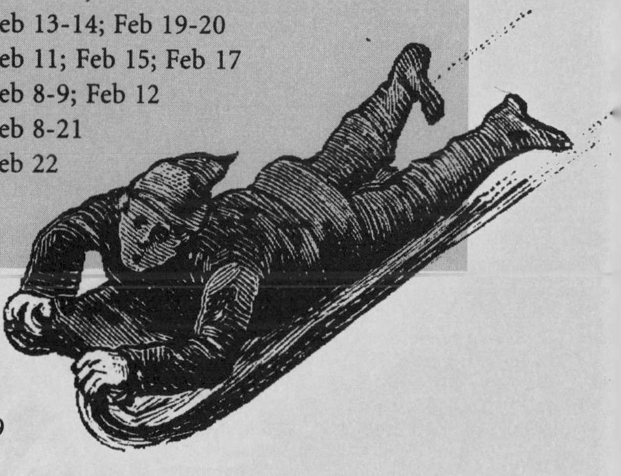

For information:

US Olympic Committee
1 Olympic Plaza
Colorado Springs, CO 80909
Phone: (719) 632-5551
Fax: (719) 578-4654
Web: http://www.nagano.olympic.org
Web: http://www.cbs.com/sports/olympics

Lisbon World Exposition: Expo '98

May 22–Sept 30, 1998

- More than 100 nations and organizations will participate in this fair dedicated to the theme "The Oceans, a Heritage for the Future." The last expo of the twentieth century, it will celebrate 500 years of Portugal's maritime heritage and the coming together of different nations by sea. It will take place in east Lisbon, on a site that stretches three miles along the river Tagus.
- Expo '98 has four major themes, each of which has several sub-themes, a few examples of which are given here.

Knowledge of the Seas, Ocean Resources

Life networks in marine ecosystems

Continental drift and the formation of the ocean depths

The Oceans and the Earth's Ecological Balance

Oceans and climate change

Natural catastrophes

The Oceans and Leisure

Technology and water sports

Sea safaris-underwater parks and reserves

Underwater archaeology

The Oceans, a Source of Artistic Expression

Seascapes (painting)

Fear of the sea (religion and myth)

The sea on stage

For information:

Portuguese National Tourist Office
590 Fifth Ave, 4th floor
New York, NY 10036
Phone:(212) 354-4403
Fax: (212) 764-6137
E-mail: info@expo98.pt
Web: http://www.expo98.pt

Spotlight on the Calendar

The Millennium

Jan 1, 2001

The clock is ticking toward the biggest New Year's celebration of all time—it's only a year away. With the excitement of the digits rolling from 19 to 20, it probably won't matter much to global partygoers in December 1999 that the beginning of the next millennium is still a year away. There has been a lot of confusion about just when the present millennium ends and the new one begins. So at the suggestion of librarian Susan Mathews of the Mead Public Library, Sheboygan, WI, here's the straight scoop as explained by the Royal Greenwich Observatory.

Why isn't it 2000?

A millennium is a period of 1,000 years. The Christian calendar is divided into two periods, BC (before Christ) and AD (anno Domini, which means 'in the year of the Lord') based on the birth of Jesus Christ. However, in ca. AD 525 when this system was instituted, there was no Year 0 designated. The monk who devised the system had only Roman numerals to work with and there was no Roman numeral for zero. So, the first year of the first western calendar millennium was AD 1 and the year 1000 was the 1,000th year, which means that Jan 1, 1001, was the first day of the second millennium and Jan 1, 2001, will be the first day of the third millennium. It is significant to note that this day has meaning only for societies where timekeeping is based on the Christian calendar. Religions such as Judaism, Islam and Buddhism that do not date time from the birth of Christ will not be reaching a new millennium.

A number of companies have sprung up to capitalize on the excitement surrounding the year 2000 with Web sites. For example, The Billennium: The Official Celebration of the Year 2000, with a Web site at http://www.billennium.com, has a countdown clock telling how many days are left until 2000 and historical information on other landmark years, such as 999 and 1899. Everything 2000: Your One-Stop Resource to Prepare for the New Millennium, at http://www.everything2000.com, has trivia about the millennium, information on the coming computer date crisis, and more.

When is the Next Leap Year?

Feb 29, 2000

The year 2000 AD will also be notable for being a leap year. The current formula for leap years comes from our use of the Gregorian calendar, instituted in 1582. Previously, under the Julian calendar, every fourth year was a leap year. However, a small discrepancy between the approximation of the length of the year (365.25 days) and the actual length of the year (365.24219 days) meant that extra days accumulated so that over time the calendar year no longer matched the seasons. To solve this problem Pope Gregory instituted a new rule for leap years: every fourth year would be a leap year, except century years would be leap years only if divisible by 400. Since the year 2000 is divisible by 400, it will be a leap year, while the year 1900 was not.

Glossary

Dominical Letter

The basis of a perpetual calendar used in the Christian church to determine the date on which Sundays fall in a particular year. Knowing the Dominical Letter (A to G) of a year gives the entire order of days in that year.

Epact

The number of days in the age of the Moon on Jan 1 of any year. Each year has an epact number that allows the dates of all full moons for the year to be calculated. It is used to determine the date of Easter. The epact is supposed to be an improvement over the Golden number (below) for this purpose.

Eras

Counting years from a particular date as year one. The era of Nabonassar, named after King Nabonassar of Babylon, dated time from the eighth century BC. The ancient Greeks counted years from the Olympics. A period of four years was called an Olympiad, so an event would be described as having occurred in the second year of the 92nd Olympiad. The Seleucid era used in the Asian part of the Roman Empire was named after a Roman general, Seleucus. Year one was 312 BC, the year he captured Babylon. The Romans counted years from the reign of an emperor or the founding of Rome. The Diocletian era, for example, was counted from AD 284. The Roman Era (AUC) had year one as 753 BC, the traditional founding date of Rome. The Byzantines dated their era back to what they thought was the creation in 5508 BC. The Roman Indiction, an era introduced by the Emperor Constantine, dated time in 15-year intervals (indictions) from AD 313. The Jewish calendar counts from the year established as the date of the creation (3760 BC) and the Muslim calendar from the flight into exile of Muhammad (AD 622). The Julian and Gregorian calendars count years from the birth of Christ. The Japanese count years from the beginning of an emperor's reign, the Chinese calendar dates time from 2637 BC and the Indian Saka era dates time from AD 78.

Golden Number

The position of any year in the 19-year Metonic cycle, a lunisolar cycle discovered by the Greek astronomer Meton. In modern times it has been used to determine the date of Easter.

Gregorian Calendar

This solar calendar, used in most countries of the world today, was designed on the order of Pope Gregory to improve on the Julian calendar, which over time had grown to exceed the seasons by ten days. In 1582, ten days were deleted from the year as a correction and the Gregorian calendar was adopted in Catholic Europe. To reflect the fact that the solar year has 365.24219 days, not 365.25 days as used in the Julian calendar, the cycle of leap years was changed so that century years must be evenly divisible by 400 to be leap years. Hence, 1600 and 2000 are leap years, 1900 was not. The Gregorian calendar is still 25 seconds longer than the true solar year but will not gain a full day for some 3,400 years.

This calendar, often called New Style as opposed to Old Style (Julian), was adopted in Roman Catholic countries in 1582, but Great Britain and its colonies (including North America) did not switch until 1752. (Great Britain also changed the beginning of the year to January at this time; it had been Annunciation Day, Mar 25.) The Gregorian calendar was not adopted in Russia and Greece until the twentieth century.

Because the 365 days in the year are not evenly divisible by the seven days in a week (there is one day left over), if one year begins on a Sunday, the next year must begin on a Monday. During a leap year, with its added day, the calendar leaps ahead from, for example, Sunday to Tuesday. Thus, a perpetual calendar has 14 possible arrangements for days of the year, seven for leap years and seven for nonleap years.

Islamic Calendar

This lunar calendar has 354 days and thus is shorter than the solar year. As a result, the fixed holidays in the Islamic calendar move "backward" about ten days each year in relation to the seasons. In roughly 36 years, Ramadan, the Islamic month of fasting, moves back through the entire solar year. If Ramadan occurs in January one year, about 18 years later it will occur in June. Many Islamic countries use the Gregorian calendar for civil purposes and the Islamic calendar determines the days of religious holidays. The Islamic era began with year one on July 16, 622, the date of the flight into exile of the Prophet Muhammad.

Jewish Calendar

This lunisolar calendar is regulated by both the moon and the sun. The average year is a lunar year with 354 days; adjustments are made by adding a leap month about every three years so that major Jewish holidays fall into their proper season. From year to year, Jewish dates vary from their Gregorian equivalents. For example, the state of Israel was founded on Iyar 5, 5708. In 1948, when this event occurred, the Gregorian date was May 14th. However, in 1998 the Gregorian equivalent is April 30th. But the addition of the extra month periodically means that this holiday will always occur in the spring. The Jewish calendar dates year one from 3761 BC, the assumed date of creation.

Julian Calendar

This solar calendar was commissioned by Julius Caesar in 46 BC. Up until that time, the Romans had used a lunar calendar. It had increasingly grown out of sync with the seasons, so the year 46 BC was lengthened to 445 days to make the adjustment. From then on, the year was 365 days long, with a leap year every fourth year days. Julian dates are now usually identified as Old Style.

The numbering of years varied, usually dating time from the reign of a Roman emperor. In the sixth century a monk named Dionysius Exiguus realized that it was the 525th year since the birth of Christ. (We now know that he was slightly off in this calculation; Christ is thought to have been born in 4 BC.) He saw an opportunity to replace the system of calculating years from pagan emperors, who often had been great persecuters of Christians, and instituted a system whereby time is calculated from the birth of Christ. Years are designated as AD (from Latin for "in the year of our Lord"). This system was not widely adopted, however, until the eighth century. The system of numbering the years before Christ's birth as BC was begun by the Venerable Bede in 731 AD. Since the system of Roman numerals available to Dionysius and Bede lacked a zero, time was divided at 1 BC and 1 AD; there was no year zero. The Julian calendar was used for more than 1,600 years and is still used by Orthodox Christian churches to determine religious holidays. See Gregorian Calendar for the successor to the Julian calendar.

Julian Period and Julian Day

This system of calculating time, which is used by astronomers, is not related to the Julian Calendar. A Frenchman, Joseph Justus Scaliger, conceived these measures in 1582 and named them after his father, Julian Scaliger. The Julian Period is composed of 7,980 years. Scaliger selected Jan 1, 4713 BC as day one of the period, which will be complete in 3267. Individual Julian days are counted from the beginning of the Julian Period and each day has its own number. Currently, more than 2,450,000 Julian days have elapsed. Astronomical reference books have tables to facilitate converting any date into its Julian-day number for calculations involving large time intervals.

Roman Calendars

Prior to the adoption of the Julian calendar in 46 BC, the Romans used various lunar calendars. The Romans, like many other civilizations, started the year in March; hence the names of the months September, October, November, and December have their roots in seven (sept), eight (oct), nine (nov) and ten (dec), when they are our ninth, tenth, eleventh and twelfth months. About 451 BC the calendar was rearranged to have the year begin in January

Solar Cycle

A cycle designed to show the relation between the day of the week and the day of the month. There are 14 possible arrangements of these days. It takes 28 years (a solar cycle) for these 14 calendars to occur in the same order.

SELECTED SPECIAL YEARS: 1957–1998

Intl Geophysical Year: July 1957-Dec 1958
World Refugee Year: July 1959-June 1960
Intl Cooperation Year: 1965
Intl Book Year: 1972
World Population Year: 1974
Intl Women's Year: 1975
Intl Year of the Child: 1979
Intl Year for Disabled Persons: 1981
World Communications Year: 1983
Intl Youth Year: 1985
Intl Year of Peace: 1986
Intl Year of Shelter for the Homeless: 1987
Year of the Reader: 1987
Year of the Young Reader: 1989
Intl Literacy Year: 1990
US Decade of the Brain: 1990-99
Intl Space Year: 1992
Intl Year for World's Indigenous Peoples: 1993
Intl Year of the Family: 1994
Year for Tolerance: 1995
Intl Year for Eradication of Poverty: 1996
Intl Year of the Ocean: 1998

CHINESE CALENDAR

The Chinese lunar year is divided into 12 months of 29 or 30 days. The calendar is adjusted to the length of the solar year by the addition of extra months at regular intervals. The years are arranged in major cycles of 60 years. Each successive year is named after one of 12 animals. These 12-year cycles are continuously repeated.

1996 . . . . Rat
1997 . . . . Ox
1998 . . . . Tiger
1999 . . . . Hare
2000 . . . . Dragon
2001 . . . . Snake
2002 . . . . Horse
2003 . . . . Sheep (Goat)
2004 . . . . Monkey
2005 . . . . Rooster
2006 . . . . Dog
2007 . . . . Pig

WEDDING ANNIVERSARY GIFTS

1st . . . . paper, plastics, clocks
2nd . . . . cotton, china, calico
3rd . . . . leather, crystal, glass
4th . . . . books, electrical appliances, silk, fruit, flowers
5th . . . . wood, silverware
6th . . . . sugar, candy, wood, iron
7th . . . . wool, copper, desk sets
8th . . . . bronze, pottery, linens, laces, electrical appliances
9th . . . . pottery, willow, leather
10th . . . . tin, aluminum, diamond jewelry
11th . . . . steel, fashion jewelry, accessories
12th . . . . silk, linen, pearls, colored gems
13th . . . . lace, textiles, furs
14th . . . . ivory, gold jewelry
15th . . . . crystal, watches, glass
16th . . . . silver hollowware
17th . . . . furniture
18th . . . . porcelain
19th . . . . bronze
20th . . . . china, platinum
21st . . . . brass, nickel
22nd . . . . copper
23rd . . . . silver plate
24th . . . . musical instruments
25th . . . . silver
26th . . . . original pictures
27th . . . . sculpture
28th . . . . orchids
29th . . . . new furniture
30th . . . . pearl, diamond
31st . . . . time pieces
32nd . . . . conveyances (including automobiles)
33rd . . . . amethyst
34th . . . . opal
35th . . . . coral, jade
36th . . . . bone china
37th . . . . alabaster
38th . . . . beryl, tourmaline
39th . . . . lace
40th . . . . ruby
41st . . . . land
42nd . . . . improved real estate
43rd . . . . trips
44th . . . . groceries
45th . . . . sapphire
46th . . . . original poetry tributes
47th . . . . books
48th . . . . optical (spectacles, microscopes, telescopes)
49th . . . . luxuries of any kind
50th . . . . gold
55th . . . . emerald
60th . . . . diamond
75th . . . . diamond

NATIONAL DAYS OF THE WORLD FOR 1998

(Compiled from publications of the U.S. Department of State, the United Nations and from information received from the countries listed.)

Most nations set aside one or more days each year as national public holidays, often recognizing the anniversary of the attainment of independence, or the birthday of the country's ruler. Below, the national days are listed alphabetically. It should be noted that in some countries the Gregorian Calendar date of observance varies from year to year. See the Index and the main chronology for further details of observance, and for numerous holidays in addition to the national days listed here.

Afghanistan	Aug 19
Albania	Nov 28
Algeria	Nov 1
Andorra	Sept 8
Angola	Nov 11
Antigua and Barbuda	Nov 1
Argentina	May 25
Armenia	Sept 21
Australia	Jan 26
Austria	Oct 26
Azerbaijan	May 28
Bahamas	July 10
Bahrain	Dec 16
Bangladesh	Mar 26
Barbados	Nov 30
Belarus	July 3
Belgium	July 21
Belize	Sept 21
Benin	Aug 1
Bhutan	Dec 17
Bolivia	Aug 6
Bosnia and Herzegovina	Mar 1
Botswana	Sept 30
Brazil	Sept 7
Brunei Darussalam	Feb 23
Bulgaria	Mar 3
Burkina Faso	Dec 11
Burundi	July 1
Cambodia	Nov 9
Cameroon	May 20
Canada	July 1
Cape Verde	July 5
Central African Republic	Dec 1
Chad	Aug 11
Chile	Sept 18
China	Oct 1
Colombia	July 20
Comoros	July 6
Congo	Aug 15
Costa Rica	Sept 15
Cote D'Ivoire	Aug 7
Croatia	May 30
Cuba	Jan 1
Cyprus	Oct 1
Czech Republic	Oct 28
Denmark	Apr 16
Djibouti	June 27
Dominica	Nov 3
Dominican Republic	Feb 27
Ecuador	Aug 10
Egypt	July 23
El Salvador	Sept 15
Equatorial Guinea	Oct 12
Eritrea	May 24
Estonia	Feb 24
Fiji	Oct 10
Finland	Dec 6
France	July 14
Gabon	Aug 17
Gambia	Feb 18
Georgia	May 26
Germany	Oct 3
Ghana	Mar 6
Great Britain*	(Tentative) June 13
Greece	Mar 25
Grenada	Feb 7
Guatemala	Sept 15
Guinea	Oct 2
Guinea-Bissau	Sept 24
Guyana	Feb 23
Haiti	Jan 1
Holy See	Oct 22
Honduras	Sept 15
Hungary	Aug 20
Iceland	June 17
India	Jan 26
Indonesia	Aug 17
Iran	Feb 11
Iraq	July 17
Ireland	Mar 17
Israel	Apr 30
Italy	June 2
Jamaica	Aug 3
Japan	Dec 23
Jordan	May 25
Kazakhstan	Oct 25
Kenya	Dec 12
Kiribati	July 12
Korea, Democratic People's Republic of	Sept 9
Korea, Republic of	Aug 15
Kuwait	Feb 25
Kyrgyzstan	Aug 31
Lao People's Democratic Republic	Dec 2
Latvia	Nov 18
Lebanon	Nov 22
Lesotho	Oct 4
Liberia	July 26
Libyan Arab Jamahiriya	Sept 1
Liechtenstein	Aug 15
Lithuania	Feb 16
Luxembourg	June 23
Madagascar	June 26
Malawi	July 6
Malaysia	Aug 31
Maldives	July 26
Mali	Sept 22
Malta	Sept 21
Marshall Islands	May 1
Mauritania	Nov 28
Mauritius	Mar 12
Mexico	Sept 16
Micronesia (Federated States of)	Nov 3
Moldova, Republic of	Aug 27
Monaco	Nov 19
Mongolia	July 11
Morocco	Mar 3
Mozambique	June 25
Myanmar	Jan 4
Namibia, Republic of	Mar 21
Nauru	Jan 31
Nepal	Dec 28
Netherlands	Apr 30
New Zealand	Feb 6
Nicaragua	Sept 15
Niger	Dec 18
Nigeria	Oct 1
Norway	May 17
Oman	Nov 18
Pakistan	Mar 23
Panama	Nov 3
Papua New Guinea	Sept 16
Paraguay	May 15
Peru	July 28
Philippines	June 12
Poland	May 3
Portugal	June 10
Qatar	Sept 3
Romania	Dec 1
Russian Federation	June 12
Rwanda	July 1
Saint Christopher (St Kitts) and Nevis	Sept 19
Saint Lucia	Feb 22
Saint Vincent and the Grenadines	Oct 27
Samoa	June 1
San Marino	Sept 3
Sao Tome and Principe	July 12
Saudi Arabia	Sept 23
Senegal	Apr 4
Seychelles	June 18
Sierra Leone	Apr 27
Singapore	Aug 9
Slovakia	Sept 1
Slovenia	June 25
Solomon Islands	July 7
Somalia	Oct 21
South Africa	Apr 27
Spain	Oct 12
Sri Lanka	Feb 4
Sudan	Jan 1
Suriname	Nov 25
Swaziland	Sept 6
Sweden	June 6
Switzerland	Aug 1
Syrian Arab Republic	Apr 17
Tajikistan	Sept 9
Tanzania, United Republic of	Apr 26
Thailand	Dec 5
The Former Yugoslav Republic of Macedonia	Aug 2
Togo	Apr 27
Tonga	June 4
Trinidad and Tobago	Aug 31
Tunisia	Mar 20
Turkey	Oct 29
Turkmenistan	Oct 27
Tuvalu	Oct 1
Uganda	Oct 9
Ukraine	Aug 24
United Arab Emirates	Dec 2
United Republic of Tanzania	Apr 26
United States of America	July 4
Uruguay	Aug 25
Uzbekistan	Sept 1
Vanuatu	July 30
Venezuela	July 5
Vietnam	Sept 2
Western Samoa	June 1
Yemen	May 22
Yugoslavia	Apr 27
Zaire (Congo)	June 30
Zambia	Oct 24
Zimbabwe	Apr 18

*Trooping of the Colour—Queen's official birthday.

1997

JAN

S	M	T	W	T	F	S
			1	2	3	4
5	6	7	8	9	10	11
12	13	14	15	16	17	18
19	20	21	22	23	24	25
26	27	28	29	30	31	

APR

S	M	T	W	T	F	S
		1	2	3	4	5
6	7	8	9	10	11	12
13	14	15	16	17	18	19
20	21	22	23	24	25	26
27	28	29	30			

JULY

S	M	T	W	T	F	S
		1	2	3	4	5
6	7	8	9	10	11	12
13	14	15	16	17	18	19
20	21	22	23	24	25	26
27	28	29	30	31		

OCT

S	M	T	W	T	F	S
			1	2	3	4
5	6	7	8	9	10	11
12	13	14	15	16	17	18
19	20	21	22	23	24	25
26	27	28	29	30	31	

FEB

S	M	T	W	T	F	S
						1
2	3	4	5	6	7	8
9	10	11	12	13	14	15
16	17	18	19	20	21	22
23	24	25	26	27	28	

MAY

S	M	T	W	T	F	S
				1	2	3
4	5	6	7	8	9	10
11	12	13	14	15	16	17
18	19	20	21	22	23	24
25	26	27	28	29	30	31

AUG

S	M	T	W	T	F	S
					1	2
3	4	5	6	7	8	9
10	11	12	13	14	15	16
17	18	19	20	21	22	23
24	25	26	27	28	29	30
31						

NOV

S	M	T	W	T	F	S
						1
2	3	4	5	6	7	8
9	10	11	12	13	14	15
16	17	18	19	20	21	22
23	24	25	26	27	28	29
30						

MAR

S	M	T	W	T	F	S
						1
2	3	4	5	6	7	8
9	10	11	12	13	14	15
16	17	18	19	20	21	22
23	24	25	26	27	28	29
30	31					

JUNE

S	M	T	W	T	F	S
1	2	3	4	5	6	7
8	9	10	11	12	13	14
15	16	17	18	19	20	21
22	23	24	25	26	27	28
29	30					

SEPT

S	M	T	W	T	F	S
	1	2	3	4	5	6
7	8	9	10	11	12	13
14	15	16	17	18	19	20
21	22	23	24	25	26	27
28	29	30				

DEC

S	M	T	W	T	F	S
	1	2	3	4	5	6
7	8	9	10	11	12	13
14	15	16	17	18	19	20
21	22	23	24	25	26	27
28	29	30	31			

1998

JAN

S	M	T	W	T	F	S
				1	2	3
4	5	6	7	8	9	10
11	12	13	14	15	16	17
18	19	20	21	22	23	24
25	26	27	28	29	30	31

APR

S	M	T	W	T	F	S
			1	2	3	4
5	6	7	8	9	10	11
12	13	14	15	16	17	18
19	20	21	22	23	24	25
26	27	28	29	30		

JULY

S	M	T	W	T	F	S
			1	2	3	4
5	6	7	8	9	10	11
12	13	14	15	16	17	18
19	20	21	22	23	24	25
26	27	28	29	30	31	

OCT

S	M	T	W	T	F	S
				1	2	3
4	5	6	7	8	9	10
11	12	13	14	15	16	17
18	19	20	21	22	23	24
25	26	27	28	29	30	31

FEB

S	M	T	W	T	F	S
1	2	3	4	5	6	7
8	9	10	11	12	13	14
15	16	17	18	19	20	21
22	23	24	25	26	27	28

MAY

S	M	T	W	T	F	S
					1	2
3	4	5	6	7	8	9
10	11	12	13	14	15	16
17	18	19	20	21	22	23
24	25	26	27	28	29	30
31						

AUG

S	M	T	W	T	F	S
						1
2	3	4	5	6	7	8
9	10	11	12	13	14	15
16	17	18	19	20	21	22
23	24	25	26	27	28	29
30	31					

NOV

S	M	T	W	T	F	S
1	2	3	4	5	6	7
8	9	10	11	12	13	14
15	16	17	18	19	20	21
22	23	24	25	26	27	28
29	30					

MAR

S	M	T	W	T	F	S
1	2	3	4	5	6	7
8	9	10	11	12	13	14
15	16	17	18	19	20	21
22	23	24	25	26	27	28
29	30	31				

JUNE

S	M	T	W	T	F	S
	1	2	3	4	5	6
7	8	9	10	11	12	13
14	15	16	17	18	19	20
21	22	23	24	25	26	27
28	29	30				

SEPT

S	M	T	W	T	F	S
		1	2	3	4	5
6	7	8	9	10	11	12
13	14	15	16	17	18	19
20	21	22	23	24	25	26
27	28	29	30			

DEC

S	M	T	W	T	F	S
		1	2	3	4	5
6	7	8	9	10	11	12
13	14	15	16	17	18	19
20	21	22	23	24	25	26
27	28	29	30	31		

1999

JAN

S	M	T	W	T	F	S
					1	2
3	4	5	6	7	8	9
10	11	12	13	14	15	16
17	18	19	20	21	22	23
24	25	26	27	28	29	30
31						

APR

S	M	T	W	T	F	S
				1	2	3
4	5	6	7	8	9	10
11	12	13	14	15	16	17
18	19	20	21	22	23	24
25	26	27	28	29	30	

JULY

S	M	T	W	T	F	S
				1	2	3
4	5	6	7	8	9	10
11	12	13	14	15	16	17
18	19	20	21	22	23	24
25	26	27	28	29	30	31

OCT

S	M	T	W	T	F	S
					1	2
3	4	5	6	7	8	9
10	11	12	13	14	15	16
17	18	19	20	21	22	23
24	25	26	27	28	29	30
31						

FEB

S	M	T	W	T	F	S
	1	2	3	4	5	6
7	8	9	10	11	12	13
14	15	16	17	18	19	20
21	22	23	24	25	26	27
28						

MAY

S	M	T	W	T	F	S
						1
2	3	4	5	6	7	8
9	10	11	12	13	14	15
16	17	18	19	20	21	22
23	24	25	26	27	28	29
30	31					

AUG

S	M	T	W	T	F	S
1	2	3	4	5	6	7
8	9	10	11	12	13	14
15	16	17	18	19	20	21
22	23	24	25	26	27	28
29	30	31				

NOV

S	M	T	W	T	F	S
	1	2	3	4	5	6
7	8	9	10	11	12	13
14	15	16	17	18	19	20
21	22	23	24	25	26	27
28	29	30				

MAR

S	M	T	W	T	F	S
	1	2	3	4	5	6
7	8	9	10	11	12	13
14	15	16	17	18	19	20
21	22	23	24	25	26	27
28	29	30	31			

JUNE

S	M	T	W	T	F	S
		1	2	3	4	5
6	7	8	9	10	11	12
13	14	15	16	17	18	19
20	21	22	23	24	25	26
27	28	29	30			

SEPT

S	M	T	W	T	F	S
			1	2	3	4
5	6	7	8	9	10	11
12	13	14	15	16	17	18
19	20	21	22	23	24	25
26	27	28	29	30		

DEC

S	M	T	W	T	F	S
			1	2	3	4
5	6	7	8	9	10	11
12	13	14	15	16	17	18
19	20	21	22	23	24	25
26	27	28	29	30	31	

2000

JAN

S	M	T	W	T	F	S
						1
2	3	4	5	6	7	8
9	10	11	12	13	14	15
16	17	18	19	20	21	22
23	24	25	26	27	28	29
30	31					

APR

S	M	T	W	T	F	S
						1
2	3	4	5	6	7	8
9	10	11	12	13	14	15
16	17	18	19	20	21	22
23	24	25	26	27	28	29
30						

JULY

S	M	T	W	T	F	S
						1
2	3	4	5	6	7	8
9	10	11	12	13	14	15
16	17	18	19	20	21	22
23	24	25	26	27	28	29
30	31					

OCT

S	M	T	W	T	F	S
1	2	3	4	5	6	7
8	9	10	11	12	13	14
15	16	17	18	19	20	21
22	23	24	25	26	27	28
29	30	31				

FEB

S	M	T	W	T	F	S
		1	2	3	4	5
6	7	8	9	10	11	12
13	14	15	16	17	18	19
20	21	22	23	24	25	26
27	28	29				

MAY

S	M	T	W	T	F	S
	1	2	3	4	5	6
7	8	9	10	11	12	13
14	15	16	17	18	19	20
21	22	23	24	25	26	27
28	29	30	31			

AUG

S	M	T	W	T	F	S
		1	2	3	4	5
6	7	8	9	10	11	12
13	14	15	16	17	18	19
20	21	22	23	24	25	26
27	28	29	30	31		

NOV

S	M	T	W	T	F	S
			1	2	3	4
5	6	7	8	9	10	11
12	13	14	15	16	17	18
19	20	21	22	23	24	25
26	27	28	29	30		

MAR

S	M	T	W	T	F	S
			1	2	3	4
5	6	7	8	9	10	11
12	13	14	15	16	17	18
19	20	21	22	23	24	25
26	27	28	29	30	31	

JUNE

S	M	T	W	T	F	S
				1	2	3
4	5	6	7	8	9	10
11	12	13	14	15	16	17
18	19	20	21	22	23	24
25	26	27	28	29	30	

SEPT

S	M	T	W	T	F	S
					1	2
3	4	5	6	7	8	9
10	11	12	13	14	15	16
17	18	19	20	21	22	23
24	25	26	27	28	29	30

DEC

S	M	T	W	T	F	S
					1	2
3	4	5	6	7	8	9
10	11	12	13	14	15	16
17	18	19	20	21	22	23
24	25	26	27	28	29	30
31						

Januarye.

JANUARY 1 — THURSDAY

Day 1 — 364 Remaining

THURSDAY, JANUARY ONE, 1998. Jan 1. First day of the first month of the Gregorian calendar year, Anno Domini 1998, being second after Leap Year, and (until July 4th) 222nd year of American independence. 1998 will be year 6711 of the Julian Period, a time frame consisting of 7,980 years, which began at noon, universal [Greenwich] time, Jan 1, 4713 BC. Astronomers will note that Julian Day number 2,450,814 begins at noon, universal time, Jan 1, 1998 (representing the number of days since the beginning of the Julian Period). New Year's Day is a public holiday in the US and in many other countries. Traditionally, it is a time for personal stocktaking, for making resolutions for the coming year, and sometimes for recovering from the festivities of New Year's Eve. Financial accounting begins anew for businesses and individuals whose fiscal year is the calendar year. Jan 1 has been observed as the beginning of the year in most English-speaking countries since the British Calendar Act of 1751, prior to which the New Year began on Mar 25 (approximating the vernal equinox). Earth begins another orbit of the sun, during which it, and we, will travel some 583,416,000 miles in 365.2422 days. New Year's Day has been called "Everyman's Birthday," and in some countries a year is added to everyone's age on Jan 1 rather than on the anniversary of each person's birth.

AUTISM AWARENESS MONTH. Jan 1–31. A month filled with events such as poster contests, a state proclamation by the governor, family activities and information on autism. This is a national celebration. Annually, the month of January. For info: Linda Ryan, Coord of Mktg and Public Relations, COSAC, 1450 Parkside Ave, Ste 22, Ewing, NJ 08638. Phone: (609) 883-8100. Fax: (609) 883-5509. Email: njautism@aol.com. WWW: http://members.aol.com/njautism

BILLIONAIRE BACHELOR BITES THE BULLET: WEDDING ANNIVERSARY. Jan 1, 1994. America's most eligible billionaire, Bill "Mr Microsoft" Gates, 38, married Marilyn French, a marketing manager at Microsoft. Under tight security to protect privacy, the wedding took place on Lanai island, Hawaii.

BONZA BOTTLER DAY™. Jan 1. (Also Feb 2, Mar 3, Apr 4, May 5, June 6, July 7, Aug 8, Sept 9, Oct 10, Nov 11 and Dec 12.) To celebrate when the number of the day is the same as the number of the month. Bonza Bottler Day™ is an excuse to have a party at least once a month. Created by the late Elaine Fremont and continued by her family, Bonza Bottler Day is now celebrated in many countries. Logo buttons are available for $2 (includes postage and handling). For info: Gail M. Berger, Bonza Bottler Day, 109 Matthew Ave, Poca, WV 25159. Phone: (304) 776-7746. Email: gberger5@aol.com.

January 1998

S	M	T	W	T	F	S
				1	2	3
4	5	6	7	8	9	10
11	12	13	14	15	16	17
18	19	20	21	22	23	24
25	26	27	28	29	30	31

CANADA: BRACKENDALE BALD EAGLE COUNT. Jan 1–31. Squamish, BC. Month-long festival focuses on the magnificence of the North American bald eagle. Workshops, raft trips, llama adventures, photo contest and lots more. Annually, the month of January. For info: Brackendale Art Gallery, Box 100, Brackendale, BC, Canada V0N 1H0. Phone: (604) 898-3333. Email: gallery@mountain-inter.net. WWW: http://www.mountain-inter.net/~gallery/

CELEBRATION OF LIFE WEEK. Jan 1–7. The purpose of this week is to impress upon people all over the world the preciousness of life and the importance of all living things. For complete information and many famous quotations about life, send $3 to cover printing, handling and postage. For info: Dr. Stanley Drake, Pres, Intl Soc of Friendship and Good Will, 412 Cherry Hills Dr, Bakersfield, CA 93309-2866.

CIRCUMCISION OF CHRIST. Jan 1. Holy day in many Christian churches. Celebrates Jesus's submission to Jewish law; on the octave day of Christmas. See also: "Solemnity of Mary, Mother of God" (Jan 1) for Roman Catholic observance since 1969 calendar reorganization.

COPYRIGHT REVISION LAW SIGNED: ANNIVERSARY. Jan 1, 1976. The first major revision since 1909 of laws governing intellectual property in the US was signed by President Ford. It took effect two years later on Jan 1, 1978. The act (Public Law 94–553) contains substantial revisions of the principles governing acquisition and duration of copyright and deals with issues that have been raised in recent years concerning photocopying and the use of copyrighted works by public broadcasting and cable television systems.

CUBA: LIBERATION DAY AND ANNIVERSARY OF THE REVOLUTION. Jan 1. A national holiday that celebrates the end of Spanish rule on Jan 1, 1899, and the overthrow of the government on Jan 1, 1959, by Fidel Castro. Cuba, largest island of the West Indies, was a Spanish possession from its discovery by Columbus (Oct 27, 1492) until 1899. Under US military control 1899–1902 and 1906–1909, a republican government took over on Jan 28, 1909, and controlled the island until it was overthrown Jan 1, 1959, by Fidel Castro's revolutionary movement (which had begun on July 26, 1953).

CZECH-SLOVAK DIVORCE: 5th ANNIVERSARY. Jan 1, 1993. As Dec 31, 1992, gave way to Jan 1, 1993, the 74-year-old state of Czechoslovakia separated into two nations—the Czech and Slovak Republics. The Slovaks held a celebration through the night in the streets of Bratislava amid fireworks, bell ringing, singing of the new country's national anthem and the raising of the Slovak flag. In the new Czech Republic no official festivities took place, but later in the day the Czechs celebrated with a solemn oath by their parliament. The nation of Czechoslovakia ended peacefully though polls showed that most Slovaks and Czechs would have preferred that Czechoslovakia survive. Before the split Czech Prime Minister Vaclav Klaus and Slovak Prime Minister Vladimir Meciar reached agreement on dividing everything from army troops and gold reserves to the art on government building walls.

DECADE OF THE BRAIN: YEAR NINE. Jan 1–Dec 31. H.J. Res. 174, Public Law 101–58 of July 25, 1989, established the period from Jan 1, 1990, through Dec 31, 1999, as the Decade of the Brain. Presidential Proclamation 6158 was issued July 17, 1990. The purpose of this decade is to enhance public awareness of the benefits to be derived from brain research. (To find the full text of the proclamation, see Contents.)

ELLIS ISLAND OPENED: ANNIVERSARY. Jan 1, 1892. Ellis Island was opened on New Year's Day in 1892. Over the years more than 20 million individuals were processed through the stations. The island was used as a point of deportation as well: in 1932 alone, 20,000 people were deported from Ellis Island. When the US entered WW II in 1941, Ellis Island became a Coast Guard Station. It closed Nov 12, 1954, and was declared a national park in 1956. After years of disuse it was restored and in 1990 reopened as a museum.

EMANCIPATION PROCLAMATION: ANNIVERSARY. Jan 1, 1863. Two of the most important presidential proclamations of American history are those of Sept 22, 1862, and Jan 1, 1863, in which Abraham Lincoln, by executive proclamation, freed the slaves in the rebelling states. "That on . . . [Jan 1, 1863] . . . all persons held as slaves within any state or designated part of a state, the people whereof shall then be in rebellion against the United States, shall be then, thenceforward, and forever, free. . . ." See also: "13th Amendment Anniversary" (Dec 18) for abolition of slavery in all states.

ENGLAND: LONDON PARADE. Jan 1. London. Begins at noon at Westminster Bridge and progresses via Trafalgar Square, Piccadilly Circus and along Piccadilly. Est attendance: 1,000,000. For info: Mr Robert Bone, Exec Dir, The London Parade, Research House, Fraser Road, Perivale, Greenford, Middlesex, England UB6 7AQ. Phone: (44) (181) 566-8586. Fax: (44) (181) 566-8494. Email: 101612.1637@compuserve.com.

FAT FREE LIVING MONTH. Jan 1–31. Healthy living is achievable. Try for at least one month to reduce the fat in your diet. Fat Free Living, Inc is devoted to helping others "take the fat out" in the hope of preventing many of the diseases associated with high fat cholesterol diets. The first month of the New Year is the perfect time to change your life. For info: Fat Free Living Inc, 15202 N 50th Place, Scottsdale, AZ 85254. Phone: (888) 328-3731. Email: fatfree@goodnet.com. WWW: http://www.fatfreeliving.com

FORSTER, E.M.: BIRTH ANNIVERSARY. Jan 1, 1879. Edward Morgan Forster, English author born at London, England, is especially remembered for his six novels: *Where Angels Fear to Tread* (1905), *The Longest Journey* (1907), *A Room with a View* (1908), *Howard's End* (1910), *A Passage to India* (1924) and the posthumously published *Maurice* (1971). He also achieved eminence for his short stories and essays, and he collaborated on the libretto for one opera, Benjamin Britten's *Billy Budd* (1951). Forster died at Coventry, England, June 7, 1970.

FRANCE: THE PARIS PARADE. Jan 1. Paris. The parade begins at 2 and its route takes in much of Montmartre and passes "Sacre Coeur." International participation of marching bands, floats, vehicles, animals, etc. Est attendance: 100,000. For info: Robert Bone, The Paris Parade Festival, Research House, Fraser Road, Perivale, Middlesex, England UB6 7AQ. Phone: (44) (181) 566-8586. Fax: (44) (181) 566-8494.

HAITI: INDEPENDENCE DAY. Jan 1, 1804. A national holiday commemorating the proclamation of independence on Jan 1, 1804. Haiti, occupying the western third of the island Hispaniola (second largest of the West Indies), was a Spanish colony from the time of its discovery by Columbus in 1492 until 1697, then a French colony until the proclamation of independence in 1804.

HANGOVER HANDICAP RUN. Jan 1. Veteran's Park, Klamath Falls, OR. Two-mile fun run at 9 AM New Year's Day morning. The 1st place male and female finishers each take home a beer-can trophy. Est attendance: 60. For info: Hangover Handicap, 1800 Fairmont, Klamath Falls, OR 97601. Phone: (541) 882-6922. Fax: (541) 883-6481.

JANUARY DIET MONTH. Jan 1–31. To promote the importance of getting back on a healthy eating plan after the winter holidays and to remind dieters that nutritious popcorn can be a part of that plan. Annually, the month of January. For info: The Popcorn Institute, 401 N Michigan Ave, Chicago, IL 60611-4267. Phone: (312) 644-6610.

JAPANESE ERA NEW YEAR. Jan 1–3. Celebration of the beginning of the year Heisei Ten, the tenth year of Emperor Akihito's reign.

JOHN E. TEAMER BLACK-EYED PEA DINNER AND AWARDS CEREMONY. Jan 1. San Francisco, CA. Annual dinner celebrating the Southern tradition of eating one's way into good luck and prosperity throughout the coming year. Named in honor of the man who introduced this tradition to MACT-SFBA. Est attendance: 100. For info: Men of All Colors Together-San Francisco Bay Area, 973 Market St, Ste 600, San Francisco, CA 94103. Phone: (415) 675-0201. Email: mactsfba@aol.com. WWW: http://users.aol.com/mactsfba/home/page.html

KLIBAN, B(ERNARD): BIRTH ANNIVERSARY. Jan 1, 1935. Cartoonist B. Kliban was born at Norwalk, CT. He was known for his satirical drawings of cats engaged in human pursuits, which appeared in the books *Cat* (1975), *Never Eat Anything Bigger than Your Head & Other Drawings* (1976) and *Whack Your Porcupine* (1977), and on T-shirts, greeting cards, calendars, bedsheets and other merchandise, creating a $50 million industry before his death at San Francisco, CA, on Aug 12, 1990.

MARCH OF DIMES BIRTH DEFECTS PREVENTION MONTH. Jan 1–31. To heighten awareness of birth defects and how they may be prevented, to inform the public about the work of the March of Dimes and to offer opportunities to new volunteers for service in the prevention of birth defects. For info: March of Dimes Birth Defects Foundation, 1275 Mamaroneck Ave, White Plains, NY 10605. Phone: (914) 428-7100.

NATIONAL BE ON-PURPOSE MONTH. Jan 1–31. An observance to encourage us to start the new year by putting our good intentions into action, personally and professionally, and to trade confusion for clarity as we balance our lives with more meaning and purpose. For info: Kevin W. McCarthy, US Partners, PO Box 1568, Winter Park, FL 32790-1568. Phone: (407) 657-6000. Fax: (407) 645-1345.

NATIONAL BOOK BLITZ MONTH. Jan 1–31. Focuses attention on improving authors' relationships with the media in order to create a bestselling book. Free book PR evaluation available. Annually, the month of January. For info: Barbara Gaughen, Media 21, 7456 Evergreen Dr, Santa Barbara, CA 93117. Phone: (805) 968-8567. Fax: (805) 968-5747. Email: barbara@rain.org.

NATIONAL ENVIRONMENTAL POLICY ACT: ANNIVERSARY. Jan 1. The National Environmental Policy Act of 1969, establishing the Council on Environmental Quality and making it federal government policy to protect the environment, took effect Jan 1, 1970.

NATIONAL EYE CARE MONTH. Jan 1–31. This month is set aside to educate the public to seek medical eye care at the earliest sign of eye trouble to prevent blindness. National Eye Care Month is sponsored by the Optic Foundation. A free kit of materials is available upon request. Please mail a self-addressed label, or fax an exact copy of your mailing label with your request. For info: Rosemary Rushka, Optic Foundation, PO Box 429098, San Francisco, CA 94142-9098. Phone: (415) 561-8500. Fax: (415) 561-8567. WWW: http://www.eyenet.org

January 1998

S	M	T	W	T	F	S
				1	2	3
4	5	6	7	8	9	10
11	12	13	14	15	16	17
18	19	20	21	22	23	24
25	26	27	28	29	30	31

NATIONAL GEOGRAPHY BEE, SCHOOL LEVEL. Jan 1–9. (Begins Dec 1, 1997.) Principals must register their schools by Oct 15, 1997. Nationwide contest involving millions of students at the school level. The Bee is designed to encourage the teaching and study of geography. There are three levels of competition. A student must win school-level Bee in order to win the right to take a written exam. The written test determines the top 100 students in each state who are eligible to go on to the state level. National Geographic brings the state winner and his/her teacher to Washington for the national level in May. Alex Trebek moderates the national level. For info: Natl Geography Bee, Natl Geographic Society, 1145 17th St NW, Washington, DC 20036. Phone: (202) 828-6635.

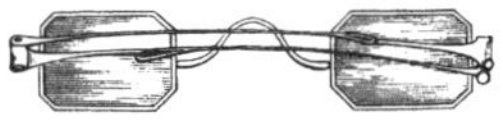

NATIONAL GLAUCOMA AWARENESS MONTH. Jan 1–31. African-Americans are 5 to 15 times more likely than the general population to go blind from glaucoma. Throughout this month, Prevent Blindness America® will provide valuable information about this "sneak thief of sight." Organizations are encouraged to educate the community through screenings, forums and programs. For info: Prevent Blindness America®, 500 E Remington Rd, Schaumburg, IL 60173. Phone: (800) 331-2020. Fax: (847) 843-8458. WWW: http://www.prevent-blindness.org

NATIONAL HIGH-TECH MONTH. Jan 1–31. Recognizing the dramatic effect high-tech products and services have had on the way we live now and how they will change the way we live in the 21st century. Promoting high-tech education and solutions in the home and in business. Annually, the month of January. For info: Kathleen Quinn, Pres, ProQuest Communications, Inc, PO Box 241, Wilmette, IL 60091-0241. Phone: (847) 998-9950. Fax: (847) 998-9945. Email: proquestpr@aol.com.

NATIONAL HOT TEA MONTH. Jan 1–31. To celebrate one of nature's most popular, soothing and relaxing beverages; the only beverage in America commonly served hot or iced, anytime, anywhere, for any occasion. For info: Joseph P. Semrany, Pres, The Tea Council of the USA, 230 Park Ave, Ste 1460, New York, NY 10169. Phone: (212) 986-6998. Fax: (212) 697-8658.

NATIONAL LOSE WEIGHT/FEEL GREAT WEEK. Jan 1–7. To inspire individuals to incorporate fitness into their daily routine and make exercise a priority, whether it be to promote weight loss or maintain overall good health and physical condition. For info: Jana Angelakis, PEX Personalized Exercise, 42 East 20 St, New York, NY 10003. Phone: (212) 254-1915.

NATIONAL PERSONAL SELF-DEFENSE AWARENESS MONTH. Jan 1–31. To educate Americans about realistic self-defense options, tactics and techniques in an increasingly aggressive world. Seminars and related events nationally focus on issues of awareness, prevention, risk reduction, confrontation avoidance and physical self-defense techniques to encourage individuals to take a pro-active role in their self-defense and in building self-confidence. For info: Natl Self-Defense Inst Inc, 300 71st St, 3rd Flr, Miami Beach, FL 33141. Phone: (305) 868-NSDI.

NATIONAL PRUNE THE FAT MONTH. Jan 1–31. To encourage Americans to cut the fat from their diets by using prune puree (a simple mixture of prunes and water) as a substitute for butter and oil in baked goods; to communicate the many benefits of prunes, their good taste, high fiber and versatility; and to dispel misconceptions about prunes. More information, recipes and telephone interviews are available. Sponsor: California Prune Board. For info: Daphne Pulver, Ketchum PR, 55 Union St, San Francisco, CA 94111. Phone: (415) 984-6307. Fax: (415) 837-0953.

NATIONAL RADIO MONTH. Jan 1–31. Celebrates 77 years of radio's role as an information and entertainment medium dedicated to serving the public. 11,000 local and national radio stations participate throughout the month. For info: Natl Assn of Broadcasters, 1771 N St NW, Washington, DC 20036-2891. Phone: (202) 429-5420. Fax: (202) 775-3523.

NATIONAL SOUP MONTH. Jan 1–31. To celebrate one of the world's favorite foods, and its relevance to today's lifestyles. For info: Public Affairs, Campbell Soup Co, Campbell Place, Camden, NJ 08103-1799. Phone: (800) 257-8443. WWW: http://www.campbellsoups.com

NATIONAL YOURS, MINE AND OURS MONTH. Jan 1–31. Blending families and creating positive step-relationships can be one of the most challenging aspects of a couple's remarriage. Each member of the family is affected in different ways. This observance focuses on what parents and children can expect as a step- or blended family and offers tips for a smooth transition and enhanced long-term relationships. Annually, the month of January. For info send SASE to: Teresa Langston, Dir, Parenting Without Pressure, 1330 Boyer St, Longwood, FL 32750-6311. Phone: (407) 767-2524.

NEW YEAR'S BLUEGRASS FESTIVAL. Jan 1–3. Convention Center, Jekyll Island, GA. 22nd annual festival. For info: Norman Adams, PO Box 98, Dahlonega, GA 30533. Phone: (706) 864-7203. Fax: (706) 864-1037.

NEW YEAR'S DAY. Jan 1. Legal holiday in all states and territories of the US and in most other countries. The world's most widely celebrated holiday.

NEW YEAR'S DISHONOR LIST. Jan 1. Since 1976, America's dishonor list of words banished from the Queen's English. Overworked words and phrases (e.g., *uniquely unique, first time ever, safe sex*). Send nominations to following address. For info: PR Office, Lake Superior State University, Sault Ste. Marie, MI 49783. Phone: (906) 635-2315. Fax: (906) 635-2111. WWW: http://www.lssu.edu

NEWPORT YACHT CLUB FROSTBITE FLEET RACE. Jan 1. Newport Yacht Club, Long Wharf, Newport, RI. Annual New Year's Day race. Sponsor: Newport Yacht Club. Est attendance: 5,000. For info: Newport Yacht Club, PO Box 488, Newport, RI 02840. Phone: (800) 326-6030. Fax: (401) 849-9060.

NOKIA SUGAR BOWL CLASSIC. Jan 1. Louisiana Superdome, New Orleans, LA. Bowl alliance championship football classic. The Sugar Bowl originated in 1935. Est attendance: 75,000. For info: Nokia Sugar Bowl, Louisiana Superdome, Mezzanine Level, 1500 Sugar Bowl Dr, New Orleans, LA 70112. Phone: (504) 528-8573 or (504) 525-4867.

OATMEAL MONTH. Jan 1–31. "Celebrate oatmeal, a low-fat, sodium-free, whole grain that when eaten daily as a part of a diet that's low in saturated fat and cholesterol may help reduce the risk of heart disease. Delicious recipes, helpful hints and tips from Quaker® Oats, The Oat Expert, will make enjoying the heart health benefits oatmeal has to offer easy, convenient and, above all, delicious." For info: The Oat Expert, 225 W Washington, Ste 1440, Chicago, IL 60606. Phone: (312) 629-1234.

OUTBACK BOWL GAME. Jan 1. Tampa Stadium, Tampa, FL. The New Year's Day Outback Bowl Game brings together top college football teams for postseason play. In addition, the bowl is highlighted by a variety of special events, sports activities, concerts and private functions. Est attendance: 65,000. For info: Mike Schulze, Tampa Bay Bowl Assn, 4511 N Himes Ave, Ste 260, Tampa, FL 33614. Phone: (813) 874-2695.

OWN YOUR SHARE OF AMERICA. Jan 1–Dec 31. A year-round campaign to promote and encourage individual investment in stocks of American companies and focus attention on individual investors' concerns and the individual's value to the securities markets. Write for a free pamphlet on investing. For info: Robert A. O'Hara, VP, Natl Assn of Investors Corp, 711 W Thirteen Mile Rd, Madison Heights, MI 48071. Phone: (810) 583-6242. Fax: (810) 583-4880.
WWW: http://www.better-investing.org

PENGUIN PLUNGE. Jan 1. Mackeral Cove, Jamestown, RI. Annual plunge into the icy waters of Narragansett Bay to benefit Rhode Island Special Olympics. Annually, Jan 1. Est attendance: 2,000. For info: Rhode Island Special Olympics, 33 College Hill Rd, Bldg 31, Warwick, RI 02886. Phone: (401) 823-7411. Fax: (401) 823-7415.

PHILIPPINES: BLACK NAZARENE FIESTA. Jan 1–9. Manila. A traditional nine-day fiesta honors Quiapo district's patron saint. Cultural events, fireworks and parades culminate in a procession with the life-size statue of the Black Nazarene. Procession begins at the historic Quiapo Church.

POLAR BEAR SWIM. Jan 1. Sheboygan Armory, Sheboygan, WI. Each New Year's Day at 1 PM, more than 450 daring swimmers brave Lake Michigan's ice floes. Most are costumed, all are crazy. Refreshments and free live entertainment from 10–6. Sponsor: Sheboygan Polar Bear Club. Est attendance: 2,000. For info: Sheboygan Conv and Visitors Bureau, 712 Riverfront Dr, Ste 101, Sheboygan, WI 53081. Phone: (414) 452-6443.

PORTLAND CENTER STAGE. Jan 1–Apr 25. (Season began Oct 3, 1997. Also Oct 3–Dec 31, 1998.) Portland, OR. A seven-month season of six plays by classical and contemporary playwrights in the Intermediate Theatre of the Portland Center for the Performing Arts. Est attendance: 90,000. For info: Portland Center Stage, PO Box 9008, Portland, OR 97207. Phone: (503) 274-6588. Fax: (503) 796-6509.

RAMADAN: THE ISLAMIC MONTH OF FASTING. Dec 31, 1997–Jan 28, 1998. Begins on Islamic lunar calendar date Ramadan 1, 1418. Ramadan, the ninth month of the Islamic calendar, is holy because it was during this month that the Holy Qur'an [Koran] was revealed. All adults of sound body and mind fast from dawn (before sunrise) until sunset to achieve spiritual and physical purification and self-discipline, abstaining from food, drink and intimate relations. It is a time for feeling a common bond with the poor and needy, of piety and prayer. Different methods for "anticipating" the visibility of the new moon crescent at Mecca are used by different Muslim groups. *Chase's* uses anticipated dates furnished by the American Muslim Council. US EST date may vary. See also: "Ramadan" (Dec 20).

REMINISCENCE MONTH. Jan 1–31. A time to recall, reminisce and record the memories of a lifetime. For info: Margaret L. Ingram, Family History Center, PO Box 1339, Albany, OR 97321. Phone: (541) 924-0268. Fax: (541) 924-0833.
Email: Margaret@matrixdm.com.
WWW: http://www.matrixdm.com/family-history

REVERE, PAUL: BIRTH ANNIVERSARY. Jan 1, 1735. American patriot, silversmith and engraver, maker of false teeth, eyeglasses, picture frames and surgical instruments. Best remembered for his famous ride on Apr 18, 1775, celebrated in Longfellow's poem, "The Midnight Ride of Paul Revere." Born at Boston, MA; died there May 10, 1818. See also: "Paul Revere's Ride Anniversary" (Apr 18).

January 1998

S	M	T	W	T	F	S
				1	2	3
4	5	6	7	8	9	10
11	12	13	14	15	16	17
18	19	20	21	22	23	24
25	26	27	28	29	30	31

ROSE BOWL GAME. Jan 1. Pasadena, CA. Football conference champions from Big Ten and Pacific-10 meet in the 84th Rose Bowl game. Tournament of Roses has been an annual New Year's Day event since 1890; Rose Bowl football game since 1902. Michigan defeated Stanford 49-0 in what was the first postseason football game. Called the Rose Bowl since 1923, it is preceded each year by the Tournament of Roses Parade. Est attendance: 100,000. For info: Pasadena Tournament of Roses Assn, 391 S Orange Grove Blvd, Pasadena, CA 91184. Phone: (818) 449-4100. Fax: (818) 449-9066.

ROSS, BETSY: BIRTH ANNIVERSARY. Jan 1, 1752. According to legend based largely on her grandson's revelations in 1870, needleworker Betsy Ross created the first stars-and-stripes flag in 1775, under instructions from George Washington. Her sewing and her making of flags were well known, but there is little corroborative evidence of her role in making the first stars-and-stripes. The account is generally accepted, however, in the absence of any documented claims to the contrary. She was born Elizabeth Griscom at Philadelphia, PA, and died there on Jan 30, 1836, at age 84.

RUSSIA: NEW YEAR'S DAY OBSERVANCE. Jan 1–2. National holiday. Modern tradition calls for setting up New Year's trees in homes, halls, clubs, palaces of culture and the hall of the Kremlin Palace. Children's parties with Granddad Frost and his granddaughter, Snow Girl. Games, songs, dancing, special foods, family gatherings and exchanges of gifts and New Year's cards.

SAINT BASIL'S DAY. Jan 1. St. Basil's or St. Vasily's feast day observed on Jan 1 by Eastern Orthodox churches. Special traditions for the day include serving St. Basil cakes, each of which contains a coin. Feast day observed on Jan 14 by those churches using Julian calendar.

SHANGHAI PARADE. Jan 1. Lewisburg, WV. A bit of Americana. Originally a spontaneous promenade that included everyone who happened by. Est attendance: 1,750. For info: Lewisburg Visitors Ctr, 105 Church St, Lewisburg, WV 24901. Phone: (304) 645-1000 or (800) 833-2068.

SILENT RECORD WEEK. Jan 1–7. To commemorate the anniversary of the invention of the silent record in 1960, which was played on Detroit jukeboxes. The following year a Silent Record Concert and Recording Session featured emcee Henry Morgan, Soupy Sales and the 120-piece Hush Symphonic Band. [Originated by the late W.T. Rabe of Sault Ste. Marie, MI.]

SNO'FLY: THE FIRST KITE FLY OF THE YEAR. Jan 1. Prairie View Park, Kalamazoo, MI. Keep the New Year's celebration in full flight at this high-flying alternative to (seemingly) endless football games. Sno'Fly takes off from the frozen lake at Prairie View Park. Est attendance: 500. For info: John Cosby, Mktg Coord, Kalamazoo County Parks Dept, 2900 Lake St, Kalamazoo, MI 49001. Phone: (616) 383-8778. Fax: (616) 383-8724.

SOLEMNITY OF MARY, MOTHER OF GOD. Jan 1. Holy Day of Obligation in Roman Catholic Church since calendar reorganization of 1969, replacing the Feast of the Circumcision, which had been recognized for more than 14 centuries. See also: "Circumcision of Christ" (Jan 1).

SOUTHWESTERN BELL COTTON BOWL CLASSIC. Jan 1. Dallas, TX. Postseason football game matching the championship team from the Big 12 with either the #2 team from the PAC-10 or the WAC champion. Est attendance: 68,000. For info: Cotton Bowl Athletic Assn, Box 569420, Dallas, TX 75356-9420. Phone: (214) 634-7525. Email: cotton@swbell.net. WWW: http://www.cottonbowl.com

STARMAN "FAMILY REUNION" YEAR. Jan 1–Dec 31. The organization Spotlight Starman International (SSI) celebrates the spirit of "Starman" by fostering the values and ethics of the show: integrity, compassion, responsibility, friendship, forgiveness, healthy parenting, life-long learning, peaceful problem-solving through honest communication, courage to change one's life for the better, social and environmental consciousness, hope for this planet and all its species. STARMAN FAMILY-CON convenes in Hollywood for a "Family Reunion" of those who created/appreciate "Starman." The dates of the convention will be available after Jan 1. For info: Vicki Werkley, Spotlight Starman Intl, 16563 Ellen Springs, Lower Lake, CA 95457. Phone: (707) 995-1228. Email: STARWERKS@aol.com.
WWW: http://www.calweb.com/~smccrory/starman.html

STOCK EXCHANGE HOLIDAY (NEW YEAR'S DAY). Jan 1. The holiday schedules for the various exchanges are subject to change if relevant rules, regulations or exchange policies are revised. If you have questions, phone: American Stock Exchange (212) 306-1000; Chicago Board of Trade (312) 435-3500; Chicago Board of Options Exchange (312) 786-5600; New York Stock Exchange (212) 656-2065; Pacific Stock Exchange (415) 393-4000; Philadelphia Stock Exchange (215) 496-5000.

SUDAN: INDEPENDENCE DAY. Jan 1. National holiday. Sudan was proclaimed a sovereign independent republic on Jan 1, 1956, ending its status as an Anglo-Egyptian condominium (since 1899).

TEXAS LIGHTS. Jan 1–15 (also Nov 15–Dec 31). Kingsville, TX. A spectacular drive-through holiday lighting display. More than 1 mile of dazzling animated displays will delight children and adults of all ages. Est attendance: 15,000. For info: Kingsville Conv and Visitors Bureau, PO Box 1562, Kingsville, TX 78364-1562. Phone: (800) 333-5032. Fax: (512) 592-3227. Email: kcvb@kingsville.org. WWW: http://www.kingsville.org

TOURNAMENT OF ROSES PARADE. Jan 1. Pasadena, CA. 109th annual parade. Theme: "Hav'n Fun." Rose Parade starting at 8:05 AM, PST, includes floats, bands and equestrians. Est attendance: 1,000,000. For info: Pasadena Tournament of Roses Assn, 391 S Orange Grove Blvd, Pasadena, CA 91184. Phone: (818) 449-4100. Fax: (818) 449-9066.

TUFF HEDEMAN PROFESSIONAL BULL RIDERS CHALLENGE. Jan 1–3. JK Northway Coliseum, Kingsville, TX. Bull riders from all over the country come to compete for national titles in this breathtaking rodeo event. Est attendance: 4,000. For info: Kingsville Conv & Visitors Bureau, PO Box 1562, Kingsville, TX 78364-1562. Phone: (800) 333-5032. Fax: (512) 592-3227. Email: kcvb@kingsville.org.
WWW: http://www.kingsville.org

UNITED KINGDOM AND REPUBLIC OF IRELAND: NEW YEAR'S HOLIDAY. Jan 1.

UNITED NATIONS: ASIAN AND PACIFIC DECADE OF DISABLED PERSONS: YEAR SIX. Jan 1–Dec 31. The decade 1993–2002 was proclaimed on Apr 23, 1992, by the Economic and Social Commission for Asia and the Pacific (ESCAP) and was endorsed by the General Assembly on Dec 16, 1992 (Res 47/88), to give further impetus to the implementation of the World Programme of Action concerning Disabled Persons in the ESCAP region and to strengthen regional cooperation in achieving the goals. Info from: United Nations, Dept of Public Info, New York, NY 10017.

UNITED NATIONS: DECADE AGAINST DRUG ABUSE: YEAR EIGHT. Jan 1–Dec 31. United Nations program for the decade 1991–2000 to strengthen international, regional and national efforts in the fight against drug abuse. Proclaimed by General Assembly on Feb 23, 1990 (Res S-17/2). Info from: United Nations, Dept of Public Info, New York, NY 10017.

UNITED NATIONS: DECADE FOR HUMAN RIGHTS EDUCATION: YEAR FOUR. Jan 1–Dec 31. On Dec 23, 1994, the General Assembly proclaimed this decade to begin on Jan 1, 1995, and welcomed the Plan of Action for the Decade submitted by the Secretary-General (Res 49/184). The Assembly expressed its conviction that human rights education should constitute a lifelong process, by which people learn respect for the dignity of others. Info from: United Nations, Dept of Public Info, New York, NY 10017.

UNITED NATIONS: DECADE FOR THE ERADICATION OF POVERTY: YEAR TWO. Jan 1–Dec 31. General Assembly on Dec 20, 1995, by Resolution 50/107 II, proclaimed 1997–2006 (the decade following the International Year for the Eradication of Poverty—1996) to be a time for governments and organizations to pursue implementation of the recommendations of the major UN conferences on this issue, particularly the World Summit for Social Development held in Copenhagen in March 1995. Info from: United Nations, Dept of Public Info, New York, NY 10017.

UNITED NATIONS: DECADE OF INTERNATIONAL LAW: YEAR NINE. Jan 1–Dec 31. The General Assembly declared this decade (1990–1999) for the purpose of promoting acceptance of and respect for international law principles; promoting peaceful settlement of disputes between states, including full respect for the International Court of Justice; encouraging development and codification of international law; and seeking to expand the teaching, study, dissemination and appreciation of international law. Info from: United Nations, Dept of Public Info, New York, NY 10017.

UNITED NATIONS: FOURTH UNITED NATIONS DEVELOPMENT DECADE: YEAR EIGHT. Jan 1–Dec 31. Major United Nations program (1991–2000) to promote world efforts to bridge enormous gap between advanced and developing countries, where two-thirds of the world's people live. (Res 45/199, Dec 21, 1990.) Info from: United Nations, Dept of Public Info, New York, NY 10017.

UNITED NATIONS: INTERNATIONAL DECADE FOR NATURAL DISASTER REDUCTION: YEAR NINE. Jan 1–Dec 31. A decade (1990–2000) in which the international community, under UN auspices, will pay special attention to fostering international cooperation in natural disaster reduction in order to reduce loss of life, property damage and social and economic disruption caused by natural hazards such as earthquakes, floods and hurricanes. Info from: United Nations, Dept of Public Info, New York, NY 10017.

UNITED NATIONS: INTERNATIONAL DECADE FOR THE ERADICATION OF COLONIALISM: YEAR NINE. Jan 1–Dec 31. On Nov 22, 1988, the General Assembly proclaimed 1990–2000 the International Decade for the Eradication of Colonialism. In December 1991 the Assembly declared the ultimate goal of the Decade to be the free exercise of the right of self-determination by the people of all remaining Non-Self-Governing Territories. 1998 marks the 38th anniversary of the adoption of the Declaration of the Granting of Independence to Colonial Countries and Peoples. Info from: United Nations, Dept of Public Info, New York, NY 10017.

UNITED NATIONS: INTERNATIONAL DECADE OF THE WORLD'S INDIGENOUS PEOPLE: YEAR FOUR (CONTINUING). Jan 1–Dec 9. (Began Dec 10, 1997.) Proclaimed by the General Assembly on Dec 21, 1993 (Res 48/163), this decade (1994–2004) focuses international attention and cooperation on the problems of indigenous people in a range of areas, such as human rights, health, education, development and environment. Governments are encouraged to include representatives of these people in planning and executing goals and activities for the decade. Info from: United Nations, Dept of Public Info, New York, NY 10017.

UNITED NATIONS: INTERNATIONAL YEAR OF THE OCEAN. Jan 1–Dec 31. On Dec 19, 1994, the General Assembly proclaimed 1998 the International Year of the Ocean to call attention to the decisive role the ocean plays in shaping the life of the planet. Info from: United Nations, Dept of Public Info, New York, NY 10017.

UNITED NATIONS: SECOND INDUSTRIAL DEVELOPMENT DECADE FOR AFRICA: YEAR SIX. Jan 1–Dec 31. On Dec 22, 1989, the General Assembly proclaimed the decade for the years 1991–2000 for the purpose of mobilizing increased political commitment to and financial and technical support for the industrialization of Africa. On Dec 22, 1992 (Res 47/177), the Assembly changed the time period for the decade to 1993–2002. Info from: United Nations, Dept of Public Info, New York, NY 10017.

UNITED NATIONS: SECOND TRANSPORT AND COMMUNICATIONS DECADE IN AFRICA: YEAR EIGHT. Jan 1–Dec 31. On Dec 20, 1988 (Res 43/179), the General Assembly proclaimed the decade 1991–2000 for the purpose of continuing the progress made in the UN's first decade (1978–1988) in solving the problems of the continent in this field and mobilizing the needed technical and financial resources. Info from: United Nations, Dept of Public Info, New York, NY 10017.

UNITED NATIONS: THIRD DISARMAMENT DECADE: YEAR NINE. Jan 1–Dec 31. United Nations General Assembly, in 1969, proclaimed the 1970s as a Disarmament Decade. Governments are urged to intensify efforts to stop the nuclear arms race, to promote nuclear disarmament and elimination of other weapons of mass destruction and to develop a treaty on complete disarmament under strict and effective international control. The observance was extended into a second decade, the 1980s, and a third, the 1990s (1990–1999). Info from: United Nations, Dept of Public Info, New York, NY 10017.

UNIVERSAL HOUR OF PEACE. Jan 1. A synchronized hour starting at noon (Greenwich Mean Time) dedicated to creating peace throughout our planet. Every man, woman and child is asked to spend the hour in meditation, prayer, conversation, listening to beautiful music or whatever it takes to help you concentrate on peace. The simple truth is "living peaceably begins by thinking peacefully." One hour of peace, a world of difference. For info: Dr. Barbara Condron, Intl Coord, School of Metaphysics, Natl HQ, HCR 1, Box 15, Windyville, MO 65783. Phone: (417) 345-8411. Fax: (417) 345-6668. Email: som@som.org. WWW: http://www.som.org

WESTERN PACIFIC HURRICANE SEASON. Jan 1–Dec 31. Most hurricanes occur from June 1 through Oct 1, though the season lasts all year. (Western Pacific: West of International Dateline.) Info from: US Dept of Commerce, Natl Oceanic and Atmospheric Admin, Rockville, MD 20852.

Z DAY. Jan 1. To give recognition on the first day of the year to all persons and places whose names begin with the letter "Z" and are always listed or thought of last in any alphabetized list. For info: Tom Zager, 4545 Kirkwood Dr, Sterling Heights, MI 48310.

ZAPATISTA REBELLION: ANNIVERSARY. Jan 1, 1994. Declaring war against the government of President Carlos Salinas de Gortari, the Zapatista National Liberation Army seized four towns in the state of Chiapas in southern Mexico on the first day of 1994. The rebel group, which took its name from the early 20th-century Mexican revolutionary Emiliano Zapata, issued a declaration stating that they were protesting discrimination against the Indian population of the region and against their severe poverty.

January 1998

S	M	T	W	T	F	S
				1	2	3
4	5	6	7	8	9	10
11	12	13	14	15	16	17
18	19	20	21	22	23	24
25	26	27	28	29	30	31

ZWINGLI, ULRICH: BIRTH ANNIVERSARY. Jan 1, 1484. Swiss humanist, author, preacher, politician and reformer, born at Wildhaus, St. Gall, Switzerland. While serving as a military chaplain in the Second War of Kappel, Zwingli was killed on Oct 11, 1531. A monument marks the place where he fell during the battle.

BIRTHDAYS TODAY

Valentina Cortese, 73, actress (*The Barefoot Contessa, Juliet of the Spirits*), born Milan, Italy, Jan 1, 1925.

Ellen DeGeneres, 40, comedienne, actress ("Ellen"), born New Orleans, LA, Jan 1, 1958.

Ernest F. Hollings, 76, US Senator (D, South Carolina), born Charleston, SC, Jan 1, 1922.

Dewey LaMarr Hoyt, 43, former baseball player, born Columbia, SC, Jan 1, 1955.

Milt Jackson, 75, jazz musician (The Modern Jazz Quartet), born Detroit, MI, Jan 1, 1923.

Helmut Jahn, 58, architect, born Nuremberg, Germany, Jan 1, 1940.

Frank Langella, 58, actor (*The Twelve Chairs*), born Bayonne, NJ, Jan 1, 1940.

Don Novello (Father Guido Sarducci), 55, actor, comedian ("The Smothers Brothers Show," "Saturday Night Live"), born Ashtabula, OH, Jan 1, 1943.

J.D. Salinger, 79, author (*Catcher in the Rye; Franny & Zooey; Seymour: An Introduction*), born New York, NY, Jan 1, 1919.

JANUARY 2 — FRIDAY

Day 2 — 363 Remaining

55-MPH SPEED LIMIT: ANNIVERSARY. Jan 2. President Richard Nixon signed a bill on Jan 2, 1974, requiring states to limit highway speeds to a maximum of 55 mph. This measure was meant to conserve energy during the crisis precipitated by the embargo imposed by the Arab oil-producing countries on the United States. A plan, used by some states, limited sale of gasoline on odd-numbered days for cars whose plates ended in odd numbers and even-numbered days for even-numbered plates. Some states limited purchases to $2–$3 per auto, and lines as long as six miles resulted in some locations. See also: "Arab Oil Embargo Lifted" (Mar 13).

GEORGIA: RATIFICATION DAY. Jan 2, 1788. By unanimous vote on Jan 2, 1788, Georgia became the fourth state to ratify the Constitution.

HAITI: ANCESTORS' DAY. Jan 2. Commemoration of the ancestors. Also known as Hero's Day. Public holiday.

JAPAN: KAKIZOME. Jan 2. Traditional Japanese festival gets under way when the first strokes of the year are made on paper with the traditional brushes.

KENNEDY ANNOUNCES FOR PRESIDENCY: ANNIVERSARY. Jan 2, 1960. Senator John F. Kennedy announced his bid for the Democratic presidential nomination.

MILLER, ROGER: BIRTH ANNIVERSARY. Jan 2, 1936. Country and western singer, songwriter and musician "King of the Road" Roger Miller was born at Ft Worth, TX. Miller won 11 Grammy Awards and a Tony (1986 for the score to the Broadway play *Big River*). Miller died Oct 25, 1992, at Los Angeles, CA.

NASHVILLE FISHING EXPO. Jan 2–4. Tennessee State Fairgrounds, Nashville, TN. Annual event featuring the latest in fishing tackle, rods, reels, boats, boating equipment, guide services and other accessories. Daily seminars by BASS pros. Est attendance: 10,000. For info: Daryl Hobby, Esau, Inc, PO Box 50096, Knoxville, TN 37950. Phone: (423) 588-1233 or (800) 588-ESAU. Fax: (423) 588-6938.

RUSSIA: PASSPORT PRESENTATION. Jan 2. A ceremony for 16-year-olds, who are recognized as citizens of the country on this day. Always on the first working day of the New Year.

SMOKY MOUNTAIN WINTERFEST BRIDGE FESTIVAL. Jan 2–4. Heartlander Country Resort, Pigeon Forge, TN. Sectional bridge tournament. For info: Pigeon Forge Dept of Tourism, 2450 Parkway, PO Box 1390, Pigeon Forge, TN 37868. Phone: (800) 251-9100.

SPACE MILESTONE: *LUNA 1* (USSR). Jan 2, 1959. First moon shot missed and became first spacecraft from Earth to orbit sun.

SPAIN CAPTURES GRANADA: ANNIVERSARY. Jan 2, 1492. Spaniards took the city of Granada from the Moors, ending seven centuries of Muslim rule in Spain.

STAMP EXPO. Jan 2–4. Travelodge Hotel, Long Beach, CA. Annual expo. Est attendance: 7,500. For info: Intl Stamp Collectors Soc, PO Box 854, Van Nuys, CA 91408. Phone: (818) 997-6496. Fax: (818) 988-4337. Email: iibick@aol.com. WWW: http://www.4free.com/bick

TAFT, HELEN HERRON: BIRTH ANNIVERSARY. Jan 2, 1861. Wife of William Howard Taft, 27th President of the US, born at Cincinnati, OH. Died May 22, 1943.

THOMAS, MARTHA CAREY: BIRTH ANNIVERSARY. Jan 2, 1857. The second president of Bryn Mawr College, Martha Carey Thomas gained a reputation for her insistence that the education of women should be as rigorous as that of men. A zealous suffragist, she served as the first president of the National College Women's Equal Suffrage League. Thomas promoted Bryn Mawr's Summer School for Women in Industry (opened in 1921) to provide a liberal education for working women. Born at Baltimore, MD, she died at Philadelphia, Dec 2, 1935.

WOLFE, JAMES: BIRTH ANNIVERSARY. Jan 2, 1727 (New Style). English general who commanded the British army's victory over Montcalm's French forces on the Plains of Abraham at Quebec City in 1759. As a result, France surrendered Canada to England. Wolfe was born at Westerham, Kent, England. He died at the Plains of Abraham, of battle wounds on Sept 13, 1759, at age 32.

BIRTHDAYS TODAY

Jim Bakker (James Orsen), 59, former TV evangelist, born Muskegon, MI, Jan 2, 1939.

Christopher Durang, 49, playwright, actor, born Montclair, NJ, Jan 2, 1949.

Cuba Gooding, Jr, 30, actor (*Jerry Maguire*), born The Bronx, NY, Jan 2, 1968.

Diane Lane, 33, actress (*A Little Romance, Rumble Fish*), born New York, NY, Jan 2, 1965.

Kay A. Orr, 59, former Governor of Nebraska (R), born Burlington, IA, Jan 2, 1939.

Wendy Philips, 46, actress (Stacey Walling on "Executive Suite"), born Brooklyn, NY, Jan 2, 1952.

Richard Riley, 65, US Secretary of Education in Clinton administration, born Greenville, SC, Jan 2, 1933.

Renata Tebaldi, 76, singer, born Pesaro, Italy, Jan 2, 1922.

Michael Tippett, 93, composer, born London, England, Jan 2, 1905.

JANUARY 3 — SATURDAY

Day 3 — 362 Remaining

ALASKA: ADMISSION DAY. Jan 3. Alaska, which had been purchased from Russia in 1867, became the 49th state on Jan 3, 1959. The area of Alaska is nearly one-fifth the size of the rest of the United States.

"THE ARSENIO HALL SHOW" TV PREMIERE: ANNIVERSARY. Jan 3, 1989. Arsenio Hall became the first African-American to host a successful syndicated late-night talk show. The show attracted a younger audience than that of Johnny Carson's "The Tonight Show" and effectively limited the impact of CBS's 1989 late-night entry, "The Pat Sajak Show." Hall was successful in booking guests with soul and rap music acts who had rarely been seen on other shows. His was also the show on which presidential candidate Bill Clinton appeared, playing the saxophone in dark glasses. Hall was named by *TV Guide* (June 1990) as its first "TV Person of the Year."

ATTLEE, CLEMENT RICHARD: BIRTH ANNIVERSARY. Jan 3, 1883. English leader of the Labour Party and prime minister (July 1945–Oct 1951). Born at London, England; died there Oct 8, 1967.

BATTLE OF STONE'S RIVER: ANNIVERSARY. Jan 3, 1863. After three days of fighting near Murfreesboro, TN, General Braxton Bragg withdrew his Confederate troops from the Battle of Stone's River on Jan 3, 1863, despite being in relative control of the battlefield on the first day's fighting. Bragg received heavy criticism for his actions at Stone's River.

CONGRESS ASSEMBLES. Jan 3. The Constitution provides that "the Congress shall assemble at least once in every year. . . ." and the 20th Amendment specifies "and such meeting shall begin at noon on the 3rd day of January, unless they shall by law appoint a different day."

COOLIDGE, GRACE ANNA GOODHUE: BIRTH ANNIVERSARY. Jan 3, 1879. Wife of Calvin Coolidge, 30th president of the US, born at Burlington, VT. Died July 8, 1957.

DAVIES, MARION: BIRTH ANNIVERSARY. Jan 3, 1897. Born at Brooklyn, NY, Marion Cecilia Douras became Marion Davies and made her first appearance on film in 1917. Her romantic and professional involvement with newspaper magnate William Randolph Hearst ensured the type of publicity that would launch her to stardom. Her films included *Runaway Romany*, *When Knighthood Was in Flower*, *The Patsy* and *Show People*. She retired from the entertainment industry in 1937. On Sept 23, 1961, Davies died of cancer at Hollywood.

EAGLE WATCH. Jan 3–4. Mississippi Valley Welcome Center, LeClaire, IA. A slide show and three 45-minute oral presentations are given by the Army Corps of Engineers regarding American bald eagles, their habits and why they migrate to the Mississippi River Valley area. Rangers are available with binoculars and telescopes to help spot the eagles along the river. Est attendance: 700. For info: Pam Black, Dir Visitor Services, Mississippi Valley Welcome Ctr, 900 Eagle Ridge Rd, LeClaire, IA 52753. Phone: (319) 289-3009. Fax: (319) 289-3159.

FIRST FEMALE CONGRESSIONAL PAGE: ANNIVERSARY. Jan 3, 1939. Gene Cox, 13, served on the House floor as aide to her father, Representative Eugene Cox (D-GA), on opening day of the 76th Congress. She was paid $4 for 3 hours of work and there were no objections to her one-day service. More than 30 years later, however, there was much debate when Senator Jacob Javits (R-NY) nominated a female to be a real Senate page.

LENNON-ONO ALBUM CONFISCATION: ANNIVERSARY. Jan 3. John Lennon and Yoko Ono posed nude for the cover of their album *Two Virgins*. On Jan 3, 1969, a shipment of 30,000 of the albums was confiscated by police in Newark, NJ, as a violation of pornography statutes.

"LOOK UP AND LIVE" TV PREMIERE: ANNIVERSARY. Jan 3, 1954. CBS broadcast this show on Sunday mornings for 24 years. Rev Lawrence McMasters appeared in the early years and Merv Griffin hosted the show in 1955. Pamela Ilott, executive producer, was also director of religious programming for CBS News.

MOTT, LUCRETIA (COFFIN): BIRTH ANNIVERSARY. Jan 3, 1793. American teacher, minister, antislavery leader and (with Elizabeth Cady Stanton) one of the founders of the women's rights movement in the US. Born at Nantucket, MA, she died near Philadelphia, PA, Nov 11, 1880.

PAPER MANIA PLUS. Jan 3–4. Hartford, CT. All types of ephemera, advertising and photography, from colonial deeds to Beatles memorablia on display and for sale. For info: Hillcrest Promotions, Box 152, Wethersfield, CT 06109. Phone: (860) 529-7582.

PAVLOVA, ANNA: BIRTH ANNIVERSARY. Jan 3, 1885. Russian ballerina Anna Pavlova, thought by some to have been the greatest dancer of all time, was born at St. Petersburg, Russia. After performing with great success with the Ballet Russe and other companies, she formed her own company in 1910 and performed on tour for enthusiastic audiences in nearly every country in the world. Pavlova died at The Hague, Netherlands, on Jan 23, 1931, at age 46.

"QUEEN FOR A DAY" TV PREMIERE: ANNIVERSARY. Jan 3, 1956. NBC/ABC game show and syndicated broadcast on which merchandise prizes were awarded to the contestant who evoked the most sympathy from the studio audience. The show began some 11 years earlier on the radio with Jack Bailey hosting. Five women were chosen from the audience to appear on stage. Each related her story of misfortune and explained what she needed to remedy the situation and the audience would vote by applause. The lucky winner was then given the royal treatment—crown, sceptre and red robe—plus a prize to help with her problem. This soon became the top-rated daytime show. Jeanne Cagney was the show's fashion commentator. In 1970 the show went into syndication with Dick Curtis as host, but it didn't last long.

January 1998

S	M	T	W	T	F	S
				1	2	3
4	5	6	7	8	9	10
11	12	13	14	15	16	17
18	19	20	21	22	23	24
25	26	27	28	29	30	31

RAUH, JOSEPH L. JR: BIRTH ANNIVERSARY. Jan 3, 1911. Political activist Joseph L. Rauh, Jr, was born at Cincinnati, OH. In 1947 he cofounded the Americans for Democratic Action (ADA), which supports liberal causes. Rauh helped create the minority civil rights plank at the 1948 Democratic National Convention—a foundation for the federal civil rights legislation in the 1960s. He served on the executive board of the NAACP and was general counsel to the Leadership Conference on Civil Rights. He died on Sept 3, 1992, at Washington, DC.

STURGES, JOHN: BIRTH ANNIVERSARY. Jan 3, 1911. Motion picture director John Sturges, born at Oak Park, IL, was known for his action movies. He received an Academy Award nomination in 1955 for *Bad Day at Black Rock*. He also directed *Gunfight at the OK Corral* (1956), *The Magnificent Seven* (1960), *The Great Escape* (1963) and his last film *The Eagle Has Landed* (1977). He died on Aug 18, 1992, at San Luis Obispo, CA.

TOLKIEN, J[OHN] R[ONALD] R[EUEL]: BIRTH ANNIVERSARY. Jan 3, 1892. Author of *The Hobbitt* (1937) and the trilogy *The Lord of the Rings*. Though best known for his fantasies, Tolkien was also a serious philologist. Born at Bloemfontein, South Africa, he died at Bournemouth, England, on Sept 2, 1973.

BIRTHDAYS TODAY

Joan Walsh Anglund, 72, author, illustrator of children's books (*Crocus in the Snow, Bedtime Book*), born Hinsdale, IL, Jan 3, 1926.

Victor Borge (Borge Rosenbaum), 89, comedian, pianist, born Copenhagen, Denmark, Jan 3, 1909.

Dabney Coleman, 66, actor ("Buffalo Bill," *Nine to Five, Tootsie*), born Austin, TX, Jan 3, 1932.

James Samuel (Jim) Everett III, 35, football player, born Emporia, KS, Jan 3, 1963.

Mel Gibson, 47, actor (*Hamlet, The Road Warrior, Lethal Weapon*), born New York, NY, Jan 3, 1951.

Carla Anderson Hills, 64, former US Trade Representative (Bush administration), born Los Angeles, CA, Jan 3, 1934.

Robert Marvin (Bobby) Hull, 59, Hockey Hall of Fame left wing, born Point Anne, Ontario, Canada, Jan 3, 1939.

Robert Loggia, 68, actor, born Staten Island, NY, Jan 3, 1930.

Victoria Principal, 48, actress (Pam Ewing on "Dallas"), born Fukuoka, Japan, Jan 3, 1950.

Stephen Stills, 53, musician, songwriter, born Dallas, TX, Jan 3, 1945.

JANUARY 4 — SUNDAY

Day 4 — 361 Remaining

AMNESTY FOR POLYGAMISTS: ANNIVERSARY. Jan 4, 1893. President Benjamin Harrison issued a proclamation granting full amnesty and pardon to all persons who had since Nov 1, 1890, abstained from unlawful cohabitation of a polygamous marriage. This was intended in the main for a specific group of elderly Mormons who had previously continued in the practice of contracting into serial marriages. Amnesty was based on the condition that those pardoned must obey the law in the future or be "vigorously prosecuted." The practice of polygamy was a factor interfering with attainment of statehood for Utah. The last attempt to prosecute polygamy in Utah occurred in 1960 when one individual was cited for illegal cohabitation, but he eluded arrest and so was never brought to trial.

BRAILLE, LOUIS: BIRTH ANNIVERSARY. Jan 4, 1809. The inventor of a widely used touch system of reading and writing for the blind was born at Coupvray, France. Permanently blinded at the age of three by a leatherworking awl in his father's saddlemaking shop, Braille developed a system of writing that used, ironically, an awl-like stylus to punch marks in paper that could be felt and interpreted by the blind. The system was largely ignored until after Braille died in poverty, suffering from tuberculosis, on Mar 28, 1852.

"THE CATHOLIC HOUR" TV PREMIERE: 45th ANNIVERSARY. Jan 4, 1953. Produced in cooperation with the National Council of Catholic Men, this show ran for 17 years, alternating from week to week with "The Eternal Light" and "Frontiers of Faith."

CELEBRATION SUNDAY. Jan 4. To help raise awareness of the rights done to correct the wrongs done to women, beginning with Christians. At 2 PM at Christian Women's Ministries and everywhere, throughout the day, we rejoice and demonstrate our gratitude to God and to one another for the good already done on behalf of our Christian sisters, by doing deliberate acts of love or justice to or on behalf of one or more of our Christian sisters. Est attendance: 100. For info send SASE: Christian Women's Ministries, 222 SW Harrison, Garden Office 9, Portland, OR 97201. Email: pastor@christianwomen.com. WWW: http://www.christianwomen.com/ministries

"COLLEGE BOWL" TV PREMIERE: ANNIVERSARY. Jan 4, 1959. Originally, a quiz show on CBS. Two colleges each sent a team of their best and brightest to the academic competition. The college received $500 for their scholarship funds for showing up and $1,500 plus another appearance if their team won. One team from a small college in the Midwest was tripped up over a question asking the types of teeth humans have and the number of each. "College Bowl" was sponsored by General Electric, produced by Jack Cleary and hosted by Allen Ludden (1959–62) and Robert Earle (1962–70). More recent incarnations of "College Bowl" have appeared on NBC and Disney with Pat Sajak and Dick Cavett as hosts.

EARTH AT PERIHELION. Jan 4. At approximately 4 PM, EST, planet Earth will reach Perihelion, that point in its orbit when it is closest to the sun (about 91,400,000 miles). The Earth's mean distance from the sun (mean radius of its orbit) is reached early in the months of April and October. Note that Earth is closest to the sun during Northern Hemisphere winter. See also: "Earth at Aphelion" (July 3).

FIRST MONDAY TRADE DAYS. Jan 4–5. (Also the 1st Monday of every month and the preceding Sunday.) Jackson County Courthouse Square, Scottsboro, AL. One of the Deep South's oldest and largest trade days where bartering, haggling and swapping of goods has not passed on with time; blend of antique shows, craft fairs, rummage sales. Believed to have begun in the mid-1850s when Jackson County Circuit Court used to meet on the first Monday of each month, thus attracting tradesmen. Est attendance: 7,500 per month. For info: Rick Roden, Tourism Exec Dir, 409 S Broad St, Scottsboro, AL 35768. Phone: (205) 259-5500. Fax: (205) 259-4447.

GENERAL TOM THUMB: BIRTH ANNIVERSARY. Jan 4, 1838. Charles Sherwood Stratton, perhaps the most famous midget in history, was born at Bridgeport, CT. His growth almost stopped during his first year, but he eventually reached a height of three feet, four inches and a weight of 70 pounds. "Discovered" by P.T. Barnum in 1842, Stratton, as "General Tom Thumb," became an internationally known entertainer and on tour performed before Queen Victoria and other heads of state. On Feb 10, 1863, he married another midget, Lavinia Warren. Stratton died at Middleborough, MA, on July 15, 1883.

GRIMM, JACOB: BIRTH ANNIVERSARY. Jan 4, 1785. Librarian, mythologist and philologist, born at Hanau, Germany. Best remembered for *Grimm's Fairy Tales* (in collaboration with his brother Wilhelm). Died at Berlin, Germany, Sept 20, 1863.

HOLLOWAY, STERLING: BIRTH ANNIVERSARY. Jan 4, 1905. Actor Sterling Holloway prospered in films and television, but he is probably best remembered as the voice of Winnie the Pooh. Holloway provided the voices for a number of characters in several full-length animated features, including *Alice in Wonderland* (the Cheshire Cat), *The Aristocats* and *The Jungle Book*. He died Nov 22, 1992, at Los Angeles, CA.

MYANMAR: INDEPENDENCE DAY. Jan 4. National Day. Formerly Burma, the country's name was changed to the Union of Myanmar in 1989 to reflect that the population is made up not just of the Burmese but of many other ethnic groups as well. The British controlled the country from 1826 until 1948 when Burma was granted independence. Since then it has been controlled primarily by military regimes despite attempts at democracy.

"NIGHT COURT" TV PREMIERE: ANNIVERSARY. Jan 4, 1984. NBC sitcom set in an urban courtroom. Initially "Night Court" centered on humorous courtroom predicaments, but over time began to focus more on the regular characters and made hilarious use of that ensemble. The original cast included Harry Anderson as Judge Harry T. Stone; John Larroquette as prosecutor Dan Fielding; Richard Moll as court officer Bull Shannon; and Selma Diamond (1984–85) as court officer Selma Hacker. Karen Austin as clerk Lana Wagner and Paula Kelly as public defender Liz Williams were gone after one season; Ellen Foley then became PD Billie Young but was replaced by Markie Post in 1985 as PD Christine Sullivan. Charles Robinson joined the cast as clerk Mack Robinson in 1985. Diamond died in 1985 and Florence Halop, who then appeared as court officer Florence Kleiner, died in 1986. The much younger actress Marsha Warfield was then brought aboard as Court Officer Roz Russell. Mel Tormé made a few appearances as himself, Harry's idol.

NIXON'S REJECTION OF SENATE ORDER: ANNIVERSARY. Jan 4, 1974. President Richard Nixon rejected the Senate Watergate Committee's subpoenas seeking White House tapes and documents.

POLISH-AMERICAN IN THE HOUSE: ANNIVERSARY. Jan 4, 1977. Maryland Democrat Barbara Mikulski took her seat in the US House of Representatives, the first Polish-American ever to do so. An able voice for female as well as working class Baltimore constituents of the 3rd District, Ms Mikulski went on to be elected to the US Senate.

SETON, ELIZABETH ANN BAYLEY: FEAST DAY. Jan 4. First American-born saint (beatified Mar 17, 1963; canonized Sept 14, 1975). Born at New York, NY, Aug 28, 1774, Seton was the founder of the American Sisters of Charity, the first American order of Roman Catholic nuns. She died at Baltimore, MD, Jan 4, 1821.

"SOMEDAY WE'LL LAUGH ABOUT THIS" WEEK. Jan 4–10. We've all used the expression, "Someday we'll laugh about this!" Why wait? It usually takes less than seven days for people to violate 90% of their New Year's resolutions. This week helps us to remember the art of laughing at ourselves. This week tickles the yoke and joke of perfectionism while encouraging people to strive for excellence at the same time. This week is a great way to start the new year—laughing at the humorous human condition. For a free information packet on the positive power of humor send a stamped ($1.01) self-addressed envelope. For info: The Humor Project, Inc, 110 Spring St, Dept C, Saratoga Springs, NY 12866. Phone: (518) 587-8770. Fax: (518) 587-8771. Email: humor@wizvax.net. WWW: http://www.wizvax.net/humor/

TRIVIA DAY. Jan 4. In celebration of those who know all sorts of facts and/or have doctorates in uselessology. For info: Robert L. Birch, Puns Corps, Box 2364, Falls Church, VA 22042-0364. Phone: (703) 533-3668.

UTAH: ADMISSION DAY: ANNIVERSARY. Jan 4, 1896. Utah became the 45th state on this day in 1896.

BIRTHDAYS TODAY

Dyan Cannon, 61, actress (Oscar nomination for *Heaven Can Wait, Bob and Carol and Ted and Alice*), born Tacoma, WA, Jan 4, 1937.

Patrick Cassidy, 37, actor ("Bay City Blues," *Longtime Companion*), born Jan 4, 1961.

Jean Chretien, 64, 20th prime minister of Canada, born Shawinigan, Quebec, Jan 4, 1934.

Clifford Eugene (Cliff) Levingston, 37, former basketball player, born San Diego, CA, Jan 4, 1961.

Ann Magnuson, 42, actress, writer, performance artist ("Anything but Love," *Desperately Seeking Susan, Tequila Sunrise*), born Charleston, WV, Jan 4, 1956.

Floyd Patterson, 63, former boxer, born Waco, NC, Jan 4, 1935.

Barbara Rush, 71, actress ("Peyton Place," *Magnificent Obsession, Hombre*), born Denver, CO, Jan 4, 1927.

Donald Francis (Don) Shula, 68, former football coach and player, born Paineville, OH, Jan 4, 1930.

Jane Wyman (Sarah Jane Fulks), 84, actress ("Falcon Crest," *My Man Godfrey, My Favorite Spy*; Oscars for *Johnny Belinda* and *Magnificent Obsession*), born St. Joseph, MO, Jan 4, 1914.

JANUARY 5 — MONDAY

Day 5 — 360 Remaining

AILEY, ALVIN: BIRTH ANNIVERSARY. Jan 5, 1931. Dancer and choreographer. Born at Rogers, TX, Alvin Ailey began his noted career as a choreographer in the late 1950s after a successful career as a dancer. He founded the Alvin Ailey American Dance Theater, drawing from classical ballet, jazz, Afro-Caribbean and modern dance idioms to create the 79 ballets of the company's repertoire. He and his work played a central part in establishing a role for blacks in the world of modern dance. Ailey died on Dec 1, 1989, at New York, NY.

"ALL MY CHILDREN" TV PREMIERE: ANNIVERSARY. Jan 5, 1970. This ABC show became TV's top-rated soap opera by the 1978–79 season, and even today the show keeps viewers glued to the screen. "All My Children" was created by Agnes Nixon, who had written for "Search for Tomorrow," "Another World" and "One Life to Live." Set in a place called Pine Valley, NY, the show focused on the Tyler and Martin families. The story includes the illegitimate child of Dr. Tyler, Erica Kane (played by Susan Lucci), who became one of daytime TV's most popular characters. Lucci has been nominated more than a dozen times for an Emmy, but has not won. This serial has included in its cast Hugh Franklin as Dr. Charles Tyler and Ruth Warrick as his wife, Phoebe; son Lincoln has been played by James Karen, Paul Dumont, Nicholas Pryor and Peter White; daughter Ann by Diana De Vegh, Joanna Miles, Judith Barcroft and Gwyn Gilliss.

CARVER, GEORGE WASHINGTON: 55th DEATH ANNIVERSARY. Jan 5, 1943. Black American agricultural scientist, author, inventor and teacher. Born into slavery at Diamond Grove, MO, probably in 1864. His research led to the creation of synthetic products made from peanuts, potatoes and wood. Carver died at Tuskegee, AL, on Jan 5, 1943. His birthplace became a national monument in 1953.

DECATUR, STEPHEN: BIRTH ANNIVERSARY. Jan 5, 1779. American naval officer (whose father and grandfather, both also named Stephen Decatur, were also seafaring men) born at Sinepuxent, MD. In a toast at a dinner in Norfolk in 1815, Decatur spoke his most famous words: "Our country! In her intercourse with foreign nations may she always be in the right; but our country, right or wrong." Mortally wounded in a duel with Commodore James Barron, at Bladensburg, MD, on the morning of Mar 22, 1820, Decatur was carried to his home in Washington where he died a few hours later.

January 1998	S	M	T	W	T	F	S
					1	2	3
	4	5	6	7	8	9	10
	11	12	13	14	15	16	17
	18	19	20	21	22	23	24
	25	26	27	28	29	30	31

FIVE-DOLLAR-A-DAY MINIMUM WAGE: ANNIVERSARY. Jan 5. Henry Ford announced on Jan 5, 1914, that all worthy Ford Motor Company employees would receive a minimum wage of $5 a day. Ford explained the policy as "profit sharing and efficiency engineering." The more cynical attributed it to an attempt to prevent unionization and to obtain a docile workforce that would accept job speedups. To obtain this minimum wage an employee had to be of "good personal habits." Whether an individual fit these criteria was determined by a new office created by Ford Motor Company—the Sociological Department.

ITALY: EPIPHANY FAIR. Jan 5. Piazza Navona, Rome, Italy. On the eve of Epiphany a fair of toys, sweets and presents takes place among the beautiful Bernini Fountains.

MONDALE, WALTER FREDERICK: 70th BIRTHDAY. Jan 5, 1928. 42nd vice president of the US and Democratic Party candidate for president in 1984. Born at Ceylon, MN.

MOON PHASE: FIRST QUARTER. Jan 5. Moon enters First Quarter phase at 9:18 AM, EST.

NEW YEAR'S RESOLUTIONS WEEK. Jan 5–9. To show people how, why and what resolutions/goals should be set and the necessary action steps to make this new year the best ever! For info: Gary Ryan Blair, Blair Leadership Group, 1201 E Fayette St, Syracuse, NY 13210. Phone: (800) 731-GOAL. Fax: (315) 474-6954. Email: GoalsGuy@aol.com.

PICCARD, JEANNETTE RIDLON: BIRTH ANNIVERSARY. Jan 5. First American woman to qualify as free balloon pilot (1934). One of first women to be ordained as Episcopal priest (1976). Pilot for record-setting balloon ascent into stratosphere (from Dearborn, MI, Oct 23, 1934) (57,579 ft) with her husband, Jean Felix Piccard. See also: "Piccard, Jean Felix: Birth Anniversary" (Jan 28). Identical twin married to identical twin. Born at Chicago, IL, Jan 5, 1895. Died at Minneapolis, MN, May 17, 1981.

ROMAN CATHOLIC/EASTERN ORTHODOX MEETING: ANNIVERSARY. Jan 5, 1964. Pope Paul VI and Patriarch Athenagoras of Jerusalem met in the Holy Land for the first meeting in five centuries between a Roman Catholic pontiff and an Eastern Orthodox patriarch.

☆ ☆ ☆

RUFFIN, EDMUND: BIRTH ANNIVERSARY. Jan 5, 1794. Born in Prince George County, VA, Edmund Ruffin was an American agriculturist whose discoveries about crop rotation and fertilizer were influential in the early agrarian culture of the US. He published the *Farmer's Register* from 1833 to 1842, a journal that promoted scientific agriculture. A noted politician as well as a farmer, he was an early advocate of Southern secession whose views were widely circulated in pamphlets. As a member of the Palmetto Guards of Charleston, he was given the honor of firing the first shot on Fort Sumter on Apr 12, 1861. According to legend, after the South's defeat he became despondent and, wrapping himself in the Confederate flag, took his own life on June 18, 1865, at Amelia County, VA.

TWELFTH NIGHT. Jan 5. Evening before Epiphany. Twelfth Night marks the end of medieval Christmas festivities and the end of Twelfthtide (the 12-day season after Christmas ending with Epiphany). Also called Twelfth Day Eve.

WYOMING INAUGURATES FIRST WOMAN GOVERNOR IN US. Jan 5. Nellie Tayloe (Mrs William B.) Ross became the first woman to serve as governor upon her inauguration as governor of Wyoming on Jan 5, 1925.

BIRTHDAYS TODAY

Robert Duvall, 67, actor ("Naked City," *The Godfather*), born San Diego, CA, Jan 5, 1931.

Alexander English, 44, former basketball player, born Columbia, SC, Jan 5, 1954.

Diane Keaton (Diane Hall), 52, actress (Oscar for *Annie Hall; Sleeper, Love and Death, Hair*), born Los Angeles, CA, Jan 5, 1946.

Ronald Dale (Ron) Kittle, 40, former baseball player, born Gary, IN, Jan 5, 1958.

Pamela Sue Martin, 44, actress (*The Poseidon Adventure*, "The Nancy Drew Mysteries," "Dynasty"), born Westport, CT, Jan 5, 1954.

Walter Frederick "Fritz" Mondale, 70, former US vice president and senator, born Ceylon, MN, Jan 5, 1928.

W.D. Snodgrass, 72, poet, born Wilkinsburg, PA, Jan 5, 1926.

JANUARY 6 — TUESDAY

Day 6 — 359 Remaining

ARMENIAN CHRISTMAS. Jan 6. Christmas is observed on this day in the Armenian Church, the oldest Christian national church.

CARNIVAL SEASON. Jan 6–Feb 24. A secular festival preceding Lent. A time of merrymaking and feasting before the austere days of Lenten fasting and penitence (40 weekdays between Ash Wednesday and Easter Sunday). The word *carnival* probably is derived from the Latin *carnem levare*, meaning "to remove meat." Depending on local custom, the carnival season may start any time between Nov 11 and Shrove Tuesday. Conclusion of the season is much less variable, being the close of Shrove Tuesday in most places. Celebrations vary considerably, but the festival often includes many theatrical aspects (masks, costumes and songs) and has given its name (in the US) to traveling amusement shows that may be seen throughout the year. Observed traditionally in Roman Catholic countries from Epiphany through Shrove Tuesday.

EPIPHANY or TWELFTH DAY. Jan 6. Known also as Old Christmas Day and Twelfthtide. On the twelfth day after Christmas, Christians celebrate the visit of the Magi, the first Gentile recognition of Christ. Epiphany of Our Lord, one of the oldest Christian feasts, is observed in Roman Catholic churches in the US on a Sunday between Jan 2 and 8. Theophany of the Eastern Orthodox Church is observed on this day in churches using the Gregorian calendar and on Jan 19 in those churches using the Julian calendar and celebrates the manifestation of the divinity of Jesus at the time of his baptism in the Jordan River by John the Baptist.

GEORGE AND BARBARA BUSH: WEDDING ANNIVERSARY. Jan 6, 1945. First Presbyterian Church, Rye, NY. George Herbert Walker Bush was 20 and Barbara Pierce was 19. Their marriage produced six children: George Walker Bush, Jr in 1946; Pauline Robinson "Robin" Bush in 1949, who died of leukemia in 1953 at age three; John "Jeb" Ellis Bush in 1953; Neil Mallon Bush in 1955, Marvin Pierce Bush in 1956 and Dorothy Walker Bush in 1959.

"HALLMARK HALL OF FAME" TV PREMIERE: ANNIVERSARY. Jan 6, 1952. Carried at different times by ABC, CBS, NBC and PBS, this was a top quality dramatic anthology series. Originally titled "Hallmark Television Playhouse," the program was sponsored by Hallmark Cards and hosted by Sarah Churchill until 1955. A few of the presentations were *Hamlet*, with Maurice Evans and Ruth Chatterton (Apr 26, 1953); *Moby Dick*, with Victor Jory (May 16, 1954); *Macbeth*, with Maurice Evans, Dame Judith Anderson and House Jameson (Nov 28, 1954); *Alice in Wonderland*, with Eva LeGallienne, Elsa Lanchester and Reginald Gardiner (Oct 23, 1955). The list goes on with splendid performances by many highly acclaimed actors and actresses.

INTERNATIONAL SNOW SCULPTING CHAMPIONSHIPS. Jan 6–11. Breckenridge, CO. Sixteen teams from around the globe create fleeting but beautiful works of art from blocks of snow 12 feet tall and weighing 20 tons. Est attendance: 30,000. For info: Intl Snow Sculpting Championships, PO Box 1567, Breckenridge, CO 80424. Phone: (970) 453-2913. Fax: (970) 453-7238. Email: gobreck@brecknet.com.

ITALY: LA BEFANA. Jan 6. Epiphany festival in which the "Befana," a kindly witch, bestows gifts on children—toys and candy for those who have been good, but a lump of coal or a pebble for those who have been naughty. The festival begins on the night of Jan 5 with much noise and merrymaking (when the Befana is supposed to come down the chimneys on her broom, leaving gifts in children's stockings) and continues with joyous fairs, parades and other activities throughout Jan 6.

JAMAICA: MAROON FESTIVAL. Jan 6. Commemorates the 18th-century Treaty of Cudjoe. While Jamaica was a Spanish colony, its native inhabitants (Arawaks) were exterminated. The Spanish then imported African slaves to work their plantations. When the Spanish were driven out (1655), the black slaves fled to the mountains. The "Maroons" (fugitive slaves) were permitted to settle in the north of the island in 1738.

JOAN OF ARC: BIRTH ANNIVERSARY. Jan 6, 1412. Born in the village of Domrémy, in the Meuse River valley of France (probably in 1412). Turned over to an ecclesiastical court by the British, she was tried for heresy and burned to death at the stake on May 30, 1431, at age 19; in reality, she was executed for the military action she'd taken against the British on behalf of Charles VII of France.

"THE LAST WORD" TV PREMIERE: ANNIVERSARY. Jan 6, 1957. CBS talk show moderated by Dr. Bergen Evans that aired Sunday afternoons and was dedicated to discussing the English language. Three guest celebrities or authorities along with John Mason Brown, permanent panelist, would discuss questions submitted by viewers about language. The half-hour show was produced by Fred Freed.

MALESKA, EUGENE T.: BIRTH ANNIVERSARY. Jan 6, 1916. *New York Times* crossword puzzle editor Eugene T. Maleska was born at Jersey City, NJ. He invented new puzzle formats and clue styles for crossword puzzles in 1977 after a career in education. Maleska died on Aug 3, 1993, at Daytona Beach, FL.

MIX, TOM: BIRTH ANNIVERSARY. Jan 6, 1880. American motion picture actor, especially remembered for western cowboy films. Born at Driftwood, PA. Died near Florence, AZ, Oct 12, 1940.

NATIONAL SMITH DAY. Jan 6. The commonest surname in the English-speaking world is Smith. There are an estimated 2,382,500 Smiths in the US. This special day honors the birthday in 1580 of Captain John Smith, the leader of the English colonists who settled in Jamestown, VA, in 1607, thus making him one of the first American Smiths. On this special day, all derivatives, such as Goldsmith, are invited to participate. For more info, send $2 to cover the cost of photocopying and postage to Adrienne Sioux Koopersmith, 1437 W Rosemont, 1W, Chicago, IL 60660-1319. Phone: (773) 743-5341. Fax: (773) 743-5395. Email: kooper@interaccess.com.

NEW MEXICO: ADMISSION DAY: ANNIVERSARY. Jan 6, 1912. Became 47th state on this day in 1912.

PAN AM CIRCLES EARTH: ANNIVERSARY. Jan 6, 1942. A Pan American Airways plane arrived in New York to complete the first around-the-world trip by a commercial aircraft.

"PRO BOWLER'S TOUR" TV PREMIERE: ANNIVERSARY. Jan 6, 1962. ABC's weekly coverage of bowling tournaments with anchorman Chris Schenkel and Nelson Burton, Jr. Schenkel was previously assisted by Jack Buck (1962–64) and Billy Welu (1964–74).

SALOMON, HAYM: DEATH ANNIVERSARY. Jan 6, 1785. American Revolutionary War patriot and financier was born at Lissa, Poland, in 1740 (exact date unknown). Salomon died at Philadelphia, PA, Jan 6, 1785.

SANDBURG, CARL: BIRTH ANNIVERSARY. Jan 6, 1878. American poet, biographer, historian and folklorist, born at Galesburg, IL. Died at Flat Rock, NC, July 22, 1967.

SMITH, JEDEDIAH STRONG: BIRTH ANNIVERSARY. Jan 6, 1799. Mountain man, fur trader and one of the first explorers of the American West, Smith helped develop the Oregon Trail. He was the first American to reach California by land and first to travel by land from San Diego, up the West Coast to the Canadian border. Smith was born at Jericho (now Bainbridge), NY, and was killed by Comanche Indians along the Santa Fe Trail in what is now Kansas on May 27, 1831, at age 32.

THOMAS, DANNY: BIRTH ANNIVERSARY. Jan 6, 1912. Comedian Danny Thomas was born Muzyad Yakhoob, later Amos Jacobs, at Deerfield, MI. Thomas began his entertainment career as a radio actor and nightclub comedian and then went on to movies in the late 1940s and early 1950s. His greatest fame came from his television show "Make Room for Daddy" (1953–64), and later as a television producer. He was also a tireless philanthropist who founded St. Jude's Children's Research Hospital at Memphis, TN. Thomas died on Feb 6, 1991, at Los Angeles, CA.

THREE KINGS DAY. Jan 6. Major festival of Christian Church observed in many parts of the world with gifts, feasting, last lighting of Christmas lights and burning of Christmas greens. Twelfth and last day of Feast of the Nativity. Commemorates visit of the Three Wise Men (Kings or Magi) to Bethlehem.

"WESTINGHOUSE PLAYHOUSE" TV PREMIERE: ANNIVERSARY. Jan 6, 1961. Short-lived NBC sitcom, sponsored by Westinghouse. The series starred Nanette Fabray as Nan McGovern, an actress married to a writer with two children from a previous marriage. In real life, Fabray was married to writer Ranald MacDougall, who had three children of his own. MacDougall created the show for Fabray using their own domestic life as inspiration. The cast featured Wendell Corey as Nan's husband, Dan McGovern; Jacklyn O'Donnell and Bobby Diamond as the children; Doris Kemper as housekeeper Mrs Harper; and Mimi Gibson as Barby. The show was also called "The Nanette Fabray Show" and "Yes Yes Nanette."

BIRTHDAYS TODAY

E.L. Doctorow, 67, writer (*Ragtime, Welcome to Hard Times*), born New York, NY, Jan 6, 1931.

Bonnie Franklin, 54, actress (Ann Romano on "One Day at a Time"; *Applause*), born Santa Monica, CA, Jan 6, 1944.

Charles Lewis Haley, 34, football player, born Gladys, VA, Jan 6, 1964.

Lou Harris, 77, public opinion analyst, author, born New Haven, CT, Jan 6, 1921.

Louis Leo (Lou) Holtz, 61, former football coach, Notre Dame, born Follansbee, WV, Jan 6, 1937.

Howard M. (Howie) Long, 38, sportscaster, former football player, born Somerville, MA, Jan 6, 1960.

Nancy Lopez, 41, golfer, born Torrance, CA, Jan 6, 1957.

Earl Scruggs, 74, musician, born Cleveland County, NC, Jan 6, 1924.

John Singleton, 30, director, screenwriter (*Boyz N the Hood*), born Los Angeles, CA, Jan 6, 1968.

Loretta Young, 85, actress (Oscar for *The Farmer's Daughter*; "The Loretta Young Show"), born Salt Lake City, UT, Jan 6, 1913.

January 1998

S	M	T	W	T	F	S
				1	2	3
4	5	6	7	8	9	10
11	12	13	14	15	16	17
18	19	20	21	22	23	24
25	26	27	28	29	30	31

JANUARY 7 — WEDNESDAY

Day 7 — 358 Remaining

EMPEROR HIROHITO: DEATH ANNIVERSARY. Jan 7, 1989. After ruling Japan for 62 years as its longest-reigning ruler, Emperor Hirohito died at Tokyo of cancer at 6:33 AM on Jan 7, 1989. His only son, Crown Prince Akihito, succeeded him to the throne later that day.

"FAME" TV PREMIERE: ANNIVERSARY. Jan 7, 1982. NBC series centered on life at New York's High School of the Performing Arts. Based on the movie, it featured four of the film's actors in the same parts: Debbie Allen as dance teacher Lydia Grant; Albert Hague as music instructor Benjamin Shorofsky; Lee Curreri as student Bruno Martelli; and Gene Anthony Ray as dancing student Leroy Johnson. Also in the cast were Erica Gimpel as Coco Hernandez; Carol Mayo Jenkins as English teacher Elizabeth Sherwood; P.R. Paul (1982) as student Montgomery; Lori Singer as cellist Julie Miller; Valerie Landsburg as student Doris Schwartz; Carlo Imperato as Danny Amatullo; Michael Thoma (1982) as drama teacher Crandall; Morgan Stevens as drama teacher Reardon; and Carmine Caridi (1982–83) as Angelo Martelli.

FILLMORE, MILLARD: BIRTH ANNIVERSARY. Jan 7, 1800. Thirteenth president of the US (July 10, 1850–Mar 3, 1853). Fillmore succeeded to the presidency upon the death of Zachary Taylor, but he did not get the hoped-for nomination from his party in 1852. He ran for president in 1856 as candidate of the "Know-Nothing Party," whose platform demanded, among other things, that every government employee (federal, state and local) should be a native-born citizen. Fillmore was born at Summerhill, NY, and died at Buffalo, NY, Mar 8, 1874. Now his birthday is often used as an occasion for parties for which there is no other reason.

FIRST BALLOON FLIGHT ACROSS ENGLISH CHANNEL: ANNIVERSARY. Jan 7. Dr. John Jeffries, a Boston physician, and Jean-Pierre Blanchard, French aeronaut, on Jan 7, 1785, crossed the English Channel from Dover, England, to Calais, France, landing in a forest after being forced to throw overboard all ballast, equipment and even most of their clothing to avoid forced landing in the icy waters of the English Channel. Blanchard's trousers are said to have been the last article thrown overboard.

FIRST US COMMERCIAL BANK: ANNIVERSARY. Jan 7, 1782. The first commercial bank in the US, the Bank of North America, was opened in Philadelphia.

GARDENIA, VINCENT (VINCENT SCOGNAMIGLIO): BIRTH ANNIVERSARY. Jan 7, 1922. Stage, screen and television performer Vincent Gardenia was born at Naples, Italy. Gardenia began performing at age 5 and once estimated he had played 500 parts in his lifetime. He received two Oscar nominations, one for playing a baseball manager in *Bang the Drum*

Slowly and again for the role of patriarch of a goofy Brooklyn family in *Moonstruck*. He won a Tony for his part in *The Prisoner of Second Avenue* and an Emmy for his portrayal in *Age Old Friends*. Vincent Gardenia died Dec 9, 1992, at Philadelphia, PA.

GERMANY: MUNICH FASCHING CARNIVAL. Jan 7–Feb 24. Munich. From Jan 7 through Shrove Tuesday is Munich's famous carnival season. Costume balls are popular throughout carnival. "High points on Fasching Sunday (Feb 22) and Shrove Tuesday (Feb 24) with great carnival doings outside at the Viktualienmarkt and on Pedestrian Mall."

JAPAN: NANAKUSA. Jan 7. Festival dates back to the 7th century and recalls the seven plants served to the emperor that are believed to have great medicinal value—shepherd's purse, chickweed, parsley, cottonweed, radish, hotoke-no-za and aona.

JAPAN: USOKAE (BULLFINCH EXCHANGE FESTIVAL). Jan 7. Dazaifu, Fukuoka Prefecture. "Good Luck" gilded wood bullfinches, mixed among many plain ones, are sought after by the throngs as priests of the Dazaifu Shrine pass them out in the dim light of a small bonfire.

MONTGOLFIER, JACQUES ETIENNE: BIRTH ANNIVERSARY. Jan 7, 1745. Merchant and inventor born at Vidalon-lez Annonay, Ardèche, France. With his older brother, Joseph Michel, in Nov 1782, conducted experiments with paper and fabric bags filled with smoke and hot air, which led to invention of the hot air balloon and human's first flight. Died at Serrieres, France, Aug 2, 1799. See also: "First Balloon Flight: Anniversary" (June 5); "Aviation History Month" (Nov 1).

OLD CALENDAR ORTHODOX CHRISTMAS. Jan 7. Some Orthodox Churches celebrate Christmas on this day, which is the "Old" (Julian) calendar date.

POL POT OVERTHROWN: ANNIVERSARY. Jan 7, 1979. Pol Pot's Cambodian government fell to combined forces of Cambodian rebels and Vietnamese soldiers.

RUSSIA: CHRISTMAS OBSERVANCE. Jan 7. National holiday.

SAN ANTONIO SPORT, BOAT AND RV SHOW. Jan 7–11. San Antonio Convention Center, San Antonio, TX. Boating, travel, hunting, fishing, camping, RVs and recreation show. 41st annual show. Sponsor: Boating Trades Assn of San Antonio, TX. For info: Mike Coffen, Double C Productions, Inc, PO Box 1678, Huntsville, TX 77342. Phone: (409) 295-9677 or (800) 574-9650. Fax: (409) 295-8859. Email: doublec@lcc.net. WWW: http://www.lcc.net/~doublec

TRANSATLANTIC PHONING: ANNIVERSARY. Jan 7, 1927. Commercial transatlantic telephone service between New York and London was inaugurated. There were 31 calls made the first day.

BIRTHDAYS TODAY

William Blatty, 70, screenwriter, born New York, NY, Jan 7, 1928.
Nicolas Cage, 34, actor (*Leaving Las Vegas*), born Long Beach, CA, Jan 7, 1964.
Katie Couric, 41, co-host ("Today Show"), born Arlington, VA, Jan 7, 1957.
Erin Gray, 46, actress (Colonel Wilma Deering in "Buck Rogers in the 25th Century"), born Honolulu, HI, Jan 7, 1952.
Douglas Kiker, 68, journalist, author ("NBC Magazine with David Brinkley"; *Death Below Deck*), born Griffin, GA, Jan 7, 1930.
Kenny Loggins, 50, singer (Loggins and Messina, 1972–76: "Your Mama Don't Dance"; solo: "Whenever I Call You 'Friend,'" "I'm Alright") songwriter ("What a Fool Believes" with Michael McDonald, which won 3 Grammys), born Everett, WA, Jan 7, 1948.
Terry Moore, 69, actress ("Empire," *Gaslight, Come Back Little Sheba*), born Los Angeles, CA, Jan 7, 1929.
Jean-Pierre Rampal, 76, musician, born Marseilles, France, Jan 7, 1922.
Jann Wenner, 51, journalist, publisher, *Rolling Stone* magazine, born New York, NY, Jan 7, 1947.

JANUARY 8 — THURSDAY

Day 8 — 357 Remaining

ALL STATES PICNIC (FOR SENIOR CITIZENS). Jan 8. Yuma, AZ. Seniors from all over the US and Canada gather for picnic lunch, entertainment and fun. Sponsor: City of Yuma Parks and Recreation Department. Est attendance: 1,000. For info: Marketing Dept, Yuma Civic and Conv Ctr, 1440 Desert Hills Dr, Yuma, AZ 85365. Phone: (520) 344-3800. Fax: (520) 344-9121.

AMERICAN HISTORICAL ASSOCIATION: ANNUAL MEETING. Jan 8–11. Seattle, WA. Approximately 140 sessions will be held covering a wide range of scholarly, professional and pedagogical topics dealing with world history. Est attendance: 4,100. For info: Sharon K. Tune, Asst Dir, American Historical Assn, 400 A St SE, Washington, DC 20003. Phone: (202) 544-2422. Fax: (202) 544-8307. Email: aha@gmu.edu. WWW: http://web.gmu.edu/chnm/aha

ASARAH B'TEVET. Jan 8. Hebrew calendar date: Tevet 10, 5758. (Also on Dec 29, Hebrew calendar date: Tevet 10, 5759.) The Fast of the 10th of Tevet begins at first morning light and commemorates the beginning of the Babylonian siege of Jerusalem in the 6th century BC.

AT&T DIVESTITURE: ANNIVERSARY. Jan 8, 1982. In the most significant antitrust suit since the breakup of Standard Oil in 1911, American Telephone and Telegraph agreed Jan 8, 1982, to give up its 22 local Bell System companies ("Baby Bells"). These companies represented 80% of AT&T's assets. This ended the corporation's virtual monopoly on US telephone service.

BATTLE OF NEW ORLEANS: ANNIVERSARY. Jan 8. British forces suffered crushing losses (more than 2,000 casualties) in an attack on New Orleans, LA, Jan 8, 1815. Defending US troops were led by General Andrew Jackson, who became a popular hero as a result of the victory. Neither side knew that the war had ended two weeks previously with the signing of the Treaty of Ghent on Dec 24, 1814. Battle of New Orleans Day is observed in Louisiana.

BIDDLE, NICHOLAS: BIRTH ANNIVERSARY. Jan 8, 1786. American lawyer, diplomat, statesman, financier and scholar (completed his university studies at age 13). Born at Philadelphia, PA, he died there on Feb 27, 1844.

CHOU EN-LAI: DEATH ANNIVERSARY. Jan 8, 1976. Anniversary of the death of Chou En-Lai, premier of the State Council of the People's Republic of China. He was born in 1898 but the exact date is unknown.

COLLINS, WILLIAM WILKIE: BIRTH ANNIVERSARY. Jan 8, 1824. English novelist, author of *The Moonstone*, *The Woman in White* and *The Dead Secret*. Born at London, England, he died there Sept 23, 1889.

DOW-JONES TOPS 2,000: ANNIVERSARY. Jan 8, 1987. The Dow-Jones Index of 30 major industrial stocks topped the 2,000 mark for the first time.

FERRER, JOSE: BIRTH ANNIVERSARY. Jan 8, 1912. Award-winning actor, producer, writer and director was born at Santurce, Puerto Rico. A promising pianist in his youth, Ferrer was expected to become a concert performer. Nominated three times for an Academy Award, he won best actor for his role in *Cyrano de Bergerac*. Additionally, Ferrer was awarded Tonys and Critics' Circle prizes during half a century in the entertainment world. He died Jan 26, 1992, at Coral Gables, FL.

FOURTEEN POINTS PROPOSED: 80th ANNIVERSARY. Jan 8, 1918. In a speech before a hastily convened joint session of Congress Jan 8, 1918, President Woodrow Wilson presented Fourteen Points for a just peace. The proposal called for reduction of armaments to the lowest point consistent with domestic safety, "open covenants openly arrived at," self-determination of governments and the creation of a League of Nations to preserve peace. Wilson was unable to obtain Allied agreement to his proposals.

GREECE: MIDWIFE'S DAY or WOMEN'S DAY. Jan 8. Midwife's Day or Women's Day is celebrated on Jan 8 each year to honor midwives and all women. "On this day women stop their housework and spend their time in cafés, while the men do all the housework chores and look after the children." In some villages, men caught outside "will be stripped . . . and drenched with cold water."

NATIONAL JOYGERM DAY. Jan 8. A day when Joygerms all over the world face those who pout and in turn smile, and tout and persevere and endear themselves to others with a hug, smile and grin, and crusty curmudgeons do win over to their positive side, with joy and great pride. Spreading Joygerms: antidote to misery. Smile check-up clinics, fun and frivolity; love and laughter; silliness and surprise. For info: Joygerm Joan E. White, Founder, Joygerms Unlimited, PO Box 219, Eastwood Station, Syracuse, NY 13206-0219. Phone: (315) 472-2779.

PRESLEY, ELVIS AARON: BIRTH ANNIVERSARY. Jan 8, 1935. Popular American rock singer. Born at Tupelo, MS; died at Memphis, TN, Aug 16, 1977, at age 42. Although his middle name was spelled incorrectly as "Aron" on his birth certificate, Elvis had it legally changed to "Aaron," which is how it is spelled on his gravestone.

SAINT GUDULA'S FEAST DAY. Jan 8. Virgin, patron saint of the city of Brussels. Died Jan 8, probably in the year 712. Her relics were transferred to the church of St. Michael in Brussels.

SIRANI, ELISABETTA: BIRTH ANNIVERSARY. Jan 8, 1638. Born at Bologna, Italy, Elisabetta Sirani was one of the few women Renaissance artists. Among the 190 pieces done by her during her short life was the 1663 *Virgin and Child*, which was chosen by the US Postal Service as the 1994 traditional holiday stamp. While in her 20s Sarani established a painting school for women. When she died at her native Bologna on Aug 28, 1665, the entire city went into mourning for her.

January 1998

S	M	T	W	T	F	S
				1	2	3
4	5	6	7	8	9	10
11	12	13	14	15	16	17
18	19	20	21	22	23	24
25	26	27	28	29	30	31

SPACE MILESTONE: *LUNA 21* (USSR): 25th ANNIVERSARY. Jan 8, 1973. Unmanned vehicle, launched Jan 8, 1973, landed on the moon Jan 16, carrying *Lunakho*, a radio-controlled vehicle that explored a 37-km distance over a four-month period.

UNIVERSAL LETTER-WRITING WEEK. Jan 8–14. The purpose of this week is for people all over the world to get the new year off to a good start by sending letters and cards to friends and acquaintances not only in their own country but to people throughout the world. For complete information and suggestions about writing good letters, send $3 to cover expense of printing, handling and postage. For info: Dr. Stanley Drake, Pres, Intl Soc of Friendship and Goodwill, 412 Cherry Hills Dr, Bakersfield, CA 93309-2866.

WAR ON POVERTY: ANNIVERSARY. Jan 8. President Lyndon Johnson declared a War on Poverty in his State of the Union message Jan 8, 1964. He stressed improved education as one of the cornerstones of the program. The following Aug 20, he signed a $947.5 million anti-poverty bill designed to assist 30-35 million citizens.

BIRTHDAYS TODAY

David Bowie (David Robert Jones), 51, musician, actor, born London, England, Jan 8, 1947.

Vladimir Feltsman, 46, Russian pianist, born Moscow, USSR, Jan 8, 1952.

Slade Gorton, 70, US Senator (R, Washington), born Chicago, IL, Jan 8, 1928.

Yvette Mimieux, 57, actress (*The Light in the Piazza, The Time Machine*, "The Most Deadly Game"), born Los Angeles, CA, Jan 8, 1941.

Charles Osgood, 65, CBS newsman, born New York, NY, Jan 8, 1933.

Soupy Sales (Morton Supman), 68, comedian, author ("The Soupy Sales Show"; may hold record for pies in the face), born Wake Forest, NC, Jan 8, 1930.

JANUARY 9 — FRIDAY

Day 9 — 356 Remaining

AVIATION IN AMERICA: ANNIVERSARY. Jan 9, 1793. A Frenchman, Jean Pierre Blanchard, made the first manned free-balloon flight in America's history on Jan 9, 1793, at Philadelphia, PA. The event was watched by President George Washington and many other high government officials. The hydrogen-filled balloon rose to a height of about 5,800 feet, traveled some 15 miles and landed 46 minutes later. Reportedly Blanchard had one passenger on the flight—a little black dog.

BAKER STREET IRREGULARS' DINNER AND COCKTAIL RECEPTION. Jan 9–10. New York, NY. Annual dinner, meeting and cocktail reception. Est attendance: 160. For info: Michael F. Whelan, PO Box 2189, Easton, MD 21601. Phone: (410) 745-5553. Fax: (410) 822-7000.

BALANCHINE, GEORGE: BIRTH ANNIVERSARY. Jan 9, 1904. Born Georgi Militonovitch Balanchivadze at St. Petersburg, Russia, George Balanchine became one of the leading influences in 20th-century ballet. He choreographed more than 200 ballets, including *Concerto Barocco, Apollo, Orpheus, Serande, Firebird, Swan Lake, The Triumph of Bacchus, Waltz Academy* and *The Nutcracker*. In 1933 he was invited to the US by Boston philanthropist Lincoln Kirstein to establish a school for American dancers. Together they founded the School of American Ballet in 1934 and then formed several ballet companies, including the New York City Ballet, which was led by Balanchine. Died at New York, NY, Apr 30, 1983.

CATT, CARRIE LANE CHAPMAN: BIRTH ANNIVERSARY. Jan 9, 1859. American women's rights leader, founder (in 1919) of National League of Women Voters, born at Ripon, WI, she died at New Rochelle, NY, Mar 9, 1947.

CONNECTICUT RATIFIES CONSTITUTION: ANNIVERSARY. Jan 9, 1788. By a vote of 128 to 40, on Jan 9, 1788, Connecticut became the fifth state to ratify the Constitution.

ENGLAND: LONDON INTERNATIONAL BOAT SHOW. Jan 9–18. Earls Court Exhibition Centre, London. One of the largest international boat shows in Europe, displaying more than 600 craft, plus accessories for the marine enthusiast. Est attendance: 185,000. For info: British Marine Industries Federation/Natl Boat Shows Ltd, Meadlake Place, Thorpe Lea Rd, Egham, Surrey, England TW20 8HE. Phone: (44) (178) 447-3377. Fax: (44) (178) 443-9678.
WWW: http://www.marinedata.co.uk/bmiflibs.html

FAKE HOWARD HUGHES BIOGRAPHY: ANNIVERSARY. Jan 9, 1972. Reclusive billionaire Howard Hughes held a telephone news conference to state that the biography about him written by Clifford Irving was a fake.

"IT TAKES A THIEF" TV PREMIERE: 30th ANNIVERSARY. Jan 9, 1968. ABC's adventure series starred Robert Wagner as Alexander Mundy, an unlikely thief who agrees to conduct secret government missions instead of serving out his prison term. Malachi Thone costarred as Noah Bain, chief of the SIA, and Mundy's employer. Fred Astaire sometimes made recurring cameo appearances as Mundy's father. The show was produced by Universal TV.

NC RV & CAMPING SHOW. Jan 9–11. Special Events Center, Greensboro Coliseum Complex, Greensboro, NC. A display of the latest in recreation vehicles and accessories by various dealers. Est attendance: 10,000. For info: Apple Rock Advertising & Promotion, 1200 Eastchester Dr, High Point, NC 27265. Phone: (910) 881-7100. Fax: (910) 883-7198.

NIXON, RICHARD MILHOUS: 85th BIRTH ANNIVERSARY. Jan 9, 1913. Richard Nixon served as 36th vice president of the US (under President Dwight D. Eisenhower) Jan 20, 1953, to Jan 20, 1961. He was the 37th president of the US, serving Jan 20, 1969, to Aug 9, 1974, when he resigned the presidency while under threat of impeachment. First US president to resign that office. He was born at Yorba Linda, CA, and died at New York, NY, Apr 22, 1994.

NORTHERN EXPOSURE/WOLF RIVER RENDEZVOUS. Jan 9–11. Shawano, WI. More than 6,000 spectators are expected to watch top sled dog racers from Europe, Canada and the US compete in four-, six- and 10-dog junior and amateur classes. The festival also features mutt sled dog races, skijoring (skiers pulled by dogs), snowshoe races, a buckskinners encampment, candlelight ski, moonlight snowmobile ride, horse-drawn sleigh rides, cross-cut saw competition and chain saw carving. Est attendance: 6,000. For info: Wisconsin Dept of Tourism, PO Box 7976, Madison, WI 53707. Phone: (715) 524-2139 or (800) 235-8528. Email: tourism@laughlin.com.
WWW: http://tourism.state.wi.us

PANAMA: MARTYRS' DAY. Jan 9. Public holiday.

PHILIPPINES: FEAST OF THE BLACK NAZARENE. Jan 9. Culmination of a nine-day fiesta. Manila's largest procession takes place in the afternoon of Jan 9, in honor of the Black Nazarene, whose shrine is at the Quiapo Church.

"RAWHIDE" TV PREMIERE: ANNIVERSARY. Jan 9, 1959. CBS western that kept them dogies [cattle] rollin' home from northern Texas to Sedalia, KS. The series featured Eric Fleming (1959–65) as trail boss Gil Favor; Clint Eastwood as Rowdy Yates, ramrod and later trail boss after Fleming's departure from the show; Jim Murdock (1959–65) as Mushy; Paul Brinegar as the cook, Wishbone; Steve Raines as Quince; Rocky Shahan (1959–65) as Joe Scarlett; Sheb Wooley (1961–65) as scout Pete Nolan; Robert Cabal (1962–65) as Hey Soos; John Ireland (1965–66) as Jed Colby; David Watson (1965–66) as Ian Cabot; and Raymond St. Jacques (1965–66) as Simon Blake (St. Jacques was the first African-American regular on the series). Creator Charles Marquis Warren's western is also fondly remembered for its rollicking theme song.

STAMP EXPO '98: WEST. Jan 9–11. Quality Hotel, Anaheim, CA. Est attendance: 4,000. For info: Intl Stamp Collectors Soc, PO Box 854, Van Nuys, CA 91408. Phone: (818) 997-6496. Fax: (818) 988-4337. Email: iibick@aol.com.
WWW: http://www.4free.com/bick

YORBA LINDA, CA: NIXON BIRTHDAY HOLIDAY. Jan 9. Yorba Linda, CA. Yorba Linda, the birthplace in 1913 of former president Richard M. Nixon, became the first community officially to declare his birth anniversary a public holiday. In announcing the declaration on Sept 20, 1989, Mayor Henry Wedaa said, "We're not here to judge history—we're here to recognize it." The first observance by Yorba Linda's municipal employees took place in 1990.

YOUNG, MURAT BERNARD "CHICK": BIRTH ANNIVERSARY. Jan 9, 1901. The comic strip "Blondie" was created by Murat Bernard "Chick" Young in 1930. Originally about a jazz-age flapper who marries a playboy from a socially prominent family, "Blondie" soon changed its direction: two children and a dog were added to the cast, Dagwood became a working stiff and the strip focused on middle-class family situations and problems. Written in a slapstick fashion, "Blondie" introduced America to the "dagwood," an enormous sandwich made during Dagwood's late-night forays in the refrigerator. Chick Young was born at Chicago, IL, and died at St. Petersburg, FL, on Mar 14, 1973.

BIRTHDAYS TODAY

Joan Baez, 57, folk singer, born Staten Island, NY, Jan 9, 1941.
Tyrone Curtis ("Muggsy") Bogues, 33, basketball player, born Baltimore, MD, Jan 9, 1965.
Bob Denver, 63, actor ("The Many Loves of Dobie Gillis," "Gilligan's Island"), born New Rochelle, NY, Jan 9, 1935.
Richard Allen (Dick) Enberg, 63, sportscaster, born Mt Clemens, MI, Jan 9, 1935.
Crystal Gayle (Brenda Gayle Webb), 47, singer ("Don't It Make My Brown Eyes Blue"), born Paintsville, KY, Jan 9, 1951.
Judith Krantz (Judith Tarcher), 70, author (*Dazzle, Scruples*), born New York, NY, Jan 9, 1928.
Byron Bartlett (Bart) Starr, 64, former football coach, Pro Football Hall of Fame quarterback, born Montgomery, AL, Jan 9, 1934.
Susannah York, 57, actress (*Tom Jones, They Shoot Horses Don't They?, Superman*), born London, England, Jan 9, 1941.

☆ ☆ ☆

JANUARY 10 — SATURDAY

Day 10 — 355 Remaining

ALLEN, ETHAN: BIRTH ANNIVERSARY. Jan 10, 1738. Revolutionary War hero and leader of the Vermont "Green Mountain Boys." Born at Litchfield, CT, he died at Burlington, VT, Feb 12, 1789.

***COMMON SENSE* PUBLISHED: ANNIVERSARY.** Jan 10, 1776. More than any other publication, *Common Sense* influenced the authors of the Declaration of Independence. Thomas Paine's 50-page pamphlet sold more than 500,000 copies within a few months of its first printing.

DeSOTO'S WINTER ENCAMPMENT. Jan 10. Tallahassee, FL. Hernando DeSoto's Winter Camp at Apalachee Village Anhyca (present-day Tallahassee) interpreted with living history, craft demonstrations, exhibits, etc. Annually, the second Saturday in January. Est attendance: 1,000. For info: DeSoto's Winter Encampment, 1022 DeSoto Park Dr, Tallahassee, FL 32301. Phone: (904) 922-6007. Fax: (904) 488-0366.

DORIS MAGER, "THE EAGLE LADY." Jan 10. Oatland Island Education Center, Savannah, GA. Known nationwide for raising funds for eagles and educating children about the plight of the bald eagle, golden eagle and other birds of prey, Doris Mager, 71, and her majestic birds will conduct two birds of prey programs. Est attendance: 700. For info: Oatland Island Education Center, 711 Sandtown Rd, Savannah, GA 31410. Phone: (912) 897-3773.

HENRIED, PAUL: 90th BIRTH ANNIVERSARY. Jan 10, 1908. Actor Paul Henried once estimated that he had played in or directed more than 300 feature or made-for-TV films. Otto Preminger discovered his talent, launching his career with Max Reinhardt's theater. His career as a dashing leading man often found him playing the Continental lover, but his career expanded when he played Prince Albert in a London production of *Victoria Regina*. Though a staunch anti-Nazi, his early film roles included a number of German roles, including *Goodbye Mr. Chips, Mad, Man of Europe* and *Night Train*. He eventually moved away from the German stereotype in such films as *Of Human Bondage, The Four Horsemen of the Apocalypse, Exorcist III* and as Victor Laslo in *Casablanca*. His film career cut short by the anti-Communist blacklist in Hollywood during the 1940s, Henried found a second calling as a director, directing more than 80 episodes of TV's "Alfred Hitchcock Presents." Born at Trieste, Austria, he died on Mar 29, 1992, at Pacific Palisades, CA, at age 84.

JEFFERS, ROBINSON: BIRTH ANNIVERSARY. Jan 10, 1887. American poet and playwright. Born at Pittsburgh, PA, he died at Carmel, CA, Jan 20, 1962.

LEAGUE OF NATIONS: ANNIVERSARY. Jan 10. Through the Treaty of Versailles, the League of Nations came into existence on Jan 10, 1920. Fifty nations entered into a covenant designed to avoid war. The US never joined the League of Nations, which was dissolved on Apr 18, 1946.

"MASTERPIECE THEATRE" TV PREMIERE: ANNIVERSARY. Jan 10, 1971. Television at its best, PBS's long-running anthology series consists of many highly acclaimed original and adapted dramatizations. Most are produced by the BBC. Alistair Cooke and Russell Baker have hosted the program. Among some of the most notable presentations are: "The First Churchills" (1971); "Jude the Obscure," "The Six Wives of Henry VIII" and "Elizabeth R" (1972); "Upstairs Downstairs" (1974-1977); "I, Claudius" (1978); "The Jewel in the Crown" (1984); "Bleak House" (1985); and "A Tale of Two Cities" (1989). "The Muppet Show" had a cute take-off of the show with Kermit the Frog playing the host.

NATIONAL WESTERN STOCK SHOW AND RODEO. Jan 10–25. Denver, CO. One of the nation's largest livestock shows with more than 30 breeds of animals, 23 rodeo performances, 11 horse shows, two Mexican rodeos and cutting horse and sheep shearing contests. 92nd annual. Est attendance: 625,000. For info: Natl Western Stock Show and Rodeo, 4655 Humboldt St, Denver, CO 80216. Phone: (303) 297-1166. Fax: (303) 292-1708.

NCAA CONVENTION. Jan 10–14. Atlanta Marriott Marquis and Hyatt Regency Atlanta (co-headquarters). For info: Sandy Linson, Publ Info, NCAA, 6201 College Blvd, Overland Park, KS 66211. Phone: (913) 339-1906. Fax: (913) 339-1950. WWW: http://www.ncaa.org

SNOW SHOVEL RIDING CONTEST. Jan 10. Old Economy Park, Economy, PA. 33rd annual. Contest begins at 1 PM. Participants ride snow shovels downhill, handles extended, instead of sleds. Best time is the winner. For info: Jack Hilfinger, Beaver Co Rec Dept, Rt 51, Fallston, PA 15066. Phone: (412) 774-0133.

SOUTHWEST ANTIQUE SHOW AND SALE. Jan 10–11. Yuma Civic and Convention Center, Yuma, AZ. A fine collection of antiques and collectibles. Sponsor: Jack Black Enterprises. Est attendance: 3,500. For info: Marketing Dept, Yuma Civic and Conv Ctr, 1440 Desert Hills Dr, Yuma, AZ 85365. Phone: (520) 344-3800. Fax: (520) 344-9121.

SPACE MILESTONE: *SOYUZ 17* (USSR). Jan 10, 1975. Launched on this date, cosmonauts A. Gubarev and G. Grechko completed a 30-day space flight, landing Feb 9. Cosmonauts spent 28 days aboard *Salyut 4*, orbiting space station.

SPACE MILESTONE: *SOYUZ 27* (USSR): 20th ANNIVERSARY. Jan 10, 1978. Launched Jan 10, 1978, Cosmonauts Vladimir Dzhanibekov and Oleg Makarov linked with *Salyut 6* space station, which was already occupied by crew of *Soyuz 26*. Returned to Earth Jan 16 in *Soyuz 26*.

UNITED NATIONS GENERAL ASSEMBLY: ANNIVERSARY. Jan 10. On the 26th anniversary of the establishment of the unsuccessful League of Nations, delegates from 51 nations met in London, England, Jan 10, 1946, for the first meeting of the UN General Assembly.

US AND VATICAN ESTABLISH DIPLOMATIC RELATIONS: ANNIVERSARY. Jan 10, 1984. The US and Vatican established full diplomatic relations after a break of 117 years.

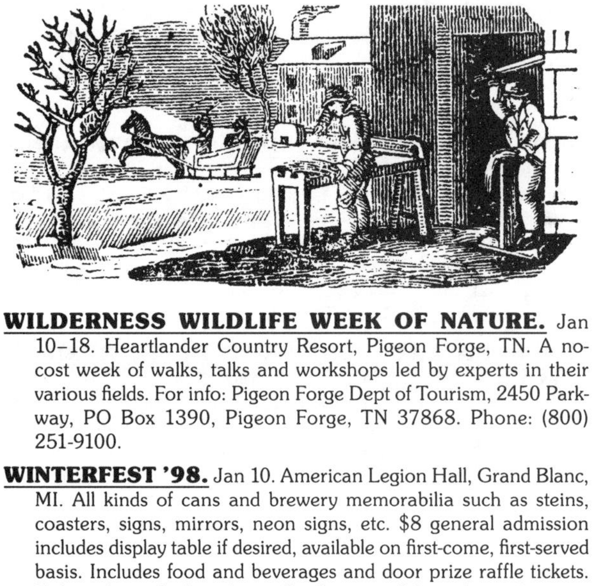

WILDERNESS WILDLIFE WEEK OF NATURE. Jan 10–18. Heartlander Country Resort, Pigeon Forge, TN. A no-cost week of walks, talks and workshops led by experts in their various fields. For info: Pigeon Forge Dept of Tourism, 2450 Parkway, PO Box 1390, Pigeon Forge, TN 37868. Phone: (800) 251-9100.

WINTERFEST '98. Jan 10. American Legion Hall, Grand Blanc, MI. All kinds of cans and brewery memorabilia such as steins, coasters, signs, mirrors, neon signs, etc. $8 general admission includes display table if desired, available on first-come, first-served basis. Includes food and beverages and door prize raffle tickets. Kids under eight free. Annually, the second Saturday in January. Est attendance: 200. For info: Gene Goulet, Pres, Mid-Michigan Chapter, Beer Can Collectors of America, 5306 Lippincott, Burton, MI 48519. Phone: (810) 742-5353. Email: davevanh@aol.com.

WOMEN'S SUFFRAGE AMENDMENT INTRODUCED IN CONGRESS: ANNIVERSARY. Jan 10, 1878. Senator A.A. Sargent of California, a close friend of Susan B. Anthony, introduced into the US Senate a women's suffrage amendment known as the Susan B. Anthony Amendment. It wasn't until Aug 26, 1920, 42 years later, that the amendment was signed into law.

January 1998

S	M	T	W	T	F	S
				1	2	3
4	5	6	7	8	9	10
11	12	13	14	15	16	17
18	19	20	21	22	23	24
25	26	27	28	29	30	31

BIRTHDAYS TODAY

Pat Benatar (Patricia Andrejewski), 45, singer, born Brooklyn, NY, Jan 10, 1953.

Gisele Mackenzie, 71, singer ("Hard To Get"; regular on "Your Hit Parade"), born Winnipeg, Manitoba, Canada, Jan 10, 1927.

Rod Stewart, 53, singer, musician ("Maggie May," "Do Ya Think I'm Sexy?"), born Glasgow, Scotland, Jan 10, 1945.

JANUARY 11 — SUNDAY

Day 11 — 354 Remaining

AFRICAN-AMERICAN ARTS FESTIVAL. Jan 11–Mar 15. Greensboro, NC. A series of arts events held in celebration of the cultural achievements of local, regional and national black artists in all disciplines of the arts (music, dance, visual arts, literature and theater). Annually, during the months of January, February and March. Sponsors: Miller Brewing Co, News and Record and WQMG-FM. Est attendance: 20,000. For info: Mary Hale, Community Events Dir, United Arts Council of Greensboro, PO Box 877, Greensboro, NC 27402. Phone: (910) 333-7440. Fax: (910) 275-2787.

CUCKOO DANCING WEEK. Jan 11–17. To honor the memory of Laurel and Hardy, whose theme, "The Dancing Cuckoos," shall be heard throughout the land as their movies are seen and their antics greeted by laughter by old and new fans of these unique masters of comedy. [Originated by the late William T. Rabe of Sault Ste. Marie, MI.]

"DESIGNATED HITTER" RULE ADOPTED: 25TH ANNIVERSARY. Jan 11, 1973. American League adopted the "designated hitter" rule, whereby an additional player was used to bat for the pitcher.

FIRST BLACK SOUTHERN LIEUTENANT GOVERNOR: ANNIVERSARY. Jan 11, 1986. L. Douglas Wilder was sworn in as lieutenant governor of Virginia. He was the first black elected to statewide office in the South since Reconstruction.

HAMILTON, ALEXANDER: BIRTH ANNIVERSARY. Jan 11. American statesman born at British West Indies, Jan 11, 1755 or 1757. Engaged in a duel with Aaron Burr the morning of July 11, 1804, at Weehawken, NJ. Mortally wounded there and died July 12, 1804.

HOSTOS, EUGENIO MARIA: BIRTH ANNIVERSARY. Jan 11, 1839. Puerto Rican patriot, scholar and author of more than 50 books. Born at Rio Canas, Puerto Rico, he died at Santo Domingo, Dominican Republic, on Aug 11, 1903. The anniversary of his birth is observed as a public holiday in Puerto Rico.

INTERNATIONAL THANK YOU DAYS©. Jan 11–18. A day to thank someone from your past or present who did something nice for you. Write, call, fax or e-mail him or her and say thank you. For info: Adrienne Sioux Koopersmith, Thanks Alot, 1437 W Rosemont, #1W, Chicago, IL 60660-1319. Phone: (773) 743-5341. Fax: (773) 743-5395. Email: kooper@interaccess.com.

☆ ☆ ☆

JAMES, WILLIAM: BIRTH ANNIVERSARY. Jan 11, 1842. American psychologist and philosopher of distinguished family that included his brother, novelist Henry James. "There is no worse lie," he wrote in *Varieties of Religious Experience* (1902), "than a truth misunderstood by those who hear it." Born at New York City, he died at Chocorua, NH, on Aug 26, 1910.

JOHN BEARGREASE SLED DOG MARATHON. Jan 11–16. Duluth, MN. To commemorate John Beargrease, a Chippewa sled dog mail carrier along the North Shore of Lake Superior from 1887–1900. A 500-mile endurance race with mushers and dogs from the US and Canada. Sponsor: Grand Portage Chippewa. Est attendance: 10,000. For info: Beargrease, Box 500, Duluth, MN 55801. Phone: (218) 722-7631. Fax: (218) 722-3675.

MacDONALD, JOHN A.: BIRTH ANNIVERSARY. Jan 11, 1815. Canadian statesman, first prime minister of Canada. Born at Glasgow, Scotland, he died June 6, 1891, at Ottawa. His birth anniversary is observed in Canada.

NEPAL: NATIONAL UNITY DAY. Jan 11. Celebration paying homage to King Prithvinarayan Shah (1723–1775), founder of the present house of rulers of Nepal and creator of the unified Nepal of today.

PAUL, ALICE: BIRTH ANNIVERSARY. Jan 11, 1885. Women's rights leader and founder of the National Woman's Party in 1913, advocate of an equal rights amendment to the US Constitution. Born at Moorestown, NJ, she died there July 10, 1977.

SWITZERLAND: MEITLISUNNTIG. Jan 11. On Meitlisunntig, the second Sunday in January, the girls of Meisterschwanden and Fahrwangen, in the Seetal district of Aargau, Switzerland, stage a procession in historical uniforms and a military parade before a female General Staff. According to tradition, the custom dates from the Villmergen War of 1712, when the women of both communes gave vital help that led to victory. Popular festival follows the procession.

THEODOSIUS I: BIRTH ANNIVERSARY. Jan 11, 347. Roman emperor known as Theodosius the Great was born at Cauca, Gallaecia, in Spain. He is best known for establishing the Nicene Creed as the defining statement of belief for Christians. In 379 Theodosius was summoned by the emperor Gratian to become emperor of the east. On Feb 28, 380, without consulting religious authorities, he issued the edict that made the Nicene Creed (in which God the Father, the Son and the Holy Spirit are all of the same substance) binding on all subjects. Only those who accepted it would be considered Christians; this was the first recorded use of that designation. Theodosius engaged in a continuing struggle with the west for power. He prohibited pagan worship, but the various emperors of the west had strong connections with pagan aristocracy. The two sides came to blows in 394. His final victory in September of that year was seen as a divine victory in which the Christian god had triumphed over the Roman gods. Theodosius died in January of 395.

US SURGEON GENERAL DECLARES CIGARETTES HAZARDOUS: ANNIVERSARY. Jan 11, 1964. US Surgeon General Luther Terry issued the first government report saying that smoking may be hazardous to one's health.

BIRTHDAYS TODAY

Clarence Clemons, 56, musician, singer, born Norfolk, VA, Jan 11, 1942.

Ben Daniel Crenshaw, 46, golfer, born Austin, TX, Jan 11, 1952.

Darryl Dawkins, 41, former basketball player, born Orlando, FL, Jan 11, 1957.

Jim Hightower, 55, radio host, author (*Hard Tomatoes, Hard Times; Eat Your Heart Out*), born Denison, TX, Jan 11, 1943.

Naomi Judd, 52, country singer ("Have Mercy," "Why Not Me"), born Ashland, KY, Jan 11, 1946.

Christine Kaufmann, 53, actress (*Taras Bulba, Bagdad Cafe*), born Lansdorf Graz, Austria, Jan 11, 1945.

Juanita Kreps, 77, government, university administrator, born Harlan County, KY, Jan 11, 1921.

Rod Taylor, 68, actor (*The Birds*; "Masquerade"), born Sydney, Australia, Jan 11, 1930.

Grant Tinker, 72, TV executive, born Stamford, CT, Jan 11, 1926.

JANUARY 12 — MONDAY

Day 12 — 353 Remaining

"ALL IN THE FAMILY" TV PREMIERE: ANNIVERSARY. Jan 12, 1971. Based on the success of the British comedy "Till Death Us Do Part," Norman Lear created CBS's controversial sitcom "All in the Family." The series was the first of its kind to realistically portray the prevailing issues and taboos of its time with a wickedly skewed and humorous bent. From bigotry to birth control, few topics were considered too sacred to discuss on air. Ultra-conservative Archie Bunker (played by Carroll O'Connor) held court from his recliner, spewing invective at any who disagreed with him. Jean Stapleton portrayed Archie's dutiful wife, Edith. Sally Struthers and Rob Reiner rounded out the cast as Archie's ultra-liberal daughter and son-in-law, Gloria and Mike "Meathead" Stivic. All three characters often fell victim to Archie's zinging one-liners and insults.

"BATMAN" TV PREMIERE: ANNIVERSARY. Jan 12, 1966. ABC's crime-fighting show gained a place in Nielsen's top 10 ratings in its first season. The series was based on the DC Comic characters created by Bob Kane in 1939. Adam West starred as millionaire Bruce Wayne and superhero alter ego, Batman. Burt Ward co-starred as Dick Grayson/Robin, the Boy Wonder. A colorful assortment of villains guest-starring each week included: Cesar Romero as the Joker; Eartha Kitt and Julie Newmar as Catwoman; Burgess Meredith as the Penguin; and Frank Gorshin as the Riddler. Some other stars making memorable appearances included Liberace, Vincent Price, Milton Berle, Tallulah Bankhead and Ethel Merman. The series played up its comic-strip roots with innovative and sharply skewed camera angles, bright bold colors and wild graphics. "Batman's" memorable theme song, composed by Neal Hefti, can be heard today with some 120 episodes in syndication.

"THE BELL TELEPHONE HOUR" TV PREMIERE: ANNIVERSARY. Jan 12, 1959. NBC's musical series ran semi-regularly for nearly 10 seasons. The Bell Telephone Orchestra was conducted by Donald Voorhees.

BURKE, EDMUND: BIRTH ANNIVERSARY. Jan 12, 1729. British orator, politician and philosopher, born at Dublin, Ireland. "Superstition is the religion of feeble minds," he wrote in 1790, but best remembered is "The only thing necessary for the triumph of evil is for good men to do nothing," not found in his writings but almost universally attributed to Burke. Died at Beaconsfield, England, July 9, 1797.

CONGRESS AUTHORIZES USE OF FORCE AGAINST IRAQ: ANNIVERSARY. Jan 12. On Jan 12, 1991, the US Congress passed a resolution authorizing the President of the US to use force to expel Iraq from Kuwait. This was the sixth congressional vote in US history declaring war or authorizing force on another nation.

"DYNASTY" TV PREMIERE: ANNIVERSARY. Jan 12, 1981. The popular ABC prime-time serial focused on the high-flying exploits of the Denver-based Carrington family. The series, created and produced by Richard and Esther Shapiro, had a weekly wardrobe budget of $10,000 with many elegant costumes designed by Nolan Miller. In addition to the juicy storylines, many tuned in worldwide to view the palatial mansions and lavish sets. John Forsythe played patriarch Blake Carrington with Linda Evans as his wife, Krystle. Joan Collins played Alexis, Blake's scheming ex-wife and arch business rival. Other cast members included Kathleen Beller, Pamela Bellwood, Diahann Carroll, Jack Coleman, John James, Heather Locklear, Pamela Sue Martin, Ted McGinley, Michael Nader, Catherine Oxenberg, Emma Samms and Gordon Thomas. Notable guest stars included William Campbell, James Farentino, George Hamilton, Charlton Heston, Rock Hudson, Billy Dee Williams and many others during the soap's long run.

ENGLAND: PLOUGH MONDAY. Jan 12. Always the Monday after Twelfth Day. Work on the farm is resumed after the festivities of the 12 days of Christmas. On preceding Sunday ploughs may be blessed in churches. Celebrated with dances and plays.

HAYES, IRA HAMILTON: BIRTH ANNIVERSARY. Jan 12, 1922. Ira Hayes was one of six US Marines who raised the American flag on Iwo Jima's Mt Suribachi on Feb 23, 1945, following a US assault on the Japanese stronghold. The event was immortalized by AP photographer Joe Rosenthal's famous photo and later by a Marine War Memorial monument at Arlington, VA. Hayes was born on a Pima Indian Reservation in Arizona. He returned home after World War II a much celebrated hero. A postage stamp depicting the flag-raising by the six Marines was issued in 1945. Hayes, a hero to everyone except himself, was unable to cope with fame. He became an alcoholic and was found dead of "exposure to freezing weather and over-consumption of alcohol" on the Sacaton Indian Reservation in Arizona, on Jan 24, 1955.

LONDON, JACK: BIRTH ANNIVERSARY. Jan 12, 1876. American author of more than 50 books: short stories, novels and travel, stories of the sea and of the far north, many marked by brutal realism. His most widely known work is *The Call of the Wild*, the great dog story published in 1903. London was born at San Francisco, CA; he died by suicide (an overdose of morphine) at age 40 on Nov 22, 1916, near Santa Rosa, CA.

MAN WATCHERS WEEK. Jan 12–17. A week of appreciation for men who are well worth watching. List of activities available. For info: Suzy Mallery, Suzy Mallery's Man Watchers Inc, 12308 Darlington Ave, Los Angeles, CA 90049. Phone: (310) 826-9101. Fax: (310) 820-3539.

MISSION SANTA CLARA DE ASIS: ANNIVERSARY. Jan 12, 1777. California mission to the Indians founded.

MOON PHASE: FULL MOON. Jan 12. Moon enters Full Moon phase at 12:24 PM, EST.

NATIONAL CLEAN-OFF-YOUR-DESK DAY. Jan 12. To provide one day early each year for every desk worker to see the top of the desk and prepare for the following year's paperwork. Annually, the second Monday in January. For info: A.C. Moeller, Box 71, Clio, MI 48420-1042.

NATIONAL THANK GOD IT'S MONDAY! DAY. Jan 12. Besides holidays, such as President's Day, being celebrated on Mondays, people everywhere start new jobs, have birthdays, celebrate promotions and begin vacations on Mondays. A day in recognition of this first day of the week. Annually, the second Monday in January. For info: Dorothy Zjawin, 61 W Colfax Ave, Roselle Park, NJ 07204. Phone: (908) 241-6241. Fax: (908) 241-6241.

TANZANIA: ZANZIBAR REVOLUTION DAY. Jan 12. National day. Zanzibar became independent in Dec 1963, under a sultan.

WINTHROP, JOHN: BIRTH ANNIVERSARY. Jan 12, 1588. American colonial governor of Massachusetts Bay Colony. Born at Edwardston, England. Governor Winthrop kept a diary of events in the Massachusetts Bay Colony, published nearly two centuries later (in 1825–1826), titled *The History of New England from 1630 to 1649*. Died at Boston, MA, on Mar 26, 1649.

WOMEN DENIED VOTE: ANNIVERSARY. Jan 12, 1915. The US House of Representatives rejected a proposal to give women the right to vote.

January 1998

S	M	T	W	T	F	S
				1	2	3
4	5	6	7	8	9	10
11	12	13	14	15	16	17
18	19	20	21	22	23	24
25	26	27	28	29	30	31

BIRTHDAYS TODAY

Kirstie Alley, 43, actress (Emmy for "Cheers"; *Star Trek: The Motion Picture, Look Who's Talking*), born Wichita, KS, Jan 12, 1955.

James Farmer, 78, civil rights leader, born Marshall, TX, Jan 12, 1920.

Joe Frazier, 54, former boxer, born Beaufort, SC, Jan 12, 1944.

HAL, 6, computer in *2001: A Space Odyssey*, by Arthur C. Clarke, "born" Urbana, IL, Jan 12, 1992.

Ray Price, 72, country singer, born Perryville, TX, Jan 12, 1926.

Luise Rainer, 86, actress (Oscars for *The Great Ziegfield* and *The Good Earth*), born Vienna, Austria, Jan 12, 1912.

Howard Stern, 44, radio and television personality ("The Howard Stern Show"), born Queens, NY, Jan 12, 1954.

Jacques Dominique Wilkins, 38, basketball player, born Paris, France, Jan 12, 1960.

JANUARY 13 — TUESDAY

Day 13 — 352 Remaining

ALGER, HORATIO, JR: BIRTH ANNIVERSARY. Jan 13, 1834. American clergyman and author of more than 100 popular books for boys (some 20 million copies sold). Born at Revere, MA, he died at Natick, MA, July 18, 1899. Honesty, frugality and hard work assured that the heroes of his books would find success, wealth and fame.

BOB HOPE CHRYSLER GOLF CLASSIC. Jan 13–18. Bermuda Dunes, CA. The nation's largest sports event for charity. It features PGA pros, celebrities and amateurs. Est attendance: 80,000. For info: Pat Bennett, PR and Production Asst, Bob Hope Chrysler Classic, 39000 Bob Hope Dr, Rancho Mirage, CA 92270. Phone: (760) 346-8184. Fax: (760) 346-6329. Email: info@bhcc.com. WWW: http://www.bhcc.com

CHASE, SALMON PORTLAND: BIRTH ANNIVERSARY. Jan 13, 1808. American statesman. Born at Cornish, NH. US senator, secretary of the treasury and chief justice of the Supreme Court. Salmon P. Chase spent much of his life fighting slavery (he was popularly known as "attorney general for runaway Negroes"). He was one of the founders of the Republican Party and his hopes for becoming candidate for president of the US in 1856 and 1860 were dashed because his unconcealed antislavery views made him unacceptable. Died at New York, NY, May 7, 1873. His portrait may be seen on US currency (the $10,000 bill).

CORRIDOR OF DEATH: 55th ANNIVERSARY. Jan 13, 1943. The suffering of the people of Leningrad during the German siege of that city was one of the greatest tragedies of World War II. More than half the population of Russia's second largest city died during the winter of 1942. On Jan 13, 1943, Soviet troops broke through German lines and opened a ten-mile wide corridor south of Lake Ladoga. Within a week supplies were arriving in the city by way of this narrow opening. Because fierce German bombardment of the passage continued for another year, the pass came to be called the "Corridor of Death." The siege finally ended Jan 27, 1944, after 880 days.

FULLER, ALFRED CARL: BIRTH ANNIVERSARY. Jan 13, 1885. Founder of the Fuller Brush Company, born at Kings County, NS, Canada. In 1906 the young brush salesman went into business on his own, making brushes at a bench between the furnace and the coal bin in his sister's basement. Died at Hartford, CT, on Dec 4, 1973.

"LIFE BEGINS AT EIGHTY" TV PREMIERE: ANNIVERSARY. Jan 13, 1950. At various times on NBC, ABC and Dumont, a panel of know-it-alls gave advice on topics previously submitted by viewers. Jack Barry hosted and produced the show. Fred Stein and Georgiana Carhart were its regular panelists.

POETRY BREAK. Jan 13. Celebrate poetry by announcing a "poetry break and reading a poem aloud—at home, at school, in the office, in the market . . . anywhere!" For info: Dr. Caroline Feller Bauer, 10155 Collins Ave, #402, Miami Beach, FL 33154-1636. Phone: (305) 868-9991. Fax: (305) 868-9992. Email: cblovesbks@aol.com.

RADIO BROADCASTING: ANNIVERSARY. Jan 13, 1910. Radio pioneer and electron tube inventor Lee De Forest arranged the world's first radio broadcast to the public—in New York, NY, on Jan 13, 1910. He succeeded in broadcasting the voice of Enrico Caruso along with other stars of the Metropolitan Opera to several receiving locations in the city where listeners with earphones marveled at wireless music from the air. Though only a few were equipped to listen, it was the first broadcast to reach the public and the beginning of a new era in which wireless radio communication became almost universal.

★**STEPHEN FOSTER MEMORIAL DAY.** Jan 13. Presidential Proclamation 2957 of Dec 13, 1951 (designating Jan 13, 1952), covers all succeeding years. (PL82–225 of Oct 27, 1951.) Observed on the anniversary of Foster's death, Jan 13, 1864, at New York, NY. See also: "Foster, Stephen: Birth Anniversary" (July 4).

BIRTHDAYS TODAY

Kevin Anderson, 38, actor (*Hoffa, Rising Sun*), born Illinois, Jan 13, 1960.

Keith Coogan, 28, actor (*Adventures in Babysitting, Cousins*), born Palm Springs, CA, Jan 13, 1970.

Patrick Dempsey, 32, actor (*Heaven Help Us, In the Mood*), born Lewiston, ME, Jan 13, 1966.

Frank Gallo, 65, artist, sculptor, born Toledo, OH, Jan 13, 1933.

Julia Louis-Dreyfus, 37, actress ("Seinfeld"), born New York, NY, Jan 13, 1961.

Edward Madigan, 62, former US secretary of agriculture in Bush administration, born Illinois, Jan 13, 1936.

Jay McInerney, 43, writer (*Bright Lights, Big City*), born Hartford, CT, Jan 13, 1955.

Penelope Ann Miller, 34, actress (*Adventures in Babysitting, The Freshman, Carlito's Way*), born Los Angeles, CA, Jan 13, 1964.

Richard Moll, 55, actor ("Night Court," *Wicked Stepmother, The Flintstones*), born Pasadena, CA, Jan 13, 1943.

Charles Nelson Reilly, 67, actor ("The Ghost and Mrs Muir," "Match Game PM"), born New York, NY, Jan 13, 1931.

Robert Stack, 79, actor (Emmy for "The Untouchables"), born Los Angeles, CA, Jan 13, 1919.

Frances Sternhagen, 68, actress (*The Tiger Makes Out, Misery*; stage: *The Good Doctor*), born Washington, DC, Jan 13, 1930.

Brandon Tartikoff, 49, broadcast executive, born Long Island, NY, Jan 13, 1949.

Gwen Verdon, 72, actress (*Damn Yankees, Cocoon*; stage: *Damn Yankees, High Button Shoes*), born Los Angeles, CA, Jan 13, 1926.

JANUARY 14 — WEDNESDAY

Day 14 — 351 Remaining

ARNOLD, BENEDICT: BIRTH ANNIVERSARY. Jan 14, 1741. American officer who deserted to the British during the Revolutionary War and whose name has since become synonymous with treachery. Born at Norwich, CT. Died June 14, 1801.

ASPEN/SNOWMASS WINTERSKOL. Jan 14–18. Snowmass Village, CO. A winter carnival—celebrating winter and having winter fun. Mad Hatter's Ball, skisplash, and ice sculpture contest. Est attendance: 5,000. For info: Randi Fox, PR, Snowmass Resort Assn, Box 5566, Snowmass Village, CO 81615. Phone: (800) SNOW-MASS.
WWW: http://www.snowmassvillage.com

CALIFORNIA APPLE DAY. Jan 14. Fresno, CA. All day event featuring educational speakers, sponsor booths, lunch and prizes for California's Apple Industry. Est attendance: 400. For info: California Apple Commission, 4974 E Clinton Way, #125, Fresno, CA 93727. Phone: (209) 456-0900. Fax: (209) 456-0125. Email: apple@cybergate.com. WWW: http://www.calapple.com

DODGSON, CHARLES LUTWIDGE (LEWIS CARROLL): 100th DEATH ANNIVERSARY. Jan 14, 1898. English mathematician and author, better known by his pseudonym, Lewis Carroll, creator of *Alice's Adventures in Wonderland,* was born at Cheshire, England, on Jan 27, 1832. *Alice* was written for Alice Liddell, daughter of a friend, and first published in 1886. *Through the Looking-Glass,* a sequel, and *The Hunting of the Snark* followed. Dodgson's books for children proved equally enjoyable to adults, and they overshadowed his serious works on mathematics. Dodgson died at Guildford, Surrey, England, on Jan 14, 1898.

FIRST CAESAREAN SECTION: ANNIVERSARY. Jan 14, 1794. Dr. Jesse Bennett, of Edom, VA, performed the first successful Caesarean section. The patient was his wife.

ILLINOIS SNOW SCULPTING COMPETITION. Jan 14–17. Rockford, IL. Teams from around the state create works of frozen art, as they compete to represent Illinois in national and international snow sculpting competition. In case of inclement weather, event may be postponed to Jan 21–24. Sponsor: Rockford Park District. Est attendance: 70,000. For info: Patricia Hayes, Rockford Park District, 1401 N Second St, Rockford, IL 61107-3086. Phone: (800) 521-0849 or (815) 987-8800. Email: rpdmail@inwave.com. WWW: http://sinnfree.org/rpd

MAURY, MATTHEW FONTAINE: BIRTH ANNIVERSARY. Jan 14, 1806. Naval officer, born at Fredericksburg, VA. Maury established oceanography as a branch of science and revolutionized the recording of oceanographic data as a superintendent of the Naval Observatory. Died at Lexington, VA, Feb 1, 1873.

OUTCAULT, RICHARD FELTON: BIRTH ANNIVERSARY. Jan 14, 1863. When Richard Felton Outcault was asked by the *New York World*'s Sunday editor to submit drawings for use with their new process for printing color pictures, colored comics or "funny papers" were born. Outcault's first color drawing, entitled "Origin of a New Species," was published Nov 18, 1894. The first regular colored strip, "Hogan's Alley," drawn by Outcault, began appearing with its main character's blustery comments written across his nightshirt. It was Outcault's famous strip "Buster Brown" that brought him celebrity and fortune. Outcault was born at Lancaster, OH, and died Sept 25, 1928, at Flushing, NY.

January 1998

S	M	T	W	T	F	S
				1	2	3
4	5	6	7	8	9	10
11	12	13	14	15	16	17
18	19	20	21	22	23	24
25	26	27	28	29	30	31

RATIFICATION DAY. Jan 14. Anniversary of the act that officially ended the American Revolution and established the US as a sovereign power. On Jan 14, 1784, the Continental Congress, meeting at Annapolis, MD, ratified the Treaty of Paris, thus fulfilling the Declaration of Independence of July 4, 1776.

ROACH, HAL: BIRTH ANNIVERSARY. Jan 14, 1892. American film writer, director and producer Harold Eugene (Hal) Roach was born at Elmira, NY. He pioneered film comedy as chief of his own studio for nearly 40 years. During that time he produced, and sometimes directed and wrote, nearly 1,000 movies. Roach is noted for originating the *Our Gang* comedies in 1922 and for introducing Laurel and Hardy to film audiences. He won Academy Awards for the short films *The Music Box* (1931) and *Bored of Education* (1936). Roach produced the film version of Steinbeck's novel *Of Mice and Men* in 1939. In 1984 he won an honorary Academy Award for career achievement. Roach died on Nov 2, 1992, at Los Angeles, CA.

"SANFORD AND SON" TV PREMIERE: ANNIVERSARY. Jan 14, 1972. NBC sitcom which gained immediate popularity depicting an African-American father and son engaged in the junkyard business. Norman Lear and Bud Yorkin developed the comedy series based on the British "Steptoe and Son." The name Sanford came from John Sanford, the real name of comedian Redd Foxx, who played Fred Sanford. His son, Lamont, was played by Demond Wilson. Others appearing on the show were Whitman Mayo as Grady; Slappy White as Melvin; LaWanda Page as Aunt Esther; Gregory Sierra as Julio; Nathaniel Taylor as Rollo; Raymond Allen as Uncle Woody; Don Bexley as Bubba Hoover; Lynn Hamilton as Donna Harris; Howard Platt and Hal Williams as Hoppy and Smitty; Pat Morita as Ah Chew; Marlene Clark as Janet; and Edward Crawford as Roger.

SCHWEITZER, ALBERT: BIRTH ANNIVERSARY. Jan 14, 1875. Alsatian philosopher, musician, physician and winner of the 1952 Nobel Peace Prize was born at Kayserberg, Upper Alsace, and died at Lambarene, Gabon, Sept 4, 1965, at age 90.

SCOTLAND: CELTIC CONNECTIONS. Jan 14–Feb 2 (tentative). Royal Concert Hall, Glasgow. Much acclaimed festival with music from around the world. For info: Glasgow Royal Concert Hall, Glasgow, Strathclyde, Scotland. Phone: (44) (141) 353-4137. Fax: (44) (141) 353-4134.

"THE SIMPSONS" PREMIERE: ANNIVERSARY. Jan 14, 1990. TV's hottest animated family, "The Simpsons," premiered as a half-hour weekly sitcom. The originator of Homer, Marge, Bart, Lisa and Maggie is cartoonist Matt Groening.

SPACE MILESTONE: *SOYUZ 4* (USSR). Jan 14, 1969. First docking of two manned spacecraft (with *Soyuz 5*) and first interchange of spaceship personnel in orbit. Launch date was Jan 14, 1969.

"TODAY" TV PREMIERE: ANNIVERSARY. Jan 14, 1952. NBC program that started the morning news format that we know today. Captained by Dave Garroway, the show was segmented with bits and pieces of news, sports, weather, interviews and other features that were repeated so that the viewer did not have to stop their morning routine to watch. The segments were brief and to the point. Sylvester Weaver devised this concept to capitalize on television's unusual qualities. What used to take three hours to broadcast live across the country was done in two with high quality videotape on a delayed basis. The addition of chimpanzee J. Fred Muggs in 1953 helped push ratings up. There have been a number of hosts over the years, from John Chancellor and Hugh Downs to Tom Brokaw and Bryant Gumbel. Female hosts (originally called "Today Girls") include Betsy Palmer, Florence Henderson, Barbara Walters, Jane Pauley and Katie Couric.

WHIPPLE, WILLIAM: BIRTH ANNIVERSARY. Jan 14, 1730. American patriot and signer of the Declaration of Independence. Born at Kittery, ME, he died at Portsmouth, NH, on Nov 10, 1785.

BIRTHDAYS TODAY

Jason Bateman, 29, actor ("Little House on the Prairie," "The Hogan Family"), born Rye, NY, Jan 14, 1969.

Julian Bond, 58, legislator, civil rights leader, born Nashville, TN, Jan 14, 1940.

Faye Dunaway, 57, actress (*Bonnie and Clyde, Chinatown, Network* [Oscar '76]), born Bascom, FL, Jan 14, 1941.

Lauch Faircloth, 70, US Senator (R, North Carolina), born Sampson County, NC, Jan 14, 1928.

Marjoe Gortner, 53, ex-evangelist, actor, singer, born Long Beach, CA, Jan 14, 1945.

Lawrence Kasdan, 49, filmmaker (*Body Heat, The Big Chill, Grand Canyon*), born Miami Beach, FL, Jan 14, 1949.

Andy Rooney, 79, writer, columnist, ("60 Minutes"; *Pieces of My Mind*), born Albany, NY, Jan 14, 1919.

Nina Totenberg, 54, broadcast journalist, correspondent ("Nightline"), born New York, NY, Jan 14, 1944.

JANUARY 15 — THURSDAY

Day 15 — 350 Remaining

ACE, GOODMAN: BIRTH ANNIVERSARY. Jan 15, 1899. Radio and TV writer, actor, columnist and humorist. With his wife, Jane, created and acted in the popular series of radio programs (1928–45) "Easy Aces." Called "America's greatest wit" by Fred Allen. Born at Kansas City, MO; died at New York, NY, Mar 25, 1982, soon after asking that his tombstone be inscribed "No flowers, please, I'm allergic."

ALPHA KAPPA ALPHA SORORITY FOUNDED: 90th ANNIVERSARY. Jan 15, 1908. Founded at Howard University at Washington, DC, by Ethel Hedgeman Lyle, Alpha Kappa Alpha was the first organization of its type for black women. It was incorporated five years and two weeks later on Jan 29, 1913.

BRITISH MUSEUM: ANNIVERSARY. Jan 15. On Jan 15, 1759, the British Museum opened its doors at Montague House in London. Incorporated by an act of Parliament in 1753, following the death of British medical doctor and naturalist Sir Hans Sloane, who had bequeathed his personal collection of books, manuscripts, coins, medals and antiquities to Britain. As the national museum and the national library of the United Kingdom, the British Museum houses many of the world's most prized treasures.

CHAMPIONSHIP SNOWMOBILE DERBY. Jan 15–18. Eagle River, WI. This annual event in northern Wisconsin is the most recognized professional snowmobile race and one of the largest gatherings of "sledders" in the world. Celebrate the 35th anniversary of the World Championship Snowmobile Derby with snowmobile fans from all over the globe as they watch more than 300 pro snowmobile racers, some from as far away as Japan, as they compete for the world championship and prizes. For info: Wisconsin Dept of Tourism, Championship Snowmobile Derby, PO Box 7976, Madison, WI 53707. Phone: (714) 479-4424. Email: tourism@laughlin.com. WWW: http://tourism.state.wi.us

ELEMENTARY SCHOOL TEACHER DAY. Jan 15. A day of recognition for these professionals who teach our children and fill their minds with knowledge and dreams. Annually, Jan 15. For info: Dawn T. Brue, 2006 NW 55th Ave, #H-5, Gainesville, FL 32653. Email: afn05660@afn.org.

"HILL STREET BLUES" TV PREMIERE: ANNIVERSARY. Jan 15, 1981. NBC police series created by Stephen Bochco and Michael Kozoll that became immensely popular, focused more on the police officers than the crimes, often depicting humorous or ludicrous incidents as well as the dramatic. The show was very realistic and highly praised by real policemen. It won a slew of Emmys. "Hill Street" ran for seven seasons before heading down memory lane. Cast: Daniel J. Travanti as Capt Frank Furillo; Veronica Hamel as PD Joyce Davenport; Michael Conrad as Sgt Phil "Let's be careful out there" Esterhaus; Barbara Bosson as Faye Furillo; and as the wonderfully drawn cops: Bruce Weitz (Mick Belker), Taurean Blacque (Neil Washington), Kiel Martin (Johnny LaRue), Joe Spano (Henry Goldblume), James B. Sikking (Howard Hunter), Rene Enriquez (Ray Calletano), Michael Warren (Bobby Hill), Betty Thomas (Lucy Bates), Ed Marinaro (Joe Coffey) plus Charles Haid as Andy Renko.

INTERNATIONAL FINALS RODEO '98. Jan 15–17. Oklahoma State Fair Grounds, Oklahoma City, OK. This is the season finale for the International Pro Rodeo Association. This rodeo pits the top cowboy/cowgirl athletes against one another in a weekend of the toughest pro rodeo competition. World championships hang in the balance until the conclusion of this pinnacle event. Televised nationally to an audience of 25 million viewers; western activities-tradeshow, IPRA Convention, dances, bucking stock sales, Miss Rodeo USA, and a Championship Awards Banquet. Est attendance: 40,000. For info: Jane Kirton, Event Coordinator, International Finals Rodeo, PO Box 83377, Oklahoma City, OK 73148. Phone: (405) 235-6540. Fax: (405) 235-6577.

JAPAN: ADULTS' DAY. Jan 15. National holiday. Day is set apart for youth of the country who have reached adulthood during the preceding year.

KING, MARTIN LUTHER, JR: BIRTH ANNIVERSARY. Jan 15, 1929. Black civil rights leader, minister and recipient of the Nobel Peace Prize (1964). Born at Atlanta, GA, he was assassinated at Memphis, TN, Apr 4, 1968. After his death many states and territories observed his birthday as a holiday. In 1983 the Congress approved HR 3706, "A bill to amend Title 5, United States Code, to make the birthday of Martin Luther King, Jr, a legal public holiday." Signed by the president on Nov 2, 1983, it became Public Law 98–144. The law sets the third Monday in January for observance of King's birthday. First observance was Jan 20, 1986. See also: "King, Martin Luther, Jr: Birthday Observed" (Jan 19).

LIVINGSTON, PHILIP: BIRTH ANNIVERSARY. Jan 15, 1716. Merchant and signer of the Declaration of Independence, born at Albany, NY. Died at York, PA, June 12, 1778.

LONGHORN WORLD CHAMPIONSHIP RODEO. Jan 15–18. Tulsa Convention Center, Tulsa, OK. More than 450 of the best cowboys and cowgirls compete in seven professional contests ranging from bronco riding to bull riding for top prize money and world championship points. Featuring colorful opening pageantry and Big, Bad BONUS Bulls. 8th annual. Est attendance: 16,000. For info: W Bruce Lehrke, Pres, Longhorn World Chmpshp Rodeo Inc, PO Box 70159, Nashville, TN 37207. Phone: (615) 876-1016. Fax: (615) 876-4685. Email: lhrodeo@idt.net. WWW: http://www.longhornrodeo.com

MACKINAW CITY WINTERFEST SNOW SCULPTING COMPETITION. Jan 15–18. Mackinaw City, MI. Professional snow sculptors will sculpt a variety of forms from large blocks of snow. Sleigh rides for the kids and a Kids' Fun Park. People's choice vote taken Sunday from 9 AM to noon. Est attendance: 5,000. For info: Mackinaw Area Tourist Bureau, PO Box 160, Mackinaw City, MI 49701. Phone: (800) 666-0160 or (616) 436-5664.

MOLIÈRE DAY: BAPTISM ANNIVERSARY. Jan 15, 1622. Most celebrated of French authors and dramatists, Jean Baptiste Poquelin, baptized at Paris, France, Jan 15, 1622, took the stage name Molière when he was about 22 years old. While playing in a performance of his last play, *Le Malade Imaginaire* (about a hypochondriac afraid of death), Molière became ill and died within a few hours at Paris, Feb 17, 1673.

QUARTERLY ESTIMATED FEDERAL INCOME TAX PAYERS' DUE DATE. Jan 15. For those individuals whose fiscal year is the calendar year and who make quarterly estimated federal income tax payments, today is one of the due dates. (Jan 15, Apr 15, June 15 and Sept 15, 1998.)

SIEGMEISTER, ELIE: BIRTH ANNIVERSARY. Jan 15, 1909. American composer Elie Siegmeister was born at New York, NY. He composed eight symphonies and eight operas, and a number of other concertos, chamber pieces and orchestral works using folk, jazz and street songs to create a contemporary American classical music. He died on Mar 10, 1991, at Manhasset, NY.

SUNDANCE FILM FESTIVAL. Jan 15–25. Park City, UT. "The premier US festival for American independent filmmakers." Est attendance: 5,000. For info: Park City Conv and Visitors Bureau, PO Box 1630, Park City, UT 84060. Phone: (800) 453-1360.

BIRTHDAYS TODAY

Lloyd Bridges, 85, actor ("Seahunt," *Roots, The Goddess*), born San Leandro, CA, Jan 15, 1913.

Charo (Maria Martinez), 47, singer, actress ("Chico and the Man"), born Murcia, Spain, Jan 15, 1951.

Chad Lowe, 30, actor ("Spencer," *Oxford Blues, Nobody's Perfect*), born Dayton, OH, Jan 15, 1968.

Rod MacLeish, 72, journalist, born Bryn Mawr, PA, Jan 15, 1926.

Margaret O'Brien, 61, actress (Beth in *Little Women*; Tootie in *Meet Me in St. Louis*), born Los Angeles, CA, Jan 15, 1937.

Edward Teller, 90, physicist, born Budapest, Hungary, Jan 15, 1908.

JANUARY 16 — FRIDAY

Day 16 — 349 Remaining

ART DECO WEEKEND FESTIVAL. Jan 16–19. Miami Beach, FL. Features parade, arts and crafts displays, jazz entertainment and plenty of food. Includes art from local talent. Est attendance: 450,000. For info: Art Deco Weekend Festival, PO Box 190180, Miami Beach, FL 33119. Phone: (305) 672-2014. Fax: (305) 672-4319.

BALD EAGLE APPRECIATION DAYS. Jan 16–18. Riverfront, Keokuk, IA. Features trained personnel stationed at observation points for viewing the American bald eagle. Indoor exhibits at Keosippi Mall and live eagle demonstrations. Est attendance: 10,000. For info: Kari Bevans, Dir of Tourism, Keokuk Area Conv and Tourism Bureau, 401 Main, Keokuk, IA 52632. Phone: (800) 383-1219 or (319) 524-5599. Fax: (319) 524-5016. Email: keochcom@interl.net.

BRITISH AIR RAID ON BERLIN: 55th ANNIVERSARY. Jan 16, 1943. In the first bombing of Germany since decisions of the Casablanca Conference, on Jan 16, 1943, the British Royal Air Force began heavy bombing of Germany by day and by night to bring about "the progressive destruction and dislocation of the German military, industrial and economic system, and for the undermining of the morale of the German people." The RAF used their new "target indicator" bombs to mark targets for their bombers.

CIVIL SERVICE CREATED: ANNIVERSARY. Jan 16, 1883. The US Congress passed a bill creating the civil service.

January 1998

S	M	T	W	T	F	S
				1	2	3
4	5	6	7	8	9	10
11	12	13	14	15	16	17
18	19	20	21	22	23	24
25	26	27	28	29	30	31

COAL CONSERVATION ORDERED: 80th ANNIVERSARY. Jan 16, 1918. In a precursor of things to come, 75 New York schools closed down for lack of coal on Jan 2, 1918. On Jan 16, by order of US Fuel Administrator Harry A. Garfield, all industry east of the Mississippi not crucial to the war effort was ordered shut down. Factories remained closed for five days. Additionally, the following nine Mondays became days of leisure for a large segment of the American work force as further attempts were made to reserve coal for troop transport, ships and merchant vessels.

DEAN, DIZZY: BIRTH ANNIVERSARY. Jan 16, 1911. Jay Hanna "Dizzy" Dean, major league pitcher (St. Louis Cardinals) and Baseball Hall of Fame member was born at Lucas, AR. Following his baseball career, Dean established himself as a radio and TV sports announcer and commentator, becoming famous for his innovative delivery. "He slud into third," reported Dizzy, who on another occasion explained that "Me and Paul [baseball player brother Paul "Daffy" Dean] . . . didn't get much education." Died at Reno, NV, July 17, 1974.

EL SALVADOR: CIVIL WAR ENDED: ANNIVERSARY. Jan 16, 1992. On Jan 16, 1992, a peace treaty was signed in Mexico City ending the 12-year civil war that had claimed 75,000 lives. On Feb 1, a cease-fire went into effect.

JAPAN: HARU-NO-YABUIRI. Jan 16. Employees and servants who have been working over the holidays are given a day off.

MERMAN, ETHEL: BIRTH ANNIVERSARY. Jan 16, 1909. Musical comedy star famous for her belting voice and brassy style. Born Ethel Agnes Zimmerman on Jan 16, 1909 (or 1912—the date changed the older she got, but most sources say 1909) at Queens, NY. Died Feb 15, 1984, at New York, NY.

MICHELIN, ANDRE: BIRTH ANNIVERSARY. Jan 16, 1853. French industrialist who, along with his brother Edouard, started the Michelin Tire Company in 1888, manufacturing bicycle tires. They were the first to use demountable pneumatic tires on cars. Born at Paris, France; died there on Apr 4, 1931.

NATIONAL NOTHING DAY: 25th ANNIVERSARY. Jan 16. Anniversary of National Nothing Day, an event created by newspaperman Harold Pullman Coffin and first observed in 1973 "to provide Americans with one national day when they can just sit without celebrating, observing or honoring anything." Since 1975, though many other events have been listed on this day, lighthearted traditional observance of Coffin's idea has continued. Coffin, a native of Reno, NV, died at Capitola, CA, Sept 12, 1981, at the age of 76.

NATIONAL WORK AT HOME WITH YOUR SPOUSE DAY. Jan 16. To encourage couples to make the most of their skills and their relationship by starting a business together and working for themselves. For info: Panda Publishing, PO Box 3834, Naperville, IL 60587-3834. Phone: (630) 357-3196. Fax: (630) 357-3197. WWW: http://www.bookhome.com

PROHIBITION AMENDMENT: ANNIVERSARY. Jan 16, 1919. Nebraska became the 36th state to ratify the prohibition amendment on Jan 16, 1919, and the 18th Amendment became part of the US Constitution. One year later, on Jan 16, 1920, the 18th Amendment took effect and the sale of alcoholic beverages became illegal in the US with the Volstead Act providing for enforcement. This was the first time that an amendment to the Constitution dealt with a social issue. The 21st Amendment, repealing the 18th, went into effect on Dec 6, 1933.

RELIGIOUS FREEDOM DAY. Jan 16. On Jan 16, 1786, the legislature of Virginia adopted a religious freedom statute that protected Virginians against any requirement to attend or support any church and against discrimination. This statute, which had been drafted by Thomas Jefferson and introduced by James Madison, later was the model for the 1st Amendment to the US Constitution.

SEATTLE BOAT SHOW. Jan 16–25. The Kingdome, Seattle, WA. Huge display of new boats, accessories and services. A second show, Seattle Boats Afloat, scheduled for Aug 1998. Large boats (35 ft or longer) on display in Puget Sound with over 70 accessories dealers on land. Est attendance: 90,000. For info: NW Marine Trade Assn, 1900 N Northlake Way, #233, Seattle, WA 98103. Phone: (206) 634-0911. Fax: (206) 632-0078.

SERVICE, ROBERT WILLIAM: BIRTH ANNIVERSARY. Jan 16, 1874. Canadian poet, born at Preston, England. Lived in the Canadian northwest for many years and perhaps is best remembered for such ballads as "The Shooting of Dan McGrew" and "The Cremation of Sam McGee" and for such books as *Songs of a Sourdough*, *Rhymes of a Rolling Stone* and *The Spell of the Yukon*. Died at France, Sept 11, 1958.

SEWARD POLAR BEAR JUMP FESTIVAL. Jan 16–18. Resurrection Bay, Seward, AK. Volunteers collect pledges to jump into bay in costumes. Festivities include golf tournament, parade, dog weight pull, dog sled race, Polar Bear Expo/Trade Show, skijoring, Bachelor/Bachelorette Auction, ice bowling, talent show, Seafood Feed and much more. Benefits local nonprofit organizations and the American Cancer Society. The actual "Plunge" takes place on Saturday, Jan 17. Est attendance: 2,500. For info: Seward Polar Bear Jump Fest, PO Box 386, Seward, AK 99664. Phone: (907) 224-5230. Fax: (907) 224-4085.

"SUPER CIRCUS" TV PREMIERE: ANNIVERSARY. Jan 16, 1949. ABC circus show that turned out to be a long-running six-year broadcast from Chicago. Heading the circus was ringmaster Claude Kirchner and assistant Mary Hartline (a lovely blonde with a terrific smile) with three clowns: Cliffy Sobier as Cliffy, Sandy Dobritch and Bardy Patton as Scampy and Nicky Frances as Nicky. Jerry Collona and Sandy Wirth took over as ringmaster and assistant after the circus moved to New York in 1955. The Big Apple was too much for it—the show only lasted a year there.

WAR AGAINST IRAQ BEGINS: ANNIVERSARY. Jan 16, 1991. On this night the Allied forces launched a major air offensive against Iraq to begin the War in the Gulf. The strike was designed to destroy Iraqi air defenses, command, control and communications centers. As Desert Shield became Desert Storm, the world was able to see and hear for the first time an initial engagement of war as CNN broadcasters stationed in Baghdad broadcast the attack live.

WINGS OVER WILLCOX/SANDHILL CRANE CELEBRATION. Jan 16–18. Willcox, AZ. Tours to the Willcox Playa to see Sandhill cranes, also to Cochise Lake to see the Waders, a hawk stalk tour, workshops on wildlife, seminars on bird watching by various experts, a banquet and much more. For info: Willcox Chamber of Commerce, 1500 N Circle "I" Rd, Willcox, AZ 85643. Phone: (800) 200-2272 or (520) 384-2272. Fax: (520) 384-0293.

WISCONSIN DELLS FLAKE OUT FESTIVAL. Jan 16–18. Tommy Bartlett Thrill Show Site, Wisconsin Dells, WI. Wisconsin-sanctioned snow sculpting competition. Winners will compete in the National Snow Sculpting Competition. Other activities include ice-carving competition, snowmobile races, sleigh rides, ice skating, glowing hot-air balloons on Saturday evening and much more. Est attendance: 20,000. For info: Wisconsin Dells Visitor and Conv Bureau, PO Box 390, Wisconsin Dells, WI 53965. Phone: (800) 223-3557. Email: wisdells@midplains.net. WWW: http://www.wisdells.com

94.7 FM WMAS RETRO PARTY. Jan 16. Pearl Street Nightclub, Northampton, MA. Listeners are invited to come dance to their favorite hits from the '70s and '80s. Watch movies from that time period on a big screen and play games for prizes. Est attendance: 300. For info: Dina Cox, PO Box 9500, Springfield, MA 01102. Phone: (413) 737-1414. Fax: (413) 737-1488.

YUMA HOME SHOW. Jan 16–18. Yuma Civic and Convention Center, Yuma, AZ. Public exhibit—home improvement, construction, renovation, remodeling and decorating. Annually, the third weekend in January. Est attendance: 15,000. For info: Yuma Civic & Convention Center, 1440 Desert Hills Dr, Yuma, AZ 85365. Phone: (520) 344-3800. Fax: (520) 344-9121.

BIRTHDAYS TODAY

Debbie Allen, 48, dancer, choreographer, singer, actress ("Fame"), born Houston, TX, Jan 16, 1950.
Anthony Joseph (A.J.) Foyt, Jr, 63, former auto racer, born Houston, TX, Jan 16, 1935.
Marilyn Horne, 64, opera singer, born Bradford, PA, Jan 16, 1934.
Katy Jurado, 71, actress (*High Noon, One-Eyed Jacks*), born Guadalajara, Mexico, Jan 16, 1927.
Eartha Kitt, 70, singer, born North, SC, Jan 16, 1928.
Jack Burns McDowell, 32, baseball player, born Van Nuys, CA, Jan 16, 1966.
Ronnie Milsap, 54, singer ("[There's] No Gettin' Over Me"), born Robinsville, NC, Jan 16, 1944.
Francesco Scavullo, 69, photographer, born Staten Island, NY, Jan 16, 1929.

JANUARY 17 — SATURDAY

Day 17 — 348 Remaining

ANTIQUE SHOW & SALE. Jan 17–18. (Also Apr 25–26 and Sept 19–20.) Mountain View Inn, Greensburg, PA. Show features fine collectibles from more than 60 dealers from 11 states. Crafts include crocks, quilts, estate jewelry, glassware, silver, linens, wicker and furniture. For info: Ruth Van Kuren, Mountain View Inn, Rte 30 East, Greensburg, PA 15601. Phone: (412) 834-5300 or (800) 537-8709. Fax: (412) 834-5304.

BALD EAGLE DAYS. Jan 17–18. High school gym, Cassville, WI. Indoor programs and exhibits. Outdoor viewing of eagles at Riverside Park (Mississippi River), Cassville, with knowledgeable attendants and at Nelson Dewey State Park. Est attendance: 1,000. For info: Mona Hudson, Tourism Coord, Cassville Tourism, PO 576, Cassville, WI 53806. Phone: (608) 725-5855. Fax: (608) 725-2192.

"BARETTA" TV PREMIERE: ANNIVERSARY. Jan 17, 1975. CBS series starring Robert Blake as Baretta, a police detective who defied his superiors and solved his cases in a most unorthodox manner—usually by figuring it out while talking to his pet cockatoo, Fred, or his informant, Rooster (played by Michael D. Roberts). Commanding officer Lt Hal Brubaker was played by Edward Grover. Viewers tuned in each week to see Fred.

CABLE CAR PATENT: ANNIVERSARY. Jan 17, 1871. Andrew Hallikie received a patent for a cable-car system that began service in San Francisco in 1873.

CANADA: MINDEN SLED DOG DERBY. Jan 17–18. Minden, Ontario. World's largest limited-class speed sled dog derby features mushers from throughout North America. Est attendance: 7,000. For info: Minden Sled Dog Derby, Box 97, Minden, Ont, Canada K0M 2K0. Phone: (800) 461-7677 or (705) 286-1288. Fax: (705) 286-4768. Email: mindentimes@halhinet.on.ca. WWW: http://www.mindentimes.on.ca

CHICAGO'S WINDY CITY JITTERBUG CLUB DANCE. Jan 17 (also Jan 31). Dance to the music of the '50s,'60s and more. Dances held twice a month at the Franklin Park American Legion Hall. Est attendance: 200. For info: CWCJC, PO Box 713, Franklin Park, IL 60131. Phone: (708) 456-6000.

EAGLE DAYS. Jan 17–18. Milford Nature Center/Fish Hatchery, Junction City, KS. Learn more about the magnificent bird that is our national emblem. Meet both a live bald eagle and a golden eagle! Guides with spotting scopes and binoculars will be waiting to show you eagles as they roost and soar around Milford Lake. Sponsor: Kansas Wildlife and Parks; US Army Corps of Engineers. Est attendance: 700. For info: Milford Nature Center, 3115 Hatchery Dr, Junction City, KS 66441. Phone: (913) 238-5323. Fax: (913) 238-5775.

ESAU'S ANTIQUE AND COLLECTIBLE MARKET. Jan 17–18. Chilhowee Park, Knoxville, TN. Popular antique fair features furniture, glassware, primitive quilts, toys, jewelry, linens and lots of other items. Monthly, on the third weekend (except December, which is on the second weekend). Est attendance: 12,000. For info: Cindy Crabtree, Esau, Inc, PO Box 50096, Knoxville, TN 37950. Phone: (423) 588-1233 or (800) 588-ESAU (3728). Fax: (423) 588-6938.

FANCY RAT AND MOUSE ANNUAL SHOW. Jan 17 or 24 (to be determined). Hacienda Heights, CA. Annual show where trophies are awarded to the winners. As urban sprawl continues to limit the space needed to keep dogs and cats, rats and mice as pets are emerging as an ideal substitute. They provide all the pleasure and satisfaction of a warm, cuddly, intelligent and friendly pet companion. The American Fancy Rat and Mouse Assn (AFRMA) was founded in 1983 to promote and encourage the breeding and exhibition of fancy rats and mice. Est attendance: 100. For info: AFRMA (CAE), 9230 64th St, Riverside, CA 92509-5924. Phone: (909) 685-2350. Fax: (818) 592-6319. Email: craigr@afrma.org. WWW: http://www.afrma.org/afrma

FIRST NUCLEAR-POWERED SUBMARINE VOYAGE: ANNIVERSARY. Jan 17. The world's first nuclear-powered submarine, the *Nautilus*, now forms part of the *Nautilus* Memorial Submarine Force Library and Museum at the Naval Submarine Base New London in Groton, CT. At 11 AM, EST, on Jan 17, 1955, her commanding officer, Commander Eugene P. Wilkerson, ordered all lines cast off and sent the historic message: "Under way on nuclear power." Highlights of the *Nautilus*: keel laid by President Harry S. Truman on June 14, 1952; christened and launched by Mrs Dwight D. Eisenhower on Jan 21, 1954; commissioned to the US Navy on Sept 30, 1954.

January 1998

S	M	T	W	T	F	S
				1	2	3
4	5	6	7	8	9	10
11	12	13	14	15	16	17
18	19	20	21	22	23	24
25	26	27	28	29	30	31

FRANKLIN, BENJAMIN: BIRTH ANNIVERSARY. Jan 17, 1706. "Elder statesman of the American Revolution," oldest signer of both the Declaration of Independence and the Constitution, scientist, diplomat, author, printer, publisher, philosopher, philanthropist and self-made, self-educated man. Author, printer and publisher of *Poor Richard's Almanack* (1733–1758). Born at Boston, MA, Franklin died at Philadelphia, PA, Apr 17, 1790. His birthday is commemorated each year by the Poor Richard Club of Philadelphia with graveside observance. In 1728 Franklin wrote a premature epitaph for himself. It first appeared in print in Ames's 1771 almanac: "The Body of BENJAMIN FRANKLIN/Printer/Like a Covering of an old Book/Its contents torn out/And stript of its Lettering and Gilding,/Lies here, Food for Worms;/But the work shall not be lost,/It will (as he believ'd) appear once more/In a New and more beautiful Edition/Corrected and amended/By the Author."

"FRONTLINE" TV PREMIERE: 15th ANNIVERSARY. Jan 17, 1983. PBS hour-long independently produced documentaries hosted by Jessica Savitch. The programs often created controversy, focusing on a variety of political, military and social issues. Judy Woodruff replaced Savitch after Savitch was killed in an auto accident in the fall of 1983.

FUN-IN-THE-SUN POSTCARD SALE. Jan 17–18. Las Palmas Hotel, Orlando, FL. Sale of antique and modern postcards by 20 dealers. Est attendance: 200. For info: John H. McClintock, Dir, Postcard Society, Inc, Box 1765, Manassas, VA 22110. Phone: (703) 368-2757.

"THE GOLDBERGS" TV PREMIERE: ANNIVERSARY. Jan 17, 1949. Originally broadcast by CBS, this show was one of the earliest TV sitcoms. The show centered around a Jewish mother and her family living in the Bronx and later moving to the suburbs. Gertrude Berg created the hit radio show before she wrote, produced and starred as Molly Goldberg in the television version. Contributing actors and actresses included Philip Loeb, Harold J. Stone, Robert H. Harris, Arlene McQuade, Larry Robinson, Tom Taylor, Eli Mintz, Menasha Skulnik and Arnold Stang.

HUTCHINS, ROBERT MAYNARD: BIRTH ANNIVERSARY. Jan 17, 1899. American educator, foundation executive and civil liberties activist, born at Brooklyn, NY. He was president and later chancellor of the University of Chicago, where he introduced many educational concepts, including the Great Books program. Died at Santa Barbara, CA, on May 14, 1977.

IKE'S FAREWELL: ANNIVERSARY. Jan 17, 1961. President Dwight D. Eisenhower, in his farewell address to the nation on national radio and television, spoke the sentences that would be the most quoted and remembered of his presidency. In a direct warning, he said, "In the councils of government, we must guard against the acquisition of unwarranted influence, whether sought or unsought, by the military-industrial complex. The potential for the disastrous rise of misplaced power exists and persists."

JAPAN SUFFERS MAJOR EARTHQUAKE: ANNIVERSARY. Jan 17, 1995. Japan suffered its second most deadly earthquake in the 20th century when a 20-second temblor left 5,500 dead and more than 21,600 people injured. The epicenter was six miles beneath Awaji Island in Osaka Bay. This was just 20 miles west of Kobe, Japan's sixth-largest city and a major port that accounted for 12% of the country's exports. Measuring 7.2 on the Richter scale, the quake collapsed or badly damaged more than 30,400 buildings and left 275,000 people homeless.

"JOHNNY OLSEN'S RUMPUS ROOM" TV PREMIERE: ANNIVERSARY. Jan 17, 1949. This Dumont daily offering was a variety show featuring Johnny Olsen as host. An early audience participation show.

MEXICO: BLESSING OF THE ANIMALS AT THE CATHEDRAL. Jan 17. Church of San Antonio in Mexico City or Xochimilco provide best sights of chickens, cows and household pets gaily decorated with flowers. (Saint's day for San Antonio Abad, patron saint of domestic animals.)

MINORITY SCIENTISTS SHOWCASE. Jan 17–19. St. Louis, MO. Open new doors to future science careers and interests during Martin Luther King Jr. weekend with hands-on activities and information available as part of a free program. Meet and talk with African-Americans working in science-related fields throughout the St. Louis area. Annually, Martin Luther King Jr. weekend. Est attendance: 2,000. For info: Bev Pfeifer-Harms, St. Louis Science Center, 5050 Oakland Ave, St. Louis, MO 63110. Phone: (314) 533-8687. Fax: (314) 289-4420. Email: bpharms@slsc.org. WWW: http://www.slsc.org

MODEL RAILROAD SHOW. Jan 17–18. Wilson Lodge, Oglebay, Wheeling, WV. Train enthusiasts will find nearly 80 train exhibitors displaying and selling their wide variety of items. Est attendance: 1,500. For info: Steve Mitch, Theater Director, Good Zoo, Oglebay, Rt 88 N, Wheeling, WV 26003. Phone: (304) 243-4034. Fax: (304) 243-4110. WWW: http://wvweb.com/oglebay

PALOMARES HYDROGEN BOMB ACCIDENT: ANNIVERSARY. Jan 17. At 10:16 AM on Jan 17, 1966, according to villagers, fire fell from the sky over Palomares, Spain. An American B-52 bomber carrying four hydrogen bombs collided with its refueling plane, spilling the bombs (two of which had "chemical explosions," scattering radioactive plutonium over the area). In a cleanup, American soldiers burned crops, slaughtered animals and removed tons of topsoil (which was sent to South Carolina for burial). More than 19 years later, in November 1985, the Nuclear Energy Board permitted villagers to see their medical reports for the first time.

PAUL BUNYAN SLED DOG RACES, WEIGHT PULL, SKIJORING AND MUTT RACES. Jan 17–18. Lake Bemidji, Bemidji, MN. 27th annual competition. For info: Bemidji Area Chamber of Commerce, Box 850, Bemidji, MN 56619-0850. Phone: (800) 458-2223.

PGA OF AMERICA FOUNDED: ANNIVERSARY. Jan 17, 1916. Golf great Walter Hagen and some 30 other pro golfers met and formed The Professional Golfers' Association of America and also developed the idea for a national championship. Rodman Wanamaker provided the trophy and $2,580 purse for the first PGA Championship, which was played on Apr 10, 1916, at the Siwanoy course in Bronxville, NY. The winner was British golfer Jim Barnes, who also won the second competition—not held until 1919 because of World War I. In 1921 Walter Hagen became the first American to win, a feat he accomplished four more times—in 1924, '25, '26 and '27.

PHILIPPINES: ATI-ATIHAN FESTIVAL. Jan 17–18. Kalibo, Aklan. One of the most colorful celebrations in the Philippines, the Ati-Atihan Festival commemorates the peace pact between the Ati of Panay (pygmies) and the Malays, who were early migrants in the islands. The townspeople blacken their bodies with soot, don colorful and bizarre costumes and sing and dance in the streets. The festival also celebrates the Feast Day of Santo Niño (the infant Jesus). Annually, the third weekend in January.

POLAND: LIBERATION DAY: ANNIVERSARY. Jan 17. Celebration of liberation from Nazi oppression on Jan 17, 1945, of the city of Warsaw by Soviet troops. Special ceremonies at the Monument to the Unknown Soldier in Warsaw's Victory Square (which had been called Adolf Hitler Platz during the German occupation).

QUEEN LILIUOKALANI DEPOSED: ANNIVERSARY. Jan 17, 1893. Hawaiian Queen Liliuokalani, the last monarch of Hawaii, lost her throne when the monarchy was abolished by the "Committee of Safety," with the foreknowledge of US minister John L. Stevens, who encouraged the revolutionaries. The Queen's supporters were intimidated by the 300 US Marines sent to protect American lives and property. Judge Sanford B. Dole became president of the republic and later was Hawaii's first governor after the US annexed it by joint resolution of Congress on July 7, 1898. Hawaii held incorporated territory status for 60 years. President Dwight D. Eisenhower signed the proclamation making Hawaii the 50th state on Aug 21, 1959.

RUSH, WILLIAM: DEATH ANNIVERSARY. Jan 17, 1833. First American-born sculptor. William Rush's work in wood and clay included busts of many notables, American and European alike; carved wooden female figureheads for ships; the masks of Tragedy and Comedy seen at the Actor's House outside Philadelphia, PA; and the *Spirit of Schuylkill* in Fairmount Park in Philadelphia. In 1805 Rush and others founded the Pennsylvania Academy of the Fine Arts. Rush was born at Philadelphia in 1756.

SAINT ANTHONY'S DAY. Jan 17. Feast day honoring Egyptian hermit who became the first Christian monk and who established communities of hermits; patron saint of domestic animals and patriarch of all monks. Lived about AD 251–354.

SENIOR BOWL FOOTBALL GAME. Jan 17. Ladd Memorial Stadium, Mobile, AL. All-star football game featuring the nation's top collegiate seniors on teams coached by National Football League coaching staffs. Proceeds go to charities. Est attendance: 40,700. For info: Vic Knight, PR Dir, Senior Bowl, 63 S Royal St, Ste 406, Mobile, AL 36602. Phone: (334) 438-2276. Fax: (334) 432-0409. Email: srbowl@dibbs.net. WWW: http://www.dibbs.net/seniorbowl/

SOUTHERN CALIFORNIA EARTHQUAKE: ANNIVERSARY. Jan 17, 1994. An earthquake measuring 6.6 on the Richter scale struck the Los Angeles area about 4:20 AM. The epicenter was at Northridge in the San Fernando Valley, about 20 miles northwest of downtown Los Angeles. A death toll of 51 was announced on Jan 20. Sixteen of the dead were killed in the collapse of one apartment building. More than 25,000 people were made homeless by the quake, and 680,000 lost electric power. Many buildings were destroyed and others made uninhabitable due to structural damage. A section of the Santa Monica Freeway, part of the Simi Valley Freeway, and three major overpasses collapsed. The highway damage caused severe commuting problems for workers in the days following the quake. Hundreds of aftershocks occurred in the following several weeks. Costs to repair the damage were estimated at 15–30 billion dollars.

TIP-UP TOWN USA. Jan 17–18. (Also Jan 24–25.) Houghton Lake, MI. Winter festival featuring a grand parade; ice-fishing contests; Ferris wheel, helicopter, pony and sleigh rides; softball on ice; tug-of-war games; concessions and Polar Bear Dip. Annually, the third and fourth weekends in January. Est attendance: 50,000. For info: Tim Romanowski, Info Mgr, Chamber of Commerce, 1625 W. Houghton Lake Dr, Houghton Lake, MI 48629. Phone: (800) 248-5253.

BIRTHDAYS TODAY

Muhammad Ali (born Cassius Marcellus Clay, Jr), 56, former heavyweight champion boxer, who changed name after converting to Islam; jailed for draft evasion when he refused the draft as a conscientious objector and then stripped of his title; born Louisville, KY, Jan 17, 1942.

Jim Carrey, 36, actor (*Dumb and Dumber, Mask, Ace Ventura*), comedian, born Ontario, Canada, Jan 17, 1962.

David Caruso, 42, actor ("NYPD Blue," *An Officer and a Gentleman*), born Queens, NY, Jan 17, 1956.

Troy Donahue, 61, actor ("Surfside 6"; "Hawaiian Eye" in its last season; *Parrish*), born New York, NY, Jan 17, 1937.

James Earl Jones, 67, actor (*The Great White Hope, Roots: The Next Generations*), born Tate County, MS, Jan 17, 1931.

Shari Lewis (Shari Hurwitz), 64, puppeteer, born New York, NY, Jan 17, 1934.

Newton Minow, 72, former head of the Federal Communications Commission (1961–1963), born Milwaukee, WI, Jan 17, 1926. Best known for his description of television as a "vast wasteland."

Sheree North (Dawn Bethel), 65, actress (*Marilyn: The Untold Story; How to Be Very Very Popular*), born New York, NY, Jan 17, 1933.

Maury Povich, 59, talk show host, born Washington DC, Jan 17, 1939.

Vidal Sassoon, 70, hair stylist, born London, England, Jan 17, 1928.

Betty White, 74, actress (Sue Ann on "Mary Tyler Moore," Rose on "The Golden Girls"), animal rights activist, born Oak Park, IL, Jan 17, 1924.

Paul Young, 42, singer ("Every Time You Go Away"), born Luton, England, Jan 17, 1956.

Donald William (Don) Zimmer, 67, baseball coach, former manager and player, born Cincinnati, OH, Jan 17, 1931.

JANUARY 18 — SUNDAY

Day 18 — 347 Remaining

BE GOOD TO YOURSELF WEEK. Jan 18–24. Created to increase public awareness of the importance of self-esteem, self-image and self-confidence. This week has seven specifically named days. See also: "Heal Old Hurts Day" (Jan 18); "Cut Yourself Some Slack Day" (Jan 19); "Lighten UP!! Day" (Jan 20); "Go for It, or Live Your Dreams Day" (Jan 21); "Love Yourself, or Be Your Own Best Friend Day" (Jan 22); "Give a Damn Day" (Jan 23); and "Be a Fool for Love Day" (Jan 24). For info: K. Diane Schutte, The Self-Renewal Project, Box 337, 5465 N Bend Rd, Cincinnati, OH 45247. Phone: (888) LUV U DAY. Email: Bgood2U@juno.com.

COCONUT GROVE BRIDAL EXPO. Jan 18. Coconut Grove, Santa Cruz, CA. Features more than 60 booths with every aspect needed for that perfect wedding, reception and honeymoon. Est attendance: 2,000. For info: Jan Bollwinkel-Smith, Pub Coord, Santa Cruz Beach Boardwalk, 400 Beach St, Santa Cruz, CA 95060-5491. Phone: (408) 423-5590.
Email: publicity@scseaside.com.
WWW: http://www.beachboardwalk.com

FIRST BLACK US CABINET MEMBER: ANNIVERSARY. Jan 18. On Jan 18, 1966, Robert Clifton Weaver was sworn in as Secretary of Housing and Urban Development, becoming the first black cabinet member in US history. He was nominated by President Lyndon Johnson.

HARDY, OLIVER: BIRTH ANNIVERSARY. Jan 18, 1892. Born at Atlanta, GA, Hardy teamed up with Stan Laurel in 1926 to form the comedy team of Laurel and Hardy. Among their most popular films: *From Soup to Nuts, Babes in Toyland, Swiss Miss.* Hardy died at Hollywood, Aug 7, 1957.

HEAL OLD HURTS DAY. Jan 18. Heal Old Hurts Day is for healing emotional wounds and scars, a day to connect with that part of ourselves that wants to forgive and forget in order to get back to that lightness of soul. Beyond that, it's about going within to forgive ourselves as well as others. Part of Be Good to Yourself Week (Jan 18–24). For info: K. Diane Schutte, The Self-Renewal Project, Box 337, 5465 N Bend Rd, Cincinnati, OH 45247. Phone: (888) LUV U DAY. Email: Bgood2U@juno.com.

January 1998

S	M	T	W	T	F	S
				1	2	3
4	5	6	7	8	9	10
11	12	13	14	15	16	17
18	19	20	21	22	23	24
25	26	27	28	29	30	31

HEALTHY WEIGHT WEEK. Jan 18–24. People who diet the first week in January and blow it the second are ready for eating and living in healthier ways by the third week—Healthy Weight Week. This is a week to learn healthy lifestyle habits that last a lifetime and prevent weight problems, rather than cause them, as dieting does. For info: Frances M. Berg, Editor/Publisher, Healthy Weight Journal, 402 S 14th St, Hettinger, ND 58639. Phone: (701) 567-2646. Fax: (701) 567-2602.
Email: fmberg@hettinger.ctctel.com.
WWW: http://www.healthyweightjournal.com

HOUSTON MARATHON. Jan 18. Houston, TX. 26th annual citywide race in conjunction with the Methodist Health Care Health & Fitness Expo (Jan 16–17). Est attendance: 7,000. For info: Greg D. Goss, Methodist Health Care, 720 North Post Oak Rd, #335, Houston, TX 77024. Phone: (713) 957-3453. Fax: (713) 957-3406. Email: marathon@ghgcorp.com.

HURWITZ, LEO: BIRTH ANNIVERSARY. Jan 18, 1909. American documentary filmmaker Leo Hurwitz was born at New York, NY. After his film *Native Land* was made in 1942 about American labor struggles in the 1930s, Hurwitz was blacklisted during the 1950s for his left-wing political ideology. He died on Jan 18, 1991, at New York, NY.

"THE JEFFERSONS" TV PREMIERE: ANNIVERSARY. Jan 18, 1975. CBS sitcom about an African-American family (formerly neighbors of the Bunkers on "All in the Family") who moved to Manhattan's East Side, thanks to the success of George Jefferson's chain of dry cleaning stores. Having a format similar to "All in the Family," the show featured a black bigot, George Jefferson, and his wife and grown child. Particularly memorable were the racial slurs Jefferson used against the mixed-marriage neighbors, Tom and Helen Willis. The show was able to humorously and tastefully introduce subjects such as mixed marriage on a prime-time series. Cast: Sherman Hemsley as George Jefferson; Isabel Sanford as Louise Jefferson; Mike Evans and Damon Evans as Lionel; Franklin Cover and Roxie Roker as the mixed couple and Berlinda Tolbert as their daughter, Jenny; and Paul Benedict as the British bachelor neighbor Bentley.

KAYE, DANNY: 85th BIRTH ANNIVERSARY. Jan 18, 1913. American entertainer Danny Kaye was born David Daniel Kaminski at Brooklyn, NY. Kaye became a star in films, international stage performances and television. His most notable films are *The Secret Life of Walter Mitty* (1947) and *Hans Christian Andersen* (1952), as well as the classic *White Christmas*. He hosted the television show *The Danny Kaye Show* in the 1960s. In addition, Kaye helped raise millions of dollars for the United Nations International Children's Emergency Fund (UNICEF) and musicians' pension plans. He died on Mar 3, 1987, at Los Angeles, CA.

LEE BIRTHDAY CELEBRATIONS. Jan 18. Alexandria, VA. The birthdays of Revolutionary War Colonel "Light Horse Harry" Lee and his son Civil War General Robert E. Lee are celebrated at the Lee-Fendall House and The Boyhood Home of Robert E. Lee. Refreshments, period music, house tours. Admission. Est attendance: 125. For info: Alexandria Conv and Visitors Assn, 221 King St, Alexandria, VA 22314. Phone: (703) 838-4200. Fax: (703) 838-4683. Email: acva@erols.com.
WWW: http://www.virginia.org

MUSICAL TRIBUTE TO DR. MARTIN LUTHER KING. Jan 18. Abraham Lincoln's Birthplace National Historical Site, Hodgenville, KY. Local Baptist and Methodist choirs present a selection of hymns and spirituals in commemoration of Dr. King's birthday. Est attendance: 200. For info: Gary V. Talley, 2995 Lincoln Farm Rd, Hodgenville, KY 42748. Phone: (502) 358-3137.

POOH DAY: A.A. MILNE BIRTH ANNIVERSARY. Jan 18, 1882. Anniversary of the birth of A(lan) A(lexander) Milne, English author, especially remembered for his children's stories: *Winnie the Pooh* and *The House at Pooh Corner*. Also the author of *Mr. Pim Passes By, When We Were Very Young* and *Now We Are Six*. Born at London, England; died at Hartfield, England, Jan 31, 1956, at age 64.

ROGET, PETER MARK: BIRTH ANNIVERSARY. Jan 18, 1779. English physician, best known as author of Roget's *Thesaurus of English Words and Phrases*, first published in 1852. Roget was also the inventor of the "log-log" slide rule. He was born at London, England, and died at West Malvern, Worcestershire, England, Sept 12, 1869.

RUFFIN, DAVIS ELI (DAVID): BIRTH ANNIVERSARY. Jan 18, 1941. American popular singer David Ruffin was born at Meridian, MS. He was one of the original members of the Motown singing group the Temptations, which began in Detroit in the 1960s. Ruffin left the group in 1968 to pursue a solo career. He and the other original members of the Temptations were inducted into the Rock and Roll Hall of Fame in 1989. Ruffin died on June 1, 1991, at Philadelphia, PA.

SIGHT-SAVING SABBATH. Jan 18. (Also Jan 24.) Religious denominations throughout the US are invited to participate in this ecumenical observance that alerts their members about the importance of periodic eye examinations and screenings to prevent blindness stemming from eye diseases, such as glaucoma. Materials that can easily be posted or distributed to the community will be provided. For info: Prevent Blindness America®, 500 E Remington Rd, Schaumburg, IL 60173. Phone: (800) 331-2020. Fax: (847) 843-8458. WWW: http//www.prevent-blindness.org

"TED MACK'S ORIGINAL AMATEUR HOUR" TV PREMIERE: 50th ANNIVERSARY. Jan 18, 1948. This immensely popular show, featuring host Ted Mack, introduced amateurs performing their talents on live television. It debuted as a regularly scheduled broadcast on the Dumont network. The show had been a long-running success on radio as "Major Bowes' Original Amateur Hour" until the death of Edward Bowes. Mack became host of the radio show a year later. While a few episodes were televised in 1947, the show did not air weekly until this date. The program also continued on radio until 1952.

WEBSTER, DANIEL: BIRTH ANNIVERSARY. Jan 18, 1782. American statesman and orator who said, on Apr 6, 1830, "The people's government, made for the people, made by the people, and answerable to the people." Born at Salisbury, NH; died at Marshfield, MA, Oct 24, 1852, at age 70.

WORLD RELIGION DAY. Jan 18. To proclaim the oneness of religion and the belief that world religion will unify the peoples of the earth. Baha'i-sponsored observance established in 1950 by the Baha'is of the US. Annually, the third Sunday in January. For info: Pamela Zivari, Baha'is of the US, Office of Public Information, 866 UN Plaza, Ste 120, New York, NY 10017-1822. Phone: (212) 803-2500. Fax: (212) 803-2573. Email: usopi-ny@bic.org.

WORLDWIDE KIWANIS WEEK. Jan 18–24. To encourage the creation of permanent relationships among Kiwanis clubs in different parts of the world. For info: Kiwanis Intl, Program Dvmt Dept, 3636 Woodview Trace, Indianapolis, IN 46268. Email: kiwanismail@kiwanis.org. WWW: http://www.kiwanis.org

BIRTHDAYS TODAY

John Boorman, 65, filmmaker (*Deliverance, Excalibur*), born Shepperton, England, Jan 18, 1933.
Kevin Costner, 43, actor (*Field of Dreams, Dances with Wolves* [Oscar for directing], *Bull Durham, Robin Hood: Prince of Thieves*), born Compton, CA, Jan 18, 1955.
Ray Dolby, 65, inventor, born Portland, OR, Jan 18, 1933.
Evelyn Lear, 67, opera singer, born New York, NY, Jan 18, 1931.
Mark Messier, 37, hockey player, New York Rangers, born Edmonton, Alberta, Canada, Jan 18, 1961.

JANUARY 19 — MONDAY

Day 19 — 346 Remaining

CONFEDERATE HEROES DAY. Jan 19. Observed on anniversary of Robert E. Lee's birthday. Official holiday in Texas.

CUT YOURSELF SOME SLACK DAY. Jan 19. For this day, we should all do unto ourselves as we would have others do unto us. We must give ourselves a break each time we're tempted to berate ourselves for making a mistake. This will be the first step toward finding a new understanding of ourselves. Part of Be Good to Yourself Week (Jan 18–24). For info: K. Diane Schutte, The Self-Renewal Project, Box 337, 5465 N Bend Rd, Cincinnati, OH 45247. Phone: (888) LUV U DAY. Email: Bgood2U@juno.com.

ENGLAND: LONDON INTERNATIONAL MIME FESTIVAL. Jan 19–31. Battersea Arts Centre, London. Features a program of theater, cabaret, literature and children's events. For info: Battersea Arts Centre, Lavender Hill, Battersea, London, England SW11 5TF. Phone: (44) (171) 223-6557. Fax: (44) (171) 978-5207.

"48 HOURS" TV PREMIERE: 10th ANNIVERSARY. Jan 19, 1988. CBS prime-time news/magazine-type program airing each week with Dan Rather as anchorman and Bernard Goldberg as its main correspondent.

HELMS, EDGAR J.: BIRTH ANNIVERSARY. Jan 19, 1863. Born near Malone, NY, Rev Dr. Helms became a minister to a parish of poor immigrants in Boston's South End. In that capacity he developed the philosophy and organization that eventually became Goodwill Industries. Helms died Dec 23, 1942, at Boston.

HISTORIC BIRTHDAY PARTIES IN LEXINGTON. Jan 19–21. Lexington, VA. Celebrates the birthdays of Robert E. Lee and Stonewall Jackson. Annually, Jan 19–21. For info: Lexington Visitors Bureau, 106 E Washington St, Lexington, VA 24450. Phone: (540) 463-3777. Fax: (540) 463-1105. Email: lexington@rockbridge.net.

JOPLIN, JANIS: 55th BIRTH ANNIVERSARY. Jan 19, 1943. Possibly the most highly regarded white female blues singer of all time, Janis Joplin was born at Port Arthur, TX. Joplin's appearance with Big Brother and the Holding Company at the Monterey International Pop Festival in August 1967 launched her to superstar status. Among her recording hits were "Get It While You Can," "Piece of My Heart" and "Ball and Chain." She died of a heroin overdose Oct 4, 1970, at Hollywood, CA, at the age of 27.

KING, MARTIN LUTHER, JR: BIRTHDAY OBSERVED. Jan 19. Public Law 98–144 designates the third Monday in January as an annual legal public holiday observing the birth of Martin Luther King, Jr. First observed in 1986. See also: "King, Martin Luther, Jr: Birth Anniversary" (Jan 15).

LEE, ROBERT E: BIRTH ANNIVERSARY. Jan 19, 1807. Greatest military leader of the Confederacy, son of Revolutionary War General Henry (Light Horse Harry) Lee. His surrender on Apr 9, 1865, to Union General Ulysses S. Grant brought an end to the Civil War. Born in Westmoreland County, VA, he died at Lexington, VA, Oct 12, 1870, at age 63. His birthday is observed on this day in Florida, Kentucky, Louisiana, South Carolina and Tennessee. Observed on third Monday in January in Alabama, Arkansas and Mississippi.

LEE-JACKSON-KING DAY IN VIRGINIA. Jan 19. Annually, the third Monday in January.

★**MARTIN LUTHER KING, JR FEDERAL HOLIDAY.** Jan 19. Presidential Proclamation has been issued without request each year for the third Monday in January since 1986.

"THE MILLIONAIRE" TV PREMIERE: ANNIVERSARY. Jan 19, 1955. The CBS drama that had all of America hoping to find Mr Michael Anthony on their doorstep. Mr John Beresford Tipton was a millionaire who made a hobby of giving away million dollar checks anonymously to some unknown people to see how they handled the sudden wealth. Michael Anthony, played by Marvin Miller, was Mr Tipton's personal secretary and the star of "The Millionaire." No one ever saw Mr Tipton but his voice (echoed by Paul Frees) would greet Anthony at the opening of each show and issue instructions for delivery of the next check. Anthony would then find the recipient and give him or her the tax-free check, explaining that the recipient had to agree never to divulge the amount or how it was acquired.

NATIONAL HANDWRITING ANALYSIS WEEK. Jan 19–25. To inform the public that handwriting is a form of behavior that can be analyzed for personality traits; that handwriting originates in the brain; that handwriting style, like personality, remains constant over a period of time while reflecting development; that personality traits can be changed by making changes in one's handwriting. Annually, a week in January to include National Handwriting Day (John Hancock's birthday). Sponsors: American Assn of Handwriting Analysts (AAHA), 820 W Maple St, Hinsdale, IL 60521. Phone: (708) 323-5647. Fax: (313) 645-2511. American Handwriting Analysis Fdtn (AHAF), PO Box 6201, San Jose, CA 95150. Phone: (408) 377-6775 or (800) 447-2637. Fax: (408) 377-3739.

Aquarius

PIER 39's SEA LION "HAUL OUT." Jan 19. Pier 39, Beach St and the Embarcadero, San Francisco, CA. Since 1990 more than 600 California sea lions yearly have been "hauling out" at the Pier and making it their yearly habitat of choice. The public can view the sea lion habitat free of charge and attend talks about the sea lions' behavior, marine habitat and migratory patterns. Annually, every Jan 19. Est attendance: 10,000. For info: Alicia Vargas, PR Dir, Pier 39, PO Box 193730, San Francisco, CA 94119. Phone: (415) 705-5500. Fax: (415) 981-8808.

POE, EDGAR ALLAN: BIRTH ANNIVERSARY. Jan 19, 1809. American poet and story writer, called "America's most famous man of letters." Born at Boston, MA, he was orphaned in dire poverty in 1811 and was raised by Virginia merchant John Allan. In 1836 he married his 13-year-old cousin, Virginia Clemm. A magazine editor of note, he is best remembered for his poetry (especially "The Raven") and for his tales of suspense. Died at Baltimore, MD, Oct 7, 1849.

SOCIETY FOR THE PRESERVATION AND ENCOURAGEMENT OF BARBER SHOP QUARTET SINGING IN AMERICA, INC (SPEBSQSA) MID-WINTER CONVENTION. Jan 19–25. Tampa, FL. Some 3,000 members meet for administrative conferences, shows and contest to select national Seniors Quartet Champion. Est attendance: 3,000. For info: Brian Lynch, PR Manager, SPEBSQSA, Inc, 6315 Third Ave, Kenosha, WI 53143-5199. Phone: (414) 653-8440. Fax: (414) 654-4048. Email: pr@spebsqsa.org. WWW: http://www.spebsqsa.org

January 1998

S	M	T	W	T	F	S
				1	2	3
4	5	6	7	8	9	10
11	12	13	14	15	16	17
18	19	20	21	22	23	24
25	26	27	28	29	30	31

THOMAS, ISAIAH: BIRTH ANNIVERSARY. Jan 19, 1749. American printer, editor, almanac publisher and historian. Born at Boston, MA; died, Apr 4, 1831, at Worcester, MA.

TIN CAN PATENT: ANNIVERSARY. Jan 19, 1825. Ezra Daggett and Thomas Kensett obtained a patent for a process for storing food in tin cans.

ULLR FEST. Jan 19–25. Breckenridge, CO. The festival celebrates Ullr, the mythical god of winter. Parade, fireworks, ski torchlight, world freestyle skiing championships and dating game. Est attendance: 30,000. For info: Gena Osborn, Breckenridge Resort Chamber, PO Box 1909, Breckenridge, CO 80424. Phone: (970) 453-2913. Fax: (970) 453-7238. Email: gobreck@brecknet.com. WWW: http://www.gobreck.com

WATT, JAMES: BIRTH ANNIVERSARY. Jan 19, 1736. Scottish engineer and inventor, born at Greenock, Scotland. The modern steam engine grew out of his efficiency-improving inventions. Died at Heathfield, England, on Aug 25, 1819.

BIRTHDAYS TODAY

Desi Arnaz, Jr, 45, singer, actor, born Los Angeles, CA, Jan 19, 1953.
Michael Crawford, 56, actor, singer (*Phantom of the Opera*), born Salisbury, Wiltshire, England, Jan 19, 1942.
Steven L. DeBerg, 44, former football player, born Oakland, CA, Jan 19, 1954.
Phil Everly, 59, singer, born Brownie, KY, Jan 19, 1939.
Roy Leonard, 67, Chicago radio personality, born Redwood Falls, MN, Jan 19, 1931.
Robert MacNeil, 67, broadcast journalist, born Montreal, Quebec, Canada, Jan 19, 1931.
Guy Madison, 76, actor (title role in "Wild Bill Hickok" radio and TV shows; *Til the End of Time*), born Bakersfield, CA, Jan 19, 1922.
Robert Palmer, 49, singer, born Babley, England, Jan 19, 1949.
Dolly Parton, 52, singer ("Jolene"), actress (*Nine to Five*), born Sevier County, TN, Jan 19, 1946.
Javier Perez de Cuellar, 78, Peruvian diplomat, former UN Secretary General, born Lima, Peru, Jan 19, 1920.
Simon Rattle, 43, British orchestra conductor, born Liverpool, England, Jan 19, 1955.
Christopher Andrew (Chris) Sabo, 36, former baseball player, born Detroit, MI, Jan 19, 1962.
Jean Stapleton (Jeanne Murray), 75, actress (*Klute*; Emmy for Edith Bunker in "All in the Family"), born New York, NY, Jan 19, 1923.
Fritz Weaver, 72, actor (*Holocaust, Marathon Man*), born Philadelphia, PA, Jan 19, 1926.

JANUARY 20 — TUESDAY

Day 20 — 345 Remaining

AQUARIUS, THE WATER CARRIER. Jan 20–Feb 19. In the astronomical/astrological zodiac, which divides the sun's apparent orbit into 12 segments, the period Jan 20–Feb 19 is identified, traditionally, as the sun-sign of Aquarius, the Water Carrier. The ruling planet is Uranus or Saturn.

BRAZIL: NOSSO SENHOR DO BONFIM FESTIVAL. Jan 20–30. Salvador, Bahia, Brazil. Our Lord of the Happy Ending Festival is one of Salvador's most colorful religious feasts. Climax comes with people carrying water to pour over church stairs and sidewalks to cleanse them of impurities.

BRAZIL: SAN SEBASTIAN'S DAY. Jan 20. Patron Saint of Rio de Janeiro.

BURNS, GEORGE: BIRTH ANNIVERSARY. Jan 20, 1896. Comedian George Burns was born at New York City. He began in vaudeville without much success until he teamed up with Gracie Allen, who became his wife. As Burns and Allen, the two had a long career on radio, in film and with their hit TV show,

"The George Burns and Gracie Allen Show." More recently he played the role of God and the Devil in the *Oh, God!* movies. He lived to be 100, and died Mar 9, 1996.

FELLINI, FEDERICO: BIRTH ANNIVERSARY. Jan 20, 1920. Director and screenwriter Federico Fellini was born at Rimini, Italy. Four of Fellini's movies won Oscars for best foreign-language film: *La Strada* (1956), *The Nights of Cabiria* (1957), *8½* (1963) and *Amarcord* (1974). He received an honorary Oscar in 1993 in recognition of his cinematic accomplishments. Fellini died Oct 31, 1993, at Rome.

GEORGE V: DEATH ANNIVERSARY. Jan 20, 1936. More than 50 years after his death it was revealed that King George V of England died, at age 71, because of lethal injections consisting of 3/4 gram of morphine and 1 gram of cocaine, administered by his physician, Lord Dawson. His last words were not "How is the Empire?" as formerly believed but "God damn you" as he lost consciousness after injection of the morphine. Lord Dawson's notes indicated that the fatal injections were given to assure death in time for announcement "in the morning papers rather than the less appropriate evening journals."

GRAY, HAROLD LINCOLN: BIRTH ANNIVERSARY. Jan 20, 1894. The creator of *Little Orphan Annie* was born at Kankakee, IL. The comic strip featuring the 12-year-old Annie, her dog Sandy and her mentor and guardian Oliver "Daddy" Warbucks began appearing in the *Chicago Tribune* in 1924. While controversial for its strong conservative views, the strip was highly popular for its stories demonstrating the values of perseverance, independence and courage. Gray created the strip for 44 years until his death on May 9, 1968, at La Jolla, CA, at age 74.

GUINEA-BISSAU: NATIONAL HEROES DAY. Jan 20. National holiday in the Republic of Guinea-Bissau.

JOHN MARSHALL APPOINTED CHIEF JUSTICE: ANNIVERSARY. Jan 20, 1801. John Marshall was appointed chief justice of the US Supreme Court.

LAILAT UL QADR: THE NIGHT OF POWER. Jan 20 (also Jan 22, 24, 26 or 28). "The Night of Power" falls on one of the last 10 days of Ramadan on an odd-numbered day (Islamic calendar dates: Ramadan 21, 23, 25, 27 or 29, 1418). The Holy Qur'an states that praying on this night is better than praying 1,000 months. Since it is not known which day it is, Muslims feel it is best to pray on each of the possible nights. Different methods for "anticipating" the visibility of the new moon crescent at Mecca are used by different Muslim sects or groups; *Chase's* uses anticipated dates furnished by the American Muslim Council. US EST date may vary.

LESOTHO: ARMY DAY. Jan 20. Lesotho, South Africa.

LIGHTEN UP!! DAY. Jan 20. Part of Be Good to Yourself Week (Jan 18–24). For info: K. Diane Schutte, The Self-Renewal Project, Box 337, 5465 N Bend Rd, Cincinnati, OH 45247. Phone: (888) LUV U DAY. Email: Bgood2U@juno.com.

MOON PHASE: LAST QUARTER. Jan 20. Moon enters Last Quarter phase at 2:40 PM, EST.

RID THE WORLD OF FAD DIETS AND GIMMICKS DAY. Jan 20. The "worst" weight loss products and programs of the year are announced—the 9th annual Slim Chance Awards—by Healthy Weight Journal and the National Council Against Health Fraud. Diet quackery defrauds, disables and kills. List of 1998 awards plus diet quackery information available. For info: Frances M. Berg, Editor/Publisher, Healthy Weight Journal, 402 S 14th St, Hettinger, ND 58639. Phone: (701) 567-2646. Fax: (701) 567-2602. Email: fmberg@hettinger.ctctel.com. WWW: http://www.healthyweightjournal.com

SOUTHWEST SENIOR INVITATIONAL GOLF CHAMPIONSHIP. Jan 20–23. Yuma Golf and Country Club, Yuma, AZ. A 36-hole medal play tournament, limited to 120 players 50 and older. For info: Caballeros de Yuma, Inc, Box 5987, Yuma, AZ 85366-5987. Phone: (520) 343-1715. Fax: (520) 783-1609.

US REVOLUTIONARY WAR: CESSATION OF HOSTILITIES: ANNIVERSARY. Jan 20, 1783. On Jan 20, 1783, the British and US Commissioners signed a preliminary "Cessation of Hostilities," which was ratified by England's King George III on Feb 14 and led to the Treaties of Paris and Versailles, Sept 3, 1783, ending the war.

BIRTHDAYS TODAY

Edwin "Buzz" Aldrin, 68, former astronaut, one of first three men on moon, born Montclair, NJ, Jan 20, 1930.

Paul D. Coverdell, 59, US Senator (R, Georgia), born Des Moines, IA, Jan 20, 1939.

Shelley Fabares, 56, actress (Mary on "The Donna Reed Show"; "Coach"; sang "Johnny Angel"), born Santa Monica, CA, Jan 20, 1942.

Arte Johnson, 64, comedian, actor (Emmy for "Rowan & Martin's Laugh-In"), born Chicago, IL, Jan 20, 1934.

DeForest Kelley, 78, actor ("Star Trek" TV series and *Star Trek* movies), born Atlanta, GA, Jan 20, 1920.

Lorenzo Lamas, 40, actor ("Falcon Crest," "Renegade"), born Los Angeles, CA, Jan 20, 1958.

David Lynch, 52, director ("Twin Peaks," *Blue Velvet*), writer, producer, born Missoula, MT, Jan 20, 1946.

Patricia Neal, 72, actress (*The Day the Earth Stood Still, Breakfast at Tiffany's, Hud, The Subject Was Roses*), born Packard, NY, Jan 20, 1926.

Natan (Anatoly) Scharansky, 50, expatriate Soviet dissident, born Donetsk, USSR, Jan 20, 1948.

Otis Dewey "Slim" Whitman, 74, singer (first country performer to play at the London Palladium), born Tampa, FL, Jan 20, 1924.

JANUARY 21 — WEDNESDAY

Day 21 — 344 Remaining

BALDWIN, ROGER NASH: BIRTH ANNIVERSARY. Jan 21, 1884. Founder of the American Civil Liberties Union, called the "country's unofficial agitator for, and defender of, its civil liberties." Born at Wellesley, MA, he died Aug 26, 1981, at Ridgewood, NJ.

BRECKINRIDGE, JOHN CABELL: BIRTH ANNIVERSARY. Jan 21, 1821. Fourteenth vice president of the US (1857–1861), serving under President James Buchanan. Born at Lexington, KY, died there May 17, 1875.

BROWNING, JOHN MOSES: BIRTH ANNIVERSARY. Jan 21, 1855. World famous gun maker and inventor who was taught gunsmithing by his Mormon pioneer father, Jonathan Browning, was born in Ogden, UT. Starting the J.M. & M.S. Browning Arms Co with his brother at Morgan, UT, he designed guns for Winchester, Remington, Stevens and Colt arms companies, as well as American and European armies. Browning had more gun patents than any other gunsmith in the world. He is best known worldwide for inventing the machine gun in 1890 and the automatic pistol in 1896. He died suddenly on Nov 26, 1926, at age 71, while in Belgium on business. The company he founded, known now as Browning Arms Co, is located in Morgan, UT.

FIRST CONCORDE FLIGHT: ANNIVERSARY. Jan 21, 1976. The supersonic Concorde airplane was put into service by Britain and France.

FITCH, JOHN: BIRTH ANNIVERSARY. Jan 21, 1743. American inventor, clockmaker, gunsmith, surveyor and steamboat developer. Born at East Windsor, CT; died at Bardstown, KY, July 2, 1798.

GO FOR IT, OR LIVE YOUR DREAMS DAY. Jan 21. Part of Be Good to Yourself Week (Jan 18–24). For info: K. Diane Schutte, The Self-Renewal Project, Box 337, 5465 N Bend Rd, Cincinnati, OH 45247. Phone: 888 LUV U DAY. Email: Bgood2U@juno.com.

JACKSON, THOMAS JONATHAN "STONEWALL": BIRTH ANNIVERSARY. Jan 21, 1824. Confederate general and one of the most famous soldiers of the American Civil War, best known as "Stonewall" Jackson. Born at Clarksburg, VA (now WV); died of wounds received in battle near Chancellorsville, VA, May 10, 1863.

KIWANIS INTERNATIONAL: ANNIVERSARY. Jan 21. First Kiwanis Club chartered Jan 21, 1915, at Detroit, MI.

MARGARET BRENT DEMANDS A POLITICAL VOICE: ANNIVERSARY. Jan 21, 1648. Margaret Brent made her claim as America's first feminist by demanding a voice and vote for herself in the Maryland colonial assembly. Brent came to America in 1638 and was the first woman to own property in Maryland. At the time of her demands she was serving as secretary to Governor Leonard Calvert. She was ejected from the meetings, but when Calvert died she became his executor and became acting governor, presiding over the General Assembly.

NATIONAL HUGGING DAY™. Jan 21. Since hugging is something everyone can do and since it is a healthful form of touching, this day should be spent hugging anyone who will accept a hug, especially family and friends. The most "Huggable People" of the year will be announced. Nominations accepted through Jan 10. For more info, please send SASE to: Rev Kevin C. Zaborney, 4900 Campau Dr, Midland, MI 48640. Phone: (517) 631-5740. Email: kzaborney@aol.com.

PONTIAC SILVERDOME CAMPER, TRAVEL AND RV SHOW. Jan 21–25. Pontiac Silverdome, Pontiac, MI. This event brings together buyers and sellers of RVs, motor homes, campers and camping accessories, as well as buyers and sellers of camping vacations and travel destinations. Est attendance: 28,000. For info: Mike Wilbraham, ShowSpan, Inc, 1400 28th St SW, Grand Rapids, MI 49509. Phone: (616) 530-1919. Fax: (616) 530-2122. WWW: http://showsmw@aol.com

SONORA SHOWCASE. Jan 21–22. Yuma, AZ. A fiesta to promote the state of Sonora, Mexico, features dancers, food and beverage samples, vacation information and curios. Est attendance: 7,000. For info: Marketing Dept, Yuma Civic and Conv Ctr, 1440 Desert Hills Dr, Yuma, AZ 85365. Phone: (520) 344-3800. Fax: (520) 344-9121.

TOPS CLUB, INC: 50th ANNIVERSARY. Jan 21. Milwaukee, WI. TOPS (Take Off Pounds Sensibly) is the leading, international, non-profit weight-loss support group. Founded in 1948 in Milwaukee, WI, by Esther Manz, a homemaker, TOPS has grown to almost 300,000 members in 11,700 chapters worldwide. It is dedicated to providing its members with information, motivation and fellowship in attaining and maintaining physician-prescribed weight-loss goals. For info: Susan Trones, TOPS Club Inc, 4575 S Fifth St, Milwaukee, WI 53207. Phone: (414) 482-4620 or (800) 932-8677. WWW: http://www.tops.org

January 1998

S	M	T	W	T	F	S
				1	2	3
4	5	6	7	8	9	10
11	12	13	14	15	16	17
18	19	20	21	22	23	24
25	26	27	28	29	30	31

***USS NAUTILUS* LAUNCHED:.** Jan 21, 1954. The world's first atomic submarine, the *USS Nautilus*, was launched at Groton, Connecticut.

WOLFMAN JACK: 60th BIRTH ANNIVERSARY. Jan 21, 1938. Wolfman Jack was born Robert Smith at Brooklyn, NY. He became famous as a disc jockey for XERF-AM in Via Cuna, Cohuilla, Mexico, from 1963 to 1966, and then for XERB in Rosarito, Mexico, from 1966. Wolfman Jack was influential as a border radio voice because XERB broadcast at 250,000 watts, which was five times the legal limit for American stations at the time, and therefore he was heard over a vast part of the US during his night shift of blues, hillbilly, and other black and white music that wasn't getting a lot of exposure. He later appeared on American radio, movies and television as an icon of 1960s radio. Wolfman Jack died on July 1, 1995, at Belvidere, NC.

BIRTHDAYS TODAY

Robbie Benson (Robert Segal), 42, actor ("Search for Tomorrow," *Ode to Billie Joe*), born Dallas, TX, Jan 21, 1956.

Geena Davis, 41, actress (Oscar for *The Accidental Tourist; Thelma and Louise*, "Buffalo Bill"), born Ware, MA, Jan 21, 1957.

Mac Davis, 56, actor, songwriter ("The Mac Davis Show," *North Dallas Forty*), born Lubbock, TX, Jan 21, 1942.

Placido Domingo, 57, opera singer, one of the "Three Tenors," born Madrid, Spain, Jan 21, 1941.

Jill Eikenberry, 51, actress (Ann Kelsey in "L.A. Law"), born New Haven, CT, Jan 21, 1947.

Gary Locke, 48, Governor of Washington (D), born Seattle, WA, Jan 21, 1950.

Jack William Nicklaus, 58, golfer, born Columbus, OH, Jan 21, 1940.

Billy Ocean, 48, musician, songwriter, born London, England, Jan 21, 1950.

Hakeem Abdul Olajuwon, 35, basketball player, born Lagos, Nigeria, Jan 21, 1963.

Detlef Schrempf, 35, basketball player, born Leverkusen, West Germany, Jan 21, 1963.

Paul Scofield, 76, actor (*A Man for All Seasons, Quiz Show*; stage: *A Man for All Seasons*), born Hurstpierpoint, England, Jan 21, 1922.

JANUARY 22 — THURSDAY

Day 22 — 343 Remaining

ALLIES TAKE NEW GUINEA: 55th ANNIVERSARY. Jan 22, 1943. In the first land victory over the Japanese in World War II, on Jan 22, 1943, American and Australian soldiers overcame the last pockets of resistance west and south of Sanananda on New Guinea. Three thousand Allies were killed in the battle. The Japanese lost 7,000. Of the 350 prisoners taken most were Chinese and Korean laborers attached to the Japanese forces. Almost no Japanese allowed themselves to be taken prisoner, preferring to commit hara-kiri.

AMPÈRE, ANDRE: BIRTH ANNIVERSARY. Jan 22, 1775. Physicist, student of electrical and magnetic phenomena, founder of the science of electrodynamics. Born at Lyons, France, from his early childhood, tragedy and depression pursued him. His father was executed during the French Revolution. His first wife died young. His second marriage was unhappy. Ampère died at Marseilles, France, on June 10, 1836. The epitaph he selected for his tombstone was *tandem felix* ("happy at last"). The ampere, a unit of electrical current, is named for him.

ANSWER YOUR CAT'S QUESTION DAY. Jan 22. If you will stop what you are doing and take a look at your cat, you will observe that the cat is looking at you with a serious question. Meditate upon it, then answer the question! Annually, Jan 22. [© 1997 by WPL] For info: Tom or Ruth Roy, Wellness Permission League, PO Box 662, Mount Gretna, PA 17064-0662. Phone: (500) 437-5104 or (717) 964-1308. Fax: (717) 964-1335. Email: wellcat@wellcat.com. WWW: http://www.wellcat.com

BACON, FRANCIS: BIRTH ANNIVERSARY. Jan 22, 1561. Statesman and essayist, born at London, England. One may guess that Bacon was of short stature as he wrote (*Apothegms*), "Wise nature did never put her precious jewels into a garret four stories high: and therefore . . . exceeding tall men had ever very empty heads." Died at London, Apr 9, 1626.

BENEDICT XV: DEATH ANNIVERSARY. Jan 22, 1922. Pope from 1914 until his death at Rome at age 67, Benedict XV was born Giacomo Della Chiesa Nov 21, 1854, at Pegli, Kingdom of Sardinia.

BYRON, GEORGE GORDON: BIRTH ANNIVERSARY. Jan 22, 1788. Romantic poet, born at London, England. Died of fever at Missolonghi, Greece, Apr 19, 1824, while fighting for Greek independence.

CHAMPAGNES FRANCE DAY. Jan 22. New York, NY. A date which coincides with Saint Vincent's Day in France, honoring the patron saint of vine growers. Champagnes France Day, held by the Champagne Wines Information Bureau, celebrates the uniqueness of Champagne wines and reminds us that Champagne only comes from La Champagne, France. The day also marks the annual culmination of the Champagnes France Challenge, a national contest aimed at creating greater awareness of, and interest in, Champagne wines. Annually, every Jan 22. Est attendance: 150. For info: Jean-Louis Carbonnier, Champagne Wines Information Bureau, 820 Second Ave, New York, NY 10017. Phone: (212) 682-6565 ext 203 or (800) 64-CHAMPagne. Fax: (212) 697-0910. Email: info@champagnes.com.
WWW: http://www.champagnes.com

"EMERGENCY!" TV PREMIERE: ANNIVERSARY. Jan 22, 1972. This NBC program was introduced in midseason up against "All in the Family." It surprised everyone by becoming quite popular. The fast-paced action of the fire department paramedics saving lives by giving victims emergency treatment and then taking them to the hospital demonstrated the steps taken during emergency situations.

INDIANA MOTORCYCLE & WATERCRAFT EXPOSITION. Jan 22–25. Indiana State Fairgrounds, Indianapolis, IN. For info: Kevin Renfro, VP, 2511 E 46th St, Ste E-2, Indianapolis, IN 46205. Phone: (800) 892-1723 or (317) 546-4344. Fax: (317) 546-3002. Email: insportshow@iquest.net.

KNOXVILLE FISHING EXPO. Jan 22–25. Jacob Building, Chilhowee Park, Knoxville, TN. Annual event featuring the latest in fishing tackle, rods, reels, boats, boating equipment, guide services and other accessories. Est attendance: 13,000. For info: Daryl Hobby, Esau, Inc, PO Box 50096, Knoxville, TN 37950. Phone: (423) 588-1233 or (800) 588-ESAU. Fax: (423) 588-6938.

"LAUGH-IN" TV PREMIERE: 30th ANNIVERSARY. Jan 22, 1968. Actually the name of this NBC comedy was "Rowan and Martin's Laugh-In." Funnymen Dan Rowan and Dick Martin hosted the show, but they seemed staid next to the show's other regulars, most of whom were young unknowns, including Dennis Allen, Chelsea Brown, Judy Carne, Ruth Buzzi, Ann Elder, Richard Dawson, Teresa Graves, Arte Johnson, Goldie Hawn, Alan Sues, Jo Anne Worley, Lily Tomlin and many others. The show moved fast from gag to gag with heads popping out of bushes or doors in the big wall. The show brought a new energy to comedy as well as new phrases to our vocabulary ("You bet your sweet bippy," "Sock it to me"). Producers were George Schlatter and Ed Friendly, followed by Paul Keyes.

LOVE YOURSELF, OR BE YOUR OWN BEST FRIEND DAY. Jan 22. Part of Be Good to Yourself Week (Jan 18–24). For info: K. Diane Schutte, The Self-Renewal Project, Box 337, 5465 N Bend Rd, Cincinnati, OH 45247. Phone: (888) LUV U DAY. Email: Bgood2U@juno.com.

NATIONAL NO-TILLAGE CONFERENCE. Jan 22–24. Indianapolis, IN. Attracts innovative farmers interested in reducing tillage to protect the environment and boost profits. Est attendance: 850. For info: Frank Lessiter, National No-Tillage Conference, PO Box 624, Brookfield, WI 53008-0624. Phone: (414) 782-4480. Fax: (414) 782-1252. Email: Lesspub@aol.com.

"OZARK JUBILEE" TV PREMIERE: ANNIVERSARY. Jan 22, 1955. ABC country and western music show hosted by Red Foley from Springfield, MO. Brenda "(Open Up Your Heart and) Let the Sunshine In" Lee appeared on the show at age 10 as one of the regulars. Other regulars included Smiley Burnette, Bobby Lord, Wanda Jackson, Suzi Arden, Webb Pierce, Uncle Cyp and Aunt Sap Brasfield.

PONSELLE, ROSA: BIRTH ANNIVERSARY. Jan 22, 1897. Formerly Rosa Melba Ponzilla, soprano Ponselle was born at Meriden, CT. Her career changed direction from vaudeville to opera when she was discovered by Enrico Caruso at the age of 21. Under the tutelage of Romano Romani, Ponselle made her operatic debut at the Met in Verdi's *La forza del destino*. Her career spanned 19 seasons at the Met, and included performances in London and Florence. After 17 years of retirement she returned to the opera in 1954, this time as artistic director for the Baltimore Civic Opera. Ponselle died on May 25, 1981, at Baltimore.

ROE V WADE DECISION: 25th ANNIVERSARY. Jan 22, 1973. On Jan 22, 1973, in the case of *Roe v Wade*, the US Supreme Court struck down state laws restricting abortions during the first six months of pregnancy. In the following two decades debate has continued to rage between those who believe a woman has a right to choose whether or not to continue a pregnancy and those who believe that aborting such a pregnancy is murder of an unborn child.

SAINT VINCENT'S FEAST DAY. Jan 22. Spanish deacon and martyr who died AD 304. Patron saint of wine growers. Old weather lore says if there is sun on this day, good wine crops may be expected in the ensuing season.

STRINDBERG, AUGUST: BIRTH ANNIVERSARY. Jan 22, 1849. Swedish novelist and dramatist often called Sweden's greatest playwright. Born at Stockholm and died there of cancer on May 14, 1912, at age 63.

UPJOHN, RICHARD: BIRTH ANNIVERSARY. Jan 22, 1802. American architect and founder of the American Institute of Architects in 1857. A Gothic revivalist, he designed many churches. Among his works were Trinity Chapel, New York, NY; Corn Exchange Bank Building, New York, NY; Central Congregational Church, Boston, MA. Born at Shaftesbury, England, he died on Aug 17, 1878, at Garrison, NY.

VINSON, FRED M.: BIRTH ANNIVERSARY. Jan 22, 1890. The 13th Chief Justice of the US, born at Louisa, KY. Served in the House of Representatives, appointed Director of War Mobilization during World War II, Secretary of the Treasury under Harry Truman. Nominated by Truman to succeed Harlan F. Stone as Chief Justice of the US Supreme Court. Died at Washington, DC, on Sept 8, 1953.

WOMEN'S HEALTHY WEIGHT DAY. Jan 22. A day to honor American women of all sizes and confirm that beauty, talent and love cannot be weighed. Corporate winners of the Women's Healthy Weight Media Contest will be announced—businesses that portray a healthy, realistic look for women. This is a day to appreciate women in all their diversity and reject the national obsession with thinness that is shattering the lives of women, young girls and their families. For info: Frances M. Berg, Editor/Publisher, Healthy Weight Journal, 402 S 14th St, Hettinger, ND 58639. Phone: (701) 567-2646. Fax: (701) 567-2602. Email: fmberg@hettinger.ctctel.com.
WWW: http://www.healthyweightjournal.com

BIRTHDAYS TODAY

Linda Blair, 39, actress (*The Exorcist, Airport*), born Westport, CT, Jan 22, 1959.
Seymour Cassel, 61, actor (*Faces, Dick Tracy, Honeymoon in Vegas*), born Detroit, MI, Jan 22, 1937.
Pete (Pierre) S. duPont IV, 63, former Governor of Delaware (R), born Wilmington, DE, Jan 22, 1935.
George Edward Foreman, 49, boxer, born Marshall, TX, Jan 22, 1949.
John Hurt, 58, actor ("And the Band Played On," *The Elephant Man*), born Lincolnshire, England, Jan 22, 1940.
Piper Laurie (Rosetta Jacobs), 66, actress, born Detroit, MI, Jan 22, 1932.
Steve Perry, 49, singer, born Hanford, CA, Jan 22, 1949.
Joseph Wambaugh, 61, author, ex-police officer (*The Blooding, Fugitive Nights*), born East Pittsburgh, PA, Jan 22, 1937.

JANUARY 23 — FRIDAY

Day 23 — 342 Remaining

AUGUSTA FUTURITY. Jan 23–31. Augusta, GA. Brings together the top cutting horses and riders in the world to compete for purse and awards of more than $600,000. Sponsors: Wrangler, John Deere, Budweiser, WRDW-TV12, Manna Pro Feed Co, Ariat Boots, Palmer & Cay Insurance, CellularOne, *Augusta Chronicle*, Gist Buckles, USAir, Montana Pride Feed, Exiss Trailers and American Hat Company. Est attendance: 42,000. For info: Skip Peterson, Dir of Mktg, Augusta Futurity, PO Box 936, Augusta, GA 30903. Phone: (706) 823-3370 or (706) 823-3417.

"BARNEY MILLER" TV PREMIERE: ANNIVERSARY. Jan 23, 1975. ABC sitcom about a New York precinct captain starred Hal Linden as Captain Barney Miller. The 12th Precinct gang included Barbara Barrie as Miller's wife, Abe Vigoda as Detective Phil Fish, Max Gail as Sergeant Stan Wojehowicz, Gregory Sierra as Sergeant Chano Amengual, Jack Soo as Sergeant Nick Yemana, Ron Glass as Detective Ron Harris and a host of others who helped make the show a pleasant memory.

January 1998

S	M	T	W	T	F	S
				1	2	3
4	5	6	7	8	9	10
11	12	13	14	15	16	17
18	19	20	21	22	23	24
25	26	27	28	29	30	31

BLACKWELL, ELIZABETH, AWARDED MD: ANNIVERSARY. Jan 23, 1849. Dr. Elizabeth Blackwell became the first woman to receive an MD degree. The native of Bristol, England, was awarded her degree by the Medical Institution of Geneva, NY.

BULGARIA: BABIN DEN. Jan 23. Celebrated throughout Bulgaria as Day of the Midwives. Traditional festivities.

CARTER CAVES CRAWLATHON. Jan 23–25. Carter Caves State Resort Park, Olive Hill, KY. Weekend of caving for beginners and experienced. Est attendance: 500. For info: Carter Caves State Resort Pk, John Tierney, Naturalist, Olive Hill, KY 41164.

CARTER REINSTATES SELECTIVE SERVICE REGISTRATION: ANNIVERSARY. Jan 23, 1980. President Jimmy Carter, saying he planned to "revitalize" the Selective Service System, reinstated registration and pledged to use military force, if necessary, to protect the Persian Gulf from Soviet aggression.

"DONNY AND MARIE" TV PREMIERE: ANNIVERSARY. Jan 23, 1976. ABC show hosted by talented brother-and-sister act Donny and Marie Osmond. There were seven other talented siblings in the Osmond family who appeared on the show at times along with regulars Jim Connell and Hank Garcia. The sister-and-brother team could sing, dance and perform on ice skates.

GIVE A DAMN DAY. Jan 23. Part of Be Good to Yourself Week (Jan 18–24). For info: K. Diane Schutte, The Self-Renewal Project, Box 337, 5465 N Bend Rd, Cincinnati, OH 45247. Phone: (888) LUV U DAY. Email: Bgood2U@juno.com.

HANCOCK, JOHN: BIRTH ANNIVERSARY. Jan 23, 1737. American patriot and statesman, first signer of the Declaration of Independence. Born at Braintree, MA; died at Quincy, MA, Oct 8, 1793. Hancock's name has become part of the American language, referring to any handwritten signature, as in "Put your John Hancock on that!"

HEWES, JOSEPH: BIRTH ANNIVERSARY. Jan 23, 1730. Signer of the Declaration of Independence. Born at Kingston, NJ, he died Nov 10, 1779.

ICE FEST. Jan 23–25. Ligonier, PA. A weekend of ice-carving demonstrations as blocks of ice are turned into works of art. For info: Julie Donovan, Ligonier Chamber of Commerce, 120 East Main St, Ligonier, PA 15601. Phone: (412) 238-4200. Fax: (412) 238-4610.

ICEBOX DAYS XVIII. Jan 23-31. International Falls, MN. Smoosh racing, "Freeze Yer Gizzard Blizzard Run," turkey bowling, ski races, mutt races and beach party. Est attendance: 5,000. For info: Shawn M. Mason, Chamber of Commerce, 301 2nd Ave, International Falls, MN 56649. Phone: (800) 325-5766 or (218) 283-9400. Fax: (218) 283-3572. WWW: http://www.intlfalls.org

"THE KING FAMILY SHOW" TV PREMIERE: ANNIVERSARY. Jan 23, 1965. ABC musical variety show featuring the singing and playing of the King sisters and other descendents of William King Driggs, who organized the family musical group in the 1930s. Including spouses, children, grandchildren and great-grandchildren, some three dozen members of the King family have appeared on camera at one time.

LONGHORN WORLD CHAMPIONSHIP RODEO. Jan 23–25. Final date available after Sept 1, 1997. Target Center, Minneapolis, MN. More than 150 of the best cowboys and cowgirls compete in six professional contests ranging from bronco riding to bull riding for top prize money and world championship points. Featuring colorful opening pageantry and Big, Bad BONUS Bulls. 6th annual. Est attendance: 16,000. For info: W. Bruce Lehrke, Pres, Longhorn World Championship Rodeo, Inc, PO Box 70159, Nashville, TN 37207. Phone: (615) 876-1016. Fax: (615) 876-4685. Email: lhrodeo@idt.net.
WWW: http://www.longhornrodeo.com

MICRO BREW REVIEW & COOL DOG BALL. Jan 23. Helena Civic Center, Helena, MT. Sponsored by the Race to the

Sky, this fourth annual kickoff party (race is 2 weeks later) features more than 30 micro brews from Montana and the northwest. Est attendance: 1,500. For info: Micro Brew Review, 2905 N Montana, Box 30-MUSH, Helena, MT 59601. Phone and fax: (406) 442-4008. WWW: http://www.race2sky.com

NATIONAL HANDWRITING DAY. Jan 23. Popularly observed on birthday of John Hancock to encourage more legible handwriting.

NATIONAL PIE DAY. Jan 23. To focus attention on pie as an American art form, culinary inheritance and taste delight through pie tastings, pie-making classes for adults and kids, pie recipe collections, competitions including the National Pie Championships and other pie-related activities. For info: John Lehndorff, Exec Dir, American Pie Council, PO Box 18793, Boulder, CO 80308-1793. Phone: (303) 402-0702. Fax: (303) 415-0164. Email: piecouncil@aol.com. WWW: http://www.piecouncil.com

NATIONAL SPIELING DAY. Jan 23. On this date America celebrates its unofficial national pastime—blathering. All citizens are encouraged to give lengthy lectures to their friends, families and workmates. Speakers should take extra care to discourse in loud, grating voices and to expand upon arcane topics. Listeners should applaud no matter how ear-wrenching the spiel. For info: Bill Donahue, Donahue Brothers Productions, 5824 SE Francis, Portland, OR 97206. Phone: (503) 788-7765. Fax: (503) 788-7173. Email: wfd13@teleport.com.

SOUTHWESTERN EXPOSITION LIVESTOCK SHOW AND RODEO. Jan 23–Feb 8. Fort Worth, TX. Western-flavored extravaganza. Observed centennial in 1996. World's first indoor rodeo added in 1918 (45 acres under roof). Prize livestock displays, horse shows, midway, commercial exhibits and quality family-oriented entertainment. Est attendance: 800,000. For info: Delbert Bailey, PO Box 150, Fort Worth, TX 76101-0150. Phone: (817) 877-2400. Fax: (817) 877-2499. WWW: http://www.ftstockshowrodeo.com

STENDHAL: BIRTH ANNIVERSARY. Jan 23, 1783. French author Marie Henri Beyle, whose best-known pseudonym was Stendhal. Best remembered are his novels *The Red and the Black* (1831) and *The Charterhouse of Parma* (1839). Born at Grenoble, France, he died at Paris, Mar 23, 1842.

STEWART, POTTER: BIRTH ANNIVERSARY. Jan 23. Associate Justice of the Supreme Court of the United States, nominated by President Eisenhower on Jan 17, 1959. (Oath of office, May 15, 1959.) Born at Jackson, MI, he retired in July 1981 and died on Dec 7, 1985, five days after suffering a stroke, at Putney, VT. Buried at Arlington National Cemetery.

TWENTIETH AMENDMENT TO US CONSTITUTION RATIFIED: 65th ANNIVERSARY. Jan 23, 1933. The 20th Amendment was ratified on Jan 23, 1933, fixing the date of the presidential inauguration at the current Jan 20 instead of the previous Mar 4. It also specified that were the president-elect to die before taking office, the vice president-elect would succeed to the presidency. In addition, it set Jan 3 as the official opening date of Congress each year.

TWENTY-FOURTH AMENDMENT TO US CONSTITUTION RATIFIED: ANNIVERSARY. Jan 23. Poll taxes and other taxes were eliminated as a prerequisite for voting in all federal elections by the 24th Amendment, ratified on Jan 23, 1964.

USS *PUEBLO* SEIZED BY NORTH KOREA: 30th ANNIVERSARY. Jan 23, 1968. North Korea seized the *USS Pueblo* in the Sea of Japan, claiming the ship was on a spy mission. The crew was held for 11 months. The vessel was confiscated. Accompanying the crew when they were released—on Dec 22, 1968—was the body of Seaman Duane D. Hodges, the only crewman killed.

BIRTHDAYS TODAY

Richard Dean Anderson, 48, actor ("General Hospital" [1976–81], "MacGyver"), born Minneapolis, MN, Jan 23, 1950.

Princess Caroline, 41, born Monte Carlo, Monaco, Jan 23, 1957.

Tom Carper, 51, Governor of Delaware (D), born Beckley, WV, Jan 23, 1947.

Gil Gerard, 55, actor ("Buck Rogers," "Sidekicks"), born Little Rock, AR, Jan 23, 1943.

Patrick Capper (Pat) Haden, 45, sportscaster, former football player, born Westbury, NY, Jan 23, 1953.

Rutger Hauer, 54, actor, born Breukelen, Netherlands, Jan 23, 1944.

Frank R. Lautenberg, 74, US Senator (D, New Jersey), born Paterson, NJ, Jan 23, 1924.

Jeanne Moreau, 70, actress (*Jules and Jim, Viva Maria*), born Paris, France, Jan 23, 1928.

Gail O'Grady, 35, actress (Donna on "NYPD Blue"), born Detroit, MI, Jan 23, 1963.

Chita Rivera (Conchita del Rivero), 65, singer, actress (*The Kiss of the Spider Woman*, "The New Dick Van Dyke Show"), born Washington, DC, Jan 23, 1933.

Tiffani-Amber Thiessen, 24, model, actress ("Beverly Hills 90210," "Saved by the Bell," *Son-in- Law*), born Long Beach, CA, January 23, 1974.

JANUARY 24 — SATURDAY

Day 24 — 341 Remaining

ACHELIS, ELISABETH: BIRTH ANNIVERSARY. Jan 24, 1880. Calendar reform advocate, editor, author, born at Brooklyn, NY. Author of *The World Calendar.* Proposed calendar made every year the same, with equal quarters, each year beginning on Sunday, Jan 1, and each date falling on same day of week every year. Died at New York, NY, Feb 11, 1973.

BE A FOOL FOR LOVE DAY. Jan 24. Part of Be Good to Yourself Week (Jan 18–24). For info: K. Diane Schutte, The Self-Renewal Project, Box 337, 5465 N Bend Rd, Cincinnati, OH 45247. Phone: (888) LUV U DAY. Email: Bgood2U@juno.com.

BOLIVIA: ALACITIS FAIR. Jan 24–26. La Paz. Traditional annual celebration by Aymara Indians on this date with prayers and offerings to god of prosperity.

CALIFORNIA GOLD DISCOVERY: 150th ANNIVERSARY. Jan 24, 1848. James W. Marshal, an employee of John Sutter, accidentally discovered gold while building a sawmill near Coloma, CA, on Jan 24, 1848. Efforts to keep the discovery secret failed, and the gold rush was quickly under way.

CHINESE NEW YEAR FESTIVAL. Jan 24–Feb 15. San Francisco, CA. North America's largest Chinese community salutes the Year of the Tiger. Activities include Chinatown Flower Market Fair; Miss Chinatown USA Pageant with Coronation Ball; Chinese New Year Parade; Chinatown Community Street Fair, which showcases the diversity of Chinese culture from Chinese opera and ballet, traditional dance and ancient dynastic costumes to martial arts. Booths feature cooking demonstrations, calligraphy and arts and crafts. Est attendance: 700,000. For info: Chinese Chamber of Commerce, New Year Festival, 730 Sacramento, San Francisco, CA 94108. Phone: (415) 391-9680. Fax: (415) 982-4720.

FDR's "UNCONDITIONAL SURRENDER" STATEMENT: 55th ANNIVERSARY. Jan 24, 1943. At the end of the Casablanca Conference, 1943, Franklin D. Roosevelt and Winston Churchill held a press conference. Roosevelt stated, "Peace can come to the world only by the total elimination of German and Japanese war power. That means the unconditional surrender of Germany, Italy and Japan." This position calling for "unconditional surrender" has subsequently been criticized by some as having prolonged the war.

"THE FIGHT OF THE WEEK" TV PREMIERE: 45th ANNIVERSARY. Jan 24, 1953. For 11 years, you could catch a boxing match every week on TV. Jack Drees announced the matches the first few seasons; Don Dunphy succeeded him.

FIRST CANNED BEER: ANNIVERSARY. Jan 24, 1935. Canned beer went on sale for the first time, in Richmond, Virginia.

FREEZE FOR FOOD 10K RACE AND 5K RUN/WALK. Jan 24. Vilas Park Shelter, Madison, WI. Fundraiser for Oxfam-America, sponsored by the Returned Peace Corps Volunteers of Wisconsin–Madison. $10 registration fee for each event. Times posted; prizes awarded for top pledge raisers and event finishers. We will never cancel the race due to weather! Est attendance: 150. For info: Dave Hamilton or Deb Hamilton, Co-Dirs, RPCVs of Wisconsin, 1160 Washington Rd, Stoughton, WI 53589. Phone: (608) 873-5437.

GOODSON, MARK: BIRTH ANNIVERSARY. Jan 24, 1915. Producer and creator of TV game shows, Mark Goodson was born in Sacramento, CA. His career in entertainment began in radio where he created his first game show, "Pop the Question." He later teamed with Bill Todman and that partnership led to "What's My Line?," "I've Got a Secret," "Password," "The Price Is Right" and "Family Feud." He died on Dec 18, 1992, at New York, NY.

LONGWOOD GARDENS WELCOMES SPRING. Jan 24–Apr 3. Kennett Square, PA. Indoor conservatory display features thousands of colorful, fragrant spring bulbs, green lawns, palm trees, orchids and roses. Organ concerts on most Sunday afternoons. Est attendance: 125,000. For info: Longwood Gardens, PO Box 501, Kennett Sq, PA 19348-0501. Phone: (610) 388-1000. WWW: http://www.longwoodgardens.org

MURDER MYSTERY WEEKEND. Jan 24 (also Mar 14, Oct 10 and Nov 14). The Groveland Hotel, Groveland, CA. This 1849 historic hotel is a perfect setting for amateur sleuth guests to unravel deep secrets. The weekend of mystery and mirth is directed by a professional theatrical company, with a script that weaves fact and fiction around a cocktail party, dinner and morning brunch. Est attendance: 200. For info: Peggy A. Mosley, Innkeeper, The Groveland Hotel, PO Box 289, Groveland, CA 95321. Phone: (209) 962-4000. Fax: (209) 962-6674. Email: peggy@groveland.com. WWW: http://www.groveland.com

January 1998

S	M	T	W	T	F	S
				1	2	3
4	5	6	7	8	9	10
11	12	13	14	15	16	17
18	19	20	21	22	23	24
25	26	27	28	29	30	31

NO BIG DEAL: THE ART OF MINIATURES. Jan 24–Mar 22. Herbert Hoover Presidential Museum, West Branch, IA. Temporary exhibit will feature regional artists, craftsmen, hobbyists and of course their miniature creations. Examples: dollhouses, dioramas and village scenes, and scale models. Est attendance: 5,000. For info: Special Events, Herbert Hoover Presidential Museum, PO Box 488, West Branch, IA 52358. Phone: (319) 643-5301. Fax: (319) 643-5825.
WWW: http://www.nara.gov./nara/president/hoover

SPACE MILESTONE: *COSMOS 954* (USSR) FALLS. Jan 24, 1978. Nuclear-equipped reconnaissance satellite launched Sept 18, 1977. Fell into Earth's atmosphere and burned over northern Canada. Some radioactive debris reached ground on Jan 24, 1978.

SPACE MILESTONE: *DISCOVERY* (US). Jan 24, 1985. Space shuttle *Discovery* launched from and returned to Kennedy Space Center, FL, deploying eavesdropping satellite in secret, all-military mission, Jan 24–27, 1985.

TOGO: ECONOMIC LIBERATION DAY. Jan 24. National holiday.

WHARTON, EDITH: BIRTH ANNIVERSARY. Jan 24, 1862. American author (*The Age of Innocence, Ethan Frome*) and Pulitzer Prize winner. Born at New York, NY. Died Aug 11, 1937.

BIRTHDAYS TODAY

Ernest Borgnine, 81, actor ("McHale's Navy," "The Single Guy"), born Hamden, CT, Jan 24, 1917.
John Beasley (Jack) Brickhouse, 82, former sportscaster, Ford Frick Award winner, born Peoria, IL, Jan 24, 1916.
Neil Diamond, 57, singer, composer ("Cracklin' Rosie," "Song Sung Blue"), born Coney Island, NY, Jan 24, 1941.
Robert Keith (Rob) Dibble, 34, former baseball player, born Bridgeport, CT, Jan 24, 1964.
Nastassja Kinski, 38, actress (*Tess; The Hotel New Hampshire; Paris, Texas*), daughter of late actor Klaus Kinski, born Berlin, Germany, Jan 24, 1960.
Michael Ontkean, 48, actor ("Twin Peaks," *Slap Shot*), born Vancouver, British Columbia, Canada, Jan 24, 1950.
Mary Lou Retton, 30, Olympic gold medal gymnast, born Fairmont, WV, Jan 24, 1968.
Oral Roberts, 80, evangelist, born Tulsa, OK, Jan 24, 1918.
Yakov Smirnoff, 47, comedian ("What a Country," "Night Court"), born Odessa, USSR, Jan 24, 1951.
Maria Tallchief, 73, former ballet dancer, born Fairfax, OK, Jan 24, 1925.

JANUARY 25 — SUNDAY

Day 25 — 340 Remaining

BOYLE, ROBERT: BIRTH ANNIVERSARY. Jan 25, 1627. Irish physicist, chemist and author who formulated Boyle's Law in 1662. Born at Lismore, Ireland, he died at London, England, Dec 30, 1691.

BURNS, ROBERT: BIRTH ANNIVERSARY. Jan 25, 1759. Beloved Scottish poet ("Oh wad some power the giftie gie us To see oursels as others see us!"). Born at Ayrshire, Scotland, he died at Dumfries, Scotland, July 21, 1796. His birthday is widely celebrated, especially in Scotland, England and Newfoundland.

CAPONE, AL: DEATH ANNIVERSARY. Jan 25, 1947. Gangster Alphonse ("Scarface") Capone, who dominated organized crime in Chicago throughout Prohibition, died at age 48 at Miami after suffering from syphilis. Capone was born Jan 17, 1899, at Naples, Italy, and moved with his family to Brooklyn, NY.

CHRIS STRATTON DART TOURNAMENT. Jan 25. Springbrook Golf Course, Battle Creek, MI. 6th annual benefit tournament dedicated to Chris Stratton, a great darter and well-liked person. Fifty percent of entry fees donated to American

Cancer Society. Est attendance: 100. For info: Bill Buckner, Springbrook Golf Course, 1600 Ave A, Battle Creek, MI 49015. Phone: (616) 965-6512.

CURTIS, CHARLES: BIRTH ANNIVERSARY. Jan 25, 1860. Thirty-first vice president of the US (1929–1933). Born at Topeka, KS, he died at Washington, DC, Feb 8, 1936.

EINSTEIN ON WINE. Jan 25. Tampa, FL. Fundraiser for MOSI Science Center held by BEAM (Be Enthusiastic About MOSI). Events include wine tastings, food, seminars, grape stomping and a silent auction. Est attendance: 1,500. For info: Mktg Dept, MOSI, 4801 E Fowler Ave, Tampa, FL 33617-2099. Phone: (813) 987-6373. Fax: (813) 987-6310.

FIRST SCHEDULED TRANSCONTINENTAL FLIGHT: ANNIVERSARY. Jan 25, 1959. American Airlines opened the jet age in the US with the first scheduled transcontinental flight on a Boeing 707, from California to New York.

FIRST TELEVISED PRESIDENTIAL NEWS CONFERENCE: ANNIVERSARY. Jan 25, 1961. Beginning a tradition that survives to this day, John F. Kennedy held the first televised presidential news conference five days after being inaugurated the 35th president.

LISTEN COMPASSIONATELY TO A SURVIVOR WEEK. Jan 25–31. When something extraordinarily calamitous like rape, street crime or domestic violence happens, most survivors feel a compelling need to tell their stories and be heard and supported by family and friends. Unfortunately, tales of trauma can make listeners uncomfortable–so much that we listeners back off, telling survivors to just "put it all behind them." This week is our opportunity to listen well to friends and family members who have survived calamity. Annually, the last week in January. For info: Veritas Programming, 111 Main St, Brattleboro, VT 05301. Phone: (802) 257-1054. Fax: (802) 257-3097. Email: veritas@sover.net. WWW: http://www.sover.net/~schwcof

MAUGHAM, W. SOMERSET: BIRTH ANNIVERSARY. Jan 25, 1874. English short story writer, novelist and playwright born at Paris, France. Among his best-remembered books: *Of Human Bondage, Cakes and Ale* and *The Razor's Edge.* Died at Cap Ferrat, France, Dec 16, 1965.

MILLS, FLORENCE: BIRTH ANNIVERSARY. Jan 25, 1896. The leading black American singer and dancer of the Jazz Age and the Harlem Renaissance was born Florence Winfree at Washington, DC. She appeared in Langston Hughes's *Shuffle Along* in 1921 and *Plantation Review* on Broadway in 1922, then at the London Pavilion in *Dover Street to Dixie* in 1923. Offered a spot in the *Ziegfeld Follies*, she turned it down and joined in creating a rival show with an all-black cast. Mills was the first black woman to appear as a headliner at the Palace Theatre on June 27, 1924. Mills was so revered for her concerted efforts to create opportunities for black entertainers and to bring the unique culture of blacks to Broadway that more than 150,000 people swarmed the streets of Harlem to mourn her when she died at New York City on Nov 1, 1927, at age 31.

NATIONAL POPCORN DAY. Jan 25. A salute to popcorn. "What's more American than a super bowl of popcorn while watching the Super Bowl?" Annually, on Superbowl Sunday. For info: Polly Peterson, WROE-FM, PO Box 1035, Neenah, WI 54957-1035. Phone: (414) 725-4447. Fax: (414) 725-0463.

NATIONAL SCOTTISH CULTURE MONTH. Jan 25–Feb 28. Month-long celebration of Scottish culture and products. ScotsFest takes place annually during this month. ScotsFest '98 kicks off with a Robert Burns Supper on Jan 25 to celebrate the birthdate of Scotland's most celebrated poet. For info: Schieffelin and Somerset, 2 Park Ave, New York, NY 10016. Phone: (212) 251-8200. Fax: (212) 251-8382.

A ROOM OF ONE'S OWN DAY. Jan 25. For anyone who knows or longs for the sheer bliss and rightness of having a private place, no matter how humble, to call one's own. [© 1997 by WPL] For info: Tom or Ruth Roy, Wellness Permission League, PO Box 662, Mt Gretna, PA 17064-0662. Phone: (500) 437-5104 or (717) 964-1308. Fax: (717) 964-1335.

SOLO-PRENEURING WEEK. Jan 25–31. Control your own destiny by taking charge of your work and your life. This week is set aside to plan and prepare for the work you were meant to do, and to celebrate those who are following a path of their own choosing. Whether you are an employee, a business owner, or just contemplating your place in the workforce, resolve to learn how you can do work that is satisfying and fulfilling, create your own job security, prepare for an uncertain future, and have fun doing work you love. For a free booklet on how you can create the career of your dreams, send a self-addressed, stamped envelope to the address below. ATTN: SP Booklet. For info: Cathy Stucker, Special Interests Publishing, 4646 Hwy 6, Ste 123, Sugar Land, TX 77478. Phone: (281) 265-7342. Fax: (281) 265-9727. Email: cstucker@flash.net.

SUPER BOWL XXXII. Jan 25. San Diego, CA. The battle between the NFC and AFC champions. Annually, the last Sunday in January. The 1999 Super Bowl will be in Miami; the 2000 Super Bowl will be in Atlanta. For info: PR Dept, The Natl Football League, 410 Park Ave, New York, NY 10022. Phone: (212) 758-1500.

WOOLF, VIRGINIA: BIRTH ANNIVERSARY. Jan 25, 1882. English writer, critic and novelist. Author of *Jacob's Room* and *To the Lighthouse.* Born at London, England. After completing her last novel, *Between the Acts,* she collapsed under the strain and drowned herself in the River Ouse near Rodmell, England, on Mar 28, 1941.

BIRTHDAYS TODAY

Corazon "Cory" Aquino, 75, former president of the Philippines, born Tarlac Province, Philippine Islands, Jan 25, 1923.

Conrad Burns, 63, US Senator (R, Montana), born Gallatin, MO, Jan 25, 1935.

Chris Chelios, 36, hockey player, Chicago, IL, Jan 25, 1962.

Mark ("Super") Duper (born Mark Kirby Dupas), 39, former football player, born Pineville, LA, on Jan 25, 1959.

Ernie Harwell, 80, sportscaster, born Washington, GA, Jan 25, 1918.

Dean Jones, 67, actor (*Tea and Sympathy, The Love Bug, Beethoven*), born Decatur, AL, Jan 25, 1931.

Dinah Manoff, 40, actress (stage: *I Ought to Be in Pictures* [Tony and Theatre World Stage Awards, 1980]; "Soap" [1978–79], "Empty Nest"), born New York, NY, Jan 25, 1958.

Edwin Newman, 79, journalist, author ("Comet," *A Civil Tongue*), born New York, NY, Jan 25, 1919.

Eduard Amvrosiyevich Shevardnadze, 70, former Russian minister of foreign affairs, born Mamati, USSR, Jan 25, 1928.

Leigh Taylor-Young, 53, actress ("Peyton Place," "Dallas," *I Love You Alice B. Toklas*), born Washington, DC, Jan 25, 1945.

JANUARY 26 — MONDAY

Day 26 — 339 Remaining

AUSTRALIA: AUSTRALIA DAY—FIRST BRITISH SETTLEMENT: ANNIVERSARY. Jan 26, 1788. A shipload of convicts arrived briefly at Botany Bay (which proved to be unsuitable) and then at Port Jackson (later the site of the city of Sydney). Establishment of an Australian prison colony was to relieve crowding of British prisons. Australia Day, formerly known as Foundation Day or Anniversary Day, has been observed since about 1817 and has been a public holiday since 1838. Observed on Jan 26 if a Monday, otherwise on the first Monday thereafter.

DENTAL DRILL PATENT: ANNIVERSARY. Jan 26, 1875. George F. Green, of Kalamazoo, MI, patented the electric dental drill.

DIRECT DEPOSIT WEEK. Jan 26–30. Encouraging people to use the faster, safer, smarter way of getting paid by using payroll direct deposit. For info: Rossana Czelusniak, Product Planning Specialist, New York Clearing House Assn, 450 W 33rd St, New York, NY 10001. Phone: (212) 613-0166. Fax: (212) 564-5109. Email: webmaster@nych.org. WWW: http://www.ezpay.org

DOMINICAN REPUBLIC: NATIONAL HOLIDAY. Jan 26. An official public holiday celebrates the birth anniversary of Juan Pablo Duarte, one of the fathers of the republic.

FRANKLIN PREFERS TURKEY: ANNIVERSARY. Jan 26, 1784. In a letter to his daughter, Benjamin Franklin expressed his unhappiness over the choice of the eagle as the symbol of America. He preferred the turkey.

GRANT, JULIA DENT: BIRTH ANNIVERSARY. Jan 26, 1826. Wife of Ulysses Simpson Grant, 18th president of the US. Born at St. Louis, MO; died Dec 14, 1902.

HITLER YOUTH DEPLOYED: 55th ANNIVERSARY. Jan 26, 1943. Due to the need for more men at the front, the Nazis began manning anti-aircraft batteries within Germany with members of the Hitler Youth who were aged fifteen and up. This was 10 days after the British had begun the heavy bombing of Berlin and other German cities. See also: "British Air Raid on Berlin" (Jan 16).

INDIA: REPUBLIC DAY. Jan 26. National holiday. Anniversary of Proclamation of the Republic, Basant Panchmi. On Jan 26, 1929, Indian National Congress resolved to work for establishment of a sovereign republic, a goal that was realized on Jan 26, 1950, when India became a democratic republic.

MacARTHUR, DOUGLAS: BIRTH ANNIVERSARY. Jan 26, 1880. US general and supreme commander of Allied forces in Southwest Pacific during World War II. Born at Little Rock, AR, he served as commander of the Rainbow Division's 84th Infantry Brigade in World War I, leading it in the St. Mihiel, Meuse-Argonne and Sedan offensives. MacArthur died at Washington, DC, Apr 5, 1964. Remembered for his "I shall return" prediction when forced out of the Philippines by the Japanese, a promise he fulfilled. Relieved of Far Eastern command by President Harry Truman on Apr 11, 1951, during the Korean War.

MICHIGAN: ADMISSION DAY: ANNIVERSARY. Jan 26, 1837. Became 26th state on this day in 1837.

"MIKE HAMMER" TV PREMIERE: ANNIVERSARY. Jan 26, 1984. Originally a TV series in the '50s, Mike Hammer was the title character in a show about a gritty, urban detective created by writer Mickey Spillane. CBS revived the series with Stacy Keach as the hard-boiled detective. Production was stopped while Keach was briefly imprisoned for a drug charge in 1984. The series returned in 1986 and currently appears as made-for-TV movies. The series also featured Don Stroud as NYPD Captain Pat Chambers; Kent Williams as Asst DA Barrington; Lindsay Bloom as Hammer's secretary Velda; Danny Goldman as "Ozzie the Answer"; Donna Denton as "The Face"; and Lee Benton as Jenny the bartender.

PEDDLER'S VILLAGE ANNUAL QUILT COMPETITION AND DISPLAY. Jan 26–Apr 5. Peddler's Village, Lahaska, PA. Handmade quilt entries, from as far away as Japan, compete for $1,500 in cash prizes in such categories as traditional, Amish, creative, clothing and amateur. A distinguished panel of judges chooses the winners, and quilts are displayed in the Village Gazebo. Open daily to public. Free admission. Est attendance: 6,000. For info: Peddler's Village, Routes 202 & 263, Lahaska, PA 18931. Phone: (215) 794-4000. Fax: (215) 794-4001. WWW: http://www.peddlersvillage.com

VAN HEUSEN, JIMMY: 85th BIRTH ANNIVERSARY. Jan 26, 1913. Jimmy Van Heusen was born Edward Chester Babcock at Syracuse, NY. He was a composer of many Hollywood film songs and other popular songs along with his lyricist partners Johnny Burke and Sammy Cahn. One of his 76 songs that Frank Sinatra recorded was "My Kind of Town." Van Heusen won four Academy Awards for his songs that were in movies such as *Going My Way* (1944). He was inducted into the Songwriters Hall of Fame when it was founded in 1971. Van Heusen died on Feb 7, 1990, at Rancho Mirage, CA.

BIRTHDAYS TODAY

Anita Baker, 40, singer ("Sweet Love," "Rhythm of Love"), born Toledo, OH, Jan 26, 1958.

Father George Harold Clements, 66, Roman Catholic priest who adopted child, civil rights leader, born Chicago, IL, Jan 26, 1932.

Angela Davis, 54, political activist, born Birmingham, AL, Jan 26, 1944.

Philip Jose Farmer, 80, science fiction writer, born North Terre Haute, IN, on Jan 26, 1918.

Jules Feiffer, 69, cartoonist, writer, born New York, NY, Jan 26, 1929.

Scott Glenn, 56, actor (*The Right Stuff, Silverado*), born Pittsburgh, PA, Jan 26, 1942.

Wayne Gretzky, 37, hockey player, born Brantford, Ontario, Canada, Jan 26, 1961.

Paul Newman, 73, actor (Oscar for *The Color of Money; Cat on a Hot Tin Roof, Exodus, Cool Hand Luke, Hud, Butch Cassidy and the Sundance Kid, The Verdict*), director (*Rachel, Rachel; Harry and Son; The Glass Menagerie*), auto racer, born Cleveland, OH, Jan 26, 1925.

Andrew Ridgeley, 35, musician, born Bushey, England, Jan 26, 1963.

Gene Siskel, 52, movie critic, born Chicago, IL, Jan 26, 1946.

Robert George (Bob) Uecker, 63, sportscaster, actor, former baseball player, born Milwaukee, WI, Jan 26, 1935.

Roger Vadim, 70, filmmaker (*Barbarella, And God Created Woman*), born Paris, France, Jan 26, 1928.

Eddie Van Halen, 41, guitarist ("Jump," "Right Now"), born Nijmegen, Netherlands, Jan 26, 1957.

JANUARY 27 — TUESDAY

Day 27 — 338 Remaining

***APOLLO I*: SPACECRAFT FIRE: ANNIVERSARY.** Jan 27, 1967. Three American astronauts, Virgil I. Grissom, Edward H. White and Roger B. Chaffee, died when fire suddenly broke out at 6:31 PM in *Apollo I* during a launching simulation test, as it stood on the ground at Cape Kennedy, FL, Jan 27, 1967. First launching in the Apollo program had been scheduled for Feb 27, 1967.

BIRMINGHAM SPORT AND BOAT SHOW. Jan 27–Feb 1. Birmingham/Jefferson Civic Center, Birmingham, AL. For info: Mike Coffen, Double C Productions, Inc, Box 1678, Huntsville, TX 77342. Phone: (409) 295-9677 or (800) 574-9650. Fax: (409) 295-8859. Email: doublec@lcc.net. WWW: http://www.lcc.net/~doublec

GOMPERS, SAMUEL: BIRTH ANNIVERSARY. Jan 27, 1850. Labor leader, first president of the American Federation of Labor, born at London, England. Died Dec 13, 1924, at San Antonio, TX.

GUNPOWDER PLOT TRIAL: ANNIVERSARY. Jan 27, 1606. The surviving conspirators in the "Gunpowder Treason," a plot to blow up Parliament and the king on Nov 5, 1605, were brought to trial and convicted at London, England, Jan 27, 1606. Four days later they were executed. An inscription on a contemporary engraving states: "The heads of Percy and Catesby after

January 1998

S	M	T	W	T	F	S
				1	2	3
4	5	6	7	8	9	10
11	12	13	14	15	16	17
18	19	20	21	22	23	24
25	26	27	28	29	30	31

they were dead, were cut off and set upon the ends of Parliament House. Friday the last of Jan, 1606, were executed in Parliament Yard: T. Winter, Rokenvood, Keys and Guido Fawkes, their quarters were placed over London gates and their heads upon London Bridge." See also: "Guy Fawkes Day" (Nov 5).

INTERNATIONAL SNOW-SCULPTING COMPETITION. Jan 27–31. Performing Arts Center, Milwaukee, WI. 13th annual. Throughout this event, more than 250,000 spectators will view world-class snow sculptures. During the first three days, the competitors, including many Olympic winners and contenders, will create a variety of art pieces ranging from abstract designs to whimsical animals to towering ice castles. The completed sculptures will be judged and awarded on Saturday. For info: Gene Kempfer, Dir, Intl Snow-Sculpting Competition, 1554 S 74th St, Milwaukee, WI 53214. Phone: (414) 476-5573. Email: tourism@laughlin.com. WWW: http://tourism@laughlin.com

KERN, JEROME: BIRTH ANNIVERSARY. Jan 27, 1885. American composer born at New York City; died there Nov 11, 1945. In addition to scores for stage and screen, Kern wrote many memorable song hits, including "Who," "Make Believe," "Ol' Man River," "Bill," "The Night Was Made for Love," "Smoke Gets in Your Eyes," "Lovely to Look At," "I Won't Dance," "The Way You Look Tonight," "All the Things You Are," "The Last Time I Saw Paris" and "Dearly Beloved."

"LAVERNE AND SHIRLEY" TV PREMIERE: ANNIVERSARY. Jan 27, 1976. Laverne and Shirley kept the laughs coming with their outrageous antics. The ABC sitcom was a spin-off of the popular TV show "Happy Days" that was also set during the late '50s in Milwaukee, WI. Penny Marshall (sister of series co-creator, Garry Marshall) starred as Laverne DeFazio with Cindy Williams as Shirley Feeney. The two friends worked at a brewery and shared a basement apartment. Also featured in the cast were: Phil Foster as Laverne's father, Frank DeFazio; David L. Lander as friend and co-worker Andrew "Squiggy" Squigman; Michael McKean as friend and co-worker Lenny Kowznovski; Betty Garrett as landlady Edna Babish; and Eddie Mekka as Carmine Ragusa, Shirley's sometime boyfriend.

MOZART, WOLFGANG AMADEUS: BIRTH ANNIVERSARY. Jan 27, 1756. One of the world's greatest music makers. Born at Salzburg, Austria, into a gifted musical family, Mozart began performing at age three and composing at age five. Some of the best known of his more than 600 compositions include the operas *Marriage of Figaro*, *Don Giovanni*, *Cosi fan tutte* and *The Magic Flute*; his unfinished Requiem Mass; his C major symphony known as the "Jupiter"; and many of his quartets and piano concertos. He died at Vienna on Dec 5, 1791, at age 35.

RICKOVER, HYMAN GEORGE: BIRTH ANNIVERSARY. Jan 27, 1900. American naval officer. Known as the "Father of the Nuclear Navy." Admiral Rickover directed development of nuclear reactor-powered submarines, the first of which was the *Nautilus*, launched in 1954. Rickover was noted for his blunt remarks: "To increase the efficiency of the Department of Defense," he said, "you must first abolish it." The four-star admiral retired (unwillingly) at the age of 81, after 63 years in the navy. Born in Russia, Rickover died at Arlington, VA, on July 9, 1986, and was buried at Arlington National Cemetery.

SCOTLAND: UP HELLY AA. Jan 27. Lerwick, Shetland Islands. Norse galley burned in impressive ceremony symbolizing sacrifice to sun. Old Viking custom. Annually, the last Tuesday in January. Tourist Information Centre, Market Cross, Bressay, Shetland, Scotland ZE2. Phone: (44) (595) 693-434. Fax: (44) (595) 695-807.

SIOUX EMPIRE FARM SHOW. Jan 27–31. Sioux Falls, SD. Winter farm and livestock show featuring all classes of livestock, commercial exhibits, horse pull, consumer programs and a women's show. Est attendance: 40,000. For info: Sioux Empire Farm Show, Chamber of Commerce, 200 N Phillips Ave, #102, Sioux Falls, SD 57102. Phone: (605) 373-2016.

THOMAS CRAPPER DAY. Jan 27, 1910. Born at Thorne, Yorkshire, England, in 1836 (exact date unknown), Crapper is said to be the prime developer of flush toilet mechanism as it is known today. Founder, London, 1861, of Thomas Crapper & Co, later patentees and manufacturers of sanitary appliances. Died Jan 27, 1910. [Editor's Note: The date of Crapper's death has been revised based on info sent by Dr. Andy Gibbons of the Intl Thomas Crapper Society, who has viewed Crapper's gravestone and obtained a copy of his death certificate. Ken Grabowski sent further info.]

VIETNAM WAR ENDED: 25th ANNIVERSARY. Jan 27, 1973. US and North Vietnam, along with South Vietnam and the Viet Cong, signed an "Agreement on ending the war and restoring peace in Vietnam." Signed at Paris, France, Jan 27, 1973, to take effect on Jan 28 at 8 AM Saigon time, thus ending US combat role in a war that had involved American personnel stationed in Vietnam since defeated French forces had departed under terms of the Geneva Accords in 1954. Longest war in US history. More than one million combat deaths (US: 46,079).

BIRTHDAYS TODAY

Mikhail Baryshnikov, 50, ballet dancer, actor (*Dancers, White Nights, The Turning Point*), born Riga, Latvia, USSR, Jan 27, 1948.

Anthony Cris Collinsworth, 39, sportscaster, former football player, born Dayton, OH, Jan 27, 1959.

Mairead Corrigan, 54, pacifist, Nobel Peace Prize winner, born Belfast, Northern Ireland, Jan 27, 1944.

Bridget Fonda, 34, actress, daughter of actor Peter Fonda, (*It Could Happen to You, Single White Female*), born Los Angeles, CA, Jan 27, 1964.

Skitch Henderson, 80, band leader (many years with "The Tonight Show"), born Halstad, MN, Jan 27, 1918.

Mimi Rogers, 42, actress (*The Doors, The Rapture*), born Coral Gables, FL, Jan 27, 1956.

JANUARY 28 — WEDNESDAY

Day 28 — 337 Remaining

"BARNABY JONES" TV PREMIERE: 25th ANNIVERSARY. Jan 28, 1973. CBS drama about a mild-mannered, milk-drinking (but don't say milquetoast) private eye who comes out of retirement following his son's murder. Produced by Quinn Martin. Cast included Buddy Ebsen as Barnaby Jones; Lee Meriwether as Barnaby's widowed daughter-in-law, Betty Jones; John Carter as Lt Biddle; and Mark Shera as Jedediah Jones.

***CHALLENGER* SPACE SHUTTLE EXPLOSION: ANNIVERSARY.** Jan 28. At 11:39 AM, EST, on Jan 28, 1986, the Space Shuttle *Challenger* exploded, 74 seconds into its flight and about 10 miles above the earth. Hundreds of millions around the world watched television replays of the horrifying event that killed seven people, destroyed the billion-dollar craft, suspended all shuttle flights and halted, at least temporarily, much of the US manned space flight program. Killed were teacher Christa McAuliffe (who was to have been the first ordinary citizen in space) and six crew members: Francis R. Scobee, Michael J. Smith, Judith A. Resnik, Ellison S. Onizuka, Ronald E. McNair and Gregory B. Jarvis. [See also individual names.]

CHINESE NEW YEAR. Jan 28. Traditional Chinese lunar year begins at sunset on day of second New Moon following the winter solstice. Begins year 4696 of the ancient Chinese calendar, designated as the Year of the Tiger. Generally celebrated until the Lantern Festival fifteen days later, but merchants usually reopen their stores and places of business on the fifth day of the first lunar month (Feb 1, 1998). See also: "China: Lantern Festival" (Feb 11).

ENGLAND: WORLD OF DRAWINGS AND WATERCOLOURS. Jan 28–Feb 1. The Dorchester Hotel, London. Original works of art are offered for sale by 50 leading galleries and dealers. The only fair of its kind in the world. Est attendance: 10,000. For info: Mrs Sally Jordan, World of Drawings and Watercolours, 7-11 Kensington High St, London, England W8 5NP. Phone: (44) (171) 411-3166. Fax: (44) (181) 752-1951.

"FANTASY ISLAND" TV PREMIERE: 20th ANNIVERSARY. Jan 28, 1978. You knew you were a bona fide "star" in the '70s when you received a casting call from "Fantasy Island." Young and old stayed home on Saturday night to watch Mr Roarke introduce us to yet another hapless lot of guest stars anxious to live out their fantasies in camp splendor. Ricardo Montalban starred as our prescient guide, Mr Roarke, with Herve Villechaize as Tattoo; Wendy Schaal as Mr Roarke's goddaughter, Julie; and Christopher Hewett as Mr Roarke's assistant, Lawrence. The show's run of 130 episodes was produced by Aaron Spelling and Leonard Goldberg. Who can forget Tattoo's opening lines each week, "De plane, de plane!"

GREAT SEAL OF THE UNITED STATES: AUTHORIZATION ANNIVERSARY. Jan 28, 1782. Congress, on Jan 28, 1782, resolved that the secretary of the Congress should "keep the public seal, and cause the same to be affixed to every act, ordinance or paper, which Congress shall direct. . . ." Although the Great Seal did not exist yet, the Congress recognized the need for it. See also: "Great Seal of the United States: Anniversary" (June 20, July 4 and Sept 16).

ISRAELI SIEGE OF SUEZ CITY ENDS: ANNIVERSARY. Jan 28, 1974. The Israeli army lifted its siege of Suez City, freed encircled Egyptian troops and turned over 300,000 square miles of Egyptian territory to the UN, thereby ending the occupation that started during the October 1973 war.

MacKENZIE, ALEXANDER: BIRTH ANNIVERSARY. Jan 28, 1822. The man who became the first Liberal prime minister of Canada (1873–78) was born at Logierait, Perth, Scotland. He died at age 70 on Apr 17, 1892, at Toronto.

MARTÍ, JOSÉ JULIAN: BIRTH ANNIVERSARY. Jan 28, 1853. Cuban author and political activist born at Havana, Cuba, Martí was exiled to Spain, where he studied law before coming to the US in 1890. He was killed in battle at Dos Rios, Cuba, May 19, 1895.

MOON PHASE: NEW MOON. Jan 28. Moon enters New Moon phase at 1:01 AM, EST.

MUSEUM OF AMERICAN GLASS: MID-WINTER EXHIBIT. Jan 28–Mar 8. Wheaton Village, Millville, NJ. "Curator's Choice" exhibit of fine glass items. Est attendance: 6,000. For info: Wheaton Village, 1501 Glasstown Rd, Millville, NJ 08332-1566. Phone: (609) 825-6800 or (800) 998-4552. Fax: (609) 825-2410. Email: mail@wheatonvillage.org. WWW: http://www.wheatonvillage.org

January 1998

S	M	T	W	T	F	S
				1	2	3
4	5	6	7	8	9	10
11	12	13	14	15	16	17
18	19	20	21	22	23	24
25	26	27	28	29	30	31

PICCARD, AUGUSTE: BIRTH ANNIVERSARY. Jan 28, 1884. Scientist and explorer, born at Basel, Switzerland. Record-setting balloon ascents into stratosphere and ocean depth descents and explorations. Twin brother of Jean Felix Piccard. Died at Lausanne, Switzerland, Mar 24, 1962. See also: "Piccard, Jean Felix: Birth Anniversary" (Jan 28).

PICCARD, JEAN FELIX: BIRTH ANNIVERSARY. Jan 28, 1884. Scientist, engineer, explorer, born at Basel, Switzerland. Noted for cosmic-ray research and record-setting balloon ascensions into stratosphere. Reached 57,579 ft in sealed gondola piloted by his wife, Jeannette, in 1934. Twin brother of Auguste Piccard. Died at Minneapolis, MN, Jan 28, 1963. See also: "Piccard, Jeannette Ridlon: Birth Anniversary" (Jan 5) and "Piccard, Auguste: Birth Anniversary" (Jan 28).

STANLEY, HENRY MORTON: BIRTH ANNIVERSARY. Jan 28, 1841. Explorer born in Wales and leader of the expedition to find the missing missionary-explorer David Livingstone, who had not been heard from for more than two years. Stanley began the search in Africa on Mar 21, 1871, finally finding the emplorer at Ujiji, near Lake Tanganyika, on Nov 10, 1871, whereupon he asked the now-famous question: "Dr. Livingstone, I presume?" Stanley died at London, England, May 10, 1904.

BIRTHDAYS TODAY

Alan Alda (born Alphonso D'Abruzzo), 62, actor (*Paper Lion, The Four Seasons*; Captain Benjamin "Hawkeye" Pierce on "M*A*S*H"), director, born New York, NY, Jan 28, 1936.

John Beck, 55, actor (Ketcham on "Nichols," Mark Graison on "Dallas," *Sleeper, The Big Bus*), born Chicago, IL, Jan 28, 1943.

Susan Howard (Jeri Lynn Mooney), 55, actress (Donna Culver Krebbs on "Dallas"), born Marshall, TX, Jan 28, 1943.

Harley Jane Kozak, 41, actress (*When Harry Met Sally . . ., Parenthood*), born Wilkes-Barre, PA, Jan 28, 1957.

Claes Oldenburg, 69, artist, sculptor (*Standing Trowel*), born Stockholm, Sweden, Jan 28, 1929.

Jeanne Shaheen, 51, Governor of New Hampshire (D), born St. Charles, MO, Jan 28, 1947.

Susan Sontag, 65, author (*Against Interpretation, The Volcano Lover: A Romance*), born New York, NY, Jan 28, 1933.

Elijah Wood, 17, actor (*Back to the Future Part II, The Good Son*), born Cedar Rapids, IA, Jan 28, 1981.

JANUARY 29 — THURSDAY

Day 29 — 336 Remaining

CHATTANOOGA BOAT SHOW. Jan 29–Feb 1. Chattanooga, TN. 13th annual show featuring more than 50,000 square feet of boats and booths displaying fishing tackle, marine equipment, water skis and much more. Thursday and Friday 5-10 PM; Saturday 10 AM-10 PM; Sunday 12-5 PM. Est attendance: 12,000. For info: Cindy Crabtree, Esau, Inc, PO Box 50096, Knoxville, TN 37950. Phone: (423) 588-1233 or (800) 588-ESAU. Fax: (423) 588-6938.

CHEKHOV, ANTON PAVLOVICH: BIRTH ANNIVERSARY. Jan 29, 1860 (New Style). Russian playwright and short story writer, especially remembered for *The Sea Gull, The Three Sisters* and *The Cherry Orchard.* Born at Taganrog, Russia; died on July 15, 1904, at the Black Forest Spa at Badenweiler, Germany.

EID-AL-FITR: CELEBRATING THE FAST. Jan 29. Islamic calendar date: Shawwal 1, 1418. This feast/festival celebrates having completed the Ramadan fasting (which began Dec 31, 1997) and usually lasts for several days. Everyone wears new clothes; children receive gifts from parents and relatives; games, folktales, plays, puppet shows, trips to amusement parks; children allowed to stay up late. Different methods for "anticipating" the visibility of the new moon crescent at Mecca are used by different Muslim groups. *Chase's* uses anticipated dates furnished by the American Muslim Council. US EST date may vary.

FREETHINKER'S DAY. Jan 29. Annual celebration of the birth of Thomas Paine. For info: Truth Seeker Co, Inc, 16935 W Bernardo Dr, Ste 103, San Diego, CA 92127. Phone: (800) 321-9054 or (760) 676-0430. Fax: (760) 676-0433. Email: tseditor@aol.com. WWW: http://freethought.com

KANSAS: ADMISSION DAY: ANNIVERSARY. Jan 29, 1861. Kansas became the 34th state on this day.

McKINLEY, WILLIAM: BIRTH ANNIVERSARY. Jan 29, 1843. 25th president of the US, born at Niles, OH. Died in office, at Buffalo, NY, Sept 14, 1901, as the result of a gunshot wound by an anarchist assassin on Sept 6, 1901, while he was attending Pan American Exposition.

MILITARY BAN ON HOMOSEXUALS EASED: 5th ANNIVERSARY. Jan 29, 1993. An interim policy on ending the ban on homosexuals in the US military is announced by President William Clinton. The policy ended the questioning of military recruits regarding their sexual orientation but allowed removal of openly homosexual members from active service. President Clinton's announced policy of "don't ask, don't tell, don't pursue" allowed homosexuals to serve in the armed forces as long as they were discreet.

MORMON BATTALION ARRIVAL IN CALIFORNIA: ANNIVERSARY. Jan 29, 1847. The 500 men of the US Mormon Battalion, along with 50 women and children, arrived at San Diego, CA, on this date, having marched 2,000 miles—the longest march in modern military history—since leaving Council Bluffs, IA, on July 16, 1846, to fight in the war against Mexico. In the course of their trek they established the first wagon route from Santa Fe to southern California. Their historic arrival is commemorated each year with a military parade in San Diego's Old Town. For info: Mormon Battalion Visitors Center, 2510 Juan St, San Diego, CA 92110. Phone: (619) 298-3317. Fax: (619) 298-5866.

NATIONAL PUZZLE DAY. Jan 29. To recognize different puzzles and games and their creators. Call or write for free information on the origins and creators of puzzles and games. For info: Carol Handz, Coord, Jodi Jill Features, 1705 14th St, Ste 321, Boulder, CO 80301. Phone: (303) 786-9849. Fax: (303) 786-9849.

PAINE, THOMAS: BIRTH ANNIVERSARY. Jan 29, 1737. American Revolutionary leader, a corset-maker by trade, author of *Common Sense*, *The Age of Reason* and many other influential works, was born at Thetford, England. "These are the times that try men's souls" are the well-known opening words of his inspirational tract *The Crisis*. Paine died at New York, NY, June 8, 1809, but 10 years later his remains were moved to England by William Cobbett for reburial there. Reburial was refused, however, and the location of Paine's bones, said to have been distributed, is unknown.

SPACE MILESTONE: *SATURN SA-5* (US). Jan 29, 1964. Orbits record 19 tons. Launched on Jan 29, 1964.

SWEDENBORG, EMANUEL: BIRTH ANNIVERSARY. Jan 29, 1688. Born at Stockholm, Sweden, Swedenborg is remembered as a scientist, inventor, writer and religious leader. He died at London, England, on Mar 29, 1772.

ZORA NEALE HURSTON FESTIVAL OF THE ARTS AND HUMANITIES. Jan 29–Feb 1. Eatonville, FL (10 miles east of Orlando). Festival celebrates Hurston, her work, her hometown, Eatonville, popularly known as the oldest incorporated African-American municipality in the country, and the cultural contributions Africa-descended people have made to the United States and to world culture, with four days of arts and humanities programming highlighting theatre, music, folklore and literature through seminars, symposia, master classes, intellectual conversations/dialogues, art exhibitions, workshops, self-tours, concert fare and performances. Festival attracts both "domestic and international travelers looking for 'the other Florida'—the Africa-descendant cultural matrix." Est attendance: 75,000. For info: Assn to Preserve Eatonville, Inc, PO Box 2586, Eatonville, FL 32751. Phone: (407) 647-3307. Fax: (407) 647-3959. Email: zora@cs.ucf.edu. WWW: http://www.cs.ucf.edu/~zora

BIRTHDAYS TODAY

John Forsythe (John Freund), 80, actor ("Bachelor Father"; Charlie's voice on "Charlie's Angels"; "Dynasty"), born Penn's Grove, NJ, Jan 29, 1918.

Sara Gilbert, 23, actress (Darlene on "Roseanne"), born at Santa Monica, CA, Jan 29, 1975.

Germaine Greer, 59, author (*Daddy We Hardly Knew You, The Female Eunuch*), born Melbourne, Victoria, Australia, Jan 29, 1939.

Martha Wright Griffiths, 86, political leader, former Lieutenant Governor of Michigan (D), former congresswoman, advocate for feminist issues, born Pierce City, MO, Jan 29, 1912.

Ann Jillian, 47, actress ("It's a Living," *The Ann Jillian Story*), born Cambridge, MA, Jan 29, 1951.

Ronald Stacey King, 31, basketball player, born Lawton, OK, Jan 29, 1967.

Gregory Efthimios (Greg) Louganis, 38, actor, Olympic gold medal diver, born San Diego, CA, Jan 29, 1960.

Bobbie Phillips, 30, actress ("Murder One," *Red Shoe Diaries*) born Charleston, SC, Jan 29, 1968.

Katharine Ross, 55, actress (Elaine Robinson in *The Graduate*), born Los Angeles, CA, Jan 29, 1943.

Stephen Louis (Steve) Sax, 38, former baseball player, born Sacramento, CA, Jan 29, 1960.

Tom Selleck, 53, actor ("Magnum, P.I."; *Three Men and a Baby; Mr. Baseball*), born Detroit, MI, Jan 29, 1945.

Oprah Winfrey, 44, TV talk show hostess (many Emmys for "The Oprah Winfrey Show"), actress (Sophia in *The Color Purple*), producer (owner of Harpo Studios in Chicago), born Kosciusko, MS, Jan 29, 1954.

JANUARY 30 — FRIDAY

Day 30 — 335 Remaining

ALL THAT JAZZ WEEKEND. Jan 30–Feb 1. Grove Park Inn Resort, Asheville, NC. One of the Inn's most popular events, the 6th annual jazz weekend features legendary jazz performers on Friday and Saturday night. Est attendance: 1,600. For info: Grove Park Inn Resort, 290 Macon Ave, Asheville, NC 28804. Phone: (800) 374-0050 or (704) 252-2711 ext 8045 or 8005. Fax: (704) 253-7053.

BEATLES LAST PUBLIC APPEARANCE: ANNIVERSARY. Jan 30, 1969. On this day the Beatles performed together in public for the last time. The show took place on the roof of their Apple Studios in London, England, but it was interrupted by police after they received complaints from the neighbors about the noise.

BLOODY SUNDAY: ANNIVERSARY. Jan 30, 1972. In Derry, Northern Ireland, on Jan 30, 1972, 13 Roman Catholics were shot dead by British troops during a banned civil rights march. During 1972, which was the first year of British direct rule, 467 people were killed in the fighting.

CANADA: ONTARIO WINTER CARNIVAL BON SOO. Jan 30–Feb 8. Sault Ste. Marie, Ontario. One of Canada's largest winter carnivals features more than 125 festive indoor and hearty outdoor events for all ages during a 10-day winter extravaganza. Annually, the last weekend in January through the first weekend in February. Est attendance: 100,000. For info: Donna Gregg, Bon Soo Winter Carnival Inc, PO Box 781, Sault Ste. Marie, Ont, Canada P6A 5N3. Phone: (705) 759-3000. Fax: (705) 759-6950.

CHARLES I EXECUTION: ANNIVERSARY. Jan 30. English king beheaded by order of Parliament under Oliver Cromwell Jan 30, 1649; considered a martyr by some.

CHOCOLATES OF THE WORLD. Jan 30–31. Cleveland, OH. Sample and learn all about chocolate and its impact on history around the globe. Silent auction, door prizes and workshops. Est attendance: 1,000. For info: Cleveland Council on World Affairs, 75 Public Sq, Cleveland, OH 44113-2001. Phone: (216) 781-3730. Fax: (216) 781-2729. Email: info@ccwa.org. WWW: http://www.ccwa.org

DAYTONA USA 2-HOUR ENDURANCE CHAMPIONSHIP. Jan 30. Daytona International Speedway, Daytona Beach, FL. 3rd annual showroom-stock endurance race. For info: Daytona Intl Speedway, PO Box 2801, Daytona Beach, FL 32120-2801. Phone: (904) 947-6782 or for tickets (904) 254-2700. Fax: (904) 947-6791. WWW: http://www.daytonausa.com

FIRST BRAWL IN THE US HOUSE OF REPRESENTATIVES: 200th ANNIVERSARY. Jan 30, 1798. The first brawl to break out on the floor of the US House of Representatives occurred in Philadelphia, PA, on Jan 30, 1798. The fight was precipitated by an argument between Matthew Lyon of Vermont and Roger Griswold of Connecticut. Lyon spat in Griswold's face. Although a resolution to expel Lyon was introduced, the measure failed and Lyon maintained his seat.

FLORIDA WILDLIFE EXPOSITION. Jan 30–Feb 1. Orlando Centroplex, Expo Centre, Orlando, FL. Featuring more than 200 of the nation's finest wildlife artists, wood sculptors, conservation groups and live wildlife exhibits. Est attendance: 9,600. For info: Michael E. Kessler, Pres, Florida Wildlife Exposition Inc, PO Box 15693, Sarasota, FL 34277. Phone: (941) 364-9453. Fax: (941) 364-9453.

GANDHI, MOHANDAS: ASSASSINATION: 50th ANNIVERSARY. Jan 30, 1948. Indian religious and political leader, assassinated at New Delhi, India, Jan 30, 1948. The assassin was a Hindu extremist, Ram Naturam. See also: "Gandhi, Mohandas Karamchand (Mahatma): Birth Anniversary" (Oct 2).

MACKINAW MUSH SLED DOG RACE. Jan 30–Feb 1. Old Railroad Depot, Mackinaw City, MI. Sanctioned ISDA event with purse and various classes. Races start at 9 each morning. Also children's events and weight pull. Annually, the first weekend in February. Est attendance: 4,000. For info: Mackinaw Area Tourist Bureau, 706 S Huron, Mackinaw City, MI 49701. Phone: (616) 436-5664. Fax: (616) 436-5991. Email: bjones@freeway.net.

MARYLAND ADOPTS ARTICLES OF CONFEDERATION: ANNIVERSARY. Jan 30, 1781. Maryland became the last of the 13 original states to adopt the Articles of Confederation.

McCALL WINTER CARNIVAL. Jan 30–Feb 8. McCall, ID. Come beat the winter blahs at this celebration of winter that includes ice sculptures, dances, food, snowmobile races, sled dog races, beard contest, parade and a sculpting contest. Est attendance: 20,000. For info: McCall Chamber of Commerce, PO Box D, McCall, ID 83638. Phone: (208) 634-7631 or (800) 260-5130. Fax: (208) 634-7752. Email: mccallcc@cyberhighway.net. WWW: http://www.mccall-1achamber.org

January 1998

S	M	T	W	T	F	S
				1	2	3
4	5	6	7	8	9	10
11	12	13	14	15	16	17
18	19	20	21	22	23	24
25	26	27	28	29	30	31

NATIONAL INANE ANSWERING MESSAGE DAY. Jan 30. Annually, the day set aside to change, shorten, replace or delete those ridiculous and/or annoying answering machine messages that waste the time of anyone who must listen to them. [© 1997 by WPL]. For info: Thomas and Ruth Roy, Wellness Permission League, PO Box 662, Mount Gretna, PA 17064-0662. Phone: (500) 437-5104 or (717) 964-1308. Fax: (717) 964-1335.

NC RV AND CAMPING SHOW. Jan 30–Feb 1. Charlotte Merchandise Mart, Charlotte, NC. A display of the latest in recreation vehicles and accessories by various dealers. Est attendance: 14,000. For info: Apple Rock Advertising & Promotion, 1200 Eastchester Dr, High Point, NC 27265. Phone: (910) 881-7100. Fax: (910) 883-7198.

RAF BOMBS HITLER CELEBRATION: 55th ANNIVERSARY. Jan 30, 1943. British Royal Air Force Mosquito bombers ran a daylight raid on Berlin timed to coincide with a speech being given by Joseph Goebbels in honor of Hitler's 10th year in power.

ROOSEVELT, FRANKLIN DELANO: BIRTH ANNIVERSARY. Jan 30, 1882. 32nd president of the US (Mar 4, 1933–Apr 12, 1945). The only president to serve more than two terms, FDR was elected four times. He supported the Allies in WW II before the US entered the struggle by supplying them with war materials through the Lend-Lease Act; he became deeply involved in broad decision making after the Japanese attack on Pearl Harbor on Dec 7, 1941. Born at Hyde Park, NY, he died a few months into his fourth term on Apr 12, 1945, at Warm Springs, GA. His birthday is observed as a holiday in Kentucky.

SAINT PAUL WINTER CARNIVAL. Jan 30–Feb 8. St. Paul, MN. Minnesota's largest tourist attraction and the nation's oldest and largest winter festival. The 112-year-old St. Paul Winter Carnival provides 10 fun-filled days with more than 100 indoor and outdoor events celebrating the thrills and chills of wintertime fun. Est attendance: 1,000,000. For info: Saint Paul Festival and Heritage Foundation, 332 Minnesota St, Ste 102E, St. Paul, MN 55101. Phone: (612) 223-4700. Fax: (612) 223-4707. Email: carnival@stpaul.gov.

TET OFFENSIVE BEGINS: 30th ANNIVERSARY. Jan 30, 1968. After calling for a cease-fire during the Tet holiday celebrations, North Vietnam and the National Liberation Front launched a major offensive throughout South Vietnam on that holiday. The attacks erupted in 36 of the 44 provincial capitals and 5 of the 6 major cities. In addition, the Viet Cong attacked the US embassy in Saigon, Tan Son Nhut Air Base, the presidential palace and South Vietnamese general staff headquarters. Costing as many as 40,000 battlefield deaths, the offensive was a tactical defeat for the Viet Cong and North Vietnam. The South Vietnamese held their ground and the US was able to airlift troops into the critical areas and quickly regain control. However, the offensive is credited as a strategic success in that it continued the demoralization of American public opinion. After Tet, American policy toward Vietnam shifted from winning the war to seeking an honorable way out.

TUCHMAN, BARBARA W.: BIRTH ANNIVERSARY. Jan 30, 1912. Historian and journalist Barbara Tuchman's most famous works were her Pulitzer Prize–winning books *The Guns of August* (1962) and *Stilwell and the American Experience in China, 1911–45* (1971). Tuchman was known for making history live, never dry. Other well-known books included *The Proud Tower* (1966) and *The First Salute* (1988). Barbara Wertheim Tuchman was born at New York, NY and died at Greenwich, CT, Feb 6, 1988.

WINTERFEST. Jan 30–Feb 1 (Also Feb 6–8). Ludington, MI. Ice and snow sculpture competition, indoor sidewalk sale, hot air balloon race, antique show and sale, marathon race and cross country ski race. Est attendance: 20,000. For info: Ludington Area Chamber of Commerce, 5827 W US 10, Ludington, MI 49431. Phone: (800) 542-4600. Fax: (616) 845-6857. Email: suelacvb@aol.com. WWW: http://www.ludingtoncvb.com

BIRTHDAYS TODAY

Brett Butler, 40, comedienne, actress ("Grace Under Fire"), born Montgomery, AL, Jan 30, 1958.

Richard B. Cheney, 57, US Secretary of Defense in Bush administration, born Lincoln, NE, Jan 30, 1941.

Phil Collins, 47, musician, singer, songwriter, born Chiswick, England, Jan 30, 1951.

Charles S. Dutton, 47, actor ("Roc," *Mississippi Masala, Menace II Society*), born Baltimore, MD, Jan 30, 1951.

Gene Hackman, 68, actor (*The French Connection, Bonnie and Clyde, Unforgiven*), born San Bernardino, CA, Jan 30, 1930.

Dorothy Malone, 73, actress ("Peyton Place"; Oscar for *Written on the Wind*), born Chicago, IL, Jan 30, 1925.

Dick Martin, 76, comedian, actor (Emmy for "Rowan & Martin's Laugh-In"), born Detroit, MI, Jan 30, 1922.

Frank O'Bannon, 68, Governor of Indiana (D), born Louisville, KY, Jan 30, 1930.

Vanessa Redgrave, 61, actress (*Mary, Queen of Scots; Julia*), born London, England, Jan 30, 1937.

Boris Spassky, 61, chess player, journalist, born Leningrad, USSR, Jan 30, 1937.

Curtis Northrop Strange, 43, golfer, born Norfolk, VA, Jan 30, 1955.

Jody Watley, 37, singer, born Chicago, IL, Jan 30, 1961.

JANUARY 31 — SATURDAY

Day 31 — 334 Remaining

BLACK HILLS STOCK SHOW AND RODEO. Jan 31–Feb 9. Rapid City, SD. Events include PRCA rodeos, ranch rodeo, timed sheepdog trials, draft horse events, livestock shows and sales, buffalo show and sale, bucking horse and bull sale, stockman banquet and ball, world champion wild-horse races and commercial exhibits. Est attendance: 250,000. For info: Central States Fair, 800 San Francisco, Rapid City, SD 57701. Phone: (605) 342-8325.

BROOKFIELD ICE HARVEST. Jan 31. Brookfield, VT. Demonstrations of ice harvesting using the original equipment near the Brookfield Floating Bridge, one of only two such bridges remaining in the US today. Annually, the last Saturday in January. Est attendance: 1,000. For info: Al Wilder, PO Box 105, Brookfield, VT 05036. Phone: (802) 276-3959.

CANADA: ROBBIE BURNS DINNER. Jan 31. Dinner honoring Scottish poet Robert Burns with bagpipe music and haggis. For info: Royal Canadian Legion, Bracebridge Chamber of Commerce, 1-1 Manitoba St, Canada P1L-1S4. Phone: (705) 645-8500.

CANADA'S COLDEST RECORDED TEMPERATURE: ANNIVERSARY. Jan 31, 1947. At Whitehorse, in Canada's Yukon Territory, a temperature of 62 degrees below zero (Fahrenheit) was recorded on Jan 31, 1947, a record low for all of Canada's provinces and territories.

GERMAN SURRENDER AT STALINGRAD: 55th ANNIVERSARY. Jan 31, 1943. Two pockets of starving German soldiers remained in Stalingrad on this date. They had received no supplies since Soviet soldiers had encircled the city the previous November. Friedrich von Paulus, whom Hitler had promoted to field marshal only the day before, was forced to seek surrender terms, thereby becoming the first German marshal to surrender. Hitler was furious with von Paulus, believing he should have preferred suicide to surrender. Two days later the last German resistance in Stalingrad ended. Approximately 160,000 Germans died in the Stalingrad Battle; 34,000 were evacuated by air. Of the 90,000 captured and sent to Siberia on foot, tens of thousands died on the way. This Allied victory is generally considered the psychological turning point of the war.

GREY, ZANE: BIRTH ANNIVERSARY. Jan 31, 1872. Zane Grey (original name Pearl Grey), American dentist and prolific author of tales of the old west, was born at Zanesville, OH. Grey eventually wrote more than 80 books that were translated into many languages and sold more than 10 million copies. The novel *Riders of the Purple Sage* (1912) was the most popular. Grey died Oct 23, 1939, at Altadena, CA.

IRONCLADS BATTLE IN CHARLESTON HARBOR: ANNIVERSARY. Jan 31, 1863. Two Confederate ironclad ships, the *Chicora* and *Palmetto State*, severely damaged two Union ships participating in the blockade of Charleston, SC, harbor. Despite the successful battle, the harbor remained under blockade, although the South declared otherwise.

McDONALD'S INVADES THE SOVIET UNION: ANNIVERSARY. Jan 31, 1990. McDonald's Corporation opened its first fast food restaurant in the Soviet Union.

McKINLEY DAY. Jan 31. McKinley Museum, Canton, OH. A celebration of the birth anniversary of President William McKinley with special activities all day. For info: McKinley Museum, 800 McKinley Monument Dr NW, Canton, OH 44711. Phone: (330) 455-7043.

MOORE, GARRY: BIRTH ANNIVERSARY. Jan 31, 1915. American television host Garry Moore was born Thomas Garrison Morfit at Baltimore, MD. His best known shows were "I've Got a Secret" (1952–67) and "To Tell the Truth" (1969–76). He gave Carol Burnett her break on TV when he made her a regular on "The Garry Moore Show." He died on Nov 28, 1993, at Hilton Head Island, SC.

NAURU: NATIONAL HOLIDAY. Jan 31. Republic of Nauru.

"NIGHT HEAT" TV PREMIERE: ANNIVERSARY. Jan 31, 1985. A joint production of the Canadian network CTV and CBS, "Night Heat" was filmed in a disguised Toronto made to represent any big city. The series, which took place mainly after hours, was about two urban cops assigned to the Mid-South precinct and the columnist assigned to cover their cases. Sonny Grosso, a former cop himself, and Larry Jacobson served as producers. Cast principals included: Scott Hylands as veteran detective Kevin O'Brien; Jeff Wincott as his partner, Frank Giambone; and Allan Royal as reporter Tom Kirkwood.

NORTHGATE MALL BRIDAL SHOW & EXPO. Jan 31–Feb 1. Northgate Mall, Cincinnati, OH. One of the longest-running bridal shows in the area. Features bridal/trousseau fashion shows throughout the weekend. Exhibitors include florists, photographers, videographers, caterers, travel agents, DJs, reception halls, limousine services and entertainment agencies. For info: Northgate Mall Information Center, 9501 Colerain Ave, Cincinnati, OH 45251. Phone: (513) 385-5600.

RAILROAD AND HOBBY SHOW. Jan 31–Feb 1. West Springfield, MA. Now expanded to two buildings, nearly 4½ acres with more than 30 operating layouts; displays; art; railroadiana; Shortline, Tourist and Class 1 railroads; flea market, dealers and more. Est attendance: 22,000. For info: Robert Buck, PO Box 718, Warren, MA 01083-0718. Phone: (413) 436-0242.

ROBINSON, JACKIE: BIRTH ANNIVERSARY. Jan 31. Jack Roosevelt Robinson, athlete and business executive, first black to enter professional major league baseball (Brooklyn Dodgers, 1947). Born at Cairo, GA, Jan 31, 1919. Played with Brooklyn Dodgers 1947–1956. Voted National League's Most Valuable Player in 1949 and elected to the Baseball Hall of Fame in 1962. Died at Stamford, CT, Oct 24, 1972. A special commemorative Jackie Robinson postage stamp was issued in the Black Heritage USA Series in 1982.

ROLEX 24 AT DAYTONA. Jan 31–Feb 1. Daytona International Speedway, Daytona Beach, FL. 36th annual running of the most prestigious endurance race in North America (exotic purpose-built race cars). Sponsor: Rolex Watch. For info: Daytona Intl Speedway, PO Box 2801, Daytona Beach, FL 32120-2801. Phone: (904) 947-6782 or for tickets (904) 253-RACE (7223). Fax: (904) 947-6791.

SCHUBERT, FRANZ: BIRTH ANNIVERSARY. Jan 31, 1797. Composer, born at Vienna, Austria, and died there of typhus on Nov 19, 1828, at age 31. Buried, at his request, near the grave of Beethoven. Schubert last worked on his "Unfinished Symphony" (No. 8) in 1822. On the 100th anniversary of his death in 1928 a $10,000 prize was offered to "finish" the work. The protests were so great that the offer was withdrawn.

SCOTCH TAPE DEVELOPED. Jan 31, 1928. Scotch tape developed by Richard Drew, of the 3M Company.

SHOW OF WHEELS. Jan 31–Feb 1. Lea County Fairgrounds, Lovington, NM. Car show presented by the Lovington Chamber of Commerce. Featuring antiques, classics, streetrods, motorcycles and minitrucks. A swapmeet, commercial exhibits and games will be an exciting part of the show. RV parking available. For info: Lovington Chamber of Commerce, PO Box 1347, Lovington, NM 88260. Phone: (505) 396-5311 or Ron Carson (505) 396-3661. Fax: (505) 396-2823.

SLOVIK, EDDIE D.: EXECUTION ANNIVERSARY. Jan 31, 1945. Anniversary of execution by firing squad of 24-year-old Private Eddie D. Slovik. Born at Detroit, MI, Feb 18, 1920, Slovik was assigned to Company G, 109th Infantry, 28th Division, US Army. His death sentence, the first for desertion since the Civil War, has been a subject of controversy since. First buried in France, Slovik's remains were exhumed in 1987 for reburial beside his wife, Antoinette, who died in 1979, after years of effort to clear Slovik's name and have his body returned to the US.

SPACE MILESTONE: *APOLLO 14* (US). Jan 31, 1971. Launch date of *Apollo 14*. Five days later on Feb 5 astronauts Alan B. Shepard, Jr, and Edgar D. Mitchell landed on the moon (Lunar Module *Antares*). Command Module *Kitty Hawk* was piloted by Stuart A. Roosa. Pacific splashdown on Feb 9.

SPACE MILESTONE: *LUNA 9* (USSR). Jan 31, 1966. Launch of mission that accomplished the first soft landing on the moon three days later on Feb 3. Transmitted photos.

SPACE MILESTONE: PROJECT MERCURY TEST (US). Jan 31, 1961. Launched on this date, Project Mercury accomplished the first US recovery of a large animal from space. Ham, the chimpanzee, successfully transmitted signals.

SPACE MILESTONE: UNITED STATES SPACE EXPLORATION BEGINS: 40th ANNIVERSARY. Jan 31, 1958. *Explorer I*, the first successful US satellite, was launched on this date. Weighing 31 lbs, *Explorer I* transmitted radio signals until May 23, 1958, and discovered the Van Allen Belt. Its orbit decayed Mar 31, 1970.

SPEEDWEEKS. Jan 31–Feb 15. Daytona International Speedway, Daytona Beach, FL. The city becomes the "World Center of Racing" with three weekends of competition, including the Daytona 500. For info: Public Relations, Daytona Intl Speedway, Box 2801, Daytona Beach, FL 32120-2801. Phone: (904) 947-6782 or for tickets (904) 253-RACE (7223). Fax: (904) 947-6791. WWW: http://www.daytonausa.com

BIRTHDAYS TODAY

Ernest (Ernie) Banks, 67, Baseball Hall of Fame shortstop, born Dallas, TX, Jan 31, 1931.

Carol Channing (Carol Channing Lowe), 75, actress (stage: *Hello, Dolly!; Thoroughly Modern Millie*), born Seattle, WA, Jan 31, 1923.

Johnny (Rotten) Lydon, 42, singer (lead with controversial yet revered band the Sex Pistols 1975–77; then formed Public Image Ltd later in 1977), born near London, England, Jan 31, 1956.

Norman Mailer, 75, author (*The Executioner's Song, The Naked and the Dead*), born Long Branch, NJ, Jan 31, 1923.

Stuart Margolin, 58, actor, director, writer ("The Rockford Files" [Emmy Awards, 1979, 1980], *The Big Blue, S.O.B.*), born Davenport, IA, Jan 31, 1940.

Suzanne Pleshette, 61, actress (Emily Hartley in "The Bob Newhart Show"), born New York, NY, Jan 31, 1937.

Lynn Nolan Ryan, 51, former baseball player, born Refugio, TX, Jan 31, 1947.

Jean Simmons, 69, actress (*Black Narcissus, The Robe, Elmer Gantry*), born London, England, Jan 31, 1929.

Jessica Walter, 54, actress ("Amy Prentiss," *Play Misty for Me, The Flamingo Kid*), born Brooklyn, NY, Jan 31, 1944.

Februarie.

FEBRUARY 1 — SUNDAY

Day 32 — 333 Remaining

AMD AWARENESS MONTH. Feb 1–28. More than 13 million Americans age 40 and older show signs of age-related macular degeneration. AMD is now a leading cause of blindness among older Americans. During this month, Prevent Blindness America (formerly known as National Society to Prevent Blindness) steps up its efforts to inform people about AMD. For info: Marketing Dept, Prevent Blindness America, 500 E Remington Rd, Schaumburg, IL 60173. Phone: (800) 331-2020.

AMERICAN HEART MONTH. Feb 1–28. Volunteers across the country spend one to four weeks canvassing neighborhoods and providing educational information about heart disease and stroke. For info: Cathy Yarbrough, News Media Relations, American Heart Association, 7272 Greenville Ave, Dallas, TX 75231. Phone: (800) AHA-USA1. Fax: (214) 369-3685. WWW: http://www.americanheart.org

★**AMERICAN HEART MONTH.** Feb 1–28. Presidential Proclamation always issued each year for February since 1964. (PL88–254 of Dec 30, 1963.)

AMERICAN HISTORY MONTH. Feb 1–28. Massachusetts.

AN AFFAIR TO REMEMBER MONTH. Feb 1–28. Make your romance sizzle by having an affair with your mate this month. Details and creative romantic ideas on having a marital (not extramarital) affair are available. Annually, in February. For info: Rose Smith, Pres, The Institute of Monogamy, 4900 Mesa Bonita Ct NW, Albuquerque, NM 87120. Phone: (505) 899-3121.

BLACK HISTORY MONTH. Feb 1–28. Traditionally the month containing Abraham Lincoln's birthday (Feb 12) and Frederick Douglass's presumed birthday (Feb 14). Observance of a special period to recognize achievements and contributions by African-Americans dates from Febuary 1926, when it was launched by Dr. Carter G. Woodson and others. Variously designated Negro History, Black History, Afro-American History, African-American History, Black Heritage and Black Expressions, the observance period was initially one week, but since 1976 the entire month of February.

BLACK MARIA STUDIO: ANNIVERSARY. Feb 1, 1893. The first moving picture studio was completed, built on Thomas Edison's laboratory compound in West Orange, NJ, at a cost of less than $700. The wooden structure of irregular oblong shape was covered with black tar paper. It had a sharply sloping roof hinged at one edge so that half of it could be raised to admit sunlight. Fifty feet in length, it was mounted on a pivot enabling it to be swung around to follow the changing position of the sun. There was a stage draped in black at one end of the single room. Though the structure was officially called a Kinetographic Theater, it was nicknamed the "Black Maria" because it resembled an old-fashioned police wagon. It was described as "hot and cramped" by "Gentleman" Jim Corbett, the pugilistic idol who was the subject of an early movie made in the studio.

February 1998	S	M	T	W	T	F	S
	1	2	3	4	5	6	7
	8	9	10	11	12	13	14
	15	16	17	18	19	20	21
	22	23	24	25	26	27	28

BOMBECK, ERMA: BIRTH ANNIVERSARY. Feb 1, 1927. Humorist and writer born at Dayton, OH. Authored many books, including *The Grass Is Always Greener Over the Septic Tank*. Bombeck died at San Francisco, CA, Apr 22, 1996.

BRIDAL FAIR AND WOMEN'S EXPO. Feb 1. New Castle, PA. Bridal vendors, wedding vendors, fashion show and giveaways. Annually, the first Sunday in February. Est attendance: 1,500. For info: Bob McCracken, Gen Mgr, 1906 Wilmington Rd, New Castle, PA 16105. Phone: (412) 656-1200. Fax: (412) 656-6397.

CAR INSURANCE FIRST ISSUED. Feb 1, 1898. Travelers Insurance Co. issued the first car insurace against accidents with horses.

CARAWAY, HATTIE WYATT: BIRTH ANNIVERSARY. Feb 1, 1878. Born in Bakersville, TN, Hattie Caraway became a US senator from Arkansas when her husband died in 1931 and she was appointed to fill out his term. The following year she ran for the seat herself and became the first woman elected to the US Senate. She served 14 years there, becoming an adept and tireless legislator (once introducing 43 bills on the same day) who worked for women's rights (once cosponsoring an equal rights amendment), supported New Deal policies as well as Prohibition and opposed the increasing influence of lobbyists. Caraway died at Falls Church, VA, Dec 21, 1950.

CELEBRATION OF CHOCOLATE. Feb 1–28. Oregon, IL. Afternoon and evening reservations for private Chocolate Tea Parties. Selection of hot cocoas, imported and domestic boxed chocolates, specialty handcrafted candy and fresh-baked goods from the 1800s, gourmet fudge collection. Est attendance: 1,000. For info: Sharon Burdick, Innkeeper, Pinehill Bed & Breakfast, 400 Mix St, Oregon, IL 61061. Phone: (815) 732-2061.

CHINESE LUNAR NEW YEAR FESTIVAL: YEAR OF THE TIGER (FU-HU, OR GIM MIEW). Feb 1. Baltimore, MD. Dragon/Lion (Mo Tze) performance, Chinese culture, indoor program, evensong and traditions. Chinese dinner by advance subscription reservation ($9) on Lunar New Year, Jan 2. Est attendance: 500. For info: Lillian Lee Kim, Grace and St. Peter's Parish, 524 Anneslie Rd, Baltimore, MD 21212-2009. Phone: (410) 539-1395 or (410) 377-8143.

☆ ☆ ☆

CIRCLE K INTERNATIONAL WEEK. Feb 1–7. To highlight the work and activities of Circle K for the general public. Circle K is a sponsored program of Kiwanis International for college students. Annually, the first full week of February. For info: Circle K Intl, 3636 Woodview Trace, Indianapolis, IN 46268-3196. Phone: (317) 875-8755. Fax: (317) 879-0204. Email: circlek@iquest.net.

CLEAR LAKE EPICUREAN EVENING. Feb 1. Webster, TX, at Baybrook Mall. Come and enjoy tasting food from area restaurants while being entertained by local performers. For info: Shari Liebman, Clear Lake Area Chamber of Commerce, 1201 Nasa Rd One, Houston, TX 77058. Phone: (281) 488-7676. Fax: (281) 488-8981.

CREATIVE ROMANCE MONTH. Feb 1–28. To encourage couples to keep the sizzle in their relationships by celebrating romance in unique ways; to remind lovers that creativity and a sprinkle of intrigue can turn any day into a romantic adventure. Free tip sheets are available. For info: Eileen Buchheim, Founder, Celebrate Romance, 18 Altimira, Coto De Caza, CA 92679. Phone: (714) 459-7620. To arrange media interviews, call Suzanne Friendly at (714) 459-7621.

DEAR BESS: LOVE LETTERS FROM THE PRESIDENT: EXHIBITION. Feb 1–28. Truman Library, Independence, MO. An exhibition highlighting the personal relationship between the Trumans as illustrated in almost 50 years of personal letters from Harry to Bess. For info: Larry J. Hackman, Dir, Harry S. Truman Library, US Hwy 24 and Delaware St, Independence, MO 64050-1798. Phone: (816) 833-1400 or (800) 833-1225. Fax: (816) 833-4368.
Email: library@truman.nara.gov.
WWW: http://sunsite.unc.edu/lia/president/truman.html

FESTIVAL OF THE NORTH. Feb 1–28. Ketchikan, AK. A cultural event encompassing an annual Wearable Art Show, performing, visual and literary arts, including a myriad of workshops. Annually, the month of February. Est attendance: 1,000. For info: Ketchikan Area Arts and Humanities Council, 338 Main St, Ketchikan, AK 99901. Phone: (907) 225-2211. Fax: (907) 225-4330.

FLAGSTAFF WINTERFEST. Feb 1–28. Flagstaff, AZ. This winter festival, now in its 12th year, showcases Flagstaff's mountain wonderland with events including sled dog races, alpine and nordic ski activities, snow games, sleigh rides, snowmobile drag races, concerts, historic walking tours, Native American storytelling and a parade. Est attendance: 20,000. For info: Ann Dunlop, Winterfest Coordinator, Flagstaff Chamber of Commerce, 101 W Rte 66, Flagstaff, AZ 86001. Phone: (800) 842-7293. Fax: (520) 779-1209. Email: chamber@flagstaff.az.us.
WWW: http://www.flagstaff.az.us

FORD, JOHN: BIRTH ANNIVERSARY. Feb 1, 1895. Film director John Ford was born at Cape Elizabeth, ME, as Sean Aloysius O'Feeney; he changed his name after moving to Hollywood. Ford won his first Academy Award in 1935 for *The Informer*. Among his many other films: *The Plough and the Stars, Stagecoach, Young Mr. Lincoln, The Grapes of Wrath, How Green Was My Valley, Rio Grande, The Quiet Man, What Price Glory?, The Searchers, Mister Roberts* and *The Man Who Shot Liberty Valance*. During World War II he served as chief of the Field Photographic Branch of the OSS. Two of his documentaries made during the war earned him Academy Awards. He died on Aug 31, 1973, at Palm Desert, CA.

FREEDOM DAY: ANNIVERSARY. Feb 1. Anniversary of President Abraham Lincoln's approval, Feb 1, 1865, of the 13th Amendment to the US Constitution (abolishing slavery): "1. Neither slavery nor involuntary servitude, except as a punishment for crime whereof the party shall have been duly convicted, shall exist within the United States or any place subject to their jurisdiction. 2. Congress shall have power to enforce this article by appropriate legislation." The amendment had been proposed by the Congress on Jan 31, 1865; ratification was completed Dec 18, 1865.

February 1998

S	M	T	W	T	F	S
1	2	3	4	5	6	7
8	9	10	11	12	13	14
15	16	17	18	19	20	21
22	23	24	25	26	27	28

GABLE, CLARK: BIRTH ANNIVERSARY. Feb 1. Actor William Clark Gable's first film was *The Painted Desert* in 1931 during the era when talking films were replacing silent films. He won an Academy Award for his role in the comedy *It Happened One Night*, which established him as a romantic screen idol. Other films included *China Seas, Mutiny on the Bounty, Saratoga, Command Decision, Run Silent Run Deep* and *Gone with the Wind*, for which his casting as Rhett Butler seemed a foregone conclusion due to his popularity as the acknowledged "King of Movies." Gable was born on Feb 1, 1901, at Cadiz, OH, and died on Nov 16, 1960, shortly after completing his last film, Arthur Miller's *The Misfits*, in which he starred with Marilyn Monroe.

"GENERAL ELECTRIC THEATER" TV PREMIERE: 45th ANNIVERSARY. Feb 1, 1953. CBS's half-hour dramatic anthology series was hosted by Ronald Reagan (in between his movie and political careers). Making their television debuts were Joseph Cotten (1954); Fred MacMurray, James Stewart and Myrna Loy (1955); Bette Davis, Anne Baxter, Tony Curtis and Fred Astaire (1957); Sammy Davis Jr (1958); and Gene Tierney (1960). Other memorable stars who appeared on the series include: Joan Crawford, Harry Belafonte, Rosalind Russell, Ernie Kovacs, the Marx Brothers, and Nancy Davis Reagan, who starred with her husband in the premonitory episode titled "A Turkey for the President" (1958).

GLOBAL FAMILY FEAST WEEK. Feb 1–7. To introduce children and families to foods of the world. Try foods from a different continent each day this week, and share your own family's ethnic recipes with other families of different national origins. To sit at another's table is truly the spice of life. Annually, the first full week in February, starting on Sunday. For info: Black Swan Enterprises Inc, 2559 N Wabel Ave, Milwaukee, WI 53211. Phone: (414) 332-5993. Fax: (414) 332-6088.

GREENSBORO SIT-IN: ANNIVERSARY. Feb 1. Commercial discrimination against blacks and other minorities provoked a nonviolent protest, Feb 1, 1960. In Greensboro, NC, four students from the Agricultural and Technical College at Greensboro (Ezell Blair, Jr, Franklin McCain, Joseph McNeill and David Richmond) sat down at a Woolworth store lunch counter and ordered coffee. Refused service, they remained all day. The following days similar sit-ins took place at the Woolworth lunch counter. Before the week was over they were joined by a few white students. The protest spread rapidly, especially in southern states. More than 1,600 persons were arrested before the year was over for participating in sit-ins. Civil rights for all became a cause for thousands of students and activists. In response, equal accommodation regardless of race reached lunch counters, hotels and business establishments in thousands of places where it had been unknown before.

INTERNATIONAL BOOST SELF-ESTEEM MONTH. Feb 1–28. A month to focus on the importance of nurturing and cultivating self-esteem to beat the winter blahs, to boost morale and to inspire yourself and others to seize new challenges. For info: Valla Dana Fotiades, M.Ed., PO Box 812, West Side Stn, Worcester, MA 01602-0812. Phone: (508) 799-9860.
Email: eblvalla@aol.com.

INTERNATIONAL EMBROIDERY MONTH. Feb 1–28. A time to promote commercial monogramming and embroidery and heighten apparel consumers' awareness of the role that this industry plays in fashion, home furnishings, advertising and sports around the world. For info: Melissa J. Thompson Maher, Editor, Stitches Magazine, 5660 Greenwood Plaza Blvd, Ste 350, Englewood, CO 80111. Phone: (303) 793-0448. Fax: (303) 793-0454.

"LATE NIGHT WITH DAVID LETTERMAN" TV PREMIERE: ANNIVERSARY. Feb 1, 1982. This is where it all began: the stupid pet tricks, stupid human tricks, and the legendary top ten lists. "Late Night" premiered on NBC as a talk/variety show appearing after "The Tonight Show with Johnny Carson." Host David Letterman was known for his irreverent sense of humor and daffy antics. The offbeat show attained cult status among college crowds and insomniacs, as many tuned in to see a Velcro-suited Letterman throwing himself to a wall. The show also featured bandleader-sidekick Paul Shaffer; writer Chris Elliott; and Calvert DeForest as geezer Larry "Bud" Melman. In 1993, Letterman made a highly publicized exit from NBC and began hosting "The Late Show" on CBS.

LOW VISION AWARENESS MONTH. Feb 1–28. Low vision can be caused by macular degeneration, diabetic retinopathy and glaucoma. While there are no cures for these conditions, low vision aids can help make the most of remaining vision. Prevent Blindness America® provides information on eye disease warning signs and on low vision aids. For info: Prevent Blindness America®, 500 Remington Rd, Schaumburg, IL 60173. Phone: (800) 331-2020. Fax: (847) 843-8458.
WWW: http://www.prevent-blindness.org

MARFAN SYNDROME AWARENESS MONTH. Feb 1–28. Volunteers across the country distribute heart-shaped objects and educational information about Marfan syndrome, and related connective tissue disorders that can result in life-threatening cardiovascular problems as well as orthopedic and ophthalmologic handicaps; it affects about 200,000 Americans. Annually, the month of February. For info: Cathie Tsuchiya, National Marfan Foundation, 382 Main St, Port Washington, NY 11050. Phone: (800) 862-7326 or (516) 883-8712. Fax: (516) 883-8040. Email: staff@marfar.org. WWW: http://www.marfar.org

NATIONAL CHERRY MONTH. Feb 1–28. To publicize the colorful red tart cherry. Recipes, posters and table tents available. For info: Jane Baker, Mktg Dir, Cherry Marketing Institute, PO Box 30285, Lansing, MI 48909-7785. Phone: (517) 669-4264. Fax: (517) 669-3354. Email: jbaker@cherrymkt.org. WWW: http://www.cherrymkt.org

NATIONAL CHILDREN'S DENTAL HEALTH MONTH. Feb 1–28. To increase dental awareness and stress the importance of regular dental care. For info: American Dental Assn, 211 E Chicago Ave, Chicago, IL 60611. To purchase materials, phone in US: (800) 947-4746. WWW: http://www.ada.org

★**NATIONAL FREEDOM DAY.** Feb 1. Presidential Proclamation 2824, Jan 25, 1949, covers all succeeding years (PL80–842 of June 30, 1948).

NATIONAL SIGN UP FOR SUMMER CAMP MONTH. Feb 1–28. Every year more than 6 million children continue a national tradition by attending day or resident camps. Building self-confidence, learning new skills and making memories that last a lifetime are just a few examples of what makes camp special and why camp does children a world of good. To find the right program, parents begin looking at summer camps during this month—and sign their children up while there are still vacancies. For info: Public Relations, American Camping Assn, 5000 State Rd 67N, Martinsville, IN 46151. Phone: (765) 342-8456. Email: bschultz@aca-camps.org. WWW: http://www.aca-camps.org. For a guide to accredited camps, call (800) 428-CAMPS.

NATIONAL WEDDINGS MONTH. Feb 1–28. As the "wedding season" gets into high gear, this observance is to call attention to the fact that approximately 2.5 million weddings are celebrated in the US each year. For info: Gerard J. Monaghan, Pres, Assn of Bridal Consultants, 200 Chestnutland Rd, New Milford, CT 06776-2521. Phone: (860) 355-0464. Fax: (860) 354-1404. Email: bridalassn@.com.
WWW: http://www.bridalnet.com

NATIONAL WILD BIRD FEEDING MONTH. Feb 1–28. To recognize that February is one of the most difficult winter months in much of the US for birds to survive in the wild, and to encourage people to provide food, water and shelter to supplement the wild birds' natural diet of weed seeds and harmful insects. For info: Sue Wells, Exec Dir, National Bird-Feeding Society, PO Box 236, Northbrook, IL 60065-0023. Phone: (847) 272-0135.

ORCHID DISPLAY. Feb 1–22. Missouri Botanical Garden, St. Louis, MO. Spectacular display of the Garden's vast orchid collection design in a surrealistic theme using life-sized "Orchid People." For info: Missouri Botanical Garden, 4344 Shaw Blvd, St. Louis, MO 63110. Phone: (314) 577-5100 or (800) 642-8842. WWW: http://www.mobot.org

PLANT THE SEEDS OF GREATNESS MONTH. Feb 1–28. Think globally—build for the future—Plant the Seeds of Greatness. If you're unhappy with your present situation, discover how you can remove the barriers and make a change in your life for the better. Use the next 28 days to put to use your own unique prosperity consciousness and plant the seeds for your new career, life objectives or goals. Make a difference for yourself, your family, your business or your community. Take a chance, help yourself, or help another unlock the potential for success and plant the seeds of greatness. Get outside of your comfort zone and take action on your ideas and dreams. For info send a SASE: Lorrie Walters Marsiglio, Lorimar Communications, PO Box 284 CC, Wasco, IL 60183-0284. Phone: (630) 584-9368.

RETURN SHOPPING CARTS TO THE SUPERMARKET MONTH. Feb 1–28. Chicago, IL. A monthlong opportunity to return stolen shopping carts, milk crates, bread trays and ice cream baskets to supermarkets and avoid the increased food prices that these thefts cause. Annually, the month of February. Sponsor: Illinois Food Retailers Assn. For info: Anthony A. Dinolfo, Grocer, "Retired," 8148 S Homan Ave, Chicago, IL 60652. Phone: (773) 737-6540.

ROBINSON CRUSOE DAY. Feb 1. Anniversary of the rescue, Feb 1, 1709, of Alexander Selkirk, Scottish sailor who had been put ashore (in Sept 1704) on the uninhabited island Juan Fernandez at his own request after a quarrel with his captain. His adventures formed the basis for Daniel Defoe's book *Robinson Crusoe*. A day to be adventurous and self-reliant.

"THE SECRET STORM" TV PREMIERE: ANNIVERSARY. Feb 1, 1954. "The Secret Storm" lathered up homes for twenty years. The soap revolved around the Ames family in fictional Woodbridge and featured a variety of actors and actresses who have moved on to bigger things. Among them are: Bibi Besch, Roy Scheider, Diana Muldaur, Nicholas Coster, Robert Loggia, Laurence Luckinbill, Audrey Landers, Christina Crawford, Diane Ladd, Troy Donahue and Frances Sternhagen.

ST. LAURENT, LOUIS STEPHEN: BIRTH ANNIVERSARY. Feb 1, 1882. Canadian lawyer and prime minister, born at Compton, Quebec. Died at Quebec City, July 25, 1973.

SWITZERLAND: HOMSTROM. Feb 1. Scuol. Burning of straw men on poles as a symbol of winter's imminent departure. Annually, the first Sunday in February.

WISCONSIN FARM WOMAN OF THE YEAR MONTH. Feb 1–28. Recognition of farm women for their great importance and role in agriculture. They milk cows, do field work, run errands, pay bills, take care of children, make meals plus perform other household chores. Because of her dedication, a program has been developed to honor the farm woman. WWIB Radio holds a contest for county winners. One farm woman is chosen from the county winners to be The West Central Wisconsin Farm Woman of the Year. For info: Steve Flater, Sales Mgr, WWIB Radio, 2396 State Hwy 53, Chippewa Falls, WI 54729. Phone: (715) 723-1037.

WISE HEALTH CONSUMER MONTH. Feb 1–28. To promote safe and healthy medicinal products. For info: American Institute for Preventive Medicine, 30445 Northwestern Hwy, Ste 350, Farmington Hills, MI 48334. Phone: (810) 539-1800.

WOMEN'S HEART HEALTH DAY. Feb 1. As American Heart Month begins, here is a day to promote awareness that heart disease is the number one killer of American women. For info: Charlotte Libov, Editor, Women's Health Hot Line, 71 Judson Lane, Bethlehem, CT 06751. Phone: (203) 266-5904. Fax: (203) 266-5465. Email: char@softwaredesign.com.
WWW: http://www.softwaredesign.com/womens-health.html

WORLDWIDE INNOVATION MONTH. Feb 1–28. To promote innovation and creativity in all organizations around the world. The George Land World Class Innovator Award will be presented to winners at the Innovation Convergence being held in Santa Barbara, CA, Feb 22–26. For info: Joyce Wycoff, Exec Dir, Innovation Network, 34 E Sola, D101, Santa Barbara, CA 93101. Phone: (805) 965-8477. Fax: (805) 963-8220. Email: staff@thinksmar.com. WWW: http://www.thinksmart.com

"YOU ARE THERE" TV PREMIERE: 45th ANNIVERSARY. Feb 1, 1953. The program began as an inventive radio show in 1947. News correspondents would comb the annals of history and "interview" the movers and shakers of times past. Walter Cronkite hosted the series on CBS for four seasons. The show's concept was revived for a season in 1971 with Cronkite gearing the program towards children.

BIRTHDAYS TODAY

Theodore Roosevelt (T.R.) Dunn, 43, former basketball player, born Birmingham, AL, Feb 1, 1955.

Michael B. Enzi, 54, US Senator (R, Wyoming), born Bremerton, WA, Feb 1, 1944.

Don Everly, 61, singer, musician ("Bye Bye Love," "Wake Up Little Susie" with brother Phil), born Brownie, KY, Feb 1, 1937.

Sherilynn Fenn, 33, actress ("Twin Peaks," *Wild at Heart*), born Feb 1, 1965.

Sherman Hemsley, 60, actor ("All in the Family," "The Jeffersons," "Amen"), born Philadelphia, PA, Feb 1, 1938.

Rick James (James Johnson), 46, singer (King of Funk in the '80s, *Street Songs*), born Buffalo, NY, Feb 1, 1952.

Bob Jamieson, 55, broadcast journalist, born Streator, IL, Feb 1, 1943.

Terry Jones, 56, actor, director ("Monty Python's Flying Circus"), born Colwyn Bay, Wales, Feb 1, 1942.

Garrett Morris, 61, comedian ("Saturday Night Live"), born New Orleans, LA, Feb 1, 1937.

Bill Mumy, 44, actor (*Palm Springs Weekend, Twilight Zone—The Movie*, "Lost in Space," "The Rockford Files"), born El Centro, CA, Feb 1, 1954.

Lisa Marie Presley, 30, daughter of Priscilla and Elvis, born Memphis, TN, Feb 1, 1968.

Stuart Whitman, 62, actor ("Cimarron Strip," *The Seekers*), born San Francisco, CA, Feb 1, 1936.

FEBRUARY 2 — MONDAY

Day 33 — 332 Remaining

AUDEN, WYSTAN HUGH: BIRTH ANNIVERSARY. Feb 2, 1907. Pulitzer Prize–winning Anglo-American poet was born at York, England. "Some books," he wrote in *The Dyer's Hand* (1962), "are undeservedly forgotten; none are undeservedly remembered." Died on Sept 28, 1973, at Vienna, Austria.

BAN ON AFRICAN NATIONAL CONGRESS LIFTED: ANNIVERSARY. Feb 2, 1990. The 30-year ban on the African National Congress was lifted by South African President F. W. de Klerk. De Klerk also vowed to free Nelson Mandela soon and lift restrictions on 33 other opposition groups.

February 1998

S	M	T	W	T	F	S
1	2	3	4	5	6	7
8	9	10	11	12	13	14
15	16	17	18	19	20	21
22	23	24	25	26	27	28

BENET, WILLIAM ROSE: BIRTH ANNIVERSARY. Feb 2. American poet and critic. Born at Fort Hamilton, NY, on Feb 2, 1886. Died at New York, NY, on May 4, 1950.

BIG LAKE ICE CLASSIC. Feb 2–Apr 15. Big Lake, AK. Annual lottery to guess the day and hour when a classic Mustang will go through the ice in the spring. Sponsors: Big Lake Chamber of Commerce and Houston Booster Club. For info: LaRae Eldridge, Chair, Big Lake Chamber of Commerce, PO Box 520067, Big Lake, AK 99652. Phone: (907) 892-7976 or (907) 892-6109.

BONZA BOTTLER DAY™. Feb 2. To celebrate when the number of the day is the same as the number of the month. Bonza Bottler Day™ is an excuse to have a party at least once a month. For further information, see Jan 1. For info: Gail M. Berger, 109 Matthew Ave, Poca, WV 25159. Phone: (304) 776-7746. Email: gberger5@aol.com.

CALIFORNIA KIWIFRUIT DAY. Feb 2. National campaign to educate Americans about the nutritional benefits of kiwifruit (they provide twice the vitamin C of oranges); ways to enjoy kiwifruit; kiwifruit's colorful history. Annually, Feb 2. For info: Laura Bachmann, Porter Novelli, 100 First St, Ste 2600, San Francisco, CA 94105. Fax: (415) 288-7421.

CANDLEMAS DAY or PRESENTATION OF THE LORD. Feb 2. Observed in Roman Catholic and Eastern Orthodox Churches. Commemorates presentation of Jesus in the Temple and the purification of Mary 40 days after his birth. Candles have been blessed on this day since the 11th century. Formerly called the Feast of Purification of the Blessed Virgin Mary. Old Scottish couplet proclaims: "If Candlemas is fair and clear/There'll be two winters in the year."

GROUNDHOG DAY. Feb 2. Old belief that if the sun shines on Candlemas Day, or if the groundhog sees his shadow when he emerges on this day, six weeks of winter will ensue.

GROUNDHOG DAY IN PUNXSUTAWNEY, PENNSYLVANIA. Feb 2. Widely observed traditional annual Candlemas Day event at which "Punxsutawney Phil, king of the weather prophets," is the object of a search. Tradition is said to have been established by early German settlers. The official trek (which began in 1887) is followed by a weather prediction for the next six weeks. [Phil made his dramatic film debut with Bill Murray in *Groundhog Day*.]

GROUNDHOG DAY IN SUN PRAIRIE, WISCONSIN. Feb 2. Sun Prairie, WI. To predict the weather for the balance of winter. Prognostication at 7:15 AM, EST, to see if Jimmy the Groundhog has seen his shadow. Persons born on this date are eligible for "official" groundhog birth certificate and/or groundhog club membership (for a small fee). Est attendance: 700. For info: Chamber of Commerce, 109 E Main St, Sun Prairie, WI 53590. Phone: (608) 837-4547. Fax: (608) 837-8765.

HALAS, GEORGE: BIRTH ANNIVERSARY. Feb 2, 1895. George ("Papa Bear") Halas, Pro Football Hall of Fame coach and owner born at Chicago, IL. After playing football at the University of Illinois and baseball with the New York Yankees, Halas helped to found the National Football League and the Chicago Bears in 1920. As coach of the Bears for 40 years, he compiled a record of 324 wins, 151 losses and 31 ties. Charter member of the Hall of Fame, 1963. Died at Chicago, IL, Oct 31, 1983.

IMBOLC. Feb 2. (Also called Imbolg, Candlemas, Lupercalia, Feast of Pan, Feast of Torches, Feast of Waxing Light, Brigit's Day and Oimelc.) One of the "Greater Sabbats" during the Wiccan year, Imbolc marks the recovery of the Goddess (after giving birth to the Sun, or the God, at Yule) and celebrates the anticipation of spring. Annually, Feb 2.

JOYCE, JAMES: BIRTH ANNIVERSARY. Feb 2, 1882. Irish novelist and poet, author of *Dubliners, A Portrait of the Artist as a Young Man, Ulysses, Finnegan's Wake* and *Chamber Music*, was born at Dublin. "A man of genius," he wrote in *Ulysses*, "makes no mistakes. His errors are volitional and are portals of discovery." Of *Finnegan's Wake* Joyce is reported to have replied to an academic whose letter had asked for clues to its meaning, "If I can throw any obscurity on the subject, let me know." (From AP story, "1000 years of Irish Memories. . . ." by Hugh A. Mulligan.) Joyce died at age 58 of peritonitis at Zurich, Switzerland, on Jan 13, 1941, and was buried there.

LINCOLN, ABRAHAM: DELAWARE AND OREGON BIRTHDAY OBSERVANCE. Feb 2. Observed annually in Delaware and Oregon on the first Monday in February. See also: "Lincoln, Abraham: Birth Anniversary" (Feb 12).

LUXEMBOURG: CANDLEMAS. Feb 2. Traditional observance of Candlemas. At night children sing a customary song wishing health and prosperity to their neighbors and receive sweets in return. They carry special candles called *Lichtebengel* symbolizing the coming of spring.

MEXICO: DIA DE LA CANDELARIA. Feb 2. All Mexico celebrates. Dances, processions, bullfights.

NATIONAL SCHOOL COUNSELING WEEK. Feb 2–6. Promotes school counseling in the school and community. For info: American School Counselor Assn, 801 N Fairfax St, Ste 310, Alexandria, VA 22314. Phone: (800) 306-4722. Fax: (703) 683-1619. Email: escaoffice@aol.com.
WWW: http://www.edge.net/asca/

PUNXSUTAWNEY KANI GROUNDHOG DAY PREDICTION. Feb 2. Springfield, MO. My Country 100.5 FM morning show cohost Kani Bud, appropriately clad in a groundhog costume, emerges from the Springfield city drainage system to issue her 4th annual prognostication on when the beginning of spring can be expected. Annually, on Groundhog Day (if a weekday). Est attendance: 100. For info: Steve Kern, Promotions Dir, My Country Radio, 840 S Glenstone, Springfield, MO 65802. Phone: (417) 869-1059. Fax: (417) 869-1000.
WWW: http://www.mycountry.com

***THE RECORD OF A SNEEZE*: ANNIVERSARY.** Feb 2, 1893. One day after Thomas Edison's "Black Maria" studio was completed in West Orange, NJ, a studio cameraman took the first "close-up" in film history. *The Record of a Sneeze*, starring Edison's assistant Fred P. Ott, was also the first motion picture to receive a copyright (1894). See also: "Black Maria Studio: Anniversary" (Feb 1).

TREATY OF GUADALUPE HIDALGO: 150th ANNIVERSARY. Feb 2, 1848. The war between Mexico and the United States formally ended with the signing of the Treaty of Guadalupe Hidalgo, signed in the village for which it was named, on Feb 2, 1848. The treaty provided for Mexico's cession to the US of the territory that became the states of California, Nevada, Utah, most of Arizona, and parts of New Mexico, Colorado and Wyoming, in exchange for $15 million from the US. In addition, Mexico relinquished all rights to Texas, north of the Rio Grande. The Senate ratified the treaty on Mar 10, 1848.

WALTON, GEORGE: DEATH ANNIVERSARY. Feb 2. Signer of the Declaration of Independence. Born at Prince Edward County, VA, 1741 (exact date unknown). Died Feb 2, 1804.

"WHAT'S MY LINE?" TV PREMIERE: ANNIVERSARY. Feb 2, 1950. This popular game show premiered on CBS and ran for 17 years in prime time. A panel of four celebrities figured out the professions of the contestants and the identities of the mystery guests by asking yes-or-no questions. The first panel consisted of Louis Untermeyer, columnist Dorothy Kilgallen, New Jersey Governor Harold Hoffman, and psychiatrist Dr. Richard Hoffman. Yankee Phil Rizzuto was the first mystery guest. Other guests included James Cagney, Ty Cobb, Walt Disney, Judy Garland, Jimmy Carter, Frank Sinatra and Alfred Hitchcock. John Daly hosted.

BIRTHDAYS TODAY

Christie Brinkley, 45, model, born Monroe, MI, Feb 2, 1953.
Sean Michael Elliott, 30, basketball player, born Tucson, AZ, Feb 2, 1968.
Farrah Fawcett, 51, actress, model ("Charlie's Angels," *The Burning Bed*), born Corpus Christi, TX, Feb 2, 1947.
Bo Hopkins, 56, actor ("The Rockford Files," "Dynasty," *The Wild Bunch, American Graffiti*), born Greenwood, SC, Feb 2, 1942.
Simon MacCorkindale, 46, actor, producer, screenwriter ("Falcon Crest," *Death on the Nile, Jaws 3-D*), born Isle-of-Ely, England, Feb 2, 1952.
Dexter Manley, 39, former football player, born Houston, TX, Feb 2, 1959.
Graham Nash, 56, musician, singer, born Blackpool, England, Feb 2, 1942.
Liz Smith, 75, journalist, author, born Fort Worth, TX, Feb 2, 1923.
Tom Smothers, 61, comedian, folksinger (brother of Dick Smothers, "The Smothers Brothers Comedy Hour"; Yo-Yo Man), born New York, NY, Feb 2, 1937.
Elaine Stritch, 73, actress (*Company*, sang "The Ladies Who Lunch"), born Birmingham, MI, Feb 2, 1925.

FEBRUARY 3 — TUESDAY

Day 34 — 331 Remaining

BLACKWELL, ELIZABETH: BIRTH ANNIVERSARY. Feb 3, 1821. First woman physician. Born near Bristol, England, she and several other members of her family were active abolitionists, women's suffrage advocates and pioneers in women's medicine. Her family moved to New York State in 1832, and she received a medical doctor's degree at Geneva, NY, in 1849. She established a hospital in New York City with an all-woman staff, where she recruited and trained nurses for service in the Civil War. Returning to England in 1869, she continued to teach and practice medicine until her death at Hastings, England, May 31, 1910. A US postage stamp was issued in her honor in 1981.

CIVIL WAR PEACE TALKS: ANNIVERSARY. Feb 3, 1865. Abraham Lincoln and his Secretary of State, William Seward, met to discuss peace with Confederate Vice President Alexander Stephens and others at Hampton Road, VA. The meeting, which took place on board the ship *River Queen*, lasted four hours and produced no positive results. The Confederates sought an armistice first and discussion of reunion later, while Lincoln was insistent that recognition of Federal authority must be the first step toward peace.

"THE DAY THE MUSIC DIED." Feb 3. The anniversary of the death of rock-and-roll pioneer and legend Charles Hardin "Buddy" Holly. "The Day the Music Died," so-called in singer Don McLean's song "American Pie," is the date on which in 1959 Holly was killed in a plane crash along with J.P. Richardson (otherwise known as "The Big Bopper") and Richie Valens. Holly was born Sept 7, 1936, at Lubbock, TX, and died in a cornfield near Mason City, IA, Feb 3, 1959.

FIFTEENTH AMENDMENT TO US CONSTITUTION RATIFIED: ANNIVERSARY. Feb 3. The 15th Amendment, ratified on Feb 3, 1870, granted that the right of citizens to vote shall not be denied on account of race, color or previous condition of servitude.

FOUR CHAPLAINS MEMORIAL DAY. Feb 3, 1943. Commemorates four chaplains (George Fox, Alexander Goode, Clark Poling, John Washington) who sacrificed their life belts and lives in torpedoing of SS *Dorchester* off Greenland.

GOLF AROUND CINCINNATI. Feb 3–Mar 11. Northgate Mall, Cincinnati, OH. 18-hole miniature golf course featuring replica Cincinnati landmarks at each hole built by local architects and building companies. Proceeds from the course to benefit the Epilepsy Council of Greater Cincinnati. Events scheduled include a Celebrity Play, Senior's Day Out for golfers 55 and over and a Corporate Challenge Tournament. For info: Northgate Mall Information Center, 9501 Colerain Ave, Cincinnati, OH 45251. Phone: (513) 385-5600, or Rob Stewart, Epilepsy Council of Greater Cincinnati, 3 Centennial Plaza, 895 Central Ave, Ste 1000, Cincinnati, OH 45202. Phone: (513) 721-2905.

GROUND FROG'S DAY. Feb 3. Knoxville, TN. Radio station WIVK's mascot is "WIVICK" the frog. On the day after Groundhog Day, if "WIVICK" sees his shadow, it's six weeks til big cash give-a-ways. Annually, Feb 3. For info: Wilhite & Wall, PO Box 11167, Knoxville, TN 37939. Phone: (423) 588-6511. Fax: (423) 656-FROG.

INCOME TAX BIRTHDAY: SIXTEENTH AMENDMENT TO US CONSTITUTION: RATIFICATION ANNIVERSARY. Feb 3, 1913. On Feb 3, 1913, the 16th Amendment was ratified, granting Congress the authority to levy taxes on income. (Church bells did not ring throughout the land, and no dancing in the streets was reported.)

JAPAN: BEAN-THROWING FESTIVAL (SETSUBUN). Feb 3. Setsubun marks the last day of winter according to the lunar calendar. Throngs at temple grounds throw beans to drive away imaginary devils.

JOHNSTON, JOSEPH: BIRTH ANNIVERSARY. Feb 3, 1807. Born near Farmville, VA, and died Mar 21, 1891, at Washington, DC. Confederate general in the Civil War whose troops were never directly defeated. Longstanding differences with Jefferson Davis, president of the Confederacy, prevented him, however, from reaching his full potential.

LAUGH AND GROW RICH DAY. Feb 3. Recognition of laughter's power to add to the bottom line. People are more effective, tend to remember things better and laughter helps to lower the turnover rate. Annually, the first Tuesday in February. For info: Rick Segel, 1 Wheatland St, Burlington, MA 01803. Phone: (617) 272-9995. Fax: (617) 272-9996.

MOON PHASE: FIRST QUARTER. Feb 3. Moon enters First Quarter phase at 5:53 PM, EST.

NAUVOO LEGION CHARTERED: ANNIVERSARY. Feb 3, 1841. Created by Illinois Charter and comprised of 5,000 Mormon men under the command of Lt General Joseph Smith, the Nauvoo Legion was considered the "largest trained soldiery in the US" except for the US Army.

ROCKWELL, NORMAN: BIRTH ANNIVERSARY. Feb 3, 1894. American artist and illustrator especially noted for his realistic and homey magazine cover art for the *Saturday Evening Post.* Born at New York, NY, he died at Stockbridge, MA, Nov 8, 1978, at age 84.

SPACE MILESTONE: *CHALLENGER STS-10* (US). Feb 3, 1984. Shuttle *Challenger* launched from Kennedy Space Center, FL, with crew of five (Vance Brand, Robert Gibson, Ronald McNair, Bruce McCandless and Robert Stewart). On Feb 7 two astronauts became first to fly freely in space (propelled by their backpack jets), untethered to any craft. Landed at Cape Canaveral, FL, on Feb 11.

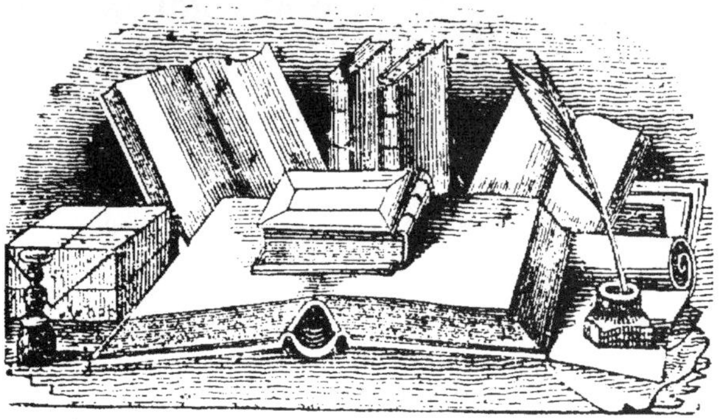

STEIN, GERTRUDE: BIRTH ANNIVERSARY. Feb 3. Avant-garde expatriate American writer, perhaps best remembered for her poetic declaration (in 1913): "Rose is a rose is a rose." Born at Allegheny, PA, Feb 3, 1874. Died at Paris, France, July 27, 1946.

ZEHNDER'S SNOWFEST (WITH ICE CARVING AND STATE OF MICHIGAN SNOW SCULPTING COMPETITIONS). Feb 3–9. Frankenmuth, MI. Annual festival also includes ice demonstrations, exhibitions by international teams from 12 countries and many children's activities such as a petting zoo and magic shows. Est attendance: 200,000. For info: Linda Kelly, Zehnder's of Frankenmuth, 730 S Main St, Frankenmuth, MI 48734. Phone: (800) 863-7999. Fax: (517) 652-3544.
WWW: http://www.zehnder's.com

BIRTHDAYS TODAY

Shelley Berman, 72, comedian ("Mary Hartman, Mary Hartman"), born Chicago, IL, Feb 3, 1926.

Joey Bishop (Joseph Abraham Gottlieb), 80, actor ("The Joey Bishop Show," "Liar's Club"), born New York, NY, Feb 3, 1918.

Blythe Danner, 55, actress (*The Miser, Butterflies Are Free, Brighton Beach Memoirs, Mr and Mrs Bridge, Alice*), born Philadelphia, PA, Feb 3, 1943.

Vlade Divac, 30, basketball player, born Prijepolje, Yugoslavia, Feb 3, 1968.

Morgan Fairchild (Patsy McClenny), 48, actress ("Dallas," "Falcon Crest," "Flamingo Road," "North and South"), born Dallas, TX, Feb 3, 1950.

Keith Gordon, 37, actor, director (*All That Jazz, Dressed to Kill, A Midnight Clear*), born Feb 3, 1961.

Robert Allen (Bob) Griese, 53, sportscaster, Pro Football Hall of Fame quarterback, born Evansville, IN, Feb 3, 1945.

James Michener, 91, author (*Journey, Space, The World Is My Home: Memoirs*), born New York, NY, Feb 3, 1907.

Bibi Osterwald, 78, actress ("Bridget Loves Bernie"), born New Brunswick, NJ, Feb 3, 1920.

Paul S. Sarbanes, 65, US Senator (D, Maryland), born Salisbury, MD, Feb 3, 1933.

Francis Asbury (Fran) Tarkenton, 58, Pro Football Hall of Fame quarterback, born Richmond, VA, Feb 3, 1940.

FEBRUARY 4 — WEDNESDAY

Day 35 — 330 Remaining

APACHE WARS BEGIN: ANNIVERSARY. Feb 4, 1861. The period of conflict known as the Apache Wars began on this date at Apache Pass, AZ, when Army Lt George Bascom arrested Apache Chief Cochise for raiding a ranch. Cochise escaped and declared war. The wars lasted 25 years under the leadership of Cochise and, later, Geronimo.

February 1998

S	M	T	W	T	F	S
1	2	3	4	5	6	7
8	9	10	11	12	13	14
15	16	17	18	19	20	21
22	23	24	25	26	27	28

CANADA: VANCOUVER INTERNATIONAL BOAT SHOW. Feb 4–8. BC Place Stadium, Vancouver, BC. Sail and powerboats, sailboards, inflatables, canoes, personal watercraft, marine electronics and accessories, marine services, charters, sailing schools, water skis, sporting goods, travel and resort destinations, fishing equipment and Marine Facts Stage. Est attendance: 45,000. For info: Canadian National Sportsmen's Shows, 703 Evans Ave, Ste 202, Toronto, Ont, Canada M9C 5E9. Phone: (416) 695-0311.

HALFWAY POINT OF WINTER. Feb 4. At 3:01 AM, EST, on Feb 4, 44 days, 11 hours and 54 minutes of winter will have elapsed and the equivalent remain before 2:55 PM, EST, on Mar 20, 1998, which is the spring equinox and the beginning of spring.

LINDBERGH, CHARLES AUGUSTUS: BIRTH ANNIVERSARY. Feb 4, 1902. American aviator Charles "Lucky Lindy" Lindbergh was the first to fly solo and nonstop over the Atlantic Ocean, New York to Paris, May 20–21, 1927. Born at Detroit, MI, Feb 4, 1902. Died at Kipahula, Maui, HI, Aug 27, 1974. See also: "Lindbergh Flight Anniversary" (May 20).

NORTHWEST FLOWER AND GARDEN SHOW. Feb 4–8. Washington State Convention Center, Seattle, WA. The 1998 theme is "Gardens of the Past: The Way We Were." Est attendance: 80,000. For info: Celice Eldred, 1515 NW 51st St, Seattle, WA 98107. Phone: (206) 789-5333. Fax: (206) 784-5545.

SRI LANKA: INDEPENDENCE DAY. Feb 4. Democratic Socialist Republic of Sri Lanka observes National Day. Public holiday.

TORTURE ABOLITION DAY: ANNIVERSARY. Feb 4, 1985. Twenty countries signed a UN document titled "Convention Against Torture and Other Cruel, Inhuman or Degrading Treatment or Punishment." Adopted Dec 10, 1984, by the UN General Assembly, it defined torture as any act "by which severe pain or suffering, whether physical or mental, is intentionally inflicted" to obtain information or a confession. Signatory countries were Afghanistan, Argentina, Belgium, Bolivia, Costa Rica, Denmark, Dominican Republic, Finland, France, Greece, Iceland, Italy, Netherlands, Norway, Portugal, Senegal, Spain, Sweden, Switzerland and Uruguay. While the US did sign the document, signing is only a preliminary stage that must be followed by ratification—which the US has never done.

USO: BIRTHDAY. Feb 4. To honor the civilian agency founded in 1941 that provides support worldwide for US service people and their families. The United Service Organizations (USO) centers have served as a home away from home for hundreds of thousands of Americans.

BIRTHDAYS TODAY

David Brenner, 53, comedian (host of "Nightlife," a short-lived talk show opposite "The Tonight Show"), born Philadelphia, PA, Feb 4, 1945.

Gary Conway, 62, actor ("Burke's Law," *I Was a Teenage Frankenstein*), born Boston, MA, Feb 4, 1936.

Alice Cooper (Vincent Damon Furnier), 50, singer, songwriter, born Detroit, MI, Feb 4, 1948.

Lisa Eichhorn, 46, actress (*The Vanishing, King of the Hill*), born Reading, PA, Feb 4, 1952.

Pamela Franklin, 48, actress (*The Prime of Miss Jean Brodie, The Legend of Hell House*), born Tokyo, Japan, Feb 2, 1950.

Betty Friedan, 77, author (*The Feminine Mystique*), founder, the National Organization for Women (NOW), born Peoria, IL, Feb 4, 1921.

Russel Hoban, 73, artist, author, born Lansdale, PA, Feb 4, 1925.

Rosa Lee Parks, 85, civil rights leader who refused to give up her seat on the bus, born Tuskegee, AL, Feb 4, 1913.

J. Danforth (Dan) Quayle, 51, 44th US Vice President, born Indianapolis, IN, Feb 4, 1947.

Donald W. Riegle, Jr, 60, former US Senator (D, Michigan), born Flint, MI, Feb 4, 1938.

Denis Joseph Savard, 37, former hockey player, born Pointe Gatineau, Quebec, Canada, Feb 4, 1961.

John Schuck, 58, actor ("McMillan and Wife," *McCabe and Mrs. Miller, Dick Tracy*), born Boston, MA, Feb 4, 1940.

Lawrence Taylor, 39, former football player, born Williamsburg, VA, Feb 4, 1959.

FEBRUARY 5 — THURSDAY

Day 36 — 329 Remaining

CARRADINE, JOHN: BIRTH ANNIVERSARY. Feb 5, 1906. American film actor John Carradine was born Richmond Reed Carradine at Greenwich Village, NY. He appeared in more than 200 films. Frequently observed wandering the streets in a velvet suit and satin cape while reciting Shakespeare, he became known as "the Bard of the Boulevard." Carradine died on Nov 27, 1988, at Milan, Italy.

FLORIDA STATE FAIR. Feb 5–16. Florida State Fair Grounds, Tampa, FL. The fair features the best arts, crafts, competitive exhibits, equestrian shows, livestock, entertainment and food found in Florida. Also not to be missed is "Cracker Country," where cultural and architectural history has been preserved. Est attendance: 500,000. For info: Kenneth Allen, PR Mktg Dir, Florida State Fair, PO Box 11766, Tampa, FL 33680. Phone: (813) 621-7821 or 24-hour hotline (813) 622-PARK. Fax: (813) 628-4902. WWW: http://www.dos.state.fl.us/statefair

HOBBY INDUSTRY ASSOCIATION ANNUAL TRADE SHOW. Feb 5–8 (classes begin Feb 4). Dallas Convention Center, Dallas, TX. 57th annual showcase for wholesale and retail buyers to view and order craft and hobby products. Est attendance: 200,000. For info: Hobby Industry Association, 319 E 54th St, Elmwood Park, NJ 07407. Phone: (201) 794-1133. Fax: (201) 797-0657. Email: hia@ix.netcom.com.
WWW: http://www.hobby.org/hia

LONGEST WAR IN HISTORY: ENDING ANNIVERSARY. Feb 5, 1985. The Third Punic War, between Rome and Carthage, started in the year 149 BC. It culminated in the year 146 BC, when Roman soldiers led by Scipio razed Carthage to the ground. The desolated site was cursed and rebuilding forbidden. On this date, 2,131 years after the war began, Ugo Vetere, mayor of Rome, and Chedli Klibi, mayor of Carthage, met at Tunis to sign a treaty of friendship officially ending the Third Punic War.

MEXICO: ANNIVERSARY OF THE CONSTITUTION. Feb 5, 1917. Present constitution, embracing major social reforms, adopted on this day, 1917.

MOBIUS ADVERTISING AWARDS. Feb 5. Chicago, IL. Selection and recognition of the world's most outstanding television and radio commercials, print advertising and package designs. Founded in 1971. Est attendance: 500. For info: J.W. Anderson, Chairman, The Mobius Advertising Awards, 841 N Addison Ave, Elmhurst, IL 60126-1291. Phone: (630) 834-7773. Fax: (630) 834-5565.
Email: MOBIUSAWARDS@compuserve.com.

NATIONAL GIRLS AND WOMEN IN SPORTS DAY. Feb 5. For info: Women's Sports Foundation, Eisenhower Park, East Meadow, NY 11554. Phone: (516) 542-4700.

NEW JERSEY CONGRESSIONAL RECEPTION AND DINNER. Feb 5. Sheraton Washington Hotel, Washington, DC. 61st annual reception and dinner in nation's capital where New Jersey business community honors the State's Congressional Delegation. Annually, the first Thursday in February. Sponsor: NJ State Chamber of Commerce. Est attendance: 1,600. For info: William E. Payne, Vice President, NJ State Chamber of Commerce, 216 W State St, Trenton, NJ 08608. Phone: (609) 989-7888. WWW: http://www.njchamber.com

PEEL, ROBERT: BIRTH ANNIVERSARY. Feb 5, 1788. English statesman, established the Irish constabulary (known as the "Peelers"). Later, as England's Home Secretary, he reorganized the London police, thereafter known as "Bobbies." Born at Lancashire, England, Feb 5, 1788. Died July 2, 1850, at London from injuries received in a fall from his horse.

SIGNING OF FAMILY-LEAVE BILL: 5th ANNIVERSARY. Feb 5, 1993. President William Clinton signed legislation requiring companies with 50 or more employees (and all government agencies) to allow employees to take up to 12 weeks unpaid leave in a 12-month period to deal with the birth or adoption of a child. The bill became operable on Aug 5, 1993.

STEVENSON, ADLAI EWING: BIRTH ANNIVERSARY. Feb 5, 1900. American statesman, governor of Illinois, Democratic candidate for president in 1952 and 1956, US representative to the UN, 1961–1965. Born at Los Angeles, CA, Feb 5, 1900. Died at London, England, July 14, 1965. (Not to be confused with his grandfather, Vice President Adlai Ewing Stevenson, born Oct 23, 1835.) See also: "Stevenson, Adlai Ewing: Birth Anniversary" (Oct 23).

WEATHERMAN'S [WEATHERPERSON'S] DAY. Feb 5. Commemorates the birth of one of America's first weathermen, John Jeffries. Born on Feb 5, 1744, and died on Sept 16, 1819, a Boston physician who kept detailed records of weather conditions, 1774–1816. See also: "First Balloon Flight Across English Channel: Anniversary" (Jan 7).

WITHERSPOON, JOHN: 275th BIRTH ANNIVERSARY. Feb 5, 1723. Clergyman, signer of the Declaration of Independence and reputed coiner of the word *Americanism* (in 1781). Born near Edinburgh, Scotland, Feb 5, 1723. Died Nov 15, 1794.

BIRTHDAYS TODAY

Henry Louis (Hank) Aaron, 64, baseball executive, Baseball Hall of Fame outfielder, all-time home-run leader, born Mobile, AL, Feb 5, 1934.

Bobby Brown, 29, singer, dancer ("My Prerogative," "Every Little Step"), born Roxbury, MA, Feb 5, 1969.

Red Buttons (Aaron Chwatt), 79, actor ("The Red Buttons Show," "The Double Life of Henry Phyfe"), born The Bronx, NY, Feb 5, 1919.

Father Andrew Greeley, 70, Roman Catholic priest and author (*Happy Are the Merciful, An Occasion of Sin*), born Oak Park, IL, Feb 5, 1928.

Christopher Guest, 50, writer, comedian (Emmy for writing *Lily Tomlin*; regular on "Saturday Night Live"), born New York, NY, Feb 5, 1948.

Barbara Hershey (Barbara Hertzstein), 50, actress (*Hannah and Her Sisters, With Six You Get Eggroll*, "The Monroes"), born Los Angeles, CA, Feb 5, 1948.

David Alan Ladd, 51, actor, producer (*A Dog of Flanders, The Day of the Locust*), born Los Angeles, CA, Feb 5, 1947.

Jennifer Jason Leigh (Morrow), 36, actress (*Miami Blues, Rush, Backdraft*), born Los Angeles, CA, Feb 5, 1962.

Charlotte Rampling, 52, actress (*Georgy Girl, Farewell My Lovely*), born Sturmer, England, Feb 5, 1946.

David Selby, 57, actor ("Falcon Crest," *Rich and Famous*), born Morgantown, WV, Feb 5, 1941.

Roger Thomas Staubach, 56, Pro Football Hall of Fame quarterback, born Cincinnati, OH, Feb 5, 1942.

☆ ☆ ☆

FEBRUARY 6 — FRIDAY

Day 37 — 328 Remaining

ACCESSION OF QUEEN ELIZABETH II: ANNIVERSARY. Feb 6. Princess Elizabeth Alexandra Mary succeeded to the British throne (becoming Elizabeth II, Queen of the United Kingdom of Great Britain and Northern Ireland and Head of the Commonwealth) upon the death of her father, King George VI, on Feb 6, 1952. Her coronation took place on June 2, 1953, in Westminster Abbey at London.

ALBANY AMERICAN WINE FESTIVAL. Feb 6–8. Desmond Hotel, Albany-Shaker Rd, Albany, NY. More than 120 of America's outstanding wineries represented, featuring more than 400 wines. Library Wine Auction, special release, reception and elegant cuisine. For info: The Desmond, 660 Albany-Shaker Rd, Albany, NY 12207. Phone: (518) 464-WINE.
WWW: http://albany.org

ARBOR DAY (ARIZONA). Feb 6. In the counties of Apache, Navajo, Coconino, Mohave and Yavapai, the Friday following Apr 1, and in all other counties the Friday following Feb 1, in each year, shall be known as Arbor Day. See also: "Arbor Day (Arizona)" (Apr 3).

BIG BAND WEEKEND. Feb 6–8. Asheville, NC. This 7th annual event salutes World War II veterans with two orchestras and a show band for a weekend of ballroom dancing. For info: Grove Park Inn Resort, 290 Macon Ave, Asheville, NC 28804. Phone: (800) 374-0050 or (704) 252-2711 ext 8005 or 8045. Fax: (704) 253-7053.

BULLNANZA. Feb 6–7. Lazy E Arena, Guthrie, OK. Present and past champions in exciting competition in bull riding. Annually, the first Friday and Saturday in February. Est attendance: 14,000. For info: Lazy E Arena, Rte 5, Box 393, Guthrie, OK 73044. Phone: (800) 595-RIDE. Fax: (405) 282-3785. Email: learena@ionet.net. WWW: http://www.lazye.com

BURR, AARON: BIRTH ANNIVERSARY. Feb 6, 1756. Third vice president of the US (Mar 4, 1801–Mar 3, 1805). While vice president, Burr challenged Alexander Hamilton to a duel and mortally wounded him on July 11, 1804, at Weehawken, NJ. Indicted for the challenge and for murder, he fled, but later returned to Washington to complete his term of office (during which he presided over the impeachment trial of Supreme Court Justice Samuel Chase). In 1807 Burr was arrested, tried for treason (in an alleged scheme to invade Mexico) and acquitted. Born at Newark, NJ, died at Staten Island, NY, on the day a final decree of divorce was issued to his second wife, Sept 14, 1836.

CANADA: BRACEBRIDGE WINTER CARNIVAL. Feb 6–8. Bracebridge, Ont. Annually, in February. Polar Bear Club dip, outdoor sports and activities, children's games. For info: Winter Carnival, Bracebridge Chamber of Commerce, 1-1 Manitoba St, Bracebridge, Ont, Canada P1L 1S4. Phone: (705) 645-8121. Fax: (705) 645-7592. Email: bracecha@muskoka.com.

CORDOVA ICEWORM FESTIVAL. Feb 6–8. Cordova, AK. A multitude of activities for all the family to enjoy: variety show; arts and crafts, basketball tournament, blessing of the fleet, survival suit race, pet show, auction and much more. The legendary 140-ft-long Iceworm, which is propelled by 40 pairs of legs, makes his annual appearance as the finale of the Grand Parade! Cor-

February 1998

S	M	T	W	T	F	S
1	2	3	4	5	6	7
8	9	10	11	12	13	14
15	16	17	18	19	20	21
22	23	24	25	26	27	28

dova is surrounded by the Chugach Mountains and the Prince William Sound on the Gulf of Alaska. Est attendance: 1,500. For info: Darrel Olson, Chair, Box 768, Cordova, AK 99574. Phone: (907) 424-5756. Fax: (907) 424-3523.
Email: beedle2@ptialaska.net.

DULCIBRRR. Feb 6–7. Falls of Rough, KY. Dulcimer workshops and concerts. Est attendance: 500. For info: Tom DeHaven, Rec Supervisor, Rough River State Resort Pk, 450 Lodge Rd, Falls of Rough, KY 40119. Phone: (502) 257-2311.

GREAT NORTHEAST HOME SHOW. Feb 6–8. Pepsi Arena and Empire State Plaza, Albany, NY. For 18 years this has been the largest consumer home show in the northeast. In addition to exhibits, informative seminars are held throughout the show on topics about the home. Annually, the first full weekend in February. Sponsor: The Times Union Newspaper. Est attendance: 30,000. For info: Heather Mabee, Show Promoter, Ed Lewi Associates, 6 Chelsea Pl, Clifton Park, NY 12065. Phone: (518) 383-6183. Fax: (518) 383-6755.

HOGGETOWNE MEDIEVAL FAIRE. Feb 6–8. Alachua County Fairgrounds, Gainesville, FL. 12th annual faire features jousting, birds of prey, medieval arts and crafts, food and continuous entertainment on five stages. Est attendance: 25,000. For info: Linda Piper, City of Gainesville, Div of Cultural Affairs, PO Box 490 Sta. 30, Gainesville, FL 32602. Phone: (352) 334-2197. Fax: (352) 334-2146.

HOT AIR AFFAIR. Feb 6–8. Hudson, WI. More than 40 hot air balloons from across the nation will launch and race over the St. Croix River Valley in northwest Wisconsin. A torchlight parade features balloon pilots and crews lighting up the night with blasts of fire from their balloon baskets. At an evening "moonglow," the balloonists fire their burners and "glow in the dark" as visitors stroll among them. Est attendance: 20,000. For info: (888) 247-2332. WWW: http://tourism.state.wi.us

ITALY: FEAST OF THE INCAPPUCCIATI. Feb 6. Gradoli (near Viterbo). On the Thursday before Ash Wednesday the members of the Confraternity of Purgatory make the rounds of the town dressed in traditional hooded robes, bearing a banner and walking to the beat of a drum. They stop at every house to collect foodstuffs in the name of the souls in purgatory; the food is then served at the banquet on Ash Wednesday.

LONGHORN WORLD CHAMPIONSHIP RODEO. Feb 6–8. Riverfront Coliseum, Cincinnati, OH. More than 200 of the best cowboys and cowgirls compete in six professional contests ranging from bronc riding to bull riding for top prize money and world championship points. Featuring colorful opening pageantry and Big, Bad BONUS Bulls. 24th annual. Est attendance: 24,000. For info: W. Bruce Lehrke, Pres, Longhorn World Chmpshp Rodeo, Inc, PO Box 70159, Nashville, TN 37207. Phone: (615) 876-1016. Fax: (615) 876-4685. Email: lhrodeo@idt.net. WWW: http://www.longhornrodeo.com

MASSACHUSETTS RATIFIES CONSTITUTION: ANNIVERSARY. Feb 6, 1788. By a vote of 187 to 168 on Feb 6, 1788, Massachusetts became the sixth state to ratify the Constitution.

MID-WINTER'S DAY CELEBRATION. Feb 6. Ann Arbor, MI. To create euphoria by fiat in celebration that winter is half over. For info: Richard Ankli, The Fifth Wheel Tavern, 639 Fifth St, Ann Arbor, MI 48103.

MILITARY AIR TRANSPORT CRASHES IN INDIANA: ANNIVERSARY. Feb 6, 1992. A Lockhead C-130 transport on training maneuvers crashed into the rear of a restaurant and a hotel in Evansville, IN. Sixteen people were killed, including the five crew members who were with the Kentucky National Guard based in Louisville, KY. The crash marked the second time in 4½ years that a military plane crashed into an Indiana hotel. On Oct 20, 1987, an Air Force fighter jet crashed into the Ramada Inn-Airport in Indianapolis, killing 10.

MOOSE STOMPERS WEEKEND. Feb 6–8. Houlton, ME. Human curling, human dog sled racing, potato peeling contest, wiffle snow ball, giant sliding hill for children, snowmobiling activities, cross country skiing, skating, bonfire, wagon rides and much more. For info: Greater Houlton Chamber of Commerce, 109 Main St, Houlton, ME 04730. Phone: (207) 532-4216.
Email: chamber@houlton.com.
WWW: http://www.mainerec.com/houlton.html

NATIONAL BASKETBALL ASSOCIATION: ALL-STAR WEEKEND. Feb 6–8. Madison Square Garden, New York, NY. For info: Brian McIntyre, VP, PR, Natl Basketball Assn, Olympic Tower, 645 Fifth Ave, New York, NY 10022. Phone: (212) 826-7000.

NATIONAL KRAUT AND FRANKFURTER WEEK. Feb 6–15. To celebrate the fabulous pair of sauerkraut and frankfurters as one of America's favorite taste combinations. Sponsor: Pickle Packers International Inc. For info: DHM Group, Inc, PO Box 767, Holmdel, NJ 07733. Fax: (908) 946-3343.

NEW ZEALAND: WAITANGI DAY. Feb 6. National Day. Commemorates signing of the Treaty of Waitangi (at Waitangi, Chatham Islands, New Zealand) on Feb 6, 1840. The treaty between the native Maori and the European peoples provided for development of New Zealand under the British Crown.

NORMAN ROCKWELL'S COLONIAL SIGN PAINTER COVER FOR *THE SATURDAY EVENING POST*: ANNIVERSARY. Feb 6, 1926. Norman Rockwell's Feb 6, 1926, cover for the *Post* was the first to appear in full color. It depicted a Rockwell kindred spirit—a Colonial sign painter.

NRA RODEO FINALS. Feb 6–8. MetraPark Arena, Billings, MT. Rodeo action at its best—23rd annual finals. A fun-filled rodeo weekend in cowboy country! Est attendance: 16,000. For info: Northern Rodeo Assn, PO Box 1122, Billings, MT 59103. Phone: (406) 252-1122. Fax: (406) 252-0300.

OPENING CEREMONY, WINTER OLYMPICS. Feb 6, 1998. The opening ceremony of the 1998 Winter Olympics will be held today at 9 PM EST. However, because of the 14-hour time difference, the ceremony will actually take place at 11 AM on Feb 7 in Japan.

PAY-A-COMPLIMENT DAY ©. Feb 6. Practice this simple act of kindness and pay a compliment to co-workers, family members or a stranger on the street or in the elevator in your office building. Go ahead, make someone feel a little happier today. For info: Adrienne Sioux Koopersmith, 1437 W Rosemont, #1W, Chicago, IL 60660-1319. Phone: (773) 743-5341. Fax: (773) 743-5395. Email: kooper@interaccess.com.

PERCHVILLE USA. Feb 6–8. Tawas Bay, East Tawas, MI. A winter festival with ice-fishing contests, polar bear swims, go-kart races on the ice, IWPA dog weight pulls, softball tournaments and many children's activities. Annually, the first weekend in February. Est attendance: 10,000. For info: Kimberly Lingo, Program Director, Tawas Area Chamber of Commerce, Box 608, Tawas City, MI 48764-0608. Phone: (517) 362-8643 or (800) 55-TAWAS.

REAGAN, RONALD WILSON: BIRTHDAY. Feb 6, 1911. Fortieth president of the US. Former sportscaster, motion picture actor, governor of California (1967–1974); he was the oldest and the first divorced person to become president. Born at Tampico, IL. Married actress Jane Wyman in 1940 and they were divorced in 1948; married actress Nancy Davis, Mar 4, 1952.

RUTH, "BABE": BIRTH ANNIVERSARY. Feb 6, 1895. One of baseball's greatest heroes, George Herman "Babe" Ruth was born at Baltimore, MD. The left-handed pitcher—"the Sultan of Swat,"—hit 14 home runs in 22 major league seasons of play and played in 10 World Series. Died at New York, NY, on Aug 16, 1948.

SIMMS, HILDA: DEATH ANNIVERSARY. Feb 6, 1994. American stage and film actress was born Hilda Moses at Minneapolis, MN. She joined the American Negro Theater at Harlem, NY, in 1943 and was given the title role in *Anna Lucasta*. When the production moved to Broadway in 1944, it became the first all-black, major production to be performed on Broadway without a racial theme. Simms was the creative arts director of New York State's human rights division, through which she was instrumental in bringing discrimination against black actors to public attention during the 1960s. She died at Buffalo, NY.

SPORTSFEST '98. Feb 6–7. Held indoors at the Myriad Convention Center, Oklahoma City, OK. Oklahoma's amateur winter sports festival includes some 5,500 athletes competing in about 14 events, including gymnastics, basketball, tumbling, table tennis, volleyball and cheerleading plus a trade show and sports celebrities. Est attendance: 10,000. For info: Sooner State Games, 100 W Main, Ste 287, Oklahoma City, OK 73102. Phone: (405) 235-4222. Fax: (405) 232-7723. Email: snrstgms@aol.com.

TENNESSEE CRAFT AND HOBBY SHOW. Feb 6–8. Chilhowee Park, Knoxville, TN. Annual show highlights a broad range of crafts and hobbies at more than 250 booths. Est attendance: 13,000. For info: Katie Parton, Esau, Inc, PO Box 50096, Knoxville, TN 37950. Phone: (423) 588-1233 or (800) 588-ESAU(3728). Fax: (423) 588-6938.

TWENTIETH AMENDMENT TO US CONSTITUTION: ADOPTION ANNIVERSARY. Feb 6. The 20th Amendment was adopted on this date in 1933. The amendment fixed the date of the presidential inauguration as Jan 20, instead of the previous date of Mar 4; specified that were the president-elect to die before taking office, the vice president-elect would succeed to the presidency. In addition, it set Jan 3 as the official opening date of Congress each year.

February 1998

S	M	T	W	T	F	S
1	2	3	4	5	6	7
8	9	10	11	12	13	14
15	16	17	18	19	20	21
22	23	24	25	26	27	28

WORLD SHOVEL RACE CHAMPIONSHIPS. Feb 6–8. Angel Fire, MN. This famous event highlights thrilling competition in production and modified divisions for several age groups. "Modified" competition reaches speeds of 75 mph. Spectator competition on stock grain scoop shovels. Est attendance: 3,000. For info: Angel Fire Resort, PO Drawer B, Angel Fire, NM 87710. Phone: (800) 633-7463 or (505) 377-4237. Fax: (505) 377-4395. Email: gmorton@angelfireresort.com. WWW: http://www.angelfireresort.com

BIRTHDAYS TODAY

Sarah Brady, 56, handgun control activist, born Alexandria, VA, Feb 6, 1942.

Tom Brokaw, 58, journalist, born Yankton, SD, Feb 6, 1940.

Natalie Cole, 48, singer ("This Will Be," "I've Got Love On My Mind"), born Los Angeles, CA, Feb 6, 1950.

Fabian (Fabian Forte), 55, singer, actor, born Philadelphia, PA, Feb 6, 1943.

Mike Farrell, 59, actor ("M*A*S*H," "The Interns"), born St. Paul, MN, Feb 6, 1939.

Walter Edward Fauntroy, 65, former Delegate to Congress (D, District of Columbia), born Washington, DC, Feb 6, 1933.

Zsa Zsa (Sari) Gabor, 79, actress (*Ninotchka, Special Tonight*), born Budapest, Hungary, Feb 6, 1919.

Gayle Hunnicut, 55, actress ("Dallas," *The Wild Angels, Marlowe*), born Fort Worth, TX, Feb 6, 1943.

Barry Miller, 40, actor (stage: *Biloxi Blues* [Tony, Theatre World, Outer Critics Circle and Drama Desk Awards, 1985]; *Saturday Night Fever, The Last Temptation of Christ*), born Los Angeles, CA, Feb 6, 1958.

Gigi Perreau, 57, actress (*Bonzo Goes to College, Tammy Tell Me True*), born Los Angeles, CA, Feb 6, 1941.

Ronald Wilson Reagan, 87, 40th US president, former sportscaster and actor (*The Winning Team*), born Tampico, IL, Feb 6, 1911.

Rip Torn (Elmore Torn, Jr), 67, actor ("The Larry Sanders Show," *The Blue and the Gray*), born Temple, TX, Feb 6, 1931.

Michael Tucker, 54, actor (Stuart Markowitz on "L.A. Law"), born Baltimore, MD, Feb 6, 1944.

Mamie Van Doren, 65, actress (*High School Confidential, The Candidate, Three Nuts in Search of a Bolt*), born Rowena, SD, Feb 6, 1933.

FEBRUARY 7 — SATURDAY

Day 38 — 327 Remaining

AMERICAN COUNCIL ON EDUCATION ANNUAL MEETING. Feb 7–10. Hyatt Regency Hotel, San Francisco, CA. Est attendance: 1,200. For info: Stephanie Marshall, Amer Council on Educ, One Dupont Circle, Washington, DC 20036. Phone: (202) 939-9410. Fax: (202) 833-4760. Email: stephanie_marshall@ace.nche.edu. WWW: http://www.acenet.edu

AMERICANA INDIAN AND WESTERN ART SHOW AND SALE. Feb 7–9. Yuma, AZ. Indian and Western paintings, rugs and jewelry. Est attendance: 6,000. For info: Marketing Dept, Yuma Civic and Conv Ctr, 1440 Desert Hills Dr, Yuma, AZ 85365. Phone: (520) 344-3800. Fax: (520) 344-9121.

ANTIQUE VALENTINE EXHIBIT. Feb 7–8 (also Feb 12–15). Surratt House and Tavern, Clinton, MD. Display of 19th-century valentines and memorabilia. Est attendance: 500. For info: Surratt House and Tavern, PO Box 427, Clinton, MD 20735. Phone: (301) 868-1121. Fax: (301) 868-8177. WWW: http://www/engr.umd.edu/clw

ARIZONA RENAISSANCE FESTIVAL. Feb 7–Mar 29. (Saturdays, Sundays and Presidents' Day [Feb 16th] only.) Apache Junction, AZ. 10th anniversary season. The king and his court, duelists and fair maidens, crafts, food and games, jousting knights and all the other fun of the days of yore. The official sister event to the Robin Hood Festival in Sherwood Forest, England. Est attendance: 250,000. For info: Arizona Renaissance Festival, 12601 E Highway 60, Apache Junction, AZ 85219. Phone: (520) 463-2700.

BALLET INTRODUCED TO THE US: ANNIVERSARY. Feb 7. Renowned French danseuse Mme Francisquy Hutin introduced ballet to the US on Feb 7, 1827, with a performance of *The Deserter*, staged at the Bowery Theater, New York, NY. A minor scandal erupted when the ladies in the lower boxes left the theatre upon viewing the light and scanty attire of Mme Hutin and her troupe.

BLAKE, EUBIE: BIRTH ANNIVERSARY. Feb 7, 1883. James Hubert "Eubie" Blake, American composer and pianist, writer of nearly 1,000 songs (including "I'm Just Wild about Harry" and "Memories of You"). Born at Baltimore, MD, on Feb 7, 1883. Recipient of the Presidential Medal of Freedom in 1981. Last professional performance was in Jan 1982. Died at Brooklyn, NY, five days after his 100th birthday, on Feb 12, 1983.

CAMELLIA FESTIVAL. Feb 7–14. Massee Lane Gardens, Fort Valley, GA. 7th annual celebration of the beautiful flower, the camellia. Events include: garden tours and workshops, art show and Senior Citizen Day, fashion show and luncheon, Family Fun Day and a tour of homes. Call for more details and ticket prices. Annually, the second week of February. Sponsor: The American Camellia Society. Est attendance: 4,000. For info: Rhonda Gatlin, Activities Dir, Massee Lane Gardens, One Massee Lane, Fort Valley, GA 31030. Phone: (912) 967-2358 or (912) 967-2722. Fax: (912) 967-2083. Email: acs@mail.peach.public.lib.ga.us. WWW: http://www.peach.public.lib.ga.us/ACS/acs.htm

CHOCOLATE FESTIVAL. Feb 7. Firehouse Art Center, Norman, OK. Tasting sessions, cooking competitions and tantalizing displays of chocolate as an art form are a treat for the eyes as well as the palate. Annually, the Saturday before Valentine's Day. Est attendance: 2,000. For info: Linda Sexton, Asst Dir, The Firehouse Art Center, 444 S Flood, Norman, OK 73069. Phone: (405) 329-4523.

DICKENS, CHARLES: BIRTH ANNIVERSARY. Feb 7, 1812. English social critic and novelist, born at Portsmouth, England. Among his most successful books: *Oliver Twist, The Posthumous Papers of the Pickwick Club, David Copperfield* and *A Christmas Carol.* Died at Gad's Hill, England, June 9, 1870, and was buried at Westminster Abbey.

DOLL SHOW. Feb 7. Yuma Civic and Convention Center, Yuma, AZ. Assorted antique, handmade and collector's item dolls on display and for sale. Also, miniature furniture and doll-making supplies on sale. Sponsor: Yuma Doll Club. Est attendance: 650. For info: Marketing Dept, Yuma Civic and Conv Ctr, 1440 Desert Hills Dr, Yuma, AZ 85365. Phone: (520) 782-5797 or (520) 344-3800. Fax: (520) 344-9121.

ELEVENTH AMENDMENT TO US CONSTITUTION (SOVEREIGNTY OF THE STATES): RATIFICATION ANNIVERSARY. Feb 7. On Feb 7, 1795, the 11th Amendment to the Constitution was ratified, curbing the powers of the federal judiciary in relation to the states. The amendment reaffirmed the sovereignty of the states by prohibiting suits against them.

ENGLAND: BRISTOL CLASSIC CAR SHOW. Feb 7–8. Royal Bath and West Showground, Shepton Mallet, Somerset. Everything for the classic car enthusiast with club stands, trade stands and autojumble. Auction at 2 PM Sunday. Est attendance: 18,000. For info: Robert Ewin, Dir, Nationwide Exhibitions (UK) Ltd, PO Box 20, Fishponds, Bristol, England BS16 5QU. Phone: (44) (117) 9701370. Fax: (44) (117) 970-1371.

EVERGLADES CITY SEAFOOD FESTIVAL. Feb 7–8. City Park, Everglades City, FL. Community raises funds to improve community center and city park. School children raise funds to pay for prom and other events. Est attendance: 60,000. For info: Betterment Assn of Everglades Area, Inc, PO Box 5029, Everglades City, FL 34139. Phone: (941) 695-4100. Fax: (941) 695-2526.

FAMILY WILDLIFE FESTIVAL. Feb 7–8. Lindsay Wildlife Museum, Walnut Creek, CA. Wildlife and nature center holds annual festival featuring remarkable live wild animals. Focus on learning to live with wildlife, fascinating differences between wild and domestic animals. Prior festivals have featured a timber wolf, cheetah, snowy leopard and coyote. Annually, the first weekend in February. Est attendance: 3,000. For info: Lindsay Wildlife Museum, 1931 First Ave, Walnut Creek, CA 94596. Phone: (510) 935-1978. Fax: (510) 935-8015.
WWW: http://www.wildlife-museum.org

FIRST SECURITY BOULDER MOUNTAIN TOUR. Feb 7. Galena Lodge, Sun Valley, ID. A 30K cross-country race from Galena Lodge to the Sawtooth National Recreation Area (SNRA) headquarters. For info: Sun Valley/Ketchum Chamber of Commerce, Box 2420, Sun Valley, ID 83353. Out-of-state phone: (800) 634-3347; Idaho phone: (208) 726-3423. Fax: (208) 726-4533. Email: sunval@micron.net. WWW: http://www.visitsunvalley.com

FIRST SECURITY WINTER GAMES OF IDAHO. Feb 7–Mar 1. Idaho Falls, Sun Valley, Boise, McCall and Kellogg, ID. Idaho's official winter sports competition—three weekends of competition in ice hockey, figure skating, alpine skiing, freestyle skiing, telemark skiing, snowboarding, cross-country skiing and snowmobiling with 3,000 participants. For info: Winter Games of Idaho, Amy McDevitt, Exec Dir, PO Box 15214, Boise, ID 83715. Phone: (208) 393-2255. Fax: (208) 393-2187.

GREAT AMERICAN PIZZA BAKE. Feb 7–14. Pizza parlors, restaurants and volunteer agencies nationwide create healthy pizza recipes to increase the public's awareness of the benefits of controlling high cholesterol levels through diet. For info: Frederick S. Mayer, Pres, Cholesterol Council of America, c/o PPSI, PO Box 1336, Sausalito, CA 94966. Phone: (415) 332-4066. Email: ppsi@aol.com.

GRENADA: INDEPENDENCE DAY. Feb 7. National Day.

INVITATIONAL SKI JUMPING TOURNAMENT. Feb 7–8. Eau Claire, WI. More than 60 top jumpers from the US and Canada will fly off the 90-meter hill to compete for a piece of the $1000 purse at this annual tournament now in its 108th year. For info: Wisconsin Dept of Tourism, Ski Jumping Tournament, PO Box 7976, Madison, WI 53707. Phone: (715) 832-2128. Email: tourism@laughlin.com. WWW: http://tourism.state.wi.us

KALEIDOSCOPE ON THE MALL. Feb 7–8. Kennedy Mall, Dubuque, IA. Ethnic food, global art and craft bazaar, continuous ethnic entertainment. Sponsor: Kaleidoscope, An Intercultural Program. Annually, the first weekend in February. Est attendance: 20,000. For info: Ruth Nash, Kaleidoscope, 422 Loras Blvd, Dubuque, IA 52001. Phone: (319) 588-9751. Fax: (319) 588-2714.

LAURA INGALLS WILDER GINGERBREAD SOCIABLE. Feb 7. Pomona, CA. The 31st annual event commemorates the birthday (Feb 7, 1867) of the renowned author of the "Little House" books. The library has on permanent display the handwritten manuscript of *Little Town on the Prairie* and other Wilder memorabilia. Entertainment by fiddlers, craft displays, apple cider and gingerbread. Annually, the first Saturday in February. Est attendance: 300. For info: Marguerite F. Raybould, Friends of the Pomona Public Library, 625 S Garey Ave, Pomona, CA 91766. Phone: (909) 620-2017. Fax: (909) 620-3713.

LEWIS, SINCLAIR: BIRTH ANNIVERSARY. Feb 7. American novelist and social critic. Recipient of Nobel Prize for Literature (1930). Among his novels: *Main Street, Babbitt* and *It Can't Happen Here.* Born Harry Sinclair Lewis at Sauk Center, MN, on Feb 7, 1885. Died at Rome, Italy, Jan 10, 1951.

MID-WINTER ANTIQUES AND COLLECTIBLE SHOW AND SALE. Feb 7–8. Millville, NJ. Snow, rain or shine, the sale will go on. Est attendance: 2,000. For info: Wheaton Village, 1501 Glasstown Rd, Millville, NJ 08332. Phone: (800) 998-4552 or (609) 825-6800. Fax: (609) 825-2410.
Email: mail@wheatonvillage.org.
WWW: http://www.wheatonvillage.org

MORE, SIR THOMAS: BIRTH ANNIVERSARY. Feb 7, 1478. Anniversary of birth of lawyer, scholar, author, Lord Chancellor of England, martyr and saint at London, England, on Feb 7, 1478. Refusing to recognize Henry VIII's divorce from Queen Catherine, the "Man for All Seasons" was found guilty of treason and imprisoned in the Tower of London, Apr 17, 1534. He was beheaded at Tower Hill on July 6, 1535, and his head displayed from Tower Bridge. Canonized in 1935. Memorial observed on June 22.

NATIONAL HOME AND GARDEN SHOW. Feb 7–15. I-X Center, Cleveland, OH. The largest show of its kind in the country with more than 35 feature gardens, 900 exhibitors and three fully decorated and landscaped walk-through model homes. Est attendance: 291,000. For info: National Home and Garden Show, PO Box 550–Edgewater Branch, Cleveland, OH 44107. Phone: (216) 529-1300.

PERRY'S "BRR" (BIKE RIDE TO RIPPEY). Feb 7. Perry, IA. Winter bike riding. Twenty-two miles of frigid fun. Annually, the first Saturday in February. Est attendance: 2,000. For info: Chamber of Commerce, Kathy Hoskinson, 1226 Second St, Perry, IA 50220. Phone: (515) 465-4601. Fax: (515) 465-2256.

SARANAC LAKE WINTER CARNIVAL. Feb 7–15. Saranac Lake, NY. Come and join the family fun with fireworks and entertainment, food booths and much more. Annually, the first two full weekends in February. For info: Saranac Lake Winter Carnival, Saranac Lake Chamber of Commerce, 30 Main St, Saranac Lake, NY 12983. Phone: (518) 891-1990 or (800) 347-1992.

SPACE MILESTONE: *SOYUZ 24* (USSR). Feb 7, 1977. Two cosmonauts docked at *Salyut 5* space lab. Returned to Earth Feb 25. Launched on Feb 7, 1977.

TOMS RIVER WILDFOWL ART AND DECOY SHOW. Feb 7–8. Toms River High School North, Toms River, NJ. 140 artists and carvers, decoy-carving competitions, decorative and gunning decoys, junior competition; free seminars on decoy carving, decoy painting and flat art painting; fine arts competition, etc. Annually, the first weekend in February. Est attendance: 4,000. For info: Janet Sellitto, Management Service Coordinator, Ocean County YMCA, PO Box 130, 1088 Whitty Rd, Toms River, NJ 08754. Fax: (908) 341-1629.
WWW: http://www.ocymca.org

TWIN CITIES' KREW OF JANUS MARDI GRAS PARADE. Feb 7. Monroe, LA. Festive parade to celebrate Mardi Gras. For info: Tourism Sales Mgr, 1333 State Farm Dr, Monroe, LA 71202. Phone: (800) 843-1872. Fax: (318) 324-1752. Email: mwmcvb@iamerica.net.
WWW: http://www.bayou.com/visitors

February 1998

S	M	T	W	T	F	S
1	2	3	4	5	6	7
8	9	10	11	12	13	14
15	16	17	18	19	20	21
22	23	24	25	26	27	28

BIRTHDAYS TODAY

Eddie Bracken, 78, actor (*Miracle of Morgan's Creek, Hail the Conquering Hero*), born New York, NY, Feb 7, 1920.

Oscar Brand, 78, singer, born Winnipeg, Manitoba, Canada, Feb 7, 1920.

Garth Brooks, 36, singer ("Friends in Low Places"), born Tulsa, OK, Feb 7, 1962.

Miguel Ferrer, 44, actor ("Twin Peaks," *Star Trek III: The Search for Spock, Hot Shots! Part Deux*), born Santa Monica, CA, Feb 7, 1954.

Juwan Howard, 25, basketball player, born Chicago, IL, Feb 7, 1973.

Herb Kohl, 63, US Senator (D, Wisconsin), born Milwaukee, WI, Feb 7, 1935.

Daniel Raymond (Dan) Quisenberry, 45, former baseball player, born Santa Monica, CA, Feb 7, 1953.

James Spader, 38, actor (*sex, lies, and videotape, Wolf*), born Boston (MA) suburbs, Feb 7, 1960.

Gay Talese, 66, author (*The Kingdom and the Power, Unto the Sons*), born Ocean City, NJ, Feb 7, 1932.

FEBRUARY 8 — SUNDAY

Day 39 — 326 Remaining

ARCA 200 LATE MODEL STOCK CAR RACE. Feb 8. Daytona International Speedway, Daytona Beach, FL. 35th annual running. Season kickoff for the Bondo/Mar-Hyde Series. For info: Daytona Intl Speedway, PO Box 2801, Daytona Beach, FL 32120-2801. Phone: (904) 947-6782. Fax: (904) 947-6791. WWW: http://www.daytonausa.com

BOY SCOUTS OF AMERICA FOUNDED: ANNIVERSARY. Feb 8. On Feb 8, 1910, the Boy Scouts of America was founded in Washington, DC, by William Boyce, based on the work of Sir Robert Baden-Powell with the British Boy Scout Association.

BUSCH CLASH OF '98. Feb 8. Daytona International Speedway, Daytona Beach, FL. Winners of Busch Pole Awards for the NASCAR Winston Cup season. Sponsor: Busch Beer. For info: Daytona Intl Speedway, PO Box 2801, Daytona Beach, FL 32120-2801. Phone: (904) 947-6782. Fax: (904) 947-6791.

CANADA: YUKON QUEST 1,000-MILE SLED DOG RACE. Feb 8–20. Whitehorse, Yukon. The 15th annual "challenge of the North" 1,000-mile dog sled race from Whitehorse, YT, to Fairbanks, AK. Top mushers from North America and around the world compete for the $125,000 purse. Est attendance: 10,000. For info: Yukon Quest Intl Assn, Box 5555, Whitehorse, YT, Canada Y1A 5H4. Phone: (403) 668-4711. Info also from: Yukon Quest, Intl, PO Box 75015, Fairbanks, AK 99707. Phone: (907) 452-7954. WWW: http://www.yukonquest.org

CARDIAC REHABILITATION WEEK. Feb 8–14. For info: American Assn of Cardiovascular and Pulmonary Rehabilitation, 7611 Elmwood Ave, Ste 201, Middleton, WI 53562. Phone: (608) 831-6989.

CELEBRATION OF LOVE WEEK. Feb 8–14. To stress the importance and value of love in making the world a much better place in which to live. For complete info, send $3 to cover expense of printing, handling and postage. Annually, the second full week of February. For info: Dr. Stanley Drake, Pres, Intl Soc of Friendship and Good Will, 412 Cherry Hills Dr, Bakersfield, CA 93309-2866.

DEAN, JAMES: BIRTH ANNIVERSARY. Feb 8, 1931. American stage, film and television actor, who achieved immense popularity during a brief career. Born at Fairmont, IN. Best remembered for his role in *Rebel Without a Cause*. Died in an automobile accident on Sept 30, 1955, at age 24. Stamp collectors made the US postal stamp bearing Dean's likeness the most popular stamp of 1996.

DESERT FOOTHILLS MUSICFEST. Feb 8–22 (Feb 9–10, 12, 14–15, 17–20). Carefree/Cave Creek, AZ in four venues. Arizona's premier winter classical music festival celebrates its 7th anniversary with 11 events over a 15-day period. Eight concerts, three daytime "Festival Insights," (lecture, mini-concerts). Features the festival chamber ensemble, Phoenix Symphony Orchestra, solo and guest artists. Artists from music centers in Arizona and across the US perform. Est attendance: 4,000. For info: Desert Foothills, Musicfest Publicity, PO Box 5254, Carefree, AZ 85377. Phone: (602) 488-0806. Fax: (602) 488-2310.

"GOOD TIMES" TV PREMIERE: ANNIVERSARY. Feb 8, 1974. A CBS spinoff from "Maude," which was a spinoff of "All in the Family." "Good Times" featured an African-American family living in the housing projects of Chicago. The series portrayed the Evans family's struggles to improve their lot. The cast featured Esther Rolle and John Amos as Florida and James Evans; Jimmie Walker as son J.J.; BernNadette Stanis as daughter Thelma; Ralph Carter as son Michael; Johnny Brown as janitor Mr. Bookman; Ja'net DuBois as neighbor Willona Woods; Janet Jackson as Willona's adopted daughter Penny; and Ben Powers as Thelma's husband, Keith Anderson. "Good Times" was created by Michael Evans and Eric Monte and initially produced by Norman Lear.

JAPAN: HA-RI-KU-YO (NEEDLE MASS). Feb 8. Ha-Ri-Ku-Yo, a Needle Mass, may be observed on either Feb 8 or Dec 8. On this day girls do no needlework; instead they gather old and broken needles, which they dedicate to the Awashima Shrine in Wakayama. Girls pray to Awashima Myozin (their protecting deity) that their needlework, symbolic of love and marriage, will be good. Participation in the Needle Mass hopefully leads to a happy marriage.

JAPAN: SNOW FESTIVAL. Feb 8–12. Sapporo, Hokkaido. Huge, elaborate snow and ice sculptures are erected on the Odori-Koen Promenade.

KURSK RETAKEN: 55th ANNIVERSARY. Feb 8, 1943. One year and three months after being taken by the Nazis, the important railroad junction of Kursk was retaken by the Red Army. This city had served as a principle center of north/south communication and was an essential post for the German army in their chain to the Ukraine.

LOVE MAY MAKE THE WORLD GO 'ROUND, BUT LAUGHTER KEEPS US FROM GETTING DIZZY WEEK. Feb 8–14. This week is dedicated to Victor Borge's notion that "Laughter is the shortest distance between two people" and Joel Goodman's notion that "Seven days without laughter makes one weak." This is a chance to lighten your relationships and to reinforce the connection between "heart" and "hearty laughter." Annually, the week leading up to and including Valentine's Day. To receive a free live-love-laugh info packet on the positive power of humor, send a stamped ($1.01), self-addressed envelope. For info: The HUMOR Project, Inc, 110 Spring St, Dept C, Saratoga Springs, NY 12866. Phone: (518) 587-8770. Fax: (518) 587-8771. Email: humor@wizvax.net. WWW: http://www.wizvax.net/humor/

MARTHA GRIFFITHS SPEAKS OUT AGAINST SEX DISCRIMINATION: ANNIVERSARY. Feb 8. On Feb 8, 1964, during the congressional debate over the 1964 Civil Rights Act, Representative Martha Griffiths delivered a memorable speech advocating the prohibition of discrimination based on sex. Her efforts resulted in adding civil rights protection for women to the 1964 Act. She later successfully led the campaign for the Equal Rights Amendment in the House of Representatives.

MARY, QUEEN OF SCOTS: EXECUTION ANNIVERSARY. Feb 8, 1587. Mary Stuart, the queen regent of Scotland, was beheaded at Fotheringhay, England, her death warrant having been sealed by Queen Elizabeth I on Feb 1. Mary, the daughter of James V of Scotland by his second wife, Mary of Guise, was born Dec 7 or 8, 1542, at Linlithgow, Scotland, and became queen a week later upon the death of her father, although she did not begin governing until after the death of her mother in 1561. She was forced to abdicate in favor of her son (James VI) when the people turned against her after she married the Earl of Bothwell, who was believed to be the murderer with Mary's knowledge of her second husband (her cousin Henry Stewart, Lord Darnley). She fled to England for protection, only to find herself a prisoner for the rest of her life. She was tried and sentenced to death in 1586 because of her involvement in a plot to assassinate Elizabeth. She was buried at Peterborough, but in 1612 her body was moved to Henry VII's Chapel at Westminster, where a tomb was erected by her son. Essentially, Mary Stuart was a victim of the political intrigue and Protestant–Roman Catholic conflicts that surrounded the Reformation and Henry VIII's ecclesiastical revolution.

★**NATIONAL CHILD PASSENGER SAFETY AWARENESS WEEK.** Feb 8–14. For info: Office of Occupant Protection, National Highway Safety Administration, 400 Seventh St SW, Washington, DC 20590. Phone: (202) 366-9550.

NATIONAL FUTURE HOMEMAKERS OF AMERICA FHA/HERO WEEK. Feb 8–14. To call the nation's attention to the activities and goals of the organization and family and consumer sciences education. Theme: "Building Strong Leaders in Families, Careers and Communities." For info: Patti Frattarola, Comm Coord, Future Homemakers of America, 1910 Association Dr, Reston, VA 21091. Phone: (703) 476-4900. Fax: (703) 860-2713.

OCEAN COUNTY BLUEGRASS FESTIVAL. Feb 8 (snow date Feb 15). Waretown, NJ. A family-oriented bluegrass festival where no alcoholic beverages or smoking are allowed. For info: Albert Music Hall, PO Box 657, Waretown, NJ 08758. Phone: (609) 971-1593.

OPERA DEBUT IN THE COLONIES: ANNIVERSARY. Feb 8. The first opera produced in the colonies was performed on Feb 8, 1735, at the Courtroom, in Charleston, SC. The opera was *Flora; or the Hob in the Well*, written by Colley Cibber.

PAPAL TREASURES FROM THE VATICAN COLLECTIONS. Feb 8–Apr 12. Cleveland, OH. An exhibition at the Cleveland Museum of Art of early Christian, Renaissance and Baroque art to coincide with the sesquicentennial of the Catholic Diocese of Cleveland. For info: Cleveland Museum of Art, 11150 East Blvd, Cleveland, OH 44106. Phone: (216) 421-7340. WWW: http://www.clemusart.com

REENACTMENT OF COWTOWN'S LAST OLD WEST GUNFIGHT. Feb 8. White Elephant Saloon, Fort Worth, TX. Annual reenactment of Fort Worth's last Old West gunfight, which took place on Feb 8, 1887, between White Elephant Saloon owner Luke Short and former Marshal T.I. "Longhaired Jim" Courtright. Annually, Feb 8. Est attendance: 400. For info: Joe Dulle, Owner, 108 E Exchange Ave, Fort Worth, TX 76106-8210. Phone: (817) 624-9712. Fax: (817) 625-9663.

SAM AND ELIZABETH COLT EXHIBITION. Feb 8–Apr 5 (also Sept 12–Dec 8). Wadsworth, Atheneum, Hartford, CT. "Sam & Elizabeth: Legend and Legacy of Colt's Empire"—an epic exhibition dramatizing the effect of industrialization through an encounter with Hartford's Sam and Elizabeth Colt. It features 250 works of art and memorabilia, including paintings, sculpture, furniture, jewelry, photos and Sam Colt's firearms collection. Est attendance: 50,000. For info: PR Dept, Wadsworth Atheneum, 600 Main St, Hartford, CT 06103. Phone: (860) 278-2670 ext 3050. Fax: (860) 527-0803.

SHERMAN, WILLIAM TECUMSEH: BIRTH ANNIVERSARY. Feb 8. Born at Lancaster, OH, Feb 8, 1820. General Sherman is especially remembered for his devastating march through Georgia during the Civil War and his statement "War is hell." Died at New York, NY, Feb 14, 1891.

SPACE MILESTONE: *ARABSAT-1*. Feb 8, 1985. League of Arab States communications satellite launched into geosynchronous orbit from Kourou, French Guiana, by ESA, Feb 8, 1985.

SPACE MILESTONE: *BRASILSAT-1* (BRAZIL). Feb 8, 1985. Brazilian communications satellite launched into geosynchronous orbit from Kourou, French Guiana, by ESA, Feb 8, 1985.

VERNE, JULES: BIRTH ANNIVERSARY. Feb 8, 1828. French writer, sometimes called "the father of science fiction." Born at Nantes, France, on Feb 8, 1828. Author of *Around the World in Eighty Days, Twenty Thousand Leagues Under the Sea* and many other novels. Died at Amiens, France, on Mar 24, 1905.

WORLD MARRIAGE DAY. Feb 8. A special day to honor all marriages. Celebrations worldwide include parades, dances, shopping mall events, balloon releases, dinners, religious services, renewing wedding vows, local contests for posters and essays and a national Couple Married Longest Search. Annually, the second Sunday in February. For info: Mark & Cheryl Stoker, World Marriage Day, 2625 S Dundee St, Tampa, FL 33629. Phone: (813) 835-0795. Fax: (813) 835-1690.

WSBA and WARM 103 EASTER CRAFT SHOW. Feb 8. York, PA. Quality craft displays will be presented with everything from miniatures and ornaments to quilts and country furniture. Admission fee. Est attendance: 6,500. For info: Gina M. Koch, Special Events Dir, PO Box 910, York, PA 17402-0619. Phone: (717) 764-1155. Fax: (717) 252-4708.

BIRTHDAYS TODAY

Brooke Adams, 49, actress (*Days of Heaven, Gas Food Lodging*), born New York, NY, Feb 8, 1949.

Gary Coleman, 30, actor ("Diff'rent Strokes," *The Kid from Left Field*), born Zion, IL, Feb 8, 1968.

John Grisham, 43, author (*The Firm, The Client*), born Jonesboro, AR, Feb 8, 1955.

Robert Klein, 56, comedian ("Comedy Tonight," "TV's Bloopers & Practical Jokes"), born New York, NY, Feb 8, 1942.

Ted Koppel, 58, journalist (anchor of "Nightline"), born Lancashire, England, Feb 8, 1940.

Jack Lemmon (John Uhler, III), 73, actor (*Mr Roberts, The Odd Couple*), born Boston, MA, Feb 8, 1925.

Nick Nolte, 57, actor (*48 Hours, Grace Quigley, Prince of Tides*, "Rich Man, Poor Man"), born Omaha, NE, Feb 8, 1941.

Mary Steenburgen, 45, actress (*Melvin and Howard, Parenthood, Back to the Future Part III*), born Newport, AR, Feb 8, 1953.

John Williams, 66, musician (pianist), conductor (formerly with Boston Pops), composer (scores for *Jaws, Star Wars, Jurassic Park, Schindler's List*), born New York, NY, Feb 8, 1932.

February 1998

S	M	T	W	T	F	S
1	2	3	4	5	6	7
8	9	10	11	12	13	14
15	16	17	18	19	20	21
22	23	24	25	26	27	28

FEBRUARY 9 — MONDAY

Day 40 — 325 Remaining

ADE, GEORGE: BIRTH ANNIVERSARY. Feb 9, 1866. American newspaperman, playwright and humorist. Born at Kentland, IN. Remembered especially for his *Fables in Slang*, published in 1900. Died at Brook, IN, May 16, 1944.

ALLIES RETAKE GUADALCANAL: 55th ANNIVERSARY. Feb 9, 1943. In a major strategic victory, the American 161st and 132nd Regiments retook Guadalcanal in the Solomon Islands on this date after a six-month- long battle. More than nine thousand Japanese and two thousand Americans were killed. The fierce resistance by the Japanese was an indication to the Allies of things to come. Guadalcanal put the Allies within striking distance of Rabaul, the major Japanese base in the area.

BEHAN, BRENDAN: 75th BIRTH ANNIVERSARY. Feb 9, 1923. Irish playwright and poet. Born at Dublin, Ireland, on Feb 9, 1923. Died there on Mar 20, 1964.

DIETARY MANAGERS' PRIDE IN FOOD SERVICE WEEK. Feb 9–13. An annual commemorative event honoring dietary managers and their employees and celebrating the important role they play in institutional food service. Annually, in February. For info: Dennis Leopold, VP, Dietary Managers Assn, One Pierce Pl, Ste 1220W, Itasca, IL 60143-1277. Phone: (800) 323-1908. Fax: (708) 775-9250.

FREELANCE WRITERS APPRECIATION WEEK. Feb 9–13. Freelance writers do more than query editors and write and submit articles and books (nonfiction and fiction). They provide overworked editors with material, as well as inform and entertain readers. Annually, the second week of February. For info: Dorothy Zjawin, Dir, 61 W Colfax Ave, Roselle Park, NJ 07204. Phone: (908) 241-6241. Fax: (908) 241-6241.

GTE SUNCOAST CLASSIC. Feb 9–15 (tentative). TPC of Tampa Bay, Tampa, FL. One of the premier stops on the Senior PGA Tour, attracting one of the strongest fields of top Senior Tour pros. The TPC of Tampa Bay affords outstanding "Stadium Golf"® viewing with amphitheater-style mounds along fairways and around greens. Pro-am event Wednesday and Thursday, followed by professional competitive rounds Fri–Sun. Est attendance: 187,000. For info: GTE Suncoast Classic, 16002 N Dale Mabry, 2nd Fl, Tampa, FL 33618. Phone: (813) 265-4653. Fax: (813) 265-4655. Email: dantram@gte.net.
WWW: http://www.classic.gte.net

GYPSY ROSE LEE: BIRTH ANNIVERSARY. Feb 9. American ecdysiast and author whose real name was Rose Louise Hovick. Born at Seattle, WA, on Feb 9, 1914. Her autobiography, *Gypsy*, was made into a Broadway musical and a motion picture. Died at Los Angeles, CA, on Apr 26, 1970.

HARRISON, WILLIAM HENRY: 225th BIRTH ANNIVERSARY. Feb 9, 1773. 9th president of the US (Mar 4–Apr 4, 1841). His term of office was the shortest in our nation's history—32 days. He was the first president to die in office (of pneumonia contracted during inaugural ceremonies). Born at Berkeley, VA, Feb 9, 1773. Died at Washington, DC, Apr 4, 1841.

ITALY: CARNIVAL WEEK. Feb 9–15. Milan. Carnival week is held according to local tradition, with shows and festive events for children on Tuesday and Thursday. Parades of floats, figures in the costume of local folk characters Meneghin and Cecca, parties and more traditional events are held on Saturday. Annually, the Sunday–Saturday of Ash Wednesday week.

LOWELL, AMY: BIRTH ANNIVERSARY. Feb 9. American poet born at Brookline, MA, Feb 9, 1874. Died there May 12, 1925.

NATIONAL "DAV" DAY. Feb 9. "DAV" stands for Develop Alternative Vices. A day to change your habits, improve yourself and become your own person so that things you do today will affect you positively tomorrow. Annually, Feb 9. For info: Kevin Davenport, 5304 Regency Way, Rockford, IL 61114.

NATIONAL FIELD TRIAL CHAMPIONSHIP. Feb 9–20. (Monday–Friday only.) Ames Plantation, Grand Junction, TN. To select the national champion all-age bird dog. Est attendance: 8,000. For info: Natl Field Trial Champion Assn, Box 389, Grand Junction, TN 38039. Phone: (901) 878-1067. Fax: (901) 878-1068.

RANDOM ACTS OF KINDNESS WEEK. Feb 9–15. A global grass roots awareness campaign and celebration of the power of Random Acts of Kindness as a counterbalance to random acts of violence. Our goal is to reverse the tide of anger and violence in our society by deepening our connection with others through the practice of simple, day-to-day kindness to our fellow humankind. Annually, Monday–Sunday including Feb 14. For info: Nancy Briggin, Dir, Random Acts of Kindness Foundation, 411 Scenic Rd, Fairfax, CA 94930. Phone: (415) 456-0480. Fax: (415) 456-0680. Email: rakday96@aol.com. WWW: http://www.ReadersNdex.com.randomacts/

RUSK, (DAVID) DEAN: BIRTH ANNIVERSARY. Feb 9, 1909. US diplomat Dean Rusk was born at Cherokee County, GA. He served as US secretary of state from 1961 to 1969, during which time he gave continual support for US involvement in the Vietnam War. He died on Dec 20, 1994, at Athens, GA.

TUBB, ERNEST: BIRTH ANNIVERSARY. Feb 9. Country and western singer, born at Crisp, TX, on Feb 9, 1914. Ernest Tubb was the sixth member to be elected to the Country Music Hall of Fame and the headliner on the first country music show ever to be presented at Carnegie Hall. His first major hit, "Walking the Floor Over You," gained him his first appearance at the Grand Ole Opry in 1942, and he attained regular membership in 1943. He died on Sept 6, 1984, at Nashville, TN.

VEECK, BILL: BIRTH ANNIVERSARY. Feb 9, 1914. William Louis (Bill) Veeck, Jr, Baseball Hall of Fame executive born at Chicago, IL. Veeck was baseball's premier promoter and showman as an owner of several teams. He integrated the American League, sent a midget to the plate to start a game and, in general, sought to provide fans with entertainment in addition to baseball. Inducted into the Hall of Fame in 1991. Died at Chicago, IL, Jan 2, 1986.

WAR TIME: ANNIVERSARY. Feb 9, 1942. US clocks were advanced one hour at 2 AM as the nation went on War Time to conserve electricity. President Roosevelt had signed this daylight savings bill on Jan 20.

BIRTHDAYS TODAY

Mia Farrow (Maria de Lourdes Villers), 53, actress ("Peyton Place," *Rosemary's Baby, Hannah and Her Sisters*), born Los Angeles, CA, Feb 9, 1945.

Kathryn Grayson (Zelma Hedrick), 75, actress (*Kiss Me Kate, The Kissing Bandit*), born Winston-Salem, NC, Feb 9, 1923.

Carole King, 56, singer, songwriter, born Brooklyn, NY, Feb 9, 1942.

John Martin Kruk, 37, former baseball player, born Charleston, WV, Feb 9, 1961.

Judith Light, 49, actress ("One Life to Live," "Who's the Boss?"), born Trenton, NJ, Feb 9, 1949.

Roger Mudd, 70, journalist (former anchorman "ABC Evening News"), born Washington, DC, Feb 9, 1928.

Joe Pesci, 55, actor (*Raging Bull, Goodfellas, My Cousin Vinny*), born Newark, NJ, Feb 9, 1943.

Charles Shaughnessy, 43, actor ("The Nanny"), born London, England, Feb 9, 1955.

Janet Suzman, 59, actress (*Nicholas and Alexandra, A Dry White Season*), born Johannesburg, South Africa, Feb 9, 1939.

Travis Tritt, 35, country and western singer (*Country Club*), born Marietta, GA, Feb 9, 1963.

Alice Walker, 54, author (*The Color Purple, The Temple of My Familiar, Possessing the Secret of Joy, Meridian*), born Eatonton, GA, Feb 9, 1944.

James Webb, 52, former US Secretary of the Navy, born St. Joseph, MO, Feb 9, 1946.

FEBRUARY 10 — TUESDAY

Day 41 — 324 Remaining

"ALL THE NEWS THAT'S FIT TO PRINT": ANNIVERSARY. Feb 10. The familiar slogan "All the News That's Fit to Print" has appeared on page one of *The New York Times* since Feb 10, 1897. Although in October 1896 *The New York Times* offered a prize of $100 to anyone who could come up with a better slogan of 10 words or less, none was found.

ANDERSON, DAME JUDITH: 100th BIRTH ANNIVERSARY. Feb 10, 1898. Australian film and stage actress Dame Judith Anderson was born Frances Margaret Anderson at Adelaide, Australia. She was nominated for an Academy Award in 1941 for her role in Alfred Hitchcock's film *Rebecca*. In 1960 she was made Dame Commander of the British Empire by Queen Elizabeth II. She died on Jan 3, 1992, at Santa Barbara, CA.

BRECHT, BERTOLT: 100th BIRTH ANNIVERSARY. Feb 10, 1898. German playwright born at Augsburg. His plays, such as *Mother Courage*, reflect his Marxist and antimilitary world view. Also wrote plays (*The Threepenny Opera*) in collaboration with composer Kurt Weill. Died at East Berlin, Aug 14, 1956.

CALIFORNIA FARM EQUIPMENT SHOW AND INTERNATIONAL EXPOSITION. Feb 10–12. Tulare, CA. The largest farm equipment show in North America. For info: PO Box 1475, 4450 S Laspina, Tulare, CA 93275. Phone: (800) 999-9186 or (209) 688-1751. Fax: (209) 686-5065. Email: agricenter@worldnet.att.net. WWW: http://www.farmshow.org

DUMP YOUR "SIGNIFICANT JERK" DAY. Feb 10. It's time to take out the garbage and get rid of that "Jerk" boyfriend or girlfriend. Annually, the Tuesday before Valentine's Day. For info: Marcus P. Melton Jr, Sharkbait Press, PO Box 11300, Costa Mesa, CA 92627. Phone: (714) 645-0139.

DURANTE, JIMMY: BIRTH ANNIVERSARY. Feb 10, 1893. "The Schnozz," Jimmy Durante, was born at New York City. Durante's barber father found money to pay for piano lessons, and Jimmy began earning money playing for neighborhood parties and dances. His first "break" into show biz came when he was 17 and got a regular job playing ragtime at Diamond Tony's Saloon at Coney Island. Later, he worked at Coney Island with his friend Eddie Cantor, who urged him to try comedy. Durante developed a unique comedic style as a short-tempered but lovable personage. His shtick included slamming down his hat and flapping his arms. His clothing, his enormous nose, craggy face, gravelly singing voice and mispronunciations were all part of the persona. Durante, whose career spanned six decades, appeared on TV, stage and screen. His television signoff, "Good night, Mrs Calabash, wherever you are!" became a trademark. Jimmy Durante died at Santa Monica, CA, Jan 29, 1980.

FIRST ACTOR TO PERFORM IN TWO CITIES ON THE SAME DAY: ANNIVERSARY. Feb 10, 1887. Nathaniel Carr Goodwin performed at an 11:30 AM matinee of *Turned Up* in Boston, MA, then, following the closing curtain, he returned to New York City on the 1 PM train and that evening performed in *The Mascot* at the Bijou Theatre at 8 PM.

FIRST WORLD WAR II MEDAL OF HONOR: ANNIVERSARY. Feb 10, 1942. Second Lt Alexander Ramsey ("Sandy") Nininger, Jr, was posthumously awarded World War II's first Medal of Honor for heroism at the Battle of Bataan. He had graduated from West Point in 1941 and was on his first assignment after being commissioned.

GRAND CENTER BOAT SHOW. Feb 10–15. Grand Center, Grand Rapids, MI. This event brings together buyers and sellers of power and sail boats, boating accessories, docks, dockominiums and vacation properties. Est attendance: 32,000. For info: Henri Boucher, ShowSpan, Inc, 1400 28th St SW, Grand Rapids, MI 49509. Phone: (616) 530-1919.

LAMB, CHARLES: BIRTH ANNIVERSARY. Feb 10. Literary critic, poet and essayist, born at London, England, on Feb 10, 1775. "The greatest pleasure I know," he wrote in 1834, "is to do a good action by stealth, and to have it found out by accident." Died at Edmonton, England, Dec 27, 1834.

MALTA: FEAST OF ST. PAUL'S SHIPWRECK. Feb 10. Valletta. Holy day of obligation. Commemorates shipwreck of St. Paul on the north coast of Malta in AD 60.

"MY FRIEND FLICKA" TV PREMIERE: ANNIVERSARY. Feb 10, 1956. CBS series about a boy and his horse based on the children's book by Mary O'Hara. The series is set in the early 1900s on the Goose Bar Ranch in Montana. Johnny Washbrook starred as Ken McLaughlin; Gene Evans as Ken's father, Rob; Anita Louise as Ken's mother, Nell; Frank Ferguson as Gus, the ranch hand; and Wahama, the beautiful Arabian horse, as Flicka. A real drooler for those horse-loving girls.

PASTERNAK, BORIS LEONIDOVICH: BIRTH ANNIVERSARY. Feb 10. Russian poet and novelist, born at Moscow, Russia, Feb 10, 1890. Best-known work: *Doctor Zhivago*. Died at Moscow, May 30, 1960.

PLIMSOLL DAY. Feb 10, 1824. A day to remember Samuel Plimsoll, "The Sailor's Friend," a coal merchant turned reformer and politician, who was elected to Parliament in 1868. He attacked the practice of overloading heavily insured ships, calling them "coffin ships." His persistence brought about amendment of Britain's Merchant Shipping Act. The Plimsoll Line, named for him, is a line on the side of ships marking maximum load allowed by law. Born at Bristol, England, Feb 10, 1824. Died at Folkestone, England, June 3, 1898.

ROENTGEN, WILHELM KONRAD: 75th DEATH ANNIVERSARY. Feb 10, 1923. German physicist, born at Lennep, Prussia, Mar 27, 1845. Discovered the X-ray and won the first Nobel Prize for physics. Died at Munich, Germany, Feb 10, 1923.

TWENTY-FIFTH AMENDMENT TO US CONSTITUTION RATIFIED (PRESIDENTIAL SUCCESSION, DISABILITY): ANNIVERSARY. Feb 10, 1967. Procedures for presidential succession were further clarified by the 25th Amendment, along with provisions for continuity of power in the event of a disability or illness of the president. The 25th Amendment was ratified on Feb 10, 1967.

WHITE, WILLIAM ALLEN: BIRTH ANNIVERSARY. Feb 10, 1868. American newspaperman, owner and editor of the *Emporia Gazette*. Coined the phrase "tinhorn politician" and, in one obituary, wrote of the deceased that he had "the talent of a meat-packer, the morals of a money changer and the manners of an undertaker." Born at Emporia, KS, Feb 10, 1868. Died there Jan 29, 1944.

BIRTHDAYS TODAY

Laura Dern, 31, actress (*Blue Velvet, Rambling Rose*), born Los Angeles, CA, Feb 10, 1967.

Donovan (Donovan P. Leitch), 52, singer, songwriter, born Glasgow, Scotland, Feb 10, 1946.

Leonard Kyle (Lenny) Dykstra, 35, baseball player, born Santa Ana, CA, Feb 10, 1963.

Roberta Flack, 59, singer, born Black Mountain, NC, Feb 10, 1939.

Kirk Fordice, 64, Governor of Mississippi (R), born Memphis, TN, Feb 10, 1934.

Dennis Louis Gentry, 39, former football player, born Lubbock, TX, Feb 10, 1959.

Frances Moore Lappe, 54, author (*Diet for a Small Planet, Rediscovering America's Values*), born Pendleton, OR, Feb 10, 1944.

Gregory John (Greg) Norman, 43, golfer, born Melbourne, Australia, Feb 10, 1955.

Leontyne Price, 71, opera singer, born Laurel, MS, Feb 10, 1927.

Mark Andrew Spitz, 48, Olympic gold medal swimmer, born Modesto, CA, Feb 10, 1950.

Robert Wagner, 68, actor ("It Takes a Thief," "Hart to Hart"), born Detroit, MI, Feb 10, 1930.

☆ ☆ ☆

FEBRUARY 11 — WEDNESDAY

Day 42 — 323 Remaining

BE ELECTRIFIC DAY. Feb 11. Connecticut Life Extension Center, Danbury, CT. A day to honor the birth of Thomas Alva Edison and discover "electricity" of the body through applied kinesiology and other body energy demonstrations. For info: Carolyn Finch, Applied Kinesiologist, Bogart Communications Inc, 51 Cedar Dr, Danbury, CT 06811. Phone: (203) 792-4833. Fax: (203) 743-5675.

CAMEROON: YOUTH DAY. Feb 11. Public holiday.

CHILD, LYDIA MARIA: BIRTH ANNIVERSARY. Feb 11, 1802. Lydia Maria Child was born on Feb 11, 1802, at Medord, MA. As a writer her works included *Hobomok*, about early Salem and Plymouth life, and *The Rebels*, which described pre-Revolutionary Boston. In addition, she produced several practical works including *The Frugal Housewife*, which enjoyed 21 editions, and *The Mother's Book*. In 1833 she and her husband, David Lee Child, published the controversial abolitionist document "An Appeal in Favor of That Class of Americans Called Africans," which called for educating the slaves. Their work for abolition continued with the weekly newspaper *The National Anti-Slavery Standard*, which they published in New York City from 1840–1844. Lydia died Oct 20, 1880, at Wayland, MA.

CHINA: LANTERN FESTIVAL. Feb 11. Traditional Chinese festival falls on 15th day of first month of Chinese lunar calendar year. Lantern processions mark end of the Chinese New Year holiday season. See also: "Chinese New Year" (Jan 28).

DUNNE, PHILIP: 90th BIRTH ANNIVERSARY. Feb 11, 1908. American screenwriter and director Philip Dunne was born at New York, NY. In 1947 he joined directors John Huston and William Wyler to found the Committee for the First Amendment, which campaigned against the "blacklisting" in Hollywood of anyone suspected of being a communist by the House Un-American Activities Committee. He was also a founder of the Screen Writers Guild. Dunne died on June 2, 1992, at Malibu, CA.

EDISON, THOMAS ALVA: BIRTH ANNIVERSARY. Feb 11, 1847. American inventive genius and holder of more than 1,200 patents (including the incandescent electric lamp, phonograph, electric dynamo and key parts of many now-familiar devices such as the movie camera, telephone transmitter, etc). Edison said, "Genius is 1 percent inspiration and 99 percent perspiration." His birthday is now widely observed as Inventor's Day. Born at Milan, OH, and died at Menlo Park, NJ, Oct 18, 1931, at age 84.

FIRST WOMAN EPISCOPAL BISHOP: ANNIVERSARY. Feb 11, 1989. The presiding bishop of the Episcopal Church, Bishop Edmond L. Browning, consecrated Rev Barbara Clementine Harris as a bishop of the Episcopal Church.

February 1998

S	M	T	W	T	F	S
1	2	3	4	5	6	7
8	9	10	11	12	13	14
15	16	17	18	19	20	21
22	23	24	25	26	27	28

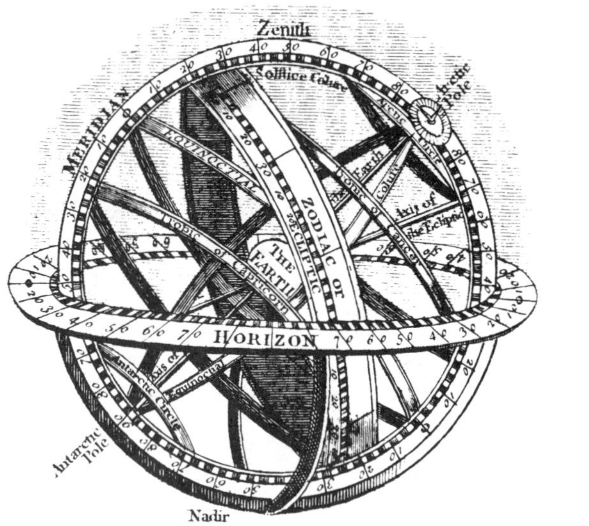

FULLER, MELVILLE WESTON: BIRTH ANNIVERSARY. Feb 11, 1833. Eighth chief justice of the US Supreme Court. Born at Augusta, ME, Feb 11, 1833. Died at Sorrento, ME, July 4, 1910.

GIBBS, JOSIAH WILLARD: BIRTH ANNIVERSARY. Feb 11, 1839. Chemist and professor of physics at Yale, born at New Haven, CT. Gibbs died at New Haven, CT, Apr 28, 1903.

IRAN, ISLAMIC REPUBLIC OF: NATIONAL DAY. Feb 11. National holiday observed in Islamic Republic of Iran.

JAPAN: NATIONAL FOUNDATION DAY: ANNIVERSARY. Feb 11. Marks the founding of the Japanese nation. In 1872 the government officially set Feb 11, 660 BC, as the date of accession to the throne of the Emperor Jimmu (said to be Japan's first emperor) and designated the day a national holiday by the name of Empire Day. The holiday was abolished after World War II, but was revived as National Foundation Day in 1966. Ceremonies are held with Their Imperial Majesties the Emperor and Empress, the Prime Minister and other dignitaries attending. National holiday.

MANDELA, NELSON: PRISON RELEASE ANNIVERSARY. Feb 11, 1990. At 4:14 PM (locally), Feb 11, 1990, after serving more than 27½ years of a life sentence (convicted, with eight others, of sabotage and conspiracy to overthrow the government), South Africa's Nelson Mandela, 71 years old, walked away from the Victor Verster prison farm at Paarl, South Africa, a free man. He had survived the cruelty accorded to blacks by a governmental system of apartheid, the legally enforced separation and oppression of non-white persons. Mandela greeted a cheering throng of well-wishers, along with hundreds of millions of television viewers worldwide, with demands for an intensification of the struggle for equality for blacks, who make up nearly 75% of South Africa's population.

MANKIEWICZ, JOSEPH L.: BIRTH ANNIVERSARY. Feb 11, 1909. Oscar-winning American film writer, director and producer was born at Wilkes-Barre, PA. He became a Hollywood screenwriter, winning an Oscar nomination for *Skippy* in 1931. He coined the famous W.C. Fields phrase "my little chickadee" for the 1932 film *If I Had a Million*. In 1935 he turned to producing and subsequently made *The Philadelphia Story, Strange Cargo* and *Woman of the Year*. He began directing in 1946 with *Dragonwyck* and his stature grew with such films as *The Late George Apley, The Ghost and Mrs Muir, A Letter to Three Wives, All About Eve, Guys and Dolls, Cleopatra* and *Sleuth*, among others. Mankiewicz won four Academy Awards for directing and screenwriting. He died Feb 5, 1993, at Mount Kisco, NY.

MOON PHASE: FULL MOON. Feb 11. Moon enters Full Moon phase at 5:23 AM, EST.

SPACE MILESTONE: FIRST SOVIET COMMERCIAL SATELLITE MISSION. Feb 11, 1990. Anatoly Solovyov and Aleksandr Balandin departed the Baikonur launching site on the Soviet Union's first satellite mission designed for profit—by producing industrial crystals in the weightlessness of space. The craft arrived at the *Mir* orbital space station on Feb 13. Launching of the *Soyuz* TM-9 capsule was witnessed by four American astronauts and televised live. The mission was hailed as initiating a new level of openness of information about Soviet space projects.

SPACE MILESTONE: *OSUMI* (JAPAN). Feb 11, 1970. First Japanese satellite launched Feb 11, 1970. Japan became fourth nation to send a satellite into space.

TAIWAN: LANTERN FESTIVAL AND TOURISM DAY. Feb 11. Fifteenth day of the First Moon of the lunar calendar marks end of New Year holiday season. Lantern processions and contests.

TU B'SHVAT. Feb 11. Hebrew calendar date: Shebat 15, 5758. The 15th day of the month of Shebat in the Hebrew calendar year is set aside as Hamishah Asar (New Year of the Trees or Jewish Arbor Day), a time to show respect and appreciation for trees and plants.

VATICAN CITY: INDEPENDENCE ANNIVERSARY. Feb 11. The Lateran Treaty, signed by Pietro Cardinal Gasparri and Benito Mussolini on Feb 11, 1929, guaranteed the independence of the State of Vatican City and recognized the sovereignty of the Holy See over it. Area is about 109 acres.

WATER CLOSET INCIDENT: ANNIVERSARY. Feb 11. Jack Paar, then host of "The Tonight Show," walked out of his late-night TV show on Feb 11, 1960. The incident was prompted by NBC's censoring of a slightly off-color "water closet" joke the previous night. After a meeting with network officials, Paar agreed to return to the show on Mar 7.

WHITE SHIRT DAY. Feb 11. Anniversary of UAW-GM agreement following 44-day sit-down strike at General Motors' Flint, MI, factories in 1937. "Blue-collar" workers traditionally wear white shirts to work on this day, symbolic of workingman's dignity won. Has been observed by proclamation in Flint, MI.

BIRTHDAYS TODAY

Lloyd Bentsen, 77, former US Secretary of Treasury in Clinton administration, born Mission, TX, Feb 11, 1921.

Paul Bocuse, 72, chef, born Collonges-au-Mont-d'Or, France, Feb 11, 1926.

Mel Carnahan, 64, Governor of Missouri (D), born Birch Tree, MO, Feb 11, 1934.

Sheryl Crow, 36, singer, musician, born Kennett, MO, Feb 11, 1962.

Virginia Johnson, 73, psychologist, born Springfield, MO, Feb 11, 1925.

Mike Leavitt, 47, Governor of Utah (R), born Cedar City, UT, Feb 11, 1951.

Tina Louise, 64, actress (Ginger Grant in "Gilligan's Island"; *The Stepford Wives*), born New York, NY, Feb 11, 1934.

Sergio Mendes, 57, musician, band leader, born Niteroi, Brazil, Feb 11, 1941.

Leslie Nielsen, 76, actor (*Naked Gun* films, *Airplane!*, "Peyton Place"), born Regina, Saskatchewan, Canada, Feb 11, 1922.

Burt Reynolds, 62, actor (*Hooper, Deliverance, Cannonball Run*, "Evening Shade"), born Waycross, GA, Feb 11, 1936.

Sidney Sheldon, 81, author (*Bloodline, The Doomsday Conspiracy*), born Chicago, IL, Feb 11, 1917.

FEBRUARY 12 — THURSDAY

Day 43 — 322 Remaining

ADAMS, LOUISA CATHERINE JOHNSON: BIRTH ANNIVERSARY. Feb 12, 1775. Wife of John Quincy Adams, sixth president of the US. Born at London, England, Feb 12, 1775. Died May 14, 1852.

AMERICAN ASSOCIATION FOR THE ADVANCEMENT OF SCIENCE ANNUAL MEETING. Feb 12–17. Philadelphia, PA. Annual meeting of the AAAS. For info: AAAS, 1333 H St NW, Washington, DC 20005. Phone: (202) 326-6640. Fax: (202) 289-4950. WWW: http://www.aaas.org

CANADA: CALGARY BOAT AND SPORTSMEN'S SHOW. Feb 12–15. Roundup Centre, Stampede Park, Calgary, Alberta. Sail, power and fishing boats; hunting, fishing and camping supplies; resort destinations and outdoor recreation; RVs and motor homes; 4-wheel-drive vehicles, motorcycles, mountain bikes; family entertainment. Est attendance: 25,000. For info: Canadian Natl Sportsmen's Shows, 703 Evans Ave, Ste 202, Toronto, Ont, Canada M9C 5E9. Phone: (416) 695-0311. Fax: (416) 695-0381.

DARWIN, CHARLES ROBERT: BIRTH ANNIVERSARY. Feb 12, 1809. Author and naturalist. Born at Shrewsbury, England, Feb 12, 1809. Best remembered for his books *On the Origin of Species by Means of Natural Selection, or the Preservation of Favoured Races in the Struggle for Life* and *The Descent of Man and Selection in Relation to Sex*. Died at Down, Kent, England, Apr 19, 1882.

ENGLAND: CHESTER ANTIQUES AND FINE ART SHOW. Feb 12–15. Chester Racecourse, Cheshire. 50 stands on three floors where all items have been vetted for authenticity and age. Est attendance: 6,000. For info: Barbara Bell, Event Mgr, PO Box 114, Haywards Heath, Sussex, England RH16 2YU. Phone: (44) (144) 448-2514. Fax: (44) (144) 448-3412.

GATORADE 125-MILE QUALIFYING RACES (FOR DAYTONA 500). Feb 12. Daytona International Speedway, Daytona Beach, FL. 39th annual qualifying races for the Daytona 500 also determine starting positions 3–30. Sponsor: Gatorade. For info: Daytona Intl Speedway, PO Box 2801, Daytona Beach, FL 32120-2801. Phone: (904) 947-6782. Fax: (904) 947-6791. WWW: http://www.daytonusa.com

HARRIS, ROY: 100th BIRTH ANNIVERSARY. Feb 12, 1898. Born at Chandler, OK, Feb 12, 1898, Harris was one of the most important composers of this century. He was known for his use of Anglo-American folk tunes. He composed more than 200 works, including 13 symphonies, several ballet scores, and much chamber and choral music. His best known work is his *Third Symphony* (1939). He died at Santa Monica, CA, Oct 1, 1979.

ITALY: PURGATORY BANQUET. Feb 12. Gradoli (near Viterbo). On Ash Wednesday, gourmands are on hand for the banquet of penitence for the souls in purgatory, held on the premises of the cooperative winery.

KOSCIUSKO, THADDEUS: BIRTH ANNIVERSARY. Feb 12, 1746. Polish patriot. Born in Lithuania, died at Solothurn, Switzerland, Oct 15, 1817.

LAWN-GARDEN AND PATIO SHOW. Feb 12–15. Omaha Civic Auditorium, Omaha, NE. For info: Robert P. Mancuso, Pres, Mid-America Expositions, 1613 Farnam St, Ste 666, Omaha, NE 68102-2142. Phone: (800) 475-SHOW or (402) 346-8003. Fax: (402) 346-5412.

LEWIS, JOHN LLEWELLYN: BIRTH ANNIVERSARY. Feb 12. American labor leader born near Lucas, IA, Feb 12, 1880. His parents came to the US from Welsh mining towns, and Lewis left school in the seventh grade to become a miner himself. Became leader of United Mine Workers of America and champion of all miners' causes. Died at Washington, DC, June 11, 1969.

February 1998

S	M	T	W	T	F	S
1	2	3	4	5	6	7
8	9	10	11	12	13	14
15	16	17	18	19	20	21
22	23	24	25	26	27	28

LINCOLN, ABRAHAM: BIRTH ANNIVERSARY. Feb 12, 1809. Sixteenth president of the US (Mar 4, 1861–Apr 15, 1865) and the first to be assassinated (on Good Friday, Apr 14, 1865, while watching a performance of *Our American Cousin* at Ford's Theatre in Washington, DC). His presidency encompassed the tragic Civil War. Especially remembered are his Emancipation Proclamation (Jan 1, 1863), his Gettysburg Address (Nov 19, 1863) and his proclamation establishing the last Thursday of November as Thanksgiving Day. Lincoln's birthday is observed on this day in most states, but on the first Monday in February in Delaware and Oregon. Born in Hardin County, KY, Feb 12, 1809. Died at Washington, DC, Apr 15, 1865. See also: "Presidents' Day." (Feb 16.)

LINCOLN'S BIRTHPLACE CABIN WREATH LAYING. Feb 12. Abraham Lincoln's Birthplace NHS, Hodgenville, KY. A wreath is placed at the door of the symbolic "Birthplace Cabin" in commemoration of the birth of Abraham Lincoln. Refreshments are also served to park visitors. Est attendance: 200. For info: Gary V. Talley, 2995 Lincoln Farm Rd, Hodgenville, KY 42748. Phone: (502) 358-3137.

LOST PENNY DAY ©. Feb 12. Today is set aside to put all of those pennies stashed in candy dishes, bowls and jars back in circulation. Take those pennies and give them to a shelter or agency that assists the homeless or your local Humane Society where they can do the most good. Annually, on President Abraham Lincoln's birthday, the man depicted on the copper penny. For info: Adrienne Sioux Koopersmith, 1437 W Rosemont, #1W, Chicago, IL 60660-1319. Phone: (773) 743-5341. Fax: (773) 743-5395. Email: kooper@interaccess.com.

LUXEMBOURG: BURGSONNDEG. Feb 12. Young people build a huge bonfire on a hill to celebrate the victorious sun, marking the end of winter. A tradition dating to pre-Christian times.

MILWAUKEE HOME IMPROVEMENT SHOW. Feb 12–15. Wisconsin State Fair Park, West Allis, WI. Cosponsored by Milwaukee/NARI Home Improvement Council and the *Milwaukee Journal Sentinel*, this show is for remodeling contractors and is of particular interest to homeowners planning a remodeling project for their home. Est attendance: 32,000. For info: Mary Fox, Exec Dir, Milwaukee/NARI Home Improvement Council, 13390 Watertown Plank Rd, PO Box 668, Elm Grove, WI 53122-0668. Phone: (414) 789-4800. Fax: (414) 789-4805.

NEW JERSEY INVENTORS HALL OF FAME INDUCTION BANQUET. Feb 12. Hazell Center Ballroom, New Jersey Institute of Technology, University Heights, Newark, NJ. Annual banquet celebrating New Jersey's inventing heritage and honoring newly inducted individual and corporate members of the

New Jersey Inventors Hall of Fame. Admission: $75 per person. Attendance: 300. For info: Paul F. Hassen, Dir PR, New Jersey Institute of Technology, University Heights, Newark, NJ 07102. Phone: (201) 596-3434. Email: hassen@admin.njit.edu.

NOTHING DAY. Feb 12. To bring dignity to the art of "nuthing" or "nothing" and to help "nothers" find imaginative ways to fill in the blanks of their job applications. For info: Bob Birch, The Puns Corps, PO Box 2364, Falls Church, VA 22042-0364. Phone: (703) 533-3668.

OGLETHORPE DAY. Feb 12. General James Edward Oglethorpe (born at London, England, Dec 22, 1696), with some 100 other Englishmen, landed at what is now Savannah, GA, on Feb 12, 1733. Naming the new colony Georgia for England's King George II, Oglethorpe was organizer and first governor of the colony and founder of the city of Savannah. Oglethorpe Day and Georgia Day observed on this date.

RACE TO THE SKY—A GREAT MONTANA TRADITION SLED DOG RACE. Feb 12–20. 13th annual race starts near Helena, MT, ends at Missoula, MT. This 350-mile race along the Continental Divide is a beautiful and challenging trail. In what is known as the most beautiful race on earth, more than 30 teams compete from the US, Canada and Europe. Est attendance: 12,000. For info: Montana Sled Dog, Inc, 2905 Montana, PO Box 30-Mush, Helena, MT 59601. Phone: (406) 442-4008. Fax: (406) 442-4008.

SAFETYPUP'S® BIRTHDAY. Feb 12. This year Safetypup®, created by the National Child Safety Council, joyously celebrates his birthday by bringing safety awareness/education messages to children in a positive, nonthreatening manner. Safetypup® has achieved a wonderful balance of safety sense, caution and childlike enthusiasm about life and helping kids "Stay Safe and Sound." For info: Barbara Handley Huggett, Dir, NCSC, Research and Development, Box 1368, Jackson, MI 49204-1368. Phone: (517) 764-6070.

SPACE MILESTONE: *VENERA 1* (USSR). Feb 12, 1961. Spacecraft launched from space platform in experiment projecting satellite into interplanetary space, Feb 12, 1961.

UTAH WOMEN GIVEN THE VOTE: ANNIVERSARY. Feb 12, 1870. The women in the Utah Territory were granted the right to vote in political elections—50 years before the 19th Amendment was ratified. For info: Public Affairs Dept, Church of Jesus Christ of Latter-Day Saints, 15 E South Temple St, Salt Lake City, UT 84150. Phone: (801) 240-4395. Fax: (801) 240-1167.

WASHINGTON'S BIRTHDAY CELEBRATION. Feb 12–22. Laredo, TX. Founded in 1898, the event celebrates the cultures of both the US and Mexico with festivities ranging from the Jalapeño Festival to parades, fireworks and a carnival. The largest celebration of George Washington's birthday in the nation. Est attendance: 500,000. For info: Washington's Birthday Celebration Assn, 1819 E Hillside Rd, Laredo, TX 78041. Phone: (210) 722-0589. Fax: (210) 722-5528. Email: wbca@tcsi.net.

BIRTHDAYS TODAY

Maud Adams, 53, actress (*Killer Force, Octopussy*), born Lulea, Sweden, Feb 12, 1945.

Joe Don Baker, 62, actor (*Charlie Varrick, Cool Hand Luke*), born Groesbeck, TX, Feb 12, 1936.

Judy Blume, 60, author (*Blubber, Superfudge*), born Elizabeth, NJ, Feb 12, 1938.

Cliff De Young, 51, actor (*Blue Collar, F/X*), born Inglewood, CA, Feb 12, 1947.

Joseph Henry (Joe) Garagiola, 72, sportscaster, former baseball player, born St. Louis, MO, Feb 12, 1926.

Arsenio Hall, 43, comedian, actor (*Coming to America*), former TV talk-show host, born Cleveland, OH, Feb 12, 1955.

Joanna Kerns, 45, actress ("Growing Pains"), former national-caliber gymnast, born San Francisco, CA, Feb 12, 1953.

William Felton (Bill) Russell, 64, Basketball Hall of Fame center and former coach, born Monroe, LA, Feb 12, 1934.

Arlen Specter, 68, US Senator (R, Pennsylvania), born Wichita, KS, Feb 12, 1930.

Franco Zeffirelli, 75, film director, born Florence, Italy, Feb 12, 1923.

FEBRUARY 13 — FRIDAY

Day 44 — 321 Remaining

AFRICAN-AMERICAN ARTISTS ANNUAL. Feb 13–28. St. Simon Island, GA. Exhibit and promotion of African-American artists, their art and artistic achievements. For info: Exec Dir or Mittie B. Hendrix, Coastal Center for the Arts, 2012 Demere Rd, St. Simons Island, GA 31522. Phone: (912) 634-0404.

ANCHORAGE FUR RENDEZVOUS. Feb 13–22. Anchorage, AK. "Alaska's largest celebration." Features four world championships in three sled dog races and dog weight-pulling contest. Carnival, native dances, Eskimo blanket toss, fur auction, snow sculpture, snow sports and much more—more than 120 events. 63rd annual Rondy! Annually, beginning the second Friday in February and running for 10 days. Est attendance: 250,000. For info: Greater Anchorage, Inc, 327 Eagle St, Anchorage, AK 99501. Phone: (907) 277-8615 or (907) 274-1177. Fax: (907) 277-2199.

BALD EAGLE CONFERENCE. Feb 13–15. Oregon Institute of Technology, Klamath Falls, OR. 19th annual conference features speakers, art exhibits, field trips and film festival centered on bald eagles and the largest wintering population of the birds in the lower 48 states. Plus 2-mile and 10K runs at wildlife area. Est attendance: 500. For info: Ralph Opp, Asst Coord, Oregon Dept of Fish and Wildlife, 1850 Miller Island Rd, West Klamath Falls, OR 97603. Phone: (800) 445-6728.

BLACK LOVE DAY. Feb 13. A national, commemorative holiday of observance, celebration, reconciliation and demonstration of love within the black community and for the black community. Annually, Feb 13. For info: African American Holiday Assn, PO Box 30967, Washington, DC 20030. Phone: (202) 310-1430. Fax: (202) 610-0222.

BLAME SOMEONE ELSE DAY. Feb 13. To share the responsibility and the guilt for the mess we're in. Blame someone else! Annually, the first Friday the 13th of the year. For info: A.C. Moeller, Box 71, Clio, MI 48420-1042.

BOSKONE 35. Feb 13–15. Framingham, MA. New England's regional science fiction convention. Includes science fiction and fantasy program, a large professional art show, booksellers and other exhibitors/vendors and numerous other activities. Est attendance: 900. For info: Boskone Chairman, New England Science Fiction Assn, PO Box 809, Framingham, MA 01701-0203. Phone: (617) 625-2311. Fax: (617) 776-3243.
WWW: http://www.panix.com/NESFA/home.html

CABIN FEVER QUILT SHOW. Feb 13–15. Independence, MO. Display of approximately 50 handmade quilts. Many original designs by club members. For info: (816) 252-0608 or Missouri Division of Tourism, Truman Office Bldg, PO Box 1055, Jefferson City, MO 65102. Phone: (573) 751-4133. Fax: (573) 751-5160.

CANADA: FESTIVAL DU VOYAGEUR. Feb 13–22. Winnipeg, Manitoba. More than 400 shows, food and "joie de vivre" of the fur-trade era. Sled dog races, snow sculptures, costumed interpreters in historic Fort Gibraltar, arts and crafts display and sale, French-Canadian cuisine and much more at Western Canada's largest winter festival. Est attendance: 200,000. For info: Festival du Voyageur, 768 Tache Ave, Winnipeg, MB, Canada R2H 2C4. Phone: (204) 237-7692. Fax: (204) 233-7576.
Email: voyageur@festivalvoyageur.mb.ca.
WWW: http://www.festivalvoyageur.mb.ca

"CAPTAIN GALLANT OF THE FOREIGN LEGION" TV PREMIERE: ANNIVERSARY. Feb 13, 1955. Buster Crabbe starred as the action hero, Captain Michael Gallant, member of the French Foreign Legion, in this NBC children's adventure series. Cullen Crabbe (Buster's son) played the roll of orphan Cuffy Sanders, with Al "Fuzzy" Knight as Private Fuzzy Knight, and Gilles Queant as Sergeant Du Val.

CHURCHILL, RANDOLPH HENRY SPENCER: BIRTH ANNIVERSARY. Feb 13, 1849. English politician and the father of Winston Churchill. Born at Blenheim, Woodstock, Oxfordshire, England, he died at London, England, on Jan 24, 1895.

COWBOY STATE GAMES WINTER SPORTS FESTIVAL. Feb 13–16. Casper, WY. The festival features a variety of winter sporting events for athletes of all ages. Est attendance: 1,600. For info: Eileen Ford, Cowboy State Games, PO Box 3485, Casper, WY 82602. Phone: (307) 577-1125. Fax: (307) 577-8111. Email: cwboygames@aol.com.

DISCOUNT AUTO PARTS 200 NASCAR GOODY'S DASH SERIES RACE. Feb 13. Daytona Beach, FL. 20th annual race is season kickoff for the NASCAR Goody's Dash Series. Sponsor: Discount Auto Parts. For info: Daytona Intl Speedway, PO Box 2801, Daytona Beach, FL 32120-2801. Phone: (904) 947-6782. Fax: (904) 947-6791. WWW: http://www.daytonausa.com

DOW-JONES TOPS 7,000: ANNIVERSARY. Feb 13, 1997. The Dow-Jones Index of 30 major industrial stocks topped the 7,000 mark for the first time. On July 16, 1997, the Dow topped 8,000.

DRESDEN FIRE BOMBING: ANNIVERSARY. Feb 13, 1945. Dresden, Germany. Allied fire bombing caused a firestorm that destroyed the city and killed 135,000 people.

FIRST MAGAZINE PUBLISHED IN AMERICA: ANNIVERSARY. Feb 13. Andrew Bradford published *The American Magazine*, Feb 13, 1741, just three days ahead of Benjamin Franklin's *General Magazine.*

FIRST PUBLIC SCHOOL IN AMERICA: ANNIVERSARY. Feb 13. The Boston Latin School opened on Feb 13, 1635, and is America's oldest public school.

FRANCE: NICE CARNIVAL. Feb 13–Feb 24. Dates from the 14th century and is celebrated each year during the 12 days ending with Shrove Tuesday. Derived from ancient rites of spring, the carnival offers parades, floats, battles of flowers and confetti, a fireworks display lighting up the entire Baie des Anges. King Carnival is burned on his pyre at the end of the event.

FRIDAY THE THIRTEENTH. Feb 13. Variously believed to be a lucky or unlucky day. Every year has at least one Friday the 13th, but never more than three. Three Fridays in 1998 fall on the 13th day, in February, March and November. Fear of the number 13 is known as triskaidekaphobia.

GET A DIFFERENT NAME DAY. Feb 13. If you dislike your name, or merely find it boring, today is the day to adopt the moniker of your choice. [© 1997 by WPL] For info: Thomas or Ruth Roy, Wellness Permission League, PO Box 662, Mt Gretna, PA 17064-0662. Phone: (500) 437-5104 or (717) 964-1308. Fax: (717) 964-1335.

GOLD RUSH DAYS. Feb 13–15. Wickenburg, AZ. 50th annual community-wide celebration of the Old West: rodeo, parade, carnival, gold panning. Named one of the top 100 events in North America by the American Bus Association. Annually, the second full weekend in February. Est attendance: 60,000. For info: Chamber of Commerce, 216 N Frontier St, Wickenburg, AZ 85390. Phone: (520) 684-5479 or (520) 684-0977. Fax: (520) 684-5470. Email: wburgcoc@primenet.com.

February 1998

S	M	T	W	T	F	S
1	2	3	4	5	6	7
8	9	10	11	12	13	14
15	16	17	18	19	20	21
22	23	24	25	26	27	28

GREATER PHILADELPHIA MID-WINTER SCOTTISH AND IRISH MUSIC FESTIVAL AND FAIR. Feb 13–15. Valley Forge Convention Center, King of Prussia, PA. Music, dance, spectacle and song celebrate Ireland and Scotland. All-star lineup of entertainment and a host of ethnic activities, foods and products. Est attendance: 6,000. For info: Wm M. Reid, Jr, Scottish & Irish Festival, PO Box 102, Plymouth Meeting, PA 19462. Phone: (610) 825-7268. Fax: (610) 825-8745.

ICESCAPE, NORTHEAST WISCONSIN'S WINTER FESTIVAL. Feb 13–15. Houdini Plaza, Appleton, WI. Winter festival featuring the Wisconsin State Ice Carving Championship, food, the "Avenue of Ice," family activities, flaming cherries jubilee, carriage rides and other winter fun. Est attendance: 35,000. For info: Brian Scharrer, c/o Appleton Downtown Inc, Icescape Committee, 103 W College Ave, Ste 1111, Appleton, WI 54911. Phone: (414) 954-9112. Fax: (414) 954-0219.

IROC XXII INTERNATIONAL RACE OF CHAMPIONS. Feb 13. Daytona International Speedway, Daytona Beach, FL. All-star race for the greatest drivers from different forms of racing in the US. Sponsor: True Value Hardware Stores presents Firebird Iroc XXII. For info: Daytona Intl Speedway, PO Box 2801, Daytona Beach, FL 32120-2801. Phone: (904) 947-6782. Fax: (904) 947-6791. WWW: http://www.daytonausa.com

IRWIN WINS FIRST MEDAL OF HONOR: ANNIVERSARY. Feb 13, 1861. Col Bernard Irwin distinguished himself while leading troops in a battle with Chiricahua Apache Indians at Apache Pass, AZ (at the time part of the territory of New Mexico). For those actions Irwin later became the first person awarded the new US Medal of Honor, although he didn't actually receive it until three years later (Jan 24, 1864).

MID-CONTINENT RAILWAY'S STEAM SNOW TRAIN. Feb 13–15. Mid-Continent Railway Museum, North Freedom, WI. Snow tours aboard authentic steam train. Coach, first class and dinner service available. Est attendance: 3,000. For info: Wisc Dells Visitor and Conv Bureau, PO Box 390, Wisconsin Dells, WI 53965. Phone: (800) 223-3557. Email: wisdells@midplains.net. WWW: http://www.wisdells.com

NC RV AND CAMPING SHOW. Feb 13–15. Charlie Rose Expo Center, Fayetteville, NC. A display of the latest in recreation vehicles and accessories by various dealers. Est attendance: 5,000. For info: Apple Rock Advertising & Promotion, 1200 Eastchester Dr, High Point, NC 27265. Phone: (910) 881-7100. Fax: (910) 883-7198.

NEWPORT WINTER FESTIVAL. Feb 13–22. Newport, RI. More than 60 individual events from food, music and entertainment to skating, hayrides, snow sculptures, ice carving, scavenger hunt and even hot-air balloon demonstrations—fun for all ages. Est attendance: 25,000. For info: Kathryn Farrington, Newport County Conv & Visitor Bureau, 23 America's Cup Ave, Newport, RI 02840. Phone: (800) 326-6030. Fax: (401) 849-0291. Email: gonewport@aol.com. WWW: http://www.travelfile.com/get?gonewport

PIAZZETTA, GIOVANNI BATTISTA: BIRTH ANNIVERSARY. Feb 13, 1682. Prominent 18th-century Venetian painter. Notable among his works are the *Ecstasy of St. Francis* and *Fortune Teller*. Born on Feb 13, 1682, at Venice, Italy, and died there Apr 28, 1754.

RECREATIONAL VEHICLE SHOW. Feb 13–16 (also Feb 20–23). Timonium State Fairgrounds, Timonium, MD. Mid-Atlantic's oldest, largest and best-attended RV show with exhibitors to display all the latest in motor homes, camping and RV accessories. Est attendance: 20,000. For info: Maryland Recreational Vehicle Assn, 8332 Pulaski Hwy, Baltimore, MD 21237. Phone: (410) 687-7200. Fax: (410) 686-1486.

SKEPTICS' DAYS. Feb 13 (also on Mar 13 and Nov 13). National celebration of skepticism. During this day examine those issues which you are most skeptical about. A day to collectively put these issues under a microscope and cut away those attachments that stand in your way of gaining greater success and freedom. Annually, held on Friday 13th. For info: Adrienne Sioux Koopersmith, 1437 W Rosemont, #1W, Chicago, IL 60660-1319. Phone: (773) 743-5341. Fax: (773) 743-5395.
Email: kooper@interaccess.com.

SOUTH COAST WRITER'S CONFERENCE AND FIREMAN'S FISH FRY. Feb 13–14. Gold Beach Resort and Gold Beach Union High School. Keynote speaker followed by a series of workshops and roundtable discussions concerning writing techniques, publishing guidelines and editorial commentary. Est attendance: 100. For info: Gold Beach Chamber of Commerce, 29279 Ellensburg Ave, #3, Gold Beach, OR 97444. Phone: (800) 525-2334. Fax: (541) 247-0188.
Email: goldbeach@harborside.com.
WWW: http://www.harborside.com/gb

SOUTHEASTERN WILDLIFE EXPOSITION. Feb 13–15. Spectacular wildlife and nature art exposition showcasing original paintings, prints, sculpture, photography, carvings, collectibles and crafts. Eleven exhibition sites throughout historic Charleston. Est attendance: 42,000. For info: Southeastern Management Co, 211 Meeting Street, Charleston, SC 29401. Phone: (803) 723-1748.

STAMP EXPO. Feb 13–15. Elks Lodge, Pasadena, CA, and Palm Springs Convention Center, Palm Springs, CA. Annual expo. Est attendance: 4,000. For info: Intl Stamp Collectors Society, PO Box 854, Van Nuys, CA 91408. Phone: (818) 997-6496. WWW: http://www.4free.com/bick

TRUMAN, BESS (ELIZABETH) VIRGINIA WALLACE: BIRTH ANNIVERSARY. Feb 13. Wife of Harry S. Truman, 33rd president of the US. Born at Independence, MO, Feb 13, 1885. Died there on Oct 18, 1982.

WHISKEY FLAT DAYS. Feb 13–16. Kernville, CA. Whiskey Flat Days commemorates the old Kernville that was called Whiskey Flat in 1860, until the name was changed to Kernville. We turn back the clock as the parade, stores and residents go back to the 1860s. Frog races, craft booths, rodeo, parade, games for small children, carnival, street dances, puppet shows, costume and whiskerino contests, melodrama and much more. Annually, the Friday–Monday of President's Day weekend. Est attendance: 25,000. For info: Kernville Chamber of Commerce, PO Box 397, Kernville, CA 93238. Phone: (760) 376-2629. Fax: (760) 376-4371. Email: kcc@kernvalley.com.
WWW: http://www.kernvalley.com/kerncofc/index.htm

WOOD, GRANT: BIRTH ANNIVERSARY. Feb 13, 1892. American artist especially noted for his powerful realism and satirical paintings of the American scene was born near Anamosa, IA. He was a printer, sculptor, woodworker and high school and college teacher. Among his best-remembered works are *American Gothic, Fall Plowing* and *Stone City*. Died at Iowa City, IA, Feb 12, 1942. Buried at the Riverside Cemetery in Anamosa, IA.

YUMA JAYCEE'S SILVER SPUR RODEO. Feb 13–15. Yuma County Fairgrounds, Yuma, AZ. Three-day rodeo features professional rodeo cowboy action, preceded by a week of activities beginning with parade on Feb 1. Annually, the second weekend in February. Sponsors: Budweiser, Dodge, Pepsi, Best Western Inn Suites and Jack-in-the-Box. Est attendance: 28,000. For info: Richard Metzler, Rodeo Chair, Silver Spur Rodeo, PO Box 2797, Yuma, AZ 85364. Phone: (520) 782-4955.

YUMA SQUARE AND ROUND DANCE FESTIVAL. Feb 13–15. Yuma Civic and Convention Center, Yuma, AZ. Square and round dance enthusiasts from Southern California and Arizona participate. Est attendance: 1,800. For info: Marketing Dept, Yuma Civic and Conv Ctr, 1440 Desert Hills Dr, Yuma, AZ 85365. Phone: (520) 344-3800. Fax: (520) 344-9121.

BIRTHDAYS TODAY

Stockard Channing (Susan Stockard), 54, actress (*Six Degrees of Separation, The House of Blue Leaves*), born New York, NY, Feb 13, 1944.
Robert J. Eaton, 58, Vice Chairman and Chief Operating Officer at Chrysler Corp, born Buena Vista, CO, Feb 13, 1940.
Carol Lynley, 56, actress (*Harlow, Bunny Lake Is Missing*), born New York, NY, Feb 13, 1942.
David Naughton, 47, singer, actor, (*An American Werewolf in London, Overexposed*), born Hartford, CT, Feb 13, 1951.
Kim Novak (Marilyn Novak), 65, actress (*Bell, Book and Candle; Vertigo*), born Chicago, IL, Feb 13, 1933.
Oliver Reed, 60, actor (*The Jokers, Women in Love*), born Wimbledon, England, Feb 13, 1938.
Edward Gay (Eddie) Robinson, 79, football coach, born Jackson, LA, Feb 13, 1919.
George Segal, 64, actor (*A Touch of Class, King Rat*), born Great Neck, NY, Feb 13, 1934.
Jerry Springer, 54, TV host ("The Jerry Springer Show"), born London, England, Feb 13, 1944.
Bo Svenson, 57, actor (*North Dallas Forty, Heartbreak Ridge*), born Goteborg, Sweden, Feb 13, 1941.
Peter Tork (Peter Thorkelson), 54, singer, actor ("The Monkees"), born Washington, DC, Feb 13, 1944.
Chuck Yeager, 75, pilot who broke sound barrier, born Myra, WV, Feb 13, 1923.

FEBRUARY 14 — SATURDAY

Day 45 — 320 Remaining

ALBRECHT-KEMPER VALENTINE DINNER. Feb 14. Albrecht-Kemper Museum of Art, St. Joseph, MO. An elegant way for "sweet'arts" to celebrate and also support the museum's major winter fund-raiser. Annually, the Saturday prior to Valentine's Day or Valentine's Day if it falls on Saturday. Est attendance: 200. For info: Information Desk, AKMA, 2818 Frederick Ave, St. Joseph, MO 64506. Phone: (816) 233-7003. Fax: (816) 233-3413. Email: AKMA@albrechtkemper.org.
WWW: http://www.albrechtkemper.org

ARIZONA: ADMISSION DAY: ANNIVERSARY. Feb 14. Became 48th state on this day in 1912.

BENNY, JACK: BIRTH ANNIVERSARY. Feb 14. American comedian. Born Benjamin Kubelsky, Jack Benny entered vaudeville in Waukegan, IL, at age 17, using the violin as a comic stage prop. His radio show first aired in 1932 and continued for 20 years with little change in format. He also had a long-running television show. One of his most well-known comic gimmicks was his purported stinginess. In 1927 Benny married Mary Livingstone (Sadie Marks). He was born Feb 14, 1894, at Chicago, IL, and died Dec 26, 1974, at Beverly Hills, CA.

BULGARIA: VITICULTURISTS' DAY (TRIFON ZAREZAN). Feb 14. Celebrated since Thracian times. Festivities are based on cult of Dionysus, god of merriment and wine.

CANADA: FROSTY FROLICS WINTER CARNIVAL. Feb 14–21. Bancroft, Ont. Sled dog races, craft show and special attractions. Easter Seals Snowmobile Snowarama. Est attendance: 5,000. For info: Bancroft and District Chamber of Commerce, PO Box 539, Bancroft, Ont, Canada K0L 1C0. Phone: (613) 332-1513. Fax: (613) 332-2119.
Email: chamber@commerce.bancroft.on.ca.
WWW: http://www.commerce.bancroft.on.ca

CHOCOLATE FESTIVAL. Feb 14–15. Browning Mansion, Galesburg, IL. A chocolate lover's dream! Homemade and commercially made chocolates, tortes, cakes, pies and creams—all you can eat for a small admission fee. Annually, the weekend closest to Valentine's Day. Est attendance: 700. For info: Galesburg Area Conv and Visitors Bureau, PO Box 749, Galesburg, IL 61402-0749. Phone: (309) 343-1194. Fax: (309) 343-1195. Email: gacvb@misslink.net. WWW: http://www.misslink.net/gacvb

ENGLAND: BOAT, CARAVAN AND LEISURE SHOW. Feb 14–22. National Exhibition Centre, Birmingham, West Midlands. A wide range of mobile homes, boating and tourism products will be on exhibit. For info: Birmingham Post and Mail Ltd, 28 Colmore Circus, Queensway, Birmingham, England B4 6AX. Phone: (44) (121) 234-5257. Fax: (44) (121) 212-1214.

ENGLAND: BRISTOL CLASSIC MOTORCYCLE SHOW. Feb 14–15. Royal Bath and West Showground, Shepton Mallet, Somerset, England. Everything for the motorcycle enthusiast with club stands, trade stands and autojumble. Est attendance: 17,000. For info: Robert Ewin, Dir, Nationwide Exhibitions (UK) Ltd, PO Box 20, Fishponds, Bristol, England BS16 5QU. Phone: (44) (117) 970-1370. Fax: (44) (117) 970-1371.

FARM TOY SHOW AND AUCTION. Feb 14. Sauk Centre, MN. More than 25 vendors display farm toy equipment from 9 AM to 4:30 PM, with a consignment auction starting at 5:30 PM. Est attendance: 800. For info: Lisa Long, Mgr, Sauk Centre Chmbr of Commerce, PO Box 222, Sauk Centre, MN 56378. Phone: (320) 352-5201, ext C.
WWW: http://www.saukcentre.com

FERRIS WHEEL DAY. Feb 14, 1859. Anniversary of the birth of George Washington Gale Ferris, American engineer and inventor, at Galesburg, IL, on Feb 14, 1859. Among his many accomplishments as a civil engineer, Ferris is best remembered as the inventor of the Ferris wheel, which he developed for the World's Columbian Exposition at Chicago, IL, in 1893. Built on the Midway Plaisance, the 250-feet-in-diameter Ferris wheel (with 36 coaches, each capable of carrying 40 passengers), proved one of the greatest attractions of the fair. It was America's answer to the Eiffel Tower of the Paris International Exposition of 1889. Ferris died at Pittsburgh, PA, on Nov 22, 1896.

FIESTA DAY. Feb 14. Ybor City, Tampa, FL. Tampa National Historic Landmark District celebrates its ethnic roots. This is a free street festival honoring the Cuban, African-American, Italian, Jewish and Spanish immigrants who first settled Ybor City. The more than 50-year-old celebration is held in harmony with the Gasparilla Festival and occurs following the pirate invasion earlier in the month. Features food, music and entertainment representing the district's culturally diverse background. Held 10–5, followed by the Illuminated Night Parade in the evening. Est attendance: 75,000. For info: Ybor City Chamber of Commerce, 1800 E 9th Ave, Tampa, FL 33605. Phone: (810) 248-3712. Fax: (810) 247-1764.

February 1998	S	M	T	W	T	F	S
	1	2	3	4	5	6	7
	8	9	10	11	12	13	14
	15	16	17	18	19	20	21
	22	23	24	25	26	27	28

FIRST PRESIDENTIAL PHOTOGRAPH: ANNIVERSARY. Feb 14, 1849. President James Polk became the first US president to be photographed while in office. The photographer was Mathew B. Brady, who would become famous for his photography during the American Civil War.

FLORIDA MANATEE FESTIVAL. Feb 14–15. Crystal River, FL. Prestigious fine arts show featuring approximately 135 artists and a seafood festival with a wide variety of foods. Other family events include live entertainment, 5K run, craft show, special children's events. Annually, the February. Est attendance: 35,000. For info: Marlon Lightfoot, Exec VP, Nature Coast Chamber at Crystal River, 28 NW Highway 19, Crystal River, FL 34428. Phone: (352) 795-3149. Fax: (352) 795-4260.

GARGOYLES 300 NASCAR BUSCH SERIES RACE. Feb 14. Daytona International Speedway, Daytona Beach, FL. 40th annual race is season kickoff for the NASCAR Busch series. Sponsor: Gargoyles. For info: Daytona Intl Speedway, PO Box 2801, Daytona Beach, FL 32120-2801. Phone: (904) 947-6782. Fax: (904) 947-6791. WWW: http://www.daytonausa.com

GEORGE WASHINGTON BIRTHNIGHT BANQUET AND BALL. Feb 14. Alexandria, VA. Recreation of dinner, dancing and toasts offered to George Washington in Alexandria. Staged in original setting—Gadsby's Tavern. Eighteenth-century dancing, clothing. Alexandrians portray historic characters including George and Martha Washington. Annually, the Saturday of the federal holiday weekend. Sponsor: George Washington Birthday Celebration Committee. Est attendance: 200. For info: Alexandria Conv and Visitors Assn, 221 King St, Alexandria, VA 22314. Phone: (703) 838-4200. Fax: (703) 838-4683. Email: acva@erols.com. WWW: http://www.virginia.org

GEORGIA HERITAGE PROGRAM HISTORY WEEK AND BLACK HISTORY MONTH CELEBRATION. Feb 14. Oatland Island Education Center, Savannah, GA. Experience a part of living history. Demonstrations of 19th-century skills by costumed staff in circa 1835 log cabins. Jazz history and jazz band, black history Civil War re-enactment of black soldiers' experiences. Est attendance: 2,000. For info: Oatland Island Education Center, 711 Sandtown Rd, Savannah, GA 31410. Phone: (912) 897-3773. Fax: (912) 898-7402.

GEORGIA WEEK PROGRAM. Feb 14. Wormsloe Historic Site, Savannah, GA. The focus is on the Colonial War with Spain in living history demonstrations related to Colonial Georgia history, militia, woodworking and farm life. Est attendance: 500. For info: Wormsloe State Historic Site, 7601 Skidaway Rd, Savannah, GA 31406. Phone: (912) 353-3023.

HANCOCK, WINFIELD SCOTT: BIRTH ANNIVERSARY. Feb 14, 1824. Born at Montgomery, PA, died Feb 9, 1886, at Governers Island, NY. After serving as Union general in the Civil War, his command of the military division of Texas and Louisiana won him much favor from the Democratic Party because he allowed local civil authorities to retain their power. He pleased the Democrats so well they made him their presidential candidate in 1880. He lost to James A. Garfield by a narrow margin.

HOMES FOR BIRDS WEEK. Feb 14–21. A week to encourage people to clean out, fix up and put up homes for wild birds. Annually, the third week in February. For info: John F. Gardner, Pres, Wild Bird Marketplace, 1891 Santa Barbara Dr, Ste 106, Lancaster, PA 17601. Phone: (717) 581-5310. Fax: (717) 581-5312.

INTERNATIONAL FLIRTING WEEK. Feb 14–20. Celebrating the ancient art of flirting and recognizing the role it plays in the lives of singles seeking a mate, couples looking to sustain their love and those simply exchanging a playful glance with a stranger, acquaintance, colleague, etc. For info: Robin Gorman Newman, 58 Grace Ave, #2J, Great Neck, NY 11021. Phone: (516) 773-0911. Email: rgnewman@aol.com.

KINDRED SPIRITS DAY. Feb 14. A celebration of the bond between humans and domestic animals and its enhancement of the quality of life of both. Educational, informational, fun. Annually, Valentine's Day. For info: Kindred Spirits Animal Sanctuary, PO Box 48, Suquamish, WA 98392. Phone: (360) 598-2545 or (888) KINDRED. Fax: (360) 598-2546.

KROGER ST. JUDE TENNIS INTERNATIONAL. Feb 14–22. Racquet Club of Memphis, Memphis, TN. The world's finest tennis players compete in one of the most prestigious tour events of the year. For info: Tom Buford, Kroger St. Jude, Racquet Club of Memphis, 5111 Sanderlin, Memphis, TN 38117. Phone: (901) 765-4400.

MARRIAGE OF THE PORT CEREMONY. Feb 14–15. Bryan, TX. (Also Feb 21–22.) Old Portuguese tradition in which a superb hearty red wine is fortified by adding brandy to the barrel. After considerable aging the result is gold medal–winning Papa Paulo Port. The ceremony takes place during each free tour of the winery and guests are treated to free tastings of port made two years prior and wedding cake. Tour schedule: weekdays 1 and 2:30 PM; Sat 11 AM, 12:30, 2:30 and 4 PM; Sun 12:30 and 2:30 PM. For info: Steve Wiley, Mktg Dir, Messina Hof Wine Cellars, 4545 Old Reliance Rd, Bryan, TX 77808. Phone: (409) 778-9463. Fax: (409) 778-1729.

NATIONAL CONDOM WEEK. Feb 14–21. To educate consumers, patients, students and professionals on the prevention of sexually transmitted diseases, including AIDS, and teenage pregnancies. For info: Frederick S. Mayer, Pres, Pharmacists Planning Service, Inc, Box 1336, Sausalito, CA 94966. Phone: (415) 332-4066. Email: ppsi@aol.com.

OREGON: ADMISSION DAY: ANNIVERSARY. Feb 14. Became 33rd state on this day in 1859.

PROUT, MARY ANN ("AUNT MARY PROUT"): BIRTH ANNIVERSARY. Feb 14, 1801. It is believed most likely that Mary Prout—social activist, humanitarian, educator—was born free on this date at Baltimore, MD. Prout became a teacher and in 1830 founded a day school. Actively involved in her church, Prout founded a secret society that became the Independent Order of St. Luke to help with the cost of medical care and burial services for needy blacks, an organization that grew to have 1,500 chapters across the nation by 1900. Prout died at Baltimore in 1884.

RACE RELATIONS DAY. Feb 14. A day designated by some churches to recognize the importance of interracial relations. Formerly was observed on Abraham Lincoln's birthday or on the Sunday preceding it. Since 1970 observance has generally been on Feb 14.

READ TO YOUR CHILD DAY. Feb 14. Motto: "Show your kids you love them: Read to them." To encourage parents, teachers and other caregivers to engage in the wonderfully beneficial and delightfully fun practice of reading to children. A packet of materials is available, including ideas for campaigns to promote literacy, plus reproducible flyers on classroom reading, family reading at home and sharing books with babies. Flyers describe the benefits of read-aloud sessions, give tips for oral reading and list books people can read for more information. Annually, on Valentine's Day. For packet send business-sized, stamped, self-addressed envelope plus two thirty-two cent stamps (to cover photocopy expenses) to Dee Anderson, 1023 25 St, #1, Moline, IL 61265.

SALMON RUSHDIE'S DEATH SENTENCE: ANNIVERSARY. Feb 14, 1989. Iranian leader Ayatollah Ruholla Khomeini, offended by *The Satanic Verses*, called on Muslims Feb 14, 1989, to kill the book's British author, Salmon Rushdie. On the following day the Ayatollah offered a $1 million reward for execution of his sentence. Rushdie, suddenly the center of international controversy and fearful for his life, went into hiding. Worldwide protests against the efforts to abridge academic and literary freedoms, countered by protests of Muslim and other religious fundamentalists, stimulated the sales of *The Satanic Verses*, but Rushdie remained virtually a prisoner unable to resume a public life because of the Ayatollah's death sentence. The reward was later increased to $2 million by an Iranian foundation.

SAN FRANCISCO CHINESE NEW YEAR GOLDEN DRAGON PARADE. Feb 14. San Francisco, CA. The largest Chinese New Year parade outside mainland China. Est attendance: 500,000. For info: Chinese Chamber of Commerce, Wayne Hu, Chair, Chinese New Year Parade, 730 Sacramento, San Francisco, CA 94108. Phone: (415) 391-9680. Fax: (415) 982-4720.

SPACE MILESTONE: *LUNA 20* (USSR). Feb 14, 1972. Launched Feb 14, 1972. Unmanned lunar probe soft-landed on Moon, Feb 21, collected samples and returned to Earth, Feb 25.

SPACE MILESTONE: SMM (US). Feb 14, 1980. Unmanned Delta rocket, a "Solar Maximum Mission Observatory," launched Feb 14, 1980. Intended to study solar flares.

VALENTINE'S DAY. Feb 14. St. Valentine's Day celebrates the feasts of two Christian martyrs of this name. One, a priest and physician, was beaten and beheaded on the Flaminian Way at Rome, Italy, on Feb 14, AD 269, during the reign of Emperor Claudius II (who died of the plague less than a year later). Another Valentine, the Bishop of Terni, is said to have been beheaded, also on the Flaminian Way at Rome, on Feb 14 (possibly in a later year). Both history and legend are vague and contradictory about details of the Valentines and some say that Feb 14 was selected for the celebration of Christian martyrs as a diversion from the ancient pagan observance of Lupercalia. An old legend has it that birds choose their mates on Valentine's Day. Now it is one of the most widely observed unofficial holidays. It is an occasion for the exchange of gifts (usually books, flowers or sweets) and greeting cards with affectionate or humorous messages. See also: "Lupercalia" (Feb 15).

VALENTINE'S DAY MASSACRE: ANNIVERSARY. Feb 14. Anniversary of Chicago gangland executions in 1929, when gunmen posing as police shot seven members of the George "Bugs" Moran gang.

WALKER LAKE FISH DERBY. Feb 14–16. Hawthorne, NV. Fishing contest for cutthroat trout, hobo dinner and liars contest. Tagged fish worth $25,000 and many more prizes. For local info: (702) 945-5896. For info: Mineral County Chamber of Commerce, PO Box 1635, Hawthorne, NV 89415. Phone: (702) 945-5896. Fax: (702) 945-1257.

WALLET, SKEEZIX: "BIRTHDAY." Feb 14. Comic strip character in "Gasoline Alley" by Frank King. First cartoon character to grow and age with the days, weeks and years of publication. Foundling child of Walt and Phyllis Wallet, discovered on doorstep Feb 14, 1921. Skeezix grew through childhood, marriage, military service in World War II, returning home to parenthood and business after the war. Comic strip began in *Chicago Tribune*, Aug 23, 1919.

WHITE, CARRIE: DEATH ANNIVERSARY. Feb 14, 1991. Carrie White, named the world's oldest person by the *Guinness Book of World Records*, died at 117 years of age at Palatka, FL. Born in 1874, she was declared the "oldest living person in the world" by Guinness in 1988. She had spent 75 years in the Florida State Hospital for post-typhoid psychosis, after being admitted by her husband one day after her 35th birthday. She was released from the hospital when she was 109 and moved to a nursing home in Palatka.

94.7 WMAS VALENTINE'S BALL. Feb 14. A semi-formal affair for both couples and singles. An evening of music, dancing and prizes. Est attendance: 700. For info: Dina Cox, PO Box 9500, Springfield, MA 01120. Phone: (413) 737-1414. Fax: (413) 737-1488.

BIRTHDAYS TODAY

Carl Bernstein, 54, journalist, author (investigated Watergate story with Bob Woodward), born Washington, DC, Feb 14, 1944.

Drew Bledsoe, 26, football player, born Ellensburg, WA, Feb 14, 1972.

Hugh Downs, 77, broadcaster ("Today," "20/20"), born Akron, OH, Feb 14, 1921.

Zach Galligan, 34, actor (*Gremlins, Gremlins II*), born New York, NY, Feb 14, 1964.

Judd Gregg, 51, US Senator (R, New Hampshire), born Nashua, NH, Feb 14, 1947.

Florence Henderson, 64, singer, actress ("The Brady Bunch"), born Dale, IN, Feb 14, 1934.

Gregory Hines, 52, dancer, actor (*Tap*), born New York, NY, Feb 14, 1946.

Edmund George Love, 86, teacher, historian, author, born Flushing, MI, Feb 14, 1912.

Andrew Prine, 62, actor (*The Miracle Worker, Chisum*), born Jennings, FL, Feb 14, 1936.

Donna Shalala, 57, US Secretary of Health and Human Services in Clinton administration, born Cleveland, OH, Feb 14, 1941.

Teller, 50, magician (Penn and Teller), name legally changed to Teller, born Philadelphia, PA, Feb 14, 1948.

Meg Tilly, 38, actress (*Agnes of God, Two Jakes*), born Long Beach, CA, Feb 14, 1960.

Ken Wahl, 45, actor ("Wiseguy"; *The Wanderers*; *Fort Apache, The Bronx*), born Chicago, IL, Feb 14, 1953.

FEBRUARY 15 — SUNDAY

Day 46 — 319 Remaining

AFGHANISTAN: SOVIET TROOP WITHDRAWAL DEADLINE: ANNIVERSARY. Feb 15, 1989. The USSR's target of withdrawal of all Soviet troops from Afghanistan by this date was essentially met.

ANTHONY, SUSAN BROWNELL: BIRTH ANNIVERSARY. Feb 15, 1820. American reformer and militant advocate of women's suffrage. She was arrested and fined in 1872 for voting—a criminal act if done by a woman! First American woman to have her likeness on coinage (1979, Susan B. Anthony dollar). Born at Adams, MA, Feb 15, 1820. Died at Rochester, NY, Mar 13, 1906. Her birthday is a legal holiday in Florida.

ARLEN, HAROLD: BIRTH ANNIVERSARY. Feb 15. American composer and songwriter. Born at Buffalo, NY, on Feb 15, 1905. Arlen wrote many popular songs, including "Over the Rainbow" (for which he won 1939 Oscar for best song), "That Old Black Magic," "Blues in the Night" and "Stormy Weather." Died at New York, NY, on Apr 23, 1986.

BARRYMORE, JOHN: BIRTH ANNIVERSARY. Feb 15, 1882. American actor of famous acting family. Born John Blythe at Philadelphia, PA, and died at Los Angeles, CA, May 29, 1942. US Postal Service stamp was issued in 1982 featuring Ethel, John and Lionel Barrymore.

CERMAK, ANTON J.: 65th ASSASSINATION ANNIVERSARY. Feb 15, 1933. At Bay Front Park, Miami, FL, an assassin aiming at President-elect Franklin D. Roosevelt had his aim deflected by a spectator. Cermak, mayor of Chicago, IL, was struck and killed instead. Giuseppe (Joe) Zangara, the 32-year-old assassin, who had emigrated from Italy in 1923, was electrocuted at the Raiford, FL, state prison on Mar 20, 1933.

February 1998

S	M	T	W	T	F	S
1	2	3	4	5	6	7
8	9	10	11	12	13	14
15	16	17	18	19	20	21
22	23	24	25	26	27	28

CLARK, ABRAHAM: BIRTH ANNIVERSARY. Feb 15, 1726. Signer of the Declaration of Independence, farmer and lawyer. Died Sept 15, 1794.

DAYTONA 500. Feb 15. Daytona International Speedway, Daytona Beach, FL. 40th annual running of the "world's greatest races" is season kickoff for the NASCAR Winston Cup season. For info: Daytona Intl Speedway, PO Box 2801, Daytona Beach, FL 32120-2801. Phone: (904) 947-6782. Fax: (904) 947-6791. WWW: http://www.daytonusa.com

ENABLED ENTREPRENEURS' WEEK. Feb 15–21. In recognition of entrepreneurs with disabilities, those who chart their own courses with determination and perseverance, creating businesses for themselves and jobs for people in the community. Show your support this week by identifying these entrepreneurs, getting to know them and their businesses. Encourage networking opportunities with other business owners in your area. Annually, the third week in February. For info: Carol MacKenzie, Communicate with Care, 10 Westwood Rd, Lexington, MA 02173. Phone: (617) 863-8436. Email: commwcare@aol.com.

GALILEI, GALILEO: BIRTH ANNIVERSARY. Feb 15, 1564. Physicist and astronomer who helped overthrow medieval concepts of the world, born at Pisa, Italy. He proved the theory that all bodies, large and small, descend at equal speed and gathered evidence to support Copernicus's theory that the earth and other planets revolve around the sun. Galileo died at Florence, Italy, Jan 8, 1642.

GIVE YOURSELF CREDIT WEEK. Feb 15–21. A week during which members of the American Collectors Association, Inc, put on seminars, contests and other events to educate consumers about the importance of financial responsibility and maintaining a good credit reputation. Annually, the third week in February. For info: American Collectors Assn, Inc, PO Box 39106, Minneapolis, MN 55439-0106. Phone: (612) 926-6547 or (612) 926-6547. Fax: (612) 926-1624. Email: comm@collector.com. WWW: http://www.collector.com

INTERNATIONAL FRIENDSHIP WEEK. Feb 15–21. Promotion of international friendship and the international language Esperanto. For complete information, send $3 to cover expense of printing, handling and postage. Annually, the last full week in February. For info: Dr. Stanley Drake, Pres, Intl Society of Friendship & Good Will, 412 Cherry Hills Dr, Bakersfield, CA 93309-2866.

LUPERCALIA. Feb 15. Anniversary of ancient Roman fertility festival. Thought by some to have been established by Romulus and Remus who, legend says, were suckled by a she-wolf at Lupercal (a cave in Palestine). Goats and dogs were sacrificed. Lupercalia celebration persisted until the fifth century of the Christian era. Possibly a forerunner of Valentine's Day customs.

McCORMICK, CYRUS H.: BIRTH ANNIVERSARY. Feb 15. Inventor of the reaper. Born Feb 15, 1809, at Rockbridge County, VA. It is said that Cyrus McCormick's invention of the reaper is second only to the railroad in the development of the US. Continuing the dream of his father, McCormick constructed a horse-operated reaper which was demonstrated for the first time in a Virginia wheat field late in July 1831. He moved his operation to Chicago, IL, in 1847 in order to be closer to the Midwest's expanding wheat fields. His business prospered despite two decades of constant litigation over patent rights, and by the time of the London World's Fair in 1851, he and his invention had achieved worldwide notoriety. He died on May 13, 1884, at Chicago, IL. In 1902–03, his McCormick Harvesting Machine Company was consolidated with other firms to become the International Harvester Company.

MENENDEZ DE AVILES, PEDRO: BIRTH ANNIVERSARY. Feb 15. Spanish explorer and naval adventurer. Born Feb 15, 1519. Explored Florida coastal regions for king of Spain and established a fort at St. Augustine in September 1565. Died Sept 17, 1574, at Santander, Spain.

POINTS OF ENTRY: A NATION OF STRANGERS. Feb 15–Apr 13. Museum of the Jimmy Carter Library, Atlanta, GA. This photography exhibit explores the topic of immigration in US history from a social and documentary standpoint. The exhibit brings together a range of images, including etchings of slave ships, daguerreotypes of Chinese gold miners in California, new arrivals at Ellis Island, and even modern-day images of Haitian rafters. The work of photographers Jacob Lewis Hine, Andreas Larsen Dahl, Don Bartletti, Audrey Gottlieb, James Newberry and Chester Higgins, Jr will be on display. For info: Nancy Clifford, Public Affairs, Museum of the Jimmy Carter Library, 441 Freedom Pkwy, Atlanta, GA 30307. Phone: (404) 331-0296. Fax: (404) 730-2215. Email: library@carter.nara.gov.

REMEMBER THE *MAINE* DAY: 100th ANNIVERSARY. Feb 15, 1898. American battleship, *Maine*, was blown up while at anchor in Havana harbor, at 9:40 PM, on this day in 1898. The ship, under the command of Captain Charles G. Sigsbee, sank quickly, and 260 members of its crew were lost. Inflamed public opinion in the US ignored the lack of evidence to establish responsibility for the explosion. "Remember the *Maine*" became the war cry, and a formal declaration of war against Spain followed on Apr 25, 1898.

REVOLUTIONARY WAR ENCAMPMENT. Feb 15. Alexandria, VA. Sunday afternoon of Washington's Birthday Weekend. Camp life demonstrated at Fort Ward Museum and Historic Site. British and Colonial uniformed troops engage in a skirmish, demonstrate camp life. Free. Est attendance: 2,000. For info: Marketing Coordinator, Alexandria Conv and Visitors Assn, 221 King St, Alexandria, VA 22314. Phone: (703) 838-4200. Fax: (703) 838-4683. Email: acva@erols.com.
WWW: http://www.virginia.org

SOVIET TROOP WITHDRAWAL FROM AFGHANISTAN: ANNIVERSARY. Feb 15, 1989. The last of the Soviet Union's troops were pulled out of Afghanistan on Feb 15, 1989, ending more than nine years of intervention in a civil war between the government and Muslim rebel groups.

SPANISH WAR MEMORIAL DAY AND *MAINE* MEMORIAL DAY. Feb 15. Massachusetts.

SUTTER, JOHN AUGUSTUS: BIRTH ANNIVERSARY. Feb 15, 1803. Born at Kandern, Germany, on Feb 15, 1803. Sutter established the first white settlement on the site of Sacramento, CA, in 1839, and owned a large tract of land there, which he named New Helvetia. The first great gold strike in the US was on his property, at Sutter's Mill, Jan 24, 1848. His land was soon overrun by gold seekers who, he claimed, slaughtered his cattle and stole or destroyed his property. Sutter was bankrupt by 1852. Died at Washington, DC, on June 18, 1880.

TIFFANY, CHARLES LEWIS: BIRTH ANNIVERSARY. Feb 15, 1812. American jeweler whose name became synonymous with high standards of quality. Born at Killingly, CT, Feb 15, 1812, and died at New York, NY, on Feb 18, 1902. Father of artist Louis Comfort Tiffany. See also: "Tiffany, Louis Comfort: Birth Anniversary" (Feb 18).

BIRTHDAYS TODAY

Adolfo (Adolfo F. Sardina), 65, fashion designer, born Havana, Cuba, Feb 15, 1933.

Marisa Berenson, 50, actress (*Cabaret, Barry Lyndon*), model, born New York, NY, Feb 15, 1948.

Claire Bloom, 67, actress (*A Doll's House, The Spy Who Came In from the Cold*), born London, England, Feb 15, 1931.

Susan Brownmiller, 63, author, feminist (*Against Our Will, Femininity*), born Brooklyn, NY, Feb 15, 1935.

Chris Farley, 34, actor ("Saturday Night Live," *Tommy Boy, Beverly Hills Ninja*), born Madison, WI, Feb 15, 1964.

Matt Groening, 44, cartoonist ("The Simpsons"), born Portland, OR, Feb 15, 1954.

Harvey Korman, 71, actor, comedian (two Emmys for "The Carol Burnett Show"; *High Anxiety*), born Chicago, IL, Feb 15, 1927.

Melissa Manchester, 47, singer ("Don't Cry Out Loud"), born Bronx, NY, Feb 15, 1951.

Kevin McCarthy, 84, actor (*Invasion of the Body Snatchers, Buffalo Bill and the Indians, Matinee*), born Seattle, WA, Feb 15, 1914.

William Mark Price, 34, basketball player, born Bartlesville, OK, Feb 15, 1964.

Jane Seymour, 47, actress (Emmy for "East of Eden," "Dr. Quinn: Medicine Woman"), born Hillingdon, England, Feb 15, 1951.

FEBRUARY 16 — MONDAY

Day 47 — 318 Remaining

BERGEN, EDGAR: BIRTH ANNIVERSARY. Feb 16, 1903. Actor, radio entertainer and ventriloquist, voice of Charlie McCarthy, Mortimer Snerd and Effie Klinker. Father of Emmy Award-winning actress Candice Bergen, star of TV's "Murphy Brown." Born at Chicago, IL, Feb 16, 1903. Died at Las Vegas, NV, Sept 30, 1978.

BROTHERHOOD/SISTERHOOD WEEK. Feb 16–20. A kickoff period for programs emphasizing a commitment to brotherhood/sisterhood. The National Program Office develops educational materials for use during this period that can be used year round. The third full week in February. Sponsor: The National Conference (founded as the National Conference of Christians and Jews). For info: The Natl Conference, 71 Fifth Ave, New York, NY 10003. Phone: (212) 206-0006.

FLAHERTY, ROBERT JOSEPH: BIRTH ANNIVERSARY. Feb 16. American filmmaker, explorer and author, called "father of the documentary film." Born at Iron Mountain, MI, Feb 16, 1884. Died at Dunnerston, VT, July 23, 1951. Films included *Nanook of the North, Moana* and *Man of Aran*.

GEORGE WASHINGTON BIRTHDAY CELEBRATION PARADE. Feb 16. Alexandria, VA. Nation's largest parade honoring George Washington. Staged by his hometown. More than 200 units. Floats, bands, antique cars, and equestrian units, bagpipers. Route through historic district. Sponsor: George Washington Birthday Celebration Committee. Free admission. Est attendance: 50,000. For info: Alexandria Conv and Vistiors Association, 221 King St, Alexandria, VA 22314. Phone: (703) 838-4200. Fax: (703) 838-4683. Email: acva@erols.com. WWW: http://www.virginia.org

HEART 2 HEART DAY. Feb 16. Confide something to your diary—start young and you'll write a whole book before you know it! Annually, two days after Valentine's Day. For info: Fine Print Publishing Co, PO Box 916401, Longwood, FL 32791-6401. Phone: (407) 865-9606. Fax: (407) 865-9607.

KING, WAYNE: BIRTH ANNIVERSARY. Feb 16, 1901. American saxophonist and band leader, widely known as "the Waltz King," born at Savannah, IL. His own composition, "The Waltz You Save for Me," was his theme song. Died at age 84 at Paradise Valley, AZ, on July 16, 1985.

LITHUANIA: INDEPENDENCE DAY. Feb 16, 1918. National Day. The anniversary of Lithuania's Feb 16, 1918, declaration of independence is observed by many Lithuanians, especially those outside Lithuania, as the Baltic state's Independence Day. In 1940, Lithuania became a part of the Soviet Union, under an agreement between Joseph Stalin and Adolf Hitler. On Mar 11, 1990, Lithuania declared its independence from the Soviet Union, holding free elections and severing ties with Moscow. Lithuania was the first of the Soviet republics to declare its independence. After demanding independence, Lithuania set up a border police force and aided young men in efforts to avoid the Soviet military draft, prompting then Soviet leader Mikhail Gorbachev to send tanks into the capital of Vilnius and impose oil and gas embargoes. In the wake of the failed coup attempt in Moscow on Aug 19, 1991, Lithuanian independence finally was recognized.

PRESIDENTS' DAY. Feb 16. The third Monday in February. Presidents' Day observes the birthdays of George Washington (Feb 22) and Abraham Lincoln (Feb 12). With the adoption of the Monday Holiday Law (which moved the observance of George Washington's birthday from Feb 22 each year to the third Monday in February), some of the specific significance of the event was lost, and added impetus was given to the popular description of that holiday as Presidents' Day. Present usage often regards Presidents' Day as a day to honor all former presidents of the US.

RICHARDS, IVOR ARMSTRONG: BIRTH ANNIVERSARY. Feb 16, 1893. Author of many books on literary criticism, himself a "critic's critic." Born at Sandbach, Cheshire, England, Feb 16, 1893. Died at Cambridge, England, Sept 7, 1979.

STOCK EXCHANGE HOLIDAY (WASHINGTON'S BIRTHDAY). Feb 16. The holiday schedules for the various exchanges are subject to change if relevant rules, regulations or exchange policies are revised. If you have questions, phone: American Stock Exchange (212) 306-1000; Chicago Board of Trade (312) 435-3500; Chicago Board of Options Exchange (312) 786-5600; New York Stock Exchange (212) 656-2065; Pacific Stock Exchange (415) 393-4000; Philadelphia Stock Exchange (215) 496-5000.

WASHINGTON, GEORGE: BIRTHDAY OBSERVANCE (LEGAL HOLIDAY). Feb 16. Legal public holiday (Public Law 90–363 sets Washington's birthday observance on the third Monday in February each year—applicable to federal employees and to the District of Columbia). Observed on this day in all states. See also: "Washington, George: Birth Anniversary" (Feb 22).

February 1998

S	M	T	W	T	F	S
1	2	3	4	5	6	7
8	9	10	11	12	13	14
15	16	17	18	19	20	21
22	23	24	25	26	27	28

WILSON, HENRY: BIRTH ANNIVERSARY. Feb 16, 1812. Eighteenth vice president of the US (1873–75). Born at Farmington, NH, died at Washington, DC, Nov 22, 1875.

BIRTHDAYS TODAY

Sonny Bono (Salvatore Bono), 63, singer ("I Got You Babe," "The Beat Goes On" [with Cher]), politician (US Representative [R-CA], former mayor of Palm Springs, CA), born Detroit, MI, Feb 16, 1935.

LeVar Burton, 41, actor ("Roots," "Star Trek: The Next Generation"), born Landsthul, Germany, Feb 16, 1957.

James Ingram, 42, singer ("Baby, Come to Me" [with Patti Austin]), songwriter, born Akron, OH, Feb 16, 1956.

William Katt, 43, actor ("The Greatest American Hero," *Perry Mason Returns* and several Perry Mason follow-ups, *Carrie*), born Los Angeles, CA, Feb 16, 1955.

George Frost Kennan, 94, historian, diplomat, born Milwaukee, WI, Feb 16, 1904.

John Patrick McEnroe, Jr, 39, tennis player, born Wiesbaden, West Germany, Feb 16, 1959.

Barry Primus, 60, actor ("Cagney and Lacey," *Absence of Malice, Down and Out in Beverly Hills*), born New York, NY, Feb 16, 1938.

Peter Kelly Tripucka, 39, former basketball player, born Glen Ridge, NJ, Feb 16, 1959.

Leonard F. Woodcock, 87, labor union official, statesman, born Providence, RI, Feb 16, 1911.

FEBRUARY 17 — TUESDAY

Day 48 — 317 Remaining

BARBER, WALTER LANIER "RED": 90th BIRTH ANNIVERSARY. Feb 17, 1908. One of the first broadcasters inducted into the Baseball Hall of Fame, "Red" Barber was born Feb 17, 1908, in Columbus, MS. Barber's first professional play-by-play experience was announcing the Cincinnati Reds opening day on radio in 1934. That game was also the first major league game he had ever seen. He broadcast baseball's first night game (in Brooklyn) on Aug 26, 1939, the game in which Jackie Robinson broke the color barrier in 1947, and while a Yankee radio announcer he called Roger Maris's 61st home run in 1961. "Red" Barber died Oct 22, 1992, at Tallahassee, FL.

CHICAGO FLAG EXHIBIT CONTROVERSY: ANNIVERSARY. Feb 17, 1989. An exhibit at the School of the Art Institute of Chicago, titled *What is the Proper Way to Display a US Flag?*, consisted of a ledger for viewers to write their impressions but required the viewers to stand on a US flag mounted on the floor to reach the ledger. The exhibit by art student Scott Tyler prompted protests from veterans' groups, a failed lawsuit, and introduction of legislation by Senator Bob Dole to make displaying a US flag on the floor or ground a crime.

CORELLI, ARCANGELO: BIRTH ANNIVERSARY. Feb 17, 1633. Italian composer and virtuoso violinist, born at Fusignano, Italy, on Feb 17, 1633. From his home in Rome, Corelli made extensive and popular concert tours throughout much of Europe. Died at Rome, Italy, on Jan 8, 1713.

FORT SUMTER RETURNED TO UNION CONTROL: ANNIVERSARY. Feb 17, 1865. After a siege that lasted almost a year and a half, Fort Sumter in South Carolina returned to Union hands on this date. The site of the first shots fired in the American Civil War, the fort had become a symbol for both sides during the war. As Union attempts to retake it by shelling diminished the fort's capacity with large bombardments, Southern forces managed to hold out with few casualties.

GERONIMO: DEATH ANNIVERSARY. Feb 17. American Indian of the Chiricahua (Apache) tribe was born about 1829 in Arizona. He was the leader of a small band of warriors whose devastating raids in Arizona, New Mexico and Mexico caused the US Army to send 5,000 men to recapture him after his first escape. He was confined at Fort Sill, OK, where he died on Feb 17, 1909, after dictating, for publication, the story of his life.

HOSPITALITY INDUSTRY CAREER FAIR. Feb 17. WA State Convention & Trade Center, Olympia, WA. 4th annual career fair open to Northwest students in high school and college interested in culinary, hotel/motel and tourism. Est attendance: 600. For info: Education Dir, Washington Restaurant Assoc, 2405 Evergreen Park Dr SW, Bldg A, Olympia, WA 98502. Phone: (360) 956-7279.

LAENNEC, RENE THEOPHILE HYACINTHE: BIRTH ANNIVERSARY. Feb 17, 1781. Famed French physician, author and inventor of the stethoscope, called "father of chest medicine." He wrote extensively about respiratory and heart ailments. Born at Quimper, France, he died there Aug 13, 1826.

MALTHUS, THOMAS: BIRTH ANNIVERSARY. Feb 17. English economist, author and demographer. Born near Dorking, England, on Feb 17, 1766. Malthusian population theories (especially that population growth exceeds growth of production) provoked great controversy when published in 1798 but have attained greater acceptance in the 20th century. Died near Bath, England, Dec 23, 1834.

McCLURE, SAMUEL SIDNEY: BIRTH ANNIVERSARY. Feb 17, 1857. Irish-American newspaper editor and publisher, founder of newspaper syndicate. Born at County Antrim, Ireland, Feb 17, 1857. Died at New York, NY, Mar 21, 1949.

NATIONAL PTA FOUNDERS' DAY: ANNIVERSARY. Feb 17. Celebrates the PTA's founding by Phoebe Apperson Hearst and Alice McLellan Birney in 1897. For info: Natl PTA, 330 N Wabash, Ste 2100, Chicago, IL 60611. Phone: (312) 670-6782. Fax: (312) 670-6783. Email: info@pta.org. WWW: http://www.pta.org

PEALE, RAPHAEL: BIRTH ANNIVERSARY. Feb 17. American painter, member of famous family of early American painters, born at Annapolis, MD, Feb 17, 1774. Died Mar 4, 1825.

BIRTHDAYS TODAY

Alan Bates (Arthur Bates), 64, actor (*An Unmarried Woman, Women in Love*), born Derbyshire, England, Feb 17, 1934.

James Nathaniel (Jim) Brown, 62, activist, actor, Pro Football Hall of Fame fullback, born St. Simons Island, GA, Feb 17, 1936.

Brenda Fricker, 53, actress (*My Left Foot,* [Academy Award, Best Supporting Actress], *The Field*), born Dublin, Ireland, Feb 17, 1945.

Lee Hoiby, 72, composer, concert pianist, born Madison, WI, Feb 17, 1926.

Hal Holbrook (Harold Rowe, Jr), 73, actor (*Magnum Force, All the President's Men*), born Cleveland, OH, Feb 17, 1925.

Michael Jeffrey Jordan, 35, basketball player, former baseball player, born New York, NY, Feb 17, 1963.

Lou Diamond Phillips, 36, actor (*La Bamba, Stand and Deliver*), born Philippines, Feb 17, 1962.

FEBRUARY 18 — WEDNESDAY

Day 49 — 316 Remaining

ARTS & CRAFTS FESTIVAL & ANTIQUE SHOW. Feb 18–23. The Grove Park Inn Resort, Asheville, NC. More than 1,000 arts & crafts collectors, dealers, architects, historians, craftsmen and curators meet for three important days of seminars, exhibits, discussions, demonstrations, tours, debates, panels and antiques. Est attendance: 2,000. For info: Bruce Johnson, PO Box 8773, Asheville, NC 28814. Phone: (704) 254-1912.

COW MILKED WHILE FLYING IN AN AIRPLANE: ANNIVERSARY. Feb 18, 1930. Elm Farm Ollie became the first cow to fly in an airplane. During the flight, which was attended by reporters, she was milked and the milk was sealed in paper containers and parachuted over St. Louis, MO.

DAVIS, JEFFERSON: INAUGURATION ANNIVERSARY. Feb 18, 1861. In the years before the Civil War, Jefferson Davis was the acknowledged leader of the Southern bloc and a champion of states' rights, but he had little to do with the secessionist movement until after his home state of Mississippi joined the Confederacy on Jan 9, 1861. Davis withdrew from the Senate that same day. He was unanimously chosen as president of the Confederacy's provisional government and inaugurated at Montgomery, AL, on Feb 18. Within the next year he was elected to a six-year term by popular vote and inaugurated a second time on Feb 22, 1862, in Richmond, VA.

ELM FARM OLLIE DAY CELEBRATION. Feb 18. Wisconsin. This day marks the first flight in an airplane by a dairy cow, Elm Farm Ollie, on Feb 18, 1930, at the St. Louis International Air Exposition. Although this brave bovine hailed from Missouri, residents of the "Dairy State" mark this festive event by consuming large amounts of cheese and ice cream and by singing the "Bovine Cantata" from Moocini's lyric opera *Madame Butterfat*. Est attendance: 200. For info: Barry Levenson, Curator, Mount Horeb Mustard Museum, PO Box 468, Mount Horeb, WI 53572. Phone: (608) 437-3986. Fax: (608) 437-4018. Email: curator@mustardweb.com. WWW: http://www.mustardweb.com

GAMBIA: INDEPENDENCE DAY. Feb 18. National holiday. Independence from Britain granted Feb 18, 1965. Referendum in April 1970 established Gambia as a republic within the Commonwealth.

LA FIESTA DE LOS VAQUEROS. Feb 18–22. Tucson, AZ. Tucson celebrates its Old West heritage with parade, PRCA rodeo and other related rodeo events. Est attendance: 55,000. For info: Tucson Rodeo Committee, Inc, PO Box 11006, Tucson, AZ 85734. Phone: (520) 741-2233. Fax: (520) 741-7273.

LUTHER, MARTIN: DEATH ANNIVERSARY. Feb 18, 1546. The Augustinian monk who put his "95 Theses" on the church door in protest and sparked the Reformation. See also: "Luther, Martin: Birth Anniversary" (Nov 10).

MILWAUKEE BOAT SHOW. Feb 18–22. Wisconsin Center, Milwaukee, WI. This event brings together buyers and sellers of sail and power boats, including fishing boats, pontoons and boating accessories, as well as vacation property and travel destinations. Est attendance: 25,000. For info: Henri Boucher, ShowSpan, Inc, 1400 28th St SW, Grand Rapids, MI 49509. Phone: (616) 530-1919. Fax: (616) 530-2122.

PEABODY, GEORGE: BIRTH ANNIVERSARY. Feb 18. American merchant and philanthropist. Born Feb 18, 1795. Died Nov 4, 1869.

PONTIAC SILVERDOME BOAT, SPORT AND FISHING SHOW. Feb 18–22. Pontiac Silverdome, Pontiac, MI. This event brings together buyers and sellers of boating, fishing and outdoor sporting products. US and Canadian hunting and fishing trips, as well as other vacation travel destinations, are featured. Est attendance: 35,000. For info: Henri Boucher, ShowSpan, Inc, 1400 28th St SW, Grand Rapids, MI 49509. Phone: (616) 530-1919. Fax: (616) 530-2122.

RABINOWITZ, SOLOMON: BIRTH ANNIVERSARY. Feb 18. Russian-born author and humorist better known by his pen name, Sholem Aleichem. Born in the Ukraine, Feb 18, 1859. Affectionately known in the US as the "Jewish Mark Twain." Died at New York, NY, May 13, 1916.

"TATTLETALES" TV PREMIERE: ANNIVERSARY. Feb 18, 1974. Three celebrity couples competed in this Q & A show hosted by Bert Convy. "Tattletales," produced by Mark Goodson and Bill Todman, appeared on CBS and in syndication.

TIFFANY, LOUIS COMFORT: 150th BIRTH ANNIVERSARY. Feb 18, 1848. American artist, son of famed jeweler Charles L. Tiffany. Best remembered for his remarkable work with decorative iridescent "favrile" glass. Born at New York, NY, on Feb 18, 1848. Died there Jan 17, 1933. See also: "Tiffany, Charles Lewis: Birth Anniversary" (Feb 15).

WILLKIE, WENDELL LEWIS: BIRTH ANNIVERSARY. Feb 18, 1892. American lawyer, author, public utility executive and politician. Born at Elwood, IN, Feb 18, 1892. Presidential nominee of the Republican Party in 1940. Remembered too for his book, *One World*, published in 1943. Died at New York, NY, Oct 8, 1944.

BIRTHDAYS TODAY

Helen Gurley Brown, 76, author (*Sex and the Office*), publisher (*Cosmopolitan*), born Green Forest, AR, Feb 18, 1922.

Aldo Ceccato, 64, conductor, born Milan, Italy, Feb 18, 1934.

Matt Dillon, 34, actor (*My Bodyguard, Drugstore Cowboy*), born Westchester, NY, Feb 18, 1964.

Milos Forman, 66, film director (Oscars for *Amadeus* and *One Flew Over the Cuckoo's Nest*), born Caslaz, Czechoslovakia, Feb 18, 1932.

George Kennedy, 71, actor (Oscar for *Cool Hand Luke*; "The Blue Knight"), born New York, NY, Feb 18, 1927.

Toni Morrison (Chloe Anthony), 67, Nobel Prize-winning novelist (*Beloved, Jazz, Tar Baby, Sula*), born Lorain, OH, Feb 18, 1931.

Juice Newton (Judy Cohen), 46, singer (platinum album *Juice*, gold album *Quiet Lives*), born Virginia Beach, VA, Feb 18, 1952.

Yoko Ono, 65, artist, musician, widow of John Lennon, born Tokyo, Japan, Feb 18, 1933.

Jack Palance, 78, actor (Oscar for *City Slickers*; "Bronk," "Ripley's Believe It or Not"), born Lattimer, PA, Feb 18, 1920.

Molly Ringwald, 30, actress (*Sixteen Candles, The Breakfast Club, Pretty in Pink*), born Roseville, CA, Feb 18, 1968.

Greta Scacchi, 38, actress (*White Mischief, Presumed Innocent*), born Milan, Italy, Feb 18, 1960.

Cybill Shepherd, 48, actress (*The Last Picture Show*; Maddie Hayes on "Moonlighting"), born Memphis, TN, Feb 18, 1950.

John Travolta, 43, actor (*Pulp Fiction, Look Who's Talking, Urban Cowboy, Saturday Night Fever*, "Welcome Back Kotter"), born Englewood, NJ, Feb 18, 1955.

John William Warner, 71, US Senator (R, Virginia), ex-husband of Elizabeth Taylor, born Washington, DC, Feb 18, 1927.

Vanna White, 41, TV personality ("Wheel of Fortune"), born Conway, SC, Feb 18, 1957.

Gahan Wilson, 68, cartoonist, author, born Evanston, IL, Feb 18, 1930.

February 1998

S	M	T	W	T	F	S
1	2	3	4	5	6	7
8	9	10	11	12	13	14
15	16	17	18	19	20	21
22	23	24	25	26	27	28

FEBRUARY 19 — THURSDAY

Day 50 — 315 Remaining

ACBL TOURNAMENT. Feb 19–22. Yuma, AZ. Bridge sectional. Annually, the second to last weekend in February. Est attendance: 600. For info: Marion Weatherwax, Yuma Innsuites Hotel, Yuma, AZ 85365. Phone: (520) 343-0270.

BIG 10 WOMEN'S SWIMMING AND DIVING CHAMPIONSHIP. Feb 19–21. Indiana University, Bloomington, IN. Est attendance: 1,500. For info: Dennis LaBissoniere, Big Ten Conference, 1500 W Higgins Rd, Park Ridge, IL 60068-6300. Phone: (847) 696-1010. Fax: (847) 696-1110.
WWW: http://www.bigten.org

BIG 12 MEN'S AND WOMEN'S INDOOR TRACK CHAMPIONSHIPS. Feb 19–21. Ames, IA. Est attendance: 5,000. For info: Dru Hancock, Championship, Big 12 Conference, 2201 Stemmons Freeway, 28th Floor, Dallas, TX 75207. Phone: (214) 774-2121. Fax: (214) 742-2045.

BOLLINGEN PRIZE AWARD: ANNIVERSARY. Feb 19. On Feb 19, 1949, the first Bollingen Prize for poetry was awarded to Ezra Pound for his collection *The Pisan Cantos.* The first award was steeped in controversy because Pound had been charged with treason after making pro-Fascist broadcasts in Italy during World War II.

CANADA: OTTAWA BOAT AND SPORTSMEN'S SHOW. Feb 19–22. Civic Centre, Coliseum and Aberdeen Pavilion, Lansdowne Park, Ottawa, Ontario. Boating, hunting, fishing and archery information. Products displayed: powerboats, runabouts, inflatables, personal watercraft, fishing tackle, travel info, hunting gear, canoes, kayaks, camping and family entertainment. Est attendance: 30,000. For info: Canadian Natl Sportsmen's Shows, 703 Evans Ave, Ste 202, Toronto, Ont, Canada M9C 5E9. Phone: (416) 695-0311. Fax: (416) 695-0381.

CANADA: YUKON SOURDOUGH RENDEZVOUS. Feb 19–22. Whitehorse, Yukon. Mad trapper competitions, flour packing, beard-growing contests, old time fiddle show, sourdough pancake breakfasts, can-can girls, talent shows, etc. Also, many family-oriented activities. Visitors welcome to participate. Est attendance: 15,000. For info: Yukon Sourdough Rendezvous, Box 5108, Whitehorse, Yukon, Canada Y1A 4S3. Phone: (403) 667-2148 or (800) FUN-N-SNO. Fax: (403) 668-6755.
Email: ysr@hypertech.yk.ca.
WWW: http://www.haylow.yk.net/rendez

COPERNICUS, NICOLAUS: 525th BIRTH ANNIVERSARY. Feb 19, 1473. Polish astronomer and priest who revolutionized scientific thought with what came to be called the Copernican theory, which placed the sun instead of the earth at the center of our planetary system. Born at Torun, Poland, Feb 19, 1473. Died in East Prussia on May 24, 1543.

DYNO AMERICAN BIRKEBEINER XXVI RACE. Feb 19–21. Cable to Hayward, WI. The largest and most prestigious cross-country ski marathon in North America attracts more than 7,500 participants for the 52K trek. Starting off with the Birkie, skiers of the 25K Kortelopet finish at the halfway point. A nordic festival of related ski events and activities begins Feb 19. Est attendance: 25,000. For info: American Birkebeiner Ski Foundation, Inc, Box 911, Hayward, WI 54843. Phone: (715) 634-5025. Fax: (715) 634-5663. Email: birkieAwin@bright.net. WWW: http://www.winona.com/birkie

ENGLAND: NORTHWEST KNITTING AND NEEDLECRAFT EXHIBITION. Feb 19–22. G-Mex Centre, Manchester, Greater Manchester. Everything for the hand and machine knitter and the needlecraft enthusiast, fashion shows, lectures, demonstrations. Est attendance: 30,000. For info: Robert Ewin, Dir, Nationwide Exhibitions (UK) Ltd, PO Box 20, Fishponds, Bristol, England BS16 5QU. Phone: (44) (117) 970-1370. Fax: (44) (117) 970-1371.

GARRICK, DAVID: BIRTH ANNIVERSARY. Feb 19, 1717. English actor and playwright. Born Feb 19, 1717. Died Jan 20, 1779.

HEDIN, SVEN: BIRTH ANNIVERSARY. Feb 19, 1865. Explorer and scientist, Sven Anders Hedin was born at Stockholm, Sweden, on Feb 19, 1865, and died there on Nov 26, 1952. His Tibetan explorations provided the first substantial knowledge of that region to the rest of the world.

JAPANESE INTERNMENT: ANNIVERSARY. Feb 19, 1942. As a result of President Franklin Roosevelt's Executive Order 9066, issued on this date, some 110,000 Japanese-Americans living in coastal Pacific areas were placed in concentration camps in remote areas of Arizona, Arkansas, inland California, Colorado, Idaho, Utah and Wyoming. The interned Japanese-Americans (two-thirds were US citizens) lost an estimated $400 million in property.

KNIGHTS OF PYTHIAS: FOUNDING ANNIVERSARY. Feb 19. The social and fraternal order of the Knights of Pythias was founded at Washington, DC, Feb 19, 1864.

MAYMONT FLOWER & GARDEN SHOW. Feb 19–22. Richmond Centre, Richmond, VA. The 9th annual Maymont Flower & Garden Show is Virginia's largest. Landscape exhibits, lectures and more. Benefits Maymont, a house museum two miles from downtown Richmond. For info: Maymont Foundation, 1700 Hampton St, Richmond, VA 23220. Phone: (804) 358-7166.

MOON PHASE: LAST QUARTER. Feb 19. Moon enters Last Quarter phase at 10:27 AM, EST.

SIMPLOT GAMES. Feb 19–21. Holt Arena, Idaho State University, Pocatello, ID. One of the nation's largest indoor high school track and field events, featuring 2,500 top high school athletes from the US and Canada. Est attendance: 20,000. For info: Carol Lish, Exec Dir, Simplot Games, PO Box 912, Pocatello, ID 83204. Phone: (800) 635-9444. Fax: (208) 238-2967. Email: clish@simplot.com. WWW: http://www.simplot.com

BIRTHDAYS TODAY

Prince Andrew, 38, Duke of York, born London, England, Feb 19, 1960.

George Edward (Eddie) Arcaro, 82, former sportscaster and jockey, born Cincinnati, OH, Feb 19, 1916.

Justine Bateman, 32, actress ("Family Ties"), born Rye, NY, Feb 19, 1966.

Jeff Daniels, 43, actor (*The Purple Rose of Cairo, Something Wild, Dumb and Dumber*), born Georgia, Feb 19, 1955.

Falco, 41, musician, born Vienna, Austria, Feb 19, 1957.

Hana Mandlikova, 35, tennis player, born Prague, Czechoslovakia, Feb 19, 1963.

Smokey Robinson (William Robinson, Jr), 58, singer, songwriter ("Cruisin'," "Being With You"), born Detroit, MI, Feb 19, 1940.

Seal, 35, British singer-songwriter ("Prayer for the Dying"), born Sealhenry Samuel, London, England, Feb 19, 1963.

Andrew Shue, 31, actor ("Melrose Place"), born South Orange, NJ, Feb 19, 1967.

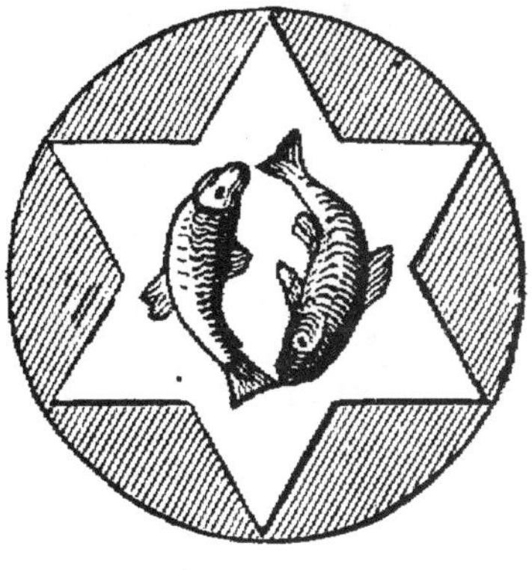

FEBRUARY 20 — FRIDAY

Day 51 — 314 Remaining

ADAMS, ANSEL: BIRTH ANNIVERSARY. Feb 20, 1902. American photographer known for his photographs of Yosemite National Park, born at San Francisco, CA. Adams died at Monterey, CA, Apr 22, 1984.

COBAIN, KURT: BIRTH ANNIVERSARY. Feb 20, 1967. American rock musician and singer Kurt Cobain was born at Aberdeen, WA. As leader of the Seattle band Nirvana, he was viewed as the founder of the genre known as grunge rock and as his generation's spokesperson, though he publicly denounced such roles. He died by his own hand on Apr 8, 1994, at Seattle, WA.

CRAZY CHILI SHOWDOWN. Feb 20–21. Behind the Crazy Water Hotel, Mineral Wells, TX. Chili cooks from across the country head to historic Mineral Wells for one of the hottest chili cookoffs in the region. From fiddlers to free chili tastings, they offer a great time to the public. Proceeds go to help needy families at Christmas. Annually, third weekend in February. Est attendance: 2,000. For info: The Mineral Wells Index, PO Box 370, Mineral Wells, TX 76068. Phone: (940) 325-4465. Fax: (940) 325-2020.

DOUGLASS, FREDERICK: DEATH ANNIVERSARY. Feb 20. American journalist, orator and antislavery leader. Born at Tuckahoe, MD, probably in February 1817. Died at Anacostia Heights, DC, Feb 20, 1895. His original name before his escape from slavery was Frederick Augustus Washington Bailey.

ENGLAND: BATH LITERATURE FESTIVAL. Feb 20–Mar 1. Various venues, Bath, Avon. A stellar line-up of some of the most celebrated and engaging authors writing today. Also, readings, discussions and creative workshops and children's events. For info: Bath Festivals Box Office, 2 Church St, Abbey Green, Bath, Avon, England BA1 1NL. Phone: (44) (122) 546-3362. Fax: (44) (122) 531-0377.

50 YEARS OF PLANTS AND PEOPLE. Feb 20. Arcadia, CA. 50th anniversary of the California Arboretum Foundation Incorporated that created the Arboretum of Los Angeles County, Feb 20, 1948. Est attendance: 500. For info: Joan Murphine, 333 E 17th St 7C, Costa Mesa, CA 92627. Phone: (714) 650-4846. Email: callcafarb@aol.com.

HOUSTON LIVESTOCK SHOW AND RODEO. Feb 20–Mar 8. Astrodome Complex, Houston, TX. Livestock show with more than 25,000 entries. "Wild rodeo action" and top-name musical entertainment. For info: Marketing Dept, Houston Livestock Show and Rodeo Assn, Box 20070, Houston, TX 77225-0070. Phone: (713) 791-9000. Fax: (713) 794-9528. WWW: http://www.hlsr.com

INDIANAPOLIS BOAT, SPORT AND TRAVEL SHOW. Feb 20–Mar 1. Indiana State Fairgrounds, Indianapolis, IN. Est attendance: 200,000. For info: Kevin Renfro, VP, Ste E-2, Corporate Sq East, 2511 E 46th St, Indianapolis, IN 46205. Phone: (317) 546-4344. Fax: (317) 546-3002. Email: insportshow@iquest.net.

JALAPEÑO FESTIVAL. Feb 20–21. Laredo, TX. Celebration of the jalapeño pepper. Events include the world famous Jalapeño Eating Contest, the "Some Like It Hot" Recipe Contest, the crowning of Ms Jalapeño, Jalapeño Olympic games, spicy food, cold drinks, big name entertainment, music and dancing. Held during Laredo's annual Washington's Birthday Celebration. Proceeds benefit youth-oriented charities. Est attendance: 25,000. For info: c/o Anselmo Castro, Jr, Jalapeño Festival, Inc, PO Drawer 1359, Laredo, TX 78042-1359. Phone: (210) 726-6697. Fax: (210) 726-6660. Email: anselmo_castro@iboc.com.

JEFFERSON, JOSEPH: BIRTH ANNIVERSARY. Feb 20. Distinguished American actor, born on Feb 20, 1829, at Philadelphia, PA. Joseph Jefferson, the fourth actor in a family of actors and the third of the same name, made his stage debut at the age of three as Cora's child in Kotzebue's *Pizarro*. After many successes, his search for a character both humorous and pathetic centered on Rip Van Winkle, about whom he wrote a short play. Later revised by Dion Boucicault, the play opened with Jefferson in the leading role at London, England, in 1865 and was an immediate success. The role of Rip Van Winkle became the signature role for which he was known. Jefferson died at Palm Beach, FL, on Apr 23, 1905. He is remembered each year in Chicago when the Joseph Jefferson Awards are presented to recognize excellence in theatrical productions.

LONGHORN WORLD CHAMPIONSHIP RODEO. Feb 20–22. The Palace of Auburn Hills, Auburn Hills, MI. More than 200 of the best cowboys and cowgirls compete in six professional contests ranging from bronc riding to bull riding for top prize money and world championship points. Featuring colorful opening pageantry and Big, Bad BONUS Bulls. 20th annual. Est attendance: 42,000. For info: W. Bruce Lehrke, Pres, Longhorn World Chmpshp Rodeo, Inc, PO Box 70159, Nashville, TN 37207. Phone: (615) 876-1016. Fax: (615) 876-4685. Email: lhrodeo@idt.net. WWW: http://www.longhornrodeo.com

MIDWINTER BLUEGRASS FESTIVAL. Feb 20–22. Holiday Inn, Hannibal, MO. Annually, the third weekend in February. Est attendance: 3,000. For info: Delbert Spray, Program Dir, Tri-State Bluegrass Assn, RR1, Kahoka, MO 63445. Phone: (573) 853-4344.

NEWPORT SEAFOOD AND WINE FESTIVAL. Feb 20–22. Newport, OR. Central coastal festival featuring seafood and wines from Oregon, Washington, California and Idaho. Est attendance: 17,500. For info: Kathy Simmons, Special Events Coordinator, Chamber of Commerce, 555 SW Coast Hwy, Newport, OR 97365. Phone: (541) 265-8801. Fax: (541) 265-5589. Email: chamber@newport.com.

NORTHERN HEMISPHERE HOODIE-HOO DAY. Feb 20. At high noon (local time) citizens are asked to go outdoors and yell "Hoodie-Hoo" to chase away winter and make ready for spring, one month away. [© 1997 by WPL] For info: Tom or Ruth Roy, Wellness Permission League, PO Box 662, Mt Gretna, PA 17064-0662. Phone: (500) 437-5104. Fax: (717) 964-1335.

OREGON SHAKESPEARE FESTIVAL. Feb 20–Nov 1. An 8-month season of 11 plays by Shakespeare, classical and contemporary playwrights on three stages: the outdoor Elizabethan Stage, the versatile Angus Bowmer Theatre and the intimate Black Swan. Est attendance: 353,000. For info: Oregon Shakespeare Festival, Box 158, Ashland, OR 97520. Phone: (541) 482-4331. WWW: http://www.mind.net/osf/

PISCES, THE FISH. Feb 20–Mar 20. In the astronomical/astrological zodiac, which divides the sun's apparent orbit into 12 segments, the period Feb 20–Mar 20 is identified, traditionally, as the sun sign of Pisces, the Fish. The ruling planet is Neptune.

PRESCOTT, WILLIAM: BIRTH ANNIVERSARY. Feb 20. American Revolutionary soldier. Born at Groton, MA, Feb 20, 1726. Died at Pepperell, MA, Oct 13, 1795. Credited with the order, "Don't fire until you see the whites of their eyes," at the Battle of Bunker Hill, June 17, 1775.

ROMMEL STRIKES FROM MARETH LINE: 55th ANNIVERSARY. Feb 20, 1943. After his defeat in Libya in January of 1943, Field Marshal Erwin Rommel retreated to the Mareth Line, an old French frontier position in Tunisia. From there Rommel took the offensive to defeat US forces at Kasserine Pass on this date. He then attacked the 8th Army at Medenine but had to pull back after losing 52 tanks. British General Sir Bernard Montgomery then took the offensive Mar 20, attacking and turning the Mareth Line. The German forces withdrew and shortly thereafter Rommel was recalled to Germany, and his command passed to Italian General Messe, who retreated to Enfidaville.

☆ ☆ ☆

SECOND HONEYMOON WEEKEND. Feb 20–22. Whether married recently or for a number of years, this weekend is set aside for all couples to spend some quality time together away from the grind and routine of their everyday lives. Take your significant other aside and experience fun, joy and closeness together. Annually, the weekend immediately after Valentine's Day. For info: Adrienne Sioux Koopersmith, 1437 W Rosemont, #1W, Chicago, IL 60660-1319. Phone: (773) 743-5341. Fax: (773) 743-5395. Email: kooper@interaccess.com.

SMOKY MOUNTAINS STORYTELLING FESTIVAL. Feb 20–21. Patriot Park, Pigeon Forge, TN. Food, bonfire and hayrides with tall tales by some of the area's best storytellers. Est attendance: 1,000. For info: Kay Powell, Pigeon Forge Dept of Tourism, 2450 Parkway, PO Box 1390, Pigeon Forge, TN 37868. Phone: (800) 251-9100 or (423) 453-8574.

SPACE MILESTONE: *FRIENDSHIP 7* (US): FIRST AMERICAN TO ORBIT EARTH: 35th ANNIVERSARY. Feb 20, 1962. John Herschel Glenn, Jr, became the first American, and the third man, to orbit Earth. Aboard the capsule *Friendship 7*, he made three orbits of Earth. Spacecraft was *Mercury-Atlas 6*.

SPACE MILESTONE: *MIR* SPACE STATION (USSR). Feb 20, 1986. A "third-generation" orbiting space station, *Mir* (Peace), was launched without crew on Feb 20, 1986, from the Baikonur space center at Leninsk, Kazakhstan. Believed to be 40 feet long, weigh 47 tons and have six docking ports.

STAMP EXPO/USA. Feb 20–22. Quality Hotel, Anaheim, CA. Annual expo. Est attendance: 5,000. For info: Intl Stamp Collectors Society, PO Box 854, Van Nuys, CA 91408. Phone: (818) 997-6496. Fax: (818) 988-4337. Email: iibick@aol.com. WWW: http://www.4free.com/bick

STOTZ, CARL E.: BIRTH ANNIVERSARY. Feb 20, 1920. Carl E. Stotz shaped the summers of millions of kids as the founder of Little League baseball. Born at Williamsport, PA, Feb 20, 1910, he organized the first three-team league there in 1939. Died June 4, 1992.

STUDENT VOLUNTEER DAY. Feb 20. To honor students who give of themselves and of their personal time to improve the lives of others and their communities. Annually, Feb 20. Est attendance: 250. For info: Susquehanna University, Center for Service Learning and Volunteer Programs, 514 University Avenue, Selinsgrove, PA 17870-1001. Phone: (717) 372-4139. Fax: (717) 372-2745. Email: woodsd@susqu.edu.

WINCHELL, WALTER: DEATH ANNIVERSARY. Feb 20, 1972. Journalist, broadcaster, reporter and gossip columnist Walter Winchell died at Los Angeles on Feb 20, 1972. He was admired for his way with turning a phrase. His show business columns were voraciously read by millions of Americans between 1924–1963.

February 1998

S	M	T	W	T	F	S
1	2	3	4	5	6	7
8	9	10	11	12	13	14
15	16	17	18	19	20	21
22	23	24	25	26	27	28

BIRTHDAYS TODAY

Edward Albert, 47, actor (*Butterflies Are Free, Terminal Entry, Guarding Tess*), born Los Angeles, CA, Feb 20, 1951.
Robert Altman, 73, film director (*M*A*S*H, Nashville*), born Kansas City, MO, Feb 20, 1925.
Charles Wade Barkley, 35, basketball player, born Leeds, AL, Feb 20, 1963.
Cindy Crawford, 32, model, actress, TV host, born DeKalb, IL, Feb 20, 1966.
Sandy Duncan, 52, actress (*Funny Face*, "The Hogan Family," *Peter Pan*), born Henderson, TX, Feb 20, 1946.
Philip Anthony (Phil) Esposito, 56, hockey executive, former coach and Hockey Hall of Fame center, born Sault Ste. Marie, Ontario, Canada, Feb 20, 1942.
Kelsey Grammer, 43, actor ("Cheers," "Frasier"), born St. Thomas, US Virgin Islands, Feb 20, 1955.
Muriel Fay Buck Humphrey, 86, widow of Hubert Humphrey, born Huron, SD, Feb 20, 1912.
Mitch McConnell, 56, US Senator (R, Kentucky), born in Colbert County, AL, Feb 20, 1942.
Jennifer O'Neill, 50, actress (*The Summer of '42*, "Cover-Up"), born Rio de Janeiro, Brazil, Feb 20, 1948.
Kenneth Olsen, 72, founder of Digital Equipment Corporation, born Bridgeport, CT, Feb 20, 1926.
Sidney Poitier, 71, actor (*In the Heat of the Night*, Oscar for *Lilies of the Field*), born Miami, FL, Feb 20, 1927.
Buffy Sainte-Marie (Beverly Sainte-Marie), 57, Native-American folksinger ("Mister Can't You See," "He's an Indian Cowboy in the Rodeo"), born Craven, Saskatchewan, Canada, Feb 20, 1941.
Patty Hearst Shaw, 44, newspaper heiress who was kidnapped by radical group Symbionese Liberation Army and later convicted and imprisoned for her participation (forced or not) in a bank robbery with her kidnappers; actress (*Cry-Baby*), born San Francisco, CA, Feb 20, 1954.
Peter Strauss, 51, actor ("Rich Man Poor Man," *Soldier Blue*), born Croton-on-Hudson, NY, Feb 20, 1947.
Robert William (Bobby) Unser, 64, auto racer, born Albuquerque, NM, Feb 20, 1934.
Gloria Vanderbilt, 74, fashion designer, artist, subject of a famous child custody battle, born New York, NY, Feb 20, 1924.
James Wilby, 40, actor (*DreamChild, Howards End*), born Rangoon, Burma, Feb 20, 1958.
Nancy Wilson, 61, singer ("Yesterday's Love Songs/Today's Blues"), born Chillicothe, OH, Feb 20, 1937.

FEBRUARY 21 — SATURDAY

Day 52 — 313 Remaining

ANDERSONVILLE REVISITED. Feb 21–22 (tentative). Andersonville National Historic Site, Andersonville, GA. Two reenactments in the stockade area. One demonstrates prisoner and guard life at Andersonville during the Civil War. The second is at night and depicts a reunion of some former prisoners who returned to visit Andersonville after the turn of the century. Est attendance: 1,200. For update and info: Alan Marsh, Park Ranger, Andersonville National Historic Site, Rte 1, Box 800 Hwy 49 N, Andersonville, GA 31711. Phone: (912) 924-0343. Fax: (912) 928-9640.

BANGLADESH: MARTYRS DAY. Feb 21. National mourning day in memory of martyrs of the Bengali Language Movement in 1952. Mourners gather at the Azimpur graveyard and proceed to Shaheed Minar.

BATTLE OF WEST POINT AND PRAIRIE. Feb 21–22. Columbus and West Point, MS. Civil War reenactment with campsites, battles, entertainment and sutler stores taking place on Windmill Rd (off Hwy 50) between Columbus and West Point. Sponsor: Possum Tour Reenactors, Inc. Est attendance: 2,500. For info: Carolyn Denton, Dir, Columbus Conv & Visitors Bureau, PO Box 789, Columbus, MS 39703. Phone: (800) 327-2686 or (601) 329-1191. Fax: (601) 329-8969. Email: ccvb@tile.com.
WWW: http://friendship.columbus.ms.us

BRAZIL: CARNIVAL. Feb 21–24. Especially in Rio de Janeiro, this carnival is said to be one of the last great folk festivals, and the big annual event in the life of Brazilians. Begins on Saturday night before Ash Wednesday and continues through Shrove Tuesday.

BRIGHTON FIELD DAY AND RODEO. Feb 21–22. Brighton Indian Reservation, Okeechobee, FL. Arts and crafts, alligator wrestling, PRCA rodeo, animal show, parade and beautiful Native American clothing. Sponsor: Seminole Tribe of Florida. Annually, the third weekend in February. Est attendance: 5,500. For info: Ellen Click, Field Day Contact Person, Rte 6, Box 666, Okeechobee, FL 34974. Phone: (813) 763-4128. Fax: (941) 763-5077.

CARDBOARD DOWNHILL DERBY. Feb 21. Arapahoe Basin Ski Area, CO. Teams design cardboard crafts to take down a ski slope. Each team has a theme and designs the craft and costumes to correspond. Past entries have included a giant Bozo head, a pirate ship, a bi-plane—all made of cardboard, tape, glue and string. Est attendance: 2,000. For info: Dave Rush, Promotions Coord, KBCO Radio, 2500 Pearl St, Ste 315, Boulder, CO 80302. Phone: (303) 444-5600. Fax: (303) 444-2929. WWW: http://www.kbcoradio.com

CHILDREN'S WESTERN JAMBOREE. Feb 21–22. Guthrie, OK. This event brings the spirit of the old west into the lives of many with a fun-filled day of activities for children of all ages. For info: Lazy E Arena, Rte 5, Box 393, Guthrie, OK 73044-9205. Phone: (800) 595-RIDE or (405) 282-RIDE. Fax: (405) 282-3785. Email: arena@lazye.com.
WWW: http://www.lazye.com

CIA AGENT ARRESTED AS SPY: ANNIVERSARY. Feb 21, 1994. Aldrich Hazen Ames and his wife Maria del Rosario Casas Ames were arrested on charges they had spied for the Soviet Union beginning in 1985 and had continued to spy for Russia after the Soviet collapse in 1991. Ames had worked as a counterintelligence officer for the CIA at its headquarters in Langley, VA. Prosecutors said that the pair had been paid about $2.5 million for their activities and were probably responsible for the deaths of at least ten CIA agents whom Ames had identified for the Soviets. The government considered this to be one of the most serious spy cases ever uncovered in the US. On Apr 28 Aldrich Ames was sentenced to life in prison. Rosario Ames was sentenced to a 63-month prison term in return for her husband's promise to cooperate with authorities.

ESA MID-WINTER SURFING CHAMPIONSHIP. Feb 21. Narragansett Town Beach, Narragansett, RI. Competition in all age categories and specialty events with prizes and trophies. Est attendance: 125. For info: Peter Pan, ESA Dir, 396 Main St, Wakefield, RI 02879. Phone: (401) 789-3399. Fax: (401) 782-0458.

FASNACHT. Feb 21. Helvetia, WV. Celebration with a Swiss flavor includes parade, masked ball and the burning of "old man winter." Annually, the Saturday before Ash Wednesday. Sponsor: Helvetia Restoration and Development Assn, Inc. Est attendance: 200. For info: Eleanor Mailloux, Swiss Village, PO Box 42, Helvetia, WV 26224. Phone: (304) 924-6435.

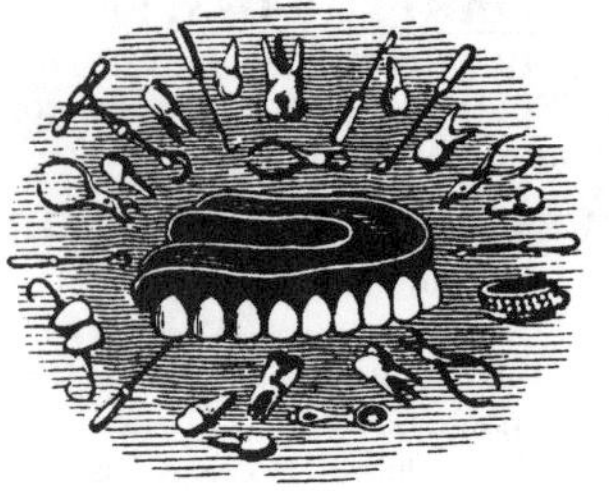

FIRST WOMAN TO GRADUATE FROM DENTAL SCHOOL: ANNIVERSARY. Feb 21. On Feb 21, 1866, Lucy Hobbs became the first woman to graduate from a dental school, in Cincinnati, OH.

FRENCH WEST INDIES: CARNIVAL. Feb 21–25. Martinique. For five days, business comes to a halt. Streets spill over with parties and parades. Carnival Queen is elected. For info: Ms Muriel Wiltord, Martinique Promo Bureau, 444 Madison Ave, 16th Floor, New York, NY 10022. Phone: (800) 391-4909. Fax: (212) 838-7855. Email: martinique@nyo.com. WWW: http://martinique.org

HATSUME FAIR. Feb 21–22. Morikami Museum, Delray Beach, FL. Celebrates the coming of spring with demonstrations and performances of Japanese taiko drums, folk dancing, martial arts, plants, orchids and bonsai exhibits. Annually, the last weekend in February. Est attendance: 16,000. For info: Melodie Shute, Dir of Mktg, The Morikami Museum, 4000 Morikami Park Rd, Delray Beach, FL 33446. Phone: (561) 495-0233. Fax: (561) 499-2557. WWW: http://www.icsi.com/ics/morikami/

KLONDIKE DAYS/WORLD CHAMPIONSHIP OVAL SPRINT. Feb 21–22. Eagle River Derby Track, Eagle River, WI. More than 72 sled dog teams from the US and Canada on the only oval sprint racing track for sled dogs in the country. Also, a re-creation of primitive camps used by early buck-skinners, pioneers, trappers and traders, complete with tomahawk throwing, logging and ceremonial dance competition. Additional attractions include a horse weight-pull reminiscent of Wisconsin's logging days, a chain saw carving exhibition and Native culture presentations. Est attendance: 12,000. For info: Klondike Days, PO Box 1166, Eagle River, WI 54521-0218. Phone: (715) 479-7428. Or obtain an informational brochure by calling (888) Dog-Sled.

KNIGHTS OF ST. YAGO ILLUMINATED NIGHT PARADE. Feb 21. Ybor City, Tampa, FL. Dozens of illuminated floats and parade units, the Gasparilla pirates, dignitaries and marching bands light up the night in the city's biggest night parade. Est attendance: 100,000. For info: Ybor City Chamber of Commerce, 1800 E 9th Ave, Tampa, FL 33605. Phone: (813) 248-3712. Fax: (813) 247-1764.

MALCOLM X: ASSASSINATION ANNIVERSARY. Feb 21. Malcolm X, a black leader who renounced the Black Muslim sect to form the Organization of Afro-American Unity, was shot and killed as he spoke to a rally at the Audubon Ballroom in New York, NY, on Feb 21, 1965. Three men were convicted of the murder in 1966 and sentenced to life in prison. Born Malcolm Little, the son of a Baptist preacher, on May 19, 1925, at Omaha, NE.

MARDI GRAS IN CAJUN COUNTRY. Feb 21–24. Lafayette, LA. Celebration before the beginning of Lent. Included festivities: parades, costume contest, annual Southwest Louisiana Mardi Gras Association Pageant and Ball. The surrounding rural areas offer the traditional Courir du Mardi Gras. Second-largest carnival celebration in Louisiana. Est attendance: 300,000. For info: Kelly Strenge, Public Relations and Special Projects Mgr, Lafayette Conv and Visitors Commission, PO Box 52066, Lafayette, LA 70505. Phone: (800) 346-1958. Fax: (318) 232-0161.

NATIONAL FFA WEEK. Feb 21–28. More than 450,000 FFA members in more than 7,200 chapters across the US, Guam, Puerto Rico and the Virgin Islands organize events and activities fostering and supporting agricultural education and the FFA. FFA is the organization for high school students studying the business, science and technology of agriculture. For info: William F. Stagg, Dir of Communications, Natl FFA Organization, 5632 Mt. Vernon Memorial Hwy, Alexandria, VA 22309-0160. Phone: (703) 360-3600 ext 243. WWW: http://www.ffa.org

***NEW YORKER* PUBLISHED: ANNIVERSARY.** Feb 21, 1925. First issue of the magazine published on this date.

OLD WEST SHOW. Feb 21–22. Garcia La Mision Civic Center, Deming, NM. (Also, Aug 15–16.) Buy, sell and trade saddles, bits, spurs, chaps, old firearms, knives, memorabilia, western bronzes, Native American artifacts, western literature and more. Annually, the third weekends of February and August. Est attendance: 1,500. For info: Howard G. Staub, PO Drawer 2249, Deming, NM 88031. Phone: (505) 546-3727. Fax: (505) 546-8810.

ORANGE HISTORICAL SOCIETY ANNUAL ANTIQUE SHOW. Feb 21–22. Amity Jr High School, Orange, CT. More than 30 antique dealers displaying quality collections. Catered luncheon served until 3 PM both days. Sat 10–5; Sun 10–4. Admission $3.50. Annually, the last weekend in February. Est attendance: 1,200. For info: Show Coord, Orange Historical Society, PO Box 784, Orange, CT 06477. Phone: (203) 795-3160.

PALMER, ALICE FREEMAN: BIRTH ANNIVERSARY. Feb 21, 1855. Born at Colesville, NY, Alice Freeman Palmer became president of Wellesley College at the age of 27. Under her leadership the school for girls grew into one of the leading women's colleges. She was also instrumental in bringing the women's school Radcliffe College into its association with Harvard University. One of the organizers of the American Association of University Women, she served as its president for two terms. She was named to the Massachusetts Board of Education in 1889 and was appointed the first dean of women at the University of Chicago when it opened in 1892. Palmer died Dec 6, 1902, at Paris.

PARKE COUNTY MAPLE FAIR. Feb 21–22. (Also Feb 28–Mar 1) Rockville, IN. Headquarters at the 4-H Fairgrounds, 1 mile north of Rockville on US 41. Pancakes, sausage and maple syrup meals. Largest indoor craft and art show. Farmers' Market, Butcher Shop, tours to the Sugar Camps featuring the unique process of making maple syrup. Held annually last weekend in February and first weekend in March. Est attendance: 50,000. For info: Anne Lynk, Covered Bridge Capital, PO Box 165, Rockville, IN 47872. Phone: (765) 569-5226. Fax: (765) 569-3900. Email: anne@ticz.com. WWW: http://www.coveredbridges.com

RICHARD NIXON'S TRIP TO CHINA: ANNIVERSARY. Feb 21, 1972. Richard Nixon became the first US president to visit any country not diplomatically recognized by the US when he went to the People's Republic of China for meetings with Chairman Mao Tse-tung and Premier Chou En-lai. Nixon arrived at Peking on this date, and departed China on Feb 28. The "Shanghai Communique" was issued Feb 27. See also: "Shanghai Communique Anniversary" (Feb 27).

SANDINO, CESAR AUGUSTO: ASSASSINATION ANNIVERSARY. Feb 21. Nicaraguan guerrilla leader after whom the Sandinistas of the present day are named. Sandino, born in 1893 (exact date unknown), was murdered along with his brother and several aides at Managua on Feb 21, 1934. He and his followers had eluded the occupying force of US Marines as well as the Nicaraguan National Guard from 1927 until 1933. Regarded by the US as an outlaw and a bandit, he is revered as a martyred patriot hero by many Nicaraguans. His successful resistance and the resulting widespread anti-US feeling were

February 1998

S	M	T	W	T	F	S
1	2	3	4	5	6	7
8	9	10	11	12	13	14
15	16	17	18	19	20	21
22	23	24	25	26	27	28

largely responsible for inauguration of a US counteraction—the "Good Neighbor Policy" toward Latin American nations during the administration of President Franklin D. Roosevelt.

SOUTHERN SPRING SHOW. Feb 21–Mar 1. Charlotte, NC. The sights and scents of springtime—everything for home and garden. Dozens of professionally landscaped gardens, judged and full flower show, outdoor furniture and all the supplies and equipment for lawn and garden. Plus designer rooms, home building products and accessories, crafts, sculptures, travel and leisure exhibits and special show features and offerings. Est attendance: 100,000. For info: Media Coordinator, Southern Shows, Inc, PO Box 36859, Charlotte, NC 28236. Phone: (800) 849-0248. Fax: (704) 376-6345.

WASHINGTON MONUMENT DEDICATED: ANNIVERSARY. Feb 21. Monument to first president was dedicated on Feb 21, 1885, at Washington, DC.

BIRTHDAYS TODAY

Christopher Atkins, 37, actor ("Dallas," *The Blue Lagoon*), born Rye, NY, Feb 21, 1961.

William Baldwin, 35, actor (*Born on the Fourth of July, Backdraft*), born Massapequa, NY, Feb 21, 1963.

Mary Chapin Carpenter, 40, musician (*Stones in the Road, Hometown Girl*), born Princeton, NJ, Feb 21, 1958.

Tyne Daly, 51, actress (Emmy for Lacey on "Cagney and Lacey"; *Gypsy*), born Madison, WI, Feb 21, 1947.

David Geffen, 54, record company executive (Geffen Records), born New York City, NY, Feb 21, 1944.

Hubert de Givenchy, 71, fashion designer, born Beauvais, France, Feb 21, 1927.

Gary Lockwood, 61, actor (*Splendor in the Grass, 2001: A Space Odyssey*), born Van Nuys, CA, Feb 21, 1937.

Rue McClanahan, 64, actress (Vivian on "Maude," Blanche on "The Golden Girls"), born Healdton, OK, Feb 21, 1934.

Nina Simone (Eunice Waymon), 65, singer ("I Loves You Porgy," "Trouble in Mind"), born Tryon, NC, Feb 21, 1933.

Alan Stuart Trammell, 40, baseball player, born Garden Grove, CA, Feb 21, 1958.

FEBRUARY 22 — SUNDAY

Day 53 — 312 Remaining

BADEN-POWELL, ROBERT: BIRTH ANNIVERSARY. Feb 22, 1857. British army officer who founded the Boy Scouts and Girl Guides. Born at London, England, Feb 22, 1857. Died at Kenya, Africa, Jan 8, 1941.

BLUES BLAST–PHOENIX BLUES SOCIETY MUSIC FESTIVAL. Feb 22. Mesa Amphitheatre, Mesa, AZ. The first national blues festival of the calendar year held annually in February outdoors at a grassy amphitheatre. Past blues performers include John Mayall, Charles Brown, Joe Louis Walker, Guitar Shorty, Lavelle White, Little Charlie and the Nightcats, Francine Reed, Red Piazza and the Mighty Flyers. Est attendance: 2,000. For info: The Phoenix Blues Society, PO Box 36874, Phoenix, AZ 85067-6874. Phone: (602) 252-0599. Email: phxblues@aztec.asu.edu. WWW: http://www.aztec.asu.edu/phxblues/

CLOSING CEREMONY, WINTER OLYMPICS. Feb 22, 1998. The closing ceremony of the 1998 Winter Olympics in Nagano, Japan, will be held today at 5 AM, EST. Because of the 14-hour time difference, the event will be taking place at 7 PM in Japan.

FASCHING SUNDAY. Feb 22. Germany and Austria. The last Sunday before Lent.

JOE CAIN PROCESSION. Feb 22. Mobile, AL. Honors the man who revived the Mardi Gras in Mobile in 1866 following the War Between the States. Annually, the Sunday before Shrove Tuesday. Est attendance: 100,000. For info: Wayne Dean, Sr, VP, Joe Cain Society, 1064 Palmetto St, Mobile, AL 36604-3041. Phone: (334) 432-3960.

LOWELL, JAMES RUSSELL: BIRTH ANNIVERSARY. Feb 22. American essayist, poet and diplomat. Born at Cambridge, MA, on Feb 22, 1819. Died there on Aug 12, 1891.

MILLAY, EDNA ST. VINCENT: BIRTH ANNIVERSARY. Feb 22, 1892. American poet ("My candle burns at both ends. . . ."), born at Rockland, ME. She died Oct 19, 1950, at Austerlitz, NY.

MONTGOMERY BOYCOTT ARRESTS: ANNIVERSARY. Feb 22, 1956. On Feb 20 white city leaders of Montgomery, AL, issued an ultimatum to black organizers of the three-month-old Montgomery bus boycott. They said if the boycott ended immediately there would be "no retaliation whatsoever." If it did not end, it was made clear they would begin arresting black leaders. Two days later, 80 well-known boycotters, including Rosa Parks, Martin Luther King, Jr and E.D. Nixon marched to the sheriff's office in the county courthouse, where they gave themselves up for arrest. They were booked, fingerprinted and photographed. The next day the story was carried by newspapers all over the world.

NATIONAL ENGINEERS WEEK. Feb 22–28. The 48th annual observance, cosponsored by 18 national engineering societies and 12 major national corporations, will feature classroom programs in elementary and secondary schools throughout the US, shopping mall exhibits, engineering workplace tours and other events. Also, the Future Cities Competition national finals held in Washington, DC. Honorary chair for this year's event is W.W. Allen, Chairman and CEO of Phillips Petroleum. The Chairing Society is the Construction Specifications Institute. For more info call: Natl Engineers Week Headquarters, 1420 King St, Alexandria, VA 22314. Phone: (703) 684-2852. Email: eweek@nspe.org. WWW: http://www.eweek.org

PEALE, REMBRANDT: BIRTH ANNIVERSARY. Feb 22, 1778. American portrait and historical painter, born at Bucks County, PA, on Feb 22, 1778. Died at Philadelphia, PA, on Oct 3, 1860.

SAINT LUCIA: INDEPENDENCE DAY. Feb 22. National holiday.

SCHOPENHAUER, ARTHUR: BIRTH ANNIVERSARY. Feb 22, 1788. Philosopher and author, born at Danzig, Germany, Feb 22, 1788, and died at Frankfurt am Main, Germany, Sept 21, 1860. Generally regarded as a misanthrope, the never-married Schopenhauer wrote, in 1819, "To marry is to halve your rights and double your duties."

SHROVETIDE. Feb 22–24. The three days before Ash Wednesday: Shrove Sunday, Monday and Tuesday—a time for confession and for festivity before the beginning of Lent.

WADLOW, ROBERT PERSHING: BIRTH ANNIVERSARY. Feb 22. Tallest man in recorded history, born on Feb 22, 1918, at Alton, IL. Though only 9 lbs at birth, by age 10 Wadlow already stood over 6 feet tall and weighed 210 lbs; Wadlow died at age 22, a remarkable 8 feet 11.1 inches tall, 490 lbs. His gentle, friendly manner in the face of constant public attention earned him the name the "Gentle Giant." Wadlow died on July 15, 1940, at Manistee, MI, of complications resulting from a foot infection.

WASHINGTON, GEORGE: BIRTH ANNIVERSARY. Feb 22, 1732. First president of the US ("First in war, first in peace and first in the hearts of his countrymen" in the words of Henry "Light-Horse Harry" Lee). Born at Westmoreland County, VA, on Feb 22 (New Style), Feb 11 (Old Style), 1732, he died at Mt Vernon, VA, Dec 14, 1799. See also: "Washington, George: Birthday Observance (Legal Holiday)" (Feb 16 in 1998).

WOOLWORTHS FIRST OPENED: ANNIVERSARY. Feb 22, 1879. First chain store, Woolworths, opened in Utica, NY.

BIRTHDAYS TODAY

Amy Strum Alcott, 42, golfer, born Kansas City, MO, Feb 22, 1956.
George Lee ("Sparky") Anderson, 64, former baseball manager and player, born Bridgewater, SD, Feb 22, 1934.
Drew Barrymore, 23, actress (Gertie in *E.T. The Extra-Terrestrial; Irreconcilable Differences, Bad Girls*), born Los Angeles, CA, Feb 22, 1975.
Michael Te Pei Chang, 26, tennis player, born Hoboken, NJ, Feb 22, 1972.
Jonathan Demme, 54, director (*Silence of the Lambs*), born Centre, MD, Feb 22, 1944.
Paul Dooley, 70, actor (*Slap Shot, Breaking Away, The Player*), born Parkersburg, WV, Feb 22, 1928.
Julius Winfield ("Dr. J") Erving, 48, former basketball player, born Roosevelt, NY, Feb 22, 1950.
Nelson Bunker Hunt, 72, business executive, born El Dorado, TX, Feb 22, 1926.
Edward Moore (Ted) Kennedy, 66, US Senator (D, Massachusetts), born Boston, MA, Feb 22, 1932.
Niki Lauda, 49, auto racer, author, born Vienna, Austria, Feb 22, 1949.
Kyle MacLachlan, 39, actor ("Twin Peaks," *Blue Velvet, The Flintstones*), born Yakima, WA, Feb 22, 1959.
Miou Miou, 48, actress (*Entre Nous, La Lectrice*), born Paris, France, Feb 22, 1950.
Julie Walters, 48, actress (*Educating Rita, Prick Up Your Ears*), born Birmingham, England, Feb 22, 1950.

FEBRUARY 23 — MONDAY

Day 54 — 311 Remaining

BRUNEI DARUSSALAM: NATIONAL DAY. Feb 23. National holiday observed in Brunei Darussalam.

CARNIVAL. Feb 23–24. Period of festivities, feasts, foolishness and gaiety immediately before Lent begins on Ash Wednesday. Ordinarily Carnival includes only Fasching (the Feast of Fools), being the Monday and Tuesday immediately preceding Ash Wednesday. The period of Carnival may also be extended to include longer periods in some areas.

DENMARK: STREET URCHINS' CARNIVAL. Feb 23. Observed on Shrove Monday.

DOW-JONES TOPS 4,000: ANNIVERSARY. Feb 23, 1995. The Dow-Jones Index of 30 major industrial stocks topped the 4,000 mark for the first time.

DUBOIS, W.E.B.: BIRTH ANNIVERSARY. Feb 23, 1868. William Edward Burghardt Dubois, American educator and leader of movement for black equality. Born at Great Barrington, MA, Feb 23, 1868. Died at Accra, Ghana, Aug 27, 1963. "The cost of liberty," he wrote in 1909, "is less than the price of repression."

FASCHING. Feb 23–24. In Germany and Austria, Fasching, also called Fasnacht, Fasnet or Feast of Fools, is a Shrovetide festival with processions of masked figures, both beautiful and grotesque. Always the two days (Rose Monday and Shrove Tuesday) between Fasching Sunday and Ash Wednesday.

GROUND WAR AGAINST IRAQ BEGINS: ANNIVERSARY. Feb 23. On Feb 23, 1991, after an air campaign lasting slightly more than a month, Allied forces launched the ground offensive against Iraqi forces. The relentless air attacks had devastated troops and targets in both Iraq and Kuwait. A world that had watched and anticipated "The Mother of All Battles" was surprised at the swiftness and ease with which Allied forces were able to subdue Iraqi forces.

GUYANA: ANNIVERSARY OF REPUBLIC. Feb 23. National holiday. Guyana became a republic Feb 23, 1970.

HANDEL, GEORGE FREDERICK: BIRTH ANNIVERSARY. Feb 23. Born at Halle, Saxony, Germany, on Feb 23, 1685. Handel and Johann Sebastian Bach (see also: "Bach, Johann Sebastian: Birth Anniversary" [Mar 21]), born the same year, were perhaps the greatest masters of Baroque music. Handel's most frequently performed work is the oratorio *Messiah*, which was first heard in 1742. He died at London, England, on Apr 14, 1759.

ICELAND: BUN DAY. Feb 23. Children invade homes in the morning with colorful sticks and receive gifts of whipped cream buns (on the Monday before Shrove Tuesday).

JAPANESE ATTACK US MAINLAND: ANNIVERSARY. Feb 23, 1942. In the first attack on the US mainland, a Japanese submarine fired 25 shells at an oil refinery at the edge of Ellwood Oil Field 12 miles west of Santa Barbara, CA. One shell made a direct hit of the rigging causing minor damage. President Roosevelt was giving a fireside chat at the time of the attack.

MILITARY COUP IN THAILAND: ANNIVERSARY. Feb 23, 1991. Thailand Prime Minister Chatichai Choonhavan was arrested in a nonviolent coup by the Thai military. The leader of the coup, General Sunthorn Kongsompong, declared martial law and then sought ideas for a new government from students and political activists.

PEPYS, SAMUEL: BIRTH ANNIVERSARY. Feb 23, 1633. Diarist, born at London, England, Feb 23, 1633. Wrote Pepys in his diary (Mar 10, 1666): "The truth is, I do indulge myself a little the more in pleasure, knowing that this is the proper age of my life to do it; and, out of my observation that most men that do thrive in the world do forget to take pleasure during the time that they are getting their estate, but reserve that till they have got one, and then it is too late for them to enjoy it." Died at London, England, May 26, 1703.

SHIRER, WILLIAM L.: BIRTH ANNIVERSARY. Feb 23, 1904. American journalist and author William L. Shirer was born at Chicago, IL. As the European correspondent from 1927 to 1934 for the *Chicago Tribune* he became a friend of Mohandas K. Gandhi, the leader of India's independence movement. As a result of this he published *Gandhi: A Memoir* in 1980. His best-known book is *The Rise and Fall of the Third Reich* (1960), in which he used his experiences in Europe with the *New York Herald Tribune*, the Universal News Service and CBS Radio as a foundation. He died on Dec 28, 1993, at Boston, MA.

SHROVE MONDAY. Feb 23. The Monday before Ash Wednesday. In Germany and Austria, this is called Rose Monday.

TAYLOR, GEORGE: DEATH ANNIVERSARY. Feb 23, 1781. Signer of the Declaration of Independence. Born 1716 (exact place and date unknown).

WILLARD, EMMA HART: BIRTH ANNIVERSARY. Feb 23, 1787. Pioneer in higher education for women, born at Berlin, CT, Emma Willard supplemented her own education through self-study. Intent on improving educational opportunities for women, she sent her *Plan for Improving Female Education* to the governor of New York. In this plan she described her ideal for a girls' school, including the instruction usually offered the girls of her day (music, drawing, painting, penmanship, dancing), as well as adding religious and moral instruction, natural philosophy and domestic science. The New York legislature granted her a charter for the Waterford Academy for Young Ladies. The school later moved to Troy, NY, where it was first named the Troy Female Seminary and later the Emma Willard School. She assisted in the founding of a teachers' training school for girls at Athens, Greece, in 1832. She began the Willard Association for the Mutual Improvement of Female Teachers in 1837, and she authored sev-

February 1998

S	M	T	W	T	F	S
1	2	3	4	5	6	7
8	9	10	11	12	13	14
15	16	17	18	19	20	21
22	23	24	25	26	27	28

eral textbooks on geography, history and astronomy. Willard died at Troy, NY, Apr 15, 1870.

BIRTHDAYS TODAY

Roberto Martin Antonio (Bobby) Bonilla, 35, baseball player, born New York, NY, Feb 23, 1963.

Sylvia Chase, 60, newscaster, born Northfield, MN, Feb 23, 1938.

Peter Fonda, 59, actor (*Easy Rider, Race with the Devil*), born New York, NY, Feb 23, 1939.

Edward Lee ("Too Tall") Jones, 47, former football player and boxer, born Jackson, TN, Feb 23, 1951.

Howard Jones, 43, singer (gold album *Dream into Action*), born Southampton, England, Feb 23, 1955.

Rodney Slater, 43, US Secretary of Transportation in Clinton administration, born Tutwyler, MS, Feb 23, 1955.

Johnny Winter (John Dawson, III), 54, singer, musician (*Still Alive and Well, Second Winter*), born Beaumont, TX, Feb 23, 1944.

FEBRUARY 24 — TUESDAY

Day 55 — 310 Remaining

ESTONIA: INDEPENDENCE DAY. Feb 24. National holiday.

GREGORIAN CALENDAR DAY: ANNIVERSARY. Feb 24, 1582. Pope Gregory XIII, enlisting the expertise of distinguished astronomers and mathematicians, issued a bull correcting the Julian calendar that was then 10 days in error. The new calendar named for him, the Gregorian calendar, became effective on Oct 4, 1582, in most Catholic countries, in 1752 in Britain and the American colonies, in 1918 in Russia and in 1923 in Greece. It is the most widely used calendar in the world today. See also: "Calendar Adjustment Day Anniversary" (Sept 2) and "Gregorian Calendar Adjustment Anniversary" (Oct 4).

GRIMM, WILHELM CARL: BIRTH ANNIVERSARY. Feb 24. Mythologist and author, born at Hanau, Germany, Feb 24, 1786. Best remembered for *Grimm's Fairy Tales,* in collaboration with his brother, Jacob. Died at Berlin, Germany, Dec 16, 1859. See also: "Grimm, Jacob: Birth Anniversary" (Jan 4).

HADASSAH: ANNIVERSARY. Feb 24, 1912. Twelve members of the Daughters of Zion Study Circle met in New York City under the leadership of Henrietta Szold. A constitution was drafted to expand the study group into a national organization called Hadassah (Hebrew for "myrtle" and the biblical name of Queen Esther) to foster Jewish education in America and to create public health nursing and nurses training in Palestine. Hadassah is now the largest women's volunteer organization in the US with 1,500 chapters here and in Puerto Rico rooted in health care delivery, education and vocational training, children's villages and services and land reclamation in Israel. See also "Szold, Henrietta: Birth Anniversary" (Dec 21).

HENDOS FAT TUESDAY AT BRECKENRIDGE. Feb 24. Breckenridge Ski Area, Breckenridge, CO. A Mardi Gras celebration at 10,000 feet—beads, face painting, costumes, Cajun music and fresh seafood at the Maggie Base of Peak 9. Est attendance: 25,000. For info: John Hendryson, PO Box 7868, Breckenridge, CO 80424. Phone: (970) 453-2913. Fax: (970) 453-7238. Email: gobreck@brecknet.com.

HOMER, WINSLOW: BIRTH ANNIVERSARY. Feb 24. American artist. Born at Boston, MA, Feb 24, 1836. Noted for the realism of his work, from the Civil War reportage to the highly regarded rugged outdoor scenes of hunting and fishing. Died at his home at Prout's Neck, ME, Sept 29, 1910.

ICELAND: BURSTING DAY. Feb 24. Feasts with salted mutton and thick pea soup. (Shrove Tuesday.)

INTERNATIONAL PANCAKE DAY. Feb 24. Liberal, KS. The 1998 International Pancake Race will be the 49th annual competition between the women of Liberal, KS, and Olney, Bucks, England. The women, wearing the traditional dress, apron and scarf, run a 415-yard "S"-shaped course, carrying a pancake in a skillet. Other events include a breakfast parade, talent show, eating and flipping contests and the Miss Liberal scholarship pageant. Annually on Shrove Tuesday, the day before Ash Wednesday. Est attendance: 5,000. For info: Rosalee Phillips, Exec Secy, PO Box 665, Liberal, KS 67905. Phone: (316) 624-6427.

MAMOU MARDI GRAS CELEBRATION. Feb 24. Mamou, LA. Country-style Courir de Mardi Gras with a band of horsemen who leave town at 8:30 AM, travel the countryside gathering various items for their gumbo and performing for the residents and return to town at 4 PM. Live Cajun music is provided from 9 AM to 6 PM downtown at no charge. A dance with live Cajun music is held at the American Legion Hall from 6 PM to midnight with a cover charge. Sponsor: Mamou Mardi Gras Assn. Est attendance: 15,000. For info: Gerald J. Fontenot, Chamber of Commerce, PO Box 490, Mamou, LA 70554. Phone: (318) 468-3272 or (318) 468-2300.

MARDI GRAS. Feb 24. Celebrated especially in New Orleans, LA, Mobile, AL, and certain Mississippi and Florida cities. Last feast before Lent. Although Mardi Gras (Fat Tuesday, literally) is properly limited to Shrove Tuesday, it has come to be popularly applied to the preceding two weeks of celebration.

NIMITZ, CHESTER: BIRTH ANNIVERSARY. Feb 24. Commander of all Allied naval, land and air forces in the southwest Pacific during a portion of WWII, Admiral Chester William Nimitz was born Feb 24, 1885, at Fredericksburg, TX. During the final assault on Japan in April 1945, Nimitz resumed command of the entire naval operation in the Pacific which he had shared with MacArthur for some time. Nimitz was one of the signers of the Japanese document of surrender Sept 2, 1945, aboard the *USS Missouri* in Tokyo Bay. Nimitz died Feb 20, 1966, at Treasure Island, San Francisco Bay, CA. The USS *Nimitz* was named in his honor.

ONCE UPON A TIME DAY. Feb 24. Fairy tales have entertained and captivated children of different cultures for hundreds of years. Read a fairy tale to a child today. On the birthday of Wilhelm Grimm (born 1786) who with his brother Jacob Grimm (born Jan 4, 1785) published several collections of German fairy tales that carried these stories far beyond the borders of Germany. For more info, send $2 to cover the costs of postage and photocopying. For info: Adrienne Sioux Koopersmith, 1437 W Rosemont, #1W, Chicago, IL 60660-1319. Phone: (773) 743-5341. Fax: (773) 743-5395. Email: kooper@interaccess.com.

PACZKI DAY. Feb 24. Food lovers pick this day to enjoy these round, sugar-coated, fruit filled Polish pre-Lenten pastries, pronounced "poonch-kee," available in bakeries nationwide. Paczki Day coincides with Shrove Tuesday or Fat Tuesday, the day before Ash Wednesday. Sponsors: RBA (The Retailer's Bakery Association) and RBA National Paczki Promotion Board. For info: RBA-The Retailer's Bakery Assoc, 14239 Park Center Dr, Laurel, MD 20707. Phone: (301) 725-2149 or (800) 884-1500 for a free promotions Paczki kit. Email: rba@rbanet.com.

PACZKI DAY IN HAMTRAMCK. Feb 24. Hamtramck, MI. Shrove Tuesday, the day before Lenten fasting begins, is the occasion for baking and selling the delicious pastry known as *paczki,* which is described as a "distant cousin of the jelly doughnut." Especially observed among Polish citizens.

RECORD LOSS FOR GENERAL MOTORS: ANNIVERSARY. Feb 24, 1992. The greatest loss by a US company was suffered by the world's largest industrial company, General Motors Corporation. The $4.45 billion loss for 1991 was announced on Feb 24, 1992.

SHROVE TUESDAY. Feb 24. Always the day before Ash Wednesday. Sometimes called Pancake Tuesday.

SHROVETIDE PANCAKE RACE. Feb 24. Olney, Buckinghamshire, England. The pancake race at Olney has been run since 1445. Competitors must be women over 16 years of age, wearing traditional housewife's costume, including apron and head-covering. With a toss and flip of the pancake on the griddle that each must carry, the women dash from marketplace to the parish church, where the winner receives a kiss from the ringer of the Pancake Bell. Shriving service follows. Starting time for the race is usually 11:45 AM. Annually, on Shrove Tuesday.

SNOWMASS MARDI GRAS. Feb 24. Snowmass Village, CO. Parade, costume contest, uphill race and masquerade ball. Est attendance: 3,000. For info: Snowmass Resort Assn, PO Box 5566, Snowmass Village, CO 81615. Phone: (970) 923-2000.

SPAY DAY USA. Feb 24. An annual, nationwide event designed to end the tragedy of pet overpopulation by encouraging every humane American to take responsibility for having at least one cat or dog spayed or neutered, be it theirs, a neighbor's or a shelter animal. Veterinary clinics, humane societies/shelters, animal protection organizations, individuals and others are encouraged to participate. Annually, the last Tuesday in February. For info: Doris Day Animal League, Spay Day USA, 227 Massachusetts Ave NE, Ste 100, Washington, DC 20002. Phone: (202) 546-1761. Fax: (202) 546-2193. Email: ddal@aol.com. WWW: http://www.ddal.org

VOTE TO IMPEACH PRESIDENT ANDREW JOHNSON: ANNIVERSARY. Feb 24. In an escalating showdown over reconstruction policy following the American Civil War, the House of Representatives voted to impeach President Andrew Johnson on Feb 24, 1867. During the two years following the end of the war, the Republican-controlled Congress had sought to severely punish the South by undoing the policies of President Johnson. Congress passed the Reconstruction Act that divided the South into five military districts headed by general officers who were to take their orders from General Grant, the head of the army, instead of from President Johnson. In addition, Congress passed the Tenure of Office Act, which required Senate approval before Johnson could remove any official whose appointment was originally approved by the Senate. Johnson vetoed this act but the veto was overridden by Congress. To test the constitutionality of the act, Johnson dismissed Secretary of War Edwin Stanton, triggering the impeachment vote.

WAGNER, HONUS: BIRTH ANNIVERSARY. Feb 24. American baseball great born John Peter Wagner at Carnegie, PA, on Feb 24, 1874. Nicknamed the "Flying Dutchman," Wagner was among the first five players elected to the Baseball Hall of Fame in 1936. Died in the town of his birth on Dec 6, 1955.

BIRTHDAYS TODAY

Barry Bostwick, 53, actor (*The Rocky Horror Picture Show, Between Love and Hate*), born San Mateo, CA, Feb 24, 1945.

James Farentino, 60, actor ("Dynasty," "Cool Million," *The Story of a Woman*), born New York, NY, Feb 24, 1938.

Rupert Holmes, 51, musician, songwriter ("Escape"), born Tenafly, NJ, Feb 24, 1947.

February 1998

S	M	T	W	T	F	S
1	2	3	4	5	6	7
8	9	10	11	12	13	14
15	16	17	18	19	20	21
22	23	24	25	26	27	28

Mark Lane, 71, lawyer, activist, author (*Rush to Judgment, Eyewitness Chicago*), assassination buff, born New York, NY, Feb 24, 1927.

Michel Legrand, 66, composer, conductor, born Paris, France, Feb 24, 1932.

Joseph I. Lieberman, 56, US Senator (D, Connecticut), born Stamford, CT, Feb 24, 1942.

Donald Vincent (Don) Majkowski, 34, football player, born Buffalo, NY, Feb 24, 1964.

Zell Miller, 66, Governor of Georgia (D), born Young Harris, GA, Feb 24, 1932.

Eddie Clarence Murray, 42, baseball player, born Los Angeles, CA, Feb 24, 1956.

Edward James Olmos, 51, actor (*Stand and Deliver*; Emmy for "Miami Vice"), born East Los Angeles, CA, Feb 24, 1947.

Renata Scotto, 62, soprano, born Savona, Italy, Feb 24, 1936.

Helen Shaver, 47, actress (*Desert Hearts, The Color of Money*), born St. Thomas, Ontario, Canada, Feb 24, 1951.

John Vernon, 66, actor (*Point Blank, Dirty Harry, I'm Gonna Git You Sucka*), born Montreal, Canada, Feb 24, 1932.

Abe Vigoda, 77, actor ("Barney Miller," "Fish"), born New York, NY, Feb 24, 1921.

FEBRUARY 25 — WEDNESDAY

Day 56 — 309 Remaining

ASH WEDNESDAY. Feb 25. Marks the beginning of Lent. Forty weekdays and six Sundays (Saturday considered a weekday) remain until Easter Sunday. Named for use of ashes in ceremonial penance.

BACKUS, JIM: 85th BIRTH ANNIVERSARY. Feb 25, 1913. Born James Gilmore Backus on Feb 23, 1913, at Cleveland, OH. An actor whose career encompassed radio, television and film, Jim Backus is most remembered as the voice behind the near-sighted bumbler, Mr Magoo, and for his portrayal of Thurston Howell III on the popular 1960s TV show, "Gilligan's Island." Backus died July 3, 1989, at Santa Monica, CA.

BASCOM, "TEXAS ROSE": BIRTH ANNIVERSARY. Feb 25, 1922. A Cherokee-Choctaw Indian born in Covington County, MS, Rose Flynt married a rodeo cowboy and learned trick roping, becoming known as the greatest female trick roper in the world. She appeared on stage, in movies and on early TV. She toured with the USO during WW II, performing at every military base and military hospital in the US. After the war she toured the world, entertaining servicemen stationed overseas. In 1981 she was inducted into the National Cowgirl Hall of Fame (located in Hereford, TX). She died Sept 23, 1993.

BURGESS, ANTHONY: BIRTH ANNIVERSARY. Feb 25, 1917. Author (*A Clockwork Orange*). Born at Manchester, England. Died Nov 25, 1993, at London.

CAMEL MOTORCYCLE WEEK. Feb 25–Mar 8. Daytona International Speedway, Daytona Beach, FL. Twelve days of action-packed motorcycle racing including the world's greatest motorcycle race (Daytona 200 by Arai on Mar 8) and the Daytona Supercross by Honda (Mar 7). Sponsor: Camel. For info: Daytona Intl Speedway, PO Box 2801, Daytona Beach, FL 32120-2801. Phone: (904) 947-6782 or for tickets (904) 253-RACE (7223). Fax: (904) 947-6791. WWW: http://www/daytonausa.com

CARUSO, ENRICO: 125th BIRTH ANNIVERSARY. Feb 25, 1873. Operatic tenor of legendary voice and fame, born at Naples, Italy, on Feb 25, 1873. Died there Aug 2, 1921.

CHAMORRO, VIOLETA: ELECTION ANNIVERSARY. Feb 25. On Feb 25, 1990, Violeta Barrios de Chamorro defeated communist leader Daniel Ortega in a free election bringing Marxist rule to an end in Nicaragua. Her election was the result of a broad-based coalition that sought an end to the communist policies and tensions between the US-backed Contras and Ortega's forces.

CLAY BECOMES HEAVYWEIGHT CHAMP: ANNIVERSARY. Feb 25, 1964. Twenty-two-year-old Cassius Clay (later Muhammed Ali) became world heavyweight boxing champion by defeating Sonny Liston. At the height of his athletic career Ali was well known for both his fighting ability and personal style. His most famous saying was, "I am the greatest!" In 1967 he was convicted of violating the Selective Service Act and was stripped of his title for refusing to be inducted into the armed services during the Vietnam War. Ali cited religious convictions as his reason for refusal. In 1971 the Supreme Court reversed the conviction. Ali is the only fighter to win the heavyweight fighting title three separate times. He defended that title nine times.

DAVIS, ADELLE: BIRTH ANNIVERSARY. Feb 25, 1905. American nutritionist and author, born at Lizton, IN. Her message "You are what you eat" found an eager readership for her books, including *Let's Cook It Right* (1947) and *Let's Eat Right to Keep Fit* (1954). Davis died of bone cancer at Palo Verdes Estates, CA, on May 31, 1974.

FENWICK, MILLICENT HAMMOND: BIRTH ANNIVERSARY. Feb 25. Former fashion model, author, editor, member NJ General Assembly and US congresswoman, Millicent Fenwick was born New York, NY, Feb 25, 1910. A champion of liberal causes, Fenwick pointed to her sponsorship of the resolution creating the commission to monitor the 1975 Helsinki accords on human rights as her proudest achievement. She fought for civil rights, peace in Vietnam, aid for the poor, reduction of military programs, gun control and restrictions on capital punishment. She was widely known because of her sense of humor and habit of smoking a pipe. Millicent Fenwick, who was the inspiration for Garry Trudeau's "Doonesbury" character Lacey Davenport, died at Bernardsville, NJ, on Sept 16, 1992.

FIRST NATIONAL BANK CHARTERED BY CONGRESS: ANNIVERSARY. Feb 25, 1791. The First Bank of the United States at Philadelphia, PA, was chartered on Feb 25, 1791. Proposed as a national bank by Alexander Hamilton, it lost its charter in 1811. The Second Bank of the United States received a charter in 1816 which expired in 1836. Since that time, the US has had no central bank. Central banking functions are carried out by the Federal Reserve System, established in 1913.

FREER, CHARLES LANG: BIRTH ANNIVERSARY. Feb 25, 1856. American art collector who built and endowed the Freer Gallery, which was presented to the Smithsonian Institution in 1906. Born at Kingston, NY, died at New York, NY, on Sept 25, 1919.

HEBRON MASSACRE: ANNIVERSARY. Feb 25, 1994. An American-born Jewish settler in Hebron, Israel, Baruch Goldstein, opened fire with an assault rifle in a crowded mosque, part of a complex sacred to both Jews and Muslims because it is believed to contain the tomb of Abraham and his wife Sarah. Of the more than 400 Muslims gathered for early morning prayers during the holy month of Ramadan, 29 were killed immediately and 150 were wounded. Others, including Goldstein, were crushed in the panic to flee or during subsequent rioting. The incident called into question the possibility of continuing the peace talks between Israel, the Palestinians, Jordan and Syria. In late 1993 Israel and the Palestinian Liberation Organization had signed an agreement designed to bring peace between the two groups. Palestinian and Israeli extremists both opposed the accord.

KUWAIT: NATIONAL DAY. Feb 25. National holiday.

LENT BEGINS. Feb 25–Apr 11. Most Christian churches observe period of fasting and penitence (40 weekdays and 6 Sundays—Saturday considered a weekday) beginning on Ash Wednesday and ending on the Saturday before Easter.

LIONEL HAMPTON JAZZ FESTIVAL. Feb 25–28. University of Idaho, Moscow, Idaho. Each year, college, high school, junior high school and elementary school vocal and instrumental jazz ensembles come from all over the US to compete in the festival and attend concerts and clinics given by the world's greatest jazz artists. Annually, Wednesday–Saturday the last full week of February. Est attendance: 35,000. For info: Dr. Lynn J. Skinner, Exec Dir, UI Lionel Hampton Jazz Fest, Lionel Hampton School of Music, Univ of Idaho, Moscow, ID 83844-4014. Phone: (208) 885-6765. Fax: (208) 885-6513. Email: beain@osprey.csrv.uidaho.edu.

RENOIR, PIERRE AUGUSTE: BIRTH ANNIVERSARY. Feb 25, 1841. Impressionist painter, born at Limoges, France, Renoir's paintings are known for their joy and sensuousness as well as the light techniques he employed in them. In his later years he was crippled by arthritis and would paint with the brush strapped to his hand. He died at Cagnes-sur-Mer, Provence, France, Dec 17, 1919.

SPACE MILESTONE: *SOYUZ 32* (USSR). Feb 25, 1979. Launched on Feb 25, 1979, from Baikonur space center in Soviet Central Asia. Cosmonauts Vladimir Lyakhov and Valery Ryumin aboard, docked at *Salyut 6* space station on Feb 26. Returned to Earth in *Soyuz 34* after record 175 days in space on Aug 19, 1979.

"YOUR SHOW OF SHOWS" TV PREMIERE: ANNIVERSARY. Feb 25, 1950. Sid Caesar and Imogene Coca starred in the NBC 90-minute variety program along with Carl Reiner and Howard Morris. The show included monologues, improvisations, parodies, pantomimes and sketches of varying length. Max Leibman produced the show. Some of its writers were: Mel Tolkin, Lucille Kallen, Mel Brooks, Larry Gelbart ("M*A*S*H"), Neil Simon and Woody Allen.

BIRTHDAYS TODAY

Tom Courtenay, 61, actor (*The Dresser, The Loneliness of the Long Distance Runner, Otley*), born Hull, England, Feb 25, 1937.

Larry Gelbart, 70, writer, producer ("M*A*S*H"), born Chicago, IL, Feb 25, 1928.

Karen Grassle, 54, actress (Caroline Ingalls on "Little House on the Prairie"), born Berkeley, CA, Feb 25, 1944.

Philip Habib, 78, diplomat, born Brooklyn, NY, Feb 25, 1920.

George Harrison, 55, musician and singer (one of The Beatles), born Liverpool, England, Feb 25, 1943.

Darrell Kurt Rambis, 40, basketball player, born Cupertino, CA, Feb 25, 1958.

Sally Jessy Raphael, 55, talk show host, born Easton, PA, Feb 25, 1943.

Bert Remsen, 73, actor (*McCabe and Mrs Miller, Nashville, Dick Tracy*), born Glen Cove, KY, Feb 25, 1925.

Faron Young, 66, singer ("Hello Walls"), born Shreveport, LA, Feb 25, 1932.

FEBRUARY 26 — THURSDAY

Day 57 — 308 Remaining

BELGIUM: CAT FESTIVAL. Feb 26. Ieper. Traditional cultural observance. Annually, on the second day of Lent.

BIG 10 MEN'S SWIMMING AND DIVING CHAMPIONSHIP. Feb 26–28. University of Minnesota, Minneapolis, MN. Est attendance: 2,000. For info: Dennis LaBissoniere, Big Ten Conference, 1500 W Higgins Rd, Park Ridge, IL 60068-6300. Phone: (847) 696-1010. Fax: (847) 696-1110. WWW: http://www.bigten.org.

BIG 12 MEN'S AND WOMEN'S SWIMMING CHAMPIONSHIPS. Feb 26–28. University of Texas, Austin, TX. Est attendance: 5,000. For info: Dru Hancock, Championships, Big 12 Conference, 2201 Stemmons Freeway, 28th Floor, Dallas, TX 75207. Phone: (214) 742-1212. Fax: (214) 742-2045.

CHARRO DAYS. Feb 26–Mar 1. Brownsville, TX. Two Nations–Twin Cultures, a true example of international harmony and cooperation between Brownsville, Texas, and Matamoros, Mexico. Starts the last Thursday in February. Colorful celebration of the charro horseman of Mexico, a man of great riding skills. Dances, parades and carnival. Est attendance: 150,000. For info: Charro Days, Inc, PO Box 3247, Brownsville, TX 78523-3247. Phone: (210) 542-4245. Fax: (210) 542-6771.

CODY, WILLIAM FREDERIC "BUFFALO BILL": BIRTH ANNIVERSARY. Feb 26. American frontiersman who claimed to have killed more than 4,000 buffaloes. Born at Scott County, IA, on Feb 26, 1846. Subject of many heroic Wild West yarns, Cody became successful as a showman and exhibitionist, taking his acts across the US and to Europe. Died on Jan 10, 1917, at Denver, CO.

COMMUNIST MANIFESTO PUBLISHED: 150th ANNIVERSARY. Feb 26, 1848. Written by Karl Marx and Friedrich Engels on the eve of the revolutions of 1848, the *Manifesto* provided ideas for socialist and communist movements.

DAUMIER, HONORE: BIRTH ANNIVERSARY. Feb 26, 1808. French painter and caricaturist famous for his satirical and comic lithographs. Once spent six months in prison for a caricature of Louis Philippe shown as Gargantua consuming the heavy taxes of the citizens. Born on Feb 26, 1808, at Marseilles, France. He died on Feb 11, 1879, at Volmondois, France.

FLORIDA STRAWBERRY FESTIVAL. Feb 26–Mar 8. Plant City, FL. Celebration of winter strawberry harvest. Est attendance: 825,000. For info: Patsy Brooks, Gen Mgr, Florida Strawberry Fest, PO Drawer 1869, Plant City, FL 33564-1869. Phone: (813) 752-9194 or (813) 754-1996. Fax: (813) 754-4297. WWW: http://www.plantcity.org

GLEASON, JACKIE: BIRTH ANNIVERSARY. Feb 26, 1916. American musician, comedian and actor, Herbert John "Jackie" Gleason was born at Brooklyn, NY. Best known for his role as Ralph Kramden in the long-running television series "The Honeymooners." Died at Fort Lauderdale, FL, June 24, 1987, at age 71.

GRAND CANYON NATIONAL PARK ESTABLISHED: ANNIVERSARY. Feb 26. By an act of Congress, Grand Canyon National Park was established Feb 26, 1919. An immense gorge cut through the high plateaus of northwest Arizona by the raging Colorado River and covering 1,218,375 acres, Grand Canyon National Park is considered one of the most spectacular natural phenomena in the world.

HUGO, VICTOR: BIRTH ANNIVERSARY. Feb 26, 1802. French author, born at Besançon, France. "An invasion of armies can be resisted," he wrote in 1852, "but not an idea whose time has come." His most well-known work was the novel *Les Misérables*. Died at Paris, May 22, 1885, age 83.

February 1998

S	M	T	W	T	F	S
1	2	3	4	5	6	7
8	9	10	11	12	13	14
15	16	17	18	19	20	21
22	23	24	25	26	27	28

ITALIAN FEAST AND CARNIVAL. Feb 26–Mar 1. Venice Airport, Venice, FL. Italian food festival, rides, games, and heritage booth. Est attendance: 25,000. For info: Carl Sellitti, Italian-American Club of Venice, 645 Michigan Dr S, Venice, FL 34293. Phone: (941) 493-6344.

JOHN AND MABLE RINGLING MUSEUM OF ART MEDIEVAL FAIR. Feb 26–Mar 1. Sarasota, FL. A benefit for the Ringling Museum of Art featuring a 14th-century European village filled with food, arts and crafts, entertainment, armored jousting and a human chess match. Annually, the first weekend in March and the prior Thursday and Friday. Est attendance: 56,000. For info: (Apr to Nov) Medieval Fair, 1244 S Canterbury Rd, Ste 306, Shakopee, MN 55379. Phone: (800) 966-8215 or (612) 445-7361. Fax: (612) 445-7380. (Dec to Mar) Medieval Fair, Ringling Museum of Art, 5401 Bay Shore Rd, Sarasota, FL 34243. Phone: (941) 351-8497.

MOON PHASE: NEW MOON. Feb 26. Moon enters New Moon phase at 12:26 PM, EST.

SOLAR ECLIPSE. Feb 26. Total eclipse of the sun. Central eclipse begins at 10:47 AM, EST, reaches greatest eclipse at 12:35 PM, EST, ends at 2:09 PM, EST. Visible in Pacific Ocean, extreme southwest and eastern parts of US, southeast Canada, Mexico, Central America, northern half of South America, West Indies, Atlantic Ocean, southern tip of Greenland, extreme western part of Iceland, Portugal, West Africa.

STRAUSS, LEVI: BIRTH ANNIVERSARY. Feb 26, 1829. Bavarian immigrant Levi Strauss created the world's first pair of jeans—Levi's 501 jeans—for California's gold miners in the 1800s. Born at Buttenheim, Bavaria, Germany, he died in 1902, at age 73.

VERCORS, JEAN: BIRTH ANNIVERSARY. Feb 26, 1902. Jean Vercors was the author of the first clandestine novel published during the Nazi occupation of France. Vercors, whose real name was Jean-Marcel de Bruller, was best known for his novel *Silence of the Sea*, which he published with Pierre de Lescure for their publishing house, Les Editions de Minuit, after the Nazis occupied France in 1941. Vercors was born at Paris, France, and died there June 10, 1991, at age 89.

WORLD TRADE CENTER BOMBING: 5th ANNIVERSARY. Feb 26, 1993. A 1,210-lb bomb packed in a van exploded in the underground parking garage of the World Trade Center in New York City, killing six people and injuring more than 1,000 (mostly from smoke inhalation). The powerful blast left a crater 200 feet wide and several stories deep. The cost for damage to the building and disruption of business for the 350 companies with offices in the Center exceeded more than $591 million. Fifteen people—the fundamentalist Moslem cleric Sheik Omar Abdul Rahman and fourteen of his followers—were indicted for the bombing. Rahman was given a life sentence and the others received prison terms of up to 240 years each.

YELTSIN FOES FREED: ANNIVERSARY. Feb 26, 1994. Former speaker of the Russian parliament Ruslan Khasbulatov and former vice president Alexander Rutskoi along with many of their followers walked out of prison, freed by general amnesty granted by the new Russian parliament. Their attempt in October 1993 to overthrow the government of Boris Yeltsin turned violent and ended with the military shelling the Russian parliament building, forcing their capitulation. The uncertain Russian political landscape was further clouded when the amnesty also ended the treason trials of the former hardliners who sought to overthrow Mikhail Gorbachev in August 1991.

☆ ☆ ☆

BIRTHDAYS TODAY

Mason Adams, 79, actor (Charlie Hume on "Lou Grant"; "Morningstar/Eveningstar"), born New York, NY, Feb 26, 1919.

Rolando Antonio Blackman, 39, basketball player, born Panama City, Panama, Feb 26, 1959.

Johnny Cash, 66, singer ("Guess Things Happen That Way," "Ring of Fire"), born Kingsland, AR, Feb 26, 1932.

Fats Domino (Antoine Domino), 70, singer, songwriter ("Ain't That a Shame," "I'm in Love Again," "Blueberry Hill," "Whole Lotta Loving"), born New Orleans, LA, Feb 26, 1928.

Marshall Faulk, 25, football player, born New Orleans, LA, Feb 26, 1973.

Betty Hutton (Elizabeth June Thornberg), 77, singer, actress (*Annie Get Your Gun*, "The Betty Hutton Show"), born Battle Creek, MI, Feb 26, 1921.

Tony Randall (Leonard Rosenberg), 78, actor (*Pillow Talk*, "The Odd Couple"), born Tulsa, OK, Feb 26, 1920.

FEBRUARY 27 — FRIDAY

Day 58 — 307 Remaining

ANDERSON, MARIAN: BIRTH ANNIVERSARY. Feb 27, 1897. Born at Philadelphia, Anderson's talent was evident at an early age. Her involvement with the Union Baptist Church choir led her to numerous venues, including a performance with the New York Philharmonic Orchestra. Her career stonewalled by the prejudice she encountered in the US, she moved to Europe where the magnificence of her voice and her versatility as a performer began to establish her as one of the world's finest contraltos. Preventing Anderson's performance at Washington's Constitution Hall in 1939 on the basis of her color, the Daughters of the American Revolution directly, though unintentionally, secured for her the publicity that would lay the foundation for her success in the States. Her performance was rescheduled, and on Apr 9 (Easter Sunday) 75,000 people showed up to hear her sing from the steps of the Lincoln Memorial and the performance was simultaneously broadcast by radio. In 1957 Anderson became the first African-American to perform with the New York Metropolitan Opera. The following year President Eisenhower named her a delegate to the United Nations. She performed at President Kennedy's inauguration and in 1963 received the Presidential Medal of Freedom. She retired the subsequent year. Anderson died on Apr 8, 1993, at Portland, OR.

BENNETT, JOAN: BIRTH ANNIVERSARY. Feb 27, 1910. American film and television actress was born at Palisades, NJ. Her film career was mostly during the 1930s and 1940s in such films as *Father of the Bride* (1950), after which she became a star of the television cult hit "Dark Shadows" (originally broadcast 1966–1971). Bennett died on Dec 7, 1990, at Scarsdale, NY.

BIG 10 MEN'S INDOOR TRACK AND FIELD CHAMPIONSHIP. Feb 27–28. Purdue University, W. Lafayette, IN. Est attendance: 1,500. For info: Dennis LaBissoniere, Big Ten Conference, 1500 W Higgins Rd, Park Ridge, IL 60068-6300. Phone: (847) 696-1010. Fax: (847) 696-1110. WWW: http://www.bigten.org

BIG 10 WOMEN'S BASKETBALL TOURNAMENT. Feb 27–Mar 2. Indianapolis, IN. Est attendance: 2,500. For info: Dennis LaBissoniere, Big 10 Conference, 1500 W Higgins Rd, Park Ridge, IL 60068-6300. Phone: (847) 696-1010. Fax: (847) 696-1110. WWW: http://www.bigten.org

BIG 10 WOMEN'S INDOOR TRACK AND FIELD CHAMPIONSHIP. Feb 27–28. Michigan State University, Lansing, MI. Est attendance: 1,500. For info: Dennis LaBissoniere, Big Ten Conference, 1500 W Higgins Rd, Park Ridge, IL 60068-6300. Phone: (847) 696-1010. Fax: (847) 696-1110. WWW: http://www.bigten.org

CARNAVAL MIAMI—1998. Feb 27–Mar 8. Little Havana, Miami, FL. Ten-day celebration includes 8K run (Feb 27), Carnaval Night (Feb 28), Carnaval in South Beach (Mar 1), Calle Ocho Cooking Contest (Mar 3), Carnaval Miami Golf Classic (Mar 5), Carnaval Miami Sports Festival and Carnaval Miami Internacional (Mar 7) and culminates with Calle Ocho: Open House (Mar 8). Endless entertainment in this 23-block party with musical stages, ethnic foods, dancing and plenty of events for the entire family. Billed as the largest block party in the world with over a million people in attendance. For info: Kiwanis Club of Little Havana, 1312 SW 27 Ave, 3rd Fl, Miami, FL 33145. Phone: (305) 644-8888. Fax: (305) 644-8693. WWW: http://www.carnavalmiami.org

DOMINICAN REPUBLIC: INDEPENDENCE DAY. Feb 27. National Day. Independence gained in 1844 at withdrawal of Haitians, who had controlled the area for the past 22 years.

FARRELL, JAMES THOMAS: BIRTH ANNIVERSARY. Feb 27. American author, novelist and short-story writer, best known for his Studs Lonigan trilogy. Born at Chicago, IL, Feb 27, 1904. Died at New York, NY, Aug 22, 1979.

HAMILTON, ALICE: BIRTH ANNIVERSARY. Feb 27, 1869. American pathologist Alice Hamilton was born at New York, NY. She contributed to the workmen's compensation laws by reporting on the dangers to workers of industrial toxic substances. She taught at Harvard Medical School from 1919 until 1935. Hamilton died on Sept 22, 1970, of a stroke at Hadlyme, CT.

KUWAIT LIBERATED AND 100-HOUR WAR ENDS: ANNIVERSARY. Feb 27, 1991. On Feb 27, 1991, Allied troops entered Kuwait City, Kuwait, four days after launching a ground offensive. President George Bush declared Kuwait to be liberated and ceased all offensive military operations. The end of military operations at midnight EST came 100 hours after the beginning of the land attack.

LONGFELLOW, HENRY WADSWORTH: BIRTH ANNIVERSARY. Feb 27, 1807. American poet and writer was born at Portland, ME. He is best remembered for his classic narrative poems, such as *The Song of Hiawatha, Paul Revere's Ride* and *The Wreck of the Hesperus*, he died at Cambridge, MA, Mar 24, 1882, at age 75.

LONGHORN WORLD CHAMPIONSHIP RODEO. Feb 27–Mar 1. UTC Arena, Chattanooga, TN. More than 200 of the best cowboys and cowgirls compete in six professional contests ranging from bronco riding to bull riding for top prize money and world championship points. Featuring colorful opening pageantry and Big, Bad BONUS Bulls. 16th annual. Est attendance: 15,000. For info: W. Bruce Lehrke, Pres, Longhorn World Championship Rodeo, Inc, PO Box 70159, Nashville, TN 37207. Phone: (615) 876-1016. Fax: (615) 876-4685. Email: lhrodeo@idt.net. WWW: http://www.longhornrodeo.com

LOST DUTCHMAN DAYS. Feb 27–Mar 1. Apache Junction, AZ. 3-Day rodeo competiton (senior pro rodeo), dance, carnival, parade, business vendors, arts and crafts booths in celebration of the legend of the Superstition Mountains and the Lost Dutchman Mine. Est attendance: 100,000. For info: Apache Junction Chamber of Commerce, PO Box 1747, Apache Junction, AZ 85217-1747. Phone: (800) 252-3141. Fax: (602) 982-2331.

NO BRAINER DAY. Feb 27. This is a day where you can slack off, play hookey or find the easy way out. If you are going to do anything at all, make it a no brainer, something you can do without any serious thought. A drop in heart attacks is found on days like this—just what the doctor ordered. You have the rest of the year for a hectic schedule. For more info, send $2 to cover the costs of photocopying and postage to: Adrienne Sioux Koopersmith, 1437 W Rosemont, 1W, Chicago, IL 60660-1319. Phone: (773) 743-5341. Fax: (773) 743-5395. Email: kooper@interaccess.com.

SAINT GABRIEL POSSENTI FEAST DAY. Feb 27. St. Gabriel of the Sorrowful Mother (Francis Possenti, 1838–1862). Italian patron saint of young seminarians.

SHANGHAI COMMUNIQUE: ANNIVERSARY. Feb 27, 1972. On this day, President Richard Nixon and Premier Chou En-Lai released a joint communique (the Shanghai Communique) after Nixon's weeklong visit to the People's Republic of China. The two nations agreed to work toward normalizing relations. Stopping short of establishing diplomatic relations, this was the first step in that direction. The two nations entered full diplomatic relations on Jan 1, 1979, during the Carter administration.

SNOWFEST. Feb 27–Mar 8. North Lake Tahoe and Truckee, CA. Snowfest is a fantastic vacation opportunity, showcasing America's largest concentration of skiing and outdoor recreation combined with the fun, sparkle and excitement of 10 full days of over 100 special and unique events. Annually, beginning the Friday before the first Sunday in March. Est attendance: 130,000. For info: Festivals at Tahoe, PO Box 7590, Tahoe City, CA 96145. Phone: (916) 583-7625.

TEXAS COWBOY POETRY GATHERING. Feb 27–Mar 1. Sul Ross State University, Alpine, TX. Cowboys from Texas and neighboring states gather for poetry readings and music. Includes Trappings of Texas Art and gear show. Est attendance: 3,000. For info: J.J. Tucker, Asst Coord of Campus Activities, Texas Cowboy Poetry Gathering Committee, Sul Ross University, Campus Activities C-190, Alpine, TX 79832. Phone: (915) 837-8191 or (915) 837-3237. Fax: (915) 837-8192.
Email: mmiller@sul-ross-1.sulross.edu.
WWW: http://www.cowboypoetry.org

TWENTY-SECOND AMENDMENT TO US CONSTITUTION (TWO-TERM LIMIT): RATIFICATION ANNIVERSARY. Feb 27. After the four successive presidential terms of Franklin Roosevelt, the 22nd Amendment, ratified on Feb 27, 1950, limited the tenure of presidential office to two terms.

BIRTHDAYS TODAY

Adam Baldwin, 36, actor (*My Bodyguard, Full Metal Jacket*), born Chicago, IL, Feb 27, 1962.

Michael Bolton, 45, singer ("How Am I Supposed to Live Without You"), born New Haven, CT, Feb 27, 1953.

Mary Frann, 55, actress (Joanna on "Newhart"), born St. Louis, MO, Feb 27, 1943.

Alan Guth, 51, physicist, born New Brunswick, NJ, Feb 27, 1947.

Howard Hesseman, 58, actor ("WKRP in Cincinnati," "Head of the Class"), born Salem, OR, Feb 27, 1940.

Charlayne Hunter-Gault, 56, broadcast journalist, born Due West, SC, Feb 27, 1942.

Ralph Nader, 64, consumer advocate, lawyer, born Winsted, CT, Feb 27, 1934.

Irwin Shaw, 85, writer (*Rich Man, Poor Man; The Young Lions*), born New York, NY, Feb 27, 1913.

Elizabeth Taylor, 66, actress (Oscar for *Who's Afraid of Virginia Woolf?; National Velvet, Cleopatra, Cat on a Hot Tin Roof*), AIDS activist, born London, England, Feb 27,1932.

Malcolm Wallop, 65, former US Senator (R, Wyoming), born New York, NY, Feb 27, 1933.

Joanne Woodward, 68, actress (Oscar for *The Three Faces of Eve; Mr and Mrs Bridge*), born Thomasville, GA, Feb 27, 1930.

James Ager Worthy, 37, former basketball player, born Gastonia, NC, Feb 27, 1961.

February 1998

S	M	T	W	T	F	S
1	2	3	4	5	6	7
8	9	10	11	12	13	14
15	16	17	18	19	20	21
22	23	24	25	26	27	28

FEBRUARY 28 — SATURDAY

Day 59 — 306 Remaining

BLACK HISTORY PARADE. Feb 28. Monroe, LA. Informative parade to celebrate Black History Month. Annually, the last Saturday in February. For info: Tourism Sales Mgr, Monroe–W Monroe CVB, PO Box 6054, Monroe, LA 71211. Phone: (800) 843-1872. Fax: (318) 324-1752. Email: mwmcvb@iamerica.net. WWW: http://www.bayou.com/visitors

BLONDIN, CHARLES: BIRTH ANNIVERSARY. Feb 28. Daring French acrobat and aerialist (whose real name was Jean Francois Gravelet). Born at St. Omer, France, Feb 28, 1824. Especially remembered for his conquest of Niagara Falls. See also: "Charles Blondin's Conquest of Niagara Falls: Anniversary" (June 30).

CANIFF, MILTON: BIRTH ANNIVERSARY. Feb 28, 1907. Creator of the comic strips "Terry and the Pirates®" and "Steve Canyon," Milton Caniff was born at Hillsboro, OH. His strips were noted for their fine draftsmanship and action/adventure story lines. Caniff died Apr 3, 1988, at New York City.

CLAM CHOWDER COOKOFF AND GREAT CHOWDER CHASE. Feb 28–Mar 1. Santa Cruz Beach Boardwalk, Santa Cruz, CA. Who makes the world's greatest clam chowder? Up to 80 teams compete to find out. Prizes for best booth encourage wacky costumes, elaborate props! Separate categories for restaurants, media and individuals, Boston and Manhattan style chowder. Free admission. Est attendance: 15,000. For info: Jan Bollwinkel-Smith, Publicity Coord, Santa Cruz Beach Boardwalk, 400 Beach St, Santa Cruz, CA 95060-5491. Phone: (408) 423-5590. Email: publicity@scseaside.com.
WWW: http://www.beachboardwalk.com

De MONTAIGNE, MICHEL: BIRTH ANNIVERSARY. Feb 28, 1533. French essayist and philosopher. "And if you have lived a day," he wrote in Book I of his *Essays*, "you have seen everything. One day is equal to all days. There is no other light, no other night. This sun, this moon, these stars, the way they are arranged, all is the very same your ancestors enjoyed and that will entertain your grandchildren. . . ." Died Sept 13, 1592.

FLORAL DESIGN DAY. Feb 28. A day to commemorate floral designing as an art form. Annually, on Feb 28. For info: Dr. Stephen Rittner, Rittners School of Floral Design, 345 Marlborough St, Boston, MA 02115. Phone: (617) 267-3824.
Email: stevrt@tiac.net.
WWW: http://www.tiac.net/users/stevrt/index.html.

HECHT, BEN: BIRTH ANNIVERSARY. Feb 28, 1894. In the course of his career Ben Hecht wrote in many genres. His newspaper column, "1001 Afternoons in Chicago," popularized human interest sketches. His play *The Front Page*, written with Charles MacArthur, was a hit on Broadway (1928) and in film (1931). He was a successful reporter and his first novel *Eric Dorn*, resulted partly from his time reporting from Berlin after World War I. Hecht wrote or co-wrote a number of successful movie scripts, including *Notorious, Scoundrel* and *Wuthering Heights*. Born at New York City, he died there Apr 18, 1964.

LEE, ANN: BIRTH ANNIVERSARY. Feb 28, 1736. The founder of Shakerism in America was born in Manchester, England. Joined the Shaking Quakers, or Shakers, in 1758, and came to US in 1774, forming a Shaker group near Albany. Became known for the gift of tongues and ability to work miracles and cure diseases. Pacifists, the Shakers refused to bear arms in the American Revolution. Branded a British sympathizer, Lee was charged with high treason and jailed for 4½ months. Known as "Ann the Word" or "Mother Ann." Died at Watervliet, NY, Sept 8, 1784, at age 48.

LYON, MARY: BIRTH ANNIVERSARY. Feb 28, 1797. Mary Lyon, born near Buckland, MA, became a pioneer in the field of higher education for women. Teaching since age 17, she founded Mount Holyoke Seminary (forerunner of Mount Holyoke College) in South Hadley, MA, in 1837 at a time when American women were educated primarily by ministers in classes held in their homes. Mount Holyoke was one of the first permanent women's colleges. She died Mar 5, 1849, at South Hadley.

"M*A*S*H": THE FINAL EPISODE: 15th ANNIVERSARY. Feb 28, 1983. Concluding a run of 255 episodes, this 2½-hour finale was the most-watched television show at that time—77% of the viewing public was tuned in. Cast members included Alan Alda as Capt Hawkeye Pierce, Wayne Rogers as Capt Trapper John McIntyre, McLean Stevenson as Lt Col Henry Blake, Harry Morgan as Col Sherman Potter, Loretta Swit as Maj Margaret "Hot Lips" Houlihan, Mike Farrell as Capt B.J. Hunnicut, Larry Linville as Maj Frank Burns, Gary Burghoff as Pvt Walter "Radar" O'Reilly, William Christopher as Father Francis Mulcahy, Jamie Farr as Cpl Maxwell Klinger and David Ogden Stiers as Maj Charles Emerson Winchester III. The show premiered on Sept 17, 1972.

NATO PLANES DOWN SERB JETS: ANNIVERSARY. Feb 28, 1994. In the first military action by the North Atlantic Treaty Organization (NATO) in the two-year-old Bosnian civil war and the first combat action by NATO in its 45-year history, UN-designated American fighter planes shot down four of six Bosnian Serb jets operating in a no-fly zone.

PALME, OLOF: ASSASSINATION ANNIVERSARY. Feb 28, 1986. The popular prime minister of Sweden was shot to death as he left a movie theatre in Stockholm with his wife. A courageous and dominant figure in Swedish politics, Palme, an aristocrat turned socialist, had earned international respect. On the day of his death he had signed (with five other world leaders) an appeal to the leaders of the United States and the Soviet Union to forgo nuclear testing until the next summit meeting. Born on Jan 30, 1927, Palme was the third European head of government to be assassinated since the beginning of World War II (the others: Prime Minister Armand Calinescu of Rumania in 1939 and Prime Minister Luis Carrero Blanco of Spain in 1973).

PIER 39'S TULIPMANIA. Feb 28–Mar 8. Pier 39, San Francisco, CA. More than 35,000 multicolored tulips in 70 different varieties of blooming colors will be on display in the 20th annual Tulipmania, a free spring tradition in San Francisco. Free guided landscaping tours are presented daily at 10 AM. Est attendance: 10,000. For info: Alicia Vargas, PR Dir, Pier 39, PO Box 193730, San Francisco, CA 94119. Phone: (415) 705-5500. Fax: (415) 981-8808.

SAINT OSWALD OF WORCESTER FEAST DAY. Feb 28. Bishop of Worcester, England, from 961, and Archbishop of York from 972. Oswald died on Feb 29, 992, but Feb 28 is generally celebrated as his Feast Day.

"SMOKELESS" CIGARETTE WITHDRAWN: ANNIVERSARY. Feb 28, 1989. The R.J. Reynolds Tobacco Company stopped marketing Premier, the "smokeless" cigarette, due to poor sales.

TENNIEL, JOHN: BIRTH ANNIVERSARY. Feb 28. Illustrator and cartoonist, born at London, England, Feb 28, 1820. Best remembered for his illustrations for Lewis Carroll's *Alice's Adventures in Wonderland.* Died at London, Feb 25, 1914.

USS *PRINCETON* EXPLOSION: ANNIVERSARY. Feb 28. On Feb 28, 1844, the newly built "war steamer," USS *Princeton*, cruising on the Potomac River with top government officials as its passengers, fired one of its guns (known, ironically, as the "Peacemaker") to demonstrate the latest in naval armament. The gun exploded, killing Abel P. Upshur, Secretary of State; Thomas W. Gilmer, Secretary of the Navy; David Gardiner, of Gardiners Island, NY; and several others. Many were injured. The president of the US, John Tyler, was on board and narrowly escaped death.

BIRTHDAYS TODAY

Joss Ackland, 70, actor (*The House That Dripped Blood, The Hunt for Red October, The Sicilian*), born London, England, Feb 29, 1928.

Svetlana Allilueva, 72, daughter of Joseph Stalin, author (*The Faraway Music*), born Moscow, USSR, Feb 28, 1926.

Mario Gabrielle Andretti, 58, auto racer, born Montona, Trieste, Italy, Feb 28, 1940.

Adrian Delano Dantley, 42, former basketball player, born Washington, DC, Feb 28, 1956.

Charles Durning, 75, actor (*Dog Day Afternoon*, "Evening Shade"), born Highland Falls, NY, Feb 28, 1923.

Arthur Franz, 78, actor (*Sands of Iwo Jima, Caine Mutiny, That Championship Season*), born Perth Amboy, NJ, Feb 29, 1920.

Frank Gehry, 69, architect, born Toronto, Ontario, Canada, Feb 28, 1929.

Robert Sean Leonard, 29, actor (*The Manhattan Project, Dead Poets Society*), born Westwood, NJ, Feb 28, 1969.

Jack Lousma, 62, astronaut, born Grand Rapids, MI, Feb 29, 1936.

Michèle Morgan (Simone Roussel), 78, actress (*The Fallen Idol*), born Neuilly, France, Feb 29, 1920.

Bernadette Peters, 54, singer/actress (*George M, Dames at Sea*), born New York, NY, Feb 28, 1944.

Alex Rocco, 62, actor ("The Famous Teddy Z," *The Godfather, The Stunt Man*), born Cambridge, MA, Feb 29, 1936.

Antonio Sabato, Jr, 26, actor ("Earth 2"), born Rome, Italy, Feb 29, 1972.

Charles Aaron ("Bubba") Smith, 53, actor, former football player, born Beaumont, TX, Feb 28, 1945.

Tommy Tune, 59, actor, singer, dancer (Tony for *My One and Only; Will Rogers Follies*, "Dean Martin Presents . . ."), musical theater director, born Wichita Falls, TX, Feb 28, 1939.

John Turturro, 41, actor (*Desperately Seeking Susan, Quiz Show*), born Brooklyn, NY, Feb 28, 1957.

March.

MARCH 1 — SUNDAY

Day 60 — 305 Remaining

★**AMERICAN RED CROSS MONTH.** Mar 1–31. Presidential Proclamation for Red Cross Month issued each year for March since 1943. Issued as American Red Cross Month since 1987.

ARTICLES OF CONFEDERATION RATIFIED: ANNIVERSARY. Mar 1, 1781. This compact made among the original 13 states had been adopted by the Congress Nov 15, 1777, and submitted to the states for ratification on Nov 17, 1777. Maryland was the last state to approve, on Feb 27, 1781, but Congress named Mar 1, 1781, as the day of formal ratification. The Articles of Confederation remained the supreme law of the nation until Mar 4, 1789.

"BELIEVE IT OR NOT" TV PREMIERE: ANNIVERSARY. Mar 1, 1949. The series was originally a radio show based on Robert L. Ripley's comic strips describing superhuman feats. Both the radio program and the NBC TV show were hosted by Robert Ripley until his death in 1949. Robert St. John became Ripley's successor. ABC recreated the show in 1982 with Jack Palance as host.

THE BETTER HALF. Mar 1–June 7. Clinton, MD. An exhibit related to the changing roles of 19th-century women. Est attendance: 2,000. For info: Laurie Verge, Dir, Surratt House & Tavern, PO Box 427, Clinton, MD 20735. Voice and TDD phone: (301) 868-1121. Fax: (301) 868-8177.
WWW: http://www.engr.umd.edu/~clwspoon/surratt.html

BIBLE WOMEN AWARENESS MONTH. Mar 1–31. To help raise awareness of the women in the Bible and the stories of their lives which are role models for women today and the heritage of all who live in our Judeo-Christian society. Bible Women Cameo Presentations (dramatic acting of their stories presented in first person monologues); Scripture and book readings; "Crash Courses" and "Get-Acquainted With Bible Women" workshops; newspaper/magazine articles, radio/TV guest interviews and Bible Women Surprise Parties. For info send SASE: Christian Women's Ministries, 222 SW Harrison, Garden Office 9, Portland, OR 97201. Email: christine@christianwomen.com.

BLACK HILLS PASSION PLAY—FLORIDA. Mar 1–Apr 12. (Note: Not performed every day—call in advance.) Lake Wales Amphitheater, Lake Wales, FL. Spectacular outdoor drama depicting the last seven days in the life of Christ. Cast of more than 200, plus live animals. Est attendance: 40,000. For info: Lake Wales Amphitheater, PO Box 71, Lake Wales, FL 33859. Phone: (800) 622-8383 or (941) 676-1495. Fax: (941) 638-2037.

March 1998

S	M	T	W	T	F	S
1	2	3	4	5	6	7
8	9	10	11	12	13	14
15	16	17	18	19	20	21
22	23	24	25	26	27	28
29	30	31				

BOSNIA AND HERZEGOVINA: NATIONAL HOLIDAY. Mar 1.

CATARACT AWARENESS MONTH. Mar 1–31. Activities during this month are designed to educate people about one of the most common types of vision loss and the treatment options now available. Materials that can easily be posted or distributed to the community will be provided. For info: Marketing Dept, Prevent Blindness America, 500 E Remington Rd, Schaumburg, IL 60173. Phone: (800) 331-2020 or (847) 843-2020.

COMMEMORATION OF THE ARRIVAL OF MARTIN PINZON: ANNIVERSARY. Mar 1, 1493. Bayona. Martin Alonzo Pinzon (1440–1493), Spanish shipbuilder and navigator (and co-owner of the *Niña* and the *Pinta*), accompanied Christopher Columbus on his first voyage, as commander of the *Pinta*. Storms separated the ships on their return voyage, and the *Pinta* first touched land at Bayona, Spain, where Pinzon gave Europe its first news of the discovery of the New World (before Columbus's landing and announcement at Palos). Pinzon's brother, Vicente Yanez Pinzon, was commander of the third caravel of the expedition, the *Niña*. Another brother, Francisco, was pilot of the *Pinta*.

CRANE WATCH '98. Mar 1–Apr 15. Kearney, NE. "World's Largest Concentration of Cranes." Each spring some 500,000 sandhill cranes (80% of the world's population of this species) gather on the Platte River "staging area" during their northward migration. For info: Kearney Visitors Bureau, PO Box 607, Kearney, NE 68847. Phone: (800) 652-9435.

ELLISON, RALPH WALDO: BIRTH ANNIVERSARY. Mar 1, 1914. American writer and educator born at Oklahoma City, OK. Author of the acclaimed novel *Invisible Man* (1952), Ellison spent seven years writing the book, the story of a young black man's struggle for his own identity in the face of rejection from both whites and blacks. Quickly recognized as a classic of 20th-century literature, it won for Ellison the National Book Award in 1953. While he wrote only one published novel, Ellison published collections of his essays, reviews and stories in *Shadow and Act* (1964) and *Going to the Territory* (1986). He died Apr 16, 1994, at New York City.

ENGLAND: CORNWALL '98– WORLD WATER-SPORTS FESTIVAL. Mar 1–Sept 30 (tentative). Many venues throughout Cornwall. Water-related sports and events including the Cutty Sark Tall Ships race and the International Sailing Championships. For info: Cornwall '98, Trevint House, Stangways Terr, Truro, Cornwall, England TR1 2PA. Phone: (44) (872) 223-527. Fax: (44) (872) 424-470.

ETHICS AWARENESS MONTH. Mar 1–31. An insurance industry educational event to increase practitioners' awareness of ethical issues within the sector. Sponsors: The American College, American Institute for CPCU, American Society of CLU & ChFC and the CPCU Society. For info: Susan Farmer, Mgr PR, Amer Soc of CLU & ChFC, 270 S Bryn Mawr Ave, Bryn Mawr, PA 19010-2195. Phone: (800) 927-2427 or (610) 526-2500. Fax: (610) 527-1499.

GAINES, WILLIAM M.: BIRTH ANNIVERSARY. Mar 1, 1922. The magazine *Mad*, especially popular in the 1960s and 1970s, was founded and published by William Gaines. Alfred E. Neuman, the loony, freckle-faced mascot of the publication, became a pop-culture hero. The magazine, known for its parodies of movies, comic strips and celebrities as well as its satire of politics and social mores, greatly influenced dozens of humorists. Gaines was born at The Bronx, NY. He died June 3, 1992, at New York City.

HELP SOMEONE SEE WEEK OBSERVANCE. Mar 1–7. Rockford, OH. Collect used eyeglasses, offer new glass cases for nursing home residents, arrange visits from guide dogs, have programs or videos about sight. For info: Dorothy Trisel, Activities Dir, Shane Hill Nursing Home, 10731 State Rte 118, Rockford, OH 45882-8947.

HEMOPHILIA MONTH. Mar 3–31. For info: National Hemophilia Foundation, 110 Greene St, Ste 303, New York, NY 10012. Phone: (800) 42-HANDI.

HUMORISTS ARE ARTISTS MONTH (HAAM). Mar 1–31. To recognize the important contributions made by various types of humorists to the high art of living. For info: Lone Star Publications of Humor, 8452 Fredericksburg Rd, Ste 103, San Antonio, TX 78229. Email: lspubs@aol.com. WWW: http://members.aol.com/lspubs/lsindex.html

★**IRISH-AMERICAN HERITAGE MONTH.** Mar 1–31. Presidential Proclamation called for by House Joint Resolution 401 (PL 103-379), before Congress stopped legislating for presidential proclamations of special observances.

JAPAN: OMIZUTORI (WATER-DRAWING FESTIVAL). Mar 1–14. Todaiji, Nara. At midnight, a solemn rite is performed in the flickering light of pine torches. People rush for sparks from the torches, which are believed to have magic power against evil. Most spectacular on the night of Mar 12. The ceremony of drawing water is observed at 2 AM on Mar 13, to the accompaniment of ancient Japanese music.

KOKOSCHKA, OSKAR: BIRTH ANNIVERSARY. Mar 1, 1886. Born at Pochlarn, Austria. Avant-garde artist, playwright, teacher and humanitarian, provoked violent reaction to his work. After viewing a 1911 exhibition of Kokoschka's work, the Archduke Franz Ferdinand is reported to have declared, "This man deserves to have every bone in his body broken." Kokoschka's work was featured in a 1937 Munich exhibit of "Degenerate Art." Became a naturalized British citizen in 1947. Died at Montreux, Switzerland, on Feb 22, 1980.

KOREA: SAMILJOL or INDEPENDENCE DAY. Mar 1. Koreans observe the anniversary of the Mar 1, 1919, independence movement against Japanese colonial rule.

LINDBERGH KIDNAPPING: ANNIVERSARY. Mar 1. 20-month-old Charles A. Lindbergh, Jr, the son of Charles A. and Anne Morrow Lindbergh, was kidnapped from their home at Hopewell, NJ, on Mar 1, 1932. Even though the Lindberghs paid a $50,000 ransom, their child's body was found in a wooded area less than five miles from the family home on May 12. As a result of the kidnapping and murder of the Lindbergh baby, the Crime Control Act was passed on May 18, 1934. It authorized the death penalty for kidnappers who take their victims across state lines.

MENTAL RETARDATION AWARENESS MONTH. Mar 1–31. To educate the public about the needs of this nation's more than 7 million citizens with mental retardation and about ways to prevent retardation. The Arc of the United States is a national organization on mental retardation, formerly the Association for Retarded Citizens. For info: Liz Moore, The Arc, 500 E Border St, Ste 300, Arlington, TX 76010. Phone: (817) 261-6003. Fax: (817) 277-3491. Email: lizmoore@metronet.com. WWW: http://thearc.org/welcome.html

MILLER, GLENN: BIRTH ANNIVERSARY. Mar 1. American band leader and composer (Alton) Glenn Miller. Born at Clarinda, IA, on Mar 1, 1904. Miller enjoyed great popularity, especially preceding and during the World War II era. His hit recordings included "Moonlight Serenade," "String of Pearls," "Jersey Bounce" and "Sleepy Lagoon." Major Miller, leader of the US Army Air Force band, disappeared Dec 15, 1944, over the English Channel, on a flight to Paris where he was scheduled to give a show. There were many explanations of his disappearance, but 41 years later, in December 1985, new accounts reported that crew members of an aborted RAF bombing said they believed they had seen Miller's plane, a Norseman D-64, go down, the victim of bombs being jettisoned by the RAF over the English Channel.

MUSIC IN OUR SCHOOLS MONTH. Mar 1–31. To draw public awareness to the importance of music education as part of a balanced curriculum. The 1998 theme is "Music Power." Additional information and awareness items are available from MENC. Approx participation: 8,000,000. For info: Judy T. Humphrey, Mgr Special Programs, Music Educators Natl Conference (MENC), 1806 Robert Fulton Dr, Reston, VA 20191. Phone: (800) 336-3768 or (703) 860-4000. Fax: (703) 860-1531.

NATIONAL CHRONIC FATIGUE SYNDROME AWARENESS MONTH. Mar 1–31. To educate patients, their families, the public and the medical profession about the nature and impact of CFS, "the Thief of Vitality," and related disorders, as well as to encourage and provide research funding. Annually, the month of March. For info: Natl Chronic Fatigue Synd and Fibromyalgia Assn, PO Box 18426, Kansas City, MO 64133. Phone: (816) 313-2001 or (816) 313-2000 (24-hour info line). Fax: (816) 524-6782.

NATIONAL CRAFT MONTH. Mar 1–31. Promoting the fun and creativity of hobbies and crafts. For info: Hobby Industry Association, National Craft Month, Richartz and Fliss, 259 Baldwin Rd, Parsippany, NJ 07054. Phone: (201) 299-0070. Fax: (201) 299-1060. WWW: http://www.i-craft.com. Info also available from: Julie Fox, Assn of Crafts and Creative Industries, 1100-H Brandywine Blvd, PO Box 2188, Zanesville, OH 43702-2188. Phone: (614) 452-4541.

NATIONAL DESIGN DRAFTING WEEK. Mar 1–7. To bring attention to the services provided by those in the profession of design and drafting. For info: Rachel Howard, Exec Dir, American Design Drafting Assn, PO Box 799, Rockville, MD 20848-0799. Phone: (301) 460-6875. Fax: (301) 460-8591. Email: national@adda.org. WWW: http://adda.org

NATIONAL EYE DONOR MONTH. Mar 1–31. For info: Eye Bank Assn of America, 1001 Connecticut Ave NW, Ste 601, Washington, DC 20036. Phone: (202) 775-4999.

NATIONAL FROZEN FOOD MONTH. Mar 1–31. Promotes a national awareness of the economical and nutritional benefits of frozen foods. Annually, the month of March. For info: Lori B. Pohlman, VP Communications & New Media, Natl Frozen Food Assn, 4755 Linglestown Rd, Ste 300, Harrisburg, PA 17112. Phone: (717) 657-8601. Fax: (717) 657-9862. Email: nffm@nffa.org. WWW: http://www.nffa.org

NATIONAL KIDNEY MONTH. Mar 1–31. For info: Natl Kidney Foundation, 30 E 33rd St, New York, NY 10016. Phone: (800) 622-9010 or (212) 889-2210.

NATIONAL NUTRITION MONTH. Mar 1–31. To educate consumers about the importance of good nutrition by providing the latest practical information on how simple it can be to eat healthfully. The "Eat Right America"® campaign. For info: The American Dietetic Assn, Natl Ctr for Nutrition and Dietetics, 216 W Jackson Blvd, Chicago, IL 60606-6995. Phone: (312) 899-0040 ext 4759. Fax: (312) 899-1739.

NATIONAL ON-HOLD MONTH. Mar 1–31. A month to recognize everyone who has been placed "on hold" after calling a place of business, and to honor those businesses who make this hold time more enjoyable by supplying informative messages and music for their callers waiting on hold. For info: Audiomax, 540 Township Line Rd, Blue Bell, PA 19422. Phone: (800) 284-4653 or (215) 643-0700. Fax: (215) 641-1287.

NATIONAL PIG DAY. Mar 1. To accord to the pig its rightful, though generally unrecognized, place as one of man's most intelligent and useful domesticated animals. Annually, Mar 1. For further information send SASE to: Ellen Stanley, 7006 Miami, Lubbock, TX 79413.

NATIONAL PROFESSIONAL PET SITTERS WEEK. Mar 1–7. A week to show pet sitters who work 365 days a year for customers. Est attendance: 2,500. For info: Pet Sitters International (PSI), 418 E King St, King, NC 27021. Phone: (910) 983-9222. Fax: (910) 983-3755. Email: petsitin@ols.net. WWW: http://www.petsit.com

NATIONAL SAUCE MONTH. Mar 1–31. Held each year in March to celebrate the diversity of sauces used in cooking. Celebrated with cooking contests, samplings and taste-offs across the country. Sponsor: Martini and Rossi Vermouth. For info: Laura Baddish, The Alden Group, 52 Vanderbilt Ave, New York, NY 10017. Phone: (212) 867-6400.

NATIONAL TALK WITH YOUR TEEN ABOUT SEX MONTH. Mar 1–31. The importance of frank talk with teenagers about sex is emphasized. Parents are encouraged to provide their teenage children with current, accurate information and open lines for communication, as well as support their self-esteem, reduce misinformation and guide teenagers toward making responsible decisions regarding sex. Annually, the month of March. For info send SASE to: Teresa Langston, Dir, Parenting Without Pressure (PWOP), 1330 Boyer St, Longwood, FL 32750-6311. Phone: (407) 767-2524.

NATIONAL UMBRELLA MONTH. Mar 1–31. In honor of one of the most versatile and underrated inventions of the human race, this month is dedicated to the purchase, use of and conversation about umbrellas. Annually, the month of March. For info: Thomas Edward Knibb, 8819 Adventure Ave, Walkersville, MD 21793-7828. Phone: (301) 898-3009.

NATIONAL WOMEN'S HISTORY MONTH. Mar 1–31. A time for reexamining and celebrating the wide range of women's contributions and achievements that are too often overlooked in the telling of US history. Information catalog available. For info: Natl Women's History Project, 7738 Bell Rd, Dept P, Windsor, CA 95492. Phone: (707) 838-6000. Fax: (707) 838-0478. Email: nwhp@aol.com. WWW: http://www.nwhp.org

NATIONAL WRITE A LETTER OF APPRECIATION WEEK. Mar 1–7. Send a letter expressing your gratitude to others, acknowledging the goodness that we find all around us. For info: Larry McManus, 127 E Main St, Barrington, IL 60010. Phone: (847) 842-0808. Fax: (847) 842-8719.
Email: mcmanus@maxx.mc.net.
WWW: http://www.appreciation.org

NEBRASKA: ADMISSION DAY: ANNIVERSARY. Mar 1, 1867. Became 37th state on this day in 1867.

OHIO: ADMISSION DAY: 195th ANNIVERSARY. Mar 1, 1803. Became 17th state on this day in 1803.

PEACE CORPS FOUNDED: ANNIVERSARY. Mar 1, 1961. Official establishment of the Peace Corps by President John F. Kennedy's signing of executive order. The Peace Corps has sent more than 148,000 volunteers to 132 developing countries to help their people help themselves. The volunteers assist in projects such as health, education, water sanitation, agriculture, nutrition and forestry. For info: Peace Corps, 1990 K St, Rm 8500, Washington, DC 20526. Phone: (800) 424-8580 or (202) 606-3010. Fax: (202) 606-3110.

POISON PREVENTION AWARENESS MONTH. Mar 1–31. To educate parents, grandparents, schoolchildren and PTAs about accidental poisoning and how to prevent it. PPSI is a nonprofit organization. There is a $15 charge for kit materials. Annually, the month of March. For info: Frederick Mayer, Pres PPSI, Pharmacists Planning Service, Inc, 200 Gate Five Rd, PO Box 1336, Sausalito, CA 94966. Phone: (800) 523-2222. Fax: (415) 332-1832.

RED CROSS MONTH. Mar 1–31. To make the public aware of American Red Cross service in the community. There are nearly 1,600 Red Cross chapters nationwide; each local chapter plans its own activities. For info on activities in your area, contact your local Red Cross chapter. For info: American Red Cross Natl HQ, Public Inquiry Center, 8111 Gatehouse Rd, Falls Church, VA 22042. Phone: (703) 206-7090. Fax: (703) 206-7507. Email: info@usa.redcross.org. WWW: http://www.redcross.org

March 1998

S	M	T	W	T	F	S
1	2	3	4	5	6	7
8	9	10	11	12	13	14
15	16	17	18	19	20	21
22	23	24	25	26	27	28
29	30	31				

RETURN THE BORROWED BOOKS WEEK. Mar 1–7. To remind you to make room for those precious old volumes that will be returned to you, by cleaning out all that worthless trash that your friends are waiting for. Annually, the first seven days of March. For info: Inter-Global Society for Prevention of Cruelty to Cartoonists, Al Kaelin, Secy, 3119 Chadwick Dr, Los Angeles, CA 90032. Phone: (213) 221-7909.

ROSACEA AWARENESS MONTH. Mar 1–31. Rosacea Awareness Month has been designated by the National Rosacea Society to raise understanding of this increasingly common disease. Rosacea is a facial skin condition that can cause permanent physical and psychological damage if it is not diagnosed and treated. For info: Sam Huff, Dir, Natl Rosacea Soc, 800 S Northwest Hwy, Ste 200, Barrington, IL 60010. Phone: (847) 382-8971. Fax: (847) 382-5567. Email: rosacea@aol.com.
WWW: http://www.rosacea.org

SAINT-GAUDENS, AUGUSTUS: 150th BIRTH ANNIVERSARY. Mar 1, 1848. Sculptor, born at Dublin, Ireland. His works include the statue of Lincoln in Lincoln Park, Chicago, and of Admiral Farragut in Madison Square, New York. Saint-Gaudens died at Cornish, NH, Aug 3, 1907.

SAVE YOUR VISION WEEK. Mar 1–7. To remind Americans that vision is one of the most vital of all human needs and its protection is of great significance to the health and welfare of every individual. Annually, the first full week in March. For info: American Optometric Assn, 243 N Lindbergh Blvd, St. Louis, MO 63141. Phone: (314) 991-4100. Fax: (314) 991-4101. WWW: http://www.aoanet.org/aoanet

★**SAVE YOUR VISION WEEK.** Mar 1–7. Presidential Proclamation issued for the first week of March since 1964, except 1971 and 1982 when issued for the second week of March. (PL88–1942, of Dec 30, 1963.)

SHORE, DINAH: BIRTH ANNIVERSARY. Mar 1, 1917. American radio and television personality Dinah Shore was born Frances Rose Shore at Winchester, TN on Mar 1, 1917. In addition to recording many hit songs in the 1930s and 1940s she was one of the first women to be successful as a television host, beginning in the 1950s with the "Dinah Shore Chevy Show." She received 10 Emmys before she died on Feb 24, 1994, at Beverly Hills, CA.

SLAYTON, DONALD "DEKE" K.: BIRTH ANNIVERSARY. Mar 1, 1924. "Deke" Slayton, longtime chief of flight operations at the Johnson Space Center, was born Mar 1, 1924, at Sparta, WI. Slayton was a member of Mercury Seven, the original group of young military aviators chosen to inaugurate America's sojourn into space. Unfortunately for Slayton, a heart problem prevented him from participating in any of the Mercury flights. When in 1971 the heart condition mysteriously went away, Slayton flew on the last Apollo Mission. This July 1975 flight involving a docking with a Soviet Soyuz spacecraft symbolized a momentary thaw in relations between the two nations. During his years as chief of flight operations, Slayton directed astronaut training and selected the crews for nearly all missions. Slayton died June 13, 1993, at League City, TX.

SWITZERLAND: CHALANDRA MARZ. Mar 1. Engadine. Springtime traditional event when costumed young people, ringing bells and cracking whips, drive away the demons of winter.

UNIVERSAL HUMAN BEINGS WEEK. Mar 1–7. The purpose of this observance is to inspire men and women to become Universal Human Beings in a world that is rapidly becoming a "global village." Annually, Mar 1–7. For complete info send $3 to cover printing, handling and postage. For info: Dr. Stanley Drake, Pres, Intl Soc of Friendship and Good Will, 412 Cherry Hills Dr, Bakersfield, CA 93309-2866.

WALES: SAINT DAVID'S DAY. Mar 1. Celebrates patron saint of Wales. Welsh tradition calls for the wearing of a leek on this day.

WORKPLACE EYE HEALTH AND SAFETY MONTH. Mar 1–31. Can you see the dangers at your workplace? Accidents at work are a major cause of preventable blindness. Find out more about Prevent Blindness America®'s workplace safety program, The Wise Owl Club, and find out how to make your work environment easier on your eyes. For info: Prevent Blindness America®, 500 Remington Rd, Schaumburg, IL 61073. Phone: (800) 331-2020. Fax: (847) 843-8458.
WWW: http://www.prevent-blindness.org

YOUTH ART MONTH. Mar 1–31. To emphasize the value and importance of participation in art in the development of all children and youth. For info: Council for Art Education, Inc, 100 Boylston St, Ste 1050, Boston, MA 02116. Phone: (617) 426-6400.

BIRTHDAYS TODAY

Catherine Bach, 44, actress ("The Dukes of Hazzard"), born Warren, OH, Mar 1, 1954.

Harry Belafonte, 71, singer ("Mary's Boy Child," "Island in the Sun," "Banana Boat Song"), born New York, NY, Mar 1, 1927.

John B. Breaux, 54, US Senator (D, Louisiana), born Crowley, LA, Mar 1, 1944.

Robert Conrad, 63, actor ("The Wild Wild West"), born Chicago, IL, Mar 1, 1935.

Roger Daltrey, 54, singer (lead singer of the Who), born London, England, Mar 1, 1944.

Timothy Daly, 42, actor (*Diner*, "Wings"), born New York, NY, Mar 1, 1956.

Ron Howard, 44, actor (Opie on "The Andy Griffith Show," "Happy Days"); director (*Cocoon, Backdraft*), born Duncan, OK, Mar 1, 1954.

Judith Rossner, 63, novelist, born New York, NY, Mar 1, 1935.

Alan Thicke, 51, actor ("Thicke of the Night," "Growing Pains"), former disc jockey, born Kirkland Lake, Ontario, Canada, Mar 1, 1947.

Richard (Purdy) Wilbur, 77, former poet laureate of the US, born New York, NY, Mar 1, 1921.

MARCH 2 — MONDAY

Day 61 — 304 Remaining

BATTLE OF BISMARCK SEA: 55th ANNIVERSARY. Mar 2–4, 1943. Protected by American and Australian fighters, 137 American Flying Fortress and Liberator bombers attacked a Japanese convoy en route from their base at Rabaul to Lae, New Guinea on Mar 2, 1943. In the convoy were eight transports carrying 7,000 reinforcements, which were escorted by eight destroyers. All the transports and four of the destroyers were sunk and 3,500 Japanese troops were drowned. Of the 150 Japanese aircraft involved in the fighting 102 were shot down. The Battle of Bismarck Sea was a major victory for the Allies, ending any efforts by the Japanese to send reinforcements to New Guinea.

CORAY, MELISSA BURTON: BIRTH ANNIVERSARY. Mar 2, 1828. Coray was born at Mersey, Ontario, Canada. At the age of 18 she accompanied her Mormon Battalion soldier husband, William Coray, on a 2,000-mile military march on foot from Council Bluffs, IA, to San Diego, CA, then 1,500 more miles across the Sierra Nevada Mountains and the Nevada desert to Salt Lake City, UT, the only woman to make the entire trip. On July 30, 1994, a mountain peak near Carson Pass was named for her, the 2nd peak in California to be named for a woman.

CYPRUS: GREEN MONDAY. Mar 2. Green, or Clean, Monday is the first Monday of Lent. Lunch in the fields, with bread, olives and uncooked vegetables and no meat or dairy products.

GEISEL, THEODOR "DR. SEUSS": BIRTH ANNIVERSARY. Mar 2, 1904. Theodor Seuss Geisel, the creator of *The Cat in the Hat* and *How the Grinch Stole Christmas*, was born on Mar 2, 1904, at Springfield, MA. Known to children and parents as Dr. Seuss, Geisel's books have sold more than 200 million copies and have been translated into 20 languages. His career began with *And to Think That I Saw It on Mulberry Street*, which was turned down by 27 publishing houses before being published by Vanguard Press. His books included many messages, from environmental consciousness in *The Lorax* to the dangers of pacifism in *Horton Hatches the Egg* and *Yertel the Turtle*'s thinly veiled references to Hitler as the title character. He was awarded a Pulitzer Prize in 1984 "for his contribution over nearly half a century to the education and enjoyment of America's children and their parents." He died on Sept 24, 1991, at La Jolla, CA.

GREEN COUNTRY JAZZ FESTIVAL. Mar 2. Northeastern State University, Tahlequah, OK. A day-long concert featuring the state's finest high school and university bands. Clinics throughout the day; an all-out gala in the evening. Est attendance: 1,000. For info: Northeastern State University, Arts and Letters College, Tahlequah, OK 74464. Phone: (918) 456-5511 ext 3600. Fax: (918) 458-2346.

GUAM: DISCOVERY DAY or MAGELLAN DAY. Mar 2. Commemorates discovery of Guam on Mar 6, 1521. Annually, the first Monday in March.

HELP SOMEONE SEE WEEK. Mar 2–9. Donate used eyeglasses for distribution in Third World countries by Medical Ministry International. Send glasses, cases and frames to MMI, 12281 SW 28th St, Miami, FL 33175. For info: Madonna Yates, 3525 Richard Drive, Columbus, IN 47203. For project info: MMI, PO Box 940207, Plano, TX 75094.

HOUSTON, SAM: BIRTH ANNIVERSARY. Mar 2, 1793. American soldier and politician born in Rockbridge County, VA, remembered for his role in Texas history. In earlier years Houston was a congressman (1823–27) and governor (1827–29) of Tennessee. He resigned his office as governor of Tennessee in 1829 and rejoined the Cherokee Indians (with whom he had lived for several years as a teenage runaway), who accepted him as a member of their tribe. Houston went to Texas in 1832 and became commander of the Texan army in the War for Texan Independence, which was secured when Houston routed the much larger Mexican forces led by Santa Ana, on Apr 21, 1836, at the Battle of San Jacinto. After Texas's admission to the Union, Houston served as US senator and later as governor of the state. He was deposed in 1861 when he refused to swear allegiance to the Confederacy. Houston, the only person to have been elected governor of two different states, failed to serve his full term of office in either. The city of Houston, TX, was named for him. He died on July 26, 1863, at Huntsville, TX.

INTERNATIONAL WEEK AT TEXAS A&M. Mar 2–6. Memorial Student Center, Texas A&M University, College Station, TX. Texas A&M's more than 2,600 international students from some 100 countries introduce their cultures to the university and community during this 19th annual International Week. Cultural displays, an international buffet, talent show and traditional dress parade are some of the week's highlights. Est attendance: 5,000. For info: Intl Student Services, Texas A&M University, 1st Flr Bizzell Hall East, College Station, TX 77843-1226. Phone: (409) 845-1825. Fax: (409) 862-4633. Email: iss@iss.tamu.edu. WWW: http://www.acs.tamu.edu/~isa

NATIONAL PROCRASTINATION WEEK. Mar 2–8. To promote the benefits of relaxing through putting off until tomorrow everything that needn't be done today. For info: Les Waas, Pres, Procrastinators' Club of America Inc, PO Box 712, Bryn Athyn, PA 19009. Phone: (215) 947-9020. Fax: (215) 947-7007.

NATIONAL SCHOOL BREAKFAST WEEK. Mar 2–6. To focus on the importance of a nutritious breakfast served in the schools, giving children a good start to their day. Annually, the first full week in March (weekdays). For info: American School Food Service Assn, 1600 Duke St, 7th Fl, Alexandria, VA 22314-3436. Phone: (703) 739-3900. WWW: http://www.asfsa.org

NEWSPAPER IN EDUCATION WEEK. Mar 2–6. A week-long celebration of using newspapers in the classroom as living textbooks. Annually, the first full week in March (weekdays). For info: René Gunder, Mgr Education Programs, NAA Foundation, 11600 Sunrise Valley Dr, Reston, VA 22091. Phone: (703) 648-1251. Fax: (703) 620-1265. Email: guntr@naa.org.

ORTHODOX LENT. Mar 2–Apr 11. Great Lent or Easter Lent, observed by Eastern Orthodox Churches, lasts until Holy Week begins on Orthodox Palm Sunday (Apr 12).

OTT, MELVIN (MEL): BIRTH ANNIVERSARY. Mar 2, 1909. Baseball Hall of Fame outfielder born at Gretna, LA. Playing for the New York Giants, Ott hit 511 home runs, a National League record until Willie Mays surpassed it in 1966. Inducted into the Hall of Fame in 1951. Died at New Orleans, LA, Nov 21, 1958.

POPE PIUS XII: BIRTH ANNIVERSARY. Mar 2, 1876. Eugenio Maria Giovanni Pacelli, 260th pope of the Roman Catholic Church. Born Mar 2, 1876, at Rome, Italy. Elected pope Mar 2, 1939. Died at Castel Gandolfo, near Rome, Oct 9, 1958.

RITT, MARTIN: BIRTH ANNIVERSARY. Mar 2, 1914. American film and television director Martin Ritt was born at New York, NY. His best-known films are *Hud* (1963), *Sounder* (1972), *The Front* (1976) and *Norma Rae* (1979). During the 1950s he was blacklisted by McCarthy's anti-Communist crusades. Ritt died on Dec 8, 1990, at Santa Monica, CA.

SCHURZ, CARL: BIRTH ANNIVERSARY. Mar 2. American journalist, political reformer and army officer in Civil War. Born near Cologne, Germany, on Mar 2, 1829. Died at New York, NY, on May 14, 1906.

SPACE MILESTONE: *PIONEER 10* (US): ANNIVERSARY. Mar 2, 1972. On Mar 2, 1972, this probe began a journey on which it was scheduled to pass and photograph Jupiter, 620 million miles from Earth, in December 1973, cross the orbit of Pluto in 1987, and then become the first known Earth object to leave our solar system. On Sept 22, *Pioneer 10* reached another space milestone at 4:19 PM, when it reached a distance 50 times farther from the sun than the sun is from Earth.

March 1998

S	M	T	W	T	F	S
1	2	3	4	5	6	7
8	9	10	11	12	13	14
15	16	17	18	19	20	21
22	23	24	25	26	27	28
29	30	31				

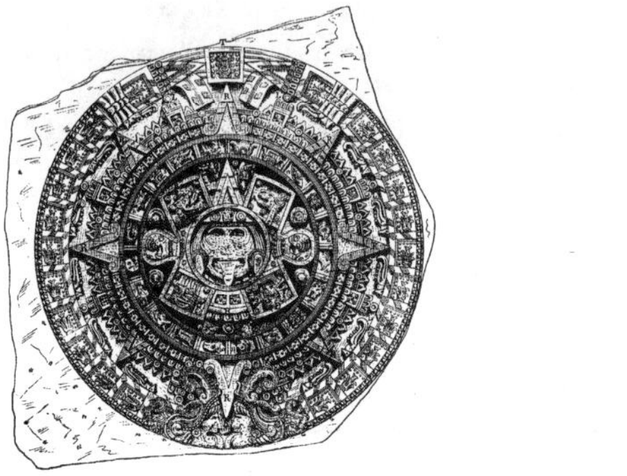

SPACE MILESTONE: *SOYUZ 28* (USSR): 20th ANNIVERSARY. Mar 2, 1978. Cosmonauts Alexi Gubarev and Vladimir Remek linked with *Salyut 6* space station Mar 3, visiting crew of *Soyuz 26*. Returned to Earth Mar 10. Remek, from Czechoslovakia, was the first person in space from a country other than the US or USSR. Launched Mar 2, 1978.

TEXAS INDEPENDENCE DAY. Mar 2. Texas adopted Declaration of Independence from Mexico on this day, 1836.

BIRTHDAYS TODAY

Jon Bon Jovi (John Bongiovi), 36, singer, musician, songwriter ("Living on a Prayer," "You Give Love a Bad Name"), born Sayreville, NJ, Mar 2, 1962.

John Cullum, 68, actor (stage: *On A Clear Day You Can See Forever, Shenandoah, On the Twentieth Century*; "Northern Exposure"), born Knoxville, TN, Mar 2, 1930.

Russell D. Feingold, 45, US Senator (D, Wisconsin), born Janesville, WI, Mar 2, 1953.

Mikhail Sergeyvich Gorbachev, 67, former Soviet political leader, born Privolnoye, Stavropol, Russia, Mar 2, 1931.

John Irving, 56, author (*Cider House Rules, The World According to Garp*), born Exeter, NH, Mar 2, 1942.

Jennifer Jones (Phyllis Isley), 79, actress (Oscar for *The Song of Bernadette*), born Tulsa, OK, Mar 2, 1919.

Eddie Money, 49, musician, born Brooklyn, NY, Mar 2, 1949.

Laraine Newman, 46, comedienne ("Saturday Night Live"), born Los Angeles, CA, Mar 2, 1952.

Doc Watson, 75, singer, musician, born Deep Gap, NC, Mar 2, 1923.

Tom Wolfe, 67, author, journalist (*The Bonfire of the Vanities, The Right Stuff*), born Richmond, VA, Mar 2, 1931.

MARCH 3 — TUESDAY

Day 62 — 303 Remaining

BELL, ALEXANDER GRAHAM: BIRTH ANNIVERSARY. Mar 3, 1847. Inventor of the telephone, born at Edinburgh, Scotland, Bell acquired his interest in the transmission of sound from his father, Melville Bell, a teacher of the deaf. Bell's use of visual devices to teach articulation to the deaf contributed to the theory from which he derived the principle of the vibrating membrane used in the telephone. On Mar 10, 1876, Bell spoke the first electrically transmitted sentence to his assistant in the next room: "Mr Watson, come here, I want you." Bell's other accomplishments include a refinement of Edison's phonograph, the first successful phonograph record, ailerons and the audiometor, and he continued exploring the nature and causes of deafness. He died near Baddeck, Nova Scotia, Canada, on Aug 2, 1922.

BETHUNE, NORMAN: BIRTH ANNIVERSARY. Mar 3, 1890. Canadian physician who worked in the front lines during World War I, the Spanish Civil War and the Chinese Revolution. Bethune was born at Gravenhurst, Ont; he died at age 49 in China while treating a soldier of Mao's Eighth Route Army, Nov 11, 1939. He is said to be the only Western man recognized as a hero of the Chinese Revolution.

BIG 12 WOMEN'S BASKETBALL TOURNAMENT. Mar 3–7. Kansas City, MO. Est attendance: 25,000. For info: Dru Hancock, Championships, Big 12 Conference, 2201 Stemmons Freeway, 28th floor, Dallas, TX 75207. Phone: (214) 742-1212. Fax: (214) 742-2045.

BONZA BOTTLER DAY™. Mar 3. To celebrate when the number of the day is the same as the number of the month. Bonza Bottler Day™ is an excuse to have a party at least once a month. For more information, see Jan 1. For info: Gail M. Berger, 109 Matthew Ave, Poca, WV 25159. Phone: (304) 776-7746. Email: gberger5@aol.com.

BULGARIA: LIBERATION DAY. Mar 3. Grateful tribute to the Russian, Romanian and Finnish soldiers and Bulgarian volunteers who, in the Russo-Turkish War, 1877–78, liberated Bulgaria from Ottoman rule and five centuries of oppression.

FLORIDA: ADMISSION DAY: ANNIVERSARY. Mar 3. Became 27th state on this day in 1845.

I WANT YOU TO BE HAPPY DAY. Mar 3. A day dedicated to reminding people to be thoughtful of others by showing love and care and concern, even if things are not going well for themselves. For info: Harriette W. Grimes, Grandmother, PO Box 545, Winter Garden, FL 34777-0545. Phone: (407) 656-3830. Fax: (407) 656-2790.

JAPAN: HINAMATSURI (DOLL FESTIVAL). Mar 3. This special festival for girls is observed throughout Japan. Annually, Mar 3.

MALAWI: MARTYR'S DAY. Mar 3. Public holiday in Malawi.

"MOONLIGHTING" TV PREMIERE: ANNIVERSARY. Mar 3, 1985. Cybill Shepherd and Bruce Willis starred in ABC's comedy-adventure hour with Allyce Beasley as rhyming receptionist Agnes DiPesto. The premise: former model Maddie Hayes (Shepherd) discovers that the Blue Moon Detective Agency is her only remaining asset after her business manager embezzled her wealth. After deciding to keep the agency, she and her sparring partner, wisecracking detective David Addison (Willis) go off on a series of madcap adventures. The show frequently broke with formula by using the show-within-a-show technique, having characters directly address the camera, shooting sequences in black and white or by going completely off-concept (as in an episode based on Shakespeare's "The Taming of the Shrew"). The show unfortunately foundered due to personality conflicts and production delays.

MOROCCO: ANNIVERSARY OF THE THRONE. Mar 3. National holiday.

"MR WIZARD" TV PREMIERE: ANNIVERSARY. Mar 3, 1951. Don Herbert as Mr Wizard explained the mysteries of science while performing experiments in front of wide-eyed children. The series ran on NBC for fourteen continuous years. In 1983, Herbert returned to host "Mr Wizard's World" on Nickelodeon.

NATIONAL ANTHEM DAY. Mar 3, 1931. The bill designating "The Star-Spangled Banner" as our national anthem was adopted by the US Senate and went to President Herbert Hoover for signature. The president signed it the same day.

PULLMAN, GEORGE: BIRTH ANNIVERSARY. Mar 3, 1831. Born on March 3, 1831, at Brocton, NY, George Mortimer Pullman was an inventor and industrialist who became famous for his design and production of the "Pullman" railroad sleeping car. His first attempt at improving railroad sleeping accommodations began in 1858, while working as a contractor for the Chicago & Alton Railroad at Chicago, IL. His initial model was not adopted, but he left Chicago only to return five years later in 1863 with a new design that was enthusiastically received. He secured a patent for the folding upper berth design in 1864, and a second patent for the lower berth design in 1865. By 1867 Pullman and his partner organized the Pullman Palace Car Company, which became the greatest railroad car-building organization in the world. Pullman died Oct 19, 1897 at Chicago, IL, at age 66.

RIDGWAY, MATTHEW BUNKER: BIRTH ANNIVERSARY. Mar 3. American Army officer, Matthew Bunker Ridgway was born Mar 3, 1895, at Fort Monroe, VA. As major general commanding the newly formed 82nd Airborne Division, he led it in the invasion of Sicily in July of 1943 and the invasion of the Italian mainland in 1944. Ridgway replaced MacArthur as commander of the US Eighth Army in Korea in 1951 and succeeded Eisenhower as Supreme Allied Commander of the North Atlantic Treaty Organization in 1952. He became US Army Chief of Staff in 1953. Ridgway retired in June of 1955. He died at Fox Chapel, PA, July 26, 1993.

TASTE OF THE TOWN. Mar 3. Multi-Purpose Events Center Exhibit Hall, Wichita Falls, TX. More than 50 restaurants and vendors gather together to show off the best food in town benefiting the Wichita County Chapter of the Red Cross. Est attendance: 2,200. For info: Wichita Falls Conv & Visitors Bureau, 1000 Fifth St, Wichita Falls, TX 76031. Phone: (817) 716-5500. Fax: (817) 716-5509.

TOWN MEETING DAY. Mar 3. Vermont. The first Tuesday in March is an official state holiday in Vermont. Nearly every town elects officers, approves budget items and deals with a multitude of other items in a day-long public meeting of the voters.

WOMAN SUFFRAGE PARADE ATTACKED: 85th ANNIVERSARY. Mar 3, 1913. A parade held by the National American Woman Suffrage Association in Washington, DC, on Mar 3, 1913—the day before Woodrow Wilson's inauguration—turned into a near riot when people in the crowd began jeering and shoving the marchers. The 5,000 women and their supporters were spit upon, struck in the face and pelted with burning cigar stubs while police looked on and made no effort to intervene. Secretary of War Henry Stimson was forced to send soldiers from Fort Myer to restore order.

BIRTHDAYS TODAY

David Faustino, 24, actor ("Married. . .With Children"), born Los Angeles, CA, Mar 3, 1974.

Jacqueline (Jackie) Joyner-Kersee, 36, Olympic gold medal heptathlete, born East St. Louis, IL, Mar 3, 1962.

Tim Kazurinsky, 48, actor, comedian, writer ("Saturday Night Live"), born Johnstown, PA, Mar 3, 1950.

Arnold Newman, 80, photographer, born New York, NY, Mar 3, 1918.

Princess Radziwill (Caroline Lee Bouvier), 65, sister of the late Jackie Kennedy Onassis, born New York, NY, Mar 3, 1933.

Herschel Walker, 36, football player, born Wrightsville, GA, Mar 3, 1962.

MARCH 4 — WEDNESDAY

Day 63 — 302 Remaining

ADAMS, JOHN QUINCY: RETURN TO CONGRESS ANNIVERSARY. Mar 4. On Mar 4, 1830, John Quincy Adams returned to the House of Representatives to represent the district of Plymouth, MA. He was the first former president to do so and served for eight consecutive terms.

CONGRESS: ANNIVERSARY OF FIRST MEETING UNDER CONSTITUTION. Mar 4. The first Congress met in New York, NY, on Mar 4, 1789. A quorum was obtained in the House on Apr 1 and in the Senate on Apr 5, and the 1st Congress was formally organized on Apr 6. Electoral votes were counted, and George Washington was declared president (69 votes) and John Adams vice president (34 votes).

"THE DICK CAVETT SHOW" TV PREMIERE: 30th ANNIVERSARY. Mar 4, 1968. Dick Cavett began his television career on ABC with a daytime talk show that subsequently became a late night program competing with Johnny Carson. Cavett, with his Yale background, had a reputation as an "intellectual" host and was particularly adept at the one-man interview. Fred Roy served as his announcer and drummer Bobby Rosengarten served as bandleader. Cavett has since appeared on the CBS, PBS and USA networks hosting a variety of shows in similar formats.

DING LING: DEATH ANNIVERSARY. Mar 4, 1986. Writer and champion of women's rights, born in Hunan Province, China, in 1904. Ding was a prolific author, having written nearly 300 novels as well as plays, short stories and essays. She received the 1951 Stalin Prize for Literature for her novel *The Sun Shines Over the Sanggan River* (1949). In the 1950s she fell from favor, was exiled and, in 1970, was imprisoned. After the death of Chairman Mao she was freed and during her last years she enjoyed renewed attention and favor. Died at age 82 at Peking, China, on Mar 4, 1986.

GREENWOOD, JOAN: BIRTH ANNIVERSARY. Mar 4, 1921. British stage and screen actress Joan Greenwood was born at Chelsea, London. With her husky voice she became best known for playing the roles of coquettes. She died on Feb 27, 1987, at London.

GROVER CLEVELAND'S SECOND PRESIDENTIAL INAUGURATION: ANNIVERSARY. Mar 4, 1893. Grover Cleveland was inaugurated for a second but nonconsecutive term as president. In 1885 he had become 22nd President of the US and in 1893 the 24th. Originally a source of some controversy, the Congressional Directory for some time listed him only as the 22nd president. The Directory now lists him as both the 22nd and 24th presidents though some historians continue to argue that one person cannot be both. Benjamin Harrison served during the intervening term, defeating Cleveland in electoral votes, though not in the popular vote.

HUG A GI DAY. Mar 4. Today is the only calendrical date which is a command—March Fourth. Therefore, today we honor all of the gallant men and women who serve in all branches of the military. It is the day we acknowledge and salute the sacrifices they make to keep this the land of the free. For info: Adrienne Sioux Koopersmith, 1437 W Rosemont, 1W, Chicago, IL 60660-1319. Phone: (773) 743-5341. Fax: (773) 743-5395.
Email: kooper@interaccess.com.

NAIA MEN'S AND WOMEN'S SWIMMING AND DIVING NATIONAL CHAMPIONSHIPS. Mar 4–7. Federal Way, WA. Individuals compete for All-America honors while teams compete for the national championship. 18th annual competitions for women and 41st annual for men. Est attendance: 3,000. For info: Natl Assn of Intercollegiate Athletics, 6120 S Yale Ave, Ste 1450, Tulsa, OK 74136. Phone: (918) 494-8828. Fax: (918) 494-8841. Email: khenry@naia.org. WWW: http://www.naia.org

OLD INAUGURATION DAY. Mar 4. Anniversary of the date set for beginning the US presidential term of office, 1789–1933. Although the Continental Congress had set the first Wednesday of March 1789 as the date for the new government to convene, a quorum was not present to count the electoral votes until Apr 6. Though George Washington's term of office began on Mar 4, he did not take the oath of office until Apr 30, 1789. All subsequent presidential terms (except successions following the death of an incumbent), until Franklin D. Roosevelt's second term, began on Mar 4. The 20th Amendment (ratified Jan 23, 1933) provided that "the terms of the President and Vice President shall end at noon on the 20th day of January . . . and the terms of their successors shall then begin."

March 1998

S	M	T	W	T	F	S
1	2	3	4	5	6	7
8	9	10	11	12	13	14
15	16	17	18	19	20	21
22	23	24	25	26	27	28
29	30	31				

PENNSYLVANIA DEEDED TO WILLIAM PENN: ANNIVERSARY. Mar 4. To satisfy a debt of £16,000, King Charles II of England granted a royal charter, deed and governorship of Pennsylvania to William Penn on Mar 4, 1681.

***PEOPLE* MAGAZINE: ANNIVERSARY.** Mar 4. The popular gossip magazine was officially launched with the Mar 4, 1974, issue featuring a cover photo of Mia Farrow.

PERKINS, FRANCES: CABINET APPOINTMENT 65th ANNIVERSARY. Mar 4, 1933. Frances Perkins became the first woman appointed to the president's cabinet on Mar 4, 1933. She was appointed Secretary of Labor by President Franklin D. Roosevelt.

PULASKI, CASIMIR: BIRTH ANNIVERSARY. Mar 4, 1747. American Revolutionary hero, General (and chief of cavalry) Kazimierz (Casimir) Pulaski, born at Winiary, Mazovia, Poland, the son of a count. He was a patriot and military leader in Poland's fight against Russia of 1770–71, who went into exile at the partition of Poland in 1772. He went to America in 1777 to join in the Revolution, fighting with General Washington at Brandywine and also serving at Germantown and Valley Forge. He organized the Pulaski Legion to wage guerrilla warfare against the British. Mortally wounded in a heroic charge at the siege of Savannah, GA, on Oct 9, 1779, he died aboard the warship *Wasp* on Oct 11, 1779. Pulaski Day is celebrated on the first Monday of March in Illinois.

ROCKNE, KNUTE: BIRTH ANNIVERSARY. March 4, 1888. Legendary Notre Dame football coach born at Voss, Norway. Known for such sayings as "Win one for the Gipper," he died at Cottonwood Falls, KS, March 31, 1931.

RONALD AND NANCY REAGAN: WEDDING ANNIVERSARY. Mar 4, 1952. Little Brown Church in the San Fernando Valley, CA. Ronald Reagan was 41 and Nancy Davis (born Anne Frances Robbins) was 30. They were both professional actors at the time, and William Holden served as best man. This was Reagan's second marriage. His first marriage to actress Jane Wyman (born Sarah Jane Fulks) in 1940 produced daughter Maureen Elizabeth Reagan in 1941, adopted son Michael Edward Reagan (born 1942) in 1945 and daughter Christina Reagan in 1947. Christina was born prematurely and died within a few days. Nancy and Ronald have two children: Patricia Ann Reagan (Patti Davis), born in 1952, and Ronald Prescott Reagan, in 1958. Reagan was the first US president who had been divorced.

SPACE MILESTONE: *OGO 5* (US): 30th ANNIVERSARY. Mar 4, 1968. Orbiting geophysical laboratory collected data on sun's influence on Earth. Launched Mar 4, 1968.

STOP BAD SERVICE DAY. Mar 4. Celebrating those companies that foster loyalty from customers by giving thorough, professional service. Consumers are encouraged to thank their favorite companies for offering a superior level of services. For info: Margo Chevers, PO Box 1584, Plainville, MA 02762. Phone: (508) 695-8687. Fax: (508) 643-2978.
Email: mcspeaker@aol.com.

TELEVISION ACADEMY HALL OF FAME: FIRST INDUCTEES ANNOUNCED. Mar 4. On Mar 4, 1984, the Television Academy of Arts and Sciences announced the formation of the Television Academy Hall of Fame in Burbank, CA. The first inductees were Lucille Ball, Milton Berle, Paddy Chayefsky, Norman Lear, Edward R. Murrow, William S. Paley and David Sarnoff.

VERMONT: ADMISSION DAY: ANNIVERSARY. Mar 4. Became 14th state on this day in 1791.

BIRTHDAYS TODAY

Emilio Estefan, 45, percussionist for The Miami Sound Machine ("Anything for You"), born Havana, Cuba, Mar 4, 1953.

Jane Goodall (Baroness Van Lawick-Goodall), 64, anthropologist known for study of chimpanzees, born London, England, Mar 4, 1934.

Kevin Maurice Johnson, 32, basketball player, born Sacramento, CA, Mar 4, 1966.

Patsy Kensit, 30, actress (*The Great Gatsby, Chicago Joe and the Showgirl, Blame It on the Bellboy*), born London, England, Mar 4, 1968.

Kay Lenz, 45, actress (*Rich Man, Poor Man*), born Los Angeles, CA, Mar 4, 1953.

Miriam Makeba, 66, actress, singer, anti-apartheid activist, born Johannesburg, South Africa, Mar 4, 1932.

Barbara McNair, 64, singer, actress ("The Barbara McNair Show"), born Racine, WI, Mar 4, 1934.

Catherine O'Hara, 44, comedienne, writer ("Second City TV," "SCTV Network 90"), actress (*Home Alone*), born Toronto, Ontario, Canada, Mar 4, 1954.

Paula Prentiss (Paula Ragusa), 59, actress ("He & She," *Man's Favorite Sport, What's New Pussycat?*), born San Antonio, TX, Mar 4, 1939.

Alice Rivlin, 67, Director, Office of Management and Budget, born Philadelphia, PA, Mar 4, 1931.

Mary Wilson, 54, singer (original member of the Supremes with Diana Ross and Florence Ballard), born Detroit, MI, Mar 4, 1944.

MARCH 5 — THURSDAY

Day 64 — 301 Remaining

AUSTRALIA: EIGHT HOUR DAY or LABOR DAY. Mar 5. Western Australia and Tasmania. Parades and celebrations commemorate trade union efforts during the 19th century to limit working hours. Their slogan: "Eight hours labor, eight hours recreation, eight hours rest!" In New South Wales it is called "Six Hour Day."

BANK HOLIDAY: 65th ANNIVERSARY. Mar 5, 1933. On his first full day in office (Sunday, Mar 5, 1933), President Roosevelt proclaimed a national "Bank Holiday" to help save the nation's faltering banking system. Most banks were able to reopen after the 10-day "holiday" (Mar 4–14), but in the meantime, "scrip" had temporarily replaced money in many American households.

BIG 10 MEN'S BASKETBALL TOURNAMENT. Mar 5–6. For info: Dennis LaBissoniere, Big 10 Conference, 1500 W Higgins Rd, Park Ridge, IL 60068-6300. Phone: (847) 696-1010. Fax: (847) 696-1110. WWW: http://www.bigten.org

BIG 12 MEN'S BASKETBALL CHAMPIONSHIP. Mar 5–8. Kansas City, MO. Est attendance: 75,000. For info: Tim Allen, Championships, Big 12 Conference, 2201 Stemmons Freeway, 28th floor, Dallas, TX 75207. Phone: (214) 742-1212. Fax: (214) 742-2045.

BLACKSTONE, WILLIAM: BIRTH ANNIVERSARY. Mar 5, 1595. William Blackstone, born at Durham County, England, was the first settler in what is now Boston, MA, and also the first in what is now Rhode Island. Blackstone came to New England with the Capt Robert Gorges expedition in 1623. When the expedition failed and most returned to England, he stayed and settled on what later became Beacon Hill. In 1634, he sold most of his Boston property and moved to the shores of the river that now bears his name. He died there at what is now Cumberland, RI, on May 26, 1675.

BOSTON MASSACRE: ANNIVERSARY. Mar 5. On Mar 5, 1770, a skirmish between British troops and a crowd in Boston, MA, became widely publicized and contributed to the unpopularity of the British regime in America before the American Revolution. Five men were killed and six more were injured by British troops commanded by Capt Thomas Preston.

CRISPUS ATTUCKS DAY: DEATH ANNIVERSARY. Mar 5. New Jersey. Honors Crispus Attucks, possibly a runaway slave, who was a leader of the American colonists involved in the Boston Massacre and the first to die in the skirmish there on Mar 5, 1770.

CULLIGAN, EMMETT J.: BIRTH ANNIVERSARY. Mar 5, 1893. Emmett J. Culligan, founder of world's largest water treatment organization, was born at Yankton, SD. Culligan first experimented with a water-softening device in the early 1920s—to soften water used to wash his baby's diapers. In 1936 he launched the company from a Northbrook, IL, blacksmith shop. Recipient of Horatio Alger Award in 1969, Culligan died at San Bernardino, CA, on June 3, 1970.

ENGLAND: CRUFTS DOG SHOW. Mar 5–8. National Exhibition Centre, Birmingham, West Midlands. The world's greatest dog show where more than 18,000 top pedigree dogs compete to achieve the title of "Best in Show," the most prestigious award in the world of dogs. Est attendance: 95,000. For info: Events Department, The Kennel Club, 1 Clarges St, London, England W1Y 8AB. Phone: (44) (171) 493-7838. Fax: (44) (171) 518-1028. Ticket info: (44) (171) 518-1012. WWW: http://www.crufts.org.uk

FESTIVAL OF NATIVE ARTS. Mar 5–7. University of Alaska, Fairbanks. Native cultural event features craft exhibits and sales, demonstrations and dances presented by Native people from all over Alaska. Est attendance: 4,000. For info: Festival of Native Arts, PO Box 756300, Univ of Alaska, Fairbanks, AK 99775-6300. Phone: (907) 474-7181 or (907) 474-6889. Fax: (907) 474-5624. Email: ttjkr@aurora.alaska.edu.

HARRISON, REX: 90th BIRTH ANNIVERSARY. Mar 5, 1908. Born Reginald Carey on Mar 5, 1908, at Huyton, England. Rex Harrison's career as an actor encompassed more than 40 films and scores of plays. He won both a Tony and an Oscar for the role of Henry Higgins in *My Fair Lady*, perhaps his most famous role. Among other films, he appeared in *Dr. Doolittle, Cleopatra, Blithe Spirit* and *Major Barbara*. He claimed he would never retire from acting, and he was appearing in a Broadway revival of Somerset Maugham's *The Circle* three weeks before his death on June 2, 1990, at his home in New York, NY.

HEMLOCK DAY. Mar 5. To honor the legendary Taffy Hemlock, supposed inventrix of a procedure for attaching padlocks around the hem of her skirt so that it would not be blown upward by inquisitive winds that might let her ankles get freckled. Celebrated by the True-Blue Law Society with patent searches to determine when/if the idea was ever patented. For info: Robert L. Birch, Puns Corps, Box 2364, Falls Church, VA 22042-0364. Phone: (703) 533-3668.

"IRON CURTAIN" SPEECH: ANNIVERSARY. Mar 5, 1946. Winston Churchill, speaking at Westminster College, Fulton, MO, established the cold war boundary with these words: "From Stettin in the Baltic to Trieste in the Adriatic an iron curtain has descended across the continent." Though Churchill was not the first to use the phrase *iron curtain*, his speech gave it a new currency and its usage has persisted.

JOHNSON IMPEACHMENT PROCEEDINGS BEGIN: ANNIVERSARY. Mar 5, 1868. On Mar 5, 1868, the Senate convened as a court to hear the charges against President Andrew Johnson. Supreme Court Chief Justice Salmon Chase was the presiding officer and the prosecution was led by radical Republicans Benjamin Butler and Thaddeus Stevens. Johnson was defended ably, and the Senate vote of 35–19 fell one vote short of the two-thirds majority necessary for impeachment.

KNOXVILLE BOAT SHOW. Mar 5–8. Knoxville Convention Center, Knoxville, TN. 15th annual show featuring more than 50,000 sq ft of boats and 70 booths displaying scuba and marine equipment, water skis and more. Est attendance: 14,000. For info: Cindy Crabtree, Event Coord, ESAU, Inc, PO Box 50096, Knoxville, TN 37950. Phone: (423) 588-1233 or (800) 588-ESAU. Fax: (423) 588-6938.

MICHIGAN HOME AND GARDEN SHOW. Mar 5–8. Pontiac Silverdome, Pontiac, MI. Products and services for home building/remodeling, home furnishings and interior design, lawn and garden and related areas. On-site constructions, theme gardens, seminars and demonstrations, plus The Standard Flower Show sponsored by The Federated Garden Clubs of Michigan, District 1. Est attendance: 45,000. For info: Mike Wilbraham, ShowSpan, Inc, 1400 28th St SW, Grand Rapids, MI 49509. Phone: (616) 530-1919. Fax: (616) 530-2122.

MOON PHASE: FIRST QUARTER. Mar 5. Moon enters First Quarter phase at 3:41 AM, EST.

NAIA MEN'S AND WOMEN'S INDOOR TRACK AND FIELD NATIONAL CHAMPIONSHIPS. Mar 5–7. Devaney Sports Center, Lincoln, NE. Individuals compete for All-America honors while teams compete for the national championship. 33rd (men) and 18th (women) annual competition. Est attendance: 2,500. For info: Natl Assn Intercollegiate Athletics, 6120 S Yale Ave, Ste 1450, Tulsa, OK 74136. Phone: (918) 494-8828. Fax: (918) 494-8841. Email: khenry@naia.org. WWW: http://www.naia.org

NORTH DAKOTA WINTER SHOW. Mar 5–15. Valley City, ND. 11-day agricultural expo featuring world's largest crop show, 10-breed cattle show, culinary arts show and competition, style and needlework show and competition, children's area, 4-performance PRCA Rodeo, state team roping and penning championships, Draft horse pulls, Old-Time tractor pull (tractors built prior to 1955), 80 vendor farm toy show and single performance headliner country concert. Annually, beginning the first Thursday in March. Est attendance: 75,000. For info: Dale Hildebrant, Mgr, ND Winter Show, PO Box 846, Valley City, ND 58072. Phone: (701) 845-1401 or (800) 437-0218. Fax: (701) 845-3914.

SAINT PIRAN'S DAY. Mar 5. This is the birth date of St. Piran, the patron saint of Cornish tinners. Cornish worldwide celebrate this day. Annually, Mar 5. For info: The Cornish American Heritage Soc, 2405 N Brookfield Rd, Brookfield, WI 53045. Phone: (414) 786-9358. Email: jjolliff@post.its.mcw.edu.

March 1998

S	M	T	W	T	F	S
1	2	3	4	5	6	7
8	9	10	11	12	13	14
15	16	17	18	19	20	21
22	23	24	25	26	27	28
29	30	31				

BIRTHDAYS TODAY

Samantha Eggar, 59, actress ("Samantha and the King," *The Collector*), born London, England, Mar 5, 1939.
Penn Jillette, 43, magician, born Greenfield, MA, Mar 5, 1955.
Paul Sand (Paul Sanchez), 54, actor ("St. Elsewhere"; Tony Award for *Story Theatre*), born Los Angeles, CA, Mar 5, 1944.
Dean Stockwell, 62, actor (*The Boy with Green Hair*, "Quantum Leap"), born Los Angeles, CA, Mar 5, 1936.
Laurence Tisch, 75, executive, born New York, NY, Mar 5, 1923.
Michael Warren, 52, actor ("Paris," "Hill Street Blues") born South Bend, IN, Mar 5, 1946.
Fred Williamson, 60, actor ("Julia," "Half Nelson"), former professional football player, born Gary, IN, Mar 5, 1938.

MARCH 6 — FRIDAY

Day 65 — 300 Remaining

AMA NATIONAL HOT-SHOE DIRT TRACK. Mar 6. Daytona Beach Municipal Stadium, Daytona Beach, FL. For info: Daytona Intl Speedway, John Story, PR, Box 2801, Daytona Beach, FL 32120-2801. Phone: (904) 254-6782 or for tickets (904) 253-RACE (7223). Fax: (904) 947-6791. WWW: http://www.daytonausa.com

BROWNING, ELIZABETH BARRETT: BIRTH ANNIVERSARY. Mar 6. English poet, author of *Sonnets from the Portuguese*, wife of poet Robert Browning and subject of the play *The Barretts of Wimpole Street,* was born near Durham, England, Mar 6, 1806. She died at Florence, Italy, June 29, 1861.

CAROLINA CRAFTSMEN'S SPRING CLASSIC. Mar 6–8. State Fairgrounds, Columbia, SC. Arts and crafts. Est attendance: 20,000. For info: The Carolina Craftsmen, 1240 Oakland Ave, Greensboro, NC 27403. Phone: (910) 274-5550. Fax: (910) 274-1084.

CHALO NITKA. Mar 6–8. Moore Haven, FL. To promote Lake Okeechobee bass fishing and bring the Seminoles and the rest of the community together for a celebration. *Chalo Nitka* means "Bass Day" in the Seminole language. Annually, the first three-day weekend in March. Est attendance: 10,000. For info: Exec Dir, Glades County Chamber of Commerce, Box 490, Moore Haven, FL 33471. Phone: (941) 946-0440. Fax: (941) 946-2282.

COMEDY CLASSIC. Mar 6–8. Asheville, NC. 10th annual Comedy Classic is a weekend to come and get your funnybone tickled and let the cares of the world dissolve in laughter. For info: Grove Park Inn Resort, 290 Macon Ave, Asheville, NC 28804. Phone: (800) 374-0050 or (704) 252-2711. Fax: (704) 253-7053.

DRESDEN'S IN BLOOM™. Mar 6–May 3. There will be many seasonal events, demonstrations and entertainment opportunities taking place throughout Dresden and in The Longaberger® Company properties. There will be shopping fun for all at The Longaberger Specialty Shops™ and great food at all of our resturants. Also look for fabulous entertainment and fun for the whole family. Est attendance: 33,000. For info: The Longaberger® Company, 1360 Main St, Dresden, OH 43821. Phone: (614) 754-5778. Fax: (614) 754-5720.

FALL OF THE ALAMO: ANNIVERSARY. Mar 6. Anniversary of the fall of the Texan fort, the Alamo, on Mar 6, 1836. The siege, led by Mexican general Santa Anna, began on Feb 23 and reached its climax on Mar 6, when the last of the defenders was slain. Texans, under General Sam Houston, rallied with the war cry "Remember the Alamo" and, at the Battle of San Jacinto, on Apr 21, defeated and captured Santa Anna, who signed a treaty recognizing Texas's independence.

FULTON OYSTERFEST. Mar 6–8. Fulton Navigation Park, Fulton, TX. This salute to the oyster industry features oyster-shucking, raw oyster-eating contests, more than 100 arts and crafts booths, food and fun, live bands and other entertainment. Annually, the first full weekend in March. Est attendance: 40,000. For info: Fulton Oysterfest, PO Box 393, Fulton, TX 78358. Phone: (512) 729-2388. Fax: (512) 729-3248.

GHANA: INDEPENDENCE DAY. Mar 6, 1957. National holiday. Received independence from Great Britain on this day, 1957.

"IN THE HEAT OF THE NIGHT" TV PREMIERE: 10th ANNIVERSARY. Mar 6, 1988. NBC's police drama was based on the 1967 movie with the same name. Carroll O'Connor played Mississippi police chief Bill Gillespie who, along with Howard Rollins as Detective Virgil Tibbs, investigated crimes in the rural South. The cast featured Alan Autry as Lt Bubba Skinner; Anne-Marie Johnson as Virgil's wife, Althea; David Hart as Deputy Parker William; Hugh O'Connor as Deputy Lonnie Jamison; Christian LeBlanc as Deputy Junior Abernathy; Geoffrey Thorne as Deputy Sweet; and Crystal Fox as dispatcher Lu Ann Corman.

LONGHORN WORLD CHAMPIONSHIP RODEO. Mar 6–8. Von Braun Civic Center, Huntsville, AL. More than 200 of the best cowboys and cowgirls compete in six professional contests ranging from bronco riding to bull riding for top prize money and world championship points. Featuring colorful opening pageantry and Big, Bad BONUS Bulls. 19th annual. Est attendance: 16,000. For info: W. Bruce Lehrke, Pres, Longhorn World Chmpshp Rodeo, Inc, PO Box 70159, Nashville, TN 37207. Phone: (615) 876-1016. Fax: (615) 876-4685. Email: lhrodeo@idt.net. WWW: http://www.longhornrodeo.com

MARYLAND HOME AND FLOWER SHOW. Mar 6–8. (Also 13–15.) Timonium Fairgrounds, Baltimore, MD. The largest display of home building, remodeling and home decorating exhibits in the Baltimore area. Includes educational exhibits, crafts, plant marketplace and displays of landscaped gardens. Est attendance: 89,000. For info: S & L Productions Inc, Crain Overlook, 1916 Crain Hwy, Ste 16, Glen Burnie, MD 21061. Phone: (410) 863-1180. Fax: (410) 863-1187.

MICHELANGELO: BIRTH ANNIVERSARY. Mar 6. Anniversary of the birth, Mar 6, 1475, at Caprese, Italy, of Michelangelo di Lodovico Buonarroti Simoni. A prolific Renaissance painter, sculptor, architect and poet, who had a profound impact on Western art. Michelangelo's fresco painting on the ceiling of the Sistine Chapel at the Vatican in Rome, Italy, is often considered the pinnacle of his achievement in painting, as well as the highest achievement of the Renaissance. Also among his works were the sculptures *David* and *The Pieta.* Appointed architect of St. Peter's in 1542, a post he held until his death on Feb 18, 1564, at Rome.

MIDNIGHT AT THE OASIS. Mar 6–8. Ray Kroc Complex/Desert Sun Stadium, Yuma, AZ. Stroll down memory lane at an incredible nostalgic festival featuring the cars and music of the '50s and '60s. Open to '72 and older American cars and trucks and foreign classics. Show & Shine, Rock 'n Roll Concert and Dance, vendors, arts and crafts, activities and entertainment for the whole family. For info: Mary Cordery, Adm Exec, Caballeros de Yuma, PO Box 5987, Yuma, AZ 85366. Phone: (520) 343-1715. Fax: (520) 783-1609.

NC RV AND CAMPING SHOW. Mar 6–8. NC State Fairgrounds, Raleigh, NC. A display of the latest in recreational vehicles and accessories by various dealers. Est attendance: 10,000. For info: Apple Rock Advertising & Promotions, 1200 Eastchester Dr, High Point, NC 27265. Phone: (910) 881-7100. Fax: (910) 883-7198.

PEALE, ANNA CLAYPOOLE: BIRTH ANNIVERSARY. Mar 6, 1791. American painter of miniatures. Born at Philadelphia, PA, Mar 6, 1791. Died on Dec 25, 1878.

ROUGH RIVER HUMOR FESTIVAL. Mar 6–7. Falls of Rough, KY. Festival includes variety shows, plus workshops on how to tell funny stories and jokes. Est attendance: 535. For info: Rough River Dam State Resort PK, Tom DeHaven, Rec Super, Falls of Rough, KY 40119. Phone: (502) 257-2311.

SAINT LOUIS VARIETY CLUB TELETHON AND DINNER WITH THE STARS. Mar 6–7. Adam's Mark Hotel, St. Louis, MO. A 10-hour telethon to raise funds for disabled and disadvantaged children in the greater St. Louis area. Aired on KMOV Channel 4 (CBS). Est attendance: 1,200. For info: St. Louis Variety Club, 1000 Des Peres Rd, Ste 120, St. Louis, MO 63131. Phone: (314) 821-8184. Fax: (314) 821-0433.

SOUTH TEXAS RANCHING HERITAGE FESTIVAL. Mar 6–8. Kingsville, TX. Cowboy storytelling, craftsmen, ranching rodeo and camp cooking. Est attendance: 7,000. For info: Kingsville Conv and Visitors Bureau, PO Box 1562, Kingsville, TX 78364-1562. Phone: (800) 333-5032. Fax: (512) 592-3227. Email: kcvb@kingsville.org. WWW: http://www.kingsville.org

WINTER CARNIVAL. Mar 6–7. Red Lodge, MT. Winter Carnival features parades, snow sculptures, King and Queen contest, Snow Ball, costume contest, Cardboard Classic Race (for which teams design crafts of carboard for downhill race), live music and prizes. Torchlight parade and spaghetti dinner. Annually, the first weekend in March. Est attendance: 2,000. For info: Red Lodge Area Chamber of Commerce, PO Box 988, Red Lodge, MT 59068. Phone: (406) 446-2610. Email: redlodge@wtp.net.

BIRTHDAYS TODAY

Marion Barry, 62, re-elected mayor of Washington, DC, born Itta Bena, MS, Mar 6, 1936.

Christopher Samuel Bond, 59, US Senator (R, Missouri), born St. Louis, MO, Mar 6, 1939.

Sarah Caldwell, 74, conductor, born Maryville, MO, Mar 6, 1924.

L. Gordon Cooper, 71, astronaut, born Shawnee, OK, Mar 6, 1927.

Gabriel Garcia-Marquez, 70, Nobel Prize-winning author (*A Hundred Years of Solitude, Love in the Time of Cholera*), born Aracaracca, Colombia, Mar 6, 1928.

Dave Gilmour, 54, singer, musician (member Pink Floyd, *The Dark Side of the Moon*), born Cambridge, England, Mar 6, 1944.

Alan Greenspan, 72, economist, Chairman of the Federal Reserve Board, born New York, NY, Mar 6, 1926.

Ed McMahon, 75, actor, TV ("Big Top" as a clown; "The Tonight Show," "Star Search"), born Detroit, MI, Mar 6, 1923.

Ben Murphy, 56, actor ("Alias Smith and Jones," *Yours, Mine and Ours*), born Jonesboro, AR, Mar 6, 1942.

Shaquille Rashan O'Neal, 26, basketball player, born Newark, NJ, Mar 6, 1972.

Rob Reiner, 53, actor ("All in the Family"), director (*When Harry Met Sally, This Is Spinal Tap*), born New York, NY, Mar 6, 1945.

Wilver Dornel (Willie) Stargell, 58, Baseball Hall of Fame outfielder and first baseman, born Earlsboro, OK, Mar 6, 1940.

Valentina Tereshkova-Nikolaeva, 61, cosmonaut, born Maslennikovo, USSR, Mar 6, 1937.

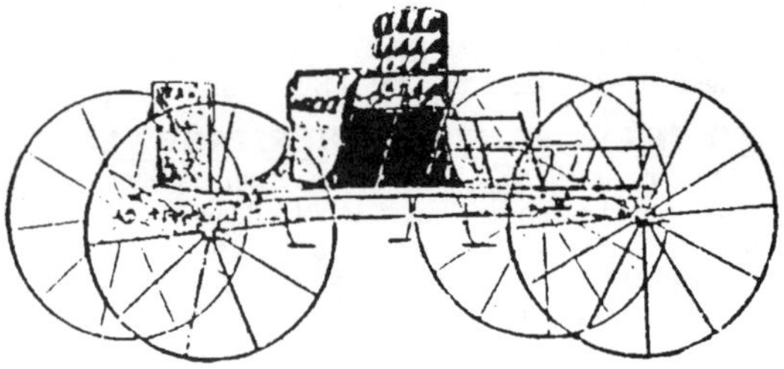

MARCH 7 — SATURDAY

Day 66 — 299 Remaining

AMA GRAND NATIONAL KICKOFF DIRT TRACK. Mar 7. Daytona Beach Municipal Stadium, Daytona Beach, FL. For info: Daytona Intl Speedway, John Story, PR, Box 2801, Daytona Beach, FL 32120-2801. Phone: (904) 254-6782 or for tickets (904) 253-RACE (7223). Fax: (904) 947-6791. WWW: http://www.daytonausa.com

AMERICAN CLUB'S TEDDY BEAR CLASSIC. Mar 7–8. The American Club, Kohler, WI. The creations of more than 60 teddy bear artists from across the country on display—bears, accessories, clothes, supplies, gifts. Many demonstrations. Annually, the first weekend in March. Est attendance: 3,500. For info: The American Club, Highland Dr, Kohler, WI 53044. Phone: (800) 344-2838. Fax: (414) 457-0299.

ANTIQUE SHOW AND SALE. Mar 7–8. West Platte High School Auditorium, 935 Washington St, Weston, MO. 30–40 selected dealers from several states display a variety of antiques (including furniture) and collectibles for sale to the general public. For info: Weston Development Co, 502 Main, Weston, MO 64098. Phone: (816) 640-2909.

BAY AREA RENAISSANCE FESTIVAL. Mar 7–8. (Also Mar 14–15, 21–22, 28–29; Apr 4–5, 11–12.) Largo, FL. A re-creation of a 16th-century village, nestled on 40 wooded acres with food, drink, entertainment, crafts, jousting, human chess match. Six consecutive weekends, rain or shine, 10 AM–6 PM. 19th annual festival. Est attendance: 90,000. For info: Bay Area Renaissance Festival, 1920 Lake Ave, Ste 5, Largo, FL 34641-3720. Phone: (813) 586-5423. Fax: (813) 587-0832.

BEACH PARTY. Mar 7. Deadwood, SD. 12th annual. Forget Ft Lauderdale for spring break! Head to the beach at the #10. Sand, hot tub, beach hats, music and limbo contests. Est attendance: 400. For info: Old Style Saloon #10, 657 Main St, Deadwood, SD 57732. Phone: (605) 578-3346 or (800) 952-9398. Fax: (605) 578-1944. Email: saloon10@deadwood.net.

BIG 10 WRESTLING CHAMPIONSHIP. Mar 7–8. Penn State, University Park, PA. Est attendance: 10,000. For info: Dennis LaBissoniere, Big Ten Conference, 1500 W Higgins Rd, Park Ridge, IL 60068-6300. Phone: (847) 696-1010. Fax: (847) 696-1110. WWW: http://www.bigten.org

BIG 12 WRESTLING CHAMPIONSHIP. Mar 7. Norman, OK. Est attendance: 2,000. For info: Dru Hancock, Championships, Big 12 Conference, 2201 Stemmons Freeway, 28th floor, Dallas, TX 75207. Phone: (214) 742-1212. Fax: (214) 742-2045.

BRUSH COUNTRY ANTIQUE SHOW & SALE. Mar 7–8. Kingsville, TX. An outstanding show and sale full of unique and antique collectibles, treasures and gifts. For info: Kingsville Conv & Visitors Bureau, PO Box 1562, Kingsville, TX 78364-1562. Phone: (800) 333-5032. Fax: (512) 592-3227. Email: kcvb@kingsville.org. WWW: http://www.kingsville.org

March 1998

S	M	T	W	T	F	S
1	2	3	4	5	6	7
8	9	10	11	12	13	14
15	16	17	18	19	20	21
22	23	24	25	26	27	28
29	30	31				

BURBANK, LUTHER: BIRTH ANNIVERSARY. Mar 7. Anniversary of birth of American naturalist and author, creator and developer of many new varieties of flowers, fruits, vegetables and trees. Luther Burbank's birthday is observed by some as Bird and Arbor Day. Born at Lancaster, MA, Mar 7, 1849. Died at Santa Rosa, CA, Apr 11, 1926.

CANADIAN-AMERICAN DAYS FEST. Mar 7–22. Myrtle Beach, SC. Concerts, square dances, beach games and sports events. Est attendance: 100,000. For info: Marilyn Chewnling, Fest Dir, Myrtle Beach Area Chamber of Commerce, PO Box 2115, Myrtle Beach, SC 29578. Phone: (803) 626-7444. Fax: (803) 626-0009. WWW: http://www.myrtlebeachlive.com

DAYTONA SUPERCROSS BY HONDA. Mar 7. Daytona International Speedway, Daytona Beach, FL. One of the most famous and toughest Supercross races in the world. Sponsor: Honda. For info: Daytona Intl Speedway, PO Box 2801, Daytona Beach, FL 32120-2801. Phone: (904) 947-6782 or for tickets (904) 253-RACE (7223). Fax: (904) 947-6791. WWW: http://www.daytonausa.com

DISTINGUISHED SERVICE MEDAL: 80th ANNIVERSARY. Mar 7, 1918. With US troops fighting in the trenches in France during the First World War, President Woodrow Wilson authorized the creation of a new bronze, beribboned medal to be given to US Army personnel who performed "exceptionally meritorious service."

HONG KONG FOOD FESTIVAL. Mar 7–22 (tentative). Hong Kong. This annual festival engages the entire territory with focus on one of its favorite pastimes: eating. Special food-related tours, exhibitions, street carnival and special events at hotels and restaurants. Organized by the Hong Kong Tourist Association with sponsorship by local businesses. For info: Hong Kong Tourist Assn, 610 Enterprise Dr, Ste 200, Oakbrook, IL 60521. Phone: (630) 575-2828. Fax: (630) 575-2829. Email: hktachi@hkta.org. WWW: http://www.hkta.org

HOPKINS, STEPHEN: BIRTH ANNIVERSARY. Mar 7, 1707. Colonial governor (Rhode Island) and signer of the Declaration of Independence. Born at Providence, RI, died July 13, 1785, at age 78.

IDITAROD SLED DOG RACE. Mar 7. Anchorage to Nome, AK. The fabled 1,049-mile race with each sled drawn by 16 Northern Breed Dogs. For info: Iditarod Trail Committee, Mile 2.2 - Knik Rd, PO Box 870800, Wasilla, AK 99687. Phone: (907) 376-5155. Fax: (907) 373-6998. WWW: http://www.iditarod.com

MONOPOLY INVENTED: 65th ANNIVERSARY. Mar 7, 1933. Monopoly was mass marketed by Parker Brothers beginning in 1935.

MUSEUM OF ART LAS OLAS ART FESTIVAL. Mar 7–8. Museum of Art, Fort Lauderdale, FL. Fine arts and crafts festival held annually. 10 AM–6 PM. Est attendance: 75,000. For info: Las Olas Art Festival, PO Box 2211, Ft Lauderdale, FL 33303. Phone: (954) 525-3838.

NATCHEZ SPRING PILGRIMAGE. Mar 7–Apr 11. Corner of Canal and State Sts, Natchez, MS. 67th annual tour of 32 antebellum mansions furnished with period antiques, set in formal gardens. Exciting Confederate Pageant "Southern Exposure" and Southern Road to Freedom performances. Carriage and bus sightseeing tours daily. Est attendance: 35,000. For info: Natchez Pilgrimage Tours, PO Box 347, Natchez, MS 39121. Phone: (800) 647-6742 or (601) 446-6631. Fax: (601) 446-8687.

NENANA TRIPOD RAISING FESTIVAL. Mar 7–8. Nenana, AK. Festival centers around the guessing of the exact time of the ice breakup on the Tanana River. Highlights include the raising of the tripod (Mar 8), Nenana Banana Eating, Weight-Pull Contest (humans and dogs), sled dog races, craft bazaar and much more. Est attendance: 4,000. For info: Nenana Ice Classic, Box 272, Nenana, AK 99760. Phone: (907) 832-5446. Fax: (907) 832-5888.

NETHERLANDS: EUROPEAN FINE ART FAIR. Mar 7–15. MECC, Maastricht. Old Master paintings, antiques, textile arts, modern paintings and sculptures, antiquities, books and prints. Annually, in March. Est attendance: 55,000. For info: The European Fine Art Fdtn, PO Box 1035, 5200 BA Den Bosch, Netherlands. Phone: (31) 73 614-5165. Email: info@tefaf.com. WWW: http://www.tefaf.com

PHILADELPHIA FLOWER SHOW. Mar 7–Mar 14. Convention Center, Philadelphia, PA. The growth of technology has enhanced the exchange of ideas, plants and practices to the benefit and delight of gardeners throughout the US. Est attendance: 220,000. For info: Lisa Stephano, Pennsylvania Horticultural Society, 100 N 20th St, 5th Floor, Philadelphia, PA 19103-1495. Phone: (215) 988-8800 or (215) 988-8899. Fax: (215) 988-8810. Email: janeteva@libertynet.org. WWW: http://www.libertynet.org/~phs

SAINT PIRAN'S DAY CELEBRATION. Mar 7. Location available after Jan 1. Celebration in honor of St. Piran, patron saint of Cornwall and Cornish peoples. Held to help preserve history and culture of Cornish people (Celtic). Annually, the Saturday nearest Mar 5. Est attendance: 50. For info: Polly Whitman, Pres, Greater Kansas City Cornish Society, 24 E 68th St, Kansas City, MO 64113-2414. Phone: (816) 444-1963.

SALVADOR DALI MUSEUM OPENING: ANNIVERSARY. Mar 7, 1982. The museum was opened in St. Petersburg, FL, by A. Reynolds and Eleanor R. Morse as a permanent home for the Morse collection, which includes 95 oils, 1,300 watercolors, drawings, graphics, sculptures and photographs. For info: Salvador Dali Museum, 1000 Third St S, St. Petersburg, FL 33701. Phone: (813) 823-3767. Fax: (813) 894-6068. Email: daliweb@mindspring.com. WWW: http://www.daliweb.com

SOUTHEAST FLORIDA SCOTTISH FESTIVAL AND GAMES. Mar 7. Heritage Park, Plantation, FL. Est attendance: 8,000. For info: Scottish-American Soc of Southeast Florida, 5901 NE 21 Rd, Ft Lauderdale, FL 33308. Phone: (954) 776-5675.

SPRING CRAFT AND GIFT SHOW: INDOOR SHOW. Mar 7–8. Wisconsin State Fair Park, Milwaukee, WI. Show combined with commercial gift exhibitors and craftsmen. Est attendance: 23,000. For info: Dir, Spring Craft and Gift Show, 9312 W National Ave, West Allis, WI 53227. Phone: (414) 321-2100.

YELLOWSTONE ART CENTER'S ART AUCTION. Mar 7. Billings, MT. Nationally advertised contemporary art auction (regional/national work). 30th annual auction. Est attendance: 500. For info: Trina Cullinan, Admin Assistant, Yellowstone Art Ctr, 401 N 27th St, Billings, MT 59101. Phone: (406) 256-6804.

BIRTHDAYS TODAY

Anthony Armstrong-Jones (Lord Snowdon), 68, photographer, born London, England, Mar 7, 1930.
Joseph (Joe) Carter, 38, baseball player, born Oklahoma City, OK, Mar 7, 1960.
Michael Eisner, 56, baseball and hockey executive, born Mount Kisco, NY, Mar 7, 1942.
Janet Guthrie, 60, auto racer, born Iowa City, IA, Mar 7, 1938.
Franco Harris, 48, Pro Football Hall of Fame running back, born Fort Dix, NJ, Mar 7, 1950.
John Heard, 52, actor (*The Milagro Beanfield War, Rambling Rose, The Pelican Brief*), born Washington, DC, Mar 7, 1946.
Ivan Lendl, 38, tennis player, born Ostrava, Czechoslovakia, Mar 7, 1960.
Willard Herman Scott, 64, weatherman ("Today Show") friend of centenarians, born Alexandria, VA, Mar 7, 1934.
Daniel J. Travanti, 58, actor ("Hill Street Blues"), born Kenosha, WI, Mar 7, 1940.
Peter Wolf, 52, singer (lead with J. Geils Band; "Centerfold"), born Boston, MA, Mar 7, 1946.

MARCH 8 — SUNDAY

Day 67 — 298 Remaining

AUTOGRAPH COLLECTING WEEK. Mar 8–14. Celebrating the fun of collecting autographs for love and money! Thousands of adults and children all over the world enjoy obtaining the signatures of the famous, infamous and nearly-famous, and almost everyone has at least one special autograph tucked away somewhere. This week honors a hobby which can be started with little or no money, and allows the hobbyist of any age to build an exciting and valuable collection. For a free brochure about how to get started in autograph collecting, send a SASE to the address below. ATTN: Autographs. For info: Cathy Stucker, On-Line Autograph Collectors Club, 4646 Hwy 6, Ste 123, Sugar Land, TX 77478. Phone: (281) 265-7342. Fax: (281) 265-9727. Email: cstucker@flash.net.

BEAVERS, LOUISE: BIRTH ANNIVERSARY. Mar 8, 1902. The Hollywood career of Louise Beavers spanned 30 years and more than 125 films. Though she was forced to play stereotypical roles, such as those of maids, her authentic talent was always apparent. Her starring role in the film *Imitation of Life* earned her high praise from critic Jimmie Fiddler "for the finest performance of 1935." Beavers was a member of the Black Filmmakers Hall of Fame. She also performed with Mae West at Las Vegas and played the title role in the TV series "Beulah" (1951–53). She died at Los Angeles on Oct 26, 1962, at age 60.

CAXTON'S *MIRROR OF THE WORLD* TRANSLATION: ANNIVERSARY. Mar 8, 1481. William Caxton, England's first printer, completed the translation from French into English of *The Mirror of the World*, a popular account of astronomy and other sciences. In print soon afterward, *Mirror of the World* became the first illustrated book printed in England.

DAYTONA 200 BY ARAI. Mar 8. Daytona International Speedway, Daytona Beach, FL. Motorcycle road race for superbikes. Sponsor: Arai Helmets. For info: Daytona Intl Speedway, PO Box 2801, Daytona Beach, FL 32120-2801. Phone: (904) 947-6782 or for tickets (904) 253-RACE (7223). Fax: (904) 947-6791. WWW: http://www.daytonausa.com

FIRST US INCOME TAX: 85th ANNIVERSARY. Mar 8, 1913. The Internal Revenue Service began to levy and collect income taxes.

GIRL SCOUT SUNDAY. Mar 8. Girl Scouts worship together in the place of worship of their choice. For info: Media Services, Girl Scouts of the USA, 420 Fifth Ave, New York, NY 10018. Phone: (212) 852-8000. Fax: (212) 852-6514. WWW: http://www.gsusa.org

GIRL SCOUT WEEK. Mar 8–14. To observe the anniversary of the founding of the Girl Scouts of the United States of America, the largest voluntary organization for girls and women in the world, which began on Mar 12, 1912. Special observances include: Girl Scout Sabbath, Mar 14, and Girl Scout Sunday, Mar 8, when Girl Scouts gather to attend religious services together; and Girl Scout Birthday, Mar 12. For info: Media Services, Girl Scouts of the USA, 420 Fifth Ave, New York, NY 10018. Phone: (212) 852-8000. Fax: (212) 852-6514. WWW: http://www.gsusa.org

INTERNATIONAL (WORKING) WOMEN'S DAY. Mar 8. A day to honor women, especially working women. Said to commemorate an 1857 march and demonstration in New York, NY, by female garment and textile workers. Believed to have been first proclaimed for this date at an international conference of women held in Helsinki, Finland, in 1910, "that henceforth March 8 should be declared International Women's Day." The 50th anniversary observance, at Peking, China, in 1960, cited Clara Zetkin (1857–1933) as "initiator of Women's Day on Mar 8." This is perhaps the most widely observed holiday of recent origin and is unusual among holidays originating in the US in having been widely adopted and observed in other nations, including socialist countries. In the USSR and the People's Republic of China it is a national holiday, and flowers or gifts are presented to women workers.

MOSBY CAPTURES STOUGHTON: ANNIVERSARY. Mar 8, 1863. In a daring raid with his commando-style raiders, Colonel John Mosby captured Union General E. H. Stoughton from his headquarters in Fairfax County Courthouse in Virginia on this date. Mosby's irregular forces patrolled a northern area of Virginia that became known as Mosby's Confederacy. Supported by the local populace and reviled by his Northern enemies, Mosby's Rangers were one of the most successful of the Southern irregular forces.

☆ ☆ ☆

NATURAL BRIDGE BATTLE RE-ENACTMENT. Mar 8. Tallahassee, FL. Re-enactment of the Confederate army's victory at the Natural Bridge site, which kept Tallahassee (the state capital) from falling into Union hands. Annually, the first full weekend in March. Est attendance: 2,500. For info: Natural Bridge Battlefield State Historic Site, 1022 DeSoto Park Dr, Tallahassee, FL 32301. Phone: (904) 922-6007. Fax: (904) 488-0366.

RUSSIA: INTERNATIONAL WOMEN'S DAY. Mar 8. National holiday.

"SEZ WHO?" FOURPLAY! MARCH MADNESS. Mar 8–30. Hooters, Chicago, IL. Two-player man-and-woman teams compete against one another, trying to complete humorous, provocative and otherwise memorable quotes made by basketball personalities. Annually, from the Sunday in March when NCAA Tournament field is announced through Monday, 22 days later, when the championship game is played. Est attendance: 600. Rich Bysina, PO Box 209, Winfield, IL 60190. Phone: (630) 682-3712.

SYRIAN ARAB REPUBLIC REVOLUTION DAY: ANNIVERSARY. Mar 8. Official public holiday commemorating assumption of power by Revolutionary National Council, Mar 8, 1963.

UNITED NATIONS: INTERNATIONAL WOMEN'S DAY. Mar 8. An international day observed by the organizations of the United Nations system. Info from: United Nations, Dept of Public Info, New York, NY 10017.

UNIVERSAL WOMEN'S WEEK. Mar 8–14. To remind ourselves and others of the value of women of all ages and classes and of their rights and dignity, and to honor outstanding women in the fields of government, business, industry, science, health, education, social work and the cultural arts by election to Universal Hall of Fame. Please send $3 to cover expense of printing, handling and postage. Annually, Mar 8–14. For info: Dr. Stanley Drake, Pres, Intl Soc of Friendship and Good Will, 412 Cherry Hills Dr, Bakersfield, CA 93309-2866.

March 1998

S	M	T	W	T	F	S
1	2	3	4	5	6	7
8	9	10	11	12	13	14
15	16	17	18	19	20	21
22	23	24	25	26	27	28
29	30	31				

VAN BUREN, HANNAH HOES: BIRTH ANNIVERSARY. Mar 8, 1783. Wife of Martin Van Buren, 8th president of the US. Born at Kinderhook, NY, Mar 8, 1783. Died Feb 5, 1819.

WARMEST US WINTER ON RECORD DECLARED: ANNIVERSARY. Mar 8. On Mar 8, 1992, the National Climatic Data Center declared the winter of 1991–92 the warmest US winter in the 97 years that the Federal Government had been keeping record of climatic conditions. The average temperature of 36.87 degrees Fahrenheit eclipsed the previous record set in 1953–54 of 36 degrees Fahrenheit.

BIRTHDAYS TODAY

George F. Allen, 46, Governor of Virginia (R), born Whittier, CA, Mar 8, 1952.

Cyd Charisse (Tula Finklea), 75, actress (*Silk Stockings*), dancer (*Grand Hotel, Singin' in the Rain*), born Amarillo, TX, Mar 8, 1923.

Susan Clark, 58, actress ("Webster," *Babe*), born Sarnia, Ontario, Canada, Mar 8, 1940.

Mickey Dolenz, 53, singer ("I'm a Believer"), actor ("The Monkees," "Circus Boy"), born Los Angeles, CA, Mar 8, 1945.

Charley Pride, 60, singer, former minor league baseball player, born Sledge, MS, Mar 8, 1938.

Aidan Quinn, 39, actor (*Desperately Seeking Susan*; stage: *A Streetcar Named Desire* [Theatre World Award]), born Chicago, IL, Mar 8, 1959.

Lynn Redgrave, 55, actress (*Georgy Girl*; Ann Anderson in "House Calls"), born London, England, Mar 8, 1943.

James Edward (Jim) Rice, 45, former baseball player, born Anderson, SC, Mar 8, 1953.

Carole Bayer Sager, 51, singer, songwriter ("That's What Friends Are For," with Burt Bacharach), born New York, NY, Mar 8, 1947.

Raynoma (Mayberry Liles) Gordy Singleton, 61, co-founder of Motown, born Detroit, MI, Mar 8, 1937.

Claire Trevor, 89, actress (*Key Largo, Stagecoach*), born New York, NY, Mar 8, 1909.

MARCH 9 — MONDAY

Day 68 — 297 Remaining

ADAMS, RICHARD C.: 10th DEATH ANNIVERSARY. Mar 9, 1988. Richard C. Adams, feeling challenged by the shortage of paintbrushes during World War II, invented the paint roller in 1940, while working in his basement. Adams died at La Mesa, CA, on this date.

AMERICAN BOWLING CONGRESS CONVENTION (WITH HALL OF FAME INDUCTION CEREMONIES). Mar 9–14. Reno, NV. Local, state and national bowling leaders gather to decide the rules of the game in a democratic setting. The week features board of directors' meetings, special seminars, dinners honoring top leaders, Hall of Fame induction ceremonies and workshops. Est attendance: 5,000. For info: Mark Miller, American Bowling Congress Conv, 5301 S 76th St, Greendale, WI 53129-0500. Phone: (414) 421-6400. Fax: (414) 421-7977.

BARBIE DEBUTS: ANNIVERSARY. Mar 9, 1959. The popular girls' doll debuted in stores. More than 800 million dolls have been sold.

BELIZE: BARON BLISS DAY. Mar 9. Official public holiday in Belize. Celebrated in honor of Sir Henry Edward Ernest Victor Bliss, a great benefactor of Belize.

CANADA: COMMONWEALTH DAY. Mar 9. Second Monday in March is observed as Commonwealth Day.

"FAMILY" TV PREMIERE: ANNIVERSARY. Mar 9, 1976. ABC drama about the Lawrence family living in Pasadena, CA, who stuck together through trials and triumphs. Cast members included: Sada Thompson as Kate Lawrence; James Broderick as her husband Douglas; Elaine Heilveil and Meredith Baxter-Birney as their divorced daughter Nancy Maitland; Gary Frank as their son Willie; and Kristy McNichol as youngest daughter Buddy (Letitia). The show was created by Jay Presson Allen and produced by Mike Nichols, Aaron Spelling.

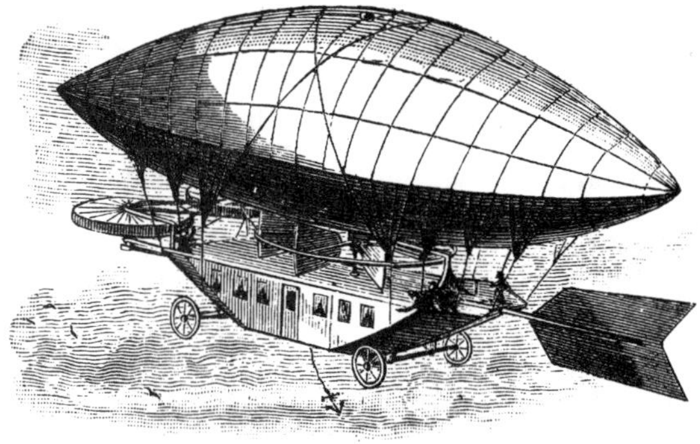

GAGARIN, YURI ALEXSEYEVICH: BIRTH ANNIVERSARY. Mar 9, 1934. Russian cosmonaut Yuri Gagarin, the first man to travel in space (Apr 12, 1961). Born at Gzhatsk, USSR, on Mar 9, 1934. The 27-year-old Soviet Air Force major made man's first flight in space, lasting 108 minutes and orbiting Earth in a rocket-propelled, five-ton space capsule, 187 miles above the Earth's surface. Gagarin was killed in an airplane crash near Moscow, USSR, on Mar 27, 1968. After his death the town in which he was born was renamed Gagarin, and the Gagarin Museum was established in the frame house where he spent his childhood.

GRANT COMMISSIONED COMMANDER OF ALL UNION ARMIES: ANNIVERSARY. Mar 9, 1863. In Washington, DC, Ulysses S. Grant accepted his commission as Lieutenant General, becoming the commander of all the Union armies.

JULIA, RAUL: BIRTH ANNIVERSARY. Mar 9, 1940. Born at San Juan, Puerto Rico, Julia became an actor after graduating from the University of Puerto Rico and moved to the US in 1964. He won acclaim and four Tony nominations for roles he played on Broadway ranging from Shakespeare's Proteus to Mack the Knife. Most widely known of his many film roles are Gomez in *The Addams Family* and *Addams Family Values* and Valentín in *Kiss of the Spider Woman*. Julia died Oct 24, 1994, at Manhasset, NY.

MOST BORING FILM AWARDS. Mar 9. 13th annual awards for the most boring films of the previous year. Categories include Comedy, Action and Big Stars-Big Flops. For info: Alan Caruba, Founder, The Boring Inst, PO Box 40, Maplewood, NJ 07040. Phone: (973) 763-6392. Fax: (973) 763-4287.

PANIC DAY. Mar 9. Run around all day in a panic, telling others you can't handle it anymore. [© 1997 by WPL] For info: Tom or Ruth Roy, Wellness Permission League, PO Box 662, Mt Gretna, PA 17064-0662. Phone: (500) 437-5104. Fax: (717) 964-1335.

SAINT FRANCES OF ROME: FEAST DAY. Mar 9. Patron of motorists and model for housewives and widows (1384–1440). After 40 years of marriage she was widowed in 1436 and later joined the community of Benedictine Oblates. Canonized in 1608.

SPACE MILESTONE: *SPUTNIK 9* (USSR). Mar 9, 1961. Dog, Chernushka (Blackie), was a passenger. Mar 9, 1961.

UNITED KINGDOM: COMMONWEALTH DAY. Mar 9. Replaces Empire Day observance recognized until 1958. Observed on second Monday in March.

VESPUCCI, AMERIGO: BIRTH ANNIVERSARY. Mar 9. Italian navigator, merchant and explorer for whom the Americas were named. Born at Florence, Italy, probably on Mar 9, 1451. He participated in at least two expeditions between 1499 and 1502, which took him to the coast of South America, where he discovered the Amazon and Plata rivers. Vespucci's expeditions were of great importance because he believed that he had discovered a new continent, not just a new route to the Orient. Neither Vespucci nor his exploits achieved the fame of Columbus, but the New World was to be named not for Columbus, but for Amerigo Vespucci, by an obscure German geographer and mapmaker, Martin Waldseemuller. See also: "Waldseemuller, Martin: Remembrance Day" (Apr 25). Ironically, in his work as an outfitter of ships, Vespucci had been personally acquainted with Christopher Columbus. Vespucci died at Seville, Spain, on Feb 22, 1512.

BIRTHDAYS TODAY

Brian Keith Bosworth, 33, former football player, born Oklahoma City, OK, Mar 9, 1965.
Robert James (Bobby) Fischer, 55, World Chess Champion (1972), born Chicago, IL, Mar 9, 1943.
Mickey Gilley, 62, singer/musician ("City Lights," "Stand by Me"), cousin of Jerry Lee Lewis, born Natchez, MS, Mar 9, 1936.
Marty Ingels, 62, actor, former comedian ("I'm Dickens . . . He's Fenster," *A Guide for the Married Man*), born Brooklyn, NY, Mar 9, 1936.
David Hume Kennerly, 51, photographer, born Rosenburg, OR, Mar 9, 1947.
Emmanuel Lewis, 27, actor ("Webster"), born Brooklyn, NY, Mar 9, 1971.
Jeffrey Osborne, 50, musician, songwriter, born Providence, RI, Mar 9, 1948.
Benito Santiago, 33, baseball player, born Ponce, Puerto Rico, Mar 9, 1965.
Mickey Spillane (Frank Morrison), 80, author (*The Killing Man, Vengeance Is Mine*), born Brooklyn, NY, Mar 9, 1918.
Trish Van Devere, 55, actress (*Where's Poppa?, One Is a Lonely Number*), born Tenafly, NJ, Mar 9, 1943.
Joyce Van Patten, 64, actress (*Monkey Shines*, "The Goodbye Guys"), born Queens, NY, Mar 9, 1934.

MARCH 10 — TUESDAY

Day 69 — 296 Remaining

"THE INCREDIBLE HULK" TV PREMIERE: 20th ANNIVERSARY. Mar 10, 1978. A wonderfully campy action series based on the popular Marvel comic books as well as a modern day Jekyll and Hyde story. Bill Bixby played the erudite scientist, Dr. David Banner, who accidentally exposed himself to gamma radiation. When provoked, Banner metamorphosed into the shirt-shredding, body-baring, green-skinned, gnarling neanderthal Hulk. The 6′5″, 275-lb former Mr Universe, Lou Ferrigno, played the largely non-speaking part of the Hulk.

JUPITER EFFECT: ANNIVERSARY. Mar 10, 1982. The much-talked-about and sometimes-feared planetary configuration of a semi-alignment of the planets on the same side of the sun occurred on this date without causing any of the disasters or unusual natural phenomena that some had predicted. See the 1982 edition of *Chase's Annual Events* for diagram and detailed description.

LUCE, CLAIRE BOOTHE: 95th BIRTH ANNIVERSARY. Mar 10, 1903. Playwright and politician Claire Boothe Luce was born at New York City. Luce wrote for and edited *Vogue* and *Vanity Fair* as well as writing plays, three of which were later adapted into motion pictures—*The Women* (1936), *Kiss the Boys Goodbye* (1938) and *Margin of Error* (1939). She served in the US House of Representatives (1943–47) and as ambassador to Italy (1953–56)—the first woman appointed ambassador to a major country. Luce died Oct 9, 1987, at Washington, DC.

MALPIGHI, MARCELLO: BIRTH ANNIVERSARY. Mar 10, 1628. Italian physician, physiologist, author and teacher, called the "father of microscopic anatomy." Born near Bologna, Italy, on Mar 10, 1628. Malpighi was a pioneer in the use of the microscope for biological and botanical study. Died at Rome, Italy, on Nov 30, 1694.

MARIO DAY. Mar 10. A day for all persons named Mario. Using the abbreviation for the month of March, i.e., MAR, with the day i.e., 10, you get the name spelled out: MAR10. Annually, Mar 10. For info: Mario Fascitelli, 6005 Osuna Rd, NE, Albuquerque, NM 87109. Phone: (505) 881-2414. Fax: (505) 889-8661. Email: C21Allied@aol.com.

PAPER MONEY ISSUED: ANNIVERSARY. Mar 10, 1862. The first paper money was issued in the US on this date. The denominations were $5 (Hamilton), $10 (Lincoln) and $20 (Liberty). They were not legal tender when first issued but became so by Act of March 17, 1862.

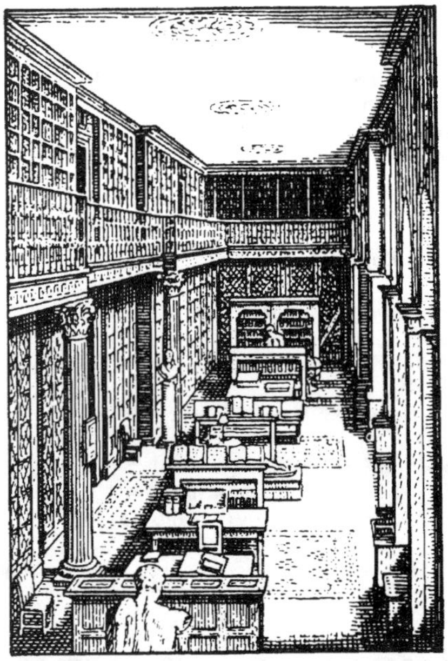

PUBLIC LIBRARY ASSOCIATION CONFERENCE. Mar 10–14. Kansas City, MO. Exhibits, panels, workshops. For info: Public Library Assn, American Library Assn, 50 E Huron St, Chicago, IL 60611. Phone: (312) 280-5028. Fax: (312) 280-5029. WWW: http://www.ala.org

SALVATION ARMY IN THE USA: ANNIVERSARY. Mar 10, 1880. On this day Commissioner George Scott Railton and seven women officers landed in New York to officially begin the work of the Salvation Army in the United States.

TELEPHONE INVENTION: ANNIVERSARY. Mar 10. Alexander Graham Bell transmitted the first telephone message to his assistant in the next room: "Mr Watson, come here, I want you," on Mar 10, 1876, at Cambridge, MA. See also: "Bell, Alexander Graham: Birth Anniversary" (Mar 3).

TRIUMPH OF AGRICULTURE EXPOSITION FARM AND RANCH MACHINERY SHOW. Mar 10–11. Civic Auditorium, Omaha, NE. For info: Robert P. Mancuso, Mid-America Expositions, Inc, 1613 Farnam Bldg, Suite 666, Omaha, NE 68102. Phone: (402) 346-8003. Fax: (402) 346-5412.

TUBMAN, HARRIET: 85th DEATH ANNIVERSARY. Mar 10, 1913. American abolitionist, Underground Railroad leader, born a slave at Bucktown, Dorchester County, MD, about 1820 or 1821. Died at Auburn, NY, Mar 10, 1913. She escaped from a Maryland plantation in 1849 and later helped more than 300 slaves reach freedom.

March 1998

S	M	T	W	T	F	S
1	2	3	4	5	6	7
8	9	10	11	12	13	14
15	16	17	18	19	20	21
22	23	24	25	26	27	28
29	30	31				

WALD, LILLIAN D.: BIRTH ANNIVERSARY. Mar 10, 1867. American sociologist, founder of the Henry Street Settlement in New York City and of the first nonsectarian public health nursing service. Born at Cincinnati, OH, died at Westport, CT, Sept 1, 1940, at age 73.

BIRTHDAYS TODAY

Heywood Hale Broun, 80, broadcaster, born New York, NY, Mar 10, 1918.

Kim Campbell, 51, first woman prime minister of Canada, born Vancouver Island, British Columbia, Mar 10, 1947.

Prince Edward, 34, son of Queen Elizabeth II, born London, England, Mar 10, 1964.

Bob Greene, 51, journalist, born Columbus, OH, Mar 10, 1947.

Chuck Norris, 58, actor (*Missing in Action*, "Walker, Texas Ranger"), born Ryan, OK, Mar 10, 1940.

David Rabe, 58, playwright, born Dubuque, IA, Mar 10, 1940.

Sharon Stone, 40, actress (*Basic Instinct, The Specialist, Casino*), born Meadville, PA, Mar 10, 1958.

MARCH 11 — WEDNESDAY

Day 70 — 295 Remaining

BUREAU OF INDIAN AFFAIRS ESTABLISHED: ANNIVERSARY. Mar 11, 1824. The US War Department created the Bureau of Indian Affairs.

CAMPBELL, MALCOLM: BIRTH ANNIVERSARY. Mar 11, 1885. Record-making British auto racer, the first man to travel five miles a minute (300 mph) in an automobile. Born at Chislehurst, Kent, England, on Mar 11, 1885. Died at his home in Surrey, England, Dec 31, 1948.

CANADA: EDMONTON BOAT AND SPORTSMEN'S SHOW. Mar 11–15. Northlands Agricom, Edmonton, Northlands, Alberta. Fishing, sailing and powerboats, hunting and camping supplies, resort destinations, outdoor recreation, RVs and motor homes, 4-wheel drive vehicles, mountain bikes and family entertainment. Est attendance: 34,700. For info: Canadian Natl Sportsmen's Shows, 703 Evans Ave, Ste 202, Toronto, Ont, Canada M9C 5E9. Phone: (416) 695-0311. Fax: (416) 695-0381.

JOHNNY APPLESEED DAY (JOHN CHAPMAN DEATH ANNIVERSARY). Mar 11. Anniversary of the death on Mar 11, 1845, of John Chapman, better known as Johnny Appleseed, believed to have been born at Leominster, MA, Sept 26, 1774. The planter of orchards and friend of wild animals was regarded by the Indians as a great medicine man. He died at Allen County, IN. See also: "Johnny Appleseed: Birth Anniversary" (Sept 26).

LEARNING DISABILITIES ASSOCIATION OF AMERICA INTERNATIONAL CONFERENCE. Mar 11–14. Washington Hilton, Washington, DC. Est attendance: 5,200. For info: Jean S. Peterson, Natl Exec Dir, Learning Disabilities Assn of America, 4156 Library Rd, Pittsburgh, PA 15234. Phone: (412) 341-1515. Fax: (412) 344-0224. Email: ldanatl@usaor.net. WWW: http://www.ldanatl.org

LEND-LEASE PROGRAM BEGINS: ANNIVERSARY. Mar 11, 1941. The Lend-Lease Bill, which enabled Britain to borrow money from the US to buy food and arms during World War II, went into effect.

NAIA MEN'S DIVISION II BASKETBALL NATIONAL CHAMPIONSHIP TOURNAMENT. Mar 11–17. Idaho Center, Nampa, ID. 32-team field competes for the national championship. 7th annual. Est attendance: 30,000. For info: Natl Assn of Intercollegiate Athletics, 6120 S Yale Ave, Ste 1450, Tulsa, OK 74136. Phone: (918) 494-8828. Fax: (918) 494-8841. Email: khenry@naia.org. WWW: http://www.naia.org

NAIA WOMEN'S DIVISION II BASKETBALL NATIONAL CHAMPIONSHIP TOURNAMENT. Mar 11–17. Sioux City, IA. 32-team field competes for the national championship. 7th annual. Est attendance: 12,500. For info: Natl

Assn of Intercollegiate Athletics, 6120 S Yale Ave, Ste 1450, Tulsa, OK 74136. Phone: (918) 494-8828. Fax: (918) 494-8841. Email: khenry@naia.org. WWW: http://www.naia.org

OUTRIGGER HOTELS HAWAIIAN MOUNTAIN TOUR. Mar 11–15. Oahu, HI. Televised, preseason, 5-stage, international mountain bike race for professionals and amateurs. Includes Prologue, Time Trial, Cross Country, Downhill, Point-to-Point and Criterium. $20,000 pro purse awarded for men's and women's stages, overall individual GC and team GC. Cytomaximizer Downhill Stage Race held in conjunction. Est attendance: 10,000. For info: Event Marketing, Inc, Pauahi Tower, 1001 Bishop St, #880, Honolulu, HI 96813. Phone: (808) 521-4322. Fax: (808) 538-0314. Email: dey@emisport.
WWW: http://www.emisport.com

PAINE, ROBERT TREAT: BIRTH ANNIVERSARY. Mar 11, 1731. Jurist and signer of the Declaration of Independence. Born at Boston, MA, died there May 11, 1814.

PANDEMIC OF 1918 HITS US: 80th ANNIVERSARY. Mar 11, 1918. The first cases of the "Spanish" influenza were reported in the US when 107 soldiers became sick at Fort Riley, KS. By the end of 1920 nearly 25% of the US population had had it. As many as 500,000 civilians died from the virus, exceeding the number of US troops killed abroad in World War I. Worldwide, more than 1% of the global population, or 22 million people, had died by 1920. The origin of the virus was never determined absolutely, though it was probably somewhere in Asia. The name "Spanish" influenza came from the relatively high number of cases in that country early in the epidemic. Due to the panic, cancellation of public events was common and many public service workers wore masks on the job. Emergency tent hospitals were set up in some locations due to overcrowding.

"SMALL FRY CLUB" TV PREMIERE: ANNIVERSARY. Mar 11, 1947. A precursor to current children's programs, "Small Fry Club" premiered on the DuMont network with "Big Brother" Bob Emery as host. The show was extremely popular and innovative in using cartoons, skits, puppets, songs and demonstrations to attract the attention of its young viewers.

SPRINGTIME TALLAHASSEE. Mar 11–Apr 11. Tallahassee, FL. This 31st annual festival celebrates Florida's capital city, Tallahassee, "the city where spring begins!" Mar 11: A.J. Breakfast in the Park; Mar 21: Springtacular: A Children's Parade and Family Festival; Apr 4: Grand Parade and Jubilee on the streets of downtown Tallahassee. Sponsored in part by Coca-Cola, Powertel, AMSOUTH Bank. Est attendance: 250,000. For info: Anita Gregory, Exec Dir, Springtime Tallahassee, PO Box 1465, Tallahassee, FL 32302-1465. Phone: (904) 224-1373. Fax: (904) 224-0833.

TA'ANIT ESTHER (FAST OF ESTHER). Mar 11. Hebrew calendar date: Adar 13, 5758. Commemorates Queen Esther's fast, in the 6th century BC, to save the Jews of ancient Persia. Ordinarily observed Adar 13, the Fast of Esther is observed on the previous Thursday (Adar 11) when Adar 13 is a Sabbath.

TASSO, TORQUATO: BIRTH ANNIVERSARY. Mar 11, 1544. Poet of the late Renaissance, born at Sorrento, Italy. His violent outbursts and acute sensitivity to criticism led to his imprisonment for seven years, during which the "misunderstood genius" continued his literary creativity. Died at Rome, Italy, Apr 25, 1595.

WELK, LAWRENCE: 95th BIRTH ANNIVERSARY. Mar 11, 1903. Bandleader Lawrence Welk was born in Strasburg, ND. He learned to play the accordion and at 17 formed his first band. He left home at the age of 21 and, after playing all over the Midwest, he moved to Los Angeles where in 1955 his show began its nationwide television broadcast of "Champagne Music." The longest-running program in TV history, "The Lawrence Welk Show" played each Saturday on ABC from 1955 until 1971 when it was dropped because sponsors thought its audience was too old. Welk managed to keep the show on a network of more than 250 independent stations for 11 more years and it still can be seen in reruns. Welk's entertainment empire expanded to include the purchase of royalty rights to songs, including the entire collection of songs by Jerome Kern and the Lawrence Welk Village in Escondido, CA. Welk died at Santa Monica, CA, on May 17, 1992.

WILSON, HAROLD: BIRTH ANNIVERSARY. Mar 11, 1916. British statesman and twice prime minister (1964–70 and 1974–76), leader of the Labor Party. Born at Huddersfield, Yorkshire. He died May 24, 1995, at London.

BIRTHDAYS TODAY

Douglas Adams, 46, author (*Hitchhiker's Guide to the Galaxy*), born England, Mar 11, 1952.
Sam Donaldson, 64, journalist, born El Paso, TX, Mar 11, 1934.
Bobby McFerrin, 48, jazz musician, singer, songwriter, born New York, NY, Mar 11, 1950.
Robert Adam Mosbacher, 71, Secretary of Commerce, born Mt Vernon, NY, Mar 11, 1927.
Rupert Murdoch, 67, newspaper publisher (*New York Post, The Boston Herald*), born Melbourne, Australia, Mar 11, 1931.
Dominique Sanda, 47, actress (*The Garden of the Finzi-Continis, 1900*), born Paris, France, Mar 11, 1951.
Antonin Scalia, 62, Associate Justice of the US Supreme Court, born Trenton, NJ, Mar 11, 1936.

MARCH 12 — THURSDAY

Day 71 — 294 Remaining

ATATÜRK, MUSTAFA KEMAL: BIRTH ANNIVERSARY. Mar 12, 1881. The founder of modern Turkey was born at Salonika, Greece (then part of the Ottoman Empire). After a distinguished army career, he led the Turkish revolution after World War I and was elected Turkey's first president. He died at Istanbul, Nov 10, 1938.

AUSTRIA INVADED BY NAZI GERMANY. Mar 12, 1938. As a test of its own war readiness and of the response of the other major powers, Germany occupied Austria. A year later Germany invaded Czechoslovakia and, in September, Poland, beginning World War II.

BERMUDA COLONIZED BY ENGLISH: ANNIVERSARY. Mar 12, 1609. The ship of Admiral Sir George Somers, taking settlers to Virginia, was wrecked on the reefs of Bermuda. The islands had been discovered in the early 1500s but were uninhabitated until 1609.

BOYCOTT, CHARLES CUNNINGHAM: BIRTH ANNIVERSARY. Mar 12, 1832. Charles Cunningham Boycott, born at Norfolk, England, Mar 12, 1832, has been immortalized by having his name become part of the English language. In County Mayo, Ireland, the Tenants' "Land League" in 1880 asked Boycott, an estate agent, to reduce rents (because of poor harvest and dire economic conditions). Boycott responded by serving eviction notices on the tenants, who retaliated by refusing to have any dealings with him. Boycott died at Suffolk, England, on June 19, 1897.

CANADA: QUEBEC CITY SPORTSMEN'S SHOW. Mar 12–15. Parc de l'Exposition, Quebec City, Quebec. Major manufacturers, distributors and retailers of the outdoors, including camping, fishing and hunting, fishing boats, canoes, kayaks and other craft; tourism, campgrounds, outfitters, lodges and entertainment. Est attendance: 16,000. For info: Canadian Natl Sportsmen's Shows, 703 Evans Ave, Ste 202, Toronto, Ont, Canada M9C 5E9. Phone: (416) 695-0311. Fax: (416) 695-0381.

CHURCH OF ENGLAND ORDAINS WOMEN PRIESTS: ANNIVERSARY. Mar 12, 1994. The Church of England for the first time ordained 32 women at Bristol Cathedral. About 700 male members of the clergy and unknown thouands of members indicated they would leave the Church of England and join the Roman Catholic Church. The Catholic Church responded to the ordination by saying that it "constitutes a profound obstacle to every hope of reunion between the Catholic Church and the Anglican Communion." This day's ordinations were not the first. In early 1994 about 1,380 women priests were ordained in churches of the Anglican Communion outside of Great Britain.

FDR'S FIRST FIRESIDE CHAT: 65th ANNIVERSARY. Mar 12, 1933. President Franklin Delano Roosevelt made the first of his Sunday evening "fireside chats" to the American people on Mar 12, 1933. Speaking by radio from the White House, he reported rather informally on the economic problems of the nation and on his actions to deal with them.

GIRL SCOUTS OF THE USA FOUNDING: ANNIVERSARY. Mar 12, 1912. Juliet Low founded Girl Scouts of the USA at Savannah, GA.

GREAT BLIZZARD OF '88: ANNIVERSARY. Mar 12, 1888. One of the most devastating blizzards to hit northeastern US began in the early hours of Monday, Mar 12, 1888. A snowfall of 40–50 inches, accompanied by gale force winds, left drifts as high as 30–40 feet. More than 400 persons died in the storm (200 in New York City alone). Some survivors of the storm, "The Blizzard Men of 1888," held annual meetings in New York City as late as 1941 to recount personal recollections of the event.

KEROUAC, JACK: BIRTH ANNIVERSARY. Mar 12, 1922. American poet and novelist Jack (Jean-Louis) Kerouac, leader and spokesman for the Beat movement, was born at Lowell, MA. Kerouac is best known for his novel *On the Road*, published in 1957, which celebrates the Beat ideal of nonconformity. In 1950 Kerouac published his first novel, *The Town and the City*, which did well critically, but its conventionality left him feeling in need of a new form for expressing himself. Kerouac published *The Dharma Bums* in 1958, followed by *The Subterraneans* the same year, *Doctor Sax* and its sequel *Maggie Cassidy* in 1959, *Lonesome Traveler* in 1960, *Big Sur* in 1962 and *Desolation Angels* in 1965. Kerouac died at St. Petersburg, FL, at age 47 on Oct 21, 1969. A previously unpublished part of *On the Road* called *Visions of Cody* was published posthumously in 1972.

LESOTHO: MOSHOESHOE'S DAY. Mar 12. National holiday.

LUNAR ECLIPSE. Mar 12–13. Penumbral eclipse of the moon. Moon enters penumbra at approximately 9:14 PM, EST, reaches middle of eclipse at 11:20 PM, EST and leaves penumbra at 1:25 AM, EST. The beginning of the penumbral phase visible in North America except Alaska and northwestern Canada, Central America, South America, Europe, western Asia, Africa, Greenland, the North Polar region, parts of Antarctica, the eastern South Pacific Ocean, the southeastern North Pacific Ocean, the Atlantic Ocean and western Indian Ocean; the end visible in North America, Central America, South America, Greenland, Iberian Peninsula, western France, British Isles, extreme western Africa, parts of Antarctica, extreme eastern Asia, the eastern half of the Pacific Ocean, the North Atlantic Ocean and the western South Atlantic Ocean.

MAURITIUS: INDEPENDENCE DAY: 30th ANNIVERSARY. Mar 12, 1968. National holiday commemorates attainment of independent nationhood (within the British Commonwealth) on Mar 12, 1968.

MOON PHASE: FULL MOON. Mar 12. Moon enters Full Moon phase at 11:34 PM, EST.

NEWCOMB, SIMON: BIRTH ANNIVERSARY. Mar 12, 1835. Astronomer, born at Wallace, NS. Newcomb investigated the orbits of Uranus, Neptune and the inner planets and devised planetary tables that were used universally by observatories. Died at Washington DC, July 11, 1909.

PIERCE, JANE MEANS APPLETON: BIRTH ANNIVERSARY. Mar 12, 1806. Wife of Franklin Pierce, 14th president of the US. Born at Hampton, NH. Died Dec 2, 1863.

PURIM. Mar 12. Hebrew calendar date: Adar 14, 5758. Feasts, gifts, charity and the reading of the Book of Esther mark this joyous commemoration of Queen Esther's intervention, in the 6th century BC, to save the Jews of ancient Persia. Haman's plot to exterminate the Jews was thwarted, and he was hanged on the very day he had set for execution of the Jews.

SAINT PATRICK'S DAY DART TOURNAMENT. Mar 12–15. Battle Creek, MI. 14th annual tournament with seven separate contests to celebrate the luck of the Irish by encouraging the fast-growing interest in the US in the sport of darting. Annually, beginning the Thursday on or before St. Patrick's Day. Est attendance: 200. For info: Bill Buckner, Owner, Springbrook Golf Course, 1600 Ave A, Battle Creek, MI 49015. Phone: (616) 965-6512.

SPACE MILESTONE: *SOYUZ T-4* (USSR). Mar 12, 1981. Launched Mar 12, 1981. Two cosmonauts (V. Kovalyonok and V. Savinykh) docked at *Salyut 6* space station (in orbit since Sept 29, 1977) on Mar 13. Returned to Earth May 26, after 75 days in space.

SUN YAT-SEN: DEATH ANNIVERSARY. Mar 12, 1925. The heroic leader of China's 1911 revolution is remembered on the anniversary of his death at Peking, China. Observed as Arbor Day in Taiwan.

WORLD'S LARGEST CONCERT. Mar 12 (tentative). To kick off Music in Our Schools Month, the World's Largest Concert will be broadcast on PBS stations nationally and over the Armed Forces Television Network overseas. Send $3 to cover shipping for "Teacher's Guide." Approx participation: 8,000,000. For info: Judy Humphrey, Mgr Special Programs, Music Educators Natl Conference, 1806 Robert Fulton Dr, Reston, VA 20191. Phone: (800) 336-3768 or (703) 860-4000. Fax: (703) 860-1531. WWW: http://www.menc.org

March 1998

S	M	T	W	T	F	S
1	2	3	4	5	6	7
8	9	10	11	12	13	14
15	16	17	18	19	20	21
22	23	24	25	26	27	28
29	30	31				

BIRTHDAYS TODAY

Edward Albee, 70, playwright, born Washington, DC, Mar 12, 1928.

Kent Conrad, 50, US Senator (D, North Dakota), born Bismarck, ND, Mar 12, 1948.

Barbara Feldon, 57, actress (played 99 on "Get Smart"; *Smile*), born Pittsburgh, PA, Mar 12, 1941.

Marlon Jackson, 41, singer (Jackson 5), born Gary, IN, Mar 12, 1957.

Al (Alwin) Jarreau, 58, singer, songwriter, born Milwaukee, WI, Mar 12, 1940.

Liza Minnelli, 52, singer ("Come Saturday Morning"), actress (Oscar for *Cabaret; The Sterile Cuckoo, Arthur*), born Los Angeles, CA, Mar 12, 1946.

Dale Bryan Murphy, 42, former baseball player, born Portland, OR, Mar 12, 1956.

Wally Schirra, 75, former astronaut, born Hackensack, NJ, Mar 12, 1923.

Darryl Eugene Strawberry, 36, baseball player, born Los Angeles, CA, Mar 12, 1962.

James Taylor, 50, singer, musician ("You've Got a Friend," "Handy Man"), born Boston, MA, Mar 12, 1948.

John D. Waihee III, 72, former Governor of Hawaii (D), born Honolulu, HI, Mar 12, 1926.

Andrew Young, 66, civil rights leader, former mayor of Atlanta, GA, born New Orleans, LA, Mar 12, 1932.

MARCH 13 — FRIDAY

Day 72 — 293 Remaining

ARAB OIL EMBARGO LIFTED: ANNIVERSARY. Mar 13, 1974. The oil-producing Arab countries agreed to lift their five-month embargo on petroleum sales to the US. During the embargo prices went up 300 percent and a ban was imposed on Sunday gasoline sales. The embargo was in retaliation for US support of Israel during the October 1973 Middle-East War.

BLACK HERITAGE FESTIVAL OF LOUISIANA. Mar 13–14. New Orleans, LA. Cultural, educational and fun activities showcasing the achievements and talents of blacks. Features an art exhibit, talent show, storytellers, national performers and exhibitors and a children's area. Est attendance: 8,000. For info: Louadrian Reed, Black Heritage Foundation, PO Box 60131, New Orleans, LA 70160. Phone: (504) 827-0112.

CANADA: SPAGHETTI BRIDGE BUILDING CONTEST. Mar 13. Kelowna, British Columbia. To challenge the world to match our expertise in Spaghetti Bridge design. World record load 176kg (388 lb), suspended from a one-meter-long bridge weighing less than 0.75kg (1.66 lb). Annually, in March. Est attendance: 500. For info: Karen Shaw, Exec Dir of Admin, Okanagan University College, 1000 KLO Rd, Kelowna, BC, Canada V1Y 4X8. Phone: (250) 862-5662. Fax: (250) 862-5476. Email: kshaw@okanagan.bc.ca. WWW: http://www.okanagan.bc.ca

CANADA: TORONTO SPORTSMEN'S SHOW. Mar 13–22. National Trade Center, Exhibition Place, Toronto, Ontario. Fishing manufacturers and retailers, fishing seminars, travel/vacation exhibits, cottages, camping products, boats and marine accessories, wildlife art, decoy championships, pet products and breeders, conservation and outdoor organizations, sporting goods, retriever trials, arena show and family entertainment. Est attendance: 180,000. For info: Canadian Natl Sportsmen's Shows, 703 Evans Ave, Ste 202, Toronto, Ont, Canada M9C 5E9. Phone: (416) 695-0311. Fax: (416) 695-0381.

CLARENCE DARROW DEATH COMMEMORATION. Mar 13. Jackson Park, Chicago, IL. Annually, on the anniversary of his death, a wreath is tossed from the Jackson Park Clarence Darrow Bridge, named in honor of the famed lawyer and civil libertarian. At 10 AM. At 11 AM a discussion follows in the Columbian Room of the Museum of Science and Industry. Est attendance: 100. For info: Herb Kraus, 875 N Michigan, Ste 2250, Chicago, IL 60611. Phone: (312) 266-7800 or (312) 640-6791. Fax: (312) 266-2874.

DEAF HISTORY MONTH. Mar 13–Apr 15. Observance of three of the most important anniversaries for deaf Americans: Apr 15, 1817, establishment of the first public school for the deaf in America, later known as The American School for the Deaf; Apr 8, 1864, charter signed by President Lincoln authorizing the Board of Directors of the Columbia Institution (now Gallaudet University) to grant college degrees to deaf students; Mar 13, 1988, the victory of the Deaf President Now movement at Gallaudet. To help set up a program at libraries, schools, and other organizations, the Friends of Libraries for Deaf Access, Inc (FOLDA, Inc) has developed resources promoting public awareness about the deaf community and its rich history. For info: Alice L. Hagemeyer, Coord of Deaf Awareness Events, FOLDA, Inc, 9126 Fowler Ln, Lanham, MD 20706. Phone: (301) 572-5168. Fax: (301) 572-4134. Email: alhagemeyer@juno.com.

DELMONICO, LORENZO: BIRTH ANNIVERSARY. Mar 13, 1813. Famed restaurateur and gastronomic authority. Born Mar 13, 1813, at Marengo, Switzerland. Operated a number of restaurants in New York, NY. Died there Sept 3, 1881.

EARMUFFS PATENTED: ANNIVERSARY. Mar 13, 1887. Chester Greenwood of Maine received a patent for earmuffs on this date.

FILLMORE, ABIGAIL POWERS: 200th BIRTH ANNIVERSARY. Mar 13, 1798. First wife of Millard Fillmore, 13th president of the US. Born at Stillwater, NY, Mar 13, 1798. Died Mar 30, 1853. It is said that the White House was without any books until Abigail Fillmore, formerly a teacher, made a room on the second floor into a library. Within a year, Congress appropriated $250 for the president to spend on library books for the White House.

GOOD SAMARITAN INVOLVEMENT DAY. Mar 13. A day to emphasize the importance of unselfish aid to those who need it. Recognized on the anniversary of the killing of Catherine (Kitty) Genovese, Mar 13, 1964, in the Kew Gardens community, Queens, NY. Reportedly no fewer than 38 of her neighbors, not wanting "to get involved," witnessed and watched for nearly 30 minutes as the fleeing girl was pursued and repeatedly stabbed by her 29-year-old attacker.

HUBBARD, L. RON: BIRTH ANNIVERSARY. Mar 13. Lafayette Ronald Hubbard, science fiction writer, recluse and founder of the Church of Scientology. Born at Tilden, NE, Mar 13, 1911. His best-known book was *Dianetics: The Modern Science of Mental Health.* Died at San Luis Obispo County, CA, on Jan 24, 1986.

"THE LARRY KING SHOW" TV PREMIERE: 15th ANNIVERSARY. Mar 13, 1983. Radio talk show host Larry King brought his topical interview program to syndicated TV in 1983. Using a telephone hook-up, viewers called in to speak to particular guests. King has been appearing on CNN since 1985 interviewing a variety of newsmakers and celebrities.

LONGHORN WORLD CHAMPIONSHIP RODEO. Mar 13–15. Show Me Center, Cape Girardeau, MO. More than 220 of the best cowboys and cowgirls compete in six professional contests ranging from bronc riding to bull riding for top prize money and world championship points. Featuring colorful opening pageantry and Big, Bad BONUS Bulls. 11th annual. Est attendance: 14,000. For info: W. Bruce Lehrke, Pres, Longhorn World Chmpshp Rodeo, Inc, PO Box 70159, Nashville, TN 37207. Phone: (615) 876-1016. Fax: (615) 876-4685. Email: lhrodeo@idt.net. WWW: http://www.longhornrodeo.com

LOWELL, PERCIVAL: BIRTH ANNIVERSARY. Mar 13. American astronomer, founder of the Lowell Observatory at Flagstaff, AZ. Born at Boston, MA, Mar 13, 1855. Died at Flagstaff on Nov 12, 1916. Lowell was initiator of the search that resulted (25 years after the search began and 14 years after his death) in discovery of the planet Pluto. The discovery was announced on Lowell's birthday, Mar 13, 1930, by the Lowell Observatory.

NAIA WRESTLING NATIONAL CHAMPIONSHIPS. Mar 13–14. Jamestown Civic Center, Jamestown, ND. Individuals compete for All-America honors in 12 weight divisions, while teams compete for the national championship. 41st annual competition. Est attendance: 4,000. For info: Natl Assn of Intercollegiate Athletics, 6120 S Yale Ave, Ste 1450, Tulsa, OK 74136. Phone: (918) 494-8828. Fax: (918) 494-8841. Email: khenry@naia.org. WWW: http://www.naia.org

NCAA MEN'S BASKETBALL CHAMPIONSHIP FIRST/SECOND ROUNDS. Mar 13 (also Mar 15). Myriad Convention Center, Oklahoma City, OK. Eight universities competing which are selected at-large or have won conference titles. Three doubleheader sessions. The two winners go to round one of the Final Four. Est attendance: 40,000. For info: Stanley Draper, Exec Secretary, Oklahoma City All Sports Assn, 100 W Main, Ste 285, Oklahoma City, OK 73102. Phone: (405) 236-5000. Fax: (405) 236-5008.

NORTHWEST CRIBBAGE TOURNAMENT. Mar 13–15. Baker City, OR. Est attendance: 200. For info: Baker County VCB, 490 Campbell St, Baker City, OR 97814. Phone: (800) 523-1235 or (541) 523-3356.

OPERATION FLASH: 55th ANNIVERSARY. Mar 13, 1943. Disillusioned German officers planned to take the life of Adolf Hitler on this date. Hitler was to stop at Smolensk on his way to his headquarters and an officer who was not involved in the plot had been commissioned to deliver a package to Hitler's plane which he was told contained two bottles of liquor for a friend in Rastenburg. A bomb in the package was timed to go off over Minsk, but it reached Rastenburg without detonating. The package was later recovered and a defective detonator was found. See also: "Gersdorff Hitler Assassination Attempt" (Mar 21).

PLANET URANUS DISCOVERY: ANNIVERSARY. Mar 13. German-born English astronomer Sir William Herschel discovered the 7th planet from the sun, Uranus, on Mar 13, 1781.

PRIESTLY, JOSEPH: BIRTH ANNIVERSARY. Mar 13, 1733. English clergyman and scientist, discoverer of oxygen. Born at Fieldhead, England, Mar 13, 1733. He and his family narrowly escaped an angry mob attacking their home because of his religious and political views. They moved to the US in 1794. Died at Northumberland, PA, Feb 6, 1804.

RATTLESNAKE ROUNDUP. Mar 13–15. Sweetwater, TX. Educational programs about rattlesnakes, flea market, gun, knife, and coin show, large cookoff, dances, numerous pounds of live rattlesnakes on display, snake meat available to eat and snake articles for sale. Snake hunts and bus tours available. Annually, the second weekend in March. Est attendance: 30,000. For info: Sweetwater Chamber of Commerce, PO Box 1148, Sweetwater, TX 79556. Phone: (915) 235-5488 or (800) 658-6757. Fax: (915) 235-1026. WWW: http://camalott.com/~sweetwater

SAINT AUBIN, HELEN "CALLAGHAN" CANDAELE: BIRTH ANNIVERSARY. Mar 13, 1929. Helen Candaele St. Aubin, known as Helen Callaghan during her baseball days, was born at Vancouver, BC, Canada. St. Aubin and her sister, Margaret Maxwell, were recruited for the All-American Girls Professional Baseball League, which flourished in the 1940s when many major league players were off fighting World War II. She first played at age 15 for the Minneapolis Millerettes, an expansion team that moved to Indiana and became the Ft Wayne Daisies. For the 1945 season the left-handed outfielder led the league with a .299 average and 24 extra base hits. In 1946 she stole 114 bases in 111 games. Her son Kelly Candaele's documentary on the women's baseball league inspired the film *A League of Their Own*. St. Aubin, who was known as the "Ted Williams of women's baseball," died Dec 8, 1992, at Santa Barbara, CA.

SAINT PATRICK'S DAY CELEBRATION BEARD-GROWING CONTEST. Mar 13–15. Shamrock, TX. All men in town must either grow a beard or purchase a permit, and they must begin growing beard after Jan 1, 1998. Celebration also includes Miss Irish Rose Pageant, chuck wagon cook off, rodeo events and dances. Est attendance: 10,000. For info: Jim Triplett, Chamber of Commerce, 207 N Main, Shamrock, TX 79079. Phone: (806) 256-2516 or (806) 256-2501. Fax: (806) 256-3739. Email: irishedb@pan-tex.net.

VIRGINIA SPRING SHOW. Mar 13–15. Showplace Exhibition Center, Richmond, VA. Features hundreds of artisans and craftspeople, food shops, spring entertainment. Holiday Cooking Theatre. 11th annual show. Est attendance: 25,000. For info: Virginia Show Productions, PO Box 305, Chase City, VA 23924. Phone: (804) 372-3996. Fax: (804) 372-3996.

March 1998

S	M	T	W	T	F	S
1	2	3	4	5	6	7
8	9	10	11	12	13	14
15	16	17	18	19	20	21
22	23	24	25	26	27	28
29	30	31				

BIRTHDAYS TODAY

Walter Annenberg, 90, publisher, born Milwaukee, WI, Mar 13, 1908.

Thomas Andrew (Andy) Bean, 45, golfer, born Lafayette, GA, Mar 13, 1953.

Adam Clayton, 38, musician (U2), born Dublin, Ireland, Mar 13, 1960.

Dana Delany, 42, actress ("China Beach," *Moon Over Parador*), born New York, NY, Mar 13, 1956.

Glenne Headly, 41, actress (*The Purple Rose of Cairo, Dick Tracy, Mortal Thoughts*), born New London, CT, Mar 13, 1957.

Vance Edward Johnson, 35, football player, born Trenton, NJ, Mar 13, 1963.

Deborah Raffin, 45, actress ("Foul Play"), born Los Angeles, CA, Mar 13, 1953.

Neil Sedaka, 59, singer, songwriter ("Breaking Up Is Hard to Do," with Howard Greenfield), born Brooklyn, NY, Mar 13, 1939.

MARCH 14 — SATURDAY

Day 73 — 292 Remaining

AMERICAN & CANADIAN SPORT, TRAVEL & OUTDOOR SHOW. Mar 14–22. I-X Center, Cleveland, OH. America's largest show of its kind with more than 700 exhibitors, including travel destinations, camping and fishing equipment, boats, RVs, canoes and more. Seminars and wildlife educational shows each day. Est attendance: 275,000. For info: American & Canadian Sport, Travel & Outdoor Show, PO Box 550–Edgewater Branch, Cleveland, OH 44107. Phone: (216) 529-1300.

BERING SEA ICE GOLF CLASSIC. Mar 14. Nome, AK. A six-hole course played on the frozen Bering Sea. The object is to land the bright-orange ricocheting golf ball into the sunken, flagged coffee cans before losing it among the built-up chunks of ice. Starts promptly at 10 AM at the Breakers Bar. Approx 60 golfers. Est attendance: 150. For info: Bering Sea Lions Club, Box 326, Nome, AK 99762. Phone: (907) 443-2494.

EINSTEIN, ALBERT: BIRTH ANNIVERSARY. Mar 14. Theoretical physicist best known for his theory of relativity. Born at Ulm, Germany, Mar 14, 1879. Nobel Prize, 1921. Died at Princeton, NJ, Apr 18, 1955.

GIRL SCOUT SABBATH. Mar 14. Girl Scouts of Jewish faith worship together in the temple of their choice. For info: Media Services, Girl Scouts of the USA, 420 Fifth Ave, New York, NY 10018. Phone: (212) 852-8000. Fax: (212) 852-6514. WWW: http://www.gsusa.org

HIGHLAND COUNTY MAPLE FESTIVAL. Mar 14–15 (also Mar 21–22). Highland County, VA. To welcome visitors to view the process of syrup making. Large craft shows. Est attendance: 60,000. For info: Highland County Chamber of Commerce, PO Box 223, Monterey, VA 24465. Phone: (540) 468-2550. Fax: (540) 468-2551. Email: highcc@cfw.com.
WWW: http://www.cfw.com/~highcc/index.html

INDIANA FLOWER AND PATIO SHOW. Mar 14–22. Indiana State Fairgrounds Event Center, Indianapolis, IN. The oldest show of its kind in the Midwest, featuring 20 landscaped gardens and products and services for home, yard and patio. Est attendance: 85,000. For info: Patrick Buchen, Pres, HSI Show Productions, Box 502797, Indianapolis, IN 46250. Phone: (317) 576-9933. Fax: (317) 576-9955.

JONES, CASEY: BIRTH ANNIVERSARY. Mar 14. Railroad engineer and hero of ballad, whose real name was John Luther Jones. Born near Cayce, KY, Mar 14, 1864. Died in railroad wreck Apr 30, 1900.

KAPPA DELTA SHAMROCK PROJECT TO PREVENT CHILD ABUSE. Mar 14. Nationwide. Since 1984, collegiate and alumnae members of Kappa Delta Sorority have gathered on the Saturday on or before St. Patrick's Day to raise monies for the National Committee to Prevent Child Abuse (NCPCA) and local beneficiaries. More than $3.1 million has been raised, with 80 percent of the funds remaining in local communities and 20 percent benefiting the NCPCA.

MARSHALL, THOMAS RILEY: BIRTH ANNIVERSARY. Mar 14. Twenty-eighth vice president of the US (1913–1921). Born at North Manchester, IN, Mar 14, 1854. Died at Washington, DC, June 1, 1925.

MARX, KARL: DEATH ANNIVERSARY. Mar 14, 1883. The German socialist, founder and father of modern communism, author of *Das Kapital* and (with Friedrich Engels) the *Communist Manifesto*. Born at Treves, Germany, May 5, 1818. Died at London, England, Mar 14, 1883, at age 64.

McGUIRE'S 5K ST. PATRICK'S DAY PREDICTION RUN. Mar 14. Pensacola, FL. The largest, most popular 5K run in the history of Pensacola, "The Nation's Largest Prediction Run." 9 AM. Est attendance: 2,800. For info: Susi Lyon, McGuire's Irish Pub, 600 E Gregory St, Pensacola, FL 32501. Phone: (904) 433-6789. Fax: (904) 434-5400.

MOTH-ER DAY. Mar 14. A day set aside to honor moth collectors and specialists. Celebrated in museums or libraries with moth collections. For info: Bob Birch, Puns Corps Grand Punscorpion, Box 2364, Falls Church, VA 22042-0364. Phone: (703) 533-3668.

NATCHITOCHES JAZZ FESTIVAL. Mar 14. Natchitoches, LA. Natchitoches will celebrate St. Patrick's Day weekend to the sounds of jazz, rhythm and blues, downtown on the banks of the Cane River Lake. The event features numerous bands, continuous music from 11 AM til 9 PM. Est attendance: 4,000. For info: Natchitoches Parish Tourism Commission, 781 Front St, Natchitoches, LA 71457. Phone: (318) 352-8072 or (800) 259-1714. Fax: (318) 352-2415.

NATIONAL SKI-JORING FINALS. Mar 14–15. Red Lodge Rodeo Grounds, Red Lodge, MT. Horsemen and skiers provide action entertainment. Derived from the Scandinavian sport of pulling a skier behind a horse, Ski-joring has evolved from a leisure winter diversion into lively, regulated competition. Annually, the second weekend in March. Est attendance: 3,000. For info: Red Lodge Chamber of Commerce, Box 988, Red Lodge, MT 59068. Phone: (406) 446-1718. Email: redlodge@wtp.net.

NEW ENGLAND SLED DOG RACES. Mar 14–15. Intown Trail, Rangeley, ME. Eight-dog, six-dog, four-dog pro and junior classes race 1–9 miles, depending on the size of the team. Annually, the second weekend in March. Sponsor: New England Sled Dog Club. Est attendance: 500. For info: Gail Spaulding, Chamber of Commerce, PO Box 317, Rangeley, ME 04970. Phone: (207) 864-5364. Fax: (207) 864-5366.
Email: mtlakes@rangeley.org.

SAINT PATRICK'S DAY CELEBRATION WITH IRISH STEW COOKOFF. Mar 14. Murphysboro, IL. Parade, 5K walk/run plus Irish stew cook off, lawn mower races. Free admission. Est attendance: 2,000. For info: The Molly-O Restaurant, 1701 Walnut St, Murphysboro, IL 62966. Phone: (618) 684-5451 or (800) 406-8774. Fax: (618) 687-1030.

SAINT PATRICK'S DAY TEA. Mar 14–15. Rockwood Museum, Wilmington, DE. Enjoy afternoon tea with a bit of Irish. Tour, tea with sandwiches and sweets. Est attendance: 120. For info: Rockwood Museum, 610 Shipley Rd, Wilmington, DE 19809. Phone: (302) 761-4340. Fax: (302) 764-4570.
Email: info@rockwood.org. WWW: http://www.rockwood.org

SAINT URHO'S DAY. Mar 14. Finland, MN. Wacky, lighthearted fest salutes the great St. Urho, who rid Finland of grasshoppers; includes spoof beauty pageant, parade, dances, ethnic food and heritage center. Est attendance: 2,000. For info: Bonnie Tikkanen, St. Urho Committee, Box 516, Finland, MN 55603. Phone: (218) 353-7359.

SAVE A SPIDER DAY. Mar 14. Don't begrudge a busy, useful spider its web; don't stomp or vacuum those little octopedal arachnids! If you *have* to, gently move your spiders to a safer place. Annually, Mar 14. Submitted by Linda Campbell Franklin. Linda Campbell Franklin, Save a Spider Day, 2716 Northfield, Charlottesville, VA 22901.

SEA LION SUDS FEST. Mar 14–15. Curry County Fairgrounds, Gold Beach, OR. Celebration of Oregon's micro-brewed suds with a slew of beers to sample. Fun games, craft booths, food from pizza to seafood and live music and dancing. Est attendance: 500. For info: Gold Beach Chamber of Commerce, 29279 S Ellensburg Ave, #3, Gold Beach, OR 97444. Phone: (800) 525-2334. Fax: (541) 247-0188.
Email: goldbeach@harborside.com.
WWW: http://www.harborside.com/gb

SEOUL RECAPTURED BY UN FORCES: ANNIVERSARY. Mar 14, 1951. Seoul, which had fallen to Chinese forces in January, 1951, was retaken by United Nations troops.

SHEEP TO SHAWL CRAFT FESTIVAL. Mar 14. Oatland Island Education Center, Savannah, GA. During this annual shearing of the Oatland sheep, members of the Fiber Guild of the Savannahs will demonstrate the carding, spinning and weaving of wool. Area craftsmen will have booths set up to sell stained glass, jewlery, pottery, country crafts, wreaths and dried arrangements. Annually, the second Saturday in March. Est attendance: 1,900. For info: Oatland Island Education Ctr, 711 Sandtown Rd, Savannah, GA 31410. Phone: (912) 897-3773. Fax: (912) 898-7402.

ST. PATRICK'S DAY PARADE. Mar 14. Downtown Hornell, NY. It's a "come as you are" line of march, open to anyone, with no entry fee, no judges, no prizes. Hornell's parade is designed as purely a fun affair, especially for those people who've always wanted to be in a parade but never had the opportunity. It has gotten larger and longer every year, with more and more "would-be Irish" strolling down Main Street. Annually, the Saturday before St. Patrick's Day except when St. Patrick's Day is a Thursday or Friday, then, the following Saturday. Est attendance: 3,000. For info: Bat Lyons, Bilbat Radio, Inc., PO Box 726, Hornell, NY 14843. Phone: (607) 324-2000. Fax: (607) 324-2001. Email: sales@wkpq.com. WWW: http://www.wkpq.com

TAYLOR, LUCY HOBBS: BIRTH ANNIVERSARY. Mar 14, 1833. Lucy Beaman Hobbs, first woman in America to receive a degree in dentistry (Ohio College of Dental Surgery, 1866) or to be admitted to membership in a state dental association. Born in New York State, Mar 14, 1833. In 1867 she married James M. Taylor, a painter for a railroad who also became a dentist (after she instructed him in the essentials). Active women's rights advocate. Died at Lawrence, KS, Oct 3, 1910.

VICTORIAN EASTER AT BELLE MEADE. Mar 14–Apr 19. Nashville, TN. Genteel Southern Mansion exhibiting Easter decorations and lore from the 19th century. Tours led by guides in period costumes. Est attendance: 12,000. For info: Belle Meade Plantation, 5025 Harding Rd, Nashville, TN 37205. Phone: (615) 356-0501 or (800) 270-3991. Fax: (615) 356-2336.

BIRTHDAYS TODAY

Frank Borman, 70, former astronaut, airline executive, born Gary, IN, Mar 14, 1928.

Michael Caine (Maurice Joseph Micklewhite), 65, actor (*Alfie, The Ipcress File, Sleuth*), born London, England, Mar 14, 1933.

Billy Crystal, 51, actor ("Soap," *When Harry Met Sally . . ., City Slickers*), born Long Beach, NY, Mar 14, 1947.

Quincy Jones, 65, composer, producer ("We Are the World"), born Chicago, IL, Mar 14, 1933.

Hank Ketcham, 78, cartoonist ("Dennis the Menace"), born Seattle, WA, Mar 14, 1920.

Kirby Puckett, 37, former baseball player, born Chicago, IL, Mar 14, 1961.

Rita Tushingham, 56, actress (*Dr. Zhivago, A Taste of Honey*), born Liverpool, England, Mar 14, 1942.

MARCH 15 — SUNDAY

Day 74 — 291 Remaining

BATTLE OF GUILFORD COURTHOUSE OBSERVANCE. Mar 15. Guilford Courthouse National Military Park, Greensboro, NC. A program to observe the 217th anniversary of the Battle of Guilford Courthouse, the largest Revolutionary War battle in North Carolina. Annually, Mar 15. Est attendance: 250. For info: Robert A. Vogel, Superintendent, Guilford Courthouse NMP, 2332 New Garden Rd, Greensboro, NC 27410-2355. Phone: (910) 288-1776. Fax: (910) 282-2296.

BUZZARD DAY. Mar 15. Hinckley, OH. Tradition says that on this day the buzzards (also known as turkey vultures or carrion crows) return to Hinckley, OH, from their winter quarters in the Great Smoky Mountains to rear their young. Pancake and sausage breakfast, crafters and exhibits. For info: Hinckley Chamber of Commerce, PO Box 354, Hinckley, OH 44233.

CAMP FIRE BOYS AND GIRLS BIRTHDAY WEEK. Mar 15–21. To celebrate the 88th anniversary of Camp Fire Boys and Girls (founded in 1910 as Camp Fire Girls). For info: Camp Fire Boys and Girls, 4601 Madison Ave, Kansas City, MO 64112. Phone: (816) 756-1950. Fax: (816) 756-0258. Email: info@campfire.org. WWW: http://www.campfire.org

CHILDREN AND HEALTHCARE WEEK™. Mar 15–21. The goal of this observance is to increase awareness among families, schools, local communities and all health care professionals of the special needs of children and their families in health care settings. A comprehensive guide of planning materials is available for $10. For info: Assn for the Care of Children's Health, 7910 Woodmont Ave, Ste 300, Bethesda, MD 20814. Phone: (301) 654-6549 or (800) 808-ACCH. Fax: (301) 986-4553. Email: acch@clark.net. WWW: http://look.net/acch

"EIGHT IS ENOUGH" TV PREMIERE: ANNIVERSARY. Mar 15, 1977. "Eight Is Enough" was a one-hour comedy-drama set in Sacramento starring Dick Van Patten as Tom Bradford, a columnist for a local paper and a widower with eight children. Diana Hyland played his wife Joan; she died from cancer after filming five shows. The children were played by Grant Goodeve, Lani O'Grady, Laurie Walters, Susan Richardson, Dianne Kay, Willie Aames, Connie Needham and Adam Rich. In the fall of 1977 Betty Buckley joined the cast as tutor Abby Abbott, who later married Tom. Most of the cast was reunited for Tom's 50th birthday on "Eight Is Enough: A Family Reunion" shown on Oct 18, 1987.

ENGLAND: CHELTENHAM GOLD CUP MEETING. Mar 15–17. Cheltenham Racecourse, Prestbury, Cheltenham, Gloucestershire. Major national hunt meeting. Est attendance: 150,000. For info: Cheltenham Racecourse, Prestbury Park, Cheltenham, Gloucestershire, England. Phone: (44)(124) 251-3014. Fax: (44)(124) 222-4227.

"GO NUTS OVER TEXAS PEANUTS WEEK." Mar 15–21. Everything's big in Texas, including the pride in its peanut industry! Texas is the nation's second largest peanut-producing state and is one of only two states that grow all four US peanut varities: Runner, Spanish, Virginia and Valencia. Part of National Peanut Month, "Go Nuts Over Peanuts Week," celebrates America's favorite nut. Annually, the third full week of March. For info: Mary Webb, Texas Peanut Producers Board, PO Box 398, Gorman, TX 76454. Phone: (817) 734-2846. Fax: (817) 734-2017.

"GUN SHY" TV PREMIERE: 15th ANNIVERSARY. Mar 15, 1983. This half-hour comedy-western set in Quake City, CA, was based on Disney's "Apple Dumpling Gang" films. Barry Van Dyke (son of Dick) appeared as Russell Donovan, a gambler stuck with two kids he won in a card game (Keith Mitchell & Adam Rich as Clovis, Bridgette Anderson as Celia); Geoffrey Lewis and Tim Thomerson as townspeople; Henry Jones as Homer McCoy, Quake City's barber and sheriff; and Pat McCormick as Mound.

IDES OF MARCH. Mar 15. Julius Caesar assassinated this day in 44 BC.

JACKSON, ANDREW: BIRTH ANNIVERSARY. Mar 15, 1767. 7th president of the US (Mar 4, 1829–Mar 3, 1837) was born in a log cabin at Waxhaw, SC. Jackson was the first president since George Washington who had not attended college. He was a military hero in the War of 1812. His presidency reflected his democratic and equalitarian values. Died at Nashville, TN, June 8, 1845, at age 78. His birthday is observed as a holiday in Tennessee.

KENNEDY CENTER IMAGINATION CELEBRATION. Mar 15–Apr 30. Colorado Springs, CO. A national festival program of the John F. Kennedy Center for the Performing Arts, this community-wide celebration has something for everyone: from hundreds of lively performances that delight the senses to friendly, small-town happenings that warm the heart. Most events are free; a nominal fee is charged for those that are not. Open to the public. Est attendance: 231,000. For info: Mary Mashburn, Coord, Pikes Peak Library Dist, 5550 N Union Blvd, Colorado Springs, CO 80918. Phone: (719) 531-6333, ext 1208. Fax: (719) 528-2820. Email: mmashbur@ppld.org. WWW: http://imagine.pple.org

MAINE: ADMISSION DAY: ANNIVERSARY. Mar 15. Became 23rd state on this day in 1820.

"MR BELVEDERE" TV PREMIERE: ANNIVERSARY. Mar 15, 1985. A sitcom about a sarcastic, talented and wise British housekeeper and his love-hate relationship with a Pittsburgh family. It starred Christopher Hewitt as Lynn Belvedere; former baseball player Bob Uecker as his employer/antagonist sportswriter George Owens; Ilene Graff as George's wife Marsha, a law student; Rob Stone as Kevin; Tracy Wells as Heather; and Brice Beckham as mischievous Wesley. At the end of each episode, Mr Belvedere narrated the day's lesson as he wrote in his journal, and ended the show on a funny note.

NATIONAL AGRICULTURE WEEK. Mar 15–21. To honor America's providers of food and fiber and to educate the general public about the US agricultural system. Annually, the week that includes the first day of spring. For info: Agriculture Council of

March 1998

S	M	T	W	T	F	S
1	2	3	4	5	6	7
8	9	10	11	12	13	14
15	16	17	18	19	20	21
22	23	24	25	26	27	28
29	30	31				

America, 927 15th St NW, Ste 800, Washington, DC 20005. Phone: (800) 982-4329.

NATIONAL BRUTUS DAY. Mar 15. No matter where you work, you must admit there's as much intrigue, plotting and back-stabbing as was found in ancient Rome or is found today inside the Beltway. [© 1997 by WPL]. For info: Thomas Roy, Wellness Permission League, PO Box 662, Mount Gretna, PA 17064-0662. Phone: (500) 437-5104 or (717) 964-1308. Fax: (717) 964-1335.

NATIONAL POISON PREVENTION WEEK. Mar 15–21. To aid in encouraging the American people to learn of the dangers of accidental poisoning and to take preventive measures against it. Annually, the third full week in March. For info: Ken Giles, Secy, Poison Prevention Week Council, Box 1543, Washington, DC 20013. Email: info@cpsc.gov. WWW: http://www.cpsc.gov

★**NATIONAL POISON PREVENTION WEEK.** Mar 15–21. Presidential Proclamation issued each year for the third week of March since 1962. (PL87–319 of Sept 26, 1961.)

PEDIATRIC NURSE PRACTITIONER WEEK. Mar 15–21. The National Association of Pediatric Nurse Associates and Practitioners, an association of more than 5,400 pediatric nurse practitioners and specialty nurses in advanced practice providing primary health care to infants, children, adolescents and young adults, proclaims this week in honor of nearly 11,000 practitioners dedicated to improving children's health. For info: Joe Casey, Dir of Membership and Coomunications, NAPNAP, 1101 Kings Highway North, Ste 206, Cherry Hill, NJ 08034-1912. Phone: (609) 667-1773. Fax: (609) 667-7181. Email: 74224.51@Compuserve.com. WWW: http://www.napnap.org

PULMONARY REHABILITATION WEEK. Mar 15–21. For info: American Assn of Cardiovascular and Pulmonary Rehabilitation, 7611 Elmwood Ave, Ste 201, Middleton, WI 53562. Phone: (608) 831-6989.

TRUE CONFESSIONS DAY. Mar 15. Confession is good for the soul. Go into work today and tell all. If you plan to stay home, make an appointment with your mirror. [© 1997 by WPL] For info: Tom and Ruth Roy, Wellness Permission League, Box 1264, Mount Gretna, PA 17064-0662. Phone: (500) 437-5104 or (717) 964-1308. Fax: (717) 964-1335.

VAN BROCKLIN, NORM: BIRTH ANIVERSARY. Mar 15, 1926. Norman Van Brocklin, Pro Football Hall of Fame quarterback and coach, born at Eagle Butte, SD. Van Brocklin played college football at Oregon and then signed with the Los Angeles Rams. He helped the Rams win their only NFL title in 1951. After finishing his playing career with the Philadelphia Eagles, he coached the Minnesota Vikings and the Atlanta Falcons. Inducted into the Pro Football Hall of Fame in 1979. Died at Social Circle, GA, May 2, 1983.

BIRTHDAYS TODAY

Harold Douglas Baines, 39, baseball player, born St. Michael's, MD, Mar 15, 1959.

Alan Bean, 66, former astronaut, born Wheeler, TX, Mar 15, 1932.

Robert Terrell (Terry) Cummings, 37, basketball player, born Chicago, IL, Mar 15, 1961.

Fabio, 37, model, born Fabio Lanzoni, Milan, Italy, Mar 15, 1961.

Ruth Bader Ginsburg, 65, Associate Justice of the US Supreme Court, born Brookyn, NY, Mar 15, 1933.

Mark Green, 53, lawyer, author, social activist (*Ronald Reagan's Reign of Error*), born Brooklyn, NY, Mar 15, 1945.

Michael Vaughn (Mickey) Hatcher, Jr, 43, former baseball player, born Cleveland, OH, Mar 15, 1955.

Judd Hirsch, 63, actor (Emmy for "Taxi"; *Ordinary People*), born New York, NY, Mar 15, 1935.

Mike Love, 57, singer, musician (member of the Beach Boys), born Los Angeles, CA, Mar 15, 1941.

Federico Peña, 51, US Secretary of Energy in the Clinton administration, born Laredo, TX, Mar 15, 1947.

Dee Snider, 43, singer (Twisted Sister), composer, born Massapequa, NY, Mar 15, 1955.

Sly Stone (Sylvester Stewart), 54, singer, musician (funk/rock leader Sly & the Family Stone), born Dallas, TX, Mar 15, 1944.

Craig Wasson, 44, actor ("Phyllis," *Body Double, Malcolm X*), born Ontario, OR, Mar 15, 1954.

MARCH 16 — MONDAY

Day 75 — 290 Remaining

AUSTRALIA: CANBERRA DAY. Mar 16. Australian Capital Territory. Public holiday the third Monday in March.

BLACK PRESS DAY: ANNIVERSARY OF THE FIRST BLACK NEWSPAPER. Mar 16. Anniversary of the founding of the first black newspaper in the US, *Freedom's Journal*, on Varick St in New York, NY, on Mar 16, 1827. Observed as "Black Press Day in New York City" by mayoral proclamation in 1977.

BONHEUR, ROSA: BIRTH ANNIVERSARY. Mar 16, 1822. French painter and sculptor best known for her paintings of animals, Rosa (Marie-Rosalie) Bonheur was born at Bordeaux and trained with her father, an art teacher. With the income from the sale of her art she purchased the castle of By near Fontainebleau where she died at age 77 on May 25, 1899. Bonheur's *The Horse Fair*, which she painted in 1849, was purchased by the American millionaire Cornelius Vanderbilt for $53,600, a record price at the time. In 1865 Bonheur was awarded the Grand Cross of the Légion d'Honneur, the first woman so honored. An early Bohemian and feminist, Bonheur defied female convention of the day by dressing in pants and smoking cigarettes.

CLYMER, GEORGE: BIRTH ANNIVERSARY. Mar 16, 1739. Signer of the Declaration of Independence and of the US Constitution. Born Mar 16, 1739. Died at Philadelphia, PA, Jan 24, 1813.

CURLEW DAY. Mar 16. Traditional arrival date for the long-billed curlew at the Umatilla (Oregon) National Wildlife Refuge. More than 500 of the long-billed curlews have been reported at this location during their nesting season.

GODDARD DAY. Mar 16. Commemorates first liquid-fuel-powered rocket flight on this day, 1926, devised by Robert Hutchings Goddard (1882–1945) at Auburn, MA.

"THE GUMBY SHOW" TV PREMIERE: ANNIVERSARY. Mar 16, 1957. This kids' show was a spinoff from "Howdy Doody," where the character of Gumby was first introduced in 1956. Gumby and his horse Pokey were clay figures whose adventures were filmed using the process of "pixillation." "The Gumby Show," created by Art Clokey, was first hosted by Bobby Nicholson and later by Pinky Lee. It was syndicated in 1966 and again in 1988.

MADISON, JAMES: BIRTH ANNIVERSARY. Mar 16. Fourth president of the US (Mar 4, 1809–Mar 3, 1817). Born at Port Conway, VA, Mar 16, 1751. He was president when British forces invaded Washington, DC, requiring Madison and other high officials to flee while the British burned the Capitol, the president's residence and most other public buildings (Aug 24–25, 1814). Died at Montpelier, VA, June 28, 1836.

MY LAI MASSACRE: 30th ANNIVERSARY. Mar 16, 1968. Most-publicized atrocity of Vietnam War. On Mar 16, 1968, according to findings of US Army's Peers investigating team, approximately 300 noncombatant Vietnamese villagers (at My Lai and Mykhe, near the South China Sea) were killed by infantrymen of the American Division.

NATIONAL FREE PAPER WEEK. Mar 16–20. To promote the contributions free circulation community newspapers make to their communities each week. For info: Deirdre Flynn, Assc Dir, Assn of Free Community Papers, 401 N Michigan, Chicago, IL 60611-4267. Phone: (312) 644-6610 or (312) 644-6610.

NATIONAL MANUFACTURING WEEK. Mar 16–19. Chicago, IL. More than 2,000 exhibits and hundreds of hours of conference seminars on what's new in manufacturing. Est attendance: 65,000. For info: James P. Carty, VP Small Manufacturers, Natl Assn of Manufacturers, 1331 Pennsylvania Ave NW, Ste 600, Washington, DC 20004. Phone: (202) 637-3047. Fax: (202) 637-3182. WWW: http://www.nam.org

NIXON, THELMA CATHERINE PATRICIA RYAN: BIRTH ANNIVERSARY. Mar 16, 1912. Wife of Richard Milhous Nixon, 37th president of the US. Born at Ely, NV, she died at Park Ridge, NJ, June 22, 1993, at age 81.

POPE, JOHN: BIRTH ANNIVERSARY. Mar 16, 1822. Pope, a Union general in the Civil War, was born in Louisville, KY, graduated from West Point in 1842 and fought under General Zachary Taylor in the Mexican War. During the Civil War President Abraham Lincoln put Pope in charge of the Army of Virginia. He led the Union forces at the second Battle of Bull Run (Aug 1862) to a disastrous defeat, losing about 15,000 troops. He was immediately relieved of his command and sent to Minnesota to handle rioting Sioux Indians. Pope continued to deal with Indian matters until 1883 and eventually espoused the goal of assimilation into white culture. Pope had become a hard-working, well-informed commander with a real understanding of and empathy for the problems of the Indians as well as the nearby white settlements. He died in Ohio at age 70 on Sept 23, 1892.

SAINT PATRICK'S DAY CELEBRATION ON THE RIVER. Mar 16–17. Rousakis Plaza, Savannah, GA. This annual celebration is widely regarded as the nation's second largest. It draws people from all around the world. Est attendance: 500,000. For info: Rick Lott, Dir, Savannah Waterfront Assn, PO Box 572, Savannah, GA 31402. Phone: (912) 234-0295. Fax: (912) 234-4904.

SAINT URHO'S DAY. Mar 16. Hood River, OR. Join the parade and party to honor the tongue-in-cheek patron saint who drove the grasshoppers out of the vineyards in Finland. Est attendance: 150. For info: Camille Hukari, 3009 Dethman Ridge, Hood River, OR 97031. Phone: (541) 386-5785. Fax: (541) 387-4657.

SPACE MILESTONE: *GEMINI 8* (US). Mar 16, 1966. Executed (with *Agena*) first docking of orbiting spacecraft. Safe emergency landing after malfunction. Launched Mar 16, 1966.

"TRUE STORY" TV PREMIERE: ANNIVERSARY. Mar 16, 1957. NBC's half-hour anthology series dramatized real-life stories for four years. It was hosted by Kathi Norris.

March 1998

S	M	T	W	T	F	S
1	2	3	4	5	6	7
8	9	10	11	12	13	14
15	16	17	18	19	20	21
22	23	24	25	26	27	28
29	30	31				

BIRTHDAYS TODAY

Bernardo Bertolucci, 57, filmmaker (Oscar for *The Last Emperor; Once Upon a Time in the West; Last Tango in Paris*), born Parma, Italy, Mar 16, 1941.

Erik Estrada, 49, actor ("CHiPS," *Honey Boy*), born New York, NY, Mar 16, 1949.

Isabelle Huppert, 43, actress (*Violette, Story of Women*), born Paris, France, Mar 16, 1955.

Jerry Lewis, 73, comedian, actor (*My Friend Irma*), director (*The Bellboy*), born Newark, NJ, Mar 16, 1925.

Leo McKern, 78, actor (*The Mouse That Roared, A Man for All Seasons, Help*, "Rumpole of the Bailey"), born New South Wales, Australia, Mar 16, 1920.

Daniel Patrick Moynihan, 71, US Senator (D, New York), born Tulsa, OK, Mar 16, 1927.

Kate Nelligan, 47, actress (*Eye of the Needle, Frankie and Johnny, The Prince of Tides*), born London, Ontario, Canada, Mar 16, 1951.

MARCH 17 — TUESDAY

Day 76 — 289 Remaining

ANN ARBOR FILM FESTIVAL. Mar 17–22. Ann Arbor, MI. Independent 16mm film festival in its 36th year. Genres represented include experimental, animation, documentary, narrative, avant-garde. No video for pre-entry. Entry deadline: Feb 15, 1998. $11,000 awarded in prizes. Est attendance: 5,000. For info: Vicki Honeyman, Festival Dir, Ann Arbor Film Festival, PO Box 8232, Ann Arbor, MI 48107. Phone: (313) 995-5356. Fax: (313) 995-5396. Email: vicki@honeyman.org.
WWW: http://www.citi.umich/edu/u/honey/aaff

BRIDGER, JIM: BIRTH ANNIVERSARY. Mar 17, 1804. American fur trader, frontiersman and scout, born at Richmond, VA, and died July 17, 1881, near Kansas City, MO. Believed to be the first white man to visit (in 1824) the Great Salt Lake, he also established Fort Bridger in southwestern Wyoming as a fur-trading post and as a way station for pioneers heading west on the Oregon Trail. Bridger National Forest in western Wyoming is named for him.

CAMP FIRE BOYS AND GIRLS. Mar 17. To commemorate the 88th anniversary of the founding of Camp Fire Boys and Girls and the service given to children and youth across the nation. Founded in 1910 as Camp Fire Girls. For info: Camp Fire Boys and Girls, 4601 Madison Ave, Kansas City, MO 64112. Phone: (816) 756-1950. Fax: (816) 756-0258. Email: info@campfire.org. WWW: http://www.campfire.org

COLE, NAT "KING" (NATHANIEL ADAMS COLE): BIRTH ANNIVERSARY. Mar 17, 1919. Nat "King" Cole was born at Montgomery, AL, and began his musical career at an early age, playing the piano at age four. His career included many highlights, among which was his role as the first black entertainer to host a national television show. His many songs included "The Christmas Song," "Nature Boy," "Mona Lisa," "Ramblin' Rose" and "Unforgettable." Although he was dogged by racial discrimination throughout his career, including the cancellation of his television show because opposition from southern white viewers decreased advertising revenue, Cole was criticized by prominent black newspapers for not joining other black entertainers in the civil rights struggle. Cole contributed more than $50,000 to civil rights organizations in response to the criticism. Nat "King" Cole died Feb 25, 1965, at Santa Monica, CA, at age 45.

EVACUATION DAY. Mar 17. A public holiday in Boston and Suffolk County, MA, celebrates anniversary of the evacuation from Boston of British troops on Mar 17, 1776.

FEMALE RELIEF SOCIETY OF NAUVOO ORGANIZED: ANNIVERSARY. Mar 17, 1842. Twenty Mormon women formally initiated this organization in Nauvoo, IL, which is now known as the Relief Society and has grown to almost four million members. Information furnished by Church of Jesus Christ of Latter-Day Saints, Public Affairs Dept.

IRELAND: NATIONAL DAY. Mar 17. St. Patrick's Day is observed in the Republic of Ireland as a legal national holiday.

JONES, BOBBY: BIRTH ANNIVERSARY. Mar 17. Golfing great Robert Tyre Jones, Jr, first golfer to win the grand slam (the four major British and American tournaments in one year). Born at Atlanta, GA, on Mar 17, 1902. Died there Dec 18, 1971.

MC VON O'SKI DAY. Mar 17. This is a salute to our Scottish, German, Irish and Polish friends and neighbors whose names begin with Mc, Von, O' or end with ski. For more info, send $2 to cover postage and photocopying. For info: Adrienne Sioux Koopersmith, 1437 W Rosemont, #1W, Chicago, IL 60660-1319. Phone: (773) 743-5341. Fax: (773) 743-5395.
Email: kooper@interaccess.com.

NAIA MEN'S DIVISION I NATIONAL BASKETBALL CHAMPIONSHIP. Mar 17–23. Mabee Center, Tulsa, OK. 61st annual tournament. Est attendance: 35,000. For info: Natl Assn of Intercollegiate Athletics, 6120 S Yale Ave, Ste 1450, Tulsa, OK 74136. Phone: (918) 494-8828. Fax: (918) 494-8841. Email: khenry@naia.org. WWW: http://www.naia.org

NORTHERN IRELAND: SAINT PATRICK'S DAY HOLIDAY. Mar 17. National Holiday.

NUREYEV, RUDOLF HAMETOVICH: 60th BIRTH ANNIVERSARY. Mar 17, 1938. Rudolf Nureyev, one of the most charismatic ballet stars of the 20th century, was born Mar 17, 1938, on a train in southeastern Siberia. Nureyev's defection from the Soviet Union on June 17, 1961, while on tour with the Kirov Ballet, made headlines worldwide. The dancer was known for his ability to combine passion with a high level of perfectionism. His long partnership with Dame Margot Fonteyn of the Royal Ballet was legendary, and he also performed frequently with the Martha Graham Dance Company. During the years Nureyev performed he also choreographed, restaged many classics and served as the Paris Opera Ballet's artistic director. Nureyev died Jan 6, 1993, at Levallois, France, a suburb of Paris.

PARKER, GEORGE: DEATH ANNIVERSARY. Mar 17. George Parker, the second Earl of Macclesfield, was born in 1697 (exact date unknown). The eminent English astronomer was president of the Royal Society from 1752 until his death on Mar 17, 1764. He was one of the principal authors of the Bill for Regulating the Commencement of the Year (British Calendar Act of 1751), which was introduced in Parliament by Lord Chesterfield. That act caused the adoption, in 1752, of the "New Style" Gregorian calendar, which is still in use today. Parker died at Shirburn Castle, England.

PIZZA EXPO '98. Mar 17–19. This show provides an opportunity for independent, chain and franchise pizza operators to meet with manufacturers and service representatives from the pizza industry. Professional seminars are provided Mar 16–19. Also includes Pizza Festiva™ recipe and Pizza World Games™ competitions. Est attendance: 6,000. For info: Gerry Durnell, Exec Dir, Natl Assn of Pizza Operators, PO Box 1347, New Albany, IN 47151. Phone: (812) 949-0909 or (800) 489-8324. Fax: (812) 941-9711.

RUSTIN, BAYARD: BIRTH ANNIVERSARY. Mar 17, 1910. Black pacifist and civil rights leader, Bayard Rustin was an organizer and participant in many of the great social protest marches—for jobs, freedom, nuclear disarmament. He was arrested and imprisoned more than 20 times for his civil rights and pacifist activities. Born at West Chester, PA, Rustin died at New York, NY, Aug 24, 1987, at age 77.

SAINT PATRICK'S DAY. Mar 17. Commemorates the patron saint of Ireland, Bishop Patrick (AD 389–461) who, about AD 432, left his home in the Severn Valley, England, and introduced Christianity into Ireland. Feast Day in the Roman Catholic Church. A national holiday in Ireland and Northern Ireland.

SAINT PATRICK'S DAY CELEBRATION. Mar 17. McMenamins Edgefield, Troutdale, OR. Bagpipes, Celtic music, wandering storyteller, Irish coffees and special Irish menus in the pub and restaurant. Annual McMenamins tradition. Est attendance: 1,000. For info: McMenamins Edgefield, 2126 SW Halsey, Troutdale, OR 97060. Phone: (800) 669-8610.
Email: edge@mcmenamins.com.
WWW: http://www.mcmenamins.com

SAINT PATRICK'S DAY CELEBRATION. Mar 17. Broadway Market Square, Baltimore, MD. Held in observance of St. Patrick's Day. Program features Irish band, Irish dance group and a Leprechaun Look-A-Like Contest. Est attendance: 250. For info: Dept of Rec and Parks Office of Adventures in Fun, Patterson Park Recreation Complex, 2601 E Baltimore St, Baltimore, MD 21224. Phone: (410) 396-9177. Fax: (410) 327-4120.

SAINT PATRICK'S DAY CELEBRATION. Mar 17. 111th St & Third Ave, Huntington, WV. Live entertainment, music and dance appropriate for St. Patrick's Day. Food, games, beverages, concessions and parade. Est attendance: 2,000. For info: Rick Abel, Greater Huntington Parks & Recreation, PO Box 2985, Huntington, WV 25728. Phone: (304) 696-5954. Fax: (304) 696-5588.

SOUTH AFRICAN WHITES VOTE TO END MINORITY RULE: ANNIVERSARY. Mar 17, 1992. A referendum proposing ending white minority rule through negotiations was supported by a whites-only ballot. The vote of 1,924,186 (68.6 percent) whites in support of President F. W. de Klerk's reform policies was greater than expected.

SPACE MILESTONE: *DISCOVERY* (US). Mar 17, 1989. Space shuttle *Discovery* landed at Edwards Air Force Base after carrying five astronauts on mission to put into orbit a $100 million tracking and data-relay satellite.

SPACE MILESTONE: *VANGUARD 1* (US): 40th ANNIVERSARY. Mar 17, 1958. Established "pear shape" of Earth. At only three pounds it was the first solar-powered satellite.

ST. PATRICK'S DAY. Mar 17. Briarwood Beach, OH. Mayor Leonard English proclaimed Mar 17 to be a legal holiday in observance of St. Patrick's Day. Annually, since 1981. For info: Leonard English, The Village of Briarwood Beach, 485 Shorefield Dr, Chippewa Lake, OH 44215.

TAIWAN: BIRTHDAY OF KUAN YIN, GODDESS OF MERCY. Mar 17. Nineteenth day of Second Moon of the lunar calendar, celebrated at Taipei's Lungshan (Dragon Mountain) and other temples.

TANEY, ROGER B.: BIRTH ANNIVERSARY. Mar 17, 1777. Fifth Chief Justice of the Supreme Court, born in Calvert County, MD. Served as Attorney General under President Andrew Jackson. Nominated as Secretary of the Treasury, he became the first presidential nominee to be rejected by the Senate. His rejection centered on his strong stance against the Bank of the United States as a central bank and his role in urging President Jackson to veto the congressional bill extending its charter. A year later, he was nominated to the Supreme Court as an associate justice by Jackson, but his nomination was stalled until the death of Chief Justice John Marshall on July 6, 1835. Taney was nominated to fill Marshall's place on the bench and after much resistance he was sworn in as Chief Justice in March 1836. His tenure on the Supreme Court is most remembered for the Dred Scott decision. He died at Washington, DC, on Oct 12, 1864, at age 87.

TOP TEN EXPERTS OF THE YEAR ANNOUNCED. Mar 17. Publisher of the *Yearbook of Experts, Authorities & Spokespersons* names the year's most influential experts in the nation. Criteria includes media recognition regarding issues and events. For info: Broadcast Interview Source, Mitchell P. Davis, CEO, 2233 Wisconsin Ave NW, Washington, DC 20007. Phone: (202) 333-4904. WWW: http://www.yearbook.com

TURKEY VULTURES RETURN TO THE LIVING SIGN. Mar 17. Entire Canisteo Valley, Canisteo, NY. Traditionally turkey vultures return on St. Pat's Day to their roosting sites in and around the world famous living sign. For info: Rick Roche, 4904 State Route 36, Canisteo, NY 14823. Phone: (607) 698-2134.

BIRTHDAYS TODAY

Daniel Ray (Danny) Ainge, 39, sportscaster, former basketball player and baseball player, born Eugene, OR, Mar 17, 1959.

Susie Allanson, 46, singer ("Baby Don't Keep Me Hangin' On"), born Minneapolis, MN, Mar 17, 1952.

Betty Allen, 68, educator at Harlem School of the Arts, former opera and concert singer, born Campbell, OH, Mar 17, 1930.

Lesley-Anne Down, 44, ("Upstairs, Downstairs," "Dallas," *The Pink Panther Strikes Again, The Great Train Robbery*), born London, England, Mar 17, 1954.

Patrick Duffy, 49, actor ("The Man from Atlantis," "Dallas"), born Townsend, MT, Mar 17, 1949.

Paul Horn, 68, composer, musician, born New York, NY, Mar 17, 1930.

Rob Lowe, 34, actor (*St. Elmo's Fire, About Last Night . . .*), born Charlottesville, VA, Mar 17, 1964.

Mercedes McCambridge, 80, actress (voice of Satan in *The Exorcist*; Oscar for *All the King's Men*), born Joliet, IL, Mar 17, 1918.

Kurt Russell, 47, actor (*Backdraft, Elvis*), born Springfield, MA, Mar 17, 1951.

Gary Sinise, 43, stage and screen actor (*Forrest Gump, Apollo 13*). Born at Chicago, IL, Mar 17, 1955.

March 1998

S	M	T	W	T	F	S
1	2	3	4	5	6	7
8	9	10	11	12	13	14
15	16	17	18	19	20	21
22	23	24	25	26	27	28
29	30	31				

MARCH 18 — WEDNESDAY

Day 77 — 288 Remaining

ARUBA: FLAG DAY. Mar 18. Aruba national holiday. Display of flags, national music and folkloric events.

BRANSON FAN FEST. Mar 18–22 (tentative). Lawrence Welk Resort Center, Branson, MO. Music lovers from throughout the nation can meet their favorite Branson entertainers and enjoy five days of concerts and outdoor entertainment. Ozark hospitality at its finest with entertainment, fabulous food and more at the largest event of the Branson Country Spring season. For info: Branson/Lakes Area Chamber of Commerce, PO Box 1897, Branson, MO 65615. Phone: (417) 334-4136.

CALHOUN, JOHN CALDWELL: BIRTH ANNIVERSARY. Mar 18, 1782. American statesman and first vice president of the US to resign that office (Dec 28, 1832). Born at Abbeville District, SC, died at Washington, DC, Mar 31, 1850, at age 68.

CLEVELAND, GROVER: BIRTH ANNIVERSARY. Mar 18, 1837. The 22nd and 24th president of the US was born Stephen Grover Cleveland at Caldwell, NJ. Terms of office as president: Mar 4, 1885–Mar 3, 1889, and Mar 4, 1893–Mar 3, 1897. He ran for president for the intervening term and received a plurality of votes cast but failed to win electoral college victory for that term. Only president to serve two nonconsecutive terms. Also the only president to be married in the White House. He married 21-year-old Frances Folsom, his ward. Their daughter, Esther, was the first child of a president to be born in the White House. Died at Princeton, NJ, June 24, 1908, at age 71.

C.M. RUSSELL AUCTION OF ORIGINAL WESTERN ART. Mar 18–21. Heritage Inn, Great Falls, MT. Western art event features auctions, seminars, 102 display/sale rooms with thousands of artworks for sale, entertainment, elegant receptions and the best of Montana hospitality. Annually, the third Wednesday–Saturday in March. Est attendance: 6,000. For info: Donna Madison, Exec Dir, Great Falls Adv Fed, PO Box 634, Great Falls, MT 59403-0634. Phone: (800) 803-3351 or (406) 761-6453.

DODGE NATIONAL CIRCUIT FINALS RODEO. Mar 18–21. Holt Arena, Pocatello, ID. The top two winners of the 12 PRCA Rodeo Circuits compete in bull riding, bareback riding, saddle bronco riding, steer wrestling, calf roping, team roping, barrel racing and wrangler bullfights. Est attendance: 50,000. For info: PR Dir, Dodge Natl Circuit Finals Rodeo, PO Box 4541, Pocatello, ID 83205. Phone: (208) 233-1546.

FIRST ELECTRIC RAZOR MARKETED: ANNIVERSARY. Mar 18. The first electric razor was marketed by Schick Inc on Mar 18, 1931.

JOHNSON, WILLIAM H.: BIRTH ANNIVERSARY. Mar 18, 1901. African-American artist born at Florence, SC; died Apr 13, 1970, at Islip, NY. Johnson spent many years in Europe painting expressionist works such as *Minnie* (1930) and *Sun Setting, Denmark* (1930–32). He was strongly influenced by the vivid styles and brushstrokes of Henry O. Tanner, Vincent van Gogh, Paul Gauguin, Edvard Munch and Otto Dix. He left Europe when Hitler began confiscating and destroying art that had primitivist or African themes. Back in the US, Johnson developed a new, flatter style and delved into subjects of his own experience as well as historical African-American figures and events. *Going to Church* (1940–41) and *Mom and Dad* (1944) are distinct examples of his later work.

JORDAN'S BACK: ANNIVERSARY. Mar 18, 1995. Michael Jordan, easily considered one of the National Basketball Association's greatest all-time players, made history again when he announced that he was returning to professional play after a 17-

month break. The 32-year-old star had retired just before the start of the 1993–94 season, following the terrible murder of his beloved father, James Jordan. Jordan, who averaged 32.3 points a game during regular season play, had led the Chicago Bulls to three successive NBA titles. While retired, he tried a baseball career, playing for the Chicago White Sox minor league team, the Birmingham Barons.

MICHIGAN'S GRANDPARENTS AND GRANDCHILDREN DAY. Mar 18. During this annual observance grandparents are invited into schools across Michigan to join with the children in special programs and events. For info: Luella Davison, Grandparents Anonymous, 1924 Beverly, Sylvan Lake, MI 48320. Phone: (800) 4-A-Child.

NAIA WOMEN'S DIVISION I NATIONAL BASKETBALL CHAMPIONSHIP TOURNAMENT. Mar 18–24. Oman Arena, Jackson, TN. 32-team field competes for the national championship. 18th annual competition. Est attendance: 38,000. For info: Natl Assn of Intercollegiate Athletics, 6120 S Yale Ave, Ste 1450, Tulsa, OK 74136. Phone: (918) 494-8828. Fax: (918) 494-8841. Email: khenry@naia.org. WWW: http://www.naia.org

NATIONAL SPORTS TRIVIA WEEK. Mar 18–24. Ask your favorite sports trivia question now! Super week of overlapping sports events: Final Four of college basketball is near, pro basketball and hockey still being played, spring training for baseball is underway. From the publishers of "Super Bowl Trivia" and "World Series Trivia." For info: Judy Colbert, Tuft Turtle Publishing, Box 3308, Crofton, MD 21114-0308. Phone: (301) 858-0196. Email: tuftturtle@aol.com.

NJCAA DIVISION II MEN'S BASKETBALL NATIONAL FINALS. Mar 18–21. Danville, IL. Junior College Division II national men's basketball finals tournament. Est attendance: 8,000. For info: Jeanie Cooke, Exec Dir, Danville Area Conv/Visitors Bureau, PO Box 992, Danville, IL 61834. Phone: (800) 383-4386.

NURSING CONFERENCE ON PEDIATRIC PRIMARY CARE. Mar 18–22. Chicago. Offers continuing education on clinical practice, professional development and legislative issues relevant to the nursing profession. Est attendance: 1,200. For info: Natl Assn of Pediatric Nurse Associates and Practitioners, 1101 Kings Hwy N, Ste 206, Cherry Hill, NJ 08034. Phone: (609) 667-1773. Fax: (609) 667-7187. WWW: http://www.napnap.org

RIO GRANDE VALLEY LIVESTOCK SHOW. Mar 18–22. Mercedes, TX. For the youth of the four counties in the valley to exhibit their projects. Est attendance: 175,000. For info: Jack D. Schwarz, Rio Grande Valley Livestock Show Inc, Box 867, Mercedes, TX 78570. Phone: (210) 565-2456. Fax: (210) 565-3005.

SPACE MILESTONE: *VOSKHOD 2* (USSR). Mar 18, 1965. Colonel Leonov stepped out of capsule for 20 minutes in special space suit. Launched Mar 18, 1965.

"TALES OF WELLS FARGO" TV PREMIERE: ANNIVERSARY. Mar 18, 1957. This half-hour western starred Dale Robertson as Jim Hardie, agent for Wells Fargo transport company. In the fall of 1961, the show expanded to an hour. Hardie bought a ranch, and new cast members were added, including Jack Ging as Beau McCloud, another agent; Virginia Christine as Ovie, a widow owning a nearby ranch; Lory Patrick and Mary Jane Saunders as Ovie's daughters; and William Demarest as Jeb, Hardie's ranch foreman. Jack Nicholson appeared in one of his first major TV roles in the episode "The Washburn Girl."

BIRTHDAYS TODAY

Bonnie Blair, 34, Olympic gold medal speed skater, born Cornwall, NY, Mar 18, 1964.
Irene Cara, 39, singer ("Fame," "The Dream"), actress (*Ain't Misbehavin'*), born Bronx, NY, Mar 18, 1959.
Frederik Willem de Klerk, 62, former president of South Africa, born Johannesburg, South Africa, Mar 18, 1936.
Kevin Dobson, 54, actor ("Kojak," "Knots Landing"), born New York, NY, Mar 18, 1944.
Brad Dourif, 48, (*One Flew Over the Cuckoo's Nest, Blue Velvet, Jungle Fever*), born Huntington, WV, Mar 18, 1950.
Peter Graves, 72, brother of James Arness, actor ("Mission: Impossible," "The Winds of War"), born Minneapolis, MN, Mar 18, 1926.
George Kander, 71, composer, born Kansas City, MO, Mar 18, 1927.
Shashi Kapoor, 60, actor (*Heat and Dust, Sammy and Rosie Get Laid*), born Calcutta, India, Mar 18, 1938.
Queen Latifah, 28, rap artist, actress (*Jungle Fever*, "Living Single"), born East Orange, NJ, Mar 18, 1970.
Wilson Pickett, 57, singer, songwriter ("The Midnight Hour," "It's Too Late"), born Prattville, AL, Mar 18, 1941.
George Plimpton, 71, author (*Paper Lion, Shadow Box*), TV host, editor, born New York, NY, Mar 18, 1927.
John Updike, 66, author (*Rabbit Run, The Witches of Eastwick*), born Shillington, PA, Mar 18, 1932.
Vanessa Williams, 35, singer, actress (*Bye, Bye Birdie, Kiss of the Spider Woman*), born New York, NY, Mar 18, 1963.

MARCH 19 — THURSDAY

Day 78 — 287 Remaining

ABSOLUTELY INCREDIBLE KID DAY. Mar 19. Camp Fire Boys and Girls, one of the nation's oldest and largest youth development organizations, holds its second annual event to encourage adults to write a letter to a child in their life to tell the child how special they are and how much they mean to them. Annually, the third Thursday in March. For info: Camp Fire Boys and Girls, 4601 Madison, Kansas City, MO 64112. Phone: (816) 756-1950. Fax: (816) 756-0258.

BRADFORD, WILLIAM: BIRTH ANNIVERSARY. Mar 19, 1589. Pilgrim father, governor of Plymouth Colony. Born at Yorkshire, England, and baptized on Mar 19, 1589. Sailed from Southampton, England, on the *Mayflower* in 1620. Died at Plymouth, MA, on May 9, 1657.

BRYAN, WILLIAM JENNINGS: BIRTH ANNIVERSARY. Mar 19. American political leader, member of Congress, Democratic presidential nominee (1896), "free silver" advocate, assisted in prosecution at Scopes trial, known as "the Silver-Tongued Orator." Born at Salem, IL, Mar 19, 1860. Died at Dayton, TN, July 26, 1925.

EARP, WYATT: 150th BIRTH ANNIVERSARY. Mar 19, 1848. Born at Monmouth, IL, and died Jan 13, 1929, at Los Angeles, CA. A legendary figure of the Old West, Earp worked as a railroad hand, saloonkeeper, gambler, lawman, gunslinger, miner and real estate investor at various times. Best known for his involvement in the gunfight at the OK Corral on Oct 26, 1881, in Tombstone, AZ.

ENGLAND: CHELSEA ANTIQUES FAIR. Mar 19–29 (also Sept 10–20). Chelsea Old Town Hall, King's Rd, London. Prestigious antiques fair with a wide range of pre-1830 furniture and other items with a pre-1860 dateline, for sale. Est attendance: 9,000. For info: Penman Antiques Fair, Haywards Heath, PO Box 114, Haywards Heath, West Sussex, England RH16 2YU. Phone: (44) (144) 448-2514. Fax: (44) (144) 448-3412.

FLORIDA STATE BOAT AND SPORTS SHOW. Mar 19–22. Florida Expo Park, Tampa, FL. Sponsor: Natl Marine Manufacturers Assn. Est attendance: 15,000. For info: Carolyn Luis, 400 Arthur Godfrey Rd, Ste 310, Miami Beach, FL 33140. Phone: (305) 531-8410. Fax: (305) 534-3139.

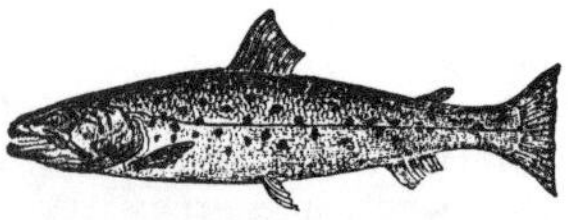

GRAND CENTER SPORT, FISHING AND TRAVEL SHOW. Mar 19–22. Grand Center, Grand Rapids, MI. This event brings together buyers and sellers of fishing boats and equipment, RVs, campers and their accessories, as well as other outdoor sporting goods. US and Canadian hunting and fishing trips and other vacation travel destinations are featured. All aspects of fishing, including tackle boats, seminars, demonstrations and displays are emphasized. Est attendance: 45,000. For info: Henri Boucher, ShowSpan, Inc, 1400 28th St SW, Grand Rapids, MI 49509. Phone: (616) 530-1919. Fax: (616) 530-2122.

LIVINGSTONE, DAVID: BIRTH ANNIVERSARY. Mar 19, 1813. Scottish physician, missionary and explorer. Born at Blantyre, Scotland, Mar 19, 1813. Subject of a famous search by Henry M. Stanley, who found him at Ujiji, near Lake Tanganyika in Africa, on Nov 10, 1871. Dr. Livingstone died in Africa, May 1, 1873. See also: "Stanley, Henry Morton: Birth Anniversary" (Jan 28).

"MARY TYLER MOORE SHOW": THE FINAL EPISODE: ANNIVERSARY. Mar 19, 1977. "Mary Tyler Moore" was the first of a new wave of sitcoms to make it big in the early '70s. It combined good writing, an effective supporting cast and contemporary attitudes. The show centered around the two most important places in Mary Richards's (Mary Tyler Moore) life—the WJM-TV newsroom and her apartment on North Waverly in Minneapolis. At home she shared the ups and downs of life with her friend Rhoda Morgenstern (Valerie Harper) and the manager of her apartment building, Phyllis Lindstrom (Cloris Leachman). At work, as the associate producer (later producer) of "The Six O'Clock News," Mary struggled to function in a man's world. Figuring in her professional life were her irascible boss Lou Grant (Ed Asner), levelheaded and softhearted news writer Murray Slaughter (Gavin MacLeod) and self-obsessed, narcissistic anchorman Ted Baxter (Ted Knight). In the last episode the unthinkable happened—everyone in the WJM newsroom except the inept Ted was fired. (Premiered fall of 1970 and ran for 168 episodes.)

A MOUNTAIN QUILTFEST. Mar 19–22. Smoky Mountain Convention Center, Pigeon Forge, TN. The Piecemakers and the Sevier Valley Quilters join forces with some world-renowned instructors. Show free; fees for lessons. Est attendance: 5,000. For info: Kay Powell, Pigeon Forge Dept of Tourism, 2450 Parkway, PO Box 1390, Pigeon Forge, TN 37868. Phone: (800) 251-9100 or (423) 453-8574.
WWW: http://www.pigeon-forge.tn.us

ROGERS, EDITH NOURSE: BIRTH ANNIVERSARY. Mar 19, 1881. Edith Nourse Rogers was a YMCA and Red Cross volunteer in France during World War I. In 1925 she was elected to the US Congress to fill the vacancy left by the death of her husband. An able legislator, she was reelected to the House of Representatives 17 times and became the first woman to have her name attached to major legislation. She was a major force in the legislation creating the Women's Army Auxiliary Corps (May 14, 1942) during World War II. Rogers was born at Saco, ME, and died Sept 10, 1960, at Boston.

RUSSELL, CHARLES M.: BIRTH ANNIVERSARY. Mar 19, 1864. Born at St. Louis, MO, Charles M. Russell moved to Montana at about age 16 and became a cowboy. Considered one of the greatest Western artists, he recorded the life of a cowboy in his artwork. He died Oct 26, 1926, at Great Falls, MT.

March 1998

S	M	T	W	T	F	S
1	2	3	4	5	6	7
8	9	10	11	12	13	14
15	16	17	18	19	20	21
22	23	24	25	26	27	28
29	30	31				

RYDER, ALBERT PINKHAM: BIRTH ANNIVERSARY. Mar 19, 1847. Painter Albert Pinkham Ryder was born at New Bedford, MA, where he gained a great love for the sea, the subject of many of his works. Even after moving with his family to New York City in 1868, Ryder was a misanthrope and recluse. He dedicated himself totally to his painting, working slowly and piling layer after layer of paint on his canvases until he achieved the look he was after. In his lifetime Ryder created only 150 paintings. Three of his best-known works are *The Race Track*, *Toilers of the Sea* and *Siegfried and the Rhine Maidens*. Ryder died at age 70 on Mar 28, 1917, at Elmhurst, NY. Because of his method of painting, many of his works have deteriorated seriously since their creation.

SCHMECKFEST. Mar 19–22. Freeman, SD. (Mar 22 Matinee performance only.) Bratwurst and sauerkraut, kuchen and pluma moos. These are just a few of the dishes served at this German "festival of tasting" where visitors can also watch cooking and craft demonstrations and an evening musical. Est attendance: 8,000. For info: LaRuth Kramer, 44147 280th St, Freeman, SD 57029. Phone: (605) 925-7362.

SIRICA, JOHN JOSEPH: BIRTH ANNIVERSARY. Mar 19, 1904. John Sirica, "the Watergate Judge," was born at Waterbury, CT. During two years of trials and hearings, Sirica relentlessly pushed for the names of those responsible for the June 17, 1972, burglary of the Democratic National Committee headquarters in Washington's Watergate Complex. Sirica's unwavering search for the truth ultimately resulted in the toppling of the Nixon administration. Judge John Sirica died Aug 15, 1992, at Washington, DC.

SPIFFS INTERNATIONAL FOLK FAIR. Mar 19–22. St. Petersburg, FL. An international folk fair with arts, crafts, music, dance and foods of 57 different ethnicities. Exhibitors are members only. Colorful, exciting Parade of Nations. Est attendance: 50,000. For info: The St. Petersburg Intl Folk Fair Soc (SPIFFS), 2201 First Ave N, St. Petersburg, FL 33713. Phone: (813) 327-7999. Fax: (813) 323-1913. Email: folkfair@aol.com.

SWALLOWS RETURN TO SAN JUAN CAPISTRANO. Mar 19. Traditional date (St. Joseph's Day) for swallows to return to old mission of San Juan Capistrano, CA, since 1776. See also: "St. John of Capistrano: Death Anniversary" (Oct 23).

US STANDARD TIME ACT: 80th ANNIVERSARY. Mar 19, 1918. Anniversary of passage by the Congress of the Standard Time Act, which authorized the Interstate Commerce Commission to establish standard time zones for the US. The Act also established "Daylight-Saving Time," to save fuel and to promote other economies in a country at war. Daylight-saving time first went into operation on Easter Sunday, Mar 31, 1918. The Uniform Time Act of 1966, as amended in 1986, by Public Law 99–359, now governs standard time in the US. See also: "Daylight-Saving Time" (Apr 5).

VAN FLEET, JAMES ALWARD: BIRTH ANNIVERSARY. Mar 19, 1892. US Army four-star general James Alward Van Fleet was born at Coytesville, NJ. He served in World War I, World War II, the Korean War and consulted the Defense Department during the Vietnam War. He was awarded the Distinguished Service Cross with three oak leaf clusters among numerous other decorations during his service. He died on Sept 23, 1992, at Polk City, FL.

WARREN, EARL: BIRTH ANNIVERSARY. Mar 19, 1891. American jurist, 14th Chief Justice of the US Supreme Court. Born at Los Angeles, CA; died at Washington, DC, July 9, 1974.

WINGS OVER THE PLATTE. Mar 19–22. Grand Island, NE. Celebrate the arrival of the world's largest concentration of sandhill cranes. Each spring up to 500,000 cranes gather along the Platte River during their northward migration. Seminars, tours, nature hikes, films. Est attendance: 1,000. For info: Theresa Kuzelka, Grand Island/Hall County Conv and Visitors Bureau, PO Box 1486, Grand Island, NE 68802. Phone: (800) 658-3178 or (308) 382-4400. Fax: (308) 382-1154. Email: cvb@gionline.net.
WWW: http://www.gionline.net/cvb

BIRTHDAYS TODAY

Ursula Andress, 62, actress (*Dr. No, What's New Pussycat?*), born Bern, Switzerland, Mar 19, 1936.

Glenn Close, 51, actress (*The Big Chill, Fatal Attraction*; stage: *Sunset Boulevard*), born Greenwich, CT, Mar 19, 1947.

Ornette Coleman, 68, composer, saxophonist, born Fort Worth, TX, Mar 19, 1930.

Patrick McGoohan, 70, director, actor ("The Prisoner"), born New York, NY, Mar 19, 1928.

Philip Roth, 65, author (*The Great American Novel, Portnoy's Complaint*), born Newark, NJ, Mar 19, 1933.

Brent Scowcroft, 73, business executive, consultant, born Ogden, UT, Mar 19, 1925.

Renee Taylor, 63, actress, writer ("Acts of Love and Other Comedies" [Emmy], "Mary Hartman, Mary Hartman," *The Producers, A New Leaf*), born New York, NY, Mar 19, 1935.

Bruce Willis, 43, actor ("Moonlighting," *In Country, Die Hard*), born Penn's Grove, NJ, Mar 19, 1955.

MARCH 20 — FRIDAY

Day 79 — 286 Remaining

BLUEGRASS MUSIC WEEKEND. Mar 20–22. Iowan Motor Lodge, Ft Madison, IA. 11th annual event. Est attendance: 2,000. For info: Delbert Spray, RR1, Kahoka, MO 63445. Phone: (573) 853-4344.

FLOWERCRAFT. Mar 20–22. Wilson Lodge, Oglebay, Wheeling, WV. A unique arts and crafts show, featuring more than 50 artisans displaying spring garden floral themed handcrafts. Est attendance: 5,000. For info: Barbara Palmer, Special Events Coord, Oglebay, Rt 88 N, Wheeling, WV 26003. Phone: (304) 243-4121. Fax: (304) 243-4110.
WWW: http://wvweb.com/oglebay

GREAT AMERICAN MEATOUT. Mar 20. America's foremost celebration of meatless eating asks consumers to "kick the meat habit, at least for the day" at 1,000 events across the country. For info: Farm Animal Reform Movement, Box 30654, Bethesda, MD 20824. Phone: (301) 530-1737 or (800) MEAT-OUT. Fax: (301) 530-5747. Email: farmusa@erols.com.
WWW: http://envirolink.org/arrs/farm

IBSEN, HENRIK: BIRTH ANNIVERSARY. Mar 20, 1828. Norwegian playwright. Born at Skien, Norway. Among his best-remembered plays: *Peer Gynt, The Pillars of Society, The Wild Duck, An Enemy of the People* and *Hedda Gabler*. Died at Oslo, Norway, May 23, 1906.

LONGHORN WORLD CHAMPIONSHIP RODEO. Mar 20–22. Celeste Center, Columbus, OH. More than 300 of the best cowboys and cowgirls compete in six professional contests ranging from bronc riding to bull riding for top prize money and world championship points. Featuring colorful opening pageantry and Big, Bad BONUS Bulls. 24th annual. Est attendance: 18,000. For info: W. Bruce Lehrke, Pres, Longhorn World Championship Rodeo, Inc, PO Box 70159, Nashville, TN 37207. Phone: (615) 876-1016. Fax: (615) 876-4685. Email: lhrodeo@idt.net. WWW: http://www.longhornrodeo.com

MACON CHERRY BLOSSOM FESTIVAL. Mar 20–29. Macon, GA. 16th annual Cherry Blossom Festival features concerts, exhibits, parades, children's events, hot-air balloons, street party, fireworks, food, fun and family entertainment. 224,000 Yoshino cherry trees. Est attendance: 600,000. For info: Debbie Smith, Macon Cherry Blossom Fest, 794 Cherry St, Macon, GA 31201. Phone: (912) 751-7429. Fax: (912) 751-7408. WWW: http://www.cherryblossom.com

NATIONAL AGRICULTURE DAY. Mar 20. A day to honor America's providers of food and fiber and to educate the general public about the US agricultural system. Week of celebration: Mar 15–21. Annually, the first day of spring. For info: Agriculture Council of America, 927 15th St NW, Ste 800, Washington, DC 20005. Phone: (800) 982-4329. Fax: (202) 289-6648. Email: agcounsil@aol.com.

NATIONAL SPRING FEVER WEEK. Mar 20. Annually, the first day of spring. Recognizing the special socialization rites single people face during this season of revitalization. For info: Robin Gorman Newman, 58 Grace Ave, #2J, Great Neck, NY 11021. Phone: (516) 773-0911. Email: rgnewman@aol.com.

NERVE-GAS ATTACK ON JAPANESE SUBWAY: ANNIVERSARY. Mar 20, 1995. Twelve people were killed and 5,000 injured in a nerve gas attack on the Tokyo subway system during rush hour. Suspected in the attack was the Japanese religious sect Aum Shinrikyo, founded and led by Shoko Asahara (real name Chizuo Matsumoto). The group, which professes belief in a hybrid of Buddhist-Hindu teachings, predicts an apocalypse. In a raid conducted against the sect's main compound in Kamikuishiki on Mar 25, police seized literature that predicted 90 percent of the people in the world would be killed by poison gas. Also seized were two tons of chemicals for making sarin, the poison used in the Mar 20 attack. Sarin is one of the most deadly compounds known. A small amount can paralyze the central nervous system and cause death. This cache was reported to contain enough materials to kill five million people. In a second raid, televised by most major Japanese television stations on May 16, Asahara was arrested. Asahara and 40 members of Aum Shinrikyo were charged with murder and attempted murder.

NEWTON, ISAAC: DEATH ANNIVERSARY. Mar 20, 1727. Sir Isaac Newton was the chief figure of the scientific revolution of the 17th century, a physicist and mathematician who laid the foundations of calculus, studied the mechanics of planetary motion and discovered the law of gravitation. Born at Woolsthorpe, England, on Dec 25, 1642, he died at London, England, on Mar 20, 1727.

NORTHEAST GREAT OUTDOORS SHOW. Mar 20–22. Empire State Plaza, Albany, NY. 12th annual expo with seminars by professional sportsmen, archery range, duck-calling contest, casting pool and lots of exhibitors. Annually, the third full weekend in March. Sponsor: Albany Times Union Newspapers. Est attendance: 20,000. For info: Heather Mabee, Exec Dir, Ed Lewi Assoc, 6 Chelsea Pl, Clifton Park, NY 12065. Phone: (518) 383-6183. Fax: (518) 383-6755.

OSTARA. Mar 20. (Also called Alban Eilir.) One of the "Lesser Sabbats" during the Wiccan year, Ostara is a fire and fertility festival that marks the beginning of spring. Annually, on the spring equinox.

PIGEONS RETURN TO THE CITY-COUNTY BUILDING. Mar 20. City-County Bldg, Ft Wayne, IN. Pigeons flock back to Ft Wayne's municipal building after the long winter. Umbrellas are recommended for viewing the event! Est attendance: 150. For info: Barb Richards, Program Dir, WAJI Radio, 347 W Berry, Ste 600, Ft Wayne, IN 46802. Phone: (219) 423-3676. Fax: (219) 422-5266. WWW: http://www.waji.com

PROPOSAL DAY!®. Mar 20 (also Sept 23). Proposal Day is a holiday for singles who are seeking marriage. Both bachelors and bachelorettes are encouraged to propose marriage to their true love on Proposal Day; the days of the vernal and autumnal equinoxes. Singles not quite ready to propose can celebrate the holiday by sending a gift to the one they hope to marry someday. List released each equinox of the 10 most eligible celebrity singles. Annually, on the first day of spring (vernal equinox). For info: John Michael O'Loughlin, 1333 W Campbell, #125, Richardson, TX 75080. Phone: (972) 721-9975.

SHAMROCK SPORTSFEST. Mar 20–21. Pavilion Convention Center, Virginia Beach, VA. Marathon 8K, Masters 8K, 5K walk, sports and fitness expo, runner's clinic and children's marathon. Friday night pasta party. Saturday night party. Est attendance: 25,000. For info: Shamrock Sportsfest, 2308 Maple St, Virginia Beach, VA 23451-1310. Phone: (757) 481-5090. Fax: (757) 481-2942. Email: sportsfest@juno.com.

SKINNER, B.F.: BIRTH ANNIVERSARY. Mar 20, 1904. American psychologist Burrhus Frederic Skinner was born at Susquehanna, PA. He was a pioneer in behaviorism, and he is best known for developing the "Skinner box" (an enclosed experimental environment). He died on Aug 18, 1990, at Cambridge, MA.

SNOWMAN BURNING. Mar 20. Reading of poetry heralding the end of winter and the arrival of spring, followed by sacrifice in effigy, toasts and cheers. Annually, on or near the first day of spring. Est attendance: 300. For info: Lake Superior State University, Sault Ste. Marie, MI 49783. Phone: (906) 635-2315. Fax: (906) 635-2111. WWW: http://www.lssu.edu

SPRING. Mar 20–June 21. In the Northern Hemisphere spring begins today with the vernal equinox, at 2:55 PM, EST. Note that in the Southern Hemisphere today is the beginning of autumn. Sun rises due east and sets due west everywhere on Earth (except near poles) and the daylight length (interval between sunrise and sunset) is virtually the same everywhere today: 12 hours, 8 minutes.

STAMP EXPO. Mar 20–22. Quality Hotel, Anaheim, CA. Annual Anaheim expo. Est attendance: 4,000. For info: Intl Stamp Collectors Soc, PO Box 854, Van Nuys, CA 91408. Phone: (818) 997-6496. Fax: (818) 988-4337.
Email: iibick@aol.com. WWW: http://www.4free.com/bick

SUGARLOAF'S SPRING FORT WASHINGTON CRAFT FESTIVAL. Mar 20–22. Fort Washington Expo Center, Fort Washington, PA. Now in its 4th year, this show features 300 nationally recognized craft designers and fine artists displaying and selling their original creations. Demonstrations, hourly gift certificate drawings and more. Est attendance: 23,000. For info: Sugarloaf Mountain Works, Inc, 200 Orchard Ridge Dr, #215, Gaithersburg, MD 20878. Phone: (800) 210-9900.

TENNESSEE OLD TIME FIDDLER'S CHAMPIONSHIP. Mar 20–21 (tentative). Clarksville, TN. A music festival you will never forget. Features many of the best "old-time" musicians competing for the title and cash prizes. Est attendance: 3,000. For info: Clarksville Tourist Information Center, 180 Holiday Rd, Clarksville, TN 37040. Phone: (615) 648-0001.

TUNISIA: INDEPENDENCE DAY. Mar 20. Commemorates treaty of Mar 20, 1956, by which France recognized Tunisian autonomy.

March 1998

S	M	T	W	T	F	S
1	2	3	4	5	6	7
8	9	10	11	12	13	14
15	16	17	18	19	20	21
22	23	24	25	26	27	28
29	30	31				

VICTORIAN HOLMES WEEKEND. Mar 20–22. Cape May, NJ. A weekend of mystery and intrigue awaits amateur sleuths when Cape May celebrates the works of Sir Arthur Conan Doyle, creator of Sherlock Holmes. Annually, the second weekend in March, Friday–Sunday. Est attendance: 200. For info: Mid-Atlantic Center for the Arts, 1048 Washington St, PO Box 340, Cape May, NJ 08204. Phone: (609) 884-5404 or (800) 275-4278 for tickets. Fax: (609) 884-2006.
Email: mac4arts@algorithms.com.
WWW: http://www.beachcomber.com/capemay/mac.html

WHOOPERS AND HOOPERS INVITATIONAL BASKETBALL TOURNAMENT. Mar 20–22. Hastings, NE. 17th annual tournament in which more than 140 teams and 1,400 invited basketball participants—former professional, collegiate and high school—compete five on five. Divided into six divisions including A (semi-pro or AAU caliber), B (upper intermediate), C (intermediate), D1 & D2 (small-town teams) and women's A (AAU caliber) and B (all others). Trophies awarded for top four places in each division. Est attendance: 3,000. For info: Whoopers and Hoopers, 606 West Fifth, Hastings, NE 68901. Phone: (402) 462-4159.

BIRTHDAYS TODAY

Holly Hunter, 40, actress (Oscar and Best Actress at Cannes for *The Piano; Broadcast News, The Firm*), born Conyers, GA, Mar 20, 1958.

William Hurt, 48, actor (*The Accidental Tourist, Broadcast News*), born Washington, DC, Mar 20 1950.

Spike Lee, 41, director, producer, writer, actor (*She's Gotta Have It* [LA Film Critics Award for best new director, 1986], *Do the Right Thing* [LA Film Critics Awards for best picture and director, 1989], *Mo' Better Blues, Jungle Fever, Malcolm X, Crooklyn, Clockers*), born Atlanta, GA, Mar 20, 1957.

Hal Linden (Harold Lipshitz), 67, actor ("Barney Miller," "Blacke's Magic"), born The Bronx, NY, Mar 20, 1931.

Marian McPartland, 78, musician (*After Hours, Ambiance, Personal Choice, In My Life*), founder of Halcyon Records, born Slough, England, Mar 20, 1920.

Brian Mulroney, 59, Canadian statesman and 18th prime minister of Canada, born Baie Comeau, Quebec, Mar 20, 1939.

Rosie O'Donnell, 36, actress (*A League of Their Own*), host ("The Rosie O'Donnell Show"), born Commack, NY, Mar 21, 1962.

Robert Gordon (Bobby) Orr, 50, Hockey Hall of Fame defenseman, born Parry Sound, Ont, Canada, Mar 20, 1948.

Jerry Reed (Jerry Hubbard), 61, singer, songwriter ("When You're Hot, You're Hot"), born Atlanta, GA, Mar 20, 1937.

Carl Reiner, 76, actor ("The Dick Van Dyke Show," "Your Show of Shows"), writer, director, born Bronx, NY, Mar 20, 1922.

Patrick James (Pat) Riley, 53, basketball coach and former player, born Schenectady, NY, Mar 20, 1945.

Fred Rogers, 70, producer, TV personality ("Mr Rogers' Neighborhood"), born Latrobe, PA, Mar 20, 1928.

Theresa Russell, 41, actress (*Straight Time, Black Widow*), born San Diego, CA, Mar 20, 1957.

Paul Junger Witt, 55, producer, director, born New York, NY, Mar 20, 1943.

MARCH 21 — SATURDAY

Day 80 — 285 Remaining

ARIES, THE RAM. Mar 21–Apr 19. In the astronomical/astrological zodiac, which divides the sun's apparent orbit into 12 segments, the period Mar 21–Apr 19 is identified, traditionally, as the sun sign of Aries, the Ram. The ruling planet is Mars.

ARTISTS' NATIONAL JURIED COMPETITION. Mar 21–Apr 18. Coastal Center for the Arts, St. Simons Island, GA. 45th annual. Artists nationwide submit work to be judged for entry and prizes. Deadline for entry is Feb 10, 1998. 45th annual exhibit opens the Saturday of the Annual Tour of Homes as a special event of the tour with official opening awards presentation. Leading floral designers interpret selected artworks. In 1996 this show attracted artists from Japan, Afghanistan, Mexico and Canada. It is considered the premier show of the region for the year. Est attendance: 2,000. For info: Coastal Center for the Arts, 2012 Demere Rd, St. Simons Island, GA 31522. Phone: (912) 634-0404.

BACH, JOHANN SEBASTIAN: BIRTH ANNIVERSARY. Mar 21. Organist and composer, one of the most influential composers in musical history. Born on Mar 21, 1685, at Eisenach, Germany. Died at Leipzig, Germany, on July 28, 1750.

BIG 10 MEN'S GYMNASTICS CHAMPIONSHIP. Mar 21–22. University of Michigan, Ann Arbor, MI. For info: Dennis LaBissoniere, Big Ten Conference, 1500 W Higgins Rd, Park Ridge, IL 60068-6300. Phone: (847) 696-1010. Fax: (847) 696-1110. WWW: http://www.bigten.org

BIG 10 WOMEN'S GYMNASTICS CHAMPIONSHIP. Mar 21. University of Iowa, Iowa City, IA. Est attendance: 1,900. For info: Dennis LaBissoniere, Big Ten Conference, 1500 W Higgins Rd, Park Ridge, IL 60068-6300. Phone: (847) 696-1010. Fax: (847) 696-1110. WWW: http://www.bigten.org

BIG 12 WOMEN'S GYMNASTICS CHAMPIONSHIP. Mar 21. Place TBA. Est attendance: 2,000. For info: Julie Dorn, Championships, Big 12 Conference, 2201 Stemmons Freeway, 28th Floor, Dallas, TX 75207. Phone: (214) 742-1212. Fax: (214) 742-2045.

BIRD DAY—IOWA. Mar 21. Iowa state observance.

CAMP FIRE BOYS AND GIRLS BIRTHDAY SABBATH. Mar 21. A day when Camp Fire Boys and Girls commemorate the organization's founding and worship together and participate in the services in their churches or temples. For info: Camp Fire Boys and Girls, 4601 Madison Ave, Kansas City, MO 64112. Phone: (816) 756-1950. Fax: (816) 756-0258. Email: info@campfire.org. WWW: http://www.campfire.org

CANADA: MAPLE FESTIVAL OF NOVA SCOTIA. Mar 21–Apr 11 (Saturdays only). Northern Nova Scotia. Promotion of the maple industry. Pancake suppers with entertainment, industry equipment displays and crafts displays. Est attendance: 5,000. For info: Lorna A. Crowe, RR1, Southampton, Cumberland Co, NS, Canada B0M 1W0. Phone: (902) 546-2844.

FLOWER DAY. Mar 21. Citizens will give or display flowers or plants in their communities and neighborhoods, schools, hospitals, businesses, memorials, shopping malls, government agencies; each state will honor the state flower at its capital. Area florists will also advertise Flower Day. For info: Fifth Street Flower Shop, 739 S 5th St, Springfiled, IL 62703.

FOUR EVENINGS OF IRISH FILM. Mar 21–23. Screenings at The Grand Opera House, Wilmington, DE. Festival of Irish films features both recent and classic films by Irish directors and studios. One feature length and short form presented on each evening followed by a discussion period. Est attendance: 650. For info: Rockwood Museum, 610 Shipley Rd, Wilmington, DE 19809. Phone: (302) 761-4340. Fax: (302) 764-4570.
Email: info@rockwood.org. WWW: http://www.rockwood.org

GALLO, JULIO: BIRTH ANNIVERSARY. Mar 21, 1910. American vintner Julio Gallo was born at Oakland, CA. He is best known for his role in the Ernest and Julio Gallo Winery, of Modesto, CA, which at one time claimed about 26 percent of the US wine industry. He died on May 2, 1993, near Tracy, CA.

GERSDORFF HITLER ASSASSINATION ATTEMPT: 55th ANNIVERSARY. Mar 21, 1943. In a suicide/assassination attempt planned for this date, Major General Baron von Gersdorff was to carry a bomb in the pocket of his greatcoat to the "Heroes Memorial Day" annual dedication to the dead of the First World War. Hitler was to attend this event to inspect some weaponry taken from captured Russian soldiers. The bomb was to go off within ten minutes of Hitler's arrival at the event as he was not expected to be there for very long. The conspirators were unable to locate the necessary short time fuse and the attempt had to be called off. This was the second serious plan to assassinate Hitler in 1943.

INTERNATIONAL ASTROLOGY DAY. Mar 21. To foster a spirit of networking among the astrological community worldwide; to build and enhance ties among individual astrologers and astrological organizations; and to educate the media and the public about the nature of serious astrology. Annually, Mar 21. For info: Assn for Astrological Networking (AFAN), 8306 Wilshire Blvd, Ste 537, Beverly Hills, CA 90211. Phone: (800) 578-AFAN. Fax: (212) 799-2748. Email: rgdreyer@aol.com.
WWW: http://www.AFAN.org

IRANIAN NEW YEAR: NORUZ. Mar 21. National celebration for all Iranians, this is the traditional Persian New Year. (In Iran spring comes on Mar 21.) It is a celebration of nature's rebirth. Every household spreads a special cover with symbols for the seven good angels on it. These symbols are sprouts, wheat germ, apples, hyacinth, fruit of the jujube, garlic and sumac heralding life, rebirth, health, happiness, prosperity, joy and beauty. A fish bowl is also customary, representing the end of the astrological year, and wild rue is burnt to drive away evil and bring about a happy New Year. For info: Mahvash Tafreshi, Librarian, Farmingdale Public Library, 116 Merritts Rd, Farmingdale, NY 11735. Phone: (516) 249-9090. Fax: (516) 694-9697 or Yassaman Djalali, Librarian, West Valley Branch Library, 1243 San Tomas Aquino Rd, San Jose, CA 95117. Phone: (408) 244-4766.

JUAREZ, BENITO PABLO: BIRTH ANNIVERSARY. Mar 21, 1806. A full-blooded Zapotec Indian, Benito Pablo Juarez was born at Oaxaca, Mexico, on Mar 21, 1806, and grew up to become the president of Mexico. He learned Spanish at age 12. Juarez became judge of the civil court in Oaxaca in 1842, a member of congress in 1846 and governor in 1847. In 1858, following a rebellion against the constitution, the presidency was passed to Juarez. He died at Mexico City July 18, 1872. A symbol of liberation and of Mexican resistance to foreign intervention, his birthday is a public holiday in Mexico.

LESOTHO: NATIONAL TREE PLANTING DAY. Mar 21. Lesotho, South Africa.

LEWIS, FRANCIS: BIRTH ANNIVERSARY. Mar 21, 1713. Signer of the Declaration of Independence. Born at Wales, Mar 21, 1713. Died Dec 31, 1802.

LUNSFORD, BASCOM LAMAR: BIRTH ANNIVERSARY. Mar 21, 1882. Folk song writer and folklorist who authored the folk song "Mountain Dew," Lunsford started the first folk music festival in 1928 in Asheville, NC. This event, which led to the formation of the National Clogging and Hoedown Council, is held to this day. He was known as the "father of clogging dance" and the "king of folk music." He memorized and recorded some 320 folk songs, tunes and stories for the Library of Congress. Born at Mars Hill, NC. Lunsford died Sept 4, 1973, at South Turkey Creek, NC.

MAPLE SYRUP SATURDAY. Mar 21. Gordon Bubolz Nature Preserve, Appleton, WI. Find out how to make maple syrup. Est attendance: 1,000. For info: Mike Brandel, Exec Dir, Gordon Bubolz Nature Preserve, 4815 N Lynndale Dr, Appleton, WI 54915. Phone: (414) 731-6041. Fax: (414) 731-9593.
Email: Bubolz@dataex.com.
WWW: http://www.geocities.com/Rainforest/4579

MARYLAND DAYS. Mar 21–22. Historic St. Mary's City, St. Mary's City, MD. Season-opening weekend for historic area, the site of Maryland's 17th-century capital. Marks the founding of the state in 1634. Pageantry, living history, food and music. Usually held on the weekend nearest Mar 25, the official state holiday. Est attendance: 6,000. For info: Public Affairs Office, Historic St. Mary's City, PO Box 39, St. Mary's City, MD 20686. Phone: (301) 862-0990 or (800) SMC-1634. Fax: (301) 862-0968.

MASTER GARDENER DAY. Mar 21. A day to recognize both Master Gardeners and The Master Gardener Program, which was begun by Dr. Dave Gibby in the state of Washington in 1972. Becoming an official Master Gardener involves completing a gardening course and serving an internship of volunteer work on various projects with a Master Gardener. Requirements vary from state to state. An international organization called MaGic was started in 1988. Annually, on the first full day of spring. For info: Master Gardeners International Corporation, 2904 Cameron Mills Road, Alexandria, VA 22302.

MEMORY DAY. Mar 21. To encourage awareness of traditional memory system using pattern t,d = 1; n = 2; m = 3; r = 4; l = 5; j,ch = 6; k,q,g-hard = 7; f,v = 8; b,p = 9. Study historic examples of the use of the memory system in the writings of Milton, Thomas Gray, Longfellow, Lincoln and others. For info: Robert L. Birch, Coord, Puns Corps, Box 2364, Falls Church, VA 22042-0364. Phone: (703) 533-3668.

MILITARY THROUGH THE AGES. Mar 21–22. Jamestown Settlement, Williamsburg, VA. Reenactment groups depicting soldiers and military encounters throughout history join forces with modern-day veterans and active units to demonstrate camp life, tactics and weaponry. Est attendance: 4,000. For info: Media Relations, Jamestown-Yorktown Fdtn, Box 1607, Williamsburg, VA 23187. Phone: (757) 253-4838.
WWW: http://www.historyisfun.org

MOON PHASE: LAST QUARTER. Mar 21. Moon enters Last Quarter phase at 2:38 AM, EST.

NAMIBIA: INDEPENDENCE DAY. Mar 21. National Day.

NAW-RUZ. Mar 21. Baha'i New Year's Day. Astronomically fixed to commence the year. One of the nine days of the year when Baha'is suspend work. For info: Pamela Zivari, Baha'is of the US, Office of Public Info, 866 UN Plaza, Ste 120, New York, NY 10017-1822. Phone: (212) 803-2500. Fax: (212) 803-2573. Email: usopi-ny@bic.org.

March 1998

S	M	T	W	T	F	S
1	2	3	4	5	6	7
8	9	10	11	12	13	14
15	16	17	18	19	20	21
22	23	24	25	26	27	28
29	30	31				

NEW JERSEY SONGWRITER'S SHOW. Mar 21. Waretown, NJ. Original music written and performed by musicians from New Jersey. No alcoholic beverages or smoking allowed. Est attendance: 400. For info: New Jersey Songwriter's Show, Albert Music Hall, PO Box 657, Waretown, NJ 08758. Phone: (609) 971-1593.

POCAHONTAS (REBECCA ROLFE): DEATH ANNIVERSARY. Mar 21, 1617. Pocahontas, daughter of Powhatan, leader of the Indian union of Algonkin nations, helped to foster good will between the colonists of the Jamestown settlement and her people. Pocahontas converted to Christianity, was baptized with the name Rebecca and married John Rolfe Apr 5, 1614. In 1616, she accompanied Rolfe on a trip to his native England, where she was regarded as an overseas "ambassador." Pocahontas's stay in England drew so much attention to the Virginia Company's Jamestown settlement that lotteries were held to help support the colony. Shortly before she was scheduled to return to Jamestown, Pocahontas died of either smallpox or pneumonia.

PURSUE THE POSSIBILITIES. Mar 21–22. Miami Valley Centre Mall, Piqua, OH. A showcase of the many festivals, events, museums and more in the upper Miami Valley area. For info: Miami County Visitors & Conv Bureau, PO Box 159, Troy, OH 45373. Phone: (800) 348-8993 or (937) 339-1044. WWW: http://www.TDN-net.com

STRANG, JAMES JESSE (KING STRANG): BIRTH ANNIVERSARY. Mar 21, 1813. Perhaps America's only crowned king was born at Scipio, NY, and christened Jesse James Strang (which he later changed to James Jesse Strang). He was crowned king of Mormons on Beaver Island, MI, July 8, 1850, and ruled his kingdom until his death. Elected to Michigan legislature in 1852 and 1854. Wounded by assassins on June 16, 1856, on Beaver Island, he died on June 19 at Voree, WI, at age 43.

UNITED NATIONS: INTERNATIONAL DAY FOR THE ELIMINATION OF RACIAL DISCRIMINATION. Mar 21. Initiated by the United Nations General Assembly in 1966 to be observed annually on Mar 21, the anniversary of the killing of 69 African demonstrators at Sharpeville, South Africa in 1960, as a day to remember "the victims of Sharpeville and those countless others in different parts of the world who have fallen victim to racial injustice" and to promote efforts to eradicate racial discrimination worldwide. Info from: United Nations, Dept of Public Info, New York, NY 10017.

UNITED NATIONS: WEEK OF SOLIDARITY WITH THE PEOPLES STRUGGLING AGAINST RACISM AND RACIAL DISCRIMINATION. Mar 21–27. Annual observance initiated by United Nations General Assembly as part of its program of the Decade for Action to Combat Racism and Racial Discrimination. Info from: United Nations, Dept of Public Info, New York, NY 10017.

WORLD WAR I: THE SECOND BATTLE OF SOMME: 80th ANNIVERSARY. Mar 21–Apr 4. General Erich Ludendorff launched the Michael offensive, the biggest German offensive of 1918, on Mar 21 with a five-hour artillery barrage. The Central Power objective was to drive a wedge between the British and French forces and drive the British to the sea. Although they did not accomplish this objective, in the south they captured Montdidier and advanced to a depth of 40 miles. They managed to create a bulge in the front south of Somme and end what had effectively been a stalemate. The Allies lost nearly 230,000 men and the Germans almost as many in the Battle of Somme.

BIRTHDAYS TODAY

Ed Broadbent (John Edward Broadbent), 62, Canadian professor and political leader (New Democratic Party), born Oshawa, Ontario, Canada, Mar 21, 1936.

Matthew Broderick, 36, actor (*War Games, The Freshman, Family Business*), born New York, NY, Mar 21, 1962.

Peter Brook, 73, theater director, born London, England, Mar 21, 1925.

Timothy Dalton, 52, actor (*Centennial, License to Kill*), born Colwyn Bay, Wales, Mar 21, 1946.

Al Freeman, Jr, 64, actor (*A Patch of Blue; Roots: The Next Generation*), born San Antonio, TX, Mar 21, 1934.

Jay Walter Hilgenberg, 38, former football player, born Iowa City, IA, Mar 21, 1960.

Phyllis McGinley, 93, poet, born Ontario, Canada, Mar 21, 1905.

Gary Oldman, 40, actor (*Sid and Nancy, JFK*), born South London, England, Mar 21, 1958.

MARCH 22 — SUNDAY

Day 81 — 284 Remaining

AS YOUNG AS YOU FEEL DAY. Mar 22. Now more than ever you are as young as you feel. So stop acting your chronological age and get out there and start feeling peppy! [© 1997 by WPL] For info: Thomas Roy, Wellness Permission League, PO Box 662, Mount Gretna, PA 17064-0662. Phone: (500) 437-5104 or (717) 964-1308. Fax: (717) 964-1335.

CAMP FIRE BOYS AND GIRLS BIRTHDAY SUNDAY. Mar 22. A day when Camp Fire Boys and Girls commemorate the organization's founding and worship together and participate in the services of their churches or temples. For info: Camp Fire Boys and Girls, 4601 Madison Ave, Kansas City, MO 64112. Phone: (816) 756-1950. Fax: (816) 756-0258. Email: info@campfire.org. WWW: http://www.campfire.org

ENGLAND: MOTHERING SUNDAY. Mar 22. Fourth Sunday of Lent, formerly occasion for attending services at Mother Church, family gatherings and visits to parents. Now popularly known as Mother's Day, and a time for visiting and taking gifts to mothers.

EQUAL RIGHTS AMENDMENT SENT TO STATES FOR RATIFICATION: ANNIVERSARY. Mar 22, 1972. On this date the Senate passed the 27th Amendment, prohibiting discrimination on the basis of sex, sending it to the states for ratification. Hawaii led the way as the first state to ratify and by the end of the year 22 of the required states had ratified it. On Oct 6, 1978, the deadline for ratification was extended to June 30, 1982, by Congress. The amendment still lacked three of the required 38 states for ratification. This was the first extension granted since Congress set seven years as the limit for ratification. The amendment failed to achieve ratification as the deadline came and passed and no additional states ratified the measure.

FIRST WOMEN'S COLLEGIATE BASKETBALL GAME: ANNIVERSARY. Mar 22, 1893. The first women's collegiate basketball game was played at Smith College in Northampton, MA. Senda Berenson, then Smith's director of physical education and "mother of women's basketball," supervised the game, in which Smith's sophomore team beat the freshman team 5–4. For info: Dir of Media Relations, Smith College, Office of College Relations, Northhampton, MA 01063. Phone: (413) 585-2190. Fax: (413) 585-2174. Email: ashanahan@colrel.smith.edu.

HIA EURO—THE INTERNATIONAL TRADE FAIR FOR CRAFT & HOBBY SUPPLIES. Mar 22–24. Maastricht Exhibition & Congress Ctr, Maastricht, The Netherlands. 4th annual trade fair. Largest European market dedicated to crafts and hobbies. A trade-only event. Classes run concurrently. Est attendance: 8,500. For info: Susan Danker, Dir of Mtgs and Expos, HIA, 319 E 54th St, PO Box 348, Elmwood Park, NJ 07407. Phone: (201) 794-1133. Fax: (201) 797-0657. Email: hia@ix.netcom.com. WWW: http://www.hobby.org/hia

INTERNATIONAL GOOF-OFF DAY. Mar 22. A day of relaxation and a time to be oneself; a day for some good-humored fun and some good-natured silliness. Everyone needs one special day each year to goof off. For info: Monica A. Dufour, 471 S Vanburen Circle, Davison, MI 48423-8535. Phone: (810) 658-3147.

JORDAN: ARAB LEAGUE DAY. Mar 22. National holiday, the Hashemite Kingdom of Jordan.

LASER PATENTED: ANNIVERSARY. Mar 22, 1960. The first patent for a laser (light amplification by stimulated emission of radiation) granted to Arthur Schawlow and Charles Townes.

LUXEMBOURG: BRETZELSONNDEG. Mar 22. Fourth Sunday in Lent is occasion for boys to give pretzel-shaped cakes to sweethearts who may respond, on Easter Sunday, with a gift of decorated egg or sweet.

NATIONAL WEEK OF THE OCEAN FESTIVAL SEA-SON. Mar 22–May 10. Fort Lauderdale, FL. Includes billfish tournament, sea chanty concerts, school marine fair, Earth Day, waterway cleanup, two seafood festivals and Mother Ocean Day. Est attendance: 300,000. For info: Cynthia Hancock, Pres, Natl Week of the Ocean, Inc, PO Box 179, Ft Lauderdale, FL 33302. Phone: (954) 462-5573.

PAGE, RUTH: BIRTH ANNIVERSARY. Mar 22, 1899. American dancer and choreographer Ruth Page was born at Indianapolis, IN. She was a leading figure in Chicago dance with the Lyric Opera of Chicago, the Chicago Opera Ballet and the Chicago Ballet. She died on Apr 7, 1991, at Chicago, IL.

SPACE MILESTONE: *SOYUZ 39* (USSR). Mar 22, 1981. Launched on Mar 22, 1981, two cosmonauts (V. Dzhanibekov and, from Mongolia, J. Gurragcha) docked at *Salyut 6* space station Mar 23, where they were greeted by the previous team of cosmonauts. Returned to Earth Mar 30.

SPACE MILESTONE: *STS-3* (US). Mar 22, 1982. Shuttle *Columbia* launched on third test flight from Kennedy Space Center, FL, with astronauts Jack Lousma and Gordon Fullerton. Landed at White Sands Missile Range, NM, Mar 30.

UNITED NATIONS: WORLD DAY FOR WATER. Mar 22. The General Asssembly declared this observance (Res 47/193) to promote public awareness of how water resource development contributes to economic productivity and social well-being.

BIRTHDAYS TODAY

George Benson, 55, singer, guitarist ("On Broadway," "Give Me the Night"), born Pittsburgh, PA, Mar 22, 1943.

Robert Quinlan (Bob) Costas, 46, sportscaster, born New York, NY, Mar 22, 1952.

Bruno Ganz, 57, actor (*The American Friend, Wings of Desire, The Last Days of Chez Nous*), born Zurich, Switzerland, Mar 22, 1941.

Orrin Grant Hatch, 64, US Senator (R, Utah), born Pittsburgh, PA, Mar 22, 1934.

Werner Klemperer, 78, actor (Emmy for "Hogan's Heroes"; *Ship of Fools*), born Cologne, Germany, Mar 22, 1920.

Andrew Lloyd-Webber, 50, composer (*Cats, Phantom of the Opera*), born London, England, Mar 22, 1948.

Karl Malden (Mladen Sekulovich), 84, actor (*A Streetcar Named Desire*, "The Streets of San Francisco"), born Gary, IN, Mar 22, 1914.

Marcel Marceau, 75, actor, pantomimist (had the only speaking part in *Silent Movie*), born Strasbourg, France, Mar 22, 1923.

Matthew Modine, 39, actor (*Married to the Mob*, "And the Band Played On"), born Loma Linda, CA, Mar 22, 1959.

Pat (Marion Gordon) Robertson, 68, TV evangelist, born Lexington, VA, Mar 22, 1930.

☆ ☆ ☆

William Shatner, 67, actor (Captain Kirk of "Star Trek"; "T.J. Hooker"), author (*Tek* novels), born Montreal, Quebec, Canada, Mar 22, 1931.

Stephen Sondheim, 68, composer (*A Little Night Music*), born New York, NY, Mar 22, 1930.

M. Emmet Walsh, 63, actor (*Serpico, Blood Simple, Raising Arizona*), born Ogdensburg, NY, Mar 22, 1935.

Bill Wendell, 74, announcer ("Tonight," "Late Night with David Letterman"), born London, England, Mar 22, 1924.

MARCH 23 — MONDAY

Day 82 — 283 Remaining

BATTLE OF KERNSTOWN: ANNIVERSARY. Mar 23. As General George McClellan began the Peninsular campaign to move on the Confederate capital of Richmond, VA, Confederate General Stonewall Jackson engaged a larger force of Union troops at Kernstown in the northern Shenandoah Valley of Virginia on Mar 23, 1862. Although he ultimately was forced to retreat, the Battle of Kernstown provided a diversion central to the South's military strategy. Fearing an attack on Washington, DC, northern troops were kept around Washington as part of its defense, leaving fewer troops available for the Peninsular campaign.

"BEAT THE CLOCK" TV PREMIERE: ANNIVERSARY. Mar 23, 1950. On this game show from the team of Mark Goodson and Bill Todman, couples performed stunts within a specified time period (usually under 60 seconds) with the winners being given a chance to try a special stunt to win a great prize. Special stunts were very difficult, and the same one was attempted every week until a couple got it right. Frank Wayne and Bob Howard created the stunts which were pre-tested by the show's staff. In 1952, James Dean got his first TV job testing stunts and warming up the audience. Bud Collyer was the host, assisted by Roxanne (her real name was Dolores Rosedale). A 1969 syndicated version was hosted by Jack Narz and then by Gene Wood, which had celebrities to help the contestants and no special stunt. A 1979 revival was hosted by Monty Hall.

"BIG BERTHA" PARIS GUN: 80th ANNIVERSARY. Mar 23, 1918. In 1918 Germany initiated use of a terrifying new weapon—the Paris Gun—so called because it was first used against that city. The great gun, with a 25-foot carriage, was first used in combat when it was fired from a wooded location near Laon on Mar 23, 1918. It took 176 seconds for a shell to reach the city from a distance of 75 miles. On that first day 15 shots killed 16 individuals. Ridiculing the designers and manufacturers of the weapon, Parisians nicknamed it "Big Bertha" after the wife of the head of the munitions corporation. On Good Friday, Mar 29, a shell from the armament struck the church of Saint Gervais, which was crowded with worshipers. The casualty toll was 88 dead and 68 injured.

"THE BOLD AND THE BEAUTIFUL" TV PREMIERE: ANNIVERSARY. Mar 23, 1987. A continuing daytime serial created by William Bell and Lee Phillip Bell to be "young and hip." It is set in the fashion industry of LA with two central families, the Logans and the Forresters. The cast has included, as the Forresters: John McCook, Susan Flannery, Clayton Norcross, Jeff Trachta, Ronn Moss, Teri Ann Linn, Colleen Dion; and as the Logans: Robert Pine, Judith Baldwin, Nancy Burnett, Nancy Sloan, Carrie Mitchum (granddaughter of Robert), Ethan Wayne (son of John), Brian Patrick Clarke, Katherine Kelly Lang and Lesley Woods. Other cast members include Jeff Conaway, Tippi Hedren and Hunter Tylo.

March 1998

S	M	T	W	T	F	S
1	2	3	4	5	6	7
8	9	10	11	12	13	14
15	16	17	18	19	20	21
22	23	24	25	26	27	28
29	30	31				

CLARK, BARNEY: 15th DEATH ANNIVERSARY. Mar 23, 1983. Barney Clark died after living almost 112 days with an artificial heart. The heart, made of polyurethane plastic and aluminum, was implanted in Clark at the University of Utah Medical Center, Salt Lake City, on Dec 2, 1982. Clark was the first person ever to receive a permanent artificial heart. Born at Provo, UT, on Jan 21, 1921, Clark was 61 at the time of the implantation and 62 when he died.

COLFAX, SCHUYLER: 175th BIRTH ANNIVERSARY. Mar 23, 1823. 17th vice president of the US (1869–73). Born at New York, NY. Died Jan 13, 1885, at Mankato, MN.

DICK CLARK RETIRES FROM "AMERICAN BANDSTAND": ANNIVERSARY. Mar 23, 1989. After 33 years, 59-year-old Dick Clark retired from hosting the television program "American Bandstand."

LIBERTY DAY: ANNIVERSARY. Mar 23. Anniversary of Patrick Henry's speech for arming the Virginia militia—at St. Johns Church, Richmond, VA, on Mar 23, 1775. "I know not what course others may take, but as for me, give me liberty or give me death."

NATIONAL CLUTTER AWARENESS WEEK. Mar 23–29. To provide a week of awareness of clutter accumulated over the summer, fall and winter months to begin that Spring Cleaning purge. From the garage to the kitchen cabinets, the hall closet to the desk drawers, the piles of magazines, clothes that don't fit, junk drawers, purses, toys and tool chest, begin to make plans to purge, sort, recycle and organize all the "nests," and piles of clutter. Let go of unused, worn out, out-of-style stuff that takes up much-needed space and have time to enjoy summer. In the office, from the storeroom to the supply cabinets, the lunchroom, desks, computers, bulletin boards, file cabinets. Creating awareness of excess and unused items will help employees to take responsible action to maintain more order and tidiness of their office and work areas. Annually, the last full week of March. For info: Gloria Schaaf, Organization Works!, 155 East 88th St, Ste 3F, New York, NY 10128. Phone: (212) 410-4937.

NEAR MISS DAY. Mar 23, 1989. A mountain-sized asteroid passed within 500,000 miles of Earth, a very close call according to NASA. Impact would have equalled strength of 40,000 hydrogen bombs, created a crater the size of the District of Columbia and devastated everything for 100 miles in all directions.

NEW ZEALAND: OTAGO AND SOUTHLAND PROVINCIAL ANNIVERSARY. Mar 23. In addition to the statutory public holidays of New Zealand, there is in each provincial district a holiday for the provincial anniversary. This is observed in Otago and Southland on Mar 23.

PAKISTAN: REPUBLIC DAY. Mar 23. National holiday. On this day in 1940 the All-India-Muslim League adopted a resolution calling for a Muslim homeland. On the same day in 1956 Pakistan declared itself a republic.

RALLY FOR DECENCY: ANNIVERSARY. Mar 23. Anita Bryant, Jackie Gleason and Kate Smith rallied with 30,000 others in Miami on this day in 1969 in reaction to Jim Morrison's arrest for indecent exposure.

UNITED NATIONS: WORLD METEOROLOGICAL DAY. Mar 23. An international day observed by meteorological services throughout the world and by the organizations of the UN system. "Natural Disaster Reduction: How Meteorological and Hydrological Services Can Help." Info from: United Nations, Dept of Public Info, New York, NY 10017.

BIRTHDAYS TODAY

Roger Bannister, 69, physician, former track athlete, born Harrow, England, Mar 23, 1929.

Chaka Khan (Yvette Marie Stevens), 45, singer (with Rufus: "Tell Me Something Good," "You Got the Love"; solo: "I Feel for You"), born Chicago, IL, Mar 23, 1953.

Jason Kidd, 25, basketball player, born San Francisco, CA, Mar 23, 1973.

Akira Kurosawa, 88, filmmaker (*Rashomon, The Seven Samurai, Ran*), born Tokyo, Japan, Mar 23, 1910.
Moses Eugene Malone, 44, former basketball player, born Petersburg, VA, Mar 23, 1954.
Amanda Plummer, 41, actress (Tony for *Agnes of God; The Fisher King*), born New York City, NY, Mar 23, 1957.

MARCH 24 — TUESDAY

Day 83 — 282 Remaining

AMERICAN DIABETES ALERT. Mar 24. A one-day "wake-up call" for those eight million Americans who have diabetes and don't even know it. During the Alert, local ADA affiliates use the diabetes risk test—a simple paper-and-pencil quiz—to communicate the risk factors and symptoms of the disease. For more information, call 1-800-DIABETES (342-2383). Annually, the fourth Tuesday in March. For info: (800) 232-3472.

EXXON VALDEZ OIL SPILL: ANNIVERSARY. Mar 24, 1989. The tanker *Exxon Valdez* ran aground in Prince William Sound. The resultant oil spill leaked 11 million gallons of oil into one of nature's richest habitats.

HOUDINI, HARRY: BIRTH ANNIVERSARY. Mar 24, 1874. Magician and escape artist. Born at Budapest, Hungary, died at Detroit, MI, on Oct 31, 1926. Lecturer, athlete, author, expert on history of magic, exposer of fraudulent mediums and motion picture actor. Was best known for his ability to escape from locked restraints (handcuffs, straitjackets, coffins, boxes and milk cans). Anniversary of his death (Halloween) has been the occasion for meetings of magicians and attempts at communication by mediums.

MELLON, ANDREW W.: BIRTH ANNIVERSARY. Mar 24, 1855. American financier, industrialist, government official (Secretary of the Treasury), art and book collector born at Pittsburgh, PA. Died Aug 26, 1937, at Southhampton, NY.

MORRIS, WILLIAM: BIRTH ANNIVERSARY. Mar 24, 1834. English poet and artist. Died at Hammersmith, London, Oct 3, 1896.

NATIONAL ORGANIZE YOUR HOME OFFICE DAY. Mar 24. To set aside one day each year for the home office professional to organize his or her office. Annually, the fourth Tuesday in March. For info: Lisa Kanarek, Organizational Consultant, 660 Preston Forest Ctr, Ste 120, Dallas, TX 75230. Phone: (214) 361-0556. Email: Lisaorgani@aol.com.

OMAHA HOME SHOW. Mar 24–29. Omaha Civic Auditorium, Omaha, NE. Annually, in March. For info: Robert P. Mancuso, Pres, Mid-America Exposition, Inc, 1613 Farnam St, Ste 666, Omaha, NE 68102-2142. Phone: (402) 346-8003 or (800) 475-SHOW. Fax: (402) 346-5412.

"ORIGINAL" WESTERN MASSACHUSETTS HOME SHOW. Mar 24–29. West Springfield, MA. The largest home show in New England with more than 700 booths and a large outside area covering more than six acres of exhibits. Annually, third or fourth week of March. Est attendance: 92,500. For info: Edward R. Pedersen, Exec VP, Home Builders Assn of Western Massachusetts, 260 Worthington St, Ste 203, Springfield, MA 01103. Phone: (413) 733-3126. Fax: (413) 781-8416. Email: HBAWM@MAP.COM.

PHILIPPINE INDEPENDENCE: ANNIVERSARY. Mar 24, 1934. President Franklin Roosevelt signed a bill granting independence to the Philippines. The bill, which took effect July 4, 1946, brought to a close almost half a century of US control of the islands.

POWELL, JOHN WESLEY: BIRTH ANNIVERSARY. Mar 24, 1834. American geologist, explorer, ethnologist. Born at Mt Morris, NY, Mar 24, 1834. Died at Haven, ME, Sept 23, 1902.

RHODE ISLAND VOTERS REJECT CONSTITUTION: ANNIVERSARY. Mar 24, 1788. In a popular referendum on Mar 24, 1788, Rhode Island rejected the new Constitution by a vote of 2,708 to 237. The state later (May 29, 1790) ratified the Constitution and on June 7, 1790, ratified the Bill of Rights.

ROSMINI-SERBATI, ANTONIO: BIRTH ANNIVERSARY. Mar 24, 1797. Italian religious philosopher was born at Rovereto, Austria. In 1828 he founded the Institute of Charity, or Rosminians, a Roman Catholic educational and charitable organization modeled on the Jesuit rule, modern political and social thought and the concept of an ideal being. He died on July 1, 1855, at Stresa, Lombardy.

SAINT GABRIEL FEAST DAY. Mar 24. Saint Gabriel the Archangel, patron saint of postal, telephone and telegraph workers.

TB BACILLUS DISCOVERED: ANNIVERSARY. Mar 24, 1882. The tuberculosis bacillus was discovered by German scientist Robert Koch.

☆ ☆ ☆

BIRTHDAYS TODAY

Lara Flynn Boyle, 28, actress ("Twin Peaks," *Dead Poets Society, Red Rock West*), born Davenport, IA, Mar 24, 1970.
Norman Fell, 74, actor (*The Graduate*, "Three's Company"), born Philadelphia, PA, Mar 24, 1924.
Lawrence Ferlinghetti, 79, poet, author (*Coney Island of the Mind*), born Yonkers, NY, Mar 24, 1919.
Byron Janis, 70, pianist, born McKeesport, PA, Mar 24, 1928.
Bob Mackie, 58, costume and fashion designer, born Monterey Park, CA, Mar 24, 1940.
Donna Pescow, 44, actress (*Saturday Night Fever*, "Angie"), born Brooklyn, NY, Mar 24, 1954.

MARCH 25 — WEDNESDAY

Day 84 — 281 Remaining

BARTOK, BELA: BIRTH ANNIVERSARY. Mar 25, 1881. Hungarian composer. Born Mar 25, 1881, at Nagyszentmiklos (now in Romania). Died at New York, NY, Sept 26, 1945.

BORGLUM, GUTZON: BIRTH ANNIVERSARY. Mar 25, 1871. American sculptor who created the huge sculpture of four American presidents (Washington, Jefferson, Lincoln and Theodore Roosevelt) at Mt Rushmore National Memorial in the Black Hills of South Dakota. Born John Gutzon de la Mothe Borglum at Bear Lake, ID, the son of Mormon pioneers, he worked the last 14 years of his life on the Mt Rushmore sculpture. He died at Chicago, IL, on Mar 6, 1941.

"CAGNEY & LACEY" TV PREMIERE: ANNIVERSARY. Mar 25, 1982. "Cagney & Lacey" broke new ground as the first TV crime show in which the central characters were both female. The series was based on a made-for-TV movie that aired Oct 8, 1981, starring Loretta Swit and Tyne Daly. Meg Foster played Swit's character, Chris Cagney, but after one season she was replaced by Sharon Gless. The combination of Gless's Cagney and Daly's Mary Beth Lacey worked well. Daly and Gless won six Emmys together for their roles.

COXEY'S ARMY MARCH ON WASHINGTON: ANNIVERSARY. Mar 25, 1894. Anniversary of a march on the nation's Capitol, begun Mar 25, 1894. Jacob S. Coxey, businessman, economic reformer, advocate of interest-free government bonds, left Massillon, OH, on foot with an "army" of about 100 followers. Arrived at Washington, DC, May 1. His hope to influence Congress was thwarted when he and part of his army were arrested for trespassing on government property. Fifty years later he spoke from the Capitol steps, reiterating his belief in non-interest-bearing government bonds.

FEAST OF ANNUNCIATION. Mar 25. Celebrated in the Roman Catholic Church in commemoration of the message of the Angel Gabriel to Mary that she was to be the Mother of Christ.

GREECE: INDEPENDENCE DAY. Mar 25. National holiday. Celebrates independence from Turkey, 1821.

HAPPY LAND SOCIAL CLUB FIRE: ANNIVERSARY. Mar 25. Julio Gonzalez, described as a jilted boyfriend, returned to the Happy Land Social Club after being evicted by a bouncer and set fire to it as an act of revenge on Mar 25, 1990. Most of the 87 victims were Honduran and Dominican immigrants who attended the unlicensed dance club in the East Tremont section of The Bronx, NY. Rejected by his girlfriend, an employee of the club, Gonzalez set fire to the only entrance and exit, cutting off escape for the assembled crowd.

JAZZ AT THE PHILHARMONIC: ANNIVERSARY. Mar 25, 1946. One of the most influential solos of jazz alto saxophonist Charlie ("Bird") Parker's career was his rendition of "Lady Be Good," performed at the Los Angeles Philharmonic Auditorium. Every aspect of the performance became part of the language of modern jazz.

LEAN, SIR DAVID: 90th BIRTH ANNIVERSARY. Mar 25, 1908. British film director Sir David Lean was born at London. He directed 16 films and won 28 Academy Awards. His films include *Bridge on the River Kwai* (1957), *Lawrence of Arabia* (1962) and *Dr. Zhivago* (1965). He died on Apr 16, 1991, at London.

MARYLAND DAY. Mar 25. Commemorates arrival of Lord Baltimore's first settlers in Maryland in 1634.

"9 to 5" TV PREMIERE: ANNIVERSARY. Mar 25, 1982. This half-hour sitcom was based on the 1980 movie of the same name about three working women in dead-end jobs in a large corporation. The three women were played by Rita Moreno, Valerie Curtin and Rachel Dennison (in the role her sister Dolly Parton had played in the movie). Also in the cast were Jeffrey Tambor and Peter Bonerz, Suzanne Stone, Mary Farrell, Peggy Pope, Ann Weldon, Peter Hobbs and Herb Edelman.

PECAN DAY. Mar 25. Anniversary of the planting by George Washington, on Mar 25, 1775, of pecan trees (some of which still survive) at Mount Vernon. The trees were a gift to Washington from Thomas Jefferson, who had planted a few pecan trees from the southern US at Monticello, VA. The pecan native to southern North America is sometimes called "America's own nut." First cultivated by American Indians, it has been transplanted to other continents but has failed to achieve wide use or popularity outside the US.

SLAVE TRADE ABOLISHED BY ENGLAND: ANNIVERSARY. Mar 25, 1807. The English Parliament abolished the slave trade, after a long campaign against it.

March 1998

S	M	T	W	T	F	S
1	2	3	4	5	6	7
8	9	10	11	12	13	14
15	16	17	18	19	20	21
22	23	24	25	26	27	28
29	30	31				

TOSCANINI, ARTURO: BIRTH ANNIVERSARY. Mar 25, 1867. Italian opera and symphony conductor Arturo Toscanini was born at Parma, Italy. He had an all-encompassing repertoire but was famous primarily for the operas of Verdi and the symphonies of Beethoven. Toscanini died at New York City on Jan 16, 1957.

TRIANGLE SHIRTWAIST FIRE: ANNIVERSARY. Mar 25, 1911. At about 4:30 PM, fire broke out at the Triangle Shirtwaist Co in New York, NY, minutes before the seamstresses were to go home. Some workers were fatally burned while others leaped to their deaths from the windows of the 10-story building. It was found that some of the deaths were a direct result of workers being trapped on the ninth floor by a locked door. The fire lasted only 18 minutes but left 146 workers dead, most of them young immigrant women. Labor law forbade locking factory doors while employees were at work, and owners of the company were indicted on charges of first- and second-degree manslaughter. The tragic fire became a turning point in labor history, bringing about reforms in health and safety laws. On the 75th anniversary of the fire (1986), survivors and others participated in a memorial ceremony at the site of the fire to honor the victims and to observe the achievements that resulted from the fire.

BIRTHDAYS TODAY

Bonnie Bedelia, 52, actress (*My Sweet Charlie, Die Hard, Die Hard 2*), born New York, NY, Mar 25, 1946.

Anita Bryant, 58, singer ("The George Gobel Show"; hit song "Paper Roses"), Miss America ('58), born Barnsdall, OK, Mar 25, 1940.

Eileen Ford, 76, model agency executive, born New York, NY, Mar 25, 1922.

Aretha Franklin, 56, singer ("Respect," "Think"), born Memphis, TN, Mar 25, 1942.

Paul Michael Glaser, 55, actor ("Starsky and Hutch"), director (*Butterflies Are Free*), born Cambridge, MA, Mar 25, 1943.

Mary Gross, 45, comedienne, actress ("Saturday Night Live"), born Chicago, IL, Mar 25, 1953.

Elton John (Reginald Kenneth Dwight), 51, musician, singer, songwriter, born Pinner, England, Mar 25, 1947.

Sarah Jessica Parker, 33, actress (*LA Story, Honeymoon in Vegas*), born Nelsonville, OH, Mar 25, 1965.

Gloria Steinem, 63, feminist (original publisher of *Ms* magazine), journalist, born Toledo, OH, Mar 25, 1935.

John Stockwell, 37, actor, writer, director (*Top Gun, Under Cover*), born Galveston, TX, Mar 25, 1961.

Debi Janine Thomas, 31, figure skater, medical student, born Poughkeepsie, NY, Mar 25, 1967.

MARCH 26 — THURSDAY

Day 85 — 280 Remaining

BANGLADESH: INDEPENDENCE DAY. Mar 26. Celebrated with parades, youth festivals and symposia.

BELLAMY, EDWARD: BIRTH ANNIVERSARY. Mar 26, 1850. American author best remembered for his novel *Looking Backward* (1888). Born at Chicopee Falls, MA, on Mar 26, 1850. Died there on May 28, 1898.

BOWDITCH, NATHANIEL: 225th BIRTH ANNIVERSARY. Mar 26, 1773. American mathematician and astronomer, author of the *New American Practical Navigator*. Born at Salem, MA, Mar 26, 1773. Died at Boston, MA, Mar 16, 1838.

CAMP DAVID ACCORD SIGNED: ANNIVERSARY. Mar 26, 1979. Israeli Prime Minister Menachem Begin and Egyptian President Anwar Sadat signed the Camp David peace treaty, ending 30 years of war between their two countries. The agreement was fostered by President Jimmy Carter.

COLLEGIATE SECRETARIES INTERNATIONAL™ and FUTURE SECRETARIES ASSOCIATION® CONFERENCE. Mar 26–28. Albuquerque, NM. Est attendance: 500. For info: Susan Fenner, PhD, Edu and Professional Devel Mgr, Professional Secretaries Intl®; The Assn for Office Professionals™, 10502 NW Ambassador Dr, PO Box 20404, Kansas City, MO 64195-0404. Phone: (816) 891-6600. Fax: (816) 891-9118. Email: bburton@psi.org. WWW: http://www.gvi.net/psi

DELANO, JANE: BIRTH ANNIVERSARY. Mar 26, 1858. Jane Arminda Delano, dedicated American nurse and teacher, superintendent of the US Army Nurse Corps, chairman of the American Red Cross Nursing Service and recipient (posthumously) of the Distinguished Service Medal of the US, was born Mar 26, 1858, near Townsend, NY. While on an official visit to review Red Cross activities, she died Apr 15, 1919, in an army hospital at Savenay, France. Her last words: "What about my work? I must get back to my work." Buried first at Loire, France, her remains were reinterred at Arlington Cemetery in 1920.

FOCH TAKES COMMAND ON WESTERN FRONT: 80th ANNIVERSARY. Mar 26, 1918. General Ferdinand Foch, Commander of the French Army at the Marne and the Somme, was appointed General-in-Chief of the joint Allied forces on the Western Front. In practice the national commanders (Haig, King Albert, Pershing) retained extensive control of the individual forces.

FROST, ROBERT LEE: BIRTH ANNIVERSARY. Mar 26. American poet who tried his hand at farming, teaching, shoemaking and editing before winning acclaim as a poet. Pulitzer Prize winner. Born at San Francisco, CA, Mar 26, 1874. Died at Boston, MA, Jan 29, 1963.

KUHIO DAY. Mar 26. Hawaii. Also known as Prince Jonah Kuhio Kalanianaole Day, honoring birthday of Hawaii's second delegate to Congress.

LEGAL ASSISTANTS DAY. Mar 26. A day recognizing the many contributions made to the legal profession by legal assistants. For info: Claudia A. Evart, 30 Park Ave, Ste 2-P, New York, NY 10016. Phone: (212) 779-2227.

LOS ANGELES MARATHON QUALITY OF LIFE EXPO. Mar 26–28. Los Angeles Convention Center, Los Angeles, CA. A three-day consumer show where Marathon Bike Tour and other participants pick up race materials. Exhibits include health, fitness, travel, biking, etc. 400 booths. Est attendance: 70,000. For info: John Wilson, Los Angeles Marathon, 11110 W Ohio Ave, Ste 100, Los Angeles, CA 90025. Phone: (310) 444-5544.

MAKE UP YOUR OWN HOLIDAY DAY. Mar 26. This day is a day you may name for whatever you wish. Reach for the stars! Make up a holiday! Annually, Mar 26. [© 1997 by WPL] For info: Thomas and Ruth Roy, Wellness Permission League, PO Box 662, Mt Gretna, PA 17064-0662. Phone: (500) 437-5104 or (717) 964-1308. Fax: (717) 964-1335.

SOVIET COSMONAUT RETURNS TO NEW COUNTRY: ANNIVERSARY. Mar 26. After spending 313 days in space in the Soviet *Mir* space station, cosmonaut Serge Krikalev returned to Earth and to what was for him a new country, on Mar 26, 1992. He left Earth on May 18, 1991, a citizen of the Soviet Union, but during his stay aboard the space station, the Soviet Union crumbled and quickly became the Commonwealth of Independent States. Originally scheduled to return in October 1991, Krikalev's return was delayed by five months due to his country's disintegration and the ensuing monetary problems.

SPRING FESTIVAL. Mar 26–Apr 5. Westville Village, Lumpkin, GA. Celebrate the arrival of spring with activities similar to those of the spring of 1850 with emphasis on music of the period. Est attendance: 5,000. For info: Patty Cannington, Westville, Box 1850, Lumpkin, GA 31815. Phone: (912) 838-6310 or (888) 733-1850. WWW: http://www.westville.org

WAYNE STATE UNIVERSITY: CELEBRATION OF THE ARTS. Mar 26. Detroit, MI. Celebration showcases arts events and programs on campus featuring music, dance, theatre, visual art, English composition and art education. Est attendance: 200. For info: Pat Borninski, MR Info Officer, Wayne State University, 3222 FAB, Detroit, MI 48202. Phone: (313) 577-2150. Fax: (313) 577-8154. Email: p.bornin@cms.cc.wayne.edu. WWW: http://www.medis.wayne.edu/

WHITMAN, WALT: DEATH ANNIVERSARY. Mar 26, 1892. American poet, born May 31, 1819. Following a short-lived and largely unsuccessful career in journalism, Whitman in 1855 published the collection of poetry for which he is now famous, *Leaves of Grass*. Widely criticized in the US and only marginally received abroad, its rhythmically rambling discourse and mystical imagery proved incomprehensible to most early readers. Although Whitman insisted that *Leaves of Grass* was only a celebration of himself as an average man, it was in fact a celebration of "the self," as defined by the inseparableness of body and soul. His exploration of the communion of body and soul and his presentation of love as longing and death as satisfaction of longing resulted in what was to his 19th-century audience decidedly indecent physiological imagery. When he died on Mar 26, 1892, his obituary was published in newspapers worldwide, finally marking his place in the history of great American literature. "No really great song," Whitman wrote, "can ever attain full purport till long after the death of its singer—till it has accrued and incorporated the many passions, many joys and sorrows, it has aroused."

WILLIAMS, TENNESSEE: BIRTH ANNIVERSARY. Mar 26, 1911. Tennessee Williams was born in Columbus, MS. He became one of America's most prolific playwrights, producing such works as *The Glass Menagerie*; *A Streetcar Named Desire*, which won a Pulitzer Prize; *Cat on a Hot Tin Roof*, which won a second Pulitzer; *Night of the Iguana; Summer and Smoke, The Rose Tattoo; Camino Real; Sweet Bird of Youth* and *Small Craft Warnings*, among others. Williams died Feb 25, 1983.

"THE YOUNG AND THE RESTLESS" TV PREMIERE: 25th ANNIVERSARY. Mar 26, 1973. "Y&R" replaced "Where the Heart Is" in 1973. This daytime serial is generally thought of as TV's most artistic soap, and has won numerous Emmys for outstanding daytime drama series. "Y&R" is set in the town of Genoa City. Its original storylines revolved around the Brooks and Foster families, but by the early '80s most of them were gone and the Abbott and Williams families were highlighted. The serial's very large and changing cast has included now famous actors David Hasselhoff, Tom Selleck, Wings Hauser, Deidre Hall and Michael Damian. In 1980, "Y&R" expanded from a half-hour to an hour. Its theme music is well known as "Nadia's Theme," as it was played during Nadia Comaneci's routine at the 1976 Olympics.

BIRTHDAYS TODAY

Marcus Allen, 38, football player, born San Diego, CA, Mar 26, 1960.
Alan Arkin, 64, actor (*Catch-22*), director (*Little Murders*), born New York, NY, Mar 26, 1934.
Uwe Konstantine Blab, 36, former basketball player, born Munich, West Germany, Mar 26, 1962.
Pierre Boulez, 73, composer, conductor, born Montbrison, France, Mar 26, 1925.
James Caan, 58, actor (*Rabbit Run, The Godfather*), director, born New York, NY, Mar 26, 1940.
Leeza Gibbons, 41, TV hostess ("Entertainment Tonight"), born Hartsville, SC, Mar 26, 1957.
Jennifer Grey, 38, actress (*Dirty Dancing, Ferris Bueller's Day Off*), Joel Grey's daughter, born New York, NY, Mar 26, 1960.
Erica Jong, 56, author, poet (*Fear of Flying, Becoming Light, How to Save Your Own Life*), born New York, NY, Mar 26, 1942.
Vicki Lawrence, 49, actress, singer ("The Carol Burnett Show," "Mama's Family"), born Inglewood, CA, Mar 26, 1949.
Leonard Nimoy, 67, actor (Spock on "Star Trek"), director (*Three Men and a Baby*), writer, born Boston, MA, Mar 26, 1931.
Sandra Day O'Connor, 68, Associate Justice of the US Supreme Court, born El Paso, TX, Mar 26, 1930.
Teddy Pendergrass, 48, singer, born Philadelphia, PA, Mar 26, 1950.
Diana Ross, 54, singer ("Keep Me Hangin' On," "Ain't No Mountain High Enough"), actress (*Lady Sings the Blues, The Wiz*), born Detroit, MI, Mar 26, 1944.
Martin Short, 48, actor (*The Three Amigos, Inner Space*), comedian ("SCTV Network 90," "Saturday Night Live"), born Hamilton, Ontario, Canada, Mar 26, 1950.

March 1998

S	M	T	W	T	F	S
1	2	3	4	5	6	7
8	9	10	11	12	13	14
15	16	17	18	19	20	21
22	23	24	25	26	27	28
29	30	31				

John Houston Stockton, 36, basketball player, born Spokane, WA, Mar 26, 1962.
Bob Woodward, 55, journalist (investigated Watergate with Carl Bernstein), born Geneva, IL, Mar 26, 1943.

MARCH 27 — FRIDAY

Day 86 — 279 Remaining

BUSINESS AND FARM EXPO. Mar 27–28. Dexter, MO. Exhibitors display their products and services during this two-day public event. Indoor and outdoor exhibition spaces available. Annually, the fourth Friday and Saturday in March. Est attendance: 1,200. For info: Business and Farm Expo, Dexter Chamber of Commerce, PO Box 21, Dexter, MO 63841. Phone: (573) 624-7458 or (800) 332-8857. Fax: (573) 624-7459.

CANARY ISLANDS PLANE CRASH. Mar 27, 1977. Worst accident in the history of civil aviation. Two Boeing 747s collided on the ground; 570 people lost their lives—249 on the KLM Airlines plane and 321 on Pan Am.

"DREAM HOUSE" TV PREMIERE: 30th ANNIVERSARY. Mar 27, 1968. On this game show, couples competed for a chance to win furniture and a house. Mike Darrow hosted the NBC version, where three couples competed in a question-and-answer format, and the winning couple received furnishings for one room; if a couple won seven times in a row, they won a dream house valued at up to $40,000.

EARTHQUAKE STRIKES ALASKA: ANNIVERSARY. Mar 27, 1964. The strongest earthquake in North American history (8.4 on the Richter scale) struck Alaska, east of Anchorage. 117 people were killed.

EDISTO INDIAN CULTURAL FESTIVAL. Mar 27–28. Summerville, SC. Craft competition, unrestricted dance competition, free camping. Annually, the fourth weekend in March. Est attendance: 4,000. For info: Matthew Creel, Chief, Edisto Tribal Council, 1125 Ridge Rd, Ridgeville, SC 29472. Phone: (803) 871-2126. Fax: (803) 871-8048.

FUNKY WINKERBEAN: ANNIVERSARY. Mar 27, 1972. Anniversary of the nationally syndicated comic strip. For info: Tom Batiuk, Creator, 2750 Substation Rd, Medina, OH 44256. Phone: (330) 722-8755.

"GENERATIONS" TV PREMIERE: ANNIVERSARY. Mar 27, 1989. "Generations" was the first daytime serial in which one of the main families was black. Set in Chicago, the series focused on the relationships between the Marshalls and the Whitmores. The cast included Lynn Hamilton, Joan Pringle, Taurean Blacque, James Reynolds, Sharon Brown, Debbi Morgan, Jonelle Allen, Kristoff St. John, Patricia Crowley, Gail Ramsey, Gerard Prendergast and Kelly Rutherford, as well as many others.

HILL, PATTY SMITH: BIRTH ANNIVERSARY. Mar 27, 1868. Patty Smith Hill, schoolteacher, author and education specialist was born at Anchorage (suburb of Louisville), KY. She was author of the lyrics of the song "Good Morning to All," which later became known as "Happy Birthday to You." Her older sister, Mildred J. Hill, composed the melody for the song which was first published in 1893 as a classroom greeting in the book *Song Stories for the Sunday School.* A stanza beginning "Happy Birthday to You" was added in 1924, and the song became arguably the most frequently sung song in the world. See also: "Hill, Mildred J.: Birth Anniversary" (June 27) and "Happy Birthday to 'Happy Birthday to You' " (June 27).

ITALY: PROCESSION OF THE ADDOLORATA AND PROCESSION OF THE MYSTERIES. Mar 27–28. Taranto. Procession of the Addolorata is held on Holy Thursday, while the Procession of the Mysteries takes place on Good Friday. Both processions have in common the very slow pace of the participants and their unusual costumes.

LUXEMBOURG: OSWEILER. Mar 27. Blessing of horses, tractors and cars.

MOON PHASE: NEW MOON. Mar 27. Moon enters New Moon phase at 10:14 PM, EST.

NORTH SEA OIL RIG DISASTER: ANNIVERSARY. Mar 27. The Alexander L. Keilland Oil Rig capsized Mar 27, 1980, during a heavy storm in the Norwegian sector of the North Sea. The pentagon-type, French-built oil rig had about 200 persons aboard and 123 lives were lost.

OLDENBERG BEER CAMP. Mar 27–29 (also Sept 11–13). Ft Mitchell, KY. For beer lovers throughout the world. Extravaganza dedicated to learning about your favorite beverage. Activities, discussions, seminars and of course beer tasting of over 200 varieties. Campers learn the Beer Camp Song, oath, do field trips and more. Biannually in March and September. Est attendance: 300. For info: Oldenberg Brewing Co, I-75 and Buttermilk Pike, Ft Mitchell, KY 41017. Phone: (606) 341-7223. Fax: (606) 341-0580.

PERIGEAN SPRING TIDES. Mar 27–28. Spring tides, the highest possible tides, occur when New Moon or Full Moon falls within 24 hours of the moment the Moon is nearest Earth (perigee) in its monthly orbit on Mar 28, at 2 AM, EST.

ROENTGEN, WILHELM KONRAD: BIRTH ANNIVERSARY. Mar 27, 1845. German scientist who discovered x-rays (1895) and won a Nobel Prize in 1901. Born at Lennep, Prussia, Mar 27, 1845. Died at Munich, Germany, Feb 10, 1923.

SAINT PETERSBURG FESTIVAL OF STATES (WITH NATIONAL BAND CHAMPIONSHIPS). Mar 27–Apr 5. To salute civic endeavors and highlight the 50 states. National band championships, art show, two parades, antique cars, jazz festival, plus one more night of concert entertainment, country-and-western concert, 5K run. Est attendance: 300,000. For info: St. Petersburg Festival of States, Box 1731, St. Petersburg, FL 33731. Phone: (813) 898-3654. Fax: (813) 821-2601.

SMITH, THORNE: BIRTH ANNIVERSARY. Mar 27, 1892. Perhaps the most critically neglected popular author of the 20th century, he was born James Thorne Smith, Jr, at Annapolis, MD, on Mar 27, 1892, and died in Florida on June 20, 1934. Author of numerous humorous supernatural fantasy novels, including *Rain in the Doorway, The Stray Lamb* and, of course, *Topper*. The "Thorne Smith" touch has inspired several motion pictures and television series, including "Bewitched." For info: George H. Scheetz, Exec Secy, The Thorne Smith Soc, 2112 W White St, #163, Champaign, IL 61821-2935. Email: scheetz@prairienet.org.

SPACE MILESTONE: *VENERA 8* (USSR). Mar 27, 1972. Launched on this date, *Venera 8* made a soft landing on Venus July 22, 1972, and sent back radio transmissions of surface data.

STEICHEN, EDWARD: BIRTH ANNIVERSARY. Mar 27, 1879. Celebrated American photographer. Born Mar 27, 1879. Died Mar 25, 1973.

SWANSON, GLORIA: BIRTH ANNIVERSARY. Mar 27. American film actress and businesswoman. Born Gloria May Josephine Svensson at Chicago, Mar 27, 1899. Author of an autobiography, *Swanson on Swanson*, published in 1980. Died at New York, NY, Apr 4, 1983.

TEMPE SPRING FESTIVAL OF THE ARTS. Mar 27–29. Downtown Tempe, AZ. Features more than 500 artists and craftspeople, continuous entertainment, Ecotopia (environmental zone) and children's activity area. Est attendance: 240,000. For info: Britt Kimball, Event Coord, Mill Avenue Merchants Assn, PO Box 3084, Tempe, AZ 85281. Phone: (602) 967-4877. Fax: (602) 967-6638.

VAUGHAN, SARAH: BIRTH ANNIVERSARY. Mar 27, 1924. Born at Newark, NJ, on Mar 27, 1924. Legendary jazz singer renowned for her melodic improvising, wide vocal range and extraordinary technique. She began her career by winning an amateur contest sponsored by New York's Apollo Theater in 1943, which she entered on a dare. She was spotted and hired by Earl Hines to accompany his band as his relief pianist as well as singer. Her solo career began in 1945. As her career took off, she was given the nickname "The Divine One" by Chicago disc jockey Dave Garroway, a moniker that would remain with her the rest of her life. She used her three-octave range to explore a repertoire including Duke Ellington, George Gershwin, Irving Berlin, Rodgers and Hammerstein and an album of poems written by Pope John Paul II, set to music by Tito Fontana and Sante Palumbo. Sarah Vaughan died at Los Angeles, CA, Apr 3, 1990.

VIGNY, ALFRED VICTOR: BIRTH ANNIVERSARY. Mar 27, 1797. Born in Loches, France, to an aristocratic family, Vigny was the most philosophical of the French Romantic writers. He died at age 74 on Sept 17, 1863, at Paris. At 17 Vigny became a second lieutenant in the Royal Guards but left military life in 1827 to pursue his literary career. This experience led to *Servitude et grandeur militaires* (1835), three stories that showed the dullness of the soldier's life during peace but also his dignity and wish for self-sacrifice. After his first collection of verse, *Poèmes* (1822), and contributions to Victor Hugo's *La Muse Française*, Vigny was lauded as a Romantic poet with elegance and intensity. His novel *Cinq-Mars* (1826) was the first important historical novel in French, and Vigny came to be viewed as the literary leader of the French Romantic movement.

BIRTHDAYS TODAY

Jesse Brown, 54, US Secretary of Veterans Affairs in Clinton administration, born Detroit, MI, Mar 27, 1944. At press time, submitted his resignation.

Mariah Carey, 28, singer ("Vision of Love," "I'll Be There"), born Long Island, NY, Mar 27, 1970.

Randall Cunningham, 35, former football player, born Santa Barbara, CA, Mar 27, 1963.

Anthony Lewis, 71, journalist, author (*Gideon's Trumpet; Make No Law: The Sullivan Case and the First Amendment*), born New York, NY, Mar 27, 1927.

Austin Pendleton, 58, actor (*Mr and Mrs Bridge, Guarding Tess*), born Warren, OH, Mar 27, 1940.

Mstislav Leopoldovich Rostropovich, 71, musician, born Baku, USSR, Mar 27, 1927.

Maria Schneider, 46, actress (*Last Tango in Paris*), born Paris, France, Mar 27, 1952.

Quentin Tarantino, 35, actor (*Pulp Fiction*), born Knoxville, TN, Mar 27, 1963.

William Caleb (Cale) Yarborough, 58, former auto racer, born Timmonsville, SC, Mar 27, 1940.

Michael York, 56, actor (*Cabaret, The Three Musketeers*), born Fulmer, England, Mar 27, 1942.

MARCH 28 — SATURDAY

Day 87 — 278 Remaining

AMERICAN BRAIN TUMOR ASSOCIATION 25th ANNIVERSARY CELEBRATION. Mar 28. Hotel Sofitel, Rosemont, IL. Prominent researchers from leading medical centers will present cutting-edge information on brain tumor treatments and wellness issues. General sessions, special interest sessions, exhibits, banquet with emcee Bill Kurtis. Est attendance: 500. For info: American Brain Tumor Assn, 2720 River Rd, Des Plaines, IL 60018. Phone: (847) 827-9910 or (800) 886-2282. Fax: (847) 827-9918. Email: info@abta.org. WWW: http://www.abta.org

ATLANTIQUE CITY ANTIQUES AND COLLECTIBLES SPRING FAIR. Mar 28–29. Atlantic City, Convention Center, Atlantic City, NJ. "World's largest" antiques and collectibles show, with more than 1,200 dealers displaying and selling an array of memorabilia from Jack Benny's violin to a first-edition Superman comic book. For info: Mark Soifer, PR, 1803 Clover Ave, Vineland, NJ 08360. Phone: (609) 691-7535. Fax: (609) 691-9458.

BARTHOLOMEW, FREDDIE: BIRTH ANNIVERSARY. Mar 28, 1924. Child star of the 1930s, Freddie Bartholomew was born Frederick Llewellyn at Great Britain. He appeared in 24 films and became the second-highest paid child star after Shirley Temple. He died on Jan 23, 1992 at Sarasota, FL.

BATTLE OF LA GLORIETTA PASS: ANNIVERSARY. Mar 28, 1862. At Pigeon's Ranch, a stagecoach stop on the Santa Fe Trail (about 19 miles southeast of Santa Fe, NM), Confederate forces briefly prevailed over Union troops in what some have called the most important battle of the Civil War in the Southwest. It was feared that if Union troops failed to hold here, the Confederate forces would proceed to Fort Union and on to control of the rich gold fields of Colorado and California. A reenactment of the battle in 1985 drew attention to the battlefield and the adobe remains of Pigeon's Ranch.

CATTLE BARON'S BALL. Mar 28. Wichita Falls, TX. A gala event featuring an evening of the finest Southwestern cuisine, a star-studded performance from a big name country and western star, live and silent auctions, casino gaming and more—all to support the fight of cancer in Wichita County. For info: Wichita Falls Conv & Visitors Bureau, 1000 5th St, Wichita Falls, TX 76301. Phone: (817) 716-5500. Fax: (817) 716-5509.

COMMUNITY RUMMAGE AND COLLECTIBLE SALE. Mar 28. Norfolk, NE. Fundraiser for the Norfolk Senior Citizens Center. Members of the community purchase space to sell rummage and collectibles. Baked goods and a lunch counter are available all day. Open 8–4. For info: Jean Atwood, Coord, Norfolk Senior Citizens Ctr, 307 Prospect, PO Box 302, Norfolk, NE 68702. Phone: (402) 371-8299.

CZECH REPUBLIC: TEACHERS' DAY. Mar 28. Celebrates birth on this day of Jan Amos Komensky (Comenius), Moravian educational reformer (1592–1671).

DAYTONA BEACH SPRING '98 SPEEDWAY SPECTACULAR. Mar 28–29. Daytona International Speedway, Daytona Beach, FL. 9th annual car show of all makes and models of collector vehicles. Many car clubs make this their largest annual event. Show includes display of antiques, classics, sportscars, muscle cars, race cars, custom and special interest vehicles on the speedway infield both days, with a large swap meet of auto parts and accessories. Collector car sales corral, crafts sale. Annually, the last or next to the last weekend in March. Est attendance: 25,000. For info: Rick D'Louhy, Exec Dir, Daytona Beach Racing and Recreational Facilities District, PO Box 1958, Daytona Beach, FL 32115-1958. Phone: (904) 255-7355.

EASTERFEST. Mar 28. Scottish Rite Cathedral, New Castle, PA. Easter craft vendors, hand-painted decorative eggs, ethnic food. Est attendance: 7,000. For info: Parish Office Chair, Parish Office, 124 N Beaver St, New Castle, PA 16101. Phone: (412) 658-2564. Fax: (412) 658-9024.

EGGSIBIT '98. Mar 28–29. Firth Youth Center, Phillipsburg, NJ. 28th annual show to encourage the art of decorating eggshells. Annually, the weekend prior to Palm Sunday. Est attendance: 2,000. For info: Dawn Slifer, Firth Youth Center, 108 Anderson St, Phillipsburg, NJ 08865. Phone: (908) 454-7281.

March 1998

S	M	T	W	T	F	S
1	2	3	4	5	6	7
8	9	10	11	12	13	14
15	16	17	18	19	20	21
22	23	24	25	26	27	28
29	30	31				

ENGLAND: HARROGATE INTERNATIONAL YOUTH MUSIC FESTIVAL. Mar 27–Apr 3 (tentative). Harrogate, North Yorkshire. Noncompetitive festival that brings together youth (up to 25 years of age) in bands, choirs, orchestras and dance groups from all over the world. Est attendance: 7,000. For info: Perform Europe, 33 Maddox St, London, England W1R 9LD. Phone: (44) (171) 491-8141. Fax: (44) (171) 629-3108.

"GREATEST SHOW ON EARTH" FORMED: ANNIVERSARY. Mar 28, 1881. P.T. Barnum and James A. Bailey merged their circuses to form the "Greatest Show on Earth."

***HAIR* BROADWAY OPENING: 30th ANNIVERSARY.** Mar 28, 1968. The controversial rock musical *Hair*, produced by Michael Butler, opened at the Biltmore Theatre in New York City on Mar 28, 1968. For those who opposed the Vietnam War and the "Establishment," this was a defining piece of work—as evidenced by some of its songs, such as "Aquarius," "Hair," "Let the Sunshine In."

LAZAR, IRVING ("SWIFTY"): BIRTH ANNIVERSARY. Mar 28, 1907. Hollywood talent agent whose clients included Ernest Hemingway, Lillian Hellman, Cole Porter, Richard Nixon and Humphrey Bogart (who nicknamed him "Swifty" after Lazar met Bogart's challenge to make him five film deals in one day in 1955). He died on Dec 30, 1993, at Beverly Hills, CA.

NATCHEZ POWWOW. Mar 28–29. Natchez, MS. Native American dancing and crafts. Est attendance: 5,000. For info: Grand Village of the Natchez Indians, 400 Jefferson Davis Blvd, Natchez, MS 39120. Phone: (601) 446-6502. Fax: (601) 446-6503. Email: gvni@bkbank.com.

NEW ENGLAND CONFERENCE ON STORYTELLING FOR CHILDREN. Mar 28. Arts Center, Keene State College, Keene, NH. Warm, supportive one-day conference for teachers and others interested in learning more about storytelling. Keynote plus two workshops and a performance. There will be workshops for children. Resources will be available. Est attendance: 100. For info: Mary Mayshark-Stavely, Keene State College, Keene, NH 03435-2503. Phone: (603) 358-2218.
Email: mmayshar@keene.edu.

SAINT JOHN NEPOMUCENE NEUMANN: BIRTH ANNIVERSARY. Mar 28, 1811. First male saint of the US. Born at Prachatice, Bohemia, came to the US in 1836. As Bishop of Philadelphia, he was affectionately known as the "Little Bishop." Died at Philadelphia, PA, Jan 5, 1860. Beatified Oct 13, 1963. Canonized June 19, 1977.

SPACE MILESTONE: *NOAA 8* (US): 15th ANNIVERSARY. Mar 28, 1983. Search and Rescue Satellite (SARSAT) launched from Vandenburg Air Force Base, CA, to aid in locating ships and aircraft in distress. *Kosmos 1383*, launched on July 1, 1982, by the USSR, in a cooperative rescue effort, is credited with saving more than 20 lives.

SPRING CRAFT FESTIVAL. Mar 28–29. St. Simons Island, GA. Seventh annual festival where 100 fine crafts artists exhibit and sell their creations. Annually, the last full weekend in March. Est attendance: 10,000. For info: Glynn Art Assn, 319 Mallory St, St. Simons Island, GA 31522. Phone: (912) 638-8770. Fax: (912) 638-8770.

THREE MILE ISLAND NUCLEAR POWER PLANT ACCIDENT: ANNIVERSARY. Mar 28, 1979. A series of accidents beginning at 4 AM, EST, Mar 28, 1979, at Three Mile Island on the Susquehanna River about 10 miles southeast of Harrisburg, PA, was responsible for extensive reevaluation of the safety of existing nuclear power generating operations. Equipment and other failures reportedly brought Three Mile Island close to a meltdown of the uranium core, threatening extensive radiation contamination.

TRIPEX-98. Mar 28–29. LaVale Fire Hall, west of Cumberland, MD. A show for stamp collectors featuring eight or nine dealers, stamp exhibits, free information on collecting stamps, door prizes and the US Postal Service. Free admission and parking. Sponsored by the Tri-State Stamp Club. Annually, the last weekend in

March unless Easter falls on that weekend. Est attendance: 200. For info: Ted Rissell, 365 Back Bay Rd, Swanton, MD 21561. Phone: (301) 387-6463.

VIETNAM MORATORIUM CONCERT: ANNIVERSARY. Mar 28. A seven-hour concert at Madison Square Garden in New York City on Mar 28, 1970, featured many stars who had donated their services for the antiwar cause. Among them were Jimi Hendrix; Dave Brubeck; Harry Belafonte; Peter, Paul and Mary; Judy Collins; the Rascals; Blood, Sweat and Tears; and the Broadway cast of *Hair.*

WURSTFEST. Mar 28–29. Hermann, MO. Contest between gourmet sausage makers. Festival celebrates the art of sausage making. Sample and purchase of home made sausage from vendors from throughout Missouri. Annually, the fourth weekend in March. Est attendance: 10,000. For info: Hermann Visitor Ctr, 306 Market St, Hermann, MO 65041. Phone: (573) 486-2744. Fax: (573) 486-5363.

BIRTHDAYS TODAY

Dirk Bogarde (Derek van Den Bogaerde), 77, actor (*The Damned, Death in Venice*), born London, England, Mar 28, 1921.

Conchata Ferrell, 55, actress ("LA Law," "Hearts Afire," *Mystic Pizza, Edward Scissorhands*), born Charleston, WV, Mar 28, 1943.

Ken Howard, 54, actor ("The White Shadow"), born El Centro, CA, Mar 28, 1944.

Reba McEntire, 44, singer ("For My Broken Heart"), born Chockie, OK, Mar 28, 1954.

Frank Hughes Murkowski, 65, US Senator (R, Alaska), born Seattle, WA, Mar 28, 1933.

Byron Antom Scott, 37, basketball player, born Ogden, UT, Mar 28, 1961.

Dianne Wiest, 50, actress (Oscars for *Hannah and Her Sisters* and *Bullets Over Broadway*), born Kansas City, MO, Mar 28, 1948.

☆ ☆ ☆

MARCH 29 — SUNDAY

Day 88 — 277 Remaining

ASPEN/SNOWMASS BANANA SEASON. Mar 29–Apr 4. Snowmass Village, CO. Events: Banana Bonanza Hunt; High Altitude Beach Party and volleyball games; Bartenders' Banana Brawl Drink Contest; Banana Sidewalk Sale. For the Banana Bonanza Hunt, hundreds of prize-filled plastic bananas are hidden on the ski slopes. Clues lead to one "Big Banana Prize." Est attendance: 3,000. For info: Snowmass Resort Assn, PO Box 5566, Snowmass Village, CO 81615. Phone: (970) 923-2000.

BAILEY, PEARL MAE: 80th BIRTH ANNIVERSARY. Mar 29, 1918. American singer and Broadway musical star Pearl Bailey was born at Newport News, VA. She began her career in vaudeville and won a special Tony Award in 1968 and the Presidential Medal of Freedom in 1988. Bailey died on Aug 17, 1990, at Philadelphia, PA.

BIGGS, EDWARD GEORGE POWER: BIRTH ANNIVERSARY. Mar 29, 1906. Baroque organist who helped establish the organ as a concert instrument. Biggs refused to perform on electronic organs, but sought and recorded on organs surviving from the era of Johann Sebastian Bach and George Frideric Handel. After arthritis forced him to retire, he published early organ music. Biggs was born at Westcliff-on-Sea, Essex, England, and came to the US in 1930 at the age of 24. He died Mar 10, 1977, at Boston.

CANADA: BRITISH NORTH AMERICA ACT: ANNIVERSARY. Mar 29, 1867. This act of the British Parliament established the Dominion of Canada, uniting Ontario, Quebec, Nova Scotia and New Brunswick. The remaining colonies in Canada were still ruled directly by Great Britain until Manitoba joined the Dominion in 1870, British Columbia in 1871, Prince Edward Island in 1873 and Alberta and Saskatchewan in 1905.

COMMITTEE ON ASSASSINATIONS REPORT: ANNIVERSARY. Mar 29, 1979. The House Select Committee on Assassinations released the final report on its investigation into the assassinations of President John F. Kennedy, Martin Luther King, Jr, and Robert Kennedy on this day. Based on available evidence, the committee concluded that President Kennedy was assassinated as a result of a conspiracy, although no trail of a conspiracy could be established. The Soviet Union, Cuba, CIA, FBI, Secret Service, anti-Castro Cuban groups and organized crime were ruled out as possible sources of a conspiracy, although in the latter two groups evidence did not preclude the possibility that members of those two groups may have been involved as individuals not representing their organizations. They also concluded that on the basis of scientific acoustical evidence two gunmen fired at the President, although no second gunman could be identified, and they found that the Warren Commission failed to investigate adequately the possibility of a conspiracy primarily because the Commission did not receive all the relevant information that was in the possession of other government agencies at the time. [Note: In Dec 1980, the FBI released a report discounting the two-gunman theory, stating that the distinguishable sounds of two separate guns were not proven scientifically.] In addition the committee concluded that the possibility of conspiracy did exist in the cases of Dr. King and Robert Kennedy, although no specific individuals or organizations could be pinpointed as being involved. See also: "Warren Commission Report: Anniversary" (Sept 27).

CONSIDER CHRISTIANITY WEEK. Mar 29–Apr 4. A week to encourage Christians to examine the evidence and reasons for their faith, and for non-Christians to take another look at the faith that has played such an important role in shaping the history and culture in which we live. Annually, beginning two Sundays before Easter. For info: Hanna Hushbeck, PR, Aletheia Publishing, 936 N Lincoln St, Redlands, CA 92374. Phone: (909) 794-8941. Fax: (909) 794-8941. Email: consider@genesisnetwork.net. WWW: http://www.genesisnetwork.net/business/consider/index.htm

ENGLAND: CARE SUNDAY. Mar 29. The fifth Sunday of Lent, also known as Carling Sunday and Passion Sunday. First day of Passiontide, remembering the sorrow and passion of Christ.

ENGLAND: SUMMER TIME. Mar 29–Oct 25. In England and much of Europe, "Summer Time" (one hour in advance of Standard Time), similar to daylight-saving time, is observed from 0100 hours on the day after the fourth Saturday in March until 0100 hours on the day after the fourth Saturday in October.

EUROPE: SUMMER DAYLIGHT SAVING TIME. Mar 29–Sept 27. Many European countries observe daylight-saving (summer) time from 2 AM on the last Sunday in March until 3 AM on the last Sunday in September.

GREECE: DUMB WEEK. Mar 29–Apr 4. The week preceding Holy Week is known as Dumb Week, as no services are held in churches throughout this period except on Friday, eve of the Saturday of Lazarus.

HOOVER, LOU HENRY: BIRTH ANNIVERSARY. Mar 29. Wife of Herbert Clark Hoover, 31st president of the US. Born Mar 29, 1875, at Waterloo, IA. Died Jan 7, 1944.

JOHN PARTRIDGE "DEATH" HOAX: ANNIVERSARY. Mar 29, 1708. English astrologer John Partridge (real name: John Hewson) so offended readers by his foolish predictions that he became the target of parodies and jokes, most serious of which was that of the satirist Jonathan Swift. Under the pseudonym Isaac Bickerstaff, Swift published his own almanac, for the year 1708, in which he predicted that Partridge would die at 11 PM, Mar 29, 1708, "of a raging fever." Poor Partridge made the mistake of trying to prove he was still alive, only to find writers, citizens and even the court were more amused by continuing the fiction of his death.

KNIGHTS OF COLUMBUS FOUNDERS' DAY. Mar 29. The first Knights of Columbus charter was granted in 1882 by the state of Connecticut. This Catholic, family, fraternal, service organization has grown into a volunteer force of Knights and family members totaling nearly six million who annually donate tens of millions of dollars and volunteer hours to countless charitable projects. For info: Ronald J. Tracz, VP, Fraternal Services, Knights of Columbus, 1 Columbus Plaza, New Haven, CT 06510-3326.

LOS ANGELES MARATHON FAMILY REUNION FESTIVAL. Mar 29. Los Angeles, CA. A multicultural athletic competition designed to foster community spirit as well as pride in one's physical well-being. Food, sampling, general merchandise. Est attendance: 100,000. For info: John Wilson, Los Angeles Marathon, 11110 W Ohio Ave, Ste 100, Los Angeles, CA 90025. Phone: (310) 444-5544.

MADAGASCAR: COMMEMORATION DAY. Mar 29, 1947. Commemoration Day for the victims of the rebellion in 1947 against French colonization.

MOUNTAIN VIEW INN SPRING CRAFT SHOW. Mar 29. (Also Holiday Craft Show Nov 29.) Mountain View Inn, Greensburg, PA. More than 90 crafters in three rooms. Celebrate the arrival of spring and view crafters selling bunnies, candy, quilts, dolls, Amish furniture, jewelry, grapevine wreaths and more. For info: Ann Nemanic, Mountain View Inn, Rte 30 East, Greensburg, PA 15601. Phone: (412) 834-5300 or (800) 537-8709. Fax: (412) 834-5304.

NATIONAL MOM AND POP BUSINESS OWNERS DAY. Mar 29. A day recognizing those very special husband and wife business owner teams that work and commune together. Take this day to strike a balance between business and love. For info: Rick/Margie Segel, 1 Wheatland St, Burlington, MA 01803. Phone: (617) 272-9995. Fax: (617) 272-9996.

PASSION WEEK. Mar 29–Apr 4. The week beginning on the fifth Sunday in Lent; the week before Holy Week.

PASSIONTIDE. Mar 29–Apr 11. The last two weeks of Lent (Passion Week and Holy Week), beginning with the fifth Sunday of Lent (Passion Sunday) and continuing through the day before Easter (Holy Saturday or Easter).

QUINLAN, KAREN ANN: BIRTH ANNIVERSARY. Mar 29. Born at Scranton, PA, on Mar 29, 1954, Karen Ann Quinlan became the center of an international legal, medical and ethical controversy over the right to die. Reportedly she became irreversibly comatose on Apr 14, 1975. A petition filed by her adoptive parents in New Jersey's Superior Court, Sept 12, 1975, sought permission to discontinue use of a respirator, allowing her to die "with grace and dignity." In 1976 the petition was upheld by New Jersey's Supreme Court. Quinlan lived nearly a decade without the respirator—until June 11, 1985. Her plight brought into focus the ethical dilemmas of advancing medical technology—the need for a new understanding of life and death; the right to die; the role of judges, doctors and hospital committees in deciding when to prolong or *not* to prolong life.

STRAW HAT WEEK. Mar 29–Apr 5. A week of celebration during which the felt hat is put aside in favor of the straw or fabric hat by both men and women. Local businesses and the media are encouraged to plan hat-related activities. Annually, one or two weeks before Easter. For info: Casey Bush, Exec Dir, Headwear Info Bureau, 302 W 12 St, PH-C, New York, NY 10014. Phone: (212) 627-8333. Email: milicase@earthlink.net. WWW: http://www.hatsny.com

SWEDENBORG, EMANUEL: DEATH ANNIVERSARY. Mar 29, 1772. Swedish scientist and theologian Emanuel Swedenborg (family name Svedberg) died at London, England. His writings interpreting most of the scriptures as the direct word of God formed the basis of the Church of the New Jerusalem, which was established by his devotees soon after his death at age 84. Swedenborg was born Jan 29, 1688, at Stockholm. He postulated new methods of construction and finding longitude by the stars. He had plans as well for machine guns, submarines and airplanes. In 1715 Swedenborg published Sweden's first scientific journal. Around 1743 Swedenborg's study of the human anatomy and his search for the soul led him to begin thinking more about religion. He published several works about his religious philosophy and determined that it was his mission to reveal the spiritual meaning in books of the Bible believed to have come immediately from God.

TAIWAN: YOUTH DAY. Mar 29. Public holiday observed annually on Mar 29.

TEXAS LOVE THE CHILDREN DAY. Mar 29. A day recognizing every child's right and need to be loved. Promoting the hope that one day all children will live in loving, safe environments and will be given proper health care and equal learning opportunities. Precedes the start of National Child Abuse Prevention Month (April). For info: Patty Murphy, 1101 Lynda Lane, Arlington, TX 76013. Phone: (817) 275-2595.

TWENTY-THIRD AMENDMENT TO US CONSTITUTION RATIFIED: ANNIVERSARY. Mar 29. District of Columbia residents were given the right to vote in presidential elections under the 23rd Amendment, ratified Mar 29, 1961.

TYLER, JOHN: BIRTH ANNIVERSARY. Mar 29. 10th president of the US (Apr 6, 1841–Mar 3, 1845). Born at Charles City County, VA, Mar 29, 1790, Tyler succeeded to the presidency upon the death of William Henry Harrison. Tyler's first wife died while he was president, and he remarried before the end of his term of office, becoming the first president to marry while in office. Fifteen children were born of the two marriages. In 1861 he was elected to the Congress of the Confederate States but died at Richmond, VA, Jan 18, 1862, before being seated. His death received no official tribute from the US government.

WALTON, SAM: BIRTH ANNIVERSARY. Mar 29, 1918. Founder of Wal-Mart discount stores, born at Kingfisher, OK. Became one of the wealthiest men in America, died at Little Rock, AR, on Apr 5, 1992.

YOUNG, DENTON TRUE (CY): BIRTH ANNIVERSARY. Mar 29, 1867. Baseball Hall of Fame pitcher born at Gilmore, OH. Young is baseball's all-time winningest pitcher, having accumulated 511 victories in his 22-year career. The Cy Young Award is given each year in his honor to major league's best pitcher. Inducted into the Hall of Fame in 1937. Died at Peoli, OH, Nov 4, 1955.

March 1998

S	M	T	W	T	F	S
1	2	3	4	5	6	7
8	9	10	11	12	13	14
15	16	17	18	19	20	21
22	23	24	25	26	27	28
29	30	31				

BIRTHDAYS TODAY

Earl Christian Campbell, 43, Pro Football Hall of Fame running back, born Tyler, TX, Mar 29, 1955.

Bud Cort, 48, actor (*Harold and Maude, Brewster McCloud*), born New Rochelle, NY, Mar 29, 1950.

Eric Idle, 55, actor ("Monty Python's Flying Circus"), author, born Durham, England, Mar 29, 1943.

Christopher Lambert, 41, actor (*Greystoke: The Legend of Tarzan, Lord of the Apes; To Kill a Priest*), born New York, NY, Mar 29, 1957.

John Major, 55, former British prime minister, born Brixton, England, Mar 29, 1943.

Eugene McCarthy, 82, former US Senator (anti-Vietnam War presidential hopeful in '68), born Watkins, MN, Mar 29, 1916.

John Joseph McLaughlin, 71, editor, columnist, TV host, born Providence, RI, Mar 29, 1927.

MARCH 30 — MONDAY

Day 89 — 276 Remaining

ANESTHETIC FIRST USED IN SURGERY: ANNIVERSARY. Mar 30, 1842. Dr. Crawford W. Long, having seen the use of nitrous oxide and sulfuric ether at "laughing gas" parties, observed that individuals under their influences felt no pain. On Mar 30, 1842, he removed a tumor from the neck of a man who was under the influence of ether.

DOCTORS' DAY. Mar 30. Traditional annual observance since 1933 to honor America's physicians on anniversary of occasion when Dr. Crawford W. Long became the first acclaimed physician to use ether as an anesthetic agent in a surgical technique.

GOYA, FRANCISCO JOSE De: BIRTH ANNIVERSARY. Mar 30, 1746. Spanish painter and etcher. It is estimated that he executed more than 1,800 paintings, drawings and lithographs during his lifetime. Born at Aragon, Spain, died at Bordeaux, France, Apr 16, 1828.

"I AM IN CONTROL" DAY: ANNIVERSARY. Mar 30, 1981. Anniversary of former Secretary of State Alexander Haig's televised announcement (while President Ronald Reagan was undergoing surgery after being shot by a would-be assassin): "As of now, I am in control here in the White House. . . ." Haig continued to say: "Constitutionally, gentlemen, you have the president, the vice president and the secretary of state in that order. . . ."

"JEOPARDY" TV PREMIERE: ANNIVERSARY. Mar 30, 1964. The "thinking person's" game show, "Jeopardy" has a reputation as a mature, intelligent and classy program. Art Fleming was the original host of the show, in which three contestants won cash by attempting to give the correct question to an answer uncovered on a board of 30 squares, with five answers each in six different categories. Contestants went through two rounds and "final jeopardy," where they could wager up to all their earnings on one question. In 1978, the format was changed so that only two contestants entered the second round, and only one played final jeopardy. When the series returned in 1984, it went back to its old format, with Alex Trebek as the popular host. By the end of the '80s, "Jeopardy" was one of the most popular shows.

O'CASEY, SEAN: BIRTH ANNIVERSARY. Mar 30, 1880. Irish playwright (*Juno and the Paycock*). Born at Dublin, Ireland, Mar 30, 1880. Died at Torquay, England, on Sept 18, 1964.

PENCIL PATENTED: ANNIVERSARY. Mar 30, 1858. First pencil with the eraser top was patented by Hyman Lipman.

REAGAN, RONALD: ASSASSINATION ATTEMPT ANNIVERSARY. Mar 30. President Ronald Reagan was shot in the chest by a 25-year-old gunman, about 2:30 PM, EST, Mar 30, 1981, in Washington, DC. John W. Hinckley, Jr, the accused attacker, was arrested at the scene. On June 21, 1982, a federal jury in the District of Columbia found Hinckley not guilty by reason of insanity and he was committed to St. Elizabeth's Hospital, at Washington, DC, for an indefinite time.

SEWARD'S DAY: ANNIVERSARY OF THE ACQUISITION OF ALASKA. Mar 30, 1867. Observed in Alaska near anniversary of its acquisition from Russia in 1867. Annually, the last Monday in March. The treaty of purchase was signed between the Russians and the Americans on Mar 30, 1867, and ratified by the Senate on May 28, 1867. The territory was formally transferred on Oct 18, 1867.

"SOMERSET" TV PREMIERE: ANNIVERSARY. Mar 30, 1970. "Somerset" was a spin-off from "Another World," but this serial had little in common with its parent, focusing on different characters and developing storylines about crime and intrigue. The two main characters from "AW" were Sam Lucas (Jordan Charney) and his wife, Lahoma Vane Lucas (Ann Wedgeworth), but new cast members included Ed Kemmer, Georgann Johnson, Ralph Clanton, Len Gochman, Nick Coster, Dorothy Stinette and Marie Wallace. Famous "Somerset" alumni include Michael Nouri, Ted Danson and Sigourney Weaver.

TRINIDAD AND TOBAGO: SPIRITUAL BAPTIST LIBERATION SHOUTER DAY. Mar 30. Public Holiday. For info: Information Dept, Tourism Div, Tourism and Industrial Development Co, 10-14 Phillips St, Port of Spain, Trinidad, West Indies.

VAN GOGH, VINCENT: BIRTH ANNIVERSARY. Mar 30, 1853. Dutch post-Impressionist painter, especially known for his bold and powerful use of color. Born at Groot Zundert, Holland, Mar 30, 1853. Died at Auvers-sur-Oise, France, July 29, 1890.

BIRTHDAYS TODAY

John Astin, 68, actor ("The Addams Family"; stage: *The Three Penny Opera*), director, born Baltimore, MD, Mar 30, 1930.

Warren Beatty, 60, actor (*Bonnie and Clyde*), director (*Reds, Dick Tracy*), producer, born Richmond, VA, Mar 30, 1938.

Tracy Chapman, 34, singer ("Fast Car"), born Cleveland, OH, Mar 30, 1964.

Eric Clapton, 53, singer (with Yardbirds, Cream), songwriter ("Layla," with Jim Gordon), born Ripley, England, Mar 30, 1945.

Celine Dion, 30, pop singer, Grammy winner, born Mar 30, 1968.

Richard Dysart, 69, actor (Leland McKenzie on "LA Law"), born Augusta, ME, Mar 30, 1929.

Frankie Laine, 85, actor, singer ("Frankie Laine Time"; *Viva Las Vegas*), born Chicago, IL, Mar 30, 1913.

Peter Marshall, 71, TV host, actor, born Huntington, WV, Mar 30, 1927.

Bob Miller, 53, Governor of Nevada (D), born Evanston, IL, Mar 30, 1945.

Paul Reiser, 41, actor (*Diner*, "Mad About You"), born New York, NY, Mar 30, 1957.

MARCH 31 — TUESDAY

Day 90 — 275 Remaining

BUNSEN BURNER DAY. Mar 31. A day to honor the inventor of the Bunsen burner, Robert Wilhelm Eberhard von Bunsen, who provided chemists and chemistry students with one of their most indispensable instruments. The Bunsen burner allows the user to regulate the proportions of flammable gas and air to create the most efficient flame. Bunsen was born at Gottingen, Germany, on Mar 31, 1811, and was a professor of chemistry at the universities at Kassel, Marburg, Breslau and Heidelberg. He died at Heidelberg, Germany, Aug 16, 1899.

CHAVEZ, CESAR ESTRADA: BIRTH ANNIVERSARY. Mar 31, 1927. Labor leader who organized migrant farm workers in support of better working conditions. Chavez initiated the National Farm Workers Association in 1962, attracting attention to the migrant farm workers' plight by organizing boycotts of products including grapes and lettuce. He was born at Yuma, AZ, and died Apr 23, 1993, at San Luis, AZ.

CHESNUT, MARY BOYKIN MILLER: 175th BIRTH ANNIVERSARY. Mar 31, 1823. Born at Pleasant Hill, SC, and died Nov 22, 1886, at Camden, SC. During the Civil War Chesnut accompanied her husband, a Confederate staff officer, on military missions. She kept a journal of her experiences and observations, which was published posthumously as *A Diary from Dixie*, a perceptive portrait of Confederate military and political leaders and insightful view of Southern life during the Civil War.

CHRYSLER OPENS DETROIT FACTORY: ANNIVERSARY. Mar 31, 1992. In an unorthodox move for recessionary times, the Chrysler Corporation opened a new plant on Jefferson Ave in Detroit, MI, on Mar 31, 1992. The opening came at a time when American automakers were scaling back and closing plants while Japanese competitors were opening facilities in mid-South rural locations to avoid unions and urban problems. Located across the street from the site of its 85-year-old predecessor that was torn down in 1991, the new plant produces Jeep Grand Cherokee utility vehicles.

DESCARTES, RENE: BIRTH ANNIVERSARY. Mar 31. French philosopher and mathematician, known as the "father of modern philosophy." Born at La Haye, Touraine, France, on Mar 31, 1596. Cartesian philosophical precepts are often remembered because of his famous proposition "I think, therefore I am" (*Cogito ergo sum . . .*). Died of pneumonia at Stockholm, Sweden, on Feb 11, 1650.

EIFFEL TOWER: ANNIVERSARY. Mar 31. Built for the Paris Exhibition of 1889, the tower was named for its architect, Alexandre Gustave Eiffel, and is one of the world's best known landmarks.

FITZGERALD, EDWARD: BIRTH ANNIVERSARY. Mar 31, 1809. English author. Born Mar 31, 1809. Perhaps best known for his translation of Omar Khayyam's *Rubaiyat*. Died June 14, 1883.

GOGOL, NIKOLAI VASILEVICH: BIRTH ANNIVERSARY. Mar 31. Russian author of plays, novels and short stories. Born at Sorochinsk, Russia, on Mar 31, 1809. Died at Moscow, Russia, Mar 4, 1852. Gogol's most famous work was the novel *Dead Souls*.

GORE, ALBERT, JR.: BIRTHDAY. Mar 31, 1948. Forty-fifth US Vice President, born at Washington, DC.

March 1998

S	M	T	W	T	F	S
1	2	3	4	5	6	7
8	9	10	11	12	13	14
15	16	17	18	19	20	21
22	23	24	25	26	27	28
29	30	31				

HAYDN, FRANZ JOSEPH: BIRTH ANNIVERSARY. Mar 31, 1732. "Father of the symphony." Born at Rohrau, Austria-Hungary, on Mar 31, 1732. Composed about 120 symphonies, more than a hundred works for chamber groups, a dozen operas and hundreds of other musical works. Died at Vienna, Austria, on May 31, 1809.

JOHNSON, JOHN (JACK) ARTHUR: BIRTH ANNIVERSARY. Mar 31, 1878. In 1908 Jack Johnson became the first black to win the heavyweight boxing championship when he defeated Tommy Burns at Sydney, Australia. Unable to accept a black's triumph, the boxing world tried to find a white challenger. Jim Jeffries, former heavyweight title holder, was badgered out of retirement. On July 4, 1919, at Reno, NV, the "battle of the century" proved to be a farce when Johnson handily defeated Jeffries. Race riots swept the US and plans to exhibit the film of the fight were canceled. Johnson was born at Galveston, TX, and died in an automobile accident June 10, 1946, at Raleigh, NC. He was inducted into the Boxing Hall of Fame in 1990. The film *The Great White Hope* is based on his life.

MARVELL, ANDREW: BIRTH ANNIVERSARY. Mar 31, 1621. English poet. Born at Winestead, Yorkshire, England. From his poem "To His Coy Mistress": "Had we but world enough and time/this coyness, lady, were no crime. . . . But at my back I always hear/time's winged chariot drawing near. . . ." Died at London, England, Aug 18, 1678.

MORGAN, HENRY: BIRTH ANNIVERSARY. Mar 31, 1915. Henry Lerner von Ost Jr (Henry Morgan) was born at New York City. In 1933, at age 18, he became the youngest radio announcer in the US. His prickly quips and frequent antics quickly won him his own show. No one, politicians, radio executives or even his own sponsors, was spared his sharp tongue. From 1963 to 1977 he was a panelist on "I've Got a Secret," and he was a frequent guest on other television shows. Henry Morgan died May 19, 1994, at New York City.

PEARSE, RICHARD: 95th FLIGHT ANNIVERSARY. Mar 31, 1903. According to claim, Richard Pearse, a farmer and inventor, flew a monoplane of his own design several hundred yards along a road near Temuka, New Zealand, and then landed it on top of a 12-foot-high hedge, on Mar 31, 1903. Pearse also built the craft, which consisted of a steerable tricycle undercarriage and an internal combustion engine. A Pearse commemorative medal was issued on Sept 19, 1971, by the Museum of Transport and Technology, Auckland, New Zealand.

SOVIET GEORGIA VOTES FOR INDEPENDENCE: ANNIVERSARY. Mar 31. On Mar 31, 1991, the Soviet Republic of Georgia voted to declare its republic independent from the Soviet Union. Georgia followed the Baltic States of Lithuania, Estonia and Latvia by becoming the fourth republic to reject Mikhail Gorbachev's new vision of the Soviet Union as espoused in a new Union Treaty. Vote totals revealed that 98.9 percent of those voting favored independence from Moscow. Hours after the election, troops were dispatched from Moscow to Georgia under a state of emergency.

TEN BEST-CENSORED STORIES OF 1997. Mar 31. To announce the top ten underreported news stories of 1997 as determined by a national panel of jurors. On Mar 31 a 250–300 page Sourcebook detailing the "Top 25 Censored Stories of 1997" will be released by Project Censored. For info: Peter Phillips, Dir, Project Censored, Sonoma State University, Rohnert Park, CA 94928. Phone: (707) 664-2500. Fax: (707) 664-2108.

VIRGIN ISLANDS: TRANSFER DAY. Mar 31, 1917. Commemorates transfer resulting from purchase of the Virgin Islands by the US from Denmark, Mar 31, 1917, for $25 million.

BIRTHDAYS TODAY

Herb Alpert, 63, musician (Tijuana Brass), born Los Angeles, CA, Mar 31, 1935.

Leo Buscaglia (Felice Leonardo Buscaglia), 73, educator, author, motivational speaker, born Los Angeles, CA, Mar 31, 1925.

Richard Chamberlain, 63, actor ("Dr. Kildare," *Shogun*; an accomplished Shakespearean actor), born Los Angeles, CA, Mar 31, 1935.

Liz Claiborne, 69, fashion designer, born Brussels, Belgium, Mar 31, 1929.

William Daniels, 71, actor (Emmy for "St. Elsewhere"; voice of KITT on "Knight Rider"), born Brooklyn, NY, Mar 31, 1927.

Gordon (Gordie) Howe, 70, Hockey Hall of Fame right wing, born Floral, Saskatchewan, Canada, Mar 31, 1928.

John Jakes, 66, author (*California Gold, In the Big Country*), born Chicago, IL, Mar 31, 1932.

Shirley Jones, 64, singer, actress ("The Partridge Family," *Elmer Gantry, Oklahoma!*), born Smithton, PA, Mar 31, 1934.

Gabe Kaplan, 52, actor ("Welcome Back Kotter"), born Brooklyn, NY, Mar 31, 1946.

Richard Kiley, 76, actor (Emmy for "The Thorn Birds;" *The Blackboard Jungle*), born Chicago, IL, Mar 31, 1922.

Patrick J. Leahy, 58, US Senator (D, Vermont), born Montpelier, VT, Mar 31, 1940.

Edward Francis (Ed) Marinaro, 48, actor ("Hill Street Blues," "Sisters"), former football player, born New York, NY, Mar 31, 1950.

Marc McClure, 41, actor (*Freaky Friday, Back to the Future*), born San Mateo, CA, Mar 31, 1957.

Octavio Paz, 84, essayist, poet *Luna silvestre*, major literary figure after World War II. Born Mexico City, Mexico, Mar 31, 1914.

Rhea Perlman, 50, actress (Carla Tortelli on "Cheers" [three Emmy Awards]; *Carwash*), born Brooklyn, NY, Mar 31, 1948.

Christopher Walken, 55, actor (*The Deer Hunter, Batman Returns*), born Queens, NY, Mar 31, 1943.

Aprill.

APRIL 1 — WEDNESDAY

Day 91 — 274 Remaining

ALCOHOL AWARENESS MONTH. Apr 1–30. To help raise awareness among community prevention leaders and citizens about the problem of underage drinking. Concentrates on community grassroots activities. For info: Public Info Dept, Natl Council on Alcoholism and Drug Dependence, Inc, 12 W 21st St, New York, NY 10010. Phone: (212) 206-6770. Fax: (212) 645-1690. WWW: http://www.ncadd.org

APRIL FOOLS' or ALL FOOLS' DAY. Apr 1. "The joke of the day is to deceive persons by sending them upon frivolous and nonsensical errands; to pretend they are wanted when they are not, or, in fact, any way to betray them into some supposed ludicrous situation, so as to enable you to call them 'An April Fool.' "—Brady's *Clavis Calendaria*, 1812. "The first of April, some do say,/Is set apart for All Fools' Day,/But why the people call it so,/Nor I nor they themselves do know."—*Poor Robin's Almanack* for 1760.

AZALEA FESTIVAL. Apr 1–30. Muskogee, OK. One of the oldest and most celebrated public parks in the southwest, 122 acres, 40 acres of manicured gardens with 30,000 azaleas of 625 varieties. Ranked in the top 100 events by the National Business Association. Annually in April since 1967. Est attendance: 300,000. For info: Ervalene Jenkins, Muskogee Conv and Tourism, PO Box 2361, Muskogee, OK 74402. Phone: (888) 687-6137. Fax: (918) 684-6364. Email: tourism@ok.azalea.net.

BRIDGE OVER THE NEPONSET: ANNIVERSARY. Apr 1. The first bridge built in the US spanned the Neponset River between Milton and Dorchester, MA. The authority to build the bridge and an adjoining mill was issued to Israel Stoughton, on Apr 1, 1634, by the Massachusetts General Court.

BULGARIA: SAINT LASARUS'S DAY. Apr 1. Ancient Slavic holiday of young girls, in honor of the goddess of spring and love.

CANADA: MONTREAL SPORTSMEN'S SHOW. Apr 1–5. Place Bonaventure, Montreal, Quebec. Major manufacturers, distributors and retailers of the outdoors: camping, fishing and hunting industries; tent trailers, fishing boats, canoes, kayaks and other craft; tourism, campgrounds, outfitters and lodges; seminars and entertainment. Est attendance: 60,000. For info: Canadian Natl Sportsmen's Shows, 703 Evans Ave, Ste 202, Toronto, Ont, Canada M9C 5E9. Phone: (416) 695-0311. Fax: (416) 695-0381.

CANADA: SHAW FESTIVAL. Apr 1–Oct 31. Niagara-on-the-Lake, Ontario. The Shaw Festival is the only theatre in the world that specializes exclusively in plays by George Bernard Shaw and his contemporaries—plays about the beginning of the modern world. Presented in three theaters in historic Niagara-on-the-Lake, The Shaw's work engages the imagination, illuminates the past and inspires debate about the future. Est attendance: 300,000. For info: Box Office, Shaw Festival, Box 774, Niagara-on-the-Lake, Ont, Canada L0S 1J0. Phone: (800) 511-7429. WWW: http://www.shawfest.com

April 1998

S	M	T	W	T	F	S
			1	2	3	4
5	6	7	8	9	10	11
12	13	14	15	16	17	18
19	20	21	22	23	24	25
26	27	28	29	30		

CANCER CONTROL MONTH. Apr 1–30. For info: American Cancer Society, 1599 Clifton Rd NE, Atlanta, GA 30329-4251. Phone: (800) ACS-2345.

CHASE'S DEADLINE APPROACHING. Apr 1. Time to plan ahead. Schedule 1999 celebrations and observances and submit information to *Chase's 1999 Calendar of Events* by May 8, 1998. Sponsors/information suppliers of events in this book should have received confirmation/revision ("reup") forms for the 1999 edition by this time. To submit new entries for consideration, use a copy of the form on the last page of this book. Send to: Chase's Editor, Chase's Calendar of Events, NTC/Contemporary Publishing, 4255 W Touhy Ave, Lincolnwood, IL 60646-1975.

COMMUNITY SERVICE MONTH IN CALIFORNIA. Apr 1–30. Focuses attention on the variety of community services provided by California cities: child care, recreation, housing, public information, social services, health services, library and art programs. Annually, the month of April. Sponsor: League of California Cities, 1400 K St, Sacramento, CA 95814. For info: INTERCOM, 10601 Magnolia Ave, Santee, CA 92071-1266. Phone: (916) 444-5790 or (619) 258-4100.

DEFEAT AT FIVE FORKS: ANNIVERSARY. Apr 1. After withdrawing to Five Forks, VA, Confederate troops under George Pickett were defeated and cut off by Union troops on Apr 1, 1865. This defeat, according to many military historians, sealed the immediate fate of Robert E. Lee's armies at Petersburg and Richmond. On Apr 2, Lee informed Confederate President Jefferson Davis that he would have to evacuate Richmond. Davis and his cabinet fled by train to Danville, VA.

"THE DOCTORS" TV PREMIERE: 35th ANNIVERSARY. Apr 1, 1963. "The Doctors" premiered on NBC on the same day as ABC's long-running soap "General Hospital," providing viewers with a double dose of medical drama. The show was set at Hope Memorial Hospital and began as an anthology series that was subsequently transformed into a serial in 1964. Created by Orin Tovrov, "The Doctors" ran for 19 years. Ellen Burstyn, Gil Gerard, Kathleen Turner, Julia Duffy and Alec Baldwin are some of its famous alums.

FRESH FLORIDA TOMATO MONTH. Apr 1–30. To publicize the Florida tomato as a versatile, nutritious, flavorful food. For info: Anita Fial, Lewis & Neale, Inc, 49 E 21st St, 8th Flr, New York, NY 10010. Phone: (212) 420-8808. Fax: (212) 254-2452. Email: laneale@aol.com.

"GENERAL HOSPITAL" TV PREMIERE: 35th ANNIVERSARY. Apr 1, 1963. "General Hospital," ABC's longest-running soap, revolves around the denizens of fictional Port Charles, NY. "GH" was created by Doris and Frank Hursley. John Boradino, who was with the show from the beginning until his death in May of 1996, played the role of Dr. Steve Hardy, upstanding director of medicine and pillar of the community. In the '80s, story lines became more unusual with plots involving international espionage, mob activity and aliens. The wedding of supercouple Luke and Laura (Anthony Geary and Genie Francis) was a ratings topper. By the '90s, stories moved away from high-powered action to more conventional romance. Many of Hollywood's actors have received their big break on the show, including Demi Moore, Janine Turner, Jack Wagner, Richard Dean Anderson, Rick Springfield, John Stamos, Emma Samms, Mark Hamill, Finola Hughes and Tia Carrere.

GOLDEN RULE WEEK. Apr 1–7. The purpose of this week is to remind everyone of the importance of the Golden Rule in making this a better world in which we all may live. For a copy of the Golden Rule of 10 religions, send $3 to cover printing and postage. For info: Dr. Stanley J. Drake, Pres, Intl Society of Friendship and Goodwill, 412 Cherry Hills Dr, Bakersfield, CA 93309-2866.

GRAND STRAND FISHING RODEO. Apr 1–Oct 31. Myrtle Beach, SC. Awards for surf, inlet, pier and deep-sea fish catches. Est attendance: 1,000. For info: Chamber of Commerce, Box 2115, Myrtle Beach, SC 29578. Phone: (803) 626-7444. Fax: (803) 626-0009. WWW: http://www.myrtlebeach-info.com

HARVEY, WILLIAM: BIRTH ANNIVERSARY. Apr 1, 1578. Physician, born at Folkestone, England. The first to discover the mechanics of the circulation of the blood. Died at Roehampton, England, June 3, 1657.

HOLY HUMOR MONTH. Apr 1–30. To recognize the healing power of Christian joy, humor and celebration; to be "Fools for Christ" on April Fools' Day (Apr 1); to celebrate the Easter Monday of Western Christianity (Apr 13) and the Easter Monday of Eastern Christianity (Apr 20). Churches and prayer groups nationwide participate. Some churches celebrate on Bright Sunday ("Holy Humor Sunday"), the Sunday after Easter. For info: George Goldtrap, The Fellowship of Merry Christians, Inc, PO Box 895, Portage, MI 49081-0895. Phone: (615) 868-1969. Fax: (616) 324-3984. Email: joyfulnz@aol.com.
WWW: http://kalamazoo.inetmi.com/cities/kazoo/tjnoise/tjnoise/html

HOME IMPROVEMENT TIME. Apr 1–Sept 30. To explain the investment advantages of spending disposable income for home improvement to create better family living and improved community environment. (May is a promotion focal point.) For info: James A. Stewart, Jr, Home Improvement Time, PO Box 247, Oakdale, PA 15701-0247. Phone: (412) 787-2881. Fax: (412) 787-3233.

INTERNATIONAL AMATEUR RADIO MONTH. Apr 1–30. To disseminate information about the important part amateur radio operators or "hams" throughout the world are playing in promoting friendship, peace and good will. To obtain complete information about becoming an International Good Will Ambassador as well as a list of amateur radio operators in many countries, send $3 to cover expense of printing, handling and postage. Annually, the month of April. For info: Dr. Stanley Drake, Pres, Intl Soc of Friendship and Good Will, 412 Cherry Hills Dr, Bakersfield, CA 93309-2866.

INTERNATIONAL TWIT AWARD MONTH. Apr 1–30. Any famous name (celebrity with the worst sense of humor) is eligible for most Tiresome Wit (TWIT) of 1998. For info: Lauren Barnett, Lone Star Publications of Humor, 8452 Fredericksburg Rd, Ste #103, San Antonio, TX 78229. Email: lspubs@aol.com. WWW: http://members.aol.com/lspubs/lsindex.html

LISTENING AWARENESS MONTH. Apr 1–30. To help raise awareness of the need for effective listening-skill building by the presentation of listening seminars, book readings, skill-building workshops, newspaper/magazine articles, radio/TV guest interviews and listening parties throughout the USA. For info and/or effective listening activities, exercises and skill-building information, send a self-addressed, stamped envelope to Christine Carpenter, Dir, Effective Listeners Assn, PO Box 8716, Portland, OR 97207-8716.

MONTH OF THE YOUNG CHILD. Apr 1–30. Michigan. To promote awareness of the importance of young children and their specific needs in today's society. Many communities celebrate with special events for children and families. For info: Michigan Assn for Education of Young Children, Beacon Pl, Ste 1-D, 4572 S Hagadorn Road, East Lansing, MI 48823-5385. Phone: (800) 336-6424 or (517) 336-9700. Fax: (517) 336-9790. WWW: http://www.miaeyc.com

NATIONAL CHILD ABUSE PREVENTION MONTH. Apr 1–30. For info: Natl Committee to Prevent Child Abuse, 332 S Michigan Ave, Ste 1600, Chicago, IL 60604. Phone: (312) 663-3520.

NATIONAL COSMETOLOGY MONTH. Apr 1–30. Encourages better personal appearance in order to increase self-awareness, self-worth and self-development. For info: Communications, Natl Cosmetology Assn, 3510 Olive St, St. Louis, MO 63103. Phone: (314) 534-7980. Fax: (314) 534-8618.
Email: nca-now@primary.net. WWW: http://www.nca-now.com

NATIONAL FUN AT WORK DAY. Apr 1. Today and every day the workplace should be spiced with fun, laughter and a playful attitude. Morale will increase, productivity will soar and the bottom line will improve. For info: Matt Weinstein, Playfair, 2207 Oregon St, Berkeley, CA 94705. Phone: (510) 540-8768. Fax: (510) 540-7638. Email: playfair1@aol.com.
WWW: http://www.playfair.com

NATIONAL HUMOR MONTH. Apr 1–30. 23rd anniversary. Focuses on the joy and therapeutic value of laughter and how it can reduce stress, improve job performance and enrich the quality of life. For info: send SASE (55¢) to: Larry Wilde, Dir, The Carmel Institute of Humor, 25470 Canada Dr, Carmel, CA 93923-8926.

NATIONAL KNUCKLES DOWN MONTH. Apr 1–30. To recognize and revive the American tradition of playing and collecting marbles and keep it rolling along. Please send self-addressed, stamped envelope with inquiries. For info: Cathy C. Runyan, The Marble Lady, 7812 NW Hampton Rd, Kansas City, MO 64152. Phone: (816) 587-8687.

NATIONAL LAWN AND GARDEN MONTH. Apr 1–30. National celebration of the joys and benefits of landscape and lawn care. Annually, the month of April. For info: Bonnie Van Fleet, Assoc Landscape Contractors of America (ALCA), 150 Elden St, Ste 270, Herndon, VA 20170. Phone: (703) 736-9666. Fax: (703) 736-9668.

NATIONAL OCCUPATIONAL THERAPY MONTH. Apr 1–30. To recognize the services and accomplishments of occupational therapy practitioners and promote awareness of the benefits of occupational therapy. For info: Suzanne Carleton, The American Occupational Therapy Assn, Inc, 4720 Montgomery Lane, PO Box 31220, Bethesda, MD 20824-1220. Phone: (301) 652-2682 or (301) 652-6611 ext. 2962. Fax: (301) 652-7711. TDD: (800) 377-8555. Consumer Line: (800) 668-8225 (April 1-30 only). WWW: http://www.aota.org

NATIONAL POETRY MONTH. Apr 1–30. Annual observance to pay tribute to the great legacy and ongoing achievement of American poets and the vital place of poetry in American culture. In a proclamation issued in honor of the first observance, President Bill Clinton called it "a welcome opportunity to celebrate not only the unsurpassed body of literature produced by our poets in the past, but also the vitality and diversity of voices reflected in the works of today's American poets. . . . Their creativity and wealth of language enrich our culture and inspire a new generation of Americans to learn the power of reading and writing at its best." Spearheaded by the Academy of American Poets, this is the largest and most extensive celebration of poetry in American history. For info: Academy of American Poets, 584 Broadway, Ste 1208, New York, NY 10012-3250. Phone: (212) 274-0343. WWW: http://www.poets.org

NATIONAL SEXUALLY TRANSMITTED DISEASES (STDs) EDUCATION AND AWARENESS MONTH. Apr 1–30. To educate consumers, patients, students and professionals about the prevention of sexually transmitted diseases. Kit of materials available for $15. For info: Frederick Mayer, Pharmacists Planning Service, Inc, PO Box 1336, Sausalito, CA 94966. Phone: (415) 332-4066. Fax: (415) 332-1832. Email: ppsi@aol.com.

NATIONAL WOODWORKING MONTH®. Apr 1–30. To focus attention on the beauty and satisfaction of working with wood. To help motivate Americans to undertake woodworking projects to improve their home and general surroundings. To increase consumers' knowledge and skill in woodworking and wood-finishing endeavors. For info: Anne Coiley, VP, Consumer PR, Gilbert Whitney and Johns, Minwax Natl Woodworking® Month Program, 110 S Jefferson Rd, Whippany, NJ 07981.

NATIONAL YOUTH SPORTS SAFETY MONTH. Apr 1–30. Bringing public attention to the prevalent problem of injuries in youth sports. This event promotes safety in sport activities and is supported by more than 60 national sports and medical organizations. For info: Michelle Glassman, Exec Dir, Natl Youth Sports Safety Fdtn, 10 Meredith Circle, Needham, MA 02192. Phone: (617) 449-2499. Fax: (617) 444-3288. Email: NYSSF@aol.com.

PREVENTION OF ANIMAL CRUELTY MONTH. Apr 1–30. The ASPCA sponsors this crucial month which is designed to prevent cruelty to animals by focusing on public awareness and public education campaigns. For info: ASPCA Public Info Dept, 424 E 92nd St, New York, NY 10128. Phone: (212) 876-7700 ext 4650 or 4655. Email: valeriea@aspca.org or press@aspca.org. WWW: http://www.aspca.org

PRO-AM SNIPE EXCURSION AND HUNT. Apr 1. Moultrie, GA. Celebrating the time-honored custom of snipe hunting. The denim snipe has come back from the brink of extinction and will be honored at the 1998 event which will include a Snipe Parade, a Snipe Ball and festivities at the Denim Wing of the Snipe Museum at New Elm, GA. New Snipe-O-Rama racing oval open! Annually, April 1. For info: Beth Gay, PO Box 1110, Moultrie, GA 31776. Phone: (912) 985-6540.

RAM, JAGJIVAN: 90th BIRTH ANNIVERSARY. Apr 1, 1908. Indian political leader and coworker with Mohandas K. Gandhi and Jawaharlal Nehru in the fight for Indian independence. Born into a family of "untouchables" at the village of Chandwa, Bihar, India, on Apr 1, 1908, Ram was one of the first of that class to attend school and university. Known as the champion and spokesman for India's 100 million untouchables, he overcame most of the handicaps of caste. He served in a number of ministerial cabinet posts and twice was a candidate for prime minister. Ram died at New Delhi, India, July 6, 1986.

ROBERT THE HERMIT: DEATH ANNIVERSARY. Apr 1, 1832. One of the most famous hermits in American history died in his hermitage at Seekonk, MA, on Apr 1, 1832. Robert was a bonded slave, the son of an African mother and probably an Anglo-Saxon father. After obtaining his freedom, he was swindled out of it and shipped to a foreign slave market, then later escaped to America. He was separated from his first wife by force and rejected by his second wife after a long sea voyage, before withdrawing from society.

SORRY CHARLIE DAY. Apr 1. To honor Charlie the Tuna, who has been rejected for 35 years and still keeps his spunk. A day to recognize anyone who has been rejected and lived through it. Join the "Sorry Charlie, No-Fan-Club-for-You Club." Please send SASE with inquiries. For info: Cathy Runyan, 7812 NW Hampton Rd, Kansas City, MO 64152. Phone: (816) 587-8687. Fax: (816) 587-8687.

April 1998

S	M	T	W	T	F	S
			1	2	3	4
5	6	7	8	9	10	11
12	13	14	15	16	17	18
19	20	21	22	23	24	25
26	27	28	29	30		

SPORTS EYE SAFETY MONTH. Apr 1–30. During this month's observance, Prevent Blindness America will encourage young athletes to wear eye/face protection when participating in sports. Materials that can easily be posted or distributed to the community will be provided. For info: Prevent Blindness America®, 500 E Remington Rd, Schaumburg, IL 60173. Phone: (800) 331-2020. Fax: (847) 843-8458.
WWW: http://www.prevent-blindness.org

STRESS AWARENESS MONTH. Apr 1–30. To promote public awareness of what stress is, what causes it to occur and what can be done about it. A month-long focus on the dangers of stress, successful coping strategies and the myths about stress that are prevalent in our society. For info: Morton C. Orman, MD, Dir, The Health Resource Network, 2936 E Baltimore St, Baltimore, MD 21224. Phone: (410) 732-1900. Fax: (410) 276-9179. WWW: http://www.stresscure.com

SWITZERLAND: EASTER FESTIVAL LUCERNE. Apr 1–5. Lucerne. Easter festival of classical music including chamber music and concerts with sacred music, which will take place in two of the most splendid churches in Lucerne, the Jesuit and Franciscan Churches. For info: Secretariat/Press Office, Easter Festival Lucerne, Hirscmattstrasse 13, PO Box CH-6002, Lucerne, Switzerland. Phone: (41) 210-3562. Fax: (41) 210-7784. Email: media@LucerneMusic.ch.
WWW: http://www.LucerneMusic.ch/

US HOUSE OF REPRESENTATIVES ACHIEVES A QUORUM: ANNIVERSARY. Apr 1. First session of Congress was held Mar 4, 1789, but not enough representatives arrived to achieve a quorum until Apr 1.

"YOU DON'T SAY" TV PREMIERE: 35th ANNIVERSARY. Apr 1, 1963. This game show premiered on NBC and has since appeared in syndication. Contestants and celebrities had to guess a person or place from clues given to them. It was originally hosted by Tom Kennedy and produced by Ralph Andrews.

ZAM! ZOO AND AQUARIUM MONTH. Apr 1–30. A national celebration to focus public attention on the role of zoos and aquariums in wildlife education and conservation. Held at 168 AZA member institutions in the US and Canada. Sponsor: American Zoo and Aquarium Association. For information, contact your local zoo or aquarium.

BIRTHDAYS TODAY

Kevin Jerome Duckworth, 34, basketball player, born Harvey, IL, Apr 1, 1964.

David Eisenhower, 51, author (*Eisenhower at War*), lawyer, grandson of former president Dwight Eisenhower, born West Point, NY, Apr 1, 1947.

Ali MacGraw, 59, actress (*Goodbye, Columbus; Love Story*), born Pound Ridge, NY, Apr 1, 1939.

Toshiro Mifune, 78, actor (*Shogun, Rashomon*), born Tsingtao, China, Apr 1, 1920.

Annette O'Toole, 45, actress (*Smile, 48HRS*), born Houston, TX, Apr 1, 1953.

Jane Powell (Suzanne Burce), 69, actress (*Seven Brides for Seven Brothers*), born Portland, OR, Apr 1, 1929.

Debbie Reynolds, 66, actress (*Singin' in the Rain, Mother*), born El Paso, TX, Apr 1, 1932.

Libby Riddles, 42, first woman to win the 1,135-mile Iditarod Alaskan dogsled race, in 1985, born Madison, WI, Apr 1, 1956.

Glenn Edward ("Bo") Schembechler, Jr, 69, former baseball executive and football coach, born Barberton, OH, Apr 1, 1929.

Daniel Joseph ("Rusty") Staub, 54, restauranteur, former baseball player, born New Orleans, LA, Apr 1, 1944.

APRIL 2 — THURSDAY

Day 92 — 273 Remaining

ANDERSEN, HANS CHRISTIAN: BIRTH ANNIVERSARY. Apr 2. Author chiefly remembered for his more than 150 fairy tales, many of which are regarded as classics of children's literature. Andersen was born at Odense, Denmark, on Apr 2, 1805, and died at Copenhagen, Denmark, on Aug 4, 1875.

ARGENTINA: NATIONAL HOLIDAY. Apr 2. Commemoration of the intent of recovery of the Malvinas Islands from Great Britain, where they are known as the Falkland Islands.

"AS THE WORLD TURNS" TV PREMIERE: ANNIVERSARY. Apr 2, 1956. One of the longest-running soaps currently on air, "ATWT" premiered on CBS. The series is set in midwestern Oakdale and revolves around the Hughes family and their neighbors. Irma Phillips was the show's creator and head writer. Some of its cast members who made it big are: Meg Ryan, Julianne Moore, Michael Nader, Steven Weber, Ming-Na Wen and John De Lancie.

BARTHOLDI, FREDERIC AUGUSTE: BIRTH ANNIVERSARY. Apr 2. French sculptor who created *Liberty Enlightening the World*, which stands in New York Harbor. Also remembered for the *Lion of Belfort* in Belfort, France. Born at Colman, in Alsace, France, on Apr 2, 1834. Died at Paris, France, Oct 4, 1904.

BREAD RIOT IN RICHMOND: ANNIVERSARY. Apr 2, 1863. Indicative of conditions in the Confederate capital of Richmond, VA, an angry mob's demands for bread from a bakery wagon escalated into the harrassment and destruction of nearby shops on Apr 2, 1863. Confederate president Jefferson Davis, in a bold move, stepped into the angry crowd and stated, "We do not desire to injure anyone, but this lawlessness must stop. I will give you five minutes to disperse, otherwise you will be fired upon." The mob dispersed without bloodshed.

CASANOVA, GIOVANNI GIACOMO GIROLAMO: BIRTH ANNIVERSARY. Apr 2, 1725. Celebrated Italian writer-librarian and, by his own account, philanderer, adventurer, rogue, seminarian, soldier and spy. Born at Venice, Italy, Apr 2, 1725. As the Chevalier de Seingalt, he died at Dux, Bohemia, June 4, 1798, while serving as librarian and working on his lively and frank *History of My Life*, a brilliant picture of 18th-century life.

"DALLAS" TV PREMIERE: 20th ANNIVERSARY. Apr 2, 1978. Oil tycoons battled for money, power and prestige in this prime-time CBS soap that ran for nearly 13 years. The Ewings and Barneses were Texas' modern day Hatfields and McCoys. Larry Hagman starred as the devious, scheming womanizer J.R. Ewing. When J.R. was shot in the 1980 season-ending cliffhanger, the revelation of the mystery shooter was the single-most watched episode of its time (it was Kristin, J.R.'s sister-in-law, played by Mary Crosby). Cast members included Jim Davis, Barbara Bel Geddes, Donna Reed, Ted Shackelford, Joan Van Ark (who, along with Shackelford, starred in spin-off "Knots Landing"), Patrick Duffy, Linda Gray, Charlene Tilton, David Wayne, Keenan Wynn, Ken Kercheval, Victoria Principal and Steve Kanaly.

"THE EDGE OF NIGHT" TV PREMIERE: ANNIVERSARY. Apr 2, 1956. "The Edge of Night" premiered on CBS along with "As The World Turns." Though the plots initially revolved around crime and courtroom drama, the serial's format soon developed along more conventional soap story lines of romance. The soap shifted to ABC in 1975 but was cancelled in 1984. Larry Hagman, Dixie Carter, Lori Laughlin, Willie Aames and Amanda Blake were some of the show's most prominent players.

ENGLAND: GRAND NATIONAL HORSERACING MEETING. Apr 2–4. Aintree Racecourse, Aintree, Liverpool. Britain's premier horse race and most famous steeplechase is run over 4.5 miles on this beautiful and legendary course. The Grand National race takes place on Apr 4, the culmination of the race meeting. Est attendance: 100,000. For info: Racecourse Mgr, Aintree Racecourse, Liverpool, Merseyside, England L9 5AS. Phone: (44) (151) 523-2600. Fax: (44) (151) 530-1512.
WWW: http://www.demon.co.uk/racenews/aintree

FALKLAND ISLANDS WAR: ANNIVERSARY. Apr 2–June 15, 1982. Argentina, claiming sovereignty over the nearby Falkland Islands (called by them the Malvinas), invaded and occupied the British Crown Colony on Apr 2, 1982. British forces defeated the Argentinians on June 15, 1982. About 250 British and 600 Argentine lives were lost in the conflict. In 1986, three military officers, including General Leopoldo Galtieri (who was president of Argentina at the time of the invasion), were convicted and sentenced for the military crime of negligence. Commemorative ceremonies are observed on Apr 2 in Argentina and on June 15 in the Falkland Islands.

FIRST WHITE HOUSE EASTER EGG ROLL: ANNIVERSARY. Apr 2, 1877. The first White House Easter Egg Roll took place on Apr 2, 1877, during the administration of Rutherford B. Hayes. The traditional event was discontinued by President Franklin D. Roosevelt in 1942 and reinstated on Apr 6, 1953, by President Dwight D. Eisenhower.

INTERNATIONAL CHILDREN'S BOOK DAY. Apr 2. Commemorates the international aspects of children's literature and observes Hans Christian Andersen's birthday. Sponsor: Intl Board on Books for Young People, Nonnenweg 12, Postfach, CH-4003 Basel, Switzerland. For info: USBBY Secretariat, c/o Intl Reading Assn, Box 8139, Newark, DE 19714-8139.

KINGSVILLE INTERNATIONAL YOUNG PERFORMERS' COMPETITIONS WITH THE ISABEL SCIONTI PIANO SOLO COMPETITIONS. Apr 2–4. Texas A&M University–Kingsville, TX. 17th annual international music competition for performers of classical music. Prodigies and aspiring concert artists under age 26 compete in separate contests for piano solo and orchestral instruments. Cash prizes total about $25,000. Performance awards with orchestra and in recital offered. All contest events—including string, woodwind and brass master classes given by concert artist–contest judges—are free and open to the public. Annual. Contestant's entry fee $30; deadline Jan 15, 1998. Sponsor: Music Club of Kingsville, Inc (affiliate of National Federation and Texas Federation of Music Clubs). Est attendance: 1,500. For info: Mary Tryer, 1222 W Lee, Kingsville, TX 78363. Phone: (512) 592-2374. Fax: (512) 592-2374.

MONTEREY WINE FESTIVAL. Apr 2–5. Monterey Conference Center, Monterey Marriott Hotel, Monterey, CA. 22nd annual featuring the finest wines from California. Tastings, lectures, educational seminars and a large bottle auction. More than 200 wineries will feature more than 800 different wines from California's diverse wine regions. Est attendance: 4,000. For info: The Monterey Wine Festival, PO Box 1749, Monterey, CA 93942. Phone: (408) 656-WINE (9463).
Email: 76543.1635@compuserve.com.
WWW: http://www.MontereyWine.com

MULE DAY. Apr 2–5. Columbia, TN. Started in 1934 as Breeders Day when mules were brought into town to be sold and traded. Today this homecoming is celebrated with arts and crafts, flea market, knife show and a huge parade. Annually, the first full weekend in April unless Easter is the first full weekend—then it moves forward one week. Est attendance: 250,000. For info: Mule Day, PO Box 66, Columbia, TN 38402. Phone: (615) 381-9557.

NASIRABAD, BANGLADESH TORNADO: ANNIVERSARY. Apr 2, 1972. An outbreak of tornadoes covering about 800 square miles swept through Bangladesh's Mymensingh district, including Nasirabad, the town worst hit by the disaster. The tornado killed around 200 people and left 25,000 others homeless.

NORWAY: VOSS JAZZ FESTIVAL. Apr 2–4. Voss. Three days of jazz as well as folk music by Norwegian, European and American performers at this major ski resort. Annually, the weekend before Easter. For info: Norwegian Tourist Bd, 655 Third Ave, New York, NY 10017. Phone: (212) 885-9700.
Email: gonorway@interport.net.
WWW: http://www.norway.org/web/norway/tourism.html

PASCUA FLORIDA DAY. Apr 2. Florida. Commemorates the sighting of Florida by Ponce de Leon in 1513. He named the land Pascua Florida because of its discovery at Easter, the "Feast of the Flowers."

PONCE DE LEON DISCOVERS FLORIDA: ANNIVERSARY. Apr 2. On Apr 2, 1513, Juan Ponce de Leon discovered Florida by landing at the site that became the city of St. Augustine. He claimed the land for the King of Spain.

RECONCILIATION DAY. Apr 2. Columnist Ann Landers writes "Since 1989, I have suggested that April 2 be set aside to write that letter or make that phone call and mend a broken relationship. Life is too short to hold grudges. To forgive can be enormously life-enhancing . . . ."

SPRING PILGRIMAGE TO ANTEBELLUM HOMES. Apr 2–12. Columbus, MS. Tours of pre–Civil War homes for visiting public. Sponsor: Columbus Historic Foundation, PO Box 46, Columbus, MS 39703. Est attendance: 5,000. For info: Columbus Conv and Visitor Bureau, PO Box 789, Columbus, MS 39703. Phone: (800) 327-2686. Fax: (601) 329-8969.
Email: ccvb@tilc.com.
WWW: http://www.friendship.columbus.ms.us

SWITZERLAND: NAFELS PILGRIMAGE. Apr 2. Canton Glarus. Commemoration of the Battle of Nafels, fought on Apr 9, 1388. Observed annually on first Thursday in April, with processions, prayers, sermon and a reading out of the names of those killed in the battle.

US MINT: ANNIVERSARY. Apr 2, 1792. The first US Mint was established at Philadelphia, PA, as authorized by an act of Congress dated Apr 2, 1792.

WHITE, CHARLES: 80th BIRTH ANNIVERSARY. Apr 2, 1918. Renowned African-American artist, born at Chicago, IL; died Oct 3, 1979. Charles White began his professional career by painting murals for the WPA during the Depression. Both White and artist Elizabeth Catlett (his wife at the time), were largely influenced by Mexican muralists Diego Rivera and David Alfaro Siquieros. Among his most notable creations are: *J'Accuse* (1966), a series of charcoal drawings depicting a variety of African-Americans from all ages and walks of life; the *Wanted* posters (c. 1969), a series of paintings based on old runaway slave posters; and *Homage to Langston Hughes* (1971).

April 1998

S	M	T	W	T	F	S
			1	2	3	4
5	6	7	8	9	10	11
12	13	14	15	16	17	18
19	20	21	22	23	24	25
26	27	28	29	30		

ZOLA, EMILE: BIRTH ANNIVERSARY. Apr 2. Prolific French novelist of the naturalist school, remembered especially for his role in the Dreyfus case (resulting in retrial and vindication of Alfred Dreyfus). Emile Edouard Charles Antoine Zola was born at Paris, France, Apr 2, 1840. Defective venting of a stove flue in his bedroom (which some believed to be the work of political enemies) resulted in his death from carbon monoxide poisoning at Paris, Sept 28, 1902.

BIRTHDAYS TODAY

Dana Carvey, 43, comedian, actor (*Wayne's World*, "Saturday Night Live"), born Missoula, MT, Apr 2, 1955.

Buddy Ebsen, 90, actor (Jed Clampett on "The Beverly Hillbillies"; "Barnaby Jones"), born Belleville, IL, Apr 2, 1908.

Sir Alec Guinness, 84, British actor (*Star Wars, A Passage to India*), born London, England, Apr 2, 1914.

Emmylou Harris, 51, singer ("Amarillo," "Till I Gain Control Again"), born Birmingham, AL, Apr 2, 1947.

Linda Hunt, 53, actress (Mother Superior on "The Flying Nun"; Oscar for *The Year of Living Dangerously*), born Morristown, NJ, Apr 2, 1945.

Camille Paglia, 51, literature professor and literary and cultural critic. Born Endicott, NY, Apr 2, 1947.

Pamela Reed, 45, actress (*The Right Stuff, The Best of Times, Bob Roberts*, "Grand"; stage: *Getting Out* [Drama Desk Award]), born Tacoma, WA, Apr 2, 1953.

Leon Russell, 57, musician, born Lawton, OK, Apr 2, 1941.

APRIL 3 — FRIDAY

Day 93 — 272 Remaining

ABRAHAM BALDWIN AGRICULTURAL COLLEGE HOMECOMING CELEBRATION. Apr 3–4. ABAC Campus, Tifton, GA. Class reunions, alumni awards banquet, dance. Est attendance: 500. For info: Nancy Coleman, Exec Secy, ABAC Alumni Assn, ABAC 13, 2802 Moore Hwy, Tifton, GA 31794-2693. Phone: (912) 386-3321. Fax: (912) 386-7144. Email: alumni@c.abac.peachnet.edu.

ALCOHOL-FREE WEEKEND. Apr 3–5. Observance to increase public awareness of the problems associated with drinking alcoholic beverages by asking Americans to refrain from drinking them for this weekend. For info: Jeffrey Hon, Public Info Office, Natl Council on Alcoholism and Drug Dependence, Inc, 12 W 21st St, New York, NY 10010. Phone: (212) 206-6770. WWW: http://www.ncadd.org

AMERICAN CROSSWORD PUZZLE TOURNAMENT AND CONVENTION. Apr 3–5. Stamford Marriott Hotel, Stamford, CT. 300 solvers from the US and Canada compete on eight puzzles during this 21st annual event. Points are awarded for accuracy and speed. The final puzzle is played on giant white boards for everyone to watch. Prizes are awarded in 21 skill, age and geographical categories and the grand prize is $1,000. The weekend also includes group word games, guest speakers and appearances by celebrity crossword solvers. Solvers can compete at home for fun and receive a ranking in all their solving categories. Est attendance: 350. For info: Will Shortz, Dir, Amer Crossword Puzzle Tournament, 55 Great Oak Lane, Pleasantville, NY 10570. Phone: (914) 769-9128. Fax: (914) 769-9128. WWW: http://www.crosswordtournament.com

AMERICAN INDIAN DANCE AND POWWOW FESTIVAL. Apr 3–5. DeSoto Caverns Park, Childersburg, AL. Artists and craftspeople from across the US. Native American dancing includes hoop, traditional, fine, fancy and many more. 23rd annual festival. Est attendance: 12,000. For info: Joe Beckham, DeSoto Caverns Park, DeSoto Caverns Pkwy, Childersburg, AL 35044. Phone: (205) 378-7252.
Email: desoto@syl.mindspring.com.

ARBOR DAY (ARIZONA). Apr 3. In the counties of Apache, Navajo, Coconino, Mohave and Yavapai, the Friday following Apr 1, and in all other counties the Friday following Feb 1, in each year, shall be known as Arbor Day. See also: "Arbor Day (Arizona)" (Feb 6).

ARMENIAN APPRECIATION DAY. Apr 3. Lighthearted look at the contribution of legendary Armenians such as Palboonian (Paul Bunyan) and Tontonian to American folklore, with special emphasis on studies of the relationship of the Smithsonian Institution Collection to the history of Armenian-American folklore. Annually, Apr 3. For info: Robert L. Birch, Puns Corps, Box 2364, Falls Church, VA 22042-0364. Phone: (703) 533-3668.

BIG MUDDY FOLK MUSIC FESTIVAL. Apr 3–4. Thespian Hall, Boonville, MO. Performing folk festival with instructional workshop by artists appearing. Est attendance: 3,000. For info: Judy Shields, Admin, Friends of Historic Boonville, PO Box 1776, Boonville, MO 65233. Phone: (816) 882-7977. Fax: (816) 882-7977. Email: friendsart@vax1.rainis.net.

BIRMINGHAM RESISTANCE: ANNIVERSARY. Apr 3, 1962. In retaliation against a black boycott of downtown stores, the Birmingham, AL, City Commission voted not to pay the city's $45,000 share of a $100,000 county program which supplied surplus food to the needy. More than 90 percent of the recipients of aid were black. When the NAACP protested the Commission's decision, Birmingham Mayor Arthur J. Hanes dismissed their complaint as a "typical reaction from New York Socialist radicals."

BLACKS RULED ELIGIBLE TO VOTE: ANNIVERSARY. Apr 3. On Apr 3, 1944, the United States Supreme Court, in an 8–1 ruling, declared that blacks could not be barred from voting in the Texas Democratic primaries. The high court repudiated the contention that political parties are private associations and held that discrimination against blacks violated the 15th Amendment.

BURROUGHS, JOHN: BIRTH ANNIVERSARY. Apr 3, 1837. American naturalist and author. Born at Roxbury, NY, Apr 3, 1837. "Time does not become sacred to us until we have lived it," he wrote in 1877. Died Mar 29, 1921.

CALICO HULLABALOO. Apr 3–5. Calico Ghost Town, Yermo, CA. Mormon pioneer Lafayette Mecham's discovery of silver ore in the 1880s resulted in a silver rush and a mining town named Calico. Activities include championship horseshoe-pitching and world championship tobacco-spitting contests, live bands, shows and more. Est attendance: 8,000. For info: Calico Ghost Town, PO Box 638, Yermo, CA 92398. Phone: (800) TO-CALICO. Fax: (619) 254-2047.

DOGWOOD ARTS FESTIVAL. Apr 3–19. Knoxville, TN. A springtime celebration with 60 miles of dogwood trails and more than 100 events featuring arts, crafts, parades and musical performances. It's the "Best 17 Days of Spring in America." Est attendance: 350,000. For info: Dogwood Arts Festival, 111 N Central Ave, Knoxville, TN 37902. Phone: (615) 637-4561. WWW: http://www.korrnet.org/dogwood

ENGLAND: NORTHEAST KNITTING AND NEEDLECRAFT EXHIBITION. Apr 3–5. Leeds University Exhibition Centre, Leeds. Everything for the hand and machine knitter and needlecraft enthusiast including fashion shows, lectures and demonstrations. For info: Robert Ewin, Dir, Nationwide Exhibitions (UK) Ltd, PO Box 20, Fishponds, Bristol, England BS16 5QU. Phone: (44) (117) 970-1370. Fax: (44) (117) 970-1371.

FALL OF RICHMOND: ANNIVERSARY. Apr 3. After the withdrawal of Robert E. Lee's troops, the Confederate capital of Richmond and nearby Petersburg surrendered to Union forces on Apr 3, 1865. Richmond had survived four years of continuous threats from the North. On Apr 4, the city was toured by President Abraham Lincoln.

GRAHAM, CALVIN "BABY VET": BIRTH ANNIVERSARY. Apr 3. The man who became known as World War II's "baby vet," Calvin Graham was born Apr 3, 1930, at Canton, TX. Graham enlisted in the Navy at the age of 12. As a gunner on the USS *South Dakota*, he was struck by shrapnel during the battle of Guadalcanal in 1942 but still helped pull fellow crew members to safety. The navy gave Graham a dishonorable discharge, revoked his disability benefits and stripped him of his decorations, including a Purple Heart and Bronze Star, after discovering his age. Eventually, through congressional efforts, he was granted an honorable discharge and won back all but the Purple Heart. His benefits were restored in 1988. Graham died Nov 6, 1992, at Fort Worth, TX.

INAUGURATION OF PONY EXPRESS: ANNIVERSARY. Apr 3. The Pony Express began on Apr 3, 1860, when the first rider left St. Joseph, MO. The following day another rider headed east from Sacramento, CA. For $5 an ounce letters were delivered within 10 days. There were 190 way stations between 10 and 15 miles apart, and each rider had a "run" of between 75 and 100 miles. The Pony Express lasted less than two years, ceasing operation in October 1861, when the overland telegraph was completed.

IRVING, WASHINGTON: BIRTH ANNIVERSARY. Apr 3, 1783. American author, attorney and one time US Minister to Spain, Irving was born at New York, NY, Apr 3, 1783. Creator of *Rip Van Winkle* and *The Legend of Sleepy Hollow*, he was also the author of many historical and biographical works, including *A History of the Life and Voyages of Christopher Columbus* and the *Life of Washington*. Died at Tarrytown, NY, Nov 28, 1859.

"JUVENILE JURY" TV PREMIERE: ANNIVERSARY. Apr 3, 1947. Appeared on NBC, CBS and in syndication. Jack Barry created and co-produced this show which had a panel of youngsters doling out advice and answers to viewers' questions.

MARSHALL PLAN: 50th ANNIVERSARY. Apr 3, 1948. Suggested by Secretary of State George C. Marshall in a speech at Harvard, June 5, 1947, the legislation for the European Recovery Program, popularly known as the Marshall Plan, was signed by President Truman on Apr 3, 1948. After distributing more than $12 billion, the program ended in 1952. The US Postal Service issued a Marshall Plan commemorative stamp in 1997.

MEDIEVAL FAIR. Apr 3–5. University of Oklahoma Brandt Park Duck Pond, Norman, OK. Arts and crafts and living history fair. The Middle Ages come alive with dancers, music, theater, jousting, knights in combat and a human chess match. Feasts and follies include games and food "fit for a king." Meet such characters as King Arthur, Sir Lancelot and Merlin. Admission is free. Annually, the second weekend in April (unless Easter weekend). Est attendance: 100,000. For info: Linda Linn, 1700 Asp, Norman, OK 73072. Phone: (405) 288-2536. Fax: (405) 325-7698. Email: llinn@cce.occe.ou.edu.

MOON PHASE: FIRST QUARTER. Apr 3. Moon enters First Quarter phase at 3:18 PM, EST.

NATIONAL GEOGRAPHY BEE STATE LEVEL. Apr 3. Site is different in each state—many are in state capital. Winners of school-level competitions who scored in the top 100 in their state on a written test compete in the State Geography Bees. The winner of each state bee will go to Washington, DC, for the national level in May. Est attendance: 450. For info: Natl Geography Bee, Natl Geographic Soc, 1145 17th St NW, Washington, DC 20036. Phone: (202) 828-6635.

PATENT GRANTED FOR HAT BLOCKING MACHINE: ANNIVERSARY. Apr 3. On Apr 3, 1866, Rudolph Eickemeyer and G. Osterheld were granted the first patent for a hat blocking and shaping machine.

POSITIVE POWER OF HUMOR AND CREATIVITY CONFERENCE. Apr 3–6. Saratoga Springs, NY. Participants will enjoy themselves while learning practical ideas they can apply both personally and on the job. Recent conferences have featured special appearances by Jay Leno, Victor Borge, Steve Allen, Sid Caesar, The Capitol Steps and The Smothers Brothers. More than 10,000 attendees from all 50 states and abroad. 13th annual conference. Est attendance: 3,600. To receive a conference brochure and free humor info packet, send SASE ($1.01) to Dr. Joel Goodman, Dir, The Humor Project, 110 Spring St, Saratoga Springs, NY 12866. Phone: (518) 587-8770. Fax: (518) 587-8771. Email: humor@wizvax.net. WWW: http://www.wizvax.net/humor/

POTEET STRAWBERRY FESTIVAL. Apr 3–5. Poteet, TX. One of the oldest and largest festivals in Texas established to promote Poteet's crop—strawberries. Great food and family entertainment. Est attendance: 100,000. For info: Nita Harvey, Festival Coord, PSFA, Poteet Strawberry Festival Assn, PO Box 227, Poteet, TX 78065. Phone: (210) 742-8144. Fax: (210) 742-3608. Email: nharvey@texas.net. WWW: http://www.strawberryfestival.com

RAINEY, MA (GERTRUDE BRIDGET): BIRTH ANNIVERSARY. Apr 3, 1888. Known as the "Mother of the Blues," Gertrude "Ma" Rainey was born at Columbus, GA. She made her stage debut at the Columbus Opera House in 1900 in a talent show called "The Bunch of Blackberries." After touring together as "Rainey and Rainey, the Assassinators of the Blues," she and her husband eventually separated and she toured on her own under the auspices of the Theater Owners Booking Association. She made her first recording in 1923 and her last on Dec 28, 1928, after being told that the rural southern blues she sang had gone out of style. She died Dec 22, 1939, at Columbus, GA.

RAND, SALLY: BIRTH ANNIVERSARY. Apr 3, 1904. American actress, ecdysiast and inventor of the fan dance (which gained fame in 1933 at the Chicago World's Fair). Born Helen Gould Beck at Hickory County, MO, on Apr 3, 1904. Died at Glendora, CA, Aug 31, 1979.

SKAGIT VALLEY TULIP FESTIVAL. Apr 3–19. Skagit County, Mount Vernon, WA. To celebrate and share the spectacular beauty of more than 1,500 acres of blooming daffodils and tulips that herald the arrival of spring in the Skagit Valley of Washington state. Est attendance: 1,000,000. For info: Audrey Smith, SVTF Exec Dir, PO Box 1784, Mt Vernon, WA 98273. Phone: (360) 428-5959. Fax: (360) 424-6237. Email: tulip@sos.net. WWW: http://www.tulipfestival.org

STAMP EXPO. Apr 3–5. Wilshire Ebell Convention Complex, Los Angeles, CA. Est attendance: 4,000. For info: Intl Stamp Collectors Soc, PO Box 854, Van Nuys, CA 91408. Phone: (818) 997-6496. Fax: (818) 988-4337. Email: iibick@aol.com. WWW: http://www.4free.com/bick

April 1998

S	M	T	W	T	F	S
			1	2	3	4
5	6	7	8	9	10	11
12	13	14	15	16	17	18
19	20	21	22	23	24	25
26	27	28	29	30		

STUDENT GOVERNMENT DAY IN MASSACHUSETTS. Apr 3. Annually, the first Friday of April.

SUGARLOAF'S SPRING GAITHERSBURG CRAFT FESTIVAL. Apr 3–5. Montgomery County Fairgrounds, Gaithersburg, MD. This show, now in its 23rd year, features 500 nationally recognized craft designers and fine artists displaying and selling their original creations. Craft demonstrations, children's entertainment, live music, hourly gift certificate drawings, large selection of delicious food and more. Est attendance: 31,000. For info: Sugarloaf Mountain Works, Inc, 200 Orchard Ridge Dr, #215, Gaithersburg, MD 20878. Phone: (800) 210-9900.

SUWANNEE RIVER JAM. Apr 3–4. Live Oak, FL. Country jams with award-winning performers in a beautiful outdoor setting. Est attendance: 30,000. For info: James Cornett, Spirit of the Suwannee Music Park, 3076 95th Dr, Live Oak, FL 32060. Phone: (904) 364-1683. Fax: (904) 364-2998. Email: spirit@musicliveshere.com. WWW: http://www.musicliveshere.com

TWEED DAY: 175th ANNIVERSARY. Apr 3, 1823. Day to consider the cost of political corruption. Birthday of William March Tweed, New York City political boss, whose "Tweed Ring" is said to have stolen $30 to $200 million from the city. Born at New York, NY, Apr 3, 1823. Died in his cell at New York's Ludlow Street Jail, Apr 12, 1878. Cartoonist Thomas Nast deserves much credit for Tweed's arrests and convictions.

WOMAN PRESIDES OVER US SUPREME COURT: ANNIVERSARY. Apr 3, 1995. Supreme Court Justice Sandra Day O'Connor became the first woman to preside over the US high court when she sat in for Chief Justice William H. Rehnquist and second in seniority Justice John Paul Stevens when both were out of town.

BIRTHDAYS TODAY

Alec Baldwin, 40, actor ("Knots Landing," *The Getaway, Miami Blues*), born Massapequa, NY, Apr 3, 1958.

Marlon Brando, 74, actor (Oscars for *On the Waterfront, The Godfather*; Emmy for *Roots: Next Generation*), born Omaha, NE, Apr 3, 1924.

Doris Day (Doris Von Kappelhoff), 74, actress, singer ("Young at Heart," *The Man Who Knew Too Much, Pillow Talk*, "The Doris Day Show"), born Cincinnati, OH, Apr 3, 1924.

Max Frankel, 68, journalist, born Gera, Germany, Apr 3, 1930.

Helmut Kohl, 68, Chancellor of Germany, born Ludwigshafen, Germany, Apr 3, 1930.

Jonathan Lynn, 55, writer, actor, director (*Into the Night, Nuns on the Run, My Cousin Vinny*), born Bath, England, Apr 3, 1943.

Marsha Mason, 56, actress (Oscar nominations for *The Goodbye Girl, Cinderella Liberty*), born St. Louis, MO, Apr 3, 1942.

Eddie Murphy, 37, comedian ("Saturday Night Live"), actor (*Trading Places, Coming to America, 48HRS; Beverly Hills Cop* movies), born Brooklyn, NY, Apr 3, 1961.

Wayne Newton, 56, singer ("Danke Schoen," "Daddy Don't You Walk So Fast"), born Norfolk, VA, Apr 3, 1942.

Tony Orlando (Michael Orlando Cassivitis), 54, singer (Tony Orlando and Dawn; "Tie a Yellow Ribbon Round the Old Oak Tree"), born New York, NY, Apr 3, 1944.

David Hyde Pierce, 39, actor (Niles on "Frasier"), born Albany, NY, Apr 3, 1959.

APRIL 4 — SATURDAY

Day 94 — 271 Remaining

SPRING CITY-WIDE GARAGE SALE. Apr 4. Electra, TX. Sales throughout the Electra area. Chamber of Commerce will provide free coffee and maps on Apr 4, 1998 at 7 AM. The Chamber of Commerce office will close at 8 AM so that we too may enjoy all of the bargains. Est attendance: 500. For info: Dawn

Dunsmore, Electra Chamber of Commerce, 112 W Cleveland, Electra, TX 76360. Phone: (817) 495-3577. Fax: (817) 495-3577.

THE BIG EVENT. Apr 4. Bryan and College Station, TX. In the nation's largest student-run service project, approximately 5,000 Texas A&M students spend a day assisting in a variety of community service projects in Bryan and College Station. Students use this as their way of saying "thanks" to the community for what it does for Texas A&M students. Annually, in the spring. Est attendance: 5,000. For info: Debbie Emminger, The Big Event, Texas A&M University, 127 John J. Koldus Bldg, College Station, TX 77843-1236. Phone: (409) 845-9618. Fax: (409) 847-8854.

BONZA BOTTLER DAY™. Apr 4. To celebrate when the number of the day is the same as the number of the month. Bonza Bottler Day™ is an excuse to have a party at least once a month. For more information, see Jan 1. For info: Gail M. Berger, 109 Matthew Ave, Poca, WV 25159. Phone: (304) 776-7746. Email: gberger5@aol.com.

CANADA: ELMIRA MAPLE SYRUP FESTIVAL. Apr 4. Elmira, Ontario. Tours of maple bush by hay wagon, sugaring-off shanty in operation, Pennsylvania Dutch cuisine, handcrafted goods, arts and crafts and antiques. Est attendance: 40,000. For info: Elmira & Woolwich Chamber of Commerce, 5 First St E, Ont, Canada N3B 2E3. Phone: (519) 669-2605. Fax: (519) 669-8251. WWW: http://www.sentex.net/maplesyrup

CLEAR LAKE CRAWFISH FESTIVAL. Apr 4. Landolt Pavilion, Seabrook, TX. 3rd annual. Come and enjoy crawfish, cajun music, silent auction, games for kids and a Crawfish Eating Contest. This event is to raise money for Fourth of July fireworks over Clear Lake. For info: Clear Lake Area Chamber of Commerce, 1201 Nasa Rd One, Houston, TX 77058. Phone: (281) 488-7676. Fax: (281) 488-8981.

DIX, DOROTHEA LYNDE: BIRTH ANNIVERSARY. Apr 4, 1802. American social reformer and author. Born at Hampden, ME, on Apr 4, 1802. Left home at age 10, was teaching at age 14 and founded a home for girls in Boston while still in her teens. In spite of frail health, she was a vigorous crusader for humane conditions in insane asylums, jails and almshouses and for the establishment of state-supported institutions to serve those needs. Named superintendent of women nurses during the Civil War. Died at Trenton, NJ, on July 17, 1887.

DOLL SHOW: THE DOLLMAKERS. Apr 4–5 (tentative). Antique and contemporary dolls on display and for sale. Visiting artists will participate. Est attendance: 1,800. For info: Wheaton Village, 1501 Glasstown Rd, Millville, NJ 08332. Phone: (609) 825-6800 or (800) 998-4552. Fax: (609) 825-2410. Email: mail@wheatonvillage.org. WWW: http://www.wheatonvillage.org

DULCIMER FESTIVAL. Apr 4–5. Lumpkin, GA. Appalachian dulcimer music, professional and amateur. Dulcimer-building workshop and teaching sessions available. Est attendance: 750. For info: Patty Cannington, PR, PO Box 1850, Lumpkin, GA 31815. Phone: (912) 838-6310 or (888) 733-1850. WWW: http://www.westville.org

FINGER LAKES CRAFTSMEN SPRING-EASTER ARTS AND CRAFTS SHOW. Apr 4–5. Monroe County Fairgrounds Dome Arena, Rochester, NY. 28th annual. All media and categories including photography and prints. Est attendance: 8,000. For info: Ronald L. Johnson, Finger Lakes Craftsmen Shows, 1 Freshour Dr, Shortsville, NY 14548. Phone: (716) 289-9439. Fax: (716) 289-9440.

FLAG ACT OF 1818: ANNIVERSARY. Apr 4, 1818. Congress approved the first flag of the United States on this day in 1818.

GIAMATTI, ANGELO BARTLETT: 60th BIRTH ANNIVERSARY. Apr 4, 1938. Baseball Commissioner and former president of Yale University. Born at Boston, MA, on Apr 4, 1938. A. Bartlett Giamatti received his education and taught at Yale University, and later became the youngest person to be named president of the university, at the age of 39, in 1978. Following his tenure at Yale he became the president of Major League Baseball's National League in 1986 and served in that capacity until he was appointed Commissioner of Baseball on Apr 1, 1989. An accomplished author, he moved freely between the worlds of literature and baseball, often linking the two in the many articles he wrote. One week prior to his death, he suspended Pete Rose for life for betting on baseball games. Giamatti died at Martha's Vineyard, MA, on Sept 1, 1989.

HATE WEEK. Apr 4–10. Recognizes the day on which the fictional character Winston Smith started his secret diary and wrote the words "DOWN WITH BIG BROTHER," Wednesday, Apr 4, 1984. From George Orwell's anti-Utopian novel, *1984*, portraying the end of human privacy and the destruction of the individual in a totalitarian state (first published in 1949). "Hates" varied from the daily two-minute concentrated hate to the grand culmination observed during Hate Week.

HERITAGE FAIR/SPRING FEST. Apr 4 (tentative). Poor Farm Park, Ashland, VA. Features demonstrations by Native American artists and craftspeople. Also, encampments trace US history from the arrival of Europeans to modern military. Cultural music and dancing, Native American Powwow and children's Easter egg hunt. Est attendance: 13,000. For info: Jeannie Chewning, Hanover Co Parks and Recreation, 200 Berkley St, Ashland, VA 23005. Phone: (804) 798-8062.

HISTORIC PENDLETON SPRING JUBILEE. Apr 4–5. Pendleton, SC. Come and join the fun in historic Pendleton with amusement rides, arts and crafts displays, food booths, entertainment and much more. Annually, the first full weekend in April. Est attendance: 45,000. For info: Historic Pendleton Spring Jubilee, PO Box 565, Pendleton, SC 29670. Phone: (803) 646-3782. Fax: (803) 646-2506. Email: pendtour@innova.net.

INDIANA GENEALOGICAL SOCIETY MEETING. Apr 4. Indianapolis, IN. Annual meeting and workshop will feature eight lectures regarding family history and geneaology. 8 AM–4 PM. Annually, the first Saturday in April unless it's Easter weekend. For info: Betty L. Warren, Registrar, Indiana Genealogical Society, 6922 Rocklane Rd, Greenwood, IN 46143-9739 or IGS, PO Box 10507, Fort Wayne, IN 46852-0507.

INTERNATIONAL WILDLIFE FILM FESTIVAL. Apr 4–11. Missoula, MT. 21st annual. A juried international wildlife film festival. This eight-day gathering will involve the world's top wildlife filmmakers and producers sharing their ideas, techniques and products to interested members of the public and filmmaking profession. The festival provides films for viewing by people of all ages with special sections for children. Community celebrations such as a wildlife parade, workshops and panel discussions are also part of this annual festival. Festival venues are located at various locations around Missoula. For info: Amy Sperry, Festival Coord, Intl Wildlife Film Festival, 802 East Front St, Missoula, MT 59802. Phone: (406) 728-9380. Fax: (406) 728-2881.

KING, MARTIN LUTHER, JR: 30th ASSASSINATION ANNIVERSARY. Apr 4, 1968. The Rev Dr. Martin Luther King, Jr, was shot at Memphis, TN, Apr 4, 1968. James Earl Ray is serving a 99-year sentence for the crime. See also: "King, Martin Luther, Jr: Birth Anniversary" (Jan 15).

KING OPPOSES VIETNAM WAR: ANNIVERSARY. Apr 4, 1967. Speaking before the Overseas Press Club in New York City, Rev Dr. Martin Luther King, Jr, announced his opposition to the Vietnam War. That same day, at the Riverside Church in Harlem, King suggested that those who saw the war as dishonorable and unjust should avoid military service. He proposed that the US take new initiatives to conclude the war.

KITE FLITE. Apr 4. Space Center, Alamogordo, NM. Annual event with kite flight. Est attendance: 300. For info: Jack Moore, Marketing Dir, Space Center, PO Box 533, Alamogordo, NM 88311. Phone: (800) 545-4021. Fax: (505) 437-7722.
Email: space-plan@nmsua.nmsu.edu.
WWW: http://abcc.nmsu.edu/~bwood/

***LADY BE GOOD* LOST: 55th ANNIVERSARY.** Apr 4, 1943. The nine-man crew of the World War II American Liberator bomber *Lady Be Good* bailed out 200 miles off course over the Sahara Desert and disappeared. They were returning to their base in Libya after a raid over southern Italy. On Nov 9, 1958, 15 years after the plane went down and more than 13 years after the war had ended, a pilot flying across the Sahara south of Tobruck sighted wreckage of an aircraft in the sand. Five skeletons and a diary describing the final days of the crew were recovered. The radio, guns and ammunition in the plane were in working order.

April 1998

S	M	T	W	T	F	S
			1	2	3	4
5	6	7	8	9	10	11
12	13	14	15	16	17	18
19	20	21	22	23	24	25
26	27	28	29	30		

MAPLE SYRUP FESTIVAL. Apr 4–5. Bradys Run County Park, Fallston, PA. Demonstrates the maple-tree-tapping process and builds a 19th-century arts, crafts and educational festival around it. Est attendance: 40,000. For info: Beaver County Conservation District, 1000 Third St, Ste 202, Beaver, PA 15009-2026. Phone: (412) 774-7090. Fax: (412) 774-9421.

MOUNT HOOD RAILHOOD: A SEASON OF FUN. Apr 4–Dec 20. Hood River, OR. 92-year-old historic railroad offers 44-mile round-trip excursions through natural beauty of the northwest Columbia River Gorge and foothills of Mount Hood, Oregon's highest peak. Special holiday events and harrowing train robberies throughout the season. For info: Mt Hood Railroad, 110 Railroad Ave, Hood River, OR 97031. Phone: (800) TRAIN-61 or (541) 386-3556. Fax: (541) 386-2141.

MULTI-CULTURAL EASTER EGG DISPLAY. Apr 4–19. Belleville, IL. A multi-cultural exhibit of Easter eggs decorated in various ethnic and modern artistic styles, and featuring daily demonstrations of individual techniques. No admission fee. Est attendance: 7,000. For info: Shrine of Our Lady of the Snows, 442 S DeMazenod Dr, Belleville, IL 62223-1094. Phone: (618) 397-6700. Fax: (618) 398-6549.
WWW: http://www.apci.net/~oblates/

NATIONAL HUG A NEWSMAN DAY. Apr 4. A chance for radio/TV news reporters to get away from the job which is often spent reporting on serious issues such as death and tragedy. For info: Mike Anthony, Pres, 3950 Hwy D, #12, Lake Ozark, MO 65049. Phone: (573) 348-0500.

NATIONAL READING A ROAD MAP WEEK. Apr 4–10. To promote map reading as an enjoyable pastime and as a survival skill for present and future drivers and all armchair travelers. Motto: Happiness is knowing how to read a road map. For info: RosaLind Schilder, 309 Florence Ave, #225N, Jenkintown, PA 19046. Email: mikenroz18@aol.com.

NORTH ATLANTIC TREATY RATIFIED: ANNIVERSARY. Apr 4, 1949. The North Atlantic Treaty Organization was created by this treaty, which was signed by 12 nations, including the US. (Four countries joined later.) The 16 NATO member nations are united for common defense.

NORWAY: EASTER FESTIVAL (WITH WORLD CHAMPIONSHIP REINDEER RACES). Apr 4–13. Kautokeino and Karasjok. Colorful traditional Norwegian celebration with Sami (Lapp) weddings, traditional fair, concerts and the World Championship Reindeer Races. For info: Norwegian Tourist Board, 655 Third Ave, New York, NY 10017. Phone: (212) 885-9700. Email: gonorway@interport.net.
WWW: http://www.norway.org/web/norway/tourism.html

PEANUT-KIDS–BASEBALL DAY. Apr 4. Edwards-Freeman Nut Co, Conshohocken, PA. In a salute to the ingredients that relate to our national pastime, an annual observance is held at which MVP (Master Vendor, Peanuts) Cheryl Spielvogel throws out the first "ball" (bag of peanuts shaped like a baseball) to Philadelphia Phillies players, then to Little League players and others present. Annually, the Saturday prior to the Phillies' home opener. Sponsors: Conshohocken Little League, Edwards-Freeman Nut Co. Est attendance: 150. For info: Abe S. Rosen, Rosen-Coren Agency, Inc, 2381 Philmont Ave, Ste 117, Huntingdon Valley, PA 19006-6294. Phone: (215) 938-1017.

PERKINS, ANTHONY: BIRTH ANNIVERSARY. Apr 4, 1932. American actor Anthony Perkins was born at New York, NY. Best known for his movie role as homicidal innkeeper Norman Bates in the film *Psycho* (1960), Perkins appeared in many Broadway plays in addition to his numerous film roles. He received an Oscar nomination for his supporting role in *Friendly Persuasion* (1956). Perkins died on Sept 12, 1992, at Hollywood, CA.

"POLICE STORY" TV PREMIERE: ANNIVERSARY. Apr 4, 1952. Produced by Jerome Robinson, directed by David Rich and narrated by Norman Rose, "Police Story" was an early anthology series on CBS depicting incidents from real-life police files.

PONY EXPRESS–JESSE JAMES WEEKEND. Apr 4–5. Patee House Museum, St. Joseph, MO. Observing the start of the Pony Express and the ending of Jesse James. Annually, the weekend nearest Apr 3 except when it falls on Easter. (Marking two events, at one location, in and around Patee House Museum and the Jesse James Home Museum.) Est attendance: 2,500. For info: Patee House Museum, 12th and Penn, Box 1022, St. Joseph, MO 64502. Phone: (816) 232-8206.

PRAIRIE DOG CHILI COOKOFF AND WORLD CHAMPIONSHIP OF PICKLED QUAIL-EGG EATING. Apr 4–5. Traders Village, Grand Prairie, TX. Tongue-in-cheek salute to the official state dish of Texas, chili con carne, or "Texas Red." World championship of pickled quail-egg eating featuring contestants devouring as many of these gourmet delights as possible in the 60-second time limit. Est attendance: 75,000. For info: Traders Village, Allan Hughes, 2602 Mayfield Rd, Grand Prairie, TX 75052-7246. Phone: (972) 647-2331.

SALTER ELECTED FIRST WOMAN MAYOR IN US: ANNIVERSARY. Apr 4, 1887. The first woman elected mayor in the US was Susanna Medora Salter, who was elected mayor of Argonia, KS, on Apr 4, 1887. Her name had been submitted for election without her knowledge by the Woman's Christian Temperance Union, and she did not know she was a candidate until she went to the polls to vote. She received a two-thirds majority vote and served one year for the salary of $1.

SCOTLAND: EDINBURGH INTERNATIONAL SCIENCE FESTIVAL. Apr 4–19. Edinburgh. More than 350 events at 35 venues. Includes workshops, talks, films and exhibitions. Est attendance: 200,000. For info: Pauline Mullin, Media and Info Officer, Edinburgh Intl Science Festival, 149 Rose St, Edinburgh, Scotland EH2 4LS. Box Office Phone: (44) (131) 220-3977. Fax: (44) (131) 220-3987. Email: esf@scifest.demon.co.uk. WWW: http://www.go-edinburgh.co.uk

SENEGAL: INDEPENDENCE DAY. Apr 4. National holiday.

SHEEP TO SHAWL. Apr 4. Jarrell Plantation, Juliette, GA. Hand shearing of sheep. Washing, dyeing, felting of wool. Carding, spinning and weaving of wool and cotton. Self-guided tour of plain-style plantation houses and mill complex. 10:30 AM– 3:30 PM. Admission fee. Sponsor: Georgia Heartland Spinners and Weavers Guild. Est attendance: 300. For info: Jarrell Plantation State Historic Site, Rte 2, Box 220, Juliette, GA 31046. Phone: (912) 986-5172.

SMOTHERS BROTHERS FIRED: ANNIVERSARY. Apr 4. CBS canceled this popular comedy series Apr 4, 1969. The hour-long show strongly influenced television humor during the two years it aired. Tom and Dick, however, frequently found themselves at odds with the censors over material that would be considered tame today. Guests and cast members frequently knocked the Vietnam War and the Nixon Administration. Acts featuring antiwar protestors such as Harry Belafonte were often cut.

SPACE MILESTONE: *STS-6* (US): 15th ANNIVERSARY. Apr 4, 1983. Shuttle *Challenger* launched from Kennedy Space Center, FL, Apr 4, 1983, with four astronauts (Paul Weitz, Karol Bobko, Story Musgrave and Donald Peterson). Four-hour spacewalk by Musgrave and Peterson. Landed at Edwards Air Force Base, CA, Apr 9.

TARPON SPRINGS ARTS AND CRAFTS FESTIVAL. Apr 4–5. Tarpon Springs, FL. Est attendance: 30,000. For info: Tarpon Springs Chamber of Commerce, 11 E Orange St, Tarpon Springs, FL 34689. Phone: (813) 937-6109. Fax: (813) 937-6100. WWW: http://www.TarponSprings.com

VITAMIN C ISOLATED: ANNIVERSARY. Apr 4, 1932. Vitamin C was first isolated by C. C. King at the University of Pittsburgh.

WATERS, MUDDY: BIRTH ANNIVERSARY. Apr 4, 1915. Born McKinley Morganfield at Rolling Fork, MS, American blues guitarist and singer Muddy Waters played a significant part in developing modern rhythm and blues that came to be known as Chicago or urban blues. It was predominately from this music that later forms such as rock and roll and soul sprang. Muddy Waters died at Westmont, IL, on Apr 30, 1983.

YALE, LINUS: BIRTH ANNIVERSARY. Apr 4, 1821. American portrait painter and inventor of the lock that is named for him was born at Salisbury, NY, Apr 4, 1821. He was creator of the Yale Infallible Bank Lock and developer of the cylinder lock. Yale died at New York, NY, Dec 25, 1868.

YAMAMOTO, ISOROKU: BIRTH ANNIVERSARY. Apr 4, 1884. Considered Japan's greatest naval strategist, Admiral Isoroku Yamamoto, who planned the attack on Pearl Harbor, was born Apr 4, 1884, at Nagaoko, Honshu. Yamamoto also devised the complex attack on Midway Island which ended in defeat for the Japanese because the Allies had the key to the Imperial fleet code and were prepared for the June 4, 1942, attack. The US intercepted reports of Yamamoto's proposed 1943 tour of the Western Solomons and shot down his plane Apr 18, while he was touring Japanese installations in the area.

BIRTHDAYS TODAY

Maya Angelou, 70, author, poet (*All God's Children Need Travelling Shoes*), born St. Louis, MO, Apr 4, 1928.

Elmer Bernstein, 76, composer of dozens of movie soundtracks, born New York, NY, Apr 4, 1922.

William C. (Bill) Bridges, 59, former basketball player, born Hobbs, NM, Apr 4, 1939.

Robert Downey, Jr, 33, actor (*Chaplin, Short Cuts, Natural Born Killers*), born New York, NY, Apr 4, 1965.

Kitty Kelley, 56, author (*Jackie Oh!, Nancy Reagan*), born Hartford, CT, Apr 4, 1942.

Christine Lahti, 48, actress ("The Harvey Korman Show," "Chicago Hope"; *Swing Shift*), born Detroit, MI, Apr 4, 1950.

Richard G. Lugar, 66, US Senator (R, Indiana), born Indianapolis, IN, Apr 4, 1932.

William Manchester, 76, author (*The Last Lion, A World Lit Only by Fire*), born Attleboro, MA, Apr 4, 1922.

Nancy McKeon, 32, actress (Jo on "The Facts of Life"), born Westbury, NY, Apr 4, 1966.

Craig T. Nelson, 52, actor ("Coach," *Private Benjamin, Poltergeist, The Killing Fields*), born Spokane, WA, Apr 4, 1946.

Michael Parks, 60, actor ("Then Came Bronson," "Twin Peaks," *The Happening*), born Corona, CA, Apr 4, 1938.

Elizabeth Wilson, 73, actress (*The Prisoner of Second Avenue, The Addams Family*; stage: *Taken in Marriage*), born Grand Rapids, MI, Apr 4, 1925.

APRIL 5 — SUNDAY

Day 95 — 270 Remaining

CURTIS EASTER PAGEANT. Apr 5. Medicine Valley High School Auditorium, Curtis, NE. "Truly an unforgettable, inspirational, touching spiritual experience!" A choir, acting cast and supporting cast of more than 200 people depict the last week in the life of Christ through music and narration. Seventeen magnificent "Living Pictures." Curtis is Nebraska's official "Easter City." Annually, 3 PM Palm Sunday afternoon. Sponsor: Curtis Community. Est attendance: 2,000. For info: Brad Welch, Easter Pageant Pres, Easter Pageant, Box 102, Curtis, NE 69025. Phone: (308) 367-4350 Day or (308) 367-4471 Evening. Fax: (308) 367-4101.

DAVIS, BETTE: 90th BIRTH ANNIVERSARY. Apr 5, 1908. American actress Bette Davis was born Ruth Elizabeth Davis at Lowell, MA. In addition to acting in more than 80 films, earning 10 Academy Award nominations and winning the best actress Academy Award twice, for *Dangerous* (1935) and *Jezebel* (1938), Davis also claimed to have nicknamed the Academy Award "Oscar" after her first husband, Harmon Oscar Nelson, Jr, whose derriere she said resembled that of the statuette. She died on Oct 6, 1989, at Neuilly-sur-Seine, France.

DISCOTHEQUE BOMBING: ANNIVERSARY. Apr 5, 1986. A bomb exploded in La Belle, a popular discotheque in West Berlin, Germany, killing two American soldiers and a Turkish woman. Although three groups claimed responsibility for the bombing, American intelligence organizations attributed it to orders from Libyan head-of-state Muammar el-Qaddafi, and President Reagan ordered a retaliatory air strike on Libya. At 7 PM, EST, on Apr 14, 1986 (1 AM, Apr 15, Libyan time), American forces launched a bombing attack on the Libyan cities of Tripoli and Benghazi, reportedly killing 37 (including a daughter of Qaddafi) and wounding another 93. Nearly two years later, on Jan 11, 1988, West German authorities arrested 27-year-old Christine Gabriele Endrigkeit, charging her with the La Belle bombing, citing "clues" that the bombing might have been ordered by Syrian agents. See also: "American Bombing of Libya: Anniversary" (Apr 14).

"FIRESIDE THEATRE" TV PREMIERE: ANNIVERSARY. Apr 5, 1949. Gene Raymond and later Jane Wyman hosted this NBC anthology program consisting of 15- and 30-minute dramas. One of its most acclaimed presentations was "The Reign of Amelika Jo" on Oct 12, 1954. It was set in the South Pacific during World War II and had a mostly black and Asian cast.

FIRST US CHAMBER OF COMMERCE FOUNDED: ANNIVERSARY. Apr 5, 1768. The first Chamber of Commerce in the US was founded at New York City.

HOLY WEEK. Apr 5–11. Christian observance dating from the fourth century, known also as Great Week. The seven days beginning on the sixth and final Sunday in Lent (Palm Sunday), consisting of: Palm Sunday, Monday of Holy Week, Tuesday of Holy Week, Spy Wednesday (or Wednesday of Holy Week), Maundy Thursday, Good Friday and Holy Saturday (or Great Sabbath or Easter Even). A time of solemn devotion to and memorializing of the suffering (passion), death and burial of Christ. Formerly a time of strict fasting.

INTERNATIONAL BUILDING SAFETY WEEK. Apr 5–11 (tentative). To make all Americans aware of the important health and life safety services available to them from their state and local professional building departments. Sponsors: Natl Conference of States on Building Codes and Standards, Inc, Council of American Building Officials, International Conference of Building Officials, Southern Building Code Congress International and Building Officials and Code Administrators International. For info: Jill Moreschi, NCSBCS, 505 Huntmar Park Dr, Ste 210, Herndon, VA 20170. Phone: (703) 437-0100. Fax: (703) 481-3596. WWW: http://www.ncsbcs.org

LISTER, JOSEPH: BIRTH ANNIVERSARY. Apr 5, 1827. English physician who was the founder of aseptic surgery. Born Apr 5, 1827, at Upton, Essex, England. Died at Walmer, England, on Feb 10, 1912.

"MARRIED . . . WITH CHILDREN" TV PREMIERE: ANNIVERSARY. Apr 5, 1987. Raunchy Fox TV show premiered as the antidote to Cosby-style family shows. Ed O'Neill starred as boorish, luckless shoe salesman Al Bundy; Katey Sagal portrayed Al's big-haired, spandex-clad, sex-starved wife Peg; Christina Applegate played airheaded bombshell daughter Kelly; and David Faustino played hormone-driven son Bud. The Bundys' neighbors were portrayed by Amanda Bearse as Marcy Rhoades; David Garrison as husband #1, Steve; and Ted McGinley as husband #2, Jefferson Darcy. The show went off the air in 1997.

April 1998

S	M	T	W	T	F	S
			1	2	3	4
5	6	7	8	9	10	11
12	13	14	15	16	17	18
19	20	21	22	23	24	25
26	27	28	29	30		

NATIONAL BIRTHPARENTS WEEK. Apr 5–11. A time to recognize and honor the 5 million mothers and fathers who, at great personal sacrifice, have been separated from their children by adoption and to focus attention on the rights of all family members to know each other. Annually, the first full week in April. For info: Concerned United Birthparents, Inc (CUB), 2000 Walker St, Des Moines, IA 50317. Phone: (800) 822-2777.

NATIONAL CRAFT-BREWERS CONFERENCE AND TRADE SHOW. Apr 5–8. Georgia World Congress Center, Atlanta, GA. To educate brewers and potential brewers on the technical and business aspects of small-scale professional microbrewing and pub brewing. Est attendance: 3,500. For info: The Institute for Brewing Studies, Box 1679, Boulder, CO 80306. Phone: (303) 447-0816. Fax: (303) 447-2825. Email: info@aob.org. WWW: http://www.beertown.org

PALM SUNDAY. Apr 5. Commemorates Christ's last entry into Jerusalem, when His way was covered with palms by the multitudes. Beginning of Holy (or Great) Week in Western Christian churches.

PALM SUNDAY EGG HUNT. Apr 5. Beach areas, Seaside Heights, NJ. 1 PM. More than 12,000 eggs are buried in the sand. Children in five different age groups dig for these plastic eggs filled with various tickets that are redeemed for prizes. Annually, Palm Sunday. Est attendance: 25,000. For info: Seaside Business Assn, PO Box 98, Seaside Heights, NJ 08751. Phone: (908) 793-1510.

PHILIPPINES: HOLY WEEK. Apr 5–11. National observance. Flagellants in the streets, *cenaculos* (passion plays) and other colorful and solemn rituals mark the country's observance of Holy Week.

RESNIK, JUDITH A.: BIRTH ANNIVERSARY. Apr 5. Dr. Judith A. Resnik, 36-year-old electrical engineer, was mission specialist on Space Shuttle *Challenger* on Jan 28, 1986. Dr. Resnik, the second American woman in space (1984), was born at Akron, OH, on Apr 5, 1949. She perished with all others aboard when *Challenger* exploded on Jan 28, 1986. See also: "*Challenger* Space Shuttle Explosion Anniversary" (Jan 28).

ROBERT PRAGER MEMORIAL DAY. A GERMAN-AMERICAN DAY OF REMEMBRANCE. Apr 5. A day to commemorate the anti-German hysteria of the two World Wars, to pay tribute to German-American heritage and recognize its contribution to the American community and to remember all people who have suffered from prejudice and hate. Annually, Apr 5. For info: Dr. Don Heinrich Tolzmann, Dir, German-American Studies Program, Univ of Cincinnati, PO Box 20113, Cincinnati, OH 45221-0113. Phone: (513) 556-1955. Fax: (513) 556-1955.

"SECRET AGENT" TV PREMIERE: ANNIVERSARY. Apr 5, 1961. Before Patrick McGoohan became "The Prisoner," he played the role of intelligence agent John Drake on this CBS adventure series. Produced in England by ATV, it also aired there as "Danger Man."

TAIWAN: NATIONAL TOMB-SWEEPING DAY. Apr 5. National holiday since 1972. According to Chinese custom, the tombs of ancestors are swept "clear and bright" on this day, and rites honoring ancestors are held. Tomb-Sweeping Day is observed on Apr 5, except in leap years, when it falls on Apr 4.

"THE TRACEY ULLMAN SHOW" TV PREMIERE: ANNIVERSARY. Apr 5, 1987. This Emmy award-winning comedy-variety show was one of the Fox network's early critical hits. Tracey Ullman starred with Julie Kavner, Dan Castellaneta, Joe Malone and Sam McMurray. The show, produced by James L. Brooks, contained sketches, songs and satire. Animated snippets in between segments introduced us to the Simpsons and were executed by Matt Groening, creator of the "Life in Hell" comic strip. "The Simpsons" spun off from the show in 1990 with Castellaneta and Kavner speaking the voices of Homer and Marge Simpson.

US: DAYLIGHT SAVING TIME BEGINS. Apr 5–Oct 25. Daylight Saving Time begins at 2 AM. The Uniform Time Act of 1966 (as amended in 1986 by Public Law 99–359), administered by the US Dept of Transportation, provides that Standard Time in each zone be advanced one hour from 2 AM on the first Sunday in April until 2 AM on the last Sunday in October (except where state legislatures provide exemption). Many use the popular rule "spring forward, fall back," to remember which way to turn their clocks. See also: "Standard Time" (Oct 25).

WASHINGTON, BOOKER TALLAFERRO: BIRTH ANNIVERSARY. Apr 5, 1856. Black educator and leader born at Franklin County, VA. "No race can prosper," he wrote in *Up from Slavery*, "till it learns that there is as much dignity in tilling a field as in writing a poem." Died at Tuskeegee, AL, on Nov 14, 1915.

BIRTHDAYS TODAY

Jane Asher, 52, actress (*DreamChild, Brideshead Revisited*), born London, England, Apr 5, 1946.

Eric Burdon, 57, singer (*Eric Burdon Declares War, Black Man's Burdon*), songwriter, born Walker-on-Tyne, England, Apr 5, 1941.

Roger Corman, 72, filmmaker (king of B horror movies), born Detroit, MI, Apr 5, 1926.

Max Gail, 55, actor ("Barney Miller," *Pearl*), born Grosse Point, MI, Apr 5, 1943.

Arthur Hailey, 78, author (*Airport, The Final Diagnosis*), born Luton, England, Apr 5, 1920.

Nigel Hawthorne, 69, actor (*Young Winston, Gandhi*), born Coventry, England, Apr 5, 1929.

Walter E. Massey, 60, physicist, former vice president at Argonne National Laboratory, former director National Science Foundation, born Hattiesburg, MS, Apr 5, 1938.

Michael Moriarty, 56, actor (*The Last Detail, Bang the Drum Slowly*, "Law & Order"), born Detroit, MI, Apr 5, 1942.

Gregory Peck, 82, actor (Oscar for *To Kill a Mockingbird; Roman Holiday, Gentleman's Agreement*), born La Jolla, CA, Apr 5, 1916.

Colin Luther Powell, 61, former Chairman US Joint Chiefs of Staff, retired, born Harlem, NY, Apr 5, 1937.

Gale Storm, 76, actress ("My Little Margie," "NBC Comedy Hour," "The Gale Storm Show"), born Bloomington, TX, Apr 5, 1922.

APRIL 6 — MONDAY

Day 96 — 269 Remaining

ASIMOV, ISAAC: DEATH ANNIVERSARY. Apr 6. Although Isaac Asimov was one of the world's best-known writers of science fiction, his almost 500 books dealt with subjects as diverse as the Bible, works for preschoolers, college textbooks, mysteries, chemistry, biology, limericks, Shakespeare, Gilbert and Sullivan and modern history, among others. During his prolific career he helped to elevate science fiction from pulp magazines to a more intellectual level. Some of his works include the *Foundation Trilogy, The Robots of Dawn, Robots and Empire, Nemesis, Murder at the A.B.A.* (in which he himself was a character), *The Gods Themselves* and *I, Robot*, in which he posited the famous Three Laws of Robotics. Asimov was born Jan 2, 1920, near Smolensk, Russia, and died on Apr 6, 1992.

BRIGHAM YOUNG'S LAST MARRIAGE: ANNIVERSARY. Apr 6, 1868. Brigham Young, Mormon Church leader, married his 27th, and last, wife on Apr 6, 1868.

BROADCASTERS INTERNATIONAL CONVENTION AND EXPOSITION AND NAB MULTIMEDIA WORLD: ANNUAL MEETING. Apr 6–9. Convention Center, Las Vegas, NV. Est attendance: 80,000. For info: Haidee Calore, Natl Assn of Broadcasters, 1771 N. St., NW, Washington, DC 20036-2891. Phone: (202) 429-5300 or (800) 342-2460. Fax: (202) 429-5343. Email: register@nab.org or exhibit@nab.org. WWW: http://www.nab.org

CHICKEN LITTLE AWARDS. Apr 6. 8th annual awards to organizations and/or individuals "who have frightened the daylights out of large numbers of people" with scientifically dubious predictions, theories and statements. The Center monitors the media for "scare campaigns." For info: Alan Caruba, Natl Anxiety Center, PO Box 40, Maplewood, NJ 07040. Phone: (973) 763-6392. Fax: (973) 763-4287.

CHING MING FESTIVAL. Apr 6. Widely observed Chinese festival (literally: "Pure and Bright"), Ching Ming is now regarded as an All Souls' Day. Families gather at graves of ancestors, leaving flowers and food after tidying the graves. A picnic spirit prevails, rather than solemnity. Set for the 106th day after the winter solstice; the Gregorian calendar date may vary slightly.

CHURCH OF JESUS CHRIST OF LATTER-DAY SAINTS: ANNIVERSARY. Apr 6, 1830. Under the leadership of Joseph Smith, Jr, The Church of Jesus Christ of Latter-Day Saints was founded with six members in a log cabin at Fayette, NY. For info: Church of Jesus Christ of Latter-Day Saints, Public Affairs Dept, 15 E South Temple St, Salt Lake City, UT 84150. Phone: (801) 240-4395. Fax: (801) 240-1167.

FIRST MODERN OLYMPICS: ANNIVERSARY. Apr 6, 1896. The first modern Olympics formally opened in Athens, Greece, after a 1500-year hiatus.

FIRST TONY AWARDS PRESENTED: ANNIVERSARY. Apr 6, 1947. The American Theatre Wing bestowed the first annual Tony awards for distinguished service to the theater.

☆ ☆ ☆

FIRST US CREDIT UNION LAW: ANNIVERSARY. Apr 6. To recognize the Apr 6, 1909, charter of the St. Canadian credit union of Manchester, NH, with the help of Alphonse Desjardins, Canadian credit union pioneer.

GLOBAL COMMUNICATIONS ERA WEEK. Apr 6–10. Various programs at various sites, including electronic forums, based on each year's planning and sponsorships. Recognizes individual and collaborative efforts of all participant organizations, their knowledge and offerings to the evolving communications marketplace. Annually, the first full week in April. For info: Carlos A. Webster, Committee for Societal Studies, BKB Enterprises, 187 Highway 513, Frenchtown, NJ 08825. Phone: (908) 996-6988. Fax: (908) 996-6930.

HENSON AND PEARY TO NORTH POLE: ANNIVERSARY. Apr 6, 1909. Matthew H. Henson, a black man hired as a servant, accompanied Commodore Robert E. Peary on his historic trip to the North Pole, reaching there on Apr 6, 1909. In 1945, Henson received a medal from the US government for "outstanding service" in the field of science.

JOYCE PAPERS RELEASED: ANNIVERSARY. Apr 6, 1992. After 51 years, many of the personal papers, letters, notes and bills of James Joyce were put on display at the National Library of Ireland in Dublin. The papers were gathered by Joyce's secretary Paul Léon during the early days of World War II in Paris. Léon, who was eventually arrested and killed at Auschwitz, gave the papers to the Irish envoy in Paris to send to the National Library in Dublin, with instructions not to allow their viewing until 50 years after Joyce's death. Some of the documents are being withheld from viewing until the year 2050.

MULLIGAN, GERRY: BIRTH ANNIVERSARY. Apr 6, 1927. American jazz saxophonist Gerry Mulligan was born at New York, NY. He performed with many great jazz musicians including Miles Davis, Dave Brubeck, Chet Baker and Duke Ellington, and is credited with helping create the cool-jazz movement with Miles Davis. Mulligan died on Jan 20, 1996, at Darien, CT.

NATIONAL PUBLIC HEALTH WEEK. Apr 6–12. Annually, the first full week in April. For info: Katherine McCarter, American Public Health Assn, 1015 15th St NW, Washington, DC 20005. Phone: (202) 789-5600.

PLAN YOUR EPITAPH DAY. Apr 6. (Also, Nov 2.) Dedicated to the proposition that a forgettable gravestone is a fate worse than death, and that everyone can be in the same league with William Shakespeare and W.C. Fields. Semiannually, coincides with Ching Ming Festival and the Day of the Dead. For info: Lance Hardie, Dead or Alive, PO Box 4595, Arcata, CA 95518. Phone: (707) 822-6924. Email: sunrise@hardiehouse.org. WWW: http://www.hardiehouse.org/epitaph

PORTLAND, OR: BIRTHDAY. Apr 6, 1853. "The City of Roses" adds a year today.

"PRIVATE BENJAMIN" TV PREMIERE: ANNIVERSARY. Apr 6, 1981. The CBS sitcom was based on the Goldie Hawn movie about a pampered young woman enlisting in the army and going through the trials of basic training. Eileen Brennan and Hal Williams reprised their movie roles as Captain Doreen Lewis and drill instructor Sergeant Ted Ross. Lorna Patterson played Private Judy Benjamin. Also featured were: Joyce Little, Joan Roberts, Lisa Raggio, Ann Ryerson, Lucy Webb, Francesca Roberts, Damita Jo Freeman, Wendie Jo Sperber, Robert Mandan and Polly Holliday.

RAPHAEL: BIRTH ANNIVERSARY. Apr 6, 1483. Raffaello Santi (Sanzio), Italian painter and architect. Probably born on Apr 6, 1483, at Urbino, Italy. Died on his 37th birthday, at Rome, Italy, Apr 6, 1520.

SCHNEIDERMAN, ROSE: BIRTH ANNIVERSARY. Apr 6, 1882. A pioneer in the battle to increase wages and improve working conditions for women, Rose Schneiderman was born at Saven, Poland, and her family immigrated to the US six years later. At age 16 she began factory work in New York City's garment district and quickly became a union organizer. Opposed to the open-shop policy, which permitted nonunion members to work in a unionized shop, Schneiderman organized a 1913 strike of 25,000 women shirtwaist makers. She worked as an organizer for the International Ladies Garment Workers Union (ILGWU) and for the Women's Trade Union League (WTUL), serving as president for more than 20 years. During the Great Depression President Roosevelt appointed her to his Labor Advisory Board—the only woman member. Died Aug 11, 1972, at New York City.

SCOTTSBORO TRIAL: ANNIVERSARY. Apr 6, 1931. In what became a *cause célèbre*, nine black youths went on trial at Scottsboro, AL, accused of raping two white women on a freight train. All were convicted in a hasty trial, but by 1950 were free by parole, appeal or escape.

SPACE MILESTONE: *CHALLENGER STS-11* (US). Apr 6, 1984. Shuttle *Challenger* launched with five astronauts (Robert Crippen, Francis Scobee, George Nelson, Terry Hart and James Van Hoften). Mission required recovery and repair of damaged satellite. Landed at Edwards Air Force Base, CA, on Apr 13.

TEFLON INVENTED: 60th ANNIVERSARY. Apr 6, 1938. Teflon coating was invented by Roy J. Plunkett.

THAILAND: CHAKRI DAY. Apr 6. Commemorates foundation of present dynasty by King Rama I (1782–1809), who also established Bangkok as capital.

THOMAS, LOWELL: BIRTH ANNIVERSARY. Apr 6, 1892. World traveler, reporter, editor and radio newscaster, whose broadcasts spanned more than half a century, 1925–1976. Born at Woodington, OH, on Apr 6, 1892. Died at Pawling, NY, on Aug 29, 1981. His radio sign-off, "So long until tomorrow," was known to millions of listeners and he is said to have been the first to broadcast from a ship, an airplane, a submarine and a coal mine.

TRAGEDY IN RWANDA: ANNIVERSARY. Apr 6, 1994. A plane carrying the presidents of Rwanda and Burundi was shot down near Kigali, the Rwandan capital, exacerbating a brutal ethnic war that led to the massacre of hundreds of thousands. Presidents Juvenal Habyarimana of Rwanda and Cyprien Ntaryamira of Burundi were returning from a summit in Tanzania where they discussed ways of ending the killing in their countries sparked by ethnic rivalries between the Hutu and Tutsi tribes. Following the attack on the two leaders, Rwanda descended into chaos as the two tribes began killing each other in a genocidal battle for power, leading to a mass exodus of civilians caught in the maelstrom.

US ENTERS WORLD WAR I: ANNIVERSARY. Apr 6, 1917. After Congress approved a declaration of war against Germany, the US entered World War I, which had begun in 1914.

US SENATE ACHIEVES A QUORUM: ANNIVERSARY. Apr 6. The US Senate was formally organized after achieving a quorum on Apr 6, 1789.

YAWM ARAFAT: THE STANDING AT ARAFAT. Apr 6. Islamic calendar date: Dhu-Hijjah 9, 1418. The day when people on the Hajj (pilgrimage to Mecca) assemble for "the Standing" at the plain of Arafat in Mina, Saudi Arabia, near Mecca. This gathering is a foreshadowing of that on the Day of Judgment. Different methods for "anticipating" the visibility of the new moon crescent at Mecca are used by different Muslim groups. *Chase's* uses anticipated dates furnished by the American Muslim Council. US EST date may vary.

April 1998

S	M	T	W	T	F	S
			1	2	3	4
5	6	7	8	9	10	11
12	13	14	15	16	17	18
19	20	21	22	23	24	25
26	27	28	29	30		

BIRTHDAYS TODAY

Rik Aalbert (Bert) Blyleven, 47, former baseball player, born Zeist, The Netherlands, Apr 6, 1951.

Candace Cameron, 22, actress ("Full House"), born Canoga Park, CA, Apr 6, 1976.

Merle Haggard, 61, singer, songwriter ("Okie from Muskogee," "If We Make It Through December"), born Bakersfield, CA, Apr 6, 1937.

Marilu Henner, 46, actress (Elaine Nardo on "Taxi"; Ava Newton on "Evening Shade"), born Chicago, IL, Apr 6, 1952.

Bruce King, 74, former Governor of New Mexico (D), born Stanley, NM, Apr 6, 1924.

Barry Levinson, 56, director, producer, writer, actor ("The Carol Burnett Show" [writer; Emmy Awards 1974, 1975], *Rain Man, Avalon, Bugsy*), born Baltimore, MD, Apr 6, 1942.

Andre Previn, 69, composer, conductor, born Berlin, Germany, Apr 6, 1929.

John Ratzenberger, 51, actor (Cliff on "Cheers"), born Bridgeport, CT, Apr 6, 1947.

John Sculley, 59, business executive, born New York, NY, Apr 6, 1939.

Roy Thinnes, 60, actor ("The Invaders," "The Outer Limits"), born Chicago, IL, Apr 6, 1938.

James Dewey Watson, 70, bio-chemist, co-discoverer (with Francis Crick) of the DNA structure, born El Paso, TX, Apr 6, 1928.

Billy Dee Williams, 61, actor (*Brian's Song, Lady Sings the Blues, Return of the Jedi*), born New York, NY, Apr 6, 1937.

APRIL 7 — TUESDAY

Day 97 — 268 Remaining

CHANNING, WILLIAM ELLERY: BIRTH ANNIVERSARY. Apr 7, 1780. Well-known abolitionist and leader of the Unitarian movement in the US, born at Newport, RI. He stood for religious liberalism and influenced such people as Longfellow, Bryant, Emerson, Lowell and Holmes. Died at Bennington, VT, Oct 2, 1842.

EID-AL-ADHA: FEAST OF THE SACRIFICE. Apr 7. Islamic calendar date: Dhu-Hijja 10, 1418. Commemorates Abraham's willingness to sacrifice his son Ishmael in obedience to God. It is part of the Hajj (pilgrimage to Mecca). For the pilgrims and many others, the day begins with the sacrifice of an animal in remembrance of the Angel Gabriel's substitution of a lamb as Abraham's offering. One-third of the meat is given to the poor and the rest is shared with friends and family. Celebrated with gifts and general merrymaking, the festival usually continues for several days. Different methods for "anticipating" the visibility of the moon crescent at Mecca are used by different Muslim groups. *Chase's* uses anticipated dates furnished by the American Muslim Council. US EST date may vary.

FAIRCHILD, DAVID GRANDISON: BIRTH ANNIVERSARY. Apr 7. American botanist, government official and explorer. Born at East Lansing, MI, Apr 7, 1869. Noted for scientific studies on importation of tropical plant species such as avocados and mangoes. Died at Miami, FL, Aug 6, 1954.

FORD, HENRY: DEATH ANNIVERSARY. Apr 7, 1947. Industrialist Henry Ford, whose assembly-line method of automobile production revolutionized the industry, died at age 83 at Dearborn, MI, where his manufacturing complex was located. His Model T made up half of the world's output of cars during its years of production. Ford was born July 30, 1863, at Wayne County, MI, on the family farm. For several years Ford built racing cars until, in 1903, he and his partners formed the Ford Motor Company. In 1908 the company presented the Model T, which was produced until 1927, and in 1913 Ford introduced the assembly line and mass production. Ford's innovations in mass, assembly-line production reduced the time it took to build each car from 12½ hours to only 1½. This lowered the unit cost and enabled him to sell cars for $500, making automobile ownership a possibility for an unprecedented percentage of the population.

HOLIDAY, BILLIE: BIRTH ANNIVERSARY. Apr 7, 1915. Billie Holiday (born Eleanora Fagan, nicknamed "Lady Day") is considered by many jazz critics to have been the greatest jazz singer ever recorded. In her 26-year career, despite having received no formal training, she demonstrated a unique style with sophisticated and dramatic phrasing. Among her best-known songs are "Lover Man," "God Bless the Child," "Don't Explain" and "Strange Fruit." Holiday was born at Philadelphia, PA. She died at New York City on July 17, 1959.

KING, WILLIAM RUFUS DEVANE: BIRTH ANNIVERSARY. Apr 7, 1786. 13th vice president of the US died on the 46th day after taking the Oath of Office, of tuberculosis, at Cahawba, AL, on Apr 18, 1853. The Oath of Office had been administered to King at Havana, Cuba, as authorized by a special act of Congress (the only presidential or vice presidential oath to be administered outside the US). Born in Sampson County, NY, King was the only vice president of the US who had served in both the House of Representatives and the Senate. Never married, King's term of office as vice president was Mar 4–Apr 18, 1853.

MALINOWSKI, BRONISLAW: BIRTH ANNIVERSARY. Apr 7. Leading British anthropologist, author and teacher. Born on Apr 7, 1884, at Krakow, Poland. His pioneering anthropological fieldwork in Melanesia inspired his colleagues and students. In 1939 he became a visiting professor at Yale University. Died at New Haven, CT, on May 16, 1942.

NEW YORK SLAVE REVOLT: ANNIVERSARY. Apr 7, 1712. Nine whites were killed in a slave revolt in New York City. Planned by 27 slaves, the rebellion was begun by setting fire to an outhouse; as whites came to put the fire out, they were shot. The state militia was called out to capture the rebels and the city of New York responded to the event by strengthening its slave codes. Twenty-one blacks were executed as participants, and six alleged participants committed suicide.

NO HOUSEWORK DAY. Apr 7. No trash. No dishes. No making of beds or washing of laundry. And no guilt. Give it a rest. [© 1997 by WPL] For info: Tom or Ruth Roy, Wellness Permission League, PO Box 662, Mt Gretna, PA 17064-0662. Phone: (500) 437-5104 or (717) 964-1308. Fax: (717) 964-1335.

UNITED NATIONS: WORLD HEALTH DAY. Apr 7. A United Nations observance commemorating the establishment of the World Health Organization on Apr 7, 1948. Info from: United Nations, Dept of Public Info, New York, NY 10017.

WINCHELL, WALTER: BIRTH ANNIVERSARY. Apr 7, 1879. Controversial American journalist, gossip columnist and radio broadcaster, singer and actor, who roused the ire of many prominent public figures. Born at New York, NY; died at Los Angeles, CA, on Feb 20, 1972.

WORDSWORTH, WILLIAM: BIRTH ANNIVERSARY. Apr 7. English Lake Poet and philosopher born on this day, 1770. "Poetry," he said, "is the spontaneous overflow of powerful feelings: it takes its origin from emotion recollected in tranquility." Wordsworth died on Apr 23, 1850.

WORLD HEALTH DAY. Apr 7. A complete planning kit available focusing on "Safe Motherhood." For info: American Assn for World Health, World Health Day, 1825 K St NW, Ste 1208, Washington, DC 20006. Phone: (202) 466-5883. Fax: (202) 466-5896. Email: aawhstaff@aol.com.
WWW: http://www.aawhworldhealth.org

WORLD HEALTH ORGANIZATION: 50th ANNIVERSARY. Apr 7, 1948. This agency of the United Nations was founded to coordinate international health systems. It is headquartered in Geneva. Among its achievements is the elimination of smallpox.

WORLD WAR I: BATTLE OF LYS RIVER: 80th ANNIVERSARY. Apr 7, 1918. Having failed to break through Allied lines at Somme in March, General Erich Ludendorff made another attempt by attacking Flanders along the Lys River. On the hot, misty, sticky mornings of Apr 7 and 8, 1918, the Germans released mustard gas. On Apr 9 the Central Powers began a high explosive bombardment along the 12-mile front from LaBasse to Armentieres. The British managed to avoid a break in their line, and finally Foch sent nine French divisions to take over a portion of it. On Apr 30, realizing that "further attacks promised no success," Ludendorff ended the offensive. As a result of this battle the British were unable to initiate an offensive for three months. The Allies suffered 240,000 casualties while the German losses exceeded 348,000.

BIRTHDAYS TODAY

(William) Hodding Carter III, 63, television and newspaper journalist, born New Orleans, LA, Apr 7, 1935.

Francis Ford Coppola, 59, filmmaker (the *Godfather* movies; *Apocalypse Now*), born Detroit, MI, Apr 7, 1939.

Anthony Drew (Tony) Dorsett, 44, Pro Football Hall of Fame running back, born Rochester, PA, Apr 7, 1954.

Daniel Ellsberg, 67, author (released the "Pentagon Papers" to the *New York Times*), born Chicago, IL, Apr 7, 1931.

David Frost, 59, entertainer ("That Was the Week That Was"), interviewer, born Tenterden, England, Apr 7, 1939.

James Garner (James Baumgardner), 70, actor (*The Americanization of Emily*, "Maverick," "The Rockford Files"), born Norman, OK, Apr 7, 1928.

John Oates, 50, singer ("Maneater" with Hall and Oates), songwriter, born New York, NY, Apr 7, 1948.

Wayne Rogers, 65, actor ("M*A*S*H," "House Calls"), born Birmingham, AL, Apr 7, 1933.

APRIL 8 — WEDNESDAY

Day 98 — 267 Remaining

BIRTHDAY OF THE BUDDHA: BIRTH ANNIVERSARY. Apr 8. Among Buddhist holidays, Apr 8 is the most important as it commemorates the birthday of the Buddha. The founder of Buddhism had the given name Siddhartha, the family name Gautama and the clan name Shaka. He is commonly called the Buddha, meaning in Sanskrit "the enlightened one." He is thought to have lived in India from c. 563 BC to 483 BC.

April 1998

S	M	T	W	T	F	S
			1	2	3	4
5	6	7	8	9	10	11
12	13	14	15	16	17	18
19	20	21	22	23	24	25
26	27	28	29	30		

BLACK SENATE PAGE APPOINTED: ANNIVERSARY. Apr 8, 1965. Sixteen-year-old Lawrence Bradford of New York City was the first black page appointed to the US Senate.

EASTER CELEBRATION. Apr 8. Broadway Market Square, Baltimore, MD. Musical entertainment and performances given in celebration of Easter. A best-decorated Easter egg contest and the Easter bunny also featured. Est attendance: 250. For info: Dept of Rec & Parks Office of Adventures in Fun, Patterson Park Recreation Complex, 2601 E Baltimore St, Baltimore, MD 21224. Phone: (410) 396-9177. Fax: (410) 327-4120.

FEDERAL GOVERNMENT SEIZURE OF STEEL MILLS: ANNIVERSARY. Apr 8, 1952. On this date President Harry S. Truman seized control of the nation's steel mills by presidential order in an attempt to prevent a shutdown by strikers. On Apr 29, a US District Court declared the seizure unconstitutional and workers immediately walked out. Production dropped from 300,000 tons a day to less than 20,000. After 53 days the strike ended on July 24, with steelworkers receiving a 16¢ hourly wage raise plus a 5.4¢ hourly increase in fringe benefits.

FIRST INTERCOLLEGIATE RODEO: ANNIVERSARY. Apr 8, 1939. The first Intercollegiate Rodeo was held at historic Godshall Ranch, Apple Valley, CA. The student cowboys and cowgirls, who hailed from California and Arizona colleges and universities, were assisted by world champion professional cowboys including Harry Carey, Dick Foran, Curley Fletcher, Tex Ritter and Errol Flynn from Hollywood. Collegiate rodeos had been held since 1919 at Texas A&M University. College cowboys and cowgirls organized a national association in Texas in 1949 named National Intercollegiate Rodeo Association, which continues today as the only national college rodeo organization. For info: Sylvia Mahoney, NIRA Alumni Natl Chair, Natl Intercollegiate Rodeo Assn, PO Box 1518, Vernon, TX 76385. Phone: (817) 552-5532. Email: smahoney@vrjc.cc.tx.us.

FISCUS, KATHY: DEATH ANNIVERSARY. Apr 8, 1949. Three-year-old Kathy Fiscus of San Marino, CA, fell while playing into an abandoned well pipe 14 inches wide and 120 feet deep. Rescue workers toiled ceaselessly for two days while thousands watched and national attention was focused on the tragedy. Her body was recovered Apr 10, 1949. An alarmed nation suddenly became attentive to other abandoned wells and similar hazards, and "Kathy Fiscus laws" were enacted in a number of places requiring new safety measures to prevent recurrence of such a tragic accident.

GAINES-SHELTON, RUTH: BIRTH ANNIVERSARY. Apr 8, 1872. African-American playwright born at Glasgow, MO. Best known for prize-winning comedy *The Church Fight*, which was published in *Crisis* (a publication of the NAACP) in May of 1926.

HOME RUN RECORD SET BY HANK AARON: ANNIVERSARY. Apr 8. Henry ("Hammerin' Hank") Aaron hit the 715th home run of his career on Apr 8, 1974, breaking the record set by Babe Ruth in 1935. Playing for the Atlanta Braves, Aaron broke the record in Atlanta in a game against the Los Angeles Dodgers. He finished his career in 1976 with a total of 755 home runs. This record remains unbroken. At the time of his retirement, Aaron also held records for first in RBIs, second in at-bats and runs scored and third in base hits.

JAPAN: FLOWER FESTIVAL (HANA MATSURI). Apr 8. Commemorates Buddha's birthday. Ceremonies in all temples.

KNIGHT, O. RAYMOND: BIRTH ANNIVERSARY. Apr 8, 1872. The "Father of Canadian Rodeo," O. Raymond Knight was born at Payson, UT. His father, the Utah mining magnate

Jesse Knight, founded the town of Raymond, Alberta in 1901. In 1902, Raymond produced Canada's first rodeo, "Raymond Stampede." He also built rodeo's first grandstand and first chute in 1903. O. Raymond Knight died on Feb 7, 1947. For info: John A. Bascom, Raymond Sports Hall of Fame, Max Court, Box 511, Raymond, Alta, Canada T0K 2S0. Phone: (403) 752-3094.

McRAE, CARMEN: BIRTH ANNIVERSARY. Apr 8, 1920. After winning an amateur contest at Harlem's legendary Apollo Theatre in her hometown New York City, McRae went on to become a noted jazz singer, singing with the Earl Hines, Mercer Ellington and Benny Carter bands among others and recording more than 20 albums. She died Nov 10, 1994, at Beverly Hills, CA.

MORRIS, LEWIS: BIRTH ANNIVERSARY. Apr 8, 1726. Signer of the Declaration of Independence, born in Westchester County, NY, Apr 8, 1726. Died Jan 22, 1798.

POLL TAX OUTLAWED: ANNIVERSARY. Apr 8, 1966. In the last of a series of moves to abolish poll taxes, a three-judge federal court in Jackson, MS, outlawed Mississippi's $2 poll tax as a voting requirement for state and local elections.

SEVENTEENTH AMENDMENT TO US CONSTITUTION RATIFIED. Apr 8, 1913. Prior to the 17th Amendment, ratified on Apr 8, 1913, members of the Senate were elected by each state's respective legislature. The advent and popularity of primary elections during the last decade of the 19th century and the early 20th century and a string of senatorial scandals, most notably a scandal involving William Lorimer, an Illinois political boss in 1909, forced the Senate to end its resistance to a constitutional amendment requiring direct popular election of senators.

WHITE, RYAN: DEATH ANNIVERSARY. Apr 8, 1990. This young man from Kokomo, IN, put the face of a child on AIDS and helped promote greater understanding of the disease. Ryan, a hemophiliac, contracted Acquired Immune Deficiency Syndrome from a blood transfusion. Banned from the public school system in Central Indiana in 1984 at the age of 10, he moved with his mother and sister to Cicero, IN, where he was accepted by students and faculty alike. Ryan once stated that he only wanted to be treated as a normal teenager, but that was not to be as media attention made him a celebrity. A few days after attending the Academy Awards in 1990, 18-year-old Ryan was hospitalized and on Palm Sunday, Apr 8, he lost his valiant fight. His funeral was attended by many celebrities, including First Lady Barbara Bush and Elton John, who sang at the service.

WILLIAMS, WILLIAM: BIRTH ANNIVERSARY. Apr 8. Signer of the Declaration of Independence. Born at Lebanon, CT, Apr 8, 1731. Died there Aug 2, 1811.

BIRTHDAYS TODAY

Gary Edmund Carter, 44, sportscaster, former baseball player, born Culver City, CA, Apr 8, 1954.

William D. Chase, 76, librarian and chronicler of contemporary civilization as cofounder and coeditor of *Chase's Annual Events*, born Lakeview, MI, Apr 8, 1922.

Mark Gregory Clayton, 37, former football player, born Indianapolis, IN, Apr 8, 1961.

Betty (Elizabeth) Ford, 80, wife of Gerald Ford, 38th president of the US. Born Chicago, IL, Apr 8, 1918.

Shecky Greene, 73, comedian, actor, born Chicago, IL, Apr 8, 1925.

John J. Havlicek, 58, Basketball Hall of Fame forward, born Lansing, OH, Apr 8, 1940.

Seymour Hersh, 61, journalist, born Chicago, IL, Apr 8, 1937.

James Augustus ("Catfish") Hunter, 52, Baseball Hall of Fame pitcher, born Hertford, NC, Apr 8, 1946.

Julian Lennon, 35, musician, singer, son of John Lennon, born Liverpool, England, Apr 8, 1963.

Stuart Pankin, 52, actor ("Not Necessarily the News," *Irreconcilable Differences, Arachnophobia*), born Philadelphia, PA, Apr 8, 1946.

Terry Porter, 35, basketball player, born Milwaukee, WI, Apr 8, 1963.

John Schneider, 44, actor ("Dukes of Hazzard," *Smokey and the Bandit*), born Mount Kisco, NY, Apr 8, 1954.

APRIL 9 — THURSDAY

Day 99 — 266 Remaining

BLACK PAGE APPOINTED TO US HOUSE OF REPRESENTATIVES: ANNIVERSARY. Apr 9, 1965. Fifteen-year-old Frank Mitchell of Springfield, IL, was the first black appointed a page to the US House of Representatives.

CIVIL RIGHTS BILL OF 1866: ANNIVERSARY. Apr 9, 1866. The Civil Rights Bill of 1866, passed by Congress over the veto of President Andrew Johnson, granted blacks the rights and privileges of American citizenship and formed the basis for the Fourteenth Amendment to the United States Constitution.

CIVIL WAR ENDING: ANNIVERSARY. Apr 9, 1865. At 1:30 PM, on Sunday, Apr 9, 1865, General Robert E. Lee, commander of the Army of Northern Virginia, surrendered to General Ulysses S. Grant, commander-in-chief of the Union Army, ending four years of civil war. The meeting took place in the house of Wilmer McLean at the village of Appomattox Court House, VA. Confederate soldiers were permitted to keep their horses and go free to their homes, while Confederate officers were allowed to retain their swords and side arms as well. Grant wrote the terms of surrender. Formal surrender took place at the Courthouse on Apr 12. Death toll for the Civil War is estimated at 500,000 men.

CONGRESS OF RACIAL EQUALITY "FREEDOM RIDERS": ANNIVERSARY. Apr 9, 1947. Testing the US Supreme Court's June 3, 1946, ban against segregation in interstate bus travel, the Congress of Racial Equality (CORE) sent "freedom riders" into the south. Founded by James Farmer in 1942, CORE pioneered the use of passive resistance tactics that were used extensively in the American Civil Rights Movement.

DOGWOOD ARTS FESTIVAL. Apr 9–26. Maryville, TN. To celebrate spring. Activities and events for all ages. Est attendance: 12,000. For info: Chamber of Commerce, Blount County Dogwood Arts Fest, 201 S Washington St, Maryville, TN 37804-5728. Phone: (423) 983-2241. Fax: (423) 984-1386.
Email: chambcom@chamber.blount.tn.us.
WWW: http://chamber.blount.tn.us

ECKERT, J(OHN) PRESPER, JR: BIRTH ANNIVERSARY. Apr 9, 1919. Co-inventor with John W. Mauchly of ENIAC (Electronic Numerical Integrator and Computer), which was first demonstrated at the Moore School of Electrical Engineering at the University of Pennsylvania in Philadelphia on Feb 14, 1946. This is generally considered the birth of the computer age. Originally designed to process artillery calculations for the Army, ENIAC was also used in the Manhattan Project. Eckert and Mauchly formed Electronic Control Co, which later became Unisys Corp. Eckert was born at Philadelphia; he died at Bryn Mawr, PA, June 3, 1995.

FIELDS, W.C.: BIRTH ANNIVERSARY. Apr 9. Claude William Dukenfield (W.C. Fields), stage and motion picture actor and expert juggler. Born at Philadelphia, PA, Apr 9, 1879. Died Dec 25, 1946, at Pasadena, CA. He wrote his own epitaph: "On the whole, I'd rather be in Philadelphia."

JENKINS'S EAR DAY: ANNIVERSARY. Apr 9, 1731. Anniversary of the day in 1731 when English master mariner Robert Jenkins lost an ear (for which a war was named). Spanish *guarda-costa* boarded and plundered the British ship *Rebecca* off Jamaica, and, among other outrages, cut off Jenkins's ear. Little notice was taken until seven years later, when Jenkins exhibited the detached ear and described the atrocity to a committee of the House of Commons. In consequence, Britain declared war on Spain in October 1739, a war that lasted until 1743 and is still known as the "War of Jenkins's Ear." Nothing else is known of him.

KING, FRANK: BIRTH ANNIVERSARY. Apr 9, 1883. Created by Frank King in 1919 as a comic strip about men's interest in autos, *Gasoline Alley* had a tremendous jump in popularity in 1921 when its main character Walt adopted a foundling called Skeezix. Devoid of melodrama, this strip sympathetically described the day-to-day lives of Walt, Skeezix and their friends and family, and it was the first American cartoon in which the characters actually aged. Frank King was born at Cashon, WI, and died at Winter Park, FL, on June 24, 1969.

MARIAN ANDERSON EASTER CONCERT: ANNIVERSARY. Apr 9. On Easter Sunday, Apr 9, 1939, black American contralto Marian Anderson sang an open-air concert from the steps of the Lincoln Memorial in Washington, DC, to an audience of 75,000, after having been denied use of the Daughters of the American Revolution (DAR) Constitution Hall. The event became an American antidiscrimination *cause célèbre* and led First Lady Eleanor Roosevelt to resign from the DAR.

MAUNDY THURSDAY or HOLY THURSDAY. Apr 9. The Thursday before Easter, originally "dies mandate," celebrates Christ's injunction to love one another, "Mandatus novum do vobis. . . ." ("A new commandment I give to you. . . .")

MUYBRIDGE, EADWEARD: BIRTH ANNIVERSARY. Apr 9. English photographer famed for his studies of animals in motion. Born Edward James Muggeridge, at Kingston-on-Thames, England, Apr 9, 1830. Died there May 8, 1904.

April 1998

S	M	T	W	T	F	S
			1	2	3	4
5	6	7	8	9	10	11
12	13	14	15	16	17	18
19	20	21	22	23	24	25
26	27	28	29	30		

PHILIPPINES: ARAW NG KAGITINGAN. Apr 9. National observance to commemorate the fall of Bataan in 1942. The infamous "Death March" is reenacted at the Mount Samat Shrine, the Dambana ng Kagitingan.

PHILIPPINES: MORIONE'S FESTIVAL. Apr 9–12. Marinduque Island. Provincewide masquerade, Lenten plays and celebrations. Annually, Holy Thursday through Easter Sunday.

ROBESON, PAUL BUSTILL: 100th BIRTH ANNIVERSARY. Apr 9, 1898. Paul Robeson was born on Apr 9, 1898, in Princeton, NJ. He was an All-American football player at Rutgers University and received his law degree from Columbia University in 1923. After being seen by Eugene O'Neill in an amateur stage production, he was offered a part in O'Neill's play, *The Emperor Jones*. His performance in that play with the Provincetown Players established him as an actor. Without ever having taken a voice lesson, he also became a popular singer. His stage credits include *Show Boat, Porgy, The Hairy Ape* and *Othello*, which enjoyed the longest Broadway run of a Shakespearean play. He displayed his talents during his tours of Europe and the Soviet Union, and in 1950 he was denied a passport by the US for refusing to sign an affidavit stating whether he was or ever had been a member of the Communist Party. The action was overturned by the Supreme Court in 1958. His film credits include *Emperor Jones, Showboat, King Solomon's Mines* and *Song of Freedom*, among others. Robeson died at Philadelphia, PA, on Jan 23, 1976.

SPACE MILESTONE: *SOYUZ 35* (USSR). Apr 9, 1980. Two cosmonauts (Valery Ryumin and Leonid Popov) launched Apr 9, 1980, from Baikonur space center in Kazakhstan, USSR. Docked at *Salyut 6* on Apr 10. Ryumin and Popov returned to Earth Oct 11, 1980, after setting a new space endurance record of 185 days.

SPRING BLUEGRASS FESTIVAL. Apr 9–12. Live Oak, FL. Four days of extraordinary bluegrass music in a beautiful outdoor setting. Est attendance: 10,000. For info: James Cornett, Spirit of the Suwannee Music Park, 3076 95th Dr, Live Oak, FL 32060. Phone: (904) 364-1683. Fax: (904) 364-2998.
Email: spirit@musicliveshere.com.
WWW: http://www.musicliveshere.com

TEXAS PANHANDLE TORNADO: ANNIVERSARY. Apr 9, 1947. A monster tornado clearing a 1½-mile-long path struck through at least twelve towns in Texas, Oklahoma and Kansas, killing 169 people and causing over $15 million in damage. The tornado traveled 221 miles across the three states.

TUNISIA: MARTYRS' DAY. Apr 9.

VOTE LAWYERS OUT OF OFFICE DAY. Apr 9. This is the day that voters renew their pledge never to vote for a lawyer for public office. A cleansing effort. Annually, the second Thursday in April. Sponsor: Sharkbait Press. For info: Marcus P. Meleton, Jr, Sharkbait Press, PO Box 11300, Costa Mesa, CA 92627-0300. Phone: (714) 645-0139.

WAYNE STATE UNIVERSITY: FUNERAL FOR WINTER. Apr 9. Detroit, MI. Events include a New Orleans-style procession with jazz band playing Dixieland music. "Miss Spring" and a local TV personality conduct an irreverent burial ceremony. Est attendance: 1,000. For info: Pat Borninski, Media Relations Officer, Wayne State University, 3222 FAB, Detroit, MI 48202. Phone: (313) 577-2150. Fax: (313) 577-8154.
Email: pbornin@cms.cc.wayne.edu.
WWW: http://www.media.wayne.edu/

WINSTON CHURCHILL DAY. Apr 9. Anniversary of enactment of legislation in 1963 that made the late British statesman an honorary citizen of the US.

BIRTHDAYS TODAY

Severiano (Seve) Ballesteros, 41, golfer, born Pedrena, Spain, Apr 9, 1957.

Jean-Paul Belmondo, 65, actor (*The Man from Rio, Is Paris Burning?*), born Neuilly-sur-Seine, France, Apr 9, 1933.

Hugh Hefner, 72, founder of *Playboy*, born Chicago, IL, Apr 9, 1926.

Paul Krassner, 66, editor, journalist, born Brooklyn, NY, Apr 9, 1932.

Michael Learned, 59, actress (*The Waltons, Nurses*; stage: *The Sisters Rosenzweig*), born Washington, DC, Apr 9, 1939.

Tom Lehrer, 70, songwriter ("Vatican Rag," "New Math"), pianist, mathematician, born New York, NY, Apr 9, 1928.

Cynthia Nixon, 32, actress (*Tattoo, Amadeus*), born New York, NY, Apr 9, 1966.

Carl Perkins, 66, singer, songwriter ("Blue Suede Shoes"), born Jackson, TN, Apr 9, 1932.

Keshia Knight Pulliam, 19, actress (Rudy Huxtable on "The Cosby Show"), born Newark, NJ, Apr 9, 1979.

Dennis Quaid, 44, actor (*Everybody's All-American*), born Houston, TX, Apr 9, 1954.

Jacque Villeneueve, 27, race car driver, winner of 1995 Indianapolis 500, born St. Jean d'Iberville, Quebec, April 9, 1971.

APRIL 10 — FRIDAY

Day 100 — 265 Remaining

AMERICA'S FAMILY PET EXPO. Apr 10–12 or Apr 17–19. Pomona, CA. As urban sprawl continues to limit the space needed to keep dogs and cats as pets, rats and mice are gradually emerging as an ideal substitute. They provide all the pleasure and satisfaction of a warm, cuddly, intelligent and friendly pet companion. The American Fancy Rat and Mouse Assn (AFRMA) was founded in 1983 to promote and encourage the breeding and exhibition of fancy rats and mice. For info: AFRMA (CAE), 9230 64th St, Riverside, CA 92509-5924. Phone: (909) 685-2350. Fax: (818) 592-6319. Email: craigr@afrma.org. WWW: http://www.afrma.org/afrma

BATAAN DEATH MARCH: ANNIVERSARY. Apr 10, 1942. On this morning American and Filipino prisoners were herded together by Japanese soldiers on Mariveles Airfield on Bataan (in the Philippine islands) and began the Death March to Camp O'Donnell, near Cabanatuan. During the six-day march they were given only one bowl of rice. More than 5,200 Americans and many more Filipinos lost their lives in the course of the march.

BOOTH, WILLIAM: BIRTH ANNIVERSARY. Apr 10, 1829. General William Booth, founder of the movement that became known, in 1878, as the Salvation Army, was born at Nottingham, England, on Apr 10, 1829. Apprenticed to a pawn-broker at the age of 13, Booth experienced firsthand the misery of poverty. He broke with conventional church religion and established a quasi-military religious organization with military uniforms and ranks. Recruiting from the poor, from converted criminals and from many other social outcasts, his organization grew rapidly and its influence spread from England to the US and to most other countries. Booth was the author of *In Darkest England* and *The Way Out*. At revivals in slum areas the itinerant evangelist offered help for the poor, homes for the homeless, sobriety for alcoholics, rescue homes for women and girls, training centers and legal aid. Booth died at London, England, Aug 20, 1912. See "Salvation Army Founder's Day" (below).

BRAHMS "REQUIEM" PREMIERE: ANNIVERSARY. Apr 10, 1868. Composer Johannes Brahms fortified his reputation as one of the leading figures in 19th-century German Romantic music with the success of his *Requiem*, which premiered at Bremen Cathedral on this date. The peaceful choral piece, at turns both melancholy and exuberant, is one of the more recognized and often-sung funerary works in the musical canon.

COMMODORE PERRY DAY. Apr 10. Matthew Calbraith Perry, commodore in the US Navy, negotiator of first treaty between US and Japan (Mar 31, 1854). Born Apr 10, 1794. Died Mar 4, 1858.

CONNORS, CHUCK (KEVIN JOSEPH): BIRTH ANNIVERSARY. Apr 10, 1921. "The Rifleman" of television fame, Chuck Connors played that role from 1958 to 1963. His portrayal of a slave owner in the miniseries *Roots* won him an Emmy nomination. Connors acted in more than 45 films and appeared on many TV series and specials. He played professional basketball and baseball before becoming an actor. Born at Brooklyn, NY; died Nov 10, 1992, at Los Angeles.

ENGLAND: DEVIZES TO WESTMINSTER INTERNATIONAL CANOE RACE. Apr 10–13. Starts from Wharf Car Park, Wharf St, Devizes, Wiltshire. Canoes race along 125 miles of the Kennet and Avon canals and the River Thames, ending at County Hall Steps, Westminster Bridge Rd, London. Est attendance: 6,000. For info: Paul Owen, 14 Milldown Ave, Goring-on-Thames, Reading, Berkshire, England RG8 0AS. Phone: (44) (149) 187-2042.

FESTIVAL OF FLOWERS. Apr 10–May 10. Biltmore Estate, Asheville, NC. A Victorian celebration of spring with floral displays filling each room of Biltmore House. Call for a schedule of events. Est attendance: 86,000. For info: The Biltmore Estate, 1 N Pack Sq, Asheville, NC 28801. Phone: (800) 543-2961. Email: www.marketing@biltmore.com. WWW: http://www.biltmore.com

FIRST PGA CHAMPIONSHIP: ANNIVERSARY. Apr 10, 1916. The recently formed Professional Golfer's Association of America held its first championship at Siwanoy golf course in Bronxville, NY. The trophy and the lion's share of the $2,580 purse were won by British golfer Jim Barnes.

GOOD EGG TREASURE HUNT. Apr 10–11. Good Zoo, Oglebay, Wheeling, WV. Treasure hunt and magic shows. Annually, the Friday and Saturday before Easter. Est attendance: 3,400. For info: Penny Miller, Zoo Dir, Good Zoo, Oglebay, Wheeling, WV 26003. Phone: (304) 243-4027. Fax: (304) 243-4110. WWW: http://wvweb.com/oglebay

GOOD FRIDAY. Apr 10. Observed in commemoration of the crucifixion. Oldest Christian celebration. Possible corruption of "God's Friday." Observed in some manner by most Christian sects and as public holiday or part holiday in Delaware, Florida, Hawaii, Illinois, Indiana, New Jersey, North Carolina, Pennsylvania and Tennessee.

☆ ☆ ☆

GREAT PLAINS ROWING CHAMPIONSHIPS XIV. Apr 10–11. Lake Shawnee, Topeka, KS. 14th annual 60-event rowing regatta for high school, college, and master age oarspeople. Annually, on income tax weekend. Sponsors: US Rowing and many other groups. Est attendance: 12,000. For info: Don Craig, 4336 SE 25th St Terrace, Topeka, KS 66605. Phone: (913) 233-9951. Fax: (913) 233-9952. Email: 74452,410@compuserve.com.

GROTIUS, HUGO: BIRTH ANNIVERSARY. Apr 10, 1583. Anniversary of the birth of Hugo Grotius, the Dutch theologian, attorney, scholar and statesman whose beliefs profoundly influenced American thinking, especially with regard to the conscience of humanity. Born at Delft, Holland, Apr 10, 1583, Grotius was long an exile from his own country. He died at Rostock, Germany, Aug 28, 1645.

LIBERATION OF BUCHENWALD CONCENTRATION CAMP: ANNIVERSARY. Apr 10, 1945. Buchenwald, north of Weimar, Germany, was entered by Allied troops on this date. It was the first of the Nazi concentration camps to be liberated. It had been established in 1937, and about 56,000 people died there.

MAJIC 95.1 BODACIOUS BUNNY HUNT. Apr 10. Franke Park, Ft Wayne, IN. Inflatable bunnies are hidden all around the park. Each bunny is worth a specific number of points. Contestants have one minute to hunt for bunnies. The one with the most points wins an Easter brunch and a chocolate bunny! Annually, the Friday prior to Easter. Est attendance: 200. For info: Barb Richards, Asst Program Dir, WAJI Radio, 347 W Berry, Ste 600, Ft Wayne, IN 46802. Phone: (219) 423-3676. Fax: (219) 422-5266. WWW: http://waji.com

NATIONAL SIBLINGS DAY. Apr 10. To honor all brothers and sisters who are living and memorialize those who have died. Created by Claudia A. Evart of New York City in memory of her sister Lisette and brother Alan. Annually, Apr 10. For info: Claudia A. Evart, The Siblings Day Committtee, 30 Park Ave, Ste Z-P, New York, NY 10016-3833. Phone: (212) 779-2227.

OZARK UFO CONFERENCE. Apr 10–12. Inn of the Ozarks Conference Center, Eureka Springs, AR. 10th annual meeting of researchers from various states and foreign countries to inform the public of the latest news concerning UFOs. Speakers include authors of books on the subject and people who have investigated UFO cases; program includes audiovisual presentations of UFO evidence. Est attendance: 500. For info: Lucius Farish, Ozark UFO Conference, # 2 Caney Valley Drive, Plumerville, AR 72127-8725. Phone: (501) 354-2558.

PASSOVER BEGINS AT SUNDOWN. Apr 10. See "Pesach" (Apr 11).

PERKINS, FRANCES: BIRTH ANNIVERSARY. Apr 10. First woman member of a US presidential cabinet. Born at Boston, MA, Apr 10, 1880. Appointed secretary of labor by President Franklin D. Roosevelt in 1933, a post in which she served until 1945. She was married in 1915 to Paul Caldwell Wilson, but used her maiden name in public life. Died at New York, NY, May 14, 1965.

PULITZER, JOSEPH: BIRTH ANNIVERSARY. Apr 10. American journalist, founder of the Pulitzer Prizes, born at Budapest, Hungary, on Apr 10, 1847. Died at Charleston, SC, Oct 29, 1911. Pulitzer Prizes awarded annually since 1917. Write for entry and deadline info. (Please specify Book, Journalism, Drama or Music Competition.) For info: Pulitzer Prize Bd, 702 Journalism, Columbia Univ, New York, NY 10027. Phone: (212) 854-3841. WWW: http://www.pulitzer.org

ROBERT GRAY BECOMES FIRST AMERICAN TO CIRCUMNAVIGATE THE EARTH: ANNIVERSARY. Apr 10, 1790. When Robert Gray docked the *Columbia* in Boston Harbor on this day, he became the first American to circumnavigate the earth. He sailed from Boston, MA, in Sept 1787, to trade with Indians of the Pacific Northwest. From there he sailed to China and then continued around the world. His 42,000-mile journey opened trade between New England and the Pacific Northwest and helped the US establish claims to the Oregon Territory.

April 1998

S	M	T	W	T	F	S
			1	2	3	4
5	6	7	8	9	10	11
12	13	14	15	16	17	18
19	20	21	22	23	24	25
26	27	28	29	30		

SAFETY PIN PATENTED: ANNIVERSARY. Apr 10, 1849. Walter Hunt of New York patented the first safety pin.

SALVATION ARMY FOUNDER'S DAY. Apr 10, 1829. Birth anniversary of William Booth, a Methodist minister who began an evangelical ministry in the East End of London in 1865 and established mission stations to feed and house the poor. In 1878 he changed the name of the organization to the Salvation Army. Booth was born at Nottingham, England; he died at London on Aug 20, 1912. See also: "Booth, William: Birth Anniversary" (Apr 10).

STOCK EXCHANGE HOLIDAY (GOOD FRIDAY). Apr 10. The holiday schedules for the various exchanges are subject to change if relevant rules, regulations or exchange policies are revised. If you have questions, phone: American Stock Exchange (212) 306-1000; Chicago Board of Trade (312) 435-3500; Chicago Board of Options Exchange (312) 786-5600; New York Stock Exchange (212) 656-2065; Pacific Stock Exchange (415) 393-4000; Philadelphia Stock Exchange (215) 496-5000.

UNITED KINGDOM: GOOD FRIDAY BANK HOLIDAY. Apr 10. Bank and public holiday in England, Wales, Scotland and Northern Ireland.

WOODWARD, ROBERT BURNS: BIRTH ANNIVERSARY. Apr 10, 1917. Nobel Prize-winning (1965) Harvard University science professor whose special field of study was molecular structure of complex organic compounds. Called "one of the most outstanding scientific minds of the century." Born at Boston, MA, Apr 10, 1917. Died July 8, 1979.

WORLD GRITS FESTIVAL. Apr 10–12. St. George, SC. Come join in the family fun at this unique festival. Plenty of food, entertainment, amusement rides, a parade, merchandise exhibits, sports events and much more. Est attendance: 45,000. For info: World Grits Festival, PO Box 787, St. George, SC 29477. Phone: (803) 563-3255.

BIRTHDAYS TODAY

Kenneth ("Babyface") Edmonds, 41, pop performer and song writer, born Indianapolis, IN, Apr 10, 1957.

David Halberstam, 64, author (*The Best and the Brightest, The Summer of Forty-Nine*), born New York, NY, Apr 10, 1934.

John Earl Madden, 62, sportscaster, former football coach, born Austin, MN, Apr 10, 1936.

Joe Don Meredith, 60, former sportscaster, actor and football player, born Mount Vernon, TX, Apr 10, 1938.

Harry Morgan (Harry Bratsburg), 83, actor (Emmy for Colonel Potter on "M*A*S*H"; Bill Gannon on "Dragnet"), born Detroit, MI, Apr 10, 1915.

Steven Seagal, 47, actor, producer (*Hard to Kill, On Deadly Ground*), born Lansing, MI, Apr 10, 1951.

Omar Sharif (Michael Shalhoub), 66, actor (*Lawrence of Arabia, Dr. Zhivago*), born Alexandria, Egypt, Apr 10, 1932.

Paul Edward Theroux, 57, author (*The Mosquito Coast, Millroy the Magician*), born Medford, MS, Apr 10, 1941.

Max Von Sydow, 69, actor (*The Seventh Seal, The Emigrants*), born Lund, Sweden, Apr 10, 1929.

APRIL 11 — SATURDAY

Day 101 — 264 Remaining

BARBERSHOP QUARTET DAY. Apr 11. Commemorates the gathering of some 26 persons in Tulsa, OK, on Apr 11, 1938, and the founding there of the Society for the Preservation and Encouragement of Barbershop Quartet Singing in America.

BLISS, LIZZIE "LILLIE": BIRTH ANNIVERSARY. Apr 11, 1864. Lizzie "Lillie" Bliss was born at Boston, MA. She was one of the three founders (all women) of the Museum of Modern Art in New York City in 1929. She died on March 12, 1931, at New York City.

BOLIN, JANE MATILDA: BIRTHDAY. Apr 11, 1908. Jane Matilda Bolin, born at Poughkeepsie, NY, was the first black woman to graduate from the Yale School of Law (1931) and went on to become the first black woman judge in the US. She served as assistant corporation counsel for the city of New York before being appointed to the city's Domestic Relations Court and the Family Court of the State of New York.

CHINCOTEAGUE ISLAND EASTER DECOY SHOW. Apr 11–12. Chincoteague Island, VA. Wildfowl carving and wildlife art exhibits. Annually, Easter weekend. Est attendance: 2,500. For info: Jackie Russell, Chincoteague Chamber of Commerce, Box 258, Chincoteague Island, VA 23336. Phone: (757) 336-6161. Fax: (757) 336-1242. Email: pony@shore.intercom.net. WWW: http://www.intercom.net/local/chincoteague

CIMARRON TERRITORY CELEBRATION. Apr 11–19. Beaver, OK. Shoot-out, parade, talent show, biggest and heaviest cow chip contest, Cow Chip Chili Cook-Off, Cow Chip Classic Races. 29th annual "World Cow Chip Throwing Championship®" Contest on Apr 19. Antiques, coins, guns and crafts show. Est attendance: 4,500. For info: Rita Marshall, Secy, Beaver Chamber of Commerce, PO Box 878, Beaver, OK 73932. Phone: (405) 625-4726.

CIVIL RIGHTS ACT OF 1968: 30th ANNIVERSARY. Apr 11, 1968. On Apr 11, 1968, exactly one week after the assassination of Martin Luther King, Jr, the Civil Rights Act of 1968 (protecting civil rights workers, expanding the rights of Native Americans and providing antidiscrimination measures in housing) was signed into law by President Lyndon B. Johnson, who said: " . . . the proudest moments of my presidency have been times such as this when I have signed into law the promises of a century."

CYPRUS: THE PROCESSION OF ICON OF SAINT LAZARUS. Apr 11. Larnaca, Cyprus. Annually, the day before Easter Sunday.

DOGWOOD FESTIVAL. Apr 11–26. Lewiston, ID. Art show, quilt show, arts and crafts fair, wine and beer tasting, garden tours, concerts and plays. Many sports and recreational events. Est attendance: 40,000. For info: Lewis-Clark Center for Arts & History, 415 Main, Lewiston, ID 83501. Phone: (208) 799-2243. Fax: (208) 799-2850.

EASTER BEACH RUN. Apr 11. Daytona Beach, FL. The 30th annual beach run on "the world's most famous beach" includes a 4-mile run for 28 age divisions and a 2-mile run for youth 11 years old and younger. Est attendance: 2,000. For info: Easter Beach Run, Daytona Beach Leisure Services Dept, PO Box 2451, Daytona Beach, FL 32115-2451. Phone: (904) 258-3169. Fax: (904) 239-6550.

EASTER BUNNY BOOGIE. Apr 11. Aiken, SC. The Easter Bunny Boogie is a noncompetitive Easter egg hunt with carnival rides and games at Virginia Acres Soccer Field. Annually, the Saturday before Easter. Est attendance: 700. For info: Easter Bunny Boogie, City of Aiken Parks and Recreation, Odell Weeks Center, 1700 Whiskey Rd, Aiken, SC 29803. Phone: (803) 642-7649. Fax: (803) 642-7639.

EASTER EVEN. Apr 11. The Saturday before Easter. Last day of Holy Week and of Lent.

EVERETT, EDWARD: BIRTH ANNIVERSARY. Apr 11, 1794. American statesman and orator, born at Dorcester, MA. It was Edward Everett who delivered the main address at the dedication of Gettysburg National Cemetery, Nov 19, 1863. President Abraham Lincoln also spoke at the dedication, and his brief speech (less than two minutes) has been called one of the most eloquent in the English language. Once a candidate for vice president of the US (1860), Everett died at Boston, MA, on Jan 15, 1865.

FORT PULASKI: ANNIVERSARY. Apr 11, 1862. Fort Pulaski National Monument, Tybee Island, GA. Commemorates the siege and reduction of the fort in 1862. On this date the age of masonry fortification ended and the era of rifled artillery began, with the surrender of the Confederate garrison after a 30-hour siege.

GOOSE POND COLONY DOGWOOD FESTIVAL. Apr 11–12. Goose Pond Colony, Scottsboro, AL. Two days of fun for everyone including a golf tournament, food, entertainment, boat show and RV show, arts and crafts, skydivers, Classic Car Show, triathlon, Dogwood Festival Ball and much more. Est attendance: 5,000. For info: Jo Reed Brumley, PO Box 973, Scottsboro, AL 35768. Phone: (800) 268-2884 or (205) 259-2884.

GREAT EASTER EGG SCRAMBLE. Apr 11. Cincinnati, OH. Ramble to the Zoo's scramble and enjoy watching two separate egg hunts for children up to five years of age. Treat stations will be set up throughout the park for older children. Event also includes Easter Bunny photos, a puppet show, wagon rides and an Easter Bonnet and Basket Contest. Est attendance: 6,000. For info: Events & Promo Dept, Cincinnati Zoo and Botanical Gardens, 3400 Vine St, Cincinnati, OH 45220. Phone: (513) 281-4701. Fax: (513) 559-7790. WWW: http://www.cincy.zoo.org

HAROLD WASHINGTON ELECTED FIRST BLACK MAYOR OF CHICAGO: 15th ANNIVERSARY. Apr 11, 1983. Harold Washington defeated Bernard Epton on Apr 11, 1983, and became the first black mayor of Chicago. Of the city's 1.6 million voters a record 82% voted. Washington won 51% of the votes, which split along racial lines. He was reelected in April 1987, but died suddenly seven months later at his office on Nov 25, 1987.

HUGHES, CHARLES EVANS: BIRTH ANNIVERSARY. Apr 11, 1862. Eleventh chief justice of US Supreme Court. Born at Glens Falls, NY, Apr 11, 1862. Died at Osterville, MA, Aug 27, 1948.

JOHN WILKES BOOTH ESCAPE ROUTE TOUR. Apr 11 and 25. (Also May 2 and 16, Sept 12 and 26, and Oct 10 and 17.) Clinton, MD. A 12-hour bus tour over the route used by Lincoln's assassin. Est attendance: 45. For info: Surratt House & Tavern, Box 427, Clinton, MD 20735. Phone: (301) 868-1121. Fax: (301) 868-8177.
WWW: http://www.engr.umd.edu/~clwspoon/surratt.html

JULIAN, PERCY: BIRTH ANNIVERSARY. Apr 11. Percy Julian, producer of a synthetic progesterone using soy beans, was born Apr 11, 1899, at Montgomery, AL. He also developed a cheaper method of producing cortisone, a drug to treat glaucoma and a chemical foam to fight petroleum fires. Percy Julian died Apr 19, 1975, at Waukegan, IL.

MERRIAM, EVE: DEATH ANNIVERSARY. Apr 11, 1992. A poet, playwright and author of more than 50 books for both adults and children. Eve Merriam's works, which often focused on feminism, include *It Doesn't Always Have to Rhyme, Blackberry Ink, After Nora Slammed the Door: The Women's Unfinished Revolution, Halloween ABC, Mommies at Work* and a book of urban poems attacked by authorities as glamorizing crime, *The Urban Mother Goose*. For the stage she penned the musical *The Club*, set in an all-male private club with conversations centering on derogatory remarks about women, in which all the male characters are played by women. Her play *Out of Our Father's House* portrayed the lives of American women, and in 1978 it was presented at the White House as well as on public television's "Great Performances" series. She also wrote the first documentary on women's rights for network TV, *We the Women*. She died at New York City.

MOON PHASE: FULL MOON. Apr 11. Moon enters Full Moon phase at 6:23 PM, EDT.

PESACH or PASSOVER. Apr 11–18. Hebrew calendar dates: Nisan 15–22, 5758. Apr 11, the first day of Passover, begins an eight-day celebration of the delivery of the Jews from slavery in Egypt. Unleavened bread (matzoh) is eaten at this time.

POLE, PEDAL, PADDLE. Apr 11. Jackson, WY. The original relay race of this kind. Alpine skiing, cross-country skiing, biking and boating from Teton Village to the Snake River. Sponsor: Jackson Hole Ski Club. For info: Jackson Hole Chamber of Commerce, Box E, Jackson, WY 83001. Phone: (307) 733-3316. Fax: (307) 733-5585.

RABBITT ROMP. Apr 11. Metro Washington Park Zoo, Portland, OR. Celebration of rabbits, eggs and spring. For info: Events Coord, Metro Washington Park Zoo, 4001 SW Canyon Rd, Portland, OR 97221-2799. Phone: (503) 226-1561. Fax: (503) 220-5754.

REMEMBRANCE DAY. Apr 11. A special day to remember a loved one who has died. A way to say "I still love you; I have not forgotten" by planting a tree, performing community service, saying a prayer, etc. Send an LSASE for info. Annually, the Saturday before Easter. For info: Chaplain Mike Miller, Happy Days Ministries, 35 Hilcreek Blvd, Charleston, SC 29412.

SPACE MILESTONE: *APOLLO 13* (US). Apr 11, 1970. Launched on this date. Astronauts Lovell, Haise and Swigert endangered when oxygen tank ruptured. Planned moon landing canceled. Details of accident made public and world shared concern for crew who splashed down successfully in Pacific Apr 17.

SPELMAN COLLEGE ESTABLISHED: ANNIVERSARY. Apr 11, 1881. Spelman College, with funding from the Rockefeller family, opened its doors for the first time with the purpose of educating young African-American women. The institution, located in Atlanta, GA, was dubbed "the Radcliffe for Negro women."

STRAWBERRY HILL RACES. Apr 11. Fairgrounds on Strawberry Hill, Richmond, VA. Annual steeplechase featuring a week of festivities leading up to the event. Elegant, yet fun, pre-race party and tailgate competition on race day. $73,000 in purses. Sponsored by Atlantic Rural Exposition, Inc. Benefits the Richmond Symphony. Est attendance: 22,000. For info: Sue Mullins, Equine Dir, Strawberry Hill Races, PO Box 26805, Richmond, VA 23261. Phone: (804) 228-3238. Fax: (804) 228-3252.

UGANDA: LIBERATION DAY. Apr 11. Republic of Uganda celebrates anniversary of "overthrow of Idi Amin's dictatorship," on Apr 11, 1979.

WHOOPING CRANE RUN. Apr 11. Fulton Navigation Park, Rockport, TX. 10th annual. Two-mile walk, 5K and 10K runs, plus ½-K run for kids seven and under. For info: Rockport Fulton YMCA, 104 N Church St, Rockport, TX 78382. Phone: (512) 790-9622. Fax: (512) 790-9696.

YMCA HEALTHY KIDS DAY. Apr 11. To promote the healthiness of children nationwide. For info: YMCA of the USA, 101 N Wacker Dr, Chicago, IL 60606. Phone: (312) 269-1198 or (312) 977-9063.

BIRTHDAYS TODAY

Tony Brown, 65, journalist, host for WLIB-AM show "Tony Brown," born Charleston, WV, Apr 11, 1933.

Oleg Cassini, 85, fashion designer, born Paris, France, Apr 11, 1913.

Joel Grey (Joe Katz), 66, actor (Oscar for *Cabaret; The Seven Per Cent Solution*), born Cleveland, OH, Apr 11, 1932.

Bill Irwin, 48, actor, choreographer (*The Regard of Flight*), born Santa Monica, CA, Apr 11, 1950.

Ethel Kennedy, 70, widow of Robert Kennedy, born Greenwich, CT, Apr 11, 1928.

April 1998

S	M	T	W	T	F	S
			1	2	3	4
5	6	7	8	9	10	11
12	13	14	15	16	17	18
19	20	21	22	23	24	25
26	27	28	29	30		

Louise Lasser, 59, actress ("Mary Hartman, Mary Hartman"), born New York, NY, Apr 11, 1939.

Peter Riegert, 51, actor (*Local Hero, Crossing Delancey*), born New York, NY, Apr 11, 1947.

Bret William Saberhagen, 34, baseball player, born Chicago Heights, IL, Apr 11, 1964.

Jean-Claude Servan-Schreiber, 80, journalist, author (*The Chosen and the Choice*), born Paris, France, Apr 11, 1918.

APRIL 12 — SUNDAY

Day 102 — 263 Remaining

ANNIVERSARY OF THE BIG WIND. Apr 12. Mount Washington, NH. The highest-velocity natural wind ever recorded occurred on the morning of Apr 12, 1934, at the Mount Washington, NH, Observatory. Three weather observers, Wendell Stephenson, Alexander McKenzie and Salvatore Pagliuca, observed and recorded the phenomenon in which gusts reached 231 miles per hour—"the strongest natural wind ever recorded on the earth's surface." The 50th anniversary was observed at the site in 1984, with the three original observers participating in the ceremony.

ATTACK ON FORT SUMTER: ANNIVERSARY. Apr 12. After months of escalating tension, Major Robert Anderson refused to evacuate Fort Sumter in Charleston, SC. On April 12, 1861, Confederate troops under the command of General P.T. Beauregard opened fire on the harbor fort at 4:30 AM and continued until Major Anderson surrendered on Apr 13. No lives were lost despite the firing of some 40,000 shells in the first major engagement of the American Civil War.

BILLINGS, JOHN SHAW: BIRTH ANNIVERSARY. Apr 12, 1838. American librarian and army physician. Born Apr 12, 1838. Died Mar 11, 1913.

BIRMINGHAM FESTIVAL OF ARTS' SALUTE TO BRAZIL. Apr 12–26. Birmingham, AL. A salute to the arts and culture of Brazil. This festival, now in its 48th year, celebrates the arts and culture of a different country each year. Est attendance: 300,000. For info: Iris Gross, Exec Dir, Festival of Arts, 205 20th St N, Birmingham, AL 35203. Phone: (205) 252-7652. Fax: (205) 252-7656. Email: office@bhamfestarts.org.
WWW: http://www.bhamfeststarts.org

CLAY, HENRY: BIRTH ANNIVERSARY. Apr 12, 1777. Statesman, born at Hanover County, VA. Was the Speaker of the House of Representatives and later became the leader of the new Whig party. He was defeated for the presidency three times. Clay died at Washington, DC, June 29, 1852.

EASTER SUNDAY. Apr 12. Commemorates the Resurrection of Christ. Most joyous festival of the Christian year. The date of Easter, a movable feast, is derived from the lunar calendar: the first Sunday following the first full moon on or after the vernal equinox (Mar 20)—always between Mar 22 and Apr 25. The Council of Nicaea (AD 325) prescribed that Easter be celebrated on the Sunday after Passover, as that feast's date had been established in Jesus' time. After 1582, when Pope Gregory XIII introduced the Gregorian calendar, Orthodox Christians continued to use the Julian calendar, so that Easter can sometimes be as much as five weeks apart in the Western and Eastern churches. Many other dates in the Christian year are derived from the date of Easter. An ecumenical group met in 1997 to propose a way that Eastern and Western Christians could set the same date for Easter, starting in 2001 (when the Eastern and Western dates for Easter happen to coincide). Easter in 1999 will be Apr 4; in 2000 will be Apr 23; in 2001 will be Apr 15. See also: "Orthodox Easter Sunday or Pascha."

EASTER SUNRISE SERVICE. Apr 12. Chimney Rock Park, Chimney Rock, NC. Celebrate the glory of Easter at this 43rd annual nondenominational community worship service overlooking beautiful Lake Lure. Gates open at 4:30 AM. No admission charge. Est attendance: 1,500. For info: Mary Jaeger-Gale,

Mktg Mgr, PO Box 39, Chimney Rock, NC 28720. Phone: (800) 277-9611 or (704) 625-9611. Fax: (704) 625-9610. Email: visit@chimneyrockpark.com. WWW: http://www.chimneyrockpark.com

FREE AFRICAN SOCIETY FOUNDED: ANNIVERSARY. Apr 12, 1787. Richard Allen and Absalom Jones were both members of St. George's Methodist Church in Philadelphia when on one particular Sunday, all of the black parishioners were ordered to leave their seats and attend segregated services from the balcony. Allen and Jones subsequently founded the Free African Society, the nation's first independent black social group. The Free African Society arranged activities, aid and relief operations and assistance for widows and orphans. Furthermore, it served as an organizational network allowing free Negroes from across the country to communicate.

HALIFAX INDEPENDENCE DAY. Apr 12. North Carolina. Anniversary of the resolution adopted by the Provincial Congress of North Carolina at Halifax, NC, Apr 12, 1776, authorizing the delegates from North Carolina to the Continental Congress to vote for a Declaration of Independence.

MARKSVILLE EASTER EGG KNOCKING CONTEST. Apr 12. Marksville, LA. Competition among owners of chicken, goose, turkey and guinea eggs, which have been boiled and dyed. Annually, on Easter Sunday 9 AM– noon. Est attendance: 300. For info: Chamber of Commerce, Box 365, Marksville, LA 71351. Phone: (318) 253-9222.

MERRIE MONARCH FESTIVAL (WITH WORLD'S LARGEST HULA COMPETITION). Apr 12–18. Hilo, HI. Cultural event honoring King David Kalakaua. Festival culminates with the world's largest hula competition. Hawaii's finest hula schools compete in ancient and modern divisions. Annually, beginning on Easter Sunday. Est attendance: 6,000. For info: Dorothy Thompson, Hawaii Naniloa Hotel, Merrie Monarch Office, 93 Banyan Dr, Hilo, HI 96720. Phone: (808) 935-9168.

MORAVIAN EASTER SUNRISE SERVICE. Apr 12. Winston-Salem, NC. Outdoor religious service featuring Moravian bands playing in streets to awaken sleepers. Service begins in Salem Square, and concludes in God's Acre, the Moravian Graveyard, at daybreak. Est attendance: 12,500. For info: Salem Congregation, 459 S Church St, Winston-Salem, NC 27101-5314. Phone: (910) 722-6504. Fax: (910) 723-1029.

NATIONAL GARDEN WEEK. Apr 12–18. To recognize and honor the 78 million Americans who eagerly garden each year. These American gardeners enhance and improve the environment with their efforts. Annually, the second full week of April. For info: Natl Garden Bureau, 1311 Butterfield Rd, Ste 310, Downers Grove, IL 60515. Phone: (630) 963-0770.

NATIONAL MINORITY CANCER AWARENESS WEEK. Apr 12–18. For info: National Cancer Information Service, 550 N Broadway, Ste 300, Baltimore, MD 21205. Phone: (800) 4-CANCER.

NATIONAL WEEK OF THE OCEAN. Apr 12–18. A week focusing on humanity's interdependence with the ocean, asking each of us to appreciate, protect and use the ocean wisely. 15th annual. For info: Pres/Co-Founder, Cynthia Hancock, Natl Week of the Ocean, Inc, PO Box 179, Fort Lauderdale, FL 33302. Phone: (954) 462-5573.

NATIONAL WOMEN'S NUTRITION WEEK. Apr 12–15. Founded by Dr. Lois M. Vanderhoof, of Applied Nutrition Concepts. To recognize the importance and value of health in all phases of a woman's life. A woman's biochemistry needs nutritional support when on the pill, during pregnancy, during lactation, when she is under stress and going through menopause. This week is designed to educate women about the importance of nutrition for their ongoing health and well-being. For info: Dr Lois M Vanderhoof, Applied Nutrition Concepts, 2828 W Parker Rd, #208, Plano, TX 75075. Phone: (972) 612-5505. Email: lmvplano@flash.net. WWW: http://www.healit.com

150 YEARS OF ROBINSON FAMILY HATS: EXHIBIT. Apr 12 (also every Sunday through May). Granville Life-Style Museum, Granville, OH. Family members of the late Hubert and Oese Robinson saved their bonnets, hats, infant caps and headwear of all descriptions from the 1820s to the 1970s. All on exhibit. Annually, the second Sunday in April through end of May. For info: Gina Hughes, Adm Asst, Granville Life-Style Museum, H.D. Robinson House, 121 S Main St, Granville, OH 43023.

ORTHODOX PALM SUNDAY. Apr 12. Celebration of Christ's entry into Jerusalem, when His way was covered with palms by the multitudes. Beginning of Holy Week in the Orthodox Church.

★**PAN AMERICAN WEEK.** Apr 12–18. Presidential Proclamation customarily issued as "Pan American Day and Pan American Week." Always issued for the week including Apr 14, except in 1965, from 1946 through 1948, 1955 through 1977, and 1979.

POLIO VACCINE: ANNIVERSARY. Apr 12, 1955. Anniversary of announcement in 1955 that the polio vaccine developed by American physician Dr. Jonas E. Salk was "safe, potent and effective." Incidence of the dreaded infantile paralysis, or poliomyelitis, declined by 95% following introduction of preventive vaccines.

ROOSEVELT, FRANKLIN DELANO: DEATH ANNIVERSARY. Apr 12, 1945. With the end of WWII only months away, the nation and the world were stunned by the sudden death of the president shortly into his fourth term of office. Roosevelt, 32nd president of the US (Mar 4, 1933–Apr 12, 1945), was the only president to serve more than two terms—he was elected to four consecutive terms. He died at Warm Springs, GA.

SPACE MILESTONE: *COLUMBIA STS 1* (US) FIRST SHUTTLE FLIGHT. Apr 12, 1981. First flight of Shuttle *Columbia*. Two astronauts (John Young and Robert Crippen), on first manned US space mission since *Apollo-Soyuz* in July 1976, spent 54 hours in space (36 orbits of Earth) before landing at Edwards Air Force Base, CA, Apr 14.

SPACE MILESTONE: *DISCOVERY* (US). Apr 12, 1985. On its 16th mission (from Kennedy Space Center, FL) shuttle *Discovery* was launched carrying a US Senator (Jake Garn) as a member of its crew of seven.

SPACE MILESTONE: *VOSTOK I*, FIRST MAN IN SPACE. Apr 12, 1961. Yuri Gagarin became the first man in space when he made a 108-minute voyage, orbiting Earth in a 10,395-lb vehicle, *Vostok I*, launched by the USSR.

"SUGAR'IN OFF." Apr 12. Somerset, PA. Celebrates the end of the traditional maple season in the Allegheny Highlands. Tasty "Spotzas," syrup, sugar and other sweets to taste. For info: Mark Ware, Somerset Historical Center, 10649 Somerset Pike, Somerset, PA 15501. Phone: (814) 445-6077.

TALKING BOOK WEEK. Apr 12–18. To recognize volunteers and descriptive organizations who provide reading and informational services for the visually impaired and physically disabled. For info: Dawn L. Jordan, Outreach Dir, Audio Descriptive Network, 115 Brenton St, Richmond, VA 23222. Phone: (804) 321-2063.

TRUANCY LAW: ANNIVERSARY. Apr 12, 1853. The first truancy law was enacted in New York. A $50 fine was charged against parents whose children between the ages of 5 and 15 were absent from school.

"21 JUMP STREET" TV PREMIERE: ANNIVERSARY. Apr 12, 1987. Youthful big city cops bust crime in the local schools and colleges in this Fox police drama. Starred Johnny Depp as Tom Hansen; Holly Robinson as Judy Hoffs; Dustin Nguyen as H.T. Ioki; Peter DeLuise as Doug Penhall; Frederic Forrest as Captain Jenko; Steven Williams as Captain Adam Fuller; and Richard Greico as Dennis Booker. It was one of the Fox network's early hits.

WORLD'S LARGEST EASTER EGG HUNT. Apr 12. Garrison Homes, Homer, GA. Approximately 150,000 hidden eggs and 100 prize eggs. Begins at 2 PM. Free and open to all—no age limit. Est attendance: 10,000. For info: Robin Chitwood, Banks County Chamber of Commerce, PO Box 57, Homer, GA 30547. Phone: (706) 677-2108 or (800) 638-5004.

"YOUR HIT PARADE" RADIO PREMIERE: ANNIVERSARY. Apr 12, 1935. This program debuted on radio in 1935 with its countdown of the week's top songs. In 1950 it became a TV program. See also: "'Your Hit Parade' TV Premiere: Anniversary" (Oct 7).

BIRTHDAYS TODAY

David Cassidy, 48, singer ("Cherish"), actor ("The Partridge Family"), born New York, NY, Apr 12, 1950.

Beverly Cleary, 82, author of the *Ramona* series for children; winner of the Newbery Medal for *Dear Mr Henshaw*. Born at McMinnville, OR, Apr 12, 1916.

Claire Danes, 19, actress, born New York, NY, Apr 12, 1979.

Shannen Doherty, 27, actress ("Beverly Hills 90210," *Night Shift, Heathers*), born Memphis, TN, Apr 12, 1971.

Andy Garcia, 42, actor (*The Untouchables, The Godfather, Part III*), born Havana, Cuba, Apr 12, 1956.

Lionel Hampton, 85, bandleader, born Louisville, KY, Apr 12, 1913.

Herbie Hancock, 58, musician, born Chicago, IL, Apr 12, 1940.

Dan Lauria, 51, actor ("The Wonder Years," *Stakeout*), born Apr 12, 1947.

David Letterman, 51, comedian, TV talk show host ("Late Show with David Letterman"), born Indianapolis, IN, Apr 12, 1947.

Ann Miller (Lucille Ann Collier), 75, actress (*Sugar Babies, You Can't Take It with You, Easter Parade*), born Houston, TX, Apr 12, 1923.

Ed O'Neill, 52, actor ("Married . . . With Children," *Deliverance, Wayne's World*), born Youngstown, OH, Apr 12, 1946.

Scott Turow, 49, writer (*Presumed Innocent, The Burden of Proof*), born Chicago, IL, Apr 12, 1949.

April 1998

S	M	T	W	T	F	S
			1	2	3	4
5	6	7	8	9	10	11
12	13	14	15	16	17	18
19	20	21	22	23	24	25
26	27	28	29	30		

APRIL 13 — MONDAY

Day 103 — 262 Remaining

BECKETT, SAMUEL: BIRTH ANNIVERSARY. Apr 13, 1906. Author, critic and playwright born at Foxrock, County Dublin, Ireland. Writing in both French and English, Samuel Beckett is best remembered for his plays, including *Waiting for Godot, Endgame, Krapp's Last Tape* and *Happy Days*. Beckett settled in Paris, France, in 1937 and served with an underground resistance group during the early years of World War II. In the years following the war he entered a period of intense creativity, producing among others the novels *Molloy, Malone Dies* and *The Unnamable* and two plays, *Eleutheria* and *Waiting for Godot*. *Waiting for Godot* received an acclaimed production at the Theatre de Babylone in Paris in January 1953, and with it Beckett achieved worldwide renown. Beckett's style involved an ever-increasing concentration on stripping writing to its bare essence. He died Dec 22, 1989, at Paris.

BUTTS, ALFRED M.: BIRTH ANNIVERSARY. Apr 13, 1899. Alfred Butts was a jobless architect in the Depression when he invented the board game Scrabble. The game was just a fad for Butts's friends until a Macy's executive saw the game being played at a resort in 1952, and the world's largest store began carrying it. Manufacturing of the game was turned over to Selchow & Righter when 35 workers were producing 6,000 sets a week. Butts received three cents per set for years. He said, "One-third went to taxes. I gave one-third away, and the other third enabled me to have an enjoyable life." Butts was born at Poughkeepsie, NY. He died Apr 4, 1993, at Rhinebeck, NY.

CASSIDY, BUTCH: BIRTH ANNIVERSARY. Apr 13, 1866. Born Robert Leroy Parker at Beaver, UT, son of Mormon pioneer Maximillian Parker, he became a notorious outlaw of the Old West, leader of The Wild Bunch gang. Some believed he died in a gun battle in Bolivia in 1909 while others are certain he returned and died in the USA. For info: Outlaw Trail History Assn and Center, 155 E Main, Vernal, UT 84078. Phone: (801) 789-0091. Fax: (801) 781-5319. Email: dburton@easilink.com.

COMPEER FRIENDSHIP WEEK. Apr 13–19. An opportunity to become a Compeer volunteer and provide a supportive friendship to a child or adult diagnosed with a mental illness. To honor friendships, Compeer affiliate programs across the country offer violets for sale to communities as well as other items that can be purchased to show support for the program. Est attendance: 4,000. For info: Katey Breen, Intl Coord, Compeer, 259 Monroe Ave, Rochester, NY 14607. Phone: (800) 836-0475. Fax: (716) 325-2558. Email: compeer@Frontiernet.net. WWW: http://www.compeer.org

EASTER MONDAY. Apr 13. Holiday or bank holiday in many places, including England, Northern Ireland, Wales, Canada and North Carolina in the US.

EASTER MONDAY CELEBRATION. Apr 13. (Also Apr 20.) Portage, MI. To resurrect the old Christian custom of celebrating Easter Monday in observance of Jesus' rising from the dead, "the practical joke that God played on Satan." (Easter Monday for Eastern Christians is celebrated on Apr 20.) Churches and prayer groups nationwide participate. Some churches celebrate on Bright Sunday ("Holy Humor Sunday"), the Sunday after Easter. For info: George Golditrap, The Fellowship of Merry Christians, Inc, PO Box 895, Portage, MI 49081-0895. Phone: (615) 868-1969. Email: joyfulnz@aol.com. WWW: http://kalamazoo.inetmi.com/cities/kazoo/tjnoise/thnoise.html

EGG SALAD WEEK. Apr 13–19. Dedicated to the many delicious uses for all of the Easter eggs that have been cooked, colored, hidden and found. Annually, the full week after Easter. For info: American Egg Bd, Elisa Maloberti, 1460 Renaissance Dr, Park Ridge, IL 60068. Email: aebnet@aol.com. WWW: http://www.aeb.org

ENGLAND: HALLATON BOTTLE KICKING. Apr 13. Hallaton, Leicestershire. Ancient custom dating back at least 600 years. Annually, on Easter Monday.

FIRST BASEBALL STRIKE ENDS: ANNIVERSARY. Apr 13. On Apr 13, 1972, major league baseball players and owners agreed on a settlement in which owners added an additional $500,000 to the players' pension fund. This ended the first baseball strike, which had begun Apr 5 when the season opener was canceled.

GOLDENBELLS FESTIVAL. Apr 13–May 3. Hamden, CT. Concerts, festivals, nature walks, athletic competitions and more. For info: Goldenbells Festival, (203) 281-4768 or Greater New Haven Conv & Visitors Bureau, One Long Wharf Dr, New Haven, CT 06511. Phone: (203) 777-8550 or (800) 332-STAY. Fax: (203) 782-7755.

GREAT CHICAGO FLOOD: ANNIVERSARY. Apr 13, 1992. On this morning Chicagoans awoke to one of the most unusual disasters of modern times: the Chicago River broke through a rupture in an old underground freight tunnel wall, sending millions of gallons of water flooding into the tunnel system of the downtown business district. The water filled the freight tunnels and began pouring into basements of buildings that previously had been connected to the tunnel system. The greater Loop area had to be evacuated as electricity was cut off ahead of the rising water. A hectic effort mounted to plug the leak in the river eventually succeeded, even though the exact nature of the damage could not be ascertained. Once the flow of water had stopped, the city began the slow and expensive process of draining the water from beneath its structures and trying to cope with the losses due to what for most Chicagoans was an invisible disaster.

JEFFERSON, THOMAS: BIRTH ANNIVERSARY. Apr 13, 1743. Third president of the US (Mar 4, 1801–Mar 3, 1809). Born at Albermarle County, VA, Apr 13, 1743. Jefferson, who died at Charlottesville, VA, on July 4, 1826, wrote his own epitaph: "Here was buried Thomas Jefferson, author of the Declaration of American Independence, of the statute of Virginia for religious freedom, and father of the University of Virginia." A holiday in Alabama and Oklahoma.

★**JEFFERSON, THOMAS: BIRTH ANNIVERSARY.** Apr 13. Presidential Proclamation 2276, of Mar 21, 1938, covers all succeeding years. (Pub Res No. 60 of Aug 16, 1937.)

LUXEMBOURG: EMAISHEN. Apr 13. Luxembourg (city). Popular traditional market and festival on the "Marche-aux-Poissons." Young lovers present each other with earthenware articles, sold only on this day. Annually, on Easter Monday.

***SILENT SPRING* PUBLICATION: ANNIVERSARY.** Apr 13, 1962. Rachel Carson's *Silent Spring*, released this date, warned humankind that for the first time in history every person is subjected to contact with dangerous chemicals from conception until death. Ms Carson painted a vivid picture of how chemicals—used in many ways but particularly in pesticides—have upset the balance of nature, undermining the survival of countless species. This enormously popular and influential book became a softspoken battle cry to protect our natural surroundings. Ms Carson's intention was to shock and stir people into action; and, indeed, the publication of this book might well have signaled the beginning of the environmental movement.

SINGAPORE: SONGKRAN FESTIVAL. Apr 13–15. Public holiday. Thai water festival. To welcome the new year the image of Buddha is bathed with holy or fragrant water, and lustral water is sprinkled on celebrants. Joyous event, especially observed at Thai Buddhist temples. (Dates of observance subject to alteration.)

SWITZERLAND: EGG RACES. Apr 13. Rural northwest Swiss Easter Monday custom. Race among competitors carrying large numbers of eggs while running to neighboring villages.

UNITED KINGDOM: EASTER MONDAY BANK HOLIDAY. Apr 13. Bank and public holiday in England, Wales and Northern Ireland. (Scotland not included.)

UNIVERSITY OF VIRGINIA FOUNDER'S DAY. Apr 13. Charlottesville, VA. Celebration marks the 255th anniversary of the birth (Apr 13, 1743) of the University's founder, Thomas Jefferson. For info: University of Virginia, Booker House, Univ News Office, Box 9018, Charlottesville, VA 22906-9018.

WHITE HOUSE EASTER EGG ROLL. Apr 13. Traditionally held at executive mansion's south lawn on Easter Monday. Custom said to have started at Capitol grounds about 1810. Transferred to White House lawn in 1870s.

BIRTHDAYS TODAY

Peabo Bryson, 47, singer, born Greenville, SC, Apr 13, 1951.
Ben Nighthorse Campbell, 65, US Senator (R, Colorado), born Auburn, CA, Apr 13, 1933.
Jack Casady, 54, musician, born Washington, DC, Apr 13, 1944.
Bill Conti, 56, composer (Oscar for *The Right Stuff*; "Dynasty," "Falcon Crest," "Inside Edition"), born Providence, RI, Apr 13, 1942.
Edward Fox, 61, actor (*The Day of the Jackal, Gandhi, The Dresser*), born London, England, Apr 13, 1937.
Al Green, 52, singer ("Let's Stay Together," "You Ought to Be with Me"), born Forrest City, AR, Apr 13, 1946.
Howard Keel (Howard Leek), 79, actor (*Annie Get Your Gun, Seven Brides for Seven Brothers*), born Gillespie, IL, Apr 13, 1919.
Madalyn Murray O'Hair, 79, atheist, lawyer, author (*Why I Am an Atheist*), born Pittsburgh, PA, Apr 13, 1919.
Ron Perlman, 48, actor ("Beauty and the Beast," *The Name of the Rose*), born New York, NY, Apr 13, 1950.
Saundra Santiago, 41, actress ("Miami Vice"), born The Bronx, NY, Apr 13, 1957.
Rick Schroder, 28, actor ("Silver Spoons," *The Champ*), born Staten Island, NY, Apr 13, 1970.
Paul Sorvino, 59, actor ("Law and Order"), born Brooklyn, NY, Apr 13, 1939.
Lyle Waggoner, 63, actor ("The Carol Burnett Show," "Wonder Woman," *Dead Women in Lingerie*), born Kansas City, KS, Apr 13, 1935.
Max M. Weinberg, 47, musician (drummer with Bruce Springsteen's E Street Band), born South Orange, NJ, Apr 13, 1951.
Eudora Welty, 89, writer (*Delta Wedding, Losing Battles*), born Jackson, MS, Apr 13, 1909.

APRIL 14 — TUESDAY

Day 104 — 261 Remaining

AMERICAN BOMBING OF LIBYA: ANNIVERSARY. Apr 14. American warplanes, on orders from President Reagan, bombed the Libyan cities of Tripoli and Benghaze at 7 PM, EST, on Apr 14, 1986 (1 AM, Apr 15, Libyan time), reportedly killing 37 persons (including the infant daughter of head of state Muammar el-Qaddafi) and wounding another 93, many of them civilians. The American raid (condemned in a US-vetoed UN resolution) was, according to President Reagan's broadcast on Apr 14, in retaliation for the Apr 5 bomb explosion at a popular West Berlin discotheque which caused the deaths of two American soldiers and a Turkish woman. See also: "Discotheque Bombing: Anniversary" (Apr 5).

CAMPBELL BECOMES FIRST AMERICAN AIR ACE: 80th ANNIVERSARY. Apr 14, 1918. Lieutenant Douglas Campbell became the first American pilot to achieve the designation of ACE when he shot down his fifth German aircraft on Apr 14, 1918.

FIRST AMERICAN ABOLITION SOCIETY FOUNDED: ANNIVERSARY. Apr 14. The first abolition organization formed in the US was The Society for the Relief of Free Negroes Unlawfully Held in Bondage, which was founded Apr 14, 1775 in Philadelphia, PA.

FIRST DICTIONARY OF AMERICAN ENGLISH PUBLISHED: ANNIVERSARY. Apr 14, 1828. Noah Webster published his *American Dictionary of the English Language* on this date.

***GRAPES OF WRATH* PUBLISHED: ANNIVERSARY.** Apr 14, 1939. John Steinbeck's novel of the Great Depression, *Grapes of Wrath*, won the 1940 Pulitzer Prize. It chronicled the mass migration to California of dispossessed farmers from the Dust Bowl region of the Great Plains.

HONDURAS: DIA DE LAS AMERICAS. Apr 14. Honduras. Pan American Day, a national holiday.

LINCOLN, ABRAHAM: ASSASSINATION ANNIVERSARY. Apr 14. President Abraham Lincoln was shot while watching a performance of *Our American Cousin* at Ford's Theatre, Washington, DC, on Apr 14, 1865. He died the following day. Assassin was John Wilkes Booth, a young actor.

NATIONAL CATHOLIC EDUCATIONAL ASSOCIATION CONVENTION AND EXPOSITION. Apr 14–17. Los Angeles Convention Center, Los Angeles, CA. Annual meeting for NCEA members and anyone working in, or interested in, the welfare of Catholic education. Est attendance: 11,000. For info: Nancy Brewer, Conv Dir, Natl Catholic Educational Assn, 1077 30th St NW, Ste 100, Washington, DC 20007. Phone: (202) 337-6232. Fax: (202) 333-6706.

★**PAN AMERICAN DAY.** Apr 14. Presidential Proclamation 1912, of May 28, 1930, had effect of covering every Apr 14 (required by Governing Board of Pan American Union). Proc 2386, Feb 12, 1940, observed Union's 50th anniversary. Proclamation issued each year since 1948.

SULLIVAN, ANNE: BIRTH ANNIVERSARY. Apr 14, 1866. Anne Sullivan became well known for "working miracles" with Helen Keller, who was blind and deaf. Nearly blind herself, Sullivan used a manual alphabet communicated by the sense of touch to teach Keller to read, write and speak and then to help her to go on to higher education. Anne Sullivan died Oct 20, 1936, at Forest Hills, NY.

April 1998

S	M	T	W	T	F	S
			1	2	3	4
5	6	7	8	9	10	11
12	13	14	15	16	17	18
19	20	21	22	23	24	25
26	27	28	29	30		

TAFT OPENED BASEBALL SEASON: ANNIVERSARY. Apr 14. On Apr 14, 1910, President William Howard Taft began a sports tradition by throwing out the first baseball of the season at an American League game between Washington and Philadelphia. Washington won 3–0.

TIN PAN SOUTH. Apr 14–18. Nashville, TN. Annual music festival sponsored by the Nashville Songwriters Association International (NSAI) celebrates songwriters and their craft. Highlights of the week include the Legendary Songwriter Concert at the historic Ryman Auditorium, related-songwriter events and golf tournament. During the rest of the week, the nation's top performing songwriters in gospel, rock and country will appear at local clubs around town. Est attendance: 5,000. For info: Tin Pan South, c/o NSAI, 15 Music Square W, Nashville, TN 37203. Phone: (615) 251-3472. Fax: (615) 256-0034. Email: nsai@edge.net. WWW: http://songs.org/nsai

TOYNBEE, ARNOLD JOSEPH: BIRTH ANNIVERSARY. Apr 14. English historian, author of monumental *Study of History*. Born at London, England, Apr 14, 1889. Died at York, England, Oct 22, 1975.

BIRTHDAYS TODAY

Julie Christie, 58, actress (*Dr. Zhivago, Petulia, Shampoo*), born Chukua, India, Apr 14, 1940.

Bradford Dillman, 68, actor (*Compulsion*, "Falcon Crest"), born San Francisco, CA, Apr 14, 1930.

Sir John Gielgud, 94, actor (*Becket, The Loved One, The Charge of the Light Brigade*), director, born London, England, Apr 14, 1904.

Anthony Michael Hall, 30, actor, comedian ("Saturday Night Live," *Sixteen Candles, The Breakfast Club*), born Boston, MA, Apr 14, 1968.

David Christopher Justice, 32, baseball player, born Cincinnati, OH, Apr 14, 1966.

Loretta Lynn, 63, singer ("Coal Miner's Daughter," "The Pill"), born Butcher's Hollow, KY, Apr 14, 1935.

Gregory Alan (Greg) Maddux, 32, baseball player, born San Angelo, TX, Apr 14, 1966.

Peter Edward (Pete) Rose, 57, former baseball player, born Cincinnati, OH, Apr 14, 1941.

Rod Steiger, 73, actor (*On the Waterfront, The Pawnbroker*; Oscar for *In the Heat of the Night*), born Westhampton, NY, Apr 14, 1925.

Emma Thompson, 39, actress (*Howard's End, Sense and Sensibility*), born London, England, Apr 14, 1959.

APRIL 15 — WEDNESDAY

Day 105 — 260 Remaining

BENTON, THOMAS HART: BIRTH ANNIVERSARY. Apr 15. Thomas Hart Benton was an artist whose work was indicative of the American style of painting known as Regionalism. His works of life in the Midwest and South were not always flattering to their subjects, but his style became known as a truly American style of painting. He was born on Apr 15, 1889, at Neosho, MO, and died at Kansas City, MO, Jan 19, 1975.

"BUCK ROGERS" TV PREMIERE: ANNIVERSARY. Apr 15, 1950. At first a radio show, "Buck Rogers" premiered on ABC with Kem Dibbs. Buck was an average American who woke up from a cave behind Niagara Falls to find himself in the year 2430. The show featured Lou Prentis as Lieutenant Wilma Deering; Harry Southern as Dr. Huer; and Harry Kingston as Black Barney Wade. Buck was later played by Robert Pastene.

CHINA: CANTON SPRING TRADE FAIR. Apr 15–May 15. The Guangzhou (Canton) Spring Trade Fair is held on the same dates each year.

FIRST MCDONALDS OPENS: ANNIVERSARY. Apr 15, 1955. The first franchised McDonalds was opened in Des Plaines, IL, by Ray Kroc, who had gotten the idea from a hamburger joint in San Bernardino, CA, run by the McDonald brothers. By the mid-1990s, there were more than 15,000 McDonalds in 70 countries.

FIRST SCHOOL FOR DEAF FOUNDED: ANNIVERSARY. Apr 15, 1817. Thomas Hopkins Gallaudet and Laurent Clerc founded the first US public school for the deaf, Connecticut Asylum for the Education and Instruction of Deaf and Dumb Persons (now the American School for the Deaf), at Hartford, CT.

"IN LIVING COLOR" TV PREMIERE: ANNIVERSARY. Apr 15, 1990. Fox's sketch comedy series was modeled after "Saturday Night Live." The show was created by Keenen Ivory Wayans. Between skits, the Fly Girls would entertain the studio audience with hip dances (actress Rosie Perez choreographed the dances before breaking into movies). The show featured Wayans, his brothers Damon and Shawn, his sister Kim, Tommy Davidson, David Alan Grier, T'Keyah "Crystal" Keymah, Kelly Coffield, Kim Coles and Jim Carrey before he was Ace Ventura. Some of the most popular recurring characters were: Homey, the embittered clown; the flammable Fire Marshall Bill; and the effeminate movie critics of "Men on Film."

INCOME TAX PAY DAY. Apr 15. A day all Americans need to know—the day by which taxpayers are supposed to make their accounting of the previous year and pay their share of the cost of government. The US Internal Revenue Service provides free forms.

LIBERACE MUSEUM FOUNDED: ANNIVERSARY. Apr 15. The Liberace Museum in Las Vegas, NV, houses "Mr Showmanship's" million-dollar stage wardrobe, rare antiques, classic cars and his collection of pianos. The museum is the key funding arm for the non-profit Liberace Foundation for the Performing and Creative Arts that provides scholarship grants for schools, colleges and universities. For info: Jamie G. James, James Agency, PR, 3630 Coldwater Canyon Ave, Studio City, CA 91604. Phone: (818) 508-4902. Fax: (818) 508-0562. Email: JamesAgy@aol.com.

LONGYEAR, JOHN MUNROE: BIRTH ANNIVERSARY. Apr 15, 1850. American capitalist, president of a bank and a button factory, landowner, philanthropist, onetime mayor of Marquette, MI. Disapproving of a railway route through Marquette, he caused his home, a stone castle-like showplace, to be torn down in 1903 and moved, stone by stone and stick by stick (in more than 190 freight cars), a distance, he said, of more than 1,300 miles, by rail, and re-erected at Brookline, MA. Born at Lansing, MI, Apr 15, 1850. Died May 28, 1922.

PEALE, CHARLES WILSON: BIRTH ANNIVERSARY. Apr 15, 1741. American portrait painter (best known for his many portraits of colonial and American Revolutionary War figures) was born in Queen Anne County, MD, Apr 15, 1741. Died at Philadelphia, PA, on Feb 22, 1827.

QUARTERLY ESTIMATED FEDERAL INCOME TAX PAYERS' DUE DATE. Apr 15. For those individuals whose fiscal year is the calendar year and who make quarterly estimated federal income tax payments, today is one of the due dates. (Jan 15, Apr 15, June 15 and Sept 15, 1998.)

SCOTTSDALE CULINARY FESTIVAL™. Apr 15–19. Scottsdale, AZ. Ten spectacular culinary events including Wine Country Brunch; Le Tour Culinaire, a progressive black-tie dinner; Culinary Authors' Luncheon featuring nationally and internationally acclaimed chefs/authors; Mayor's Culinary Cup Appetizer Competition; Great Arizona Picnic featuring 50 of the Valley's best restaurants; and more. Proceeds benefit arts education programs for youth in the community. Est attendance: 64,000. For info: Scottsdale Culinary Festival, Box 9431, Scottsdale, AZ 85252. Phone: (602) 991-6252. Fax: (602) 991-6269. Email: xcellen@aol.com.

SINKING OF THE *TITANIC*: ANNIVERSARY. Apr 15, 1912. The "unsinkable" luxury liner *Titanic* on its maiden voyage (from Southampton, England, to New York, NY) struck an iceberg just before midnight on Apr 14, 1912, and sank at 2:27 AM, Apr 15. The *Titanic* had 2,224 persons aboard. Of these, more than 1,500 were lost. About 700 people were rescued from the icy waters off Newfoundland by the liner *Carpathia*, which reached the scene about two hours after the *Titanic* went down. The sunken *Titanic* was located and photographed in Sept 1985. In July 1986, an expedition aboard the *Atlantis II*, headed by Dr. Robert D. Ballard, descended to the deck of the *Titanic* in a submersible craft, *Alvin*, and guided a robot named Jason, Jr, in a search of the ship. Two memorial bronze plaques were left on the deck of the sunken ship.

SMITH, BESSIE: BIRTH ANNIVERSARY. Apr 15, 1894. The "Empress of the Blues," Bessie Smith, was born at Chattanooga, TN (year varies as late as 1900). She was assisted in her efforts to break into show business by Ma Rainey, the first great blues singer. Her first recording was made in February 1923. Smith died of injuries she sustained in an automobile accident at Clarksdale, MS, Sept 26, 1937. It has been said that had she been white she would have received earlier medical treatment. The black hospital to which Bessie was taken after the accident is now the Riverside Hotel where legendary bluesmen have stayed since 1944.

THANK YOU SCHOOL LIBRARIAN DAY. Apr 15. Recognizes the unique contribution made by school librarians who are resource people extraordinaire, supporting the myriad educational needs of faculty, staff, students and parents *all year long*! Three cheers to all the public, private and parochial school infomaniacs whose true love of reading and lifelong learning make them great role models for kids of all ages. To help celebrate, take your school librarian to lunch, donate a book in his/her honor to the library, tell your librarian what a difference he/she has made in your life. Sponsor: "Carpe Libris" (Seize the Book), a loosely knit group of underappreciated librarians. Press packet available for $5. For info: Judyth Lessee, Organizer, Carpe Libris, PO Box 40503, Tucson, AZ 85717-0503. Phone: (520) 318-2954. Email: rinophyl@rtd.com.

WASHINGTON, HAROLD: BIRTH ANNIVERSARY. Apr 15, 1922. Illinois legislator and Mayor of Chicago (1983–1987). Born at Chicago, IL, and died there on Nov 25, 1987. Harold Washington was one of the first African-Americans to head a major US city. He was instrumental in tearing down Chicago's famed Democratic Machine, a holdover from the many decades of domination by the Richard J. Daley administration.

ZANZIBAR HURRICANE: ANNIVERSARY. Apr 15, 1872. Beginning at 6 AM, Zanzibar's most powerful hurricane ripped through as many as 150 ships in its harbor and killed about 200 people.

BIRTHDAYS TODAY

Evelyn Ashford, 41, Olympic gold medal track athlete, born Shreveport, LA, Apr 15, 1957.

Linda Bloodworth-Thomason, 51, producer, writer ("Designing Women," "Evening Shade"), born Popular Bluff, MO, Apr 15, 1947.

Claudia Cardinale, 60, actress (*The Pink Panther, Once Upon a Time in the West*), born Tunis, Italy, Apr 15, 1938.

Roy Clark, 65, singer and guitarist ("Yesterday, When I Was Young"; regular on "Hee Haw"), born Meherrin, VA, Apr 15, 1933.

Michael Jerome Cooper, 42, former basketball player, born Los Angeles, CA, Apr 15, 1956.

Heloise Cruse Evans, 47, newspaper columnist ("Hints from Heloise"), born Waco, TX, Apr 15, 1951.

Amy Wright, 48, actress (*Breaking Away, Wise Blood, The Accidental Tourist*), born Chicago, IL, Apr 15, 1950.

APRIL 16 — THURSDAY

Day 106 — 259 Remaining

AMERICANA SPRING SAMPLER. Apr 16–18. Tennessee State Fairgrounds, Nashville, TN. 15th annual retail and wholesale folk art fair with 200 country craft, folk art, fine art and antique professionals exhibiting and selling their wares. For info: Americana Sampler, Inc, PO Box 160009, Nashville, TN 37216-0009. Phone: (615) 227-2080. Fax: (615) 741-7225.

AMIS, KINGSLEY: BIRTH ANNIVERSARY. Apr 16, 1922. Author (*The Crime of the Century, Lucky Jim*), born London, England. Died Oct 22, 1995.

CHAPLIN, CHARLES SPENCER: BIRTH ANNIVERSARY. Apr 16, 1889. Celebrated film comedian who portrayed "The Little Tramp" was born at London, England. Film debut in 1914. Knighted in 1975. Died at Vevey, Switzerland, Dec 25, 1977. In his autobiography Chaplin wrote: "There are more valid facts and details in works of art than there are in history books."

DENMARK: QUEEN MARGRETHE'S BIRTHDAY. Apr 16. Thousands of children gather to cheer the queen at Amalienborg Palace, and the Royal Guard wears scarlet gala uniforms.

DIEGO, JOSE de: BIRTH ANNIVERSARY. Apr 16, 1867. Puerto Rican patriot and political leader Jose de Diego born on this day.

FORT LAUDERDALE SPRING BOAT SHOW. April 16–19. Greater Fort Lauderdale/Broward Co Conv Center. Everything from small boats to mega-yachts to boating equipment. For info: Greater Fort Lauderdale Conv/Visitors Bureau, 1850 Eller Dr, Ste 303, Fort Lauderdale, FL 33316. Phone: (954) 765-4466.

ICELAND: "FIRST DAY OF SUMMER." Apr 16. A national public holiday, *Sumardagurinn fyrsti*, with general festivities, processions and much street dancing, especially in Reykjavik, greets the coming of summer. Flags are flown on this day. Annually, the third Thursday in April.

INTERNATIONAL WHISTLERS CONVENTION. Apr 16–19. Louisburg, NC. Music festival. Assemblage and contest of professional and amateur whistlers and whistle collectors. Contests for children, teens and adults. Est attendance: 2,500. For info: Allen de Hart, Dir, Franklin County Arts Council, Inc, PO Box 758, Louisburg, NC 27549. Phone: (919) 496-2521 or (919) 496-4771. Fax: (919) 496-1191.

MANCINI, HENRY: BIRTH ANNIVERSARY. Apr 16, 1924. Born at Cleveland, OH, Mancini made his mark in Hollywood composing film scores and songs. He won 20 Grammy Awards and four Oscars (song "Moon River" and score for *Breakfast at Tiffany's*; song "Days of Wine and Roses" for the film; score for *Victor/Victoria*). He also composed *The Pink Panther*, "Peter Gunn" and "Mr Lucky" themes. Died June 14, 1994, at Beverly Hills, CA.

MASIH, IQBAL: DEATH ANNIVERSARY. Apr 16, 1995. Twelve-year-old Iqbal Masih, who reportedly had received death threats after speaking out against Pakistan's child labor practices, was shot to death. Masih, who was sold into labor as a carpet weaver at the age of four, spent the next six years of his life shackled to a loom. He began speaking out against child labor after escaping from servitude at the age of ten. In November of 1994 he spoke at an international labor conference in Sweden, and he received a $15,000 Reebok Youth in Action Award a month later. There were reports after the shooting that Masih's death was arranged by a "carpet mafia."

April 1998

S	M	T	W	T	F	S
			1	2	3	4
5	6	7	8	9	10	11
12	13	14	15	16	17	18
19	20	21	22	23	24	25
26	27	28	29	30		

NATIONAL STRESS AWARENESS DAY. Apr 16. To focus public awareness on one of the leading health problems in the world today. Health-related organizations throughout the country are encouraged to sponsor stress education programs and events. Annually, the first day after income taxes due. For info: Morton C. Orman, MD, Dir, The Health Resource Network, 2936 E Baltimore St, Baltimore, MD 21224. Phone: (410) 732-1900. WWW: http://www.stresscure.com

NATURAL BRIDGES NATIONAL MONUMENT: 90th ANNIVERSARY. Apr 16, 1908. Utah. Natural Bridges National Monument was established Apr 16, 1908.

NORTH CAROLINA AZALEA FESTIVAL. Apr 16–19. Wilmington, NC. This flower festival features a parade, fireworks, food booths, a circus and entertainment for the whole family. Est attendance: 100,000. For info: North Carolina Azalea Festival, PO Box 51, Wilmington, NC 28402. Phone: (910) 763-0905. Fax: (910) 251-8282.

SLAVERY ABOLISHED IN DISTRICT OF COLUMBIA: ANNIVERSARY. Apr 16, 1862. Congress abolished slavery in the District of Columbia. One million dollars was appropriated to compensate owners of freed slaves, and $100,000 was set aside to pay district slaves who wished to emigrate to Haiti, Liberia or any other country outside the US.

SLOANE, HANS: BIRTH ANNIVERSARY. Apr 16, 1660. British medical doctor and naturalist whose personal collection became the nucleus of the British Museum. Born at County Down, Ireland, on Apr 16, 1660. Upon his death at Chelsea, England, on Jan 11, 1753, his collections of books, manuscripts, medals and antiquities were bequeathed to Britain and accepted by an act of Parliament that incorporated the British Museum. It was opened to the public at London, England, on Jan 15, 1759. It is the national museum and library of the United Kingdom.

SPACE MILESTONE: *APOLLO 16* (US). Apr 16, 1972. Astronauts John W. Young, Charles M. Duke, Jr, and Thomas K. Mattingly II (command module pilot) began 11-day mission that included 71-hour exploration of moon (Apr 20–23). Landing module (LM) named *Orion*. Splashdown in Pacific Ocean within a mile of target, Apr 27.

SYNGE, JOHN MILLINGTON: BIRTH ANNIVERSARY. Apr 16, 1871. Irish dramatist and poet, most of whose plays were written in the brief span of six years before his death at age 37 of lymphatic sarcoma. His best-known work was *The Playboy of the Western World* (1907), which caused protests and rioting at early performances. Synge (pronounced "Sing") was born near Dublin and died there on Mar 24, 1909.

WILLIAM INGE FESTIVAL. Apr 16–18. Independence Community College, Independence, KS. Seminars, presentations, lectures and banquet with nationally known playwrights honoring the Pulitzer Prize– and Academy Award–winning author of *Picnic* and *Splendor in the Grass*. Annually, the third Thursday and Saturday of April. Est attendance: 5,000. For info: Jill Warford, Festival Director, Independence Community College, PO Box 708, Independence, KS 67301. Phone: (800) 842-6063.

WRIGHT, WILBUR: BIRTH ANNIVERSARY. Apr 16, 1867. Aviation pioneer born at Millville, IN. Died at Dayton, OH, May 30, 1912.

BIRTHDAYS TODAY

Kareem Abdul-Jabbar (born Lewis Ferdinand Alcindor, Jr), 51, former basketball player, born New York, NY, Apr 16, 1947.

Edie Adams (Elizabeth Edith Enke), 67, singer, actress, born Kingston, PA, Apr 16, 1931.

Ellen Barkin, 43, actress (*Tender Mercies, Diner*), born New York, NY, Apr 16, 1955.

Jon Cryer, 33, actor ("Partners," *Pretty in Pink, Hot Shots!*), born New York, NY, Apr 16, 1965.

Merce Cunningham, 79, dancer, choreographer, born Centralia, WA, Apr 16, 1919.

Lukas Haas, 22, actor (*Witness, Rambling Rose*), born West Hollywood, CA, Apr 16, 1976.

Barry Nelson, 75, actor (*Pete 'n Tillie, The Shining*), born Oakland, CA, Apr 16, 1923.

Jay O. Sanders, 45, actor ("Crime Story," *Tucker: The Man and His Dream*), born Austin, TX, Apr 16, 1953.

Peter Ustinov, 77, actor (Oscars for *Spartacus, Topkapi*), born London, England, Apr 16, 1921.

Bobby Vinton, 63, singer ("Mr Lonely," "Roses Are Red [My Love]"), born Canonsburg, PA, Apr 16, 1935.

APRIL 17 — FRIDAY

Day 107 — 258 Remaining

AMERICAN SAMOA: FLAG DAY. Apr 17. National holiday commemorating first raising of American flag in what was formerly Eastern Samoa, on Apr 17, 1900. Public holiday with singing, dancing, costumes and parades.

CANADA: EDSON TRADE SHOW. Apr 17–19. Edson, Alta. Trade and sports show. Est attendance: 5,000. For info: Edson and District Chmbr of Commerce, 5433 3rd Ave, Edson, Alta, Canada T7E 1L5. Phone: (403) 723-4918. Fax: (403) 723-5545.

CANADA: MUSKOKA ARTS AND CRAFTS SPRING MEMBER SHOW. Apr 17–19. Bracebridge, Ont. For info: Bracebridge Chamber of Commerce, 1-1 Manitoba St, Bracebridge, Ont, Canada P1L 1S4. Phone: (705) 645-5501.

DOGWOOD MUSIC FESTIVAL. Apr 17–18. Camdenton, MO. This annual rite of spring features Flat Pickin' music competition, arts and crafts, bluegrass music, art exhibitions, displays of antique wooden boats and more. For info: (800) 769-1004 or Missouri Division of Tourism, Truman State Office Bldg, PO Box 1055, Jefferson City, MO 65102. Phone: (573) 751-4133. Fax: (573) 751-5160.

DOLLY'S MUSIC ON PARADE. Apr 17. Pigeon Forge, TN. Dolly Parton serves as grand marshal in the 13th annual parade. Theme-based parade kicks off the spring season. For info: Kay Powell, Pigeon Forge Dept of Tourism, 2450 Parkway, PO Box 1390, Pigeon Forge, TN 37868. Phone: (800) 251-9100 or (423) 453-8574.

DOW-JONES TOPS 3,000: ANNIVERSARY. Apr 17, 1991. The Dow-Jones Index of 30 major industrial stocks topped the 3,000 mark for the first time.

ENGLAND: MORPETH NORTHUMBRIAN GATHERING. Apr 17–19. Morpeth. Concerts, crafts, films, barn dance, competitions and street entertainment. For info: Westgate House, Dogger Bank, Morpeth, Northumberland, England. Phone: (44) (91) 274-7756.

FIESTA SAN ANTONIO. Apr 17–26. San Antonio, TX. Ten days of culture, heritage, beauty and remembrance. Parades, carnivals, sports, fireworks, music, ethnic feasts, art exhibits, dances—more than 150 events. This colorful fiesta originated in 1891 with the Battle of Flowers parade honoring the memory of Texas heroes who fought against General Santa Anna for Texan independence at the Alamo and San Jacinto. Est attendance: 3,500,000. For info: Mktg Coord, Fiesta San Antonio Commission, Inc, 122 Heiman, San Antonio, TX 78205. Phone: (210) 227-5191. Fax: (210) 227-1139.

"THE FRED WARING SHOW" TV PREMIERE: ANNIVERSARY. Apr 17, 1949. Fred Waring was leader of the big band called the Pennsylvanians, which featured about sixty-five musicians and singers. The show was produced and directed by Bob Banner and aired on Sunday nights until 1954.

FRENCH QUARTER FESTIVAL. Apr 17–19. New Orleans, LA. This festival focuses on all that makes the Quarter special—art, antiques, food, music, shopping, lifestyles and the people. Free concerts on 13 stages, historic patio tours, parade, children's activities, fireworks, 5K race and other family activities. Est attendance: 250,000. For info: Amy Hymel, Event Coord, 100 Conti St, New Orleans, LA 70130. Phone: (504) 522-5730. Fax: (504) 522-5711. Email: info@fqfestivals.org.
WWW: http://www.FQFestivals.org

HOLIDAY IN DIXIE. Apr 17–26. Shreveport and Bossier City, LA. Ten days in April celebrating the beginning of spring with over 50 events including carnival, tournaments, a treasure hunt, parades; also Barksdale AFB Open House. Takes place throughout both cities. Est attendance: 300,000. For info: Kay Pierson, Exec Dir, Holiday in Dixie, PO Box 44067, Shreveport, LA 71134-4406. Phone: (318) 865-5555.

KENTUCKY DERBY FESTIVAL. Apr 17–May 3. Louisville, KY. Civic celebration as Louisville warms up for the derby. About 70 events, two-thirds of which are free to the public. Est attendance: 1,500,000. For info: Kentucky Derby Festival, Inc, 1001 South Third St, Louisville, KY 40203. Phone: (502) 584-6383. Fax: (502) 589-4674. WWW: http://www.kdf.org

KING RANCH WILD GAME LUNCH & TEXAS CACTUS FESTIVAL. Apr 17–19. Kingsville, TX. Cactus symposium on Friday at Texas A&M Campus. Nilgai Carne Guisada Lunch, cooked and served outdoors on King Ranch. Cactus Fiesta on Saturday and Sunday in historic downtown Kingsville with arts and crafts booths, music (Tejano, country, mariachi and other types), children's rides, Folkloric dancers, "Taste of South Texas" food booths and cactus cooking competition. For info: Kingsville Conv and Visitors Bureau, PO Box 1562, Kingsville, TX 78364-1562. Phone: (800) 333-5032. Fax: (512) 592-3227. Email: kcvb@kingsville.org. WWW: http://www.kingsville.org

LAKE, ARTHUR: BIRTH ANNIVERSARY. Apr 17, 1905. American actor Arthur Lake was born Arthur Silverlake at Corbin, KY. He portrayed Dagwood Bumstead in the many *Blondie* films from 1939 to 1950. Lake died on Jan 9, 1987, at Indian Wells, CA.

MENNONITE RELIEF SALE. Apr 17–18. Kansas State Fair Grounds, Hutchinson, KS. More than 70 Mennonite, Brethren in Christ and Amish congregations in Kansas sponsor this annual festival and benefit auction for the worldwide hunger relief and community aid programs of the Mennonite Central Committee. Auctions of quilts, grandfather clocks, furniture, tools and crafts. Great food and lots more. No vendors. Est attendance: 30,000. For info: Richard Ediger, Pres, Box 488, Buhler, KS 67522. Phone: (316) 543-2787.

MORGAN, JOHN PIERPONT: BIRTH ANNIVERSARY. Apr 17, 1837. American financier and corporation director born at Hartford, CT, Morgan died on Mar 31, 1913, leaving an estate valued at more than $70 million.

NATIONAL ASSOCIATION OF COLLEGE STORES MEETING & CAMPUS MARKET EXPO. Apr 17–21. Baltimore, MD. The only national conference and trade exhibit designed exclusively for collegiate retailers. The NACS 75th Annual Meeting/CAMEX brings college store managers and buyers together with publishing companies and other suppliers in this yearly exposition of the products to be seen on college campuses next fall. Est attendance: 8,000. For info: Jerry Buchs, PR Dir, Natl Assn of College Stores, 500 E Lorain St, Oberlin, OH 44074. Phone: (216) 775-7777. Email: info@nacs.org. WWW: http://www.nacs.org

NEEDHAM, THERESA: BIRTH ANNIVERSARY. Apr 17, 1912. Owner of Chicago's legendary South Side blues bar, Theresa's Lounge, Theresa Needham was born at Meridian, MS. Especially memorable at the bar were "Blue Monday" all-day jams at which the city's top blues performers locked horns in musical battles. Needham, who was bartender, bouncer and talent agent, came to be known as "the Godmother of Chicago Blues." Died at Chicago, IL, Oct 16, 1992.

NETHERLANDS AND SCILLY ISLES PEACE: ANNIVERSARY. Apr 17. The 335-year "state of war" that had existed between the Netherlands and the Scilly Isles came to an end on Apr 17, 1986. On that date Dutch ambassador Jonkheer Huydecoper flew to the Scilly Isles to deliver a proclamation terminating the war that had started in 1651. Though hostilities had ceased three centuries earlier, a standing joke in the islands was that no one had bothered to declare an end to the war—until 1986. One of history's longer wars thus was concluded.

PUYALLUP SPRING FAIR. Apr 17–19. Puyallup Fairgrounds, Puyallup, WA. Fair to celebrate spring, including exhibits, animals, flowers, rides, demonstrations, gardening, recycling, lots of entertainment, food and much more. Est attendance: 85,000. For info: Puyallup Spring Fair, PO Box 430, Puyallup, WA 98371-0162. Phone: (253) 841-5045. Email: fairpr@thefair.com. WWW: http://www.thefair.com

REASONER, HARRY: 75th BIRTH ANNIVERSARY. Apr 17, 1923. American television journalist Harry Reasoner was born at Dakota City, IA. In 1956 Reasoner joined CBS News, where he anchored the "CBS Sunday News" (1963–70) and was one of the two original anchors, along with Mike Wallace, of the news magazine show "60 Minutes." He was co-anchor of the "ABC Evening News" from 1970 until 1978, when he returned to CBS and "60 Minutes." He died on Aug 6, 1991, at Norwalk, CT.

THE ROARING 20s. Apr 17–May 10 (Fri–Sun only). Mount Hope Estate, Manheim, PA. Mount Hope Mansion turns speakeasy as the Philadelphia Renaissance Faire's acting company lights the fires that made the 1920s roar. Wine served for medicinal purposes, of course. Est attendance: 7,000. For info: Michelle Cunningham, Mgr, Mount Hope Estate and Winery, PO Box 685, Cornwall, PA 17016. Phone: (717) 665-7021. Fax: (717) 664-3466. Email: prfscrib@postoffice.net. WWW: http://www.parenaissancefaire.com

SEATTLE CHERRY BLOSSOM & JAPANESE CULTURAL FESTIVAL. Apr 17–19. Seattle, WA. Come and enjoy Japanese culture with fireworks, entertainment, arts and crafts, food booths and much more. Est attendance: 30,000. For info: Seattle Cherry Blossom & Japanese Cultural Festival, PO Box 9055, Seattle, WA 98109. Phone: (206) 524-7870. Fax: (206) 524-7870.

SOLIDARITY GRANTED LEGAL STATUS: ANNIVERSARY. Apr 17, 1989. After nearly a decade of struggle and suppression the Polish labor union Solidarity was granted legal status, clearing the way for the downfall of the Polish Communist Party. Solidarity and the Polish people surprised the government by winning 99 of the 100 parliamentary seats in the election. General Wojciech Jaruzelski was elected president on July 19 and nominated Czelaw Kiszczak prime minister, enraging the Lech Walesa–led Solidarity. On Aug 7 Walesa swayed the traditional allies of the Communist Party—the United Peasant and Democratic Parties—to switch sides. Kiszczak resigned as prime minister a week later after failing to form a government, forcing Jaruzelski to accept the principal of a government led by Solidarity.

SPACE MILESTONE: *SURVEYOR 3* (US). Apr 17, 1967. Launch date of lunar probe vehicle, which then made soft landing on Moon on Apr 20 and with its digging apparatus established surface qualities.

SPRING VICTORIAN WEEKEND. Apr 17–19. Cape May, NJ. Spring into the Victorian lifestyle with a weekend of tours and events celebrating the coming of spring in the nation's first seashore resort. Features a restoration house tour and exposition, brass band concert, authentic Victorian dinner and more. Annually, the third weekend in April, Friday–Sunday. Est attendance: 4,000. For info: Mid-Atlantic Center for the Arts, 1048 Washington St, PO Box 340, Cape May, NJ 08204. Phone: (609) 884-5404 or (800) 275-4278 for tickets. Fax: (609) 884-2006. Email: mac4arts@algorithms.com. WWW: http://www.beachcomber.com/capemay/mac.html

SUGARLOAF'S SPRING NOVI ART FAIR. Apr 17–19. Novi Expo Center, Novi, MI. This show, now in its 4th year, features 300 nationally recognized craft designers and fine artists displaying and selling their original creations. Craft demonstrations, children's entertainment, hourly gift certificate drawings, and more. Est attendance: 19,000. For info: Sugarloaf Mountain

April 1998

S	M	T	W	T	F	S
			1	2	3	4
5	6	7	8	9	10	11
12	13	14	15	16	17	18
19	20	21	22	23	24	25
26	27	28	29	30		

Works, Inc, 200 Orchard Ridge Dr, #215, Gaithersburg, MD 20878. Phone: (800) 210-9900.

SYRIAN ARAB REPUBLIC: INDEPENDENCE DAY. Apr 17. Official holiday.

VERRAZANO DAY. Apr 17. Celebrates discovery of New York harbor, 1524, by Giovanni Verrazano, Florentine navigator, 1480(?)–1527.

WILDER, THORNTON: BIRTH ANNIVERSARY. Apr 17, 1897. Pulitzer Prize–winning American playwright (*Our Town*) and novelist, born at Madison, WI. Died at Hamden, CT, Dec 7, 1975.

WORLD'S LARGEST TRIVIA CONTEST. Apr 17–19. Stevens Point, WI. More than 12,000 players including more than 530 teams compete to answer eight questions every hour for 54 hours straight. Prize: Oscar-like trophy. Est attendance: 12,000. For info: Jim Oliva, University of Wisconsin, Rm 105 CAC, WWSP-Radio (89.9 FM), Stevens Point, WI 54481. Phone: (715) 346-3755. Email: theoz@free.org.
WWW: http://www.easy-axcess.com/trivia

BIRTHDAYS TODAY

Lindsay Anderson, 75, director, born Bangalore (*If . . ., O Lucky Man!*), India, Apr 17, 1923.

Sean Bean, 40, actor (*Stormy Monday, The Field, Patriot Games*), born Sheffield, Yorkshire, England, Apr 17, 1958.

Norman Julius ("Boomer") Esiason, 37, football player, born West Islip, NY, Apr 17, 1961.

Anna Marie Holmes, 55, dancer, born Mission City, British Columbia, Canada, Apr 17, 1943.

Olivia Hussey, 47, actress (Juliet in Franco Zeffirelli's *Romeo and Juliet*), born Buenos Aires, Argentina, Apr 17, 1951.

Don Kirshner, 64, music publisher, promoter, born The Bronx, NY, Apr 17, 1934.

Cynthia Ozick, 70, feminist, writer, born New York, NY, Apr 17, 1928.

APRIL 18 — SATURDAY

Day 108 — 257 Remaining

BLOCK HOUSE STEEPLECHASE RACES. Apr 18. Foothills Equestrian Nature Center, Tryon, NC. 52nd annual running of the Block House Steeplechase. Est attendance: 15,000. For info: Mitzi Lindsey, Tryon Riding & Hunt Club, PO Box 1095, Tryon, NC 28782. Phone: (800) 438-3681. Fax: (704) 859-5598. Email: trhc@teleplex.net.

CANADA: CONSTITUTION ACT OF 1982: ANNIVERSARY. Apr 18, 1982. Replacing the British North America Act of 1867, the Canadian Constitution Act of 1982 provides Canada with a new set of fundamental laws and civil rights. Signed by Queen Elizabeth II, at Parliament Hill, Ottawa, Canada, on Saturday, Apr 18, 1982, it went into effect at 12:01 AM, Sunday, Apr 18, 1982.

CHOCO-MAS DAY. Apr 18 (also Aug 14). Hernando Cortes (1485–1547) Spanish Conqueror and explorer called it the "Divine Drink that builds up resistance and fights Fatigue." Other ancient people called it the "Food of the Gods." What is it? Chocolate of course! Today we recognize the divine and heavenly qualities of chocolate by indulging in the purchase/making of our favorite confection. For info: Adrienne Sioux Koopersmith, 1437 W Rosemont, #1W, Chicago, IL 60660-1319. Phone: (773) 743-5341. Fax: (773) 743-5395. Email: kooper@interaccess.com.

COIN SHOW. Apr 18–19 (also Nov 14–15). LaVale, MD. Features US and foreign coins and currency, precious metals, sports cards and supplies. Est attendance: 450. For info: Western Maryland Coin Club, 1260 Vocke Rd, La Vale, MD 21502-7716. Phone: (301) 729-0777.

COMMUNITY SPIRIT DAYS. Apr 18–25. Coinciding with National Volunteer Week, these eight days are driven by three concepts intended to help local people in need. Each community will collect items at a central point for distribution to local charities; conduct special projects geared to helping the local populace; and hold a community gathering of the town's nonprofit groups, at which participants are thanked. Each gathering will culminate with the presentation of the municipality's Spirit of America Foundation Awards for outstanding volunteerism. For info: Jennifer Connolly, Spirit of America Foundation, PO Box 5637, Augusta, ME 04332. Phone: (207) 622-7311. Fax: (207) 854-0809.

COOKING IN PARADISE. Apr 18–25. Yuana Hotel, St. Barthelemy. Renowned cooking instructor and James Beard Award winner Steven Raichlen offers his 10th annual "Cooking in Paradise" class, focusing on healthy Creole and Caribbean cuisine in sophisticated St. Barts. The course also includes visits to restaurants, a gourmet picnic and sailing cruise. Est attendance: 15. For info: Barbara Raichlen, PO Box 331597, Coconut Grove, FL 33133. Phone: (305) 854-9550. Fax: (305) 854-9717. Email: 102333.1603@compuserve.

CRAWFORD, SAMUEL EARL "WAHOO SAM": BIRTH ANNIVERSARY. Apr 18, 1880. Major league baseball player with the Detroit Tigers, born Apr 18, 1880, at Wahoo, NE. Wahoo Sam played pro ball for 20 years, racking up a career batting average of .309. His record of 312 career triples still stands. He was inducted into the Baseball Hall of Fame in 1957. Crawford died on June 15, 1968, at Hollywood, CA.

DAFFODIL FESTIVAL PARADE. Apr 18. Tacoma, Puyallup, Sumner and Orting, WA. 65th annual parade, featuring a myriad of floats decorated with freshly cut flowers, primarily daffodils. Est attendance: 140,000. For info: Daffodil Fest, Inc, PO Box 1824, Tacoma, WA 98401. Phone: (206) 627-6176.

DARROW, CLARENCE SEWARD: BIRTH ANNIVERSARY. Apr 18, 1857. American attorney often associated with unpopular causes, from the Pullman strike in 1894 to the Scottsboro case in 1932, born at Kinsman, OH. At the Scopes trial, July 13, 1925, Darrow said: "I do not consider it an insult, but rather a compliment, to be called an agnostic. I do not pretend to know where many ignorant men are sure—that is all that agnosticism means." Darrow died at Chicago, IL, on Mar 13, 1938.

DRAGOON ENCAMPMENT AND FORT LEAVENWORTH HISTORIC HOMES TOUR. Apr 18. Fort Leavenworth, KS. Step back in time at the oldest fort in continuous operation west of the Mississippi for a living history interpretation of the Mexican War–period soldier's life. Encampment will include dragoon soldiers acting out their daily routines and laundresses doing laundry and making soap. Tour Leavenworth vintage homes including the oldest residence in Kansas. Annually, the third weekend in April. Est attendance: 1,500. For info: Connie Hachenberg, Dir, Leavenworth-Lansing Conv & Visitors Bureau, 518 Shawnee, PO Box 44, Leavenworth, KS 66048. Phone: (800) 844-4114. Fax: (913) 682-8170.

☆ ☆ ☆

EARTH DAY. Apr 18. Burritt Museum and Park, Huntsville, AL. An all-day festival of workshops, games, hikes and exhibits. Discuss global environmental issues, learn new lifestyle alternatives and be immersed in nature itself. This festival stresses how each individual can impact the environment. Adults and children are encouraged to explore the wonders and workings of this fascinating planet we call "home." Admission charged. Est attendance: 700. For info: Jeff Hughes, Dir Ed, Burritt Museum and Park, 3101 Burritt Dr, Huntsville, AL 35801. Phone: (205) 536-2882. Fax: (205) 532-1784.

FEAST OF THE RAMSON. Apr 18. Richwood, WV. A dinner dedicated to the ramp, a wild leek, which grows wild in the mountains. Arts and crafts; mountain song and dance. Est attendance: 1,500. For info: Maxine Corbet, Exec Secy, Richwood Area Chamber of Commerce, 50 Oakford Ave, Richwood, WV 26261. Phone: (304) 846-6790.

FIRST FAMILIES: MAKING A HOME AT THE WHITE HOUSE. Apr 18–Nov 1. West Branch, IA. An exhibit focusing on the first families and their domestic lives inside the White House. Est attendance: 500,000. For info: Special Events Coord, Herbert Hoover Presidential Museum, PO Box 488, 210 Parkside Dr, West Branch, IA 52358. Phone: (319) 643-5301. Fax: (319) 643-5825. WWW: http://www.nara.gov./nara/president/hoover

FLOWER & GARDEN FESTIVAL. Apr 18–19. Lahaska, PA. Devoted to gardening and horticultural enthusiasts. Exhibitors include nurseries, florists, nature centers, landscape architects, lawn and garden equipment and supplies businesses, garden clubs and environmental groups. Crafts and artwork on nature topics for sale. Lectures and demonstrations on topics related to theme. Live entertainment, children's activities. Free admission. Est attendance: 10,000. For info: Peddler's Village, Routes 202 & 263, Lahaska, PA 18931. Phone: (215) 794-4000. Fax: (215) 794-4001. WWW: http://www.peddlersvillage.com

GEORGIA RENAISSANCE SPRING FESTIVAL. Apr 18–May 31. (Saturdays, Sundays and Memorial Day.) Atlanta, GA. Theme park features "the entertainment, romance and art of the Renaissance." More than 100 performances daily on 10 stages; thousands of unique craft items for sale. Est attendance: 200,000. For info: Sarah Waters, Georgia Renaissance Festival, PO Box 986, Fairburn, GA 30213. Phone: (770) 964-8575. Fax: (770) 964-1477.

HISTORIC GARDEN WEEK IN VIRGINIA. Apr 18–25. This annual statewide event, celebrating its 65th anniversary, is billed as "America's Largest Open House." It showcases more than 250 of Virginia's finest homes, gardens, plantations and landmark properties on more than 30 separate tours. A brochure is available. A 200-page guidebook will be available in early March 1998. Please mail a contribution of $3 to cover postage and handling. Est attendance: 50,000. For info: Garden Club of Virginia, 12 E Franklin St, Richmond, VA 23219. Phone: (804) 644-7776. Fax: (804) 644-7778. WWW: http://www.VAGardenweek.org

HOOD RIVER VALLEY BLOSSOM FESTIVAL. Apr 18–19. Hood River, OR. Breathtaking views of the Hood River Valley's orchards in bloom. Arts and crafts, dinners, seasonal opening of the Mount Hood Railroad. 44th annual festival. Est attendance: 20,000. For info: Hood River Co Chamber of Commerce, 405 Portway, Hood River, OR 97031. Phone: (800) 366-3530.

THE HOUSE THAT RUTH BUILT: 75th ANNIVERSARY. Apr 18, 1923. More than 74,000 fans attended Opening Day festivities as the New York Yankees inaugurated their new stadium in the Bronx. Babe Ruth christened it with a game-winning three-run homer into the right-field bleachers. In his coverage of the game for the *New York Evening Telegram* sportswriter Fred Lieb described Yankee Stadium as "The House That Ruth Built," and the name stuck.

INDIAN DAY. Apr 18. Russell Cave National Monument, Bridgeport, AL. Programs on Native American culture with demonstrations of how everyday things were done in the past presented by expert volunteers. Activities may include flint knapping, pipe carving, bows, arrows, fire, pottery, finger weaving, petroglyphs and much more. Est attendance: 2,500. For info: Park Ranger, 3729 County Rd 98, Bridgeport, AL 35740. Phone: (205) 495-2672.

JAPAN BOMBED: ANNIVERSARY. Apr 18, 1942. For the first time during WW II, the mainland of Japan was bombed. Brigade General James Doolittle led a squadron of B-25s from the US carrier *Hornet*. Cities bombed included Tokyo, Yokohama, Kobe and Nagoya. Doolittle said they flew so low that "one of our party observed a ball game in progress." Although the bombers did little damage, the psychological victory was enormous.

April 1998

S	M	T	W	T	F	S
			1	2	3	4
5	6	7	8	9	10	11
12	13	14	15	16	17	18
19	20	21	22	23	24	25
26	27	28	29	30		

JUST PRAY NO: WORLDWIDE WEEKEND PRAYER. Apr 18–19. Churches throughout the world. Prayer breakfasts, lunches, street rallies and marches to gain media attention. Bible studies and sermons concerning alcoholism and drug abuse and revival meetings aimed at those bound by addiction. For info: "Just Pray No," Ltd, 124 Garfield Pl, E Rockaway, NY 11518. Phone: (516) 599-7399.

KENDUSKEAG STREAM CANOE RACE. Apr 18. Bangor, ME. A 16.5-mile whitewater open canoe race. Est attendance: 1,500. For info: Bangor Parks and Recreation Dept, 647 Main St, Bangor, ME 04401. Phone: (207) 947-1018. Fax: (207) 947-1605.

LONGWOOD GARDENS ACRES OF SPRING. Apr 18–May 22. Kennett Square, PA. Thousands of spring bulbs, flowering shrubs and trees bloom throughout 1,050 acres of formal gardens, woodlands and meadows. Sunday afternoon organ and chamber music concerts. Est attendance: 150,000. For info: Longwood Gardens, PO Box 501, Kennett Square, PA 19348-0501. Phone: (610) 388-1000. WWW: http://www.longwoodgardens.org

MOSSY CREEK BARNYARD FESTIVAL. Apr 18–19. (Also Oct 17–18.) Warner Robins, GA. Arts and crafts chosen from best in the nation; heritage crafts, country and folk music and folk tales in relaxed atmosphere. Semiannually, the third weekend of April (usually) and of October. Est attendance: 20,000. For info: Carolyn Chester, Mossy Creek Barnyard Festival, Inc, 106 Anne Dr, Warner Robins, GA 31093. Phone: (912) 922-8265.

MUSEUM OPEN HOUSE. Apr 18–19. (Also Nov 14–15). Clinton, MD. Annual open house at historic site features free tours, special gift shop sales, refreshments. Est attendance: 500. For info: Surratt House and Tavern, PO Box 427, Clinton, MD 20735. Phone: (301) 868-1121. Fax: (301) 868-8177. WWW: http://www.engr.umd.edu/clwspoon/surratt.html

NORTHERN CALIFORNIA CHERRY BLOSSOM FESTIVAL (WITH PARADE). Apr 18–19. (Also Apr 25–26.) Japantown, San Francisco, CA. More than 2,000 Californians of Japanese descent and performers from Japan participate in this most elaborate offering of Japanese culture and customs this side of the Pacific, highlighted by colorful parade. Sponsors: Japanese-American communities of Northern California and several corporations. Media contact address: Norm Ishimoto, Ki Associates, 182 Second St, Fourth Fl, San Francisco, CA 94105-3801. Phone: (415) 227-0402. Fax: (415) 227-0403. Est attendance: 100,000. For info: Cherry Blossom Festival, PO Box 15147, San Francisco, CA 94115-0147. Phone: (415) 776-4304. Fax: (415) 776-4402. WWW: http://www.e-media.com/sakura

PACKY'S BIRTHDAY PARTY. Apr 18. Metro Washington Park Zoo, Portland, OR. A party to celebrate the 36th birthday of the zoo's famous elephant. Est attendance: 3,000. For info: Events Coord, Metro Washington Park Zoo, 4001 SW Canyon Rd, Portland, OR 97221-2799. Phone: (503) 226-1561. Fax: (503) 220-5754.

PAUL REVERE'S RIDE: ANNIVERSARY. Apr 18. The "Midnight Ride" of Paul Revere and William Dawes started at about 10 PM on Apr 18, 1775, to warn American patriots between Boston, MA, and Concord, MA, of the approaching British.

PENNSYLVANIA MAPLE FESTIVAL. Apr 18–19 (also Apr 24–26). Meyersdale, PA. To celebrate the miracle of the maple. Est attendance: 50,000. For info: Pennsylvania Maple Festival, Box 222, Meyersdale, PA 15552. Phone: (814) 634-0213. Fax: (814) 634-0147. Email: maple@shol.com. WWW: http://www.shol.com/maple

PET OWNERS INDEPENDENCE DAY. Apr 18. Dog and cat owners take day off from work and the pets go to work in their place, since most pets are jobless, sleep all day and do not even take out the trash. [© 1997 by WPL] For info: Tom and Ruth Roy, Wellness Permission League, PO Box 662, Mt Gretna, PA 17064-0662. Phone: (500) 437-5104 or (717) 964-1308. Fax: (717) 964-1335.

"REAL PEOPLE" TV PREMIERE: ANNIVERSARY. Apr 18, 1979. Real people do the darndest things—from making paintings out of lint to making houses out of aluminum cans. NBC developed the program to spotlight the achievements, funny inventions and extraordinary stunts of ordinary Americans. Hosts of the show included: Fred Willard, Sarah Purcell, John Barbour, Skip Stephenson, Bill Rafferty, Byron Allen, Peter Billingsley, Kerry Millerick and David Ruprecht.

SAN FRANCISCO 1906 EARTHQUAKE: ANNIVERSARY. Apr 18, 1906. Business section of San Francisco, some 10,000 acres, destroyed by earthquake, Apr 18, 1906. First quake occurred at 5:13 AM, followed by fire. Nearly 4,000 lives were lost.

SPACE MILESTONE: *TITAN 34-D* ROCKET FAILURE. Apr 18, 1986. Launched from Vandenburg Air Force Base, CA, on Apr 18, 1986, the $65 million *Titan* exploded when it was only a few hundred feet into flight, destroying the $500 million KH-11 reconnaissance satellite payload. Poisonous fumes were released by the explosion, causing concern for the safety of persons in nearby communities.

SURRENDER AT DURHAM STATION: ANNIVERSARY. Apr 18. On Apr 18, 1865, Union General William Tecumseh Sherman and Confederate General Joseph Johnston signed a broad political peace agreement at Durham Station, NC. The agreement promised a general amnesty for all Southerners and pledged federal recognition of all Southern state governments after their officials took an oath of allegiance to the United States. Sherman was roundly criticized for his role in drawing up the agreement, although he based it on an earlier conversation with Lincoln and Grant. The agreement was rejected by President Andrew Johnson, and Sherman and Johnston were forced to reach a new agreement with terms virtually the same as those given Robert E. Lee.

"THIRD WORLD" DAY: ANNIVERSARY. Apr 18, 1955. Anniversary of the first use of the phrase "third world," which was used by Indonesia's President Sukarno in his opening speech at the Bandung Conference. Representatives of nearly 30 African and Asian countries (2,000 attendees) heard Sukarno praise the American war of independence, "the first successful anticolonial war in history." More than half the world's population, he said, was represented at this "first intercontinental conference of the so-called colored peoples, in the history of mankind." The phrase and the idea of a "third world" rapidly gained currency, generally signifying the aggregate of nonaligned peoples and nations—generally the nonwhite and underdeveloped portion of the world.

WALKER LAKE BIRD AND NATURAL HISTORY FESTIVAL. Apr 18. Walker Lake, Hawthorne, NV. Migration of the loon, plus more than 150 species of birds. Program includes: local artists, photo exhibit, museum curator, history of Walker Lake, Audubon Society, tour and luncheon. Est attendance: 350. For local chamber of commerce: Mineral Point Chamber of Commerce, PO Box 1635, Hawthorne, NV 89415. Phone: (702) 945-5896. Fax: (702) 945-1257.

WINE AND ROSES FESTIVAL. Apr 18. Bryan, TX. This event features the 15th annual Texas artists' competition. The winning painting becomes the focal point for next year's private reserve wine label. Team grape-stomping competition, dozens of food and craft booths, a petting zoo, vineyard hayrides and tours, classic and antique cars plus a variety of live music performances. Est attendance: 6,000. For info: Steve Wiley, Mktg Dir, Messina Hof Wine Cellars, 4545 Old Reliance Rd, Bryan, TX 77808. Phone: (409) 778-1729. Fax: (409) 778-1729.

ZIMBABWE: INDEPENDENCE DAY. Apr 18. National holiday commemorates the recognition by Great Britain of Zimbabwean independence in 1980. Prior to this, the country had been the British colony of Southern Rhodesia.

ZOOBILATION! CONSERVATION FESTIVAL. Apr 18–19. Mill Mountain Zoological Park, Roanoke, VA. A festival dedicated to making everyone aware of the fragile state of the environment. Nationally known conservationists will conduct seminars and programs that both entertain and inform. Activities celebrating the arrival of spring with special exhibitors, speakers, live music, children's activities and more! Sponsors: The Roanoke Special Events committee and the Mill Mountain Zoo. Est attendance: 5,000. For info: Special Events Dept, Mill Mountain Zoo, PO Box 13484, Roanoke, VA 24034. Phone: (540) 343-3241. Email: zoo@roanoke.infi.net. WWW: http://www.mmzoo.org

BIRTHDAYS TODAY

Ed Garvey, 58, lawyer, union official, labor negotiator, born Burlington, WI, Apr 18, 1940.

Barbara Hale, 76, actress (Della Street on "Perry Mason"), born De Kalb, IL, Apr 18, 1922.

Melissa Joan Hart, 22, actress ("Twisted Desire," "Sabrina the Teenage Witch"), born Long Island, NY, Apr 18, 1976.

Robert Hooks, 61, actor, director, producer (*Star Trek III: The Search for Spock* ; stage: *Day of Absence, Where's Daddy?* [Theatre World Awards for both]), born Washington, DC, Apr 18, 1937.

John James, 42, actor ("Search for Tomorrow," "Dynasty"), born Minneapolis, MN, Apr 18, 1956.

Dorothy Lyman, 51, actress (Opal on "All My Children"; "Mama's Family"), director, born Minneapolis, MN, Apr 18, 1947.

Wilber Buddyhia Marshall, 36, football player, born Titusville, FL, Apr 18, 1962.

Hayley Mills, 52, actress (*Pollyana, The Parent Trap, The Moon Spinners*), born London, England, Apr 18, 1946.

Rick Moranis, 44, actor, writer ("SCTV," *Ghostbusters, Honey I Shrunk the Kids, My Blue Heaven*), born Toronto, Canada, Apr 18, 1954.

Conan O'Brien, 35, host ("Late Night with Conan O'Brien"), born Brookline, MA, Apr 18, 1963.

Eric Roberts, 42, actor (*Runaway Train, Star 80*), born Biloxi, MS, Apr 18, 1956.

James Woods, 51, actor (*Holocaust, The Onion Field*), born Vernal, UT, Apr 18, 1947.

APRIL 19 — SUNDAY

Day 109 — 256 Remaining

AMERICA'S KIDS/AMERICAN HERO COMMEMORATIVE STAMP. Apr 19. Elementary school teachers all across America are invited to have their students complete petitions to persuade the US Postal Service to issue a commemorative stamp honoring the 19 children and volunteer nurse, Rebecca Anderson, who perished in the Oklahoma City bombing, Apr 19, 1995. For info: Rich Bysina, Winfield Chamber of Commerce, PO Box 209, Winfield, IL 60190. Phone: (630) 682-3712.

BATTLE OF LEXINGTON AND CONCORD: ANNIVERSARY. Apr 19, 1775. Massachusetts. Start of the American Revolution as the British fired the "shot heard 'round the world."

BIG BROTHERS/BIG SISTERS APPRECIATION WEEK. Apr 19–25. To honor the men and women who serve on a ONE-TO-ONE® basis as Big Brother and Big Sister volunteers who provide much needed guidance and support to at-risk children, primarily from one-parent families, in need of an adult mentor and role model. For info: Mktg/Communications, Big Brothers/Big Sisters of America, 230 N 13th St, Philadelphia, PA 19107. Phone: (215) 567-7000. Fax: (215) 567-0394.

BRANCH DAVIDIAN FIRE AT WACO: 5th ANNIVERSARY. Apr 19, 1993. After a 51-day standoff between the Branch Davidians and law-enforcement groups, the compound of the religious cult burned to the ground with 86 of its members inside on Apr 19, 1993, near Waco, TX, after federal agents began battering the compound with armored vehicles. Nine cultists escaped, but the 86 that perished included 17 children and the cult's leader, David Koresh.

EXPLOSION ON THE *USS IOWA*: ANNIVERSARY. Apr 19. In one of the worst naval disasters since the war in Vietnam, a freak explosion rocked the battleship, USS *Iowa*, killing 47 sailors, on Apr 19, 1989. The explosion occurred in the No. 2 gun turret as the *Iowa* was participating in gunnery exercises about 300 miles northeast of Puerto Rico.

GARFIELD, LUCRETIA RUDOLPH: BIRTH ANNIVERSARY. Apr 19, 1832. Wife of James Abram Garfield, 20th president of the US, born at Hiram, OH. Died Mar 14, 1918.

JIMMY STEWART RELAY MARATHON. Apr 19. Griffith Park, Los Angeles, CA. Team relay with five people, each running 5.2 miles. Funds raised go to benefit the Saint John's Child and Family Development Center, 17th annual marathon. Est attendance: 20,000. For info: Jimmy Stewart Relay Marathon, St. John's Health Ctr, 1328 22nd Street, Santa Monica, CA 90404. Phone: (310) 829-8968. Fax: (310) 315-6167.

April 1998

S	M	T	W	T	F	S
			1	2	3	4
5	6	7	8	9	10	11
12	13	14	15	16	17	18
19	20	21	22	23	24	25
26	27	28	29	30		

JOHN PARKER DAY. Apr 19. Remembering John Parker's order, at Lexington Green, Apr 19, 1775: "Stand your ground. Don't fire unless fired upon; but if they mean to have a war, let it begin here." John Parker, revolutionary soldier, captain of minutemen, born at Lexington, MA, July 13, 1729. Died Sept 17, 1775.

LAUREL HIGHLANDS DOLL SHOW. Apr 19. Greensburg, PA. Three rooms filled with dolls and toys for the avid collector. Must-see show for the doll enthusiast. For info: Mountain View Inn, Rte 30 East, Greensburg, PA 15601. Phone: (412) 834-5300 or (800) 537-8709. Fax: (412) 834-5304.

LOCAL COLORS. Apr 19. Roanoke, VA. An international event celebrating the cultural richness of the Roanoke Valley and surrounding areas. The event begins with an international parade at noon and the celebration continues until 5 PM. Included in the day's activities are an international fashion show, storytelling, crafts and displays from more than 40 countries, entertainment on stage, games for children and ethnic foods from around the world. For info: Center in the Square, One Market Square, SE, 5th Floor, Roanoke, VA 24011-1434. Phone: (540) 342-5700. Fax: (540) 224-1238. Email: CTIS@CTIS.org.

MOON PHASE: LAST QUARTER. Apr 19. Moon enters Last Quarter phase at 3:53 PM, EDT.

NATIONAL COIN WEEK. Apr 19–25. To promote the history and lore of numismatics and the hobby of coin collecting. For info: James Taylor, Dir of Educ, American Numismatic Assn, 818 N Cascade Ave, Colorado Springs, CO 80903. Phone: (800) 367-9723. Fax: (719) 634-4085. Email: anaedu@money.org. WWW: http://www.money.org

NATIONAL COUNTY GOVERNMENT WEEK. Apr 19–25. Started in 1991 to raise public awareness and understanding about the role and responsibilities of the nation's counties. Counties hold open houses and tours of their facilities; hold special programs for students and young people; recognize the contribution of volunteers and county employees; and speak to civic and community groups. The goal is to give citizens a better idea of the programs and services that counties provide and to encourage citizens to become involved in the local governmental process. County government week is sponsored by the National Association of Counties. For info: Tom Goodman, Public Affairs Dir, National Assn of Counties, 440 First St, NW, Washington, DC 20001. Phone: (202) 942-4222 or (202) 393-2630. Email: tgoodman@naco.org.

NATIONAL INFANTS IMMUNIZATION WEEK. Apr 19–25. To increase parents awareness of immunizing their children to hamper the effects of some diseases. For info: Kim Crumly, Centers for Disease Control and Prevention, National Immunization Program, 1600 Clifton Rd, Mail Stop E2, Atlanta, GA 30333. Phone: (404) 639-8226.

NATIONAL LIBRARY WEEK. Apr 19–25. A nationwide observance sponsored by the American Library Association. Celebrates libraries and librarians, the pleasures and importance of reading and invites library use and support. For info: American Library Assn, Public Info Office, 50 E Huron St, Chicago, IL 60611. Phone: (312) 280-5044. Fax: (312) 944-8520. Email: pio@ala.org. WWW: http://www.ala.org

NATIONAL ORGAN AND TISSUE DONOR AWARENESS WEEK. Apr 19–25. To encourage Americans to consider organ and tissue donation and to sign donor cards when getting a driver's license. For info: National Kidney Foundation, 30 E 33rd St, New York, NY 10016. Phone: (800) 622-9010 or (212) 889-2210.

NATIONAL PTA EARTH WEEK. Apr 19–25. In 1990, the National PTA recognized the importance of the environment to the health and safety of our children and designated the week in

Mail to: NTC/Contemporary Publishing Co.,
4255 W. Touhy Ave., Lincolnwood, IL 60646-1975

YES! Send me ________ copies of
Chase's 1999 Calendar of Events at $59.95 each*
Quantity Discounts:
Deduct 10% per copy for 3–9 copies
Deduct 20% per copy for 10 or more copies $ ______

YES! Send me ________ copies of
Chase's 1999 Sports Calendar of Events at $29.95 each*
Quantity Discounts:
Deduct 10% per copy for 3–9 copies
Deduct 20% per copy for 10 or more copies $ ______

Sales Tax:
Add applicable tax in AL, CA, FL, IL, NC, NJ, NY, OH, PA, TX, WA $ ______

Shipping and Handling:
Add $5.00 for first copy, $3.50 for each additional copy $ ______

☐ Check ☐ Money Order
(payable to NTC/Contemporary Publishing Co.) TOTAL $ ______

☐ VISA ☐ MasterCard ☐ AmEx ☐ Discover

Acct. ______________________ Exp. ___/___

X ______________________
Signature if charging to bank card

____
Name (please print)

SHIP TO:

____
Name

____
Address

____
Address

____
City State Zip

STANDING ORDER/Authorization

To ensure that I receive each year's new annual edition(s) of ***Chase's*** calendars, please accept this Standing Order Authorization to ship me _______ copies of each edition of ***Chase's Calendar of Events*** and _______ copies of each edition of ***Chase's Sports Calendar of Events***, beginning with the 1999 editions, and to bill me at the address shown above.

Signature ______________________ Date
Name ______________________ (please print)
Phone (   ) ______________________

*Prices subject to change without notice. F98

which Earth Day falls (Apr 22) as Earth Week. During Earth Week, PTA members and others work to improve the environment in their homes, schools and communities. For info: Natl PTA Awareness Program, Natl PTA, 330 N Wabash Ave, Ste 2100, Chicago, IL 60611-3690. Phone: (312) 670-6782. Fax: (312) 670-6783. Email: info@pta.org. WWW: http://www.pta.org

NATIONAL VOLUNTEER WEEK. Apr 19–25. National Volunteer Week honors those who reach out to others through volunteer community service and calls attention to the need for more community services for individuals, groups and families to help solve serious social problems that affect our communities. For info: Customer Information Center, Points of Light Foundation, 1737 H Street, NW, Washington, DC 20006. Phone: (202) 223-9186. Fax: (202) 223-9256. Email: volnet@aol.com.

NETHERLANDS–UNITED STATES DIPLOMATIC RELATIONS: ANNIVERSARY. Apr 19, 1782. Anniversary of establishment of America's oldest continuously peaceful diplomatic relations. On this date, the States General of the Netherlands United Provinces admitted John Adams (later to become second president of the US) as minister plenipotentiary of the young American republic. This was the second diplomatic recognition of the US as an independent nation. Within six months Adams had succeeded in bringing about the signing of the first Treaty of Amity and Commerce between the two countries (Oct 8, 1782).

NEWSPAPER ASSOCIATION OF AMERICA CONVENTION. Apr 19–22. Dallas, TX. For info: Newspaper Assn of America, 1921 Gallows Rd, Ste 600, Vienna, VA 22182. Phone: (703) 902-1600. WWW: http://www.naa.org

OKLAHOMA CITY BOMBING: ANNIVERSARY. Apr 19, 1995. A car bomb exploded outside the Alfred P. Murrah Federal Building in Oklahoma City, OK, at 9:02 AM, killing 168 people, 19 of them children at a day-care center; a nurse died of head injuries sustained while helping in rescue efforts. The bomb, estimated to have weighed 5,000 pounds, had been placed in a rented truck. The blast ripped off the north face of the 9-story building, leaving a 20-foot-wide crater and debris two stories high. Timothy J. McVeigh, a decorated Gulf War army vet who is alleged to have been deeply angered by the Bureau of Alcohol, Tobacco and Firearms (ATF) attack on the Branch Davidian compound at Waco, TX, exactly 2 years before, has been convicted of the bombing. The ATF had offices in the OK federal building. At press time, Terry L. Nicholls, an army buddy of McVeigh, is awaiting trial.

ORTHODOX EASTER SUNDAY OR PASCHA. Apr 19. Observed by Eastern Orthodox Churches on this date. See also: "Easter Sunday."

PROFESSIONAL SECRETARIES WEEK. Apr 19–25. Acknowledgment of the contributions of all office professionals and their vital roles in business, industry, education and government. Annually, the last full week (from Sunday–Saturday) in April. Professional Secretaries Day is observed on Wednesday of this week (Apr 22 in 1998). For info: Rick Stroud, Communications Dir, Professional Secretaries Intl®-The Assn for Office Professionals™, 10502 NW Ambassador Dr, PO Box 20404, Kansas City, MO 64195-0404. Phone: (816) 891-6600. Fax: (816) 891-9118. Email: psihq@psi.org. WWW: http://www.gvi.net/psi

READING IS FUN WEEK. Apr 19–25. To highlight the importance and fun of reading. For info: Rachael Walker, Spec Projects Mgr, Reading Is Fundamental, Inc, 600 Maryland Ave SW, Rm 600, Washington, DC 20024-2569. Phone: (202) 287-3371. Fax: (202) 287-3196.

RICARDO, DAVID: BIRTH ANNIVERSARY. Apr 19, 1772. Economist David Ricardo, whose writings greatly influenced later economic theory, was born at London. He is recognized as the man who first systematized economics. In his best-known work, *Principles of Political Economy and Taxation* (1817), he discussed wages and rent and the economic relationships among landlords, workers and owners of capital. In 1819 Ricardo purchased his own seat in the House of Commons and became a member of Parliament. He died at age 51 on Sept 11, 1823, at Gatcombe Park, Gloucestershire.

SHERMAN, ROGER: BIRTH ANNIVERSARY. Apr 19, 1721. American statesman, member of the Continental Congress (1774–81 and 1783–84), signer of the Declaration of Independence and of the Constitution, was born at Newton, MA. He also calculated astronomical and calendar information for an almanac. Sherman died at New Haven, CT, July 23, 1793.

SIERRA LEONE: NATIONAL HOLIDAY. Apr 19. Sierra Leone became a republic on Apr 19, 1971.

SKY AWARENESS WEEK. Apr 19–25. A celebration of the sky and an opportunity to appreciate its natural beauty, to understand sky and weather processes and to work together to protect the sky as a natural resource (it's the only one we have). Events are held at schools, nature centers, etc, all across the US. Annually, during National Science and Technology Week. For info: Barbara G. Levine, How The Weather Works, 1522 Baylor Ave, Rockville, MD 20850. Phone: (301) 762-7669 or (301) 251-0242. Fax: (301) 762-7669. Email: skyweek@weatherworks.com. WWW: http://www.weatherworks.com

SPACE MILESTONE: *SALYUT 7* (USSR). Apr 19, 1982. New space station launched from Tyuratam, USSR, to replace the aging *Salyut 6*.

WARSAW GHETTO REVOLT: 55th ANNIVERSARY. Apr 19, 1943. A prolonged revolt began in Warsaw, Poland, when German troops tried to resume deportation of Jewish residents of the Warsaw Ghetto to the Treblinka concentration camp. With only 17 rifles and hand-made grenades, for almost a month, 1,200 Jewish fighters resisted 2,100 German troops who were armed with machine guns. When the uprising ended on May 16, 300 Germans and 7,000 Jews had died and the Warsaw Ghetto lay in ruins.

WEEK OF THE YOUNG CHILD. Apr 19–25. To focus on the importance of quality early childhood education. For info: Pat Spahr, Dir of Info Development, Natl Assn for the Educ of Young Children, 1509 16th St, NW, Washington, DC 20036. Phone: (800) 424-2460. Fax: (202) 328-1846. Email: naeyc@naeyc.org. WWW: http://www.naeyc.org/naeyc

WORLD COW CHIP-THROWING CHAMPIONSHIP® CONTEST. Apr 19. Beaver, OK. 29th annual. A highly specialized international organic sporting event which draws dung flingers from around the world. Annually, the final day of Cimarron Territory Celebration (Apr 11–19 in 1998). Est attendance: 4,500. For info: Rita Marshall, Secy, Beaver County Chamber of Commerce, PO Box 878, Beaver, OK 73932-0878. Phone: (405) 625-4726.

WSBA and WARM 103 SPRING CRAFT SHOW. Apr 19. York Fairgrounds, York, PA. More than 250 crafts, from country to contemporary, Victorian and southwestern, handcrafted furniture, wood carvings, dolls, jewelry, pottery, collectibles, quilts, baskets and much more. Admission fee. Est attendance: 7,000. For info: Gina M. Koch, Spec Events Dir, PO Box 910, York, PA 17402-0619. Phone: (717) 764-1155. Fax: (717) 252-4708.

BIRTHDAYS TODAY

Don Adams, 71, actor (Emmy for "Get Smart"), born New York, NY, Apr 19, 1927.

Tim Curry, 52, actor (*The Rocky Horror Picture Show*; stage: *Hair, Amadeus, My Favorite Year*), born Cheshire, England, Apr 19, 1946.

Elinor Donahue, 61, actress ("Father Knows Best," "The Andy Griffith Show"), born Tacoma, WA, Apr 19, 1937.

Kenneth (Kenneth Everette Battelle), 71, hairdresser, born Syracuse, NY, Apr 19, 1927.

Dudley Moore, 63, actor (*Arthur, Bedazzled*), composer, born London, England, Apr 19, 1935.

Hugh O'Brian, 68, actor ("The Life and Legend of Wyatt Earp," *Broken Lance, Ten Little Indians*), born Rochester, NY, Apr 19, 1930.

Alan Price, 56, singer, songwriter, born Fairfield, England, Apr 19, 1942.

Al Unser Jr, 36, auto racer, Indy Car national champion, born Albuquerque, NM, Apr 19, 1962.

Frank John Viola, Jr, 38, baseball player, born Hempstead, NY, Apr 19, 1960.

APRIL 20 — MONDAY

Day 110 — 255 Remaining

BIG 12 WOMEN'S GOLF CHAMPIONSHIP. Apr 20–22. Norman, OK. Est attendance: 1,000. For info: Dru Hancock, Big 12 Conference, 2201 Stemmons Freeway, 28th Floor, Dallas, TX 75207. Phone: (214) 742-1212. Fax: (214) 742-2045.

BOSTON MARATHON—102nd RUNNING. Apr 20. Boston, MA. The marathon begins in the rural New England town of Hopkinton, winds through eight cities and towns and finishes near downtown Boston. 1998 will be the 102nd year of this historic running event. 15,000 participants. Est attendance: 2,000,000. For info: Marja Bakker, Boston Athletic Assn, Boston Marathon, PO Box 1998, Hopkinton, MA 01748. Phone: (508) 435-6905. Email: mile27@star.net.
WWW: http://www.bostonmarathon.org

CANADA: NEWFOUNDLAND: SAINT GEORGE'S DAY. Apr 20. Holiday observed in Newfoundland on Monday nearest Feast Day (Apr 23) of St. George.

EXPLORE YOUR CAREER OPTIONS WEEK. Apr 20–24. Maybe you're aspiring to a new career or merely interested in more opportunities in your present career. Get a fresh start by taking stock of all available options. For info: Dorothy Zjawin, Dir, 61 W Colfax Ave, Roselle Park, NJ 07204. Phone: (908) 241-6241. Fax: (908) 241-6241.

FORDYCE ON THE COTTON BELT FESTIVAL. Apr 20–25. Fordyce, AR. 17th annual railroad event includes arts and crafts, quilt show and sale, train rides, musical entertainment, rodeo, parade, railroad displays, beauty pageants, gospel singing and more. Est attendance: 10,000. For info: Chamber of Commerce, PO Box 588, Fordyce, AR 71742. Phone: (501) 352-3520. Fax: (501) 352-8090.

FRENCH, DANIEL CHESTER: BIRTH ANNIVERSARY. Apr 20, 1850. American sculptor born at Exeter, NH. One of the most important artists of the 19th and early 20th centuries as a sculptor of public monuments, French is best known for his 1875 "Minute Man" statue at Concord, MA, and his 1922 statue of the seated Abraham Lincoln in the Lincoln Memorial at Washington, DC. His home and studio in Stockbridge, MA, were donated to the National Trust for Historic Preservation and are open to the public. For info: Chesterwood, PO Box 827, Stockbridge, MA 01262-0827.

April 1998

S	M	T	W	T	F	S
			1	2	3	4
5	6	7	8	9	10	11
12	13	14	15	16	17	18
19	20	21	22	23	24	25
26	27	28	29	30		

HERITAGE WEEK. Apr 20–25. New Harmony, IN. Head to this historic village and watch crafters create 19th-century-style chairs, candles, baskets and pottery. Annually, Monday through Saturday of the third week in April. Est attendance: 4,000. For info: Special Projects Coord, Historic New Harmony, PO Box 579, New Harmony, IN 47631. Phone: (812) 682-4488. Fax: (812) 682-4313. Email: cknudson.ucs@smtp.usi.edu.

HITLER, ADOLF: BIRTH ANNIVERSARY. Apr 20, 1889. German dictator, frustrated artist, obsessed with superiority of the "Aryan race" and the evil of Marxism (which he saw as a Jewish plot), Hitler was born at Braunau am Inn, Austria. Turning to politics, despite a five-year prison sentence (writing *Mein Kampf* during the nine months he served), his rise was predictable and, on Aug 19, 1934, a German plebiscite vested sole executive power in Führer Adolf Hitler. Facing certain defeat by the Allied Forces, on Apr 30, 1945, he shot himself while his mistress, Eva Braun, took poison in a Berlin bunker where they had been hiding for more than three months.

LUDLOW MINE INCIDENT: ANNIVERSARY. Apr 20. Miners struggling for recognition of their United Mine Workers Union were attacked in Ludlow, CO, by National Guard troops on Apr 20, 1914. The Guardsmen were paid by the mining company. A tent colony was destroyed, five men and one boy were killed by machine-gun fire, and 11 children and two women were burned to death.

NATIONAL ORGANIZE YOUR FILES WEEK. Apr 20–26. To provide a week (after tax season and in conjunction with spring cleaning) for corporations, offices and home offices to annually review and organize their files and file systems. From purging, reorganizing and creating new systems to upgrading files and tabbing—creating more effective files will save time and money for every business, not to mention alleviate the frustration of not being able to retrieve files in a timely manner. Annually, third full week of April. For info: Gloria Schaaf, Organization Works!, 155 E 88th Street, Ste. 3F, New York, NY 10128. Phone: (212) 410-4937.

PATRIOT'S DAY IN MASSACHUSETTS AND MAINE. Apr 20. Commemorates Battles of Lexington and Concord, 1775. Annually, the third Monday in April.

SMITH, HOLLAND: BIRTH ANNIVERSARY. Apr 20, 1882. Considered the father of amphibious warfare, Holland "Howling Mad" Smith was born at Hatchechubie, AL. Smith developed techniques for amphibious assaults that involved coordination of land, sea and air forces. During WWII he led troops in assaults in the Marshall and Mariana Islands and also directed forces at Guam, Iwo Jima and Okinawa. Smith died Jan 12, 1967, at San Diego, CA.

TAURUS, THE BULL. Apr 20–May 20. In the astronomical/astrological zodiac that divides the sun's apparent orbit into 12 segments, the period Apr 20–May 20 is identified, traditionally, as the sun sign of Taurus, the Bull. The ruling planet is Venus.

WORLD'S BIGGEST FISH FRY. Apr 20–25. Paris, TN. Huge festival with parades, arts and crafts, midway, antique car show, rodeo, catfish races and over 13,000 lbs. of catfish with all the trimmings. 45th annual. Events held the last full week of April every year. Est attendance: 100,000. For info: World's Biggest Fish Fry, PO Box 444, Paris, TN 38242. Phone: (901) 644-1143. Fax: (901) 642-3431.

BIRTHDAYS TODAY

Nina Foch, 74, actress (*Scaramouche*), born Leyden, Holland, Apr, 20, 1924.

Jessica Lange, 49, actress (Oscars for *Tootsie* and *Blue Skies*; *Frances, Country, Sweet Dreams*), born Cloquet, MN, Apr 20, 1949.

Joey Lawrence, 22, actor ("Blossom," "Brotherly Love"), born Strawbridge, PA, Apr 20, 1976.

David Leland, 51, actor (*Time Bandits*), writer, director (*Mona Lisa, Wish You Were Here*), born Cambridge, England, Apr 20, 1947.

Donald Arthur (Don) Mattingly, 37, former baseball player, born Evansville, IN, Apr 20, 1961.

Ryan O'Neal, 57, actor ("Peyton Place," *Love Story, Paper Moon*), born Los Angeles, CA, Apr 20, 1941.

Pat Roberts, 62, US Senator (R, Kansas), born Topeka, KS, Apr 20, 1936.

John Paul Stevens, 78, Associate Justice of the US Supreme Court, born Chicago, IL, Apr 20, 1920.

Luther Vandross, 47, singer, songwriter ("Never Too Much"), born New York, NY, Apr 20, 1951.

APRIL 21 — TUESDAY

Day 111 — 254 Remaining

BRAZIL: TIRADENTES DAY. Apr 21. National holiday commemorating execution of national hero, dentist Jose da Silva Xavier, nicknamed Tiradentes (tooth-puller), a conspirator in revolt against the Portuguese in 1789.

BRONTE, CHARLOTTE: BIRTH ANNIVERSARY. Apr 21. English novelist born Apr 21, 1816, at Hartshead, Yorkshire, England. "Conventionality," she wrote in the preface to *Jane Eyre*, "is not morality. Self-righteousness is not religion. To attack the first is not to assail the last." She died on Mar 31, 1855.

EIGHTY-NINER CELEBRATION. Apr 21–26. Guthrie, OK. In celebration of its heritage, this historically restored town features Old West gunfights, chuckwagon feed, professional rodeo and Oklahoma's largest parade of bands, floats and roundup clubs from across the state. Est attendance: 10,000. For info: Frankie Smith, Dir, Chamber of Commerce, Box 995, Guthrie, OK 73044. Phone: (800) 299-1889 or (405) 282-1948 or (405) 282-2589. Fax: (405) 282-0061.

FESTIVAL INTERNATIONAL DE LOUISIANE. Apr 21–26. Lafayette, LA. Celebrates the cultural connections between French Louisiana and the French-speaking world. Visual and performing artists of Louisiana and several francophone countries provide open air concerts, exhibits, theater, film and international cuisine. Est attendance: 150,000. For info: Mktg Coord, Festival Intl de Louisiane, PO Box 4008, Lafayette, LA 70502. Phone: (318) 232-8086. Fax: (318) 291-5480. Email: fil@net-connect.net. WWW: http://www.fil.net-connect.net

FESTIVAL OF RIDVAN. Apr 21–May 2. Annual Baha'i festival commemorating the 12 days (Apr 21–May 2, 1863) when Baha'u'llah, the prophet-founder of the Baha'i Faith, resided in a garden called Ridvan (Paradise) in Baghdad, at which time He publicly proclaimed His mission as God's messenger for this age. The first, ninth (Apr 29 in 1997) and twelfth days are celebrated as holy days and are three of the nine days of the year when Baha'is suspend work. For info: Pamela Zivari, Baha'is of the US, Office of Public Information, 866 UN Plaza, Ste 120, New York, NY 10017-1822. Phone: (212) 803-2500. Fax: (212) 803-2573. Email: usopi-ny@bic.org.

FREDERICKSBURG DAY. Apr 21. Fredericksburg, VA. Spring tour of historic homes and gardens. To fund one historic garden restoration in Virginia per year. Est attendance: 2,000. For info: Visitor Center, 706 Caroline St, Fredericksburg, VA 22401. Phone: (800) 678-4748. Fax: (540) 372-6587. Email: fburg@illuminet.net.

FROEBEL, FRIEDRICH: BIRTH ANNIVERSARY. Apr 21, 1782. German educator and author Friedrich Froebel, who believed that play is an important part of a child's education, was born at Oberwiessbach, Thuringia. Froebel invented the kindergarten, founding the first one at Blankenburg, Germany, in 1837. Froebel also invented a series of toys which he described as "gifts" intended to stimulate learning. (The American architect Frank Lloyd Wright as a child received these toy "gifts" [maplewood blocks] from his mother and spoke throughout his life of their value.) Froebel's ideas about the role of directed play, toys and music in children's education had a profound influence in England and the US, where the nursery school became a further extension of his ideas. Froebel died at Marienthal, Germany, on June 21, 1852.

INDONESIA: KARTINI DAY. Apr 21. Republic of Indonesia. Honors Raden Adjeng Kartini, pioneer in the emancipation of the women of Indonesia.

ITALY: BIRTHDAY OF ROME. Apr 21. National celebration of the founding of Rome. Traditionally in 753 BC.

KINDERGARTEN DAY. Apr 21. A day to recognize the importance of play, games and "creative self-activity" in children's education and to note the history of the kindergarten. Observed on anniversary of the birth of Friedrich Froebel (Apr 21, 1782) who established the first kindergarten in 1837. German immigrants brought Froebel's ideas to the US in the 1840s. The first kindergarten in a public school in the US was started in 1873, at St. Louis, MO.

MANGANO, SILVANA: BIRTH ANNIVERSARY. Apr 21, 1930. Italian actress Silvana Mangano was born at Rome, Italy. She is best known for her role in the film *Bitter Rice* (1948). Mangano died on Dec 16, 1989, at Madrid, Spain.

MUIR, JOHN: BIRTH ANNIVERSARY. Apr 21, 1838. American naturalist, explorer, conservationist and author for whom the 550-acre Muir Woods National Monument (near San Francisco, CA) is named. Muir, born at Dunbar, Scotland, on Apr 21, 1838, emigrated to the US in 1849, where he urged establishment of national parks and profoundly influenced US forest conservation. Died at Los Angeles, CA, on Dec 24, 1914.

RED BARON SHOT DOWN: 80th ANNIVERSARY. Apr 21, 1918. German flying ace Baron Manfred von Richtofen was shot down and killed during the battle of the Somme on Apr 21, 1918. The "Red Baron," so named for the color of his Fokker triplane, was credited with 80 kills in less than two years. Royal Flying Corp pilots recovered his body and the Allies buried him with full military honors. Asked about his fighting philosophy he was quoted as saying, "I am a hunter. My brother Lothar is a butcher. When I have shot down an Englishman, my hunting passion is satisfied for a quarter of an hour."

SAN JACINTO DAY. Apr 21. Texas. Commemorates Battle of San Jacinto, Apr 21, 1836, in which Texas won independence from Mexico. A 570-foot monument, dedicated on the 101st anniversary of the battle, marks the site on the banks of the San Jacinto River, about 20 miles from present city of Houston, TX, where General Sam Houston's Texans decisively defeated the Mexican forces led by Santa Anna in the final battle between Texas and Mexico.

SPACE MILESTONE: *COPERNICUS, OAO 4* (US). Apr 21, 1972. Launch of Orbiting Astronomical Observer, named in honor of the Polish astronomer.

BIRTHDAYS TODAY

David Boren, 57, former US Senator (D, Oklahoma), born Washington, DC, Apr 21, 1941.

Tony Danza, 47, actor ("Taxi," "Who's the Boss"), born Brooklyn, NY, Apr 21, 1951.

Queen Elizabeth II, 72, Queen of the United Kingdom, born London, England, Apr 21, 1926.

Charles Grodin, 63, actor (*Midnight Run, Beethoven*), director, host ("The Charles Grodin Show"), born Pittsburgh, PA, Apr 21, 1935.

Patti LuPone, 49, actress (*Evita*; "Life Goes On"), born Northport, NY, Apr 21, 1949.

Andie MacDowell, 40, former model, actress (*sex, lies, and videotape* [Best Actress Award, LA Film Critics], *The Player, Groundhog Day*), born Gaffney, SC, Apr 21, 1958.

Elaine May, 66, actress, writer (comedy with Mike Nichols), director (*A New Leaf*), born Philadephia, PA, Apr 21, 1932.

Iggy Pop, 51, singer, born Ann Arbor, MI, Apr 21, 1947.

Anthony Quinn, 82, actor (Oscars for *Viva Zapata, Lust for Life*), born Chihuahua, Mexico, Apr 21, 1916.

APRIL 22 — WEDNESDAY

Day 112 — 253 Remaining

BABE'S PITCHING DEBUT: ANNIVERSARY. April 22, 1914. Babe Ruth made his professional pitching debut, playing for the Baltimore Orioles in his own hometown. Allowing just six hits and contributing two singles himself, Ruth shut out the Buffalo Bisons, 6–0.

BRAZIL: DISCOVERY OF BRAZIL DAY. Apr 22. Commemorates discovery by Pedro Alvarez Cabral, 1500.

COINS STAMPED "IN GOD WE TRUST": ANNIVERSARY. Apr 22. By Act of Congress, the phrase "In God We Trust" began to be stamped on all US coins on Apr 22, 1864.

EARTH DAY. Apr 22. The original Earth Day, first observed Apr 22, 1970, with message "Give Earth a Chance" and attention to reclaiming the purity of the air, water and living environment. Special 10th anniversary observance on Apr 22, 1980, with assistance from US Environmental Protection Agency. Annually, Apr 22. Note: Earth Day activities have been held by many groups and on various dates, often on the weekend closest to Apr 22. The vernal equinox has been chosen by some for this observance.

FIRST SOLO TRIP TO NORTH POLE: ANNIVERSARY. Apr 22, 1994. Norwegian explorer Borge Ousland became the first person to make the trip to the North Pole alone. The trip took 52 days, during which he pulled a 265-pound sled. Departing from Cape Atkticheskiy in Siberia on Mar 2, he averaged about 18½ miles per day over the 630-mile journey. Ousland had traveled to the Pole on skis with Erling Kagge in 1990.

KGBX TYPEWRITER TOSS. Apr 22. KGBX /FM Radio, Springfield, MO. Participating secretaries toss a typewriter from a lift-truck nearly 50 feet in the air. The typewriter landing closest to the bull's-eye wins an array of prizes. Definitely a "smashing" success! Annually, Secretaries Day. 9th annual toss. Est attendance: 250. For info: Pamela Cooper, KGBX Radio, 1856 S Glenstone, Springfield, MO 65807. Phone: (417) 890-5555. Fax: (417) 869-1000. WWW: http://www.kgbx.com

LENIN, NIKOLAI: BIRTH ANNIVERSARY. Apr 22, 1870. Russian socialist and revolutionary leader (real name: Vladimir Ilyich Ulyanov), ideological follower of Karl Marx. Born at Simbirst, on the Volga, Russia, Apr 22, 1870 (New Style) (Apr 10, 1870, Old Style). Leader of the Great October Socialist Revolution of 1917. Lenin died at Gorky, near Moscow, on Jan 21, 1924. His embalmed body, in a glass coffin at the Lenin Mausoleum, has been viewed by millions of visitors to Moscow's Red Square.

April 1998

S	M	T	W	T	F	S
			1	2	3	4
5	6	7	8	9	10	11
12	13	14	15	16	17	18
19	20	21	22	23	24	25
26	27	28	29	30		

OKLAHOMA DAY. Apr 22. Oklahoma.

OKLAHOMA LAND RUSH: ANNIVERSARY. Apr 22. At twelve o'clock noon on Apr 22, 1889, a gun shot signaled the start of the Oklahoma land rush as thousands of settlers rushed into the territory to claim land. Under pressure from cattlemen, the federal government opened 1,900,000 acres of central Oklahoma that had been bought from the Creek and Seminole tribes.

PROFESSIONAL SECRETARIES DAY. Apr 22. Annually, the Wednesday of Professional Secretaries Week. For info: Rick Stroud, Communications Dir, Professional Secretaries Intl®-The Assn for Office Professionals™, 10502 NW Ambassador Dr, PO Box 20404, Kansas City, MO 64195-0404. Phone: (816) 891-6600. Fax: (816) 891-9118. Email: psihq@psi.org. WWW: http://www.gvi.net/psi

RACKING HORSE SPRING CELEBRATION. Apr 22–25. Decatur, AL. Racking horses from throughout the country are shown each night, culminating with the selection of award winners. Est attendance: 25,000. For info: Jacklyn Bailey, Decatur Conv and Visitors Bureau, 719 6th Ave SE, PO Box 2349, Decatur, AL 35602. Phone: (205) 350-2028 or (800) 524-6181. Email: dcvb@hiwaay.net.

SPALDING UNIVERSITY RUNNING OF THE RODENTS. Apr 22. Louisville, KY. 26th annual. To celebrate the prefinals "Rat Race" that occurs each year, to develop community spirit and to unofficially kick off the Kentucky Derby festivities. Est attendance: 300. For info: Public Relations, Spalding University, 851 S Fourth St, Louisville, KY 40203. Phone: (502) 585-7140 or (800) 896-8941. Fax: (502) 585-7158. Email: pr@spalding13.win.net. WWW: http://www.spalding.edu

BIRTHDAYS TODAY

Eddie Albert (Edward Albert Heimberger), 90, actor ("Green Acres," *Teahouse of the August Moon, Roman Holiday*), born Rock Island, IL, Apr 22, 1908.

Byron Allen, 37, comedian, TV host ("Byron Allen Show," "Real People"), actor (*Case Closed*, which he also co-wrote and co-produced), born Detroit, MI, Apr 22, 1961.

Glen Campbell, 63, singer ("Gentle on My Mind," "By the Time I Get to Phoenix," "Country Boy"), born Billstown, AR, Apr 22, 1935.

Peter Frampton, 48, singer ("Show Me the Way," "Do You Feel Like We Do"), songwriter, born Beckenham, England, Apr 22, 1950.

Chris Makepeace, 34, actor (*My Bodyguard*), born Montreal, Quebec, Canada, Apr 22, 1964.

Yehudi Menuhin, 82, violinist, born New York, NY, Apr 22, 1916.

Jason Miller, 59, playwright (*That Championship Season* [winner of NY Drama Critics Best Play Award, 1972, Tony Award, 1973, and Pulitzer Prize for Drama]); actor (*The Exorcist, The Ninth Configuration*), born Scranton, PA, Apr 22, 1939.

Jack Nicholson, 62, actor (Oscars for *One Flew Over the Cuckoo's Nest* and *Terms of Endearment; Five Easy Pieces, The Last Detail*), born Neptune, NJ, Apr 22, 1936.

Aaron Spelling, 70, writer, producer ("Fantasy Island," "Melrose Place"), born Dallas, TX, Apr 22, 1928.

John Waters, 52, filmmaker (*Pink Flamingoes*), born Baltimore, MD, Apr 22, 1946.

APRIL 23 — THURSDAY

Day 113 — 252 Remaining

AMERICAN QUILTER'S SOCIETY QUILT SHOW. Apr 23–26. Paducah, KY. More than 400 quilts are exhibited with $85,000 awarded in prizes. Seminars, workshops. Est attendance: 30,000. For info: American Quilter's Soc, PO Box 3290, Paducah, KY 42002. Phone: (502) 898-7903.

BERMUDA: PEPPERCORN CEREMONY: ANNIVERSARY. Apr 23. St. George. Commemorates the payment of one peppercorn in 1816 to the governor of Bermuda for rental of Old State House by the Masonic Lodge.

BIG 12 MEN'S AND WOMEN'S TENNIS CHAMPIONSHIP. Apr 23–26. Kansas City, MO. Est attendance: 1,000. For info: Dru Hancock, Big 12 Conference, 2201 Stemmons Freeway, 28th Floor, Dallas, TX 75207. Phone: (214) 742-1212. Fax: (214) 742-2045.

BUCHANAN, JAMES: BIRTH ANNIVERSARY. Apr 23. The 15th president of the US, born at Cove Gap, PA, on Apr 23, 1791, was the only president who never married. He served one term in office, Mar 4, 1857–Mar 3, 1861, and died at Lancaster, PA, on June 1, 1868.

CERVANTES SAAVEDRA, MIGUEL DE: DEATH ANNIVERSARY. Apr 23. Spanish poet, playwright and novelist died in his 69th year, at Madrid, Spain, on Apr 23, 1616 (also the day of William Shakespeare's death). The exact date of Cervantes's birth at Alcala de Henares is unknown, but he was baptized Oct 9, 1547, and some believe he was born on Michaelmas, Sept 29. As soldier and tax collector, Cervantes traveled widely. He spent more than five years in prisons in Spain, Italy and North Africa. His greatest creation was Don Quixote, the immortal Knight of La Mancha whose profession was chivalry. Riding his nag, Rozinante, and accompanied by Squire Sancho Panza, Don Quixote tilts at windmills of the mind in the world's best-known novel. Nearly a thousand editions of *Don Quixote* (a bestseller since its first appearance in 1605) have been published, and it has been translated into more languages than any other book except the Bible.

CIVIL WAR REENACTMENT. Apr 23–26. Rand Park, Keokuk, IA. Battle reenactment, military ball, theater production, historic encampment, ladies' tea and style show and military band concert. Est attendance: 25,000. For info: Kari Bevans, Keokuk Area Conv and Tourism Bureau, 401 Main, Keokuk, IA 52632. Phone: (800) 383-1219 or (319) 524-5599. Email: keochcom@interl.net.

ENGLAND: CHELSEA ART FAIR. Apr 23–26. London. Dynamic event for all art lovers with paintings, drawings, etchings, prints, sculpture and studio pottery and glass dating from the year 1500 to the present. Est attendance: 4,000. For info: Barbara Bell, Event Mgr, PO Box 114, Haywards Heath, Sussex, England RH16 2YU. Phone: (44)(144) 448-2514.

ENGLAND: HARROGATE SPRING FLOWER FESTIVAL. Apr 23–26. Great Yorkshire Showground, Harrogate, North Yorkshire. Spectacular exhibits and displays at Britain's largest spring show. Est attendance: 60,000. For info: Alan Ravenscroft, Show Dir, North of England Horticultural Soc, 4A South Park Rd, Harrogate, North Yorkshire, England HG1 5QU. Phone: (44) (142) 356-1049. Fax: (44) (142) 353-6880.

ENGLAND: SOUTHERN KNITTING AND NEEDLECRAFT EXHIBITION. Apr 23–26. Royal Bath and West Showground, Shepton Mallet, Somerset. Everything for the hand and machine knitter and needlecraft enthusiast, fashion shows, lectures, demonstrations. Est attendance: 18,000. For info: Robert Ewin, Dir, Nationwide Exhibitions (UK) Ltd, PO Box 20, Fishponds, Bristol, England BS16 5QU. Phone: (44) (117) 970-1370. Fax: (44) (117) 970-1371. Email: nationwideexhibitions.co.uk.

HOLOCAUST DAY (YOM HASHOAH). Apr 23. Hebrew calendar date: Nisan 27, 5758. A day established by Israel's Knesset as a memorial to the Jewish dead of World War II. Anniversary in Jewish calendar of Nisan 27, 5705 (corresponding to Apr 10, 1945, in the Gregorian calendar), the day on which Allied troops liberated the first Nazi concentration camp, one of the most notorious, Buchenwald, north of Weimar, Germany, established in 1937, where about 56,000 prisoners, many of them Jewish, perished.

INTERNATIONAL HOME FURNISHINGS MARKET. Apr 23–May 1. (Also Oct 15–23.) High Point and Thomasville, NC. The largest wholesale home furnishings market in the world. (Not open to the general public.) Est attendance: 70,000. For info: Intl Home Furnishings Mktg Assn, PO Box 5687, High Point, NC 27262. Phone: (910) 889-0203. Fax: (910) 889-7460.

INTERNATIONAL SPECIAL LIBRARIANS DAY. Apr 23. Recognition for the important role that special librarians play in the international sharing of information. For info: Dir PR, SLA, 1700 18th St NW, Washington, DC 20009-2514. WWW: http://www.sla.org

NEW BEGINNING FESTIVAL. Apr 23–25. Coffeyville, KS. A multistate arts and crafts festival; cheese festival, carnival, entertainment. Est attendance: 15,000. For info: Chamber of Commerce, Box 457, Coffeyville, KS 67337. Phone: (316) 251-2550. Fax: (316) 251-5448. Email: chamber@terraworld.net.

PEARSON, LESTER B.: BIRTH ANNIVERSARY. Apr 23, 1897. 14th prime minister of Canada, born at Toronto, Canada. He was Canada's chief delegate at the San Francisco conference where the UN charter was drawn up and later served as president of the General Assembly. He wrote the proposal that resulted in the formation of the North Atlantic Treaty Organization (NATO). He was awarded the Nobel Peace Prize. Died at Rockcliffe, Canada, Dec 27, 1972.

PHYSICISTS DISCOVER TOP QUARK: ANNIVERSARY. Apr 23, 1994. Physicists at the Department of Energy's Fermi National Accelerator Laboratory found evidence for the existence of the subatomic particle called the top quark, the last undiscovered quark of the six predicted to exist by current scientific theory. The discovery provides strong support for the quark theory of the structure of matter. Quarks are subatomic particles that make up protons and neutrons found in the nuclei of atoms. The five other quark types that had already been proven to exist are the up quark, down quark, strange quark, charm quark and bottom quark. Further experimentation over many months confirmed the discovery, and it was publicly announced on Mar 2, 1995.

PLANCK, MAX: BIRTH ANNIVERSARY. Apr 23, 1858. Formulator of the quantum theory which revolutionized physics, born at Kiel, Germany. Einstein's application of quantum theory to light led to the theories of relativity. Planck died at Gottingen, Germany, Oct 3, 1947.

PURSUE THE CHALLENGE: LEADERSHIP TRAINING FOR SELF-ADVOCATES. Apr 23–25. Anchorage, AK. The fourth annual International People First Conference will be a gathering of self-advocates and people with disabilities from around the world. The three-day conference will feature workshops in the areas of: living in the community, removing barriers, working across groups, understanding the law and international disability rights. Self-advocates are people with developmental disabilities who advocate on their own behalf. Est attendance: 1,000. For info: People First Alaska, 2330 Nichols St, Anchorage, AK 99508. Phone: (907) 272-8270. Fax: (907) 274-4802. Email: AYPPLFA@uaa.alaska.edu.

SAINT GEORGE FEAST DAY. Apr 23. Martyr and patron saint of England, who died Apr 23, AD 303. Hero of the George and the dragon legend. The story says that his faith helped him slay a vicious dragon that demanded daily sacrifice after the king's daughter became the intended victim.

SAINT GEORGE'S DAY ANNUAL CELEBRATION. Apr 23. New York, NY. Celebration of the birth of St. George, the patron saint of England, at an authentic British pub featuring coloring contests, prizes and appearances of St. George and the dragon. Annually, Apr 23. Est attendance: 200. For info: Deven Black, Genl Mgr, North Star Pub, 93 South St, New York, NY 10038. Phone: (212) 509-6757. WWW: http://www.goodeating.com/northstar

SHAKESPEARE, WILLIAM: BIRTH AND DEATH ANNIVERSARY. Apr 23. England's most famous and most revered poet and playwright. He was born at Stratford-on-Avon, England, Apr 23, 1564, baptized there three days later and died there on his birthday, Apr 23, 1616. Author of at least 36 plays and 154 sonnets, Shakespeare created the most influential and lasting body of work in the English language, an extraordinary exploration of human nature. His epitaph: "Good frend for Jesus sake forbeare, To digg the dust enclosed heare. Blese be ye man that spares thes stones, And curst be he that moves my bones."

SPACE MILESTONE: *SOYUZ 10* (USSR). Apr 23, 1971. Launch date of Soviet mission in which Cosmonauts V.A. Shatalov, A.S. Yeliseyev and N.N. Rukavishnikov docked Apr 24 with *Salyut 1* orbital space station. Return Earth landing at Kazakhstan, USSR, Apr 24.

SPAIN: BOOK DAY AND LOVER'S DAY. Apr 23. Barcelona. Saint George's Day and the anniversary of the death of Spanish writer Miguel de Cervantes have been observed with special ceremonies in the Palacio de la Disputacion and throughout the city since 1714. Book stands are set up in the plazas and on street corners. This is Spain's equivalent of Valentine's Day. Women give books to men; men give roses to women.

TAKE OUR DAUGHTERS TO WORK DAY. Apr 23. A national public education campaign sponsored by the Ms Foundation for Women in which girls aged 9–15 go to work with adult hosts—parents, grandparents, cousins, aunts, uncles, friends. Take Our Daughters to Work Day has succeeded in mobilizing parents, educators, employers and other caring adults to take action to redress the inequalities in girls' lives and focus national attention on the concerns, hopes and dreams of girls. Annually, the fourth Thursday in April. For info: Lauren Wechsler, Natl Media Mgr, Take Our Daughters to Work Day, Ms Foundation for Women, 120 Wall St, 33rd Fl, New York, NY 10005. Phone: (800) 676-7780 or (212) 742-2300. Fax: (212) 742-1531. Email: todtwcom@ms.foundation.org. WWW: http://www.msfoundation.org

April 1998

S	M	T	W	T	F	S
			1	2	3	4
5	6	7	8	9	10	11
12	13	14	15	16	17	18
19	20	21	22	23	24	25
26	27	28	29	30		

TEXAS STATE CHAMPIONSHIP FIDDLERS FROLICS. Apr 23–26. Hallettsville, TX. Old-time fiddling championship of Texas. The best tasting sausage in Texas contest. Proceeds to various charities. Est attendance: 12,000. For info: Knights of Columbus, Box 46, Hallettsville, TX 77964. Phone: (512) 798-2311. Fax: (512) 798-4365. Email: arjo9286@cvtv.net. WWW: http://www.hallettsville.com

TURKEY: NATIONAL SOVEREIGNTY AND CHILDREN'S DAY. Apr 23. Commemorates Grand National Assembly's inauguration on Apr 23, 1923.

UNITED NATIONS: WORLD BOOK AND COPYRIGHT DAY. Apr 23. Observed throughout the United Nations system.

WASHINGTON STATE APPLE BLOSSOM FESTIVAL. Apr 23–May 3. Wenatchee, WA. To showcase the greater Wenatchee Valley, its people and heritage by producing an ongoing community celebration. Parades, arts and crafts, gem and mineral show, theatrical productions, Youth Day and carnival. More than 40 events. Est attendance: 100,000. For info: Washington State Apple Blossom Festival Assn, Box 2836, Wenatchee, WA 98807. Phone: (509) 662-3616. Fax: (509) 665-0347.

WOODS, GRANVILLE T.: BIRTH ANNIVERSARY. Apr 23. Granville T. Woods was born in Columbus, OH, on Apr 23, 1856. He invented the induction telegraph known as the Synchronous Multiplex Railway Telegraph which allowed communication between dispatchers and trains while the trains were in motion. The communication avenues opened by his invention decreased the number of train accidents. In addition, Woods is credited with a number of other electrical inventions and was compared favorably to Thomas Edison.

BIRTHDAYS TODAY

Valerie Bertinelli, 38, actress ("One Day at a Time," *Silent Witness*), born Wilmington, DE, Apr 23, 1960.

David Birney, 58, actor (Theatre World Award for *Summertree*; "Love Is a Many Splendored Thing," "Bridget Loves Bernie," "The Long Journey Home"), born Washington, DC, Apr 23, 1940.

Shirley Temple Black, 70, former ambassador to Ghana, child star with dimples and curls (*Heidi, Curly Top, Little Miss Marker, The Bachelor and the Bobbysoxer*), TV hostess ("Shirley Temple's Storybook" and "Shirley Temple Theatre"), born Santa Monica, CA, Apr 23, 1928.

Sandra Dee (Alexandra Zuck), 56, actress (*Imitation of Life, A Summer Place, Gidget*), born Bayonne, NJ, Apr 23, 1942.

Joyce Dewitt, 49, actress ("Three's Company"), born Wheeling, WV, Apr 23, 1949.

Jan Hooks, 41, actress ("Saturday Night Live," "Designing Women"), born Atlanta, GA, Apr 23, 1957.

Lee Majors, 58, actor ("The Six Million Dollar Man," "The Fall Guy"), born Wyandotte, MI, Apr 23, 1940.

Bernadette Devlin McAliskey, 51, political activist, born Cookstown, Northern Ireland, Apr 23, 1947.

Warren Edward Spahn, 77, Baseball Hall of Fame pitcher, born Buffalo, NY, Apr 23, 1921.

Narada Michael Walden, 46, drummer (with Mahavishnu Orchestra), singer, songwriter and record producer ("Freeway of Love" with Aretha Franklin; "Where Do Broken Hearts Go" with Whitney Houston), born Kalamazoo, MI, Apr 23, 1952.

APRIL 24 — FRIDAY

Day 114 — 251 Remaining

ARBOR DAY. Apr 2. Nebraska. Observed on the last Friday in April. First observance of Arbor Day was in this state on Apr 10, 1872. Now observed on many different dates in many states and countries.

ARMENIAN MARTYRS DAY. Apr 24. Commemorates the massacre of Armenians under the Ottoman Turks in 1915. On this day, deportations from Turkey began. Also called Armenian Liberation Day. Adolf Hitler, in a speech at Obersalzberg on Aug

22, 1939, is reported to have said, "Who today remembers the Armenian extermination?" in an apparent justification of the Nazi's use of genocide.

A(UGUSTA) BAKER'S DOZEN—A CELEBRATION OF STORIES. Apr 24–25. Columbia, SC. Annual event honors Augusta Baker and recognizes her distinguished career as librarian, storyteller, teacher and author. It features outstanding authors, illustrators and storytellers. Sponsors: Richland County Public Library and the College of Library and Information Science, Univ of South Carolina. Est attendance: 4,000. For info: Judy McClendon, PR Librarian, Richland County Public Library, 1431 Assembly St, Columbia, SC 29201. Phone: (803) 929-3440. Fax: (803) 929-3459.

BASCOM, GEORGE N.: BIRTH ANNIVERSARY. Apr 24, 1836. West Point Graduate Lieutenant George N. Bascom was assigned to search out Apache chief Cochise, believed to be responsible for an 1861 raid on an Arizona ranch. He arrested Cochise at Apache Pass, but the chief escaped and declared war, launching a reign of terror known as the Apache Wars. Bascom was born at Owingsville, KY, and died the year following his Apache adventure when he became a casualty of the Civil War battle at Fort Craig, Valverde, NM, on Feb 21, 1862.

CARTWRIGHT, EDMUND: BIRTH ANNIVERSARY. Apr 24, 1743. English cleric and inventor (developed the power loom and other weaving inventions) was born at Nottinghamshire, England, Apr 24, 1743. He died at Hastings, Sussex, England, Oct 30, 1823.

CONNECTICUT STORYTELLING FESTIVAL. Apr 24–26. Connecticut College, New London, CT. 17th annual festival features performances for families and adults, plus workshops and story-sharing by Connecticut and nationally renowned storytellers. Annually, the last full weekend in April. Est attendance: 300. For info: Christine Tagg, Adm, Connecticut Storytelling Center, Connecticut College Box 5295, 270 Mohegan Ave, New London, CT 06320. Phone: (860) 439-2764. Fax: (860) 439-5431. Email: cltag@conncoll.edu. WWW: http://ourworld.compuserve.com/homepages/insalowitz/stories.htm

DAFFODIL FESTIVAL. Apr 24–27. Nantucket Island, MA. Daffodil show, shop window displays, antique car parade, tailgate picnic, flower show (Sunday and Monday). Est attendance: 15,000. For info: Nantucket Island Chamber of Commerce, 48 Main St, Nantucket, MA 02554-3595. Phone: (508) 228-1700.

DOGWOOD ARTS AND CRAFTS FESTIVAL. Apr 24–26. Huntington Civic Arena, Huntington, WV. 28th annual. Craft and food booths plus live entertainment for all ages. Annually, the last full weekend in April. Est attendance: 15,000. For info: Matt Franco, Huntington Civic Arena, PO Box 2767, One Civic Center Plaza, Huntington, WV 25701. Phone: (304) 696-5990. Fax: (304) 696-4463.

EIGHTEENTH-CENTURY MARKET FAIR AND RIFLE FROLIC. Apr 24–26. Big Pool, MD. A gathering of the best 18th-century-style artisans and craftsmen amidst a historical encampment. Est attendance: 6,000. For info: Fort Frederick State Park, 11100 Fort Frederick Rd, Big Pool, MD 21711. Phone: (301) 842-2155. Fax: (301) 842-0028.

FIDDLER'S FROLICS. Apr 24–26. Knights of Columbus Hall, Hallettsville, TX. Competition to determine the Texas state champion fiddler and inductees to the Texas Fiddlers Hall of Fame. Est attendance: 15,000. For info: Kenneth Henneke, Co-chair, PO Box 46, Hallettsville, TX 77964. Phone: (512) 798-5934 or (512) 798-2311. Fax: (512) 798-4365. WWW: http://www.hallettsville.com

FIRST THANKSGIVING FESTIVAL. Apr 24–26. Chamizal National Memorial, El Paso, TX. This is the 400th anniversary of the First Thanksgiving. The Spanish government plans to send His Majesty, King Juan Carlos I or HRH Felipe, the Crown Prince of Spain, to be the honored guest at this quadricentennial celebration. They will dedicate a statue of Juan de Oñate on horseback. In April 1598 Juan de Oñate arrived at the Rio Grande with 600 colonists and 8,000 head of livestock. After what had been a four-month journey across harsh desert, he ordered a feast of thanksgiving. This festival includes colorful reenactments with conquistadors, Spanish soldiers, monks, women and children as well as vendors, food, arts and crafts. Annually, the last full weekend in April. Est attendance: 20,000. For info: Sheldon Hall, Pres, El Paso Mission Trail Assn, 1 Civic Center Plaza, El Paso, TX 79901. Phone: (800) 351-6024. Fax: (915) 532-2105.

FORT MOORE ESTABLISHED: ANNIVERSARY. Apr 24, 1847. At the conclusion of the Mexican War, the Mormon Battalion of the Army of the West established Fort Moore overseeing the pueblo of Los Angeles. The fort was named in honor of their captain who had perished in the Battle of San Pascual.

HUG A PROM SPONSOR DAY. Apr 24. A day honoring all the teachers across the US who successfully help to organize, promote and chaperone their high school's prom. Annually, the fourth Friday in April. For info: Shep Moyle, Pres, Stumps, One Party Place, South Whitley, IN 46787. Phone: (800) 22-Party. Fax: (219) 723-6976. Email: promnet@www.stumpsparty.com. WWW: http://www.stumpsparty.com

IRELAND: EASTER RISING. Apr 24, 1916. Irish nationalists seized key buildings in Dublin and proclaimed an Irish republic. The rebellion collapsed, however, and it wasn't until 1922 that the Irish Free State, the predecessor of the Republic of Ireland, was established.

LIBRARY OF CONGRESS: ANNIVERSARY. Apr 24, 1800. Congress approved an act providing "for the purchase of such books as may be necessary for the use of Congress . . . and for fitting up a suitable apartment for containing them." Thus began one of the world's greatest libraries.

NATIONAL ARBOR DAY. Apr 24. The Committee for National Arbor Day has as its goal the observance of Arbor Day in all states on the same day, the last Friday in April. This unified Arbor Day date would provide our citizenry with the opportunity to better learn the importance of trees to our way of life. This date is a good planting date for many states throughout the country. National Arbor Day has been observed in 1970, 1972, 1988, 1990, 1991 and 1993 by Presidential Proclamation. More than half the states now observe Arbor Day on the proposed April Friday. Sponsors include: International Society of Arboriculture; Society of Municipal Arborists; American Assn of Nurserymen; National Arborist Assn; National Recreation and Park Assn; Arborists Assn of New Jersey. For info: Committee for Natl Arbor Day, 63 Fitzrandolph Rd, West Orange, NJ 07052. Phone: (201) 731-0840. Fax: (201) 731-6020.

NATIONAL DREAM HOTLINE®. Apr 24–26. The National Dream Hotline is sponsored by the School of Metaphysics as an educational service to people throughout the world. Faculty and staff of the College and School of Metaphysics Centers throughout the midwest will offer the benefits of 30 years of research into the significance and meaning of dreams by manning the hotline phones from 6 PM, EDT, Friday until midnight Sunday. Annually, the last weekend in April. For info: Dr. Barbara Condron, Natl Advisor, or Dr. Laurel Clark, Media Coordinator, School of Metaphysics, HCR 1, Box 15, Windyville, MO 65783. Phone: (417) 345-8411. Fax: (417) 345-6668. Email: som@som.org. WWW: http://www.som.org

NEW ORLEANS JAZZ AND HERITAGE FESTIVAL. Apr 24–May 3. New Orleans, LA. A two-weekend festival with thousands of musicians playing. Evening concerts, outdoor daytime activities, Louisiana specialty foods and handmade crafts. Est attendance: 400,000. For info: New Orleans Jazz and Heritage Festival, PO Box 53407, New Orleans, LA 70153-3407. Phone: (504) 522-4786. WWW: http://www.nojazzfest.com

PANOPLY '98. Apr 24–26. Big Spring International Park, Huntsville, AL. Comprehensive arts festival celebrating the performing arts through a variety of music, theatre and dance. Visual arts are presented in a juried art show. Est attendance: 120,000. For info: The Arts Council, 700 Monroe St, Huntsville, AL 35801. Phone: (205) 533-6565. Fax: (205) 533-3811. Email: hsv.tis.net/arts/council. WWW: http://www.panoply.com

RATTLESNAKE DERBY. Apr 24–26. Mangum, OK. Hunters stalk these wily reptiles and attempt to bring in the most snakes and the longest snake. Snakeskins and meat will be sold, and entertainment will include live music, a carnival and flea market. A herpetologist will be on hand to educate festival-goers. Est attendance: 40,000. For info: Chamber of Commerce, 222 W Jefferson, Mangum, OK 73554. Phone: (405) 782-2444.

SOUTH CAROLINA FESTIVAL OF ROSES. Apr 24–26. Edisto Memorial Gardens, Orangeburg, SC. To celebrate the beauty of the roses and the gardens. Est attendance: 30,000. For info: Carol P. Whisenhunt, Orangeburg County Chamber of Commerce, PO Box 328, Orangeburg, SC 29116-0328. Phone: (803) 534-6821. Fax: (803) 531-9435.

SPACE MILESTONE: *CHINA 1* (PEOPLE'S REPUBLIC OF CHINA). Apr 24, 1970. China becomes fifth nation to orbit satellite with launch of its own rocket. Broadcast Chinese song "Tang Fang Hung" ("The East Is Red") and telemetric signals.

SPRING FLING. Apr 24–26. Wichita Falls, TX. A celebration of the arts. Artists from all over the US display their art. Food booths, demonstrations and entertainment. Est attendance: 21,000. For info: Wichita Falls Conv and Visitors Bureau, PO Box 1860, Wichita Falls, TX 76307. Phone: (817) 716-5500. Fax: (817) 716-5509.

SPRINGFEST. Apr 24–26. Heber Springs, AR. 11th annual festival features arts and crafts, children's activities, sports show, food concessions and more. Est attendance: 10,000. For info: Dianne Williams, Exec Dir, Chamber of Commerce, 1001 W Main, Heber Springs, AR 72543. Phone: (501) 362-2444. Fax: (501) 362-9953. Email: hebercoc@arkansas.net. WWW: http://www.Heber-Springs.com

STAMP EXPO '98: SOUTH. Apr 24–26. Quality Hotel, Anaheim, CA. Est attendance: 4,000. For info: Intl Stamp Collectors Soc, PO Box 854, Van Nuys, CA 91408. Phone: (818) 997-6496. Fax: (818) 988-4337. Email: iibick@aol.com. WWW: http://www.4free.com/bick

SUGARLOAF'S SPRING TIMONIUM CRAFT FESTIVAL. Apr 24[-]26. Maryland State Fairgrounds, Timonium, MD. This show, now in its 21st year, features 340 nationally recognized craft designers and fine artists displaying and selling their original creations. Craft demonstrations, live music, children's entertainment, food, hourly gift certificate drawings and more. Est attendance: 24,000. For info: Sugarloaf Mountain Works, Inc, 200 Orchard Ridge Dr, #215, Gaithersburg, MD 20878. Phone: (800) 210-9900.

THOMAS, ROBERT BAILEY: BIRTH ANNIVERSARY. Apr 24, 1766. Founder and editor of *The Farmer's Almanac* (first issue for 1793) was born at Grafton, MA, Apr 24, 1766. Thomas died May 19, 1846, while working on the 1847 edition.

TROLLOPE, ANTHONY: BIRTH ANNIVERSARY. Apr 24, 1815. English novelist, born at London, England, Apr 24, 1815. Died there Dec 6, 1882. "Of the needs a book has," he wrote in his autobiography, "the chief need is that it be readable."

April 1998

S	M	T	W	T	F	S
			1	2	3	4
5	6	7	8	9	10	11
12	13	14	15	16	17	18
19	20	21	22	23	24	25
26	27	28	29	30		

WARD WORLD CHAMPIONSHIP WILDFOWL CARVING COMPETITION. Apr 24–26. Ocean City Convention Center, Ocean City, MD. Judging of contemporary wildfowl wood sculpture. Est attendance: 20,000. For info: Jane Rollins, Events Coord, Ward Museum of Wildfowl Art, 909 S Schumaker Dr, Salisbury, MD 21804. Phone: (410) 742-4988 ext 106. Fax: (410) 742-3107.

WARREN, ROBERT PENN: BIRTH ANNIVERSARY. Apr 24. American poet, novelist, essayist and critic. America's first official poet laureate, 1986–88, Robert Penn Warren was born at Guthrie, KY, on Apr 24, 1905. Warren was awarded the Pulitzer Prize for his novel *All the King's Men*, as well as for his poetry in 1958 and 1979. He died of cancer Sept 15, 1989, at Stratton, VT.

BIRTHDAYS TODAY

Eric Balfour, 21, actor, musician, born Los Angeles, CA, Apr 24, 1977.

Eric Bogosian, 45, actor, playwright, performance artist, born Boston, MA, Apr 24, 1953.

Vince Ferragamo, 44, former football player, born Torrance, CA, Apr 24, 1954.

Chipper Jones, 26, baseball player, born DeLand, FL, Apr 24, 1972.

Stanley J. Kauffmann, 82, critic, born New York, NY, Apr 24, 1916.

Shirley MacLaine, 64, author, actress (Emmy for "Gypsy in My Soul"; Oscar for *Terms of Endearment; Irma La Douce, The Turning Point, Being There*), born Richmond, VA, Apr 24, 1934.

Michael O'Keefe, 43, actor (*The Great Santini, Caddyshack*; stage: *Mass Appeal* [Theatre World Award]), born Larchmont, NY, Apr 24, 1955.

Barbra Streisand, 56, singer, actress (Oscar for *Funny Girl; The Way We Were, Yentl*), director (*Prince of Tides*), born New York, NY, Apr 24, 1942.

Rudolph (Rudy) Tomjanovich, 50, basketball coach and former player, born Hamtramck, MI, Apr 24, 1948.

APRIL 25 — SATURDAY

Day 115 — 250 Remaining

ABORTION FIRST LEGALIZED: ANNIVERSARY. Apr 25, 1967. The first law legalizing abortion in the US was signed by Colorado Governor John Arthur Love. The law allowed therapeutic abortions in cases in which a three-doctor panel unanimously agreed.

AMERICAN HERITAGE MUSIC FESTIVAL. Apr 25–26. Yorktown Victory Center, Yorktown, VA. Various performers will present interpretations of 17th- and 18th-century period music and instruments throughout the day and during special evening concerts. Est attendance: 1,500. For info: Media Relations, Jamestown-Yorktown Fdtn, PO Box 1607, Williamsburg, VA 23187. Phone: (757) 253-4838. Fax: (757) 253-5299. WWW: http://www.historyisfun.org

ANTIQUE AND COLLECTIBLE FLEA MARKET. Apr 25–26. Weston, MO. 16th annual flea market sponsored by the Weston Lions Club, with antiques, collectibles and food available. For info: Weston Development, 502 Main, Weston, MO 64098. Phone: (816) 640-2909.

ANZAC DAY. Apr 25. Australia, New Zealand and Western Samoa. Memorial day and veterans' observance, especially to mark World War I Anzac landing at Gallipoli, Turkey, on Apr 25, 1915 (ANZAC: Australia and New Zealand Army Corps).

ART IN THE PARK FESTIVAL. Apr 25. Oakland Park Library, Oakland Park, FL. Annual celebration of National Library Week, features a juried, fine-arts-only show with cash awards. Activities for all ages, including "Create Your Own Book," professional storytelling, facepainting, and sidewalk chalk art contest for children, plant displays, used book sale, live music and more. Annually, the Saturday before National Library Week. For info:

Joanne Fischer, Art In The Park Coord, Oakland Park Library, 1298 NE 37 St, Oakland Park, FL 33334-4576. Phone: (954) 561-6289. Fax: (954) 561-6146.
Email: f600546k@bcfreenet.seflin.org.

BIRDWATCHING WEEKEND. Apr 25–26. Madison, MN. More than 225 birdwatchers check out the birds at Salt Lake, a small saltwater lake just west and south of Madison where more than 150 species of birds have been spotted in past years. Sponsor: Minnesota Ornithologists' Union and the Prairie Woods Nature Society. Housing sponsored by Madison Ambassadors, Saturday evening meal sponsored by Sons of Norway in Madison. Continental breakfast and noon lunch on Saturday sponsored by American Legion Club of Marietta. Annually, the fourth weekend in April. Est attendance: 225. For info: Donna Ventrella, Chamber of Commerce, 404 6th Ave, Madison, MN 56256. Phone: (320) 598-7373 ext 14. Fax: (320) 598-7376.

CHAUTAUQUA FESTIVAL. Apr 25. DeFuniak Springs, FL. Annually, the fourth Saturday in April. Est attendance: 7,000. For info: Florida Chautauqua, Chautauqua Festival, PO Box 847, DeFuniak Springs, FL 32435. Phone: (904) 892-9494. Fax: (904) 892-9494.

CRAFT FAIR USA: INDOOR SHOW. Apr 25–26. Wisconsin State Fair Park, Milwaukee, WI. Sale of handcrafted items—jewelry, pottery, weaving, leather, wood, glass and sculpture. Est attendance: 13,000. For info: Director, Craft Fair USA, 9312 W National Ave, West Allis, WI 53227. Phone: (414) 321-2100.

DAYTON COWBOY POETRY & WESTERN ART SHOW. Apr 25. Dayton, NV. 8th annual chowder cook-off, plus cowboy poetry and western art. Annually, the last Saturday in April. For info: Nevada Commission on Tourism, Capitol Complex, Carson City, NV 89701. Phone: (702) 246-7909 or (702) 246-0188. Fax: (702) 687-6779.

DOVE AWARDS PRESENTATION. Apr 25. Telecast live on The Family Channel, the Gospel Music Association presents the 28th annual Dove Awards for gospel music in a two-hour show. Est attendance: 4,000. For info: Gospel Music Assn (GMA), 1205 Division St, Nashville, TN 37203-4011. Phone: (615) 242-0303. Fax: (615) 254-9755.

EAST MEETS WEST: ANNIVERSARY. Apr 25, 1945. US Army Lieutenant Albert Kotzebue encountered a single Soviet soldier near the German village of Lechwitz, 75 miles south of Berlin. Patrols of General Leonard Gerow's V Corps saluted the advance guard of Marshall Ivan Konev's Soviet 58th Guards Division. Soldiers of both nations embraced and exchanged toasts. The Allied armies of East and West had finally met.

FARRAGUT CAPTURES NEW ORLEANS: ANNIVERSARY. Apr 25, 1862. Union forces under the command of Flag Officer David Farragut seized the city of New Orleans, LA, resulting in the surrender of several Confederate forts along the Mississippi in subsequent days. This action removed any Confederate resistance to Northern action on the Mississippi River as far north as New Orleans. General Benjamin Butler arrived on Apr 27 and took command of the management of the captured city.

FIRST BLOOM FESTIVAL. Apr 25–May 2. American Rose Center, Shreveport, LA. Annual festival celebrating the first spring bloom of more than 20,000 roses, camellias, azaleas, daffodils and other flowering plants. Entertainment, mini-rose sale and refreshments. Est attendance: 10,000. For info: American Rose Center, PO Box 30000, Shreveport, LA 71130-0030. Phone: (318) 938-5402. Fax: (318) 938-5405. Email: ars@ars-hg.org.
WWW: http://www.ars.org

FIRST LICENSE PLATES: ANNIVERSARY. Apr 25, 1901. New York began requiring license plates on automobiles on this date, the first state to do so.

FITZGERALD, ELLA: BIRTH ANNIVERSARY. Apr 25, 1917. "First Lady of Song," born at Newport News, VA. Jazz singer known for her treatments of Gershwin, Cole Porter, Duke Ellington and Rogers and Hart. Fitzgerald died at Beverly Hills, CA, June 15, 1996.

FOXFIELD RACES. Apr 25 (also Sept 27). Charlottesville, VA. Steeplechase horse racing. Est attendance: 20,000. For info: W. Patrick Butterfield, Racing Mgr, Foxfield Racing Assn, PO Box 5187, Charlottesville, VA 22905. Phone: (804) 293-9501. Fax: (804) 293-8169.

GREAT CARDBOARD BOAT REGATTA. Apr 25. SIUC Campus Lake, Carbondale, IL. Teams and individuals design, build and race person-powered boats made of corrugated cardboard. "Titanic Award" for most spectacular sinking plus trophies for team spirit, most creative use of cardboard, best-dressed team, most spectacular-looking boat. Prizes for top finishers in three boat classes: Class I, propelled by oars or paddles; Class II, propelled by mechanical means such as paddlewheels, propellors; Class III, "Instant Boats" made from "Secret Kits" by spectators-turned-participants. Registration 10 AM; races begin 12 noon. 25th annual regatta. Additional competition at other locations across the country on various dates. Est attendance: 13,500. For info: Southern Illinois University, School of Art and Design, Carbondale, IL 62901. Phone: (618) 867-2346.
Email: commodore@GCBR.com.
WWW: http://www.GCBR.com

KITEFEST. Apr 25–26. River Oaks Park, Kalamazoo, MI. Family-oriented kite-flying event includes children's kite-making workshop, kite competitions, an indoor fly and lots of kite flying. Est attendance: 5,000. For info: John D. Cosby, Mktg Coord, Kalamazoo County Parks Dept, 2900 Lake St, Kalamazoo, MI 49001. Phone: (616) 383-8778. Fax: (616) 383-8724.

LEWIS, ROBERT Q.: BIRTH ANNIVERSARY. Apr 25, 1920. American comedian Robert Q. Lewis was born at New York, NY. He is best known for his many appearances on television quiz shows such as "What's My Line," "To Tell the Truth" and "Call My Bluff." He died on Dec 11, 1991, at Los Angeles, CA.

LIVINGSTON RAILROAD SWAP MEET. Apr 25. Northern Pacific Passenger Depot, Livingston, MT. Railroad hobby items and collectibles for sale at this 8th annual swap. Est attendance: 750. For info: Livingston Depot Center, Box 1319, Livingston, MT 59047. Phone: (406) 222-2300 or 2304.

MACAU: ANNIVERSARY OF THE PORTUGUESE REVOLUTION. Apr 25. Anniversary of the 1974 revolution.

MAIN STREET FESTIVAL. Apr 25–26. Downtown Franklin, TN. 15th annual festival features more than 220 of the South's leading craftspersons. Food, entertainment (blues, pop, country, classical and rock), children's area and carnival. Showcases historical downtown. Est attendance: 100,000. For info: Melanie Gentry, Main Street Festival, PO Box 807, Franklin, TN 37065. Phone: (615) 791-9924. Email: peterjordan@mindspring.com. WWW: http://www.phoenix.wl.com/franklin/dfa/mainfest.htm

MARCH OF DIMES WALKAMERICA. Apr 25–26. The March of Dimes' largest fundraiser takes place in communities nationwide the last weekend in April with more than one million volunteers participating. Funds raised support research, education and community-based programs to prevent birth defects and to help lower the rate of premature births and infant mortality. Call your local chapter to learn how to participate. For info: March of Dimes Birth Defects Fdtn, Natl HQ, 1275 Mamaroneck Ave, White Plains, NY 10605. Phone: (914) 997-4574.

MARCONI, GUGLIELMO: BIRTH ANNIVERSARY. Apr 25. Inventor of wireless telegraphy (1895) born at Bologna, Italy, on this date, 1874. Died at Rome, July 20, 1937.

MAYMONT'S HERBS GALORE. Apr 25. Richmond, VA. Annual celebration of herbs at Maymont, Richmond's house museum. A variety of speakers, cooking demonstrations, garden walks and more than 40 plant and craft vendors. For info: Maymont Foundation, 1700 Hampton St, Richmond, VA 23220. Phone: (804) 358-7166.

MISSISSIPPI RIVER VALLEY SCENIC DRIVE. Apr 25–26. Mississippi River valley of southeast Missouri. Homemade goodies, quilt shows, tours, entertainment, demonstrations; various small towns participate. For info: Frank Nickell, One University Plaza, Southeastern Missouri University, Cape Girardeau, MO 63701. Phone: (573) 651-2555. Fax: (573) 651-2200.

NATIONAL GOOD TELEPHONE DAY. Apr 25. One day each year when people answer the phone by the third ring; don't leave anyone on hold for a millennium; don't make rude remarks about the caller unless the call is put on hold; don't slam the phone on any surface during a call; and, if you are responsible for providing "help" on a help-line, take calls and don't leave lines interminably on hold. And last but not least, thank the person for calling at the conclusion of the call. For info: W.B. DeNeen, Pres, TELE-COR, PO Box 1149, Waterford, CT 06385. Phone: (860) 444-2522.

OUTDOOR QUILT SHOW. Apr 25. Kechi, KS. 3rd annual show in which 250-500 quilts are displayed throughout the community in storefronts and at local churches. Some quilts are for sale. Only outdoor quilt show in south central Kansas. All proceeds from the show go to support the cost of the following year's show. Est attendance: 1,200. For info: Kechi Area Chamber of Commerce, PO Box 578, Kechi, KS 67067-0578. Phone: (316) 744-9403. Fax: (316) 744-1337. Email: kechirick@feist.com.

PERIGEAN SPRING TIDES. Apr 25–26. Spring tides, the highest possible tides, occur when New Moon or Full Moon falls within 24 hours of the moment the Moon is nearest Earth (perigee) in its monthly orbit, on Apr 25 at 2 PM, EDT.

POLK COUNTY RAMP TRAMP FESTIVAL. Apr 25. Polk County 4-H Camp, (Greasy Creek Community) near Benton, TN. A tribute to the ramp, a wild onionlike plant that grows only in the Appalachian Mountains. Bluegrass music and feast of the ramps. Est attendance: 800. For info: Wm Don Ledford, Extension Leader, Box 189, Benton, TN 37307. Phone: (615) 338-4503.

April 1998

S	M	T	W	T	F	S
			1	2	3	4
5	6	7	8	9	10	11
12	13	14	15	16	17	18
19	20	21	22	23	24	25
26	27	28	29	30		

PORTUGAL'S DAY. Apr 25. Portugal. Public holiday.

REDBUD TRAIL RENDEZVOUS. Apr 25–26. Rochester, IN. Reenactment of a pre-1840 gathering to trade furs on the Tippecanoe River, tepee village, traditional music and crafts, pioneer and Indian dances, foods cooked over wood fires. Museum, round barn and Living History Village at north end of grounds. Est attendance: 2,000. For info: Fulton County Historical Soc, 37 E 375 N, Rochester, IN 46975. Phone: (219) 223-4436.

SFCC SPRING ARTS FESTIVAL. Apr 25–26. Thomas Center, Gainesville, FL. Artists and craftsmen from all areas of the US display their work. Also, the Children's Rainbow Garden—a complete art fest for kids. 29th annual festival. Est attendance: 124,000. For info: Santa Fe Community College, Spring Arts Fest, 3000 NW 83rd St, Gainesville, FL 32606. Phone: (352) 395-5355. Fax: (352) 395-5918. Email: kathryn.lehman@santafe.cc.fl.us.

SHRIMPFEST. Apr 25. Salem Civic Center Fairgrounds, Salem, VA. Fifth annual all-you-can-eat shrimp, baked beans, corn on the cob, slaw and dessert. Outdoors; advance tickets $16. Also includes live band concerts. Est attendance: 2,500. For info: Wendi Schultz, CFE Exec Dir, Roanoke Festival in the Park, PO Box 8276, Roanoke, VA 24014. Phone: (540) 342-2640.

SOUTHERN MARYLAND CELTIC FESTIVAL. Apr 25. Jefferson Patterson Park, St. Leonard, MD. Scottish fiddling championship, bagpipe competition, Scottish heptathlon, Highland dancing competition, Celtic marketplace and crafts, parade of clans and nations, Celtic harp workshop, Celtic folk music, demonstrations and Celtic foods. Annually, the last Saturday in April. Est attendance: 7,000. For info: Mary Beth Dent, Celtic Society of Southern Maryland, 992 Breakwater Dr, Annapolis, MD 21403. Phone: (410) 257-9003.

SPACE MILESTONE: HUBBLE SPACE TELESCOPE DEPLOYED (US). Apr 25, 1990. Deployed this date by *Discovery*, the telescope is the largest on-orbit observatory to date and is capable of imaging objects up to 14 billion light-years away. The resolution of images was expected to be seven to ten times greater than images from Earth-based telescope's, since the Hubble Space Telescope is not hampered by Earth's atmospheric distortion. Launched Apr 12, 1990, from Kennedy Space Center, FL. Unfortunately, the telescope's lenses were defective so that the anticipated high quality of imaging was not possible. In 1993, however, the world watched as a shuttle crew successfully retrieved the Hubble from orbit, executed the needed repair and replacement work and released it into orbit once more.

VIRGINIA WINE FESTIVAL. Apr 25–26. Charlottesville, VA. Wine tastings from the vineyards of central Virginia. Gourmet foods, music, house tour and craft demonstrations. Est attendance: 2,000. For info: Ash Lawn–Highland, Wine Festival, James Monroe Parkway, Charlottesville, VA 22902. Phone: (804) 293-9539. Fax: (804) 293-8000. Email: ashlawn@comet.net. WWW: http://www.avenue.org/ashlawn

WALDSEEMULLER, MARTIN: REMEMBRANCE DAY. Apr 25, 1507. Little is known about the obscure scholar now called the "godfather of America," the German geographer and mapmaker Martin Waldseemuller, who gave America its name. In a book titled *Cosmographiae Introductio*, published on Apr 25, 1507, Waldseemuller wrote: "Inasmuch as both Europe and Asia received their names from women, I see no reason why any one should justly object to calling this part Amerige, i.e., the land of Amerigo, or America, after Amerigo, its discoverer, a man of great ability." Believing it was the Italian navigator and merchant Amerigo Vespucci (see also: "Vespucci, Amerigo: Birth Anniversary" [Mar 9]) who had discovered the new continent, Waldseemuller sought to honor Vespucci by placing his name on the map. First applied only to the South American continent, it soon was used for both the American continents. Waldseemuller did not learn about the voyage of Christopher Columbus until several years later. Of the thousand copies of his map that were printed, only one is known to have survived. Waldseemuller probably was born at Radolfzell, Germany, about 1470. He died at St. Die, France, about 1517–1520.

WILDFLOWER WALK. Apr 25. Blairsville, GA. Vogel State Park. Nestled in the heart of the Chattahoochee National Forest, Vogel provides a perfect setting for a wide variety of flowering plants and bushes such as Trillium, Jack in the Pulpit, Star Grass, Indian Pipes, Lady Slippers, Rhododendron, Wild and Flaming Azalea, Mountain Laurel and Sarvis. The hike is led by an experienced naturalist, so if you're interested in learning the names of some of the beautiful wildflowers, or would just like to experience the beauty of the mountains, come join us for a walk in the park. For info: David Foot, Vogel State Park, 7485 Vogel State Park Rd, Blairsville, GA 30512. Phone: (706) 745-2628.

BIRTHDAYS TODAY

William J. Brennan, Jr, 92, former Associate Justice of the US Supreme Court, born Newark, NJ, Apr 25, 1906. Died July 25, 1997.

David John (Dave) Corzine, 42, former basketball player, born Arlington Heights, IL, Apr 25, 1956.

Jeffrey De Munn, 51, actor (*Ragtime, Frances*), born Buffalo, NY, Apr 25, 1947.

Meadow George ("Meadowlark") Lemon III, 66, former basketball player, born Lexington, SC, Apr 25, 1932.

Paul Mazursky, 68, director (*Harry and Tonto, An Unmarried Woman, Scenes from a Mall, The Pickle*), born Brooklyn, NY, Apr 25, 1930.

Al Pacino, 58, actor (Oscar for *Scent of a Woman; Dog Day Afternoon*, the *Godfather* movies), born East Harlem, NY, Apr 25, 1940.

Talia Shire, 52, actress (Connie in the *Godfather* movies and Adrian in the *Rocky* movies), born Jamaica, NY, Apr 25, 1946.

APRIL 26 — SUNDAY

Day 116 — 249 Remaining

ASTRONOMY WEEK. Apr 26–May 2. To take astronomy to the people. Astronomy Week is observed during the calendar week in which Astronomy Day falls. See also: "Astronomy Day" (May 2).

AUDUBON, JOHN JAMES: BIRTH ANNIVERSARY. Apr 26. American artist and naturalist, born at Haiti, Apr 26, 1785. Died Jan 27, 1851, at New York, NY.

BECKWOURTH, JIM: 200th BIRTH ANNIVERSARY. Apr 26, 1798. Black American mountain man was born in Virginia and died in 1867(?) at Denver, Colorado Territory. Marrying a series of Indian women, Beckwourth lived with the Crow Indians for about six years. He apparently abandoned his wives, however, and went further west, establishing a route through the Sierras to the newly discovered gold fields of California, where he was immortalized by journalist Thomas Bonner. He later served as a guide and interpreter for US troops in the Cheyenne War of 1864. He died mysteriously during a return visit to the Crow.

BLOSSOMTIME FESTIVAL OF SOUTHWESTERN MICHIGAN. Apr 26–May 3. Benton Harbor, MI. To promote the abundant fruit industry and tourism in Michigan. Spring comes alive as the blossoms announce the forthcoming arrival of the season's most delectable fruits. Est attendance: 250,000. For info: Gretchen Schalon, Exec Dir, Blossomtime, Inc, 151 E Napier Ave, Benton Harbor, MI 49022. Phone: (616) 926-7397.

CANADA–UNITED STATES GOODWILL WEEK. Apr 26–May 2. To bring about a better understanding of the American and Canadian ways of life and to recognize the anniversary of the signing of the Rush-Bagot treaty on Apr 28, 1817, which limited US and British armaments on the Great Lakes. Annually, the full week including Apr 28. For info: Kiwanis Intl, 3636 Woodview Trace, Indianapolis, IN 46268.
Email: Kiwanismail@kiwanis.org.
WWW: http://www.Kiwanis.org

CHERNOBYL NUCLEAR REACTOR DISASTER: ANNIVERSARY. Apr 26, 1986. At 1:23 AM, local time, an explosion occurred at the Chernobyl atomic power station at Pripyat in the Ukraine. The resulting fire burned for days, sending radioactive material into the atmosphere. More than 100,000 persons were evacuated from a 300-square-mile area around the plant. Three months later 31 people were reported to have died and thousands exposed to dangerous levels of radiation. Estimates projected an additional 1,000 cancer cases in nations downwind of the radioactive discharge. The plant was encased in a concrete tomb in an effort to prevent the still-hot reactor from overheating again and to minimize further release of radiation.

"CHINA BEACH" TV PREMIERE: 10th ANNIVERSARY. Apr 26, 1988. The stories of "China Beach" revolved around the lives of the women serving at a Da Nang armed forces hospital during the Vietnam War. The theme and background music of the series evoked plenty of nostalgia from the turbulent era. The ABC drama was created by William Boyles, Jr, and John Sacret Young. The cast featured Dana Delany, Michael Boatman, Nancy Giles, Jeff Kober, Robert Picardo, Concetta Tomei, Brian Wimmer, Marg Helgenberger, Chloe Webb, Nan Woods, Megan Gallagher, Ned Vaughn and Ricki Lake.

CONFEDERATE MEMORIAL DAY IN FLORIDA AND GEORGIA. Apr 26. See also: Confederate Memorial Day entries for Apr 27, May 10 and May 25.

EARTH FAIR '98. Apr 26. San Diego, CA. A free public event featuring more than 250 exhibitors representing nonprofit, for-profit and government organizations. Events foster public education and awareness of contemporary environmental issues. Included are seven stages of live entertainment, a special edition "Earth Times" newspaper, speakers, natural food and a popular Kids Area with numerous activities. Fair will be kicked off by the Earth Parade at 10:30 AM. Est attendance: 70,000. For info: San Diego Earth Day, PO Box 9827, San Diego, CA 92169-9827. Phone: (619) 496-6666. Fax: (619) 272-2933.
Email: earthday@qualcomm.com.

FAUSET, JESSIE REDMON: BIRTH ANNIVERSARY. Apr 26, 1882. African-American poet, editor and novelist, born at Fredericksville, NJ, and died in 1961. Fauset, as literary editor of *Crisis* (a publication of the NAACP), was a patron to so many writers of the Harlem Renaissance that her efforts prompted Langston Hughes to dub her the "midwife of the so-called New Negro Literature." Along with W.E.B. Du Bois, Fauset also published and edited the children's magazine *The Brownie Book*. Her novels about the African-American middle-class experience dealt with issues of identity, autonomy and struggles for fulfillment. Her most recognized works include *The Chinaberry Tree* (1931) and *Comedy, American Style* (1933).

GUERNICA MASSACRE: ANNIVERSARY. Apr 26, 1937. Late in the afternoon of Monday, Apr 26, 1937, the ancient Basque town of Guernica, in northern Spain, was attacked without warning by German-made airplanes. Three hours of intensive bombing left the town in flames, and citizens who fled to the fields and ditches around Guernica were machine-gunned from the air. This atrocity inspired Pablo Picasso's mural *Guernica*. Responsibility for the bombing was never officially established, but the suffering and anger of the victims and their survivors are still evident at anniversary demonstrations.

HELENA RAILROAD FAIR. Apr 26. Civic Center, Helena, MT. Largest railroad hobby event in Montana features a mix of scale and tin-plate trains; railroad memorabilia and collectibles; real-life train watching at the MRL Helena depot. Est attendance: 4,000. For info: Helena Railroad Fair, PO Box 4914, Helena, MT 59604. Phone: (406) 442-6118.

HESS, RUDOLF: BIRTH ANNIVERSARY. Apr 26, 1894. One of the most bizarre figures of World War II Germany, Walter Richard Rudolf Hess was born at Alexandria, Egypt. He was a close friend, confidant and personal secretary to Adolf Hitler who had dictated much of *Mein Kampf* to Hess while both were prisoners at Landsberg Prison. Third in command in Nazi Germany, Hess surprised the world on May 10, 1941, by flying alone to Scotland and parachuting from his plane on what he called a "mission of humanity": offering peace to Britain if she would join Germany in attacking the Soviet Union. He was immediately taken prisoner of war. At the Nuremberg Trials (1946), after questions about his sanity, he was convicted and sentenced to life imprisonment at Spandau Allied War Crimes Prison in Berlin, Germany. Outliving all other prisoners there, he was the only inmate from 1955 until he succeeded (in his fourth attempt) in committing suicide. He died at age 93, on Aug 17, 1987.

INDUSTRY DAY. Apr 26. Beatrice, NE. Features industries of Gage County and their products. Antique gas engine demonstrations, exhibits of stationary engine equipment. Est attendance: 300. For info: Kent Wilson, Dir, Gage County Historical Soc, PO Box 793, Beatrice, NE 68310. Phone: (402) 228-1679. WWW: http://www4.infoanalytic.com/h/beatrice.html#gage

LOOS, ANITA: BIRTH ANNIVERSARY. Apr 26, 1893. American author and playwright, born at Sisson, CA, on Apr 26, 1893. She is best remembered for her book *Gentlemen Prefer Blondes*, published in 1925. Loos, a brunette, died at New York, NY, on Aug 18, 1981.

MONTGOMERY WARD SEIZED: ANNIVERSARY. Apr 26. Montgomery Ward Chairman Sewell Avery was physically removed from his office on Apr 26, 1944, when federal troops seized Ward's Chicago offices after the company refused to obey President Franklin D. Roosevelt's order to recognize a CIO union. Government control ended May 9, shortly before the National Labor Relations Board announced the United Mail Order Warehouse and Retail Employees Union had won an election to represent the company's workers.

MOON PHASE: NEW MOON. Apr 26. Moon enters New Moon phase at 7:41 AM, EDT.

MOTHER, FATHER DEAF DAY. Apr 26. A day to honor deaf parents and recognize the gifts of culture and language they give to their hearing children. Annually, the last Sunday of April. Sponsored by Children of Deaf Adults International Inc (CODA). For info: Trudy Schafer-Jeffers, CODA, PO Box 30715, Santa Barbara, CA, 93130-0715. Phone: (617) 789-3862 (TTY or Voice). Fax: (301) 572-4134.

NATIONAL LINGERIE WEEK. Apr 26–May 2. Celebrating the Spirit of a Woman and importance of lingerie through a series of special events and promotions. Spirit of a Woman Awards—Monday, Apr 27. For info: Karen Bromley, c/o The Bromley Group, Intimate Apparel Council, 150 Fifth Ave, Ste 510, New York, NY 10011. Phone: (212) 807-0878. Fax: (212) 673-3534. WWW: http://www.bromley-group.com

NATIONAL WELDING WEEK. Apr 26–May 2. America's construction, manufacturing, transportation, aerospace, food processing, electronics, nuclear power and petrochemical industries rely on the proven capability of more than 90 different welding and allied process technologies. The ability to weld science's newest materials, such as composites, is a real challenge to welding equipment manufacturers. This challenge is being met by American scientists, engineers, inspectors, radiographers, welders and designers. This week is dedicated to these professionals and the work they do. For info: Mktg Communications, American Welding Society, 550 NW LeJeune Rd, Miami, FL 33126. Phone: (800) 443-9353.

OLMSTED, FREDERICK LAW: BIRTH ANNIVERSARY. Apr 26, 1822. Known as the "father of landscape architecture in America," Olmsted participated in the designing of Yosemite National Park, New York City's Central Park and parks for Boston, Hartford and Louisville. Born at Hartford, CT, died at Waverly, MA, Aug 28, 1903. Olmsted's home and studio, Fairsted Estate outside of Boston, is now preserved as a National Historic Site and is open to the public: 99 Warren St, Brookline, MA 02146.

RAILROAD MEMORABILIA AND MODEL SHOW. Apr 26. National Farm Toy Museum, Dyersville, IA. Features railroad collectibles and all scales of model railroad equipment. Annually, the final Sunday in April. Est attendance: 900. For info: Dyersville Area Chamber of Commerce, PO Box 187, Dyersville, IA 52040. Phone: (319) 875-2311. Fax: (319) 875-8391.
Email: dacc@juno.com.
WWW: http://www.rcww.com/dyersville/

RICHTER SCALE DAY. Apr 26. A day to recognize the importance of Charles Francis Richter's research and his work in development of the earthquake magnitude scale that is known as the Richter scale. Richter, an American author, physicist and seismologist, was born on Apr 26, 1900, near Hamilton, OH. An Earthquake Awareness Week was observed in recognition of his work. Richter died at Pasadena, CA, on Sept 30, 1985.

SIRK, DOUGLAS: BIRTH ANNIVERSARY. Apr 26, 1900. Film director Douglas Sirk was born Detlef Sierck at Skagen, Denmark. His films include *Magnificent Obsession* (1954), *Written on the Wind* (1956) and *Imitation of Life* (1959), which became cult classics in Europe. He died on Jan 14, 1987, at Lugano, Switzerland.

April 1998

S	M	T	W	T	F	S
			1	2	3	4
5	6	7	8	9	10	11
12	13	14	15	16	17	18
19	20	21	22	23	24	25
26	27	28	29	30		

SOUTH AFRICAN MULTIRACIAL ELECTIONS: ANNIVERSARY. Apr 26–29, 1994. For the first time in the history of South Africa, the nation's approximately 18 million blacks voted in multiparty elections. This event marked the definitive end of apartheid, the system of racial separation that had kept blacks and other minorities out of the political process. The election resulted in Nelson Mandela of the African National Congress being elected president and F.W. de Klerk (incumbent president) of the National Party vice president.

SPRING TASTING BUFFET. Apr 26. De Witt, IA. Tasting buffet of recipes that are to be featured in an upcoming nationally released recipe book. For info: Gina Griep, Special Events Coord, Healthy Exchanges, PO Box 124, De Witt, IA 52742. Phone: (319) 659-8234. Fax: (319) 659-2126.

TANZANIA: UNION DAY. Apr 26. Celebrates union between mainland Tanzania (formerly Tanganyika) and the islands of Zanzibar and Pemba, in 1964.

UNITED STATES HOLOCAUST MUSEUM: 5th ANNIVERSARY. Apr 26, 1993. Washington, DC. After the Museum opened to the public, over two million visitors toured the permanent exhibition during its first year of operation.

WARBIRDS IN ACTION AIR SHOW. Apr 26–27. Minter Field, Shafter, CA. 15th annual air show features flybys of up to 100 WWII trainers, fighters, bombers and reconnaissance aircraft. Also includes aerobatics, air racers, pilots' barbecue, dance and rides. Annually, the fourth weekend in April. Est attendance: 20,000. For info: Minter Field Air Museum, PO Box 445, Shafter, CA 93263-0445. Phone: (805) 393-0291 or (805) 746-3305. Fax: (805) 746-3143.

BIRTHDAYS TODAY

Carol Burnett, 62, actress ("Garry Moore Show," "Carol Burnett Show," *The Four Seasons*), born San Antonio, TX, Apr 26, 1936.

Duane Eddy, 60, musician, born Corning, NY, Apr 26, 1938.

Bambi Linn, 72, dancer, born Brooklyn, NY, Apr 26, 1926.

Boyd Matson, 51, TV journalist (host of "National Geographic Explorer"), born Oklahoma City, OK, Apr 26, 1947.

Bobby Rydell, 56, singer ("Wild One," "Volare"), born Philadelphia, PA, Apr 26, 1942.

Gary Wright, 55, musician, born Englewood, NJ, Apr 26, 1943.

APRIL 27 — MONDAY

Day 117 — 248 Remaining

AMERICAN DESIGN DRAFTING ASSOCIATION CONFERENCE. Apr 27–May 1. Minneapolis, MN. Est attendance: 200. For info: Aileen Worrell, Program Manager, American Design Drafting Assn, PO Box 799, Rockville, MD 20848-0799. Phone: (301) 460-6875. Fax: (301) 460-8591. Email: national@adda.org. WWW: http://www.adda.org

BABE RUTH DAY: ANNIVERSARY. Apr 27, 1947. Babe Ruth Day was celebrated in every ballpark in organized baseball in the US as well as Japan. Mortally ill with throat cancer, Ruth appeared at Yankee Stadium to thank his former club for the honor.

BEGINNING OF THE END OF THE CIVIL WAR: ANNIVERSARY. Apr 27, 1864. Union General Ulysses S. Grant issued orders to his armies that would lead to the end of the American Civil War. The plan called for Sherman to advance on Confederate forces through Georgia, Siegal to move through the Shenandoah Valley, Butler to advance up the James River toward Richmond and Meade to follow and engage the Army of Northern Virginia under Robert E. Lee.

BIG 12 MEN'S GOLF CHAMPIONSHIP. Apr 27–28. Hutchinson, KS. Est attendance: 1,000. For info: Dru Hancock, Big 12 Conference, 2201 Stemmons Freeway, 28th Floor, Dallas, TX 75207. Phone: (214) 742-1212. Fax: (214) 742-2045.

CONFEDERATE MEMORIAL DAY IN MISSISSIPPI. Apr 27. Annually, last Monday in April. Observed on other dates in some states: the fourth Monday in April in Alabama, Apr 26 in Florida and Georgia, May 10 in North Carolina and South Carolina, last Monday in May in Virginia; and with Jefferson Davis's birthday on June 3 in Kentucky.

DENNIS, SANDY: BIRTH ANNIVERSARY. Apr 27, 1937. American actress Sandy Dennis was born Sandra Dale Dennis at Hastings, NE. In addition to two Tony Awards she won an Academy Award for her supporting role in *Who's Afraid of Virginia Woolf* (1966). She died on Mar 2, 1992, at Westport, CT.

FAST DAY IN NEW HAMPSHIRE. Apr 27. Dates from the days of "public humiliation, fasting and prayer" proclaimed by royal governors during the 17th-century settlement of New England. Annually, the fourth Monday in April.

GIBBON, EDWARD: BIRTH ANNIVERSARY. Apr 27, 1737. English historian and author. His *History of the Decline and Fall of the Roman Empire* remains a model of literature and historical writing. From his description of the Roman emperor Gordianus II: "Twenty-two acknowledged concubines, and a library of sixty-two thousand volumes, attested the variety of his inclinations; and from the productions which he left behind him, it appears that the former as well as the latter were designed for use rather than for ostentation." Born at Putney, Surrey, England, Gibbon died at London, on Jan 6, 1794. The remains of his magnificent library, left by Gibbon at Lausanne, Switzerland, were sold at auction in London on Dec 20, 1934.

GODWIN, MARY WOLLSTONECRAFT: BIRTH ANNIVERSARY. Apr 27, 1759. English writer whose best-known book was *Vindication of the Rights of Women*, published in 1792. Born at London, England, Apr 27, 1759, and died there Sept 10, 1797. Her daughter, Mary, was the wife of poet Percy Bysshe Shelley but is best remembered as the author of *Frankenstein*, published in 1818.

GRANT, ULYSSES SIMPSON: BIRTH ANNIVERSARY. Apr 27, 1822. 18th president of the US (Mar 4, 1869–Mar 3, 1877), born Hiram Ulysses Grant at Point Pleasant, OH. He graduated from the US Military Academy in 1843. President Lincoln promoted Grant to lieutenant general in command of all the Union armies on Mar 9, 1864. On Apr 9, 1865, Grant received General Robert E. Lee's surrender, at Appomattox Court House, VA, which he announced to the secretary of war as follows: "General Lee surrendered the Army of Northern Virginia this afternoon on terms proposed by myself. The accompanying additional correspondence will show the conditions fully." Nicknamed "Unconditional Surrender Grant," he died at Mount McGregor, NY, July 23, 1885, just four days after completing his memoirs. He was buried in Riverside Park, New York, NY, where Grant's Tomb was dedicated in 1897.

ISLAMIC NEW YEAR. Apr 27. Islamic calendar date: Muharram 1, 1419. The first day of the first month of the Islamic calendar. Different methods for "anticipating" the visibility of the new moon crescent at Mecca are used by different groups. *Chase's* uses anticipated dates furnished by the American Muslim Council. US EST date may vary.

LANTZ, WALTER: BIRTH ANNIVERSARY. Apr 27, 1900. Originator of Universal Studios' animated opening sequence for their first major musical film, *The King of Jazz*. Walter Lantz is best remembered as the creator of Woody Woodpecker, the bird with the wacky laugh and the taunting ways. Lantz received a lifetime achievement Academy Award for his animation in 1979. He was born at New Rochelle, NY, and died Mar 22, 1994, at Burbank, CA.

MAGELLAN, FERDINAND: DEATH ANNIVERSARY. Apr 27. Portuguese explorer Ferdinand Magellan was probably born near Oporto, Portugal, about 1480, but neither the place nor the date is certain. Usually thought of as the first man to circumnavigate the earth, he died before completing the voyage; thus his co-leader, Basque navigator Juan Sebastian de Elcano, became the world's circumnavigator. The westward, 'round-the-world expedition began on Sept 20, 1519, with five ships and about 250 men. Magellan was killed by natives of the Philippine island of Mactan, Apr 27, 1521.

MATANZAS MULE DAY. Apr 27, 1898. In one of the first naval actions of the Spanish-American War, US naval forces, on Apr 27, 1898, bombarded the Cuban village of Matanzas. It was widely reported that the only casualty of the bombardment was one mule. "The Matanzas Mule" became instantly famous and remains a footnote in the history of the Spanish-American War.

MORSE, SAMUEL FINLEY BREESE: BIRTH ANNIVERSARY. Apr 27, 1791. American artist and inventor, after whom the Morse code is named, was born at Charlestown, MA, and died at New York, NY, Apr 2, 1872. Morse conceived the idea of an electromagnetic telegraph while on shipboard, returning from art instruction in Europe in 1832, and he proceeded to develop his idea. With financial assistance approved by Congress, the first telegraph line in the US was constructed, between Washington, DC, and Baltimore, MD. The first message tapped out by Morse from the Supreme Court Chamber at the US Capitol building on May 24, 1844, was: "What hath God wrought?"

NATIONAL PLAYGROUND SAFETY WEEK. Apr 27–May 1. An opportunity for families, community parks, schools and child-care facilities to focus on preventing public playground-related injuries. Sponsored by the National Program for Playground Safety (NPPS), this event helps educate the public about the more than 200,000 children (that's one child every 2½ minutes) that require emergency room treatment for playground-related injuries each year. For info: Natl Program for Playground Safety, School of HPELS, UNI, Cedar Falls, IA 50614-0618. Phone: (800) 554-PLAY. Fax: (319) 273-7308. WWW: http://www.uni.edu/playground

NICKERSON, CAMILLE ("THE LOUISIANA LADY"): DEATH ANNIVERSARY. Apr 27, 1982. Camille Nickerson, music arranger, composer, musician and educator is remembered for her broad musical talent and her work as a music collector who gathered and transcribed the Creole music of her native New Orleans. Of Creole extraction herself, Nickerson performed for a time in the US and Europe using the stage name "The Louisiana Lady." She was born Mar 30, 1888, and died at Washington, DC, at age 94.

SIERRA LEONE: INDEPENDENCE DAY. Apr 27. National Day.

SOUTH AFRICA: FREEDOM DAY. Apr 27. National holiday.

SULTANA STEAMSHIP EXPLOSION: ANNIVERSARY. Apr 27. Early in the morning of Apr 27, 1865, America's worst steamship disaster occurred. The *Sultana*, heavily overloaded with an estimated 2,300 passengers, exploded in the Mississippi River, just north of Memphis, en route to Cairo, IL. Most of the passengers were Union soldiers who had been prisoners of war and were eagerly returning to their homes. Although there was never an accurate accounting of the dead, estimates range from the Naval History Division's 1,450 to nearly 2,000. Cause of the explosion was not determined, but the little-known event is unparalleled in US history.

April 1998

S	M	T	W	T	F	S
			1	2	3	4
5	6	7	8	9	10	11
12	13	14	15	16	17	18
19	20	21	22	23	24	25
26	27	28	29	30		

TOGO: INDEPENDENCE DAY. Apr 27. National holiday.

WOMEN'S INTERNATIONAL BOWLING CONGRESS ANNUAL MEETING. Apr 27–29. Quad Cities, IL, IA. Est attendance: 3,500. For info: Mark Miller, WIBC, 5301 S 76th St, Greendale, WI 53129. Phone: (414) 421-9000. Fax: (414) 421-7977.

YUGOSLAVIA: NATIONAL DAY. Apr 27.

BIRTHDAYS TODAY

Anouk Aimee, 64, actress (*A Man and a Woman, The Golden Salamander*), born Paris, France, Apr 27, 1934.

Sheena Easton (Sheena Shirley Orr), 39, singer ("Morning Train"), born Bellshill, Scotland, Apr 27, 1959.

Casey Kasem, 66, radio/TV host ("America's Top 40"), born Detroit, MI, Apr 27, 1932.

Coretta Scott King, 71, lecturer, writer, widow of Martin Luther King, Jr, born Marion, AL, Apr 27, 1927.

Jack Klugman, 76, actor ("The Odd Couple," "Quincy, ME"), born Philadelphia, PA, Apr 27, 1922.

APRIL 28 — TUESDAY

Day 118 — 247 Remaining

BARRYMORE, LIONEL: BIRTH ANNIVERSARY. Apr 28. Famed American actor of celebrated acting family, Lionel Barrymore was born Lionel Blythe, at Philadelphia, PA, Apr 28, 1878. He died at Van Nuys, CA, Nov 15, 1954. US Postal Service stamp issued in 1982 honored Ethel, John and Lionel Barrymore.

BIOLOGICAL CLOCK GENE DISCOVERED: ANNIVERSARY. Apr 28, 1994. Northwestern University announced that the so-called biological clock, that gene governing the daily cycle of waking and sleeping called the circadian rhythm, had been found in mice. Never before pinpointed in a mammal, the biological clock gene was found on mouse chromosome #5.

CANADA: NATIONAL DAY OF MOURNING. Apr 28. A national day of mourning for workers killed or injured on the job in Canada. The Canadian Labour Congress first officially recognized the day in 1986. Pointing to the nearly one million workplace injuries each year in Canada, the CLC has called for stricter health and safety regulations and for annual recognition of this day throughout Canada. Federal legislation (Bill D–223) first recognized this day in 1991.

CONTRABAND DAYS (PIRATE FESTIVAL). Apr 28–May 10. Lake Charles, LA. A major 13-day festival celebrating Jean Lafitte, "The Gentleman Pirate," and the contraband treasures he is supposed to have hidden along the shores of Lake Charles. Events include a mock invasion by pirates, a night boat parade, concerts, fireworks, water events, children's area. Est attendance: 250,000. For info: Marlene C. Hobbs, Exec Dir, Contraband Days, Inc, PO Box 679, Lake Charles, LA 70602. Phone: (318) 436-5508. Fax: (318) 436-1126.

GIBBS, MIFFLIN WISTER: BIRTH ANNIVERSARY. Apr 28, 1828. Mifflin Wister Gibbs was born at Philadelphia, PA, Apr 28, 1828. In 1873 he became the first black man to be elected a judge in the US, winning an election for City Judge in Little Rock, AR.

GREAT POETRY READING DAY. Apr 28. Read some great poetry/The world better to see. For further info send SASE to: Robert A. Stevens, Clio Area High School, One Mustang Dr, Clio, MI 48420.

HOMER, LOUISE DILWORTH: BIRTH ANNIVERSARY. Apr 28, 1871. The mesmerizing Louise Dilworth Homer was one of the most formidable contraltos of her time. Her plum roles in *Aïda, Tristan und Isolde, Orfeo ed Euridice, Hänsel und Gretel* and *Samson et Dalilah* (with the legendary Caruso), brought her tremendous acclaim. She was born at Sewickley, PA, and died at Winter Park, FL on May 6, 1947.

KISS-YOUR-MATE DAY. Apr 28. Show your mate how much you care. Share the pleasure of a kiss when he or she least expects it. Annually, Apr 28. For info: Alan W. Brue, 2006 NW 55th Ave, #H-5, Gainesville, FL 32653.

MARYLAND CONSTITUTION RATIFICATION: ANNIVERSARY. Apr 28, 1788. Maryland became the seventh state to ratify the Constitution, by a vote of 63 to 11.

MONROE, JAMES: BIRTH ANNIVERSARY. Apr 28, 1758. The 5th president of the US was born at Westmoreland County, VA, Apr 28, 1758, and served two terms in that office (Mar 4, 1817–Mar 3, 1825). Monrovia, the capital city of Liberia, is named after him, as is the Monroe Doctrine, which he enunciated at Washington, DC, on Dec 2, 1823. Last of three presidents to die on US Independence Day, Monroe died at New York, NY, July 4, 1831.

MUSSOLINI EXECUTED: ANNIVERSARY. Apr 28, 1945. Italian partisans shot Benito Mussolini near the lakeside village of Dongo. Leaders of the Fascist Party, several of his friends and his mistress Clara Petacci also were executed. The 23-year-long Fascist rule of Italy was ended.

MUTINY ON THE *BOUNTY*: ANNIVERSARY. Apr 28, 1789. The most famous of all naval mutinies occurred on board HMS *Bounty*. Captain of the *Bounty* was Lieutenant William Bligh, an able seaman and a mean-tempered disciplinarian. The ship, with a load of breadfruit tree plants from Tahiti, was bound for Jamaica. Fletcher Christian, leader of the mutiny, put Bligh and 18 of his loyal followers adrift in a 23-foot open boat. Miraculously Bligh and all of his supporters survived a 47-day voyage of more than 3,600 miles, before landing on the island of Timor, June 14, 1789. In the meantime, Christian had put all of the remaining crew (excepting eight men and himself) ashore at Tahiti where he picked up 18 Tahitians (6 men and 12 women) and set sail again. Landing at Pitcairn Island in 1790 (probably uninhabited at the time), they burned the *Bounty* and remained undiscovered for 18 years, when an American whaler, the *Topaz*, called at the island (1808) and found only one member of the mutinous crew surviving. However, the little colony had thrived and, when counted by the British in 1856, numbered 194 persons.

BIRTHDAYS TODAY

Ann-Margret (Ann-Margaret Olsson), 57, actress (Oscar nominations for *Carnal Knowledge* and *Tommy*), born Stockholm, Sweden, Apr 28, 1941.

Saddam Hussein, 61, Iraqi dictator, born Takrit, Iraq, Apr 28, 1937.

Bruno Kirby, 49, actor (*When Harry Met Sally, City Slickers*), born Apr 28, 1949.

Barry Louis Larkin, 34, baseball player, born Cincinnati, OH, Apr 28, 1964.

Harper Lee (Nelle Harper), 72, author (*To Kill a Mockingbird*), born Monroeville, AL, Apr 28, 1926.

Jay Leno, 48, TV talk show host ("Tonight Show"), comedian, born New Rochelle, NY, Apr 28, 1950.

Madge Sinclair, 60, actress ("Gabriel's Fire," *Conrack, Coming to America*), born Kingston, Jamaica, Apr 28, 1938.

Marcia Strassman, 50, actress (Julie Kotter in "Welcome Back Kotter"), born New York, NY, Apr, 28, 1948.

Chris Young, 27, actor ("Falcon Crest," *The Great Outdoors*), born Chambersburg, PA, Apr 28, 1971.

APRIL 29 — WEDNESDAY

Day 119 — 246 Remaining

"COKE TIME" TV PREMIERE: 45th ANNIVERSARY. Apr 29, 1953. A bi-weekly fifteen-minute musical series hosted by Eddie Fisher on NBC. Fisher's back-up group, The Echoes, consisted of Ralph Brewster, Marilyn Jackson, Norma Zimmer and Don Williams.

ELLINGTON, "DUKE" (EDWARD KENNEDY ELLINGTON): BIRTH ANNIVERSARY. Apr 29, 1899. "Duke" Ellington, one of the most influential individuals in jazz history, was born Apr 29, 1899, at Washington, DC. Ellington's professional career began when he was 17, and by 1923 he was leading a small group of musicians at the Kentucky Club in New York City who became the core of his big band. Ellington is credited with being one of the founders of big band jazz. He used his band as an instrument for composition and orchestration to create big band pieces, film scores, operas, ballets, Broadway shows and religious music. Ellington was responsible for more than 1,000 musical pieces. He drew together instruments from different sections of the orchestra to develop unique and haunting sounds such as that of his famous "Mood Indigo." "Duke" Ellington died May 24, 1974, at New York City.

ELLSWORTH, OLIVER: BIRTH ANNIVERSARY. Apr 29. Third chief justice of the US Supreme Court, born at Windsor, CT, on Apr 29, 1745. Died there, Nov 26, 1807.

EWELL, TOM: BIRTH ANNIVERSARY. Apr 29, 1909. Born Samuel Yewell Tompkins at Owensboro, KY, Ewell acted in many films and TV series. He won a Tony Award for his Broadway role as the husband in *The Seven Year Itch*, a role he reprised in the film version costarring with Marilyn Monroe. In the '60s he starred in his own TV show, "The Tom Ewell Show." He died Sept 12, 1994, at Woodland Hills, CA.

FRIENDSHIP SEES NO COLOR WEEK. Apr 29–May 7. A week to "see beyond color" and to make at least one friend of another race. Dates set to coincide with the anniversary of the Los Angeles riots of 1992. For info: Brian Harris, PO Box 74, Stanton, CA 90680. Phone: (714) 236-0805.

HEARST, WILLIAM RANDOLPH: BIRTH ANNIVERSARY. Apr 29, 1863. American newspaper editor and publisher, born at San Francisco, CA, Apr 29, 1863. Died at Beverly Hills, CA, Aug 14, 1951.

HIROHITO MICHI-NO-MIYA, EMPEROR: BIRTH ANNIVERSARY. Apr 29, 1901. Former Emperor of Japan, born at Tokyo. Hirohito's death on Jan 27, 1989, ended the reign of the world's longest ruling monarch. He became the 124th in a line of monarchs when he ascended to the Chrysanthemum Throne in 1926. Hirohito presided over perhaps the most eventful years in the 2,500 years of recorded Japanese history, including the attempted military conquest of Asia; the attack on the US that brought that country into World War II, leading to Japan's ultimate defeat after the US dropped atomic bombs on Hiroshima and Nagasaki; and the amazing economic restoration following the war that led Japan to a preeminent position of economic strength. Although he opposed initiating hostilities with the US, he signed a declaration of war, allowing Japan's militarist Prime Minister, Hideki Tojo, to begin the fateful campaign. During the war's final days he overruled Tojo and advocated surrender. Hirohito broadcast a taped message to the Japanese people to stop fighting and "endure the unendurable." This radio message was the first time the emperor's voice had ever been heard outside the imperial household and inner circle of government. After the war, Hirohito was allowed to remain on his throne. He denounced his divinity in 1946, bestowed upon him by Japanese law, and became a "symbol of the state" in Japan's new parliamentary democracy. Hirohito turned his energies to his real passion, marine biology, becoming a recognized world authority in the field.

LOS ANGELES RIOTS: ANNIVERSARY. Apr 29. On Apr 29, 1992, a jury in Simi Valley, CA, failed to convict four Los Angeles police officers accused in the videotaped beating of Rodney King, providing the spark that set off rioting, looting and burning in South Central Los Angeles, CA, and other areas across the country. The anger unleashed during and after the violence was attributed to widespread racism, lack of job opportunities and the resulting hopelessness of inner-city poverty.

MOMENT OF LAUGHTER DAY. Apr 29. Laughter is a potent and powerful way to deal with the difficulties of modern living. Since the physical, emotional and spiritual benefits of laughter are widely accepted, this day is set aside for everyone to take the necessary time to experience the power of laughter. For info: Izzy Gesell, Head Honcho of Wide Angle Humor, PO Box 962, Northampton, MA 01061. Phone: (413) 586-2634.

SAINT CATHERINE OF SIENA: FEAST DAY. Apr 29. Youngest of 20 children, St. Catherine of Siena was born in 1347. Patron saint of Italy. She died Apr 29, 1380, a week after suffering a stroke.

April 1998

S	M	T	W	T	F	S
			1	2	3	4
5	6	7	8	9	10	11
12	13	14	15	16	17	18
19	20	21	22	23	24	25
26	27	28	29	30		

SHENANDOAH APPLE BLOSSOM FESTIVAL. Apr 29–May 4. Winchester, VA. Springtime extravaganza celebrating the blooming of apple trees. Est attendance: 300,000. For info: Shenandoah Apple Blossom Festival, 135 N Cameron St, Winchester, VA 22601. Phone: (540) 662-3863. Fax: (540) 662-7274. WWW: http://www.apple-blossom.com

SPACE MILESTONE: *CHALLENGER* (US). Apr 29, 1985. *Challenger* launched from Kennedy Space Center, FL, with crew of seven and animal menagerie including monkeys and rats. Landed after 111 orbits of Earth on May 6, 1985, at Edwards Air Force Base, CA.

SUNFEST '98. Apr 29–May 3. West Palm Beach, FL. Florida's largest music, art and waterfront festival features some of the best acts in jazz, pop, blues and more. Family-oriented event includes a juried art show, hand-made crafts, fireworks, water and youth park activities and fabulous foods. Est attendance: 300,000. For info: SunFest of Palm Beach County, Inc, PO Box 279, West Palm Beach, FL 33402-0279. Phone: (561) 659-5980. 24-hour hotline: (561) 659-5992. Fax: (561) 659-3567. Email: sunfester@aol.com. WWW: http://www.sunfest.org

TAIWAN: CHENG CHENG KUNG LANDING DAY. Apr 29. Commemorates landing in Taiwan on this day in 1661 of Ming Dynasty loyalist Cheng Cheng Kung (Koxinga), who ousted Dutch colonists who had occupied Taiwan for 37 years. Main ceremonies held at Tainan, in south Taiwan, where Dutch had their headquarters and where Cheng is buried. Cheng's birthday is also joyously celebrated, but according to the lunar calendar—on the 14th day of the seventh moon, Sept 4 in 1998.

BIRTHDAYS TODAY

Andre Kirk Agassi, 28, tennis player, born Las Vegas, NV, Apr 29, 1970.

George Herbert Allen, 76, former football coach, born Detroit, MI, Apr 29, 1922.

Daniel Day-Lewis, 41, actor (Oscar for *My Left Foot; The Unbearable Lightness of Being*), born London, England, Apr 29, 1957.

Robert Gottlieb, 67, editor, born New York, NY, Apr 29, 1931.

Celeste Holm, 79, actress (*All About Eve*; Oscar for *Gentleman's Agreement*), born New York, NY, Apr 29, 1919.

Rod McKuen, 65, poet, singer, born San Francisco, CA, Apr 29, 1933.

Zubin Mehta, 62, conductor, born Bombay, India, Apr 29, 1936.

Kate Mulgrew, 43, actress (Captain Janeway on "Star Trek: Voyager"; Kate Ryan on "Ryan's Hope"; Kate Columbo on "Mrs Columbo"), born Dubuque, IA, Apr 29, 1955.

Michelle Pfeiffer, 40, actress (*Batman Returns, Dangerous Liaisons, The Fabulous Baker Boys*), born Orange County, CA, Apr 29, 1958.

Jerry Seinfeld, 44, comedian ("Seinfeld"), born Brooklyn, NY, Apr 29, 1954.

Uma Thurman, 28, actress (*Henry and June, Pulp Fiction*), born Boston, MA, Apr 29, 1970.

APRIL 30 — THURSDAY

Day 120 — 245 Remaining

BELTANE. Apr 30. (Also called Bealtaine, May Eve, Walpurgis Night, Cyntefyn, Roodmass and Cethsamhain.) One of the "Greater Sabbats" during the Wiccan year, it celebrates the union or marriage of the Goddess and God. In Scotland, Beltane was one of the quarter days or terms when rents were due and debts settled. On the eve of Beltane, two fires were built close together and cattle driven between them to ward off disease prior to putting them out to pasture for the new season. Annually, on Apr 30.

BIG TEN WOMEN'S TENNIS CHAMPIONSHIP. Apr 30–May 3. University of Michigan, Ann Arbor, MI. For info: Dennis LaBissoniere, Big 10 Conference, 1500 W Higgins Rd, Park Ridge, IL 60068-6300. Phone: (847) 696-1010. Fax: (847) 696-1110. WWW: http://www.bigten.org

CINCO DE MAYO FESTIVAL. Apr 30–May 3. World Trade Center and Tom McCall Waterfront Park. Portland, OR. A Mexican celebration with ethnic foods, continuous entertainment, dancing, arts and crafts booths. Part of Portland's Sister City program with Guadalajara, Mexico. Est attendance: 200,000. For info: Portland-Guadalajara Sister City Assn, PO Box 728, Portland, OR 97207. Phone: (503) 222-9807. Fax: (503) 292-9315. WWW: http://www.cincodemayoppx.com

COLEMAN, BESSIE: DEATH ANNIVERSARY. Apr 30, 1926. Bessie Coleman would not take no for an answer, especially where it concerned her dreams of flying. Because of her race and gender, she was denied admission to aviation school programs in the US. She therefore worked as a manicurist earning her way to Paris. There she received an international pilot's license from the Fédération Aéronautique Internationale in 1921. Upon return, "Queen Bess" took part in numerous acrobatic air exhibitions where her stunt-flying and "figure eights" won her many admirers. She avidly encouraged others to follow in her footsteps. Coleman, however, perished in a plane crash during a practice session.

FESTIVAL OF NATIONS. Apr 30–May 3. St. Paul Civic Center, St. Paul, MN. Celebration by more than 95 ethnic groups, each presenting food specialties, folk dances and folk arts to the public. Est attendance: 95,000. For info: Intl Institute of Minnesota, 1694 Como Ave, St. Paul, MN 55108. Phone: (612) 647-0191. Fax: (612) 647-9268.
WWW: http://www.iimn.org/festnations

HAIRSTYLIST APPRECIATION DAY. Apr 30. The personalized service of hairstylists makes customers look great and feel great about themselves. Hairstyling is the art of creating a self-image to help boost self-esteem while lending an ear to customers' problems, thereby lessening their stress. For info: Anne Camilleri, 1220 Arroyo St, San Carlos, CA 94070. Phone: (415) 593-3733 or (415) 568-0565.

HARRISON, MARY SCOTT LORD DIMMICK: BIRTH ANNIVERSARY. Apr 30, 1858. Second wife of Benjamin Harrison, 23rd president of the US, born at Honesdale, PA, Apr 30, 1858. Died Jan 5, 1948.

INTERNATIONAL SCHOOL SPIRIT SEASON. Apr 30–Sept 30. To recognize everyone who has helped to make school spirit better and to provide time to plan improved spirit ideas for the coming school year. For info: Jim Hawkins, Chairman, Pepsters, Committee for More School Spirit, P.O. Box 2652, San Diego, CA 92112. Phone: (619) 280-0999.

INTERNATIONAL WALK DAYS ©. Apr 30 (also Dec 26). Long before humankind could fly, drive or in-line skate we walked. Today is the day to get primal, leave the car at home and whenever possible walk to your destination. Touted as the best exercise, walking is an undertaking that is not only non-discriminatory, aerobically correct, vital for work-outs and a great method to pass the time, but it enables a person to get out (of himself and his home) and enjoy the weather and surroundings. For info: Adrienne Sioux Koopersmith, 1437 W Rosemont, #1W, Chicago, IL 60660-1319. Phone: (773) 743-5341. Fax: (773) 743-5395. Email: kooper@interaccess.com.

ISRAEL: YOM HA'ATZMA'UT (INDEPENDENCE DAY): 50th ANNIVERSARY. Apr 30, 1948. Hebrew calendar date: Iyar 5, 5758. Celebrates proclamation of independence from British mandatory rule by Palestinian Jews and establishment of the state of Israel and the provisional government on May 14, 1948 (Hebrew calendar date: Iyar 5, 5708). Dates in the Hebrew calendar vary from their Gregorian equivalents from year to year, so, while Iyar 5 in 1948 was May 14, in 1998 it is April 30.

ITALY: FEAST OF SAN PELLEGRINO. Apr 30–May 1. Gualdo Tadino (near Perugia). Ceremony with elements of history and folklore, called also "Festa del Maggio" (May Festival), which dates back to the 15th century and is celebrated on the night of Apr 30–May 1. At the end of several rituals, a huge poplar, formerly barked, is heaved with quick and expert movements in the middle of the square.

JOSEY'S WORLD CHAMPION JUNIOR BARREL RACE. Apr 30–May 3. Josey's Ranch, Marshall, TX. Youth barrel-racing competition. Annually, the first weekend in May. Est attendance: 4,000. For info: Pam Whisenant, Dir of Conv and Visitor Development, Marshall Chamber of Commerce, PO Box 520, Marshall, TX 75671. Phone: (903) 935-7868. Fax: (903) 935-9982. Email: cvd@internetwork.net.

LEWIS FAMILY HOMECOMING AND BLUEGRASS FESTIVAL. Apr 30–May 2. 11th annual. Lincolnton, GA. For info: Norman Adams, PO Box 98, Dahlonega, GA 30533. Phone: (706) 864-7203. Fax: (706) 864-1037.

LILLY, WILLIAM: BIRTH ANNIVERSARY. Apr 30, 1602. English astrologer, author and almanac compiler, born at Diseworth, Leicestershire. His almanacs were among the most popular in Britain from 1644 until his death, June 9, 1681, at Hersham, Surrey, England.

LOUISIANA: ADMISSION DAY: ANNIVERSARY. Apr 30, 1812. Became 18th state on this day in 1812.

LOUISIANA PURCHASE: ANNIVERSARY. Apr 30, 1803. Purchased from France, it doubled the size of the US, extending the Western border to the Rocky Mountains.

LOYALTY DAYS AND SEAFAIR FESTIVAL. Apr 30–May 3. Newport, OR. Celebration of loyalty to America. Parade, queen and court, sports car races, Navy ships in port and other activities. Est attendance: 5,000. For info: Chamber of Commerce, 555 SW Coast Hwy, Newport, OR 97365. Phone: (541) 265-8801 or (800) 262-7844. Fax: (541) 265-5589.
Email: chamber@newport.com.

MUHAMMAD ALI STRIPPED OF TITLE: ANNIVERSARY. Apr 30, 1967. Muhammad Ali was stripped of his world heavyweight boxing championship when he refused to be inducted into military service. Said Ali, "I have searched my conscience, and I find I cannot be true to my belief in my religion by accepting such a call." He had claimed exemption as a minister of the Black Muslim religion.

NATIONAL HONESTY DAY (WITH HONEST ABE AWARDS). Apr 30. To celebrate honesty and those who are honest and honorable in their dealings with others. Nominations accepted for most honest people and companies. Winners to be awarded "Honest Abe" awards and given "Abies" on National Honesty Day. Annually, Apr 30. For info: M. Hirsh Goldberg, Author of *The Book of Lies*, 3103 Szold Dr, Baltimore, MD 21208. Phone: (410) 486-4150.

NATIONAL PLAYGROUND SAFETY DAY. Apr 30. An opportunity for families, community parks, schools and child-care facilities to focus on preventing public playground-related injuries. Sponsored by the National Program for Playground Safety (NPPS), this event helps educate the public about the more than 200,000 children (that's one child every 2½ minutes) that require emergency room treatment for playground-related injuries each year. For info: National Program for Playground Safety, School of HPELS, UNI, Cedar Falls, IA 50614-0618. Phone: (800) 554-PLAY. Fax: (319) 273-7308.
WWW: http://www.uni.edu/playground

NETHERLANDS: QUEEN'S BIRTHDAY. Apr 30. A public holiday in celebration of the Queen's birthday, and the Dutch National Day. The whole country parties as young and old participate in festivities such as markets, theater, music and games.

NORTHERN EUROPE: WALPURGIS NIGHT. Apr 30. Witches' Sabbath. Eve of May Day. Celebrated particularly by university students.

ORGANIZATION OF AMERICAN STATES FOUNDED: 50th ANNIVERSARY. Apr 30, 1948. This regional alliance was founded by 21 nations of the Americas at Bogota, Colombia. Its purpose is to further economic development and integration among nations of the Western hemisphere; to promote representative democracy; and to help overcome poverty. The Pan-American Union, with offices in Washington, DC, serves as the General Secretariat for the OAS.

SEIZURE OF IRANIAN EMBASSY IN LONDON: ANNIVERSARY. Apr 30. On Apr 30, 1980, three dissident Arabs from Khuzestan Province of Iran seized the Iranian Embassy in London, England, and took about 20 people hostage. British commandos of the Special Air Service (SAS) stormed the embassy on May 5, 1980, freeing the 19 remaining hostages and killing or capturing the perpetrators of the seizure.

SMITH, MICHAEL J.: BIRTH ANNIVERSARY. Apr 30, 1945. Michael J. Smith, 40-year-old pilot of the Space Shuttle *Challenger* on Jan 28, 1986. It was to have been Commander Smith's first space flight. Born at Beaufort, NC, Smith perished with all others on board when the Space Shuttle *Challenger* exploded on Jan 28, 1986. See also: "*Challenger* Space Shuttle Explosion Anniversary" (Jan 28).

SPANK OUT DAY USA. Apr 30. A day on which all caretakers of children—parents, teachers and daycare workers—are asked not to use corporal punishment as discipline and to become aquainted with positive, effective disciplinary alternatives. For info: Nadine Block, EPOCH-USA, 155 W Main St, Ste 100-B, Columbus, OH 43215. Phone: (614) 221-8829. Email: nblock@infinet.com.

SWEDEN: FEAST OF VALBORG. Apr 30. An evening celebration in which Sweden "sings in the spring" by listening to traditional hymns to the spring, often around community bonfires. Also known as Walpurgis Night, the Feast of Valborg occurs annually on Apr 30.

TENNIS STAR SELES STABBED AT COURTSIDE: 5th ANNIVERSARY. Apr 30, 1993. While resting at courtside during a match at Hamburg, Germany, 19-year-old Yugoslavian tennis player Monica Seles was stabbed between her shoulder blades with a five-inch steak knife by a 38-year-old German, Guenter P. (his last name was not identified under German privacy laws), on Apr 30, 1993. Seles suffered a half-inch puncture wound and was released from the hospital on May 2.

THEATER IN NORTH AMERICA FIRST PERFORMANCE: 400th ANNIVERSARY. Apr 30, 1598. On the banks of the Rio Grande, near present day El Paso, TX, the first North American theatrical performance was acted. The play was a Spanish commedia featuring an expedition of soldiers. On July 10 of the same year, the same group produced *Moros y Los Cristianos* (Moors and Christians), an anonymous play.

WASHINGTON, GEORGE: PRESIDENTIAL INAUGURATION ANNIVERSARY. Apr 30. In New York, NY, on Apr 30, 1789, George Washington was inaugurated as the first president of the US under the new Constitution. Robert R. Livingston administered the oath of office to Washington on the balcony of Federal Hall, at the corner of Wall and Broad streets.

WILSON, ELLIS: BIRTH ANNIVERSARY. Apr 30, 1899. African-American artist born at Mayfield, KY, and died at New York, NY, Jan 1, 1977. Wilson painted realistic portrayals of African-Americans at work and at play. He studied the elongated style of El Greco and used his techniques in depicting the effortless grace and musculature of male and female subjects. In 1944, his work was awarded a Guggenheim fellowship—a prize that accorded him more recognition. He then visited South Carolina, painting city scenes and fishing towns. *The Open Market at Charleston* was one of his favorite paintings of the period. In the 1950s, Wilson took a revelatory trip to Haiti which changed the way he painted. Unable to note any facial features on the Haitians he painted from a distance, Wilson began painting flat, stylized silhouettes. *Haitian Funeral Procession* (c 1950s) remains Wilson's most popular and accessible painting.

BIRTHDAYS TODAY

Queen Beatrix, 60, Queen of the Netherlands, born Apr 30, 1938.

Lawton Chiles, 68, Governor of Florida (D), born Lakeland, FL, Apr 30, 1930.

Jill Clayburgh, 54, actress (*An Unmarried Woman, Luna*), born New York, NY, Apr 30, 1944.

Gary Collins, 60, actor, born Boston, MA, Apr 30, 1938.

Perry King, 50, actor (*Slaughterhouse Five, The Lords of Flatbush, Switch*), born Alliance, OH, Apr 30, 1948.

Cloris Leachman, 68, actress (Oscar for *The Last Picture Show*; Phyllis on "The Mary Tyler Moore Show"), born Des Moines, IA, Apr 30, 1930.

Willie Nelson, 65, singer ("Always on My Mind," "Woman," "On the Road Again"), actor (*Honeysuckle Rose, The Electric Horseman*), born Abbott, TX, Apr 30, 1933.

Al Lee Toon, Jr, 35, former football player, born Newport News, VA, Apr 30, 1963.

Burt Young, 58, writer, actor (*Chinatown, Rocky, Once upon a Time in America*), born New York, NY, Apr 30, 1940.

Maye.

MAY 1 — FRIDAY

Day 121 — 244 Remaining

ADDISON, JOSEPH: BIRTH ANNIVERSARY. May 1, 1672. English essayist born at Milston, Wiltshire, England. Died at London, June 17, 1719. "We are," he wrote in *The Spectator*, "always doing something for Posterity, but I would fain see Posterity do something for us."

★**ASIAN PACIFIC AMERICAN HERITAGE MONTH.** May 1–31. Presidential Proclamation issued honoring Asian Pacific Americans each year since 1979. Public Law 102-450 of Oct 28, 1992, designated the observance for the month of May each year.

BELGIUM: PLAY OF SAINT EVERMAAR. May 1. Annual performance (for more than 1,000 years) by the village inhabitants of a real "mystery" play, in its original form.

BETTER SLEEP MONTH. May 1–31. Emphasizes the importance of good sleep to good health and encourages Americans to reevaluate their bedtime habits and check bedding for signs of old age. Sponsor: The Better Sleep Council. For info: Ms Andrea Herman, Dir, Better Sleep Council, 333 Commerce St, Alexandria, VA 22314. Phone: (703) 683-8371. Fax: (703) 683-4503.

BIG 10 WOMEN'S GOLF CHAMPIONSHIP. May 1–3. Penn State University, University Park, PA. For info: Dennis LaBissoniere, Big Ten Conference, 1500 W Higgins Rd, Park Ridge, IL 60068-6300. Phone: (847) 696-1010. Fax: (847) 696-1110. WWW: http://www.bigten.org

BIG 12 WOMEN'S SOFTBALL CHAMPIONSHIP. May 1–3. ASA Hall of Fame Stadium, Oklahoma City, OK. Third conference championship in newly formed Big 12 Conference with the winner automatically qualifying for regionals in Women's College World Series. Est attendance: 15,000. For info: Stanley Draper, Jr, Exec Secy, Oklahoma City All Sports Assn, 100 W Main, Ste 285, Oklahoma City, OK 73102. Phone: (405) 236-5000. Fax: (405) 236-5008.

BREAD PUDDING RECIPE EXCHANGE. May 1–7. A week dedicated to the exchange of creative bread pudding recipes. For sample recipes send a SASE. For info: Bread Pudding Update, PO Box 416, Denver, CO 80201. Phone: (303) 575-5676.

BREATHE EASY MONTH. May 1–31. A public awareness campaign to educate the public on the American Lung Association's mission to prevent lung disease and promote lung health. Areas of public concern include the dangers of secondhand smoke, air pollution—both indoors and outdoors—and how asthma can be controlled with proper education. For info: Phone: (800) LUNG-USA.

May 1998

S	M	T	W	T	F	S
					1	2
3	4	5	6	7	8	9
10	11	12	13	14	15	16
17	18	19	20	21	22	23
24	25	26	27	28	29	30
31						

CARTOON ART APPRECIATION WEEK. May 1–7. To create a greater public awareness of and appreciation for cartoon art and its creators, the Museum schedules a variety of special events that celebrate the contribution of cartoons to the artistic, social and historic fabric of Americana. Also, to promote literacy using cartoon art as an educational tool, classroom activity kits for all ages are available to teachers and parents. Est attendance: 300. For info: CAAW Director, Cartoon Art Museum, 814 Mission St, 2nd Fl, San Francisco, CA 94103. Phone: (415) 227-8666. Fax: (415) 243-8666.

CINCO DE MAYO FIESTA NEVADA. May 1–3 (tentative). Sparks, NV. 7th annual outdoor Hispanic and Latin celebration featuring musical groups, mariachis, dance performances, food, arts and crafts booths. For info: Nevada Commission on Tourism, Capitol Complex, Carson City, NV 89710. Phone: (702) 353-2284 or (800) 237-0774. Fax: (702) 687-6779.

CLARK, MARK: BIRTH ANNIVERSARY. May 1, 1896. US general who served in both World Wars, Mark Clark was born at Madison Barracks, NY. In November 1942, he commanded the US forces taking part in the invasion of North Africa, and in January 1943, he became commander of the US Fifth Army, which invaded Italy in September 1943, taking Rome in June of 1944. After the Germans capitulated in Italy, Clark was appointed commander of US occupation forces in Austria. Clark died at Charleston, SC, Apr 17, 1984.

COLUMBIAN EXPOSITION OPENING: ANNIVERSARY. May 1, 1893. At 12:08 PM President Grover Cleveland, in the presence of nearly a quarter of a million people, placed his finger on a golden key opening the Columbian Exposition in Chicago, IL. Amid the unfurling of thousands of flags, sounding of trumpets and booming of cannons, the key caused a magnet connected with an electric valve to be energized, steam rushed into great cylinders and the immense pump, 50 feet high, began its enormous burden of pumping 15,000,000 gallons of water a day to supply the 685-acre fair and its visitors with an ample water supply.

☆ ☆ ☆

CREATIVE BEGINNINGS MONTH. May 1–31. Are you creative? Have you tapped into your full potential? Enjoy the budding month of May while discovering something new about yourself. Enroll in a course, write a poem, plant a garden, coordinate a social event. While developing your gifts, encourage others to also cultivate their own creative beginnings. For info: Christina Bergenholtz, PO Box 301, Grafton, MA 01519. Phone: (508) 839-5139. Email: chrismhb@aol.com

DATE YOUR MATE MONTH. May 1–31. May is the month to make your romance sizzle. Get back into the dating game by making a date with your mate this month. Annually, in May. For info: Rose Smith, Pres, Institute of Monogamy, 4900 Mesa Bonita Ct NW, Albuquerque, NM 87120. Phone: (505) 899-3121.

DENMARK: TIVOLI GARDENS SEASON. May 1–Sept 20. Copenhagen. World-famous for its variety of entertainment, symphony concerts, pantomime and ballet. Beautiful flower arrangements and excellent restaurants. Traditional season: May 1 until the third Sunday in September.

DOOR COUNTY FESTIVAL OF BLOSSOMS. May 1–31. Door County, WI. This month-long festival celebrates the May blooming of more than 1 million wildflowers and tulips, as well as the apple and cherry blossoms, in Door County. The area, famous for its lighthouses, offers walking and boat tours of several lighthouses at the 4th annual Door County Lighthouse Walk, May 17–18. For info: Wisconsin Dept of Tourism, Festival of Blossoms, PO Box 7976, Madison, WI 53707. Phone: (800) 52-RELAX or (414) 743-4456. Email: tourism@laughlin.com. WWW: http://tourism.state.wi.us

EMMETT KELLY CLOWN FESTIVAL. May 1–3. Houston, MO. Special appearances by Emmett Kelly, Jr, and Joey as well as clowns from across the Midwest. Events include a parade and a huge arts and crafts fair. Est attendance: 10,000. For info: Emmett Kelly Clown Festival, 103 N Grand, Houston, MO 65483. Phone: (417) 967-2220. Fax: (417) 967-3583.

FAMILY SUPPORT MONTH. May 1–31. The purpose of this observance is to support families with children during divorce, separation and custody issues. Promotes respect for mother/child relationships. Media: Kathleen Quinn, Proquest Communications, Ltd, 626 Carriage Hill Dr, Glenview, IL 60025. For info: Children Hurt in Legal Disputes (CHILD), PO Box 241, Wilmette, IL 60091-0241. Phone: (847) 998-9950. Fax: (847) 998-9945. Email: proquestkq@aol.com.

FIBROMYALGIA EDUCATION AND AWARENESS MONTH. May 1–31. To promote education and awareness of the dangers of fibromyalgia which is also known as the fibromyalgia syndrome (FSM), fibrositis or chronic muscle pain syndrome. Fibromyalgia affects more than 10 million American women. Kit of material available for $15. For info: Frederick S. Mayer, Pres, PPSI, PO Box 1336, Sausalito, CA 94933. Phone: (415) 332-4066. Fax: (415) 332-1832. Email: ppsi@aol.com.

GARDENING WEEKEND IN THE QUIET CORNER. May 1–3. Northeastern Connecticut. More than 30 shops offer special displays, discounts and demonstrations throughout the region. Annually, the first weekend in May. Est attendance: 1,000. For info: Northeast Connecticut Visitors District, PO Box 598, Putnam, CT 06260. Phone: (860) 928-1228. Fax: (860) 928-4720. Email: quietcorner@snet.net.
WWW: http://www.webtravels.com/quietcorner

GAZPACHO AFICIONADO TIME. May 1–Oct 31. A time to appreciate one of Spain's finest contributions to international cuisine: gazpacho, a nutritious cold soup made from fresh tomatoes and other vegetables. Observed while tomatoes are ripe.

GENEVA ON THE RIVER. May 1–3. Geneva, IL. A celebration of generations. Celebrate our rich historical heritage. Teas, street entertainment and Geneva's 200 landmark buildings are highlights. Annually, the first full weekend in May. For info: Geneva Chamber of Commerce, 8 S Third St, PO Box 481, Geneva, IL 60134. Phone: (630) 232-6060. Fax: (630) 232-6083.

GREAT BRITAIN FORMED: ANNIVERSARY. May 1, 1707. A union between England and Scotland resulted in the formation of Great Britain. (Wales had been part of England since the 1500s.) Today's United Kingdom consists of Great Britain and Northern Ireland.

GREECE: LABOR DAY. May 1. A general exodus to the countryside is customary on this national holiday.

HEPATITIS AWARENESS MONTH. May 1–31. For info: Hepatitis Foundation Intl, 30 Sunrise Terr, Cedar Grove, NJ 07009. Phone: (201) 239-1035.

HUNTINGTON'S DISEASE AWARENESS MONTH. May 1–31. For info: Huntington's Disease Society of America, 140 W 22nd St, 6th floor, New York, NY 10011-2420. Phone: (800) 345-4372 or (212) 242-1968.

INTERNATIONAL TUBA DAY. May 1. To recognize tubists in musical organizations around the world who have to go through the hassle of handling a tuba in order to make beautiful music. Annually, the first Friday in May. For info: Dr. Sy Brandon, Music Dept, Millersville University, PO Box 1002, Millersville, PA 17551-0302. Phone: (717) 872-3439. Fax: (717) 871-2304.
Email: sbrandon@marander.millersv.edu.

May 1998

S	M	T	W	T	F	S
					1	2
3	4	5	6	7	8	9
10	11	12	13	14	15	16
17	18	19	20	21	22	23
24	25	26	27	28	29	30
31						

ISLE OF EIGHT FLAGS SHRIMP FESTIVAL. May 1–3. Fernandina Beach, FL. Commemorates Fernandina's role as the birthplace of the modern shrimping industry. Multi-event festival includes juried arts and crafts show, entertainment, antiques, pirates and food. Est attendance: 150,000. For info: Isle of Eight Flags Shrimp Festival, PO Box 6146, Fernandina Beach, FL 32035. Phone: (904) 261-0203.

ITALY: FESTIVAL OF SAINT EFISIO. May 1–4. Cagliari. Said to be one of the biggest and most colorful processions in the world. Several thousand pilgrims on foot, in carts and on horseback wearing costumes dating from the 17th century accompany the statue of the saint through the streets.

JONES, MARY HARRIS (MOTHER JONES): BIRTH ANNIVERSARY. May 1, 1830. Irish-born American labor leader. After the death of her husband and four children (during the Memphis yellow fever epidemic of 1867) and loss of her belongings in the Chicago Fire, 1871, Jones devoted her energies and her life to organizing and advancing the cause of labor. It seemed she was present wherever there were labor troubles. She gave her last speech on her 100th birthday. Born at Cork, Ireland. Died Nov 30, 1930.

KANSAS BARBED WIRE SWAP/SELL. May 1–2. LaCrosse, KS. Barbed Wire Collectors Association show and meeting. Est attendance: 200. For info: Bradley Penka, Kansas Barbed Wire Collectors Assn, PO Box 716, LaCrosse, KS 67548. Phone: (913) 222-9900.

LANDON AZALEA GARDEN FESTIVAL AND ANTIQUE SHOW. May 1–3. Bethesda, MD. Garden stroll amid 15,000 blooming azaleas. Plant sale, flower show, historic farmhouse tour, lunch, musical entertainment and 40 antique dealers. Annually. Est attendance: 30,000. For info: Landon School, 6101 Wilson Lane, Bethesda, MD 20817. Phone: (301) 320-3200. Fax: (301) 320-2787.
Email: jeanne_hamrick@landon.net.
WWW: http://www.landon.net

LAW DAY. May 1. To advance equality and justice under law; to encourage citizen support of law observance and law enforcement; and to foster respect for law and understanding of its essential place in the life of every citizen of the US. For info: American Bar Assn, Division for Public Education, 541 N Fairbanks Court, Chicago, IL 60611-3314. Phone: (312) 988-5735.

★**LAW DAY.** May 1. Presidential Proclamation issued each year for May 1 since 1958 at request. (PL87–20 of Apr 7, 1961.)

LEI DAY. May 1. Hawaii. On this special day—the Hawaiian version of May Day—leis are made, worn, given, displayed and entered in lei-making contests. One of the most popular Lei Day celebrations takes place in Honolulu at Kapiolani Park in Waikiki. Includes the state's largest lei contest, the crowning of the Lei Day Queen, Hawaiian music, hula and flowers galore.

★**LOYALTY DAY.** May 1. Presidential Proclamation issued annually for May 1 since 1959 at request. (PL85–529 of July 18, 1958.) Note that an earlier proclamation was issued in 1955.

LUCY STONE MARRIED: ANNIVERSARY. May 1, 1855. When nationally known public speaker and feminist Lucy Stone married Henry Blackwell, a marriage contract written by the bride and groom was read at the wedding that disavowed the gross inequity married women suffered under American law, and the word "obey" was omitted from their marriage vows. A year after the ceremony the bride further shocked society by taking back her maiden name, which she kept for the rest of her life.

MARSHALL ISLANDS, REPUBLIC OF THE: CONSTITUTION DAY. May 1. National holiday.

MAY BREAKFASTS. May 1–31. Rhode Island. This unique annual state-wide event originated in 1867 and features Rhode Island favorites, including Jonnycakes and other native dishes. Locations vary from bird sanctuaries, to church and grange halls, yacht clubs, schools and veteran's posts. In-state phone: (401) 277-2601; out-of-state phone: (800) 556-2484. Est attendance:

20,000. For info: Rhode Island Tourism, 1 W Exchange St, Providence, RI 02903. WWW: http://www.visitrhodeisland.com

MAY DAY. May 1. Lumpkin, GA. Celebration of the planting season with traditional May Day activities and the May Pole Dance. Est attendance: 800. For info: Westville Village, Patty Cannington, PR Dir, PO Box 1850, Lumpkin, GA 31815. Phone: (912) 838-6310 or (888) 733-1850. WWW: http://www.westville.org

MAY DAY. May 1. The first day of May has been observed as a holiday since ancient times. Spring festivals, maypoles and maying still are common, but the political importance of May Day has grown since the 1880s, when it became a workers' day in the US. Now widely observed in socialist countries as a workers' holiday or as Labor Day. In most European countries, when May Day falls on Saturday or Sunday, the Monday following is observed as a holiday, with bank and store closings, parades and other festivities.

MAY DAY BASKET GIVE-AWAY. May 1–3. Minneapolis-St Paul, MN. Singles with Heart, a group that brings single people together to do volunteer work, distributes May Day baskets full of surprises in the Twin Cities. Annually, the first weekend in May. For info: Singles with Heart, 3620 Regal Oak, Minnetonka, MN 55305.

MAY IN MONTCLAIR. May 1–31. Montclair Township, NJ. 20th annual month-long festival celebrating the wealth of cultural, artistic, historic and recreational opportunities in Montclair for residents, merchants and visitors. Est attendance: 4,000. For info: Jean H. Kidd, Chair, May in Montclair, 91 Central Ave, Montclair, NJ 07042. Phone: (201) 744-7660.

MAY IS BETTER HEARING AND SPEECH MONTH. May 1–31. A nationwide public information campaign held each May to inform the 41 million Americans with hearing and speech problems that help is available. Annually, the month of May. For info: Georgia Biggs, Publication Asst, Natl Grange, 1616 H St NW, Washington, DC 20006. Phone: (202) 628-3507. Fax: (202) 347-1091.

MEMPHIS IN MAY INTERNATIONAL FESTIVAL. May 1–31. Memphis,TN. Month-long celebration of international business and fun. Events are on the weekends and include International Weekend, Beale Street Musical Festival and more than 125 sanctioned events throughout the city. For info: Memphis in May Intl Festival, 245 Wagner Pl, Memphis, TN 38103. Phone: (901) 525-4611.

NATIONAL ALLERGY/ASTHMA AWARENESS MONTH. May 1–31. Kit of materials available for $15 from this non-profit organization. For info: Frederick S. Mayer, Pres, Pharmacist Planning Services, Inc, c/o Allergy Council of America (ACA), PO Box 1336, Sausalito, CA 94966. Phone: (415) 332-4066. Fax: (415) 332-1832. Email: ppsi@aol.com.

NATIONAL ANTIQUE BOTTLE COLLECTING WEEK. May 1–7. A week-long celebration to honor the individuals, clubs, groups and organizations who study and research the preservation and care of historical bottles. Annually, the first week of May. For info: Federation of Historical Bottle Collectors, 88 Sweetbriar Branch, Longwood, FL 32750-2783. Phone: (407) 332-7689. Email: glassman.carl@mci2000.com.
WWW: http://www.av.qnet.com/~glassman/

NATIONAL ARTHRITIS MONTH. May 1–31. Increases awareness of the more than 100 diseases known as arthritis and increases support for the 40 million Americans with arthritis. For info: Arthritis Foundation, 1330 W Peachtree St NW, Atlanta, GA 30309. Phone: (800) 283-7800 or (404) 872-7100. Fax: (404) 872-0457.

NATIONAL BARBECUE MONTH. May 1–31. To encourage people to start enjoying barbecuing early in the season when Daylight Saving Time lengthens the day. Annually, the month of May. Sponsor: Barbecue Industry Assn. For info: Donna H. Myers, DHM Group, Inc, PO Box 767, Holmdel, NJ 07733. Fax: (908) 946-3343.

NATIONAL BIKE MONTH. May 1–31. 42nd annual celebration of bicycling for recreation and transportation. Local activities sponsored by bicycling organizations, environmental groups, PTAs, police departments, health organizations and civic groups. About 5 million participants nationwide. Annually, the month of May. For info: League of American Bicyclists, 190 W Ostend St, Ste 120, Baltimore, MD 21230-3755. Phone: (410) 539-3399. WWW: http://www.bikeleague.org

NATIONAL DIGESTIVE DISEASES AWARENESS MONTH. May 1–31. For info: Digestive Disease National Coalition, 507 Capitol Ct NE, Ste 200, Washington, DC 20002. Phone: (202) 544-7494.

NATIONAL EGG MONTH. May 1–31. Dedicated to the versatility, convenience, economy and good nutrition of "The incredible edible egg." Annually, the month of May. For info: American Egg Board, Linda Braun, Consumer Services Mgr, 1460 Renaissance Dr, Park Ridge, IL 60068. Email: aebnet@aol.com. WWW: http://www.aeb.org

NATIONAL GOOD CAR-KEEPING MONTH. May 1–31. To promote increased safety and value through good car maintenance. For info: Sander Allen, Good Car-Keeping Institute, 230 N Michigan Ave, Ste 1630, Chicago, IL 60601.

NATIONAL HAMBURGER MONTH. May 1–31. Sponsored by White Castle, the original fast-food hamburger chain, founded in 1921, to pay tribute to one of America's favorite foods. With or without condiments, on or off a bun or bread, hamburgers have grown in popularity since the early 1920s and are now an American meal mainstay. For info: White Castle System, Inc, Marketing Dept, 555 W Goodale St, Columbus, OH 43215-1171. Phone: (614) 228-5781. Fax: (614) 228-8841.
WWW: http://www.whitecastle.com

NATIONAL HIGH BLOOD PRESSURE EDUCATION MONTH. May 1–31. To promote the control and treatment of high blood pressure. Church Blood Pressure Sunday, May 3. Annually, the month of May. For info: Natl High Blood Pressure Education Program Info Ctr, Natl Heart, Lung and Blood Institute, PO Box 30105, Bethesda, MD 20824-0105. Phone: (301) 251-1222. Fax: (301) 251-1223. Email: nhlbiic@dgsys.com.

NATIONAL MELANOMA/SKIN CANCER DETECTION AND PREVENTION MONTH. May 1–31. For info: American Academy of Dermatology, PO Box 681069, Schaumburg, IL 60168. Phone: (847) 330-0230.

NATIONAL MENTAL HEALTH MONTH. May 1–31. For info: Natl Mental Health Assn, 1021 Prince St, Alexandria, VA 22314-2971. Phone: (800) 969-6642 or (703) 684-7722.

NATIONAL MOVING MONTH. May 1–31. Recognizing America's mobile roots and kicking off the busiest moving season of the year. Each year more than 21 million Americans move between Memorial Day and Labor Day, with the average American moving every seven years. During this month moving experts will be educating Americans on how to plan a successful move, to pack efficiently and handle the uncertainties and questions that moving children may have. For info: Allied Van Lines, PO Box 9569, Downers Grove, IL 60515. Phone: (630) 241-2538. Fax: (630) 241-4343. WWW: http://www.alliedvan.com

NATIONAL NEUROFIBROMATOSIS MONTH. May 1–31. For info: Natl Neurofibromatosis Foundation, 120 Wall St, 16th Fl, New York, NY 10005. Phone: (800) 323-7938 or (212) 344-6633.

NATIONAL PHYSICAL FITNESS AND SPORTS MONTH. May 1–31. Encourages individuals and organizations to promote fitness activities and programs. For info: President's Council on Physical Fitness and Sports, HHH Building, 200 Independence Ave, SW, Room 738H, Washington, DC 20201-0004. Phone: (202) 690-9000. Fax: (202) 690-5211.

NATIONAL SALSA MONTH. May 1–31. Recognizing salsa as America's favorite condiment, used more often than even ketchup as a topping, dip, marinade and to spice up countless recipes. National Salsa Month celebrates more than 50 years of picante sauce, a salsa created in 1947, and celebrates Cinco de Mayo, a major Mexican holiday now recognized across North America. For info: Pace Foods, PO Box 12636, San Antonio, TX 78212-0636. Phone: (800) 433-PACE.
WWW: http://www.pacefoods.com

NATIONAL SELF-DISCOVERY MONTH. May 1–31. May is the month for men and women of all walks of life across America (and the world) to begin to become more aware of themselves; to appreciate their uniqueness as individuals as well as their natural equality and oneness as human beings. For info: Christian Fisher, Inner Power Technologies, 691 Chilton Ave, Ste 2, Niagara Falls, NY 14301.

NATIONAL SENIOR TRAVEL MONTH. May 1–31. Combining the spirit of Older Americans Month (May) and National Tourism Week (May 4–10), this month celebrates the many opportunities for the 50+ traveler. For info: Iliana Carlo, Promotion Dir, New Choices Magazine, 28 W 23rd St, New York, NY 10010. Fax: (212) 366-8899. Email: newchoices@aol.com.
WWW: http://seniornews.com/new-choices

NATIONAL SIGHT-SAVING MONTH. May 1–31. Prevent Blindness America, formerly National Society to Prevent Blindness, annually devotes this observance to a different topic in the fields of vision health or vision safety. Each topic reflects the latest developments in the specific area of focus. For info: Prevent Blindness America, 500 E Remington Rd, Schaumburg, IL 60173. Phone: (800) 331-2020 or (847) 843-2020.

NATIONAL STROKE AWARENESS MONTH. May 1–31. For info: Natl Stroke Assn, 96 Inverness Dr East, Ste 1, Englewood, CO 80112-5112. Phone: (800) STR-OKES.

NATIONAL TRAUMA AWARENESS MONTH. May 1–31. Each year no fewer than 150,000 Americans die as a result of traumatic injury. Annual campaign focusing on a different aspect of trauma (injury), providing a sober reminder that we must each work to create a healthier and safer society. For info: American Trauma Society, 8903 Presidential Pkwy, Ste 512, Upper Marlboro, MD 20772-2656. Phone: (301) 420-4189 or (800) 556-7890. Fax: (301) 420-0617.

May 1998

S	M	T	W	T	F	S
					1	2
3	4	5	6	7	8	9
10	11	12	13	14	15	16
17	18	19	20	21	22	23
24	25	26	27	28	29	30
31						

NEW HOMEOWNER'S DAY. May 1. You have faced all the challenges—now take the time as a new homeowner to stand back and reflect on your new home and savor the feeling. For info: Dorothy Zjawin, Dir, 61 W Colfax Ave, Roselle Park, NJ 07204. Phone: (908) 241-6241. Fax: (908) 241-6241.

★**OLDER AMERICANS MONTH.** May 1–31. Presidential Proclamation; from 1963 through 1973 this was called "Senior Citizens Month." In May 1974 it became Older Americans Month. In 1980 the title included Senior Citizens Day, which was observed on May 8, 1980. Always has been issued since 1963.

PEN-FRIENDS WEEK INTERNATIONAL. May 1–7. To encourage everyone to have one or more pen-friends not only in their own country but in other countries. For complete information on how to become a good pen-friend and information about how to write good letters, send $3 to cover expense of printing, handling and postage. Annually, May 1–7. For info: Dr. Stanley J. Drake, Pres, Intl Soc of Friendship and Good Will, 412 Cherry Hills Dr, Bakersfield, CA 93309-2866.

PERSONAL HISTORY AWARENESS MONTH. May 1–31. To educate individuals and families about the importance of compiling a personal history. Plan local events to include workshops, classes and lectures. Write or call for sample newsletter. For info: Margaret L. Ingram, Family History Center, PO Box 1339, Albany, OR 97321. Phone: (541) 924-0268. Fax: (541) 924-0833.
Email: Margaret@matrixdm.com.
WWW: http://www.matrixdm.com/family-history

PHILIPPINES: FEAST OF OUR LADY OF PEACE AND GOOD VOYAGE. May 1–31. Pilgrimage to the shrine of Nuestra Sra de la Paz y Buen Viaje in Antipolo, Rizal.

PHILIPPINES: SANTACRUZAN. May 1–31. Maytime pageant-procession that recalls the quest of Queen Helena and Prince Constantine for the Holy Cross.

PROJECT SAFE BABY MONTH. May 1–31. Dedicated to raising awareness of correct child safety seat use, to increasing the availability of child safety seats and to educating parents, teachers and health professionals about child safety in the car. Sponsor: Midas Intl, Inc. For info: Golin/Harris Communications, Inc, Project Safe Baby Team, 500 N Michigan Ave, Chicago, IL 60611. Phone: (312) 836-7100.

☆ ☆ ☆

REACT MONTH. May 1–31. Highlights safety education in the correct emergency use of CB radio by travelers. Recognizes the contributions of REACT volunteers to safety communications within their communities for public events or local emergencies. Encourages the public to join a REACT Team and further its safety communications initiatives in the community. For info: REACT International Inc, Box 998, Wichita, KS 67201. Phone: (316) 263-2100. Fax: (316) 263-2118.
WWW: http://www.reactintl.org/

REOPENING OF THE 1743 PALATINE HOUSE MUSEUM. May 1. Schoharie, NY. Open Thursday through Monday 1–5 PM, May through October. The Palatine House is a living museum and is the oldest existing building in Schoharie County. Est attendance: 900. For info: Diane Szabo, Program Dir, Schoharie Colonial Heritage Assn, PO Box 554, Schoharie, NY 12157. Phone: (518) 295-7505 or (518) 295-7585.

REVISE YOUR WORK SCHEDULE MONTH. May 1–31. To increase awareness, exploration and implementation of nontraditional work schedules such as flextime, telecommuting, job sharing and compressed work weeks. Annually, the month of May. For info: Maggi Payment, Dir, Center for Worktime Options, 1286 University Ave, #192, San Diego, CA 92103. Phone: (619) 232-0404.

RICHMOND'S MUSHROOM FESTIVAL. May 1–3. Richmond, MO. Parade, arts and crafts, carnival, bands and beer gardens. Est attendance: 15,000. For info: Sally Familiner, Exec Dir, Chamber of Commerce, 170 N Thornton, Richmond, MO 64085. Phone: (816) 776-6916. Fax: (816) 776-6917.

RUSSIA: INTERNATIONAL LABOR DAY. May 1–2. Public holiday in Russian Federation. "Official May Day demonstrations of working people."

SAINT TAMENEND'S DAY. May 1. Colonial American joyous May Day celebration, recently revived. Legendary American Indian sage, Chief Tamenend, canonized by fun-loving young colonists asserting independence from old-world patrons. Modern celebrants, tired of overly serious political observances, identify selves by pinning dollar bill to their jackets. For info: Dr. Nicholas Varga, Dept of History, Loyola College, 4501 N Charles St, Baltimore, MD 21210-2699. Phone: (410) 617-2554.

SAVE THE RHINO DAY. May 1. May day! May day! Rhinos still in danger! Help save the world's remaining rhinos on the verge of extinction! Get involved with local, national and international conservation efforts to stop the senseless slaughter of these gentle pachyderms. Call your local zoo or write Really, Rhinos! for a $5 information packet. For info: Judyth Lessee, Founder, Really, Rhinos!, PO Box 40503, Tucson, AZ 85717-0503. Phone: (520) 327-9048. Email: rinophyl@rtd.com.

SCOTLAND: PITLOCHRY FESTIVAL THEATRE SEASON. May 1–Oct 10. Pitlochry Festival Theatre, Pitlochry, Tayside. Annual festival of drama, music and the arts, with plays performed in repertory, plus concerts, exhibitions and fringe events. For info: Marketing Dept, Pitlochry Festival Theatre, Pitlochry, Perthshire, Scotland PH16 5DR. Phone: (17) 96 472680. Fax: (17) 96 473054.

SENIOR CITIZENS MONTH. May 1–31. Massachusetts.

SEQUIM IRRIGATION FESTIVAL. May 1–10. Sequim, WA. Come and join the fun at this unique festival. Includes amusement rides, fireworks, a parade, arts and crafts displays, entertainment, food booths and much more. Est attendance: 15,000. For info: Sequim Chamber of Commerce, Sequim Irrigation Festival, PO Box 907, Sequim, WA 98382. Phone: (360) 683-6197. Fax: (360) 683-6349. Email: sequimchamber@daka.com.

SIGHT-SAVING MONTH—ULTRAVIOLET AWARENESS. May 1–31. While the damage ultraviolet (UV) causes to skin is obvious, the damage it can do to eyes may not be. Not enough attention is paid to the damage UV can do to the eyes. Exposure to UV can burn delicate eye tissue and raise the risk of developing cataracts and cancers of the eye. For info: Prevent Blindness America®, 500 E Remington Rd, Schaumburg, IL 60173. Phone: (800) 331-2020. Fax: (847) 843-8458. WWW: http://www.prevent-blindness.org

SMITH, KATE: BIRTH ANNIVERSARY. May 1. One of America's most popular singers. Kate Smith, who never took a formal music lesson, recorded more songs than any other performer (more than 3,000), made more than 15,000 radio broadcasts and received more than 25 million fan letters. On Nov 11, 1938, she introduced a new song during her regular radio broadcast, written especially for her by Irving Berlin: "God Bless America." It soon became the unofficial national anthem. Born Kathryn Elizabeth Smith at Greenville, VA, on May 1, 1909. She began her radio career on May 1, 1931, with "When the Moon Comes Over the Mountain," a song identified with her throughout her career. She died at Raleigh, NC, June 17, 1986.

SOWERBY, LEO: BIRTH ANNIVERSARY. May 1, 1895. Pulitzer prize–winning composer of more than 550 compositions, born at Grand Rapids, MI, and died July 7, 1968, at Port Clinton, OH.

STRIKE OUT STROKES MONTH. May 1–31. Dedicated to the prevention of strokes. Factors resulting from heredity or natural processes can't be changed but with proper medical treatment and healthful lifestyle adjustments, some risk factors can be eliminated. Kit materials available for $15. For info: Frederick S Mayer, Pres, Pharmacy Council on Stroke Prevention, PO Box 1336, Sausalito, CA 94966. Phone: (415) 332-4066. Fax: (415) 332-1832. Email: ppsi@aol.com.

STROKE AWARENESS MONTH. May 1–31. American Heart Association and other organizations across the nation work together to conduct awareness campaigns about stroke, the leading cause of disability in the US. Observance is designed to alert the public about stroke's warning signs, how it might be prevented and resources available to help stroke survivors and their care givers. During 1998, the American Heart Association's 50th anniversary as a voluntary health agency, the observance focuses upon stroke's impact on women. For info: Cathy Yarbrough, News Media Relations, American Heart Assn, Natl Center, 7272 Greenville Ave, Dallas, TX 75231. Phone: (800) AHA-USA1. Fax: (214) 369-3685. WWW: http://www.americanheart.org

SUGARLOAF'S SPRING MANASSAS CRAFT FESTIVAL. May 1–3. Prince William County Fairgrounds, Manassas, VA. This show, now in its 3rd year, features 300 nationally recognized craft designers and fine artists displaying and selling their original creations. Craft demonstrations, children's entertainment, live music, drawings, food, hourly gift certificate drawings and more. Est attendance: 15,000. For info: Sugarloaf Mountain Works, Inc, 200 Orchard Ridge Dr, #215, Gaithersburg, MD 20878. Phone: (800) 210-9900.

TAOS SPRING ARTS FESTIVAL. May 1–17. Taos, NM. Featuring arts and crafts from all around New Mexico. Est attendance: 20,000. For info: Taos Spring Arts Festival, PO Drawer 1, Taos, NM 87571. Phone: (800) 732-8267. Fax: (505) 758-3872. Email: taos@taoswebb.com.

TEILHARD DE CHARDIN, PIERRE: BIRTH ANNIVERSARY. May 1. French Jesuit author, paleontologist and philosopher, born at Sarcenat, France, May 1, 1881. He died at New York, NY, Apr 10, 1955.

TENNESSEE RIVER FIDDLERS CONVENTION. May 1–2. McFarland Park, Florence, AL. The lazy Tennessse River will be the backdrop to the sounds of banjos, dobros, guitars and fiddles during this Bluegrass celebration. Musicians, both young and old, compete for more than $5,000 in prize money in 16 categories. Annually, the first full weekend in May. Est attendance: 5,000. For info: City of Florence, Park and Recreation Dept, 2500 Chisholm Rd, PO Box 2040, Florence, AL 35630. Phone: (205) 760-6416. Fax: (205) 760-6497. Email: RGres33403@aol.com.

TOAD SUCK DAZE. May 1–3. Downtown, Conway, AR. 17th annual event features toad jumping contests, concerts, parade, street dancing, tug-o-war, softball tournament, bike race, 5 and 10K runs, arts and crafts and more. Annually, the first weekend in May. Est attendance: 125,000. For info: Janiece Driscoll, c/o Conway Chamber of Commerce, PO Box 1492, Conway, AR 72033. Phone: (501) 327-7788. Fax: (501) 327-7790. Email: janieced.conwayarkcc.org. WWW: http://www.conwayarkcc.org/daze

U-2 INCIDENT: ANNIVERSARY. May 1, 1960. On the eve of a summit meeting between US President Dwight D. Eisenhower and Soviet Premier Nikita Khrushchev, a U-2 espionage plane flying at about 60,000 feet was shot down over Sverdlovsk, in central USSR. The pilot, CIA agent Francis Gary Powers, survived the crash, as did large parts of the aircraft, a suicide kit and sophisticated surveillance equipment. The sensational event, which US officials described as a weather reconnaissance flight gone astray, resulted in cancellation of the summit meeting. Powers was tried, convicted and sentenced to 10 years in prison, by a Moscow court. In 1962 he was returned to the US in exchange for an imprisoned Soviet spy but found an unfriendly American public, which apparently believed he should have used his suicide kit. He died in a helicopter crash in 1977. See also: "Powers, Francis Gary: Birth Anniversary" (Aug 17).

VEGETARIAN RESOURCE GROUP'S ESSAY CONTEST FOR KIDS. May 1. Baltimore, MD. Children ages 18 and under are encouraged to submit 2–3-page essays on topics related to vegetarianism. Essays accepted beginning May 1. Winners announced Sept 15 and will receive a $50 savings bond. For info: The Vegetarian Resource Group, PO Box 1463, Baltimore, MD 21203. Phone: (410) 366-8343. Email: thevrg@aol.com. WWW: http://www.vrg.org

WILLIAMS, ARCHIE: BIRTH ANNIVERSARY. May 1, 1915. Archie Williams, along with Jesse Owens and others, debunked Hitler's theory of the superiority of the Aryan athletes at the 1936 Berlin Olympics. As a black member of the US team Williams won a gold medal by running the 400-meter in 46.5 seconds (.4 second slower than his own record of earlier that year). Williams, who was born May 1, 1915, at Oakland, CA, earned a degree in mechanical engineering from the University of California-Berkeley in 1939, but had to dig ditches for a time because they weren't hiring black engineers. In time Williams became an airplane pilot and for 22 years he trained Tuskegee Institute pilots including the black air corp of WW II. He joined the Army Air Corps in 1942. When asked during a 1981 interview about his treatment by the Nazis during the 1936 Olympics, he replied, "Well, over there at least we didn't have to ride in the back of the bus." Archie Williams died June 24, 1993, at Fairfax, CA.

WOMEN'S HEALTH CARE MONTH. May 1–31. To initiate a public education campaign devoted to increasing awareness of the many health concerns unique to women. Focus will be on the prevention of the major causes of death and poor health among women—heart disease, cancer, arthritis, osteoporosis and bone fractures, as well as on depression and alcoholism in women. There is a $15 charge for kit materials. Annually, the month of May. For info: Pharmacists Planning Service, Inc, 200 Gate Five Rd, PO Box 1336, Sausalito, CA 94966. Phone: (415) 332-4066. Fax: (415) 332-1832. Email: ppsi@aol.com.

May 1998	S	M	T	W	T	F	S
						1	2
	3	4	5	6	7	8	9
	10	11	12	13	14	15	16
	17	18	19	20	21	22	23
	24	25	26	27	28	29	30
	31						

WORLD CHAMPIONSHIP CRIBBAGE TOURNAMENT. May 1–3. Plumas County Fairgrounds, Quincy, CA. Founded in 1972, the country's oldest cribbage tournament now draws entrants from all over the country during the two-day event. Annually, the first weekend in May. Est attendance: 700. For info: Mike Taborski, Tournament Chair, PO Box B, Quincy, CA 95971. Phone: (916) 283-0800. Fax: (916) 283-3952. Email: featherpub@aol.com.

BIRTHDAYS TODAY

Charles (Chuck) Bednarik, 73, Pro Football Hall of Fame center and linebacker, born Bethlehem, PA, May 1, 1925.

Harry Caray (born Harry Christopher Carabini), 79, sportscaster, Ford Frick Award winner, born St. Louis, MO, May 1, 1919.

Steve Cauthen, 38, jockey, born Walton, KY, May 1, 1960.

Judy Collins, 59, singer ("Both Sides Now," "Chelsea Morning"), born Seattle, WA, May 1, 1939.

Rita Coolidge, 53, singer ("[Your Love Has Lifted Me] Higher and Higher," "We're All Alone"), born Nashville, TN, May 1, 1945.

Glenn Ford, 82, actor (*The Blackboard Jungle, The Fastest Gun Alive*, "The Family Holvak"), born Quebec, Canada, May 1, 1916.

Joseph Heller, 75, writer (*Catch-22, God Knows*), born Brooklyn, NY, May 1, 1923.

Sonny James (Jimmy Loden), 69, singer ("Young Love"), born Hackleburg, AL, May 1, 1929.

Bobbie Ann Mason, 58, writer (*In Country, Spence and Lila*), born Mayfield, KY, May 1, 1940.

Jack Paar, 80, entertainer, born Canton, OH, May 1, 1918.

☆ ☆ ☆

MAY 2 — SATURDAY

Day 122 — 243 Remaining

ANN ARBOR SPRING ART FAIR. May 2–3. Ann Arbor, MI. To give the public the opportunity to view and invest in the finest arts and crafts. 20th annual. Est attendance: 15,000. For info: Audree Levy, 10629 Park Preston, Dallas, TX 75230. Phone: (214) 369-4345. Fax: (214) 369-3236. WWW: http://www.annarbor.org

APPLE BLOSSOM FESTIVAL. May 2–3. Gettysburg, PA. An annual event held the first weekend in May at the South Mountain Fairgrounds, 10 mi. NW of Gettysburg on PA Rt 234. For info: Gettysburg Convention & Visitors Bureau, 35 Carlisle St, Gettysburg, PA 17325. Phone: (717) 334-6274. Fax: (717) 334-1166. WWW: http://www.gettysburg.com

ASTRONOMY DAY. May 2. To take astronomy to the people. International Astronomy Day is observed on a Saturday near the first quarter moon between mid-April and mid-May. See Apr 26 for Astronomy Week. Co-sponsored by 15 astronomical organizations. For info: Gary E. Tomlinson, Coord, Astronomy Day Headquarters, c/o Chaffee Planetarium, 272 Pearl NW, Grand Rapids, MI 49504. Phone: (616) 456-3532. Email: gtomlinson@wingsbbs.com. WWW: http://www.mcs.net/~bstevens/al

BARK IN THE PARK. May 2. Lincoln Park, Chicago, IL. In recognition of Be Kind to Animals Week, thousands of paws and feet will hit the ground running or walking for this 5K event. Entrance fee. Est attendance: 2,000. For info: The Anti-Cruelty Society, 157 W Grand Ave, Chicago, IL 60610. Phone: (312) 644-8338.

CERTIFIED PROFESSIONAL® SECRETARY EXAMINATION. May 2 (also Nov 7). The examinations are given at various locations throughout the world. The first Saturday of May and the first Saturday of November. For info: Kathy Schoneboom, CPS Mgr, Professional Secretaries Intl®—The Assn for Office Professionals ™, 10502 NW Ambassador Dr, PO Box 20404, Kansas City, MO 64195-0404. Phone: (816) 891-6600. Fax: (816) 891-9118. Email: cps@psi.org. WWW: http://www.gvi.net/psi

CHERRY BLOSSOM ARTS WEEKEND/TOUR OF THE INNS. May 2–3. Bay Head, NJ. Galleries host fine art. Artists and crafters demonstrate a variety of activities celebrating the arts and architecture. The Annual Cherry Blossom Tour of Inns includes Bay Head Gables, Bay Head Sands, Conovers Bay Head Inn, Bay Head Harbor Inn, The Bentley Inn and The Grenville Hotel. Est attendance: 600. For info: Janice Eskesen, Chairperson, 676 Main Ave, Bay Head, NJ 08742-5346. Phone: (732) 899-0767 or (800) 4-BAYHED.

CHOWDER FESTIVAL, FLOWER AND ART SHOW. May 2–3. Gold Beach, OR. Curry County Fairgrounds. The Curry County Historical Society, Innominata Garden Club and Curry Arts Association put together a weekend of food, fun, flowers and fine art. Est attendance: 800. For info: Gold Beach Chamber of Commerce, 29279 Ellensburg Ave, #3, Gold Beach, OR 97444. Phone: (800) 525-2334. Fax: (541) 247-0188.
Email: goldbeach@harborside.com.
WWW: http://www.harborside.com/gb

COTTON PICKIN' FAIR. May 2–3. Also Oct 3–4. Gay, GA. At the old cotton gin complex, this award-winning festival features 300 exhibitors of antiques and arts and crafts, on-going entertainment, great country cooking, children's activities and demonstrations by craftspeople. Biannually, the first weekend of May and Oct. Est attendance: 60,000. For info: Lana Miles, Fair Coord, PO Box 1, Gay, GA 30218. Phone: (706) 538-6814.

CROSBY, HARRY LILLIS "BING": BIRTH ANNIVERSARY. May 2. American singer, composer and actor, born at Tacoma, WA, May 2, 1904. Died while playing golf near Madrid, Spain, Oct 14, 1977.

DANDELION MAY FEST. May 2. Der Marktplatz, Dover, OH. Old-fashioned festival includes finals in a nationwide dandelion recipe contest, live entertainment, slides and presentations about dandelions and food booths featuring dishes made from dandelions, including dandelion coffee ice cream, dandelion pizza, dandelion bread and dandelion omelettes. Also, dandelion wine and jelly tasting, family entertainment and 5K fun run. Festival includes 5th National Dandelion Cook-Off, for entry forms for cook-off call: (800) 697-4858. Est attendance: 8,000. For info: Anita Davis, Coord, Der Marktplatz-Breitenbach Wine Cellars, 5934 Old Route 39 NW, Dover, OH 44622. Phone: (330) 343-3603. Fax: (330) 343-8290. Email: bdavis@Tusco.net.

DEPOT LANE SINGERS. May 2 (also Dec 5). Schoharie, NY. 75–100 singers celebrate the seasons in song. Est attendance: 700. For info: Frances Tripp, Dir, Schoharie Colonial Heritage Assn, PO Box 554, Schoharie, NY 12157. Phone: (518) 295-7168 or (518) 295-7505.

ENGLAND: BRIGHTON FESTIVAL. May 2–24. Various venues, Brighton, East Sussex. Annual international festival which includes all aspects of the performing arts. For info: Lisa Wolfe, Mktg Dept, Brighton Festival, 21-22 Old Steine, Brighton, East Sussex, England BN1 1EL. Phone: (44) (127) 367-6926. Fax: (44) (127) 362-2453.

FLEMINGTON SPEEDWAY RACING SEASON. May 2–Nov 7 (Saturday nights). Flemington Fairgrounds, Flemington, NJ. Racing by various types of stock cars and other vehicles. 6 PM starting time. Est attendance: 5,000. For info: Paul Kuhl, Flemington Fairgrounds, PO Box 293, Rt 31, Flemington, NJ 08822. Phone: (908) 782-2413. Fax: (908) 806-8432.

IRVINE ANIMAL CARE CENTER OPEN HOUSE. May 2. Irvine, CA. As urban sprawl continues to limit the necessary space needed to keep dogs and cats, rats and mice as pets are gradually emerging as an ideal substitute. They provide all the pleasures and satisfaction of a warm, cuddly, intelligent and friendly pet companion. The American Fancy Rat and Mouse Association (AFRMA) was founded in 1983 to promote and encourage the breeding and exhibition of fancy rats and mice. For info: AFRMA (CAE), 9230 64th St, Riverside, CA 92509-5924. Phone: (909) 685-2350. Fax: (818) 592-6319. Email: craigr@afrma.org. WWW: http://www.afrma.org/afrma

JEAN LAKE FESTIVAL. May 2–3. Pike Pioneer Museum, Troy, AL. An arts and crafts show with over 80 vendors displaying oil and watercolor paintings along with woodworking and textiles, food and entertainment. Annually, the first full weekend in May. Est attendance: 3,500. For info: Charlotte Gibson, Jean Lake Festival, PO Box 871, Troy, AL 36081. Phone: (334) 566-3597.

KBCO KINETICS SCULPTURE CHALLENGE. May 2. Boulder Reservoir, Boulder, CO. Participants make human powered crafts that must travel over water, land and mud. Kinetics also features a concert starring nationally acclaimed acts as well as food, drinks, volleyball tournament and a hot-air balloon festival. Est attendance: 200,000. For info: Kate Culligan, Jacor Marketing Director, 2500 Pearl St, Ste 315, Boulder, CO 80302. Phone: (303) 899-4201. WWW: http://www.kbcoradio.com

KENTUCKY DERBY. May 2. Churchill Downs, Louisville, KY. The running of America's premier thoroughbred horse race, inaugurated in 1875. First jewel in the "Triple Crown," traditionally followed by the Preakness (the second Saturday after Derby) and the Belmont Stakes (the fifth Saturday after Derby). Annually, the first Saturday in May. Est attendance: 135,000. For info: Churchill Downs, 700 Central Ave, Louisville, KY 40208. Phone: (502) 636-4400. WWW: http://kentuckyderby.com

LANSING DAZE. May 2. Lansing High School and Lansing City Hall, Lansing, KS. Features pancake breakfast, ice cream social, car show, craft show, quilt show, square dancing and entertainment. Annually, the first weekend in May. Est attendance: 5,000. For info: Connie Hachenberg, Dir, Leavenworth-Lansing Conv and Visitors Bureau, 518 Shawnee, PO Box 44, Leavenworth, KS 66048. Phone: (800) 844-4114. Fax: (913) 682-8170.

LEE, PINKY (PINCUS LEFF): BIRTH ANNIVERSARY. May 2, 1907. Born at St. Paul, MN. When young, Leff had dreams of becoming an attorney, but abandoned the idea when classmates laughed at his lisp. His show business debut was in burlesque in the 1930s. He is best remembered for "The Pinky Lee Show" which telecast from Los Angeles in the early 1950s. Pinky Lee died Apr 3, 1993, at Mission Viejo, CA.

LEE-JACKSON LACROSSE CLASSIC. May 2. Washington and Lee University, Lexington, VA. Community-wide event when the Washington and Lee lacrosse team meets the Virginia Military Institute team. 2 PM. For info: Lexington Visitors Bureau, 106 E Washington St, Lexington, VA 24450. Phone: (540) 463-3777. Fax: (540) 463-1105. Email: lexington@rockbridge.net.

LEONARDO DA VINCI: DEATH ANNIVERSARY. May 2, 1519. Italian artist, scientist and inventor. Painter of the famed *The Last Supper*, perhaps the first painting of the High Renaissance and of the *Mona Lisa*. Inventor of the first parachute. Died May 2, 1519, at age 67.

LILAC TIME. May 2–17. Lilacia Park, Lombard, IL. The world-renowned Lilacia Park, an 8.5 acre horticulture showcase with 1,100 lilacs and 40,000 tulips, is the site of Lilac Time, Lombard's annual celebration of spring. The festival includes horticulture seminars, Lilacia Park tours, concerts, luncheons in the park, an art show, kids' activities, Lilac Queen Coronation, Lilac Ball and the annual Lilac Parade. Annually, the first two weeks in May. Est attendance: 15,000. For info: Lilac Time Hotline, Phone: (630) 953-6000 ext 411.

LOW COUNTRY SHRIMP FESTIVAL. May 2. McClellanville, SC. Seafood, arts, crafts, civic display, entertainment and Blessing of the Fleet. Annually, the first Saturday in May. Est attendance: 4,000. For info: The Archibald Rutledge Academy, PO Box 520, McClellanville, SC 29458. Phone: (803) 887-3323.

MAINE STATE PARADE. May 2. Lewiston, ME. A giant parade with floats, food, music and fun. The parade is broadcast live on WCSH-TV and WLBZ-TV statewide. Annually, the first Saturday in May. Est attendance: 28,000. For info: WCSH-TV, One Congress Square, Portland, ME 04101. Phone: (207) 828-6666 or (207) 784-0599. Fax: (207) 828-6620.

MALTA: CARNIVAL. May 2–3. Valletta. Festival dates from 1535 when Knights of St. John introduced Carnival in Malta. Dancing, bands, decorated trucks and grotesque masks. Annually, the first weekend after May 1.

MARYLAND SHEEP AND WOOL FESTIVAL. May 2–3. Howard County Fairgrounds, West Friendship, MD. 25th anniversary. Sheep and Fleece show plus over 200 craftspeople, shearing, sheepherding and weaving demonstrations and crafts seminars. Free admission and parking. For info: Leslie Bauer, Maryland Sheep & Wool, PO Box 99, Glenwood, MD 21738. Phone: (410) 531-3647.
WWW: http://www.sheepandwoolfestival.org

MICAJAH AUTRY DAY. May 2. Autryville, NC. Patriotic festival with parade, arts and crafts, food, personalities, music and dance. Est attendance: 2,000. For info: Donna Cashwell, Micajah Autry Society, PO Box 52, Autryville, NC 28318. Phone: (910) 525-4621. Fax: (910) 525-4567.

MILLFEST. May 2. Old Mill Museum Complex, Lindsborg, KS. Annual running of the restored flour mill with guided tours of the mill (visitors must be over 12 years old to tour the mill), plus entertainment and pioneer arts and crafts fair. Noon Bar-B-Que. Charge for Bar-B-Que and Museum/Mill tours. Annually, the first Saturday in May. Est attendance: 600. For info: McPherson County Old Mill Museum, PO Box 94, 120 Mill St, Lindsborg, KS 67456. Phone: (913) 227-3595.
WWW: http://www.lindsborg.org

NATIONAL BABY'S DAY. May 2. Churches unite to celebrate babies as a blessing from God. Baby's Day is a day when the laughter of babies will ring throughout the nation to change the hearts of people. Annually, the first Saturday in May. For info: Tender Hearts Family Ministries, 2004 N Tustin Ave, Orange, CA 92665. Phone: (714) 283-4777.

NATIONAL HEADACHE FOUNDATION FUNDRAISER. May 2. New York, NY. Annual black tie silent auction and dinner serves as the major fundraiser for the National Headache Foundation. Proceeds from the evening are used for research, education and service. Est attendance: 200. For info: Suzanne E. Simons, Exec Dir, Natl Headache Fdtn, 428 W St. James Place, 2nd Floor, Chicago, IL 60614-2750. Phone: (773) 388-6395. Fax: (773) 525-7357.

May 1998

S	M	T	W	T	F	S
					1	2
3	4	5	6	7	8	9
10	11	12	13	14	15	16
17	18	19	20	21	22	23
24	25	26	27	28	29	30
31						

NORTHEAST NEBRASKA ANNUAL PLANT FAIR. May 2. Northeast Community College Auditorium, Norfolk, NE. Educational programs on plants; show features plants from various nurseries and latest trends on growing plants. Open 9–3. Est attendance: 4,000. For info: Chris Carlson, UNL Madison County Extension Office, PO Box F, Battle Creek, NE 68715. Phone: (402) 675-2785.

POPE LEO XIII: BIRTH ANNIVERSARY. May 2, 1810. Giocchino Vincenzo Pecci, 256th pope of the Roman Catholic Church, born at Carpineto, Italy. Elected pope Feb 20, 1878. Died July 20, 1903, at age 93.

RAY, SATYAJIT: BIRTH ANNIVERSARY. May 2, 1921. Film director Satyajit Ray was born at Calcutta, India. Possibly India's best known film director, he made more than 30 films and won numerous international awards, including an Academy Award for lifetime achievement. His films include the trilogy *Pather Panchali* (1956), *Aparajito* (1956) and *The World of Apu* (1959). Ray died on Apr 23, 1992, at Calcutta.

ROAN MOUNTAIN WILDFLOWER TOURS AND BIRD-WALKS. May 2–3. Roan Mountain State Park, Roan Mountain, TN. Wildflower and nature identification and inspiration. Annually, the first full weekend in May. Est attendance: 1,200. For info: Jennifer Laughlin, Ranger Naturalist, Roan Mtn State Park, Rte 1, Box 236, Roan Mountain, TN 37687. Phone: (423) 772-3303.

ROBERT'S RULES DAY. May 2, 1837. Anniversary of the birth of Henry M. Robert (General, US Army), author of *Robert's Rules of Order*, a standard parliamentary guide. Born May 2, 1837. Died May 11, 1923.

SPRING GALA. May 2–3. Lovington, NM. Arts and crafts show at the Lea County Fairgrounds. For info: Nancy Moore, Promotions, Lovington Chamber of Commerce, PO Box 1347, Lovington, NM 88260. Phone: (505) 396-5311. Fax: (505) 396-2823.

TOWSONTOWN SPRING FESTIVAL. May 2–3. Towson, MD. Five stages with continuous entertainment. 400 food, craft and display vendors on the street. Art exhibit, flea market and antique auto display. Annually, the first Saturday and Sunday in May. Est attendance: 250,000. For info: Towsontown Spring Fest, PO Box 10116, Towson, MD 21285-0116. Phone: (410) 825-1144. Fax: (410) 832-5863.

VIRGINIA GOLD CUP. May 2. Great Meadow, The Plains, VA. Steeplechasing began in Ireland in 1762 when two horsemen held a cross-country match race to a far away church steeple. Great Meadow is the largest steeplechase course in the country with a spectacular hillside amphitheater. The Virginia Gold Cup race, sponsored by BMW and Land Rover, is run over a challenging 4-mile post and rail course of 23 fences. Advance tickets only. Benefits free year-round use of Great Meadow by non-profit community organizations. Annually, the first Saturday in May. Est attendance: 40,000. For info: Virginia Gold Cup Assn, PO Box 840, Warrenton, VA 20188. Phone: (540) 347-2612. Fax: (540) 349-1829. WWW: http://www.vagoldcup.com

VIRGINIA STATE CHAMPIONSHIP CHILI COOK-OFF. May 2. Farmers Market area, Roanoke, VA. Live entertainment, pepper eating contest and the best chili samples from across the Commonwealth of Virginia. All compete for the state title. Annually, the first Saturday in May. Est attendance: 20,000. For info: Gayle Williams, Downtown Roanoke Inc, 310 First St, Roanoke, VA 24011. Phone: (540) 342-2028. Fax: (540) 344-1452.
Email: dai@roanoke.org. WWW: http://downtown.roanoke.org

YWCA FESTIVAL OF RACES. May 2. Cedar Rapids, IA. A festival of family fun with an 8K and 5K run, a 5K health walk, two children's races and a carnival with entertainment for kids. Annually, the first Saturday in May. Est attendance: 3,000. For info: Marcie Hosch, YWCA, 318 Fifth St SE, Cedar Rapids, IA 52401. Phone: (319) 365-1458. Fax: (319) 365-2263.

BIRTHDAYS TODAY

Theodore Bikel, 74, singer, actor, born Vienna, Austria, May 2, 1924.

Larry Gatlin, 49, singer, songwriter ("Broken Lady," "All the Gold in California"), born Odessa, TX, May 2, 1949.

Lesley Gore, 52, singer ("I'll Cry If I Want To"), born Tenafly, NJ, May 2, 1946.

Bianca Jagger, 53, actress, political activist, ex-wife of Mick Jagger, born Managua, Nicaragua, May 2, 1945.

Benjamin Spock, 95, pediatrician, author, born New Haven, CT, May 2, 1903.

MAY 3 — SUNDAY

Day 123 — 242 Remaining

ACKNOWLEDGE YOUR SUPPORTIVE SPOUSE WEEK. May 3–9. If you are a married entrepreneur or self-employed professional, and the ongoing support of your "behind the scenes" spouse has been critical to your success, this is the week to publicly acknowledge your spouse for helping you achieve your entrepreneurial dream. Write us to nominate your spouse for a National Award. Annually, the first full week in May. For info: Azriela Jaffe, Anchored Dreams, PO Box 209, Bausman, PA 17504. Phone: (717) 872-1890. Fax: (717) 872-0963. Email: azjaffe@aol.com. WWW: http://www.isquare.com/crlink.htm

BE KIND TO ANIMALS WEEK®. May 3–9. To promote kindness and humane care toward animals. Annually, the first full week of May. Features "Be Kind to Animals Kid Contest." For info: Joyce Briggs, Mktg/PR, American Humane Assn, 63 Inverness Dr E, Englewood, CO 80112. Phone: (800) 227-4645 or (303) 792-9900. Fax: (303) 792-5333.
Email: joyce@amerhumane.org.
WWW: http://www.amerhumane.org/aha

"CBS EVENING NEWS" TV PREMIERE: 50th ANNIVERSARY. May 3, 1948. The news program began as a fifteen-minute telecast with Douglas Edwards as anchor. Walter Cronkite succeeded him in 1962 and expanded the show to thirty minutes; Eric Sevareid served as commentator. Dan Rather anchored the newscasts upon Cronkite's retirement in 1981. At one point, to boost sagging ratings, Connie Chung was added to the newscast as Rather's co-anchor, but she left in 1995 in a well-publicized dispute. Rather remains solo, and, as Cronkite would say, ". . . that's the way it is."

CITY OF PITTSBURGH MARATHON AND 10K. May 3. Point State Park, Pittsburgh, PA. The cheering crowds filling the streets make this race an event. More than 3,000 participants race over bridges and through 12 of the city's neighborhoods toward the finish line in Point State Park. Co-sponsored by the University of Pittsburgh Medical Center. For info: Greater Pittsburgh Conv & Visitors Bureau, Four Gateway Center, Pittsburgh, PA 15222-1259. Phone: (412) 647-7866 or (800) 359-0758. Fax: (412) 644-5512.

CONSERVE WATER/DETECT-A-LEAK WEEK. May 3–9. To help everyone learn why it is important to conserve our water and how to help accomplish this goal. For info: American Leak Detection, c/o S&S Public Relations, Inc, 400 Skokie Blvd, Ste 200, Northbrook, IL 60062. Phone: (847) 291-1616. Fax: (847) 291-1758.

CORN PLANTING CEREMONY. May 3. Museum of Indian Culture, Allentown, PA. Lenape (Delaware Indian) ceremony, arts, crafts, demonstrations, foods and family fun. Annually, the first Sunday in May. Est attendance: 3,000. For info: Lenni Lenape Historical Soc, Museum of Indian Culture, 2825 Fish Hatchery Rd, Allentown, PA 18103-9801. Phone: (610) 797-2121. Fax: (610) 797-2801. WWW: http://www.lenape.org

FLEXIBLE WORK ARRANGEMENTS WEEK. May 3–9. To promote experimentation with rearranged work schedules and working at home or at a neighborhood work center. Annually, the week beginning with the first Sunday in May. For info: Maggi Payment, 1286 University Ave, #192, San Diego, CA 92103. Phone: (619) 232-0404.

FRANKENMUTH SKYFEST. May 3. Frankenmuth, MI. To encourage participation in a healthy outdoor sport that adapts to all age groups. 1998 will be the 17th annual Skyfest. Annually, the first Sunday in May. Est attendance: 4,500. For info: Audrey Fischer, Kite Kraft, 576 S Main St, Frankenmuth, MI 48734. Phone: (517) 652-2961.

GOODWILL INDUSTRIES WEEK. May 3–9. To call international attention to Goodwill Industries as a leader in job training and employment services for people with disabilities and other barriers to employment. Annually, the first full week in May. For info: Goodwill Industries Intl, Communications Dept, 9200 Rockville Pike, Bethesda, MD 20814-3896. Phone: (301) 530-6500. Fax: (301) 530-1516. WWW: http://www.goodwill.org

GOSPEL SING—BLACK AND WHITE/NOW AND THEN. May 3. Arrow Rock, MO. A celebration of gospel music with mid-Missouri choirs, quartets, duets and soloists performing music from black and spiritual traditions all the way to contemporary songs of praise. Recognizing the vast array of music written in praise of the same Lord. Est attendance: 200. For info: HARC, PO Box M, Arrow Rock, MO 65320.
Email: tmcglaughlin@vaxl.rain.gen.mo.us.

GREEK FOOD FESTIVAL. May 3–8. St. Nicholas Greek Orthodox Cathedral, Oakland, PA. More than 20,000 people stop in for an appetizing dose of Greek food and culture. A 32-year tradition, the festival includes dancing and live entertainment each evening. For info: Greater Pittsburgh Conv & Visitors Bureau, Four Gateway Center, Pittsburgh, PA 15222-1259. Phone: (412) 682-3866 or (800) 359-0758. Fax: (412) 644-5512.

☆ ☆ ☆

HONG KONG: BIRTHDAY OF LORD BUDDHA. May 3. Religious observances are held in Buddhist temples, and Buddha's statue is bathed. Po Lin Monastery and the other monasteries on Lantau Island are visited by many worshipers during the festival. Annually, the eighth day of fourth lunar month.

HOWARD OLD-FASHIONED DAY. May 3. Community Building, Howard, NY. Taking you back in history. Horse-pulled homemade ice cream, butter churning, antique plowing and fitting with horses. Annually, the first Sunday in May. Est attendance: 1,000. For info: Phil Bennett, Farmer, RD #3, Hornell, NY 14843. Phone: (607) 324-0735 or (607) 566-2487.

INTERNATIONAL UNMOTHERS DAY. May 3. A 21st-century organization bringing appropriate recognition to the millions of women world-wide who have been ignored during decades of attention to mothers and motherhood. For info: Denise Marquardt, Pres, Unmothers Intl, 8678 Meade St, Montague, MI 49437-1350.

JAPAN: CONSTITUTION MEMORIAL DAY. May 3. National holiday.

LUMPY RUG DAY. May 3. To encourage the custom of teasing bigots and trigots for shoving unwelcome facts under the rug. When many cans of worms have been shoved under the rug, the defenders of the status quo obtain a new rug high enough to cover the unwanted facts. For info: Robert L. Birch, Coord, Puns Corps, Box 2364, Falls Church, VA 22042-0364. Phone: (703) 533-3668.

MACHIAVELLI, NICCOLO: BIRTH ANNIVERSARY. May 3, 1469. Italian writer and statesman, born at Florence, Italy. Author of *The Prince*, a book of advice for a ruler that prescribes strong, absolute government. Died at Florence, June 22, 1527.

MEIR, GOLDA: 100th BIRTH ANNIVERSARY. May 3, 1898. Born at Kiev, Russia, Meir was prime minister of Israel from 1969 to 1974. She died at Jerusalem on Dec 8, 1978.

MEXICO: DAY OF THE HOLY CROSS. May 3. Celebrated especially by construction workers and miners, a festive day during which anyone who is building must give a party for the workers. A flower-decorated cross is placed on every piece of new construction in the country.

MONTPELIER SPRING FESTIVAL. May 3. Laurel, MD. 28th annual free cultural arts festival at the Montpelier Mansion grounds with four stages of continuous entertainment, music and dance, also 100 booths of artists and crafters, children's parade, clowns, free train and pony rides, displays and food. Free shuttle buses. Annually, the first Sunday in May. Est attendance: 25,000. For info: Diane Sills, Pres, South Laurel Recreation Council, 8710 Granite Lane, Laurel, MD 20708. Phone: (301) 776-2805. Fax: (301) 206-9682.

MOON PHASE: FIRST QUARTER. May 3. Moon enters First Quarter phase at 6:04 AM, EDT.

NATIONAL FAMILY WEEK. May 3–9. Traditionally the first Sunday and the first full week in May are observed as National Family Week in many Christian churches.

NATIONAL PET WEEK. May 3–9. To promote public awareness of veterinary medical service for animal health and care. Annually, the first full week in May. For info: The American Veterinary Medical Assn, 1931 N Meacham Rd, Schaumburg, IL 60173. Phone: (800) 248-2862. Fax: (847) 925-1329.

NATIONAL POSTCARD WEEK. May 3–9. To advertise use of picture postcards for correspondence and collecting. Annually, the first full week of May since 1984. For info: John H. McClintock, Founder, Postcard History Society, Box 1765, Manassas, VA 22110. Phone: (703) 368-2757.

NATIONAL PTA TEACHER APPRECIATION WEEK. May 3–9. PTAs across the country conduct activities to strengthen respect and support for teachers and the teaching profession. For info: Natl PTA, 330 N Wabash Ave, Ste 2100, Chicago, IL 60611. Phone: (312) 670-6782. Fax: (312) 670-6783.
Email: info@pta.org. WWW: http://www.pta.org

NATIONAL PUBLIC RADIO FIRST BROADCAST: ANNIVERSARY. May 3, 1971. National noncommercial radio network, financed by Corporation for Public Broadcasting, began programming.

NATIONAL SAFE KIDS WEEK. May 3–9. For info: National SAFE KIDS Campaign, 111 Michigan Ave NW, Washington, DC 20010-2970. Phone: (202) 662-0600.

NATIONAL SUICIDE AWARENESS WEEK. May 3–9. For info: American Assn of Suicidology, 4201 Connecticut Ave NW, Washington, DC 20009. Phone: (202) 237-2280.

May 1998

S	M	T	W	T	F	S
					1	2
3	4	5	6	7	8	9
10	11	12	13	14	15	16
17	18	19	20	21	22	23
24	25	26	27	28	29	30
31						

NATIONAL TOURISM WEEK. May 3–9. To promote and enhance awareness of travel and tourism's importance to the economic, social and cultural well-being of the US. Annually, beginning the first Sunday in May. For info: Tourism Works for America Council, 1100 New York Ave NW, Ste 450, Washington, DC 20005-3934. Phone: (202) 408-8422. Email: ckeefe@tia.org.

NATIONAL WILDFLOWER WEEK. May 3–9. A week dedicated to encouraging observation, cultivation and study of native wildflowers as a way to deepen humankind's relationship and responsibility to creation and Creator. Annually, the first full week in May. Sponsor: Secular Franciscan Order, USA. For info: Charles Spencer, SFO, Chairman, National Ecology Commission, 107 Jensen Circle, West Springfield, MA 01089-4451. Phone: (413) 737-7600. Fax: (413) 737-7600.
Email: cspencer@mail.map.com.
WWW: http://pages.map.com/SecularFranciscanEcology

O. HENRY PUN-OFF (WORLD CHAMPIONSHIP). May 3. The O. Henry Museum, Austin, TX. Pundits and punographers match wits for a wordy cause in two separate pun-filled competitions (Punniest of Show and High Lies & Low Puns). Sponsors: The City of Austin Parks and Recreation Department, Friends of the O. Henry Museum and Punsters United Nearly Yearly (PUNY). Est attendance: 2,000. For info: Valerie Bennett, Curator, O. Henry Museum, 409 E Fifth St, Austin, TX 78701. Phone: (512) 453-4431 or (512) 472-1903. Fax: (512) 472-7102. WWW: http://www.ci.austin.tx.us/parks/ohenry.html

PALM HARBOR DAY ARTS, CRAFTS AND MUSIC FESTIVAL. May 3. "Pop" Stansell Park, Palm Harbor, FL. Juried arts and crafts show to celebrate the 120th birthday of Palm Harbor. Est attendance: 3,000. For info: Connie Davis, Exec Dir, Palm Harbor Chamber of Commerce, 32845 US 19N, Ste 210, Palm Harbor, FL 34684-3123. Phone: (813) 784-4287. Fax: (813) 786-2336.

POLAND: CONSTITUTION DAY (SWIETO TRZECIEGO MAJO). May 3. National Day. Celebrates ratification of Poland's first constitution, 1791.

SIEGE OF YORKTOWN OUSTS REBELS: ANNIVERSARY. May 3, 1862. After nearly a month's siege, General Joseph Johnston's outnumbered Confederate forces evacuated Yorktown, VA, and moved back to Richmond. General McClellan's Army of the Potomoc occupied Yorktown the following day. With the capture of Yorktown, President Abraham Lincoln left Washington, DC, for Fort Monroe, VA, to observe the ongoing Peninsula Campaign.

SOUTHERN APPALACHIAN DULCIMER FESTIVAL. May 3. Tannehill Historical State Park, McCalla, AL. Festival highlighting old-time dulcimer music. Est attendance: 2,000. For info: Vicki Gentry, Tannehill Historical State Park, 12632 Confederate Parkway, McCalla, AL 35111. Phone: (205) 477-5711. Fax: (205) 477-9400.

☆ ☆ ☆

SPACE MILESTONE: *DELTA 3914* ROCKET FAILURE. May 3, 1986. Launched from Cape Canaveral, FL, the rocket failed, flew out of control and was intentionally destroyed by explosives 90 seconds after launch to avoid the risk of having it land in a populated area.

TRADITIONAL PLOWING MATCH. May 3. Woodstock, VT. This 13th annual event features a horse- and oxen-drawn plowing competition as well as demonstrations of different plowing techniques. Est attendance: 1,050. For info: Deborah Bulissa, Exec Asst, Billings Farm and Museum, PO Box 489, Woodstock, VT 05091. Phone: (802) 457-2355. Fax: (802) 457-4663. Email: billings.farm@valley.net.

UNITED NATIONS: WORLD PRESS FREEDOM DAY. May 3. A day to recognize that a free, pluralistic and independent press is an essential component of any democratic society and to promote press freedom in the world.

BIRTHDAYS TODAY

James Brown, 65, singer, songwriter, ("Papa's Got a Brand New Bag"), born Augusta, GA, May 3, 1933.

Christopher Cross, 47, musician, songwriter, born Anston, TX, May 3, 1951.

Doug Henning, 51, magician, born Fort Gary, Manitoba, Canada, May 3, 1947.

Jeffrey John Hornacek, 35, basketball player, born Elmhurst, IL, May 3, 1963.

Engelbert Humperdinck (Gerry Dorsey), 62, singer ("Release Me [And Let Me Love Again]," "After the Lovin' "), born Madras, India, May 3, 1936.

Pete Seeger, 79, folksinger (was with The Weavers), songwriter ("Where Have All the Flowers Gone?"), born New York, NY, May 3, 1919.

Frankie Valli, 61, singer ("Can't Take My Eyes Off You," "Grease"), born Newark, NJ, May 3, 1937.

MAY 4 — MONDAY

Day 124 — 241 Remaining

"ANOTHER WORLD" TV PREMIERE: ANNIVERSARY. May 4, 1964. Created by Irna Phillips and sponsored by P&G, this soap is set in fictional Bay City. It was the first soap to air for a full hour and the first to beget two spin-offs ("Somerset" and "Texas"). Charles Durning, Ted Shackelford, Eric Roberts, Ray Liotta, Kyra Sedgwick, Faith Ford, Morgan Freeman, Jackee Harry and Valerie Pettiford are some of its well-known alums.

CHINA: YOUTH DAY. May 4. Annual public holiday "recalls the demonstration on May 4, 1919, by thousands of patriotic students in Beijing's Tiananmen Square to protest imperialist aggression in China."

CURACAO: MEMORIAL DAY. May 4. Victims of World War II are honored on this day. Military ceremonies at the War Monument. Not an official public holiday.

DISCOVERY OF JAMAICA BY CHRISTOPHER COLUMBUS: ANNIVERSARY. May 4, 1494. Christopher Columbus discovered Jamaica on this day. The Arawak Indians were its first inhabitants.

GRAND BAZAR DE CHARITÉ FIRE: ANNIVERSARY. May 4, 1897. The Grand Bazar—one of Parisian society's most attended charity events—drew more than 1,500 people, mainly upper class women, who crowded into a building that was only 220 × 300 feet. When a kinematograph lamp ignited, pandemonium ensued as many women turned into human torches unable to escape or manuever around their booths, as they were hindered by their fashion accoutrements. About 150 of Paris's grande dames perished in the flames.

HAYMARKET SQUARE RIOT: ANNIVERSARY. May 4, 1886. Labor union unrest in Chicago in 1886 led to violence when a crowd of unemployed men tried to enter the McCormick Reaper Works, where a strike was underway. Although no one was killed, anarchist groups called a mass meeting in Haymarket Square to avenge the "massacre." When the police advanced on the demonstrators, a bomb was thrown and several policemen were killed. Four leaders of the demonstration were hanged and another committed suicide in jail. Three others were given jail terms. The case aroused considerable controversy around the world. See also: "Haymarket Pardon: Anniversary (June 26)."

HEPBURN, AUDREY (EDDA VAN HEEMSTRA HEPBURN-RUSTEN): BIRTH ANNIVERSARY. May 4, 1929. Audrey Hepburn, whose first major movie role in *Roman Holiday* (1953) won her an Academy Award as best actress, was born near Brussels, Belgium. Hepburn made 26 movies during her career and received four additional Oscar nominations. During the latter years of her life Hepburn served as spokesperson for the United Nations Children's Fund. She traveled worldwide raising money for the organization. Audrey Hepburn died Jan 20, 1993, at Tolochenaz, Switzerland.

☆ ☆ ☆

KENT STATE STUDENTS' MEMORIAL DAY: ANNIVERSARY. May 4, 1970. Four students (Allison Krause, 19; Sandra Lee Scheuer, 20; Jeffrey Glenn Miller, 20; and William K. Schroeder, 19) were killed by National Guard during demonstrations against the Vietnam War at Kent (Ohio) State University.

MANN, HORACE: BIRTH ANNIVERSARY. May 4, 1796. American educator, author, public servant, known as the "father of public education in the US," was born at Franklin, MA. Founder of Westfield (MA) State College and editor of the influential *Common School Journal.* Mann died at Yellow Springs, OH, on Aug 2, 1859.

NATIONAL HERB WEEK. May 4–10. A time to focus on the use and history of herbs—past and present. Annually, the Monday–Sunday in May ending on Mother's Day. For info: Intl Herb Assn (IHA), PO Box 317, Mundelein, IL 60060. Phone: (847) 949-4372. Fax: (847) 949-5896. Email: ihacathy@aol.com.

NATIONAL WEATHER OBSERVER'S DAY. May 4. For those people, amateurs and professionals alike, who love to follow the everyday phenomenon known as weather. Annually, May 4. For info: Alan W. Brue, 2006 NW 55th Ave, #H-5, Gainesville, FL 32653.

PUBLIC SERVICE RECOGNITION WEEK. May 4–10. Take this opportunity to thank the "Unsung Heroes and Heroines" of the public work force who perform a range of vital services. Public employees are scientists and police officers, teachers and doctors, astronauts and zoologists, engineers and food inspectors, forest rangers and claims representatives, researchers and foreign service agents. Free resource materials to promote the celebration available. Annually, the first Monday–Sunday in May. For info: Jo Wright, Exec Dir, Public Employees Roundtable, PO Box 44801, Washington, DC 20026-4801. Phone: (202) 927-5000. Fax: (202) 927-5001. Email: permail@patriot.net. WWW: http://www.patriot.net/users/permail

READ ME WEEK. May 4–8. National and local celebrities and other volunteers read in classrooms wearing readable clothing with school appropriate messages. For info: Lee Fairbend, Exec Dir, Book'Em!, 624 Grassmere Business Park, Ste 14, Nashville, TN 37211. Phone: (615) 834-7323.

RELATIONSHIP RENEWAL DAY. May 4. To salute and strengthen committed couples who value change and acceptance in the context of an ongoing relationship. Celebrants will mutually cite the challenges and changes met in the past year and offer each other well-deserved congratulations. For info: Peter Rosenzweig, PhD, Cheerleader, Nondisposable Relationships, 713 Golf Mill Professional Bldg, Niles, IL 60714. Phone: (847) 297-5750.

RHODE ISLAND INDEPENDENCE DAY. May 4. Rhode Island abandoned allegiance to Great Britain on this day, 1776.

SPACE MILESTONE: *ATLANTIS* (US). May 4, 1989. First American planetary expedition in 11 years. Space shuttle *Atlantis* was launched on this date, its major objective to deploy the *Magellan* spacecraft on its way to Venus to map the planet's surface. The shuttle was on its 65th orbit when it landed on May 8, mission accomplished.

TYLER, JULIA GARDINER: BIRTH ANNIVERSARY. May 4, 1820. Second wife of John Tyler, 10th president of the US, born at Gardiners Island, NY. Died July 10, 1889.

UNITED KINGDOM: MAY DAY BANK HOLIDAY. May 4. Bank and public holiday in England, Wales, Scotland and Northern Ireland.

WADE-DAVIS RECONSTRUCTION BILL PASSES THE HOUSE: ANNIVERSARY. May 4, 1864. Over the objections of President Lincoln, the House of Representatives on this date passed the Wade-Davis Reconstruction bill, containing stiff punitive measures against the South that if put into law would have destroyed Lincoln's more moderate reconstruction aims. The bill was also adamantly opposed by Radical Republicans, led by Thaddeus Stevens for whom it was insufficiently severe in its treatment of the Southern rebels. Lincoln eventually killed the bill by using the pocket veto.

ZAMBIA: LABOR DAY. May 4. Dedicated to "Freedom and Labor," the motto of Zambia's only political party, UNIP. A day of mobilization for maximum productivity. Annually, the first Monday in May.

BIRTHDAYS TODAY

Nickolas Ashford, 56, singer, songwriter ("Ain't No Mountain High Enough" with Valerie Simpson), born Fairfield, SC, May 4, 1942.

Maynard Ferguson, 70, musician, born Verdun, Quebec, Canada, May 4, 1928.

David Guterson, 42, writer (*The Country Ahead of Us, the Country Behind, Snow Falling on Cedars*), born Seattle, WA, May 4, 1956.

Jackie Jackson (Sigmund Esco Jackson), 47, singer (Jackson 5), born Gary, IN, May 4, 1951.

Roberta Peters, 68, opera singer (retired), born the Bronx, NY, May 4, 1930.

Randy Travis, 39, country and western musician ("Forever and Ever, Amen"), born Marshville, NC, May 4, 1959.

George F. Will, 57, editor, columnist, baseball executive, born Champaign, IL, May 4, 1941.

MAY 5 — TUESDAY

Day 125 — 240 Remaining

AMERICAN BOWLING CONGRESS BUD LIGHT MASTERS TOURNAMENT. May 5–9. Reno, NV. Top professional and nonprofessional bowlers from across the country and several foreign nations compete for $235,000 in prize money and one of the sport's most prestigious titles. Each player rolls 10 qualifying games before a cut is made to the top 120 bowlers. Then another five qualifying games cut the field to 63, who join the defending champion in a unique 3-game, double-elimination match play format. Est attendance: 10,000. For info: Mark Miller, American Bowling Congress, 5301 S 76th St, Greendale, WI 53129-1127. Phone: (414) 421-6400. Fax: (414) 421-7977.

BASEBALL'S FIRST PERFECT GAME: ANNIVERSARY. May 5, 1904. Denton T. "Cy" Young pitched baseball's first perfect game, not allowing a single opposing player to reach first base. Young's outstanding performance led the Boston Americans in a 3–0 victory over Philadelphia in the American League. The Cy Young Award for pitching was named in his honor.

BLY, NELLIE: BIRTH ANNIVERSARY. May 5, 1867. Nellie Bly was the pseudonym used by pioneering American journalist Elizabeth Cochrane Seaman (born May 5, 1867). Like her namesake which came from a Stephen Foster song, Nellie Bly was a social reformer and human rights advocate. As a journalist, she is best known for her exposé on conditions in what were then known as "insane asylums," where she posed as an "inmate." As an adventuress, she is best known for her 1889–90 tour around-the-world in 72 days, in which she bettered the time of Jules Verne's fictional character Phileas Fogg by eight days. She died Jan 27, 1922, at age 54. It wasn't until 56 years after her death that a marker was placed at her grave.

May 1998

S	M	T	W	T	F	S
					1	2
3	4	5	6	7	8	9
10	11	12	13	14	15	16
17	18	19	20	21	22	23
24	25	26	27	28	29	30
31						

BONZA BOTTLER DAY™. May 5. To celebrate when the number of the day is the same as the number of the month. Bonza Bottler Day™ is an excuse to have a party at least once a month. For more information, see Jan 1. For info: Gail M. Berger, 109 Matthew Ave, Poca, WV 25159. Phone: (304) 776-7746. Email: gberger5@aol.com.

CRASH OF 1893: ANNIVERSARY. May 5, 1893. Wall Street stock prices took a sudden drop. By the end of the year 600 banks had closed. The Philadelphia and Reading, the Erie, the Northern Pacific, the Union Pacific and also the Atchison, Topeka and Santa Fe railroads had gone into receivership. 15,000 other businesses went into bankruptcy. Other than the "Great Depression" of the 1930s, this was the worst economic crisis in US history; 15–20 percent of the work force was unemployed.

JAPAN: CHILDREN'S DAY. May 5. National holiday. Observed on the fifth day of the fifth month each year.

JOHNSON, AMY: FLIGHT ANNIVERSARY. May 5, 1930. Yorkshire born Amy Johnson began the first successful solo flight by a woman from England to Australia. Leaving Croydon Airport in a de Havilland D.H. 60 Gypsy Moth named *Jason*, she flew 9,960 miles to Port Darwin, Australia, arriving May 28. The song "Amy, Wonderful Amy" celebrated the fame of this "wonder girl of the air," who became a legend in her own lifetime. Serving as an air ferry pilot during WW II, she was lost over the Thames Estuary in 1941.

KOREA: CHILDREN'S DAY. May 5. A time for families to take their children on excursions. The various parks and children's centers throughout the country are packed with excited and colorfully dressed children. A national holiday since 1975.

MARX, KARL: BIRTH ANNIVERSARY. May 5, 1818. German socialist, founder and father of modern communism, author of *Das Kapital* and (with Friedrich Engels) *The Communist Manifesto*, was born at Treves, Germany; died at London, England, Mar 14, 1883.

MEXICO: CINCO DE MAYO: ANNIVERSARY. May 5. Mexican national holiday recognizing anniversary of Battle of Puebla, May 5, 1862, in which Mexican troops under General Ignacio Zaragoza, outnumbered three to one, defeated invading French forces of Napoleon III. Anniversary is observed by Mexicans everywhere with parades, festivals, dances and speeches.

NATIONAL TEACHER DAY. May 5. To pay tribute to American educators, sponsored by the National Education Association, Teacher Day falls during the National PTA's Teacher Appreciation Week. Local communities and organizations are encouraged to use this opportunity to honor those who influence and inspire the next generation through their work. Annually, the Tuesday of the first full week in May. For info: Natl Education Assn (NEA), 1201 16th St NW, Washington, DC 20036. Phone: (202) 822-7200.

NETHERLANDS: LIBERATION DAY. May 5. Marks liberation of the Netherlands from Nazi Germany, May 5, 1945.

POWER, TYRONE: BIRTH ANNIVERSARY. May 5, 1914. American actor, best known for his motion-picture action-adventure roles, Tyrone Power was born at Cincinnati, OH. Power died Nov 15, 1958, at Madrid, Spain.

SPACE MILESTONE: *FREEDOM 7* (US). May 5, 1961. First US astronaut in space, second man in space, Alan Shepard, Jr, projected 115 miles into space in suborbital flight reaching a speed of more than 5,000 miles per hour.

"STOP THE MUSIC" TV PREMIERE: ANNIVERSARY. May 5, 1949. ABC's prime-time musical-game show hosted by Bert Parks. Featured the singing talents of Kay Armen, Jimmy Blaine, Betty Ann Grove, Estelle Loring, Jaye P. Morgan and June Valli, and the dancing numbers of Sonja and Courtney Van Horne. Harry Salter conducted the band.

THAILAND: CORONATION DAY. May 5. Thailand.

BIRTHDAYS TODAY

Pat Carroll, 71, actress (Emmy for "Caesar's Hour"; "The Ted Knight Show"), born Shreveport, LA, May 5, 1927.

Alice Faye (Ann Leppert), 83, actress (*In Old Chicago, Lillian Russell*), born New York, NY, May 5, 1915.

Richard E. Grant, 41, actor (*Henry and June, LA Story, The Age of Innocence*), born Mbabane, Swaziland, May 5, 1957.

Lance Henriksen, 55, actor (*Dog Day Afternoon, The Terminator, Near Dark*), born New York, NY, May 5, 1943.

Jean-Pierre Leaud, 54, actor (at 14 chosen to play Antoine Doinel in Truffaut's *The 400 Blows* and subsequent autobiographical films *Love at 20, Stolen Kisses, Bed and Board, Love on the Run*), born Paris, France, May 5, 1944.

Michael Murphy, 60, actor (*Nashville, Manhattan, Salvador*), born Los Angeles, CA, May 5, 1938.

Michael Palin, 55, actor, comedian ("Monty Python's Flying Circus," *Life of Brian*), born Sheffield, Yorkshire, England, May 5, 1943.

Roger Rees, 54, actor, born Aberystwyth, Wales, May 5, 1944.

Tammy Wynette (Virginia Wynette Pugh), 56, singer ("Stand by Your Man"), born Red Bay, MS, May 5, 1942.

Tina Yothers, 25, actress (Jennifer on "Family Ties"), born Whittier, CA, May 5, 1973.

MAY 6 — WEDNESDAY

Day 126 — 239 Remaining

ASHURA: TENTH DAY. May 6. Islamic calendar date: Muharram 10, 1419. Commemorates death of Muhammad's grandson and the Battle of Karbala. A time of fasting, reflection and meditation. Jews of Medina fasted on the tenth day in remembrance of their salvation from Pharoah. The Prophet Muhammad desired to fast two days instead of one in remembrance, but he died the next year. Different methods for "anticipating" the visibility of the new moon crescent at Mecca are used by different sects groups. *Chase's* uses anticipated dates furnished by the American Muslim Council. US EST date may vary.

BABE RUTH'S FIRST MAJOR LEAGUE HOME RUN: ANNIVERSARY. May 6, 1915. George Herman "Babe" Ruth of the Boston Red Sox hit his first major league home run in a game against the New York Yankees in New York.

BONNIE BLUE NATIONAL HORSE SHOW. May 6–9. Virginia Horse Center, Lexington, VA. Major all-breed event, "A"-rated show of the American Horse Show Association. For info: Lexington Visitors Bureau, 106 E Washington St, Lexington, VA 24450. Phone: (540) 463-3777. Fax: (540) 463-1105. Email: lexington@rockbridge.net.

FREUD, SIGMUND: BIRTH ANNIVERSARY. May 6, 1856. Austrian physician, born at Freiberg, Moravia. Founder of psychoanalysis. Freud died at London, England, Sept 23, 1939.

HALFWAY POINT OF SPRING. May 6. At 12:59 AM, EDT, on May 6, 1998, 46 days, 9 hours and 4 minutes of spring will have elapsed, and the equivalent will remain before June 21, 9:03 AM, EDT, which is the summer solstice and the beginning of summer.

HINDENBURG DISASTER: ANNIVERSARY. May 6, 1937. At 7:20 PM, the dirigible *Hindenburg* exploded as it approached the mooring mast at Lakehurst, NJ, after a trans-Atlantic voyage. Of its 97 passengers and crew, 36 died in the accident, which ended the dream of mass transportation via dirigible.

NATIONAL ANXIETY DISORDERS SCREENING DAY. May 6. For info: National Mental Illness Screening Project, 1 Washington St, Ste 304, Wellesley Hills, MA 02181-1706. Phone: (617) 239-0071.

NATIONAL NURSES DAY AND WEEK. May 6–12. A week to honor the outstanding efforts of nurses everywhere to strengthen the health of the nation. Annually, beginning on May 6, National Nurses Day, and ending on May 12, Florence Nightingale's birthday. Call or write for a free catalog. For info: American Nurses Assn, 600 Maryland Ave SW, Ste 100W, Washington, DC 20024. Phone: (800) 274-4262. Fax: (202) 651-7003. Email: jstanish@ana.org. WWW: http://www.nursingworld.org

NATIONAL TOURIST APPRECIATION DAY. May 6. Emphasizes the fact that tourism is the second-largest employer in the US. Annually, a Wednesday early in May. For info: Tourism Works for America Council, 1100 New York Ave NW, Ste 450, Washington, DC 20005-3934. Phone: (202) 408-8422. Email: ckeefe@tia.org.

PEARY, ROBERT E.: BIRTH ANNIVERSARY. May 6, 1856. Born at Cresson, PA. Peary served as a cartographic draftsman in the US Coast and Geodetic Survey for two years, then joined the US Navy's Corp of Civil Engineers in 1881. He first worked as an explorer in tropical climates as he served as subchief of the Inter-Ocean Canal Survey in Nicaragua. After reading of the inland ice of Greenland, Peary became attracted to the Arctic. He organized and led eight Arctic expeditions and is credited with the verification of Greenland's island formation, proving that the polar ice cap extended beyond 82° north latitude, and the discovery of the Melville meteorite on Melville Bay, in addition to his famous discovery of the North Pole on Apr 6, 1909. Peary died on Feb 20, 1920, at Washington, DC.

PENN, JOHN: BIRTH ANNIVERSARY. May 6, 1740. Signer of the Declaration of Independence, born at Caroline County, VA. Died Sept 14, 1788.

SACK OF ROME: ANNIVERSARY. May 6, 1527. The Renaissance ended with the Sack of Rome beginning on this date. As part of a series of wars between the Hapsburg Empire and the French monarchy, German troops killed some 4,000 inhabitants of Rome, looted works of art and libraries. Pope Clement VII, who supported the French, was imprisoned at the Castel St. Angelo. Nearly a year passed before order could be restored in the city.

TAGORE, RABINDRANATH: BIRTH ANNIVERSARY. May 6, 1861. Hindu poet, mystic and musical composer was born at Calcutta, India. Received Nobel Prize (literature) in 1913. Died at Calcutta, Aug 7, 1941. His birthday is observed in Bangladesh on the 25th day of the Bengali month of Baishakha (second week of May), when the poet laureate is honored with songs, dances and discussions of his works.

VALENTINO, RUDOLPH: BIRTH ANNIVERSARY. May 6, 1895. Rodolpho Alfonzo Rafaello Pietro Filiberto Guglieimi Di Valentina D'Antonguolla, whose professional name was Rudolph Valentino, was born at Castellaneta, Italy. Popular cinema actor. Press reports claimed that "at least one weeping veiled woman in black brought flowers to his tomb" (at Hollywood Memorial Park) every year on the anniversary of his death at New York, NY, Aug 23, 1926.

BIRTHDAYS TODAY

Tony Blair, 45, British prime minister, born Edinburgh, Scotland, May 6, 1953.

George Clooney, 37, actor (Dr. Douglas Ross on "ER"), son of broadcast journalist Nick Clooney, nephew of singer Rosemary Clooney, born Augusta, KY, May 6, 1961.

Ben Masters, 51, actor (*All That Jazz, Making Mr. Right*), born Corvallis, OR, May 6, 1947.

Willie Howard Mays, 67, Baseball Hall of Fame outfielder, born Westfield, AL, May 6, 1931.

Bob Seger, 53, musician, singer ("Night Moves," "Travelin' Man"), born Ann Arbor, MI, May 6, 1945.

Richard C. Shelby, 64, US Senator (D, Alabama), born Birmingham, AL, May 6, 1934.

MAY 7 — THURSDAY

Day 127 — 238 Remaining

BEAUFORT SCALE DAY. May 7, 1774. A day to honor the British naval officer, Sir Francis Beaufort, who devised (1805) a scale of wind force from 0 (calm) to 12 (hurricane) that was based on observation, not requiring any special instruments. The scale was adopted for international use in 1874 and has since been enlarged and refined. Beaufort was born at Flower Hill, Meath, Ireland, on May 7, 1774, and died at Brighton, England, on Dec 17, 1857.

BEETHOVEN'S NINTH SYMPHONY PREMIERE: ANNIVERSARY. May 7, 1824. Beethoven's 9th Symphony in D Minor was performed for the first time at Vienna, Austria. Known as the *Choral* because of his use of voices in symphonic form for the first time, the Ninth was his musical interpretation of Schiller's *Ode to Joy*. Beethoven was completely deaf when he composed it, and it was said a soloist had to tug on his sleeve when the performance was over to get him to turn around and see the enthusiastic response he could not hear.

BIG 10 MEN'S TENNIS CHAMPIONSHIP. May 7–10. University of Minnesota, Minneapolis, MN. For info: Dennis LaBissoniere, Big Ten Conference, 1500 W Higgins Rd, Park Ridge, IL 60068-6300. Phone: (847) 696-1010. Fax: (847) 696-1110. WWW: http://www.bigten.org

BRAHMS, JOHANNES: BIRTH ANNIVERSARY. May 7, 1833. Regarded as one of the greatest composers of 19th-century music, Johannes Brahms was born at Hamburg, Germany. Brahms wrote in most areas of music and is especially noted for his vocal *Requiem, Symphony No 1 in C minor* and *Symphony No 4 in E minor*. While on a national concert tour in 1850, Brahms met the composer Robert Schumann and his wife Clara Schumann, who was also a composer and "the most brilliant concert pianist of her day." The endorsement and support of the Schumanns quickly established his musical reputation. After Schumann's death in 1856, Brahms became devoted to Clara, supporting her and her children. He and Clara remained close friends for the rest of their lives. Brahms died Apr 3, 1897, at age 64 at Vienna.

BROWNING, ROBERT: BIRTH ANNIVERSARY. May 7, 1812. English poet and husband of poet Elizabeth Barrett Browning, born at Camberwell, near London. Known for his dramatic monologues. Died at Venice, Italy, Dec 12, 1889.

CANADA: TRADE SHOW. May 7–9. Canadian Lakehead Exhibition Hall, Thunder Bay, Ontario. From security systems to cosmetics, this trade show displays the gamut of Thunder Bay's industry. Est attendance: 30,000. For info: Trade Show, 857 N May St, Thunder Bay, Ont, Canada P7C 3S2. Phone: (807) 622-9882. Fax: (807) 622-7752.
Email: chamber@tb-chamber.on.ca.

COOPER, GARY: BIRTH ANNIVERSARY. May 7, 1901. Frank James Cooper was born at Helena, MT. He changed his name to Gary at the start of his movie career. He is best known by baseball fans for his portrayal of Lou Gehrig in *The Pride of the Yankees*. Other films included *Wings, The Virginian, Desire, The Plainsman, Beau Geste, Meet John Doe, Sergeant York* (for which he won his first Academy Award), *High Noon* (winning his second Oscar for best actor), *The Court Martial of Billy Mitchell* and *The Wreck of the Mary Deare,* among others. He died May 13, 1961, at Hollywood, CA.

DIEN BIEN PHU FALLS: ANNIVERSARY. May 7, 1954. Vietnam's victory over France ends the Indochina War. This battle is considered one of the greatest victories won by a former colony over a colonial power.

ENGLAND: MITSUBISHI MOTORS BADMINTON HORSE TRIALS. May 7–10. Badminton, Glos. Famous international horse trials consisting of showjumping, cross country and dressage. Est attendance: 200,000. For info: Box Office, Badminton Horse Trials, Badminton, Glos, England GL9 1DF. Phone: (44) (145) 421-0272. WWW. http://www.badminton horse.co.uk

FIRST PRESIDENTIAL INAUGURAL BALL: ANNIVERSARY. May 7, 1789. Celebrating the inauguration of George Washington, the first Presidential Inaugural Ball was held in New York, NY.

GERMANY: HAMBURG HARBOR BIRTHDAY. May 7, 1189. Hamburg. "Hafengeburtstag" celebrates establishment of Hamburg as a free city.

GERMANY'S FIRST SURRENDER: ANNIVERSARY. May 7, 1945. Russian, American, British and French ranking officers crowded into a second-floor recreation room of a small red-brick schoolhouse (which served as Eisenhower's headquarters) in Reims, Germany. Representing Germany, Field Marshall Alfred

May 1998

S	M	T	W	T	F	S
					1	2
3	4	5	6	7	8	9
10	11	12	13	14	15	16
17	18	19	20	21	22	23
24	25	26	27	28	29	30
31						

Jodl signed an unconditional surrender of all German fighting forces. After a signing that took almost 40 minutes, Jodl was ushered into Eisenhower's presence. The American general asked the German if he fully understood what he had signed and informed Jodl that he would be held personally responsible for any deviation from the terms of the surrender, including the requirement that German commanders sign a formal surrender to the USSR at a time and place determined by that government.

"KRAFT TELEVISION THEATRE" TV PREMIERE: ANNIVERSARY. May 7, 1947. Live theatrical programs appeared on both the NBC and ABC networks. The show was a gold mine for discovering new talents. Among the playwrights getting their big breaks were: Rod Serling; Paddy Chayefsky; Reginald Rose; and Tad Mosel. Some of the show's most notable plays included: "Double Door" (1947); "Feathers in a Gale" (1950) with George Reeves; "The Easy Mark" (1951) with Jack Lemmon; "Double in Ivory" (1953) with Lee Remick and Beverly Whitney; "To Live in Peace" (1953) with Anne Bancroft; "The Missing Years" (1954) with Anthony Perkins and Mary Astor; "Alice in Wonderland" (1954) with Robin Morgan, Art Carney, Edgar Bergen and Charlie McCarthy; and "A Profile in Courage" (1956) with James Whitmore. The last play was based on a book by Senator John F. Kennedy who also appeared on the program to introduce the drama.

***LUSITANIA* SINKING: ANNIVERSARY.** May 7, 1915. British passenger liner *Lusitania*, on its return trip from New York to Liverpool, carrying nearly 2,000 passengers, was torpedoed by a German submarine off the coast of Ireland, sinking within minutes; 1,198 lives lost. US President Wilson sent note of protest to Berlin on May 13, but Germany, which had issued warning in advance, pointed to *Lusitania*'s cargo of ammunition for Britain. US maintained "neutrality," for the time being.

MacLEISH, ARCHIBALD: BIRTH ANNIVERSARY. May 7, 1892. American poet and Librarian of Congress (1939–44) was born at Glencoe, IL, 1892. MacLeish, who was also a playwright, Pulitzer Prize winner, editor, lawyer, professor and farmer, died at Boston, MA, on Apr 20, 1982.

MARTIN Z. MOLLUSK DAY. May 7. Moorlyn Terrace Beach, Ocean City, NJ. If Martin Z. Mollusk, a hermit crab, sees his shadow at 11 AM, EST, summer comes a week early—if he doesn't, summer begins on time. Est attendance: 300. For info: Mark Soifer, City Hall, 9th St and Asbury Ave, Ocean City, NJ 08226. Phone: (609) 525-9300 or (609) 399-0272. Fax: (609) 399-0374.

★ **NATIONAL DAY OF PRAYER.** May 7. Presidential Proclamation always issued for the first Thursday in May since 1981. (PL100–307 of May 5, 1988.) Beginning in 1957, a day in October was designated, except in 1972 and 1975 through 1977.

NATIONAL PRIVY DIGGERS DAY. May 7. A celebration to honor those individuals who choose to dig up the past in an unconventional way. Many important historical artifacts are found through this exploration of old outhouses. For info: Prospect Heights Public Library Dist, 12 N Elm St, Prospect Heights, IL 60070.

PASTE-UP DAY. May 7. Honors all paste-up artists who work for newspaper, magazine, book and desktop publishers. For info: Sugar Sweet Designs, 5883 A Old Clarksville Pike, Joelton, TN 37080. Email: ssdesign96@aol.com.

PELLA TULIP TIME FESTIVAL. May 7–9. Pella, IA. To pay homage to the founders of this predominately Dutch community. Activities include coronation of queen, parades, flowers, Dutch singing and dancing. Est attendance: 100,000. For info: Pella Historical Society, 507 Franklin, Pella, IA 50219. Phone: (515) 628-4311. Fax: (515) 628-9192. Email: pellatt@kdsi.net. WWW: http://www.kdsi.net/~pellatt

"STRIKE IT RICH" TV PREMIERE: ANNIVERSARY. May 7, 1951. The downtrodden and the poverty-stricken showed up on this game show to tell their sob stories. Whoever received the most votes from the studio audience was declared the winner. The losers were able to receive help from sympathetic viewers through a telephone "heart line." The show got in trouble with the New York City Welfare Department in 1954 when 55 of the show's hopeful contestants remained in New York and went on welfare.

BIRTHDAYS TODAY

Theresa Brewer, 67, singer ("[Open Up Your Heart and] Let the Sun Shine In"), born Toledo, OH, May 7, 1931.

Pete V. Domenici, 66, US Senator (R, New Mexico), born Albuquerque, NM, May 7, 1932.

Amy Heckerling, 44, filmmaker, born New York, NY, May 7, 1954.

Traci Lords, 30, actress ("Melrose Place"), born Steubenville, OH, May 7, 1968.

Darren McGavin, 76, actor (*The Man with the Golden Arm*, "Mickey Spillane's Mike Hammer"), born Spokane, WA, May 7, 1922.

Tim Russert, 48, TV news talk show moderator ("Meet the Press"), born Buffalo, NY, May 7, 1950.

John Constantine (Johnny) Unitas, 65, Pro Football Hall of Fame quarterback, born Pittsburgh, PA, May 7, 1933.

MAY 8 — FRIDAY

Day 128 — 237 Remaining

ALBANY TULIP FESTIVAL. May 8–10. Albany, NY. 50th annual. To celebrate Albany's Dutch heritage. Reenactment of old world tradition of scrubbing the streets, tulip flower show, Kinderkermis (children's fair in Dutch) and Pinksterfest (celebrating spring). Annually, Mother's Day weekend. For info: Phone: (800) 258-3582. WWW: http://www.albany.org

APPLE BLOSSOM FESTIVAL. May 8–10. St. Joseph, MO. Citywide festival celebrating spring includes concerts, dances, softball tournaments and the ever popular Apple Blossom Parade. Annually, the second weekend in May. Est attendance: 15,000. For info: Ron Rosenauer, 411 Jules St, St. Joseph, MO 64501. Phone: (816) 233-8549 or (816) 271-1442.

AUSTRIA: VIENNA FESTIVAL. May 8–June 14. Held since 1951, this festival features 1,000 events, including opera, ballet, chamber and symphonic music. For info: Wiener Festwochen, Lehargasse 11, A-1060 Vienna, Austria. Phone: (43) 1 589 220. Fax: (43) 1 589 2249. Email: festwochen@netway.at. WWW: http://www.festwochen.or.at

BATTLE OF McDOWELL: ANNIVERSARY. May 8, 1862. In a major engagement in the Shenandoah Valley Campaign of the Civil War, General Stonewall Jackson's rebel forces repulsed an attack by Union forces at McDowell, VA.

BATTLE OF THE CORAL SEA: ANNIVERSARY. May 8, 1942. Beginning on this date, the Battle of the Coral Sea impeded Japanese expansion and introduced a new form of naval warfare. None of the surface vessels exchanged fire—the entire battle was waged by aircraft. The US lost a carrier, destroyer and tanker. The Japanese lost seven warships, including a carrier.

BIG TEN MEN'S GOLF CHAMPIONSHIP. May 8–10. University of Illinois, Champaign, IL. For info: Dennis LaBissoniere, Big Ten Conference, 1500 W Higgins Rd, Park Ridge, IL 60068-6300. Phone: (847) 696-1010. Fax: (847) 696-1110. WWW: http://www.bigten.org

BIG TEN SOFTBALL TOURNAMENT. May 8–9. TBA. Est attendance: 1,500. For info: Dennis LaBissoniere, Big 10 Conference, 1500 W Higgins Rd, Park Ridge, IL 60068-6300. Phone: (847) 696-1010. Fax: (847) 696-1110.
WWW: http://www.bigten.org

CANADA: CANADIAN TULIP FESTIVAL. May 8–18. Ottawa, Ontario. The world's largest tulip festival with 3 million tulips in bloom. See a parade of decorated boats, floral sculptures, non-stop entertainment and fireworks. This event grew out of a thank you gift of bulbs for providing refuge to the Dutch Royal Family. The 48th annual festival will honor horticulture and floral artistry. Est attendance: 600,000. For info: Canadian Tulip Festival, 360 Albert St, Ste 1120, Ottawa, Ont, Canada K1R 7X7. Phone: (613) 567-5757. Fax: (613) 567-6216.
WWW: http://www.tulipfestival.ca

CELEBRATION OF SHAWNEE TOWN. May 8–9. Yellville, AR. Yellville's city park is transformed into living history celebrating the town's Native American roots. More than 50 skilled craftspeople display and demonstrate their skills in flint knapping, basket weaving, wood carving and bow and arrow making. Native American dancers and drummers perform Friday and Saturday. Annually, the second weekend in May. Est attendance: 5,000. For info: Chamber of Commerce, PO Box 369, Yellville, AR 72687. Phone: (870) 449-4676.

CZECH REPUBLIC: LIBERATION DAY. May 8. Commemorates the liberation of Czechoslovakia from the Germans in 1945.

DENMARK: COMMON PRAYER DAY. May 8. Public holiday. The fourth Friday after Easter, known as "Store Bededag," is a day for prayer and festivity.

DUNANT, JEAN HENRI: BIRTH ANNIVERSARY. May 8, 1828. Author and philanthropist, founder of the Red Cross Society, was born at Geneva, Switzerland. Nobel prize winner in 1901. Died at Heiden, Switzerland, Oct 30, 1910.

May 1998

S	M	T	W	T	F	S
					1	2
3	4	5	6	7	8	9
10	11	12	13	14	15	16
17	18	19	20	21	22	23
24	25	26	27	28	29	30
31						

ENGLAND: HELSTON FURRY DANCE. May 8. The world-famous Helston Furry Dance is held each year on May 8 (except when the 8th is a Sunday or Monday, in which case it is held on the previous Saturday). Dancing around the streets of Helston, Cornwall, begins early in the morning and continues throughout the day. The "Furry" dance leaves Guildhall at the stroke of noon and winds its way in and out of many of the larger buildings. Final dance at 5 PM.

FASHION SHOW. May 8. Mount Mary College, Milwaukee, WI. Student designer fashion show. Est attendance: 1,500. For info: Mary Cain, Mount Mary College, 2900 N Menomonee River Parkway, Milwaukee, WI 53222-4545. Phone: (414) 256-1210. Fax: (414) 256-1205. Email: mktg@mtmary.edu.
WWW: http://www.mtmary.edu

GERMANY'S SECOND SURRENDER: ANNIVERSARY. May 8, 1945. Stalin refused to recognize the document of unconditional surrender signed at Reims, so a second signing was held at Berlin. The event was turned into an elaborate formal ceremony by the Soviets who had lost some ten million lives during the war. As in the Reims document, the end of hostilities was set for 12:01 AM local time on May 9.

GOTTSCHALK, LOUIS MOREAU: BIRTH ANNIVERSARY. May 8, 1829. American pianist of international fame who toured the US during the Civil War. Gottschalk composed for the piano combining American and Creole folk themes and rhythms in his work. Born at New Orleans, LA, he died Dec 18, 1869, at Rio de Janeiro, Brazil.

JOHNSON, ROBERT: BIRTH ANNIVERSARY. May 8, 1911. Born in Hazelhurst, MS, and murdered at age 27 on Aug 16, 1938, at Greenwood, MS (poisoned by a jealous husband), in his short life Johnson was a master blues guitarist, a singer and songwriter of such influence that he is still one of the most studied and celebrated blues musicians. He developed a unique guitar style of such skill that it was said he acquired his ability by selling his soul to the Devil—the film *Crossroads* is based very loosely on this myth. A musical genius of great magnetism and intensity, he is considered an important inspiration in the development of blues and rock. Johnson's only two recording sessions captured for us the classics "Sweet Home Chicago," "I Believe I'll Dust My Broom," "Cross Road Blues," "Hell Hound on My Trail," "Me and the Devil Blues" and others. Johnson was inducted posthumously into the Blues Hall of Fame in 1980 and the Rock & Roll Hall of Fame in 1986.

LAUMEIER CONTEMPORARY ART FAIR. May 8–10. St. Louis, MO. A huge art fair at the Laumeier Sculpture Park with 160 artists' booths, entertainment and children's activities. Annually, Mother's Day weekend. Est attendance: 18,000. For info: Laumeier Sculpture Park, 12580 Rott Rd, St. Louis, MO 63127. Phone: (314) 821-1209. Fax: (314) 821-1248.

LAVOISIER, ANTOINE LAURENT: EXECUTION ANNIVERSARY. May 8. French chemist and the "father of modern chemistry." Especially noted for having first explained the real nature of combustion and for showing that matter is not destroyed in chemical reactions. Born at Paris, France on Aug 26, 1743, Lavoisier was guillotined on May 8, 1794, at the Place de la Revolution for his former position as a tax collector. The Revolutionary Tribunal is reported to have responded to a plea to spare his life with the statement: "We need no more scientists in France."

LISTON, SONNY: BIRTH ANNIVERSARY. May 8, 1932. Charles ("Sonny") Liston, boxer born at St. Francis County, AR. Liston rose above a record of criminal activity to defeat Floyd Patterson for the heavyweight title on Sept 25, 1962. He defeated Patterson in a rematch but then lost the title to Cassius Clay, who later changed his name to Muhammad Ali. In a rematch Ali knocked out Liston with a punch few observers saw. Died at Las Vegas, NV, Dec 30, 1970.

NO SOCKS DAY. May 8. If we give up wearing socks for one day, it will mean a little less laundry, thereby contributing to the betterment of the environment. Besides, we will all feel a bit freer, at least for one day. Annually, May 8. [© 1997 by WPL] For info: Thomas and Ruth Roy, Wellness Permission League, PO Box 662, Mt Gretna, PA 17064-0662. Phone: (500) 437-5104 or (717) 964-1308. Fax: (717) 964-1335.

OUIMET, FRANCIS DESALES: BIRTH ANNIVERSARY. May 8, 1893. American amateur golfer, stockbroker and philanthropist who is credited with establishing the popularity of golf in the US. Born at Brookline, MA, his golfing career began as a caddy. In 1913, at age 20, he generated national enthusiasm for the game of golf when he became the first American and first amateur to win the US Open Golf Championship. He won the US Amateur Championship in 1914 and 1931, and was a member of the US Walker Cup team from its first tournament in 1922 until 1949, serving as its nonplaying captain for six of those years. In 1949, he established the Francis Ouimet Caddy Scholarship Fund, and in 1951, he became the first American to be elected Captain of the Royal and Ancient Golf Club (established in 1754) of St. Andrews, Scotland. Ouimet died at Newton, MA, Sept 2, 1967. The US Postal Service issued a commemorative postage stamp honoring him in 1988.

POKE SALAD FESTIVAL. May 8–9. Blanchard, LA. Events include a parade, street dance, carnival, craft show, cloggers, country and western music and dinner with poke salad. Est attendance: 5,000. For info: Pete Copes, PO Box 207, Blanchard, LA 71009. Phone: (318) 929-3219.

RHODODENDRON FESTIVAL. May 8–17. Port Townsend, WA. Enjoy the lovely flowers. Festival includes amusement rides, a parade, arts and crafts display and plenty of food. Est attendance: 25,000. For info: Rhododendron Festival, PO Box 766, Port Townsend, WA 98368. Phone: (360) 385-2722. Fax: (360) 697-1156.

TRUMAN, HARRY S.: BIRTH ANNIVERSARY. May 8, 1884. The 33rd president of the US, succeeded to that office upon the death of Franklin D. Roosevelt, Apr 12, 1945, and served until Jan 20, 1953. Born at Lamar, MO, Truman was the last of the nine US presidents who did not attend college. Affectionately nicknamed "Give 'em Hell Harry" by admirers. The only employment of atomic bombs on populated areas during war occurred during his presidency (Aug 6 and Aug 9, 1945, at Hiroshima and Nagasaki, Japan). Truman died at Kansas City, MO, on Dec 26, 1972. His birthday is a holiday in Missouri.

V-E DAY: ANNIVERSARY. May 8, 1945. Victory in Europe Day commemorates unconditional surrender of Germany to Allied Forces. The surrender document was signed by German representatives at General Dwight D. Eisenhower's headquarters at Reims to become effective, and hostilities to end, at one minute past midnight on May 9, 1945. President Harry S. Truman on May 8 declared May 9, 1945, to be "V-E Day." A separate German surrender to the USSR was signed at Karlshorst, near Berlin, on May 8. See also: "Russia: Victory Day" (May 9).

☆ ☆ ☆

BIRTHDAYS TODAY

David Attenborough, 72, author, naturalist (*Life on Earth, Trials of Life*), born London, England, May 8, 1926.

Peter Benchley, 58, author, journalist (*Rummies, Jaws*), born New York, NY, May 8, 1940.

Melissa Gilbert, 34, actress (Laura on "Little House on the Prairie"; *The Miracle Worker*), born Los Angeles, CA, May 8, 1964.

David Keith, 44, actor, director (*The Great Santini, Take This Job and Shove It, An Officer and a Gentleman*), born Knoxville, TN, May 8, 1954.

Ronald Mandel (Ronnie) Lott, 39, former football player, born Albuquerque, NM, May 8, 1959.

Thomas Pynchon, 61, writer (*V, Gravity's Rainbow*), born Glen Cove, NY, May 8, 1937.

Don Rickles, 72, comedian, actor (*Blazing Saddles*, "The Dean Martin Show"), born New York, NY, May 8, 1926.

Toni Tennille, 55, singer (along with husband Daryl Dragon made up singing duo Captain and Tennille), born Montgomery, AL, May 8, 1943.

James R. Thompson, 62, former Governor of Illinois (R), born Chicago, IL, May 8, 1936.

MAY 9 — SATURDAY

Day 129 — 236 Remaining

AMERICAN BOWLING CONGRESS SENIORS TOURNAMENT. May 9–10. Reno, NV. State and provincial senior champions compete for titles in four divisions at the American Bowling Congress Tournament site. For info: Mark Miller, ABC, 5301 S 76th St, Greendale, WI 53129. Phone: (414) 423-3224. Fax: (414) 421-7977.

BOYD, BELLE: BIRTH ANNIVERSARY. May 9, 1843. Notorious Confederate spy who later became an actress and lecturer was born at Martinsburg, VA. Author of the book *Belle Boyd in Camp and Prison*, she died June 11, 1900.

BRAILLE INSTITUTE–OPTIMIST TRACK AND FIELD OLYMPICS. May 9. Braille Institute Youth Center, Los Angeles, CA. To offer athletic competition to blind and visually impaired youths. Annually, the second Saturday in May. Co-sponsored by the Optimist Clubs of Southern California. Est attendance: 1,000. For info: Braille Institute, Communications Dept, 741 N Vermont Ave, Los Angeles, CA 90029. Phone: (213) 663-1111.

BROWN, JOHN: BIRTH ANNIVERSARY. May 9, 1800. Abolitionist leader born at Torrington, CT, and hanged Dec 2, 1859, at Charles Town, WV. Leader of attack on Harpers Ferry, Oct 16, 1859, which was intended to give impetus to movement for escape and freedom for slaves. His aim was frustrated and in fact resulted in increased polarization and sectional animosity. Legendary martyr of the abolitionist movement.

BUZZARD DAYS FESTIVAL. May 9. Glendive, MT. Just as the swallows return to Capistrano each year, so do the turkey vultures come back to perch on the gnarled trees of the dramatic badlands in Makoshika State Park nestled next to Glendive, MT. The festival includes a parade and family-oriented activities and food at the park. The key to attending a buzzard festival is to keep moving . . . if you're still the buzzards are soon to visit you with a meal in mind. For info: Chuck Carbert, Park Ranger, Box 1242, Glendive, MT 59330. Phone: (406) 365-6256.

CCC REUNION AND LUNCHEON. May 9. Blairsville, GA. Vogel State Park. A program on the Civilian Conservation Corps will be presented by Park Manager, David Foot. The CCC museum will be open for viewing. The CCC was responsible for constructing many of the facilities at Vogel State Park. For info: David Foot, Vogel State Park, 7485 Vogel State Park Rd, Blairsville, GA 30512. Phone: (706) 745-2628.

CELEBRATE '98! May 9. Lawrence University, Appleton, WI. Celebrate spring with music, entertainment, food and crafts. Five stages and more than 200 booths. Est attendance: 40,000. For info: Carla Krueger, Lawrence Univ, PO Box 599, Appleton, WI 54912. Phone: (414) 832-6600. Fax: (414) 832-7695.

ELECTRA GOAT BBQ COOK-OFF. May 9. Electra Goat Grounds, Electra, TX. Goat Brisket, Pork Ribs, Chicken Cook-Off, Cow Patty Drop, live band, Jackpot Steak & Beans Competition, tug-o-war, eating contest, children's games and crafts. Little Mr. and Miss Goat Competition and Friday Night Cookie Toss. Dance 9 PM–1 AM after cook-off. Annually, the Saturday before Mother's Day. Est attendance: 1,500. For info: Dawn Dunsmore, Electra Chamber of Commerce, 112 W Cleveland, Electra, TX 76360. Phone: (817) 495-3577. Fax: (817) 495-3577.

EUROPEAN UNION: ANNIVERSARY OBSERVANCE. May 9. Member countries of the European Union commemorate the May 9, 1950, announcement by French statesman Robert Schuman of the "Schuman Plan" for establishing a single authority for production of coal, iron and steel in France and Germany. This organization was a forerunner of the European Economic Community, founded in 1957, which later became the European Union.

FEMINIST BOOKSTORE WEEK. May 9–17. Visit your favorite feminist bookstore for author signings and other special events. For info: Feminist Bookstore News, PO Box 882554, San Francisco, CA 94188. Phone: (415) 642-9993. Fax: (414) 642-9995. Email: carol@FemBkNews.com.

GONZALES, PANCHO: BIRTH ANNIVERSARY. May 9, 1928. Richard Alonzo ("Pancho") Gonzales, tennis player born at Los Angeles, CA. A self-taught player, Gonzales won the 1948 US National Singles Championship and repeated in 1949. He turned pro and won the world's championship from 1954 through 1962. Gonzales was an aggressive, temperamental player who rarely trained. Died at Las Vegas, NV, July 3, 1995.

GOODWILL EMBASSY TOUR. May 9. Washington, DC. Eight embassies (ambassadors' residences) and chanceries (ambassadors' offices) open their doors to visitors on this self-guided tour. Experience the culture and history of each place as each building contains architecture, furnishings and fine arts native to each of the countries. Tickets: $25 in advance, $30 on day of tour. Est attendance: 2,500. For info: Public Relations Mgr, Davis Memorial Goodwill Industries Inc, 2200 South Dakota Ave NE, Washington, DC 20018. Phone: (202) 636-4225, ext 1220.

GUM TREE FESTIVAL. May 9–10. Tupelo, MS. A juried art show with arts, crafts and live entertainment. 10K run. Annually, the second weekend in May. Est attendance: 15,000. For info: Tupelo Conv and Visitors Bureau, PO Drawer 47, Tupelo, MS 38802. Phone: (800) 533-0611 or (601) 844-2787. Fax: (601) 844-2787.

HOMEFEST. May 9–10. Bald Knob, AR. School reunions, homecomings, sports events, 5K run-walk, basketball, horseshoe pitching, checkers, antique autos, crafts, street dance, parade, beauty pageant and more. Est attendance: 5,000. For info: Bald Knob Area Chamber of Commerce, PO Box 338, Bald Knob, AR 72010. Phone: (501) 724-3140.

	S	M	T	W	T	F	S
May 1998						1	2
	3	4	5	6	7	8	9
	10	11	12	13	14	15	16
	17	18	19	20	21	22	23
	24	25	26	27	28	29	30
	31						

HUNTER FREES THE SLAVES: ANNIVERSARY. May 9, 1862. At Hilton Head, SC, General David Hunter, commander of the Department of the South, issued orders freeing slaves in South Carolina, Florida and Georgia. Not having congressional or presidential approval, the orders were countermanded by President Lincoln on May 19.

INTERNATIONAL MIGRATORY BIRD CELEBRATION. May 9–10. Chincoteague, VA. Two days of walks, talks, workshops, boat tours, children's activities and an art celebration all conducted outdoors with the birds. Annually, Mother's Day weekend. Est attendance: 6,000. For info: Chincoteague Chamber of Commerce, PO Box 258, Chincoteague, VA 23336. Phone: (757) 336-6161. Fax: (757) 336-1242.
Email: pony@shore.intercom.net.
WWW: http://www.intercom.net/local/chincoteague/

IROQUOIS STEEPLECHASE. May 9. Percy Warner Park, Nashville, TN. Nashville's original "Rite of Spring." This event is the oldest continuously run, weight-for-age steeplechase in the United States. The steeplechase has a seven-race card with the featured Iroquois Memorial. Annually, the second Saturday in May. Est attendance: 30,000. For info: Elizabeth Wilson, Steeplechase Office, 2424 Garland Ave, Nashville, TN 37212. Phone: (615) 332-7284. Fax: (615) 322-6453.

JAMESTOWN FOUNDING WEEKEND. May 9–10. Jamestown, VA. Anniversary of the founding of Jamestown, first permanent English colony in North America, in May of 1607. Est attendance: 3,000. For info: Activities Coord, Colonial Natl Historical Park, PO Box 210, Yorktown, VA 23690. Phone: (757) 898-3400. WWW: http://www.nps.gov/colo/

JAMESTOWN LANDING DAY. May 9. Jamestown Settlement, Williamsburg, VA. Celebration of the anniversary of the establishment of America's first permanent English settlement at Jamestown, VA, in 1607. Militia presentations and sailing demonstrations. Est attendance: 1,200. For info: Media Relations, Jamestown-Yorktown Fdtn, PO Box 1607, Williamsburg, VA 23187. Phone: (757) 253-4838. Fax: (757) 253-5299. WWW: http://www.historyisfun.org

JUBILEE. May 9. Bennettsville, SC. Arts and crafts festival with entertainment, children's events and juried art show. Annually, the second Saturday in May. Est attendance: 6,000. For info: Ken Harmon, 701 W Main St, Bennettsville, SC 29512. Phone: (803) 479-9721.

MARKET SQUARE FAIR. May 9. Fredericksburg, VA. To create an awareness of Fredericksburg's historic heritage. Arts, crafts, food and entertainment. Est attendance: 6,000. For info: Visitor Center, 706 Caroline St, Fredericksburg, VA 22401. Phone: (800) 678-4748. Fax: (540) 372-6587. Email: fburg@illuminet.net.

MOTHER'S DAY ANNUAL RHODODENDRON SHOW. May 9–10. Crystal Springs Rhododendron Gardens, Portland, OR. Spectacular display of rhododendron and azalea blooms and plant sale. Est attendance: 6,000. For info: Ted Van Veen, Garden Chair, American Rhododendron Society, Portland Chapter, PO Box 86424, Portland, OR 97286. Phone: (503) 777-1734.

NATIONAL SMALL BUSINESS DAY. May 9. To honor small business and entrepreneurial spirit in the US. Tips for promoting your small business will be provided. For info: Nancy Michaels, Impression Impact, 369 Lindsay Pond Rd, Concord, MA 01742. Phone: (508) 287-0718. Fax: (508) 287-0410.

NETHERLANDS: NATIONAL WINDMILL DAY. May 9. Second Saturday in May each year. About 950 windmills still survive, and some 300 still are used occasionally and have been designated national monuments by the government. As many windmills as possible are in operation on National Windmill Day for the benefit of tourists.

PENINSULA CAMPAIGN INTENSIFIED: ANNIVERSARY. May 9, 1862. Confederate forces in Norfolk, VA, evacuated the city in a costly move, leaving valuable material for the Union army. Norfolk and Portsmouth were occupied on May 10 and the naval yard at Gosport, VA, was burned. President Abraham Lincoln was personally involved in this action, supervising the Federal expeditionary force.

PETER PADDLEFISH DAY FESTIVAL. May 9. Sidney, MT. The legend of Peter Paddlefish and his girlfriend, Paula, is to Sidney what groundhogs are to Punxsutawney, PA. This family-oriented festival marks the opening of paddlefish season on Montana's Yellowstone River. Family activities and games, a parade and food highlight the event. Interestingly, paddlefish are a prehistoric fish species whose roe (fish eggs) is sold as caviar on the international market. Who would have thought Montana—the land of cows and cowboys—also was a world supplier of caviar! For info: Sharon Rau, Sidney Chamber of Commerce, 909 S Central Ave, Sidney, MT 59270. Phone: (406) 482-1916.

PRATER'S MILL COUNTRY FAIR. May 9–10 (also Oct 10–11). Dalton, GA. Arts and crafts show in the atmosphere of an old-fashioned country fair. Est attendance: 25,000. For info: Judy Alderman, Prater's Mill Fdtn, Inc, 848 Shugart Rd, Dalton, GA 30720-2429. Phone: (706) 275-6455. Fax: (706) 275-6455.

RENO, NEVADA: BIRTHDAY. May 9, 1868. First known as Fullers Crossing, then Lakes Crossing, on this date it officially became Reno, known today as "The Biggest Little City in the World." Its six-week residency requirement for divorce became law on May 1, 1931.

ROCK-A-THON. May 9. Senior citizens and their friends, family and local businesses commit to rocking in rocking chairs to raise money for area children's hospitals. Money raised is often used by the neonatal and pediatrics units of these hospitals to purchase rocking chairs to be used to rock and comfort sick children. For info: Rock-A-Thon/Mktg Dept, National Guest Homes, LLC, 8550 Katy Freeway, Ste 201, Houston, TX 77024. Phone: (713) 464-4884. Fax: (713) 464-4891.

RUSSIA: VICTORY DAY. May 9. National holiday observed annually to commemorate the 1945 Allied Forces defeat of Nazi Germany in World War II and to honor the 20 million Soviet people who died in that war. Among the traditional rituals of this celebration, veterans renew wartime friendships, reminisce and swap stories, sing some of the frontline songs and visit national cemeteries. Hostilities ceased and the German surrender became effective at one minute after midnight on May 9, 1945. See also: "V-E Day" (May 8).

SAVANNAH SCOTTISH GAMES AND HIGHLAND GATHERING. May 9. Old Fort Jackson, Savannah, GA. Clan tents, geological information, highland regimental pipe bands, Southeast Regional Scottish Highland Dancing Championship, single malt Scotch whiskey tasting, kilted golf, entertainment by Scotland's finest musicians and children's games. Est attendance: 6,000. For info: Savannah Scottish Games and Highland Gathering, PO Box 13435, Savannah, GA 31416. Phone: (912) 897-5781 or (912) 234-6579. Fax: (912) 234-0447.

SHEEP SHEAR FEST. May 9. Second Baptist Church, Walworth, NY. Setting depicts a biblical market place with event personnel dressed in period costumes. Activities include shearing a sheep every half hour and demonstrators carding, spinning and weaving the raw wool; a petting zoo; a storyteller; children's activities; food; arts and crafts; souvenirs and live music. Everything held under large tents come rain or come shine. Annually, the Saturday before Mother's Day. Est attendance: 1,000. For info: Sheep Shear Committee, Second Baptist Church, 3689 Walworth Palmyra Rd, PO Box 68, Walworth, NY 14568. Phone: (315) 986-1288.

TRADITIONAL MUSIC WEEKEND. May 9–10. Pricketts Fort State Park, Fairmont, WV. Appalachian mountain music with banjo pickers, fiddle players and ballad singers. Annually, the second weekend in May. For info: Pricketts Fort State Park, Rte 3, Box 407, Fairmont, WV 26554. Phone: (304) 363-3030. Fax: (304) 363-3857. WWW: http://www.dmssoft.com/pfort

"VAST WASTELAND" SPEECH: ANNIVERSARY. May 9, 1961. Speaking before the bigwigs of network TV at the annual convention of the National Association of Broadcasters, Newton Minow, the new chairman of the Federal Communications Commission, exhorted those executives to sit through an entire day of their own programming. He suggested to them they "will observe a vast wasteland." Further, he urged them to try for "imagination in programming, not sterility; creativity, not imitation; experimentation, not conformity; excellence, not mediocrity."

BIRTHDAYS TODAY

Candice Bergen, 52, actress (*Starting Over, The Group*, "Murphy Brown"), daughter of ventriloquist Edgar Bergen, born Beverly Hills, CA, May 9, 1946.
James L. Brooks, 58, screenwriter, producer ("Taxi," "The Mary Tyler Moore Show"), born Brooklyn, NY, May 9, 1940.
Albert Finney, 62, actor (*Tom Jones, Shoot the Moon, Annie, The Dresser*), born Salford, England, May 9, 1936.
Anthony Keith (Tony) Gwynn, 38, baseball player, born Los Angeles, CA, May 9, 1960.
Glenda Jackson, 61, actress (Oscars for *Women in Love* and *Touch of Class*), born Cheshire, England, May 9, 1937.
Billy Joel, 49, singer, composer ("It's Still Rock and Roll to Me," "Just the Way You Are"), born Hicksville, NY, May 9, 1949.
Mike Wallace, 80, TV journalist ("60 Minutes"), born Brookline, MA, May 9, 1918.

MAY 10 — SUNDAY

Day 130 — 235 Remaining

ALCOHOL AND OTHER DRUG-RELATED BIRTH DEFECTS WEEK. May 10–16. To increase public awareness of the risks associated with alcohol and other drug use during pregnancy. For info: Publ Info Office, Natl Council on Alcoholism and Drug Dependence, Inc, 12 W 21st St, New York, NY 10010. Phone: (212) 206-6770. Fax: (212) 645-1690. WWW: http://www.ncadd.org

ASTOR PLACE RIOT: ANNIVERSARY. May 10, 1889. A riot erupted outside the Astor Place Opera House in New York, NY, where the British actor William Charles Macready was performing. Led by the American actor Edwin Forrest, angry crowds revolted against dress requirements for admission and against Macready's public statements on the vulgarity of American life. On May 8, Macready's performance of *Macbeth* was stopped by Forrest's followers. Two days later, a mob led by Ned Buntline shattered the windows of the theater during a performance. Troops were summoned and they were ordered to fire, killing 22 and wounding 26.

CONFEDERATE MEMORIAL DAY IN NORTH AND SOUTH CAROLINA. May 10. See also Apr 26, Apr 27 and May 25 for Confederate Memorial Day observances in other southern states.

COOS BAY HUMMINGBIRD GOOSE DAY (NORTHBOUND). May 10. Coos Bay, OR. This is the traditional day to watch for those benevolent geese who allow the tiny hummingbirds to snuggle deep in their goose down to migrate north. The believers in the Hummingbird Geese gather in all of Coos Bay to "Humhonk" them in for close scrutiny, to watch as the little Hummers disembark. (Best Humhonker trophy awarded.) For info: Doug Benton, Head Humhonker, K-Light Radio, 580 Kingwood Ave, Coos Bay, OR 97420. Phone: (503) 269-2020 or (800) 447-7664. Fax: (541) 267-0114. Email: lrg@ucinet.com. WWW: http://www.k-light.com

GIRLS INCORPORATED WEEK. May 10–16. To focus national and local attention on the goals of Girls Incorporated as an organization for the rights and needs of girls. Annually, beginning the second Sunday in May. For info: Amy Sutnick-Plotch, Girls Inc, 30 E 33rd St, 7th Fl, New York, NY 10016. Phone: (212) 689-3700. Fax: (212) 683-1253.

GOLDEN SPIKE DRIVING: ANNIVERSARY. May 10. Anniversary of the meeting of Union Pacific and Central Pacific railways, at Promontory Point, UT, May 10, 1869. On that day a golden spike valued at about $400 was driven by Leland Stanford, president of the Central Pacific, to celebrate the linkage. Long called the final link in the ocean-to-ocean railroad, this event cannot be accurately described as completing the transcontinental railroad, but it did complete continuous rail tracks between Omaha and Sacramento. See also: "Transcontinental US Railway Completion: Anniversary" (Aug 15).

KITEDAY. May 10. Charlottesville, VA. Fly a kite at Ash Lawn-Highland. Est attendance: 300. For info: Ash Lawn-Highland, James Monroe Parkway, Charlottesville, VA 22902. Phone: (804) 293-9539.
Email: ashlawn@comet.net. WWW: http://avenue.org/ashlawn

KIWANIS PRAYER WEEK. May 10–16. Encourages Kiwanis Clubs to promote religious activities throughout their communities and to recognize individuals for their contributions to spiritual welfare. Annually, the second full week in May. For info: Kiwanis Intl, Program Development Dept, 3636 Woodview Trace, Indianapolis, IN 46268. Email: kiwanismail@kiwanis.org. WWW: http://www.kiwanis.org

MANDELA INAUGURATION: ANNIVERSARY. May 10, 1994. In a dramatic and historic exchange of power, former political prisoner Nelson Mandela was inaugurated as President of South Africa. Long the focal point of apartheid foes' attempts to end the enforced policy of discrimination in South Africa, Mandela handily won the first free election in South Africa.

MOTHER OCEAN DAY. May 10. To celebrate the wonder, the vastness and beauty of the ocean. Casting of roses into the sea from the beach and from the water. Annually, on Mother's Day. For info: Cynthia Hancock, Pres, Natl Week of the Ocean, Inc, PO Box 179, Ft Lauderdale, FL 33302. Phone: (954) 462-5573.

★**MOTHER'S DAY.** May 10. Presidential Proclamation always issued for the second Sunday in May. (Pub Res No. 2 of May 8, 1914.)

MOTHER'S DAY. May 10. Observed first in 1907 at the request of Anna Jarvis of Philadelphia, PA, who asked her church to hold service in memory of all mothers on the anniversary of her mother's death. Annually, the second Sunday in May.

MOTHER'S DAY HOUSEWALK. May 10. Evanston, IL. 23rd annual tour of historic homes as a fund-raiser for the Evanston Historical Society. Annually, on Mother's Day. For info: Evanston Historical Society, 225 Greenwood St, Evanston, IL 60201. Phone: (847) 475-3410.

MUDDER'S DAY OFF ROAD CHALLENGE. May 10. Rhinelander, WI. 22K mountain bike race on the scenic Mudder's Day Trail at Holiday Acres Resort. Annually, on Mother's Day. Est attendance: 300. For info: Rhinelander Area Chamber of Commerce, PO Box 795, Rhinelander, WI 54501. Phone: (800) 236-4386. Fax: (715) 365-7467.

NATIONAL FAMILY MONTH™. May 10–June 21. A month-long national observance to celebrate and promote strong, supportive families. Sponsored by KidsPeace®, a private, not-for-profit organization that has been helping kids overcome crisis since 1882. Annually, Mother's Day through Father's Day. For info: Paula Knouse, Kids Peace, 5100 Tilghamn St, Ste 010, Allentown, PA 18104. Phone: (610) 799-8325.
WWW: http://kidspeace.org

NATIONAL HISTORIC PRESERVATION WEEK. May 10–16. To draw public attention to historic preservation including neighborhoods, districts, landmark buildings, open space and maritime heritage. Annually, the second full week in May. For info: Lori Schuman, Natl Trust for Historic Preservation, 1785 Massachusetts Ave NW, Washington, DC 20036. Phone: (202) 588-6141. Fax: (202) 588-6299. Email: pr@nthp.org. WWW: http://www.nationaltrust.org

NATIONAL NURSING HOME WEEK. May 10–16. A community outreach program designed to familiarize the public with long-term care facilities and the services they provide. Activities are conducted locally by individual long-term care facilities. Annually, Mother's Day through the following Saturday. For info: American Health Care Assn, Natl Nursing Home Week, 1201 L St NW, Washington, DC 20005. Phone: (202) 842-4444. Fax: (202) 842-3860.

NATIONAL POLICE WEEK. May 10–16. See also "Peace Officer Memorial Day" (May 15). For info: American Police Hall of Fame and Museum, 3801 Biscayne Blvd, Miami, FL 33137. Phone: (305) 573-0070.

★**NATIONAL TRANSPORTATION WEEK.** May 10–16. Presidential Proclamation issued for week including third Friday in May since 1960. (PL 86–475 of May 20, 1960, first requested; PL87–449 of May 14, 1962, requested an annual proclamation.)

★**POLICE WEEK.** May 10–16. Presidential Proclamation 3537 of May 4, 1963, covers all succeeding years. (PL87–726 of Oct 1, 1962.) Always the week including May 15 since 1962.

RACE FOR THE CURE®. May 10. Schenley Park, Pittsburgh, PA. 5K walk/run and one-mile fun walk to raise awareness of breast cancer and help fund research for a cure. One of 63 around the country founded by the Susan G Komen Breast Cancer Foundation. Annually, on Mother's Day. Est attendance: 11,000. For info: Race for the Cure®, 1620 Murray Ave, Pittsburgh, PA 15217. Phone: (412) 521-2873. Fax: (412) 421-1121.
WWW: http://race4cure.lm.com

ROSS, GEORGE: BIRTH ANNIVERSARY. May 10. Lawyer and signer of the Declaration of Independence, born at New Castle, DE, May 10, 1730. Died at Philadelphia, PA, July 14, 1779.

TRUST YOUR INTUITION DAY ©. May 10. As our society grows more hectic and out of control, today is the day we pay homage to the wonderful gift of sixth sense, "gut" feelings or that still small voice which is sometimes the only clue we have to go on in this ever-changing world. For info: Adrienne Sioux Koopersmith, 1437 W Rosemont, #1W, Chicago, IL 60660-1319. Phone: (773) 743-5341. Fax: (773) 743-5395.
Email: kooper@interaccess.com.

UNIVERSAL FAMILY WEEK. May 10–16. To stress the importance of the fundamental role of good families in strengthening humankind. For complete info, send $3 to cover expense of printing, handling and postage. Annually, the second full week in May. For info: Dr. Stanley Drake, Pres, Intl Society of Friendship and Goodwill, 412 Cherry Hills Dr, Bakersfield, CA 93309-2866.

May 1998

S	M	T	W	T	F	S
					1	2
3	4	5	6	7	8	9
10	11	12	13	14	15	16
17	18	19	20	21	22	23
24	25	26	27	28	29	30
31						

VANCOUVER, GEORGE: 200th DEATH ANNIVERSARY. May 10, 1798. English navigator, explorer and author for whom Vancouver Island and the cities of Vancouver (British Columbia and Washington) are named was born in 1758 (exact date unknown) and joined the navy at the age of 13. He surveyed the coasts of Australia, New Zealand and western North America and sailed with Captain James Cook to the Arctic in 1780. Vancouver died at Petersham, Surrey, England, on May 10, 1798, just as he was correcting the final pages of his *Journal*, which was published in three volumes at London later that year.

VEAL BAN ACTION DAY. May 10. (Mother's Day) To publicize the inhumane and unsanitary conditions under which "milk-fed veal" calves are raised. Local actions include picketing of veal restaurants, leafletting and information tables. For info: Farm Animal Reform Movement, Box 30654, Bethesda, MD 20824. Phone: (301) 530-1737. Fax: (301) 530-5747. Email: farmusa@erols.com. WWW: http://www.envirolink.org/arrs/farm

BIRTHDAYS TODAY

Bono, 38, singer (U2), born Dublin, Ireland, May 10, 1960.
T. Berry Brazleton, 80, pediatrician, author, born Waco, TX, May 10, 1918.
Jason Brooks, 32, actor ("Days of Our Lives"), born Colorado Springs, CO, May 10, 1966.
Judith Jamison, 54, dancer and choreographer, born Philadelphia, PA, May 10, 1944.
Dave Mason, 52, singer, musician, songwriter ("We Just Disagree," "So High"), born Worcester, England, May 10, 1946.
Gary Owens, 62, actor ("Rowan & Martin's Laugh-In," "The Gong Show"), born Mitchell, SD, May 10, 1936.
Ara Raoul Parseghian, 75, former football coach and sportscaster, born Akron, OH, May 10, 1923.
Marie-France Pisier, 54, actress (*Cousin Cousine, French Postcards*), born Indochina, May 10, 1944.
Ronald F. (Rony) Seikaly, 33, basketball player, born Beirut, Lebanon, May 10, 1965.

MAY 11 — MONDAY

Day 131 — 234 Remaining

BATTLE OF HAMBURGER HILL BEGINS: ANNIVERSARY. May 11, 1969. One of the most infamous battles that signified the growing frustration with America's involvement in the Vietnam war began. Attempting to seize Dong Ap Bia mountain, American troops repeatedly scaled the hill over a 10-day period, often engaging in bloody hand-to-hand combat with the North Vietnamese. After finally securing the objective, American military decision makers chose to abandon it and the North Vietnamese retook it shortly thereafter. The heavy casualties in the struggle to take the hill inspired the name "Hamburger Hill."

BERLIN, IRVING: BIRTH ANNIVERSARY. May 11, 1888. Songwriter. Born Israel Isidore Baline at Tyumen, Russia. Irving Berlin moved to New York, NY, with his family when he was four years old. After the death of his father, he began singing in saloons and on street corners in order to help his family and worked as a singing waiter as a teenager. Berlin became one of America's most prolific songwriters, authoring such songs as "Alexander's Ragtime Band," "White Christmas," "God Bless America," "There's No Business Like Show Business," "Doin' What Comes Naturally," "Puttin' On the Ritz," "Blue Skies" and "Oh! How I Hate to Get Up in the Morning" among others. He could neither read nor write musical notation. Berlin died at the age of 101 on Sept 22, 1989, at New York, NY.

DALI, SALVADOR: BIRTH ANNIVERSARY. May 11. Born at Figueras, Spain, on May 11, 1904. A leading painter in the Surrealist movement, Salvador Dali was equally well known for his sometimes baffling antics and attempts to shock his audiences. The largest collection of his works resides in the Salvador Dali Museum in St. Petersburg, FL. Dali died on Jan 23, 1989, at his hometown of Figueras.

EAT WHAT YOU WANT DAY. May 11. Here's a day you may actually enjoy yourself. Ignore all those on-again/off-again warnings. [© 1997 by WPL] For info: Tom and Ruth Roy, Wellness Permission League, PO Box 662, Mt Gretna, PA 17064-0662. Phone: (500) 437-5104 or (717) 964-1308. Fax: (717) 964-1335.

ELKIN, STANLEY: BIRTH ANNIVERSARY. May 11, 1930. Born at Brooklyn, NY, Stanley Elkin became a professor at Washington University, in St. Louis, MO, where he lectured on fiction writing for more than 30 years. In addition to his teaching, Elkin was a novelist of particular acclaim. A prolific writer, the author of 17 books, he was awarded the National Book Critics Circle Award in 1983 for his novel, *George Mills*. Elkin, who suffered from multiple sclerosis, died of a heart attack at St. Louis, MO in 1995.

FAIRBANKS, CHARLES WARREN: BIRTH ANNIVERSARY. May 11, 1852. Twenty-sixth vice president of the US (1905–1909) born at Unionville Center, OH, May 11, 1852. Died at Indianapolis, IN, June 4, 1918.

GRAHAM, MARTHA: BIRTH ANNIVERSARY. May 11. Martha Graham was born on May 11, 1894, at Allegheny, PA, and became one of the giants of the modern dance movement in the US. She began her dance career at the comparatively late age of 22 and joined the Greenwich Village Follies in 1923. Her new ideas began to surface in the late '20s and '30s, and by the mid-1930s she was incorporating the rituals of the southwestern American Indians in her work. She is credited with bringing a new psychological depth to modern dance by exploring primal emotions and ancient rituals in her work. She performed until the age of 75, and she premiered her 180th ballet, *The Maple Leaf Rag,* in the fall of 1990. Martha Graham died Apr 1, 1991, at the age of 96 at New York City.

HART, JOHN: DEATH ANNIVERSARY. May 11. Signer of the Declaration of Independence, farmer and legislator, born about 1711 (exact date unknown), at Stonington, CT. Died on May 11, 1779.

INTERNATIONAL ONLINE ROMANCE WEEK. May 11–15. This week singles are encouraged to use the Internet to meet new friends in an effort to eventually find romance. Married and other established couples are encouraged to express their love through e-mail love notes. Annually, the second week in May. For info: Lorilyn Bailey, LORMAZ Communications, PO Box 40304, Raleigh, NC 27629. Phone: (919) 878-9108. Email: lorilynb@online-romance.com.

JAPAN: CORMORANT FISHING FESTIVAL. May 11–Oct 15. Cormorant fishing on the Nagara River, Gifu. "This ancient method of catching Ayu, a troutlike fish, with trained cormorants, takes place nightly under the light of blazing torches."

MARLEY, BOB: DEATH ANNIVERSARY. May 11, 1981. Anniversary of the death, at Miami, FL, on May 11, 1981, of Bob Marley. With his group, The Wailers, he was one of the most popular and influential performers of reggae music, an "off-beat-accented Jamaican" music closely associated with the political/religious Rastafarian movement (admirers of the late Ethiopian emperor Haile Selassie, who was formerly called Ras Tafari). Marley, who died of cancer, was born Feb 6, 1945, at Rhoden Hall in northern Jamaica.

***MERRIMAC* DESTROYED: ANNIVERSARY.** May 11, 1862. After the spectacular standoff with the Union ironclad *Monitor* on Mar 9, the Confederate ironclad *Merrimac* was destroyed by the Confederate navy on May 11. In the wake of advancing Union troops in the Peninsular Campaign, the South was forced to destroy the valuable vessel to prevent its capture by Union forces.

MINNESOTA: ADMISSION DAY: ANNIVERSARY. May 11, 1858. Became 32nd state on this day in 1858.

MOON PHASE: FULL MOON. May 11. Moon enters Full Moon phase at 10:29 AM, EDT.

Equus

NATIONAL STUTTERING AWARENESS WEEK. May 11–17. For info: Stuttering Foundation of America, 3100 Walnut Grove Rd, Ste 603, Memphis, TN 38111-0749. Phone: (800) 992-9392 or (901) 452-7343.

SEATTLE BLACKOUT: ANNIVERSARY. May 11. On May 11, 1942, Seattle, WA, became the first US city to institute outside blackout control during WW II. All outdoor lighting became subject to permit.

BIRTHDAYS TODAY

Louis Farrakhan, 65, leader Nation of Islam, born New York, NY, May 11, 1933.

Robert Jarvik, 52, physician, inventor of artificial heart that went into Barney Clark, born Midland, MI, May 11, 1946.

James M. Jeffords, 64, US Senator (R, Vermont), born Rutland, VT, May 11, 1934.

Denver Pyle, 78, actor ("The Life and Legend of Wyatt Earp"; Uncle Jesse on "The Dukes of Hazzard"), born Bethune, CO, May 11, 1920.

Natasha Richardson, 35, actress (*The Handmaid's Tale, Nell*), born London, England, May 11, 1963.

Mort Sahl, 71, actor (*Don't Make Waves, Doctor You've Got to be Kidding*), born Montreal, Quebec, Canada, May 11, 1927.

MAY 12 — TUESDAY

Day 132 — 233 Remaining

DONIZETTI'S *L'ELISIR D'AMORE* PREMIERE: ANNIVERSARY. May 12, 1832. Italian composer Gaetano Donizetti's famed comic opera *L'Elisir d'amore* (*The Elixir of Love*) premiered on this date. With a libretto written by Felice Romani, the opera is about a poor peasant's attempts to woo a wealthy and spirited girl. It remains among Donizetti's best known works.

GEORGE VI'S CORONATION: ANNIVERSARY. May 12, 1937. George VI was crowned at Westminster Abbey in London, following the abdication of his brother, Edward VIII. Born Dec 14, 1895, King George died Feb 6, 1952. He was succeeded by his daughter Elizabeth, the current reigning monarch.

LEAR, EDWARD: BIRTH ANNIVERSARY. May 12, 1812. English artist and author, best remembered for his light verse and limericks. Lear was born at Highgate, England, and died at San Remo, Italy, Jan 29, 1888. See also: "Limerick Day" (May 12).

LIMERICK DAY. May 12. Observed on the birthday of one of its champions, Edward Lear. The limerick, which dates from the early 18th century, has been described as the "only fixed verse form indigenous to the English language." It gained its greatest popularity following the publication of Edward Lear's *Book of Nonsense* (and its sequels). Write a limerick today! Example: There was a young poet named Lear/Who said, it is just as I fear/Five lines are enough/For this kind of stuff/Make a limerick each day of the year. See also: "Lear, Edward: Birth Anniversary" (May 12).

NIGHTINGALE, FLORENCE: BIRTH ANNIVERSARY. May 12, 1820. English nurse and public health activist who, through her unselfish devotion to nursing, contributed perhaps more than any other single person to the development of modern nursing procedures and dignity of nursing as a profession. Founder of the Nightingale training school for nurses. Author of *Notes on Nursing*. Born at Florence, Italy. Died at London, England, on Aug 13, 1910.

PORTUGAL: PILGRIMAGE TO FATIMA. May 12–13. Commemorates first appearance of the Virgin of the Rosary to little shepherd children May 13, 1917. Pilgrims come to Cova da Iria, religious center, candlelit procession, Mass of the sick, for annual observance.

SPITTING PROHIBITION IN NEW YORK CITY: ANNIVERSARY. May 12, 1896. The New York City Department of Health passed a health ordinance prohibiting spitting on sidewalks or in other public places.

VIRGIN ISLANDS: NURSE OF THE YEAR AWARD. May 12. Annually, on anniversary of birth of Florence Nightingale (May 12, 1820), the Virgin Islands Nurses' Assn selects two nurses for special recognition. Awards are named in honor of deceased outstanding Virgin Island nurses.

WOODMEN RANGER'S DAY. May 12. To celebrate the founding of the Woodmen Youth Program in 1903—Woodmen Rangers®. For info: Woodmen of the World/Omaha Woodmen Life Insurance Society, John S. Manna, 1700 Farnam, Omaha, NE 68102. Phone: (402) 271-7258.

BIRTHDAYS TODAY

Burt Bacharach, 69, composer ("Walk On By," "Close to You," "Raindrops Keep Fallin' on My Head"); many film scores, born Kansas City, MO, May 12, 1929.

Lawrence Peter ("Yogi") Berra, 73, former baseball coach and manager, Baseball Hall of Fame catcher, born St. Louis, MO, May 12, 1925.

Bruce Boxleitner, 47, actor (*How the West Was Won*, "Scarecrow and Mrs King"), born Elgin, IL, May 12, 1951.

Gabriel Byrne, 48, actor (*The Usual Suspects*), born Dublin, Ireland, May 12, 1950.

George Carlin, 61, comedian ("That Girl," "The George Carlin Show"), born New York, NY, May 12, 1937.

Lindsay Crouse, 50, actress (*House of Games, Slap Shot, The Verdict, Places in the Heart*), born New York, NY, May 12, 1948.

Emilio Estevez, 36, actor (*Breakfast Club, Repo Man*), born New York, NY, May 12, 1962.

Kim Fields, 29, actress (Tootie Ramsey on "The Facts of Life"), born Los Angeles, CA, May 12, 1969.

Kim Greist, 40, actress (*Brazil, Throw Momma from the Train*), born Stamford, CT, May 12, 1958.

Katharine Hepburn, 91, actress (Oscars for *Morning Glory, Guess Who's Coming to Dinner, Lion in Winter, On Golden Pond, Adam's Rib, Pat and Mike, The African Queen*), born Hartford, CT, May 12, 1907.

May 1998

S	M	T	W	T	F	S
					1	2
3	4	5	6	7	8	9
10	11	12	13	14	15	16
17	18	19	20	21	22	23
24	25	26	27	28	29	30
31						

Samuel Daniel Nujoma, 69, President of Namibia, born Ongandjeia, Namibia, May 12, 1929.
Millie Perkins, 60, actress ("Knots Landing," *The Diary of Anne Frank, Wall Street*), born Passaic, NJ, May 12, 1938.
Howard K. Smith, 84, journalist, born Ferriday, LA, May 12, 1914.
Tom Snyder, 62, broadcast journalist, TV personality, born Milwaukee, WI, May 12, 1936.
Frank Stella, 62, artist (*Empress of India*), born Malden, MA, May 12, 1936.
Louis Rodman Whitaker, 41, former baseball player, born New York, NY, May 12, 1957.
Steve Winwood, 50, musician, singer, born Birmingham, England, May 12, 1948.

MAY 13 — WEDNESDAY

Day 133 — 232 Remaining

ATTEMPTED ASSASSINATION OF POPE JOHN PAUL II: ANNIVERSARY. May 13, 1981. Pope John Paul II was shot twice at close range while riding in an open automobile at St. Peter's Square in Rome, Italy. Two other persons also were wounded. An escaped terrorist, Mehmet Ali Agca (already under sentence of death for the murder of a Turkish journalist), was arrested immediately and was convicted July 22, 1981, of attempted murder of the pope. After convalescence Pope John Paul II was pronounced recovered by his doctors on Aug 14, 1981.

THE DAY OF THE TEACHER (EL DIA DEL MAESTRO). May 13. California honors its teachers every year on The Day of the Teacher. Patterned after "El Dia Del Maestro" celebrated in Mexico, The Day of the Teacher was originated by the Association of Mexican-American Educators and the California Teachers Association and designated by the California legislature. A tribute to all teachers and their lasting influence on children's lives. Annually, the second Wednesday of May. For info: CTA, 1705 Murchison Dr, Burlingame, CA 94010. Phone: (415) 697-1400. Fax: (415) 697-0786. WWW: http://www.cta.org

DOUGLAS, VIRGINIA O'HANLON: DEATH ANNIVERSARY. May 13, 1971. Virginia O'Hanlon Douglas lived a long and productive life as an educator and a loving mother. However, to the reading public she is re-introduced year after year at Christmas-time, as the disheartened eight-year old who asked the staff of *The New York Sun* whether Santa Claus exists. In a famous 1897 editorial Francis P. Church answered her question and reassured Virginia that yes, indeed ". . . there is a Santa Claus." Douglas died at Valatie, NY, on May, 13, 1971, at the age of 81.

LOUIS, JOE: BIRTH ANNIVERSARY. May 13. World heavyweight boxing champion, 1937–1949, nicknamed the "Brown Bomber," Joseph Louis Barrow was born near Lafayette, AL, May 13, 1914. He died Apr 12, 1981, at Las Vegas, NV. Burial at Arlington National Cemetery. (Louis's burial there, by presidential waiver, was the 39th exception ever to the eligibility rules for burial in Arlington National Cemetery.)

MACAU: PROCESSION OF OUR LADY OF FATIMA. May 13. To commemorate the miracle of 1917, when the Madonna appeared to residents of Fatima, Portugal, an image of Our Lady is carried in pilgrimage from Sao Domingos Church to Penha Church, generally around 6 PM.

MEXICAN WAR DECLARED: ANNIVERSARY. May 13, 1846. Although fighting had begun days earlier, Congress officially declared war on Mexico on this date. The struggle cost the lives of 11,300 American soldiers and resulted in the annexation by the US of land that became parts of Oklahoma, New Mexico, Arizona, Nevada, California, Utah and Colorado. The war ended in 1848. See also "Treaty of Guadalupe Hidalgo (Feb 2)."

NATIONAL RECEPTIONIST DAY. May 13. Day of recognition for our nation's frontline personnel in business, because you only get one chance to make a good first impression. Receptionists may go by other names such as host/hostess, maitre d', front desk clerk, operator, customer service representative, information desk personnel or anyone responsible for creating or maintaining a favorable image for the company by greeting clients and guests. There are some 892,000 receptionists in the US. Annually, the second Wednesday in May. For info: Jennifer Alexander, Dir, Natl Receptionist Society, 51 Oakwood Trail, Sparta, NJ 07871. Phone: (201) 729-1903. Fax: (201) 729-2769.

NATIONAL THIRD SHIFT WORKERS DAY. May 13. To show appreciation for and to honor those often-forgotten workers who toil through the night to keep countless companies and businesses running smoothly. Annually, the second Wednesday in May. For info: Jeff Corbett, PO Box 2, Statesville, NC 28687.

NORTHERN IRELAND: ROYAL ULSTER AGRICULTURAL SOCIETY BALMORAL SHOW. May 13–15. The Showgrounds, Balmoral, Belfast. The premier agricultural show on Northern Ireland's calendar. Est attendance: 70,000. For info: Mr Rees, Royal Ulster Agricultural Society, Balmoral Showgrounds, Belfast, Northern Ireland BT9 6GW. Phone: (44) (123) 266-5225. Fax: (44) (123) 266-1264.

PHILADELPHIA POLICE BOMBING: ANNIVERSARY. May 13. On May 13, 1985, during the siege of a "radical group" in Philadelphia, PA, police in a helicopter reportedly dropped a bomb containing the powerful military plastic explosive C-4 on the building in which the group was housed. The bomb and the resulting fire left 11 persons dead (including four children) and destroyed 61 homes.

PREAKNESS FROG HOP. May 13. Patterson Park, Baltimore, MD. Event determines Baltimore's entry to the international frog jumping contest. Frogs must be four inches in length from the nose to where the tail should be (not counting the legs). Trophies awarded to the 1st-, 2nd- and 3rd-place winners, plus the 1st-place frog only (not the owner) is flown to California to represent the City of Baltimore in the Calaveras County Frog Jumping Jubilee. Est attendance: 300. For info: Office of Adventures in Fun, Patterson Park Recreation Complex, 2601 E Baltimore St, Baltimore, MD 21224. Phone: (410) 396-9177. Fax: (410) 327-4120.

SAINT LAWRENCE SEAWAY ACT: ANNIVERSARY. May 13, 1954. President Dwight D. Eisenhower signed legislation authorizing US–Canadian construction of a waterway that would make it possible for ocean-going ships to reach the Great Lakes.

SPACE MILESTONE: *ENDEAVOUR* (US). May 13, 1992. Three astronauts from the shuttle *Endeavour* simultaneously walked in space for the first time.

SULLIVAN, ARTHUR: BIRTH ANNIVERSARY. May 13, 1842. English composer best known for light operas (with Sir William Gilbert), born May 13, 1842. Died Nov 22, 1900.

WELLS, MARY: 55th BIRTH ANNIVERSARY. May 13, 1943. Motown's first big star, Mary Wells was born May 13, 1943 at Detroit, MI. Wells was known for such hits as "The One Who Really Loves You," "You Beat Me to the Punch," "Two Lovers" and her signature song, "My Guy." She was one of a group of black artists of the '60s, along with Smokey Robinson, the Supremes, the Temptations and the Four Tops, who helped end musical segregation by getting played on white radio stations. Mary Wells died July 26, 1992, at Los Angeles.

WORLD WAR II: TUNIS CAMPAIGN VICTORY: 55th ANNIVERSARY. May 13, 1943. General Sir Harold Alexander telegraphed Winston Churchill, who was in Washington attending a conference, "It is my duty to report that the Tunis campaign is over. All enemy resistance has ceased. We are masters of the North African shores." About 250,000 Germans and Italians surrendered in the last few days of the campaign. This Allied victory in North Africa helped open Mediterranean shipping lanes.

BIRTHDAYS TODAY

Franklyn Ajaye, 49, actor ("Keep on Truckin'," *Car Wash*), born Brooklyn, NY, May 13, 1949.

Beatrice Arthur (Bernice Frankel), 72, actress (*Mame, Fiddler on the Roof*, "Maude," "Golden Girls"), born New York, NY, May 13, 1926.

Frances Barber, 41, actress (*Sammy and Rosie Get Laid, We Think the World of You*), born Wolverhampton, England, May 13, 1957.

Clive Barnes, 71, critic, born London, England, May 13, 1927.

Peter Gabriel, 48, singer, songwriter (former lead singer of Genesis), born London, England, May 13, 1950.

Harvey Keitel, 59, actor (*Mean Streets, Blue Collar, Bugsy, The Piano*), born Brooklyn, NY, May 13, 1939.

Tim Pigott-Smith, 52, actor ("The Jewel in the Crown," *Remains of the Day*), born Rugby, England, May 13, 1946.

Dennis Keith ("Worm") Rodman, 37, basketball player, born Trenton, NJ, May 13, 1961.

Herbert Ross, 71, actor, choreographer, director on stage and screen, born New York, NY, May 13, 1927.

Darius Rucker, 30, lead singer for Hootie and the Blowfish, born Charleston, SC, May 13, 1968.

Stevie Wonder (Steveland Morris Hardaway), 47, singer, musician (16 Grammy Awards; "I Just Called to Say I Love You"), born Saginaw, MI, May 13, 1951.

MAY 14 — THURSDAY

Day 134 — 231 Remaining

BALANCHINE-GRAHAM COLLABORATION: ANNIVERSARY. May 14, 1959. In a melding of classical ballet and modern dance, George Balanchine's and Martha Graham's *Episodes* premiered. A new experience for ballet enthusiasts, half of the program was choreographed by Balanchine and the other half by Graham.

BIG 12 MEN'S BASEBALL CHAMPIONSHIP. May 14–17. All Sports Stadium, Oklahoma City, OK (tentative site). Second annual Big 12 Baseball Championship. Most successful conference championship in the USA. Est attendance: 50,000. For info: OK City All Sports Assn, 100 W Main, Ste 285, Oklahoma City, OK 73102. Phone: (405) 236-5000. Fax: (405) 236-5008.

BOYNE CITY NATIONAL MUSHROOM HUNTING CHAMPIONSHIP. May 14–17. Boyne City, MI. Morel Mushroom Hunting Championship, arts and crafts, Taste of Boyne, live entertainment and carnival. Est attendance: 13,500. For info: Chamber of Commerce, 28 S Lake St, Boyne City, MI 49712. Phone: (616) 582-6222.

CALAVERAS COUNTY FAIR AND JUMPING FROG JUBILEE. May 14–17. Calaveras Fairgrounds, Angels Camp, CA. County fair and reenactment of Mark Twain's "Celebrated Jumping Frog of Calaveras County." This "Superbowl" of the sport of frog jumping attracts more than 3,000 frogs annually from around the world. Est attendance: 45,000. For info: 39th District Agricultural Assn, S Highway 49, PO Box 489, Angels Camp, CA 95222. Phone: (209) 736-2561. Fax: (209) 736-2476. Email: info@frogtown.org. WWW: http://www.frogtown.org

"ERNIE KOVACS" TV PREMIERE: ANNIVERSARY. May 14, 1951. Comedian Ernie Kovacs first hosted "It's Time for Ernie," a fifteen-minute afternoon program on NBC in May of 1951 before replacing the "Kukla, Fran and Ollie Show" with "Ernie in Kovacsland." Kovacs also appeared on a variety of daytime and prime-time series and was a fill-in for Steve Allen on the "Tonight!" show. His early shows featured Andy McKay, Trigger Lund, Eddie Hatrak and his wife, Edie Adams.

FAHRENHEIT, GABRIEL DANIEL: BIRTH ANNIVERSARY. May 14, 1686. German physicist whose name is attached to one of the major temperature measurement scales. He introduced the use of mercury in thermometers and greatly improved their accuracy. Born at Danzig, Germany, he died at Amsterdam, Holland, on Sept 16, 1736.

FIRST REAL FEMALE HOUSE PAGE APPOINTMENT: 25th ANNIVERSARY. May 14, 1973. The House of Representatives received formal approval of the appointment of female pages in 1972. On May 14, 1973, in the 93rd Congress, Felda Looper was appointed as the successor to Gene Cox who, for three hours, had served as the first female page 34 years earlier.

GAINSBOROUGH, THOMAS: BIRTH ANNIVERSARY. May 14, 1727. English landscape and portrait painter. Among his most remembered works: *The Blue Boy, The Watering Place* and *The Market Cart*. Born at Sudbury, Suffolk, England, he died at London, on Aug 2, 1788.

GETTYSBURG BLUEGRASS FESTIVAL. May 14–17. Gettysburg, PA. Granite Hill Campground on Rt 116. For info: Gettysburg Conv & Visitors Bureau, 35 Carlisle St, Gettysburg, PA 17325. Phone: (717) 334-6274. Fax: (717) 334-1166. WWW: http://www.gettysburg.com

JAMESTOWN, VIRGINIA: FOUNDING ANNIVERSARY. May 14, 1607. The first permanent English settlement in what is now the US took place at Jamestown, VA (named for England's King James I), on this date. Captains John Smith and Christopher Newport were among the leaders of the group of royally chartered Virginia Company settlers who had traveled from Plymouth, England, in three small ships: *Susan Constant, Godspeed* and *Discovery*.

LAG B'OMER. May 14. Hebrew calendar date: Iyar 18, 5758. Literally, the 33rd day of the omer (harvest time), the 33rd day after the beginning of Passover. Traditionally a joyous day for weddings, picnics and outdoor activities.

LEWIS AND CLARK EXPEDITION BEGAN: ANNIVERSARY. May 14, 1804. Charged by President Thomas Jefferson with finding a route to the Pacific, Meriwether Lewis and Capt William Clark left St. Louis on this date. They arrived at the Pacific coast of Oregon in Nov 1805 and returned to St. Louis, Sept 23, 1806.

LITTLE NORWAY FESTIVAL. May 14–17. Petersburg, AK. Celebration of Norwegian Independence Day. The majestic natural beauty that gives Petersburg its nickname ("Little Norway"), the rich Norwegian traditions and spirit and the combination of visitors from near and far and friendly residents form the backdrop to the gala celebration. Food and craft booths, kids activities, dancing, melodrama, pageant, Fish-O-Rama Seafood Feast. Est attendance: 3,000. For info: Petersburg Chamber of Commerce, Box 649, Petersburg, AK 99833. Phone: (907) 772-3646. Fax: (907) 772-3646. WWW: http://www.petersburg.org

NATIONAL ROAD FESTIVAL. May 14–17. Washington, Fayette and Somerset counties, PA. Wagon train encampments, food and entertainment. Festival celebrates the first national road commissioned by Thomas Jefferson. For info: Bob Grenoble, National Road Festival, US Rt 40, c/o 3543 National Pike, Farmington, PA 15437. Phone: (412) 329-1560.

NORWAY: MIDNIGHT SUN AT NORTH CAPE. May 14–July 30. North Cape. First day of the season with around-the-clock sunshine. At North Cape, the sun never dips below the horizon from May 14 to July 30, but the night is bright long before and after these dates.

OWEN, ROBERT: BIRTH ANNIVERSARY. May 14, 1771. English progressive owner of spinning works, philanthropist, Utopian socialist, founder of New Harmony, IN, born at Newtown, Wales. Died there Nov 17, 1858.

May 1998

S	M	T	W	T	F	S
					1	2
3	4	5	6	7	8	9
10	11	12	13	14	15	16
17	18	19	20	21	22	23
24	25	26	27	28	29	30
31						

PHILIPPINES: CARABAO FESTIVAL. May 14–15. Pulilan, Bulacan; Nueva Ecija; Angono, Rizal. Parade of farmers to honor their patron saint, San Isidro, with hundreds of "dressed up" carabaos participating.

SMALLPOX VACCINE DISCOVERED: ANNIVERSARY. May 14, 1796. In the 18th century, smallpox was a widespread and often fatal disease. Edward Jenner, a physician in rural England, heard reports of dairy farmers who apparently became immune to smallpox as a result of exposure to cowpox, a related but milder disease. On May 14, 1796, after two decades of studying the phenomenon, Jenner injected cowpox into a healthy eight-year-old boy, who subsequently developed cowpox. Six weeks later, Jenner inoculated the boy with smallpox. He remained healthy. Jenner called this new procedure *vaccination*, from *vaccinia*, another term for cowpox. Within 18 months, 12,000 people in England had been vaccinated and the number of smallpox deaths dropped by two-thirds.

SPACE MILESTONE: *SOYUZ 40* (USSR). May 14, 1981. Launched with two cosmonauts (L. Popov and, from Rumania, D. Prunariu); docked at *Salyut 6* space station on May 15. Returned to Earth on May 22.

"THE STARS AND STRIPES FOREVER" DAY: ANNIVERSARY. May 14, 1897. Anniversary of the first public performance of John Philip Sousa's march, "The Stars and Stripes Forever," at Philadelphia, PA. The occasion was the unveiling of a statue of George Washington, and President William McKinley was present. A bill was introduced in the Congress in 1985 to make "The Stars and Stripes Forever" the official national march of the US.

UNDERGROUND AMERICA DAY. May 14. Underground America Day is one man's (Malcolm Wells) attempt to get others to think of designing and building structures underground. Mr Wells publishes illustrations and humorous suggestions for celebrating Underground America Day. Annually, May 14. For info: Malcolm Wells, 673 Satucket Rd, Brewster, MA 02631. Phone: (508) 896-6850. Fax: (508) 896-5116.

WAAC: ANNIVERSARY. May 14, 1942. During WW II women became eligible to enlist for noncombat duties in the Women's Auxiliary Army Corps (WAAC) by an act of Congress on May 14, 1942. Women also served as Women Appointed for Voluntary Emergency Service (WAVES), Women's Auxiliary Ferrying Squadron (WAFS), and Coast Guard or Semper Paratus Always Ready Service (SPARS), the Women's Reserve of the Marine Corp.

BIRTHDAYS TODAY

Walter Berry, 34, former basketball player, born New York, NY, May 14, 1964.

Jack Bruce, 55, musician, born Glasgow, Scotland, May 14, 1943.

David Byrne, 46, singer (with Talking Heads), composer (songs, film scores), born Dumbarton, Scotland, May 14, 1952.

Byron L. Dorgan, 56, US Senator (D, North Dakota), born Dickinson, ND, May 14, 1942.

Meg Foster, 50, actress ("Cagney & Lacey," *The Emerald Forest, They Live*), born Reading, PA, May 14, 1948.

George Lucas, 54, filmmaker (*Star Wars* trilogy; director *American Graffiti*), born Modesto, CA, May 14, 1944.

Jose Dennis Martinez, 43, baseball player, born Granada, Nicaragua, May 14, 1955.

Patrice Munsel, 73, singer, born Spokane, WA, May 14, 1925.

Ralph Neas, 52, Executive Director of the Leadership Conference on Civil Rights, born Brookline, MA, May 14, 1946.

Michael Anthony (Mike) Quick, 39, former football player, born Hamlet, NC, May 14, 1959.

MAY 15 — FRIDAY

Day 135 — 230 Remaining

ART FAIR AND WINE FEST. May 15–17. Washington, MO. The largest Missouri wine tasting of state wines as well as a juried art show featuring 60 midwestern artists. Art fair is free. Admission to the wine pavilion includes a commemorative wine glass. For info: Downtown Washington Inc, PO Box 144, Washington, MO 63090. Phone: (314) 239-1743. Fax: (314) 239-4832.

ASPHALT COWBOY PANCAKE BREAKFAST. May 15. Roaring Gulch, Redding, CA. Annual 4-city-block breakfast serving more than 11,000 breakfasts in five hours. Annually, Friday of the third weekend in May. Est attendance: 11,400. For info: Asphalt Cowboys, PO Box 801, O'Brien, CA 96070. Phone: (916) 238-2341. Fax: (916) 238-2386.

BARABOO CIRCUS HERITAGE. May 15–17. Sauk County Fairgrounds, Baraboo, WI. A weekend of circus fun for Boy Scouts, Girl Scouts, 4-H, church youth groups and other organized youth groups. Hiking, camping, team skills competition, Pinewood Derby race, Circus World Museum and of course, the circus! Annually, the weekend after Mother's Day. Est attendance: 2,000. For info: Baraboo Circus Heritage, Boy Scouts of America, Four Lakes Council, 34 Schroeder Ct, Madison, WI 53711-6222. Phone: (608) 273-1005.

BAUM, LYMAN FRANK: BIRTH ANNIVERSARY. May 15, 1856. American newspaperman who wrote the Wizard of Oz stories was born at Chittenango, NY. Although *The Wonderful Wizard of Oz* is the most famous, Baum also wrote many other books for children, including more than a dozen about Oz. He died at Hollywood, CA, May 6, 1919.

CARFERRY FESTIVAL. May 15–17. Ludington, MI. Nautical festival celebrating maiden voyage of passenger ferry SS *Badger* featuring fireworks, Classic Car Show, Grand Parade, Pageants, James Street Bed Race, Blessing of the Fleet and Coast Guard Open House. Est attendance: 30,000. For info: Ludington Area Chamber of Commerce, 5827 W US 10, Ludington, MI 49431. Phone: (800) 542-4600. Fax: (616) 845-6857. Email: suelacvb@aol.com. WWW: http://www.ludingtoncvb.com

COTTEN, JOSEPH: BIRTH ANNIVERSARY. May 15, 1905. Stage and screen star Joseph Cotten was born at Petersburg, VA. Among Cotten's movie credits were *Citizen Kane, The Magnificent Ambersons* and *The Third Man*. Among his most noted performances on Broadway were *The Philadelphia Story* and *Once More with Feeling*. Joseph Cotten died Feb 6, 1994, at Los Angeles.

DUBUQUEFEST/VERY SPECIAL ARTS FESTIVAL. May 15–17. Dubuque, IA. A celebration of folk and fine arts. Dance, opera, music, mime, arts, crafts, poetry, drama and historic architecture. Annually, the third weekend in May, Friday–Sunday. Est attendance: 65,000. For info: DubuqueFest/Very Special Arts Festival, PO Box 1713, Dubuque, IA 52004-1713. Phone: (319) 588-9751. Fax: (319) 588-2714.

DULCIMER DAYS. May 15–17. Coshocton, OH. Dulcimer competition, exhibits, open stage, jam sessions, Saturday evening concert and more. Est attendance: 1,400. For info: Cheryl Oswald, Roscoe Village, 381 Hill St, Coshocton, OH 43812. Phone: (800) 877-1830 or (614) 622-9310. Fax: (614) 623-6555.

EASTERN PACIFIC HURRICANE SEASON. May 15–Nov 30. Eastern Pacific defined as: Coast to 140 degrees west longitude. Info from: US Dept of Commerce, Natl Oceanic and Atmospheric Admin, Rockville, MD 20852.

ENGLAND: BATH INTERNATIONAL MUSIC FESTIVAL. May 15–31. Bath (various venues). International arts festival which will include jazz, classical early and contemporary performances, concerts, talks and exhibitions. Est attendance: 50,000. For info: Bath Festivals Office, 2 Church St, Abbey Green, Bath, England BA1 1NL. Phone: (44) (122) 546-3362. Fax: (44) (122) 531-0377.

FIRST FLIGHT ATTENDANT: ANNIVERSARY. May 15, 1930. Ellen Church became the first airline stewardess (today's flight attendant), flying on a United Airlines flight from San Francisco to Cheyenne, WY.

FRISCH, MAX: BIRTH ANNIVERSARY. May 15. Max Frisch was one of Europe's leading post–World War II literary figures. His work includes the novels *Homo Faber, I'm Not Stiller, Juerg Reinhardt* and plays *The Firebugs, Andorra* and many others. In addition to his writing, he was a controversial critic of his native Switzerland, its government and its people. Frisch was born on May 15, 1911, and died on Apr 4, 1991.

GASOLINE RATIONING: ANNIVERSARY. May 15, 1942. Seventeen eastern states initiated gasoline rationing as part of the war effort. By Sept 25, rationing was nationwide. A limit of three gallons a week for nonessential purposes was set and a 35 mph speed limit was imposed.

GATLINBURG SCOTTISH FESTIVAL AND HIGHLAND GAMES. May 15–17. Gatlinburg, TN. Celebration of Scotland, its people and traditions. Music, food and fun. Est attendance: 12,000. For info: Gatlinburg Chamber of Commerce, PO Box 527, Gatlinburg, TN 37738. Phone: (800) 568-4748 or (423) 436-2392. Fax: (423) 436-3704.
WWW: http://www.gatlinburg.com

☆ ☆ ☆

GEORGE WALLACE SHOT: ANNIVERSARY. May 15, 1972. George Wallace was shot by Arthur Bremer while Wallace was in Laurel, MD, campaigning for the US presidency. For the remainder of his life Wallace was paralyzed from the waist down. On Aug 4, 1972, Bremer was sentenced to 67 years in prison for the shooting.

HOT AIR BALLOON CLASSIC. May 15–17. Live Oak, FL. Spectacular fun, color and music. Est attendance: 10,000. For info: Vicki Bass, Spirit of the Suwannee Music Park, 3076 95th Dr, Live Oak, FL 32060. Phone: (904) 364-1683. Fax: (904) 364-2998. Email: spirit@musicliveshere.com.
WWW: http://www.musicliveshere.com

May 1998

S	M	T	W	T	F	S
					1	2
3	4	5	6	7	8	9
10	11	12	13	14	15	16
17	18	19	20	21	22	23
24	25	26	27	28	29	30
31						

INTERNATIONAL PICKLE WEEK. May 15–25. To give national recognition to the world's most humorous vegetable. Sponsor: Pickle Packers Intl, Inc. For info: Donna H. Myers, DHM Group, Inc, PO Box 767, Holmdel, NJ 07733. Fax: (908) 946-3343.

JAPAN: AOI MATSURI (HOLLYHOCK FESTIVAL). May 15. Kyoto. The festival features a pageant reproducing imperial processions of ancient times that paid homage to the shrine of Shimogamo and Kamigamo.

LILAC FESTIVAL. May 15–25. Highland Park, Rochester, NY. Developed by renowned park designer Frederick Law Olmstead, Highland Park is the site of the Lilac Festival, the largest celebration of its kind in North America. In addition to the spectacle of more than 500 varieties of lilacs in bloom, the festival provides free admission, free entertainment, a free concert with the Rochester Philharmonic Orchestra, a parade, a 10K race, two juried art shows, a senior citizens day and music festivals. Est attendance: 500,000. For info: Cherie Bevona, PR Coord, Lilac Festival, 171 Reservoir Ave, Rochester, NY 14620. Fax: (716) 256-4968. Email: lilacfestival@roch.com.
WWW: http://www.roch.com/lilacfestival

LOST IN THE '50s. May 15–17. Sandpoint, ID. Dance and show with '50s stars, vintage car parade, car show, car rally and 5K run. Est attendance: 3,000. For info: Festival at Sandpoint, Carolyn Gleason, Chair, 215 S 2nd Ave, Sandpoint, ID 83864. Phone: (208) 263-9321 or (208) 265-LOST.

MAIFEST '98. May 15–17. MainStrasse Village, Covington, KY. MainStrasse celebrates the German tradition of welcoming the first spring wines and the beginning of the festival season. Artist and craftsman exhibits, international food and drink, live music and entertainment. Est attendance: 275,000. For info: Cindy Scheidt, MainStrasse Village, 616 MainStrasse, Covington, KY 41011. Phone: (606) 491-0458. Fax: (606) 655-7932.

MEXICO: SAN ISIDRO DAY. May 15. Day of San Isidro Labrador celebrated widely in farming regions to honor St. Isidore, the Plowman. Livestock gaily decorated with flowers. Celebrations usually begin about May 13 and continue for about a week.

MILES CITY BUCKING HORSE SALE. May 15–17. Miles City, MT. Miles City is real "Lonesome Dove" country and its annual bucking horse sale is where rodeo stock operators from around the west come to purchase their bucking horses for the coming rodeo season. A festive event, the sale not only involves cowboys trying to ride some of the wildest horses in the country, but western artists displaying and creating works in a weekend art show, an antique show featuring guns and coins, a western trade show featuring practical and gift items, a Saturday morning parade and Miles City's western attractions like the Range Riders Museum which chronicles the life of the cowboy on the northern Great Plains. (Miles City is the community featured in the novel and the two television mini series about "Lonesome Dove.") Est attendance: 3,200. For info: Susan Sanderson, Miles City Chamber of Commerce, Box 127, Miles City, MT 59301. Phone: (406) 232-6585.

MINT JULEP SCALE MEET. May 15–17. Rough River Dam State Resort Park, Falls of Rough, KY. A weekend for radio-controlled airplane enthusiasts. Est attendance: 400. For info: Tom DeHaven, Rec Supervisor, Rough River Dam State Resort Park, 450 Lodge Rd, Falls of Rough, KY 40119. Phone: (502) 257-2311.

MOREL MUSHROOM FESTIVAL. May 15–17. Muscoda, Wisconsin's "Morel Mushroom Capital," celebrates the end of the morel mushroom's two-week peak season. The 15th annual celebration includes a contest with mushrooms judged in five categories: heaviest, tallest, biggest around, most on one stem (cluster) and oddest. Mushrooms available to sample and purchase. Many fun activities for the whole family. Annually, the weekend after Mother's Day. Est attendance: 1,000. For info: Muscoda Civic Pride Organization, Morel Mushroom Fest, PO Box 706, Muscoda, WI 53573. Phone: (608) 739-3770. Fax: (608) 739-3941. Email: glm@mwt.net.

MORMON TRAIL RIDE. May 15–17. Las Flores Ranch, Summit Valley, CA. Open trail ride retraces the trails of the Mormon pioneers who crossed the deserts and mountains of California and settled the valley of San Bernardino in 1851. Annually, the third weekend of May. Est attendance: 250. For info: Ken Schroeder, Trail Boss, Mormon Trail Ride Assn, Apple Valley Sheriff's Posse, PO Box 338, Victorville, CA 92392. Phone: (760) 247-2558 evenings.

★**NATIONAL DEFENSE TRANSPORTATION DAY.** May 15. Presidential Proclamation customarily issued as "National Defense Transportation Day and National Transportation Week." Issued each year for the third Friday in May since 1957. (PL85–32 of May 16, 1957.)

NATIONAL PIKE FESTIVAL. May 15–17. Along Route 40 in Clear Spring, Hagerstown, Funkstown and Boonsboro, MD. National Pike was the first federally funded interstate highway in 1800s. Conestoga wagons, buggies, mules and horses. Activities at each stop. Est attendance: 6,000. For info: Hagerstown/Washington County Conv and Visitors Bureau, Elizabeth Hager Center, 16 Public Sq, Hagerstown, MD 21740. Phone: (301) 791-3246 or (800) 228-STAY. Fax: (301) 791-2601.

NATIONALITY DAYS FESTIVAL. May 15–17 (tentative). Ambridge, PA. 33rd year. Crafts, entertainment and a huge variety of ethnic foods. For info: (412) 266-3040 or Beaver County Tourist Promotion Agency, 215 B Ninth St, Monaca, PA 15061-2028. Phone: (412) 728-0212. Fax: (412) 728-0456.

NYLON STOCKINGS: ANNIVERSARY. May 15. On May 15, 1940, nylon hose went on sale at stores throughout the country. Competing producers bought their nylon yarn from E.J. du Pont de Nemours. W.H. Carothers of Du Pont developed nylon, called "Polymer 66," in 1935. It was the first totally man-made fiber and over time substituted for other materials and came to have widespread application.

OCONALUFTEE INDIAN VILLAGE. May 15–Oct 25. Cherokee Indian Reservation, Cherokee, NC. To portray the Cherokee lifestyle of the 1750 period. Also featuring *Unto These Hills* (mid-June–late-August), a drama portraying history of eastern band of Cherokees. Est attendance: 150,000. For info: Cherokee Historical Assn, Margie Douthit, PR, PO Box 398, Cherokee, NC 28719. Phone: (704) 497-2111. Fax: (704) 497-6987.

O'CONNELL, DANIEL: DEATH ANNIVERSARY. May 15, 1847. Irish Catholic political leader Daniel O'Connell, known as "the Liberator" for his role in achieving the right of Catholics to sit in Parliament, died at age 81 at Genoa, Italy. O'Connell was born Aug 6, 1775, near Cahirciveen, County Kerry.

PARAGUAY: INDEPENDENCE DAY. May 15. Commemorates independence from Spain, attained 1811.

★**PEACE OFFICER MEMORIAL DAY.** May 15. Presidential Proclamation 3537, of May 4, 1963, covers all succeeding years. (PL87–726 of Oct 1, 1962.) Always May 15 of each year since 1963; however, first issued in 1962 for May 14.

PEACE OFFICER MEMORIAL DAY. May 15. An event honored by some 21,000 police departments nationwide. Memorial ceremonies at 10 AM in American Police Hall of Fame and Museum, Miami, FL. See also: "National Police Week" (May 10–16). Sponsor: Natl Assn of Chiefs of Police. Est attendance: 1,000. For info: American Police Hall of Fame and Museum, 3801 Biscayne Blvd, Miami, FL 33137. Phone: (305) 573-0070. WWW: http://www.aphf.org

PORTER, KATHERINE ANNE: BIRTH ANNIVERSARY. May 15, 1890. American prose writer Katherine Anne Porter was born at Indian Creek, TX. Her one long novel, *Ship of Fools* (1962), is considered by some to be one of the greatest allegorical works in English. She won the Pulitzer Prize and the National Book Award in 1965 for *Collected Short Stories*. Porter died on Sept 18, 1980, at Silver Spring, MD.

SCHNITZLER, ARTHUR: BIRTH ANNIVERSARY. May 15. Austrian playwright, novelist and medical doctor, Arthur Schnitzler was born at Vienna, Austria, on May 15, 1862. Noted for his psychoanalytical examination of Viennese society. Schnitzler died Oct 21, 1931.

SEASPACE '98. May 15–17. Hyatt Regency Downtown Hotel, Houston, TX. Scuba diving symposium featuring seminars, photo and video courses, photo contest and exhibit, film festival, environmental awareness area, free intro to scuba and snorkel, hall of exhibits and receptions. Sponsor: Houston Underwater Club. For more info send SASE. Est attendance: 8,000. For info: Seaspace, PO Box 3753, Houston, TX 77253-3753. Phone: (713) 721-8533 or (713) 467-6675. Fax: (713) 721-8533. WWW: http://www.seaspace.ycg.org

SPACE MILESTONE: *FAITH 7* (US): 35th ANNIVERSARY. May 15, 1963. Launched with Major Gordon Leroy Cooper and orbited the Earth 22 times.

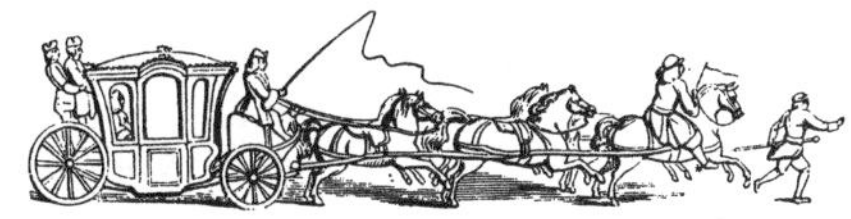

STAGECOACH DAYS. May 15–17. Marshall, TX. Arts and craft booths, Wild West shootouts, stagecoach rides, historic home tours, children's events, parade, Miss Loose Caboose Contest, live entertainment, cultural potpourri, lip synch contest, pet show, barbeque cook-off and Bull Plop contest. Annually, the third weekend in May. Est attendance: 30,000. For info: Pam Whisenant, Dir, Convention & Visitor Development, PO Box 520, Marshall, TX 75671. Phone: (903) 935-7868. Fax: (903) 935-9982. Email: cvd@internetwork.net.

SUGARLOAF'S SPRING SOMERSET CRAFT FESTIVAL. May 15–17. Garden State Exhibit Center, Somerset, NJ. This show, now in its 5th year, features 250 nationally recognized craft designers and fine artists displaying and selling their original creations. Craft demonstrations, children's entertainment, hourly gift certificate drawings and more! Est attendance: 15,000. For info: Sugarloaf Mountain Works, Inc, 200 Orchard Ridge Dr, #215, Gaithersburg, MD 20878. Phone: (800) 210-9900.

SYTTENDE MAI. May 15–17. Stoughton, WI. This is the longest-running Norwegian Independence Day festival held outside of Norway. Syttende Mai commemorates the signing of the Norwegian Constitution on May 17, 1814. The celebration is also an affirmation of a cultural heritage that remains strong after more than a century in the New World. Today, Stoughton honors its Norwegian roots with parades, folk dancing, arts and crafts, Norwegian costumes, rosemailing exhibitions, an ugly troll contest and Norwegian foods. For info: Wisconsin Dept of Tourism, Syttende Mai, PO Box 7976, Madison, WI 53707. Phone: (608) 873-7912. Email: tourism@laughlin.com.
WWW: http://tourism.state.wi.us

TOWN POINT JAZZ AND BLUES FESTIVAL. May 15–17. Norfolk, VA. Temperatures will rise a little higher than normal with the hottest jazz and blues sounds on the East Coast! Relax by the serene waterfront as jazz and blues masters alike gather on the Elizabeth River. Free and open to the public. For info: Marketing Director, Norfolk Festevents, Ltd, 120 W Main St, Norfolk, VA 23510. Phone: (757) 441-2345. Fax: (757) 441-5198.

UNITED NATIONS: INTERNATIONAL DAY OF FAMILIES. May 15. The general assembly (res 47/237) on Sept 20, 1993, voted this as an annual observance beginning in 1994.

VIKING FEST. May 15–17. Poulsbo, WA. Celebrating Poulsbo's Norwegian heritage, festival features Scandinavian luncheon, pancake breakfast, road race, food booths, entertainment, arts and crafts, outdoor concerts, flea market and more. Coincides with "Syttende Mai" (17th of May)—the Norwegian Constitution Day. Est attendance: 40,000. For info: Viking Fest, PO Box 1125, Poulsbo, WA 98370. Phone: (360) 779-4848. Fax: (360) 779-3115.

WILLAMETTE VALLEY FOLK FESTIVAL. May 15–17. Eugene, OR. 28th annual folk festival with multiple stages of musical performances, workshops and folk dancing. Sponsor: EMU Cultural Forum. Free. Est attendance: 10,000. For info: Debby Martin, Program Mgr, EMU Cultural Forum, University of Oregon, Eugene, OR 97403. Phone: (541) 346-4373. Fax: (541) 346-4400. WWW: http://darkwing.uoregon.edu/~cultural

May 1998

S	M	T	W	T	F	S
					1	2
3	4	5	6	7	8	9
10	11	12	13	14	15	16
17	18	19	20	21	22	23
24	25	26	27	28	29	30
31						

WILSON, ELLEN LOUISE AXSON: BIRTH ANNIVERSARY. May 15, 1860. First wife of Woodrow Wilson, 28th president of the US, born at Savannah, GA. Died Aug 6, 1914.

BIRTHDAYS TODAY

Anna Marie Alberghetti, 62, singer, actress (*Cinderfella, Carnival*), born Pesaro, Italy, May 15, 1936.
Madeleine Albright, 61, US Secretary of State (Clinton administration), born Prague, Czechoslovakia, May 15, 1937.
Eddy Arnold, 80, the "Tennessee Plowboy" singer ("Make the World Go Away"), born Henderson, TN, May 15, 1918.
Richard Avedon, 75, photographer, born New York, NY, May 15, 1923.
George Howard Brett, 45, baseball executive and former player, born Glen Dale, WV, May 15, 1953.
Joey Matthew Browner, 38, former football player, born Warren, OH, May 15, 1960.
David Cronenberg, 55, filmmaker, born Toronto, Ontario, Canada, May 15, 1943.
Brian Eno, 50, avant-garde musician, born Woodbridge, England, May 15, 1948.
Lee Horsley, 43, actor ("Nero Wolfe," "Matt Houston"), born Muleshoe, TN, May 15, 1955.
Jasper Johns, 68, artist (Neo-Dada Encaustic and collage composition *Flag*), born Augusta, GA, May 15, 1930.
Lainie Kazan, 56, singer, actress (*My Favorite Year, Beaches*), born New York, NY, May 15, 1942.
Trini Lopez, 61, actor, singer (*Marriage on the Rocks, The Dirty Dozen*), born Dallas, TX, May 15, 1937.
Emmitt Smith, 29, football player, born Pensacola, FL, May 15, 1969.
Paul Zindel, 62, writer (*The Effect of Gamma Rays on Man-in-the-Moon Marigolds*), born New York, NY, May 15, 1936.

MAY 16 — SATURDAY

Day 136 — 229 Remaining

★**ARMED FORCES DAY.** May 16. Presidential Proclamation 5983, of May 17, 1989, covers the third Saturday in May in all succeeding years. Originally proclaimed as "Army Day" for Apr 6, beginning in 1936 (S.Con.Res. 30 of Apr 2, 1936). S.Con.Res. 5 of Mar 16, 1937, requested annual Apr 6 issuance, which was done through 1949. Always the third Saturday in May since 1950. Traditionally issued once by each Administration.

ARMED FORCES DAY MILITARY VEHICLE RALLY AND SWAP MEET. May 16–17. Hawthorne, NV. Rally and swap meet of military vehicles from WW II to the present. For local info: Mineral County Chamber of Commerce, PO Box 1635, Hawthorne, NV 89415. Phone: (702) 945-5896. Fax: (702) 945-1257.

ARTS IN THE PARK. May 16. Demopolis, AL. Annual arts and crafts festival held in downtown Confederate Park. Vendors display for sale hand made wares, art exhibits, entertainment, food and children's activities. Fun for all ages. 8 AM to 4 PM. Free admission. Est attendance: 8,000. For info: Jane Gross, Demopolis Chamber of Commerce, PO Box 667, Demopolis, AL 36732. Phone: (334) 289-0270. Fax: (334) 289-1382.

ATWOOD EARLY ROD RUN. May 16–17. Atwood, KS. Classic car show with several states represented. Includes downtown festival, remote-control car races, drag races, barbecue and '50s dance. Est attendance: 1,500. For info: Atwood Ambassadors, 410 N 5th, PO Box 341, Atwood, KS 67730. Phone: (913) 626-3144.

AUTOMOTION '98. May 16–17. Wisconsin Dells, WI. 800 cars on display, including street machines, classics and antiques. Event includes swap meet, live entertainment, "Car Cruise" and other activities. Est attendance: 15,000. For info: Wisc Dells Visitor and Conv Bureau, Box 390, Wisconsin Dells, WI 53965. Phone: (800) 223-3557. Email: wisdells@midplains.net.
WWW: http://www.wisdells.com

BATTLE OF CHAMPION'S HILL: ANNIVERSARY. May 16, 1863. After a standoff of nearly a year around the strategic Mississippi River city of Vicksburg, MS, Union forces under Ulysses S. Grant defeated Southern forces under General John Pemberton at Champion's Hill, MS, on this date. Pemberton's forces withdrew into Vicksburg, and the seige of Vicksburg began on May 19.

BEVERLY HILLS: AFFAIRE IN THE GARDENS. May 16–17 (also Oct 17–18). Beverly Gardens Park at Rodeo Drive, Beverly Hills, CA. To foster an appreciation of arts in the community. Juried show; only fine arts and crafts considered. Garden setting. Biannually, the third weekends in May and October. Est attendance: 50,000. For info: Brad Meyerowitz, Sr Rec Supr, Beverly Hills Recreation and Parks Dept, 8400 Gregory Way, Beverly Hills, CA 90211. Phone: (310) 550-4628. Fax: (310) 659-1620.

BIOGRAPHERS DAY. May 16. Anniversary of the meeting, in London, England, on May 16, 1763, of James Boswell and Samuel Johnson, beginning history's most famous biographer-biographee relationship. Boswell's *Journal of a Tour to the Hebrides* (1785) and his *Life of Samuel Johnson* (1791) are regarded as models of biographical writing. Thus, this day is recommended as one on which to start reading or writing a biography.

BUTLER ISSUES "WOMAN ORDER": ANNIVERSARY. May 16, 1862. General Benjamin Butler, military governor of New Orleans, issued what became known as the "Woman Order." The text of General Order Number 28 read, in part, "As the officers and soldiers of the United States have been subjected to repeated insults from women (calling themselves ladies) of New Orleans . . . when any female shall . . . show contempt for the United States, she shall be regarded as a woman of the town plying her avocation." This order typified Butler's attitude toward the captured city and its populace and, along with other controversial acts as military governor, set the stage for his dismissal as military governor in December of 1862.

CALIFORNIA STRAWBERRY FESTIVAL. May 16–17. Strawberry Meadows of College Park, Oxnard, CA. This weekend event features a variety of gourmet strawberry foods, live musical entertainment, a 200-booth juried arts and crafts show. Strawberryland for children and the Strawberry Shortcake Eating Competition. Annually, the third weekend in May. Est attendance: 80,000. For info: Bill Garlock, Festival Mgr, 1621 Pacific Ave, #127, Oxnard, CA 93033. Phone: (805) 385-7578.

CANADA: UPPER CANADA VILLAGE. May 16–Oct 12. Morrisburg, Ontario (9:30–5 daily). One of Canada's premiere attractions. Visitors enter the world of the 1860s. Costumed interpreters bring history to life in this fully operational rural community as they perform period activities, entertain as townsfolk or as tradesmen apply their skills in restored buildings ranging from homes to trade shops. Many special events and programs offered throughout the season. Est attendance: 200,000. For info: Upper Canada Village, Parks of the St. Lawrence, RR 1, Morrisburg, Ont, Canada K0C 1X0. Phone: (800) 437-2233 or (613) 543-3704.

CELEBRATION OF QUILTS XII. May 16–17. Burton, OH. Quilting guilds and shops set up in Century Village homes to demonstrate a variety of quilting techniques. Antique, contemporary and Amish quilts and quilting supplies. Lectures; museum quilts on display. Est attendance: 3,200. For info: Joan Campbell, Sheauga Quilters, PO Box 462, Chardon, OH 44024. Phone: (216) 286-3763.

CIVIL WAR EVENT. May 16–17. Hammonasset State Park, Madison, CT. 8th annual living history encampment with fun for the whole family. Est attendance: 10,000. For info: C. Quist, 233 Main St, Deep River, CT 06417. Phone: (860) 526-4993.

A DAY IN OLD NEW CASTLE. May 16. New Castle, DE. Many of the historic homes, gardens and buildings of New Castle exhibit rare and beautiful pieces of colonial furniture and charming specimens of the builder's art. Annually, the third Saturday in May. Est attendance: 5,000. For info: A Day in Old New Castle, Box 166, New Castle, DE 19720. Phone: (302) 328-2413.

DO DAH DAY. May 16. Birmingham, AL. Free music, arts and crafts festival and more to raise funds for the Greater Birmingham Humane Society and the Metro Humane Shelter. A mile-long parade kicks off the event. Est attendance: 20,000. For info: Betsy Stout-Jones, Do Dah Day Committee, 900 Essex Rd, Birmingham, AL 35222. Phone: (205) 595-3771. Fax: (205) 595-3464. Email: dodah1998@aol.com.

DON MACLEOD COOKOUT (WITH ELK ANTLER AUCTION). May 16. Town Square, Jackson, WY. Hot barbecue beef, hot dogs and baked goods in conjunction with the annual Elk Antler Auction. Boy Scouts harvest the dropped antlers and the proceeds from the auction benefit the BSA and the Natl Elk Refuge. Annually, the third Saturday in May. Est attendance: 1,000. For info: Jackson Hole Historical Society & Museum, Box 1005, Jackson, WY 83001. Phone: (307) 733-9605. Fax: (307) 739-9019.

EARTH DAY COMMUNITY FESTIVAL. May 16–17. St. Louis, MO. An educational event with hundreds of exhibitors related to environmental issues and their solutions. Est attendance: 50,000. For info: Jerry Klamon, Alliance for a Livable World, PO Box 63350, St Louis, MO 63163. Phone: (314) 776-4442. Email: earthdystl@aol.com.

EIGHTEENTH-CENTURY SPRING MARKET FAIR. May 16–17 (also July 18–19 and Oct 17–18). McLean, VA. Learn 18th-century crafts, music and games. Period wares for sale. Est attendance: 3,000. For info: Publicist, Claude Moore Colonial Farm at Turkey Run, 6310 Georgetown Pike, McLean, VA 22101. Phone: (703) 442-7557. Fax: (703) 442-0714.

FIRST ACADEMY AWARDS: ANNIVERSARY. May 16, 1929. About 270 people attended a dinner at the Hollywood Roosevelt Hotel at which the first Academy Awards were given in 12 categories. The silent film *Wings* won Best Picture. A committee of only 20 members selected the winners that year. By the third year, the entire membership of the Academy voted.

FISHING HAS NO BOUNDARIES—MONTICELLO. May 16–17. Freeman Lake, Monticello, IN. A new two-day event for disabled persons to experience fishing on the lake. Any disability, sex, age, race, etc, are eligible. Expected attendance will be 50 participants and 130 volunteers. For info: FHNB, 7805 N Harrison, PO Box 325, Battleground, IN 47920. Phone: (765) 567-2567.

FONDA, HENRY: BIRTH ANNIVERSARY. May 16, 1905. American stage and screen actor, Motion Picture Academy Award winner, born Henry Jaynes Fonda at Grand Island, NE. Began his acting career at the Omaha (NE) Playhouse. Fonda died at Los Angeles, CA, Aug 12, 1982.

GETTYSBURG OUTDOOR ANTIQUE SHOW. May 16. Gettysburg, PA. Features 180 dealers in antiques with exhibits and displays. Annually, the third Saturday in May. Est attendance: 25,000. For info: Gettysburg Conv and Visitors Bureau, 35 Carlisle St, Gettysburg, PA 17325-1899. Phone: (717) 334-6274. Fax: (717) 334-1166. WWW: http://www.gettysburg.com

GWINNETT, BUTTON: DEATH ANNIVERSARY. May 16, 1777. Signer of the Declaration of Independence, born at Down Hatherley, Gloucestershire, England, about 1735 (exact date unknown). Died following a duel, May 16, 1777.

HUMANATEE/ST. MARKS FESTIVAL. May 16. San Marcos de Apalache State Historic Site, St. Marks, FL. Celebrate and welcome manatees back to St. Marks and Wakulla Rivers. Food, displays, music, walk and much more. Annually, the third Saturday in May. Est attendance: 1,500. For info: Tom King, HuManatee, PO Box 52, St. Marks, FL 32355. Phone: (904) 926-1215 or San Marcos Fort at (904) 925-6216.

JOHNSON, MARV: 5th DEATH ANNIVERSARY. May 16, 1993. Soul music pioneer. Born at Detroit, MI, and died on May 16, 1993, at Columbia, SC.

LEWIS AND CLARK RENDEZVOUS. May 16–17. St. Charles, MO. Authentic reenactment of Lewis and Clark's encampment in 1804 prior to embarking on the exploration of the Louisiana Purchase. Activities include parades with fife and drum corps, court martial reenactment, black powder shoot, church service and 19th-century crafts, food and demonstrations. Annually, the third weekend in May. Est attendance: 25,000. For info: St. Charles Conv and Visitors Bureau, 230 S Main, St. Charles, MO 63301. Phone: (800) 366-2427 or (314) 946-7776. WWW: http://www.st-charles.mo.us

LIBERACE: BIRTH ANNIVERSARY. May 16, 1919. Wladziu Valentino Liberace, concert pianist who began with a piano, a candelabra, a brother named George and a huge engaging smile, threw in extravagant clothes and jewels and became a Las Vegas headliner and the winner of two Emmy Awards, six gold albums and two stars on the Hollywood Walk of Fame. Liberace was born at West Allis, WI; he died Feb 4, 1987, at Palm Springs, CA.

LIBERACE'S 79th BIRTHDAY CELEBRATION. May 16. The Liberace Museum, Las Vegas, NV. Featuring a Liberace Impersonator Competition. To celebrate Liberace's birthday, the museum will share a giant piano-shaped birthday cake with museum guests. And Mr Showmanship's most inspired fans will have the opportunity to demonstrate their talent, humor and passion for fashion in a competition. Contestants vying for the title of World's Greatest Liberace Impersonator 1998 are invited to use the piano in their presentations and/or sing one of Liberace's well-known songs or offer their best rendition of one of Liberace's trademark lines. Impersonators will be judged on costuming, showmanship and material selection. Winners will receive a Rhinestone Candelabra trophy. For info: Jamie G. James, The James Agency, 3630 Coldwater Canyon Ave, Studio City, CA 91604. Phone: (818) 508-4902. Fax: (818) 508-0562. Email: JamesAgy@aol.com.

LIBERTY SPRING ON THE SQUARE FESTIVAL. May 16. Liberty, MO. Festival highlights farmers market, handcrafts, arts and antiques booths and exhibits, entertainment, food, children's activities and a re-enactment of the town's first daylight bank robbery. Est attendance: 10,000. For info: Spring on the Square Festival, PO Box 159, Liberty, MO 64068. Phone: (816) 792-6033. Fax: (816) 792-6091.

MAIFEST. May 16–17. Hermann, MO. A German celebration of spring. Winery tours and wine tasting, stage show, volksplatz (craft area), parade, museum tours, children's activities, great German food, beer and wine gardens and German bands and dancing. Annually, the third weekend of May. Est attendance: 20,000. For info: Visitor Info Center, Hermann Tourism Group, 306 Market St, P.O. Box 104, Hermann, MO 65041. Phone: (800) 932-8687. Fax: (573) 486-5363.

May 1998

S	M	T	W	T	F	S
					1	2
3	4	5	6	7	8	9
10	11	12	13	14	15	16
17	18	19	20	21	22	23
24	25	26	27	28	29	30
31						

MARTIN, BILLY: 70th BIRTH ANNIVERSARY. May 16, 1928. Baseball player and manager. Born at Berkeley, CA. Billy Martin's baseball career included managerial stints with five major league teams: the New York Yankees, Minnesota Twins, Detroit Tigers, Texas Rangers and the Oakland Athletics. After a successful playing career, he compiled a record of 1,258 victories to 1,018 losses in his 16 seasons as a manager. His combative and fiery style both on and off the field kept him in the headlines, and he will long be remembered for his on-again/off-again relationship with Yankees' owner George Steinbrenner, for whom he managed the Yankees five different times. Martin died in an auto accident on Dec 25, 1989.

MEET THE ARTISANS AND ARTISANS SHOW. May 16–17 (also Oct 3–4). Milford Green, CT. 36th annual. More than 200 juried, award-winning artists and crafters from throughout the nation. For info: Meet the Artisans & Artisans Show, (203) 874-5672 or Greater New Haven Conv & Visitors Bureau, One Long Wharf Dr, New Haven, CT 06511. Phone: (203) 777-8550 or (800) 332-STAY. Fax: (203) 782-7755.

MIFFLIN-JUNIATA ARTS FESTIVAL. May 16–17. Lewistown Rec Park, Lewistown, PA. 75 juried arts and craft vendors; professional and amateur performances; free children's crafts and special exhibits. Admission free. Est attendance: 12,000. For info: Jenny Landis, Co-Chair, c/o Mifflin-Juniata Arts Council, PO Box 1126, Lewistown, PA 17044. Phone: (717) 248-8711. Email: jenny @acsworld.net.

MORTON, LEVI PARSONS: BIRTH ANNIVERSARY. May 16, 1824. Twenty-second vice president of the US (1889–93) born at Shoreham, VT. Died at Rhinebeck, NY, May 16, 1920.

NATIONAL RESTAURANT ASSOCIATION: RESTAURANT, HOTEL, MOTEL SHOW. May 16–May 20. McCormick Place, Chicago, IL. Est attendance: 100,000. For info: Richard Gaven, National Restaurant Association, 150 N Michigan Ave, Ste 2000, Chicago, IL 60601. Phone: (312) 853-2525. Fax: (312) 853-2548.

NATIONAL SAFE BOATING WEEK. May 16–24. Brings boating safety to the public's attention, decreases the number of boating fatalities and makes the waterways safer for all boaters. Sponsor: US Coast Guard. For info: Jo Calkin, Commandant (G-OPB-2), US Coast Guard, 2100 Second St SW, Washington, DC 20593. Phone: (800) 368-5647.

★**NATIONAL SAFE BOATING WEEK.** May 16-22. Presidential Proclamation during May since 1995. From 1958 through 1977, issued for a week including July 4 (PL85–445 of June 4, 1958). From 1981 through 1994, issued for the first week in June (PL96–376 of Oct 3, 1980). Not issued from 1978 through 1980.

NATIONAL STATIONERY SHOW. May 16–19. Javits Center, New York, NY. Sponsored by the Greeting Card Association. For info: George Little Management, 10 Bank St, White Plains, NY 10606. Phone: (914) 421-3200.

PEABODY, ELIZABETH PALMER: BIRTH ANNIVERSARY. May 16, 1804. Born at Billerica, MA, Peabody was an innovative educator, author and publisher. She opened her first school in Lancaster, MA, when only 16, her second two years later in Boston. In 1839 Peabody opened a bookstore that quickly became the intellectuals' hangout. With her own printing press Peabody became the first woman publisher in Boston and possibly the US. She published three of her brother-in-law Nathaniel Hawthorne's earliest books. For two years she published and wrote for *The Dial*, the literary magazine and voice of the Transcendental movement. Peabody's enduring accomplishment was the establishment of the first kindergarten in the US, in 1860 in Boston. She promoted the concept vigorously, even creating a magazine, *Kindergarten Messenger*, in 1873. Died Jan 3, 1894, at Jamaica Plain, MA.

"PEC THING." May 16–17 (also Sept 19–20). Pecatonica, IL. Semi-annual antique show with more than 400 exhibitors. Est attendance: 15,000. For info: Lisa Rosenkrans, Winnebago Country Fair Assn, PO Box K, Pecatonica, IL 61063-0670. Phone: (815) 239-1641. Fax: (815) 239-1653.

POLE, PEDAL, PADDLE. May 16. Bend, OR. Five-stage iron-man-type race for singles, teams and couples; includes downhill skiing, nordic skiing, biking, canoeing and running. Annually, the third Saturday in May. Sponsors: US Bank, Pepsi, Bud Light, Teva, Cellular One, Z21TV. Est attendance: 12,000. For info: Mt Bachelor Ski Education Foundation, PO Box 388, Bend, OR 97709. Phone: (541) 388-0002. Fax: (541) 388-7848. Email: mbsef@bendnet.com. WWW: http://www.bendnet.com/ppp

PREAKNESS STAKES. May 16. Pimlico Race Course, Baltimore, MD. Running of the Preakness Stakes, middle jewel in the Triple Crown, was inaugurated in 1873. Annually, the third Saturday in May—two Saturdays after the Kentucky Derby—and followed, three Saturdays later, by the Belmont Stakes. Est attendance: 100,000. For info: Maryland Jockey Club, Pimlico Race Course, Baltimore, MD 21215. Phone: (410) 542-9400. WWW: http://www.marylandracing.com

RAF BOMBS RUHR DAMS: 55th ANNIVERSARY. May 16–17, 1943. Over these two days, Royal Air Force Lancasters attacked three dams in the German Ruhr Valley. They dropped 4.5 ton bombs designed specifically for this mission. The Mohne and the Eder (the largest dam in Europe at the time) were both damaged. These two dams provided drinking water for four million people and supplied 75% of the electrical power for industry. Widespread flooding and many deaths resulted.

RHUBARB FESTIVAL. May 16. Intercourse, PA. A light-hearted celebration honoring rhubarb, which grows abundantly in the Pennsylvania Dutch country. Food, games and contests all featuring rhubarb—recipe contest, rhubarb pie throw, rhubarb pick-up sticks and more—plus entertainment. Est attendance: 10,000. For info: Mel Hauser, Kitchen Kettle Village, Box 380, Intercourse, PA 17534. Phone: (800) 732-3538 or (717) 768-8261.

ROAD CHURCH MISSIONARY FAIR. May 16. Road Congregational Church, Stonington, CT. Bake sale, crafts, white elephants and more. Homemade food available at noon. For info: Libby Kennedy, 21 Roosevelt Ave, Mystic, CT 06355. Phone: (860) 536-1514.

SANTA FE TRAIL ANTIQUE MARKET. May 16–17. Arrow Rock, MO. 50–75 antique merchants, some dressed in period costumes, line the streets of this 19th-century village and sell their wares. Performances by the "sacred harp" singers and the Missouri Cloggers. Est attendance: 3,000. For info: Betty Kusgen, "Rose Hill" Antiques, 21495 Hwy 41, Blackwater, MO 65322. Phone: (816) 846-3031.

SEND A KID TO KAMP RADIOTHON. May 16. Masterson Station Park, Lexington, KY. Annually, the third Saturday in May since 1988. Est attendance: 15,000. For info: Dennis Smith, 770 AM, WCGW, Lexington Green, Ste 600, 3191 Nicholasville, Lexington, KY 40503. Phone: (606) 245-1900. Fax: (606) 245-1806. Email: MortensonB@aol.com.

UNIVERSAL SOLDIERS/PIONEER DAYS. May 16–17 (tentative). Raccoon State Park, Hookstown, PA. 8th annual. A living history encampment presenting units from all the wars. Also musical entertainment and crafts. For info: (412) 899-2200 or Beaver County Tourist Promotion Agency, 215 B Ninth St, Monaca, PA 15061-2028. Phone: (412) 728-0212. Fax: (412) 728-0456.

WASHINGTON FINE ART FAIR AND WINEFEST. May 16–18. Rennick Riverfront, Washington, MO. More than 50 of the Midwest's best fine artists displaying original drawings, paintings, and sculptures in conjunction with twelve of mid-Missouri's wineries presenting more than 50 wines. For info: (314) 239-1743 or Missouri Division of Tourism, Truman State Office Bldg, PO Box 1055, Jefferson City, MO 65102. Phone: (573) 751-4133. Fax: (573) 751-5160.

WEAR PURPLE FOR PEACE DAY: THE FIRST INTERGLACTICAL [SIC] HOLIDAY. May 16. The Moderns theorize that people of space will not communicate with people of Earth because of our violent nature. This day is an attempt to convey the idea to the people of space that we, the people of Earth, are making an attempt to attain more peace on our planet. The Moderns believe this is essential to making contact with the people of space. For info: Jon E. Mod, The Moderns, 4915 8th Ave, Kenosha, WI 53140. Phone: (414) 653-0230.

WEBSTER COUNTY WOODCHOPPING FESTIVAL (WITH WOODCHOPPING AND TURKEY-CALLING CHAMPIONSHIPS). May 16–24. Webster Springs, WV. South Eastern US World Championship Woodchopping Contest and State Championship Turkey-Calling Contest. Est attendance: 10,000. For info: Woodchopping Festival Committee, PO Box 227, Webster Springs, WV 26288. Phone: (304) 847-7666. Fax: (304) 847-5117.

WRIGHT PLUS. May 16. Oak Park, IL. The Frank Lloyd Wright Home and Studio Foundation's annual housewalk features guided tours of the interiors of 10 buildings designed by Frank Lloyd Wright and his architectural contemporaries, including Unity Temple and Wright's own home and studio. Reservations are required. Tickets limited. (Tickets available Mar 1.) Annually, third Saturday in May. Est attendance: 3,000. For info: Director of Public Relations, Frank Lloyd Wright Home and Studio, 951 Chicago Ave, Oak Park, IL 60302. Phone: (708) 848-1976 or (708) 848-9518. Fax: (708) 848-1248.

YOU GOTTA HAVE PARK. May 16–17. Prospect Park, Brooklyn, NY. This annual weekend-long celebration of Brooklyn's Prospect Park is dedicated to cleaning, greening and bringing the Park's neighbors and volunteers together. Annually, the third weekend in May. Est attendance: 150,000. For info: Prospect Park Alliance, Public Info Office, External Affairs, Litchfield Villa, 5 Prospect Park W, Brooklyn, NY 11215. Phone: (718) 965-8954 or (718) 965-8951. Fax: (718) 965-8972.
Email: prospect1@juno.com.
WWW: http://www.prospectpark.org

☆ ☆ ☆

BIRTHDAYS TODAY

Pierce Brosnan, 46, actor ("Remington Steele," James Bond in *GoldenEye*), born County Meath, Ireland, May 16, 1952.

Dan Coats, 55, US Senator (R, Indiana), born Jackson, MI, May 16, 1943.

Tracey Gold, 29, actress ("Shirley," "Goodnight Beantown," "Growing Pains"), born New York, NY, May 16, 1969.

James B. Hunt, Jr, 61, Governor of North Carolina (D), born Greensboro, NC, May 16, 1937.

Janet Jackson, 32, singer ("What Have You Done for Me Lately"), actress ("Fame"), born Gary, IN, May 16, 1966.

Olga Korbut, 43, Olympic gold medal gymnast, born Grodno, USSR, May 16, 1955.

John Scott (Jack) Morris, 43, former baseball player, born St. Paul, MN, May 16, 1955.
Gabriela Sabatini, 28, tennis player, born Buenos Aires, Argentina, May 16, 1970.
John Thomas Salley, 34, basketball player, born New York, NY, May 16, 1964.
Joan (Benoit) Samuelson, 41, Olympic gold medal runner, born Cape Elizabeth, ME, May 16, 1957.
Bill Smitrovich, 51, actor ("Crime Story," *Splash, Manhunter*), born Bridgeport, CT, May 16, 1947.
Tori Spelling, 25, actress ("Beverly Hills 90210"), born Beverly Hills, CA, May 16, 1973.
Studs Terkel (Louis Terkel), 86, author, journalist (*Hard Times, Working*), born New York, NY, May 16, 1912.
Lowell P. Weicker, Jr, 67, former Governor of Connecticut (CP), born Paris, France, May 16, 1931.
Debra Winger, 43, actress (*Terms of Endearment, Shadowlands*), born Columbus, OH, May 16, 1955.
Mare Winningham, 39, actress (*The Thornbirds*), born Phoenix, AZ, May 16, 1959.

MAY 17 — SUNDAY

Day 137 — 228 Remaining

BELL, JAMES (COOL PAPA): 95th BIRTH ANNIVERSARY. May 17, 1903. Negro League baseball player James "Cool Papa" Bell was born at Starkville, MS. He played 25 seasons from 1922 to 1946 (one year before Jackie Robinson broke the "color barrier" in major league baseball) with a career average of .338. Regarded as the fastest man ever to play the game—he could round the bases in 13 seconds—he was inducted into the Baseball Hall of Fame in 1974. Bell died on Mar 7, 1991, at St. Louis, MO.

BLESSING OF THE BIKES. May 17. Litchfield, CT. Mass and blessing of motorcycles at the Grotto of Our Lady of Lourdes Shrine. Annually, the third Sunday in May. For info: Grotto of Our Lady of Lourdes Shrine, PO Box 667, Litchfield, CT 06759. Phone: (860) 567-1041.

BROWN v BOARD OF EDUCATION DECISION: ANNIVERSARY. May 17, 1954. The US Supreme Court ruled unanimously that segregation of public schools "solely on the basis of race" denied black children "equal educational opportunity" even though "physical facilities and other 'tangible' factors may have been equal. Separate educational facilities are inherently unequal." The case was argued before the Court by Thurgood Marshall, who would go on to become the first black appointed to the Supreme Court.

CAPE MAY MUSIC FESTIVAL. May 17–June 28. Cape May, NJ. A dazzling array of sounds and styles—from Vivaldi to Stravinski, from the Renaissance to the Jazz Era, from ethnic folk to world music and more. The world's finest chamber ensembles and special guest artists perform in the elegant Victorian setting of Cape May. Est attendance: 5,000. For info: Mid-Atlantic Center for the Arts, PO Box 340, Cape May, NJ 08204. Phone: (800) 275-4278 or 609-884-5404.
WWW: http://www.beachcomber.com/capemay/mac.html

EXAMINER BAY TO BREAKERS RACE. May 17. San Francisco, CA. Largest footrace in the world attracts 80,000 runners each year, from world-class athletes to fun runners; post-race festival, live concert, food and beverages. Annually, the third Sunday in May. Est attendance: 200,000. For info: *Examiner* Bay to Breakers, PO Box 429200, San Francisco, CA 94142. Phone: (415) 808-5000, ext 2222.

May 1998

S	M	T	W	T	F	S
					1	2
3	4	5	6	7	8	9
10	11	12	13	14	15	16
17	18	19	20	21	22	23
24	25	26	27	28	29	30
31						

FIRST KENTUCKY DERBY: ANNIVERSARY. May 17, 1875. The first running of the Kentucky Derby took place at Churchill Downs, Louisville, KY. Jockey Oliver Lewis rode the horse Aristides to a winning time of 2:37.25.

HOPA ART FESTIVAL. May 17. Wisconsin Rapids, WI. 32nd annual festival featuring fine art by 60 Midwest artists. Music, refreshments, prizes and children's activities. Admission $1 with proceeds supporting Artists-In-Education and scholarships. Est attendance: 2,500. For info: Mary Beth Rokus, Arts Council of South Wood County, PO Box 818, Wisconsin Rapids, WI 54495. Phone: (715) 421-4552. Fax: (715) 422-3882.

INTERNATIONAL AIDS CANDLELIGHT MEMORIAL AND MOBILIZATION. May 17. The world's largest grassroots AIDS event has four goals: to commemorate those who have died of AIDS, to show support for those living with HIV/AIDS, and to raise awareness of the disease's impact and of the opportunities to respond to HIV/AIDS. The 15th annual Memorial and Mobilization will be observed in more than 45 nations. For info: Mobilization Against AIDS, 584-B Castro St, San Francisco, CA 94114-1465. Phone: (415) 863-4676. Fax: (415) 863-4740. Email: mobilization@out.org.

JENNER, EDWARD: BIRTH ANNIVERSARY. May 17, 1749. English physician, born at Berkeley, England. He was the first to establish a scientific basis for vaccination with his work on smallpox. Jenner died at Berkeley, England, Jan 26, 1823.

NATIONAL EMERGENCY MEDICAL SERVICES (EMS) WEEK. May 17–23. Honoring EMS providers nationwide who provide life-saving care in a multitude of circumstances. Also a time for the public to learn about injury prevention, safety awareness and emergency preparedness. For info: American College of Emergency Physicians, 1111 19th St NW, Ste 650, Washington, DC 20036-3603. Phone: (800) 320-0610, ext 3006.

NEW YORK STOCK EXCHANGE ESTABLISHED: ANNIVERSARY. May 17. On May 17, 1792, some two dozen merchants and brokers agreed to establish what is now known as the New York Stock Exchange. In fair weather they operated under a buttonwood tree on Wall Street, in New York, NY. In bad weather they moved to the shelter of a coffeehouse to conduct their business.

NORWAY: CONSTITUTION DAY OR INDEPENDENCE DAY. May 17. National holiday. Constitution signed and Norway separated from Denmark on this day, 1814. Parades and children's festivities.

PHILIPPINES: FERTILITY RITES. May 17–19. Obando, Bulacan. A triple religious fete in honor of San Pascual, Santa Clara and the Virgin of Salambao marked by dancing of childless couples.

RESEARCH/STUDY TEAM ON NONVIOLENT LARGE SYSTEMS CHANGE ANNUAL MEETING. May 17–19. Asiloman Conference Center, Pacific Grove, CA. Discussions and

recommendations on better ways of solving problems without violence. We bring people from Eastern Europe and the Middle East and South Africa and other areas in conflict to the conferences. Presentations are invited. Registration is free. Est attendance: 60. For info: Dr. Donald W. Cole, RODC, The Org Dev Institute, 11234 Walnut Ridge Rd, Chesterland, OH 44026. Phone: (216) 729-7419 or (216) 461-4333. Fax: (216) 729-9319.
Email: DonWCole@aol.com.
WWW: http://members.aol.com/odinst

ROGATION SUNDAY. May 17. The fifth Sunday after Easter is the beginning of Rogationtide (Rogation Sunday and the following three days before Ascension Day). Rogation Day rituals date from the fifth century.

RUNNING AND FITNESS WEEK. May 17–23. Educational campaign designed to introduce more Americans to the pleasures and benefits of participating in a regular exercise program. For info: Barbara Baldwin, American Running and Fitness Assn, 4405 East-West Hwy, Ste 405, Bethesda, MD 20814. Phone: (800) 776-2732. Fax: (301) 913-9520.

RURAL LIFE SUNDAY OR SOIL STEWARDSHIP SUNDAY. May 17. With an increase in ecological and environmental concerns, Rural Life Sunday emphasizes the concept that Earth belongs to God, who has granted humanity the use of it, along with the responsibility of caring for it wisely. At the suggestion of the Intl Assn of Agricultural Missions, Rural Life Sunday was first observed in 1929, under plans adopted by the Home Missions Council of North America and the Federal Council of Churches. The day is observed annually by churches of many Christian denominations and includes pulpit exchanges by rural and urban pastors. Under the auspices of the Natl Assn of Soil and Water Conservation Districts, the week beginning with Rural Life Sunday is now widely observed as Soil Stewardship Week, with the Sunday itself alternatively termed Soil Stewardship Sunday. As environmental issues loom larger, observances now feature calls for individual action on the problems of air, water and noise pollution, in addition to problems associated with the conservation of open spaces. Traditionally, Rural Life Sunday is the Sunday preceding Ascension Day (Rogation Sunday).

SAINT LOUIS WALK OF FAME INDUCTION CEREMONY. May 17. St. Louis, MO. Outdoor free-admission ceremony with ragtime band. Famous St. Louisans are honored. Nonprofit organization provides a showcase for the cultural heritage of St. Louis. In addition to stars in the sidewalks are plaques describing the achievements and contributions each creative St. Louisan made to our country's culture (Chuck Berry, Miles Davis, T.S. Eliot, Betty Grable, Vincent Price, Tennessee Williams, Scott Joplin, Charles Lindbergh, Buddy Ebsen, etc). Annually, the third Sunday in May. Est attendance: 1,200. For info: Joe Edwards, Chair, St. Louis Walk of Fame, 6504 Delmar, St. Louis, MO 63130. Phone: (314) 727-0110.

SANTA CRUZ BEACH BOARDWALK GIANT DIPPER: ANNIVERSARY. May 17. The Giant Dipper roller coaster opened at Santa Cruz Beach Boardwalk in Santa Cruz, CA, on May 17, 1924, and quickly became the park's most popular ride. The Dipper was built by Arthur Looff, the son of master carousel-horse carver Charles I.D. Looff. In June of 1987, the Giant Dipper and the Looff carousel were designated National Historic Landmarks by the US National Park Service.

SHEEP SHEARING FESTIVAL. May 17. North Andover, MA. Festival takes place on the North Andover Common and features sheep shearing, sheepdog demonstrations, crafts fair, live music, rides, games and food booths. Est attendance: 10,000. For info: American Field Services Intercultural Program, c/o Connie Chabot, 62 Kingston St, North Andover, MA 01845. Phone: (508) 689-8014. Email: lchabot@mdc.net.

UNITED NATIONS: WORLD TELECOMMUNICATION DAY. May 17. A day to draw attention to the necessity and importance of further development of telecommunications in the global community. Info from: United Nations, Dept of Public Info, New York, NY 10017.

USS *STARK* ATTACKED: ANNIVERSARY. May 17, 1987. The US Navy's guided missile frigate *Stark*, sailing off the Iranian coast in the Persian Gulf, was struck and set afire by two Exocet sea-skimming missiles fired from an Iraqi warplane at 2:10 PM, EDT, May 17, 1987. Also struck was a Cypriot flag tanker. At least 28 American naval personnel were killed. Only hours earlier a Soviet oil tanker in the Gulf had struck a mine.

★**WORLD TRADE WEEK.** May 17–23. Presidential Proclamation has been issued each year since 1948 for the third week of May with three exceptions: 1949, 1955 and 1966.

YOUTH AGAINST VIOLENCE. May 17. Westboro, MA. Youth raising awareness about domestic violence through education and an annual Walk Against Violence. Annually, the third Sunday in May. Est attendance: 100. For info: Westboro Youth & Family Services, Explorer Post 24, Town Hall, 34 W Main St, Westboro, MA 01581. Phone: (508) 366-3090. Fax: (508) 366-3047.

BIRTHDAYS TODAY

Mia Hamm, 26, soccer player for US National Soccer Team, born Selma, AL, May 17, 1972.

Dennis Hopper, 62, actor (*Easy Rider, Giant, Rebel Without a Cause*), born Dodge City, KS, May 17, 1936.

Christian Lacroix, 48, French couturier, born Arles, France, May 17, 1950.

Ray Charles ("Sugar Ray") Leonard, 42, former boxer, born Washington, DC, May 17, 1956.

Daniel Ricardo (Danny) Manning, 32, basketball player, born Hattiesburg, MS, May 17, 1966.

E. Benjamin Nelson, 57, Governor of Nebraska (D), born McCook, NE, May 17, 1941.

Maureen O'Sullivan, 87, actress (Jane in the Tarzan films; *Hannah and Her Sisters*), born Voyle, Ireland, May 17, 1911.

Bill Paxton, 43, actor (*Aliens, One False Move, Twister*), born Fort Worth, TX, May 17, 1955.

Trent Reznor, 33, rock singer for Nine Inch Nails, born Mercer, PA, May 17, 1965.

Bob Saget, 42, actor ("Full House"), host ("America's Funniest Home Videos"), born Philadelphia, PA, May 17, 1956.

MAY 18 — MONDAY

Day 138 — 227 Remaining

BIRTHDAY OF MOTHER'S WHISTLER. May 18. To celebrate the birthday of the world's most melodious human whistler, who cannot only duplicate the songs of rare, exotic and extinct birds, but in many cases, do so through his nose. For info: Mother's Whistler, Warfield and Twin Silo Lanes, Huntingdon Valley, PA 19006. Phone: (215) 947-7007.

BUCKLE UP AMERICA! WEEK. May 18–25. An observance to remind Americans of the importance of wearing seat belts. For info: Office of Occupant Protection, National Highway Safety Administration, 400 Seventh St SW, Washington, DC 20590. Phone: (202) 366-9550.

CANADA: VICTORIA DAY. May 18. Commemorates the birth of Queen Victoria on May 24, 1819. Observed annually on the first Monday preceding May 25.

CAPRA, FRANK: BIRTH ANNIVERSARY. May 18, 1897. The Academy Award–winning director whose movies were suffused with affectionate portrayals of the common man and the strengths and foibles of American democracy. Capra was born at Palermo, Sicily. He bluffed his way into silent movies in 1922 and, despite total ignorance of movie making, directed and produced a profitable one-reeler. He was the first to win three directorial Oscars—for *It Happened One Night* (1934), *Mr Deeds Goes to Town* (1936) and *You Can't Take It with You* (1938). The motion picture academy voted the first and third of these as best picture. Capra said his favorite of the films he made was *It's a Wonderful Life* (1946). He died Sept 3, 1991.

FONTEYN, MARGOT: BIRTH ANNIVERSARY. May 18, 1919. Born Margaret Hookman in Reigate, Surrey, England, Dame Margot Fonteyn thrilled ballet audiences for 45 years. She emerged from the Sadler's Wells company during the 1930s and 1940s as a solo artist and followed those successes by partnering with Soviet exile Rudolph Nureyev in the 1960s. She died Feb 21, 1991, in Panama City, Panama.

HAITI: FLAG AND UNIVERSITY DAY. May 18. Public holiday.

INTERNATIONAL MUSEUM DAY. May 18. To pay tribute to museums of the world. "Museums are an important means of cultural exchange, enrichment of cultures and development of mutual understanding, cooperation and peace among people." Annually, May 18. Sponsor: Intl Council of Museums, Paris, France. For info: AAM/ICOM, 1575 Eye St NW, 4th Fl, Washington, DC 20005. Phone: (202) 289-1818. Fax: (202) 289-6578.

INTERNATIONAL SALUTE TO PUBLIC RELATIONS WEEK. May 18–24. Recognition of the positive role public relations practitioners play in disseminating relevant information to the news media and the general public. The strategic counseling provided to companies is another invaluable component of the practice. Annually, the third full week of May. For info: Robin Gorman Newman, RGN Communications, 58 Grace Ave, #2J, Great Neck, NY 11021. Phone: (516) 773-0911. Email: rgnewman@aol.com.

MARQUETTE, JACQUES: DEATH ANNIVERSARY. May 18. Father Jacques Marquette (Père Marquette), Jesuit missionary-explorer of the Great Lakes region. Died May 18, 1675, near Ludington or Frankfort, MI.

MOUNT SAINT HELENS ERUPTION: ANNIVERSARY. May 18, 1980. A major eruption of Mount St. Helens volcano, in southwestern Washington blew steam and ash more than 11 miles into the sky. First major eruption of Mount St. Helens since 1857, though on Mar 26, 1980, there had been a warning eruption of smaller magnitude.

NAIA BASEBALL WORLD SERIES. May 18–23. Drillers Stadium, Tulsa, OK. 42nd annual competition. Est attendance: 20,000. For info: Natl Assn of Intercollegiate Athletics, 6120 S Yale Ave, Ste 1450, Tulsa, OK 74136. Phone: (918) 494-8828. Fax: (918) 494-8841. Email: khenry@naia.org. WWW: http://www.naia.org

NAIA MEN'S AND WOMEN'S OUTDOOR TRACK AND FIELD NATIONAL CHAMPIONSHIPS. May 18–20. Tulsa, OK. 47th annual men's and 18th annual women's competition. Est attendance: 2,500. For info: Natl Assn of Intercollegiate Athletics, 6120 S Yale Ave, Ste 1450, Tulsa, OK 74136. Phone: (918) 494-8828. Fax: (918) 494-8841. Email: khenry@naia.org. WWW: http://www.naia.org

NAIA MEN'S TENNIS NATIONAL CHAMPIONSHIPS. May 18–23. Shadow Mountain Tennis Club, Tulsa, OK. 47th annual competition. Est attendance: 1,500. For info: Natl Assn of Intercollegiate Athletics, 6120 S Yale Ave, Ste 1450, Tulsa, OK 74136. Phone: (918) 494-8828. Fax: (918) 494-8841. Email: khenry@naia.org. WWW: http://www.naia.org

NAIA SOFTBALL NATIONAL CHAMPIONSHIP. May 18–22. Arrowhead Softball Complex, Broken Arrow, OK. 18th annual competition. Est attendance: 2,000. For info: Natl Assn of Intercollegiate Athletics, 6120 S Yale Ave, Ste 1450, Tulsa, OK 74136. Phone: (918) 494-8828. Fax: (918) 494-8841. Email: khenry@naia.org. WWW: http://www.naia.org

NAIA WOMEN'S TENNIS NATIONAL CHAMPIONSHIPS. May 18–23. Tulsa Southern Tennis Club, Tulsa, OK. 18th annual tournament. Individuals compete for All-America honors, while teams compete for the national championship. Est attendance: 1,500. For info: Natl Assn of Intercollegiate Athletics, 6120 S Yale Ave, Ste 1450, Tulsa, OK 74136. Phone: (918) 494-8828. Fax: (918) 494-8841. Email: khenry@naia.org. WWW: http://www.naia.org

NATIONAL EDUCATIONAL BOSSES WEEK. May 18–22. A special week to honor bosses in the field of education such as principals and school superintendents. Annually, the third week in May. For info: National Assn of Educational Office Personnel, PO Box 12619, Wichita, KS 67277. Fax: (316) 942-7100.

POPE JOHN PAUL II: BIRTHDAY. May 18, 1920. Karol Wojtyla, 264th pope of the Roman Catholic Church, born at Wadowice, Poland, May 18, 1920. Elected pope on Oct 16, 1978. He was the first non-Italian to be elected pope in 456 years (since the election of Pope Adrian VI, in 1522) and the first Polish pope.

SPACE MILESTONE: *APOLLO 10* (US). May 18, 1969. Launched with astronauts Colonel Thomas Stafford and Commander Eugene Cernan, who brought lunar module (LM) "Snoopy" within 9 miles of moon's surface on May 22. *Apollo 10* circled moon 31 times and returned to Earth May 26.

SWITZERLAND: PACING THE BOUNDS. May 18. Liestal. Citizens set off at 8 AM and march along boundaries to the beating of drums and firing of pistols and muskets. Occasion for fetes. Annually, the Monday before Ascension Day.

VISIT YOUR RELATIVES DAY. May 18. A day to renew family ties and joys by visiting often-thought-of-seldom-seen relatives. Annually, May 18. For info: A.C. Moeller, Box 71, Clio, MI 48420-1042.

WOMAN INDUCTED INTO NATIONAL INVENTORS HALL OF FAME: ANNIVERSARY. May 18, 1991. Gertrude Belle Elion, co-recipient of the 1988 Nobel Prize in Medicine, became the first woman inducted as a member of the National Inventors Hall of Fame. Elion's research led to the development of leukemia-fighting drugs and immunosuppressant Imuran which is used in kidney transplants.

BIRTHDAYS TODAY

Perry Como (Pierino Como), 86, singer ("Catch a Falling Star"), actor, born Canonsburg, PA, May 18, 1912.

Reginald Martinez (Reggie) Jackson, 52, Baseball Hall of Fame outfielder, born Wyncote, PA, May 18, 1946.

Robert Morse, 67, actor (*The Loved One, A Guide for the Married Man*; stage: *Say Darling* [Theatre World Award]), *How to Succeed in Business Without Really Trying* [Tony Award]), born Newton, MA, May 18, 1931.

Yannick Simone Camille Noah, 38, tennis player, born Sedan, France, May 18, 1960.

Pope John Paul II (Karol Wojtyla), 78, Roman Catholic leader, born Wadowice, Poland, May 18, 1920.

May 1998

S	M	T	W	T	F	S
					1	2
3	4	5	6	7	8	9
10	11	12	13	14	15	16
17	18	19	20	21	22	23
24	25	26	27	28	29	30
31						

Pernell Roberts, 70, actor (*Ride Lonesome*, "Bonanza," "Trapper John, M.D."), born Waycross, GA, May 18, 1928.
Warren Bruce Rudman, 68, lawyer, former US Senator (R, New Hampshire), born Boston, MA, May 18, 1930.
James Stephens, 47, actor ("The Paper Chase"), born Mt Kisco, NY, May 18, 1951.

MAY 19 — TUESDAY

Day 139 — 226 Remaining

BOYS' CLUBS FOUNDED: ANNIVERSARY. May 19, 1906. The Federated Boys' Clubs, which later became the Boys' Clubs of America, was founded.

DARK DAY IN NEW ENGLAND: ANNIVERSARY. May 19, 1780. At midday near-total darkness unaccountably descended on much of New England. Candles were lit, fowls went to roost and many fearful persons believed that doomsday had arrived. At New Haven, CT, Colonel Abraham Davenport opposed adjournment of the town council in these words: "I am against adjournment. The day of judgment is either approaching or it is not. If it is not, there is no cause for an adjournment. If it is, I choose to be found doing my duty. I wish therefore that candles may be brought." No scientifically verifiable cause for this widespread phenomenon was ever discovered.

HANSBERRY, LORRAINE: BIRTH ANNIVERSARY. May 19, 1930. American playwright Lorraine Hansberry was born at Chicago, IL. For her now classic play *A Raisin in the Sun* (1959), she became the youngest American and first black to win the Best Play Award from the New York Critics' Circle. The play, based on an incident in Hansberry's life and titled after the Langston Hughes poem, deals with issues such as racism, cultural pride and self-respect and was the first stage production written by a black woman to appear on Broadway (1959). *To Be Young, Gifted, and Black*, a book of excerpts from her journals, letters, speeches and plays, was published posthumously in 1969. Tragically, Lorraine Hansberry died of cancer on Jan 12, 1965, at the age of 34.

HO CHI MINH: BIRTH ANNIVERSARY. May 19. Vietnamese leader and first president of the Democratic Republic of Vietnam, born in central Vietnamese village of Kim Lien (Nghe An Province), probably on May 19, 1890. His original name was Nguyen That Thanh. Died at Hanoi, Vietnam, Sept 3, 1969.

MALCOLM X: BIRTH ANNIVERSARY. May 19, 1925. Black nationalist and civil rights activist Malcolm X was born Malcolm Little at Omaha, NE. While serving a prison term he resolved to transform his life. On his release in 1952 he changed his name to Malcolm X and worked for the Nation of Islam until he was suspended by Black Muslim leader Elijah Muhammed on Dec 4, 1963. Malcolm X later made the pilgrimage to Mecca and became an orthodox Muslim. He was assassinated as he spoke to a meeting at the Audubon Ballroom in New York, NY, on Feb 21, 1965.

MAY RAY DAY. May 19. To celebrate the beginning of the warm outside days the sun gives us. Also, a day for people named Ray. Annually, May 19. For info: Richard Ankli, The Fifth Wheel Tavern, 639 Fifth St, Ann Arbor, MI 48103.

MOON PHASE: LAST QUARTER. May 19. Moon enters Last Quarter phase at 12:35 AM, EDT.

NAIA MEN'S GOLF NATIONAL CHAMPIONSHIPS. May 19–23. Southern Hills Country Club, Tulsa, OK. 47th annual. Est attendance: 500. For info: Natl Assn of Intercollegiate Athletics, 6120 S Yale Ave, Ste 1450, Tulsa, OK 74136. Phone: (918) 494-8828. Fax: (918) 494-8841. Email: khenry@naia.org. WWW: http://www.naia.org

NAIA WOMEN'S GOLF NATIONAL CHAMPIONSHIPS. May 19–21. White Hawk Golf Club, Bixby, OK. 4th annual. Est attendance: 300. For info: Natl Assn of Intercollegiate Athletics, 6120 S Yale Ave, Ste 1450, Tulsa, OK 74136. Phone: (918) 494-8828. Fax: (918) 494-8841. Email: khenry@naia.org. WWW: http://www.naia.org

NATIONAL BIKE TO WORK DAY. May 19. At the state or local level, Bike to Work events are conducted by small and large businesses, city governments, bicycle clubs and environmental groups. About two million participants nationwide. Annually, the third Tuesday in May. For info: Bonnie McClun, Education Dir, League of American Bicyclists, 190 W Ostend St, Ste 120, Baltimore, MD 21230-3755. Phone: (410) 539-3399. Fax: (410) 539-3496. Email: bikeleague@aol.com. WWW: http://www.bikeleague.org

NATIONAL GEOGRAPHY BEE: NATIONAL FINALS. May 19–20. National Geographic Society Headquarters, Washington, DC. The first place winner from each state-level competition on Apr 3 advances to the national level. Alex Trebek of "Jeopardy!" fame moderates the finals which are televised on PBS stations. They compete for scholarships and prizes totaling more than $50,000. Est attendance: 400. For info: Natl Geography Bee, Natl Geographic Society, 1145 17th St NW, Washington, DC 20036. Phone: (202) 828-6635.

ORGANIZATION DEVELOPMENT INSTITUTE ANNUAL INFORMATION EXCHANGE. May 19–22. Asilomar Conference Center, Pacific Grove, CA. Organization development professionals exchange ideas on changes and new developments in the field at this 27th annual conference. Est attendance: 100. For info: Dr. Donald W. Cole, RODC, The Org Dev Institute, 11234 Walnut Ridge Rd, Chesterland, OH 44026. Phone: (216) 461-4333 or (216) 729-7419. Fax: (216) 729-9319. Email: DonWCole@aol.com. WWW: http://members.aol.com/odinst

PEALE, SARAH MIRIAM: BIRTH ANNIVERSARY. May 19, 1800. American portrait painter, member of famous early American family of painters, born at Philadelphia, PA. Died there on Feb 4, 1885.

SCOBEE, FRANCIS R.: BIRTH ANNIVERSARY. May 19, 1939. Commander of the ill-fated space shuttle *Challenger*, 46-year-old pilot Francis R. Scobee had been in the astronaut program since 1978 and had been pilot of the *Challenger* in 1984. Born at Cle Elum, WA, Scobee perished with all others on board when the *Challenger* exploded on Jan 28, 1986. See also: "*Challenger* Space Shuttle Explosion Anniversary" (Jan 28).

SIMPLON TUNNEL OPENING: ANNIVERSARY. May 19, 1906. Tunnel officially opened on this day. Construction started in 1898. From Brig, Switzerland, to Iselle, Italy.

SPACE MILESTONE: *MARS 2* AND *MARS 3* (USSR). May 19 and 28, 1971. Entered Martian orbits on Nov 27 and Dec 2, respectively. *Mars 3* sent down a TV-equipped capsule that soft-landed and transmitted pictures for 20 seconds. Launch dates: May 19 and 28, 1971.

TURKEY: YOUTH AND SPORTS DAY. May 19. Public holiday commemorating beginning of national movement for independence in 1919, led by Mustafa Kemal Ataturk.

27th AMENDMENT RATIFIED: ANNIVERSARY. May 19, 1992. The 27th amendment to the Constitution was ratified, prohibiting Congress from giving itself pay raises.

ZOO'S FOR YOU DAY. May 19. Metro Washington Park Zoo, Portland, OR. Free admission to the zoo for people with disabilities. Est attendance: 3,500. For info: Events Coord, Metro Washington Park Zoo, 4001 SW Canyon Rd, Portland, OR 97221-2799. Phone: (503) 226-1561. Fax: (503) 220-5754.

BIRTHDAYS TODAY

Richard Aldo (Rick) Cerone, 44, former baseball player, born Newark, NJ, May 19, 1954.
Nora Ephron, 57, writer (*Heartburn* [made into a movie]), born New York, NY, May 19, 1941.
James Fox, 59, actor (*A Passage to India, The Russia House, Patriot Games*), born London, England, May 19, 1939.
David Hartman, 61, actor (Emmy for "Good Morning America"; *Hello Dolly*), born Pawtucket, RI, May 19, 1937.

Grace Jones, 46, model, singer ("Sorry," "I Need a Man"), actress, born Spanishtown, Jamaica, May 19, 1952.

William (Bill) Laimbeer, Jr, 41, former basketball player, born Boston, MA, May 19, 1957.

James Lehrer, 64, journalist (co-anchor "MacNeil/Lehrer NewsHour"), born Wichita, KS, May 19, 1934.

Pete Townshend, 53, musician (The Who; "I Can See for Miles," "Let My Love Open the Door"), born London, England, May 19, 1945.

MAY 20 — WEDNESDAY

Day 140 — 225 Remaining

AMELIA EARHART ATLANTIC CROSSING: ANNIVERSARY. May 20, 1932. Leaving Harbor Grace, Newfoundland, Canada at 7 PM, Amelia Earhart landed near Londonderry, Ireland, on May 20. The 2,026-mile flight took 13 hours and 30 minutes. She was the first woman to fly solo across the Atlantic. Earhart, along with her navigator Fred Noonan, disappeared on July 2, 1937, between Lae, New Guinea, and Howland Island while trying to fly her Lockheed twin-engine plane around the equator to gather scientific data.

BALZAC, HONORE DE: BIRTH ANNIVERSARY. May 20, 1799. French novelist born at Tours, France. "It is easier," Balzac wrote in 1829, "to be a lover than a husband for the simple reason that it is more difficult to be witty every day than to say pretty things from time to time." Died at Paris, on Aug 18, 1850.

CAMEROON: NATIONAL HOLIDAY. May 20. Republic of Cameroon. Commemorates declaration of the republic on May 20, 1972.

COUNCIL OF NICAEA I: ANNIVERSARY. May 20–Aug 25, 325. First ecumenical council of Christian Church, called by Constantine I, first Christian emperor of Roman Empire. Nearly 300 bishops are said to have attended this first of 21 ecumenical councils (latest, Vatican II, began Sept 11, 1962), which was held at Nicaea, Bithynia, in Asia Minor in the year 325. Dates are approximate. The council condemned Arianism (which denied divinity of Christ), formulated the Nicene Creed and fixed the date of Easter.

ELIZA DOOLITTLE DAY. May 20. To honor Miss Doolittle (heroine of Bernard Shaw's *Pygmalion*) for demonstrating the importance and the advantage of speaking one's native language properly. Est attendance: 15. For info: H. M. Chase, Doolittle Day Committee, 2460 Devonshire Rd, Ann Arbor, MI 48104-2706.

FESTIVAL OF FLAGS. May 20–24. Killeen Special Events Ctr and Rodeo Grounds. Killeen, TX. The Festival of Flags is a celebration of Killeen's multi-cultural heritage. The Festival includes an arts and crafts show, international food booths, PRCA rodeo, outdoor concert, bowling tournament, parade, military static display, carnival, petting zoo and more. Annually, Memorial Day weekend. Est attendance: 40,000. For info: Killeen Festival of Flags, PO Box 11599, Killeen, TX 76547-1599. Phone: (254) 286-4626.

May 1998

S	M	T	W	T	F	S
					1	2
3	4	5	6	7	8	9
10	11	12	13	14	15	16
17	18	19	20	21	22	23
24	25	26	27	28	29	30
31						

GIGLI, BENIAMINO: BIRTH ANNIVERSARY. May 20, 1890. Celebrated Italian tenor born at Recanati, Italy. Died at Rome, on Nov 30, 1957.

HERZL, THEODOR: BIRTH ANNIVERSARY. May 20, 1860. Founder of the modern Zionist movement, born at Budapest, Hungary. Herzl died at Edlach, Austria, July 3, 1904.

HOMESTEAD ACT: ANNIVERSARY. May 20, 1862. President Lincoln signed the Homestead Act on this date, opening millions of acres of government-owned land in the West to settlers or "homesteaders," who had to reside on the land and cultivate it for five years.

JULIA A. MOORE POETRY FESTIVAL. May 20. Flint Public Library, Flint, MI. The public is invited to submit bad poems to this poetry festival and contest dedicated to the memory of America's worst poet. Winners' poems will be read at the library May 24. See also: "Moore, Julia A.: Birth Anniversary" (Dec 1). Est attendance: 150. For info: Julia A. Moore Poetry Festival, c/o Flint Public Library, 1026 E Kearsley St, Flint, MI 48502. Phone: (810) 232-7111 ext 205. Fax: (810) 232-8360.
Email: tpowers@flint.lib.mi.us.
WWW: http://www.flint.lib.mi.us/fpl.html

LAFAYETTE DAY. May 20. Massachusetts.

LINDBERGH FLIGHT: ANNIVERSARY. May 20–21, 1927. Anniversary of the first solo trans-Atlantic flight. Captain Charles Augustus Lindbergh, 25-year-old aviator, departed from rainy, muddy Roosevelt Field, Long Island, NY, alone at 7:52 AM, May 20, 1927, in a Ryan monoplane named *Spirit of St. Louis*. He landed at Le Bourget airfield, Paris, at 10:24 PM Paris time (5:24 PM, NY time), on May 21, winning a $25,000 prize offered by Raymond Orteig for the first nonstop flight between New York City and Paris, France (3,600 miles). The "flying fool" as he had been dubbed by some doubters became "Lucky Lindy," an instant world hero. See also: "Lindbergh, Charles Augustus: Birth Anniversary" (Feb 4).

MADISON, DOLLY (DOROTHEA) DANDRIDGE PAYNE TODD: BIRTH ANNIVERSARY. May 20, 1768. Wife of James Madison, 4th president of the US, born at Guilford County, NC, May 20, 1768. Died July 12, 1849.

MECKLENBURG DAY. May 20. North Carolina. Commemorates claimed signing of a declaration of independence from England by citizens of Mecklenburg County on this day, 1775.

MOTOR VOTER BILL SIGNED: 5th ANNIVERSARY. May 20, 1993. The latest effort to remove barriers to voter registration resulted in the passage of the Motor Voter Bill, which was signed into law by President William Clinton on this date. This bill requires the states to allow voter registration by mail or when a citizen applies for or renews a driver's license.

NATIONAL BE A MILLIONAIRE DAY. May 20. A global celebration of the joys of achieving millionaire status. This day launches a year-long series of activities to teach people the premier skills, habits, attitudes, and strategies used by the 400 richest Americans. It motivates people to use their own unique talents to convert paycheck skills to wealth. Annually, the third Wednesday in May. For info: Dee Wright, 106 Long Pine Place, #3B, Baltimore, MD 21244.

NATIONAL EMPLOYEE HEALTH AND FITNESS DAY. May 20. To focus on the importance of fitness and healthy lifestyles at the worksite. For info: Natl Assn of Governor's Councils on Physical Fitness/Sports, 201 S Capitol Ave, Ste 560, Indianapolis, IN 46225-1072. Phone: (317) 237-5630. Fax: (317) 237-5632. Email: Govcouncil@aol.com.
WWW: http://www.fitnesslink.com/govcouncil

NCAA DIVISION I WOMEN'S GOLF CHAMPIONSHIPS. May 20–23. Madison, WI. University Ridge Golf Course. For info: NCAA, 6201 College Blvd, Overland Park, KS 66211-2422. Phone: (913) 339-1906. Fax: (913) 339-0026. WWW: http://www.ncaa.org

NORMAN ROCKWELL'S FIRST *SATURDAY EVENING POST* COVER: ANNIVERSARY. May 20, 1916. Norman Rockwell's first cover for the *Post*, depicting a boy having to care for his infant sibling—pushing the baby carriage while his buddies set off to play ball—appeared on the May 20 edition.

NORWAY: BERGEN INTERNATIONAL FESTIVAL. May 20–May 31. Bergen. World-class music festival features artists from Norway and abroad. One of the largest annual musical events in Scandinavia. For info: Norwegian Tourist Board, 655 Third Ave, New York, NY 10017. Phone: (212) 885-9700. WWW: http://www.norway.org/web/norway/tourism.htm

PENNSYLVANIA AVENUE CLOSED: ANNIVERSARY. May 20, 1995. Barricades were erected to close off a two-block stretch of Pennsylvania Avenue, a six-lane street with a sidewalk that passes within 150 feet of the north face of the White House. A review of security procedures had been initiated after an attempt by an unemployed truck driver to land a small airplane on the South Lawn in September of 1994, but the closing of Pennsylvania Avenue was a direct response to the bombing of the Alfred P. Murrah Federal Building in Oklahoma City, OK, Apr 19, 1995.

ROUSSEAU, HENRI JULIEN FELIX: BIRTH ANNIVERSARY. May 20. Henri Rousseau, nicknamed Le Douanier because of his onetime post as customs toll-keeper. Celebrated French painter born at Laval, Mayenne, France, May 20, 1844. Clarinet player in a regimental band, painter of deceptively "primitive" pictures of exotic foliage, flowers and fruit of the jungle, with stilted human and animal figures. Died at Hospital Necker, Paris, Sept 4, 1910.

SPACE MILESTONE: PIONEER *VENUS I* (US): 20th ANNIVERSARY. May 20, 1978. Launched this date, became first Venus orbiter the following Dec 4.

WEIGHTS AND MEASURES DAY. May 20. Anniversary of international treaty, signed May 20, 1875, providing for the establishment of an International Bureau of Weights and Measures. The bureau was founded on international territory at Sevres, France.

BIRTHDAYS TODAY

Danny Aiello, Jr, 65, actor ("Lady Blue," *Do the Right Thing*), born New York, NY, May 20, 1933.

Cher (Cherilyn Sarkisian), 52, singer ("Half Breed," "Dark Lady"), actress (*Moonstruck*), born El Centro, CA, May 20, 1946.

Joe Cocker, 54, singer ("You Are So Beautiful"), born Sheffield, England, May 20, 1944.

John R. McKernan, Jr, 50, former Governor of Maine (R), born Bangor, ME, May 20, 1948.

Bronson Pinchot, 39, actor ("Perfect Strangers," *Beverly Hills Cop*), born New York, NY, May 20, 1959.

Ronald Prescott Reagan, 40, dancer, talk show host, son of former President Ronald Reagan, born Los Angeles, CA, May 20, 1958.

James "Jimmy" Stewart, 90, actor (*Rear Window, Philadelphia Story, It's a Wonderful Life*), born Indiana, PA, May 20, 1908. Died July 2, 1997.

Constance Towers, 65, actress, born Whitefish, MT, May 20, 1933.

Anthony Zerbe, 62, actor ("Harry-O," *Cool Hand Luke, Papillon*), born Long Beach, CA, May 20, 1936.

MAY 21 — THURSDAY

Day 141 — 224 Remaining

AMERICAN RED CROSS: FOUNDING ANNIVERSARY. May 21, 1881. Commemorates the founding of the American Red Cross by Clara Barton, its first president. The Red Cross had been founded in Switzerland in 1864 by representatives from 16 European nations. The organization is a voluntary, not-for-profit organization governed and directed by volunteers and provides disaster relief at home and abroad. 1.1 million volunteers are involved in community services such as collecting and distributing donated blood and blood products, teaching health and safety classes and acting as a medium for emergency communication between Americans and their armed forces.

ASCENSION DAY. May 21. Commemorates Christ's ascension into heaven. Observed since AD 68. Ascension Day is the 40th day after the Resurrection, counting Easter as the 1st day.

BELGIUM: PROCESSION OF THE HOLY BLOOD. May 21. Religious historical procession. Recalls heroic, adventurous crusaders, including Count Thierry of Alsace, who carried back relic of the Holy Blood. Always on Ascension Day.

BIG 10 BASEBALL TOURNAMENT. May 21–24. Location TBA. Est attendance: 1,500. For info: Dennis LaBissoniere, Big 10 Conference, 1500 W Higgins Rd, Park Ridge, IL 60068-6300. Phone: (847) 696-1010. Fax: (847) 696-1110. WWW: http://www.bigten.org

BURR, RAYMOND WILLIAM STACY: BIRTH ANNIVERSARY. May 21, 1917. Stage, film and TV actor best known for the role of Perry Mason in the series of the same name. He was born at New Westminister, British Columbia, and died near Healdsburg, CA, on Sept 12, 1993.

CANADA: GOLDEN SHEAF AWARDS/YORKTON SHORT FILM AND VIDEO FESTIVAL. May 21–24. Yorkton, Saskatchewan. The prestigious "Golden Sheaf" awards are presented at North America's longest continuous running short film festival. Free public screenings, film and video mini-cinema for distributors and buyers and workshops. Est attendance: 2,000. For info: Tourism Saskatchewan, 500–1900 Albert St, Regina, Sask, Canada S4P 4L9. Phone: (800) 667-7191 or (306) 782-7077. Email: travel.info@sasktourism.sk.ca. WWW: http://www.sasktourism.com

CURTISS, GLENN HAMMOND: BIRTH ANNIVERSARY. May 21, 1878. American inventor and aviator, born at Hammondsport, NY, on May 21, 1878. The aviation pioneer died at Buffalo, NY, on July 23, 1930.

DURER, ALBRECHT: BIRTH ANNIVERSARY. May 21, 1471. German painter and engraver, one of the greatest artists of the Renaissance, was born at Nuremberg, Germany, and died there Apr 6, 1528.

"FAITH FOR TODAY" TV PREMIERE: ANNIVERSARY. May 21, 1950. Religious series hosted by Reverend William J. Fagal in cooperation with the Seventh Day Adventist Church. Stories were dramatized with a sermon explaining the lessons learned at the end of the program. In 1971 the show changed format and was set in a hospital. It was also known as "Westbrook Hospital" in some markets.

FRY, ELIZABETH GURNEY: BIRTH ANNIVERSARY. May 21, 1780. English reformer who dedicated her life to improving the condition of the poor and especially of women in prison, born at Earlham, Norfolk, England. Died at Ramsgate, on Oct 12, 1845.

GATEWAY FARM EXPO. May 21–23. Buffalo County Fairgrounds, Kearney, NE. Est attendance: 20,000. For info: Kearney Area Chamber of Commerce, PO Box 607, Kearney, NE 68847. Phone: (800) 652-9435.

GEMINI, THE TWINS. May 21–June 20. In the astronomical/astrological zodiac, which divides the sun's apparent orbit into 12 segments, the period May 21–June 20 is identified, traditionally, as the sun sign period of Gemini, the Twins. The ruling planet is Mercury.

HAMMER, ARMAND: 100th BIRTH ANNIVERSARY. May 21, 1898. American industrialist Armand Hammer was born at New York, NY. He built the Occidental Petroleum Co into a $20 billion conglomerate after he invested $100,000 in it in 1956 and it was awarded two oil concessions in Libya. He was a trained physician who was sympathetic to the Soviet economy and people and gave away millions of dollars through philanthropy to cancer research. Hammer died on Dec 10, 1990, at Los Angeles, CA.

HUMMEL, SISTER MARIA INNOCENTIA: BIRTH ANNIVERSARY. May 21, 1909. Born at Massing, Bavaria, Sister Maria Innocentia Hummel cultivated an early interest in drawing and attended Munich's Academy of Fine Arts. She entered Siessen Convent run by the Sisters of the Third Order of St. Francis, a teaching order, and began teaching art to kindergarten children. In 1934 Franz Goebel obtained an exclusive license to translate her drawings into three-dimensional figurines. The first M.I. Hummel figurines were displayed at the Leipzig Trade Fair in 1935; they made their first appearance in the American market in May 1935. She died on Nov 6, 1946, at Siessen, Germany. Many M.I. Hummel Clubs across the country commemorate her birth date with special events and fund-raisers for local charities.

KODIAK CRAB FESTIVAL. May 21–25. Kodiak, AK. A celebration of spring and the Emerald Isle. Featured are parades, carnival booths and midway, running events, a golf tournament, bicycle and survival suit races, a blessing of the fleet ceremony and memorial services. Annually, Memorial Day weekend. Est attendance: 15,000. For info: Kodiak Chamber of Commerce, Box 1485, Kodiak, AK 99615. Phone: (907) 486-5557. Fax: (907) 486-7605. Email: chamber@kodiak.org.
WWW: http://www.kodiak.org/kodiak

MEMORY DAYS. May 21–25. Grayson, KY. Parade, art show and horse show. Est attendance: 10,000. For info: Robert L. Caummisar, Chamber of Commerce, 301 W Main St, Grayson, KY 41143. Phone: (606) 474-9522.

NATIONAL WAITSTAFF DAY. May 21. A day for restaurant managers and patrons to recognize and to express their appreciation for the many fine and dedicated waitresses and waiters. For info: Gaylord F. Ward, Promotion Dir, 1505 E Bristol Rd, Burton, MI 48529-2214.

NCAA WOMEN'S COLLEGE WORLD SERIES. May 21–25. Amateur Softball Association Hall of Fame Stadium, Oklahoma City, OK. 17th annual. The top eight universities qualify by winning one of eight NCAA Regionals. Double elimination. Est attendance: 25,000. For info: Stanley Draper, Exec Secretary, Oklahoma City All Sports Association, 100 W Main St, Ste 285, Oklahoma City, OK 73102. Phone: (405) 236-5000. Fax: (405) 236-5008.

***PIETA* ATTACKED: ANNIVERSARY.** May 21, 1972. Lazlo Toth, a Hungarian native, attacked Michelangelo's centuries-old sculpture *The Pieta* while screaming, "I am Jesus Christ!" The Madonna's left arm was severed, her veil and nose were smashed and her left eye was disfigured.

POPE, ALEXANDER: BIRTH ANNIVERSARY. May 21, 1688. English poet born at London, England. "A man," Pope wrote in 1727, "should never be ashamed to own he has been in the wrong, which is but saying, in other words, that he is wiser today than he was yesterday." Died at Twickenham, May 30, 1744.

RAJIV GANDHI ASSASSINATED: ANNIVERSARY. May 21, 1991. Former Indian Prime Minister Rajiv Gandhi was assassinated in the midst of a reelection campaign. He was killed when a bomb, hidden in a bouquet of flowers given by admirers, exploded as he approached a dais to begin a campaign rally. He had served as prime minister between 1984 and 1989 after succeeding his mother, Indira Gandhi, who was assassinated in 1984.

ROANOKE FESTIVAL IN THE PARK. May 21–31. Roanoke, VA. A celebration of life and the arts. Three-day juried fine art and craft show, 2-day juried wearable art show, children's activities, children's theatre, parade, river boat races, volleyball and soccer tournaments, USCF bike races, USSSA softball tournament, in-line skate race, 5K and 10K races, concerts, product and service area and expo area. Est attendance: 375,000. For info: Wendi Schultz, CFE Dir, Roanoke Festival in the Park, PO Box 8276, Roanoke, VA 24014. Phone: (540) 342-2640.

SAKHAROV, ANDREI DMITRIYEVICH: BIRTH ANNIVERSARY. May 21. Soviet physicist, human rights activist and environmentalist Andrei Sakharov was born at Moscow, Russia, on May 21, 1921. A collaborator in producing the first Soviet atomic bomb, and later the hydrogen bomb, Sakharov later denounced shortcomings of his country's government and was exiled to Gorky, Russia, 1980–1986. He was a formulator of the reform and restructuring concept known as *perestroika* and of *glasnost* (freedom). He was named to the Soviet Congress of Peoples Deputies eight months before his death at Moscow on Dec 14, 1989. As a physicist, he was the developer of destructive weapons; as a humanitarian, he was courageous as a dissident from militarism and super-governments and an advocate of human rights and conservation.

BIRTHDAYS TODAY

Peggy Cass, 74, actress (Elinore Hathaway on "The Hathaways"; panelist on "To Tell the Truth"), born Boston, MA, May 21, 1924.

Robert Creeley, 72, author, poet (*Have a Heart, Windows*), born Arlington, MA, May 21, 1926.

Janet Dailey, 54, writer and novelist (romance novels—*Tangled Vines*), born Storm Lake, IA, May 21, 1944.

Al Franken, 47, comedian, writer (*Rush Limbaugh Is A Big Fat Idiot and Other Observations*), actor ("Saturday Night Live"), born New York, NY, May 21, 1951.

Heinz Holliger, 59, oboist, composer, conductor, born Langenthal, Switzerland, May 21, 1939.

William "Spike" O'Dell, 45, Chicago radio personality, born Moline, IL, May 21, 1953.

Judge Reinhold, 41, actor (*Beverly Hills Cop*), born Wilmington, DE, May 21, 1957.

Harold Robbins, 82, author (*The Piranhas, Stiletto*), born New York, NY, May 21, 1916.

Leo Sayer, 50, singer ("You Make Me Feel Like Dancing"), songwriter, born Shoreham, England, May 21, 1948.

Mr T (Lawrence Tero or Tureaud), 46, actor (*Rocky III*, "The A-Team"), born Chicago, IL, May 21, 1952.

May 1998

S	M	T	W	T	F	S
					1	2
3	4	5	6	7	8	9
10	11	12	13	14	15	16
17	18	19	20	21	22	23
24	25	26	27	28	29	30
31						

MAY 22 — FRIDAY

Day 142 — 223 Remaining

ALMA HIGHLAND FESTIVAL AND GAMES. May 22–24. Alma College, Alma, MI. Old-world pageantry honoring Scottish traditions—Highland dancing, piping, drumming, athletic competitions, clan tents and grand parade. 30th annual festival. Annually, Memorial Day weekend. Est attendance: 60,000. For info: Chamber of Commerce, 110 W Superior St, PO Box 516, Alma, MI 48801. Phone: (517) 463-8979.

BIG TEN MEN'S/WOMEN'S OUTDOOR TRACK AND FIELD CHAMPIONSHIPS. May 22–24. Ohio State University, Columbus, OH. Est attendance: 1,500. For info: Dennis LaBissioniere, Big Ten Conference, 1500 W Higgins Rd, Champaign, IL 60068-6300. Phone: (847) 696-1010. Fax: (847) 696-1110. WWW: http://www.bigten.org

BROOKINGS-HARBOR AZALEA FESTIVAL. May 22–25. Brookings, OR. Parade, street fair, art shows, seafood, 10K run, Bonsai exhibit, regional quilt show, crafts fair, Coast Guard demonstration, old-time fiddlers, live music. 59th festival. Annually, Memorial Day weekend. Est attendance: 12,000. For info: Brookings-Harbor Chamber of Commerce, PO Box 940, Brookings, OR 97415. Phone: (800) 535-9469. Fax: (541) 469-4094. Email: chamber@wave.net.

CANADA: GUELPH SPRING FESTIVAL. May 22–31. Guelph, Ontario. Music, theatre, dance, opera and jazz with celebrated performers. Est attendance: 20,000. For info: Guelph Spring Festival, Box 1718, Guelph, Ont, Canada N1H 6Z9. Phone: (519) 821-3210. Fax: (519) 821-4403.
Email: gsf@freespace.net.
WWW: http://www.freespace.net/~gsf

CANADA: IMMIGRANT'S DAY. May 22. A day to celebrate and recognize the contributions made by immigrants to Canada and to discuss the Canadian Immigration policy and experience. For info: Sergio R. Karas, BA, LLB, Barrister and Solicitor, Karas & Assoc, 212 King St W, Ste 410, Toronto, Ont, Canada M5H 1K5. Phone: (416) 506-1800. Fax: (416) 599-5582. Email: karas@karas.ca. WWW: http://www.karas.ca

CASSATT, MARY: BIRTH ANNIVERSARY. May 22, 1844. Leading American artist of the Impressionist school, Mary Cassatt was born May 22, 1844 (some sources give 1845), at Allegheny City, PA (now part of Pittsburgh). She settled in Paris in 1874 where she was influenced by Degas and the Impressionists. She was later instrumental in their works becoming well known in the US. The majority of her paintings and pastels were based on the theme of mother and child. After 1900 her eyesight began to fail, and by 1914 she was no longer able to paint. Cassatt died at Chateau de Beaufresne near Paris, France, June 14, 1926.

DOYLE, ARTHUR CONAN: BIRTH ANNIVERSARY. May 22, 1859. English physician Sir Arthur Conan Doyle is best remembered as a detective story writer, especially for the creation of Sherlock Holmes and Dr. Watson. Doyle was born at Edinburgh, Scotland. He was deeply interested in and lectured on the subject of spiritualism. Died at Crowborough, Sussex, England, on July 7, 1930.

DRESDEN'S HOMETOWN SUMMER ™. May 22–July 19. Dresden, OH. There will be many seasonal events, demonstrations and entertainment opportunities taking place throughout Dresden and in The Longaberger® Company properties. There will be shopping fun for all at The Longaberger Specialty Shops™ and great food at its restaurants. Est attendance: 72,000. For info: Salle Schlesselman, The Longaberger® Company, 1360 Main St, Dresden, OH 43821. Phone: (614) 754-5778. Fax: (614) 754-5720.

ENGLAND: ENGLISH RIVIERA DANCE FESTIVAL. May 22–June 6. Torquay, Devon. Demonstrations by world champions and participatory events including Modern, Ballroom, Disco and Latin American dance styles. Est attendance: 2,000. For info: Philip Wylie, Ickenham, 73 Hoylake Crescent, Middlesex, England UB10 8JQ. Phone: (44) (189) 563-2143. Fax: (44) (189) 563-8015.

GETTYSBURG SQUARE DANCE ROUND-UP. May 22–23. Gettysburg, PA. 39th annual event held at Gettysburg College with nationally known callers. For info: Gettysburg Conv & Visitors Bureau, 35 Carlisle St, Gettysburg, PA 17325. Phone: (717) 334-6274. Fax: (717) 334-1166.
WWW: http://www.gettysburg.com

GRUBSTAKE DAYS. May 22–25. Yucca Valley, CA. Includes parade, carnival, PCRA rodeo, dances, tug-of-war, horseshoe tournament, food and community booths, arts and craft booths and breakfasts offered by local service organizations. Annually, Memorial Day weekend. Est attendance: 30,000. For info: Yucca Valley Chamber of Commerce, 56300 29 Palms Hwy, Ste D, Yucca Valley, CA 92284. Phone: (760) 365-6323. Fax: (760) 365-0763. Email: yvcc@desertgold.com. WWW: http://www.desertgold.com

HAWAII STATE FAIR. May 22–June 14. Aloha Stadium, Oahu, Hawaii. Entertainment, rides, booths with commercial exhibits. For info: Hawaii Visitors and Conv Bureau, 2270 Kalakaua Ave, Ste 801, Honolulu, HI 96815. Phone: (808) 595-4606. Fax: (808) 922-8991.

MEMORIAL DAY BURLINGTON BLUEGRASS FESTIVAL. May 22–24. Annually, Memorial Day Weekend. Est attendance: 3,000. For info: Delbert Spray, RR1, Kahoka, MO 63445. Phone: (573) 853-4344.

MEMORIAL WEEKEND FUN. May 22–25. Live Oak, FL. A great family weekend filled with activities. Est attendance: 3,000. For info: James Cornett, Spirit of the Suwannee Music Park, 3076 95th Dr, Live Oak, FL 32060. Phone: (904) 364-1683. Fax: (904) 364-2998. Email: spirit@musicliveshere.com.
WWW: http://www.musicliveshere.com

MEMORIAL WEEKEND SALMON DERBY. May 22–25. Petersburg, AK. Four days of fishing with more than $30,000 in prizes awarded! Est attendance: 400. For info: Petersburg Chamber of Commerce, PO Box 649, Petersburg, AK 99833. Phone: (907) 772-3646. Fax: (907) 772-3646.
WWW: http://www.petersburg.org

"MISTER ROGERS NEIGHBORHOOD" TV PREMIERE: ANNIVERSARY. May 22, 1967. Presbyterian minister Fred Rogers hosted this long-running PBS children's program. Puppets and human characters interacted in the neighborhood of make-believe. Rogers played the voices of many of the puppets and educated young viewers on a variety of important and/or offbeat subjects. The human cast members included: Betty Aberlin, Joe Negri, David Newell, Don Brockett, Francois Clemmons, Robert Trow, Audrey Roth, Elsie Neal and Yoshi Ito.

MUSICAL INSTRUMENT PREVIEW AND AUCTION. May 22–25. Seattle Center, Seattle, WA. 17th annual auction of consigned musical instruments, paraphernalia and memorabilia at the Northwest Folklife Festival. Preview of the items to be auctioned will be on May 22–25. Est attendance: 10,000. For info: Sandy Bradley, Auctioneer, 313 18th Ave, Seattle, WA 98122. Phone: (206) 548-9622. Fax: (206) 548-9623.
Email: sandy@potluck.com. WWW: http://www.potluck.com

★**NATIONAL MARITIME DAY.** May 22. Presidential Proclamation always issued for May 22 since 1933. (Pub Res No. 7 of May 20, 1933.)

NATIONAL MARITIME DAY. May 22. Anniversary of departure for first steamship crossing of Atlantic from Savannah, GA, to Liverpool, England, by steamship *Savannah* in 1819.

NIXON FIRST AMERICAN PRESIDENT TO VISIT MOSCOW: ANNIVERSARY. May 22, 1972. President Richard Nixon became the first American president to visit Moscow. Four days later on May 26, Nixon and Soviet leader Leonid Brezhnev signed a treaty on antiballistic missile systems and an interim agreement on limitation of strategic missiles.

NORTHWEST FOLKLIFE FESTIVAL. May 22–25. Seattle Center, Seattle, WA. Ethnic and traditional arts event celebrating world cultures in the Northwest Region. Includes music, dance, food, crafts, visual arts exhibits, children's programs, demonstrations, films and more. More than 6,000 performers. Annually, Friday–Monday on Memorial Day weekend. Est attendance: 200,000. For info: Northwest Folklife Fest, 305 Harrison St, Seattle, WA 98109-1695. Phone: (206) 684-7300 or (206) 684-7327. Fax: (206) 684-7190. Email: marym@folklife.org. WWW: http://www.nwfolklife.org/folklife/

OLIVIER, LAURENCE: BIRTH ANNIVERSARY. May 22, 1907. Actor, director and theater manager. Born at Dorking, England, on May 22, 1907. Thought by many to be the most influential actor of this century, Laurence Olivier's theatrical and film career in many ways shaped the art forms within which he participated. Honored with nine Academy Award nominations, three Oscars and five Emmy awards, his repertoire included most of the prime Shakespearean roles, Archie Rice in John Osborne's *The Entertainer* and roles in such films as *Rebecca, Pride and Prejudice, The Boys from Brazil, Sleuth, Marathon Man* and *Wuthering Heights*. Olivier was an innovative and tireless theater manager with London's Old Vic company and the National Theatre of Great Britain. The National Theatre's largest auditorium and Britain's equivalent of Broadway's Tony awards carry his name. He was knighted in 1947 and made a peer of the throne in 1970. Olivier died at Ashurst, England, on July 11, 1989.

PITTSBURGH FOLK FESTIVAL. May 22–24. David Lawrence Convention Center, Pittsburgh, PA. Pittsburgh's 20-plus nationalities celebrate their heritage with colorful costumes, authentic folk dancing and mouth-watering delicacies. For info: Greater Pittsburgh Conv & Visitors Bureau, Four Gateway Center, Pittsburgh, PA 15222-1259. Phone: (412) 281-4882 or (800) 359-0758. Fax: (412) 644-5512.

PITTSBURGH RIVER FEST. May 22–25. IC Light Amphitheatre, Station Square, Pittsburgh, PA. This festival brings the sights and sounds of the Louisiana bayou right to Pittsburgh's own three rivers. It features a colorful array of Zydeco and Dixieland music and a Cajun and Creole menu, as well as dancing and entertainment. For info: Greater Pittsburgh Conv & Visitors Bureau, Four Gateway Center, Pittsburgh, PA 15222-1259. Phone: (412) 837-6800 or (800) 359-0758. Fax: (412) 644-5512.

POSTCARD SALE. May 22–23. Howard Johnson Hotel, Hagerstown, MD. 36 tables filled with antique and modern postcards. Est attendance: 200. For info: John H. McClintock, Dir, Postcard History Society, PO Box 1765, Manassas, VA 22110. Phone: (703) 368-2757.

RA, SUN: BIRTH ANNIVERSARY. May 22, 1914. Born Herman (Sonny) Blount, Sun Ra was a pioneering and innovative jazz musician whose avant garde performances mixed elements of theater with his surreal composition and performance style. Ra was born at Birmingham, AL, and died there on May 30, 1993.

May 1998

S	M	T	W	T	F	S
					1	2
3	4	5	6	7	8	9
10	11	12	13	14	15	16
17	18	19	20	21	22	23
24	25	26	27	28	29	30
31						

RHODODENDRON FESTIVAL. May 22–24. Florence, OR. Abundance of springtime rhododendron blooms celebrated with a Grand Floral parade, arts and crafts show and carnival. Est attendance: 35,000. For info: Chamber of Commerce, Box 26000, Florence, OR 97439. Phone: (541) 997-3128. Fax: (541) 997-4101.

RIVERFEST. May 22–24. Riverfront Park, Little Rock, AR. 21st annual outdoor festival of the visual and performing arts with non-stop entertainment, food vendors, visual artists, kid stuff. Est attendance: 150,000. For info: Van Tilbury, PO Box 3232, Little Rock, AR 72203. Phone: (501) 376-4781. Fax: (501) 370-3292.

SACRAMENTO JAZZ JUBILEE. May 22–25. Sacramento, CA. More than 100 bands from the US, Canada and foreign countries perform American traditional jazz music in approximately 40 venues around Sacramento at the world's largest traditional jazz festival. Est attendance: 100,000. For info: Roger Krum, Exec Dir, Sacramento Traditional Jazz Society, 2787 Del Monte Blvd, Sacramento, CA 95691. Phone: (916) 372-5277. Fax: (916) 372-3429. Email: stjs@earthlink.net. WWW: http://www.sacjazz.com/jazz/jubilee.htm

SOUTH SHORE SINGLES FOUNDING ANNIVERSARY. May 22. First Parish Church, Norwell, MA. Nonprofit singles group started in a living room in 1979 and now has more than 600 members. Provides support, social and educational programs to singles, new and seasoned. Celebrated with dinner/dancing at VFW Hall, Abington, MA. Annually, the fourth Friday in May. Sponsor: South Shore Singles. Est attendance: 300. For info: Terry Kleine, 15 Franklin Rd, Hanover, MA 02339. Phone: (617) 878-3289.

SPOLETO FESTIVAL USA. May 22–June 7. Comprehensive arts festival with a mix of more than 100 performances of opera, dance, theater, chamber and symphonic music, jazz, literary and visual arts set in one of America's most beautiful and historic cities. For info: Spoleto Festival USA, PO Box 157, Charleston, SC 29402. Phone: (803) 722-2764. WWW: http://www.charleston.net/spoleto

SUMMER CELEBRATION. May 22–25. Florence, AL. Four days filled with sporting events for the entire family. All events focus on summer fun and safety and include tennis, golf, frisbee golf tournament, 5K run, century bike ride, mountain bike race, waverunner races, BBQ cook-off and Veteran's Memorial Celebration complete with a fireworks show. Annually, Memorial Day weekend. Est attendance: 10,000. For info: Florence/Lauderdale Tourism, One Hightower Place, Florence, AL 35630. Phone: (205) 740-4141 or (888) FLO-TOUR. Fax: (205) 740-4142. Email: dwilson@floweb.com. WWW: http://www.flo-tour.org

"THERE WENT JOHNNY!" NIGHT: ANNIVERSARY. May 22, 1992. After almost 30 years as host of the "Tonight" show, Johnny Carson hosted his last show. Carson became host of the late-night talk show, which began as a local New York program hosted by Steve Allen, on Oct 1, 1962. Over the years Carson occasionally made headlines with such extravaganzas as the marriage of Tiny Tim and Miss Vicki. Johnny received Emmys for his work four years in a row, 1976–79. Ed McMahon, his sidekick of 30 years, and Doc Severinsen, longtime bandleader, left the show with Carson. Jay Leno, the show's exclusive guest host, became the new regular host.

TRUMAN DOCTRINE: ANNIVERSARY. May 22, 1947. In order to contain Communism after World War II, the US furnished aid to Greece and Turkey. Congress approved the Truman Doctrine on this day. A corollary of this doctrine was the Marshall Plan, which began sending aid to war-torn European countries in 1948.

WAGNER, RICHARD: BIRTH ANNIVERSARY. May 22, 1813. German composer born at Leipzig who made revolutionary changes in the structure of opera. Best known for his Ring Cycle (*Der Ring des Nibelungen*). Died at Italy, Feb 13, 1883.

WORLD CHAMPIONSHIP OLD-TIME PIANO PLAYING CONTEST. May 22–25. Holiday Inn, Decatur, IL. Competition and festival of ragtime, honky-tonk and old-time music. Annually, Memorial Day weekend. Sponsor: Old-Time Music Preservation Assn (OMPA) Inc. Est attendance: 1,000. For info: Judy Leschewski, PO Box 4714, Decatur, IL 62525. Phone: (217) 428-2403.

YEMEN: NATIONAL DAY. May 22. Public holiday.

BIRTHDAYS TODAY

Charles Aznavour, 74, singer, songwriter, actor (*Shoot the Piano Player, Candy, The Tin Drum*), born Paris, France, May 22, 1924.
Richard Benjamin, 60, actor (*Goodbye Columbus, Diary of a Mad Housewife*, "He and She"), born New York, NY, May 22, 1938.
Naomi Campbell, 28, model, born London, England, May 22, 1970.
Frank Converse, 60, actor ("Movin' On," *Hurry Sundown*), born St. Louis, MO, May 22, 1938.
Judith Crist, 76, critic, born New York, NY, May 22, 1922.
Thomas Edward (Tommy) John, 55, former baseball player, born Terre Haute, IN, May 22, 1943.
Barbara Parkins, 55, actress ("Peyton Place," *Valley of the Dolls*), born Vancouver, British Columbia, Canada, May 22, 1943.
Michael Sarrazin, 58, actor (*The Flim Flam Man, The Reincarnation of Peter Proud*), born Quebec City, Quebec, Canada, May 22, 1940.
Susan Strasberg, 60, actress ("The Marriage," "Toma," *Picnic*), born New York, NY, May 22, 1938.
Paul Winfield, 58, actor (*Sounder, Star Trek II: The Wrath of Khan, Presumed Innocent*), born Los Angeles, CA, May 22, 1940.

MAY 23 — SATURDAY

Day 143 — 222 Remaining

ALABAMA JUBILEE. May 23–25. Point Mallard, Decatur, AL. Hot-air balloon races, arts, crafts, antique cars, water and air shows. Annually, Memorial Day weekend. Est attendance: 100,000. For info: Jacklyn Bailey, Decatur Conv and Visitors Bureau, Box 2349, 719 6th Ave SE, Decatur, AL 35602. Phone: (205) 350-2028 or (800) 524-6181. Email: dcvb@hiwaay.net.

CARNIVAL '98. May 23–24. San Francisco, CA. Mardi Gras-like revel embraces a parade, street festival and costume contest where people indulge their fantasies through masquerade, music and dance. Annually, Memorial Day weekend. Est attendance: 500,000. For info: Marcus Gordon, Mission Economic and Cultural Assn, 3007 24th St, San Francisco, CA 94110. Phone: (415) 826-1401. Fax: (415) 824-2242.

CHESTERTOWN TEA PARTY FESTIVAL. May 23–24. Chestertown, MD. Reenactment of 1774 tea dumping, crafts, music, food and games. Est attendance: 15,000. For info: Chestertown Tea Party Festival, Inc, Box 526, Chestertown, MD 21620. Phone: (410) 778-0416.

CIVIL WAR WEEKEND. May 23–25. Yorktown Battlefield, Yorktown, VA. 100 reenactors present a recreated Civil War encampment, Confederate field hospital and military drills performed on the battlefield in Colonial National Historical Park. Est attendance: 3,000. For info: Activities Coord, Colonial Natl Historical Park, PO Box 210, Yorktown, VA 23690. Phone: (757) 898-3400. WWW: http://www.nps.gov/colo/

DAKOTA COWBOY POETRY GATHERING. May 23–24. Medora, ND. Local and national cowboy poets reunion. Includes western art show. Sponsor: Theodore Roosevelt Medora Foundation, PO Box 198, Medora, ND 58645. Est attendance: 4,000. For info: North Dakota Tourism, HC01 Box 25, Sentinel Butte, ND 58654. Phone: (800) 435-5663 or (701) 872-4746.

DECLARATION OF THE BAB. May 23. Baha'i commemoration of May 23, 1844, when the Bab, the prophet-herald of the Baha'i Faith, announced in Shiraz, Persia, that he was the herald of a new messenger of God. One of the nine days of the year when Baha'is suspend work. For info: Pamela Zivari, Dir, Baha'is of the US, Office of Public Information, 866 UN Plaza, Ste 120, New York, NY 10017-1822. Phone: (212) 803-2500. Fax: (212) 803-2573. Email: usopi-ny@bic.org.

1836 ENCAMPMENT. May 23–24. Westville-Lumpkin, GA. Reenactment of an encampment of soldiers who had been dispatched to protect local citizens against Indian attacks. An Indian camp will also be demonstrated. Est attendance: 1,000. For info: Patty Cannington, Westville, PO Box 1850, Lumpkin, GA 31815. Phone: (912) 838-6310 or (888) 733-1850.
WWW: http://www.westville.org

FAIRBANKS, DOUGLAS ELTON: BIRTH ANNIVERSARY. May 23, 1883. Douglas Fairbanks was born at Denver, CO, May 23, 1883. He made his professional debut as an actor in Richmond, VA, on Sept 10, 1900, in *The Duke's Jester.* His theatrical career turned to Hollywood, and he became a movie idol appearing in such films as *The Americano, He Comes Up Smiling, The Mark of Zorro, The Three Musketeers, Robin Hood, The Thief of Bagdad, The Black Pirate* and *The Gaucho.* He married "America's Sweetheart," Mary Pickford, in 1918, and in 1919 he joined with D.W. Griffith and Charlie Chaplin to form the production company United Artists. He died at Santa Monica, CA, on Dec 12, 1939.

FARMINGTON INVITATIONAL BALLOON FESTIVAL. May 23–24. Farmington, NM. Hot-air balloons launch off the banks of Farmington Lake. Famous Splash and Dash and Hare and Hound races included in the two-day event. Est attendance: 2,000. For info: Farmington Conv and Visitors Bureau, 203 W Main, Ste 401, Farmington, NM 87401. Phone: (800) 448-1240 or (505) 326-7602. Fax: (505) 327-0577.
Email: fmncub@cyberport.com.
WWW: http://www.farmingtonnm.org

FULLER, MARGARET: BIRTH ANNIVERSARY. May 23, 1810. Journalist and author Sarah Margaret Fuller, born at Cambridgeport, MA, began reading Virgil at age six. Her conversational powers won her the admiration of students at Harvard University, and she was befriended by Ralph Waldo Emerson. She shared editorial duties with Emerson on the Transcendentalist quarterly *The Dial* after a move to New York in 1844, and was hired by Horace Greeley as literary critic for the *New York Tribune.* Her book *Women in the Nineteenth Century*, the first feminist statement by an American writer, brought her international acclaim. In 1846, as a foreign correspondent for the *Tribune*, she became caught up in the Italian revolutionary movement and secretly married a young Roman nobleman, the Marquis Giovanni Angelo Ossoli. Enroute to the US, Fuller and her husband and child died on July 19, 1850, when their ship was wrecked off Fire Island near New York, NY.

GEM, MINERAL AND JEWELRY SHOW AND SALE. May 23–25. Clayton Recreation Park Arena, Clayton, NY. Show includes fluorescent mineral light show, jewelry, dealers' supplies, crystals, beads, fossils, mineral specimens, gemstones and craft books. Archaeology clubs and lapidary societies will also be present. The clubs will be doing slide shows, giving out information and selling items. Annually, Memorial Day weekend. For info: Thousand Islands Museum, PO Box 27, 403 Riverside Dr, Clayton, NY 13624. Phone: (315) 686-5794.

GUTHRIE JAZZ BANJO FESTIVAL. May 23–25. Downtown Guthrie, OK. Jazz banjo bands and soloists from all over the US perform music from the gay '90s, as well as the roaring '20s and contemporary selections at various venues around historic Guthrie. Also antique autos on parade. Annually, on Memorial Day weekend. Sponsor: Mr Brady Hunt/Guthrie CVB. Est attendance: 10,000. For info: Chamber of Commerce, Guthrie Conv & Visitors Bureau, PO Box 995, Guthrie, OK 73044. Phone: (405) 282-1948 or (800) 299-1889 or (800) OK-BANJO. Fax: (405) 282-0061.

HALFWAY PARK DAYS. May 23–24. Martin L. (Marty) Snook Memorial Park, Hagerstown, MD. Family fun in the park with arts and crafts, free entertainment, food and children's rides. Annually, Memorial Day weekend. Est attendance: 8,000. For info: Lions Club of Halfway, 10923 Holly Terrace, Hagerstown, MD 21740-7804. Phone: (301) 739-3219.

HEAD-OF-THE-MON-RIVER HORSESHOE TOURNAMENT. May 23–25. Fairmont, WV. Open to horseshoe pitchers with a 1998 State/National Horseshoe Pitchers Assn membership card. Est attendance: 300. For info: Tri-County Horseshoe Club Dir, Davis "Catfish" Woodward, 1133 Sunset Dr, Fairmont, WV 26554. Phone: (304) 366-3819.

INTERNATIONAL JAZZ DAY. May 23. Jazz lovers worldwide celebrate jazz every May, on the Saturday of the Memorial Day weekend. Originated by the New Jersey Jazz Society, and sanctioned by the American Federation of Jazz Societies, the United Nations Jazz Society and the Sacramento Traditional Jazz Society. For info: D. Michael Denny, New Jersey Jazz Society, 136 River Rd, East Hanover, NJ 07936. Phone: (201) 887-3167. Fax: (201) 503-0126.
Email: jazzday@geocities.com.
WWW: http://www.geocities.com/BourbonStreet/4270

JIM BUTLER DAYS. May 23–26. Tonopah, NV. Street dance, vendors, parade, arm wrestling, BBQ, chili cook-off, horseshoe and volleyball tourney, stock car races, pancake breakfast, teen dance and arts and crafts.

LOBSTERFEST. May 23–25. Mystic Seaport, Mystic, CT. A New England lobster bake on the banks of the Mystic River over the Memorial Day weekend. Est attendance: 10,000. For info: Mystic Seaport, 75 Greenmanville Ave, PO Box 6000, Mystic, CT 06355-0990. Phone: (203) 572-5315.

LONGWOOD GARDENS FESTIVAL OF FOUNTAINS. May 23–Sept 5. Kennett Square, PA. A magical mixture of rainbow-hued fountains, alfresco garden concerts, fireworks and leisurely evenings in the conservatory. Est attendance: 275,000. For info: Longwood Gardens, PO Box 501, Kennett Square, PA 19348-0501. Phone: (610) 388-1000.
WWW: http://www.longwoodgardens.org

MANSFIELD, ARABELLA: BIRTH ANNIVERSARY. May 23, 1846. Arabella Mansfield, born Belle Aurelia Babb near Burlington, IA, was the first woman admitted to the legal profession in the US. In 1869 while teaching at Iowa Wesleyan College, Mansfield was certified as an attorney and admitted to the Iowa bar. According to the examiners, "she gave the very best rebuke possible to the imputation that ladies cannot qualify for the practice of law." Mansfield never did practice law, however, continuing her career as an educator. She joined the faculty of DePauw University, in Greencastle, IN, where she became dean of the schools of art and music. One of the first woman college professors and administrators in the US, Mansfield was also instrumental in the founding of the Iowa Woman Suffrage Society in 1870. She died Aug 2, 1911, at Aurora, IL.

MAYFEST. May 23. Main St, Bennington, VT. A juried craft fair with more than 130 craft vendors, food booths, entertainment and raffle while Main St closed to traffic. Annually, the Saturday of Memorial Day weekend. Est attendance: 8,000. For info: Better Bennington Corp, PO Box 704, Bennington, VT 05201. Phone: (802) 442-5758. WWW: http://www.thisisvermont.com

MEMORIAL WEEKEND BBQ. May 23–24. Jarbidge, NV. 29th annual Memorial Day weekend BBQ. Dance to live music both nights. For info: Nevada Commission on Tourism, Capitol Complex, Carson City, NV 89701. Phone: (702) 482-8267 or (702) 687-4322. Fax: (702) 687-6779.

MESMER, FRIEDRICH ANTON: BIRTH ANNIVERSARY. May 23, 1734. German physician after whom Mesmerism was named. Magnetism and hypnotism were used by him in treating disease. Died on Mar 5, 1815.

NEW YORK PUBLIC LIBRARY: ANNIVERSARY. May 23, 1895. New York's then-governor Samuel J. Tilden was the driving force that resulted in the combining of the private Astor and Lenox libraries with a $2 million endowment and 15,000 volumes from the Tilden Trust to become the New York Public Library, incorporated this day in 1895.

OFF STREET ARTS AND CRAFTS FESTIVAL. May 23–25. Prescott, AZ. Arts and crafts. For info: Joanne Welton, Tourism Admin, Prescott Chamber of Commerce, PO Box 1147, Prescott, AZ 86302-1147. Phone: (520) 445-2000.

PAYNE, JOHN: BIRTH ANNIVERSARY. May 23, 1912. American actor John Payne was born at Roanoke, VA. He is best-known as the idealistic lawyer who helps Santa Claus in *Miracle on 34th Street* (1947). He died on Dec 6, 1989, at Malibu, CA.

PENNSYLVANIA ARTS & CRAFTS COUNTRY FESTIVAL. May 23–25. Washington County Fairgrounds, Irwin, PA. More than 150 art and craft exhibits from six different states. Crafts include woodworking, pottery, jewelry, glass, quilts and folk art. Food, children's entertainment and live demonstrations. For info: Debbie or Dave Stoner, Family Festivals Assn, PO Box 166, Irwin, PA 15642. Phone: (412) 863-4577. Fax: (412) 863-4577.

PORTUGUESE FESTA. May 23–24. Lovelock, NV. Mass, parade, sopa, baked goods and crafts. For local info: Phone: (702) 273-2566. For Nevada Tourism: Nevada Commission on Tourism, Capitol Complex, Carson City, NV 89710. Phone: (702) 687-4322 or (800) 227-0774. Fax: (702) 687-6779.

RIVERSPREE FESTIVAL. May 23–24. Elizabeth City, NC. A celebration of life on the river. Sporting events, food, crafts, entertainment. Annually, Memorial Day weekend. Est attendance: 75,000. For info: River Spree, Elizabeth City Area Chamber of Commerce, 502 E Ehringhaus St, PO Box 426, Elizabeth City, NC 27907-0426. Phone: (919) 335-4365. Fax: (919) 335-5732.

SLOVO, JOE: BIRTH ANNIVERSARY. May 23, 1926. South African Communist Party leader Joe Slovo was a long-

May 1998

S	M	T	W	T	F	S
					1	2
3	4	5	6	7	8	9
10	11	12	13	14	15	16
17	18	19	20	21	22	23
24	25	26	27	28	29	30
31						

time friend and ally of Nelson Mandela. The first white to become a member of the African National Congress Executive Committee, Slovo was one of the most prominent white men involved in South Africa's antiapartheid movement. He lived in exile from 1963 to 1990, serving as head of the military arm of the ANC during that period. Born at Obelai, Lithuania, he died Jan 6, 1995, at Johannesburg.

SOUTH CAROLINA CONSTITUTION RATIFICATION: ANNIVERSARY. May 23, 1788. By a vote of 149 to 73, South Carolina became the eighth state to ratify the Constitution, on May 23, 1788.

SUPREME COURT UPHOLDS BAN ON ABORTION COUNSELING: ANNIVERSARY. May 23, 1991. In the case *Rust vs Sullivan*, the Supreme Court, in a 5–4 ruling, on May 23, 1991, upheld federal regulations that barred federally funded family planning clinics from providing any information about abortion.

SWEDEN: LINNAEUS DAY. May 23, 1707. Stenbrohult. Commemorates birth, May 23, 1707, of Carolus Linnaeus (Carl von Linne), Swedish naturalist. Died at Uppsala, Sweden, Jan 10, 1778.

TASTE OF CINCINNATI. May 23–25. Cincinnati, OH. Greater Cincinnati is famous for its fine food, from elegant five-star dining to five-way chili. This popular eating extravaganza presents a taste of the most delicious culinary delights available. Est attendance: 400,000. For info: Downtown Council, 300 Carew Tower, 441 Vine, Cincinnati, OH 45202. Phone: (513) 579-3191. Fax: (513) 579-3101. WWW: http://www.gccc.com

TIVOLI FEST. May 23–24. Elk Horn, IA. Annual Danish celebration with parade, Danish Folk Dancers, Danish foods, unique giftshops, historical tours and much more. Annually, Memorial Day weekend. Sponsors: Better Elk Horn Club. Est attendance: 5,000. For info: Lisa Riggs, Danish Windmill, PO Box 245, Elk Horn, IA 51531. Phone: (712) 764-7472 or (800) 451-7960. Fax: (712) 764-7475.

TRASH FEST. May 23–25. Toledo Bend Reservoir, Anacoco, LA. Scuba divers gather to retrieve more than two tons of debris from bottom of lake. Bands, spearfishing tournament, crawfish boil and fireworks display. Est attendance: 300. For info: Toledo Divers Assn, Dick Wilgus, 55 Perch Dr, Anacoco, LA 71403. Phone: (318) 286-5395. Fax: (318) 286-9362.

UTICA OLD-FASHIONED ICE CREAM FESTIVAL. May 23–25. Utica, OH. Saluting "America's favorite dessert," ice cream, with a weekend of fun and entertainment—parade, queen contest, arts and crafts, antique gas engines, sheep herding with border collies and plenty of delicious ice cream. Est attendance: 26,000. For info: Michael Dager, Utica Ice Cream Festival, PO Box 588, Utica, OH 43080. Phone: (614) 892-3921.

WAR OF JENKIN'S EAR: LIVING HISTORY. May 23. Wormsloe Historic Site, Savannah, GA. The focus is on the Colonial war with Spain in living history demonstrations related to Colonial Georgia history, militia, woodworking and farm life. Museum, film and trails. Est attendance: 500. For info: Wormsloe State Historic Site, 7601 Skidaway Rd, Savannah, GA 31406. Phone: (912) 353-3023.

WILLIAM CARNEY RECEIVES CONGRESSIONAL MEDAL OF HONOR: ANNIVERSARY. May 23. Sergeant William H. Carney, of the 54th Massachusetts Colored Infantry, was the first black to win the Congressional Medal of Honor. He was cited for his efforts, although wounded twice, during the Battle of Fort Wagner, SC, on June 18, 1863. He was issued the medal on May 23, 1900.

BIRTHDAYS TODAY

Barbara Barrie, 67, actress ("Barney Miller," *One Potato, Two Potato* [Best Actress award at 1964 Cannes Film Festival], *Breaking Away*), born Chicago, IL, May 23, 1931.

Drew Carey, 37, actor ("The Drew Carey Show"), born Cleveland, OH, May 23, 1961.

Rosemary Clooney, 70, singer ("Mangos"; "The Rosemary Clooney Show"), actress (*White Christmas*), born Maysville, KY, May 23, 1928.

Joan Collins, 65, actress (Alexis Carrington Colby on "Dynasty"), born London, England, May 23, 1933.

Marvelous Marvin Hagler, 44, former boxer, born Newark, NJ, May 23, 1954.

Robert Moog, 64, inventor of first commercially viable keyboard synthesizer, born Flushing, NY, May 23, 1934.

Artie Shaw, 88, musician, born New York, NY, May 23, 1910.

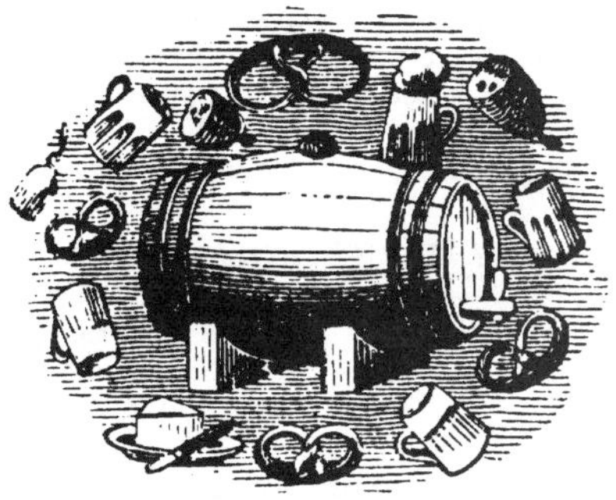

MAY 24 — SUNDAY

Day 144 — 221 Remaining

ANTI-SALOON LEAGUE FOUNDED: ANNIVERSARY. May 24, 1893. Anti-Saloon League was founded by Howard H. Russell at Oberlin, OH. Efforts in that state were so successful the Anti-Saloon League of America was organized in 1895. The League's permanent home became Otterbein College in Westerville, OH, in 1909.

BASEBALL FIRST PLAYED UNDER THE LIGHTS: ANNIVERSARY. May 24, 1935. The Cincinnati Reds defeated the Philadelphia Phillies by a score of 2–1, as more than 20,000 fans enjoyed the first night baseball game in the major leagues. The game was played at Crosley Field, Cincinnati, OH.

BELIZE: COMMONWEALTH DAY. May 24. Public holiday.

BROOKLYN BRIDGE OPENED: ANNIVERSARY. May 24, 1883. Nearly 14 years in construction, the $16 million Brooklyn Bridge over the East River opened May 24, 1883. Designed by John A. Roebling, the steel suspension bridge has a span of 1,595 feet.

BULGARIA: ENLIGHTENMENT AND CULTURE DAY. May 24. National holiday festively celebrated by schoolchildren, students, people of science and art. Manifestations and concerts to express love for education and culture.

COAL MINER DAYS. May 24–25. Downtown and the fairgrounds. Novinger, MO. Turn-of-the-century coal mining boom town celebrates its heritage with old-time contests, music, dancing and displays. Est attendance: 3,000. For info: Glenna Daniels, Novinger Renewal Inc, Rt 3, Box 31, Novinger, MO 63559. Phone: (816) 488-5280.

ERITREA: INDEPENDENCE DAY. May 24. National Day. Gained independence from Ethiopia in 1993 after 30-year civil war.

INDIANAPOLIS 500-MILE RACE. May 24. Indianapolis, IN. Recognized as the world's largest single-day sporting event. First race was in 1911. Annually, the Sunday of Memorial Day weekend. For info: Indianapolis Motor Speedway Corp, 4790 W 16th St, Indianapolis, IN 46222. Phone: (317) 481-8500. WWW: http://brickyard.com

ITALY: WEDDING OF THE SEA. May 24. Venice. The feast of the Ascension is the occasion of the ceremony recalling the "Wedding of the Sea" performed by Venice's Doge, who cast his ring into the sea from the ceremonial ship known as the *Bucintoro*, to symbolize eternal dominion. Annually, on the Sunday following Ascension.

LEUTZE, EMANUEL: BIRTH ANNIVERSARY. May 24, 1816. Obscure itinerant painter, born in Germany, May 24, 1816, came to the US when he was nine years old, began painting by age 15. Painted some of most famous American works, such as *Washington Crossing the Delaware, Washington Rallying the Troops at Monmouth* and *Columbus Before the Queen*. Died July 18, 1868.

MANNOCK, "MICK" EDWARD: BIRTH ANNIVERSARY. May 24, 1887. Edward Mannock, British flying ace credited with 73 hits during World War I, was born at Preston Cavalry Barracks, Brighton, England. Mannock most likely would not have been considered eligible to fly due to an astigmatism in one eye, but probably memorized the chart prior to having his eyesight tested. Although it was the custom of the time, Mannock refused to attend the funerals of enemies. Edward Mannock died during a flight on July 26, 1918.

MEMORIAL DAY CEREMONIES. May 24. Andersonville, GA. Ceremonies pay tribute to our country's men and women who paid for our freedom with their lives. For info: Alan Marsh, Park Ranger, Andersonville National Historic Site, Rte 1, Box 800, Hwy 49 North, Andersonville, GA 31711. Phone: (912) 924-0343.

MILLS, WILBUR D.: BIRTH ANNIVERSARY. May 24, 1909. Born in Kensett, AR, Wilbur D. Mills became one of the most powerful members of Congress, serving as Chair of the House of Representatives Ways and Means Committee for 16 years. A Harvard graduate, Mills was first elected to Congress in 1939 at the age of 29. After a scandal involving a burlesque dancer known as Fanne Fox, "the Argentine Firecracker," he lost his position heading the Ways and Means Committee but was reelected. He served one final term and retired in 1976. Mills died May 2, 1992, in Searcy, AR.

MORSE OPENS FIRST US TELEGRAPH LINE: ANNIVERSARY. May 24, 1844. The first US telegraph line was formally opened between Baltimore, MD, and Washington, DC. Samuel F.B. Morse sent the first officially telegraphed words "What hath God wrought?" from the Capitol building to Baltimore. Earlier messages had been sent along the historic line during testing, and one, sent on May 1, contained the news that Henry Clay had been nominated as president by the Whig party, meeting in Baltimore. This message reached Washington one hour prior to a train carrying the same news.

NEWHOUSE, SAMUEL I.: BIRTH ANNIVERSARY. May 24, 1895. Multimillionaire businessman who built family publishing and communications empire. Born to immigrant parents in a New York City tenement, Newhouse became "America's most profitable publisher." He accumulated 31 newspapers, 7 magazines, 6 television stations, 5 radio stations and 20 cable television systems. His success with the "bottom line" in publishing and communications was without parallel. He died at New York, NY, Aug 29, 1979.

PALMER, LILLI: BIRTH ANNIVERSARY. May 24, 1914. Stage, screen and television actress Lilli Palmer was born Lillie Marie Peiser, at Poznan, Poland. She also painted and was the author of several novels and an autobiography titled *Change Lobsters—And Dance*. She died at Los Angeles, CA, on Jan 27, 1986.

PEALE, JAMES: DEATH ANNIVERSARY. May 24, 1831. American portrait and miniature painter (painted portraits of George and Martha Washington and General Sir Thomas Shirley) was born at Chestertown, MD, in 1749 (exact date unknown).

PIKE PLACE MARKET STREET FESTIVAL. May 24–25. Seattle, WA. 27th annual "thank you" party for the citizens of Seattle who voted to save the market from being razed in 1971, thus preserving it as a historic landmark. Activities include Kids Alley, two music stages, crafts, roving artists and musicians and much more. Est attendance: 65,000. For info: Pam Audette, Pike Place Market Merchants Assn, 93 Pike St, #312, Seattle, WA 98101. Phone: (206) 587-0351. Fax: (206) 624-6960.

SMITH VALLEY STRAWBERRY FESTIVAL. May 24. Wellington, NV. Strawberry shortcake fest and music. Annually, the fourth Sunday of May. For local info: Phone (702) 465-2452. For info: Mason Valley, Chamber of Commerce, 227 S Main St, Yerington, NV 89447. Phone: (702) 463-2245. Fax: (702) 463-3369.

SPACE MILESTONE: *AURORA 7* MERCURY SPACE CAPSULE (US). May 24, 1962. With this launch Scott Carpenter became second American to orbit Earth, circling it three times.

***VICTORIA* BOAT DISASTER: ANNIVERSARY.** May 24, 1881. One of Canada's worst marine disasters occurred on the Thames River (near London, Ontario). "The *Victoria*, a small, double-decked stern-wheeler, was conducting holiday excursion trips between London and Springbank Park. On a return trip to London the boat was dangerously overcrowded with more than 600 passengers. The crowd shifted from side to side, resulting in a precarious rocking motion of the boat. It finally keeled over and the boiler crashed through the bulwarks, bringing the upper deck and large awning down upon the struggling crowd. The *Victoria* sank immediately, and at least 182 people, the majority from London, lost their lives.

BIRTHDAYS TODAY

Gary Burghoff, 55, actor (Emmy "M*A*S*H"), born Bristol, CT, May 24, 1943.

Roger Caras, 70, nature writer, born Methuen, MA, May 24, 1928.

Tommy Chong, 60, actor (*Up in Smoke, The Corsican Brothers* [also wrote screenplay and directed]), born Edmonton, Canada, May 24, 1938.

Joe Dumars III, 35, basketball player, born Shreveport, LA, May 24, 1963.

Bob Dylan (Robert Zimmerman), 57, composer, singer, born Duluth, MN, May 24, 1941.

Patti LaBelle (Patricia Louise Holte), 54, singer ("Since I Don't Have You"), born Philadelphia, PA, May 24, 1944.

Alfred Molina, 45, actor (*Raiders of the Lost Ark, Letter to Brezhnev*), born London, England, May 24, 1953.

May 1998

S	M	T	W	T	F	S
					1	2
3	4	5	6	7	8	9
10	11	12	13	14	15	16
17	18	19	20	21	22	23
24	25	26	27	28	29	30
31						

Frank Oz, 54, puppeteer, born Hereford, England, May 24, 1944.

Priscilla Beaulieu Presley, 53, actress (Jenna on "Dallas"; *Naked Gun* movies), ex-wife of Elvis, born Brooklyn, NY, May 24, 1945.

Coleman Alexander Young, 52, former mayor of Detroit, MI, born Tuscaloosa, AL, May 24, 1946.

MAY 25 — MONDAY

Day 145 — 220 Remaining

AFRICAN FREEDOM DAY: ANNIVERSARY. May 25. Public holiday in Chad, Zambia and some other African states. Members of the Organization for African Unity (formed May 25, 1963) commemorate their independence from colonial rule. Sports contests, political rallies and tribal dances.

ARGENTINA: INDEPENDENCE DAY. May 25. Anniversary of establishment of independent republic, following revolt of the provinces against Spanish rule, May 25, 1810.

BOLDER BOULDER 10K. May 25. Boulder, CO. A 10K race of walkers, joggers and world-class runners through the streets of Boulder. Annually, on Memorial Day. Est attendance: 40,000. For info: Bolder Boulder, PO Box 9125, Boulder, CO 80301-9125. Phone: (303) 444-7223. Fax: (303) 938-4863.

CARVER, RAYMOND: 60th BIRTH ANNIVERSARY. May 25, 1938. American poet and short story writer who chronicled the lives of America's working poor. Born on May 25, 1938, at Clatskanie, OR, died Aug 2, 1988, at his home at Port Angeles, WA, soon after finishing a book of poetry entitled *A New Path to the Waterfall.*

CONFEDERATE MEMORIAL DAY IN VIRGINIA. May 25. Annually, the last Monday in May.

CONSTITUTIONAL CONVENTION: ANNIVERSARY. May 25, 1787. At Philadelphia, PA, the delegates from seven states, forming a quorum, opened the Constitutional Convention, which had been proposed by the Annapolis Convention on Sept 11–14, 1786. Among those who were in attendance: George Washington, Benjamin Franklin, James Madison, Alexander Hamilton and Elbridge Gerry. See also: "Annapolis Convention Anniversary" (Sept 11).

DAVIS, MILES: BIRTH ANNIVERSARY. May 25, 1926. Jazz trumpeter Miles Davis was born at Alton, IL. He was influenced by the be-bop music style of Charlie Parker and Dizzy Gillespie and ended up leaving the Julliard School of Music to join Parker's quintet in 1945 at the age of 19. He experimented with different styles throughout his career, exploring new voicings in jazz with arranger Gil Evans and musicians John Coltrane and Red Garland, delving into "modal" music with Tony Williams and Wayne Shorter and moving into a fusion sound in the '60s. His career was beset with bouts of drug addiction, but in the 1970s his return to the music scene found him creating a sound that melded his be-bop origins, modal chord progressions and driving rock rhythms. He died on Sept 28, 1991.

DOWIE, JOHN ALEXANDER: BIRTH ANNIVERSARY. May 25, 1847. Evangelist and claimant of the title "Elijah the Restorer" was born at Edinburgh, Scotland. He established the Christian Catholic Church in Zion, IL, where some 5,000 followers created a unique community without pharmacies, physicians, theaters or dance halls and where smoking, drinking and the eating of pork were prohibited. Dowie's ostentatiously expensive personal lifestyle and his unsuccessful attempt to convert New York City were partially responsible for the falling away of his followers. He was expelled from the church in 1906 and died at Chicago, IL, Mar 9, 1907.

ELIZABETH BOWER DAY. May 25. Oklahoma. To honor the Nursing Home Queen who promoted nursing homes statewide. (Ms Bower passed away in December 1994.) Annually, May 25. For info: Cheryl Hankins, Social Services or Peaches Grayson, Activities Dir, McMahon Tomlinson Nursing Center, 3126 Arlington, Lawton, OK 73505. Phone: (405) 357-3240. Fax: (405) 585-5483.

EMERSON, RALPH WALDO: BIRTH ANNIVERSARY. May 25, 1803. American author and philosopher born at Boston, MA, and died there Apr 27, 1882. It was Emerson who wrote (in his essay "Self-Reliance," 1841), "A foolish consistency is the hobgoblin of little minds, adored by little statesmen and philosophers and divines. With consistency a great soul has simply nothing to do."

JORDAN: INDEPENDENCE DAY. May 25. National holiday. Commemorates treaty of May 25, 1946, proclaiming autonomy and establishing monarchy.

MEMORIAL DAY. May 25. Legal public holiday. (PL90–363 sets Memorial Day on last Monday in May. Applicable to federal employees and District of Columbia.) Also known as Decoration Day because of the tradition of decorating with flowers the graves of servicemen. Especially an occasion for honoring those who have died in battle. (Observance dates from Civil War years in US: first documented observance at Waterloo, NY, May 5, 1865.) See also: "Confederate Memorial Day" (Apr 26, Apr 27, May 10 and May 25).

MEMORIAL DAY PARADE AND CEREMONIES. May 25. Gettysburg National Cemetery, Gettysburg, PA. 2,000 schoolchildren scatter flowers over the unknown graves. Memorial services follow parade. For info: Gettysburg Conv and Visitors Bureau, 35 Carlisle St, Gettysburg, PA 17325-1899. Phone: (717) 334-6274. Fax: (717) 334-1166.
WWW: http://www.gettysburg.com

★**MEMORIAL DAY, PRAYER FOR PEACE.** May 25. Presidential Proclamation issued each year since 1948. PL81–512 of May 11, 1950, asks President to proclaim annually this day as a day of prayer for permanent peace. PL90–363 of June 28, 1968, requires that beginning in 1971 it will be observed the last Monday in May. Often entitled "Prayer for Peace Memorial Day," and traditionally requests the flying of the flag at half-staff "for the customary forenoon period."

MOON PHASE: NEW MOON. May 25. Moon enters New Moon phase at 3:32 PM, EDT.

MURRAY, PHILIP: BIRTH ANNIVERSARY. May 25, 1886. American labor leader and founder of the Congress of Industrial Organizations, also active in and a leader of the United Mine Workers, was born near Blantyre, Scotland. Murray died at San Francisco, CA, on Nov 9, 1952.

NATIONAL MISSING CHILDREN'S DAY. May 25. To promote awareness of the problem of missing children; to offer a forum for change; and to offer safety information for children in school and community. Annually, May 25. For info: Child Find of America, Inc, PO Box 277, New Paltz, NY 12561-0277. Phone: (914) 255-1848. National toll-free hotline phone numbers: (800) I-AM-LOST or (800) A-WAY-OUT.

NATIONAL TAP DANCE DAY. May 25. To celebrate this unique American art form that represents a fusion of African and European cultures and to transmit tap to succeeding generations through documentation and archival and performance support. Held on the anniversary of the birth of Bill "Bojangles" Robinson to honor his outstanding contribution to the art of tap dancing on stage and in films through the unification of diverse stylistic and racial elements.

PAICH MEMORIAL DAY AUCTION. May 25. (Also Labor Day Auction Sept 7.) Mountain View Inn, Greensburg, PA. Annual Memorial Day auction featuring glassware, rugs, furniture, pictures and many other items. For info: Mountain View Inn, Rte 30 East, Greensburg, PA 15601. Phone: (412) 834-5300 or (800) 537-8709. Fax: (412) 834-5304.

ROBINSON, BILL "BOJANGLES": BIRTH ANNIVERSARY. May 25, 1878. Born at Richmond, VA, the grandson of a slave, Robinson is considered one of the greatest tap dancers. He is best known for a routine in which he tap-danced up and down a staircase. He appeared in several films with Shirley Temple and taught Gene Kelly, Sammy Davis, Jr, Gregory Hines, and others. Died at New York City, Nov 25, 1949.

SIKORSKY, IGOR: BIRTH ANNIVERSARY. May 25, 1889. Aeronautical engineer best remembered for his development of the first successful helicopter in 1939. Also pioneered in multi-engine airplanes and large flying boats that made transoceanic air transportation possible. Born at Kiev, Russia, and died Oct 26, 1972, at Easton, CT.

SOLZHENITSYN GOES HOME: ANNIVERSARY. May 25, 1994. After 20 years living in exile, mostly in the US, Russian author Alexander Solzhenitsyn returned to his homeland. The author had been expelled from the Soviet Union in 1974 after his three-volume work exposing the Soviet prison camp system, *The Gulag Archipelago*, was published in the West. After the collapse of the Soviet Union late in 1991, he announced his intention to go back.

May 1998

S	M	T	W	T	F	S
					1	2
3	4	5	6	7	8	9
10	11	12	13	14	15	16
17	18	19	20	21	22	23
24	25	26	27	28	29	30
31						

SPACE MILESTONE: *SKYLAB 2* (US). May 25, 1973. Joseph P. Kerwin, Paul J. Weitz and Charles (Pete) Conrad, Jr, spent 28 days in space experimentation. Pacific splashdown occurred June 22. Launched May 25, 1973.

STOCK EXCHANGE HOLIDAY (MEMORIAL DAY). May 25. The holiday schedules for the various exchanges are subject to change if relevant rules, regulations or exchange policies are revised. If you have questions, phone: American Stock Exchange (212) 306-1000; Chicago Board of Trade (312) 435-3500; Chicago Board of Options Exchange (312) 786-5600; New York Stock Exchange (215) 656-2065; Pacific Stock Exchange (415) 393-4000; Philadelphia Stock Exchange (215) 496-5000.

TITO (JOSIP BROZ): BIRTH ANNIVERSARY. May 25, 1892. Josip Broz, Yugoslavian soldier and political leader, born near Zagreb, Yugoslavia. Died May 4, 1980, and was interred in garden of his home at Belgrade. Funeral was attended by leaders of most of the world's major nations.

TOUR OF SOMERVILLE. May 25. Somerville, NJ. The oldest continuously run major bicycle race in America. 1998 marks the 55th running. Attracts more than 600 top amateur cyclists for seven events. Annually, on Memorial Day. Est attendance: 40,000. For info: Dan Puntillo, Admin, PO Box 125, Somerville, NJ 08876. Phone: (908) 725-0461.

TUNNEY, JAMES JOSEPH (GENE): 100th BIRTH ANNIVERSARY. May 25, 1898. Heavyweight boxing champion, business executive. The famous "long count" occurred in seventh round of Jack Dempsey–Gene Tunney world championship fight, Sept 22, 1927, at Soldier Field, Chicago, IL. Tunney was born at New York, NY, and died at Greenwich, CT, Nov 7, 1978.

UNITED KINGDOM: SPRING BANK HOLIDAY. May 25. Bank and public holiday in England, Wales, Scotland and Northern Ireland.

USS *NORTH CAROLINA* MEMORIAL DAY OBSERVANCE. May 25. Wilmington, NC. Annual Memorial Day observance held at 5:45 PM. For info: USS *North Carolina* Battleship Memorial, Susan Pope, Box 480, Wilmington, NC 28402. Phone: (910) 251-5797. Fax: (910) 251-5807. Email: NCBB55@aol.com. WWW: http://www.city-info.com/NCBB55.html

VIRGIN ISLANDS: MEMORIAL DAY. May 25. Parades and ceremonies take place throughout the islands. Yacht races featured on St. Croix. Observed annually on last Monday in May.

BIRTHDAYS TODAY

Dixie Carter, 59, actress (Julia Sugarbaker on "Designing Women"), born McLemoresville, TN, May 25, 1939.

Jessi Colter (Miriam Johnson), 51, singer, songwriter, born Phoenix, AZ, May 25, 1947.

Tom T. Hall, 62, singer ("P.S. I Love You"), songwriter ("Harper Valley PTA"), born Olive Hill, KY, May 25, 1936.

Justin Henry, 27, actor (*Kramer vs. Kramer, Sixteen Candles*), born May 25, 1971.

K.C. Jones, 66, former basketball coach and player, born Tyler, TX, May 25, 1932.

Robert Ludlum, 71, author (*The Aquitaine Progression, The Parsifal Mosaic*), born New York, NY, May 25, 1927.

Sir Ian McKellen, 59, actor (stage: *Amadeus* [Tony Award]; *Last Action Hero, Six Degrees of Separation*), born Burnley, England, May 25, 1939.

Mike Myers, 35, actor/comedian ("Saturday Night Live," *Wayne's World, Austin Powers: International Man of Mystery*), born Scarsborough, Canada, May 25, 1963.

Connie Sellecca, 43, actress ("Hotel"), born The Bronx, NY, May 25, 1955.

Beverly Sills, 69, opera singer (retired), born Brooklyn, NY, May 25, 1929.

Gordon Smith, 46, US Senator (R, Oregon), born Pendleton, OR, May 25, 1952.

Sheryl Swoopes, 27, basketball player, US Olympic Basketball Team, born Brownfield, TX, May 25, 1971.

Leslie Uggams, 55, singer ("Sing Along with Mitch"), actress, born New York, NY, May 25, 1943.

Karen Valentine, 51, actress ("Room 222"), born Sebastopol, CA, May 25, 1947.

MAY 26 — TUESDAY

Day 146 — 219 Remaining

DUNKIRK EVACUATED: ANNIVERSARY. May 26, 1940. The British Expeditionary Force had become trapped by advancing German armies near this port on the northern coast of France. On this date, the evacuation of 200,000 British and 140,000 French and Belgian soldiers began. Sailing on every kind of transport available, including fishing boats and recreational craft, these men were safely across the English Channel by June 2.

ENGLAND: INTERNATIONAL TT MOTORCYCLE RACES. May 26–June 6. Isle of Man. World-famous motorcycle road races held over a 38-mile course. Practice sessions will be held from May 26–30. Est attendance: 40,000. For info: Auto Cycle Union, Road Race Dept, Wood St, Rugby, Warwickshire, England CV21 2YX. Phone: (44) (178) 854-0519. Fax: (44) (178) 857-3585.

FEAST OF SAINT AUGUSTINE OF CANTERBURY. May 26. Pope Gregory sent Augustine to convert the pagan English. Augustine became the first archbishop of Canterbury. Augustine died May 26, 604 AD.

GEORGIA: INDEPENDENCE DAY. May 26. National Day.

JOLSON, AL: BIRTH ANNIVERSARY. May 26, 1886. Actor, singer (born Asa Yoelson at St. Petersburg, Russia). Died at San Francisco, CA, Oct 23, 1950.

MONTAGU, LADY MARY WORTLEY: BAPTISM ANNIVERSARY. May 26, 1689. English author baptized May 26, 1689. Died Aug 21, 1762.

MORLEY, ROBERT: 90th BIRTH ANNIVERSARY. May 26, 1908. British actor Robert Morley was born at Semley, England. Among his best known film credits are *Major Barbara* (1939) and *The African Queen* (1951). He died on June 3, 1992, at Reading, England.

PRINCE JONAH KUHIO KALANIANOLE DAY. May 26. Hawaii. Commemorates the man, who as Hawaii's delegate to the US Congress, introduced the first bill for statehood in 1919. Not until 1959 did Hawaii become a state.

PUSHKIN, ALEXANDER: BIRTH ANNIVERSARY. May 26, 1799. Russian author born May 26, 1799. Died Jan 29, 1837.

RIDE, SALLY KRISTEN: BIRTHDAY. May 26. Dr. Sally Ride, one of first seven women in the US astronaut corps and the first American woman in space, was born at Encino, CA, May 26, 1951. She was married in 1982 to another astronaut, Steve Hawley. Her flight aboard the space shuttle, *Challenger*, was launched from Cape Canaveral, FL, on June 18 and landed at Edwards Air Force Base, CA, on June 24, 1983. The six-day flight was termed "nearly a perfect mission."

SPACE MILESTONE: *SOYUZ 36* (USSR). May 26, 1980. *Soyuz 36* launched with cosmonauts Bertalan Farkas, of Hungary, and Valery Kubasov of the USSR, and docked at *Salyut 6* the next day for a week-long visit with Ryumin and Popov before returning to Earth.

VIETNAM AND US RESUME RELATIONS: ANNIVERSARY. May 26, 1994. Nearly 20 years after the end of the Vietnam War, the US and Vietnam agreed to resume diplomatic relations. In the early 1990s Vietnam had become one of the fastest growing economies in Asia after giving up Communist controls and allowing economic reform. Earlier in 1994 President Bill Clinton had lifted the American embargo that hindered Americans from doing business in Vietnam.

WAYNE, JOHN: BIRTH ANNIVERSARY. May 26, 1907. American motion picture actor, born Marion Michael Morrison, at Winterset, IA. He died at Los Angeles, CA, June 11, 1979. "Talk low, talk slow and don't say too much" was his advice on acting.

BIRTHDAYS TODAY

James Arness, 75, actor ("Gunsmoke," "How the West Was Won"), born Minneapolis, MN, May 26, 1923.

Helena Bonham Carter, 32, actress (*A Room With a View*, *Howard's End*), born Golders Green, London, England, May 26, 1966.

Genie Francis, 36, actress (Laura Vining on "General Hospital"), born Englewood, NJ, May 26, 1962.

Lenny Kravitz, 34, singer ("Circus"), musician, song writer ("Justify My Love"), born New York, NY, May 26, 1964.

Peggy Lee (Norma Delores Egstrom), 78, singer ("Fever," "Is That All There Is?"), actress, born Jamestown, ND, May 26, 1920.

Brent Musburger, 59, sportscaster, born Portland, OR, May 26, 1939.

Stevie Nicks, 50, singer (with Fleetwood Mac; "Don't Stop"), songwriter ("Edge of Seventeen"), born Phoenix, AZ, May 26, 1948.

Sally K. Ride, 47, astronaut, first American woman in space, born Los Angeles, CA, May 26, 1951.

Philip Michael Thomas, 49, actor ("Miami Vice," *Hair*), born Los Angeles, CA, May 26, 1949.

Wesley Darcel Walker, 43, former football player, born San Bernardino, CA, May 26, 1955.

Hank Williams, Jr, 49, singer ("All for the Love of Sunshine," "I Fought the Law"), born Shreveport, LA, May 26, 1949.

☆ ☆ ☆

MAY 27 — WEDNESDAY

Day 147 — 218 Remaining

BENNETT, ARNOLD: BIRTH ANNIVERSARY. May 27, 1867. English novelist, playwright and critic (Enoch) Arnold Bennett was born at Hanley, in the pottery-manufacturing district of North Staffordshire, England. Best known of his novels is *The Old Wives' Tale* (1908), and most harshly criticized (by the literati) of his books was the popular *How to Live on Twenty-Four Hours a Day* (1908). His *Journals* from 1896 until near the time of his death in 1931 provide insight into Bennett's life, thought and his writing methods. "The price of justice," Arnold wrote, "is eternal publicity." He contracted typhoid fever in France and died at London, on May 27, 1931.

BLOOMER, AMELIA JENKS: BIRTH ANNIVERSARY. May 27, 1818. American social reformer and women's rights advocate, born at Homer, NY, May 27, 1818. Her name is remembered especially because of her work for more sensible dress for women and her recommendation of a costume that had been introduced about 1849 by Elizabeth Smith Miller but came to be known as the "Bloomer Costume," or "Bloomers." Amelia Bloomer died at Council Bluffs, IA, Dec 30, 1894.

CARSON, RACHEL (LOUISE): BIRTH ANNIVERSARY. May 27, 1907. American scientist and author, born at Springdale, PA. Author of *Silent Spring* (1962), a book that provoked widespread controversy over the use of pesticides. Died Apr 14, 1964.

DUNCAN, ISADORA: BIRTH ANNIVERSARY. May 27, 1878. American-born interpretive dancer who revolutionized the entire concept of dance. Bare-footed, freedom-loving, liberated woman and rebel against tradition, she experienced worldwide professional success and profound personal tragedy (her two children drowned, her marriage failed and she met a bizarre death when the long scarf she was wearing caught in a wheel of the open car in which she was riding, strangling her). Born at San Francisco, CA, May 27, 1878. Died at Nice, France, Sept 14, 1927.

ENGLAND: ROYAL BATH AND WEST OF ENGLAND SHOW. May 27–30. Royal Bath and West Showground, Shepton Mallet, Somerset. One of the oldest and largest agricultural shows in the country. Est attendance: 150,000. For info: Royal Bath and West of England Society, The Showground, Shepton Mallet, Somerset, England BA4 6QN. Phone: (44) (174) 982-2200. Fax: (44) (174) 982-3169.

FIRST RUNNING OF PREAKNESS: 125th ANNIVERSARY. May 27, 1873. The first running of the Preakness Stakes in Pimlico, MD, was won by Survivor with a time of 2:43. The winning jockey was G. Barbee.

GOLDEN GATE BRIDGE OPENED: ANNIVERSARY. May 27, 1937. 200,000 people crossed San Francisco's Golden Gate Bridge on its first day.

HAMMETT, (SAMUEL) DASHIELL: BIRTH ANNIVERSARY. May 27. The man who brought realism to the genre of mystery writing, Dashiell Hammett was born May 27, 1894, at St. Marys County, MD. Hammett's first two novels, *Red Harvest* (1929) and *The Dain Curse* (1929), were based on his eight years spent as a Pinkerton detective. Hammett is recognized as the founder of the "hard-boiled" school of detective fiction. Three of his novels have been made into films: *The Maltese Falcon* (1930), considered by many to be his finest work; *The Thin Man* (1932), which provided the basis for a series of five movies starring William Powell and Myrna Loy; and *The Glass Key* (1931). Hammett, who refused to name members of an alleged subversive organization during House Un-American Activities Committee hearings, was jailed for six months in 1951, and later was charged with tax delinquency by the Bureau of Internal Revenue. He never resumed writing and died Jan 10, 1961, at New York City.

HICKOCK, WILD BILL: BIRTH ANNIVERSARY. May 27, 1837. Born at Troy Grove, IL, and died Aug 2, 1876, at Deadwood, SD. American frontiersman, legendary marksman, lawman, army scout and gambler. Hickock's end came when he was shot dead at a poker table by a drunk in the Number Ten saloon.

HUMPHREY, HUBERT HORATIO: BIRTH ANNIVERSARY. May 27, 1911. Born at Wallace, SD, May 27, 1911. 38th vice president of the US. Died at Waverly, MN, Jan 13, 1978.

NATIONAL SENIOR HEALTH AND FITNESS DAY. May 27. Local sites in all 50 states. Fifth annual event to promote the value of fitness and exercise for older adults. During this day—as part of Older Americans Month activities—seniors across the country are involved in locally organized health promotion activities. Call the toll-free number for further info and a list of local sites. Annually, the last Wednesday in May. In 1997 more than 90,000 older adults participated in fitness activities at more than 900 sites nationwide. Est attendance: 100,000. For info: Tina Godin, Program Coord, Mature Market Resource Center, 621 E Park Ave, Libertyville, IL 60048. Phone: (800) 828-8225. Fax: (847) 816-8662.
Email: maturemkt@aol.com. WWW: http://www.fitnessday.com

PRICE, VINCENT: BIRTH ANNIVERSARY. May 27, 1911. Actor, best known for his portrayal of sinister villains in horror films and as host for the TV series "Mystery." Born at St. Louis, MO, and died at Los Angeles, CA, on Oct 25, 1993.

RMS *QUEEN MARY*: MAIDEN VOYAGE: ANNIVERSARY. May 27, 1936. Anniversary of the maiden voyage from Southampton, England, to New York Harbor.

May 1998

S	M	T	W	T	F	S
					1	2
3	4	5	6	7	8	9
10	11	12	13	14	15	16
17	18	19	20	21	22	23
24	25	26	27	28	29	30
31						

BIRTHDAYS TODAY

John Barth, 68, author (*Last Voyage of Somebody the Sailor, Letters*), born Cambridge, MD, May 27, 1930.
Pat Cash, 33, tennis player, born Melbourne, Australia, May 27, 1965.
Christopher J. Dodd, 54, US Senator (D, Connecticut), born Willimantic, CT, May 27, 1944.
Louis Gossett, Jr, 62, actor (Emmy for "Roots"; Oscar for *An Officer and a Gentleman; Sadat, Enemy Mine*), born Brooklyn, NY, May 27, 1936.
Henry Kissinger, 75, former secretary of state, author, born Fuerth, Germany, May 27, 1923.
Christopher Lee, 76, actor (*Dracula, The Mummy*), born London, England, May 27, 1922.
Ramsey Lewis, 63, musician, winner of three Grammy awards, born Chicago, IL, May 27, 1935.
Lee Meriwether, 63, actress (Cat Woman on TV "Batman"; former Miss America ('55), born Los Angeles, CA, May 27, 1935.
William Sessions, 68, former director of the FBI, born Fort Smith, AK, May 27, 1930.
Samuel Jackson (Sam) Snead, 86, golfer, born Hot Springs, May 27, 1912.
Frank Thomas, 30, baseball player, born Columbus, GA, May 27, 1968.
Bruce Weitz, 55, actor ("Hill Street Blues," "Death of a Centerfold: The Dorothy Stratton Story"), born Norwalk, CT, May 27, 1943.
Herman Wouk, 83, writer (*Marjorie Morningstar, The Winds of War*), born New York, NY, May 27, 1915.

MAY 28 — THURSDAY

Day 148 — 217 Remaining

AGASSIZ, LOUIS: BIRTH ANNIVERSARY. May 28, 1807. Professor of zoology and geology at Harvard, born at Motier, Switzerland. He was a major influence in spawning American interest in natural history and helped to establish the Harvard Museum of Comparative Zoology. "The eye of the trilobite," Agassiz wrote in 1870, "tells us that the sun shone on the old beach where he lived; for there is nothing in nature without a purpose, and when so complicated an organ was made to receive the light, there must have been light to enter it." Agassiz died at Cambridge, MA, Dec 14, 1873.

AMNESTY INTERNATIONAL FOUNDED: ANNIVERSARY. May 28, 1961. This Nobel Prize winning human rights organization was founded by London lawyer Peter Berenson when he read about the arrest of a group of students in Portugal. He launched a one-year campaign called Appeal for Amnesty. Today Amnesty International has over one million members in 150 countries who work to free all prisoners of conscience (those imprisoned for their beliefs), abolish the use of torture and the death penalty and guarantee human rights for women. For info: Amnesty USA, 322 8th Ave, New York, NY 10001. Phone: (800) AMNESTY or (212) 807-8400.
WWW: http://www.amnesty-usa.org

AZERBAIJAN: NATIONAL DAY. May 28. Public holiday.

CALIFORNIA SENIOR GAMES SACRAMENTO. May 28–31. Sacramento, CA. Athletic competition for men and women age 50 and older. Compete in five-year age divisions. Twenty-one sports. Est attendance: 1,000. For info: Pamela Rhodes, Coord, 6005 Folsom Blvd, Sacramento, CA 95819. Phone: (916) 277-6094. Fax: (916) 277-6074.

CANADA: ANNAPOLIS VALLEY APPLE BLOSSOM FESTIVAL. May 28–June 1. Windsor to Digby, Nova Scotia. Annual festival with barbecues, sports events, art show, Princess Tea, coronation ceremonies, dances, concerts, fireworks, craft fair, children's parade, Grand Street Parade and "Sunday in the Park" (family entertainment). Annually, since 1933. Est attendance: 125,000. For info: Festival Office, 37 Cornwallis St, Kentville, NS, Canada B4N 2E2. Phone: (902) 678-8322. Fax: (902) 678-3710. WWW: http://www.valleyweb.com

DIONNE QUINTUPLETS: BIRTHDAY. May 28, 1934. Five daughters (Marie, Cecile, Yvonne, Emilie and Annette) were born to Oliva and Elzire Dionne, near Callander, Ont, Canada. They were the first quints known to have lived for more than a few hours after birth. Emilie died in 1954, Marie in 1970. The other three sisters are still living.

FLEMING, IAN: BIRTH ANNIVERSARY. May 28, 1908. English novelist, creator of the James Bond series. Born at London, died Aug 12, 1964, at Sandwich, England.

GUILLOTIN, JOSEPH IGNACE: BIRTH ANNIVERSARY. May 28, 1738. French physician and member of the Constituent Assembly who urged the use of a machine that was sometimes called the "Maiden" for the execution of death sentences—in a less painful, more certain way of dispatching those sentenced to death. The guillotine was first used on Apr 25, 1792, for the execution of a highwayman, Nicolas Jacques Pelletier. Other machines for decapitation had been in use from time to time in other countries since the Middle Ages. Guillotin was born at Saintes, France and died at Paris, Mar 26, 1814.

MAINLY MOZART FESTIVAL. May 28–June 14. San Diego County and Baja, CA. David Atherton conducts world-class artists in a bi-national celebration of Mozart and his contemporaries in San Diego and Escondido, CA, and Tijuana, Rosarito, Mexicali and Ensenada, Mexico. Chamber orchestra, chamber music and recitals are presented. Est attendance: 20,000. For info: Public Relations, Mainly Mozart, PO Box 124705, San Diego, CA 92112-4705. Phone: (619) 239-0100. Fax: (619) 233-4292. Email: admin@mainlymozart.com. WWW: http://www.mainlymozart.com

ORTHODOX ASCENSION DAY. May 28. Observed by Eastern Orthodox Churches on this date.

PITT, WILLIAM: BIRTH ANNIVERSARY. May 28, 1759. British prime minister from 1783 to 1801 and from 1804 to 1806, Pitt was influenced by Adam Smith's economic theories and reduced England's large national debt caused by the American Revolution. Born at Hayes, Kent, England, he died Jan 23, 1806, at Putney. He was the son of William Pitt, first earl of Chatham, for whom the city of Pittsburgh was named.

PORTLAND ROSE FESTIVAL. May 28–June 21. Portland, OR. Celebration includes more than 70 events featuring grand floral parade, hot air balloons, band festivals, auto and dragon boat races, carnival, air show and Navy ship visits. Est attendance: 2,000,000. For info: Clarence Moriwaki, Portland Rose Festival Assn, 220 NW Second Ave, Portland, OR 97209. Phone: (503) 227-2681. Fax: (503) 227-6603. Email: info@rosefestival.org. WWW: http://www.rosefestival.org

SAINT BERNARD OF MONTJOUX FEAST DAY. May 28. Patron saint of mountain climbers, founder of Alpine hospices of the Great and Little St. Bernard, died at age 85, probably on May 28, 1081.

SAKHALIN ISLAND QUAKE: ANNIVERSARY. May 28, 1995. At 1:03 AM, the island of Sakhalin, off the east coast of Russia, was struck by an earthquake that measured 7.5 on the Richter scale. The town of Neftegorsk at the epicenter was almost completely flattened. More than 2,000 of the town's 3,200 citizens were buried in rubble while they slept. Although rescue efforts were severely hampered by frigid weather and the remoteness of the area, the Russian government nevertheless turned down offers of help from South Korea and Japan. It was determined that the city will not be rebuilt and that survivors will be relocated to southern Sakhalin.

SIERRA CLUB FOUNDED: ANNIVERSARY. May 28, 1892. Founded by famed naturalist John Muir, the Sierra Club promotes conservation of the natural environment by influencing public policy. It has been especially important in the founding of and protection of our national parks. For info: Sierra Club, 85 Second St, 2d flr, San Francisco, CA 94105-3441. Phone: (415) 977-5500. WWW: http://www.sierraclub.org

SLUGS RETURN FROM CAPISTRANO DAY. May 28. It's a little known secret that slimy slugs spend their winters in lovely Capistrano and return to our patios and gardens on this date. Bare feet not a good idea now through first frost. [© 1997 by WPL] For info: Tom or Ruth Roy, Wellness Permission League, PO Box 662, Mt Gretna, PA 17064-0662. Phone: (500) 437-5104 or (717) 964-1308. Fax: (717) 964-1335.

SUMMER LIGHTS. May 28–31. Nashville, TN. Art, dance, theatre and more than 250 live entertainment acts covering a wide variety of musical genres work together to make this Nashville's largest festival. Est attendance: 150,000. For info: Shannon White, Festival Coord, 209 10th Ave S, Ste 347, Nashville, TN 37203. Phone: (615) 259-0900. Fax: (615) 259-0651. Email: summerlights@mindspring.com. WWW: http://www.summerlights.org

THORPE, JAMES FRANCIS: BIRTH ANNIVERSARY. May 28, 1888. Jim Thorpe, distinguished American athlete, winner of pentathlon and decathlon events at the 1912 Olympic Games, professional baseball and football player, American Indian, born near Prague, OK, and died at Lomita, CA, Mar 28, 1953.

"ZOO PARADE" TV PREMIERE: ANNIVERSARY. May 28, 1950. NBC's half-hour program on animals and animal behavior was hosted by Marlin Perkins and Jim Hurlbut. Initially, it was broadcast from Lincoln Park Zoo in Chicago, but after 1955, the show was broadcast from other locales throughout the country.

BIRTHDAYS TODAY

Carroll Baker, 67, actress (*Baby Doll, Harlow*), born Johnstown, PA, May 28, 1931.

Barry Commoner, 81, biologist, politician, born Brooklyn, NY, May 28, 1917.

Kirk Harold Gibson, 41, former baseball player, born Pontiac, MI, May 28, 1957.

Armon Louis Gilliam, 34, basketball player, born Pittsburgh, PA, May 28, 1964.

Rudolph Giuliani, 54, Mayor of New York City, born Brooklyn, NY, May 28, 1944.

Gladys Knight, 54, singer (and the Pips; "Neither One of Us," "If I Were Your Woman"), born Atlanta, GA, May 28, 1944.

Sondra Locke, 51, actress (*The Heart Is a Lonely Hunter, Bronco Billy*), director (*Ratboy*), born Shelbyville, TN, May 28, 1947.

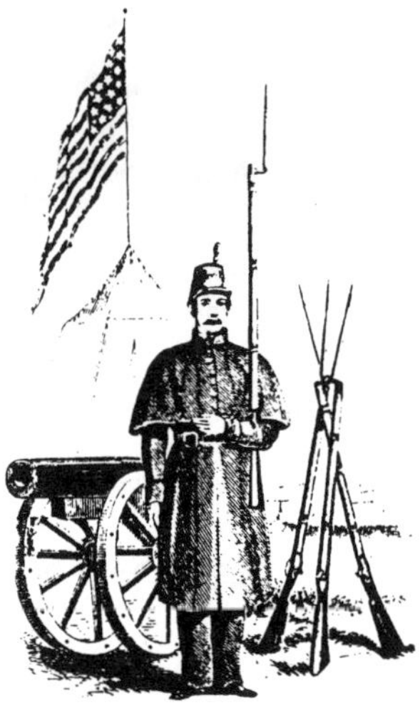

MAY 29 — FRIDAY

Day 149 — 216 Remaining

AMNESTY ISSUED FOR SOUTHERN REBELS: ANNIVERSARY. May 29, 1865. President Andrew Johnson issued a proclamation giving a general amnesty to all who participated in the rebellion against the United States. High ranking members of the Confederate government and military and those who owned more than $20,000 worth of property were excepted and had to apply individually to the President for a pardon. Once an oath of allegience was taken, all former property rights, except those in slaves, were returned to the former owners.

ASCENSION OF BAHA'U'LLAH: ANNIVERSARY. May 29. Baha'i observance of the anniversary of the death in exile of Baha'u'llah (the prophet-founder of the Baha'i Faith), May 29, 1892. One of the nine days of the year when Baha'is suspend work. For info: Pamela Zivari, Dir, Baha'is of the US, Office of Public Information, 866 UN Plaza, Ste 120, New York, NY 10017-1822. Phone: (212) 803-2500. Fax: (212) 803-2573. Email: usopi-ny@bic.org.

CHARLES II: RESTORATION AND BIRTH ANNIVERSARY. May 29, 1660. Restoration of Charles II to English throne. Also his birthday (May 29, 1630). English monarchy restored after Commonwealth period under Oliver Cromwell.

CHESTERTON, GILBERT KEITH: BIRTH ANNIVERSARY. May 29, 1874. English author. Died June 14, 1936.

CONSTANTINOPLE FELL TO THE TURKS: ANNIVERSARY. May 29, 1453. The city of Constantinople was captured by the Turks, who renamed it Istanbul. This conquest marked the end of the Byzantine Empire; the city became the capital of the Ottoman Empire.

FISHING HAS NO BOUNDARIES—EAGLE RIVER. May 29–31. "T" Docks, Dock Park, Eagle River, WI. A three-day fishing experience for disabled persons on the Eagle River Chain of 28 beautiful lakes. Any disability, age, sex, race, etc, eligible. Attended by 75 participants and 200 volunteers. For info: Wil Campbell, Fishing Has No Boundaries, PO Box 2200, Eagle River, WI 54521. Phone: (715) 479-9309. Fax: (715) 479-4782. Email: wbc1@newnorth.net.

HENRY, PATRICK: BIRTH ANNIVERSARY. May 29, 1736. American revolutionary leader and orator, born at Studley, VA, and died near Brookneal, VA, June 6, 1799. Especially remembered for his speech (Mar 23, 1775) for arming the Virginia militia, at St. Johns Church, Richmond, VA, when he declared: "I know not what course others may take, but as for me, give me liberty or give me death."

May 1998	S	M	T	W	T	F	S
						1	2
	3	4	5	6	7	8	9
	10	11	12	13	14	15	16
	17	18	19	20	21	22	23
	24	25	26	27	28	29	30
	31						

KENNEDY, JOHN FITZGERALD: BIRTH ANNIVERSARY. May 29, 1917. Thirty-fifth president of the US, born at Brookline, MA, May 29, 1917. Assassinated while riding in an open automobile, in Dallas, TX, Nov 22, 1963. (Accused assassin Lee Harvey Oswald was killed at the Dallas police station by a gunman, Jack Rubenstein [Ruby], two days later.) Kennedy was the youngest man ever elected to the presidency, the first Roman Catholic, and the first president to have served in the US Navy. He was the fourth US president to be killed by an assassin, and the second to be buried at Arlington National Cemetery (first was William Howard Taft).

MORNING RADIO WISE GUY DAY. May 29. To honor all morning radio disc jockeys who get your day started with humor, music and information. Annually, last Friday in May. For info: Leroy and Mark, 98 KISC FM, 300 E. Third, Spokane, WA 99202. Phone: (509) 459-9800. Fax: (509) 459-9850. Email: mholman@iea.com. WWW: http://98kiss.fm.net

MOSCOW COMMUNIQUE: ANNIVERSARY. May 29, 1972. President Richard Nixon and Soviet Party leader Leonid Brezhnev released a joint communique after Nixon's week-long visit to Moscow. During the visit the two men acknowledged their major differences on the Vietnam War, signed a treaty on antiballistic missile systems as well as an interim agreement on limitation of strategic missiles and an agreement for a joint space flight in 1975. This was the first visit ever to Moscow by a US president (May 22–30, 1972).

MOUNT EVEREST SUMMIT REACHED: ANNIVERSARY. May 29, 1953. New Zealand explorer Sir Edmund Hillary and Tensing Norgay, a Sherpa guide, became the first team to reach the summit of Mt Everest, the world's highest mountain.

RHODE ISLAND: RATIFICATION DAY. May 29. Thirteenth state to ratify Constitution, on this day in 1790.

SOCCER TRAGEDY: ANNIVERSARY. May 29, 1985. A riot at Heysel stadium in Brussels, Belgium, killed 39 people. Fans attending the European Cup Final, between Liverpool and Juventus of Turin, clashed before the match started. Some 400 persons were injured in the riot. The incident was televised and viewed by millions throughout Europe. More than two years later, Sept 2, 1987, the British government announced that 26 British soccer fans (identified from television tapes) would be extradited to Belgium for trial. Hooliganism at soccer matches became the target of increased security measures for most of England's more than 90 professional teams following the 1985 tragedy.

SPENGLER, OSWALD: BIRTH ANNIVERSARY. May 29, 1880. German historian, author of *The Decline of the West*, born at Blankenburg-am-Harz, Germany. Died at Munich, Germany, May 8, 1936.

VIRGINIA PLAN PROPOSED: ANNIVERSARY. May 29, 1787. Just five days after the Constitutional Convention met at Philadelphia, PA, the "Virginia Plan" was proposed. It called for establishment of a new governmental organization consisting of a legislature with two houses, an executive (chosen by the legislature) and a judicial branch.

WISCONSIN: ADMISSION DAY: 150th ANNIVERSARY. May 29, 1848. Became 30th state on this day in 1848. At noon, every community in the state will ring bells to mark the occasion and the governor will host the state celebration of its sesquicentennial at Capitol Square in Madison.

BIRTHDAYS TODAY

Annette Bening, 40, actress (*The American President, Bugsy, The Grifters, Valmont*), born Topeka, KS, May 29, 1958.

Kevin Conway, 56, actor (*When You Comin' Back, Red Ryder?, Of Mice and Men, Other People's Money*), born New York, NY, May 29, 1942.

Eric Davis, 36, baseball player, born Los Angeles, CA, May 29, 1962.

Paul Ehrlich, 66, population biologist, born Philadelphia, PA, May 29, 1932.

Melissa Etheridge, 37, singer/guitarist, born Leavenworth, KS, May 29, 1961.

Anthony Geary, 50, actor (Luke on "General Hospital"), born Coalville, UT, May 29, 1948.

Bob Hope (Leslie Townes), 95, comedian ("Road" movies with Bing Crosby; entertained US troops abroad), born Eltham, England, May 29, 1903.

Adrian Paul, 39, actor ("Highlander" series), born London, England, May 29, 1959.

Felix Rohatyn, 70, investment banker (developed strategy to keep New York City solvent), born Vienna, Austria, May 29, 1928.

Alfred (Al) Unser, Sr, 59, auto racer, born Albuquerque, NM, May 29, 1939.

Francis Thomas (Fay) Vincent, Jr, 60, former commissioner of baseball, born Waterbury, CT, May 29, 1938.

Lisa Whelchel, 35, actress (Blair on "Facts of Life"), born Fort Worth, TX, May 29, 1963.

MAY 30 — SATURDAY

Day 150 — 215 Remaining

CHINA: DRAGON BOAT FESTIVAL. May 30. An important Chinese observance, the Dragon Boat Festival commemorates a hero of ancient China, poet Qu Yuan, who drowned himself in protest against injustice and corruption. It is said that rice dumplings were cast into the water to lure fish away from the body of the martyr, and this is remembered by the eating of zhong zi, glutinous rice dumplings filled with meat and wrapped in bamboo leaves. Dragon boat races are held on rivers. The Dragon Boat Festival is observed in many countries by their Chinese populations. Also called Fifth Month Festival or Summer Festival. Annually, the fifth day of the fifth lunar month.

CMN CHAMPIONS. May 30–31. The largest televised fundraiser in history. More than $150 million was raised in 1997. Benefits 165 hospitals for children. For info: Children's Miracle Network, 4525 S 2300 E, Ste 202, Salt Lake City, UT 84117. Phone: (801) 278-8900.

CROATIA: NATIONAL DAY. May 30. Public holiday.

FAIRMOUNT ACADEMY 1800s FESTIVAL. May 30. Fairmount, MD. Rain date the following Saturday. Restored school, spelling bees, square dancing, quilt show, folk arts and crafts, music and plenty of good food. For info: Nevette Muir, Fairmount Academy Historical Assn, PO Box 134, Upper Fairmount, MD 21867. Phone: (410) 651-0351 or (410) 651-3945.

FIRST AMERICAN DAILY NEWSPAPER PUBLISHED: ANNIVERSARY. May 30, 1783. *The Pennsylvania Evening Post* became the first daily newspaper published in the US on May 30, 1783. The paper was published in Philadelphia, PA, by Benjamin Towne.

GERMANY: MARBURG UNIVERSITY FOUNDING: ANNIVERSARY. May 30. University of Marburg was founded May 30, 1527.

GREAT FLOOD OF 1889 COMMEMORATIVE WEEKEND. May 30–31. Johnstown Flood Museum, Johnstown, PA. The Johnstown Flood Museum recreates the shocking catastrophe in which 2,209 people died, tens of thousands were left homeless and a prospering city was left a wasteland. "The Johnstown Flood" documentary, winner of Best Documentary, Short Subject in 1989, is shown hourly. For info: Katherine A. Morris, Johnstown Flood Museum, PO Box 1889, Johnstown, PA 15907-1889. Phone: (814) 539-1889 or (888) 222-1889. Fax: (814) 599-4885.

HALL OF FAME FOR GREAT AMERICANS: OPENING ANNIVERSARY. May 30, 1901. The Hall of Fame for Great Americans at New York University, New York, NY, was dedicated and opened to the public on this day.

HEIRLOOM SEED DAY. May 30. Woodstock, VT. Learn about the importance of heirloom vegetables and the many seed varieties available. Take home a packet of select seeds saved from the museum's 19th-century garden. For info: Deborah Bulissa, Billings Farm & Museum, Box 489, Woodstock, VT 05091. Phone: (802) 457-2355. Fax: (802) 457-4663. Email: billings.farm@valley.net.

KOREA: TANO DAY. May 30. Fifth day of fifth lunar month. Summer food offered at the household shrine of the ancestors. Also known as Swing Day, since girls dressed in their prettiest clothes often compete in swinging matches. The Tano Festival usually lasts from the third through eighth day of the fifth lunar month: May 28–June 2.

LINCOLN MEMORIAL DEDICATION: ANNIVERSARY. May 30, 1922. The memorial is made of marble from Colorado and Tennessee and limestone from Indiana. It stands in West Potomac Park in Washington, DC. The outside columns are Doric, the inside, Ionic. The Memorial was designed by architect Henry Bacon and its cornerstone was laid in 1915. A skylight lets light into the interiors where the compelling statue "Seated Lincoln," by sculptor Daniel Chester French, is situated.

LOOMIS DAY. May 30. To honor Mahlon Loomis, a Washington, DC, dentist who received a US patent on wireless telegraphy in 1872 (before Marconi was born). Titled "An Improvement in Telegraphing," the patent described how to do without the wires; this patent was backed up by experiment on the Massanutten Mountains of Virginia. For info: Robert L. Birch, Puns Corps, Box 2364, Falls Church, VA 22042-0364. Phone: (703) 533-3668.

MEMORIAL DAY (TRADITIONAL). May 30. This day honors the tradition of making memorial tributes to the dead, especially remembering those who have died in battle. Observed as a legal public holiday on the last Monday in May.

PALATINE MUSEUM SPRING EVENT. May 30. Sheep shearing festival at Palatine House Museum, Schoharie, NY. This event is fun for the whole family. Est attendance: 1,700. For info: Diane Szabo, Program Dir, Schoharie Colonial Heritage Assn, Box 554, Schoharie, NY 12157. Phone: (518) 295-7505 or (518) 295-7585.

PEACHTREE JUNIOR. May 30. Atlanta, GA. A 3K noncompetitive run for children ages 7–12. Entries limited to 2,500. Est attendance: 2,500. Send SASE for info: Atlanta Track Club, Peachtree Jr, 3097 E Shadowlawn Ave, Atlanta, GA 30305. Phone: (404) 231-9064.

PETER I: BIRTH ANNIVERSARY. May 30, 1672. Peter I (Peter the Great) Tzar and Emperor of Russia. His primary aim was to make Russia a major power equal to its size and potential, and the way he saw to do this was through education and technology. He established printing presses and published translations of foreign books, particularly scientific and technical material. The Russian alphabet was simplified, and Arabic numerals were introduced. Peter encouraged trade with foreign countries, mercantilism within Russia and the entrepreneurial skills of resident foreigners; he allowed industrialists to own serfs, a right previously limited to landholders. He completely overhauled the government, the Greek Orthodox Church, the military system and the structure of taxes, ultimately increasing the power of the monarchy at the expense of the nobility and the national church. Upon his death at age 52 on Jan 28, 1725, he was succeeded by his wife Catherine.

POPE NIXES ORDAINING OF WOMEN: ANNIVERSARY. May 30, 1994. Pope John Paul II, in a letter to Roman Catholic bishops, declared the debate on the ordination of women closed. He stated that, based on New Testament practices and tradition, the church could not ordain women to the priesthood. This announcement put the Roman Catholic church at odds with the Anglican Communion, which had ordained a group of women earlier in the year. Several other Christian denominations have had an ordained female clergy for years. The announcement also went against the hopes of a large segment of Roman Catholics around the world. Many Catholics had long petitioned that clergy be allowed to marry, and many felt that the ordination of women was necessary to relieve an increasingly desperate shortage of priests.

PRINTERS ROW BOOK FAIR. May 30–31. South Dearborn Street between Congress and Polk in Chicago, IL. More than 150 booksellers and publishers from all over the U.S. and Canada fill the streets with new, used, rare and antiquarian books for sale; demonstrations of paper making, paper marbling and book binding; author readings, panel discussions, poetry tent and an elaborate children's program are all part of the free programs. Food, music and much more at the largest book event in the Midwest. Est attendance: 75,000. For info: Elizabeth Kramer, Program Coord, Near South Planning Bd, 1727 S Indiana, #104, Chicago, IL 60616. Fax: (312) 987-9215.

SAINT JOAN OF ARC: FEAST DAY. May 30. French heroine and martyr, known as the Maid of Orleans, led French against English invading army. Captured, found guilty of heresy and burned at the stake in 1431 (at age 19). Innocence declared in 1456. Canonized in 1920.

SEASIDE FINE ART SHOW. May 30–31. Neptune Park, St. Simons Island, GA. Strictly juried fine art festival attracts top artists from all over the country. Prestigious judges, top prize money. Annually, the last full weekend of May. Est attendance: 15,000. For info: The Glynn Art Assn, PO Box 20673, St. Simons Island, GA 31522. Phone: (912) 638-8770. Fax: (912) 638-8770.

SHAVUOT BEGINS AT SUNDOWN. May 30. Jewish Pentecost. See "Shavuot" (May 31).

SPACE MILESTONE: *ARIANE-2* (ESA). May 30, 1986. European Space Agency unmanned rocket carrying Intelsat V communications satellite was launched from Kourou space center in French Guiana. It was destroyed during launch because of a malfunction.

SPACE MILESTONE: *MARINER 9* (US). May 30, 1971. Unmanned spacecraft was launched, which entered Martian orbit the following Nov 13. The craft relayed temperature and gravitational fields and sent back spectacular photographs of both the surface of Mars and of her two moons. First spacecraft to orbit another planet.

SPACE MILESTONE: *NASA ATS-6* (US). May 30, 1974. Launch of communications satellite with expected six-year life in stationary orbit.

SPRING FESTIVAL. May 30. Worthington, MN. Celebrating the end of the school year this program is for children third grade and under. Festival coincides with the opening of Pioneer Village. A special attraction is planned and there will be drawings for prizes for the children in attendance. Lunch will be provided for everyone. For info: Alan Swanson, Nobles County Historical Society, 1210 Duba St, Worthington, MN 58187. Phone: (507) 376-4011.

May 1998

S	M	T	W	T	F	S
					1	2
3	4	5	6	7	8	9
10	11	12	13	14	15	16
17	18	19	20	21	22	23
24	25	26	27	28	29	30
31						

TRINIDAD: INDIAN ARRIVAL DAY. May 30. Port of Spain, West Indies. Public holiday. For info: Info Dept, Tourism Div, Tourism and Industrial Development Co, Trinidad and Tobago Ltd, 10–14 Phillips St, West Indies. Phone: (800) 595-1868.

WHIPPOORWILL MORGAN HORSE OPEN BARN. May 30–31. Old Lyme, CT. Visitors can pet newborn foals and watch stallions and mares perform. There will also be an informative and informal introduction to the Morgan Horse. Est attendance: 250. For info: McCulloch Farm, Whippoorwill Morgan, 100 Whippoorwill Rd, Old Lyme, CT 06371. Phone: (860) 434-7355.

WORLD WAR II: BATTLE OF THE ALEUTIAN ISLANDS: 55th ANNIVERSARY. May 30, 1943. The islands of Kiska and Attu in the Aleutian Islands off the coast of Alaska were retaken by the US 7th Infantry Division on May 30, 1943. The battle (Operation Landgrab) began when an American force of 11,000 landed on Attu May 12. In three weeks of fighting US casualties numbered 552 killed and 1,140 wounded. Only 28 wounded Japanese were taken prisoner. Their dead amounted to 2,352, of whom 500 committed suicide.

ZOO BABIES. May 30–June 30. Cincinnati Zoo and Botanical Garden, Cincinnati, OH. The adorable new offspring are made easy to find with eight-foot storks placed at baby animal areas. Special weekend family entertainment. Est attendance: 180,000. For info: Events/Promo Dept, Cincinnati Zoo and Botanical Garden, 3400 Vine St, Cincinnati, OH 45220. Phone: (513) 281-4701 ext 8316. Fax: (513) 559-7790. WWW: http://www.cincyzoo.org

BIRTHDAYS TODAY

Blake Bashoff, 17, actor (*Bushwhacked, Big Bully*), born Philadelphia, PA, May 30, 1981.
Keir Dullea, 62, actor (*David and Lisa, 2001: A Space Odyssey*), born Cleveland, OH, May 30, 1936.
Bob Evans, 80, restaurant executive, born Sugar Ridge, OH, May 30, 1918.
Wynonna Judd, 34, singer ("Wynonna," "Tell Me Why"), winner of six Grammy awards, born Ashland, KY, May 30, 1964.
Ted McGinley, 40, actor ("Married. . . With Children," *Revenge of the Nerds*), born Newport Beach, CA, May 30, 1958.
Colm Meaney, 45, actor ("Star Trek: The Next Generation"), born Dublin, Ireland, May 30, 1953.
Michael J. Pollard, 59, actor (*Bonnie and Clyde*, "Leo & Liz in Beverly Hills"), born Passaic, NJ, May 30, 1939.
Manny Ramirez, 26, baseball player, born Santo Domingo, Dominican Republic, May 30, 1972.
Gale Eugene Sayers, 55, Pro Football Hall of Fame running back, born Wichita, KS, May 30, 1943.
Stephen Tobolowsky, 47, actor (*The Grifters, Groundhog Day*), born Dallas, TX, May 30, 1951.
Clint Walker, 71, actor (*The Dirty Dozen*, "Cheyenne"), born Hartford, IL, May 30, 1927.

MAY 31 — SUNDAY

Day 151 — 214 Remaining

AMECHE, DON: 90th BIRTH ANNIVERSARY. May 31, 1908. Film, stage, radio and TV actor. Born Dominic Felix Amici at Kenosha, WI, and died Dec 6, 1993, at Scottsdale, AZ.

BATTLE OF SEVEN PINES: ANNIVERSARY. May 31, 1862. Confederate General Joseph Johnston's troops defeated McClellan's Army of the Potomac at the Battle of Seven Pines (or Fair Oaks, VA). Although the Confederates scored a major battlefield victory and McClellan's forces withdrew the next day, the effect of the battle did little to ease the pressure on the besieged Confederate capital of Richmond. During the battle Johnston was wounded, and Robert E. Lee was named commander of the Army of Northern Virginia.

FREDERICKSBURG MUSIC FESTIVAL. May 31–June 7. Final date available after Apr 1. A series of concerts featuring some of the nation's top musicians with musical styles from Dixieland to symphony and jazz to chamber. Occasionally, dance performances are offered. Annually, around the first week of June. Est attendance: 4,500. For info: Fredericksburg Festival of the Arts, Inc, PO Box 7816, Fredericksburg, VA 22404. Phone: (540) 374-5040. Fax: (540) 374-1866.

FRENCH WEST INDIES: JUNE REGATTAS. May 31–June 6. Martinique. Innovative sailing event leaving from Le Marin Marina. For info: Ms Muriel Wiltord, Martinique Promo Bureau, 444 Madison Ave, 16th Fl, New York, NY 10022. Phone: (800) 391-4909. Fax: (212) 838-7855.
Email: martinique@nyo.com.
WWW: http://www.martinique.org

ITALY: PALIO DEI BALESTRIERI. May 31. Gubbio. The last Sunday in May is set aside for a medieval crossbow contest between Gubbio and Saensepolcro; medieval costumes, arms.

JOHNSTOWN FLOOD: ANNIVERSARY. May 31. Heavy rains in May, 1889, caused the Connemaugh River Dam to burst on May 31 of that year. At nearby Johnstown, PA, the resulting flood killed more than 2,300 persons and destroyed the homes of thousands more. Nearly 800 unidentified drowning victims were buried in a common grave at Johnstown's Grandview Cemetery. So devastating was the flood and so widespread the sorrow for its victims that "Johnstown Flood" entered the language as a phrase to describe a disastrous event. The valley city of Johnstown, in the Allegheny Mountains, has been damaged repeatedly by floods, but that of 1889 took the greatest number of lives. Floods in 1936 (25 deaths) and 1977 (85 deaths) were next most destructive.

NATIONAL SAVE YOUR HEARING DAY. May 31. A public awareness campaign on the importance of saving your hearing featuring presentation of free hearing screening tests. Annually, May 31 (last day of Better Hearing and Speech Month). For info: Robert D. Bruce, Chair, National Save Your Hearing Foundation, 15835 Park Ten Pl, Ste 105, Houston, TX 77084-5131. Phone: (281) 492-2784. Fax: (281) 492-1434. Email: 71530,2600@compuserve.com.

PEALE, NORMAN VINCENT: 100th BIRTH ANNIVERSARY. May 31, 1898. American religious leader Norman Vincent Peale was born at Bowersville, OH. He is best known for his book *The Power of Positive Thinking* (1952), which combines religion and psychiatry. He was a minister at the Marble Collegiate Church at New York, NY, and served as president of the Council of Churches of the City of New York for four terms. He died on Dec 24, 1993, at Pawling, NY.

PENTECOST. May 31. The Christian feast of Pentecost commemorates descent of the Holy Spirit unto the Apostles, 50 days after Easter. Observed on the seventh Sunday after Easter. Recognized since the third century. See also: "Whitsunday" (below).

POPE PIUS XI: BIRTH ANNIVERSARY. May 31, 1857. Ambrogio Damiano Achille Ratti, 259th pope of the Roman Catholic Church, born at Desio, Italy. Elected pope Feb 6, 1922. Died Feb 10, 1939.

"SEINFELD" TV PREMIERE: ANNIVERSARY. May 31, 1990. "Seinfeld"—the show about nothing—premiered on NBC to wide acclaim. The show revolves around the lives and exploits of its four main leads whose storylines are usually intertwined for some surprising plot twists. Comedian Jerry Seinfeld uses his stand-up routines as an introduction to the show; some of the programs concerned relationships, valet parking, annoying dogs, waiting for Chinese food and just about anything else. The cast features Seinfeld as himself; Julia Louis-Dreyfus as his ex-girlfriend, Elaine Bennett; Jason Alexander as his best friend, George Costanza; and Michael Richards as his neighbor, Cosmo Kramer.

SHAVUOT or FEAST OF WEEKS. May 31. Jewish Pentecost holy day. Hebrew date, Sivan 6, 5758. Celebrates giving of Torah (the Law) to Moses on Mount Sinai.

★**SMALL BUSINESS WEEK.** May 31–June 6. To honor the 22 million small businesses in the US. Annually, the first full week in June. For info: Small Business Administration, Info Services, 409 3rd St SW, 7th Fl, Washington, DC 20416. Phone: (202) 205-6606 or (202) 205-6531. WWW: http://www.sba.gov

STEVENSON DEPOT DAYS. May 31–June 6 (tentative dates). Stevenson, AL. Depot Days bring back the days when the Iron Horse of the Rails was the King of Transportation. Activities are focused around the historic Stevenson Depot, an important junction during the Civil War now listed on the National Register of Historic Places. Activities include wagon rides to Civil War fort, square dancing, storytelling contests, clogging, museum tours and big band entertainment. Annually, the first week in June. Est attendance: 10,000. For info: Stevenson Depot Museum, PO Box 894, Stevenson, AL 35772. Phone: (205) 437-3012.

SUNFLOWER MUSIC FESTIVAL. May 31–June 14. White Concert Hall, Washburn University, Topeka, KS. Nationally renowned chamber music students gather to perform a series of free concerts featuring ensembles and orchestras. No admission charge. For info: Washburn University Relations, 1700 SW College, Topeka, KS 66621. Phone: (785) 231-1010. Fax: (785) 231-1009. Email: zzdpmu@acc.wuacc.edu.

WHITMAN, WALT: BIRTH ANNIVERSARY. May 31, 1819. Poet and journalist Whitman's best known work, *Leaves of Grass,* is a classic of American poetry. His poems celebrated all of modern life, concealing nothing, including subjects that were considered taboo at the time. Died Mar 26, 1892, at Camden, NJ, at age 72. He was elected to the Hall of Fame of Great Americans in 1930.

WHITSUNDAY. May 31. Whitsunday, the seventh Sunday after Easter, is a popular time for baptism. "White Sunday" is named for the white garments formerly worn by the candidates for baptism and occurs at the Christian feast of Pentecost. See also: "Pentecost" (above).

WORLD NO-TOBACCO DAY. May 31. Intended to discourage tobacco users from consuming tobacco and to encourage governments, communities, groups and individuals to become aware of the challenge and to take action. For info: World No-Tobacco Day, American Assn for World Health, 1825 K St NW, Ste 1208, Washington, DC 20006. Phone: (202) 466-5883. Fax: (202) 466-5896. Email: aawhstaff@aol.com.
WWW: http://aawhworldhealth.org

BIRTHDAYS TODAY

Tom Berenger, 48, actor (*Born on the Fourth of July, The Field, Gettysburg*), born Chicago, IL, May 31, 1950.

Clint Eastwood, 68, actor, director (Oscar *Unforgiven*), former mayor of Carmel, CA, born San Francisco, CA, May 31, 1930.

Chris Elliott, 38, writer ("Late Night with David Letterman"), actor ("Get a Life"), born New York, NY, May 31, 1960.

Sharon Gless, 55, actress (Emmy for Cagney on "Cagney & Lacey"), born Los Angeles, CA, May 31, 1943.

Gregory Harrison, 48, actor ("Logan's Run," "Trapper John, MD"), born Avalon, Catalina Island, CA, May 31, 1950.

Joseph William (Joe) Namath, 55, Pro Football Hall of Fame quarterback, former sportscaster and actor, born Beaver Falls, PA, May 31, 1943.

Johnny Paycheck (Don Lytle), 57, singer ("Mr Lovemaker," "Take This Job and Shove It"), songwriter, born Greenfield, OH, May 31, 1941.

Brooke Shields, 33, actress (*Pretty Baby, The Blue Lagoon*, "Suddenly Susan"), born New York, NY, May 31, 1965.

Lea Thompson, 37, actress ("Caroline in the City," *Back to the Future, Howard the Duck*), born Rochester, MN, May 31, 1961.

Terry Waite, 59, Church of England special envoy, former hostage in Lebanon ('87–'91), born May 31, 1939.

Peter Yarrow, 60, composer, singer (Peter, Paul and Mary), born New York, NY, May 31, 1938.

☆ ☆ ☆

Iune.

JUNE 1 — MONDAY

Day 152 — 213 Remaining

ATLANTIC, CARIBBEAN AND GULF HURRICANE SEASON. June 1–Nov 30. For info: US Dept of Commerce, Natl Oceanic and Atmospheric Admin, Rockville, MD 20852.

CANCER FROM THE SUN MONTH. June 1–30. To promote education and awareness of the dangers of skin cancer from too much exposure to the sun. Kit of materials available for $15 from this nonprofit organization. For info: Frederick Mayer, Pres, Pharmacy Council on Dermatology (PCD), PO Box 1336, Sausalito, CA 94966. Phone: (415) 332-4066. Fax: (415) 332-1832. Email: ppsi@aol.com.

CENTRAL PACIFIC HURRICANE SEASON. June 1–Oct 31. Central Pacific is defined as 140 West Longitude to the International Date Line (180 West Longitude). For info: Natl Dept of Commerce, Natl Oceanic and Atmospheric Admin, Rockville, MD 20852.

ENGLAND: DICING FOR BIBLES. June 1. An old Whitmonday ceremony at All Saints Church, St. Ives, Huntingdonshire. A bequest (in 1675) with the intent of providing Bibles for poor children of the parish required winning them at a dice game played in the church. In recent years the dicing has been moved from the altar to a "more suitable" place. Six Bibles are given on Whitmonday each year.

FIREWORKS SAFETY MONTH. June 1–July 4. Activities during this month are designed to warn and educate parents and children about the dangers of playing with fireworks. Prevent Blindness America will offer suggestions for safer ways to celebrate the Fourth of July. Materials that can easily be posted or distributed to the community will be provided. For info: Prevent Blindness America®, 500 E Remington Rd, Schaumburg, IL 60173. Phone: (800) 331-2020. Fax: (847) 843-8458. WWW: http://www.prevent-blindness.org

GAY AND LESBIAN BOOK MONTH. June 1–30. Celebrating the publication of gay and lesbian literary works. For info: Michele Karlsberg, 47 Dongan Hills Ave, 1st Fl, Staten Island, NY 10306. Phone: (718) 351-9599. Fax: (718) 980-4262. Email: mlpubcorp@aol.com.

GAY AND LESBIAN HISTORY MONTH. June 1–30. Observed this month because on June 28, 1969, the clientele of a gay bar, the Stonewall Inn in New York City, rioted after being harassed by the police. Stonewall is now recognized as the start of the gay liberation movement.

June 1998

S	M	T	W	T	F	S
	1	2	3	4	5	6
7	8	9	10	11	12	13
14	15	16	17	18	19	20
21	22	23	24	25	26	27
28	29	30				

HOWARD, LESLIE: 55th DEATH ANNIVERSARY. June 1, 1943. During the return trip from a British government-sponsored tour of Spain, on June 1, 1943, a plane transporting 50-year-old actor Leslie Howard was shot down by German raiders. Rumors that he was serving on a spy mission for his government circulated at the time. In her biography about her father (*A Quite Remarkable Father*) his daughter expressed doubt that her father was the sort to get involved in espionage. Howard's most-remembered film role is that of Ashley Wilkes in *Gone with the Wind*.

IDAHO SHAKESPEARE FESTIVAL. June 1–Sept 30. Boise, ID. Idaho's renowned professional repertory theater company presents a full summer season of The Bard, plus one contemporary work, in its outdoor amphitheater along the Boise River. Bring your picnic dinner and enjoy "Shakespeare Under the Stars." Est attendance: 28,000. For info: Kristen Robertson DeAngeli, Dir of Mktg, Idaho Shakespeare Festival, PO Box 9365, Boise, ID 83707. Phone: (208) 323-9700. Fax: (208) 323-0700. Email: idshakes@micron.net.
WWW: http://www.idahoshakespeare.org

INTERNATIONAL VOLUNTEERS WEEK. June 1–7. To honor men and women throughout the world who serve as volunteers, rendering valuable service without compensation to the communities in which they live, and to honor nonprofit organizations dedicated to making the world a better place in which to live. For complete info, send $3 to cover expense of printing, handling and postage. Annually, the first seven days of June. For info: Dr. Stanley Drake, Pres, Intl Soc of Friendship and Good Will, 412 Cherry Hills Dr, Bakersfield, CA 93309-2866.

JUNE DAIRY MONTH. June 1–30. Since 1937, the dairy industry has set aside June as a time to pay tribute to the vital role milk and dairy products play in the American diet, and the outstanding contribution of America's dairy farmers. For info: Gloria Pope, Dir of Consumer Communications, Dairy Management, Inc, 10255 W Higgins Rd, Ste 900, Rosemont, IL 60018. Phone: (847) 803-2000 ext 261.

JUNE IS NATIONAL BEEF-STEAK MONTH. June 1–30. Celebrate one of America's favorite foods—beef-steak! Beef is the number-one protein choice in America, and steak leads the pack when it comes to how consumers eat beef at home. It's also a popular choice when dining out—consumers are ordering over 8.7 million servings of steak a year. For info: Marlys Bielunski, National Cattlemen's Beef Assn, 444 N Michigan Ave, Chicago, IL 60611. Phone: (312) 670-9250. Fax: (312) 467-1672. Email: bielunski@beefusa.org.

KENTUCKY: ADMISSION DAY: ANNIVERSARY. June 1, 1792. Became 15th state on this day in 1792.

KENYA: MADARAKA DAY. June 1. Madaraka Day (Self-Rule Day) is observed as a national public holiday.

LITTLE, CLEAVON: BIRTH ANNIVERSARY. June 1. Best known for his role as the black sheriff who cleaned up a town of bumbling redneck toughs in the movie *Blazing Saddles*, Cleavon Little was born June 1, 1939, in Chickasha, OK. Little was the winner of a Tony award for the 1970 musical *Purlie* and an Emmy in 1989 for a guest appearance on the television series "Dear John." Little died Oct 22, 1992, near Sherman Oaks, CA.

MONROE, MARILYN: BIRTH ANNIVERSARY. June 1, 1926. American actress and sex symbol of the '50s. Born in Los Angeles as Norma Jean Mortensen or Baker. She had an unstable childhood in a series of orphanages and foster homes. A nude photo of her led to her film debut in 1948. Her remarkable film career came to epitomize Hollywood glamour. In 1954 she wed Yankee legend "Jolting Joe" DiMaggio, but the marriage didn't last. Monroe remained fragile and insecure, tormented by the pressures of Hollywood life. Her death from an overdose on Aug 5, 1962, in Los Angeles shocked the world. Among her films: *The Seven Year Itch, Bus Stop, Some Like It Hot, Gentlemen Prefer Blondes* and *The Misfits*.

MOON PHASE: FIRST QUARTER. June 1. Moon enters First Quarter phase at 9:45 PM, EDT.

NATIONAL ACCORDION AWARENESS MONTH. June 1–30. To increase public awareness of this multicultural instrument and its influence and popularity in today's music. For info: Permanent Press Publicity, 3551 Pierce St, San Francisco, CA 94123. Phone: (415) 440-0800. Email: belloblade@aol.com.

NATIONAL BATHROOM READING WEEK. June 1–7. To promote America's favorite reading room as the foremost seat of learning. For info: Jack Kreismer, Pres, Red-Letter Press, Box 393, Saddle River, NJ 07458. Phone: (201) 652-4402.

NATIONAL BURGLARY PREVENTION MONTH. June 1–30. The Burglary Prevention Council, during the month of June, distributes a variety of burglary-prevention information to the media. It also conducts a special mailing to police chiefs and crime prevention officers around the nation and provides material that can be used in their crime-prevention programs. Annually, the month of June. For info: Mike Bruening, Exec Dir, Burglary Prevention Council, c/o Selz/Seabolt Communications, 221 N LaSalle St, Ste 3500, Chicago, IL 60601-1520. Phone: (312) 372-7090. Fax: (312) 372-6160.

NATIONAL FISHING WEEK. June 1–7. Annual celebration providing opportunities for youths to experience recreational fishing, learn about the environment firsthand and practice conservation ethics. We encourage all to take a friend fishing. Annually, the first full week in June beginning on Monday. Est attendance: 250,000. For info: National Fishing Week Steering Committee, 1033 N Fairfax St, Ste 200, Alexandria, VA 22314-1540. Phone: (703) 684-3201.

NATIONAL ICED TEA MONTH. June 1–30. To celebrate one of the most widely consumed beverages in the world and one of nature's most perfect beverages, and to encourage Americans to refresh themselves with this all-natural, low-calorie, refreshing thirst-quencher. For info: Joseph P. Simrany, Pres, The Tea Council of the USA, 230 Park Ave, Ste 1460, New York, NY 10169. Phone: (212) 986-6998. Fax: (212) 697-8658.

NATIONAL ROVING WITH ROVER MONTH. June 1–30. Educational, informational and celebrational events promoting the joys of sharing outdoor activities like hiking, camping and backpacking with your dog. Annually, the month of June. For info: Kindred Spirits™, Animal Sanctuary, PO Box 48, Suquamish, WA 98392. Phone: (360) 598-2545 or (888) KINDRED. Fax: (360) 598-2546.

NATIONAL SAFETY MONTH. June 1–30. For info: American Society of Safety Engineers, 1800 E Oakton, Des Plaines, IL 60018-2187. Phone: (847) 699-2929.

NATIONAL SCLERODERMA AWARENESS MONTH. June 1–30. The United Scleroderma Foundation is committed to increasing awareness of this devastating disease and raising essential research dollars to determine its cause, enhance treatment and find a cure. Call or write for more information, chapter and physician referrals, quarterly newsletter, annual conference and workshop and other info. Sponsor: United Scleroderma Fdtn (USF), PO Box 399, Watsonville, CA 95077-0399. Phone: (800) 722-HOPE. Fax: (408) 728-3328. Email: outreach@scleroderma.com.

PEOPLE'S REPUBLIC OF CHINA: INTERNATIONAL CHILDREN'S DAY. June 1. Shanghai.

PHARMACISTS DECLARE WAR ON ALCOHOLISM. June 1–30. To encourage pharmacists, health care professionals and consumers to better educate and counsel the public on alcoholism and other substance abuse illnesses. By promoting alcohol abuse awareness and education to health care professionals and the general public, PCAA strives to break the stereotype surrounding alcoholism that keeps millions of Americans from receiving proper treatment. There is a $15 charge for kit materials. For info: Pharmacists Planning Service, Inc, Pharmacy Council on Alcohol Abuse, 200 Gate Five Rd, PO Box 1336, Sausalito, CA 94966. Phone: (415) 332-4066. Fax: (415) 332-1832. Email: ppsi@aol.com.

PLYMOUTH PLANTATION EARTHQUAKE: ANNIVERSARY. June 1, 1638. The first earthquake in the US to have been recorded and described in writing occurred at Plymouth, MA, at 2 PM. Governor William Bradford described the event in his *History*: ". . . it was very terrible for ye time; and as ye men were set talking in ye house, some women and others were without ye doors, and ye earth shooke with ye violence as they could not stand without catching hold of ye posts . . . but ye violence lasted not long. And about halfe an hower, or less, came an other noyse & shaking, but neither so loud nor strong as ye former, but quickly passed over, and so it ceased."

"THE PRISONER" TV PREMIERE: 30th ANNIVERSARY. June 1, 1968. "The Prisoner" was one of the most imaginative shows on TV, regarded by some as the finest dramatic series in TV history. Patrick McGoohan, who produced and starred in the series, also wrote and directed some episodes. In the series, McGoohan, who had played John Drake on "Secret Agent," found himself in a self-contained community known as "the village" where he was referred to, not by name, but as Number 6. Number 6 realized he was a prisoner, and spent most of the series trying to escape or to learn the identity of the leader, Number 1. In the last episode, he learned that he was Number 1. Angelo Muscat played his mute manservant.

SAMOA: INDEPENDENCE DAY. June 1.

SHUTTLE CAMP. June 1–Aug 1. Space Center, Alamogordo, NM. Annual series of week-long residential and day space science camps. Rocket building classes, field trips and astronomy classes. Est attendance: 940. For info: Jackie Diehl, Shuttle Camp Dir, Space Center, PO Box 533, Alamogordo, NM 88311-0533. Phone: (800) 545-4021. Fax: (505) 437-7722. Email: space-plan@nmsua.nmsu.edu. WWW: http://abcc.nmsu.edu/~bwood/

SPACE MILESTONE: *SOYUZ 9* (USSR). June 1, 1970. Cosmonauts Nikolayev and Sevastyanov set space endurance record of 17 days, 16 hours and 59 minutes. Launched June 1, 1970.

STEP PARENTS' WEEK ©. June 1–7. The shocking statistics on family life in the '90s are: 50% of all marriages end in divorce and 67% of all second marriages end in divorce. This week is in recognition of those brave souls who flaunt convention and plow forward despite the statistics. Annually, the first week in June. For info: Adrienne Sioux Koopersmith, 1437 W Rosemont, #1W, Chicago, IL 60660-1319. Phone: (773) 743-5341. Fax: (773) 743-5395. Email: kooper@interaccess.com.

TENNESSEE ADMISSION DAY: ANNIVERSARY. June 1. Became 16th state on this day in 1796. Observed as a holiday in Tennessee.

UPPERVILLE COLT AND HORSE SHOW. June 1–7. A week-long "A-rated" horse show involving hundreds of horse and rider combinations from 8- to 10-year-old children in the pony divisions to leading Olympic and World Cup riders and horses in the Hunter, Jumper and Grand Prix divisions. Sunday's highlight is the prestigious $50,000 Budweiser/Upperville Jumper Classic sponsored by Budweiser. Est attendance: 6,000. For info: Tommy L. Jones, Upperville Colt and Horse Show, PO Box 1288, Warrenton, VA 22186. Phone: (540) 592-3858. Fax: (540) 253-5761. WWW: http://www.upperville.com

VISION RESEARCH MONTH. June 1–30. Millions of Americans have healthy sight because of the work of medical and scientific researchers investigating vision-related problems. During this observance, Prevent Blindness America® encourages people to support vision research letter-writing campaigns to Congress. Success in vision research is highlighted. Materials are available. For info: Mktg Dept, Prevent Blindness America®, 500 E Remington Rd, Schaumburg, IL 60173. Phone: (800) 331-2020. Fax: (847) 843-8458. WWW: http://prevent-blindness.org

WHITMONDAY. June 1. The day after Whitsunday is observed as a public holiday in many countries.

YOUNG, BRIGHAM: BIRTH ANNIVERSARY. June 1, 1801. Mormon church leader born at Whittingham, VT. Known as "the American Moses," having led and directed thousands of religious followers across 1,000 miles of wilderness to settle more than 300 towns in the West. He died at Salt Lake City, UT, on Aug 29, 1877, and was survived by 17 wives and 47 children. Utah observes, as a state holiday, the anniversary of his entrance into the Salt Lake Valley, July 24, 1847.

BIRTHDAYS TODAY

Rene Auberjonois, 58, actor (*M*A*S*H, McCabe and Mrs Miller*, "Benson"; stage: *Coco* [Tony Award]), born New York, NY, June 1, 1940.

James Hadley Billington, 69, Librarian of Congress, born Bryn Mawr, PA, June 1, 1929.

Pat Boone, 64, singer, actor (*State Fair*), author, born Jacksonville, FL, June 1, 1934.

Pat Corley, 68, actor ("Bay City Blues"; Phil on "Murphy Brown"), born Dallas, TX, June 1, 1930.

Morgan Freeman, 61, stage and film actor (*Driving Miss Daisy*), born Memphis, TN, June 1, 1937.

Andy Griffith, 72, actor (*No Time for Sergeants*, "The Andy Griffith Show"), born Mt Airy, NC, June 1, 1926.

Lisa Hartman Black, 42, actress (Tabitha Stephens on "Tabitha"; "Knots Landing"), born Houston, TX, June 1, 1956.

Alexi Lalas, 28, soccer player, born Detroit, MI, June 1, 1970.

Alanis Morissette, 24, pop singer, born at Ottawa, Canada, June 1, 1974.

Jonathan Pryce, 51, actor (*Barbarians at the Gate, The Age of Innocence, Glengarry Glen Ross, Brazil*; stage: *Julius Caesar, Miss Saigon*; Tony Award for *Comedians*; Tony Award and Olivier Award for *Hamlet*), born Holywell, North Wales, June 1, 1947.

Frederica von Stade, 53, opera mezzo-soprano, born Somerville, NJ, June 1, 1945.

Ron Wood, 51, musician (2nd guitarist with the Rolling Stones), born London, England, June 1, 1947.

Edward Woodward, 68, actor, singer ("The Equalizer," *Wicker Man, Breaker Morant*), born Croydon, England, June 1, 1930.

JUNE 2 — TUESDAY

Day 153 — 212 Remaining

BELGIUM: PROCESSION OF THE GOLDEN CHARIOT. June 2. Mons. Horse-drawn coach carrying a reliquary of St. Waudru circles the town of Mons. Procession commemorates delivery of Mons from the plague in 1349. In the town square, in afternoon, St. George fights the dragon. Lumecon symbolizes triumph of good over evil, and when victory is won the spectators sing traditional songs.

BLACK HILLS PASSION PLAY—SOUTH DAKOTA. June 2–Aug 30. Passion Play Amphitheater, Spearfish, SD. Spectacular outdoor drama on a huge stage depicts the last seven days in the life of Christ. It features a cast of more than 200 and live animals. Annually, Sunday, Tuesday and Thursday evenings. Est attendance: 65,000. For info: Black Hills Passion Play—South Dakota, PO Box 489, Spearfish, SD 57783. Phone: (605) 642-2646 or (800) 457-0160. Fax: (941) 638-2037. Email: BHPP@blackhills.com.
WWW: http://www.blackhills.com/~BHPP

BULGARIA: HRISTO BOTEV DAY: ANNIVERSARY. June 2. Poet and national hero Hristro Botev fell fighting Turks, 1876.

GERMANY: WALDCHESTAG. June 2. Frankfurt. Since the 19th century Frankfurters have spent the Tuesday after Whitsunday in their forest. See also: "Whitsunday" above.

ITALY: REPUBLIC DAY. June 2. National holiday. Commemorates referendum on June 2, 1946, in which republic status was selected instead of return to monarchy.

MAINE LAW: ANNIVERSARY. June 2. America's first statewide statute prohibiting the sale of alcoholic beverages was enacted in the state of Maine, June 2, 1851. The following Independence Day the mayor of Bangor showed his support of the new law by smashing 10 kegs of confiscated booze.

MARQUIS DE SADE: BIRTH ANNIVERSARY. June 2, 1740. Donatien-Alphonse-François, Comte de Sade, was born at Paris, France, June 2, 1740. French military man, governor-general and author, who spent much of his life in prison because of his acts of cruelty and violence, outrageous behavior and debauchery. The word *sadism* was created from his name to describe cruelty and gratification in inflicting pain. He died near Paris, at the Charenton lunatic asylum, on Dec 2, 1814.

SAINT PIUS X: BIRTH ANNIVERSARY. June 2. Giuseppe Melchiorre Sarto, 257th pope of the Roman Catholic Church, born June 2, 1835, at Riese, Italy. Elected pope Aug 4, 1903. Died Aug 20, 1914. Canonized May 29, 1954.

YELL "FUDGE" AT THE COBRAS IN NORTH AMERICA DAY. June 2. Anywhere north of the Panama Canal. In order to keep poisonous cobra snakes out of North America, all citizens are asked to go outdoors at noon, local time, and yell "Fudge." Fudge makes cobras gag, and the mere mention of it makes them skeedaddle. Annually, June 2. [© 1997 by WPL] For info: Thomas or Ruth Roy, Wellness Permission League, PO Box 662, Mt Gretna, PA 17064-0662. Phone: (500) 437-5104 or (717) 964-1308. Fax: (717) 964-1335.

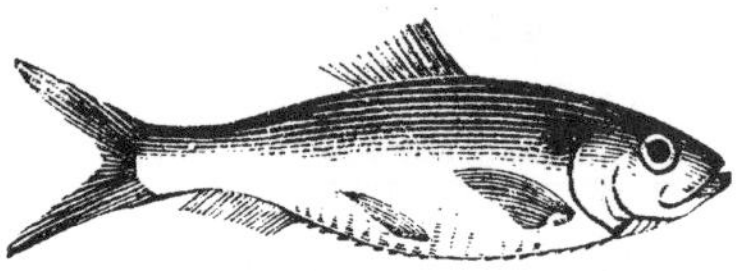

BIRTHDAYS TODAY

Diana Canova, 45, actress (Corrine on "Soap"; "I'm a Big Girl Now"), born West Palm Beach, FL, June 2, 1953.

Gary Grimes, 43, actor (*Summer of '42, Class of '44*), born San Francisco, CA, June 2, 1955.

Charles Haid, 55, actor (Renko on "Hill Street Blues"; "Delvecchio"), producer, born San Francisco, CA, June 2, 1943.

Marvin Hamlisch, 54, composer (Oscars for *The Sting, The Way We Were*; Tony for *A Chorus Line*), born New York, NY, June 2, 1944.

Stacy Keach, Jr, 57, actor (*Conduct Unbecoming*, "Mickey Spillane's Mike Hammer"), born Savannah, GA, June 2, 1941.

Sally Kellerman, 62, actress (*M*A*S*H, Back to School*), born Long Beach, CA, June 2, 1936.

Jerry Mathers, 50, actor ("Leave It to Beaver"), born Sioux City, IA, June 2, 1948.

Milo O'Shea, 72, actor (*The Purple Rose of Cairo*), born Dublin, Ireland, June 2, 1926.

Charlie Watts, 57, musician (drummer with the Rolling Stones; "[I Can't Get No] Satisfaction"), born Islington, England, June 2, 1941.

June 1998

S	M	T	W	T	F	S
	1	2	3	4	5	6
7	8	9	10	11	12	13
14	15	16	17	18	19	20
21	22	23	24	25	26	27
28	29	30				

JUNE 3 — WEDNESDAY

Day 154 — 211 Remaining

BEEF EMPIRE DAYS. June 3–14. Finney County Fairgrounds, Garden City, KS. 30th annual celebration of the beef industry. Live and carcass show; PRCA rodeo (three nights); parade; beef tasting for the public; cowboy poetry; Professional Western Art Show; feedlot roping and riding; walk/run; golf, softball and tennis tournaments; children's events. Annually, in June. Est attendance: 100,000. For info: Kelly Goss, Beef Empire Days, 1511 E Fulton Ter, Garden City, KS 67846-6165. Phone: (316) 275-6807. Fax: (316) 276-3290. Email: ctb@gcnet.com. WWW: http://gcnet.com/chamber/ctb

CANADA: THE NATIONAL TOURNAMENT. June 3–7. Spruce Meadows, Calgary, Alberta. The National Tournament features the Canadian Show Jumping Championship, including the Canadian Pacific World Cup and the Shell Cup. Enjoy country atmosphere in the Spruce Meadows Marketplace on the Plaza. Live entertainment and activities daily. Est attendance: 85,000. For info: Spruce Meadows, RR #9, Calgary, Alta, Canada T2J 5G5. Phone: (403) 974-4200. Fax: (403) 974-4270. Email: smeadows@telusplanet.net. WWW: http://www.sprucemeadows.com

CHIMBORAZO DAY. June 3. To bring the shape of the earth into focus by publicizing the fact that Mount Chimborazo, Ecuador, near the equator, pokes further out into space than any other mountain on earth, including Mount Everest. (The distance from sea level at the equator to the center of the earth is 13 miles greater than the radius to sea level at the north pole. This means that New Orleans is about six miles further from the center of the earth than is Lake Itasca at the headwaters of the Mississippi, so the Mississippi flows uphill.) For info: Robert L. Birch, Puns Corps, Box 2364, Falls Church, VA 22042-0364. Phone: (703) 533-3668.

DAVIS, JEFFERSON: BIRTH ANNIVERSARY. June 3, 1808. American statesman, US senator, only president of the Confederate States of America. Imprisoned May 10, 1865–May 13, 1867, but never brought to trial, deprived of rights of citizenship after the Civil War. Davis was born at Todd County, KY, and died at New Orleans, LA, Dec 6, 1889, at age 81. His citizenship was restored, posthumously, on Oct 17, 1978, when President Carter signed an Amnesty Bill. This bill, he said, "officially completes the long process of reconciliation that has reunited our people following the tragic conflict between the states." Davis's birth anniversary is observed in Florida, Kentucky and South Carolina on this day; in Alabama on the first Monday in June; and in Mississippi on the last Monday in May. Davis's birth anniversary is observed as Confederate Memorial Day in Tennessee.

DEWHURST, COLLEEN: BIRTH ANNIVERSARY. June 3, 1924. Colleen Dewhurst was born at Quebec, Canada, on June 3, 1924. Her 40-year career as an actress spanned stage, screen and television. After making her Broadway debut in Eugene O'Neill's *Desire Under the Elms* in 1952, she became the actress most associated with O'Neill's works in the later part of this century, also performing in *Long Day's Journey into Night; Mourning Becomes Electra; Ah, Wilderness!* and *A Moon for the Misbegotten*, for which she won her second Tony award. At the time of her death on Aug 22, 1991, she was president of Actor's Equity Association, the union for professional actors and stage managers. She won three Emmy awards, including one for her role as Murphy Brown's mother on the TV show "Murphy Brown" (1989). She died Aug 22, 1991 at South Salem, NY.

DUKE OF WINDSOR MARRIAGE: ANNIVERSARY. June 3, 1937. The Duke of Windsor who, as King Edward VIII, had abdicated the British throne on Dec 11, 1936, was married to Mrs Wallis Warfield Simpson of Baltimore, MD. The marriage took place in Monts, France, on June 3, 1937. The couple made their home in France after their marriage and had little contact with the Royal family. The Duke died at Paris on May 28, 1972, and was buried near Windsor Castle in England.

FIRST WOMAN RABBI IN US: ANNIVERSARY. June 3. Sally Jan Priesand was ordained a rabbi on June 3, 1972, making her the first woman rabbi in the US. On Aug 1, 1972, she became assistant rabbi at the Stephen Wise Free Synagogue, New York City.

GINSBERG, ALLEN: BIRTH ANNIVERSARY. June 3, 1926. Poet of the Beat Generation ("Howl"), born Newark, NJ, June 3, 1926. Died April 5, 1997 at New York, NY.

HOBART, GARRET AUGUSTUS: BIRTH ANNIVERSARY. June 3. 24th vice president of the US (1897–99), born at Long Branch, NJ, June 3, 1844. Died at Paterson, NJ, Nov 21, 1899.

HONE, WILLIAM: BIRTH ANNIVERSARY. June 3, 1780. English author and bookseller born at Bath, June 3, 1780. Died at Tottenham, Nov 6, 1842. Compiler of *The Every-Day Book, or Everlasting Calendar of Popular Amusements* (1826). It was William Hone who said: "A good lather is half the shave."

JAZZ FESTIVAL. June 3 (also June 10, 17, 24 and July 1). St. Louis, MO. Some of the best jazz in Missouri simmering on cool summer nights under the stars at the Garden. Est attendance: 15,000. For info: Public Events Office, Missouri Botanical Garden, PO Box 299, St. Louis, MO 63166-0299. Phone: (314) 577-5125 or (800) 642-8842. Email: dwillett@ridgway.mobot.org. WWW: http://www.mobot.org

KHOMEINI, AYATOLLAH RUHOLLAH: DEATH ANNIVERSARY. June 3, 1989. The Ayatollah Ruhollah Khomeini, leader of the Islamic Revolution, lifelong foe of the Shah of Iran, was arrested in 1963 after giving a speech accusing the Shah of seeking to destroy Islam. He was exiled to Turkey in 1964, following which he spent 13 years in Iraq, later moving to Paris, where he gained exposure to the world press for his cause. On Jan 16, 1979, the Shah of Iran left the country for a supposed vacation, setting the stage for Khomeini's triumphant return on Jan 31. The monarchy fell on Feb 11, 1979. Khomeini proceeded to reorganize the government based on Islamic principles. On Nov 11, 1979, a group of students loyal to Khomeini occupied the American Embassy in Teheran after the Shah was given admittance to the US for medical treatment, placing the Ayatollah at the center of a diplomatic crisis that consumed the presidency of Jimmy Carter. Khomeini focused attention on the US as the "Great Satan" and blamed many of his country's problems on imperialistic intervention. Khomeini died on June 3, 1989.

MIGIITY CASEY HAS STRUCK OUT: ANNIVERSARY. June 3, 1888. The famous comic baseball ballad "Casey at the Bat" was printed in the Sunday *San Francisco Examiner*. Appearing anonymously, it was written by Ernest L. Thayer. Recitation of "Casey at the Bat" became part of the repertoire of actor William DeWolf Hopper. The recitation took 5 minutes and 40 seconds. Hopper claimed to have recited it more than 10,000 times, the first being at Wallack's Theater in New York, NY, in 1888. The Library of Congress reissued "Casey at the Bat" in text and recording in 1986. See also: "Thayer, Ernest Lawrence: Birth Anniversary" (Aug 14).

MISSION SAN CARLOS BORROMEO DE CARMELO FOUNDING: ANNIVERSARY. June 3. California mission to the Indians founded June 3, 1770.

NCAA DIVISION I MEN'S AND WOMEN'S OUTDOOR TRACK CHAMPIONSHIPS. June 3–6. State University of New York at Buffalo, Buffalo, NY. Est attendance: 20,000. For info: NCAA, 6201 College Blvd, Overland Park, KS 66211-2422. Phone: (913) 339-1906. Fax: (913) 339-1950.
WWW: http://www.ncaa.org

SCOTT JOPLIN RAGTIME FESTIVAL. June 3–7. Historic downtown Sedalia, MO. Features both free and admission events indoors and out, including concerts, symposiums, tea dances, ragtime ball, sheet music swap, antiques and collectibles, piano rolls and player pianos, historic walking tours. Est attendance: 3,500. For info: Karen Pabst, Adm, Scott Joplin Fdtn, 116 E Main, Sedalia, MO 65301. Phone: (816) 826-2271. Fax: (816) 826-5054.

SPACE MILESTONE: *GEMINI 4* (US). June 3, 1965. Major McDivitt and Major White made 66 orbits. White took a space walk and maneuvered 20 minutes outside capsule. Launched June 3, 1965.

BIRTHDAYS TODAY

Tom Arnold, 39, actor ("Roseanne," *McHale's Navy, True Lies*), born Ottumwa, IA, June 3, 1959.
Chuck Barris, 69, TV producer ("Dating Game," "Newlywed Game," "Gong Show"), born Philadelphia, PA, June 3, 1929.
Tony Curtis (Bernard Schwartz), 73, actor ("Vega$," *Some Like It Hot*), born New York, NY, June 3, 1925.
Charles Hart, 37, lyricist, composer, born London, England, June 3, 1961.
Curtis Mayfield, 56, singer, songwriter ("Freddie's Dead"; score *Superfly*), born Chicago, IL, June 3, 1942.
Scott Valentine, 40, actor ("Family Ties"), born Saratoga Springs, NY, June 3, 1958.
Deniece Williams, 47, singer ("Free," "It's Gonna Take a Miracle"), born Gary, IN, June 3, 1951.

JUNE 4 — THURSDAY

Day 155 — 210 Remaining

ANGELA DAVIS ACQUITTAL: ANNIVERSARY. June 4, 1972. Angela Davis, black activist and professor, was found not guilty by an all-white jury of murder, kidnapping and conspiracy charges resulting from the Aug 7, 1970, fatal shooting of Judge Harold Haley during an attempted escape and kidnapping. While Davis was not present at the crime, the murder weapon had been purchased by her and she knew the perpetrators. Based upon these facts, she was arrested and charged. During her trial she told the court she bought guns to protect herself. "For a black person growing up in violence-filled Alabama," she said, "guns were a normal way of life."

CANADA: MOSAIC FESTIVAL OF CULTURES. June 4–6. Regina, Saskatchewan. City-wide festival with 24 pavilions featuring the crafts of skilled artisans, energetic folk dances, lively music and song, traditional costumes and food from around the world. Est attendance: 30,000. For info: Tourism Saskatchewan, 500-1900 Albert St, Regina, Sask, Canada S4P 4L9. Phone: (800) 667-7191 or (306) 757-5990.
Email: travel.info@sasktourism.sk.ca.
WWW: http://www.sasktourism.com

CANADA: SHELBURNE COUNTY LOBSTER FESTIVAL. June 4–7. Shelburne County, Nova Scotia. Four days of activities in celebration of the lobster-fishing industry. Local community groups and businesses throughout the county host lobster suppers, sporting events, craft shows, yacht and boat races and much more. "Shelburne County—The Lobster Capital of Canada." Annually, the first full weekend in June. Est attendance: 10,000. For info: Marilyn Johnston, Lobster Fest Secy, PO Box 280, Shelburne, NS, Canada B0T 1W0. Phone: (902) 875-3544. Fax: (902) 875-1278. Email: munshel@atcon.com.

"CAVALCADE OF STARS" TV PREMIERE: ANNIVERSARY. June 4, 1949. Although the Dumont network itself was not very successful, it was around long enough to launch this popular show. The one-hour variety show was hosted by Jack Carter (1949–50), Jackie Gleason (1950–52) and then Larry Storch in the summer of 1952. It also served as a showcase for the fledgling but soon-to-be immortal "The Honeymooners" with Gleason and Pert Kelton starring as the Kramdens.

CHINA: TIANANMEN SQUARE MASSACRE: ANNIVERSARY. June 4, 1989. After almost a month and a half of student demonstrations for democracy, the Chinese government ordered its troops to open fire on the unarmed protestors in Tiananmen Square in Beijing. The demonstrations began on Apr 18 as several thousand students marched to mourn the death of Hu Yaobang, a pro-reform leader within the Chinese government. A ban was imposed on such demonstrations; on Apr 22, 100,000 gathered in Tiananmen Square in defiance of the ban. On May 13, 2,000 of the students began a hunger strike and on May 20, the government imposed martial law and began to bring in troops. On June 2, the demonstrators turned back an advance of unarmed troops in the first clash with the People's Army. Under the cover of darkness, early on June 4, troops opened fire on the assembled crowds and armored personnel carriers rolled into the square crushing many of the students as they lay sleeping in their tents. Although the government claimed that few died in the attack, estimates range from several hundred to several thousand casualties. In the following months thousands of demonstrators were rounded up and jailed.

CURWOOD FESTIVAL. June 4–7. Owosso, MI. Homecoming celebration commemorating James Oliver Curwood, Owosso-born author and conservationist (June 12, 1878–Aug 13, 1927). The Curwood castle was built for a studio. Open to the public. 50 events including parades, races and music. Annually, the first full weekend in June. Est attendance: 75,000. For info: Curwood Festival, Box 461, Owosso, MI 48867. Phone: (517) 723-2161. Fax: (517) 723-8353.

EVERETT SALTY SEA DAYS. June 4–7. Everett, WA. Family events to celebrate Everett, Funtastic Shows Carnival, food, novelty, arts and crafts and commercial booths, live entertainment, fireworks, grand parade, classic car show, limited hydro races and Hawaiian Outrigger Boat Races. Sponsors: City of Everett, Dwayne Lane's Family of Auto Centers, Cascade Savings Bank, Key Bank, Frontier Bank, Roy Robinson Chevrolet-Geo. Est attendance: 100,000. For info: Marion Pope, Exec Dir, Salty Sea Days Assn, PO Box 7050, Everett, WA 98201. Phone: (425) 339-1113. Fax: (425) 252-6630 or (425) 259-0131.
Email: saltysea@aol.com.

June 1998

S	M	T	W	T	F	S
	1	2	3	4	5	6
7	8	9	10	11	12	13
14	15	16	17	18	19	20
21	22	23	24	25	26	27
28	29	30				

FINLAND: FLAG DAY. June 4. Finland's armed forces honor the birth anniversary of Carl Gustaf Mannerheim, born June 4, 1867.

FIRST FREE FLIGHT BY A WOMAN: ANNIVERSARY. June 4. Marie Thible, of Lyons, France, accompanied by a pilot (Monsieur Fleurant), on June 4, 1784, became the first woman in history to fly in a free balloon. According to her pilot, Madame Thible gave voice to her high spirits by "singing like a bird" as she drifted across Lyons in a balloon named *Le Gustave* (for King Gustav III of Sweden, who was watching the ascent). The balloon reached a height of 8,500 feet in a flight that lasted about 45 minutes. The event occurred one day short of a year after the first flight in history by a man. See also: "First Balloon Flight: Anniversary" (June 5).

GEORGE III: BIRTH ANNIVERSARY. June 4, 1738. The English king against whom the American Revolution was directed. Born June 4, 1738; died Jan 29, 1820.

"IT COULD BE YOU" TV PREMIERE: ANNIVERSARY. June 4, 1956. Bill Leyden was the host and Wendell Niles the announcer of this audience participation show. Its regular feature included three audience members, one of whom would be reunited with a loved one or long-lost friend. The creator of the show was Ralph Edwards.

JESSORE RAILWAY CRASH: ANNIVERSARY. June 4, 1972. An express train packed with more than 600 people rammed into a standing train at full speed in the main station of Jessore, Bangladesh. In the crash 76 people were killed on impact, while more than 500 others sustained serious injuries.

MINIATURES INTERNATIONAL. June 4–July 4. St. Simons Island, GA. A juried show of two- and three-dimensional miniature art created to provide exposure of quality miniature artwork to a large and knowledgeable audience in a recognized arts facility at the height of the visitor season. For info: Coastal Center For The Arts, 2012 Demere Rd, St. Simons Island, GA 31522. Phone: (912) 634-0404.

NURSE ASSISTANTS DAY AND WEEK. June 4–11. Recognizes those nurse assistants who provide care to all ill, elderly and long-term residents in nursing homes and other long-term nursing care centers. Begins on Career Nurse Assistants' Day, June 4. 1998 theme is: "Career Directions." For info: Genevieve Gipson, RN M Ed, Dir, Career Nurse Assistant Programs Inc, 3577 Easton Rd, Norton, OH 44203. Phone: (330) 825-9342. Email: cnajeni@aol.com.

OLEPUT FESTIVAL. June 4–6. Downtown Tupelo, MS. A Mardi Gras-style festival with music, entertainment, parade, sports competitions, hot air balloon events and great food. Est attendance: 30,000. For info: Tupelo Conv and Visitors Bureau, PO Drawer 47, Tupelo, MS 38802-1485. Phone: (800) 267-3104. Fax: (601) 841-6550.

PULITZER PRIZES FIRST AWARDED: ANNIVERSARY. June 4, 1917. The first Pulitzer Prizes were awarded on this date: biography, *Julia Ward Howe* by Laura E. Richards and Maude H. Elliott assisted by Florence H. Hall; history, *With Americans of Past and Present Days* by Jean Jules Jusserand, the French ambassador to the US. Prizes were also awarded for journalistic achievement.

ROME LIBERATED: ANNIVERSARY. June 4, 1944. The US 9th Army, commanded by General Mark Clark, entered the southern suburbs of Rome as the last of the German rearguard retreated from Mussolini's former capital. Fearful of a last-ditch effort by the Germans to hold the city, the populace remained behind closed doors as Clark's forces entered the Eternal City.

SCOTLAND: ROYAL SCOTTISH AUTOMOBILE CLUB INTERNATIONAL SCOTTISH RALLY. June 4–6. Throughout Scotland with base at Perth. Scotland's only international rally that attracts many of the world's leading drivers. Est attendance: 200,000. For info: Jonathan Lord, Royal Scottish Automobile Club (Motor Sport) Ltd, 11 Blythswood Sq, Glasgow, Scotland G2 4AG. Phone: 441412044999. Fax: 441412044949. Email: 101662.1035@compuserve.com.

TONGA: NATIONAL DAY. June 4. National holiday.

UNITED NATIONS: INTERNATIONAL DAY OF INNOCENT CHILDREN VICTIMS OF AGGRESSION. June 4. On Aug 19, 1982, the General Assembly decided to commemorate June 4 of each year as the International Day of Innocent Children Victims of Aggression.

WORLD PORK EXPO. June 4–6. Iowa State Fairgrounds, Des Moines, IA. This is the world's largest pork-specific event, featuring free pork barbecue and musical entertainment, hog shows and sales, educational seminars and a trade show with more than 500 companies represented. Pork producers cook pork on the 250-foot-long Big Grill. Some of the nation's best barbecuers compete in the Great Pork BarbeQlossal™. Est attendance: 60,000. For info: Charles Harness, VP of Communications, Natl Pork Producers Council, PO Box 10383, Des Moines, IA 50306. Phone: (515) 223-2600. Fax: (515) 223-2646.
WWW: http://www.nppc.org/

BIRTHDAYS TODAY

Gene Barry (Eugene Klass), 77, actor (*War of the Worlds*, "Bat Masterson"), born New York, NY, June 4, 1921.
Keith David, 44, actor (*Platoon, Bird*), born New York, NY, June 4, 1954.
Eldra DeBarge, 37, singer, musician (lead singer of the family group DeBarge), born Grand Rapids, MI, June 4, 1961.
Bruce Dern, 62, actor (*Coming Home, The Burbs*), born Chicago, IL, June 4, 1936.
Bettina Gregory, 52, journalist, born New York, NY, June 4, 1946.
Andrea Jaeger, 33, former tennis player, born Chicago, IL, June 4, 1965.
Xavier Maurice McDaniel, 35, basketball player, born Columbia, SC, June 4, 1963.
Robert Merrill, 79, singer, born New York, NY, June 4, 1919.
Michelle Phillips, 53, singer (with The Mamas and the Papas; "California Dreamin' "), actress ("Knots Landing"), born Long Beach, CA, June 4, 1945.
Parker Stevenson, 45, actor ("Falcon Crest," "Baywatch," *Lifeguard*), born Philadelphia, PA, June 4, 1953.
Dennis Weaver, 74, actor ("Gunsmoke," "McCloud"), born Joplin, MO, June 4, 1924.
Dr. Ruth Westheimer, 69, TV, radio host for shows on sexual relationships, born Frankfurt am Main, Germany, June 4, 1929.
Noah Wyle, 27, actor (*A Few Good Men*, "ER"), born Hollywood, CA, June 4, 1971.

JUNE 5 — FRIDAY

Day 156 — 209 Remaining

AMERICAN BAHA'I COMMUNITY: ANNIVERSARY. June 5. On this date in 1894 the first formal classes on the Baha'i were held in Chicago, IL.

AMERICAN ROSE SOCIETY NATIONAL SHOW. June 5–6. Hyatt Regency Hotel, Albuquerque, NM. Amateur growers from all over the US display thousands of their roses in this major competition. Est attendance: 2,000. For info: Robert Ardini, Chairman, American Rose Soc Publicity Committee, 230 Central Park West, 15B, New York, NY 10024. Phone: (212) 595-0353. Email: rardini@aol.com.

BACK TO RATH'S TRAIL. June 5–7. Hamlin, TX. Historical event focusing on the period of the great buffalo hunts, in particular, Rath City or Camp Reynolds (circa 1876-1879), located just north of Hamlin. During its three-year lifespan, more than 1.1 million buffalo hides were shipped out of the old post. Event features tours of the site with interpretive living history camps, archaeological research, historical symposiums, artifacts exhibits, art show, frontier balls, entertainment, poets and storytelling. Est attendance: 3,500. For info: Hamlin Chamber of Commerce, PO Box 402, Hamlin, TX 79520. Phone: (915) 576-3501.

BAHAMAS: LABOR DAY. June 5. Public holiday. First Friday in June celebrated with parades, displays and picnics.

BILLY BOWLEGS PIRATE FESTIVAL. June 5–13. Fort Walton Beach, FL. Captain Billy Bowlegs and his krewe, portrayed by local businessmen, storm the city in the pirate ship *Blackhawk* for a week of fun and frolicking. Two treasure hunts for valuable prizes will take place during the festival. Fireworks on Friday night. Est attendance: 10,000. For info: Chamber of Commerce, PO Box 640, Ft Walton Beach, FL 32549. Phone: (904) 244-8191. Fax: (904) 244-1935.

BOYD, WILLIAM: BIRTH ANNIVERSARY. June 5, 1895. Born at Hendrysburg, OH, Boyd went to Hollywood in 1919 and got a job as a film extra. His first major starring role was in *The Volga Boatman* (1926). In 1935, he got the role of Hopalong Cassidy in a series of popular westerns. He made 66 of these films between 1935 and 1948. Some of them were edited and shown on television; Boyd then made some episodes especially for TV. Died Sept 12, 1972. See also "Hopalong Cassidy TV Premiere (June 24)."

BRAZOS NIGHTS. June 5–July 11 (Fridays and Saturdays only). Indian Spring Park, Waco, TX. A family concert series with music of all types, children's activities and Saturday night laser light show. Annually, Friday and Saturday nights for six weeks during summer. Est attendance: 65,000. For info: Lisa Spinazzola, Special Events Coord, City of Waco Recreation Dept, PO Box 2570, Waco, TX 76702. Phone: (817) 750-5980. Fax: (817) 750-5782.

BROOKFIELD SUMMER FUN DAYS. June 5–7. Brookfield, MO. Celebration of summer with sidewalk sales, craft booths, concession stands, parade, games, carnival and an adult dance on Saturday night. Annually, the first full weekend in June. Est attendance: 10,000. For info: Brookfield Chamber of Commerce, 120 N Main, Brookfield, MO 64628. Phone: (816) 258-7255 or (816) 258-5217.

CANISTEO CRAZEE DAZE. June 5–7. Canisteo, NY. Sanctioned 5K walk and 10K run Friday. Famous canoe regatta Saturday. 200 canoes, rafts and tubes. Yard sales and food booths. Annually, the first weekend in June. Est attendance: 3,000. For info: Mike Price, 62 Russell St, Canisteo, NY 14823. Phone: (607) 698-4994.

CELEBRATE THE RIVER. June 5–7. Reno, NV. Stroll along the expanded Raymond I. Smith Truckee River Walk and enjoy entertainment and other events. For local info: Phone: (702) 334-2077. For Nevada Tourism: Nevada Commission on Tourism, Capitol Complex, Carson City, NV 89710. Phone: (702) 687-4322 or (800) 227-0774. Fax: (702) 687-6779.

CHURCH POINT BUGGY FESTIVAL. June 5–7. Church Point, LA. Pageants, carnival, arts and crafts, Cajun food, Cajun French music and authentic parade including buggies, horse-drawn carriages and antique cars. Est attendance: 12,000. For info: "Teasie" Cary, Mgr, Church Point Buggy Festival, 837 E Ebey, Church Point, LA 70525. Phone: (318) 684-2739 or (318) 684-5435. Fax: (318) 684-5449.

June 1998

S	M	T	W	T	F	S
	1	2	3	4	5	6
7	8	9	10	11	12	13
14	15	16	17	18	19	20
21	22	23	24	25	26	27
28	29	30				

CLARK, CHARLES JOSEPH (JOE): BIRTHDAY. June 5, 1939. Canadian politician, born at High River, Alta, Canada, June 5, 1939. Clark became Canada's 16th prime minister (and the youngest ever) on June 4, 1979, and served in that post until Mar 3, 1980.

DENMARK: CONSTITUTION DAY. June 5. National holiday. Offices and stores close at noon.

DONUT DAY. June 5–6. Chicago, IL. Founded in 1938 by the Salvation Army for fund-raising during the Great Depression, Donut Day is now an annual tradition. Recalling the donuts served to doughboys by the Salvation Army during World War I, symbolic paper "donuts" are given to contributors. Annually, the first Friday and Saturday in June. For info: Robert Bonesteel, Dir of Communications, The Salvation Army, Metro Div HQ, 5040 N Pulaski, Chicago, IL 60630. Phone: (773) 205-3546. Fax: (773) 725-2822.

FARMINGTON COUNTRY DAYS. June 5–7. Farmington, MO. Three-day event featuring amusement rides, concerts (a free "oldies" concert and a Nashville country star concert), talent show and lots more fun for the whole family. Est attendance: 30,000. For info: Farmington Chamber of Commerce, 302 N Washington, Farmington, MO 63640. Phone: (573) 756-3615. Fax: (573) 756-1003. Email: lbkerr@knights.farmington.kiz.mo.us. WWW: http://www.farmington.k12.mo.us/econdev/

FIRST BALLOON FLIGHT: ANNIVERSARY. June 5, 1783. The first public demonstration of a hot-air balloon flight took place at Annonay, France, on June 5, 1783, where the co-inventor brothers, Joseph and Jacques Montgolfier, succeeded in launching their 33-foot-diameter *globe aerostatique*. It rose an estimated 1,500 feet and traveled, windborne, about 7,500 feet before landing after the 10-minute flight—the first sustained flight of any object achieved by man.

FISHING HAS NO BOUNDARIES—THERMOPOLIS. June 5–7. Boysen Reservoir, Thermopolis, WY. A three-day fishing experience for disabled persons. Any disability, age, sex, race, etc, eligible. Fishing with experienced guides, attended by 80 participants and 100 volunteers. Annually, first full weekend in June. Est attendance: 75. For info: Fishing Has No Boundaries, HSC C of C, Box 768, Thermopolis, WY 82443. Phone: (307) 864-3192 or (800) 786-6772. Fax: (307) 864-9463. Email: wbentel@trib.com.

GREAT WISCONSIN CHEESE FESTIVAL. June 5–7. Little Chute, WI. Festival features cheese breakfast, parade, cheese tasting, cheese-carving demo and cheesecake contest. Est attendance: 10,000. For info: Little Chute Parks and Rec, 1940 Buchanan St, Little Chute, WI 54140-1414. Phone: (414) 788-7390. Fax: (414) 788-7820.

HARBORFEST. June 5–7. Nantucket Island, MA. Islandwide activities. Blessing of the fleet, boat parade, children's pirate parade, best chowder contest, windsurfing, kayak events, boat tour, marine exhibitions, demonstrations and tours. Est attendance: 10,000. For info: Nantucket Island Chamber of Commerce, 48 Main St, Nantucket, MA 02554. Phone: (508) 228-1700.

HARBORFEST. June 5–7. Norfolk, VA. Live entertainment, sailboat races, water demonstrations, tall sailing ships from around the world, military displays, Chesapeake Bay seafood, special entertainment for children and seniors and a spectacular fireworks display. Annually, the first full weekend in June. Est attendance: 500,000. For info: Harborfest, 120 W Main St, Norfolk, VA 23510. Phone: (757) 441-2345. Fax: (757) 441-5198.

HARVARD MILK DAYS FESTIVAL. June 5–7. Harvard, IL. This salute to the dairy farmer includes a parade, evening entertainment, arts and crafts fair, Avenue of Display, milk drinking contest, farm tours, tractor pull, carnival, fireworks, prince and princess contest, Milk Run (2-mile and 10K races), cattle show, talent show and Wee Farm. Est attendance: 100,000. For info: Harvard Milk Days Office, 201 W Front Street, PO Box 310, Harvard, IL 60033. Phone: (815) 943-4614. Fax: (815) 943-4556.

INTERNATIONAL OLD-TIME FIDDLERS CONTEST. June 5–6. International Peace Garden, Dunseith, ND. The International Old Time Fiddlers Contest draws young and old fiddlers alike from both Canada and the US. Contestants compete for two days performing a required list of fiddle music in pursuit of cash prizes and trophies. Est attendance: 3,000. For info: Joseph T. Alme, 1725 11th St SW, Minot, ND 58701. Phone: (701) 838-8472. Fax: (701) 838-8472. Email: imc@minot.com.

INTERNATIONAL STRANGE MUSIC WEEKEND. June 5–6. Carter Caves States Resort Park, Olive Hill, KY. Two evening concerts in an outdoor amphitheater feature "strange musicians" who play music on anything from disassembled washing machines to vacuum cleaners and stethoscopes. Daytime activities include a strange musical instrument demonstration and a "Strange Music Hall of Fame" exhibit. Est attendance: 500. For info: John Tierney, Carter Caves State Resort Park, Rte 5, Box 1120, Olive Hill, KY 41164. Phone: (606) 286-4411.

KENNEDY, ROBERT F.: 30th ASSASSINATION ANNIVERSARY. June 5, 1968. Senator Kennedy was shot while campaigning for the Democratic presidential nomination in Los Angeles, CA, June 5, 1968; he died the following day. Sirhan Sirhan was convicted of his murder.

KEYNES, JOHN MAYNARD: BIRTH ANNIVERSARY. June 5, 1883. British economist born at Cambridge, England. Author of *Treatise on Money* and *The General Theory of Employment, Interest and Money* that focused on "expansionist" economic policy. Died at Firle, England, Apr 21, 1946.

KNIM RADIO'S BIG FISH. June 5–6. Nodaway Lake, Maryville, MO. The world's largest free fishing contest attracts hundreds of fishermen from a wide area. Participants in this 18th annual 18-hour contest compete for thousands of dollars in prizes, including a grand prize boat, motor and trailer. Est attendance: 2,000. For info: KNIM Radio, 1618 S Main, PO Box 278, Maryville, MO 64468. Phone: (816) 582-2151. Fax: (816) 582-3211.

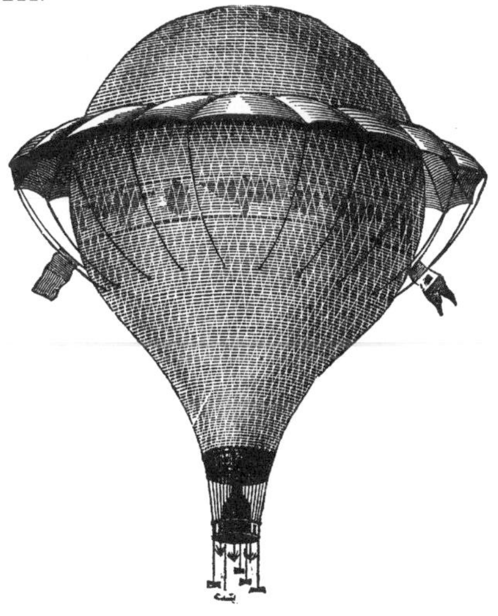

LAKE CHAMPLAIN BALLOON FESTIVAL. June 5–7. Champlain Valley Exposition, Essex Jct, VT. Fifty hot-air balloons, including spectacular special shapes, will participate in five scheduled launches. Also a juried arts and crafts show, an "evening Balloon Glow." Est attendance: 75,000. For info: Lake Champlain Balloon and Craft Festival, PO Box 115, Charlotte, VT 05445-0115. Phone: (802) 425-4884. Fax: (802) 425-4884. Email: lcbf@together.net. WWW: http://www.balloonfest.together.com

LILAC FESTIVAL. June 5–14. Mackinac Island, MI. This summer festival provides an excellent chance to see the various lilacs on Mackinac Island. Includes fireworks, a parade and entertainment. Est attendance: 30,000. For info: Mackinac Island Chamber of Commerce, PO Box 457, Mackinac Island, MI 49757. Phone: (906) 847-6418 or (800) 4LI-LACS. Fax: (906) 847-3571.

MAMOU CAJUN MUSIC FESTIVAL. June 5–6. Mamou, LA. Festival celebration with various authentic games, a Cajun Queen contest and live Cajun music on Friday night from six until midnight. On Saturday, live Cajun music is provided all day from 9–10, while various authentic Cajun games are held. Annually, the first Friday and Saturday in June. Est attendance: 5,000. For info: Eric M. Fontenot, PO Box 490, Mamou, LA 70554. Phone: (318) 948-2194 or (318) 468-2258.

MEDORA MUSICAL. June 5–Sept 6. Medora, ND. Folks whoop it up at this Broadway-class variety show held nightly in a natural amphitheatre in the Badlands. Spectacular sunsets on painted buttes and ravines compete for attention with Western song and dance, all paying tribute to our Roughriding Conservation President, Theodore Roosevelt. Est attendance: 80,000. For info: Pat Hertz, Publications Asst, North Dakota Tourism, Liberty Memorial Bldg, State Captiol Grounds, Bismarck, ND 58505. Phone: (701) 328-2525. WWW: http://www.ndtourism.com

MIAMI/BAHAMAS GOOMBAY FESTIVAL. June 5–7. Miami, FL. 22nd annual celebration of the black culture and heritage of Bahamian settlers in Miami's Coconut Grove area in the 1800s. Largest black heritage special event in the US. More than 400 vendor booths. Pre-festival events include golf tournament, beauty pageant, sailing regatta. Annually, the first full weekend in June. Est attendance: 600,000. For info: Susan Neuman, Miami/Bahamas Goombay Festival, 555 NE 15th St, #25-K, Miami, FL 33132. Phone: (305) 372-9966. Fax: (305) 372-9967. Email: susan-neuman@juno.com.

NATIONAL ATTITUDE DAY. June 5. To recognize those individuals who know who they are, what they stand for, and aren't afraid to walk a little on the wild side to maintain their identity. Celebrated by naming the top ten public figures with attitude for the year and presenting them with an attitude award and a special pair of Larry Mahan boots. A day for everyone to dress and act differently, demonstrating what it takes to stand out in a crowd. For info: Larry Mahan Boots, 209 Seventh Ave N, Nashville, TN 37219. Phone: (615) 244-1818. Fax: (615) 780-3301.

NONGAME WILDLIFE WEEKEND. June 5–7. Blackwater Falls State Park, Davis, WV. Presentations by wildlife professionals regarding nongame wildlife and endangered species. Highlight on Saturday with morning workshops and afternoon field trips such as birdwatching, visiting a snake den, interpretive plant walks, caving, forest ecology, streamlife surveys and how to attract wildlife to the backyard. Annually, the first weekend in June. Est attendance: 300. For info: Kathleen C. Leo, Project Leader, WV Nongame Wildlife Program, WV Dept of Natural Resources, PO Box 67, Ward Rd, Elkins, WV 26241. Phone: (304) 637-0245. Fax: (304) 637-0250.

ORIGINAL OZARK FESTIVAL. June 5–6. Westside Park, Ozark, AR. Festival celebrates the oldest US city incorporated with the name Ozark. Features old-time artists and craftsmen demonstrating various "lost arts" such as shingle-making, rail-splitting, quilting, soap-making and more. Food, fun, music, contests and events. Annually, the first Friday night and Saturday of June. Est attendance: 4,000. For info: Diana Wilson, Dir, Ozark Area Chamber of Commerce, 300 Airport Rd, Ozark, AR 72949. Phone: (501) 667-2525.

ROCKWOOD SUMMER CONCERT SERIES. June 5 (also June 12, 19 and 26). Outdoor summer concert series featuring folk, blues, Irish and bluegrass performers. Picnicking is encouraged. Annually, the four Fridays in June. Est attendance: 5,000. For info: Rockwood Museum, 610 Shipley Rd, Wilmington, DE 19809. Phone: (302) 761-4340. Fax: (302) 764-4570. Email: info@rockwood.org. WWW: http://www.rockwood.org

SCARRY, RICHARD McCLURE: BIRTH ANNIVERSARY. June 5, 1919. Author and illustrator of children's books was born at Boston, MA. Two widely known books of the more than 250 Scarry authored are *Richard Scarry's Best Word Book Ever* (1965) and *Richard Scarry's Please & Thank You* (1973). Often depicting small animal characters who lived like humans, over 100 million copies of his books sold worldwide. Richard Scarry died Apr 30, 1994, at Gstaad, Switzerland.

SITKA SUMMER MUSIC FESTIVAL. June 5–26. (Tuesdays and Fridays, plus Saturdays June 13, 20.) Sitka, AK. Sitka hosts a highly acclaimed chamber music festival that attracts performers and spectators from all over the world. Est attendance: 4,000. For info: Sitka Summer Music Festival, PO Box 3333, Sitka, AK 99835. Phone: (907) 277-4852. Fax: (907) 272-3035.
Email: sitkamus@ptialaska.net.
WWW: http://www.ptialaska.net/~sitkamus

SMITH, ADAM: 275th BIRTH ANNIVERSARY. June 5, 1723. Scottish economist and philosopher, author of *An Enquiry into the Nature and Causes of the Wealth of Nations* (published in 1776), born June 5, 1723, at Kirkaldy, Fifeshire, Scotland. Died at Edinburgh, Scotland, July 17, 1790. "Consumption," he wrote, "is the sole end and purpose of production; and the interest of the producer ought to be attended to only so far as it may be necessary for promoting that of the consumer."

SOONER STATE SUMMER GAMES. June 5–6 (also June 13–14, 20–21 and 27–28). Oklahoma City, OK. Oklahoma amateur sports festival. More than 10,000 athletes of all ages from every county in the state. More than 34 sports competitions. Est attendance: 35,000. For info: Sooner State Games, 100 W Main, Ste 285, Oklahoma City, OK 73102. Phone: (405) 235-4222. Fax: (405) 232-7723. Email: snrstgms@aol.com.

SPACE MILESTONE: *SOYUZ T-2* (USSR). June 5, 1980. Launched on June 5, 1980, cosmonauts Yuri Malyshev and Vladimir Aksenov docked at *Salyut 6* on June 6 and returned to Earth June 9.

SUMMER FARM TOY SHOW. June 5–7. Beckman HS and National Farm Toy Museum, Dyersville, IA. Features tours of the Ertl, Spec Cast, The Toy Factory, and Scale Models toy companies, city-wide garage sales, antique tractors and farm machinery and indoor/outdoor farm toy show. Annually, the first full weekend in June. Est attendance: 9,000. For info: Dyersville Area Chamber of Commerce, PO Box 187, Dyersville, IA 52040. Phone: (319) 875-2311. Fax: (319) 875-8391.
Email: dacc@juno.com.
WWW: http://www.rcww.com/dyersville/

SUN FUN FESTIVAL. June 5–8 (tentative dates). Myrtle Beach, SC. Air show, beauty contests, sporting events, live television shows, sandcastle-building contest, parade, greet visitors along the Grand Strand. Est attendance: 300,000. For info: Marilyn Chewning, Myrtle Beach Area Chamber of Commerce, PO Box 2115, Myrtle Beach, SC 29578. Phone: (803) 626-7444. Fax: (803) 626-0009. WWW: http://www.myrtlebeachlive.com

THREE RIVERS ARTS FESTIVAL. June 5–21. Pittsburgh, PA. Celebration of visual and performing arts. Juried visual arts exhibitions, musical performances, artists' market, children's activities and food. Est attendance: 600,000. For info: Three Rivers Arts Festival, 207 Sweetbriar St, Pittsburgh, PA 15211. Phone: (412) 481-7040. Fax: (412) 481-8505.
WWW: http://www.artswire.org/traf

UNITED NATIONS: WORLD ENVIRONMENT DAY. June 5. Observed annually on June 5, the anniversary of the opening of the UN Conference on the Human Environment held in Stockholm in 1972, which led to establishment of UN Environment Programme, based in Nairobi. The General Assembly has urged marking the day with activities reaffirming concern for the preservation and enhancement of the environment. For info: United Nations, Dept of Public Info, New York, NY 10017.

VERMONT DAIRY FESTIVAL. June 5–7. Enosburg Falls, VT. Come and join in the family fun. Festival includes amusement rides, a parade, fireworks, arts and crafts displays, entertainment, food booths and much more. Est attendance: 25,000. For info: Vermont Dairy Festival, PO Box 282, Enosburg Falls, VT 05450. Phone: (802) 933-2513. Fax: (802) 933-2513.

WOLF POINT'S HOTTEST CHILI WEEKEND. June 5–7. Sherman Park, Stampede Ground, Wolf Point, MT. Carnival, demolition derby, chili cook-off. Annually, first weekend in June. Est attendance: 4,000. For info: Wolf Point Optimist Club, PO Box 486, Wolf Point, MT 59201. Phone: (406) 653-2222. Fax: (406) 653-2221.
Email: rboysun@midrivers.com.
WWW: http://www.wolfpoint.com/chili

WORLD CAMPAIGN FOR THE BIOSPHERE. June 5. In observance of World Environment Day. To awaken people to their responsibilities toward the biosphere, which is the only known source of life in the universe and our sole planetary life-support system, of which we humans constitute an integral part and yet threaten increasingly by our ever-expanding population and profligate activities. Meetings subsequently of the World Council For The Biosphere and its sponsoring organization. For info: Dr. Nicholas Polunin, Pres, The Foundation for Environmental Conservation, 7 Chemin Taverney, 1218 Grand-Saconnex, 7th & 8th Floors, Geneva, Switzerland.

BIRTHDAYS TODAY

Chad Allen, 24, actor ("Dr. Quinn, Medicine Woman"), cartoon voice (Charlie Brown), born Cerritos, CA, June 5, 1974.
Bosin Blackbear, 77, artist, born Anadarko, OK, June 5, 1921.
Jacques Demy, 67, filmmaker (*The Umbrellas of Cherbourg*), born Pont-Chateau, France, June 5, 1931.
Margaret Drabble, 59, Canadian novelist (*The Needle's Eye*), born Sheffield, Yorkshire, England, June 5, 1939.
Ken Follett, 49, British novelist (*The Eye of the Needle*), born Wales, UK, June 5, 1949.
Spalding Gray, 57, performance artist, actor, writer (*The Killing Fields, Swimming to Cambodia, Beyond Rangoon*), born Barrington, RI, June 5, 1941.
Robert Lansing, 69, actor (*Under the Yum Yum Tree*, "The Man Who Never Was"), born San Diego, CA, June 5, 1929.
Marky Mark, 27, rapper (Marky Mark and the Funky Bunch, "Good Vibrations"), born Dorchester, MA, June 5, 1971.
Bill Moyers, 64, journalist ("Bill Moyers' Journal"), born Hugo, OK, June 5, 1934.

JUNE 6 — SATURDAY

Day 157 — 208 Remaining

AMERICAN SOCIETY OF RADIOLOGIC TECHNOLOGISTS (ASRT) ANNUAL CONFERENCE. June 6–11. Houston, TX. Conference for radiologic sciences professionals offering technical exhibits, continuing education courses, busi-

June 1998

S	M	T	W	T	F	S
	1	2	3	4	5	6
7	8	9	10	11	12	13
14	15	16	17	18	19	20
21	22	23	24	25	26	27
28	29	30				

ness meetings, House of Delegates, scientific displays and many other special events. Est attendance: 800. For info: American Soc of Radiologic Technologists, 15000 Central Ave SE, Albuquerque, NM 87123-3917. Phone: (505) 298-4500. Fax: (505) 298-5063.

ANTIQUE AUTO SWAP MEET. June 6–7. Grand Prairie, TX. More than 600 vendors from across the US gather to sell, trade or buy automobiles, parts and accessories. Est attendance: 65,000. For info: Traders Village, 2602 Mayfield Rd, Grand Prairie, TX 75052. Phone: (972) 647-2331.

"ARMSTRONG CIRCLE THEATER": ANNIVERSARY. June 6, 1950. This half-hour weekly anthology series was commonly known as "Circle Theater," and specialized in dramatizations of actual events. In 1955, the format was extended to an hour and the program began running biweekly. Hosts of "ACT" included John Cameron Swayze, Douglas Edwards, Ron Cochran and Henry Hamilton. Many stars acted their first TV roles here, including John Cassavetes, Robert Duvall, Anne Jackson and Telly Savalas.

BONZA BOTTLER DAY™. June 6. To celebrate when the number of the day is the same as the number of the month. Bonza Bottler Day™ is an excuse to have a party at least once a month. For more information, see Jan 1. For info: Gail M. Berger, 109 Matthew Ave, Poca, WV 25159. Phone: (304) 776-7746. Email: gberger5@aol.com.

BRUSH CREEK CIVIL WAR WEEKEND. June 6–7. Brush Creek Park Area 10, North Sewickley, PA. 9th annual. Civil War encampment, demonstrations, battle reenactments and more. For info: (412) 266-0256 or Beaver County Tourist Promotion Agency, 215 B Ninth St, Monaca, PA 15061-2028. Phone: (412) 728-0212. Fax: (412) 728-0456.

BUFFALO DAYS CELEBRATION (WITH BUFFALO CHIP THROWING). June 6–7. Luverne, MN. Parade, Arts in the Park, free barbecued buffalo burgers (while they last) and unique buffalo-chip throwing contest. Annually, the first weekend in June. Est attendance: 8,000. For info: Norma De Jongh, Exec Dir, Luverne Area Chamber of Commerce, 102 E Main, Luverne, MN 56156. Phone: (507) 283-4061. Fax: (507) 283-4061.

CALIFORNIA FREE-FISHING DAYS IN PUBLIC WATERS. June 6 (also Sept 26). In observance of National Fishing Week. These days are fishing days in all California waters. A fishing license is not required on these days but all other rules and regulations must be followed. For info: Conservation Education, Dept of Fish and Game, 1416 Ninth St, Sacramento, CA 95814. Fax: (916) 653-1856. Email: lbrechei@hg.dfg.ca.gov.

CAPITOL HILL PEOPLE'S FAIR. June 6–7. Civic Center Park, Denver, CO. More than 500 arts and crafts and other exhibit booths; live entertainment featuring local talent on six stages. Est attendance: 250,000. For info: Capitol Hill United Neighborhoods, 1490 Lafayette, #401, Denver, CO 80218. Phone: (303) 830-1651. Fax: (303) 830-1782. Email: chun@centralaccess.com.

COUNTRYSIDE VILLAGE ART FAIR. June 6–7. Omaha, NE. Exhibits by 140 artists from 15 states. Juried fine arts show. 28th annual show. Est attendance: 10,000. For info: Judy Drawbaugh, Countryside Merchants Assn, 2336 S 138th St, Omaha, NE 68144. Phone: (402) 333-9629.

COUPLE APPRECIATION DAY. June 6. To show thanks for each others' love and emotional support. Do something special to reinforce and celebrate your relationship. Annually, the first Saturday of June. For info: Donald Etkes, MFCC, 112 Harvard Ave, Ste 148, Claremont, CA 91711. Phone: (909) 981-7333.

COWS ON THE CONCOURSE. June 6. Madison, WI. Pet a cow on the capitol square to celebrate June Dairy Month. All major breeds of cows will be on display. Ample samplings of all types of dairy products made in Wisconsin. Antique tractors, dairy-related crafts demonstrations and displays. Annually, the first Saturday in June. Est attendance: 26,000. For info: Norman Maier, 6101 Queens Way, Madison, WI 53716. Phone: (608) 221-6898.

D-DAY: ANNIVERSARY. June 6, 1944. In the early-morning hours Allied forces landed in Normandy on the north coast of France. In an operation that took months of planning, a fleet of 2,727 ships of every description converged from British ports from Wales to the North Sea. Operation *Overlord* involved 2,000,000 tons of war materials, including more than 50,000 tanks, armored cars, jeeps, trucks, and half-tracks. The US alone sent 1,700,000 fighting men. The Germans believed the invasion would not take place under the adverse weather conditions of this early June day. But as the sun came up the village of Saint Mèere Eglise was liberated by American parachutists, and by nightfall the landing of 155,000 Allies attested to the success of D-Day. The long-awaited second front had at last materialized.

DENMARK: EEL FESTIVAL. June 6–7. Jyllinge (near Roskilde). Festival celebrated since 1968. Every restaurant and pub in town serves delicious fried eel. Other entertainments include theater, sports, tattoo bands, sailing competitions, flea markets and fireworks. Annually, the first weekend in June.

DO-DAH PARADE. June 6. Kalamazoo, MI. "Salute to Silliness." Since 1981, offbeat entries have included a precision grill team (complete with spatulas) and a herbie curbie brigade. Annually, the first Saturday in June. Est attendance: 60,000. For info: Lisa Theisen, WKMI/WKFR Radio, 4154 Jennings Dr, Kalamazoo, MI 49005-0911. Phone: (616) 344-0111. Fax: (616) 344-4223. Email: LTheisen@wkfr.com.
WWW: http://www.wkfr.com

EDGAR LEE MASTERS DAY. June 6. Lewistown, IL. Honoring poet/author of *Spoon River Anthology* with celebration of small town life: parade, auction, baking contest, poetry contest, dramatized readings of *Spoon River Anthology*, masters auto show, antiques, crafts and quilts. Est attendance: 3,000. For info: Joan Johnson, Lewistown Chamber of Commerce, PO Box 308, Lewistown, IL 61542. Phone: (309) 547-3234 or (309) 547-4300.

FORT SISSETON HISTORICAL FESTIVAL. June 6–7. Fort Sisseton State Park, Lake City, SD. Fort Sisseton comes alive the first weekend in June every year. See life as it was in 1864 when the fort was established. Cavalry drills, military costume ball, Indian dancing, Dakota Dan's medicine show, wagon train, muzzle-loader shoot, rendezvous, draft-horse pulls, fiddlers, square dancing, melodramas and arts and crafts are popular features of the festival. Est attendance: 46,000. For info: Dave Daberkow, Fort Sisseton State Park, Dept of Game, Fish and Parks, 11545 Northside Dr, Lake City, SD 57247-6142. Phone: (605) 448-5701. Fax: (605) 448-5572. WWW: http://www.state.sd.us/gfp/

FRONTIER DAYS. June 6–7. Culbertson, MT. Two days of parades, rodeos, a barn dance, talent show and genuine Western hospitality. Annually, the first weekend in June. Est attendance: 2,000. For info: Ila Mae Forbregd, PO Box 639, Culbertson, MT 59218.

GETZ, STAN: DEATH ANNIVERSARY. June 6, 1991. American jazz saxophonist Stan Getz was born at Philadelphia, PA, in 1927. He introduced the cool-jazz style, which became a major movement in the 1950s, and the bossa nova (new wave) style of the 1960s. Getz received 11 Grammy Awards, and was the first jazz musician to win the Grammy Award for Record of the Year (1965) for "The Girl from Ipanema."

GHOST TOURS. June 6. New Hope, PA. (Also every Saturday, June–August, and every Friday and Saturday, September–November) Tours meet at 8 PM sharp at the Cannon on Main St. No reservations required. Rain or shine. $8 per person. Private walks and gift certificates available. For info: Ghost Tours, PO Box 3354, Warminster, PA 18974. Phone: (215) 957-9988.

GOVERNOR'S CUP. June 6. Helena, MT. Montana's premier running event. Includes a marathon, marathon relay, 20K, 10K and 5K. Corporate entries. Approximately 7,000 runners. Annually, the first Saturday in June. Sponsor: Blue Cross/Blue Shield. Est attendance: 7,000. For info: Trish Bloom, Race Dir, Blue Cross & Blue Shield, Box 451, Helena, MT 59624. Phone: (406) 447-3414. Fax: (406) 442-6946.
WWW: http://www.govcup.bcbsmt.com

☆ ☆ ☆

GREAT CHUNKY RIVER RAFT RACE. June 6. Chunky, MS. Raft builders compete in four raft divisions in race held along the Chunky River. Cash prizes for most creative rafts. Live entertainment noon–4 PM. Raft divisions: flat-bottom boat, canoe, inflatable raft (store-bought), homemade raft. Est attendance: 3,000. For info: Lisa Cowart, Special Project/Market Coord, PO Box 4177, Meridian, MS 39304-4177. Phone: (601) 482-6161. Fax: (601) 485-9941.

GREAT WISCONSIN DELLS BALLOON RALLY. June 6–7. Wisconsin Dells, WI. More than 90 vividly colored balloons compete in this annual event. Est attendance: 100,000. For info: Wisc Dells Visitor and Conv Bureau, PO Box 390, Wisconsin Dells, WI 53965. Phone: (800) 223-3557.
Email: wisdells@midplains.net. WWW: http://www.wisdells.com

HALE, NATHAN: BIRTH ANNIVERSARY. June 6. American patriot Nathan Hale was born at Coventry, CT, on June 6, 1755. During the battles for New York during the American Revolution, he volunteered to seek military intelligence behind enemy lines and was captured on the night of Sept 21, 1776. In an audience before General William Howe, Hale admitted he was an American officer and was ordered hanged the following morning. Although some question them, his dying words, "I only regret that I have but one life to lose for my country," have become a famous symbol of American patriotism. He was hanged on Sept 22, 1776, at Manhattan, NY.

THE HIGHLANDS GLYNDEBOURNE CONCERT. June 6. The Highlands, Fort Washington, PA. An outdoor concert and picnic on the grounds of The Highlands, an 18th-century country estate. The mansion and gardens, owned by the Commonwealth of Pennsylvania, are open for touring all year round. For info: The Highlands, 7001 Sheaff Ln, Ft Washington, PA 19034. Phone: (215) 641-2687. Fax: (215) 641-2556.

HOOSIER HERITAGE ART EXHIBIT AND SALE. June 6–7. Rochester, IN. Est attendance: 1,000. For info: Fulton County Historical Society, 37 E 375 N, Rochester, IN 46975. Phone: (219) 223-4436. Email: WWillard@townsquare.net.

JACK JOUETT'S RIDE: ANNIVERSARY OBSERVANCE. June 6. Jack Jouett made a heroic 45-mile ride on horseback during the night of June 3–4, 1781, to warn Virginia Governor Thomas Jefferson and the legislature that the British were coming. Jouett rode from a tavern in Louisa County to Charlottesville, VA, in about 6½ hours, arriving at Jefferson's home at dawn on June 4. Lieutenant Colonel Tarleton's British forces raided Charlottesville, but Jouett's warning gave the Americans time to escape. Jouett was born at Albemarle County, VA, on Dec 7, 1754, and died at Bath, KY, in 1822 (exact date unknown). Reportedly, Jack Jouett Day, commemorating the historic and heroic ride, is observed annually on the first Saturday in June in the Charlottesville area.

June 1998

S	M	T	W	T	F	S
	1	2	3	4	5	6
7	8	9	10	11	12	13
14	15	16	17	18	19	20
21	22	23	24	25	26	27
28	29	30				

JUNE JUNQUE JAMBOREE. June 6. Lovington, NM. Townwide garage sale with merchants, clubs and individuals all participating. For info: Nancy Moore, Lovington Chamber of Commerce, PO Box 1347, Lovington, NM 88260. Phone: (505) 396-5311. Fax: (505) 396-2823.

KHACHATURIAN, ARAM (ILICH): BIRTH ANNIVERSARY. June 6, 1903. Armenian musician and composer, noted for compositions based on folk music and legend, born at Tbilisi, Georgia, USSR, June 6, 1903. Died May 1, 1978.

KIDS FEST. June 6–7. Central riverfront, Cincinnati, OH. Largest free event for kids and their families in the country. More than 100 activities in 14 venues. Est attendance: 200,000. For info: Leslie Keller, Event Producer, Jacor Communications, Inc, 1111 St. Gregory St, Cincinnati, OH 45202. Phone: (513) 763-5745. Fax: (513) 677-8113. Email: lgkeller@aol.com.

KOREA: MEMORIAL DAY. June 6. Nation pays tribute to the war dead, and memorial services are held at the National Cemetery in Seoul. Legally recognized Korean holiday.

MARBLE MEET AT AMANA. June 6–7. Holiday Inn, Amana, IA. Seminar, banquet and exhibits. Collectors buy, sell and trade marbles. Est attendance: 800. For info: Marbles Collectors Unltd, Box 206, Northboro, MA 01532. Phone: (319) 642-3891.

McHENRY HIGHLAND FESTIVAL. June 6. Garrett County Fairgrounds, Route 219, McHenry (Deep Creek Lake), MD. Traditional Scottish event with bagpipe bands, sheepdog exhibitions, open Scottish athletic solo piping and Highland dancing competitions, shops, foods and more. Est attendance: 2,000. For info: Promotion Council, Deep Creek Lake-Garrett County Courthouse, 200 S Third St, Oakland, MD 21550. Phone: (301) 334-1948. Fax: (301) 334-1919.
Email: gctourism@garrett.ncin.com.
WWW: http://www.gcnet.net/gctourism/gct.html

MISSISSIPPI BROILER FESTIVAL. June 6. Gaddis Recreational Park, Forest, MS. A variety of entertainment, arts, crafts. Also, tennis tournaments, youth league baseball tournament, carnival, coronation of Broiler Festival Queen, Mississippi Track Grand Prix Race, concert and fireworks. Est attendance: 5,000. For info: Patsy Nicholson, Forest Area Chamber of Commerce, PO Box 266, Forest, MS 39074. Phone: (601) 469-4332. Fax: (601) 469-3224.

NATIONAL FAMILY DAY™. June 6. A special day to recognize the importance of family in raising physically and emotionally healthy kids. Sponsored by KidsPeace®, The National Center for Kids Overcoming Crisis, a private, not-for-profit organization that has been providing hope and healing to kids in crisis since 1882. KidsPeace offers the country's widest array of children's critical care services under a "single roof" and crisis education to families across the US. Annually, the first Saturday in June. For info: Paula Knouse, KidsPeace, 5300 KidsPeace Dr, Orefield, PA 18069-9101. Phone: (610) 799-8325.
WWW: http://www.kidspeace.org

NEW BRIGHTON SUMMER FESTIVAL. June 6. New Brighton, PA. 9th annual. Come and join in the family fun with arts and crafts, entertainment, food booths and more. For info: (412) 843-1743 or Beaver County Tourist Promotion Agency, 215 B Ninth St, Monaca, PA 15061-2028. Phone: (412) 728-0212. Fax: (412) 728-0456.

OLDIESFEST. June 6. Cincinnati, OH. A free all-day music festival featuring national Oldies artists (6-10 groups/performers) performing throughout the day. The festival also has children's activities area, plenty of food and beverages, exhibition tent and more. The event is free but you must obtain a free ticket to be admitted by sending a SASE to WGRR-FM. Est attendance: 80,000. For info: Toni Mason, Promotions & Mktg Dir, WGRR Oldies 103.5FM, 3656 Edwards Rd, Cincinnati, OH 45208. Phone: (513) 321-8900. Fax: (513) 321-1175.
Email: promote@wgrr1035.com.
WWW: http://www.wgrr1035.com

OPERATION YOUTH. June 6–13. Xavier University, Cincinnati, OH. To provide a hands-on exercise in democracy for teenagers. Students elect, from their ranks, city officials who join their real counterparts in a Cincinnati council meeting. Speakers from education, industry and government. Est attendance: 100. For info: William Smith, CPA, Prof of Accounting, Dir of Operation Youth, Xavier University, 3800 Victory Pkwy, Cincinnati, OH 45207-5161. Phone: (513) 745-3504. Fax: (513) 745-4383.

OUR LOVELADIES FAIR. June 6–7. Loveladies, NJ. 9th annual preseason introduction to Island and mainland merchants. Sponsored by Long Beach Island Foundation of Arts & Sciences. Est attendance: 1,200. For info: Long Beach Island Foundation of Arts & Sciences, 120 Long Beach Blvd, Loveladies, NJ 08008. Phone: (609) 494-1241. Fax: (609) 494-0662.

PEDDLER'S VILLAGE ANNUAL ART FAIRE. June 6–7. Juried competition of paintings, prints, photography and more created by fine artists. Regional museums and cultural institutions offer hands-on fun educational programs for children. Shops offer various in-store exhibits and arts-related events. Live music, face painting and balloons. Free admission. Est attendance: 7,000. For info: Judy Goldschmidt, PR Mgr, Peddler's Village, Routes 202 & 263, Lahaska, PA 18931. Phone: (215) 794-4000. Fax: (215) 794-4001. WWW: http://www.peddlersvillage.com

PET APPRECIATION WEEK (PAW) ©. June 6–12. A purr-fect time to thoughtfully remember our pet companions who share so much with us. Do something special for your own pet or pets this week. Each day of the week has a special focus: June 7: Honor Thy Veterinarian Day ©95; June 8: VIP: Very Important Pet Day; June 9: Nine Lives Day ©95; June 10: Animal Stories Day ©95; June 11: The Three Monkeys Day©95; June 12: ToTo Times ©95. For detailed description, send $2 to cover postage and copying costs. For info: Adrienne Sioux Koopersmith, Pawsters United, 1437 W Rosemont, #1W, Chicago, IL 60660-1319. Phone: (773) 743-5341. Fax: (773) 743-5395.
Email: kooper@interaccess.com.

PET PARADE. June 6. LaGrange, IL. Children and their pets parade through the streets of LaGrange in costume, accompanied by clowns, floats, celebrities and marching bands. Trophies awarded to the most original entries in 10 costume categories. Est attendance: 80,000. For info: West Suburban Chamber of Commerce, PO Box 187, LaGrange, IL 60525. Phone: (708) 352-0494. Fax: (708) 352-0620.
Email: info@westsuburbanchamber.org.
WWW: http://www.westsuburbanchamber.org

PROPOSITION 13: 20th ANNIVERSARY. June 6, 1978. California voters (65% of them) supported a primary election ballot initiative, June 6, 1978, to cut property taxes 57 percent. Regarded as a possible omen of things to come across the country—a taxpayer's revolt against high taxes and government spending.

REOPENING OF THE RAILROAD CAR MUSEUM. June 6. Depot Lane Complex, Schoharie, NY. Open each weekend, 1–5 PM, June through October. Est attendance: 500. For info: Schoharie Colonial Heritage Assn, PO Box 554, Schoharie, NY 12157. Phone: (518) 295-7505.

SMALL CRAFT WEEKEND. June 6–7. Mystic Seaport, Mystic, CT. The 29th annual weekend when small-craft enthusiasts gather at the museum with their boats. Traditional small boats of every type sail from docks of Mystic Seaport on the Mystic River. Annually, first weekend in June. Est attendance: 4,000. For info: Mystic Seaport, 75 Greenmanville Ave, Box 6000, Mystic, CT 06355. Phone: (203) 572-0711.

SOUTH JERSEY CANOE AND KAYAK CLASSIC. June 6. Ocean County Park, Rt 88, Lakewood, NJ. Canoe and Kayak vendors from around the country set up on a beach to show the public the thrill of watersports. You may test-paddle the boats of your choice and attend a clinic about canoeing or kayaking throughout the day. Event is free. Annually, the first Saturday in June. Est attendance: 3,000. For info: Lillian Hoey, Recreation Leader, Wells Mills County Park, 905 Wells Mills Rd, Waretown, NJ 08758. Phone: (609) 971-3085. Fax: (609) 971-9540.

SOUTHERN CALIFORNIA CAJUN AND ZYDECO FESTIVAL. June 6–7. Rainbow Lagoon, Long Beach, CA. 12th annual. To celebrate Cajun and Creole cultures. Est attendance: 4,000. For info: Franklin Zawacki, 915 Sanchez St, San Francisco, CA 94114. Phone: (415) 643-9336.

SPACE MILESTONE: *SOYUZ 11* (USSR). June 6, 1971. Launched on this date with Cosmonauts G.T. Dobrovolsky, V.N. Volkov and V.I. Patsayev, who died during return landing on June 30, 1971, after 24-day space flight. *Soyuz 11* had docked at *Salyut* orbital space station June 7–29, where scientific experiments were conducted. First humans to die in space.

SPECIAL LIBRARIES ASSOCIATION ANNUAL CONFERENCE. June 6–11. Indianapolis, IN. Networking, educational activities, annual board meeting; exhibits for librarians at companies, government agencies, academic institutions, etc. Est attendance: 6,000. For info: SLA, 1700 18th St NW, Washington, DC 20009-2514. Phone: (202) 234-4700.
WWW: http://www.sla.org

STRAWBERRY FESTIVAL. June 6. Vaile Mansion, Independence, MO. Outdoor Victorian-type festival featuring strawberry treats, crafts, antiques, children's activities, carriage rides, flea market and entertainment. Annually, first Saturday in June. For info: Cathy Bennett, Tourism Dir, 111 E Maple, Independence, MO 64050. Phone: (816) 325-7430.

SURRENDER OF MEMPHIS: ANNIVERSARY. June 6, 1862. Confederate gunboats engaged a Union flotilla near Memphis, TN. As crowds of spectators watched from the riverbanks, the outgunned Confederates were defeated. The city of Memphis surrendered shortly before noon of that day, effectively opening up the Mississippi region.

SUSAN B. ANTHONY FINED FOR VOTING: ANNIVERSARY. June 6. Seeking to test for women the citizenship and voting rights extended to black males under the 14th and 15th Amendments, Susan B. Anthony led a group of women who registered and voted in a Rochester, NY, election in 1872. She was arrested, tried and sentenced to pay a fine. She refused to do so and was allowed to go free by a judge who feared she would appeal to a higher court.

SWEDEN: FLAG DAY. June 6. Commemorates the day upon which Gustavus I (Gustavus Vasa) ascended the throne of Sweden in 1523.

TAKE A KID FISHING WEEKEND. June 6–7. St. Paul, MN. Resident adults may fish without a license on these days when fishing with a child under age 16. For info: Jack Skrypek, Fisheries Chief, DNR, Box 12, 500 Lafayette Rd, St. Paul, MN 55155. Phone: (612) 296-0792 or Fisheries Info (612) 296-3325. Fax: (612) 297-4916. WWW: http://www.dnr.state.mn.us/

TOPPENISH MURAL SOCIETY'S "MURAL-IN-A-DAY." June 6. Pioneer Park, Toppenish, WA. 12 professional artists paint a complete, historically authentic mural, 14′ × 48′, in eight hours. Starting at 9 AM they work until finished, usually until 4 PM. Accompanied by an arts and crafts show and an ethnic food fair. Annually, the first Saturday in June. Est attendance: 12,000. For info: Toppenish Mural Society, PO Box 1172, Toppenish, WA 98948. Phone: (509) 865-6516.
Email: murals@wolfenet.com.
WWW: http://www.wolfenet.com/~murals/

	S	M	T	W	T	F	S
June 1998		1	2	3	4	5	6
	7	8	9	10	11	12	13
	14	15	16	17	18	19	20
	21	22	23	24	25	26	27
	28	29	30				

"20/20" TV PREMIERE: 20th ANNIVERSARY. June 6, 1978. "20/20" is an hourly newsmagazine developed by ABC to compete with CBS's "60 Minutes." Its original hosts, Harold Hayes and Robert Hughes, were cut after the first show and replaced by Hugh Downs. Barbara Walters became co-anchor in 1984. The show consisted of investigative and background reports. Contributors to the show included Tom Jarriel, Sylvia Chase, Geraldo Rivera, Thomas Hoving, Bob Brown, John Stossel, Lynn Sherr and Stone Phillips.

WORLD'S LARGEST GARAGE SALE. June 6. South Bend, IN. Annually, the first Saturday in June. Est attendance: 12,000. For info: The City of South Bend, Parks & Recreation, 301 S St. Louis Blvd, South Bend, IN 46617. Phone: (219) 235-7641 or (219) 235-9952. Fax: (219) 235-9331.

BIRTHDAYS TODAY

Sandra Bernhard, 43, actress ("Roseanne"), born Flint, MI, June 6, 1955.
Gary U.S. Bonds (Gary Anderson), 59, singer ("Quarter to Three"), songwriter, born Jacksonville, FL, June 6, 1939.
Bjorn Rune Borg, 42, tennis player, born Sodertalje, Sweden, June 6, 1956.
George Deukmejian, 70, former governor of California (R), born Menands, NY, June 6, 1928.
David Dukes, 53, actor ("Sisters," *The Handmaid's Tale*), born San Francisco, CA, June 6, 1945.
Marian Wright Edelman, 59, president of Children's Defense Fund, lawyer, civil rights activist, born Bennettsville, SC, June 6, 1939.
Kenny G, 42, sax player, born Seattle, WA, June 6, 1956.
Rueben Mayes, 35, former football player, born North Battleford, Saskatchewan, Canada, June 6, 1963.
Cam Neely, 33, former hockey player, born Comox, BC, June 6, 1965.
Amanda Pays, 39, actress ("Max Headroom," *Exposure*), born Berkshire, England, June 6, 1959.
Billie Whitelaw, 66, actress (*The Dressmaker*, "Masterpiece Theater"), born Coventry, England, June 6, 1932.

JUNE 7 — SUNDAY

Day 158 — 207 Remaining

APGAR, VIRGINIA: BIRTH ANNIVERSARY. June 7, 1909. Dr. Apgar developed the simple assessment method that permits doctors and nurses to evaluate newborns while they are still in the delivery room to identify those in need of immediate medical care. The Apgar score was first published in 1953, and the Perinatal Section of the American Academy of Pediatrics is named for Dr. Apgar. Born at Westfield, NJ, Apgar died Aug 7, 1974.

BOONE DAY. June 7. Each year on June 7, the Kentucky Historical Society celebrates the anniversary of the day in 1767 when Daniel Boone, America's most famous frontiersman, reportedly first sighted the land that would become Kentucky. The June 7 date is taken from the book *The Discovery, Settlement and Present State of Kentucky*, by John Filson, published in 1784, with an appendix titled "The Adventures of Colonel Daniel Boone." The information in the appendix supposedly originated with Boone, although Filson is the actual author. The work is not considered completely reliable by historians.

BRUMMELL, GEORGE BRYAN "BEAU": BIRTH ANNIVERSARY. June 7, 1778. Born at London, England, on June 7, 1778, Beau Brummell was, early in his life, a popular English men's fashion leader, the "arbiter elegantarium" of taste in dress. His extravagance and lack of tact (it was he who reportedly said—indicating the Prince of Wales, later George IV—"Who's your fat friend?") led him from wealth and popularity to poverty and disrepute. Once imprisoned for debt, he became careless of dress and personal appearance. He died in a charitable asylum at Caen, France, on Mar 30, 1840.

GAUGUIN, (EUGENE HENRI) PAUL: 150th BIRTH ANNIVERSARY. June 7, 1848. French painter born at Paris, France, on June 7, 1848. Formerly a stockbroker, he became a painter in his middle age and three years later renounced his life in Paris to move to Tahiti. He is remembered best for his broad, flat tones and bold colors. Gauguin died May 8, 1903, at Atoana on the island of Hiva Oa in the Marquesas.

INTERNATIONAL MUSIC CAMP. June 7–July 28. International Peace Garden, Dunseith, ND. In its 43rd season, more than 3,000 students from 62 countries enjoy the many different programs of IMC. Music camps include concert band, piping and drumming, jazz, choir, vocal jazz, orchestra, piano, guitar, marimba and total percussion. Also visual arts, dance, drama and creative-writing sessions. Est attendance: 3,000. For info: Joseph T. Alme, Dir, Intl Music Camp, 1725 11th St SW, Minot, ND 58701. Phone: (701) 838-8472. Fax: (701) 838-8472. Email: imc@minot.com.

☆ ☆ ☆

INTERNATIONAL PBX TELECOMMUNICATORS WEEK. June 7–13. To honor the switchboard operators of private businesses, to acknowledge their dedicated professionalism and the vital role they play in the modern business world. Annually, the first full week in June. For info: Mary Bohl, Secretary, Intl PBX Telecommunicators Clubs, 2505 Paul St, Eau Claire, WI 54701. Phone: (715) 839-6075. Fax: (715) 839-6015. Email: bohlrm@eau.net.

ITALY: GIOCO DEL PONTE. June 7. Pisa. The first Sunday in June is set aside for the Battle of the Bridge, a medieval parade and contest for possession of the bridge.

JAPAN: DAY OF THE RICE GOD. June 7. Chiyoda. Annual rice-transplanting festival observed on first Sunday in June. Centuries-old rural folk ritual revived in 1930s and celebrated with colorful costumes, parades, music, dancing and prayers to the Shinto rice god Wbai-sama.

KORN KLUB MUD DRAGS. June 7 (also Sept 13). River Rd, Plattsmouth, NE. Modified cars race in pits of mud in this annual fundraiser. Est attendance: 2,000. For info: Patricia Baburek, Coord, Kass Kounty King Korn Klub, PO Box 40, Plattsmouth, NE 68048. Phone: (402) 296-4155. Fax: (402) 296-4082.

NATIONAL ERGONOMICS WEEK. June 7–13. A commemoration to increase awareness of the benefits of ergonomics; to encourage consumers to make choices based on function, comfort, convenience, health factors and ease of use. The week is sponsored by the engineer and inventor who designed and developed the world's first ergonomically engineered underwear for men. For info: Cynthia Dunning Michels, ERGO, Inc, PO Box 162177, Altamonte Springs, FL 32716-2177. Phone: (800) 568-5982 or (407) 774-8044. Fax: (407) 774-8183. Email: ergoinc@worldnet.att.net. WWW: http://www.ezu.com

NATIONAL HEADACHE AWARENESS WEEK. June 7–13. Educating the public about the reality and severity of headache pain as a legitimate condition. Encouraging sufferers to consult with a physician for proper diagnosis and treatment, and to let sufferers know that there are new treatments available. For info: Suzanne E. Simons, Exec Dir, National Headache Foundation, 438 W St. James Place, 2nd Fl, Chicago, IL 60614-2750. Phone: (773) 388-6395. Fax: (773) 525-7357.

NATIONAL HUG HOLIDAY WEEK. June 7–13. To honor, recognize and express our appreciation for one another through the simple form of a hug, huggers across the country are invited to help increase hug abundance on the planet in an effort to increase awareness, support and involvement in Hugs for Health programs. The Hugs for Health Foundation provides hug therapy as a facet of the overall care plan for the elderly, terminally ill and long-term care residents. Send $1 for Holiday Huggers package. For info: Jo Lindberg, Hugs for Health Foundation, PO Box 1704, Tustin, CA 92681. Phone: (714) 832-4847.

ORTHODOX PENTECOST. June 7. Observed by Eastern Orthodox churches on this date.

RED CLOUD INDIAN ART SHOW. June 7–Aug 14. Pine Ridge, SD. Encourages Native American artists and gives their artwork exposure to the general public. Juried Art Show with cash awards. Est attendance: 12,500. For info: Brother C.M. Simon, Red Cloud Indian School, Pine Ridge, SD 57770. Phone: (605) 867-5491. Fax: (605) 867-1291.

ROSE SHOW. June 7 (tentative). Long Island, NY. More than 1,000 roses, entered by amateur growers in competition for awards, and an educational display staffed by experts to answer questions. Est attendance: 2,000. For info: Donald M. Stitt, Publicity, Long Island Rose Soc, 7 Ivy St, Oyster Bay, NY 11771. Phone: (516) 922-5341. Fax: (212) 977-6691. Email: saint2@ix.netcom.com.

ROSES INDOORS AND OUT. June 7 (also every Sunday in June). Granville, OH. Granville Life-Style Museum. Robinson family possessions featuring rose motifs: embroidered tablecloths, linens, hand-painted china, greeting cards and other memorabilia and roses growing in Oese's garden. Annually, the month of June celebrating National Rose Month. For info: Gina Hughes, Adm. Asst, Granville Life-Style Museum, H.D. Robinson House, 121 S Main St, Granville, OH 43023.

"THE $64,000 QUESTION" TV PREMIERE: ANNIVERSARY. June 7, 1955. This game show was a big hit, and the first of prime-time's big money shows. Contestants, each an expert in one area, answered questions; each time a question was answered correctly, contestants doubled their money and the questions became harder. Players, if successful, could come back the following week. For the $64,000 question, a player could bring along an expert, but if neither got the correct answer, the player left with $4,000. The host was Hal March, assisted by Lynn Dollar and later Pat Donovan, and questions were compiled by Dr. Bergen Evans. Some famous contestants were Dr. Joyce Brothers, Barbara Feldon and Jack Benny (as a joke). The show was dropped in 1958 amid the game show scandals, though no specific allegations were ever substantiated.

STATE PARKS OPEN HOUSE AND FREE FISHING DAY. June 7. Wisconsin. Free admission to state parks and forests. No fishing license is required to fish in inland lakes and Lake Michigan accessed through Wisconsin. (Free to in-state as well as out-of-state residents.) Annually, the first Sunday of the first full weekend in June. Est attendance: 8,000. For info: Bureau of Parks and Recreation, Dept of Natural Resources, PO Box 7921, Madison, WI 53707-7921. Phone: (608) 266-2181. Fax: (608) 267-7474. Email: wiparks@dnr.state.wi.us. WWW: http://www.dnr.state.wi.us/

SUPPORT GROUP RECOGNITION WEEK. June 7–13. Honoring the members of all the various support groups for their valiant endeavor to improve their lives using the educational, spiritual and motivational techniques available through their group. Annually, the second week of June. For info: Anita Heyman, Marian Health Ctr Community Advisory Board for the Disabled, 801 5th St, Sioux City, IA 51101. Phone: (712) 279-2115. Fax: (712) 279-2943.

SUPREME COURT STRIKES DOWN CONNECTICUT LAW BANNING CONTRACEPTION. June 7, 1965. In Griswold v. Connecticut, the Supreme Court guaranteed the right to privacy, including the freedom from government intrusion into matters of birth control.

TAIWAN: BIRTHDAY OF CHENG HUANG. June 7. Thirteenth day of fifth moon. Celebrated with a procession of actors on stilts doing dragon and lion dances.

TEACHER'S DAY IN MASSACHUSETTS. June 7. Annually, the first Sunday in June.

TRINITY SUNDAY. June 7. Christian Holy Day on the Sunday after Pentecost commemorates the Holy Trinity, the three divine persons—Father, Son and Holy Spirit—in one God. See also: "Pentecost" (May 31).

TURNER, JOHN NAPIER: BIRTHDAY. June 7. Canadian politician, sworn in as Canada's 17th prime minister on June 30, 1984, serving until Sept 17, 1984, when he was succeeded by Brian Mulroney. Born on June 7, 1929, at Richmond, Surrey, England.

BIRTHDAYS TODAY

Gwendolyn Brooks, 81, poet, author (Pulitzer for *Annie Allen*), born Topeka, KS, June 7, 1917.

Louise Erdrich, 44, author whose works include *Love Medicine* and *The Beet Queen*, born at Little Falls, MN, June 7, 1954.

Tom Jones (Thomas Woodward), 58, singer ("It's Not Unusual," "She's a Lady"), born Pontypridd, Wales, UK, June 7, 1940.

Bill Kreutzmann, Jr, 52, drummer/singer, co-founder of The Grateful Dead, born Palo Alto, CA, June 7, 1946.

Liam Neeson, 46, actor (*Excalibur, Ethan Frome, Schindler's List*), born Ballymena, Northern Ireland, June 7, 1952.

The Artist Formerly Known as Prince (Prince Rogers Nelson), 40, musician, singer, born Minneapolis, MN, June 7, 1958.

JUNE 8 — MONDAY

Day 159 — 206 Remaining

AMERICAN HEROINE REWARDED: ANNIVERSARY. June 8. On Mar 16, 1697, in an attack on Haverhill, MA, Indians captured Hannah Duston and killed her one-week-old baby, in addition to killing or capturing 39 others. After being taken to an Indian camp, she escaped on Apr 29 after killing 10 Indians with a tomahawk and scalping them as proof of her deed. On June 8, 1697, her husband was awarded, on her behalf, the sum of 25 pounds for her heroic efforts, the first public award to a woman in America.

ATTACK ON THE *USS LIBERTY*: ANNIVERSARY. June 8. At 2 PM local time on June 8, 1967, the unescorted US intelligence ship USS *Liberty*, sailing in international waters off the Egyptian coast, was attacked without warning by Israeli jet planes and three Israeli torpedo boats. She was strafed and hit repeatedly by rockets, cannon, napalm and finally a torpedo. Casualties: out of a crew of 294 Americans, there were 34 dead and 171 wounded. Israel apologized, claiming mistaken identity, but surviving crew members charged deliberate attack by Israel and cover-up by US authorities.

BILL OF RIGHTS PROPOSAL: ANNIVERSARY. June 8. Bill of Rights, which led to the first 10 amendments to the US Constitution, was first proposed by James Madison on June 8, 1789.

June 1998

S	M	T	W	T	F	S
	1	2	3	4	5	6
7	8	9	10	11	12	13
14	15	16	17	18	19	20
21	22	23	24	25	26	27
28	29	30				

BOLIVIAN EARTHQUAKE: ANNIVERSARY. June 8, 1994. A "deep focus" earthquake registering 8.2 on the Richter scale erupted 400 miles beneath the earth's surface in a remote area of Bolivia. The quake is believed to be the largest ever recorded in the Bolivian area. It was felt as far north as Minneapolis, MN.

COCHISE: DEATH ANNIVERSARY. June 8, 1874. Born around 1810 in the Chiricahua Mountains of Arizona, Cochise became a fierce and courageous leader of the Apache. After his arrest in 1861, he escaped and launched the Apache Wars, which lasted for 25 years. He died 13 years later near his stronghold in southeastern Arizona.

LAKI VOLCANO ERUPTION: ANNIVERSARY. June 8, 1783. One of the most violent and important volcanic eruptions of recorded history began on this date. Laki, or Skafta, volcano in southern Iceland continued eruption for eight months, expelling an estimated 4½ cubic miles of lava, ultimately causing a famine and the deaths of nearly 10,000 persons. Acid rain reached western Europe, and other climatic and atmospheric changes were worldwide. English naturalist Gilbert White described some of the "horrible phenomena" of the summer of 1783, including the "peculiar haze, or smokey fog . . . unlike anything known within the memory of man." The effects of this volcanic eruption and its possible long-term consequences are still being studied by scientists. See also: "White, Gilbert: Birth Anniversary" (July 18).

McGOWAN, WILLIAM: DEATH ANNIVERSARY. June 8. William McGowan, the chair of MCI Communications Corporation, changed the shape of the telecommunications industry by bringing lower-cost long-distance service into the marketplace. MCI's 1974 antitrust suit against AT&T, which was joined by the Justice Department, led to the breakup of AT&T 10 years later. McGowan died on June 8, 1992, at Washington, DC.

McKINLEY, IDA SAXTON: BIRTH ANNIVERSARY. June 8. Wife of William McKinley, 25th president of the US, born at Canton, OH, June 8, 1847. Died May 26, 1907.

★**NATIONAL FLAG WEEK.** June 8–14. Presidential Proclamation issued each year since 1966 for the week including June 14. (PL89–443 of June 9, 1966.) In addition, the president often calls upon the American people to participate in public ceremonies in which the Pledge of Allegiance is recited.

★**NATIONAL LITTLE LEAGUE BASEBALL WEEK.** June 8–14. Presidential Proclamation 3296, of June 4, 1959, covers all succeeding years. Always the week beginning with the second Monday in June. (H.Con.Res. 17 of June 1, 1959.)

NATIONAL MEN'S HEALTH WEEK. June 8–14. For info: National Men's Health Week, 14 E Minor St, Emmaus, PA 18098. Phone: (800) 955-2002. WWW: http://www.menshealth.com

SPACE MILESTONE: *VENERA 9* AND *10* (USSR). June 8 and 14, 1975. Launched on this date, exploration vehicles landed on Venus Oct 22 and 25. Sent first pictures ever transmitted from another planet, atmospheric analysis, temperature (905°F) and other data.

WRIGHT, FRANK LLOYD: BIRTH ANNIVERSARY. June 8, 1867. American architect born at Richland Center, WI. In his autobiography Wright wrote: "No house should ever be *on* any hill or on anything. It should be *of* the hill, belonging to it, so hill and house could live together each the happier for the other." Wright died at Phoenix, AZ, Apr 9, 1959.

WYTHE, GEORGE: DEATH ANNIVERSARY. June 8. Signer of the Declaration of Independence. Born at Elizabeth County, VA, about 1726 (exact year unknown). Died at Richmond, VA, June 8, 1806.

BIRTHDAYS TODAY

Scott Adams, 41, cartoonist, creator of *Dilbert*, born Windham, NY, June 8, 1957.

Kathy Baker, 48, actress ("Picket Fences," *The Right Stuff*), born Midland, TX, June 8, 1950.

Barbara Pierce Bush, 73, former First Lady, born Rye, NY, June 8, 1925.

Bernie Casey, 59, former football player, actor (*I'm Gonna Git You Sucka, Bill & Ted's Excellent Adventure, Roots—The Next Generation*), born Wyco, WV, June 8, 1939.

James Darren, 62, singer ("Goodbye Cruel World"), actor (*Gidget*), born Philadelphia, PA, June 8, 1936.

Griffin Dunne, 43, actor (*Straight Talk*), producer, born New York, NY, June 8, 1955.

Don Grady, 54, actor ("My Three Sons," "Mickey Mouse Club"), born San Diego, CA, June 8, 1944.

Juliana Margulies, 51, actress (Nurse Carol Hathaway on "ER"), born Spring Valley, NY, June 8, 1947.

Sara Paretsky, 51, writer (*Killing Orders, Burn Marks*), born Ames, IA, June 8, 1947.

Joan Rivers, 61, comedienne, talk-show host, born New York, NY, June 8, 1937.

Boz Scaggs, 54, singer, musician, songwriter (*Silk Degress, Middle Man*), born Dallas, TX, June 8, 1944.

Nancy Sinatra, 58, singer ("These Boots Are Made for Walkin'," "Something Stupid"), born Jersey City, NJ, June 8, 1940.

Jerry Stiller, 69, comedian, actor (Shakespearian actor; *Hairspray*, "Seinfeld"), born Brooklyn, NY, June 8, 1929.

Keenen Ivory Wayans, 40, actor ("In Living Color"), born New York, NY, June 8, 1958.

Andrew Weil MD, 56, physician and writer on natural healing, born Philadelphia, PA, June 8, 1942.

Byron Raymond ("Whizzer") White, 81, former associate justice of the US Supreme Court, former football player, born Fort Collins, CO, June 8, 1917.

JUNE 9 — TUESDAY

Day 160 — 205 Remaining

CUMMINGS, ROBERT: 90th BIRTH ANNIVERSARY. June 9, 1908. American actor Robert Cummings was born Charles Clarence Robert Orville Cummings at Joplin, MO. His best-known role was in the film *Dial M for Murder* (1954). He won an Emmy for his role in the television version of *Twelve Angry Men* (1954) and starred in the popular comedy "The Bob Cummings Show" (1955–59). He died on Dec 2, 1990 at Woodland Hills, CA.

DONALD DUCK: BIRTHDAY. June 9, 1934. Donald Duck was "born" June 9, 1934.

HONG KONG: 100th LEASE SIGNING ANNIVERSARY. June 9, 1898. Hong Kong, consisting of about 400 square miles (islands and mainland) with more than five million persons, was administered as a British Crown Colony after a 99-year lease was signed on June 9, 1898. In 1997, Hong Kong's sovereignty reverted to the People's Republic of China.

KUTNER, LUIS: 90th BIRTH ANNIVERSARY. June 9, 1908. Human rights attorney Luis Kutner was born June 9, 1908, at Chicago, IL. Kutner, who was responsible for the release of many unjustly confined prisoners, came to be known as "The Springman." He helped free Hungarian Cardinal Josef Mindszenty, poet Ezra Pound and former Congo President Moise Tshombe. He was the author of the living will and founded the World Habeas Corpus. Kutner was nominated nine times for the Nobel Peace Prize. He died Mar 1, 1993, at Chicago.

LOLOMA, CHARLES: BIRTH ANNIVERSARY. June 9, 1921. Charles Loloma was a major influence on modern Indian art and was famous for changing the look of American Indian jewelry. A painter, sculptor and potter, he was best known for his jewelry, which broke tradition with previous Indian styles using bold mosaics and materials such as coral, fossilized ivory, pearls, diamonds, charolite and sugilite. One of his trademarks was to line the inside of a bracelet or ring with stones more valuable than those on the outside. Charles Loloma was born at Hotevilla on the Hopi Indian Reservation and died June 9, 1991, at Scottsdale, AZ.

NIELSEN, CARL: BIRTH ANNIVERSARY. June 9. Danish composer born June 9, 1865. Died Oct 3, 1931. Funen Quartet plays birthday concert in the composer's childhood home at Lyndelse, near Odense, Denmark.

PAYNE, JOHN HOWARD: BIRTH ANNIVERSARY. June 9, 1791. American author, actor, diplomat, born at New York, NY, June 9, 1791. Died at Tunis, Apr 9, 1852. Author of opera libretto (*Clari*, or *The Maid of Milan*), which contained the song "Home, Sweet Home."

PORTER, COLE: BIRTH ANNIVERSARY. June 9, 1891. Cole Porter published his first song, "The Bobolink Waltz," at the age of ten. His career as a composer and lyricist for Broadway was launched in 1928 when five of his songs were used in the musical play *Let's Do It.* His prolific contributions to the Broadway stage include *Fifty Million Frenchmen, Wake Up and Dream, The Gay Divorcée, Anything Goes, Leave It to Me, Du Barry Was a Lady, Something for the Boys, Kiss Me Kate, Can Can* and *Silk Stockings.* Porter was born at Peru, IN, and died at Santa Monica, CA, Oct 15, 1964.

SENIOR CITIZENS DAY. June 9. Oklahoma.

STEPHENSON, GEORGE: BIRTH ANNIVERSARY. June 9, 1781. English inventor, developer of the steam locomotive, born near Newcastle, England, June 9, 1781. Died near Chesterfield, England, Aug 12, 1848.

THAYER, SYLVANUS: BIRTH ANNIVERSARY. June 9, 1785. A military engineer and educator, born at Braintree, MA. He was appointed superintendent of West Point at 32 and became known as the "Father of the Military Academy." Thayer died at Braintree, MA, Sept 7, 1872.

BIRTHDAYS TODAY

George Axelrod, 76, writer (screenplays *Bus Stop, Breakfast at Tiffany's*), born New York, NY, June 9, 1922.

Patricia Cornwell, 42, best-selling mystery writer, born Miami, FL, June 9, 1956. Dr Kay Scarpetta, medical examiner, is her sleuth.

Johnny Depp, 35, actor ("21 Jump Street," *Edward Scissorhands, Ed Wood*), born Owensboro, KY, June 9, 1963.

Michael J. Fox, 37, actor ("Family Ties"; *Back to the Future* films), born Edmonton, Alberta, Canada, June 9, 1961.

Marvin Kalb, 68, educator, journalist, born New York, NY, June 9, 1930.

Jackie Mason (Yacov Moshe Maza), 64, comedian ("Chicken Soup," *The World According to Me*), born Sheboygan, WI, June 9, 1934.

Robert S. McNamara, 82, banker, former cabinet member, born San Francisco, CA, June 9, 1916.

David Gene (Dave) Parker, 47, former baseball player, born Calhoun, MS, June 9, 1951.

Les Paul, 82, musician, singer (with the late Mary Ford; "Hummingbird"), born Waukesha, WI, June 9, 1916.

Wayman Lawrence Tisdale, 34, basketball player, born Tulsa, OK, June 9, 1964.

Dick Vitale, 59, sportscaster, ESPN and ABC analyst, born East Rutherford, NJ, June 9, 1939.

JUNE 10 — WEDNESDAY

Day 161 — 204 Remaining

ALCOHOLICS ANONYMOUS: FOUNDING ANNIVERSARY. June 10, 1935. On this day in Akron, OH, Dr. Robert Smith completed his first day of permanent sobriety. "Doctor Bob" and William G. Wilson are considered to have founded Alcoholics Anonymous on that day.

CZECHOSLOVAKIA: RAPE OF LIDICE: ANNIVERSARY. June 10. On June 10, 1942, Nazi German troops executed, by shooting, all male inhabitants of the Czechoslovakian village of Lidice (total population about 500 persons), burned every house and deported the women and children to Germany for "re-education." One of the most-remembered atrocities of World War II. June 10, Lidice Memorial Day, is observed in New Jersey.

GARLAND, JUDY: BIRTH ANNIVERSARY. June 10. American actress and singer born Frances Gumm at Grand Rapids, MN, June 10, 1922. While Ms Garland played in many films and toured widely as a singer, she is probably most remembered for her portrayal of Dorothy Gale in the now-classic *The Wizard of Oz.*

JOHN HULL OPENS FIRST MINT IN AMERICA: ANNIVERSARY. June 10. In defiance of English colonial law, John Hull, a silversmith, established the first mint in America, on June 10, 1652. The first coin issued was the Pine Tree Shilling, designed by Hull.

JORDAN: GREAT ARAB REVOLT AND ARMY DAY: ANNIVERSARY. June 10. Commemorates the beginning of the Great Arab Revolt on June 10, 1916. National holiday.

KIDS' DINO-DIG. June 10–11 (also July 15–16 and Aug 12–13). Thermopolis, WY. Kids dig for dinosaur fossils with professionals, along with workshops, classes on dinosaur drawings, meet the paleontologists and artists. Sponsored by Big Horn Basin Foundation. For info: The Wyoming Dinosaur Center, PO Box 868, Thermopolis, WY 82443. Phone: (307) 864-2997. Fax: (307) 864-5762. Email: Bonznrocks@aol.com. WWW: http://www.wyoming.com/dino

McDANIEL, HATTIE: BIRTH ANNIVERSARY. June 10. Hattie McDaniel was the first African-American to win an Academy Award. She won it in 1940 for her role in the 1939 film *Gone With the Wind.* Her career spanned radio and vaudeville in addition to her screen roles in *Judge Priest, The Little Colonel, Showboat* and *Saratoga*, among others. She was born on June 10, 1889, at Wichita, KS, and died Oct 26, 1952.

June 1998

S	M	T	W	T	F	S
	1	2	3	4	5	6
7	8	9	10	11	12	13
14	15	16	17	18	19	20
21	22	23	24	25	26	27
28	29	30				

MOON PHASE: FULL MOON. June 10. Moon enters Full Moon phase at 12:18 AM, EDT.

PORTUGAL: DAY OF PORTUGAL. June 10. National holiday. Anniversary of the death of Portugal's national poet, Luis Vas de Camoes (Camoens), born in 1524 (exact date unknown) at either Lisbon or possibly Coimbra. Died at Lisbon, Portugal, June 10, 1580.

RED RIVER RODEO. June 10–13. Wichita Falls, TX. Professional circuit rodeo held at the Wichita County Mounted Patrol Arena, this event features all of the traditional rodeo attractions. Est attendance: 20,000. For info: Wichita Falls Conv & Visitors Bureau, 1000 5th St, Wichita Falls, TX 76301. Phone: (817) 716-5500. Fax: (817) 716-5509.

ROCK CREEK PARK NATIONALIZED: 65th ANNIVERSARY. June 10, 1933. Rock Creek Park, authorized Sept 27, 1890, was transferred to the National Park Service. For further park info: Rock Creek Park, 5000 Glover Rd NW, Washington, DC 20015.

***TEXAS* MUSICAL DRAMA.** June 10–Aug 22. Palo Duro Canyon State Park, Canyon, TX. Paul Green outdoor drama set beneath 600-foot cliffs. History of area told by cast of 80, accented by song, dance and latest sound and light. 33rd season. Nightly except Sundays at 8:30 PM. Sponsor: Texas Panhandle Heritage Fdtn, Inc. Est attendance: 100,000. For info: Patty Bryant, Pres, TEXAS, Box 268, Canyon, TX 79015. Phone: (806) 655-2181. Fax: (806) 655-4730. WWW: http://www.spindle.net/texas

US INTERNATIONAL FILM AND VIDEO FESTIVAL AWARDS PRESENTATIONS. June 10–11. Chicago, IL. World's largest awards competition honoring business, television, informational and industrial productions. Founded in 1968. Est attendance: 300. For info: Patricia Meyer, Exec Dir, US Intl Film and Video Festival, 841 N Addison Ave, Elmhurst, IL 60126-1291. Phone: (630) 834-7773. Fax: (630) 834-5565. Email: FILMFESTIVALandMOBIUSAWARDS@compuserve.com.

VIRGINIA PORK FESTIVAL. June 10. Emporia, VA. One of the east coast's largest food festivals promoting the pork industry and featuring 37 different products that are available on an all-you-can-eat basis. Festival also features five stages of live entertainment. The 1997 event featured an appearance by NASCAR driver Terry Labonte. Est attendance: 20,000. For info: Kendra Perkins, Admit One Festivals, 425-E South Main St, PO Box 1001, Emporia, VA 23847-1001. Phone: (800) 482-7675. Fax: (804) 348-0119. Email: kperkins@admit1fest.com. WWW: http://www.admit1fest.com

BIRTHDAYS TODAY

F. Lee Bailey, 65, lawyer, born Waltham, MA, June 10, 1933.

Linda Evangelista, 33, model, born St. Catharines, Canada, June 10, 1965.

Jeff Greenfield, 55, author, journalist, born New York, NY, June 10, 1943.

Nat Hentoff, 73, music critic, journalist, born Boston, MA, June 10, 1925.

Doug McKeon, 32, actor (*On Golden Pond*), born Pomptain Plains, NJ, June 10, 1966.

Rose Mofford, 76, former governor of Arizona (D), born Globe, AZ, June 10, 1922.

Prince Philip, 77, Duke of Edinburgh, husband of Queen Elizabeth II, born Corfu, Greece, June 10, 1921.

Maurice Sendak, 70, author, illustrator (*Chicken Soup with Rice, Where the Wild Things Are*), born Brooklyn, NY, June 10, 1928.

Samuel Knox Skinner, 60, former White House Chief of Staff (Bush administration), born Chicago, IL, June 10, 1938.

JUNE 11 — THURSDAY

Day 162 — 203 Remaining

BATTLE CREEK FESTIVAL/WORLD'S LARGEST BREAKFAST TABLE. June 11–13. Battle Creek, MI. On Thursday, the Miss Cereal City Pageant will be held at Lakeview High School. Friday and Saturday events include parades, arts and crafts, 5K and 10K races, family fun walk, food bank fundraiser, farmer's market and Funland amusements, rides and games. The World's Largest Breakfast Table will be on Saturday 8 AM–noon. Annually, the second weekend in June. Est attendance: 60,000. For info: Battle Creek Cereal Festival, Greater Battle Creek Visitor and Conv Bureau, 34 W Jackson St, Ste 4, Battle Creek, MI 49017. Phone: (616) 962-2240.

CONSTABLE, JOHN: BIRTH ANNIVERSARY. June 11. English landscape painter. Born at East Bergholt, Suffolk, England, on June 11, 1776. He died at London, on Mar 31, 1837.

CORPUS CHRISTI. June 11. Roman Catholic festival celebrated in honor of the Eucharist. A solemnity observed on the Thursday following Trinity Sunday since 1246. In the US Corpus Christi is celebrated on the Sunday following Trinity Sunday. See also: "Corpus Christi (US Observance)" (June 14).

DISCOVERYLAND'S *OKLAHOMA!*. June 11–Aug 22 (nightly except Sundays). Tulsa, OK. Discoveryland was proclaimed the "National Home of Rodgers and Hammerstein's *Oklahoma!*" by the children of that duo. Discoveryland presents the state's favorite musical in a beautiful 2,000-seat amphitheatre complex, complete with horses, wagons and a real surrey with a fringe on top. Barbecue dinner, Indian dancing, gift shops and ice cream parlor top the evening for the whole family. Est attendance: 75,000. For info: Bill Jeffers, Managing Dir, Discoveryland! Business Office, 6400 S Lewis, Ste 200, Tulsa, OK 74136. Phone: (918) 245-OKLA (for tickets) or (918) 742-5255 (business office).

FESTIVAL OF THE BLUEGRASS. June 11–14. Lexington, KY. Up to 25 bands perform bluegrass music in an outdoor setting. Est attendance: 20,000. For info: James Cornett, Spirit of the Suwannee Music Park, 3076 95th Dr, Live Oak, FL 32060. Phone: (904) 364-1683. Fax: (904) 364-2998.

GLENN MILLER BIRTHPLACE SOCIETY FESTIVAL. June 11–14. Clarinda, IA. To commemorate Glenn Miller's contribution to big band music through exhibits, concerts, films, performances by winners of Glenn Miller scholarships and a big band dance. Annually, the second weekend in June. Est attendance: 3,000. For info: Glenn Miller Birthplace Soc, PO Box 61, Clarinda, IA 51632. Phone: (712) 542-2461. Fax: (712) 542-2461.

JONSON, BEN: BIRTH ANNIVERSARY. June 11. English playwright and poet, born June 11, 1572. "Talking and eloquence," he wrote, "are not the same: to speak and to speak well, are two things." Jonson died at London, England, on Aug 6, 1637. The epitaph written on his tombstone in Westminister Abbey: "O rare Ben Jonson."

KING KAMEHAMEHA I DAY. June 11. Designated state holiday in Hawaii honors memory of Hawaiian monarch (1737–1819). Governor appoints state commission to plan annual celebration.

LOMBARDI, VINCE: BIRTH ANNIVERSARY. June 11, 1913. Vincent Thomas (Vince) Lombardi, Pro Football Hall of Fame coach born at New York, NY. Lombardi played football for Fordham's famed "Seven Blocks of Granite" line in the mid-1930s, became a teacher and began to coach high school football. He became offensive line coach at West Point in 1949 and moved to the New York Giants in 1954. Five years later, he was named head coach of the Green Bay Packers, a position that lofted him to the peak of his profession. His Packers won five NFL titles and two Super Bowls in nine years, and Lombardi was generally regarded as the greatest coach and the finest motivator in pro football history. He retired in 1968, but was lured back into coaching the Washington Redskins a year later. He contracted cancer after coaching the Redskins only one season. Inducted into the Pro Football Hall of Fame in 1971. Died at Washington, DC, Sept 3, 1970.

MOUNT PINATUBO ERUPTS IN PHILIPPINES: ANNIVERSARY. June 11, 1991. Long-dormant volcano Mount Pinatubo in the Philippines erupted with a violent explosion, spewing ash and gases that could be seen for more than 60 miles, into the air. The surrounding areas were covered with ash and mud created by rainstorms. US Military bases Clark and Subic Bay were also damaged. On July 6, 1992, Ellsworth Dutton of the National Oceanic and Atmospheric Administration's Climate Monitoring and Diagnostics Laboratory announced that a layer of sulfuric acid droplets released into the Earth's atmosphere by the eruption had cooled the planet's average temperature by about 1 degree Fahrenheit. The greatest difference was noted in the Northern Hemisphere with a drop of 1.5 degrees. Although the temperature drop was temporary, the climate trend made determining the effect of greenhouse warming on the Earth more difficult through its duration.

RANKIN, JEANNETTE: BIRTH ANNIVERSARY. June 11, 1880. First woman elected to the US Congress, a reformer, feminist and pacifist, was born at Missoula, MT, June 11, 1880. She was the only member of Congress to vote against a declaration of war against Japan in December 1941. Died May 18, 1973.

RED ARMY DEPARTS BERLIN: ANNIVERSARY. June 11, 1994. After 49 years, the Russian military occupation of the region once called East Germany ended. At one time there had been 337,800 Soviet troops stationed in Germany. More than 300,000 Russian troops died in the World War II battle for Berlin in 1944–45. The departure was celebrated with a parade in Wupnsdorf south of Berlin, which was the Soviet Union's military headquarters in the former German Democratic Republic.

RED EARTH NATIVE AMERICAN CULTURAL FESTIVAL. June 11–14. Oklahoma City, OK. Named to ABA Top 100 Events in North America for 1997. Thousands of Native Americans representing more than 100 tribes from across North America celebrate their proud heritage at one of the largest intertribal gatherings in the world. Dance competitions, art exhibits, film and video showings, lectures, storytelling and parade. Est attendance: 125,000. For info: Eric Oesch, PR Dir, Red Earth, Inc, 2100 NE 52, Oklahoma City, OK 73111. Phone: (405) 427-5228. Fax: (405) 427-8079.

"SPACE ODDITY" SONG RELEASE: ANNIVERSARY. June 11, 1969. This single recorded by David Bowie was released to coincide with the *Apollo 11*'s trip to the moon, during which Neil Armstrong and Edwin Aldrin, Jr, landed and walked on the surface of the moon.

STRAUSS, RICHARD GEORG: BIRTH ANNIVERSARY. June 11, 1864. German composer, musician and conductor whose best-remembered works are *Till Eulenspiegel* (1895), *Also Sprach Zarathustra* (1896) and *Don Quixote* (1898). Born at Munich, he died at Garmisch-Partenkirchen, Germany, after a heart attack on Sept 8, 1949, at age 85.

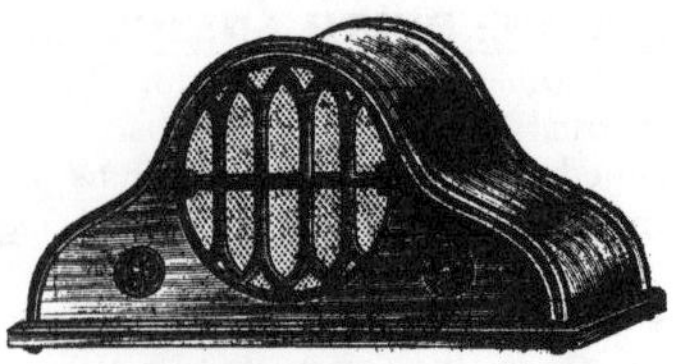

SUPERMAN CELEBRATION. June 11–14. Metropolis, IL. Weekend full of Super activities. See 15ft Superman Statue, parade, live entertainment, super museum, road race, tennis tourney, Supertrek bicycle ride, super car show, children's games and food fair. Est attendance: 30,000. For info: Metropolis Area Chamber of Commerce, Tourism & Economic Development, PO Box 188, Metropolis, IL 62960. Phone: (618) 524-2714 or (800) 949-5740. Fax: (618) 524-4780.

BIRTHDAYS TODAY

Adrienne Barbeau, 53, actress ("Maude"), born Sacramento, CA, June 11, 1945.

Henry Cisneros, 51, former US Secretary of Housing and Urban Development in Clinton administration, born San Antonio, TX, June 11, 1947.

Jacques Cousteau, 88, explorer, scientist (awarded French Legion of Honor for work in the Resistance in 1945), born St. André-de-Cubzac, France, June 11, 1910. Died June 25, 1997.

Chad Everett (Raymond Cramton), 62, actor ("The Dakotas," "Medical Center"), born South Bend, IN, June 11, 1936.

John Gary Fencik, 44, former football player, born Chicago, IL, June 11, 1954.

Joseph C. (Joe) Montana, Jr, 42, former sportscaster and football player, born New Eagle, PA, June 11, 1956.

Jackie Stewart, 59, auto racer, born Dunbartonshire, Scotland, June 11, 1939.

William Styron, 73, author (*The Confessions of Nat Turner, Sophie's Choice*), born Newport News, VA, June 11, 1925.

Gene Wilder, 59, actor (*The Producers, Willy Wonka & the Chocolate Factory, Blazing Saddles, Young Frankenstein*), director, born Milwaukee, WI, June 11, 1939.

JUNE 12 — FRIDAY

Day 163 — 202 Remaining

BADGER STATE SUMMER GAMES. June 12–14. (Finals June 25–28.) Regional competition in eight Wisconsin communities, finals in Madison. 14th annual Olympic-style competition for Wisconsin residents of all ages and abilities, featuring 26 sports and opening ceremonies. Major sponsors: AT&T, Ameritech, GTE, Wisconsin Milk Marketing Board, WPS Health Insurance Corp, Oscar Mayer Foods Corp and Tombstone Pizza. Member of the National Congress of State Games. 25,000 participants. Est attendance: 60,000. For info: Jack Eich, PR Dir, Badger State Games, PO Box 1377, Madison, WI 53701-1377. Phone: (608) 251-3333 or (608) 283-6407. Fax: (608) 283-6412.

"BIG MAC" SHORELINE SPRING SCENIC TOUR. June 12–14. Mackinaw City and Harbor Springs, MI. Also Sept 11–13. Bike tours of 25-, 50-, 75- and 100-mile routes between Mackinaw City and Harbor Springs. Each scenic tour will take you along the Lake Michigan shoreline past sparkling water, windswept dunes, through the renowned "Tunnel of Trees," over rolling hills and through quaint resort towns and old Native American villages steeped in legend and charm. Registration fee. Est attendance: 1,500. For info: Mackinaw Area Tourist Bureau, PO Box 160, Mackinac City, MI 49701. Phone: (800) 666-0160 or (616) 436-5664.

June 1998

S	M	T	W	T	F	S
	1	2	3	4	5	6
7	8	9	10	11	12	13
14	15	16	17	18	19	20
21	22	23	24	25	26	27
28	29	30				

CENTER OF THE NATION ALL-CAR RALLY. June 12–14. Belle Fourche, SD. This three-day event includes Friday evening "Cruise Night"; Saturday's big "Show 'n Shine," held all day in Hermann Park, plus food booths, vendors, live '50's and '60's music; on Sunday, poker run and demolition derby. Annually, the second weekend in June. Est attendance: 5,000. For info: Belle Fourche Chamber of Commerce, 415 5th Ave, Belle Fourche, SD 57717. Phone: (605) 892-2676. Fax: (605) 892-4633. Email: belchmbr@iwayl.iw.net.

CHISHOLM TRAIL ROUND-UP FESTIVAL. June 12–14 (tentative). Fort Worth, TX. Events include trail ride, Quanah Parker Comanche Indian Powwow and Honor Dance, Tarrant County Fair, street fair, chili and barbecue cook-offs, chuckwagon cooks' races, live armadillo and pig races, gunfighters, parade, children's area with Western-theme carnival rides and five live stages with music. Est attendance: 150,000. For info: Chisholm Trail Round-Up, PO Box 4815, Fort Worth, TX 76164-0815. Phone: (817) 625-7005. Fax: (817) 625-4036.
Email: trailboss@chisholmtrail.org.
WWW: http://www.chisholmtrail.org

CONNECTICUT EARLY MUSIC FESTIVAL. June 12–29. New London, CT. Concert Series of 17th and 18th century music performed on period instruments in historically informed styles. Annually, the last three weekends in June. Est attendance: 3,000. For info: Connecticut Early Music Festival, PO Box 329, New London, CT 06320. Phone: (860) 444-2419.

COWBOY STATE SUMMER GAMES. June 12–15. Casper, WY. The Summer Games feature more than 30 different events including everything from archery to wrestling, basketball to volleyball. Participation is open to Wyoming's amateur athletes of all ages. The Summer Games also feature a spectacular Opening Ceremony that will take place Friday evening, June 12. Est attendance: 4,000. For info: Eileen Ford, Cowboy State Games, PO Box 3485, Casper, WY 82602. Phone: (307) 577-1125. Fax: (307) 577-8111. Email: cwboygames@aol.com.

DELMARVA CHICKEN FESTIVAL. June 12–13. Millsboro Civic Center and Sussex Central Middle School, Millsboro, DE. 50th annual. A family event focusing on chicken, the leading agricultural enterprise on the Delmarva Peninsula. Food, entertainment and consumer information are featured. Est attendance: 25,000. For info: Connie Parvis, Delmarva Poultry Industry, Inc, R.D. 6, Box 47, Georgetown, DE 19947-9575. Phone: (302) 856-9037.

FIRST MAN-POWERED FLIGHT ACROSS ENGLISH CHANNEL: ANNIVERSARY. June 12. Bryan Allen, 26-year-old Californian, pedaled the 70-pound *Gossamer Albatross* 22 miles across the English Channel, from Folkestone, England, to Cape Gris-Nez, France, in 2 hours, 49 minutes on June 12, 1979, winning (with the craft's designer, Paul MacCready of Pasadena, CA) the £100,000 prize that had been offered Nov 30, 1977, by British industrialist Henry Kremer, for the first man-powered flight across the English Channel.

FRANK, ANNE: BIRTH ANNIVERSARY. June 12, 1929. Born at Frankfurt, Germany. Anne Frank's family moved to Amsterdam to try and escape the Nazis but after Holland was invaded by Germany, they had to go into hiding. In 1942, Anne began to keep a diary. She died at Bergen-Belsen concentration camp in 1945. After the war, her father published her diary, on which a stage play and movie were later based.

FRANKENMUTH BAVARIAN FESTIVAL. June 12–20. Frankenmuth, MI. To celebrate the German heritage of Frankenmuth with good food, great entertainment events for all ages, parades, craft show, children's activities, fun special events, "Michigan's Largest Chicken Dance" and much more. Est attendance: 50,000. For info: Frankenmuth Civic Events Council, PO Box 333, Frankenmuth, MI 48734. Phone: (517) 652-8155.

GREAT AMERICAN BRASS BAND FESTIVAL. June 12–14. Centre College Campus, Danville, KY. Brass bands and ensembles from throughout the country in concert Friday and Saturday. Free to the public. Est attendance: 55,000. For info: George Foreman, Dir of Programs, Great American Brass Band Festival, PO Box 429, Danville, KY 40423. Phone: (606) 236-4692. Fax: (606) 238-5448. WWW: http://www.gabbf.com

HEARTLAND ART FEST. June 12–14. St. Joseph, MO. Art festival featuring artists from five states exhibiting in all media—from pottery to watercolors, acrylics and jewelry. Also, a children's workshop, musical entertainment and specialty foods are available for your enjoyment. Annually, the second weekend in June. Est attendance: 5,000. For info: Tish Haynes, 2106 N 35th Terrace, St. Joseph MO, 64506. Phone: (816) 232-3778.

HONOR THY VETERINARIAN DAY ©. June 12. These creatures, both great and small, cannot speak and tell us "where it hurts." This event is to honor all the veterinarians and assistants who give our beloved pets the compassionate and thorough care they deserve. This date is part and parcel of PAW: Pet Awareness Week©. For info: Adrienne Sioux Koopersmith, 1437 W Rosemont, 1W, Chicago, IL 60660-1319. Phone: (773) 743-5341. Fax: (773) 743-5395. Email: kooper@interaccess.com.

HOORAY FOR YEAR-ROUND SCHOOL DAY. June 12. To promote the benfits of a year-round school calendar which makes learning a continuous process and better suits the demanding educational needs of today's world. Annually, the second Friday in June. For more info, send 9½" SASE to: Hooray for Year-Round School Day, Horace Mann Choice School, 3530-38th Ave, Rock Island, IL 61201.
WWW: http://www.augustana.edu:80/library/horacemann/HMCS_Principal.html

KUSTOM KEMPS OF AMERICA CAR SHOW. June 12–14. Oakside Community Park, Biglerville, PA. For info: Gettysburg Conv & Visitors Bureau, 35 Carlisle St, Gettysburg, PA 17325. Phone: (717) 637-5229.

***LOVING v VIRGINIA*: ANNIVERSARY.** June 12. On June 12, 1967, the US Supreme Court decision in *Loving v Virginia* swept away all 16 remaining state laws prohibiting interracial marriages.

MARKET SQUARE DAYS CELEBRATION. June 12–13. Portsmouth, NH. A dinner reception and benefit auction, historic tours, arts and crafts, a 10K road race, open-air concerts and fireworks are all part of the festivities. One of the biggest celebrations held each June on New Hampshire's picturesque seacoast. Free admission. Charge for dinner and road race. Est attendance: 100,000. For info: Pro Portsmouth, PO Box 1008, Portsmouth, NH 03802-1008. Phone: (603) 431-5388. Fax: (603) 431-3415.

MILLIGAN JUNE JUBILEE. June 12–14. Milligan, NE. Music all weekend in Nebraska's largest beer garden; classic Rock & Roll June 12 and 13; Polka Music June 14. Carnival, tournament games, antique tractor pull Saturday and parade on Sunday. Est attendance: 10,000. For info: Scott Oliva, PO Box 218, Milligan, NE 68406. Phone: (402) 629-4446. Fax: (402) 629-4446.

MINNESOTA INVENTORS CONGRESS. June 12–14. Redwood Falls, MN. To promote creativity and development of ideas into marketable products, to educate inventors and to bring the inventor to experts in the appropriate field, including a test market of up to 10,000 viewers. Highlights include more than 170 inventions from around the world on display, 100 student inventors, the Minnesota Inventors Hall of Fame and the Market Place with inventions for sale. Est attendance: 10,000. For info: Minnesota Inventors Congress, Box 71, Redwood Falls, MN 56283-0071. Phone: (507) 637-2344 or (800) INVENT-1. Fax: (507) 637-5929. Email: mic@means.net.

NATIONAL BASEBALL HALL OF FAME: ANNIVERSARY. June 12. The National Baseball Hall of Fame and Museum, Inc, was dedicated at Cooperstown, NY, June 12, 1939. Nearly 200 individuals have been honored for their contributions to the game of baseball by induction into the Baseball Hall of Fame. The first players chosen for membership (1936) were Ty Cobb, Honus Wagner, Babe Ruth, Christy Mathewson and Walter Johnson. Relics and memorabilia from the history of baseball are housed at this "shrine" of America's national sport.

OKLAHOMA MOZART INTERNATIONAL FESTIVAL. June 12–20. Bartlesville, OK. Festival features world-class artists performing with Solisti New York Orchestra, Ransom Wilson conducting. Est attendance: 40,000. For info: Jeanette Swindell, Press Relations, OK Mozart Intl Festival, Box 2344, Bartlesville, OK 74005. Phone: (918) 336-9900. Fax: (918) 336-9525. WWW: http://webtck.com/okmozart

OLDSMOBILE BALLOON CLASSIC. June 12–14. Vermilion County Airport, Danville, IL. More than 100 hot-air balloons in five morning and evening races, continuous entertainment, familyland, Balloon Glo and activities all day long. Annually, the second weekend in June. Sponsor: Oldsmobile. Est attendance: 100,000. For info: Jeanie Cooke, Exec Dir, Danville Area Conv & Visitors Bureau, Towne Centre, PO Box 992, Danville, IL 61832. Phone: (217) 442-2096.

PHILIPPINES: INDEPENDENCE DAY: 100th ANNIVERSARY. June 12, 1898. National holiday. Declared independence from Spain on this day, 1898.

POTOMAC RIVER FESTIVAL. June 12–14 (tentative). Colonial Beach, VA. 47th annual festival to promote the attractions of Colonial Beach and historic Westmoreland County. Est attendance: 25,000. For info: Chamber of Commerce, PO Box 475, Colonial Beach, VA 22443. Phone: (804) 224-8145.

RIVERFEST. June 12–13. Cape Girardeau, MO. Celebration of Mississippi River heritage. Includes professional entertainment, regional food, working crafters, children's activities, fireworks and contests. All activities take place on the streets of the historic downtown on the riverfront. Annually, second weekend in June. Est attendance: 40,000. For info: Benita Curtis, Office Mgr, Cape Girardeau Riverfest Assn, 2148 Broadway, Ste 114, Cape Girardeau, MO 63701. Phone: (573) 335-1388. Fax: (573) 335-1388.

ROUND BARN RENDEZVOUS. June 12–14. Rochester, IN. Includes teepees and tents of frontier Indiana, set up beside the Fulton County Museum, round barn and Living History Village. Open 9 AM to 7 PM Fri and Sat, 9 AM to 5 PM Sun. Est attendance: 1,000. For info: Fulton County Historical Society, 37 East 375 N, Rochester, IN 46975. Phone: (219) 223-4436.

ROUND BARN CELEBRATION AND MARKET. June 12–14. Rochester, IN. Living history village called Loyal depicts life in 1900–25. Also 5K run, restored round barn with old-time farm tools, crafts and antiques, food, music, farm demonstrations in round barn and antique tractors and railcars. Est attendance: 1,000. For info: Fulton County Historical Society, 37 East 375 N, Rochester, IN 46975. Phone: (219) 223-4436.

RUSSIA: INDEPENDENCE DAY. June 12. National holiday.

RUSSIAN FEDERATION: NATIONAL HOLIDAY. June 12.

SEA MUSIC FESTIVAL. June 12–14. Mystic, CT. World-famous folksingers and musicians performing from Mystic Seaport's tall ships or in formal concert. 19th annual. Est attendance: 7,500. For info: Mystic Seaport, 75 Greenmanville Ave, Box 6000, Mystic, CT 06355. Phone: (203) 572-5315.

SPACE MILESTONE: *VENERA 4* (USSR). June 12, 1967. Launched on this date, this instrumental capsule landed on Venus by parachute on Oct 18 and reported a temperature of 536°F.

STRAWBERRY FESTIVAL. June 12–14. Crawfordsville, IN. Festival at Lane Place includes 2½ days of arts and crafts, food, music and children's activities. All-day entertainment, car show (Sunday), softball and tennis tournaments, antique tractor exhibits and 10K run. All city museums open. Est attendance: 30,000. For info: Montgomery County Visitors & Conv Bureau, Inc, 412 E Main St, Crawfordsville, IN 47933. Phone: (800) 866-3973. Fax: (317) 362-5215. Email: mcvcb@tctc.com. WWW: http://www.tctc.com/nmcvcb

STUART'S FIRST RIDE AROUND McCLELLAN: ANNIVERSARY. June 12, 1862. In a flamboyant move Confederate J.E.B. "Beauty" Stuart led a force of cavalry and artillery to reconnoiter Federal positions on the Peninsula. Stuart and his men completely encircled McClellan's forces, disrupting communications and supply lines and leading the Union forces to believe they were threatened by a much larger force. The large boost to Confederate morale was strengthened when Stonewall Jackson's forces were reinforced under orders by Robert E. Lee.

***TECUMSEH!*: THE EPIC OUTDOOR DRAMA.** June 12–Sept 5. Chillicothe, OH. Witness the spectacular reenactment of the life and death of the great Shawnee leader Tecumseh. Held in the large, tiered amphitheater nestled in the hardwood forest of Sugarloaf Mountain. Take a backstage tour, visit the Prehistoric Museum, dine in the open-air Tecumseh Restaurant Terrace. Est attendance: 85,000. For info: Tecumseh!, PO Box 73, Chillicothe, OH 45601-0073. Phone: (614) 775-0700. Fax: (614) 775-4349. Email: Tecumseh@bright.net. WWW: http://www.bright.net/~tecumseh/index.html

WILL ROGERS STAMPEDE SUMMER CELEBRATION. June 12–20. For info: Will Rogers Stampede Summer Celebration, 419 Will Rogers Blvd, Claremore, OK 74017. Phone: (918) 341-2818. Fax: (918) 342-0663.

BIRTHDAYS TODAY

Marvin Philip (Marv) Albert (born Marvin Philip Aufrichtig), 55, sportscaster, born New York, NY, June 12, 1943.

Timothy Busfield, 41, actor ("thirtysomething," *Field of Dreams*), born Lansing, MI, June 12, 1957.

George Herbert Walker Bush, 74, 41st US president, amateur golfer, former college baseball player, born Milton, MA, June 12, 1924.

Chick Corea, 57, musician, born Chelsea, MA, June 12, 1941.

Vic Damone (Vito Farinola), 70, singer ("On the Street Where You Live"), born New York, NY, June 12, 1928.

James Houston, 77, author (*Ghost Fox*), illustrator, designer, filmmaker, born Toronto, Ontario, Canada, June 12, 1921.

Jim Nabors, 66, actor ("The Andy Griffith Show," "Gomer Pyle, U.S.M.C."), born Sylacauga, AL, June 12, 1932.

David Rockefeller, 83, banker, born New York, NY, June 12, 1915.

Rory Darnell Sparrow, 40, former basketball player, born Suffolk, VA, June 12, 1958.

Sherry Stringfield, 31, actress ("NYPD Blue," "ER"), born Colorado Springs, CO, June 12, 1967.

June 1998

S	M	T	W	T	F	S
	1	2	3	4	5	6
7	8	9	10	11	12	13
14	15	16	17	18	19	20
21	22	23	24	25	26	27
28	29	30				

JUNE 13 — SATURDAY

Day 164 — 201 Remaining

ALL ABOUT ALLIGATORS. June 13. Florence Marina State Park, Omaha, GA. Features guest speakers who work with alligators and boat tours that explore the alligator's habitat. Food and entertainment. Est attendance: 500. For info: Florence Marina State Park, Rte 1, Box 36, Omaha, GA 31821. Phone: (912) 838-4706. Fax: (912) 838-6113. Email: florence.marina@internetmci.com.

ANTIQUES ON THE DIAMOND. June 13 (also Aug 22). Ligonier, PA. 70 quality antique dealers from six states set up their products along the Diamond. For info: Julie Donovan, Ligonier Chamber of Commerce, 120 East Main St, Ligonier, PA 15658. Phone: (412) 238-4200. Fax: (412) 238-4610.

ART FAIR ON THE COURTHOUSE LAWN. June 13 (tentative). Rhinelander, WI. Original artwork and crafts, food, music and refreshments on the Oneida County Courthouse lawn. Annually, the second Saturday in June. Est attendance: 10,000. For info: Rhinelander Area Chamber of Commerce, PO Box 795, Rhinelander, WI 54501. Phone: (800) 236-4386. Fax: (715) 365-7467.

ART IN THE PARK. June 13. Bay Head, NJ. Annual juried outdoor art show. Annually, the second Saturday in June. Est attendance: 300. For info: Anne Neff, Chair, Anchor and Palette Gallery, 45 Mount St, Bay Head, NJ 08742-5346. Phone: (732) 892-7776 or (800) 4-BAYHED.

BETTY PICNIC. June 13. Tom Pierce Park, Grants Pass, OR. To celebrate the Bettys of this world for their vivacity, impulsiveness and similarities. Annually, the second Saturday in June. Send SASE, since this is a nonprofit organization. Est attendance: 55. For info: Betty Wilder and Betty Patterson, c/o Betty Picnic, 1012 NE Madrone, Grants Pass, OR 97526. Phone: (541) 476-4104.

BOLLES, DON: DEATH ANNIVERSARY. June 13. Don Bolles, investigative reporter for *The Arizona Republic*, died June 13, 1976, as a result of injuries received when a bomb exploded in his automobile, June 2, 1976, while he was engaged in journalistic investigation of alleged Mafia story. Bolles was awarded, posthumously, the University of Arizona's John Peter Zenger Award, Dec 9, 1976.

CARS IN THE PARK. June 13. Dexter, MO. 15th annual. Experience the pleasure of a walk in the park among mint-condition vintage cars. Annually, the second Saturday in June. Est attendance: 1,400. For info: Annual Cars in the Park, PO Box 21, Dexter, MO 63841. Phone: (573) 624-7458 or (800) 332-8857. Fax: (573) 624-7459.

CHINCOTEAGUE HOMESTYLE MUSIC AND SHRIMP FEST. June 13. Chincoteague, VA. Family-type entertainment with folk music on two stages and all the shrimp and charcoal pit beef you can eat. For info: Chincoteague Chamber of Commerce, PO Box 258, Chincoteague, VA 23336. Phone: (757) 336-6161. Fax: (757) 336-1242. Email: pony@shore.intercom.net. WWW: http://www.intercom.net/local/chinoteague/

EVERS, MEDGAR: 35th ASSASSINATION ANNIVERSARY. June 13, 1963. Civil rights leader Medgar Wiley Evers was active in seeking integration of schools and voter registration. He was assassinated by Byron de la Beckwith on June 13, 1963. The public outrage following his death was one of the factors that led President John F. Kennedy to propose a comprehensive civil rights law.

FINLAND: JOENSUU FESTIVAL. June 13–20. Joensuu. International event with concerts of symphonic and popular music and solo concerts, dance and theater performances, art exhibitions, films. Est attendance: 50,000. For info: Finnish Tourist Board, 655 Third Ave, New York, NY 10017. Phone: (212) 949-2333.

FOUNDERS' DAY—THE GOOD LIFE. June 13 (rain date June 14). Toms River, NJ. Street fair for local non-profit organizations with a parade, entertainment, prizes, food, literature, games and a "Crafters Corner." Est attendance: 30,000. For info: Toms River-Ocean County Chamber of Commerce, 1200 Hooper Ave, Toms River, NJ 08753. Phone: (908) 349-0220. Fax: (908) 349-1252. WWW: http://www.oc-chamber.com

FUN FLY. June 13–14 (tentative; call for firm info). Model Hobby Park, Alamogordo, NM. Friday—a workshop where kids (no age limit) build model rockets (which they get to keep); on Saturday and Sunday they launch them in the 7th annual Fun Flight. Est attendance: 100. For info: Bob Turner, Curator, Space Center, PO Box 533, Alamogordo, NM 88311-0533. Phone: (800) 545-4021. Fax: (505) 437-7722.
Email: space-plan@nmsua.nmsu.edu.
WWW: http://abcc.nmsu.edu/~bwood/

GRANGE, RED: BIRTH ANNIVERSARY. June 13, 1903. Harold Edward ("Red") Grange, Pro Football Hall of Fame halfback and sportscaster born at Forskville, PA. Perhaps the most famous football player of all time, Grange had a spectacular college career at the University of Illinois, being named an All-American in 1923, 1924, and 1925. When Illinois dedicated its Memorial Stadium on Oct 18, 1924, against Michigan, Grange scored four touchdowns in the game's first 12 minutes. Known as the "Galloping Ghost," Grange joined the Chicago Bears in 1925 for what amounted to a barnstorming tour, the start of a professional career dictated by Grange and his manager, Charles C. ("Cash and Carry") Pyle. He retired in 1934 following a knee injury, having put pro football on the sports map. Grange entered business and did announcing work on radio and television. In retirement, he lived quietly and humbly. Inducted into the Pro Football Hall of Fame as a charter member in 1963. Died at Lake Wales, FL, Jan 28, 1991.

GREAT PLAINS BALLOON RACE. June 13–14. Tea, SD. Approximately 50 hot-air balloons from five states (Iowa, Minnesota, Nebraska, North and South Dakota) take to the sky. The event features skydivers, display of stunt planes and other fun activities. Est attendance: 20,000. For info: Aerostar, PO Box 5057, Sioux Falls, SD 57117-5057. Phone: (605) 331-3500.

HERITAGE DAY CELEBRATION. June 13. Wisconsin Dells, WI. A return to the past featuring a craft fair, old-fashioned exhibits and displays, music and antique flea market. Annually, the second weekend following Memorial Day. Est attendance: 2,500. For info: Wisc Dells Visitor & Conv Bureau, PO Box 390, Wisconsin Dells, WI 53965. Phone: (800) 223-3557.
Email: wisdells@midplains.net. WWW: http://www.wisdells.com

HERITAGE DAYS FESTIVAL. June 13–14. Cumberland, MD. 30th annual. Held in historic downtown Cumberland, the festival showcases over 300 arts and crafts booths. Also, music, entertainment, children's activities, carnivals, tours of historic homes and buildings as well as historic re-enactments. Annually, the second weekend in June. Est attendance: 25,000. For info: Allegany Arts Council, WMSC/3 Canal St, Cumberland, MD 21502. Phone: (301) 777-2787.

HOME OWNERS LOAN ACT: 65th ANNIVERSARY. June 13, 1933. The Federal Savings and Loan Association was authorized on June 13, 1933, with the passage of the Home Owners Loan Act. The purpose of the legislation was to provide a convenient place for investment and to lend money on first mortgages. The first association was the First Federal Savings and Loan Association of Miami, FL, which was chartered on Aug 8, 1933.

MELROSE PLANTATION ARTS AND CRAFTS FESTIVAL. June 13–14. Melrose, LA. Held on the grounds of Historic Melrose Plantation, this event features quality handcrafted items from more than 150 juried exhibitors. Food, including the famous meat pies and soft drinks, will be available. Annually, the second full weekend in June. Est attendance: 20,000. For info: Calendar of Events, Natchitoches Parish Tourist Commission, 781 Front St, Natchitoches, LA 71457. Phone: (318) 352-8072 or (800) 259-1714. Fax: (318) 352-2415.

MIDDLE OF NOWHERE TRAIL RIDE. June 13–14. Ainsworth, NE. Trail ride along the Niobrara River. Limit 100 horses. Place to keep horses available. 10th annual ride. Est attendance: 100. For info: Mrs Mary Jo Curtis, Organizer, 340 W 3rd, Ainsworth, NE 69210. Phone: (402) 387-2488.

***MIRANDA* DECISION: ANNIVERSARY.** June 13, 1966. The US Supreme Court rendered a 5–4 decision in the case of *Miranda v Arizona*, holding that the Fifth Amendment of the Constitution "required warnings before valid statements could be taken by police." The decision has been described as "providing basic legal protections to persons who might otherwise not be aware of their rights." Ernesto Miranda, the 23-year-old whose name became nationally known, was retried after the Miranda Decision, convicted and sent back to prison. Miranda was stabbed to death in a card game dispute in Phoenix, AZ, in 1976. A suspect in the killing was released by police after he had been read his "Miranda rights." Police procedures now routinely require the reading of a prisoner's constitutional rights ("Miranda") before questioning.

MISSION SAN LUIS REY DE FRANCIA FOUNDING: 200TH ANNIVERSARY. June 13, 1798. California mission to the Indians founded June 13, 1798. Abandoned by 1846; restoration begun in 1892.

NATIONAL HERMIT WEEK. June 13–20. Celebrates the important contributions hermits, and other off-the-grid types, make to our society. Annually, beginning the 13th of June. For info: Ashton Productions, Prince St Sta-Box 668, New York, NY 10012. Phone: (212) 982-5170. Fax: (212) 260-6744.

NATIONAL POTTERY GAMES. June 13–14. Cambridge, WI. Potters from all over the country meet to exhibit and sell. Visitors can throw and fire their own creations. Also pottery competitions and demonstrations and creative children's activities at West Side park. For info: Wisconsin Dept of Tourism, National Pottery Games, PO Box 7976, Madison, WI 53707. Phone: (608) 423-3780. Email: tourism@laughlin.com.
WWW: http://tourism.state.wi.us

RENDEZVOUS FESTIVAL. June 13–14. Icelandic State Park, Cavalier, ND. A festival of culture and art celebrating the history of North Dakota's Rendezvous Region. Activities include a muzzleloader's shoot, ethnic singers, dancers and performers, pioneer demonstrations and trades. There will also be a buckskinner's encampment, ceremonies and a Chautauqua. For info: (701) 265-4561 or North Dakota Tourism, 604 East Boulevard, Bismarck, ND 58505. Phone: (701) 328-2525 or (800) 435-5663.

ROGUE RIVER JET BOAT MARATHON. June 13–14. Gold Beach, OR. Watch jet boats ply the twisted, rushing whitewater rapids of the mighty Rogue at speeds faster than your eyes can focus, starting from Jot's Resort at the mouth of the Rogue in Gold Beach, about 30 miles upriver to Agness, and back again. Other events include hydroplane racing and sprint-boat maneuvers. Est attendance: 4,000. For info: Gold Beach Chamber of Commerce, 29279 Ellensburg Ave, #3, Gold Beach, OR 97444. Phone: (800) 525-2334. Fax: (541) 247-0188.
Email: goldbeach@harborside.com.
WWW: http://www.harborside.com/gb

SAINT ANTHONY OF PADUA: FEAST DAY: DEATH ANNIVERSARY. June 13. Born at Lisbon, Portugal, Aug 15, 1195, St. Anthony is patron of the illiterate and the poor. Died at Padua, June 13, 1231. Public holiday, Lisbon.

SCOTT, WINFIELD: BIRTH ANNIVERSARY. June 13. American army general, negotiator of peace treaties with Indians and twice nominated for president (1848 and 1852). Leader of brilliant military campaign in Mexico in 1847. Scott was born at Petersburg, VA, on June 13, 1786, and died at West Point, NY, on May 29, 1866.

SHADES OF DEATH ENCAMPMENT. June 13–14. Somerset, PA. Military encampment depicting the life of the soldier and Native Americans in western Pennsylvania during the French and Indian War. Tactical and weapons demonstrations. For info: Somerset Historical Society, 10649 Somerset Pike, Somerset, PA 15501. Phone: (814) 445-6077.

SPRING CRAFTFEST. June 13. Dexter, MO. 6th annual. Exhibitors display and sell their handcrafted products in an outdoor setting under shade trees. Concession stands. Annually, the second Saturday in June. Est attendance: 1,000. For info: Spring Craftfest, PO Box 21, Dexter, MO 63841. Phone: (573) 624-7458 or (800) 332-8857. Fax: (573) 624-7459.

TERRITORIAL DAYS. June 13–14. Prescott, AZ. A celebration of arts, crafts and music. Est attendance: 15,000. For info: Chamber of Commerce, PO Box 1147, Prescott, AZ 86302. Phone: (800) 266-7534 or (520) 445-2000, ext 22. Fax: (520) 445-0068.

UNITED KINGDOM: TROOPING THE COLOUR—QUEEN'S OFFICIAL BIRTHDAY PARADE. June 13 (tentative). National holiday in the United Kingdom. Horse Guards Parade, Whitehall, London. Colorful ceremony with music and pageantry during which Her Majesty The Queen takes the salute. Starts at 11 AM. When requesting info, send stamped, self-addressed envelope. [Final date not set at press time.] The Queen's real birthday is Apr 21. Est attendance: 10,000. For info: The Ticket Office, HQ Household Division, 1 Chelsea Barracks, London, England SW1H 8RF. Phone: (44) (171) 414-2357.

UNTO THESE HILLS CHEROKEE INDIAN DRAMA. June 13–Aug 22. Cherokee Indian Reservation, Cherokee, NC. Nightly (except Sundays), an outdoor pageant, with a cast of 130 performers, portraying the history of the Eastern Band of Cherokee Indians. Est attendance: 90,000. For info: Margie Douthit, Mktg Dir, Cherokee Historical Assn, PO Box 398, Cherokee, NC 28719. Phone: (704) 497-2111. Fax: (704) 497-6987.

VIEIRA DA SILVA, MARIA-HELENA: 90th BIRTH ANNIVERSARY. June 13, 1908. Portuguese-born painter Maria Helena Vieira da Silva was born on June 13, 1908, at Lisbon. Although a French citizen, she was considered by many as Portugal's greatest contemporary artist. Her work spanned the Parisian School and Abstract Expressionism. She died Mar 6, 1992, at Paris, France.

June 1998

S	M	T	W	T	F	S
	1	2	3	4	5	6
7	8	9	10	11	12	13
14	15	16	17	18	19	20
21	22	23	24	25	26	27
28	29	30				

VIRGINIA INDIAN HERITAGE FESTIVAL. June 13. Jamestown Settlement, Williamsburg, VA. Native Americans from Virginia and other states assemble to celebrate their culture with dance, storytelling and demonstrations and sales of traditional crafts and foods. Est attendance: 3,500. For info: Media Relations, Jamestown-Yorktown Fdtn, PO Box 1607, Williamsburg, VA 23187. Phone: (757) 253-4838. Fax: (757) 253-5299. WWW: http://www.historyisfun.org

WORLD'S GREATEST YARD SALE. June 13–14. Fairgrounds, York, PA. Fundraising for York Unit, American Cancer Society. Est attendance: 30,000. For info: American Cancer Soc, 924 N Colonial Ave, York, PA 17403. Phone: (717) 848-1841. Fax: (717) 852-0919.

WYATT EARP BIRTHDAY CELEBRATION. June 13. Monmouth, IL. Luncheon with "Wyatt Earp" and Earp cousins at Meling's Restaurant. Tours of Birthplace, Pioneer Cemetery and other Earp sites 1 PM to 4 PM. Annually, the second Saturday in June. Est attendance: 150. For info: Wyatt Earp Birthplace Historic House Museum, Office: 1020 E Detroit Ave, Monmouth, IL 61462. Phone: (309) 734-6419 or Chamber of Commerce (309) 734-3181. Fax: (309) 734-6419.

YEATS, WILLIAM BUTLER: BIRTH ANNIVERSARY. June 13. Nobel prize-winning Irish poet and dramatist, born at Dublin, Ireland, on June 13, 1865. He once wrote: "If a poet interprets a poem of his own he limits its suggestibility." Yeats died at France on Jan 28, 1939. After World War II his body was returned, as he had wished, for reburial in a churchyard at Drumcliff, Ireland.

BIRTHDAYS TODAY

Tim Allen, 45, comedian, actor ("Home Improvement"), born Denver, CO, June 13, 1953.

Bettina Bunge, 35, tennis player, born Adliswick, Switzerland, June 13, 1963.

Christo (Christo Javacheff), 63, conceptual artist (*Running Fence, Valley Curtain*), born Babrovo, Bulgaria, June 13, 1935.

Sarunas Marciulionis, 34, basketball player, born Kaunas, USSR, June 13, 1964.

Malcolm McDowell, 55, actor (*A Clockwork Orange, O Lucky Man*), born Leeds, England, June 13, 1943.

Ally (Alexandra Elizabeth) Sheedy, 36, actress (*St. Elmo's Fire, The Breakfast Club, War Games*), born New York, NY, June 13, 1962.

Richard Thomas, 47, actor ("The Waltons," *Roots: The Next Generation*), born New York, NY, June 13, 1951.

JUNE 14 — SUNDAY

Day 165 — 200 Remaining

ALZHEIMER, ALOIS: BIRTH ANNIVERSARY. June 14. The German psychiatrist and pathologist Alois Alzheimer was born on June 14, 1864, at Markbreit am Mainz, Germany. In 1907 an article by Alzheimer appeared in *Allgemeine Zeitschrift für Psychiatrie*, first describing the disease that was named for him. It was thought of as a kind of presenile dementia, usually beginning at age 40–60, but whether Alzheimer's disease is an entity separate from senile dementia remains unanswered. Alzheimer died on Dec 19, 1915, at Breslau, Germany.

BARTLETT, JOHN: BIRTH ANNIVERSARY. June 14. American editor and compiler (Bartlett's *Familiar Quotations* [1855] and other works) was born at Plymouth, MA, on June 14, 1820. Though he had little formal education, he created one of the most-used reference works of the English language. No quotation of his own is among the more than 22,000 listed today, but in the preface to the first edition he wrote that the object of this work "originally made without any view of publication" was to show "the obligation our language owes to various authors for numerous phrases and familiar quotations which have become 'household words.' " Bartlett died at age 85 at Cambridge, MA, on Dec 3, 1905.

BELGIUM: MILITARY MUSIC FESTIVAL. June 14. Tournai. Traditional cultural observance. Annually, the second Sunday in June.

BOURKE-WHITE, MARGARET: BIRTH ANNIVERSARY. June 14, 1906. Margaret Bourke was born at New York City. One of the original photojournalists, she developed her personal style while photographing the Krupp Iron Works in Germany and the Soviet Union during the first Five-Year Plan. Bourke-White was one of the four original staff photographers for *Life* magazine in 1936. The first woman attached to the US armed forces during World War II, she covered the Italian campaign, the siege of Moscow and the American soldiers' crossing of the Rhine into Germany, and she shocked the world with her photographs of the concentration camps. Bourke-White photographed Mahatma Gandhi and covered the migration of millions of people after the Indian subcontinent was divided into Hindu India and Muslim Pakistan. She served as a war correspondent during the Korean War. Among her several books, the most famous was her collaboration with her second husband, novelist Erskine Caldwell, a study of rural poverty in the American South called *You Have Seen Their Faces.* She died Aug 27, 1971, at Stamford, CT.

CHILDREN'S DAY IN MASSACHUSETTS. June 14. Annually, the second Sunday in June.

CHILDREN'S SUNDAY. June 14. Traditionally the second Sunday in June is observed as Children's Sunday in many Christian churches.

CORPUS CHRISTI (US OBSERVANCE). June 14. A movable Roman Catholic celebration commemorating the institution of the Holy Eucharist. The solemnity has been observed on the Thursday following Trinity Sunday since 1246, except in the US, where it is observed on the Sunday following Trinity Sunday.

DONNA REED FESTIVAL FOR THE PERFORMING ARTS. June 14–20 (tentative). Denison, IA. Performing arts festival in Donna Reed's hometown. Focus of the festival is educational workshops in various areas of the performing arts taught by Hollywood and New York professionals. Also included are celebrity golf tournament, street fair and theatrical performances for the general public. Annually, a week in June. Est attendance: 10,000. For info: Sandra Bailen-Scott, Dir, Donna Reed Foundation, 1305 Broadway, Denison, IA 51442. Phone: (800) 336-4692. Fax: (712) 263-8026. Email: dreedfpa@pionet.net. WWW: http://www.frii.com/donna_reed/

☆ ☆ ☆

FAMILY HISTORY DAY. June 14. Every summer family reunions are so busy with games and activities that most of us forget the true purpose: to share the folklore, legends and myths that bind us together. Each participant should share at least one good recollection (fact or fiction). Don't forget the hot dogs and lemonade. [© 1997 by WPL] For info: Tom or Ruth Roy, Wellness Permission League, PO Box 662, Mt Grenta, PA 17064-0662. Phone: (500) 437-5104 or (717) 964-1308. Fax: (717) 964-1335.

FIRST NONSTOP TRANSATLANTIC FLIGHT: ANNIVERSARY. June 14–15. Captain John Alcock and Lieutenant Arthur W. Brown flew a Vickers Vimy bomber 1,900 miles nonstop from St. Johns, Newfoundland, to Clifden, County Galway, Ireland, June 14–15, 1919. In spite of their crash landing in an Irish peat bog, their flight inspired public interest in aviation and led to many other flights. See also: "Lindbergh Flight Anniversary" (May 20).

FIRST US BREACH OF PROMISE SUIT: 375th ANNIVERSARY. June 14, 1623. The first breach of promise suit in the US was filed on June 14, 1623, in the Virginia Council of State, in Charles City, VA. Reverend Greville Pooley brought suit against Cicely Jordan, who had jilted him in favor of another man.

★**FLAG DAY.** June 14. Presidential Proclamation issued each year for June 14. Proclamation 1335, of May 30, 1916, covers all succeeding years. Has been issued annually since 1941. (PL81–203 of Aug 3, 1949.) Customarily issued as "Flag Day and National Flag Week," as in 1986; the president usually mentions "a time to honor America," Flag Day to Independence Day (89 Stat. 211). See also: "National Flag Day USA: Pause for the Pledge" (this date).

FLAG DAY CEREMONIES. June 14. Betsy Ross House, Philadelphia, PA. 11 AM program followed by band concert in Atwater Kent Gardens of Betsy Ross House. Est attendance: 1,000. For info: Betsy Ross House, 239 Arch St, Philadelphia, PA 19106. Phone: (215) 627-5343. Fax: (215) 627-0591.

FLAG DAY: ANNIVERSARY OF THE STARS AND STRIPES. June 14. On this day in 1777, John Adams introduced the following resolution before the Continental Congress, meeting at Philadelphia, PA: "Resolved, That the flag of the thirteen United States shall be thirteen stripes, alternate red and white; that the union be thirteen stars, white on a blue field, representing a new constellation." Legal holiday in Pennsylvania and Florida.

GERMANFEST. June 14–21. Fort Wayne, IN. A celebration of German heritage with folk music, folk dancing, beer tents, German food, beer and wine tastings, Männerchor (men's choir) singing, Gottesdienste (masses), genealogy workshops, classical organ music, Children's Day, German films, lectures and demonstrations. Est attendance: 80,000. For info: German Heritage Soc, PO Box 12651, Fort Wayne, IN 46864. Phone: (800) 767-7752. Fax: (219) 449-7495. Email: kscheib@mail.fwi.com. WWW: http://www.fwi.com/germanfest

GINA BACHAUER INTERNATIONAL PIANO COMPETITION & FESTIVAL. June 14–27. Assembly Hall on Temple Square, Abravanel Hall, Salt Lake City, UT. Competition (Ages 19-32). Master classes, seminars, recitals and concerts. Est attendance: 10,000. For info: Massimiliano Frani, Assoc Art Dir, Gina Bachauer Intl Foundation, PO Box 11664, Salt Lake City, UT 84147. Phone: (801) 521-9200. Fax: (801) 521-9202. Email: gina@bachauer.com. WWW: http://bachauer.com

"THE GONG SHOW" TV PREMIERE: ANNIVERSARY. June 14, 1976. This popular show featured a panel of three celebrities judging amateur and professional acts, from the ordinary to the unusual. At any time, a judge could bang a gong to end the act; this was often done with gusto. Completed acts were then rated and the winner received a cash prize. Chuck Barris created (along with Chris Bearde) and hosted the show for all seasons and in syndication with the exception of one syndicated season hosted by Gary Owens. Celebrities who frequently appeared were Jaye P. Morgan, Rex Reed, Arte Johnson, Michele Lee and Jamie Farr.

GRANT WOOD ART FESTIVAL. June 14. Stone City-Anamosa, IA. Juried art exhibits, demonstrations, stage entertainment, tours of historic Stone City, quilt show and more. Annually the second Sunday in June. Est attendance: 8,000. For info: Marguerite Stoll, Media Coordinator, Grant Wood Art Festival, Inc, 124 E Main St, Anamosa, IA 52205. Phone: (319) 462-4267 or (319) 462-3988.

HARD ROCK CAFE 5K. June 14. Hard Rock Cafe, Chicago, IL. This 8th annual 5K (3.1 miles) is a family fun run with proceeds benefiting a to-be-designated charity. The race begins and ends at the cafe, and all runners are invited to join postrace festivities. Annually, a Sunday in June. Sponsor: Hard Rock Cafe, Chicago, IL. Est attendance: 4,000. For info: c/o Chicago Event Mgmt, Inc, 900 W Jackson, Ste #8-W, Chicago, IL 60607. Phone: (312) 243-3274. Fax: (312) 243-5652.

IVES, BURL: BIRTH ANNIVERSARY. June 14, 1909. American singer and actor Burl Icle Ivanhoe Ives was born at Hunt, IL. He helped to reintroduce Anglo-American folk music in the '40s and '50s. Ives won an Academy Award for his supporting role in *The Big Country* (1958), and he is well known for his role as Big Daddy in both the film and Broadway productions of *Cat On a Hot Tin Roof*. He died on April 14, 1995 at Anacortes, WA.

JAPAN: RICE PLANTING FESTIVAL. June 14. Osaka. Ceremonial transplanting of rice seedlings in paddy field at Sumiyashi Shrine, Osaka.

LEVITT PAVILION PERFORMING ARTS/MUSIC FESTIVAL. June 14–Aug 23. Levitt Pavilion, Westport, CT. 25th annual. Performing Arts/Music Festival conducts more than 50 nights of high-quality entertainment offered free to the general public. An additional seven nights of concerts are presented and a nominal admission is charged to raise money to underwrite the free nights of the festival. Est attendance: 120,000. For info: Freda Welsh, Exec Dir, Levitt Pavilion, Town Hall, 110 Myrtle Ave, Westport, CT 06880. Phone: (203) 226-7600. Fax: (203) 226-2330 Concert Line: (203) 221-4422.

MEET A MATE WEEK. June 14–20. To inspire singles seeking a mate to take advantage of summer by pursuing warm weather meeting opportunities. Options include singles travel, sports activities, New Blood parties and volunteer work. For info: Robin Gorman Newman, 58 Grace Ave, 2J, Great Neck, NY 11021. Phone: (516) 773-0911. Email: rgnewman@aol.com.

June 1998

S	M	T	W	T	F	S
	1	2	3	4	5	6
7	8	9	10	11	12	13
14	15	16	17	18	19	20
21	22	23	24	25	26	27
28	29	30				

NATIONAL FLAG DAY USA: PAUSE FOR THE PLEDGE. June 14. Held simultaneously across the country at 7 PM, EDT. Public law 99–54 recognizes the Pause for the Pledge as part of National Flag Day ceremonies. The concept of the Pause for the Pledge of Allegiance was conceived as a way for all citizens to share a patriotic moment. National ceremony at Fort McHenry National Monument and Historic Shrine.

ORTHODOX FESTIVAL OF ALL SAINTS. June 14. Observed by Eastern Orthodox churches on the Sunday following Orthodox Pentecost (June 7 in 1998). Marks the end of the 18-week Triodion cycle.

RACE UNITY DAY. June 14. Baha'i-sponsored observance promoting racial harmony and understanding and the essential unity of mankind. Annually, the second Sunday in June. Established in 1957 by the Baha'is of the US. For info: Pamela Zivari, Dir, Baha'is of the US, Office of Public Information, 866 UN Plaza, Ste 120, New York, NY 10017-1822. Phone: (212) 803-2500. Fax: (212) 803-2573. Email: usopi-ny@bic.org.

RADIO TALK SHOW WEEK. June 14–21. A salute to all those in the radio talk show industry, who give us something to talk about! Annually, upon the meeting dates of the National Association of Talk Show Hosts. For more info, send $2 to cover the costs of postage and photocopying. For info: Adrienne Sioux Koopersmith, 1437 W Rosemont, #1W, Chicago, IL 60660-1319. Phone: (773) 743-5341. Fax: (773) 743-5395. Email: kooper@interaccess.com.

SPACE MILESTONE: *MARINER 5* (US). June 14, 1967. Launched on this date, interplanetary probe of Venus established 72½–87½ percent carbon dioxide content of atmosphere on Oct 18 flyby of planet.

SPACE MILESTONE: *VOSTOK 5* (USSR): 35th ANNIVERSARY. June 14, 1963. Launched this date, *Vostok 5* with Lieutenant Colonel Valery Bykovsky orbited Earth 81 times, 2,046,000 miles. Landed June 19.

STOWE, HARRIET BEECHER: BIRTH ANNIVERSARY. June 14, 1811. American writer Harriet Beecher Stowe, daughter of the Reverend Lyman Beecher and sister of Henry Ward Beecher. Author of *Uncle Tom's Cabin*, an antislavery novel that provoked a storm of protest and resulted in fame for its author. Two characters in the novel attained such importance that their names became part of the English language—the Negro slave, Uncle Tom, and the villainous slaveowner, Simon Legree. The bitter reaction to *Uncle Tom's Cabin* and its profound political impact are without parallel in American literature. It is said that during the Civil War, when Harriet Beecher Stowe was introduced to President Abraham Lincoln, his words to her were "So you're the little woman who wrote the book that made this great war." Stowe was born at Litchfield, CT and died at Hartford, CT, on July 1, 1896, at age 85.

TAG SALE ON THE GREEN. June 14. The Colchester Green, Colchester, CT. Largest tag sale event in the state, with more than 200 vendors. Free to the public. Open 9 AM-4 PM. Est attendance: 10,000. For info: Colchester Business Assn, PO Box 453, Colchester, CT 06415. Phone: (860) 537-0340.

TO HAVE AND TO HOLD. June 14–Aug 30. Clinton, MD. A special exhibit on 19th-century wedding customs. On June 14th, there will be a reenactment of a mid-19th-century home wedding. Est attendance: 2,000. For info: Surratt House and Tavern, PO Box 427, Clinton, MD 20735. Phone: (301) 868-1121. Fax: (301) 868-8177.
WWW: http://www.engr.umd.edu/~clwspoon/surratt.html

UNIVAC COMPUTER: BIRTHDAY. June 14. Univac 1, the world's first commercial computer, designed for the US Bureau of the Census, was unveiled, demonstrated and dedicated at Philadelphia, PA, June 14, 1951. Though this milestone of the computer age was the first commercial electronic computer, it had been preceded by ENIAC (Electronic Numeric Integrator and Computer), completed under the supervision of J. Presper Eckert, Jr, and John W. Mauchly, at the Moore School of Electrical Engineering, University of Pennsylvania, in 1946.

US ARMY ESTABLISHED BY CONGRESS: ANNIVERSARY. June 14. Anniversary of Congressional Resolution of June 14, 1775, establishing the army as the first US military service.

WARREN G. HARDING BECOMES FIRST PRESIDENT TO BROADCAST ON RADIO: ANNIVERSARY. June 14. On June 14, 1922, Warren G. Harding became the first president to broadcast a message over the radio. The event was the dedication of the Francis Scott Key Memorial in Baltimore, MD. The first official government message was broadcast on Dec 6, 1923.

BIRTHDAYS TODAY

Boy George (George Alan O'Dowd), 37, singer (lead singer with Culture Club; "Do You Really Want to Hurt Me?"), born London, England, June 14, 1961.

Marla Gibbs, 52, actress (Mary on "227"; Florence on "The Jeffersons"), born Chicago, IL, June 14, 1946.

Stephanie Maria (Steffi) Graf, 29, tennis player, born Bruhl, West Germany, June 14, 1969.

Eric Arthur Heiden, 40, Olympic gold medal speed skater, born Madison, WI, June 14, 1958.

Dorothy McGuire, 80, actress (*A Tree Grows in Brooklyn, Gentlemen's Agreement*, "Rich Man, Poor Man"), born Omaha, NE, June 14, 1918.

Eddie Mekka, 46, actor (Carmine on "Laverne and Shirley"), born Worcester, MA, June 14, 1952.

Will Patton, 44, actor (*Silkwood, Desperately Seeking Susan*; stage: *Tourists and Refugees #2* [Obie Award]), born Charleston, SC, June 14, 1954.

Samuel Bruce (Sam) Perkins, 37, basketball player, born New York, NY, June 14, 1961.

Donald Trump, 52, real estate mogul, born New York City, NY, June 14, 1946.

JUNE 15 — MONDAY

Day 166 — 199 Remaining

ARKANSAS: ADMISSION DAY: ANNIVERSARY. June 15. Became 25th state on this day in 1836.

ASPEN MUSIC FESTIVAL. June 15–Aug 16. Aspen, CO. Nine weeks of concerts performed by highly acclaimed artists. Est attendance: 100,000. For info: Aspen Music Festival, 2 Music School Rd, Aspen, CO 81611. Phone: (970) 925-3254. Fax: (970) 920-1643. WWW: http://www.aspen.com/musicfestival

BEAVER FESTIVAL. June 15–20 (tentative). Third and Market Streets, Beaver, PA. 17th annual. Food, games, amusement rides, concerts in Quay Square and more. For info: (412) 773-6700 or Beaver County Tourist Promotion Agency, 215 B Ninth St, Monaca, PA 15061-2028. Phone: (412) 728-0212. Fax: (412) 728-0456.

FIRST FATAL AVIATION ACCIDENT: ANNIVERSARY. June 15. Two French aeronauts, Jean François Pilatre de Rozier and P.A. de Romain, attempting to cross the English Channel from France to England in a balloon, were killed June 15, 1785, when their balloon caught fire and crashed to the ground. Pilatre de Rozier, the first man to fly, thus became a fatality in the first fatal accident in aviation history.

GRIEG, EDVARD: BIRTH ANNIVERSARY. June 15, 1843. Pianist, composer, conductor and teacher, the first Scandinavian to compose nationalistic music. Born at Bergen, Norway, and died there Sept 4, 1907.

"HEE HAW" TV PREMIERE: ANNIVERSARY. June 15, 1969. "Hee Haw" has been described as a country-western version of "Laugh-In," composed of fast-paced sketches, silly jokes and songs. Though critics didn't like it, it had popular appeal and did well as a syndicated show. It was cohosted by Buck Owens and Roy Clark, who began to appear only occasionally in the '80s, alternating with guest hosts. Regular performers included Louis M. "Grandpa" Jones, Junior Samples, Jeannine Riley, Lulu Roman, David "Stringbean" Akeman, Sherry Miles, Lisa Todd, Minnie Pearl and Gordie Tapp.

INTERNATIONAL COUNTRY MUSIC FAN FAIR. June 15–20. State Fairgrounds and Opryland, Nashville, TN. A week-long musical celebration for fans of country music. Fan Fair schedules more than 35 hours of stage shows and other musical events, along with picture and autograph sessions with country music stars, as well as the Grand Masters Fiddling Championship. Est attendance: 24,000. For info: Fan Fair, 2804 Opryland Dr, Nashville, TN 37214. Phone: (615) 889-7503.

JACKSON, RACHEL DONELSON ROBARDS: BIRTH ANNIVERSARY. June 15, 1767. Wife of Andrew Jackson, 7th president of the US, born at Halifax County, NC, June 15, 1767. Died Dec 22, 1828.

MAGNA CARTA DAY: ANNIVERSARY. June 15. Anniversary of King John's sealing, in 1215, of the Magna Carta "in the meadow called Ronimed between Windsor and Staines on the fifteenth day of June in the seventeenth year of our reign." This document is regarded as the first charter of English liberties and one of the most important documents in the history of political and human freedom as understood today. Four original copies of the 1215 charter survive.

"MY LITTLE MARGIE" TV PREMIERE: ANNIVERSARY. June 15, 1952. "My Little Margie" was a half-hour sitcom about a "womanizing widower and his meddlesome daughter." Margie was played by Gale Storm and Charles Farrell played her father, Vern Albright. Also in the cast were Don Hayden, Clarence Kolb, Hillary Brooke, Gertrude Hoffman and Willie Best.

NEBRASKALAND DAYS AND BUFFALO BILL RODEO. June 15–23. North Platte, NE. To relive the Old West. Parades, contests, shoot-outs, art shows, frontier revue, top country-western stars. Est attendance: 100,000. For info: Nebraskaland Days, Box 706, North Platte, NE 69103. Phone: (308) 532-7939. Fax: (308) 532-3789. Email: nld@nque.com. WWW: http://www.nque.com/nld

QUARTERLY ESTIMATED FEDERAL INCOME TAX PAYERS' DUE DATE. June 15. For those individuals whose fiscal year is the calendar year and who make quarterly estimated federal income tax payments, today is one of the due dates. (Jan 15, Apr 15, June 15 and Sept 15, 1998.)

RAVINIA FESTIVAL. June 15–Sept 7 (tentative). Highland Park, IL. Summer home of the Chicago Symphony Orchestra. This 63rd annual season also includes chamber music, jazz, pop, kids' concerts and dance. For info: Ravinia Festival, PO Box 896, Highland Park, IL 60035. Phone: (847) 266-5100. Fax: (847) 266-0641. WWW: http://www.ravinia.org

ROANOKE VALLEY HORSE SHOW. June 15–20. Salem Civic Center, Salem, VA. Multibreed horse show. Est attendance: 30,000. For info: Salem Civic Ctr, John Saunders, Box 886, Salem, VA 24153. Phone: (540) 375-3004.

SPACE MILESTONE: *SOYUZ 29* (USSR): 20th ANNIVERSARY. June 15, 1978. Launched on June 15, 1978, cosmonauts Vladimir Kovalyonok and Alexander Ivanchenkov docked with *Salyut 6* space station on June 17. Returned to Earth in *Soyuz 31*, Nov 2, after 4½ months' stay and visits by two pairs of cosmonauts while there. Return landing in Kazakhstan, USSR.

TWELFTH AMENDMENT TO US CONSTITUTION RATIFIED: ANNIVERSARY. June 15. The 12th Amendment to the Constitution was ratified on June 15, 1804. It changed the method of electing the president and vice president after a tie in the electoral college during the election of 1800. Rather than each elector voting for two candidates with the candidate receiving the most votes elected president and the second-place candidate elected vice president, each elector was now required to designate his choice for president and vice president, respectively.

VIRGIN ISLANDS: ORGANIC ACT DAY: ANNIVERSARY. June 15. Commemorates the enactment by the US Congress, on July 22, 1954, of the Revised Organic Act, under which the government of the Virgin Islands is organized. Observed annually on the third Monday in June.

WORLD WALK FOR BREASTFEEDING. June 15–Sept 15. Members and friends of La Leche League International walk in different locations around the world in celebration of World Breastfeeding Week. Est attendance: 10,000. For info: World Walk Committee, La Leche League International, 1400 N Meacham, Schaumburg, IL 60173-4840. Phone: (847) 519-7730 ext 233. Fax: (847) 519-0035. WWW: http://www.lalecheleague.org/

BIRTHDAYS TODAY

Jim Belushi, 44, actor ("Saturday Night Live," *Men at Work*), born Chicago, IL, June 15, 1954.

Wade Anthony Boggs, 40, baseball player, born Omaha, NE, June 15, 1958.

Brett Morgan Butler, 41, baseball player, born Los Angeles, CA, June 15, 1957.

Simon Callow, 49, actor (*A Room with a View, Mr and Mrs Bridge, Howards End*); author (*Orson Welles*), born London, England, June 15, 1949.

Courteney Cox, 34, actress (the young woman who jumps out of the audience and dances in Bruce Springsteen's music video *Dancing in the Dark*, "Family Ties," "Friends"), born Birmingham, AL, June 15, 1964.

Mario M. Cuomo, 66, former governor of New York (D), born New York, NY, June 15, 1932.

Julie Hagerty, 43, actress (*Airplane!, Lost in America, Reversal of Fortune*; stage: *The House of Blue Leaves* [Theatre World Award]), born Cincinnati, OH, June 15, 1955.

Neil Patrick Harris, 25, actor ("Doogie Howser, MD," *Clara's Heart*), born Albuquerque, NM, June 15, 1973.

Helen Hunt, 35, actress ("Mad About You," *Peggy Sue Got Married, Twister*), born Los Angeles, CA, June 15, 1963.

Waylon Jennings, 61, singer ("Amanda," "Luckenbach, Texas"), born Littlefield, TX, June 15, 1937.

Nicola Pagett, 53, actress ("Upstairs Downstairs," *There's a Girl in My Soup, Privates on Parade*), born Cairo, Egypt, June 15, 1945.

Saul Steinberg, 84, artist, cartoonist, born Rimnicu-Sarat, Romania, June 15, 1914.

Jim Varney, 49, actor ("Hey Vern, It's Ernest," *Ernest Goes to Camp, The Beverly Hillbillies*), born Lexington, KY, June 15, 1949.

June 1998

S	M	T	W	T	F	S
	1	2	3	4	5	6
7	8	9	10	11	12	13
14	15	16	17	18	19	20
21	22	23	24	25	26	27
28	29	30				

JUNE 16 — TUESDAY

Day 167 — 198 Remaining

BLOOMSDAY: ANNIVERSARY. June 16, 1904. Anniversary of events in Dublin (June 16, 1904) recorded in James Joyce's *Ulysses*, whose central character is Leopold Bloom.

BURLINGTON STEAMBOAT DAYS/AMERICAN MUSIC FESTIVAL. June 16–21 (tentative). Mississippi Riverfront at Port of Burlington, IA. 36th annual. Week-long event offers community and visitors a chance to enjoy top-name entertainment and a carnival setting. Est attendance: 100,000. For info: Steamboat Days, PO Box 271, Burlington, IA 52601. Phone: (319) 754-4334.

GRIFFIN, JOHN HOWARD: BIRTH ANNIVERSARY. June 16. American author and photographer deeply concerned about racial problems in US. To better understand blacks in the American South, Griffin blackened his skin by the use of chemicals and ultraviolet light, keeping a journal as he traveled through the South, resulting in his best-known book, *Black Like Me*. Born at Dallas, TX, June 16, 1920. Died at Fort Worth, TX, Sept 9, 1980.

LADIES' DAY INITIATED IN BASEBALL: ANNIVERSARY. June 16, 1883. The New York Giants hosted the first Ladies' Day baseball game on June 16, 1883. Both escorted and unescorted ladies were admitted to the game free.

LAST DUSKY SEASIDE SPARROW: DEATH ANNIVERSARY. June 16, 1987. The last survivor of dusky seaside sparrows, whose habitat was a 10-mile stretch of marshland on Florida's east coast (near Titusville), died at age 12, on June 16, 1987. The last specimen, named "Orange Band," lived its last days in a cage at Walt Disney World. For possible experimental cloning its heart and lungs were frozen and preserved.

LAUREL, STAN: BIRTH ANNIVERSARY. June 16, 1890. Worked with Oliver Hardy as Laurel & Hardy for more than 30 years. Known for the comedy sketch "Who's On First?" Born at Ulverston, England. Laurel died Feb 23, 1965 at Santa Monica, CA.

NATIONAL CLAY WEEK FESTIVAL. June 16–20. City Park, Uhrichsville, OH. The fest commemorates the heritage of the valley as the "Clay Center of the World." Midway and parade. For info: Barbara Roberts, 3360 Simpson Rd SE, Dennison, OH 44621.

PETIT JEAN ANTIQUE AUTO SHOW AND SWAP MEET. June 16–21. Petit Jean Mountain, Morrilton, AR. 40th annual show and meet with more than 100 antique and classic cars competing for awards, from turn-of-the-century to 1972 models. More than 1,400 vendor spaces filled with antique cars, parts and related items. Also, arts and crafts. Est attendance: 90,000. For info: Buddy Hoelzeman, Museum of Automobiles, 8 Jones Lane, Morrilton, AR 72110. Phone: (501) 727-5427. Fax: (501) 727-5427.

"THE ROWAN AND MARTIN SHOW" TV PREMIERE: ANNIVERSARY. June 16, 1966. "The Rowan and Martin Show" was an hour-long variety series hosted by "Laugh-In" comedians Dan Rowan and Dick Martin. It was a summer replacement for "The Dean Martin Show." Also on the show were Lainie Kazan, Frankie Randall, Judi Rolin, Dom DeLuise, the Wisa D'Orso Dancers and Les Brown and his band.

SPACE MILESTONE: FIRST WOMAN IN SPACE, *VOSTOK 6* (USSR): 35th ANNIVERSARY. June 16, 1963. Valentina Tereshkova, 26, former cotton-mill worker, born on collective farm near Yaroslavl, USSR, became the first woman in space when her spacecraft, *Vostok 6*, took off from the Tyuratam launch site on June 16, 1963. She manually controlled *Vostok 6* during the 70.8-hour flight through 48 orbits of Earth and landed by parachute (separate from her cabin) on June 19, 1963. In November 1963 she married cosmonaut Andrian Nikolayev, who had piloted *Vostok 3* through 64 earth orbits, Aug 11–15, 1962. Their child Yelena (1964) was the first born to space-traveler parents.

BIRTHDAYS TODAY

Billy "Crash" Craddock, 59, singer ("Don't Destroy Me," "Ruby, Baby"), born Greensboro, NC, June 16, 1939.
Roberto Duran, 47, boxer, born Chorillo, Panama, June 16, 1951.
Neil Goldschmidt, 58, former governor of Oregon (D), born Eugene, OR, June 16, 1940.
Katharine Graham, 81, newspaper executive (*The Washington Post*), born New York, NY, June 16, 1917.
Cobi Jones, 28, soccer player, played in 1994 World's Cup, born Westlake Village, CA, June 16, 1970.
Laurie Metcalf, 43, actress ("Roseanne" [Emmy Award, 1992], *Desperately Seeking Susan*), born Edwardsville, IL, June 16, 1955.
Joyce Carol Oates, 60, writer (*Triumph of the Spider Monkey, The Time Traveler*), born Lockport, NY, June 16, 1938.
Irving Penn, 81, photographer, born Plainfield, PA, June 16, 1917.
Wayne Monte ("Tree") Rollins, 43, basketball player, born Winter Haven, FL, June 16, 1955.
Erich Segal, 61, author (*Acts of Faith; Man, Woman and Child; Love Story*), born Brooklyn, NY, June 16, 1937.
Joan Van Ark, 55, actress (Val on "Knots Landing"), born New York, NY, June 16, 1943.

JUNE 17 — WEDNESDAY

Day 168 — 197 Remaining

AMISH COUNTRY GOSPEL JUBILEE. June 17–20. Tuscarawas County Fairgrounds, Dover, OH. The largest gospel music event held in Ohio. Thousands of gospel music fans from the US and Canada will converge on Dover, in the heart of Amish territory. Days will be filled exploring the nostalgic sights of beautiful Amish country and evenings will be filled with the joyous sounds of great Gospel music. Annually, beginning the third Wednesday in June. Est attendance: 15,000. For info: Spencer Ministries, 2225 Amoy West Rd, Mansfield, OH 44903. Phone: (419) 747-3669. Fax: (419) 747-3668.

BELLAMY, RALPH: BIRTH ANNIVERSARY. June 17, 1904. American actor Ralph Rexford Bellamy was born at Chicago, IL. He appeared in more than 100 films and was best known for his stage and film portrayals of President Franklin D. Roosevelt. He was a founder of the Screen Actors' Guild and president of Actors' Equity. Bellamy was awarded an honorary Academy Award in 1987. He died on Nov 29, 1991 at Los Angeles, CA.

BUNKER HILL DAY. June 17. Suffolk County, MA. Legal holiday in the county in commemoration of the Battle of Bunker Hill that took place on this day in 1775.

CANADA: WESTERN CANADA FARM PROGRESS SHOW. June 17–20. Regina Exhibition Park, Regina, Saskatchewan. Newest innovations in agriculture and technology for farmers, manufacturers and distributors. Commercial displays, lectures and demonstrations, seminars, fashion shows. Est attendance: 40,000. For info: Tourism Saskatchewan, 500-1900 Albert St, Regina, Sask, Canada S4P 4L9. Phone: (800) 667-7191 or (306) 781-9200. Email: travel.info@sasktourism.sk.ca. WWW: http://www.sasktourism.com

CHICKEN CLUCKING CONTEST. June 17. Broadway Market Square, Baltimore, MD. Amateur chicken cluckers compete for trophies and "poultry-related" prizes. Country music band performs throughout the event. Est attendance: 250. For info: Office of Adventures in Fun, Dept of Recreation and Parks, Patterson Park Recreation Complex, 2601 E Baltimore St, Baltimore, MD 21224. Phone: (410) 396-9177. Fax: (410) 327-4129.

EVENING CONCERTS AT THE ZOO. June 17–Aug 13 (Wednesdays and Thursdays only). Metro Washington Park Zoo, Portland, OR. "Your Zoo and All That Jazz" on Wednesdays; "Rhythm & Zoo" on Thursdays. Send a SASE for schedule (available early June). Est attendance: 64,000. For info: Events Coord, Metro Washington Park Zoo, 4001 SW Canyon Rd, Portland, OR 97221-2799. Phone: (503) 226-1561. Fax: (503) 220-5754.

FAIN, SAMMY: BIRTH ANNIVERSARY. June 17, 1902. American composer Sammy Fain was born Samuel Feinberg at New York, NY. He won an Academy Award for his song "Secret Love" from *Calamity Jane* (1953) and for "Love Is a Many-Splendored Thing" from the film of the same name (1955). He died on Dec 6, 1989 at Los Angeles, CA.

"HAWKINS FALLS" TV PREMIERE: ANNIVERSARY. June 17, 1950. This serial was originally titled "Hawkins Falls, Pop. 6200," and it was broadcast first in the evening for the summer and then in the daytime for the rest of its run. It was about life in a small town. It featured Bernadine Flynn as Lona Drewer Carey, Michael Golda as her husband Dr. Floyd Carey, Win Stracke as Laif Flaigle, Ros Twohey as Millie Flaigle, Helen Bernie as Betty Sawtel, Russ Reed as Spec Bassett, featuring Elmira Roessler as Elmira Cleebe.

HERSEY, JOHN: BIRTH ANNIVERSARY. June 17, 1914. American novelist, born at Tientsin, China, who wrote *A Bell for Adano*, which won the Pulitzer Prize in 1945. *The Wall* and *Hiroshima* are both based on fact and set in Poland and Japan in World War II. Died at Key West, FL, Mar 24, 1993.

HOOPER, WILLIAM: BIRTH ANNIVERSARY. June 17. Signer of the Declaration of Independence, born at Boston, MA, June 17, 1742. Died Oct 14, 1790.

ICELAND: INDEPENDENCE DAY. June 17. Anniversary of founding of republic is major festival, especially in Reykjavik. Parades, competitions, street dancing.

JEFFERSON AWARDS. June 17–19. US Supreme Court, Washington, DC. The Jefferson Awards were founded in 1972 by Jacqueline Kennedy Onassis and Senator Robert Taft, Jr, to honor the highest ideals and achievements in the field of public service in the United States. Each year in the US Supreme Court nine winners are selected in the following categories: US Senator John Heinz Award for Greatest Public Service by an Elected or Appointed Official, S. Roger Horchow Award for Greatest Public Service by a Private Citizen, Greatest Public Service Benefiting the Disadvantaged, Greatest Public Service by an Individual Thirty-Five Years and Under and Jacqueline Kennedy Onassis Award for Outstanding Public Service Benefiting Local Communities. One winner receives the award in each of the first four categories, and five unsung heroes are selected in the last category. For info: Mike Hyland, Exec Dir, American Institute for Public Service, 621 Delaware St, Ste 300, New Castle, DE 19720. Phone: (302) 323-9659. Fax: (302) 323-9352. Email: info@aips.org. WWW: http://www.dca.net/clients/aips/

KIAMICHI OWA-CHITO FESTIVAL OF THE FOREST. June 17–20. Beavers Bend State Park, Broken Bow, OK. A celebration of American Indian culture and of the forest industry. Compete in ax throwing, cross-buck sawing, pole climbing, pole filling and logging to become the "Bull of the Woods." Also kids' games, food booths, princess contest, arts and crafts show, photography contest, battle of the bands, golf tournament, canoe races, archery contest, turkey-calling contest, 5K road race, talent contest and more. Est attendance: 50,000. For info: Chamber of Commerce, PO Box 249, Broken Bow, OK 74728. Phone: (405) 584-3393.

MARTIN, DEAN: BIRTH ANNIVERSARY. June 17, 1917. Actor/singer Dean Martin was born Dino Paul Crocetti, at Steubenville, OH. Martin's career was barely moving in 1946, when he met Jerry Lewis. Together they formed an unforgettable comedy act that carried them both to dizzying heights of success. When the team broke up, Martin found continued success as a singer as well as a Hollywood film star. Unlike so many others in the industry, Dean Martin bowed out of show biz before it became too late to do so gracefully. He died on Dec 25, 1995, at Beverly Hills, CA.

MOON PHASE: LAST QUARTER. June 17. Moon enters Last Quarter phase at 6:38 AM, EDT.

SMACKOVER OIL TOWN FESTIVAL. June 17–20 (tentative). Smackover, AR. A celebration of the impact the oil industry has had on Smackover and the surrounding area. Included is an oil run, arts and crafts, music, an ice cream social and events for all ages. Est attendance: 8,000. For info: Smackover Chamber of Commerce, 206 E 8th, Smackover, AR 71762. Phone: (501) 725-3521. Fax: (501) 725-3624.

SOCCER'S WORLD CUP HELD IN US: ANNIVERSARY. June 17–July 17, 1994. The World Cup soccer games were played in the US for the first time. The international championship is held every four years. The 1994 games began in Chicago on June 17 with a match between Germany and Bolivia and ended in Los Angeles with a final between Brazil and Italy on July 17 with Brazil taking the Cup. Soccer, generally known as football outside the US, is the most popular spectator sport in the world, though it has never achieved great status in the US above the amateur level. The games were watched on television by billions of fans around the world.

SONOMA-MARIN FAIR. June 17–21. Petaluma Fairgrounds, Petaluma, CA. Annual country fair with livestock exhibitions, flowers, carnival and entertainment. Est attendance: 64,000. For info: Sonoma-Marin Fair, 100 Gnoss Concourse, Petaluma, CA 94952. Phone: (707) 763-0931. Fax: (707) 763-0212.
Email: ehirsch@pacbell.net.

SOUTH AFRICA REPEALS LAST APARTHEID LAW: ANNIVERSARY. June 17. On June 17, 1991, the Parliament of South Africa repealed the Population Registration Act, removing the law that was the foundation of apartheid. The law, first enacted in 1950, required the classification by race of all South Africans at birth. It established four compulsory racial categories: white, mixed race, Asian and black. Although this marked the removal of the last of the apartheid laws, blacks in South Africa still could not vote.

STRAVINSKY, IGOR FYODOROVICH: BIRTH ANNIVERSARY. June 17, 1882. Russian composer and author, born at Oranienbaum (near Leningrad). Among his best-known music: the ballets *The Firebird, Petrushka* and *The Rite of Spring*; the choral work *Symphony of Psalms*; and the serialist *Abraham and Isaac, A Sacred Ballet.* Died at New York, NY, on Apr 6, 1971.

June 1998

S	M	T	W	T	F	S
	1	2	3	4	5	6
7	8	9	10	11	12	13
14	15	16	17	18	19	20
21	22	23	24	25	26	27
28	29	30				

WATERGATE DAY. June 17. Anniversary of arrests at Democratic Party Headquarters (in Watergate complex, Washington, DC) on June 17, 1972, which led to revelations of political espionage, threats of imminent impeachment of the president and, on Aug 9, 1974, the resignation of President Richard M. Nixon.

WESLEY, JOHN: BIRTH ANNIVERSARY. June 17, 1703. Born at Epworth, England. Wesley, along with his younger brother Charles, was the founder of Methodism. John Wesley died Mar 2, 1791.

WHITEWATER WEDNESDAY. June 17. Kernville, CA. One-hour and two-hour raft trips on the wild and scenic Kern River. Lunch included. Est attendance: 800. For info: Kernville Chamber of Commerce, PO Box 397, Kernville, CA 93238. Phone: (619) 376-2629. Fax: (619) 376-4371. Email: kcc@kernvalley.com.

BIRTHDAYS TODAY

Newt Gingrich, 55, Speaker of the House, born Harrisburg, PA, June 17, 1943.

Elroy Leon ("Crazylegs") Hirsch, 75, Pro Football Hall of Fame end/halfback, born Wausau, WI, June 17, 1923.

Guy Hunt, 65, former governor of Alabama (R), born Holly Pond, AL, June 17, 1933.

Dan Jansen, 33, speed skater, sportscaster, born West Allis, WI, June 17, 1965.

Greg Kinnear, 35, actor (*Sabrina*), born Logansport, IN, June 17, 1963.

Mark Linn-Baker, 45, actor ("Perfect Strangers," *My Favorite Year*), born St. Louis, MO, June 17, 1953.

Barry Manilow, 52, singer ("Mandy," "I Write the Songs"), songwriter, born Brooklyn, NY, June 17, 1946.

Joe Piscopo, 47, comedian (former "Saturday Night Live" regular), born Passaic, NJ, June 17, 1951.

☆ ☆ ☆

JUNE 18 — THURSDAY

Day 169 — 196 Remaining

BATTLE OF WATERLOO: ANNIVERSARY. June 18. Commemorates decisive defeat of Napoleon by Wellington and Blucher, near Waterloo in central Belgium, in 1815.

BOARDWALK ART SHOW. June 18–21. Virginia Beach, VA. 43rd annual. The works of nearly 400 artists are displayed along the boardwalk in this nationally ranked fine art and crafts show and sale. Annually, on Father's Day weekend. Est attendance: 300,000. For info: Virginia Beach Center for the Arts, 2200 Parks Ave, Virginia Beach, VA 23451. Phone: (757) 425-0000. Fax: (757) 425-8186.

CAHN, SAMMY: 85th BIRTH ANNIVERSARY. June 18, 1913. Tin Pan Alley legend Sammy Cahn was born Samuel Cohen, June 18, 1913, at New York City. His first songwriting hit was "Rhythm Is Our Business," which he wrote in collaboration with Saul Chaplin. He was nominated for 26 Academy Awards and won four times for "Three Coins in the Fountain" (1954), "All the Way" (1957), "High Hopes" (1959) and "Call Me Irresponsible" (1963). In the late 1940s he began working with composer Jimmy Van Heusen, and the two in essence were the personal songwriting team for Frank Sinatra for a time. Cahn wrote the greatest number of Sinatra hits, including "Love and Marriage," "The Second Time Around," "High Hopes" and "The Tender Trap." His autobiography, *I Should Care*, was published in 1974. Sammy Cahn died Jan 15, 1993, at Los Angeles.

CANADA: SAM STEELE DAYS. June 18–21. Cranbrook, British Columbia. Parade, Sweetheart Pageant, banquet and ball, Tug-Of-War, elephant hunt, railway museum tours and much more. Est attendance: 19,000. For info: Sam Steele Society, PO Box 115, Cranbrook, BC, Canada V1C 4H6. Phone: (250) 426-4161. Fax: (250) 426-3873.
Email: cbkchamber@cyberlink.bc.ca.

CHIPPEWA VALLEY COUNTRY FEST. June 18–21. Cadott, WI. Country music's best. On-site camping available. Annually, the third weekend in June. Est attendance: 120,000. For info: Chippewa Valley Music Festivals, 2309 W Cameron St, Eau Claire, WI 54703. Phone: (800) 326-FEST. Fax: (715) 832-8556. Email: cvmf@discover-net.net.

DAHLONEGA BLUEGRASS FESTIVAL. June 18–20. Cherokee, NC. 24th annual festival featuring bluegrass music. For info: Norman Adams, Dahlonega Bluegrass Fest, PO Box 98, Dahlonega, GA 30533. Phone: (706) 864-7203. Fax: (706) 864-1037.

FIRST AMERICAN WOMAN IN SPACE: 15th ANNIVERSARY. June 18, 1983. Dr. Sally Ride, 32-year-old physicist and pilot, functioned as a "mission specialist" and became the first American woman in space on June 18, 1983, when she began a six-day mission aboard the space shuttle *Challenger*. The "near-perfect" mission was launched from Cape Canaveral, FL, and landed, June 24, 1983, at Edwards Air Force Base, CA. See also: "Ride, Sally Kristen: Birthday" (May 26) and "Space Milestone: First Woman in Space" (June 16).

FOLGER, HENRY CLAY, JR: BIRTH ANNIVERSARY. June 18. American businessman and industrialist who developed one of the finest collections of Shakespeareana in the world and bequeathed it (The Folger Shakespeare Library, Washington, DC) to the American people. Born at New York, NY, on June 18, 1857. Died June 11, 1930.

FORT UNION TRADING POST RENDEZVOUS. June 18–21. Williston, ND. Re-creation of the furtrade era. Fur trade fair, music, blacksmith and craft demonstrations. Sponsor: National Park Service, Fort Union Trading Post. Est attendance: 5,600. For info: Fort Union Trading Post, RR 3 Box 71, Williston, ND 58801. Phone: (701) 572-9083. Fax: (701) 572-7321.

HUCKLEBERRY HOUSE FOUNDED: ANNIVERSARY. June 18, 1967. San Francisco, CA. The nation's first teenage runaway service originally opened at 1 Broderick St in San Francisco on June 18, 1967. Celebrating 30 years of assisting runaway and at-risk youth as well as providing family preservation counseling. For info: Bruce Fisher, Exec Dir, Youth Advocacy, Inc, 285 12th Ave, San Francisco, CA 94118.

ILLINOIS SHAKESPEARE FESTIVAL. June 18–Aug 8 (tentative). Ewing Manor, Bloomington, IL. Productions of three Shakespeare plays presented under the stars on alternating nights. This professional summer theater company hires creative talent from throughout the US. Est attendance: 12,500. For info: Illinois Shakespeare Festival, Campus Box 5700, Normal, IL 61790-5700. Phone: (309) 438-2535 (ticket office).
Email: theatre@oratmail.cfa.ilstu.edu.
WWW: http://www.orat.ilstu.edu/shakespeare

INLAND SEA SYMPOSIUM. June 18–21. Bayfield, WI. 11th annual. Annual freshwater celebration at the Red Cliff Chippewa Reservation that draws people from around the world. Participants can choose from 12 paddle excursions, five "on water" classes, family programs and various workshops covering camping, eco-systems management and environmental ethics topics. For info: Wisconsin Dept of Tourism, Inland Sea Symposium, PO Box 7976, Madison, WI 53707. Phone: (715) 779-3320. Email: tourism@laughlin.com. WWW: http://tourism.state.wi.us

JIM GIBBONS MEMORIAL 5K RUN/WALK. June 18. Columbia Yacht Club, Chicago, IL. Races for men and women and a noncompetitive walk in the memory of WLS-TV investigative reporter Jim Gibbons, who succumbed to leukemia in 1994. Proceeds benefit the Leukemia Research Foundation. Annually, the third Thursday in June. Est attendance: 2,000. For info: Merton G. Silbar, PR, 1812 Glenview Rd, Glenview, IL 60025. Phone: (847) 729-7333. Fax: (847) 729-4208.

JUNE SUWANNEE RIVER JUBILEE. June 18–20. Live Oak, FL. Join the Dixie Echoes, Florida Boys and other great and talented music groups at the beautiful amphitheater. Est attendance: 10,000. For info: Spirit of the Suwannee Music Park, 3076 95th Dr, Live Oak, FL 32060. Phone: (904) 364-1683. Fax: (904) 364-2998. Email: spirit@musicliveshere.com.
WWW: http://www.musicliveshere.com

KYSER, KAY: BIRTH ANNIVERSARY. June 18. American bandleader whose band, "Kay Kyser's Kollege of Musical Knowledge," enjoyed immense popularity in the swing era. He was born James King Kern Kyser at Rocky Mount, NC, on June 18, 1906. Kyser, a shrewd showman and performer, said he never learned to read music or play an instrument. Among his hit recordings were "Three Little Fishes" and "Praise the Lord and Pass the Ammunition," a World War II favorite. Kyser retired from show business in 1951 and died at Chapel Hill, NC, July 23, 1985.

MALLORY, GEORGE LEIGH: BIRTH ANNIVERSARY. June 18. English explorer and mountain climber born at Mobberley, Cheshire, England, June 18, 1886. Last seen climbing through the mists toward the summit of the highest mountain in the world, Mount Everest, on the morning of June 8, 1924. Best remembered for his answer when asked why he wanted to climb Mount Everest: "Because it is there."

MISS LOUISIANA PAGEANT. June 18–20. Monroe Civic Center, Monroe, LA. Preliminaries followed by the main event of crowning the new Miss Louisiana. For info: Tourism Sales Mgr, Monroe-W Monroe CVB, PO Box 6054, Monroe, LA 71211. Phone: (318) 322-5161.

NATIONAL SPLURGE DAY ©. June 18. Today is the day to go out and do something indulgent. Have fun! For info: Adrienne Sioux Koopersmith, 1437 W Rosemont, #1W, Chicago, IL 60660-1319. Phone: (773) 743-5341. Fax: (773) 743-5395. Email: kooper@interaccess.com.

OLD FORT RIVER FESTIVAL. June 18–20. Fort Smith, AR. Multifaceted festival including juried arts and crafts, large all-free children's area, two stages with continuous international touring entertainment, ethnic foods and beverages. Annually, Father's Day weekend. Sponsor: Old Fort River Festival, Inc. Est attendance: 30,000. For info: Kathy Liggett, Exec Dir, Old Fort River Fest, PO Box 3025, Fort Smith, AR 72913. Phone: (501) 783-6363.

PAPILLION DAYS. June 18–21. City Park, Papillion, NE. Carnival, arts and crafts, food, games, fireworks, kiddie parade, road rally, baby races, grand parade, adult dance, teen pool party, barbecue, pancake breakfast and free entertainment under a "Big Top Tent." Gospel sing, band concert and ice cream social conclude the weekend festivities. Annually, Father's Day weekend. Est attendance: 30,000. For info: Papillion Days, 146 N Adams, Papillion, NE 68046. Phone: (402) 597-1111.

PORTER, SYLVIA: 85th BIRTH ANNIVERSARY. June 18, 1913. American financial journalist Sylvia Feldman Porter was born June 18, 1913, at Patchogue, NY. Her column was syndicated by the *Los Angeles Times*, reaching 450 newspapers worldwide. She also wrote more than 20 books and was noted for her ability to turn complex economic language into readable prose. Porter died on June 5, 1991, at Pound Ridge, NY.

PRAIRIE VILLA RENDEZVOUS. June 18–21. Prairie du Chien, WI. Rendezvous with history and learn about life during the fur trading days and experience the fur trader lifestyle firsthand. Many participants come from around the country to display furs, others demonstrate the cumbersome process of loading a rifle with gunpowder and some prepare Indian fry bread and buffalo burgers. Workshops offer information on a variety of subjects including plants and medicines, basket weaving and beadworking. With more than 600 lodges and teepees, this is one of the largest Midwest trading rendezvous. Est attendance: 25,000. For info: Wisconsin Dept of Tourism, Prairie Villa Rendezvous, PO Box 7976, Madison, WI 53707. Phone: (800) 732-1673. Email: tourism@laughlin.com. WWW: http://tourism.state.wi.us

SEYCHELLES: CONSTITUTION DAY. June 18. National holiday.

SHAKESPEARE ON THE GREEN. June 18–21 (also June 15–28; July 2–5). Elmwood Park, Univ of Nebraska, Omaha, NE. Nonprofit professional presentations of the works of William Shakespeare in a beautiful outdoor setting for the families of the Great Plains region. One of a handful of "free" festivals across the country. Includes pre-show seminars and workshops. Picnic area and concessions, Elizabethan entertainment featuring music, dancing, singing, juggling and acrobatics. Help to support the festival is welcome. Est attendance: 30,000. For info: Michael Markey, Managing Dir, Nebraska Shakespeare Festival, Dept of Fine Arts, Creighton Univ, Omaha, NE 68178. Phone: (402) 280-2391. Email: neshakes@creighton.edu.

SPACE MILESTONE: *CHALLENGER STS-7* (US). June 18, 1983. Shuttle *Challenger*, launched from Kennedy Space Center, FL, with crew of five, including Sally K. Ride (first American woman in space), Robert Crippen, Norman Thagard, John Fabian and Frederick Houck. Landed at Edwards Air Force Base, CA, on June 24 after a near-perfect six-day mission.

SUMMERFEST ART FAIRE & JAZZ FESTIVAL. June 18–20. Tabernacle Square, Logan, UT. Celebrating the arts events include live musical theater, benefit evening and children's activities. The three-day art fair features various arts demonstrations, exhibiting artists and artisans and a fine arts exhibit. Call for jazz festival lineup. Annually, Father's Day weekend. Est attendance: 25,000. For info: Cache Valley Health Care Foundation, 1400 North 500 E, Logan, UT 84341. Phone: (801) 750-5430. Email: Lokexcel@ihc.com.

TOPS INTERNATIONAL RECOGNITION DAYS. June 18–20. Milwaukee, WI. TOPS (Take Off Pounds Sensibly), the leading non-profit international weight management group, will draw thousands of people throughout the world to celebrate 50 years of weight-loss support and success. Features include numerous group seminars and workshops, celebration activities and ceremonial events honoring members' weight-loss successes. Est attendance: 4,000. For info: Susan Trones, TOPS Club, Inc, 4575 S Fifth St, Milwaukee, WI 53207. Phone: (414) 482-4620. WWW: http://www.tops.org

US OPEN (GOLF) CHAMPIONSHIP. June 18–21. Congressional Country Club, Bethesda, MD. For info: US Golf Assn, Golf House, Championship Dept, Far Hills, NJ 07931. Phone: (908) 234-2300. Fax: (908) 234-9687. Email: usga@ix.netcom.com. WWW: http://www.usga.org

WAR OF 1812: DECLARATION ANNIVERSARY. June 18. After much debate in Congress between "hawks" such as Henry Clay and John Calhoun, and "doves" such as John Randolph, Congress issued a declaration of war on Great Britain on June 18, 1812. The action was prompted primarily by Britain's violation of America's rights on the high seas and British incitement of Indian warfare on the frontier. War was seen by some as a way to acquire Florida and Canada. The hostilities ended with the signing of the Treaty of Ghent on Dec 24, 1814, at Ghent, Belgium.

BIRTHDAYS TODAY

Roger Joseph Ebert, 56, film critic ("Siskel and Ebert"), born Urbana, IL, June 18, 1942.

Carol Kane, 46, actress (*Hester Street, The Princess Bride*, "Taxi"), born Cleveland, OH, June 18, 1952.

Donald Keene, 76, literary critic, translator, educator, born New York, NY, June 18, 1922.

Paul McCartney, 56, singer, songwriter (the Beatles, Wings), born Liverpool, England, June 18, 1942.

John D. Rockefeller IV, 61, US Senator (D, West Virginia), born New York, NY, June 18, 1937.

Isabella Rossellini, 46, model, actress (*Blue Velvet, Cousin*), born Rome, Italy, June 18, 1952.

Tom Wicker, 72, journalist, author (*One of Us: Richard Nixon & the American Dream*), born Hamlet, NC, June 18, 1926.

JUNE 19 — FRIDAY

Day 170 — 195 Remaining

AEROSPACE AMERICA. June 19–21. Will Rogers World Airport, Oklahoma City, OK. Considered one of the top five air shows in the world. More than 100 military aircraft, 85 warbirds, top aerobatic performers in the world, trade show. Annually, Father's Day weekend. Est attendance: 100,000. For info: Oklahoma City All Sports Assn, 100 W Main, Ste 285, Oklahoma City, OK 73102. Phone: (405) 236-5000. Fax: (405) 236-5008.

ANTIQUES ON THE BAY. June 19–20. St. Ignace, MI. 2nd annual show for antique and classical original vehicles 1973 or older. Special tours and awards plus auto world celebrities. For info: Nostalgia Productions, Inc, 268 Hillcrest Blvd, St. Ignace, MI 49781. Phone: (906) 643-8087 or (906) 643-0313. Fax: (906) 643-9784. Email: EDREAVIE@NOSTALGAPROD.COM.

BASCOM, EARL W.: BIRTH ANNIVERSARY. June 19, 1906. Rodeo showman and pioneer, Earl W. Bascom was born at Vernal, UT. During his career he developed the first side-delivery rodeo chute (1916), the first hornless bronc saddle (1922) and the first one-handed bareback rigging (1924). He produced the

June 1998

S	M	T	W	T	F	S
	1	2	3	4	5	6
7	8	9	10	11	12	13
14	15	16	17	18	19	20
21	22	23	24	25	26	27
28	29	30				

first rodeo in Mississippi and also produced the first rodeo performed at night under electric lights (1935). Bascom died Aug 28, 1995, at Victorville, CA.

BAYOU BOOGALOO AND CAJUN FOOD FESTIVAL. June 19–21. Town Point Park, Norfolk, VA. For this 9th annual festival Town Point Park transforms itself into the big bayou complete with hot cajun and zydeco music, spicy foods and even hotter dancing and entertainment. Est attendance: 50,000. For info: Marketing Dir, Festevents, 120 W Main St, Norfolk, VA 23510. Phone: (757) 441-2345. Fax: (757) 441-5198.

CANADA: JAZZ CITY INTERNATIONAL MUSIC FESTIVAL. June 19–28. Edmonton, Alberta. The Jazz City Festival is an annual 10-day celebration of jazz, blues and world-beat music featuring local, national and international artists. Est attendance: 125,000. For info: Jazz City Festival Soc, 10516 77 Ave NW, Edmonton, Alta T6E 1N1, Canada. Phone: (403) 432-7166. Fax: (403) 433-3779. Email: jazzcity@worldweb.com. WWW: http://www.discoveredmonton.com/jazzcity/

CANADA: MIDNIGHT MADNESS. June 19. Inuvik. Celebrates the summer solstice (24 hours of sunlight) with a variety of community events including the Midnight Sun Fun Run, walk or jog, music, midnight swim and dancing in Jim Koe Park, latenight sidewalk sales and other events. Annually, the Friday closest to summer solstice. For info: Recreation Coord, Box 1160, Inuvik, Canada X0E 0T0. Phone: (403) 979-2607. Fax: (403) 979-2071. Email: townrecl@inuvik.net.
WWW: http://www.inuvik.net

CANADA: SASKTEL SASKATCHEWAN JAZZ FESTIVAL. June 19–28. Saskatoon, Sask. 12th annual. Emphasis on mainstream jazz and a wide variety of other styles from Dixieland and blues to contemporary fusion and gospel. More than 370 musicians and 125 performances (most free), plus workshops, seminars and videos. Live jazz and blues in a number of lounges. Est attendance: 45,000. For info: Tourism Saskatchewan, 500-1900 Albert St, Regina, Sask, Canada S4P 4L9. Phone: (800) 667-7191 or (306) 652-1421.
Email: travel.info@sasktourism.sk.ca.
WWW: http://www.sasktourism.com

CITY STAGES MUSIC FESTIVAL. June 19–21. Linn Park, Birmingham, AL. Music and heritage festival featuring local and nationally known talent on 16 stages, folklife festival, children's festival, jazz camp and classical music oasis. Annually, Father's Day weekend. Est attendance: 265,000. For info: City Stages, PO Box 2266, Birmingham, AL 35201. Phone: (205) 251-1272. Fax: (205) 323-7074. Email: jennifer@citystages.org.
WWW: http://www.citystages.org

CZECH DAYS. June 19–20. Tabor, SD. Czechs dressed in their festive costumes gather with people from all parts of the world in this gala celebration. Fine Czech foods, dancing, music and entertainment. Also in conjunction with this 50th annual Czech Days celebration, the town of Tabor will be celebrating its 125th anniversary. Est attendance: 15,000. For info: Tabor Area Chamber of Commerce, Inc, Box 21, Tabor, SD 57063. Phone: (605) 463-2476.

DALESBURG MIDSUMMER FESTIVAL. June 19. Dalesburg Lutheran Church, rural Vermillion, SD. Celebration of Scandinavian and rural heritage. Dances to raise the Midsummer Pole, a smorgasbord, arts and crafts area, band concert and more. Est attendance: 1,000. For info: Ronald Johnson, Midsummer Committee, Dalesburg Midsummer Festival, 30595 University Rd, Vermillion, SD 57069-6507. Phone: (605) 253-2575.

DENMARK: VIKING FESTIVAL. June 19–July 5. Frederiksund (about 25 miles northwest of Copenhagen). Famous outdoor plays based on Danish legends. Annually, the next-to-last Friday in June through the first Sunday in July.

DOLLARS AGAINST DIABETES (DAD'S) DAY. June 19–21. DAD's Day is a national fundraising event conducted in more than 300 cities to help the Diabetes Research Institute find a permanent cure for the disease. Annually, on Father's Day weekend. Sponsor: Building and Construction Trades Dept of the AFL-CIO. Participation 30,000. For info: Dan Feller, VP, The Kamber Group, 1920 L St NW, Ste 700, Washington, DC 20036. Phone: (800) 804-3237 or (202) 223-8700. Fax: (202) 659-5559.

EMANCIPATION DAY IN TEXAS. June 19. In honor of the emancipation of the slaves in Texas on June 19, 1865.

FIRST RUNNING OF THE BELMONT STAKES: ANNIVERSARY. June 19, 1867. The first running of the Belmont Stakes took place at Jerome Park, NY. The team of jockey J. Gilpatrick and his horse Ruthless finished in a time of 3:05. The Belmont Stakes continued at Jerome Park until 1889, then moved to Morris Park, NY, between 1890–1905, and in 1906 settled at Belmont Park, NY, where it has continued to the present day. The Belmont Stakes is the oldest event of horse racing's Triple Crown.

FORTAS, ABE: BIRTH ANNIVERSARY. June 19. Abe Fortas was born June 19, 1910, at Memphis, TN. He was appointed to the Supreme Court by President Lyndon Johnson in 1965. Prior to his appointment he was known as a civil libertarian, having argued cases for government employees and other individuals accused by Senator Joe McCarthy of having communist affiliations. He argued the 1963 landmark Supreme Court case of *Gideon v Wainwright*, which established the right of indigent defendants to free legal aid in criminal prosecutions. In 1968, he was nominated by Johnson to succeed Chief Justice Earl Warren, but his nomination was withdrawn after much conservative opposition in the Senate. In 1969 Fortas became the first Supreme Court Justice to be forced to resign after revelations about questionable financial dealings were made public. Fortas died Apr 5, 1982, at Washington, DC.

FRONTIER ARMY DAYS. June 19–21. Fort Abraham Lincoln State Park, Mandan, ND. Frontier Army re-creation groups reenact frontier military life with demonstrations and living history by infantry, cavalry and "Old Scouts" groups, along with others who populated the fort during its heyday. Est attendance: 3,000. For info: Chuck Erickson, Park Mgr, Fort Abraham Lincoln State Park, Rt 2, Box 139, Mandan, ND 58554. Phone: (701) 663-4758. Fax: (701) 663-9234.

GARFIELD: 20th BIRTHDAY. June 19, 1978. America's favorite lasagna-loving cat is 20. *Garfield*, a modern classic comic strip created by Jim Davis, first appeared on June 19, 1978, and has brought laughter to millions. For info: Paws, Inc, Kim Campbell, 5440 E Co Rd 450 N, Albany, IN 47320.

GEHRIG, LOU: 95th BIRTH ANNIVERSARY. June 19, 1903. Baseball great Henry Louis Gehrig (lifetime batting average of .341), who played in seven World Series, was born at New York, NY, and died there June 2, 1941, from the degenerative muscle disease amyotropic lateral sclerosis, which has become known as Lou Gehrig's disease.

HOWARD, MOE: BIRTH ANNIVERSARY. June 19, 1897. The head stooge in the Three Stooges, Moe Howard was born Moses Horwitz in Bensonhurst, NY. He died at age 77 on May 4, 1975, at Hollywood, CA. Howard began his show business career at age 12 by running errands at Vitagraph studios. He worked with Ted Healy in various comedy and singing acts, and together they teamed with Shemp Howard and Larry Fine in the mid-1920s for an early Stooges act. In 1930 the Stooges made their film debut in *Soup to Nuts*. Although the members of the Three Stooges changed over the years, Moe Howard was one of the constants. Howard appeared in four feature films without the other Stooges. These include *Space Master X-7* and *Doctor Death, Seeker of Souls*.

HUBBARD, ELBERT: BIRTH ANNIVERSARY. June 19. Born at Bloomington, IL, on June 19, 1856, Elbert Green Hubbard, aspiring American author and craftsman, founded the Roycroft Press at East Aurora, NY. Best known of his writings were *A Message to Garcia* and a series of essays titled *Little Journeys*. Hubbard lost his life with the sinking of the *Lusitania*, May 7, 1915.

HUCKFINN JUBILEE. June 19–21. Mojave Narrows Regional Park, Victorville, CA. A Huckfinn celebration with river raft building, country and bluegrass music, hay rides, old time tent circus, crafts and food, plus Route 66 car show and the California Arm Wrestling Championships. Annually, on Father's Day weekend. Est attendance: 12,000. For info: DVT Marketing Enterprises, Inc, PO Box 56419, Riverside, CA 92517. Phone: (909) 780-8810. Email: huckfinn@huckfinn.com. WWW: http://www.huckfinn.com

INTERNATIONAL FESTIVAL OF ARTS AND IDEAS. June 19–28. New Haven Green, New Haven, CT. Hundreds of performers and dozens of events from around the world. For info: Intl Festival of Arts & Ideas, (203) ART-IDEA or Greater New Haven Conv & Visitors Bureau, One Long Wharf Dr, New Haven, CT 06511. Phone: (203) 777-8550 or (800) 332-STAY. Fax: (203) 782-7755.

"I'VE GOT A SECRET" TV PREMIERE: ANNIVERSARY. June 19, 1952. Celebrity panelists tried to guess the guests' secrets on this popular game show; celebrity guests also came on to baffle the panel. Guests whispered their secret to the host and the audience saw it on the screen. The cash prize was so low that the game was played for laughs. Garry Moore hosted the show, followed by Steve Allen and Bill Cullen. Allen Sherman ("My Son the Folk Singer") created the show and most of the celebrity "secrets." Celebrity panelists included Bill Cullen, Betsy Palmer, Henry Morgan, Bess Myerson, Steve Allen and Jayne Meadows.

JUNETEENTH. June 19. Celebrated in Texas and other parts of the Deep South in memory of this day in 1865 when Union General Granger proclaimed the slaves of Texas free.

LAKEFRONT FESTIVAL OF ARTS. June 19–21. Milwaukee Art Museum, Milwaukee, WI. Juried art fair with 185 artists from around the US and Canada. Artist demonstrations, children's activities, food and more. Fundraiser for Milwaukee Art Museum. Museum is open admission-free during the festival. Est attendance: 50,000. For info: Beth Hoffman, Milwaukee Art Museum, Friends of Art, 750 N Lincoln Memorial Dr, Milwaukee, WI 53202. Phone: (414) 224-3850. Fax: (414) 271-7588. Email: hoffman@mam.org. WWW: http://www.mam.org

MEEKER DAYS HOEDOWN & BLUEGRASS FESTIVAL. June 19–21. Downtown Puyallup, WA. Largest street fair in Pierce County features a bluegrass, country, kids and community stage, arts and crafts show, Pontiac/Buick antique car show, farmer's market, children's activities, microbrew garden and much more! Annually, the third week in June. Est attendance: 100,000. For info: Diane Picha, Meeker Days, PO Box 476, Puyallup, WA 98371. Phone: (206) 840-2631. Fax: (206) 840-2943.

MIDNIGHT SUN BASEBALL GAME. June 19. Fairbanks, AK. To celebrate the summer solstice. Game is played without artificial lights at 10:35 PM. Est attendance: 4,000. For info: Alaska Goldpanners, Box 71154, Fairbanks, AK 99707. Phone: (907) 451-0095.

NATIONAL JUGGLING DAY. June 19. Juggling clubs affiliated with the International Jugglers Association in cities all over the world hold local festivals to demonstrate, teach and celebrate their art. For info: Intl Jugglers' Assn, PO Box 218, Montague, MA 01351. Phone: (413) 367-2290. Fax: (413) 367-0259. Email: IJugglersA@aol.com.

NOVA SCOTIA MULTICULTURAL FESTIVAL. June 19–21. Dartmouth, NS. Cultural events include nine tents housing exhibits, food booths, children's tent, performances, beer tent with live bands and fashion show. 14th annual. Annually, the third full weekend in June. Est attendance: 40,000. For info: Barbara Campbell, Exec Dir, Multicultural Assn of Nova Scotia, 1809 Barrington St, Ste 901, Halifax, NS, Canada B3J 3K8. Phone: (902) 423-6534. Fax: (902) 422-0881. Email: multicul@fox.nstn.ca. WWW: http://Fox.NSTN.Ca/~multicul/

PASCAL, BLAISE: 375th BIRTH ANNIVERSARY. June 19, 1623. French philosopher, physicist and mathematician born at Clermont-Ferrand and died at Paris on Aug 19, 1662, at age 39. It was Pascal who said, "Had Cleopatra's nose been shorter, the whole history of the world would have been different." And, in his *Provincial Letters*, he wrote, "I have made this letter longer than usual because I lack the time to make it short."

RED RIVER VALLEY FAIR. June 19–28. Fargo, ND. One of the largest fairs in the state with 4-H and commercial exhibits, horse shows, car shows, large carnival midway, free entertainment. Big-name country western and rock entertainers perform all seven days. For info: (701) 282-2200 or North Dakota Tourism, 604 East Boulevard, Bismarck, ND 58505. Phone: (701) 328-2525 or (800) 435-5663.

ROSENBERG EXECUTION: 45th ANNIVERSARY. June 19, 1953. Anniversary of the electrocution of the only married couple ever executed together in the US. Julius (35) and Ethel (37) Rosenberg were executed for espionage at Sing Sing Prison, Ossining, NY. Time for the execution was advanced several hours to avoid conflict with the Jewish Sabbath. Their conviction has been a subject of controversy over the years.

SOUTH CAROLINA FESTIVAL OF FLOWERS. June 19–21. Greenwood, SC. Come and see the beautiful flowers of South Carolina. Includes arts and crafts displays, entertainment, sports events and more. Est attendance: 25,000. For info: Greenwood Chamber of Commerce, SC Festival of Flowers, PO Box 980, Greenwood, SC 29648. Phone: (864) 223-8411. Fax: (864) 229-9785.

SPACE MILESTONE: *ARIANE* (ESA). June 19, 1981. Launched from Kourou, French Guiana, *Ariane* carried two satellites into orbit: *Meteostat 2*, an ESA weather satellite, and *Apple*, a geostationary communications satellite for India, to be stationed over Sumatra.

SPLINTER FEST. June 19–21. Amana, IA. A woodcraft show with displays, products, demonstrations, equipment, supplies, entertainment, food and fellowship. Annually, the third weekend in June. Sponsors: Personalized Wood Products, Inc. Est attendance: 6,000. For info: Box 193, Amana, IA 52203. Phone: (319) 622-3100. Fax: (319) 622-6395. Email: pwp@www.jeonet.com. WWW: http://www.jeonet.com/amanas/pwp/

WATERFEST WEEKEND. June 19–20. South Sioux City, NE and Sioux City, IA. Festival on the river includes hot-air balloon races, waterski exhibitions, speedboat races, live bands, street hockey tournament, Mighty Mud Mania obstacle course, car show, volleyball tournament, kids' events and concessions/beer garden. Annually, the third weekend in June, unless there are five weekends in June—then the festival is held on the fourth weekend. Est attendance: 5,000. For info: South Sioux City Convention and Visitors Bureau, 2700 Dakota Ave, South Sioux City, NE 68776. Phone: (800) 793-6327. Fax: (402) 494-5010. Email: CVB@siouxland-freenet.com.

WONAGO WORLD CHAMPIONSHIP RODEO. June 19–20. Milwaukee, WI. More than 200 of the best cowboys and cowgirls compete in six professional contests ranging from bronc riding to bull riding for top prize and world championship points. Featuring colorful opening pageantry and Big, Bad BONUS Bulls. Held in conjunction with West Allis Western Days and North America's Largest Horse Drawn Parade on June 18. 41st annual. Est attendance: 10,000. For info: W. Bruce Lehrke, Pres, Longhorn World Chmpshp Rodeo Inc, Natl HQ, PO Box 70159, Nashville, TN 37207. Phone: (615) 876-1016. Fax: (615) 876-4685. Email: lhrodeo@idt.net. WWW: http://www.longhornrodeo.com

June 1998

S	M	T	W	T	F	S
	1	2	3	4	5	6
7	8	9	10	11	12	13
14	15	16	17	18	19	20
21	22	23	24	25	26	27
28	29	30				

WORLD SAUNTERING DAY. June 19. A day to revive the lost art of Victorian sauntering and discourage jogging, lollygagging, sashaying, fast walking and trotting. [Originated by the late W.T. Rabe of Saulte Ste. Marie, MI.]

BIRTHDAYS TODAY

Paula Abdul, 36, singer ("Forever Your Girl"), dancer, choreographer, born Los Angeles, CA, June 19, 1962.

Alan Cranston, 84, former US senator (D, California), born Palo Alto, CA, June 19, 1914.

Charles Gwathmey, 60, architect, born Charlotte, NC, June 19, 1938.

Pauline Kael, 79, critic, born Sonoma County, CA, June 19, 1919.

Nancy Marchand, 70, actress (Mrs Pynchon on "Lou Grant"; *Brain Donors*), born Buffalo, NY, June 19, 1928.

Marisa Pavan, 66, actress (*The Diary of Anne Frank*), born Cagliari, Sardinia, June 19, 1932.

Phylicia Rashad, 50, actress (Claire Huxtable on "The Cosby Show"), born Houston, TX, June 19, 1948.

Gena Rowlands, 62, actress (Adrienne Van Leyden on "Peyton Place"; *A Woman Under the Influence*), born Cambria, WI, June 19, 1936.

Salman Rushdie, 51, author (*The Jaguar Smile, Satanic Verses, Midnight's Children*), born Bombay, India, June 19, 1947.

Kathleen Turner, 44, actress (*Body Heat, Peggy Sue Got Married, Romancing the Stone*), born Springfield, MO, June 19, 1954.

Ann Wilson, 47, singer, musician (lead singer with Heart), born San Diego, CA, June 19, 1951.

JUNE 20 — SATURDAY

Day 171 — 194 Remaining

BOB DAY FESTIVAL. June 20 (tentative). Final date available after Jan 5, 1998. Library Park, Talent, OR. Parade of Bobs, Bob formation, live entertainment, Swell Bob Contest, Bobbyque. Fun for Bobs, families, friends, all those who've ever known a Bob or want to meet one. Est attendance: 1,000. For info: Judy Bunch, Bob Day Headquarters, 2305 S Pacific Hwy, Talent, OR 97540. Phone: (541) 535-7251 or (541) 488-1059.

CANADA: BAZAART. June 20. MacKenzie Art Gallery, Regina, Saskatchewan. Juried outdoor art show and sale with over 100 exhibitors. Broad range of arts and crafts. Stage entertainment, food concession. Est attendance: 20,000. For info: Tourism Saskatchewan, 500-1900 Albert St, Regina, Sask, Canada S4P 4L9. Phone: (800) 667-7191 or (306) 522-4242.
Email: travel.info@sasktourism.sk.ca.
WWW: http://www.sasktourism.com

CANADA: FRIENDSHIP FESTIVAL. June 20–July 5. Fort Erie, Ontario, and Buffalo, NY. Stage entertainment, highland games, horse show, air show, sports tournaments, arts and crafts, custom cars, fireworks, midway, food court and children's festival. Est attendance: 300,000. For info: Tracy Leblanc, Gen Mgr, Friendship Festival, PO Box 1241, Fort Erie, Ont, Canada L2A 5Y2. Phone: (888) 333-1987 or (905) 871-6454. Fax: (905) 871-1266. Email: festival@niagara.com.

CHESNUTT, CHARLES W.: BIRTH ANNIVERSARY. June 20, 1858. Born at Cleveland, OH, Chesnutt was considered by many as the first important black novelist. His collections of short stories included *The Conjure Woman* (1899) and *The Wife of His Youth and Other Stories of the Color Line* (1899). *The Colonel's Dream* (1905) dealt with the struggles of the freed slave. His work has been compared to later writers such as William Faulkner, Richard Wright and James Baldwin. He died Nov 15, 1932, at Cleveland.

CHICAGO BULLS WIN THIRD CONSECUTIVE NBA CHAMPIONSHIP: 5th ANNIVERSARY. June 20, 1993. With a four-games-to-two victory over the Phoenix Suns in the National Basketball Association (NBA) finals the Chicago Bulls earned their third straight NBA title on June 20, 1993. The Bulls became the first team to win three in a row since 1966, when the Boston Celtics won their eighth in a row. In 1996 they won the NBA title for a fourth time and in 1997 for a fifth.

COYOTE CHASE. June 20. Wellington, NV. Annual Beta Sigma Phi 10K and 5K runs and a two mile walk. Pancake breakfast, art, crafts and more. Annually, the third Saturday in June. For info: Mason Valley, Chamber of Commerce, 227 S Main St, Yerington, NV 89447. Phone: (702) 463-2245. Fax: (702) 463-3369.

EASTERN MUSIC FESTIVAL. June 20–Aug 1. Guilford College, Greensboro, NC. 37th annual summer festival of classical concerts and recitals performed by resident professionals and a corps of talented young students from the United States and abroad. Est attendance: 63,000. For info: Evelyn Cottam, Mktg Dir, Eastern Music Festival, PO Box 22026, Greensboro, NC 27420. Phone: (910) 333-7450. Fax: (910) 333-7454. Email: emf@nr.infi.net. WWW: http://www.greensboro.com/emf

"THE ED SULLIVAN SHOW" ("TOAST OF THE TOWN") TV PREMIERE: 50th ANNIVERSARY. June 20, 1948. "The Ed Sullivan Show" was officially titled "Toast of the Town" until 1955. It was the longest-running variety show and the most popular for decades. Ed Sullivan was the host, and he signed all types of acts, both well known and new, trying to have something to please everyone. Thousands of performers appeared, many making their television debut, such as Irving Berlin, Victor Borge, Hedy Lamarr, Walt Disney, and Fred Astaire and Jane Powell. Two acts attracted the largest audience of the time: Elvis Presley and the Beatles.

ENGLAND: BROADSTAIRS DICKENS FESTIVAL. June 20–27. Broadstairs, Kent. Commemorates the association of the famous novelist Charles Dickens to the town of Broadstairs. For info: Mrs Lee Ault, Honorary Festival Organiser, 58 High St, Rooftops, Broadstairs, Kent, England CT10 1JT. Phone: (44) (184) 386-3453.

FIRST BALLOON HONEYMOON: ANNIVERSARY. June 20. Roger Burnham and Eleanor Waring took the first balloon honeymoon on June 20, 1909, ascending at 12:40 PM in the balloon *Pittsfield*. They began their trip at Woods Hole, Cape Cod, MA, and landed at 4:30 PM in an orchard at Holbrook, MA.

FIRST DOCTOR OF SCIENCE DEGREE EARNED BY A WOMAN: ANNIVERSARY. June 20, 1895. Caroline Willard Baldwin became the first woman to earn a doctor of science degree at Cornell University, Ithaca, NY.

FORD THEATER FLOOR COLLAPSE: ANNIVERSARY. June 20, 1893. The floor of the Ford Theater in Washington, DC (the location where John Wilkes Booth shot President Abraham Lincoln), collapsed, killing more than 20 government workers. It was rebuilt as a national monument.

FORT SEWARD WAGON TRAIL. June 20–27. Jamestown, ND. Relive an important part of western history as you travel in a covered wagon across the great prairies region of North Dakota. This year's ride is called the "Prairie Rose Trail" and follows a historic route. Enjoy fresh air, good campfire cooking and sleep under the stars in the great North Dakota sky. For info: (701) 252-6844 or North Dakota Tourism, 604 East Boulevard, Bismarck, ND 58505. Phone: (701) 328-2525 or (800) 435-5663.

GREAT SEAL OF THE UNITED STATES: ANNIVERSARY. June 20, 1782. Charles Thomson, first official record keeper of the US, submitted his report to Congress, recommending a design for the Great Seal, on June 20, 1782. The Congress adopted his report on the same day. See also: "Great Seal of the US: Anniversary" (Jan 28, July 4 and Sept 16).

JAMES RIVER BATTEAU FESTIVAL. June 20–27. Lynchburg, VA to 40 miles west of Richmond, VA. A folklife festival that seeks to combine many different disciplines and community interests into one cultural event. Events include the building, and operation of authentic replicas of the James River Batteaux and arts, crafts and history of the cultural heritage of the James River community. Annually, the Saturday before Father's Day. Est attendance: 10,000. For info: Dian McNaught, James River Batteau Festival, 8667 Sudley Rd, Ste 210, Manassas, VA 20110. Phone: (703) 257-0707. Fax: (703) 257-9498. WWW: http://www.inmind.com/batteau

LIZZIE BORDEN VERDICT: ANNIVERSARY. June 20, 1893. Spectators at her trial cheered when the "not guilty" verdict was read by the jury foreman in the murder trial of Lizzy Borden on this date. Elizabeth Borden had been accused of and tried for the hacking to death of her father and stepmother in their Fall River, MA, home on Aug 4, 1892.

LONGEST DAM RUN. June 20. Glascow, MT. 4th annual. This is a sanctioned 5K and 10K run. There are also 5K and one mile walks. It crosses 1.8 miles of Fort Peck Dam. After two miles into the 10K race, the course rises in elevation from the low point at starting some 350 feet over a distance of approximately two miles. The 5K is flat. Both distances finish running downhill grade from the top of the dam. Annually, the third weekend in June. Est attendance: 550. For info: Glascow Chamber of Commerce and Agriculture, Box 832, Glascow, MT 59230. Phone: (406) 228-2222. Fax: (406) 228-2244.

MADAM LOU BUNCH DAY (WITH "THE ORIGINAL BED RACE"). June 20. Central City, CO. The "richest square mile on earth" celebrates the Madams and Sporting House Girls of a bygone era with "The Original Bed Race," "The Madams and Miners Ball" and much more. Annually, the third Saturday in June. Est attendance: 11,000. For info: Central City Casino Assn, PO Box 773, Central City, CO 80427. Phone: (303) 582-5251. Fax: (303) 642-0429.

MID-AMERICAN SPORT KITE CLASSIC. June 20–21. River Oaks Park, Kalamazoo, MI. A family-oriented sport kite competition, with events for Junior, Novice, Intermediate, Experienced and Master classes. Competitions for Individuals, Teams and Pairs in Precision and Ballet. Sponsors: Kazoo Stringfellows and Battle Creek Cloud Cutters Kite Clubs. Est attendance: 1,500.

June 1998

S	M	T	W	T	F	S
	1	2	3	4	5	6
7	8	9	10	11	12	13
14	15	16	17	18	19	20
21	22	23	24	25	26	27
28	29	30				

For info: John Cosby, Coord, PO Box 2241, Kalamazoo, MI 49003. Phone: (616) 345-5432. Fax: (616) 383-8778.

MIDNIGHT SUN FESTIVAL. June 20–21. Nome, AK. A celebration of the summer solstice, which is when Nome experiences the midnight sun with more than 22 hours of direct sunlight. The festival usually includes a parade, raft race and barbecue. Est attendance: 500. For info: Nome Conv & Visitors Bureau, PO Box 240, Nome, AK 99762. Phone: (907) 443-5535. Fax: (907) 443-5832. WWW: http://www.alaska.net/~nome

MURPHY, AUDIE: BIRTH ANNIVERSARY. June 20, 1924. Born at Kingston, TX, Murphy was the most decorated soldier in World War II and later became an actor in western and war movies. He died May 28, 1971, in a plane crash near Roanoke, VA.

NATIONAL JOUSTING HALL OF FAME JOUSTING TOURNAMENT. June 20. Natural Chimneys Regional Park, Mount Solon, VA. Ring jousting for novice, amateur, semiprofessional and professional jousters. Medieval jousting and Robin Hood skit. Annually, the third Saturday in June. Est attendance: 500. For info: Upper Valley Regional Park Authority, Box 478, Grottoes, VA 24441. Phone: (540) 350-2510. Fax: (540) 350-2140.

NEW OXFORD OUTDOOR ANTIQUE SHOW. June 20. New Oxford, PA. Arts, crafts, antiques and flea market. Annually, the third Saturday in June. Est attendance: 20,000. For info: Gettysburg Conv and Visitors Bureau, 35 Carlisle St, Gettysburg, PA 17325-1899. Phone: (717) 334-6274. Fax: (717) 334-1166. WWW: http://www.gettysburg.com

OPERA FESTIVAL OF NEW JERSEY. June 20–July 18. Kirby Arts Center, The Lawrenceville School, Lawrenceville, NJ. A professional organization founded in 1984 to present opera productions that are accessible to audiences of all ages and backgrounds. New Jersey's leading producer of professional opera, known for creating artistically focused new productions of opera that feature young American artists of excellence. 1998 season will feature three operas, one of which will be a 20th-century work. Est attendance: 11,000. For info: Opera Festival of New Jersey, 228 Alexander St, Princeton, NJ 08540. Phone: (609) 279-1750. Fax: (609) 279-1832. Email: adminop@operafest.org. WWW: http://www.operafest.org/nj

RENO RODEO. June 20–28. Reno, NV. 79th annual. Top professional cowboys ride in one of the west's richest rodeos. Est attendance: 120,000. For info: Reno Rodeo Assn, Box 12335, Reno, NV 89510. Phone: (702) 329-3877 or for tickets: (800) 842-7633.

SOLSTICE CELEBRATION. June 20. State Fairgrounds, Haines, AK. Party to the music of popular regional bands. Enjoy a variety of foods provided by local vendors and savor cold beer on tap in the beer garden adjacent to the stage area. Be ready for lots of entertainment beginning at 5 PM in the "Land of the Midnight Sun." For info: SE Alaska State Fair, Box 385, Haines, AK 99827. Phone: (907) 766-2476. Fax: (907) 766-2478. Email: seasfair@seaknet.alaska.edu.

SPANISH NIGHT WATCH WEEKEND. June 20–22. St. Augustine, FL. Weekend event that includes eighteenth-century historical reenactments, entertainment and storytelling. For info: Patti Rang, (904) 824-9550 or Gilbert & Manjura Marketing, 346 Freeman St, Longwood, FL 33780-4171. Phone: (407) 261-5700. Fax: (407) 261-5710.

SPANISH-AMERICAN WAR SURRENDER OF GUAM TO US: 100th ANNIVERSARY. June 20, 1898. Having not known that a war was in progress and having no ammunition on the island, the Spanish commander of Guam surrendered to Captain Glass of the USS *Charleston* on June 20, 1898.

STONE MOUNTAIN VILLAGE ARTS AND CRAFTS FESTIVAL. June 20–21. Stone Mountain Village, GA. 26th annual juried arts and crafts show featuring over 200 of the southeast's finest artists and crafters. With down-home entertainment and the best country cooking around. Est attendance: 10,000.

For info: Gayle A. Boutin, Dir, Village Festivals, PO Box 667, Stone Mountain Village, GA 30086. Phone: (770) 498-2097.

WEST VIRGINIA: ADMISSION DAY: ANNIVERSARY. June 20, 1863. Became 35th state on this day in 1863. Observed as a holiday in West Virginia.

WMAS 94.7 FM FIRST NIGHT OF SUMMER PARTY. June 20. Northampton, MA. To celebrate the first night of summer, listeners are invited to attend a pool party, including traditional aspects such as hot dogs, hamburgers, volleyball, etc. Est attendance: 400. For info: Dina Cox, PO Box 9500, Springfield, MA 01102. Phone: (413) 737-1414. Fax: (413) 737-1477.

WOMAN RUNS THE HOUSE: ANNIVERSARY. June 20. Miss Alice Robertson of Oklahoma became the first woman to preside in the US House of Representatives on June 20, 1921. Miss Robertson presided for half an hour.

BIRTHDAYS TODAY

Chet Atkins, 74, musician (guitarist who has played all styles; country music legend), born Luttrell, TN, June 20, 1924.

Olympia Dukakis, 67, actress, theatrical director (Oscar for *Moonstruck; Steel Magnolias*), born Lowell, MA, June 20, 1931.

John Goodman, 46, actor ("Roseanne," *The Flintstones*), born Afton, MO, June 20, 1952.

Nicole Kidman, 31, actress (*The Portrait of a Lady, To Die For*), born Hawaii, June 20, 1967.

Martin Landau, 67, actor (*Tucker: The Man and His Dream, Crimes and Misdemeanors* [Golden Globe Award], *Ed Wood* [Academy Award, Best Supporting Actor]), born Brooklyn, NY, June 20, 1931.

Michael Landon, Jr, 34, actor ("Bonanza: The Return" and "Bonanza: The Ghosts"), born Encino, CA, June 20, 1964.

Cyndi Lauper, 45, singer ("Girls Just Want to Have Fun"), born Brooklyn, NY, June 20, 1953.

John Mahoney, 58, actor ("Frasier"), born Manchester, England, June 20, 1940.

Anne Murray, 53, singer (gold album *Country*; "Snowbird," "Could I Have This Dance"), born Springhill, NS, Canada, June 20, 1945.

Lionel Richie, 49, singer ("Truly"), songwriter, born Tuskegee, AL, June 20, 1949.

James Tolkan, 67, actor (*Serpico, Back to the Future, Dick Tracy*), born Calumet, MI, June 20, 1931.

Andre Watts, 52, musician, born Nuremburg, Germany, June 20, 1946.

Brian Wilson, 56, singer (the Beach Boys), songwriter, born Hawthorne, CA, June 20, 1942.

JUNE 21 — SUNDAY

Day 172 — 193 Remaining

AMATEUR RADIO WEEK. June 21–28. To bring amateur radio to the attention of the public. Annually, the week culminating in the fourth weekend of June. For info: PR Coord, American Radio Relay League, 225 Main St, Newington, CT 06111. Phone: (860) 594-0328. Email: jgagne@arrl.org. WWW: http://www.arrl.org

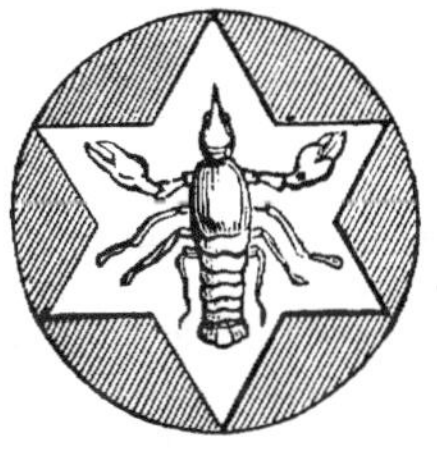

CANCER, THE CRAB. June 21–July 22. In the astronomical/astrological zodiac, which divides the sun's apparent orbit into 12 segments, the period June 21–July 22 is identified, traditionally, as the sun sign of Cancer, the Crab. The ruling planet is the moon.

CARPENTER ANT AWARENESS WEEK. June 21–27. Wood-destroying organisms cause Americans to spend $3.5 billion annually. This week will focus attention on the identification, biology and habits of carpenter ants, and provide consumers with information on the elimination of these costly pests. Annually, the last full week of June. For info: Jerry Batzner, Pres, Batzner Pest Management, Inc, 16700 W Victor Rd, New Berlin, WI 53151. Phone: (414) 797-4160. Fax: (414) 797-4166.

CIVIL RIGHTS WORKERS DISAPPEAR: ANNIVERSARY. June 21, 1964. James Chaney, Andrew Goodman and Michael Schwerner left Meridian, MS, at 9 AM on June 21, 1964, to investigate a church burning at Philadelphia, MS. They were expected back by 4 PM. When they failed to return, a search was begun. Their murdered bodies were found on Aug 4.

DEAF-BLINDNESS AWARENESS WEEK. June 21–27. A week to observe the birth anniversary of Helen Keller who was born on June 27, 1880. Annually, the full week that includes Helen Keller's birthday. For info: Alice L. Hagemeyer, Coordinator of Deaf Awareness Events, FOLDA Inc, 9126 Fowler Ln, Ste 200, Lanham, MD 20706. Phone: (301) 572-5168. Fax: (301) 572-4134. Email: alhagemeyer@juno.com.

EIGHTEENTH-CENTURY WHEAT HARVEST. June 21. The Claude Moore Colonial Farm at Turkey Run, McLean, VA. Help the colonial farm family cut and bind wheat, the farmer's second most important cash crop. Light refreshments and 18th-century games. Annually, the third Sunday in June. Est attendance: 500. For info: Gretchen Brodtman, The Claude Moore Colonial Farm, Turkey Run, 6310 Georgetown Pike, McLean, VA 22101. Phone: (703) 442-7557. Fax: (703) 442-0714.

★**FATHER'S DAY.** June 21. Presidential Proclamation issued for third Sunday in June in 1966 and annually since 1971. (PL 92–278 of Apr 24, 1972.)

FATHER'S DAY. June 21. Recognition of the third Sunday in June as Father's Day occurred first at the request of Mrs John B. Dodd of Spokane, WA, on June 19, 1910. It was proclaimed for that date by the mayor of Spokane and recognized by the governor of Washington. The idea was publicly supported by President Calvin Coolidge in 1924, but not presidentially proclaimed until 1966. It was assured of annual recognition by Public Law 92–278 of Apr 1972.

HURRICANE AGNES: ANNIVERSARY. June 21–26, 1972. Hurricane Agnes hit the eastern seaboard wreaking havoc across seven Atlantic Coast states. Casualties included 118 lives and 116,000 homes, leaving more than 200,000 homeless after Agnes dumped 28.1 trillion gallons of water over 5,000 square miles.

MIDSUMMER. June 21. One of the "Lesser Sabbats" during the Wiccan year, celebrating the peak of the Sun God in his annual cycle. Annually, on the summer solstice.

NEW HAMPSHIRE RATIFIES CONSTITUTION: ANNIVERSARY. June 21, 1788. By a vote of 57 to 47, New Hampshire became the ninth state to ratify the Constitution.

NOME RIVER RAFT RACE. June 21. Nome, AK. Homemade rafts paddle their way down the 1–2 mile course on the Nome River. The victorious team claims first place recognition and the ownership of the fur-lined Honey-Bucket which is handed down from year to year. This event draws the entire town out for a fun afternoon at Nome's largest summer event. Annually, Sunday closest to summer solstice. Est attendance: 300. For info: Bering Sea Lions Club, Box 326, Nome, AK 99762. Phone: (907) 443-2219. Email: nnbao@aurora.alaska.edu.

SARTRE, JEAN-PAUL: BIRTH ANNIVERSARY. June 21, 1905. French philosopher, "father of existentialism," born at Paris, France, June 21, 1905. In 1964, Sartre rejected the Nobel Prize for Literature when it was awarded to him. He died at Paris, Apr 15, 1980. In *Being and Nothingness*, he wrote: "Man can will nothing unless he has first understood that he must count on no one but himself; that he is alone, abandoned on earth in the midst of his infinite responsibilities, without help, with no other aim than the one he sets for himself, with no other destiny than the one he forges for himself on this earth."

SUMMER. June 21–Sept 23. In the Northern Hemisphere summer begins today with the summer solstice, at 10:03 AM, EDT. Note that in the Southern Hemisphere today is the beginning of winter. Anywhere between the Equator and Arctic Circle, the sun rises and sets farthest north on the horizon for the year, and length of daylight is maximum (12 hours, 8 minutes at equator, increasing to 24 hours at Arctic Circle).

TANNER, HENRY OSSAWA: BIRTH ANNIVERSARY. June 21, 1859. Henry Ossawa Tanner was one of the first black artists to be exhibited in galleries in the US. His works were exhibited in New York City, Washington, DC, Chicago, New Orleans and Louisville, among other cities. He was born on June 21, 1859, at Pittsburgh, PA. He died May 25, 1937, at Paris.

TOMPKINS, DANIEL D.: BIRTH ANNIVERSARY. June 21. Sixth vice president of the US (1817–25), born at Fox Meadows, NY, June 21, 1774. Died at Staten Island, NY, June 11, 1825.

UNIVERSAL FATHER'S WEEK. June 21–27. The purpose of this week, which is celebrated throughout the world the third full week in June, is to stress the importance of fatherhood in family life. For complete info and quotations about the importance of the father, send $3 to cover expense of printing, handling and postage. For info: Dr. Stanley Drake, Pres, Intl Society of Friendship and Goodwill, 412 Cherry Hills Dr, Bakersfield, CA 93309.

WASHINGTON, MARTHA DANDRIDGE CUSTIS: BIRTH ANNIVERSARY. June 21,1731. Wife of George Washington, first president of the US, born at New Kent County, VA, June 21, 1731. Died May 22, 1802.

BIRTHDAYS TODAY

Meredith Baxter, 51, actress ("Bridget Loves Bernie," "Family," "Family Ties"), born Los Angeles, CA, June 21, 1947.

Benazir Bhutto, 45, Pakistani political leader, born Karachi, Pakistan, June 21, 1953.

Thomas Doane (Tom) Chambers, 39, former basketball player, born Ogden, UT, June 21, 1959.

Derrick D. Coleman, 31, basketball player, born Mobile, AL, June 21, 1967.

Sammi Davis-Voss, 34, actress ("Homefront," *Hope and Glory, The Lair of the White Worm*), born Kidderminster, Worcestershire, England, June 21, 1964.

Joe Flaherty, 58, writer, actor ("Second City TV," "SCTV Network 90"), born Pittsburgh, PA, June 21, 1940.

Michael Gross, 51, actor ("Family Ties"), born Chicago, IL, June 21, 1947.

Mariette Hartley, 57, actress ("Peyton Place"; Polaroid commercials with James Garner), born New York, NY, June 21, 1941.

Bernie Kopell, 65, actor ("Get Smart," "The Love Boat," "When Things Were Rotten"), born New York, NY, June 21, 1933.

Juliette Lewis, 25, actress (*Cape Fear, From Dusk to Dawn*), born Los Angeles, CA, June 21, 1973.

June 1998

S	M	T	W	T	F	S
	1	2	3	4	5	6
7	8	9	10	11	12	13
14	15	16	17	18	19	20
21	22	23	24	25	26	27
28	29	30				

Nils Lofgren, 47, musician, singer, songwriter, born Chicago, IL, June 21, 1951.

Monte Markham, 60, actor ("Mr Deeds Goes to Town," "Dallas"), born Manatee, FL, June 21, 1938.

Jane Russell, 77, actress (*The Outlaw, Gentlemen Prefer Blondes*; Howard Hughes designed a special bra for her), born Bemidji, MN, June 21, 1921.

Maureen Stapleton, 73, actress (Oscar for *Reds*; stage: *The Little Foxes*), born Troy, NY, June 21, 1925.

Rick Sutcliffe, 42, former baseball player, born Independence, MO, June 21, 1956.

Prince William (William Arthur Philip Louis), 16, of Wales, son of Prince Charles and Princess Diana, born London, England, June 21, 1982.

JUNE 22 — MONDAY

Day 173 — 192 Remaining

ASSISTANT PRINCIPALS WEEK. June 22–26. Recognizing and saluting assistant principals and all that they do. Annually, the week after Father's Day. For info: Sheila Carey Jones, PO Box 150066, Brooklyn, NY 11215. Phone: (908) 964-0741.

***CHESAPEAKE-LEOPARD* AFFAIR: ANNIVERSARY.** June 22, 1807. One of the events leading to the War of 1812 occurred June 22, 1807, about 40 miles east of Chesapeake Bay. The US frigate *Chesapeake* was fired upon and boarded by the crew of the British man-of-war *Leopard*. The *Chesapeake*'s commander, James Barron, was court-martialed and convicted of not being prepared for action. Later Barron killed one of the judges (Stephen Decatur) in a duel fought at Bladensburg, MD, Mar 22, 1820.

CIRCUS TRAIN WRECK: 80th ANNIVERSARY. June 22, 1918. A Michigan Central Railroad troop train, after several days shuttling soldiers to New York from Chicago, was deadheading back to the Midwest when it struck the rear of the Hagenbeck–Wallace Circus train. The circus train had stopped to have its brake box overhauled in Ivanhoe, IN. Fifty-three circus performers were killed. Of the circus animals not killed outright, many that were crippled and maimed had to be destroyed by police officers. The performers, of whom only three could be identified, were buried in a mass grave. The engineer, A.K. Sargent, who was accused of falling asleep at the throttle, was tried and acquitted.

JOE LOUIS VS BRADDOCK/SCHMELING FIGHT ANNIVERSARIES. June 22, 1937. At Chicago's Comiskey Park, on June 22, 1937, Joe Louis won the World Heavyweight Championship title by knocking out James J. Braddock (eighth round). Louis retained the title until his retirement in 1949. Exactly one year after the Braddock fight, on June 22, 1938, Louis met Germany's Max Schmeling, at New York City's Yankee Stadium. Louis knocked out Schmeling in the first round.

LINDBERGH, ANNE MORROW: BIRTHDAY. June 22. American author and aviator, born June 22, 1907. In *Gift from the Sea*, she wrote: "By and large, mothers and housewives are the only workers who do not have regular time off. They are the great vacationless class."

MALTA: MNARJA. June 22–23. Buskett Gardens. A folk-cum-harvest festival. An all-night traditional Maltese "festa" with folk music, dancing and impromptu Maltese folk singing (ghana). This festival originated in the Middle Ages, and the word *Mnarja* is derived from *luminarja* because the countryside and the bastions around Mdina, Malta's ancient capital, used to be illuminated by "Fjakkoli" (torches made of sand mixed with oil and animal fat) on the eve of and on the feast day itself.

PAPP, JOSEPH: BIRTH ANNIVERSARY. June 22, 1921. Born Yosl Papirofsky at Brooklyn, NY, Joe Papp became one of the leading figures in American theatre. At the helm of the New York Public Theatre, Papp produced a wide range of work from the classical to that of the newest American dramatists, including *Hair, Two Gentlemen of Verona, The Pirates of Penzance, The Mystery of Edwin Drood, That Championship Season* and *A Chorus Line*, among others. He began in 1954 with the Shakespearean Theatre Workshop (which became the New York Shakespeare Festival), taking touring productions around the city on a flatbed truck. When the truck broke down in Central Park, Papp turned his touring company into Shakespeare-in-the-Park. Producing and directing more than 400 productions, Papp garnered 3 Pulitzer Prizes, 6 New York Critics Circle Awards and 28 Tonys. He died on Oct 31, 1991.

PIONEER WEEK. June 22–26. Historic Jefferson College, Washington, MS. A hands-on program for children to learn through talks, demonstrations and activities how children lived 200 years ago (fee $25). Annually, usually in June. Est attendance: 20. For info: Anne L. Gray, Historian, Historic Jefferson College, PO Box 700, Washington, MS 39190. Phone: (601) 442-2901.

SWITZERLAND: MORAT BATTLE ANNIVERSARY. June 22, 1476. The little, walled town of Morat played a decisive part in Swiss history. There, the Confederates were victorious over Charles the Bold of Burgundy, laying the basis for French-speaking areas to become Swiss. Now an annual children's festival.

TEXAS OKLAHOMA JUNIOR GOLF TOURNAMENT. June 22–26. Weeks Parks Golf Center, Wichita Falls, TX. More than 1,000 golfers eighteen years old and under from 33 states and several foreign countries participate each year. Est attendance: 2,400. For info: Wichita Falls Conv & Visitors Bureau, 1000 5th St, Wichita Falls, TX 76301. Phone: (817) 716-5500. Fax: (817) 716-5509.

US DEPARTMENT OF JUSTICE: ANNIVERSARY. June 22. Established by act of June 22, 1870, the Department of Justice is headed by the attorney general. Prior to 1870, the attorney general (whose office had been created Sept 24, 1789) had been a member of the president's cabinet but had not been the head of a department.

V-MAIL DELIVERY: ANNIVERSARY. June 22, 1942. The first V-Mail (V for victory) was dispatched from New York on this date. The system was devised during WW II to conserve cargo space for war materials and supplies. Special paper was used for writing the letters. At post offices, the letters were opened, censored and photographed in reduced proportions. The film was then transported overseas. A complete roll of film contained 1,600 letters.

BIRTHDAYS TODAY

Bill Blass, 76, fashion designer, born Fort Wayne, IN, June 22, 1922.

Ed Bradley, 57, broadcast journalist ("60 Minutes"), born Philadelphia, PA, June 22, 1941.

Klaus Maria Brandauer, 54, actor, born Altausse, Austria, June 22, 1944.

Clyde Austin Drexler, 36, basketball player, born Houston, TX, June 22, 1962.

Diane Feinstein, 65, US senator (D, California), born San Francisco, CA, June 22, 1933.

Kris Kristofferson, 62, singer, actor (*Alice Doesn't Live Here Anymore, A Star Is Born*), born Brownsville, TX, June 22, 1936.

Michael Lerner, 57, actor (*The Candidate, Eight Men Out, Barton Fink*), born Brooklyn, NY, June 22, 1941.

Tracy Pollan, 38, actress ("Family Ties," *Bright Lights, Big City*), born New York, NY, June 22, 1960.

Todd Rundgren, 50, singer (*Something/Anything*), producer, born Upper Darby, PA, June 22, 1948.

Meryl Streep, 49, actress (Oscars for *Kramer vs. Kramer* and *Sophie's Choice*), born Summit, NJ, June 22, 1949.

Lindsay Wagner, 49, actress (Jamie Sommers on "The Bionic Woman"; *The Paper Chase*), born Los Angeles, CA, June 22, 1949.

JUNE 23 — TUESDAY

Day 174 — 191 Remaining

BREAKFAST CLUB: 65th ANNIVERSARY. June 23, 1933. It was corny, but it was loved. "The Breakfast Club with Don McNeil," which hit radio airwaves on this date, had a 35-year run. It was carried by 400 affiliates and tickets became as sought-after as those for a taping of "The Tonight Show" are today. The hour-long show included celebrities such as Fran Allison of "Kukla, Fran and Ollie" fame. Its popularity, however, stemmed mainly from regular features such as "Memory Time," when McNeil read poems and letters from listeners. During World War II "Prayer Time" was started. McNeil's "Call to Breakfast," which was announced every 15 minutes, invited listeners to get up and march around the breakfast table. McNeil died in 1996.

DENMARK: MIDSUMMER EVE. June 23. Celebrated all over the country with bonfires and merrymaking.

FIRST TYPEWRITER: ANNIVERSARY. June 23, 1868. First US typewriter was patented by Luther Sholes.

FOSSE, ROBERT LOUIS (BOB): BIRTH ANNIVERSARY. June 23, 1927. Bob Fosse was born June 23, 1927, at Chicago, IL. The son of a vaudeville singer, he began his show business career at the age of 13. He was the only director in history to win an Oscar, an Emmy and a Tony for his work. As a choreographer he was known for his unique dance style that focused on explosive angularity of the human body in its movement. His body of work included the plays *Pippin, Sweet Charity, Pajama Game, Chicago, Dancin', Redhead* and *Damn Yankees*. His films included *Cabaret, Lenny* and the autobiographical *All That Jazz*. Fosse died Sept 23, 1987, at Washington, DC.

LAST FORMAL SURRENDER OF CONFEDERATE TROOPS: ANNIVERSARY. June 23, 1865. The last formal surrender of Confederate troops took place in the Oklahoma Territory. Cherokee leader and Confederate Brigadier General Waite surrendered his command of a battalion formed by Indians.

LUXEMBOURG: NATIONAL HOLIDAY. June 23. Official birthday of His Royal Highness Grand Duke Jean. Also, Luxembourg's independence is celebrated on this day.

MIDSUMMER DAY CELEBRATIONS. June 23. Celebrates the beginning of summer with maypoles, music, dancing and bonfires. Observed mainly in northern Europe, especially Scandinavian countries. Day of observance is sometimes St. John's Day (June 24), with celebration on St. John's Eve (June 23) as well. Time approximates the summer solstice. See also: "Summer" (June 21).

MOON PHASE: NEW MOON. June 23. Moon enters New Moon phase at 11:50 PM, EDT.

NATIONAL COLUMNIST'S DAY. June 23. Newspaper columnists, who bring you joy all year long, deserve to be celebrated by their readers at least once a year. Now you can send your favorite columnists, local or nationally syndicated, your own wishes for a Happy Columnist's Day and make him or her feel wonderful. Annually, the fourth Tuesday in June. For info: Jim Six, Columnist, *The Gloucester County Times*, 309 S Broad St, Woodbury, NJ 08096. Phone: (609) 845-3300. Fax: (609) 845-5480. Email: jimsix@reporters.net.

NATIONAL LEFT-HANDED GOLF TOURNAMENT. June 23–26. 63rd annual tournament; location to be determined. Est attendance: 1,200. For info: Ed Martin, NALG Sec/Treas, 6448 Shawnee Ct, Independence, KY 41051. Phone: (800) 844-6254. Email: nalgoffice@aol.com.

NORWAY: MIDSUMMER NIGHT. June 23. Celebrated with bonfires, fireworks and open-air dancing throughout the country. For info: Norwegian Tourist Board, 655 Third Ave, New York, NY 10017. Phone: (212) 885-9700.
Email: gonorway@interport.net.
WWW: http://www.norway.org/web/norway/tourism.html

SWEDEN: MIDSUMMER. June 23–24. Celebrated throughout Sweden. Maypole dancing, games and folk music.

SWEDISH DAYS FESTIVAL. June 23–28. Geneva, IL. Geneva celebrates its Swedish heritage with this midsummer festival. Six days of craft, art, rosemailing display, music competitions, entertainment, carnival, Kids' Day activities and parade provide unlimited opportunities. Annually, begins the Tuesday after Father's Day. For info: Geneva Chamber of Commerce, 8 South Third St, PO Box 481, Geneva, IL 60134. Phone: (630) 232-6060. Fax: (630) 232-6083.

June 1998

S	M	T	W	T	F	S
	1	2	3	4	5	6
7	8	9	10	11	12	13
14	15	16	17	18	19	20
21	22	23	24	25	26	27
28	29	30				

BIRTHDAYS TODAY

Bryan Brown, 51, actor (*A Town Like Alice, Breaker Morant, F/X*), born Sydney, Australia, June 23, 1947.

June Carter Cash, 69, singer (Grammy with husband Johnny for "Jackson"), born Maces Spring, VA, June 23, 1929.

James Levine, 55, conductor, born Cincinnati, OH, June 23, 1943.

Frances McDormand, 41, actress (*Fargo, Mississippi Burning*), born Illinois, June 23, 1957.

Ted Schackelford, 52, actor ("Knots Landing," "Dallas"), born Oklahoma City, OK, June 23, 1946.

Clarence Thomas, 50, Supreme Court Justice, born Pinpoint, GA, June 23, 1948.

JUNE 24 — WEDNESDAY

Day 175 — 190 Remaining

AM DYNAMO DAY. June 24. AM DynAMo Day salutes those deejays who rise and shine earlier than farmers in order to keep us entertained as we begin our day. They begin their days at dawn and help us to wake up with a smile. For more info, send $2 to cover the costs of postage and photocopying. For info: Adrienne Sioux Koopersmith, 1437 W Rosemont, #1W, Chicago, IL 60660-1319. Phone: (773) 743-5341. Fax: (773) 743-5395. Email: kooper@interaccess.com.

BEECHER, HENRY WARD: BIRTH ANNIVERSARY. June 24, 1813. Famous American clergyman and orator was born at Litchfield, CT, June 24, 1813. Died Mar 8, 1887. His dying words were "Now comes the mystery."

BERLIN AIRLIFT: 50th ANNIVERSARY. June 24, 1948. In the early days of the Cold War the Soviet Union challenged the West's right of access to Berlin. The Soviets created a blockade June 24, 1948, and an airlift to supply some 2,250,000 people resulted. The airlift lasted a total of 321 days and brought into Berlin 1,592,787 tons of supplies. Joseph Stalin finally backed down and the blockade ended May 12, 1949.

CANADA: NEWFOUNDLAND DISCOVERY DAY. June 24. Commemorates the discovery of Newfoundland by John Cabot on June 24, 1497.

CELEBRATION OF THE SENSES. June 24. Treat yourself to a stimulation of the five senses—taste, touch, scent, sight and sound—and you may experience the elevation known to many mystics as the elusive sixth sense. [© 1997 by WPL] For info: Tom or Ruth Roy, Wellness Permission League, PO Box 662, Mt Gretna, PA 17064-0662. Phone: (500) 437-5104 or (717) 964-1308. Fax: (717) 964-1335.

CIARDI, JOHN: BIRTH ANNIVERSARY. June 24, 1916. American poet, critic, translator, teacher, etymologist and author of children's books, born at Boston, MA. John Anthony Ciardi's criticism and other writings were often described as honest and sometimes as harsh. Ciardi died at Edison, NJ, on Mar 30, 1986.

DEMPSEY, JACK: BIRTH ANNIVERSARY. June 24, 1895. William Harrison Dempsey, known as "The Manassa Mauler," was world heavyweight boxing champion from 1919 to 1926. Following his boxing career Dempsey became a successful New York restaurant operator. Born at Manassa, CO, Dempsey died on May 31, 1983, at New York, NY.

"HAPPY DAYS" TV PREMIERE: ANNIVERSARY. June 24, 1970. This show was an hour of nostalgia. It was hosted by Louis Nye, with Chuck McCann, Bob Elliott, Ray Goulding and other bandleaders from the 1930s.

"HOPALONG CASSIDY" TV PREMIERE: ANNIVERSARY. June 24, 1949. A western series starring William Boyd in the title role as a hero who wore black and rode a white horse. The original episodes were segments edited from 66 movie features of Hopalong Cassidy and his sidekick, Red Connors (Edgar Buchanan). The films were so popular that Boyd produced more episodes especially for TV.

ITALY: GIOCO DEL CALCIO. June 24–28. Florence. Revival of a 16th-century football match in medieval costumes. Fireworks also on June 24.

LATVIA: JOHN'S DAY (MIDSUMMER NIGHT DAY). June 24. The festival of Jani, which commemorates the summer solstice and the name day of (Janis) John, is one of Latvia's most ancient as well as joyous rituals. This festival is traditionally celebrated in the countryside, as it emphasizes fertility and the beginning of summer. Festivities begin on June 23. For info: Embassy of Latvia, 4325 17th St. NW, Washington, DC 20011. Phone: (202) 729-8213.

MACAU: MACAU DAY. June 24. Celebrates defeat of the Dutch invasion forces of 1622 and pays homage to patron saint of Macau, Saint John the Baptist.

MONTANA TRADITIONAL JAZZ FESTIVAL. June 24–28. Helena, MT. Top-name Dixieland jazz bands from all over the nation take over Helena's historic Last Chance Gulch. Features concerts, a jazz mass, Las Vegas style shows, big bands, youth bands, sidewalk art sale and food fair. Est attendance: 6,500. For info: Don West, PO Box 856, Helena, MT 59624. Phone: (406) 449-7969. Email: dondixie@aol.com.

ONIZUKA, ELLISON S.: BIRTH ANNIVERSARY. June 24, 1946. Lieutenant Colonel Ellison S. Onizuka, 39-year-old aerospace engineer, was mission specialist aboard the Space Shuttle *Challenger* when it exploded on Jan 28, 1986 (killing all aboard). Onizuka was born on June 24, 1946, at Kealakekua, Kona, HI. See also: "*Challenger* Space Shuttle Explosion Anniversary" (Jan 28).

OUTDOOR SUMMER THEATER. June 24–Aug 22. Farmington, NM. Featuring *Anasazi, The Ancient Ones*. Performances are held in a natural sandstone amphitheater at the Lion's Wilderness park, with an optional southwest-style dinner served prior to each performance at 6:30 PM. Performances Wednesday through Saturday at 8 PM. Est attendance: 9,000. For info: Farmington Conv and Visitors Bureau, 203 W Main, Ste 401, Farmington, NM 87401. Phone: (800) 448-1240 or (505) 326-7602. Fax: (505) 327-0577. Email: fmncub@cyberport.com. WWW: http://www.farmingtonnm.org

PERU: COUNTRYMAN'S DAY. June 24. Half-day public holiday.

SAINT JOHN THE BAPTIST DAY. June 24. Celebrates birth of saint.

SCANDINAVIAN HJEMKOMST FESTIVAL. June 24–28. Civic Center and Trollwood Park, Fargo, ND, and Hjemkomst Center and Concordia College, Moorhead, MN. (Plus various minifests in both cities.) Celebration of Scandinavian heritage with traditional Icelandic, Norwegian, Finnish, Swedish and Danish crafts and foods. Reindeer to pet. Music and dance performed by guest artists from Scandinavia, Canada and USA. Authentic folk costume style show. Grandparent-Grandchild Fun Tour with passports, prizes and pictures as elves. Annual folk art juried exhibition at Concordia College. Annually, the last full weekend in June. Chosen one of the Top 100 Events in North America in 1995 by the American Bus and North American Motorcoach Assns. Est attendance: 25,000. For info: Bev Paulson, Pres, 3107 S Rivershore Dr, Moorhead, MN 56560-4963. Phone: (800) 235-7654 or (218) 233-8484.

SMITHSONIAN INSTITUTION FESTIVAL OF AMERICAN FOLKLIFE. June 24–28. (Also July 1–5.) National Mall, Washington, DC. The 32nd annual festival features programs on the Wisconsin sesquicentennial. Est attendance: 1,500,000. For info: Smithsonian Institution, 900 Jefferson Dr SW, Washington, DC 20560. Phone: (202) 357-2700.

SPACE MILESTONE: *SOYUZ T-6* (USSR). June 24, 1982. Three-man crew (V. Dzhanibekov, A. Ivanchenkov and Jean-Loup Chretien) docked at *Salyut 7*, visiting two other cosmonauts in residence there before returning to Earth on July 2. Launched June 24, 1982.

WINDJAMMER DAYS. June 24–25. Boothbay Harbor, ME. Windjammer Days, the premier maritime event along the coast of Maine. Parades, concerts, waterfront food court, live music, fireworks, visiting military vessels, windjammers sailing into harbor under full sail and much more. Fun for the whole family. Est attendance: 20,000. For info: Boothbay Harbor Chamber of Commerce, PO Box 356, Boothbay Harbor, ME 04538. Phone: (207) 633-2353. Fax: (207) 633-7448.
Email: seamaine@boothbayharbor.com.
WWW: http://www.boothbayharbor.com

BIRTHDAYS TODAY

Nancy Allen, 48, actress (*Carrie, Blow Out, Robocop*), born New York, NY, June 24, 1950.

Claude Chabrol, 68, filmmaker (*La Femme Infidèle, The Cousins*), born Sardent, France, June 24, 1930.

Mick Fleetwood, 56, musician (drummer with Fleetwood Mac; "Dreams," "Don't Stop"), born Cornwall, England, June 24, 1942.

Phyllis George, 49, former sportscaster, former Miss America, born Denton, TX, June 24, 1949.

Michele Lee, 56, actress (Karen Fairgate MacKenzie on "Knots Landing"), born Los Angeles, CA, June 24, 1942.

Robert Reich, 52, former US Secretary of Labor in Clinton administration, born Scranton, PA, June 24, 1946.

Peter Weller, 51, actor (*Adventures of Buckaroo Banzai Across the Eighth Dimension, Naked Lunch*), born Stevens Point, WI, June 24, 1947.

JUNE 25 — THURSDAY

Day 176 — 189 Remaining

AMERICAN NURSES ASSOCIATION CONVENTION. June 25–July 2. Convention Center, San Diego, CA. For info: American Nurses Association, 600 Maryland Ave SW, Washington, DC 20024. Phone: (202) 651-7203.
WWW: http://www.ana.org

AMERICAN LIBRARY ASSOCIATION ANNUAL CONFERENCE. June 25–July 2. Washington, DC. For info: Public Information Office, American Library Assn, 50 E Huron St, Chicago, IL 60611. Phone: (312) 280-5044. Fax: (312) 944-8520. Email: pro@ala.org.

ANTIQUE AUTO SHOW AND COLLECTOR CAR FESTIVAL. June 25–27. St. Ignace, MI. Parade, cruise night and swap meet. Entries from 25 states and Canada. Est attendance: 107,000. For info: Edward K. Reavie, 268 Hillcrest Blvd, St. Ignace, MI 49781. Phone: (906) 643-8087 or (906) 643-1USA. Fax: (906) 643-9784. Email: edreavie@nostalgia_prod.com. WWW: http://www.nostalgiaprod.com

ARNOLD, HENRY H. "HAP": BIRTH ANNIVERSARY. June 25, 1886. US general and commander of the Army Air Force in all theaters throughout WWII, Arnold was born at Gladwyne, PA. Although no funds were made available, as early as 1938 Arnold was persuading the US aviation industry to step up manufacturing of airplanes. Production grew from 6,000 to 262,000 per year from 1940–44. He supervised pilot training and by 1944 Air Force personnel strength had grown to 2 million from a prewar high of 21,000. He served on the US Joint Chiefs of Staff Committee and the Combined Chiefs of Staff Committee for the Allies. A popular individual with the brass and his subordinates, his nickname of "Hap" was appropriate. Made a full general in 1944, he became the US Army Air Force's first five-star general when the Air Force was made a separate military branch equal to the Army and Navy. Arnold died Jan 15, 1950, at Sonoma, CA.

BATTLE OF LITTLE BIGHORN: ANNIVERSARY. June 25, 1876. Lieutenant Colonel George Armstrong Custer, leading military forces of more than 200 men, attacked an encampment of Sioux Indians led by Chiefs Sitting Bull and Crazy Horse near Little Bighorn River, MT. Custer and all men in his immediate command were killed in the brief battle (about two hours) of Little Bighorn. One horse, named Comanche, is said to have been the only survivor among Custer's forces.

BOISE RIVER FESTIVAL. June 25–28. Boise, ID. "America's Finest Family Festival" is an international award-winning citywide celebration of the river, parks, greenbelt and people of Boise. Features more than 300 events including entertainment, children's activities, sporting competitions, food and specialty events (parades, balloon rally, international exchange, fireworks, etc). Est attendance: 1,000,000. For info: Steven Wood Schmader, CFE, Pres, Boise River Festival, 7032 S Eisenman Rd, Boise, ID 83716. Phone: (208) 338-8887. Fax: (208) 338-3833. WWW: http://www.boiseriverfestival.org

CANADA: THE NORTH AMERICAN TOURNAMENT. June 25–July 5. Spruce Meadows, Calgary, Alberta. Show jumping tournament featuring the Spruce Meadows North American Show Jumping Championships. Est attendance: 85,000. For info: Spruce Meadows, RR #9, Calgary, Alta, Canada T2J 5G5. Phone: (403) 974-4200. Fax: (403) 974-4270.
Email: smeadows@telusplanet.net.
WWW: http://www.sprucemeadows.com

CBS SENDS FIRST COLOR TV BROADCAST OVER THE AIR: ANNIVERSARY. June 25, 1951. Columbia Broadcast System broadcast the first color television program. The four-hour program was carried by stations in New York City, Baltimore, Philadelphia, Boston and Washington, DC, although no color sets were owned by the public. At the time CBS, itself, owned fewer than 40 color receivers.

CENTRAL CHINA FLOOD: ANNIVERSARY. June 25, 1991. The Huai River flooded its banks and ravaged major portions of the central Chinese province of Anhui. The poor agricultural region was devastated and approximately 3,000 people were killed. The Anhui region sustained enormous damages when the government ordered dikes broken and sluice gates opened in the rural area to prevent flooding of economically important rivers farther downstream.

CIVIL WAR IN YUGOSLAVIA: ANNIVERSARY. June 25. In an Eastern Europe freed from the iron rule of communism and the USSR, separatist and nationalist tensions suppressed for decades rose to a violent boiling point. On June 25, 1991, the republics of Croatia and Slovenia declared their independence, sparking a fractious and bitter war that spread throughout what was formerly Yugoslavia. Ethnic rivalries between Serbians and Croatians began the military conflicts that spread to Slovenia, and in 1992 fighting began in Bosnia-Herzegovina between Serbians and ethnic Muslims. Although the new republics were recognized by the UN and sanctions passed to stop the fighting, it raged on through 1995 despite the efforts of UN peacekeeping forces in the various regions.

CLARKSON CZECH FESTIVAL. June 25–28. Main St, Clarkson, NE. Czech food, entertainment, music, polkas, cooking, demonstrations, carnival, rodeo, arts and crafts. Annually, the fourth full weekend in June. Sponsor: Clarkson Commercial Club. Est attendance: 10,000. For info: Robert Brabec, 515 Elm St, Clarkson, NE 68629. Phone: (402) 892-3331 or (402) 892-3561. Fax: (402) 892-3318.

June 1998

S	M	T	W	T	F	S
	1	2	3	4	5	6
7	8	9	10	11	12	13
14	15	16	17	18	19	20
21	22	23	24	25	26	27
28	29	30				

GILLARS, MILDRED "AXIS SALLY" E.: 10th DEATH ANNIVERSARY. June 25, 1988. Mildred E. Gillars received the nickname "Axis Sally" during World War II, when she broadcast Nazi propaganda to US troops in Europe. An American citizen, she was arrested after the war and tried and convicted of treason. She was sentenced to 10 to 30 years in prison and fined $10,000. She was released after 12 years and later taught music in a convent school in Columbus, OH. She died on June 25, 1988.

HOMESTEAD DAYS. June 25–28. Beatrice, NE. This community-wide celebration recognizes the importance of the Homestead Act of 1862 to the settlement of Nebraska. Entertainment and special museum exhibits. Est attendance: 10,000. For info: Kent Wilson, Dir, Gage County Historical Society, PO Box 793, Beatrice, NE 68310. Phone: (402) 228-1679.
WWW: http://www4.infoanalytic.com/h/beatrice.html#gage

IDAHO DAYS. June 25–27. Franklin, ID. Celebration of Idaho's first settlement with melodrama, games, craft fair and a public pioneer dinner. Est attendance: 5,000. For info: Travel Rep, City of Preston, PO Box 472, Preston, ID 83263. Fax: (208) 852-0158.

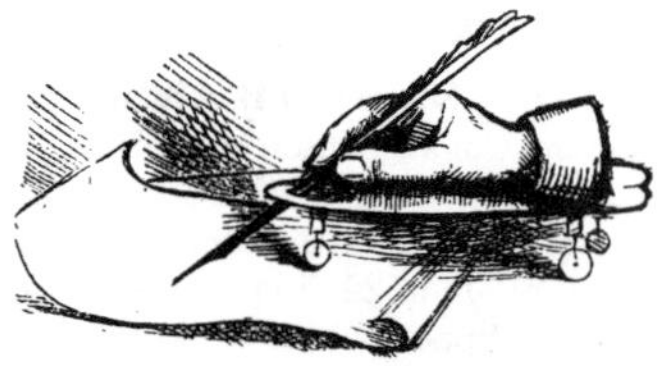

INTERNATIONAL SING-OUT DAY™. June 25. Break out in song today like they do in the musicals. Sing out your words in conversations instead of speaking them. You can even add a few dance steps if you like. In 1998, Sing Out Day ™ happens on Carly Simon's birthday. For info: Adrienne Sioux Koopersmith, 1437 W Rosemont, #1W, Chicago, IL 60660. Phone: (773) 743-5341. Fax: (773) 743-5395. Email: kooper@interaccess.com.

JAZZ IN JUNE. June 25–28. Norman, OK. Four outdoor, free jazz concerts featuring national headliners and regional up-and-coming groups. Annually, the weekend beginning with the fourth Thursday in June. Est attendance: 30,000. For info: Jazz in June, Inc, c/o Shelly Hogan, 1126 Classen Blvd, Norman, OK 73071. Phone: (405) 325-5568.
WWW: http://zoom1.telepath.com/jazzjune

JUDY JUBILEE. June 25–28. Citywide, Grand Rapids, MN. 23rd annual Judy Garland Festival. *The Wizard of Oz* will be shown on the big screen on Friday and four of the original Munchkins will be on hand. Saturday will be Children's Day at the Garland Birthplace with free hands-on activities and Ruby Slipper Contest, walkway drawing, Oz Karaoke and more. Seminars throughout the weekend and other special guests. Plus Garland/Oz Collector's Exchange. Annually, the fourth weekend in June. For info: Judy Garland Children's Museum and Birthplace, PO Box 724, Grand Rapids, MN 55744. Phone: (218) 327-9276 or toll free (800) 664-JUDY. Fax: (218) 327-9302.

KIM CAMPBELL SWORN IN AS CANADIAN PRIME MINISTER: 5th ANNIVERSARY. June 25, 1993. After winning the June 13 election to the leadership of the ruling Progressive-Conservative Party, Kim Campbell became Canada's 19th prime minister and its first woman prime minister. However, in the general election held Oct 25, 1993, the Liberal Party routed the Progressive-Conservatives in the worst defeat for a governing political party in Canada's 126-year history, reducing the former government's seats in the House of Commons from 154 to 2. Campbell was among those who lost their seats.

KOREAN WAR BEGINS: ANNIVERSARY. June 25. Forces from northern Korea invaded southern Korea on June 25, 1950, beginning a civil war. US ground forces entered the conflict on June 30. An armistice was signed at Panmunjom on July 27, 1953, formally dividing the country into two—North Korea and South Korea.

MERAMEC COMMUNITY FAIR. June 25–27. Fairgrounds, Sullivan, MO. 12th annual. Ticket price includes big-name entertainment, huge carnival, truck and tractor pulls, Mod-Bog, pageants and commercial booths. Est attendance: 10,000. For info: Meramec Community Fair, PO Box 386, Sullivan, MO 63080. Phone: (573) 860-2861.

MISS VIRGINIA PAGEANT. June 25–27. Roanoke Civic Center Auditorium, Roanoke, VA. For info: The Miss Virginia Pageant Inc, 212 S Jefferson St SW, Roanoke, VA 24011-1702. Phone: (540) 983-0700.

MOZAMBIQUE: NATIONAL DAY. June 25. National holiday.

NORTHERN IRELAND: GAME AND COUNTRY FAIR. June 25–27. Shane's Castle, Antrim, County Antrim. Ireland's premier field sports event covering all aspects of outdoor sports and country life. Est attendance: 35,000. For info: Mr John Beach, Dir, Kynes Cottage, Shanes Castle, Antrim, Northern Ireland BT41 4NE. Phone: (01) (849) 463282. Fax: (01) (849) 463282.

O'NEILL, ROSE CECIL: BIRTH ANNIVERSARY. June 25. Rose O'Neill was born on June 25, 1874, at Wilkes-Barre, PA. Her career included work as an illustrator, author and doll designer, the latter gaining her commercial success with the Kewpie Doll. In 1910, *The Ladies Home Journal* devoted a full page to her Kewpie Doll designs, which turned into a marketing phenomenon for three decades. Died at Springfield, MO, on Apr 6, 1944.

ORWELL, GEORGE: 95th BIRTH ANNIVERSARY. June 25, 1903. English satirist, author of *Animal Farm, 1984* and other works, was born at Motihari, Bengal, on June 25, 1903. George Orwell was the pseudonym of Eric Arthur Blair. Died at London, England, Jan 21, 1950.

POINT PLEASANT STERNWHEEL REGATTA. June 25–28. Point Pleasant, WV. Sternwheel boat races, entertainment, activities and arts and crafts on the street, fireworks. Annually, the last weekend in June. Est attendance: 25,000. For info: Bob Taylor, Chairman, Point Pleasant Regatta, 305 Main St, Point Pleasant, WV 25550. Phone: (304) 675-3844. Fax: (304) 675-2838. Email: sternwheel@aol.com.
WWW: http://members.aol.com/sternwheel

RABI' I: THE MONTH OF THE MIGRATION. June 25. Begins on Islamic calendar date Rabi' I 1, 1419. The third month of the Islamic calendar, the month of the migration of the Prophet Muhammad from Mecca to Medina, the event that was used as the starting year of the Islamic lunar calendar in history (622 AD). Different methods for "anticipating" the visibility of the new moon crescent at Mecca are used by different Muslim groups. *Chase's* dates are furnished by the American Muslim Council. US EST date may vary.

REVERE, ANNE: 95th BIRTH ANNIVERSARY. June 25, 1903. American actress Anne Revere was born at New York, NY. She won an Academy Award for her supporting role in *National Velvet* (1944), but was barred from films for 20 years after she refused to testify before the House Committee on Un-American Activities in the 1950s. In 1960 she won a Tony Award for her role in *Toys in the Attic*. Revere died on Dec 18, 1990 at Locust Valley, NY.

SEVEN DAYS CAMPAIGN BEGINS: ANNIVERSARY. June 25, 1862. In an effort to prevent the assumed attack on Richmond, VA, Confederate General Robert E. Lee launched a series of engagements on this date that became known as the Seven Days Campaign. Battles at Oak Grove, Gaine's Mills, Garnett's Farm, Golding's Farm, Savage's Station, White Oak Swamp and finally Malvern Hill left more than 36,000 casualties on both sides. Despite losing the final assault at Malvern Hill, the Confederates succeeded in preventing the Union army from taking Richmond.

SLOVENIA: NATIONAL DAY. June 25. Public holiday.

SUMMERFEST. June 25–July 5. Milwaukee, WI. Music festival. Est attendance: 900,000. For info: Marketing Dir, Summerfest, 200 N Harbor Dr, Milwaukee, WI 53202. Phone: (800) 273-3378 or (414) 273-2680. Fax: (414) 287-4495.
WWW: http://www.summerfest.com

SUPREME COURT ABORTION NOTIFICATION RULING: ANNIVERSARY. June 25, 1990. The Supreme Court ruled, in a 5–4 decision, that it was unconstitutional for a state to require, without providing other options, that a minor notify both her parents before obtaining an abortion.

SUPREME COURT BANS OFFICIAL PRAYER: ANNIVERSARY. June 25, 1962. The US Supreme Court ruled that a prayer read aloud in public schools violated the 1st Amendment's separation of church and state. On June 1, 1985, the court again struck down a law pertaining to the 1st Amendment when it disallowed an Alabama law that permitted a daily one-minute period of silent meditation or prayer in public schools. (Vote 6–3.)

SUPREME COURT UPHOLDS RIGHT TO DIE: ANNIVERSARY. June 25, 1990. In the case *Cruzan vs Missouri*, the Supreme Court, in a 5–4 ruling, on June 25, 1990, upheld the constitutional right of a person whose wishes are clearly known to refuse life-sustaining medical treatment.

TWO YUGOSLAV REPUBLICS DECLARE INDEPENDENCE: ANNIVERSARY. June 25, 1991. The republics of Slovenia and Croatia formally declared independence from Yugoslavia on June 25, 1991. The two northwestern European republics did not, however, secede outright.

VIRGINIA RATIFICATION DAY. June 25, 1788. Tenth state to ratify Constitution, on this day in 1788.

VIRGINIA STATE HORSE SHOW ALL-BREED EVENT. June 25–28. Fairgrounds on Strawberry Hill, Richmond, VA. Competition for Arabians, Half-Arabians, Morgans, Miniatures, saddlebreds, jumpers, walking and driving horses. The most inclusive all-breed event in the state with the most divisions of competition. "A" rated by the American Horse Shows Association. Highlights include "Championship Night" and Jumper "High Jump" class. Est attendance: 10,000. For info: Sue Mullins, Equine Dir, PO Box 26805, Richmond, VA 23261. Phone: (804) 228-3238. Fax: (804) 228-3252.

WATERMELON THUMP (WITH WORLD CHAMPION SEED-SPITTING CONTEST). June 25–27. Luling, TX. Features World Champion Seed-Spitting Contest, street dance each night, giant parade on Saturday, free live entertainment in the Beer Garden, car rally, champion melon auction, arts and crafts exhibit and sales, food, games, fun run, rides and rodeo. Annually, the last Thursday, Friday and Saturday in June. Est attendance: 35,000. For info: Susan H. Ward, Secretary, Luling Watermelon Thump Assn, Box 710, Luling, TX 78648. Phone: (830) 875-3214. Fax: (830) 875-2082. Email: lulingcc@bcsnet.net.
WWW: http://www.bcsnet.net/lulingcc/thump.htm

BIRTHDAYS TODAY

June Lockhart, 73, actress (mom in 2nd "Lassie" series and in "Lost in Space"), born New York, NY, June 25, 1925.

Sidney Lumet, 74, director (*12 Angry Men, Serpico, Deathtrap, Dog Day Afternoon, Network*), born Philadelphia, PA, June 25, 1924.

George Michael, 35, singer (Wham!; "Wake Me Up Before You Go-Go," "Faith," "Father Figure"), born Radlett, England, June 25, 1963.

Willis Reed Jr, 56, basketball executive and former coach, Basketball Hall of Fame center, born Hico, LA, June 25, 1942.

Carly Simon, 53, singer ("You're So Vain," "Nobody Does It Better"), songwriter, born New York, NY, June 25, 1945.

Jimmie Walker, 50, actor, comedian ("Good Times," "B.A.D. Cats"), born New York, NY, June 25, 1948.

JUNE 26 — FRIDAY

Day 177 — 188 Remaining

AUDI-MOUNT WASHINGTON HILLCLIMB—THE CLIMB TO THE CLOUDS. June 26–28. Gorham, NH. The "Climb to the Clouds" hillclimb is America's oldest hillclimb, originating in 1904. An SCCA-sanctioned Sportscar Hillclimb, which benefits the DARE programs in northern New Hampshire. Est attendance: 7,000. For info: Paul Giblin, Dir, PO Box 278, Gorham, NH 03581. Phone: (603) 466-3988. Email: greatgln@mt-washington. WWW: http://www.mt-washington.com

BORDEN, SIR ROBERT LAIRD: BIRTH ANNIVERSARY. June 26, 1854. Canadian statesman and prime minister, born at Grand Pre, NS. Died at Ottawa, June 10, 1937.

BUCK, PEARL SYDENSTRICKER: BIRTH ANNIVERSARY. June 26, 1892. American author, noted authority on China. Nobel Prize winner for *The Good Earth*. Born at Hillsboro, WV, June 26, 1892. Died Mar 6, 1973.

COUNTRY JAM USA. June 26–29. Grand Junction, CO. Est attendance: 110,000. For info: Paul Novitzke, Country Jam USA, 1711 S Hastings Way, Eau Claire, WI 54701. Phone: (715) 839-7500 or (800) 7800-JAM. Fax: (715) 839-7553. Email: paul@countryjam.com. WWW: http://www.countryjam.com

CUSTER'S LAST STAND REENACTMENT. June 26–28 (tentative). Hardin, MT. Reenactment of the Battle of the Little Bighorn based on an historical outline by Joe Medicine Crow, anthropologist and historian of the Crow Indian tribe. Reenacted by more than 200 Indian and cavalry riders in an outdoor arena near the site of the original battle. Est attendance: 10,000. For info: Charlene Steinmetz, Hardin Area Chamber of Commerce & Agriculture, 200 N Center, Hardin, MT 59034. Phone: (406) 665-1672. Fax: (406) 665-2917.

June 1998

S	M	T	W	T	F	S
	1	2	3	4	5	6
7	8	9	10	11	12	13
14	15	16	17	18	19	20
21	22	23	24	25	26	27
28	29	30				

DOUBLEDAY, ABNER: BIRTH ANNIVERSARY. June 26, 1819. Abner Doubleday served in the US Army during the Mexican War and against the Seminole Indians in Florida prior to his service in the American Civil War. He was stationed at Charleston, SC, where he manned the first of Fort Sumter's guns to fire back at the South after its initial bombardments. His service found him at the battle of Second Bull Run, Antietam, Fredricksburg and as a major general commanding a division at Gettysburg. As a schoolboy in Cooperstown, NY, he constantly organized ball games. He was credited with inventing the game of baseball in the year of 1839, and this fact was confirmed by a committee set up to investigate the origins of baseball by sporting goods manufacturer Albert Spaulding. Abner Doubleday was born at Ballston Spa, NY, and died at Mendham, NJ, on Jan 26, 1893, at age 73.

DOWNTOWN DENVER INTERNATIONAL BUSKERFEST. June 26–28. Denver, CO. An international street performers' festival featuring more than 200 lively, colorful shows by world-class jugglers, mimes, sword swallowers, magicians, tightrope artists, singers, dancers and more on the 16th Street Mall in downtown Denver. Est attendance: 150,000. For info: Susan Rogers-Kark, Downtown Denver Partnership, Inc, Downtown Denver Buskerfest, 511 16th St, Ste 200, Denver, CO 80202-4250. Phone: (303) 534-6161. Fax: (303) 534-2803.

ENGLAND: SHREWSBURY INTERNATIONAL MUSIC FESTIVAL. June 26–July 3. Shrewsbury, Shropshire. Non-competitive festival that brings together music and dance groups from all over the world. Est attendance: 2,700. For info: Nichola Stokes, Fest Mgr, Festival Office, Victoria Court, Ste 3, Bexton Rd, Knutsford, Cheshire, England WA16 OPF. Phone: (44) (156) 565- 2667. Fax: (44) (156) 565- 2062.

FESTIVAL IN THE PINES. June 26–28. Mormon Lake Lodge, Mormon Lake, AZ. Features 250 national artists and craftspeople, ethnic and traditional foods, continuous entertainment on three stages and a children's activity area. Annually, the last weekend in June. Est attendance: 35,000. For info: Britt Kimball, Events Coord, Mill Avenue Merchants Assn, 520 S Mill Ave, Ste 201, PO Box 3084, Tempe, AZ 85281. Phone: (602) 967-4877. Fax: (602) 967-6638.

FINLAND: KUOPIO DANCE AND MUSIC FESTIVAL. June 26–July 4. Kuopio, Finland. Some 70 events centering on classical ballet, dance theatre and jazz dance, plus other types depending on the theme for the festival. World-renowned dance and music companies; seminars, lectures, exhibits and films; selection of dance courses with internationally known dance teachers. Est attendance: 40,000. For info: Finnish Tourist Board, 655 Third Ave, New York, NY 10017. Phone: (212) 949-2333 or (358) (17) 261-8103. Fax: (358) (17) 261-1990. Email: kuopio.dance.festival@travel.fi. WWW: http://www.travel.fi/kuopiodancefestival

FLAG AMENDMENT DEFEATED: ANNIVERSARY. June 26, 1990. The Senate rejected a proposed constitutional amendment on June 26, 1990, that would have permitted states to prosecute those who destroyed or desecrated American flags.

"THE GARRY MOORE SHOW" TV PREMIERE: ANNIVERSARY. June 26, 1950. Garry Moore hosted many programs which aired at various times; this daytime show proved longest lasting. Moore was the host, with his sidekick Durward Kirby, of a show blending singing, joking and talking with guests and regulars. Regulars included Ken Carson and Denise Lor. Guest performers included Don Adams, George Gobel, Don Knotts, Jonathan Winters, Leslie Uggams and Carol Burnett. Animals also appeared on the show.

HAYMARKET PARDON: ANNIVERSARY. June 26, 1893. Illinois Governor John Peter Altgeld pardoned Samuel Fielden, Michael Schwab and Oscar Neebe, three of the anarchists who had been convicted in the violence connected with the Haymarket Riot on May 4, 1886. At a protest meeting at Haymarket Square an unknown individual threw a bomb which caused the death of several policemen. Eight anarchists were tried and convicted of the bombing. Of those one committed suicide the day before he was to be hanged; three were hanged; and Fielden, Schwab and Neebe were imprisoned. In 1893, the newly elected Altgeld, at the urging of Clarence Darrow, reviewed the transcripts of the trial of these men and concluded that they had been railroaded. The pardon was widely criticized. It was an act of political suicide for Altgeld.

HELEN KELLER FESTIVAL. June 26–28. Tuscumbia, AL. Commemorates the remarkable life of Helen Keller with stage shows for all ages, arts and crafts fair, free musical entertainment, races, historic tours of Helen Keller's Birthplace and other beautiful homes and much more. *The Miracle Worker* play performed evenings during festival and for 5 weekends following. Annually, the last weekend in June. Est attendance: 100,000. For info: Debbie Wilson, Dir, Florence/Lauderdale Tourism, One Hightower Pl, Florence, AL 35630. Phone: (205) 740-4141 or (888) FLO-TOUR. Fax: (205) 740-4142. Email: compuserve102100. 1767. WWW: http://www.flo-tour.org.1767

IDAHO REGATTA. June 26–28. Burley, ID. A speedboat spectacular on the Snake River featuring 90 of the nation's fastest flat-bottom race boats. Annually, the last weekend in June. For info: Mini Cassia Chamber of Commerce, 324 Scott Ave, Rupert, ID 83350. Phone: (208) 436-4793 or (800) 333-3408. Fax: (208) 436-4794. Email: mcid@cyberhighway.net.
WWW: http://www.cyberhighway.net/~mcidcham/

INDIANA FIDDLERS' GATHERING. June 26–28. Tippecanoe Battlefield, Battle Ground, IN. Under the huge trees that surround the Tippecanoe Battlefield, clusters of musicians will gather. Enjoy listening to these impromptu concerts, or bring your instruments and play along. Stage performances are scheduled throughout the weekend, and draw musicians and audiences from all around the Midwest. There's music, food and fun for all ages. Annually the last weekend in June. Est attendance: 10,000. For info: Indiana Fiddlers' Gathering Inc, PO Box 49, Battle Ground, IN 47920. Phone: (317) 742-1419. Fax: (317) 742-5707. WWW: http://www.dcwl.com

KLAMATH KRUISE & VINTAGE CAR SHOW. June 26–28. Klamath Falls, OR. Includes Saturday night cruise on Main St, show 'n shine, poker run, sock hop and more. Est attendance: 40,000. For info: Klamath Kruisers, PO Box 7363, Klamath Falls, OR 97602. Phone: (541) 884-0452.

LAURA INGALLS WILDER PAGEANT. June 26–28. (Also July 3–5 and 10–12.) De Smet, SD. An outdoor pageant depicting events from the book *By the Shores of Silver Lake*. See the surveyors' house, the Ingalls' home and 16 other places in De Smet mentioned in the books by author Laura Ingalls Wilder. Est attendance: 10,000. For info: The Laura Ingalls Wilder Pageant, PO Box 154, De Smet, SD 57231. Phone: (605) 692-2108.

LEWIS AND CLARK FESTIVAL. June 26–28 (tentative). Great Falls, MT. This festival takes visitors back to 1805 when the Corps of Discovery camped for one month along this section of the Missouri River. The expedition's camp is re-created and actors in historic dress talk of their four-year journey, their experiences, their tools and their view of the world—all based on the writings of the explorers. This three-day festival also features tours of other historic Lewis and Clark sites near Great Falls and around north central Montana. There are daily dramatic readings from the explorers' diaries, re-enactments of the Corps' daily activities, floats down the Missouri River and food. Annually, the last weekend in June. For info: Great Falls Chamber of Commerce, 815 2nd St South, Great Falls, MT 59405. Phone: (406) 761-4434.

MADAGASCAR: INDEPENDENCE DAY. June 26. National holiday.

MICHIGAN SUGAR FESTIVAL. June 26–28. Sebewaing, MI. In recognition of the importance of sugar beet growing and processing to Michigan and the US, this 32nd annual festival offers three days of parades, competition for the Michigan Sugar Queen (the "sweetest girl in the world"), three-on-three basketball, road race and walkathon, historical events recognition, live entertainment, day and evening carnival, music, food demonstration, sales and contests. Est attendance: 50,000. For info: Sebewaing Chamber of Commerce, Michigan Sugar Festival, PO Box 622, Sebewaing, MI 48759. Phone: (517) 883-2150. Fax: (517) 883-9367.

MIDDLETON, ARTHUR: BIRTH ANNIVERSARY. June 26. American Revolutionary leader and signer of the Declaration of Independence, born near Charleston, SC, June 26, 1742. Died at Goose Creek, SC, Jan 1, 1787.

MONTGOLFIER, JOSEPH MICHEL: DEATH ANNIVERSARY. June 26. French merchant and inventor, born at Vidalonlez-Annonay, France, in 1740 (exact date unknown) who, with his brother Jacques Etienne in Nov 1782, conducted experiments with paper and fabric bags filled with smoke and hot air, which led to invention of the hot air balloon and man's first flight. Died at Balaruc-les-Bains, France, June 26, 1810. See also: "Montgolfier, Jacques Etienne: Birth Anniversary" (Jan 7), "First Balloon Flight: Anniversary" (June 5) and "Aviation History Month" (Nov 1).

OREGON BACH FESTIVAL. June 26–July 11. Hult Center for the Performing Arts and the University of Oregon, Eugene, OR. Artistic Director Helmuth Rilling and international music forces celebrate the music of Bach and other classical composers. A new work from Krzysztof Penderecki, the Polish composer who has been at the forefront of contemporary music for 35 years, will receive its world premiere at the Festival in 1998. Est attendance: 30,000. For info: George Evano, Oregon Bach Fest, 1257 University of Oregon, Eugene, OR 97403. Phone: (800) 457-1486 or (541) 346-5666. Fax: (541) 346-5669.
WWW: http://music1.uoregon.edu/obf/obfhome.html

PIZARRO, FRANCESCO: DEATH ANNIVERSARY. June 26, 1541. Spanish conqueror of Peru, born at Extremadura, Spain, ca. 1471. Pizarro died at Lima, Peru, June 26, 1541.

PLUNKETT, ROY: BIRTH ANNIVERSARY. June 26, 1910. Polytetrafluoroethylene resin was accidentally discovered by Roy Plunkett in 1938 while he was employed by E.I. Du Pont de Nemours & Co. Commonly known as Teflon, it revolutionized the cookware industry. This substance or something similar coated three-quarters of the pots and pans in America at the time of Plunkett's death. Roy Plunkett was born at New Carlisle, OH. He died May 12, 1994, at Corpus Christi, TX.

REGGAEFEST. June 26–27. River West Festival Park, Tulsa, OK. The sounds of Jamaica fill the park as the 13th annual Reggaefest returns to the west bank of the river. Nationally known entertainers will be featured, as well as a variety of foods, import items for sale and a carnival. Annually, the last weekend in June. Est attendance: 30,000. For info: River Parks Authority, 707 S Houston, Ste 202, Tulsa, OK 74127-9033. Phone: (918) 596-2001 or (918) 665-8345. Fax: (918) 596-2004 or (918) 664-8351. Email: reggae@ionet.net. WWW: http://www.reggaefest.com

SAINT LAWRENCE SEAWAY: DEDICATION ANNIVERSARY. June 26, 1959. President Dwight D. Eisenhower and Queen Elizabeth II jointly dedicated the St. Lawrence Seaway in formal ceremonies held at St. Lambert, Que, Canada, on June 26, 1959. A project undertaken jointly by Canada and the US, the waterway (which provides access between the Atlantic Ocean and the Great Lakes) had been opened to traffic on Apr 25, 1959.

SCOTLAND: GLASGOW INTERNATIONAL JAZZ FESTIVAL. June 26–July 5. This largest jazz festival in Britain offers traditional and modern performances. 12th annual. For info: Glasgow Intl Jazz Festival, 18 Albion St, Glasgow G1 1LH, Scotland. Phone: (44) (141) 552-3552. Fax: (44) (141) 552-3592. Email: gijf@glasgow.almac.co.uk.

SHOW-ME STATE CHAMPIONSHIP BBQ COOKOFF. June 26–27. Delta Fairgrounds, Kennett, MO. Event features live music, a carnival, demolition derby and is highlighted by a tasty barbeque. Annually, the last weekend in June. For info: Kennett Jaycees, PO Box 165, Kennett, MO 63857. Phone: (573) 888-3808.

SIGNING OF THE FEDERAL CREDIT UNION ACT: ANNIVERSARY. June 26, 1934. Commemorates signing by President Franklin Delano Roosevelt of the Federal Credit Union Act, thus enabling the formation of credit unions anywhere in the US.

SNOWMASS HOT AIR BALLOON FESTIVAL. June 26–28. Snowmass Village, CO. 45 beautifully colored hot air balloons fill the sky over Snowmass Village while the pilots compete in a race and other contests. Est attendance: 6,000. For info: Snowmass Village Resort Assn, PO Box 5566, Snowmass Village, CO 81615. Phone: (970) 923-2000.

STAMP EXPO. June 26–28. Radisson Hotel, Sherman Oaks, CA. Est attendance: 5,000. For info: Intl Stamp Collectors Soc, PO Box 854, Van Nuys, CA 91408. Phone: (818) 997-6496. Fax: (818) 988-4337. Email: iibick@aol.com. WWW: http://www.4free.com/bick

STERNWHEEL DAYS. June 26–28. Augusta, KY. 21st annual. Sternwheelers grace the shore of the Ohio River. Antique car show; Kentucky arts and crafts market. Onstage and strolling entertainment all weekend. Fun for the whole family. Est attendance: 8,000. For info: City of Augusta, Sternwheel Days Committee, Betty McClanahan, PO Box 85, Augusta, KY 41002. Phone: (606) 756-2183. Fax: (606) 756-2185.

STERNWHEELER DAYS. June 26–28. Port Marina Park, Cascade Locks, OR. Return of the 599-passenger sternwheeler *Columbia Gorge* to home port for the summer. Salmon Bake, Mountain Men Encampment, bingo, children's rides, parade, food, crafts, live bluegrass music. Annually, the fourth weekend in June. Est attendance: 10,000. For info: Columbia Gorge Lions, PO Box 522, Cascade Locks, OR 97014. Phone: (541) 374-8313.

TREK FEST. June 26–27. Riverside, IA. Riverside welcomes all for a small town celebration with a Star Trek theme. Events: Star Trek swap meet, BBQ meal, Trek costume contest, free Star Trek videos, continuous free entertainment for all ages at "Enterprise Theater," including country dancers, kids' tractor pull, tumblers, magic show and state fair talent search. Trek truck pull and street dance. Parade at 10 AM Saturday. Est attendance: 7,500. For info: Riverside Area Community Club, Trek Fest, Box 55, Riverside, IA 52327. Phone: (319) 648-5475. Fax: (319) 648-2341. WWW: http://www.trekfest.com

TRUMBALL DAYS. June 26–27. Hillcrest Middle School and Trumball High School, New Haven, CT. 150 vendors, rides, puppet and magic shows for the children. For info: Trumball Days, (203) 377-2858 or Greater New Haven Conv & Visitors Bureau, One Long Wharf Dr, New Haven, CT 06511. Phone: (203) 777-8550 or (800) 332-STAY. Fax: (203) 782-7755.

UNITED NATIONS CHARTER SIGNED: ANNIVERSARY. June 26. The United Nations Charter was signed in San Francisco by 50 nations on June 26, 1945.

UNITED NATIONS: INTERNATIONAL DAY AGAINST DRUG ABUSE AND ILLICIT TRAFFICKING. June 26. Following a recommendation of the 1987 International Conference on Drug Abuse and Illicit Trafficking, the United Nations General Assembly on June 26, 1987 (Res 42/112), expressed its determination to strengthen action and cooperation for an international society free of drug abuse and proclaimed June 26 as an annual observance to raise public awareness. For info: United Nations, Dept of Public Info, Public Inquiries Unit, RM GA-57, New York, NY 10017. Phone: (212) 963-4475. Fax: (212) 963-0071. Email: inquiries@un.org.

June 1998

S	M	T	W	T	F	S
	1	2	3	4	5	6
7	8	9	10	11	12	13
14	15	16	17	18	19	20
21	22	23	24	25	26	27
28	29	30				

ZAHARIAS, MILDRED "BABE" DIDRIKSON: BIRTH ANNIVERSARY. June 26, 1914. Born Mildred Ella Didrikson at Port Arthur, TX, the great athlete was nicknamed "Babe" after legendary baseball player, Babe Ruth. She was named to the women's All-America basketball team when she was 16. At the 1932 Olympic Games, she won two gold medals—and also set world records in the javelin throw and the 80-meter high hurdles; only a technicality prevented her from obtaining the gold in the high jump. Didrikson married professional wrestler George Zaharias in 1938, six years after she began playing golf casually. In 1946 Babe won the US Women's Amateur tournament, and in 1947 she won 17 straight golf championships and became the first American winner of the British Ladies' Amateur Tournament. Turning professional in 1948, she won the US Women's Open in 1950 and 1954, the same year she won the All-American Open. Babe also excelled in softball, baseball, swimming, figure skating, billiards—even football. In a 1950 Associated Press poll she was named the woman athlete of the first half of the 20th century. She died of cancer at age 42 on Sept 27, 1956, at Galveston, TX.

BIRTHDAYS TODAY

Claudio Abbado, 65, conductor, born Milan, Italy, June 26, 1933.
Greg LeMond, 37, cyclist, born Lakewood, CA, June 26, 1961.
Chris O'Donnell, 28, actor (*Dead Poet's Society, Scent of a Woman*), born Winnetka, IL, June 26, 1970.
Eleanor Parker, 76, actress (Baroness in *The Sound of Music*), born Cedarsville, OH, June 26, 1922.
Charles Robb, 59, US senator (D, Virginia), married Lynda Bird Johnson (1967), born Phoenix, AZ, June 26, 1939.
Charlotte Zolotow, 83, author of children's books (*The Moon Was the Best, Peter and the Pigeons*), born Norfolk, VA, June 26, 1915.

JUNE 27 — SATURDAY

Day 178 — 187 Remaining

BEARTOOTH RUN. June 27. Red Lodge, MT. 8.2-mile or 4.4-mile foot race up scenic Beartooth Pass. Race will start at 7,000 feet and finish at 9,000 feet. Annually, last Saturday in June. Est attendance: 350. For info: Joan Cline, Box 988, Red Lodge, MT 59068. Phone: (406) 446-1718. Email: redlodge@wtp.net. WWW: http://www.wtp.net/redlodge

BULLWHACKER DAYS. June 27–28. Mahaffie Farmstead, Olathe, KS. A celebration of Olathe's Santa Fe Trail heritage with 1800s-period demonstrations, music, crafts, children's games and stagecoach rides. The Mahaffie Farmstead on the Santa Fe Trail near the Oregon Trail served warm meals for travelers as a stagecoach stop from 1863 to 1869. "Bullwhackers" were the men who drove teams of oxen. Annually, the fourth weekend in June. Est attendance: 8,000. For info: Mktg Dept, PO Box 768, Olathe, KS 66051-0768. Phone: (913) 782-6972.

"CAPTAIN VIDEO" TV PREMIERE: ANNIVERSARY. June 27, 1949. "Captain Video" was the first and longest running of several TV space shows. The show was based in the 22nd century and starred Richard Coogan as Captain Video, a human who led a squad of agents (the Video Rangers) fighting villains from their own and other worlds. Al Hodge replaced Coogan in 1949. Also featured were Don Hastings and Hal Conklin; with Ernest Borgnine, Jack Klugman and Tony Randall as guest villains. A second "Captain Video" series, "The Secret Files of Captain Video," began in 1953 but was dropped in 1955.

CIVIL WAR DAYS. June 27–28. Rockford, IL. Troops from Union and Confederate armies meet at Midway Village performing military drills, skirmishes and battle reenactment, camp-life demonstrations and period fashion show. Est attendance: 8,000. For info: Midway Village and Museum Center, 6799 Guilford Rd, Rockford, IL 61107. Phone: (815) 397-9112. Fax: (815) 397-9156.

CORVETTE AND HIGH PERFORMANCE SUMMER MEET. June 27–28. Puyallup, WA. Buy, sell and show cars and parts—new, used and reproductions. Est attendance: 3,250. For info: Larry W. Johnson, Show Organizer, PO Box 7753, Olympia, WA 98507. Phone: (360) 786-8844. Fax: (360) 754-1498.

"DARK SHADOWS" TV PREMIERE: ANNIVERSARY. June 27, 1966. This soap opera was completely different from all others because it featured vampires as main charactors and had a dark, Gothic feel to it. The show focused on the Collins family living in Collinsport, ME, mainly Barnabas Collins (Jonathan Frid), a 200-year-old vampire. Other cast members included Alexandra Moltke, Louis Edmonds, David Hennessy, Joan Bennett, Grayson Hall, David Selby, Kate Jackson, Lara Parker and Jerry Lacy. Action shifted between the 1800s and the 1960s. This show was very popular with teenagers, and was remade as a short-lived series in 1991.

DJIBOUTI: NATIONAL HOLIDAY. June 27.

EIGHTEENTH-CENTURY RENDEZVOUS. June 27–July 5. Pricketts Fort State Park, Fairmont, WV. Re-enactors and buckskinners weekend encampment at Fort. For info: Pricketts Fort State Park, Rte 3, Box 407, Fairmont, WV 26554. Phone: (304) 363-3030. Fax: (304) 363-3857.
WWW: http://www.dmssoft.com/pfort

EXPERIENCE AIKEN CRAFT SHOW. June 27–28. Aiken, SC. Large craft show featuring 140 crafters from all over the southeast. Carnival rides, juggler, unicyclist and a puppet show. Annually, the last weekend in June. Est attendance: 10,000. For info: Lisa J. Hall, Rec Prog Supervisor, City of Aiken Parks & Rec Dept, PO Box 1177, Aiken, SC 29802. Phone: (803) 642-7648. Fax: (803) 642-7639.

FIREFALL. June 27. Springfield/Branson Regional Airport, Springfield, MO. The Springfield Symphony provides live music choreographed to the fireworks. Also other live entertainment and concert performances. Est attendance: 60,000. For info: Springfield Convention & Visitors Bureau, 3315 E Battlefield Rd, Springfield, MO 65804. Phone: (417) 881-5300 or (800) 678-8767. WWW: http://www.springfieldmo.org

FISHING HAS NO BOUNDARIES—BEMIDJI. June 27–28. Paul Bunyan Park, Bemidji, MN. A two-day fishing experience for disabled persons. Any disability, age, sex, race, etc, eligible. Fishing with experienced guides attended by 75 participants and 130 volunteers. For info: Carol Olson, Bemidji Chamber of Commerce, Fishing Has No Boundaries, 300 Bemidji Ave, PO Box 850, Bemidji, MN 56619-0850. Phone: (800) 458-2223, ext 100. Fax: (218) 759-0810.

FOUNTAIN SQUARE ARTS FESTIVAL. June 27–28. Evanston, IL. 19th annual juried outdoor art show. For info: Evanston Chamber of Commerce, 1560 Sherman Ave, Evanston, IL 60201. Phone: (847) 328-1500.

GALESBURG RAILROAD DAYS. June 27–28. Galesburg, IL. 21st annual festival celebrating the city's railroad heritage that dates back to 1854. Carnival, street fair, railroad exhibits and displays, railyard tours, 5K run, concerts and basketball. Includes more than 40 events. Annually, the fourth weekend in June. Est attendance: 55,000. For info: Galesburg Area CVB, PO Box 749, Galesburg, IL 61402-0749. Phone: (309) 343-1194. Fax: (309) 343-1195. Email: gacvb@misslink.net.
WWW: http://www.misslink.net/gacvb/

GARDEN PARTY. June 27. Roseland Cottage, Bowen House, Woodstock, CT. A recreation of Henry Bowen's patriotic celebration from 1870–1894, attended by four US Presidents. Includes light supper, music, dancing beneath a tent and illuminated gardens. Annually, the last Saturday in June. Est attendance: 300. For info: Roseland Cottage, Bowen House, PO Box 186, Woodstock, CT 06281. Phone: (860) 928-4074. Fax: (860) 963-2208.

GETTYSBURG CIVIL WAR HERITAGE DAYS. June 27–July 5. Gettysburg, PA. Commemorates the Battle of Gettysburg. Living history encampment with both Union and Confederate army campsites, concerts, Civil War lecture series, a battle of Gettysburg reenactment, firefighter's festival, encampment church service and Civil War book fair. Est attendance: 37,500. For info: Gettysburg Conv and Visitors Bureau, 35 Carlisle St, Gettysburg, PA 17325-1899. Phone: (717) 334-6274. Fax: (717) 334-1166. WWW: http://www.gettysburg.com

GREATER PITTSBURGH RENAISSANCE FESTIVAL. June 27–28. (Also July 4–5, 11–12, 18–19, and 25–26.) West Newton, PA. A re-creation of a 16th-century marketplace where the king and queen come on holiday. Featured are more than 100 craft shops, five themed stages, games, food and armoured contact jousting. For info: David Pearson, Greater Pittsburgh Renaissance Festival, PO Box 1670, Greensburg, PA 15601-7670. Phone: (412) 872-1670.

HAPPY BIRTHDAY TO "HAPPY BIRTHDAY TO YOU." June 27, 1859. The melody of probably the most often sung song in the world, "Happy Birthday to You," was composed by Mildred J. Hill, a schoolteacher born at Louisville, KY, on this date. Her younger sister, Patty Smith Hill, was the author of the lyrics which were first published in 1893 as "Good Morning to All," a classroom greeting published in the book *Song Stories for the Sunday School.* The lyrics were amended in 1924 to include a stanza beginning "Happy Birthday to You." Now it is sung thousands of times each day—somewhere in the world every minute of the day. Although the authors are believed to have earned very little from the song, reportedly it later generated about $1 million a year for its copyright owner. The song is expected to enter public domain upon expiration of copyright in 2010. Mildred Hill died in 1916 without knowing that her melody would become the world's most popular song. See also: "Hill, Mildred J.: Birth Anniversary" (June 27) and "Hill, Patty Smith: Birth Anniversary" (Mar 27).

HEARN, LAFCADIO: BIRTH ANNIVERSARY. June 27. Author, born on the Greek island of Santa Maura, June 27, 1850. Hearn, who had been a newspaper reporter in Cincinnati, OH, and in New Orleans, LA, went to Japan in 1890 as a magazine writer. Deeply attracted to the country and to the Japanese people, he stayed there as a writer and teacher until his death at Okubo, Japan, on Sept 26, 1904. Though his writings are little remembered in America, he remains a popular figure in Japan, where his books are still used, especially in language classes. His home at Matsue is a tourist shrine.

HILL, MILDRED J.: BIRTH ANNIVERSARY. June 27, 1859. Mildred J. Hill, American musician, composer and schoolteacher, was born at Louisville, KY. She composed the melody for "Good Morning to All," a song intended to be sung by teachers and students in school classrooms. It was first published in *Song Stories for the Sunday School* in 1893. The lyrics were written by Mildred Hill's younger sister, Patty Smith Hill, and were amended in 1924 to include a stanza beginning "Happy Birthday to You." Mildred Hill died at Chicago, IL, at midnight, June 4/5, 1916, without knowing that her melody would become the world's most popular song. See also: "Happy Birthday to 'Happy Birthday to You,' . . . " (June 27) and "Hill, Patty Smith: Birth Anniversary" (Mar 27).

JUNE DAIRY FESTIVAL & TILLAMOOK CO RODEO. June 27–28. Downtown Fairgrounds, Tillamook, OR. Come and join the summer fun with amusement rides, a parade, country music entertainment, sports events, rodeo, food booths and much more. Annually, the fourth weekend in June. Est attendance: 10,000. For info: June Dairy Festival, 3705 Hwy 101 North, Tillamook, OR 97141. Phone: (503) 842-7525. Fax: (503) 842-7526.

KANSAS STATE BARBECUE CHAMPIONSHIP. June 27. Sar-Ko-Par Trails Park, Lenexa, KS. Annually, the fourth Saturday in June. Sample BBQ in nine different categories, recipe tips, and children's activities. Over 160 teams compete. $1 Admission for 12-year-olds and over. Est attendance: 25,000. For info: Bill Nicks, Lenexa Parks & Rec, 13240 Oak St, Lenexa, KS 66215. Phone: (913) 541-8592. Fax: (913) 492-8118.

"LOVING" TV PREMIERE: 15th ANNIVERSARY. June 27, 1983. This half-hour daytime serial was first introduced in prime-time as a two-hour movie the day before its daytime premiere. The show takes place at Alden University in the town of Corinth. Famous alumni include Randolph Mantooth and Luke Perry. The show was renamed "The City" in 1996 and has shifted locale to Soho in New York City.

MIDDLE OF NOWHERE CELEBRATION. June 27–28. Town Square, Ainsworth, NE. Ainsworth was christened the "Middle of Nowhere" by pro bowler Walter Ray Williams on national TV before coming here for the 1986 world horseshoe tournament. The name stuck and was given to this weekend of activities leading up to the bowling/horseshoe tournament on Sunday. Also official alumni weekend for high school graduates of Ainsworth and nearby Johnstown, a Little Miss Middle of Nowhere contest for 5-year-old girls, a parade Saturday afternoon, fireworks Sunday night and many other events. Annually, the last weekend in June. Est attendance: 450. For info: Jo Lowe, Sec, Ainsworth Area Chamber of Commerce, PO Box 112, Ainsworth, NE. Phone: (402) 387-2740. Email: jolone@aol.com. WWW: http://www.co.brown.ne.us

MONTEREY BAY BLUES FESTIVAL. June 27–28. Monterey Fairgrounds, Monterey, CA. One of the most popular festivals in California, the Blues Festival offers quality performers, food and arts and crafts. Past performers have included Etta James, Dr. John, Patti LaBelle, John Mayall, Albert King, Ruth Brown, Betty Wright, Clarence Carter, Charles Brown, Robert Cray, B.B. King, the Neville Brothers, Gladys Knight, Bobby Womack and many others. This festival is dedicated to preserving blues as an American art form. Est attendance: 30,000. For info: Bostrom Management, PO Box 1400, Seaside, CA 93955. Phone: (408) 394-2652. Fax: (408) 649-4124.

June 1998

S	M	T	W	T	F	S
	1	2	3	4	5	6
7	8	9	10	11	12	13
14	15	16	17	18	19	20
21	22	23	24	25	26	27
28	29	30				

MUSCLECAR MANIA. June 27. St. Igance, MI. 3rd annual at the Cheboygan County Fairgrounds after the St. Ignace car show. Flame throwers, burnout contests, neon, hopper and muffler rapping competition. For info: Nostalgia Productions, Inc, 268 Hillcrest Blvd, St Ignace, MI 49781. Phone: (906) 643-8087 or (906) 643-0313. Fax: (906) 643-9784.
Email: edreavie@nostalgiaprod.com.

MUSEUM COMES TO LIFE DAY. June 27. Court House Park, Ainsworth, NE. Cowboy poets, an original pioneer play, demonstrations and vendors. Pioneer dress suggested at this 6th annual festival. Annually, the last Saturday in June. Est attendance: 300. For info: Mary Jo Curtis, Chair, Sellors-Barton Museum Committee, 340 W Third St, Ainsworth, NE 69210. Phone: (402) 387-2488.

NORSKEDALEN'S MIDSUMMER FEST. June 27–28. Norskedalen Nature and Heritage Center, Coon Valley, WI. Celebrate the summer solstice and Sankt Hans Dag (Saint John's Day) in Scandinavian style. Pioneer crafts and demonstrations; children's activities, entertainment, food and raffle; nature hikes, animal presentations and horse-drawn wagon rides. Woodcarving show and competition at Skumsrud Heritage Farm; open air museum; artisans demonstrating and selling their works. Est attendance: 2,000. For info: Tammy Potaracke, Norskedalen, PO Box 225, Coon Valley, WI 54623. Phone: (608) 452-3424. Fax: (608) 452-3157.

OLD MINER'S DAY. June 27. Chloride, AZ. Parade, live music, horseshoe pitching contest, street dance, swap meet, melodrama, vaudeville, burro/mule pack and obstacle event, games and shootouts. Annually, the last Saturday in June. Est attendance: 2,000. For info: Chloride Chamber of Commerce, PO Box 268, Chloride, AZ 86431. Phone: (520) 565-2204.

PARNELL, CHARLES STEWART: BIRTH ANNIVERSARY. June 27. Irish nationalist leader and home-rule advocate born at Avondale, County Wicklow, Ireland, on June 27, 1846. Politically ruined as a result of an affair with Katherine O'Shea, the estranged wife of a member of Parliament. She was divorced by her husband (who named Parnell correspondent), and on June 25, 1891, she married Parnell. Less than a month later Parnell was defeated in a by-election. He made his last public speech on Sept 27, 1891, and died in the arms of his wife, at Brighton on Oct 6, 1891. Reportedly he was given "a magnificent funeral" by the city of Dublin, where he was buried. The anniversary of Parnell's death is observed by some as Ivy Day when a sprig of ivy is worn on the lapel to remember him. See also: "Ivy Day" (Oct 6).

PENNSYLVANIA DUTCH KUTZTOWN FOLK FESTIVAL. June 27–July 5. Summit Station, PA. To perpetuate the life and customs of the Pennsylvania Dutch people. Working craftspeople, special events and 800 handmade quilts. Est attendance: 75,000. For info: Ann Burrows, Ursinus College, Festival Associates, 461 Vine Ln, Kutztown, PA 19530. Phone: (610) 683-8707. Fax: (610) 683-5707.

PRE-OPERA LECTURE SERIES. June 27–28 (also July 4–5, 11–12, 18–19 and 25–26). Ash Lawn–Highland Summer Festival, Charlottesville, VA. Scholars present lectures during the opera season on the season's productions. Annually, the last Saturday and Sunday of June and every Saturday and Sunday in July. Est attendance: 10,000. For info: Judith H. Walker, Genl Mgr, James Monroe Parkway, Charlottesville, VA 22902. Phone: (804) 293-4500 or (804) 979-0122. Fax: (804) 293-0736.
Email: summerfestival@avenue.gen.va.us.
WWW: http://monticello.avenue.gen.va.us

QUILT SHOW. June 27–28. Hermann, MO. Large quilt show and contest. Antique and new quilts and vendors selling quilt-related items. Annually, the last weekend in June. Est attendance:

2,500. For info: Hermann Visitor Center, 306 Market St, Hermann, MO 65041. Phone: (573) 486-2744. Fax: (573) 486-5363.

SAND PLUM FESTIVAL. June 27–28. Downtown Guthrie, OK. Guthrie celebrates the ripening of the Sand Plum, used in Victorian cooking since the turn of the century. Juried fine arts show, children's activities, live entertainment, bed races, pet parade and more. Annually, the last weekend in June. Est attendance: 10,000. For info: Rick Roberts, Dir, Guthrie Conv & Visitors Bureau, PO Box 995, Guthrie, OK 73044. Phone: (800) 299-1889 or (405) 282-1947. Fax: (405) 282-0061.

SEWANEE CONCERTS AND FESTIVAL. June 27–Aug 2. Sewanee, TN. Intensive training for serious students in orchestra and chamber music with private instruction. Also composition, theory and conducting. Est attendance: 20,000. For info: Martha McCrory, Dir, Sewanee Summer Music Ctr, Univ of the South, 735 Univ Ave, Sewanee, TN 37383-1000. Phone: (615) 598-1225. Fax: (615) 598-1706.

SMITH, JOSEPH, JR, AND HYRUM: DEATH ANNIVERSARY. June 27, 1844. The founding prophet of The Church of Jesus Christ of Latter-Day Saints and his brother Hyrum were shot to death by an armed mob in Carthage, IL. At the time, Joseph Smith was the presidential candidate of the National Reform Party, the first US presidential candidate to be assassinated. For info: Public Affairs Dept, Church of Jesus Christ of Latter-Day Saints, 15 E South Temple St, Salt Lake City, UT 84150. Phone: (801) 240-4395. Fax: (801) 240-1167.

SMITHSON, JAMES: DEATH ANNIVERSARY. June 27, 1829. Scientist and founder of the Smithsonian Institution, James Smithson was born in France in 1765 (exact date unknown). His will, dated Oct 23, 1826, bequeathed his great wealth to a nation he had never visited, to found "at Washington under the name of the Smithsonian Institution, establishment for the increase and diffusion of knowledge among men." In spite of opposition, the Congress approved, on Aug 10, 1846, an act to establish the Smithsonian Institution. Most of Smithson's personal documents, books and collections were destroyed by fire in 1865. Smithson died at Genoa, Italy, June 27, 1829. His remains were removed from there to Washington, DC, in 1904.

SNAKE HUNT. June 27–28. Cross Fork, PA. To raise funds for the fire company. Est attendance: 5,000. For info: Barry Gipe, Chmn, Kettle Creek Hose Co #1, Box 264, Cross Fork, PA 17729. Phone: (717) 923-0848.

SPACE MILESTONE: *COLUMBIA STS-4* (US). June 27, 1982. Shuttle *Columbia* launched from Kennedy Space Center, FL, with astronauts K. Mattingly and Henry Hartsfield along with 22,000 lbs of cargo, landed at Edwards Air Force Base, California, on July 4.

SPACE MILESTONE: *SOYUZ T-9* (USSR): 15th ANNIVERSARY. June 27, 1983. Launched from Tyuratam June 27, 1983, with two cosmonauts (V. Lyakhov and A. Aleksandrov). The 40-ton *Soyuz T-9* docked at *Salyut 7* the next day and returned to Earth nearly five months later, Nov 23.

SPACE MILESTONE: *SOYUZ 30* (USSR): 20th ANNIVERSARY. June 27, 1978. Launched on June 27, 1978, cosmonauts Pyotr Klimuk and Miroslav Hernaszewski (from Poland) linked with *Salyut 6* on June 28, greeting crew of *Soyuz 29*. Returned to Earth July 5.

THURGOOD MARSHALL RESIGNS FROM SUPREME COURT: ANNIVERSARY. June 27, 1991. Signaling an end to the era of a liberal Supreme Court, Associate Justice Thurgood Marshall announced his resignation from the United States Supreme Court, effective once his successor was confirmed by the US Senate. Marshall was a pioneering civil rights lawyer who helped lead the fight to end racial segregation and served as US Solicitor General prior to his appointment to the high court by President Lyndon Johnson in 1967 as the first black ever to sit on the Supreme Court. As an attorney for the NAACP, he successfully argued the case of *Brown vs Board of Education* before the Supreme Court, ending the doctrine of "separate but equal." Marshall's 24-year tenure on the bench was marked by his strong liberal voice championing the rights of criminal defendants and defending abortion rights, his opposition to the death penalty and his commitment to civil rights. On July 1, 1991, President George Bush selected Clarence Thomas, a conservative black jurist, to succeed Marshall.

YOUTH SING PRAISE PERFORMANCE. June 27. Belleville, IL. Talented high school students from all over the country gather at the Shrine to perform a musical in the outdoor amphitheatre. Saturday, 7 PM. Est attendance: 2,000. For info: Shrine of Our Lady of the Snows, 442 S De Mazenod Dr, Belleville, IL 62223-1094. Phone: (618) 397-6700. Fax: (618) 398-6549. WWW: http://www.apci.net/~oblates/

BIRTHDAYS TODAY

Isabelle Adjani, 43, actress (*The Story of Adele H., Camille Claudel*), born Germany, June 27, 1955.
Bruce Babbitt, 60, US Secretary of Interior (Clinton administration), born Los Angeles, CA, June 27, 1938.
Julia Duffy, 47, actress ("Newhart," "Designing Women"), born St. Paul, MN, June 27, 1951.
Shirley-Anne Field, 60, actress (*Alfie, My Beautiful Laundrette, Getting It Right*), born London, England, June 27, 1938.
Craig Anthony Hodges, 38, former basketball player, born Park Forest, IL, June 27, 1960.
Brereton C. Jones, 59, governor of Kentucky (D), born Point Pleasant, WV, June 27, 1939.
Norma Kamali, 53, fashion designer, born New York, NY, June 27, 1945.
Captain Kangaroo (Bob Keeshan), 71, TV personality, born Lynbrook, NY, June 27, 1927.
Anna Moffo, 64, opera singer, born Wayne, PA, June 27, 1934.
H. Ross Perot, 68, philanthropist, businessman, 1992 presidential candidate (United We Stand), born Texarkana, TX, June 27, 1930.
Chuck Connors Person, 34, basketball player, born Brantley, AL, June 27, 1964.
Americo Peter (Rico) Petrocelli, 55, former baseball player, born New York, NY, June 27, 1943.

JUNE 28 — SUNDAY

Day 179 — 186 Remaining

"AMOS AND ANDY" TV PREMIERE: ANNIVERSARY. June 28, 1951. This show was based on the popular radio show about black characters played by white dialecticians Freeman Gosden and Charles Correll. In fact, it was the first dramatic series with an all-black cast. The cast included Tim Moore, Spencer Williams, Alvin Childress, Ernestine Wade, Amanda Randolph, Johnny Lee, Nick O'Demus and Jester Hairston. The series was widely syndicated until pressure from civil rights groups, who claimed the show was stereotypical and prejudicial, caused CBS to withdraw it from syndication.

ASHFSA ANNUAL MEETING AND EDUCATIONAL CONFERENCE. June 28–July 1. Orlando, FL. 31st annual. Excellent educational and networking event for all healthcare food and nutrition management professionals and exhibitors with products and services geared to healthcare food service and/or multi-department managers. Annually. Sponsor: American Society for Healthcare Food Service Administrators of the American Hospital Assn. Est attendance: 1,000. For info: Leona Zanetti, Amer Soc for Healthcare Food Service Admins, One N Franklin, 31st Floor, Chicago, IL 60606. Phone: (312) 422-3870. Fax: (312) 422-4581. Email: sarmist1@aha.org.
WWW: http://www.ashfsa.org

CLARA MAASS DAY: BIRTH ANNIVERSARY. June 28, 1876. New Jersey. Commemorates the birth in 1876 of Clara Louise Maass, the heroic nurse who gave her life in the yellow fever experiments of 1901. Created by Clara Maass Foundation.

COMECON AND WARSAW PACT DISBAND: ANNIVERSARY. June 28, 1991. The last vestiges of the Cold War–era Soviet bloc, the Council for Mutual Economic Assistance (COMECON) and the Warsaw Pact, formally disbanded on June 28 and July 1, 1991, respectively.

CYPRUS: SAINT PAUL'S FEAST. June 28–29. Kato Paphos, Cyprus. Religious festivities at Kato Paphos at which the archbishop officiates. Procession of the icon of Saint Paul through the streets.

DESCENDANTS DAY. June 28. The day in each year when all the world's citizens take an accounting of their activities during the preceding year which have impacted our descendants and our neighbors across time. Annually, last Sunday in June. For info: Charles A. Howell, Trust for the Future, 2704 12th Ave S, Nashville, TN 37204. Phone: (615) 297-2269. Fax: (615) 298-1611. Email: chowell@edge.net. WWW: http://techpoint.com/TFTF

FRANCE: FESTIVAL OF THE TARASQUE. June 28. Tarascon (Bouches du Rhone). Re-enactment of legendary monstrous beast that lurked near banks of the Rhone, capsizing boats and devouring flocks and men. Saint Martha is credited with having tamed the monster.

GAY AND LESBIAN PRIDE PARADE AND RALLY. June 28. Chicago, IL. Chicago's 29th annual parade begins at 2 PM; the rally begins at 3:30 PM. Est attendance: 200,000. For info: Gay and Lesbian Pride Parade, PO Box 14131, Chicago, IL 60614. Phone: (773) 348-8243.

INDEPENDENCE SUNDAY IN IOWA. June 28. Sunday preceding July 4, by proclamation of the governor.

INTERNATIONAL SIT-ON-THE-FRONT-PEW SUNDAY. June 28. An event that can be fun for the whole family, designed to fill churches from the front pew back so that clergy will feel encouraged that their people really do care and do want to see and hear them. Annually, the fourth Sunday in June. For info: Rebecca Stimpert, Dir of Communications, KJIL—Great Plains Christian Radio, PO Box 991, Meade, KS 67864. Phone: (316) 873-2991. Fax: (316) 873-2755. Email: kjil@kjil.com. WWW: http://www.kjil.com

JESSE JAMES ROUNDUP. June 28. Splitrock City Park, Garretson, SD. Arts in the Park with fifth annual Dutch Oven Cook-Off. Chuck Wagon Feed at supper followed by a two-act play presented by the Jesse James Players. Annually, the fourth Sunday in June. Sponsor: Jesse James Players. Est attendance: 1,000. For info: Jesse James Players, PO Box 162, Garretson, SD 57030. Phone: (605) 594-3479. Fax: (605) 594-2361.

JUSTICE BYRON R. WHITE RETIRES: 5th ANNIVERSARY. June 28, 1993. After 31 years of serving on the Supreme Court, Justice Byron R. White retired from the Supreme Court. President William Clinton nominated Ruth Bader Ginsburg to fill the vacated seat.

LATVIA: SONG FESTIVAL AND DANCE FESTIVAL. June 28–July 5. Riga, Latvia. 22nd annual song festival and 12th annual dance festival. For info: Embassy of Latvia, 4325 17th St. NW, Washington DC, 20011. Phone: (202) 726-8213.

LOG CABIN DAY. June 28. Michigan. Commemorates log cabins with tours, open houses and special festivities throughout the state. Est attendance: 11,000. For info: Virginia Handy, Sec/Treas, Log Cabin Soc of Michigan, 3503 Edwards Rd, Sodus, MI 49126. Phone: (616) 944-5719.

MAYER, MARIA GOEPPERT: BIRTH ANNIVERSARY. June 28, 1906. German-American physicist Maria Goeppert Mayer was born at Kattowitz, Germany. A participant in the Manhattan Project, she worked on the separation of uranium isotopes for the atomic bomb. Mayer became the first American woman to win the Nobel Prize when she shared the 1963 prize for physics with J. Hans Daniel Jensen and Eugene P. Wigner for their explanation of the atomic nucleus, known as the nuclear shell theory. Mayer died Feb 20, 1972, at San Diego, CA.

June 1998	S	M	T	W	T	F	S
		1	2	3	4	5	6
	7	8	9	10	11	12	13
	14	15	16	17	18	19	20
	21	22	23	24	25	26	27
	28	29	30				

MONDAY HOLIDAY LAW: 30th ANNIVERSARY. June 28, 1968. On June 28, 1968, President Lyndon B. Johnson approved Public Law 90–363, which amended section 6103(a) of title 5, United States Code, establishing Monday observance of Washington's Birthday, Memorial Day, Labor Day, Columbus Day and Veterans Day. The new holiday law took effect on Jan 1, 1971. Veterans Day observance subsequently reverted to its former observance date, Nov 11. See individual holidays for further details.

NATIONAL PREVENTION OF EYE INJURIES AWARENESS WEEK. June 28–July 4. For info: US Eye Injury Registry, Box 55565, Birmingham, AL 35255. Phone: (205) 933-0064.

NORFOLK CHAMBER MUSIC FESTIVAL. June 28–Aug 23. Norfolk,CT. Concerts by world-class artists in the historic Music Shed on an elegant old estate nestled in the Litchfield Hills. Performances are given each week on Thur, Fri, Sat and Sun. *The New York Times* said that "no concert site is more beautiful than Norfolk, Connecticut." Arrive early and picnic or stroll the estate grounds. Est attendance: 20,000. For info: Norfolk Chamber Music Festival, Ellen Battell Stoeckel Estate, Rts 44 & 272, PO Box 545, Norfolk, CT 06058-0545. Phone: (860) 542-3000. WWW: http://www.yale.edu/norfolk/

PUNXSUTAWNEY GROUNDHOG FESTIVAL. June 28–July 4. Punxsutawney, PA. Provides residents and visitors a festive week of free entertainment. Music, crafts, food, entertainers, contests, live theater. Est attendance: 12,000. For info: Roger Steele, Groundhog Festival Committee, 124 W Mahoning St, Punxsutawney, PA 15767-2017. Phone: (814) 938-7700. WWW: http://www.groundhog.org

ROUSSEAU, JEAN-JACQUES: BIRTH ANNIVERSARY. June 28, 1712. Philosopher, born at Geneva, Switzerland, June 28, 1712. Died July 2, 1778. "Man is born free," he wrote in *The Social Contract*, "and everywhere he is in chains."

RUBENS, PETER PAUL: BIRTH ANNIVERSARY. June 28. Flemish painter and diplomat born June 28, 1577, at Siegen, Westphalia. Died of gout at Antwerp, Belgium, May 30, 1640.

SIEGE OF VICKSBURG: ANNIVERSARY. June 28, 1862. The siege of the Confederate city of Vicksburg, MS, began in earnest when Admiral David Farragut succeeded in taking a fleet past the Mississippi River stronghold on this date. The siege continued for over a year.

SINGING ON THE MOUNTAIN. June 28. Grandfather Mountain, Linville, NC. Modern and traditional gospel music featuring top groups and nationally known speakers. 74th annual sing. Annually, the fourth Sunday in June. Free admission. Est attendance: 12,000. For info: Grandfather Mountain, US Highway 221 N, Linville, NC 28646. Phone: (704) 733-4337. WWW: http://www.grandfather.com

SOCIETY FOR THE PRESERVATION & ENCOURAGEMENT OF BARBER SHOP QUARTET SINGING IN AMERICA, INC (SPEBSQSA) INTERNATIONAL CONVENTION. June 28–July 4. Atlanta, GA. More than 10,000 members attend a week of shows, meetings, chorus and quartet contests. Est attendance: 10,000. For info: Brian Lynch, PR Mgr, 6315 3rd Ave, Kenosha, WI 53143-5199. Phone: (414) 653-8440. Fax: (414) 654-4048. Email: pr@spebsqsa.org. WWW: http://www.spebsqsa.org

SPECIAL RECREATION DAY. June 28. To focus attention on the recreation abilities, aspirations, needs and rights of people with disabilities—see Special Recreation Week (June 28–July 6). For info: John A. Nesbitt, Ed.D, Pres, SRI; Recreation for the

Disabled, 362 Koser Ave, Iowa City, IA 52246-3038. Phone: (319) 337-7578. Email: john-nesbitt@uiowa.edu.

SPECIAL RECREATION WEEK. June 28–July 6. To focus attention on the recreation rights, needs, aspirations and abilities of people with disabilities—infants, children, youth, young adults, adults and seniors; living in the community, in residential services and in institutions; in 40 types of play, recreation and leisure pursuits. (Special Recreation Day: July 28.) For info: John A. Nesbitt, Pres, Special Recreation, Inc, 362 Koser Ave, Iowa City, IA 52246-3038. Phone: (319) 337-7578.
Email: john-nesbitt@uiowa.edu.

WORLD WAR I: BEGINNING AND ENDING ANNIVERSARY. June 28. Archduke Francis Ferdinand and his wife assassinated at Sarajevo, Bosnia, on June 28, 1914, touching off the conflict that became World War I. Also, the anniversary of signing of the Treaty of Versailles, on June 28, 1919, formally ending the war.

BIRTHDAYS TODAY

Eric Ambler, 89, author (*The Dark Frontier, Journey into Fear*), born London, England, June 28, 1909.

Kathy Bates, 50, actress (Oscar for *Misery; Fried Green Tomatoes*), born Memphis, TN, June 28, 1948.

Donald Edward (Don) Baylor, 49, baseball manager, former player, born Austin, TX, June 28, 1949.

Danielle Brisebois, 29, actress (Stephanie on "All in the Family"; Mary-Frances on "Knots Landing"), born Brooklyn, NY, June 28, 1969.

Mel Brooks (Melvyn Kaminsky), 70, actor, director (*The Producers, Blazing Saddles*), born New York, NY, June 28, 1928.

John Cusack, 32, actor (*Say Anything, The Grifters, Bullets Over Broadway*), born Chicago, IL, June 28, 1966.

Bruce Davison, 52, actor (*Ulzana's Raid, Longtime Companion, Six Degrees of Separation*), born Philadelphia, PA, June 28, 1946.

John Albert Elway, 38, football player, born Port Angeles, WA, June 28, 1960.

Mark Eugene Grace, 34, baseball player, born Winston-Salem, NC, June 28, 1964.

Alice Krige, 44, actress (*Chariots of Fire, Barfly*), born Upington, South Africa, June 28, 1954.

Carl Levin, 64, former US senator (D, Michigan), born Detroit, MI, June 28, 1934.

Mary Stuart Masterson, 32, actress (*Fried Green Tomatoes, Benny & Joon*), born June 28, 1966.

Noriyuki "Pat" Morita, 66, entertainer, actor ("Sanford and Son," "Happy Days," *The Karate Kid, Honeymoon in Vegas*), born Isleton, CA, June 28, 1932.

JUNE 29 — MONDAY

Day 180 — 185 Remaining

DEATH PENALTY BANNED: ANNIVERSARY. June 29, 1972. In a decision that spared the lives of 600 individuals then sitting on death row, the US Supreme Court, in a 5–4 vote, found capital punishment a violation of the Eighth Amendment, which prohibits "cruel and unusual punishment." Overruling themselves, the court determined on July 2, 1976, that the death penalty was not cruel and unusual punishment and on Oct 4, 1976, lifted the ban on the death penalty in murder cases. On Jan 15, 1977, Gary Gilmore became the first individual executed in the US in more than 10 years.

ELVIS PRESLEY BOULEVARD NAMED: ANNIVERSARY. June 29, 1971. The City of Memphis, TN, voted to name a road in honor of Elvis—a 12-mile portion of the highway that passes Graceland.

FINLAND: SATA-HAME ACCORDION FESTIVAL. June 29–July 7. Ikaalinen. Est attendance: 48,000. For info: Finnish Tourist Board, 655 Third Ave, New York, NY 10017. Phone: (212) 949-2333 or (358) (3) 440-0224. Fax: (358) (3) 450-1365.

GOETHALS, GEORGE WASHINGTON: BIRTH ANNIVERSARY. June 29, 1858. American engineer and army officer, chief engineer of the Panama Canal and first civil governor of the Canal Zone, born at Brooklyn, NY, June 29, 1858. Died at New York, NY, Jan 21, 1928.

LATHROP, JULIA C.: BIRTH ANNIVERSARY. June 29, 1858. A pioneer in the battle to establish child-labor laws, Julia C. Lathrop was the first woman member of the Illinois State Board of Charities and in 1900 was instrumental in establishing the first juvenile court in the US. In 1912, President Taft named Lathrop chief of the newly created Children's Bureau, then part of the US Dept of Commerce and Labor. In 1925 she became a member of the Child Welfare Committee of the League of Nations. Julia Lathrop died Apr 15, 1932, at Rockford, IL.

MAYO, WILLIAM JAMES: BIRTH ANNIVERSARY. June 29. American surgeon, one of the Mayo brothers, establishers of the Mayo Foundation, born at LeSeuer, MN, June 29, 1861. Died July 28, 1939.

MESA VERDE NATIONAL PARK ESTABLISHED: ANNIVERSARY. June 29, 1906. Area of southwest Colorado established as national park. For further park info: Mesa Verde Natl Park, Mesa Verde Natl Park, CO 81330.

PETER AND PAUL DAY. June 29. Feast day for Saint Peter and Saint Paul. Commemorates dual martyrdom of Christian apostles Peter (by crucifixion) and Paul (by beheading) during persecution by Roman Emperor Nero. Observed since third century.

SAINT PETER'S DAY. June 29. Antakya, Turkey. Peter first preached Christianity at this place. Ceremonies at Saint Peter's Grotto, early Christian cave near Antakya.

BIRTHDAYS TODAY

Gary Busey, 54, musician, actor ("The Texas Wheelers," *The Buddy Holly Story*), born Goose Creek, TX, June 29, 1944.

Elizabeth Hanford Dole, 62, president, American Red Cross, born Salisbury, NC, June 29, 1936.

Fred Grandy, 50, former congressman (R, Iowa), former actor (Gopher on "Love Boat"), born Sioux City, IA, June 29, 1948.

Pedro Guerrero, 42, former baseball player, born San Pedro de Macoris, Dominican Republic, June 29, 1956.

Harmon Clayton Killebrew, 62, Baseball Hall of Fame third baseman, born Payette, ID, June 29, 1936.

Kwame Toure (Stokeley Carmichael), 57, civil rights leader, born Port of Spain, British West Indies, June 29, 1941.

Ruth Warrick, 83, actress (*Citizen Kane*; Phoebe Tyler on "All My Children"), born St. Louis, MO, June 29, 1915.

JUNE 30 — TUESDAY

Day 181 — 184 Remaining

BOSTON HARBORFEST. June 30–July 5. Boston, MA. Waterfront festival with fireworks, entertainment, food booths and much more. Est attendance: 1,000,000. For info: Boston Harborfest, 45 School St, Boston, MA 02108. Phone: (617) 227-1528. Fax: (617) 227-1886.

CANADA: RAYMOND STAMPEDE. June 30–July 1. Ray Knight Arena, Raymond, Alberta. Annual rodeo held at the home of Canada's first and oldest rodeo, started in 1902 by Ray Knight, founder of the town of Raymond. Est attendance: 3,500. For info: Al Heggie, Raymond Stampede Committee Chair, PO Box 335, Raymond, Alta, Canada T0K 2S0. Phone: (403) 752-3661.

CHARLES BLONDIN'S CONQUEST OF NIAGARA FALLS: ANNIVERSARY. June 30, 1859. Charles Blondin, a French acrobat and aerialist (whose real name was Jean François Gravelet), in view of a crowd estimated at more than 25,000 persons, walked across Niagara Falls on a tightrope. The walk required only about five minutes. On separate occasions he crossed blindfolded, pushing a wheelbarrow, carrying a man on his back and even on stilts. Blondin was born Feb 28, 1824, at St. Omer, France, and died at London, England, Feb 19, 1897.

GRAND TETON MUSIC FESTIVAL. June 30–Aug 22. Walk Festival Hall, Teton Village, WY. Eiji Oue, Music Director. Full symphony orchestra concerts on Friday and Saturday evenings, chamber music Tuesday through Thursday, performed by professional musicians from America's finest symphony orchestras with internationally acclaimed guest soloist and conductor 8 PM each night. Est attendance: 22,000. For info: Grand Teton Music Festival, Box 490, Teton Village, WY 83025. Phone: (307) 733-3050. Fax: (307) 739-9043. Email: gtmf@gtmf.org.

GUATEMALA: ARMED FORCES DAY. June 30. Guatemala observes public holiday.

"THE GUIDING LIGHT": ANNIVERSARY. June 30, 1952. Previously on radio, "The Guiding Light" joined the ranks of television soap operas on June 30, 1952. It holds the title of longest-lasting daytime show and longest-lasting series. The Bauer family members were played by Charita Bauer as Bertha (Bert) Bauer, Theo Goetz as Papa Bauer and Lyle Sudro as Bill Bauer. The Grants were Susan Douglas as Kathy Grant, James Lipton as Dr. Richard Grant and Alice Yourman as Laura Grant. Jone Allison played Meta Banning and Herb Nelson played the part of Joe Roberts.

LAST HURRAH FOR BRITISH HONG KONG: ANNIVERSARY. June 30, 1997. The crested flag of the British Crown Colony was officially lowered at midnight and replaced by a new flag (marked by the bauhinia flower) representing China's sovereignty and the official transfer of power. Though Britain owned Hong Kong in perpetuity, the land areas surrounding the city were leased from China and the lease expired July 1, 1997. Rather than renegotiate a new lease, Britain ceded its claim to Hong Kong.

LEAP SECOND ADJUSTMENT TIME. June 30. June 30 is one of the times that has been favored for the addition or subtraction of a second from our clock time (to coordinate atomic and astronomical time). The determination to adjust is made by the Central Bureau of the International Earth Rotation Service, in Paris, France. See also: "Note about Leap Seconds" (see Contents).

MONROE, ELIZABETH KORTRIGHT: BIRTH ANNIVERSARY. June 30, 1768. Wife of James Monroe, fifth president of the US, born at New York, NY, June 30, 1768. Died Sept 23, 1830.

NATIONAL EDUCATION ASSOCIATION MEETING. June 30–July 5. Anaheim, CA. For info: Natl Education Assoc, 1201 16th St NW, Washington, DC 20036-3290. Phone: (202) 822-7769. WWW: http://www.nea.org

SIBERIAN EXPLOSION: 90th ANNIVERSARY. June 30, 1908. Early on the morning of June 30, 1908, a spectacular explosion occurred over central Siberia. The seismic shock, firestorm, ensuing "black rain" and the illumination that was reportedly visible for hundreds of miles led to speculation about whether a meteorite or an extraterrestrial visitor was the most probable cause. Said to have been the most powerful explosion in history.

TWENTY-SIXTH AMENDMENT RATIFIED: ANNIVERSARY. June 30, 1971. The 26th Amendment to the Constitution granted the right to vote in all federal, state and local elections to all persons 18 years or older. On the date of ratification the United States gained an additional 11 million voters. Up until this time, the minimum voting age was set by the states; in most states it was 21.

TWINS FOUNDATION FOUNDING: ANNIVERSARY. June 30. Celebrating its 15th anniversary, The Twins Foundation is the country's primary research information center on the subject of twins. An international nonprofit membership organization, it was established by a group of prominent twins in New York City in 1983. The Foundation serves twins, their families, the media, medical and social scientists and the general public through its publications, its National Twins Registry and its multimedia resource center. For info: The Twins Foundation, PO Box 6043, Providence, RI 02940-6043. Phone: (401) 729-1000. Fax: (401) 751-4642. Email: twins@twinsfoundation.com. WWW: http://www.twinsfoundation.com

WHEELER, WILLIAM ALMON: BIRTH ANNIVERSARY. June 30. Nineteenth vice president of the US (1877–81), born at Malone, NY, June 30, 1819. Died there June 4, 1887.

ZAIRE (CONGO): INDEPENDENCE DAY. June 30. National holiday.

☆ ☆ ☆

BIRTHDAYS TODAY

William Atherton, 51, actor (*The Day of the Locust, Ghostbusters, Die Hard, Die Hard 2*), born New Haven, CT, June 30, 1947.

Nancy Dussault, 62, actress ("Too Close for Comfort," "The Ted Knight Show"), born Pensacola, FL, June 30, 1936.

Rupert Graves, 35, actor (*A Room with a View, Maurice*), born Weston-Super-Mare, England, June 30, 1963.

David Alan Grier, 43, actor (*A Soldier's Story, I'm Gonna Git You Sucka*), born Detroit, MI, June 30, 1955.

Lena Horne, 81, singer, actress (*Stormy Weather, Jamaica, Death of a Gunfighter, The Wiz*), born Brooklyn, NY, June 30, 1917.

Mitchell James (Mitch) Richmond, 33, basketball player, born Fort Lauderdale, FL, June 30, 1965.

Michael Gerard (Mike) Tyson, 32, boxer, born New York, NY, June 30, 1966.

Iulye.

JULY 1 — WEDNESDAY

Day 182 — 183 Remaining

ANTI-BOREDOM MONTH. July 1–31. 13th annual sponsorship of a "self-awareness" event to encourage people to examine whether they, co-workers, family or friends are experiencing "an extended period of boredom" in their lives. The Boring Institute identifies this as "a warning sign" of problems that include depression, self-destructive behavior and even suicide. Advice is offered on how to avoid and overcome boredom. For info: The Boring Institute, Alan Caruba, Founder, Box 40, Maplewood, NJ 07040. Phone: (973) 763-6392. Fax: (973) 763-4287.

ARAFAT RETURNS TO PALESTINE: ANNIVERSARY. July 1, 1994. Yasir Arafat, head of the Palestine Liberation Organization (PLO), returned to Palestine for the first time in 33 years. Israel's control of Palestine had prevented his visiting the region because he was a sworn enemy of the State of Israel and was regarded by Israelis as a terrorist. The agreement between Israel and the PLO, signed in September 1993, made possible Arafat's return. He went first to Gaza City in the Gaza Strip, where he was welcomed by a crowd estimated at 200,000. Three days later he flew by helicopter to the city of Jericho. Both areas were granted Palestinian rule by the treaty.

BATTLE OF GETTYSBURG: ANNIVERSARY. July 1, 1863. After the Southern success at Chancellorsville, VA, Confederate General Robert E. Lee led his forces on an invasion of the North, initially targeting Harrisburg, PA. As Union forces moved to counter the invasion, the battle lines were eventually formed at Gettysburg, PA, in one of the Civil War's most crucial battles, beginning on July 1, 1863. On the climactic third day of the battle (July 3), Lee ordered an attack on the center of the Union line, later to be known as Pickett's Charge. The 15,000 rebels were repulsed, ending the Battle of Gettysburg. After the defeat, Lee's forces retreated back to Virginia, listing more than one-third of the troops as casualties in the failed invasion. Union General George Meade initially failed to pursue the retreating rebels, allowing Lee's army to escape across the rain-swollen Potomac River.

"BIG TOP" TV PREMIERE: ANNIVERSARY. July 1, 1950. Charles Vanda produced this CBS kiddie circus program that broadcast weekly for seven years from Camden, NJ. Jack Sterling played ringmaster. The show also featured Dan Luri and Ed McMahon (as a clown, in his first TV appearance).

BLERIOT, LOUIS: BIRTH ANNIVERSARY. July 1. Louis Bleriot, aviation pioneer and first man to fly an airplane across the English Channel (July 25, 1909), was born at Cambrai, France, July 1, 1872. He died at Paris, Aug 2, 1936.

July 1998

S	M	T	W	T	F	S
			1	2	3	4
5	6	7	8	9	10	11
12	13	14	15	16	17	18
19	20	21	22	23	24	25
26	27	28	29	30	31	

BUREAU OF INTERNAL REVENUE ESTABLISHED: ANNIVERSARY. July 1. The Bureau of Internal Revenue was established on July 1, 1862, by act of Congress.

BURUNDI: INDEPENDENCE DAY. July 1. National holiday. Anniversary of establishment of independence, July 1, 1962.

CANADA: CANADA DAY. July 1. National holiday. Canada's national day, formerly known as Dominion Day. Observed on following day when July 1 is a Sunday. Commemorates the confederation of Upper and Lower Canada and some of the Maritime Provinces into the Dominion of Canada on July 1, 1867.

CANADA: CANADA DAY CELEBRATION. July 1. Rotary Peace Park, Whitehorse, Yukon. Birthday cake, parade, concession stands, music and entertainment, face decorating and much more. Est attendance: 3,000. For info: Dept of Canadian Heritage, 300 Main St, Room 205, Whitehorse, Yukon, Canada Y1A 2B5. Phone: (403) 667-3970. Fax: (403) 393-6702. Email: cathy_mcfadyen@pch.gc.ca.

CANADA: CANADA DAY CELEBRATION. July 1. Lucky Lake Waterslide Park, Watson Lake, Yukon. Outdoor concert, triathlon, canoe jousting, stick gambling, helicopter peanut drop, water slide, races and games, birthday cake and lots more. Est attendance: 900. For info: Tracy Durocher, Recreation Programmer, Watson Lake Canada Day Celebration, Box 590, Watson Lake, Yukon, Canada Y0A 1C0. Phone: (403) 536-2246. Fax: (403) 536-2498. Email: towl@watson.net.
WWW: http://www.yukon.net/northernlights

CANADA: CANADA DAY PARTY IN THE PARK. July 1. Bancroft, Ontario. Canada Day fireworks. Craft show, kids' games and local musicians. Est attendance: 5,000. For info: Bancroft and Dist Chmbr of Commerce, PO Box 539, Bancroft, Ont, Canada K0L 1C0. Phone: (613) 332-1513. Fax: (613) 332-2119. Email: chamber@commerce.bancroft.on.ca.
WWW: http://www.commerce.bancroft.on.ca

CANADA: MONTRÉAL JAZZ FESTIVAL. July 1–12. Close to 2,000 musicians from more than 20 countries in one of the most important jazz events in the world. Est attendance: 1,500,000. For info: Montréal Jazz Festival, 822 Sherbrooke East, Montréal, Quebec, Canada H2L 1K4. Phone: (888) 515-0515.
WWW: http://www.montrealjazzfestival.wordlinx.com

CANADA: NOVA SCOTIA INTERNATIONAL TATTOO. July 1–7. Halifax, Nova Scotia. The Tattoo combines more than 2,000 international military and civilian performers in bands, singing, dancing, marching, gymnastics and comedy. Annually, July 1–7. Est attendance: 60,000. For info: The Nova Scotia Intl Tattoo, PO Box 3233 South, Halifax, NS, Canada B3J 3H5. Phone: (902) 420-1114. Fax: (902) 423-6629.
Email: nstattoo@fox.nstn.ca. WWW: http://www.nstattoo.ca

CANADA: SOURIS VALLEY THEATRE. July 1–Aug 2 (Wednesdays through Sundays). Estevan, Saskatchewan. Enjoy professional live theatre in the big top tent adjacent to Woodlawn Regional Park. Two hilarious shows. Est attendance: 10,000. For info: (306) 634-6044 or Tourism Saskatchewan, 500-1900 Albert St, Canada S4P 4L9. Phone: (800) 667-7191.
Email: travel.info@sasktourism.sk.ca.
WWW: http://www.sasktourism.com

CLEMSON, THOMAS GREEN: BIRTH ANNIVERSARY. July 1, 1807. The man for whom Clemson University was named was born at Philadelphia, PA, on July 1, 1807. The mining engineer and agriculturist married John C. Calhoun's daughter, Anna. Clemson bequeathed the old Calhoun plantation to South Carolina, and Clemson Agricultural College (now Clemson University) was founded there in 1889. Clemson died at Clemson, SC, Apr 6, 1888.

CLEVELAND'S SECRET SURGERY: ANNIVERSARY. July 1, 1893. President Grover Cleveland boarded the yacht *Oneida* owned by his friend and neighbor Commodore E.C. Benedict, for surgery to be performed in secret on a cancerous growth in his mouth. As this was during the 1893 depression, secrecy was thought desirable to avoid further panic by the public. The whole left side of Cleveland's jaw was removed as well as a small portion of his soft palate. A second, less extensive operation was performed July 17. He was later fitted with a prosthesis of vulcanized rubber that he wore until his death June 24, 1908. A single leak of the secret was plugged by Cleveland's Secretary of War, Daniel Lamont, the only member of the administration to know about the surgery. The illness did not become public knowledge until an article appeared Sept 22, 1917, in the *Saturday Evening Post*, written by William W. Keen, who assisted in the surgery.

COURT TV DEBUT: ANNIVERSARY. July 1, 1991. The continuing evolution of home television entertainment brought on by the advent of cable television added another twist on July 1, 1991, with the advent of Court TV. Trials are broadcast in their entirety, with occasional commentary from the channel's anchor desk and switching between several trials in progress. Trials with immense popular interest, such as the William Kennedy Smith rape trial, the sentencing hearing of Marlon Brando's son and the Jeffrey Dahmer and O.J. Simpson trials, are broadcast along with more low-profile cases.

CULTIVATE YOUR CHARACTER MONTH. July 1–31. Energize your personal power and stand above the crowd. Dare to be original. Polish your pizzazz and bring your true character to life with sparkle. Character often determines whether we see opportunities for success, or blindly trip ourselves into failure. You can choose to be the character you want to be. Pull your own strings, groom your genius, tap into your talent and take charge of your character. For info: Judy Buch-Ventriloquist, Ventriloquist Assn of New England, 46 Barbara Rd, Tolland, CT 06084. Phone: (860) 871-8786. Fax: (860) 870-9246. Email: judybuch@aol.com.

DENMARK: AALBORG AND REBILD FESTIVAL (AMERICAN INDEPENDENCE DAY CELEBRATION). July 1–4. Aalborg. This celebration of the American Independence Day, at the Rebild National Park, Aalborg, Denmark, is described as "the largest single gathering for this occasion in the world." Guest speakers and Danish and American entertainment. Est attendance: 10,000. For info: 4 July Committee, Aalborg Tourist and Conv Bureau, PO Box 1862, Oesteraagade 8, DK-9100 Aalborg, Denmark. Phone: (45) (98) 12-6022. Fax: (45) (98) 16-6922. Email: tourist@pip.dknet.dk. WWW: http://www.iesd.auc.dk/aalborg/rebild/

July 1998

S	M	T	W	T	F	S
			1	2	3	4
5	6	7	8	9	10	11
12	13	14	15	16	17	18
19	20	21	22	23	24	25
26	27	28	29	30	31	

DINO-CELEBRATION. July 1–3. Thermopolis, WY. Fossil identification workshops, seminars on fossil collecting, geology for non-experts. Displays by dino-artists, meet-the-author gatherings and dig-site tours. Est attendance: 2,000. For info: The Wyoming Dinosaur Center, PO Box 868, Thermopolis, WY 82443. Phone: (307) 864-2997. Fax: (307) 864-5762. WWW: http://www.wyoming.com/dino

DIXON, WILLIE: BIRTH ANNIVERSARY. July 1. Blues legend Willie Dixon was born in Vicksburg, MI, on July 1, 1915. He moved to Chicago in 1936 and began his career as a musician with the Big Three Trio. With the advent of instrument amplification Dixon migrated away from his acoustic upright bass into producing and song writing with Chess Studios. His style of writing and producing established him as one of the primary architects of the classic Chicago sound in the 1950s. His songs were performed by Elvis Presley, the Everly Brothers, the Rolling Stones, Led Zeppelin, the Doors, Cream, the Yardbirds, Aerosmith, Jimi Hendrix and the Allman Brothers, among many others. Willie Dixon died Jan 29, 1992, at Burbank, CA.

DORSEY, THOMAS A.: BIRTH ANNIVERSARY. July 1, 1899. Thomas A. Dorsey, who was widely known as the father of gospel music, was born July 1, 1899, at Villa Rica, GA. Originally a blues composer and pianist, Dorsey eventually combined blues and religious music to develop the gospel music for which he became well known. It was Dorsey's composition "Take My Hand, Precious Lord" that Rev. Dr. Martin Luther King, Jr, had asked to have performed just moments before his assassination. Dorsey, who composed more than 1,000 gospel songs and hundreds of blues songs in his lifetime, died Jan 23, 1993, at Chicago, IL.

ENGLAND: HENLEY ROYAL REGATTA. July 1–5. Henley-on-Thames, Oxfordshire. International rowing event that is one of the big social events of the year. Est attendance: 100,000. For info: The Secretary, Henley Royal Regatta, Regatta Headquarters, Henley-on-Thames, Oxfordshire, England RG9 2LY. Phone: (44) (149) 157-2153. Fax: (44) (149) 157-5509.

FIRST ADHESIVE US POSTAGE STAMPS ISSUED: ANNIVERSARY. July 1. On July 1, 1847, the first adhesive US postage stamps were issued by the US Postal Service.

GHANA: REPUBLIC DAY. July 1. National holiday.

GUATEMALA: BANKER'S DAY. July 1. National holiday.

HEMOCHROMATOSIS SCREENING AWARENESS MONTH. July 1–31. To promote the awareness and prevention of the disorder of iron metabolism characterized by excess deposits of iron in the tissues. For info: Hemochromatosis Foundation, PO Box 8569, Albany, NY 12208. Phone: (518) 489-0972.

INTERNATIONAL "HUMP" DAY. July 1. Celebrates Wednesday, the middle day or "hump" day of the week. The American Heritage Dictionary defines "hump" as *a difficult stage*. This day also commemorates and acknowledges the struggle and contributions of all workers. For info: Clyde E. Ward, Chair, and Linda Euell, Chair, 1709 Forest Park Dr, Forestville, MD 20747. Phone: (888) 732-5933.

INTERNATIONAL JOKE DAY. July 1. International Joke Day marks the first day of the International Joke Contest, which runs through Oct 1. Participants can mail or fax their best jokes. Prizes are awarded in three catagories: funniest, most original and largest collection (please mail). For info: Wayne Reinagel, Pres, Knightraven Books, PO Box 100, Collinsville, IL 62234-0100. Phone: (618) 345-7436. Fax: Same as Phone.

"THE LIBERACE SHOW" TV PREMIERE: ANNIVERSARY. July 1, 1952. Liberace was a pianist known for his outrageous style and a candelabra on his piano, but he also hosted popular shows in the '50s and '60s. The first was a 15-minute summer replacement show. That did so well that he began a half-hour syndicated series which featured his brother George as violinist and orchestra leader. After a brief leave, he returned to TV in 1958 with a half-hour show that featured Joan O'Brien, Erin O'Brien, Dick Roman, Steve Dunne and the Gordon Robinson Orchestra. Liberace also hosted a British series and a summer series which was produced in London.

LINCOLN SIGNS INCOME TAX: ANNIVERSARY. July 1. President Abraham Lincoln signed into law a bill levying a 3% income tax on annual incomes of $600–$10,000, and 5% on incomes over $10,000. This tax law of July 1, 1862, actually went into effect, unlike an earlier law passed in August 1861, making it the first income tax levied by the United States.

"MAMA" TV PREMIERE: ANNIVERSARY. July 1, 1949. One of TV's first popular sitcoms, "Mama" told the story of a Norwegian family living in San Francisco in 1917. The show aired live through 1956; after it was cancelled, a second, filmed version lasted only 13 weeks. Cast members included Peggy Wood, Judson Laire, Rosemary Rice, Dick Van Patten, Iris Mann, Robin Morgan, Ruth Gates, Malcolm Keen, Carl Frank, Alice Frost, Patty McCormack and Kevin Coughlin. Toni Campbell replaced Robin Morgan in the revival.

MANDAN JAYCEE RODEO DAYS. July 1–4. Mandan, ND. Watch the region's top cowboys and cowgirls compete. In addition to the parade and the carnival midway, wander through local arts and crafts exhibits at Art in the Park. Est attendance: 50,000. For info: Bismarck/Mandan Conv & Visitors Bureau, Box 2274, Bismarck, ND 58502. Phone: (800) 767-3555 or (701) 222-4308. Fax: (701) 222-0647.

MOON PHASE: FIRST QUARTER. July 1. Moon enters First Quarter phase at 2:43 PM, EDT.

MORRILL LAND GRANT ACT PASSED: ANNIVERSARY. July 1, 1862. Led to the creation of the Land Grant universities in each state and Agricultural Experiment Stations.

NATIONAL BAKED BEAN MONTH. July 1–31. To pay tribute to one of America's favorite and most healthful and nutritious foods, baked beans, made with dry or canned beans. For info: Michigan Bean Commission, 1031 S US27, St. Johns, MI 48879. Phone: (517) 224-1361. Fax: (517) 224-6374.

NATIONAL BLUEBERRY MONTH. July 1–31. To promote the greater appreciation and use of cultivated blueberries. For info: Ruth Lowenberg, Lewis & Neale, Inc, 49 E 21st St, New York, NY 10010. Phone: (212) 420-8808. Fax: (212) 254-2452. Email: laneale@aol.com.

NATIONAL FINANCIAL FREEDOM DAY. July 1. Don't gamble with your financial future by leaving your finances to chance. A day dedicated to starting on the path to being debt free and finding ways to build your personal wealth. For info: Jamie K. Urick, Debt Free Intl, Inc, PO Box 705, Frankfort, IL 60423. Phone: (815) 469-7662. Fax: (815) 469-7664. Email: urickdfi@aol.com.

NATIONAL GET ALONG WITH YOUR EX MONTH. July 1–31. This month is designed to help encourage divorced, separated and never-married parents who are now living apart to improve their relationships for the sake of the children. For info: Taking the High Road, 15127 NE 24th St, #161, Dept A, Redmond, WA 98052. Phone: (206) 882-0126.

NATIONAL POSTAL WORKER DAY. July 1. To express appreciation to all past and present postal employees for their service and dedication in serving the American people. Annually, July 1. For info: Connie Totten-Oldham, 475 L'Enfant Plaza SW, Rm 10546, HQ US Postal Service, Washington, DC 20260-3100.

NATIONAL PURPOSEFUL PARENTING MONTH. July 1–31. Encourages parents to incorporate "purpose" in their parenting. Designed to elevate the level of parental effectiveness by building awareness and providing interested participants with tips for positive, conscientious parenting. For info send SASE to: Teresa Langston, Dir, Parenting Without Pressure (PWOP), 1330 Boyer St, Longwood, FL 32750-6311. Phone: (407) 767-2524.

NICK AT NITE PREMIERE: ANNIVERSARY. July 1, 1985. The first broadcast of Nick at Nite, the creation of the kids' network Nickelodeon, occurred on this day. Owned and operated by MTV Networks, Nick at Nite presents many of the old classic television series.

PLAY TACOMA DAYS™. July 1–31. Tacoma, WA. July is packed full of fun, including swimming, sailing, dancing, camping and musical entertainment. This annual event includes festivals, concerts, splash parties, salmon bakes, a golf tournament and more. Annually, the month of July. Est attendance: 280,000. For info: Metro Parks Tacoma, Jana Brown, 4702 S 19th St, Tacoma, WA 98405. Phone: (253) 305-1036. Fax: (253) 305-1014.

PROFESSIONAL SPEAKERS DAY: CELEBRATING FREEDOM OF SPEECH. July 1. Professional speakers celebrate the National Speakers Association's 25th anniversary by donating hundreds of free speeches. For info: Marsha Mardock, Mgr of Communications & Online Programs, Natl Speakers Association, 1500 S Priest Dr, Tempe, AZ 85281. Phone: (602) 968-2552. Fax: (602) 968-0911. Email: nsamardock@aol.com. WWW: http://www.nsaspeaker.org

RIVERFEST. July 1–5. Riverside Park, LaCrosse, WI. 15th annual Riverfest—the city's premier summer event! Top-name entertainers, river activities and continuous musical entertainment highlight this free fest. A food fair, beverage tent, clowns, children's activities and various athletic events held daily. Est attendance: 40,000. For info: Riverfest, Inc, PO Box 1745, LaCrosse, WI 54602. Phone: (608) 782-6000. Fax: (608) 784-1580.

RUSSIAN RUBLE BECOMES CONVERTIBLE: ANNIVERSARY. July 1, 1992. The Russian ruble became convertible with other currencies worldwide. Convertibility had long been held to be an important first move toward bringing the Russian economy into the mainstream of the world's economy. The official rate on July 1 was approximately 125 rubles to the dollar, and authorities hoped that it would eventually stabilize at approximately 80 rubles to the dollar. Previously it was illegal to convert rubles, although they traded briskly on the black market.

RWANDESE REPUBLIC: INDEPENDENCE DAY. July 1. National holiday.

SALMON BAKE SERIES. July 1 (also July 8, 15, 22, 29). Owen Beach, Pt. Defiance Park, Tacoma, WA. 36th annual. This tradition features tasty outdoor salmon or chicken dinners, lively music and lots of fun along the shores of Commencement Bay. Annually, each Wednesday evening in July. Est attendance: 2,200. For info: Metro Parks Tacoma, Jana Brown, 4702 S 19th St, Tacoma, WA 98405. Phone: (253) 305-1036. Fax: (253) 305-1014.

SALMON RIVER DAYS. July 1–4. Salmon, ID. Fourth of July celebration with a triathlon, parade, boat races, auction, family reunions, rodeo and arts and crafts festival. Annually, the first full weekend in July. Est attendance: 8,000. For info: Cathy Hemminger, Salmon Valley Chamber of Commerce, 200 Main, Ste 1, Salmon, ID 83467. Phone: (208) 756-2100.

SAND, GEORGE: BIRTH ANNIVERSARY. July 1. French novelist, author of more than 100 volumes, whose real name was Amandine Aurore Lucile (Dupin) Dudevant, was born at Paris, France, on July 1, 1804. Died at Nohant, France, on June 8, 1876. She is better remembered for having been a liberated woman during a romantic epoch than for her literary works.

SPACE MILESTONE: *KOSMOS 1383* (USSR). July 1, 1982. First search and rescue satellite—equipped to hear distress calls from aircraft and ships—launched in cooperative project with the US and France.

US'S FIRST ZOO: ANNIVERSARY. July 1. The Philadelphia Zoological Society, the first US zoo, opened July 1, 1874. On that day, 3,000 visitors traveled by foot, horse and carriage and steamboat to visit the exhibits. Price of admission was 25 cents for adults and 10 cents for children. There were 1,000 animals in the zoo when it opened.

BIRTHDAYS TODAY

Dan Aykroyd, 46, actor (*Driving Miss Daisy, The Blues Brothers, Dragnet, Ghostbusters*, "Saturday Night Live" [1975–79]), born Ottawa, Ontario, Canada, July 1, 1952.

Karen Black, 56, actress (*Five Easy Pieces, Nashville*), born Park Ridge, IL, July 1, 1942.

Genevieve Bujold, 56, actress (*Choose Me, Trouble in Mind, Dead Ringers*), born Montreal, Quebec, Canada, July 1, 1942.

Leslie Caron, 67, actress (*Gigi, An American in Paris*), dancer, born Paris, France, July 1, 1931.

Olivia DeHavilland, 82, actress (Oscar for *To Each His Own* and *The Heiress; Gone with the Wind*), born Tokyo, Japan, July 1, 1916.

Princess Diana, 37, Princess of Wales, born Sandringham, England, July 1, 1961.

Jamie Farr (Jameel Farah), 62, actor (Klinger on "M*A*S*H"; *The Blackboard Jungle*), born Toledo, OH, July 1, 1936.

Estee Lauder, 90, cosmetics executive, born New York, NY, July 1, 1908.

Frederick Carlton (Carl) Lewis, 37, Olympic gold medal track athlete, born Birmingham, AL, July 1, 1961.

Jean Marsh, 64, writer, actress (Rose on *Upstairs, Downstairs*), born Stoke Newington, England, July 1, 1934.

Sydney Pollack, 64, filmmaker (*Tootsie, The Way We Were, The Fabulous Baker Boys*), born South Bend, IN, July 1, 1934.

Twyla Tharp, 57, dancer, choreographer, born Portland, IN, July 1, 1941.

JULY 2 — THURSDAY

Day 183 — 182 Remaining

"THE ANDY WILLIAMS SHOW" TV PREMIERE: ANNIVERSARY. July 2, 1957. Andy Williams was a singer who hosted many variety shows, including "The Andy Williams-June Valli Show," "The Chevy Showroom" and "The Andy Williams Show." His shows have featured Dick Van Dyke and the Bob Hamilton Trio, the New Christy Minstrels, the Osmond Brothers, Charlie Callas, Irwin Corey and Janos Prohaska. Mike Post was hired as musical director in order to appeal to a younger audience; he introduced the practice of prerecording band arrangements rather than recording them during the taping of the show. In 1976, Williams hosted "Andy," a syndicated show.

BELGIUM: OMMEGANG PAGEANT. July 2. Splendid historic festival of medieval pageantry at the illuminated Grand-Palace in Brussels. The annual event (first Thursday in July) re-creates an entertainment given in honor of Charles V and his court.

July 1998

S	M	T	W	T	F	S
			1	2	3	4
5	6	7	8	9	10	11
12	13	14	15	16	17	18
19	20	21	22	23	24	25
26	27	28	29	30	31	

BLACK HILLS ROUNDUP. July 2–4. Roundup Grounds, Belle Fourche, SD. This 79th annual Independence Day celebration includes an exciting PRCA rodeo each day, the Miss Rodeo South Dakota pageant, western South Dakota's largest fireworks display at dusk on the shore of Orman Dam, a big Fourth of July parade downtown at 10 AM and a thrilling carnival and midway. Est attendance: 10,000. For info: Belle Fourche Chamber of Commerce, 415 Fifth Ave, Belle Fourche, SD 57717. Phone: (605) 892-2676. Fax: (605) 892-4633. Email: Belchmbr@iway1.iw.net.

CANADA: MINERAL COLLECTING FIELD TRIPS. July 2–Aug 27 (all Tuesdays and Thursdays). Bancroft, Ont. Geologist-led mineral collecting field trips visit nearby rock dumps, abandoned mines and collecting sites. Participants are educated about mineral identification, collecting techniques and earth sciences. Annually, every Tuesday and Thursday in July and August. Est attendance: 1,400. For info: Bancroft and Dist Chamber of Commerce, PO Box 539, Bancroft, Ont, Canada K0L 1C0. Phone: (613) 332-1513. Fax: (613) 332-2119.
Email: chamber@commerce.bancroft.on.ca.
WWW: http://www.commerce.bancroft.on.ca

CANADA: SHAKESPEARE ON THE SASKATCHEWAN FESTIVAL. July 2–Aug 16. Saskatoon, Saskatchewan. Innovative contemporary and traditional Shakespearean productions at this award-winning festival. Est attendance: 13,000. For info: Tourism Saskatchewan, 500-1900 Albert St, Regina, Sask, Canada S4P 4L9. Phone: (800) 667-7191 or (306) 653-2300.
Email: travel.info@sasktourism.sk.ca.
WWW: http://www.sasktourism.com

CIVIL RIGHTS ACT OF 1964 PASSED: ANNIVERSARY. July 2. On July 2, 1964, President Lyndon Johnson signed the Voting Rights Act of 1964 into law, prohibiting discrimination on the basis of race in public accommodations, in publicly owned or operated facilities, in employment and union membership and in the registration of voters. The bill included Title VI, which allowed for the cutoff of federal funding in areas where discrimination persisted.

CONSTITUTION OF THE US TAKES EFFECT: ANNIVERSARY. July 2, 1788. Cyrus Griffin of Virginia, the president of the Congress, announced on July 2, 1788, that the Constitution had been ratified by the required nine states (the ninth being New Hampshire on June 21, 1788), and a committee was appointed to make preparations for the change of government.

CRANMER, THOMAS: BIRTH ANNIVERSARY. July 2. English clergyman, reformer and martyr, born at Aslacton, Nottinghamshire, England, July 2, 1489. One of the principal authors of *The English Book of Common Prayer.* Archbishop of Canterbury. Tried for treason and burned at the stake, Oxford, England, Mar 21, 1556.

DECLARATION OF INDEPENDENCE RESOLUTION: ANNIVERSARY. July 2. Anniversary of adoption by the Continental Congress, Philadelphia, PA, July 2, 1776, of a resolution introduced on June 7, 1776, by Richard Henry Lee of Virginia: "Resolved, That these United Colonies are, and of right ought to be, free and independent States, that they are absolved from all allegiance to the British Crown, and that all political connection between them and the State of Great Britain is, and ought to be, totally dissolved. That it is expedient forthwith to take the most effectual measures for forming foreign Alliances. That a plan of confederation be prepared and transmitted to the respective Colonies for their consideration and approbation." This resolution prepared the way for adoption, on July 4, 1776, of the Declaration of Independence. See also: "Declaration of Independence: Anniversary" (July 4).

ENGLAND: EXETER FESTIVAL. July 2–19. Various venues, Exeter, Devon. Major annual music and arts festival featuring the best of British arts and culture. Est attendance: 37,000. For info: Lesley Maynard, Fest Organizer, Exeter City Council, Festival Office, Paris Street, Exeter, England EX1 1JN. Phone: (44) (139) 226-5200. Fax: (44) (139) 226-5366.

GARFIELD, JAMES ABRAM: ASSASSINATION ANNIVERSARY. July 2. President James A. Garfield was shot as he entered the railway station at Washington, DC, July 2, 1881. He died Sept 19, 1881, never having recovered from the wound. The assassin, Charles J. Guiteau, was hanged June 30, 1882.

HALFWAY POINT OF 1998. July 2. At noon on July 2, 1998, 182½ days of the year will have elapsed and 182½ will remain before Jan 1, 1999.

I FORGOT DAY. July 2. A day to make up for all the birthdays, anniversaries, new births, graduations, etc, that you forgot to acknowledge with a greeting or gift. Annually, the 183rd day of the year—exact center. For info: Gaye Andersen, Davenport College, 8200 Georgia St, Merrillville, IN 46410. Phone: (219) 769-5556. Fax: (219) 756-8911.
Email: gandersen@davenport.edu.

"THE LAWRENCE WELK SHOW" TV PREMIERE: ANNIVERSARY. July 2, 1955. This musical series, hosted by Lawrence Welk, an accordionist and bandleader, lasted for almost three decades. In its early years it was known as "The Dodge Dancing Party." The format included music, dancing and guest stars. Regulars included the Lennon Sisters, Alice Lon, Norma Zimmer, Tanya Falan, Arthur Duncan, Joe Feeney, Guy Hovis, Jim Roberts, Ralna English, Larry Hooper, Jerry Burke and Bobby Burgess. During 1956-1959, this show was on concurrently with either "Lawrence Welk's Top Tunes and New Talent" or "The Plymouth Show Starring Lawrence Welk (Lawrence Welk's Little Band)."

MANISTEE NATIONAL FOREST FESTIVAL. July 2–5. Manistee, MI. "The largest Fourth of July Celebration in the state." Grand Parade, a Venetian boat parade, fireworks over Lake Michigan and children's parade. Tours of historic buildings, Lake Bluff Audubon Center, the Big Manistee River by canoe, North Country Trail and other local attractions. Juried arts and crafts show, band concerts, entertainment, dancing, flea market, races, sports tournament and many other special events. Annually, on the Fourth of July and a weekend. Est attendance: 40,000. For info: Manistee Area Chamber of Commerce, 11 Cypress St, Manistee, MI 49660. Phone: (616) 723-2575 or (800) 288-2286.
Email: chamber@manistee.com.
WWW: http://www.manistee.com:80/~edo/chamber/

MARSHALL, THURGOOD: 90th BIRTH ANNIVERSARY. July 2, 1908. Thurgood Marshall, the first African-American on the US Supreme Court, was born July 2, 1908, at Baltimore, MD. For more than 20 years, he served as director-counsel of the NAACP Legal Defense and Educational Fund. He experienced his greatest legal victory on May 17, 1954, when the Supreme Court decision on *Brown vs Board of Education* declared an end to the "separate but equal" system of racial segregation in public schools in 21 states. Marshall argued 32 cases before the Supreme Court, winning 29 of them, before becoming a member of the high court himself. Nominated by President Lyndon Johnson, he began his 24-year career on the high court Oct 2, 1967, becoming a voice of dissent in an increasingly conservative court. Marshall announced his retirement June 27, 1991, and he died Jan 24, 1993, at Washington, DC.

MISSISSIPPI DEEP SEA FISHING RODEO. July 2–5. Gulfport, MS. 50th annual celebration, featuring fishing events, entertainment, rides, games and family fun. Sponsor: MS Deep Sea Rodeo, Inc. Est attendance: 150,000. For info: Ken Ernst, MS Deep South Rodeo, Box 1289, Gulfport, MS 39502. Phone: (601) 388-2271.

MISSISSIPPI VALLEY BLUES FESTIVAL. July 2–5. LeClaire Park, Davenport, IA. Outstanding in its quality, quantity and variety of blues; enjoy great jams, performances and workshops on the banks of the Mississippi River. Annually, the first full weekend of July. Est attendance: 35,000. For info: Mississippi Valley Blues Soc, 318 Brady St, Davenport, IA 52801. Phone: (319) 32B-LUES. WWW: http://www.mvbs.org

MOUNTAIN DANCE AND FOLK FESTIVAL. July 2–4. Asheville, NC. More than 400 performers compete in this three-day fest, which celebrates the cultural heritage of the Southern Appalachian Mountains. Includes dance teams, mountain fiddlers, banjo pickers, old-time string bands, storytellers, bluegrass bands and dulcimer sweepers. 71st annual festival. Oldest of its kind, founded in 1927 by Bascom Lamar Lunsford. Free outdoor festival, downtown. Est attendance: 5,000. For info: Asheville Area Chamber of Commerce, Folk Heritage, PO Box 1010, Asheville, NC 28802. Phone: (800) 257-5583 or (704) 258-6107. Fax: (704) 254-6054. Email: sbanjoc@aol.com.

NATIONAL TOM SAWYER DAYS (WITH FENCE PAINTING CONTEST). July 2–5. Hannibal, MO. Frog jumping, mud volleyball, Tom and Becky Contest, parade, Tomboy Sawyer Contest, 10K run, arts & crafts show and fireworks launched from the banks of the Mississippi River. Highlight is the National Fence Painting Contest. Sponsor: Hannibal Jaycees. Est attendance: 65,000. For info: Hannibal Visitors Bureau, 505 N 3rd St, Hannibal, MO 63401. Phone: (573) 221-2477.

NEBRASKA: BIG RENDEZVOUS AND HISTORICAL FESTIVAL. July 2–5. Burwell, NE. Camp site near Calamus Lake. Re-enactment of early 1800's fur trade encampment. Historical craft demos, period shelters and costumes. Early American frontier crafts and foods for sale. Blackpowder contest. Public welcome 9 AM to 7 PM daily. Admission charge. Est attendance: 1,000. For info: Peggy Haskell, Nebraska Big Rendezvous, PO Box 747, Burwell, NE 68823. Phone: (308) 346-5210. WWW: http://www.adverworld.com/id/0016/6410

RED LODGE HOME OF CHAMPIONS RODEO AND PARADE. July 2–4. Red Lodge, MT. This rodeo is part of the Professional Rodeo Cowboys Assn circuit and brings nearly all of the national champions to Red Lodge each year. At noon each day the Home of Champions Parade struts its way through downtown Red Lodge with colorful floats, antique cars, horses, dancing girls, wagons and more. Annually, July 2–4. Sponsor: Red Lodge Rodeo Assn. Est attendance: 6,000. For info: Red Lodge Area Chamber of Commerce, Box 988, Red Lodge, MT 59068. Phone: (406) 446-1718. Email: redlodge@wtp.net.
WWW: http://www.net.wtp/redlodge

ROUGHRIDER DAYS. July 2–5. Dickinson, ND. Classic western celebration featuring rodeo performances, a parade, demolition derby, concerts, dances, displays and the Fourth of July fireworks show. For info: (701) 225-5115 or North Dakota Tourism, 604 East Boulevard, Bismarck, ND 58505. Phone: (701) 328-2525 or (800) 435-5663.

SAINT LOUIS RACE RIOTS: ANNIVERSARY. July 2, 1917. Between 20 and 75 blacks were killed in a race riot in St. Louis, MO; hundreds more were injured. To protest this violence against blacks, W.E.B. DuBois and James Weldon Johnson, of the NAACP, led a silent march down Fifth Avenue in New York City.

SALEM FAIR AND EXPOSITION. July 2–11. Salem Civic Center Complex, Salem, VA. Fastest-growing and second largest state fair in Virginia. Wholesome family fun. Featuring agricultural exhibits, crafts, food, games and carnival rides. Est attendance: 350,000. For info: John Saunders, Salem Civic Center, Box 886, Salem, VA 24153. Phone: (540) 375-3004 or (540) 375-4013. Fax: (540) 375-4011. WWW: http://www.salem-va.com

SPAM TOWN USA FESTIVAL. July 2–5. Austin, MN. This 13th annual festival includes bike races and runs, recipe contests, fishing contests, family relay games, a treasure hunt and lots of entertainment. For info: Spam Town USA Festival, 329 N Main St, Ste 102, Austin, MN 55912. Phone: (507) 437-3448.

VESEY, DENMARK: DEATH ANNIVERSARY. July 2, 1822. Planner of what would have been the biggest slave revolt in US history, Denmark Vesey was executed at Charleston, SC. He had been born around 1767, probably in the West Indies, where he was sold at around age 14 to Joseph Vesey, captain of a slave ship. Vesey purchased his freedom in 1800 with $600 he won in a lottery. In 1818 Vesey and others began to plot an uprising; he held secret meetings, collected disguises and firearms and chose a date in July 1822. An earlier date was set when a slave divulged the plot, but again white authorities were warned, and police and the military were out in full force. Over the next two months 130 blacks were taken into custody; 35, including Vesey, were hanged and 31 were exiled. As a result of the plot Southern legislatures passed more rigorous slave codes.

WESTMORELAND ARTS & HERITAGE FESTIVAL. July 2–5. Twin Lakes Park, Latrobe, PA. Listed as one of ABA's Top 100 events for 1997. Multi-cultural celebration of the arts. Food booths, ethnic area, children's area, crafts, fine art exhibition, continuous entertainment on five stages. For info: Olga Gera, RD 2, Box 355 A, Latrobe, PA 15650. Phone: (412) 834-7474.

BIRTHDAYS TODAY

Jose Canseco, Jr, 34, baseball player, born Havana, Cuba, July 2, 1964.

Polly Holliday, 61, actress (Flo Castleberry in "Alice" and in "Flo"), born Jasper, AL, July 2, 1937.

Cheryl Ladd, 46, actress (Kris Munroe on "Charlie's Angels"; "Grace Kelly"), born Huron, SD, July 2, 1952.

Jimmy McNichol, 37, actor ("The Fitzpatricks," "California Fever"), born Los Angeles, CA, July 2, 1961.

Ron Silver, 52, actor, director (*Silkwood, Enemies, a Love Story*; stage: *Speed-the-Plow*), born New York, NY, July 2, 1946.

John H. Sununu, 59, former governor of New Hampshire (R), White House Chief of Staff in Reagan administration, born Havana, Cuba, July 2, 1939.

Dave Thomas, 66, founder of Wendy's (stars in TV ads), Horatio Alger Award winner, adoption advocate, born Camden, NJ, July 2, 1932.

July 1998

S	M	T	W	T	F	S
			1	2	3	4
5	6	7	8	9	10	11
12	13	14	15	16	17	18
19	20	21	22	23	24	25
26	27	28	29	30	31	

JULY 3 — FRIDAY

Day 184 — 181 Remaining

AIR CONDITIONING APPRECIATION DAYS. July 3–Aug 15. Northern Hemisphere. During Dog Days, the hottest time of the year in the Northern Hemisphere, to acknowledge the contribution of air conditioning to a better way of life. Annually, July 3–Aug 15. For info: Air-Conditioning and Refrig Institute, 4301 N Fairfax Dr, Ste 425, Arlington, VA 22203. Phone: (703) 524-8800. Fax: (703) 528-3816. Email: ari@dgsys.com. WWW: http://www.ari.org.

ALL-AMERICAN BIRTHDAY PARTY. July 3–5. Central riverfront, Cincinnati, OH. "Old-fashioned" family picnic, national talent and spectacular fireworks. Est attendance: 200,000. For info: Leslie Keller, Jacor Communications, Inc, 1111 St. Gregory St, Cincinnati, OH 45202. Phone: (513) 677-8028. Fax: (513) 677-8113. Email: lgkeller@aol.com.

ART A LA CARTE. July 3–5. Point Defiance Park, Tacoma, WA. A juried fine art and craft show and sale held in conjunction with the Seafirst Taste of Tacoma. This free event will feature more than 100 artists selling their special creations. Est attendance: 130,000. For info: Metro Parks Tacoma, Jana Brown, 4702 S 19th St, Tacoma, WA 98405. Phone: (253) 305-1036. Fax: (253) 305-1014.

BELARUS: INDEPENDENCE DAY. July 3. National holiday.

BENNETT, RICHARD BEDFORD: BIRTH ANNIVERSARY. July 3, 1870. Former Canadian prime minister, born at Hopewell Hill, NB. Died at Mickelham, England, June 26, 1947.

CANADA: DRUMMONDVILLE WORLD FOLKLORE FESTIVAL. July 3–12. Drummondville, Quebec. Groups from more than 20 countries participate in the singing and dancing of folkloric songs and themes. Est attendance: 250,000. For info: Drummondville World Folklore Festival, 405 Saint-Jean St, Drummondville, Que, Canada J2B 5L7. Phone: (819) 472-1184. Fax: (819) 474-6585. Email: folklore@drummond.com. WWW: http://www.festivalfolklore.qc.ca

CANADA: HARRISON FESTIVAL OF THE ARTS. July 3–12. Harrison Hot Springs, British Columbia. A celebration of world music, dance, theatre and visual art including a large outdoor art market. Various venues throughout the village. Variety of activities for the entire family. Est attendance: 12,000. For info: Ed Stenson, Gen Mgr, Harrison Fest, Box 399, Harrison Hot Springs, BC, Canada V0M 1K0. Phone: (604) 796-3664. Fax: (604) 796-3694. Email: harrfest@uniserve.com. WWW: http://www.echoisland.com/harrfest

COMPLIMENT-YOUR-MIRROR DAY. July 3. Participation consists of complimenting your mirror on having such a wonderful owner and keeping track of whether other mirrors you meet during the day smile at you. For info: Bob Birch, Grand Punscorpion, Puns Corps, Box 2364, Falls Church, VA 22042-0364. Phone: (703) 533-3668.

DOG DAYS. July 3–Aug 15. Hottest days of the year in Northern Hemisphere. Usually about 40 days, but variously reckoned at 30–54 days. Popularly believed to be an evil time "when the sea boiled, wine turned sour, dogs grew mad, and all creatures became languid, causing to man burning fevers, hysterics and phrensies" (from Brady's *Clavis Calendarium*, 1813). Originally the days when Sirius, the Dog Star, rose just before or at about the same time as sunrise (no longer true owing to precession of the equinoxes). Ancients sacrificed a brown dog at beginning of Dog Days to appease the rage of Sirius, believing that star was the cause of the hot, sultry weather.

EARTH AT APHELION. July 3. At approximately 8 PM, EDT, planet Earth will reach aphelion, that point in its orbit when it is farthest from the sun (about 94,510,000 miles). The Earth's mean distance from the sun (mean radius of its orbit) is reached early in the months of April and October. Note that Earth is farthest from the sun during Northern Hemisphere summer. See also: "Earth at Perihelion" (Jan 4).

ELLWOOD CITY ARTS, CRAFTS AND FOOD FESTIVAL. July 3–5. Ewing Park, Ellwood City, PA. 18th annual. More than 200 crafts booths, food, juried art show, entertainment and more. 11 AM–10 PM. For info: (412) 758-5630 or Beaver County Tourist Promotion Agency, 215 B Ninth St, Monaca, PA 15061-2028. Phone: (412) 728-0212. Fax: (412) 728-0456.

ENNIS RODEO AND PARADE. July 3–4. Ennis, MT. Billed as the fastest two-day rodeo in Montana, this is a non-stop weekend of excitement. Parade with clowns, bucking broncos and everything imaginable. Annually, July 3–4. Est attendance: 4,000. For info: Pat Hamilton, PR, Ennis Rodeo Club, PO Box 236, Ennis, MT 59729. Phone: (406) 682-4700.

FAIR SAINT LOUIS. July 3–6. Saint Louis, MO. This annual fair celebrates America's birthday with concerts, air shows, amusement rides, ethnic food and nationally known entertainers under the Gateway Arch along the Mississippi River. Fabulous firework displays under the Arch each evening are a highlight of America's biggest birthday party. For info: (314) 434-3434 or Missouri Division of Tourism, Truman State Office Bldg, PO Box 1055, Jefferson City, MO 65102. Phone: (573) 751-4133. Fax: (573) 751-5160.

FIDDLERS JAMBOREE AND CRAFTS FESTIVAL. July 3–4. Smithville, TN. Home of Joe L. Evins Appalachian Regional Crafts Center and Edgar Evins State Park. Clogging, buck dancing, dobro guitar, dulcimer, banjo, gospel singing and old-time fiddle band. More than 300 craft booths. Est attendance: 75,000. For info: Darlene Willingham, Secy, Chamber of Commerce, Box 64, Smithville, TN 37166. Phone: (615) 464-6444.

FIREWORKS ON THE FJORD. July 3. Waterfront, Poulsbo, WA. Family event featuring displays, food booths, entertainment and a giant fireworks display on picturesque Liberty Bay. Voted "Best in the West Sound (Puget)"; only fireworks display on July 3rd in the Puget Sound area, it's a great way to celebrate Independence Day early! Est attendance: 25,000. For info: Fireworks on the Fjord, Community Events Productions, PO Box 1976, Poulsbo, WA 98370. Phone: (360) 779-8018.
Email: mgraves@silverlink.net.

FOURTH OF JULY CELEBRATION. July 3–4. Thompson Park, Firemen's Park, Laurel, MT. American Legion baseball tournament, street dance, pancake breakfast, parade, Chamber of Commerce parade, barbeque in the park and the largest fireworks display in Montana at dusk. For info: Laurel Chamber of Commerce, PO Box 395, Laurel, MT 59044. Phone: (406) 628-8105.

FREEDOM DAYS. July 3–5. Farmington, NM. Celebration with a variety of special events, including spectacular fireworks, free outdoor concert, food fair, auction, street dance, parade, triathlon. Est attendance: 65,000. For info: Farmington Conv and Visitors Bureau, 203 W Main, Ste 401, Farmington, NM 87401. Phone: (800) 448-1240 or (505) 326-7602. Fax: (505) 327-0577. Email: fmncub@cyberport.com. WWW: http://www.farmingtonnm.org

GEORGE WASHINGTON TAKES COMMAND OF THE CONTINENTAL ARMY. July 3. On July 3, 1775, George Washington took command of the Continental Army in Cambridge, MA.

GETTYSBURG CIVIL WAR BOOK FAIR. July 3–4. Gettysburg, PA. More than 60 major Civil War book dealers selling new, used, out-of-print and rare books, documents, prints and photographs. Est attendance: 1,000. For info: GBPA, Box 4087, Gettysburg, PA 17325. Phone: (717) 337-0031.

GETTYSBURG CIVIL WAR RELIC AND COLLECTOR'S SHOW. July 3–5. Gettysburg, PA. 23rd annual. Accoutrements, weapons, uniforms and personal effects from American military history, 1865 and earlier. Leading collectors and dealers of Civil War material. Est attendance: 2,000. For info: Gettysburg Conv and Visitors Bureau, 35 Carlisle St, Gettysburg, PA 17325-1899. Phone: (717) 334-6274. Fax: (717) 334-1166.
WWW: http://www.gettysburg.com

HAYNES–APPERSON FESTIVAL. July 3–5. Kokomo, IN. Celebrate Kokomo's rich automotive heritage with car show, sports festival, parade, carnival, live music, food, crafts and fireworks. Stop by the Elwood Haynes Museum to learn about the inventor of the horseless carriage. Est attendance: 100,000. For info: Kokomo/Howard County Conv & Visitors Bureau, 112 N Washington St, Kokomo, IN 46901. Phone: (317) 457-6802 or (800) 837-0971. Fax: (317) 452-4564.

HUNTINGTON, SAMUEL: BIRTH ANNIVERSARY. July 3, 1731. President of Continental Congress, Governor of Connecticut, signer of the Declaration of Independence, born at Windham, CT, died at Norwich, CT, Jan 5, 1796.

IDAHO: ADMISSION DAY. July 3. Became 43rd state on this day in 1890.

IRAN AIR FLIGHT 655 DISASTER: 10th ANNIVERSARY. July 3, 1988. At 10:54 AM in the Persian Gulf, the US Navy warship *Vincennes* fired two surface-to-air missiles at Iran Air Flight 655 which destroyed the airbus, killing all 290 passengers aboard. The *Vincennes*, boasting the world's most sophisticated radar detection equipment, reportedly misread location, speed, direction, altitude, dimensions and radio signals of the airbus, mistaking it for a hostile F-14 fighter plane. A self-conducted military inquiry blamed human failure—stress on the tense crew rather than equipment malfunction—for the disaster. In summer of 1992 the public learned that the ship had been in Iranian waters at the time in the course of an operation aimed at preventing Iranian boats from laying mines.

LAURA INGALLS WILDER PAGEANT. July 3–19. Walnut Grove, MN. Performed the first three weekends in July, the pageant attempts to catch the spirit of pioneer life as told in *On the Banks of Plum Creek* by Laura Ingalls Wilder. The live production tells the story of the Charles Ingalls family in Walnut Grove in the 1870s. For info: Wilder Pageant Committee, Box 385, Walnut Grove, MN 56180. Phone: (507) 859-2114.

LIVELY LIBERTY FESTIVITIES. July 3–5. Suwannee Music Park, Live Oak, FL. Mixture of fun, music and fireworks. Est attendance: 8,000. For info: James Cornett, Spirit of the Suwannee Music Park, 3076 95th Dr, Live Oak, FL 32060. Phone: (904) 364-2998. Fax: (904) 364-2998.
Email: spirit@musicliveshere.com.
WWW: http://www.musicliveshere.com

McDERMITT RANCH HAND RODEO. July 3–5. McDermitt, NV. Ranch hands from Nevada, Oregon and Idaho compete for prize money in a number of working events. Street contest and dances add to the festive weekend. Annually, the first weekend in July. For info: Nevada Commission on Tourism, Capitol Complex, Carson City, NV 89710. Phone: (702) 687-4322 or (800) 227-0774. Fax: (702) 687-6779.

"MR PEEPERS" TV PREMIERE: ANNIVERSARY. July 3, 1952. This sitcom was broadcast live and focused on mild-mannered junior high school science teacher, Robinson J. Peepers (Wally Cox). The cast also included Tony Randall, Georgann Johnson, Patricia Benoit, Marion Lorne, Reta Shaw, Jack Warden, Ernest Truex and Sylvia Field. This half-hour series was a summer replacement, but it earned such positive reviews that it was brought back as a regular series. In 1954, TV Guide wrote that "Mr Peepers . . . comes close to being the perfect TV show."

NEW HAVEN HARBORFEST. July 3–5. New Haven Harbor and Lighthouse, New Haven, CT. Three days of fun during the Fourth of July holiday. Ship tours, fireworks displays, live music, food court, arts and crafts show, water sports exhibitions, harbor cruises, reenactment of the British invasion of New Haven. For info: New Haven Harborfest, (203) 946-7821 or Greater New Haven Conv & Visitors Bureau, One Long Wharf Dr, New Haven, CT 06511. Phone: (203) 777-8550 or (800) 332-STAY. Fax: (203) 782-7755.

OLD-TIME FIDDLER'S JAMBOREE AND CRAFTS FESTIVAL. July 3–4. Smithville, TN. Twenty-eight categories of old-time bluegrass including clogging, buck dancing, old-time fiddle band, five-string banjo, dulcimer, dobro, flat-top guitar and fiddle-off to decide the Grand Champion Fiddler. Est attendance: 100,000. For info: Smithville Fiddlers' Jamboree, PO Box 83, Smithville, TN 37166. Phone: (615) 597-8500.
WWW: http://www.public.usit.net/tngenweb/dekalb.htm or Dekalb Chamber of Commerce. Phone: (615) 597-4163.

RAID ON ENTEBBE: ANNIVERSARY. July 3, 1976. An Israeli commando unit staged a raid on Entebbe airport in Uganda and rescued 103 hostages on a hijacked Air France airliner. Three of the hostages, seven hijackers and twenty Ugandan soldiers were killed in the raid. The plane had been en route from Tel Aviv to Paris when taken over by the pro-Palestinian guerrillas.

RENDEZVOUS IN THE PARK. July 3–4 (also July 10–11). Moscow, ID. Four nights of concerts, dining and dancing under the stars. Also, children's events on the first weekend. Quality family entertainment. Est attendance: 1,000. For info: Moscow Chamber of Commerce, Rendezvous in the Park, PO Box 9004, Moscow, ID 83843. Phone: (208) 882-1800.

SPACE MILESTONE: *SOYUZ 14* (USSR). July 3, 1974. Launched on this date, cosmonauts P. Popovich and Y. Artyukhin linked with *Salyut 3* space station during 15-day mission.

SPIRIT OF AMERICA (WITH FREEDOM AND AUDIE MURPHY PATRIOTISM AWARDS). July 3–4. Point Mallard, Decatur, AL. Event was started in 1966 to lift patriotic spirits during the tragedy of the Vietnam War. Presentation of Freedom Award and Audie Murphy Patriotism Award. Also includes the crowning of Miss Point Mallard and a booming fireworks display. Est attendance: 50,000. For info: Jacklyn Bailey, Decatur Conv and Visitors Bureau, PO Box 2349, 719 6th Ave SE, Decatur, AL 35602. Phone: (205) 350-2028 or (800) 524-6181. Email: dcvb@hiwaay.net.

STAY OUT OF THE SUN DAY. July 3. For health's sake, give your skin a break today. [© 1997 by WPL] For info: Tom and Ruth Roy, Wellness Permission League, PO Box 662, Mt Gretna, PA 17064-0662. Phone: (500) 437-5104 or (717) 964-1308. Fax: (717) 964-1335.

July 1998

S	M	T	W	T	F	S
			1	2	3	4
5	6	7	8	9	10	11
12	13	14	15	16	17	18
19	20	21	22	23	24	25
26	27	28	29	30	31	

SUNDOWN SALUTE. July 3–4. Junction City, KS, with fireworks over Milford Lake. Free Independence Day Celebration includes Coors 10K Freedom Run, parade, Veterans Ceremony, family activities, music, crafts and much more. Sundown Salute Inc is a nonprofit organization made up of citizens in the interest of freedom. The Celebration is run completely from corporate, private and individual donations. Est attendance: 35,000. For info: Connie Hall, Marketing Dir, Geary County Conv & Visitors Bureau, 425 N Washington, PO Box 1846, Junction City, KS 66441-1846. Phone: (800) 528-2489 or (913) 238-2885. Fax: (913) 238-2313.

SUNSHINE FESTIVAL. July 3–5. Neptune Park on St. Simons Island, GA. Festival includes exhibits by more than 100 fine arts and crafts artists, rides, entertainment, food booths and a fireworks display. Annually, the three or four days around July 4th. Est attendance: 30,000. For info: Glynn Art Assn, 319 Mallory St, PO Box 20673, St. Simons Island, GA 31522. Phone: (912) 638-8770. Fax: (912) 638-8770.

SWITZERLAND: MONTREUX JAZZ FESTIVAL. July 3–18. Montreux, Switzerland. 32nd annual fesitval of jazz, rock, blues, folk and world music. For info: Montreux Jazz Festival, CP 1325, Switzerland. Phone: (21) (6) 234567.
WWW: http://www.grolier.fr/festival/montreux

"TONY ORLANDO AND DAWN" TV PREMIERE: ANNIVERSARY. July 3, 1974. Tony Orlando and Dawn (Telma Hopkins and Joyce Vincent Wilson) were a recording trio in the early '70s who hosted a summer replacement show for "The Sonny and Cher Show" and then a series. Regulars during the 1975–76 season included Alice Nunn, Lonnie Schorr and Lynn Stuart. In fall of 1976 the show was renamed "Tony Orlando and Dawn Rainbow Hour" and included George Carlin, Edie McClurg and Susan Lanier.

VICKSBURG SURRENDERS: ANNIVERSARY. July 3, 1863. After weeks of immediate siege at the end of a year-long campaign, Vicksburg, MS, surrendered to General Ulysses S. Grant. Formal surrender was consummated on July 4, and on July 8 the besieged city of Port Hudson also surrendered, giving the Union complete control of the Mississippi River.

VIRGIN ISLANDS: DANISH WEST INDIES EMANCIPATION DAY: 150th ANNIVERSARY. July 3, 1848. Commemorates freeing of slaves in the Danish West Indies. Ceremony in Frederiksted, St. Croix, where actual proclamation was first read by Governor-General Peter Von Scholten.

WALES: BEYOND THE BORDER—INTERNATIONAL FESTIVAL OF STORYTELLING. July 3–5. St. Donats Castle, Vale of Glamorgan. Traditional stories and music in the grounds of a medieval castle by the sea. Est attendance: 2,500. For info: David Ambrose, Dir, St. Donats Arts Centre, St. Donats Castle, Vale of Glamorgan, Wales CF61 1WF. Phone: (44) (144) 679-2151. Fax: (44) (144) 679-4711.

BIRTHDAYS TODAY

Lamar Alexander, 58, former US Secretary of Education in Bush administration, born July 3, 1940.

Laura Branigan, 41, singer ("Gloria," "How Am I Supposed to Live Without You"), born Brewster, NY, July 3, 1957.

Betty Buckley, 51, actress (*Cats, Sunset Boulevard*; Sandra Sue Abbott "Abby" Bradford on "Eight Is Enough"), born Big Springs, TX, July 3, 1947.

Tom Cruise, 36, actor (*Taps, Rain Man, The Color of Money, Born on the Fourth of July*), born Syracuse, NY, July 3, 1962.

Taylor Dayne, 35, singer ("Love Will Send You Back"), born Long Island, NY, July 3, 1963.

Pete Fountain, 68, jazz musician, born New Orleans, LA, July 3, 1930.

Kurtwood Smith, 56, actor (*Robocop, Dead Poets Society*), born New Lisbon, WI, July 3, 1942.

Tom Stoppard, 61, playwright (*Travesties, On the Razzle, The Real Thing, Arcadia*), born Zlin, Czechoslovakia, July 3, 1937.

Montel Williams, 42, talk show host ("Montel Williams Show"), born Baltimore, MD, July 3, 1956.

JULY 4 — SATURDAY

Day 185 — 180 Remaining

AIR SHOW AND FIREWORKS DISPLAY. July 4. Aransas County Airport and Rockport Beach Park, Rockport, TX. A display of military, antique and aerobatic planes on display at the Aransas County Airport and a dazzling show of aerobatic flying over Beach Park. In the evening a beautiful fireworks show will be reflected off the serene waters at Beach Park. Est attendance: 40,000. For info: Rockport-Fulton Area Chamber of Commerce, 404 Broadway, Rockport, TX 78382. Phone: (512) 729-6445 or (800) 826-6441. Fax: (512) 729-7681. WWW: http://www.rockport-fulton.org

AMERICA THE BEAUTIFUL PUBLISHED: ANNIVERSARY. July 4. The poem "America the Beautiful" by Katherine Lee Bates, a Wellesley College professor, was first published in the *Congregationalist*, a church publication, on July 4, 1895.

AMERICAN REDNECK DAY. July 4. To celebrate the work-hard, play-hard, independent spirit of the rural working class. Est attendance: 350. For info: Ed Mason, Natl Dir, American Redneck Trading Post, 317 Fogwell Rd, Centreville, MD 21617. Phone: (410) 758-0777.

ANVIL MOUNTAIN RUN. July 4. Nome, AK. At 8 AM the 17K run up 1,134-ft Anvil Mountain and return to the city of Nome starts the day's activities. Record time: 1 hr, 11 min, 23 sec. 20th running. Annually, July 4. Est attendance: 500. For info: Rasmussen's Music Mart, PO Box 2, Nome, AK 99762-0002. Phone: (907) 443-2798. Fax: (907) 443-5777.

ARMSTRONG, LOUIS: NOT BORN THIS DAY. July 4, 1901. Although he often said he was born July 4, 1900, according to personnel at the Louis Armstrong Archives of Queens College, Flushing, NY, documents in their collection indicate that Armstrong was actually born Aug 4, 1901.

BIGGEST ALL-NIGHT GOSPEL SINGING IN THE WORLD. July 4. Memorial Field, Bonifay, FL. Sponsor: Bonifay Kiwanis Club. Est attendance: 10,000. For info: Rickey Callahan, Chair, PO Box 425, Bonifay, FL 32425. Phone: (904) 547-3613. Fax: (904) 547-9223.

BOOM BOX PARADE. July 4. Main St, Willimantic, CT. Connecticut's unique people's parade. Anyone can march, enter a float or watch; only requirement—bring a radio. No "real" bands allowed. (Marching music broadcast on WILI-AM Radio and played by "boom boxes" along the parade route.) 11 AM. Est attendance: 10,000. For info: Wayne Norman, Prog Dir, WILI-AM, 720 Main St, Willimantic, CT 06226. Phone: (860) 456-1111. Fax: (860) 456-9501. Email: am@wili.com. WWW: http://www.wili.com

BRISTOL CIVIC, MILITARY AND FIREMEN'S PARADE. July 4. Bristol, RI. The nation's oldest 4th of July parade. Features floats, bands, veteran and patriotic organizations and military units. Patriotic exercises, a tradition dating to 1785, are held prior to the parade. Annually, July 4. Est attendance: 175,000. For info: Bristol County Chamber of Commerce, 654 Metacom Ave, PO Box 250, Warren, RI 02885-0250. Phone: (401) 245-0750.

CALITHUMPIAN PARADE. July 4. Biwabik, MN. Funny parade, clowns and bands; Biwabik's population of 1,000 jumps to more than 15,000 for a day. Annually, on the Fourth of July. For info: Darlene Jackson, Committe Co-Chair, Biwabik Area Civic Assn, Box 309, Biwabik, MN 55708. Phone: (218) 865-4183 or (218) 865-6033.

CANADA: BUSINESS AND PROFESSIONAL WOMEN'S FLEA MARKET AND CRAFT SALE. July 4. Bracebridge, Ont. Annually, the first Saturday in July. For info: Bracebridge Chamber of Commerce, 1-1 Manitoba St, Bracebridge, Ont, Canada P1L 1S4. Phone: (705) 645-4600.

CANADA: SASKATOON EXHIBITION. July 4–11. Exhibition Centre, Saskatoon, Saskatchewan. Free stage entertainment, concessions, horse racing, midway, kidsville, 4-H Jr activities, casino, exhibits; beef, dairy, sheep, swine shows; Saskatchewan Youth Talent Search, parade on July 6 (annually on Monday of Exhibition week). Est attendance: 185,000. For info: (306) 931-7149 or Tourism Saskatchewan, 500-1900 Albert St, Regina, Sask, Canada S4P 4L9. Phone: (800) 667-7191. Email: travel.info@sasktourism.sk.ca. WWW: http://www.sasktourism.com

CELEBRATION ON THE CANE: AN OLD FASHIONED FOURTH OF JULY. July 4. Natchitoches, LA. Featuring hot dogs, apple pie, lemonade and a variety of traditional Fourth of July fare. Musical entertainment including string bands, brass bands, Sousa marches and patriotic choir presentations. Est attendance: 10,000. For info: Calendar of Events, Natchitoches Parish Tourist Commission, 781 Front St, Natchitoches, LA 71457. Phone: (318) 352-8072 or (800) 259-1714. Fax: (318) 352-2415.

CHILDREN'S COLONIAL FAIR. July 4–5. Yorktown Victory Center, Yorktown, VA. 18th-century games and entertainment and crafts to make and take home are among a variety of activities planned for young people. Est attendance: 1,500. For info: Jamestown-Yorktown Fdtn, PO Box 1607, Williamsburg, VA 23187. Phone: (757) 253-4838. Fax: (757) 253-5299. WWW: http://www.historyisfun.org

☆ ☆ ☆

COOLIDGE, CALVIN: BIRTH ANNIVERSARY. July 4, 1872. The 30th President of the US was born John Calvin Coolidge at Plymouth, VT, July 4, 1872. He succeeded to the presidency Aug 3, 1923, following the death of Warren G. Harding. Coolidge was elected president once, in 1924, but did "not choose to run for president in 1928." Nicknamed Silent Cal, he is reported to have said, "If you don't say anything, you won't be called on to repeat it." Coolidge died at Northampton, MA, on Jan 5, 1933.

CRAFT DAY BY THE BAY. July 4. Harvey Cedars, NJ. More than 100 crafters and artists displaying and selling their handcrafted goods. Est attendance: 2,000. For info: Harvey Cedars Activity Committee, PO Box 3185, Harvey Cedars, NJ 08008. Phone: (609) 494-2843 or (609) 494-3107. Fax: (609) 494-2335.

DECLARATION OF INDEPENDENCE APPROVAL AND SIGNING: ANNIVERSARY. July 4, 1776. The Declaration of Independence was approved by the Continental Congress: "Signed by Order and in Behalf of the Congress, John Hancock, President, Attest, Charles Thomson, Secretary." The official signing occurred on Aug 2, 1776. The manuscript journals of the Congress for that date state: "The declaration of independence being engrossed and compared at the table was signed by the members."

ENGLAND: CHELTENHAM INTERNATIONAL FESTIVAL OF MUSIC. July 4–19. Cheltenham, Gloucestershire. The best of contemporary British music including symphony and chamber music, opera, dance, and jazz. Est attendance: 32,000. For info: Mr Kim Sargeant, Festival Organiser, Town Hall, Imperial Square, Cheltenham, Gloucestershire, England GL50 1QA. Phone: (44) (1242) 52-1621. Fax: (44) (1242) 57-3902.

FINLAND: SAVONLINNA OPERA FESTIVAL. July 4–Aug 2. Savonlinna. One of Europe's most important and best known music festivals. The 1998 season includes works from Wagner, Mascagni, Verdi, Britten and guest performances by the Royal Opera House Covent Garden. Est attendance: 55,000. For info: Savonlinna Opera Festival, Box Office, Olavinkatu 27, Savonlinna, Finland SF-57130. Phone: (358) 15-47 67 511. Fax: (358) 15-47 67 450. Email: helena.kontiainen@operafestival.fi.

FIRESTORM '98. July 4. Lakemont Park, Altoona, PA. The region's largest Fourth of July celebration with live entertainment on stage all day and a spectacular fireworks show. For info: Melissa Albarano, Lakemont Park, 700 Park Ave, Altoona, PA 16602. Phone: (814) 949-7275 or (800) 434-8006. Fax: (814) 949-9207.

FIREWORKS CELEBRATION. July 4. Demopolis, AL. Each year the Demopolis Area Chamber of Commerce presents a spectacular array of fireworks in celebration of Independence Day. The fireworks celebration is held at the Demopolis City Landing and begins at 9 PM. Est attendance: 10,000. For info: Jane Gross, Exec Dir, Demopolis Area Chamber of Commerce, Box 667, Demopolis, AL 36732. Phone: (334) 289-0270. Fax: (334) 289-1382. WWW: http://www.chamber.dempolis.us

FIREWORKS SPECTACULAR. July 4. Truman Dam, Warsaw, MO. Commemorating America's independence, this gigantic fireworks display can be viewed at the Truman Dam. Est attendance: 10,000. For info: Warsaw Chamber of Commerce, PO Box 264, Warsaw, MO 65355. Phone: (816) 438-5922.

FOSTER, STEPHEN: BIRTH ANNIVERSARY. July 4. Stephen Collins Foster, one of America's most famous and best-loved song writers, was born at Lawrenceville, PA, on July 4, 1826. Among his nearly 200 songs: "Oh! Susanna," "Camptown Races," "Old Folks at Home" ("Swanee River"), "Jeanie with the Light Brown Hair," "Old Black Joe," "Beautiful Dreamer." Foster died in poverty at Bellevue Hospital at New York, NY, on Jan 13, 1864. The anniversary of his death has been observed as Stephen Foster Memorial Day by Presidential Proclamation since 1952.

FOURTH OF JULY EXTRAVAGANZA AND BUFFALO-RAMA. July 4–5. Hettinger, ND. An old-fashioned Fourth at the site of the "Last Great Buffalo Hunt" and "t." Most events are free: beef barbecue, parade, variety show, pie bake-off, wild west show, fishing derby, wagon train, music, fireworks and more. Plus living history tours to the site of the "Last Great Buffalo Hunt" on June 20, 1882, when 2,000 Teton Sioux Indians in full hunting regalia killed 5,000 buffalo. Black powder cartridge shoot at site. Est attendance: 2,000. For info: Terri Thiel, Dir, Community Promotions, Box 1323, Hettinger, ND 58639. Phone: (701) 567-2531. Fax: (701) 567-2348.
Email: adamsdv@hettinger.ctctel.com.
WWW: http://www.hettingernd.com

FREDERICKSBURG HERITAGE FESTIVAL. July 4–5. Fredericksburg, VA. To create an awareness of Fredericksburg's historic heritage. Parade, raft race, street festival, country music, jazz, rock and roll, fireworks and Civil War battle reenactment. Est attendance: 15,000. For info: Visitor Center, 706 Caroline St, Fredericksburg, VA 22401. Phone: (800) 678-4748. Fax: (540) 372-6587. Email: fburg@illuminet.net.

July 1998

S	M	T	W	T	F	S
			1	2	3	4
5	6	7	8	9	10	11
12	13	14	15	16	17	18
19	20	21	22	23	24	25
26	27	28	29	30	31	

FREEDOM FEST. July 4 (rain date July 5). Lake of the Woods, Mahomet, IL. Annual celebration of patriotism. Family activities capped off by a spectacular fireworks display. Admission charged. Est attendance: 7,000. For info: Andee Chestnut, PR Coord, Champaign Co Forest Preserve District, PO Box 1040, Mahomet, IL 61853. Phone: (217) 586-3360. Fax: (217) 586-5020. Email: ccfpd@prairienet.org. WWW: http://www.prairienet.org/ccfpd

FREEDOM WEEK. July 4–10. To disseminate throughout the world information about freedom and liberty. For complete info and many famous quotations about freedom and liberty, send $3 to cover expense of printing, handling and postage. Annually, July 4–10. For info: Dr. Stanley Drake, Pres, Intl Soc of Friendship and Good Will, 412 Cherry Hills Dr, Bakersfield, CA 93309-2866.

GOLDBERG, RUBE: BIRTH ANNIVERSARY. July 4, 1883. The cartoonist with an engineering degree who put his education to work inventing elaborate machines with involved steps to accomplish ludicrously simple tasks. He is best remembered for the creative inventions of his cartoon character Lucifer Gorgonzola Butts. Born at San Francisco, Goldberg died Dec 7, 1970, at New York City.

GREAT CARDBOARD BOAT REGATTA. July 4. Rotary Riverview Park, Sheboygan, WI. The most spectacular and hilarious races of somewhat seaworthy craft ever launched in Wisconsin. Person-powered cardboard boats compete in various classes for prizes. Awards for the most spirited team, the most beautiful boats, boats following a theme and the most spectacular sinking (Titanic Award). Prizes for top finishers in three boat classes: propelled by oars or paddles; propelled by mechanical means such as paddle wheels or propellers and "Instant Boats" made from "Secret Kits" by spectators-turned-participants. Est attendance: 16,000. For info: John Michael Kohler Arts Center, 608 New York Ave, PO Box 489, Sheboygan, WI 53082-0489. Phone: (414) 458-6144. Fax: (414) 458-4473.

GREAT HOUSEBOAT/CRUISER PARADE AND FIREWORKS CELEBRATION. July 4. Rough River State Resort Park, Falls of Rough, KY. Decorated boats, cruisers and houseboats, fireworks and parade. Est attendance: 19,000. For info: Tom DeHaven, Rec Supr, Rough River Dam State Resort Park, 450 Lodge Rd, Falls of Rough, KY 40119. Phone: (502) 257-2311.

GREAT SEAL OF THE UNITED STATES PROPOSED: ANNIVERSARY. July 4, 1776. The Continental Congress, meeting at Philadelphia, PA, after voting to adopt the Declaration of Independence, went on to approve the following: "Resolved, that Dr. Franklin, Mr J. Adams and Mr Jefferson, be a committee, to bring in a device for a seal for the United States of America," thus beginning the history of the Great Seal of the US on the first day of independence.

HAWTHORNE, NATHANIEL: BIRTH ANNIVERSARY. July 4, 1804. Novelist and short-story writer (*The Scarlet Letter*), born at Salem, MA. Other works included *The House of the Seven Gables* and *The Blithedale Romance*. Hawthorne died at Plymouth, NH, May 19, 1864.

HOOD RIVER OLD-FASHIONED FOURTH OF JULY. July 4. Port Marina Park, Hood River, OR. Parade, barbecue, fun run, entertainment and fireworks over the Columbia River. For info: Hood River Chamber of Commerce, 405 Portway Dr, Hood River, OR 97031. Phone: (800) 366-3530.

ICE CREAM SOCIAL. July 4. Indianapolis, IN. Independence Day celebration. Music, lawn games and living history. Est attendance: 1,000. For info: President Benjamin Harrison Home, PR Dept, 1230 N Delaware St, Indianapolis, IN 46202. Phone: (317) 631-1898.

INDEPENDENCE DAY (FOURTH OF JULY): ANNIVERSARY. July 4, 1776. The US commemorates adoption of the Declaration of Independence by the Continental Congress on

July 4, 1776. The nation's birthday. Legal holiday in all states and territories.

INDEPENDENCE DAY CELEBRATION. July 4. Washington, DC. The nation's capital celebrates the Fourth of July with a parade past many historic monuments on the Mall. National Symphony Orchestra concert in the evening followed by spectacular fireworks display over the Washington Monument. Est attendance: 450,000. For info: Washington, DC Conv and Visitors Assn, 1212 New York Ave NW, Washington, DC 20005. Phone: (202) 789-7000 or (202) 619-7222.
WWW: http://www.washington.org

INDEPENDENCE DAY CELEBRATION. July 4–5. Eastside Park, Trenton, MO. 3rd annual all-day event with games, organized competitions, booths, an evening music show and a fireworks display at dusk. Est attendance: 1,200. For info: Linda Kennebeck, 617 Main St, Trenton, MO 64683. Phone: (816) 359-5305 or (816) 359-4324. Fax: (816) 359-4325.

INDEPENDENCE DAY SYMPHONY CONCERT AND FIREWORKS. July 4. Wheeling, WV. Independence Day celebration on the Wheeling waterfront. For info: Wheeling Conv and Visitors Bureau, 1310 Market St, Wheeling, WV 26003. Phone: (800) 828-3097 or (304) 233-7709.

INTERNATIONAL CHERRY PIT SPITTING CONTEST. July 4. Tree-Mendus Fruit Farm, Eau Claire, MI. A nutritious sport—is there a better way to dispose of the pits once you have eaten the cherry? Entrants eat a cherry and then spit the pit as far as possible on a blacktop surface. The entrant who spits the pit the farthest including the roll is the champ. Annually, the first Saturday in July. Est attendance: 1,000. For info: Lynn Sage, Adv and Promo Mgr, Tree-Mendus Fruit Farm, 9351 E Eureka Rd, Eau Claire, MI 49111. Phone: (616) 782-7101.

JULY 4th FAMILY CELEBRATION. July 4. Fort Lauderdale, FL. Featuring live music, fireworks and food. 6 PM–4:30 PM. Annually, July 4. Est attendance: 300,000. For info: Greater Fort Lauderdale Conv & Visitors Bureau, 1850 Eller Dr, Ste 303, Fort Lauderdale, FL 33316. Phone: (954) 489-3255.

JULY 4th FIREWORKS FESTIVAL. July 4. Hartsville, SC. An afternoon of family games, picnic, music and fireworks at dark. Est attendance: 8,000. For info: Tina Kissiah, Admin Asst, Greater Hartsville Chamber of Commerce, PO Box 578, Hartsville, SC 29551. Phone: (803) 332-6401.

KINGSTON OLD-FASHIONED 4th OF JULY. July 4–5. Waterfront, at Port of Kingston. Mike Wallace Park and Kola Kola Park, Kingston, WA. Family event featuring displays, food booths, children's rides, games, Classic Car Show, Touch a Truck, Kingston's Farmer's Market, Kingston's Business Fair, Tiny Town made just for children, logging contest, Slug races and more. Fireworks display over Puget Sound from the beautiful Kingston Marina. The only big display on the Peninsula. Est attendance: 15,000. For info: Greater Kingston Chamber of Commerce, PO Box 78, Kingston, WA 98346. Phone: (360) 297-3813. Fax: (360) 779-8018. Email: mgraves@silverlink.net.
WWW: http://www.kingstonwa.com

KSNT GO 4th. July 4–5. Topeka, KS. A fundraiser for nonprofit groups and a fireworks display synchronized to music. Est attendance: 100,000. For info: KSNT-TV, PO Box 2700, Topeka, KS 66601. Phone: (913) 582-4000. Fax: (913) 582-4783. Email: 27news@ksnt.com.

LAST GREAT BUFFALO HUNT: ANNIVERSARY. July 4–5. By 1882 most of the estimated 60–75 million buffalo had been killed by white hide hunters, the meat left to rot. Buffalo numbered only about 50,000 when "The Last Great Buffalo Hunt" took place on Indian reservation lands near Hettinger, ND. Some 2,000 Teton Sioux Indians in full hunting regalia killed about 5,000 buffalo. The occasion is also referred to as "The Last Stand of the American Buffalo" as within 16 months the last of the free-ranging buffalo were gone. For info: Terri Thiel, Dir Community Promotions, Box 1323, Hettinger, ND 58639. Phone: (701) 567-2531. Fax: (701) 567-2348.
Email: adamsdv@hettinger.ctctel.com.
WWW: http://hettingernd.com

LENEXA FREEDOM RUN. July 4. Old Town, Lenexa, KS. 20th annual 10K & 5K runs. Est attendance: 1,500. For info: Lenexa Parks and Recreation, 13420 Oak, Lenexa, KS 66215-3652. Phone: (913) 541-8592. Fax: (913) 492-8118.
WWW: http://www.ci.lenexa.ks.us

LEWISTOWN 4th PARADE AND CELEBRATION. July 4. Lewistown, MT. Parade, breakfast, bingo, barbecue, baseball and games. The Shrine Circus (two performances), fireworks. Est attendance: 2,000. For info: Lewistown Chamber of Commerce, PO Box 818, Lewistown, MT 59457. Phone: (406) 538-5436. Fax: (406) 538-5437. Email: lewchamb@lewistown.net. WWW: http://www.lewistown.net/~lewchamb

MARYLAND SYMPHONY AT ANTIETAM. July 4. Antietam Battlefield, Sharpsburg, MD. Maryland Symphony Orchestra features patriotic music and light classics in its salute to independence. Features fireworks and cannon fire. Annually, the Saturday closest to July 4. Est attendance: 35,000. For info: Bethany Latham, Maryland Symphony Orchestra, 13 S Potomac St, Hagerstown, MD 21740-5512. Phone: (301) 797-4000. Fax: (301) 797-2314. WWW: http://www.mdsymphony.com or http://www.culturefinder.com

MONETT OLD-FASHIONED FOURTH OF JULY CELEBRATION. July 4. Monett, MO. Parade, games, children's carnival, bands, gospel music, steam engine display, hot air balloon rides, air stunts, skydivers, National Guard helicopter and vehicle display, food and a fireworks display. Annually, the Fourth of July. Est attendance: 5,000. For info: Monett Chamber of Commerce, PO Box 47, Monett, MO 65708. Phone: (417) 235-7919. Fax: (417) 235-4076.

MOUNT MARATHON RACE. July 4. Seward, AK. Grueling footrace begins in downtown Seward, then ascends and descends 3,022-ft Mt Marathon. Race began as a wager between two sourdoughs. 71st running. Est attendance: 20,000. For info: Seward Chamber of Commerce, PO Box 749, Seward, AK 99664. Phone: (907) 224-8051. Fax: (907) 224-5353.
WWW: http://www.alaskaone.com/seward

MYSTIC SEAPORT INDEPENDENCE DAY CELEBRATION. July 4. Mystic, CT. Visitors can participate in a recreation of an 1870s Fourth of July with costumed staff. There are patriotic ceremonies and a parade of the "Antiques and Horribles." Kids, old-fashioned spelling bee. Est attendance: 3,500. For info: Mystic Seaport, 75 Greenmanville Ave, Box 6000, Mystic, CT 06355. Phone: (203) 572-5315.
WWW: http://www.mystic.org

NATIONAL COUNTRY MUSIC DAY. July 4. A day for those who love to listen to America's favorite kind of music—country music. Annually, July 4. For info: Alan W. Brue, 2006 NW 55th Ave, #H-5, Gainesville, FL 32653.

OATMAN SIDEWALK EGG FRYING CONTEST. July 4. Oatman, AZ. Contest held at high noon on the downtown streets of old Rt 66. Also, Old West gun fights, wild burros roaming the streets, food, entertainment and more. Note: Only solar heat may be used to fry the eggs. 15-minute time limit. Annually, July 4. Est attendance: 2,500. For info: Spirit Mountain Productions, 1255 Hancock Rd, Bullhead City, AZ 86442. Phone: (520) 763-5885. Fax: (520) 763-3545.

OLD-FASHIONED PICNIC IN THE PARK. July 4–5. Lincoln Park, Pittsburg, KS. Old-fashioned picnic with families gathering for contests, games, food, carnival, live music, night golf with lighted golf balls and a giant fireworks display set to music. Annually, July 4. Est attendance: 15,000. For info: Pittsburg Parks & Recreation Dept, PO Box 688, Pittsburg, KS 66762. Phone: (316) 231-8310. Fax: (316) 231-2103.

OLD GLORY JUBILEE. July 4. Elsberry, MO. Old-time picnic, parade, entertainment, games, crafts and lots of food. Est attendance: 1,000. For info: Elsberry City Hall, 201 Broadway, Elsberry, MO 63343. Phone: (573) 898-5588. Fax: (573) 898-2249.

OLD VERMONT FOURTH. July 4. Woodstock, VT. A traditional Fourth of July with patriotic speeches and debates, making "1890" flags, a spelling bee for adults, ice cream making, sack race and more. Est attendance: 750. For info: Deborah Bullissa, Exec Asst, Billings Farm and Museum, PO Box 489, Woodstock, VT 05091. Phone: (802) 457-2355. Fax: (802) 457-4663. Email: billings.farm@valley.net.

PEACHTREE ROAD RACE. July 4. Atlanta, GA. 10K run. 50,000-runner limit; advance registration only. Send self-addressed stamped envelope by Mar 1, 1998. 40,000 entrants on first-come basis and 10,000 selected by lottery from other entries postmarked in March 1998. Est attendance: 50,000. For info: Atlanta Track Club, 3097 E Shadowlawn Ave, Atlanta, GA 30305. Phone: (404) 231-9064. WWW: http://www.atlantatrackclub.org

PEPSI 400. July 4. Daytona International Speedway, Daytona Beach, FL. 40th running of NASCAR Winston Cup's "Mid-Summer Classic." Sponsor: Pepsi. For info: Daytona Intl Speedway, PO Box 28014, Daytona Beach, FL 32120-2801. Phone: (904) 947-6782 or for tickets (904) 253-RACE (7223). Fax: (904) 947-6791. WWW: http://www.daytonausa.com

PHILIPPINES: FIL-AMERICAN FRIENDSHIP DAY. July 4. National. Formerly the National Independence Day, now celebrated as Fil-American Friendship Day.

PLANTATION DAYS AT HIGHLAND. July 4–5. Ash Lawn-Highland, Charlottesville, VA. An Independence Day celebration with 18th-century crafts, living history, music, dance, food and games. Est attendance: 2,000. For info: Ash Lawn-Highland, James Monroe Parkway, Charlottesville, VA 22902. Phone: (804) 293-9539. Fax: (804) 293-8000. Email: ashlawn@comet.net. WWW: http://avenue.org/ashlawn

PRAIRIE PIONEER DAYS. July 4. Arapahoe, NE. Parade, games for kids, food booths, free swimming, watermelon bust, quilt show, horseshoe pitching, black powder shoot, model airplane event, baseball games, fireworks and more. For info: Tammie Middagh, Secy, Arapahoe Chamber of Commerce, PO Box 624, Arapahoe, NE 68922.

ROAN MOUNTAIN STATE PARK'S FIREWORKS JAMBOREE. July 4. Roan Mountain, TN. Bluegrass music, clogging and fireworks. Est attendance: 15,000. For info: Jennifer Laughlin, Ranger Naturalist, Roan Mtn State Park, 527 Hwy 143, Roan Mountain, TN 37687. Phone: (615) 772-3303. Fax: (423) 772-0142.

ROCKPORT ART FESTIVAL. July 4–5. Rockport Festival Grounds, Rockport, TX. The work of top artists from across the southwestern US lines the waterfront for two days. Jazz and plenty of good food. Est attendance: 25,000. For info: Rockport Center for the Arts, 902 Navigation Circle, Rockport, TX 78382. Phone: (512) 729-5519 or (800) 242-0071. Fax: (512) 729-4438. WWW: http://www.rockport-fulton.org

SAUK TRAIL HERITAGE DAYS POWWOW RENDEZVOUS. July 4–6. Johnson's Sauk Trail State Park, Kewanee, IL. Three-day event features artifact display, powwow, Native American crafts, circa 1800 fur traders rendezvous, voyager canoe rides and tours of the Ryan Round Barn, one of the largest in the state of Illinois. Est attendance: 20,000. For info: Mark Mikenas, Exec VP, Kewanee Chamber of Commerce, 113 E 2nd St, Kewanee, IL 61443. Phone: (309) 852-2175. Fax: (309) 852-2176. Email: kchamber@inw.net.

"THE SOUPY SALES SHOW" TV PREMIERE: ANNIVERSARY. July 4, 1955. Soupy Sales hosted a number of national and local children's shows from 1955 to 1979. All of his programs have included some of these features: jokes, puns, songs, sketches, puppets, silent films and pies in the face. Sales's humor occasionally went over the edge and got him in trouble; for example, in 1965 his show was suspended for a week because he asked his viewers to send him the green paper in their parents' wallets! His 1979 show was his return after not having a show for 12 years.

SOUTH AFRICA: ROTHMANS JULY. July 4. Durban. Premier horse racing event in South Africa with stakes of one million rand. Annually, the first Saturday in July. Est attendance: 40,000. For info: Durban Turf Club, PO Box 924, Durban, 4000, South Africa. Phone: (27) (31) 309-4545. Fax: (27) (31) 309-2553.

STOCK EXCHANGE HOLIDAY (INDEPENDENCE DAY). July 4. The holiday schedules for the various exchanges are subject to change if relevant rules, regulations or exchange policies are revised. If you have questions, phone: American Stock Exchange (212) 306-1000; Chicago Board of Trade (312) 435-3500; Chicago Board of Options Exchange (312) 786-5600; New York Stock Exchange (212) 656-2065; Pacific Stock Exchange (415) 393-4000; Philadelphia Stock Exchange (215) 496-5000.

SULLIVAN FREEDOM FESTIVAL. July 4. Sullivan Fairgrounds, Sullivan, MO. Festival open 4 PM–10 PM. Features children's activities, contests, games, entertainment, food and fireworks. Est attendance: 5,000. For info: Sullivan Chamber of Commerce, PO Box 536, Sullivan, MO 63080. Phone: (573) 860-2313. Email: chamber@fidnet.com.
WWW: http://www.ne3.com/vs

TEN THOUSAND CRESTONIANS. July 4. Downtown and McKinley Park, Creston, IA. Parade, fireworks, flea market, talent show, historical village, carnival and food. All to celebrate US founding. Est attendance: 5,000. For info: Creston Chamber of Commerce, PO Box 471, Creston, IA 50801. Phone: (515) 782-7021.

July 1998

S	M	T	W	T	F	S
			1	2	3	4
5	6	7	8	9	10	11
12	13	14	15	16	17	18
19	20	21	22	23	24	25
26	27	28	29	30	31	

TRUMAN LIBRARY INDEPENDENCE DAY CELEBRATION. July 4. Truman Library, Independence, MO. Food, games, music and fireworks. Est attendance: 8,000. For info: Larry J. Hackman, Dir, Harry S. Truman Library, US Hwy 24 and Delaware St, Independence, MO 64050. Phone: (816) 833-1400. Fax: (816) 833-4368. Email: library@truman.nara.gov. WWW: http://sunsite.unc.edu/lia/president/truman.html

TUSKEGEE INSTITUTE OPENING: ANNIVERSARY. July 4, 1881. Booker T. Washington's famed agricultural-industrial institution was built from the ground up by dedicated students seeking academic and vocational training. The institute started as a shanty before Washington purchased an abandoned plantation in Tuskegee, AL. The students built the dormitories, classrooms and chapel from bricks out of their own kiln.

WESTON JAYCEE'S ANNUAL JULY 4TH CELEBRATION. July 4. Weston, MO. The evening begins with an ice cream social and a presentation by the Missouri Valley Skydivers with fireworks beginning at 9 PM. For info: Weston Development Co, 502 Main St, Weston, MO 64098. Phone: (816) 640-2909.

WHITEFISH ART FESTIVAL. July 4–5. Whitefish, MT. Nonjuried arts and crafts show and sale. One of the valley's finest presentations of art. Proceeds go to Cross Currents School. Est attendance: 1,200. For info: Cross Currents School, PO Box 131, Whitefish, MT 59937. Phone: (406) 862-0814 or (406) 752-9099.

WOOD RADIO/SPARTAN STORES FIREWORKS GALA. July 4 (rain date July 5). Ah-Nab-Awen Park (Bicentennial Park), downtown Grand Rapids, MI. The 16th annual fireworks gala held for the Grand Rapids community—the biggest and brightest fireworks display in western Michigan. Family and musical entertainment provided for spectators. Sponsors: Spartan Brand, WOOD-AM 1300, EZ-105.7 FM. Est attendance: 350,000. For info: Juli Agacinski, Promo Dir, WOOD Radio, 77 Monroe Center, Grand Rapids, MI 49503. Phone: (616) 459-1919. Fax: (616) 732-3330. Email: juli@ez1057.com
WWW: http://www.woodradio.com or
WWW: http://www.ez1057.com

WORLD'S GREATEST LIZARD RACE. July 4. Chaparral Park, Lovington, NM. Participants and observers cheer as their lizards and iguanas race down a 16-ft ramp; winners are awarded trophies. Many other lizard events will be held throughout the day. Entertainment and other games are also featured. Annually, July 4. For info: Lovington Chamber of Commerce, PO Box 1347, Lovington, NM 88260. Phone: (505) 396-5311. Fax: (505) 396-2823.

WROK/WZOK/WXXQ ANYTHING THAT FLOATS ROCK RIVER RAFT RACE. July 4. Rock River, Rockford, IL. More than 100 rafts compete for prizes in speed and creativity. Annually, July 4. Est attendance: 60,000. For info: WROK/WZOK/WXXQ Radios, 3901 Brendenwood Rd, Rockford, IL 61107. Phone: (815) 399-2233. Fax: (815) 399-8148.

ZOOBALEE. July 4. Lee Richardson Zoo, Garden City, KS. Old fashioned Independence Day celebration featuring duck races, dunk tank, ethnic foods, dart throw, moon walk and more. Est attendance: 5,000. For info: Dianne Trankel Schwien, Dvmt Dir, Friends of Lee Richardson Zoo, Box 1638, Garden City, KS 67846. Phone: (316) 276-6243. Fax: (316) 276-0910.

BIRTHDAYS TODAY

Signy Coleman, 38, actress (Hope Newman on "The Young and the Restless"), born Marin County, CA, July 4, 1960.
Allen (Al) Davis, 69, football executive, born Brockton, MA, July 4, 1929.
Harvey Grant, 33, basketball player, born Augusta, GA, July 4, 1965.
Horace Grant, 33, basketball player, born Augusta, GA, July 4, 1965.
Leona Helmsley, 78, former hotel executive, born Brooklyn, NY, July 4, 1920.
Ann Landers (Esther Pauline Friedman), 80, advice columnist, born Sioux City, IA, July 4, 1918.
Gina Lollobrigida, 70, actress, photographer (*Belles de Nuit; Bread, Love and Dreams*), born Auviaco, Italy, July 4, 1928.
Jawann Oldham, 41, former basketball player, born Seattle, WA, July 4, 1957.
Geraldo Rivera, 55, journalist, talk-show host ("Geraldo"; *Exposing Myself*), born New York, NY, July 4, 1943.
Eva Marie Saint, 74, actress (Oscar for *On the Waterfront*; *North by Northwest, Exodus*), born Newark, NJ, July 4, 1924.
Pamela Howard (Pam) Shriver, 36, tennis player, born Baltimore, MD, July 4, 1962.
Neil Simon, 71, playwright (*The Odd Couple, Barefoot in the Park*), born New York, NY, July 4, 1927.
George Michael Steinbrenner III, 68, baseball executive, born Rocky River, OH, July 4, 1930.
Abigail Van Buren (Pauline Esther Friedman), 80, advice columnist, born Sioux City, IA, July 4, 1918.

☆ ☆ ☆

JULY 5 — SUNDAY

Day 186 — 179 Remaining

BARNUM, PHINEAS TAYLOR: BIRTH ANNIVERSARY. July 5, 1810. Promoter of the bizarre and unusual. Barnum's American Museum opened in 1842, promoting unusual acts including the Feejee Mermaid, Chang and Eng (the original Siamese Twins) and General Tom Thumb. In 1850 he began his promotion of Jenny Lind, "The Swedish Nightingale," and parlayed her singing talents into a major financial success at the nation's box offices. Barnum also cultivated a keen interest in politics, from his early days as a founder of the newspaper *Herald of Freedom*. His outspoken editorials resulted not only in lawsuits but also in at least one jail sentence. In 1852 he declined the Democratic nomination for governor of Connecticut but did serve two terms in the Connecticut legislature beginning in 1865. He was defeated in a bid for US Congress in 1866 but served as mayor of Bridgeport, CT, from 1875 to 1876. In 1871 "The Greatest Show on Earth" opened in Brooklyn, NY; Barnum merged with his rival J.A. Bailey in 1881 to form the Barnum and Bailey Circus. P.T. Barnum was born at Bethel, CT, and died at Bridgeport, CT, on Apr 7, 1891.

BE NICE TO NEW JERSEY WEEK. July 5–11. A time to recognize the assets of the state most maligned by American comedians. Annually, the first full week of July. For info: Lauren Barnett, Lone Star Publications of Humor, 8452 Fredericksburg Rd, Ste 103, San Antonio, TX 78229. Email: lspubs@aol.com. WWW: http://members.aol.com/lspubs/lsindex.html

CAPE VERDE: NATIONAL DAY. July 5. Commemorates independence from Portugal.

DIETARY MANAGERS ASSOCIATION ANNUAL MEETING AND EXPO. July 5–9. Opryland Hotel, Nashville, TN. 38th annual. Est attendance: 800. For info: Dennis Leopold, VP, Dietary Mgrs Assn, One Pierce Pl, Ste 1220W, Itasca, IL 60143-1277. Phone: (630) 775-9200. Fax: (630) 775-9250.

DUCKTONA 500. July 5. Riverview Park, Sheboygan Falls, WI. Plastic duck race in the park lagoon. "Kiss the Pig" contest, antique car show, games for children, five-mile run and live bands. Pancake breakfast, burgers, brats, beverages. Annually, the first Sunday in July. Est attendance: 3,000. For info: Lisa Wegener, Exec Dir, Sheboygan Falls Chamber Main St Office, 641 Monroe, Ste 108, Sheboygan Falls, WI 53085. Phone: (414) 467-6206. Fax: (414) 467-9571.

FARRAGUT, DAVID: BIRTH ANNIVERSARY. July 5, 1801. Born near Knoxville, TN, and died Aug 14, 1870, at Portsmouth, NH. Admiral in the American Civil War who was famous for his incredible naval victories. At Mobile Bay, AL, in a disastrous attack on his entire fleet by the Confederates' Fort Morgan, Farragut proclaimed the infamous cry, "Damn the torpedoes, full speed ahead!" They escaped the attack and Mobile Bay surrendered.

FUTURE HOMEMAKERS OF AMERICA NATIONAL LEADERSHIP MEETING. July 5–9. New Orleans, LA. This meeting is a unique opportunity to gain a national perspective on FHA/HERO activities and issues, elect officers, receive specialized leadership training and enhance chapter activities. Est attendance: 4,400. For info: Patti Frattarola, Future Homemakers of America, Inc, 1910 Association Dr, Reston, VA 20191. Phone: (703) 476-4900. Fax: (703) 860-2713. Email: natlhdqtrs@fhahero.org. WWW: http://www.fhahero.org

GREAT SPANGLED BUTTERFLY DAYS. July 5–11. A weeklong event to celebrate the diversity of Michigan's butterflies. Est attendance: 8,000. For info: Hoffmaster State Park, Gillette Visitor Center, 6585 Lake Harbor Rd, Muskegon, MI 49441. Phone: (616) 798-3573. Fax: (616) 798-4336.

ISLE OF MAN: TYNWALD DAY. July 5. Tynwald Hill at St. John's. Traditionally, on July 5, Old Midsummer Day, the island's parliament of Tynwald assembles at the meeting place of the Vikings to promulgate new laws.

LAVALLETTE INDEPENDENCE EXTRAVAGANZA. July 5. Lavallette, NJ. 45-piece orchestra plays patriotic music during an outstanding fireworks display on the bay. Very suitable for boaters to watch from the water. Always the first Sunday in July. Est attendance: 30,000. For info: Lavallette Heritage Committee, Inc, Ocean County Public Affairs, PO Box 2191, Toms River, NJ 08754. Phone: (732) 793-3652. Email: jgroskol@juno.com.

NATIONAL FAMILY FITNESS WEEK. July 5–11. Parents and children are encouraged to initiate family-oriented activities such as hiking, biking, walking, rollerblading, swimming or camping. As parents, make a commitment to help your children develop good habits including a well-balanced diet and exercise by setting good examples. National Family Fitness Week is set aside to promote the physical well-being of the family unit. Consider the future effects of a lifestyle of poor habits versus a lifestyle of healthy habits and commit to family fitness. For info: Michelle Saari & Kelly Hendershot, Mikela Corp, PO Box 571, Minot, ND 58702. Phone: (701) 857-6080. Fax: (701) 857-6081. Email: mikela@minot.ndak.net.

NATIONAL LABOR RELATIONS ACT OF 1935 (THE WAGNER ACT): ANNIVERSARY. July 5. This bill, signed into law July 5, 1935, guaranteed workers the right to organize and bargain collectively with their employers. It also prohibited the formation of company unions. An enforcement agency, the National Labor Relations Board, was created by the Act.

RAFFLES, STAMFORD: BIRTH ANNIVERSARY. July 5, 1781. Sir Stamford Raffles, English colonial official, founder of Singapore, where he is supposed to have landed on Jan 29, 1819, was born at sea, off Jamaica. He discovered with Joseph Arnold an East Indian fungus that is named after them, *Rafflesia Arnoldi*. Raffles died near London, England, on his birthday, July 5, in 1826.

RHODES, CECIL JOHN: BIRTH ANNIVERSARY. July 5, 1853. English-born, South African millionaire politician. Said to have controlled at one time 90% of the world's diamond production. His will founded the Rhodes Scholarships at Oxford University for superior scholastic achievers, aged 18–25. Rhodesia was named for him. Born at Bishop's Stortford, Hertfordshire, Rhodes died Mar 26, 1902, at Cape Town, South Africa.

SLOVAKIA: SAINT CYRIL AND METHODIUS DAY. July 5. This day is dedicated to the Greek priests and scholars from Thessalonniki, who were invited by Prince Rastislav of Great Moravia to introduce Christianity and the first Slavic alphabet to the pagan people of the kingdom in 863 AD.

SUNDAYS IN THE GARDEN. July 5–Aug 9 (Sundays only). Hamilton House, Vaughan's Lane, South Berwick, ME. Concerts in the formal gardens overlooking 1785 Georgian mansion and Salmon Falls River. Lawn chairs provided, families welcome, but no dogs, please. Admission $5. Annually, Sundays 4–5:30 PM. Est attendance: 400. For info: Soc for Preservation of New England Antiquities, 143 Pleasant St, Portsmouth, NH 03801. Phone: (603) 436-3205. Fax: (603) 436-4651.

VENEZUELA: INDEPENDENCE DAY. July 5. National holiday. Commemorates Proclamation of Independence from Spain on this date in 1811.

ZETKIN, CLARA: BIRTH ANNIVERSARY. July 5, 1857. Women's rights advocate, born at Wiederau, Germany. Zetkin has been credited with being the initiator of International Women's Day, which has been observed on Mar 8 at least since 1910. She died at Arkhangelskoe, Russia, June 20, 1933. See also: "International (Working) Women's Day" (Mar 8).

BIRTHDAYS TODAY

Eliot Feld, 56, dancer, born Brooklyn, NY, July 5, 1942.
Richard Michael ("Goose") Gossage, 47, former baseball player, born Colorado Springs, CO, July 5, 1951.
Katherine Helmond, 64, actress (stage: *The House of Blue Leaves*; "Soap," "Who's the Boss"), born Galveston, TX, July 5, 1934.
Shirley Knight, 62, actress (stage: *Kennedy's Children* [Tony Award, 1976]; *The Dark at the Top of the Stairs, Sweet Bird of Youth, Petulia*), born Goessell, KS, July 5, 1936.
Huey Lewis (Hugh Anthony Cregg III), 47, singer (Huey Lewis and the News), born San Francisco, CA, July 5, 1951.
James David Lofton, 42, former football player, born Fort Ord, CA, July 5, 1956.
Robbie Robertson, 54, musician (guitarist with the Band), born Toronto, Ontario, Canada, July 5, 1944.
Janos Starker, 74, musician, born Budapest, Hungary, July 5, 1924.

JULY 6 — MONDAY

Day 187 — 178 Remaining

CANADA: KIMBERLEY INTERNATIONAL OLD-TIME ACCORDION CHAMPIONSHIPS. July 6–12. Kimberley, British Columbia. Jam sessions, play-downs, finals and trophy presentation. Social evenings dance and entertainment; pancake breakfast. Est attendance: 15,000. For info: Jean Irvin, PO Box 473, Kimberley, BC, Canada V1A 3B9. Phone: (250) 427-4547. Fax: (250) 427-4547.

CARIBBEAN OR CARICOM DAY. July 6. The anniversary of the treaty establishing the Caribbean Community (also called the Treaty of Chaguaramas), signed by the prime ministers of Barbados, Guyana, Jamaica, and Trinidad and Tobago on July 4, 1973. Observed as a public holiday by the participating nations. Annually, the first Monday in July.

COMOROS: INDEPENDENCE DAY. July 6. Federal and Islamic Republic of Comoros commemorates Declaration of Independence on July 6, 1975.

CZECH REPUBLIC: COMMEMORATION DAY OF BURNING OF JOHN HUS. July 6. In honor of Bohemian

July 1998

S	M	T	W	T	F	S
			1	2	3	4
5	6	7	8	9	10	11
12	13	14	15	16	17	18
19	20	21	22	23	24	25
26	27	28	29	30	31	

religious reformer John Hus, who was condemned as a heretic and burned at the stake on July 6, 1415.

FIRST AIRSHIP CROSSING OF ATLANTIC: ANNIVERSARY. July 6. The first airship crossing of the Atlantic was completed as a British dirigible landed at New York's Roosevelt Field on July 6, 1919.

FIRST BLACK US STATE'S ATTORNEY: ANNIVERSARY. July 6. On July 6, 1961, Cecil Francis Poole became the first black US attorney when he was sworn in as US attorney for the Northern District of California. He served until his retirement on Feb 3, 1970.

FIRST SUCCESSFUL ANTIRABIES INOCULATION: ANNIVERSARY. July 6. On July 6, 1885, Louis Pasteur gave the first successful antirabies inoculation to a boy who had been bitten by an infected dog.

JONES, JOHN PAUL: BIRTH ANNIVERSARY. July 6, 1747. American naval officer born at Kirkbean, Scotland. Remembered for his victory in the battle of his ship, the *Bonhomme Richard*, with the British frigate *Serapis*, Sept 23, 1779. When Jones was queried: "Do you ask for quarter?" he made his famous reply: "I have not yet begun to fight!" Jones was victorious, but the *Bonhomme Richard*, badly damaged, sank two days later. Jones died at Paris, France, July 18, 1792.

LUXEMBOURG: ETTELBRUCK REMEMBRANCE DAY: ANNIVERSARY. July 6. In honor of US General George Patton, Jr, liberator of the Grand-Duchy of Luxembourg in 1945, who is buried at the American Military Cemetery in Hamm, Germany, among 5,100 soldiers of his famous Third Army.

MAJOR LEAGUE BASEBALL HOLDS FIRST ALL-STAR GAME: 65th ANNIVERSARY. July 6, 1933. The first midsummer All-Star Game was held at Comiskey Park, Chicago, IL. Babe Ruth led the American League with a home run, as they defeated the National League 4–2. Prior to the summer of 1933, All-Star contests consisted of pre- and postseason exhibitions that often found teams made up of a few stars playing beside journeymen and even minor leaguers.

MALAWI: REPUBLIC DAY. July 6. National holiday. Commemorates attainment of independence from Britain on July 6, 1964, and Malawi's becoming a republic on July 6, 1966.

MAN WATCHERS' COMPLIMENT WEEK. July 6–11. What the world needs now is love, kindness and appreciation. Pass out compliments copiously. List of activities available. For info: Suzy Mallery, Pres, Man Watchers, Inc, 12308 Darlington Ave, Los Angeles, CA 90049. Phone: (310) 826-9101 or (310) 826-9101. Fax: (310) 820-3539.

MAWLID AL NABI: THE BIRTHDAY OF THE PROPHET MUHAMMAD. July 6. Mawlid al-Nabi (Birth of the Prophet Muhammad) is observed on Muslim calendar date Rabi al-Awal 12, 1419. Different methods for calculating the visibility of the new moon crescent at Mecca are used by different Muslim groups. *Chase's* uses anticipated dates furnished by the American Muslim Council.

MUSIC FOR LIFE WEEK. July 6–10. To be observed to promote functional music in individuals and communities throughout the country; to encourage everyone to use music for consolation and comfort at times of loss; to implement humor; to accompany and ease work; and for inspiration and nurture. Also includes Music Workshop for Creativity. For info: Ann Fabe Isaacs, Pres, Composer, Music For Life, 8080 Springvalley Dr, Cincinnati, OH 45236-1395. Phone: (513) 631-1777.

"NAME THAT TUNE" TV PREMIERE: 45th ANNIVERSARY. July 6, 1953. "Name That Tune" was a musical identification show that appeared in different formats in the '50s and the '70s. Red Benson was the host of the NBC series and Bill Cullen (and later George DeWitt) was the CBS host. Two contestants listened while an orchestra played a musical selection, and the first contestant who could identify it raced across the stage to ring a bell. The winner of the round then tried to identify a number of tunes within a specific time period. After 11 years, the show was brought back with Richard Hayes as host. In 1974, new network and syndicated versions appeared.

NUDE RECREATION WEEK. July 6–12. To promote acceptance of the body and understanding of the nude recreation movement as a natural solution to many problems of modern living. For info: The Naturist Society, Box 132, Oshkosh, WI 54902. Phone: (414) 231-9950. Fax: (414) 231-9977.
Email: naturist@peter.atw.fullfeed.com.
WWW: http://www.naturist.com

OPERATION OVERCAST: ANNIVERSARY. July 6, 1945. As the end of the war approached, the US Army had begun to move German scientists and scientific equipment from the German territory designated for Russian occupation. On this date, the American Joint Chiefs of Staff authorized Operation Overcast, under which 350 German and Austrian scientists were transported to the US in a matter of months.

"THE QUIZ KIDS" TV PREMIERE: ANNIVERSARY. July 6, 1949. This show began on radio and continued on TV with the original host, Joe Kelly. He was followed by Clifton Fadiman. The format was a panel of five child prodigies who answered questions sent in by viewers. Four were regulars, staying for weeks or months, while the fifth was a "guest child." The ages of the panelists varied from six to sixteen.

REPUBLICAN PARTY FORMED: ANNIVERSARY. July 6. The Republican Party formally originated at a convention in Ripon, WI, on July 6, 1854.

SPACE MILESTONE: *SOYUZ 21* (USSR). July 6, 1976. Launched this date. Two cosmonauts, Colonel B. Volynov and Lieutenant Colonel V. Zholobov, traveled to *Salyut 5* space station (launched June 22, 1976) to study Earth's surface and conduct zoological-botanical experiments. Forty-eight-day stay on space station. Return landing on Aug 24.

SPAIN: RUNNING OF THE BULLS. July 6–14. Pamplona, Spain. Event made famous by Hemingway in which young men run through the streets of Pamplona with bulls from the bull ring. Part of the festival of San Fermin.

SWITZERLAND: SEMPACH BATTLE COMMEMORATION. July 6. On the morning of the first Monday after July 4, the Lucerne government, military and student delegations and historical groups make their way in solemn procession to the battlefield of 1386. Commemorative address, battle report and solemn service in the chapel. Also an evening procession.

TAKE CHARGE OF CHANGE WEEK. July 6–12. To increase awareness of the individual's power to control his own destiny, ChangeWorks will sponsor a series of events demonstrating the principles of taking charge of the changes that affect each of us. You can reduce stress and improve the quality of your life when you put yourself in the driver's seat. Learn how to accept the change you cannot control, manage the change you can and make change a positive force in your life. For more information and a free booklet on how you can take charge of change, send a self-addressed, stamped envelope to the address below. For info: Cathy Stucker, ChangeWorks, 4646 Hwy 6, Ste 123, Sugar Land, TX 77478. Phone: (281) 265-7342. Fax: (281) 265-9727. Email: cstucker@flash.net.

ZAMBIA: HEROES DAY. July 6. First Monday in July is Zambian national holiday—memorial day for Zambians who died in the struggle for independence. Political rallies stress solidarity.

BIRTHDAYS TODAY

Allyce Beasley, 44, actress (Agnes on "Moonlighting"), born Brooklyn, NY, July 6, 1954.

Ned Beatty, 61, actor (*Deliverance*, "Homicide," *Hear My Song*), born Lexington, KY, July 6, 1937.

Donal Donnelly, 67, actor (*The Knack, The Dead, Godfather Part III*), born Bradford, England, July 6, 1931.

Grant Goodeve, 46, actor ("Eight Is Enough," "Dynasty"), born New Haven, CT, July 6, 1952.

Merv Griffin, 73, TV host, business executive, born San Mateo, CA, July 6, 1925.

Janet Leigh, 71, actress (*That Forsyte Woman, Psycho*), born Merced, CA, July 6, 1927.

Nancy Davis Reagan, 77, former First Lady, born New York, NY, July 6, 1921.

Della Reese (Deloreese Patricia Early), 66, singer ("Don't You Know," "And That Reminds Me"), actress ("Touched by an Angel"), born Detroit, MI, July 6, 1932.

Sylvester Stallone, 52, actor (Rocky films; *Cliffhanger; Rambo* films) director, born New York, NY, July 6, 1946.

Burt Ward, 53, actor (Robin in "Batman"), born Los Angeles, CA, July 6, 1945.

July 1998

S	M	T	W	T	F	S
			1	2	3	4
5	6	7	8	9	10	11
12	13	14	15	16	17	18
19	20	21	22	23	24	25
26	27	28	29	30	31	

JULY 7 — TUESDAY

Day 188 — 177 Remaining

BONZA BOTTLER DAY™. July 7. To celebrate when the number of the day is the same as the number of the month. Bonza Bottler Day™ is an excuse to have a party at least once a month. For more information, see Jan 1. For info: Gail M. Berger, 109 Matthew Ave, Poca, WV 25159. Phone: (304) 776-7746. Email: gberger5@aol.com.

HAWAII ANNEXED BY US: 100th ANNIVERSARY. July 7, 1898. President William McKinley signs a resolution annexing Hawaii. No change in government took place until 1900, when Congress passed an act making Hawaii an "incorporated" territory of the US. This act remained in effect until Hawaii became a state in 1959.

JAPAN: TANABATA (STAR FESTIVAL). July 7. As an offering to the stars, children set up bamboo branches to which colorful strips of paper bearing poems are tied.

JIMMY AND ROSALYNN CARTER WEDDING: ANNIVERSARY. July 7, 1946. Plains Methodist Church, Plains, GA. James Earl Carter, Jr, was 21 and Eleanor Rosalynn Smith was 18. They have four children: John William "Jack" Carter was born in 1947, James Carl "Chip" Carter, 1950, Donnell Jeffrey Carter, 1952, and Amy Lynn Carter, 1968.

KUNSTLER, WILLIAM: BIRTH ANNIVERSARY. July 7, 1919. Radical attorney, defense lawyer for the Chicago Seven, born New York, NY. Died Sept 4, 1995, at New York, NY.

LINCOLN ASSASSINATION CONSPIRATORS: HANGING ANNIVERSARY. July 7. Four persons convicted of complicity with John Wilkes Booth in the assassination of President Abraham Lincoln (Apr 14, 1865) were hanged at Washington, DC, on July 7, 1865. The four: Mary E. Surratt, Lewis Payne, David E. Harold and George A. Atzerodt.

MOTHER FRANCES XAVIER CABRINI CANONIZED: ANNIVERSARY. July 7, 1946. Pope Pius XII presided over the canonization ceremonies for Mother Frances Xavier Cabrini, as she became the first American to be canonized. She was the founder of the Missionary Sisters of the Sacred Heart of Jesus, and her principal shrine is at Mother Cabrini High School, New York, NY. Her feast day is celebrated on Dec 22.

PAIGE, LEROY ROBERT (SATCHEL): BIRTH ANNIVERSARY. July 7, 1906. Baseball Hall of Fame pitcher born at Mobile, AL. Paige was the greatest attraction in the Negro Leagues and was also, at age 42, the first black pitcher in the American League. Inducted into the Hall of Fame in 1971. Died at Kansas City, MO, July 7, 1906.

"RYAN'S HOPE" TV PREMIERE: ANNIVERSARY. July 7, 1975. This ABC soap ran until 1989 and was set mostly at the fictional Ryan's Tavern or Riverside Hospital in New York City. The show depicted the lives of the ardently Irish Ryan family. Claire Labine and Paul Avila Mayer created the show. The original cast included Faith Catlin, Justin Deas, Bernard Barrow, Helen Gallagher, Michael Hawkins, Ilene Kristen, Malcom Groome and Kate Mulgrew as members of the Ryan family. Daniel Hugh-Kelly, Ana Alicia, Nana Visitor, Marg Helgenberger, James Sloyan, Christine Ebersole, Nell Carter, Yasmine Bleeth, Gloria DeHaven, Corbin Bernsen, Christian Slater, Grant Show and Regis Philbin have been among the show's many other regulars over the years.

SOLOMON ISLANDS: NATIONAL HOLIDAY. July 7.

"THE STORK CLUB" TV PREMIERE: ANNIVERSARY. July 7, 1950. "The Stork Club" ran for four years on CBS and for one year on ABC. Sherman Billingsley served as host and producer of this variety show which was set in a fictional bistro (where he also played the proprietor).

SURRATT, MARY: EXECUTION ANNIVERSARY. July 7. Mary E. Surratt, who had been convicted by a military commission of conspiracy in the assassination of President Abraham Lincoln, was hanged on July 7, 1865, becoming the first woman executed for a crime in the US. Her conviction was and is a subject of controversy, as the only crime she appeared to have committed was to own the boarding house where John Wilkes Booth planned the assassination.

TANZANIA: SABA SABA DAY. July 7. Marks the day in 1954 when Tanzania's mainland ruling party, TANU, was formed.

WALES: LLANGOLLEN INTERNATIONAL MUSICAL EISTEDDFOD. July 7–12. Eisteddfod Field, Llangollen, Clwyd. Thousands of singers and folk dancers from more than 30 countries take part in this annual international music festival. Friendly rivalry among amateur groups performing amid the Welsh rivers and mountains. Est attendance: 120,000. For info: Maureen A. Jones, Mktg Dir, Llangollen Intl Musical Eisteddfod, Llangollen, North Wales, UK LL20 8NG. Phone: (44) (1978) 8620236. Fax: (44) (1978) 861300. Email: lime@celtic.co.uk. WWW: http://www.llangollen.org.uk

ZAMBIA: UNITY DAY. July 7. First Tuesday in July. Memorial day for Zambians who died in the struggle for independence. Political rallies stressing solidarity throughout country.

BIRTHDAYS TODAY

Pierre Cardin, 76, fashion designer, born Venice, Italy, July 7, 1922.

Alan J. Dixon, 71, former US Senator (D, Illinois), born Belleville, IL, July 7, 1927.

Shelley Duvall, 49, actress (*Popeye, Nashville, Roxanne*), born Houston, TX, July 7, 1949.

Jessica Hahn, 39, model, born Massapequa, NY, July 7, 1959.

Gian Carlo Menotti, 87, composer, born Cadigliano, Italy, July 7, 1911.

Wally Phillips, 73, Chicago radio personality, born Portsmouth, OH, July 7, 1925.

Ralph Lee Sampson, 38, former basketball player, born Harrisonburg, VA, July 7, 1960.

Doc Severinsen, 71, composer, conductor, musician (band leader on "The Tonight Show"), born Arlington, OR, July 7, 1927.

Ringo Starr (Richard Starkey), 58, singer, musician (drummer with the Beatles), born Liverpool, England, July 7, 1940.

Matthew Jerome (Matt) Suhey, 40, former football player, born Bellefonte, PA, July 7, 1958.

JULY 8 — WEDNESDAY

Day 189 — 176 Remaining

ASPINWALL CROSSES US ON HORSEBACK: ANNIVERSARY. July 8, 1911. On July 8, 1911, Nan Jane Aspinwall rode into New York City carrying a letter to Mayor William Jay Gaynor from San Francisco Mayor Patrick Henry McCarthy, becoming the first woman to cross the US on horseback. She began her trip in San Francisco on Sept 1, 1910, and covered 4,500 miles in 301 days.

BOCA GRANDE TARPON TOURNAMENT ("WORLD'S RICHEST"). July 8–9. Boca Grande Pass, Boca Grande, FL. Tarpon fishing; field limited to 60 boats; entry fee $3,500 per boat. With 60 entries, first place (largest tarpon) pays off $100,000. Annually, the week after the Fourth of July. Est attendance: 800. For info: Boca Grande Chamber of Commerce, PO Box 704, Boca Grande, FL 33921. Phone: (941) 964-0568. Fax: (941) 964-0620. Email: bgcc@ewol.com. WWW: http://www.charlotte-online.com/bocagrande/

CANADA: DUST AND DREAMS. July 8–Aug 3. Station Arts Centre/Seager Wheeler Place, Rosthern, Saskatchewan. Presentation of an original "Prairie Musical" depicting life in small town Saskatchewan during the 1930s. It is written by Saskatchewan's own singer and songwriter, Connie Kaldor. Shows are Tuesday to Sunday. Est attendance: 10,000. For info: Tourism Saskatchewan, 500—1900 Albert St, Regina, Sask, Canada S4P 4L9. Phone: (800) 667-7191 or (306) 232-5332. Email: travel.info@sasktourism.sk.ca. WWW: http://www.sasktourim.com

CANADA: FORESTRY AND FLORA TOURS. July 8–Aug 26 (All Wednesdays). Bancroft, Ontario. A registered professional forester leads tours through local forests, identifying species, describing forestry practices and the forestry industry. Trips include tours of sawmill or fiberboard plant. Annually, every Wednesday in July and August (except July 1). For info: Bancroft and District Chamber of Commerce, PO Box 539, Bancroft, Ontario, Canada K0L 1C0. Phone: (613) 332-1513. Fax: (613) 332-2119. Email: chamber@commerce.bancroft.on.ca. WWW: http://www.commerce.bancroft.on.ca

CENTRAL PENNSYLVANIA FESTIVAL OF THE ARTS. July 8–12. University Park, State College, PA. A celebration of the arts—visual, performing, film—with 325 artists on hand. Est attendance: 100,000. For info: Central Pennsylvania Festival of the Arts, Box 1023, State College, PA 16804-1023. Phone: (814) 237-3682. Fax: (814) 237-0708. Email: cpfa@connectek.com.

CHESAPEAKE TURTLE DERBY. July 8. Baltimore, MD. Ten races, with winner of each race competing in special grand sweepstakes race to determine the grand champ. Trophies and prizes awarded to the winners. Est attendance: 300. For info: Office of Adventures in Fun, Patterson Park Recreation Complex, 2601 E Baltimore St, Baltimore, MD 21224. Phone: (410) 396-9177. Fax: (410) 327-4120.

DECLARATION OF INDEPENDENCE FIRST PUBLIC READING: ANNIVERSARY. July 8, 1776. Colonel John Nixon read the Declaration of Independence to the assembled residents at Philadelphia's Independence Square.

ECKSTINE, BILLY: BIRTH ANNIVERSARY. July 8, 1914. Band leader and bass-baritone singer Billy Eckstine was born William Clarence Eckstein at Pittsburgh, PA. After performing with the Earl Hines band for almost 20 years, Eckstine formed his own band in 1944. At one time or another the band's ranks included Charlie Parker, Dizzy Gillespie, Miles Davis, Fats Navarro, Dexter Gordon, Gene Ammons, Art Blakey and vocalist Sarah Vaughan—some of the greatest be-bop musicians of all time. Among Eckstine's hits were "Fools Rush In," "Everything I Have Is Yours," "I Apologize," "My Foolish Heart," "Blue Moon" and "Body and Soul." Billy Eckstine died Mar 8, 1993, at Pittsburgh.

ENGLAND: WAYS WITH WORDS LITERATURE FESTIVAL. July 8–15. Dartington Hall, Dartington, Devon. Some 100 writers give lectures, seminars, interviews, discussions and readings. Book stalls, workshops and plays are also included. Est attendance: 6,500. For info: Steven Bristow, Dir, Ways With Words Literature Festival, Droridge Farm, Dartington, Totnes, Devon, England TQ9 6JQ. Phone: (44) (180) 386-7311. Fax: (44) (180) 386-3688.

FINLAND: TIME OF MUSIC. July 8–15. Viitasaari. Festival in a town of 300 lakes focuses on contemporary music with top international and Finnish artists performing more than 100 works from some of the most interesting composers of our time, many being performed for the first time ever. Also, a sizable program for children. Est attendance: 8,000. For info: Finnish Tourist Board, 655 Third Ave, New York, NY 10017. Phone: (212) 949-2333. or Time of Music, Kesleitie 10, Finland 44500 Viitasaari. Phone: (358) (14) 573195 or Fax: (358) (14) 5793515. Email: time.music@festivals.fi. WWW: http://www.festivals.fi/tom/

KIM IL SUNG: DEATH ANNIVERSARY. July 8, 1994. President Kim Il Sung, the only leader in the history of North Korea, died just a few weeks before an historic summit with the president of South Korea was to take place. A Stalinist-styled dictator, Kim had created a godlike personality cult surrounding himself and his son and presumed heir apparent Kim Jong Il. His death came at a crucial time in world politics. North Korea and the US had recently cooled rhetoric regarding North Korea's nuclear program and had begun further talks just hours prior to the announcement of Kim's death. The North–South Summit and the US–North Korean talks were postponed.

MONTANA GOVERNOR'S CUP WALLEYE TOURNAMENT. July 8–11. Fort Peck, MT. Two-person team event, limited to 200 teams. First place award of $10,000. There is an 80% payback of $260 entry fee. Kids' fishing event also. Annually, the second weekend in July. Est attendance: 2,000. For info: Glasgow Area Chamber of Commerce & Agriculture, Box 832, Glasgow, MT 59230. Phone: (406) 228-2222. Fax: (406) 228-2244.

MOULIN, JEAN: 55th DEATH ANNIVERSARY. July 8, 1943. Jean Moulin, a Free French representative, was parachuted into occupied France on Jan 1, 1942, with the task of uniting the underground resistance. Moulin had with him (in the false bottom of a matchbox) a personal message of admiration for the resistance from General Charles DeGaulle. On May 27, 1943, the underground agreed to the creation of a National Resistance Council with Moulin as president. A short month later, in June, he was arrested in Lyon by the Gestapo. He was tortured for eleven days but betrayed no one. Moulin died on or about July 8, on a train while being transferred by the Nazis to a concentration camp.

OLIVE BRANCH PETITION: ANNIVERSARY. July 8. Representatives of New Hampshire, Massachusetts Bay, Rhode Island, Providence, Connecticut, New York, New Jersey, Pennsylvania, Delaware, Maryland, Virginia, North Carolina and South Carolina signed, on July 8, 1775, a petition from the Congress to the King (George III), a final attempt by moderates in the Second Continental Congress to avoid a complete break with England.

ROCKEFELLER, NELSON ALDRICH: 90th BIRTH ANNIVERSARY. July 8, 1908. Born at Bar Harbor, ME, July 8, 1908. Governor of New York state (1958–73). Nominated as vice president by President Ford on Aug 20, 1974, under provisions of the 25th Amendment. Sworn in on Dec 19, 1974, after confirmation by the Senate and served until Jan 20, 1977. Died at New York, NY, Jan 26, 1979. Rockefeller was the second person to become vice president without having been elected (Gerald R. Ford was the first).

SHELLEY, PERCY BYSSHE: DEATH ANNIVERSARY. July 8, 1822. Poet Percy Bysshe Shelley, one of the leading English Romantic poets and embodiment of a free spirit was born at Warnham, Sussex, on Aug 4, 1792. He lived abroad in Italy until his death at sea off the coast of Viareggio in 1822, just a month before his 30th birthday. Shelley's important works include "Ozymandias" published in 1818; "Ode to the West Wind," "The Cloud," "To a Skylark" and *Prometheus Unbound* in 1819; and *Adonais* (an elegy for John Keats) in 1821.

WYANDOTTE STREET ART FAIR. July 8–11. Downtown Wyandotte, MI. More than 350 artists and craftspeople display and sell their wares. Also, music, street entertainers, Children's Emporium and sidewalk sales. Sponsored by Anheuser Busch and Pepsi Co. Est attendance: 250,000. For info: Leslie Lupo, Dir, 3131 Biddle Ave, Wyandotte, MI 48192. Phone: (313) 246-4505. Fax: (313) 246-4519.

July 1998

S	M	T	W	T	F	S
			1	2	3	4
5	6	7	8	9	10	11
12	13	14	15	16	17	18
19	20	21	22	23	24	25
26	27	28	29	30	31	

Cepheus

BIRTHDAYS TODAY

Roone Arledge, 67, TV executive, born Forest Hills, NY, July 8, 1931.

Kevin Bacon, 40, actor (stage: *Forty Deuce* [Obie Award]; *Diner, A Few Good Men, Apollo 13*), born Philadelphia, PA, July 8, 1958.

Raffi Cavoukian, 50, children's singer and songwriter, born Cairo, Egypt, July 8, 1948.

Kim Darby, 50, actress ("Rich Man, Poor Man," *True Grit*), born Los Angeles, CA, July 8, 1948.

Phil Gramm, 56, US Senator (R, Texas), born Fort Benning, GA, July 8, 1942.

Cynthia Gregory, 52, ballerina, born Los Angeles, CA, July 8, 1946.

Anjelica Huston, 47, actress (Oscar for *Prizzi's Honor; The Grifters, The Addams Family*), born Los Angeles, CA, July 8, 1951.

Steve Lawrence (Sidney Liebowitz), 63, singer ("Party Doll," "Go Away Little Girl"), born New York, NY, July 8, 1935.

Sarah Newcomb McClendon, 88, journalist (50+ years with White House press corps), columnist, born Tyler, TX, July 8, 1910.

Jeffrey Tambor, 54, actor ("Hill Street Blues," "The Larry Sanders Show," *City Slickers*), born San Francisco, CA, July 8, 1944.

Alyce Faye Wattleton, 55, former executive director of Planned Parenthood Federation of America, born St. Louis, MO, July 8, 1943.

JULY 9 — THURSDAY

Day 190 — 175 Remaining

BASTILLE DAYS FESTIVAL (LA KERMESSE DE LA BASTILLE). July 9–12. Milwaukee, WI. Celebrated "on the streets" of East Town in the heart of downtown Milwaukee. "Storm the Bastille" 5K run, sidewalk cafes, bicycle races, French marketplace, continuous entertainment on four stages, waiters'/waitresses' race, New France encampment, dancing in the streets. Admission is free. Est attendance: 200,000. For info: East Town Assn, 770 N Jefferson, Milwaukee, WI 53202. Phone: (414) 271-7400. Fax: (414) 271-6401.

FINLAND: JYVASKYLA ARTS FESTIVAL. July 9–12. Jyvaskyla. Annual festival begun in 1955 for the purpose of stimulating discussion of contemporary philosophical and social concerns and building a bridge between different national and ethnic traditions. About 50 events including seminars, music, visual arts and film. Est attendance: 10,000. For info: Finnish Tourist Board, 655 Third Ave, New York, NY 10017. Phone: (212) 949-2333 or (358) (14) 624385. Fax: (358) (14) 214808.
WWW: http://www.jkl.fi/festivaalit/kesa/

FIRST OPEN-HEART SURGERY: ANNIVERSARY. July 9, 1893. In Provident Hospital on Chicago's south side, black surgeon Dr. Daniel Hale Williams performed the first successful open-heart surgery.

FOURTEENTH AMENDMENT TO US CONSTITUTION RATIFIED: ANNIVERSARY. July 9, 1868. The 14th Amendment, ratified on July 9, 1868, defined United States citizenship and provided that no State shall have the right to abridge the rights of any citizen without due process and equal protection under the law. Coming three years after the Civil War, the 14th Amendment also included provisions for barring individuals who assisted in any rebellion or insurrection against the United States from holding public office, and releasing federal and state governments from any financial liability incurred in the assistance of rebellion or insurrection against the United States.

HOWE, ELIAS: BIRTH ANNIVERSARY. July 9. American inventor of the sewing machine. Born on July 9, 1819, at Spencer, MA. He died on Oct 3, 1867, at Brooklyn, NY.

LOGGER DAYS. July 9–12. Libby, MT. Celebration of logging heritage. Est attendance: 4,000. For info: Libby Chamber of Commerce, PO Box 704, Libby, MT 59923. Phone: (406) 293-4167. Fax: (406) 293-3222. Email: libbyacc@libby.org. WWW: http://www.libby.org/libbyacc/

MARION COUNTY FAIR. July 9–12. State Fairgrounds, Salem, OR. Exceptional food and entertainment, carnival, commercial exhibits, open class exhibits, horse and llama shows and livestock. Est attendance: 40,000. For info: Mary Boedigheimer, Coord, PO Box 703, Salem, OR 97308. Phone: (503) 585-9998.

MARTYRDOM OF THE BAB. July 9. Baha'i observance of the anniversary of the execution by a firing squad, July 9, 1850, in Tabriz, Persia, of the 30-year-old Mirza Ali Muhammed, the Bab (prophet-herald of the Baha'i Faith). One of the nine days of the year when Baha'is suspend work. For info: Pamela Zivari, Dir, Baha'is of the US, Office of Public Information, 866 UN Plaza, Ste 120, New York, NY 10017-1822. Phone: (212) 803-2500. Fax: (212) 803-2573. Email: usopi-ny@bic.org.

MOON PHASE: FULL MOON. July 9. Moon enters Full Moon phase at 12:01 PM, EDT.

NATIONAL MARFAN FOUNDATION ANNUAL CONFERENCE. July 9–11. New York Hospital/Cornell Medical Center, New York, NY. 14th annual conference features clinic, medical panels and consumer workshops, all relating to the Marfan syndrome. Est attendance: 500. For info: Natl Marfan Foundation, 382 Main St, Port Washington, NY 11050-3121. Phone: (800) 8-MARFAN. Fax: (516) 883-8040. Email: staff@marfan.org. WWW: http://www.marfan.org.

OREGON TRAIL DAYS. July 9–12. Gering, NE. Oldest continuing celebration in state of Nebraska commemorating Oregon Trail. Parades, barbecues, street dances, Intl Food Fair, concert, Nebraska State CASI Chili Cookoff, musical plays and a western art show highlight the 77th annual celebration. Annually, the second full weekend in July. Est attendance: 30,000. For info: Event Coord, PO Box 222, Gering, NE 69341. Phone: (308) 436-4457. Fax: (308) 436-6888.

RADCLIFFE, ANN WARD: BIRTH ANNIVERSARY. July 9, 1764. English novelist famous for her gothic novels (fiction works especially popular in the late 18th and early 19th centuries). Among her works are *The Romance of the Forest, The Mysteries of Udolpho* and *The Italian*. She was born on July 9, 1764, at London, England, and died there on Feb 7, 1823.

RESPIGHI, OTTORINO: BIRTH ANNIVERSARY. July 9. Italian composer born at Bologna, Italy, on July 9, 1879. He died at Rome, Apr 18, 1936.

SOVIET ROCKET THREAT: ANNIVERSARY. July 9. On this day in 1960, Soviet Premier Nikita Krushchev threatened military action against the US if Washington were to attempt an overthrow of the Castro regime in Cuba.

BIRTHDAYS TODAY

Barbara Cartland, 97, world's top-selling romance novelist, born Hatfield, England, July 9, 1901.

Brian Dennehy, 60, actor ("Star of the Family"), born Bridgeport, CT, July 9, 1938.

Margaret Gillis, 45, dancer, choreographer, born Montreal, Quebec, Canada, July 9, 1953.

James Hampton, 62, actor ("F Troop," "Love, American Style"), born Oklahoma City, OK, July 9, 1936.

Tom Hanks, 42, actor (*Forrest Gump, Sleepless in Seattle*; Oscars for *Philadelphia, Forrest Gump*), born Concord, CA, July 9, 1956.

David Hockney, 61, artist, born Bradford, England, July 9, 1937.

Mathilde Krim, 72, geneticist, philanthropist, born Como, Italy, July 9, 1926.

Courtney Love, 33, singer ("Live Through This"), actress (*The People vs. Larry Flynt*), born San Francisco, CA, July 9, 1965.

Kelly McGillis, 41, actress (*Witness, Top Gun, The Accused*), born Newport Beach, CA, July 9, 1957.

Richard Roundtree, 56, actor (*Shaft, Shaft's Big Score, Q, Once upon a Time When We Were Colored*), born New Rochelle, NY, July 9, 1942.

Fred Savage, 22, actor ("The Wonder Years," *The Princess Bride, The Wizard*), born Highland Park, IL, July 9, 1976.

Orenthal James (O.J.) Simpson, 51, former sportscaster and actor, Pro Football Hall of Fame running back, born San Francisco, CA, July 9, 1947.

Jimmy Smits, 40, actor (*Glitz*, "LA Law," "NYPD Blue"), born New York, NY, July 9, 1958.

John Tesh, 46, TV host ("Entertainment Tonight"), born Garden City, NY, July 9, 1952.

☆ ☆ ☆

JULY 10 — FRIDAY

Day 191 — 174 Remaining

ALLIED INVASION OF SICILY: 55th ANNIVERSARY. July 10, 1943. Operation Husky, the Allied infantry attack on Italy, began on the island of Sicily. The British entry into Syracuse was the first Allied success in Europe. General Dwight D. Eisenhower, the Allied Commander-in-Chief, described the invasion as "the first page in the liberation of the European Continent."

ASHE, ARTHUR: 55th BIRTH ANNIVERSARY. July 10, 1943. Born in Richmond, VA, Arthur Ashe became a legend for his list of firsts as a black tennis player. Ashe was chosen for the US Davis Cup team in 1963 and became captain in 1980. He won the US men's singles championship and US Open in 1968 and in 1975 the men's singles at Wimbledon. Ashe won a total of 33 career titles. In 1985 he was inducted into the International Tennis Hall of Fame. A social activist, Ashe worked to eliminate racism and stereotyping. He was arrested numerous times while protesting. He helped create inner-city tennis programs for youths and wrote the three-volume *A Hard Road to Glory: A History of the African-American Athlete*. Aware that *USA Today* intended to publish an article revealing that he was infected with the AIDS virus, Ashe announced on Apr 8, 1992, that he probably contracted HIV through a transfusion during bypass surgery in 1983. In September of 1992 he began a $5 million fundraising effort on behalf of the Arthur Ashe Foundation for the Defeat of AIDS and during his last year campaigned for public awareness regarding the AIDS epidemic. He died at New York City on Feb 6, 1993, from pneumonia.

BAHAMAS: INDEPENDENCE DAY: 25th ANNIVERSARY. July 10, 1973. Public holiday. At 12:01 AM, on July 10, 1973, the Bahamas gained their independence after 250 years as a British Crown Colony.

BASTILLE DAY CELEBRATION. July 10. Boston, MA. A street celebration with typical Parisian joie de vivre; dining and dancing under the stars. This is the 24th year for the largest Bastille Day celebration in the US. Est attendance: 3,000. For info: The French Library and Cultural Center, 53 Marlborough St, Boston, MA 02116-2099. Phone: (617) 266-4351. Fax: (617) 266-1780. Email: info@frenchlib.org. WWW: http://www.frenchlib.org

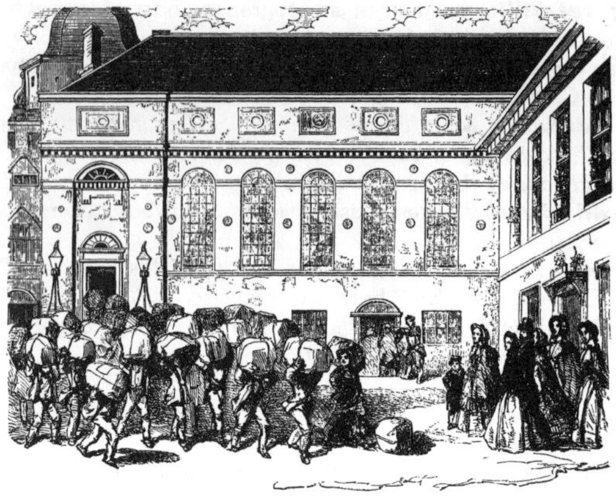

BEREA CRAFT FESTIVAL. July 10–12. Berea, KY. Craftspeople from 20 states gather to exhibit, demonstrate and sell their work. Est attendance: 12,000. For info: Lila Bellanda, Pres, Berea Craft Enterprises, Box 128, Berea, KY 40403. Phone: (606) 986-2540 or (606) 986-1585.

BETHUNE, MARY McLEOD: BIRTH ANNIVERSARY. July 10, 1875. Mary Jane McLeod Bethune was born in Mayesville, SC, the first in her family to be born free. Bethune became a teacher and in 1904 founded her own school in Florida, the Daytona Normal and Industrial School for Negro Girls. In 1931, the school merged with a local men's college, Cookman Institute, and was renamed Bethune-Cookman College. An adviser on minority affairs under President Franklin D. Roosevelt, she directed the Division of Negro Affairs of the National Youth Administration. She died May 18, 1955, at Daytona Beach, FL.

BLISSFESTIVAL. July 10–12. Cross Village, MI. Traditional, acoustic and folk music, two stages, workshops, camping, kids' area and activities. Music styles from jazz to bluegrass. Est attendance: 5,000. For info: Blissfest, Box 441, Harbor Springs, MI 49740. Phone: (616) 348-2815. WWW: http://www.blissfest.org

BORIS YELTSIN INAUGURATED AS RUSSIAN PRESIDENT: ANNIVERSARY. July 10. 1991. Boris Yeltsin took the oath of office as the first popularly elected president in Russia's 1,000-year history. He defeated the Communist Party candidate resoundingly, establishing himself as a powerful political counterpoint to Mikhail Gorbachev, the president of the Soviet Union, of which Russia was the largest republic. Yeltsin had been dismissed from the Politburo in 1987 and resigned from the Communist Party in 1989. His popularity forced Gorbachev to make concessions to the republics in the new union treaty forming the Confederation of Independent States.

CALVIN, JOHN: BIRTH ANNIVERSARY. July 10, 1509. Theologian, born at Noyon, France. Reformer and founder of Presbyterianism. Calvin died at Geneva, Switzerland, May 27, 1564.

CANADA: ABBOTSFORD BERRY FESTIVAL. July 10–11. Abbottsford, BC. July heralds the height of the Raspberry Capital of Canada's berry season. Sample delicious local berries and berry products. Linger to cheer the musicians, magicians and clowns; play bingo; angle at the fishing pond; take the kids on fun rides and browse through local craft and market-style food stands. Est attendance: 25,000. For info: Lynn Wickens, Abbotsford Downtown Business Assn, 33780 Hazel St, Abbotsford, BC, Canada V2S 2M6. Phone: (604) 850-6547. Fax: (604) 850-6547. Email: lwickens@rapidnet.net. WWW: http://bia.bc.ca/abbotsford

July 1998

S	M	T	W	T	F	S
			1	2	3	4
5	6	7	8	9	10	11
12	13	14	15	16	17	18
19	20	21	22	23	24	25
26	27	28	29	30	31	

CANADA: CANADIAN TURTLE DERBY. July 10–12. Boissevain, Manitoba. A fun-filled family weekend, adjacent to the famous International Peace Garden. Live turtle races. Curling Bonspiel, ball and volleyball tourneys, mini-triathlon, fireworks and children's entertainment. Outdoor Art Gallery with more than 17 murals! Ample camping available. 27th annual derby. Est attendance: 5,000. For info: Ivan Strain, Canadian Turtle Derby, PO Box 122, Boissevain, Man, Canada R0K 0E0. Phone: (204) 534-6000. Fax: (204) 534-6825.

CANADA: EDMONTON INTERNATIONAL STREET PERFORMERS FESTIVAL. July 10–19. Sir Winston Churchill Square, Edmonton, Alta, Canda. Family-oriented busking festival. More than 50 acts from around the world. Est attendance: 200,000. For info: E.I.S.P.F., #901 10136 100 St, Edmonton, Alberta, Canada T5J 0P1. Phone: (403) 425-5162. Fax: (403) 426-0853. Email: street@worldweb.com. WWW: http://www.discoveredmonton.com/

CANADA: GREAT RENDEZVOUS. July 10–19. Old Fort Williams, Thunder Bay, Ontario. Join hundreds of re-enactors as they celebrate the arrival of the partners, clerks and voyageurs to the inland headquarters of the North West Company. Take part in Rendezvous games and activities with colorful fur trade characters! Annually, mid-July. Est attendance: 14,000. For info: Marty Mascarin, Communications Officer, Vickers Heights Post Office, Thunder Bay, Ont, Canada P0T 2Z0. Phone: (807) 473-2344 or (807) 577-8461. Fax: (807) 473-2312. WWW: http://www.oldfortwilliam.on.ca

CLERIHEW DAY. July 10. A day recognized in remembrance of Edmund Clerihew Bentley, journalist and author of the celebrated detective thriller *Trent's Last Case* (1912), but perhaps best known for his invention of a popular humorous verse form, the clerihew, consisting of two rhymed couplets of unequal length:/Edmund's middle name was Clerihew/A name possessed by very few,/But verses by Mr Bentley/Succeeded eminently./Bentley was born at London on July 10, 1875, and died there on Mar 30, 1956.

CORNSTOCK. July 10–12. Pat's Corn Place, north of New London, WI. 7th annual. A weekend of camping, live music and outdoor fun. Annually, the weekend following the Fourth of July. Est attendance: 300. For info: Clay Duval, 418 W Pine St, New London, WI 54961. Phone: (414) 982-3964. Email: dval-des@athenet.net.

DALLAS, GEORGE MIFFLIN: BIRTH ANNIVERSARY. July 10, 1792. Eleventh Vice President of the US (1845–49), born at Philadelphia, PA. Died there Dec 31, 1864.

DINOSAUR ROUNDUP RODEO. July 10–12. Vernal, UT. 45th annual presentation of one of the top PRCA rodeos, plus wrangler bull fights and fun for the entire family. Annually, the second weekend in July. Est attendance: 10,000. For info: Dinosaurland Travel Board, 25 E Main St, Vernal, UT 84078. Phone: (800) 421-9635 or (801) 789-1352.

DON'T STEP ON A BEE DAY. July 10. Seven-year-old Michael Roy of the Wellness Permission League reminds kids and grown-ups that now is the time of year when going barefoot can mean getting stung by a bee. If you get stung tell Mom. [© 1997 by WPL] For info: Michael Roy, Wellness Permission League, PO Box 662, Mt Gretna, PA 17064-0662. Phone: (500) 437-5104 or (717) 964-1308. Fax: (717) 964-1335.

ELEPHANT STAMPEDE: ANNIVERSARY. July 10, 1972. Due to drought and a massive heat wave, herds of thirst-crazed wild elephants went on a rampage through five villages near the Chandka Forest of India killing 24 people.

GILBERT, JOHN: BIRTH ANNIVERSARY. July 10, 1897. Silent film star John Gilbert was born John Pringle at Logan, UT, and subsequently adopted his stepfather's name, Gilbert. In 1916 Gilbert had his billed screen debut in *Bullets and Brown Eyes*. For several years he continued to write, act and help direct for small studios. In the early 1920s Gilbert contracted with Fox and then with MGM and had leading roles in several films, such as *The Merry Widow* and *The Big Parade*. Although he was a popular leading man in the early '20s, he was unable to succeed when sound came to movies and MGM released him from his contract in 1934. He suffered a heart attack and died Jan 9, 1936, at the age of 41.

GWYNNE, FREDERICK HUBBARD: BIRTH ANNIVERSARY. July 10, 1926. Stage, screen and TV actor, best known for the TV roles Herman Munster in "The Munsters" and Officer Muldoon in "Car 54, Where Are You?" Gwynne was born at New York, NY, and died at Taneytown, MD, on July 2, 1993.

HERITAGEFEST. July 10–12, also 17–19. New Ulm, MN. This unique Old World celebration features continuous entertainment on five stages, including performers from Europe and storytellers, jugglers and mimes. Ethnic food and beverages. For info: Heritagefest, PO Box 461, New Ulm, MN 56073-0461. Phone: (507) 354-8850.

HISTORIC FARM DAYS. July 10–12. Penfield, IL. This weekend-long event features antique farm machinery displays, agricultural demonstrations, square dancing, a tractor parade, children's pedal tractor pull, food and entertainment. Admission charged. Est attendance: 5,000. For info: Dave Berbaum, I&I Antique Tractor Club, PO Box 65, Penfield, IL 61862. Phone: (217) 863-2681.

HODAG COUNTRY FESTIVAL. July 10–12. Hodag "50" Track, Rhinelander, WI. 21st anniversary country music festival, one of the oldest open-air festivals in the Midwest. Annually, the second full weekend in July. Est attendance: 70,000. For info: Bernie or Diane Eckert, Hodag Country Fest, 4743 Bus Hwy 8, Rhinelander, WI 54501-9202. Phone: (715) 369-1300. Fax: (715) 362-3919. WWW: http://www.hodag.com

HOGG, IMA: BIRTH ANNIVERSARY. July 10, 1882. American collector and philanthropist Ima Hogg was born at Mineola, TX. She founded the Houston Symphony and created the Bayou Bend Collection of the Museum of Fine Arts. She was the only daughter of Texas Governor (1891–95) James Stephen Hogg who, some have suggested, deliberately named his daughter "Ima" for political attention. Contrary to folklore, she did not have a sister named Ura Hogg. She died at age 93, on Aug 19, 1975, following an auto accident at London, England.

INTERN APPRECIATION DAY. July 10. A day to extend appreciation and gratitude to all the student interns who expend their time and energies for a plethora of different organizations during the summer months. Annually, in July. For info: Phillip Harris, 201 S 4th St, #616, San Jose, CA 95112. Phone: (408) 947-0418. Fax: (408) 947-0418. Email: pwh@worldnet.att.net.

LITCHFIELD OPEN HOUSE TOUR. July 10–11. Litchfield, CT. Preview tour and cocktail reception on Friday. Open house tour features an assortment of homes as well as additional attractions of historical and architectural significance. Annually, the second weekend in July. Est attendance: 1,500. For info: Connecticut Junior Republic, PO Box 161, Goshen Road, Litchfield, CT 06759. Phone: (860) 567-9423. Fax: (860) 567-9792.

MAINE: SCHOONER DAYS. July 10–12. Harbor Park Memorial Landing, Rockland, ME. Parade of sail, maritime demonstrations, water events. Maine craft show, fireworks, North Atlantic Blues Festival. For info: Rockland-Thomaston Area Chamber of Commerce, P.O. Box 508, Harbor Park Public Landing, Rockland, ME 04841. Phone: (207) 596-0376. Fax: (207) 596-6549. Email: rtacc@midcoast.com.
WWW: http://www.midcoast.com/~rtacc

NETHERLANDS: NORTH SEA JAZZ FESTIVAL. July 10–12. Nederlands Congresgebouw (Dutch Congress Building), The Hague. Live jazz festival with top-name entertainment. Annually, the second weekend in July. Est attendance: 70,000. For info: North Sea Jazz Fest, PO Box 3325, 2601 DH Delft, Netherlands. Phone: (31) (10) 591-9000. Fax: (31) (10) 592-6130.

PROSPECT PARK FISHING CONTEST. July 10–18. Prospect Park, Brooklyn, NY. A contest for young anglers, 15 and under, with prizes for the largest or most fish. At the Rustic Shelter Lakeside near the Kate Wollman Rink parking lot. Groups must register ahead of time. Est attendance: 700. For info: Public Info Mgr, Public Info Office—Hitchfield Villa, 95 Prospect Park W, Prospect Park, Brooklyn, NY 11215. Phone: (718) 965-8954. Fax: (718) 965-8972. Email: prospect1@juno.com.
WWW: http://www.prospectpark.org

PROUST, MARCEL: BIRTH ANNIVERSARY. July 10, 1871. Anniversary of birth of famed French author (July 10, 1871–Nov 19, 1922). "Happiness," he wrote in *The Past Recaptured*, "is beneficial for the body but it is grief that develops the powers of the mind."

***RAINBOW WARRIOR* SINKING: ANNIVERSARY.** July 10. The 160-ft ship, the *Rainbow Warrior*, operated by Greenpeace, an environmentalist organization, was sunk and a photographer aboard was killed while the ship was at Marsden Wharf, Auckland, New Zealand, on July 10, 1985. Reportedly it was caused by a bomb attached to the underside of the ship by saboteurs. The ship had been scheduled for use in a protest against nuclear tests in the South Pacific Ocean by the French government.

SCHOONER DAYS. July 10–12. Harbor Park, Rockland, ME. Celebrates historic and landmark schooners engaged in the windjammer trade. Featuring the Tall Ships Parade of Sail, fireworks, Maine arts and crafts, maritime displays and demonstrations, entertainment and more. Est attendance: 20,000. For info: Paul "Gil" Merriam, Rockland Tomaston Area Chamber of Commerce, PO Box 508, Rockland, ME 04841. Phone: (207) 596-0376. Fax: (207) 596-6549. Email: rtacc@midcoast.com.

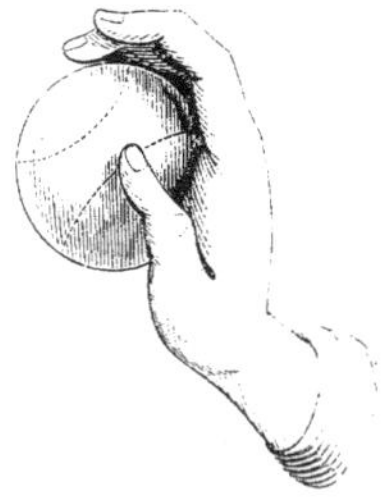

SLOW PITCH SOFTBALL TOURNAMENT. July 10–12. Elm Park, Williamsport, PA. 25th annual charitable tournament with 64 teams. Sponsor: Miller Lite. Est attendance: 8,500. For info: Don Phillips, Mid-State Beverage Co, 532 Sylvan Dr, South Williamsport, PA 17701. Phone: (717) 322-3331.

SPACE MILESTONE: *TELSTAR* (US): 35th ANNIVERSARY. July 10, 1962. First privately owned satellite (American Telephone and Telegraph Company) and first satellite to relay live TV pictures across the Atlantic. Launched on July 10, 1962.

STAMP EXPO. July 10–12. Elks Lodge, Pasadena, CA. Est attendance: 4,000. For info: Intl Stamp Collectors Soc, Box 854, Van Nuys, CA 91408. Phone: (818) 997-6496. Fax: (818) 988-4337. Email: iibick@aol.com. WWW: http://www/4free.com/bick

STATE GAMES OF OREGON. July 10–12. Portland, OR. Oregon's Olympic-style amateur sports festival. Normally, the first weekend after July 4th. Est attendance: 16,000. For info: Kerry Duffy, Exec Dir, 4840 SW Western Ave, Ste 900, Beaverton, OR 97005. Phone: (503) 520-1319. Fax: (503) 520-9747.

TURKEY RAMA. July 10–12. McMinnville, OR. This annual event in McMinnville, once known as the Turkey Capital of the world, continues to include traditional turkey BBQ, Biggest Turkey contest, street sales, fun run, carnival, car show, entertainment. Est attendance: 25,000. For info: Greater McMinnville Chamber of Commerce, 417 N Adams, McMinnville, OR 97128. Phone: (503) 472-6196. Fax: (503) 472-6198.

US LIFTS SANCTIONS AGAINST SOUTH AFRICA: ANNIVERSARY. July 10, 1991. President George Bush lifted US trade and investment sanctions against South Africa on July 10, 1991. The sanctions had been imposed through the Comprehensive Anti-apartheid Act of 1986, which Congress had passed to punish South Africa for policies of racial separation.

WESTERN HERITAGE DAYS. July 10–12. Grant-Kohrs National Historic Site, Deer Lodge, MT. Demonstrations of blacksmithing, chuckwagon cooking and draft horse use. Calf branding and special programs for children. Free admission. Annually, the second full weekend in July. Est attendance: 1,800. For info: Superintendent, Grant-Kohrs Ranch NHS, PO Box 790, Deer Lodge, MT 59722. Phone: (406) 846-2070.

WHALING CITY FESTIVAL. July 10–12. Veterans Memorial Buttonwood Park, New Bedford, MA. Features numerous exhibitors, amusement rides, arts and crafts displays and eight stages of music. Est attendance: 300,000. For info: Whaling City Festival, 220 Union St, New Bedford, MA 02740. Phone: (508) 996-3348. Fax: (508) 990-2367.

WHISTLER, JAMES ABBOTT McNEILL: BIRTH ANNIVERSARY. July 10, 1834. American painter (especially known for painting of his mother), born at Lowell, MA, July 10, 1834. Died at London, England, July 17, 1903. When a woman declared that a landscape reminded her of Whistler's paintings, he reportedly said, "Yes, madam, Nature is creeping up."

WILD HORSE STAMPEDE. July 10–12. Wolf Point, MT. 75th Jubilee. The "Granddaddy" of all Montana rodeos features a wild-horse race, three rodeos, three parades and Native American culture. This is the oldest PRCA rodeo in Montana. Est attendance: 12,000. For info: Clint Long, Chairman, Wolf Point Chamber of Commerce, 217 3rd Ave S, Wolf Point, MT 59201. Phone: (406) 653-2200. Fax: (406) 653-2200.

WORLD CHAMPIONSHIP DOMINO TOURNAMENT. July 10–11. Community Bldg, Andalusia, AL. Prizes and trophies total $35,000. All profits from the tournament go to charity and to sponsor future tournaments. The primary charity is ASCCA, a camp for children and adults with disabilities. Annually, the second weekend in July. Sponsors: Andalusia Rotary Club, GTE, Henderson Sewing Machine Co and Coca-Cola. For info: World Championship Domino Tournament, PO Box 276, Andalusia, AL 36420. Phone: (334) 222-5673 or (334) 222-8466.

WYOMING: ADMISSION DAY: ANNIVERSARY. July 10. Became 44th state on this day in 1890.

BIRTHDAYS TODAY

Saul Bellow, 83, author (*Herzog, The Bellarosa Connection*), born Lachine, Quebec, Canada, July 10, 1915.
David Brinkley, 78, ABC TV journalist, born Wilmington, NC, July 10, 1920.
Roger Timothy Craig, 38, former football player, born Davenport, IA, July 10, 1960.
Andre Nolan Dawson, 44, former baseball player, born Miami, FL, July 10, 1954.
David Norman Dinkins, 71, former and first black Mayor of New York City (D), born Trenton, NJ, July 10, 1927.
Arlo Guthrie, 51, singer (Woody Guthrie's son; "The City of New Orleans," "Alice's Restaurant"), born Brooklyn, NY, July 10, 1947.
Jerry Herman, 65, composer, lyricist, born New York, NY, July 10, 1933.
Jean Kerr, 75, author (*Finishing Touches, Please Don't Eat the Daisies*), born Scranton, PA, July 10, 1923.
Sue Lyon, 52, actress (*Lolita, The Flim Flam Man*), born Davenport, IA, July 10, 1946.
Lawrence Pressman, 59, actor ("Doogie Howser MD," *The Hanoi Hilton*), born Cynthiana, NY, July 10, 1939.
Virginia Wade, 53, tennis player, born Bournemouth, England, July 10, 1945.

July 1998

S	M	T	W	T	F	S
			1	2	3	4
5	6	7	8	9	10	11
12	13	14	15	16	17	18
19	20	21	22	23	24	25
26	27	28	29	30	31	

JULY 11 — SATURDAY

Day 192 — 173 Remaining

ADAMS, JOHN QUINCY: BIRTH ANNIVERSARY. July 11, 1767. Sixth president of the US, and the son of the second president, John Quincy Adams was born at Braintree, MA. After his single term as president, he served 17 years as a member of Congress from Plymouth, MA. He died Feb 23, 1848, at the House of Representatives (in the same room in which he had taken the presidential Oath of Office on Mar 4, 1825). John Quincy Adams was the only president whose father had also been president of the US.

ALL AMERICAN PET PHOTO DAY. July 11. A day designed to celebrate the American families' interest in taking pictures of the family pet. This day is also used to promote responsible pet ownership. It is held as part of the annual summertime "All American" Pet Photo Contest. Sponsored by CPI Photo and FOX Photo in cooperation with The Humane Society of the United States (HSUS). A free booklet by a world-renowned animal photographer featuring tips on taking pictures of the family pet is available. Annually, the second Saturday in July. For info: Robyn Frankel, Frankel Public Relations, 8026 Venetian Dr, St. Louis, MO 63105. Phone: (314) 863-3373.
WWW: http://www.cpiphoto.com

ANTHONY WAYNE DAY. July 11. To recognize the contributions of American Revolutionary War general Anthony Wayne (Jan 1, 1745–Dec 15, 1796). Observed in Michigan since governor's proclamation of 1971. Est attendance: 30,000. For info: Pat Borninski, MR Info Officer, Wayne State University, Detroit, MI 48202. Phone: (313) 577-2150. Fax: (313) 577-8154.
Email: pbornin@cms.cc.wayne.edu.
WWW: http://www.media.wayne.edu

ART FAIR ON THE SQUARE. July 11–12. Madison, WI. This is one of the largest and most popular juried art fairs in the Midwest, with nearly 500 artists from around the country selling their works. The fair occupies eight blocks around Madison's state Capitol building and attracts large crowds. There's also entertainment and lots of food. For info: Wisconsin Dept of Tourism, Art Fair on the Square, PO Box 7976, Madison, WI 53707. Phone: (608) 257-0158. Email: tourism@laughlin.com.
WWW: http://tourism.state.wi.us

BARN DAY. July 11–12. Two miles south of Filley, NE. Threshing demonstration, antique farm equipment, entertainment. The barn is on the National Register of Historic Sites and is the largest limestone barn in Nebraska. Est attendance: 700. For info: Kent

Wilson, Dir, Gage County Historical Soc, PO Box 793, Beatrice, NE 68310. Phone: (402) 228-1679. WWW: http://www.infoanalytic.com/h/beatrice.html#gage

BON ODORI "FESTIVAL OF THE LANTERNS." July 11. Chicago, IL. 500 performers, most clad in colorful kimonos, dance in celebration to music of different prefectures of Japan. The beat of the huge *taiko* (drum) helps keep tempo. Dances are performed outdoors, and public participation is encouraged. 8 PM. Annually, mid-July. Est attendance: 750. For info: Office Secretary, Midwest Buddhist Temple, 435 W Menomonee St, Chicago, IL 60614. Phone: (312) 943-7801. Fax: (312) 943-8069.

BOWDLER'S DAY. July 11. A day to remember the prudish medical doctor, Thomas Bowdler, born near Bath, England, on July 11, 1754. He gave up the practice of medicine and undertook the cleansing of the works of Shakespeare by removing all the words and expressions he considered to be indecent or impious. His *Family Shakespeare*, in 10 volumes, omitted all those words "which cannot with propriety be read aloud in a family." He also "purified" Edward Gibbon's *History of the Decline and Fall of the Roman Empire* and selections from the Old Testament. So offensive was his censorship that his name became synonymous with self-righteous expurgation, and the word *bowdlerize* has become part of the English language. Bowdler died at Rhydings, in South Wales, Feb 24, 1825.

BRAILLE RALLYE. July 11. Braille Institute Youth Center, Los Angeles, CA. Blind or visually impaired students from Braille Institute use braille or large-print instructions to navigate sighted drivers through more than 80 miles of LA streets. Celebrity drivers from television, radio and film help make this a special event. Annually, in July. For info: Braille Institute Communications Dept, 741 N Vermont Ave, Los Angeles, CA 90029. Phone: (213) 663-1111, ext 276. Fax: (213) 663-0867.

BROOKINGS SUMMER ARTS FESTIVAL. July 11–12. Brookings, SD. Features artists from all over the US participating in a juried art show, with a wide variety of food booths and entertainment. Est attendance: 60,000. For info: Director, Brookings Summer Arts Festival Committee, PO Box 4, Brookings, SD 57006. Phone: (605) 692-6125.

CANADA: ANTIQUE AND CLASSIC BOAT SHOW. July 11. Sagamo Park, Lake Muskoka, Gravenhurst, Ont. Largest in-water boat display (more than 100 boats) in Canada. Greatest variety of turn-of-the-century boats in North America. Antique Boat Flea Market, Field of Dreams and numerous boat-related land displays. Est attendance: 10,000. For info: The Antique and Classic Boat Society Inc, PO Box 305, Islington, Ontario, Canada M9A 4X3. Phone: (416) 299-3311. Fax: (416) 748-9767.

CIRCUS CITY FESTIVAL. July 11–18. Peru, IN. Youth amateur circus performed by children 7 to 21 years of age helping to preserve the circus heritage of Miami County, IN. Circus parade, July 18, 10 AM. Annually, beginning the Saturday before and ending the Saturday after the third Wednesday of July. Est attendance: 75,000. For info: Circus City Festival Inc, 154 N Broadway, Peru, IN 46970. Phone: (765) 472-3918.

DAY OF THE FIVE BILLION: ANNIVERSARY. July 11, 1987. An eight-pound baby boy, Matej Gaspar, born at 1:35 AM, EST, July 11, 1987, at Zagreb, Yugoslavia, was proclaimed the five billionth inhabitant of Earth. The United Nations Fund for Population Activities, hoping to draw attention to population growth, proclaimed July 11 as "Day of the Five Billion," noting that 150 babies are born each minute. The US Census Bureau has estimated that the world's population will reach 6.2 billion by the year 2000.

ELKHART GRAND PRIX AND MOTOR SPORTS WEEKEND. July 11–12. Elkhart, IN. The largest karting event race in the world follows a 4,900-ft course through downtown streets. More than 700 competitors from all over the world. Also features top-name race car drivers, antique and hot rod car show and swap meet, racing car displays, carnival and celebrity entertainment at the 10th annual race. Annually, the second weekend in July. Est attendance: 70,000. For info: Curt Paluzzi, Natl Kart News, 51535 Bittersweet Rd, Granger, IN 46530. Phone: (219) 277-0033. Fax: (219) 277-4279. Email: nkartnews@aol.com. WWW: http://www.nkn.com

FINLAND: INTERNATIONAL JAZZ FESTIVAL. July 11–19. Pori. 33rd international festival presenting the jazz music of today with top-name performances. 12 different venues; some go on all night. Est attendance: 120,000. For info: Finnish Tourist Board, 655 Third Ave, New York, NY 10017. Phone: (212) 949-2333 or (358) (2) 550-5550. Fax: (358) (2) 550-5525. Email: elina.yrjola@porijazz.fi. WWW: http://www.porijazz.fi

MIDSUMMER YULE FESTIVAL. July 11. Chadds Ford, PA. Open air Christmas-in-July festival with crafts, Santa makers, museum tour, kids' rides, food. Est attendance: 2,000. For info: American Christmas Museum, PO Box 735, Chadds Ford, PA 19317. Phone: (610) 388-0600. Fax: (610) 388-6599.

MONGOLIA: NAADAM NATIONAL HOLIDAY. July 11. Public holiday; commemorates overthrow of the feudal monarch in 1921.

NAPALM USED: ANNIVERSARY. July 11, 1945. The US dropped several thousand pounds of the recently developed weapon napalm on Japanese forces still holed up on Luzon in the Philippines. Napalm, which was later used heavily as a defoliant in Vietnam, was a thickener consisting of a mixture of aluminum soaps used to jell gasoline.

NEW ENGLAND ARTS & CRAFTS FESTIVAL. July 11–12. Milford Green, Milford, CT. 12th annual. More than 100 artists and crafters from New England to Florida. For info: New England Arts & Crafts Festival, (203) 878-6647 or Greater New Haven Conv & Visitors Bureau, One Long Wharf Dr, New Haven, CT 06511. Phone: (203) 777-8550 or (800) 332-STAY. Fax: (203) 782-7755.

"THE NEWLYWED GAME" TV PREMIERE: ANNIVERSARY. July 11, 1966. Four newly married couples competed for prizes on this game show created by the inimitable Chuck Barris (mastermind of "The Gong Show"). The winners were determined by the couple that could best predict the responses of their respective spouses. Barris, Bob Eubanks and Paul Rodriguez have served as hosts.

NEWPORT MUSIC FESTIVAL. July 11–26. Newport, RI. Unique chamber music programs, American debuts and international artists with special guest artists from the Festival's 30-year history. Three concerts daily held in Newport's fabled mansions. Est attendance: 23,000. For info: Dr. Mark P. Malkovich III, Gen Dir, The Newport Music Festival, PO Box 3300, Newport, RI 02840-0992. Phone: (401) 846-1133 or (401) 849-0700. Fax: (401) 849-1857. Email: staff@newportmusic.org. WWW: http://www.newportmusic.org

OLD-FASHIONED ICE CREAM FESTIVAL. July 11–12. Rockwood Museum, Wilmington, DE. Old-fashioned ice cream social. Hot-air balloons, craft show, antique show, Victorian fashion show, old-time music, high-wheeled bicycles, games and homemade ice cream. Est attendance: 14,000. For info: Rockwood Museum, 610 Shipley Rd, Wilmington, DE 19809. Phone: (302) 761-4340. Fax: (302) 764-4570. Email: info@rockwood.org. WWW: http://www.rockwood.org

RENAISSANCE FAIRE. July 11–12. University of Great Falls, Great Falls, MT. Enter a world of the sights, sounds, tastes and activities of 16th-century Europe. Costumed village folk greet and entertain you. The Royal Retinue proceeds through the Faire, welcoming one and all to enjoy the sounds of madrigals, folk songs, dancers, minstrels, crafters and artisans demonstrating their skills. To add to the ambience the streets are filled with banners, pennants and coats of arms. Est attendance: 2,000. For info: Lana Furdell, Faire Dir, University of Great Falls, 1301 20th St South, Great Falls, MT 59405. Phone: (406) 791-5255. Fax: (406) 791-5393. Email: lfurdell@ugf.edu.

ROAR FAIRE/WALK ON THE WILD SIDE. July 11. Metro Washington Park Zoo, Portland, OR. Roar Faire focuses on the things we're all doing to make the world a better place for animals—and people. Games, crafts and things to take home. Est attendance: 4,000. For info: Metro Washington Park Zoo, 4001 SW Canyon Rd, Portland, OR 97221-2799. Phone: (503) 226-1561. Fax: (503) 226-6836.

ROCKIN' THE TETONS MUSIC FESTIVAL. July 11–12. Alta, WY. 8th annual. A weekend of rock, blues and reggae held under the beautiful blue skies of the western slope of the Teton mountain range. Nationally acclaimed musicians as well as regional favorites descend upon this cozy, self-contained resort. Weekend activities include great music, arts and crafts and food and beverages. Past performers have included Elvin Bishop, Commander Cody and Jefferson Starship. Est attendance: 6,000. For info: Grand Targhee Ski & Summer Resort, PO Box SKI, Alta, WY 83422. Phone: (800) TAR-GHEE. Fax: (307) 353-8148. Email: targhee@pdt.net.
WWW: http://www.idahonews.com/targhee

SANTA FE CHAMBER MUSIC FESTIVAL. July 11–Aug 17. St. Francis Auditorium, Museum of Fine Arts, Santa Fe, NM. Highly acclaimed chamber music festival celebrates its 26th season. Draws on international talent, featuring works from the baroque, romantic and classical periods, including world premiere performances. Annually, beginning during the first full week in July through the third week in August. Est attendance: 15,000. For info: Alan Silow, Dir of PR, Santa Fe Chamber Music Fest, PO Box 853, Santa Fe, NM 87504. Phone: (505) 983-2075. Fax: (505) 986-0251. WWW: http://www.santafechambermusic.org

SHINDIG-ON-THE-GREEN. July 11. (Also July 18, Aug 1, 8, 15, 22, 29, Sept 5.) Downtown Asheville, NC. A free open-air festival held on the City-County Plaza. Clogging, bluegrass bands, dulcimer players, balladeers, banjo players and all kinds of traditional mountain entertainment. Shindig begins each evening at 7 PM. 29th annual. Est attendance: 24,000. For info: Folk Heritage, Asheville Chamber of Commerce, PO Box 1010, Asheville, NC 28802-1010. Phone: (800) 257-5583 or (704) 258-6107. Fax: (704) 254-6054. Email: sbanjoc@aol.com.

SMITH, JAMES: DEATH ANNIVERSARY. July 11. Signer of the Declaration of Independence, born in Ireland about 1719 (exact date unknown). Died July 11, 1806.

SMITH RIVER KIWANIS FESTIVAL & LOGGING SHOW. July 11–12. Smith River, CA. Featuring a larger sanctioned logging show and gala celebration of the lily bulb industry in the Easter lily capital of the world. Annually, the second weekend in July. Est attendance: 9,000. For info: Rowdy Creek Fish Hatchery, PO Box 328, Smith River, CA 95567. Phone: (707) 487-3443.

July 1998

S	M	T	W	T	F	S
			1	2	3	4
5	6	7	8	9	10	11
12	13	14	15	16	17	18
19	20	21	22	23	24	25
26	27	28	29	30	31	

SODBUSTER DAYS. July 11–12. Fort Ransom State Park, Fort Ransom, ND. Remember the way things were done in rural North Dakota during the early 1920s with shelling corn by hand, rope weaving, horse-drawn plowing and haying. Est attendance: 4,000. For info: Ft Ransom State Park, 5981 Walt Hjelle Parkway, Ft Ransom, ND 58033-9712. Phone: (701) 973-4331. Fax: (701) 973-4271.

SPACE MILESTONE: *SKYLAB* (US): FALLS TO EARTH. July 11, 1979. The 82-ton spacecraft that was launched May 14, 1973, re-entered Earth's atmosphere on July 11, 1979. Expectation was that 20–25 tons probably would survive to hit Earth, including one piece of about 5,000 pounds. This generated intense international public interest in where it would fall. The chance that some person would be hit by a piece of *Skylab* was calculated at one in 152. Targets were drawn, *Skylab* parties were held and the media swarmed to cover the largest man-made object to fall to Earth from orbit. *Skylab* broke up and fell to Earth in a shower of pieces over the Indian Ocean and Australia, with no known or reported casualties.

STONE HOUSE DAY. July 11. Hurley, NY. Tour six to nine privately-owned, 250-plus year-old stone houses. Annually, the second Saturday in July. Est attendance: 800. For info: Stone House Day, Hurley Reformed Church, PO Box 328, Hurley, NY 12443. Phone: (914) 331-4121.

TALKEETNA MOOSE DROPPING FESTIVAL (WITH MOOSE DROPPING TOSS GAME). July 11–12. Talkeetna, AK. Parade, booths, entertainment, 5K fun run, Mountain Mother contest and the famous moose dropping toss game. Est attendance: 5,500. For info: Sue Denver, Talkeetna Historical Soc, PO Box 76, Talkeetna, AK 99676. Phone: (907) 733-2487 or (907) 733-1478. Email: hc89bx585@matnet.com.

THREE RIVERS FESTIVAL. July 11–19. Fort Wayne, IN. A citywide extravaganza of more than 200 events including parades, food, juried art show, juried craft show, concerts, children's events and fireworks. Est attendance: 500,000. For info: Three Rivers Festival, 2301 Fairfield Ave, Ste 107, Ft Wayne, IN 46807. Phone: (219) 745-3378 or (219) 745-5556. Fax: (219) 744-1453.

TIVOLI—VIKING DAYS AT THE NORDIC HERITAGE MUSEUM. July 11–12. Nordic Heritage Museum, Seattle, WA. A two-day outdoor Scandinavian festival featuring crafts, foods, entertainment and children's activities. Swedish pancake breakfast Saturday morning, barbecued salmon in afternoon, roast pig and cafe Sunday morning and food booths throughout both days. Est attendance: 3,500. For info: Marianne Forssblad, Dir, Nordic Heritage Museum, 3014 NW 67th St, Seattle, WA 98117. Phone: (206) 789-5707. Fax: (206) 789-3271.

TUPPER LAKE WOODSMEN'S DAYS (WITH CHAINSAW SCULPTURING CONTEST). July 11–12. Tupper Lake, NY. Competitions for woodsmen and lumberjacks. Includes the 7th annual Northeast Regional Chainsaw Sculpturing Contest. Annually, the second weekend in July. Est attendance: 25,000. For info: Tupper Lake Woodsmen's Assn, PO Box 759, 19 Front St, Tupper Lake, NY 12986. Phone: (518) 359-9444.

TWO THOUSAND DAYS BEFORE "2000"™. July 11. Today is the 538th day before the year 2,000. Now is the time to do all those things you've wanted to do but put off for way too long. Although the countdown began on July 11, 1994, it is not too late to participate, by just taking a moment each day to do something you ordinarily wouldn't. That way, when the clock strikes midnight on Dec 31, 1999, you can say you've accomplished 2,000 things before 2000 and 805 new, enriching feats and gestures of goodwill and brotherhood—if you start today! For info: Adrienne Sioux Koopersmith, 1437 W Rosemont, 1W, Chicago, IL 60660-1319. Phone: (773) 743-5341. Fax: (773) 743-5395. Email: kooper@interaccess.com.

UGLY TRUCK CONTEST. July 11. Pelican Rapids, MN. Farm trucks and beat-up pickups, the worse the better, are put on display and judged. The only requirements are that the vehicle must be licensed and be able to travel under its own power. Owner of the ugliest truck wins a cash prize. A flea market is also held in conjunction with the contest. Est attendance: 100. For info: c/o Len Zierke, Ugly Truck Contest, PO Box 435, Pelican Rapids, MN 56572-0435. Phone: (218) 863-6693. Fax: (218) 863-6695.

UNITED NATIONS: WORLD POPULATION DAY. July 11. In June 1989, the Governing Council of the United Nations Development Programme recommended that July 11 be observed by the international community as World Population Day. An outgrowth of the Day of Five Billion (July 11, 1987), the Day seeks to focus public attention on the urgency and importance of population issues, particularly in the context of overall development plans and programs and the need to create solutions to these problems. For info: United Nations, Dept of Public Info, Public Inquiries Unit, RM GA-57, New York, NY 10017. Phone: (212) 963-4475. Fax: (212) 963-0071. Email: inquiries@un.org.

WHITE, E.B.: BIRTH ANNIVERSARY. July 11, 1899. Versatile author of books for adults and children (*Charlotte's Web*), born at Mount Vernon, NY. *New Yorker* editor. White died at North Brooklyn, ME, Oct 1, 1985.

WORLD FOLKFEST. July 11–18. Springville, UT. Large international folk dance event. No dance performances on the 12th or 15th. Est attendance: 30,000. For info: Springville World Folkfest, PO Box 306, 50 S Main, Springville, UT 84663. Phone: (801) 489-2700 or (801) 489-3657. Fax: (801) 489-2709. WWW: http://www.AVPRO.com/folkfest

BIRTHDAYS TODAY

Giorgio Armani, 62, fashion designer, born Romagna, Italy, July 11, 1936.

Harold Bloom, 68, literary critic, born New York, NY, July 11, 1930.

Debbie Harry, 53, singer (lead singer of Blondie; "The Tide Is High"), born Miami, FL, July 11, 1945.

Tab Hunter (Arthur Gelien), 67, actor (*Damn Yankees, Judge Roy Bean*, "The Tab Hunter Show"), born New York, NY, July 11, 1931.

Stephen Lang, 46, actor (*Last Exit to Brooklyn, Tombstone*), born Queens, NY, July 11, 1952.

Mark Lester, 40, actor (*Fahrenheit 451, Oliver*), born Oxford, England, July 11, 1958.

Theodore Maiman, 71, physicist, developed first working laser, born Los Angeles, CA, July 11, 1927.

Bonnie Pointer, 47, singer (Pointer Sisters; "Steam Heat"), born East Oakland, CA, July 11, 1951.

Leon Spinks, 45, former boxer, born St. Louis, MO, July 11, 1953.

Beverly Todd, 52, actress, director, producer (*Baby Boom, Clara's Heart*), born Chicago, IL, July 11, 1946.

Sela Ward, 42, actress (Teddy on "Sisters," *The Fugitive*), born Meridian, MS, July 11, 1956.

JULY 12 — SUNDAY

Day 193 — 172 Remaining

BATTLE OF KURSK: 55th ANNIVERSARY. July 12, 1943. The largest tank battle in history took place outside the small village of Prohorovka, Russia. Nine hundred Russian tanks attacked an equal number of German Panther and Porsche tanks. Though the German equipment was larger, that advantage was lost in a close range battle where they lacked maneuverability. When Hitler ordered a cease-fire, 300 German tanks remained strewn over the field.

De RITA, JOE: BIRTH ANNIVERSARY. July 12, 1909. American comedian Curly Joe DeRita was born on July 12, 1909. He was the last surviving member of the Three Stooges comedy team. Curly Joe joined the team in 1959 after Joe Besser left. He appeared in *Have Rocket, Will Travel* (1959), *Snow White and the Three Stooges* (1961) and *The Outlaw is Coming* (1965). DeRita died on July 3, 1993, at Los Angeles, CA.

"EVENING AT POPS" TV PREMIERE: ANNIVERSARY. July 12, 1970. PBS's popular concert series premiered with conductor Arthur Fiedler heading the Boston Pops Orchestra. Conductor/composer John Williams took over the post upon Fiedler's death in 1979.

"FAMILY FEUD" TV PREMIERE: ANNIVERSARY. July 12, 1976. From the production team of Mark Goodson and Bill Todman, this game show set two families against each other to raise the greater number of points. The contestants had to predict the most common answers to a given survey. Richard Dawson, TV's famous kissing host, and the late Ray Combs served as hosts of the show.

FAST OF TAMMUZ. July 12. Jewish holiday. Hebrew calendar date: Tammuz 17, 5758. Shiva Asar B'Tammuz begins at first light of day and commemorates the first-century Roman siege that breached the walls of Jerusalem. Begins a three-week time of mourning.

GERMANY ENDS MILITARY BAN: ANNIVERSARY. July 12, 1994. Germany's Constitutional Court ended the ban on sending German troops to fight outside the country. The ban had been in effect since shortly after World War II, when Germany was disarmed. (Japan has a similar ban.) The ruling would allow German troops to join in peacekeeping missions of the United Nations or the North Atlantic Treaty Organization (NATO). As if to signal the change in status, German military units marched in the Bastille Day celebration in Paris on July 14, the first time German troops had appeared in France since the German occupation ended in 1945.

KIRIBATI: INDEPENDENCE DAY. July 12. Republic of Kiribati attained independence July 12, 1979.

NATIONAL FARRIER'S WEEK. July 12–18. A salute from horse owners to the men and women who keep their horses shod and equine feet and legs in top-notch condition. Annually, the third week in July. For info: Frank Lessiter, American Farriers Journal, PO Box 624, Brookfield, WI 53008-0624. Phone: (414) 782-4480. Fax: (414) 782-1252. Email: Lesspub@aol.com.

NATIONAL THERAPEUTIC RECREATION WEEK. July 12–18. To increase awareness of therapeutic recreation programs and services, and to expand leisure opportunities for individuals with disabilities in their local communities. Annually, the second week in July. For info: Natl Therapeutic Recreation Society, Ahren's NRPA Institute, 22377 Belmont Ridge Rd, Ashborn, VA 20148. Phone: (800) 626-NRPA. Email: NTRSNRPA@aol.com. WWW: http://www.nrpa.org

"NORTHERN EXPOSURE" TV PREMIERE: ANNIVERSARY. July 12, 1990. CBS's comedy-drama was essentially a fish-out-of-water (or rather a New Yorker out of Manhattan) series. Dr. Joel Fleischman (Rob Morrow) was forced to practice medicine in remote Cicely, Alaska, to pay off his student loans. He gradually accepted his lot through the help of the town's quirky citizens who needed him because he was the only doctor in town. The show's principal cast featured Barry Corbin as Maurice Minnefield, a former NASA astronaut and Cicely's most prominent businessman; Janine Turner as bush pilot Maggie O'Connell; Elaine Miles as Joel's assistant/receptionist Marilyn; Darren E. Burrows as Ed Chigliak, a half-Indian aspiring filmmaker; John Cullum as Cicely's mayor and tavern owner Holling Vincoeur; Cynthia Geary as Holling's girlfriend and waitress Shelley Tambo; Peg Phillips as store proprietor Ruth Anne; and John Corbett as deejay and philosopher Chris Stevens.

OSLER, SIR WILLIAM: BIRTH ANNIVERSARY. July 12. Anniversary of birth at Tecumseh, Ontario, Canada, on July 12, 1849, of William Osler, physician, teacher and author of *Principles and Practice of Medicine*. Osler died at Oxford, England, Dec 29, 1919.

SAO TOME AND PRINCIPE: NATIONAL DAY. July 12. National holiday observed.

SPACE MILESTONE: *PHOBOS 2* (USSR). July 12, 1988. Sent back the first close-up photos of Phobos, one of two small moons of Mars. Launched from Soviet space probe in central Asia on July 12, 1988.

THOREAU, HENRY DAVID: BIRTH ANNIVERSARY. July 12, 1817. American author and philosopher, born at Concord, MA. Died there May 6, 1862. In *Walden* he wrote, "I frequently tramped eight or ten miles through the deepest snow to keep an appointment with a beechtree, or a yellow birch, or an old acquaintance among the pines."

TURNER'S FRONTIER ADDRESS: ANNIVERSARY. July 12, 1893. Historian Frederick Jackson Turner delivered his paper,"The Significance of the Frontier in American History," at a meeting of the American Historical Association in Chicago during the Columbian Exposition. Stating that the frontier was a spawning ground for many of the social and intellectual traits that made Americans different from Europeans, Turner saw the end of the frontier as a major break in the psychology of the nation. Turner's formalization of this idea came in part from his reading the *Extra Census Bulletin No. 2: Distribution of Population According to Density: 1890* which said that, "Up to and including 1890 the country had a frontier of settlement, but at present the unsettled area has been so broken into by isolated bodies of settlement that there can hardly be said to be a frontier line."

VICTORIAN NEEDLEWORK. July 12 (also Sundays through Oct). H.D. Robinson House, Granville, OH. Robinson-family needle-work; quilts, lace, embroidery spanning more than 100 years. For info: Gina Hughes, Adm Asst, Life-Style Museum, H.D. Robinson House, 121 S Main St, Granville, OH 43023. Phone: (614) 587-0373.

WEDGWOOD, JOSIAH: BIRTH ANNIVERSARY. July 12. Famed English pottery designer and manufacturer, born at Burslem, Staffordshire, England, July 12, 1730. Died at Etruria, Staffordshire, England, Jan 3, 1795.

WSBA and WARM 103 SUMMER CRAFT SHOW. July 12. York Fairgrounds, York, PA. More than 250 crafts, from country to contemporary, Victorian and southwestern, handcrafted furniture, wood carvings, dolls, jewelry, pottery, collectibles, quilts, baskets and much more. Admission fee. Est attendance: 5,000. For info: Gina M. Koch, Spec Events Dir, PO Box 910, York, PA 17402-0619. Phone: (717) 764-1155. Fax: (717) 252-4708.

BIRTHDAYS TODAY

Van Cliburn (Harvey Lavan, Jr), 64, pianist, born Shreveport, LA, July 12, 1934.
Bill Cosby, 60, comedian, actor (Emmys for "I Spy," "The Cosby Show"), born Philadelphia, PA, July 12, 1938.
Mel Harris, 41, actress ("Something So Right," "thirtysomething"), born Bethlehem, PA, July 12, 1957.
Mark O. Hatfield, 76, Former US Senator (R, Oregon), born Dallas, OR, July 12, 1922.
Christine McVie, 55, singer, musician (member of Fleetwood Mac; "Got a Hold On Me"), born Birmingham, England, July 12, 1943.
Denise Nicholas, 53, actress ("Room 222," "In the Heat of the Night," *Let's Do It Again*), born Detroit, MI, July 12, 1945.
Jamey Sheridan, 47, actor ("Shannon's Deal," *The House on Carroll Street*), born Pasadena, CA, July 12, 1951.
Richard Simmons, 50, TV personality, weight loss guru, author, born New Orleans, LA, July 12, 1948.
Roger Smith, 73, former chair of General Motors, born Columbus, OH, July 12, 1925.

July 1998

S	M	T	W	T	F	S
			1	2	3	4
5	6	7	8	9	10	11
12	13	14	15	16	17	18
19	20	21	22	23	24	25
26	27	28	29	30	31	

Kristi Tsuya Yamaguchi, 27, Olympic gold medal figure skater, born Hayward, CA, July 12, 1971.

JULY 13 — MONDAY

Day 194 — 171 Remaining

"BROTHERS" TV PREMIERE: ANNIVERSARY. July 13, 1984. This sitcom was rejected by ABC and NBC before airing on Showtime, partly because one of its characters was openly gay. "Brothers" thus became the first original sitcom made for cable television. Robert Walden starred as Joe Waters, an ex-football player and restaurant owner; Brandon Maggart as eldest brother Lou, a conservative construction worker; and Paul Regina as youngest brother Clifford, who disclosed his orientation in the very first episode. Other regulars included: Philip Charles MacKenzie as Clifford's friend Donald, a stereotypically gay man; Hallie Todd as Joe's daughter, Penny; Robin Riker as Joe's waitress, Kelly; and Mary Ann Pascal as Samantha, Joe's girlfriend/wife. The series dealt with sensitive topics such as gay-bashing, AIDS and male-to-male intimacy. "Brothers" was set in Philadelphia.

FORREST, NATHAN BEDFORD: BIRTH ANNIVERSARY. July 13, 1821. Confederate cavalry commander whose birthday is observed in Tennessee, Forrest was also one of the founders of the short-lived original Ku Klux Klan. Forrest was born July 13, 1821, at Bedford County, TN, and died Oct 29, 1877, at Memphis, TN.

FRANCE: NIGHT WATCH OR LA RETRAITE AUX FLAMBEAUX. July 13. France. Celebrates eve of the Bastille's fall.

INTERNATIONAL TOWN CRIERS DAY. July 13. A day recognizing the ancient and honorable art and tradition of town crying and the significant contribution town criers make to promoting their respective towns and cities. Annually, the second Monday in July. For info: Scott O. Fraser, Official Town Crier, 42 Clarke St N, Woodstock, Ont, Canada, N4S 7M5. Phone: (519) 537-8675.

JAPAN: BON FESTIVAL (FEAST OF LANTERNS). July 13–15. Religious rites throughout Japan in memory of the dead who, according to Buddhist belief, revisit Earth during this period. Lanterns are lighted for the souls. Spectacular bonfires in the shape of the character *dai* are burned on hillsides on the last day of the Bon or O-Bon Festival, bidding farewell to the spirits of the dead.

"LIVE AID" CONCERTS: ANNIVERSARY. July 13, 1985. Concerts at Philadelphia, PA, and London, England (Kennedy and Wembley stadiums), on July 13, 1985, were seen by 162,000 attendees and an estimated 1.5 billion television viewers. Organized to raise funds for African famine relief; the musicians performed without fee, and nearly $100 million was pledged toward aid to the hungry.

NORTHERN IRELAND: ORANGEMEN'S DAY. July 13. National holiday commemorates Battle of Boyne, July 1 (Old Style), 1690, in which the forces of King William III of England, Prince of Orange, defeated those of James II, at Boyne River in Ireland. Ordinarily observed on July 12. If July 12 is a Saturday or a Sunday the holiday observance is on the following Monday.

NORTHWEST ORDINANCE: ANNIVERSARY. July 13, 1787. On this date the Northwest Ordinance, providing for government of the territory north of the Ohio River, became law. The ordinance guaranteed freedom of worship and the right to trial by jury, and it prohibited slavery.

NORWAY: MOLDE INTERNATIONAL JAZZ FESTIVAL. July 13–18. Molde. 35th annual festival, attracting international stars from both sides of the Atlantic. For info: Norwegian Tourist Board, 655 Third Ave, New York, NY 10017. Phone: (212) 885-9700 or (212) 573-9061. Fax: (212) 885-9710. Email: gonorway@interport.net. WWW: http://www.norway.org

WOOLLEY, MARY E.: BIRTH ANNIVERSARY. July 13, 1863. Mary Woolley was born at South Norwalk, CT. The first woman to attend classes and graduate from Brown University (1894), Woolley pursued a career in education, serving on the faculty of Wellesley College. In 1901 she was named president of Mount Holyoke College, where her impact was enormous as she not only upgraded the school's faculty and curriculum but also raised the funds to add 16 major buildings to the campus. In 1932 she became the first female representative of the US at a major diplomatic conference, serving as a delegate to the Conference on Reduction and Limitation of Armaments. Woolley died Sept 5, 1947, at Westport, CT.

BIRTHDAYS TODAY

Harrison Ford, 56, actor (*American Graffiti, Star Wars* and *Indiana Jones* films), born Chicago, IL, July 13, 1942.
Robert Forster, 57, actor ("Banyon," *Reflections in a Golden Eye*), born Rochester, NY, July 13, 1941.
John French (Jack) Kemp, 63, former US Secretary of Housing and Urban Development, former football player, born Los Angeles, CA, July 13, 1935.
Louise Mandrell, 44, country western singer, born Corpus Christi, TX, July 13, 1954.
Cheech Marin, 52, writer (*My Name Is Cheech the School Bus Driver*), actor (Cheech and Chong films), born Los Angeles, CA, July 13, 1946.
Roger McGuinn (James Joseph McGuinn), 56, musician, born Chicago, IL, July 13, 1942.
Erno Rubik, 54, inventor of the Rubik's Cube, born in a hospital air raid shelter at Budapest, Hungary, July 13, 1944.
Wole Soyinka, 64, author (*The Lion and the Jewel, The Strong Breed*), born Abeokuta, Nigeria, July 13, 1934.
Michael Spinks, 42, boxer, born St. Louis, MO, July 13, 1956.
Patrick Stewart, 58, actor ("Star Trek: The Next Generation," *Excalibur, LA Story*), born Mirfield, England, July 13, 1940.
David Storey, 65, author, playwright (*The Performance of Small Firms*), born Wakefield, England, July 13, 1933.
Anthony Jerome ("Spud") Webb, 35, basketball player, born Dallas, TX, July 13, 1963.

JULY 14 — TUESDAY

Day 195 — 170 Remaining

BASCOM, FLORENCE: BIRTH ANNIVERSARY. July 14, 1862. After receiving her third bachelor's degree from the University of Wisconsin in 1884 and a master's degree in 1887, Florence Bascom entered Johns Hopkins University and became the first woman to receive a doctorate in 1893. She taught at Ohio State and became a professor at Bryn Mawr. She also was the first woman appointed a geologist with the US Geological Survey, was Associate Editor of "American Geologist" (1890–1905) and became the first woman elected a Fellow of the Geological Society of America. She died on June 18, 1945.

BASTILLE DAY MOONLIGHT GOLF TOURNAMENT. July 14. Greenleaf Point Golf Course, Fort McNair, Washington, DC. After a cookout, teams of four tee off wearing glow-in-the-dark necklaces and hitting glow-in-the-dark balls. Participants are given membership into the Natl Capital Moonlight Golf Assn. Annually, July 14. For info: Ft McNair Sports Center, Bldg 17, 4th & P St SW, Washington, DC 20319-5050. Phone: (202) 685-3138.

CHANCELLOR, JOHN: BIRTH ANNIVERSARY. July 14, 1927. Television broadcast journalist John Chancellor was born at Chicago, IL. He rose through the ranks at the *Chicago Sun-Times*, from copy boy to feature writer. Chancellor spent more than four decades with the NBC network, beginning in 1950. During that time, he took a two-year respite from journalism to serve President Lyndon Johnson as director of the Voice of America. Chancellor retired in 1993, but his distinctive, familiar voice was still heard, for example, when he narrated a PBS documentary in 1996. He battled cancer for several years, but died July 12, 1996, at Princeton, NJ.

"THE EDDY ARNOLD SHOW" TV PREMIERE: ANNIVERSARY. July 14, 1952. Country and western singer Eddy Arnold hosted his first series on CBS as a summer replacement for "The Perry Como Show."

EDWARDS, DOUGLAS: BIRTH ANNIVERSARY. July 14, 1917. American television journalist Douglas Edwards was born at Ada, OK. He began his career in radio, but in 1947 he became the first major announcer to move to television. He was anchor for CBS's first nightly news program, "Douglas Edwards with the News" (1948-62), where he gave memorable on-scene coverage of such events as the sinking of the *Andrea Doria* in 1956. Edwards worked for CBS until his retirement two years before he died on Oct 13, 1990, at Sarasota, FL.

ENGLAND: BIRMINGHAM RIOT: ANNIVERSARY. July 14, 1791. Following a dinner celebrating the second anniversary of the fall of the Bastille, an angry mob rioted in Birmingham, England. The main target of their wrath was the home of scientist (discoverer of oxygen) Joseph Priestley, who was unpopular because of his religious views and his approval of the American and French revolutionary causes. The mob ruled Birmingham for three days, burning Priestly's home and laboratory as well as the homes of his friends. Priestly, in disguise, and his family narrowly escaped with their lives. They lived for a time in London before moving, in 1794, to America. See also: "Priestley, Joseph: Birth Anniversary" (Mar 13).

FORD, GERALD RUDOLPH: 85th BIRTHDAY. July 14, 1913. Thirty-eighth president of the US. Born Leslie King, at Omaha, NE, July 14, 1913. Ford became 41st vice president of the US on Dec 6, 1973, by appointment, following the resignation of Spiro T. Agnew from that office on Oct 10, 1973. Ford became president on Aug 9, 1974, following the resignation from that office on that day of Richard M. Nixon. He was the first non-elected vice president and president of the US.

FRANCE: BASTILLE DAY OR FETE NATIONAL. July 14. Public holiday commemorating the fall of the Bastille at the beginning of the French Revolution, on July 14, 1789. Also celebrated or observed in many other countries.

GUTHRIE, WOODROW WILSON "WOODY": BIRTH ANNIVERSARY. July 14, 1912. American folksinger, songwriter ("This Land Is Your Land," "Union Maid," "Hard Traveling"), born at Okemah, OK. Traveled the country by freight train, singing and listening. Became a strong union supporter. Died Oct 3, 1967, at New York City. Father of Arlo Guthrie.

"MASQUERADE PARTY" TV PREMIERE: ANNIVERSARY. July 14, 1952. Variations of this game show have appeared all over the TV schedule on NBC, CBS, ABC and in syndication. A panel of celebrities tried to guess the identity of a guest celebrity, who usually appeared in costume or under heavy makeup. Hosts of the show include: Bud Collyer, Douglas Edwards, Peter Donald, Eddie Bracken, Robert Q. Lewis, Bert Parks and Richard Dawson.

MISSION SAN ANTONIO DE PADUA: ANNIVERSARY. July 14. California. Mission to the Indians founded July 14, 1771.

MURRAY, KEN: BIRTH ANNIVERSARY. July 14, 1903. American comedian Ken Murray was born at New York, NY. He began in vaudeville, then moved to films and television. He died Oct 12, 1988, at Beverly Hills, CA.

NATIONAL BABY FOOD FESTIVAL. July 14–19. Fremont, MI. One of western Michigan's largest family festivals. Featured throughout the week will be arts and crafts, sporting events, spectacular midway and nationally renowned entertainment. A summertime festival highlighting the Great American lifestyle. Sponsor: Fremont Chamber of Commerce. Toll-free phone: (800) 592-BABY. Est attendance: 165,000. For info: Fremont Chamber of Commerce, 33 W Main, Fremont, MI 49412. Phone: (616) 924-2270. Fax: (616) 924-9248.

ORGANIZATION DEVELOPMENT WORLD CONGRESS. July 14–18. University of Dublin, Trinity College, Dublin, Ireland. Organization development professionals exchange ideas on changes and new developments in the field. Est attendance: 100. For info: Dr. Donald W. Cole, RODC, Organization Development Institute, 11234 Walnut Ridge Rd, Chesterland, OH 44026. Phone: (216) 461-4333 or (216) 729-7419. Fax: (216) 729-9319. Email: DonWCole@aol.com. WWW: http://members.aol.com/odinst

SARTO, ANDREA DEL: BIRTH ANNIVERSARY. July 14, 1486. Celebrated Italian painter was born near Florence, Italy. "Sarto," a nickname referring to his father's trade as a tailor, was the name he chose during his lifetime, though the real surname was probably either Vanucchi or di Francesco. One of the most renowned artists of his time, his paintings hang in the great galleries of the world. He died at Florence, Jan 22, 1531.

SNAKE RIVER STAMPEDE. July 14–18. Nampa, ID. In its 83rd year this is one of the top 20 professional rodeo events in the nation featuring the world's top cowboys and cowgirls in action. Events include bareback bronc riding, saddle bronc riding, bull riding, calf roping, team roping, steer wrestling, barrel racing and the Wrangler bull fight. Est attendance: 40,000. For info: Jimmy Hurley, Snake River Stampede, PO Box 231, Nampa, ID 83653. Phone: (208) 466-8497. Fax: (208) 465-4438.

BIRTHDAYS TODAY

Polly Bergen, 68, actress ("To Tell the Truth," *The Winds of War*), singer, born Knoxville, TN, July 14, 1930.

Ingmar Bergman, 80, filmmaker (*The Seventh Seal, Wild Strawberries, Cries and Whispers*), born Uppsala, Sweden, July 14, 1918.

Gerald Rudolph Ford (born Leslie King), 85, 38th US President, amateur golfer, born Omaha, NE, July 14, 1913.

Missy Gold, 28, actress (Katie Gatling on "Benson"), born Great Falls, MT, July 14, 1970.

Roosevelt (Rosey) Grier, 66, actor, former football player, born Cuthbert, GA, July 14, 1932.

Harry Dean Stanton, 72, actor (*Two-Lane Blacktop; Repo Man; Paris, Texas; Wild at Heart*), born West Irvine, KY, July 14, 1926.

Steven Michael (Steve) Stone, 51, sportscaster, former baseball player, born Euclid, OH, July 14, 1947.

July 1998

S	M	T	W	T	F	S
			1	2	3	4
5	6	7	8	9	10	11
12	13	14	15	16	17	18
19	20	21	22	23	24	25
26	27	28	29	30	31	

JULY 15 — WEDNESDAY

Day 196 — 169 Remaining

ANN ARBOR SUMMER ART FAIR AND STREET FAIR. July 15–18. Ann Arbor, MI. Juried art fair with more than 560 of the nation's finest artists and contemporary craftspeople. Free family art activity area, specialty shops and restaurants. Also, the 38th annual Street Fair of 1,000 visual and 50 performing arts. For Street Fair Info: Ann Arbor Street Art Fair, Inc, Box 1352, Ann Arbor, MI 48106. Est attendance: 500,000. For Summer Art Fair info: Shary Brown, Art Fair Dir, Michigan Guild of Artists and Artisans, 118 N Fourth Ave, Ann Arbor, MI 48104-1402. Phone: (313) 662-3382. Fax: (313) 662-0339. WWW: http://www.artfair.org

CANADA: JUST FOR LAUGHS: THE MONTREAL INTERNATIONAL COMEDY FESTIVAL. July 15–26. Montreal, Quebec. Make the trip to the worldwide capital of comedy! More than 650 artists from 14 countries play in more than 1,000 shows and performances at indoor and outdoor venues that blanket the entire city. In the past, Just for Laughs has featured some of today's top comedy draws including David Schwimmer, Tim Allen, Jerry Seinfeld, Brett Butler and Kelsey Grammer, Rowan "Mr Bean" Atkinson, Jim Carrey, Lily Tomlin and John Candy, to name but a few. Est attendance: 500,000. For info: Robin Altman, Dir of Press Relations and Corporate Affairs, Just for Laughs Comedy Festival, 51 rue Sherbrooke Ouest, Montreal, Quebec, Canada H2X 1X2. Phone: (514) 845-3155 ext 2259. Fax: (514) 845-4140. WWW: http://www.hahaha.com

CANADA: SAINT SWITHUN'S SOCIETY ANNUAL CELEBRATION. July 15. Toronto, Ontario. Goals include the promotion of feelings of goodwill, the celebration of St. Swithun's Day on July 15 and the patterning of members' lives after the example of our Patron. Organizes spontaneous celebrations throughout the year and creates Honourary Members. Affiliated with the Friends of Winchester Cathedral. Publishes "The Water Spout" newsletter, free upon request. Annually, July 15. Est attendance: 100. For info: Norman A. McMullen, Pres, St. Swithun's Soc, 427 Lynett Crescent, Richmond Hill, Ont, Canada L4C 2V6. Phone: (905) 883-0984.

COMMERCIAL AIR FLIGHT BETWEEN THE US AND USSR BEGINS: 30th ANNIVERSARY. July 15, 1968. On July 15, 1968, a Soviet Aeroflot jet landed at Kennedy Airport in New York, NY, marking the start of direct commercial air flight between the US and the then USSR.

CRAB AND CLAM BAKE. July 15. Somers Cove Marina, Crisfield, MD. One of Maryland's finest seafood festivals, featuring steamed crabs and clams, fried fish, raw clams, fried clams and side dishes—all you can eat! Entertainment. 1–5 PM. Tickets must be purchased in advance. Annually, the third Wednesday in July. Est attendance: 5,000. For info: Crisfield Area Chamber of Commerce, PO Box 292, Crisfield, MD 21817-0292. Phone: (800) 782-3913 or (410) 968-2500. Fax: (410) 968-0524.

GLENDALE HEIGHTS SUMMERFEST. July 15–19. Glendale Heights, IL. A five-day festival of entertainment for all age groups, a spectacular 24-ride carnival, a Show & Shine car show, crafts, food vendors. The festival concludes with one of the best fireworks displays in the western suburbs. The Village takes pride in having been recognized by the Illinois Festival Association as one of the 10 best festivals in the state. Est attendance: 100,000. For info: Paula Sabatino, Chairman, Village of Glendale Heights, 300 E Civic Center Plaza, Glendale Heights, IL 60139. Phone: (630) 260-6000. Fax: (630) 260-9728.

HOG CALLING CONTEST. July 15. Broadway Market Square, Baltimore, MD. Amateur hog callers compete for prizes. Country music entertainment. Live hogs on display. Est attendance: 250. For info: Office of Adventures in Fun, Patterson Park Recreation Complex, 2601 E Baltimore St, Baltimore, MD 21224. Phone: (410) 396-9177. Fax: (410) 327-4120.

MOORE, CLEMENT CLARKE: BIRTH ANNIVERSARY. July 15, 1779. American author and teacher, best remembered for his popular verse, "A Visit from Saint Nicholas" (" 'Twas the Night Before Christmas"), which was first published anonymously and without Moore's knowledge in a newspaper on Dec 23, 1823. Moore was born at New York, NY, July 15, 1779, and died at Newport, RI, on July 10, 1863.

"ONE LIFE TO LIVE" TV PREMIERE: 30th ANNIVERSARY. July 15, 1968. Set in the fictional Pennsylvania town of Llanview, the show was created by Agnes Nixon to depict the class and ethnic struggles of the town's denizens. The initial cast featured many Jewish, Polish and African-American characters. The show departed from inter-ethnic storytelling in the 1980s for far more fantastic adventures set in locales such as heaven, the old west and a futuristic mountain silo called Eternia. Since then, the show has returned to its strengths of traditional storytelling by featuring Latino and African-American actors as integral characters in new storylines. Award-winning actress Erika Slezak heads the cast as the venerable Viki Lord Riley Buchanan Carpenter, the town's matron with five alternate personalities. Among those who have appeared on "OLTL" are Tom Berenger, Judith Light, Robert Desiderio, John Cullum, Tommy Lee Jones, Laurence Fishburne, Jane Badler, Jameson Parker, Leigh McCloskey, Phylicia Rashad, Christine Ebersole, Richard Grieco, Marcia Cross, Blair Underwood, Jessica Tuck, Joe Lando, Audrey Landers and Yasmine Bleeth.

REMBRANDT: BIRTH ANNIVERSARY. July 15, 1606. Dutch painter and etcher, born at Leiden, Holland. One of the undisputed giants of western art. Known for *The Night Watch* and many portraits and self-portraits, died at Amsterdam, Holland, Oct 4, 1669.

RESPECT CANADA DAY. July 15. To show our friends to the north that we really do know they are not just some strange northern province of America. [© 1997 by WPL] For info: Thomas and Ruth Roy, Wellness Permission League, PO Box 662, Mt Gretna, PA 17064-0662. Phone: (500) 437-5104 or (717) 964-1308. Fax: (717) 964-1335.

SAINT FRANCES XAVIER CABRINI: BIRTH ANNIVERSARY. July 15. First American saint, last of 13 children, founder of schools, orphanages, convents and hospitals, born at Lombardy, Italy, July 15, 1850. Died of malaria at Chicago, IL, Dec 22, 1917. Canonized July 7, 1946.

SAINT SWITHIN'S DAY. July 15. Swithun (Swithin), Bishop of Winchester (AD 852–862), died July 2, 862. Little is known of his life, but his relics were transferred into Winchester Cathedral on July 15, 971, a day on which there was a heavy rainfall. According to old English belief, it will rain for 40 days thereafter when it rains on this day. "St. Swithin's Day, if thou dost rain, for 40 days it will remain; St. Swithin's Day, if thou be fair, for 40 days, –will rain nea mair."

SINCLAIR LEWIS DAYS. July 15–19. Sauk Centre, MN. Parade, park activities, park dance, Miss Sauk Centre pageant, Fun Golf Tournament, flea market, craft sale, Heart of Lakes Bike Tour, milk carton boat races, softball tournament, kiddie caravan and volleyball tournament in Sinclair Lewis's hometown. Est attendance: 10,000. For info: Lisa Long, Mgr, Sauk Centre Chamber of Commerce, PO Box 222, Sauk Centre, MN 56378. Phone: (320) 352-5201 ext C. WWW: http://www.saukcentre.com

SPACE MILESTONE: *APOLLO-SOYUZ* TEST PROJECT (US, USSR): ANNIVERSARY. July 15, 1975. After three years of planning, negotiation and preparation, the first US–USSR joint space project reached fruition with the linkup in space of *Apollo 18* (crew: T. Stafford, V. Brand, D. Slayton; landed in Pacific Ocean July 24, during 136th orbit) and *Soyuz 19* (crew: A.A. Leonov, V.N. Kubasov; landed July 21, after 96 orbits). *Apollo 18* and *Soyuz 19* were linked 47 hours (July 17–19) while joint experiments and transfer of personnel and materials back and forth between craft took place. Launch date was July 15, 1975.

WORLD WAR I: BATTLE OF THE MARNE: 80th ANNIVERSARY. July 15, 1918. General Erich Ludendorff launched Germany's fifth, and last, offensive to break through the Chateau-Thierry salient. This all-out effort involved three armies branching out from Rheims to cross the Marne River. The Germans were successful in crossing the Marne near Chateau-Thierry before American, British and Italian divisions stopped their progress. On July 18 General Foch, Commander-in-Chief of the Allied troops, launched a massive counteroffensive that resulted in a German retreat that continued for four months until they sued for peace in November.

BIRTHDAYS TODAY

Willie Aames, 38, actor ("Eight Is Enough," "Charles in Charge"), born Newport Beach, CA, July 15, 1960.

Kim Alexis, 38, model, born Lockport, NY, July 15, 1960.

Julian Bream, 65, musician (classical guitar, lute), born London, England, July 15, 1933.

Lolita Davidovich, 37, actress (*Indictment, Cobb*), born London, Ontario, Canada, July 15, 1961.

Alex George Karras, 63, former football player, actor (dad on "Webster"; *Babe, Victor/Victoria*), born Gary, IN, July 15, 1935.

Ken Kercheval, 63, actor ("Dallas," "Search for Tomorrow"), born Wolcottville, IN, July 15, 1935.

Linda Ronstadt, 52, singer ("Heart Like a Wheel," "Simple Dreams"), songwriter, born Tucson, AZ, July 15, 1946.

Jan-Michael Vincent, 54, actor ("The Winds of War," "Airwolf"), born Denver, CO, July 15, 1944.

George V. Voinovich, 62, Governor of Ohio (R), born Cleveland, OH, July 15, 1936.

Forest Whitaker, 37, actor, director (*Platoon, Bird, The Crying Game*; directed *Jason's Lyric, Waiting to Exhale*), born Longview, TX, July 15, 1961.

JULY 16 — THURSDAY

Day 197 — 168 Remaining

AMUNDSEN, ROALD: BIRTH ANNIVERSARY. July 16, 1872. Norwegian explorer born near Oslo, author Roald Amundsen was the first man to sail from the Atlantic to the Pacific Ocean via the Northwest Passage (1903–05). He discovered the South Pole (Dec 14, 1911) and flew over the North Pole in a dirigible in 1926. He flew, with five companions, from Norway, June 18, 1928, in a daring effort to rescue survivors of an Italian Arctic expedition. No trace of the rescue party or the airplane was ever located. See also: "South Pole: Discovery Anniversary" (Dec 14).

ATOMIC BOMB TESTED: ANNIVERSARY. July 16, 1945. In the New Mexican desert at Alamogordo Air Base, 125 miles southeast of Albuquerque, the experimental atomic bomb was set off at 5:30 AM. Dubbed "Fat Boy" by its creator, the plutonium bomb vaporized the steel scaffolding holding it as the immense fireball rose 8,000 ft in a fraction of a second—ultimately creating a mushroom cloud to a height of 41,000 ft. At ground zero the bomb emitted heat three times the temperature of the interior of the sun. All plant and animal life for a mile around had ceased to exist. When informed by President Truman at Potsdam of the successful experiment, Winston Churchill responded, "It's the Second Coming in wrath!"

BOLIVIA: LA PAZ DAY: 450th ANNIVERSARY. July 16, 1548. Founding of city, now capital of Bolivia, on this day, 1548.

CANADA: EDMONTON'S KLONDIKE DAYS EXPOSITION. July 16–25. Edmonton, Alberta. Edmonton's early days as a frontier community and gateway to the Yukon in the rush for gold set the stage for the city's annual Klondike Days festival. Parades, pancake breakfasts, gambling casinos, entertainment, gold panning and the World Championship Sourdough Raft Race. Est attendance: 700,000. For info: Cheryl Herchen, Public Relations, Northlands Park, Box 1480, Edmonton, Alta, Canada T5J 2N5. Phone: (403) 471-7210. Fax: (403) 477-9536.
Email: npmarket@planet.eon.net.
WWW: http://www.northlands.com

CANADA: JULYFEST. July 16–19. Kimberley, British Columbia. Platzl entertainment, sports events (soccer, bocce ball), refreshment garden at arena, events for all ages at Rotary Park; parade. Annually, the third weekend in July. Est attendance: 3,000. For info: Kimberley Bavarian Soc, 350 Ross St, Kimberley, BC, Canada V1A 2Z9. Phone: (250) 427-3666. Fax: (250) 427-5378.

CANADA: SHELBURNE FOUNDERS' DAYS. July 16–19. Shelburne, Nova Scotia. To commemorate the settlement of Shelburne by the United Empire Loyalists in 1783. Community groups and volunteers organize canoe and yacht races, canoe jousting, greased pole games, fireworks, canteens, craft demonstrations, musical entertainment, a Loyalist Garden Party and re-enactment regiments: camps, parades, battles. Annually, the weekend closest to July 21. Est attendance: 7,000. For info: Jerry Locke, Parks/Recreation Dept Dir, PO Box 699, Shelburne, NS, Canada B0T 1W0. Phone: (902) 875-3873. Fax: (902) 875-3932.

CANADA: VANCOUVER FOLK MUSIC FESTIVAL. July 16–19. Vancouver, British Columbia. Come and join in the musical festival which also features a parade, food booths, entertainment and much more. Est attendance: 30,000. For info: Vancouver Folk Music Festival, Box 381, 916 W Broadway, Vancouver, BC, Canada V5Z 1K7. Phone: (604) 602-9798. Fax: (604) 602-9790. Email: vfmf@axionet.com.

COMET CRASHES INTO JUPITER: ANNIVERSARY. July 16, 1994. The first fragment of the comet Shoemaker-Levy crashed into the planet Jupiter, beginning a series of spectacular collisions, each unleashing more energy than the combined effect of an explosion of all our world's nuclear arsenal. Video imagery from earthbound telescopes as well as the Hubble telescope provided vivid records of the explosions and their aftereffects. In 1993 the comet had shattered into a series of about a dozen large chunks that resembled "pearls on a string" after its orbit brought it within the gravitational effects of our solar system's largest planet.

July 1998

S	M	T	W	T	F	S
			1	2	3	4
5	6	7	8	9	10	11
12	13	14	15	16	17	18
19	20	21	22	23	24	25
26	27	28	29	30	31	

COUNTRY JAM USA. July 16–19. Eau Claire, WI. The country stars will shine. Today's hottest stars playing the music that is the heart and soul of America. Food and beverage tents, campgrounds. Est attendance: 120,000. For info: Paul Novitzke, Exec Dir, Country Jam USA, 1711 S Hastings Way, Eau Claire, WI 54701. Phone: (800) 7800-JAM or (715) 839-7500. Fax: (715) 839-7553.

CRAFT FAIR OF THE SOUTHERN HIGHLANDS. July 16–19. (Also Oct 15–18.) Asheville Civic Center, Asheville, NC. In 1948 this fair started the crafts revival so evident today. More than a craft fair, this event includes demonstrations, children's workshops and traditional mountain music—all in addition to the 150 craft exhibits by the finest craftspeople in a nine-state region. Est attendance: 12,000. For info: Katherine Caldwell, PR, Southern Highland Craft Guild, PO Box 9545, Asheville, NC 28815. Phone: (704) 298-7928. Fax: (704) 298-7962.

DESTINY IN DAYTON. July 16–19. Bryan College, Dayton, TN. Five performances of an original drama written from the actual transcript of the Scopes trial—"the world's most famous court trial." Also, an arts and crafts fair, an antique car show and much more. Est attendance: 3,000. For info: Tom Davis, Bryan College, Scopes Festival, PO Box 7000, Dayton, TN 37321-7000. Phone: (423) 775-7206. Fax: (423) 775-7220.
Email: davisto@bryannet.bryan.edu.

DISTRICT OF COLUMBIA: ESTABLISHING LEGISLATION ANNIVERSARY. July 16. On July 16, 1790, George Washington signed legislation that selected the District of Columbia as the permanent capital of the US. Boundaries of the district were established in 1792. Plans called for the government to remain housed at Philadelphia, PA, until 1800, when the new national capital would be ready for occupancy.

EARTHQUAKE JOLTS PHILIPPINES: ANNIVERSARY. July 16. An earthquake measuring 7.7 on the Richter scale struck the Philippines on July 16, 1990, killing an estimated 1,621 persons and leaving approximately 1,000 missing. The quake struck in an area north of Manila, and heavy damage was reported in Cabanatuan, Baguio and on Luzon island. The quake was the worst in the Philippines in 14 years.

EDDY, MARY BAKER: BIRTH ANNIVERSARY. July 16, 1821. Founder of Christian Science; born near Concord, NH, she died at Chestnut Hill, MA, Dec 3, 1910.

ENGLAND: GOLF OPEN CHAMPIONSHIP. July 16–19. Royal Birkdale Golf Club, England. Major event on the golfing calendar. Est attendance: 170,000. For info: D. Hill, St. Andrews, Royal and Ancient Golf Club, Fife, Scotland KY16 9JD. Phone: (44) (1334) 472-2112. Fax: (44) (1334) 447-7580.

ENGLAND: SOUTHERN CATHEDRALS FESTIVAL. July 16–19. Chichester Cathedral, Chichester, Sussex. Festival of church music and concerts performed by the Cathedral Choirs of Chichester, Salisbury and Winchester. Est attendance: 1,000. For info: Alan Thurlow, 2 St. Richard's Walk, Chichester, Sussex, England SP1 3EF. Phone: (012) (43) 784790.

FESTA ITALIANA. July 16–19. Milwaukee, WI. America's #1 Italian festival is a combination of romantic music, authentic food and "street festival" spirit. At the Summerfest grounds, this fest offers Sicilian brass bands, Italian music, entertainment and gondola rides. A Sunday Mass features a religious procession reminiscent of Sicily's past. Italian heritage is displayed with sacred church art, vintage photos of Italian neighborhoods and the musical scores and song sheets from the Golden Age of Opera. For info: Wisconsin Dept of Tourism, Festa Italiana, PO Box 7976, Madison, WI 53707. Phone: (414) 223-2180 or (414) 223-2194. Email: tourism@laughlin.com. WWW: http://tourism.state.wi.us

FOLKMOOT USA: THE NORTH CAROLINA INTERNATIONAL FOLK FESTIVAL. July 16–26. Waynesville, NC. A festival of international folk dance featuring groups from 10 countries. Est attendance: 75,000. For info: Folkmoot USA, PO Box 658, Waynesville, NC 28786. Phone: (704) 452-2997. Fax: (704) 452-5762. Email: folkmoot@pobox.com. WWW: http://www.pobox.com/~folkmoot

FOUNDER'S DAY PICNIC. July 16–18. El Dorado Springs, MO. Three-day festival featuring carnival, crafters, entertainment, friends and family reunions. Annually, the Thursday, Friday and Saturday closest to third weekend in July. Est attendance: 8,000. For info: Founder's Day Picnic Chairperson, City Hall, 127- W Spring, El Dorado Springs, MO 64744. Phone: (417) 876-2521.

HOT DOG NIGHT. July 16. Luverne, MN. More than 12,000 hot dogs are served free of charge; free orange drink is also provided. Various demonstrations. Est attendance: 5,000. For info: Norma De Jongh, Exec Dir, Luverne Area Chamber of Commerce, 102 E Main, Luverne, MN 56156. Phone: (507) 283-4061. Fax: (507) 283-4061.

JAMBOREE IN THE HILLS. July 16–19. St. Clairsville, OH. 22nd anniversary. Billed as the "Super Bowl of Country Music," this festival is a four-day outdoor country music show featuring the top names in country music today. Sponsors: Jamboree USA and WWVA Radio. Annually, the third weekend in July. Est attendance: 90,000. For info: Terri A. Phillips, Publicity Dir, Jamboree in the Hills, 1015 Main St, Wheeling, WV 26003. Phone: (800) 624-5456. Fax: (304) 234-0067. WWW: http://www.jamboreeusa.com

MICAJAH. July 16–18 (also July 23–25, 30–Aug 1). Autryville, NC. To promote patriotism, local history and heritage. *Micajah* is an outdoor drama depicting the life of Micajah Autry, local hero of the Battle of the Alamo. Est attendance: 200. For info: Donna N. Cashwell, Pres, Micajah Autry Society, Inc, PO Box 52, Autryville, NC 28318. Phone: (910) 525-4621. Fax: (910) 525-4567.

MINERAL BLUEGRASS FESTIVAL. July 16–18. Mineral, VA. 15th annual festival. For info: Norman Adams, PO Box 98, Dahlonega, GA 30533. Phone: (706) 864-7203. Fax: (706) 864-1037.

MISSION SAN DIEGO DE ALCALA FOUNDING: ANNIVERSARY. July 16. First of 21 California missions to the Indians, founded July 16, 1769.

MOON PHASE: LAST QUARTER. July 16. Moon enters Last Quarter phase at 11:13 AM, EDT.

NATCHITOCHES/NORTHWESTERN STATE UNIVERSITY FOLK FESTIVAL. July 16–18. Northwestern State University, Natchitoches, LA. The festival is a "purist" folk festival in that folk artists who are reviving a traditional Louisiana folk art or still working a Louisiana tradition are invited. Music, food, crafts and storytellers. Annually, the third weekend in July. Est attendance: 24,000. For info: Don Hatley, Louisiana Folklife Center, Natchitoches/NSU Folk Fest, NSU PO Box 3663, Natchitoches, LA 71497. Phone: (318) 357-4332. Fax: (318) 357-4331. Email: folklife@alpha.nsula.edu. WWW: http://www.nsula.edu/departments/folklife/

REYNOLDS, JOSHUA: 275th BIRTH ANNIVERSARY. July 16, 1723. English portrait painter whose paintings of 18th-century English notables are among the best of the time. Born at Plympton, Devon, England, Sir Joshua died at London on Feb 23, 1792, at age 68. "He who resolves never to ransack any mind but his own," Reynolds told students of the Royal Academy in 1774, "will be soon reduced, from mere barrenness, to the poorest of all imitations; he will be obliged to imitate himself, and to repeat what he has before often repeated."

ROGERS, GINGER: BIRTH ANNIVERSARY. July 16, 1911. Ginger Rogers is best remembered as Fred Astaire's dance partner in a series of romantic musicals. She appeared in 70 films during her six-decade career, winning an Oscar for her leading role in the 1940 film *Kitty Foyle*. Rogers was born at Independence, MO, and died Apr 25, 1995, at Rancho Mirage, CA.

SPACE MILESTONE: *APOLLO 11* (US): MAN SENT TO THE MOON. July 16, 1969. Launched on July 16, 1969, and resulted in man's first moon landing. Lunar module *Eagle* landed on moon, 4:17 PM, EDT, July 20. Commander Neil Armstrong descended from *Eagle* to moon's surface, followed shortly by Colonel Edwin Aldrin, Jr. After rejoining spaceship *Columbia*, piloted by Lieutenant Colonel Michael Collins, astronauts returned to Earth on July 24, bringing firsthand reports of lunar surface, photographs and rock samples. Man's first landing on an extraterrestrial body.

STANWYCK, BARBARA: BIRTH ANNIVERSARY. July 16, 1907. Actress Barbara Stanwyck was born Ruby Stevens in the Flatbush section of Brooklyn, NY. She began her career at the age of 15 as a chorus girl, and at the age of 18 she won a leading role in the Broadway melodrama *Noose*, appearing for the first time as Barbara Stanwyck. She appeared in 82 films including *Stella Dallas*; *Double Indemnity*; *Sorry, Wrong Number*; *The Lady Eve* and the television series "The Big Valley." In 1944, the government listed her as the nation's highest paid woman, earning $400,000 per year. Stanwyck died at Santa Monica, CA, on Jan 21, 1990.

WELLS, IDA B.: BIRTH ANNIVERSARY. July 16, 1862. African American journalist and anti-lynching crusader Ida B. Wells was born the daughter of slaves at Holly Springs, MS, during the Civil War and grew up as Jim Crow and lynching were becoming prevalent. Wells argued that lynchings occurred not to defend white women but because of whites' fear of economic competition from blacks. She traveled extensively, founding anti-lynching societies and black women's clubs. Wells's *Red Record* (1895) was one of the first accounts of lynchings in the South. She died Mar 25, 1931, at Chicago, IL.

BIRTHDAYS TODAY

Ruben Blades, 50, singer (two Grammy Awards in 1986 and 1988), actor (*Crossover Dreams, The Milagro Beanfield War*), born Panama City, Panama, July 16, 1948.

Richard H. Bryan, 61, US Senator (D, Nevada), born Washington, DC, July 16, 1937.

Phoebe Cates, 35, actress (*Fast Times at Ridgemont High, Gremlins, Gremlins 2: The New Batch*), born New York, NY, July 16, 1965.

Stewart Copeland, 46, musician (drummer with the Police), songwriter, born McLean, VA, July 16, 1952.

Alexis Herman, 51, Secretary of Labor in the Clinton administration, born Mobile, AL, July 16, 1947.

Barnard Hughes, 83, actor (*Sisters*, "Doc"), born Bedford Hills, NY, July 16, 1915.

Bess Myerson, 74, former Miss America ('45), former government official, born New York, NY, July 16, 1924.

Barry Sanders, 30, football player, born Wichita, KS, July 16, 1968.

Richard L. Thornburgh, 66, former US Attorney General, born Pittsburgh, PA, July 16, 1932.

Pinchas Zukerman, 50, violinist, born Tel Aviv, Israel, July 16, 1948.

JULY 17 — FRIDAY

Day 198 — 167 Remaining

ABBOTT, BERENICE: 100th BIRTH ANNIVERSARY. July 17, 1898. Berenice Abbott was born at Springfield, OH, and went on to become a pioneer of American photography. She is best remembered for her black and white photographs of New York City in the 1930s, many of which appeared in the book *Changing New York*. After publishing this collection she began photographing scientific experiments that illustrated the laws and processes of physics. She died at Monson, ME, on Dec 11, 1991.

BIG SKY STATE GAMES. July 17–19. Billings, MT. An Olympic-styled festival for Montana citizens. This statewide multisport program is designed to inspire people of all ages and skill levels to develop their physical and competitive abilities to the height of their potential through participation in fitness activities. Est attendance: 12,000. For info: Big Sky State Games, Box 7136, Billings, MT 59103-7136. Phone: (406) 254-7426. Fax: (406) 254-7439.

CANADA: COUNTRY GOOD TIMES. July 17–19. Wilberforce, Ont. Family fun celebrating music and local musicians featuring amateur contest, flea market, carnival midway, vendors and bingo. Annually, the third weekend in July. Est attendance: 5,000. For info: Bancroft and Dist Chamber of Commerce, PO Box 539, Bancroft, Ont, Canada K0L 1C0. Phone: (613) 332-1513. Fax: (613) 332-2119. Email: chamber@commerce.bancroft.on.ca. WWW: http://www.commerce.bancroft.on.ca

CANADA: GREAT NORTHERN ARTS FESTIVAL. July 17–26. Inuvik, Northwest Territory. Exhibition and sale by more than 75 Northern artists. Workshops, demonstrations and seminars on printmaking, drawing, painting, tapestry and carving. Nightly entertainment and special presentations—drumming and dancing, storytelling, throat singing, fashion show, jam sessions. Est attendance: 7,500. For info: Genl Mgr, Great Northern Arts Festival, Box 2921Z, Inuvik, NWT, Canada X0E 0T0. Phone: (403) 979-3536. Email: greatart@internorth.com. WWW: http://www.greatart.nt.ca

July 1998

S	M	T	W	T	F	S
			1	2	3	4
5	6	7	8	9	10	11
12	13	14	15	16	17	18
19	20	21	22	23	24	25
26	27	28	29	30	31	

CANADA: KINSMEN BIG VALLEY JAMBOREE. July 17–19. Craven, Saskatchewan. Ranked by the American Bus Association in 1995 as one of the Top 100 events in North America, the Big Valley Jamboree is renowned for its world class line up of country music stars, set in the beautiful Qu'Appelle Valley. The event also includes a main stage saloon, concessions, souvenirs and free camping. Est attendance: 12,000. For info: (306) 352-2300 or Tourism Saskatchewan, 500-1900 Albert St, Regina, Sask, Canada S4P 4L9. Phone: (800) 667-7191.
Email: travel.info@sasktourism.sk.ca.
WWW: http://www.sasktourism.com

CANADA: SASKATCHEWAN HANDCRAFT FESTIVAL. July 17–19. Battleford Arena and Alex Dillabough Centre, Battleford, Saskatchewan. Features the finest in Saskatchewan crafts. Juried craft exhibition, children's pavilion, craft market and demonstrations, food pavilion. Est attendance: 9,000. For info: Tourism Saskatchewan, 500–1900 Albert St, Regina, Sask, Canada S4P 4L9. Phone: (800) 667-7191 or (306) 653-3616.
Email: travel.info@sasktourism.sk.ca.
WWW: http://www.sasktourism.com

CANADA: SPORTSMAN RIVER ROAR POWER BOAT RACES. July 17–19. South Saskatchewan River, downtown Saskatoon, Saskatchewan. Formula One powerboats race in this internationally acclaimed Professional Outboard Performance Race Tour. Professional racers compete with boats capable of reaching speeds of 130 mph. Held in conjunction with Saskatchewan Place's Taste of Saskatchewan where more than 20 restaurants and organizations serve up their finest cuisine. Est attendance: 60,000. For info: (306) 665-2001 or Tourism Saskatchewan, 500-1900 Albert St, Regina, Sask, Canada S4P 4L9. Phone: (800) 667-7191. Email: travelinfo@sasktourism.sk.ca.
WWW: http://www.sasktourism.com

CANADA: WINNIPEG FRINGE THEATRE FESTIVAL. July 17–26. Winnipeg, Manitoba. A 10-day, noon-to-midnight, nonstop theatrical smorgasbord with more than 100 theatre companies from around the world. The Winnipeg Fringe Festival: Pushing the envelope in theatrical entertainment since 1988. Est attendance: 70,000. For info: The Winnipeg Fringe Festival, 174 Market Ave, Winnipeg, Manitoba, Canada R3B 0P8. Fax: (204) 947-3741. Email: fringe@mtc.mb.ca.
WWW: http://www.mtc.ma.ca

CRUISIN' INTO MOONLIGHT MADNESS. July 17. Springfield, VT. Street festival with classic car rally and competition, sock hop, hula hoop contest, best-dressed couple contest, lots of food and much more. Est attendance: 3,000. For info: Springfield Chamber of Commerce, 14 Clinton St, Springfield, VT 05156. Phone: (802) 885-2779.
Email: spfldcoc@vermontel.com.

DECOY AND WILDLIFE ART SHOW. July 17–19. Clayton Recreation Park Arena, Clayton, NY. 30th annual. World championship carvers of duck decoys, songbirds, birds of prey, animals, fish and related wildlife. Buying, trading and selling all take place. Events include hunting decoy contest, head whittling, decoy painting, vintage decoy contest and auction. Displays of handcrafted wildlife from wood, silver, gold and pewter. Est attendance: 5,000. For info: Thousand Islands Museum, PO Box 27, 403 Riverside Dr, Clayton, NY 13624. Phone: (315) 686-5794.

ENGLAND: BBC HENRY WOOD PROMENADE CONCERTS. July 17–Sept 12. London. "The Proms" consists of more than 70 concerts at the Royal Albert Hall, including symphonic and chamber music, choral music, opera and jazz. For info: BBC Henry Wood Promenade Concerts, Broadcasting House, London, England W1A 1AA. Phone: (44) (171) 765-4791. Fax: (44) (171) 765-5445. Email: proms@bbc.co.uk. WWW: http://www.bbc.co.uk/proms/

GARDNER, ERLE STANLEY: BIRTH ANNIVERSARY. July 17. American author of detective fiction, born at Malden, MA, July 17, 1889. Best remembered for his detective story series about lawyer-detective Perry Mason, Gardner also wrote novels under the pen name A.A. Fair. Gardner died at Temecula, CA, Mar 11, 1970.

GERRY, ELBRIDGE: BIRTH ANNIVERSARY. July 17. Fifth vice president of the US (1813–14), born at Marblehead, MA, July 17, 1744. Died at Washington, DC, Nov 23, 1814. His name became part of the language (gerrymander) after he signed a redistricting bill while governor of Massachusetts in 1812.

IRAQ: NATIONAL DAY. July 17. National holiday.

KALAMAZOO COUNTY FLOWERFEST. July 17–19. Bronson Park, Library Lane, Kalamazoo and Portage, MI. Celebration of color and beauty, highlighting the Kalamazoo County bedding plant industry, the largest producer of bedding plants in the nation. Three-dimensional sculptures, floral mounds, flower show, landscape seminars, AAS garden winners and entertainment. Annually, the third weekend in July. Est attendance: 20,000. For info: Kalamazoo County Flowerfest, Inc, PO Box 986, Portage, MI 49081-0986. Phone: (616) 381-3597. Fax: (616) 381-0311.

KANSAS CITY BLUES AND JAZZ FESTIVAL. July 17–19. Penn Valley Park, Kansas City, MO. The largest music festival in the region representing one of four world-renowned blues and jazz cities. During the 1920s and 1930s Kansas City was known for its blues-based, riff-oriented sound and was at the top of the jazz world. Annually, the third weekend in July. Est attendance: 160,000. For info: Peter Horak, Exec Dir, Kansas City Blues and Jazz Festival, 423 Westport Rd, Ste 204, Kansas City, MO 64111. Phone: (816) 753-3378. Fax: (816) 531-2583. Email: kcbnj@qni.com.
WWW: http://www.unicom.net/kcbluesjazz

KANSAS CITY HOTEL DISASTER: ANNIVERSARY. July 17, 1981. Anniversary of the collapse of aerial walkways at the Hyatt Regency Hotel in Kansas City, MO. About 1,500 people were attending the popular weekly tea dance when, at about 7 PM, two concrete and steel skywalks that were suspended from the ceiling of the hotel's atrium broke loose and fell on guests in the crowded lobby, killing 114 people. In 1986, a state board revoked the licenses of two engineers convicted of gross negligence for their part in designing the hotel.

KENTUCKY STATE CHAMPIONSHIP OLD-TIME FIDDLER'S CONTEST. July 17–18. Rough River Dam State Resort Park, Falls of Rough, KY. Old-time and bluegrass music competition; Governor's cup trophy is awarded to the champion fiddler. More than $4,000 in prize money. Annually, the third Friday and Saturday in July. Est attendance: 3,000. For info: Brent L. Miller, PO Box 4042, Leitchfield, KY 42755. Phone: (502) 259-3578. Fax: (502) 259-5221.

KOREA: CONSTITUTION DAY: 50th ANNIVERSARY. July 17, 1948. Legal national holiday. Commemorates the proclamation of the constitution of the republic of Korea on July 17, 1948. Ceremonies at Seoul's capitol plaza and all major cities.

MIDSUMMER NIGHTS' FAIR. July 17–18. Lions Park, Norman, OK. Juried and invited artists and craftspeople display their work for show and sale in booths under the stars. A pottery auction, dalmatian mascot contest, festival foods, free entertainment and free art activities for the whole family are set for this 21st annual event, 6 PM–midnight. Est attendance: 8,000. For info: Asst Dir, Firehouse Art Center, 444 S Flood, Norman, OK 73069. Phone: (405) 329-4523.

MINNEAPOLIS AQUATENNIAL. July 17–26. Minneapolis, MN. Major civic water festival to celebrate Minnesota's 10,000 lakes and quality of life. Some 30 events, including sports competitions, musical entertainment, pageants, parades and fireworks. Traditional family fun and community spirit in a completely volunteer-run and sponsor-driven festival. Annually, the third week in July. Est attendance: 1,000,000. For info: DaleAnn Murphy, The Murphy Group, c/o Minneapolis Aquatennial, Riverplace, 43 Main St SE, Ste 145, Minneapolis, MN 55414. Phone: (612) 331-8371 or (612) 512-1155. Fax: (612) 512-1144.
Email: aquatenn@aquatennial.mpls.mn.us/
WWW: http://www.acquatennial.org

MURDER MYSTERY WEEKEND. July 17–19. Moodus, CT. "Deadful Delights" Murder Mysteries of New York's C2JR Enterprises produce this most entertaining three-day event. Rates for Friday dinner through Sunday lunch start at $154 per adult and include meals, activities, entertainment, lodging and even a little blood. For info: Sunrise Resort, PO Box 415, Moodus, CT 06469. Phone: (860) 873-8681 or (800) 225-9033.

OLD-TIME THRESHMAN'S SHOW. July 17–19. Adams, TN. Blacksmithing, storytelling, antique cars, steam engines and much more. Est attendance: 12,000. For info: Tennessee-Kentucky Threshman's, PO Box 115, Adams, TN 37010. Phone: (615) 696-2383.

PUERTO RICO: MUÑOZ-RIVERA DAY. July 17. Public holiday on the anniversary of the birth of Luis Muñoz-Rivera. The Puerto Rican patriot, poet and journalist was born at Barranquitas, Puerto Rico, on July 17, 1859. He died at Santurce, a suburb of San Juan, Puerto Rico, Nov 15, 1916.

SALEM ART FAIR AND FESTIVAL. July 17–19. Bush's Pasture Park, Salem, OR. A celebration of the arts with 200 arts/crafts booths, artist demonstrations, continuous performing arts, food, children's parade and art activities, historic Bush House Museum and living history performances, special art exhibition, 5K walk and run for the arts. Annually, the third full weekend in July. Est attendance: 100,000. For info: Salem Art Assn, 600 Mission St SE, Salem, OR 97302. Phone: (503) 581-2228.

SHERWOOD ROBIN HOOD FESTIVAL. July 17–18. Sherwood, OR. Parade, archery contest, dance, music, beer garden, game booths, food and arts and crafts. Annually, the third weekend in July. Est attendance: 5,000. For info: Robin Hood Festival Assn, PO Box 496, Sherwood, OR 97140. Phone: (503) 625-6873.

SONG OF HIAWATHA PAGEANT. July 17–19 (also July 24–26 and July 31–Aug 2). Pipestone, MN. 50th annual presentation of pageant based on Longfellow's poem, held in a natural outdoor amphitheater. Elaborate lighting, lovely costumes and cast of 200 help make an unforgettable event. Annually, last two weekends in July and first weekend in August. Sponsor: The Hiawatha Club. Est attendance: 15,000. For info: Mick Myers, Exec Dir, Pipestone Chmbr Comm, PO Box 8 CAE, Pipestone, MN 56164. Phone: (507) 825-3316. Fax: (507) 825-3317. Email: pipecham@rconnect.com. WWW: http://www.pipestone.mn.us

SPACE MILESTONE: *SOYUZ T-12* (USSR). July 17, 1984. Launched on July 17, 1984, cosmonaut Svetlana Savitskaya became the first woman to walk in space (July 25) and the first woman to make more than one space voyage. With cosmonauts V. Dzhanibekov and I. Volk. Docked at *Salyut 7* on July 18 and returned to Earth July 29.

STEALTH BOMBER FLIGHT: ANNIVERSARY. July 17, 1989. The B-2 Stealth bomber airplane was flown successfully over the desert near Palmdale, CA, for almost two hours. A decade of work and $22 billion reportedly were spent on the project prior to the first flight. Designed to penetrate Soviet radar, the B-2 Stealth bomber was said to be capable of delivering up to 25 tons of nuclear or other bombs. Average cost of the 132 bombers requested by the Air Force was estimated to be $530 million each. On this first test flight the plane flew at speeds of up to 180 knots (200 mph) and was put through several types of turns. Higher speeds and retraction of the landing gear were left for subsequent test flights.

STEAMBOAT'S RAINBOW WEEKEND. July 17–19. Steamboat Springs, CO. 18th annual Hot-Air Balloon Rodeo; 24th annual Art-in-the-Park; Strings in the Mountains Chamber Music Festival; PRCA Rodeo; kids' tent and entertainment. Est attendance: 15,000. For info: Steamboat Springs Chamber Resort Assn, PO Box 774408, Steamboat Springs, CO 80477. Phone: (970) 879-0880. Fax: (970) 879-2543. Email: info@steamboat-chamber.com. WWW: http://www.steamboat-chamber.com

SYRACUSE ARTS & CRAFTS FESTIVAL. July 17–19. Syracuse, NY. Features a plethora of art and craft displays, food booths, entertainment. Fun for the whole family. Est attendance: 60,000. For info: Syracuse Arts & Crafts Festival, 1900 State Tower Bldg, Syracuse, NY 13202. Phone: (315) 422-8284. Fax: (315) 471-4503. Email: downtown@emi.com.

TWIN-O-RAMA. July 17–19. Cassville, WI. Celebration honoring twin and other multiple births. Est attendance: 7,500. For info: Twin-O-Rama, Inc, PO Box 545, Cassville, WI 53806. Phone: (608) 725-5180 or (608) 725-5102.

VIRGINIA LAKE FESTIVAL. July 17–19. Clarksville, VA. Fun-filled weekend with Pig Pickin, opening ceremonies on Friday; arts and crafts show, flea market, balloons, five-mile run, fish fry and fireworks on Saturday; beach music festival, live entertainment for children and adults on Sunday. Annually, the third weekend in July (Friday–Sunday). Est attendance: 50,000. For info: Clarksville Lake Country Chamber of Commerce, 105 2nd St, Box 1017, Clarksville, VA 23927. Phone: (804) 374-2436. Fax: (804) 374-8174. Email: clarksville@kerrlake.com. WWW: http://kerrlake.com/clarksville

July 1998

S	M	T	W	T	F	S
			1	2	3	4
5	6	7	8	9	10	11
12	13	14	15	16	17	18
19	20	21	22	23	24	25
26	27	28	29	30	31	

WRONG DAYS. July 17–18. Wright, MN. 32nd annual festival with teen and adult dances, coronation, amateur contest, smorgasbord, flea and crafts market, softball and horseshoe tournaments, dunk tank, parade, kids' games and more. Est attendance: 2,000. For info: Bonnie Adams, Wrong Days in Wright, PO Box 125, Wright, MN 55798. Phone: (218) 357-3901.

"WRONG WAY" CORRIGAN DAY. July 17, 1938. Douglas Groce Corrigan, an unemployed airplane mechanic, left Brooklyn, NY's Floyd Bennett field, ostensibly headed for Los Angeles, CA, in a 1929 Curtiss Robin monoplane. He landed 28 hours, 13 minutes later at Dublin, Ireland's Baldonnell airport after a 3,150-mile nonstop flight without radio or special navigation equipment and in violation of American and Irish flight regulations. Born at Galveston, TX, on Jan 22, 1907, Corrigan received a hero's welcome home; he was nicknamed "Wrong Way" Corrigan because he claimed he accidentally followed the wrong end of his compass needle.

YARMOUTH CLAM FESTIVAL. July 17–19. Yarmouth, ME. 33rd annual. Family-oriented festival featuring clams and more. Annually, the third weekend in July. Est attendance: 150,000. For info: Yarmouth Chamber of Commerce, Linda A. Gray, Executive Dir, 374 US Route 1, Yarmouth, ME 04096. Phone: (207) 846-3984. Fax: (207) 846-5419. Email: ycc@omnisystem.com. WWW: http://www.propel.com/clamfest

ZIPPO/CASE INTERNATIONAL SWAP MEET. July 17–18. Zippo/Case Visitors Center, Bradford, PA. Annual gathering of fans and collectors of Zippo windproof lighters and Case knives. Hosted by Zippo Manufacturing Company and its subsidiary W.R. Case & Sons Cutlery Co, festivities include two days of buying, selling and trading Zippo lighters and Case knives. Friday, July 17, is the celebration of the fifth National Zippo Day, highlighted by a live national radio broadcast hosted by Jim Zippo and Maria Danza on the ABC Pure Gold Network. Zippo/Case Store will feature special sales and Zippo/Case Swap Meet commemoratives. Est attendance: 5,000. For info: Peggy J. Errera, Communications Coord, Zippo Manufacturing Co, 33 Barbour St, Bradford, PA 16701. Phone: (814) 368-2786. Fax: (814) 368-2874. WWW: http://www.zippomfg.com

BIRTHDAYS TODAY

Lucie Arnaz, 47, actress ("Here's Lucy," "The Lucy Arnaz Show," *Lost In Yonkers*), born Los Angeles, CA, July 17, 1951.

Diahann Carroll (Carol Diahann Johnson), 63, singer, actress ("Julia," "Dynasty"), born New York, NY, July 17, 1935.

Phyllis Diller (Phyllis Driver), 81, actress ("The Beautiful Phyllis Diller Show," *Boy, Did I Get a Wrong Number!*), born Lima, OH, July 17, 1917.

David Hasselhoff, 46, actor ("The Young and the Restless," "Knight Rider," "Bay Watch"), born Baltimore, MD, July 17, 1952.

Aaron Lansky, 43, founder of National Yiddish Book Center, born New Bedford, MA, July 17, 1955.

Pat McCormick, 64, writer, actor ("Jack Paar Show," "The Tonight Show"; *Buffalo Bill and the Indians*), born July 17, 1934.

Phoebe Snow, 46, singer ("Poetry Man"), born New York, NY, July 17, 1952.

Donald Sutherland, 63, actor (*M*A*S*H, Klute, Backdraft*), born St. John, New Brunswick, Canada, July 17, 1935.

Robert Thomas (Bobby) Thigpen, 35, former baseball player, born Tallahassee, FL, July 17, 1963.

Alex Winter, 33, actor (*Bill & Ted's Excellent Adventure*), born London, England, July 17, 1965.

JULY 18 — SATURDAY

Day 199 — 166 Remaining

ABRAHAM LINCOLN BIRTHPLACE NATIONAL HISTORIC SITE: FOUNDER'S DAY WEEKEND. July 18–19. Hodgenville, KY. Special pioneer demonstrations, drama and musical programs commemorating the anniversary of the park and the founding of the National Park Service. Annually, weekend closest to July 17. Est attendance: 4,000. For info: Gary

V. Talley, Natl Park Service, 2995 Lincoln Farm Rd, Hodgenville, KY 42748. Phone: (502) 358-3137.

ANTI-CRUELTY SOCIETY DOGWASH. July 18. Chicago, IL. A fun annual event for all dog owners in the city to have their dogs washed by Society volunteers. Cost depends on size of dog. Est attendance: 200. For info: The Anti-Cruelty Soc, 157 W Grand Ave, Chicago, IL 60610. Phone: (312) 644-8338.

ANTIQUE AUTO SHOW. July 18. Wheaton Village, Millville, NJ. 16th annual show, held rain or shine. For info: Wheaton Village, 1501 Glasstown Rd, Millville, NJ 08332. Phone: (609) 825-6800 or (800) 998-4552. Fax: (609) 825-2410. Email: mail@wheatonvillage.org. WWW: http://www.wheatonvillage.org

BANNACK DAYS. July 18–19. Bannack, MT. Montana's first territorial capital, now a living ghost town, comes to life with a celebration of Montana's mining, ranching and farming history. Stage coach rides, main street gunfights, old-time dancing, lots of music and fun are provided during this two-day celebration along Grasshopper Creek each year. Operated as a state park, Bannack features a town from the mid-1800s now held in a state of "arrested decay." It is open year round to the public. For info: Cindy Staszak, Montana Fish, Wildlife and Parks, 4200 Bannack Rd, Dillon, MT 59725. Phone: (406) 834-3413.

CARVER DAY COMMEMORATIVE CELEBRATION. July 18. Diamond, MO. Family-oriented educational programs, gospel singing, storytelling, environmental education and guided historic tours at the George Washington Carver National Monument. Est attendance: 1,300. For info: George Washington Carver Natl Monument, 5646 Carver Rd, Diamond, MO 64840. Phone: (417) 325-4151. Fax: (417) 325-4231.

CHICAGO GOLF CLUB: ANNIVERSARY. July 18, 1893. The first 18-hole golf course in America, laid out by Charles Blair MacDonald, was incorporated in Wheaton, IL. MacDonald was the architect of many of the early US courses which he attempted to model on the best in Scotland and England. It was his belief that at each tee a golfer should face a hazard at the average distance of his shot.

COLTON COUNTRY DAY. July 18. Main St, Colton, NY. Annual flea market, live entertainment, museum exhibits. Special programs to be announced. Annually, the third weekend in July. Sponsor: Colton Historical Soc. Est attendance: 1,200. For info: Dennis Eickhoff, Town Historian, PO Box 109, Colton, NY 13625-0109. Phone: (315) 262-2800.
Email: eickhoff@northnet.org.

COW APPRECIATION DAY. July 18. Woodstock, VT. A "cowledge bowl" competition, dairy education programs, butter and ice cream making and more. Est attendance: 300. For info: Deborah Bulissa, Billings Farm & Museum, Box 489, Woodstock, VT 05091. Phone: (802) 457-2355. Fax: (802) 457-4663. Email: billings.farm@valley.net.

CRAFT FAIR USA: INDOOR SHOW. July 18–19. Wisconsin State Fair Park, Milwaukee, WI. Sale of handcrafted items: jewelry, pottery, weaving, leather, wood, glass, yulecraft and sculpture. Est attendance: 13,000. For info: Director, Craft Fair USA, 9312 W National Ave, West Allis, WI 53227. Phone: (414) 321-2100.

EIGHTEENTH-CENTURY SUMMER MARKET FAIR. July 18–19. McLean, VA. 18th-century games, music and crafts. Militia will drill. Est attendance: 4,000. For info: Publicist, Claude Moore Colonial Farm at Turkey Run, 6310 Georgetown Pike, McLean, VA 22101. Phone: (703) 442-7557. Fax: (703) 442-0714.

ENGLAND: THE ROYAL INTERNATIONAL AIR TATTOO. July 18–19. The world's most spectacular military airshow celebrates the 80th anniversary of the Royal Air Force with an eight-hour Theatre of the Air flying display. More than 400 aircraft from many nations, two-mile static park, military bands and exhibitions. Est attendance: 150,000. For info: RIAT Info Officer, PO Box 1940, Fairford, Gloucestershire, England GL7 4NA. Phone: (44) (128) 571-3456.
Email: rafbfe@rafbfe.telme.com.

EVANS, CHICK: BIRTH ANNIVERSARY. July 18, 1890. Charles (Chick) Evans, Jr, golfer born at Indianapolis, IN. Evans competed as an amateur against the best professionals in the early 20th century, winning the US Open in 1916. In the 1920s he established the Chick Evans Caddie Foundation, later called the Evans Scholarship Fund, that has helped send over 4,000 people to college. Died at Chicago, IL, Nov 6, 1979.

EVANSTON ETHNIC ARTS FESTIVAL. July 18–19. Evanston, IL. A lakefront festival of music, dance, crafts and ethnic foods. For info: Evanston Arts Council, 927 Noyes St, Evanston, IL 60201. Phone: (847) 491-0266.

FINLAND: KAUSTINEN FOLK MUSIC FESTIVAL. July 18–26. Kaustinen. Scandinavia's largest annual international festival of folk music and dance. Thousands of Finnish and hundreds of foreign artists perform. Every visitor has the opportunity to join in the music, dance and song. First organized in 1968. Est attendance: 100,000. For info: Finnish Tourist Board, 655 Third Ave, New York, NY 10017. Phone: (212) 949-2333 or (358) (6) 860-4111. Fax: (358) (6) 860-4222.
Email: folk.fest@kaustinen.inet.fi.

FLEA MARKET/ANTIQUE/CRAFT SALE. July 18. Sauk Centre, MN. 27th year for this sale, sponsored by St. Michael's Auxiliary in conjunction with Sinclair Lewis Days. Sale features 90 exhibitors. The Auxiliary offers lunches at their food stand for a fee, also bake sale and raffle. Annually, the third Saturday in July. Est attendance: 2,000. For info: Joyce C. Lyng, St. Michael's Auxiliary, 1725 Sinclair Lewis Ave, Sauk Centre, MN 56378. Phone: (320) 352-2624.

FRIENDSVILLE FIDDLE AND BANJO CONTEST. July 18. Friendsville, MD. Fiddlers from Garrett County and surrounding region participate in event. Old-time bluegrass entertainment. Cloggers welcome. Est attendance: 1,000. For info: Friendsville Fiddle and Banjo Contest, 133 Claude Fike Rd, Accident, MD 21520.

FULLER, BOBBY: DEATH ANNIVERSARY. July 18, 1966. Bobby Fuller, leader of the rock group Bobby Fuller Four, was found dead in his car at Los Angeles, CA. No definite cause of death was ever proven. The Bobby Fuller Four is best remembered for their 1966 hit song "I Fought the Law," which was written by Sonny Curtis, a member of Buddy Holly's Crickets.

HAYAKAWA, SAMUEL ICHIYE: BIRTH ANNIVERSARY. July 18, 1906. Samuel Ichiye Hayakawa was born at Vancouver, British Columbia, and came to the US in 1927. An academic, in 1968 he was appointed acting president of San Francisco State College. During student demonstrations on his first day in office he climbed atop a sound truck and disconnected the wires, silencing the demonstrators. His actions gained him enormous popularity among conservatives and he was promoted to permanent president by then-Governor Ronald Reagan. As his popularity grew he switched from the Democratic to the Republican party and ran for the US Senate in 1974, but the courts ruled he had not been a Republican for the required 12 months. He ran again in 1976 and was elected, serving one term in the Senate. He then led the successful California initiative to declare English the state's official language in 1986. Hayakawa wrote nine textbooks on language and semantics, newspaper columns and articles ranging from jazz history to mental retardation. He died Feb 27, 1992, at Greenbrae, CA.

HIGHLIGHTS FOUNDATION WRITERS WORKSHOP AT CHAUTAUQUA. July 18–25. Chautauqua, NY. A seven-day immersion in study, peer exchange and individual professional guidance for those interested in writing for children. Est attendance: 125. For info: Jan Keen, Conf Dir, Highlights Fdtn, Inc, 814 Court St, Honesdale, PA 18431. Phone: (717) 253-1192. Fax: (717) 253-0179.

JAPAN'S RULING PARTY SINCE 1955 LOSES PARLIAMENT MAJORITY: 5th ANNIVERSARY. July 18, 1993. Japan's Liberal Democratic Party, the ruling conservative branch of the government, lost the majority in the general elections. They only won 223 seats in the 511-seat lower house, the more powerful of Japan's two houses. The party had held majority since its inception in 1955. On July 22 Premier Kiichi Miyazawa resigned.

KOHLER OUTDOOR ARTS FESTIVAL. July 18–19. Sheboygan, WI. A multiarts extravaganza featuring the works of 130 artists, demonstrations, live entertainment, children's workshops and exhibition tours. Est attendance: 16,000. For info: John Michael Kohler Arts Center, 608 New York Ave, PO Box 489, Sheboygan, WI 53082-0489. Phone: (414) 458-6144. Fax: (414) 458-4473.

MANDELA, NELSON: 80th BIRTHDAY. July 18, 1918. South African President Nelson Rolihlahla Mandela was born the son of a Tembu tribal chieftain on July 18, 1918, at Qunu, near Umtata, in the Transkei territory of South Africa. Giving up his hereditary rights, Mandela chose to become a lawyer and earned his degree at the University of South Africa. He joined the African National Congress (ANC) in 1944, eventually becoming deputy national president in 1952. His activities in the struggle against apartheid resulted in his conviction for sabotage in 1964. During his 28 years in jail, Mandela remained a symbol of hope to South Africa's nonwhite majority, the demand for his release a rallying cry for civil rights activists. That release finally came on Feb 11, 1990, as millions watched via satellite television. In 1994 Mandela was elected President of South Africa in the first all-race election there. See also: "Mandela, Nelson: Prison Release Anniversary" (Feb 11).

NATIONAL SPORTING GOODS ASSOCIATION WORLD SPORTS EXPO. July 18–20. McCormick Place, Chicago, IL. The international kickoff of the exposition where sporting goods retailers will see 1999 products. Est attendance: 90,000. For info: Larry Weindruch, Dir of Communications, Natl Sporting Goods Assn, 1699 Wall St, Mt Prospect, IL 60056-5780. Phone: (847) 439-4000. Fax: (847) 849-0111.
Email: nsga1699@aol.com.
WWW: http://www.nsgachicagoshow.com

ODETS, CLIFFORD: BIRTH ANNIVERSARY. July 18, 1906. Clifford Odets began his writing career as a poet before turning to acting. He helped found the Group Theatre in 1931. In 1935 he returned to writing with works for the Group Theatre such as *Waiting for Lefty, Awake and Sing!* and *Golden Boy*. His proletarian views helped make him a popular playwright during the Depression years. Other plays include *The Big Knife, The Country Girl* and *The Flowering Peach*. Odets was born at Philadelphia, PA, and died at Los Angeles, CA, on Aug 15, 1963.

OIL HERITAGE WEEK. July 18–26. Oil City, PA. Sporting events, food fair, concerts, parades, arts and crafts, sales, tours, train rides and car show. Honoring the birthplace of the world's oil industry. Est attendance: 50,000. For info: Oil City Area Chamber of Commerce, PO Box 376, Oil City, PA 16301. Phone: (814) 676-8521 or (800)-2-Oil City. Fax: (814) 676-8185.
Email: msullivan@oilcitychamber.org.
WWW: http://www.oilcitychamber.org

OSCAR MAYER WIENERMOBILE: BIRTHDAY. July 18, 1936. Invented in 1936 by Carl Mayer, nephew of Oscar Mayer, the Oscar Mayer Wienermobile was built by General Body Company in Chicago, IL. Today a fleet of six Wienermobiles tours the country. For info: Hotdogger Advisor, PO Box 7188, Madison, WI 53707. Phone: (608) 285-6793 or (608) 285-3204. Fax: (608) 242-6108. Email: ksuto@kraft.com.
WWW: http://www.oscar-mayer.com

PRESIDENTIAL SUCCESSION ACT: 50th ANNIVERSARY. July 18, 1947. President Harry S. Truman signed an Executive Order determining the line of succession should the president be temporarily incapacitated or die in office. The speaker of the house and president pro tem of the senate are next in succession after the vice president. This line of succession became the 25th Amendment to the Constitution, which was ratified on Feb 10, 1967.

RUTLEDGE, JOHN: DEATH ANNIVERSARY. July 18. American statesman, associate justice on the Supreme Court, born at Charleston, SC, in September 1739. Nominated second Chief Justice of the Supreme Court to succeed John Jay, and served as Acting Chief Justice until his confirmation was denied because of his opposition to the Jay Treaty. He died at Charleston, SC, on July 18, 1800.

SAWTOOTH MOUNTAIN MAMAS ARTS & CRAFTS FAIR. July 18–19. Stanley, ID. More than 150 artists and artisans, nine food vendors and live music throughout the day. Pancake breakfast on Sunday. Annually, the third weekend in July. Est attendance: 2,500. For info: Stanley/Sawtooth Chamber of Commerce, Box 8, Stanley, ID 83278. Phone: (208) 774-3411.

SPACE MILESTONE: *ROHINI 1* (INDIA). July 18, 1980. First successful launch from India, orbited 77-lb satellite. July 18, 1980.

SUMMERFAIR. July 18–19. Rocky Mountain College Campus, Billings, MT. Major regional craft fair with arts and crafts, food, music, dance, drama and children's activities on the campus green. Est attendance: 20,000. For info: Trina Cullinan or Barbara Anderson, Yellowstone Art Center, 401 N 27th, Billings, MT 59101. Phone: (406) 256-6804. Fax: (406) 256-6817.

SUMMERSWAP. July 18. Heritage Park, Frankenmuth, MI. A beer can collectors and breweriana trade show. Breweriana is the collection of brewery memorabilia, including steins, signs, coasters, mirrors, neon signs, etc. The show is attended by collectors from a 10–12-state area and Canada. Admission includes display table. Tables available on first-come, first-served basis. Annually, the third Saturday in July. Est attendance: 300. For info: Dave Van Hine, Show Chairman, Beer Can Collectors of America, Mid-Michigan Chapter, 357 N Harvest Lane, Frankenmuth, MI 48734. Phone: (517) 652-9818. Email: davevanh@aol.

July 1998

S	M	T	W	T	F	S
			1	2	3	4
5	6	7	8	9	10	11
12	13	14	15	16	17	18
19	20	21	22	23	24	25
26	27	28	29	30	31	

TEDDY BEAR'S PICNIC. July 18–19. Lahaska, PA. Bring your teddy bear for the festivities: competitions, teddy bear craftspeople from across the country, puppet shows, parades, a backyard circus, live entertainment. Est attendance: 7,000. For info: Judy Goldschmidt, PR Mgr, Peddler's Village, Routes 202 & 263, Lahaska, PA 18931. Phone: (215) 794-4000. Fax: (215) 794-4001. WWW: http://www.peddlersvillage.com

THACKERAY, WILLIAM MAKEPEACE: BIRTH ANNIVERSARY. July 18, 1811. English author, best remembered for his novels, especially *Pendennis* and *Vanity Fair*, was born at Calcutta, India, and died at London, England, Dec 23, 1863.

WHITE, GILBERT: BIRTH ANNIVERSARY. July 18, 1720. Born at Selborne, Hampshire, England, on July 18, 1720. Gilbert White has been called the "father of British naturalists." His book *The Natural History of Selborne*, published in 1788, enjoyed immediate success and is said to never have been out of print. White died near his birthplace, June 26, 1793. His home survives as a museum.

***WILD* ABOUT WILDLIFE.** July 18–Aug 15. Coastal Center for the Arts, St. Simons Island, GA. A juried exhibit designed to give opportunity for focus on one of the most popular subjects for all ages—wildlife. Two- and three-dimensional. For info: Coastal Center for the Arts, 2012 Demere Rd, St. Simons Island, GA 31522. Phone: (912) 634-0404.

WOODCRAFT FESTIVAL. July 18–19. Grand Rapids, MN. Northern Minnesota woodcrafters demonstrate traditional woodcrafting techniques, discussions with artisans and hands-on activities. Est attendance: 1,000. For info: Robert Drake, Forest History Center, 2609 Cnty Rd 76, Grand Rapids, MN 55744. Phone: (218) 327-4482. Fax: (218) 327-4483.

WORLD CHAMPIONSHIP CARDBOARD BOAT RACE. July 18. Sandy Beach, Heber Springs, AR. Cardboard boats that defy natural laws float and race on Greers Ferry Lake; open to all comers; winner may compete in the Annual America's International Cardboard Cup Challenge; other activities scheduled all day. 11th annual race. Est attendance: 6,500. For info: Dianne Williams, Exec Dir, Chamber of Commerce, 1001 W Main, Heber Springs, AR 72543. Phone: (501) 362-2444 or (800) 77-HEBER. Fax: (501) 362-9953.
Email: hebercoc@arkansas.net.
WWW: http://www.Heber-Springs.com

BIRTHDAYS TODAY

James Brolin, 57, actor ("Hotel"), born Los Angeles, CA, July 18, 1941.

Richard Totten (Dick) Button, 69, sportscaster, Olympic gold medal figure skater, born Englewood, NJ, July 18, 1929.

Hume Cronyn, 87, actor (*The Seventh Cross, Sunrise at Campobello, Cocoon*), director, born London, Ontario, Canada, July 18, 1911.

Dion Di Mucci, 59, singer (Dion and the Belmonts), born the Bronx, NY, July 18, 1939.

John Glenn, 77, US Senator (D, Ohio), first American astronaut to orbit Earth, born Cambridge, OH, July 18, 1921.

Anfernee "Penny" Hardaway, 26, basketball player, born Memphis, TN, July 18, 1972.

Elizabeth McGovern, 37, actress (*Ordinary People, Racing with the Moon*), born Evanston, IL, July 18, 1961.

Calvin Peete, 55, golfer, born Detroit, MI, July 18, 1943.

Martha Reeves, 57, singer (lead of Martha & The Vandellas; "Power of Love"), born Detroit, MI, July 18, 1941.

Ricky Skaggs, 44, musician (bluegrass guitar), singer ("I Don't Care"), born Cordell, KY, July 18, 1954.

Red Skelton, 85, comedian, actor ("The Red Skelton Show"), born Vincennes, IN, July 18, 1913.

Hunter S. Thompson, 59, journalist, editor, born Louisville, KY, July 18, 1939.

Yevgeny Alelesandrovich Yevtushenko, 65, poet, born Zima, USSR, July 18, 1933.

JULY 19 — SUNDAY

Day 200 — 165 Remaining

ART FESTIVAL. July 19. Harvey Cedars, NJ. More than 75 artists participate in this festival. Est attendance: 1,500. For info: Harvey Cedars Activity Committee, PO Box 3185, Harvey Cedars, NJ 08008. Phone: (609) 494-2843 or (609) 494-3107. Fax: (609) 494-2335.

ATTACK ON FORT WAGNER: ANNIVERSARY. July 19, 1863. In a second attempt to capture Fort Wagner on June 19, 1863, outside Charleston, SC, Federal troops were repulsed after losing 1,515 men as opposed to Southern losses of only 174. The attack was led by the 54th Massachusetts Colored Infantry, commanded by Colonel Robert Gould Shaw, who was killed in the action. This was the first use of black troops in the war. The film *Glory* was based on the Massachusetts 54th, and this was the attack featured in the film. Fort Wagner was never taken by the Union.

★**CAPTIVE NATIONS WEEK.** July 19–25. Presidential proclamation issued each year since 1959 for the third week of July. (PL86–90 of July 17, 1959.)

CHRISTMAS IN JULY. July 19–26. Moodus, CT. Experience the joy of Christmas in July. The "real meaning" of Christmas in July is Santa Claus, unwrapping presents, making a special craft, putting up a tree and watching someone else take it down!! For info: Sunrise Resort, PO Box 415, Moodus, CT 06469. Phone: (860) 873-8681 or (800) 225-9033.

DEGAS, EDGAR: BIRTH ANNIVERSARY. July 19. French Impressionist painter, especially noted for his paintings of dancers in motion, was born at Paris, France, July 19, 1834. Degas died Sept 26, 1917.

ITALY: FEAST OF THE REDEEMER. July 19. Venice. Procession of gondolas and other craft commemorating the end of the epidemic of 1575. Annually, the third Sunday in July.

LUXEMBOURG: BEER FESTIVAL. July 19. At Diekirch an annual beer festival is held on the third Sunday in July.

MANILA FLOODS: ANNIVERSARY. July 19, 1972. A 30-hour rainfall flooded much of the Philippine Archipelago leaving as many as 289 dead and thousands without shelter, 45,000 in one province alone. Starvation in highly populated areas like Manila caused President Ferdinand Marcos to send troops after profiteers who were stockpiling food.

MARILYN MONROE'S FIRST SCREEN TEST: ANNIVERSARY. July 19, 1946. Marilyn Monroe was given her first screen test at Twentieth Century-Fox Studios. Even with no sound, this test was all they needed to sign her first contract. Beginning with *Scudda-Hoo! Scudda-Hay!* in 1948 and ending with *The Misfits* in 1961, Monroe made a total of 29 films during her short career.

MAYO, CHARLES HORACE: BIRTH ANNIVERSARY. July 19. American surgeon, one of the Mayo brothers, founders of the Mayo Clinic and Mayo Foundation, born at Rochester, MN, July 19, 1865. Died at Chicago, IL, May 26, 1939.

NICARAGUA: NATIONAL LIBERATION DAY. July 19. Following the National Day of Joy (July 17—anniversary of date in 1979 when dictator Anastasio Somoza Debayle fled Nicaragua) is annual July 19 observance of National Liberation Day, anniversary of day the National Liberation Army claimed victory over the Somoza dictatorship.

REGISTER'S ANNUAL GREAT BICYCLE RIDE ACROSS IOWA. July 19–25. A weeklong bicycle ride across Iowa with 7,500 riders from around the country. Annually, the last full week of July. After Nov 1 and before Mar 1 send a business-size self-addressed, stamped envelope to address below. Sponsor: *Des Moines Register*. Est attendance: 7,500. For info: Event Mktg Mgr, Des Moines Register, 715 Locust, Des Moines, IA 50309. Phone: (515) 284-8282. Fax: (515) 284-8138. WWW: http://www.ragbrai.org

SAINT CYRIL'S PARISH FESTIVAL. July 19. Kiwanis Park, Sheboygan, WI. Slovenian foods, music, games, raffle 10:30 AM–7 PM. Polka Mass at 10:30 AM, $3,000 bingo at 1 PM under the Big Top tent. Est attendance: 5,000. For info: St. Cyril & Methodius Parish, 822 New Jersey Ave, Sheboygan, WI 53081. Phone: (414) 457-7110.

SAINT VINCENT DE PAUL: OLD FEAST DAY. July 19. A day remembering the founder of the Vincentian Congregation and the Sisters of Charity, born in France in 1581 (exact date unknown). He died Sept 27, 1660. His Feast Day was formerly observed on July 19 but is now observed on the anniversary of his death, Sept 27.

SPACE WEEK. July 19–25. The calendar week containing July 20 has been observed in a number of communities and states as Space Week, commemorating the July 20, 1969, landing on the moon by two US astronauts, Neil Alden Armstrong and Edwin Eugene Aldrin, Jr. See also: "Space Milestone: Moon Day" (July 20).

UNITED AIRLINES FLIGHT 232 CRASHED IN IOWA CORNFIELD: ANNIVERSARY. July 19, 1989. Chicago-bound United Airlines flight 232 crashed into a cornfield in Sioux City, IA. The DC-10 aircraft was carrying 293 people when it slammed into the runway and flipped over, bursting into a fireball. Miraculously, 181 of the passengers and crew survived the crash. Emergency personnel at the airport and in Sioux City had been alerted to the situation approximately one-half hour before the crash when the pilot reported an uncontained engine failure and a complete hydraulic system failure. The rear engine failed when a turbine disintegrated, sending shards of metal through the tail cone section, which dislodged from the aircraft and was later found in Alta, IA, approximately 70 miles east of the crash site.

WOMEN'S RIGHTS CONVENTION AT SENECA FALLS: 150th ANNIVERSARY. July 19, 1848. A convention concerning the rights of women, called by Lucretia Mott and Elizabeth Cady Stanton, was held at Seneca Falls, NY, on July 19–20, 1848. The issues discussed included voting, property rights and divorce. The convention drafted a "Declaration of Sentiments" that paraphrased the Declaration of Independence, addressing man instead of King George, and called for women's "immediate admission to all the rights and privileges which belong to them as citizens of the United States." This convention was the beginning of an organized women's rights movement in the US. The most controversial issue was Stanton's demand for women's right to vote. See also: "Women's Rights Convention Called" (July 14).

YALOW, ROSALYN: BIRTHDAY. July 19, 1921. Medical physicist Rosalyn Yalow was born at New York City. Along with Andrew V. Schally and Roger Guillemin, in 1977 Yalow was awarded the Nobel Prize for Physiology or Medicine. Through her research on medical applications of radioactive isotopes, Yalow developed RIA, a sensitive and simple technique used to measure minute concentrations of hormones and other substances in blood or other body fluids. First applied to the study of insulin concentration in the blood of diabetics, RIA was soon used in hundreds of other applications.

BIRTHDAYS TODAY

Philip Agee, 63, former CIA agent, author (*Inside the Company: CIA Diary*), born Tacoma Park, FL, July 19, 1935.

Vikki Carr (Florencia Bisenta deCasilla), 57, singer ("It Must Be Him," "With Pen In Hand"), born El Paso, TX, July 19, 1941.

Anthony Edwards, 36, actor ("Northern Exposure," "ER," *Fast Times at Ridgemont High, Top Gun*), born July 19, 1962.

Clea Lewis, 33, actress (Audrey on "Ellen"; *The Rich Man's Wife*), born Cleveland Heights, OH, July 19, 1965.

George Stanley McGovern, 76, former US senator and '72 Democratic presidential nominee, born Avon, SD, July 19, 1922.

Ilie Nastase, 52, tennis player, born Bucharest, Romania, July 19, 1946.

July 1998

S	M	T	W	T	F	S
			1	2	3	4
5	6	7	8	9	10	11
12	13	14	15	16	17	18
19	20	21	22	23	24	25
26	27	28	29	30	31	

JULY 20 — MONDAY

Day 201 — 164 Remaining

"ARTHUR MURRAY PARTY" TV PREMIERE: ANNIVERSARY. July 20, 1950. This ballroom dancing show appeared on all four networks (ABC, DuMont, CBS and NBC) and was hosted by Kathryn Murray, wife of famed dance school founder Arthur Murray.

BASEBALL DECLARED NON-ESSENTIAL OCCUPATION: 80th ANNIVERSARY. July 20, 1918. Secretary of War Newton D. Baker ruled that baseball was a non-essential occupation. He stated that all players of draft age should seek "employment to aid successful prosecution of the war or shoulder guns and fight." On July 26, Baker allowed baseball to continue until Sept 1. Nearly 250 ballplayers entered the armed services.

COLOMBIA: INDEPENDENCE DAY. July 20. National holiday. Commemorates the beginning of the independence movement with an uprising against Spanish officials on this day in 1810 in Bogota. Colombia gained independence from Spain in 1819 when Simon Bolivar decisively defeated the Spanish.

GENEVA ACCORDS. July 20. An agreement covering cessation of hostilities in Vietnam, signed at Geneva, Switzerland, July 20, 1954, on behalf of the commanders-in-chief of French forces in Vietnam and the People's Army of Vietnam. A further declaration of the Geneva Conference was released July 21, 1954. Partition, foreign troop withdrawal and elections for a unified government, within two years, were among provisions.

HILLARY, SIR EDMUND PERCIVAL: BIRTHDAY. July 20, 1919. Explorer, mountaineer born at Auckland, New Zealand, on July 20, 1919. With Tenzing Norgay, a Sherpa guide, became first to ascend summit of highest mountain in the world, Mt Everest (29,028 ft), at 11:30 AM on May 29, 1953. "We climbed because nobody climbed it before," he said.

RIOT ACT: ANNIVERSARY. July 20. To "read the riot act" now usually means telling children to be quiet or less boisterous, but in 18th-century England reading the riot act was a more serious matter. On July 20, 1715, the Riot Act took effect. By law, in England, if 12 or more persons were unlawfully assembled to the disturbance of the public peace an authority was required "with a loud voice" to command silence and read the riot act proclamation: "Our sovereign lord the king chargeth and commandeth all persons, being assembled, immediately to disperse themselves, and peaceably to depart to their habitations, or to their lawful business, upon the pains contained in the act made in the first year of King George, for preventing tumults and riotous assemblies. God save the king." Any persons who failed to obey within one hour were to be seized, apprehended and carried before a justice of the peace.

SAINT ANN'S ITALIAN STREET FESTIVAL. July 20–26. Hoboken, NJ. 88th annual festival features live entertainment nightly with top stars. Also, rides, games of chance, international foods, crafts and much more. Est attendance: 150,000. For info: Church of St. Ann's, 704 Jefferson St, Hoboken, NJ 07030-2010. Phone: (201) 659-1114. Fax: (201) 659-1416.

SPACE MILESTONE: MOON DAY. July 20, 1969. Anniversary of man's first landing on moon. Two US astronauts (Neil Alden Armstrong and Edwin Eugene Aldrin, Jr) landed lunar module *Eagle* at 4:17 PM, EDT, July 20, 1969, and remained on lunar surface 21 hours, 36 minutes and 16 seconds. The landing was made from the *Apollo XI*'s orbiting command and service module, code named *Columbia*, whose pilot, Michael Collins, remained aboard. Armstrong was first to set foot on the moon. Armstrong and Aldrin were outside the spacecraft, walking on the moon's surface, approximately 2¼ hours.

WALES: ROYAL WELSH SHOW. July 20–23. Royal Welsh Showground, Llanelwedd, Builth Wells, Powys. National agricultural show incorporating exhibitions of livestock, farm machinery, horticulture and forestry displays. Est attendance: 230,000. For info: The Secretary, Royal Welsh Agricultural Soc, Llanelwedd, Builth Wells, Powys, Wales, UK LD2 3SY. Phone: (1) (982) 553683. Fax: (1) (982) 553563.

BIRTHDAYS TODAY

Kim Carnes, 52, singer ("Bette Davis Eyes"), songwriter (cowrote score *Flashdance*), born Hollywood, CA, July 20, 1946.

Judy Chicago (Judy Cohen), 59, artist, feminist, born Chicago, IL, July 20, 1939.

Larry E. Craig, 53, US Senator (R, Idaho), born Council, ID, July 20, 1945.

Charles Joseph (Chuck) Daly, 68, sportscaster and former basketball coach, born St. Mary's, PA, July 20, 1930.

Donna Dixon, 41, actress ("Bosom Buddies," *Dr. Detroit*), born Alexandria, VA, July 20, 1957.

Nelson Doubleday, 65, baseball executive, publisher, born Long Island, NY, July 20, 1933.

Peter Forsberg, 25, hockey player, born Ornskoldvik, Sweden, July 20, 1973.

Sir Edmund Hillary, 79, explorer (first to climb Mt Everest), born Auckland, New Zealand, July 20, 1919.

Sally Ann Howes, 64, actress (*Dead of Night, The History of Mr Polly*), singer, born London, England, July 20, 1934.

Michael Ilitch, 69, sports executive, former minor league baseball player, born Detroit, MI, July 20, 1929.

Barbara Ann Mikulski, 62, US senator (D, Maryland), born Baltimore, MD, July 20, 1936.

Diana Rigg, 60, actress ("The Avengers"; Tony for *Medea; King Lear, Witness for the Prosecution*), born Doncaster, Yorkshire, England, July 20, 1938.

Carlos Santana, 51, musician, born Autlan, Mexico, July 20, 1947.

JULY 21 — TUESDAY

Day 202 — 163 Remaining

BAGELFEST. July 21–25. Mattoon, IL. The World's Biggest Bagel Breakfast with free bagels and toppings, entertainment, Big Band Sounds, Bagel Beauties, arts and crafts. Annually, in July. Est attendance: 60,000. For info: Rachel Doeding, Exec Asst, Mattoon Chamber of Commerce, 1701 Wabash, Mattoon, IL 61938. Phone: (217) 235-5661. Fax: (217) 234-6544.

BELGIUM: NATIONAL HOLIDAY. July 21. Marks accession of first Belgian king, Leopold I, at independence from Netherlands on this day, 1831.

CLEVELAND, FRANCES FOLSOM: BIRTH ANNIVERSARY. July 21, 1864. Wife of Grover Cleveland, 22nd president of the US, born at Buffalo, NY, July 21, 1864. Died Oct 29, 1947.

FIRST ROBOT HOMICIDE: ANNIVERSARY. July 21. The first reported killing of a human by a robot occurred at Jackson, MI. On July 21, 1984, a robot turned and caught a 34-year-old worker between it and a safety bar, crushing him. He died of the injuries on July 26. According to the National Institute for Occupational Safety and Health, it was "the first documented case of a robot-related fatality in the US."

GARFIELD COUNTY FAIR. July 21–25. Burwell, NE. County fair, carnival, rodeo and flea market. Est attendance: 10,000. For info: Peggy Haskell, Garfield County Frontier Fair Assn, Box 747, Burwell, NE 68823. Phone: (308) 346-5210.

GUAM: LIBERATION DAY. July 21. Guam ceded to US by Spain, 1898. US forces returned to Guam on this day, 1944.

HEMINGWAY, ERNEST: BIRTH ANNIVERSARY. July 21. American short story writer and novelist born at Oak Park, IL, July 21, 1899. Made his name with such works as *The Sun Also Rises* (1926), *A Farewell to Arms* (1929), *For Whom the Bell Tolls* (1940) and *The Old Man and the Sea* (1952). He was awarded the Nobel Prize in 1954 and wrote little thereafter; he shot himself on July 2, 1961, at Ketchum, ID, having been seriously ill for some time.

LEBRIJA RAILWAY WRECK: ANNIVERSARY. July 21, 1972. A Madrid-Cadiz Express train packed with more than 500 people crashed head-on into a local train—which had ignored a red light—outside the Spanish town of Lebrija. All 76 passengers on the local train were killed, and more than 100 passengers on board the express train were injured.

McLUHAN, MARSHALL: BIRTH ANNIVERSARY. July 21, 1911. (Herbert) Marshall McLuhan, university professor and author, called "the Canadian sage of the electronic age," was born at Edmonton, Alberta, Canada. *Understanding Media* and *The Medium is the Massage* (not to be confused with his widely quoted aphorism: "The medium is the message"), among other books, were widely acclaimed for their fresh view of communication. McLuhan is reported as saying: "Most people are alive in an earlier time, but you must be alive in our own time." He died at Toronto, Ontario, Dec 31, 1980.

NATIONAL WOMEN'S HALL OF FAME: ANNIVERSARY. July 21, 1979. Seneca Falls, NY. Founded to honor American women whose contributions "have been of the greatest value in the development of their country" and located in the community known as the "birthplace of women's rights," where the first Women's Suffrage Movement convention was held in 1848, the Hall of Fame was dedicated with 23 inductees. Earlier National Women's Hall of Fame, honoring "Twenty outstanding women of the Twentieth Century," was dedicated at New York World's Fair, on May 27, 1965.

ROCKBRIDGE REGIONAL FAIR. July 21–25. Lexington, VA. Held at the Virginia Horse Center. 4-H Show, rodeo, carnival, exhibits (commercial and crafts), activities of all kinds. For info: Lexington Visitors Bureau, 106 E Washington St, Lexington, VA 24450. Phone: (540) 463-3777. Fax: (540) 463-1105. Email: lexington@rockbridge.net.

TERRY, ELLEN: 70th DEATH ANNIVERSARY. July 21, 1928. Popular English actress (Alice) Ellen Terry was born at Coventry, Warwickshire. Terry is best known for her portrayal of Shakespeare's heroines, especially Portia, and as theatrical partner of English actor Henry Irving. Together she and Irving dominated both the British and American theater of their day. She died at Small Hythe, Kent, on July 21, 1928.

BIRTHDAYS TODAY

Lance Guest, 38, actor ("Lou Grant," *The Last Starfighter*), born Saratoga, CA, July 21, 1960.

Edward Herrmann, 55, actor (*The Paper Chase, Eleanor and Franklin*), born Washington, DC, July 21, 1943.

Norman Jewison, 72, producer, director (*Moonstruck, Fiddler on the Roof*), born Toronto, Ontario, July 21, 1926.

Don Knotts, 74, actor, comedian ("The Andy Griffith Show," *The Ghost and Mr Chicken*), born Morgantown, WV, July 21, 1924.

Jon Lovitz, 41, actor (*A League of Their Own*), born Tarzana, CA, July 21, 1957.

Matt Mulhern, 38, actor ("Major Dad," *Biloxi Blues*), born Philadelphia, PA, July 21, 1960.

Janet Reno, 60, US Attorney General in Clinton administration, born Miami, FL, July 21, 1938.

Isaac Stern, 78, violinist, born Kreminiecz, USSR, July 21, 1920.

Cat Stevens (Stephen Demetri Georgiou, chosen Muslim name is Yusuf Islam), 50, singer, songwriter, born London, England, July 21, 1948.

Paul D. Wellstone, 54, US Senator (D, Minnesota), born Washington, DC, July 21, 1944.

Robin Williams, 46, actor (Mork on "Mork and Mindy"; *The Fisher King, Mrs Doubtfire, Popeye, Hook*), born Chicago, IL, July 21, 1952.

JULY 22 — WEDNESDAY

Day 203 — 162 Remaining

DILLINGER, JOHN: DEATH ANNIVERSARY. July 22. Bank robber, murderer, prison escapee and the first person to receive the FBI's appellation "Public Enemy No. 1" (July 1934). After nine years in prison (1924–33), Dillinger traveled, in 1933–34, through Indiana, Illinois, Ohio, Wisconsin, Minnesota and Iowa, leaving a path of violent crimes. Reportedly betrayed by the "Lady in Red," he was killed by FBI agents as he left Chicago's Biograph movie theater (where he had watched *Manhattan Melodrama*, starring Clark Gable and Myrna Loy), on July 22, 1934. He was born at Indianapolis, IN, on June 28, 1902.

FAIRFEST. July 22–26. Adams County Fairgrounds, Hastings, NE. Annual county fair featuring midway; open-class competitions in culinary arts, needlework, floral culture, woodworking and the visual arts; Adams County 4-H competition, livestock show (with auction the last day of fair); and live entertainment in the Grand Stand. Est attendance: 70,000. For info: Sandy Himmelberg, Genl Mgr, 947 South Baltimore, Hastings, NE 68901. Phone: (402) 462-3247. Fax: (402) 462-4731.

FARMERS' FESTIVAL. July 22–26. Pigeon, MI. 25th anniversary. To recognize and honor farmers for their unique contribution to rural life in Michigan's "thumb area." Features parades, barbecues, stage shows, crafts and sidewalk sales. Sponsor: Pigeon Chamber of Commerce. Est attendance: 10,000. For info: Linda Clabuesch, Chairman, 58 S Caseville Rd, Pigeon, MI 48755. Phone: (517) 453-2330.

MENDEL, GREGOR JOHANN: BIRTH ANNIVERSARY. July 22, 1822. Botanist Gregor Mendel (original name Johann Mendel) was born of peasant parents at Heinzendorf, Austria. His pioneering work in genetics became the basis for the modern science of genetics and heredity. Around 1856 Mendel began experiments in the small monastery garden, crossing different varieties of the garden pea. The import of Mendel's work was not seen until many years after his death at age 61 on Jan 6, 1884, at Brünn. In 1900 other European botanists discovered his papers and confirmed and extended his theories, which formed the basis of the study of heredity and genetics.

July 1998

S	M	T	W	T	F	S
			1	2	3	4
5	6	7	8	9	10	11
12	13	14	15	16	17	18
19	20	21	22	23	24	25
26	27	28	29	30	31	

MENNINGER, KARL: BIRTH ANNIVERSARY. July 22, 1893. American psychiatrist Karl Augustus Menninger was born at Topeka, KS. Along with his father and brother, he founded the Menninger Clinic and Foundation at Topeka in the 1920s, which provided a caring environment to ease emotional troubles. He died on July 18, 1990, at Topeka.

PIED PIPER OF HAMELIN: ANNIVERSARY—MAYBE. July 22, 1376. According to legend, the German town of Hamelin, plagued with rats, bargained with a piper who promised to, and did, pipe the rats out of town and into the Weser River. Refused payment for his work, the piper then piped the children out of town and into a hole in a hill, never to be seen again. All on this day in 1376, according to 16th-century accounts. More recent historians suggest that the event occurred in 1284 when young men of Hamelin left the city on colonizing adventures.

RAT-CATCHERS DAY. July 22. A day to recognize the rat-catchers who labor to exterminate members of the genus *Rattus*, disease-carrying rodents that infest most of the "civilized" world. Observed on anniversary of the extraordinary feat of the Pied Piper of Hamelin on July 22, 1376 (according to 16th-century chronicler Richard Rowland Verstegen).

RILEY, JAMES WHITCOMB: DEATH ANNIVERSARY. July 22, 1916. American "Hoosier" poet, born at Greenfield, IN, on Oct 7 probably in 1853, but possibly several years earlier. Riley died at Indianapolis on July 22, 1916.

SPACE MILESTONE: *SOYUZ TM-3* (USSR). July 22, 1987. Two Soviet cosmonauts, Aleksandr Viktorenko and Aleksandr Aleksandrov, along with the first Syrian space traveler, Mohammed Faris, were launched on a projected 10-day mission, on July 22, 1987. Launched from the Baikonur base in Central Asia, the spacecraft orbited Earth for two days before linking with Soviet space station *Mir*.

SPOONER'S DAY (*WILLIAM SPOONER BIRTH ANNIVERSARY*). July 22. A day named for the Reverend William Archibald Spooner (born at London, England, July 22, 1844, warden of New College, Oxford, 1903–24, died at Oxford, England, Aug 29, 1930), whose frequent slips of the tongue led to coinage of the term *spoonerism* to describe them. A day to remember and emulate the scholarly man whose accidental transpositions gave us blushing crow (for crushing blow), tons of soil (for sons of toil), queer old dean (for dear old queen), swell foop (for fell swoop) and half-warmed fish (for half-formed wish).

BIRTHDAYS TODAY

Orson Bean (Dallas Frederick Burroughs), 70, actor ("To Tell the Truth," "Mary Hartman, Mary Hartman"), born Burlington, VT, July 22, 1928.

Irene Bedard, 31, actress ("Lakota Woman: Siege at Wounded Knee," "Grand Avenue," "Crazy Horse," *Squanto: A Warrior's Tale*; voice of Pocahontas in the Disney film), born Anchorage, AK, July 22, 1967.

Albert Brooks (Albert Einstein), 51, comedian, actor (*Broadcast News, Mother*), born Los Angeles, CA, July 22, 1947.

Willem Dafoe, 43, actor (*Platoon, Mississippi Burning*), born Appleton, WI, July 22, 1955.

Oscar De La Renta, 66, fashion designer, born Santo Domingo, Dominican Republic, July 22, 1932.

Robert J. Dole, 75, former US Senator (R, Kansas), born Russell, KS, July 22, 1923.

Jim Edgar, 52, Governor of Illinois (R), born Vinita, OK, July 22, 1946.

Danny Glover, 51, actor ("Chiefs," *Lethal Weapon, The Color Purple*), born San Francisco, CA, July 22, 1947.

Don Henley, 51, musician (drummer; The Eagles), songwriter (cowrote "The Boys of Summer"), born Linden, TX, July 22, 1947.

Kay Bailey Hutchison, 55, US Senator (R, Texas), born Galveston, TX, July 22, 1943.

John Leguizamo, 33, actor (*Carlito's Way*; stage: *Mambo Mouth* [also writer; Obie & Outer Critics Circle Awards], *Spic-O-Rama* [also writer; Theatre World Award]), born Bogota, Colombia, July 22, 1965.

William V. Roth, Jr, 77, US Senator (R, Delaware), born Great Falls, MT, July 22, 1921.

Bobby Sherman, 53, singer, actor, born Santa Monica, CA, July 22, 1945.

Alex Trebek, 58, game show host ("Concentration," "Jeopardy"), born Sudbury, Canada, July 22, 1940.

Margaret Whiting, 74, singer ("The Money Tree," "The Wheel of Hurt"), born Detroit, MI, July 22, 1924.

☆ ☆ ☆

JULY 23 — THURSDAY

Day 204 — 161 Remaining

AHA NATIONAL HOMEBREWERS CONFERENCE. July 23–26. Portland, OR. A conference and trade show for the beer enthusiast and homebrewer. Est attendance: 700. For info: Jim Parker, Dir, American Homebrewers Assn, PO Box 1679, Boulder, CO 80306-1679. Phone: (303) 447-0816.

BIX BEIDERBECKE MEMORIAL JAZZ FESTIVAL. July 23–26. Davenport, IA. Annually, the last full weekend of July. Est attendance: 10,000. For info: Bix Beiderbecke Memorial Society, PO Box 3688, Davenport, IA 52808. Phone: (319) 324-7170. Fax: (319) 326-1732.

BROWNE, CORAL: 85th BIRTH ANNIVERSARY. July 23, 1913. British actress Coral Edith Browne was born at Melbourne, Australia. In the 1950s she worked with the Old Vic theater in London. Her films include *Auntie Mame* (1958). She was married to actor Vincent Price. Browne died on May 29, 1991, at Los Angeles, CA.

CURRY COUNTY FAIR & RODEO. July 23–26. Gold Beach, OR. A traditional, family-style celebration of food, fun and frolic. For 12 consecutive years, it has been awarded the Gold Medal Medallion by the Oregon's State Fair Association and rated #1 Small County Fair on numerous occasions. Est attendance: 15,000. For info: Gold Beach Chamber of Commerce, 29279 Ellensburg Ave, #3, Gold Beach, OR 97444. Phone: (800) 525-2334. Fax: (541) 247-0188.
Email: goldbeach@harborside.com.
WWW: http://www.harborside.com/gb

DELAWARE STATE FAIR. July 23–Aug 1. Harrington, DE. Fireworks, country, gospel and pop talent, rodeos, demolition derby, amusement rides and harness racing. Plenty of food and entertainment. Est attendance: 216,000. For info: Delaware State Fair, PO Box 28, Harrington, DE 19952. Phone: (302) 398-3269. Fax: (302) 398-5030.

DRYSDALE, DON: BIRTH ANNIVERSARY. July 23, 1936. Elected to the Baseball Hall of Fame in 1984, Don Drysdale was a pitcher for the Brooklyn and Los Angeles Dodgers from 1956 to 1969, compiling a won-lost record of 209–166 with a career ERA of 2.95. Following his playing career he became a successful and popular broadcast announcer for the Chicago White Sox and then for the Los Angeles Dodgers. He was born at Van Nuys, CA, and died at Montreal, Canada, on July 3, 1993.

EGYPT, ARAB REPUBLIC OF: 45th ANNIVERSARY NATIONAL DAY. July 23, 1952. Anniversary of the Revolution of July 23, 1952, which was launched by army officers and changed Egypt from a monarchy to a republic.

ENGLAND: SUSSEX COUNTRY ANTIQUES AND ART FAIR. July 23–26. Barkham Manor Vineyard, Piltdown, Sussex. Small oak and country event of quality, plus an adjacent art fair encompassing art of all kinds dating from the year 1500 to 1997 with another marquee with a further 23 general antique stands. In idyllic surroundings with excellent food and wine. Est attendance: 5,000. For info: Barbara Bell, Event Mgr, PO Box 114, Haywards Heath, Sussex, England RH16 2YU. Phone: (44) (144) 448-2514.

FIRST US SWIMMING SCHOOL: OPENING ANNIVERSARY. July 23, 1827. The first swimming school in the US opened in Boston, MA. Its pupils included John Quincy Adams and James Audubon.

"THE GENE AUTRY SHOW" TV PREMIERE: ANNIVERSARY. July 23, 1950. Popular CBS western ran for six years starring movie actor Gene Autry. Along with sidekick Pat Buttram, Autry helped bring criminals to justice.

GREAT TEXAS MOSQUITO FESTIVAL. July 23–25. Clute, TX. More than 100 booths: arts and crafts, food, entertainment, novelty-games and carnival. Meet "Willie Man Chew," a 25-ft inflatable mosquito dressed in cowboy boots and hat. Annually, the last Thursday–Saturday in July. Est attendance: 30,000. For info: City of Clute Pks and Rec Dept, PO Box 997, Clute, TX 77531. Phone: (409) 265-8392 or (800) 371-2971. Fax: (409) 265-8767.

GRIFFITH, DAVID (LEWELYN) WARK: 50th DEATH ANNIVERSARY. July 23, 1948. D.W. Griffith, pioneer producer-director in the American motion picture industry, best remembered for his film *Birth of a Nation* (1915). Born at LaGrange, KY, Jan 22, 1875. Died at Hollywood, CA, July 23, 1948.

JAPAN: SOMA NO UMAOI (WILD HORSE CHASING). July 23–25. Hibarigahara, Haramachi, Fukushima Prefecture, Japan. 1,000 horsemen clad in ancient armor compete for possession of three shrine flags shot aloft on Hibarigahara Plain, and men in white costumes attempt to catch wild horses corralled by the horsemen.

LEO, THE LION. July 23–Aug 22. In the astronomical/astrological zodiac, which divides the sun's apparent orbit into 12 segments, the period July 23–Aug 22 is identified, traditionally, as the sun sign of Leo, the Lion. The ruling planet is the sun.

MOON PHASE: NEW MOON. July 23. Moon enters New Moon phase at 9:44 AM, EDT.

NATIONAL HOMEBREWERS COMPETITION AND CONFERENCE (WITH HOMEBREWER OF THE YEAR SELECTION). July 23–26. Denver, CO. Evaluation and judging of more than 2,000 homebrewed beers in order to improve their quality. "Homebrewer of the Year" will be chosen. Lectures, seminars, exhibits and demonstrations to promote the brewing of quality beer. Est attendance: 500. For info: The American Homebrewers Assn, PO Box 1679, Boulder, CO 80306. Phone: (303) 447-0816.

NEBRASKA'S BIG RODEO. July 23–25. Fairgrounds, Burwell, NE. Professional rodeo. Contestants compete in four exciting performances in historic, outdoor rodeo arena. Added thrills—chuckwagon races, wild horse races, Dinnerbell Derby, bull fighting-Burwell style, quilt and art shows, parade, flea market, llama and longhorn cattle show, c/w music and dancing and Miss Burwell Rodeo Pageant. Est attendance: 10,000. For info: Peggy Haskell, Garfield County Frontier Fair Assn, Box 747, Burwell, NE 68823. Phone: (308) 346-5210.

SAINT APOLLINARIS: FEAST DAY. July 23. First bishop of Ravenna, and a martyr, of unknown date. Observed July 23.

SPACE MILESTONE: *SOYUZ 37* (USSR). July 23, 1980. Launched on July 23, 1980, cosmonauts Viktor Gorbatko and, the first non-Caucasian in space, Lieutenant Colonel Pham Tuan (Vietnam), docked at *Salyut 6* on July 24. Returned to Earth July 31.

US SENIOR OPEN (GOLF) CHAMPIONSHIP. July 23–26. Olympia Fields Country Club, Olympia Fields, IL. For info: US Golf Assn, Golf House, Championship Dept, Far Hills, NJ 07931. Phone: (908) 234-2300. Fax: (908) 234-9687. Email: usga@ix.netcom.com. WWW: http://www.usga.org

BIRTHDAYS TODAY

Ronny Cox, 60, actor (*Deliverance, Bound for Glory, Total Recall*), born Cloudcroft, NM, July 23, 1938.

Gloria DeHaven, 73, actress (*Two Girls and a Sailor*, "Nakia"), born Los Angeles, CA, July 23, 1925.

Nicholas Gage, 59, journalist, film producer, writer (*Eleni*), born Lia, Greece, July 23, 1939.

Woody Harrelson, 37, actor ("Cheers" [Emmy Award, 1989], *White Men Can't Jump, Natural Born Killers*), born Midland, TX, July 23, 1961.

Don Imus, 50, radio talk show host, media icon and author, born Riverside, CA, July 23, 1948.

Arata Isozaki, 67, architect, born Oita, Japan, July 23, 1931.

Anthony M. Kennedy, 62, Supreme Court Justice, born Sacramento, CA, July 23, 1936.

Edie McClurg, 47, actress ("Martin Mull's History of White People in America"; "WKRP in Cincinnati"; *Planes, Trains and Automobiles; Eating Raoul; A River Runs Through It*), born Kansas City, MO, July 23, 1951.

Belinda Montgomery, 48, actress ("Man From Atlantis"), born Winnipeg, Manitoba, Canada, July 23, 1950.

Gary Dwayne Payton, 30, basketball player, born Oakland, CA, July 23, 1968.

Harold Henry ("Pee Wee") Reese, 80, Baseball Hall of Fame shortstop, born Ekron, KY, July 23, 1918.

July 1998

S	M	T	W	T	F	S
			1	2	3	4
5	6	7	8	9	10	11
12	13	14	15	16	17	18
19	20	21	22	23	24	25
26	27	28	29	30	31	

JULY 24 — FRIDAY

Day 205 — 160 Remaining

ANNIE OAKLEY DAYS. July 24–26. Greenville, OH. To keep alive the memory of Annie Oakley. Visit the newly dedicated Annie Oakley Memorial Park. Est attendance: 40,000. For info: Tim Gade, Pres, Annie Oakley Days Committee, Inc, PO Box 129, Greenville, OH 45331. Phone: (937) 547-0400. Fax: (937) 548-6711.

ANTIQUE POWER EXHIBITION. July 24–26. Burton, OH. More than 100 old-time engines toot whistles and puff smoke as they demonstrate yesterday's feats such as wood sawing and grain threshing. Daily parades, slow races, tractor pulls. Est attendance: 2,600. For info: Marlene F. Collins, Geauga County Historical Soc, PO Box 153, Burton, OH 44021. Phone: (216) 834-4012.

ARCADIA DAZE. July 24–26. Arcadia MI. The scenic village of Arcadia is the setting for this midsummer event. Activities include a parade on Sunday at 1:30 PM on Lake Street. An art fair, steak fry, fishing contest, games for the children, pancake breakfast, 5K and 10K running race on Saturday and a street dance. An old-fashioned good time for the whole family. Annually, the fourth weekend in July. Sponsor: Arcadia Lion's Club. Est attendance: 2,500. For info: Wesley Hall, Arcadia Daze, 3269 Lake St, Arcadia, MI 49613. Phone: (616) 889-5555.

ARTS IN THE PARK. July 24–26. Kalispell, MT. Annual juried arts and crafts show and fair, food and entertainment. Est attendance: 15,000. For info: PR Dept, Hockaday Center for the Arts, PO Box 83, 2nd Ave E at 3rd St, Kalispell, MT 59903. Phone: (406) 755-5268. Fax: (406) 755-2023.

BELE CHERE. July 24–26. Asheville, NC. A community celebration featuring a variety of food, music, children's activities and events. Annually, the last full weekend in July. Est attendance: 350,000. For info: Denise Hedges, Festival Coord, Bele Chere Festival, PO Box 7148, Asheville, NC 28802. Phone: (704) 253-1009.

BERNE SWISS DAYS. July 24–25. Berne, IN. Discover Switzerland in Indiana with Swiss food, dancing, yodeling and a parade. Visit the Swiss Heritage Village, complete with 19th-century houses, a church and cheese house. Est attendance: 75,000. For info: Berne Chamber of Commerce, PO Box 85, Berne, IN 46711. Phone: (219) 589-8080.

BLUE RIVER FESTIVAL. July 24–26. Crete, NE. Weekend of activities including arts and craft booths, sidewalk sales, children's parade and games, music, car show, food, airport open house, fireworks, high school alumni banquet and class reunions. Annually, the weekend of the fourth Saturday in July. Est attendance: 5,500. For info: Crete Chamber of Commerce, 1341 Main St, Crete, NE 68333. Phone: (402) 826-2136. Fax: (402) 826-4152.

BOLIVAR, SIMON: BIRTH ANNIVERSARY. July 24, 1783. "The Liberator," born at Caracas, Venezuela. Commemorated in Venezuela and other Latin American countries. Died Dec 17, 1830, at Santa Marta, Colombia.

BRIGHAM YOUNG ENTERS SALT LAKE VALLEY: ANNIVERSARY. July 24, 1847. Utah state holiday commemorating this event.

CANADA: NOVA SCOTIA BLUEGRASS AND OLD-TIME MUSIC FESTIVAL. July 24–26. Ardoise, Nova Scotia. 27th annual family event featuring acoustic music by groups from the US and Canada's Atlantic area. Annually, the last full weekend in July. Est attendance: 3,000. For info: Jerry Murphy, Dir, Downeast Bluegrass Oldtime Music Soc, PO Box 546, Elmsdale, NS, Canada B0N 1M0. Phone: (902) 883-7189.

CEDAR GROVE HOLLAND FEST. July 24–25. Cedar Grove, WI. Residents celebrate with street scrubbing, klompen dancing, films, wooden shoe races for children, parade, art fair and traditional Dutch foods. The Holland Fest Players perform each evening. Also Holland Festival Run/Walk. Annually, the last Friday and Saturday in July. Est attendance: 10,000. For info: Cedar Grove Holland Fest, PO Box HF, Cedar Grove, WI 53013. Phone: (414) 668-6982 or (414) 668-6523.

CENTRAL NEBRASKA ETHNIC FESTIVAL. July 24–26. Downtown Grand Island, NE. The streets come alive with color, music and foods from all ethnic cultures in the Central Nebraska area. Singing, dancing, eating, laughter and enjoyment for the whole family. Annually, the fourth weekend in July. Est attendance: 40,000. For info: Dianne Kelley, Downtown Dvmt Dir, PO Box 1968, Grand Island, NE 68802. Phone: (308) 385-5444 ext 230. Fax: (308) 385-5423.

COUSINS DAY. July 24. A day to honor all cousins who are living and to pay homage to those who have passed on. For info: Claudia A. Evart, 30 Park Ave, Ste 2P, New York, NY 10016-3833. Phone: (212) 779-2227.

DAYS OF '47 PIONEER PARADE. July 24. Salt Lake City, UT. One of the largest and oldest parades in the US celebrates the arrival of the first pioneers in Salt Lake Valley in 1847. Televised throughout the intermountain west. Est attendance: 300,000. For info: Frank T. Hales, Days of '47 Pioneer Parade Chair, PO Box 11687, Salt Lake City, UT 84147-0687. Phone: (801) 560-0047.

DETROIT'S BIRTHDAY. July 24. Anniversary of the landing, on July 24, 1701, at the site of Detroit, by Antoine de la Mothe Cadillac, in the service of Louis XIV of France. Fort Pontchartrain du Detroit was first settlement on site.

DODGE CITY DAYS. July 24–Aug 2. Dodge City, KS. Western heritage celebration with concerts, arts and crafts, parades, PRCA rodeo, street dances, cookouts, art show, antique car show. Est attendance: 75,000. For info: Dodge City Conv & Visitors Bureau, Third & W Wyatt Earp, PO Box 1474, Dodge City, KS 67801. Phone: (316) 225-8186. Fax: (316) 227-2957.
Email: dcvb@pld.com.
WWW: http://banzai.neosoft.com/citylink/dodge or
WWW: http://trails.net/dqcity//

DUMAS, ALEXANDRE: BIRTH ANNIVERSARY. July 24, 1802. French playwright and novelist, born at Villers-Cotterets, France. He is said to have written more than 300 volumes, including *The Count of Monte Cristo* and *The Three Musketeers*. Father of Alexandre Dumas (Dumas fils), also a novelist and playwright (1824–95). Dumas died near Dieppe, France, Dec 5, 1870.

EARHART, AMELIA: 100th BIRTH ANNIVERSARY. July 24, 1898. American aviatrix lost on flight from New Guinea to Howland Island, in the Pacific Ocean, July 3, 1937. First woman to cross the Atlantic solo and fly solo across the Pacific from Hawaii to California. Born at Atchison, KS.

FAIRBANKS SUMMER ARTS FESTIVAL. July 24–Aug 9. University of Alaska, Fairbanks, AK. Two weeks of workshops and concerts involving music, dance, theater, opera theater, ice skating theater and the visual arts. More than 60 guest artists and instructors from across the nation are featured. Est attendance: 12,500. For info: Jo Scott, Fairbanks Summer Arts Fest, Box 80845, Fairbanks, AK 99708. Phone: (907) 479-6778. Fax: (907) 479-4329. WWW: http://www.alaskabest.com/festival

GERMAN FEST. July 24–26. Milwaukee, WI. Featuring bands from Milwaukee, the US and Germany. Cultural exhibition with a genealogy section and travelogue of Germany, Trachtenschau, a "style show" of ethnic costumes, sheepshead and Marketplace. Beverages and food including Spanferkel (roasted pig). Schnitzel, bratwurst and desserts. Est attendance: 100,000. For info: German Fest Milwaukee Inc, 8229 W Capitol Dr, Milwaukee, WI 53222. Phone: (800) 355-9067 or (414) 464-9444. Fax: (414) 464-3164.

GILROY GARLIC FESTIVAL. July 24–26. Gilroy, CA. Midsummer harvest celebration in the "Garlic Capital of the World." Great garlic recipe contest/cookoff. Ethnic foods, continuous entertainment on three stages, arts, crafts and children's area. Est attendance: 130,000. For info: Gilroy Garlic Festival Assn, PO Box 2311, Gilroy, CA 95021. Phone: (408) 842-1625.

GOLD DISCOVERY DAYS. July 24–26. Custer, SD. Parade, historic "Pageant of Paha Sapa," park festival, carnival, pancake breakfast, bed races, boat regatta, fun run/walk and hot-air balloon rally. Est attendance: 6,000. For info: Cindy Mayes, Gold Discovery Days Committee, 615 Washington St, Custer, SD 57730. Phone: (605) 673-2244.

GRAND CELEBRATION RODEO AND POWWOW. July 24–26. Hinckley, MN. Largest Powwow in the Midwest, with over 1,200 dancers, drummers and singers from nearly every tribe in the US and Canada. Native American merchandise and food vendors plus a carnival. For info: Grand Casino, 777 Lady Luck Dr, Hinckley, MN 55037. Phone: (320) 384-7101.

INDIANA HUNTING & OUTDOOR SHOW. July 24–26. Indiana State Fairgrounds, Indianapolis, IN. For info: Kevin Renfro, VP, 2511 E 46th St, Ste E-2, Indianapolis, IN 46205. Phone: (317) 546-4344 or (800) 892-1723. Fax: (317) 546-3002. Email: insportshow@iquest.net.

IOWA STORYTELLING FESTIVAL. July 24–25. City Park, Clear Lake, IA. This 10th annual storytelling event is held in a scenic lakeside setting. Friday evening "Stories After Dark." Two performances Saturday plus story exchange for novice tellers. Annually, the last Friday and Saturday in July. Est attendance: 800. For info: Jean Casey, Dir, Clear Lake Public Library, 200 N 4th St, Clear Lake, IA 50428. Phone: (515) 357-6133. Fax: (515) 357-4645.

LUMBERJACK WORLD CHAMPIONSHIPS. July 24–26. Hayward, WI. Professional male and female lumberjacks and logrollers from around the world compete in speed sawing, pole climbing, logrolling and chopping events in the Northwoods town of Hayward. Amateurs can also participate; there are logrolling events for kids and chopping and sawing competitions for adults. Est attendance: 7,700. For info: Wisconsin Dept of Tourism, Lumberjack World Championships, PO Box 7976, Madison, WI 53707. Phone: (715) 634-2484. Email: tourism@laughlin.com. WWW: http://tourism.state.wi.us

MOUNTAIN MAN RENDEZVOUS. July 24–Aug 2. Red Lodge, MT. Montana's fur trapping era is recreated at an authentic mountain men rendezvous camp outside of Red Lodge. The camp residents are from around the country and they offer historical goods and crafts for sale as well as provide an opportunity for visitors to join in their rendezvous celebrations. There is music, dancing, games and food. Est attendance: 6,000. For info: Joan Cline, Red Lodge Chamber of Commerce, PO Box 988, Red Lodge, MT 59068. Phone: (406) 446-1718.

NORTH DAKOTA STATE FAIR. July 24–Aug 1. Minot, ND. For nine days the State Fair features the best in big-name entertainment, farm and home exhibits, displays, the Midway and NPRA rodeo. Est attendance: 250,000. For info: North Dakota State Fair, Box 1796, Minot, ND 58702. Phone: (701) 857-7620. Fax: (701) 857-7622. Email: ndsf@minot.com.

OWATONNA FESTIVAL OF ARTS. July 24–26. Owatonna, MN. More than 70 exhibitors in a juried show plus vendors, entertainment, a hog roast and a duck race on the Straight River. For info: Owatonna Festival of Arts, Box 6, Owatonna, MN 55060. Phone: (507) 451-2250.

PIONEER DAY: ANNIVERSARY. July 24. Utah. Commemorates first settlement on this day, 1847, by Brigham Young.

PONY GIRLS SOFTBALL NATIONAL CHAMPIONSHIPS. July 24–Aug 4 (tentative). Site TBA. Slow- and fast-pitch National Championships for girls ages 9–18. Est attendance: 11,000. For info: Pony Baseball, PO Box 225, Washington, PA 15301. Phone: (412) 225-1060. Fax: (412) 225-9852. Email: pony@pulsenet.com. WWW: http://www.pony.org

POTSDAM DECLARATION: ANNIVERSARY. July 24, 1945. As the Potsdam Conference came to a close in Germany, Churchill, Truman and China's representatives fashioned a communique to Japan offering them an opportunity to end the war. It demanded that Japan completely disarm, allowed them sovereignty to the four main islands and to minor islands to be determined by the Allies, and insisted that all Japanese citizens be given immediate and complete freedom of speech, religion and thought. The Japanese would be allowed to continue enough industry to maintain their economy. The communique concluded with a demand for unconditional surrender. Unaware these demands were backed up by an atomic bomb, on July 26 Japanese Prime Minister Admiral Kantaro Suzuki rejected the Potsdam Declaration.

RAF JAMS NAZI RADAR IN OPERATION GOMORRAH: 55th ANNIVERSARY. July 24, 1943. On the first of the Royal Air Force Operation Gomorrah raids on Hamburg, Germany, "windows" (bales of ten-and-a-half-inch strips of aluminum foil) were pushed out of the bombers causing the German radar screens to see a snowstorm of false echo "aircraft" on their screens. As a result only twelve of the 791 bombers sent on the mission were shot down.

SCHUYLER COLFAX DAYS. July 24–26. Schuyler, NE. Sidewalk sale, bands, craft show, antique tractor show, milk jug race, fireworks, sand volleyball tournament (couples) and a baseball tournament. Est attendance: 2,000. For info: Marlene Moore, Exec Secy, Chamber of Commerce, 1107 B St, Schuyler, NE 68661. Phone: (402) 352-5472. Fax: (402) 352-2754. Email: sd45455@ltec.net.

SNOWBIRD UTAH JAZZ & BLUES FESTIVAL. July 24–25. Snowbird, UT. Come and join the fun with plenty of jazz and blues music. Festival also includes food booths and much more. Annually, the last weekend in July. Est attendance: 6,000. For info: Snowbird & Ski Summer Resort, Snowbird, UT 84092. Phone: (801) 521-6040. Fax: (801) 742-3344.

SPAIN: SAN SEBASTIAN JAZZ FESTIVAL. July 24–28. This 33rd annual festival is the oldest surviving jazz festival in Europe. For info: Festival de Jazz San Sebastian, 2 Calle Camino, 20004 Donostia-San Sebastian, Spain. Phone: (34-43) 481179. Fax: (34-43) 481743. WWW: http://www.jazzaldia.com

UFO DAYS. July 24–26. Elmwood, WI. Starts Friday evening at 6: ends Sunday evening at 6. Annually, the last full weekend in July. Est attendance: 3,000. For info: Jerome Hofacker, Pres, Elmwood Community Club, UFO Days, 323 Winter Ave, PO Box 207, Elmwood, WI 54740. Phone: (715) 639-4132.

WORLD'S LARGEST GARAGE SALE. July 24–26. Evanston, IL. More than 500 vendors selling everything imaginable at the 27th annual sale. For info: Evanston Chamber of Commerce, 1560 Sherman Ave, Evanston, IL 60201. Phone: (847) 328-1500.

BIRTHDAYS TODAY

Bella Abzug, 78, lawyer, feminist, former congresswoman (famous for her many hats), born New York, NY, July 24, 1920.
Kevin Gregory Butler, 36, football player, born Savannah, GA, July 24, 1962.
Ruth Buzzi, 62, comedienne, actress ("Rowan & Martin's Laugh-In," "Sesame Street"), born Westerly, RI, July 24, 1936.
Joseph (Joe) Barry Carroll, 40, former basketball player, born Pine Bluff, AR, July 24, 1958.
Lynda Carter, 47, actress ("Wonder Woman," "Partners in Crime") former Miss World–USA, singer, born Phoenix, AZ, July 24, 1951.
Robert Hays, 51, actor (*Airplane!*, "Starman"), born Bethesda, MD, July 24, 1947.
Julie A. Krone, 35, jockey, born Benton Harbor, MI, July 24, 1963.
Karl Malone, 35, basketball player, born Summerfield, LA, July 24, 1963.
Pat Oliphant, 63, cartoonist, born Adelaide, Australia, July 24, 1935.
Marc Racicot, 50, Governor of Montana (R), born Thompson Falls, MT, July 24, 1948.
Chris Sarandon, 56, actor (*Dog Day Afternoon, The Princess Bride*), born Beckley, WV, July 24, 1942.
Peter Serkin, 51, musician, born New York, NY, July 24, 1947.
Billy Taylor, 77, musician, born Greenville, NC, July 24, 1921.

JULY 25 — SATURDAY

Day 206 — 159 Remaining

ALLEGANY COUNTY INVITATIONAL DRUM AND BUGLE CORPS CHAMPIONSHIPS. July 25. Cumberland, MD. Eastern Regional Senior Drum and Bugle Corps Championship featuring 10 drum and bugle corps competing for top honors. Annually, the last Saturday in July. Est attendance: 7,000. For info: Drumfest, PO Box 3571, LaVale, MD 21504. Phone: (301) 777-8325.

July 1998

S	M	T	W	T	F	S
			1	2	3	4
5	6	7	8	9	10	11
12	13	14	15	16	17	18
19	20	21	22	23	24	25
26	27	28	29	30	31	

ANDREA DORIA SINKS: ANNIVERSARY. July 25, 1956. The Italian luxury liner collided with the *Stockholm*, a Swedish liner, on its way to New York. Other ships in the area came to the rescue of the *Andrea Doria*. 1,634 people were rescued during the ordeal, including the captain and the crew.

ANTIQUE AND CLASSIC BOAT RENDEZVOUS. July 25–26. Mystic Seaport, Mystic, CT. Pre-1952 power and sailing yachts on view for Mystic Seaport visitors. Mystic River parade on Sunday. Est attendance: 4,000. For info: Mystic Seaport, 75 Greenmanville Ave, Box 6000, Mystic, CT 06355. Phone: (203) 527-5315.

BLACK HILLS JAZZ AND BLUES FESTIVAL. July 25. Memorial Park, Rapid City, SD. Outdoor music festival features national recording jazz and blues musicians and bands in a beautiful park setting. Est attendance: 2,500. For info: Ruth Brennan, Rapid City Arts Council, 713 Seventh St, Rapid City, SD 57701. Phone: (605) 394-4101. Email: rbrennan@tmn.com.

BLUE RIDGE DRAFT HORSE AND MULE SHOW. July 25. Ferrum, VA. One of the largest shows in the mid-Atlantic region, the event features 52 competitive classes for horses and mules. Show features major breeds of draft horses, more than 100 horses and mules from five states as well as crafts, music and food. Annually, the fourth Saturday in July. Est attendance: 2,000. For info: Blue Ridge Institute, c/o Ferrum College, Rt 40 West, Ferrum, VA 24088. Phone: (540) 365-4416.

CANADA: BENSON & HEDGES SYMPHONY OF FIRE. July 25 (also July 29, Aug 1 and 5). English Bay, Vancouver, BC. The largest international musical fireworks competition in the world is held 1,000 ft offshore. Each show is a minimum of 25 min. Est attendance: 1,150,000. For info: Tourism BC, Visitor Services, Box 9830, Stn Prov Gov't, Victoria, BC, Canada V8W 9W5. Phone: (604) 688-1992. Fax: (604) 738-4307.

CANADA: PION–ERA. July 25–26. Western Development Museum grounds, Saskatoon, Saskatchewan. This event includes demonstrations of various pioneer skills including ice cream making, butter churning, quilting, spinning and threshing, a parade of engines, children's activities, concessions, interfaith church service and musical entertainment. Est attendance: 6,000. For info: (306) 931-1910 or Tourism Saskatchewan, 500-1900 Albert St, Regina, Sask, Canada S4P 4L9. Phone: (800) 667-7191. Email: travel.info@sasktourism.sk.ca. WWW: http://www.sasktourism.com

CENTRAL MAINE EGG FEST. July 25. Pittsfield, ME. Features "World's Largest Egg" competition, an early morning breakfast, parade, games, crafts, fireworks. Annually, the fourth Saturday in July. Est attendance: 25,000. For info: Central Maine Egg Festival Committee, Box 82, Pittsfield, ME 04967. Phone: (207) 487-5416 or (207) 487-5282.

FIRST AIRPLANE CROSSING OF ENGLISH CHANNEL: ANNIVERSARY. July 25. On Sunday, July 25, 1909, Louis Bleriot, after asking from the cockpit, "Where is England?" took off from Les Baraques (near Calais), France, and landed on English soil at Northfall Meadow, near Dover, where he was greeted first by English police and customs officers. This, the world's first international overseas airplane flight, was accomplished in a 28-hp monoplane with a wingspan of 23 ft. Bleriot was born at Cambrai, France, July 1, 1872. See also: "Bleriot, Louis: Birth Anniversary" (July 1).

FIRST ASSEMBLY DAY. July 25–26. Jamestown, Colonial Natl Historical Park, Yorktown, VA. Living history interpreters commemorate the beginning of representative government in the new world. Est attendance: 2,000. For info: Activities Coord, Colonial Natl Historical Park, PO Box 210, Yorktown, VA 23690. Phone: (757) 898-3400. WWW: http://www.nps.gov/colo

GERMANY: WAGNER FESTSPIELE. July 25–Aug 28. Bayreuth. The works of Richard Wagner are performed daily at the Festival Theatre, which Wagner had built in 1872–76. For info: Bayreuther Festspiele, Pressebüro, Postfach 100262, Bayreuth, Germany D-95402.

GILFORD, JACK: BIRTH ANNIVERSARY. July 25, 1907. American actor Jack Gilford was born Jacob Gellman at New York, NY. Though he was blacklisted for 10 years following refusal to answer questions before the House Un-American Activities Committee in the 1950s, he appeared in many films, stage productions and television programs including an Academy Award-nominated role opposite Jack Lemmon in *Save the Tiger* (1973) and his best-known role as Hysterium in the stage and film versions of *A Funny Thing Happened on the Way to the Forum*. He died on June 4, 1990, at New York, NY.

GREAT HEARTLAND TRAILS FESTIVAL. July 25–26. Lenexa, KS. This time-travel festival includes an 1800s Kansas prairie with settlers, traders, soldiers and emigrants setting up an encampment on their journey west. Also, a living history museum, entertainment, period concessions and an educational fair. Annually, the last weekend in July. Est attendance: 5,000. For info: Bill Nicks, Lenexa Parks & Rec, 13240 Oak St, Lenexa, KS 66215. Phone: (913) 541-8592. Fax: (913) 492-8118.

HANOVER DUTCH FESTIVAL. July 25. Hanover, PA. Handmade crafts, ethnic foods, music, entertainment, children's carnival, petting zoo, antique car show. 15th annual festival. Est attendance: 5,000. For info: Hanover Area Chamber of Commerce, 146 Carlisle St, Hanover, PA 17331. Phone: (717) 637-6130.

HARRISON, ANNA SYMMES: BIRTH ANNIVERSARY. July 25. Wife of William Henry Harrison, 9th president of the US, born at Morristown, NJ, July 25, 1775. Died Feb 25, 1864.

HARVEST WEEKENDS. July 25–26. (Also Aug 1–2, Aug 8–9, Aug 15–16) Bryan, TX. Step into the romance of winemaking by joining the Harvest Pickers Club and participate in hand-harvesting. A typical harvest weekend begins with a walk through the vines followed by the leisurely hand-harvesting of grapes. Afterward, you're invited to attend a classic European-style harvest luncheon which is followed by a wine and food pairing seminar. On Saturday evenings a concert features a variety of musical styles from jazz, country and rock. Annually, late-July to mid-August to coincide with the grape harvest. For info: Steve Wiley, Mktg Dir, Messina Hof Wine Cellars, 4545 Old Reliance Rd, Bryan, TX 77808. Phone: (409) 778-9463. Fax: (409) 778-1729.

KANSAS RIVER VALLEY ART FAIR. July 25–26. Gage Park, Topeka, KS. 19th annual juried fine arts festival. Nearly 100 artists from several-state area. Entertainment, children's activities. Est attendance: 5,000. For info: Anita Wolgast, Historic Ward-Meade Park, 124 NW Fillmore, Topeka, KS 66606. Phone: (913) 368-3888. Fax: (913) 368-3890.

MID-SUMMER ANTIQUES AND COLLECTIBLES SHOW AND SALE. July 25–26. Millville, NJ. Rain or shine. Est attendance: 2,000. For info: Wheaton Village, 1501 Glasstown Rd, Millville, NJ 08332. Phone: (609) 825-6800 or (800) 998-4552. Fax: (609) 825-2410. Email: mail@wheatonvillage.org. WWW: http://www.wheatonvillage.org

MILITARY FIELD DAYS. July 25–26. Big Pool, MD. Reactivated military units from French and Indian War, Revolutionary War and Civil War set up encampments, perform tactical demonstrations and do living history programs. Period sutlers offer their wares for sale. Entrance fee. Annually, the last full weekend in July. Est attendance: 3,500. For info: Ft Frederick State Park, 11100 Ft Frederick Rd, Big Pool, MD 21711. Phone: (301) 842-2155.

MONTANA STATE FAIR. July 25–Aug 2. Great Falls, MT. Horse racing, petting zoo, carnival, discount days, nightly entertainment and plenty of food. Est attendance: 202,000. For info: Kelly Michel, State Fair, Box 1888, Great Falls, MT 59403. Phone: (406) 727-8900. Fax: (406) 452-8955.

MUSSOLINI OUSTED: 55th ANNIVERSARY. July 25, 1943. Two weeks after the Allied attack on Sicily began, the Fascist Grand Council met for the first time since December of 1939 and took a confidence vote resulting in Mussolini's being removed from office and placed under arrest. Italy's King Victor Emmanuel ordered Marshal Pietro Badoglio to form a new government.

NORFOLK PUBLIC LIBRARY YOUTH LITERATURE FESTIVAL. July 25. Johnny Carson Theatre, Norfolk, NE. Presentations by award-winning, nationally known authors, book reviews, book displays and sales and autograph sessions. Est attendance: 300. For info: Karen Drevo, Youth Services Librarian, Norfolk Public Library, 308 Prospect Ave, Norfolk, NE 68701. Phone: (402) 644-8710. Fax: (402) 370-3260. Email: kdrevo@ncfcomm.com.

PUERTO RICO: CONSTITUTION DAY ANNIVERSARY. July 25. Also called Commonwealth Day or Occupation Day. Commemorates proclamation of constitution on July 25, 1952.

PUERTO RICO: LOIZA ALDEA FIESTA. July 25–28. Best known of Puerto Rico's patron saint festivities. Villagers of Loiza Aldea, 20 miles east of San Juan, don devil masks and colorful costumes for a variety of traditional activities.

SAINT SPYRIDON GREEK ORTHODOX FESTIVAL. July 25–26. Kiwanis Park, Sheboygan, WI. Greek music and dancing. Festival foods include Greek pastries, shish kabobs, gyros. Annually, the last weekend (Sat and Sun) of July. Est attendance: 5,000. For info: St. Spyridon Greek Orthodox Church, PO Box 1210, Sheboygan, WI 53082-1210. Phone: (414) 452-3096.

SILVER HOOPS. July 25. Kellogg, ID. Three-on-three basketball tournament. For info: Thresa McCoy, Mgr, Kellogg Chamber of Commerce, 608 Bunker Ave, Kellogg, ID 83837. Phone: (208) 784-0821. Fax: (208) 783-4343. Email: kellogg@nidlink.com. WWW: http://www.nidlink.com/~kellogg

SUMMERFEST. July 25. Hillandale Park, Harrisonburg, VA. To provide a showcase of talent in western Virginia to highlight the uniqueness of the history, nature and arts of the Shenandoah Valley. Arts and crafts, drama, dance and music. 10 AM–5 PM. Est attendance: 4,000. For info: Dept of Parks and Recreation, 305 S Dogwood Dr, Harrisonburg, VA 22801. Phone: (540) 433-9168.

TAYLOR HORSEFEST. July 25. Taylor, ND. This annual celebration is highlighted by a parade of horses and horse-drawn equipment, ethnic food fest, craft vendors, exhibits, demonstrations, music and cowboy poetry. Horse drawn taxis provide transportation throughout the town during the day. For info: (701) 974-2355 or North Dakota Tourism, 604 East Boulevard, Bismarck, ND 58505. Phone: (701) 328-2525 or (800) 435-5663.

July 1998

S	M	T	W	T	F	S
			1	2	3	4
5	6	7	8	9	10	11
12	13	14	15	16	17	18
19	20	21	22	23	24	25
26	27	28	29	30	31	

TEST-TUBE BABY: 20th BIRTHDAY. July 25, 1978. Anniversary of the birth of Louise Brown, on this date in 1978, at Oldham, England. First documented birth of a baby conceived outside the body of a woman. Parents: Gilbert John and Lesley Brown, of Bristol, England. Physicians: Patrick Christopher Steptoe and Robert Geoffrey Edwards.

TIDEWATER ARCHAEOLOGY WEEKEND. July 25–26. St. Mary's City, MD. Hands-on opportunity to dig at an archaeology site at Maryland's first capital. Special behind-the-scenes tours. Annually, usually the last weekend in July. Est attendance: 1,000. For info: Public Affairs Office, Historic St. Mary's City, PO Box 39, St. Mary's City, MD 20686. Phone: (301) 862-0981 or (800) SMC-1634. Fax: (301) 862-0968.

VERMONT FORESTRY EXPO. July 25–26. Fairgrounds, Barton, VT. Features amateur and professional lumberjack competitions plus an equipment expo and parade, tug-o-war, children's events and games. Educational displays and videos provide information about Vermont's timber industry. Est attendance: 5,000. For info: Vermont Forest Products Assn, 24 Sparhawk Rd, Greensboro Bend, VT 05824. Phone: (802) 533-9212. Fax: (802) 533-9222.

BIRTHDAYS TODAY

Louise Joy Brown, 20, first test-tube baby, born Oldham, England, July 25, 1978.
Midge Decter, 71, journalist, born St. Paul, MN, July 25, 1927.
Douglas Dean Drabek, 36, baseball player, born Victoria, TX, July 25, 1962.
Janet Margolin, 55, actress (stage: *Daughter of Silence* [Theatre World Award]; screen: *David and Lisa, Take the Money and Run, Annie Hall*), born New York, NY, July 25, 1943.
Walter Jerry ("Sweetness") Payton, 44, Pro Football Hall of Fame running back, born Columbia, MS, July 25, 1954.
Nathaniel (Nate) Thurmond, 57, Basketball Hall of Fame center, born Akron, OH, July 25, 1941.

☆ ☆ ☆

JULY 26 — SUNDAY

Day 207 — 158 Remaining

ATOMIC BOMB DELIVERED: ANNIVERSARY. July 26, 1945. The US cruiser *Indianapolis* arrived at Tinian Island in the Marianas with a deadly cargo. Aboard were the makings of the atomic bomb. On the island waited scientists prepared to complete the assembly.

CATLIN, GEORGE: BIRTH ANNIVERSARY. July 26, 1796. American artist famous for his paintings of Native American life. In 1832 he toured North and South American tribes, recording their lives in his work. He died on Dec 23, 1872, at Jersey City, NJ.

CHURCH AND SYNAGOGUE LIBRARY ASSOCIATION CONFERENCE. July 26–28. Marriot-Cleveland Airport, Cleveland, OH. Est attendance: 250. For info: Judith Janzen, Exec Secy, Church and Synagogue Library Assn, Box 19357, Portland, OR 97280-0357. Phone: (503) 244-6919 or (800) LIB-CSLA. Fax: (503) 977-3734. Email: csla@worldaccessnet.com.

CLINTON, GEORGE: BIRTH ANNIVERSARY. July 26, 1739. Fourth vice president of the US (1805–12), born at Little Britain, NY. Died at Washington, DC, Apr 20, 1812.

CUBA: NATIONAL HOLIDAY: ANNIVERSARY OF REVOLUTION. July 26. Anniversary of 1953 beginning of Fidel Castro's revolutionary "26th of July Movement."

CURACAO: CURACAO DAY. July 26. "Although not officially recognized by the government as a holiday, various social entities commemorate the fact that on this day Alonso de Ojeda, a companion of Christopher Columbus, discovered the Island of Curaçao in 1499, sailing into Santa Ana Bay, the entrance of the harbor of Willemstad."—tourism info. Festivities on this day.

HUXLEY, ALDOUS: BIRTH ANNIVERSARY. July 26, 1894. English author, satirist, mystic and philosopher, Aldous Leonard Huxley was born at Godalming, Surrey, England. Best known of his works are *Brave New World, Crome Yellow* and *Point Counter Point.* Huxley died at Los Angeles, CA, Nov 22, 1963.

JOHN HUNT MORGAN CAPTURED: ANNIVERSARY. July 26, 1863. After harrassing Union forces in Tennessee and Ohio throughout the Civil War, Confederate raider John Hunt Morgan was captured at New Lisbon, OH, on July 26, 1863. Morgan was imprisoned in the Ohio Penitentiary, from which he later escaped.

LAVALLETTE HERITAGE ARTS AND CRAFTS SHOW. July 26 (rain date Aug 2). Lavallette, NJ. Juried arts, crafts and antiques show. Only the best of the best welcome to exhibit. One of the best shows on the eastern seaboard. 3 PM to dark. Annually, the last Sunday in July. Est attendance: 20,000. For info: Joy Grosko, Heritage Committee of Lavallette, 86 Dickman Dr, Lavallette, NJ 08735. Phone: (732) 793-3652 Joy Grosko or (732) 793-7317 Ginny Shreve.

LIBERIA: INDEPENDENCE DAY. July 26. National holiday. Became republic on this day, 1847, under aegis of the US societies for repatriating former slaves in Africa.

MALDIVES: NATIONAL DAY. July 26. National holiday.

NEW YORK RATIFICATION DAY. July 26, 1788. Eleventh state to ratify Constitution, on this day in 1788.

PUBLICATION OF FIRST ESPERANTO BOOK: ANNIVERSARY. July 26, 1887. To commemorate the anniversary of the publication of Dr. Zamenhof's first textbook about the international language Esperanto. For complete information about Esperanto and this worldwide organization, please send $3 to cover expense of printing and postage. For info: Dr. Stanley J. Drake, Intl Soc of Friendship and Good Will (ISFGW), 412 Cherry Hills Dr, Bakersfield, CA 93309-2866.

RANCH RODEO. July 26. Burwell, NE. A new concept in rodeo where ranch hands compete against the clock while performing tasks that are part of their everyday life. Est attendance: 500. For info: Conv and Visitors Bureau, PO Box 747, Burwell, NE 68823. Phone: (308) 346-5210.

SHAW, GEORGE BERNARD: BIRTH ANNIVERSARY. July 26. Irish playwright, essayist, vegetarian, socialist, antivivisectionist and, he said, ". . . one of the hundred best playwrights in the world." Born at Dublin, Ireland, on July 26, 1856. Died at Ayot St. Lawrence, England, Nov 2, 1950.

SPACE MILESTONE: *APOLLO 15* (US). July 26, 1971. Launched this date. Astronauts David R. Scott and James B. Irwin landed on moon (lunar module *Falcon*) while Alfred M. Worden piloted command module *Endeavor*. *Rover 1*, a four-wheel vehicle, was used for further exploration. Departed moon Aug 2, after nearly three days. Pacific landing Aug 7.

US ARMY FIRST DESEGREGATION: ANNIVERSARY. July 26, 1944. During World War II the US Army ordered desegregation of its training camp facilities. Later the same year black platoons were assigned to white companies in a tentative step toward integration of the battlefield. However, it was not until after the War—July 26, 1948—that President Harry Truman signed an order officially integrating the armed forces.

BIRTHDAYS TODAY

Blake Edwards, 76, producer, writer, director (*Victor/Victoria, The Pink Panther*), born Tulsa, OK, July 26, 1922.

Susan George, 48, actress (*Straw Dogs*), born London, England, July 26, 1950.

Mick (Michael Philip) Jagger, 55, singer, musician (lead singer of the Rolling Stones), born Dartford, England, July 26, 1943.

Jason Robards, 76, actor (*All the President's Men, Julia, Quick Change*; stage: *The Iceman Cometh* [Obie Award], *Long Day's Journey into Night* [Theatre World Award]), born Chicago, IL, July 26, 1922.

Kevin Spacey, 39, actor (*The Usual Suspects, Working Girl, Henry and June*; stage: *Lost in Yonkers*), born South Orange, NJ, July 26, 1959.

JULY 27 — MONDAY

Day 208 — 157 Remaining

ATLANTIC TELEGRAPH CABLE LAID: ANNIVERSARY. July 27, 1866. Cable laying successfully completed on this date.

DUMAS, ALEXANDRE (DUMAS FILS): BIRTH ANNIVERSARY. July 27, 1824. French novelist and playwright, as was his father. Author of *La Dame aux Camélias.* Dumas fils was born at Paris, France, July 27, 1824, and died at Marly-le-Roi, France, on Nov 27, 1895.

DUROCHER, LEO: BIRTH ANNIVERSARY. July 27, 1905. Leo Durocher was born at West Springfield, MA. He began his major league baseball career with the New York Yankees in 1925. He also played for the St. Louis Cardinals' "Gashouse Gang" and the Brooklyn Dodgers, where he first served as player-manager in 1939. It was during that season that he used the phrase "Nice guys finish last," which would become his trademark. As a manager, he guided the New York Giants into two World Series. Following a five-year period away from baseball, he resurfaced as a coach with the Los Angeles Dodgers in 1961. In 1966 he signed with the Chicago Cubs as manager. After leaving the Cubs, he spent one season with the Houston Astros, then retired from baseball in 1973. He died Oct 7, 1991.

GREAT CIRCUS PARADE WEEK. July 27–Aug 2. Baraboo/Milwaukee, WI. Circus wagons make their annual journey to Milwaukee from Baraboo, home of the nation's largest collection of antique circus wagons, arriving in Milwaukee on July 28. Visit the parade showgrounds off the shores of Lake Michigan, July 29–Aug 1 at noon, for a free viewing of a 40-tent display of circus wagons and performances under the Big Top. The Great Circus Parade, winding its way through the streets of Milwaukee on Aug 2, is the only parade of its kind in the world—an authentic recreation of a 19th-century parade complete with 65 restored circus wagons, 750 horses, clowns, animals and marching bands. Est attendance: 500,000. For info: Great Circus Parade, 606 E Wisconsin Ave, Milwaukee, WI 53202. Phone: (414) 273-7877. Fax: (414) 273-4941. WWW: http://circus.compuware.com

KOREAN WAR ARMISTICE: 45th ANNIVERSARY. July 27, 1953. Armistice agreement ending war that had lasted three years and 32 days was signed at Panmunjom, Korea, July 27, 1953 (July 26, US time), by US and North Korean delegates. Both sides claimed victory at conclusion of two years, 17 days of truce negotiations.

US DEPARTMENT OF STATE BIRTHDAY. July 27. The first presidential cabinet department, called the Department of Foreign Affairs, was established by the Congress on July 27, 1789. Later the name was changed to Department of State.

USA PEANUT CONGRESS. July 27–30. Westin Hotel, Hilton Head, SC. Open to all members of the peanut industry. For info: Jeannette Anderson, Exec Dir, National Peanut Council, Inc, 1500 King St, Ste 301, Alexandria, VA 22314. Phone: (703) 838-9500. Fax: (703) 838-9089.

VIRGIN ISLANDS: HURRICANE SUPPLICATION DAY. July 27. Legal holiday. Population attends churches to pray for protection from hurricanes. Annually, the fourth Monday in July.

BIRTHDAYS TODAY

Peggy Gale Fleming, 50, Olympic gold medal figure skater, sportscaster, born San Jose, CA, July 27, 1948.

Bobbie Gentry (Roberta Streeter), 56, singer, songwriter ("Ode to Billie Joe"), born Chicasaw County, MS, July 27, 1942.

Norman Lear, 76, TV scriptwriter, producer ("All In the Family," "Maude"), born Haven, CT, July 27, 1922.

Maureen McGovern, 49, singer ("The Morning After"), actress, born Youngstown, OH, July 27, 1949.

Betty Thomas, 50, director, actress ("Hill Street Blues"), born St. Louis, MO, July 27, 1948.

James Victor, 59, actor (*Fuzz, Stand and Deliver*), born Santiago, Dominican Republic, July 27, 1939.

JULY 28 — TUESDAY

Day 209 — 156 Remaining

CANADA: BUFFALO DAYS. July 28–Aug 2. Regina Exhibition Park, Regina, Saskatchewan. Midway rides, grandstand shows, livestock exhibits, casino, fashion show, home-craft displays, parade, exhibits. Est attendance: 200,000. For info: (306) 781-9200, Tourism Saskatchewan, 500-1900 Albert St, Regina, Sask, Canada S4P 4L9. Phone: (800) 667-7191. Email: travel.info@sasktourism.sk.ca. WWW: http://www.sasktourism.com

CELEBRATION OF OUR LADY OF THE SNOWS. July 28–Aug 5. Belleville, IL. This annual Eucharistic Celebration invites the public to come and celebrate the patroness of the Shrine at the Outdoor Amphitheatre. A candlelight procession will close the services. Est attendance: 2,500. For info: Shrine of Our Lady of the Snows, 442 S DeMazenod Dr, Belleville, IL 62223-1094. Phone: (618) 397-6700. Fax: (618) 398-6549. WWW: http://www.apci.net/~oblates/

HAMBURG FIRESTORM: 55th ANNIVERSARY. July 28, 1943. More than 42,000 civilians were killed when 2,326 tons of bombs, predominately incendiaries, were dropped on Hamburg, Germany, by the Allies on this date. At the center of the firestorm the winds uprooted trees, and flames burned eight square miles in the eight hours the fire lasted. A firestorm occurs when the fires in a given area become so intense they devour all the oxygen nearby and suck more into themselves creating hurricane-force winds which feed the fires and move them at great speeds.

HEYWARD, THOMAS: BIRTH ANNIVERSARY. July 28, 1746. American Revolutionary soldier, signer of the Declaration of Independence. Died Mar 6, 1809.

ONASSIS, JACQUELINE LEE BOUVIER KENNEDY: BIRTH ANNIVERSARY. July 28, 1929. Editor, widow of John Fitzgerald Kennedy (35th president of the US), born at Southampton, NY. Later married (Oct 20, 1968) Greek shipping magnate Aristotle Socrates Onassis, who died Mar 15, 1975. The widely admired and respected former First Lady died May 19, 1994, at New York City.

July 1998

S	M	T	W	T	F	S
			1	2	3	4
5	6	7	8	9	10	11
12	13	14	15	16	17	18
19	20	21	22	23	24	25
26	27	28	29	30	31	

PERU: INDEPENDENCE DAY. July 28. San Martin declared independence on July 28, 1821. After the final defeat of Spanish troops by Simon Bolivar in 1824, Spanish rule ended.

POTTER, (HELEN) BEATRIX: BIRTH ANNIVERSARY. July 28, 1866. Creator of the Peter Rabbit stories for children, born at London, England. Died at Sawrey, Lancashire, Dec 22, 1943.

"THE SAMMY KAYE SHOW" TV PREMIERE: ANNIVERSARY. July 28, 1951. CBS's musical program hosted by bandleader Sammy Kaye swayed audiences to swinging tunes on Saturday nights.

SINGING TELEGRAM: 65th ANNIVERSARY. July 28, 1933. Anniversary of the first singing telegram, said to have been delivered to singer Rudy Vallee on his 32nd birthday, July 28, 1933. Early singing telegrams often were delivered in person by uniformed messengers on bicycle. Later they were usually sung over the telephone.

SPACE MILESTONE: *RANGER 7* (US). July 28, 1964. Televised back to Earth 4,308 close-up photographs of moon. Launched July 28, 1964.

SPACE MILESTONE: *SKYLAB 3* (US): 25th ANNIVERSARY. July 28, 1973. Launched on July 28, 1973, Alan L. Bean, Owen K. Garriott and Jack R. Lousma started record 59-day mission to test man's space flight endurance. Pacific splashdown Sept 25.

TERRY FOX DAY: 40th BIRTH ANNIVERSARY. July 28, 1958. With cancer requiring amputation of his right leg at age 18, Fox determined to devote his life to a fight against the disease. His "Marathon of Hope," a planned 5,200-mile run westward across Canada, started Apr 12, 1980, at St. John's, Newfoundland, and continued 3,328 miles to Thunder Bay, Ontario, Sept 1, 1980, when he was forced to stop by spread of the disease. During the run (on an artificial leg) he raised $24 million for cancer research and inspired millions with his courage. Terry

Fox was born at Winnipeg, Manitoba, and died at New Westminster (near Vancouver), British Columbia, Canada, June 28, 1981.

VALLEE, RUDY: BIRTH ANNIVERSARY. July 28, 1901. American singer, saxophone player and radio idol of millions during the 1930s. Born Hubert Prior Vallee, at Island Pond, VT, the crooner used a megaphone to amplify his voice and introduced his performances with the salutation, "Heigh-ho-everybody!" Vallee appeared in a number of movies, including *How to Succeed in Business Without Really Trying*. Among his best-remembered songs are "I'm Just a Vagabond Lover," "Cheerful Little Earful," "If I Had a Talking Picture of You," "Say It Isn't So" and his signature song, "My Time Is Your Time." Vallee died at age 84 at North Hollywood, CA, on July 3, 1986, while watching Statue of Liberty centennial ceremonies on television.

VETERANS BONUS ARMY EVICTION: ANNIVERSARY. July 28, 1932. Some 15,000 unemployed veterans of World War I marched on Washington, DC, in the summer of 1932, demanding payment of a war bonus. After two months' encampment in Washington's Anacostia Flats, eviction of the bonus marchers by the US Army was ordered by President Herbert Hoover. Under the leadership of General Douglas MacArthur, Major Dwight D. Eisenhower and Major George S. Patton, Jr (among others), cavalry, tanks and infantry attacked. Fixed bayonets, tear gas and the burning of the veterans' tents hastened the end of the confrontation. One death was reported.

ZENGER, JOHN PETER: DEATH ANNIVERSARY. July 28, 1746. German-born John Peter Zenger emigrated to New York at age 13 and in 1726 established his own printing business. His acquittal in a libel suit because what he wrote was based on fact is recognized as the earliest victory for freedom of the press in the British colonies of North America. Truth has been a key defense in libel cases ever since. Zenger went on to serve as public printer in the colonies of New York and New Jersey. He died at about age 49, at New York City.

BIRTHDAYS TODAY

William Warren (Bill) Bradley, 55, former US senator, Basketball Hall of Fame forward, born Crystal City, MO, July 28, 1943.

Darryl Hickman, 67, actor ("The Many Loves of Dobie Gillis," "The Americans"), born Los Angeles, CA, July 28, 1931.

Linda Kelsey, 52, actress (Billie on "Lou Grant"), born Minneapolis, MN, July 28, 1946.

Lori Loughlin, 34, actress ("The Edge of Night," *Back to the Beach*), born Long Island, NY, July 28, 1964.

Jacques Piccard, 76, inventor, explorer, born Brussels, Belgium, July 28, 1922.

Sally Anne Struthers, 50, actress (Gloria on "All in the Family"), born Portland, OR, July 28, 1948.

Rick Wright, 53, singer, musician (keyboard player with Pink Floyd), born London, England, July 28, 1945.

☆ ☆ ☆

JULY 29 — WEDNESDAY

Day 210 — 155 Remaining

CANADA: MUSKOKA DISTRICT KENNEL CLUB CHAMPIONSHIP SHOW. July 29–31. James D. Lang Activity Park, Bracebridge, Ont. For info: Muskoka Dist Kennel Club, Bracebridge C of C, 1-1 Manitoba St, Bracebridge, Ont, Canada P1L-1S4. Phone: (705) 645-5801 or (705) 645-8121. Fax: (705) 645-7592. Email: bracecha@muskoka.com.

CANADA: TRIAL OF LOUIS RIEL. July 29–Aug 28 (Wednesdays, Thursdays and Fridays). Shumiatcher Theatre at the MacKenzie Art Gallery, Regina, Saskatchewan. Now in its 31st season this play presents a reenactment of the dramatic events surrounding Louis Riel, the Metis leader in the North West Rebellion of 1885. One of the longest-running stage shows in Canada. Est attendance: 5,000. For info: (306) 584-8890 or Tourism Saskatchewan, 500–1900 Albert St, Regina, Sask, Canada S4P 4L9. Phone: (800) 667-7191. Email: travel.info@sasktourism.sk.ca. WWW: http://www.sasktourism.com

CHINCOTEAGUE PONY PENNING. July 29–30. Chincoteague Island, VA. To round up the 150 wild ponies living on Assateague Island and swim them across the inlet to Chincoteague, where about 50–60 of them are sold. Est attendance: 50,000. For info: Jacklyn Russell, Chamber of Commerce, Box 258, Chincoteague, VA 23336. Phone: (757) 336-6161. Fax: (757) 336-1242. Email: pony@shore.intercom.net.
WWW: http:///www.intercom.net/local/chincoteague

DOLL SHOW. July 29. Baltimore, MD. Open to girls and boys 14 years of age and under. 12 different categories of dolls. Trophies and prizes for winners. Overall Doll Show Queen & King are selected from the winners of the different doll categories. The Doll Show King & Queen are presented additional prizes and crowned at the conclusion of the show. Est attendance: 300. For info: Office of Adventures and Fun, Patterson Park Recreation Complex, 2601 E Baltimore St, Baltimore, MD 21224. Phone: (410) 396-9177. Fax: (410) 327-4120.

EAA FLY-IN CONVENTION. July 29–Aug 4. Wittman Regional Airport, Oshkosh, WI. World's largest sport aviation event. More than 12,000 airplanes annually fly in for this Experimental Aircraft Association event. Daily air shows, special programs, more than 500 forums, workshops and seminars. Est attendance: 850,000. For info: Dick Knapinski, Corporate Communications, Experimental Aircraft Assn, PO Box 3086, Oshkosh, WI 54903-3086. Phone: (414) 426-4800.
WWW: http://www.eea.org

HOOD RIVER COUNTY FAIR. July 29–Aug 1. Hood River, OR. From 4-H activities to the excitement of the carnival, this annual old-fashioned country fair is bustling with things to do! Est attendance: 15,000. For info: Hood River Chamber of Commerce, Box 385, Odell, OR 97044. Phone: (541) 354-2865. Fax: (541) 354-2875.

***INDIANAPOLIS* SUNK: ANNIVERSARY.** July 29, 1945. After delivering the atomic bomb to Tinian Island, the American cruiser *Indianapolis* was headed for Okinawa to train for the invasion of Japan when it was torpedoed by a Japanese submarine. Of 1,196 crew members, more than 350 were immediately killed in the explosion or went down with the ship. There were no rescue ships nearby, and those fortunate enough to survive endured the next 84 hours in ocean waters. By the time they were spotted by air on Aug 2, only 318 sailors remained alive, the others either having drowned or been eaten by sharks. This is the US Navy's worst-ever loss at sea.

MUSSOLINI, BENITO: BIRTH ANNIVERSARY. July 29, 1883. The anniversary of birth of Italian Fascist leader, at Dovia, Italy. Self-styled "Il Duce" (the leader), Mussolini governed Italy, first as prime minister and later as absolute dictator, 1922–43. Reportedly, under his regime "the trains ran on time." It was Mussolini who said: "War alone . . . puts the stamp of nobility upon the peoples who have the courage to face it." But military defeat of Italy in World War II was Mussolini's downfall. Repudiated and arrested by the Italian government, he was temporarily rescued by German paratroops in 1943. Later, as they attempted to flee in disguise to Switzerland, he and his mistress, Clara Petacci, were shot and killed by Italian partisans near Lake Como, Italy, Apr 28, 1945.

NEW JERSEY STATE FAIR. July 29–Aug 9. Cherry Hill, NJ. Reithoffer Shows, book fair, various types of music entertainment, circus, food booths and sports events. Est attendance: 206,000. For info: New Jersey State Fair, 406 Richard Rd, Rockledge, FL 32955. Phone: (407) 633-4028. Fax: (407) 633-6930.

NORWAY: OLSOK EVE. July 29. Commemorates Norway's Viking king St. Olav, who fell in battle at Stiklestad near Trondheim, Norway, July 29, 1030. Bonfires, historical pageants.

PERU: NATIONAL HOLIDAY. July 29. Public holiday in Peru celebrated with a military parade and a gala horse race in Monterrico Race Track.

RAIN DAY IN WAYNESBURG, PENNSYLVANIA. July 29. Legend has it that rain will fall in Waynesburg, PA, on July 29 as it has most years for the last century, according to local records in this community, which was laid out in 1796 and incorporated in 1816.

ROOSEVELT, ALICE HATHAWAY LEE: BIRTH ANNIVERSARY. July 29. First wife of Theodore Roosevelt, 26th President of the US, born at Chestnut Hill, MA, July 29, 1861. Died Feb 14, 1884.

TARKINGTON, BOOTH: BIRTH ANNIVERSARY. July 29. American novelist, born at Indianapolis, IN, July 29, 1869. Died there May 19, 1946.

ZAMBIA: MUTOMBOKO CEREMONY. July 29. Ancient annual ceremony to honor Senior Chief, the traditional leader of the Luunda peoples of the Luapula Province in north-central Zambia. Joyous communal party and cultural get-together.

BIRTHDAYS TODAY

Ken Burns, 45, documentary filmmaker ("Civil War" series), born New York, NY, July 29, 1953.

Peter Jennings, 60, journalist (anchorman for "ABC Evening News"), born Toronto, Ontario, Canada, July 29, 1938.

Alexandra Paul, 35, actress ("Baywatch," *Dragnet*), born New York, NY, July 29, 1963.

Marilyn Tucker Quayle, 49, former Second Lady, born Indianapolis, IN, July 29, 1949.

Patty Scialfa, 42, singer, born Deal, NJ, July 29, 1956.

Paul Taylor, 68, dancer, choreographer, born Allegheny, NY, July 29, 1930.

David Warner, 57, actor ("Holocaust," *Tron*), born Manchester, England, July 29, 1941.

Wil Wheaton, 26, actor ("Star Trek: The Next Generation," *Stand by Me*), born Burbank, CA, July 29, 1972.

JULY 30 — THURSDAY

Day 211 — 154 Remaining

BRONTE, EMILY: BIRTH ANNIVERSARY. July 30, 1818. English novelist, one of the Brontë sisters, best known for *Wuthering Heights*. Died Dec 19, 1848.

CANADA: AGRIFAIR. July 30–Aug 4. Abbotsford, British Columbia. Fun for everyone with attractions like draft horses, dairy, beef, llama and poultry; hands-on milking display; motor sports; home variety trade show; antique farm display bursting with antique toys; children's midway; plus everything from national and international stage entertainment to a rodeo and nightly fireworks. Est attendance: 55,000. For info: Harvey Carroll, Abbotsford Agrifair, PO Box 2334, Abbotsford, BC, Canada V2T 4X2. Phone: (604) 852-6674. Fax: (604) 852-6631.

CANADA: BIG VALLEY JAMBOREE. July 30–Aug 2. Camrose, Alta. One of the largest country music festivals in Canada, featuring top-name entertainers and more than 60 acts. Beer gardens, trade shows, unserviced camping and parking. Est attendance: 15,000. For info: Glen Vinet, PO Box 1418, Camrose, Alta, Canada T4V 1X3. Phone: (403) 672-0224 or (888) 404-1234. Fax: (403) 672-9530. Email: bvj@ccinet.ab.ca.

CANADA: ROCKHOUND GEMBOREE. July 30–Aug 2. Bancroft, Ontario. Daily expeditions to prime mineral locations, dealers, demonstrations and displays, swapping. Est attendance: 14,000. For info: Bancroft and District Chamber of Commerce, PO Box 539, Bancroft, Ont, Canada K0L 1C0. Phone: (613) 332-1513. Fax: (613) 332-2119.
Email: chamber@commerce.bancroft.on.ca.
WWW: http://www.commerce.bancroft.on.ca

FORD, HENRY: BIRTH ANNIVERSARY. July 30, 1863. Automotive pioneer, born in Dearborn Township, MI, remembered especially for developing an assembly-line production system, for introducing a $5-a-day wage for automotive workers and for his statement: "History is bunk." Ford died at Dearborn, MI, on Apr 7, 1947, at age 83.

HILL, ANITA FAYE: BIRTHDAY. July 30. Law professor Anita Hill, born on an Oklahoma farm, July 30, 1956, shocked the nation and forever changed public attitudes toward sexual harassment of women in October 1991. Her nationally televised testimony accused now-Justice Clarence Thomas of sexual harassment before the all-male Senate Judiciary Committee during that committee's confirmation hearings concerning President Bush's nomination of Thomas as a justice of the Supreme Court. From a rural upbringing in relative obscurity, youngest of 13 children, Yale graduate, she abruptly became one of the nation's best-known and most-admired women as a result of her televised testimony.

HOFFA, JAMES: DISAPPEARANCE ANNIVERSARY. July 30. Former Teamsters Union leader, 62-year-old James Riddle Hoffa was last seen July 30, 1975, outside a restaurant in Bloomfield Township, near Detroit, MI. His 13-year federal prison sentence had been commuted by former President Richard M. Nixon in 1971. On Dec 8, 1982, seven years and 131 days after his disappearance, an Oakland County judge declared Hoffa officially dead as of July 30, 1982.

MAINE LOBSTER FESTIVAL. July 30–Aug 2. Harbor Park, Public Landing, Rockland, ME. Annual celebration and promotion of the lobster industry featuring lobster dinners, arts, crafts, exhibits, live entertainment, parade, contests and a road race. Est attendance: 65,000. For info: Rockland Thomaston Area Chamber of Commerce, PO Box 508, Rockland, ME 04841. Phone: (207) 596-0376. Fax: (207) 596-6549.
Email: rtacc@midcoast.com.
WWW: http://www.midcoast.com/~rtacc

MOORE, HENRY: 100th BIRTH ANNIVERSARY. July 30, 1898. English sculptor born at Castleford, Yorkshire. Died at Hertfordshire, Aug 31, 1986.

ROCKINGHAM OLD HOME DAYS. July 30–Aug 2. Bellows Falls and Rockingham, VT. Sidewalk sales. Fireworks on Saturday evening. Sunday pilgrimage to the Old Rockingham Meeting House with ceremonies and speeches. Annually, the first weekend in August. Est attendance: 12,000. For info: Great Falls Chamber of Commerce, PO Box 554, Bellows Falls, VT 05101. Phone: (802) 463-4280. Email: gfrcc@sover.net.
WWW: http://www.sover.net/~daxtell/bf

SAUERKRAUT FESTIVAL. July 30–Aug 2. Phelps, NY. Firemen's Field. As its name implies, this unique festival serves sauer-

July 1998

S	M	T	W	T	F	S
			1	2	3	4
5	6	7	8	9	10	11
12	13	14	15	16	17	18
19	20	21	22	23	24	25
26	27	28	29	30	31	

kraut but also has other food booths. Also features amusement rides, fireworks, a parade, arts and crafts display and different kinds of entertainment. Est attendance: 15,000. For info: Sauerkraut Festival, 21 E Main St, Clifton Springs, NY 14432. Phone: (315) 462-3376.

SAVIN ROCK FESTIVAL. July 30–Aug 2. Old Grove Park, West Haven, CT. Nightly entertainment, crafts fair, shopping mart, food and rides. For info: Savin Rock Festival, (203) 937-3511 or Greater New Haven Conv & Visitors Bureau, One Long Wharf Dr, New Haven, CT 06511. Phone: (203) 777-8550 or (800) 332-STAY. Fax: (203) 782-7755.

STENGEL, CHARLES DILLON (CASEY): BIRTH ANNIVERSARY. July 30, 1890. Baseball Hall of Fame outfielder and manager born at Kansas City, MO. His success as manager of the New York Yankees (ten pennants and seven World Series titles in 12 years) made him one of the game's enduring stars. Inducted into the Hall of Fame in 1966. Died at Glendale, CA, Sept 29, 1975.

THAT FAMOUS PRESTON NIGHT RODEO. July 30–Aug 1. Preston, ID. The second under-the-lights rodeo in America, this 57-year-old RCA-approved rodeo has top national cowboys. Est attendance: 16,000. For info: Travel Rep, City of Preston, PO Box 472, Preston, ID 83263. Fax: (208) 852-0158.

"TIC TAC DOUGH" TV PREMIERE: ANNIVERSARY. July 30, 1956. Game show premiered on CBS with Jay Jackson, Jack Barry, Gene Rayburn and Bill Wendell serving as hosts during its three-year run. Two contestants play tic-tac-toe by answering questions in a selected category. The show was resurrected in 1978 with Wink Martindale as host.

VANUATU: INDEPENDENCE DAY. July 30. Vanuatu became an independent republic on July 30, 1980, and observes its national holiday on this day.

VEBLEN, THORSTEIN: BIRTH ANNIVERSARY. July 30, 1857. American economist, born at Valders, WI, and died at Menlo Park, CA, Aug 3, 1929. "Conspicuous consumption," he wrote in *The Theory of the Leisure Class*, "of valuable goods is a means of reputability to the gentleman of leisure."

BIRTHDAYS TODAY

Paul Anka, 57, singer, songwriter ("Diana"; "My Way" for Frank Sinatra), born Ottawa, Ontario, July 30, 1941.

Peter Bogdanovich, 59, producer, director (*The Last Picture Show, Paper Moon*), born Kingston, NY, July 30, 1939.

Delta Burke, 42, actress (played Suzanne Sugarbaker on "Designing Women"; former Miss Florida), born Orlando, FL, July 30, 1956.

Kate Bush, 40, singer ("The Man with the Child in His Eyes"), songwriter, born Lewisham, England, July 30, 1958.

Edd Byrnes, 65, actor ("Kookie" on "77 Sunset Strip"; *Darby's Rangers*), born New York, NY, July 30, 1933.

James William (Bill) Cartwright, 41, former basketball player, born Lodi, CA, July 30, 1957.

Laurence Fishburne, 37, actor (*Boyz N the Hood, Deep Cover, What's Love Got to Do with It, Higher Learning*; stage: *Two Trains Running* [Tony, Theatre World Awards]), born Augusta, GA, July 30, 1961.

Anita Faye Hill, 42, law professor (the Clarence Thomas hearings), born on an Oklahoma farm, July 30, 1956.

Christopher Paul (Chris) Mullin, 35, basketball player, born New York, NY, July 30, 1963.

Ken Olin, 44, actor ("Hill Street Blues," "Falcon Crest," "thirtysomething"), born Chicago, IL, July 30, 1954.

David Sanborn, 53, saxophonist, composer, born Tampa, FL, July 30, 1945.

Arnold Schwarzenegger, 51, bodybuilder, actor (*The Terminator, Twins, True Lies, Last Action Hero*), born Graz, Austria, July 30, 1947.

Eleanor Marie Cutri Smeal, 59, feminist (former president of NOW), born Ashtabula, OH, July 30, 1939.

JULY 31 — FRIDAY

Day 212 — 153 Remaining

AMERICAN LUMBERJACK CHAMPIONSHIPS AT LOG BOOM. July 31–Aug 2. Pettibone Park on the Mississippi River, La Crosse, WI. Historical family event featuring the best log rollers, axmen, sawyers, tree climbers in the world. Prairie La Crosse Rendezvous with more than 150 primitive camps of woodworkers, blacksmiths, spinners, weavers and more. Traditional music, food, art, children's games. Est attendance: 20,000. For info: Mississippi River Log Boom, PO Box 801, La Crosse, WI 54601. Phone: (608) 782-1003. Fax: (608) 782-4275.

AMERICOVER. July 31–Aug 2. Somerset DoubleTree, Somerset, NJ. 43rd annual convention and exhibition. The AFDCS is the only not-for-profit, noncommercial, international philatelic (stamp collector) society devoted exclusively to First Day Covers and First Day Cover collecting. AMERICOVER will be the largest single philatelic event (stamp show and sale) this year dealing primarily with First Day Covers, their collectors, cachet makers and dealers. A fun time for all! Est attendance: 1,500. For info: American First Day Cover Society, PO Box 1335, Maplewood, NJ 07040-0456. Phone: (201) 762-2012. Fax: (201) 762-7916. Email: americover@aol.com.

BRATWURST DAYS. July 31–Aug 1. Sheboygan, WI. Sheboygan celebrates bratwurst at Kiwanis Park with music, national entertainment, Bratozica, parade, flea market and, of course, bratwurst-eating contest. Since 1953. Est attendance: 40,000. For info: Sheboygan Jaycees, PO Box 561, Sheboygan, WI 53081. Phone: (414) 457-9495 or (414) 458-2137. Fax: (414) 458-5922.

CANADA: PIONEER DAYS. July 31–Aug 3. Mennonite Heritage Village, Steinbach, Manitoba. Pioneer demonstrations and related activities in a heritage village setting. Est attendance: 14,000. For info: Harv Klassen, Exec Dir, Box 1136, Steinbach, Manitoba, Canada R0A 2A0. Phone: (204) 326-9661. Fax: (204) 326-5046.

DECATUR CELEBRATION. July 31–Aug 2. Decatur, IL. A free family street festival within 22 city blocks of fun with 13 entertainment stages, arts, crafts and commercial vendors, 66 one-of-a-kind food vendors. Est attendance: 300,000. For info: Decatur Celebration, 132 S Water, Ste 418, Decatur, IL 62523. Phone: (217) 423-4222. Fax: (217) 423-4271.

FEAST OF SAINT IGNATIUS OF LOYOLA. July 31. 1491–1556. Founder of the Society of Jesus and Jesuits. Canonized in 1622.

FIRST US GOVERNMENT BUILDING: ANNIVERSARY. July 31. The cornerstone of the Mint, the first US government building, was laid on this day in 1792.

KENNEDY INTERNATIONAL AIRPORT DEDICATION: 50th ANNIVERSARY. July 31, 1948. New York's International Airport at Idlewild Field was dedicated by President Harry S. Truman on July 31, 1948. It was later renamed John F. Kennedy International Airport.

KENNEDY-CHENG UNITED NATIONS MEMBERSHIP SUMMIT: ANNIVERSARY. July 31. President John F. Kennedy agreed during talks held with General Chen Cheng July 31–Aug 1, 1961, to support Nationalist China in its bid for UN membership and oppose the admission of Communist China to the United Nations.

MELVILLE MARATHON. July 31–Aug 1. Mystic Seaport, Mystic, CT. Marathon reading of the classic *Moby Dick* in celebration of Herman Melville's birthday. Reading takes place on deck and in foc's'le of the last wooden whaler, *Charles W. Morgan*. Annually, 24-hour reading from noon July 31 to noon Aug 1. Est attendance: 6,000. For info: Mystic Seaport, 75 Greenmanville Ave, PO Box 6000, Mystic, CT 06355-0990. Phone: (203) 572-5315.

MOON PHASE: FIRST QUARTER. July 31. Moon enters First Quarter phase at 8:05 AM, EDT.

NATIONAL BALLOON CLASSIC. July 31–Aug 8. Indianola, IA. A spectator-oriented balloon extravaganza involving fun events utilizing up to 100 balloons. It is held on the Classic's specially designed balloon field with a natural amphitheater for perfect viewing. Balloons fly morning and evening, weather permitting. The Classic stage features live local & regional entertainment. Est attendance: 75,000. For info: Gerald Knoll, PO Box 346, Indianola, IA 50125. Phone: (800) FLY-IOWA or (515) 961-8415. Fax: (515) 961-8415. Email: classic@www.balloon.weather.net. WWW: http://www.balloon.weather.net

OHIO STATE FAIR. July 31–Aug 16 (tentative). Columbus, OH. Family fun, amusement rides, games, food booths, parades, entertainment, rodeos, circus, auto thrill show and tractor pulls. Est attendance: 900,000. For info: Ohio State Fair, 717 E 17th Ave, Columbus, OH 43211. Phone: (614) 644-4000. Fax: (614) 644-4031.

OZARK EMPIRE FAIR. July 31–Aug 9. Springfield, MO. Regional fair with carnival, exhibits, livestock and entertainment. Est attendance: 230,000. For info: Ozark Empire Fair, PO Box 630, Springfield, MO 65801. Phone: (417) 833-2660. Fax: (417) 833-3769.

REEVES, JIM: DEATH ANNIVERSARY. July 31. Country music star Jim Reeves died at age 41, July 31, 1964, when the single-engine plane in which he was traveling crashed in a dense fog. Reeves's biggest hit was "He'll Have to Go" (1959), and he was inducted into the Country Music Hall of Fame in 1967.

SALVADOR, FRANCIS: DEATH ANNIVERSARY. July 31, 1776. The first Jew to die in the American Revolution, Salvador was also the first Jew elected to office in colonial America. He was voted a member of the South Carolina Provincial Congress in January 1775.

SQUARE FAIR. July 31–Aug 2. Lima Town Square, Lima, OH. Outdoor performing and visual arts festival. Est attendance: 50,000. For info: Martin Porter, Exec Dir, Council for the Arts of Greater Lima, Box 1124, Lima, OH 45802. Phone: (419) 222-1096. Fax: (419) 222-3871. Email: limaarts@bright.net. WWW: http://www.bright.net/~limaarts

SUSSEX COUNTY FARM AND HORSE SHOW. July 31–Aug 9. Augusta, NJ. "New Jersey's Best Fair." The state's largest livestock and horse show also includes educational exhibits, amusements, commercial exhibits and entertainment. Located off Rt 206 Plains Rd. Gate opens 5 PM Friday and closes 5 PM Sun. Est attendance: 240,000. For info: Howard Worts, Mgr, PO Box M, Branchville, NJ 07826. Phone: (201) 948-5500. Fax: (201) 948-0903. WWW: http://www.sussex-county-fair.org

TELLURIDE JAZZ CELEBRATION. July 31–Aug 2. Telluride, CO. Some of jazz's hottest rising stars and most accomplished musicians team up in the town park by day and in intimate nightclubs at night. Annually, the first weekend in August. Sponsor: American Express. Est attendance: 1,500. For info: Holly Henry, Mktg Mgr, Telluride Central Reservations, 666 W Colorado Ave, PO Box 653, Telluride, CO 81435. Phone: (800) 525-3455. Fax: (970) 728-6475. WWW: http://www.tvs.org

TRINIDAD: SIGHTED BY COLUMBUS: 500th ANNIVERSARY. July 31, 1498. Christopher Columbus first sighted the island that he called La Trinidad. The island was inhabited by two tribes of "Indians," the Arawaks, who were peaceful fishermen and farmers, and the more beligerent Caribs. Upon his return to Spain, Columbus described the islands to the King as very lush and pleasant, and soon the Spaniards began to colonize them. Trinidad and Tobago remained under Spanish rule from 1498 until Feb 18, 1797, when the Spanish Governor, Chacon, surrendered the islands to the British Navy. British rule continued until 1962 when Trinidad and Tobago gained their independence, after having been self-governing since 1956. (Info provided by the Tourism Development Authority.)

US PATENT OFFICE OPENS: ANNIVERSARY. July 31. On July 31, 1790, the first US Patent Office opened its doors, and the first US patent was issued to Samuel Hopkins of Vermont for a new method of making pearlash and potash. The patent was signed by George Washington and Thomas Jefferson.

WHITE OAK RENDEZVOUS. July 31–Aug 2. Deer River, MN. Voted one of the top 25 Festivals by the Minnesota office of tourism. One big weekend for re-enactment of fur trade history placed in a setting of 80 acres of pasture and wilderness. 200 tipis and white canvas lodges placed around a North West Company Fur Post from 1798. Blacksmith shop, root cellar, clerk's quarters and store, birchbark canoe–building shed, Ojibwe village. Country, bluegrass and old-time music, dance, puppetry and one-mile-long nature trail with plants labeled to explain their use in 1798 for medicine, shelter or food. 18th-century craft demonstrations and sales. Also, specialty foods from the fur trade period. Est attendance: 8,000. For info: Perry Vining, Rendezvous Bourgeois, Box 306, Deer River, MN 56636. Phone: (218) 246-9393. Fax: (218) 246-9393. Email: pvining@northernnet.com. WWW: http://northernnet.com/white_oak/index.html

BIRTHDAYS TODAY

Dean Cain, 32, actor ("Lois & Clark: The New Adventures of Superman"), born Mount Clemens, MI, July 31, 1966.

Geraldine Chaplin, 54, actress (*Nashville, Roseland, Chaplin*), born Santa Monica, CA, July 31, 1944.

Milton Friedman, 86, economist, journalist, born Brooklyn, NY, July 31, 1912.

Evonne Goolagong, 47, former tennis player, born Griffith, Australia, July 31, 1951.

Irv Kupcinet, 86, former TV talk-show host, columnist, born Chicago, IL, July 31, 1912.

Sherry Lansing, 54, producer (*Fatal Attraction, The Accused*), born Chicago, IL, July 31, 1944.

Gary Lewis, 52, singer ("This Diamond Ring"), born New York, NY, July 31, 1946.

Don Murray, 69, actor (*Bus Stop*, "Knots Landing"), born Hollywood, CA, July 31, 1929.

Wesley Snipes, 36, actor (*Jungle Fever, White Men Can't Jump, Rising Sun*), born Orlando, FL, July 31, 1962.

William F. Weld, 53, Governor of Massachusetts (R), born Smithtown, NY, July 31, 1945. As *Chase's* went to press, Weld was nominated to be US ambassador to Mexico and resigned as governor.

August.

AUGUST 1 — SATURDAY

Day 213 — 152 Remaining

AMERICAN HERITAGE GLASS AND CRAFTS FESTIVALS. Aug 1–2. Good Childrens Zoo, Oglebay, Wheeling, WV. A grand gathering of the best glass and craft artisans from a three-state area in the beautiful outdoors with food and entertainment. Annually, the first weekend in August. Sponsored by the Wheeling Park Commission (Oglebay). Est attendance: 5,000. For info: Barbara Palmer, Special Events Coord, Oglebay, Wheeling, WV 26003. Phone: (304) 243-4010. Fax: (304) 243-4110.

AMHERST'S TEDDY BEAR RALLY. Aug 1. Amherst, MA. Teddy bear parade, official bear appraiser, coloring event, Teddy Bear Hospital, UMass Oompah Band, Winnie-the-Pooh readings and more than 165 teddy bear dealers and exhibits. Entertainment and refreshments; free. 16th annual rally. Est attendance: 20,000. For info: Amherst Rotary Club, Teddy Bear Rally Committee, PO Box 542, Amherst, MA 01004. Phone: (413) 256-8983.

BATTLE OF BUSHY RUN: 235th ANNIVERSARY. Aug 1–2. Harrison City, PA. This re-enactment commemorates the decisive battle of Pontiac's War on Aug 5 and 6, 1763. Event includes a guided tour through the battle's historic camp and demonstrations of military crafts. For info: John Giblin, PO Box 468, Harrison City, PA 15636-0468. Phone: (412) 527-5584.

BENIN, PEOPLE'S REPUBLIC OF: NATIONAL DAY. Aug 1. Public holiday.

BROWN, RONALD H.: BIRTH ANNIVERSARY. Aug 1, 1941. Born at Washington, DC, Ronald H. Brown grew up in Harlem and studied at Middlebury College in Vermont. After serving in the Army he returned to New York and worked for the Urban League. After graduating from St. John's University law school, Brown served as chief council for the Senate Judiciary Committee. Although his early business involvements were of a rather suspicious nature, he went on to become the first African-American partner at the law firm of Patton Boggs & Blow, the first African-American leader of the Democratic National Committee and later served as the US Secretary of Commerce during the Clinton administration. Brown died in a plane crash at Dubrovnik, Croatia, Apr 3, 1996.

BROWNIES AT BRUNCH. Aug 1–31. Oregon, IL. Celebrate 100+ years of the American brownie. Exotic flavors, served with seasonal berries, juice bar, New Salem cider. For info: Prairie Confections, 400 Mix St, Oregon, IL 61061. Phone: (815) 732-2061.

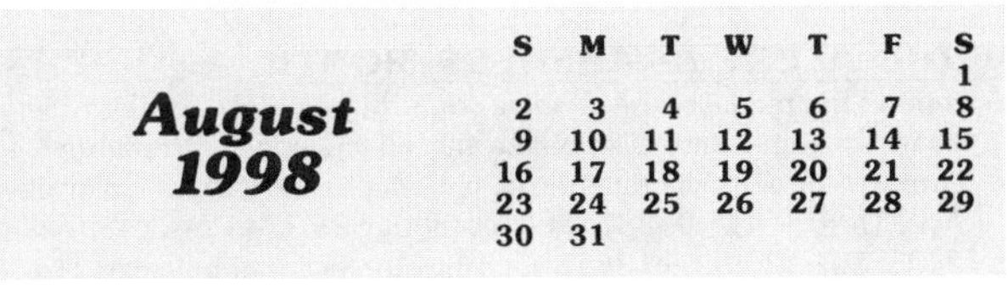

August 1998

S	M	T	W	T	F	S
						1
2	3	4	5	6	7	8
9	10	11	12	13	14	15
16	17	18	19	20	21	22
23	24	25	26	27	28	29
30	31					

BURK, MARTHA (CALAMITY JANE): 95th DEATH ANNIVERSARY. Aug 1. Known as a frontierswoman and companion to Wild Bill Hickock, Calamity Jane Burk was born Martha Jane Canary in Princeton, MO, probably in the year 1852. As a young girl living in Montana, she became an excellent markswoman. She went to the Black Hills of South Dakota as a scout for a geological expedition in 1875. Several opposing traditions account for her nickname, one springing from her kindness to the less fortunate, while another attributes it to the harsh warnings she would give men who would offend her. She died on Aug 1, 1903, and was buried at Deadwood, SD, next to Wild Bill Hickock.

CALIFORNIA DRY BEAN FESTIVAL. Aug 1–2. Tracy, CA. 12th annual. To promote the California dry bean industry, to raise funds for nonprofit organizations and to highlight the City of Tracy. Est attendance: 50,000. For info: Leslie Hamrick, Coord, c/o Tracy Chamber of Commerce, California Dry Bean Festival, 223 E 10th St, Tracy, CA 95376. Phone: (209) 835-2131. Fax: (209) 833-9526.

CANADA: ICELANDIC FESTIVAL OF MANITOBA (ISLENDINGADAGURINN). Aug 1–3. Gimli, Manitoba. Celebration of Gimli's Icelandic heritage features parade, poetry, music and traditional Icelandic cuisine. Est attendance: 30,000. For info: Lenore Good, Icelandic Festival of Manitoba, 79 McNulty Crescent, Winnipeg, Manitoba, Canada R2M 5J4. Phone: (204) 257-2765.

CANADA: MOOSE MOUSE DAYS. Aug 1–4. Sicamous, British Columbia. Parade, baseball, crafts, dance, mud bog and many other festival events. For info: Doreen Favel, Sicamous Chamber of Commerce, PO Box 346, Sicamous, BC, Canada V0E 2V0. Phone: (604) 836-3313. Fax: (604) 836-4368. Email: sicamous.chamber@resont.com.

CANADA: YORKTON THRESHERMEN'S SHOW AND SENIORS' FESTIVAL. Aug 1–2. Western Development Museum grounds, Yorkton, Saskatchewan. Old-fashioned entertainment, arts and crafts; demonstrations of steam gas engines, threshing, stoking, bag tying, clay-oven baking and antique cars. Est attendance: 6,000. For info: (306) 783-8361 or Tourism Saskatchewan, 500–1900 Albert St, Regina, Sask, Canada S4P 4L9. Phone: (800) 667-7191 or (306) 787-2328.
Email: travel.info@sasktourism.sk.ca.
WWW: http://www.sasktourism.com

CHEROKEE DAYS OF RECOGNITION. Aug 1–2. Red Clay State Park, Cleveland, TN. Traditional and contemporary Cherokee dances, storytelling, Native American food, Cherokee arts and crafts and the annual blowgun contest are featured. Annually, the first weekend in August. Sponsor: Tennessee Dept of Environment and Conservation. Est attendance: 15,000. For info: Lois I. Osborne, Park Mgr, Red Clay State Hist Park, 1140 Red Clay Park Rd SW, Cleveland, TN 37311. Phone: (423) 478-0339.

CHILDREN'S LAWN PARTY. Aug 1 (Aug 2 rain date). Roseland Cottage, Bowen House, Woodstock, CT. Popular Victorian games from the 1800s such as hoop rolling, games of graces, ninepins and bilboquet along with croquet, spinning tops, marbles and jacks will delight young and old. The original peanut hunt will also be held and a hat-making table for children to create their own hats to wear during the day will be available. Roseland Cottage is owned and operated by the Society for the Preservation of New England Antiquities and is a National Historic Landmark. Annually, the first Saturday in August. Est attendance: 200. For info: Pam Russo, Site Mgr, Roseland Cottage, PO Box 186, Woodstock, CT 06281. Phone: (860) 928-4074. Fax: (860) 963-2208.

CHILDREN'S VISION AND LEARNING MONTH. Aug 1–31. A monthlong campaign encouraging parents to have their children's vision examined by an eye-care professional prior to the start of the new school year. For info: Huck Roberts, Exec Dir, American Fdtn for Vision Awareness (AFVA), 243 N Lindbergh Blvd, St. Louis, MO 63141. Phone: (800) 927-AFVA. Fax: (314) 991-4101. Email: afva@aol.com.

CROP DAY. Aug 1. Greenwood, MS. Features cotton row tours—remembering when cotton was king. Civil War encampment, cannon shoot, Rubber Duck Race, volleyball and in-line hockey tournaments and a basketball shoot. Also arts and crafts sales, children's activities, entertainment and barbecue. Annually, the first Saturday in August. Est attendance: 15,000. For info: Janice Moor, Exec VP, Greenwood-Leflore County Chamber of Commerce, PO Box 848, Greenwood, MS 38935-0849. Phone: (601) 453-4152. Fax: (601) 453-8003.

DIARY OF ANNE FRANK: THE LAST ENTRY: ANNIVERSARY. Aug 1. To escape deportation to concentration camps, the Jewish family of Otto Frank hid for two years in the back-room office and warehouse of his food products business in Amsterdam. Gentile friends smuggled in food and other supplies during their confinement. Thirteen-year-old Anne Frank, who kept a journal during the time of their hiding, penned her last entry in the diary Aug 1, 1944: "[I] keep on trying to find a way of becoming what I would like to be, and what I could be, if . . . there weren't any other people living in the world." Three days later (Aug 4, 1944) Grüne Polizei raided the "Secret Annex" where the Frank family was hidden. Anne and her sister were sent to Bergen-Belsen concentration camp where Anne died at age 15, two months before the liberation of Holland. Young Anne's diary, later found in the family's hiding place, has been translated into 30 languages and has become a symbol of the indomitable strength of the human spirit.

EMANCIPATION OF 500: ANNIVERSARY. Aug 1. Virginia planter Robert Carter III confounded his family and friends by filing a deed of emancipation for his 500 slaves Aug 1, 1791. One of the wealthiest men in the state, Carter owned 60,000 acres over 18 plantations. The deed included the following words: "I have for some time past been convinced that to retain them in Slavery is contrary to the true principles of Religion and Justice and therefore it is my duty to manumit them." The document established a schedule by which 15 slaves would be freed each Jan 1, over a 21-year period, plus slave children would be freed at age 18 for females and 21 for males. It is believed this was the largest act of emancipation in US history and predated the Emancipation Proclamation by 70 years.

ENGLAND: SKANDIA LIFE COWES WEEK. Aug 1–8. Cowes, Isle of Wight. Yachting festival covering all classes of yacht racing. Est attendance: 14,000. For info: Cowes Week Organizers, Cowes Combined Clubs, 18 Bath Rd, Cowes, Isle of Wight, England PO31 7QN. Phone: (44) (198) 329-5744. Fax: (44) (198) 329-5329.

FESTIVAL OF NATIONS. Aug 1–8. Red Lodge, MT. A nine-day extravaganza. All events are free, following the philosophy of festival founders that the festival should be a fun, educational experience including information on cooking, crafts, customs, dances and languages. Est attendance: 15,000. For info: Joan Cline, Exec Secy, Red Lodge Chamber of Commerce, PO Box 988, Red Lodge, MT 59068. Phone: (406) 446-1718.

FORGOTTEN PAST STEAM AND GAS SHOW. Aug 1–2. Benton, KY. Antique steam and gas engines, fully preserved and working. Crafts, flea market and swap meet. Annually, the first Saturday and Sunday in August. For info: Bill Luebker, 3390 US Hwy 68 E, Benton, KY 42025. Phone: (502) 527-9244.

GARCIA, JERRY: BIRTH ANNIVERSARY. Aug 1, 1942. Jerome John Garcia was born at San Francisco, CA. Country, bluegrass and folk musician, a guitar player of remarkable ability, Garcia was the leading force behind the legendary Grateful Dead, the band that sustained a veritable industry for its legion of followers. He died Aug 9, 1995, at Forest Knolls, CA, ending a musical career that spanned more than three decades.

August 1998

S	M	T	W	T	F	S
						1
2	3	4	5	6	7	8
9	10	11	12	13	14	15
16	17	18	19	20	21	22
23	24	25	26	27	28	29
30	31					

HALEAKALA NATIONAL PARK AUTHORIZED: ANNIVERSARY. Aug 1, 1916. Summit of a volcano on Maui in the Hawaiian Islands was authorized as a part of Hawaii Natl Park. For further park info: Haleakala Natl Park, PO Box 369, Makawao, HI 96768.

HERB AND PLANT DAY. Aug 1. Somerset, PA. Features the historic uses of plants and herbs as food and medicines. Also a farmer's market with local produce. For info: Mark Ware, Somerset Historical Center, 10649 Somerset Pike, Somerset, PA 15501. Phone: (814) 445-6077.

HILL, JAMES: BIRTH ANNIVERSARY. Aug 1, 1916. British film director James Hill was born at Jeffersonville, IN. He is best known for his film *Born Free* (1966), but he also won an Academy Award for *Giuseppina* (1961). He died on Oct 9, 1994, at London, England.

HOME OF THE HAMBURGER CELEBRATION. Aug 1. Seymour, WI. Giant parade, Bun Run, live music, kid's games and entertainment, Hamburger Meet. Est attendance: 10,000. For info: Home of the Hamburger Inc, PO Box 173, Seymour, WI 54165. Phone: (414) 833-9522 or (414) 833-2663.

INTERNATIONAL CLOWN WEEK. Aug 1–7. To call public attention to the charitable activities of clowns and the wholesome entertainment they provide. Annually, Aug 1–7. Est attendance: 2,500. For info: Jim Roberts, Chair, Intl Clown Week, Clowns of America Intl Inc, 532 W Dixie, Frankun, KY 42701. Phone: (502) 769-3188.

JAMAICA: ABOLITION OF SLAVERY. Aug 1, 1838. National day. Spanish settlers introduced the slave trade into Jamaica in 1509 and sugar cane in 1640. Slavery continued until Aug 1, 1838, when it was abolished.

JONATHAN HAGER FRONTIER CRAFT DAYS. Aug 1–2. Jonathan Hager House, City Park, Hagerstown, MD. Featuring dozens of demonstrating craftsmen, great bluegrass music and great food. Annually, the first weekend in August. Est attendance: 10,000. For info: John Nelson, Jonathan Hager House and Museum, 110 Key St, Hagerstown, MD 21740. Phone: (301) 739-8393.

KEY, FRANCIS SCOTT: BIRTH ANNIVERSARY. Aug 1, 1779. American attorney, social worker, poet and author of the US national anthem. Key was on shipboard off Baltimore during the British bombardment of Fort McHenry on the night of Sept 13–14, 1814. Thrilled to see the American flag still flying over the fort at daybreak, Key wrote the poem "The Star-Spangled Banner." Born at Frederick County, MD, he died at Baltimore, MD, on Jan 11, 1843.

LEAGUE OF NEW HAMPSHIRE CRAFTSMEN ANNUAL CRAFTMEN'S FAIR. Aug 1–9. Mt Sunapee State Park, Newbury, NH. "America's oldest crafts fair"—65th annual fair. More than 170 crafts booths, Living with Crafts exhibit, CraftWear exhibit, New Hampshire Art Assn exhibit, daily performing arts, children's activities and more. Admission: $6 adults, $4 seniors. Est attendance: 50,000. For info: League of NH Craftsmen, 205 N Main St, Concord, NH 03301. Phone: (603) 224-3375. Fax: (603) 225-8452.

LUGHNASADH. Aug 1. (Also called August Eve, Lammas Eve, Lady Day Eve and Feast of Bread.) One of the "Greater Sabbats" during the Wiccan year, Lughnasadh marks the first harvest. Annually, Aug 1.

MEDIC ALERT AWARENESS MONTH. Aug 1–31. To remind the public of the positive steps they can take for their own peace of mind and to enhance the effectiveness of emergency care. For info: Public Relations Dept, Medic Alert, 2323 Colorado Ave, Turlock, CA 95381. Phone: (800) 825-3785 or (209) 669-2403. Fax: (209) 669-2457. Email: roth_david@medicalert.org.

MELVILLE, HERMAN: BIRTH ANNIVERSARY. Aug 1. American author, best known for his novel *Moby Dick*, born at New York, NY, Aug 1, 1819. Died Sept 28, 1891.

MITCHELL, MARIA: BIRTH ANNIVERSARY. Aug 1, 1818. An interest in her father's hobby and an ability for mathematics resulted in Maria Mitchell's becoming the first female professional astronomer. In 1847, while assisting her father in a survey of the sky for the US Coast Guard, Mitchell discovered a new comet and determined its orbit. She received many honors because of this, including being elected to the American Academy of Arts and Sciences—its first woman. Mitchell joined the staff at Vassar Female College in 1865—the first US female professor of astronomy—and in 1873 was a cofounder of the Association for the Advancement of Women. Born at Nantucket, MA, Mitchell died June 28, 1889, at Lynn, MA.

NATIONAL CERTIFIED REGISTERED NURSE ANESTHETIST WEEK. Aug 1–7. To provide recognition for the nation's certified registered nurse anesthetists (CRNAs) who administer more than 65% of the anesthesia in the US each year. For info: Betty Colitti-Stuffers, PR Dir, Amer Assn of Nurse Anesthetists, 222 S Prospect, Park Ridge, IL 60068. Phone: (847) 692-7050. Fax: (847) 692-6968. WWW: http://www.aana.com

NATIONAL CZECHOSLOVAKIAN FESTIVAL. Aug 1–2. Wilber, NE. Festival to promote preservation of Czech culture, foods, traditions—accordion, polka and Czech band music, parades, national queen contest, museum, art show, Czech dinners, programs, contests, fellowship, reunions. Annually, the first weekend in August. Cosponsored by Nebraska Czechs of Wilber. Est attendance: 40,000. For info: Wilber Chamber of Commerce, PO Box 1164, Wilber, NE 68465. Phone: (402) 821-2732 or (888) 4-WILBER.

NATIONAL HAIR-ITAGE MONTH. Aug 1–31. Hail hair! This month salutes all those involved in the beauty/hair care industry. Indulge yourself this month and explore a whole new you. Curl. Color. Trim and texturize. Take "before and after" photos. Only your hairdresser knows for sure! For more info, send $2 to cover the cost of photocopying and postage to Adrienne Sioux Koopersmith, 1437 W Rosemont, 1W, Chicago, IL 60660-1319. Phone: (773) 743-5341. Fax: (773) 743-5395.
Email: kooper@interaccess.com.

NATIONAL MUSTARD DAY. Aug 1. Mustard lovers across the nation pay tribute to the condiment of kings—and the king of condiments—by lathering their favorite spread on hot dogs, pretzels, licorice and even ice cream (an acquired taste)! The Mount Horeb Mustard Museum ("If you collect us, they will come") contains the world's largest collection of prepared mustards and mustard memorabilia. Annually, the first Saturday in August. Est attendance: 1,000. For info: Barry M. Levenson, Curator, The Mount Horeb Mustard Museum, 109 E Main St, Mount Horeb, WI 53572. Phone: (608) 437-3986. Fax: (608) 437-4018. Email: curator@mustardweb.com. WWW: http://www.mustardweb.com

OAK RIDGE ATOMIC PLANT BEGUN: 55th ANNIVERSARY. Aug 1, 1943. Ground was broken in Oak Ridge, TN, for the first plant built to manufacture the uranium 235 needed to build an atomic bomb. The plant was largely completed by July of 1944 at a final cost of $280 million. By August 1945 the total cost for development of the A-bomb ran to $1 billion.

OKLAHOMA ALL-NIGHT SINGING. Aug 1. Veterans' Memorial Park, Konawa, OK. Famous quartets, trios, duets and soloists from across the nation entertain and share their style of gospel song in this 35th annual gospel music event. An Oklahoma summer tradition. Campers begin arriving on Thursday and Friday. The park is usually filled by noon on Saturday for the evening presentation that concludes Gospel Music Festival. Food available; free parking and admission. Bring lawn chairs for this all-night, outdoor event. Est attendance: 15,000. For info: Oklahoma All-Night Gospel Singing Assn, PO Box 55, Konawa, OK 74849. Phone: (405) 759-3129.

OWENSBORO SHOW. Aug 1–2. Owensboro, KY. To promote the art and culture of prehistoric Indians and to display outstanding collections of relics; buying, selling and trading. Est attendance: 3,000. For info: Kathy Gerber, Box 7, Tell City, IN 47586-0007. Phone: (812) 547-4881. Fax: (812) 547-2525. Email: agerber@psci.net.

PENNSYLVANIA RENAISSANCE FAIRE. Aug 1–Oct 11. Manheim, PA. Recreation of 16th-century Elizabethan village. Lords and ladies, mongers, merchants, jousting, human chess match, medieval foods and crafts. Fair takes place Saturday–Monday from Aug 1 until Labor Day; Saturdays and Sundays only thereafter. Est attendance: 100,000. For info: Michelle Cunningham, Mgr of PR, Mount Hope Estate and Winery, PO Box 685, Cornwall, PA 17016. Phone: (717) 665-7021. Fax: (717) 664-3466. Email: prfscrib@postoffice.net.
WWW: http://www.parenaissancefaire.com/

PITTSBURGH THREE RIVERS REGATTA. Aug 1–2 (also Aug 6–9). Pittsburgh, PA. The country's largest inland river regatta featuring air, land and water events. Est attendance: 1,500,000. For info: Ida D'Errico, 530 William Penn Pl, Pittsburgh, PA 15219. Phone: (412) 261-7055. Fax: (412) 261-4009.

PRESIDENT'S ENVIRONMENTAL YOUTH AWARD NATIONAL COMPETITION. Aug 1–July 31, 1999. Young people in all 50 states are invited to participate in the President's Environmental Youth Awards program, which offers them, individually and collectively, an opportunity to become an environmental force with their community. The program encourages individuals, school classes, schools, summer camps and youth organizations to promote local environmental awareness and positive community involvement. For info: Doris Gillespie, Environmental Education Coord, US Environmental Protection Agency, 401 M St, #1707, Washington, DC 20460. Phone: (202) 260-8749. Fax: (202) 260-0790.

QUILT SHOW. Aug 1–25. Woodstock, VT. A juried showing of quilts made by Windsor County quilters, displayed with selected 19th-century Vermont quilts. Daily quilting demonstrations and activities. Est attendance: 9,700. For info: Deborah Bulissa, Exec Asst, Billings Farm and Museum, PO Box 489, Woodstock, VT 05091. Phone: (802) 457-2355. Fax: (802) 457-4663. Email: billings.farm@valley.net.

ROMANCE AWARENESS MONTH. Aug 1–31. To educate couples about how romance can improve their relationships. To encourage couples to display romance throughout the year rather than just on Valentine's Day. Free tip sheets are available. For info: Eileen Buchheim, Founder, Celebrate Romance, 18 Altimira-West Tower, Coto De Caza, CA 92679. Phone: (714) 459-7620. To arrange media interviews, call Suzanne Friendly at (714) 459-7621.

SAWYER TRIATHLON XV. Aug 1. Tom Sawyer State Park, Louisville, KY. Participants swim ½ mile, bicycle 28 miles and run 5K cross-country. Est attendance: 500. For info: Tim Curtis, Recreation Dir, E.P. Tom Sawyer Park, 3000 Freys Hill Rd, Louisville, KY 40241-2172. Phone: (502) 426-8950.

SIMPLIFY YOUR LIFE WEEK. Aug 1–7. A week to encourage people to simplify their lives and reduce clutter, thereby reducing stress and acquiring a happier and more peaceful lifestyle. For information about this worldwide organization and 100 ways to simplify one's life, send $3 to cover expenses of printing, handling and postage. For info: Dr. Stanley Drake, Pres, Intl Soc of Friendship and Good Will (ISFGW), 412 Cherry Hills Dr, Bakersfield, CA 93309-2866.

SOUTHEASTERN SOUTH DAKOTA THRESHING SHOW. Aug 1–2. Lennox, SD. Threshing, corn shelling, hay bailing, stone grinding flour, parade, tractor pull and flea market. Est attendance: 3,500. For info: Threshing Assn, PO Box 356, Lennox, SD 57039. Phone: (605) 647-5688.

SPINAL MUSCULAR ATROPHY AWARENESS MONTH. Aug 1–31. To promote awareness and prevention of the deterioration of the muscles surrounding the spinal area. For info: Families of Spinal Muscular Atrophy, PO Box 196, Libertyville, IL 60048. Phone: (800) 886-1762 or (847) 367-7620.

SWITZERLAND: NATIONAL DAY. Aug 1. Anniversary of the founding of the Swiss Confederation. Commemorates a pact made in 1291. Parades, patriotic gatherings, bonfires and fireworks. Young citizens' coming-of-age ceremonies. Observed since 600th anniversary of Swiss Confederation was celebrated in 1891.

TALL TIMBER DAYS FESTIVAL. Aug 1–2. Grand Rapids, MN. Festival features the Sheer Brothers Lumberjack Show, chainsaw carvers, arts and crafts, Applecords Quartet, competitions, YMCA run, Native American dance and storytelling, canoeing and bed racing. Families welcome. Annually, the first full weekend in August. Est attendance: 30,000. For info: Tall Timber Days, PO Box 134, Grand Rapids, MN 55744. Phone: (218) 326-5618. Fax: (218) 326-5618.

August 1998

S	M	T	W	T	F	S
						1
2	3	4	5	6	7	8
9	10	11	12	13	14	15
16	17	18	19	20	21	22
23	24	25	26	27	28	29
30	31					

TRINIDAD AND TOBAGO: EMANCIPATION DAY. Aug 1. Public holiday.

UPTOWN ART FAIR. Aug 1–2. Minneapolis, MN. The midwest's largest outdoor juried arts and crafts festival featuring 525 national artists, food and beverage booths, a children's art activities booth and entertainment. Est attendance: 350,000. For info: Uptown Art Fair, 3013 Holmes Ave South, Minneapolis, MN 55408. Phone: (612) 823-4581.

US CUSTOMS: ANNIVERSARY. Aug 1. "The first US customs officers began to collect the revenue and enforce the Tariff Act of July 4, 1789, on Aug 1, 1789. Since then, the customhouse and the customs officer have stood as symbols of national pride and sovereignty at ports of entry along the land and sea borders of our country." (From Presidential Proclamation 4306.)

VIRGINIA STATE HORSE SHOW—QUARTER HORSE DIVISION. Aug 1–2. Fairgrounds on Strawberry Hill, Richmond, VA. Open, amateur, novice and youth competition for registered quarter horses. Est attendance: 1,000. For info: Sue Mullins, Equine Dir, PO Box 26805, Richmond, VA 23261. Phone: (804) 228-3238. Fax: (804) 228-3252.

WALES: ROYAL NATIONAL EISTEDDFOD. Aug 1–8. Bridgend, South Wales. A cultural event with competitive festivals of music, drama, literature, arts and crafts. All events conducted in Welsh with simultaneous translation into English available. Est attendance: 160,000. For info: Royal Natl Eisteddfod, Cardiff, South Glamorgan, 40 Parc Ty Glas, Llanshien, Wales CF4 5WU. Phone: (44) (122) 276-3777. Fax: (44) (122) 226-3737. WWW: http://www.eisteddfod.org.uk

WARSAW UPRISING: ANNIVERSARY. Aug 1, 1944. Having received radio reports from Moscow promising aid from the Red Army, the Polish Home Army rose up against the Nazi oppressors. At 5 PM thousands of windows were thrown open and Polish patriots, 40,000 strong, began shooting at German soldiers in the streets. The Germans responded by throwing eight divisions into the battle. Despite appeals from the London-based Polish government-in-exile, no assistance was forthcoming from the Allies, and after two months of horrific fighting the rebellion was quashed.

WHITE RIVER WATER CARNIVAL. Aug 1–8. Batesville, AR. Public receptions, Miss White River pageant, bass classic tournament, four-mile run, four-ball golf tournament, arts, crafts, parade, children's activities, entertainment in the park, ski show. Est attendance: 9,000. For info: Chamber of Commerce, 409 Vine, Batesville, AR 72501. Phone: (870) 793-2378. Fax: (870) 793-3061. Email: BACofC@intellinet.com.
WWW: http://batesville.dina.org

WORLD BREASTFEEDING WEEK. Aug 1–7. Commemoration of signing of Innocenti Declaration. Includes a World Walk for Breastfeeding. Breastfeeding advocates, health care professionals and social service agencies focus attention on the importance and benefits of breastfeeding. Fairs, picnics, fund-raising and government proclamations highlight the week. Annually, the first week of August. For info: La Leche League Intl, 1400 N Meacham, Schaumburg, IL 60168-4079. Phone: (847) 519-7730 or (800) LA LECHE. Fax: (847) 519-0035.
WWW: http://www.lalecheleague.org/

WYATT EARP WESTERN DAY. Aug 1. Monmouth, IL. "OK Corral Reenactment" and "Life of Wyatt Earp" show 2 PM to 3 PM. Birthplace tours 11 AM to 4 PM, Pioneer Cemetery tours and music. Est attendance: 250. For info: Wyatt Earp Birthplace, Historic House Museum, Office: 1020 E Detroit Ave, Monmouth, IL 61462. Phone: (309) 734-6419 or Chamber of Commerce (309) 734-3181. Fax: (309) 734-6419.

BIRTHDAYS TODAY

Tempestt Bledsoe, 25, talk-show host, actress ("Tempestt," "The Cosby Show"), born Chicago, IL, Aug 1, 1973.

Robert Cray, 45, singer, guitarist, songwriter, born Columbus, GA, Aug 1, 1953.

Alfonse M. D'Amato, 61, US Senator (R, New York), born Brooklyn, NY, Aug 1, 1937.

Dom DeLuise, 65, comedian, actor, born Brooklyn, NY, Aug 1, 1933.

Giancarlo Giannini, 56, actor (*Swept Away . . . By an Unusual Destiny in the Blue Sea of August, Seven Beauties*), born Spezia, Italy, Aug 1, 1942.

Arthur Hill, 76, actor (*Harper, The Andromeda Strain,* "Owen Marshall"), born Melfort, Saskatchewan, Canada, Aug 1, 1922.

Yves Saint Laurent, 62, fashion designer, born Oran, Algeria, Aug 1, 1936.

Tom Wilson, 67, cartoonist ("Ziggy"), born Grant Town, WV, Aug 1, 1931.

AUGUST 2 — SUNDAY

Day 214 — 151 Remaining

ALBERT EINSTEIN'S ATOMIC BOMB LETTER: ANNIVERSARY. Aug 2. Albert Einstein, world-famous scientist, a refugee from Nazi Germany, wrote a letter to US President Franklin D. Roosevelt, Aug 2, 1939, first mentioning a possible "new phenomenon . . . chain reactions . . . vast amounts of power" and "the construction of bombs." "A single bomb of this type," he wrote, "carried by boat and exploded in a port, might very well destroy the whole port together with some of the surrounding territory." An historic letter that marked the beginning of atomic weaponry. Six years and four days later, Aug 6, 1945, the Japanese port of Hiroshima was destroyed by the first atomic bombing of a populated place.

AMERICAN FAMILY DAY. Aug 2. Observed on the first Sunday in August in Arizona. The observance date is designated by statute.

BALDWIN, JAMES ARTHUR: BIRTH ANNIVERSARY. Aug 2, 1924. Black American author noted for descriptions of black life in the US. Born at New York, NY. His best-known work, *Go Tell It on the Mountain*, was published in 1953. Died at Saint Paul-de-Vence, France, Nov 30, 1987.

CANADA: CANMORE HERITAGE DAY FOLK FESTIVAL. Aug 2–3. Centennial Park, Canmore, Alberta. 20th annual. Alberta's longest-running folk festival. Featuring food booths, entertainment, workshops and pancake breakfast. Est attendance: 6,500. For info: Beate Hanna-West, Office Administrator, Canmore Folk Festival, PO Box 8098, Canmore, Alberta, Canada K0L 1C0. Phone: (403) 678-3561. Fax: (403) 678-3561.

CANADA: FOLKLORAMA—CANADA'S CULTURAL CELEBRATION. Aug 2–15. Winnipeg, Manitoba. More than 35 pavilions representing various cultures offer traditionally prepared cuisine, exhilarating entertainment and captivating cultural displays for 14 prairie summer nights. Folklorama is the largest multicultural celebration of its kind in the world and has been named the #1 Event in Canada by the American Bus Assn. Est attendance: 500,000. For info: Claudette Leclerc, Exec Dir, Folklorama, 300—180 King St, Winnipeg, Man, Canada R3B 3G8. Phone: (204) 982-6210 or (800) 665-0234. Fax: (204) 943-1956. Email: information@Folklorama.ca.
WWW: http://www.folklorama.ca

CHERRY RIVER FESTIVAL. Aug 2–9. Richwood, WV. A landlocked Navy of Admirals parades as a climax to this weeklong world-famous event which features pageants, contests, athletic events, parades and dances. Est attendance: 4,000. For info: Maxine Corbett, Board of Directors, Cherry River Festival, Box 482, Richwood, WV 26261. Phone: (304) 846-6790.

COLUMBUS SAILING ANNIVERSARY ON THE SANTA MARIA. Aug 2. Battelle Park, Columbus, OH. Special observances for the anniversary of Christopher Columbus sailing from Spain in search of India held aboard the *Santa Maria*, the only full-size replica of Columbus's flagship on permanent display in North America. For info: Columbus Santa Maria, 109 N Front St, Columbus, OH 43215. Phone: (614) 645-8760. Fax: (614) 645-8748. WWW: http://www.SantaMaria.org

☆ ☆ ☆

DECLARATION OF INDEPENDENCE: OFFICIAL SIGNING ANNIVERSARY. Aug 2. Contrary to widespread misconceptions, the 56 signers did not sign as a group and did not do so on July 4, 1776. John Hancock and Charles Thompson signed only draft copies that day, the official day the Declaration was adopted by Congress. The signing of the official declaration occurred on Aug 2, 1776, when 50 men probably took part. Later that year, five more apparently signed separately and one added his name in a subsequent year. (From "Signers of the Declaration . . ." US Dept of the Interior, 1975.) See also: "Declaration of Independence" (July 4).

FINLAND: LAHTI ORGAN FESTIVAL. Aug 2–9. Lahti. Annual festival emphasizing organ music. Also, choirs, orchestras, instrumental groups and solo artists. Plus master classes, seminars and panel discussions. Est attendance: 15,000. For info: Finnish Tourist Board, 655 Third Ave, New York, NY 10017. Phone: (212) 949-2333 or (358) (3) 782-3184. Fax: (358) (3) 783-2190.

FRIENDSHIP DAY. Aug 2. A day to heed the advice of 18th-century English philosopher Samuel Johnson: "A man should keep his friendships in constant repair." A time to acknowledge old friends and celebrate new ones. Please enclose SASE if you write in. For info: Linda Gorin, The Best To You, 7920 Silverton Ave #F, San Diego, CA 92126.

HARDING, WARREN GAMALIEL: 75th DEATH ANNIVERSARY. Aug 2, 1923. The 29th president of the US, and the first to have a radio, was born at Corsica, OH, Nov 2, 1865. His term of office: Mar 4, 1921–Aug 2, 1923 (died in office). His undistinguished administration was tainted by the Teapot Dome scandal, and his sudden death while on a western speaking tour (San Francisco, CA, Aug 2, 1923) prompted many dark rumors. In 1927, the book *The President's Daughter* by Nan Britton, dedicated "to all unwedded mothers, and to their innocent children whose fathers are usually not known to the world," added doubts about morality in high political places.

IRAQ INVADES KUWAIT: ANNIVERSARY. Aug 2, 1990. On orders of President Saddam Hussein, the Iraqi army invaded Kuwait. Hussein claimed that Kuwait presented a serious threat to Iraq's economic existence by overproducing oil and driving prices down on the world market. After conquering the capital, Kuwait City, Hussein installed a military government in Kuwait, prior to annexing it to Iraq on the claim that Kuwait was historically part of Iraq. This led to the 100-hour war against Iraq, Operation Desert Storm.

ITALY: JOUST OF THE QUINTANA. Aug 2. Ascoli/Piceno. The first Sunday in August is set aside for the Torneo della Quintana, an historical pageant with 15th-century costumes.

L'ENFANT, PIERRE CHARLES: BIRTH ANNIVERSARY. Aug 2. The architect, engineer and Revolutionary War officer who designed the plan for the city of Washington, DC, Pierre Charles L'Enfant was born at Paris, France, on Aug 2, 1754. He died at Prince Georges County, MD, on June 14, 1825.

LOY, MYRNA (WILLIAMS): BIRTH ANNIVERSARY. Aug 2, 1905. Actress known for her film roles in the "Thin Man" series and for speaking out against the House Committee on Un-American Activities. Born near Helena, MT, and died at New York City on Dec 14, 1993.

MACEDONIA, FORMER YUGOSLAV REPUBLIC OF: NATIONAL DAY. Aug 2.

PROFESSIONAL SECRETARIES INTERNATIONAL: ANNUAL CONVENTION. Aug 2–5. Atlanta, GA. Est attendance: 2,000. For info: Dale Shuter, Conv Mgr, Professional Secretaries Intl–® The Assn for Office Professionals™, 10502 NW Ambassador Dr, PO Box 20404, Kansas City, MO 64195-0404. Phone: (816) 891-6600. Fax: (816) 891-9118.
Email: psihq@psi.org. WWW: http://www.gvi.net/psi

SAINT ELIAS DAY (ILLINDEN): 95th ANNIVERSARY OF MACEDONIAN UPRISING. Aug 2, 1903. Most sacred, honored and celebrated day of the Macedonian people. Anniversary of the uprising of Macedonians against Turkey. Turkish reprisals against the insurgents were ruthless, including the destruction of 105 villages and the execution of more than 1,700 noncombatants.

SISTERS' DAY. Aug 2. Celebrating the spirit of sisterhood—sisters nationwide show appreciation and give recognition to one another for the special relationship they share. Send a card, make a phone call, share memories, photos, flowers, candy, etc. Annually, the first Sunday in August each year. For info: Tricia Eleogram, 666 Hawthorne, Memphis, TN 38107. Phone: (901) 725-5190 or (901) 7550751. Fax: (901) 754-9923. Email: sistersday@aol.com.

TISHA B'AV OR FAST OF AB. Aug 2. Hebrew calendar date: Ab 9, 5758. Commemorates and mourns the destruction of the first and second Temples in Jerusalem (586 BC and AD 70).

VOLKSFEST. Aug 2. New Glarus, WI. Celebration of Swiss Independence Day. Annually, the first Sunday in August. Est attendance: 2,000. For info: Volksfest, Box 713, New Glarus, WI 53574. Phone: (608) 527-2095 or (800) 527-6838.

W.C. HANDY FESTIVAL. Aug 2–8. Florence, AL. A weeklong street-strutting, toe-tapping and hand-clapping celebration of the musical heritage of Florence native W.C. Handy—"the father of the blues"—culminating in a spectacular Saturday-evening concert. Also includes 5K DaDoo Run Run, Century Bike Ride, polo match and volleyball tournament. Est attendance: 150,000. For info: Nancy Gonce, Exec Dir, Music Preservation Soc, PO Box 1827, Florence, AL 35631. Phone: (205) 766-7642 or (800) 47-BLUES.

YUGOSLAVIA: SINJSKA ALKA. Aug 2. Near Split. Sinj spear-throwing chivalric contest, a game on horses, founded in 1715 to commemorate victory over Turkish army. Weapons and colorful costumes from the 18th century.

BIRTHDAYS TODAY

Joanna Cassidy, 54, actress ("Buffalo Bill," *Under Fire*), born Camden, NJ, Aug 2, 1944.

James Fallows, 49, journalist, editor (*US News & World Report*), born Philadelphia, PA, Aug 2, 1949.

Linda Sue Fratianne, 38, figure skater, born Los Angeles, CA, Aug 2, 1960.

Kathryn Harrold, 48, actress ("I'll Fly Away," "The Larry Sanders Show," *Modern Romance*), born Tazewell, VA, Aug 2, 1950.

Carroll O'Connor, 74, actor (*Marlowe*, "All in the Family," "In the Heat of the Night"), born New York, NY, Aug 2, 1924.

Peter O'Toole, 65, actor (*Lawrence of Arabia, Becket*), born Connemara, Ireland, Aug 2, 1933.

Beatrice Straight, 80, actress (Oscar for *Network*), born Old Westbury, NY, Aug 2, 1918.

August 1998

S	M	T	W	T	F	S
						1
2	3	4	5	6	7	8
9	10	11	12	13	14	15
16	17	18	19	20	21	22
23	24	25	26	27	28	29
30	31					

☆ ☆ ☆

AUGUST 3 — MONDAY

Day 215 — 150 Remaining

ANTIGUA AND BARBUDA: AUGUST MONDAY. Aug 3–4. The first Monday in August and the day following form the August Monday Public Holiday in Antigua and Barbuda.

ARMY NURSES PAY RAISE: ANNIVERSARY. Aug 3, 1861. Although it had been known from the time the Second Continental Congress authorized the Continental Army (June 14, 1775) that " . . . the sick suffered much for want of good female nurses. . . ." (General Washington had asked the Congress to authorize a matron and nurses), progress was slow. The pay of a nurse, originally $2 per month and one ration per day, was increased to $8 per month and one ration per day on Apr 7, 1777. Congress, 84 years later, authorized the Surgeon General to employ women as nurses for army hospitals at a salary of $12 per month plus one ration per day.

AUSTRALIA: PICNIC DAY. Aug 3. The first Monday in August is a bank holiday in New South Wales and Picnic Day in Northern Territory, Australia.

BAHAMAS: EMANCIPATION DAY. Aug 3. Public holiday in Bahamas. Annually, the first Monday in August.

CANADA: CHOCOLATE FESTIVAL. Aug 3–8. St. Stephen, New Brunswick. Events include chocolate meals, chocolate teas, chocolate-eating contests, "Choctail hour" and the ever-popular Ganong Chocolate Factory tours. (Tours must be booked in advance.) Est attendance: 5,000. For info: Mr Derek O'Brien, Chair, Chocolate Fest '98, PO Box 5002, St. Stephen, NB, Canada E3L 2X5. Phone: (506) 465-5616. Fax: (506) 465-5610.

CANADA: CIVIC HOLIDAY. Aug 3. The first Monday in August is observed as a holiday in seven of Canada's 10 provinces. Civic Holiday in Manitoba, New Brunswick, Northwest Territories, Ontario and Saskatchewan; British Columbia Day in British Columbia; and Heritage Day in Alberta.

COLORADO DAY. Aug 3. Colorado. Annually, the first Monday in August. Commemorates Admission Day, Aug 1, 1876, when Colorado became the 38th state.

COLUMBUS SAILS FOR THE NEW WORLD: ANNIVERSARY. Aug 3. Christopher Columbus, "Admiral of the Ocean Sea," set sail half an hour before sunrise from Palos, Spain, on Friday, Aug 3, 1492. With three ships, *Niña*, *Pinta* and *Santa Maria*, and a crew of 90, he sailed "for Cathay" but found instead a New World of the Americas, first landing at Guanahani (San Salvador Island in the Bahamas) on Oct 12. See also: "Columbus Day" (Oct 12).

DRUG ADDICTED BABY AWARENESS WEEK. Aug 3–9. A week to open our eyes to the reality and severity of a serious problem affecting hundreds of thousands of innocent babies. Adopt, become a foster parent, volunteer to hold/cuddle newborn addicted babies in local hospitals. For info: Barbara Harris, PO Box 74, Stanton, CA 90680. Phone: (714) 236-0217.

GRENADA: EMANCIPATION DAY. Aug 3. Grenada observes public holiday annually on the first Monday in August.

GUINEA-BISSAU: COLONIZATION MARTYR'S DAY. Aug 3. National holiday is observed.

ICELAND: SHOP AND OFFICE WORKERS' HOLIDAY. Aug 3. In Iceland an annual holiday for shop and office workers is observed on the first Monday in August.

JAMAICA: INDEPENDENCE DAY. Aug 3. National holiday observing achievement of Jamaican independence on Aug 6, 1962. Annually, the first Monday in August.

KELLY, GENE: BIRTH ANNIVERSARY. Aug 3, 1912. Actor, dancer born at Pittsburgh, PA. His movies included *Singin' in the Rain* and *American in Paris*. Kelly died at Beverly Hills, CA, Feb 2, 1996.

KUHN, MARGARET (MAGGIE): BIRTH ANNIVERSARY. Aug 3, 1905. When she was forced into retirement because she'd reached the age of 65, Maggie Kuhn founded the Gray Panthers organization to fight age discrimination. Subsequently she waged a battle that resulted in mandatory retirement being banned. Born at Buffalo, NY, Kuhn died Apr 22, 1995, at Philadelphia, PA.

NATIONAL BARGAIN HUNTING WEEK. Aug 3–9. Founded by Debbie Keri-Brown, author of two books on bargain hunting. The week is a time when businesses and shoppers can celebrate the thrill of the hunt for those bargains and the triumph of the "find." This can be accomplished through their own personal celebrations, sales and other special ways of saying, "I am proud to be a bargain hunter" or "This deal's for you." For a free listing of ways to celebrate, enclose a self-addressed, stamped envelope with your request or visit the website. For info: Debbie Keri-Brown, 959 Harborview Dr, Westerville, OH 43081. WWW: http://www.angelfire.com/free/BARGAINS.html

NATIONAL SMILE WEEK. Aug 3–9. "Share a smile and it will come back to you, bringing happiness to you and the giver." Annually, the first Monday in August through the following Sunday. For info: Heloise, Newspaper Columnist, Box 795000, San Antonio, TX 78279. Fax: (210) 435-6473.
Email: heloise@cis.compuserve.com.
WWW: http://www.heloise.com

"PRIMETIME LIVE" TV PREMIERE: ANNIVERSARY. Aug 3, 1989. Sam Donaldson and Diane Sawyer host this magazine show that features investigative and consumer reports as well as human interest stories.

PSYCHIC WEEK. Aug 3–7. To utilize the power of the psyche to bring peace, find lost individuals and concentrate "psychic power" on beneficial causes. Annually, the first week in August (Monday–Friday). [Created by the late Richard R. Falk.]

PYLE, ERNEST TAYLOR: BIRTH ANNIVERSARY. Aug 3, 1900. Ernie Pyle was born at Dana, IN, and began his career in journalism in 1923. After serving as managing editor of the Washington *Daily News*, he returned to his first journalistic love of working as a roving reporter in 1935. His column was syndicated by nearly 200 newspapers and often focused on figures behind the news. His reports of the bombing of London in 1940 and subsequent reports from Africa, Sicily, Italy and France earned him a Pulitzer Prize in 1944. He was killed by machine-gun fire at the Pacific island of Ie Shima Apr 18, 1945.

SANTA CRUZ BEACH BOARDWALK LOOFF CAROUSEL: ANNIVERSARY. Aug 3. Danish woodcarver Charles I.D. Looff delivered the classic carousel on Aug 3, 1911. A furniture-maker by trade, Looff began carving carousel animals as a hobby after immigrating to America. His first carousel was installed at Coney Island in New York in 1875. The Boardwalk carousel features jeweled horses and a 342-pipe Ruth band organ built in 1894. The carousel and the park's Giant Dipper roller coaster were designated National Historic Landmarks by the US National Park Service in June of 1987.

SCOPES, JOHN T.: BIRTH ANNIVERSARY. Aug 3. Central figure in a cause célèbre (the "Scopes Trial" or the "Monkey Trial"), John Thomas Scopes was born Aug 3, 1900, at Paducah, KY. An obscure 24-year-old schoolteacher at the Dayton, TN, high school in 1925, he became the focus of world attention. Scopes never uttered a word at his trial, which was a contest between two of America's best-known lawyers (William Jennings Bryan and Clarence Darrow). The trial, July 10–21, 1925, resulted in Scopes's conviction. He was fined $100 "for teaching evolution" in Tennessee. The verdict was upset on a technicality, and the statute he was accused of breaching was repealed in 1967. Scopes died at Shreveport, LA, Oct 21, 1970.

STURGIS RALLY AND RACES. Aug 3–9. Sturgis, SD. The granddaddy of all motorcycle rallies and races. For 58 years the small community of Sturgis has welcomed motorcycle enthusiasts from around the world to a week of varied cycle racing, tours of the beautiful Black Hills, old and new cycles at the National Motorcycle Museum, trade shows and thousands of bikes on display. Annually, beginning the Monday after the first full weekend in August. Est attendance: 215,000. For info: Sturgis Rally & Races, Inc, PO Box 189, Sturgis, SD 57785. Phone: (605) 347-6570. Fax: (605) 347-3245. Email: srr@rally.sturgis.sd.us. WWW: http://www.rally.sturgis.sd.us

TUNISIA: HABIB BOURGUIBA BIRTH ANNIVERSARY. Aug 3, 1902. Public holiday commemorating the birth of Tunisia's first elected president. Bourguiba was elected twice, then made president for life, but was forced out on Nov 6, 1987.

WORLD FOOTBAG CHAMPIONSHIPS. Aug 3–9. Denver, CO. Seven-day sports event spotlights competition of foot-skills—the Super Bowl of footbag! Now in its 19th year, it attracts the world's top footbag competitors from the US and six other countries. Prize money exceeds $10,000. Sponsors: Mattel Sports, Adidas, Sipa Sipa Footbags and The World Footbag Association. Est attendance: 3,000. For info: Bruce Guettich, Dir, World Footbag Assn, PO Box 775208, Steamboat Springs, CO 80477. Phone: (800) 878-8797. Fax: (970) 870-2846.
Email: wfa@worldfootbag.com.
WWW: http://www.worldfootbag.com

ZAMBIA: YOUTH DAY. Aug 3. First Monday in August. National holiday. Youth activities are order of the day. Focal point is Lusaka's Independence Stadium.

BIRTHDAYS TODAY

Tony Bennett (Anthony Dominick Benedetto), 72, singer ("I Left My Heart in San Francisco," "In the Middle of an Island"), born New York, NY, Aug 3, 1926.

Steven Berkoff, 61, actor, director, writer (*A Clockwork Orange, Beverly Hills Cop, The Krays*), born London, England, Aug 3, 1937.

P. D. (Phyllis Dorothy) James, 78, mystery novelist (*Devices and Desires, Innocent Blood*), born Oxford, England, Aug 3, 1920.

John McGinley, 39, actor (*Platoon, Born on the Fourth of July*), born New York, NY, Aug 3, 1959.

Martin Sheen (Ramon Estevez), 58, actor (*Badlands, Apocalypse Now*), born Dayton, OH, Aug 3, 1940.

Martha Stewart, 57, lifestyle consultant, TV personality, writer, born Nutley, NJ, Aug 3, 1941.

Leon Uris, 74, author (*Mitla Pass, Exodus*), born Baltimore, MD, Aug 3, 1924.

AUGUST 4 — TUESDAY

Day 216 — 149 Remaining

ARMSTRONG, LOUIS: BIRTH ANNIVERSARY. Aug 4, 1901. Jazz musician extraordinaire born this day at New Orleans, LA. Died at New York, NY, July 6, 1971. Asked to define jazz, Armstrong reportedly replied, "Man, if you gotta ask, you'll never know." The trumpet player was also known as Satchmo. He appeared in many films. Popular singles included "It's a Wonderful World" and "Hello, Dolly" (with Barbra Streisand).

CIVIL RIGHTS WORKERS FOUND SLAIN: ANNIVERSARY. Aug 4, 1964. After disappearing on June 21, three civil rights workers were found murdered and buried in an earthen dam outside Philadelphia, MS. The three young men were workers on the Mississippi Summer Project organized by the Student Nonviolent Coordinating Committee (SNCC) to increase black voter registration. Prior to their disappearance, James Chaney, Andrew Goodman and Michael Schwerner were detained by Neshoba County police on charges of speeding. When their car was found, burned, on June 23, President Johnson ordered an FBI search for the men.

COAST GUARD DAY. Aug 4. Celebrates anniversary of founding of the US Coast Guard, Aug 4, 1790.

COLT LEAGUE WORLD SERIES. Aug 4–11 (tentative dates). Lafayette, IN. International young adult baseball World Series for players of league ages 15 and 16. Est attendance: 2,500. For info: Pony Baseball Inc, PO Box 225, Washington, PA 15301. Phone: (412) 225-1060. Fax: (412) 225-9852. Email: pony@pulsenet.com. WWW: http://www.pony.org

CUNNINGHAM, GLENN: BIRTH ANNIVERSARY. Aug 4, 1909. Glenn Clarence Cunningham, the "Kansas Ironman," American track athlete and 1934–37 world record holder for the mile, member of the US Olympic teams in 1932 and 1936, was born at Atlanta, KS. On June 16, 1934, at Princeton, NJ, Cunningham set a world record for the mile (4:06.7 min). Cunningham died at Menifee, AR, on Mar 10, 1988.

HONG KONG: BIRTHDAY OF LU PAN. Aug 4. The birthday of Lu Pan, the Master Builder, is a holiday for everybody connected with the building trades. Ceremonies sponsored by the Builders' Guilds are held at Lu Pan Temple in Kennedy Town. Festive dinner parties. Annually, the 13th day of 6th lunar month.

MANDELA, NELSON: ARREST ANNIVERSARY. Aug 4, 1962. Nelson Rolihlahla Mandela, charismatic black South African leader, was born in 1918, the son of the Tembu tribal chief, at Umtata, Transkei territory of South Africa. A lawyer and political activist, Mandela, who in 1952 established the first black law partnership in South Africa, had been in conflict with the white government there much of his life. Acquitted of a treason charge after a trial that lasted from 1956 to 1961, he was apprehended again by security police on Aug 4, 1962. The subsequent trial, widely viewed as an indictment of white domination, resulted in Mandela's being sentenced to five years in prison. In 1963 he was taken from the Pretoria prison to face a new trial—for sabotage, high treason and conspiracy to overthrow the government—and in June 1964 he was sentenced to life in prison. See also: "Mandela, Nelson: Prison Release Anniversary" (Feb 11).

August 1998

S	M	T	W	T	F	S
						1
2	3	4	5	6	7	8
9	10	11	12	13	14	15
16	17	18	19	20	21	22
23	24	25	26	27	28	29
30	31					

NATIONAL NIGHT OUT. Aug 4. Designed to heighten crime prevention awareness and to promote police-community partnerships. Annually, the first Tuesday in August. For info: Matt A. Peskin, Dir, Natl Assn of Town Watch, PO Box 303, Wynnewood, PA 19096. Phone: (610) 649-7055 or (800) 648-3688. Fax: (610) 649-5456. WWW: http://www.nationaltownwatch.org

SCALIGER, JOSEPH JUSTUS: BIRTH ANNIVERSARY. Aug 4. French scholar who has been called the founder of scientific chronology. Born at Agen, France, Aug 4, 1540, the 10th son of classical scholar Julius Caesar Scaliger. In 1582 he suggested a new system for measuring time and numbering years. His "Julian Period" (named for his father), which consisted of 7,980 consecutive years (beginning Jan 1, 4713 BC), is still in use. He died at Leiden, Netherlands, Jan 21, 1609.

SCHUMAN, WILLIAM HOWARD: BIRTH ANNIVERSARY. Aug 4, 1910. American composer who won the first Pulitzer Prize for composition and founded the Julliard School of Music, was born Aug 4, 1910, in New York. His compositions include *American Festival Overture, Symphony No. 3, New England Triptych*, the baseball opera *The Mighty Casey* and *On Freedom's Ground*, which was written for the centennial of the Statue of Liberty in 1986. He was instrumental in the conception of the Lincoln Center for the Performing Arts and served as its first president during the 1960s. In 1985 he was awarded a special Pulitzer Prize for his contributions. He also received a National Medal of Arts in 1985 and a Kennedy Center Honor in 1989. Schuman died at New York City, Feb 15, 1992.

TEXAS COUNTY FAIR/OLD SETTLERS REUNION. Aug 4–8 (tentative). Fair Grounds, Houston, MO. A fun festival with arts and crafts, carnival midway, gospel music concert, country bands, truck pulls, tractor pulls and demolition derby. Est attendance: 8,000. For info: Texas County Fair/Old Settlers Reunion, 103 N Grand Ave, Houston, MO 65483. Phone: (417) 967-2220. Fax: (417) 967-3583.

US GIRLS' JUNIOR (GOLF) CHAMPIONSHIP. Aug 4–9. Legends Club of Tennessee, Franklin, TN. For info: US Golf Assn, Golf House, Championship Dept, Far Hills, NJ 07931. Phone: (908) 234-2300. Fax: (908) 234-9687. Email: usga@ix.netcom.com. WWW: http://www/usga.org

VIRGIN ISLANDS: NICOLE ROBIN DAY. Aug 4. Commemorates the safe return of the *Nicole Robin* and her crew on Aug 4, 1973, after a harrowing 23-day experience. Nicole Robin Day is celebrated by appropriate ceremonies and festivities throughout the Virgin Islands.

WALLENBERG, RAOUL: BIRTH ANNIVERSARY. Aug 4, 1912. Swedish architect Raoul Gustaf Wallenberg was born at Stockholm, Sweden. He was the second person in history (Winston Churchill was the first) to be voted honorary American citizenship (US House of Representatives 396–2, Sept 22, 1981). Little is known of his architectural achievements, but he is credited with saving 100,000 Jews from almost certain death at the hands of the Nazis during World War II. Wallenberg was arrested by Soviet troops at Budapest, Hungary, on Jan 17, 1945, and according to the official Soviet press agency Tass died in prison in 1947 (exact date undisclosed).

BIRTHDAYS TODAY

Richard Belzer, 54, comedian, actor (*Mad Dog and Glory*, "Homicide: Life on the Streets"), born Bridgeport, CT, Aug 4, 1944.

William Roger Clemens, 36, baseball player, born Dayton, OH, Aug 4, 1962.

Elizabeth, the Queen Mother (Elizabeth Angela Marguerite), 98, born Hertfordshire, England, Aug 4, 1900.

Joseph Henri Maurice ("Rocket") Richard, 77, Hockey Hall of Fame right wing, born Montreal, Quebec, Canada, Aug 4, 1921.

Kristofer Tabori, 46, actor ("Seventh Avenue," "Chicago Story"), born Los Angeles, CA, Aug, 4, 1952.

Helen Thomas, 78, journalist (long-time White House correspondent), born Winchester, KY, Aug 4, 1920.

AUGUST 5 — WEDNESDAY

Day 217 — 148 Remaining

ABBOTT'S MAGIC GET-TOGETHER (WITH TALENT CONTESTS). Aug 5–8. Colon, MI. Magic convention. Est attendance: 1,200. For info: Abbott's Magic Co, 124 St. Joseph St, Colon, MI 49040. Phone: (616) 432-3235. Fax: (616) 432-3357. Email: GBORD98968@aol.com.

AIKEN, CONRAD: BIRTH ANNIVERSARY. Aug 5, 1899. American poet, short-story writer, critic and Pulitzer Prize winner (poetry, 1916). He was born at Savannah, GA and died there Aug 17, 1973.

"AMERICAN BANDSTAND" TV PREMIERE: ANNIVERSARY. Aug 5, 1957. "American Bandstand" and Dick Clark are synonyomous; he hosted the show for more than 30 years. "AB" started out as a local show in Philadelphia. Clark, then a disk jockey, took over as host at the age of 26. The format was simple: teens dancing, performers doing their latest hits, Clark introducing songs and listing the top 10 songs each week. This hour-long show was not only TV's longest-running musical series, but also the first one devoted exclusively to rock and roll. Twenty-six weeks after Clark turned over the hosting duties to David Hirsch in 1989, the show was dropped.

BEARD, MARY R.: BIRTH ANNIVERSARY. Aug 5, 1876. American historian Mary Ritter Beard was born at Indianapolis, IN. Many of her books were written in collaboration with her husband, Charles A. Beard. She died at Phoenix, AZ, on Aug 14, 1958.

BEVIER HOMECOMING. Aug 5–8. Bevier, MO. Make yourself right at home as you enjoy a carnival, top country entertainers, a parade and lots more fun for folks of all ages. For info: Donny Roberts, Bevier Homecoming, 109 Gentry, Bevier, MO 63532. Phone: (816) 773-6902.

BURKINA FASO: REPUBLIC DAY. Aug 5, 1960. Burkina Faso (formerly Upper Volta) gained autonomy from France.

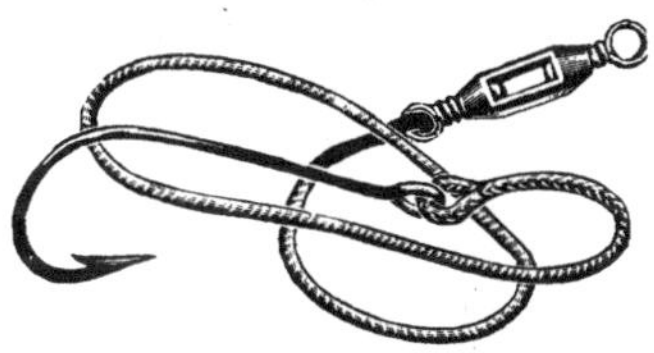

CANADA: DIGBY SCALLOP DAYS FESTIVAL. Aug 5–9. Digby, Nova Scotia. A celebration of our seafaring heritage, honoring the fishermen of the world-famous Digby Scallop Fleet. Savor the marvelous mollusks of the deep. Cheer the scallop shuckers in competition. Enjoy local talent. Take in our grand street parade and children's events. Est attendance: 12,000. For info: Digby Scallop Days Assn, PO Box 983, Digby, NS, Canada B0V 1A0. Phone: (902) 245-4531. Fax: (902) 245-2121. WWW: http://www.valleyweb.com/digby/scallop.html

CANADA: THE FLIGHT BEGINS. Aug 5. Abbotsford, British Columbia. The week preceding Airshow, Abbotsford takes flight with an aeronautical theme. The entire city bursts with frivolty in anticipation of airshow weekend. Join us for an old-fashioned picnic in the park which includes a tug-of-war, mascots, entertainment, variety of food booths, fun fair, Ronald McDonald Stage Show and other children's activities and so much more. Come soar with us during The Flight Begins Festival! Est attendance: 1,500. For info: Abbotsford Chamber of Commerce, 2462 McCallum Rd, Abbotsford, BC, Canada V2S 3P9. Phone: (604) 859-9651. Fax: (604) 850-6880.

ELIOT, JOHN: BIRTH ANNIVERSARY. Aug 5. John Eliot, American "Apostle to the Indians," translator of the Bible into an Indian tongue (the first Bible to be printed in America), was born at Hertfordshire, England, on Aug 5, 1604. He died at Roxbury, MA, on May 21, 1690.

FEDERAL INCOME TAX: ANNIVERSARY. Aug 5, 1861. Abraham Lincoln signed into law the first federal income tax, to become effective Jan 1, 1862. It was a 3% tax levied on incomes of more than $800, as an emergency wartime measure only. It was never really put into effect and was rescinded in 1872.

FIRST ENGLISH COLONY IN NORTH AMERICA: FOUNDING ANNIVERSARY. Aug 5, 1583. Sir Humphrey Gilbert, English navigator and explorer, aboard his sailing ship, the *Squirrel*, sighted the Newfoundland coast and took possession of the area around St. John's harbor in the name of the Queen, thus establishing the first English colony in North America. Gilbert was lost at sea, in a storm off the Azores, on his return trip to England.

GEORGIA MOUNTAIN FAIR. Aug 5–16. Georgia Mountain Fairgrounds, Hiawassee, GA. Authentic mountain demonstrations including corn millin', board splittin', soap and hominy makin' and others. Pioneer village with re-created one-room school, log cabin, barn and corncrib. Nashville talent, clogging, midway, arts and crafts and much more. Est attendance: 130,000. For info: Hilda Thomason, Mgr, Georgia Mountain Fair, PO Box 444, Hiawassee, GA 30546. Phone: (706) 896-4191.

KIDS' DAY. Aug 5. Patterson Park, Baltimore, MD. All kids 12 years of age and under enjoy an hour of free fun, games, refreshments and entertainment. Est attendance: 300. For info: Office of Adventures and Fun, Patterson Park Recreation Complex, 2601 E Baltimore St, Baltimore, MD 21224. Phone: (410) 396-9177. Fax: (410) 327-4120.

LYNCH, THOMAS: BIRTH ANNIVERSARY. Aug 5. Signer, Declaration of Independence, born Prince George's Parish, SC, Aug 5, 1749. Died 1779 (lost at sea, exact date of death unknown).

MISS CRUSTACEAN USA BEAUTY PAGEANT AND OCEAN CITY CREEP. Aug 5. 6th St Beach, Ocean City, NJ. Participants are hermit tree crabs. To determine most beautiful tree crab and fastest tree crab on earth. Begins at 1 PM, EST. Est attendance: 500. For info: Mark Soifer, PR Dir, City of Ocean City, City Hall, Ocean City, NJ 08226. Phone: (609) 525-9300. Fax: (609) 399-0374.

MONROE, MARILYN: DEATH ANNIVERSARY. Aug 5, 1962. The world fell in love with Monroe's unique combination of sensuality and approachability. She was the epitome of Hollywood glamour, making 29 films in her career. Her tragic death at age 36 from an overdose of sleeping pills was shocking to all and is shrouded in controversy. She was born June 1, 1926, at Los Angeles.

MUSTANG LEAGUE WORLD SERIES. Aug 5–8. Irving, TX. International youth baseball World Series for players of league ages 9 and 10. Est attendance: 3,000. For info: Pony Baseball, Inc, PO Box 225, Washington, PA 15301. Phone: (412) 225-1060. Fax: (412) 225-9852.
Email: pony@pulsenet.com. WWW: http://www.pony.org

OLD FIDDLERS' CONVENTION. Aug 5–8. Galax, VA. 63rd annual event features dance, folk songs, old-time and bluegrass music competition. Est attendance: 25,000. For info: Edward F. Carico, Box 655, Galax, VA 24333. Phone: (540) 236-8541. Fax: (540) 236-8681.

SCOTLAND: ABERDEEN INTERNATIONAL YOUTH FESTIVAL. Aug 5–15. Aberdeen, Scotland. Talented young people from all areas of the performing arts come from around the world to participate in this festival. Est attendance: 30,000. For info: Nicola Wallis, 3 Nuborn House, Clifton Rd, London, England SW19 4QT. Phone: (44) (181) 946-2995. Fax: (44) (181) 944-6507.

SEASHORE OPEN HOUSE TOUR. Aug 5. Loveladies, NJ. 32nd annual. Come and enjoy the fabulous shoreline houses. For info: Long Beach Island Foundation of the Arts and Sciences, 120 Long Beach Blvd, Loveladies, NJ 08008. Phone: (609) 494-1241. Fax: (609) 494-0662.

BIRTHDAYS TODAY

Loni Anderson, 52, actress ("WKRP in Cincinnati," *The Jayne Mansfield Story*), born St. Paul, MN, Aug 5, 1946.

Neil Alden Armstrong, 68, former astronaut (first man to walk on moon), born Wapakoneta, OH, Aug 5, 1930.

Josie Bissett, 28, actress (played Jane on "Melrose Place"), born Seattle, WA, Aug 5, 1970.

Patrick Aloysius Ewing, 36, basketball player, born Kingston, Jamaica, Aug 5, 1962.

Samantha Sang, 45, singer ("Emotion"), born Melbourne, Australia, Aug 5, 1953.

John Saxon, 62, actor ("Falcon Crest," *Enter the Dragon, Nightmare on Elm Street*), born Brooklyn, NY, Aug 5, 1936.

Jonathan Silverman, 32, actor (*Brighton Beach Memoirs, Weekend at Bernie's*), born Los Angeles, CA, Aug 5, 1966.

Erika Slezak, 52, actress ("One Life to Live"), born Los Angeles, CA, Aug 5, 1946.

Sammi Smith, 55, singer ("Help Me Make It Through the Night"), born Orange, CA, Aug 5, 1943.

AUGUST 6 — THURSDAY

Day 218 — 147 Remaining

AMISH ACRES ARTS & CRAFTS FESTIVAL. Aug 6–9. Nappanee, IN. Displays of Amish arts and crafts including furniture and other objects. Also features a variety of entertainment. Est attendance: 60,000. For info: Amish Acres Arts & Crafts Festival, 1600 Market St, Nappanee, IN 46550. Phone: (219) 773-4189. Fax: (219) 773-4180.

ATOMIC BOMB DROPPED ON HIROSHIMA: ANNIVERSARY. Aug 6, 1945. At 8:15 AM, local time, an American B-29 bomber, the *Enola Gay*, dropped an atomic bomb named "Little Boy" over the center of the city of Hiroshima, Japan. The bomb exploded about 1,800 ft above the ground, killing more than 105,000 civilians and destroying the city. It is estimated that another 100,000 persons were injured and died subsequently as a direct result of the bomb and the radiation it produced. This was the first time in history that such a devastating weapon had been used by any nation.

BALL, LUCILLE: BIRTH ANNIVERSARY. Aug 6, 1911. Film and television pioneer and comedian born at Butte, MT. In addition to her many other film and television credits, Lucille Ball always will be remembered for her role in the 1950s CBS sitcom "I Love Lucy." As Lucy Ricardo, the wife of bandleader Ricky Ricardo (her real-life husband, Desi Arnaz), she exhibited a comedic style that became a trademark of early television comedy.

BOLIVIA: INDEPENDENCE DAY. Aug 6. National holiday. Gained freedom from Spain, 1825.

August 1998

S	M	T	W	T	F	S
						1
2	3	4	5	6	7	8
9	10	11	12	13	14	15
16	17	18	19	20	21	22
23	24	25	26	27	28	29
30	31					

BRONCO LEAGUE WORLD SERIES. Aug 6–13 (tentative dates). Monterey, CA. International youth baseball World Series for players of league ages 11 and 12. Est attendance: 4,350. For info: Pony Baseball, Inc, PO Box 225, Washington, PA 15301. Phone: (412) 225-1060. Fax: (412) 225-9852. Email: pony@pulsenet.com. WWW: http://www.pony.org

CANADA: HALIFAX INTERNATIONAL BUSKER FESTIVAL. Aug 6–16. Halifax, Nova Scotia. Street performers and artists from around the world, vaudeville nights and international street food fair. Annually, beginning the first Thursday in August. Est attendance: 500,000. For info: Kim Kelley, Exec Dir, Halifax Intl Busker Fest, 1679 Bedford Row, Guelph, Ont, Canada B3J 1T1. Phone: (902) 429-3910. Fax: (902) 429-7554. Email: buskers@ns.sympatico.ca.

ELECTROCUTION FIRST USED TO CARRY OUT DEATH PENALTY: ANNIVERSARY. Aug 6. On Aug 6, 1890, at Auburn Prison, Auburn, NY, William Kemmler of Buffalo, NY, became the first man to be executed by electrocution. He had been convicted of the hatchet murder of his common-law wife, Matilde Ziegler, on Mar 28, 1889. This first attempt at using electrocution to carry out the death penalty was a botched affair. As reported by George Westinghouse, Jr, "It has been a brutal affair. They could have done better with an axe."

FIRST WOMAN SWIMS THE ENGLISH CHANNEL: ANNIVERSARY. Aug 6, 1926. The first woman to swim the English Channel was 19-year-old Gertrude Ederle of New York, NY. Her swim was completed in 14 hours and 31 minutes.

FLEMING, ALEXANDER: BIRTH ANNIVERSARY. Aug 6, 1881. Sir Alexander Fleming, Scottish bacteriologist, discoverer of penicillin and 1954 Nobel Prize recipient, was born at Lochfield, Scotland. He died at London, England, Mar 11, 1955.

GREAT ARKANSAS PIG-OUT. Aug 6–8. Morrilton, AR. Focus is on food of all kinds: barbecue, chicken, homemade ice cream, catfish, funnel cakes, hamburgers, spaghetti dinners. Activities include pig chase, hog calling, children's fairy-tale park, rides, arts, crafts, entertainment, games, street dance, gospel singing. 10th annual pig-out. Est attendance: 20,000. For info: Chamber of Commerce, 120 N Division, Morrilton, AR 72110. Phone: (501) 354-2393. Fax: (501) 354-8642. Email: mcc@mev.net.

"GREAT DEBATE": ANNIVERSARY. Aug 6–Sept 10, 1787. The Constitutional Convention engaged in the "Great Debate" over the draft constitution, during which it determined that Congress should have the right to regulate foreign trade and interstate commerce, established a four-year term of office for the president and appointed a five-man committee to prepare a final draft of the Constitution.

HIROSHIMA DAY. Aug 6. Memorial observances in many places for victims of the first atomic bombing of a populated place, which occurred at Hiroshima, Japan, Aug 6, 1945, when an American B-29 bomber dropped an atomic bomb over the center of the city. More than 205,000 civilians died either immediately in the explosion or subsequently of radiation.

INTERNATIONAL FESTIVAL. Aug 6–9. Calais, ME, and St. Stephen, New Brunswick, Canada. Festival of international cooperation between St. Stephen and Calais with the theme "The Spirit of International Friendship and Goodwill." Celebrating the friendship of two countries joining as one. Est attendance: 14,000. For info: Keith Guttormsen, Exec Chamber Dir, Intl Fest Committee, PO Box 368, Calais, ME 04619. Phone: (207) 454-2308. Email: calcham@nemaine.com. WWW: http://www.mainerec.com/calais.html

JAMAICA: INDEPENDENCE ACHIEVED: ANNIVERSARY. Aug 6, 1962. Jamaica attained its independence after centuries of British rule. Sir Alexander Bustamante became the first Jamaican Prime Minister.

JAPAN: PEACE FESTIVAL. Aug 6. Hiroshima, Japan. The festival held annually at Peace Memorial Park is observed in memory of the victims of the Aug 6, 1945, atomic bomb explosion there.

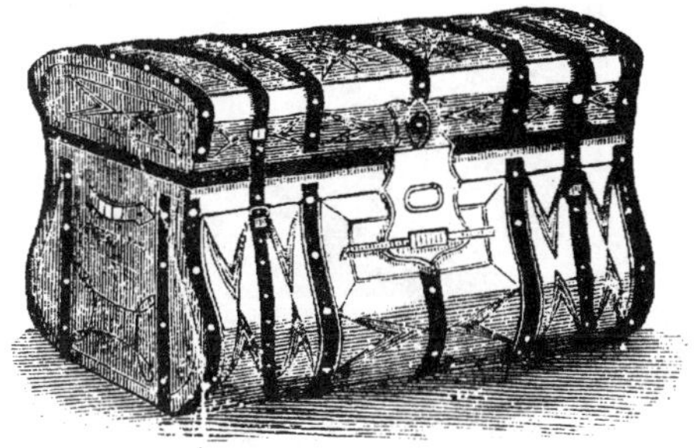

JUDGE CRATER DAY. Aug 6. Anniversary of mysterious disappearance at age 41, on Aug 6, 1930, of Joseph Force Crater, justice of the New York State Supreme Court. Never seen or heard from after disappearance on this date. Declared legally dead in 1939.

MAINE FESTIVAL. Aug 6–9. Brunswick, ME. Maine's premier art and cultural event, with more than 1,000 artists and craftspersons on site. Features seven stages of country, traditional and contemporary music, dance, theater and literary presentations. A juried art/craft market, giant paintings and art installations, a Maine products show, art workshops for all ages, musical instrument builders, fine woodworking, a microbrew festival, traditional Maine seafood and ethnic foods. Tickets: $6–$12. Family pass: (2a & 3c) $30. Campsites: $20. Est attendance: 24,000. For info: Maine Arts, Inc, 582 Congress St, Portland, ME 04101. Phone: (207) 772-9012. Fax: (207) 772-3995.

NATIONAL COUNTRY MUSIC FESTIVAL. Aug 6–9. East City Park, Ainsworth, NE. "Country Music Capital of Nebraska." 27th annual festival features country music contest judged in these categories: fiddlers, pickers, female singers, male singers, vocal groups, juniors, preteens and 55+ group. Free pancakes on the weekend. Also, NE State Auctioneer's Bid-Calling contest, square dancing and more. Camping facilities are available, first come first served. Contestants may register by mail or phone. Annually, the second weekend in August (Thursday–Sunday). Est attendance: 2,700. For info: Jo Lowe, Exec Secy, or Kathy Worrell, Co-Chair, Ainsworth Area Chamber of Commerce, PO Box 112, Ainsworth, NE 69210. Phone: (402) 387-2740 or (402) 387-2844. Email: jolone@aol.com. WWW: http://www.co.brown.ne.us

NATIONAL HOBO CONVENTION. Aug 6–9. Britt, IA. The 98th annual convention and accompanying events honor the hobo—a traveling laborer who pursues jobs via the rail lines. Visit the Hobo Jungle and the Hobo Museum. Join the hoboes for storytelling, parade, the traditional mulligan stew and the Coronation of the Hobo King and Queen, as well as entertainment, carnival, gospel concert, six-block craft and flea market, 5K walk, 5K & 10K runs, fine-arts show, classic and antique car show and more. Annually, the weekend of the second Saturday in August (Thursday–Sunday). Est attendance: 30,000. For info: Britt Chamber of Commerce, PO Box 63, Britt, IA 50423. Phone: (515) 843-3867.

NEARING, SCOTT: BIRTH ANNIVERSARY. Aug 6, 1883. American sociologist, antiwar crusader, back-to-the-land advocate and author, with his wife Helen, of *Living the Good Life* (1954). He was born at Morris Run, PA, and died a century later at his farm at Harborside, ME, on Aug 24, 1983.

PURGING PESTILENCE: DEALING WITH DISEASE IN THE 19th CENTURY. Aug 6–Nov 8. Belle Meade Plantation, Nashville, TN. An exhibit in a restored Southern mansion, which explores the ignorance, superstition and medical practices of the 1800s. Tours led by guides in period costumes. For info: Belle Meade Plantation, 5025 Harding Rd, Nashville, TN 37205. Phone: (800) 270-3991 or (615) 356-0501. Fax: (615) 356-2336.

ROOSEVELT, EDITH KERMIT CAROW: BIRTH ANNIVERSARY. Aug 6, 1861. Second wife of Theodore Roosevelt, 26th president of the US, born at Norwich, CT, died Sept 30, 1948.

SPACE MILESTONE: *VOSTOK 2* (USSR). Aug 6, 1961. Launched on Aug 6, 1961, Gherman Titov orbited Earth 17 times over period of 25 hours, 18 minutes. Titov broadcast messages in passage over countries, controlled spaceship manually for two hours.

SPAIN: QUINCENA MUSICAL DE SAN SEBASTIAN. Aug 6–Sept 2. Spain's oldest festival includes orchestral and choral music. For info: Quincena Musical, Reina Regente, s/n 20003 San Sebastian, Spain. Fax: 34-43 43 07 02.

TENNYSON, ALFRED, LORD: BIRTH ANNIVERSARY. Aug 6. English poet born at Somersby, Lincolnshire, England, Aug 6, 1809. Appointed English poet laureate in succession to William Wordsworth. Died at Aldworth, England, Oct 6, 1892.

TEXAS FOLKLIFE FESTIVAL. Aug 6–9. San Antonio, TX. Provides an entertaining and historic understanding of the crafts, art, food, music, history and heritage of the more than 40 different cultures and ethnic groups that settled and developed the state of Texas. Est attendance: 70,000. For info: Lynn Catalina, Dir of Comm & Mktg, Institute of Texan Cultures, 801 S Bowie St, San Antonio, TX 78205-3296. Phone: (210) 458-2300. Fax: (210) 458-2205. Email: lcatalin@itcpost1.utsa.edu.
WWW: http://www.utsa.edu/itc

VOTING RIGHTS ACT OF 1965 SIGNED: ANNIVERSARY. Aug 6, 1965. Signed into law by President Lyndon Johnson, the Voting Rights Act of 1965 was designed to thwart attempts to discriminate against minorities at the polls. The act suspended literacy and other disqualifying tests, authorized appointment of federal voting examiners and provided for judicial relief on the federal level to bar discriminatory poll taxes. Congress has voted to extend the Act in 1975, 1984 and 1991.

WISCONSIN STATE FAIR. Aug 6–16. State Fair Park, Milwaukee, WI. Wisconsin celebrates its rural heritage at the state's largest and oldest annual event. Features giant midway, concessions, livestock, food and flower judging and top-name entertainment. [Call 24-hour recorded information line at (414) 266-7188 for performance times and dates, updated weekly.] Est attendance: 930,000. For info: PR Dept, Wisconsin State Fair Park, PO Box 14990, West Allis, WI 53214-0990. Fax: (414) 266-7007. Email: state.fair@wsfp.state.wi.us.
WWW: http://www.wsfp.state.wi.us

BIRTHDAYS TODAY

Paul Bartel, 60, director, writer, actor (*Rock 'n' Roll High School, Eating Raoul, Gremlins 2: The New Batch*), born New York, NY, Aug 6, 1938.

Peter Bonerz, 60, actor ("Bob Newhart Show," "9 to 5"), director, born Portsmouth, NH, Aug 6, 1938.

Soleil Moon Frye, 22, actress ("Punky Brewster"), born Glendora, CA, Aug 6, 1976.

Dorian Harewood, 48, actor (*The Falcon and the Snowman, Full Metal Jacket*), born Dayton, OH, Aug 6, 1950.

Catherine Hicks, 47, actress (Marilyn Monroe in TV movie *Marilyn; Peggy Sue Got Married*), born Scottsdale, AZ, Aug 6, 1951.

Freddie Laker, 76, former airline executive, born Canterbury, England, Aug 6, 1922.

Robert Mitchum, 81, actor (*The Night of the Hunter, The Story of G.I. Joe*), born Bridgeport, CT, Aug 6, 1917.

David Maurice Robinson, 33, basketball player, born Key West, FL, Aug 6, 1965.

AUGUST 7 — FRIDAY

Day 219 — 146 Remaining

ALABAMA PRO NATIONAL TRUCK AND TRACTOR PULL. Aug 7–8. Lexington, AL. Six different classes compete: Pro National 7500 Superstock, Pro National 6200 2-Wheel Drive Trucks, Pro National 7200 Modified Tractors (multiengine), State Level 6200 4-Wheel Drive Truck, Local Level 4×4 Street Class and Local Level 15,200 Farm Class. Est attendance: 20,000. For info: Debbie Wilson, Dir, Florence/Lauderdale Tourism, One Hightower Pl, Florence, AL 35630. Phone: (205) 740-4141 or (888) FLO-TOUR. Fax: (205) 740-4142.
WWW: http://www.flo-tour.org

BLUEBERRY FESTIVAL. Aug 7–8. Library Lawn and Village Green, Montrose, PA. 19th annual fund-raiser for the Susquehanna County Library and Historical Society. Two days filled with food, fun and festivity. Raffles, book sale, children's games, silent auction, handstitched quilt, commemorative items and more. Annually, the first Friday and Saturday in August. Est attendance: 5,000. For info: Susquehanna Co Historical Soc & Free Library Assn, 2 Monument Sq, Montrose, PA 18801. Phone: (717) 278-1881. Fax: (717) 278-9336. Email: suspuliv@epix.net. WWW: http://www.epix.net/~suspulib

BLUEGRASS FESTIVAL. Aug 7–9. Grand Targhee Ski and Summer Resort, Alta, WY. 11th annual. Set in a beautiful outdoor venue on a pristine mountainside on the gorgeous western slopes of the Grand Teton Mountains, this festival is three days of incredible bluegrass music featuring national, regional and local talent such as Alison Krauss, Del McCoury Band, Peter Rown and David Grisman. Also, arts and crafts, food and beverages. Est attendance: 7,000. For info: Grand Targhee Ski & Summer Resort, PO Box SKI, Alta, WY 83422. Phone: (800) TAR-GHEE. Fax: (307) 353-8148. Email: targhee@pdt.net.
WWW: http://www.idahonews.com/targhee

BOOM DAYS. Aug 7–9. Leadville, CO. The city's oldest annual celebration features a large parade, street races, mining events, pack burro race and arts and crafts. Fun for the whole family. Est attendance: 35,000. For info: Gloria Cheshier, Chamber of Commerce, PO Box 861, Leadville, CO 80461. Phone: (719) 486-3900 or (800) 933-3901. Fax: (719) 486-8478. Email: leadville@sni.net.
WWW: http://www.colorado.com/leadville

BUNCHE, RALPH JOHNSON: BIRTH ANNIVERSARY. Aug 7. American statesman, UN official, Nobel Peace Prize recipient, born at Detroit, MI, Aug 7, 1904. Died Dec 9, 1971.

CANADA: ABBOTSFORD INTERNATIONAL AIRSHOW. Aug 7–9. Abbotsford Airport, Abbotsford, British Columbia. Leading air show in North America attracts the world's top aeronautical performers. Thrill to the grace of the Canadian Snowbirds, the raw power of the international air demonstration squadrons, dramatic teams of daring performers and soloists. Static displays and food booths. Open daily 8–5; aerial show 11–5. Airshow camping facilities. Est attendance: 250,000. For info: Abbotsford Intl Airshow, 30470 Approach Dr, Abbotsford, BC, Canada V2T 6H5.

CANADA: FESTIVAL BY THE SEA. Aug 7–16. Saint John, New Brunswick. This waterfront festival features food booths, entertainment and much more. Est attendance: 50,000. For info: Festival by the Sea, PO Box 6848, Station A, Saint John, NB, Canada E2L 4S3. Phone: (506) 632-0086. Fax: (506) 632-0994.

August 1998

S	M	T	W	T	F	S
						1
2	3	4	5	6	7	8
9	10	11	12	13	14	15
16	17	18	19	20	21	22
23	24	25	26	27	28	29
30	31					

CARNATION CITY FESTIVAL. Aug 7–16. Alliance, OH. To honor the scarlet carnation, Ohio's state flower. Alliance is home of the carnation. 10 days of activities. Est attendance: 100,000. For info: Carnation Fest Bd of Directors, 210 E Main St, Alliance, OH 44601. Phone: (330) 823-6260. Fax: (330) 823-4434.
Email: allcham@alliancelink.com.
WWW: http://www.rodman.lib.oh.us/rpl/home.htm

CAROLINA CRAFTSMEN'S SUMMER CLASSIC. Aug 7–9. Convention Center, Myrtle Beach, SC. Arts and crafts. Est attendance: 20,000. For info: The Carolina Craftsmen, 1240 Oakland Ave, Greensboro, NC 27403. Phone: (910) 274-5550. Fax: (910) 274-1084.

COTE D'IVOIRE: NATIONAL DAY. Aug 7.

DESERT SHIELD: ANNIVERSARY. Aug 7, 1990. Five days after the Iraqi invasion of Kuwait, US President George Bush ordered the military buildup that would become known as Desert Shield, to prevent further Iraqi advances.

FINLAND: TURKU MUSIC FESTIVAL. Aug 7–16. Turku. One of Finland's oldest music festivals in its oldest city. Music ranges from the medieval era to present day, performed by world-famous artists and groups in halls with fine acoustics, churches and even museums. Est attendance: 15,000. For info: Finnish Tourist Board, 655 Third Ave, New York, NY 10017. Phone: (212) 949-2333.

FIRST PICTURE OF EARTH FROM SPACE: ANNIVERSARY. Aug 7. US satellite *Explorer VI* transmitted the first picture of Earth from space Aug 7, 1959, and for the first time man had a likeness of his planet based on more than Earth measurements, projections and conjectures.

GOLD COAST ART FAIR. Aug 7–9. Chicago, IL. Features the work of 600 artists of painting and sculpture in a large outdoor exhibit. Est attendance: 800,000. For info: Gold Coast Art Fair, c/o *Near North News*, 222 W Ontario, Ste 502, Chicago, IL 60610-3695.

GRAND PRAIRIE WESTERN DAYS. Aug 7–8. Grand Prairie, TX. Tribute to western heritage featuring PRCA rodeo performances, free pancake breakfast, western art show, Old West gunfights, parade, barbecue, C & W dance and free lunches. Est attendance: 60,000. For info: Doug Beich, City of Grand Prairie, 326 W Main St, Grand Prairie, TX 75053-4045. Phone: (972) 237-8112. Fax: (972) 237-8267.

GREAT SALMON VALLEY BALLOONFEST. Aug 7–9. City Park, Salmon, ID. Arts and crafts, sidewalk sales, tethered rides, BBQs, Dutch oven tailgate brunch, whitewater float trips, fun flights and much more. For info: Salmon Chamber of Commerce, 200 Main St, Ste 1, Salmon, ID 83467. Phone: (208) 756-2100.

GREENE, NATHANIEL: BIRTH ANNIVERSARY. Aug 7, 1742. Born at Patowomut, RI, American Revolutionary War General Nathaniel Greene was described as the "ablest military officer of the Revolution under Washington." Greene died at Savannah, GA, June 19, 1786.

GULF OF TONKIN RESOLUTION: ANNIVERSARY. Aug 7, 1964. Congress approved the "Gulf of Tonkin Resolution," pertaining to the war in Vietnam, which gave President Lyndon Johnson authority "to take all necessary measures to repel any armed attack against the forces of the United States and to prevent further aggression."

HALFWAY POINT OF SUMMER. Aug 7. At 5:20 AM, EDT, on Aug 7, 1998, 46 days, 9 hours and 42 minutes will have elapsed and the equivalent will remain before 1:37 AM, EDT, Sept 23, 1998, the autumnal equinox and the beginning of autumn.

HOT CAJUN NITES. Aug 7–9. Live Oak, FL. A weekend filled with Cajun music, dancing, food and fun. Est attendance: 4,000. For info: Vicki Bass, Spirit of the Suwannee Music Park, 3076 95th Dr, Live Oak, FL 32060. Phone: (904) 364-1683. Fax: (904) 364-2998. Email: spirit@musicliveshere.com.
WWW: http://www.musicliveshere.com

ISING, RUDOLF C.: 95th BIRTH ANNIVERSARY. Aug 7, 1903. Rudolf C. Ising, cocreator with Hugh Harmon of "Looney Tunes" and "Merrie Melodies," was born at Kansas City, MO. Ising and Harmon's initial production, *Bosko the Talk-Ink Kid* (1929), was the first talkie cartoon synchronizing dialogue on the soundtrack with the action on screen. Ising received an Academy Award in 1948 for *Milky Way*, a cartoon about three kittens. Ising, who emphasized the musical element of cartoons, was the primary developer of "Merrie Melodies." His greatest strengths were in writing and producing rather than illustration. During WWII he headed the animation division for the Army Air Forces movie unit developing training films. Rudolf Ising died July 18, 1992, at Newport Beach, CA.

"LIL" MARGARET'S BLUEGRASS AND OLD TIME MUSIC FESTIVAL. Aug 7–9. Leonardtown, MD. Bluegrass music, crafts, old-time cars and tractors, plenty of home-cooked meals and lots of fun. Annually, the second weekend in August. Est attendance: 1,000. For info: Joseph H. Goddard, Lil Margaret's Bluegrass, 20529 White Point Rd, Leonardtown, MD 20650. Phone: (301) 475-8191. WWW: http://www.gotech.com/

LUNAR ECLIPSE. Aug 7. Penumbral eclipse of the moon. Moon enters penumbra at 9:31 PM, EDT, reaches middle of eclipse at 10:24 PM and leaves penumbra at 11:18 PM, EDT. The beginning of the penumbral phase visible in eastern North America, Central America, South America, southern Greenland, Europe, extreme western Asia, Africa, most of Antarctica, western Indian Ocean, eastern South Pacific Ocean, southeastern North Pacific Ocean, Atlantic Ocean; the end of phase visible in North America except northern and western Canada and Alaska, Central America, South America, most of Europe, southern Greenland, Africa except the extreme east, most of Antarctica, the eastern South Pacific Ocean, southeastern North Pacific Ocean, Atlantic Ocean.

☆ ☆ ☆

MATA HARI: BIRTH ANNIVERSARY. Aug 7, 1876. Mata Hari (child of the dawn) was born Margaret Gertrude Zelle at Leewarden, Netherlands. Her spectacular career as a dancer, courtesan and spy made her name a part of languages around the world. Probably an ineffective double agent, she nevertheless fascinated royalty and high officials of several countries. Arrested as a German spy (Agent H-21) in a Paris hotel on Feb 13, 1917, she was tried, convicted and sentenced to death. The greatest of her many roles was the final one—when she refused a blindfold and threw a kiss to the firing squad at Vincennes, France, on Oct 15, 1917. See also: "Mata Hari: Execution Anniversary" (Oct 15).

MOON PHASE: FULL MOON. Aug 7. Moon enters Full Moon phase at 10:10 PM, EDT.

PURPLE HEART: ANNIVERSARY. Aug 7, 1782. At Newburgh, NY, on this date, General George Washington ordered the creation of a Badge of Military Merit. The badge consisted of a purple cloth heart with silver braided edge. Only three are known to have been awarded during the Revolutionary War. The award was reinstituted on the bicentennial of Washington's birth, Feb 22, 1932, and recognizes those wounded in action.

ROCKY GAP COUNTRY BLUE GRASS MUSIC AND CRAFTS FESTIVAL. Aug 7–9. Cumberland, MD. Arts and crafts, food, music workshops and country bluegrass music. Annually, the first full weekend in August. Est attendance: 22,000. For info: Rocky Gap Foundation Inc, PO Box 1998, Western Maryland Station, Cumberland, MD 21502. Phone: (301) 722-5200. WWW: http://www.mcclarran_williams.com

SCOTLAND: EDINBURGH MILITARY TATTOO: THE MAIN EVENT. Aug 7–29. Edinburgh Castle, Edinburgh, Lothian. Display of military color and pageantry held at night on the floodlit esplanade of Edinburgh Castle. A unique blend of music, ceremony, entertainment and theater. Est attendance: 200,000. For info: The Edinburgh Military Tattoo, The Tattoo Office, 32 Market St, Edinburgh, Scotland EH1 1QB. Phone: (44) (131) 225-1188. Fax: (44) (131) 225-8627. WWW: http://edintattoo.co.uk/

SHANTY DAYS: CELEBRATION OF THE LAKE. Aug 7–9. Legion Park, Algoma, WI. Three-day festival to celebrate lakeshore heritage. Entertainment, ethnic food, arts and crafts, street fair, 5K walk/run, fishing contest, kids' area, minnow racing, book sale, community parade, photo contest and fireworks finale. Est attendance: 23,000. For info: Carol Wiese, Exec Dir, Algoma Area Chamber of Commerce, 1226 Lake St, Algoma, WI 54201. Phone: (920) 487-2041 or (800) 498-4888. Fax: (920) 487-5519. Email: aacofc@itol.com.
WWW: http://www.algoma.org

STAMP EXPO '98: CALIFORNIA. Aug 7–9. Pasadena Convention Center, Pasadena, CA. Est attendance: 4,000. For info: Intl Stamp Collectors Society, PO Box 854, Van Nuys, CA 91408. Phone: (818) 997-6496. Fax: (818) 988-4337.
Email: iibick@aol.com. WWW: http://www.4free.com/bick

STOWE ANTIQUE AND CLASSIC CAR MEET. Aug 7–9. Nichols Field, Stowe, VT. A festival and parade of antique cars that attracts entrants and spectators from throughout the US. Est attendance: 8,000. For info: Stowe Area Assn, Box 1320, Stowe, VT 05672. Phone: (802) 253-7321.

TRADITIONAL JAZZ FESTIVAL. Aug 7–9. North Branford, CT. Est attendance: 12,000. For info: The Great Connecticut Traditional Jazz Festival, PO Box 380, North Branford, CT 06471. Phone: (203) 483-9343 or (800) HOT-EVENT. Fax: (203) 483-9343.

US HOT-AIR BALLOON CHAMPIONSHIPS. Aug 7–15. Columbia, MO. 200 hot-air balloons fill the skies of Columbia, as 100 pilots compete for $100,000 and the right to represent the US in the World Championships. Some 100 fiesta balloons and special-shaped balloons are expected to fly during this event. Plus carnival, children's area, live music and crafts exhibits. Est attendance: 250,000. For info: Missouri Balloon Corp, 1400 Forum Blvd, Ste 20, Columbia, MO 65203. Phone: (573) 446-5566.

US WAR DEPARTMENT: ESTABLISHMENT ANNIVERSARY. Aug 7. The second presidential cabinet department, the War Department was established by Congress on Aug 7, 1789.

WORLD FREEFALL CONVENTION. Aug 7–16. Quincy, IL. Skydivers converge in Quincy and fill the skies with their brilliant-colored parachutes. Spectators can enjoy the sights and take part in helicopter rides, biplane rides and hot-air balloon rides. Those wishing to skydive may purchase a tandem skydive or take lessons and skydive on their own. Est attendance: 20,000. For info: Rob Ebbing, World Freefall Convention, 1515 Kentucky, Quincy, IL 62301. Phone: (217) 222-5867. Fax: (217) 222-5867. Email: wffc@freefall.com. WWW: http://www.freefall.com

BIRTHDAYS TODAY

Lana Cantrell, 55, singer, actress, born Sydney, Australia, Aug 7, 1943.

Stan Freberg, 72, satirist, born Pasadena, CA, Aug 7, 1926.

John Glover, 54, actor (stage: *Great God Brown*, *Julia*, *Melvin and Howard*), born Kingston, NY, Aug 7, 1944.

Garrison Keillor, 56, humorist, producer (host "The Prairie Home Companion"), writer (*Radio Days*), born Anoka, MN, Aug 7, 1942.

DeLane Matthews, 37, actress ("Dave's World"), born Rockledge, FL, Aug 7, 1961.

Alberto Salazar, 41, marathon runner, born Havana, Cuba, Aug 7, 1957.

B.J. Thomas (Billy Joe Thomas), 56, singer ("Hooked on a Feeling," "Raindrops Keep Falling on My Head"), born Houston, TX, Aug 7, 1942.

AUGUST 8 — SATURDAY

Day 220 — 145 Remaining

ALL-AMERICAN SOAP BOX DERBY. Aug 8. Derby Downs, Akron, OH. A weeklong festival culminating in world championship race by regional champs from US, Canada, Germany, Ireland, Australia and Philippines. 61st annual derby. Est attendance: 15,000. For info: Jeff Iula, Genl Mgr, Intl Soap Box Derby, Inc, PO Box 7233, Derby Downs, Akron, OH 44306. Phone: (330) 733-8723. Fax: (330) 733-1370. Email: 2077607@mcimail.com. WWW: http://pages.prodigy.com/soapbox

ANTIQUE FLEA MARKET. Aug 8. Somerset, PA. 28th annual. More than 90 vendors dealing in quality antiques and collectibles. For info: Sandy Berkebile, Antique Flea Market, 601 N Center Ave, Somerset, PA 15501. Phone: (814) 445-6431.

ARTS AND CRAFTS FESTIVAL. Aug 8–9. Loveladies, NJ. Featuring arts and crafts displays, entertainment, food and more. For info: Long Beach Island Foundation of the Arts and Sciences, 120 Long Beach Blvd, Loveladies, NJ 08008. Phone: (609) 494-1241. Fax: (609) 494-0662.

BEAVER COUNTY AIRSHOW. Aug 8–9. Beaver County Airport, Chippewa, PA. 14th annual. For info: (412) 846-9922, (412) 843-8170 or Beaver County Tourist Promotion Agency, 215 B Ninth St, Monaca, PA 15061-2028. Phone: (412) 728-0212. Fax: (412) 728-0456.

BEN & JERRY'S NEWPORT FOLK FESTIVAL. Aug 8–9. Ft Adams State Park, Newport, RI. Nationally-known and up-and-coming performers. For info: Newport County Conv and Visitors Bureau, 23 America's Cup Ave, Newport, RI 02840. Phone: (800) 326-6030. Fax: (401) 849-0291. Email: gonewport@aol.com. WWW: http://www.travelfile.com

August 1998

S	M	T	W	T	F	S
						1
2	3	4	5	6	7	8
9	10	11	12	13	14	15
16	17	18	19	20	21	22
23	24	25	26	27	28	29
30	31					

BLUEBERRY ARTS FESTIVAL. Aug 8. State Office Building, Methodist Church and Main Street Gallery and Theatre, Ketchikan, AK. A street fair featuring arts and crafts, food, games and contests for all ages, performing arts events and poetry and prose reading. Annually, the second Saturday in August. Est attendance: 5,000. For info: Ketchikan Area Arts and Humanities Council, 338 Main St, Ketchikan, AK 99901. Phone: (907) 225-2211. Fax: (907) 225-4330.

BONZA BOTTLER DAY™. Aug 8. To celebrate when the number of the day is the same as the number of the month. Bonza Bottler Day™ is an excuse to have a party at least once a month. For more information, see Jan 1. For info: Gail M. Berger, 109 Matthew Ave, Poca, WV 25159. Phone: (304) 776-7746. Email: gberger5@aol.com.

BUD BILLIKEN PARADE. Aug 8. Chicago, IL. A parade especially for children begun in 1929 by Robert S. Abbott. The second largest parade in the US, it features bands, floats, drill teams and celebrities. Annually, the second Saturday in August. For info: Michael Brown, PR Dir, Chicago Defender Charities, 2400 S Michigan, Chicago, IL 60616. Phone: (312) 225-2400. Fax: (312) 255-9231.

CAPITOL AF'AIR. Aug 8–9. Bismarck, ND. The state capitol grounds provide the backdrop for this capital arts and crafts show. More than 90 exceptional artisans display and sell their artwork on the great mall of the capitol gorunds. Other highlights include music and dance performances, children's activities and several food booths. For info: (701) 223-5986 or Bismarck Conv & Visitors Bureau, PO Box 2274, Bismarck, ND 58501. Phone: (701) 222-4308 or (800) 767-3555. Fax: (701) 222-0647.

COLUMBUS DAYS. Aug 8–16. Columbus, NE. Citywide. Band concert, prayer breakfast, coronation ball, baby show, arts and crafts, archery, horseshoes, lip-synch, talent show, community picnic, quilt show, teen dance, book sale, big-wheel races, volleyball, tennis, pie-eating contest, etc. Est attendance: 12,500. For info: Dale Collinsworth, Exec VP, Columbus Area Chamber of Commerce, PO Box 515, Columbus, NE 68602-0515. Phone: (402) 564-2769. Fax: (402) 564-2026.
Email: chamber@megavision.com.

CRATER LAKE RIM RUNS AND MARATHON. Aug 8. Crater Lake National Park, OR. One of the toughest and most spectacular races you'll ever run! Race routes are around Crater Lake, the deepest lake in the US. Included are a 6.7-mile, a 13-mile and a full marathon. Est attendance: 500. For info: Crater Lake Rim Runs, 5830 Mack Ave, Klamath Falls, OR 97603. Phone: (541) 884-6939.

ELVIS WEEK. Aug 8–16. Memphis, TN. Each year Elvis fans from around the world visit Memphis as Aug 16 marks the anniversary of Elvis Presley's death (Aug 16, 1977) at his beloved home, Graceland Mansion. More than 35 events occur throughout the city with special events sponsored by Graceland. The tribute known as "Elvis Week" includes the candlelight vigil on the evening of Aug 15 at Graceland Mansion. Free brochure on all events available. Est attendance: 40,000. For info: Graceland, 3734 Elvis Presley Blvd, Memphis, TN 38186-0508. Phone: (800) 238-2000. WWW: http://www.elvis-presley.com

FOUNDER'S DAY. Aug 8. The Atheneum, New Harmony, IN. Civic-pride celebration of this communal utopian town's founding in 1814. Fun activities and free tours. Admission: free. Annually, Aug 8. For info: Public Programs Mgr, Historic New Harmony, PO Box 579, New Harmony, IN 47631. Phone: (812) 682-4488. Fax: (812) 682-4313.
Email: cknudson.ucs@smtp.usi.edu.

FRENCH WEST INDIES: FÊTE DES CUISINIÈRES. Aug 8. Guadeloupe. Women in Creole costumes carry baskets of decorated stuffed lobsters and other island specialties. For info: Guadeloupe Tourist Office, 161 Washington Valley Rd, Warren, NJ 07059-7121. Phone: (888) 4-GUADELOUPE. Fax: (908) 302-0809.

GIFT OF THE WATERS PAGEANT. Aug 8–9. Hot Springs Park, Thermopolis, WY. Reenactment of the treaty that sold the US a tract of reservation almost 10 miles square, which includes Big Horn Hot Springs. Est attendance: 2,000. For info: Pageant Day Committee, PO Box 768, Thermopolis, WY 82443. Phone: (307) 864-3192. Fax: (307) 864-3192.
Email: hotspot@wyoming.com.
WWW: http://www.wyoming.com/~hotspot

GORE, TIPPER: BIRTHDAY. Aug 8, 1948. Second Lady, born Mary Elizabeth Aitcheson at Washington, DC.

HENSON, MATTHEW A.: BIRTH ANNIVERSARY. Aug 8, 1866. American black explorer, born at Charles County, MD. Orphaned as a youth, Henson, at the age of 12, served as a cabin boy on the sailing ship *Katie Hines*. He met Robert E. Peary while working in a Washington, DC, store in 1888 and was hired to be Peary's valet. He accompanied Peary on his seven subsequent Arctic expeditions. During the successful 1908–9 expedition to the North Pole, Henson and two of the four Eskimo guides reached their destination on Apr 6, 1909. Peary arrived minutes later and verified the location. Henson's account of the expedition, *A Negro Explorer at the North Pole*, was published in 1912. In addition to the Congressional medal awarded all members of the North Pole expedition, Henson received the Gold Medal of the Geographical Society of Chicago and, at 81, was made an honorary member of the Explorers Club in New York, NY.

INTERNATIONAL AEROBATIC CHAMPIONSHIPS. Aug 7–10. Start your day at the airport with pancake breakfast and plane rides. Aerobatic competition, free forums and exhibits at FDL County Airport. Est attendance: 10,000. For info: Fond du Lac Conv Bureau, 19 W Scott St, Fond du Lac, WI 54935. Phone: (800) 937-9123. Fax: (414) 929-6846.
Email: fdlcvb@uscyber.com.
WWW: http://www.visitwisconsin.com/fdl

INTER-STATE FAIR AND RODEO. Aug 8–16. Coffeyville, KS. "Largest outdoor fair and rodeo event in southeast Kansas and northeast Oklahoma." Est attendance: 60,000. For info: Montgomery County Fair Assn, Box 457, Coffeyville, KS 67337. Phone: (316) 251-2550. Fax: (316) 251-5448.
Email: chamber@terraworld.net.

JOURS DE FÊTE (DAYS OF CELEBRATION). Aug 8–9. Ste. Genevieve, MO. Celebration of town's French heritage. Tours of historic homes dating to the 1700s that exemplify some of the finest French Creole architecture. Also more than 600 arts and crafts booths and colonial crafts demonstrations by authentically costumed crafters. Est attendance: 40,000. For info: Ste. Genevieve Tourist Info Center, 66 S Main, Ste. Genevieve, MO 63670. Phone: (573) 883-7097 or (800) 373-7007.

KNIGHTS OF COLUMBUS FAMILY WEEK. Aug 8–16. Held annually in August as a celebration of the importance of the family. Local councils throughout the countries in which the K of C is present hold family-oriented activities throughout this observance. The birth (Aug 12) and death (Aug 14) of Father Michael J. McGivney, founder of the Knights of Columbus, fall during this event. For info: Ronald J. Tracz, VP, Fraternal Services, Knights of Columbus, 1 Columbus Plaza, New Haven, CT 06510-3326.

KRXL CAR CRUISE. Aug 8. Kirksville, MO. Motorcycles, cars, antiques, hot rods, classics, originals and street rods. Est attendance: 3,000. For info: Steve Lloyd, General Mgr, KRXL, 1308 N Baltimore St, Kirksville, MO 63501. Phone: (816) 665-9841.

LAVENDER LIBERTY DAY. Aug 8. Baker Beach, San Francisco, CA. For everybody, especially nudist bisexuals, transgender persons, greens, feminist libertarians. Remembering birthday of pioneer gay-libber Karl Heinrich Ulrichs (Aug 28, 1825). Annually, the second Saturday in August. Est attendance: 100. For info: SUN (Senior Unlimited Nudes), c/o Tahanga Research Assn, PO Box 495, Berkeley, CA 94701-0495. Email: danr@holonet.net.

LEITERSBURG PEACH FESTIVAL. Aug 8–9. Leitersburg Ruritan Community Park, Leitersburg, MD. This peach-oriented event features crafts, pony rides, bluegrass and country music and a quilt raffle. Annually, the second weekend in August. Est attendance: 10,000. For info: Leitersburg Ruritan Club, 21378 Leiters Mill Rd, Hagerstown, MD 21742-1633. Phone: (301) 797-6387.

MARCH, FREDRIC: BIRTH ANNIVERSARY. Aug 8, 1897. Academy and Tony Award–winning actor Fredric March was born Frederick McIntyre Bickel at Racine, WI. Over the course of his long and distinguished career, March performed on both the stage and screen. He made more than 65 movies and was nominated for five Academy Awards, winning in 1932 for his role in *Dr. Jekyll and Mr. Hyde* and in 1947 for *The Best Years of Our Lives*. In 1956 he appeared on stage in the world premiere of Eugene O'Neill's *Long Day's Journey into Night*. He received the Tony Award for that performance. He died at age 77 on Apr 14, 1975, at Los Angeles, CA.

MARKERT, RUSSELL: BIRTH ANNIVERSARY. Aug 8, 1899. American choreographer Russell Markert was born at Jersey City, NJ. He founded and directed the Radio City Music Hall Rockettes from 1932 to 1971. He died on Dec 1, 1990, at Waterbury, CT.

MONDALE, JOAN ADAMS: BIRTHDAY. Aug 8. Wife of 42nd vice president of the US, Walter F. Mondale, born at Eugene, OR, on Aug 8, 1930. Married Dec 27, 1955.

MONTANAFAIR. Aug 8–15. MetraPark, Billings, MT. Montana's biggest event featuring exhibits, livestock events, carnival, rodeo and entertainment. Est attendance: 240,000. For info: MetraPark, PO Box 2514, Billings, MT 59103. Phone: (406) 256-2400.

MORRIS, ESTHER HOBART McQUIGG: BIRTH ANNIVERSARY. Aug 8, 1814. Esther Hobart McQuigg Morris was born at Tioga County, NY, but eventually moved to the Wyoming Territory, where she worked in the women's rights movement and had a key role in getting a women's suffrage bill passed. Morris became justice of the peace of South Pass City, WY, in 1870, one of the first times a woman held public office in the US. She represented Wyoming at the national suffrage convention in 1895. She died Apr 2, 1902, at Cheyenne, WY.

NATIONAL SCRABBLE CHAMPIONSHIP. Aug 8–13. Players compete for the national championship in the popular game invented by unemployed architect Alfred Butts in 1931. Est attendance: 500. For info: Kathy Hummel, Natl Scrabble Assn, Box 700, Front St Garden, Greenport, NY 11944. Phone: (516) 477-0033. Fax: (516) 477-0294. Email: info@scrabble-assoc.com.

NEW OXFORD RAGTIME FESTIVAL. Aug 8. New Oxford, PA. Festival includes piano competition, ragtime pianists and instrumental ragtime. Events are held come rain or shine from 10 AM–5 PM. For info: Gettysburg Conv & Visitors Bureau, 35 Carlisle St, Gettysburg, PA 17325. Phone: (717) 334-6274. Fax: (717) 334-1166. WWW: http://www.gettysburg.com

NORTH GEORGIA HERBAL FAIRE. Aug 8. Rabun Gap Nacoochee School, Rabun Gap, GA. A day of herbal celebration featuring nationally known speakers, demonstrations, food, children's activities and craftspeople selling their own herbal creations. Est attendance: 2,000. For info: Penny's Garden, PO Box 573, Mountain City, GA 30562. Phone: (706) 746-6918. Fax: (706) 746-7120. Email: pennysgarden@stc.net.

ODIE: 20th BIRTHDAY. Aug 8, 1978. Commemorates the birthday of Odie, Garfield's sidekick, who first appeared in the Garfield comic strip on this date. For info: Paws, Inc, Kim Campbell, 5440 E Co Rd, 450 N, Albany, IN 47320. WWW: http://www.garfield.com

PILOT PEN INTERNATIONAL TENNIS TOURNAMENT. Aug 8–16. CT Tennis Center, Yale University, New Haven, CT. Fifty-six of the world's top men's singles players and 28 doubles teams will compete for more than $1 million in prize money. For info: CT Tennis Center (888) 99-PILOT or Greater New Haven Conv & Visitors Bureau, One Long Wharf Dr, New Haven, CT 06511. Phone: (203) 777-8550 or (800) 332-STAY. Fax: (203) 782-7755.

RAILROADER'S FESTIVAL (WITH SPIKE-DRIVING CONTEST). Aug 8. Promontory, UT. Visitors relive the rush to complete the transcontinental railroad. Professionals vie for the world's record in a spike-driving contest. Annually, the second Saturday in August. Sponsor: Golden Spike National Historic Site, PO Box 897, Brigham City, UT 84302. Phone: (801) 471-2209. Est attendance: 4,000. For info: Utah Travel Council, Council Hall, Capitol Hill, Salt Lake City, UT 84114. Phone: (801) 538-1030. Fax: (801) 538-1399. WWW: http://www.utah.com

RAWLINGS, MARJORIE KINNAN: BIRTH ANNIVERSARY. Aug 8, 1896. American short-story writer and novelist (*The Yearling*), born at Washington, DC. Rawlings died at St. Augustine, FL, Dec 14, 1953.

ROCK CITY'S FAIRY TALE FESTIVAL. Aug 8–9 (also Aug 15–16 and 22–23). Rock City Gardens, Lookout Mountain, TN. Memories are made and dreams come true each year as Rock City holds its 12th annual Fairy Tale Festival where storybook characters come to life. Cinderella, Little Red Riding Hood, Sleeping Beauty and others will greet visitors as they enter the gardens. Est attendance: 40,000. For info: Shelda Spencer Rees, PR Dept, See Rock City Inc, PO Box 2315, Chattanooga, TN 37409. Phone: (706) 820-2531. Fax: (706) 820-9623.

SEWARD SILVER SALMON DERBY. Aug 8–16. Seward, AK. Alaska's largest salmon derby. Fishermen vie for cash prizes, including tagged fish, daily top fish awards and sweepstakes drawing. 43rd annual. Est attendance: 10,000. For info: Seward Chamber of Commerce, PO Box 749, Seward, AK 99664. Phone: (907) 224-8051. Fax: (907) 224-5353. WWW: http://www.alaskaone.com/seward

SHILTS, RANDY: BIRTH ANNIVERSARY. Aug 8, 1951. Journalist known for his reporting on the AIDS epidemic. One of the first openly homosexual journalists to work for a mainstream newspaper and the author of *And the Band Played On: Politics, People and the AIDS Epidemic.* Born at Davenport, IA, and died at Guerneville, CA, on Feb 17, 1994.

SILVER VALLEY CLASSIC HORSESHOE TOURNAMENT. Aug 8–9. City Park, Kellogg, ID. Annually, the second weekend of August. Saturday, sanctioned National Horseshoe Association singles tournament. Sunday, doubles fun tournament. Est attendance: 120. For info: Don Heidt, 304 E Cameron Ave, Apt A, Kellogg, ID 83837.

SNEAK SOME ZUCCHINI ONTO YOUR NEIGHBORS' PORCH NIGHT. Aug 8. Due to overzealous planting of zucchini, citizens are asked to drop off baskets of the squash on neighbors' doorsteps. Annually, Aug 8. [© 1997 by WPL] For info: Tom or Ruth Roy, Wellness Permission League, PO Box 662, Mt Gretna, PA 17064-0662. Phone: (500) 437-5104 or (717) 964-1308. Fax: (717) 964-1335.

SPACE MILESTONE: *PIONEER VENUS* MULTIPROBE (US): 20th ANNIVERSARY. Aug 8, 1978. Second craft in *Pioneer Venus* program. Split into five and probed Venus atmosphere Dec 9. Launched on Aug 8, 1978.

STATE WILD GAME COOKOFF. Aug 8. Oakwood Lakes State Park, SD. Open to any cook with a pot to cook in. Categories include porridge and roasted meat. Contestants are also judged on their best "true fabrication" of how they caught the critter for the pot. Est attendance: 100. For info: Dave & Julie Huebner, Brookings Renegade Muzzleloaders, 47826 Main St, Bushnell, SD 57276. Phone: (605) 693-4589.

STREETSCENE. Aug 8. Covington, VA. Car Show, open to all types of vehicles! 10–4. Entertainment throughout the day. Annually, the second Saturday in August. Est attendance: 12,500. For info: Kars Unlimited, Inc, PO Box 851, Covington, VA 24426. Phone: (540) 962-3642.

VICARY DAY. Aug 8. Freedom, PA. 7th annual. Historical crafters, water battles, parade, food, crafts, car cruise and more. For info: (412) 728-5744 or Beaver County Tourist Promotion Agency, 215 B Ninth St, Monaca, PA 15061-2028. Phone: (412) 728-0212. Fax: (412) 728-0456.

WATERMELON FESTIVAL. Aug 8. Rush Springs, OK. Beginning with watermelon judging and ending with the crowning of the festival queen, the highlight of the celebration is the serving of 50,000 pounds of free watermelon at Jeff Davis Park. Est attendance: 20,000. For info: Chamber of Commerce, Box 298, Rush Springs, OK 73082. Phone: (405) 476-3277.

WILD WEST DAYS. Aug 8–9. Rockford, IL. Bank robbery reenactment, cowboy music, roping demonstrations, gunfights and great grub. Est attendance: 5,000. For info: Midway Village & Museum Center, 6799 Guilford Rd, Rockford, IL 61107. Phone: (815) 397-9112. Fax: (815) 397-9156.

WORLD WAR I: SECOND BATTLE OF AMIENS: 80th ANNIVERSARY. Aug 8, 1918. Two days after the Battle of Marne ended, the British Fourth Army mounted an offensive at Amiens with the objective of freeing the Amiens-Paris railway

August 1998

S	M	T	W	T	F	S
						1
2	3	4	5	6	7	8
9	10	11	12	13	14	15
16	17	18	19	20	21	22
23	24	25	26	27	28	29
30	31					

from bombardment by the German Second and Eighteenth Armies. More than 16,000 German prisoners were taken in two hours of fighting the first day. The German forces were forced back to the Hindenburg line by Sept 3. This battle is considered a turning point by many historians because of its impact on the psyche of Germany. Aug 8 was described by General Erich Ludendorff as a "Black Day" for Germany.

BIRTHDAYS TODAY

Beatrice, 10, Princess of York, born London, England, Aug 8, 1988.
Keith Carradine, 48, actor (*Nashville, Will Rogers Follies*), singer, born San Mateo, CA, Aug 8, 1950.
Benny Carter, 91, jazz musician, composer, born New York, NY, Aug 8, 1907.
Dino DeLaurentiis, 79, producer, born Torre Annunziata, Italy, Aug 8, 1919.
The Edge (David Evans), 37, musician (U2), born Dublin, Ireland, Aug 8, 1961.
Dustin Hoffman, 61, actor (Oscars for *Rain Man, Kramer vs Kramer; The Graduate, Midnight Cowboy, Outbreak*), born Los Angeles, CA, Aug 8, 1937.
Deborah Norville, 40, TV hostess ("Today Show"), born Dalton, GA, Aug 8, 1958.
Roberta Cooper Ramo, 56, first woman president of the American Bar Association, born Denver, CO, Aug 8, 1942.
Edward T. Schafer, 52, governor of North Dakota (R), born Bismark, ND, Aug 8, 1946.
Connie Stevens, 60, actress (Cricket Blake on "Hawaiian Eye"), born Brooklyn, NY, Aug 8, 1938.
Mel Tillis, 66, singer, songwriter, born Pahokee, FL, Aug 8, 1932.
Esther Williams, 75, swimmer, actress (*Take Me Out to the Ball Game, Dangerous When Wet*), born Los Angeles, CA, Aug 8, 1923.

AUGUST 9 — SUNDAY

Day 221 — 144 Remaining

ATOMIC BOMB DROPPED ON NAGASAKI: ANNIVERSARY. Aug 9, 1945. Three days after the atomic bombing of Hiroshima, an American B-29 bomber named *Bock's Car* left its base on Tinian Island carrying a plutonium bomb nicknamed "Fat Man." Its target was the Japanese city of Kokura, but because of clouds and poor visibility the bomber headed for a secondary target, Nagasaki, where at 11:02 AM, local time, it dropped the bomb, killing an estimated 70,000 persons and destroying about half the city. In 1985, it was said that the bombardier who pushed the button releasing the bomb would like to apologize to the survivors (called *hibakusha*), but the mayor of Nagasaki declined, saying he could not find it in his heart to meet him. Memorial services are held annually at Nagasaki and also at Kokura, where those who were spared because of the bad weather also grieve for those at Nagasaki who suffered in their stead.

BOOK LOVERS DAY. Aug 9. Borrow or buy a book and start reading it! Lend or give a book to somebody you love. Annually, Aug 9. Sponsor: "A writer, on behalf of all writers, readers, librarians, booksellers and publishers." For info: Linda Campbell Franklin, Book Lovers Day, 2716 Northfield, Charlottesville, VA 22901.

BURRO RACE. Aug 9. Leadville, CO. International Pack Burro Race leaves from Main St up Mosquito Pass and back. Est attendance: 35,000. For info: Gloria Cheshier, Chamber of Commerce, Box 861, Leadville, CO 80461. Phone: (719) 486-3900 or (800) 933-3901. Fax: (719) 486-8478. Email: leadville@sni.net. WWW: http://www.colorado.com/leadville

CATALINA WATER SKI RACE. Aug 9. Long Beach, CA. International water-ski racing teams race 62 miles across open seas, round-trip from Long Beach to Catalina Island and back. Est attendance: 9,000. For info: Long Beach Boat and Ski Club, PO Box 2370, Long Beach, CA 90801. Phone: (714) 894-3498. Fax: (714) 893-2363.

COCHRAN, JACQUELINE: DEATH ANNIVERSARY. Aug 9, 1980. American pilot Jacqueline Cochran was born at Pensacola, FL, in 1910. She began flying in 1932 and by the time of her death she had set more distance, speed and altitude records than any other pilot, male or female. She was founder and head of the WASPs (Women's Air Force Service Pilots) during World War II; she won the Distinguished Service Medal in 1945 and the US Air Force Distinguished Flying Cross in 1969. She died on Aug 9, 1980, at Indio, CA.

COUNTRY JAMBOREE. Aug 9. Trollwood Park, Fargo, ND. A full day of country music featuring the region's finest country music performers. Sponsor: Froggy 99.9 FM. Est attendance: 5,000. For info: Carolyn Boutain, Dir, Trollwood Park, PO Box 1796, Fargo, ND 58107. Phone: (701) 241-8160. Fax: (701) 241-8266.

EXETER ROAD RALLY. Aug 9. Exeter City Park, Exeter, NE. Participants decipher clues which take them throughout the countryside and into neighboring communities. Evening meal served. Registration 1 PM. 14th annual rally. Annually, the second Sunday in August. Est attendance: 150. For info: Norene Fitzgerald, Box 368, Exeter, NE 68351. Phone: (402) 266-2691.

FAMILY DAY. Aug 9. To focus attention on family solidarity and its potential as the best teacher of basic beliefs and values. Annually, the second Sunday in August. See also: "American Family Day" observed on the first Sunday in August in Arizona and "Family Day" observed on the last Sunday in August in Tennessee. For info: Kiwanis Intl, Program Dvmt Dept, 3636 Woodview Trace, Indianapolis, IN 46268. Email: kiwanismail@kiwanis.org. WWW: http://www.kiwanis.org

HERBERT HOOVER DAY. Aug 9. Iowa. Annually, the Sunday nearest Aug 10th.

INTERNATIONAL ART APPRECIATION DAY. Aug 9. A day to applaud and appreciate the abundance of art in all of its splendorous variety. For info: Adrienne Sioux Koopersmith, 1437 W Rosemont, #1W, Chicago, IL 60660-1319. Phone: (773) 743-5341. Fax: (773) 743-5395. Email: kooper@interaccess.com.

ITALY: PALIO DEL GOLFO. Aug 9. La Spezia. A rowing contest over a 2,000-meter course is held on the second Sunday in August.

JAPAN: MOMENT OF SILENCE. Aug 9. Nagasaki. Memorial observance held at Peace Memorial Park for victims of second atomic bomb, which was dropped on Nagasaki by an American bomber, Aug 9, 1945.

LASSEN VOLCANIC NATIONAL PARK ESTABLISHED: ANNIVERSARY. Aug 9, 1916. California's Lassen Peak and Cinder Cone National Monument, proclaimed May 6, 1907, and other wilderness land were combined and established as a national park. For further park info: Lassen Volcanic Natl Park, Mineral, CA 96063.

MORTON, WILLIAM THOMAS GREEN: BIRTH ANNIVERSARY. Aug 9, 1819. Dentist, born at Charlton, MA. Morton was the first to use ether as a general anesthetic. Died at New York, NY, July 15, 1868.

NATIONAL HAND-HOLDING DAY©. Aug 9. A day to take the opportunity to hold the hand of someone you hold dear. For info: Adrienne Sioux Koopersmith, 1437 W Rosemont, #1W, Chicago, IL 60660-1319. Phone: (773) 743-5341. Fax: (773) 743-5395. Email: kooper@interaccess.com.

NATIONAL NO-TILLAGE WEEK. Aug 9–15. The country's most innovative farmers demonstrate use of conservation tillage practices to provide consumers with an abundant, healthy food supply while protecting the environment. For info: Frank Lessiter, No-Till Farmer, PO Box 624, Brookfield, WI 53008-0624. Phone: (414) 782-4480. Fax: (414) 782-1252. Email: Lesspub@aol.com.

NATIONAL RESURRECT ROMANCE WEEK. Aug 9–15. Event focuses on celebrating noncommercialized romanticism by paying tribute to those persons who are romantic year-round, not just on Valentine's Day or Sweetest Day. Event encourages all persons, especially men, to find ways to be romantic every day of the year. Annually, six months after Valentine's Day. For info: Michael Webb, Editor, The RoMantic Newsletter, 2291 Avent Ferry, Ste 215, Raleigh, NC 27606. Phone: (888) 476-6268 or (919) 462-0900. Fax: (919) 461-9933. Email: romantc@aol.com. WWW: http://www.TheRomantic.com

PERSEID METEOR SHOWERS. Aug 9–13. Among the best-known and most spectacular meteor showers are the Perseids, peaking about Aug 10–12. As many as 50–100 may be seen in a single night. Wish upon a "falling star"!

PRESIDENTIAL RESIGNATION: ANNIVERSARY. Aug 9, 1974. The resignation from the presidency of the US by Richard Milhous Nixon, which had been announced in a speech to the American people the night before, became effective at noon on this day. Nixon, under threat of impeachment as a result of the Watergate scandal, became the first US president to resign.

PYROTECHNICS GUILD INTERNATIONAL FIREWORKS CONVENTION. Aug 9–14. Gillette, WY. The world's finest fireworks are displayed and members compete for the title of Grand Master during this annual international pyrotechnic convention. The Pyrotechnics Guild promotes the design, construction and safe display of the highest-quality pyrotechnics. Annually, a week in August. Est attendance: 50,000. For info: Mark Wray, Pyrotechnics Guild International Inc, 11144 Claire Ave, Northridge, CA 91326-2333. Phone: (818) 363-6277. Email: mlwray@aol.com. WWW: http://www.pacificnet.net/~pgi/

ROASTING EARS OF CORN FOOD FEST. Aug 9. The Museum of Indian Culture, Allentown, PA. Traditional American Indian event with activities for the whole family. Est attendance: 3,000. For info: Lenni Lenape Historical Soc, 2825 Fish Hatchery Rd, Allentown, PA 18103-9801. Phone: (610) 797-2121. Fax: (610) 797-2801. WWW: http://www.lenape.org

SCOTLAND: EDINBURGH FESTIVAL FRINGE. Aug 9–31. Edinburgh, Scotland. More than 10,000 performances of more than 1,000 shows in 150 venues, including theater, dance, music and children's shows. Takes place at the same time and on the fringes of the Edinburgh International Festival. For info: Edinburgh Festival Fringe Society, 180 High St, Edinburgh, Scotland EH1 1QS. Phone: (44) (131) 226-5257. Fax: (44) (131) 220-4205. Email: admin@edfringe.org.uk.
WWW: http://www.presence.co.uk/fringe

August 1998

S	M	T	W	T	F	S
						1
2	3	4	5	6	7	8
9	10	11	12	13	14	15
16	17	18	19	20	21	22
23	24	25	26	27	28	29
30	31					

SCOTLAND: EDINBURGH INTERNATIONAL FESTIVAL. Aug 9–31. Edinburgh, Lothian. One of the world's largest arts festivals, attracting many international stars. Now in its 51st year, the festival includes symphonic music, opera and ballet. Est attendance: 620,000. For info: Mktg Dept, Edinburgh Festival Society, 21 Market St, Edinburgh, Scotland EH1 1BW. Phone: (44) (131) 473-2001. Fax: (44) (131) 473-2002.

SINGAPORE: INDEPENDENCE DAY. Aug 9, 1965. Most festivals in Singapore are Chinese, Indian or Malay, but celebration of national day is shared by all to commemorate the withdrawal of Singapore from Malaysia and its becoming an independent state in 1965. Music, parades, dancing.

UNITED NATIONS: INTERNATIONAL DAY OF THE WORLD'S INDIGENOUS PEOPLE. Aug 9. On Dec 23, 1994, the General Assembly decided that the International Day of the World's Indigenous People shall be observed on Aug 9 every year during the International Decade of the World's Indigenous People (1994–2004) (Res 49/214). The date marks the anniversary of the first day of the meeting in 1992 of the Working Group on Indigenous Populations of the Subcommission on Prevention of Discrimination and Protection of Minorities. For info: United Nations, Dept of Public Info, Public Inquiries Unit, RM GA-57, New York, NY 10017. Phone: (212) 963-4475. Fax: (212) 963-0071. Email: inquiries@un.org.

VEEP DAY. Aug 9. Recalling the day in 1974 when Richard Nixon's resignation let Gerald Ford succeed to the presidency of the US. This was the first time the new Constitutional provisions for presidential succession took effect. For info: c/o Bob Birch, The Puns Corps, PO Box 2364, Falls Church, VA 22042-0364. Phone: (703) 533-3668.

WALTON, IZAAK: BIRTH ANNIVERSARY. Aug 9, 1593. English author of classic treatise on fishing, *The Compleat Angler*, published in 1653, was born at Stafford, England. Died at Winchester, England, Dec 15, 1683. "Angling," Walton wrote, "may be said to be so like the mathematics, that it can never be fully learnt."

WEBSTER-ASHBURTON TREATY SIGNED: ANNIVERSARY. Aug 9. The treaty delimiting the eastern section of the Canadian-American border was negotiated in 1842 by the US Secretary of State, Daniel Webster, and Alexander Baring, president of the British Board of Trade. The treaty established the boundaries between the St. Croix and Connecticut rivers, between Lake Superior and the Lake of the Woods, and between Lakes Huron and Superior. The treaty was signed in Washington, DC, on Aug 9, 1842.

BIRTHDAYS TODAY

Amanda Bearse, 40, actress ("Married . . . with Children"), born Atlanta, GA, Aug 9, 1958.

Robert Joseph (Bob) Cousy, 70, former coach and Basketball Hall of Fame guard, born New York, NY, Aug 9, 1928.

William Daley, 50, US Secretary of Commerce (Clinton administration), born Chicago, IL, Aug 9, 1948.

Sam Elliott, 54, actor ("Mission Impossible," *Gettysburg*), born Sacramento, CA, Aug 9, 1944.

Melanie Griffith, 41, actress (*Working Girl, Something Wild, Smile*), born New York, NY, Aug 9, 1957.

Whitney Houston, 35, singer ("And I Will Always Love You"), actress (*Waiting to Exhale*), born Newark, NJ, Aug 9, 1963.

Brett Hull, 34, hockey player, born Belleville, Ontario, Canada, Aug 9, 1964.

Rodney George (Rod) Laver, 60, former tennis player, born Rockhampton, Australia, Aug 9, 1938.

Kenneth Howard (Ken) Norton, Sr, 53, former boxer, born Jacksonville, IL, Aug 9, 1945.

Deion Sanders, 31, football player, born Fort Meyers, FL, Aug 9, 1967.

David Steinberg, 56, comedian ("The Music Scene," "The David Steinberg Show"), born Winnipeg, Manitoba, Canada, Aug 9, 1942.

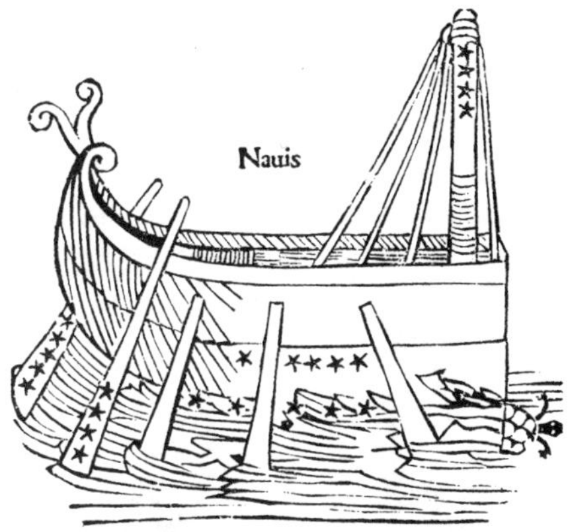

AUGUST 10 — MONDAY

Day 222 — 143 Remaining

CAMPBELL, ANGUS: BIRTH ANNIVERSARY. Aug 10. Professor of psychology and sociology, author and director of the Institute for Social Research at the University of Michigan, called a "man with a scientist's mind and a humanist's heart," born Aug 10, 1910, at Leiters, IN. He was one of the principal researchers in studies of social and racial problems and attitudes. Campbell died Dec 15, 1980, at Ann Arbor, MI.

"CANDID CAMERA" TV PREMIERE: 50th ANNIVERSARY. Aug 10, 1948. This show—which appeared at various times on the big three networks and in syndication—was created and hosted by Allen Funt. The show was initially an Armed Forces Radio program based on Funt's success in recording and broadcasting soldiers' gripes. The show's modus operandi was to catch people unawares on camera—either as part of a practical joke or just being themselves. It spawned numerous imitators such as "Totally Hidden Video," "People Do the Craziest Things" and "America's Funniest Home Videos."

DON'T WAIT—CELEBRATE! WEEK. Aug 10–16. To encourage frequent festivities acknowledging small but significant accomplishments such as team wins, good grades, completed projects, new neighbors, braces off, balanced checkbooks. Gathering for these minigalas will enhance and nurture relationships while raising the self-esteem of the honorees. Annually, the second full week in August. For info: Patty Sachs, Celebration Creations, 73-729 Manzanita Ct, Palm Desert, CA 92260. Phone: (619) 341-2066. Fax: (619) 341-2066.
Email: partysachs@internetmci.com.
WWW: http://www.angelfire.com/biz/celebrationsplus/dont.html

ECUADOR: INDEPENDENCE DAY. Aug 10. National holiday. Celebrates declaration of independence, Aug 10, 1809.

GINSBURG SWORN IN AS 107th JUSTICE: 5th ANNIVERSARY. Aug 10, 1993. One week after her confirmation by the Senate, Judge Ruth Bader Ginsburg was sworn in as the 107th Supreme Court justice. Ginsburg, a former leading women's-rights advocate, became the court's second woman justice.

HOOVER, HERBERT CLARK: BIRTH ANNIVERSARY. Aug 10, 1874. The 31st president of the US was born at West Branch, IA. Hoover was the first president born west of the Mississippi River and the first to have a telephone on his desk (installed Mar 27, 1929). "Older men declare war. But it is youth that must fight and die," he said in Chicago, IL, at the Republican National Convention, June 27, 1944. Hoover died at New York, NY, Oct 20, 1964. The Sunday nearest Aug 10th is observed in Iowa as Herbert Hoover Day.

JAPAN'S UNCONDITIONAL SURRENDER: ANNIVERSARY. Aug 10, 1945. A gathering to discuss surrender terms took place in Emperor Hirohito's bomb shelter; the participants were stalemated. Hirohito settled the question, believing continuation of the war would only result in further loss of Japanese lives. A message was transmitted to Japanese ambassadors in Switzerland and Sweden to accept the terms issued at Potsdam on July 26, 1945, except that the Japanese emperor's sovereignty must be maintained. The Allies devised a plan under which the emperor and the Japanese government would administer under the rule of the Supreme Commander of the Allied Powers, and the Japanese surrendered.

MISSOURI: ADMISSION DAY: ANNIVERSARY. Aug 10. Became 24th state on this day in 1821.

SMITHSONIAN INSTITUTION FOUNDED: ANNIVERSARY. Aug 10, 1846. Founding of the Smithsonian Institution at Washington, DC. For info: Smithsonian Institution, 900 Jefferson Dr SW, Washington, DC 20560. Phone: (202) 357-2700.

SPACE MILESTONE: *DISCOVERER 13* (US). Aug 10, 1960. Ejected space capsule, first object recovered after orbiting. Launched Aug 10, 1960.

VICTORY DAY. Aug 10. Rhode Island. State holiday commemorating President Truman's announcement of the surrender of the Japanese to the Allies on Aug 14, 1945. Annually, the second Monday in Aug.

BIRTHDAYS TODAY

Ian Anderson, 51, musician, singer (leader of Jethro Tull; "Bungle in the Jungle"), born Blackpool, England, Aug 10, 1947.
Rosanna Arquette, 39, actress (*Desperately Seeking Susan, New York Stories*), born New York, NY, Aug 10, 1959.
Antonio Banderas, 38, actor (*Too Much, Four Rooms*), born Malaga, Spain, Aug 10, 1960.
Riddick Bowe, 31, boxer, born Brooklyn, NY, Aug 10, 1967.
Jimmy Dean (Seth Ward), 70, singer ("Big Bad John," "P.T. 109"), born Plainview, TX, Aug 10, 1928.
Eddie Fisher, 70, singer ("Heart," "Cindy, Oh Cindy"), born Philadelphia, PA, Aug 10, 1928.
Rhonda Fleming (Marilyn Lewis), 75, actress ("Stage Door," *The Best of Broadway*), born Los Angeles, CA, Aug 10, 1923.
Betsy Johnson, 56, fashion designer, born Wethersfield, CT, Aug 10, 1942.
Benjamin Ward, 72, police administrative official, born Brooklyn, NY, Aug 10, 1926.

AUGUST 11 — TUESDAY

Day 223 — 142 Remaining

ATCHISON, DAVID R.: BIRTH ANNIVERSARY. Aug 11. Missouri legislator who was president of the US for one day. Born at Frogtown, KY, on Aug 11, 1807, Atchison's strong proslavery opinions made his name prominent in legislative debates. He served as president pro tempore of the Senate a number of times, and he became president of the US for one day—Sunday, Mar 4, 1849—pending the swearing in of President-elect Zachary Taylor on Monday, Mar 5, 1849. The city of Atchison, KS, and the county of Atchison, MO, are named for him. He died at Gower, MO, on Jan 26, 1886.

BAHAMAS: FOX HILL DAY. Aug 11. Nassau. Annually, the second Tuesday in August.

BEATLES' NATIONAL APPLE WEEK: ANNIVERSARY. Aug 11–18. The Beatles proclaimed this week to be "National Apple Week" in 1965, when they launched their Apple recording label. Presentation boxes of "Our First Four" releases were sent to the Queen, the Queen Mother and Princess Margaret. In return, the Queen Mother sent a thank you note saying that she was "greatly touched by this kind thought from the Beatles" and "much enjoyed listening to these recordings."

BOND, CARRIE JACOBS: BIRTH ANNIVERSARY. Aug 11, 1862. American composer of well-known songs, including "I Love You Truly" and "A Perfect Day," and of scores for motion pictures, Carrie Jacobs Bond was born at Janesville, WI; she died at Hollywood, CA, at age 84, on Dec 28, 1946.

CHAD: INDEPENDENCE DAY. Aug 11. National holiday.

FINLAND: TAMPERE INTERNATIONAL THEATRE FESTIVAL. Aug 11–16. Tampere. 30th annual festival includes approximately 60 productions from abroad and Finland in about 200 performances, plus about 150 other events. Seminars, OFF Tampere, festival club's exhibitions, etc. Est attendance: 100,000. For info: Raija-Liisa Seilo, Exec Dir, Tampere Intl Theatre Festival Office, Tullikamarinaukio 2, Tampere, Finland FIN-33100. Phone: (358) (3) 222-8536. Fax: (358) (3) 223-0121.

FIRST FOREIGN-BORN OFFICER APPOINTED CHAIR OF JOINT CHIEFS: 5th ANNIVERSARY. Aug 11, 1993. President Bill Clinton appointed Army General John Shalikashvili to succeed Colin Powell as Chairman of the Joint Chiefs of Staff. Shalikashvili was born in Poland, but his family fled to Germany in 1944 to escape advancing Soviet troops. After moving to the US, his family lived in Peoria, IL. "General Shali" has a distinguished military record and is a Vietnam war veteran.

FREDERICK DOUGLASS SPEAKS: ANNIVERSARY. Aug 11, 1841. Having escaped from slavery only three years earlier, Frederick Douglass was legally a fugitive when he first spoke before an audience. At an antislavery convention on Nantucket Island Douglass spoke simply but eloquently about his life as a slave. His words were so moving that he was asked to become a full-time lecturer for the Massachusetts Anti-Slavery Society. Douglass became a brilliant orator, writer and abolitionist who championed the rights of blacks as well as the rights of all humankind.

HALEY, ALEX PALMER: BIRTH ANNIVERSARY. Aug 11, 1921. Born at Ithaca, NY, Alex Palmer Haley was raised by his grandmother in Henning, TN. In 1939 he entered the US Coast Guard and served as a cook, but eventually he became a writer and college professor. His interview with Malcolm X for *Playboy* led to his first book, *The Autobiography of Malcolm X*, which sold six million copies and was translated into eight languages. *Roots*, his Pulitzer Prize–winning novel published in 1976, sold millions, was translated into 37 languages and was made into an eight-part TV miniseries in 1977. Its airing set records as millions of Americans of all hues tuned in to see its portrayal of the horrors of slavery and the humanity and nobility of spirit of its victims. The story also generated an enormous interest in family ancestry. Haley died at Seattle, WA, Feb 13, 1992.

INGERSOLL, ROBERT GREEN: BIRTH ANNIVERSARY. Aug 11, 1833. American author, orator, lawyer, politician and agnostic was born at Dresden, NY, and died at Dobbs Ferry, NY, on July 21, 1899, at age 65. "An honest God," he wrote, "is the noblest work of man."

INTERTRIBAL INDIAN CEREMONIAL. Aug 11–16. Red Rock State Park, Gallup, NM. A major Indian festival with more than 50 tribes from the US and Mexico. Parades, Indian dances, rodeos, arts and crafts and foods. Est attendance: 32,500. For info: Intertribal Indian Ceremonial Assn, Box 1, Church Rock, NM 87311. Phone: (800) 233-4528 or (505) 863-3896. Fax: (505) 722-5158.

PRESIDENTIAL JOKE DAY: ANNIVERSARY. Aug 11, 1984. Anniversary of President Ronald Reagan's voice-test joke. In preparation for a radio broadcast, during a thought-to-be-off-the-record voice level test, instead of counting "one, two, three . . ." the president said: "My fellow Americans, I am pleased to tell you I just signed legislation which outlaws Russia forever. The bombing begins in five minutes." The statement was picked up by live television cameras and was seen and heard by millions worldwide. The incident provoked national and international reactions, including a news network proposal of new ground rules concerning the use of "off-the-record" remarks.

SAINT CLARE OF ASSISI: FEAST DAY. Aug 11, 1253. Chiara Favorone di Offreduccio, a religious leader inspired by St. Francis of Assisi, was the first woman to write her own religious order rule. Born at Assisi, Italy, in 1193, she died there Aug 11, 1253. A "Privilege of Poverty" freed her order from any constraint to accept material security, making the "Poor Clares" totally dependent on God.

SIOUX EMPIRE FAIR. Aug 11–16. Sioux Falls, SD. Grandstand concerts, livestock exhibits, 4-H activities, flower and vegetable displays and craft exhibits. Est attendance: 200,000. For info: Sioux Empire Fair, W.H. Lyon Fairgrounds, Sioux Falls, SD 57107. Phone: (605) 367-7178.

SPACE MILESTONE: *VOSTOK 3* (USSR). Aug 11, 1962. Launched on this date, Andrian Nikolayev orbited Earth 64 times over a period of 94 hours, 25 minutes, covering distance of 1,242,500 miles. Achieved radio communication with *Vostok 4* and telecast from spacecraft.

TONTITOWN GRAPE FESTIVAL. Aug 11–15 (tentative). Tontitown, AR. 100th annual festival features more than 100 crafts exhibitors, a carnival and more than 6,000 lbs of homemade pasta and sauce served at Italian spaghetti dinners. Est attendance: 25,000. For info: Tontitown Grape Festival, PO Box 39, Tontitown, AR 72770. Phone: (501) 361-2612.

WATTS RIOT: ANNIVERSARY. Aug 11, 1965. A minor clash between the California Highway Patrol and two young blacks set off six days of riots in the Watts area of Los Angeles. Thirty-four deaths were reported and more than 3,000 people were arrested. Damage to property was listed at $40 million. The less-immediate cause of the disturbance and the others that followed was racial tension between whites and blacks in American society.

BIRTHDAYS TODAY

Joanna Coles, 54, children's author, born Newark, NJ, Aug 11, 1944.

Arlene Dahl, 70, actress ("One Life to Live," "Fantasy Island"), mother of actor Lorenzo Lamas, born Minneapolis, MN, Aug 11, 1928.

Mike Douglas (Michael Delaney Dowd, Jr), 73, TV host, singer, born Chicago, IL, Aug 11, 1925.

Jerry Falwell, 65, clergyman (head of Moral Majority PAC), born Lynchburg, VA, Aug 11, 1933.

Hulk Hogan (born Terry Gene Bollea), 45, wrestler, actor, born Augusta, GA, Aug 11, 1953.

Tim Hutchinson, 49, US Senator (R, Arkansas), born Gravette, AR, Aug 11, 1949.

Joe Jackson, 43, musician, songwriter, born Burton-on-Trent, England, Aug 11, 1955.

Anna Massey, 61, actress (*Bunny Lake Is Missing, A Doll's House*), born Thankeham, England, Aug 11, 1937.

Carl Rowan, 73, journalist, author (*Breaking Barriers*), born Ravenscraft, TN, Aug 11, 1925.

August 1998

S	M	T	W	T	F	S
						1
2	3	4	5	6	7	8
9	10	11	12	13	14	15
16	17	18	19	20	21	22
23	24	25	26	27	28	29
30	31					

AUGUST 12 — WEDNESDAY

Day 224 — 141 Remaining

BEWICK, THOMAS: BIRTH ANNIVERSARY. Aug 12, 1753. English artist, wood engraver and author, remembered especially for his book illustrations in *History of Quadrupeds*, *British Birds* and *Fables of Aesop*. Born at Cherryburn, Northumberland, and died at Gateshead, Durham, England, on Nov 8, 1828, at age 75.

CANTINFLAS: BIRTH ANNIVERSARY. Aug 12, 1911. Mexico's most famous comic actor, Cantinflas, was born at Mexico City as Mario Moreno Reyes. Particularly popular with the poor of Mexico because he most often portrayed the underdog, Cantinflas got his start in Mexico City *carpas*, the equivalent of vaudeville. He became internationally known for his role in *Around the World in 80 Days*. The name Cantinflas was invented by the comic to prevent his parents from learning he was in show business, which they considered a shameful endeavor. Died on Apr 20, 1993, at Mexico City.

DeMILLE, CECIL B.: BIRTH ANNIVERSARY. Aug 12, 1881. Film pioneer, born at Ashfield, MA. Cecil Blount DeMille was a film showman extraordinaire known for lavish screen spectacles. He produced more than 70 major films which were noted more for their large scale than for their subtle artistry. He produced one of the earliest four-reel films, *The Squaw Man*, in 1913, which boasted the first use of indoor lighting on an actor and was the first film to publicize the names of its stars. His other innovations included the sneak preview and the idea of producing different versions of a popular film. His films include *The Crusades, The Sign of the Cross, King of Kings, Cleopatra, The Plainsman, The Buccaneer, Reap the Wild Wind* and *The Ten Commandments*, which was made in 1923 and then in a new version in 1956. De Mille was awarded an Oscar for *The Greatest Show on Earth* in 1953. He died on Jan 21, 1959, at Hollywood, CA.

FLOOD VICTIMS RECEIVE $6.2 BILLION: 5th ANNIVERSARY. Aug 12, 1993. President Bill Clinton signed a bill Aug 12, 1993, providing $6.2 billion in federal relief to victims of floods in July and August for nine states from North Dakota to Missouri. Due to the record rains in the spring of up to 200% above average, the Midwest suffered 50 deaths, 70,000 left homeless and an estimated $12 billion in damage as of Aug 9, 1993.

INDIAN DAY. Aug 12. Massachusetts.

INDIANA STATE FAIR. Aug 12–23. Indiana State Fairgrounds Event Center, Indianapolis, IN. Top-rated livestock exhibition, world-class harness racing, top country music, giant midway and Pioneer Village. Est attendance: 700,000. For info: Jeff Fites, Publicity Coord, Indiana State Fair, 1202 E 38th St, Indianapolis, IN 46205-2869. Phone: (317) 927-7500. Fax: (317) 927-7578. WWW: http://www.iquest.net/statefair

KAHOKA FESTIVAL OF BLUEGRASS MUSIC. Aug 12–15. Kahoka, MO. Top bluegrass bands, clogging workshops and shows, Fiddlers Frolic, jam sessions, Miss Kahoka pageant, clogging contest and old-fashioned square dance. 26th annual festival. Est attendance: 4,000. For info: Delbert Spray, Program Dir, RR 1, Kahoka, MO 63445. Phone: (573) 853-4344.

KING PHILIP ASSASSINATION: ANNIVERSARY. Aug 12, 1676. Native American, Philip, son of Massasoit, chief of the Wampanog tribe, was killed near Mt Hope, RI, by a renegade Indian of his own tribe, bringing to an end the first and bloodiest war between American Indians and white settlers of New England, a war that had raged for nearly two years and was known as King Philip's War.

MATHEWSON, CHRISTY: BIRTH ANNIVERSARY. Aug 12, 1880. Famed American baseball player Christopher (Christy) Mathewson, one of the first players named to Baseball's Hall of Fame, was born at Factoryville, PA. Died at Saranac Lake, NY, Oct 7, 1925. He pitched three complete games during the 1905 World Series without allowing opponents to score a run. In 17 years he won 372 games while losing 188 and striking out 2,499 players.

MOUNT OGURA PLANE CRASH: ANNIVERSARY. Aug 12, 1985. A Japan Airlines plane crashed into the side of Mount Ogura, Japan, claiming 475 lives. The worst air disaster involving a single plane.

PALOMINO LEAGUE WORLD SERIES. Aug 12–15 (tentative dates). Greensboro, NC. International young adult baseball World Series for players of league ages 17 and 18. Est attendance: 6,650. For info: Pony Baseball, Inc, Box 225, Washington, PA 15301. Phone: (412) 225-1060. Fax: (412) 225-9852. Email: pony@pulse.net.com. WWW: http://www.pony.org

SEWING MACHINE INVENTED. Aug 12, 1851. Isaac Singer developed the sewing machine for use in homes.

SOUTHEAST ALASKA STATE FAIR AND ALASKAN BALD EAGLE MUSIC FESTIVAL. Aug 12–16. Haines, AK. Agricultural fair on the SE Alaska State Fair Grounds. Past entertainers have included Taj Mahal, Tuck & Patti, Leo Kottke, Karla Bonoff, Dan Hicks, Tony Rice and more. Est attendance: 10,000. For info: SE Alaska State Fair, PO Box 385, Haines, AK 99827. Phone: (907) 766-2476. Fax: (907) 766-2478. Email: seafair@seaknet.alaska.edu.

SPACE MILESTONE: *ECHO I* (US). Aug 12, 1960. First successful communications balloon, launched on this date.

SPACE MILESTONE: *ENTERPRISE* (US). Aug 12, 1977. Reusable orbiting vehicle (space shuttle) makes first successful flight on its own within Earth's atmosphere. Launched from Boeing 747 on Aug 12, 1977.

SWEDEN: CRAYFISH PREMIERE. Aug 12. Crayfish may be sold and served in restaurants the following day after the season opens. Annually, the second Wednesday in August.

THAILAND: BIRTHDAY OF THE QUEEN. Aug 12. The entire kingdom of Thailand celebrates the birthday of Queen Sirikit.

BIRTHDAYS TODAY

Dale Bumpers, 73, US Senator (D, Arkansas), born Charleston, AR, Aug 12, 1925.

John Derek (Dereck Harris), 72, actor (*All the King's Men, Prince of Players*), born Hollywood, CA, Aug 12, 1926.

William Goldman, 67, writer (*The Princess Bride, Marathon Man*), born Chicago, IL, Aug 12, 1931.

George Hamilton, 59, actor (*Love at First Bite, Act One*, "The Survivors"), born Memphis, TN, Aug 12, 1939.

Sam J. Jones, 44, actor (*Flash Gordon, "10"*), born Chicago, IL, Aug 12, 1954.

Michael Kidd (Milton Greenwald), 79, choreographer, born Brooklyn, NY, Aug 12, 1919.

Pat Metheny, 44, jazz guitarist ("Song X," "Letter from Home"), born Lee's Summit, MO, Aug 12, 1954.

"Buck" (Alvis Edgar) Owens, 69, singer ("Hee Haw," "Act Naturally"), songwriter, born Sherman, TX, Aug 12, 1929.

Pete Sampras, 27, tennis player, born Washington, DC, Aug 12, 1971.

George Soros, 68, billionaire, financier and philanthropist in Eastern Europe and the US, born Budapest, Hungary, Aug 12, 1930.

Fife Symington III, 53, Governor of Arizona (R), born New York, NY, Aug 12, 1945.

Porter Wagoner, 68, singer ("The Carroll County Accident"), born West Plains, MO, Aug 12, 1930.

Jane Wyatt, 85, actress (mother in "Father Knows Best"; Spock's mom on "Star Trek"), born New York, NY, Aug 12, 1913.

AUGUST 13 — THURSDAY

Day 225 — 140 Remaining

BEAVER COUNTY RIVERFEST. Aug 13–16. Riverfront Park, Rochester, PA. 24th annual. Join in the family fun with entertainment, food and much more. For info: (412) 846-6750 or Beaver County Tourist Promotion Agency, 215 B Ninth St, Monaca, PA 15061-2028. Phone: (412) 728-0212. Fax: (412) 728-0456.

BERLIN WALL ERECTED: ANNIVERSARY. Aug 13. Early in the morning of Sunday, Aug 13, 1961, the East German government closed the border between east and west sectors of Berlin with barbed wire fence to discourage further population movement to the west. Telephone and postal services were interrupted, and, later in the week, a concrete wall was built to strengthen the barrier between official crossing points. The dismantling of the wall was begun on Nov 9, 1989. See also: "Berlin Wall: Dismantling Anniversary" (Nov 9).

CANADA: CENTRAL CANADA EXHIBITION. Aug 13–23. Ottawa, Ontario. Amusement rides, food booths, various theme entertainment and circus. Plenty of fun for the whole family. Est attendance: 580,000. For info: Central Canada Exhibition, Lansdowne Park, Coliseum Bldg, Ottawa, Ontario, Canada K1S 3W7. Phone: (613) 237-7222. Fax: (613) 230-1748.

CAXTON, WILLIAM: BIRTH ANNIVERSARY. Aug 13. First English printer, born Aug 13, 1422. Died at London, England, 1491. Caxton produced first book printed in English (while he was still at Bruges), the *Recuyell of the Histories of Troy*, in 1476, and in the autumn of 1476 set up a print shop in Westminster, becoming the first printer in England.

August 1998

S	M	T	W	T	F	S
						1
2	3	4	5	6	7	8
9	10	11	12	13	14	15
16	17	18	19	20	21	22
23	24	25	26	27	28	29
30	31					

CENTRAL AFRICAN REPUBLIC: INDEPENDENCE DAY. Aug 13. Commemorates Proclamation of Independence of the Central African Republic, Aug 13, 1960.

COBBLESTONE FESTIVAL. Aug 13–16. Falls City, NE. Includes games, races, contests, carnival rides, flea market, food concessions, car show, demolition derby, tractor pull, parade, craft demos and more. Annually, mid-August. Est attendance: 2,500. For info: Chamber of Commerce, 107 E 17th, PO Box 146, Falls City, NE 68355. Phone: (402) 245-4228. Fax: (402) 245-4254.

CROW INDIAN FAIR. Aug 13–16. Crow Agency, MT. Members of Indian Tribes from around the US and Canada join the Crow Nation in this annual celebration. Crow Fair features the largest teepee village of any celebration among western tribes along with four days of traditional dancing, ceremonies, arts, crafts and food. A western rodeo is held in conjunction with the Crow Fair which is located near the Little Big Horn Battlefield National Historic Site. For info: Burton Pretty On Top, Crow Tribal Bldg, Crow Agency, MT 59022. Phone: (406) 638-2601.

ELWOOD GLASS FESTIVAL. Aug 13–15. Elwood, IN. Glass factory tours, parade, craft market, flea market, quilt show. Est attendance: 30,000. For info: Pat Bollinger, Chamber of Commerce, 108 S Anderson St, Elwood, IN 46036. Phone: (765) 552-0180.

HITCHCOCK, ALFRED (JOSEPH): BIRTH ANNIVERSARY. Aug 13, 1899. English film director and master of suspense born at London, made a string of classics including *The 39 Steps, Rebecca, Suspicion, Notorious, Rear Window, To Catch a Thief, The Birds, Psycho* and *Frenzy*, in addition to his TV series "Alfred Hitchcock Presents." He died on Apr 29, 1980, at Beverly Hills, CA.

HOPE WATERMELON FESTIVAL. Aug 13–16. Hope, AR. An event in which the entire family can participate while promoting the city of Hope and having fun. Hope is the birthplace of 42nd President of the US Bill Clinton. Annually, the third weekend in August. Est attendance: 50,000. For info: Mktg Dept, Hope–Hempstead County Chamber of Commerce, 108 W 3rd, PO Box 250, Hope, AR 71802-0250. Phone: (501) 777-3640.

INTERNATIONAL LEFTHANDERS DAY. Aug 13. To recognize the needs and frustrations of left-handers and celebrate the good life of left-handedness. For info: Lefthanders Intl, Box 8249, Topeka, KS 66608. Phone: (913) 234-2177. Fax: (913) 232-3999.

IOWA STATE FAIR. Aug 13–23. Iowa State Fairgrounds, Des Moines, IA. One of America's oldest and largest state fairs with one of the world's largest livestock shows. Ten-acre carnival, superstar grandstand stage shows, track events, spectacular free entertainment. 160-acre campgrounds. Est attendance: 900,000. For info: Kathie Swift, Mktg Dir, Iowa State Fair, Statehouse, 400 E 14th St, Des Moines, IA 50319-0198. Phone: (515) 262-3111. Fax: (515) 262-6906. WWW: http://iowastatefair.com

MISSOURI STATE FAIR. Aug 13–22. Sedalia, MO. Livestock shows, commercial and competitive exhibits, horse show, car races, tractor pulls, carnival and headline musical entertainment. Economical family entertainment. Est attendance: 350,000. For info: Deanna Alleger, PR Dir, Missouri State Fair, 2503 W 16th, Sedalia, MO 65301. Phone: (816) 530-5600. Fax: (816) 530-5609.

OAKLEY, ANNIE: BIRTH ANNIVERSARY. Aug 13. Annie Oakley was born at Darke County, OH, Aug 13, 1860. She developed an eye as a markswoman early as a child, becoming so proficient that she was able to pay off the mortgage on her family farm by selling the game she killed. A few years after defeating vaudeville marksman Frank Butler in a shooting match, she married him and they toured as a team until joining Buffalo Bill's Wild West Show in 1885. She was one of the star attractions for 17 years. She died Nov 3, 1926, at Greenville, OH.

PGA CHAMPIONSHIP. Aug 13–16. Sahalee Country Club, Redmond, WA. The 80th championship conducted by the Professional Golfers' Association of America. Est attendance:

150,000. For info: Kerry Haigh, Senior Dir of Tournaments, PGA of America, Box 109601, Palm Beach Gardens, FL 33410-9601. Phone: (561) 624-8495. Fax: (561) 624-8429.

RIBFEST. Aug 13–15. Kalamazoo, MI. Features the smell of sizzling ribs as rib-burners from throughout the US tantalize the taste buds of West Michigan. Festival will feature live entertainment, family-oriented events, food booths and the "Sponsors Choice Award" for best ribs. Annually, the second full weekend in August (Thursday–Saturday). Est attendance: 22,000. For info: Deborah Droppers, Comm Advocates for Persons with Developmental Disabilities, 806 S Westnedge St, Kalamazoo, MI 49008-1162. Phone: (616) 342-9801.

SKOWHEGAN STATE FAIR. Aug 13–22. Fairgrounds, Skowhegan, ME. 180th annual. Huge fair with horse pulling, tractor pulls, harness racing, carnival midway, exhibits, flower show, grandstand shows, coliseum events, truck pulls, demolition derby and much more. Annually, three weeks before Labor Day. Est attendance: 100,000. For info: Fred Lunt, Skowhegan State Fair Assn, PO Box 39, Skowhegan, ME 04976. Phone: (207) 474-2947.

STONE, LUCY: BIRTH ANNIVERSARY. Aug 13, 1818. American women's rights pioneer, born near West Brookfield, MA, Lucy Stone dedicated her life to the abolition of slavery and the emancipation of women. Although she graduated from Oberlin College, she had to finance her education by teaching for nine years because her father did not favor college education for women. An eloquent speaker for her causes, she headed the list of 89 men and women who signed the call to the first national Woman's Rights Convention, held in Worcester, MA, in Oct 1850. On May 1, 1855, she married Henry Blackwell. She and her husband aided in the founding of the American Suffrage Association, taking part in numerous referendum campaigns to win suffrage amendments to state constitutions. She died on Oct 18, 1893, at Dorchester, MA.

SUN PRAIRIE'S SWEET CORN FESTIVAL. Aug 13–16. Sun Prairie, WI. Family-oriented fun. Carnival, midget auto races, parade, beer, brats, food, exhibits and all the hot, buttered sweet corn you can eat. Est attendance: 100,000. For info: Chamber of Commerce, 109 E Main, Sun Prairie, WI 53590. Phone: (608) 837-4547. Fax: (608) 837-8765.

TUNISIA: WOMEN'S DAY. Aug 13. General holiday. Celebration of independence of women.

WE LOVE ERIE DAYS!. Aug 13–16. Erie, PA. The scenic waterfront is the setting for Erie's largest celebration. Activities include continuous live onstage entertainment, rides, food, boat races and ship tours. Est attendance: 300,000. For info: August Schiava, 1006 State St, Erie, PA 16501. Phone: (814) 454-7191. Fax: (814) 459-0241. Email: erie-tourism@erie.net.
WWW: http://www.eriepa.com

BIRTHDAYS TODAY

Fidel Castro, 71, President of Cuba, former amateur baseball player, born Mayari, Oriente Province, Cuba, Aug 13, 1927.

Quinn Cummings, 31, actress (*The Goodbye Girl,* Annie on "Family"), born Los Angeles, CA, Aug 13, 1967.

M. Joycelyn Elders, MD, 65, former Surgeon General of the US in Clinton administration, born Schaal, AR, Aug 13, 1933.

Dan Fogelberg, 47, composer, singer ("Same Old Lang Syne," "Leader of the Band"), born Peoria, IL, Aug 13, 1951.

Pat Harrington, Jr, 69, actor, comedian ("The Jack Paar Show," "One Day at a Time"), born New York, NY, Aug 13, 1929.

Don Ho, 68, singer ("Tiny Bubbles"), born Kakaako, HI, Aug 13, 1930.

William Benjamin (Ben) Hogan, 86, former golfer, born Dublin, TX, Aug 13, 1912. Died July 25, 1997, at Ft Worth, TX.

Kevin Tighe, 54, actor ("Emergency," *The Graduate, Matewan, What's Eating Gilbert Grape?*), born Los Angeles, CA, Aug 13, 1944.

☆ ☆ ☆

AUGUST 14 — FRIDAY

Day 226 — 139 Remaining

AMERICAN PSYCHOLOGICAL ASSOCIATION ANNUAL MEETING. Aug 14–18. San Francisco, CA. For info: Convention Office, American Psychological Assn, 750 First St NE, Washington, DC 20002-4242. WWW: http://www.apa.org

ATLANTIC CHARTER SIGNING: ANNIVERSARY. Aug 14, 1941. The eight-point agreement was signed by US President Franklin D. Roosevelt and British Prime Minister Winston S. Churchill. The charter grew out of a three-day conference aboard ship in the Atlantic Ocean, off the Newfoundland coast, and stated policies and hopes for the future agreed to by the two nations.

CANADA: SOURDOUGH RENDEZVOUS GOLD RUSH BATHTUB RACE. Aug 14–16. Beginning in Whitehorse, Yukon Territory. 7th annual 462-mile bathtub race from Whitehorse to Dawson. Est attendance: 1,500. For info: Derek Charlton, Mktg Dept, Yukon Sourdough Rendezvous Society, Box 5108, Whitehorse, YT, Canada Y1A 4S3. Phone: (403) 667-2148 or (800) 386-8786. Fax: (403) 668-6755.
Email: ysr@hypertech.yk.ca.
WWW: http://www.haylow.yk.net/rendez

COLOGNE CATHEDRAL: COMPLETION ANNIVERSARY. Aug 14, 1880. The largest Gothic church in northern Europe, the Cologne Cathedral in Cologne, Germany, was completed Aug 14, 1880, just 632 years after rebuilding began on Aug 14, 1248. In fact, there had been a church on its site since 873, but a fire in 1248 made rebuilding necessary. The cathedral was again damaged, by bombing, during World War II.

CONNECTICUT RIVER VALLEY BLUEGRASS FESTIVAL. Aug 14–16. Moodus, CT. Featuring 11 great bluegrass bands. For ticket information call: (860) 347-5007. For info: Sunrise Resort, PO Box 415, Moodus, CT 06469. Phone: (860) 873-8681 or (800) 225-9033.

COSHOCTON CANAL FESTIVAL. Aug 14–16. Coshocton, OH. Celebrates the arrival of first canal boat in Roscoe. Crafts, parades and old-time entertainment. Annually, the third weekend in August. Est attendance: 13,000. For info: Roscoe Village Fdtn, 381 Hill St, Coshocton, OH 43812. Phone: (800) 877-1830 or (614) 622-9310. Fax: (614) 623-6555.

ELVIS PRESLEY SALUTE. Aug 14. Broadway Market Square, Baltimore, MD. Salutes rock and roll singer Elvis Presley. Elvis impersonator, live musical entertainment, Elvis memorabilia on display and available for purchase and "Let Me Be Your Teddy Bear" and Elvis look-alike contests featured. Est attendance: 300. For info: Office of Adventures and Fun, Patterson Park Recreation Complex, 2601 E Baltimore St, Baltimore, MD 21224. Phone: (410) 396-9177. Fax: (410) 327-4120.

GINZA HOLIDAY: JAPANESE CULTURAL FESTIVAL. Aug 14–16. Midwest Buddhist Temple, Chicago, IL. Experience the Waza (National Treasures tradition) by viewing 300 years of Edo craft tradition and seeing it come alive as master craftsmen from Tokyo demonstrate their arts. Japanese folk and classical dancing, martial arts, taiko (drums), flower arrangements and cultural displays. Chicken teriyaki, sushi, udon, shaved ice, corn on the cob and refreshments. Annually, the third weekend in August. Est attendance: 5,000. For info: Office Secretary, Midwest Buddhist Temple, 435 W Menomonee St, Chicago, IL 60614. Phone: (312) 943-7801. Fax: (312) 943-8069.

HOLZFEST. Aug 14–16. Amana, IA. Woodcrafters of all types display and sell their products. Fellowship, entertainment, food and demonstrations. Annually, the third weekend in August. Est attendance: 12,000. For info: R.C. Eichacker, Personalized Wood Products, Box 193, Amana, IA 52203. Phone: (319) 622-3100. Fax: (319) 622-6395. Email: pwp@www.jeonet.com. WWW: http://www.jeonet.com/amanas/pwp/

ILLINOIS STATE FAIR. Aug 14–23. Springfield, IL. Amusement rides, food booths, parade, various types of entertainment, rodeos and tractor pulls. For info: Joe Saputo, Illinois State Fair, PO Box 19427, Springfield, IL 62794. Phone: (217) 782-6661. Fax: (217) 782-9115.

JUST, ERNEST E.: BIRTH ANNIVERSARY. Aug 14, 1883. American marine biologist Ernest E. Just was born at Charleston, SC. He was the first recipient of the NAACP's Spingarn Medal and was a professor at Howard University from 1907 to 1941, where he was head of physiology at the medical school (1912–20) and head of zoology (1912–41). He died on Oct 27, 1941, at Washington, DC.

LIBERTY TREE DAY. Aug 14. Massachusetts.

MACHIAS WILD BLUEBERRY FESTIVAL. Aug 14–16. Machias, ME. Harvest festival includes crafts sale, lobster boil, five-mile race, entertainment, children's parade, blueberry foods and a wild blueberry pie-eating contest. Annually, the third weekend in August. Est attendance: 15,000. For info: Machias Wild Blueberry Festival, PO Box 265, Machias, ME 04654. Phone: (207) 255-6665.

MILWAUKEE IRISH FEST. Aug 14–16. Milwaukee, WI. World's largest and most comprehensive Irish music and cultural event, featuring 14 stages of Irish and Irish-American music, dance and theater. Activities include sports, contests, parades, displays, food, marketplace, dance and children's activities. Weeklong summer school precedes the festival with lectures and demonstrations in Irish music, dance and culture. Annually, the third weekend in August. Est attendance: 100,000. For info: Milwaukee Irish Fest, 515 N Glenview Ave, Milwaukee, WI 53213. Phone: (414) 476-3378. Fax: (414) 476-7712. Email: ifest@execpc.com.

MISSOURI RIVER FESTIVAL OF THE ARTS. Aug 14–22. Thespian Hall, Boonville, MO. Performing arts festival with major symphony, opera, jazz, children's program, Broadway music and folk music. Est attendance: 5,000. For info: Judy Shields, Admin, Friends of Historic Boonville, PO Box 1776, Boonville, MO 65233. Phone: (816) 882-7977. Fax: (816) 882-7977. Email: friendsart@vax1.rainis.net.

MONTANA COWBOY POET GATHERING. Aug 14–16. Lewistown, MT. Gathering of cowboy poets to share lyrics and poetry. Est attendance: 1,500. For info: Lewistown Area Chamber of Commerce, Cowboy Poetry Committee, PO Box 818, Lewistown, MT 59457. Phone: (406) 538-5436. Fax: (406) 538-5437. Email: lewchamb@lewistown.net. WWW: http://www.lewistown.net/~lewchamb

August 1998

S	M	T	W	T	F	S
						1
2	3	4	5	6	7	8
9	10	11	12	13	14	15
16	17	18	19	20	21	22
23	24	25	26	27	28	29
30	31					

MOON PHASE: LAST QUARTER. Aug 14. Moon enters Last Quarter phase at 3:48 PM, EDT.

NATIONAL FINANCIAL AWARENESS DAY. Aug 14. To educate the public in the basic financial guidelines to form the foundations for financially sound practices from early adulthood through retirement. For info: Jamie K. Urick, Debt Free International, Inc, PO Box 705, Frankfort, IL 60423. Phone: (815) 469-7662. Fax: (815) 469-7664. Email: urickdfi@aol.com.

NEWPORT JVC JAZZ FESTIVAL. Aug 14–16. Ft Adams State Park, Newport, RI. This festival is considered one of the premier jazz events in the country, with legendary performers and rising stars. For info: Newport County Conv and Visitors Bureau, 23 America's Cup Ave, Newport, RI 02840. Phone: (800) 326-6030. Fax: (401) 849-0291. Email: gonewport@aol.com. WWW: http://www.travelfile.com

SHADYSIDE ARTS FESTIVAL. Aug 14–16. Pittsburgh, PA. With nightly outdoor jazz performances, workshops and more than 200 designers of American collectibles exhibiting their arts, it is not amazing that this festival attracts more than 200,000 people each year. For serious art and music lovers only. Est attendance: 200,000. For info: Greater Pittsburgh Conv & Visitors Bureau, Four Gateway Center, Pittsburgh, PA 15222-1259. Phone: (412) 681-2809 or (800) 359-0758. Fax: (412) 644-5512.

SOCIAL SECURITY ACT: ANNIVERSARY. Aug 14. The Congress approved, on Aug 14, 1935, the Social Security Act, which contained provisions for the establishment of a Social Security Board to administer federal old-age and survivors insurance in the US. By signing the bill into law, President Franklin D. Roosevelt was fulfilling a 1932 campaign promise.

TEXAS RANCH ROUNDUP. Aug 14–15. Wichita Falls, TX. Cowboys from prestigious ranches in Texas compete in the events that make up their daily work. Cattle roping and penning and other rodeo-type events plus ranch cooking contests, ranch talent contests. Est attendance: 18,000. For info: Wichita Falls Conv and Visitors Bureau, 1000 5th St, Wichita Falls, TX 76301. Phone: (800) 799-6732 or (817) 716-5500. Fax: (817) 716-5509.

THAYER, ERNEST LAWRENCE: BIRTH ANNIVERSARY. Aug 14, 1863. The man who wrote the famous comic baseball ballad "Casey at the Bat" was born at Lawrence, MA. He wrote a series of comic ballads for the *San Francisco Examiner*, of which "Casey at the Bat" was the last. It was published on Sunday, June 3, 1888, and Thayer received $5 in payment for it. Recitations of the ballad by the actor William DeWolf Hopper greatly increased its popularity, and it is said that by 1900 there were few Americans who had not heard of "Casey at the Bat." In 1986 the Library of Congress reissued it in text and in recording. Ernest L. Thayer, who regarded the ballad's fame as a nuisance, and whose other writings are widely forgotten, died at Santa Barbara, Ca, on Aug 21, 1940.

365-INNING SOFTBALL GAME: ANNIVERSARY. Aug 14–15, 1976. The Gager's Diner softball team played the Bend'n Elbow Tavern in a 365-inning softball game in 1976. Starting at 10 AM Aug 14, the game was called because of rain and fog at 4 PM, Aug 15. The 70 players, including 20 women, raised $4,000

for construction of a new softball field and for the Monticello, NY, Community General Hospital. The Gagers beat the Elbows 491–467. To date, this remains the longest softball game on record.

TRAILS WEST!® Aug 14–16. Civic Center Park, St. Joseph, MO. Arts festival celebrating St. Joseph's unique cultural heritage. Fine arts, crafts and heritage folk art, zany stick horse racing, wide variety of taste-tempting food, beer saloon and wine garden, children's games, re-enactors and big-name entertainment. Annually, the third weekend in August. Est attendance: 80,500. For info: Wally Bloss, Allied Arts Council, 118 S 8th, St. Joseph, MO 64501. Phone: (800) 216-7080 or (816) 233-0231. Fax: (816) 233-6704. Email: wbloss@stjoearts.org.
WWW: http://stjoearts.org

VICTORY DAY or V-J DAY. Aug 14. Anniversary of President Truman's announcement, on Aug 14, 1945, that Japan had surrendered to the Allies, setting off celebrations across the nation. Official ratification of surrender occurred aboard the USS *Missouri* in Tokyo Bay, on Sept 2 (Far Eastern time).

WESTERN IDAHO FAIR. Aug 14–22. Boise, ID. 101st annual. Largest fair in the state, including four stages of entertainment on the grounds with local and regional talent, seven nights of grandstand concerts, two days of Idaho Cowboy Assn Rodeo finals, carnival midway, 70 food booths and a power equipment display. Annually, the third full week of August. Est attendance: 250,000. For info: Don Bich, Manager, Western Idaho Fair, 5610 Glenwood, Boise, ID 83714. Phone: (208) 376-3247.

WYANDOTTE WATERFEST. Aug 14–16. Bishop Park, Wyandotte, MI. Outdoor boat show, Great Lakes jet ski competition, fireworks, parade of boats, boat rides and professional band. Est attendance: 35,000. For info: Leslie Lupo, Dir, 3131 Biddle Ave, Wyandotte, MI 48192. Phone: (313) 246-4505. Fax: (313) 246-4519.

BIRTHDAYS TODAY

Charles Neal Anderson, 34, former football player, born Graceville, FL, Aug 14, 1964.

Russell Baker, 73, journalist, author, born Loudoun County, VA, Aug 14, 1925.

Halle Berry, 30, actress (*Living Dolls, Boomerang*), born Cleveland, OH, Aug 14, 1968.

Julia Child, 86, food authority, author (*The French Chef*), born Pasadena, CA, Aug 14, 1912.

David Crosby, 57, singer (Crosby, Stills & Nash), songwriter, born Los Angeles, CA, Aug 14, 1941.

Antonio Fargas, 52, actor (*Shaft, I'm Gonna Git You Sucka!, Car Wash*), born Bronx, NY, Aug 14, 1946.

Alice Ghostley, 72, actress (Bernice on "Designing Women"; Esmeralda on "Bewitched"), born Eve, MO, Aug 14, 1926.

Buddy Greco, 72, singer ("Mr Lonely"), composer, musician, born Philadelphia, PA, Aug 14, 1926.

Earvin ("Magic") Johnson, Jr, 39, basketball player, born Lansing, MI, Aug 14, 1959.

Arthur Betz Laffer, 58, economist, born Youngstown, OH, Aug 14, 1940.

Gary Larson, 48, cartoonist ("The Far Side"), born Tacoma, WA, Aug 14, 1950.

Steve Martin, 53, comedian, actor ("Saturday Night Live," *All of Me, Roxanne, LA Story, Parenthood*), born Waco, TX, Aug 14, 1945.

Susan Saint James, 52, actress ("MacMillan and Wife," "Kate and Allie"), born Long Beach, CA, Aug 14, 1946.

Robyn Smith, 54, jockey, born San Francisco, CA, Aug 14, 1944.

Danielle Steel, 51, author (*Vanished, Wanderlust*), born New York, NY, Aug 14, 1947.

AUGUST 15 — SATURDAY

Day 227 — 138 Remaining

ASSUMPTION OF THE VIRGIN MARY. Aug 15. Greek and Roman Catholic churches celebrate Mary's ascent to Heaven.

BARRYMORE, ETHEL: BIRTH ANNIVERSARY. Aug 15. Celebrated award-winning actress of stage, screen and television, born Ethel Blythe at Philadelphia, PA, Aug 15, 1879. Died at Beverly Hills, CA, June 18, 1959. US Postal Service stamp was issued in 1982 featuring Ethel, John and Lionel Barrymore.

BATTLE OF BLUE LICKS CELEBRATION. Aug 15–16. Blue Licks Battlefield State Park, Mount Olivet, KY. Commemorates the anniversary of Revolutionary War Battle of Blue Licks (which involved Daniel Boone). Living-history demonstrations, arts, crafts, games, competitions and battle reenactment. Annually, the third weekend in August. Est attendance: 3,000. For info: Bill Stevens, Park Mgr, Blue Licks Battlefield State Pk, PO Box 66, Mt Olivet, KY 41064-0066. Phone: (606) 289-5507. Fax: (606) 289-5409.

BIKE VAN BUREN XII. Aug 15–16. Van Buren County, IA. A laid-back bicycle tour of the villages, landmarks and landscape of this rural Iowa county. The "red carpet of hospitality" is rolled out for the bikers as they pass through. Est attendance: 600. For info: Mary E. Muir, Exec Dir, Villages of Van Buren, Inc, PO Box 9, Keosauqua, IA 52565. Phone: (800) 868-7822.
Email: villages@netins.net.
WWW: http://www.netins.net/showcase/villages

BLUE CLAW CRAB CRAFT SHOW & CRAB RACE. Aug 15. Harvey Cedars, NJ. Crafters displaying their goods at Sunset Park. Crab race determines fastest crab on Long Beach Island. For info: Harvey Cedars Activity Committee, PO Box 3185, Harvey Cedars, NJ 08008. Phone: (609) 494-2843 or (609) 494-3107. Fax: (609) 494-2335.

BONANZAVILLE USA PIONEER DAYS. Aug 15–16. Bonanzaville USA, West Fargo, ND. The 43 buildings in the Victorian-era pioneer village come to life. Ice cream and lemonade are sold at the drugstore, log cabin residents turn out lefse and jellies for sample and sale, a country market sells garden produce, threshing machines crank up, church services are performed in both German and Norwegian, and the highlights of the weekend are the old-time vehicle parades. Est attendance: 10,000. For info: Exec Dir, Bonanzaville USA, PO Box 719, West Fargo, ND 58078. Phone: (701) 282-2822 or (800) 700-5317.
Email: bville1@juno.com.

BONAPARTE, NAPOLEON: BIRTH ANNIVERSARY. Aug 15. Anniversary of birth of French emperor Napoleon Bonaparte on island of Corsica, Aug 15, 1769. He died in exile at 5:49 PM, May 5, 1821, on the island of St. Helena. Public holiday in Corsica, France.

CANADA: DISCOVERY DAYS CELEBRATION. Aug 15–17. Watson Lake, Yukon Territory. Celebration of the discovery of gold in the Yukon includes pool party, wild game barbecue, whipped cream slide, tug o' war, Peterbilt Truck Pull, square dancing, mini-triathlon, parade, Ride and Tyke-cycling, stuffed animal and run event, bubble gum-blowing contest, fancy hatmaking, 5th annual rubber duck race, children's events and more. Est attendance: 1,200. For info: Tracy Durocher, Recreation Programmer, Town of Watson Lake Recreation Dept, Box 590, Watson Lake, YT, Canada Y0A 1C0. Phone: (403) 536-2246. Fax: (403) 536-2498. Email: towl@watson.net.
WWW: http://www.yukon.net/northernlights

CANADA: PAINT THE TOWN©. Aug 15–16. Annapolis Royal, Nova Scotia. 30 artists from across the province "paint the town," sketching at designated sites in Annapolis Royal. Work is auctioned off each evening. Entertainment. Est attendance: 700. For info: Susan Tileston, Exec Dir, Annapolis Region Canadian Arts Council, Box 534, Annapolis Royal, Nova Scotia, Canada B0S 1A0. Phone: (902) 532-7069. Fax: (902) 532-7357. Email: arcac@clan.tartanNET.ns.ca.
WWW: http://www.valleyweb.com/artsplace/

CHAUVIN DAY. Aug 15. A day named for Nicholas Chauvin, French soldier from Rochefort, France, who idolized Napoleon and who eventually became a subject of ridicule because of his blind loyalty and dedication to anything French. Originally referring to bellicose patriotism, chauvinism has come to mean blind or absurdly intense attachment to any case. Observed on Napoleon's birth anniversary because Chauvin's birth date is unknown.

CONGO: NATIONAL HOLIDAY. Aug 15. Congolese national day.

ELVIS PRESLEY REMEMBERED. Aug 15. St. Louis, MO. Singer Elvis Presley, his entire family and Col Tom Parker are impersonated in a live display titled "From Tupelo to Graceland" to mark the anniversary week of his death. Later a two-hour live music show featuring Steve Davis and the TCB Band will be held in the Elvis Room at Blueberry Hill. Est attendance: 800. For info: Blueberry Hill, 6504 Delmar, St. Louis, MO 63130. Phone: (314) 727-0880.

ENGLAND: THREE CHOIRS FESTIVAL. Aug 15–22. Gloucester Cathedral, Gloucester. Europe's oldest music festival, with performances by the three cathedral choirs of Hereford, Worcester and Gloucester. Est attendance: 20,000. For info: Mr Anthony Boden, Three Choirs Festival, Community House, College Green, Gloucester, England GL1 2LZ. Phone: (44) (145) 252-9819.

August 1998

S	M	T	W	T	F	S
						1
2	3	4	5	6	7	8
9	10	11	12	13	14	15
16	17	18	19	20	21	22
23	24	25	26	27	28	29
30	31					

FERBER, EDNA: BIRTH ANNIVERSARY. Aug 15, 1887. Edna Ferber was born at Kalamazoo, MI. She wrote her first novel, *Dawn O'Hara*, in 1911 and became a prolific writer, producing many popular magazine stories. Her novel *So Big* brought her a huge commercial success in 1924 as well as a Pulitzer Prize. Her other novels include *Show Boat, Cimarron, Saratoga Trunk, Giant* and *Ice Palace*, all of which were made into successful films. Ferber collaborated with George Kaufman in writing for the stage on *The Royal Family, Dinner at Eight, Stage Door* and *Bravo*. Ferber died at New York, NY, on Apr 16, 1968.

GREAT PIKES PEAK COWBOY POETRY GATHERING. Aug 15. Pikes Peak Center, Colorado Springs, CO. Fundraising event for the library district featuring cowboy poetry and music, children's programs, Western art auction and a concert with special guests. Est attendance: 5,000. For info: Pikes Peak Library Dist, Public Relations Office, 5550 N Union Blvd, Colorado Springs, CO 80918. Phone: (719) 531-6333 ext 1201. Fax: (719) 528-2820.

HARDING, FLORENCE KLING DeWOLFE: BIRTH ANNIVERSARY. Aug 15. Wife of Warren Gamaliel Harding, 29th president of the US, born at Marion, OH, Aug 15, 1860. Died Nov 21, 1924.

HOMETOWN DAYS. Aug 15–16. Strasburg, CO. To remind people of the first continuous chain of rails from an Atlantic to a Pacific port. The rails were joined Aug 15, 1870, at Comanche, which was later renamed Strasburg. Annually, the third weekend in August. Est attendance: 1,000. For info: Sandy Miller, Curator-Comanche Crossing Museum, 7433 S Rd 157, Strasburg, CO 80136. Phone: (303) 622-4690.

INDIA INDEPENDENCE DAY: ANNIVERSARY. Aug 15, 1947. Anniversary of Indian independence.

KOREA: LIBERATION DAY. Aug 15. National holiday commemorates acceptance by Japan of Allied terms of surrender in 1945, thereby freeing Korea from 36 years of Japanese domination. Also marks formal proclamation of the Republic of Korea in 1948. Military parades and ceremonies throughout country.

LEADVILLE TRAIL 100 BIKE RACE. Aug 15 (tentative). Leadville, CO. Some 500 cyclists compete in this 100-mile off-road bike race over Colorado's high peaks—out 50 miles to a peak above Twin Lakes and back to Leadville. Sponsor: Leadville Trail 100, Inc. Est attendance: 1,000. For info: Gloria Cheshier, Exec Dir, Greater Leadville Area Chamb of Comm, PO Box 861, Leadville, CO 80461. Phone: (719) 486-3900 or (800) 933-3901. Fax: (719) 486-8478. Email: leadville@sni.net.
WWW: http://www.colorado.com/leadville

LIECHTENSTEIN: NATIONAL DAY. Aug 15. Public holiday.

MAINE HIGHLAND GAMES. Aug 15. Thomas Point Beach, Brunswick, ME. Presented by the Saint Andrew's Society of Maine. Bagpipe bands, Highland and Scottish dancing, Scottish arts and crafts fair, folksingers, Scottish fiddling, children's games, adult athletics including tossing of the caber, wheat sheaf toss and putting of the stone, border collie herding demonstrations, Highland cattle and individual piping contests. American and Scottish foods galore. The only Scottish event of its kind held in Maine! Scots and non-Scots will enjoy the color, pageantry and friendly atmosphere. 20th annual. Adults $8, children under 12 $4. For info: Thomas Point Beach, 29 Meadow Rd, Brunswick, ME 04011. Phone: (207) 725-6009.
WWW: http://www.thomaspointbeach.com

MARYLAND STATE CHILI COOK-OFF CHAMPIONSHIP. Aug 15. Cumberland, MD. Ali Ghan Shrine Picnic Grounds. Chili contest, 5K run and two-mile walk, car show auction, arts and crafts, train rides, entertainment, food and beverages, games and beauty contest. Est attendance: 2,000. For info: Ali Ghan Shrine Temple, PO Box 1416, Cumberland, MD 21501. Phone: (301) 722-5970. Fax: (301) 777-5276.

MICHIGAN RENAISSANCE FESTIVAL. Aug 15–Sept 27 (weekends and Labor Day only). Holly, MI. Continuous entertainment on 15 stages featuring comedy, drama, bawdy and clas-

sical music and folk dance at this re-creation of a 16th-century village harvest festival. More than 400 costumed participants join in theater, games and equestrian events. Also, more than 130 crafts booths. Est attendance: 250,000. For info: PR Dir, Michigan Renaissance Fest, 120 S Saginaw, Holly, MI 48442. Phone: (800) 601-4848 or (248) 634-5552 ext 107.
Email: Renfestmi@aol.com.
WWW: http://members.aol.com/Renfestmi

MILFORD OYSTER FESTIVAL. Aug 15. Downtown Milford and Fowler Field, Milford, CT. 250 arts and crafts, headline entertainment, classic car show, canoe race, harbor activities, health fair, corporate row and food court. For info: Milford Oyster Festival, (203) 878-5363 or Greater New Haven Conv & Visitors Bureau, One Long Wharf Dr, New Haven, CT 06511. Phone: (203) 777-8550 or (800) 332-STAY. Fax: (203) 782-7755.

MINNESOTA RENAISSANCE FESTIVAL. Aug 15–Sept 27 (weekends and Labor Day only). Shakopee, MN. A celebration of 16th-century Renaissance Europe with entertainment on 10 lively stages, food, arts and crafts, games and live jousting. Est attendance: 350,000. For info: Minnesota Renaissance Festival, 1244 S Canterbury Rd, Ste 306, Shakopee, MN 55379. Phone: (800) 966-8215 or (612) 445-7361. Fax: (612) 445-7380.

NATIONAL HOMELESS ANIMALS DAY AND CANDLELIGHT VIGILS. Aug 15. A day to call attention to the fact that 12–17 million healthy dogs and cats are killed each year in the US in animal shelters because of overpopulation—a problem that has a solution: Spay/Neuter! It Stops the Killing! The vigils memorialize the animals killed in the preceding year and sympathize with the caring shelter personnel who must take the lives of the animals. Vigils will be held throughout the US and beyond. For info: Intl Society for Animal Rights, Inc, 421 S State St, Clarks Summit, PA 18411-1015. Phone: (717) 586-2200. Fax: (717) 586-9580.

NATIONAL I LOVE COWBOYS AND COWGIRLS DAY. Aug 15. Cowbys and cowgirls of all ages are America's best loved heros and heroines. In our own way, let's show our admiration, our appreciation and our affection for them today. For info: Thomas Danaher, PO Box 85565, Las Vegas, NV 89185. WWW: http://www.poets.com/vip/artist/ThomasDanaher.html

NATIONAL RELAXATION DAY. Aug 15. Everyone should have a special day during the year for total relaxation. Today is a time to think about and encourage new ideas for enjoyment of a relaxation day. Annually, Aug 15. For info: Sean M. Moeller, PO Box 71, Clio, MI 48420-1042.

NATURAL CHIMNEYS JOUSTING TOURNAMENT. Aug 15. Natural Chimneys Regional Park, Mt Solon, VA. A modern version of a medieval contest, believed to be the oldest continuously held sporting event in America. Annually, the third Saturday in August. Est attendance: 500. For info: Upper Valley Regional Park Authority, Box 478, Grottoes, VA 24441. Phone: (540) 350-2510. Fax: (540) 350-2140.

NORTHEASTERN WISCONSIN THRESHEREE AND ANTIQUE MACHINERY SHOW. Aug 15–16. Sturgeon Bay, WI. Continuous display of operating antique machinery, antique tractor pull, barefoot horse pull, crafts and games for kids, food and refreshments. Annually, the third weekend in August. Est attendance: 3,500. For info: Josephine Bochek, Northeastern Wisconsin Antique Power Assn, 4376 Rudy Rd, Sturgeon Bay, WI 54235. Phone: (414) 743-5251.

O-BON FESTIVAL. Aug 15. Morikami Museum, Delray Beach, FL. Traditional Japanese summer festival welcomes the ancestral spirits back to Earth with folk dancing, music, games and amusements, culminating with the floating of paper lanterns on Morikami pond at dusk and a fireworks display. Est attendance: 8,000. For info: Melodie Shute, Dir of Mktg, The Morikami Museum, 4000 Morikami Park Rd, Delray Beach, FL 33446. Phone: (561) 495-0233. Fax: (561) 499-2557.
WWW: http://www.icsi.com/ics/morkami/

PANAMA CANAL OPENS. Aug 15, 1914. The first official trip across the Panama Canal, taken by the *Ancon*, from Limon Bay to Panama Bay. The treaty between the US and the Republic of Panama to build the canal was signed in February, 1904. Ten years later the canal was officially open.

PANAMA: PANAMA CITY FOUNDATION DAY. Aug 15. Traditional annual cultural observance recognizes foundation of Panama City.

POLISH AMERICAN WEEKEND. Aug 15–16. Penn's Landing, Philadelphia, PA. Two-day festival of Polish food, music and dance. For info: Polish American Congress, Eastern Pennsylvania District, 308 Walnut St, Philadelphia, PA 19106. Phone: (215) 739-3408. Fax: (215) 922-1518.

PONY LEAGUE WORLD SERIES. Aug 15–22 (tentative dates). Washington, PA. International youth baseball World Series for teams of players ages 13 and 14. Est attendance: 16,500. For info: Pony Baseball, Inc, PO Box 225, Washington, PA 15301. Phone: (412) 225-1060. Fax: (412) 225-9852.
Email: pony@pulsenet.com. WWW: http://www.pony.org

PRESIDENT BENJAMIN HARRISON'S BIRTHDAY CELEBRATION. Aug 15 (tentative date). Indianapolis, IN, Harrison's hometown. Also free tours of the Victorian mansion. Est attendance: 500. For info: PR Dept, President Benjamin Harrison Home, 1230 N Delaware St, Indianapolis, IN 46202. Phone: (317) 631-1898. Fax: (317) 236-1688.

SANTA MARIA DAY. Aug 15–16. Dayton, NV. Parade, crafts, food, games and street dance. For local info: (702) 246-3993 or Nevada Commission on Tourism, Capitol Complex, Carson City, NV 89710. Phone: (702) 687-4322 or (800) 227-0774. Fax: (702) 687-6779.

SCOTLAND: EDINBURGH BOOK FESTIVAL. Aug 15–31. Charlotte Square Gardens, Edinburgh, Lothian. Europe's biggest book event for the public—with more than 250 international authors, an extensive program for children, plus thousands of books to buy. Est attendance: 80,000. For info: Edinburgh Book Festival, Scottish Book Centre, 137 Dundee St, Edinburgh, Scotland EH111BG. Phone: (44) (131) 228-5444. Fax: (44) (131) 228-4333.

SCOTT, SIR WALTER: BIRTH ANNIVERSARY. Aug 15, 1771. Born at Edinburgh, Scotland. Famed poet and novelist. "But no one shall find me rowing against the stream," he wrote in the introduction to *The Fortunes of Nigel*; "I care not who knows it—I write for the general amusement." Died at Abbotsford, Scotland, Sept 21, 1832.

TRANSCONTINENTAL US RAILWAY COMPLETION: ANNIVERSARY. Aug 15. The Golden Spike ceremony at Promontory Point, UT, May 10, 1869, was long regarded as the final link in a transcontinental railroad track reaching from an Atlantic port to a Pacific port. In fact, that link occurred unceremoniously on another date in another state. Diaries of engineers working at the site establish "the completion of a transcontinental track at a point 928 feet east of today's milepost 602, or 3,812 feet east of the present Union Pacific depot building at Strasburg (formerly Comanche)," CO. The final link was made at 2:53 PM, Aug 15, 1870 (see: Robert A. LeMassena's ". . . The True Transcontinental Hook-up" in *Kansas Quarterly*, Vol III, No 2). Annual celebration at Strasburg, CO, on a weekend in August. See also: "Golden Spike Day" (May 10).

WATERMELON DAY. Aug 15. Vining, MN. "The Biggest Small Town Celebration in Ottertail County." There is a large arts and crafts show (at least 75 vendors), farmers and flea market. Old-time musical jamboree, kids' games. Crowning of King and Queen. Evening features a large parade at 7 PM followed by a street dance and drawings for prizes. Annually, the third Saturday in August. Est attendance: 3,500. For info: Watermelon Day Committee, PO Box 101, Vining, MN 56588-0101. Phone: (218) 769-4218.

WCSH 6 SIDEWALK ART FESTIVAL. Aug 15. Portland, ME. More than 350 artists from across the country display their works from Congress Square to Monument Square in downtown Portland. This is the largest one-day festival on the East Coast. Prize money of more than $20,000 awarded. Annually, the third Saturday in August. Est attendance: 50,000. For info: WCSH 6, 1 Congress Sq, Portland, ME 04101. Phone: (207) 828-6666. Fax: (207) 828-6620.

WOODSTOCK: ANNIVERSARY. Aug 15. The Woodstock Music and Art Fair opened on this day in 1969 on an alfalfa field on or near Yasgur's Farm at Bethel, NY. The three-day rock concert featured 24 bands and drew a crowd of more than 400,000 people.

BIRTHDAYS TODAY

Stephen G. Breyer, 60, US Supreme Court justice, born San Francisco, CA, Aug 15, 1938.
Mike Connors (Krekor Ohanian), 73, actor ("Mannix"), born Fresno, CA, Aug 15, 1925.
Linda Ellerbee, 54, journalist, born Bryan, TX, Aug 15, 1944.
Vernon Eulion Jordan, Jr, 63, civil rights leader, born Atlanta, GA, Aug 15, 1935.
Debra Messing, 30, actress ("Ned and Stacey," "NYPD Blue"), born Brooklyn, NY, Aug 15, 1968.
Phyllis Stewart Schlafly, 74, antifeminist, author, born St. Louis, MO, Aug 15, 1924.
Eugene (Gene) Upshaw, 53, union executive and former football player, born Robstown, TX, Aug 15, 1945.
Kathryn Whitmire, 52, first woman mayor of Houston, TX, born Houston, TX, Aug 15, 1946.

AUGUST 16 — SUNDAY

Day 228 — 137 Remaining

AMERICAN SOCIETY OF ASSOCIATION EXECUTIVES ANNUAL MEETING AND EXPOSITION. Aug 16–18. Nashville, TN. Major meeting for ASAE members, nonmembers and suppliers including education sessions, board meetings and awards presentations. Est attendance: 5,000. For info: Lorri Lee, American Soc of Assn Executives, 1575 Eye St NW, Washington, DC 20005-1168. Phone: (202) 626-2798.

ANTIQUE FIRE APPARATUS MUSTER AND SHOW. Aug 16. Wheaton Village, Millville, NJ. Sponsored by the Glasstown Antique Fire Brigade. Held rain or shine. Est attendance: 2,000. For info: Wheaton Village, 1501 Glasstown Rd, Millville, NJ. Phone: (609) 825-6800 or (800) 998-4552. Fax: (609) 825-2410. Email: mail@wheatonvillage.org. WWW: http://www.wheatonvillage.org

BABE RUTH DIES: 50th ANNIVERSARY. Aug 16, 1948. Baseball fans of all ages and all walks of life mourned when the great Bambino died of cancer at New York City at the age of 53. The left-handed pitcher and "Sultan of Swat" hit 714 home runs in 22 major league seasons of play and had played in 10 World Series. His body lay in state at the main entrance of Yankee Stadium where people waited in line for hours to march past the coffin. On Aug 19, countless numbers of people surrounded St. Patrick's Cathedral for the funeral mass and lined the streets along the route to the cemetery as America bade farewell to one of baseball's greatest legends.

August 1998

S	M	T	W	T	F	S
						1
2	3	4	5	6	7	8
9	10	11	12	13	14	15
16	17	18	19	20	21	22
23	24	25	26	27	28	29
30	31					

BATTLE OF CAMDEN: ANNIVERSARY. Aug 16. Revolutionary War battle fought near Camden, SC, on Aug 16, 1780. American troops led by General Horatio Gates suffered disastrous losses. Nearly 1,000 Americans killed and another 1,000 captured by the British. British losses about 325. One of America's worst defeats in the war.

BEGIN, MENACHEM: 85th BIRTH ANNIVERSARY. Aug 16, 1913. Menachem Begin was born at Brest-Litovsk, Poland. Exposed at an early age to Zionism, Begin attended a Zionist Hebrew school for his early education and joined the Zionist Revisionists' youth movement at 15, an organization he later headed after obtaining a law degree at Warsaw University. A militant Zionist and anticommunist, he fled to Russia in 1939 ahead of the advancing Nazis, where he was soon arrested and sent to Siberia. Freed in 1941, Begin found his way to Palestine and quickly became a leader in the Jewish underground fighting for Israel's independence; by 1943 he headed the national military organization. While he was successful on the radical periphery of power, Begin's election as Prime Minister of Israel in 1977 quickly introduced him to the necessary compromises of governing a nation, and over time he became less outspoken and dramatic. In 1979 at Camp David, MD, he signed a peace treaty between Israel and Egypt with President Jimmy Carter and President Anwar el Sadat of Egypt. In this precedent-setting treaty with Egypt, Begin surrendered the Sinai Desert, which had been captured in the 1967 Six Day War. Once the peace with Egypt finally was cemented, Begin became embroiled in the continuing international controversy over the future of the Israeli-occupied West Bank and Gaza Strip. Begin spent the last eight years of his life as a virtual recluse, never fully recovering from the death of his wife, Aliza. He died Mar 9, 1992.

BENNINGTON BATTLE DAY: ANNIVERSARY. Aug 16, 1777. Anniversary of battle is legal holiday in Vermont.

CHAMBERSFEST. Aug 16–22. Chambersburg, PA. Annual Civil War festival including Old Market Day, Celebrate the Arts, Civil War Seminar, Pet Parade, Almost Anything Goes Games and a local talent fest. Est attendance: 9,000. For info: Melissa Knepper, Dir of Member Services, Greater Chambersburg Chamber of Commerce, 75 South Second St., Chambersburg, PA 17201. Phone: (717) 264-7101.

COMEDY CELEBRATION DAY. Aug 16. Golden Gate Park, San Francisco, CA. A comedy extravaganza from local and nationally known comics to say thank you to the city that's nurtured so many comedic artists. Sponsors: *The San Francisco Chronicle*, Robin Williams, local comedy clubs. Est attendance: 50,000. For info: Jose Simon, Exec Producer, 178 Dellabrook Ave, San Francisco, CA 94131. Phone: (415) 643-9009.

DOG DAY ROAD RACE. Aug 16. Harvey Cedars, NJ. 20th annual. More than 800 runners will participate in this five-mile run. Sponsored by the High Point Volunteer Fire Dept. For info: Dog Day Race, High Point Fire Co, 80th and Compass Ave, Harvey Cedars, NJ 08008. Phone: (609) 361-9364.

DOMINICAN REPUBLIC: RESTORATION OF THE REPUBLIC. Aug 16. The anniversary of the Restoration of the Republic is celebrated as an official public holiday.

ENGLAND: MANCHESTER MASSACRE or BATTLE OF PETERLOO: ANNIVERSARY. Aug 16. Anniversary of demonstration by more than 50,000 persons protesting unemployment, starvation wages, overcrowding, high costs and British government policies. The mass meeting, Aug 16, 1819, was held in St. Peter's Fields, Manchester, England. Police and cavalry charged the unarmed crowd with sabres. Casualty estimates for the 10-minute battle varied widely, but several deaths and up to 500 injuries were claimed.

HARMONIC CONVERGENCE: ANNIVERSARY. Aug 16, 1987. At about 20 designated "sacred sites" around the world (including Lake Titicaca, Bolivia; Boulder, CO, Niagara Falls and the Grand Canyon in the US) believers gathered to harmonize and meditate about peace and to ward off any impending doom. The harmonic convergence, projected from ancient Mayan and Aztec calendars to begin on this date, was said to signal the beginning of a period of cleansing that would last until 1992, in preparation for alien intelligence to be confronted in the next century.

JOE MILLER'S JOKE DAY. Aug 16. A day to tell a joke in honor of the English comic actor Joseph (or Josias) Miller, who was born in 1684 (exact date unknown). Miller acted at the Drury Lane Theatre in London, England, starting in 1709, and was a popular favorite for many years. It is probable that his family had established "Miller's Droll Booth" at Bartholomew's Fair. Joe Miller is remembered mainly because of a book with which he had no direct connection: *Joe Miller's Jests*, compiled by John Mottley and first published in 1739. It consisted of only 70 pages, containing 247 jokes. Republished, revised and expanded hundreds of times, it reached more than 1,500 jokes in the ensuing two centuries. Joe Miller died at London on Aug 16, 1738, never having heard of the celebrated book of *Joe Miller's Jests*. From *Joe Miller's Jests*, London, 1739: "A melting Sermon being preached in a country Church, all fell a weeping but one Man, who being asked, why he did not weep with the rest? O! said he. I belong to another Parish."

KLONDIKE GOLD DISCOVERY: ANNIVERSARY. Aug 16, 1896. According to the oral tradition of the Tagish First Nations People, Skookum Jim, Dawson Charlie and George Carmack found gold in Rabbit Creek, a tributary of the Klondike River, lying "thick between the flaky slabs like cheese sandwiches." This event that led to the great Klondike Gold Rush is celebrated in the Yukon each year with a public holiday, Discovery Day, observed on the nearest Monday (see Aug 17).

LAWRENCE (OF ARABIA), T.E.: BIRTH ANNIVERSARY. Aug 16, 1888. British soldier, archaeologist and writer, born at Tremadoc, North Wales. During World War I, led the Arab revolt against the Turks and served as a spy for the British. His book, *Seven Pillars of Wisdom*, is a personal account of the Arab revolt. He was killed in a motorcycle accident at Dorset, England, May 19, 1935.

LUXEMBOURG: OUR LADY OF GIRSTERKLAUS PROCESSION. Aug 16. Rosport. Tradition since 1328. Annually, the Sunday after Aug 15.

MacFADDEN, BERNARD: BIRTH ANNIVERSARY. Aug 16, 1868. Physical culture enthusiast and publisher, born at Mill Springs, MO. He was once publisher of *Physical Culture Magazine, True Story Magazine, True Romances, True Detective Mysteries Magazine* and many others. MacFadden made parachute jumps on his 81st, 83rd and 84th birthdays. He died at Jersey City, NJ, of jaundice, following a three-day fast, on Oct 12, 1955.

MEANY, GEORGE: BIRTH ANNIVERSARY. Aug 16, 1894. American labor leader George Meany was born at New York, NY. A plumber by trade, he became president of the AFL (American Federation of Labor) in 1952, and when he merged the AFL with the CIO (Congress of Industrial Organizations) he became the leading labor spokesperson in the US. In 1957 he expelled Jimmy Hoffa's Teamsters Union from the AFL-CIO and lost the United Auto Workers in 1967. His tenure as president lasted until 1979. He died on Jan 10, 1980, at Washington, DC.

NEWSPAPERS TAKEN TO COURT FOR PRO-CONFEDERATE SYMPATHIES: ANNIVERSARY. Aug 16. Beginning on Aug 16, 1861, several newspapers in Union states were brought to court for alleged pro-Confederate sympathies, including the Brooklyn *Eagle*, the New York *Journal of Commerce* and the New York *Daily News*. On Aug 19, an editor for the *Essex County Democrat*, in Haverhill, MA, was tarred and feathered for his Southern leanings expressed in the newspaper.

PRESLEY, ELVIS: DEATH ANNIVERSARY. Aug 16. One of America's most popular singers, Elvis Presley was pronounced dead at the Memphis Baptist Hospital at 3:30 PM, Aug 16, 1977, at age 42. The 10th anniversary (1987) of his death was an occasion for pilgrimages by admirers to Graceland, his home and gravesite at Memphis, TN, when an estimated 20,000 persons participated in a candlelight tribute to Presley. See also: "Presley, Elvis: Birth Anniversary" (Jan 8).

SCOTLAND: EDINBURGH INTERNATIONAL FILM FESTIVAL. Aug 16–30. Edinburgh. Festival includes documentaries, world premieres, special events and lectures. Est attendance: 30,000. For info: Marketing Manager, Edinburgh International Film Festival, 88 Lothian Rd, Filmhouse, Edinburgh, Scotland EH3 9BZ. Phone: (44) (131) 228-4051. Fax: (44) (131) 229-5501. Email: info@edfilmfest.org.uk.

SCOTTS BLUFF COUNTY FAIR. Aug 16–23. County Fairgrounds, Mitchell, NE. County fair including stock displays and shows, special events such as large-name country and western concert, largest amateur rodeo in Nebraska, tractor pull, free stage acts, grounds act, rubber-check races, demolition derby. Beef sale on Monday, Aug 24. Est attendance: 40,000. For info: Leon Meyer, Fair Mgr, Scotts Bluff County Fair, Box 157, Mitchell, NE 69357. Phone: (308) 623-1828. Fax: (308) 623-1328.

STAGG, AMOS ALONZO: BIRTH ANNIVERSARY. Aug 16, 1862. Amos Alonzo Stagg, football player and coach born at West Orange, NJ. Stagg played baseball and football at Yale and then forsook the ministry for physical education. He built the football program at the University of Chicago as an integral part of William Rainey Harper's plan to build a great university. Over 40 years at Chicago, he became the game's greatest innovator and master strategist. When Chicago de-emphasized football, he moved to the College of the Pacific, finishing his career with a record of 314-181-15. Died at Stockton, CA, Mar 17, 1965.

THANKS FOR ALL THE GIFTS WEEK. Aug 16–22. A time to catch up on all the thank you notes and cards for birthdays, graduations, weddings, etc, that you forgot to send. Annually, the third week in August. For info: Eva Rosenberg, Giftech Corp, 2961 Industrial Rd, Ste 731, Las Vegas, NV 89109. Phone: (888) 443-8547.

TOBACCO HARVEST. Aug 16. McLean, VA. Help cut and hang tobacco to dry. Enjoy 18th-century games and light refreshment afterward. Est attendance: 400. For info: Claude Moore Colonial Farm at Turkey Run, 6310 Georgetown Pike, McLean, VA 22101. Phone: (703) 442-7557. Fax: (703) 442-0714.

BIRTHDAYS TODAY

Angela Bassett, 40, actress (*Boyz N the Hood, Malcolm X, What's Love Got to Do with It, Waiting to Exhale*), born New York, NY, Aug 16, 1958.

Robert Culp, 68, actor (Kelly Robinson on "I Spy"; *Bob and Carol and Ted and Alice*), born Berkeley, CA, Aug 16, 1930.

Frank Newton Gifford, 68, sportscaster, Pro Football Hall of Fame halfback/end, born Santa Monica, CA, Aug 16, 1930.

Kathie Lee Gifford, 45, TV personality, singer, married to football great Frank Gifford, born Paris, France, Aug 16, 1953.

Eydie Gorme (Edith Gormezano), 66, singer ("Blame It on the Bossa Nova"), born New York, NY, Aug 16, 1932.

Timothy Hutton, 38, actor (*Taps, Made in Heaven*), born Malibu, CA, Aug 16, 1960.

Madonna (Madonna Louise Veronica Ciccone), 40, singer ("Material Girl"), actress (*Desperately Seeking Susan, A League of Their Own, Evita*), born Bay City, MI, Aug 16, 1958.

Carol Moseley-Braun, 51, US Senator (D, Illinois), born Chicago, IL, Aug 16, 1947.

Julie Newmar, 63, actress (Cat Woman on TV's "Batman"; *Li'l Abner*), born Hollywood, CA, Aug 16, 1935.

Fess Parker, 71, actor ("Daniel Boone," *Davy Crockett*), born Ft Worth, TX, Aug 16, 1927.

Reginald VelJohnson, 46, actor (*Ghostbusters, Die Hard, Die Hard 2*), born Queens, NY, Aug 16, 1952.

Lesley Ann Warren, 52, actress (*Victor/Victoria, Choose Me*, "Cinderella"), born New York, NY, Aug 16, 1946.

AUGUST 17 — MONDAY

Day 229 — 136 Remaining

ALLIES TAKE SICILY: 55th ANNIVERSARY. Aug 17, 1943. After only 39 days, the entire island of Sicily was under the control of Allied forces. The official total of Germans and Italians captured was put at 130,000.

BALLOON CROSSING OF ATLANTIC OCEAN: 20th ANNIVERSARY. Aug 17, 1978. Three Americans—Max Anderson, 44; Ben Abruzzo, 48; and Larry Newman, 31—all of Albuquerque, NM, became first to complete transatlantic trip in a balloon. Starting from Presque Isle, ME, Aug 11, they traveled some 3,200 miles in 137 hours, 18 minutes, landing about 60 miles west of Paris, in their craft, named the *Double Eagle II*.

CANADA: YUKON DISCOVERY DAY: ANNIVERSARY. Aug 17. In the Klondike region of the Yukon, at Bonanza Creek (formerly known as Rabbit Creek), George Washington Carmack discovered gold on Aug 16 or 17, 1896. During the following year more than 30,000 people joined the gold rush to the area. Anniversary is celebrated as a holiday (Discovery Day) in the Yukon, on nearest Monday.

CROCKETT, DAVID "DAVY": BIRTH ANNIVERSARY. Aug 17. American frontiersman, adventurer and soldier, born Aug 17, 1786, in Hawkins County, TN. Died during final heroic defense of the Alamo, Mar 6, 1836. In his *Autobiography* (1834), Crockett wrote, "I leave this rule for others when I'm dead, Be always sure you're right—then go ahead."

FORT SUMTER SHELLED BY NORTHERN FORCES: ANNIVERSARY. Aug 17, 1863. In what would become a long siege, Union forces began shelling Fort Sumter in Charleston, SC. The site of the first shots fired during the Civil War, Sumter endured the siege for a year and a half before being returned to Union hands.

FULTON SAILS STEAMBOAT: ANNIVERSARY. Aug 17, 1807. Robert Fulton began the first American steamboat trip between Albany and New York, NY, on a boat later called the *Clermont*. After years of promoting submarine warfare, Fulton engaged in a partnership with Robert R. Livingston, the US minister to France, allowing Fulton to design and construct a steamboat. His first success came in August 1803 when he launched a steam-powered vessel on the Seine. That same year the US Congress granted Livingston and Fulton exclusive rights to operate steamboats on New York waters during the next 20 years. The first Albany-to-New York trip took 32 hours to travel the 150-mile course. Although his efforts were labeled "Fulton's Folly" by his detractors, his success allowed the partnership to begin commercial service the next year on Sept 4, 1808.

August 1998

S	M	T	W	T	F	S
						1
2	3	4	5	6	7	8
9	10	11	12	13	14	15
16	17	18	19	20	21	22
23	24	25	26	27	28	29
30	31					

GABON: NATIONAL DAY. Aug 17. National holiday.

GOLDWYN, SAMUEL: BIRTH ANNIVERSARY. Aug 17, 1882. Motion picture producer and industry pioneer, born Samuel Goldfish, at Warsaw, Poland. Goldwyn died at Los Angeles, CA, Jan 31, 1974. Attributed to Goldwyn is the observation: "Anybody who goes to see a psychiatrist ought to have his head examined."

INDONESIA: INDEPENDENCE DAY. Aug 17. National holiday. Republic proclaimed on this day, 1945. It was only after several years of fighting, however, that Indonesia was formally granted its independence by the Netherlands, Dec 27, 1949.

NATIONAL AVIATION WEEK. Aug 17–23. A celebration of flight designed to increase public awareness, knowledge and appreciation of aviation. Annually, the week of Orville Wright's birthday, Aug 19. For info: Lafayette Natural History Museum and Planetarium, 637 Girard Park Dr, Lafayette, LA 70503. Phone: (318) 291-5544. Fax: (318) 291-5464.

POWERS, FRANCIS GARY: BIRTH ANNIVERSARY. Aug 17. One of America's most famous aviators, Francis Gary Powers was born at Jenkins, KY, Aug 17, 1929. The CIA agent, pilot of a U-2 overflight across the Soviet Union, was shot down May 1, 1960, near Sverdlovsk, USSR. He was tried, convicted and sentenced to 10 years' imprisonment in August 1960. Returned to the US in 1962, in exchange for an imprisoned Soviet spy, he found an unwelcoming homeland. Powers died in a helicopter crash near Los Angeles, CA, on Aug 2, 1977.

WEIRD CONTEST WEEK. Aug 17–21. Music Pier, Boardwalk and Moorlyn Terr, Ocean City, NJ. One contest daily. Contests include artistic pie eating (chewing something meaningful out of a TastyKake Pie), saltwater taffy sculpting, french fry sculpting, animal and celebrity impersonation and Miss Miscellaneous Contest. 11 AM. Annually, the third week in August. Sponsors: The City of Ocean City, TastyKake Baking Company, Shriver's Saltwater Taffy. Est attendance: 4,500. For info: Mark Soifer, PR Dir, City of Ocean City, City Hall, 9th Asbury Ave, Ocean City, NJ 08226. Phone: (609) 525-9300. Fax: (609) 399-0374.

WEST MICHIGAN FAIR. Aug 17–23. West Michigan Fairgrounds, Ludington, MI. Traditional county fair, complete with carnival rides and games, livestock judging, 4-H exhibits, live entertainment and food. Annually, the third week in August. Est attendance: 20,000. For info: Sue Brillhart, Exec VP, Ludington Area Conv and Visitors, 5827 W US 10, Ludington, MI 49431. Phone: (800) 542-4600.

WYOMING STATE FAIR. Aug 17–22. Douglas, WY. Recognizing the products, achievements and cultural heritage of the people of Wyoming. Bringing together rural and urban citizens for an inexpensive, entertaining and educational experience. Features Livestock show for beef, swine, sheep and horses; Junior Livestock show for beef, swine, sheep, horses, dogs and rabbits; competitions and displays for culinary arts, needlework, visual arts, and floriculture; 4-H and FFA County Chapters State qualifications competitions; Youth Talent Show; Demo Derby; live entertainment; midway; rodeos and an All Girl Rodeo (rough stock). Est attendance: 82,000. For info: Wyoming State Fair, Drawer 10, Douglas, WY 82633. Phone: (307) 358-2398. Fax: (307) 358-6030.

BIRTHDAYS TODAY

Belinda Carlisle, 40, singer ("Mad About You"), born Hollywood, CA, Aug 17, 1958.

Harrison V. Chase, 85, associate professor emeritus (Florida State University–Tallahassee), cofounder and coeditor of *Chase's Annual Events* (1957–70), born Big Rapids, MI, Aug 17, 1913.

Robert DeNiro, 55, actor (Oscars for *Raging Bull, The Godfather II; Taxi Driver*), born New York, NY, Aug 17, 1943.

Robert Joy, 47, actor (*Atlantic City, Desperately Seeking Susan, Longtime Companion*), born Montreal, Canada, Aug 17, 1951.

Maureen O'Hara, 78, actress (*The Quiet Man, Miracle on 34th Street, The Hunchback of Notre Dame*), born Dublin, Ireland, Aug 17, 1920.

Sean Penn, 38, actor (*Fast Times at Ridgemont High, Casualties of War*), born Santa Monica, CA, Aug 17, 1960.

Nelson Piquet, 46, auto racer, born Brasilia, Brazil, Aug 17, 1952.

Larry Rivers, 75, artist, born New York, NY, Aug 17, 1923.

Guillermo Vilas, 46, tennis player, born Mar del Plata, Argentina, Aug 17, 1952.

AUGUST 18 — TUESDAY

Day 230 — 135 Remaining

AMERICAN NEUTRALITY APPEAL: ANNIVERSARY. Aug 18. President Woodrow Wilson, on Aug 18, 1914, followed his Aug 4th Proclamation of Neutrality with an appeal to the American people to remain impartial in thought and deed with respect to the war that was raging in Europe (World War I).

BAD POETRY DAY. Aug 18. After all the "good" poetry you were forced to study in school, here's a chance for a payback. Invite some friends over, compose some really rotten verse and send it to your old high school English teacher. [© 1997 by WPL] For info: Tom or Ruth Roy, Wellness Permission League, PO Box 662, Mt Gretna, PA 17064-0662. Phone: (500) 437-5104 or (717) 964-1308. Fax: (717) 964-1335.

CANADA: ROYAL RED ARABIAN HORSE SHOW. Aug 18–22. Regina Exhibition Park, Regina, Saskatchewan. Royal Red Canadian International Arabian Horse Show showcases the best Arabian and Half-Arabian horses in North America. Est attendance: 15,000. For info: (306) 781-9216 or Tourism Saskatchewan, 500-1900 Albert St, Regina, Sask, Canada S4P 4L9. Phone: (800) 667-7191. Email: travel.info.@sasktourism.sk.ca. WWW: http://www.sasktourism.com

CLEMENTE, ROBERTO: BIRTH ANNIVERSARY. Aug 18, 1934. Professional National League baseball player, born at Carolina, Puerto Rico; died Dec 31, 1972, at San Juan, Puerto Rico. Drafted by the Pittsburgh Pirates in 1954, he played his entire major league career with them. Clemente died in a plane crash Dec 31, 1972, while on a mission of mercy to Nicaragua to deliver supplies he had collected for survivors of an earthquake. He was elected to the Baseball Hall of Fame in 1973.

DARE, VIRGINIA: BIRTH ANNIVERSARY. Aug 18, 1587. Virginia Dare, the first child of English parents to be born in the New World, was born to Ellinor and Ananias Dare, at Roanoke Island, NC, Aug 18, 1587. When a ship arrived to replenish their supplies in 1591, the settlers (including Virginia Dare) had vanished, without leaving a trace of the settlement.

HOOKSTOWN FAIR. Aug 18–22. Hookstown, PA. 51st annual. Exhibits, rides and entertainment. Main arena activities include tractor pulls, demolition derby and fireworks. For info: (412) 573-4512 or Beaver County Tourist Promotion Agency, 215 B Ninth St, Monaca, PA 15061-2028. Phone: (412) 728-0212. Fax: (412) 728-0456.

LEWIS, MERIWETHER: BIRTH ANNIVERSARY. Aug 18. American explorer (of Lewis and Clark expedition), born Aug 18, 1774. Died Oct 11, 1809.

NINETEENTH AMENDMENT TO US CONSTITUTION RATIFIED: ANNIVERSARY. Aug 18. The 19th Amendment, ratified on Aug 18, 1920, extended the right to vote to women.

PENN STATE'S AG PROGRESS DAYS. Aug 18–20. The Larson Agricultural Research Center, Rock Springs, PA. To provide the public with the latest information on agricultural industries and developments Penn State has made in the field of agriculture. More than 300 commercial exhibitors. Est attendance: 50,000. For info: Robert Oberheim, Penn State Univ, 420 Agricultural Admin Bldg, University Park, PA 16802. Phone: (814) 865-2081. Fax: (814) 863-2704.
WWW: http://www.cas.psu.edu/docs/agis/apd/apd.html

SAINT LOUIS BLUES HERITAGE FESTIVAL. Aug 18–23. St. Louis County Buder Park, St. Louis, MO. Five outdoor stages will feature prominent national and St. Louis artists from all blues music genres. Est attendance: 65,000. For info: St. Louis Blues Heritage Festival, Inc, PO Box 190605, St. Louis, MO 63119. Phone: (888) 211-3784. Fax: (314) 644-2485. Email: bluesfest@mo.net. WWW: http://www.stlbluesfest.org

BIRTHDAYS TODAY

Rosalynn (Eleanor) Smith Carter, 71, former First Lady, wife of President Jimmy Carter, born Plains, GA, Aug 18, 1927.

Lafayette ("Fat") Lever, 38, former basketball player, born Pine Bluff, AR, Aug 18, 1960.

Luc Montagnier, 66, virologist, born Chabris, France, Aug 18, 1932.

Martin Mull, 55, actor, comedian ("Mary Hartman, Mary Hartman," "Roseanne"), born Chicago, IL, Aug 18, 1943.

Roman Polanski, 65, filmmaker (*Rosemary's Baby, Macbeth, Chinatown*), born Paris, France, Aug 18, 1933.

Robert Redford, 61, actor (*Butch Cassidy and the Sundance Kid, The Sting, The Natural*), director (*A River Runs Through It*, Oscar for *Ordinary People*), born Santa Monica, CA, Aug 18, 1937.

Christian Slater, 29, actor (*Heathers, Broken Arrow, Pump Up the Volume*), born New York, NY, Aug 18, 1969.

Madeleine Stowe, 40, actress (*The Last of the Mohicans, Short Cuts*), born Los Angeles, CA, Aug 18, 1958.

Patrick Swayze, 44, dancer, actor ("North and South," *Dirty Dancing*), born Houston, TX, Aug 18, 1954.

Malcolm-Jamal Warner, 28, actor ("The Cosby Show"), born Jersey City, NJ, Aug 18, 1970.

Caspar Willard Weinberger, 81, former Secretary of Defense, born San Francisco, CA, Aug 18, 1917.

Shelley Winters (Shelly Schrift), 76, actress (Oscars for *A Patch of Blue, The Diary of Anne Frank*), born St. Louis, MO, Aug 18, 1922.

AUGUST 19 — WEDNESDAY

Day 231 — 134 Remaining

AFGHANISTAN: INDEPENDENCE DAY. Aug 19. National day.

ARTISTS IN THE PARK. Aug 19. Cate Park, Wolfeboro, NH. 18th annual juried exhibit and sale including 42 artists and craftspeople, demonstrations throughout the day and family entertainment shows at noon, 2:30 and 3:30 PM. Held rain or shine, 10 AM–5 PM. Sponsors: Governor Wentworth Arts Council. Est attendance: 4,000. For info: Deborah Hopkins, Co-Chair, PO Box 1322, Wolfeboro, NH 03894. Phone: (603) 569-4994.

CANADA: QUEBEC EXPO. Aug 19–30. Quebec. A spectacular expo which features entertainment, a circus, ice shows and harness racing. For info: Expo Quebec, 2205 Ave du Colissee, Quebec, Canada G1L 4W7. Phone: (418) 691-7110. Fax: (418) 691-7249.

CLINTON, WILLIAM JEFFERSON (BILL): BIRTHDAY. Aug 19, 1946. Forty-second US President, born at Hope, AR. Elected to a second term in 1996.

COUP ATTEMPT IN THE SOVIET UNION: ANNIVERSARY. Aug 19, 1991. A Soviet coalition of hard-line communists staged a coup d'état, removing President Mikhail Gorbachev from power. Gorbachev had been on vacation in the Crimea and was due to return to Moscow the next day to sign a treaty that would have taken much of the power away from the Central USSR government and given it to the republics signing the treaty. On the third day, Aug 21, in the face of massive public resistance, the conspirators gave up, flew to the Crimea hoping to negotiate with Gorbachev and were taken into custody, but Gorbachev returned to Moscow in an extremely weakened position. The independence of the republics, the dissolution of the Soviet Union and the loss of power by Gorbachev soon followed.

500 DAY COUNT UP TO ONE DAY IN PEACE. Aug 19. Individuals, organizations, institutions and governments around the world have declared One Day in Peace on Jan 1, 2000. On Apr 6, 1997—the 1,000 day count up—celebrations took place worldwide. Concerts, parades, fairs, festivals and celebrations will herald the remaining 500 days to build a brighter future, one day at a time. For info: Robert Alan Silverstein, CountUp 2000, Box 1475, Highstown, NJ 08520-1475. Email: countUP@aol.com. WWW: http://www.countUP2000.com

FORBES, MALCOLM: BIRTH ANNIVERSARY. Aug 19. Publisher, born Aug 19, 1919, at New York, NY. Malcolm Forbes was an unabashed proponent of capitalism, and his beliefs led to his colorful and successful climb to the top of the magazine-publishing industry. Known as much for his lavish lifestyle as his publishing acumen, Forbes was also an avid motorcyclist and hot-air balloonist. He died on Feb 24, 1990, at Far Hills, NJ.

August 1998

S	M	T	W	T	F	S
						1
2	3	4	5	6	7	8
9	10	11	12	13	14	15
16	17	18	19	20	21	22
23	24	25	26	27	28	29
30	31					

GERMAN PLEBISCITE: ANNIVERSARY. Aug 19. In a plebiscite, Aug 19, 1934, 89.9% of German voters approved giving Chancellor Adolf Hitler the additional office of president, placing the Führer in uncontestable and supreme command of that country's destiny.

NASH, OGDEN: BIRTH ANNIVERSARY. Aug 19, 1902. American writer, best remembered for his humorous verse. Born at Rye, NY; died May 19, 1971. "Undeniably brash/Was young Ogden Nash/Whose notable verse/Was admirably terse/And written with panache."

★**NATIONAL AVIATION DAY.** Aug 19. Presidential Proclamation 2343, of July 25, 1939, covers all succeeding years. Always Aug 19 of each year since 1939. Observed annually on anniversary of birth of Orville Wright, who piloted "first self-powered flight in history," Dec 17, 1903. First proclaimed by President Franklin D. Roosevelt.

RODDENBERRY, GENE: BIRTH ANNIVERSARY. Aug 19. The creator of the popular TV series "Star Trek," Gene Roddenberry was born at El Paso, TX, on Aug 19, 1921. Turning from his first career as an airline pilot to writing, he created one of the most successful TV science fiction series ever. The original series, which ended its run in 1969, lives on in reruns, and the "Star Trek: The Next Generation," "Star Trek: Deep Space Nine" and "Star Trek: Voyager" series have continuing popularity. Eight feature films also have been spawned from the original concept. Roddenberry died on Oct 24, 1991, at Santa Monica, CA.

SPACE MILESTONE: *SOYUZ T-7* (USSR). Aug 19, 1982. Launched from Tyuratam, USSR, with second woman in space (test pilot Svetlana Savitskaya) and two other cosmonauts. Docked at *Salyut 7* and visited the cosmonauts in residence there for the three previous months before returning to Earth on Aug 27 in the *Soyuz T-5* vehicle that had been docked there. The *Soyuz T-7* returned to Earth Dec 10 with the remaining two cosmonauts.

SPACE MILESTONE: *SPUTNIK 5* (USSR). Aug 19, 1960. Space menagerie satellite launched on this date. The dog passengers, Belka and Strelka, became first living organisms recovered from orbit.

SWITZERLAND: INTERNATIONAL FESTIVAL OF MUSIC. Aug 19–Sept 16. Lucerne. A classical music festival considered to have the most spectacular scenery of any music festival in Europe. Features more than 60 events including symphony concerts, chamber music, concerts presenting young artists and choral concerts. Annually, in August and September. Est attendance: 55,000. For info: Rosmarie Hohler-Welti, Mgr Public Affairs, Intl Festival of Music, PO Box CH-6002, Lucerne, Switzerland. Phone: (41) (41) 210-3562. Fax: (41) (41) 210-7784. Email: media@LucerneMusic.ch.
WWW: http://www.LucerneMusic.ch/

WRIGHT, ORVILLE: BIRTH ANNIVERSARY. Aug 19, 1871. Aviation pioneer born at Dayton, OH, on Aug 19, 1871, and died there Jan 30, 1948.

BIRTHDAYS TODAY

Adam Arkin, 42, actor ("Chicago Hope," "Northern Exposure") born Brooklyn, NY, Aug 19, 1956.

Ronald Maurice (Ron) Darling, Jr, 38, former baseball player, born Honolulu, HI, Aug 19, 1960.

Kevin Dillon, 33, actor (*Platoon, The Doors*), born Mamaroneck, NY, Aug 19, 1965.

Peter Gallagher, 43, actor (*sex, lies and videotape, Short Cuts, The Hudsucker Proxy*), born New York, NY, Aug 19, 1955.

Ring Lardner, Jr, 83, screenwriter and member of blacklisted Hollywood Ten (Oscar for *Woman of the Year; M*A*S*H*), born Chicago, IL, Aug 19, 1915.

Gerald McRaney, 50, actor ("Simon & Simon," "Major Dad"), born Collins, MS, Aug 19, 1948.

Diana Muldaur, 60, actress ("Star Trek: The Next Generation," "LA Law," *The Swimmer*), born New York, NY, Aug 19, 1938.

Cindy Nelson, 43, alpine skier, born Lutsen, MN, Aug 19, 1955.

Jill St. John (Jill Oppenheim), 58, actress (*Diamonds Are Forever*), born Los Angeles, CA, Aug 19, 1940.

Kyra Sedgwick, 33, actress (*Born on the Fourth of July*), born New York, NY, Aug 19, 1965.

William Lee (Willie) Shoemaker, 67, former jockey, born Fabens, TX, Aug 19, 1931.

John Stamos, 35, actor ("General Hospital," "Full House"), born Los Angeles, CA, Aug 19, 1963.

AUGUST 20 — THURSDAY

Day 232 — 133 Remaining

"ANDY'S GANG" TV PREMIERE: ANNIVERSARY. Aug 20, 1955. This children's program was originally known as "Smilin' Ed's Gang," which ran for five years until host Ed McConnell's death in 1955. Andy Devine took over the show which was retitled "Andy's Gang." The gangs of both shows included Midnight the Cat, Squeaky the Mouse, Froggy the Gremlin and Gunga Ram, the Indian boy.

CHEROKEE'S BLUEGRASS FESTIVAL. Aug 20–22. Cherokee, NC. 16th annual. For info: Norman Adams, PO Box 98, Dahlonega, GA 30533. Phone: (706) 864-7203. Fax: (706) 864-1037.

COCKROACH DERBY. Aug 20. Rutgers University Cook Campus, New Brunswick, NJ. The 11th annual "Roach Derby" sponsored by the New Jersey Pest Control Association. Pits the fastest roaches in the Garden State against one another to determine the best. Est attendance: 500. For info: Alan Caruba, New Jersey Pest Control Assn, PO Box 40, Maplewood, NJ 07040. Phone: (973) 763-6392. Fax: (973) 763-4287.

DELCAMBRE SHRIMP FESTIVAL. Aug 20–23. Delcambre, LA. Features a variety of shrimp dishes, with other food and beverages served. Family fun with amusement rides and music entertainment. Est attendance: 45,000. For info: Delcambre Shrimp Festival, PO Box 286, Delcambre, LA 70528. Phone: (318) 364-0780. Fax: (318) 685-2653.

ENGLAND: KENSINGTON ART FAIR. Aug 20–23. Kensington Town Hall, London. 40 stands offer mainly contemporary art—paintings, sculpture, original prints, studio pottery, etc. Est attendance: 3,500. For info: Barbara Bell, Event Mgr, PO Box 114, Haywards Heath, Sussex, England RH16 2YU. Phone: (44) (144) 448-2514. Fax: (44) (144) 448-3412.

GUEST, EDGAR ALBERT: BIRTH ANNIVERSARY. Aug 20, 1881. Newspaperman and author of folksy, homespun verse that enjoyed great popularity and was syndicated in more than 100 newspapers. Born at Birmingham, England; died at Detroit, MI, Aug 5, 1959. "Eddie Guest Day" usually proclaimed on birth anniversary in Detroit.

HARRISON, BENJAMIN: BIRTH ANNIVERSARY. Aug 20, 1833. The 23rd president of the US, born at North Bend, OH. He was the grandson of William Henry Harrison, ninth president of the US. His term of office, Mar 4, 1889–Mar 3, 1893, was preceded and followed by the presidential terms of Grover Cleveland (who thus became the 22nd and 24th president of the US). Harrison died at Indianapolis, IN, Mar 13, 1901.

HUNGARY: NATIONAL DAY. Aug 20. National holiday.

LITTLESTOWN GOOD OLE DAYS CELEBRATION. Aug 20–22. Gettysburg, PA. Annual antique show; arts and crafts, flea market, music and entertainment. Est attendance: 20,000. For info: Gettysburg Conv & Visitors Bureau, 35 Carlisle St, Gettysburg, PA 17325-1899. Phone: (717) 334-6274. Fax: (717) 334-1166. WWW: http://www.gettysburg.com

LOVECRAFT, H.P.: BIRTH ANNIVERSARY. Aug 20. Howard Phillips Lovecraft, American author of horror tales of the supernatural, a pioneering science fiction writer and a notable epistolarian, was born at Providence, RI, on Aug 20, 1890. He died there Mar 15, 1937.

O'HIGGINS, BERNARDO: BIRTH ANNIVERSARY. Aug 20, 1778. First ruler of Chile after its declaration of independence. Called the "Liberator of Chile." Born at Chillan, Chile. Died at Lima, Peru, Oct 24, 1842.

PLUTONIUM FIRST WEIGHED: ANNIVERSARY. Aug 20. University of Chicago scientist Glenn Seaborg and his colleagues first weighed plutonium, the first man-made element, on Aug 20, 1942.

SAARINEN, (GOTTLIEB) ELIEL: 125th BIRTH ANNIVERSARY. Aug 20, 1873. Famed architect. Born at Helsinki, Finland. Died at Bloomfield Hills, MI, July 1, 1950.

SOLDIERS' REUNION CELEBRATION. Aug 20. Newton, NC. Parade climaxes the 109th annual soldiers' reunion celebration—"oldest patriotic event of its kind in the US, honoring all veterans." Annually, the third Thursday in August. Concerts, arts, crafts, food and games. Est attendance: 27,500. For info: Soldiers' Reunion Committee, Box 267, Newton, NC 28658. Phone: (704) 464-2383.

SPACE MILESTONE: *VIKING 1* AND *2* (US). Aug 20 and Sept 9, 1975. Sister ships launched toward Mars from Cape Canaveral, FL, on Aug 20 and Sept 9, 1975. *Viking 1*'s lander touched down on Mars July 20, 1976, and *Viking 2*'s lander on Sept 3, 1976. Sent back to Earth high-quality photographs, analysis of atmosphere, weather information and results of sophisticated experiments intended to determine whether life may be present on Mars.

SPACE MILESTONE: *VOYAGER 2* (US). Aug 20, 1977. Launched this date, this unmanned spacecraft journeyed past Jupiter in 1979, Saturn in 1981, Uranus in 1986 and Neptune in 1989, sending photographs and data back to scientists on Earth.

SWEDEN: SOUR HERRING PREMIERE. Aug 20. By ordinance, the year's supply of sour herring may begin to be sold on the third Thursday in August.

WISCONSIN FOLKLIFE FESTIVAL. Aug 20–23. Madison, WI. A restaging of the Smithsonian Institution's Festival of American Folklife, the nation's largest annual cultural event, will take place in Madison on the Capitol Square, as well as adjoining streets, parks and the Monona Terrace Convention Center. Exhibits will explore the state's rich ethnic, regional and cultural traditions as well as Wisconsin's worklore. For info: Wisconsin Dept of Tourism, Wisconsin Folklife Festival, PO Box 7976, Madison, WI 53707. Phone: (800) 236-PLAY. Email: tourism@laughlin.com. WWW: http://tourism.state.wi.us

XEROX 914 DONATED TO SMITHSONIAN: ANNIVERSARY. Aug 20. On Aug 20, 1985, the original Xerox 914 copying machine (which had been introduced to the public 25 years earlier—in March 1960) was formally presented to the Smithsonian Institution's National Museum of American History in Washington, DC. Invented by Chester Carlson, a patent lawyer, the quick and easy copying of documents by machine revolutionized the world's offices.

BIRTHDAYS TODAY

Joan Allen, 42, actress (*Searching for Bobby Fischer, Nixon* [Academy Award, Best Supporting Actress]), born Rochelle, IL, Aug 20, 1956.

Connie Chung (Constance Yu-Hwa), 52, journalist, born Washington, DC, Aug 20, 1946.

Isaac Hayes, 56, musician, singer, songwriter, born Covington, TN, Aug 20, 1942.

Michael Jeter, 46, actor ("Evening Shade" [Emmy Award, 1992], *Miller's Crossing, The Fisher King*), born Lawrenceberg, TN, Aug 20, 1952.

Donald (Don) King, 67, boxing promoter, born Cleveland, OH, Aug 20, 1931.

Mark Edward Langston, 38, baseball player, born San Diego, CA, Aug 20, 1960.

Alfonso Raymond (Al) Lopez, 90, Baseball Hall of Fame manager and catcher, born Tampa, FL, Aug 20, 1908.

George John Mitchell, 65, former US Senator (D, Maine), born Waterville, ME, Aug 20, 1933.

Graig Nettles, 54, former baseball player, born San Diego, CA, Aug 20, 1944.

Ron Paul, 63, former congressman from Texas, Libertarian Party candidate for president of US, born Pittsburgh, PA, Aug 20, 1935.

Robert Plant, 50, singer, born Bromwich, England, Aug 20, 1948.

Al Roker, 44, meteorologist on "Today Show," born Brooklyn, NY, Aug 20, 1954.

AUGUST 21 — FRIDAY

Day 233 — 132 Remaining

ALASKA STATE FAIR/EXPO 98. Aug 21–Sept 7. Palmer, AK. Cows and critters, music and dancing, rides, excitement and family fun at the state's largest summer extravaganza. More than 500 events including demonstrations, high-caliber entertainment, rodeos, horse shows, homemaking and agricultural exhibits. The 1998 Fair is a three-week celebration honoring the Gold Rush and is known as Expo '98. Est attendance: 280,000. For info: Alaska State Fair, Inc, 2075 Glenn Hwy, Palmer, AK 99645. Phone: (907) 745-4827. Fax: (907) 745-7173. Email: akstatefair@corecom.net.

AMERICAN BAR ASSOCIATION FOUNDING: ANNIVERSARY. Aug 21, 1878. Organized at Sarasota, NY.

AQUINO, BENIGNO: 15th ASSASSINATION ANNIVERSARY. Aug 21, 1983. Filipino opposition leader Benigno S. Aquino, Jr, was shot and killed at the Manila airport on his return to the Philippines on Aug 21, 1983. The killing precipitated greater anti-Marcos feeling and figured significantly in the Feb 7, 1986, election that brought about the collapse of the government administration of Ferdinand E. Marcos and the inauguration of Corazon C. Aquino, widow of the slain man, as president.

BEARDSLEY, AUBREY VINCENT: BIRTH ANNIVERSARY. Aug 21, 1872. English artist and illustrator born at Brighton. Died at Menton, France, Mar 16, 1898.

BLACK HILLS STEAM AND GAS THRESHING BEE. Aug 21–23. Sturgis, SD. Held annually one mile east of the Sturgis Airport. The pioneer heritage of our country comes alive with old steam and gas tractors, threshing machine demonstrations, flea market, parade, antique automobiles and dozens of other demonstrations related to yesteryear. Est attendance: 4,000. For info: Ranae Pickar, Receptionist/Secretary, Chamber of Commerce, Box 504, Sturgis, SD 57785. Phone: (605) 347-2556. Fax: (605) 347-6682.

CALIFORNIA STATE FAIR. Aug 21–Sept 7. Sacramento, CA. Top-name entertainment, fireworks, California counties exhibits, livestock nursery, culinary delights, carnival rides, demolition derbies and award-winning wines and microbrews. For info: Cal Expo, PO Box 15649, Sacramento, CA 95852. Phone: (916) 263-3000.

CANADA: COE HILL AGRICULTURAL FAIR. Aug 21–22. Coe Hill, Ontario. Competitions for best vegetables and animals, along with kid's games, Hell Driver's auto demonstration and music. Annually, the second to last weekend in August. Est attendance: 5,000. For info: Bancroft and District Chamber of Commerce, PO Box 539, Bancroft, Ont, Canada K0L 1C0. Phone: (613) 332-1513. Fax: (613) 332-2119. Email: chamber@commerce.bancroft.on.ca. WWW: http://www.commerce.bancroft.on.ca

CANADA: EDSON SIDEWALK JAMBOREE. Aug 21–23. Edson, Alberta. Townwide sidewalk sale. Est attendance: 8,000. For info: Edson and District Chamber of Commerce, 5433 Third Ave, Edson, Alta, Canada T7E 1L5. Phone: (403) 723-4918. Fax: (403) 723-5545.

CANADA: MORDEN CORN AND APPLE FESTIVAL. Aug 21–23. Morden, Manitoba. It's fun and it's free! Est attendance: 35,000. For info: Morden Chamber of Commerce, 102-195 Stephen St, Morden, Man, Canada R6M 1V3. Phone: (204) 822-5630. Fax: (204) 822-6404.

CHARLESTON STERNWHEEL REGATTA FESTIVAL. Aug 21–30. Charleston, WV. A 10-day festival celebrating Charleston's river heritage. Est attendance: 400,000. For info: Charleston Festival Commission, Inc, PO Box 2749, Charleston, WV 25330. Phone: (304) 348-6419. Fax: (304) 348-0737.

CORVETTE SHOW. Aug 21–23. State Dock, Mackinaw City, MI. Parade of Corvettes on Friday at 7 PM. Show and visitor viewing, awards and Sunset Boat Cruise on Saturday. For info: Corvette Show, 708 S Huron, Mackinaw City, MI 49701. Phone: (616) 436-5574.

EVANSTON/GLENBROOK HOSPITALS AMERICAN CRAFT EXPOSITION. Aug 21–23. Evanston, IL. A juried show of works by American craftworkers to benefit the Evanston and Glenbrook Hospitals. For info: Evanston/Glenbrook Hospitals Auxiliary, 1301 Central St, Evanston, IL 60201. Phone: (847) 570-5096.

FESTIVAL OF THE LITTLE HILLS. Aug 21–23. Frontier Park and South Main, St. Charles, MO. The largest festival of the year; activities include demonstrations by craftspeople and artisans. Annually, the third weekend in August. Est attendance: 300,000. For info: St. Charles Conv and Visitors Bureau, 230 S Main, St. Charles, MO 63301. Phone: (800) 366-2427 or (314) 946-7776. WWW: http://www.st-charles.mo.us

HAWAII ADMISSION DAY HOLIDAY. Aug 21. The third Friday in August is observed as a state holiday each year, recognizing the anniversary of Hawaii's statehood. Hawaii became the 50th state on Aug 21, 1959.

HAWAII STATEHOOD: ANNIVERSARY. Aug 21, 1959. President Dwight Eisenhower signed a proclamation admitting Hawaii to the Union. The statehood bill had passed the previous March with a stipulation that statehood should be approved by a vote of Hawaiian residents. The referendum passed by a huge margin in June and Eisenhower proclaimed Hawaii the 50th state on Aug 21.

MOON PHASE: NEW MOON. Aug 21. Moon enters New Moon phase at 10:03 PM, EDT.

PRAIRIE VILLAGE JAMBOREE. Aug 21–23. Prairie Village, Madison, SD. Come and join the fun with arts and crafts displays, a parade, entertainment, tractor pulls and much more. Est attendance: 35,000. For info: Prairie Village Jamboree, PO Box 256, Madison, SD 57042. Phone: (605) 256-3644.

QUANTRILL'S RAID ON LAWRENCE, KANSAS: ANNIVERSARY. Aug 21, 1863. Confederate raider William

August 1998

S	M	T	W	T	F	S
						1
2	3	4	5	6	7	8
9	10	11	12	13	14	15
16	17	18	19	20	21	22
23	24	25	26	27	28	29
30	31					

Clarke Quantrill launched a predawn terrorist raid on Lawrence, KS, leaving 150 civilians dead and much of the town ruined. Quantrill had been denied a commission in the Southern army for his barbaric approach to war.

SMOKY MOUNTAIN FIDDLERS CONVENTION. Aug 21–22. Loudon, TN. Come and join in the fun with entertainment, food booths, arts and crafts displays and much more. Est attendance: 6,000. For info: Smoky Mountain Fiddlers Conv, PO Box 309, Loudon, TN 37774. Phone: (423) 458-4352. Fax: (423) 458-2845.

SMOKY MOUNTAIN WOODWORKING SHOW. Aug 21–23. Gatlinburg Convention Center, Knoxville, TN. Annual show featuring woodworking tools, supplies and seminars. For info: Cindy Crabtree, Event Coordinator, Smoky Mountain Woodworking Show, PO Box 50096, Knoxville, TN 37950. Phone: (423) 588-1233 or (800) 588-3728. Fax: (423) 588-6938.

SOLAR ECLIPSE. Aug 21. Annular eclipse of the sun. Central eclipse begins at 8:15 PM, EDT, reaches greatest eclipse at 10:14 PM, EDT, and ends at 11:56 PM, EDT. Visible in North Indian Ocean, India, southeast Asia, southern China, Indonesia, Malaysia, Philippine Republic, southern Japan, Australasia, South Pacific Ocean.

SPACE MILESTONE: *GEMINI 5* (US). Aug 21, 1965. Launched on this date, this craft carrying astronauts Lieutenant Colonel Cooper and Lieutenant Commander Conrad orbited Earth 128 times for new international record of eight days. First launch of a satellite from a manned spacecraft.

YANKTON RIVERBOAT DAYS AND SUMMER ARTS FESTIVAL. Aug 21–23. Riverside Park, Yankton, SD. Parades, water ski show and competition, tug-o-war, giant beach ball volleyball, antique tractor pull, continuous entertainment, juried arts fair, food vendors, rodeo and square dancing. Est attendance: 110,000. For info: Riverboat Days, PO Box 483, Yankton, SD 57078. Phone: (605) 665-1657 or (800) 888-1460. Fax: (605) 665-7501. Email: visitorinfo@yanktonsd.com. WWW: http://www.yanktonsd.com

BIRTHDAYS TODAY

Steve Case, 40, founder of America Online, born Oahu, HI, Aug 21, 1958.

Kim Cattrall, 42, actress (*Police Academy, Bonfire of the Vanities*), born Liverpool, England, Aug 21, 1956.

Wilton Norman (Wilt) Chamberlain, 62, Basketball Hall of Fame center, born Philadelphia, PA, Aug 21, 1936.

Jackie DeShannon, 54, singer, songwriter ("Put a Little Love in Your Heart"), born Hazel, KY, Aug 21, 1944.

Princess Margaret, 68, Countess of Snowdon, sister of Queen Elizabeth II, born Glamis, Scotland, Aug 21, 1930.

James Robert (Jim) McMahon, 39, football player, born Jersey City, NJ, Aug 21, 1959.

Kenny Rogers, 60, singer ("Lucille," "Lady"), born Houston, TX, Aug 21, 1938.

Melvin Van Peebles, 66, playwright (*Ain't Supposed to Die a Natural Death*), born Chicago, IL, Aug 21, 1932.

Clarence Williams III, 59, actor ("The Mod Squad," *Purple Rain*), born New York, NY, Aug 21, 1939.

Alicia Witt, 23, actress ("Cybill") born Worcester, MA, Aug 21, 1975.

AUGUST 22 — SATURDAY

Day 234 — 131 Remaining

ANTIQUE MARINE ENGINE EXPOSITION. Aug 22–23. Mystic Seaport, Mystic, CT. Collectors from across the US and Canada gather for the 7th annual exposition of pre-World War II marine engines and engine models. Unique engines power watercraft in a boat parade on the Mystic River. For info: Mystic Seaport, 75 Greenmanville Ave, PO Box 6000, Mystic, CT 06355-0990. Phone: (203) 572-5315.

BALLUNAR LIFTOFF. Aug 22–24 (tentative). Nassau Bay, TX. Come and enjoy a festive weekend with hot-air balloon, air show and NASA/Johnson Space Center. Sponsored by Space Center Houston/Clear Lake Area Chamber of Commerce. For info: Shari Liebman, Clear Lake Area Chamber of Commerce, 1201 Nasa Rd One, Houston, TX 77058. Phone: (281) 488-7676. Fax: (281) 488-8981.

BE AN ANGEL DAY. Aug 22. A day to do "one small act of service for someone. Be a blessing in someone's life." Annually, Aug 22. For info: Angel Heights Healing Center, Rev Jayne M. Howard, PO Box 95, Upperco, MD 21155. Phone: (410) 833-6912. Fax: (410) 429-4077. Email: blessing@erols.com. WWW: http://drwnet.com/angel

CAMEROON: VOLCANIC ERUPTION: ANNIVERSARY. Aug 22, 1986. Deadly fumes from a presumed volcanic eruption under Lake Nios in Cameroon killed more than 1,500 persons. A similar occurrence two years earlier had killed 37 persons.

CANADA: OJIBWA KEESHIGUN. Aug 22–23. Old Fort William, Thunder Bay, Ontario. A celebration of Old Fort William's native culture. Taste historic foods, enjoy unique demonstrations and join in crafts and games. Experience the atmosphere of a powwow with traditional singing and dancing. Annually, late August. Est attendance: 6,000. For info: Marty Mascarin, Communications Officer, Vickers Heights PO, Thunder Bay, Ont, Canada P0T 2Z0. Phone: (807) 473-2344 or (807) 577-8461. Fax: (807) 473-2312.

CHRISTMAS BAZAAR. Aug 22–23. Trollwood Park, Fargo, ND. A two-day arts and crafts festival featuring more than 300 booths. All items handmade. Concessions available. Strolling and staged entertainment is also scheduled. Est attendance: 50,000. For info: Carolyn Boutain, Dir of Trollwood Park, PO Box 1796, Fargo, ND 58107. Phone: (701) 241-8160. Fax: (701) 241-8266.

DANKFEST. Aug 22–23. Harmony Museum, Harmony, PA. Pioneer crafts, historic-district tours, food and entertainment. Est attendance: 3,000. For info: Kathy Luek, Administrator, Historic Harmony, 218 Mercer St, PO Box 524, Harmony, PA 16037. Phone: (412) 452-7341. WWW: http://www.novard.com/harmonymuseum

DEBUSSY, CLAUDE: BIRTH ANNIVERSARY. Aug 22, 1862. (Achille) Claude Debussy, French musician and composer, especially remembered for his impressionistic "tone poems," was born at St. Germain-en-Laye, France. He died at Paris, France, on Mar 25, 1918.

GREAT AMERICAN DUCK RACE. Aug 22–23. Deming, NM. "World's richest duck race." Also Duck Queen and Darling Duckling contests, Tortilla Toss, parade and other festivities. Est attendance: 24,000. For info: The Great American Duck Race, PO Box 1402, Deming, NM 88031. Phone: (800) 848-4955.

HERRIMAN, GEORGE: BIRTH ANNIVERSARY. Aug 22, 1880. In 1910 when George Herriman introduced a cat and mouse as subplot characters to his comic strip "The Dingbat Family," their non-sequitur dialogue gained enough attention to result in a spin-off strip of their own. The superbly drafted "Krazy Kat and Ignatz" had as its central theme unrequited love. Kat loved Ignatz, but the malevolent mouse took every opportunity to throw bricks at the devoted cat. Carried out against a surrealistic backdrop fashioned after the Arizona desert, "Krazy Kat" was popular with a mass audience as well as artists and intellectuals, and it remained enormously popular after Herriman's death. Born at New Orleans, LA, he died at Hollywood, CA, Apr 25, 1944.

ICE CREAM SOCIAL. Aug 22. Shane Hill Nursing Home, Rockford, OH. Employees, residents and their families gather for games, music and entertainment at family-night ice cream social. Annually, the fourth Saturday of August. Est attendance: 500. For info: Dorothy Trisel, Shane Hill Nursing Home, 10731 State Rte 118, Rockford, OH 45882-8947.

INTERNATIONAL YACHT RACE: ANNIVERSARY. Aug 22, 1851. A silver trophy (then known as the "Hundred Guinea Cup," and offered by the Royal Yacht Squadron) was won in a race around the Isle of Wight by the US yacht *America*. The trophy, later turned over to the New York Yacht Club, became known as the America's Cup.

ITALY: STRESA MUSICAL WEEKS. Aug 22–Sept 19. Stresa. International festival includes concerts by symphonic orchestras, chamber music, recitals and a series by young winners of international musical contests. 36th annual festival. For info: Assn Settimane Musicali di Stresa, Via R Bonghi 4, Stresa (Lago Maggiore), Italy 28049. Phone: (39) (323) 31095 or (39) (323) 30459. Fax: (39) (323) 33006.

KGB FOUNDER STATUE DISMANTLED: ANNIVERSARY. Aug 22. In the wake of the popular revolt that smashed the right-wing Soviet coup, a crowd of 10,000 Muscovites watched on Aug 22, 1991, as cranes dismantled a 14-ton statue of Felix Dzerzhinsky, a Polish intellectual tapped by Vladimir Lenin to organize the fledgling Soviet Union's secret police. After trucks had hauled away the massive likeness of Dzerzhinsky, Moscow residents adorned the statue's pedestal and the nearby KGB headquarters with graffiti.

LANGLEY, SAMUEL PIERPONT: BIRTH ANNIVERSARY. Aug 22. American astronomer, physicist and aviation pioneer for whom Langley Air Force Base, VA, is named. Born at Roxbury, MA, Aug 22, 1834, Langley died at Aiken, SC, on Feb 27, 1906.

LEADVILLE TRAIL 100 ULTRAMARATHON. Aug 22–23 (tentative). Leadville, CO. One of the toughest 100-mile footraces in the country, the course goes through the Rocky Mountains 50 miles to the ghost town of Winfield and back. Runners begin at 4 AM and must complete race in 30 hours. Sponsor: Leadville Trail 100, Inc. Est attendance: 2,000. For info: Gloria Cheshier, Exec Dir, Greater Leadville Chamber of Commerce, PO Box 861, Leadville, CO 80461. Phone: (719) 486-3900 or (800) 933-3901. Fax: (719) 486-8478. Email: leadville@sni.net. WWW: http://www.colorado.com/leadville

MORMON CHOIR FIRST PERFORMANCE: ANNIVERSARY. Aug 22, 1847. What would later become the world-famous Mormon Tabernacle Choir gave its first public performance in Salt Lake City, UT, for an outdoor meeting of The Church of Jesus Christ of Latter-Day Saints. Widely known for its concert tours, recordings and weekly radio and television broadcasts from Temple Square, the choir's radio program "Music and the Spoken Word" is the longest continuously running radio program in network history, dating back to 1929. For info: Church of Jesus Christ of Latter-Day Saints, Public Affairs Dept, 15 E South Temple St, Salt Lake City, UT 84150. Phone: (801) 240-4395. Fax: (801) 240-1167.

PEOPLE'S REPUBLIC OF CHINA: FESTIVAL OF HUNGRY GHOSTS. Aug 22–Sept 20. Important Chinese festival, also known as Ghosts Month. According to Chinese legend, during the 7th lunar month the souls of the dead are released from purgatory to roam the Earth. Joss sticks are burnt in homes; prayers, food and "ghost money" are offered to appease the ghosts. Market stallholders combine to hold celebrations to ensure that their businesses will prosper in the coming year. Wayang (Chinese street opera) and puppet shows are performed, and fruit and Chinese delicacies are offered to the spirits of the dead. Chung Yuan (All Souls' Day) is observed on the 15th day of the 7th lunar month: Sept 5 in 1998.

ROCKBRIDGE COMMUNITY FESTIVAL. Aug 22. Lexington, VA. Fun for all ages—crafts, exhibits, live music, food and games. For info: Lexington Visitors Bureau, 106 E Washington St, Lexington, VA 24450. Phone: (540) 463-3777. Fax: (540) 463-1105. Email: lexington@rockbridge.net.

STONE, MELVILLE ELIJAH: 150th BIRTH ANNIVERSARY. Aug 22, 1848. Influential American journalist Melville Stone was born at Hudson, IL, and died at New York, NY, Feb 15, 1929. His autobiography, *Fifty Years a Journalist*, was published in 1921.

VIETNAM CONFLICT BEGINS: ANNIVERSARY. Aug 22, 1945. Less than a week after the Japanese surrender ended World War II, a team of Free French parachuted into southern Indochina in response to a successful coup by a Communist guerrilla named Ho Chi Minh in Vietnam.

WALES: LLANDRINDOD WELLS VICTORIAN FESTIVAL. Aug 22–30. Llandrindod Wells, Powys. The whole town turns the clocks back to the Victorian age. For info: Festival Office, Old Town Hall, Temple St, Llandrindod Wells, Powys, Wales LD1 5DL. Phone: (59) 782-3441. Fax: (59) 782-5905.

WILLARD, ARCHIBALD M.: BIRTH ANNIVERSARY. Aug 22, 1836. American artist, best known for his painting *The Spirit of '76*, was born at Bedford, OH. Willard died at Cleveland, OH, Oct 11, 1918.

☆ ☆ ☆

BIRTHDAYS TODAY

Ray Bradbury, 78, author (*The Toynbee Convector, Fahrenheit 451*), born Waukegan, IL, Aug 22, 1920.

Gerald Paul Carr, 66, former astronaut, born Denver, CO, Aug 22, 1932.

Henri Cartier-Bresson, 90, photographer, born Chanteloup, France, Aug 22, 1908.

Valerie Harper, 57, actress (Rhoda on "The Mary Tyler Moore Show" and "Rhoda"), born Suffern, NY, Aug 22, 1941.

John Lee Hooker, 81, singer ("Boom, Boom"), born Clarksdale, MS, Aug 22, 1917.

Sylva Koscina, 65, actress (*Juliet of the Spirits, The Secret War of Harry Frigg*), born Yugoslavia, Aug 22, 1933.

Steve Kroft, 53, coeditor, correspondent ("60 Minutes"), born Kokomo, IN, Aug 22, 1945.

Paul Leo Molitor, 42, baseball player, born St. Paul, MN, Aug 22, 1956.

Duane Charles (Bill) Parcells, 57, football coach, born Englewood, NJ, Aug 22, 1941.

Norman H. Schwarzkopf, 64, retired army general, born Trenton, NJ, Aug 22, 1934.

Cindy Williams, 50, actress (*American Graffiti*, "Laverne & Shirley"), born Van Nuys, CA, Aug 22, 1948.

Carl Michael Yastrzemski, 59, Baseball Hall of Fame outfielder, born Southampton, NY, Aug 22, 1939.

August 1998

S	M	T	W	T	F	S
						1
2	3	4	5	6	7	8
9	10	11	12	13	14	15
16	17	18	19	20	21	22
23	24	25	26	27	28	29
30	31					

AUGUST 23 — SUNDAY

Day 235 — 130 Remaining

BELGIUM: WEDDING OF THE GIANTS. Aug 23. Traditional cultural observance. Annually, the fourth Sunday in August.

FIRST MAN-POWERED FLIGHT: ANNIVERSARY. Aug 23. At Schafter, CA, Aug 23, 1977, Bryan Allen pedaled the 70-lb *Gossamer Condor* for a mile at a "minimal altitude of two pylons" in a flight certified by the Royal Aeronautical Society of Britain, winning a £50,000 prize offered by British industrialist Henry Kremer. See also: "First Man-Powered Flight Across English Channel: Anniversary" (June 12).

LUXEMBOURG: SCHUEBERMESS SHEPHERD'S FAIR. Aug 23–Sept 5. Fair dates from 1340. (Two weeks beginning on the next to last Sunday of August.)

MASTERS, EDGAR LEE: BIRTH ANNIVERSARY. Aug 23. American poet, author of the *Spoon River Anthology*, was born at Garnett, KS, Aug 23, 1869. He died at Melrose Park, PA, Mar 5, 1950.

PERRY, OLIVER HAZARD: BIRTH ANNIVERSARY. Aug 23, 1785. American naval hero. Born Aug 23, 1785. Died Aug 23, 1819. Best remembered is his announcement of victory at the Battle of Lake Erie on Sept 10, 1813: "We have met the enemy, and they are ours."

SACCO-VANZETTI MEMORIAL DAY: ANNIVERSARY. Aug 23, 1927. Nicola Sacco and Bartolomeo Vanzetti were electrocuted at the Charlestown, MA, prison on this date. Convicted of a shoe factory payroll robbery during which a guard had been killed, Sacco and Vanzetti maintained their innocence to the end. Six years of appeals marked this American cause célèbre during which substantial evidence was presented to show that both men were elsewhere at the time of the crime. However, on the 50th anniversary of their execution, Massachusetts governor Michael S. Dukakis proclaimed Aug 23, 1977, a memorial day, noting that the 1921 trial had been "permeated by prejudice."

SPACE MILESTONE: *INTELSAT-4 F-7* (US); 25th ANNIVERSARY. Aug 23, 1973. International Communications Satellite Consortium's *Intelsat* launched Aug 23, 1973, to relay communications from North and South America to Europe and Africa.

VIRGO, THE VIRGIN. Aug 23–Sept 22. In the astronomical/astrological zodiac, which divides the sun's apparent orbit into 12 segments, the period Aug 23–Sept 22 is identified, traditionally, as the sun sign of Virgo, the Virgin. The ruling planet is Mercury.

BIRTHDAYS TODAY

Tony Bill, 58, actor (*You're a Big Boy Now, Pee-wee's Big Adventure*), director (*My Bodyguard*), born San Diego, CA, Aug 23, 1940.

Michael James (Mike) Boddicker, 41, former baseball player, born Cedar Rapids, IA, Aug 23, 1957.

Barbara Eden (Barbara Huffman), 64, actress ("I Dream of Jeannie," *The Wonderful World of the Brothers Grimm*), born Tucson, AZ, Aug 23, 1934.

Sonny Jurgensen, 64, Pro Football Hall of Fame quarterback, born Wilmington, NC, Aug 23, 1934.

Shelley Long, 49, actress (Diane Chambers on "Cheers"; *Irreconcilable Differences*), born Fort Wayne, IN, Aug 23, 1949.

Patricia McBride, 56, dancer, born Teaneck, NJ, Aug 23, 1942.

Vera Miles, 68, actress (*The Wrong Man, Psycho*), born Boise City, OK, Aug 23, 1930.

Mark Russell (Mark Ruslander), 66, political comedian ("Real People"), born Buffalo, NY, Aug 23, 1932.

Richard Sanders, 58, actor ("WKRP in Cincinnati," "Berrengers"), born Harrisburg, PA, Aug 23, 1940.

Rick Springfield, 49, singer, actor, born Sydney, Australia, Aug 23, 1949.

AUGUST 24 — MONDAY

Day 236 — 129 Remaining

DUFF, HOWARD: 85th BIRTH ANNIVERSARY. Aug 24, 1913. American actor Howard Duff was born at WA. He played detective Sam Spade on radio in the 1940s and then went on to films and television. He died on July 9, 1990, at Santa Barbara, CA.

"THE FACTS OF LIFE" TV PREMIERE: ANNIVERSARY. Aug 24, 1979. This NBC sitcom was spun off from "Dif-f'rent Strokes" with Drummond family housekeeper Edna Garrett (Charlotte Rae) moving to Peekskill, NY, to take over as housemother at Eastland, a boarding school for girls. During the first season, the cast included John Lawlor as Headmaster Steven Bradley, Jenny O'Hara as Miss Mahoney, Lisa Welchel as Blair Warner, Mindy Cohn as Natalie Green, Kim Fields as Dorothy "Tootie" Ramsey, Felice Schacter as Nancy Olson, Julie Piekarski as Sue Ann Weaver, Julie Anne Haddock as Cindy Webster and Molly Ringwald as Molly Parker.

ITALY: VESUVIUS DAY. Aug 24. Anniversary of the eruption of Vesuvius, an active volcano in southern Italy, on Aug 24, AD 79, which destroyed the cities of Pompeii, Stabiae and Herculaneum.

JARVIS, GREGORY B.: BIRTH ANNIVERSARY. Aug 24, 1944. Gregory B. Jarvis, a civilian engineer with Hughes Aircraft Co, was born in Detroit, MI. Jarvis was the 41-year-old payload specialist who perished with other crew members and Christa McAuliffe in the Space Shuttle *Challenger* explosion on Jan 28, 1986. See also: "*Challenger* Space Shuttle Explosion: Anniversary" (Jan 28).

LITTLE LEAGUE BASEBALL WORLD SERIES. Aug 24–29 (tentative). Williamsport, PA. Eight teams from the US and foreign countries compete for the World Championship. Est attendance: 100,000. For info: Little League Baseball HQ, Box 3485, Williamsport, PA 17701. Phone: (717) 326-1921. Fax: (717) 326-1074. WWW: http://www.littleleague.org

SAINT BARTHELEMY: PATRON SAINT DAY. Aug 24. The festival of St. Barthelemy is celebrated for several days, beginning on Aug 24. The "look and feeling of a French country fair."

SAINT BARTHOLOMEW'S DAY MASSACRE: ANNIVERSARY. Aug 24, 1572. Anniversary of the massacre in Paris and throughout France of thousands of Protestant Huguenots. The massacre began when the church bells tolled at dawn on St. Bartholomew's Day, Aug 24, 1572, and continued for several days. Pope Gregory XIII ordered a medal struck to commemorate the event, but Protestant countries abhorred the killings, estimated at 2,000 to 70,000.

SOUTHERN CYCLONE: ANNIVERSARY. Aug 24, 1893. A hurricane hit Savannah, GA, and Charleston, SC, on Aug 24, 1893, killing between 1,000 and 2,000 people.

SPACE MILESTONE: *VOYAGER 2* (US). Aug 24, 1989. Launched in 1977, *Voyager 2* had its first close encounter with Neptune.

UKRAINE: INDEPENDENCE DAY. Aug 24. National day.

WARNER WEATHER QUOTATION: 100th ANNIVERSARY. Aug 24, 1897. Charles Dudley Warner, American newspaper editor for the *Hartford Courant*, published this now famous and oft-quoted sentence, "Everybody talks about the weather, but nobody does anything about it." The quotation is often mistakenly attributed to his friend and colleague Mark Twain. Warner and Twain were part of the most notable American literary circle during the late 19th century. Warner was a journalist, essayist, novelist, biographer and author who collaborated with Mark Twain in writing *The Gilded Age* in 1873. Warner was also a contributing editor to the *Hartford Courant, Harper's New Monthly Magazine* and the *Library of the World's Best Literature*.

WASHINGTON, DC: INVASION ANNIVERSARY. Aug 24–25. British forces briefly invaded and raided Washington, DC, burning the Capitol, the president's house and most other public buildings on Aug 24–25, 1814. President James Madison and other high US government officials fled to safety until British troops (not knowing the strength of their position) departed the city two days later.

BIRTHDAYS TODAY

Max Cleland, 56, US Senator (D, Georgia), born Atlanta, GA, Aug 24, 1942.

Gerry Cooney, 42, former boxer, born New York, NY, Aug 24, 1956.

Steve Guttenberg, 40, actor ("Billy," "No Soap, Radio"), born Brooklyn, NY, Aug 24, 1958.

Marlee Matlin, 33, actress (Oscar for *Children of a Lesser God*), born Morton Grove, IL, Aug 24, 1965.

Reginald Wayne (Reggie) Miller, 33, basketball player, born Riverside, CA, Aug 24, 1965.

Michael Richards, 48, actor (Kramer on "Seinfeld," *Trial and Error*), born Culver City, CA, Aug 24, 1950.

Calvin Edward (Cal) Ripken, Jr, 38, baseball player, born Havre de Grace, MD, Aug 24, 1960.

Louis Teicher, 74, pianist, composer, born Wilkes-Barre, PA, Aug 24, 1924.

Mason Williams, 60, composer, born Abilene, TX, Aug 24, 1938.

AUGUST 25 — TUESDAY

Day 237 — 128 Remaining

BERNSTEIN, LEONARD: 80th BIRTH ANNIVERSARY. Aug 25, 1918. American conductor and composer Leonard Bernstein was born at Lawrence, MA. One of the greatest conductors in American music history, he first conducted the New York Philharmonic Orchestra at age 25 and was its director from 1959 to 1969. His musicals include *West Side Story* and *On the Town*, and his operas and operettas include *Candide*. He died five days after his retirement on Oct 14, 1990, at New York, NY.

August 1998

S	M	T	W	T	F	S
						1
2	3	4	5	6	7	8
9	10	11	12	13	14	15
16	17	18	19	20	21	22
23	24	25	26	27	28	29
30	31					

HARTE, BRET: BIRTH ANNIVERSARY. Aug 25. Francis Bret(t) Harte, journalist, poet, printer, teacher and novelist, especially remembered for his early stories of California ("The Luck of Roaring Camp," "The Outcasts of Poker Flat" and "How Santa Claus Came to Simpson's Bar"), was born at Albany, NY, Aug 25, 1836. He died at London, England, May 5, 1902.

KELLY, WALT: 85th BIRTH ANNIVERSARY. Aug 25, 1913. American cartoonist and creator of the comic strip "Pogo" was born at Philadelphia, PA, on Aug 25, 1913. It was Kelly's character Pogo who paraphrased Oliver Hazard Perry to say, "We has met the enemy, and it is us." Kelly died at Hollywood, CA, Oct 18, 1973. See also: "Perry, Oliver Hazard: Birth Anniversary" (Aug 23).

MICHIGAN STATE FAIR. Aug 25–Sept 7. State Fairgrounds, Detroit, MI. Est attendance: 400,000. For info: State of Michigan, Dept of Commerce, 1120 W State Fair Ave, Detroit, MI 48203. Phone: (313) 368-1000.

NATIONAL PARK SERVICE ANNIVERSARY OBSERVANCE. Aug 25. Colonial Natl Historical Park, Jamestown and Yorktown, VA. Est attendance: 1,700. For info: Activities Coord, Colonial National Historical Park, PO Box 210, Yorktown, VA 23690. Phone: (757) 898-3400.
WWW: http://www.nps.gov/colo/

PINKERTON, ALLAN: BIRTH ANNIVERSARY. Aug 25. Scottish-born American detective, founder of detective agency in Chicago, IL, in 1850, first chief of US Army's secret service, remembered now because of his strike-breaking employments and his lack of sympathy for working people. Pinkerton was born at Glasgow, Scotland, Aug 25, 1819, and died at Chicago, IL, July 1, 1884.

SMITH, SAMANTHA: DEATH ANNIVERSARY. Aug 25. American schoolgirl whose interest in world peace drew praise and affection from people around the world. In 1982, the 10-year-old wrote a letter to Soviet leader Yuri Andropov asking him, "Why do you want to conquer the whole world, or at least our country?" The letter was widely publicized in the USSR and Andropov replied personally to her. Samantha Smith was invited to visit and tour the Soviet Union. On Aug 25, 1985, the airplane on which she was riding crashed in Maine, killing all aboard, including Samantha and her father. In 1986, minor planet No 3147, an asteroid between Mars and Jupiter, was named Samantha Smith in her memory.

URUGUAY: INDEPENDENCE DAY. Aug 25. National holiday. Declared independence from Brazil on this day, 1825.

BIRTHDAYS TODAY

Cecil D. Andrus, 67, former Governor of Idaho (D), born Hood River, OR, Aug 25, 1931.

Anne Archer, 51, actress ("Falcon Crest"; stage: *A Couple of White Chicks Sitting Around Talking*), born Los Angeles, CA, Aug 25, 1947.

Cornelius O'Landa Bennett, 32, football player, born Birmingham, AL, Aug 25, 1966.

Sean Connery, 68, actor (James Bond movies; *The Man Who Would Be King*), born Edinburgh, Scotland, Aug 25, 1930.

Elvis Costello, 44, musician, songwriter ("Oliver's Army"), born London, England, Aug 25, 1954.

Billy Ray Cyrus, 37, country singer ("Achy Breaky Heart"), born Flatwoods, KY, Aug 25, 1961.

Mel Ferrer, 81, actor (*Scaramouche, The Sun Also Rises*), born Elberon, NJ, Aug 25, 1917.

Monty Hall, 75, former TV host ("Let's Make a Deal"), born Winnipeg, Manitoba, Canada, Aug 25, 1923.

Anthony Heald, 54, actor (*The Silence of the Lambs, Searching for Bobby Fischer*), born New Rochelle, NY, Aug 25, 1944.

Regis Philbin, 65, talk show host ("Live with Regis and Kathie Lee"), born New York, NY, Aug 25, 1933.

John Savage, 49, actor (*The Deer Hunter, Hair*), born Long Island, NY, Aug 25, 1949.

Claudia Schiffer, 28, model, restauranteur (partner in the Fashion Cafe, New York), born Rheinberg, Germany, Aug 25, 1970.

Wayne Shorter, 65, jazz musician ("High Life"), born Newark, NJ, Aug 25, 1933.

Tom Skerritt, 65, actor ("Picket Fences," *Steel Magnolias*), born Detroit, MI, Aug 25, 1933.

Blair Underwood, 34, actor ("One Life to Live," "LA Law"), born Tacoma, WA, Aug 25, 1964.

Joanne Whalley, 34, actress ("The Singing Detective"; stage: *What the Butler Saw; Dance with a Stranger*), born Manchester, England, Aug 25, 1964.

AUGUST 26 — WEDNESDAY

Day 238 — 127 Remaining

DeFOREST, LEE: 125th BIRTH ANNIVERSARY. Aug 26, 1873. American inventor of the electron tube, radio knife for surgery and the photoelectric cell and a pioneer in the creation of talking pictures and television. Born at Council Bluffs, IA, De Forest was holder of hundreds of patents but perhaps best remembered by the moniker he gave himself in the title of his autobiography, *Father of Radio*, published in 1950. So unbelievable was the idea of wireless radio broadcasting that De Forest was accused of fraud and arrested for selling stock to underwrite the invention that later was to become an essential part of daily life. De Forest died at Hollywood, CA, on June 30, 1961.

ENGLAND: INTERNATIONAL BEATLES FESTIVAL. Aug 26–Sept 1. Liverpool, Merseyside. Music and entertainment connected with the Beatles. Est attendance: 120,000. For info: Mr Bill Heckle, Cavern City Tours Ltd, The Cavern Club, 10 Mathew St, Liverpool, Merseyside, England L2 6RE. Phone: (44) (151) 236-9091. Fax: (44) (151) 236-8081.

FIRST BASEBALL GAMES TELEVISED: ANNIVERSARY. Aug 26, 1939. WXBS television, in New York City, broadcast the first major league baseball games—a doubleheader between the Cincinnati Reds and the Brooklyn Dodgers at Ebbets Field. Announcer Red Barber interviewed Leo Durocher, manager of the Dodgers, and William McKechnie, manager of the Reds, between games.

ISHERWOOD, CHRISTOPHER: BIRTH ANNIVERSARY. Aug 26. Author of short stories, plays and novels, Christopher William Isherwood was born at High Lane, Cheshire, England, on Aug 26, 1904. The play and motion picture *I Am a Camera* and the musical *Cabaret* were based on a short story, "Sally Bowles," in his collection from the 1930s titled *Goodbye to Berlin*, which contained the line "I am a camera with its shutter open, quite passive, recording, not thinking." Isherwood died at Santa Monica, CA, Jan 4, 1986.

KRAKATOA: ERUPTION ANNIVERSARY. Aug 26, 1883. Anniversary of the biggest explosion in historic times. The eruption of the Indonesian volcanic island, Krakatoa (Krakatau), on Aug 26, 1883, was heard 3,000 miles away, created tidal waves 120 ft high (killing 36,000 persons), hurled five cubic miles of earth fragments into the air (some to a height of 50 miles) and affected the oceans and the atmosphere for years.

MAKE YOUR OWN LUCK DAY. Aug 26. A day to take affirmative actions in your life to direct events and take control of your destiny for a happier, more productive and successful life by making your own luck and creating opportunities. Remember, the welcome mat is always out at the door to opportunity. For info: J. Richard Falls, PO Box 165090, Irving, TX 75016-5090.

NEVADA STATE FAIR. Aug 26–30. Reno Livestock Events Center, Reno, NV. State entertainment and carnival, with home arts, agriculture and commercial exhibits. Est attendance: 73,000. For info: Gary Lubra, CEO, Nevada State Fair, 1350-A N Wells Ave, Reno, NV 89512. Phone: (702) 688-5767. Fax: (702) 688-5763. Email: nvstatefair@inetworld.com.
WWW: http://www.aztech-cs.com/nsfl

SABIN, ALBERT BRUCE: BIRTH ANNIVERSARY. Aug 26, 1906. American medical researcher Albert Bruce Sabin was born at Bialystok, Poland. He is most noted for his oral vaccine of the polio virus, which replaced Jonas Salk's injected vaccine because Sabin's provided lifetime protection. He was awarded the US National Medal of Science in 1971. Sabin died on Mar 3, 1993, at Washington, DC.

SPACE MILESTONE: *SOYUZ 15* (USSR). Aug 26, 1974. Launched on Aug 26, 1974, cosmonauts G. Sarafanov and L. Demin returned to Earth Aug 28, making an emergency night landing.

SPACE MILESTONE: *SOYUZ 31* (USSR): 20th ANNIVERSARY. Aug 26, 1978. Launched on Aug 26, Valery Bykovsky and Sigmund Jaehn docked at *Salyut 6* on Aug 27, stayed for a week, then returned to Earth in *Soyuz 29* vehicle, leaving their *Soyuz 31* docked at space station. Earth landing on Sept 3.

SUSAN B. ANTHONY DAY. Aug 26. Massachusetts.

★**WOMEN'S EQUALITY DAY.** Aug 26. Presidential Proclamation issued in 1973 and 1974 at request and since 1975 without request.

WOMEN'S EQUALITY DAY. Aug 26. Anniversary of certification as part of US Constitution, in 1920, of the 19th Amendment, prohibiting discrimination on the basis of sex with regard to voting. Congresswoman Bella Abzug's bill to designate Aug 26 of each year as "Women's Equality Day" in August 1974 became Public Law 93–382.

BIRTHDAYS TODAY

Benjamin Crowninshield Bradlee, 77, journalist, editor, born Boston, MA, Aug 26, 1921.

Macaulay Culkin, 18, actor (*Home Alone, My Girl*), born New York, NY, Aug 26, 1980.

Geraldine Anne Ferraro, 63, first woman vice-presidential candidate, born Newburgh, NY, Aug 26, 1935.

Ronny Graham, 79, actor, composer ("Chico and the Man"), born Philadelphia, PA, Aug 26, 1919.

Irving R. Levine, 76, broadcast journalist, born Pawtucket, RI, Aug 26, 1922.

Branford Marsalis, 38, musician, born New Orleans, LA, Aug 26, 1960.

Robert G. Torricelli, 47, US Senator (D, New Jersey), born Paterson, NJ, Aug 26, 1951.

AUGUST 27 — THURSDAY

Day 239 — 126 Remaining

ACTON FAIR. Aug 27–30. Acton, ME. A country fair featuring horse and ox pulls, firemen's muster, 4-H projects, flowers, arts and crafts, stage shows and handicraft. Vendors call Douglas Roberts at (207) 324-1250. Est attendance: 20,000. For info: Lista C. Staples, Secy, RR1, Box 3140, Shapleigh, ME 04076. Phone: (207) 636-2026.

BROOKLYN FAIR. Aug 27–30. Brooklyn, CT. The oldest continuously active fair in the US celebrating its 147th anniversary. Annually, the weekend before Labor Day. Est attendance: 110,000. For info: Sandy Eggers, Sec, Brooklyn Fair, PO Box 410, Brooklyn, CT 06234. Phone: (860) 779-0012. Fax: (860) 779-1822.

DAWES, CHARLES GATES: BIRTH ANNIVERSARY. Aug 27. Thirtieth vice president of the US (1925–1929), born at Marietta, OH, Aug 27, 1865. Won the Nobel Peace Prize in 1925 for the "Dawes Plan" for German reparations. Died at Evanston, IL, Apr 23, 1951.

DREISER, THEODORE: BIRTH ANNIVERSARY. Aug 27, 1871. American novelist Theodore Dreiser was born at Terre Haute, IN. As part of the Chicago group he was an exponent of American naturalism in literature. His first novel, *Sister Carrie* (1900), was suppressed by his publisher on moral grounds. Dreiser's finest achievement is widely considered to be his novel *An American Tragedy* (1925). He died on Dec 28, 1945, at Hollywood, CA.

"THE DUCHESS" WHO WASN'T DAY. Aug 27. At least once on Aug 27 (her birthdate in 1850), repeat the following quotation from the novel *Molly Bawn*, which has passed into the English language: "Beauty is in the eye of the beholder." Margaret Wolfe Hungerford often wrote under the pseudonym "The Duchess," which was the title of her most popular novel—hence the name of this event. Her novels were read in Ireland, England, Canada, the US, Australia and continental Europe. A popular romance novelist with about 40 books published, Hungerford was born at Rosscarbery, County Cork, Ireland, on Aug 27, 1850; she died at Bandon, County Cork, in 1897. For info: Peggy Shirley, Chambrel, 3800 Treyburn, Williamsburg, VA 23185. Phone: (757) 220-1839. Fax: (757) 229-9367.

EAST COAST SURFING CHAMPIONSHIPS AND SPORTS FESTIVAL. Aug 27–30. Oceanfront to 12th St, Virginia Beach, VA. 36th annual championship. Pro and amateur surfing and volleyball, 5K run, skimboarding, outrigger canoe racing, team tug-of-war, bands, food. Est attendance: 100,000. For info: Virginia Beach Jaycees, PO Box 62041, Virginia Beach, VA 23466. Phone: (800) 861-7873. WWW: http://www.ECSC1.com

FIRST COMMERCIAL OIL WELL: ANNIVERSARY. Aug 27. On Aug 27, 1859, W.A. "Uncle Billy" Smith discovered oil in a shaft being sunk in western Pennsylvania. Drilling had reached 69 ft, 6 inches when Smith saw a dark film floating on the water below the derrick floor. Soon 20 barrels of crude were being pumped each day.

FIRST PLAY PRESENTED IN NORTH AMERICAN COLONIES. Aug 27. Acomac, VA, was the site of the first play presented in the North American colonies on Aug 27, 1655. The play was *Ye Bare and Ye Cubb*, by Phillip Alexander Bruce. Three local residents were arrested and fined for acting in the play. At the time, most colonies had laws prohibiting public performances; Virginia, however, had no such ordinance.

GETTYSBURG FALL BLUEGRASS FESTIVAL. Aug 27–30. Gettysburg, PA. Festival features some of the country's best stars of bluegrass music. Annually, the fourth weekend of August or the weekend prior to the Labor Day weekend. For info: Gettysburg Conv & Visitors Bureau, 35 Carlisle St, Gettysburg, PA 17325. Phone: (717) 334-6274. Fax: (717) 334-1166. WWW: http://www.gettysburg.com

"GOOD SEX! WITH DR. RUTH WESTHEIMER" TV PREMIERE: ANNIVERSARY. Aug 27, 1984. This program premiered on the Lifetime Cable Channel with sex therapist Ruth Westheimer counseling actors appearing as her patients. The show was renamed several times as "Dr. Ruth," "The All New Dr. Ruth Show," "What's Up, Dr. Ruth?" and "On the Air with Dr. Ruth." The show's format also changed to include celebrity and physician interviews and call-ins.

August 1998

S	M	T	W	T	F	S
						1
2	3	4	5	6	7	8
9	10	11	12	13	14	15
16	17	18	19	20	21	22
23	24	25	26	27	28	29
30	31					

HAMLIN, HANNIBAL: BIRTH ANNIVERSARY. Aug 27. Fifteenth vice president of the US (1861–1865) born at Paris, ME, Aug 27, 1809. Died at Bangor, ME, July 4, 1891.

HOTTER 'N HELL HUNDRED WEEKEND. Aug 27–30. Wichita Falls, TX. To encourage bicycling and to benefit the city of Wichita Falls and its parks and green spaces. Spaghetti dinner and consumer show on Friday in conjunction with packet pickup. Also festival and consumer show all day Saturday. The largest sanctioned century ride in the US—more than 10,000 riders. Est attendance: 25,000. For info: Wichita Falls Bicycling Club, Inc, PO Box 2096, Wichita Falls, TX 76307. Phone: (817) 692-2925. Fax: (817) 322-1118. WWW: http://www.wtr.com/hhh

JOHNSON, LYNDON BAINES: 90th BIRTH ANNIVERSARY. Aug 27, 1908. The 36th president of the US succeeded to the presidency following the assassination of John F. Kennedy. Johnson's term of office: Nov 22, 1963–Jan 20, 1969. In 1964, he said: "The challenge of the next half-century is whether we have the wisdom to use [our] wealth to enrich and elevate our national life—and to advance the quality of American civilization." Johnson was born Aug 27, 1908, near Stonewall, TX, and died at San Antonio, TX, Jan 22, 1973. His birthday is observed as a holiday in Texas.

MINNESOTA STATE FAIR. Aug 27–Sept 7. St. Paul, MN. Major entertainers, agricultural displays, arts, crafts, food, carnival rides, animal judging and performances. Est attendance: 1,600,000. For info: Minnesota State Fair, 1265 Snelling Ave N, St. Paul, MN 55108-3099. Phone: (612) 642-2200. Email: fairinfo@statefair.gen.mn.us.

MONTREUX DETROIT JAZZ FESTIVAL. Aug 27–31. Detroit, MI. Celebration for jazz lovers and festival fans. Features Detroit groups as well as international stars and reflects Detroit's roots in the development of American jazz. 100 sets performed on four stages. Est attendance: 750,000. For info: Montreux Detroit Jazz Festival, Music Hall Ctr, 350 Madison Ave, Detroit, MI 48226. Phone: (313) 963-7622. Fax: (313) 963-2462. WWW: http://www. montreuxdetroitjazz.com

NEW YORK STATE FAIR. Aug 27–Sept 7. Empire Expo Center, Syracuse, NY. Agriculture and livestock competitions, top-name entertainment, the International Horse Show, business and industrial exhibits, the midway and ethnic presentations. Est attendance: 900,000. For info: Joseph LaGuardia, Dir of Mktg, NY State Fair, Empire Expo Ctr, Syracuse, NY 13209. Phone: (315) 487-7711. Fax: (315) 487-9260.

OREGON STATE FAIR. Aug 27–Sept 7. Salem, OR. Exhibits, products and displays illustrate Oregon's role as one of the nation's major agricultural and recreational states. Floral gardens, carnival, big-name entertainment, horse show and food. Annually, 12 days ending on Labor Day. Est attendance: 730,000. For info: Oregon State Fair, 2330 17th St NE, Salem, OR 97310-0140. Phone: (503) 378-3247.

RAYE, MARTHA: BIRTH ANNIVERSARY. Aug 27, 1916. Born at Butte, MT, Martha Raye began singing when she was three. Raye performed for American servicemen during three wars and received the Jean Hersholt Humanitarian Award from the Academy of Motion Picture Arts and Sciences (1969) for that service. She appeared in her first film, *Rhythm on the Range*, in 1936. She had several TV shows, including "The Martha Raye Show" (1955–56). In 1993 Raye was awarded the Presidential Medal of Freedom. Martha Raye died Oct 19, 1994, at Los Angeles, CA.

REPUBLIC OF MOLDOVA: NATIONAL DAY. Aug 27. Public holiday.

TELLURIDE MUSHROOM FESTIVAL. Aug 27–30. Telluride, CO. To educate people about the types of wild mushrooms—edible, poisonous, psychoactive—and their cultivation. Est attendance: 150. For info: Fungophile, Inc, Box 480503, Denver, CO 80248-0503. Phone: (303) 296-9359. Fax: (303) 296-9359. Email: ladomyco@dnvr.uswest.com. WWW: http://www.telluridemm.com

TENNESSEE WALKING HORSE NATIONAL CELEBRATION. Aug 27–Sept 5. Celebration Grounds, Shelbyville, TN. More than 3,800 entries compete for more than $600,000 in prizes and awards—and the World Grand Championship titles. A 10-day festival for the whole family, plus trade show. Est attendance: 250,000. For info: Barbara Simmon, Public Relations Dir, Tennessee Walking Horse Natl Celebration, Calhoun and Evans, PO Box 1010, Shelbyville, TN 37160. Phone: (615) 684-5915. Fax: (615) 684-5949.

BIRTHDAYS TODAY

Sarah Chalke, 22, actress (the second Becky on "Roseanne"), born Ottawa, Ontario, Canada, Aug 27, 1976.

Daryl Dragon, 56, musician (Captain and Tennille), songwriter, born Studio City, CA, Aug 27, 1942.

J. Robert Kerrey, 55, US senator (D, Nebraska), born Lincoln, NE, Aug 27, 1943.

Mother Teresa (Agnes Gonxha Bojaxhiu), 88, nun, missionary, born Skopje, Yugoslavia, Aug 27, 1910.

Paul Rubens (Pee-wee Herman), 46, actor, writer ("Pee-wee's Playhouse," "Murphy Brown"; *Pee-wee's Big Adventure, Big Top Pee-wee*), born Peekskill, NY, Aug 27, 1952.

Tommy Sands, 61, singer ("Teen-Age Crush," "Goin' Steady"), born Chicago, IL, Aug 27, 1937.

Tuesday Weld (Susan Kerr), 55, actress ("The Many Loves of Dobie Gillis," *Looking for Mr Goodbar*), born New York, NY, Aug 27, 1943.

AUGUST 28 — FRIDAY

Day 240 — 125 Remaining

BOYER, CHARLES: BIRTH ANNIVERSARY. Aug 28, 1889. American film star born at Figeac, France. Died at Scottsdale, AZ, Aug 26, 1978.

CLASSIC CAR SHOW AND SWAP MEET. Aug 28–30. Site One, Oglebay, Wheeling, WV. Car enthusiasts can view a wide assortment of antique, sports and specialty cars and motorcycles at this event sponsored by the Good Zoo and the Ohio Valley Street Survivor's Car Club. Est attendance: 5,000. For info: John Hargleroad, Operations Dir, Good Zoo, Oglebay, Rt 88 N, Wheeling, WV 26003. Phone: (304) 243-4028. Fax: (304) 243-4110. WWW: http://wvweb.com/oglebay

COMMERCIAL RADIO BROADCASTING: ANNIVERSARY. Aug 28, 1922. Broadcasters realized radio could earn profits from the sale of advertising time. WEAF in New York ran a commercial "spot" on Aug 28, which was sponsored by the Queensboro Realty Corporation of Jackson Heights in New York City to promote Hawthorne Court, a group of apartment buildings in Queens. The commercial rate was $100 for 10 minutes.

COOS BAY HUMMINGBIRD GOOSE DAY (SOUTHBOUND). Aug 28. Coos Bay, OR. The traditional day to watch for those benevolent geese who allow tiny hummingbirds to snuggle into their goose down to migrate south. Believers in the hummingbird geese gather all over Coos County to "humhonk" them close enough to see the little hummers climb aboard. (Best humhonker trophy awarded.) Est attendance: 1,200. For info: Doug Benton, Head Humhonker, K-Light Radio, 580 Kingwood Ave, Coos Bay, OR 97420. Phone: (800) 447-7664. Fax: (541) 267-0114. Email: lrg@ucinet.com. WWW: http://www.k light.com

DRESDEN'S HARVEST GATHERING. Aug 28–Nov 1. Dresden, OH. There will be many seasonal events, demonstrations and entertainment opportunities taking place throughout Dresden and in The Longaberger® Company properties. There will be shopping fun for all at The Longaberger Specialty Shops™ and great food at all our restaurants. Look for fabulous entertainment and fun for the whole family. Est attendance: 63,000. For info: Salle Schlesselman, The Longaberger® Company, 1360 Main St, Dresden, OH 43821. Phone: (614) 754-5778. Fax: (614) 754-5720.

FEAST OF SAINT AUGUSTINE. Aug 28. Bishop of Hippo, author of *Confessions* and *The City of God*, died Aug 28, AD 430.

GOETHE, JOHANN WOLFGANG von: BIRTH ANNIVERSARY. Aug 28. German author-philosopher born Aug 28, 1749. Died Mar 22, 1832.

HAYES, LUCY WARE WEBB: BIRTH ANNIVERSARY. Aug 28, 1831. Wife of Rutherford Birchard Hayes, 19th president of the US, born at Chillicothe, OH, Aug 28, 1831. Died June 25, 1889. She was nicknamed "Lemonade Lucy" because she and the president, both abstainers, served no alcoholic beverages at White House receptions.

KETCHUM WAGON DAYS CELEBRATION. Aug 28–30. Ketchum, ID. Mining history celebration featuring the largest non-motorized parade in the West. Flapjack breakfast, band concerts, dancers and a car auction. Est attendance: 15,000. For info: Sun Valley/Ketchum Chamber, Box 2420, Sun Valley, ID 83353. Phone: (800) 634-3347. Fax: (208) 726-4533.
Email: sunval@micron.net.
WWW: http://www.visitsunvalley.com

MARCH ON WASHINGTON: 35th ANNIVERSARY. Aug 28, 1963. More than 250,000 people attended this Civil Rights rally in Washington, DC, at which Rev. Dr. Martin Luther King, Jr, made his famous "I have a dream" speech.

NEBRASKA STATE FAIR. Aug 28–Sept 7. Lincoln, NE. Book fair, food booths, variety of entertainment, rodeos, amusement rides and tractor pulls. For info: Nebraska State Fair, PO Box 81223, Lincoln, NE 68501. Phone: (402) 473-4110. Fax: (402) 473-4114. Email: nestatefair@statefair.org.

PETERSON, ROGER TORY: BIRTH ANNIVERSARY. Aug 28, 1908. Naturalist, author of *A Field Guide to Birds*, born at Jamestown, NY. Peterson died at Old Lyme, CT, July 28, 1996.

PORT ROYAL HURRICANE: ANNIVERSARY. Aug 28, 1722. The hapless Jamaican town of Port Royal was devastated twice within a 30-year span by two natural disasters—an earthquake in 1692 and a hurricane in 1722. The hurricane killed 400 townspeople and sunk 26 merchant ships.

POTATO FEAST DAYS. Aug 28–30. Houlton, ME. Potato Feast supper, Parade of Dolls, potato games for kids, entertainment, townwide sales, fun run, classic car show, arts and crafts fair, potato barrel rolling contest and much more. Annually, the last full weekend in August. For info: Greater Houlton Chamber of Commerce, 109 Main St, Houlton, ME 04730. Phone: (207) 532-4216. Email: chamber@houlton.com.
WWW: http://www.mainerec.com/houlton.html

SETON, ELIZABETH ANN BAYLEY: BIRTH ANNIVERSARY. Aug 28. First American-born saint was born on this day in 1774. See also: "Seton, Elizabeth Ann Bayley: Feast Day" (Jan 4).

SPIRIT OF WOVOKA DAYS POWWOW. Aug 28–30. Yerington, NV. Powwow held in honor of Wovoka, sponsored by the Mason Valley Wind Spirit dancers. For local info: (702) 463-7123 or (702) 463-2350 or call Mason Valley Chamber of Commerce. Phone: (702) 463-2245. Fax: (702) 463-3369.

TOTAH FESTIVAL. Aug 28–30. Farmington, NM. Native American juried fine arts and crafts show and marketplace—highlighted by an Indian rug auction. Est attendance: 10,000. For info: Farmington Conv and Visitors Bureau, 203 W Main, Ste 401, Farmington, NM 87401. Phone: (800) 448-1240 or (505) 326-7602. Fax: (505) 327-0577. Email: fmncub@cyberport.com. WWW: http://farmingtonnm.org

BIRTHDAYS TODAY

William S. Cohen, 58, US Secretary of Defense (Clinton administration), born Bangor, ME, Aug 28, 1940.

Ben Gazzara, 68, actor (*Anatomy of a Murder*, "Run for Your Life"), born New York, NY, Aug 28, 1930.

Ronald Ames (Ron) Guidry, 48, former baseball player, born Lafayette, LA, Aug 28, 1950.

Scott Hamilton, 40, Olympic gold medal figure skater, born Toledo, OH, Aug 28, 1958.

Donald O'Connor, 73, actor, dancer ("Donald O'Connor Texaco Show," *Singin' in the Rain*), born Houston, TX, Aug 28, 1925.

Jason Priestley, 29, actor ("Beverly Hills 90210," *Tombstone*), born Vancouver, British Columbia, Canada, Aug 28, 1969.

Rick Rossovich, 41, actor (*The Terminator, Roxanne*), born Palo Alto, CA, Aug 28, 1957.

Emma Samms (Emma Samuelson), 38, actress ("General Hospital"; Fallon Carrington Colby on "Dynasty"), born London, England, Aug 28, 1960.

David Soul, 52, actor (Hutch on "Starsky and Hutch"; *Salem's Lot*), born Chicago, IL, Aug 28, 1946.

AUGUST 29 — SATURDAY

Day 241 — 124 Remaining

"ACCORDING TO HOYLE" DAY (EDMOND HOYLE DEATH ANNIVERSARY). Aug 29, 1769. A day to remember Edmond Hoyle and a day for fun and games *according to the rules*. For many years Hoyle lived in London, England, and gave instructions in the playing of games. His name became synonymous with the idea of correct play according to the rules, and the phrase "according to Hoyle" became a part of the English language. Hoyle died at London.

BEHEADING OF SAINT JOHN THE BAPTIST. Aug 29. Commemorates the martyrdom of Saint John the Baptist, beheaded upon order from King Herod, about AD 29.

BERGMAN, INGRID: BIRTH ANNIVERSARY. Aug 29. One of cinema's greatest actresses. Bergman was born at Stockholm, Sweden, Aug 29, 1915, and died at London, England, on her 67th birthday, Aug 29, 1982. Three times a winner of Academy Awards. Controversy over her personal life made her and her films unpopular to American audiences during an interval of several years between periods of awards and adulation.

CALVERT COUNTY JOUSTING TOURNAMENT. Aug 29. Christ Church grounds, Port Republic, MD. The 132nd annual tournament of Maryland's official state sport, steeped in colorful pageantry. Country supper, bazaar, organ recitals, children's activities, one-room schoolhouse, colonial church. Admission fee. Est attendance: 1,500. For info: Christ Church, 3100 Broomes Island Rd, Port Republic, MD 20676. Phone: (410) 586-0565.

CANADA: MAYNOOTH MADNESS. Aug 29. Maynooth, Ontario. An exciting, fun-filled day for the whole family, with loggers' games and parade, children's activities, petting zoo, pony rides and a craft show featuring original arts and crafts. Annually, the last Saturday in August. Est attendance: 7,000. For info: Bancroft and District Chamber of Commerce, PO Box 539, Bancroft, Ont, Canada K0L 1C0. Phone: (613) 332-1513. Fax: (613) 332-2119. Email: chamber@commerce.bancroft.on.ca. WWW: http://www.commerce.bancroft.on.ca

August 1998

S	M	T	W	T	F	S
						1
2	3	4	5	6	7	8
9	10	11	12	13	14	15
16	17	18	19	20	21	22
23	24	25	26	27	28	29
30	31					

CANADA: WELLING FAMILY FUN DAY. Aug 29. Welling, Alberta. The town of Welling is noted in rodeo history as the home of the first side-delivery rodeo chute and arena, constructed in 1916. (Side-delivery chutes are now standard at all rodeos worldwide.) Family Day—a day of fun and activities—is celebrated with an annual cowboy boot-throwing contest. For info: Craig Watson, Pres, Welling Recreation Society, Box 57, Welling, Alta, Canada T0K 2N0. Phone: (403) 752-4539. Email: rwilde@upanet.uleth.ca.

CARROLL, ANNA ELLA: BIRTH ANNIVERSARY. Aug 29. American writer and publicist for the Union cause during the Civil War, she was born in Somerset County, MD, on Aug 29, 1815. Her actions in the Civil War were the subject of several books. She died at Washington, DC, Feb 18, 1894.

CHAMPLAIN VALLEY FAIR. Aug 29–Sept 7. Essex Junction, VT. Vermont's largest fair. Agricultural exhibits and competitions, variety of entertainment, arts and crafts, midway rides, commercial exhibits, great food and much more. Est attendance: 300,000. For info: George Rousseau, Dir of Sales and Mktg, PO Box 209, Essex Junction, VT 05453. Phone: (802) 878-5545. Fax: (802) 879-5404.

CHILDREN'S DAY. Aug 29. Woodstock, VT. Traditional farm activities from corn shelling to sawing firewood—19th-century games, traditional spelling bee, ice cream and butter making, wagon rides. For info: Deborah Bulissa, Exec Asst, Billings Farm Museum, PO Box 489, Woodstock, VT 05091. Phone: (802) 457-2355. Fax: (802) 457-4663. Email: billings.farm@valley.net.

CHILE CHALLENGE OFF-ROAD BIKE RACE. Aug 29–30. Angel Fire, NM. Annual bike race held on the ski mountain in this beautiful alpine setting. All skill levels. Est attendance: 400. For info: Angel Fire Resort, PO Drawer B, Angel Fire, NM 87710. Phone: (800) 633-7463 or (505) 377-4237. Fax: (505) 377-4395. Email: gmorton@angelfireresort.com. WWW: http://www.angelfireresort.com

DENMARK: HO SHEEP MARKET. Aug 29. The village of Ho, near Esbjerg, holds its annual sheep market on the last Saturday in August, when some 50,000 people visit the fair.

EASTERN IDAHO STATE FAIR. Aug 29–Sept 5. Blackfoot, ID. Family fun, amusement rides, food booths, entertainment, tractor pulls and more. Est attendance: 202,000. For info: Eastern Idaho State Fair, PO Box 250, Blackfoot, ID 83221. Phone: (208) 785-2480. Fax: (208) 785-2483.

HOLMES, OLIVER WENDELL: BIRTH ANNIVERSARY. Aug 29. Physician and author, born at Cambridge, MA, Aug 29, 1809. Died at Boston, MA, Oct 7, 1894. "A moment's insight," he wrote, "is sometimes worth a life's experience."

LARBAUD, VALERY NICOLAS: BIRTH ANNIVERSARY. Aug 29. Novelist, essayist and translator of English literature. Born at Vichy, France, Aug 29, 1881; died there Feb 2, 1957.

LOCKE, JOHN: BIRTH ANNIVERSARY. Aug 29, 1632. English philosopher, founder of philosophical liberalism, born at Wrington, England. His ideas influenced the American colonists and were enshrined in the Constitution. Locke died at Essex, England, Oct 28, 1704.

MARYLAND RENAISSANCE FESTIVAL. Aug 29–Oct 25 (Saturdays, Sundays and Labor Day). Annapolis, MD. A 16th-century English festival with Henry VIII, sword swallowers, magicians, authentic jousting, juggling, music, theater, games, food and crafts. Est attendance: 245,000. For info: Jules Smith, Maryland Renaissance Festival, PO Box 315, Crownsville, MD 21032. Phone: (410(266-7304 TDD or (410) 573-1509. Fax: (410) 573-1508. Email: rennfest@erols.com. WWW: http://www.rennfest.com

MORE HERBS, LESS SALT DAY. Aug 29. It's healthier, zestier and lustier! [© 1997 by WPL] For info: Tom or Ruth Roy, Wellness Permission League, PO Box 662, Mt Gretna, PA 17064-0662. Phone: (500) 437-5104 or (717) 964-1308. Fax: (717) 964-1335.

OMAHA CACTUS AND SUCCULENT SOCIETY SHOW AND SALE. Aug 29–30. Southroads Mall, Bellevue, NE. Hundreds of plants on display Saturday and Sunday, with a huge selection of unusual succulents for sale both days. Club members' plant entries are evaluated by accredited judges. Est attendance: 2,000. For info: Kathy Bokelman, 320 N Washington, Papillion, NE 68046. Phone: (402) 592-9913. Fax: (402) 592-6901. Email: kbokelma@monarch.papillion.ne.

PARKER, CHARLIE: BIRTH ANNIVERSARY. Aug 29, 1920. Jazz saxophonist Charlie Parker was born at Kansas City, KS. He earned the nickname "Yardbird" (later "Bird") from his habit of sitting in the backyard of speakeasies, fingering his saxophone. His career as a jazz saxophonist took him from jam sessions in Kansas City to New York, where he met Dizzy Gillespie, Chubby Jackson and others who were creating a style of music that would become known as bop or bebop. Although his musical genius was unquestioned, Parker's addiction to heroin (begun at age 15) constantly haunted his life. He died at Rochester, NY, Mar 12, 1955, at the age of 34.

***ROYAL GEORGE* SINKS AT SEA: ANNIVERSARY.** Aug 29, 1792. Prized British battleship *Royal George* sank due to fatal human error in one of the worst maritime disasters in history. While the ship was being repaired at Spithead, the port side was tilted too close to the waterline. A gust of wind lowered the ship even further, allowing tons of water to flood into its open gunports. The ship sank within minutes before many of the 1,300 on board realized what was happening and more than 900 people drowned.

SEPTEMBER SKIRMISH. Aug 29–30. Point Mallard, Decatur, AL. Staged in honor of local Confederate generals John Hunt Morgan and Joe Wheeler. More than 200 authentically clad Yankee and Rebel soldiers meet in daily battles. Visitors may join a young recruit and follow his life as a soldier during the Candlelight Camp Tour on Saturday night or join the Civil War roundtable discussion. For info: Jacklyn Bailey, Decatur Conv/Visitors Bureau, 719 6th Ave SE, PO Box 2349, Decatur, AL 35602. Phone: (205) 350-2028 or (800) 524-6181. Email: dcvb@hiwaay.net.

SHAYS REBELLION: ANNIVERSARY. Aug 29, 1786. Daniel Shays, veteran of Lexington, Bunker Hill, Ticonderoga, Saratoga and Stony Point, after whom rebellion was named, was one of the leaders of more than 1,000 rebelling discontents who sought redress of grievances during depression days of 1786–87. On Aug 29, 1786, they prevented the general court sessions and on Sept 26 they prevented the Supreme Court sessions at Springfield, MA. On Jan 25, 1787, they attacked the federal arsenal at Springfield; on Feb 2, Shays's troops were routed and fled. Shays was sentenced to death but pardoned June 13, 1788. Later received small pension for services in American Revolution.

SOVIET COMMUNIST PARTY SUSPENDED: ANNIVERSARY. Aug 29, 1991. The day on which the Supreme Soviet, the parliament of the USSR, suspended all activities of the Communist Party, seizing its property and bringing to an end the institution that ruled the Soviet Union for nearly 75 years. The action followed an unsuccessful coup Aug 19–21 that sought to overthrow the government of Soviet President Mikhail Gorbachev but instead prompted a sweeping wave of democratic change. Gorbachev quit as party leader on Aug 24.

TOOLS AND SKILLS THAT BUILT THE COLONY. Aug 29. Wormsloe Historic Site, Savannah, GA. The focus is the Colonial war with Spain in living history demonstrations related to Colonial Georgia history, militia, woodworking and farm life. Museum, film and trails. 11–4. Est attendance: 500. For info: Wormsloe State Historic Site, 7601 Skidaway Rd, Savannah, GA 31406. Phone: (912) 353-3023.

WEST VIRGINIA ITALIAN HERITAGE FESTIVAL PASTA COOKOFF. Aug 29. Clarksburg, WV. Participants cook a pasta dish to compete for prizes. For info: Rosalyn B. Queen, Exec Dir, WV Italian Heritage Fest, 227 Washington Ave, Schroath Bldg, Ste 2H, PO Box 1632, Clarksburg, WV 26302-1632. Phone: (304) 622-7314. Fax: (304) 622-7314. Email: wvihf@wvonline.com. WWW: http://www.wvonline.com/wvihf

WESTFEST. Aug 29–30. West, TX. West celebrates its Czech heritage with folk dances, Czech pastries, sausage, polka music, arts and crafts, children's area, 5K run, parade. Est attendance: 40,000. For info: Westfest, Box 65, West, TX 76691. Phone: (817) 826-5058. WWW: http://www.westfest.com

BIRTHDAYS TODAY

Sir Richard Attenborough, 75, filmmaker (*In Which We Serve, The Great Escape*), born Cambridge, England, Aug 29, 1923.

Carl Banks, 36, football player, born Flint, MI, Aug 29, 1962.

Rebecca De Mornay, 36, actress (*Risky Business, The Hand That Rocks the Cradle*), born Santa Rosa, CA, Aug 29, 1962.

Jim Florio, 61, former Governor of New Jersey (D), born Brooklyn, NY, Aug 29, 1937.

William Friedkin, 59, filmmaker (Oscar for *The French Connection, The Exorcist*), born Chicago, IL, Aug 29, 1939.

Elliott Gould (Elliott Goldstein), 60, actor (*M*A*S*H, The Long Good-Bye*), born Brooklyn, NY, Aug 29, 1938.

Michael Jackson, 40, singer, songwriter ("We Are the World," *Bad, Thriller, Beat It*), born Gary, IN, Aug 29, 1958.

Robin Leach, 57, TV host ("Lifestyles of the Rich and Famous"), born London, England, Aug 29, 1941.

John Sidney McCain III, 62, US senator (R, Arizona), born Panama Canal Zone, Aug 29, 1936.

Mark Morris, 42, choreographer, dancer, born Seattle, WA, Aug 29, 1956.

William Edward (Will) Perdue III, 33, basketball player, born Melbourne, FL, Aug 29, 1965.

Robert Rubin, 60, US Secretary of the Treasury in Clinton administration, born New York, NY, Aug 29, 1938.

AUGUST 30 — SUNDAY

Day 242 — 123 Remaining

ANNAPOLIS RUN. Aug 30. Navy-Marine Corps Memorial Stadium, Annapolis, MD. Maryland's premier 10-mile foot race, through historic Annapolis and along Naval Academy seawalls; designer premium for all finishers; entries limited to 4,000. Annually, the last Sunday of August since 1976. (Non-Labor Day weekend.) Est attendance: 4,000. For info: Annapolis Striders, Inc, PO Box 187, Annapolis, MD 21404-0187. Phone: (410) 268-1165.

ARTHUR, ELLEN LEWIS HERNDON: BIRTH ANNIVERSARY. Aug 30. Wife of Chester Alan Arthur, 21st president of the US, born at Fredericksburg, VA, Aug 30, 1837. Died Jan 12, 1880.

BARNEGAT BAY CRAB RACE AND SEAFOOD FESTIVAL. Aug 30. Seaside Heights, NJ. Crab race, seafood festival and craft fair. Est attendance: 5,000. For info: Lucy Greene, Pres, Barbara Morgan, Admin Asst, Toms River–Ocean Co Chmbr of Com, 1200 Hooper Ave, Toms River, NJ 08753. Phone: (908) 349-0220. Fax: (908) 349-1252. WWW: http://www.oc-chamber.com

DELICATO CHARITY GRAPE STOMP. Aug 30. Delicato Vineyards, Manteca, CA. Wine, food and entertainment. Est attendance: 7,000. For info: Dorothy Indelicato, Delicato Vineyards, 12001 S Hwy 99, Manteca, CA 95336-9209. Phone: (209) 825-6213. Fax: (209) 825-6207. Email: wine@delicato.com. WWW: http://www.delicato.com

FAMILY DAY IN TENNESSEE. Aug 30. Observed annually on the last Sunday in August.

FIRST WHITE HOUSE PRESIDENTIAL BABY: BIRTH ANNIVERSARY. Aug 30, 1893. Frances Folsom Cleveland (Mrs Grover Cleveland) was the first presidential wife to have a baby at the White House when she gave birth to a baby girl (Esther) on Aug 30, 1893. The first child ever born in the White House was a granddaughter to Thomas Jefferson in 1806.

HUEY P. LONG DAY. Aug 30. Louisiana.

MacMURRAY, FRED: 90th BIRTH ANNIVERSARY. Aug 30, 1908. Fred MacMurray was born at Kankakee, IL. His film and television career included a wide variety of roles, ranging from comedy (*The Absent-Minded Professor, Son of Flubber, The Shaggy Dog, The Happiest Millionaire*) to serious drama (*The Caine Mutiny, The Miracle of the Bells, Fair Wind to Java, Double Indemnity*). During 1960–72 he portrayed Steven Douglas, the father on "My Three Sons," which was second only to "Ozzie and Harriet" as network TV's longest running family sitcom. He died on Nov 5, 1991.

MOON PHASE: FIRST QUARTER. Aug 30. Moon enters First Quarter phase at 1:06 AM, EDT.

NATIONAL VETERINARY WEEK. Aug 30–Sept 5. Celebrating the veterinary profession's role in the long and healthy life of companion animals and in the unparalleled safety of our food supply. Observed in conjunction with the Central Veterinary Conference in Kansas City, MO. For info: Leslie Craven, Project Mgr, Veterinary Medicine Publishing Group, 15333 W 95th St, Lenexa, KS 66219. Phone: (913) 492-4300. Fax: (913) 492-4157. Email: leslie_craven@medec.com.

PERU: SAINT ROSE OF LIMA'S DAY. Aug 30. Saint Rose of Lima was the first saint of the western hemisphere. She lived at the time of the colonization by Spain in the 16th century. Patron saint of the Americas and the Philippines. Public holiday in Peru.

PONY EXPRESS FESTIVAL. Aug 30. Hollenberg Pony Express Station, State Historic Site, Hanover, KS. Reenactment of Pony Express ride with mochila exchange, pioneer living-history demonstrations, 1860s historic dress group, circuit-rider church service, noon meal on the grounds and a reenactment of the arrival of an Oregon Trail wagon train. Annually, the last Sunday in August. Sponsor: Kansas State Historical Society, Friends of Hollenberg Station. Est attendance: 5,000. For info: Duane Durst, Curator, Hollenberg Pony Express Station, State Historic Site, RR1, 2889, 23rd Rd, Hanover, KS 66945. Phone: (913) 337-2635.

RUTHERFORD, ERNEST: BIRTH ANNIVERSARY. Aug 30, 1871. Physicist, born at Nelson, New Zealand. He established the nuclear nature of the atom, the electrical structure of matter and achieved the transmutation of elements, research which later resulted in the atomic bomb. Rutherford died at Cambridge, England, Oct 19, 1937.

SHELLEY, MARY WOLLSTONECRAFT: BIRTH ANNIVERSARY. Aug 30, 1797. English novelist Mary Shelley, daughter of the philosopher William Godwin and the feminist Mary Wollstonecraft and wife of the poet Percy Bysshe Shelley, was born at London and died there Feb 1, 1851. In addition to being the author of the famous novel *Frankenstein*, Shelley is important in literary history for her work in the editing and publishing of her husband Percy's unpublished work after his tragic early death.

SPACE MILESTONE: *DISCOVERY* (US). Aug 30, 1984. Space shuttle *Discovery* was launched from Kennedy Space Center, FL, on this date for its maiden flight with six-member crew. During the flight the crew deployed three satellites and used a robot arm before landing at Edwards Air Force Base, CA, on Sept 5.

SPACE MILESTONE: *STS-8* (US): 15th ANNIVERSARY. Aug 30, 1983. Shuttle *Challenger* with five astronauts (Richard Truly, Daniel Brandenstein, Guion Bluford, Jr, Dale Garner and William Thornton) was launched from Kennedy Space Center, FL, on this date. Return landing six days later on Sept 5 at Edwards Air Force Base, CA.

STRAITH, CLAIRE, MD: BIRTH ANNIVERSARY. Aug 30, 1891. Innovator in plastic and cosmetic surgery, born at Southfield, MI. After attending an international meeting in Paris, France, at the end of World War I to discuss and share information regarding reconstructive surgical techniques used on the battlefield, Dr. Claire Straith returned to the US and dedicated his career to the new field of plastic surgery. He developed many of the techniques used in plastic and cosmetic surgery, designed new surgical instruments and led a campaign that convinced automakers, in 1930, to use safety glass and remove dangerous projections from the interior of cars. He founded the Straith Memorial Hospital in Detroit, MI, which is now the Straith Clinic and Hospital in Southfield, MI. Dr. Straith died on July 13, 1958.

TURKEY: VICTORY DAY. Aug 30. Commemorates victory in War of Independence in 1922. Military parades, performing of the Mehtar band (the world's oldest military band), fireworks.

WILKINS, ROY: BIRTH ANNIVERSARY. Aug 30. Roy Wilkins, grandson of a Mississippi slave, civil rights leader, active in the National Association for the Advancement of Colored People (NAACP), retired as its executive director in 1977. Born at St. Louis, MO, Aug 30, 1901. Died at New York, NY, Sept 8, 1981.

August 1998

S	M	T	W	T	F	S
						1
2	3	4	5	6	7	8
9	10	11	12	13	14	15
16	17	18	19	20	21	22
23	24	25	26	27	28	29
30	31					

BIRTHDAYS TODAY

Elizabeth Ashley (Elizabeth Ann Cole), 57, actress (*Agnes of God, Cat on a Hot Tin Roof*, "Evening Shade"), born Ocala, FL, Aug 30, 1941.

Timothy Bottoms, 47, actor (*The Last Picture Show, The Paper Chase*), born Santa Barbara, CA, Aug 30, 1951.

Jean-Claude Killy, 55, Olympic gold medal alpine skier, born Saint Cloud, France, Aug 30, 1943.

Peggy Lipton, 51, actress ("The Mod Squad" [Golden Globe Award, 1971], "Twin Peaks"), born New York, NY, Aug 30, 1947.

Robert Lee Parish, 45, basketball player, born Shreveport, LA, Aug 30, 1953.

David Paymer, 44, actor (*City Slickers, Mr Saturday Night*), born Long Island, NY, Aug 30, 1954.

Theodore Samuel (Ted) Williams, 80, Baseball Hall of Fame outfielder, born San Diego, CA, Aug 30, 1918.

AUGUST 31 — MONDAY

Day 243 — 122 Remaining

CHARLESTON EARTHQUAKE: ANNIVERSARY. Aug 31, 1886. Charleston, SC. The first major earthquake in the recorded history of the eastern US occurred on this date. It is believed that about 100 persons perished in the quake, centered near Charleston but felt up to 800 miles away. The first shock was at 9:51 PM, EST. Though a number of smaller eastern US quakes had been described and recorded since 1638, this was the most terrible and affected persons living in an area of some two million square miles.

"CRANKSHAFT": ANNIVERSARY. Aug 31. Celebrating the anniversary of the nationally syndicated comic strip. For info: Tom Batiuk, 2750 Substation Rd, Medina, OH 44256. Phone: (330) 722-8755.

HONG KONG: LIBERATION DAY. Aug 31. Public holiday. Annually, the last Monday in August.

IRA DECLARES TRUCE: ANNIVERSARY. Aug 31, 1994. The Irish Republican Army (IRA) announced a cease-fire in its 25-year-old war against British control of Northern Ireland. The conflict, which had taken 3,167 lives, started with Roman Catholic protests against discrimination by the Protestant majority in the country. British authorities sent in heavily armed troops to patrol the country, especially its capital, Belfast. The Catholic goal was reunification with the predominately Catholic Republic of Ireland, while the Protestant majority in Northern Ireland steadfastly opposed such a reunion. The IRA gave no timetable for the duration of the cease-fire, nor were any weapons turned in. Two earlier cease-fires, in 1972 and 1975, both failed to last.

KLONDIKE ELDORADO GOLD DISCOVERY: ANNIVERSARY. Aug 31, 1896. Two weeks after the Rabbit/Bonanza Creek claim was filed, gold was discovered on Eldorado Creek, a tributary of Bonanza. More than $30 million worth of gold (worth some $600–$700 million in today's dollars) was mined from the Eldorado Claim in 1896.

KYRGYZSTAN: INDEPENDENCE DAY. Aug 31. National holiday.

MALAYSIA: NATIONAL DAY. Aug 31. National holiday.

MONTESSORI, MARIA: BIRTH ANNIVERSARY. Aug 31, 1870. Italian physician and educator, born at Chiaraville, Italy. Founder of the Montessori method of teaching children. Montessori died at Noordwijk, Holland, May 6, 1952.

NATIONAL OLD-TIME COUNTRY MUSIC CONTEST, FESTIVAL & EXPO. Aug 31–Sept 8. Pottowattamie County Fairgrounds, Avoca, IA. Country music fans come from all around to hear their favorites. Also arts and crafts displays, other musical entertainment and food booths. Est attendance: 50,000. For info: Natl Old-Time Country Music Contest, Fest & Expo, PO Box 438, Walnut, IA 51577. Phone: (712) 784-3001.

POLAND: SOLIDARITY FOUNDED ANNIVERSARY. Aug 31. The Polish trade union Solidarity was formed at the Baltic Sea port of Gdansk, Poland, on Aug 31, 1980. The union was outlawed by the government, and many of its leaders were arrested. Led by Lech Walesa, Solidarity persisted in its opposition to the Communist-controlled government, and on Aug 19, 1989, Polish president Wojcieck Jaruzelski astonished the world by nominating for the post of prime minister Tadeusz Mazowiecki, "a longtime Catholic activist," a deputy in the Polish Assembly, 1961–72, and editor-in-chief of *Tygodnik Solidarnosc*, Solidarity's weekly newspaper, bringing to an end 42 years of Communist Party domination.

SAROYAN, WILLIAM: 90th BIRTH ANNIVERSARY. Aug 31, 1908. American writer of Armenian descent, author of *The Human Comedy* and of Pulitzer Prize–winning play *The Time of Your Life*, was born at Fresno, CA, and died there on May 18, 1981. In April 1981, he gave reporters a final statement for publication after his death: "Everybody has got to die, but I have always believed an exception would be made in my case. Now what?"

SHAWN, WILLIAM: BIRTH ANNIVERSARY. Aug 31. William Shawn, editor of *The New Yorker* for 35 years, was born at Chicago, IL, Aug 31, 1907. A quiet, considerate and courteous man, Shawn was virtual dictator of editorial policy for the magazine, which in turn had an impact on the literary and reportorial styles of writers throughout the country. Nonfiction pieces in *The New Yorker* contributed to public opinion on important issues during Shawn's tenure. William Shawn died Dec 8, 1992, at New York, NY.

TRINIDAD AND TOBAGO: INDEPENDENCE DAY. Aug 31. National holiday. Became Commonwealth nation Aug 31, 1962.

UNITED KINGDOM: SUMMER BANK HOLIDAY. Aug 31. Bank and public holiday in England, Wales and Northern Ireland. (Scotland not included.)

BIRTHDAYS TODAY

James Coburn, 70, actor (*Our Man Flint, The President's Analyst*), born Laurel, NE, Aug 31, 1928.

Richard Gere, 49, actor (*An Officer and a Gentleman, Pretty Woman*), born Philadelphia, PA, Aug 31, 1949.

Debbie Gibson, 28, singer ("Only in My Dreams," "Foolish Beat"), born Brooklyn, NY, Aug 31, 1970.

Buddy Hackett (Leonard Hacker), 74, comedian, actor (*The Love Bug, The Music Man*; many cartoon voices), born New York, NY, Aug 31, 1924.

Van Morrison, 53, singer, songwriter ("Brown Eyed Girl," "Domino"), born Belfast, Northern Ireland, Aug 31, 1945.

Edwin Corley Moses, 43, Olympic gold medal track athlete, born Dayton, OH, Aug 31, 1955.

Hideo Nomo, 30, baseball player, born Osaka, Japan, Aug 31, 1968.

Itzhak Perlman, 53, violinist, born Tel Aviv, Israel, Aug 31, 1945.

Frank Robinson, 63, former baseball executive and manager, Baseball Hall of Fame outfielder, born Beaumont, TX, Aug 31, 1935.

Daniel Schorr, 82, journalist, born New York, NY, Aug 31, 1916.

G.D. Spradlin, 78, actor (*The Godfather Part II, North Dallas Forty, The War of the Roses*), born Garvin County, OK, Aug 31, 1920.

Jack Thompson, 58, actor (*The Chant of Jimmie Blacksmith, Breaker Morant*), born Sydney, Australia, Aug 31, 1940.

Glenn Tilbrook, 41, singer, musician, born London, England, Aug 31, 1957.

September.

SEPTEMBER 1 — TUESDAY

Day 244 — 121 Remaining

AMERICAN HERITAGE MONTH. Sept 1–30. September is an important month in our nation's heritage. The name "United States" replaced "United Colonies" by an act of Congress on Sept 9, 1776. The Revolutionary War ended Sept 3, 1783 with the signing of the Treaty of Peace in Paris. The US Constitution was signed on Sept 17, 1787. The National Society, Sons of the American Revolution has a museum and library that honors the men and women who won our independence in the Revolutionary War. For info: National Society, Sons of the American Revolution, 1000 S Fourth St, Louisville, KY 40203. Phone: (502) 589-1776. Fax: (502) 589-1671.

"ART LINKLETTER'S HOUSE PARTY" TV PREMIERE: ANNIVERSARY. Sept 1, 1952. Television's longest-running daytime variety show was hosted by Art Linkletter. This blend of talk and audience participation started on radio. In 1968, the show was renamed "The Linkletter Show" and moved from the afternoon to a morning slot. The series was well-known for its daily interview with four schoolchildren.

BABY SAFETY MONTH. Sept 1–30. The Juvenile Products Manufacturers Association, Inc (JPMA), a national trade organization of juvenile product manufacturers devoted to helping parents keep baby safe, is disseminating information to parents, grandparents and other child caregivers about baby safety. The information from JPMA pertains to safe selection of juvenile products through the Association's Safety Certification Program and tips on correct use of products such as cribs, car seats, infant carriers and decorative accessories. For a free copy of JPMA's brochure "Safe and Sound for Baby," write to the address below and mark ATTN: JPMA Safety Brochure. Enclose a self-addressed stamped envelope and specify whether you want the brochure in English or Spanish. For info: JPMA, PR Dept, 236 Rte 38-W, Ste 100, Moorestown, NJ 08057.

BE KIND TO EDITORS AND WRITERS MONTH. Sept 1–30. A time for editors and writers to show uncommon courtesy toward each other. For info: Lauren Barnett, Lone Star Publications of Humor, 8452 Fredericksburg Rd, Ste 103, San Antonio, TX 78229. Email: lspubs@aol.com.
WWW: http://members.aol.com/lspubs/lsindex.html

BIG KNOB GRANGE FAIR. Sept 1–5. New Sewickley, PA. 56th annual. For info: (412) 843-7863 or Beaver County Tourist Promotion Agency, 215 B Ninth St, Monaca, PA 15061-2028. Phone: (412) 728-0212. Fax: (412) 728-0456.

September 1998

S	M	T	W	T	F	S
		1	2	3	4	5
6	7	8	9	10	11	12
13	14	15	16	17	18	19
20	21	22	23	24	25	26
27	28	29	30			

BRAZIL: INDEPENDENCE WEEK. Sept 1–7. The independence of Brazil is commemorated with civic and cultural ceremonies promoted by federal, state and municipal authorities. On Sept 7, a grand military parade takes place and the National Defense League organizes the Running Race in Honor of the Symbolic Torch of the Brazilian Nation.

BURROUGHS, EDGAR RICE: BIRTH ANNIVERSARY. Sept 1, 1875. US novelist (*Tarzan of the Apes*), born at Chicago, IL. Correspondent for the *Los Angeles Times*, died at Encino, CA, Mar 19, 1950.

CARTIER, JACQUES: DEATH ANNIVERSARY. Sept 1. French navigator and explorer who sailed from St. Malo, France, Apr 20, 1534, in search of a northwest passage to the Orient. Instead, he discovered the St. Lawrence River, explored Canada's coastal regions and took possession of the country for France. Cartier was born at St. Malo, about 1491 (exact date unknown) and died there Sept 1, 1557.

CHICKEN BOY'S BIRTHDAY. Sept 1. Chicken Boy is a 22-foot-tall statue of a boy with a chicken's head, holding a bucket of chicken. Formerly the signage for the restaurant for which he is named, he was rescued from destruction when the restaurant went out of business by Future Studio of Los Angeles, a graphic design studio. Chicken Boy has since become a pop culture icon. (Some call him the Statue of Liberty of Los Angeles.) For info: Amy Inouye, Owner of Future Studio, PO Box 292000, Los Angeles, CA 90029. Phone: (213) 660-0620. Fax: (213) 660-2571.

CHILD INJURY PREVENTION WEEK. Sept 1–7. Tot Lot Children's Center, New Hyde Park, NY. We will host a local child safety fair on Saturday, Sept 5, 1998 to provide information on injury prevention, safety issues and life saving and to serve as a resource for activity and media information for all interested groups on a national level. Est attendance: 4,000. For info: Safety By Design® Ltd, PO Box 4312, Great Neck, NY 11023. Phone: (516) 488-5395. Fax: (516) 482-1475.

CHILDREN'S EYE HEALTH AND SAFETY MONTH. Sept 1–30. Prevent Blindness America® directs its educational efforts to common causes of eye injuries and common eye problems among children. Materials that can easily be posted or distributed to the community will be provided. For info: Prevent Blindness America®, 500 E Remington Rd, Schaumburg, IL 60173. Phone: (800) 331-2020. Fax: (847) 843-8458. WWW: http://www.prevent-blindness.org

CHILDREN'S GOOD MANNERS MONTH. Sept 1–30. Starts the school year with a national program of teachers and parents encouraging good manners in children. The year-long program includes monthly objectives that work in conjunction with a reinforcing home program. For info: Dr. Fleming Allaire, 35 Eastfield St, Manchester, CT 06040. Phone: (860) 643-0051.

CHILE: NATIONAL MONTH. Sept 1–30. A month of special significance in Chile: arrival of spring, Independence of Chile anniversary (proclaimed Sept 18, 1810), anniversary of the armed forces rising of Sept 11, 1973, to overthrow the government and celebration of the 1980 Constitution and Army Day, Sept 19.

DUGALD RAILWAY WRECK: ANNIVERSARY. Sept 1, 1947. Two Canadian National trains collided head-on at Dugald, Ontario, killing 31 people, including the engineering crew of the train, in one of Canada's worst railway accidents.

EMMA M. NUTT DAY. Sept 1. A day to honor the first woman telephone operator, Emma M. Nutt, who reportedly began her professional career at Boston, MA, Sept 1, 1878, and continued working as a telephone operator for some 33 years.

FLEMINGTON AGRICULTURAL FAIR. Sept 1–7. Flemington, NJ. Est attendance: 200,000. For info: Karlene Pisarcik, Flemington Fair Grounds, PO Box 293, Rt 31, Flemington, NJ 08822. Phone: (908) 782-2413. Fax: (908) 806-8432.

INTERNATIONAL GAY SQUARE DANCE MONTH. Sept 1–30. Emphasis on square-dancing as a healthy, fun, recreational activity. For info: Intl Assn of Gay Square Dance Clubs (IAGSDC),

PO Box 15428, Crystal City, VA 22215-0428. Phone: (800) 835-6462. Email: iagsdc@glyphic.com.
WWW: http://www.glyphic.com/IAGSDC

JAPAN: KANTO EARTHQUAKE MEMORIAL DAY. Sept 1, 1923. A day to remember the 57,000 people who died during Japan's greatest earthquake.

KOREAN AIR LINES FLIGHT 007 DISASTER: 15th ANNIVERSARY. Sept 1, 1983. Korean Air Lines Flight 007, en route from New York, NY, to Seoul, Korea, reportedly strayed more than 100 miles off course, flying over secret Soviet military installations on the Kamchatka Peninsula and Sakhalin Island. Two and one-half hours after it was said to have entered Soviet airspace, at 3:26 AM, Korean time (Aug 31 at 1:26 PM, EST), a Soviet interceptor plane destroyed the Boeing 747 with 269 persons on board (240 passengers and 29 crew members) which then crashed in the Sea of Japan. There were no survivors. President Reagan, in Proclamation 5093, appointed Sunday, Sept 11, 1983, as a National Day of Mourning and recommended "homage to the memory of those who died."

LIBYA: REVOLUTION DAY. Sept 1. Commemorates the revolution of Sept 1, 1969. National holiday.

MARCIANO, ROCKY: BIRTH ANNIVERSARY. Sept 1, 1923. Rocky Marciano, boxer born Rocco Francis Marchegiano at Brockton, MA. Marciano used superb conditioning to fashion an impressive record that propelled him to fight against Jersey Joe Walcott for the heavyweight title on Sept 23, 1952. Marciano knocked Walcott out and in 1956 he retired as the only undefeated heavyweight champion. Died in a plane crash at Newton, IA, Aug 31, 1969. The film *Somebody Up There Likes Me* recounts his life story.

MARRIAGE HEALTH MONTH. Sept 1–30. A month to promote a program designed to help married couples improve the health of their marriage. Having a healthy intimate relationship is an important part of mental well-being. Write for a free quiz on the health status of your marriage. Annually, the month of September. For info: Rose Smith, Co-Founder, Institute of Monogamy, 4900 Mesa Bonita Ct, NW, Albuquerque, NM 87120. Phone: (505) 899-3121.

MISSION SAN LUIS OBISPO DE TOLOSA: FOUNDING ANNIVERSARY. Sept 1, 1772. California mission to the Indians.

NATIONAL CHICKEN MONTH. Sept 1–30. Focuses consumer attention on chicken as the most nutritious, convenient, economical and versatile food available. For info: Bill Roenigk, Sr VP, Natl Broiler Council, 1155 15th St NW, Ste 614, Washington, DC 20005. Phone: (202) 296-2622. Fax: (202) 293-4005. Email: 76263.462@compuserve.com.

NATIONAL CHOLESTEROL EDUCATION MONTH. Sept 1–30. Promoting education about and treatment of high blood cholesterol. Annually, the month of September. For info: Info Center Mgr, Natl Heart, Lung and Blood Institute, Natl Cholesterol Education Program, PO Box 30105, Bethesda, MD 20824-0105. Phone: (301) 251-1222. Fax: (301) 251-1223. Email: nhlbiic@dgsys.com.
WWW: http://www.nhlbi.nih.gov/nhlbi/nhlbi.htm

NATIONAL FOOD EDUCATION SAFETY MONTH. Sept 1–30. An initiative sponsored by the Industry Council on Food Safety, a coalition of food service industry suppliers and associations. The goals are to encourage food safety training among all food service workers, to heighten awareness about the importance of food safety education and to showcase to the public the food service industry's expertise in food service and its commitment to serving safe food. For info: Cindy Wilson, Industry Council on Food Safety, 250 S Wacker Dr, Ste 1400, Chicago, IL 60606-5834. Phone: (312) 715-6770. Fax: (312) 715-0807. Email: cwilson@foodtrain.com.

NATIONAL HONEY MONTH. Sept 1–30. To honor the US's 211,600 beekeepers and 2.5 million colonies of honey bees, which produce more than 198 million pounds of honey each year. For info: Mary Humann, Natl Honey Board, 390 Lashley St, Longmont, CO 80501. Phone: (303) 776-2337.
WWW: http://www.nhb.org

NATIONAL HUMOR IN BUSINESS MONTH. Sept 1–30. Month is dedicated to creating awareness of the constructive and profitable ways that humor in business can contribute to organizational success. Encouraging business to inject humor into all aspects of their goal achievement processes so that their employees and customers laugh their way to productivity and profit. Annually, the month of September. For info: Darren J. La Croix, The Humor Institute, PO Box 557, Auburn, MA 01501. Phone: (617) 289-7632. Fax: (617) 289-7158.
WWW: http://www.humorinst.com

NATIONAL MINDMAPPING MONTH. Sept 1–30. To promote creativity and innovation in business through the use of mindmapping, a visual form of outlining. For info: Joyce Wycoff, Exec Dir, Innovation Network, 34 E Sola, Ste D101, Santa Barbara, CA 93101. Phone: (805) 965-8477. Fax: (805) 963-8220. Email: staff@thinksmart.com. WWW: http://www.thinksmart.com

NATIONAL MUSHROOM MONTH. Sept 1–30. To promote the greater appreciation and use of cultivated mushrooms. For info: Ruth Lowenberg, Lewis & Neale, Inc, 49 E 21st St, New York, NY 10010. Phone: (212) 420-8808. Fax: (212) 254-2452. Email: lanshrooms@aol.com.
WWW: http://www.mushroomcouncil.com

NATIONAL ORGANIC HARVEST MONTH. Sept 1–30. National celebration to educate all ages about organic food and agriculture, sponsored by Organic Trade Association. Local and regional events organized by retailers, manufacturers, distributors and consumer groups include food fairs, tastings, farm tours, cooking demonstrations and meet-the-farmer days. Annually, the month of September. For info: Holly Givens, Organic Trade Assn, PO Box 1078, Greenfield, MA 01302. Phone: (413) 774-7511. Fax: (413) 774-6432. Email: ota@igc.apc.org.

NATIONAL PEDICULOSIS PREVENTION MONTH. Sept 1–30. To promote awareness of how to prevent pediculosis (lice). For info: Natl Pediculosis Assn, PO Box 610189, Newton, MA 02161. Phone: (617) 449-NITS.

NATIONAL PIANO MONTH. Sept 1–30. Recognizes America's most popular instrument and its more than 20 million players; also encourages piano study by people of all ages. For info: Donald W. Dillon, Exec Dir, Natl Piano Fdtn, 4020 McEwen, Ste 105, Dallas, TX 75244-5019. Phone: (972) 233-9107. Fax: (972) 490-4219. Email: dwdillon@aol.com.

NATIONAL RICE MONTH. Sept 1–30. To focus attention on the importance of rice to the American diet and to salute the US rice industry. For info: Dir of Information Services, USA Rice Council, PO Box 740123 Dept NRM, Houston, TX 77274. Phone: (713) 270-6699. Fax: (713) 270-9021.

NATIONAL SCHOOL SUCCESS MONTH. Sept 1–30. Today's young people have many distractions from school and are sometimes overwhelmed when it comes to academics. Parents are often unskilled at effectively redirecting the attention of their children, especially their teenagers. This observance is to recognize parents who want to support and encourage their children to succeed in school and to explore ways to do that. Annually, the month of September. For info send SASE to: Teresa Langston, Dir, Parenting Without Pressure, 1330 Boyer St, Longwood, FL 32750-6311. Phone: (407) 767-2524.

NATIONAL SICKLE CELL MONTH. Sept 1–30. For info: Natl Assn for Sickle Cell Disease, 200 Corporate Pointe, Ste 495, Culver City, CA 90230-7633. Phone: (800) 421-8453 or (310) 216-6363.

NATIONAL VETERINARY MONTH. Sept 1–30. Celebrating the veterinary profession's role in the long and healthy life of companion animals and in the unparalleled safety of our food supply. Observed in conjunction with the Central Veterinary Conference in Kansas City, MO. For info: Leslie Craven, Project Coord, Veterinary Medicine Publishing Group, 15333 W 95th St, Lenexa, KS 66219. Phone: (913) 492-4300. Fax: (913) 492-4157.

PICATINNY PEAK FALL HAWKWATCH. Sept 1–Dec 1. Picatinny Arsenal, Lake Hopatong, NJ. Fall hawkwatch to count migrating raptors. Between 8,000 and 10,000 raptors per year are counted. Member site of Hawk Migration Association of North America (HMANA). Annually, Sept 1 through Dec 1. For info: John J. Reed, 31 Croft Rd, Lake Hopatcong, NJ 07849-1023. Phone: (201) 724-2703. Email: jjreed@army.pica.mil.

PLEASURE YOUR MATE MONTH. Sept 1–30. To promote love and show appreciation to your mate. Look for new ways to create happiness together. Use this event to establish a life-long habit of sharing pleasure. Annually, the month of September. For info: Donald Etkes, MFCC, 112 Harvard Ave, Ste 148, Claremont, CA 91711. Phone: (909) 981-7333.

PTA MEMBERSHIP ENROLLMENT MONTH IN TEXAS. Sept 1–30. Texas PTA is the largest child-advocacy organization in Texas with more than 750,000 members. National PTA is the largest child-advocacy organization in the nation with nearly 6.5 million members. For info: Linda Y. Jackson, Texas PTA, 408 W 11th St, Austin, TX 78701-2199. Phone: (512) 476-6769 or (800) TALK-PTA. Fax: (512) 476-8152. Email: txpta@onr.com. WWW: http://www.onr.com/tpta

REUTHER, WALTER PHILIP: BIRTH ANNIVERSARY. Sept 1, 1907. American labor leader who began work in a steel factory at age 16 and later became president of the United Automobile Workers (UAW) and the Congress of Industrial Organizations (CIO). Born at Wheeling, WV, Reuther spent several years traveling and worked for two years in a Russian automobile factory. Often at the center of controversy, he was the target of an assassin in 1948. Reuther and his wife died in an airplane crash on May 9, 1970, near the UAW Family Education Center at Black Lake, MI. The Family Education Center, a project which he had cherished, was later named for Walter and May Reuther.

SELF-IMPROVEMENT MONTH. Sept 1–30. To disseminate information about the importance of life-long learning and self-improvement. For complete information and lists of books, materials and cassettes, send $3 to cover expense of printing, handling and postage. Annually, the month of September. For info: Dr. Stanley Drake, Pres, Intl Soc of Friendship and Good Will, 412 Cherry Hills Dr, Bakersfield, CA 93309-2866.

SELF-UNIVERSITY WEEK. Sept 1–7. Reminds adults (in or out of school) that each of us has a responsibility to help shape the future by pursuing life-long learning. Committed to self-education as the lifeblood of democracy and the key to living life to its fullest. Dedicated to furthering education not as something you get but as something you take. Annually, the first seven days of September. For info: Autodidactic Press, PO Box 872749, Wasilla, AK 99687. Phone: (907) 376-2932. Fax: (907) 376-2932. Email: autpress@alaska.net.

September 1998

S	M	T	W	T	F	S
		1	2	3	4	5
6	7	8	9	10	11	12
13	14	15	16	17	18	19
20	21	22	23	24	25	26
27	28	29	30			

"SHAZAM!/ISIS" TV PREMIERE: ANNIVERSARY. Sept 1, 1974. "Shazam!" and "Isis" were two half-hour segments of "The Shazam!/Isis Hour" that made up the last two seasons of "Shazam!" and the first two of "Isis." "Shazam!" was based on the Marvel Comics hero, a young man named Billy Batson (Michael Gray) who could transform himself into Captain Marvel (John Davey and Jackson Bostwick) by uttering the title word. Les Tremayne was featured as Batson's traveling companion, Mentor. "Isis" was an adventure series about Andrea Thomas (JoAnna Cameron), a high-school science teacher who learns how to transform herself into the Egyptian goddess Isis. Also featured were Brian Cutler and Joanna Pang. Lous Scheimer and Norm Prescott produced both shows.

SIGOURNEY, LYDIA: BIRTH ANNIVERSARY. Sept 1, 1791. Prolific American author, Lydia Howard Huntley Sigourney was born at Norwich, CT. Her writings, mainly moral and religious works, included such titles as *How to Be Happy, Letters to Young Ladies* and *Pleasant Memories of Pleasant Lands.* She wrote more than 65 books before her death June 10, 1865, at Hartford, CT.

SLOVAKIA: NATIONAL DAY. Sept 1. Anniversary of the adoption of the Constitution of the Slovak Republic.

SOUTH DAKOTA STATE FAIR. Sept 1–7. Huron, SD. Grandstand entertainment nightly, 10 free stages with multiple shows daily, hundreds of commercial exhibits and thousands of livestock exhibits. One of the largest agricultural fairs in the US. Est attendance: 250,000. For info: Jewel Tschetter, Mgr, South Dakota State Fair, PO Box 1275, Huron, SD 57350-1275. Phone: (605) 353-7340. Fax: (605) 353-7348.

SUBLIMINAL MARKETING MONTH. Sept 1–30. Put to use your entrepreneurial thinking to achieve your goals and increase your visibility. Recognize and apply the prosperity-building opportunities for increasing your networking, marketing and publicity goals through the use of color, scents and language. Identify and take action on success strategies to attract more clients, income and media attention. Finish the last quarter of the year successfully by using the powerful resources you already possess. For info send a LSASE to: Lorrie Walters Marsiglio, PO Box 284-CC, Wasco, IL 60183-0284. Phone: (630) 584-9368.

TWITTY, CONWAY: 65th BIRTH ANNIVERSARY. Sept 1, 1933. Country and western music star who began his career as a rock 'n roll performer in the style of Elvis Presley, born at Friars Point, MS. Died June 5, 1993, at Springfield, MO.

UZBEKISTAN: INDEPENDENCE DAY. Sept 1. National holiday.

BIRTHDAYS TODAY

Gloria Estefan, 41, singer (Miami Sound Machine, "Don't Want to Lose You"), born Havana, Cuba, Sept 1, 1957.

Barry Gibb, 52, singer (with the Bee Gees; "Staying Alive"), songwriter, born Manchester, England, Sept 1, 1946.

Ron O'Neal, 61, actor (*Super Fly, Red Dawn*; stage: *No Place To Be Somebody* [Obie Award]), born Utica, NY, Sept 1, 1937.

Seiji Ozawa, 63, conductor, born Hoten, Japan, Sept 1, 1935.

Ann W. Richards, 65, former Governor of Texas (D), born Waco, TX, Sept 1, 1933.

Don Stroud, 61, actor ("Mike Hammer," *The Buddy Holly Story, Licence to Kill*), born Honolulu, HI, Sept 1, 1937.

Lily Tomlin, 59, actress ("Laugh-In," *The Search for Signs of Intelligent Life in the Universe*), born Detroit, MI, Sept 1, 1939.

SEPTEMBER 2 — WEDNESDAY

Day 245 — 120 Remaining

BISON-TEN-YELL DAY. Sept 2. Honoring the "bicentennial" of the imaginary birth of Bison-Ten-Yell, imaginary inventor of a set of ten battle yells as signals, based on the traditional memory aid system eventually adopted by football players. For info: Bob Birch, Grand Punscorpion, Puns Corps, Box 2364, Falls Church, VA 22042-0364. Phone: (703) 533-3668.

CALENDAR ADJUSTMENT DAY: ANNIVERSARY. Sept 2. Pursuant to the British Calendar Act of 1751, Britain (and the American colonies) made the "Gregorian Correction" on Sept 2, 1752. The Act proclaimed that the day following Wednesday, Sept 2, should become Thursday, Sept 14, 1752. There was rioting in the streets by those who felt cheated and who demanded the eleven days back. The Act also provided that New Year's Day (and the change of year number) should fall on Jan 1 (instead of Mar 25) in 1752 and every year thereafter. See also: "Gregorian Calendar Adjustment: Anniversary" (Feb 24, Oct 4).

CANADA: GRAND FORKS INTERNATIONAL BASEBALL TOURNAMENT. Sept 2–7. James Donalson Park, Grand Forks, British Columbia. Twelve-team invitational tournament draws from the four corners of North America, Cuba and from the Pacific Rim. Annually, Labor Day weekend, beginning Wednesday. Est attendance: 35,000. For info: Larry Seminoff, Box 1214, Grand Forks, BC, Canada V0H 1H0. Phone: (250) 442-2110. Fax: (250) 442-3788.

DAYS OF MARATHON: ANNIVERSARY. Sept 2–9, 490 BC. Anniversary of the event during the Persian Wars from which the marathon race is derived. Phidippides, "an Athenian and by profession and practice a trained runner," according to Herodotus, was dispatched from Marathon to Sparta (26 miles), Sept 2 to seek help in repelling the invading Persian army. Help being unavailable by religious law until after the next full moon, Phidippides ran the 26 miles back to Marathon on Sept 4. Without Spartan aid, the Athenians defeated the Persians at the Battle of Marathon on Sept 9. According to legend Phidippides carried the news of the battle to Athens and died as he spoke the words, "Rejoice, we are victorious." The marathon race was revived at the 1896 Olympic Games in Athens. Course distance, since 1924, is 26 miles, 385 yards. See also: "Battle of Marathon: Anniversary" (Sept 9).

ENGLAND: GREAT FIRE OF LONDON: ANNIVERSARY. Sept 2–5, 1666. The fire generally credited with bringing about our system of fire insurance started Sept 2, 1666, in the wooden house of a baker named Farryner, in London's Pudding Lane, near the Tower. During the ensuing three days more than 13,000 houses were destroyed, though it is believed that only six lives were lost in the fire.

FORTEN, JAMES: BIRTH ANNIVERSARY. Sept 2, 1766. James Forten was born of free black parents at Philadelphia, PA. As a powder boy on an American Revolutionary warship, he escaped being sold as a slave when his ship was captured due to the intervention of the son of the British commander. While in England he became involved with abolitionists. On his return to Philadelphia, he became an apprentice to a sailmaker and eventually purchased the company for which he worked. He was active in the abolition movement, and in 1816, his support was sought by the American Colonization Society for the plan to settle American blacks in Liberia. He rejected their ideas and their plans to make him the ruler of the colony. From the large profits of his successful sailmaking company, he contributed heavily to the abolitionist movement and was a supporter of William Lloyd Garrison's anti-slavery journal, *The Liberator*. Died at Philadelphia, PA, Mar 4, 1842.

IRANIAN EARTHQUAKE: ANNIVERSARY. Sept 2, 1962. Iran's biggest earthquake since 1775 destroyed 31 villages covering 8,000 square miles. More than 10,000 people died in the massive quake, 10,000 were injured and 25,000 people were left homeless.

McAULIFFE, CHRISTA: 50th BIRTH ANNIVERSARY. Sept 2, 1948. Christa McAuliffe, a 37-year-old Concord, NH, high-school teacher, was to have been the first "ordinary citizen" in space. Born Sharon Christa Corrigan at Boston, MA, she perished with six crew members in the Space Shuttle *Challenger* explosion on Jan 28, 1986. See also: "Challenger Space Shuttle Explosion Anniversary" (Jan 28).

NATIONAL STEARMAN FLY-IN. Sept 2–5. Galesburg, IL. The largest gathering of Stearman airplanes—the biplane trainers that gave wings to more military pilots than any other series of aircraft in the world. Est attendance: 7,500. For info: Tourism Associate, Galesburg Area CVB, PO Box 749, Galesburg, IL 61402-0749. Phone: (309) 343-1194. Fax: (309) 343-1195. Email: gacvb@misslink.net. WWW: http://www.misslink.net/gacvb/

PRIME BEEF FESTIVAL. Sept 2–5. Monmouth Park, Monmouth, IL. Princess Pageant, parade, carnival from noon-midnight, Beef and Pork Show, judging, music, food and exhibitors. Sponsor: Monmouth Area Chamber of Commerce and the Wyatt Earp Birthplace Association, phone: (309) 734-6419. Est attendance: 5,000. For info: Monmouth Chamber of Commerce, PO Box 857, 620 S Main St, Monmouth, IL 61462. Phone: (309) 734-3181. Fax: (309) 734-8579.

SHERMAN ENTERS ATLANTA: ANNIVERSARY. Sept 2, 1864. After a four-week siege, Union General William Tecumseh Sherman entered Atlanta, GA. The city had been evacuated on the previous day by Confederate troops under General John B. Hood. Hood had mistakenly assumed Sherman was ending the siege on Aug 27, when actually Sherman was beginning the final stages of his attack. Hood then sent troops to attack the Union forces at Jonesboro. Hood's troops were defeated, opening the way for the capture of Atlanta.

SOUTH MOUNTAIN FAIR. Sept 2–6. Gettysburg, PA. Display of agricultural products, arts, crafts and industrial and agricultural exhibits. Est attendance: 12,500. For info: Gettysburg Conv and Visitors Bureau, 35 Carlisle St, Gettysburg, PA 17325-1899. Phone: (717) 334-6274. Fax: (717) 334-1166. WWW: http://www.gettysburg.com

SWEET CORN FESTIVAL. Sept 2–5. Millersport, OH. All concessions are operated by more than 80 non-profit charitable organizations. Wide variety of food, four entertainment stages, giant midway, exhibits, numerous contests and games. For info: Sweet Corn Fest, Inc, PO Box 337, Millersport, OH 43046. Phone: (614) 467-3943.

US TREASURY DEPARTMENT: ANNIVERSARY. Sept 2, 1789. The third presidential cabinet department, the Treasury Department, was established by Congress.

"THE VERDICT IS YOURS" TV PREMIERE: ANNIVERSARY. Sept 2, 1957. This courtroom drama was a popular show performed without scripts. An outline prepared for each case by the writers was the starting point for the performers. Actors played the witnesses, defendants and plaintiffs; the judges and lawyers were played by real lawyers. This was an audience participation show with jurors chosen from the studio audience. "Verdict's" first court reporter was Jim McKay; Bill Stout succeeded him.

VICTORY DAY or V-J DAY. Sept 2. Official ratification of Japanese surrender to the Allies occurred aboard the USS *Missouri* in Tokyo Bay on Sept 2 (Far Eastern time) in 1945, thus prompting President Truman's declaration of this day as Victory-over-Japan Day. Japan's initial, informal agreement of surrender was announced by Truman and celebrated in the US on Aug 14.

VIETNAM: INDEPENDENCE DAY. Sept 2, 1945. Ho Chi Minh formally proclaimed the independence of Vietnam and the establishment of the Democratic Republic of Vietnam. National holiday.

BIRTHDAYS TODAY

Cleveland Amory, 81, author (*The Cat and the Curmudgeon, The Cat Who Came for Christmas*), born Nahant, MS, Sept 2, 1917.

Nathaniel ("Tiny") Archibald, 50, Basketball Hall of Fame guard, born New York, NY, Sept 2, 1948.

Terry Paxton Bradshaw, 50, sportscaster, Pro Football Hall of Fame quarterback, born Shreveport, LA, Sept 2, 1948.

Marge Champion, 75, dancer, actress ("Marge and Gower Champion Show," *Show Boat, The Swimmer*), born Los Angeles, CA, Sept 2, 1923.

Jimmy Connors, 46, tennis player, born East St. Louis, IL, Sept 2, 1952.

Eric Demetric Dickerson, 38, former football player, born Sealy, TX, Sept 2, 1960.

Mark Harmon, 47, actor ("St. Elsewhere," "Eleanor and Franklin: The White House Years"), born Burbank, CA, Sept 2, 1951.

k.d. lang, 37, singer ("Constant Craving"), born Consort, Canada, Sept 2, 1961.

Linda Purl, 43, actress (Ashley Pfister on "Happy Days"; Charlene Matlock on "Matlock"), born Greenwich, CT, Sept 2, 1955.

Keanu Reeves, 34, actor (*Bill and Ted's Excellent Adventure, My Own Private Idaho, Speed*), born Beirut, Lebanon, Sept 2, 1964.

John Thompson, 57, college basketball coach, former player, born Washington, DC, Sept 2, 1941.

Peter Victor Ueberroth, 61, former commissioner of baseball and Olympic organizer, born Evansville, IL, Sept 2, 1937.

SEPTEMBER 3 — THURSDAY

Day 246 — 119 Remaining

AMATI, NICOLO: BIRTH ANNIVERSARY. Sept 3. Celebrated Italian violin maker. Sept 3, 1596–Aug 12, 1684.

BEGINNING OF THE PENNY PRESS: ANNIVERSARY. Sept 3, 1833. Benjamin H. Day launched the *New York Sun* on Sept 3, 1833. This was the first truly successful penny newspaper to originate in the US. The *Sun* was sold on sidewalks by newspaper boys. By 1836 the paper was the largest seller in the country with a circulation of 30,000. It was possibly Day's concentration on human-interest stories and sensationalism that made his publication a success while efforts at penny papers in Philadelphia, New York and Boston had failed.

BLUE HILL FAIR. Sept 3–7. Blue Hill, ME. A "down-to-earth" country fair. Annually, Labor Day weekend. Est attendance: 55,000. For info: Blue Hill Fair, PO Box 390, Blue Hill, ME 04614. Phone: (207) 374-3701. Fax: (207) 374-3702.

CRANDALL, PRUDENCE: BIRTH ANNIVERSARY. Sept 3, 1803. Born to a Quaker family at Hopkinton, RI, this American schoolteacher sparked controversy in the 1830s with her efforts to educate black girls. When her private academy for girls was boycotted because she admitted a black girl, she started a school for "young ladies and misses of colour." Died on Jan 28, 1890.

September 1998

S	M	T	W	T	F	S
		1	2	3	4	5
6	7	8	9	10	11	12
13	14	15	16	17	18	19
20	21	22	23	24	25	26
27	28	29	30			

ESCAPE TO FREEDOM: ANNIVERSARY. Sept 3, 1838. Dressed as a sailor and carrying identification papers borrowed from a retired merchant seaman, Frederick Douglass boarded a train in Baltimore, MD, a slave state, and rode to Wilmington, DE, where he caught a steamboat to the free city of Philadelphia. He then transferred to a train headed for New York City where he entered the protection of the underground railway network. Douglass later became a great orator and one of the leaders of the antislavery struggle.

FILENE, EDWARD ALBERT: BIRTH ANNIVERSARY. Sept 3. American merchant and philanthropist who established the US credit union movement in 1921, born Salem, MA, Sept 3, 1860. Died Paris, France, Sept 26, 1937.

ITALY SURRENDERS: 55th ANNIVERSARY. Sept 3, 1943. General Giuseppe Castellano signed three copies of the "short armistice," effectively surrendering "unconditionally" for the Italian government. That same day the British Eighth Army, commanded by General Bernard Montgomery, invaded the Italian mainland.

LOUISIANA SHRIMP AND PETROLEUM FESTIVAL AND FAIR. Sept 3–7. Morgan City, LA. Free Admission to this event that recognizes and celebrates the importance of the shrimp and oil industry to the area. Arts, crafts, water and street parades, Cajun culinary classic, antique show, shrimp cook-off, music in the park, unique children's village (a magical adventureland), gospel tent, coronation pageant and ball, carnival, blessing of the fleet. American Bus Association's "Top 100 Event." Est attendance: 150,000. For info: Louisiana Shrimp and Petroleum Festival and Fair Assn, Box 103, Morgan City, LA 70381. Phone: (504) 385-0703. Fax: (504) 384-4628.

MIDWEST OLD THRESHERS REUNION. Sept 3–7. McMillan Park, Mount Pleasant, IA. The reunion began in 1950. Old Threshers is a celebration of our rich agricultural heritage. Attractions range from displays of steam engines and agricultural exhibits to turn-of-the-century living and antique cars, tractors and gas engines. There are also steam trains, trolleys, crafts, museums, music and camping. Annually, five days ending on Labor Day. Est attendance: 125,000. For info: Midwest Old Threshers, 1887 Threshers Rd, Mt Pleasant, IA 52641. Phone: (319) 385-8937. Fax: (319) 385-0563.

NATIONAL SWEETCORN FESTIVAL. Sept 3–7. McFerron Park, Hoopeston, IL. 54th annual festival includes 29 tons of free corn on the cob, nationally sanctioned beauty pageant, carnival, flea market, horse show, demolition derby, bands and talent shows. Est attendance: 50,000. For info: Jeanie Cooke, Exec Dir, Danville Area Conv/Visitors Bureau, PO Box 992, Danville, IL 61834. Phone: (217) 442-2096.

QATAR: INDEPENDENCE DAY. Sept 3. National holiday.

SAN MARINO: NATIONAL DAY. Sept 3. Public holiday.

"SEARCH FOR TOMORROW" TV PREMIERE: ANNIVERSARY. Sept 3, 1951. This soap lasted for 35 years. It began as a fifteen-minute program and expanded to thirty minutes in 1968, when it also began to videotape performances instead of doing them live. "Search" was set in the town of Henderson, and its central character was Joanne Gardner Barron Tate Vincente Tourneur (played by Mary Stuart). Other notable cast members have included: Don Knotts, Robert Mandan, Ken Kercheval, Jill Clayburgh, Natalie Schafer, Susan Sarandon, Robert Loggia, Hal Linden, Morgan Fairchild, Joe Morton, Robby Benson, Kevin Kline, Cynthia Gibb and Olympia Dukakis.

TELLURIDE FILM FESTIVAL. Sept 3–6. Telluride, CO. 25th annual film festival attracts film lovers, artists and scholars from all over the globe. National and international premiers, world archive treasures, innovative or experimental filmmaking and retrospectives. Annually, Labor Day weekend. Est attendance: 5,000. For info: The Natl Film Preserve, Box B 1156, Hanover, NH 03755. Phone: (603) 643-1255. Fax: (603) 643-5938.
Email: tellufilm@aol.com.
WWW: http://telluridemm.com/filmfest.html

TREATY OF PARIS: SIGNING ANNIVERSARY. Sept 3, 1783. Treaty between Britain and the United States, ending the Revolutionary War, signed at Paris, France, Sept 3, 1783. American signatories: John Adams, Benjamin Franklin and John Jay.

UNITED TRIBES INTERNATIONAL POWWOW. Sept 3–6. Bismarck, ND. Enjoy one of the largest Native American cultural events in the nation. This colorful pageant includes dancers competing from 30 tribes throughout the country and has been named one of the American Bus Association's top 100 events four times. The event includes the area's largest Indian Arts Exposition and Sales plus the Miss Indian Nations Pageant. For info: Bismarck/Mardan Conv & Visitors Bureau, PO Box 2274, Bismarck, ND 58502. Phone: (800) 767-3555. Fax: (701) 222-0647.

UTAH STATE FAIR. Sept 3–13. Salt Lake City, UT. Est attendance: 360,000. For info: Utah State Fair Park, 155 N 1000 W, Salt Lake City, UT 84116. Phone: (801) 538-8440. Fax: (801) 538-8455. Email: utstdonna@fiber.net.

VICTORIAN DOO-DADS. Sept 3–Nov 29. Clinton, MD. A display of unusual items of the Victorian era including such things as cup plates, invalid feeders and more. Est attendance: 2,000. For info: Laurie Verge, Dir, Surratt House & Tavern, PO Box 427, Clinton, MD 20735. Phone: (301) 868-1121. Fax: (301) 868-8177.
WWW: http://www.engr.umd.edu/~clwspoon/surratt.html

BIRTHDAYS TODAY

Eileen Brennan, 61, actress (*The Last Picture Show, Private Benjamin*), born Los Angeles, CA, Sept 3, 1937.

Kitty Carlisle, 83, actress, (*A Night at the Opera*; "To Tell the Truth") singer, born New Orleans, LA, Sept 3, 1915.

Pauline Collins, 58, actress (played Sarah in "Upstairs, Downstairs"; stage: *Shirley Valentine* [in London won Olivier Award as best actress, in NY won Tony, Drama Desk and Outer Critics Circle Awards]), born Exmouth, England, Sept 3, 1940.

Anne Jackson, 72, actress (*Lovers and Other Strangers*; many stage roles), born Allegheny, PA, Sept 3, 1926.

Valerie Perrine, 55, actress (*Lenny, W.C. Fields and Me*), born Galveston, TX, Sept 3, 1943.

Charlie Sheen (Carlos Irwin Estevez), 33, actor (*Platoon, Hot Shots*), born New York, NY, Sept 3, 1965.

Damon Stoudamire, 25, basketball player, born Portland, OR, Sept 3, 1973.

Mort Walker (Mortimer Walker Addison), 75, cartoonist ("Beetle Bailey"), born El Dorado, KS, Sept 3, 1923.

SEPTEMBER 4 — FRIDAY

Day 247 — 118 Remaining

AUTUMN MAGIC (WITH TOM MIX FESTIVAL). Sept 4–6. Guthrie, OK. Features the Guthrie Tom Mix festival, antique/collectible market, Western Legends memorabilia market, classic car show, western re-enactors, live entertainment. Est attendance: 12,000. For info: Guthrie Conv & Visitors Bureau, PO Box 995, Guthrie, OK 73044-0995. Phone: (800) 299-1889 or (405) 282-1947. Fax: (405) 282-0061.

BENTON NEIGHBOR DAY. Sept 4–5. Benton, MO. Large festival that includes exhibits, greased pole climb, indoor dance, amusement park, Little Mr and Miss contest, greased pig contest, live bands, antique car show, horseshoe tournament, sky divers, queen contest, kid tractor pull, parade and talent show. Annually, the Friday and Saturday before Labor Day. Est attendance: 3,000. For info: Benton Chamber of Commerce, PO Box 477, Benton, MO 63736. Phone: (573) 545-3125.

BRITT DRAFT HORSE SHOW. Sept 4–6. Hancock County Fairgrounds, Britt, IA. Largest draft horse hitch show in North America, featuring 16 draft six-horse hitches from the US and Canada representing the very best of the Belgian, Percheron and Clydesdale performance horses. Annually, Labor Day weekend. Est attendance: 10,000. For info: Randel or Melodie Hiscocks, Britt Draft Horse Assn, PO Box 312, Britt, IA 50423. Phone: (515) 843-4181.

BRUCKNER, ANTON: BIRTH ANNIVERSARY. Sept 4. Austrian composer born at Ansfelden, Austria, Sept 4, 1824. Died at Vienna, Austria, Oct 11, 1896.

BURNHAM, DANIEL: BIRTH ANNIVERSARY. Sept 4. American architect and city planner, Daniel Hudson Burnham, born Sept 4, 1846, at Henderson, NY. Burnham was an advocate of tall, fireproof buildings, probably the first to be called "skyscrapers." In 1909 he proposed a long-range city plan for Chicago, IL, that was a key factor in the "forever open, clear and free" policy which resulted in Chicago having the most beautiful lakefront of any major urban city in the US. Died June 1, 1912.

"CAPTAIN MIDNIGHT" TV PREMIERE: ANNIVERSARY. Sept 4, 1954. A children's show starring Richard Webb as Captain Midnight, a World War I flying ace who battled crime as part of the Secret Squadron. Webb was joined by Sid Melton as Ichabod (Ikky) Mudd, his assistant, and Olan Soule as Tut, an eccentric scientist. "Captain Midnight" moved to TV from radio, where it was sponsored by Ovaltine. In reruns, the name was changed to "Jet Jackson, Flying Commando" because Ovaltine owned the rights to the Captain Midnight name.

CHATEAUBRIAND, FRANCOIS RENE DE: BIRTH ANNIVERSARY. Sept 4, 1768. French poet, novelist, historian, explorer and statesman, witness to the French Revolution. Born at St. Malo, France, Sept 4, 1768. Died at Paris, France, July 4, 1848.

CURACAO: ANIMALS' DAY. Sept 4. In Curaçao the Association for the Protection of Animals organizes an animal show for this day and the best-kept animals are awarded prizes.

DANIEL BOONE PIONEER FESTIVAL. Sept 4–6. Winchester, KY. Take yourself back to the days of Daniel Boone and the pioneers. Features entertainment, arts and crafts displays and food booths. Est attendance: 35,000. For info: Daniel Boone Pioneer Festival, 2 S Maple St, Ste A, Winchester, KY 40391. Phone: (606) 744-0556. Fax: (606) 744-9229.

ENGLAND: BLACKPOOL ILLUMINATIONS. Sept 4–Nov 9. The Promenade, Blackpool, Lancashire. "A five-mile spectacle of lighting." Est attendance: 8,000,000. For info: Tourism and Services Dept, 1 Clifton St, Blackpool, Lancashire, England FY1 1LY. Phone: (44) (112) 532-1623. Fax: (44) (112) 532-6368. WWW: http://www.blackpool.gov.uk

FALL FOLK DANCE CAMP. Sept 4–7. Camp Russel, Wheeling, WV. Nationally recognized folk-dance instructors lead participants in ethnic, international and national dances. Est attendance: 100. For info: Oglebay Institute Visual and Creative Arts Dept, Oglebay Institute, Stifel Fine Arts Ctr, 1330 National Rd, Wheeling, WV 26003. Phone: (304) 242-7700. Fax: (304) 242-7700.

FESTIVAL OF MOUNTAIN AND PLAIN: A TASTE OF COLORADO. Sept 4–7. Civic Center Park, Denver, CO.

Region's largest free outdoor festival, this four-day food and entertainment extravaganza features more than 50 of Colorado's best restaurants, musical acts on six outdoor stages, gourmet cooking demonstrations, 170 arts and crafts booths, educational exhibits, children's music and activities, carnival rides and games. Est attendance: 350,000. For info: Susan Rogers Kark, Downtown Denver Partnership, Taste of Colorado, 511 16th St, Ste 200, Denver, CO 80202-4250. Phone: (303) 534-6161. Fax: (303) 534-2803.

FORT BRIDGER RENDEZVOUS. Sept 4–7. Evanston, WY. Come and join in the family fun with entertainment, food booths, merchandise exhibits and much more. Est attendance: 30,000. For info: Fort Bridger Rendezvous, 230 High Ridge Pt, Evanston, WY 82930-4664. Phone: (307) 789-7559.

FREDERICKSBURG HINKELFEST. Sept 4–6. Fredericksburg, PA. Stage entertainment, rides, food, arts and crafts and more. Est attendance: 20,000. For info: Rainbow Region Vacation Bureau, Box 329, Lebanon, PA 17042. Phone: (717) 272-8555.

A GATHERING OF FRIENDS CONFERENCE. Sept 4. Lithopolis, OH. Storytellers share what they have learned with each other and the public. Est attendance: 150. For info: Donna Foster, Program Dir, Creative Arts Institute, Inc, 8021 Kennedy Rd, Blacklick, OH 43004. Phone: (614) 759-9407. Fax: (614) 759-8480.

HOG CAPITAL OF THE WORLD FESTIVAL. Sept 4–7. Kewanee, IL. World's largest pork chop BBQ. Also features professional entertainment, carnival, flea market, Model T races, parade, four-mile run (Hog Stampede) and the Hogatta Regatta. Annually, Labor Day weekend. Est attendance: 60,000. For info: Mark Mikenas, Exec VP, Kewanee Chamber of Commerce, 113 East 2nd St, Kewanee, IL 61443. Phone: (309) 852-2175. Fax: (309) 852-2176. Email: kchamber@inw.net.

HOISINGTON CELEBRATION. Sept 4–7. Bicentennial Park, Hoisington, KS. 101st annual event includes dances, demolition derby, horseshoe tournament, parade, talent contest, car show, carnival, kiddie events, royalty and baby contests, float contest. Annually, Labor Day weekend. Est attendance: 35,000. For info: Hoisington Labor Day Committee, 123 N Main, Hoisington, KS 67544. Phone: (316) 653-4311.

INDIAN SUMMER FESTIVAL. Sept 4–6. Maier Festival Park, Milwaukee, WI. Festival dedicated to promoting the unique culture of the American Indian. Cultural events and exhibits, competition powwow, arts and crafts, traditional and contemporary entertainment and traditional food. Est attendance: 75,000. For info: Indian Summer Festivals, Inc, 7441 W Greenfield Ave, Ste 109, Milwaukee, WI 53214. Phone: (414) 774-7119. Fax: (414) 774-6810.
WWW: http://www.execpc.com/~indsumr/index.html#markets

September 1998

S	M	T	W	T	F	S
		1	2	3	4	5
6	7	8	9	10	11	12
13	14	15	16	17	18	19
20	21	22	23	24	25	26
27	28	29	30			

ITALIAN STREET FAIR. Sept 4–7. Riverfront Park, downtown Nashville, TN. 44th annual affair benefits the Nashville Symphony Orchestra. Annually, Labor Day weekend. Est attendance: 100,000. For info: Nashville Symphony Guild, 209 Tenth Ave S, Nashville, TN 37203. Phone: (615) 255-5600.

JOHNSTOWN FOLKFEST. Sept 4–6. Johnstown, PA. A three-day heritage festival held over Labor Day weekend, incorporates three performance stages featuring Grammy-winning entertainers, more than 50 ethnic food vendors, children's entertainment and tours of the magnificent churches that surround the festival grounds. For info: Kelly I. Shaffer, Johnstown Area Heritage Assn, PO Box 1889, Johnstown, PA 15907-1889. Phone: (814) 539-1889.

LITTLE BALKANS DAYS/PAACA LITTLE BALKANS FOLKLIFE FESTIVAL. Sept 4–6. Pittsburg, KS. This event attracts more than 100 arts and crafts booths, is spread all over Pittsburg from the mall on the south to the Historical Museum on the north and in the parks in between. Contests, tournaments, food, live entertainment, street dances, displays, hot-air balloon races and much more. Annually, Labor Day weekend. Est attendance: 40,000. For info: Pittsburg Area Festival Assn, PO Box 1115, Pittsburg, KS 66762. Phone: (316) 231-1000 or (800) 879-1212. Fax: (316) 231-3178. Email: pittcofc@pitton.com. WWW: http://chamber.pitton.com

LOS ANGELES, CALIFORNIA: BIRTHDAY. Sept 4. Los Angeles founded, by decree, on Sept 4, 1781, and called "El Pueblo de Nuestra Senora La Reina de Los Angeles de Porciuncula."

MARFA LIGHTS FESTIVAL. Sept 4–6. Marfa, TX. Family-oriented festival with big-name music stars, arts and crafts and more. Annually, Friday–Sunday of Labor Day weekend. Est attendance: 4,000. For info: Marfa Chamber of Commerce, PO Box 635, Marfa, TX 79843. Phone: (915) 729-4942. Fax: (915) 729-4956.

NATIONAL CHAMPIONSHIP CHUCKWAGON RACES. Sept 4–6. Clinton, AR. Five divisions of chuckwagon races, bronc fanning race, Snowy River race, live entertainment, barn dance, western show, western art, saddles, tack-clothing vendors. 13th annual races. Annually, Labor Day weekend. Est attendance: 20,000. For info: Dan Eoff, Rt 6, Box 187-1, Clinton, AR 72031. Phone: (501) 745-8407. Fax: (501) 745-4416.

NATIONAL CHAMPIONSHIP INDIAN POWWOW. Sept 4–6. Traders Village, Grand Prairie, TX. Hundreds of Indians gather for colorful traditional dance contests, Indian arts and crafts shows, homemade tepee competition and Indian food. Est attendance: 75,000. For info: Dallas-Fort Worth Inter-Tribal Assn, Traders Village, 2602 Mayfield Rd, Grand Prairie, TX 75052-7246. Phone: (972) 647-2331.

NEW MEXICO STATE FAIR. Sept 4–20. Albuquerque, NM. Fireworks, blues, country, gospel, pop and rock entertainment. Rodeos, circus, auto thrill show, tractor pulls, horse racing and free grandstand shows. For info: New Mexico State Fair, PO Box 8546, Albuquerque, NM 87198. Phone: (505) 265-1791 or (505) 842-9918. Fax: (505) 247-9101.

NEWSPAPER CARRIER DAY. Sept 4. Anniversary of the hiring of the first "newsboy" in the US, 10-year-old Barney Flaherty, who is said to have answered the following classified advertisement which appeared in *The New York Sun*, Sept 4, 1833: "To the Unemployed—a number of steady men can find employment by vending this paper. A liberal discount is allowed to those who buy to sell again."

NORTH CAROLINA APPLE FESTIVAL. Sept 4–7. Hendersonville, NC. Festival includes arts and crafts displays, entertainment, food booths, sports events and much more. Est attendance: 200,000. For info: North Carolina Apple Festival, PO Box 886, Hendersonville, NC 28793. Phone: (704) 697-4557.

NORTHERN PLAINS HERITAGE FESTIVAL. Sept 4–6. Dickinson, ND. Celebrate the Russian, German and Scandinavian heritage of our local homesteaders at this annual event. A horse and buggy pioneer parade starts out the weekend and ethnic foods, dress, music, demonstrations and displays round it out. Est attendance: 3,000. For info: Northern Plains Heritage Festival, 24 Second St W, Dickinson, ND 58602. Phone: (800) 279-7391 or (701) 225-4988. Fax: (701) 225-9261.

NUGGET BEST IN THE WEST RIB COOK-OFF. Sept 4–7. Victorian Square, Sparks, NV. Rib cookers from across the country compete for the title of Nugget Best in the West Rib Cooker. Competing cookers sell ribs to the crowd over the four-day Labor Day weekend. Free concerts nightly feature groups like Bad Company, Mumbo Gumbo or Steve Wariner. Other music groups presented throughout the day—all free. Hundreds of craft booths and activities for the kids. Est attendance: 200,000. For info: John Ascuaga's Nugget, 1100 Nugget Ave, Sparks, NV 89431. Phone: (800) 648-1177. WWW: http://www.janugget.com

OATMEAL FESTIVAL. Sept 4–5. Bertram/Oatmeal, TX. To celebrate the town of Oatmeal being put back on the state map years after being left off. Fun, food and foolishness. Observed annually Labor Day weekend. Est attendance: 7,000. For info: Oatmeal Fest, PO Box 70, Bertram/Oatmeal, TX 78605. Phone: (512) 355-2197. Fax: (512) 355-3182.

ODYSSEY–A GREEK FESTIVAL. Sept 4–7. Orange, CT. An indoor/outdoor festival celebrating Greek culture, featuring authentic Greek cuisine, live music and marketplace. For info: St. Barbara Greek Orthodox Church, 480 Racebrook Rd, Orange, CT 06477. Phone: (203) 795-1347 or Greater New Haven Conv & Visitors Bureau, One Long Wharf Dr, New Haven, CT, 06511. Phone: (203) 777-8550 or (800) 332-STAY. Fax: (203) 782-7755.

OFFICE OLYMPICS. Sept 4. Downtown Shreveport, LA. A one-day event that spotlights the office employee! 100 teams of five (men and women) office workers compete in such zany events as The Water Break Relay, The Office Chair Roll-off, Toss the Boss, Memo Mania, Beat the Clock and Corporal Chaos, The Human Post-it-Note and Musical Office Chairs. Sponsor: KVKI Radio. Est attendance: 6,000. For info: Melinda R. Coyer, Office Olympics Founder, KVKI Radio, PO Box 31130, Shreveport, LA 71130-1130. Phone: (318) 688-1130. Fax: (318) 687-8574.

ON THE WATERFRONT. Sept 4–6. Rockford, IL. Largest street food and music festival in the region. Eight music stages, more than 50 specialty foods, dozens of special events. Est attendance: 350,000. For info: On the Waterfront, Inc, PO Box 437, Rockford, IL 61105-0437. Phone: (815) 968-5600. WWW: http://www.onthewaterfront.com

PAYSON GOLDEN ONION DAYS. Sept 4–7. Payson, UT. This unique festival includes amusement rides, fireworks, a parade, arts and crafts displays, entertainment, food booths, a demolition derby and much more. Annually, Labor Day weekend. Est attendance: 10,000. For info: Payson Chamber of Commerce, PO Box 21, Payson, UT 84651. Phone: (801) 465-2634.

PENNSYLVANIA ARTS & CRAFTS COLONIAL FESTIVAL. Sept 4–7. Westmoreland Fairgrounds, Greensburg, PA. Step back to colonial times with more than 160 exhibits of hand-crafted furniture, floral arrangements, ceramics, tole, decorative paintings and wrought iron. Civil War encampment, fife and drum music and food booths. For info: Debbie or Dave Stoner, Family Festivals Assoc, Inc, PO Box 166, Irwin, PA 15642. Phone: (412) 863-4577. Fax: (412) 863-4577.

POLISH FEST. Sept 4–6. Wisconsin Dells, WI. Traditional Polish celebration with festive and colorful dance, dress, food and live music. Est attendance: 9,000. For info: Polish Fest, 400 City at Highway 12, Wisconsin Dells, WI 53965-0390. Phone: (800) 659-6811 or (608) 253-4451.

POLK, SARAH CHILDRESS: BIRTH ANNIVERSARY. Sept 4, 1803. Wife of James Knox Polk, 11th president of the US. Born at Murfreesboro, TN, Sept 4, 1803, and died, Aug 14, 1891.

SANTA-CALI-GON DAYS FESTIVAL. Sept 4–7. Historic Square, Independence, MO. Regional celebration for the three trails—Santa Fe, California, Oregon—which all started in Independence. Huge arts and crafts show, live Nashville performers, large carnival midway and free admission. Largest Labor Day weekend event in Kansas City metropolitan area. Est attendance: 225,000. For info: Santa-Cali-Gon Days, 210 W Truman Rd, Independence, MO 64051. Phone: (816) 252-4745. WWW: http://www.kcmo.com/icc

STEAMBOAT DAYS FESTIVAL. Sept 4–6. Jeffersonville, IN. Nonprofit community festival that includes a parade, arts and crafts, food booths, games, air show and a variety of whimsically styled competitive races. Est attendance: 100,000. For info: Jack Alexander, Pres, PO Box Steamboat, Jeffersonville, IN 47131-0764. Phone: (812) 284-2628.

STONEWALL JACKSON HERITAGE ARTS AND CRAFTS JUBILEE. Sept 4–7. Jackson's Mill 4-H Camp, Weston, WV. Historic and contemporary celebration of Appalachian heritage with music, dancing, arts and crafts, photo and quilt shows, Civil War reenactment, living history on the site of Stonewall Jackson's childhood home. Est attendance: 45,000. For info: Stonewall Jackson Heritage Arts and Crafts Jubilee, PO Box 956, Weston, WV 26452. Phone: (304) 269-1863 or (800) 296-1863.

TAIWAN: CHENG CHENG KUNG BIRTH ANNIVERSARY. Sept 4. Joyous celebration of birth of Cheng Cheng Kung (Koxinga), the Ming Dynasty loyalist who ousted the Dutch colonists from Taiwan in 1661. Dutch landing is commemorated annually on Apr 29, but Cheng's birthday is honored on 14th day of seventh moon according to the Chinese lunar calendar.

TENNESSEE STATE FAIR. Sept 4–13. Nashville, TN. A huge variety of exhibits, carnival midway, animal and variety shows, live stage presentations, livestock, agricultural and craft competitions and food and game booths. Est attendance: 316,000. For info: Tennessee Fair Office, PO Box 40208, Melrose Station, Nashville, TN 37204. Phone: (615) 862-8980.

THOMAS POINT BEACH BLUEGRASS FESTIVAL. Sept 4–6. Brunswick, ME. Featuring world-class bluegrass musicians on the southern coast of Maine. Swimming, playground, picnic area, snack bar, free camping, Sunday-morning worship service on the beach. Fun for the whole family! 20th annual festival. Enjoy an end-of-summer family outing and terrific bluegrass music. Est attendance: 4,000. For tickets and info: Thomas Point Beach, 29 Meadow Rd, Brunswick, ME 04011. Phone: (207) 725-6009. WWW: http//www.thomaspointbeach.com

TOPEKA RAILROAD DAYS FESTIVAL. Sept 4–7. Topeka, KS. A celebration of Topeka's railroad heritage with exhibits, arts and crafts, big-name entertainment, food and excursion-train trips, many complete with entertainment. Annually, Labor Day weekend. Est attendance: 92,000. For info: Topeka Railroad Days, Inc, 605 S Kansas Ave, Topeka, KS 66603. Phone: (913) 232-5533. Fax: (913) 232-6259. Email: rrdays@kspress.com. WWW: http://www.tyrell.net/~rrdays

VERMONT STATE FAIR. Sept 4–13. Fairgrounds, Rutland, VT. Est attendance: 100,000. For info: Vermont State Fair, 175 S Main St, Rutland, VT 05701. Phone: (802) 775-5200.

VINTAGE AUTO RACE AND CONCOURS D'ELEGANCE. Sept 4–6. Steamboat Springs, CO. Street race and display of classic vintage automobiles. Annually, Labor Day weekend. Sponsors: Bridgestone, Sheraton, ITT. Est attendance: 15,000. For info: Special Events Coord, Steamboat Springs Chamber Resort Assn, PO Box 774408, Steamboat Springs, CO 80477. Phone: (970) 879-0880. Fax: (970) 879-2543. Email: info@steamboat-chamber.com. WWW: http://www.steamboat-chamber.com

WEST VIRGINIA ITALIAN HERITAGE FESTIVAL. Sept 4–6. Clarksburg, WV. Est attendance: 150,000. For info: West Virginia Italian Heritage Festival Office, Box 1632, Clarksburg, WV 26301. Phone: (304) 622-7314. Fax: (304) 622-7314. Email: wvihf@wvonline.com. WWW: http://www.wvonline.com/wvihf

WISCONSIN STATE COW-CHIP THROW. Sept 4–5. Prairie du Sac, WI. Cow-Chip Throw, 5K and 10K runs, arts and crafts fair, live music, parade, Cow-Pie-Eating Contest. Est attendance: 50,000. For info: Wisconsin State Cow-Chip Throw, PO Box 3, Prairie du Sac, WI 53578. Phone: (608) 643-4317. Fax: (608) 643-5421. Email: toolsmkt@bankpds.com.

WOODSTOCK FAIR. Sept 4–7. Woodstock, CT. Annually, Labor Day weekend. Est attendance: 250,000. For info: Woodstock Fair, PO Box 1, South Woodstock, CT 06267. Phone: (860) 928-3246.

WRIGHT, RICHARD: BIRTH ANNIVERSARY. Sept 4, 1908. Novelist and short-story writer whose works included *Native Son, Uncle Tom's Children* and *Black Boy*, born at Natchez, MS. Wright died at Paris, France, Nov 28, 1960.

BIRTHDAYS TODAY

Carlos Romero Barcelo, 66, US Resident Commissioner (D, Commonwealth of Puerto Rico), born San Juan, PR, Sept 4, 1932.

Craig Claiborne, 78, editor, author, born Sunflower, MS, Sept 4, 1920.

Mitzi Gaynor (Franchesca Mitzi Marlene de Charney von Gerber), 67, singer, dancer, actress (*South Pacific*), born Chicago, IL, Sept 4, 1931.

Paul Harvey, 80, broadcaster/commentator ("The Rest of the Story"), born Tulsa, OK, Sept 4, 1918.

Judith Ivey, 47, actress (*Compromising Positions, Brighton Beach Memoirs*; stage: *Steaming*), born El Paso, TX, Sept 4, 1951.

Alexander Liberman, 86, editor, painter, photographer, sculptor, born Kiev, USSR, Sept 4, 1912.

Jennifer Salt, 54, actress (Eunice Tate on "Soap"), born Los Angeles, CA, Sept 4, 1944.

Thomas Sturges (Tom) Watson, 49, golfer, born Kansas City, MO, Sept 4, 1949.

SEPTEMBER 5 — SATURDAY

Day 248 — 117 Remaining

AMERICAN LEGION LABOR DAY CELEBRATION. Sept 5–7. Downtown Schuyler, NE. 78th annual celebration. Carnival, Hole-in-One Contest, Alumni Dance. Annually, the first weekend in September. Sponsor: American Legion. Est attendance: 10,000. For info: Marlene Moore, Exec Secy, Chamber of Commerce, 1107 B St, Schuyler, NE 68661. Phone: (402) 352-5472. Fax: (402) 352-2754. Email: sd45455@tec.net.

BANKS COUNTY FESTIVAL. Sept 5–6. Homer, GA. 26th annual. On the historic courthouse lawn. Featuring parade, arts and crafts, square dancing contests, street dance, cake walk, food and children's activities. Free admission. For info: Banks County Chamber of Commerce, PO Box 57, Homer, GA 30547. Phone: (706) 677-2108 or (800) 638-5004.

BE LATE FOR SOMETHING DAY. Sept 5. To create a release from the stresses and strains resulting from a consistent need to be on time. For info: Les Waas, Pres, Procrastinators' Club of America, Inc, Box 712, Bryn Athyn, PA 19009. Phone: (215) 947-9020. Fax: (215) 947-7007.

September 1998

S	M	T	W	T	F	S
		1	2	3	4	5
6	7	8	9	10	11	12
13	14	15	16	17	18	19
20	21	22	23	24	25	26
27	28	29	30			

BOX CAR DAYS. Sept 5–7. Tracy, MN. To celebrate the city's heritage as a railroad community. Annually, Labor Day weekend. Est attendance: 10,000. For info: Con Rettmer, Exec Dir, Chamber of Commerce, 372 Morgan St, Tracy, MN 56175. Phone: (507) 629-4021. Fax: (507) 629-4345.

CAGE, JOHN: BIRTH ANNIVERSARY. Sept 5, 1912. American composer John Cage was born at Los Angeles, CA. An avant-garde composer, he pioneered the experimental music and performance art schools. He used non-traditional instruments such as flower pots and cowbells in innovative situations, such as performances governed by chance, in which the *I Ching* was consulted to determine the direction of the performance. In 1978, he was elected to the American Academy of Arts and Sciences, and in 1982 was awarded France's highest honor for cultural contributions, *Commandeur de l'Ordre des Arts et des Lettres*. He died on Aug 12, 1992, at New York, NY.

CAPITAL DISTRICT SCOTTISH GAMES. Sept 5–6. Altamont, NY. Celtic festival features the Northeastern US Pipe Band and Open Highland Dancing Championships, Highland athletics, Scottish dogs, country dancers, Celtic goods, Scottish/American food/beverages. Est attendance: 10,000. For info: Donald Martin, Capital District Scottish Games, 7 Lori Lane, Latham, NY 12110. Phone: (518) 785-5951.

CARNOVSKY, MORRIS: BIRTH ANNIVERSARY. Sept 5, 1897. American actor Morris Carnovsky was born at St. Louis, MO. In 1931 with actor Lee Strasberg and others he founded the Group Theater at New York, NY. He was blacklisted in the 1950s by the House Un-American Activities Committee, but was still asked by John Houseman to perform in the American Shakespeare Festival in 1956 and began a successful Shakespearean career. He was elected to the Theater Hall of Fame in 1979. Carnovsky died on Sept 1, 1992, at Easton, CT.

CHARLESTON DISTANCE RUN. Sept 5. Charleston, WV. To provide an amateur 15-mile race of professional quality for residents and visitors to Charleston. A 5K (3.1 miles) race also will be held. Est attendance: 1,500. For info: Danny Wells, Race Dir, Charleston Festival Commission, Inc, PO Box 2749, Charleston, WV 25330. Phone: (304) 348-6419 or (304) 348-5122. Fax: (304) 348-1740.

CLEVELAND NATIONAL AIR SHOW. Sept 5–7. Burke Lakefront Airport, Cleveland, OH. Country's oldest air show, featuring extensive military and foreign aircraft participation. Est attendance: 200,000. For info: Cleveland Natl Air Show, Burke Lakefront Airport, Cleveland, OH 44114. Phone: (216) 781-0747. Fax: (216) 781-7810. Email: cknacle@aol.com. WWW: http://www.webohio.com/airshow.html

CLOTHESLINE FAIR. Sept 5–7. Prairie Grove Battlefield State Park, Prairie Grove, AR. 47th annual fair with more than 200 arts and crafts exhibitors; parade; folk, bluegrass, gospel and country music; square-dancing exhibitions and competitions; living history programs and tours. Annually, Labor Day weekend. Est attendance: 45,000. For info: Rhonda Escobedo, Prairie Grove Battlefield State Park, PO Box 306, Prairie Grove, AR 72753. Phone: (501) 846-2990. Fax: (501) 846-4035.

DENMARK: AARHUS FESTIVAL WEEK. Sept 5–14. Observed from the first Saturday in September and for nine days after, since 1965, with theater, ballet, opera, sports, exhibitions and special programs for children.

ELDRIDGE, FLORENCE: BIRTH ANNIVERSARY. Sept 5, 1901. American actress Florence Eldridge was born at Brooklyn, NY. She is best-known for her stage performances in the 1920s with her husband, Frederic March. She died on Aug 1, 1988, at Santa Barbara, CA.

EVERLY BROTHERS HOMECOMING. Sept 5. Central City, KY. The homecoming celebration features top artists. Est attendance: 20,000. For info: Everly Brothers Foundation, PO Box 309, Central City, KY 42330. Phone: (502) 754-9603. Fax: (502) 754-5745.

FAIR AT NEW BOSTON. Sept 5–6. George Rogers Clark Park, Springfield, OH. An authentic re-creation of an 18th-century trades fair with period crafts, military encampments, food and entertainment. Annually, the Saturday and Sunday of Labor Day weekend. Est attendance: 12,000. For info: Fairmaster, George Rogers Clark Heritage Assn, PO Box 1251, Springfield, OH 45501. Phone: (937) 882-9216 or (937) 864-2526.

FAIRE ON THE SQUARE ARTS AND CRAFTS FESTIVAL. Sept 5–7. Prescott, AZ. 180 craft vendors displaying and selling their wares. Annually, Labor Day weekend. Est attendance: 30,000. For info: Joanne Welton, Tourism Adm, Prescott Chamber of Commerce, PO Box 1147, Prescott, AZ 86302-1147. Phone: (520) 445-2000 ext 22.

FIRST CONTINENTAL CONGRESS ASSEMBLY: ANNIVERSARY. Sept 5. The first assembly of this forerunner of the US Congress took place at Philadelphia, PA, on Sept 5, 1774. Peyton Randolph, delegate from Virginia, was elected president.

GERALD FORD: ASSASSINATION ATTEMPTS: ANNIVERSARY. Sept 5. Lynette A. "Squeaky" Fromme, a follower of convicted murderer Charles Manson, attempted to shoot President Gerald Ford on Sept 5, 1975. On Sept 22 of the same year, another attempt on Ford's life occurred when Sara Jane Moore shot at him.

GERMANY: BERLINER FESTWOCHEN. Sept 5–29. Berlin. Music and theatre festival. For info: Berliner Festspiele, Budapester Strasse 50, D-10787, Berlin 30, Germany. Phone: (49) (30) 25489100. Fax: (49) (30) 25489111. WWW: http://www.berlinerfestpiele.be

HISTORIC NORWICHTOWN DAYS. Sept 5–6. Norwich, CT. Experience and explore living history on one of the country's most pristine 18th century town greens. Colonial and Native American craft, trade and military demonstrations; lectures and colonial music. Also, Patriot Parade with famous figures from history. Est attendance: 25,000. For info: Susan Ponder, Chair, Historic Norwichtown Days, PO Box 6010, Yantic, CT 06389. Phone: (860) 886-1874. Fax: (860) 886-7820. Email: HND@aol.com.

IROQUOIS INDIAN FESTIVAL. Sept 5–7. Iroquois Indian Museum, Howes Cave, NY. Performances of social dancing by the "Jim Sky Dancers" in traditional Iroquois clothing. Demonstrations of crafts such as moccasin making, basket weaving, pottery making, silversmithing and stone carving. Archaeology and art exhibits, Iroquois foods, films and videos, children's activities and lectures. Est attendance: 6,000. For info: Iroquois Indian Museum, PO Box 7, Howes Cave, NY 12092. Phone: (518) 296-8949. Fax: (518) 296-8955. Email: iroquois@telenet.net.

ISRAELI OLYMPIAD MASSACRE: ANNIVERSARY. Sept 5–6, 1972. Eleven members of the Israeli Olympic Team were killed in an attack on the Olympic Village in Munich and attempted kidnapping of team members. Four of seven guerrillas, members of the Black September faction of the Palestinian Liberation Army, were also killed. In retaliation, Israeli jets bombed Palestinian positions in Lebanon and Syria on Sept 8, 1972.

JAMES, JESSE: BIRTH ANNIVERSARY. Sept 5, 1847. Western legend and bandit Jesse Woodson James was born at Centerville (now Kearney), MO. His criminal exploits were glorified and romanticized by writers for Eastern readers looking for stories of Western adventure and heroism. After the Civil War, James and his brother, Frank, formed a group of eight outlaws who robbed banks, stagecoaches and stores. In 1873, the James gang began holding up trains. The original James gang was put out of business on Sept 7, 1876, while attempting to rob a bank in Northfield, MN. Every member of the gang except for the James brothers was killed or captured. The brothers formed a new gang and resumed their criminal careers in 1879. Two years later, the governor of Missouri offered a $10,000 reward for their capture, dead or alive. On Apr 3, 1882 at St. Joseph, MO, Robert Ford, a member of the gang, shot 34-year-old Jesse in the back of the head and claimed the reward.

JAZZ FESTIVAL. Sept 5. Pahrump Valley Vineyard, Pahrump, NV. Free jazz concerts. For local info: (702) 727-6900. Nevada Commission on Tourism, Capitol Complex, Carson City, NV 89710. Phone: (800) 227-0774. Fax: (702) 687-6779.

JUBILEE DAYS FESTIVAL. Sept 5–7. Zion, IL. 50th annual communitywide festival featuring an arts and crafts festival, Queen's Pageant, Illinois's largest Labor Day parade and fireworks. Annually, Labor Day weekend. Est attendance: 10,000. For info: Jubilee Days Fest, Inc, Richard Walker, Exec Dir, PO Box 23, Zion, IL 60099. Phone: (847) 746-5500.

KEEP THE FLAME ALIVE STORYTELLING CONTEST. Sept 5. Millersport, OH. Official National Storyteller of the Year® named at this contest. Sponsored by the Creative Arts Institute of America, Adventures in Storytelling Magazine and the Ohio Arts Council. Annually, the Saturday before Labor Day. Est attendance: 500. For info: Donna Foster, Creative Arts Institute, 8021 Kennedy Rd, Blacklick, OH 43004. Phone: (614) 759-9407. Fax: (614) 759-8480.

KINGSTON'S BLUEGRASS FESTIVAL. Sept 5. Waterfront Park, Port of Kingston, Kingston, WA. Family event with traditional bluegrass live bands. The largest bluegrass festival in the Peninsula. Joining together the region's biggest and most popular market, Kingston's Farmers Market. Featuring great food, crafts and local arts. Est attendance: 5,000. For info: Community Event Productions, PO Box 1976, Poulsbo, WA 98370. Phone: (360) 779 8018. Email: mgraves@silverlink.net.

"THE MacNEIL-LEHRER NEWSHOUR" TV PREMIERE: 15th ANNIVERSARY. Sept 5, 1983. Originally, this PBS news show was called "The MacNeil-Lehrer Report" and was on every weeknight for a half hour. Robert MacNeil and Jim Lehrer were joined by Charlayne Hunter-Gault and Judy Woodruff. In 1983, the show was expanded to an hour and became TV's first regularly scheduled daily hour news show. The show has been praised for its depth and objectivity. In 1995, Robert MacNeil retired.

MAGIC CIRCLE BIKE CHALLENGE. Sept 5. Willcox, AZ. A 109-mile bicycle challenge with a 66-mile loop and 33-mile bike races. Annually, the Saturday of Labor Day Weekend. Sponsor: Rex Allen Days, Inc. Est attendance: 500. For info: Willcox Chamber of Commerce and Agriculture, 1500 N Circle I Rd, Willcox, AZ 85643. Phone: (520) 384-2272. Fax: (520) 384-0293. or Rex Allen Days, Inc, PO Box 429, Willcox, AZ 85643.

MARSHALL COUNTY BLUEBERRY FESTIVAL. Sept 5–7. Plymouth, IN. Over 600 craft and commercial booths, parade, circus, fireworks, 15K run, antique car show, horse pull and luscious blueberry treats. Est attendance: 500,000. For info: Marshall County Conv & Visitors Bureau, 220 N Center St, PO Box 669, Plymouth, IN 46563-0669. Phone: (219) 936-5020 or (800) 626-5353. Fax: (219) 936-9845.

MICHIGAN'S GREAT FIRE OF 1881: ANNIVERSARY. Sept 5. According to Michigan Historical Commission, "Small fires were burning in the forests of the 'Thumb area of Michigan,' tinder-dry after a long, hot summer, when a gale swept in from the southwest on Sept 5, 1881. Fanned into an inferno, the fire raged for three days. A million acres were devastated in Sanilac and Huron counties alone. At least 125 persons died, and thousands more were left destitute. The new American Red Cross won support for its prompt aid to the fire victims. This was the first disaster relief furnished by this great organization."

MONTANA STATE CHOKECHERRY FESTIVAL. Sept 5. Lewistown, MT. Taste of Lewistown, tasting and judging of jam, jelly and wine; pancake breakfast, race and run-walk, parade, farmers market, 100 mile Bike-a-thon, art festival and street dance. Est attendance: 1,500. For info: Lewistown Chamber of Commerce, PO Box 818, Lewistown, MT 59457. Phone: (406) 538-5436. Fax: (406) 538-5437. Email: lewchamb@lewistown.net. WWW: http://www.lewistown.net/~lewchamb

NIELSEN, ARTHUR CHARLES: BIRTH ANNIVERSARY. Sept 5, 1897. Marketing research engineer, founder of A.C. Nielsen Co, in 1923, known for radio and TV audience surveys, was born this date and died at Chicago, IL, June 1, 1980.

OHIO WILDERNESS FRONTIER PIQUA HERITAGE FESTIVAL. Sept 5–7. Piqua, OH. To promote and celebrate our local history and that of Ohio. Annually, Labor Day weekend. Est attendance: 90,000. For info: Piqua Heritage Fest, Inc, PO Box 1418, Piqua, OH 45356. Phone: (937) 778-0441. WWW: http://www.wesnet.com/phf

OREGON TRAIL RODEO. Sept 5–7. Hastings, NE. PRCA-sponsored rodeo. Annually, Saturday–Monday of Labor Day weekend. Est attendance: 5,500. For info: Sandy Himmelberg, Genl Mgr, Oregon Trail Rodeo, 947 S Baltimore, Hastings, NE 68901. Phone: (402) 462-3247. Fax: (402) 462-4731.

POWERS' CROSSROADS COUNTRY FAIR AND ART FESTIVAL. Sept 5–7. Newnan, GA. 300 top US and Canadian artists and craftsmen. Old plantation skills revived including using a gristmill and sorghum syrup mill. Patriotic entertainment, country music and down-home country cooking. Est attendance: 60,000. For info: Coweta Festivals, Inc, Box 899, Newnan, GA 30264. Phone: (770) 253-2011. Fax: (770) 253-8180.

PRAIRIE ARTS FESTIVAL. Sept 5. West Point, MS. 5K run, 600 arts and crafts exhibitors, juried fine arts competition, Kidsville, train rides, four stages with entertainment and evening concert in the park. 9 AM–5 PM. Annually, the Saturday before Labor Day. Est attendance: 30,000. For info: Louise Campbell, Coord, Prairie Arts Festival, PO Box 177, West Point, MS 39773. Phone: (601) 494-5121. Fax: (601) 494-6396.

RIVERFEST USA. Sept 5–6. Cincinnati, OH and northern Kentucky. Three-city end-of-summer celebration; entertainment on six stages. The event is capped off with one of the country's best fireworks displays. Est attendance: 500,000. For info: Leslie Keller, Event Producer, Jacor Communications, Inc, 1111 St. Gregory St, Cincinnati, OH 45202. Phone: (513) 677-8028. Fax: (513) 677-8113. Email: lgkeller@aol.com.

September 1998

S	M	T	W	T	F	S
		1	2	3	4	5
6	7	8	9	10	11	12
13	14	15	16	17	18	19
20	21	22	23	24	25	26
27	28	29	30			

SCOTLAND: BRAEMAR ROYAL HIGHLAND GATHERING. Sept 5. Princess Royal and Duke of Fife Memorial Park, Braemar, Grampian. Kilted clansmen from all over the world gather. Traditional activities including tossing cabers, dancing and playing bagpipes. Est attendance: 17,000. For info: Mr W.A. Meston, Coilacriech, Ballater, Aberdeenshire, Scotland AB35 5UH. Phone: (44) (133) 975-5377.

SPACE MILESTONE: *VOYAGER 1* (US). Sept 5, 1977. Launched on Sept 5, 1977, twin of *Voyager 2* which was launched Aug 20.

STA-BIL NATIONALS CHAMPIONSHIP LAWN MOWER RACE. Sept 5. Rockford MetroCentre, Rockford, IL. Three classes of races for winners of regional races held across the US. Mowers will travel at speeds ranging from 10 mph to more than 50 mph. Held in conjunction with the On the Waterfront Festival. Est attendance: 2,000. For info: US Lawn Mower Racing Assn, 1812 Glenview Rd, Glenview, IL 60025. Phone: (847) 729-7363. Fax: (847) 729-4208. Email: letsmow@aol.com. WWW: http://letsmow.com/uslmra

SWITZERLAND: SAINT GOTTHARD AUTOMOBILE TUNNEL: OPENING ANNIVERSARY. Sept 5. The longest underground motorway in the world, the St. Gotthard Auto Tunnel in Switzerland was opened to traffic on Sept 5, 1980. More than 10 miles long, requiring $417,000,000 and 10 years for construction, it became the most direct route from Switzerland to the southern regions of the continent. The St. Gotthard Pass, the main passage since the Middle Ages, was closed much of every year by massive snow drifts.

TASTE OF MADISON. Sept 5–6. Capitol Concourse, Madison, WI. Food and entertainment fest, including booths from more than 60 restaurants, five stages, waiters' race and Kiddie Korner. Est attendance: 200,000. For info: Madison Festivals, Inc, PO Box 628103, Middleton, WI 53562. Phone: (608) 831-1725. Fax: (608) 831-1727.

WILHELM TELL FESTIVAL. Sept 5–7. New Glarus, WI. Presentation of Schiller's Wilhelm Tell drama in German and English in natural outdoor theater. Alpine festival with Swiss entertainment. Annually, Labor Day weekend. Est attendance: 2,000. For info: Dan Gartzke, Mktg Dept, Wilhelm Tell Guild, Box 456, New Glarus, WI 53574. Phone: (800) 527-6838.

WOOLLEY, MARY: DEATH ANNIVERSARY. Sept 5, 1947. Mary Woolley was born at South Norwalk, CT. The first woman to graduate from Brown University (1894), she served on the faculty of Wellesley College, was named president of Mount Holyoke College, and became the first female representative of the US at a major diplomatic conference as a delegate to the Conference on Reduction and Limitation of Armaments. Woolley died at Westport, CT.

WORLD CHAMPIONSHIP BARBECUE GOAT COOKOFF AND ARTS AND CRAFTS FAIR. Sept 5. Richards Park, Brady, TX. 25th annual cook-off to promote Brady and the sheep and goat industry. Arts and crafts fair featuring local and statewide artists. Est attendance: 17,000. For info: Brady Chamber of Commerce, 101 E First St, Brady, TX 76825. Phone: (915) 597-3491.

ZANUCK, DARRYL F.: BIRTH ANNIVERSARY. Sept 5, 1902. Born at Wahoo, NE, Darryl F. Zanuck became a celebrated—and controversial—movie producer. He was also a co-founder of Twentieth Century Studios, which later merged with Fox. His film credits include *The Jazz Singer* (the first sound picture), *Forever Amber, The Snake Pit* and *The Grapes of Wrath.* He died on Dec 21, 1979, at Palm Springs, CA.

BIRTHDAYS TODAY

John Claggett Danforth, 62, former US Senator (R, Missouri) born St. Louis, MO, Sept 5, 1936.

William Devane, 59, actor (*From Here to Eternity*, "Knots Landing"), born Albany, NY, Sept 5, 1939.

Dennis Dugan, 52, actor (*The Howling, Parenthood, Problem Child*), born Wheaton, IL, Sept 5, 1946.
Willie James Gault, 38, former football player, born Griffin, GA, Sept 5, 1960.
Cathy Lee Guisewite, 48, cartoonist ("Cathy"), born Dayton, OH, Sept 5, 1950.
Arthur Koestler, 93, author (*The Thirteenth Tribe, Scum of the Earth*), born Budapest, Hungary, Sept 5, 1905.
Carol Lawrence (Carol Maria Laraia), 63, singer, actress, born Melrose Park, IL, Sept 5, 1935.
Bob Newhart, 69, comedian ("The Bob Newhart Show," "Newhart"), born Chicago, IL, Sept 5, 1929.
Raquel Welch, 56, actress (*The Three Musketeers, Woman of the Year*), model, born Chicago, IL, Sept 5, 1942.

SEPTEMBER 6 — SUNDAY

Day 249 — 116 Remaining

ADDAMS, JANE: BIRTH ANNIVERSARY. Sept 6. American worker for peace, social welfare, rights of women, founder of Hull House (Chicago), co-winner of Nobel Prize, 1931. Born at Cedarville, IL, Sept 6, 1860. Died May 21, 1935, at Chicago, IL.

ART IN THE GARDEN. Sept 6. Washington, PA. For info: Kara Bradstock, Washington County Historical Society, 49 East Maiden St, Washington, PA 15301. Phone: (412) 225-6740. Fax: (412) 225-8495.

BALTIC STATES' INDEPENDENCE RECOGNIZED: ANNIVERSARY. Sept 6. The Soviet government recognized the independence of the Baltic states—Latvia, Estonia and Lithuania—on Sept 6, 1991. The action came 51 years after the Baltic states were annexed by the Soviet Union. All three Baltic states had earlier declared their independence, and many nations had already recognized them diplomatically, including the US on Sept 2, 1991.

BEECHER, CATHARINE ESTHER: BIRTH ANNIVERSARY. Sept 6, 1800. Catharine Esther Beecher was born at East Hampton, NY. In addition to teaching herself mathematics, philosophy and Latin, Beecher had been formally educated in art and music. An early advocate for equal education for women, she founded the Hartford Female Seminary, which was widely recognized for its advanced curriculum. She was also instrumental in the founding of women's colleges in Iowa, Illinois and Wisconsin. Beecher died May 12, 1878, at Elmira, NY.

BELGIUM: HISTORICAL PROCESSION. Sept 6. Tournai. Traditional cultural observance. Annually, the Sunday closest to Sept 8.

CHEETAH RUN. Sept 6. Throughout the Cincinnati Zoo in Ohio. The Cheetah Run is a 2.5-mile course throughout the beautiful zoo grounds. The race is followed by a Fun Run for children around Swan Lake. An awards ceremony follows the race. Est attendance: 1,500. For info: Events and Promotions Dept, Cincinnati Zoo and Botanical Garden, 3400 Vine St, Cincinnati, OH 45220. Phone: (513) 281-4701, ext 8316. Fax: (513) 559-7790. WWW: http://www.cincyzoo.org

DALTON, JOHN: BIRTH ANNIVERSARY. Sept 6. English chemist, physicist, teacher and developer of atomic theory, was born at Eaglesfield, near Cockermouth, England, on Sept 6, 1766. Dalton died at Manchester, England, on July 27, 1844.

FIREWORKS DISPLAY. Sept 6. On the banks of the Ohio River, Cincinnati, OH. Nationally acclaimed 30-minute display of fireworks with a synchronized soundtrack broadcast on WEBN 102.7 FM. Blast-off is at 9:05 PM concluding the Riverfest USA activities. Sponsored by Toyota and WEBN-FM. Annually, the Sunday before Labor Day. Est attendance: 500,000. For info: WEBN-FM, 1111 Saint Gregory St, Cincinnati, OH 45202. Phone: (513) 621-9326. Fax: (513) 784-1249.

FIRST RADIO BROADCAST OF A PRIZEFIGHT: ANNIVERSARY. Sept 6, 1920. The first boxing match broadcast on radio—Jack Dempsey knocked out Billy Miske in the third round of a scheduled ten-round fight.

FOX VALLEY FOLK FEST. Sept 6–7. Geneva, IL. Music, dance and storytelling festival. Features food, folk art, concerts, jam sessions and an old-time community barn dance. For info: Geneva Chamber of Commerce, 8 South Third St, PO Box 481, Geneva, IL 60134. Phone: (630) 232-6060. Fax: (630) 232-6083.

HARVEST WINE CELEBRATION. Sept 6–7. Livermore, CA. The Harvest Wine Celebration acts as an open-house event offering the public an opportunity to visit 15 wineries, listen to live music, sample Livermore Valley wines, shop for arts and crafts and learn more about this historic wine region. Free shuttle service is provided to and from each of the wineries on both days. Annually, Labor Day weekend. Est attendance: 10,000. For info: Michael Perry, Livermore Valley Winegrowers Assn, 1984 Railroad Ave, Ste A, Livermore, CA 94550. Phone: (510) 447-WINE or (510) 370-9777. Fax: (510) 447-0433. Email: LVWA@aol.com. WWW: http://www.onai.com/~lvwa

ITALY: HISTORICAL REGATTA. Sept 6. Venice. Traditional competition among two-oar racing gondolas, preceded by a procession of Venetian ceremonial boats of the epoch of the Venetian Republic. Annually, the first Sunday in September.

ITALY: JOUST OF THE SARACEN. Sept 6. Arezzo. The first Sunday in September is set aside for the Giostra del Saracino, a tilting contest of the 13th century, with knights in armor.

JEWISH RENAISSANCE FAIR. Sept 6. Morristown, NJ. Simultaneous stages of theater, music and comedy all day long, the artists' quarter, cafes and restaurants, arts and crafts expo, carnival games, golf course and storybook hay ride. Star-studded show on main stage late in the day. Annually, the Sunday of Labor Day weekend. Est attendance: 10,000. For info: Rabbi Boruch Klar, Dir of Community Outreach, Rabbinical College of America, 226 Sussex Ave, PO Box 1996, Morristown, NJ 07960. Phone: (201) 267-9404. Fax: (201) 731-6821.

LAFAYETTE, MARQUIS DE: BIRTH ANNIVERSARY. Sept 6, 1757. French general and aristocrat, the Marquis de Lafayette, whose full name was Marie-Joseph-Paul-Yves-Roch-Gilbert du Motier, came to America to assist in the revolutionary cause and volunteered to serve without compensation. He was awarded a major-generalship and began a lasting friendship with the American commander-in-chief, George Washington. After an alliance was signed with France, he returned to his native country and persuaded Louis XVI to send a 6,000-man force to assist the Americans. On his return, he was given command of an army in Virginia and was instrumental in forcing the surrender of Lord Cornwallis at Yorktown, leading to the end of the war and American independence. He was hailed as "The Hero of Two Worlds," and was appointed a brigadier general on his return to France in 1782. He became a leader of the liberal aristocrats during the early days of the French revolution, presenting to the National Assembly his draft of "A Declaration of the Rights of Man and of the Citizen." As the commander of the newly formed national guard of Paris, he rescued Louis XVI and Marie-Antoinette from a crowd that stormed Versailles on Oct 6, 1789, returning them to Paris where they became hostages of the revolution. His popularity waned after his guards opened fire on angry demonstrators demanding abdication of the king in 1791. He fled to Austria with the overthrow of the monarchy in 1792, returning when Napoleon Bonaparte came to power. He again served as captain of the guard in 1830 during the overthrow of King Charles X. Born at Chavaniac, died at Paris, on May 20, 1834, at age 76.

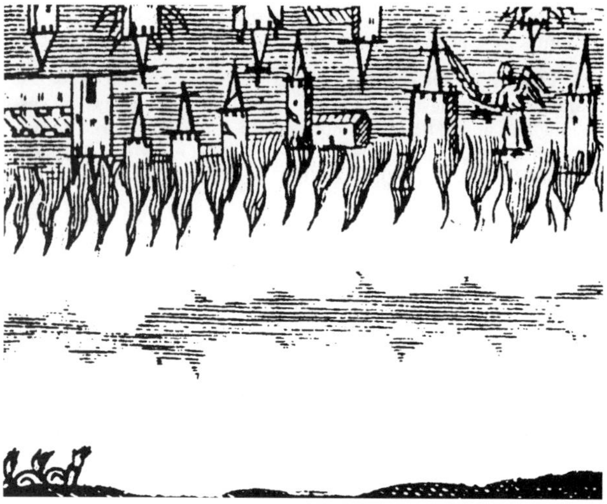

LUNAR ECLIPSE. Sept 6. Penumbral eclipse of the moon. Moon enters penumbra at 5:14 AM, EDT, reaches middle of eclipse at 7:10 AM, and leaves penumbra at 9:06 AM. Beginning of penumbral phase visible in North America except the extreme east, Central America, South America except the extreme east, Australia except the extreme west, New Zealand, most of Antarctica, extreme eastern Asia, most of the Pacific Ocean, extreme western Atlantic Ocean; end of phase visible in western North America, Australia, New Zealand, eastern half of Asia, most of Antarctica, Pacific Ocean except eastern South Pacific, eastern half of Indian Ocean.

MIND MAPPING FOR THE LEARNING ORGANIZATION WEEK. Sept 6–12. Mind Map applications and Brain Club presentations of Mind Maps in the workplace. Est attendance: 100. For info: Quirino Blasco, Buzan Centre, 415 Federal Hwy, Lake Park, FL 33403. Phone: (561) 881-0188. Fax: (561) 845-3210.

MISSOURI RIVER BLUEGRASS AND OLD TIME MUSIC FESTIVAL. Sept 6–7. Cross Ranch State Park, Cross Ranch, ND. The location of this primitive state park along the Missouri River offers a perfect setting for a picking and fiddling get-together for local, regional and national bluegrass groups. Other activities include a children's fest with games and entertainment, gospel concerts and a Sunday church service. For info: (701) 794-3731 or North Dakota Tourism, 604 East Boulevard, Bismarck, ND 58505. Phone: (701) 328-2525 or (800) 435-5663.

MOON PHASE: FULL MOON. Sept 6. Moon enters Full Moon phase at 7:21 AM, EDT.

NATIONAL 5-A-DAY WEEK. Sept 6–12. To encourage all Americans to increase the amount of fruits and vegetables they eat to five servings per day, to better their health and reduce their risk of cancer. For info: Produce for Better Health Fdtn, 1500 Casho Mill Rd, PO Box 6035, Newark, DE 19711. Phone: (302) 738-7100 or (800) 4-CANCER. Fax: (302) 738-4825.

POTATO BOWL. Sept 6–12. Grand Forks, ND. This year featuring the 1998 North Central Hot Air Balloon Championships. Potato Bowl USA salutes the potato featuring queen contest, concert, football game, a parade and other events. For info: Grand Forks Conv and Visitors Bureau, 4251 Gateway Drive, Grand Forks, ND 58203. Phone: (800) 866-4566. Fax: (701) 746-0775. WWW: http://www.grandforksCVB.org

September 1998

S	M	T	W	T	F	S
		1	2	3	4	5
6	7	8	9	10	11	12
13	14	15	16	17	18	19
20	21	22	23	24	25	26
27	28	29	30			

ROSE, BILLY: BIRTH ANNIVERSARY. Sept 6. Billy Rose (William S. Rosenberg), American theatrical producer, author, songwriter and husband of Fanny Brice, was born at New York, NY, on Sept 6, 1899. His songs include: "That Old Gang of Mine," "Me and My Shadow," "Without a Song," "It's Only a Paper Moon" and hundreds of others. Rose died at Montego Bay, Jamaica, Feb 10, 1966.

"RUNNING OF THE SHEEP" DRIVE FESTIVAL. Sept 6. Reedpoint, MT. Hundreds of Montana-bred woolies charge down the six blocks of Main St. Also a parade, Egg Toss and contests, such as the ugliest sheep and the prettiest ewe. Annually, Sunday of Labor Day weekend. Est attendance: 8,500. For info: Russ Schlievert, 201 N Division, Reedpoint, MT 59069. Phone: (406) 326-2288.

SAINT PETERSBURG NAME RESTORED: ANNIVERSARY. Sept 6, 1991. Russian legislators on Sept 6, 1991, voted to restore the name Saint Petersburg to the nation's second largest city. The city had been known as Leningrad for 67 years in honor of the Soviet Union's founder, Vladimir I. Lenin. The city, founded in 1703 by Peter the Great, has had three names in the 20th century with Russian leaders changing its German-sounding name to Petrograd at the beginning of World War I in 1914 and Soviet Communist leaders changing its name to Leningrad in 1924 following their leader's death.

SUNDAE IN THE PARK. Sept 6. Swimming Pool Park, Yerington, NV. YTA presents a celebration of Mason Valley with an art and food festival featuring arts, crafts and food produced in the Mason Valley area. All-day entertainment and free ice cream sundaes for everyone. Est attendance: 300. For info: Mason Valley, Chamber of Commerce, 227 So Main St, Yerington, NV 89447. Phone: (702) 463-2245. Fax: (702) 463-3369.

SWAZILAND: INDEPENDENCE DAY: 30th ANNIVERSARY. Sept 6. Commemorates attainment of national independence on Sept 6, 1968. National holiday.

"WYATT EARP" TV PREMIERE: ANNIVERSARY. Sept 6, 1955. Officially titled "The Life and Legend of Wyatt Earp," this half-hour series marked the beginning of the trend toward "adult westerns." It was loosely based on fact, with Hugh O'Brien as Earp, marshall of Dodge City, KS, and later of Tombstone, AZ. Also featured were Douglas Fowley, Myron Healey, Morgan Woodward, Randy Stuart, Damian O'Flynn, Steve Brodie and Trevor Bardette.

BIRTHDAYS TODAY

Jane Curtin, 51, actress ("Saturday Night Live," "Kate and Allie"), comedienne, born Cambridge, MS, Sept 6, 1947.

Jeff Foxworthy, 40, comedian (album *You Know You're a Redneck*), actor ("The Jeff Foxworthy Show"), author (*No Shirt, No Shoes . . . No Problem*), born Atlanta, GA, Sept 6, 1958.

Swoosie Kurtz, 54, actress (*The World According to Garp*; Tony for *The House of Blue Leaves*; "Sisters"), born Omaha, NE, Sept 6, 1944.

Jo Anne Worley, 61, comedienne, actress ("Rowan & Martin's Laugh-In"), born Lowell, IA, Sept 6, 1937.

SEPTEMBER 7 — MONDAY

Day 250 — 115 Remaining

BANGOR LABOR DAY ROAD RACE. Sept 7. Bass Park, Bangor, ME. Five-mile road race. Annually, on Labor Day. Est attendance: 200. For info: Bangor Parks and Rec Dept, Parks and Rec, 647 Main St, Bangor, ME 04401. Phone: (207) 947-1018. Fax: (207) 947-1605.

BRAZIL: INDEPENDENCE DAY. Sept 7, 1822. Declared independence from Portugal on this date. National holiday.

BUHL DAY. Sept 7. Buhl Farm, Sharon, PA. To honor the laboring man. Observed annually on Labor Day. Est attendance: 25,000. For info: Nancy D. Emmett, Box 709, Sharon, PA 16146. Phone: (412) 981-5522.

CANADA: LABOR DAY. Sept 7. Annually, the first Monday in September.

COLUMBIA RIVER CROSS CHANNEL SWIM. Sept 7. Hood River, OR. The annual swim across the mighty Columbia River draws 550 contestants each year to swim the approximately one mile distance for fun. Est attendance: 550. For info: Hood River County Chamber of Commerce, Columbia River Cross Channel Swim, 405 Portway, Hood River, OR 97031. Phone: (800) 366-3530. Fax: (541) 386-2057.

CORBETT-SULLIVAN PRIZE FIGHT: ANNIVERSARY. Sept 7, 1892. John L. Sullivan was knocked out by James J. Corbett in the 21st round of a prize fight at New Orleans, LA. It was the first major fight under the Marquess of Queensberry Rules.

"THE FLYING NUN" TV PREMIERE: ANNIVERSARY. Sept 7, 1967. This sitcom about a nun at a convent in Puerto Rico who discovers that she can fly starred Sally Field as Elsie Ethrington (Sister Betrille) and featured Madeline Sherwood, Marge Redmond, Shelley Morrison, Alejandro Rey and Vito Scotti.

FULL EMPLOYMENT WEEK. Sept 7–14. An extension of Labor Day to include the full week beginning with that holiday.

GRANDMA MOSES DAY. Sept 7. Anna Mary (Robertson) Moses, modern primitive American painter born at Greenwich, NY, Sept 7, 1860. Started painting at the age of 78. Her 100th birthday was proclaimed Grandma Moses Day in New York state. Died at Hoosick Falls, NY, Dec 13, 1961.

GREAT BATHTUB RACE. Sept 7. Nome, AK. 21st annual. Lets people know that participants can bathe at least once a year. Further, when politicians participate, they can let their constituents know that they clean up their act yearly. Bathtubs mounted on wheels are raced down Front Street. Each team has five members, one in the tub, with bubbles apparent in the bath water. Tub must be full of water at beginning and have at least 10 gallons at the finish line. The other four team members must wear large-brim hats and suspenders and carry either a bar of soap, washcloth, towel or bath mat for the entire race. Winning team claims trophy, a statue of Miss Piggy and Kermit taking a bath, which is handed down from year to year. Annually, at noon on Labor Day. Est attendance: 1,000. For info: Rasmussen's Music Mart, PO Box 2, Nome, AK 99762-0002. Phone: (907) 443-2798 or (907) 443-2219. Fax: (907) 443-5777.

HOLLY, BUDDY: BIRTH ANNIVERSARY. Sept 7. American popular music performer, composer and band leader. Called one of the most innovative and influential musicians of his time, he was a pioneer of rock 'n roll. His hits included "That'll Be the Day" and "Peggy Sue." Born Charles Harden Holley, at Lubbock, TX, on Sept 7, 1936. Buddy Holly died at age 22, in an airplane crash near Mason City, IA, on Feb 3, 1959.

"JIM BOWIE" TV PREMIERE: ANNIVERSARY. Sept 7, 1956. Also known as "The Adventures of Jim Bowie," this half-hour western about the inventor of the Bowie knife starred Scott Forbes as the title character. He was also the only regular on the show. As a result of criticism, the violence was decreased on the show. Louis Edelman produced the series.

LABOR DAY. Sept 7. Legal public holiday. Public Law 90–363 sets Labor Day on the first Monday in September. Observed on this day in all states and in Canada. First observance believed to have been a parade at 10 AM, on Tuesday, Sept 5, 1882, in New York, NY, probably organized by Peter J. McGuire, a Carpenters and Joiners Union secretary. In 1883, a union resolution declared "the first Monday in September of each year a Labor Day." By 1893, more than half of the states were observing Labor Day on one or another day, and a bill to establish Labor Day as a federal holiday was introduced in Congress. On June 28, 1894, President Grover Cleveland signed into law an act making the first Monday in September a legal holiday for federal employees and the District of Columbia.

LABOR DAY BREAKOUT. Sept 7. The Old Jail Museum, Crawfordsville, IN. An annual event to commemorate the transfer of the deed of title of the old county jail from the county to the Montgomery County Cultural Foundation. The Foundation was organized in 1975 as a bicentennial project to preserve the unique rotary jail and operate the structure as a museum of local history and culture. Annually, on Labor Day. Est attendance: 600. For info: Montgomery County Cultural Foundation, Inc, The Old Jail Museum, 222 N Washington St, PO Box 771, Crawfordsville, IN 47933. Phone: (765) 362-5222.

MENTAL HEALTH WORKERS' WEEK. Sept 7–13. A special week set aside to appreciate mental health workers. Annually, beginning on Labor Day. For info: George Blake, PhD, Pres, American Assn of Psychiatric Technicians, 336 Johnson Rd, Michigan City, IN 46360. Phone: (219) 879-2911. Fax: (219) 879-1887.

NATIONAL VEGETARIAN AWARENESS WEEK. Sept 7–13. To increase Americans' consumptions of fruits and vegetables to five or more servings per day in order to reduce the risk of cancer.

NEITHER SNOW NOR RAIN DAY. Sept 7. Anniversary of the opening to the public, on Labor Day, 1914, of the New York Post Office Building at Eighth Avenue between 31st and 33rd Streets. On the front of this building was an inscription supplied by William M. Kendall of the architectural firm that planned the building. The inscription, a free translation from Herodotus, reads: "Neither snow nor rain nor heat nor gloom of night stays these couriers from the swift completion of their appointed rounds." This has been long believed to be the motto of the US Post Office and Postal Service. They have, in fact, no motto . . . but the legend remains. [Info from: New York Post Office, Public Info Office and US Postal Service.]

NEW HAVEN LABOR DAY ROAD RACE. Sept 7. New Haven Green, New Haven, CT. Men's 20K national championship, 5K race and ½ mile children's fun run. Annually, on Labor Day. For info: New Haven Labor Day Road Race, (203) 481-5933 or Greater New Haven Conv & Visitors Bureau, One Long Wharf Dr, New Haven, CT 06511. Phone: (203) 777-8550 or (800) 332-STAY. Fax: (203) 782-7755.

QUEEN ELIZABETH I: BIRTH ANNIVERSARY. Sept 7, 1533. Queen of England, daughter of Henry VIII and Anne Boleyn, after whom the "Elizabethan Era" was named, was born in Greenwich Palace on Sept 7, 1533. She ascended the throne in 1558 at the age of 25. During her reign, the British defeated the Spanish Armada in July 1588, the Anglican Church was essentially established and England became a world power. She died at Richmond, England, Mar 24, 1603.

SOUTH AFRICA: SETTLER'S DAY. Sept 7. Republic of South Africa. Annually, the first Monday in September.

STOCK EXCHANGE HOLIDAY (LABOR DAY). Sept 7. The holiday schedules for the various exchanges are subject to change if relevant rules, regulations or exchange policies are revised. If you have questions, phone: American Stock Exchange (212) 306-1000; Chicago Board of Trade (312) 435-3500; Chicago Board of Options Exchange (312) 786-5600; New York Stock Exchange (212) 656-2065; Pacific Stock Exchange (415) 393-4000; Philadelphia Stock Exchange (215) 496-5000.

SUBSTITUTE TEACHER APPRECIATION WEEK. Sept 7–12. Although substitute teachers get no sick days or respect, they teach when the regular teacher cannot and continually adjust to different classroom situations. Annually, the second week of September. For info: Dorothy Zjawin, Dir, 61 W Colfax Ave, Roselle Park, NJ 07204. Phone: (908) 241-6241. Fax: (908) 241-6241.

"TRUTH OR CONSEQUENCES" TV PREMIERE: ANNIVERSARY. Sept 7, 1950. This game show lasted for many years on both radio and TV. The half-hour show was based on a parlor game: contestants who failed to answer a question before the buzzer (nicknamed Beulah) went off had to perform stunts (i.e. pay the consequences). Ralph Edwards created and hosted the show until 1954, then it became a prime-time show hosted by Jack Bailey. Bob Barker succeeded him in 1956 and hosted it through its syndicated run. In 1977, the show was revived as "The New Truth or Consequences" with Bob Hilton as host.

WAIKIKI ROUGHWATER SWIM. Sept 7. Waikiki Beach, Honolulu, HI. The 28th annual swim is 2.4 miles from Sans Souci Beach to Duke Kahanamoku Beach. "The World's Largest Open Water Swimming Event." Preregistration is required. Annually, Labor Day. Est attendance: 1,200. For info: Jim Anderson, One Keahole Place #1607, Honolulu, HI 96825-3414. Fax: (808) 396-8868. Email: waikikijim@aol.com.

WOMEN'S WORK IN COLONIAL TIMES. Sept 7. New London, CT. The everyday work of women in the 17th and 18th centuries is interpreted by costumed role-players, with hands-on demonstrations of open-hearth cooking, health and medicine programs, spinning, dyeing, weaving, candle-making, etc. Hours: Noon–4 PM. Admission: $4 adults, $1 children; free to working women. Annually, on Labor Day. Est attendance: 50. For info: The Hempsted Houses, 11 Hempstead St, New London, CT 06320. Phone: (860) 443-7949 or Antiquarian & Landmarks Society Phone: (860) 247-8996.

BIRTHDAYS TODAY

Corbin Bernsen, 44, actor ("LA Law," "Ryan's Hope," *Major League*), born North Hollywood, CA, Sept 7, 1954.

September 1998

S	M	T	W	T	F	S
		1	2	3	4	5
6	7	8	9	10	11	12
13	14	15	16	17	18	19
20	21	22	23	24	25	26
27	28	29	30			

Susan Blakely, 48, actress (*The Way We Were, The Lords of Flatbush, Shampoo*), born Frankfurt, Germany, Sept 7, 1950.

Michael DeBakey, 90, distinguished heart surgeon, born Lake Charles, LA, Sept 7, 1908.

Michael Feinstein, 42, singer, pianist, born Columbus, OH, Sept 7, 1956.

Arthur Ferrante, 77, pianist (Ferrante and Teicher; "Exodus," "Tonight"), composer, born New York, NY, Sept 7, 1921.

Chrissie Hynde, 47, singer, songwriter (lead singer of the Pretenders), born Akron, OH, Sept 7, 1951.

Daniel Ken Inouye, 74, US Senator (D, Hawaii), born Honolulu, HI, Sept 7, 1924.

Julie Kavner, 47, actress (*Radio Days*, "Rhoda," Marge Simpson's voice on "The Simpsons"), born Los Angeles, CA, Sept 7, 1951.

Elia Kazan (Elia Kazanjoglou), 89, filmmaker (*On the Waterfront, East of Eden, Viva Zapata!*), born Constantinople, Turkey, Sept 7, 1909.

John Philip Law, 61, actor (*The Russians Are Coming, the Russians Are Coming; Barbarella*), born Hollywood, CA, Sept 7, 1937.

SEPTEMBER 8 — TUESDAY

Day 251 — 114 Remaining

ANDORRA: NATIONAL HOLIDAY. Sept 8.

ANOTHER LOOK UNLIMITED DAY. Sept 8. Your house, garage, barn, shed, attic or yard. Encourages everyone to look over their possessions and give surplus to charity or reuse in other projects. Lessen the flow to landfills. Annually, the day after Labor Day. For info: N VIRA MYNTL, PO Box 220, Holts Summit, MO 65043.

CLINE, PATSY: BIRTH ANNIVERSARY. Sept 8, 1932. Country and western singer, born Virginia Patterson Hensley at Winchester, VA. Patsy Cline got her big break in 1957 when she won an Arthur Godfrey Talent Scout show, singing "Walking After Midnight." Her career took off and she became a featured singer at the Grand Ole Opry, attaining the rank of top female country singer. She died in a plane crash on Mar 5, 1963, at Camden, TN, along with singers Hawkshaw Hawkins and Cowboy Copas.

GALVESTON HURRICANE: ANNIVERSARY. Sept 8, 1900. The worst national disaster in US history in terms of lives lost. More than 6,000 people were killed.

LONG, HUEY P.: ASSASSINATION ANNIVERSARY. Sept 8. Louisiana senator Huey P. Long was shot at Baton Rouge, LA, Sept 8, 1935. The assassin, Dr. Carl A. Weiss, was killed by Long's bodyguards.

MALTA: SIEGE BROKEN: ANNIVERSARY. Sept 8. "Two Sieges and Regatta Day" festivities now commemorate victory over the Turks, Sept 8, 1565, when the siege that began in May 1565 was broken by the Maltese and the Knights of St. John after a loss of nearly 10,000 lives. Also commemorated is survival of the 1943 siege by the Axis Powers. Parades, fireworks, boat races, etc, especially at the capital, Valleta, and the Grand Harbour.

MISS AMERICA FIRST CROWNED: ANNIVERSARY. Sept 8. Margaret Gorman of Washington, DC, was crowned the first Miss America at the end of a two-day pageant in Atlantic City, NJ, on Sept 8, 1921.

MISSION SAN GABRIEL ARCHANGEL: FOUNDING ANNIVERSARY. Sept 8. California mission to the Indians founded Sept 8, 1771.

NIXON PARDON DAY: ANNIVERSARY. Sept 8. Anniversary of the "full, free, and absolute pardon unto Richard Nixon, for all offenses against the United States which he, Richard Nixon, has committed or may have committed or taken part in during the period from January 20, 1969, through August 9, 1974." (Presidential Proclamation 4311, Sept 8, 1974, by Gerald R. Ford.)

NORTHERN PACIFIC RAILROAD COMPLETED: ANNIVERSARY. Sept 8, 1883. After 19 years of construction, the Northern Pacific Railroad became the second railroad to link the two coasts. The Union Pacific and Central Pacific lines met at Utah in 1869.

"THE OPRAH WINFREY SHOW" TV PREMIERE: ANNIVERSARY. Sept 8, 1986. This daytime talk show has been the top-rated talk show for years and also has the distinction of being the first talk show hosted by a black woman, Oprah Winfrey. Her show is taped in front of a studio audience who are solicited for their questions and feedback. In the mid-1990s, fed up with the plethora of trashy talk shows that had sprung up everywhere, Winfrey decided to upgrade the quality of topics that her show presented.

PEPPER, CLAUDE DENSON: BIRTH ANNIVERSARY. Sept 8. US Representative and former Senator, born near Dudleyville, AL, on Sept 8, 1900. Claude Pepper's career in politics spanned 53 years and 10 presidents, and he became the champion for America's senior citizens. He was elected to the US Senate in 1936, where he was a principal architect of many of the nation's "safety net" social programs including Social Security, the minimum wage and medical assistance for the elderly and for handicapped children. After a 14-year career in the Senate, he returned to Congress in the House of Representatives where he served 14 terms. A staunch advocate for senior citizens, he served as chairman of the House Select Committee on Aging, drafted legislation banning forced retirement and fought against cutting Social Security benefits to retired workers. Pepper died at Washington, DC, on May 30, 1989.

PLAY DAYS. Sept 8–12. In a world filled with downsizing, rightsizing and shaftsizing, we need humor to reaffirm our humanity and sanity. This week the HUMOR Project will be spreading the word on 1,001 ways to add humor to your life and work. Jest for success—humor works. Annually, the Tuesday through Saturday after Labor Day. For info: Dr. Joel Goodman, Dir, The HUMOR Project, Dept C, 110 Spring St, Sarasota Springs, NY 12866. Phone: (518) 587-8770. Fax: (518) 587-8771.
Email: humor@wizvax.net.
WWW: http://www.wizvax.net/humor/

SELLERS, PETER (RICHARD HENRY): BIRTH ANNIVERSARY. Sept 8. Award-winning British comedian and film star, especially remembered for his role as the bumbling character Inspector Clouseau in the *Pink Panther* films. Born Sept 8, 1925. Died at London, England, July 24, 1980.

☆ ☆ ☆

"STAR TREK" FIRST BROADCAST: ANNIVERSARY. Sept 8. The first of 79 episodes of the TV series "Star Trek" was aired on the NBC network on Sept 8, 1966. Although the science fiction show set in the future only lasted a few seasons, it has remained enormously popular through syndication reruns. It has been given new life through six motion pictures, a cartoon TV series and the very popular TV series "Star Trek: The Next Generation" and "Star Trek: Deep Space Nine." It has consistently ranked among the biggest titles in the motion picture, television, home video and licensing divisions of Paramount Pictures.

"TARZAN" TV PREMIERE: ANNIVERSARY. Sept 8, 1966. This hour adventure series was based on Edgar Rice Burroughs' character, who appeared for the first time on TV. Tarzan, an English lord who preferred the jungle, was played by Ron Ely. Manuel Padilla, Jr was Jai, a jungle orphan; Alan Caillou was Jason Flood, Jai's tutor; and Rockne Tarkington was Rao, a veterinarian. There was no Jane.

"THAT GIRL" TV PREMIERE: ANNIVERSARY. Sept 8, 1966. "That Girl" was a half-hour sitcom starring Marlo Thomas as Ann Marie, an independent aspiring actress in New York City. Ted Bessell also starred as her boyfriend Don Hollinger; they were finally engaged in 1970. Also featured were Lew Parker, Rosemary DeCamp and Bonnie Scott. Well-known performers who appeared on the show include Dabney Coleman, George Carlin and Bernie Kopell.

BIRTHDAYS TODAY

Sid Caesar, 76, comedian, actor ("Your Show of Shows"), born Yonkers, NY, Sept 8, 1922.

Alan Feinstein, 57, actor ("Edge of Night," "Love of Life," "Search for Tomorrow"), born New York, NY, Sept 8, 1941.

Wendell Hampton Ford, 74, US Senator (D, Kentucky), born Davies County, KY, Sept 8, 1924.

Marilyn (Williamson) Mims, 44, opera singer, born Collins, MS, Sept 8, 1954.

Heather Thomas, 41, actress (Jody Banks on "The Fall Guy"), born Greenwich, CT, Sept 8, 1957.

Henry Thomas, 27, actor (*E.T. The Extra Terrestrial, Legends of the Fall*), born San Antonio, TX, Sept 8, 1971.

Rogatien (Rogie) Vachon, 53, hockey executive and former player, born Palmarolle, Quebec, Canada, Sept 8, 1945.

SEPTEMBER 9 — WEDNESDAY

Day 252 — 113 Remaining

BATTLE OF MARATHON: ANNIVERSARY. Sept 9. On the day of the ninth month's full moon in the year 490 BC, the numerically superior invading army of Persia was met and defeated on the Plain of Marathon by the Athenian army, led by Miltiades. More than 6,000 men died in the day's battle which drove the Persians to the sea and the mound of earth covering the dead is still visible at the site. See also: "Days of Marathon: Anniversary" (Sept 2) for the legendary running of Phidippides and the origin of the marathon race.

BONZA BOTTLER DAY™. Sept 9. To celebrate when the number of the day is the same as the number of the month. Bonza Bottler Day™ is an excuse to have a party at least once a month. For more information, see Jan 1. For info: Gail M. Berger, 109 Matthew Ave, Poca, WV 25159. Phone: (304) 776-7746. Email: gberger5@aol.com.

BULGARIA: SOCIALIST REVOLUTION ANNIVERSARY. Sept 9. National holiday in Bulgaria.

CALIFORNIA: ADMISSION DAY. Sept 9. Became 31st state on this day in 1850.

CANADA: THE MASTERS. Sept 9–13. Spruce Meadows, Calgary, Alta. World-class show jumping competition, along with Equi-Fair, Breeds for the World and Festival of Nations. Feature events are the Bank of Montreal Nations' Cup and the $725,000 du Maurier International, the world's most prestigious Grand Prix. Est attendance: 150,000. For info: Spruce Meadows, RR #9, Calgary, AB, Canada T2J 5G5. Phone: (403) 974-4200. Fax: (403) 974-4270. Email: smeadows@telusplanet.net.
WWW: http://www.sprucemeadows.com

DEFEAT OF JESSE JAMES DAYS. Sept 9–13. Northfield, MN. Bank raid reenactment, 5K and 15K runs, arts, crafts, bike race, parade and professional rodeo. Est attendance: 150,000. For info: Kathy Feldbrugge, Exec VP, Northfield Chamber of Commerce, Promotion Dept, PO Box 198, Northfield, MN 55057. Phone: (507) 645-5604. Fax: (507) 663-7782.

DO IT! DAY (aka FIGHT PROCRASTINATION DAY). Sept 9. Organizationally challenged? Today is your day. No excuses—Do It! Annually, the first Wednesday after Labor Day. For info: Ethel M. Cook, Productivity Consultant, 4 Hilda Rd, Bedford, MA 01730. Phone: (617) 275-2326. Fax: (617) 275-7136. Email: ethelcook@aol.com.

FARMERS AND THRESHERMENS JUBILEE. Sept 9–13. New Centerville, PA. Many steam engines, threshing demonstrations using man power, horses and steam, quilt show, crafts, truck and tractor pulls. Live entertainment, good food. For info: Clark Brocht, Farmers & Threshermens Jubilee, 1428 Casselman Rd, Rockwood, PA 15557. Phone: (814) 926-3142.

"FAT ALBERT AND THE COSBY KIDS" TV PREMIERE: ANNIVERSARY. Sept 9, 1972. This cartoon series was hosted by Bill Cosby, with characters based on his childhood friends in Philadelphia. Its central characters—Fat Albert, Weird Harold, Mush Mouth and Donald—were weird-looking but very human. The show sent messages of tolerance and harmony. In 1979 the show was renamed "The New Fat Albert Show."

KOREA, DEMOCRATIC PEOPLE'S REPUBLIC OF: NATIONAL DAY. Sept 9. National holiday in the Democratic People's Republic of [North] Korea.

LUXEMBOURG: ANNIVERSARY LIBERATION CEREMONY. Sept 9. Petange. Commemoration of liberation of Grand-Duchy by the Allied forces in 1944. Ceremony at monument of the American soldier.

MAO TSE-TUNG: DEATH ANNIVERSARY. Sept 9. People's Republic of China pays tribute to memory of late Chinese leader, who died on Sept 9, 1976. Memorial Hall, where his flag-draped body lies encased in crystal, was opened at Tiananmen Square in Beijing on the first anniversary of his death.

OUTRIGGER HOTELS ANNUAL HAWAIIAN OCEAN-FEST. Sept 9–13. Oahu, HI. A variety of events celebrating Hawaii's ocean sports. The Hawaiian International Ocean Challenge Sept 5–6, competition between six-person teams of the world's best lifeguards in kayak, surf rescue, paddleboard, and outrigger canoe. Ocean Challenge includes a "World Team" selected from individual competition at the Walmea Open Ocean Challenge Sept 9; Outrigger's Waikiki Kings Race held Sept 13, an ocean ironman event with four continuous disciplines—run, kayak, swim, and paddleboard. Est attendance: 10,000. For info: Pauahi Tower, Event Marketing, 1001 Bishop St, Ste 880, Honolulu, HI 96813. Phone: (808) 521-4322. Fax: (808) 538-0314. Email: dey@emisport.com. WWW: http://www.emisport.com

"RHODA" TV PREMIERE: ANNIVERSARY. Sept 9, 1974. This spinoff from "The Mary Tyler Moore Show" starred Valerie Harper as Rhoda Morgenstern, who returns to New York, finds a job and gets married (she also gets separated and divorced). Other characters included her husband Joe Gerard (David Groh), her sister Brenda (Julie Kavner), her mother Ida (Nancy Walker), her father Martin (Harold Gould) and Carlton, the heard-but-not-seen doorman (Lorenzo Music). Other regulars included Richard Masur, Wes Stern, Barbara Sharma, Scoey Mitchell, Ron Silver, Anne Meara, Michael DeLano and Kenneth McMillan.

SANDERS, COLONEL HARLAND DAVID: BIRTH ANNIVERSARY. Sept 9. Founder of Kentucky Fried Chicken, born near Henryville, IN, Sept 9, 1890. Died Dec 16, 1980.

TAJIKISTAN: INDEPENDENCE DAY. Sept 9. National holiday.

"WELCOME BACK, KOTTER" TV PREMIERE: ANNIVERSARY. Sept 9, 1975. In this half-hour sitcom, Gabe Kotter (Gabriel Kaplan) returns to James Buchanan High School, his alma mater, to teach the "sweathogs," a group of hopeless underachievers. Other featured cast members included Marcia Strassman, John Travolta, Robert Hegyes, Ron Palillo, Lawrence Hilton-Jacobs, John Sylvester White and James Wood. Later in the series, Julie Kotter had twins, and two new sweathogs were added, played by Melonie Haller and Stephen Shortridge. The theme song, "Welcome Back," was sung by John Sebastian.

WILLIAM, THE CONQUEROR: DEATH ANNIVERSARY. Sept 9, 1087. Anniversary of the death of William I, The Conqueror, King of England and Duke of Normandy, whose image is portrayed in the Bayeux Tapestry. Victorious over Harold at the Battle of Hastings (the Norman Conquest) in 1066, William was crowned King of England at Westminster Abbey on Christmas Day of that year. Later, at age 60, while waging war in France, William met his death at Rouen, on Sept 9, 1087.

WORLD WAR II: BATTLE OF SALERNO: 55th ANNIVERSARY. Sept 9–16, 1943. US General Mark Clark's Fifth Army made an amphibious assault on Salerno, Italy (Operation Avalanche), at 3:30 AM. The British 1st Airborne Division seized the southern Italian port of Taranto (Operation Slapstick) without opposition. Initial gains along the western coast of Italy were checked by strong German forces by Sept 12. In some places, the Allied forces were pushed back to within two miles of the coast. On Sept 15, US 82nd Airborne and British 7th Armoured counter-attacked and on Sept 16, units of the American 5th Army and the British 8th Army joined up near Vallo di Lucania.

BIRTHDAYS TODAY

Benjamin Roy ("BJ") Armstrong, 31, basketball player, born Detroit, MI, Sept 9, 1967.

Hugh Grant, 38, actor (*Impromptu, Sense and Sensibility, Four Weddings and a Funeral*), born London, England, Sept 9, 1960.

Jane Greer, 74, actress (*Out of the Past, Prisoner of Zenda, Against All Odds*), born Washington, DC, Sept 9, 1924.

Michael Keaton (Michael Douglas), 47, actor ("Report to Murphy," *Batman, The Dream Team*), born Pittsburgh, PA, Sept 9, 1951.

Daniel Lewis (Dan) Majerle, 33, basketball player, born Traverse City, MI, Sept 9, 1965.

Kristy McNichol, 36, actress ("Family" [Emmy Awards: 1977, 1979], "Empty Nest," *Little Darlings, Two Moon Junction*), born Los Angeles, CA, Sept 9, 1962.

Sylvia Miles, 64, actress (*Midnight Cowboy, Farewell My Lovely, She-Devil*), born New York, NY, Sept 9, 1934.

Billy Preston, 52, musician, songwriter, singer ("Will It Go Round in Circles," "Nothing From Nothing"), born Houston, TX, Sept 9, 1946.

Cliff Robertson, 73, actor ("Falcon Crest," *Brainstorm, Charly, PT-109*), born La Jolla, CA, Sept 9, 1925.

Joseph Robert (Joe) Theisman, 49, sportscaster, Pro Football Hall of Fame quarterback, born New Brunswick, NJ, Sept 9, 1949.

Tom Wopat, 47, actor ("The Dukes of Hazzard," "Cybill") born Lodi, WI, Sept 9, 1951.

SEPTEMBER 10 — THURSDAY

Day 253 — 112 Remaining

ANVIL MOUNTAIN 59 MINUTE 37 SECOND CHALLENGE. Sept 10. Nome, AK. A running event that starts at the base of Anvil Mountain, where runners must run 834 ft up the face of the mountain and return in less than 59 minutes and 37 seconds or be disqualified from the competition. Trophies awarded for first–third finishers, first woman finisher and first finisher 16 years of age and under. Record time is 25 minutes 37 seconds. Annually, the second Thursday in September. Est attendance: 1,000. For info: Rasmussen's Music Mart, PO Box 2, Nome, AK 99762-0002. Phone: (907) 443-2798 or (907) 443-2919. Fax: (907) 443-5777.

BELGIUM: FLANDERS FESTIVAL. Sept 10–Oct 31. Brussels, Belgium. Ancient music, classical music and choral music. For info: Sophie Cocquyt, Ravensteinstraat 60, Brussels, Belgium B-1000. Phone: (32) (0) 2-548-95-95. Fax: (32) (0) 2-548-95-90.

BELIZE: SAINT GEORGE'S CAYE DAY. Sept 10. Public holiday celebrated in honor of the battle between the European Baymen Settlers and the Spaniards for the territory of Belize.

BRAXTON, CARTER: BIRTH ANNIVERSARY. Sept 10. American revolutionary statesman and signer of the Declaration of Independence. Born on Sept 10, 1736, at Newington, VA. Died on Oct 10, 1797, at Richmond, VA.

September 1998

S	M	T	W	T	F	S
		1	2	3	4	5
6	7	8	9	10	11	12
13	14	15	16	17	18	19
20	21	22	23	24	25	26
27	28	29	30			

CANADA: TORONTO INTERNATIONAL FILM FESTIVAL. Sept 10–19. Toronto, Ont. A 10-day festival of contemporary Canadian and international cinema at various downtown theatres. Call or write for info or to be put on mailing list. Est attendance: 250,000. For info: Toronto Intl Film Festival, 2 Carlton St, Ste 1600, Toronto, Ont, Canada M5B 1J3. Phone: (416) 967-7371. Fax: (416) 967-9477. Email: tiffg@torfilmfest.ca. WWW: http://www.bell.ca/filmfest

CHILI AND BLUEGRASS FESTIVAL. Sept 10–12. Tulsa, OK. Free concerts from the best in bluegrass and country music and tantalizing chili during the International Chili Society Mid-America Regional Chili Cookoff. Open car show, children's Kiddie Korral and 5K "Pepper Run" (run event). Annually, Thursday, Friday and Saturday following Labor Day. Est attendance: 65,000. For info: Dell Davis, Fest Dir, Chili and Bluegrass Festival, 320 S Boston Ave, Ste 101, Tulsa, OK 74103. Phone: (918) 583-2617. Fax: (918) 587-7721.

DANVILLE HARVEST JUBILEE. Sept 10–12. Auctioneers Park, Danville, VA. A celebration of the harvest season with arts, crafts, entertainment, contests, Home and Garden show, Shrimp Fest, cheerleading jamboree, children's activity area, 5K run, clogging contest, model train exhibits, special displays by Science Museum of VA. Est attendance: 40,000. For info: Tish Lindsey, Danville Harvest Jubilee, Box 3300, Danville, VA 24543-3300. Phone: (804) 799-5200. Fax: (804) 799-6562. Email: parksrec@ci.danville.va.us.

ENGLAND: CHELSEA ANTIQUES FAIR. Sept 10–20. Chelsea Old Town Hall, King's Rd, London. Antiques fair with a wide range of pre-1830 furniture and other items with a pre-1860 dateline for sale. Est attendance: 9,000. For info: Penman Antiques Fair, PO Box 114, Haywards Heath, West Sussex, England RH16 2YU. Phone: (44) (144) 448-2514. Fax: (44) (144) 448-3412.

FUNK, ISAAC KAUFFMAN: BIRTH ANNIVERSARY. Sept 10. American publisher born at Clifton, OH, Sept 10, 1839. Partner in Funk and Wagnalls. Died at Montclair, NJ, Apr 4, 1912.

"GENTLE BEN" TV PREMIERE: ANNIVERSARY. Sept 10, 1967. This show was about the adventures of a boy, Mark Wedloe (Clint Howard) and his pet bear, Ben (Bruno). Also featured were Dennis Weaver as his father Tom, a game warden; Beth Brickell as his mother Ellen; Jack Worley as Tom's friend Spencer; and Angelo Rutherford as his friend Willie. It was filmed on location in Florida.

GREAT PEANUT TOUR. Sept 10–13. Skippers, VA. Assorted bicycle rides from 13 to 125 miles. Special peanut tour ride to examine peanuts growing, method of harvesting and a sampling of more than 40 peanut goodies. Unique water stops, nature walks, music, campfires with marshmallow roast. Annually, the weekend following Labor Day. Est attendance: 1,500. For info: Robert C. Wrenn, Emporia Bicycle Club, PO Box 668, Emporia, VA 23847. Phone: (804) 348-4215. Fax: (804) 348-4020.

"GUNSMOKE" TV PREMIERE: ANNIVERSARY. Sept 10, 1955. "Gunsmoke" was TV's longest-running western, moving from the radio to TV. John Wayne turned down the role of Marshall Matt Dillon but recommended James Arness, who got the role. Other regulars included Amanda Blake as Kitty Russell, saloon-owner; Dennis Weaver as Chester B. Goode, Dillon's deputy; and Milburn Stone as Doc Adams. In 1962, a fifth character was added—the "rugged male." Burt Reynolds played Quint Asper, followed by Roger Ewing as Thad Greenwood, and Buck Taylor as Newly O'Brian. In 1964, Ken Curtis was added as funnyman Festus Haggen, the new deputy. "Gunsmoke" was incredibly popular, both as a half-hour and hour-long show, as the number-one rated series for four seasons, and a top ten hit for six seasons.

KASS KOUNTY KING KORN KARNIVAL AND MUD DRAGS. Sept 10–13. Plattsmouth, NE. Krowning of a King and Queen of Kornland, three large parades. Free street entertainment—fire department Wall of Water, flower show, Korn Palace, museum exhibits, Hauf Brau Garten, Ugly Pickup Contest, Cow Chip Bingo, fun run, scarecrow contest, flea market, go cart, two-wheel bicycle race, Mud Drag races on Sunday and much more. Annually, the second weekend in September. Est attendance: 20,000. For info: Patricia Baburek, Coord, 141 S 3rd St, PO Box 40, Plattsmouth, NE 68048. Phone: (402) 296-4155. Fax: (402) 296-4082.

"KIDS ARE PEOPLE TOO" TV PREMIERE: 20th ANNIVERSARY. Sept 10, 1978. This ABC series was a Sunday morning magazine show for kids. Hosts included Bob McAllister, Michael Young and Randy Hamilton.

LONGS PEAK SCOTTISH HIGHLAND FESTIVAL. Sept 10–13. Estes Park, CO. Scottish-Irish celebration day with pipe bands, highland and Irish dancing, athletic championships and gathering of the clans. Featuring the US/International Invitational Championship Jousting, Professional Scottish Athletics, pipe bands and darts. Annually, the first weekend after Labor Day. Est attendance: 30,000. For info: Longs Peak Scottish Highland Festival Inc, Box 1820, Estes Park, CO 80517. Phone: (970) 586-6308. Fax: (970) 586-6308. Email: scotfest@frii.com. WWW: http://www.frii.com/~scotfest

MARION POPCORN FESTIVAL. Sept 10–12. Marion, OH. Performances by nationally known entertainers every evening; parade, athletic competition, arts and crafts. 11 AM to midnight daily. Annually, the Thursday, Friday and Saturday after Labor Day. Est attendance: 350,000. For info: Marion Popcorn Festival, PO Box 1101, Marion, OH 43301-1101. Phone: (614) 387-3378.

NEWPORT INTERNATIONAL BOAT SHOW. Sept 10–13. Newport, RI. More than 250 new sail and power boats in the water and displays of accessories, equipment and services. New product information, free sail/power boat rides in Newport harbor. Est attendance: 30,000. For info: Newport Exhibition Group, PO Box 698, 366 Thames St, Johnston, RI 02919. Phone: (401) 846-1115. WWW: http://www.newportboatshow.com

NORTH HAVEN FAIR. Sept 10–13. North Haven Fairgrounds, North Haven, CT. Large agricultural fair featuring animal and agricultural exhibits, entertainment, food and rides. For info: Greater New Haven Conv & Visitors Bureau, One Long Wharf Dr, New Haven, CT 06511. Phone: (203) 777-8550 or (800) 332-STAY. Fax: (203) 782-7755.

"THE ROAD RUNNER SHOW" TV PREMIERE: ANNIVERSARY. Sept 10, 1966. Meep! Meep! The Road Runner, a clever bird who always outwitted Wile E. Coyote and his Acme schemes, had his own cartoon series for three seasons. Other times, this character was on a show with Bugs Bunny called "The Bugs Bunny/Road Runner Hour."

ROCHESTER FAIR. Sept 10–20. Rochester, NH. Agricultural Fair. Est attendance: 170,000. For info: Rochester Fair Assn, 72 Lafayette St, Rochester, NH 03867. Phone: (603) 332-6585. Fax: (603) 332-1896.

SEW BE IT! DAY. Sept 10. Celebrating the anniversary of the patent of the sewing machine on Sept 10, 1846. Recognizing that when a hem may loosen or a button pops off, Sew Be It! For info: Adrienne Sioux Koopersmith, 1437 W Rosemont, #1W, Chicago, IL 60660-1319. Phone: (773) 743-5341. Fax: (773) 743-5395. Email: kooper@interaccess.com.

SWAP IDEAS DAY. Sept 10. To encourage people to explore ways in which their ideas can be put to work for the benefit of humanity, and to encourage development of incentives that will encourage use of creative imagination. For info: Robert L. Birch, Publicity Chair, Puns Corps, Box 2364, Falls Church, VA 22042-0364. Phone: (703) 533-3668.

WERFEL, FRANZ: BIRTH ANNIVERSARY. Sept 10. Austrian author, born at Prague, Czechoslovakia, on Sept 10, 1890. Died at Hollywood, CA, Aug 26, 1945.

WILLIAMSBURG OLD-FASHIONED TRADING DAYS. Sept 10–12. Courthouse Square, Williamsburg, KY. Arts and crafts, bluegrass and gospel singing, 8K run, antique car show and more. Annually, the first Thursday, Friday and Saturday after Labor Day. Est attendance: 35,000. For info: Theresa Estes, Coord, 522 Main St, Williamsburg, KY 40769. Phone: (606) 549-2285. Fax: (606) 549-5565.

WOLLSTONECRAFT, MARY: DEATH ANNIVERSARY. Sept 10, 1797. Writer and advocate of equality for women, Mary Wollstonecraft died at age 38 at London 11 days after giving birth to her second daughter (Mary Wollstonecraft Shelley, the author of *Frankenstein*). Wollstonecraft was born Apr 27, 1759, at London. Rebelling against her father, she left home at age 18 and served as a lady's companion, opened a school and worked as a governess before returning to London to write for publisher Joseph Johnson. Beginning with *Thoughts on the Education of Daughters* in 1787, Wollstonecraft attracted notice as a writer in favor of women's rights. Her *A Vindication of the Rights of Woman* (1792) argued that women should be given an education that would allow them to gain economic independence.

BIRTHDAYS TODAY

Jose Feliciano, 53, singer, musician ("Light My Fire," "Hi-Heel Sneakers"), born Larez, Puerto Rico, Sept 10, 1945.

Colin Firth, 38, actor (*Apartment Zero, Valmont*, "Pride and Prejudice"), born Grayshott, Hampshire, England, Sept 10, 1960.

Judy Geeson, 50, actress (*To Sir with Love, The Eagle Has Landed*), born Arundel, Sussex, England, Sept 10, 1948.

Amy Irving, 45, actress (*Carrie, Honeysuckle Rose*; singing voice of Jessica Rabbit), born Palo Alto, CA, Sept 10, 1953.

Charles Bishop Kuralt, 64, journalist (retired from "Sunday Morning"), born Wilmington, NC, Sept 10, 1934. Died July 4, 1997.

Karl Lagerfeld, 60, fashion designer, born Hamburg, Germany, Sept 10, 1938.

Arnold Daniel Palmer, 69, golfer, born Latrobe, PA, Sept 10, 1929.

Yma Sumac, 70, singer, born Ichocan, Peru, Sept 10, 1928.

Jennifer Tilly, 40, actress (*Johnny Be Good, Made in America*), born Texada, Canada, Sept 10, 1958.

Robert Wise, 84, filmmaker (*The Curse of the Cat People, The Sound of Music*), born Winchester, IN, Sept 10, 1914.

September 1998

S	M	T	W	T	F	S
		1	2	3	4	5
6	7	8	9	10	11	12
13	14	15	16	17	18	19
20	21	22	23	24	25	26
27	28	29	30			

SEPTEMBER 11 — FRIDAY

Day 254 — 111 Remaining

AFRMA FANCY RAT AND MOUSE DISPLAY. Sept 11–27. LA Fair, Pomona, CA. American Fancy Rat and Mouse Association show exhibits rats and mice of "fancy" species that make good pets. For info: AFRMA, 9230 64th St, Riverside, CA 92509-5924. Phone: (909) 685-2350. Fax: (818) 592-6319. Email: craigr@afrma.org. WWW: http://www.afrma.org/afrma

ANNAPOLIS CONVENTION: ANNIVERSARY. Sept 11–14. Twelve delegates from New York, New Jersey, Delaware, Pennsylvania and Virginia met at Annapolis, MD, Sept 11–14, 1786, to discuss commercial matters of mutual interest. The delegates voted, on Sept 14, to adopt a resolution prepared by Alexander Hamilton asking all states to send representatives to a convention at Philadelphia, PA, in May 1787 "to render the constitution of the Federal Government adequate to the exigencies of the Union."

BALD IS BEAUTIFUL CONVENTION. Sept 11–13. Morehead City, NC. To cultivate a sense of pride for all bald-headed men (folks) everywhere and eliminate the vanity associated with the loss of one's hair. As seen on national television; Bald is Beautiful Contests, family events. Annually, the second weekend in September. Est attendance: 200. For info: John T. Capps III, Founder, Bald Headed Men of America, 102 Bald Dr, Morehead City, NC 28557. Phone: (919) 726-1855. Fax: (919) 726-6061. Email: jcapps4102@aol.com.

CANADA: BRACEBRIDGE FALL FAIR AND HORSE SHOW. Sept 11–13. James D. Lang Activity Park, Bracebridge, Ontario. Flower show, produce, poultry, livestock, homecrafts, horsepull and culinary arts. Light and heavy horse show. For info: Bracebridge Chamber of Commerce, 1-1 Manitoba, Bracebridge, Ont, Canada P1L1S4. Phone: (705) 645-8121. Fax: (705) 645-7542.

CANADA: TRAIL OF '98 INTERNATIONAL ROAD RELAY. Sept 11–12. Whitehorse, Yukon. Mixed, men, ladies and masters categories with teams consisting of six to ten members race the 176 km (110 mi) from tidewater in Skagway, Alaska, to Whitehorse. Est attendance: 1,500. For info: Sport Yukon, 4061 4th Ave, Whitehorse, Yukon, Canada Y1A 1H1. Phone: (403) 668-4236. Fax: (403) 667-4237.

"THE CAROL BURNETT SHOW" TV PREMIERE: ANNIVERSARY. Sept 11, 1967. This popular comedy/variety show starred comedienne Carol Burnett, who started the show by taking questions from the audience and ended with an ear tug. Sketches and spoofs included recurring characters like "The Family" (later to be spun off as "Mama's Family") and "As the Stomach Turns." Talented regular cast members included Harvey Korman, Lyle Waggoner and Vicki Lawrence. Later, Tim Conway joined the cast. Dick Van Dyke briefly joined after Korman left in 1977.

CZECH REPUBLIC: PRAGUE AUTUMN INTERNATIONAL MUSIC FESTIVAL. Sept 11–27. Symphonic and chamber orchestras, instrumental concerts, cantatas, oratoria and recitals. For info: Prague Autumn International Music Festival, 130 00 - CZ, Prague 3, Pribenicka 20, Czech Republic. Phone: (42) (2) 627 87 40. Fax: (42) (2) 627 86 42.

DANK BAVARIAN OKTOBERFEST. Sept 11–13. IC Light Amphitheatre, Pittsburgh, PA. Celebrate the German heritage with a frothy mug of ale. Enjoy a bratwurst sandwich and stomp your feet with Bavarian dancers. Germany comes alive with culture, music and food. For info: Greater Pittsburgh Conv & Visitors Bureau, Four Gateway Center, Pittsburgh, PA 15222-1259. Phone: (412) 837-6800 or (800) 359-0758. Fax: (412) 644-5512.

DIAMOND GEM CITY DAYS AND PRAIRIE DAY. Sept 11–12. Diamond, MO. A host of activities are planned in the city of Diamond on Friday and Saturday. GEM City events include a craft fair, antique show, old-fashioned games, musical entertainment and much more. On Saturday, George Washington Carver National Monument is joining with GEM City Days for the park's annual Prairie Day event. Come take a walk back into history and celebrate life on the Missouri Prairie during the 1860s and 1870s. There will be prairie walks, wagon rides, wood carving, basket weaving, candle-making, Dutch oven cooking, spinning, weaving and numerous other activities. Est attendance: 1,300. For info: George Washington Carver Natl Monument, 5646 Carver Rd, Diamond, MO 64840. Phone: (417) 325-4151. Fax: (417) 325-4231.

FESTIVAL OF THE VINE. Sept 11–13. Geneva, IL. Autumn harvest is celebrated with a festival featuring food, music, wine tasting, craft show and antique carriage rides. Annually, the second weekend in September. For info: Geneva Chamber of Commerce, 8 South Third St, PO Box 481, Geneva, IL 60134. Phone: (630) 232-6060. Fax: (630) 232-6083.

GOAT DAYS. Sept 11–13. USA Stadium, Millington, TN. Goat contests with large cash prizes and trophies, children's area, camping, fishing, goat races, dancing, music, food, rodeo, crafts, chili and Dutch oven cook-offs and bluegrass competition. Annually, the second weekend in September. Est attendance: 12,000. For info: Goat Days Intl, 4880 Navy Rd, Millington, TN 38053. Phone: (901) 872-4559. Fax: (901) 872-7700.

GREEK FESTIVAL. Sept 11–13. Hellenic Cultural Center, Salt Lake City, UT. An annual showcase of Greek culture and heritage. Encompasses church tours, tour of Hellenic Museum, dancing by Greek youth groups and a la carte food and pastries with a boutique and gourmet shop featured. Annually, the first weekend after Labor Day. Est attendance: 30,000. For info: William (Bill) Kandas, Festival Chair, Greek Orthodox Community of Salt Lake City, 279 S 300 West, Salt Lake City, UT 84101.

HILLTOP FESTIVAL. Sept 11–13. Huntington Museum of Art, Huntington, WV. Bookfair, arts and crafts and demonstrations, children's activities, popular performing groups and food booths. Annually, first weekend after Labor Day. Est attendance: 10,000. For info: Huntington Museum of Art, 2033 McCoy Rd, Huntington, WV 25701. Phone: (304) 529-2701. Fax: (304) 529-7447.

HONEY, I WANT TO START MY OWN BUSINESS DAY. Sept 11. Take the plunge! With the support and encouragement of your spouse, take the first step toward fulfilling your entrepreneurial dream today. Join the millions of Americans who are breaking free from the tedium of corporate life and choosing the unique challenges and benefits of self-employment. Annually, the first Friday after Labor Day. For info: Azriela Jaffe, Anchored Dreams, PO Box 209, Bausman, PA 17504. Phone: (717) 872-1890. Fax: (717) 872-0963. Email: azjaffe@aol.com. WWW: http://isquare.com/crlink.htm

HOSS'S KEYSTONE COUNTRY FESTIVAL. Sept 11–13. Altoona, PA. More than 30 arts and crafts vendors, an ethnic food village. Admission includes Lakemont Park's amusement rides. For info: Allegheny Mountains Conv & Visitors Bureau, Logan Valley Mall, Rt 220 & Goods Lane, Altoona, PA 16602. Phone: (814) 943-4183 or (800) 84-ALTOONA.

INDIAN HERITAGE FESTIVAL AND POWWOW. Sept 11–12. Martinsville, VA. 14th annual traditional powwow, crafts, food and dancing. Annually, the Friday and Saturday after Labor Day. Est attendance: 5,000. For info: Carolyn Seay, Virginia Museum of Natural History, 1001 Douglas Ave, Martinsville, VA 24112. Phone: (540) 666-8600. Fax: (540) 632-6487. Email: 75143.3166@compuserve.com. WWW: http://www.vmnh.com

KANSAS STATE FAIR. Sept 11–20. Hutchinson, KS. Commercial and competitive exhibits, entertainment, carnival, car racing and other special attractions. Annually, beginning the first Friday after Labor Day. Est attendance: 335,000. For info: Robert A. Gottschalk, Gen Mgr, Kansas State Fair, 2000 N Poplar, Hutchinson, KS 67502. Phone: (316) 669-3600.

LAWRENCE, DAVID HERBERT: BIRTH ANNIVERSARY. Sept 11. English novelist, author of *Lady Chatterley's Lover.* Born at Eastwood, Nottinghamshire, England, Sept 11, 1885. Died on Mar 2, 1930.

LIGONIER HIGHLAND GAMES. Sept 11–13. Ligonier, PA. Bagpipe bands on parade, Highland dancers and athletes in daylong performances. Clan gatherings, dog show. Offers imported woolens, china, jewelry, records and foods. Mail SASE for schedule of events. For info: David L. Peet, Ligonier Highland Games, PO Box 884, Bethel Park, PA 15102-0884. Phone: (412) 851-9900.

LIND, JENNY: US PREMIERE: ANNIVERSARY. Sept 11. Jenny Lind, the "Swedish Nightingale," gave her first American performance in the Castle Garden Theatre, New York, NY, on this day in 1850.

"LITTLE HOUSE ON THE PRAIRIE" TV PREMIERE: ANNIVERSARY. Sept 11, 1974. This hour-long family drama was based on the books by Laura Ingalls Wilder. It focused on the Ingalls family and their neighbors living in Walnut Grove, MN: Michael Landon as Charles (Pa); Karen Grassle as Caroline (Ma); Melissa Sue Anderson as daughter Mary; Melissa Gilbert as daughter Laura, from whose point of view the stories were told; Lindsay and Sidney Greenbush as daughter Carrie; Wendi and Brenda Turnbeaugh as daughter Grace. Others featured were: Victor French, Bonnie Bartlett, Richard Bull, Katherine MacGregor, Jonathan Gilbert, Alison Arngrim, Charlotte Stewart, Dabbs Greer, Merlin Olsen, Patrick Laborteaux. The series spent one season in Winoka, Dakota, 1978-79. In its last season (1982), the show's name was changed to "Little House: A New Beginning," Landon appeared less often and the show centered around Laura and her husband.

MARCOS, FERDINAND EDRALIN: BIRTH ANNIVERSARY. Sept 11, 1917. Former ruler of the Philippines, born at Sarrat, Philippines. Ferdinand Marcos served as head of state from 1966 until his ouster in 1986. His authoritarian regime came under criticism for widespread corruption and suppression of democratic processes. Marcos imposed martial law in 1972 beginning a period when he wrote the constitution and laws to consolidate his power. His later years in office were marred by corruption and economic turmoil. After the assassination of Benigno Aquino, Jr, in 1983, anti-government protests increased and Marcos called for a new election in 1986, hoping to reassert his mandate. Although he defeated Corazon Aquino in the election, it was widely asserted he did so through massive vote fraud, leading to a greater decline in support at home, and Corazon Aquino became the new president of the Philippines. Marcos's health continued to decline in exile and he died on Sept 28, 1989, at Honolulu, HI.

MARIGOLD FESTIVAL. Sept 11–13. Pekin, IL. Parade, flower show, arts, crafts, paddle boat rides, golf, cardboard boat races, Civil War reenactment, carnival, three-on-three basketball, Festive Foods, "Saturday Night Event" and other family-oriented activities. Est attendance: 100,000. For info: Chamber of Commerce, PO Box 636, Pekin, IL 61555-0636. Phone: (309) 346-2106. Fax: (309) 346-2104.

MICHIGAN WINE AND HARVEST FESTIVAL. Sept 11–13. Kalamazoo and Paw Paw, MI. An annual celebration with grape stomping, winery tours, arts and crafts, carnival rides, champagne races, a midway and a grand parade (Paw Paw). Est attendance: 80,000. For info: Michigan Wine and Harvest Festival, Inc, 128 N Kalamazoo Mall, Kalamazoo, MI 49007. Phone: (616) 657-5395 or (616) 381-4003 or (800) 530-9192. Fax: (616) 343-0430.

MOUNTAIN CRAFT DAYS. Sept 11–13. Somerset, PA. Southwestern Pennsylvania's premier traditional craft festival along the Somerset Historical Center's trails. Entertainment, food, trades and crafts. For info: Mark Ware, Mountain Craft Days, 10649 Somerset Pike, Somerset, PA 15501. Phone: (814) 445-6077.

MOUNTAINEER FOLK FESTIVAL. Sept 11–13. Fall Creek Falls State Park, Pikeville, TN. Handmade crafts, traditional mountain music and pioneer skills demonstrations are just part of the fun. Country cooking, bluegrass music and different exhibits round out the jam-packed schedule. Sponsored by Friends of Fall Creek Falls State Park. Est attendance: 8,000. For info: Fall Creek Falls State Park, Betty Dunn Nature Center, Rte 3, Pikeville, TN 37367. Phone: (423) 881-5708. Fax: (423) 881-5103.

911 DAY. Sept 11. This 11th day of the ninth month is set aside to honor 911 emergency phone operators and the emergency medical technicians who respond to their calls. For more info, send $2 to cover the cost of postage and photocopying. For info: Adrienne Sioux Koopersmith, 1437 W Rosemont, #1W, Chicago, IL 60660-1319. Phone: (773) 743-5341. Fax: (773) 743-5395. Email: kooper@interaccess.com.

NO NEWS IS GOOD NEWS DAY. Sept 11. Don't read, listen to or watch the news today and you'll feel better tonight. [© 1997 by WPL] For info: Tom and Ruth Roy, Wellness Permission League, PO Box 662, Mt Gretna, PA 17064-0662. Phone: (500) 437-5104 or (717) 964-1308. Fax: (717) 964-1335.

NORDICFEST. Sept 11–13. Libby, MT. Scandinavian festival with food booths, dinners, cultural exhibits, craft shows, quilt show, art show, parade, folk dance performances, big name performances and the international Fjord horse show. Est attendance: 30,000. For info: Libby Nordicfest, Inc, Box 791, Libby, MT 59923. Phone: (800) 785-6541. WWW: http://www.libby.org

NORWALK SEAPORT OYSTER FESTIVAL. Sept 11–13. Norwalk, CT. Huge festival with vintage ships on display, 225 juried crafters, main stage with entertainment, oyster shucking and slurping contests and Kids Coves (children's entertainment). Annually, the weekend following Labor Day. Est attendance: 95,000. For info: Norwalk Seaport Assn, 132 Water St, Norwalk, CT 06854. Phone: (203) 838-9444. Fax: (203) 855-1017.

O HENRY (WILLIAM S. PORTER): BIRTH ANNIVERSARY. Sept 11, 1862. William Sydney Porter, American author, who wrote under the pen name O Henry. Best known for his short stories, including "Gift of the Magi." Born at Greensboro, NC; died at New York, NY, June 5, 1910.

September 1998

S	M	T	W	T	F	S
		1	2	3	4	5
6	7	8	9	10	11	12
13	14	15	16	17	18	19
20	21	22	23	24	25	26
27	28	29	30			

OHIO RIVER STERNWHEEL FESTIVAL. Sept 11–13. Ohio River Levee, Marietta, OH. A three-day riverfront extravaganza. More than two dozen sternwheelers line the Ohio River shore in Marietta, OH. Continuous musical entertainment for all ages, food concessions, queen coronation, sternwheel races, fireworks. Annually, the weekend following Labor Day. Est attendance: 75,000. For info: Ohio River Sternwheel Festival Committee, 316 Third St, Marietta, OH 45750. Phone: (614) 373-5178 or (614) 374-4913. Fax: (614) 374-4959. Email: mtourist@ee.net. WWW: http://www.rivertowns.org

OKTOBERFEST. Sept 11–13. MainStrasse Village, Covington, KY. Celebration of the German "storybook wedding reception" kicks off with a beer-tapping ceremony. Features include German and American food, live Bavarian music and dancing, arts and crafts, contests, children's rides and much more. Est attendance: 275,000. For info: Cindy Scheidt, Promotions Coord, MainStrasse Village, 616 Main St, Covington, KY 41011. Phone: (606) 491-0458. Fax: (606) 655-7932.

ON THE WATERFRONT SWAP MEET AND CAR SHOW. Sept 11–13. Downtown St. Ignace, MI. Car show, Corvette and Chevy judging. Plus toy show and truck display. Est attendance: 5,500. For info: Ed Reavie, President, Nostalgia Prod, Inc., 268 Hillcrest Blvd, St. Ignace, MI 49781. Phone: (906) 643-8087 or (906) 643-1USA. Fax: (906) 643-9784. Email: edreavie@nostalgia-prod.com or sales@nostalgia-prod.com. WWW: http://www.nostalgia-prod.com

PAKISTAN: FOUNDER'S 50th DEATH ANNIVERSARY. Sept 11, 1948. Pakistan observes the death anniversary in 1948 of Quaid-i-Azam Mohammed Ali Jinnah (founder of Pakistan).

REGGAE ON THE RIVER. Sept 11–12. Town Point Park, Norfolk, VA. Move to the island beat as the sounds and rhythm of reggae music sweep through Town Point Park. There will be plenty of cool, refreshing beverages and delicious island fare to round out your day in the sun. A nonstop lineup will include both regionally and nationally acclaimed artists. Est attendance: 30,000. For info: Mktg Dir, Norfolk Festevents, 120 W Main St, Norfolk, VA 23510. Phone: (757) 441-2345. Fax: (757) 441-5198. WWW: http://www.festevents.com

RICHARD CRANE MEMORIAL TRUCK SHOW. Sept 11–13. St. Ignace, MI. 3rd annual show featuring 18-wheeler competition. $1000 cash Best of Show. Parade of Lights across the Mackinac Bridge. For info: Nostalgia Productions, Inc, 268 Hillcrest Blvd, St. Ignace, MI 49781. Phone: (906) 643-8087 or (906) 643-0313. Fax: (906) 643-9784. Email: edreavie@nostalgiaprod.com.

RIVERFEST IN MANCHESTER. Sept 11–13. Stark Landing, Manchester, NH. 18th annual. Festival on the bank of the Merrimack River includes entertainment for the whole family, well-known national music groups, arts and crafts, special events, rowing regatta and other water activities, plus a fireworks extravaganza. Annually, the weekend following Labor Day. Admission charged. Est attendance: 100,000. For info: Riverfest, Inc, PO Box 21, Manchester, NH 03105. Phone: (603) 623-2623. Fax: (603) 625-9255.

"THE ROOKIES" TV PREMIERE: ANNIVERSARY. Sept 11, 1972. This hour crime show focused on three young police recruits: Michael Ontkean as Willis Gates, Georg Stanford Brown as Terry Webster and Sam Melville as Mike Danko. Also featured were Gerald S. O'Loughlin as Lieutenant Ed Ryker; Kate Jackson as nurse Jill Danko, Mike's wife; and Bruce Fairbairn as Chris Owens. The show was produced by Aaron Spelling and Leonard Goldberg.

SCOTTISH HIGHLANDS DINNER. Sept 11. Mountain View Inn, Greensburg, PA. This Friday night dinner is a kick-off to the renowned Ligonier Highland Games held the following day. Enjoy authentic Scottish buffet, spirited entertainment, bagpipes and scotch tasting. $25 per person. For info: Ann Nemanic, Scottish Highlands Dinner, 1001 Village Dr, Greensburg, PA 15601. Phone: (412) 834-5300.

"SPACE PATROL" TV PREMIERE: ANNIVERSARY. Sept 11, 1950. This children's space show was set in the 30th century. Jack Narz was the announcer. Cast included: Ed Kemmer as Commander Buzz Corry; Lyn Osborn as his assistant, Cadet Happy; Ken Mayer as Major Robbie Robertson; Paul Cavanaugh as Colonel Henderson; Virginia Hewitt as Carol, Henderson's daughter; and Nina Bara as Tonga, an enemy-turned-friend. "SP" changed from a fifteen-minute daily series to a half-hour, once-weekly format in 1951.

STAMP EXPO. Sept 11–13. Quality Hotel, Anaheim, CA. Est attendance: 4,000. For info: Intl Stamp Collectors Society, PO Box 854, Van Nuys, CA 91408. Phone: (818) 997-6496. Fax: (818) 988-4337. Email: iibick@aol.com. WWW: http://www.4free.com/bick

SUGARLOAF'S FALL MANASSAS CRAFT FESTIVAL. Sept 11–13. Prince William County Fairgrounds, Manassas, VA. This show, now in its 18th year, features 340 nationally recognized craft designers and fine artists displaying and selling their original creations. Craft demonstrations, children's entertainment, live music, food, hourly gift certificate drawings and more. Est attendance: 34,000. For info: Sugarloaf Mt Works, Inc, 200 Orchard Ridge Dr #215, Gaithersburg, MD 20878. Phone: (800) 210-9900.

TYLER'S CABINET RESIGNS: ANNIVERSARY. Sept 11. In protest of President John Tyler's veto of the Banking Bill all of his cabinet except Secretary of State Daniel Webster resigned on this day in 1841.

WESTERN WASHINGTON FAIR. Sept 11–27. Puyallup, WA. Entertainment, animals, rides, displays and food. Est attendance: 1,300,000. For info: Western Washington Fair, PO Box 430, Puyallup, WA 98371-0162. Phone: (253) 841-5045. Email: fairpr@thefair.com. WWW: http://www.thefair.com

WO-ZHA-WA DAYS FALL FESTIVAL. Sept 11–13. Wisconsin Dells, WI. Celebrates the beginning of the fall season. Arts, crafts, 100-unit parade, Maxwell Street Days and antique flea market. Est attendance: 100,000. For info: Wisconsin Dells Visitor and Convention Bureau, PO Box 390, Wisconsin Dells, WI 53965. Phone: (800) 223-3557. Email: wisdells@midplains.net. WWW: http://www.wisdells.com

WYANDOTTE HERITAGE DAYS. Sept 11–13. Bishop Park Area, Wyandotte, MI. Outdoor craft show, living history encampments, Teddy Bear picnic, costume show, Historic Home and Church Tours and colonial dinners. Est attendance: 50,000. For info: Marc Partin, Museum Dir, 2610 Biddle Ave, Wyandotte, MI 48192. Phone: (313) 246-4520. Fax: (313) 246-4552.

BIRTHDAYS TODAY

Daniel K. Akaka, 74, US Senator (D, Hawaii), born Honolulu, HI, Sept 11, 1924.

Harry Connick, Jr, 31, singer (Grammy Award for *We Are in Love*), actor (*When Harry Met Sally . . ., Copycat*), born New Orleans, LA, Sept 11, 1967.

Brian DePalma, 58, filmmaker (*The Untouchables, Bonfire of the Vanities, Carrie*), born Newark, NJ, Sept 11, 1940.

Lola Falana, 55, actress ("The New Bill Cosby Show," "Ben Vereen—Comin' at Ya"), born Camden, NJ, Sept 11, 1943.

William Xavier Kienzle, 70, author (*Body Count, The Rosary Murders*), former priest, born Detroit, MI, Sept 11, 1928.

Thomas Wade Landry, 74, Pro Football Hall of Fame coach and former player, born Mission, TX, Sept 11, 1924.

Amy Madigan, 47, actress (*Places in the Heart, Field of Dreams, Uncle Buck*), born Chicago, IL, Sept 11, 1951.

Virginia Madsen, 35, actress (*Dune, The Hot Spot, Candyman*), born Winnetka, IL, Sept 11, 1963.

SEPTEMBER 12 — SATURDAY

Day 255 — 110 Remaining

ANNUAL CAR SHOW. Sept 12. West Platte High School, Weston, MO. Enjoy classic cars in the school parking lot. For info: Weston Development Co, 502 Main, Weston, MO 64098. Phone: (816) 640-2909.

AUTORAMA. Sept 12–13. Cincinnati Zoo and Botanical Garden, Cincinnati, OH. Antique, classic or custom built hotrods compete for trophies in numerous categories. Registration fee includes family admission. 9 AM-4 PM both days. Est attendance: 5,000. For info: Events/Promo Dept, Cincinnati Zoo and Botanical Garden, 3400 Vine St, Cincinnati, OH 45220. Phone: (513) 281-4701. Fax: (513) 559-7790. WWW: http://www.cincy.zoo.org

BELGIUM: FLANDERS FESTIVAL. Sept 12–Oct 31. Gent, Belgium. Featuring ancient music, classical music and choral music. For info: Sophie Cocquyt, Klein Gentstraat 46, Gent, Belgium B-9051. Phone: (32) (0) 9-243-94-94. Fax: (32) (0) 9-243-94-90.

BOONESBOROUGH DAYS. Sept 12–13. Shafer Memorial Park, Boonsboro, MD. Crafts, antiques, living history, demonstrations, food. Boonesborough was the original spelling of the town's name. Est attendance: 10,000. For info: Boonsboro Historical Society, PO Box 213, Boonsboro, MD 21713. Phone: (301) 432-5889.

BOONSLICK FOLK FESTIVAL. Sept 12. Stolberg-Jackson Community Bldg, Arrow Rock, MO. Morning workshops on traditional folk instruments and afternoon concert. Contra dance in evening. Est attendance: 250. For info: Tempe McGlaughlin, HARC, PO Box M, Arrow Rock, MO 65320. Phone: (816) 837-3425. Email: tmcglaughlin@vaxl.rain.gen.mo.us.

CALIFORNIA PRUNE FESTIVAL. Sept 12–13. Yuba-Sutter Fairgrounds, Yuba City, CA. Food festival with celebrity chefs, six stages of entertainment, arts and crafts, children's area, photography contest, antique auto show and more. Annually, the second weekend in September. Est attendance: 30,000. For info: California Prune Festival, PO Box 3006, Yuba City, CA 95992. Phone: (916) 671-3100. Fax: (916) 751-8469.

CANADA: BINDER TWINE FESTIVAL. Sept 12. Kleinburg, Ont. Outdoor arts and crafts show, pioneer skills demonstrations, old-fashioned food and entertainment. Est attendance: 25,000. For info: Kleinburg and Area, Binder Twine Festival Inc, PO Box 6, Kleinburg, Ont, Canada LOJ 1C0. Phone: (905) 893-3083.

CEDARHURST CRAFT FAIR. Sept 12–13. Mitchell Museum, Mount Vernon, IL. National juried invitational show featuring more than 150 artists. Est attendance: 20,000. For info: Libby Jackson, Dir, Cedarhurst Craft Fair, Mitchell Museum, PO Box 923, Mount Vernon, IL 62864. Phone: (618) 242-1236. Fax: (618) 242-9530.

CHADDS FORD DAYS. Sept 12–13. Chadds Ford, PA. Open-air colonial fair with 18th-century craft demonstrations, Brandywine Valley art, live old-time music, country rides and games, Colonial crafts for sale, good food. Est attendance: 11,500. For info: Chadds Ford Historical Society, Box 27, Chadds Ford, PA 19317. Phone: (610) 388-7376. Fax: (610) 388-7480.

CHARLES LEROUX'S LAST JUMP: ANNIVERSARY. Sept 12. American aeronaut of French extraction, born in New York, NY, about 1857, claimed by *Soviet Life* to have been a nephew of President Abraham Lincoln, achieved world fame as a parachutist. After his first public performance (Philadelphia, PA, 1887) he toured European cities where his parachute jumps attracted wide attention. Credited with 238 successful jumps. On Sept 12, 1889, he jumped from a balloon over Tallinn, Estonia, and perished in the Bay of Reval. A monument to his memory was erected at Tallinn five years after his death.

ETHIOPIA: NATIONAL REVOLUTION DAY. Sept 12. Observed as a national holiday.

FALL ARTS FESTIVAL. Sept 12–Oct 12. Jackson, WY. Featuring Arts for the Parks Awards Ceremony, special shows by more than 35 major galleries, program presentations, working demonstrations, special exhibits, concerts, dance and theatre. Est attendance: 15,000. For info: Jackson Hole Chamber of Commerce, Box E, Jackson, WY 83001. Phone: (307) 733-3316. Fax: (307) 733-5585.

★**FEDERAL LANDS CLEANUP DAY.** Sept 12. Presidential Proclamation 5521, of Sept 5, 1986, covers all succeeding years. The first Saturday after Labor Day. (PL99–402 of Aug 27, 1986.)

FESTA ITALIA. Sept 12–13. Custom House Plaza, Monterey, CA. A 61-year tradition dedicated to Santa Rosalia, patron saint of the Sicilian fishermen in Monterey, the Festival includes parade, outdoor mass, blessing of the fleet, entertainment, arts and crafts and Italian food. Benefits the Italian Heritage Society of the Monterey Peninsula. Est attendance: 10,000. For info: Bostrom Management, 140 Franklin, Ste 202, Monterey, CA 93940. Phone: (408) 649-6544. Fax: (408) 649-4124.

FESTIVAL OF ADVENTURES. Sept 12–13. Aitkin, MN. This 7th annual festival celebrates the area's fur trading history. Rendezvous at Depot Museum with trappers, traders, ethnic dancers, bluegrass music and food. Est attendance: 5,000. For info: Aitkin Area Chamber of Commerce, PO Box 127, Aitkin, MN 56431. Phone: (218) 927-2316 or (800) 526-8342. Fax: (218) 927-4494. Email: upnorth@aitkin.com. WWW: http://www.aitkin.com

FESTIVAL OF THE ARTS. Sept 12. Means & Clark Park, Weatherford, OK. More than 100 booths involving artists from all over the country as well as crafters from surrounding states. Concession booths and live entertainment all day long. 25th annual. Annually, the second Saturday in September. Est attendance: 2,000. For info: Randy Hacker, Exec Dir, Weatherford Chamber of Commerce, PO Box 729, Weatherford, OK 73096. Phone: (800) 725-7744. Email: chamber@weatherford.net.

FLAX SCUTCHING FESTIVAL. Sept 12–13. Stahlstown, PA. Demonstrations of the art of making linen from the flax plant. Second oldest continuous complete flax demonstration festival in the world. Annually, the second weekend in September. Est attendance: 15,000. For info: Frank Newell, Flax Scutching Festival, RD #1, Rt 130W, Box 216, Stahlstown, PA 15687. Phone: (412) 593-2119.

"FRAGGLE ROCK" TV PREMIERE: ANNIVERSARY. Sept 12, 1987. This children's show was a cartoon version of the live Jim Henson puppet production on HBO. It was set in the rock underneath a scientist's house and featured characters such as the Fraggles, the Doozers and the Gorgs.

GARDENFEST AT LONGWOOD GARDENS. Sept 12–Oct 4. Kennett Square, PA. Longwood celebrates the beauty and bounty of late summer and early fall with harvest displays, flower shows, gardening, demonstrations and weekend performances. Est attendance: 35,000. For info: Longwood Gardens, PO Box 501, Kennett Square, PA 19348-0501. Phone: (610) 388-1000. WWW: http://www.longwoodgardens.org

September 1998

S	M	T	W	T	F	S
		1	2	3	4	5
6	7	8	9	10	11	12
13	14	15	16	17	18	19
20	21	22	23	24	25	26
27	28	29	30			

GUINEA-BISSAU: NATIONAL HOLIDAY. Sept 12. Amilcar Cabral's birthday, Sept 12, is observed as a national holiday.

HARVEST SHOW. Sept 12–13. Horticulture Center, Fairmount Park, Philadelphia, PA. More than 700 gardeners enter more than 350 horticultural and artistic categories. Educational exhibits and samples of freshly harvested crops and homemade preserved products judged. A series of special events, including live music and a children's activity tent. Est attendance: 5,000. For info: The Pennsylvania Horticultural Soc, 100 N 20th St, 5th Fl, Philadelphia, PA 19103-1495. Phone: (215) 988-8800. Fax: (215) 988-8810. Email: janeteva@libertynet.org. WWW: http://www.libertynet.org/phs

HERITAGE DAY FESTIVAL. Sept 12 (rain date Sept 13). Lavallette, NJ. Clowns, antique cars, bands, games, food, children's games, pony rides, train rides and finale with Ocean County String Band performing. 10 AM–dusk. Annually, the second Saturday in September. Est attendance: 30,000. For info: Joy Grosko, Dir, Heritage Committee Inc, 13 Camden Ave, Lavallette, NJ 08735. Phone: (732) 793-3652.

HOG WILD DAY IN PIGEON. Sept 12. Pigeon, MI. Pigeon goes "hog wild" for this event featuring a "muscle car" giveaway, a visit by "Harley Hogs" motorcyclists, T-shirts, merchant sales and drawings and lots of food. Sponsored by: Pigeon Chamber of Commerce. Annually, the second Saturday in September. Est attendance: 3,000. For info: Paul Picklo, Mgr, Thumb Cellular, 15 S Main St, Pigeon, MI 48755. Phone: (517) 453-4333. Fax: (517) 453-4363.

INDIAN DAY. Sept 12. Oklahoma. Observed on the first Saturday after the Full Moon in September.

KID'RIFIC. Sept 12–13. Hartford, CT. A two-day children's festival in downtown Hartford, produced by the Hartford Downtown Council. Kid'rific will feature hands-on art and science activities, storytelling, master teaching artists' workshops, continuous stage entertainment, a petting zoo with a 13' tall giraffe and lots more. Annually, the first weekend after Labor Day. Est attendance: 50,000. For info: Steven A. Lazaroff, Dir for Events Programming, Hartford Downtown Council, 250 Constitution Plaza, Hartford, CT 06103. Phone: (860) 728-3089. Fax: (860) 527-9696.

KING TURKEY DAYS (WITH TURKEY RACE). Sept 12. Worthington, MN. Festival to thank farm people for their patronage. On Sept 12 there is a parade and a turkey race down the 150-yard Main Street race course. Est attendance: 30,000. For info: King Turkey Days, Inc, 1121 Third Ave, Worthington, MN 56187. Phone: (800) 279-2919 or (507) 372-2919. Fax: (507) 372-2827.

"LASSIE" TV PREMIERE: ANNIVERSARY. Sept 12, 1954. This long-running series was originally about a boy and his courageous and intelligent dog, Lassie (played by more than six different dogs, all male). For the first few seasons, Lassie lived on the Miller farm and had lots of adventures. The family included Jeff (Tommy Rettig), his widowed mother Ellen (Jan Clayton), and George Cleveland as Gramps. Throughout the years there were many format and cast changes, as Lassie was exchanged from one family to another in order to have a variety of new perils and escapades. Other featured performers over the years include Cloris Leachman, June Lockhart and Larry Wilcox.

LEAVENWORTH RIVER FEST. Sept 12–13. Leavenworth, KS. Arts and crafts, outhouse races, antique car exhibits, parade, aircraft display and rides, Harley-Davidson motorcycle exhibit and children's carnival. Plenty of entertainment, food, races and competitions and several feature attractions. Annually, the second weekend in September. Est attendance: 20,000. For info: Connie Hatchenburg, Leavenworth-Lansing Conv/Visitors, 518 Shawnee, Box 44, Leavenworth, KS 66048. Phone: (913) 682-3924. Fax: (913) 682-3928. Email: (800) 844-4114.

LENEXA SPINACH FESTIVAL. Sept 12. Sar-Ko-Par Trails Park, Lenexa, KS. Celebrating Lenexa's agricultural history. Exhibits, food, games and over 200 arts and crafts booths. Est attendance: 5,000. For info: Bill Nicrs, Lenexa Parks & Rec, 13240 Oak St, Lenexa, KS 66215. Phone: (913) 541-8592. Fax: (913) 492-8118.

LITTLE FALLS ARTS AND CRAFTS FAIR. Sept 12–13. Little Falls, MN. 1,000 artists, craftspeople and hobbyists displaying and selling their items. Est attendance: 100,000. For info: Chamber of Commerce, 200 NW First St, Little Falls, MN 56345. Phone: (320) 632-5155. Fax: (320) 632-2122.
Email: chamber@upstel.net.
WWW: http://www.upstel.net/~falls/tour7.html

LOON LAKE HARVEST FESTIVAL. Sept 12–13. Aurora, MN. Demonstrations of old farm machinery, farmers market, crafts, log sawing, horse playday, activities for kids, music, ugly farmer couple contest, lots of good food. Annually, the weekend after Labor Day. Est attendance: 1,400. For info: Howard G. Meacham, Loon Lake Harvest Festival, 3871 Lane 48, Aurora, MN 55705. Phone: (218) 638-2651.

MARYLAND: DEFENDERS DAY. Sept 12. Maryland. Annual re-enactment of bombardment of Fort McHenry in 1814 which inspired Francis Scott Key to write the "Star-Spangled Banner."

MARYLAND RECREATIONAL VEHICLE SHOW. Sept 12–13 (also Sept 18–20). Timonium State Fairgrounds, Timonium, MD. 6th annual outdoor show of motorhomes, trailers, fifth-wheel trailers and pickup campers, campground booths, accessories and related items. Annually, beginning the first Saturday after Labor Day. Est attendance: 8,000. For info: Richard T. Albright, Pres, Maryland Rec Vehicle Dealers Assn, Inc, 8332 Pulaski Hwy, Baltimore, MD 21237. Phone: (410) 687-7200. Fax: (410) 686-1486.

"MAUDE" TV PREMIERE: ANNIVERSARY. Sept 12, 1972. Bea Arthur's character, Maude Findlay, was first introduced as Edith Bunker's cousin on "All in the Family." She was a loud, opinionated liberal, living with her husband Walter (Bill Macy). Other characters on the show were her divorced daughter by a previous marriage, Carol Traynor (Adrienne Barbeau), Conrad Bain as Dr. Arthur Harmon, Rue McClanahan as Arthur's wife Vivian (Bea Arthur and McClanahan would later star in another sitcom, "The Golden Girls"), Esther Rolle as Florida Evans, Maude's maid, and John Amos as her husband, James (in 1974 they left the series to star in "Good Times"). This was one of the first shows to tackle the controversial issue of abortion.

MENCKEN, HENRY LOUIS: BIRTH ANNIVERSARY. Sept 12. American newspaperman, lexicographer and critic, "the Sage of Baltimore" was born at Baltimore, MD, Sept 12, 1880, and died there Jan 29, 1956. "If, after I depart this vale," he wrote in 1921 (Epitaph, *Smart Set*), "you ever remember me and have thought to please my ghost, forgive some sinner and wink your eye at some homely girl."

"THE MONKEES" TV PREMIERE: ANNIVERSARY. Sept 12, 1966. This half-hour show featured a blend of comedy and music, with light and repetitive plots. It was based on a rock and roll group that was supposed to be an American version of the Beatles. Four young actors were chosen from over 400 to play the group members: Mickey Dolenz, Davy Jones, Mike Nesmith and Peter Tork. Dolenz and Jones had previous acting experience and Tork and Nesmith had previous musical experience. Their first songs on the show were lip-synched but enjoyed immense popularity; later the Monkees insisted on writing and performing their own music. A Monkees album, "Headquarters" and Monkees tours were very successful. In 1986, the Monkees, except for Nesmith, were reunited for a 20th Anniversary tour and the show was broadcast in reruns on MTV. The Monkees sans Nesmith also toured in 1996 for the 30th reunion celebration.

MOON PHASE: LAST QUARTER. Sept 12. Moon enters Last Quarter phase at 9:58 PM, EDT.

NANTICOKE INDIAN POWWOW. Sept 12–13. Millsboro, DE. Annual gathering of Native Americans during which Native American dances and music are presented and Native American foods and arts and crafts are sold. Dance sessions: Saturday, noon–5 PM, Sunday, 2–4:30 PM. Sunday worship service from 11 AM–noon. Annually, the weekend after Labor Day. Est attendance: 40,000. For info: Cecile Coursey, Prog Coord, Nanticoke Indian Assn, Rte 24, Box 107, Millsboro, DE 19966. Phone: (302) 945-3400.

NORDICFEST PARADE. Sept 12. Libby, MT. Parade showcases a large contingent of Norwegian fjord horses plus a variety of floats and entertainments, many of which celebrate the ethnic origins of the area's earliest settlers. For info: Nordicfest, Inc, PO Box 791, Libby, MT 59923-0791. Phone: (406) 293-2440, ext 43. Fax: (406) 293-8814.

OLD TIMER'S DAY. Sept 12–13. Vogel State Park, Blairsville, GA. If you like listening to Old Time Mountain, Bluegrass, Country, Gospel, Folk, Dulcimer and Indian Flute music, story telling and dancing, then don't miss this. Est attendance: 1,200. For info: David Foot, Mgr, Vogel State Park, Georgia Dept of Natural Resources, 7485 Vogel State Park Rd, Blairsville, GA 30512. Phone: (706) 745-2628.

OWENS, JESSE: 85th BIRTH ANNIVERSARY. Sept 12, 1913. James Cleveland (Jesse) Owens, American athlete, winner of four gold medals at the 1936 Olympic Games in Berlin, Germany, was born at Oakville, AL. Owens set 11 world records in track and field. During one track meet, at Ann Arbor, MI, Owens, representing Ohio State University, broke five world records and tied a sixth in the space of 45 minutes, on May 23, 1935. Died at Tucson, AZ, Mar 31, 1980.

QUADRANGLE FESTIVAL. Sept 12–13 (tentative). Downtown Texarkana, TX and AR. 17th annual festival features 5K run around Texarkana Historical Museum that sits on the TX-AR state line. Also, antiques, crafts, collectibles, antique autos, pet shows; country/western, traditional and contemporary music; folk artists and craftspeople; street dancing and food vendors. Est attendance: 45,000. For info: Dir of Mktg, Texarkana Museums System, PO Box 2343, Texarkana, TX 75504. Phone: (903) 793-4831. Fax: (903) 793-7108.

ROAD CHURCH COUNTY FAIR. Sept 12. Road Congregational Church, Stonington, CT. White elephants, bake table, harvest table, crafts and children's midway. Famous Barnes's Chowder Luncheon at noon (served in Civil War kettles). Auction at 2 PM. Est attendance: 300. For info: Libby Kennedy, 21 Roosevelt Ave, Mystic, CT 06355. Phone: (860) 536-1514.

ROAN MOUNTAIN STATE PARK FALL FESTIVAL. Sept 12–13. Roan Mountain, TN. Crafts, exhibits, music and clogging. Est attendance: 20,000. For info: Fall Fest, Ranger Naturalist, Roan Mt State Park, 527 Hwy 143, Roan Mountain, TN 37687. Phone: (615) 772-3303. Fax: (423) 772-0142.

SODBUSTER DAYS—THE HARVEST. Sept 12–13. Sunne Farm, Fort Ransom State Park, Fort Ransom, ND. Demonstrations of life on a small family farm of the 1920s during the fall harvest. Activities include threshing, fall field work, gathering prairie hay, ladies' demonstrations, kids games, food, music. Most farm machinery is horse-drawn. Annually, the weekend after Labor Day. Est attendance: 3,500. For info: Fort Ranson State Park, 5981 Walt Hjelle Pkwy, Ft Ransom, ND 58033-9712. Phone: (701) 973-4331. Fax: (701) 973-4271.

SPACE MILESTONE: *LUNA 16* (USSR). Sept 12, 1970. First unmanned spacecraft to land on moon (Sea of Fertility), collect samples and return to Earth was launched on this date.

SPACE MILESTONE: *LUNA 2* (USSR). Sept 12, 1959. First spacecraft to land on moon was launched on this date.

VACAVILLE ONION FESTIVAL. Sept 12–13. Vacaville, CA. Celebrity entertainment, cooking demonstrations, cuisine center, kiddie korner, onion patch, arts and crafts and more to promote the pungent bulb. Annually, the weekend following Labor Day. Est attendance: 13,000. For info: Colleen Duke, Sec, Vacaville Onion Festival, PO Box 5263, Vacaville, CA 95696. Phone: (707) 448-4613. Fax: (707) 448-4630.

VALPARAISO POPCORN FESTIVAL. Sept 12. Valparaiso, IN. Celebration of popcorn with a parade, the Popcorn Panic and Little Kernal Puff running races, arts, crafts, food booths, music and entertainment, kiddie carnival, children's play and a hot-air balloon show. Annually, the first Saturday after Labor Day. Est attendance: 65,000. For info: Glennas Kueck, Exec Dir, 204 E Lincolnway, PO Box 189, Valparaiso, IN 46384. Phone: (219) 464-8332. Fax: (219) 464-2343.

VIDEO GAMES DAY. Sept 12. A day for kids who love video games to celebrate the fun they have playing them and to thank their parents for all the cartridges and quarters they have provided to indulge this enthusiasm.

WARNER, CHARLES DUDLEY: BIRTH ANNIVERSARY. Sept 12, 1829. American newspaperman, born at Plainfield, MA, authored many works, but is perhaps best remembered for a single sentence (in an editorial, *Hartford Courant*, Aug 24, 1897): "Everybody talks about the weather, but nobody does anything about it." The quotation is often mistakenly attributed to his friend, Mark Twain. Died at Hartford, CT, Oct 20, 1900.

WATERMELON SEED-SPITTING & SPEED-EATING CHAMPIONSHIP. Sept 12–13. Pardeeville, WI. This national competition, held at Chandler Park on Park Lake, attracts thousands of visitors each year—some from as far away as New York, Australia and Algeria. The current speed-eating record is 2.5 pounds of watermelon in 3.5 seconds. Participants will need plenty of napkins and a big appetite. The event also features melon sculptures, a parade, entertainment and an evening band performance on Saturday. On Sunday, there are speed-eating and seed-spitting championships, free watermelon, a pancake breakfast and a water-ski show. For info: Wisconsin Dept of Tourism, PO Box 7976, Madison, WI 53707. Phone: (608) 429-2873. Email: tourism@laughlin.com. WWW: http://tourism.state.wi.us

WILLOW TREE FESTIVAL. Sept 12–13. Gordon, NE. This festival is a cornucopia of arts and crafts, three quality performing stages including a children's stage, children's activities, fun and food. Annually, the second weekend in September. Est attendance: 4,000. For info: Willow Tree Festival, PO Box 303, Gordon, NE 69343-0303. Phone: (308) 327-2917. Fax: (308) 327-2166. Email: rwbuchan@gpcom.net.

September 1998

S	M	T	W	T	F	S
		1	2	3	4	5
6	7	8	9	10	11	12
13	14	15	16	17	18	19
20	21	22	23	24	25	26
27	28	29	30			

WORLD WAR I: BATTLE OF SAINT-MIHIEL: 80th ANNIVERSARY. Sept 12, 1918. Under the command of General John J. Pershing, the First US Army attacked the Germans at the Saint-Mihiel salient. This was the first major US offensive of the war. Sixteen army divisions, coupled with French II Colonial Corps tanks and artillery support forced back the Germans after 36 hours of heavy fighting and reclaimed 200 square miles of French territory that had been in the hands of the Germans since 1914. The First US Army lost about 7,000 soldiers in the Battle of Saint-Mihiel.

BIRTHDAYS TODAY

Sam Brownback, 42, US Senator (R, Kansas), born Garnett, KS, Sept 12, 1956.
Deron Leigh Cherry, 39, former football player, born Riverside, NJ, Sept 12, 1959.
Irene Dailey, 78, actress (the 4th Liz Matthews on "Another World"), born New York, NY, Sept 12, 1920.
Linda Gray, 57, actress (Sue Ellen on "Dallas"), born Santa Monica, CA, Sept 12, 1941.
Timothy Duane (Tim) Hardaway, 32, basketball player, born Chicago, IL, Sept 12, 1966.
George Jones, 67, singer ("White Lightning," "Race Is On," "He Stopped Loving Her Today"), born Saratoga, TX, Sept 12, 1931.
Maria Muldaur, 55, singer ("Midnight at the Oasis," "I'm a Woman"), born New York, NY, Sept 12, 1943.
Joe Pantoliano, 44, actor (*Risky Business, The Fugitive*; stage: *Orphans*), born Jersey City, NJ, Sept 12, 1954.
Peter Scolari, 44, actor ("Bosom Buddies," "Newhart"), born New Rochelle, NY, Sept 12, 1954.
Rachel Ward, 41, actress ("The Thorn Birds," *Against All Odds*), born London, England, Sept 12, 1957.
Barry White, 54, singer ("Can't Get Enough of Your Love, Babe"), born Galveston, TX, Sept 12, 1944.

☆ ☆ ☆

SEPTEMBER 13 — SUNDAY

Day 256 — 109 Remaining

ANDERSON, SHERWOOD: BIRTH ANNIVERSARY. Sept 13. American author and newspaper publisher, born at Camden, OH, Sept 13, 1876. His best remembered book is *Winesburg, Ohio*. Anderson died at Colon, Panama, Mar 8, 1941.

"BANACEK" TV PREMIERE: ANNIVERSARY. Sept 13, 1972. This series began as a segment on "The NBC Wednesday Movie." It starred George Peppard as the title character, an independent insurance investigator working freelance for the Boston Casualty Company. Also featured were Murray Matheson as Felix Mullholland, Banacek's confidante; Ralph Manza as Jay Drury, Banacek's chauffeur; and Christine Belford as insurance investigator Carlie Kirkland.

BARRY, JOHN: DEATH ANNIVERSARY. Sept 13, 1803. Commemorates day in 1803 on which Commodore John Barry died. First American commodore who fought in Revolutionary War.

BOYER, ERNEST L.: BIRTH ANNIVERSARY. Sept 13, 1928. Educator, US Commissioner of Education; president, Carnegie Foundation for the Advancement of Teaching, was born at Dayton, OH. Died Dec 8, 1995.

BUCKEYE TREE FESTIVAL. Sept 13. Utica, OH. Ohio's only festival recognizing the Ohio State tree, celebrating Ohio's heritage. For info: Buckeye Tree Festival, PO Box 588, Utica, OH 43080. Phone: (614) 892-3921.

CANADA: INTERNATIONAL TEXAS HOLDEM POKER TOURNAMENT. Sept 13. Dawson City, Yukon. Most Northern Holdem Tournament hosted by White Ram Bed and Breakfast. Annually, the Sunday after Labor Day. For info: White Ram Manor B&B, Box 302, Dawson City, Yukon, Canada Y0B 1G0. Phone: (403) 993-5772. Fax: (403) 993-6509.

CANYON CREEK BATTLE. Sept 13. Laurel, MT. 121st anniversary. In past years, members of the Nez Perce Indian tribe and others held a peace pipe ceremony at Canyon Creek to commemorate the battle that took place between the US Cavalry and the Nez Perce led by Chief Joseph. The Nez Perce were trying to flee to freedom in Canada. For info: Laurel Chamber of Commerce, PO Box 395, Laurel, MT 59044. Phone: (406) 628-8105.

"CHICO AND THE MAN" TV PREMIERE: ANNIVERSARY. Sept 13, 1974. This sitcom starred Jack Albertson as Ed Brown, a cranky garage owner and Freddie Prinze as Chico Rodriguez, his Mexican-American employee. It was set in the barrio of East Los Angeles. However, the show was widely criticized for its use of the term "Chico," which was derogatory to many Chicanos, and for the lack of Mexican-Americans in the cast or crew. To remedy this, the cast was expanded to include Issac Ruiz as Chico's friend, Ramon, and Rodolfo Hoyos as Ed's friend, Rudy. Also added were Scatman Crothers as Louie Wilson, the garbage collector; Bonnie Boland as Mabel, the letter carrier; Ronny Graham as Reverend Bemis; and Della Reese as Della Rogers, Ed's landlady. Prinze committed suicide in 1977 but the series continued with Gabriel Melgar as Raul Garcia, a Mexican kid adopted by Ed. Charo also joined the show as Aunt Charo.

COLBERT, CLAUDETTE: 95th BIRTH ANNIVERSARY. Sept 13, 1903. Actress and comedienne Colbert, born Lily Claudette Chauchoin in Paris, France, was a beloved movie star of the '30s. She was best known for her films *Midnight, Cleopatra* and *It Happened One Night,* for which she won an Oscar in 1934. In addition to more than 60 movies, she appeared in Broadway shows and won a Golden Globe award for her role in the 1986 miniseries "The Two Mrs Grenvilles." She also received a Life Achievement Award from the Kennedy Center for Performing Arts in 1989. She died on July 30, 1996, at Bridgetown, Barbados, at the age of 92.

CORVETTE SHOW. Sept 13 (rain date Sept 20). Wheaton Village, Millville, NJ. Presented by Corvettes Unlimited Corvette Club. Est attendance: 1,500. For info: Wheaton Village, 1501 Glasstown Rd, Millville, NJ 08332. Phone: (609) 825-6800. Fax: (609) 825-2410. Email: mail@wheatonvillage.org.
WWW: http://www.wheatonvillage.org

"DICK TRACY" TV PREMIERE: ANNIVERSARY. Sept 13, 1950. Chester Gould's famous detective appeared in the comics, on radio, and in the movies before coming to TV in 1950. Ralph Byrd played Dick Tracy in the short-lived series (and in the films, too); his death in 1952 ended the series. Also featured were Joe Devlin as his partner, Sam Catchem and Angela Greene as Tess Trueheart, Tracy's wife. Warren Beatty, Madonna, Dustin Hoffman and Al Pacino starred in a 1990 feature film revival.

ENCHANTED CIRCLE CENTURY BIKE TOUR. Sept 13. Red River, NM. 100-mile scenic ride and one of the longest and most difficult bicycle tours in the Southwest. Est attendance: 1,000. For info: Red River Chamber of Commerce, PO Box 870, Red River, NM 87558. Phone: (800) 348-6444.
Email: rrinfo@newmex.com.
WWW: http://taoswebb.com/RedRiverInfo

ENGLAND: BATTLE OF BRITAIN WEEK. Sept 13–19. Annually, the third week of September—the week containing Battle of Britain Day (Sept 15).

FALL HAT WEEK. Sept 13–20. A week of celebration during which the straw hat is put aside in favor of the felt or fabric hat by both men and women. Local businesses and the media are encouraged to plan hat-related activities. Annually, in September. For info: Casey Bush, Exec Dir, Headwear Info Bureau, 302 W 12 St, PH-C, New York, NY 10014. Phone: (212) 627-8333. Email: milicase@earthlink.net. WWW: http://www.hatsny.com

FESTIVAL-IN-THE-PARK. Sept 13 (rain date Sept 27). Memorial Park, Nutley, NJ. 25th annual festival, a craft and collectibles show to benefit the Nutley Historical Society and the Historic Restoration Trust. Annually, the first Sunday after Labor Day. Est attendance: 16,000. For info: Douglas J. Eisenfelder, Festival-in-the-Park, 51 Enclosure, Nutley, NJ 07110. Phone: (201) 667-3013.

HUDSON SAILED *HALF MOON*: ANNIVERSARY. Sept 13, 1609. Henry Hudson, sailing in the *Half Moon* down the river west of Manhattan Island that is named for him, realized that the river was not an outlet to the Orient.

INTERNATIONAL HOUSEKEEPERS WEEK. Sept 13–19. A week to recognize housekeeping staff; let them know that they are appreciated and that the work they do is worthwhile, vital, commendable and acknowledged by all. Annually, the second full week in September. For info: IEHA, 1001 Eastwind Dr, Ste 301, Westerville, OH 43081-3361. Phone: (800) 200-6342. Fax: (614) 895-1248. Email: excel@ieha.org. WWW: http://www.ieha.org

ITALY: GIOSTRA DELLA QUINTANA. Sept 13. Foligno. A revival of a 17th-century joust of the Quintana, featuring 600 knights in full costume. Annually, the second Sunday in September.

JCBC CENTURY RIDE. Sept 13. Junction City, Milford Lake, Fort Riley, KS. 100-mile bicycle ride (in loops) of various course routes and optional stopping points. Annually, the second Sunday in September. Sponsor: Bicycle Club. Est attendance: 200. For info: Casey Thomas, 2206 Prospect Circle, Junction City, KS 66441. Phone: (913) 762-3310. Fax: (913) 238-8351. Email: kspetdr@tfsksu.net.

LISCO OLD-TIMERS DAY. Sept 13. Lisco, NE. Local talent puts on program and skits about an honored old-timer or couple. Parade, barbecue (free will offering), horseshoe tournament, antique tractor pull and more. Annually, Sunday after Labor Day. Sponsor: Lisco Old-timers Day Committee. Est attendance: 2,000. For info: Lisco State Bank, Lisco Old-Timers Day Committee, Lisco, NE 69148.

MARRIAGE CELEBRATION. Sept 13. Belleville, IL. An evening honoring married couples celebrating 10, 25, 40, 50, 60 and 60 plus years of marriage in 1998. Sunday, 7 PM. Est attendance: 500. For info: Shrine of Our Lady of the Snows, 442 S De Mazenod Dr, Belleville, IL 62223-1094. Phone: (618) 397-6700. Fax: (618) 398-6549.
WWW: http://www.apci.net/~oblates/

★**NATIONAL GRANDPARENTS DAY.** Sept 13. Presidential Proclamation 4679, of Sept 6, 1979, covers all succeeding years. First Sunday in September following Labor Day (PL96–62 of Sept 6, 1979). First issued in 1978 (Proc 4580 of Aug 3, 1978), requested by Public Law 325 of July 28, 1978.

NATIONAL MINDMAPPING AND BRAINSTORMING WEEK. Sept 13–19. To promote creativity and innovation in business and organizations through brainstorming and mindmapping, a visual form of outlining. For info: Joyce Wycoff, Exec Dir, Innovation Network, 34 E Sola, Ste D101, Santa Barbara, CA 93101. Phone: (805) 965-8477. Fax: (805) 963-8220. Email: staff@thinksmart.com. WWW: http://www.thinksmart.com

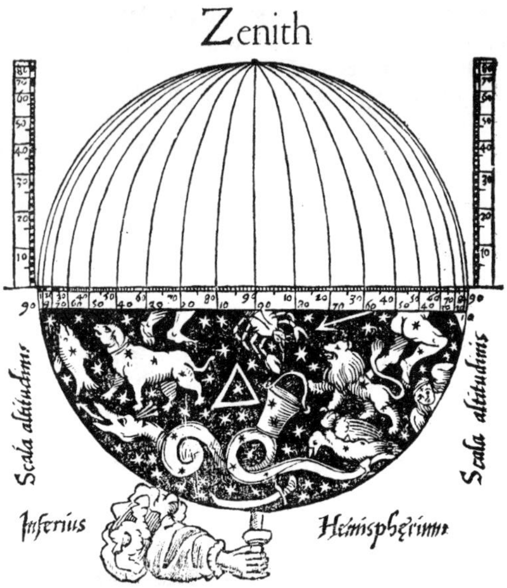

NATIONAL REHABILITATION WEEK. Sept 13–19. An opportunity to celebrate the determination of more than 43 million people with disabilities in America. It is also a time to salute the dedicated health care professionals who provide rehabilitation care and an occasion to call attention to the unmet needs of our nation's disabled citizens. For info: Natl Rehabilitation Awareness Foundation, PO Box 71, Scranton, PA 18501. Phone: (717) 341-4637. Fax: (717) 341-4331.

NEW JERSEY RESTAURANT AND HOSPITALITY EXPO. Sept 13–14. Meadowlands Exposition Center, Secaucus, NJ. Showcase for more than 300 booths featuring the latest in products and services for the food service industry. Est attendance: 7,500. For info: Diane DiNuzzo, Expo Mgr, NJ Restaurant Assn, 1 Executive Dr, Somerset, NJ 08873. Phone: (908) 302-1800. Fax: (908) 302-1804. Email: njrest@ix.netcom.com. WWW: http://www.njra.org

NORTHEAST MISSOURI TRIATHLON CHAMPIONSHIP. Sept 13. Thousand Hills State Park, Kirksville, MO. Swim 3/4 mile, bike 18 miles, run five miles. USA Triathlon Federation certified. Qualifier for International Course Nationals. Annually, the Sunday after Labor Day. Est attendance: 800. For info: KRXL Radio, Box 130, Kirksville, MO 63501. Phone: (816) 626-2213. Fax: (816) 626-2483.

OCEAN COUNTY BLUEGRASS FESTIVAL. Sept 13. Waretown, NJ. An indoor bluegrass festival where no alcoholic beverages or smoking is allowed. Est attendance: 400. For info: Albert Music Hall, PO Box 657, Waretown, NJ 08758. Phone: (609) 971-1593.

OLDER ADULT LIVING CENTER CELEBRATION WEEK. Sept 13–18. York, PA. "Great to Be a Senior Citizen" party in conjunction with National Adult Services Week. A week of special events including a pot-luck family picnic and open house. For info: Claire Brosse, Program Coord, Elderly Activities Program, 501 N Pershing Ave, York, PA 17404. Phone: (717) 846-1719.

PERSHING, JOHN J.: BIRTH ANNIVERSARY. Sept 13, 1860. US Army general who commanded the American Expeditionary Force (AEF) during World War I, Pershing was born at Laclede, MO. The AEF, as part of the inter-Allied offensive, successfully assaulted the Saint-Mihiel salient in Sept 1918 and later that month quickly regrouped for the Meuse-Argonne operation that led to the Armistice of Nov 11, 1918. Pershing died at age 87 on July 15, 1948, at Washington, DC.

September 1998

S	M	T	W	T	F	S
		1	2	3	4	5
6	7	8	9	10	11	12
13	14	15	16	17	18	19
20	21	22	23	24	25	26
27	28	29	30			

REED, WALTER: BIRTH ANNIVERSARY. Sept 13. American army physician (especially known for his Yellow Fever research). Born at Gloucester County, VA, on Sept 13, 1851. Served as an army surgeon for more than 20 years and as a professor at the Army Medical College. He died at Washington, DC, Nov 22, 1902. The US Army's general hospital in Washington, DC, is named in his honor.

"SOAP" TV PREMIERE: ANNIVERSARY. Sept 13, 1977. "Soap" was a prime-time comedy that parodied soap operas. It had plots that were funny (e.g. Corinne's baby is possessed by the devil), controversial (e.g. Billy joins a cult) and downright bizarre (e.g. Burt is abducted by aliens). The show focused on two families, the wealthy Tates and the middle-class Campbells, in Dunn's River, CT. It starred Katherine Helmond, Robert Mandan, Jennifer Salt, Diana Canova, Jimmy Baio, Robert Guillaume, Cathryn Damon, Richard Mulligan, Ted Wass, Billy Crystal, Richard Libertini, Katherine Reynolds, Robert Urich, Arthur Peterson, Roscoe Lee Browne and Jay Johnston. Rod Roddy was the announcer who recapped what had happened previously.

SOUTHEAST MISSOURI DISTRICT FAIR. Sept 13–19. Arena Park Fairgrounds, Cape Girardeau, MO. Oldest outdoor fair in the state. Celebrating its 142nd year with beauty pageants, livestock exhibition, horse show, entertainment, carnival, food and 4-H displays. Annually, the week after Labor Day. Est attendance: 92,000. For info: SEMO District Fair Assn, PO Box 234, Cape Girardeau, MO 63702-0234. Phone: (800) 455-FAIR or (573) 334-9250.

"STAR-SPANGLED BANNER" INSPIRED: ANNIVERSARY. Sept 13–14. On the night of Sept 13, 1814, Francis Scott Key was aboard a ship that was delayed in Baltimore harbor by the British attack there on Fort Henry. Key had no choice but to anxiously watch the battle. That experience and seeing the American flag still flying over the fort the next morning inspired him to pen the verses that, coupled with the tune of a popular drinking song, became our national anthem.

US CAPITAL ESTABLISHED AT NEW YORK CITY: ANNIVERSARY. Sept 13, 1788. On Sept 13, 1788, the Congress picked New York, NY, as the location of the new US government.

BIRTHDAYS TODAY

Jacqueline Bisset, 54, actress (*Rich & Famous, The Deep*), born Weybridge, England, Sept 13, 1944.

Nell Carter, 50, actress (Tony for *Ain't Misbehavin'*; "Gimme a Break"), born Birmingham, AL, Sept 13, 1948.

Peter Cetera, 54, singer (former lead singer of Chicago; solo hit "Glory of Love"), songwriter, born Chicago, IL, Sept 13, 1944.

Robert Indiana, 70, artist (*As I Opened Fire*), born New Castle, IA, Sept 13, 1928.

Michael Johnson, 31, track athlete, born Dallas, TX, Sept 13, 1967.

Richard Kiel, 59, actor (*The Longest Yard, Silver Streak, The Spy Who Loved Me*), born Detroit, MI, Sept 13, 1939.

Judith Martin, 60, author, journalist ("Miss Manners"), born Washington, DC, Sept 13, 1938.

Fred Silverman, 61, TV producer, born New York, NY, Sept 13, 1937.

Jean Smart, 39, actress ("Designing Women"), born Seattle, WA, Sept 13, 1959.

Mel Torme, 73, singer ("Comin' Home Baby"), composer ("The Christmas Song"), born Chicago, IL, Sept 13, 1925.

SEPTEMBER 14 — MONDAY

Day 257 — 108 Remaining

AMERICAN TINNITUS ASSOCIATION SCIENTIFIC ADVISORY COMMITTEE MEETING. Sept 14. San Antonio, TX. Est attendance: 24. For info: Patricia Daggett, Asst Dir, American Tinnitus Assn, Box 5, Portland, OR 97207. Phone: (503) 248-9985. Fax: (503) 248-0024. Email: tinnitus@ata.org. WWW: http//www.teleport.com/ata

"THE BOB CROSBY SHOW" TV PREMIERE: 45th ANNIVERSARY. Sept 14, 1953. Bob Crosby, Bing's younger brother, was a bandleader who hosted two shows. The first was a half-hour daytime show featuring the Modernaires, Joan O'Brien, Jack Narz and Cathy Crosby (his daughter). The second was a one-hour prime-time show with Gretchen Wyler, the Peter Gennaro dancers, the Clay Warnick singers, the Carl Hoff Orchestra and clown Emmett Kelly.

DANTE ALIGHIERI: DEATH ANNIVERSARY. Sept 14. Italian poet, author of the *Divine Comedy*, died Sept 14, 1321 at Ravenna, Italy. He was born in May 1265 (exact date unknown) at Florence, Italy.

GEMAYEL, BASHIR, ASSASSINATION: ANNIVERSARY. Sept 14, 1982. Although first government reports described his rescue and quoted him as saying "Thank God I survived this one," later news dispatches indicated that Bashir Gemayel, 34-year-old president-elect of Lebanon, died along with at least eight other persons when a bomb exploded at his Phalange party headquarters in Beirut, Lebanon, on Sept 14, 1982. On Sept 21, the Lebanese parliament elected his 39-year-old brother, Amin Gemayel, to succeed him.

"HAVE GUN WILL TRAVEL" TV PREMIERE: ANNIVERSARY. Sept 14, 1957. "Have Gun, Will Travel . . ." so read the business card of Paladin (Richard Boone), a loner whose professional services were available for a price. This half-hour western also featured Kam Tong as his servant, Hey Boy, and Lisa Lu as Hey Girl in the 1960-61 season. The show was extremely popular and ranked in the top five for most of its run.

INTERNATIONAL CROSS-CULTURAL DAY. Sept 14. People all over the world are asked to observe this day in remembrance of cultural differences that give their nations their important distinctive attributes and heritages. Also, people should renew efforts to know and understand differences of other cultures as a means of promoting international goodwill. For info: Suzanne Collier, Window on the World Inc., 123 N Third St, Ste 303, Minneapolis, MN 55401. Phone: (612) 338-3690. Fax: (612) 338-3037. Email: wowintl@aol.com.

"IRONSIDE" TV PREMIERE: ANNIVERSARY. Sept 14, 1967. This crime series starred Raymond Burr as Robert T. Ironside, Chief of Detectives for the San Francisco Police Department (he was in a wheelchair, paralyzed from an assassination attempt). Also featured were Don Galloway as his assistant, Lieutenant Ed Brown; Barbara Anderson as Officer Eve Whitfield; Don Mitchell as Mark Sanger, Ironside's personal assistant; Gene Lyons as Commissioner Dennis Randall; Elizabeth Baur as Officer Fran Belding; and Joan Pringle as Diana, Mark's wife.

McKINLEY, WILLIAM: DEATH ANNIVERSARY. Sept 14. President William McKinley was shot at Buffalo, NY, Sept 6, 1901. He died eight days later on Sept 14, 1901. Assassin Leon Czolgosz was executed Oct 29, 1901.

MOTLEY, CONSTANCE BAKER: BIRTHDAY. Sept 14, 1921. New York's first black woman state senator and federal judge, and the first woman elected borough president of Manhattan, Constance Baker Motley became interested in law and civil rights when she was barred from a public beach at age 15. She went on to become one of the top civil rights lawyers of the '50s and '60s. She presented arguments before the US Supreme Court for seven cases and won them all. Motley was born at New Haven, CT.

NATIONAL ANTHEM DAY. Sept 14. Maryland.

NATIONAL BOSS/EMPLOYEE EXCHANGE DAY. Sept 14. To help bosses and employees appreciate each other by sharing each other's point of view for a day. Annually, the first Monday after Labor Day. For info: A.C. Moeller, Box 71, Clio, MI 48420-1042.

NATIONAL SCHOOL INTERNET SAFETY WEEK. Sept 14–18. Supports safe internet usage for schools K-12 to shield students from dangerous or inappropriate web sites. For info: Seattle Software Labs, 316 Occidental S, Ste 300, Seattle, WA 98109. Phone: (206) 521-8340. Fax: (206) 521-8341. WWW: http://www.sealabs.com

PRINCESS GRACE: DEATH ANNIVERSARY. Sept 14, 1982. Princess Grace of Monaco (neé Grace Kelly) was killed in an automobile accident, when her car plunged off a mountain road in Monte Carlo. Her daughter Stephanie, who was with her, was treated for shock and bruises. Grace Kelly met Prince Rainier III while she was making her third Hitchcock film, *To Catch a Thief*. They were married in 1956.

SANGER, MARGARET (HIGGINS): BIRTH ANNIVERSARY. Sept 14. Feminist, nurse and founder of the birth control movement in the US. Born at Corning, NY, Sept 14, 1879. (Note: birth year not entirely certain because, apparently, Sanger often used a later date when obliged to divulge her birthday. Best evidence now points to Sept 14, 1879, rather than the frequently used 1883 date.) She died at Tucson, AZ, Sept 6, 1966.

SCARECROW CONTEST AND OUTDOOR DISPLAY. Sept 14–Oct 25. Peddler's Village, Lahaska, PA. Contestants compete for $4900 in cash prizes. Categories include: "A Scarecrow Whirligig"—a scarecrow that makes noise and moves with the wind; "An Extraordinary Contemporary Scarecrow"—an imaginative piece created to give a good scare in the garden; "A Traditional Scarecrow"—an outstanding example of the American Scarecrow; and "The Amateur Scarecrow"—for those who haven't won previously. Public votes for their favorites. Free admission. Est attendance: 75,000. For info: Judy Goldschmidt, PR Mgr, Peddler's Village, Routes 202 and 263, Lahaska, PA 18931. Phone: (215) 794-4000. Fax: (215) 794-4001. WWW: http://www.peddlersvillage.com

SETON, ELIZABETH ANN: CANONIZATION ANNIVERSARY. Sept 14. Elizabeth Ann Seton became the first native-born American to be canonized on Sept 14, 1975. She was declared a saint in 1974 by Pope Paul VI.

SOLO TRANSATLANTIC BALLOON CROSSING: ANNIVERSARY. Sept 14–18, 1984. Joe W. Kittinger, 56-year-old balloonist left Caribou, ME, in a 10-story-tall helium-filled balloon named *Rosie O'Grady's Balloon of Peace* on Sept 14, 1984, crossed the Atlantic Ocean and reached the French coast, above the town of Capbreton, in bad weather on Sept 17 at 4:29 PM, EDT. He crashlanded amid wind and rain near Savone, Italy, at 8:08 AM, EDT, Sept 18. Kittinger suffered a broken ankle when he was thrown from the balloon's gondola during the landing. His nearly 84-hour flight, covering about 3,535 miles, was the first solo balloon crossing of the Atlantic Ocean and a record distance for a solo balloon flight.

US SENIOR AMATEUR (GOLF) CHAMPIONSHIP. Sept 14–19. Shadow Creek Golf Club, North Las Vegas, NV. For info: US Golf Assn, Golf House, Championship Dept, Far Hills, NJ 07931. Phone: (908) 234-2300. Fax: (908) 234-9687. Email: usga@ix.netcom.com. WWW: http://www.usga.org

US SENIOR WOMEN'S AMATEUR (GOLF) CHAMPIONSHIP. Sept 14–19. Yeamans Hall Club, Charleston, SC. For info: US Golf Assn, Golf House, Championship Dept, Far Hills, NJ 07931. Phone: (908) 234-2300. Fax: (908) 234-9687. Email: usga@ix.netcom.com. WWW: http://www.usga.org

"THE WALTONS" TV PREMIERE: ANNIVERSARY. Sept 14, 1972. The epitome of the '70s family drama spawning nearly a dozen knock-offs during its nine-year run on CBS. The drama was based on creator/writer Earl Hammer Jr's experiences growing up during the Depression in rural Virginia. It began as the TV movie "The Homecoming," which was so well-received that it was turned into a weekly series covering the years 1933–43. The cast went through numerous changes through the years; the principals were: Michael Learned as Olivia Walton, mother of the clan; Ralph Waite as John Walton, father; Richard Thomas as John-Boy, eldest son; Jon Walmsley as son Jason; Judy Norton as daughter Mary Ellen; Eric Scott as son Ben; Mary Elizabeth McDonough as daughter Erin; David W. Harper as son Jim-Bob; and Kami Cotler as daughter Elizabeth. The Walton grandparents were played by Ellen Corby (Esther) and Will Geer (Zeb).

BIRTHDAYS TODAY

Zoe Caldwell, 65, actress (*Medea, The Prime of Miss Jean Brodie*), born Melbourne, Australia, Sept 14, 1933.

Mary Crosby, 39, actress ("Dallas," *Tapeheads*), born Los Angeles, CA, Sept 14, 1959.

Faith Ford, 34, actress ("Murphy Brown"), born Alexandria, LA, Sept 14, 1964.

Joey Heatherton, 54, actress (*Cry Baby, Bluebeard*, "Dean Martin and the Golddiggers"), born Rockville Centre, NY, Sept 14, 1944.

Walter Koenig, 62, actor, writer, director, producer (played Chekov in "Star Trek" and *Star Trek* movies), born Chicago, IL, Sept 14, 1936.

Kate Millett (Katherine Murray Millett), 64, feminist, writer (*Sexual Politics, Flying, The Basement*), sculptor, born St. Paul, MN, Sept 14, 1934.

Clayton Moore, 84, actor ("The Lone Ranger"), born Chicago, IL, Sept 14, 1914.

Sam Neill, 51, actor (*My Brilliant Career, Jurassic Park, The Piano*), born Ireland, Sept 14, 1947.

Nicol Williamson, 60, actor (*Robin and Marian, Excalibur*), born Hamilton, Scotland, Sept 14, 1938.

SEPTEMBER 15 — TUESDAY

Day 258 — 107 Remaining

ACUFF, ROY: 95th BIRTH ANNIVERSARY. Sept 15, 1903. Grand Ole Opry "King of Country Music" Roy Acuff was born Sept 15, 1903, at Maynardville, TN. Singer and fiddler Acuff (who was co-founder of Acuff-Rose Publishing Company, the leading publisher of country music) was a regular host on weekly Grand Ole Opry broadcasts. He frequently appeared at the Opry with his group, the Smoky Mountain Boys. In December of 1991 Acuff became the first living member elected to the Country Music Hall of Fame. Some of his more famous songs were "The Wabash Cannonball" (his theme song), "Pins and Needles (In My Heart)" and "Night Train to Memphis." Roy Acuff died Nov 23, 1992, at Nashville, TN.

"BACHELOR FATHER" TV PREMIERE: ANNIVERSARY. Sept 15, 1957. John Forsythe (Bentley Gregg) and Noreen Corcoran (Kelly Gregg) starred in this sitcom about a bachelor attorney's life turning upside-down after his orphaned niece moves in with him. The series aired at different times on all three networks. Supporting players included: Sammee Tong as Peter Tong, the butler; Jimmy Boyd as Kelly's boyfriend, Howard Meachum; Bernadette Withers as Kelly's friend Ginger; Whit Bissell as Ginger's father, Bert Loomis; Alice Backes as Bentley's secretary, Vicki; Sue Ann Langdon as Bentley's secretary, Kitty Marsh; and Victor Sen Yung as Peter's cousin, Charlie Fong.

September 1998

S	M	T	W	T	F	S
		1	2	3	4	5
6	7	8	9	10	11	12
13	14	15	16	17	18	19
20	21	22	23	24	25	26
27	28	29	30			

BALANCE AWARENESS WEEK. Sept 15–20. To develop public awareness of balance and disorders of balance system (vestibular disorders); to unite professionals, educators, support groups, medical facilities in a week-long effort to focus attention to the public and the media. For info: Vestibular Disorders Assn, PO Box 4467, Portland, OR 97208-4467. Phone: (800) 837-8428. Fax: (503) 229-8064.

"CHiPS" TV PREMIERE: ANNIVERSARY. Sept 15, 1977. A popular action-packed NBC police series depicting cases and chases of the motorcycle-riding California Highway Patrol. The show starred Erik Estrada as Francis "Ponch" Poncherello and Larry Wilcox as Jonathan Baker, two quick-witted cops. Wilcox left the show, and Estrada's new partner, Bobby "Hot Dog" Nelson, was played by Tom Reilly. Other regulars included Robert Pine, Paul Linke, Lou Wagner, Brodie Greer, Brianne Leary, Randi Oakes, Michael Dorn, Bruce Jenner, Bruce Penhall and Tina Gayle.

CHRISTIE, AGATHA: BIRTH ANNIVERSARY. Sept 15. English author of nearly a hundred books (mysteries, drama, poetry and nonfiction), born at Torquay, England, Sept 15, 1890. Died at Wallingford, England, Jan 12, 1976. "Every murderer," she wrote, in *The Mysterious Affair at Styles*, "is probably somebody's old friend."

COOPER, JAMES FENIMORE: BIRTH ANNIVERSARY. Sept 15, 1789. American novelist, historian and social critic, born at Burlington, NJ, on Sept 15, 1789, James Fenimore Cooper was one of the earliest American writers eager to develop a native American literary tradition. His most popular works are the five novels comprising *The Leatherstocking Tales,* featuring the exploits of one of the truly unique American fictional characters, Natty Bumppo. These novels, *The Deerslayer, The Last of the Mohicans, The Pathfinder, The Pioneers* and *The Prairie,* chronicle Natty Bumppo's continuing flight away from the rapid settlement of America. Other works, including *The Monikins* and *Satanstoe,* reveal him as an astute critic of American life both socially and politically. He died Sept 14, 1851, at Cooperstown, NY, the town founded by his father.

COSTA RICA: INDEPENDENCE DAY. Sept 15. National holiday. Gained independence from Spain on this day, 1821.

EL SALVADOR: INDEPENDENCE DAY. Sept 15. National holiday. Gained independence from Spain on this day, 1821.

ENGLAND: BATTLE OF BRITAIN DAY. Sept 15. Commemorates end of biggest daylight bombing raid of Britain by German Luftwaffe, on Sunday, Sept 15, 1940. Said to have been the turning point against Hitler's siege of Britain in World War II.

FIRST NATIONAL CONVENTION FOR BLACKS: ANNIVERSARY. Sept 15. The first national convention for blacks was held at Bethel Church, Philadelphia, PA, on Sept 15, 1830. The convention was called to find ways to better the condition of black people and was attended by delegates from seven states. Bishop Richard Allen was elected as the first convention president.

GRANT COUNTY HOME PRODUCTS DINNER. Sept 15. Grant County Civic Center, Ulysses, KS. 36th annual public dinner grown, prepared and served by Grant County residents. Annually, the third Tuesday of September. Est attendance: 1,800. For info: Dennis Zimmerman, Pres/CEO, Grant County Chamber of Commerce, 115 W Grant, Ulysses, KS 67880. Phone: (316) 356-4700. Fax: (316) 356-4840. Email: gchamber@pld.com.

GREENPEACE FOUNDED: ANNIVERSARY. Sept 15, 1971. The environmental organization Greenpeace, committed to a green and peaceful world, was founded by 12 members of the Don't Make a Wave committee of Vancouver, BC, Canada, when the boat *Phyllis Cormack* sailed to Amchitka, AK, to protest US nuclear testing. Greenpeace's basic principle is "that determined individuals can alter the actions and purposes of even the overwhelmingly powerful by 'bearing witness'—drawing attention to an environmental abuse through their mere unwavering presence, whatever the risk."

GUATEMALA: INDEPENDENCE DAY. Sept 15. National holiday. Gained independence from Spain on this day, 1821.

HONDURAS: INDEPENDENCE DAY. Sept 15. National holiday. Gained independence from Spain on this day, 1821.

"I SPY" TV PREMIERE: ANNIVERSARY. Sept 15, 1965. Bill Cosby made television history as the first African-American actor starring in a major dramatic role in this spy series. Cosby played Alexander "Scotty" Scott, an intellectual spy with a cover as a tennis trainer. Robert Culp played Kelly Robinson, the "tennis pro" and Scotty's partner in espionage. The series was notable for filming worldwide.

JAPAN: OLD PEOPLE'S DAY OR RESPECT FOR THE AGED DAY. Sept 15. National holiday.

LOCKWOOD, MARGARET: BIRTH ANNIVERSARY. Sept 15, 1916. British actress Margaret Lockwood was born at Pakistan. Her films include *The Lady Vanishes* (1938), *Night Train* (1940) and *The Slipper and The Rose* (1976). She died on July 15, 1990, at London, England.

"THE LONE RANGER" TV PREMIERE: ANNIVERSARY. Sept 15, 1949. "The Lone Ranger" became synonymous with the music of Rossini's "William Tell Overture." The character was created for a radio serial in 1933 by George W. Trendle. The famous masked man was the alter ego of John Reid, a Texas Ranger who was the only survivor of an ambush. He was nursed back to health by his Native-American friend, Tonto. Both men traveled around the West on their trusty steeds, Silver and Scout, fighting injustice. Clayton Moore played the Lone Ranger/John Reid and Jay Silverheels co-starred as Tonto.

NATIONAL CAREGIVERS DAY. Sept 15. A day to applaud and recognize the persons who care for the elderly, the physically and mentally challenged and the terminally ill. There are countless thousands who live each day loving, nurturing and supporting those people who are entrusted to their care. For info: Ann R. Noons, Connecting Care Resources, PO Box 645, South Dennis, MA 02660. Phone: (800) 765-0648 or (508) 432-5457. Fax: (508) 432-7808.

★**NATIONAL HISPANIC HERITAGE MONTH.** Sept 15–Oct 15. Presidential Proclamation. Beginning in 1989, always issued for Sept 15–Oct 15 of each year (PL 100–402 of Aug 17, 1988). Previously issued each year for the week including Sept 15 and 16 since 1968 at request (PL90–498 of Sept 17, 1968).

NETHERLANDS: PRINSJESDAG. Sept 15. Official opening of parliament at The Hague. On the third Tuesday in September, the queen of the Netherlands, by tradition, rides in a golden coach to the hall of knights for the annual opening of parliament.

NICARAGUA: INDEPENDENCE DAY. Sept 15. National holiday. Gained independence from Spain on this day, 1821.

QUARTERLY ESTIMATED FEDERAL INCOME TAX PAYER'S DUE DATE. Sept 15. For those individuals whose fiscal year is the calendar year and who make quarterly estimated federal income tax payments, today is one of the due dates. (Jan 15, Apr 15, June 15 and Sept 15, 1998.)

SENIOR SAFARI DAY. Sept 15. Metro Washington Park Zoo, Portland, OR. Free zoo admission for seniors and companions; music, dancing and animal talks. Est attendance: 3,500. For info: Events Coord, Metro Washington Park Zoo, 4001 SW Canyon Rd, Portland, OR 97221-2799. Phone: (503) 226-1561. Fax: (503) 220-5754.

SPACE MILESTONE: *ARIANE-3* (ESA). Sept 15, 1987. European Space Agency rocket carrying two (Australian and European) communications satellites into earth orbit marked the re-entry of western nations into commercial space projects. Launched this date from Kourou, French Guiana, with Arianespace, a private company operating the rocket for the 13-nation European Space Agency.

SPACE MILESTONE: *SOYUZ 22* (USSR). Sept 15, 1976. Launched this date with Cosmonauts V. Bykovsky and V. Asenov, *Soyuz 22* entered Earth orbit for the study of "geological and geographical characteristics on Earth's surface in the interests of the national economy." Returned to Earth on Sept 23.

TAFT, WILLIAM HOWARD: BIRTH ANNIVERSARY. Sept 15. The 27th president of the US was born at Cincinnati, OH, Sept 15, 1857. His term of office: Mar 4, 1909–Mar 3, 1913. Following his presidency he became a law professor at Yale University until his appointment as Chief Justice of the US Supreme Court in 1921. Believed to have been the heaviest US president (weighed 225 pounds at age 20). Died at Washington, DC, Mar 8, 1930, and was buried at Arlington National Cemetery.

TEXAS/OKLAHOMA FAIR. Sept 15–19. Multi-Purpose Events Center & J.S. Bridwell Agricultural Center, Wichita Falls, TX. Old-fashioned county fair with exhibits, games, food, rides and more! Est attendance: 40,000. For info: Wichita Falls Conv & Visitors Bureau, 1000 5th St, Wichita Falls, TX 76301. Phone: (817) 716-5500. Fax: (817) 716-5509.

US TROOPS ENTER GERMANY: ANNIVERSARY. Sept 15, 1944. US troops of the VII and V Corps reached the southwestern frontier of Germany. The war had finally moved into the Third Reich's backyard.

"WORLD'S LARGEST" WEATHER VANE ANNIVERSARY. Sept 15. At the edge of White Lake in Montague, MI, on Sept 15, 1984, the "world's largest" weather vane was dedicated. Forty-eight feet high with a 26-foot wind arrow, the weather vane weighing 3,500 lbs is adorned with a 14-foot replica of a 19th-century Great Lakes schooner.

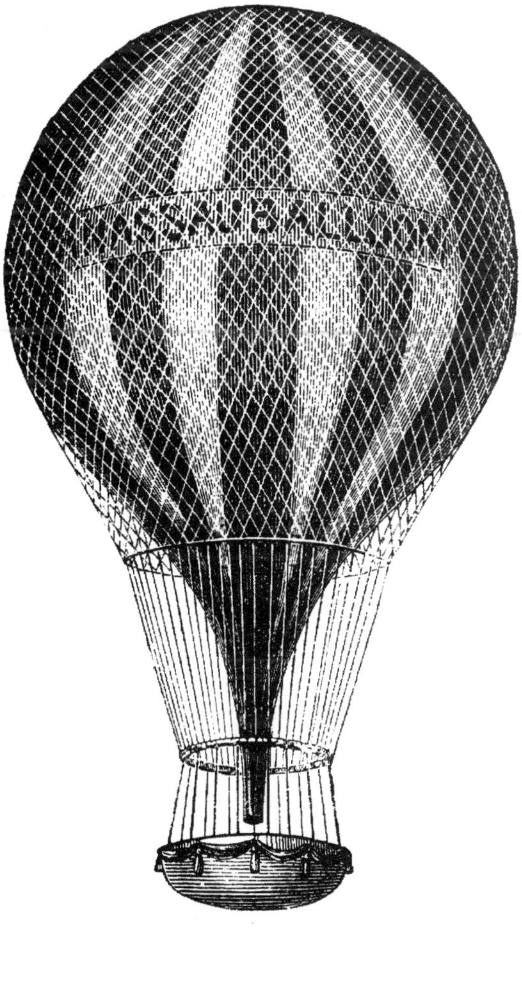

BIRTHDAYS TODAY

Jackie Cooper, 76, actor (*Our Gang* shorts, Skippy; "The People's Choice") producer, born Los Angeles, CA, Sept 15, 1922.
Norm Crosby, 71, comedian (hosted "The Comedy Shop"), born Boston, MA, Sept 15, 1927.
Sherman Douglas, 32, basketball player, born Washington, DC, Sept 15, 1966.
Prince Harry (Henry Charles Albert David), 14, of Wales, son of Prince Charles and Princess Diana, second in line to the British throne, born London, England, Sept 15, 1984.
Tommy Lee Jones, 52, actor (Oscar for *The Fugitive; Coal Miner's Daughter*), born San Saba, TX, Sept 15, 1946.
Daniel Constantine (Dan) Marino, Jr, 37, football player, born Pittsburgh, PA, Sept 15, 1961.
Carmen Maura, 53, actress (*What Have I Done to Deserve This?, Law of Desire, Women on the Verge of a Nervous Breakdown*), born Madrid, Spain, Sept 15, 1945.
Jessye Norman, 53, soprano, born Augusta, GA, Sept 15, 1945.
Merlin Jay Olsen, 58, Pro Football Hall of Fame defensive tackle, sportscaster, actor, born Logan, UT, Sept 15, 1940.
Gaylord Jackson Perry, 60, Baseball Hall of Fame pitcher, born Williamston, NC, Sept 15, 1938.
Bobby Short (Robert Waltrip), 72, singer-pianist (as a child he was called "The Midget King of Swing"; cafe song stylist), born Danville, IL, Sept 15, 1926.
Oliver Stone, 52, director (*Platoon, JFK, Wall Street*), screenwriter, born New York, NY, Sept 15, 1946.

SEPTEMBER 16 — WEDNESDAY

Day 259 — 106 Remaining

AMERICAN BUSINESS WOMEN'S ASSOCIATION NATIONAL CONVENTION. Sept 16–20. Phoenix, AZ. Businesswomen gather to learn, network and elect ABWA's national board of directors for the coming year. Seminars, speakers and the announcement of the Top Ten Business Women of ABWA and the American Business Woman of ABWA are featured. Est attendance: 3,000. For info: Carolyn Elman, American Business Women's Assn, 9100 Ward Parkway, PO Box 8728, Kansas City, MO 64114-0728. Phone: (816) 361-6621. Fax: (816) 361-4991. Email: abwa@sky.net. WWW: http://www.abwahq.org

"THE BIG STORY" TV PREMIERE: ANNIVERSARY. Sept 16, 1949. William Sloane, Norman Rose, Ben Grauer and Burgess Meredith all played host to this anthology program profiling the stories and exploits of daring journalists. The show aired for eight years on NBC.

☆ ☆ ☆

CHEROKEE STRIP DAY: ANNIVERSARY. Sept 16, 1893. Optional holiday, Oklahoma. Greatest "run" for Oklahoma land in 1893.

GENERAL MOTORS: 90th FOUNDING ANNIVERSARY. Sept 16, 1908. The giant automobile manufacturing company was founded Sept 16, 1908, by William Crapo "Billy" Durant, a Flint, MI, entrepreneur.

GOLDEN ASPEN MOTORCYCLE RALLY. Sept 16–20. Ruidoso, NM. Trade show, bike shows, riding tours, skill events, parade, awards banquet, stunt shows and thousands in prizes. Est attendance: 15,000. For info: Golden Aspen Rally Assn, PO Box 1458, Ruidoso, NM 88345. Phone: (800) 452-8045. Email: gara@usa.net. WWW: http://www.motorcyclerally.com

September 1998

S	M	T	W	T	F	S
		1	2	3	4	5
6	7	8	9	10	11	12
13	14	15	16	17	18	19
20	21	22	23	24	25	26
27	28	29	30			

GREAT SEAL OF THE UNITED STATES: FIRST USE ANNIVERSARY. Sept 16, 1782. On this date the Great Seal of the United States was, for the first time, impressed upon an official document. That document authorized George Washington to negotiate a prisoner of war agreement with the British. See also: "Great Seal of the United States: Anniversary" (Jan 28, June 20 and July 4).

"MANNIX" TV PREMIERE: ANNIVERSARY. Sept 16, 1967. Mike Connors starred as Joe Mannix, a Los Angeles private investigator working for the computer organization, Intertect, in this long-running CBS crime series. Joe Campanella played his boss, Lew Wickersham, during the first season. The show then changed format with Mannix setting up his own agency. The new cast members were Gail Fisher as Peggy Fair, his secretary; Robert Reed as Lieutenant Adam Tobias; and Ward Wood as Lieutenant Art Malcolm.

MAYFLOWER DAY: ANNIVERSARY. Sept 16. Anniversary of the departure of the *Mayflower* from Plymouth, England, Sept 16, 1620, with 102 passengers and a small crew. Vicious storms were encountered en route which caused serious doubt about the wisdom of continuing, but she reached Provincetown, MA, on Nov 21, and discharged the Pilgrims at Plymouth, MA, on Dec 26, 1620.

MEXICO: INDEPENDENCE DAY. Sept 16. National Day. The official celebration begins at 11 PM, Sept 15 and continues through Sept 16.

MIDDLEMARK, MARVIN: BIRTH ANNIVERSARY. Sept 16. Marvin Middlemark was born on Sept 16, 1919, at Long Island, NY. His passion for inventing and tinkering led to many inventions, most of which enjoyed little commercial success, like the water-driven automatic potato peeler. But it was as the inventor of a device to improve TV reception, known as "rabbit ears," that he became successful. He died on Sept 14, 1989 at Old Westbury, NY.

MORTON PUMPKIN FESTIVAL. Sept 16–19. Morton, IL. Carnival, parade, entertainment and fantastic food to celebrate the pumpkin in the "Pumpkin Capital of the World." Est attendance: 50,000. For info: Chamber of Commerce, 415 W Jefferson St, Morton, IL 61550. Phone: (309) 263-2491. Fax: (309) 263-2401. Email: pumpkin@mtco.com.

NATIONAL VISION REHABILITATION DAY. Sept 16. Because of the documented lack of knowledge about both vision loss and the availability of vision rehabilitation services, this observance has been created to promote aggressive education and treatment for people with vision problems. It is sponsored by The Lighthouse Inc, a leading resource on vision impairment, and is commemorated throughout the nation by national organizations, eye care professionals and member agencies of The National Vision Rehabilitation Cooperative. For info: Vernice Williams,

Media Mgr, The Lighthouse Inc, 111 E 59th St, New York, NY 10022. Phone: (212) 821-9555. Fax: (212) 821-9702. Email: inbox@lighthouse.org. WWW: http://www.lighthouse.org

"OWEN MARSHALL: COUNSELOR AT LAW" TV PREMIERE: ANNIVERSARY. Sept 16, 1971. "Owen Marshall" was an hour-long drama with Arthur Hill as the title character, a widowed attorney in Santa Barbara. Lee Majors, Reni Santoni and David Soul played his associates. Also featured were Joan Darling as Marshall's secretary and Christine Matchett as his daughter. This show aired on ABC.

PALESTINIAN MASSACRE: ANNIVERSARY. Sept 16, 1982. Christian militiamen (the Phalangists) entered Sabra and Shatila, two Palestinian refugee camps in West Beirut. They began open shooting and by Sept 18 hundreds of Palestinians, including elderly men, women and children, were dead. Phalangists had demanded blood of Palestinians since the assassination of their president, Bashir Gemayel, on Sept 14. Survivors of the massacre said they had not seen Israeli forces inside the camp; however, they claimed Israelis sealed off boundaries to the camps and allowed Christian militiamen to enter.

PANIZZI, ANTHONY: BIRTH ANNIVERSARY. Sept 16, 1797. Sir Anthony Panizzi, the only librarian ever hanged in effigy, was born Antonio Genesio Maria Panizzi at Brescello, Italy, on Sept 16, 1797. As a young man he joined a forbidden Italian patriotic society which advocated the overthrow of the oppressive Austrians who then controlled most of northern Italy. Tried in absentia by an Austrian court in 1820, he was sentenced to death and all his property was confiscated. He fled to England in 1823, learned the language and by 1831 was employed in the British Museum where, in 1856, he was named principal librarian. Later described as the "prince of librarians," Panizzi died at London, England, on Apr 8, 1879.

PAPUA NEW GUINEA: INDEPENDENCE DAY. Sept 16. National holiday.

PARKMAN, FRANCIS: 175th BIRTH ANNIVERSARY. Sept 16, 1823. American historian, author of *The Oregon Trail*, was born at Boston, MA, on Sept 16, 1823, and died there on Nov 8, 1893.

PENDLETON ROUND-UP. Sept 16–19. Pendleton, OR. America's classic rodeo. An 87-year-old western tradition, with participating Indian tribes from the Pacific Northwest. Plus historical Happy Canyon, an outdoor pageant each evening. Est attendance: 54,000. For info: Pendleton Round-up Assn, Box 609, Pendleton, OR 97801. Phone: (800) 457-6336.

"SKY KING" TV PREMIERE: ANNIVERSARY. Sept 16, 1951. This half-hour children's adventure series began on radio in 1947. Kirby Grant starred as Schuyler J. (Sky) King, owner of the Flying Crown Ranch, who used his plane, The Songbird, to help victims and capture criminals. To help him was a cast that included Gloria Winters as his niece, Penny; Ron Hagerthy as his nephew Clipper; Ewing Mitchell as the sheriff, Mitch; Norman Ollstead as Bob Carey; and Gary Hunley as Mickey.

STAY AWAY FROM SEATTLE DAY. Sept 16. Observed worldwide, except in Seattle, WA, to give America's "Best Place to Live" city a break from the influx of people moving to the area. On this day every year, the rest of us will try to keep the appeal of Seattle from haunting us with its siren call. [© 1997 by WPL] For info: Thomas and Ruth Roy, Wellness Permission League, PO Box 662, Mt Gretna, PA 17064-0662. Phone: (500) 437-5104 or (717) 964-1308. Fax: (717) 964-1335.

STEAMBOAT MOTORCYCLE WEEKEND. Sept 16–20. Steamboat Springs, CO. Vintage and Modern street races. Pre-weekend includes motorcross, trials race and dirt track. Display of classic motorcycles. 18th annual. Est attendance: 10,000. For info: Special Events Dept, Steamboat Springs Chamber Resort Assn, PO Box 774408, Steamboat Springs, CO 80477. Phone: (970) 879-0880. Fax: (970) 879-2543.
Email: info@steamboat-chamber.com.
WWW: http://www.steamboat-chamber.com

TORQUEMADA, TOMAS DE: 500th DEATH ANNIVERSARY. Sept 16, 1498. One of history's most malevolent persons, feared and hated by millions. As Inquisitor-General of Spain, he ordered burning at the stake for more than 10,000 persons and burning in effigy for another 7,000 (according to 18th-century estimates). Torquemada persuaded Ferdinand and Isabella to rid Spain of the Jews. More than a million families were driven from the country and Spain suffered a commercial decline from which it never recovered. Torquemada was born at Valladolide, Spain, in 1420 (exact date unknown) and died at Avila, Spain, Sept 16, 1498.

UNITED NATIONS: INTERNATIONAL DAY FOR THE PRESERVATION OF THE OZONE LAYER. Sept 16. On Dec 19, 1994, the General Assembly proclaimed this day to commemorate the date in 1987 on which Montreal Protocol on Substances that Deplete the Ozone Layer was signed (Res 49/114). States are invited to devote the Day to promote, at the national level, activities in accordance with the objectives of the Protocol. The ozone layer filters sunlight and prevents the adverse effects of ultraviolet radiation from reaching the Earth's surface, thereby preserving life on the planet. For info: United Nations, Dept of Public Info, Public Inquiries Unit, Rm GA-57, New York, NY 10017. Phone: (212) 963-4475. Fax: (212) 963-0071. Email: inquiries@un.org.

BIRTHDAYS TODAY

Lauren Bacall (Betty Joan Perske), 74, actress (*Applause, Woman of the Year, Key Largo, How to Marry a Millionaire*), born New York, NY, Sept 16, 1924.

Elgin Gay Baylor, 64, former coach and Basketball Hall of Fame forward, born Washington, DC, Sept 16, 1934.

Ed Begley, Jr, 49, actor ("St. Elsewhere"), born Los Angeles, CA, Sept 16, 1949.

Charlie Byrd, 73, musician ("Meditation"; "Desafinado" with Stan Getz), born Chuckatuck, VA, Sept 16, 1925.

David Copperfield (Kotkin), 42, illusionist, born Metuchen, NJ, Sept 16, 1956.

Peter Falk, 71, actor (*The Great Race*, "Columbo"), born New York, NY, Sept 16, 1927.

Anne Francis, 66, actress (*Bad Day at Black Rock, Blackboard Jungle, Forbidden Planet*), born Ossining, NY, Sept 16, 1932.

Allen Funt, 84, TV producer, host ("Candid Camera"), born Brooklyn, NY, Sept 16, 1914.

Henry Louis Gates, Jr, 48, professor of African-American studies at Harvard, editor of the *Norton Anthology of African American Literature*, born Keyser, WV, Sept 16, 1950.

Orel Leonard Hershiser IV, 40, baseball player, born Buffalo, NY, Sept 16, 1958.

B.B. King, 73, singer ("Rock Me Baby," "The Thrill is Gone"), born Itta Bena, MS, Sept 16, 1925.

John Knowles, 72, writer (*A Separate Peace*), born Farmont, WV, Sept 16, 1926.

Richard Marx, 35, singer, born Chicago, IL, Sept 16, 1963.

Mark McEwen, 44, weatherman, music editor, born San Antonio, TX, Sept 16, 1954.

Janis Paige, 75, singer, actress (stage: *The Pajama Game; Silk Stockings*), born Tacoma, WA, Sept 16, 1923.

Timothy ("Rock") Raines, 39, baseball player, born Sanford, FL, Sept 16, 1959.

Mickey Rourke, 42, actor (*9½ Weeks, Bar Fly*), born Schenectady, NY, Sept 16, 1956.

Molly Shannon, 34, actress ("Saturday Night Live"), born Shaker Heights, OH, Sept 16, 1964.

Robin R. Yount, 43, former baseball player, born Danville, IL, Sept 16, 1955.

SEPTEMBER 17 — THURSDAY

Day 260 — 105 Remaining

BATTLE OF ANTIETAM: ANNIVERSARY. Sept 17, 1862. This date has been called America's bloodiest day in recognition of the high casualties suffered in the Civil War battle between General Robert E. Lee's Confederate forces and General George McClellan's Union army. Estimates vary, but more than 25,000 Union and Confederate soldiers were killed or wounded in this battle on the banks of the Potomac River in Maryland.

BURGER, WARREN E.: BIRTH ANNIVERSARY. Sept 17, 1907. Former Chief Justice of the US Warren E. Burger was born at St. Paul, MN. A conservative on criminal matters, but a progressive on social issues, he had the longest tenure (1969-86) of any chief justice in this century. Appointed by President Nixon, he voted in the majority on *Roe vs Wade* (1973), which upheld a woman's right to an abortion, and on *US vs Nixon* (1974), which forced Nixon to surrender audio tapes to the Watergate special prosecutor. He died on June 25, 1995 at Washington, DC.

CANADA: ARTS FESTIVAL XV. Sept 17–20. Annapolis Royal, Nova Scotia. Performance, workshops, art exhibits, a costume arts ball and readings by famous Canadian writers. Annually, the third weekend in September. Est attendance: 2,500. For info: Susan Tileston, Exec Dir, ARCAC, Annapolis Royal Community Arts Council, Box 534, Annapolis Royal, NS, Canada B0S 1A0. Phone: (902) 532-7069. Fax: (902) 532-7357.
Email: arcoc@clan.tartannet.ns.ca.
WWW: http://www.valleyweb.com/artspeace/

★**CITIZENSHIP DAY.** Sept 17. Presidential Proclamation always issued for Sept 17 at request (PL82-261 of Feb 29, 1952). Customarily issued as "Citizenship Day and Constitution Week."

CONNOLLY, MAUREEN: BIRTH ANNIVERSARY. Sept 17, 1934. Maureen ("Little Mo") Catherine Connolly Brinker, tennis player born at San Diego, CA. Connolly became the second-youngest woman to win the US National championship at Forest Hills, NY when she captured that title in 1951. She repeated in 1952 and won Wimbledon, too. In 1953, she became the first woman to win the Grand Slam, taking the US, French, Australian and Wimbledon championships. After winning a second straight French title and a third straight Wimbledon, she suffered a crushed leg in a horseback riding accident and never competed again. Died at Dallas, TX, June 21, 1969.

CONSTITUTION OF THE US: ANNIVERSARY. Sept 17, 1787. On this date delegations from 12 states at the Constitutional Convention in Philadelphia, PA, voted unanimously to approve the proposed document. Thirty-nine of the 42 delegates present signed it and the Convention adjourned, after drafting a letter of transmittal to the Congress. The proposed constitution stipulated that it would take effect when ratified by nine states.

September 1998

S	M	T	W	T	F	S
		1	2	3	4	5
6	7	8	9	10	11	12
13	14	15	16	17	18	19
20	21	22	23	24	25	26
27	28	29	30			

★**CONSTITUTION WEEK.** Sept 17–23. Presidential Proclamation always issued for the period of Sept 17–23 each year since 1955 (PL 84–915 of Aug 2, 1956).

CONSTITUTION DAY IN ARIZONA. Sept 17. Arizona. This state holiday commemorates the signing of the US Constitution on September 17, 1787.

FOLKFEST. Sept 17–20. Bismarck, ND. Join one of the American Bus Association's top 100 events. There is something for everyone: a parade, Gumi Race, Renaissance Feast, queen coronation, national entertainment, downtown street fair and local events celebrating North Dakota's culture and heritage. For info: Bismarck/Mandan Conv & Visitors Bureau, PO Box 2274, Bismarck, ND 58502. Phone: (800) 767-3555. Fax: (701) 222-0647.

FOSTER, ANDREW (RUBE): BIRTH ANNIVERSARY. Sept 17, 1879. Rube Foster's efforts in baseball earned him the title of "The Father of Negro Baseball." He was a manager and star pitcher, pitching 51 victories in one year. In 1919, he called a meeting of black baseball owners and organized the first black baseball league, the Negro National League. He served as its president until his death in 1930. Foster was born at Calvert, TX, the son of a minister. He died Dec 9, 1930, at Kankakee, IL.

"THE FUGITIVE" TV PREMIERE: 35th ANNIVERSARY. Sept 17, 1963. A nail-biting adventure series on ABC. Dr. Richard Kimble (David Janssen) was wrongly convicted and sentenced to death for his wife's murder, but escaped from his captors in a train wreck. This popular program aired for four years detailing Kimble's search for the one-armed man (Bill Raisch) who had killed his wife, Helen (Diane Brewster). In the meantime, Kimble himself was being pursued by Lieutenant Philip Gerard (Barry Morse). The final episode aired Aug 29, 1967, and featured Kimble extracting a confession from the one-armed man as they struggled from the heights of a water tower in a deserted amusement park. That single episode was the highest-rated show ever broadcast until 1976. The TV series generated a hit movie in 1993 with Harrison Ford as Kimble and Oscar-winner Tommy Lee Jones as Gerard.

"HEAD OF THE CLASS" TV PREMIERE: ANNIVERSARY. Sept 17, 1986. This ABC sitcom was billed as the antithesis of "Welcome Back, Kotter." It ran for five years, depicting the travails and triumphs of brainy students in the Individual Honors Program (IHP) of New York's Fillmore High School. One episode in 1988 was noteworthy as the first American prime-time program filmed entirely in the Soviet Union. Howard Hesseman starred as part-time actor and substitute teacher Charlie Moore (a man more adept at teaching life's lessons than history). The cast also featured William G. Schilling as Principal Samuels; Jeannetta Arnette as Assistant Principal Bernadette Meara; Leslie Bega as Maria; Dan Frischman as Arvid; Robin Givens as Darlene; Khrystyne Haje as Simone; Jory Husain as Jawaharlal; Tony O'Dell as Alan; Brian Robbins as Eric; Kimberly Russell as Sarah; Dan Schneider as Dennis; Tannis Vallely as Janice; Rain Pryor, daughter of comedian Richard Pryor, as T.J.; Michael DeLorenzo as Alex; Lara Piper as Viki; De'Voreaux White as Aristotle; and Jonathan Ke Quan as Jasper. After Hesseman left the show in 1990, Scottish comedian Billy Connolly took over the class. The series ended with the graduation of all the characters.

HENDRICKS, THOMAS ANDREWS: BIRTH ANNIVERSARY. Sept 17. Twenty-first vice president of the US (1885) born Muskingum County, OH, Sept 17, 1819. Died at Indianapolis, IN, Nov 25, 1885.

HERZOG, CHAIM: BIRTH ANNIVERSARY. Sept 17, 1918. President of Israel, an ex-general and chief delegate to the UN, author, lawyer, born at Belfast, Northern Ireland Sept 17, 1918. He was a British army officer in World War II, died at Tel Aviv, Israel, Apr 17, 1997.

HUMMER/BIRD CELEBRATION. Sept 17–20. Rockport and Fulton, TX. To celebrate the spectacular fall migration of the ruby-throated hummingbird and other birds from their summer nesting grounds in the north along the eastern Gulf Coast on the way to their winter grounds in Mexico and Central America, and its 500-mile journey across the Gulf. There are programs, workshops, booths, concessions, bus and boat tours. Est attendance: 5,000. For info: Rockport Fulton Area Chamber of Commerce, Hummer/Bird Celebration, 404 Broadway, Rockport, TX 78382. Phone: (800) 242-0071 or (512) 729-6445. Fax: (512) 729-7681. WWW: http://www.rockport-fulton.org

INDIANAPOLIS FALL BOAT SHOW. Sept 17–20. Indiana State Fairgrounds, Indianapolis, IN. For info: Kevin Renfro, VP, 2511 E 46th St., Ste E-2, Indianapolis, IN 46205. Phone: (317) 546-4344 or (800) 892-1723. Fax: (317) 546-3002. Email: insportshow@iquest.net.

LOS ANGELES COUNTY FAIR. Sept 17–Oct 4 (tentative). Pomona, CA. "America's Fair," world's largest county fair, features free stage acts and attractions, livestock, thoroughbred racing, carnival, flower and garden show, home arts, nightly fireworks, horse shows, commercial exhibits, photography and much more. Est attendance: 1,400,000. For info: Fairplex, Sid Robinson, Communications Mgr, Box 2250, Pomona, CA 91769. Phone (909) 623-3111. Fax: (909) 629-2067.
Email: robinson@fairplex.com. WWW: http://www.fairplex.com

"M*A*S*H" TV PREMIERE: ANNIVERSARY. Sept 17, 1972. This popular CBS series was based on the 1970 Robert Altman movie and a book by Richard Hooker. The show aired for 11 years, set during the Korean War (actually, the show lasted longer than the war). It followed the lives of doctors and nurses on the war front with both humor and pathos. The cast included: Alan Alda as Captain Benjamin Franklin "Hawkeye" Pierce; Wayne Rogers as Captain John "Trapper John" McIntyre; McLean Stevenson as Lieutenant Colonel Henry Blake; Loretta Swit as Major Margaret "Hot Lips" Houlihan; Larry Linville as Major Frank Burns; Gary Burghoff as Corporal Walter "Radar" O'Reilly; William Christopher as Father Francis Mulcahy; Jamie Farr as Corporal Max Klinger; Harry Morgan as Colonel Sherman Potter; and Mike Farrell as Captain B. J. Hunnicut. The show won numerous awards during its run. Its final episode, "Goodbye, Farewell and Amen" was the highest-rated program of all time, topping the "Who Shot J.R.?" revelation on "Dallas." The show generated two spin-offs: "Trapper John, M.D." and "AfterM*A*S*H."

"MISSION: IMPOSSIBLE" TV PREMIERE: ANNIVERSARY. Sept 17, 1966. This action-adventure espionage series was produced by Bruce Geller, appearing on CBS for seven years. The premise of the show was simple: each week the IMF (Impossible Missions Force) leader would receive instructions on a super-secret mission to be carried out by the crew. Steven Hill played the first IMF leader, Dan Briggs. He was replaced by Peter Graves who played Jim Phelps. The crew included: Martin Landau as Rollin Hand, master of disguise; Barbara Bain, real-life wife of Landau, as Cinnamon Carter; Greg Morris as Barney Collier, technical expert; Peter Lupus as Willy Armitage, tough guy; Leonard Nimoy as Hand's replacement, Paris; Lesley Warren as Dana Lambert; Sam Elliott as Doug; Lynda Day George as Casey; and Barbara Anderson as Mimi Davis. The show was remade for ABC in 1988; it lasted two seasons. Graves reprised his role with a new team featuring Phil Morris as Grant Collier, son of Barney. The latest incarnation of "Mission: Impossible" recently turned up on the silver screen in 1996, starring Tom Cruise.

NATIONAL CONSTITUTION CENTER CONSTITUTION WEEK. Sept 17–23. To celebrate and commemorate the signing of the US Constitution on Sept 17, 1787. The National Constitution Center sponsors ceremonial signings of the Constitution nationwide. Everyone is invited to participate and receive educational materials about the world's oldest working Constitution. Est attendance: 1,000,000. For info: Natl Constitution Center, The Bourse, 111 S Independence Mall East, Ste 560, Philadelphia, PA 19106. Phone: (215) 923-0004. Fax: (215) 923-1749. WWW: http://www.libertynet.org/~ncc

ATHLETICS

NATIONAL FOOTBALL LEAGUE FORMED: ANNIVERSARY. Sept 17, 1920. The National Football League was formed in Canton, OH.

NATIONAL GUITAR FLAT-PICKING CHAMPIONSHIPS AND WALNUT VALLEY FESTIVAL. Sept 17–20. Cowley County Fairgrounds, Winfield, KS. The Walnut River is the site of this 27th annual family event featuring four stages with eight contests, at least 14 workshops and many first-class concerts. The Walnut Valley Arts and Crafts Festival features handmade instruments and a large variety of art and craft items, both ornamental and functional. All-weather facilities. Est attendance: 13,000. For info: Walnut Valley Assn, Bob Redford, PO Box 245, Winfield, KS 67156. Phone: (316) 221-3250. Fax: (316) 221-3109.
WWW: http://www.southwind.net/walnut-valley

NATIONAL STUDENT DAY™. Sept 17. Created to recognize all students from preschool through postgraduate, this is the perfect day to show the students in our lives how proud we are of them, to recognize their hard work and to show support for their efforts. For info: Ralph E. Williams, Exec Dir, National Assn of College Students, 8695 College Pkwy, Ste 300, Ft Myers, FL 33919. Phone: (800) 500-4255 or (941) 489-1530. Fax: (941) 489-1142. Email: nacs@collegeknowledge.com.
WWW: http://www.collegeknowledge.com

NORTHERN APPALACHIAN STORYTELLING FESTIVAL. Sept 17–19. Straughn Hall, Mansfield University, Mansfield, PA. Showcases the talent of the nation's top storytellers who share through their performances a sense of roots and cultural diversity. There are performances Friday and Saturday evening, plus a ghost story session late Friday night. In addition, there are storytelling master classes Saturday morning and a workshop on Thursday and Friday. 18th annual. Annually, the third weekend in September. Est attendance: 1,700. For info: Dr. Priscilla M. Travis, N Appalachian Storytelling Fest, PO Box 434, Mansfield, PA 16933. Phone: (717) 662-4785. Fax: (717) 662-4112. Email: ptravis@mnsfld.edu.

SELFRIDGE, THOMAS E.: 90th DEATH ANNIVERSARY. Sept 17, 1908. Lieutenant Thomas E. Selfridge, 26-year-old passenger in 740-lb biplane piloted by Orville Wright, was killed when, after four minutes in the air, the plane fell from a height of 75 feet. Nearly 2,000 spectators witnessed the crash at Fort Myer, VA, on Sept 17, 1908. The plane was being tested for possible military use by the Army Signal Corps. Orville Wright was seriously injured in the crash. Selfridge Air Force Base, MI, was named after the young lieutenant, a West Point graduate, who was the first fatality of powered airplane travel.

SEVEN SWEETS AND SEVEN SOURS FESTIVAL. Sept 17–19. Intercourse, PA. The biggest time of the year is when we put up our fruits and vegetables for the long winter. The whole Village is invaded with Wonderful End-of-the-Garden Creations. Est attendance: 10,000. For info: Mel Hauser, Kitchen Kettle Village, Box 380, Intercourse, PA 17534. Phone: (800) 732-3538 or (717) 768-8261.

SPACE MILESTONE: *PEGASUS 1* (US): 20th ANNIVERSARY. Sept 17, 1978. 23,000-pound research satellite broke up over Africa and fell to Earth. Major pieces are believed to have fallen into Atlantic Ocean off the coast of Angola on this date. The satellite had been orbiting Earth for more than 13 years since being launched Feb 16, 1965.

"SUGARFOOT" TV PREMIERE: ANNIVERSARY. Sept 17, 1957. One of three ABC westerns produced by Warner Brothers in the late fifties. The show alternated with "Cheyenne" and "Bronco." Will Hutchins starred as Tom (Sugarfoot) Brewster, an Easterner with designs on becoming a lawyer in the Wild West. All three shows later aired under the "Cheyenne" appellation in 1960.

SUNFEST. Sept 17–20. Ocean City, MD. Come and join in the family fun. Festival includes amusement rides, a parade, arts and crafts displays, various forms of musical entertainment, food booths and much more. Est attendance: 250,000. For info: Sunfest, 200 125th St, Ocean City, MD 21842. Phone: (800) 626-2326 or (410) 250-0125. Fax: (410) 250-5409.

WEST VIRGINIA OIL AND GAS FESTIVAL. Sept 17–20. Sistersville, WV. To honor the oil and gas industry—past, present and future. 30th annual. Est attendance: 20,000. For info: Mrs Carroll Vincent, West Virginia Oil and Gas Festival, Box 25, Sistersville, WV 26175. Phone: (304) 652-2939.

WILLIAMS, HANK, SR: 75th BIRTH ANNIVERSARY. Sept 17, 1923. Hiram King Williams, country and western singer, born at Georgia, AL, on Sept 17, 1923. He achieved his first major hit with "Lovesick Blues," which brought him a contract with the Grand Ole Opry. His string of hits included "Cold, Cold Heart," "Honky Tonk Blues," "Jambalaya," "Your Cheatin' Heart," "Take These Chains From My Heart" and "I'll Never Get Out of This World Alive," which was released prior to his death on Jan 1, 1953, at Oak Hill, VA.

BIRTHDAYS TODAY

Anne Bancroft (Anna Maria Italiano), 67, actress (Tony and Oscar for *The Miracle Worker; The Graduate, The Turning Point*), born New York, NY, Sept 17, 1931.

Paul Benedict, 60, actor ("The Jeffersons"; many stage roles), born Silver City, NM, Sept 17, 1938.

George Blanda, 71, Pro Football Hall of Fame quarterback and placekicker, born Youngwood, PA, Sept 17, 1927.

Anthony Carter, 38, football player, born Riviera Beach, FL, Sept 17, 1960.

Charles Ernest Grassley, 65, US Senator (R, Iowa), born New Hartford, IA, Sept 17, 1933.

Philip D. (Phil) Jackson, 53, basketball coach, former player, born Deer Lodge, MT, Sept 17, 1945.

Ken Kesey, 63, author (*One Flew Over the Cuckoo's Nest*), born LaJunta, CO, Sept 17, 1935.

Dorothy Loudon, 65, actress, singer ("The Garry Moore Show"), born Boston, MA, Sept 17, 1933.

Jeff MacNelly, 51, cartoonist ("Shoe"), born New York, NY, Sept 17, 1947.

Roddy McDowall, 70, actor (*How Green Was My Valley, Planet of the Apes*; Tony for *The Fighting Cock*), born London, England, Sept 17, 1928.

Cassandra Peterson, 47, actress (movie hostess Elvira), born Manhattan, KS, Sept 17, 1951.

John Ritter, 50, actor (Emmy for "Three's Company"; *Problem Child*), born Burbank, CA, Sept 17, 1948.

Rita Rudner, 42, comedienne, actress (*Peter's Friends*), born Miami, FL, Sept 17, 1956.

David H. Souter, 59, Associate Justice of the US Supreme Court, born Melrose, MA, Sept 17, 1939.

SEPTEMBER 18 — FRIDAY

Day 261 — 104 Remaining

"THE ADDAMS FAMILY" TV PREMIERE: ANNIVERSARY. Sept 18, 1964. Charles Addams' quirky *New Yorker* cartoon creations were brought to life in this ABC sitcom about a family full of oddballs. John Astin played lawyer Gomez Addams; with Carolyn Jones as his morbid wife Morticia; Ken Weatherwax as son Pugsley; Lisa Loring as daughter Wednesday; Jackie Coogan as Uncle Fester; Ted Cassidy as both Lurch, the butler, and Thing, a disembodied hand; Blossom Rock as Grandmama; and Felix Silla as Cousin Itt.

September 1998

S	M	T	W	T	F	S
		1	2	3	4	5
6	7	8	9	10	11	12
13	14	15	16	17	18	19
20	21	22	23	24	25	26
27	28	29	30			

ANTIQUE AND CLASSIC CAR SHOW. Sept 18–20. Willow Park, Bennington, VT. Brass cars, Woodies, costume judging and events of skill and dexterity in handling these wonderful machines of yesteryear are all part of this car show. A flea market with auto-related parts and memorabilia entices collectors seeking that elusive fender or gas running lamp. A display and demonstration of antique motorcycles, tractor and farm machinery are also featured. Est attendance: 10,000. For info: Michael Williams, Bennington Area Chamber of Commerce, Veterans Memorial Dr, Bennington, VT 05201. Phone: (802) 447-3311. Fax: (802) 447-1163. Email: bennchamb@sover.net.

BAYFEST. Sept 18–20. Corpus Christie, TX. Plenty of fun at this waterfront festival. Festival includes amusement rides, a parade, fireworks, arts and crafts displays, various musical entertainment, food booths, merchandise exhibitors and much more. Est attendance: 160,000. For info: Bayfest, PO Box 1858, Corpus Christie, TX 78403. Phone: (512) 887-0868. Fax: (512) 887-9773.

THE BIG E. Sept 18–Oct 4. West Springfield, MA. New England's Fall Classic and one of the nation's largest fairs. Each September, The Big E features all free entertainment including top-name talent, a big-top circus and horse show. Also children's attractions, daily parade, historic village, Avenue of States, Better Living Center and much more. Annually, beginning the second Friday after Labor Day. Est attendance: 1,000,000. For info: Catherine Pappas, Comm Mgr, Eastern States Exposition, 1305 Memorial Ave, West Springfield, MA 01089. Phone: (413) 737-2443. Fax: (413) 787-0127. Email: mkt@thebige.com.
WWW: http://www.thebige.com

BRAZZI, ROSSANO: BIRTH ANNIVERSARY. Sept 18, 1916. Hollywood actor Rossano Brazzi was born at Bologna, Italy. A leading romantic figure in the 1950s and 1960s, he appeared in more than 200 films. He died on Dec 24, 1994 at Rome, Italy.

CAROLINA CRAFTSMEN'S FALL CLASSIC. Sept 18–20. Benton Convention Center, Winston-Salem, NC. Arts and crafts. Est attendance: 20,000. For info: The Carolina Craftsmen, 1240 Oakland Ave, Greensboro, NC 27403. Phone: (910) 274-5550. Fax: (910) 274-1084.

CENTRAL WASHINGTON STATE FAIR. Sept 18–27. Yakima, WA. Family fun, amusement rides, food booths, parades, arts and crafts displays, entertainment, auto thrill show and demolition derby. Est attendance: 320,000. For info: Central Washington State Fair, PO Box 1381, Yakima, WA 98907. Phone: (509) 248-7160. Fax: (509) 248-8093.

CHILE: INDEPENDENCE DAY. Sept 18. National holiday. Gained independence from Spain, 1810.

DEMILLE, AGNES: BIRTH ANNIVERSARY. Sept 18, 1905. Dancer, choreographer for ballet and Broadway shows such as *Oklahoma*, born at New York City, NY. DeMille died at New York City, NY, Oct 7, 1993.

DETROIT FESTIVAL OF ARTS. Sept 18–20. Detroit, MI. Detroit Cultural Center and Wayne State University become a 15-block kaleidoscope of visual, performing and literary arts: live entertainment forum with more than 300 stage and street performers, 100 visual artists. Children's Fair, Poetry Festival and more. Est attendance: 250,000. For info: Pat Borninski, MR Officer, Wayne State Univ, 3222 FAB, Detroit, MI 48202. Phone: (313) 577-2150. Fax: (313) 577-8154.
Email: pbornin@cms.cc.wayne.edu.
WWW: http://www.media.wayne.edu/

DIEFENBAKER, JOHN: BIRTH ANNIVERSARY. Sept 18. Canadian lawyer, statesman and Conservative prime minister (1957–63). Born at Normandy Township, Ont, Canada, on Sept 18, 1895. Died at Ottawa, Ont, Aug 16, 1979. Diefenbaker was a member of the Canadian Parliament from 1940 until his death.

ENGLAND: HARROGATE AUTUMN FLOWER SHOW. Sept 18–20. Great Yorkshire Showground, Harrogate, N Yorkshire. See Britain's first blooms, talk to the experts and witness the giants in the National Onion Championship. Est attendance: 35,000. For info: Alan Ravenscroft, Show Dir, North of England Horticultural Society, 4A South Park Rd, Harrogate, North Yorkshire, England HG1 5QU. Phone: (44) (142) 356-1049.

GARBO, GRETA: BIRTH ANNIVERSARY. Sept 18, 1905. International film actress Greta Garbo was born Greta Lovisa Gustafsson at Stockholm, Sweden. A famous recluse, she retired temporarily, then permanently, from films after 19 years and 27 films, which spanned the late-silent era and beginning of sound movies. Her on-screen roles and her off-screen life were both characterized by an image of a seductress involved in tragic love affairs. She died on Apr 15, 1990 at New York, NY.

GEIGER, RAY: BIRTH ANNIVERSARY. Sept 18. Born in Irvington, NJ, on Sept 18, 1910, Ray Geiger became editor of the *Farmer's Almanac* in 1934, shortly after graduating from Notre Dame. He remained editor until completing the 1994 edition in the fall of 1993 (when his son Peter became editor), the longest running almanac editor in American history. He died Apr 1, 1994, at Auburn, ME. *The Farmer's Almanac* offices are in Lewiston, ME.

"GET SMART" TV PREMIERE: ANNIVERSARY. Sept 18, 1965. A spy-thriller spoof appearing on both NBC (1965-69) and CBS (1969-70). Don Adams starred as bumbling CONTROL Agent 86, Maxwell Smart. His mission was to thwart the evildoings of the KAOS organization. Agent Smart was usually successful with the help of his friends: Barbara Feldon as Agent 99 (whom Smart eventually married); Edward Platt as The Chief; Robert Karvelas as Agent Larraby; Dick Gautier as Hymie the Robot; and David Ketchum as Agent 13.

HAITI INVASION AVERTED: ANNIVERSARY. Sept 18, 1994. Just as military forces of the US were poised to invade Haiti, an agreement was reached with an American negotiating team to restore President Jean-Bertrand Aristide to power. The team consisted of former president Jimmy Carter, former chairman of the joint chiefs of staff, General Colin Powell and Senator Sam Nunn, Democrat of Georgia.

HULL HOUSE OPENS: ANNIVERSARY. Sept 18, 1889. This settlement house was founded in Chicago by Jane Addams and Ellen Gates Starr. It soon became the heart of one of the country's most influential social reform movements, offering a mix of cultural and education programs to new immigrants. See also: "Addams, Jane: Birth Anniversary" (Sept 6).

IRON HORSE OUTRACED BY HORSE: ANNIVERSARY. Sept 18, 1830. In a widely celebrated race, the first locomotive built in America, the Tom Thumb, lost to a horse. Mechanical difficulties plagued the steam engine over the nine-mile course between Riley's Tavern and Baltimore, MD, and a boiler leak prevented the locomotive from finishing the race. In the early days of trains, engines were nicknamed "Iron Horses."

JOHNSON, SAMUEL: BIRTH ANNIVERSARY. Sept 18. English lexicographer and literary lion, creator of the first great dictionary of the English language (1755) and author of poems and essays. Less well known is his novel *Rasselas: Prince of Abyssinia* (1759) written to pay for his mother's funeral. It begins with what has been called "the most beautiful sentence ever written": "Ye who listen with credulity to the whispers of fancy, and pursue with eagerness the phantoms of hope; who expect that age will perform the promises of youth, and that the deficiencies of the present day will be supplied by the morrow; attend to the history of Rasselas, Prince of Abyssinia." Johnson was born at Lichfield, in Staffordshire, England, Sept 18, 1709, and died at London, England, on Dec 13, 1784.

LOUISIANA NATIVE & CONTEMPORARY CRAFTS FESTIVAL. Sept 18–20. Lafayette. LA. A celebration of Louisiana's history through its native crafts, music, food and folklore. More than 300 juried Louisiana craftspeople, musicians, dancers, chefs, artisans and storytellers offer an inside look at the original artistry and cultural history of Louisiana, while also recognizing traditions and crafts still viable today. Est attendance: 2,000. For info: Lafayette Natural History Museum & Planetarium, 637 Girard Park Dr, Lafayette, LA 70503. Phone: (318) 291-5544. Fax: (318) 291-5464.

"LOVE IS A MANY SPLENDORED THING" TV PREMIERE: ANNIVERSARY. Sept 18, 1967. A soap opera created by veteran writer, Irna Phillips, airing on CBS for five years. It was based on the 1955 film starring William Holden and Jennifer Jones. Irna Phillips left the show after the network nixed inter-racial romance in favor of political storylines. David Birney, Leslie Charleson, Bibi Besch and Donna Mills have all appeared on the show.

MONTEREY JAZZ FESTIVAL. Sept 18–20. Monterey, CA. Celebrating its 41st year, the country's oldest continuous jazz festival features the sounds of some of the world's finest jazz musicians. Fax: (408) 373-0244. Est attendance: 35,000. For info: Monterey Jazz Festival, PO Box Jazz, Monterey, CA 93942. Phone: (408) 373-3366 or (800) 307-3378. Fax: (408) 373-0244.

NEW HAMPSHIRE HIGHLAND GAMES. Sept 18–20. Loon Mountain, Lincoln, NH. From the tossing of the caber to the lilting melodies of the clarsach plus massed pipe bands on parade, there's something for everyone at New Hampshire's Highland Games: a three-day Scottish festival crammed with music, dance, crafts, athletic events, Scottish food and more. For those of Scottish heritage, there's also a chance to look up one's clan connection, as more than 60 Scottish clans and societies have tents with displays. Admission charged. Est attendance: 35,000. For info: New Hampshire Highland Games, PO Box 495, Dublin, NH 03444-0495. Phone: (603) 563-8801. Fax: (603) 563-8549. Email: nhscot@top.monad.net.
WWW: http://newww.com/org/nhhg

RACKING WORLD CELEBRATION. Sept 18–26. Decatur, AL. Week-long event featuring racking horses from across the nation. The highlight of the 75-class event is the crowning of the World Grand Racking Horse Champion on the last night. Annually, the last full week in September. Est attendance: 25,000. For info: Jacklyn Bailey, Decatur Conv and Visitors Bureau, 719 6th Ave SE, PO Box 2349, Decatur, AL 35602. Phone: (205) 350-2028 or (800) 524-6181. Email: dcvb@hiwaay.net.

READ, GEORGE: BIRTH ANNIVERSARY. Sept 18, 1733. Lawyer and signer of the Declaration of Independence, born at Cecil County, MD, Sept 18, 1733. Died on Sept 21, 1798.

SAINT FRANCIS RIVER POWWOW. Sept 18–20. Farmington, MO, 65 miles south of St. Louis. Native American Powwow and competitive dancing. Est attendance: 5,000. For info: Linda Schlicter, Chair, 502 S Carleton, Farmington, MO 63640. Phone: (573) 756-6703 or (573) 756-3658.

"SHIRLEY TEMPLE THEATRE" TV PREMIERE: ANNIVERSARY. Sept 18, 1960. An NBC children's anthology of specials appearing on Sundays, hosted by Shirley Temple. Reruns were broadcast on ABC on the following Mondays. "Beauty and the Beast," "Rumplestiltskin," "Rapunzel," "Mother Goose," "The Land of Oz" and "Babes in Toyland" were among the stories presented.

SOUTHSIDE FALL FESTIVAL. Sept 18–20. St. Joseph, MO. The highlight of this event is a professional rodeo the United Rodeo Association named "Rodeo of the Year." Also featured are a parade, arts and crafts, street dances, food and much more. Annually, the third weekend in September. Est attendance: 30,000. For info: Dan Garvin, Shelter Insurance, 318 Illinois, St. Joseph, IL 64504. Phone: (816) 238-1450 or (816) 238-3515.

SPACE MILESTONE: *SOYUZ 38* (USSR). Sept 18, 1980. Launched on this date with Cosmonauts Arnaldo Tamayo Mendes (Cuba) and Yuri Romanenko aboard and docked at *Salyut 6* for week-long mission, returning to Earth Sept 26.

"THE SPEIDEL SHOW" TV PREMIERE: ANNIVERSARY. Sept 18, 1950. Ventriloquist Paul Winchell was featured with his dummies, Mahoney and Knucklehead Smiff, on this NBC comedy-variety series which ran for four years. Dorothy Claire, Hilda Vaughn and Jimmy Blaine also made appearances on the show, which included the quiz segment "What's My Name?" Winchell later hosted a variety of programs such as "Circus Time," "The Paul Winchell Show," "Cartoonies," "Winchell and Mahoney Time" and "Runaround."

STATE FAIR OF OKLAHOMA. Sept 18–Oct 4. Fairgrounds, Oklahoma City, Oklahoma. Third largest fair in North America includes seven buildings of commercial exhibits; Walt Disney's World on Ice, Ringling Bros and Barnum & Bailey Circus, PRCA championship rodeo, livestock competitions, top-name concerts and motorsports events. Annually, second Friday after Labor Day. Est attendance: 1,300,000. For info: Scott Munz, State Fair of Oklahoma, PO Box 74943, Oklahoma City, OK 73147. Phone: (405) 948-6700.

STORY, JOSEPH: BIRTH ANNIVERSARY. Sept 18, 1779. Associate justice of the US Supreme Court (1811–45) was born at Marblehead, MA. "It is astonishing," he wrote a few months before his death, "how easily men satisfy themselves that the Constitution is exactly what they wish it to be." Story died on Sept 10, 1845, having served 33 years on the Supreme Court bench.

US AIR FORCE ESTABLISHED: ANNIVERSARY. Sept 18, 1947. Although its heritage dates back to 1907 when the Army first established military aviation, the US Air Force became a separate military service on this date. Responsible for providing an Air Force that is capable, in conjunction with the other armed forces, of preserving the peace and security of the United States, the department is separately organized under the Secretary of the Air Force and operates under the authority, direction and control of the Secretary of Defense.

US CAPITOL CORNERSTONE LAID: ANNIVERSARY. Sept 18, 1793. President George Washington on Sept 18, 1793, laid the Capitol cornerstone in Washington, DC, in a Masonic ceremony. That event was the first and last recorded occasion at which the stone with its engraved silver plate was seen. In 1958, during the extension of the east front of the Capitol, an unsuccessful effort was made to find it.

US TAKES OUT ITS FIRST LOAN: ANNIVERSARY. Sept 18. The first loan taken out by the US was negotiated and secured by Alexander Hamilton on Feb 17, 1790. After beginning negotiations with the Bank of New York and the Bank of North America on Sept 18, 1789, Hamilton obtained the sum of $191,608.81 from the two banks in what became known as the Temporary Loan of 1789. The loan was obtained without authority of law and was used to pay the salaries of the president, senators, representatives and officers of the first Congress. Repayment was completed on June 8, 1790.

"WAGON TRAIN" TV PREMIERE: ANNIVERSARY. Sept 18, 1957. "Wagon Train" was a popular western on NBC and ABC, airing for eight years. The series was about a journey along the wagon trail from Missouri to California. Each week the travelers encountered new surroundings and interacted with different guest stars. Ward Bond played wagonmaster Major Seth Adams until his death in 1960. He was replaced by John McIntire as Chris Hale. Other regulars were: Robert Horton as scout Flint McCullough; Frank McGrath as cook Charlie Wooster; Terry Wilson as Bill Hawks; Denny (Scott) Miller as scout Duke Shannon; Michael Burns as Barnaby West, a teen passenger; and Robert Fuller as scout Cooper.

September 1998

S	M	T	W	T	F	S
		1	2	3	4	5
6	7	8	9	10	11	12
13	14	15	16	17	18	19
20	21	22	23	24	25	26
27	28	29	30			

WHITE WOMAN MADE AMERICAN INDIAN CHIEF: ANNIVERSARY. Sept 18. On Sept 18, 1891, Harriet Maxwell Converse was made a chief of the Six Nations Tribe at the Tonawanda Reservation, NY. She was given the name Ga-is-wanoh, which means "The Watcher." She had been adopted as a member of the Seneca tribe in 1884 in appreciation of her efforts on behalf of the tribe.

BIRTHDAYS TODAY

Frankie Avalon, 58, singer ("Venus," "Dede Dinah"), actor (teen flicks with Annette Funicello), born Philadelphia, PA, Sept 18, 1940.

Robert F. Bennett, 65, US Senator (R, Utah), born Salt Lake City, UT, Sept 18, 1933.

Robert Blake (Michael Gubitosi), 60, actor ("Baretta," *In Cold Blood, Little Rascals*), born Nutley, NJ, Sept 18, 1938.

Ryne Dee Sandberg, 39, baseball player, born Spokane, WA, Sept 18, 1959.

Jack Warden, 78, actor ("NYPD," "Bad News Bears," "Crazy Like a Fox"; Emmy for *Brian's Song*), born Newark NJ, Sept 18, 1920.

SEPTEMBER 19 — SATURDAY

Day 262 — 103 Remaining

ALABAMA COASTAL CLEANUP. Sept 19. Mobile and Baldwin County, AL. Volunteers convene to "get the trash out of the splash" by cleaning up Alabama's beaches. This event provides participants with a first hand experience that improves the ecosystem. Annually, the third Saturday in September. Est attendance: 3,000. For info: Alabama Coastal Foundation, PO Box 1760, Fairhope, AL 36533. Phone: (334) 621-1541. Fax: (334) 621-1382.

APPLEJACK FESTIVAL. Sept 19–20. Nebraska City, NE. To promote local orchards and their abundant apple harvest. Est attendance: 30,000. For info: Nebraska City Chamber of Commerce, 806 First Ave, Nebraska City, NE 68410. Phone: (402) 873-3000. Fax: (402) 873-3000. Email: necity@nebraskacity.com. WWW: http://www.nebraskacity.com

BARNESVILLE BUGGY DAYS. Sept 19–20. Barnesville, GA. 25th annual. Arts and crafts festival with more than 180 exhibitors, food, entertainment, a parade at 4 PM and fireworks at 9:30 PM on Saturday. Annually, the third full weekend in September. Est attendance: 60,000. For info: Barnesville-Lamar Chamber of Commerce, PO Box 506, Barnesville, GA 30204. Phone: (404) 358-2732.

BELLE MEADE PLANTATION FALL FEST. Sept 19–20. Belle Meade Plantation, Nashville, TN. Annual fundraiser, crafts, antiques, music, food, market, garden, garage treasures and children's fest. Annually, the third weekend of September. Est attendance: 20,000. For info: Belle Meade Plantation, 5025 Harding Rd, Nashville, TN 37205. Phone: (615) 356-0501. Fax: (615) 356-2336.

BIG WHOPPER LIAR'S CONTEST. Sept 19. Murphy Auditorium, New Harmony, IN. Thirty "story tellers" compete to see who can tell the BIGGEST Whopper. Annually, the third Saturday in September. Est attendance: 425. For info: Jeff Fleming, PO Box 598, Olney, IL 62450. Phone: (618) 395-8491. Fax: (618) 392-3174.

BROUGHAM, HENRY PETER: BIRTH ANNIVERSARY. Sept 19, 1778. Scotch jurist and orator born at Edinburgh, Scotland, Sept 19, 1778. Died at Cannes, France, May 7, 1868. Brougham carriage named after him. "Education," he said, "makes a people easy to lead, but difficult to drive; easy to govern, but impossible to enslave."

CANDLELIGHT WALKING TOUR OF HISTORIC CHESTERTOWN. Sept 19. Chestertown, MD. To view the interiors of historic buildings and houses in a colonial town. Annually, the third Saturday in September. Est attendance: 1,000. For info: Nancy Nunn, Curator, Historical Society of Kent County, PO Box 665, Chestertown, MD 21620. Phone: (410) 778-3499.

CARROLL, CHARLES: BIRTH ANNIVERSARY. Sept 19, 1737. American Revolutionary leader and signer of the Declaration of Independence, born at Annapolis, MD. The last surviving signer of the Declaration, he died Nov 14, 1832.

"CELEBRATE DIVERSITY" TWO RIVERS ETHNIC FESTIVAL. Sept 19. Central Memorial Park, Two Rivers, WI. A celebration of diverse cultures by bringing to Northeast Wisconsin representative musical and dance groups from around our world. Groups present a taste of these rich traditions in their music and costumes. Also included are ethnic foods, demonstrations of varied traditions, crafts and arts. As the ceremonial keg is being tapped on this date in Munich, an Oktoberfest will be held in conjunction with the festival with German food and music. Annually, the third Saturday in September. Est attendance: 11,000. For info: Nan Webster, "Celebrate Diversity," 3605 Adams St, Two Rivers, WI 54241. Phone: (920) 793-4833. Fax: (920) 793-3818. WWW: http://www.wisconline.com

CHAUTAUQUA OF THE ARTS. Sept 19–20. Columbus, IN. Fine artists and craftsmen gather to demonstrate and sell their works. Est attendance: 25,000. For info: Dixie McDonough, 1119 W Main St, Madison, IN 47250-3013. Phone: (812) 265-5080 or for lodging info: (800) 468-6564. Fax: (812) 265-5080. Email: jmcdonou@seidata.

CHEROKEE STRIP CELEBRATION. Sept 19. Perry, OK. To commemorate the opening of the Cherokee Strip to settlement on Sept 16, 1893. Annually, the Saturday or weekend nearest Sept 16. Est attendance: 10,000. For info: Cheryle Leach, Chamber of Commerce, Box 426, Perry, OK 73077. Phone: (405) 336-4684. Fax: (405) 336-4685.

CORN ISLAND STORYTELLING FESTIVAL. Sept 19–20. Louisville, KY. More than 50 storytellers. Festival includes an "olio," mixture of tales, "Fest of Storytelling" and "ghost tales" told at Long Run Park. Est attendance: 16,000. For info: Joy Pennington, Intl Order of EARS, Inc, 12019 Donohue Ave, Louisville, KY 40243. Phone: (502) 245-0643. Fax: (502) 245-7542.

COUNTRY FALL FESTIVAL. Sept 19. Downtown Lost Creek, WV. Entertainment and games for all ages, a parade, food, crafts and hot air balloon rides followed by kings and queens coronation. Est attendance: 10,000. For info: Sandra Gaston Pres, Country Fall Festival, PO Box 342, Lost Creek, WV 26385. Phone: (304) 745-4790.

COVERED BRIDGE FESTIVAL. Sept 19–20. Washington County, PA. Arts and crafts, entertainment and lots of homestyle food at each of eight covered bridges. Annually, the third weekend in September. Est attendance: 140,000. For info: Washington Co Tourism, Franklin Mall, 1500 W Chestnut St, Washington, PA 15301. Phone: (800) 531-4114 or (412) 228-5220. Email: tourism@pulsenet.com. WWW: http://www.pulsenet.com/tourism

CRAFT FAIR USA: INDOOR SHOW. Sept 19–20. Wisconsin State Fair Park, Milwaukee, WI. Sale of handcrafted items: jewelry, pottery, weaving, leather, wood, glass, yulecraft and sculpture. Est attendance: 15,000. For info: Dir, Craft Fair USA, 9312 W National Ave, West Allis, WI 53227. Phone: (414) 321-2100.

FALL CRAFTFEST. Sept 19. Dexter, MO. 7th annual. An indoor show where exhibitors display their all-hand-crafted products for sale to the public. Annually, the third Saturday in September. Est attendance: 750. For info: Annual Fall Craftfest, PO Box 21, Dexter, MO 63841. Phone: (573) 624-7458 or (800) 332-8857. Fax: (573) 624-7459.

"FLIPPER" TV PREMIERE: ANNIVERSARY. Sept 19, 1964. An adventure series starring Flipper (actually played by Susie), the intelligent, communicative and helpful dolphin. The human cast members included Brian Kelly as Chief Ranger Porter Ricks; Luke Halpin as his son Sandy; Tommy Norden as his son Bud; and Ulla Stromstedt as biochemist Ulla Norstrand. In the '90s, this series has been recreated under the same title.

FLY-IN/DRIVE-IN. Sept 19–20. Arapahoe Airport, Arapahoe, NE. Nebraska Antique Airplane Assn members and Antique and Classic Car owners fly or drive their craft/vehicles to the airport to display. Open to public. Breakfast on Saturday morning, banquet Saturday night. Annually, the third weekend in September. Est attendance: 500. For info: Araphoe Chamber of Commerce, Fly-In/Drive-In, PO Box 624, Arapahoe, NE 68922. Phone: (308) 962-7872.

GETTYSBURG OUTDOOR ANTIQUE SHOW. Sept 19. Gettysburg, PA. More than 175 dealers displaying their wares on the sidewalk. Annually, in September. Est attendance: 25,000. For info: Gettysburg Conv & Visitors Bureau, 35 Carlisle St, Gettysburg, PA 17325-1899. Phone: (717) 334-6274. Fax: (717) 334-1166. WWW: http://www.gettysburg.com

GOLDING, SIR WILLIAM: BIRTH ANNIVERSARY. Sept 19, 1911. Born at Columb Minor in Cornwall, England, this celebrated author was recognized for his contributions to literature with a Nobel Prize in 1983. His first and most popular novel was *Lord of the Flies*. He died June 19, 1993, near Truro, Cornwall.

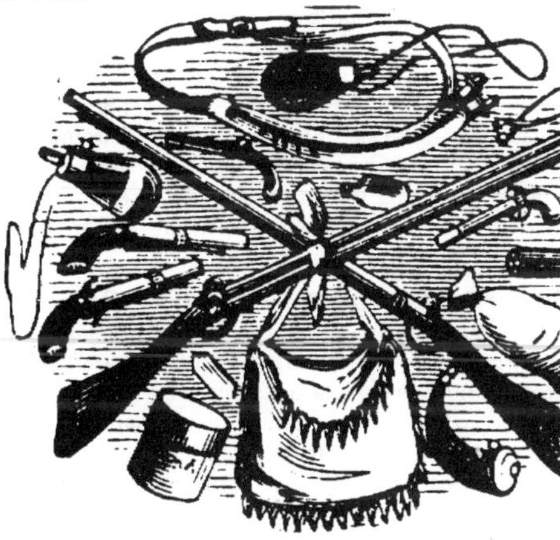

HODAG MUSKIE CHALLENGE. Sept 19–20 (tentative). Rhinelander, WI. $20,000 catch and release Muskie Tournament. Annually, the third weekend in September. Est attendance: 200 Teams. For info: Rhinelander Area Chamber of Commerce, PO Box 795, Rhinelander, WI 54501. Phone: (800) 236-4386. Fax: (715) 365-7467.

JACKSON HILL CIDER DAY. Sept 19. Jackson House, Portsmouth, NH. Noon–4 PM. A harvest celebration for families and children in the orchards of the oldest house in New Hampshire. Children can wield picking poles and assist in pressing cider and cranking the paring machines. Fiddle music, beekeeping, samples of traditional sauce and pie and tours of the house are included in the celebration. Annually, third Saturday in September. Admission: Adults $4; children $2. Est attendance: 100. For info: Society for Preservation of New England Antiquities, 143 Pleasant St, Portsmouth, NH 03801. Phone: (603) 436-3205. Fax: (603) 436-4651.

JAMESTOWN BURNED BY BACON'S REBELLION: ANNIVERSARY. Sept 19, 1676. The Virginia colony was a land of small farmers where every adult male could vote. When Charles II was restored to the English throne, he and his cronies sought to exploit the colony to the fullest for their own enrichment. Virginia Governor Sir William Berkeley, supporting the king, adopted new laws to facilitate these efforts including measures allowing only property holders to vote, raising taxes to build up the town of Jamestown and raising the cost of shipping while lowering the price for tobacco. The resulting discontent exploded when the frontier of the colony was attacked by Indians and the governor refused to defend the settlers. Nathaniel Bacon, a colonist on the governor's council, was made leader by the frontier farmers, and his troops successfully defeated the Indians. Denounced by Berkeley as rebels, Bacon and his men occupied Jamestown, forcing the governor to call an election, the first in 15 years. The Berkeley laws were repealed and election and tax reforms were instituted. While Bacon and his troops were gone on a raiding party against the Indians, Berkeley returned and again denounced them. They returned and attacked Berkeley's forces, defeating them and burning Jamestown on Sept 19, 1676. Berkeley again fled and Bacon became ruler of Virginia. When he died suddenly a short time later, the rebellion collapsed. Berkeley returned to power and Bacon's followers were hunted down, some executed and their property confiscated. Berkeley was replaced the next year and peace was restored.

JERSEY SHORE SEA KAYAK AND BAY CANOEING SHOW. Sept 19. Bayville, NJ. Canoe and sea kayak vendors from around the country set up on a beach and share the joys of watersport with the public. Test paddling is allowed all day and there are clinics to teach about canoeing and kayaking. At this show you may sign up for a trip for the following day. There is no fee. Annually, the third Saturday in September. Est attendance: 1,000. For info: Lillian Hoey, Rec Leader, Wells Mills County Park, 905 Wells Mills Rd, Waretown, NJ 08758. Phone: (609) 971-3085. Fax: (609) 971-9540.

JOHNNY APPLESEED FESTIVAL. Sept 19–20. Fort Wayne, IN. A return to the pioneer spirit of the early 1800s, at the gravesite of John Chapman, known as the "Johnny Appleseed" who planted hundreds of apple orchards along the early Indiana frontier. Crafts, music, food and demonstrators. Annually, the third full weekend in September. Est attendance: 350,000. For info: Parks and Recreation Dept, 705 E State Blvd, Fort Wayne, IN 46805. Phone: (219) 427-6003. Fax: (219) 427-6020.

September 1998

S	M	T	W	T	F	S
		1	2	3	4	5
6	7	8	9	10	11	12
13	14	15	16	17	18	19
20	21	22	23	24	25	26
27	28	29	30			

KRAZY WITH KUDZU. Sept 19–20. Chimney Rock Park, Chimney Rock, NC. Workshops, speakers, "Kudzu Queen" and others to highlight the vivacious vine. Taste kudzu and learn to make kudzu "krafts." For info: Mary Ritter, PR, Chimney Rock Park, PO Box 39, Chimney Rock, NC 28720. Phone: (800) 277-9611. Fax: (704) 625-9610.
Email: visit@chimneyrockpark.com.
WWW: http://www.chimneyrockpark.com

LAURA INGALLS WILDER FESTIVAL. Sept 19–20. Pepin, WI. 7th annual. Experience life in the mid-1800s with demonstrations of blacksmithing, woodworking, ironworking, weaving, quilting and wool-spinning by individuals dressed in period costumes. Stories and songs cited in "Little House" books are also performed and there's a Laura Ingalls look-alike contest. Additional attractions include a traveling exhibit of Wilder's written materials, sanctioned horse-pull, Civil War encampment, children's games from the period, parade, crafts and antiques at Laura Ingalls Wilder Memorial Park. For info: Wisconsin Dept of Tourism, Laura Ingalls Festival, PO Box 7976, Madison, WI 53707. Phone: (715) 442-2461 or (715) 442-2147.
Email: tourism@laughlin.com. WWW: http://tourism.state.wi.us

LUYTS, JAN: BIRTH ANNIVERSARY. Sept 19. Dutch scholar, physicist, mathematician and astronomer, Jan Luyts was born at Hoorn in western Netherlands on Sept 19, 1655. Little remembered except for his books: *Astronomica Institutio . . .* (1689) and *Introductio ad Geographiam . . .* (1690).

MEXICO CITY EARTHQUAKE: ANNIVERSARY. Sept 19–20. Nearly 10,000 persons perished in the earthquakes (8.1 and 7.5 respectively, on the Richter Scale) that devastated Mexico City Sept 19 and 20, 1985. Damage to buildings was estimated at more than $1 billion, and 100,000 homes were destroyed or severely damaged.

MITCHELL PERSIMMON FESTIVAL. Sept 19–26. Main Street, Mitchell, IN. 52nd annual. Persimmon pudding and novelty contests, parade, carnival, arts and crafts, fine arts and photography shows, antique autos and machinery, pioneer village candlelight tour, free entertainment nightly. Annually, the last full week in September. Est attendance: 90,000. For info: Greater Mitchell Chamber of Commerce, P.O. Box 216, Mitchell, IN 47446. Phone: (800) 580-1985.

NATIONAL KIDSDAY®. Sept 19. A national holiday to recognize the value, dignity and inherent worth of children everywhere (also known as National Children's Day™). Supervised and licensed by KidsPeace®, The National Center for Kids Overcoming Crisis, a private, not-for-profit organization that has been providing hope and healing to kids in crisis since 1882. KidsPeace offers the country's widest array of children's critical care services available under a "single roof" and crisis education to families across the US. Annually, the third Saturday in September. For info: Paula Knouse, KidsPeace, 5300 KidsPeace Dr, Orefield, PA 18069-9101. Phone: (610) 799-8325.
WWW: http://www.kidspeace.org

NORSKEDALEN'S THRESHING BEE. Sept 19. Norskedalen Nature and Heritage Center, Coon Valley, WI. Antique engines and pioneer demonstrations, such as winnowing, threshing, corn shredding, cream separating and more. 'All you care to eat' threshers meal, reservations required. Est attendance: 500. For info: Tammy Potaracke, Norskedalen, PO Box 225, Coon Valley, WI 54623. Phone: (608) 452-3424. Fax: (608) 452-3157.

OKTOBERFEST-ZINZINNATI. Sept 19–20. Cincinnati, OH. Events featuring oom-pah-pah bands, dancing, German foods, pastries and more. Est attendance: 500,000. For info: Downtown Council, 300 Carew Tower, 441 Vine, Cincinnati, OH 45202. Phone: (513) 579-3196. Fax: (513) 579-3101.
Email: llobsige@gccc.com.

OLD TIME MUSIC FEST. Sept 19–20. Coshocton, OH. A celebration of 19th-century music and musical instruments. A variety of stringed instrumental groups and barbershop quartets perform. A flat picking guitar contest is held on Sunday. Est attendance: 1,000. For info: Cheryl Oswald, Roscoe Village Fdtn, 381 Hill St, Coshocton, OH 43812. Phone: (614) 622-9310 or (800) 877-1830. Fax: (614) 623-6555.

OZARK HAM AND TURKEY FESTIVAL. Sept 19. California, MO. Held each year in appreciation of the two largest industries in the country. The festival includes sand volleyball tournament, car races, R/C vehicle races, parade, craft and food booths, BBQ contest, car show, folk art, live entertainment on three stages, twins contest and much more. Annually, the third Saturday in September. Est attendance: 20,000. For info: Ozark Ham and Turkey Festival, PO Box 85, California, MO 65018. Phone: (573) 796-3040. Fax: (573) 796-8309.

PAN, HERMES: DEATH ANNIVERSARY. Sept 19. American choreographer Hermes Pan was born Hermes Panaglotopulos in Tennessee in 1910. He is best known for choreographing nine of the 10 films starring Fred Astaire and Ginger Rogers, for which he won the Academy Award in choreography for *A Damsel in Distress* (1937). He died on Sept 19, 1990 at Beverly Hills, CA.

"PEOPLE ARE FUNNY" TV PREMIERE: ANNIVERSARY. Sept 19, 1954. This half-hour show combined audience participation and stunts. One feature was a Univac computer that played matchmaker for eligible men and women. Art Linkletter hosted the show until 1958; reruns were shown for the next few seasons. The show was revived for a short time in 1984; Flip Wilson was the host.

POWELL, LEWIS F., JR: BIRTHDAY. Sept 19. Retired associate justice of the Supreme Court of the United States, nominated by President Nixon on Oct 21, 1971. (Took office on Jan 7, 1972.) Justice Powell was born at Suffolk, VA, on Sept 19, 1907. In 1987, he announced his retirement from the Court.

RELIGIOUS FREEDOM WEEK. Sept 19–27. As proclaimed by Congressional Resolution and Presidential Proclamation the week of Sept 25th each year is celebrated as Religious Freedom Week. This date commemorates the anniversary of the Bill of Rights and the right to believe and practice the religion of one's own choice as laid out in the First Amendment. Annually, to include anniversary date. For info: Rev Susan Taylor, Religious Freedom Week Committee, c/o Church of Scientology, 1701 20th St NW, Washington, DC 20009. Phone: (202) 667-6404. Fax: (202) 667-6314.

ROYKO, MIKE: BIRTH ANNIVERSARY. Sept 19, 1932. Syndicated columnist to more than 600 newspapers nationwide, Pulitzer prize winner and author (*Boss*, *Slats Grobnick*). Born at Chicago, IL, Sept 19, 1932. Died at Chicago, Apr 29, 1997.

SAINT CHRISTOPHER (SAINT KITTS) AND NEVIS: INDEPENDENCE DAY. Sept 19. National holiday.

SAINT JANUARIUS (GENNARO): FEAST DAY. Sept 19. Fourth-century bishop of Benevento, martyred near Naples, Italy, whose relics in the Naples Cathedral are particularly famous because on his feast days the blood in a glass vial is said to liquefy in response to prayers of the faithful. In Sept 1979, the Associated Press reported that some 5,000 persons gathered at the cathedral at dawn, and that "the blood liquefied after 63 minutes of prayers." This phenomenon is said to occur also on the first Saturday in May.

SCARECROW FESTIVAL. Sept 19–20. Peddler's Village, Lahaska, PA. Weekend festival includes scarecrow making, pumpkin painting workshops, jack-o'-lantern and gourd art contest, musical entertainment and scarecrow competition display. Free admission. Charge for workshops. Est attendance: 10,000. For info: Judy Goldschmidt, PR Mgr, Peddler's Village, Routes 202 & 263, Lahaska, PA 18931. Phone: (215) 794-4000. Fax: (215) 794-4001. WWW: http://www.peddlersvillage.com

SOUTHWEST IOWA PROFESSIONAL HOT AIR BALLOON RACES. Sept 19–20. Creston, IA. Hare and hound races held at sunrise and sunset; parade and marching band contest and much more. Annually, the third weekend in September. Est attendance: 7,000. For info: Chamber of Commerce, Box 471, Creston, IA 50801. Phone: (515) 782-7021.

STRATTON ARTS FESTIVAL. Sept 19–Oct 18. Base Lodge, Stratton Ski Resort, Stratton, VT. In its 35th year, this Festival features the finest of Vermont's artists and artisans. The showcase is presented gallery style in the 10,000-sq-ft base lodge. Established and emerging artists' work is sold in a casual yet elegant setting. The work covers a very broad range of styles and media. Sponsor: Stratton Arts Festival. Est attendance: 12,000. For info: Ann Spencer, Asst Dir, PO Box 576, Stratton Mtn, VT 05155. Phone: (802) 297-3265. Fax: (802) 297-2358.
Email: artsfest@sover.net.
WWW: http://www.sover.net/~artsfest/

A TASTE OF FALL FEST. Sept 19–20. Cumberland, MD. Ninth annual festival featuring more than 65 craft exhibitors, entertainment, children's activities and food. Festival helps raise money to pay for equipment for the volunteer fire dept. Annually, the third weekend in September. Est attendance: 5,000. For info: Bowling Green Volunteer Fire Dept, 12420 McMullen Hwy SW, Cumberland, MD 21502. Phone: (301) 729-1522.

TEMPE EPICUREAN FESTIVAL. Sept 19–20. Tempe, AZ. 5th annual. 20 food vendors, cooking demonstrations, continuous main stage entertainment and children's area. Est attendance: 20,000. For info: Mill Avenue Merchants Assoc, 520 S Mill Ave, Ste 201, Tempe, AZ 85281. Phone: (602) 967-4877. Fax: (602) 967-6638.

TITAN II MISSILE EXPLOSION: ANNIVERSARY. Sept 19. The third major accident involving America's most powerful single weapon occurred near Damascus, AR, Sept 19, 1980. The explosion, at 3 AM, came nearly 11 hours after a fire had started in the missile silo. The multi-megaton nuclear warhead (a hydrogen bomb) reportedly was briefly airborne, but came to rest a few hundred feet away. One dead, 21 injured in accident. Previous major Titan Missile accidents: Aug 9, 1965, near Searcy, AR (53 dead); and Aug 24, 1978, near Rock, KS (2 dead, 29 injured).

TRAIL OF COURAGE LIVING-HISTORY FESTIVAL. Sept 19–20. Rochester, IN. Portrayal of life in frontier Indiana when it was Indian territory. Historic skits, music, dancing, wigwam and tepee villages, historic encampments for Revolutionary War, French and Indian War, Voyageurs, Western Fur Trade and Plains Indians; recreated 1832 Chippeway Village, also Woodland Indian village, pioneer foods and crafts, muzzleloading and tomahawk contests. Museum, roundbarn and Living History Village on grounds. Special honored Potawatomi family from county's history each year. Trail of Death Commemorative Caravan from Indiana to Kansas will be Sept 21–30. Est attendance: 18,000. For info: Fulton County Historical Society, 37 E 375N, Rochester, IN 46975. Phone: (219) 223-4436.
Email: wwillard@townsquare.net.

TRAIL OF TEARS COMMEMORATION AND MOTORCYCLE RIDE. Sept 19. Waterloo, AL. A day to gather and remember the tragic Trail of Tears when Native Americans were removed from their homes in the 1830s and were forced to walk a trail out west. Arts and crafts, museum exhibits and great entertainment. An organized motorcycle ride begins in Chattanooga the same morning and arrives in Waterloo for afternoon activities. Annually, the third Saturday in September. Est attendance: 10,000. For info: Florence/Lauderdale Tourism, One Hightower Place, Florence, AL 35630. Phone: (205) 740-4141 or (888) FLO-TOUR. Fax: (205) 740-4142. Email: dwilson@floweb.com. WWW: http://www.flo-tour.org

"THE VIRGINIAN" TV PREMIERE: ANNIVERSARY. Sept 19, 1962. TV's first ninety-minute western starred James Drury as the Virginian, a foreman trying to come to terms with the westward expansion of technology and civilization. It was set on the Shiloh Ranch, in Wyoming. Key players included Doug McClure (with Drury, the only cast members to stay for the entire run), Lee J. Cobb, Roberta Shore, Pippa Scott, Gary Clarke, Randy Boone, L.Q. Jones, Harlan Warde, Clu Gulagher, Diane Roter, John Dehner, Charles Bickford, Don Quine, Sara Lane, Ross Elliot, John McIntire, Jeanette Nolan, David Hartman and Tim Matheson. In the last season, the title was changed to "The Men From Shiloh," and Stewart Granger and Lee Majors joined the cast.

WINGS 'N' WATER FESTIVAL. Sept 19–20. Wetlands Institute, Stone Harbor, NJ. A wildfowl arts festival, spread throughout the seaside towns of Avalon and Stone Harbor, featuring wildlife art, carvings, decoys, Duck Stamps, water colors, photography, crafts, quilts, music, seafood and more. Est attendance: 8,000. For info: Cindy O'Connor, Exec Dir, Wetlands Institute, 1075 Stone Harbor Blvd, Stone Harbor, NJ 08247-1424. Phone: (609) 368-1211. Fax: (609) 368-3871.

BIRTHDAYS TODAY

James Anthony (Jim) Abbott, 31, baseball player, born Flint, MI, Sept 19, 1967.
Kevin Hooks, 40, actor, director ("The White Shadow," *Sounder*), born Philadelphia, PA, Sept 19, 1958.
Jeremy Irons, 50, actor (*Moonlighting, Dead Ringers*), born Cowes, Isle of Wight, England, Sept 19, 1948.
Joan Lunden, 47, broadcast journalist (co-host of "Good Morning America"), born Sacramento, CA, Sept 19, 1951.
Randolph Mantooth, 53, actor ("Emergency"), born Sacramento, CA, Sept 19, 1945.
David McCallum, 65, actor ("The Man From U.N.C.L.E.," *The Great Escape*), born Glasgow, Scotland, Sept 19, 1933.
Lewis Franklin Powell, Jr, 91, Associate Justice of the US Supreme Court (retired), born Suffolk, VA, Sept 19, 1907.
Twiggy (Leslie Hornby), 49, actress (*The Boy Friend, The Blues Brothers, My One and Only*), former model, born London, England, Sept 19, 1949.
Adam West, 70, actor ("Batman," "The Last Precinct"), born Walla Walla, WA, Sept 19, 1928.
Paul Williams, 58, singer, composer ("Love Boat" theme song), born Omaha, NE, Sept 19, 1940.

SEPTEMBER 20 — SUNDAY

Day 263 — 102 Remaining

ARTS/QUINCY RIVERFEST. Sept 20. Quincy, IL. Celebration of the arts and the Mississippi River in the riverfront parks. Fine arts and crafts, Dixieland Jazz stage, Country-Western stage, along with children's area featuring hands-on activities and performances. Annually, the third Sunday in September. Est attendance: 20,000. For info: Jane Blazel, Coord, Quincy Soc of Fine Arts, 300 Civic Center Plaza, Ste 244, Quincy, IL 62301-4162. Phone: (217) 222-3432. Fax: (217) 228-2787.
Email: info@artsqcy.org. WWW: http://www.artqcy.org

BEL AIR FESTIVAL FOR THE ARTS. Sept 20. Bel Air, MD. Arts, crafts, photography exhibits and entertainment. Application deadline Apr 15. Est attendance: 40,000. For info: Donna Clauer, Bel Air Rec Committee, 1909 Wheel Rd, Bel Air, MD 21015. Phone: (410) 836-2395. Email: MrsCsWkshp@aol.com.

September 1998

S	M	T	W	T	F	S
		1	2	3	4	5
6	7	8	9	10	11	12
13	14	15	16	17	18	19
20	21	22	23	24	25	26
27	28	29	30			

BILLIE JEAN KING WINS THE "BATTLE OF THE SEXES": 25TH ANNIVERSARY. Sept 20, 1973. Billie Jean King defeated Bobby Riggs in the nationally televised "Battle of the Sexes" tennis match in three straight sets.

CABRILLO FESTIVAL. Sept 20–27. San Diego, CA. Colorful pageant reenacts the historic landing of Portuguese explorer Juan Rodriguez Cabrillo who sailed into San Diego Bay on Sept 28, 1542, and discovered California. Historical events; Portuguese, Spanish, Native American and Mexican dances and food. Pageant, annually the last Sunday in September. Est attendance: 9,000. For info: Cabrillo Natl Monument, 1800 Cabrillo Memorial Dr, San Diego, CA 92106. Phone: (619) 557-5450. Fax: (619) 557-5469. WWW: http://www.nps.gov/cabr/

DEAF AWARENESS WEEK. Sept 20–26. Nationwide celebration to promote deaf culture, American Sign Language and deaf heritage. Activities include library displays, interpreted story hours, Open Houses in residential schools and mainstream programs, exhibit booths in shopping malls with "Five Minute Sign Language Lessons," material distribution. For info: Natl Assn of the Deaf, 814 Thayer Ave, Silver Spring, MD 20910-4500. Fax: (301) 587-1791.
Email: nadhq@juno.com. WWW: http://www.nad.org

EQUAL RIGHTS PARTY FOUNDING: ANNIVERSARY. Sept 20. San Francisco, CA. On Sept 20, 1884, the Equal Rights Party was formed. Their candidate for president, nominated in convention, was Mrs Belva Lockwood. The vice-presidential candidate was Marietta Stow.

FINANCIAL PANIC OF 1873: 125TH ANNIVERSARY. Sept 20, 1873. For the first time in its history, the New York Stock Exchange was forced to close Sept 20, 1873, because of a banking crisis. Although the worst of the panic and crisis was over within a week, the psychological effect on businessmen, investors and the nation at large was more lasting.

FOUNDER'S DAY CORN ROAST. Sept 20. Pacific University, Forest Grove, OR. 11:30 AM–4:30 PM. Mountain men, interactive pioneer displays, Native and other entertainment, Tug-O-War, chalk art, family activities and lots of CORN!!! Est attendance: 2,000. For info: Founder's Day Corn Roast, 2417 Pacific Ave, Forest Grove, OR 97116. Phone: (503) 357-3006.

"THE LORETTA YOUNG SHOW" TV PREMIERE: 45th ANNIVERSARY. Sept 20, 1953. NBC show (initially titled "A Letter to Loretta") hosted by and frequently starring Oscar-winning actress Loretta Young was a half-hour dramatic anthology series on Sunday nights. At the beginning of each episode Young would swirl through a door in a spectacular gown. Young garnered two Emmys during the show's eight-year run. In 1972 it was reported that Young had been awarded $559,000 in a suit against NBC for syndicating reruns of the show without her permission. Young did not want them shown because her clothes and hairstyles in the shows were long out of date by the '70s.

"LOU GRANT" TV PREMIERE: ANNIVERSARY. Sept 20, 1977. This hour-long dramatic series was a spin-off from "The Mary Tyler Moore Show." Ed Asner reprised his role as newspaper editor Lou Grant, now a city editor for the *Los Angeles Tribune*. The show tackled many serious and controversial issues, including child abuse, gun control and the plight of Vietnamese refugees. The cast included Mason Adams, Nancy Marchand, Jack Bannon, Robert Walden, Daryl Anderson, Rebecca Balding, Linda Kelsey, Allen Williams and Emilio Delgado. This series was an unusual spin-off because it was the first time a character left a sitcom to headline a drama.

"M SQUAD" TV PREMIERE: ANNIVERSARY. Sept 20, 1957. This half-hour crime series had both a catchy theme song composed by Count Basie and Lee Marvin as Lieutenant Frank Ballinger, a Chicago cop assigned to a unit that investigates murders (the M Squad). Paul Newlan played his supervisor Captain Grey. In one episode, "The Teacher," (1959), Burt Reynolds played one of his first major roles.

MIND MAP IN EDUCATION WEEK. Sept 20–26. Lake Park, FL. Mind Map competition at different grade levels and in different subjects. Summaries of past year's work or overview of year's curriculum to come. Displays, books and prizes. Est attendance: 100. For info: Vanda North, Managing Dir, Buzan Centres, 415 Federal Hwy, Lake Park, FL 33403. Phone: (561) 881-0188. Fax: (561) 845-3210.
Email: 100737.747@compuserve.com.

MOON PHASE: NEW MOON. Sept 20. Moon enters New Moon phase at 1:01 PM, EDT.

MORTON, FERDINAND "JELLY ROLL": BIRTH ANNIVERSARY. Sept 20. American jazz pianist, composer, singer and orchestra leader, was born at New Orleans, LA, Sept 20, 1885. Morton, subject of a biography titled *Mr Jelly Roll* by Alan Lomax, died July 10, 1941, at Los Angeles, CA.

NATIONAL DOG WEEK. Sept 20–26. To promote the relationship of dogs to mankind and emphasize the need for the proper care and treatment of dogs. Annually, the last full week in September. For info: Morris Raskin, Secy, Dogs on Stamps Study Unit (DOSSU), 202 A Newport Rd, Cranbury, NJ 08512. Phone: (609) 655-7411.

NATIONAL FARM ANIMALS AWARENESS WEEK. Sept 20–26. A week to promote awareness of farm animals and their natural behaviors. Each day of the week is dedicated to learning about a specific group of farm animals and to appreciating their many interesting and unique qualities. Annually, the third full week in September. For info: David Kuemmerle, Project Coord, The Humane Society of the US, Farm Animal Section, 2100 L St NW, Washington, DC 20037. Phone: (202) 452-1100. Email: hsusfarm@ix.netcom.com.

★**NATIONAL FARM SAFETY WEEK.** Sept 20–26. Presidential Proclamation issued since 1982 for the third week in September. Previously, from 1944, for one of the last two weeks in July.

NATIONAL RESEARCH COUNCIL: FIRST MEETING ANNIVERSARY. Sept 20. Anniversary of first meeting of National Research Council, at New York, NY, Sept 20, 1916. Formed at request of President Woodrow Wilson for ". . . encouraging the investigation of natural phenomena. . . ." for American business and national security. Sept 20 also marks the anniversary of the first meeting of the American Association for the Advancement of Science at Philadelphia, PA, in 1848.

NATIONAL REYE'S SYNDROME WEEK. Sept 20–26. To promote awareness and prevention of Reye's Syndrome, the acute and often fatal childhood syndrome marked by deterioration of the liver, rapid brain swelling, disturbed consciousness and seizures. For info: Natl Reye's Syndrome Foundation, PO Box 829, Bryan, OH 43506. Phone: (419) 636-2679.

NATIONAL SINGLES WEEK. Sept 20–26. To celebrate single life; to recognize singles and their associations; to present dignified options for finding a partner or living fully without one. For info: Singles Press Assn, Box 6243, Scottsdale, AZ 85261-6243. Phone: (602) 788-6001. Email: singles@primenet.com.

NATIONAL SURGICAL TECHNOLOGIST WEEK. Sept 20–26. A week sponsored by the Association of Surgical Technologists to recognize the important role of surgical technologists in the provision of quality surgical patient care. Annually, beginning with the third Sunday in September. For info: Assn of Surgical Technologists, 7108-C S Alton Way, Ste 100, Englewood, CO 80112. Phone: (303) 694-9130. Email: ast@ast.org.

"THE PHIL SILVERS SHOW" TV PREMIERE: ANNIVERSARY. Sept 20, 1955. This popular half-hour sitcom starred Phil Silvers as Sergeant Ernie Bilko, a scheming but good-natured con man whose schemes rarely worked out. Members of the command and platoon included Harvey Lembeck, Allan Melvin, Paul Ford, Elisabeth Fraser, Maurice Gosfield, Herbie Faye, Billy Sands, Mickey Freeman, Hope Sansberry, Joe E. Ross, Jimmy Little, Beatrice Pons and Nicholas Saunders. Guest stars included Fred Gwynne, Dody Goodman, Margaret Hamilton, Dick Van Dyke and Alan Alda in his first major TV role. The character of Sergeant Bilko was featured in a movie of the same title in the mid-90s.

REVOLUTIONARY TIMES AT BRANDYWINE. Sept 20. Brandywine Battlefield Park, Chadds Ford, PA. Reenactments of the Battle of Brandywine, an 18th-century tavern, children's activities; plus sutlers and crafters perform, display and sell their crafts. Plenty of good food. Est attendance: 5,000. For info: Richard Wolfe, Educ Coord, Brandywine Battlefield Park, PO Box 202, Chadds Ford, PA 19317. Phone: (610) 459-3342. Fax: (610) 459-9586.

ROCK OF CHICKAMAUGA: ANNIVERSARY. Sept 20, 1863. After disastrous moves by Union General William Starke Rosecrans, Confederate forces appeared to be carrying the day at the Battle of Chickamauga in Tennessee. With Rosecrans in flight to Chattanooga, Union General Henry Thomas and his men maintained their position and repeatedly turned back Southern attacks until they were reinforced. Thomas's actions saved the Union forces from a complete rout and earned him the nickname, "Rock of Chickamauga." Rosecrans was relieved of his command.

ROSH HASHANAH BEGINS AT SUNDOWN. Sept 20. Jewish New Year. See "Rosh Hashanah" (Sept 21).

SINCLAIR, UPTON (BEALL): BIRTH ANNIVERSARY. Sept 20, 1878. American novelist and politician born at Baltimore, MD, Sept 20, 1878. Died at Bound Brook, NJ, Nov 25, 1968. He worked for political and social reforms, and his best-known novel, *The Jungle*, prompted one of the nation's first pure food laws.

"THE THIN MAN" TV PREMIERE: ANNIVERSARY. Sept 20, 1957. The famous crimesolving duo of Nick and Nora was brought to TV after appearing in a novel by Dashiell Hammett and a film series. This half-hour crime series featured Peter Lawford as Nick Charles, a former private eye who still engaged in it for fun, and Phyllis Kirk as his wife and partner Nora. Jack Albertson played Lieutenant Evans, and their pet dog Asta was played by Asta.

TOLKIEN WEEK. Sept 20–26. To promote appreciation and enjoyment of the works of J.R.R. Tolkien. For info: Phil Helms, American Tolkien Society, Box 373, Highland, MI 48357-0373. Phone: (813) 585-0985. Fax: (813) 462-6473.

WALES: NORTH WALES MUSIC FESTIVAL. Sept 20–26. St. Asaph Cathedral, North Wales. Events include recitals, services, orchestral, choral, vocal, organ and chamber concerts. For info: Geraint Lewis, Artistic Dir, Festival Offices, High Street, St. Asaph, Denbighshire, Wales, UK.

WOOL DAY: SHEEP TO SHAWL AND BORDER COLLIES. Sept 20. Billings Farm and Museum, Woodstock, VT. This day-long event focuses on the many aspects of wool production, including a "sheep to shawl" demonstration and sheep herding, as well as many hands-on activities for all ages to enjoy. These activities include carding wool, drop spindle spinning, weaving, knitting and rug hooking. Border Collie demonstrations will show how these natural shepherds efficiently round up sheep, drive them from one area to another and corral them. Est attendance: 1,000. For info: Deborah Bulissa, Exec Asst, Billings Farm & Museum, PO Box 489, Woodstock, VT 05091. Phone: (802) 457-2355. Fax: (802) 457-4663. Email: billings.farm@valley.net.

BIRTHDAYS TODAY

Arnold Jacob ("Red") Auerbach, 81, Basketball Hall of Fame coach, born New York, NY, Sept 20, 1917.

Donald A. Hall, 70, poet, author (*Lucy's Christmas, Ox Cart Man*), born New Haven, CT, Sept 20, 1928.

Guy Damien LaFleur, 47, Hockey Hall of Fame right wing, born Thurso, Quebec, Canada, Sept 20, 1951.

Sophia Loren (Sofia Scicoloni), 64, actress (Oscar for *Two Women; Black Orchid, Marriage Italian Style*, "Brief Encounter"), born Rome, Italy, Sept 20, 1934.

Anne Meara, 74, actress ("Fame"), comedienne (Stiller and Meara), born New York, NY, Sept 20, 1924.

SEPTEMBER 21 — MONDAY

Day 264 — 101 Remaining

ARMENIA: NATIONAL DAY. Sept 21. Public holiday.

BELIZE: INDEPENDENCE DAY. Sept 21. National holiday.

BIOSPHERE DAY. Sept 21. A day to remind all humanity annually of the fragility of our only life-support, with the consequent need to safeguard it our foremost human imperative. The Biosphere is that layer of our planet's periphery (solid, liquid and gaseous) in which any form of life exists naturally. Participants are resolved to spread fundamental information worldwide concerning the Biosphere and how to preserve it. It is the Biosphere that is gravely threatened by human overpopulation and profligacy, not the inert and more solid Planet Earth. A major Biosphere fund and substantial Biosphere Prizes are planned to support Biosphere Day and spread its vital message. For info: Dr. Nicholas Polunin, Pres, The Foundation for Environmental Conservation, 7 Chemin Taverney 1218, Grand-Saconnex, Geneva, Switzerland. Phone: (41) (22) 798-2383. Fax: (41) (22) 798-2344.

September 1998

S	M	T	W	T	F	S
		1	2	3	4	5
6	7	8	9	10	11	12
13	14	15	16	17	18	19
20	21	22	23	24	25	26
27	28	29	30			

HURRICANE HUGO HITS AMERICAN COAST: ANNIVERSARY. Sept 21. After ravaging the Virgin Islands, Hurricane Hugo hit the American coast at Charleston, SC, on Sept 21, 1989. In its wake, Hugo left destruction totaling at least eight billion dollars.

JOSEPH, CHIEF: DEATH ANNIVERSARY. Sept 21, 1904. Admirable Nez Percé chief, whose Indian name was In-Mut-Too-Yah-Lat-Lat, was born about 1840 in Wallowa Valley, Oregon Territory, and died on the Colville Reservation in Washington. Faced with war or resettlement to a reservation, Chief Joseph led a dramatic attempt to escape to Canada. After three months and more than 1,000 miles, he and his people were surrounded 40 miles from Canada and sent to a reservation in Oklahoma. Though the few survivors were later allowed to relocate to another reservation in Washington, they never regained their ancestral lands.

LOVE A MENSCH WEEK. Sept 21–27. Mensches are decent, responsible men or women. During this week singles look to meet a mensch as well as take time to appreciate how mensches enhance our lives. For info: Robin Gorman Newman, Mensch Finders, 58 Grace Ave, #2J, Great Neck, NY 11021. Phone: (516) 773-0911. Email: rgnewman@aol.com.

MALTA: INDEPENDENCE DAY. Sept 21. National Day.

NATIONAL FOOD SERVICE EMPLOYEES WEEK. Sept 21–25. To promote public awareness of the contributions and importance of food service employees to life in America. Annually, the fourth week in September. For info: Women and Infants Hospital of Rhode Island, Dietary Dept, 101 Dudley St, Providence, RI 02908.

NATIONAL IMPERFECTION WEEK. Sept 21–25. A celebration of the right to be imperfect. For info: Dan Verdick, Fairview Press, Minneapolis, MN 55454. Phone: (800) 544-8207. Email: dvfair01@intxxnet.com.

NATIONAL QUARTET CONVENTION. Sept 21–26. Freedom Hall, Kentucky Fair and Exposition Center, Louisville, KY. Six-day event with focus on the nightly Southern Gospel concerts. Daytime activities include special seminars and record company showcases, celebrity golf tournament, daily Bible study and chapel service and three-hour cruise on the Belle of Louisville. Est attendance: 75,000. For info: Clarke Beasley, Exec Dir, PO Box 197406, Louisville, KY 40259. Phone: (502) 961-0988. Fax: (502) 961-0987. Email: natqc@aol.com.

"PERRY MASON" TV PREMIERE: ANNIVERSARY. Sept 21, 1957. The outstanding acting of Raymond Burr will forever associate him with Perry Mason, a highly skilled criminal lawyer who won the great majority of his cases. Episodes followed a similar format: the action took place in the first half, with the killer's identity unknown, and the courtroom drama took place in the latter half. Mason was particularly adept at eliciting confessions from the guilty parties. Regulars and semi-regulars included Barbara Hale, William Hopper, William Talman, Raymond Collins, Wesley Lau, Richard Anderson, Lee Miller, Carl Held and Connie Cezon. Following the series' end, a number of successful "Perry Mason" TV movies have aired.

ROSH HASHANAH or JEWISH NEW YEAR. Sept 21-22. Jewish holy day; observed on following day also. Hebrew calendar date: Tishri 1, 5759. Rosh Hashanah is beginning of 10 days of repentance and spiritual renewal. (Began at sundown of previous day.)

TAYLOR, MARGARET SMITH: BIRTH ANNIVERSARY. Sept 21, 1788. Wife of Zachary Taylor, 12th president of the US, born at Calvert County, MD, Sept 21, 1788. Died on Aug 18, 1852.

"THE TEXACO STAR THEATER" TV PREMIERE: 50th ANNIVERSARY. Sept 21, 1948. Also known as "The Milton Berle Show" and sponsored by Texaco until 1953, this variety show was popular, successful and a good sign for the fledgling TV industry. Milton Berle became a superstar. The show featured singing and comedy, especially sight gags and outrageous costumes. Guest stars also came on the show. Sid Stone was the pitchman, responsible for speaking the commercials. Changes were made in the fourth season: Berle cut back his appearances, new writers and a new director were added and the format was changed to a show-within-a-show. Ruth Gilbert, Fred Clark and Arnold Stang were featured, along with the new pitchman, ventriloquist Jimmy Nelson and his dummy Danny O'Day.

WATTICISM DAY: 15th ANNIVERSARY. Sept 21, 1983. Anniversary of speech by then US Interior Secretary James Watt to trade association executives at the US Chamber of Commerce, Sept 21, 1983. Referring to his advisory committee, Watt said: "We have every kind of mixture you can have. I have a black, I have a woman, two Jews and a cripple. And we have talent." He later apologized for an "unfortunate choice of words."

WELLS, HERBERT GEORGE: BIRTH ANNIVERSARY. Sept 21. English novelist and historian, born at Bromley, in Kent, England, on Sept 21, 1866. Among his books: *The Time Machine, The Invisible Man, The War of the Worlds* and *The Outline of History*. Wells died at London, Aug 13, 1946. "Human history," he wrote, "becomes more and more a race between education and catastrophe."

WORLD GRATITUDE DAY. Sept 21. To unite all people in a positive emotion of gratitude, creating a world community. Gratitude gatherings, any assemblage aware of the spirit of gratitude, are encouraged. Annual international children's poster exhibit. For info: World Gratitude Day, Edna Lemle, Pres, 132 W 31st St, New York, NY 10001.

BIRTHDAYS TODAY

Leonard Cohen, 64, singer, songwriter, born Montreal, Quebec, Canada, Sept 21, 1934.

Cecil Grant Fielder, 35, baseball player, born Los Angeles, CA, Sept 21, 1963.

Henry Gibson, 63, comedian ("Rowan and Martin's Laugh-In"), actor (*Nashville*), born Germantown, PA, Sept 21, 1935.

Artis Gilmore, 49, former basketball player, born Chipley, FL, Sept 21, 1949.

Larry Hagman, 67, actor ("I Dream of Jeannie," "Dallas"), born Fort Worth,TX, Sept 21, 1931.

Stephen King, 61, author (*Christine, Pet Sematary, The Shining, Misery, The Stand*), born Portland, ME, Sept 21, 1937.

Bill Kurtis, 58, journalist (Chicago CBS anchorman), born Pensacola, FL, Sept 21, 1940.

Ricki Lake, 30, talk-show host, actress (*Hairspray, Serial Mom*), born New York, NY, Sept 21, 1968.

Rob Morrow, 36, actor ("Northern Exposure," *Quiz Show*), born New Rochelle, NY, Sept 21, 1962.

Bill Murray, 48, comedian ("Saturday Night Live"), actor (*Ghostbusters, Groundhog Day, Mad Dog and Glory, What About Bob?, Scrooged, Caddy Shack*), born Evanston, IL, Sept 21, 1950.

Nancy Travis, 37, actress ("Almost Perfect," *Married to the Mob, Chaplin*), born New York, NY, Sept 21, 1961.

SEPTEMBER 22 — TUESDAY

Day 265 — 100 Remaining

AMERICAN BUSINESS WOMEN'S DAY. Sept 22. A day on which all Americans can recognize the important contributions more than 55 million American working women have made and are continuing to make to this nation. Annually, Sept 22. For info: Carolyn Elman, American Business Women's Assn, 9100 Ward Pkwy, Kansas City, MO 64114. Phone: (816) 361-6621. Email: c.elman@abwa.hq.org. WWW: http://www.abwahq.org

"CHARLIE'S ANGELS" TV PREMIERE: ANNIVERSARY. Sept 22, 1976. This extremely popular show of the '70s featured three attractive women solving crimes, usually scantily-dressed. Sabrina Duncan (Kate Jackson), Jill Munroe (Farrah Fawcett-Majors) and Kelly Garrett (Jaclyn Smith) signed on with detective agency Charles Townsend Associates. Their boss was never seen, only heard (the voice of John Forsythe); messages were communicated to the women by his associate John Bosley (David Doyle). During the course of the series, Cheryl Ladd replaced Fawcett, Shelley Hack and Tanya Roberts succeeded Kate Jackson.

DEAR DIARY DAY. Sept 22. Put it on paper. You'll feel better. No need to be a professional writer. [© 1997 by WPL] For info: Tom or Ruth Roy, Wellness Permission League, PO Box 662, Mt Gretna, PA 17064-0662. Phone: (500) 437-5104 or (717) 964-1308. Fax: (717) 964-1335.

ELEPHANT APPRECIATION DAY. Sept 22. Celebrate the earth's largest, most interesting and most noble endangered land animal. Free info kit from: Wayne Hepburn, Wild Heart Productions, PO Box 4710, Sarasota, FL 34230-4710. Phone: (941) 955-2950. Fax: (941) 955-5723. Email: mail@wildheart.com. WWW: http://www.wildheart.com

"FAMILY TIES" TV PREMIERE: ANNIVERSARY. Sept 22, 1982. This popular 80s sitcom was set in Columbus, OH and focused on the Keaton family: Ex-hippies Elyse (Meredith Baxter-Birney), an architect, and Steven (Michael Gross), a station manager of the local public TV station; Alex (Michael J. Fox), their smart, conservative and financially-driven son; Mallory (Justine Bateman), their materialistic, ditzy daughter; and Jennifer (Tina Yothers), their tomboy youngest daughter. Later in the series Elyse gave birth to Andrew (played by Tyler and Grant Merriman and later Brian Bonsall). Marc Price played Irwin "Skippy" Handleman, the nerdy next-door neighbor who adored the Keatons, and Mallory in particular.

☆ ☆ ☆

FARADAY, MICHAEL: BIRTH ANNIVERSARY. Sept 22. English scientist and early experimenter with electricity, born Sept 22, 1791. Died Aug 25, 1867.

FIRST ALL-WOMAN JURY EMPANELED IN COLONIES. Sept 22. The General Provincial Court in Patuxent, MD, empaneled the first all-woman jury in the colonies on Sept 22, 1656. The jury heard the case of Judith Catchpole, accused of murdering her child. The defendant claimed she had never even been pregnant, and after all the evidence was heard, the jury acquitted her.

HOBBIT DAY. Sept 22. To commemorate the birthdays of Frodo and Bilbo Baggins and their creator J.R.R. Tolkien. For info: American Tolkien Society, Box 373, Highland, MI 48357-0373. Phone: (813) 585-0985. Fax: (813) 462-6473.

HOUSEMAN, JOHN: BIRTH ANNIVERSARY. Sept 22, 1902. American actor and producer John Houseman was born Jacques Haussmann at Bucharest. He is best known for his collaboration with Orson Welles on the 1938 radio production of *War of the Worlds* and for his role as Professor Kingsfield in the film and television version of *The Paper Chase*. He won an Oscar for that film role in 1974 and helped establish the Juilliard drama school and the Acting Company repertory group. He died on Oct 30, 1988 at Malibu, CA.

ICE CREAM CONE: 95th BIRTHDAY. Sept 22, 1903. Italo Marchiony emigrated from Italy in the late 1800s and soon thereafter went into the portable restaurant business in New York, NY, with a pushcart dispensing lemon ice. Success soon led to a small fleet of pushcarts, and the inventive Marchiony was inspired to develop a cone, first made of paper, later of pastry, to hold the tasty delicacy. On Sept 22, 1903, his application for a patent for his new mold was filed, and US Patent No. 746971 was issued to him on Dec 15, 1903.

JACKSON COUNTY APPLE FESTIVAL. Sept 22–26. Jackson County, OH. Mountains of apples and barrels of cider. Homemade apple butter, apple pies and candy apples. Est attendance: 210,000. For info: Jackson County Apple Festival, Inc, PO Box 8, Jackson, OH 45640-0008. Phone: (614) 286-1339.

LONG COUNT DAY: ANNIVERSARY. Sept 22, 1927. Anniversary of world championship boxing match between Jack Dempsey and Gene Tunney, at Soldier Field, Chicago, IL. It was the largest fight purse ($990,446) in the history of boxing to that time. Nearly half the population of the US is believed to have listened to the radio broadcast of this fight. In the seventh round of the 10-round fight, Tunney was knocked down. Following the rules, Referee Dave Barry interrupted the count when Dempsey failed to go to the farthest corner. The count was resumed and Tunney got to his feet at the count of nine. Stopwatch records of those present claimed the total elapsed time from the beginning of the count until Tunney got to his feet at 12–15 seconds. Tunney, awarded seven of the 10 rounds, won the fight and claimed the world championship. Dempsey's appeal was denied and he never fought again. Tunney retired the following year after one more (successful) fight.

MALI: INDEPENDENCE DAY. Sept 22. National holiday commemorating independence from France on Sept 22, 1960. Mali, in West Africa, was known as the French Sudan while a colony of France.

"MAVERICK" TV PREMIERE: ANNIVERSARY. Sept 22, 1957. This popular western, which has since been remade into a popular movie, starred James Garner as Bret Maverick, a clever man who preferred card playing to fighting. A second Maverick was introduced when production was behind schedule—Jack Kelly played his brother Bart. Garner and Kelly played most episodes separately, and when Garner left in 1961, Kelly was in almost all the episodes. Other performers included Roger Moore, Robert Colbert and Diane Brewster. This western distinguished itself by its light touch and parody of others westerns.

NATIONAL CENTENARIANS DAY. Sept 22. A day to recognize and honor elderly individuals who have lived a century or longer. A day not only to recognize these individuals, but to listen to them discuss the memories—filled with historical information—that they have of their rich lives. Take time today to listen to a Centenarian. Special celebration held annually at Williamsport Retirement Village. For info: Meg Cliber, Mktg Dir, Williamsport Retirement Village, Founders, A Division of Brooke Grove Fdtn, 154 N Artizan St, Williamsport, MD 21795. Phone: (301) 223-7971. Fax: (301) 223-6966.

September 1998

S	M	T	W	T	F	S
		1	2	3	4	5
6	7	8	9	10	11	12
13	14	15	16	17	18	19
20	21	22	23	24	25	26
27	28	29	30			

NATIONAL YOUTH OF THE YEAR. Sept 22–26 (tentative). Washington, DC. Each year a Boys and Girls Club member is selected by a panel of judges from among five regional finalists to be the National Youth of the Year and spokesperson for Boys and Girls Clubs of America. This selection is open to Boys and Girls Club members only—ages 18 and under. Finalists are selected based on leadership qualities and service exhibited to home and family, spiritual values, service to community and Club, excellence in school and obstacles overcome. Winners are presented at a Congressional breakfast and to the president at the White House. For info: Kevin W. Davis, Dir of Program Services, Boys and Girls Clubs of America, 1230 W Peachtree St NW, Atlanta, GA 30309.

STANHOPE, PHILIP DORMER: BIRTH ANNIVERSARY. Sept 22, 1694. Philip Dormer Stanhope, the 4th Earl of Chesterfield, was born at London, England. He was a brilliant politician and orator. On Feb 20, 1751, he brought a bill into the House of Lords that caused the "New Style" Gregorian calendar to replace the "Old Style" Julian calendar in 1752. His influential political career was eclipsed by the fame of the letters he wrote to his son from when Philip was five years old until the son's death at age 36, giving shrewd counsel on manners, morals and the ways of the world. Published less than a year after his own death at London, Mar 24, 1773, the *Letters* became immensely popular, were translated and republished in many editions and in many countries. The Chesterfield, a kind of sofa, is said to be named for him.

TACY RICHARDSON'S RIDE: ANNIVERSARY. Sept 22, 1777. Courageous 23-year-old Tacy Richardson (Jan 1, 1754–June 18, 1807) rode her favorite horse, "Fearnaught," several perilous miles from the family farm in Montgomery County, PA to the James Vaux mansion to warn General George Washington of the approach of British troops led by General William Howe. As it turned out, the British crossing of the Schuylkill at Gordon's Ford was a feint to deceive Washington who indeed hastily withdrew to Pottstown, clearing the way for General Howe to spend that night in the quarters Washington had occupied only a few hours earlier.

US POSTMASTER GENERAL ESTABLISHED: ANNIVERSARY. Sept 22. Congress established office of postmaster general—Sept 22, 1789, following the departments of state, war and treasury.

BIRTHDAYS TODAY

Walter Wayne (Wally) Backman, 39, former baseball player, born Hillsboro, OR, Sept 22, 1959.

Scott Baio, 37, actor ("Happy Days," "Stoned," "Charles in Charge"), born Brooklyn, NY, Sept 22, 1961.

Shari Belafonte-Harper, 44, model, actress, born New York, NY, Sept 22, 1954.

Debbie Boone, 42, singer ("You Light Up My Life," "Baby, I'm Yours"), born Hackensack, NJ, Sept 22, 1956.

Joan Jett, 38, singer ("I Love Rock 'n' Roll," "Crimson and Clover"), musician, born Philadelphia, PA, Sept 22, 1960.

Thomas Charles (Tommy) Lasorda, 71, former baseball manager, former player, born Norristown, PA, Sept 22, 1927.

Paul Le Mat, 53, actor (*American Graffiti, Melvin and Howard, Strange Invaders*), born Rahway, NY, Sept 22, 1945.

Catherine Oxenberg, 37, actress (Amanda in "Dynasty"), born New York, NY, Sept 22, 1961.

Eugene Roche, 70, actor ("Soap," "Webster"), born Boston, MA, Sept 22, 1928.

Mike Sullivan, 59, former Governor of Wyoming (D), born Omaha, NE, Sept 22, 1939.

Arthur O. Sulzberger, 47, publisher (*New York Times*), born Mount Kisco, NY, Sept 22, 1951.

SEPTEMBER 23 — WEDNESDAY

Day 266 — 99 Remaining

AUTUMN. Sept 23–Dec 21. In the Northern Hemisphere, autumn begins today with the autumnal equinox, at 1:37 AM, EDT. Note that in the Southern Hemisphere today is the beginning of spring. Everywhere on Earth (except near the poles) the sun rises due east and sets due west, and daylight length is nearly identical—about 12 hours, 8 minutes.

BASEBALL'S GREATEST DISPUTE: 90th ANNIVERSARY. Sept 23, 1908. In the decisive game between the Chicago Cubs and the New York Giants, the National League pennant race erupted in controversy during the bottom of the ninth with the score tied 1–1, at the Polo Grounds, New York, NY. New York was at bat with two men on. The batter hit safely to centerfield, scoring the winning run. Chicago claimed that the runner on first, Fred Merkle, seeing the winning run scored, headed toward the dugout without advancing to second base, thus invalidating the play. The Chicago second baseman, Johnny Evers, attempted to get the ball and tag Merkle out, but was prevented by the fans streaming onto the field. Days later Harry C. Pulliam, head of the National Commission of Organized Baseball, decided to call the game a tie. The teams were forced to play a post-season playoff game, which the Cubs won 4–2. Fans invented the terms "boner" and "bonehead" in reference to the play and it has gone down in baseball history as "Merkle's Boner."

BLACK WALNUT FESTIVAL. Sept 23–26. Stockton, MO. 37th annual. Tours of the largest, in fact the only, black walnut processing plant in the world. Also included are a parade, craft demonstrations, queen contest, carnival and musical entertainment. Est attendance: 10,000. For info: Stockton Area Chamber of Commerce, PO Box 410, Stockton, MO 65785. Phone: (417) 276-5213.

CHASE'S 1999 CALENDAR OF EVENTS PUBLISHED. Sept 23, 1998. The 1999 *Chase's* is now available in bookstores or by calling 1-800-323-4900.

CHECKERS DAY: ANNIVERSARY. Sept 23. Anniversary of the nationally televised "Checkers Speech" by then vice-presidential candidate Richard M. Nixon, on Sept 23, 1952. Nixon was found "clean as a hound's tooth" in connection with a private fund for political expenses, and he declared he would never give back the cocker spaniel dog, Checkers, which had been a gift to his daughters. Other dogs prominent in American politics: Abraham Lincoln's dog, Fido; Franklin D. Roosevelt's much-traveled terrier, Fala; Harry S. Truman's dogs, Mike and Feller; Dwight D. Eisenhower's dog, Heidi; Lyndon Johnson's beagles, Him and Her; Ronald Reagan's dogs, Lucky and Rex; and George Bush's dog, Millie.

FAST OF GEDALYA. Sept 23. Jewish holiday. Hebrew calendar date: Tishri 3, 5759. Tzom Gedalya begins at first light of day and commemorates the 6th-century BC assassination of Gedalya Ben Achikam.

FERDINAND VI OF SPAIN: BIRTH ANNIVERSARY. Sept 23, 1713. King of Spain from 1746 to 1759, his greatest claim to fame was keeping Spain at peace. Born at Madrid, Spain, on Sept 23, 1713, he died at Villaviciosa de Odon, Spain, on Aug 10, 1759.

INNERGIZE. Sept 23. A day set aside for anyone who has said "I don't have time to do the personal things I want to do for myself." Today is the day to set time aside for yourself to do anything you want to do. For info: Michelle Porchia, inner dimensions, 4 Daniels Farm Rd, Ste 137, Trumbull, CT 06611. Phone: (203) 336-6516. Fax: (203) 336-6516.

"THE JETSONS" TV PREMIERE: ANNIVERSARY. Sept 23, 1962. "Meet George Jetson. His boy Elroy. Daughter Judy. Jane, his wife. . . . " These words introduced us to the Jetsons, a cartoon family living in the twenty-first century, the Flintstones of the Space Age. We followed the exploits of George and his family, as well as his unstable work relationship with his greedy, ruthless boss Cosmo Spacely. Voices were provided by George O'Hanlon as George, Penny Singleton as Jane, Janet Waldo as Judy, Daws Butler as Elroy, Don Messick as Astro, the family dog, and Mel Blanc as Spacely. New episodes were created in 1985 which also introduced a new pet, Orbity.

LIBRA, THE BALANCE. Sept 23–Oct 22. In the astronomical/astrological zodiac that divides the sun's apparent orbit into twelve segments, the period Sept 23–Oct 22 is identified traditionally as the sun sign of Libra, the Balance. The ruling planet is Venus.

LIPPMANN, WALTER: BIRTH ANNIVERSARY. Sept 23. American journalist, political philosopher and author. Born at New York, NY, on Sept 23, 1889, he died there on Dec 14, 1974. As a syndicated newspaper columnist he was the foremost and perhaps the most influential commentator in the nation. "Without criticism," he said in an address to the International Press Institute in 1965, "and reliable and intelligent reporting, the government cannot govern."

MABON. Sept 23. (Also called Alban Elfed.) One of the "Lesser Sabbats" during the Wiccan year, Mabon marks the second harvest as Nature prepares for the coming of winter. Annually, on the autumnal equinox.

McGUFFEY, WILLIAM HOLMES: BIRTH ANNIVERSARY. Sept 23, 1800. American educator and author of the famous *McGuffey Readers*, born at Washington County, PA, Sept 23, 1800. Died at Charlottesville, VA, May 4, 1873.

NATIONAL FOOD SERVICE EMPLOYEES DAY. Sept 23. To promote public awareness of the contributions and importance of food service employees to life in America. Annually, the Wednesday of Natl Food Service Employees Week. For info: Women and Infants Hospital of Rhode Island, Dietary Dept, 101 Dudley St, Providence, RI 02908.

PAULUS, FRIEDRICH: BIRTH ANNIVERSARY. Sept 23, 1890. The German commander of the Sixth Army who led the advance on Stalingrad in 1942, Friedrich von Paulus was born at Breitenau, Germany. Paulus' troops succeeded in taking most of Stalingrad in November 1942, but eventually became trapped within the city they had captured. Paulus surrendered to the Russians Jan 31, 1943, the same day that Hitler promoted him to field marshal. He appeared as a key witness for the Soviet prosecution at the Nuremberg trials. Paulus died on Feb 1, 1957, age 66, at Dresden, East Germany.

PIDGEON, WALTER: BIRTH ANNIVERSARY. Sept 23, 1897. Actor Walter Pidgeon was born at East St. John, New Brunswick, Canada. He died at age 87 on Sept 25, 1984, at Santa Monica, CA. In the early 1920s he made several stage appearances. He made his film debut in 1925 in *Mannequin*. Among his films are *Saratoga* and *Mrs Miniver*.

PLANET NEPTUNE DISCOVERY: ANNIVERSARY. Sept 23. First observed on Sept 23, 1846. Neptune is 2,796,700,000 miles from the sun (about 30 times as far from the sun as Earth). Eighth planet from the sun, Neptune takes 164.8 years to revolve around the sun. Diameter is about 31,000 miles compared to Earth at 7,927 miles.

PROPOSAL DAY®. Sept 23. Proposal Day® is a holiday for singles who are seeking marriage. Both bachelors and bachelorettes are encouraged to propose marriage to their true love on Proposal Day; the day of the autumnal equinox. Singles not quite ready to propose can celebrate the holiday by sending a gift to the one they hope to marry someday. List released each equinox of the 10 most eligible celebrity singles. Annually, on the first day of autumn (Autumnal Equinox). For info: John Michael O'Loughlin, 1333 W Campbell #125, Richardson, TX 75080. Phone: (972) 721-9975.

RIVER CITY ROUNDUP AND RODEO. Sept 23–28. Omaha, NE. Take a moment to reflect on the Midwest's proud past. A celebration of Omaha's agricultural and western heritage; PRCA rodeo, hot-air balloon races, barbecue and chili contests, trail rides, the world's largest 4-H Livestock Expo and a downtown parade. Est attendance: 300,000. For info: Danelle Goldsmith, Mktg Dir, River City Roundup and Rodeo, 6800 Mercy Rd, Ste 206, Omaha, NE 68106. Phone: (402) 554-9610. Fax: (402) 554-9609. Email: knights@adnet.net. WWW: http://www.RiverCityRoundup.com

SAUDI ARABIA: ANNIVERSARY KINGDOM UNIFICATION. Sept 23, 1932. National holiday. Commemorates unification on this date.

WOODHULL, VICTORIA CHAFLIN: BIRTH ANNIVERSARY. Sept 23, 1838. American feminist, reformer and first female candidate for the presidency of the US. Born at Homer, OH, on Sept 23, 1838; died at Norton Park, Bremmons, Worcestershire, England, on June 10, 1927.

BIRTHDAYS TODAY

Jason Alexander, 39, actor (*Pretty Woman, Bye, Bye, Birdy*; stage: *Jerome Robbins' Broadway*; George on "Seinfeld"), born Newark, NJ, Sept 23, 1959.

Ray Charles (Robinson), 68, singer ("Georgia on My Mind," "I Can't Stop Loving You," "What'd I Say"), composer, born Albany, GA, Sept 23, 1930.

Julio Iglesias, 55, singer ("To All the Girls I've Loved Before" with Willie Nelson), songwriter, born Madrid, Spain, Sept 23, 1943.

Tony Joseph Mandarich, 32, football player, born Oakville, Ontario, Canada, Sept 23, 1966.

Larry Hogan Mize, 40, golfer, born Augusta, GA, Sept 23, 1958.

Elizabeth Pena, 37, actress (*Down and Out in Beverly Hills, Jacob's Ladder*, "Shannon's Deal"), born Cuba, Sept 23, 1961.

Paul Petersen, 53, actor ("The Donna Reed Show," *Houseboat*), born Glendale, CA, Sept 23, 1945.

Mary Kay Place, 51, writer, actress (Loretta Haggers on "Mary Hartman, Mary Hartman"; *The Big Chill*), born Tulsa, OK, Sept 23, 1947.

Mickey Rooney (Joe Yule, Jr), 78, actor (the *Andy Hardy* movies; *The Human Comedy, The Black Stallion*), born Brooklyn, NY, Sept 23, 1920.

Bruce Springsteen, 49, singer, songwriter ("Born in the USA"), born Freehold, NJ, Sept 23, 1949.

SEPTEMBER 24 — THURSDAY

Day 267 — 98 Remaining

BABE RUTH'S FAREWELL TO THE YANKEES: ANNIVERSARY. Sept 24, 1934. On this date Babe Ruth played his last game with the New York Yankees at Yankee Stadium.

"BULLWINKLE SHOW" FIRST BROADCAST: ANNIVERSARY. Sept 24, 1961. On this day in 1961 "The Bullwinkle Show" featuring Bullwinkle the Moose and Rocky the Flying Squirrel first aired.

"DANIEL BOONE" TV PREMIERE: ANNIVERSARY. Sept 24, 1964. A successful show based loosely on the life of pioneer Daniel Boone, who helped settle Kentucky in the 1770s. Fess Parker starred as the American hero. Ed Ames played Mingo, Boone's friend, an educated Cherokee and Pat Blair played his wife, Rebecca. Also featured were Albert Salmi, Jimmy Dean, Roosevelt Grier, Darby Hinton, Veronica Cartwright and Dallas McKennon.

"A DIFFERENT WORLD" TV PREMIERE. Sept 24, 1987. In this spinoff from "The Cosby Show," Denise Huxtable (Lisa Bonet) goes off to Hillman College. The first season's cast included Marisa Tomei, Dawnn Lewis, Jasmine Guy, Loretta Devine, Amir Williams, Kadeem Hardison, Darryl Bell, Marie-Alise Recasner, Mary Alice and Sinbad. Bonet left the series and returned to "The Cosby Show." Returning for a second season were Lewis, Guy, Hardison, Bell, Alice and Sinbad, plus Charnele Brown, Cree Summer and Glynn Turman. Aretha Franklin (Turman's wife) sang the show's theme song.

FANEUIL HALL OPENED TO THE PUBLIC: ANNIVERSARY. Sept 24, 1742. On this date Faneuil Hall in Boston, MA, opened to the public. Designed by painter John Smibiert, it was enlarged in 1805 according to plans by Charles Bulfinch.

FITZGERALD, F. SCOTT: BIRTH ANNIVERSARY. Sept 24. American short story writer and novelist; author of *This Side of Paradise, The Great Gatsby* and *Tender Is the Night*. Was born Francis Scott Key Fitzgerald, at St. Paul, MN, on Sept 24, 1896. He died at Hollywood, CA, Dec 21, 1940.

GUINEA-BISSAU: INDEPENDENCE DAY. Sept 24. National holiday is observed.

HENSON, JIM: BIRTH ANNIVERSARY. Sept 24, 1936. Puppeteer, born Sept 24, 1936, at Greenville, MS. Jim Henson created a unique brand of puppetry known as the Muppets. Kermit the Frog, Big Bird, Rowlf, Bert and Ernie, Gonzo, Animal, Miss Piggy and Oscar the Grouch are a few of the puppets that captured the hearts of children and adults alike in television and film productions including "Sesame Street," "The Jimmy Dean Show," "The Muppet Show," *The Muppet Movie, The Muppets Take Manhattan, The Great Muppet Caper* and *The Dark Crystal*. Henson began his career in 1954 as producer of the TV show "Sam and Friends" in Washington, DC. He introduced the Muppets in 1956. His creativity was rewarded with 18 Emmy Awards, seven Grammy Awards, four Peabody Awards and five ACE Awards from the National Cable Television Association. Henson died unexpectedly at the age of 53 on May 16, 1990, at New York, NY.

LAVITSEF. Sept 24–27. City-wide, Norfolk, NE. Concerts, pet show, quilt show, flower show, pancake feed, 10K run, craft fair, softball/basketball tournaments, sand volleyball, ice cream social, baby contest. Parade at 10 AM on Saturday. Est attendance: 10,000. For info: LaVitsef, Inc, PO Box 1512, Norfolk, NE 68702-1512.

"THE LOVE BOAT" TV PREMIERE: ANNIVERSARY. Sept 24, 1977. This one hour comedy-drama featured guest stars in intermingling story lines aboard a cruise ship, the Pacific Princess. All stories had to do with finding or losing love, hence the title "The Love Boat." The ship's crew were the only regulars (though there were occasional recurring roles, like Charo as April):

September 1998

S	M	T	W	T	F	S
		1	2	3	4	5
6	7	8	9	10	11	12
13	14	15	16	17	18	19
20	21	22	23	24	25	26
27	28	29	30			

Gavin MacLeod as Captain Merrill Stubing; Bernie Kopell as the often-divorced Doctor Adam Bricker; Fred Grandy as assistant purser Burl "Gopher" Smith; Ted Lange as bartender Isaac Washington; and Lauren Tewes as cruise director Julie McCoy. Also featured were Jill Whelan as Vicki, Stubing's daughter; Pat Klous as Julie, who replaced Tewes; Ted McGinley as photographer Ashley Covington "Ace" Evans. The series ended in Fall 1986, but three two-hour specials were broadcast the next year. MacLeod, Lange, Kopell and Whelan were reunited in a Love Boat special in 1990.

"LOVE OF LIFE" TV PREMIERE: ANNIVERSARY. Sept 24, 1951. This serial, which began as a fifteen-minute show, ran for 28 years. It was set in the town of Barrowsville at first and later moved to Rosehill; the story lines also shifted from a focus on two sisters to a larger number of characters. The diverse cast included such notables as Christopher Reeve, Paul Michael Glaser, Roy Scheider, Ja'net DuBois, John Aniston, Marsha Mason, Bert Convy, Warren Beatty and Peter Falk.

MARSHALL, JOHN: BIRTH ANNIVERSARY. Sept 24. Fourth Chief Justice of Supreme Court, born at Germantown, VA, on Sept 24, 1755. Served in House of Representatives and as secretary of state under John Adams. Appointed by President Adams to the position of chief justice in January 1801, he became known as "The Great Chief Justice." Marshall's court was largely responsible for defining the role of the Supreme Court and basic organizing principles of government in the early years after adoption of the Constitution in such cases as *Marbury vs Madison, McCulloch vs Maryland, Cohens vs Virginia* and *Gibbons vs Ogden.* He died at Philadelphia, PA, on July 6, 1835.

MID-SOUTH FAIR. Sept 24–Oct 4. Fairgrounds, Memphis, TN. Regional fair featuring concerts, free entertainment, midway, rodeo, livestock, exhibits and special events. Est attendance: 500,000. For info: Michael Todd, Mid-South Fair, 940 Early Maxwell Blvd, Memphis, TN 38104. Phone: (901) 274-8800. Fax: (901) 274-8804. Email: liberty@mem.net.
WWW: http://www.midsouthfair.com

"THE MUNSTERS" TV PREMIERE: ANNIVERSARY. Sept 24, 1964. "The Munsters" was a half-hour sitcom about an unusual family that thought they were ordinary. Each family member resembled a different type of monster: Herman Munster (Fred Gwynne) was Frankenstein's monster; Lily, his wife (Yvonne DeCarlo) and Grandpa, her father (Al Lewis) were vampires; and his son Eddie (Butch Patrick) was a werewolf. Only their niece, Marilyn (Beverly Owen and Pat Priest), looked normal, and they considered her the unattractive family member. Most of the show's laughs came from the family's interactions with outsiders.

OHIO PUMPKIN FESTIVAL. Sept 24–27. Downtown Barnesville, OH. This 35th annual festival features King Pumpkin contest, Queen Pageant, Giant Pumpkin Parade, classic car show, banjo & fiddle contest and more. Annually, the last full weekend of September. Est attendance: 100,000. For info: Eugene "Doc" Householder, President, Ohio Pumpkin Festival, Inc, PO Box 5, Barnesville, OH 43713. Phone: (614) 695-4359. Fax: (614) 695-6437.

POSSUM TOWN PIG FEST. Sept 24–26. Columbus Fairgrounds, Columbus, MS. Gigantic barbeque cooking contests with awards for food, theme and decor of booths. Also: Miss Possum Town Pig Contest, Pigs in Review Parade, Wine Race, Hog Calling Contest, games and children's rides and live music all weekend. Proceeds support Mississippi Sheriff's Boys and Girls Ranches and other local charities. Thousands come to enjoy the competition, food and fun. Annually, the fourth weekend in September. Est attendance: 15,000. For info: Beverly Norris, Dill & Norris Co, Inc, PO Box 2099, Columbus, MS 39704-2099. Phone: (601) 328-4532.

PRESTON COUNTY BUCKWHEAT FESTIVAL. Sept 24–27. Kingwood, WV. Celebrating the fall harvest, with coronations, parades, exhibits, arts and crafts, antique cars, livestock, carnival, country music and Buckwheat Cake Dinners. 56th annual festival. Annually, beginning the last Thursday in September. Est attendance: 100,000. For info: Lucille H. Crogan, Fest Secy, Kingwood Volunteer Fire Dept, PO Box 74, Kingwood, WV 26537. Phone: (304) 329-0021 or (304) 329-0101. Fax: (304) 329-0021.

SCHWENKFELDER THANKSGIVING. Sept 24. On this day in 1734 members of the Schwenkfelder Society gave thanks for their deliverance from Old World persecution as they prepared to take up new lives in the Pennsylvania-Dutch counties of Pennsylvania. Still celebrated.

STATE FAIR OF VIRGINIA ON STRAWBERRY HILL. Sept 24–Oct 4. Richmond, VA. The pride of Virginia's industry of agriculture can be seen in more than 3,000 exhibitions, competitions and shows. Virginia's greatest annual educational and entertainment event. Est attendance: 600,000. For info: Keith T. Hessey, Genl Mgr, 600 E Laburnum Ave, Richmond, VA 23222. Phone: (804) 228-3200. Fax: (804) 228-3252.
WWW: http://www.statefair.com

BIRTHDAYS TODAY

Arne H. Carlson, 64, Governor of Minnesota (R), born New York City, Sept 24, 1934.

Phil Hartman, 50, actor ("Saturday Night Live," "News Radio"), born Ontario, Canada, Sept 24, 1948.

Sheila MacRae, 75, singer, actress, born London, England, Sept 24, 1923.

Linda McCartney, 56, singer ("Admiral Halsey" with Paul McCartney), photographer, born New York, NY, Sept 24, 1942.

James Kenneth (Jim) McKay (born James Kenneth McManus), 77, sportscaster, born Philadelphia, PA, Sept 24, 1921.

Anthony Newley, 67, actor, singer (*Oliver Twist, No Time to Die*), born London, England, Sept 24, 1931.

Rafael Corrales Palmeiro, 34, baseball player, born Havana, Cuba, Sept 24, 1964.

SEPTEMBER 25 — FRIDAY

Day 268 — 97 Remaining

"BEAUTY AND THE BEAST" TV PREMIERE: ANNIVERSARY. Sept 25, 1987. This updated version of the fairy tale was a romantic hit and acquired a cult following. It followed the experiences of Catherine Chandler (Linda Hamilton), a Manhattan lawyer who is beaten and abandoned and subsequently found and cared for by Vincent (Ron Perlman), a man-beast living under the city. Other cast members included Roy Dotrice, Jay Acovone, Ren Woods, Cory Danziger and David Greenlee. Hamilton left the series at the beginning of the third season and Jo Anderson was added as police investigator Diana Bennett; the series ended shortly thereafter.

"BROKEN ARROW" TV PREMIERE: ANNIVERSARY. Sept 25, 1956. This half-hour western was one of the few to portray Native Americans in a positive light. It starred Michael Ansara as Cochise, Apache chief, and John Lupton as Indian Agent Tom Jeffords, Cochise's blood brother. The show was syndicated under the name "Cochise."

CANADA: CALGARY INTERNATIONAL ORGAN FESTIVAL. Sept 25–Oct 3. Organ concerts and organ with full symphony orchestra. Held every four years. For info: Calgary Centre for Performing Arts, 116 Eighth Ave, SE, Calgary, Alta, Canada T2G 0K6. Phone: (403) 543-5129. Fax: (403) 543-5115. Email: info@ciof.com. WWW: http://www.ciof.com

COMMON GROUND COUNTRY FAIR. Sept 25–27. Windsor Fairgrounds, Windsor, ME. Old-time country fair celebrating rural life with the revival of forgotten skills and demonstrations of technology appropriate for the future. Features Maine-produced food, crafts, entertainment, farming demonstrations and talks, a very special Children's Area with daily and ongoing participatory activities. Annually, the third weekend after Labor Day. Sponsor: Maine Organic Farmers and Gardeners Assn. Est attendance: 60,000. For info: Susan Pierce, Special Events Dir, PO Box 2176, Augusta, ME 04338. Phone: (207) 623-5115.

DURHAM FAIR. Sept 25–27. Durham, CT. 79th annual fair features agricultural exhibits, demonstrations and competitions; name country western entertainers, craft show, rides, amusements and food. Est attendance: 250,000. For info: Durham Agricultural Fair Assn, Inc, Box 225, Durham, CT 06422. Phone: (860) 349-9495.

FABULOUS 1890s WEEKEND. Sept 25–26 (tentative). Mansfield, PA. Night football in America began in 1892 with a game between Mansfield University and Wyoming Seminary. Annually, Mansfield celebrates a "Fabulous 1890s Weekend" to commemorate the event. Motorless parade, period exhibits, crafts and other events, including the re-creation of the first night football game. Sponsors: Mansfield University of Pennsylvania and Greater Area Mansfield Chamber of Commerce. Est attendance: 10,000. For info: Dennis Miller, Dir PR, Mansfield University, Mansfield, PA 16933. Phone: (717) 662-4293. Fax: (717) 662-4965. Email: dmiller@mnsfld.edu. WWW: http://www.mnsfld.edu

September 1998

S	M	T	W	T	F	S
		1	2	3	4	5
6	7	8	9	10	11	12
13	14	15	16	17	18	19
20	21	22	23	24	25	26
27	28	29	30			

FAIRMOUNT MUSEUM DAYS/REMEMBERING JAMES DEAN FESTIVAL. Sept 25–27. Fairmount, IN. The town where James Dean grew up honors Dean and other celebrated former citizens such as Jim Davis, creator of Garfield, journalist Phil Jones and Robert Sheets, retired director of the National Hurricane Center. The Fairmount Museum boasts "the Authentic James Dean Exhibit" of memorabilia and personal items of Dean's and it sponsors the festival that also includes a parade, James Dean Look-Alike Contest, custom car show featuring the James Dean Run for pre-1970 autos, Garfield Cat Photo and Art Contest, Garfield Great Run, carnival, games, live '50s entertainment and more. Annually, the last full weekend in September. Est attendance: 25,000. For info: Fairmount Historical Museum, Inc, 203 E Washington St, PO Box 92, Fairmount, IN 46928. Phone: (765) 948-4555.

FAULKNER, WILLIAM CUTHBERT: BIRTH ANNIVERSARY. Sept 25, 1897. American novelist and short story writer William Faulkner (born Falkner) was born at New Albany, MS. A Nobel Prize winner who changed the style and structure of the American novel in this century, he died at Byhalia, MS, at age 64 on July 6, 1962. Faulkner's first novel, *Soldiers' Pay* was published in 1926. His best-known book, *The Sound and the Fury*, appeared in 1929. Shunning literary circles, Faulkner moved to a pre-Civil War house called Rowan Oak at the outskirts of Oxford, MS in 1930. From 1930 until the onset of World War II Faulkner published an incredible body of work. *The Portable Faulkner* appeared in 1946 and *Collected Stories* in 1950. In June of 1962 Faulkner published his last novel, *The Reivers*, and in July he died of a heart attack.

FIRST AMENDMENTS TO THE US CONSTITUTION SUBMITTED TO STATES: ANNIVERSARY. Sept 25, 1789. Twelve amendments to the Constitution (in response to requests of immediate changes by five of the state ratifying conventions) were submitted to the states for consideration.

FIRST AMERICAN NEWSPAPER PUBLISHED: ANNIVERSARY. Sept 25, 1690. The first (and only) edition of *Publick Occurrences Both Foreign and Domestick* was published on this date by Benjamin Harris, at the London-Coffee-House, Boston, MA. Authorities considered this first newspaper published in the US offensive and ordered immediate suppression.

"FOUR STAR PLAYHOUSE" TV PREMIERE: ANNIVERSARY. Sept 25, 1952. The actors who founded Four Star Films—Dick Powell, Charles Boyer, Joel McCrea and Rosalind Russell—starred in this dramatic anthology series. David Niven and Ida Lupino replaced McCrea and Russell, who left shortly after the series began. Other guest actors included Nigel Bruce in his only US TV role ("A String of Beads," 1954); Ronald Colman in his first TV dramatic appearance ("The Lost Silk Hat," 1952); and Joan Fontaine in her first major dramatic TV role ("The Girl on the Park Bench," 1953).

"THE KATE SMITH HOUR" TV PREMIERE: ANNIVERSARY. Sept 25, 1950. Kate Smith was a talented singer who hosted radio before beginning a successful but short TV career. This late afternoon show was the most successful (she also had two prime-time shows, "The Kate Smith Evening Hour" (Sept 1951–June 1952) and "The Kate Smith Show" (Jan–July 1960) that were less well-received). It was divided into segments, the contents of which changed over the years, but included interviews, musical numbers and comedy or drama sketches. The sketches spun-off many series, including "The World of Mr Sweeney" and "Ethel and Albert."

LAUREL HERBSTFEST. Sept 25–27. Laurel, MT. 27th annual. Celebration of the town's German heritage. Activities include arts and crafts fair, dances, parade, fun run, two full days of musical entertainment, variety of food booths, beer garden with lots of polka music and dancing. Est attendance: 4,000. For info: Laurel Herbstfest Committee, PO Box 1192, Laurel, MT 59044.

MAJOR LEAGUE BASEBALL'S FIRST DOUBLE HEADER: ANNIVERSARY. Sept 25, 1882. On this date the first major league baseball double header was played between the Providence and Worcester teams.

MOUNT PLEASANT GLASS & ETHNIC FESTIVAL. Sept 25–27. Mount Pleasant, PA. Large outdoor street festival featuring glass blowing demos, arts and crafts, parade, entertainment and ethnic foods. Entertainment on two stages, a carnival and unique activities. For info: Jeff Landy, Mount Pleasant Glass and Ethnic Festival, Municipal Bldg, Mt Pleasant, PA 15666. Phone: (412) 547-7738. Fax: (412) 547-0115.

NATIONAL ONE-HIT WONDER DAY. Sept 25. Honors the one-hit wonders of rock-n-roll. Anyone who ever had a hit single deserves eternal remembrance. For info: Steven Rosen, Editor and Publisher, *One Shot* Magazine, 11667 Elkhead Range Rd, Littleton, CO 80127. Phone: (303) 979-2318.

NEPTUNE FESTIVAL BOARDWALK WEEKEND. Sept 25–27. Virginia Beach, VA. Virginia Beach's final, fond farewell to summer features boardwalk music and entertainment, the Sandcastle Classic, athletic competitions, a parade and fireworks. Est attendance: 650,000. For info: Neptune Festival, 265 Kings Grant Rd, Ste 102, Virginia Beach, VA 23452. Phone: (757) 427-3580 or (757) 498-0215. Fax: (757) 498-1355.

NORTHERN PLAINS TRIBAL ARTS FESTIVAL. Sept 25–27. Sioux Falls, SD. Art created by members of 33 Northern Plains tribes. Community education forums, juried art show, market days, powwow and artist award ceremony. Est attendance: 4,000. For info: American Indian Services, PO Box 1720, Sioux Falls, SD 57101-1720. Phone: (605) 334-4060.

PACIFIC OCEAN DISCOVERED: ANNIVERSARY. Sept 25, 1513. On Sept 25, 1513, Vasco Núñez de Balboa, a Spanish conquistador, stood high atop a peak in the Darien, becoming the first European to look upon the Pacific Ocean, claiming it as the South Sea in the name of the King of Spain.

PACIFIC RIM WILDLIFE ART SHOW. Sept 25–27. Seattle Center Exhibition Hall, Seattle, WA. Wildlife fine art by some of the most renowned artists in North America. The show offers booth sale, competition and auction pieces and informative seminars for the entire family. Annually, the last weekend in September. Est attendance: 10,000. For info: Bob Farrelly, Pres, WES Productions, PO Box 11225, Tacoma, WA 98411. Phone: (206) 596-6728. Fax: (206) 593-4152. Email: wespro@nwrain.net.

PROWSE, JULIET: BIRTH ANNIVERSARY. Sept 25, 1936. Dancer, actress, born Bombay, India. Died Sept 14, 1996.

RAMEAU, JEAN PHILLIPPE: BIRTH ANNIVERSARY. Sept 25, 1863. Birthday of French composer Jean Phillippe Rameau. Baptised at Dijon, France, Sept 25, 1683. Called by some the greatest French composer and musical theorist of the 18th century, Rameau died at Paris, France, Sept 12, 1764.

SHOSTAKOVICH, DMITRI: BIRTH ANNIVERSARY. Sept 25. Russian composer born at St. Petersburg, Russia, Sept 25, 1906. Died at Moscow, USSR, Aug 9, 1975.

"SILVER SPOONS" TV PREMIERE: ANNIVERSARY. Sept 25, 1982. This half-hour sitcom was about a weathy, immature toy company owner and his sensible son. Joel Higgins was Edward Stratton III; Ricky Schroeder played his son Ricky, who left military school to be with his divorced father; Erin Gray was Kate Summers, Edward's secretary and later, his new wife; Leonard Lightfoot was his lawyer, Leonard Rollins; Franklyn Seales played his business manager, Dexter Stuffins; Alfonso Ribeiro was Ricky's friend and Dexter's nephew, Alfonso Speers; Jason Bateman played Derek Taylor, Ricky's sneaky friend; and Corky Pigeon played geeky Freddie Lippincottleman. Ray Walston appeared as Kate's uncle, and John Houseman had a recurring role as Edward's stuffy father.

SMITH, WALTER WESLEY "RED": BIRTH ANNIVERSARY. Sept 25, 1905. Pulitzer Prize-winning sports columnist and newspaperman for 54 years, Walter Wesley (Red) Smith was born at Green Bay, WI, on Sept 25, 1905. Called the "nation's most respected sportswriter," Smith's columns appeared in some 500 newspapers. He died at Stamford, CT, Jan 15, 1982.

STATE FAIR OF TEXAS. Sept 25–Oct 18. Fair Park, Dallas, TX. Features a Broadway musical, college football games, laser shows, concerts, livestock shows and traditional events and entertainment including exhibits, creative arts and parades. Est attendance: 3,200,000. For info: Nancy Wiley, State Fair of Texas, PO Box 150009, Dallas, TX 75315. Phone: (214) 421-8716. Fax: (214) 421-8710. Email: Info@texfair.com.
WWW: http://www.texfair.com/

TACA FALL CRAFTS FAIR. Sept 25–27. Centennial Park, Nashville, TN. Festival of fine crafts featuring 170 selected American craft artists. 20th annual fair. Annually, the last weekend in September. Est attendance: 40,000. For info: Alice C. Merritt, Exec Dir, Tennessee Assn of Craft Artists, PO Box 120066, Nashville, TN 37212. Phone: (615) 665-0502.

TOUR OF CHAMPIONS. Sept 25–26. Maui, HI. Invitational pro mountain bike race for cross country and downhill riders. Winners of select pro races throughout the season will make up the elite field of 25 cross country and downhill riders. Televised. Pro purse $100,000. Est attendance: 10,000. For info: Events Marketing, 1001 Bishop St, Pauahi Tower #880, Honolulu, HI 96813. Phone: (808) 521-4322. Fax: (808) 538-0314. Email: dey@emisport. WWW: http://www.emisport.com

VIRGINIA PEANUT FESTIVAL. Sept 25–27. Emporia, VA. Annual celebration promoting peanuts and harvesting. Features musical concerts, arts and crafts, parade, corporate village, luncheon/fashion show, carnival, car show, canoe races and fireworks. Sponsored by Emporia-Greensville Chamber of Commerce. Est attendance: 20,000. For info: Kendra Perkins, Admit One Festivals, 425-E S Main St, PO Box 868, Emporia, VA 23847-0868. Phone: (804) 348-3378. Fax: (804) 348-0119. Email: kperkins@admit1fest.com.
WWW: http://www.admit1fest.com

WILD WEST FILM FEST. Sept 25–27. Tuolumne County, CA. A Friday-night gala honors Western movie stars, followed by two days of Western film showings, celebrity/film making panel discussions, autograph signing, live entertainment, film actor guests, arts and crafts and other family-oriented activities held in an historic 1850 gold rush community. Est attendance: 15,000. For info: Tuolumne County Visitors Bureau, PO Box 4020, Sonora, CA 95370. Phone: (800) 446-1333.
WWW: http://www.mlode.com/~nsierra/visitor.html

WILLOW TRADING POST POTATO FESTIVAL. Sept 25. Willow, AK. Competition for the largest potato sculpture made with whole potatoes. There will also be a free potato buffet and live music. Annually, the last Friday in September. Est attendance: 150. For info: Willow Trading Post, PO Box 49, Willow, AK 99688. Phone: (907) 495 6457. Email: keby@matnet.com.

BIRTHDAYS TODAY

Michael Douglas, 54, actor ("The Streets of San Francisco," *Fatal Attraction, Basic Instinct*), director, born New York, NY, Sept 25, 1944.

Mark Hamill, 47, actor ("General Hospital"; Luke in *Star Wars*), born Oakland, CA, Sept 25, 1951.

Heather Locklear, 37, actress ("T.J. Hooker," "Dynasty," "Melrose Place"), born Los Angeles, CA, Sept 25, 1961.

Scottie Pippen, 33, basketball player, born Hamburg, AR, Sept 25, 1965.

Christopher Reeve, 46, actor (*Superman*), born New York, NY, Sept 25, 1952.

Philip Francis (Phil) Rizzuto, 81, Baseball Hall of Fame shortstop, born New York, NY, Sept 25, 1917.

Will Smith, 30, actor (*Independence Day* and star of TV's "The Fresh Prince of Bel-Air"), born Philadelphia, PA, Sept 25, 1968.

Robert Walden, 55, actor ("Lou Grant," *All the King's Men*), born New York, NY, Sept 25, 1943.

Barbara Walters, 67, journalist, interviewer, former "Today" host, born Boston, MA, Sept 25, 1931.

SEPTEMBER 26 — SATURDAY

Day 269 — 96 Remaining

APPLESEED, JOHNNY: BIRTH ANNIVERSARY. Sept 26. John Chapman, better known as Johnny Appleseed, believed to have been born at Leominster, MA, on Sept 26, 1774. Died at Allen County, IN, Mar 11, 1845. Planter of orchards and friend of wild animals, he was regarded as a great medicine man by the Indians.

BANNED BOOKS WEEK—CELEBRATING THE FREEDOM TO READ. Sept 26–Oct 3. Brings to the attention of the general public the importance of the freedom to read and the harm censorship causes to our society. Sponsors: American Library Association, American Booksellers Association, American Society of Journalists and Authors, Association of American Publishers, National Association of College Stores, American Association of University Presses. For info: Judith F. Krug, American Library Assn, Office for Intellectual Freedom, 50 E Huron St, Chicago, IL 60611. Phone: (312) 280-4223. Fax: (312) 280-4227. Email: oif@ala.org. WWW: http://www.ala.org/bbooks

BEATLES LAST ALBUM RELEASED: ANNIVERSARY. Sept 26. The Beatles' 13th album, *Abbey Road*, was released in the United Kingdom on Sept 26, 1969. The album zoomed to number one on the record charts and stayed there for 11 weeks. It was the last album The Beatles made together.

"THE BEVERLY HILLBILLIES" TV PREMIERE: ANNIVERSARY. Sept 26, 1962. This half-hour comedy was one of the most successful "rural" comedies on TV; in addition, according to Nielsen, the eight most watched half-hour shows are episodes of this series. "The Beverly Hillbillies" was about an Appalachian man, Jed Clampett (Buddy Ebsen) who found oil on his property, so he moved his family to a better life in Beverly Hills, CA. Most of its jokes were based on its fish-out-of-water premise. Also in the cast were Irene Ryan as Granny, Jed's mother-in-law; Donna Douglas as his daughter Elly May; Max Baer, Jr as his nephew Jethro Bodine; Raymond Bailey as neurotic Milburn Drysdale, Jed's neighbor and the owner of the bank where Jed kept his money; Nancy Kulp as Jane Hathaway, Drysdale's secretary and right-hand-woman; and Harriet MacGibbon as Margaret Drysdale, Milburn's wife.

BRECKENRIDGE OKTOBERFEST. Sept 26–27. Breckenridge, CO. For two days the streets of Breckenridge are transformed into a little bit of Munich with Bavarian food, entertainment, children's activities, beer gardens and much more. Annually, the end of September. Est attendance: 8,000. For info: Gena Osborn, Breckenridge Resort Chamber, PO Box 1909, Breckenridge, CO 80424. Phone: (970) 453-2913. Fax: (970) 453-7238. Email: gobreck@brecknet.com.

September 1998

S	M	T	W	T	F	S
		1	2	3	4	5
6	7	8	9	10	11	12
13	14	15	16	17	18	19
20	21	22	23	24	25	26
27	28	29	30			

BRIGGS AND STRATTON/AL'S RUN AND WALK FOR CHILDREN'S HOSPITAL OF WISCONSIN. Sept 26. Milwaukee, WI. Choose from an 8K run, 4-mile walk or 2.5-mile walk along the lake and through the streets. Benefit fundraiser named after Al McGuire, network basketball announcer. Finish line party on Summerfest grounds with free entertainment and fitness expo. Est attendance: 22,000. For info: Children's Hospital Foundation, Briggs & Stratton/Al's Run & Walk, PO Box 1997 MS#3060, Milwaukee, WI 53201. Phone: (414) 266-6320. Fax: (414) 266-6139.

CANADA: MUSKOKA AUTUMN STUDIO TOUR. Sept 26–27. Muskoka, Ontario. 20th annual tour. Local artists and crafts people display their studios as well as their work. For info: Bracebridge Chamber of Commerce, 1-1 Manitoba St, Canada P1L-1S4. Phone: (705) 685-5801 or (705) 645-8121. Fax: (705) 645-7592. Email: bracecha@muskoka.com.

CIVIL WAR WEEKEND. Sept 26–27. Wade House Stagecoach Inn, Greenbush, WI. 8th annual. This is the second largest Civil War re-enactment in the Midwest, drawing visitors from 15 states. Throughout the 280-acre grounds, visitors can see, hear and smell Civil War times. Each morning there are artillery, cavalry and infantry drill demonstrations. Afternoons feature a full-scale battle re-enactment at 2PM. Est attendance: 7,500. For info: Wisconsin Dept of Tourism, PO Box 7976, Madison, WI 53707. Phone: (414) 526-3271. Email: tourism@laughlin.com. WWW: http://tourism.state.wi.us

COPPER MAGNOLIA FESTIVAL. Sept 26–27. Washington, MS. Demonstration and sale of handmade crafts, family entertainment. Annually, the last full weekend in September. Est attendance: 3,000. For info: Anne L. Gray, Historian, Historic Jefferson College, Box 700, Washington, MS 39190. Phone: (601) 442-2901.

CORNISH FESTIVAL. Sept 26–27. Mineral Point, WI. Celebrates miners who came to southwest Wisconsin from Cornwall, England. Bus tours of historic sites, restored Cornish stone cottages, museum tours. Plus entertainment, speakers, Cornish food at "Taste of Mineral Point" and more. Est attendance: 200. For info: Mineral Point Chamber of Commerce, 225 High St, PO Box 78, Mineral Point, WI 53565. Phone: (608) 987-3201. Email: minpt@mhtc.net. WWW: http://www.mhtc.net/~minipt

DONIZETTI'S "LUCIA DI LAMMERMOOR" PREMIERE: ANNIVERSARY. Sept 26, 1835. *Lucia di Lammermoor*, one of opera's greatest tragic love stories, premiered in Naples, Italy on Sept 26, 1835. The opera was composed by Gaetano Donizetti with a libretto by Salvatore Cammarano. The plot was based on Sir Walter Scott's *The Bride of Lammermoor* and takes place in 17th-century Scotland. Lucia, thwarted by a blood feud from marrying the man she loves, kills her husband and then herself.

DYERSVILLE FESTIVAL OF THE ARTS. Sept 26–27. Beckman High School and National Farm Toy Museum, Dyersville, IA. The "Farm Toy Capital of the World," near the film site of the movie *Field of Dreams*. Features the Dyersville Quilt & Craft Show, with more than 100 quilted items on display. Midwestern crafts booths, art and crafts demonstrations, art on display and for sale, food and entertainment. Annually the last full weekend in September. Est attendance: 5,000. For info: Dyersville Area Chamber of Commerce, PO Box 187, Dyersville, IA 52040. Phone: (319) 875-2311. Fax: (319) 875-8391.
Email: dacc@juno.com.
WWW: http://www.rcww.com/dyersville/

ELIOT, T.S.: BIRTH ANNIVERSARY. Sept 26, 1888. Thomas Stearns Eliot, Nobel Prize winner, poet, playwright and critic, was born at St. Louis, MO, on Sept 26, 1888. "There never was a time," he believed, "when those that read at all, read so many more books by living authors than books by dead authors; there never was a time so completely parochial, so shut off from the past." Eliot died at London, England, on Jan 4, 1965.

EVERYBODY'S DAY FESTIVAL. Sept 26. Thomasville, NC. A true hometown street festival for "everybody." Crafts, food vendors and live entertainment. Est attendance: 35,000. For info: Thomasville Area Chamber of Commerce, Box 1400, Thomasville, NC 27361. Phone: (910) 475-6134. Fax: (910) 475-4802. Email: tvillecoc@infoave.net. WWW: http://www.vcoml.com/thomasville

FALL FESTIVAL OF THE ARTS. Sept 26–27. Washington, MO. Festival featuring the creative talents of two and three dimensional artists. Free children's area, wine garden, specialty foods, music and live entertainment. Est attendance: 4,000. For info: Downtown Washington, Inc, PO Box 144, Washington, MO 63090. Phone: (314) 239-1743. Fax: (314) 239-4832.

FALL FOLIAGE FESTIVAL AND BREW FEST. Sept 26. Steamboat Springs, CO. German Oktoberfest with tasting of "home brews" from the surrounding four state area. Also includes a Kindergarten, polka bands, arts and crafts fair, food fair, and more. Est attendance: 7,000. For info: Steamboat Springs Chamber Resort Assn, Special Events Info, PO Box 774408, Steamboat Springs, CO 80477. Phone: (303) 879-0880. Fax: (970) 879-2543. Email: info@steamboat.chamber.com. WWW: http://www.steamboat-chamber.com

FESTIVAL OF THE SINGING RIVER. Sept 26–27. Florence, AL. A weekend to honor and celebrate Native American culture at its best with authentic crafts, demonstrations, story telling and dancing. Held along the beautiful banks of the Tennessee River at McFarland Park. Free to the public. Annually, the fourth weekend in September. Est attendance: 30,000. For info: Florence/Lauderdale Tourism, One Hightower Place, Florence, AL 35630. Phone: (205) 740-4141 or (888) FLO-TOUR. Fax: (205) 740-4142. Email: dwilson@floweb.com. WWW: http://www.flo-tour.org

FIRST TELEVISED PRESIDENTIAL DEBATE: ANNIVERSARY. Sept 26, 1960. The debate between presidential candidates John F. Kennedy and Richard Nixon was televised from a Chicago TV studio.

FLATLANDER FALL FESTIVAL. Sept 26–27. Goodland, KS. Classic on Friday and Saturday features mini-sprint stock car races; Fall Festival on Saturday on Main Street is a street festival featuring crafts, food, games, entertainment; Saturday motorcycle show; also Saturday and Sunday, the Early Iron Car Club Rod Run on Highways 24 and 27. Est attendance: 5,000. For other info: Goodland Chamber of Commerce, 104 W 11th, PO Box 628, Goodland, KS 67735. Phone: (913) 899-7130. Fax: (913) 899-3061.

GAYS MILLS APPLE FESTIVAL. Sept 26–27. Gays Mills, WI. 39th annual. Located in southwest Wisconsin, Gays Mills is in the center of the largest and most concentrated apple orchard area in the Midwest. This area has been famous for its apples since 1905, when it won first-place honors at the apple show in New York. Today, more than 1,000 acres in Gays Mills produce apples that are nationally known for their high-quality color and flavor. Enjoy a variety of events and activities including the Wisconsin State Apple Recipe Contest, arts and crafts, a flea market, parade and fireworks. Est attendance: 20,000. For info: Wisconsin Dept of Tourism, PO Box 7976, Madison, WI 53707. Phone: (608) 735-4341. Email: tourism@laughlin.com. WWW: http://tourism.state.wi.us

GENEVA AREA GRAPE JAMBOREE. Sept 26–27. Geneva, OH. Grape harvest and products. 34th annual Jamboree. Annually, the last full weekend in September. Est attendance: 250,000. For info: Geneva Grape Jamboree, Box 92, Geneva, OH 44041. Phone: (216) 466-5262.

GERSHWIN, GEORGE: 100th BIRTH ANNIVERSARY. Sept 26, 1898. American composer remembered for his many enduring songs and melodies, including: "The Man I Love," "Strike Up the Band," "Funny Face," "I Got Rhythm" and the opera *Porgy and Bess*. Many of his works were in collaboration with his brother, Ira. Born at Brooklyn, NY, on Sept 26, 1898, he died of a brain tumor at Beverly Hills, CA, July 11, 1937. See also: "Gershwin, Ira: Birth Anniversary" (Dec 6).

GOVERNOR'S INVITATIONAL FIRELOCK MATCH. Sept 26–27. Fort Frederick State Park, Big Pool, MD. Reactivated 18th-century military units from several states participate in both individual and team competition. Annually, the last full weekend in September. Est attendance: 2,000. For info: Fort Frederick State Park, 11100 Fort Frederick Rd, Big Pool, MD 21711. Phone: (301) 842-2155. Fax: (301) 842-0028.

HARVEST FESTIVAL. Sept 26–27. Cincinnati Zoo and Botanical Garden, Cincinnati, OH. Festival features a variety of crafts, demonstrations, Appalachian music, art, storytelling, lumberjack shows, a crafts village and much more. Est attendance: 12,000. For info: Events/Promo Dept, Cincinnati Zoo and Botanical Garden, 3400 Vine St, Cincinnati, OH 45220. Phone: (513) 281-4701. Fax: (513) 559-7790. WWW: http://www.cincy.zoo.org

KIWANIS KIDS' DAY. Sept 26. To honor and assist youth—our greatest resource. Annually, the fourth Saturday in September. For info: Kiwanis Intl, Program Dvmt Dept, 3636 Woodview Trace, Indianapolis, IN 46268. Email: kiwanismail@kiwanis.org. WWW: http://www.kiwanis.org

"KNIGHT RIDER" TV PREMIERE: ANNIVERSARY. Sept 26, 1982. David Hasselhoff starred in this one-hour adventure series about a cop who was nearly killed, then brought back to life with a new identity (Michael Knight), by a mysterious millionaire. Together with a car that talked, a Pontiac Trans Am called KITT (Knight Industries Two Thousand), Knight had various adventures and missions. Other cast members included: Edward Mulhare as Devon Miles, aide to the deceased millionaire; Patricia McPherson as mechanic Bonnie Barstow; Rebecca Holden as April Curtis; William Daniels as the voice of KITT; and Peter Barros as Reginald Cornelius III, truck driver/chauffeur for KITT.

MARION COUNTY COUNTRY HAM DAYS. Sept 26–27. Lebanon, KY. Country ham breakfast, served in the streets of Lebanon. Pokey pig 10K run, pigasus parade and other specialties. Est attendance: 50,000. For info: Kathy Browning, Lebanon-Marion County Chamber of Commerce, 21 Court Sq, Lebanon, KY 40033. Phone: (502) 692-9594. Fax: (502) 692-2661. Email: chamber@eagleweb.net. WWW: http://www.eagleweb.net/chamber/marion

MOTORCYCLISTS' OPERATION SANTA CLAUS, INC, TOY RUN. Sept 26. Baltimore, MD. (Site to be announced.) The 17th annual gathering of motorcyclists from across the country. The event features live music, vendors, food and drink. Admission to the event is a new toy or $5. All proceeds benefit Salvation Army and child-oriented charities across Maryland. Annually the fourth Saturday in September. Est attendance: 20,000. For info: Motorcyclists' Operation Santa Claus, Inc, 1602 Frederick Rd, Catonsville, MD 21228. Phone: (410) 788-3222 or (410) 581-3056. Fax: (410) 788-1117.

MOUNTAIN STATE FOREST FESTIVAL. Sept 26–Oct 4. Elkins, WV. Promotes the natural resources of the area with emphasis on forests. Est attendance: 100,000. For info: Mountain State Forest Festival, Box 369, Elkins, WV 26241. Phone: (304) 636-1824. Fax: (304) 636-1824.

★**NATIONAL HUNTING AND FISHING DAY.** Sept 26. Presidential Proclamation 4682, of Sept 11, 1979, covers all succeeding years. Annually, the fourth Saturday of September.

NORTHEAST MONTANA THRESHING BEE AND ANTIQUE SHOW. Sept 26–27. Culbertson, MT. See how grandma and grandpa worked and lived. At the threshing grounds one mile southeast of town. Annually, the fourth full weekend in September. Est attendance: 2,000. For info: Rodney Iverson or Clifford Johnson, Northeast Montana Threshing Bee/Antique Show, Culbertson, MT 59218. Phone: (406) 787-5265.

OKTOBERFEST. Sept 26. Lawrence University, Appleton, WI. Come enjoy a family event with ethnic foods, fun and entertainment. Annually, the last Saturday in September. Est attendance: 100,000. For info: Campus Activities, Lawrence University, PO Box 599, Appleton, WI 54912.

OLD-TIME BARNEGAT BAY DECOY AND GUNNING SHOW. Sept 26–27. Pinelands High & Middle Schools and Tip Seaman County Park, Tuckerton, NJ. Gathering to celebrate the local waterfowling heritage. Emphasizes traditional skills such as decoy carving, working decoy rigs, sneakbox building, gunning, retrieving and goose calling contests. More than 500 vendors. Est attendance: 50,000. For info: Michael T. Mangum, Show Coord, Wells Mills County Park, 905 Wells Mills Rd, Waretown, NJ 08758. Phone: (609) 971-3085. Fax: (609) 971-9540.

PANCAKE DAY. Sept 26. Centerville, IA. Free pancakes, entertainment and two-mile long parade. Est attendance: 30,000. For info: Chamber of Commerce, 128 N 12th, Centerville, IA 52544. Phone: (515) 437-4102 or (800) 611-3800. Fax: (515) 437-0527. Email: cntrvlle@se_iowa.net.

POPE PAUL VI: BIRTH ANNIVERSARY. Sept 26, 1897. Giovanni Battista Montini, 262nd pope of the Roman Catholic Church, born at Concesio, Italy. Elected pope June 21, 1963. Died at Castel Gandolfo, near Rome, Italy, Aug 6, 1978.

RAINBOW OF ARTS CRAFT FESTIVAL. Sept 26 (rain or shine). Rockwood Park, Chesterfield, VA. 21st annual fest includes crafts, children's Imagination Station and live entertainment. Est attendance: 7,000. For info: Laura Dalton, Chesterfield County Parks and Rec, PO Box 40, Chesterfield, VA 23832. Phone: (804) 748-1623.

"ROBIN HOOD" TV PREMIERE: ANNIVERSARY. Sept 26, 1955. This series was officially titled "The Adventures of Robin Hood" and told the story of the British hero who led a group of outlaws to steal from the rich and give to the poor. Many episodes focused on Robin Hood and his enemy, Prince John, the evil ruler of Nottingham. Cast included Richard Greene as Robin Hood; Alexander Gauge as Friar Tuck; Archie Duncan and Rufus Cruikshank as Little John; Bernadette O'Farrell (1955–57) and Patricia Driscoll (1957–58) as Maid Marian; Paul Eddington and John Dearth as Will Scarlett; Alan Wheatley as the Sheriff of Nottingham; and Donald Pleasence as Prince John.

SEPTEMBER FEST. Sept 26–27. DeSoto Caverns Park, Childersburg, AL. Civil War reenactment, Civil War music, bluegrass and gospel entertainment and country craft vendors. 23rd annual. Est attendance: 8,000. For info: DeSoto Caverns Park, DeSoto Caverns Pkwy, Childersburg, AL 35044. Phone: (205) 378-7252. Email: desoto@spl.mindspring.com.

SEQUANOTA'S HERITAGE FESTIVAL. Sept 26. Jennerstown, PA. Crafts, entertainment, children's booths, food booths and quilt auction. For info: Cecilia Williams, Sequanota's Heritage Festival, Box 245, Jennerstown, PA 15547. Phone: (814) 629-6627.

SHAMU'S BIRTHDAY. Sept 26. Shamu was born at Sea World in Orlando, FL, on Sept 26, 1985, and is the first killer whale born in captivity to survive. Shamu is now living at Sea World's Texas park.

SHEYENNE VALLEY ARTS & CRAFTS FESTIVAL. Sept 26–27. Fort Ransom, ND. This 31st annual festival is one of the oldest and best in the area. Artists and crafters from several states join local people in offering 150 displays, church bazaar and dinner, turkey barbecue, cavalry performance—all in a rustic historic atmosphere. Annually, the last full weekend in September. Sponsor: Sheyenne Valley Arts and Crafts Association, Inc, a non-profit organization. Est attendance: 7,500. For info: SVACA, PO Box 21, Fort Ransom, ND 58033. Phone: (701) 973-4461.

September 1998

S	M	T	W	T	F	S
		1	2	3	4	5
6	7	8	9	10	11	12
13	14	15	16	17	18	19
20	21	22	23	24	25	26
27	28	29	30			

THRESHING BEE AND ANTIQUE SHOW. Sept 26–27. Culberston, MT. The Culberston community invites friends and neighbors from around the region to celebrate this country's heritage. Eighty plus antique tractors, many steam driven, parade through town on their way to the threshing grounds. This celebration includes demonstrations of grain threshing, steam-powered sawing of lumber, tractor races, kids games and old time fiddler music. The steam powered equipment dates back to the late 1800s and turn-of-the-century farming. For info: Rodney Iverson, Threshing Bee and Antique Show, Box 168, Culberston, MT 59218. Phone: (406) 787-5265.

TRI-STATE BAND FESTIVAL. Sept 26. Luverne, MN. 48th annual festival with more than 2,500 high school students from Minnesota, South Dakota and Iowa; trophies awarded in four classes. Annually, the last Saturday in September. Est attendance: 10,000. For info: Norma De Jongh, Exec Dir, Luverne Area Chamber of Commerce, 102 E Main, Luverne, MN 56156. Phone: (507) 283-4061. Fax: (507) 283-4061.

VICTORIAN FAIR. Sept 26–27. Winona, MN. Southeastern Minnesota fall festival celebrating Winona's golden Victorian era. Food, music and entertainment from a time long past. Est attendance: 6,000. For info: Mark Peterson, Exec Dir, Winona County Historical Soc, 160 Johnson St, Winona, MN 55987. Phone: (507) 454-2723. Fax: (507) 454-0006. Email: wchs@luminet.net.

WORLD WAR I: BATTLE OF MEUSE-ARGONNE FOREST: 80th ANNIVERSARY. Sept 26, 1918. As part of four major efforts to break the Hindenburg line, a Franco-American offensive began on this date, with the US First Army striking between the Meuse River and the Argonne Forest and the French Fourth Army to their west. After four taxing weeks of attack, the Germans were gradually pushed back. By Oct 31, the Americans had advanced 10 miles, the French had reached the Aisne River 20 miles away and the Argonne Forest was rid of the Central Power forces.

WORLD WAR II RE-ENACTMENT. Sept 26–27. Midway Village and Museum Center, Rockford, IL. Tanks, halftracks and more than 100 Allied and German re-enactors will be on the battlefield. Est attendance: 5,000. For info: Midway Village and Museum Center, 6799 Guilford Rd, Rockford, IL 61107. Phone: (815) 397-9112. Fax: (815) 397-9156.

BIRTHDAYS TODAY

Lynn Anderson, 51, singer ("Rose Garden"), born Grand Forks, ND, Sept 26, 1947.

Melissa Sue Anderson, 36, actress (Mary Ingalls Kendall on "Little House on the Prairie"), born Berkeley, CA, Sept 26, 1962.

Bryan Ferry, 53, singer (lead with Roxy Music; "Heart on My Sleeve"), songwriter, born Durham, England, Sept 26, 1945.

Mary Beth Hurt, 50, actress (*The World According to Garp, Six Degrees of Separation*), born Marshalltown, IA, Sept 26, 1948.

Julie London, 72, singer ("Cry Me a River"), actress (Dixie on "Emergency"), born Santa Rosa, CA, Sept 26, 1926.

Olivia Newton-John, 50, singer ("You're the One That I Want," "Physical"), actress (*Grease*), born Cambridge, England, Sept 26, 1948.

Christine T. Whitman, 52, Governor of New Jersey (R), raised Hunterdon County, NJ, born Sept 26, 1946.

SEPTEMBER 27 — SUNDAY

Day 270 — 95 Remaining

ADAMS, SAMUEL: BIRTH ANNIVERSARY. Sept 27, 1722. Revolutionary leader and Massachusetts state politician Samuel Adams, cousin to President John Adams (1797–1801), was born at Boston. He died there at age 81 on Oct 2, 1803. As a delegate to the First and Second Continental Congresses Adams urged a vigorous stand against England. He signed the Declaration of Independence and the Articles of Confederation and supported the war for independence. Adams served as lieutenant governor of Massachusetts under John Hancock from 1789 to 1793 and then as governor until 1797.

ANCESTOR APPRECIATION DAY. Sept 27. A day to learn about and appreciate one's forebears. For info: W. D. Chase, A.A.D. Assn, PO Box 3, Montague, MI 49437-0003.

BUFFALO WALLOW CHILI COOKOFF. Sept 27. Custer State Park, Custer, SD. Musical entertainment, art fair and lots of chili cooking and tasting. Est attendance: 3,000. For info: Custer Co Chamber of Commerce, 615 Washington St, Custer, SD 57730. Phone: (605) 673-2244. Fax: (605) 673-3726.

CONRAD, WILLIAM: BIRTH ANNIVERSARY. Sept 27, 1920. Actor, best known for his roles in the TV series "Cannon" and "Jake and the Fat Man." Born at Louisville, KY, and died at North Hollywood, CA, Feb 11, 1994.

CRUIKSHANK, GEORGE: BIRTH ANNIVERSARY. Sept 27, 1792. English illustrator, especially known for caricatures and for illustration of Charles Dickens's books. Died Feb 1, 1878.

FALL FOLIAGE FESTIVAL. Sept 27–Oct 4. Marshfield, Walden, Cabot, Plainfield, Peacham, Barnet, Groton and St. Johnsbury, VT. Eight towns welcome visitors during Vermont's famous fall foliage season. Send self-addressed stamped envelope (SASE). Est attendance: 900. For info: Fall Festival Committee, PO Box 54, West Danville, VT 05873. Phone: (802) 563-2472.

FAMILY HEALTH AND FITNESS—USA. Sept 27. Second annual event promoting the value of health and fitness for families. During this day families across the country will be involved in locally organized health promotion activities. Est attendance: 50,000. For info: Pat Henze, Exec Dir, Health Info Resource Center, 621 E Park Ave, Libertyville, IL 60048. Phone: (800) 828-8225. Fax: (847) 816-8662. Email: hlthinfo@aol.com. WWW: http://www.fitnessday.com

FESTIFALL. Sept 27. Friendship Hill National Historic Site, Point Marion, PA. To celebrate the 19th-century arts, crafts and music of the Allegheny Plateau. Historic foods are available for purchase. Tours of the Albert Gallatin house also provided. Annually, the last Sunday in September. Est attendance: 2,000. For info: Friendship Hill Assn and Natl Park Service, RD 1 Box 149-A, Point Marion, PA 15474. Phone: (412) 725-9190. Fax: (412) 725-1999. WWW: http://www.nps.gov/frhi/

★**GOLD STAR MOTHER'S DAY.** Sept 27. Presidential Proclamation always for last Sunday of each September since 1936. Proclamation 2424 of Sept 14, 1940, covers all succeeding years.

MILLIGAN MINI-POLKA DAY. Sept 27. Milligan Auditorium, Milligan, NE. Four bands play polka music from 11 AM–11 PM. Roast pork, dumpling, kraut dinner served all day. Beer, kolaches and dancing. Annually, the last Sunday in September. Est attendance: 600. For info: Leonard Kassik, PO Box 128, Milligan, NE 68406. Phone: (402) 629-4446 or (402) 629-4381. Fax: (402) 629-4446.

MORRIS, GREG: BIRTH ANNIVERSARY. Sept 27, 1934. Actor ("Mission Impossible," "Vega$"), born Cleveland, OH. Died Aug 27, 1996.

NAST, THOMAS: BIRTH ANNIVERSARY. Sept 27. American political cartoonist born Sept 27, 1840. Died Dec 7, 1902.

NATIONAL GOOD NEIGHBOR DAY. Sept 27. To build a nation and world that cares by increasing appreciation and understanding of our fellow man. Annually, the fourth Sunday in September. For info: Good Neighbor Day Fdtn, Rebecca E. Mattson, Box 379, Lakeside, MT 59922. Phone: (406) 844-3000.

RICHARD S. CALIGUIRI, CITY OF PITTSBURGH GREAT RACE. Sept 27. Frick Park to Point State Park, Pittsburgh, PA. 10K, 5K run and walk. About 11,000 runners from around the world, many wearing costumes, compete in this race, one of the largest of its kind in the country. For info: Greater Pittsburgh Conv & Visitors Bureau, Four Gateway Center, Pittsburgh, PA 15222-1259. Phone: (412) 255-2493 or (800) 359-0758. Fax: (412) 644-5512.

SAINT VINCENT DE PAUL: FEAST DAY. Sept 27. French priest, patron of charitable organizations, and co-founder of the Sisters of Charity. Canonized 1737 (lived 1581?–1660).

SEMMES, RAPHAEL: BIRTH ANNIVERSARY. Sept 27, 1809. Born at St. Charles County, MD, and died Aug 30, 1877, at Mobile, AL. Daring Confederate naval officer, best-known for his incredible raids on Union merchant ships during the middle two years of the Civil War. As commander of the *Alabama*, he captured, sank or burned 82 Union ships valued at more than $6,000,000.

SORROW SUNDAY. Sept 27. To help raise awareness of the need to right the wrongs done to women, beginning with Christians. At 2 PM at Christian Women's Ministries and everywhere, throughout the day, on Sorrow Sunday we mourn and repent for not adequately caring for our Christian sisters and for not standing with our sisters when they needed someone to be light in their darkness. On this day we wear black ribbons. For info send SASE: Christian Women's Ministries, 222 SW Harrison, Garden Office 9, Portland, OR 97201.
Email: pastor@christianwomen.com.
WWW: http://www.christianwomen.com/ministries

SPACE MILESTONE: *SOYUZ 12* (USSR): 25th ANNIVERSARY. Sept 27, 1973. Two Soviet cosmonauts (V.G. Lazarev and O.G. Makarov) made this two-day flight. Launched on this date.

"THE TONIGHT SHOW" TV PREMIERE: ANNIVERSARY. Sept 27, 1954. "The Tonight Show" has gone through numerous changes over the years it has aired, yet it has remained a top-rated show which has set the standards for all variety/talk shows to come. Steve Allen served as host from 1954–57. He introduced the format of the show with an opening monologue, games or segments for the studio audience, and then the interview on a simple desk and couch set. Jack Paar hosted from 1957–62 and Johnny Carson reigned as the king of comedy from 1962–92. Comedian Jay Leno serves as its current host.

WARREN COMMISSION REPORT: ANNIVERSARY. Sept 27. On this day in 1964, the Warren Commission issued a report stating that Lee Harvey Oswald acted alone in the assassination of President John F. Kennedy on Nov 23, 1963. Congress reopened the investigation and in 1979 the House Select Committee on Assassinations issued a report stating a conspiracy was most likely involved. See also: "Committee on Assassinations Report: Anniversary" (Mar 29).

WORLD WAR I: BATTLE OF CAMBRAISAINT–SAINT-QUENTIN: 80th ANNIVERSARY. Sept 27, 1918. British General Sir Douglas Haig moved his armies toward Cambrai and St. Quentin as part of four major efforts to break the Hindenburg line in the German salient that extended from Verdun to the sea. To the south the New Zealand and Canadian divisions smashed through the Hindenburg line on Oct 6. German General Erich Ludendorff resigned Oct 16, and the line was taken between Oct 18 and 20.

BIRTHDAYS TODAY

Wilford Brimley, 64, actor (*Cocoon*, "Our House"), born Salt Lake City, UT, Sept 27, 1934.

Shaun Cassidy, 39, singer ("Da Doo Ron Ron," "That's Rock 'n' Roll"), actor ("The Hardy Boys," "General Hospital"), born Los Angeles, CA, Sept 27, 1959.

Claude Jarman, Jr, 64, actor (*The Yearling, Rio Grande*), born Nashville, TN, Sept 27, 1934.

Stephen Douglas (Steve) Kerr, 33, basketball player, born Beirut, Lebanon, Sept 27, 1965.

Jayne Meadows, 74, actress ("I've Got a Secret," "The Steve Allen Show," *Lady in the Lake, David and Bathsheba*), born Chang, China, Sept 27, 1924.

Meat Loaf (Marvin Lee Aday), 51, singer, musician (Eddie in *The Rocky Horror Picture Show*), born Dallas, TX, Sept 27, 1947.

Arthur Heller Penn, 76, filmmaker (*Bonnie and Clyde, Alice's Restaurant, The Miracle Worker*), born Philadephia, PA, Sept 27, 1922.

Michael Jack (Mike) Schmidt, 49, Baseball Hall of Fame third baseman, born Dayton, OH, Sept 27, 1949.

Delores Taylor, 59, actress, writer, producer (*Billy Jack, The Trial of Billy Jack*), born Winner, SD, Sept 27, 1939.

Sada Thompson, 69, actress (*Twigs*; Kate Lawrence on "Family"), born Des Moines, IA, Sept 27, 1929.

SEPTEMBER 28 — MONDAY

Day 271 — 94 Remaining

CABRILLO DAY: ANNIVERSARY OF DISCOVERY OF CALIFORNIA. Sept 28, 1542. California. Commemorates discovery of California by Portuguese navigator Juan Rodriguez Cabrillo who reached San Diego Bay on this date. Cabrillo died at San Miguel Island, CA, Jan 3, 1543. His birth date is unknown. The Cabrillo National Monument marks his landfall and Cabrillo Day is still observed in California (in some areas on the Saturday nearest Sept 28).

CAPP, AL: BIRTH ANNIVERSARY. Sept 28, 1909. The creator of the fictitious village of Dogpatch, KY, Al Capp was born Alfred Gerald Caplin at New Haven, CT. The comic strip "Li'l Abner" appeared in daily newspapers from 1934 until its final episode was published Nov 13, 1977. Along with the misadventures of Abner Yokum, Capp lampooned famous public figures. The minor American institution of "Sadie Hawkins Day" made its debut in "Li'l Abner." Al Capp died Nov 5, 1979, at Cambridge, MA.

"HAZEL" TV PREMIERE: ANNIVERSARY. Sept 28, 1961. "Hazel" was based on a comic strip of the same name about a maid working for the Baxter family who gets into everyone's business. Hazel was played by Shirley Booth, and the Baxters were played by Don Defore, Whitney Blake and Bobby Buntrock. Other characters were played by Cathy Lewis, Robert P. Lieb, Maudie Prickett, Howard Smith, Norma Varden and Donald Foster. "Hazel" moved from NBC to CBS after the third season and Hazel switched families from George to younger brother, Steve Baxter. These Baxters were played by Ray Fulmer, Lynn Borden and Julia Benjamin. Buntrock and Booth remained. This was a very successful series which also featured Mala Powers and Ann Jillian.

September 1998

S	M	T	W	T	F	S
		1	2	3	4	5
6	7	8	9	10	11	12
13	14	15	16	17	18	19
20	21	22	23	24	25	26
27	28	29	30			

MASTROIANNI, MARCELLO: BIRTH ANNIVERSARY. Sept 28, 1924. Actor (*White Nights; Yesterday, Today and Tomorrow*), born Fontana Liri. Died at Paris, France, Dec 19, 1996.

MOON PHASE: FIRST QUARTER. Sept 28. Moon enters First Quarter phase at 5:11 PM, EDT.

TAIWAN: CONFUCIUS'S BIRTHDAY AND TEACHERS' DAY. Sept 28. National holiday, designated as Teachers' Day. Confucius is the Latinized name of Kung-futzu, born in Shantung province on the 27th day of the tenth moon (lunar calendar) in the 22nd year of Kuke Hsiang of Lu (551 BC). He died at age 72, having spent some 40 years as a teacher. Teachers' Day is observed annually on Sept 28.

VAN BUREN COUNTY LITERACY DAY. Sept 28. Van Buren County, IA. Children from three local districts will make and distribute bookmarks. Jim Aylesworth, noted children's author, (*Old Black Fly, My Son John*), will visit at all elementary centers. Annually, Sept 28. For info: Tomorrow's Literate Children (TLC), A Van Buren Co Reading Project, Rte 2, Box 95A, Keosauqua, IA 52565.

WIGGIN, KATE DOUGLAS: BIRTH ANNIVERSARY. Sept 28, 1856. Kate Wiggin was born Kate Douglas Smith Sept 28, 1856, at Philadelphia, PA. She helped organize the first free kindergarten on the west coast in 1878 in San Francisco, and in 1880 she and her sister established the California Kindergarten Training School. After moving back to the east coast she devoted herself to writing, producing a number of children's books including *The Birds' Christmas Carol, Timothy's Quest, Polly Oliver's Problem* and *Rebecca of Sunnybrook Farm*. She died at Harrow, England, on Aug 24, 1923.

WILLARD, FRANCES ELIZABETH CAROLINE: BIRTH ANNIVERSARY. Sept 28, 1839. American educator and reformer, president of the Women's Christian Temperance Union, 1879–98 and women's suffrage leader, born at Churchville, NY, Sept 28, 1839. Died at New York, NY, Feb 18, 1898.

BIRTHDAYS TODAY

Brigitte Bardot (Camille Javal), 64, actress (*And God Created Woman, Viva Maria*), animal rights activist, born Paris, France, Sept 28, 1934.

Jerry Clower, 72, comedian ("Nashville on the Road"), born Liberty, MS, Sept 28, 1926.

Johnny Earl Dawkins, Jr, 35, basketball player, born Washington, DC, Sept 28, 1963.

Jeffrey Jones, 51, actor (*Beetlejuice, Stay Tuned*), born Buffalo, NY, Sept 28, 1947.

Ben E. King, 60, singer, musician (wrote lyrics to "There Goes My Baby"), born Henderson, NC, Sept 28, 1938.

Madeleine M. Kunin, 65, former Governor of Vermont (D), born Zurich, Switzerland, Sept 28, 1933.

Steve M. Largent, 44, Pro Football Hall of Fame wide receiver, born Tulsa, OK, Sept 28, 1954.

William Windom, 75, actor (Emmy for "My World and Welcome to It"; "Murder She Wrote"), born New York, NY, Sept 28, 1923.

SEPTEMBER 29 — TUESDAY

Day 272 — 93 Remaining

"ALICE" TV PREMIERE: ANNIVERSARY. Sept 29, 1976. Linda Lavin played the title role in this CBS comedy that was based on the 1975 film *Alice Doesn't Live Here Anymore*. Alice Hyatt was the new girl in town—a widow raising her son while trying to make ends meet by waitressing at a diner. She also had dreams of making it big as a singer. Nine years later, Alice was able to leave her "temp" job for a gig. Lavin's co-stars were: Vic Tayback as diner owner Mel Sharples; Philip McKeon as Alice's son, Tommy; Beth Howland as waitress Vera Gorman; and Polly Holliday as sassy waitress Flo Castleberry; Diane Ladd as Flo's replacement Belle Dupree; Celia Weston as waitress Jolene Hunnicut; Martha Raye as Mel's mother, Carrie; and Marvin Kaplan as customer Henry Beesmyer.

AMERICAN INDIAN CEREMONIAL DANCING. Sept 29–30. Taos, NM. Sundown dance is performed at dusk each Sept 29, followed the next day (San Geronimo's Day) with foot races, high pole climb, clowning, feasting and dancing.

ENGLAND: SCOTLAND YARD: FIRST APPEARANCE ANNIVERSARY. Sept 29. The first public appearance of Greater London's Metropolitan Police occurred on Sept 29, 1829, amid jeering and abuse from disapproving political opponents. Public sentiment turned to confidence and respect in the ensuing years. The Metropolitan Police had been established by an act of Parliament in June 1829, at the request of Home Secretary Sir Robert Peel, after whom the London police officers became more affectionately known as "bobbies." Scotland Yard, the site of their first headquarters near Charing Cross, soon became the official name of the force.

FERMI, ENRICO: BIRTH ANNIVERSARY. Sept 29, 1901. Nuclear physicist, born at Rome, Italy. Played a prominent role in the splitting of the atom and the construction of the first American nuclear reactor. Died at Chicago, IL, Nov 16, 1954.

GOOSE DAY. Sept 29. Lewistown, PA. Traditionally based on Michaelmas Day, the religious holiday on which the Feast of St. Michael and All Angels is celebrated, Goose Day began as a day of honor and respect for the Archangel Michael, prince of guardian angels. Today, Central Pennsylvanians everywhere go out of their way to indulge themselves in a good goose dinner, heeding the old English proverb: "If you eat goose on Michaelmas Day, you will never want money all the year round." Annually, Sept 29. For info: Juniata Valley Area Chamber of Commerce, 3 W Monument Sq, Ste 204, Lewistown, PA 17044. Phone: (717) 248-6713. Fax: (717) 248-6714.

HOWARD, TREVOR: BIRTH ANNIVERSARY. Sept 29, 1916. British actor Trevor Howard was born at Cliftonville, England. He appeared in more than 70 films including *The Third Man* (1950) and *Mutiny on the Bounty* (1962). He died on Jan 7, 1988 at Bushey, England.

"MAKE ROOM FOR DADDY" TV PREMIERE: 45th ANNIVERSARY. Sept 29, 1953. Danny Thomas starred as Danny Williams, a nightclub singer and comedian, in this family sitcom. The series was renamed "The Danny Thomas Show" in 1956 after Jean Hagen (who played his wife, Margaret) left the show. Many cast members returned for the show's sequel, "Make Room for Granddaddy" in 1970. Thomas' co-stars were: Sherry Jackson and Penney Parker as Danny's daughter Terry; Rusty Hamer as son Rusty; Amanda Randolph as housekeeper Louise; Horace McMahon as Danny's agent, Phil Arnold; Jesse White as agent Jesse Leeds; Sid Melton as Charlie Halper, owner of the Copa Club; Ben Lessy as Danny's pianist, Ben; Mary Wickes as his publicist, Liz O'Neal; Hans Conried as Uncle Tonoose; Nan Bryant as Danny's mother-in-law; and Marjorie Lord as his new wife Kathy O'Hara.

MICHAELMAS. Sept 29. The feast of St. Michael and All Angels in the Greek and Roman Catholic Churches.

NELSON, HORATIO: BIRTH ANNIVERSARY. Sept 29, 1758. English naval hero of the Battle of Trafalgar born Sept 29, 1758. Died Oct 21, 1805.

SPACE MILESTONE: *DISCOVERY* (US): 10th ANNIVERSARY. Sept 29, 1988. Space Shuttle *Discovery*, after numerous reschedulings, launched from Kennedy Space Center, FL, with a five-member crew on board, and landed on Oct 3 at Edwards AFB, CA. It marked the first American manned flight since the Challenger tragedy in 1986. See also: "Challenger, Space Shuttle Explosion Anniversary" (Jan 28).

SPACE MILESTONE: *SALYUT 6* (USSR). Sept 29, 1977. Soviet space station launched this date. Burned up when it reentered Earth's atmosphere after nearly five years on July 29, 1982.

"THIRTYSOMETHING" TV PREMIERE: ANNIVERSARY. Sept 29, 1987. This ABC drama series about a group of seven baby-boomers was created by baby-boomers Ed Zwick and Marshall Herskovitz. The show's characters were very real to many viewers who were able to identify with their struggles—such as the death of a parent, disease, relationships, singlehood, marriage, divorce, career setbacks and the birth of a child. The cast featured Ken Olin as Michael Steadman; Mel Harris as his wife, Hope; Jade Mortimer and the Craven twins, Brittany and Lacey, as their daughter Jane; Timothy Busfield as Michael's business partner, Elliot Weston; Patricia Wettig (Olin's real-life wife) as Elliot's wife, Nancy; Luke Rossi as their son Ethan; Jordana Shapiro as their daughter Brittany; Polly Draper as Hope's friend Ellyn Warren; Melanie Mayron as Michael's cousin, Melissa Steadman; and Peter Horton as family friend Gary Shepherd.

TYLENOL DEATHS: ANNIVERSARY. Sept 29, 1982. On this date the first of seven deaths, including that of a 10-year-old child, occurred as a result of the individuals unknowingly taking Tylenol capsules that had been deliberately contaminated with cyanide. After a California man was poisoned taking Tylenol laced with strychnine, Johnson and Johnson, the manufacturer of the product, recalled all capsules of the pain-reliever, some 264,000 bottles. Many lawsuits resulted. The killer has never been identified.

WCVL/WIMC SENIOR CITIZENS HEALTH FAIR & EXPO. Sept 29. Montgomery County Fairgrounds, Crawfordsville, IN. An expo and trade show highlighting products and services of interest to seniors. Nearly 20 display booths, free health screenings for glaucoma, blood pressure, cholesterol, etc. Food service, travel logs. Annually, the last Tuesday in September. Est attendance: 1,000. For info: Mr Dick Munro, Gen Mgr, WCVL/WIMC Radio, PO Box 603, Crawfordsville, IN 47933. Phone: (317) 362-8200. Fax: (317) 364-1550.

YOM KIPPUR BEGINS AT SUNDOWN. Sept 29. Jewish Day of Atonement. See "Yom Kippur" (Sept 30).

BIRTHDAYS TODAY

Michelangelo Antonioni, 86, filmmaker (*Blowup, Zabriskie Point*), born Ferrara, Italy, Sept 29, 1912.

Gene Autry (Orvon Gene), 91, cowboy actor ("Gene Autry Show"), singer ("You Are My Sunshine," "Mexicali Rose"), baseball executive, born Tioga, TX, Sept 29, 1907.

Anita Ekberg, 67, actress (*La Dolce Vita*), born Malmo, Sweden, Sept 29, 1931.

Bryant Gumbel, 50, former TV host ("Today"), sportscaster, born New Orleans, LA, Sept 29, 1948.

Hersey R. Hawkins, Jr, 32, basketball player, born Chicago, IL, Sept 29, 1966.

Patricia Hodge, 52, actress ("Rumpole of the Bailey," *The Elephant Man, Betrayal*), born Cleethorpes, Lincolnshire, England, Sept 29, 1946.

Madeline Kahn, 56, actress (Tony for *The Sisters Rosenzweig; Blazing Saddles, Young Frankenstein*), born Boston, MA, Sept 29, 1942.

Jerry Lee Lewis, 63, singer, musician ("Whole Lot of Shakin' Goin' On," "Great Balls of Fire"), born Ferriday, LA, Sept 29, 1935.

Larry Linville, 59, actor (Frank on "M*A*S*H"; "Grandpa Goes to Washington"), born Ojai, CA, Sept 29, 1939.

Emily Lloyd, 28, actress (*Wish You Were Here, In Country, A River Runs Through It*), born North London, England, Sept 29, 1970.

Ian McShane, 56, actor ("Lovejoy," *The Last of Sheila*), born Blackburn, England, Sept 29, 1942.

John MacBeth Paxson, 38, former basketball player, born Dayton, OH, Sept 29, 1960.

SEPTEMBER 30 — WEDNESDAY

Day 273 — 92 Remaining

BABE SETS HOME RUN RECORD: ANNIVERSARY. Sept 30, 1927. George Herman "Babe" Ruth hit his 60th home run of the season off Tom Zachary, of the Washington Senators. Ruth's record for the most homers in a single season stood for 24 years—until Roger Maris hit 61 in 1961.

BOTSWANA: INDEPENDENCE DAY. Sept 30. National holiday. The former Bechuanaland Protectorate (British Colony) became the independent Republic of Botswana on Sept 30, 1966.

CAPOTE, TRUMAN: BIRTH ANNIVERSARY. Sept 30. American novelist and literary celebrity, was born Truman Streckfus Persons at New Orleans, LA, on Sept 30, 1924. He later took the name of his stepfather and became Truman Capote. Among his best-remembered books: *Other Voices, Other Rooms; Breakfast at Tiffany's* and *In Cold Blood*. He was working on a new novel, *Answered Prayers*, at the time of his death at Los Angeles, CA, on Aug 25, 1984.

"CHEERS" TV PREMIERE: ANNIVERSARY. Sept 30, 1982. NBC sitcom revolving around the owner, employees and patrons of a Beacon St bar in Boston. Original cast: Ted Danson as owner Sam Malone; Shelley Long and Rhea Perlman as waitresses Diane Chambers and Carla Tortelli; Nicholas Colasanto as bartender Ernie "Coach" Pantusso; John Ratzenberger as mailman Cliff Claven and George Wendt as accountant Norm Peterson. Later cast members: Woody Harrelson as bartender Woody Boyd; Kelsey Grammar as Dr. Frasier Crane; Kirstie Alley as Rebecca Howe; and Bebe Newirth as Dr. Lillith Sternin. The theme song "Where Everybody Knows Your Name," was sung by Gary Portnoy and written by him and Judy Hart Angelo. Created by Glen Charles, Les Charles and James Burrows.

FEAST OF SAINT JEROME. Sept 30. Patron saint of scholars and librarians.

FIRST ANNUAL FAIR IN AMERICA: ANNIVERSARY. Sept 30. According to the Laws and Ordinances of New Netherlands (now New York and New Jersey), on Sept 30, 1641, authorities declared that "henceforth there shall be held annually at Fort Amsterdam" a Cattle Fair (Oct 15) and a Hog Fair (Nov 1), and that "whosoever hath any things to sell or buy can regulate himself accordingly."

FIRST CRIMINAL EXECUTION IN AMERICAN COLONIES: ANNIVERSARY. Sept 30. John Billington, one of the first pilgrims to land in America, was hanged for murder on Sept 30, 1630, becoming the first criminal to be executed in the American Colonies.

MEREDITH ENROLLS AT OLE MISS: ANNIVERSARY. Sept 30, 1962. Rioting broke out when James Meredith became the first black to enroll in the all-white University of Mississippi. President Kennedy sent US troops to the area to force compliance with the law. Three people died in the fighting and 50 were injured. On June 6, 1966, Meredith was shot while participating in a civil rights march in Mississippi. On June 25 Meredith, barely recovered, rejoined the marchers near Jackson, MS.

NECKER, JACQUES: BIRTH ANNIVERSARY. Sept 30, 1732. French banker and statesman, born at Geneva, Switzerland. His dismissal from his post as head of France's Department of Finance was the immediate cause of the storming of the Bastille, July 14, 1789. Necker died near Geneva, Apr 9, 1804.

"THE RED SKELTON SHOW" TV PREMIERE: ANNIVERSARY. Sept 30, 1951. Vaudevillian and radio performer Red Skelton hosted several popular variety shows on NBC and CBS in a career that spanned 20 years. He was a gifted comedian, famous for his loony characters, sight gags, pantomimes and ad-libs. His show was also notable for introducing Johnny Carson and the Rolling Stones to a national audience.

"TWO FOR THE MONEY" TV PREMIERE: ANNIVERSARY. Sept 30, 1952. A prime-time quiz show from the Mark Goodson-Bill Todman production team appearing on NBC and CBS. Herb Shriner, Walter O'Keefe, Dennis James and Sam Levenson all served as hosts during the show's five-year run.

WORLD DAIRY EXPO. Sept 30–Oct 4. Madison, WI. World's largest dairy cattle exhibition and trade show features more than 1,200 exhibits and 1,800 head of cattle in seven breed shows at the Dane County Expo Center. About 200 animals offered for sale in four cattle breed sales. Educational forum. Open to the public. Est attendance: 68,750. For info: Marjorie Stieve, Mktg Mgr, World Dairy Expo, 2820 Walton Commons East, Ste 101, Madison, WI 53704. Phone: (608) 224-6455. Fax: (608) 224-0300. Email: wde@wdexpo.com.
WWW: http://www.world-dairy-expo.com

YOM KIPPUR OR DAY OF ATONEMENT. Sept 30. Holiest Jewish observance. A day for fasting, repentance and seeking forgiveness. Hebrew calendar date: Tishri 10, 5759.

BIRTHDAYS TODAY

Deborah Allen, 45, singer ("Baby I Lied"), songwriter ("Don't Worry 'Bout Me"), born Memphis, TN, Sept 30, 1953.

Crystal Bernard, 34, actress ("Wings"), born Garland, TX, Sept 30, 1964.

Angie Dickinson (Angeline Brown), 67, actress (Emmy for "Police Woman"; *Rio Bravo, Dressed to Kill*), born Kulm, ND, Sept 30, 1931.

Deborah Kerr, 77, actress (*From Here to Eternity, The King and I*), born Helensburgh, Scotland, Sept 30, 1921.

Lester Garfield Maddox, 83, former Governor of Georgia, born Atlanta, GA, Sept 30, 1915.

Johnny Mathis, 63, singer ("It's Not for Me to Say," "Chances Are"), born San Francisco, CA, Sept 30, 1935.

Marilyn McCoo, 55, singer (Fifth Dimension; "Up, Up and Away," "One Less Bell to Answer"), actress, born Jersey City, NJ, Sept 30, 1943.

Dominique Moceanu, 17, gymnast, born Hollywood, CA, Sept 30, 1981.

James Ralph Sasser, 62, former US Senator (D, Tennessee), born Memphis, TN, Sept 30, 1936.

Eric Stoltz, 37, actor (*Fast Times at Ridgemont High, Pulp Fiction*), born at Los Angeles, CA, Sept 30, 1961.

Victoria Tennant, 45, actress ("Winds of War," *All of Me, LA Story*), born London, England, Sept 30, 1953.

October.

OCTOBER 1 — THURSDAY

Day 274 — 91 Remaining

ADOPT-A-SHELTER-ANIMAL MONTH. Oct 1–31. To promote the adoption of animals from local shelters, the ASPCA sponsors this important observance. For info: ASPCA Public Information Dept, 424 E 92nd St, New York, NY 10128. Phone: (212) 876-7700 ext 4650 or 4655. Email: valeriea@aspca.org or press@aspca.org. WWW: http://www.aspca.org

AUTO BATTERY SAFETY MONTH. Oct 1–31. How to properly jump-start a dead vehicle battery should be a topic for students in drivers' education classes—and something every driver should know. Prevent Blindness America will offer safety tips and instructions to new and beginning drivers. For info: Prevent Blindness America®, 500 E Remington Rd, Schaumburg, IL 60173. Phone: (800) 331-2020. Fax: (847) 843-8458. Email: WWW: http://www.prevent-blindness.org

BABE CALLS HIS SHOT? ANNIVERSARY. Oct 1, 1932. In the fifth inning of game three of the World Series, with a count of two balls and two strikes and with hostile Cubs fans shouting epithets at him, Babe Ruth pointed to the center-field bleachers in Chicago's Wrigley Field and followed up by hitting a soaring home run high above the very spot to which he had just gestured. With that homer Ruth squashed the Chicago Cubs' hopes of winning the game, and the Yankees went on to sweep the Series with four straight victories. For more than half a century the question has remained: Did Ruth actually call his shot that day? Even eyewitnesses disagree. Joe Williams of *The New York Times* wrote, "In no mistaken motions, the Babe notified the crowd that the nature of his retaliation would be a wallop right out of the confines of the park." But Cubs pitcher Charlie Root said, "Ruth did *not* point at the fence before he swung. If he'd made a gesture like that, I'd have put one in his ear and knocked him on his ass." Ruth's daughter has said that he denied it. But the Babe himself also claimed he had. Fact or folklore? Either way, legend!

BAYOU HURRICANE: ANNIVERSARY. Oct 1–2, 1893. Approximately 2,000 persons died Oct 1–2, 1893, when the Louisiana Bayou country was submerged in a storm that raged from the Gulf of Mexico. The unexpected arrival of this storm caught thousands of residents off guard. The coast was swept by a 10–12-ft tidal wave.

BRAZIL: FESTIVAL OF PENHA. Oct 1–31. Rio de Janeiro. Pilgrimages, especially on Saturdays during October, to the Church of Our Lady of Penha, which is built on top of a rock, requiring a climb of 365 steps (representing the days of the year), or ride in car on inclined plane (for children, invalids and aged), for those troubled and sick who seek hope or cure.

October 1998

S	M	T	W	T	F	S
				1	2	3
4	5	6	7	8	9	10
11	12	13	14	15	16	17
18	19	20	21	22	23	24
25	26	27	28	29	30	31

BREAST CANCER CONTROL MONTH. Oct 1–31. For info: American Cancer Society, 1599 Clifton RD NE, Atlanta, GA 30329-3333. Phone: (800) ACS-2345 or (404) 320-3333.

CAMPAIGN FOR HEALTHIER BABIES MONTH. Oct 1–31. A month-long concentrated effort to focus attention on the March of Dimes Birth Defects Foundation and its community health programs, public awareness messages, advocacy and fundraising efforts. This month is designated to raise awareness of how to prevent birth defects and infant mortality. For info: Andrea Ziltzer, March of Dimes Birth Defects Fdtn, 1275 Mamaroneck Ave, White Plains, NY 10605. Phone: (914) 428-7100. Fax: (914) 997-4763. WWW: http://www.modimes.org

CHILD HEALTH MONTH. Oct 1–31. For info: American Academy of Pediatrics, 141 Northwest Point Blvd, Elk Grove Village, IL 60007. Phone: (847) 228-5005.

CHINA: PEOPLE'S REPUBLIC OF CHINA: NATIONAL DAY. Oct 1. Commemorates the founding of the People's Republic of China, Oct 1, 1949.

CHRISTMAS SEAL CAMPAIGN. Oct 1–Dec 31. An American tradition dating back to 1907 when the first Christmas Seals® were made available in the US, the annual campaign is a major support of American Lung Association programs dedicated to fighting lung diseases such as asthma, emphysema, tuberculosis and lung cancer, as well as their causes. For info: American Lung Assn, Communications Div, 1740 Broadway, New York, NY 10019-4374. Phone: (800) LUN-GUSA.
WWW: http://www.lungusa.org

COLLINS, ALBERT: BIRTH ANNIVERSARY. Oct 1, 1932. Blues guitarist Albert Collins was born at Leona, TX. An exciting, improvisational musician, he won a Grammy for *Showdown!* (1985), which was recorded with blues guitarists Robert Cray and Johnny Copeland. He was inducted into the Blues Hall of Fame in 1989. He died on Nov 24, 1993, at Las Vegas, NV.

COMPUTER LEARNING MONTH. Oct 1–31. A month-long focus of events and activities for learning new uses of computers and software, sharing ideas and helping others gain the benefits of computers and software. Numerous national contests are held to recognize students, educators and parents for their innovative ideas; computers and software are awarded to winning entries. Annually, the month of October. For info: Computer Learning Fdtn, Dept CHS, PO Box 60007, Palo Alto, CA 94306-0007. Phone: (415) 327-3347. Fax: (415) 327-3349.
Email: clf@computerlearning.org.
WWW: http://www.computerlearning.org

CO-OP AWARENESS MONTH. Oct 1–31. Co-op Awareness Month was created to remind retailers of their co-op advertising funds in time for them to research and spend these remaining funds by the end of the calendar year. For info: Elaine Stewart, Dir Client Svcs, Sales Development Services, 1335 Dublin Rd, Ste 200A, Columbus, OH 43215. Phone: (800) MOR-EADS. Fax: (614) 548-0397. Email: estewart@sdsinc.com.
WWW: http://sdsinc.com

COWBOY HALL OF FAME CEREMONY AND BANQUET. Oct 1. Willcox Community Center, Willcox, AZ. Est attendance: 150. For info: Willcox Chamber of Commerce, 1500 N Circle I Rd, Willcox, AZ 85643. Phone: (520) 384-2272 or (800) 200-2272. Fax: (520) 384-0293.

CYPRUS: INDEPENDENCE DAY. Oct 1. National holiday.

DIVERSITY AWARENESS MONTH. Oct 1–31. Celebrating, promoting and appreciating the diversity of our society. Also, a month to foster and further our understanding of the inherent value of all races, genders, nationalities, age groups, religions, sexual orientations, classes and disabilities. Annually, in October. For info: Carole Copeland Thomas, C. Thomas & Assoc, 400 W Cummings Park, Ste 1725-154, Woburn, MA 01801. Phone: (617) 938-5502. Fax: (617) 938-5504.

ENERGY MANAGEMENT IS A FAMILY AFFAIR—IMPROVE YOUR HOME. Oct 1–Mar 31, 1998. Replace energy-consuming units with new efficient home conveniences and remodel to prevent heating and cooling loss. For info: James A. Stewart, Jr, Home Improvement Time Inc, PO Box 247, Oakdale, PA 15071-0247. Phone: (412) 787-2881. Fax: (412) 787-3233.

ENGLAND: NOTTINGHAM GOOSE FAIR. Oct 1–3. Forest Recreation Ground, Nottingham. Held annually since 1284 (except during the Great Plague in 1665 and the two World Wars), the fair formerly lasted three weeks and boasted as many as 20,000 geese on display. Now lasting three days, the Nottingham Goose Fair always begins on the first Thursday in October. A traditional fair with modern amusements.

FALL IN LOVE WITH FOND DU LAC! Oct 1–31. Fond du Lac, WI. Hike, bike or birdwatch in the Horicon National Wildlife Refuge, home to more than 260 species of birds. 200,000 Canada geese migrate to the Horicon Marsh each fall on their trip from Canada to their winter grounds. Horicon Marsh viewing area is located 12 miles south of Fond du Lac on Hwy 49. Also explore colorful Kettle Moraine State Forest. Enjoy harvest specialties, orchard hayrides, wildlife galleries and more. For info: Fond du Lac Conv and Visitors Bureau, 19 W Scott St, Fond du Lac, WI 54935. Phone: (800) 937-9123. Fax: (920) 929-6846.
Email: fdlcvb@visitwisconsin.com.
WWW: http://www.visitwisconsin.com/fdl

FALL SUWANEE RIVER JUBILEE. Oct 1–3. Live Oak, FL. Featuring well-known musical groups for a weekend of music outdoors. Est attendance: 5,000. For info: Spirit of the Suwanee Music Park, 3076 95th Dr, Live Oak, FL 32060. Phone: (904) 364-1683. Fax: (904) 364-2998.
Email: spirit@musicliveshere.com.
WWW: http://www.musicliveshere.com

FIREPUP'S BIRTHDAY. Oct 1. Firepup spends his time teaching fire safety awareness to children in a fun-filled and non-threatening manner. For info: Natl Fire Safety Council, Inc, PO Box 378, Michigan Center, MI 49254-0378. Phone: (517) 764-2811.

FLU AND PNEUMONIA CAMPAIGN. Oct 1–31. To promote flu vaccination. For info: American Lung Assn, 1740 Broadway, New York, NY 10019-4374. Phone: (800) LUNG-USA. WWW: http://www.lungusa.org

GREAT AMERICAN BEER FESTIVAL. Oct 1–3. Currigan Hall, Denver, CO. To celebrate the depth, variety and distinctiveness of beers brewed by American breweries. More than 1,700 beers from most of America's breweries. 16th annual festival. Est attendance: 30,000. For info: The Assn of Brewers, Box 1679, Boulder, CO 80306. Phone: (303) 447-0816. Fax: (303) 447-2825. Email: info@aob.org.
WWW: http://www.beertown.org

HARRISON, CAROLINE LAVINIA SCOTT: BIRTH ANNIVERSARY. Oct 1, 1832. First wife of Benjamin Harrison, 23rd president of the US, born at Oxford, OH, Oct 1, 1832. Died Oct 25, 1892.

October 1998

S	M	T	W	T	F	S
				1	2	3
4	5	6	7	8	9	10
11	12	13	14	15	16	17
18	19	20	21	22	23	24
25	26	27	28	29	30	31

HEALTHY LUNG MONTH. Oct 1–31. The American Lung Association conducts a series of public awareness campaigns to promote lung health with a focus on childhood asthma, influenza and pneumonia and indoor air pollution, including secondhand smoke and radon. These programs are supported by the American Lung Association's annual Christmas Seal Campaign which follows Healthy Lung Month. For info: Communications Div, American Lung Assn, 1740 Broadway, New York, NY 10019-4374. Fax: (212) 315-8872. Email: info@lungusa.org. WWW: http://www.lungusa.org

HISPANIC HERITAGE FESTIVAL. Oct 1–31. Dade County, Miami, FL. A series of special, cultural, educational and sporting events to celebrate and enhance Hispanic culture and traditions. Est attendance: 350,000. For info: Eloy Vazquez, Hispanic Heritage Council, Inc, 4011 W Flagler St, #204, Miami, FL 33134. Phone: (305) 541-5023. Fax: (305) 541-5176.

HOROWITZ, VLADIMIR: BIRTH ANNIVERSARY. Oct 1, 1904. Virtuoso pianist, born at Berdichev, Russia, on Oct 1, 1904 (Sept 18, old style). Horowitz was widely hailed as one of the world's greatest pianists, renowned for his masterful technique. His first public debut was in Kiev in 1920, and at the age of 20 he played a series of 23 recitals in Leningrad, performing a total of more than 200 works with no duplications. He made his US debut in 1928 with the New York Philharmonic. He settled in the US in 1940 and became a citizen in 1944. His career swung full circle on Apr 20, 1986, when he performed his first concert in his native Russia after a self-imposed absence of 60 years. He died on Nov 5, 1989, at New York, NY.

INTERNATIONAL FIRED UP MONTH. Oct 1–25. A month focusing on enthusiasm and joy, where people learn what gets them fired up and incorporate that into their lives. Seminars, workshops, parties, services, community events—especially in New England where people take action and celebrate. For info: Snowden McFall, c/o Fired Up!, 74 Northeastern Blvd, Unit 20, Nashira, NH 03062. Phone: (603) 882-0600. Fax: (603) 882-5979. Email: smcfall@tiac.net.
WWW: http://www.firedup-takeaction-now.com

INTERNATIONAL STARMAN MONTH. Oct 1–31. Celebrates the TV series "Starman," which first aired in 1986 and inspired many people around the world to change their lives in positive ways. Spotlight Starman International is a group of people who appreciate the quality, consciousness and themes of the show and continue to gather annually to celebrate that spirit while raising funds for environmental, social and/or educational causes. (The organization is open to all without membership dues.) For info: Vicki Werkley, Spotlight Starman Intl, 16563 Ellen Springs, Lower Lake, CA 95457. Phone: (707) 995-1228.
Email: starwerks@aol.com.
WWW: http://www.calweb.com/~smccrory/starman.html

JAPAN: NEWSPAPER WEEK. Oct 1–7. During this week newspapers make an extensive effort to acquaint the public with their functions and attempt to carry out the role of a newspaper in a free society. Annually, the first week in October.

KOREA: ARMED FORCES DAY. Oct 1. National holiday marked by many colorful military parades, aerial acrobatics and honor guard ceremonies, held around the reviewing plaza at Yoido, an island in the Han River.

"KUNG FU" TV PREMIERE: ANNIVERSARY. Oct 1, 1972. David Carradine starred in this unusual ABC western as Kwai Chang Caine, a half-Chinese martial arts master drifter who was exiled from China. Appearing in flashback were: Keye Luke as Master Po; Philip Ahn as Master Kan; and Radames Pera as the younger Caine. The show ran for three years. "Kung Fu" returned as a 1986 TV movie introducing the late Brandon Lee as Caine's son. A sequel series currently appears in syndication starring a much older Carradine.

LAWRENCE, JAMES: BIRTH ANNIVERSARY. Oct 1, 1781. Brilliant American naval officer, whose last battle was a defeat, but whose dying words became a most honored naval motto. Lawrence, born at Burlington, NJ, was commander of the USS *Hornet*, and later captain of the *Chesapeake* when she engaged in a naval duel with HMS *Shannon* off Boston, on June 1, 1813. The *Chesapeake* was captured and towed to Halifax as a British prize. Lawrence was mortally wounded by a musket ball during the engagement and uttered his famous last words, "Don't give up the ship," as he was being carried off the ship's deck.

LE MOIS DU CAFÉ. Oct 1–31. La Madeleine French Bakery & Cafe will promote nationally one of the world's oldest beverages with a series of promotions, tips and new coffee products. For info: Patty Sullivan, Senior Mgr of PR, La Madeleine French Bakery & Cafe, 6060 N Central Expwy, Ste 138, Dallas, TX 75206. Phone: (214) 696-6962. Fax: (214) 696-0485.
Email: psullivan@why.net.

LONGWOOD GARDENS AUTUMN'S COLORS. Oct 1–23. Kennett Square, PA. Outdoor display features a harvest rainbow of brilliant foliage on 1,050 acres. Est attendance: 50,000. For info: Longwood Gardens, PO Box 501, Kennett Sq, PA 19348-0501. Phone: (610) 388-1000.
WWW: http://www.longwoodgardens.org

LUPUS AWARENESS MONTH. Oct 1–31. To promote public awareness of lupus symptoms to aid in early diagnosis and treatment of this disease. For info: Duane Peters, Dir of Communications & Dvmt, Lupus Foundation of America, 1300 Piccard Dr, Ste 200, Rockville, MD 20850-4303. Phone: (301) 670-9292. Fax: (301) 670-9486.
WWW: http://www.lupus.org/lupus

☆ ☆ ☆

"THE MERV GRIFFIN SHOW" TV PREMIERE: ANNIVERSARY. Oct 1, 1962. Singer and game show king Merv Griffin's first effort as an afternoon talk-show host premiered on NBC but was later dropped for syndication. The afternoon show continued until 1969 when Griffin was tapped to host a late-night program on CBS to compete with "The Tonight Show with Johnny Carson."

MONTH OF THE DINOSAUR. Oct 1–31. Promoting scientific awareness and educating everyone about our environment both present and past. Special on-line forums and activities as well as educational materials available to educators. For info: Ellen Sue Blakey, Big Horn Basin Geological Reseach and Educ Fdtn, PO Box 71, Thermopolis, WY 82443.
WWW: http://www.wyoming.com/dino

NATIONAL APPLE JACK MONTH. Oct 1–31. A month during which Apple Jack will be honored as America's oldest native distilled spirit, established in the early 1700s. Sponsor: Laird's Apple Jack. For info: Ted Worner, 7064 Charleston Point Dr, Lake Worth, FL 33467. Phone: (561) 439-4937.

NATIONAL BREAST CANCER AWARENESS MONTH. Oct 1–31. Entering its second decade of public and professional education and awareness. This month is promoted by several major national nonprofit cancer organizations to ensure that the media and communities everywhere focus a spotlight on the problem of breast cancer. For info: call the American Cancer Society (800) ACS-2345.

NATIONAL CAMPAIGN FOR HEALTHIER BABIES MONTH. Oct 1–31. For info: March of Dimes Birth Defects Foundation, 1275 Mamaroneck Ave, White Plains, NY 10605. Phone: (914) 997-4600.

NATIONAL CAR CARE MONTH. Oct 1–31. To educate motorists about the importance of maintaining their cars in an effort to improve air quality, highway safety and fuel conservation. For info: Car Care Council, One Grande Lake Dr, Port Clinton, OH 43452. Phone: (419) 734-5343. Fax: (419) 732-3780.
Email: carcare@infinet.com.
WWW: http://www.peoplevision.com/carcare/

NATIONAL COMMUNICATE WITH YOUR KID MONTH. Oct 1–31. The generation gap—parents and teens are often on different wavelengths and complain that they cannot talk to each other. The purpose of this observance is to open the doors to better communication between parents and teens and to build positive teen/parent relationships. Annually, the month of October. For info send SASE to: Teresa Langston, Dir, Parenting Without Pressure, 1330 Boyer St, Longwood, FL 32750-6311. Phone: (407) 767-2524.

NATIONAL COOKIE MONTH. Oct 1–31. Remember the aroma and tradition of fresh baked cookies? Remember how the delicious scent filled the house? Celebrate the All-American favorite treat, the cookie, during National Cookie Month. Make, bake or buy a batch of fresh homemade cookies in any of your favorite flavors this month. Share a little love today—share a fresh baked cookie! For info: Cookies For You, 117 S Main, Minot, ND 58701. Phone: (701) 839-4975 or (800) 814-5334. WWW: http://www.tradecorridor.com/cookies

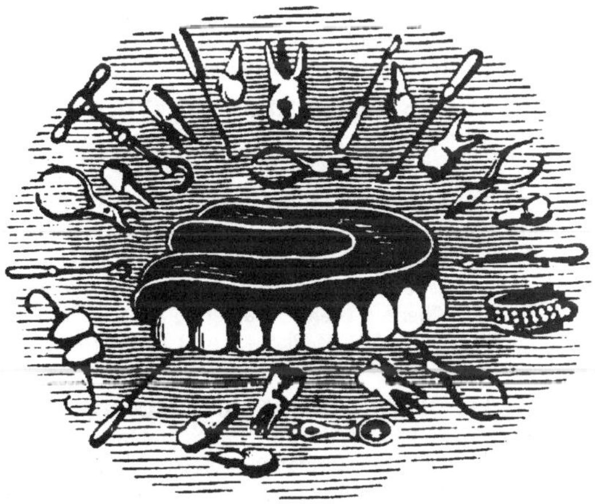

NATIONAL DENTAL HYGIENE MONTH. Oct 1–31. To increase public awareness of the importance of preventive oral health care and the dental hygienist's role as the preventive professional. Annually, during the month of October. For info: Public Relations, American Dental Hygienists' Assn, 444 N Michigan Ave, Ste 3400, Chicago, IL 60611. Phone: (312) 440-8900.
WWW: http://www.adha.org

NATIONAL DEPRESSION EDUCATION AND AWARENESS MONTH. Oct 1–31. A nonprofit campaign to educate patients, the elderly and professionals about depression disorders. Kit of materials available for $15. Annually, the month of October. For info: Frederick Mayer, Pres, Pharmacists Planning Service, Inc, PO Box 1336, Sausalito, CA 94966. Phone: (800) 421-4211. Fax: (415) 332-1832. Email: ppsi@aol.com.

NATIONAL DESSERT MONTH. Oct 1–31. Held each year to focus on the pleasures of sweet and fanciful desserts. For info: c/o The Alden Group, Martini & Rossi Asti, 52 Vanderbilt Ave, New York, NY 10017. Phone: (212) 867-6400. Fax: (212) 986-4784. Email: baddish.aol.com.

★**NATIONAL DISABILITY EMPLOYMENT AWARENESS MONTH.** Oct 1–31. Presidential Proclamation issued for the month of October (PL100–630, Title III, Sec 301a of Nov 7, 1988). Previously issued as "National Employ the Handicapped Week" for a week beginning during the first week in October since 1945.

NATIONAL FAMILY SEXUALITY EDUCATION MONTH. Oct 1–31. A national coalition effort to support parents as the first and primary sexuality educators of their children by providing information for parents and young people. For info: Planned Parenthood Federation of America, Education Dept, 810 Seventh Ave, New York, NY 10019. Phone: (800) 829-7732. Fax: (212) 247-6269. Email: education@ppfa.org. WWW: http://www.ppfa.org/ppfa

NATIONAL LIVER AWARENESS MONTH. Oct 1–31. To increase understanding of the importance of liver functions, to promote healthful practices and to encourage research into the causes and cures of liver disease. Annually, the month of October. For info: American Liver Fdtn, 1425 Pompton Ave, Cedar Grove, NJ 07009. Phone: (800) 223-0179 ext 228. Fax: (201) 256-3214. WWW: http://www.liverfoundation.org

NATIONAL LUPUS AWARENESS MONTH. Oct 1–31. For info: Lupus Foundation of America, 4 Research Pl, Ste 180, Rockville, MD 20850. Phone: (800) 558-0121 or (301) 670-9292.

NATIONAL MAKE A WILL MONTH. Oct 1–31. To encourage more Americans to make or update their will, the month is designated to focus attention on the importance of making a will—to make your wishes known, make bequests and leave a legacy. For info: Angie Niehoff, Niehoff Marketing Assoc, 858 NE 97th St, Miami Shores, FL 33138. Phone: (305) 758-2476. Fax: (305) 758-3442. Email: makeawill@aol.com.

NATIONAL MEDICAL LIBRARIANS MONTH. Oct 1–31. Recognizes and celebrates the importance and the achievements of these health sciences information professionals. Because more medical and health literature has been published in the past 10 years than in all previous years combined, medical librarians offer efficient access to quality medical and health-related information within a wide variety of health care settings. Librarians representing 23 specialty groups and 14 regional chapters of the Medical Library Association (MLA) will sponsor several meetings and educational opportunities throughout the month of October. For info: Medical Library Assn, 6 N Michigan Ave, Ste 300, Chicago, IL 60602. Phone: (312) 419-9094. Fax: (312) 419-8950. Email: info@mlahg.org. WWW: http://www.kumc.edu/MLA

NATIONAL PHYSICAL THERAPY MONTH. Oct 1–31. To increase awareness of the role of physical therapy in health care, physical therapists celebrate by hosting special activities such as fitness clinics, open houses, hotlines, athletic events, health seminars and exhibits. Annually, the month of October. For info: The American Physical Therapy Assn, 1111 N Fairfax St, Alexandria, VA 22314. Phone: (800) 999-2782 or (703) 706-3248.

October 1998

S	M	T	W	T	F	S
				1	2	3
4	5	6	7	8	9	10
11	12	13	14	15	16	17
18	19	20	21	22	23	24
25	26	27	28	29	30	31

NATIONAL PIZZA MONTH. Oct 1–31. To promote the good fun and nutrition of pizza—"America's Number One Fun Food." *Pizza Festival*, an international pizza recipe contest, is held during October, and participants are encouraged to submit recipes in categories ranging from the exotic to the traditional. Winners will be announced at the Pizza Expo in March 1999. Sponsor: *Pizza Today* Magazine and the National Association of Pizza Operators. For info: Gerry Durnell, Exec Dir, Natl Assn of Pizza Operators, 137 E Market St, New Albany, IN 47151. Phone: (812) 949-0909. Fax: (812) 941-9711.

NATIONAL POPCORN POPPIN' MONTH. Oct 1–31. To celebrate the wholesome, economical, natural food value of popcorn, America's native snack. For info: The Popcorn Institute, 401 N Michigan Ave, Chicago, IL 60611-4267. Phone: (312) 644-6610.

NATIONAL PORK MONTH. Oct 1–31. The National Pork Producers Council, in cooperation with state pork producers associations, marks October as National Pork Month. While pork promotions are conducted throughout the year, special emphasis is placed on Pork: The Other White Meat® during October. For info: Charles Harness, VP Communications, Natl Pork Producers Council, PO Box 10383, Des Moines, IA 50306. Phone: (515) 223-2600. Fax: (515) 223-2646. Email: pork@nppc.org. WWW: http://www.nppc.org/

NATIONAL ROLLER SKATING MONTH. Oct 1–31. A month-long celebration recognizing the health benefits and recreational enjoyment of this long-loved pastime. Also includes an emphasis on Safe Skating. For info: Roller Skating Assn, 6905 Corporate Dr, Indianapolis, IN 46278. Phone: (317) 875-3390. Fax: (317) 875-3394. Email: asa@oninternet.com.

NATIONAL SARCASTICS AWARENESS MONTH. Oct 1–31. To help people everywhere understand the positive and negative aspects of sarcasm. For info: Virginia Tooper, Dir of Barbs, Sarcastics Anonymous, Box 10944, Pleasanton, CA 94588. Phone: (510) 786-4567.

NATIONAL SPINA BIFIDA PREVENTION MONTH. Oct 1–31. Promoting public awareness of current scientific, medical and educational issues related to spina bifida—the second most common birth defect. For info: Info & Referral Coord, Natl Spina Bifida Assn of America, 4590 McArthur Blvd NW, Ste 250, Washington, DC 20007-4226. Phone: (202) 944-3285 or (800) 621-3141. Fax: (202) 944-3295.

NATIONAL SPINAL HEALTH MONTH. Oct 1–31. For info: American Chiropractic Assn, 1701 Clarendon Blvd, Arlington, VA 22209. Phone: (703) 276-8800.

NATIONAL STAMP COLLECTING MONTH. Oct 1–31. Sponsored by the US Postal Service. For info: Stamp Services, US Postal Service, 475 L'Enfant Plaza SW, Rm 4474-EB, Washington, DC 20260.

NATIONAL SUDDEN INFANT DEATH SYNDROME AWARENESS MONTH. Oct 1–31. Month-long focus on sudden infant death syndrome (also called crib death, the nation's major cause of death for infants beyond one week of age) promotes the BACK TO SLEEP CAMPAIGN to increase public awareness and funds available for medical research and family services. For info: Phipps Y. Cohe, Natl Public Affairs Dir, SIDS Alliance, 1314 Bedford Ave, Ste 210, Baltimore, MD 21208. Phone: (800) 221-7437. Fax: (410) 653-8709. Email: sidshg@charm.net.

NATIONAL TOILET TANK REPAIR MONTH. Oct 1–31. Month-long observance dedicated to the value and benefits of a properly tuned toilet with special emphasis on do-it-yourself repairs and water conservation. For info: Sara Romspert, Mktg Mgr, Fluidmaster, Inc, 1800 Via Burton, Anaheim, CA 92806. Phone: (714) 774-1444. Fax: (714) 774-5764.

NIGERIA: INDEPENDENCE DAY. Oct 1. National holiday. Became independent on this day in 1960, and a republic on this day in 1963.

NO SALT WEEK. Oct 1–5. Give no-salt cooking and food preparation a try! This celebration will help with recipes and combinations. Annually, the first week in October. For ideas send a large self-addressed stamped envelope. For info: Make It Tasty Spice Co, Box 416, Denver, CO 80201. Phone: (303) 575-5676.

NORWAY: PAGEANTRY IN OSLO. Oct 1. The Storting (Norway's Parliament) convenes on first weekday in October, when it decides date for the ceremonial opening of the Storting—usually the following weekday—and the parliamentary session is then opened by King Herald V in the presence of Corps Diplomatique, preceded and followed by a military procession between the Royal Palace and the Storting.

ORPHAN TRAIN HERITAGE SOCIETY OF AMERICA: ANNUAL REUNION. Oct 1–5. To be held at the Holiday Inn, Springdale, AR. Between 1854 and 1929, more than 150,000 homeless children and poor families were transported out of New York City, Boston and Chicago aboard trains accompanied by "agents." Agents for the New York Children's Aid Society arranged for midwestern families to take the children under a contract agreement. Infants placed by the New York Foundling Hospital were indentured. Annual reunion, plus regional reunions in Oklahoma, Missouri, Kansas, Texas, Iowa, Illinois, Indiana, California, Louisiana, Nebraska and Minnesota bring together survivors of the Orphan Trains era, their descendants and interested persons. All gatherings are open to the public, with a small registration fee charged at each. Books containing stories of the Orphan Train Riders are available at each reunion. Est attendance: 250. For info: Mary Ellen Johnson, Exec Dir, OTHSA, Inc, 1614 E Emma Ave, #115, Springdale, AR 72764. Phone: (501) 756-2780. Fax: (501) 756-0769.

POLISH AMERICAN HERITAGE MONTH. Oct 1–31. A national celebration of Polish history, culture and pride, in cooperation with the Polish American Congress and Polonia Across America. For info: Michael Blichasz, Chair, Polish American Cultural Center, Natl HQ, 308 Walnut St, Philadelphia, PA 19106. Phone: (215) 922-1700. Fax: (215) 922-1518.

"REMINGTON STEELE" TV PREMIERE: ANNIVERSARY. Oct 1, 1982. Laura Holt (played by Stephanie Zimbalist, daughter of Efrem Zimbalist, Jr), an imaginative private detective, could not get a case of her own—not until she made up a partner, Remington Steele, who was conveniently out of the office when clients came-a-calling. Then she met the suave stranger (Pierce Brosnan) with a foreign accent who called himself Remington Steele. They began a working partnership . . . which ended in marriage. The show aired on NBC for five years with James Read, Janet DeMay and Doris Roberts costarring.

RILEY FESTIVAL. Oct 1–4. Greenfield, IN. To celebrate the birth of Hoosier poet James Whitcomb Riley. Est attendance: 75,000. For info: Nancy Alldredge, Riley Fest Assn, PO Box 554, Greenfield, IN 46140. Phone: (317) 462-2141. Fax: (317) 462-8871.

SA'FEST 98 (SAFEty FESTival): CARTOONISTS AGAINST CRIME INTERNATIONAL CARTOON ART COMPETITION. Oct 1–31. Chicago, IL. Held in conjunction with National Crime Prevention Month and Domestic Violence Awareness Month, competition is designed to draw attention to humankind's vulnerability to random and violent crimes both in the US and abroad. The emphasis is on "How to Play It Safe® in the 90s." Cartoons propose unique safety measures, precautions and tips for avoiding crime, showing that cartoons can be educational as well as entertaining. Exhibition will be held in downtown Chicago. For info: Adrienne Sioux Koopersmith, Cartoonists Against Crime™, 1437 W Rosemont, 1W, Chicago, IL 60660-1319. Phone: (773) 743-5341. Fax: (773) 743-5395. Email: kooper@interaccess.com.

SALEM APPLE BUTTER FESTIVAL. Oct 1–4. Depot Park, Salem, WV. Old-fashioned apple butter making—canned to take home. Festival features live entertainment, bicycle poker run, 5K run, talent show, pageants, parade, food, arts and crafts, celebrity auction, bingo and fireworks. Annually, the first weekend in October (includes Thursday). Est attendance: 20,000. For info: Salem Apple Butter Festival, PO Box 293, Salem, WV 26426. Phone: (304) 782-3565. WWW: http://stulib.salem-teikyo.wvnet.edu/

STOCKTON, RICHARD: BIRTH ANNIVERSARY. Oct 1. Lawyer and signer of the Declaration of Independence, born at Princeton, NJ, Oct 1, 1730. Died there, Feb 8, 1781.

SUBSTANCE ABUSE PREVENTION MONTH. Oct 1–31. Santee, CA. Distribution of materials concerning alcohol and drug abuse. Distribution of red ribbon decals as well as attachment of red ribbons to the trees along the main thoroughfare in the city of Santee. For info: City of Santee, Santee CASA (Community Against Substance Abuse), 10601 Magnolia Ave, Santee, CA 92071-1222.

TALK ABOUT PRESCRIPTIONS MONTH. Oct 1–31. For info: National Council on Patient Information and Education, 666 11th St NW, Ste 810, Washington, DC 20001. Phone: (202) 347-6711.

"THIS IS YOUR LIFE" TV PREMIERE: ANNIVERSARY. Oct 1, 1952. Ralph Edwards hosted this program that lured unsuspecting guests on the show and surprised them by detailing their lives and achievements with their family and friends.

TUVALU: NATIONAL HOLIDAY. Oct 1.

UNITED NATIONS: INTERNATIONAL DAY OF OLDER PERSONS. Oct 1. On Dec 14, 1990, the General Assembly designated Oct 1 as the International Day for the Elderly. It appealed for contributions to the Trust Fund for Aging (which supports projects in developing countries in implementation of the Vienna International Plan of Action on Aging adopted at the 1982 World Assembly on Aging) and endorsed an action program on aging for 1992 and beyond as outlined by the Secretary-General. (Resolution 45/106.) On Dec 21, 1995, the Assembly changed the name from "for the Elderly" to "of Older Persons" to conform with the 1991 UN Principles for Older Persons. Info from: United Nations, Dept of Public Info, Public Inquiries Unit, Rm GA-57, New York, NY 10017. Phone: (212) 963-4475. Fax: (212) 963-0071. Email: inquiries@un.org.

☆ ☆ ☆

UNITED STATES 1998 FEDERAL FISCAL YEAR BEGINS. Oct 1, 1998–Sept 30, 1999.

UNIVERSAL CHILDREN'S WEEK. Oct 1–7. To disseminate throughout the world info on the needs of children and to distribute copies of the Declaration of the Rights of the Child. For complete info, send $3 to cover expense of printing, handling and postage. Annually, the first seven days of October. For info: Dr. Stanley Drake, Pres, Intl Soc of Friendship and Good Will, 412 Cherry Hills Dr, Bakersfield, CA 93309-2866.

UNIVERSITY OF CHICAGO FIRST DAY OF CLASSES: ANNIVERSARY. Oct 1, 1892. Chicago, IL. On Oct 1, 1892, the University of Chicago opened with an enrollment of 594 and a faculty of 103, including eight former college presidents.

"THE VISE" TV PREMIERE: ANNIVERSARY. Oct 1, 1954. A dramatic anthology series running for three years on ABC. It was produced in England and hosted by Ron Randell.

WORLD VEGETARIAN DAY. Oct 1. Celebration of vegetarianism's benefits to humans, animals and our planet. In addition to individuals, participants include libraries, schools, colleges, restaurants, food services, health-care centers, health food stores, workplaces and many more. For info: North American Vegetarian Society, Box 72, Dolgeville, NY 13329. Phone: (518) 568-7970. Email: navs@telenet.net. WWW: http://cyberveg.org/navs

BIRTHDAYS TODAY

Julie Andrews (Julia Wells), 63, actress, singer (Emmy for "The Julie Andrews Hour"; Oscar for *Mary Poppins*), born Walton-on-Thames, England, Oct 1, 1935.

Tom Bosley, 71, actor ("Happy Days," "Father Dowling Mysteries"), born Chicago, IL, Oct 1, 1927.

Rodney Cline (Rod) Carew, 53, Baseball Hall of Fame infielder, born Gatun, Canal Zone, Oct 1, 1945.

Jimmy Carter (born James Earl Carter, Jr), 74, 39th US President, born Plains, GA, Oct 1, 1924.

Stephen Collins, 51, actor ("Tales of the Gold Monkey," "Tattinger's" [revamped as "Nick & Hillary"]; *All the President's Men*), born Des Moines, IA, Oct 1, 1947.

Richard Harris, 68, singer ("MacArthur Park"), actor (*Camelot, Hawaii, Juggernaut, Wrestling Ernest Hemingway*), born Limerick, Ireland, Oct 1, 1930.

Walter Matthau, 78, actor (*The Odd Couple, Kotch, Grumpy Old Men*), born New York, NY, Oct 1, 1920.

Philippe Noiret, 68, actor (*The Day of the Jackal, Coup de Torchon, Il Postino*), born Lille, France, Oct 1, 1930.

Randy Quaid, 48, actor (*The Last Picture Show, Dead Solid Perfect*), born Houston, TX, Oct 1, 1950.

William Hubbs Rehnquist, 74, Chief Justice of the US Supreme Court, born Milwaukee, WI, Oct 1, 1924.

Stella Stevens, 62, actress (Jane Hancock on "Ben Casey"; Lute-Mac Sanders on "Flamingo Road"), born Hot Coffee, MS, Oct 1, 1936.

Grete Waitz, 45, marathoner, born Oslo, Norway, Oct 1, 1953.

OCTOBER 2 — FRIDAY

Day 275 — 90 Remaining

"THE ALDRICH FAMILY" TV PREMIERE: ANNIVERSARY. Oct 2, 1949. One of TV's first all-American family sitcoms, "The Aldrich Family" was originally a radio show during the '30s. The cast featured: Bob Casey, Richard Tyler, Henry Girard, Kenneth Nelson and Bob Ellis as teenager, Henry Aldrich; House Jameson as his father, Sam; Lois Wilson, Nancy Carroll and Barbara Robbins as his mother, Alice; June Dayton and Mary Malone as his sister, Mary; Jackie Kelk, Robert Barry and Jackie Grimes as Henry's best friend, Homer Brown; and Loretta Leversee as his girlfriend, Eleanor. Paul Newman also appeared regularly on the show.

"ALFRED HITCHCOCK PRESENTS" TV PREMIERE: ANNIVERSARY. Oct 2, 1955. Alfred Hitchcock was already an acclaimed director when he began hosting his mystery anthology series that aired on CBS and NBC for 10 years. Each episode began with an introduction by Hitchcock, the man with the world's most recognized profile. Hitchcock directed about 22 episodes of the series. Robert Altman was another director of note. Among the many stars who appeared on the show are: Barbara Bel Geddes, Brian Keith, Gena Rowlands, Dick York, Cloris Leachman, Joanne Woodward, Steve McQueen, Peter Lorre, Dick Van Dyke, Robert Redford, Katherine Ross and Peter Fonda.

APPLEFEST. Oct 2–4. Bayfield, WI. 37th annual. This festival offers a heritage and talent show, an apple-peeling contest, a pet parade, Big Top Chautauqua performances and arts and crafts. Additionally, fairgoers can attend events, such as the apple pie and apple cider contests, carnival rides, kids' contests and country dancing. Gourmet apple pies, strudels and frosted apple cuts, sundaes, cider, cheese pie and fresh apples are available. Every Bayfield-area orchard sets up a stand to sell apple products, with more than 11 varities of apples. For info: Wisconsin Dept of Tourism, Applefest, PO Box 7976, Madison, WI 53707. Phone: (715) 779-3335. Email: tourism@laughlin.com.
WWW: http://tourism.state.wi.us

October 1998

S	M	T	W	T	F	S
				1	2	3
4	5	6	7	8	9	10
11	12	13	14	15	16	17
18	19	20	21	22	23	24
25	26	27	28	29	30	31

ARKANSAS APPLE FESTIVAL. Oct 2–4. Lincoln, AR. Boasting the largest apple orchard in the state, the town of Lincoln celebrates its crop with a three-day fun fest. Events include the Apple Harvest Queen Contest, apple core throwing, antique cars, apple cider and plenty of free sliced apples. Annually, first weekend in October. Est attendance: 25,000. For info: Lincoln Chamber of Commerce, 106 Arthur Ave, Lincoln, AR 72744. Phone: (501) 824-5100.

CHARLIE BROWN AND SNOOPY: BIRTHDAY. Oct 2. Charles M. Schulz's "Peanuts" comic strip celebrates its 48th anniversary. Syndicated by United Feature Syndicate, the "Peanuts" comic strip now appears in 2,600 newspapers and is translated into 21 languages in 75 countries. For info: Lili Root, PR Mgr, United Media, 200 Madison Ave, New York, NY 10016. Phone: (212) 293-8520. Fax: (212) 293-8550.
WWW: http://www.unitedmedia.com

CITY STAGE. Oct 2–4. Greensboro, NC. A free two-day street festival featuring the performing and visual arts, with food vendors, arts and crafts exhibitors and demonstrators, local, regional and national performers on three stages, kiddie activities, beer gardens, concessions, souvenirs, parties and the 10K run and 5K walk for the arts. Annually, the first full weekend in October. Sponsored by Miller Brewing Company. Est attendance: 100,000. For info: Mary Hale, Community Events Dir, United Arts Council of Greensboro, PO Box 877, Greensboro, NC 27402. Phone: (910) 333-7440. Fax: (910) 275-2787.

COHOCTON FALL FOLIAGE FESTIVAL. Oct 2–4. Cohocton, NY. World-famous tree-sitting contest. Parade, more than 100 food, antiques, arts and crafts booths. 33rd annual. Est attendance: 10,000. For info: Bob Fleishman, RD #2, Cohocton, NY 14826. Phone: (716) 384-5227 or (716) 384-5312.

COME AND TAKE IT DAY. Oct 2–4. Gonzales, TX. This celebration commemorating the first shot fired for Texas independence in 1835 is named for the defiant battle cry of the colonists when the Mexican military demanded the return of a cannon. Est attendance: 30,000. For info: Chamber of Commerce, Box 134, Gonzales, TX 78629. Phone: (830) 672-6532. Fax: (830) 672-6533. Email: gonzcti@connecti.com.

DALTON DEFENDERS DAY. Oct 2–3. Coffeyville, KS. Event to honor citizens killed during Dalton Gang's robbery of two banks on Oct 5, 1892. Est attendance: 10,000. For info: Conv and Visitors Bureau, PO Box 457, Coffeyville, KS 67337. Phone: (316) 251-1194 or (800) 626-3357. Fax: (316) 251-5448. Email: ccvb@terraworld.net.

GANDHI, MOHANDAS KARAMCHAND (MAHATMA): BIRTH ANNIVERSARY. Oct 2, 1869. Indian political and spiritual leader who achieved world honor and fame for his advocacy of nonviolent resistance as a weapon against tyranny was born Oct 2, 1869, at Porbandar, India. He was assassinated in the garden of his home at New Delhi on Jan 30, 1948. On the anniversary of Gandhi's birth (Gandhi Jayanti) thousands gather at the park on the Jumna River in Delhi where Gandhi's body was cremated. Hymns are sung, verses from the Gita, the Koran and the Bible are recited, and cotton thread is spun on small spinning wheels (one of Gandhi's favorite activities). Other observances held at his birthplace and throughout India.

"THE GEORGE GOBEL SHOW" TV PREMIERE: ANNIVERSARY. Oct 2, 1954. George Gobel hosted this comedy-variety show for five years on NBC. Chanteuse Peggy King and Jeff Donnell were also on the show, with Eddie Fisher as "permanent guest star." In 1959 Gobel switched networks to CBS and appeared for a year with Joe Flynn, Anita Bryant and Harry Von Zell.

GREENE, GRAHAM: BIRTH ANNIVERSARY. Oct 2, 1904. British author Graham Greene was born at Berkhamsted, Hertfordshire, England. He centered his works around characters facing salvation and damnation in a world of chaos, often with complex Catholic settings. His works include *The Power and The Glory* (1940) and *The Third Man* (1950). He died on Apr 3, 1991, at Vevey, Switzerland.

GUINEA: INDEPENDENCE DAY. Oct 2. National Day.

GUNN, MOSES: BIRTH ANNIVERSARY. Oct 2, 1929. The 1981 winner of the NAACP Image Award for his performance as Booker T. Washington in the film *Ragtime* was born in St. Louis, MO, and grew up to be one of America's finest actors. His appearances on stage ranged from the title role in *Othello* to Jean Genet's *The Blacks*. He received an Emmy nomination for his role in *Roots* and was awarded several Obies for off-Broadway performances. In film he appeared in *Shaft* and *The Great White Hope*. He died Dec 17, 1993, at Guilford, CT.

HOLIDAY CRAFT AND GIFT SHOW. Oct 2–4. Jacob Building, Chilhowee Park, Knoxville, TN. 8th annual show featuring holiday-themed handmade crafts with an emphasis on home decor. Friday 11 AM–8 PM; Saturday 9 AM–6 PM; Sunday 12–5 PM. Est attendance: 13,000. For info: Katie Parton, Esau, Inc, PO Box 50096, Knoxville, TN 37950. Phone: (423) 588-1233 or (800) 588-ESAU. Fax: (423) 588-6938.

HULL, CORDELL: BIRTH ANNIVERSARY. Oct 2, 1871. American statesman who served in both houses of the Congress and as secretary of state was born at Pickett County, TN. Noted for his contributions to the "Good Neighbor" policies of the US with regard to countries of the Americas and to the establishment of the United Nations. Hull died at Bethesda, MD, July 23, 1955.

"THE JIMMY DURANTE SHOW" TV PREMIERE: ANNIVERSARY. Oct 2, 1954. Affectionately known as "The Schnozz," Durante hosted a Saturday night variety show with his former vaudeville partner, Eddie Jackson, pianist Jules Baffano and drummer Jack Roth. It alternated with "The Donald O'Connor Show" on NBC and aired for two years.

KENTUCKY APPLE FESTIVAL. Oct 2–3. Paintsville, KY. Apple blossom beauty pageants, apple auction, country music show, arts and crafts, flea market, antique car show, Corvette show, Apple Bowl, Terrapin Trot, amusement rides, food booths and an AKC-sanctioned dog show. Est attendance: 75,000. For info: Kentucky Apple Festival, Inc, Ray Tosti, Chairman, PO Box 879, Paintsville, KY 41240. Phone: (606) 789-4355.

LITERALLY, A HAUNTED HOUSE. Oct 2–3. (Also Oct 9–10, 16–17, 23–24 & 30–31.) New Albany, IN. Friends of Culbertson Mansion fundraiser. Est attendance: 7,500. For info: Culbertson Mansion, 914 E Main, New Albany, IN 47150. Phone: (812) 944-9600. Fax: (812) 949-6134.

"LUX VIDEO THEATRE" TV PREMIERE: ANNIVERSARY. Oct 2, 1950. James Mason, Otto Kruger and Gordon MacRae hosted this half-hour dramatic anthology series that aired for seven years on both CBS and NBC. Its famed guest stars included: Robert Stack in "Inside Story" (1951); Peter Lorre in "The Taste" (1952); Grace Kelly in "A Message for Janice" (1952); Edward G. Robinson in "Witness for the Prosecution" (1953); and Esther Williams in "The Armed Venus" (1957).

***MAPLE LEAF RAG* PREMIERE: ANNIVERSARY.** Oct 2, 1990. The last work choreographed by Martha Graham premiered at City Center in New York City. One of the 181 works created by Graham, *The Maple Leaf Rag* appeared on stage for the first time just six months before the dancer and choreographer died at the age of 96.

MARSHALL, THURGOOD, SWORN IN TO SUPREME COURT: ANNIVERSARY. Oct 2, 1967. Thurgood Marshall was sworn in as the first black associate justice to the US Supreme Court. On June 27, 1991, he announced his resignation, effective upon the confirmation of his successor.

McFARLAND, GEORGE (SPANKY): 70th BIRTH ANNIVERSARY. Oct 2, 1928. Chubby child star of the "Our Gang" comedy film shorts. Born at Dallas, TX, and died at Grapevine, TX, June 30, 1993.

NATCHEZ FALL PILGRIMAGE. Oct 2–25. Natchez, MS. Tours of 24 antebellum mansions furnished with fine antiques and surrounded by lovely gardens. Carriage and bus sightseeing tours, evening entertainment. Est attendance: 10,000. For info: Natchez Pilgrimage Tours, PO Box 347, Corner of Canal and State Streets, Natchez, MS 39121. Phone: (800) 647-6742 or (601) 446-6631. Fax: (601) 446-8687.

NATIONAL CUSTODIAL WORKERS DAY. Oct 2. A day to honor custodial workers—those who clean up after us. For info: Bette Tadajewski, Saint John the Baptist Church, 2425 Frederick, Alpena, MI 49707. Phone: (517) 354-3019.

NATIONAL STORYTELLING FESTIVAL. Oct 2–4. Jonesborough, TN. Tennessee's oldest town plays host to the most dynamic storytelling event dedicated to the oral tradition. This three-day celebration showcases storytellers, stories and traditions from across America and around the world. Annually, the first full weekend in October. Est attendance: 10,000. For info: Natl Storytelling Assn (NSA), PO Box 309, Jonesborough, TN 37659. Phone: (800) 525-4514. Fax: (423) 753-9331.

NEMONT/AGRIBITION. Oct 2–3. Wolf Point, MT. Home and agribusiness show: two days of exhibits and featured speakers. Est attendance: 2,000. For info: Sally Paulson, Exec Dir, Wolf Point Chamber of Commerce, Box 237, Wolf Point, MT 59201. Phone: (406) 653-2012. Fax: (406) 653-3240. Email: 2sallyp@3rivers.net.

OHIO SWISS FESTIVAL. Oct 2–3. Sugarcreek, OH. Swiss music, yodeling, games, costumes, parades. Continuous entertainment and tons of Swiss cheese. Annually, the fourth Friday and Saturday following Labor Day. Est attendance: 50,000. For info: Particia Kaser, Info Coord, Ohio Swiss Festival, PO Box 158, Sugarcreek, OH 44681. Phone: (330) 852-4113.

OKTOBERFEST. Oct 2–4 (also Oct 9–11). New Ulm, MN. Celebrating Minnesota's German heritage, with musical entertainment, food, horse drawn trolley rides, craft shows and dancing. For info: New Ulm Chamber of Commerce, Box 384, New Ulm, MN 56073. Phone: (507) 354-4217 or (888) 4-NEWULM.

OKTOBERFEST. Oct 2–4. Amana Colonies, Amana, IA. Traditional German festival with ethnic food and drink, craft displays and entertainment. Est attendance: 20,000. For info: Merchants of Amana, B9-38th Ave, Ste 100, PO Box 10, Amana, IA 52203. Phone: (800) 245-5465.

OKTOBERFEST. Oct 2–8. LaCrosse, WI. German fall festival featuring family events, live entertainment, lots of food, Torchlight Parade on Thursday night and Maple Leaf Parade on Saturday. Fun for the whole family. For info: Kristin Olson, Tour/Member Serv Coord, LaCrosse Area Conv & Visitors Bureau, 410 E Veterans Memorial Dr, LaCrosse, WI 54601. Phone: (800) 658-9424. Fax: (608) 782-4082. Email: lacvb@centuryinter.net. WWW: http://www.wi.centuryinter.net/lacvb

OKTOBERFEST ON THE RIVER. Oct 2–4. Savannah, GA. One giant celebration of Savannah's German heritage. Festival includes food, dancing and activities for the whole family. Annually, the first or second weekend of October. Est attendance: 200,000. For info: Savannah Waterfront Assn, PO Box 572, Savannah, GA 31402. Phone: (912) 234-0295. Fax: (912) 234-4904.

OLD SEDGWICK COUNTY FAIR. Oct 2–4. Old Cowtown Museum, Wichita, KS. Re-creation of an 1870s fair with horse-drawn carriages, craft demonstrations and sales, livestock, music and reenactments. Annually, the first full weekend in October. Est attendance: 6,000. For info: Michael S. Knecht, Dir, Old Cowtown Museum, 1871 Sim Park Dr, Wichita, KS 67203. Phone: (316) 264-0671. Fax: (316) 264-2937.

OZARK NATIVE ARTS AND CRAFTS FESTIVAL. Oct 2–4. Finley River Park, Ozark, MO. An event of all handmade crafts only. Annually, the first full weekend in October. For info: Ozark Area Chamber of Commerce, PO Box 450, Ozark, MO 65721. Phone: (417) 581-6139.

PAUL BUNYAN SHOW. Oct 2–4. Hocking College Campus, Nelsonville, OH. Live demonstrations of forestry equipment, lumberjack contests, professional timber harvester competitions, forest industry trade show, chainsaw sculptors, Robbins Crossing interpretive history program and activities and steam show exhibits. Est attendance: 60,000. For info: Judy Sinnott, Public Info Dir, Hocking College, 3301 Hocking Pkwy, Nelsonville, OH 45764. Phone: (614) 753-3591 ext 2102. Fax: (614) 753-9018. Email: sinnot_j@ccmgate.hocking.cc.oh.us.

PHILEAS FOGG'S WAGER DAY: ANNIVERSARY. Oct 2, 1872. Anniversary, from Jules Verne's *Around the World in Eighty Days*, of the famous wager of Oct 2, 1872, upon which the book is based: "I will bet twenty thousand pounds against any one who wishes, that I will make the tour of the world in eighty days or less." Then, consulting a pocket almanac, Phileas Fogg said: "As today is Wednesday, the second of October, I shall be due in London, in this very room of the Reform Club, on Saturday, the twenty-first of December, at a quarter before nine PM; or else the twenty thousand pounds . . . will belong to you." See also: "Phileas Fogg Wins a Wager Day" (Dec 21).

REDWOOD NATIONAL PARK ESTABLISHED: 30th ANNIVERSARY. Oct 2, 1968. California's Redwood National Park was established. For further park info: Redwood Natl Park, 1111 Second St, Crescent City, CA 95531.

REX ALLEN DAYS. Oct 2–4. Willcox, AZ. Annual celebration honors hometown boy Rex Allen, who gained fame as a singer, cowboy movie star and narrator for Walt Disney Productions. Celebration also honors Rex Allen, Jr, famed singer, who appeared on TNN's Yesteryears and Statler Brothers' Show. He is currently performing at the Orleans Hotel & Casino in Las Vegas. Activities include golf tournament, parade, country fair, PRCA rodeo, General Willcox Turtle Race, arts and crafts, country western concert, carnival, softball tournament, cowboy dances and miniature art show. Est attendance: 20,000. For info: Willcox Chamber of Commerce, 1500 N Circle I Rd, Willcox, AZ 85643. Phone: (520) 384-2272 or (800) 200-2272. Fax: (520) 384-0293.

SPACE MILESTONE: RECORD TIME IN SPACE. Oct 2, 1984. Three Soviet cosmonauts returned to Earth after setting a record of 237 days in space—at *Salyut* 7 space station since Feb 9.

October 1998

S	M	T	W	T	F	S
				1	2	3
4	5	6	7	8	9	10
11	12	13	14	15	16	17
18	19	20	21	22	23	24
25	26	27	28	29	30	31

SPRINGS FOLK FESTIVAL. Oct 2–3. Springs, PA. 41st annual festival during the peak of fall in Amish country. 125 craftsmen, Dutch food and continuous live music. For info: Harriet Hershberger, Springs Folk Festival, PO Box 293, Springs, PA 15562. Phone: (814) 622-2051 or (814) 662-4158.

STREETER, RUTH CHENEY: BIRTH ANNIVERSARY. Oct 2, 1895. Born at Brookline, MA, Ruth Cheney Streeter was the first director of the US Marine Corps Women's Reserve. She was active in unemployment relief, public health, welfare and old-age assistance in New Jersey during the 1930s. A student of aeronautics, she learned to fly while serving as an adjutant of a flight group in the Civil Air Patrol during the early years of World War II and became the only female member of the Committee on Aviation of the New Jersey Defense Council. Ruth Cheney Streeter died Sept 30, 1990, at Morristown, NJ.

SUGARLOAF'S FALL SOMERSET CRAFT FESTIVAL. Oct 2–4. Garden State Exhibit Center, Somerset, NJ. This show, now in its 5th year, features 250 nationally recognized craft designers and fine artists displaying and selling their original creations. Craft demonstrations, children's entertainment, hourly gift certificate drawings and more. Est attendance: 20,000. For info: Sugarloaf Mountain Works, Inc, 200 Orchard Ridge Dr, #215, Gaithersburg, MD 20878. Phone: (800) 210-9900.

"TOM CORBETT, SPACE CADET" TV PREMIERE: ANNIVERSARY. Oct 2, 1950. This space show was set in the 2350s at the Space Academy and starred Frankie Thomas in the title role as an eager cadet. Also featured were Edward Bryce, Jan Merlin, Jack Grimes, Patricia Ferris, Margaret Garland, John Fiedler and Al Markim. "Tom Corbett" was one of the few shows to be aired on all four major networks, including running on two different networks (NBC and ABC) at the same time.

"THE TWILIGHT ZONE": THE FIRST EPISODE. Oct 2, 1959. "The Twilight Zone" went on the air with these now-familiar surreal words: "There is a fifth dimension, beyond that which is known to man. It is a dimension as vast as space and as timeless as infinity. It is the middle ground between light and shadow, between science and superstition, and it lies between the pit of man's fear and the summit of his knowledge. This is the dimension of imagination. It is an area which we call The Twilight Zone." The program ran five seasons for 154 installments, with a one-year hiatus between the third and fourth seasons. It now is considered to have had some of the best drama ever to appear on television. It is noted for its scripts with twists of fate and fine lines between reality and illusion.

US OPEN STOCK DOG CHAMPIONSHIP. Oct 2–4. Hubert Bailey Farm, Dawsonville, GA. In the foothills of the Appalachian mountains, handlers from across the country will work both sheep and cattle. Also a petting zoo for children. Est attendance: 3,000. For info: Dawson County Chamber of Commerce, PO Box 299, Dawsonville, GA 30534. Phone: (706) 265-6278. Fax: (706) 265-6279. Email: chamber@dawson.org. WWW: http://www.dawson.org

VIRGINIA-CAROLINA CRAFTSMEN'S FALL CLASSIC. Oct 2–4. Roanoke Civic Center, Roanoke, VA. Arts and crafts. Est attendance: 20,000. For info: The Virginia-Carolina Craftsmen, 1240 Oakland Ave, Greensboro, NC 27403. Phone: (910) 274-5550. Fax: (910) 274-1084.

WEST VIRGINIA PUMPKIN FESTIVAL. Oct 2–4. Little League Complex, Fairgrounds Rd, Milton, WV. Crafts and demonstrations, pumpkin contests, exhibits, pageants, entertainment and outstanding concessions. Est attendance: 25,000. For info: West Virginia Pumpkin Festival, PO Box 358, Milton, WV 25541. Phone: (304) 743-9222 or (304) 696-5954.

WORLD FARM ANIMALS DAY. Oct 2. (Gandhi's birthday.) To memorialize through mock funerals, memorial services, vigils and similar activities the needless suffering and death of billions of farm animals each year. For info: Farm Animal Reform Movement, Box 30654, Bethesda, MD 20824. Phone: (301) 530-1737. Fax: (301) 530-5747. Email: farmusa@erols.com. WWW: http://www.envirolink.org/arrs/farm

BIRTHDAYS TODAY

Clay S. Felker, 70, publisher, born St. Louis, MO, Oct 2, 1928.
Donna Karan, 50, fashion designer, born Forest Hills, NY, Oct 2, 1948.
Don McLean, 53, singer ("Crying"), songwriter ("American Pie," "Vincent"), born New Rochelle, NY, Oct 2, 1945.
Rex Reed, 59, movie critic, born Fort Worth, TX, Oct 2, 1939.
Sting (Gordon Sumner), 47, musician (lead singer with the Police), songwriter ("Every Breath You Take"), actor (*Dune*), born London, England, Oct 2, 1951.

OCTOBER 3 — SATURDAY

Day 276 — 89 Remaining

ALZHEIMER'S ASSOCIATION MEMORY WALK. Oct 3–4. Memory Walk is a fun, family-oriented event developed to raise funds and generate awareness for Alzheimer's Association chapters across the country. More than 200 communities participate. Est attendance: 150,000. For info: Nicolette Coorlas, Alzheimer's Assn, 919 N Michigan Ave, Ste 1000, Chicago, IL 60611. Phone: (312) 335-5708. Fax: (312) 335-1110. Email: nicolette.coorlas@alz.org. WWW: http://www.alz.org

AMERICAN HEART WALK. Oct 3–4. This annual event is an opportunity to promote exercise as well as to educate people about heart disease and stroke. Participants in more than 900 US cities and towns ask their families and friends for a flat donation to the American Heart Association for walking the course. Annually, the first weekend in October. Est attendance: 300,000. For info: Greg Hunicutt, PR Dept, American Heart Assn, Natl Center, 7272 Greenville Ave, Dallas, TX 75231. Phone: (800) AHA-USA1. Fax: (214) 369-3685. WWW: http://www.americanheart.org

AMERICAN ROSE SOCIETY NATIONAL SHOW. Oct 3. Adams Mark Hotel, Charlotte, SC. Amateur growers from all over the US display thousands of their roses in this major competition. Est attendance: 2,000. For info: Robert Ardini, Chairman, American Rose Society Publicity Committee, 230 Central Park West, 15B, New York, NY 10024. Phone: (212) 595-0353. Email: rardini@aol.com.

ANDERSONVILLE LIVING HISTORY AND CEMETERY DEDICATION. Oct 3–4. Andersonville, GA. Re-enactment of post-Civil War Andersonville prison. Union encampment and portrayals of Clara Barton and others demonstrate efforts to identify almost 13,000 Union soldiers interred in the national cemetery. For info: Andersonville Natl Historic Site, Alan Marsh, Park Ranger, Rte 1, Box 800, Hwy 49 N, Andersonville, GA 31711. Phone: (912) 924-0343.

"THE ANDY GRIFFITH SHOW" TV PREMIERE: ANNIVERSARY. Oct 3. Marks the airing of the first episode on Oct 3, 1960. The 12,000+ members of "The Andy Griffith Show" Rerun Watchers Club and others celebrate this day with festivities every year.

APPLE HARVEST FESTIVAL. Oct 3–4. (Also Oct 10–11.) 34th annual. South Mountain Fairgrounds, Gettysburg, PA. Celebration includes tours of orchards, apple-butter boiling and antique cider press. Est attendance: 100,000. For info: Gettysburg Conv & Visitors Bureau, 35 Carlisle St, Gettysburg, PA 17325-1899. Phone: (717) 334-6274. Fax: (717) 334-1166. WWW: http://www.gettysburg.com

APPLEFEST. Oct 3–4. Downtown Weston, MO. Pressing apple cider, cooking apple butter, music, parade and Lost Arts demonstrations on Main Street. For info: Weston Development Co, 502 Main, Weston, MO 64098. Phone: (816) 640-2909.

BANCROFT, GEORGE: BIRTH ANNIVERSARY. Oct 3. American historian, born at Worcester, MA, Oct 3, 1800. Died at Washington, DC, Jan 27, 1891.

BATTLE OF GERMANTOWN REENACTMENT. Oct 3. Philadelphia, PA. Annual re-enactment of the Oct 4, 1777, Battle of Germantown. Featured are more than 400 authentically costumed troops recreating the events of the original battle twice during the day, at noon and at 3 PM. Visit the nearby Germantown Country Fair for food and fun. Annually, the first Saturday in October. Est attendance: 4,000. For info: Public Relations, Cliveden of the National Trust, 6401 Germantown Ave, Philadelphia, PA 19144. Phone: (215) 848-1777. Fax: (215) 438-2892.

BIG ISLAND RENDEZVOUS. Oct 3–4. Bancroft Bay City Park, Albert Lea, MN. Named one of the top 25 festivals in Minnesota by Office of Tourism and nominated for Top 100 Festivals in North America. Fur-trade-era festival with old-time bluegrass and country music, black powder shoot, tipi village, traders' row, workshops, traditional and ethnic foods. Est attendance: 13,000. For info: Big Island Rendezvous and Festival, Inc, 202 N Broadway, Albert Lea, MN 56007. Phone: (800) 658-2526. Fax: (507) 373-0344. Email: pvining@northernnet.com.

BIG PIG JIG: GEORGIA BARBECUE CHAMPIONSHIP. Oct 3 (also Oct 8–10). Vienna, GA. Festival features a parade, pageants, arts and crafts, 5K "Hog Jog" run, carnival, plus big stage shows. $12,000 in cash and trophies awarded to pork-cooking contest winners. Sponsored by Budweiser. Est attendance: 33,000. For info: Big Pig Jig, PO Box 308, Vienna, GA 31092. Phone: (912) 268-8275. Fax: (912) 268-8200. Email: jledford@mail.mgb.com.

BROOKFIELD OKTOBERFEST. Oct 3. Brookfield, MO. One day festival celebrating the end of summer events and activities. Est attendance: 1,000. For info: Brookfield Community Dvmt Committee, 114 W Brooks, Brookfield, MO 64628. Phone: (816) 258-7278. Fax: (816) 258-7279.

BUFFALO ROUNDUP ARTS FESTIVAL. Oct 3–5. Custer, SD. South Dakota artists and craftsmen display and sell their arts and crafts. Also, entertainment, pancake feeds, chili cookoff, bike races and much more. Est attendance: 6,000. For info: Craig Pugsley, Visitor Services Coord, Custer State Park, HC 83, Box 70, Custer, SD 57730. Phone: (605) 255-4515. Fax: (605) 255-4460.

BURLINGTON OLD-FASHIONED APPLE HARVEST FESTIVAL. Oct 3–4. Burlington, WV. Celebrate the apple harvest in the beautiful Potomac Highlands of West Virginia. Est attendance: 40,000. For info: Auxiliary of Burlington United Methodist Family Services, PO Box 96, Burlington, WV 26710-0096. Phone: (304) 289-3511 or (304) 788-1953.

CANADA: ADAMS RIVER SOCKEYE SALMON RUN. Oct 3–30. Roderick Haig-Brown Provincial Park, Adams River, British Columbia. More than 1 million sockeye salmon leave the Pacific in September and migrate up the Fraser and Thompson Rivers to their birthplace in the Adams River drainage to spawn. The salmon only run once every four years. For info: Eau Sinclair, BC Parks/Visitor Services, 1210 McGill Rd, Kamloops, BC, Canada V2C 6N6. Fax: (250) 828-4633.

CELEBRATION OF FINE CRAFTS. Oct 3–4. Riverfront Parkway, Chattanooga, TN. Marketing the creative work of the hand by 100 select American craft artists. Second annual fair. Annually, the first weekend in October. Est attendance: 15,000. For info: Alice C. Merritt, Exec Dir, Tennessee Assn of Craft Artists, PO Box 120066, Nashville, TN 37212. Phone: (615) 665-0502.

CHESAPEAKE WILDLIFE SHOWCASE. Oct 3–4. Ward Museum of Wildfowl Art, Salisbury, MD. Buy, sell and trade at the War Museum's spectacular largest decoy auction. For info: Jane Rollins, Events Coord, Ward Museum of Wildfowl Art, 909 S Schumaker Dr, Salisbury, MD 21804. Phone: (410) 742-4988. Fax: (410) 742-3107.

CIRCLE CITY CLASSIC. Oct 3. RCA Dome, Indianapolis, IN. Bowl-style football game between two predominantly black universities is preceded by several days of related activities, including concerts, Coronation, College Fair and parade. Est attendance: 6,200. For info: Indiana Sports Corp, 201 S Capitol Ave, Ste 1200, Indianapolis, IN 46225. Phone: (317) 237-5000. Fax: (317) 237-5041. Email: isc@indianasportscorp.com. WWW: http://www.indianasportscorp.com

COTTON PICKIN' FAIR. Oct 3–4. Turn-of-the-century plantation, Gay, GA. Award-winning festival featuring 300 exhibits of antiques, arts and crafts, ongoing entertainment, great country cooking, children's activities and demonstrating craftspeople. Biannually, the first weekends in May and October. For info: Ellen McEwen, Dir, or Lana Miles, Fair Coord, Cotton Pickin' Fair, PO Box 1, Gay, GA 30218. Phone: (706) 538-6814.

COUNTRY DAY CELEBRATION. Oct 3. Dent County Courthouse, Salem, MO. Features handmade crafts, food, information and display booths and all-day entertainment. Est attendance: 6,500. For info: Salem Chamber of Commerce, 409 N Main St, PO Box 385, Salem, MO 65560. Phone: (573) 729-6900. Fax: (573) 729-8780. Email: salcofc@fidnet.com. WWW: http://www.somo.com/salem

CRANBERRY FEST—A BERRY GOOD TIME. Oct 3–4. Eagle River, WI. 19th annual tribute to the cranberry, where the "World's Largest Cranberry Cheesecake" will be served. Visitors can eat, drink, wear, bake and decorate with cranberries; tour the cranberry bogs and area winery; participate in cranberry cook-off events; and visit all kinds of exhibits. Weekend activities and entertainment also include a craft show, photo contest, weaving and quilt exhibits, auction and a variety of musical performances. Est attendance: 15,000. For info: Wisconsin Dept of Tourism, Cranberry Fest-A Good Time, PO Box 7976, Madison, WI 53707. Phone: (715) 479-8575 or (800) 359-6315. Email: tourism@laughlin.com. WWW: http://tourism.state.wi.us

October 1998

S	M	T	W	T	F	S
				1	2	3
4	5	6	7	8	9	10
11	12	13	14	15	16	17
18	19	20	21	22	23	24
25	26	27	28	29	30	31

"THE DICK VAN DYKE SHOW" TV PREMIERE: ANNIVERSARY. Oct 3, 1961. This sitcom wasn't an immediate success but soon became a hit. It starred Dick Van Dyke as Rob Petrie, a TV show writer, and Mary Tyler Moore as his wife Laura, a former dancer. This was one of the first shows revolving around the goings-on at a TV series. Other cast members included: Morey Amsterdam, Rose Marie, Richard Deacon, Carl Reiner, Jerry Paris, Ann Morgan Guilbert and Larry Matthews. Carl Reiner created the series.

FALL CITYWIDE GARAGE SALE. Oct 3. Electra, TX. Sales throughout the Electra area. Chamber of Commerce will provide free coffee and maps on Oct 3, 1998, at 7 AM. The Chamber of Commerce office will close at 8 AM so that we too may enjoy all of the bargains. Est attendance: 500. For info: Dawn Dunsmore, Electra Chamber of Commerce, 112 W Cleveland, Electra, TX 76360. Phone: (817) 495-3577. Fax: (817) 495-3577.

FALL HARVEST FESTIVAL. Oct 3–4. Veteran's Memorial Park, Boyne City, MI. Historic encampment, arts and crafts show, large farmers' market, Scarecrow Contest and Lumberjack Competition. Est attendance: 8,500. For info: Deborah Thompson, Executive Dir, Fall Harvest Festival, 28 S Lake, Boyne City, MI 49712.

FAYETTE COUNTY COOKOFF & FALL FESTIVAL. Oct 3. Uniontown, PA. This autumn festival features food, entertainment, People's Choice Awards, prizes and drawings. For info: Central Fayette Chamber of Business & Industry, 11 Pittsburgh St, PO Box 2124, Uniontown, PA 15401. Phone: (412) 437-4571 or (800) 916-9365.

FELL'S POINT FUN FESTIVAL. Oct 3–4. Fell's Point National Historic District, Baltimore, MD. 32nd annual popular outdoor street festival held in Baltimore's original seaport. 300 arts and crafts vendors, antiques, four stages, family and children's area, two beer gardens, International Food Row and more. Annually, the first full weekend in October. Sponsor: The Preservation Society. Est attendance: 325,000. For info: Karen Moul, Fest Coord, Fell's Point Fun Festival, 812 S Ann St, Baltimore, MD 21231. Phone: (410) 675-6756. Fax: (410) 675-6769.

FIESTA de COLORES. Oct 3–4. JK Northway Exposition Center, Kingsville, TX. Arts and crafts show and sale. Est attendance: 5,000. For info: Kingsville Conv and Visitors Bureau, PO Box 1562, Kingsville, TX 78364-1562. Phone: (800) 333-5032. Fax: (512) 592-3227. Email: kcvb@kingsville.org. WWW: http://www.kingsville.org

GEORGIA RENAISSANCE FALL FESTIVAL. Oct 3–Nov 1 (Saturdays and Sundays only). Atlanta, GA. Theme park presents "the entertainment, romance and art of the Renaissance." More than 100 performances daily on 10 stages, thousands of unique craft items. Holiday shopping and Haunted Castle. Est attendance: 201,000. For info: Sarah Waters, Georgia Renaissance Festival, PO Box 986, Fairburn, GA 30213. Phone: (770) 964-8575. Fax: (770) 964-1477.

GERMANY: REUNIFICATION: ANNIVERSARY. Oct 3. After 45 years of division, East and West Germany reunited on Oct 3, 1990, just four days short of East Germany's 41st founding anniversary (Oct 7, 1949). Originally scheduled to coincide with the all-German parliamentary elections on Dec 2, 1990, reunification was rescheduled for the earlier date by East Germany's parliament in response to the deterioration of the economy. The new united Germany took the name the Federal Republic of Germany, the formal name of the former West Germany, and adopted the constitution of the former West Germany.

GOPHER HILL FESTIVAL. Oct 3. Old School Grounds, Ridgeland, SC. Celebrate Gopher Hill (area known as Ridgeland), named for gopher tortoise that lives here and is on South Carolina's endangered species list. Est attendance: 5,000. For info:

Jasper County Chamber of Commerce, Box 1267, Ridgeland, SC 29936. Phone: (803) 726-8126. Fax: (803) 726-6290.

GORGAS, WILLIAM CRAWFORD: BIRTH ANNIVERSARY. Oct 3, 1854. Physician and sanitary engineer, born at Toulminville, AL. He eradicated yellow fever from Havana, and the Panama Canal, allowing the completion of the canal. Gorgas died at London, England, July 4, 1920.

HEAD OF THE OHIO REGATTA. Oct 3. Allegheny River banks, Clement Park, Pittsburgh, PA. Rowing teams from local area as well as from various parts of the US and Canada race on Pittsburgh's rivers to benefit Mercy Hospital's Burn Center. For info: Greater Pittsburgh Conv & Visitors Bureau, Four Gateway Center, Pittsburgh, PA 15222-1259. Phone: (412) 232-7506 or (800) 359-0758. Fax: (412) 644-5512.

HERRIOT, JAMES (JAMES ALFRED WIGHT): BIRTH ANNIVERSARY. Oct 3, 1916. Author and veterinarian James Herriot was born at Glasgow, Scotland. Herriot wrote more than 12 books chronicling his life as a veterinarian in northern England. His *All Creatures Great and Small* (1974) was made into a TV series that became an international hit. He was made a member of the Order of the British Empire in 1979. Herriot died Feb 23, 1995, at Yorkshire, England.

HONDURAS: FRANCISCO MORAZAN HOLIDAY. Oct 3. Public holiday in honor of Francisco Morazan, national hero, who was born in 1799.

INSECT FESTIVAL. Oct 3–4. Lindsay Wildlife Museum, Walnut Creek, CA. Wildlife and nature center site for bug bash featuring native and exotic insects, craft activities, fascinating presentations. Annually, the first weekend in October. Est attendance: 3,000. For info: Lindsay Wildlife Museum, 1931 First Ave, Walnut Creek, CA 94596. Phone: (510) 935-1978. Fax: (510) 935-8015. WWW: http://www.wildlife-museum.org

ISSAQUAH SALMON DAYS FESTIVAL. Oct 3–4. Issaquah, WA. To celebrate the return of the spawning salmon to the hatchery. Annually, the first weekend in October. Est attendance: 200,000. For info: Issaquah Salmon Days Festival, 155 NW Gilman Blvd, Issaquah, WA 98027. Phone: (425) 270-2532. Fax: (425) 392-8101.

KNOX COUNTY SCENIC DRIVE. Oct 3–4 (also Oct 10–11). Knox County, IL. A self-conducted 100-mile driving tour through rural Spoon River Valley resplendent with fall colors. Different attractions at every stop feature food, crafts, art, antiques, fresh produce, old skills demonstrations, flea markets or games. Annually, the first two full weekends in October. Est attendance: 75,000. For info: Galesburg Area CVB, PO Box 749, Galesburg, IL 61402-0749. Phone: (309) 343-1194. Fax: (309) 343-1195. Email: gacvb@misslink.net. WWW: http://www.misslink.net/gacvb/

KOREA: NATIONAL FOUNDATION DAY. Oct 3. National holiday also called Tangun Day, as it commemorates day when legendary founder of the Korean nation, Tangun, established his kingdom of Chosun in 2333 BC.

KURTZMAN, HARVEY: BIRTH ANNIVERSARY. Oct 3, 1902. Cartoonist and founder of *Mad* magazine, Harvey Kurtzman was born at Brooklyn, NY. At the age of 14 he had his first cartoon published, and he began his career in comic books in 1943. His career led him to EC (Educational Comics), and with the support of William Gaines, he created *Mad* magazine, which first appeared in 1952. He died Feb 21, 1993, at Mount Vernon, NY.

LONG BEACH ISLAND CHOWDER COOK-OFF. Oct 3–4. Bayfront Park, Beach Haven, NJ. Weekend-long festival featuring unlimited tasting of up to 30 different red/white clam chowders prepared by area restaurants. Entertainment; other food/beverages available. Annually, the first weekend in October. Est attendance: 18,000. For info: Jeanne Di Paola, Exec Dir, Long Beach Island Chamber of Commerce, 265 W 9th St, Ship Bottom, NJ 08008. Phone: (800) 292-6372. Fax: (609) 494-5807. Email: sochamber@aol.com.

MAKOTI THRESHING BEE SHOW. Oct 3–4. Makoti, ND. To acquire, rebuild and maintain antique farm machinery and motor vehicles. Threshing and other demonstrations. Annually, the first weekend in October. Est attendance: 8,000. For info: Loren Quandt, Makoti Threshers, Inc, PO Box 124, Makoti, ND 58756. Phone: (701) 726-5649.

MANSON, PATRICK: BIRTH ANNIVERSARY. Oct 3. British parasitologist and surgeon sometimes called the "father of tropical medicine." Sir Patrick's research into insects as carriers of parasites was instrumental in later understanding of mosquitoes as transmitters of malaria. Born in Scotland on Oct 3, 1844, Manson died Apr 9, 1922.

MAUI SPORTS FESTIVAL. Oct 3–11. Wailea, Maui, HI. Celebration of sports includes 10K run, golf, tennis, food and wine festival, X-Terra off-road triathlon, outrigger sailing canoe race and Pacific International Sports Conference and Expo. Est attendance: 7,500. For info: Event Marketing, 1001 Bishop St, Pauahi Tower #880, Honolulu, HI 96813. Phone: (808) 521-4322. Fax: (808) 538-0314. Email: dey@emisport.com.
WWW: http://www.emisport.com

MORRO BAY HARBOR FESTIVAL. Oct 3–4. Morro Bay, CA. Celebrates a working waterfront at play! Officially launches "October Is National Seafood Month." Showcases seafood, fishing industry and diversity of marine life and coastal lifestyles. Features California Seafood Faire, wine and premium beer tasting and a flotilla of family-oriented attractions. Annually, the first full weekend in October. Phone in California: (800) 366-6043. Est attendance: 45,000. For info: Exec Dir, Morro Bay Harbor Festival, Inc, PO Box 1869, Morro Bay, CA 93443. Phone: (805) 772-1155. Email: 76660.67@compuserve.com.
WWW: http://www.morrobay.com/harborfestival

"MR AND MRS NORTH" TV PREMIERE: ANNIVERSARY. Oct 3, 1952. This half-hour murder mystery show began as a comedy radio show based on stories by Richard and Frances Lockridge. A pilot program was released in 1949, but the TV series didn't begin until 1952. It starred Richard Denning as Jerry North and Barbara Britton as his wife Pamela, a New York couple who investigated unsolved murders. Francis DeSales was also featured as Lt Bill Weigand.

MRS W.H. FELTON BECOMES FIRST WOMAN US SENATOR: ANNIVERSARY. Oct 3, 1922. Mrs W.H. Felton, 87, of Cartersville, GA, was appointed on Oct 3, 1922, by Governor Thomas Hardwick of Georgia to the Senate seat vacated by the death of Thomas E. Watson.

NATIONAL HUMAN SERVICES PROFESSIONAL AWARENESS WEEK. Oct 3–9. Acknowledging all professionals in the human services industry and their contributions to society. Programs include career exploration day on high school and college campuses; seminars, workshops and award ceremonies in communities nationally. Press kits available. For info: Cathy Cousear, Pres, Inst for Human Services Resources, 164-11 89th Ave, Ste 1131, Jamaica, NY 11432. Phone: (718) 591-0142. Email: IHSR@aol.com.

NETHERLANDS: RELIEF OF LEIDEN DAY. Oct 3. Celebration of the liberation of Leiden in 1574.

OCTOBERFEST. Oct 3–4 (also Oct 10–11, 17–18 and 24–25). Hermann, MO. First four full weekends in October. Riverfront Park and five area wineries. Live German music, international Polkafest, beer and wine gardens, German food and dancing. Winery tours and tasting and live entertainment at each winery. Special events each weekend. Est attendance: 70,000. For info: Visitor Info Center, Hermann Tourism Group, PO Box 104, Hermann, MO 65041. Phone: (800) 932-8687 or (573) 486-2772. Fax: (573) 486-5363.

OGLEBAYFEST. Oct 3–4. Oglebay, Wheeling, WV. A free parkwide celebration thanking the public for its support. Fireworks, music, dances and artists' market. Country fair, festival contests and ethnic foods. Est attendance: 100,000. For info: John Hargleroad, Operations Dir, Oglebay, Wheeling, WV 26003. Phone: (304) 243-4028. Fax: (304) 243-4110.
WWW: http://wvweb.com/oglebay

OKTOBERFEST. Oct 3–4. St. Charles, MO. A citywide celebration of French and German heritage. Activities include a parade, German bands, foods and costumes. Annually, the first full weekend in October. Est attendance: 40,000. For info: Convention and Visitors Bureau, 230 S Main St, St. Charles, MO 63301. Phone: (800) 366-2427 or (314) 946-7776.
WWW: http://www.st-charles.mo.us

OLD TRAILS FOLKLIFE FESTIVAL. Oct 3–4. Ray County Fairgrounds, Richmond, MO. Festival includes a horse-drawn parade, costumed heritage crafters and artisans, musicians, civil war drills and encampments, outlaw skirmishes, fiddles, guitar and banjo music, puppet shows, poetry readings, storytelling, quilt show, Native American heritage arts and dances, Olde Towne storefront walk and more. For info: Sally Famuliner, Exec Dir, Richmond Chamber of Commerce, 107 N Thornton, Richmond, MO 64085. Phone: (816) 776-6916. Fax: (816) 776-6917.

"OUR MISS BROOKS" TV PREMIERE: ANNIVERSARY. Oct 3, 1952. This half-hour sitcom began on the radio, and unlike many radio programs that moved to TV, most of the original radio cast was retained. It was about a favorite high school English teacher named Connie Brooks (played by Eve Arden). Also featured were Gale Gordon, Richard Crenna, Gloria McMillan and Jane Morgan. Robert Rockwell was added to the TV cast. In the fall of 1955, the setting was changed, and some regulars left. Newcomers included Nana Bryant, Bob Sweeney, Ricky Vera, Gene Barry, William Ching and Isabel Randolph.

"THE PAT BOONE SHOW" TV PREMIERE: ANNIVERSARY. Oct 3, 1957. Cleancut singer Pat Boone hosted three shows between 1957 and 1969. The first was a prime-time variety series with the McGuire Sisters and the Mort Lindsey Orchestra as regulars. The second show featured the Paul Smith Orchestra and was a daytime variety and talk show. "Pat Boone in Hollywood" was the title of the third, a 90-minute talk show.

PIONEER POWER DAY THRESHING BEE. Oct 3–4. Lewistown, MT. An old-fashioned Threshing Bee. Old steam engines at work, threshing machines, all types of steam power machines and other old restored engines. Est attendance: 500. For info: Brian H. Sallee, Central MT Flywheelers Assn, 1015 W Washington, Lewistown, MT 59457. Phone: (406) 538-5236.

PUMPKIN DAY. Oct 3. Woodstock, VT. Learn about the many uses and varieties of pumpkin through activities and programs and take home a miniature pumpkin. Also harvest activities and wagon rides. For info: Deborah Bulissa, Billings Farm & Museum, Box 489, Woodstock, VT 05091. Phone: (802) 457-2355. Fax: (802) 457-4663. Email: billings.farm@valley.net.

October 1998

S	M	T	W	T	F	S
				1	2	3
4	5	6	7	8	9	10
11	12	13	14	15	16	17
18	19	20	21	22	23	24
25	26	27	28	29	30	31

"QUINCY" TV PREMIERE: ANNIVERSARY. Oct 3, 1976. This medically-oriented crime show starred Jack Klugman as Dr. R. Quincy (we never knew his first name), a medical examiner for the LA coroner's office. Quincy's curiosity about his cases led to investigative work which often solved them. Cast members included John S. Ragin, Garry Walberg, Robert Ito, Val Bisoglio, Joseph Roman and Lynnette Mettey. Later in the series the show focused on social issues that were unrelated to forensic medicine. In the final season, Quincy got married to Dr. W. Emily Hanover (Anita Gillette).

"THE REAL McCOYS" TV PREMIERE: ANNIVERSARY. Oct 3, 1957. This first successful rural comedy program was one of the most popular, predating similar shows such as "The Beverly Hillbillies" by many seasons. It was set in rural California and featured the McCoys (played by Walter Brennan, Richard Crenna, Kathy Nolan, Michael Winkelman and Lydia Reed) and their friends (played by Tony Martinez, Andy Clyde, Madge Blake, Janet DeGore, Butch Patrick and Joan Blondell). The show switched networks for its last season.

ROBINSON NAMED BASEBALL'S FIRST BLACK MAJOR LEAGUE MANAGER: ANNIVERSARY. Oct 3, 1974. The only major league player selected most valuable player in both the American and National Leagues, Frank Robinson was hired by the Cleveland Indians as baseball's first black major league manager on this date. During his playing career Robinson represented the American League in four World Series playing for the Baltimore Orioles, led the Cincinnati Reds to a National League pennant and hit 586 home runs in 21 years of play.

SAINT SIMONS BY THE SEA: AN ARTS FEST. Oct 3–4. St. Simons Island, GA. Sponsored by the Coastal Center for the Arts, now nearing a half-century of operation. Free admission for visitors; "juried to a quality level." Annually, the first full weekend in October. For info: Mittie B. Hendrix, Exec Dir, Coastal Center for the Arts, 2012 Demere Rd, St. Simons Island, GA 31522. Phone: (912) 634-0404.

"SCARECROW AND MRS. KING" TV PREMIERE: 15th ANNIVERSARY. Oct 3, 1983. A one-hour adventure series starring Bruce Boxleitner as Lee Stetson (code name "Scarecrow"), a government agent working with Mrs Amanda King (Kate Jackson), a housewife-turned-agent. The cast also included Beverly Garland, Paul Stout, Greg Morton, Mel Stewart and Martha Smith. Mr King, played by Sam Melville, appeared once, but he was out of the picture when Mrs King and Scarecrow were married in the final season. King also became a trainee agent, and two characters were added, played by Raleigh Bond and Myron Natwick.

SKAT-TRAK [JET SKI] WORLD FINALS (IJSBA). Oct 3–10. Nautical Inn Resort, Lake Havasu City, AZ. Est attendance: 50,000. For info: Tourism Bureau, 314 London Bridge Rd, Lake Havasu City, AZ 86403. Phone: (800) 242-8278.

SPOON RIVER VALLEY SCENIC DRIVE. Oct 3–4 (also Oct 10–11). Fulton County, IL. Fall festival with fall foliage, arts and crafts, antiques and collectibles, demonstrations, exhibits, food and the beauty of the 140-mile-long Spoon River Valley. *Spoon River Anthology* in Lewistown. Annually, the first two weekends in October. Est attendance: 110,000. For info: Joan Johnson, Publicity Chair, Spoon River Scenic Drive Assn, PO Box 308, Lewistown, IL 61542. Phone: (309) 547-3234 or (309) 647-8980.

VIRGINIA CHILDREN'S FESTIVAL. Oct 3. Town Point Park, Norfolk, VA. 9th annual. An all-day family program hosted by nationally famous children's entertainers, costumed characters and five stages of entertainment. Also, magic, giant puppets, creative dance and many other activities for a day of fantasy and fun. Est attendance: 45,000. For info: Norfolk Festevents, Ltd, 120 W Main St, Norfolk, VA 23510. Phone: (757) 441-2345. Fax: (757) 441-5198.

"WHEEL OF FORTUNE" TV PREMIERE: ANNIVERSARY. Oct 3, 1952. This was a human interest show rewarding people who had done good deeds. It was hosted by Todd Russell. It was originally a morning replacement show, but in the summer of 1953 it was moved to prime time.

WINFIELD ART-IN-THE-PARK FESTIVAL. Oct 3. Scenic Island Park, Winfield, KS. More than 100 artists and craftspersons display and sell their wares. Entertainment; food services available. Annually, the first Saturday in October. Est attendance: 8,000. For info: Ann Moore Laws, Adm Asst, Winfield Arts and Humanities Council, 700 Gary, Winfield, KS 67156-3731. Phone: (316) 221-2160. Fax: (316) 221-7232.

WOODLAND INDIAN CULTURAL DAY. Oct 3. St. Mary's City, MD. Explore the lifeways of the Yaocomaco Indian people at the Woodland Indian Hamlet. Hands-on demonstrations, storytelling and more. Annually, the first Saturday in October. Est attendance: 800. For info: Public Affairs Office, Historic St. Mary's City, PO Box 39, St. Mary's City, MD 20686. Phone: (301) 862-0990 or (800) SMC-1634. Fax: (301) 862-0968.

WROK/WZOK/WXXQ ANNUAL CHILI SHOOT-OUT. Oct 3. Rockford, IL. Area cooks see who can make the best chili in the county. Chili-pepper-eating and cow-chip-throwing contests. Sponsor: WROK/WZOK-FM. Est attendance: 8,000. For info: WROK/WZOK/WXXQ, 3901 Brendenwood Road, Rockford, IL 61107. Phone: (815) 399-2233.

BIRTHDAYS TODAY

Jeff Bingaman, 55, US senator (D, New Mexico), born El Paso, TX, Oct 3, 1943.

Lindsey Buckingham, 51, musician, singer, songwriter (with Fleetwood Mac; "Go Your Own Way"), born Palo Alto, CA, Oct 3, 1947.

Chubby Checker (Ernest Evans), 57, musician, singer ("The Twist"), born South Philadelphia, PA, Oct 3, 1941.

Dennis Lee Eckersley, 44, baseball player, born Oakland, CA, Oct 3, 1954.

Madlyn Rhue, 64, actress (*It's a Mad Mad Mad Mad World*, "Executive Suite"), born Washington, DC, Oct 3, 1934.

Gore Vidal, 73, writer (*Burr, Myra Breckinridge*), born West Point, NY, Oct 3, 1925.

David Mark (Dave) Winfield, 47, former baseball player, born St. Paul, MN, Oct 3, 1951.

OCTOBER 4 — SUNDAY

Day 277 — 88 Remaining

"THE ALVIN SHOW" TV PREMIERE: ANNIVERSARY. Oct 4, 1961. This prime-time cartoon was based on Ross Bagdasarian's novelty group called The Chipmunks, which were actually speeded-up vocals. In the series, The Chipmunks were three chipmunks, Alvin, Simon and Theodore, who sang and had adventures along with their songwriter-manager David Seville. Bagdasarian supplied the voices. Part of the show featured the adventures of inventor Clyde Crashcup (voiced by Shepard Menken). "Alvin" was more successful as a Saturday morning cartoon. It returned in reruns in 1979 and also prompted a sequel, called "Alvin and the Chipmunks," in 1983.

APPLE FESTIVAL. Oct 4. Historic Ward-Meade Park, Topeka, KS. Celebration of harvest and heritage of Kansas located in 5½-acre historical park. Ethnic foods, live entertainment, special shows, turn-of-the century town square activities, more than 100 craft booths. Annually, the first Sunday in October. Est attendance: 10,000. For info: Anita Wolgast, Historic Ward-Meade Park, 124 NW Fillmore, Topeka, KS 66606. Phone: (913) 368-3888. Fax: (913) 368-3890.

BIG "C" ATTUS DAY. Oct 4. Cattus Island County Park, Toms River, NJ. Environmental organizations fair with natural history programs throughout the day. Annually, the first Sunday in October. Est attendance: 500. For info: Shaun O'Rourke, Cooper Environmental Center, 1170 Cattus Island Blvd, Toms River, NJ 08753. Phone: (908) 270-6960.

BLESSING OF THE FISHING FLEET. Oct 4. Church of Saints Peter and Paul and Fisherman's Wharf, San Francisco, CA. Annually, the first Sunday in October.

CORSICA LIBERATED: 55th ANNIVERSARY. Oct 4, 1943. The Island of Corsica became the first French territory in Europe freed from Nazi control when Free French troops entered the city of Bastia, thereby completing the retaking of the island, the culmination of a French uprising that had begun on the island on Sept 19.

"DECEMBER BRIDE" TV PREMIERE: ANNIVERSARY. Oct 4, 1954. This sitcom was filmed before a live audience at Desilu Studios and took place mainly in a living room. It starred Spring Byington as widow Lily Ruskin; Frances Rafferty as her daughter Ruth Henshaw; Dean Miller as Ruth's husband, Matt; Harry Morgan as wise-cracking next-door neighbor, Pete Porter (his wife Gladys was talked about but never seen); Verna Felton as Lily's friend Hilda Crocker; and Arnold Stang as Pvt Marvin Fisher, Pete's brother-in-law. This series spun off "Pete and Gladys" in 1960.

★ **FIRE PREVENTION WEEK.** Oct 4–10 (approximate). Presidential Proclamation issued annually for the first or second week in October since 1925. For many years prior to 1925, National Fire Prevention Day was observed in October.

FIRE PREVENTION WEEK. Oct 4–10. To increase awareness of the dangers of fire and to educate the public on how to stay safe from fire. For info: Natl Fire Protection Assn, One Batterymarch Park, Quincy, MA 02269. Phone: (617) 770-3000.

FRYEBURG FAIR. Oct 4–11. Rte 5, Fryeburg, ME. Agricultural exposition, draft horse competitions, oxen and horse pulling, midway, country shows each evening, harness racing, Woodsmen's Day (always Monday), tractor pulling, baking contests, Forestry Resource Center, Firemans Muster, sheep dog trials and juried crafts show. Annually, the week that includes the first Wednesday in October. Est attendance: 325,000. For info: June Hammond, Secy, PO Box 78, Fryeburg, ME 04037. Phone: (207) 935-3268. Fax: (207) 935-3662.

GERMANY: ERNTEDANKFEST. Oct 4. A harvest thanksgiving festival, or potato harvest festival, Erntedankfest (or Erntedanktag) is generally observed on the first Sunday in October.

GET ORGANIZED WEEK. Oct 4–10. This is an opportunity to streamline your life, create more time, lower your stress and increase your profit. Simplify your situation and make it more manageable by taking advantage of this time to get organized. Annually, the first week in October. For info: Phyllis Pilger, Exec Dir, Natl Assn of Professional Organizers, 1033 LaPosada Dr, Ste 220, Austin, TX 78752-3880. Phone: (512) 206-0151. Email: napo@assnmgmt.com.

GRANDPARENTS' DAY IN MASSACHUSETTS. Oct 4. Annually, the first Sunday in October.

GREGORIAN CALENDAR ADJUSTMENT: ANNIVERSARY. Oct 4, 1582. Pope Gregory XIII, on Feb 24, 1582, issued a bulletin that decreed that the day following Thursday, Oct 4, 1582, should be Friday, Oct 15, 1582, thus correcting the previously used Julian Calendar, then 10 days out of date. This reform was effective in most Catholic countries, though the Julian Calendar continued in use in Britain and the American colonies until 1752, in Japan until 1873, in China until 1912, in Russia until 1918 and in Greece until 1923. See also: "Gregorian Calendar Adjustment Anniversary" (Feb 24, Sept 2).

HARVEST FESTIVAL. Oct 4. Mahomet, IL. 6th annual. A day packed full of harvest activities for the whole family. Craft show and flea market, pumpkin patch, hayrides, nature programs, face painting, games, storytelling, entertainment, food sales and more. For info: PR Coord, Champaign County Forest Preserve Dist, PO Box 1040, Mahomet, IL 61853. Phone: (217) 586-3360. Fax: (217) 586-5020. Email: ccfpd@prairienet.org.
WWW: http://www.prairienet.org/ccfpd

HAYES, RUTHERFORD BIRCHARD: BIRTH ANNIVERSARY. Oct 4, 1822. Rutherford Birchard Hayes, 19th president of the US (Mar 4, 1877–Mar 3, 1881), was born at Delaware, OH, Oct 4, 1822. In his inaugural address, Hayes said: "He serves his party best who serves the country best." He died at Fremont, OH, Jan 17, 1893.

JOHNSON, ELIZA McCARDLE: BIRTH ANNIVERSARY. Oct 4. Wife of Andrew Johnson, 17th president of the US, born at Leesburg, TN, Oct 4, 1810. Died Jan 15, 1876.

"LEAVE IT TO BEAVER" TV PREMIERE: ANNIVERSARY. Oct 4, 1957. This family sitcom was a stereotypical portrayal of American family life. It focused on Theodore "the Beaver" Cleaver (Jerry Mathers), his misadventures and his family: his patient, understanding, all-knowing and firm father, Ward (Hugh Beaumont); impeccably dressed and all-knowing housewife June (Barbara Billingsley); and Wally (Tony Dow), Beaver's good-natured all-American brother. The "perfectness" of the Cleaver family was balanced by other, less than perfect characters played by Ken Osmond, Frank Bank, Richard Deacon, Diane Brewster, Sue Randall, Doris Packer, Rusty Stevens, Madge Blake and Burt Mustin. "Leave It to Beaver" remained popular in reruns and as a made-for-TV-movie in the '80s.

LESOTHO: NATIONAL DAY. Oct 4. National holiday.

MENTAL ILLNESS AWARENESS WEEK. Oct 4–10. To increase public awareness of the causes of, symptoms of and treatments for mental illnesses. Annually, the first full week in October. For info: Div of Public Affairs, American Psychiatric Assn, 1400 K St NW, Washington, DC 20005. Phone: (202) 682-6220. Fax: (202) 682-6255. Email: whill@psych.org.
WWW: http://www.psych.org

October 1998

S	M	T	W	T	F	S
				1	2	3
4	5	6	7	8	9	10
11	12	13	14	15	16	17
18	19	20	21	22	23	24
25	26	27	28	29	30	31

★**MINORITY ENTERPRISE DEVELOPMENT WEEK.** Oct 4–10. Presidential Proclamation issued without request since 1983 for the first full week in October except in 1991 when issued for Sept 22–28 and in 1992 for Sept 27–Oct 3, to coincide with the National Conference.

"MODERN ROMANCES" TV PREMIERE: ANNIVERSARY. Oct 4, 1954. Stories adapted from those in *Modern Romances* magazine appeared in this daily 15-minute series, with a new five-part story every week. The original host and narrator was Martha Scott; she was succeeded by Mel Brandt and later by guest celebrities.

MYSTERY SERIES WEEK. Oct 4–10. A celebration of continuing characters in mystery novels. Two-thirds of all new mysteries each year currently feature a series detective. The series tradition has been alive and well for more than 100 years. Series readers today can choose from more than 7,500 adult mysteries featuring more than 1,500 continuing characters from living writers. Mystery Series Week will celebrate fictional cops, private eyes and amateur sleuths from all walks of life—solving crimes from 55 BC to the 22nd century. Annually, the first full week in October. For info: Purple Moon Press, 3319 Greenfield Rd, Ste 317, Dearborn, MI 48120-1212. Phone: (313) 593-1033. Fax: (313) 593-4087. Email: PurpleMoon@prodigy.net.

NATIONAL CHILI WEEK. Oct 4–10. National observance and celebration of chili, one of the most historical and traditional American dishes. For info: Williams Foods, Inc, 13301 W 99th St, Lenexa, KS 66215. Phone: (913) 888-4343. Fax: (913) 888-0727.

NATIONAL HEALTH CARE FOOD SERVICE WEEK. Oct 4–10. A week in recognition of the contributions of health care food service workers in providing food and nutrition services to patients who are hospitalized or institutionalized. Annually, the first full week in October. Sponsor: American Society for Healthcare Food Service Administrators of the American Hospital Association. For info: Shirley Armistead, Amer Soc for Healthcare Food Service Admins, One N Franklin, 31st Flr, Chicago, IL 60606. Phone: (312) 422-3870. Fax: (312) 422-4581. Email: sarmist1@aha.org. WWW: http://www.ashfsa.org

NATIONAL METRIC WEEK. Oct 4–10. To maintain an awareness of the importance of the metric system as the primary system of measurement for the US. For info: Natl Council of Teachers of Mathematics, 1906 Assn Dr, Reston, VA 20191-1593. Phone: (703) 620-9840 ext 113. Fax: (703) 476-2970.
Email: infocentral@nctm.org. WWW: http://www.nctm.org

NATIONAL SKIN CARE AWARENESS WEEK. Oct 4–10. Renée Rouleau Skin Spa, Dallas, TX. This special week focuses on providing education on caring for your skin. Topics include protecting your skin from the dangers of the sun, how diet and lifestyle affect your skin, developing a proper skin care routine and myths and facts about skin care products. All important knowledge for great-looking skin. For info: Renée Rouleau Skin Spa, 19009 Preston Rd, Ste 206, Dallas, TX 75252. Phone: (972) 248-6131. Fax: (972) 248-5826.

NATIONAL SPINNING AND WEAVING WEEK. Oct 4–10. To celebrate the timeless craft of weaving and spinning and to honor craftsmen and women past and present who perpetuate a legacy of fine handmade textiles. Fax: (770) 495-7703. For info: Handweavers Guild of America, Inc, 3327 Duluth Hwy, Ste 201, Duluth, GA 30096. Phone: (770) 495-7702.

PULASKI DAY PARADE. Oct 4. Philadelphia, PA. Parade honoring the Polish patriot known as the "Father of the American Cavalry." Begins at 18th and Benjamin Franklin Parkway. For info: Polish American Congress, Eastern Pennsylvania District, 308 Walnut St, Philadelphia, PA 19106. Phone: (215) 739-3408. Fax: (215) 922-1518.

REMINGTON, FREDERIC S.: BIRTH ANNIVERSARY. Oct 4, 1861. Born in Canton, NY. Frederic Remington, an artist and writer, studied at Yale Art School. He travelled extensively throughout North America and is best known for the work he did in the western US, capturing life on the plains—Indians, cowboys, horses and more. He owned a ranch near Peabody, KS. He died Dec 26, 1909, age 48, at Ridgefield, CT, following an appendectomy. Much of his work is on display at the Frederic Remington Art Museum at Ogdensburg, NY. For museum info: Frederic Remington Art Museum, 303 Washington St, Ogdensburg, NY 13669. Phone: (315) 393-2425. Fax: (315) 393-4464. Email: broncho@northnet.org.
WWW: http://www.northnet.org/broncho

RUNYAN, DAMON: BIRTH ANNIVERSARY. Oct 4, 1884. American newspaperman and author, born at Manhattan, KS, and died at New York, NY, Dec 10, 1946. ". . . always try to rub up against money," he wrote, "for if you rub up against money long enough, some of it may rub off on you."

SAINT FRANCIS OF ASSISI: FEAST DAY. Oct 4. Giovanni Francesco Bernardone, religious leader, founder of the Friars Minor (Franciscan Order), born at Assisi, Umbria, Italy, in 1181. Died at Porziuncula on Oct 3, 1226. One of the "most attractive and best-loved saints of all time."

SMITH VALLEY FUN DAYS. Oct 4. Smith Valley, NV. Car show, arts, crafts, BBQ, hay ride and more. For local info: (702) 465-2354. For info: Mason Valley, Chamber of Commerce, 227 S Main St, Yerington, NV 89447. Phone: (702) 463-2245. Fax: (702) 463-3369.

SPACE MILESTONE: *LUNA 3* (USSR). Oct 4, 1959. First satellite to photograph moon's distant side was launched on this date.

SPACE MILESTONE: *SPUTNIK*. Oct 4, 1957. Anniversary of launching of first successful man-made earth satellite. *Sputnik I* ("fellow traveller of earth") weighing 184 lbs was fired into orbit from the USSR's Tyuratam launch site on this date. Transmitted radio signal for 21 days, decayed Jan 4, 1958. Beginning of Space Age and man's exploration beyond Earth. This first-in-space triumph by the Soviets resulted in a stepped-up emphasis on the teaching of science in American classrooms.

STRATEMEYER, EDWARD L.: BIRTH ANNIVERSARY. Oct 4, 1862. American author of children's books, Stratemeyer was born at Elizabeth, NJ. He created numerous series of popular children's books including "The Bobbsey Twins," "The Hardy Boys," "Nancy Drew" and "Tom Swift." He and his Stratemeyer Syndicate, using 60 or more pen names, produced more than 800 books. More than four million copies were in print in 1987. Stratemeyer died at Newark, NJ, on May 10, 1930, at age 68.

SUKKOT BEGINS AT SUNDOWN. Oct 4. Jewish Feast of Tabernacles. See "Sukkot" (Oct 5).

A TASTE OF THE WORLD WEEK. Oct 4–10. To promote interest in world cuisines and cultures. Eat a meal from a different country each day this week. When we break bread together, tolerance and understanding naturally follow. Annually, the first full week in October, starting with Sunday. For info: Black Swan Enterprises Inc, 2559 Wabel Ave, Milwaukee, WI 53211. Phone: (414) 332-5993. Fax: (414) 332-6088.

TEN-FOUR DAY. Oct 4. The fourth day of the tenth month is a day of recognition for radio operators, whose code words, "Ten-Four," signal an affirmative reply.

YELTSIN SHELLS WHITE HOUSE: 5th ANNIVERSARY. Oct 4, 1993. In a violent spectacle, the Russian military loyal to President Boris Yeltsin shelled the Russian White House, the symbol of Russian independence from communist rule. The parliament building had been seized by Yeltsin opponents led by Ruslan Khasbulatov and Alexander Rutskoi, who in the August 1992 coup had stood with Yeltsin on the White House balcony as he proclaimed that Russia should not submit to the coup plotters' attempts to turn back history. These former-allies-turned-foes reacted to Yeltsin's Sept 21 decision to dissolve the Russian parliament by seizing the parliament building. Yeltsin and his supporters succeeded in isolating them inside, cutting electricity and the flow of information to the building. But Rutskoi urged his followers to seize the Kremlin and other institutions, precipitating a day of bloody fighting in the streets of Moscow before the attackers retreated back into the White House.

BIRTHDAYS TODAY

Michael David (Mike) Adamle, 49, sportscaster, former football player, born Euclid, OH, Oct 4, 1949.
Armand Assante, 49, actor (*Belizaire the Cajun, The Mambo Kings, Fatal Instinct*), born New York, NY, Oct 4, 1949.
Clifton Davis, 53, singer, actor ("That's My Mama," "Amen"), composer, born Chicago, IL, Oct 4, 1945.
Chuck Hagel, 52, US Senator (R, Nebraska), born North Platte, NE, Oct 4, 1946.
Charlton Heston, 76, actor (*The Ten Commandments, Ben-Hur, Planet of the Apes*), born Evanston, IL, Oct 4, 1922.
Jan Murray (Murry Janofsky), 81, comedian (emcee of "Dollar a Second," "Treasure Hunt"), born New York, NY, Oct 4, 1917.
Buddy Roemer, 55, former Governor of Louisiana (D), born Shreveport, LA, Oct 4, 1943.
Susan Sarandon (born Susan Tomaling), 52, actress (Oscar for *Dead Man Walking; Atlantic City, Thelma and Louise, Lorenzo's Oil*), born New York, NY, Oct 4, 1946.
Alicia Silverstone, 22, actress (*Phenomenon, Born on the Fourth of July*), born San Francisco, CA, Oct 4, 1976.
Alvin Toffler, 70, author (*Future Shock, Power Shift*), born New York, NY, Oct 4, 1928.

OCTOBER 5 — MONDAY

Day 278 — 87 Remaining

ARTHUR, CHESTER ALAN: BIRTH ANNIVERSARY. Oct 5. The 21st president of the US, Chester Alan Arthur, was born at Fairfield, VT, Oct 5, 1830, and succeeded to the presidency following the death of James A. Garfield. Term of office: Sept 20, 1881–Mar 3, 1885. Arthur was not successful in obtaining the Republican party's nomination for the following term. He died at New York, NY, Nov 18, 1886.

BUFFALO ROUND-UP. Oct 5–8. Custer, SD. To round up, brand and separate 1,500 buffalo before auction in November. Est attendance: 4,000. For info: Craig Pugsley, Custer State Park, HC 83, Box 70, Custer, SD 57730. Phone: (605) 255-4515. Fax: (605) 255-4460.

CHIEF JOSEPH SURRENDER: ANNIVERSARY. Oct 5, 1877. After a 1,700-mile retreat, Chief Joseph and the Nez Perce Indians surrendered to US Cavalry troops at Bear's Paw near Chinook, MT, on Oct 5, 1877. Chief Joseph made his famous speech of surrender, "From where the sun now stands, I will fight no more forever."

★**CHILD HEALTH DAY.** Oct 5. Presidential Proclamation always issued for first Monday of October. Proclamation has been issued since 1928. In 1959 Congress changed celebration day from May 1 to the present observance (Pub Res No. 46 of May 18, 1928, and PL86–352 of Sept 22, 1959).

CHILDREN'S DAY. Oct 5. Established by the United Nations and observed on the first Monday in October.

CIVIL WAR "SUBMARINE" ATTACK: ANNIVERSARY. Oct 5, 1863. In an attempt to disrupt the Union blockade of Charleston Harbor, the Confederate semi-submersible *David* rammed the Federal ironclad *New Ironsides* with a spar torpedo on Oct 5, 1863. This was the first successful Southern attack using a submersible craft. Although both sides experimented with submarine warfare during the Civil War, the results were far from encouraging, as the submarines caused more fatalities to their own crews than to the opposing side.

DOLLYWOOD HARVEST CELEBRATION. Oct 5–Nov 5 (closed Thursdays). Dollywood, Pigeon Forge, TN. The oldest, largest and only authentic outdoor harvest festival comes alive to celebrate the fall season in the Smokies. For info: Dollywood, 1020 Dollywood Ln, Pigeon Forge, TN 37863. Phone: (423) 428-9488 or (800) DOLLYWOOD.

EDWARDS, JONATHAN: BIRTH ANNIVERSARY. Oct 5, 1703. Theologian and leader of the "Great Awakening," the religious revival in the colonies, born at East Windsor, CT. He later became president of the college of Princeton. Edwards died at Princeton, NJ, Mar 22, 1758, when he contracted smallpox from an inoculation.

ENRICO FERMI ATOMIC POWER PLANT ACCIDENT: ANNIVERSARY. Oct 5. A radiation alarm and Class I alert at 3:09 PM, EST, on Oct 5, 1966, signaled a problem at the Enrico Fermi Atomic Power Plant, Lagoona Beach, near Monroe, MI. The accident was contained, but nearly a decade was required to complete the decommissioning and disassembly of the plant.

FESTIVAL IN THE SCHOOLS. Oct 5–9 (tentative). Nashville, and Davidson County, TN, public and private schools. An artist-in-residence program brings area authors, storytellers, poets, songwriters, illustrators and cartoonists into classrooms to talk to children about their work. Est attendance: 6,000. For info: Galyn Martin, Program Officer, Tennessee Humanities Council, 1003 18th Ave S, Nashville, TN 37212. Phone: (615) 320-7001 ext 15. Fax: (615) 321-4586.

GODDARD, ROBERT HUTCHINGS: BIRTH ANNIVERSARY. Oct 5, 1882. The "father of the Space Age." Born at Worcester, MA. Largely ignored or ridiculed during his lifetime because of his dreams of rocket travel, including travel to other planets. Launched a liquid-fuel-powered rocket on Mar 16, 1926, at Auburn, MA. Died Aug 10, 1945. See also: "Goddard Day" (Mar 16) and "Anniversary Day" (Oct 19).

HARVEST MOON. Oct 5. So called because the full moon nearest the autumnal equinox extends the hours of light into the evening and helps the harvester with his long day's work. Moon enters Full Moon phase at 4:12 PM, EDT.

HASENFUS, EUGENE, CAPTURED: ANNIVERSARY. Oct 5, 1986. A plane carrying arms for the Nicaraguan rebels (contras) was shot down over Nicaragua on Oct 4. The only survivor was Eugene Hasenfus, ex-US Marine, of Marinette, WI, who parachuted from the doomed plane and was captured by Nicaraguan Sandinistas the following day. The US administration at first denied "any link" to the mission. Hasenfus was put on trial for violating Nicaraguan security laws. He was convicted and sentenced to 30 years in prison on Nov 15, 1986. On request of President Daniel Ortega, the Nicaraguan National Assembly pardoned Hasenfus on Dec 17, 1986, and he was flown back to the US. This episode commenced the unravelling and exposure of covert operations and possible violations of US law which in turn led to Congressional "Iran Contra" hearings and investigation by a special prosecutor.

October 1998

S	M	T	W	T	F	S
				1	2	3
4	5	6	7	8	9	10
11	12	13	14	15	16	17
18	19	20	21	22	23	24
25	26	27	28	29	30	31

KOREA: CHUSOK. Oct 5. Gala celebration by Koreans everywhere. Autumn harvest thanksgiving moon festival. Observed on 15th day of eighth lunar month (eighth full moon of lunar calendar) each year. Koreans pay homage to ancestors and express gratitude to guarding spirits for another year of rich crops. A time to visit tombs, leave food and prepare for coming winter season. Traditional food is "moon cake," made on eve of Chusok, with rice, chestnuts and jujube fruits. Games, dancing and gift exchanges. Observed since Silla Dynasty (beginning of First Millennium).

MOON FESTIVAL or MID-AUTUMN FESTIVAL. Oct 5. This festival, observed on the 15th day of the eighth moon of the lunar calendar year, is called by different names in different places, but is widely recognized throughout the Far East, including People's Republic of China, Taiwan, Korea, Singapore and Hong Kong. An important harvest festival at the time the moon is brightest, it is also a time for homage to ancestors. Special harvest foods are eaten, especially "moon cakes."

MOON PHASE: FULL MOON. Oct 5. Moon enters Full Moon phase at 4:12 PM, EDT.

NATIONAL CUSTOMER SERVICE WEEK. Oct 5–9. A weeklong opportunity for businesses to focus on the importance of the customer and the customer service profession. For info: Carrie Collins, Intl Customer Service Assn, 401 N Michigan Ave, Chicago, IL 60611-4267. Phone: (800) 360-4272. Email: icsa@sba.com. WWW: http://www.icsa.com

PEOPLE'S REPUBLIC OF CHINA: MID-AUTUMN FESTIVAL. Oct 5. To worship the moon god. According to folk legend this day is also the birthday of the earth god T'u-ti Kung. The festival indicates the year's hard work in the fields will soon end with the harvest. People express gratitude to heaven as represented by the moon and earth as symbolized by the earth god for all good things from the preceding year. 15th day of eighth month of Chinese lunar calendar.

PERIGEAN SPRING TIDES. Oct 5–6. Spring tides, the highest possible tides, occur when New Moon or Full Moon takes place within 24 hours of the moment the Moon is nearest Earth (perigee) in its monthly orbit, on Oct 6, at 9 AM, EDT.

"SCHLITZ PLAYHOUSE OF STARS" TV PREMIERE: ANNIVERSARY. Oct 5, 1951. This half-hour dramatic anthology on CBS gave many actors their first dramatic or TV role, including Amanda Blake (first major TV role), Lee Van Cleef (first major TV role), James Dean (last dramatic TV appearance), Gene Kelly (TV dramatic debut) and Janet Leigh (first dramatic American TV role). For several seasons Irene Dunne was the host; Robert Paige succeeded her.

SPACE MILESTONE: *CHALLENGER*. Oct 5, 1984. Space shuttle *Challenger* makes sixth mission with crew of seven, including two women. Launched from Kennedy Space Center, FL, on this date and landed there on Oct 13, 1984. Kathryn D. Sullivan became the first American woman to walk in space.

STONE, THOMAS: DEATH ANNIVERSARY. Oct 5, 1787. Signer of the Declaration of Independence, born 1743 (exact date unknown) in Charles County, MD. Died at Alexandria, VA, at about age 44.

SUKKOT, SUCCOTH or FEAST OF TABERNACLES, FIRST DAY. Oct 5. Hebrew calendar date: Tishri 15, 5759, begins nine-day festival in commemoration of Jewish people's 40 years of wandering in the desert and thanksgiving for the fall harvest. This high holiday season closes with Shemini Atzeret (see entry on Oct 12) and Simchat Torah (see entry on Oct 13).

SUPREME COURT 1998–1999 TERM BEGINS. Oct 5. Traditionally, the Supreme Court's annual term begins on the first Monday in October and continues with seven two-week sessions of oral arguments. Between the sessions are six recesses during which the opinions are written by the Justices. Ordinarily, all cases are decided by the following June or July.

TECUMSEH: DEATH ANNIVERSARY. Oct 5, 1813. Shawnee Indian chief and orator, born at Old Piqua near Springfield, OH, in March 1768. Tecumseh is regarded as one of the greatest of American Indians. He came to prominence between the years 1799 and 1804 as a powerful orator, defending his people against whites. He denounced as invalid all treaties by which Indians ceded their lands and condemned the chieftains who had entered into such agreements. With his brother Tenskwatawa, the Prophet, he established a town on the Tippecanoe River near Lafayette, IN, and then embarked on a mission to organize an Indian confederation to stop white encroachment. Although he advocated peaceful methods and negotiation, he did not rule out war as a last resort as he visited tribes throughout the country. While he was away, William Henry Harrison defeated the Prophet at the Battle of Tippecanoe on Nov 7, 1811, and burned the town. Tecumseh organized a large force of Indian warriors and assisted the British in the War of 1812. Tecumseh was defeated and killed at the Battle of the Thames on Oct 5, 1813.

TELLER APPRECIATION WEEK. Oct 5–10. An opportunity for bank management to express appreciation to the ever-pleasant and hard-working tellers who provide services to our valued customers. Expect to see flowers at the teller stations, cakes and other treats in the breakroom and expressions of thanks all around. A great time for customers to write a note of appreciation to their favorite tellers. For info: Easy Systems, Inc, 9757 NE Juanita Dr, Ste 304, Kirkland, WA 98034. Phone: (425) 821-8697. WWW: http://www.easysystems.com

UNITED NATIONS: WORLD HABITAT DAY. Oct 5. The United Nations General Assembly, by a resolution of Dec 17, 1985, has designated the first Monday of October each year as World Habitat Day. The first observance of this day, Oct 5, 1986, marked the 10th anniversary of the first international conference on the subject. (Habitat: United Nations Conference on Human Settlements, Vancouver, Canada, 1976.) Info from: United Nations, Dept of Public Info, Public Inquiries Unit, Rm GA-57, New York, NY 10017. Phone: (212) 963-4475. Fax: (212) 963-0071. Email: inquiries@un.org.

"YOU BET YOUR LIFE" TV PREMIERE: ANNIVERSARY. Oct 5, 1950. This funny game show began on radio in 1947 and moved to TV with Groucho Marx as the host and George Fenneman as the announcer and scorekeeper. Players tried to answer questions in the category of their choice, but Groucho's improvised interviews stole the show. Many unusual guests appeared, both professional and nonprofessional (including Phyllis Diller and Candice Bergen, who would later become famous). Players could also win money by uttering the secret word, an everyday word suspended above the stage on a duck that dropped when the word was spoken. This was one of the few shows to be filmed, because the interviews needed to be edited. Two short-lived revivals of the series aired, with Buddy Hackett as host and Ron Husmann as announcer in 1980, and with Bill Cosby in the 1990s.

"ZANE GREY THEATER" TV PREMIERE: ANNIVERSARY. Oct 5, 1956. Officially titled "Dick Powell's Zane Grey Theater," this western anthology series was hosted by Powell and featured both stories by Grey and original telecasts. Powell occasionally starred in an episode. Guest stars included Hedy Lamarr (in her only dramatic TV role), Ginger Rogers, Claudette Colbert and Esther Williams.

BIRTHDAYS TODAY

Karen Allen, 47, actress (*The Wanderers, Raiders of the Lost Ark, Starman*), born Carrollton, IL, Oct 5, 1951.

Michael Andretti, 36, race car driver, son of Mario Andretti, born Oct 5, 1962.

Raymond Lester ("Trace") Armstrong, 33, football player, born Bethesda, MD, Oct 5, 1965.

Jeff Conaway, 48, actor ("Taxi," *Grease*), born New York, NY, Oct 5, 1950.

Bill Dana, 74, actor, comedian ("The Steve Allen Show," "The Bill Dana Show"), born Quincy, MA, Oct 5, 1924.

Laura Davies, 35, golfer, 1994 LPGA Championship winner, born Coventry, England, Oct 5, 1963.

Bob Geldof, 47, singer, songwriter (lead singer and songwriter of Boomtown Rats), born Dublin, Ireland, Oct 5, 1951.

Vaclav Havel, 62, dramatist, President of the Czech Republic, born Prague, Czechoslovakia, Oct 5, 1936.

Grant Henry Hill, 26, basketball player, born Dallas, TX, Oct 5, 1972.

Glynis Johns, 75, actress (*Mary Poppins, The Ref, A Little Night Music*), born Pretoria, South Africa, Oct 5, 1923.

Steve Miller, 55, musician, singer (Steve Miller Band; "The Joker," "Abracadabra"), born Dallas, TX, Oct 5, 1943.

Walter Dale Miller, 73, former governor of South Dakota (R), born New Underwood, SD, Oct 5, 1925.

OCTOBER 6 — TUESDAY

Day 279 — 86 Remaining

AMERICAN LIBRARY ASSOCIATION FOUNDING: ANNIVERSARY. Oct 6. Founded at Philadelphia, PA, Oct 6, 1876.

EL-SADAT, ANWAR: ASSASSINATION ANNIVERSARY. Oct 6, 1981. Egyptian president and Nobel Peace Prize recipient Anwar el-Sadat was killed by assassins at Cairo while he was reviewing a military parade commemorating the 1973 Egyptian-Israeli War. At least eight other persons were reported killed in the attack on Sadat. Anwar el-Sadat was born Dec 25, 1918, at Mit Abu Al-Kom, a village near the Nile River delta.

IRELAND: IVY DAY. Oct 6. The anniversary of the death of Irish nationalist leader and Home Rule advocate Charles Stewart Parnell (q.v.) is observed, especially in Ireland, as Ivy Day. A sprig of ivy is worn on the lapel to remember Parnell. James Joyce's short story "Ivy Day in the Committee Room," published in the collection titled *Dubliners*, addresses this event.

LIND, JENNY: BIRTH ANNIVERSARY. Oct 6. Swedish opera singer born at Stockholm, Sweden, Oct 6, 1820. She died at Malvern, England, Nov 2, 1887.

NATIONAL GERMAN-AMERICAN DAY. Oct 6. Celebration of German heritage and contributions German Americans have made to the building of the nation. A Presidential Proclamation has been issued each year since 1987. Annually, Oct 6. For info: Society for German-American Studies, University of Cincinnati, PO Box 20113, Cincinnati, OH 45221. Phone: (513) 556-1955. Fax: (513) 556-2113.

NOBEL CONFERENCE XXXIV. Oct 6–7. Gustavus Adolphus College, St. Peter, MN. Annual two-day scientific symposium (34th year), and the only one sanctioned by the Nobel Foundation, Stockholm. Annually, the first Tuesday and Wednesday in October. Est attendance: 5,000. For info: Dean Wahlund, Dir of Public Affairs, Gustavus Adolphus College, 800 W College Ave, St. Peter, MN 56082-1498. Phone: (507) 933-7550.

"THE PEOPLE'S CHOICE" TV PREMIERE: ANNIVERSARY. Oct 6, 1955. This half-hour sitcom starred Jackie Cooper as Socrates (Sock) Miller, a government naturalist who becomes a politician and a real estate agent in New City, OK. Pat Breslin starred as Sock's girlfriend, Amanda (Mandy) Peoples; Paul Maxey as John Peoples, New City's mayor; Margaret Irving as Sock's Aunt Gus; Leonid Kinskey as the artist Pierre; and Dick Wesson as Sock's friend Rollo. A unique characteristic of the show was a "talking" basset hound named Cleo (voice of Mary Jane Croft) who made comments during the episode.

PHYSICIAN ASSISTANT (PA) DAY. Oct 6. To acknowledge the unique contribution of Physician Assistants to medical care on the anniversary of the graduation of the first class of PAs from Duke University. For info: Nancy Hughes, VP of Info Research Services, American Academy of Physician Assistants, 950 N Washington St, Alexandria, VA 22314-1534. Phone: (703) 836-2272. Fax: (703) 684-1924. Email: aapa@aapa.org. WWW: http://www.aapa/org

SEIBERT, FLORENCE: BIRTH ANNIVERSARY. Oct 6, 1897. American physician Florence B. Seibert was born at Easton, PA. She developed the test for tuberculosis that has been adopted by the US and the World Health Organization used worldwide. She died on Aug 23, 1991, at St. Petersburg, FL.

SZYMANOWSKI, KAROL: BIRTH ANNIVERSARY. Oct 6, 1882. Birthday of one of Poland's outstanding composers, whose art has played a role in Polish 20th-century music. Born at Timoshovka, Ukraine, on Oct 6, 1882. Died on Mar 28, 1937.

TENNYSON, ALFRED, LORD: DEATH ANNIVERSARY. Oct 6, 1892. English poet, born at Somersby, Lincolnshire, England, on Aug 6, 1809, the fourth son of a rector. At Trinity College, Cambridge, he became part of a group of young men including Arthur Hallam, whose early death prompted Tennyson to write his elegiac poem "In Memoriam." His most celebrated works include the poems "The Lady of Shalott" and "The Lotus-eaters" and the verse novelettes *Maud, Enoch Arden, Locksley Hall Sixty Years After* and *The Idylls of the King*. Tennyson was named Poet Laureate of England in 1850 to succeed William Wordsworth, and he became a peer in 1884. Died at Aldworth, Sussex, Oct 6, 1892.

WESTINGHOUSE, GEORGE: BIRTH ANNIVERSARY. Oct 6, 1846. Engineer and inventor of the air brake for railroads, born at Central Bridge, NY. He was the first employer to give his employees paid vacations. Westinghouse died at New York, NY, Mar 12, 1914.

BIRTHDAYS TODAY

Shana Alexander, 73, journalist (formerly of "60 Minutes" Point-Counterpoint segment), author, born Boston, MA, Sept 6, 1925.
Britt Ekland, 56, actress (*The Night They Raided Minsky's*), born Stockholm, Sweden, Oct 6, 1942.
Thor Heyerdahl, 84, anthropologist, explorer, author (*Kon Tiki*), born Larvik, Norway, Oct 6, 1914.
Elisabeth Shue, 35, actress (*Adventures in Babysitting, Leaving Las Vegas*), born Wilmington, DE, Oct 6, 1963.
Ruben Angel Sierra, 33, baseball player, born Rio Piedras, Puerto Rico, Oct 6, 1965.
Fred Travalena, 56, actor ("Keep On Truckin'," "ABC Comedy Hour"), born New York, NY, Oct 6, 1942.
Stephanie Zimbalist, 42, actress (Laura Holt on "Remington Steele"), born Encino, CA, Oct 6, 1956.

October 1998

S	M	T	W	T	F	S
				1	2	3
4	5	6	7	8	9	10
11	12	13	14	15	16	17
18	19	20	21	22	23	24
25	26	27	28	29	30	31

OCTOBER 7 — WEDNESDAY

Day 280 — 85 Remaining

"THE FRANK SINATRA SHOW" TV PREMIERE: ANNIVERSARY. Oct 7, 1950. Crooner Frank Sinatra's first series was a musical variety show featuring regulars Erin O'Brien and comic Ben Blue. However, this show never became popular, and during its last season it was cut from an hour to 30 minutes and could not compete with "The Texaco Star Theater," the most popular show of the time.

GERMANY: FRANKFURT BOOK FAIR: 50th ANNIVERSARY. Oct 7–12. Fairgrounds, Frankfurt. World's largest international book fair; also important event for electronic media. Best place for international rights and licenses. Open to trade for six days and to the public for two. Est attendance: 320,000. For info: Ausstellungs-und Messe (Frankfurt Book Fair), Postfach 100 116, D 60001 Frankfurt am Main, Germany.
Email: weber@book-fair.com.
WWW: http://www.frankfurt-book-fair.com

MISSISSIPPI STATE FAIR. Oct 7–18. Jackson, MS. Features nightly professional entertainment, livestock show, midway carnival, domestic art exhibits. Est attendance: 620,000. For info: Mississippi Fair Commission, PO Box 892, Jackson, MS 39205. Phone: (601) 961-4000. Fax: (601) 354-6545.

WALLACE, HENRY AGARD: BIRTH ANNIVERSARY. Oct 7, 1888. 33rd vice president of the US (1941–45) born at Adair County, IA, Oct 7, 1888. Died at Danbury, CT, Nov 18, 1965.

WISE, THOMAS JAMES: BIRTH ANNIVERSARY. Oct 7. English bibliophile and literary forger, born at Gravesend, Oct 7, 1859. One of England's most distinguished bibliographic experts, he was revealed, in 1934, to have forged dozens of "first editions" and "unique" publications over a period of more than 20 years. Many of them had been sold at high prices to collectors and libraries. The forgeries in some cases purported to predate the real first editions. Wise, whose health was broken when the exposure came, died at Hampstead, England, May 13, 1937.

"YOUR HIT PARADE" TV PREMIERE: ANNIVERSARY. Oct 7, 1950. "Your Hit Parade" began as a radio show in 1935. When it finally made it to TV, the format was simple: the show's cast performed the week's top musical hits. To sustain interest, since many of the same songs appeared weekly, eye-catching production sequences were created. "YHP" was the starting point for many famous choreographers and dancers, including Tony Charmoli, Ernie Flatt, Peter Gennaro and Bob Fosse. Regulars included Dorothy Collins, Eileen Wilson, Snooky Lanson and Sue Bennett. The show was overhauled many times and switched networks before leaving the air in 1959. A summer revival in 1974 was short-lived. See also: " 'Your Hit Parade' Radio Premiere" (Apr 12).

BIRTHDAYS TODAY

June Allyson (Ella Geisman), 81, actress (*Little Women, The Shrike*, "The June Allyson Show"), born Lucerne, NY, Oct 7, 1917.

Imamu Amiri Baraka (Leroi Jones), 64, poet, dramatist, born Newark, NJ, Oct 7, 1934.

Charles Dutoit, 62, Swiss conductor, born Lausanne, Switzerland, Oct 7, 1936.

Thomas Keneally, 63, novelist, born New South Wales, Australia, Oct 7, 1935.

Yo-Yo Ma, 43, cellist, born Paris, France, Oct 7, 1955.

Al Martino (Alfred Cini), 71, actor, singer (*Hello Dolly, Phantom of the Opera*), born Philadelphia, PA, Oct 7, 1927.

John Mellencamp, 47, singer (*American Fool, Uh-Huh*), born Seymour, IN, Oct 7, 1951.

Oliver Laurence North, 55, US Marine Corps Lieutenant Colonel, center of Iran-Contra controversy, born San Antonio, TX, Oct 7, 1943.

OCTOBER 8 — THURSDAY

Day 281 — 84 Remaining

ALVIN C. YORK DAY. Oct 8. On this day in 1918, Sergeant Alvin C. York (in the Argonne Forest, France, and separated from his patrol) killed 20 enemy soldiers and captured a hill, 132 enemy soldiers and 35 machine guns. He was awarded the US Medal of Honor and French Croix de Guerre. Ironically, York had petitioned for exemption from the draft as a conscientious objector, but was turned down by his local draft board.

AUTUMN GLORY FESTIVAL. Oct 8–11. Oakland, MD. Foliage celebration with state banjo and fiddle contests, parade, arts and crafts and antique show. Est attendance: 50,000. For info: Deep Creek Lake–Garrett County Promotion Council, Festival HQ, Court House, 200 S Third St, Oakland, MD 21550. Phone: (301) 334-1948. Fax: (301) 334-1919.
Email: GCTourism@garrett.NCIN.com.
WWW: http://www.gcnet.net/gctourism/gct.html

FALL BLUEGRASS FESTIVAL. Oct 8–11. Spirit of the Suwannee Music Park, Live Oak, FL. Weekend filled with bluegrass music and other great activities. Est attendance: 7,000. For info: Spirit of Suwannee Music Park, 3076 95th Dr, Live Oak, FL 32060. Phone: (904) 364-1683. Fax: (904) 364-2998. Email: spirit@musicliveshere.com.
WWW: http://www.musicliveshere.com

GREAT CHICAGO FIRE: ANNIVERSARY. Oct 8, 1871. Great fire of Chicago began, according to legend, when Mrs O'Leary's cow kicked over the lantern in her barn on DeKoven St. The fire leveled 3½ sq miles, destroying 17,450 buildings and leaving 98,500 people homeless and about 250 people dead. Financially, the loss was $200 million. On the same day a fire destroyed the entire town of Peshtigo, WI, killing more than 1,100 people.

JERUSALEM RIOT: ANNIVERSARY. Oct 8, 1990. When a crowd of Palestinian protesters gathered around Jerusalem's Temple Mount grew violent and began throwing stones, police responded by firing into the crowd, killing at least 17 Arabs and wounding over 100 more. Jerusalem had not seen such bloodshed since the 1967 Mideast war, when Isreal took the eastern part of the city.

KING BISCUIT BLUES FESTIVAL. Oct 8–11. Downtown Historic District, Helena, AR. 13th annual festival. Four days of the best in Delta Blues. Many of the Blues "Greats" got their start in Helena on the 1940s "King Biscuit Time" radio show and return to perform. "King Biscuit Time" first aired on station KFFA in Helena in 1941. Other activities include gospel music stage, 5K run, arm wrestling, barbecue cook-off, arts and crafts booth and games and Mississippi riverboat cruise. Annually, the second weekend in October, Columbus Day weekend. Est attendance: 80,000. For info: Main Street Helena, PO Box 247, Helena, AR 72342. Phone: (501) 338-8798. Fax: (501) 338-7397. WWW: http://www.kingbiscuitfest.org

NATIONAL DEPRESSION SCREENING DAY. Oct 8. To increase the awareness that many suffer from depression, but it can be treated. Annually, the Thursday of the first full week in October. For info: National Mental Illness Screening Project, One Washington St, Ste 304, Wellesley Hills, MA 02181-1706. Phone: (617) 239-0071.

NATIONAL DESSERT DAY. Oct 8. To focus on the pleasures of sweet and fanciful desserts. Annually, the second Thursday of October. Est attendance: 250. For info: The Alden Group, Martini & Rossi Asti, 52 Vanderbilt Ave, New York, NY 10017. Phone: (212) 867-6400.

NORMAN ROCKWELL'S SELF-PORTRAIT: 60th ANNIVERSARY. Oct 8, 1938. For the *Saturday Evening Post* cover for this date Norman Rockwell chose to portray himself in a quandary he frequently had to grapple with—trying to come up with a cover for the *Post* on deadline.

OZZIE AND HARRIET SHOW RADIO DEBUT: ANNIVERSARY. Oct 8. On their ninth wedding anniversary, Oct 8, 1944, Ozzie and Harriet Nelson made their CBS Radio debut in "The Adventures of Ozzie and Harriet." Although their sons David and Ricky were referred to frequently on air and eventually played by others, it was not until Feb 20, 1949, that David (age 12) and Rick (age 8) first appeared playing themselves on the show. "The Adventures of Ozzie and Harriet" hit television airwaves Oct 3, 1952, on ABC. The show was cancelled at the end of the 1965-66 season after 435 episodes, 409 of which were in black and white and 26 in color.

PERU: DAY OF THE NAVY. Oct 8. Public holiday in Peru.

PESHTIGO FOREST FIRE: ANNIVERSARY. Oct 8, 1871. One of the most disastrous forest fires in history began at Peshtigo, WI, on this day, the same day the Great Chicago Fire began. The Wisconsin fire burned across six counties, killing more than 1,100 persons.

"THE RAY BOLGER SHOW" TV PREMIERE: 45th ANNIVERSARY. Oct 8, 1953. Originally titled "Where's Raymond?," the format of this half-hour sitcom allowed Bolger to play a character like himself. With Bolger playing Ray Wallace, a Broadway star living in the suburbs, there was plenty of music, dancing and comedy. The cast included Richard Erdman, Allyn Joslyn, Claire Dubrey, Frances Karath and Betty Lynn. The second season's cast included Bolger, Erdman, Marjie Millar, Charles Cantor, Christine Nelson, Sylvia Lewis and Maureen Stevenson.

RICKENBACKER, EDWARD V.: BIRTH ANNIVERSARY. Oct 8, 1890. American aviator, auto racer, war hero. Born Oct 8, 1890. Died July 23, 1973.

SCHUTZ, HEINRICH: BIRTH ANNIVERSARY. Oct 8, 1585. German musician and composer sometimes called the father of German music. Born at Kostritz, Saxony, on Oct 8, 1585. Schutz died at Dresden on Nov 6, 1672. His works enjoyed renewed attention on the occasions of the bicentennials (1885) and tricentennials (1985) of two of his most devoted followers: George Frederick Handel and Johann Sebastian Bach.

SOUTH CAROLINA STATE FAIR. Oct 8–18. Columbia, SC. Conklin Shows, musical entertainment, food booths and children's activities. Est attendance: 576,000. For info: South Carolina State Fair, PO Box 393, Columbia, SC 29202. Phone: (803) 799-3387. Fax: (803) 799-1760. Email: geninfo@scsn.net.

TRAIL OF TERROR. Oct 8–11, 15–18, 22–25, 29–31. Renaissance Festival Grounds, Shakopee, MN. A family event featuring a 3/4-mile maze through spooky corridors and haunted rooms. The night is not complete without a Boo-Bash featuring games, rides, treats and much more. Est attendance: 25,000. For info: Mid-America Festivals, 1244 S Canterbury Rd, Ste 306, Shakopee, MN 55379. Phone: (800) 966-8215 or (612) 445-7361. Fax: (612) 445-7380.

BIRTHDAYS TODAY

Rona Barrett, 62, gossip columnist, born New York, NY, Oct 8, 1936.

David Carradine, 58, actor (*Boxcar Bertha*; "Kung-Fu" series), born Hollywood, CA, Oct 8, 1940.

Chevy Chase (Cornelius Crane), 55, comedian, actor ("Saturday Night Live," *Caddyshack*), born New York, NY, Oct 8, 1943.

Clodagh (Clodagh Aubry), 61, designer, born Galway, Ireland, Oct 8, 1937.

Paul Hogan, 59, actor, writer (*Crocodile Dundee, Crocodile Dundee II*), born Lightning Ridge, Australia, Oct 8, 1939.

Jesse Jackson, 57, civil rights leader ("I am somebody"; "Keep hope alive"), DC "Shadow" Senator, born Greenville, NC, Oct 8, 1941.

Sarah Purcell, 50, TV personality ("Real People"), born Richmond, IN, Oct 8, 1948.

Faith Ringgold, 68, artist, writer (*Tar Beach, My Dream of Martin Luther King*), born New York, NY, Oct 8, 1930.

Rashaan Salaam, 24, football player, born San Diego, CA, Oct 8, 1974.

Sigourney (Susan) Weaver, 49, actress (*Ghostbusters, Gorillas in the Mist, Aliens*), born New York, NY, Oct 8, 1949.

OCTOBER 9 — FRIDAY

Day 282 — 83 Remaining

ALABAMA NATIONAL FAIR. Oct 9–17. Garrett Coliseum/Fairgrounds, Montgomery, AL. A midway filled with exciting rides and games, arts and crafts, exhibits, racing pigs, a circus, a petting zoo, food and entertainment. Est attendance: 226,000. For info: Hazel Ashmore, PO Box 3304, Montgomery, AL 36109-0304. Phone: (334) 272-6831. Fax: (334) 272-6835.

ALGONQUIN MILL FALL FESTIVAL. Oct 9–11. Four miles south of Carrollton, OH. Presented by the Carroll County Historical Society. The event is an 1800s pioneer festival. Features include steam-powered grist and sawmill in operation. Also featured are antique tools and farm machinery and quilting, spinning and weaving demonstrations. Log buildings include a book store, print shop, souvenir shop and a two-story home. A one-room school, railroad station and stage coach station are on exhibit. More than 70 quality craftsmen will be demonstrating and selling their products. Est attendance: 35,000. For info: Jeanie Stevens, 3007 Mayham Rd NE, Carrollton, OH 44615. Phone: (330) 627-2946.

AMERICA'S SEXY WIVES CONTEST. Oct 9. Radio contest to pick the sexiest wife in America. Wives will be judged on their commitment to their marriages; the reason they feel they represent sexiness; and their creative expression. Annually, the second Friday in October. For info: Rose Smith, Pres, Institute of Monogamy, 4900 Mesa Bonita Ct NW, Albuquerque, NM 87120. Phone: (505) 899-3121.

APPLE BUTTER MAKIN' DAYS. Oct 9–11. Mt Vernon, MO. A huge festival highlighting the making of apple butter in large copper kettles on the courthouse lawn. Also, 375 crafters displaying and selling handmade goods, free entertainment all three days, apple pie eating contest, hairy legs contest, log sawing contest, bubble gum blowing contest, nail driving contest, pet parade, terrapin race and fiddlers. Annually, the second full weekend in October. Est attendance: 45,000. For info: Chamber of Commerce, PO Box 373, Mt Vernon, MO 65712. Phone: (417) 466-7654.

ARKANSAS STATE FAIR AND LIVESTOCK SHOW. Oct 9–18. Barton Coliseum and State Fairground, Little Rock, AR. Est attendance: 400,000. For info: Arkansas State Fair, PO Box 166660, Little Rock, AR 72216. Phone: (501) 372-8341. Fax: (501) 372-4197.

October 1998

S	M	T	W	T	F	S
				1	2	3
4	5	6	7	8	9	10
11	12	13	14	15	16	17
18	19	20	21	22	23	24
25	26	27	28	29	30	31

AUTUMN FESTIVAL. Oct 9–11 (also Oct 16–18). Ludington, MI. Pumpkin patch, haunted forest, hayrides, Moonlight Madness Sale. Events are held at different times and locations, so call or write for specifics. Est attendance: 12,000. For info: Ludington Area Chamber of Commerce, 5827 W US 10, Ludington, MI 49431. Phone: (800) 842-4600. Fax: (616) 845-6857. Email: suelacvb@aol.com. WWW: http://www.ludingtoncvb.com

BANNEKER, BENJAMIN: DEATH ANNIVERSARY. Oct 9, 1806. American astronomer, mathematician, clockmaker, surveyor and almanac author, called "first black man of science." Born near Baltimore, MD, in 1736. Died at Baltimore County, MD. Took part in original survey of city of Washington. Benjamin Banneker's *Almanac* was published 1792–97. A fire that started during his funeral destroyed his home, library, notebooks, almanac calculations, clocks and virtually all belongings and documents related to his life.

COLUMBUS DAY FESTIVAL AND HOT-AIR BALLOON REGATTA. Oct 9–11. Downtown square and Industrial Park, Columbus, KS. Hot-Air Balloon Regatta starts with Balloon Glow Friday evening; prizes are awarded for both Saturday and Sunday races. Also, car show, arts and crafts fair, entertainment, children's festival and more. Est attendance: 9,000. For info: Jean Pritchett, Mgr, Columbus Chamber of Commerce, 320 E Maple, Columbus, KS 66725. Phone: (316) 429-1492. Fax: (316) 429-1704.

FALL FESTIVAL (WITH OLE TIME FIDDLERS CONVENTION). Oct 9–18. Georgia Mountain Fairgrounds, Hiawassee, GA. The Fall Music Festival and the Ole Time Fiddlers Convention have been combined into a 10-day event. The first weekend will be the Fall Music Festival with country music, arts and crafts and a carnival. Open invitation to any single performers or bands who wish to participate. Amateur talent. Arts, crafts and carnival continue during the week with the Ole Time Fiddlers Convention the last weekend. Est attendance: 75,000. For info: Hilda Thomason, Fall Festival, PO Box 444, Hiawassee, GA 30546. Phone: (706) 896-4191.

FIREANT FESTIVAL. Oct 9–11. Marshall, TX. Arts and crafts, chili cook-off, Tour de FireAnt bike ride, 5K run, fireant calling contest, fireant roundup, rubber chicken chunking, gurning contest (ugly face), Diaper Derby Contest (crawling), parade and street dance. Sponsored by American Cyanamid. Est attendance: 50,000. For info: Pam S. Whisenant, Marshall Chamber of Commerce, PO Box 520, Marshall, TX 75671. Phone: (903) 935-7868. Fax: (903) 935-9982. Email: cvd@internetwork.net.

FORT LIGONIER DAYS. Oct 9–11. Ligonier, PA. Commemorates the Battle of Ligonier. Re-enactments, parade, outdoor entertainment, craft booths and food booths. For info: Julie Donovan, Ligonier Chamber of Commerce, 120 E Main St, Ligonier, PA 15658. Phone: (412) 238-4200. Fax: (412) 238-4610.

GEORGIA NATIONAL FAIR. Oct 9–18. Georgia National Fairgrounds, Perry, GA. Traditional state agricultural fair features thousands of entries in horse, livestock, horticultural, youth, home and fine arts categories. Family entertainment, education and fun. Sponsored by the State of Georgia. Annually, beginning the fifth Friday after Labor Day. Est attendance: 335,000. For info: Georgia National Fair, PO Box 1367, 401 Larry Walker Pkwy, Perry, GA 31069. Phone: (912) 987-3247. Fax: (912) 987-7218. Email: mtreptow@gnat.net. WWW: http://www.gnfa.com

GUMBO FESTIVAL. Oct 9–11. Bridge City, LA. To promote Cajun-French culture and provide the opportunity for people from everywhere to enjoy continuous Cajun entertainment on an outdoor stage and cuisine. Gumbo cooking contests and 5K Bridge Run. Annually, the second weekend in October. Est attendance: 150,000. For info: Rev Msgr J. Anthony Luminais, Pastor, Holy Guardian Angels Church, Box 9069, Bridge City, LA 70096. Phone: (504) 436-4712. Fax: (504) 436-4070.

HERITAGE PARADE AND FESTIVAL. Oct 9–10. Kraemer and Bradford Parks, Placentia, CA. 34th annual parade and fair featuring entertainment, food, game and craft booths. Special car show featured. Annually, the second Saturday of October. Sponsor: Heritage Committee. Est attendance: 10,000. For info: Steve Pischel, City of Placentia, 401 E Chapman Ave, Placentia, CA 92870. Phone: (714) 993-8232. Fax: (714) 961-0283.

HOOD RIVER VALLEY HARVEST FEST. Oct 9–11. Hood River, OR. The valley welcomes visitors for three days of continuous entertainment, crafts, fresh locally grown produce and fruits. 16th annual festival. Est attendance: 30,000. For info: Hood River Chamber of Commerce, 405 Portway Dr, Hood River, OR 97031. Phone: (800) 366-3530.

ICELAND: LEIF ERIKSON DAY. Oct 9. Celebrates discovery of North America in the year 1000 by Norse explorer.

INTERNATIONAL ALAN DAY. Oct 9. Celebrating the Alans of the world, marked by the announcement of "Alan of the Year" and inductees into the "Alan Hall of Fame." The Forum encourages parents to name their children with any of the many forms of the name: Alan, Allan, Allen, Allana, Alaina, Alain, etc. For info: Intl Forum of Alans, PO Box 40, Maplewood, NJ 07040. Phone: (973) 763-6392. Fax: (973) 763-4287.

KOREA: ALPHABET DAY (HANGUL): ANNIVERSARY. Oct 9. Celebrates anniversary of promulgation of Hangul (24-letter phonetic alphabet) by King Sejong of the Yi Dynasty, in 1446.

★**LEIF ERIKSON DAY.** Oct 9. Presidential Proclamation always issued for Oct 9 since 1964 (PL88–566 of Sept 2, 1964) at request.

LENNON, JOHN: BIRTH ANNIVERSARY. Oct 9. John Winston Lennon, English composer, musician, member of "The Beatles," a sensationally popular group of musical performers who captivated audiences first in England and Germany, and later throughout the world. Born at Liverpool, England, Oct 9, 1940. Murdered at New York City, NY, Dec 8, 1980.

LONGHORN WORLD CHAMPIONSHIP RODEO. Oct 9–10 (tentative). Final date available after Dec 1, 1997. Charlotte Coliseum, Charlotte, NC. More than 200 of the best cowboys and cowgirls compete in six professional contests ranging from bronc riding to bull riding for top prize money and world championship points. Featuring colorful opening pageantry and Big, Bad BONUS Bulls. 5th annual. Est attendance: 16,000. For info: W. Bruce Lehrke, Longhorn World Chmpshp Rodeo, Inc, PO Box 70159, Nashville, TN 37207. Phone: (615) 876-1016. Fax: (615) 876-4685. Email: lhrodeo@idt.net.
WWW: http://www.longhornrodeo.com

MEDFORD JAZZ JUBILEE. Oct 9–11. Medford, OR. Twelve nationally known bands will play in five Medford locations. 150 performances along with fun, food and music for all ages. Est attendance: 5,500. For info: Patti Bills, Visitors and Conv Bureau, 101 E 8th St, Medford, OR 97501. Phone: (541) 779-4847 or (800) 469-6307.

MISSION DELORES FOUNDING: ANNIVERSARY. Oct 9. The oldest building in San Francisco, CA. Formerly known as Mission San Francisco de Asis, the mission survived the great earthquake and fire of 1906. Founded Oct 9, 1776.

NATIONAL SCHOOL CELEBRATION. Oct 9. The National School Celebration will provide a high-profile celebration uniting our nation's youth during regular school hours for a patriotic observance. Every school in the nation is invited to participate. This event perpetuates the original spirit of the 1892 National School Celebration declared by President Benjamin Harrison, for which the first Pledge of Allegiance was written. Annually, the second Friday in October. For info: Paula Burton, Pres, Celebration USA, 17853 Santiago Blvd, Ste 107, Villa Park, CA 92667. Phone: (714) 283-1892.

NATIONAL WILD TURKEY CALLING CONTEST AND TURKEY TROT FESTIVAL. Oct 9–11. Town Square, Yellville, AR. 52nd annual. Wild turkey calling contest, turkey shoot, Miss Turkey Trot pageant, turkey dinner, arts, crafts, musical entertainment, Gospel Sing Sunday, parade. Annually, the second weekend in October. Est attendance: 14,000. For info: Chamber of Commerce, PO Box 369, Yellville, AR 72687. Phone: (870) 449-4676.

OZARK TRAIL AND TROUT FESTIVAL. Oct 9–11. Heber Springs, AR. Arts and crafts, pioneer parade, 5K race, fly tying and casting demonstrations, antique car show, children's activities, food concessions and much more. 33rd annual festival. Est attendance: 20,000. For info: Dianne Willams, Exec Dir, Chamber of Commerce, 1001 W Main, Heber Springs, AR 72543. Phone: (501) 362-2444. Fax: (501) 362-9953.
Email: hebercoc@arkansas.net.
WWW: http://www.Heber-Springs.com

PARKE COUNTY COVERED BRIDGE FESTIVAL. Oct 9–18. Rockville, IN. Covered bridge capital of the world, 32 historic covered bridges. Headquarters: Courthouse Lawn, Rockville. Guided bus tours on covered bridge routes. Hundreds of booths of arts, crafts, demonstrations, old-fashioned homemade foods and a farmers' market. Est attendance: 2,000,000. For info: Anne Lynk, Exec Secy, Covered Bridge Capital, PO Box 165, Rockville, IN 47872-0165. Phone: (765) 569-5226. Fax: (765) 569-3900. Email: alynk@ticz.com. WWW: http://www.coverbridges.com

PLANET FRIENDS WEEKS. Oct 9–15. Today's technology has moved children and teens out of their neighborhoods and on to a large multicultural playground called Planet Earth. Planet Friends Week encourages young people to think globally, experiencing new cultures and languages and to create their own network of Planet Friends all over the world. For info: Barbara Fowkes, 479 Grace St, Pittsburgh, PA 15236.

RED WING SHEEP DOG TRIAL. Oct 9–11. Red Wing, MN. Farmers' and ranchers' dogs compete. Est attendance: 700. For info: Charles O'Reilly, Course Dir, Red Wing Sheep Dog Trial Assn, 33933 200 Ave, Red Wing, MN 55066-7204. Phone: (800) 852-4422. Email: oreillyc@aol.com.

RHINELANDER'S OKTOBERFEST. Oct 9–11. Rhinelander, WI. The entire weekend enjoy German music, dancers, food and many activities. Est attendance: 9,000. For info: Rhinelander Area Chamber of Commerce, PO Box 795, Rhinelander, WI 54501. Phone: (800) 236-4386. Fax: (715) 365-7467.

SOUTHERN FESTIVAL OF BOOKS: A CELEBRATION OF THE WRITTEN WORD. Oct 9–10 (tentative). War Memorial, Nashville, TN. To promote reading, writing, the literary arts and a broader understanding of the language and culture of the South, this annual festival will feature readings, talks and panel discussions by up to 200 authors; exhibit booths of publishing companies and bookstores; autographing sessions; a comprehensive children's program; and the Cafe Stage, a performance corner for authors, storytellers and musicians. Est attendance: 30,000. For info: Galyn Martin, Program Officer, Tennessee Humanities Council, 1003 18th Ave S, Nashville, TN 37212. Phone: (615) 320-7001 ext 15. Fax: (615) 321-4586.

SPACE MILESTONE: *SOYUZ 25* (USSR). Oct 9, 1977. Cosmonauts Vladimir Kovalyonok and Valery Ryumin launched. Their intended link with *Salyut 6* was unsuccessful. Craft returned to Earth Oct 11.

STAMP EXPO. Oct 9–11. Quality Hotel, Anaheim, CA. Est attendance: 4,000. For info: Intl Stamp Collectors Society, PO Box 854, Van Nuys, CA 91408. Phone: (818) 997-6496. Fax: (818) 988-4337. Email: iibick@aol.com.
WWW: http://www.4free.com/bick

SUGARLOAF'S FALL TIMONIUM CRAFT FESTIVAL. Oct 9–11. Maryland State Fairgrounds, Timonium, MD. This show, now in its 22nd year, features 400 professional fine artists and craft designers displaying and selling their creations. Craft demonstrations, children's entertainment, live music, food, hourly gift certificate drawings and more. Est attendance: 35,000. For info or application: Sugarloaf Mountain Works, Inc, 200 Orchard Ridge Dr, Ste 215, Gaithersburg, MD 20878. Phone: (800) 210-9900.

"TOPPER" TV PREMIERE: 45th ANNIVERSARY. Oct 9, 1953. In this sitcom a man moves into a new home with his wife, only to discover that it's haunted by ghosts only he can see. Leo G. Carroll starred as Cosmo Topper and Anne Jeffreys and Robert Sterling starred as Marion and George Kirby, who had been killed in a skiing accident and returned to their former home as ghosts. Other cast members included Lee Patrick, Thurston Hall, Edna Skinner and Kathleen Freeman. The show was based on Thorne Smith's novel and used trick photography for some of the ghost scenes.

UGANDA: INDEPENDENCE DAY. Oct 9, 1962. National holiday commemorating achievement of autonomy.

UNITED NATIONS: WORLD POST DAY. Oct 9. An annual special observance of Postal Administrations of the Universal Postal Union (UPU). For info: United Nations, Dept of Public Info, Public Inquiries Unit, Rm GA-57, New York, NY 10017. Phone: (212) 963-4475. Fax: (212) 963-0071.
Email: inquiries@un.org.

VICTORIAN WEEK. Oct 9–18. Cape May, NJ. A 10-day celebration of Cape May's Victorian heritage, with self-guided tours of Victorian homes, antiques and crafts shows, vaudeville show and brass band concert, boisterous sing-alongs, entertaining and educational lectures. Annually, the 10 days beginning the Friday before Columbus Day. Est attendance: 15,000. For info: Mid-Atlantic Center for the Arts, PO Box 340, Cape May, NJ 08204. Phone: (609) 884-5404. Email: mac4arts@algorithms.com. WWW: http://www.beachcomber.com/capemay/mac.html

October 1998

S	M	T	W	T	F	S
				1	2	3
4	5	6	7	8	9	10
11	12	13	14	15	16	17
18	19	20	21	22	23	24
25	26	27	28	29	30	31

BIRTHDAYS TODAY

Scott Bakula, 43, actor ("Quantum Leap," "Murphy Brown"), born St. Louis, MO, Oct 9, 1955.
Jackson Browne, 48, singer, songwriter ("Running on Empty," "Lawyers in Love"), born Heidelberg, Germany, Oct 9, 1950.
Trent Lott, 57, US senator (R, Mississippi), born Duck Hill, MS, Oct 9, 1941.
Russell Myers, 60, cartoonist ("Broom-Hilda"), born Pittsburg, KS, Oct 9, 1938.
Michael Pare, 39, actor (*Streets of Fire, The Philadelphia Experiment*), born Brooklyn, NY, Oct 9, 1959.
Joseph Anthony (Joe) Pepitone, 58, former baseball player, born New York, NY, Oct 9, 1940.
Donald Sinden, 75, actor (*The Day of the Jackal*), born Plymouth, England, Oct 9, 1923.
Michael (Mike) Singletary, 40, former football player, born Houston, TX, Oct 9, 1958.
Robert Wuhl, 47, actor, writer (*Bull Durham, Cobb*), born Union, NJ, Oct 9, 1951.

OCTOBER 10 — SATURDAY

Day 283 — 82 Remaining

AGNEW RESIGNATION: 25th ANNIVERSARY. Oct 10, 1973. Spiro Theodore Agnew became the second person to resign the office of Vice President of the United States. Agnew entered a plea of no contest to a charge of income tax evasion (on contract kickbacks received while he was governor of Maryland and after he became vice president). He was sentenced to pay a $10,000 fine and serve three years probation. On Apr 27, 1981, following a class-action suit, a Maryland circuit court ruled that Agnew must pay the state $248,735 ($147,500 in kickbacks plus $101,235 in interest) for violating the public trust. Agnew was elected vice president twice, serving under President Richard M. Nixon. He died in 1996.

ALL-SPECIES HALLOWEEN GALA. Oct 10–31. St. Louis, MO. An educational program to teach children about local endangered plants and animals and engaging them in creative processes designing costumes for a performance and community-involving conclusion "gala" event. Est attendance: 15,000. For info: Laura Neuman, Alliance for a Livable World, PO Box 63350, St. Louis, MO 63163. Phone: (314) 776-4442. Email: earthdystl@aol.com.

AMERICAN INDIAN GATHERING POW-WOW. Oct 10–11. Community College Beaver County Dome, Monaca, PA. 10th annual. Indian dancing, crafts, traders food and much more. For info: (412) 775-8561 ext 157 or Beaver County Tourist Promotion Agency, 215 B Ninth St, Monaca, PA 15061-2028. Phone: (412) 728-0212. Fax: (412) 728-0456.

ANNUAL ARTS AND CRAFTS FAIR. Oct 10–11. Base Lodge, Jay Peak Ski Resort, Jay, VT. This annual event features more than 60 statewide artisans. The show is nonjuried, providing many local crafters the opportunity to display their wares. Foliage tramway rides, German Bavarian buffet and entertainment are all part of this fall foliage event. Est attendance: 6,000. For info: Jay Peak Resort, Rte 242, Jay, VT 05859. Phone: (802) 988-2611. Fax: (802) 988-4049. Email: jaypeak@together.net. WWW: http://www.jaypeakresort.com

ANNUAL PINE BARRENS JAMBOREE. Oct 10. Toms River, NJ. 4th annual. Music of the Pine Barrens, crafts, food, children's games, canoe rentals and much more. For info: Ocean County Public Affairs, PO Box 2191, Toms River, NJ 08754. Phone: (609) 971-3085. Fax: (609) 971-9540.

APPLE BUTTER FESTIVAL. Oct 10–11. Burton, OH. Enjoy the beautiful Geauga autumn with the aroma of fresh apple butter simmering in real copper kettles over outdoor fires, while visiting the antique and craft shows. Est attendance: 10,000. For info: Marlene F. Collins, Geauga County Historical Soc, PO Box 153, Burton, OH 44021. Phone: (216) 834-4012. Fax: (216) 834-4012.

APPLE BUTTER FESTIVAL. Oct 10–11. Berkeley Springs, WV. Fall festival with spicy apple butter simmering in copper kettles in the town square. A parade, two days of mountain music and old-fashioned contests. Fine crafts, farmer's market, down-home cooking and fall foliage. Annually, Columbus Day weekend. Est attendance: 40,000. For info: Apple Butter Festival, 304 Fairfax St, Berkeley Springs, WV 25411. Phone: (304) 258-3738.

ARROW ROCK HERITAGE CRAFT FESTIVAL. Oct 10–11. Arrow Rock, MO. 1850s crafters demonstrate and sell crafts of daily living: bobbin lace making, rope braiding, candle dipping, cornshuck dolls, blacksmithing and more. Historic buildings open to tour. Annually, the second full weekend in October. Est attendance: 6,500. For info: Historic Arrow Rock Council, PO Box M, Arrow Rock, MO 65320.
Email: tmcglaughlin@vaxl.rain.gen.mo.us.

BENTONSPORT ARTS FESTIVAL. Oct 10–11. Bentonsport National Historic District, IA. Juried art show held as part of a countywide scenic drive. Variety of media represented. Held on river bank in historic and picturesque restored 1840s village. Food and lodging available locally. Guided tours via horse-drawn wagon. Demonstrations. Annually, the second full weekend in October. Est attendance: 12,000. For info: Greef General Store, Bentonsport, PO Box 9, Keosauqua, IA 52565. Phone: (319) 592-3579.

BONZA BOTTLER DAY™. Oct 10. To celebrate when the number of the day is the same as the number of the month. Bonza Bottler Day™ is an excuse to have a party at least once a month. For more information, see Jan 1. For info: Gail M. Berger, 109 Matthew Ave, Poca, WV 25159. Phone: (304) 776-7746. Email: gberger5@aol.com.

CATOCTIN COLORFEST ARTS AND CRAFTS SHOW. Oct 10–11. Thurmont, MD. Live music, food, 350 arts and crafts booths featuring artists from Maryland, Virginia and Pennsylvania. Annually, the second weekend in October. Est attendance: 100,000. For info send a SASE to: Catoctin ColorFest, Inc, Box 33, Thurmont, MD 21788. Phone: (301) 271-4432.

CHOWDERFEST. Oct 10–12. Mystic Seaport, Mystic, CT. Columbus Day weekend. A riverfront festival of New England chowders. Est attendance: 9,000. For info: Mystic Seaport, 75 Greenmanville Ave, PO Box 6000, Mystic, CT 06355-0990. Phone: (203) 572-5315.

CLERGY APPRECIATION DAY. Oct 10–11. "Clergy Appreciation Day" (known to some as "Clergy Appreciation Weekend") was established five years ago. For info: Jerry Frear, Jr, Under His Wing Inc, 1500 Warren Ave, Williamsport, PA, 17701. Phone: (800) 875-4388.

COLUMBUS DAY ON THE *SANTA MARIA*. Oct 10. Battelle Park, Columbus, OH. Columbus Day observances planned on board the *Santa Maria*, the only full-size replica of Columbus's flagship on permanent display in North America. Annually, Columbus Day weekend. For info: Columbus Santa Maria, 109 N Front St, Columbus, OH 43215. Phone: (614) 645-8760. Fax: (614) 645-8748. WWW: http://www.SantaMaria.org

DOUBLE TENTH DAY: ANNIVERSARY. Oct 10, 1911. Tenth day of 10th month, Double Tenth Day, is observed by many Chinese as the anniversary of the outbreak of the revolution against the imperial Manchu dynasty, Oct 10, 1911. Sun Yat-sen and Huan Hsing were among the revolutionary leaders.

ELDON TURKEY FESTIVAL. Oct 10. Eldon, MO. 13th annual. A celebration of Miller County's state and national ranking as a top producer of wild and domestic turkeys. Event includes more than 200 crafters and exhibitors, turkey events, food, quilt show and old-time machinery show. Annually, the second Saturday in October. Est attendance: 12,500. For info: Eldon Chamber of Commerce, PO Box 209, Eldon, MO 65026. Phone: (573) 392-3752. Fax: (573) 392-0634.

FEAST OF THE HUNTERS' MOON. Oct 10–11. Fort Ouiatenon Historic Park, Lafayette, IN. Re-creation of French and Native American life at mid-1700s fur-trading outpost. 6,000 participants. Est attendance: 65,000. For info: Fern H. Martin, Dir of PR, Tippecanoe County Historical Assn, 909 South St, Lafayette, IN 47901. Phone: (765) 476-8401. Fax: (765) 476-8414. WWW: http://www.holli.com/tcha

FIJI: INDEPENDENCE DAY. Oct 10. National holiday.

FOREST CRAFTS/SCENIC DRIVE FESTIVAL. Oct 10–11. Van Buren County, IA. Scenic landscapes, historic architecture, wood carvers, buckskinners camp, flea market, quilt show, arts festival, country music show, food fair, crafts and more. Annually, the second full weekend in October. Est attendance: 18,000. For info: Mary E. Muir, Exec Dir, Villages of Van Buren, Inc, PO Box 9, Keosauqua, IA 52565. Phone: (800) 868-7822.
Email: villages@netins.net.
WWW: http://www.netins.net/showcase/villages

GOLDEN ISLES ARTS FESTIVAL. Oct 10–11. St. Simons Island, GA. 29th annual. 200 fine art and fine craft artists on exhibit. Also, local foods and entertainment. Annually, the second full weekend in October. Est attendance: 20,000. For info: The Glynn Art Assn, 319 Mallory St, St. Simons Island, GA 31522. Phone: (912) 638-8770. Fax: (912) 638-8770.

GRAPE STOMP. Oct 10–11. Pahrump, NV. Stompin' grapes the old-fashioned way is a juicy tradition at the Pahrump Valley Vineyards, Nevada's only winery. For local info: (702) 727-6900 Nevada Commission on Tourism, Capitol Complex, Carson City, NV 89710. Phone: (702) 687-4322. Fax: (702) 687-6779.

GREAT ITALIAN FESTIVAL. Oct 10–11. Reno, NV. 17th annual. Activities include a grape stomp, cooking demos, spaghetti eating contest, food and entertainment. Annually, the Saturday and Sunday before Columbus Day. For local info: (702) 786-5700. For Nevada Tourism: Nevada Commission on Tourism, Capitol Complex, Carson City, NV 89710. Phone: (702) 687-4322 or (800) 227-0774. Fax: (702) 687-6779.

HARVEST FESTIVAL. Oct 10. Bay Head, NJ. Family fun throughout historic village by the sea. Kite flying, face painting, pumpkin carving, roller blade demo, model airplane exhibit. Annually, the second Saturday in October. Est attendance: 300. For info: Bay Head Business Assn, PO Box 135, Bay Head, NJ 08742-5346. Phone: (800) 4-BAY-HED or (732) 899-0068.

HAUNTED TRAIL. Oct 10–26. Ritter Park Amphitheater, Huntington, WV. A 15-minute haunted walk on a scary trail. Also features a spooky trail for small kids. Est attendance: 8,000. For info: Rick Abel, Greater Huntington Park and Rec District, PO Box 2985, Huntington, WV 25728. Phone: (304) 696-5954. Fax: (304) 696-5588.

HAYES, HELEN: BIRTH ANNIVERSARY. Oct 10, 1900. Actress Helen Hayes, often called the First Lady of the American theater, was born at Washington, DC. Hayes's greatest stage triumph was her role as the long-lived British monarch Queen Victoria in the play *Victoria Regina*. Her first great success was in *Coquette* (1927). She won an Academy Award for best actress for her first major film role in *The Sin of Madelon Claudet* (1931) and also won best supporting actress for her role in *Airport* (1971). Helen Hayes died Mar 17, 1993, at Nyack, NY.

INTERPLANETARY CONFEDERATION DAYS. Oct 10–11. A celebration to promote worldwide recognition of our brother planets in the Milky Way galaxy—32 worlds waiting to join ours in an Interplanetary Confederation. Est attendance: 175. For info: Charles Spiegel, Unarius Academy of Science, 145 S Magnolia Ave, El Cajon, CA 92020-4522. Phone: (619) 447-4170 or (800) 475-7065. Fax: (619) 447-6485.
Email: uviel@unavius.org. WWW: http://www.unavius.org

JAPAN: HEALTH-SPORTS DAY ANNIVERSARY. Oct 10. National holiday to encourage physical activity for building sound body and mind. Created in 1966 to commemorate the day of the opening of the 18th Olympic Games in Tokyo on Oct 10, 1964.

KRUGER, PAUL: BIRTH ANNIVERSARY. Oct 10. Stephanus Johannes Paulus Kruger, former president of the South African Republic and a leader of the Boers, was born Oct 10, 1825. His birthday is commemorated in South Africa. Kruger died in Switzerland on July 14, 1904.

MOUNTAIN GLORY FESTIVAL. Oct 10. Marion, NC. A celebration of mountain heritage in western North Carolina. Arts, crafts, children's area and continuous entertainment. Also, "Mountain Glory Metric Century" bicycle ride. Annually, the second Saturday in October. Est attendance: 20,000. For info: John R. Birdsong, Exec Dir, Chamber of Commerce, 629 Tate St, Marion, NC 28752. Phone: (704) 652-4240. Fax: (704) 659-9620.

NORTHEAST MARBLE MEET. Oct 10–11. Radisson Inn, Marlborough, MA. Auction, lunch and exhibits; collectors buy, sell and trade marbles. Annually, Columbus Day weekend. Est attendance: 500. For info: Bert Cohen, 169 Marlborough St, Boston, MA 02116. Phone: (617) 247-4754. Fax: (617) 247-9093. Email: marblebert@aol.com.

NORTHERN INTERNATIONAL LIVESTOCK EXPOSITION. Oct 10–17. MetraPark, Billings, MT. Rodeo, trade show exhibits, cattle and horse sales. Est attendance: 75,000. For info: Kevin Dawe, Genl Mgr, NILE Office, PO Box 1981, Billings, MT 59103. Phone: (406) 256-2495 or (888) NILE-TIX. Fax: (406) 256-2494. Email: NILE@truewest.com.
WWW: http://www.truewest.com/NILE

OKLAHOMA HISTORICAL DAY. Oct 10. Oklahoma.

OKTOBERFEST ART & CRAFT FAIR. Oct 10. Sauk County Courthouse Square Park, Downtown Baraboo, WI. 12th annual outdoor event. Features all handmade work of 120 artists and crafters, local cuisine food stands, farmers' market, live entertainment, carnival, kids' activities. Held during peak fall color time for travelers in this area of scenic Wisconsin. Visit local orchards and browse the unique specialty shops in historic downtown Baraboo. Annually, the second Saturday in October. Est attendance: 5,000. For info: Cindy Doescher, Fan Faire Promotions, LLC, 1801 Jefferson St, Baraboo, WI 53913.

OYSTER FESTIVAL. Oct 10. Chincoteague Island, VA. Oysters fixed every way possible—all you can eat. Annually, Saturday of Columbus Day weekend. Tickets can be obtained in advance by contacting Chincoteague Chamber of Commerce. Est attendance: 2,500. For info: Jackie Russell, Chincoteague Chamber of Commerce, Box 258, Chincoteague Island, VA 23336. Phone: (757) 336-6161. Fax: (757) 336-1242. Email: pony@shore.intercom.net.
WWW: http://www.intercom.net/local/chincoteague

"OZZIE AND HARRIET" TV PREMIERE: ANNIVERSARY. Oct 10, 1952. "Ozzie and Harriet" was TV's longest-running sitcom. The successful radio-turned-TV show about the Nelson family starred the real-life Nelsons—Ozzie, his wife Harriet and their sons David and Ricky. Officially titled "The Adventures of Ozzie and Harriet," this show was set in the family's home. The boys were one reason the show was successful, and Ricky used the advantage to become a pop star. Cast members included Don DeFore, Parley Baer, Lyle Talbot, Mary Jane Croft, Frank Cady, Skip Young, Charlene Salerno, Connie Harper, Sean Morgan, Greg Dawson, Karl George, Jack Wagner and Kent McWhirter (later known as Kent McCord on "Adam-12"). David and Rick's real-life wives—June Blair and Kris Nelson—also joined the cast.

PINE BARRENS JAMBOREE. Oct 10. Wells Mills County Park, Waretown, NJ. Music of the Pines, crafts, wood carvers, nature walks, canoeing, basket weavers, children's games, food and more. Est attendance: 5,000. For info: Michael T. Mangum, Chief Naturalist, Wells Mills County Park, 905 Wells Mills Rd, Waretown, NJ 08758. Phone: (609) 971-3085. Fax: (609) 971-9540.

October 1998

S	M	T	W	T	F	S
				1	2	3
4	5	6	7	8	9	10
11	12	13	14	15	16	17
18	19	20	21	22	23	24
25	26	27	28	29	30	31

SEDONA ARTS FESTIVAL. Oct 10–11. Sedona, AZ. Annual celebration of visual, performing and culinary arts. Creative artisans present a unique collection of fine arts, crafts, foods, music and entertainment, surrounded by the scenic grandeur of towering red rocks. Featured events include Patrons Purchase Program. Admission $5; children 12 and under free with paid adult. Proceeds will benefit the cultural arts of Sedona. Rated best arts festival in Northern Arizona, 1995 Art Fair Source Book. Est attendance: 6,000. For info: Sedona Arts Festival, PO Box 2729, Sedona, AZ 86339-2729. Phone: (520) 204-9456. Fax: (520) 204-9456.

SEWARD, WILLIAM HENRY: DEATH ANNIVERSARY. Oct 10, 1872. US politician and statesman William Henry Seward, who is most often remembered for the purchase of Alaska from Russia in 1867, referred to as "Seward's Folly," was born in Florida, NY, on May 16, 1801. He died in Auburn, NY, following a trip around the world. Seward served in the New York State Senate from 1830 to 1834. Seward was governor of New York from 1839 to 1843 and became known for his antislavery stand. In 1849 he was elected to the US Senate and was reelected in 1855. In March 1861, President Lincoln named Seward secretary of state. On the evening of Lincoln's assassination, Apr 14, 1865, Seward was stabbed in the throat by Lewis Posell, a fellow conspirator of John Wilkes Booth. He recovered and maintained his cabinet position under President Andrew Johnson until 1869.

T.O.O.T. (TASTE OF OUR TOWN) FESTIVAL. Oct 10. Lewisburg, WV. A food fair with 60 food booths, two free entertainment stages, roaming musicians and art exhibit, etc. All to benefit the regional cultural center, Carnegie Hall (a gift from Andrew Carneige in 1902). Est attendance: 4,000. For info: Lewisburg Visitors Center, 105 Church St, Lewisburg, WV 24901. Phone: (800) 833-2068.

TUXEDO CREATED: ANNIVERSARY. Oct 10, 1886. Griswold Lorillard of Tuxedo Park, NY, fashioned the first tuxedo for men.

VERDI, GIUSEPPI: BIRTH ANNIVERSARY. Oct 10, 1813. Italian composer. Born at Le Roncole, Italy. His 26 operas include *Rigoletto*, *Il Trovatore*, *La Traviata* and *Aida*, and are among the most popular of all operatic music today. Died at Milan, Italy, on Jan 27, 1901.

VERMONT APPLE FESTIVAL. Oct 10–11. Riverside Middle School, Springfield, VT. Craft fair, apples, apple cider press and other family entertainment. Annually, Columbus Day weekend. Est attendance: 5,500. For info: Springfield Chamber of Commerce, 14 Clinton St, Springfield, VT 05156. Phone: (802) 885-2779. Email: spfldcoc@vermontel.com.
WWW: http://www.vermontel.com/neis/springfield.htm

"WINKY-DINK AND YOU" TV PREMIERE: 45th ANNIVERSARY. Oct 10, 1953. A popular weekend children's show, this half-hour featured sketches and cartoons (in many of which Winky-Dink, a little boy, was the star). Jack Barry hosted and Dayton Allen played Mr Bungle, Barry's assistant. The show is best remembered for the Winky-Dink Kit, bought through the mail, which was a piece of plastic, crayons and a cloth for children to use to participate in the show.

"ZORRO" TV PREMIERE: ANNIVERSARY. Oct 10, 1957. "Zorro" was a familiar character before coming to TV; he appeared in a McCulley novel and several films. The story is about Don Diego de la Vega (Guy Williams), a Spanish nobleman who is summoned to California by his father, Don Alejandro (George J. Lewis), to fight for the people. Diego's alter ego is Zorro, a dashing and assertive defender of the people. The series also starred Gene Sheldon, Henry Calvin, Britt Lomond, Don Diamond and Jolene Brand. The series reappeared in later years, first as a remake and then as a sequel.

BIRTHDAYS TODAY

Charles Dance, 52, actor (*The Jewel in the Crown, White Mischief*), born Worcestershire, England, Oct 10, 1946.
Brett Favre, 29, quarterback, born Gulfport, MS, Oct 10, 1969.
Jessica Harper, 49, actress (*Stardust Memories, Pennies from Heaven, My Favorite Year*), born Chicago, IL, Oct 10, 1949.
Harold Pinter, 68, director (*Butley*), playwright (*Betrayal, The Birthday Party*), born London, England, Oct 10, 1930.
David Lee Roth, 43, singer/musician (lead, Van Halen; "Jump," *Eat 'Em and Smile*), born Bloomington, IN, Oct 10, 1955.
Tanya Tucker, 40, singer ("Delta Dawn," "Lizzie and the Rain Man"), born Seminole, TX, Oct 10, 1958.
Ben Vereen, 52, actor, singer, dancer (Tony for *Pippin; Roots, All That Jazz,* "Webster"), born Miami, FL, Oct 10, 1946.

OCTOBER 11 — SUNDAY

Day 284 — 81 Remaining

AMERICAN INDIAN TIME OF THANKSGIVING. Oct 11. Allentown, PA. American Indian ceremony with activities for the whole family. Annually, the second Sunday in October. Est attendance: 3,000. For info: Lenni Lenape Historical Soc, Museum of Indian Culture, 2825 Fish Hatchery Rd, Allentown, PA 18103-9801. Phone: (610) 797-2121. Fax: (610) 797-2801. WWW: http://www.lenape.org

AMERICAN SAMOA: WHITE SUNDAY. Oct 11. Second Sunday in October is "children's day" on the island. Children demonstrate skits, prayers, songs and special presentations for parents, friends and relatives. A feast is prepared by the parents and served to the children.

"AMERICAN WHEELS" CAR SHOW. Oct 11 (rain date Oct 25). Wheaton Village, Millville, NJ. Features cars from the '50s, '60s and '70s. Est attendance: 1,500. For info: Wheaton Village, 1501 Glasstown Rd, Millville, NJ 08332. Phone: (609) 825-6800. Fax: (609) 825-2410. Email: mail@wheatonvillage.org. WWW: http://www.wheatonvillage.org

APPLE FESTIVAL. Oct 11. Mississippi Valley Welcome Center, LeClaire, IA. Apple vendors display and sell the freshest apples of the season along with apple desserts; caramel apples, cider donuts, apple pie, apple chips, cider and much more. Demonstrations on how to make special apple desserts, entertainment and bake sale. Est attendance: 2,250. For info: Pam Black, Dir of Visitor Services, Mississippi Valley Welcome Center, 900 Eagle Ridge Rd, LeClaire, IA 52753. Phone: (319) 289-3009. Fax: (319) 289-3159.

BILL AND HILLARY CLINTON WEDDING: ANNIVERSARY. Oct 11, 1975. Their new house, Fayetteville, AR. William Jefferson (Blythe) Clinton was 29 and Hillary Rodham was 27. They have one child: Chelsea Victoria Clinton, born in 1980.

"THE BOB NEWHART SHOW" TV PREMIERE: ANNIVERSARY. Oct 11, 1961. This half-hour variety series was hosted by Bob Newhart, a successful stand-up comedian famous for his trademark "telephone conversation" monologues. Regulars included Jackie Joseph, Kay Westfall, Jack Grinnage, Mickey Manners, Pearl Shear, June Ericson, Andy Albin and announcer Dan Sorkin. The show was critically acclaimed, winning both an Emmy and a Peabody in its short time on the air.

BRAZIL: CIRIO DE NAZARE. Oct 11–24. Greatest festival of northern Brazil, the Feast of Cirio starts on second Sunday of October in city of Belem (St. Mary of Bethlehem), capital of the state of Para. Festival lasts two weeks.

BURGOO FESTIVAL. Oct 11. Downtown, North Utica, IL. Only the "Burgoomeister" knows the secret recipe for this pioneer stew, burgoo, served outdoors at this annual Utica festival. Other events include arts and crafts, antiques, food, a reenactment of Civil War living conditions by uniformed volunteers and the firing of a Civil War cannon. Annually, the second Sunday in October. Est attendance: 30,000. For info: Burgoo Chairman, LaSalle Co Historical Museum, PO Box 278, Utica, IL 61373. Phone: (815) 667-4861.

CHICAGO MARATHON. Oct 11. Grant Park, Chicago, IL. Both the 21st annual marathon (26.2 miles) and the 8th annual 5K (3.1 miles) have reputations for attracting an international field of top athletes, and this marathon is ranked as one of the fastest in the world. Annually, a Sunday in October. Est attendance: 16,000. For info: Chicago Marathon, c/o Chicago Event Mgmt, Inc, 900 W Jackson, Ste #8-W, Chicago, IL 60607. Phone: (312) 243-3274. Fax: (312) 243-5652.
WWW: http://www.chicagomarathon.com

CIVIL WAR GARRISON DAY. Oct 11. Historic Fort Mifflin, Philadelphia, PA. Civil War reenactment and encampment with living history programs, tactical displays, medical demonstrations, costumed reenactors, 19th-century clothing displays and music. Est attendance: 500. For info: Lori Dillard Rech, Education Dir, Fort Mifflin on the Delaware, Fort Mifflin Rd, Philadelphia, PA 19153. Phone: (215) 685-4192. Fax: (215) 492-1608.

"DAVID BRINKLEY'S JOURNAL" TV PREMIERE: ANNIVERSARY. Oct 11, 1961. Newscaster David Brinkley anchored this NBC public affairs show which covered a range of issues, both serious and light. There were also filmed features. "Journal" won both an Emmy and a Peabody in 1962 and was widely respected by the critics.

★**GENERAL PULASKI MEMORIAL DAY.** Oct 11. Presidential Proclamation always issued for Oct 11 since 1929. Requested by Congressional Resolution each year from 1929–1946. (Since 1947 has been issued by custom.) Note: Proclamation 4869, of Oct 5, 1981, covers all succeeding years.

HARVEST CELEBRATION. Oct 11. Woodstock, VT. Traditional celebration of the harvest featuring a husking bee, barn dance and the arrival of the giant pumpkins. Also, farm harvest activities including food preservation, traditional toy making and cider pressing. Est attendance: 1,600. For info: Deborah Bulissa, Exec Asst, Billings Farm and Museum, PO Box 489, Woodstock, VT 05091. Phone: (802) 457-2355. Fax: (802) 457-4663. Email: billings.farm@valley.net.

☆ ☆ ☆

HOME-BASED BUSINESS WEEK. Oct 11–17. To celebrate, recognize and promote the home-based entrepreneur. Annually, the week including the second Tuesday of October. For info: Beverley Williams, American Assn of Home-Based Businesses, PO Box 10023, Rockville, MD 20849-0023. Phone: (800) 447-9710. Fax: (301) 963-7042. Email: aahbb@crosslink.net.
WWW: http://www.aahbb.org

NATIONAL ADULT IMMUNIZATION AWARENESS WEEK. Oct 11–17. To increase adults awareness that it is never to late to prevent disease. For info: Alison Roth, National Coalition for Adult Immunization, 4733 Bethesda Ave, Ste 750, Bethesda, MD 20814-5228. Phone: (301) 656-0003.

★**NATIONAL SCHOOL LUNCH WEEK.** Oct 11–17. Presidential Proclamation issued for the week beginning with the second Sunday in October since 1962 (PL87–780 of Oct 9, 1962). Note: Not issued in 1981.

PATENT ISSUED FOR FIRST ADDING MACHINE: ANNIVERSARY. Oct 11, 1887. A patent was granted to Dorr Eugene Felt for the Comptmeter, which was the first adding machine known to be absolutely accurate at all times.

ROBINSON, ROSCOE, JR: 70th BIRTH ANNIVERSARY. Oct 11, 1928. The first black American to achieve the Army rank of four-star general. Born at St. Louis, MO, and died at Washington, DC, on July 22, 1993.

ROOSEVELT, ANNA ELEANOR: BIRTH ANNIVERSARY. Oct 11. Wife of Franklin Delano Roosevelt, 32nd president of the US, was born at New York, NY, Oct 11, 1884. She led an active and independent life and was the first wife of a president to give her own news conference in the White House (1933). Widely known throughout the world, she was affectionately called "the first lady of the world." She served as US delegate to the United Nations General Assembly for a number of years before her death at New York, NY, Nov 7, 1962. A prolific writer, she wrote in *This Is My Story*, "No one can make you feel inferior without your consent."

"SATURDAY NIGHT LIVE" TV PREMIERE: ANNIVERSARY. Oct 11, 1975. Through the years this show has been through numerous cast, writing, producing and musical staff changes. However, its format has remained more or less the same: skits, commercial parodies, recurring characters and news parodies, with a different guest host and musical guest performing every week—live. It used to be known for its outrageous comedy topics and parodies that almost bordered on slander, and for having the best in controversial and unusual musical groups. Its title was originally "NBC's Saturday Night." "Live" was added and "NBC's" dropped. Notable cast members included: Chevy Chase, Dan Aykroyd, John Belushi, Jane Curtin, Garrett Morris, Laraine Newman, Gilda Radner, Bill Murray, Joe Piscopo, Eddie Murphy, Mary Gross, Tim Kazurinsky, Julia Louis-Dreyfus, Jim Belushi, Billy Crystal, Martin Short, Christopher Guest, Harry Shearer, Joan Cusack, Robert Downey, Jr, Nora Dunn, Jon Lovitz, Dana Carvey, Phil Hartman, Jan Hooks, Victoria Jackson, Dennis Miller and Kevin Nealon. The current cast is almost a complete overhaul, with only a few returning cast members. This has happened in just about every season in the network's attempt to recapture the true wit and hilarity of the early days of the show. Some critics blame a bloated staff of too many writers all whittling away at each idea for the lack of freshness and comedy in the show.

STONE, HARLAND FISKE: BIRTH ANNIVERSARY. Oct 11, 1872. Former associate justice and later chief justice of the US Supreme Court who wrote more than 600 opinions and dissents for that court, Stone was born at Chesterfield, NH. He served on the Supreme Court from 1925 until his death, at Washington, DC, on Apr 22, 1946, at age 73.

VATICAN COUNCIL II MEETS: ANNIVERSARY. Oct 11, 1962. The 21st ecumenical council of the Roman Catholic Church was convened by Pope John XXIII. It met in four annual sessions, concluding on Dec 8, 1965. It dealt with the renewal of the Church and introduced sweeping changes, such as the use of the vernacular in the Mass.

WEEMS, PARSON (MASON LOCKE): BIRTH ANNIVERSARY. Oct 11. Mason Locke Weems, 19th child of David Weems, was born in Anne Arundel County, MD, on Oct 11, 1759. An Episcopal clergyman and traveling bookseller, Weems is remembered for the fictitious stories he presented as historical fact. Best known of his "fables" is the story describing George Washington cutting down his father's cherry tree with a hatchet. Weems's fictionalized histories, however, delighted many readers who accepted them as true. They became immensely popular and were best sellers for many years. Weems died May 23, 1825, at Beaufort, SC.

October 1998

S	M	T	W	T	F	S
				1	2	3
4	5	6	7	8	9	10
11	12	13	14	15	16	17
18	19	20	21	22	23	24
25	26	27	28	29	30	31

WEST, DOTTIE: BIRTH ANNIVERSARY. Oct 11, 1932. American singer Dottie West was born at McMinnville, TN. In 1964 she won the first Grammy ever by a country vocalist for "Here Comes My Baby." She died on Sept 4, 1991, at Nashville, TN.

WESTERN SAMOA: WHITE SUNDAY. Oct 11. The second Sunday in October. For the children of Samoa, this is the biggest day of the year. On this day, traditional roles are reversed, as children lead church services, are served special foods and receive gifts of new church clothes and other special items. All the children dress in white. The following Monday is an official holiday.

XTERRA. Oct 11. Wailea, Maui, HI. Televised championship off-road triathlon. Includes 1.5K roughwater swim, 30K mountain bike race and 10K cross-country run. $30,000 pro purse. Est attendance: 5,000. For info: Event Marketing, 1001 Bishop St, Pauahi Tower #880, Honolulu, HI 96813. Phone: (808) 521-4322. Fax: (808) 538-0314. Email: dey@emisport.com. WWW: http://www.emisport.com

BIRTHDAYS TODAY

Joseph Alsop, 88, journalist, author, born Avon, CT, Oct 11, 1910.
Art Blakey, 79, jazz musician, born Pittsburgh, PA, Oct 11, 1919.
Joan Cusack, 36, actress (*Working Girl, Sixteen Candles*), born Evanston, IL, Oct 11, 1962.
Robert Gale, 53, physician, cofounder of the International Bone Marrow Registry, born Brooklyn Heights, NY, Oct 11, 1945.
Daryl Hall, 50, singer, musician (Hall and Oates), born Pottstown, PA, Oct 11, 1948.
Ron Leibman, 61, actor (*The Hot Rock, Norma Rae*; stage: *We Bombed in New Haven* [Theatre World Award], *Angels in America* [Tony Award]), born New York, NY, Oct 11, 1937.
David Morse, 45, actor ("St. Elsewhere," *The Indian Runner*), born Beverly, MA, Oct 11, 1953.
Patty Murray, 48, US Senator (D, Washington), born Seattle, WA, Oct 11, 1950.
Luke Perry, 32, actor ("Beverly Hills 90210," *Buffy the Vampire Slayer*), born Fredricktown, MO, Oct 11, 1966.
William Perry, 71, former US Secretary of Defense in Clinton administration, born Vandergrift, PA, Oct 11, 1927.
Jerome Robbins, 80, choreographer, born New York, NY, Oct 11, 1918.
Roy Scheider, 63, actor (*Jaws, All That Jazz, Cold Comfort Farm*, "Seaquest"), born Orange, NJ, Oct 11, 1935.
Steve Young, 37, football player, born Salt Lake City, UT, Oct 11, 1961.

OCTOBER 12 — MONDAY

Day 285 — 80 Remaining

BAHAMAS: DISCOVERY DAY. Oct 12. Commemorates the landing of Columbus in the Bahamas, Oct 12, 1492.

"THE BOB HOPE SHOW" TV PREMIERE: 45th ANNIVERSARY. Oct 12, 1953. Premier funnyman, well-known and loved Bob Hope made monthly appearances on TV in the 1950s. During the first season he hosted "The Colgate Comedy Hour," and during the later seasons his show was seen replacing and then alternating with Milton Berle (and in 1955-56 with Martha Raye and Dinah Shore). Leo Robin and Ralph Rainger wrote Hope's trademark and show-closing song, "Thanks for the Memory."

"THE BURNS AND ALLEN SHOW" TV PREMIERE: ANNIVERSARY. Oct 12, 1950. The comedic husband and wife duo of George Burns and Gracie Allen starred as themselves in this comedy series in which Burns was often the straight man and Allen was known for her ditziness. The show employed the technique of speaking directly to the camera ("breaking the fourth wall"); Burns often commented on the plot, told jokes or tried to make sense of Allen's actions and statements. Also on the show were their real-life son, Ronnie Burns, Bea Benaderet, Hal March, John Brown (until blacklisted by McCarthyites in the "red scare"), Fred Clark, Larry Keating, Bill Goodwin and Harry Von Zell. The show was done live for the first two seasons and included vaudeville scenes at the end of each episode.

CANADA: THANKSGIVING DAY. Oct 12. Observed on second Monday in October each year.

★**COLUMBUS DAY.** Oct 12. Presidential Proclamation always the second Monday in October. Observed on Oct 12 from 1934 to 1970 (Pub Res No 21 of Apr 30, 1934). PL90–363 of June 28, 1968, required that beginning in 1971 it would be observed on the second Monday in October.

COLUMBUS DAY OBSERVANCE. Oct 12. Public Law 90–363 sets observance of Columbus Day on the second Monday in October. Applicable to federal employees and to the District of Columbia, but observed also in most states on this day. Commemorates the landfall of Columbus in the New World, Oct 12, 1492. See also: "Columbus Day (Traditional)" (Oct 12).

COLUMBUS DAY (TRADITIONAL). Oct 12, 1492. Public holiday in most countries in the Americas and in most Spanish-speaking countries. Observed under different names and on different dates (most often, as in US, on the second Monday in October). Anniversary of Christopher Columbus's arrival, Oct 12, 1492, after a dangerous voyage across "shoreless Seas," at the Bahamas (probably the island of Guanahani), which he renamed El Salvador and claimed in the name of the Spanish crown. In his *Journal*, he wrote: "As I saw that they (the natives) were friendly to us, and perceived that they could be much more easily converted to our holy faith by gentle means than by force, I presented them with some red caps, and strings of beads to wear upon the neck, and many other trifles of small value, wherewith they were much delighted, and becamed wonderfully attached to us." See also: "Columbus Day Observance" (Oct 12).

DESTINY DAY. Oct 12. Honoring the Dutch sailor Piet de Stuini, or DeStynie, who persuaded Columbus to change the log and make it seem that Oct 12 was the date of the first New World landing. The real date, Oct 13, might have caused superstitious fear in the other sailors or in potential investors in later voyages. The change was detected by an Italian history study group named the Colombiani. For info: Bob Birch, The Puns Corps, PO Box 2364, Falls Church, VA 22042-0364. Phone: (703) 533-3668.

DISCOVERERS' DAY IN HAWAII. Oct 12. Honors all discoverers, including Pacific and Polynesian navigators. Second Monday in October.

EQUATORIAL GUINEA: INDEPENDENCE DAY. Oct 12. National holiday.

FOREST GROVE ARTS AND CRAFTS SHOW. Oct 12. Forest Grove Community Club, Forest Grove, MT. 18th annual craft show and sale, indoors, tables available, 11 AM–4 PM. Lunch available. Est attendance: 650. For info: May Charbonneau, Forest Grove Community Club, Box 6, Forest Grove, MT 59441. Phone: (406) 538 3510.

GORDONE, CHARLES: BIRTH ANNIVERSARY. Oct 12, 1925. First black playwright to win the Pulitzer Prize for drama, for his play *No Place to Be Somebody*. Born at Cleveland, OH. Died Nov 17, 1995 at College Station, TX.

INTERNATIONAL MOMENT OF FRUSTRATION SCREAM DAY. Oct 12. To share any or all of our frustrations, all citizens of the world will go outdoors at twelve hundred hours Greenwich time and scream for 30 seconds. We will all feel better or Earth will go off its orbit. Annually, Oct 12. [© 1997 by WPL] For info: Thomas and Ruth Roy, Wellness Permission League, PO Box 662, Mt Gretna, PA 17064-0662. Phone: (500) 437-5104 or (717) 964-1308. Fax: (717) 964-1335.

MacDONALD, ANNE THOMPSON: DEATH ANNIVERSARY. Oct 12, 1993. Born in 1896, MacDonald founded a nonprofit organization, Recording for the Blind, that produces audio tapes of books to benefit blind and learning disabled people. MacDonald founded the organization in 1948; its library currently contains more than 80,000 titles. She died at Huntington, NY.

McNAIR, RONALD E.: BIRTH ANNIVERSARY. Oct 12. Ronald E. McNair, a 35-year-old physicist, was the second black American astronaut in space (Feb 1984). He was born at Lake City, SC, on Oct 12, 1950. As mission specialist for the crew, he perished in the space shuttle *Challenger* explosion on Jan 28, 1986. See also: "Challenger Space Shuttle Explosion Anniversary" (Jan 28).

MEXICO: DIA DE LA RAZA. Oct 12. Columbus Day is observed as the "Day of the Race," a fiesta time to commemorate the discovery of America as well as the common interests and cultural heritage of the Spanish and Indian peoples and the Hispanic nations.

MOON PHASE: LAST QUARTER. Oct 12. Moon enters Last Quarter phase at 7:11 AM, EDT.

NATIONAL SCHOOL LUNCH WEEK. Oct 12–16. To celebrate good nutrition and wholesome, low-cost school lunches. Annually, the second full week in October. For info: Communications Dept, American School Food Service Assn, 1600 Duke St, 7th Fl, Alexandria, VA 22314-3436. Phone: (703) 739-3900 x133.

NATIVE AMERICANS' DAY (SOUTH DAKOTA). Oct 12. Observed in the state of South Dakota as a legal holiday, dedicated to the remembrance of the great Native American leaders who contributed so much to the history of South Dakota. Annually, the second Monday in October.

ONLINE WORLD CONFERENCE & EXPO. Oct 12–14. Washington Hilton Hotel, Washington, DC. Est attendance: 7,000. For info: Online Inc, 462 Danbury Rd, Wilton, CT 06897-2126. Phone: (203) 761-1466. Email: info@onlineinc.com. WWW: http://www.onlineinc.com/olworld

RACIAL BRAWL ON KITTY HAWK: ANNIVERSARY. Oct 12–13, 1972. 46 black and caucasian sailors were injured in a racial fight that broke out on the *Kitty Hawk* while the aircraft carrier was stationed off North Vietnam. According to the *New York Times*, Oct 14, 1972, "The Navy has had the reputation in the black community of being a service in which blacks are limited to stewards' jobs." The previous year, 1971, the Navy had begun a five-year program to increase the numbers of black recruits to match what was their 12% level in the general population.

SHEMINI ATZERET. Oct 12. Hebrew calendar date: Tishri 22, 5759. The eighth day of Solemn Assembly, part of the Sukkot Festival (see entry on Oct 5), with memorial services and cycle of Biblical readings in the synagogue.

SPAIN: NATIONAL HOLIDAY. Oct 12.

TRUMBULL, JONATHAN: BIRTH ANNIVERSARY. Oct 12. American patriot, counselor and friend of George Washington, governor of Connecticut Colony, born Oct 12, 1710. Died Aug 17, 1785.

VIRGIN ISLANDS–PUERTO RICO FRIENDSHIP DAY. Oct 12. Columbus Day (second Monday in October) also celebrates historical friendship between peoples of Virgin Islands and Puerto Rico.

WILLIAMS, RALPH VAUGHAN: BIRTH ANNIVERSARY. Oct 12, 1872. English composer and conductor Ralph Vaughan Williams was born at Down Ampney, Gloucestershire. He is considered England's first great truly national composer, having rooted "modern" composition techniques in traditional English folk and Tudor music and themes to create a uniquely English style. Among his many works are nine symphonies, church and choral music, film and stage music and several operas. Williams studied at the Royal College of Music as well as in Berlin under Max Bruch and in Paris under Maurice Ravel. His major compositions include the *Mass in G Minor*, *Fantasia on a Theme of Tallis* and the opera *The Pilgrim's Progress*. He died Aug 26, 1958, at London.

YORKTOWN VICTORY DAY. Oct 12. Observed as a holiday in Virginia. Annually, the second Monday in Oct.

BIRTHDAYS TODAY

Susan Anton, 48, singer ("Killin' Time" with Fred Knoblock), actress (*Goldengirl*), born Yucaipa, CA, Oct 12, 1950.

Kirk Cameron, 28, actor ("Growing Pains"), born Panorama City, CA, Oct 12, 1970.

John Engler, 50, Governor of Michigan (R), born Mt Pleasant, MI, Oct 12, 1948.

Dick Gregory, 66, comedian, author, activist, born St. Louis, MO, Oct 12, 1932.

Anthony Christopher (Tony) Kubek, 62, sportscaster, former baseball player, born Milwaukee, WI, Oct 12, 1936.

Jean Nidetch, 75, founder of Weight Watchers, born Brooklyn, NY, Oct 12, 1923.

Luciano Pavarotti, 63, opera singer, one of the "Three Tenors," born Modena, Italy, Oct 12, 1935.

Adam Rich, 30, actor (Nicholas Bradford on "Eight Is Enough"), born Brooklyn, NY, Oct 12, 1968.

Chris Wallace, 51, broadcaster ("Dateline"), White House correspondent, born Chicago, IL, Oct 12, 1947.

OCTOBER 13 — TUESDAY

Day 286 — 79 Remaining

BROWN, JESSE LEROY: BIRTH ANNIVERSARY. Oct 13, 1926. Jesse Leroy Brown was the first black American naval aviator and also the first black naval officer to lose his life in combat when he was shot down over Korea on Dec 4, 1950. On Mar 18, 1972, USS *Jesse L. Brown* was launched as the first ship to be named in honor of a black naval officer. Brown was born at Hattiesburg, MS.

MONTAND, YVES: BIRTH ANNIVERSARY. Oct 13, 1921. French actor Yves Montand was born Ivo Livi at Monsummano Alto, Italy. His career was successful in both France and America, including more than 50 films. He died on Nov 9, 1991, at Senlis, France.

NORSK HOSTFEST. Oct 13–17. State Fairgrounds, Minot, ND. The Northern Plains' biggest ethnic festival draws thousands of people to Minot for Scandinavian and American entertainment, Scandinavian delicacies, arts and crafts exhibits and dignitaries representing Sweden, Norway, Denmark, Iceland and Finland with big-name entertainment nightly. Est attendance: 65,000. For info: Bret Taylor, Minot Conv & Visitors Bureau, PO Box 2066, Minot, ND 58702. Phone: (800) 264-2626 or (701) 857-8206. Fax: (701) 857-8228.

PITCHER, MOLLY: BIRTH ANNIVERSARY. Oct 13, 1754. "Molly Pitcher," heroine of the American Revolution, was a water carrier at the Battle of Monmouth (Sunday, June 28, 1778) where she distinguished herself by loading and firing a cannon after her husband, John Hays, was wounded. Affectionately known as "Sergeant Molly" after General Washington issued her a warrant as a noncommissioned officer. Her real name was Mary Hays McCauley (née Ludwig). Born near Trenton, NJ, Oct 13, 1754. Died at Carlisle, PA, on Jan 22, 1832.

SAINT EDWARD, THE CONFESSOR: FEAST DAY. Oct 13. King of England, 1042–1066, Edward was the son of King Ethelred the Unready. Born in 1003, he died on Jan 5, 1066. On Oct 13, 1163, his remains were transported in a ceremony that was of national interest. Since then Oct 13 has been observed as his principal feast day.

SIMCHAT TORAH. Oct 13. Hebrew calendar date: Tishri 23, 5759. Rejoicing in the Torah concludes the nine-day Sukkot Festival (see entry on Oct 5). Public reading of the Pentateuch is completed and begun again, symbolizing the need for ever-continuing study.

SPACE MILESTONE: US NATIONAL COMMISSION ON SPACE. Oct 13, 1984. President Reagan signed executive order creating a National Commission on Space to prepare 20-year agenda for civilian space program. Oct 13, 1984.

US NAVY: AUTHORIZATION ANNIVERSARY. Oct 13. Commemorates legislation passed by Second Continental Congress Oct 13, 1775, authorizing the acquisition of ships and establishment of a navy.

VIRCHOW, RUDOLF: BIRTH ANNIVERSARY. Oct 13, 1821. German political leader, scientist, teacher and author. Called "the founder of cellular pathology." Born at Schivelbein, Prussia, died at Berlin, Sept 5, 1902.

WHITE HOUSE CORNERSTONE LAID: ANNIVERSARY. Oct 13, 1792. The presidential residence at 1600 Pennsylvania Ave NW, Washington, DC, designed by James Hoban (q.v.), observes its birthday on Oct 13. The cornerstone was laid Oct 13, 1792, and the first presidential family to occupy it was that of John Adams, in November 1800. With three stories and more than 100 rooms, the White House is the oldest building in Washington. First described as the "presidential palace," it acquired the name "White House" about 10 years after construction was completed. Burned by British troops in 1814, it was reconstructed, refurbished and reoccupied by 1817.

BIRTHDAYS TODAY

Chris Carter, 41, creator of "The X-Files," born Bellflower, CA, Oct 13, 1957.

Melinda Dillon, 59, actress (*Close Encounters of the Third Kind, Absence of Malice, A Christmas Story*), born Hope, AR, Oct 13, 1939.

Sammy Hagar, 49, singer, musician ("Your Love Is Driving Me Crazy"), born Monterrey, CA, Oct 13, 1949.

October 1998

S	M	T	W	T	F	S
				1	2	3
4	5	6	7	8	9	10
11	12	13	14	15	16	17
18	19	20	21	22	23	24
25	26	27	28	29	30	31

Marie Osmond, 39, actress, singer (Donny and Marie, "Ripley's Believe It or Not"), born Ogden, UT, Oct 13, 1959.
Kelly Preston, 36, actress (*Christine, Twins*), born Honolulu, HI, Oct 13, 1962.
Jerry Lee Rice, 36, football player, born Starkville, MS, Oct 13, 1962.
Glenn Anton ("Doc") Rivers, 37, basketball player, born Maywood, IL, Oct 13, 1961.
Nipsey Russell, 74, comedian, actor, born Atlanta, GA, Oct 13, 1924.
Paul Simon, 57, singer/songwriter (with Art Garfunkel: "The Sounds of Silence," "Mrs Robinson"; solo album: *Graceland*), born Newark, NJ, Oct 13, 1941.
Margaret Hilda Roberts Thatcher, 73, former Prime Minister of England, born Grantham, England, Oct 13, 1925.
Reggie Wayne Theus, 41, former basketball player, born Inglewood, CA, Oct 13, 1957.
Pamela Tiffin, 56, actress (*Harper*; stage: *Dinner at Eight* [Theatre World Award]), born Oklahoma City, OK, Oct 13, 1942.

OCTOBER 14 — WEDNESDAY

Day 287 — 78 Remaining

BE BALD AND BE FREE DAY. Oct 14. For those who are bald and who either do wear or do not wear a wig or toupee, this is the day to go "shiny" and be proud. Annually, Oct 14. [© 1997 by WPL] For info: Thomas or Ruth Roy, Wellness Permission League, PO Box 662, Mt Gretna, PA 17064-0662. Phone: (500) 437-5104 or (717) 964-1308. Fax: (717) 964-1335.

BELIZE: COLUMBUS DAY. Oct 14. Public holiday.

EISENHOWER, DWIGHT DAVID: BIRTH ANNIVERSARY. Oct 14, 1890. The 34th president of the US, Dwight David Eisenhower, was born at Denison, TX, Oct 14, 1890. Serving two terms as president, Jan 20, 1953–Jan 20, 1961, Eisenhower was the first president to be baptized after taking office (Sunday, Feb 1, 1953). Nicknamed "Ike," he held the rank of five-star general of the army (resigned in 1952, and restored by act of Congress in 1961). He served as supreme commander of the Allied forces in western Europe during WWII. In his Farewell Address (Jan 17, 1961), speaking about the "conjunction of an immense military establishment and a large arms industry," he warned: "In the councils of government, we must guard against the acquisition of unwarranted influence, whether sought or unsought, by the military-industrial complex. The potential of the disastrous rise of misplaced power exists and will persist." An American hero, Eisenhower died at Washington, DC, Mar 28, 1969.

FODOR, EUGENE: BIRTH ANNIVERSARY. Oct 14, 1905. Travel writer Eugene Fodor was born at Leva, Hungary. His first travel book was published in 1936, after which he published more than 140, hoping to bring a human element previously lacking in travel books. He died on Feb 18, 1991, at Torrington, CT.

GISH, LILLIAN: BIRTH ANNIVERSARY. Oct 14, 1893. American actress Lillian Diana Gish was born at Springfield, OH. Her film and stage career spanned more then 85 years, 100 films, the silent and sound eras of film and numerous stage productions. She was awarded an honorary Oscar in 1970 and made her last film appearance in *The Whales of August* (1987). She died on Feb 27, 1993, at New York, NY.

JAPAN: MEGA KENKA MATSURI or ROUGHOUSE FESTIVAL. Oct 14–15. Himeji. Palanquin bearers jostle one another to demonstrate their skill and balance in handling their burdens.

KING AWARDED NOBEL PEACE PRIZE: ANNIVERSARY. Oct 14. Martin Luther King, Jr, became the youngest recipient of the Nobel Peace Prize when awarded the honor on Oct 14, 1964. Dr. King donated the entire $54,000 prize money to furthering the causes of the civil rights movement.

NATIONAL TRAIN YOUR BRAIN DAY. Oct 14. Clean out the cobwebs, blast through the barriers and click on the light bulbs! Give your brain a boost today. Humans use only a small percentage of their brain power. Today is dedicated to expanding our mental capabilities by learning new thinking tools and techniques. For info: Joyce Wycoff, Exec Dir, Innovation Network, 34 E Sola, Ste D101, Santa Barbara, CA 93101. Phone: (805) 965-8477. Fax: (805) 963-8220.
Email: staff@thinksmart.com.
WWW: http://www.thinksmart.com

NORTHERN IRELAND PLOUGHING CONTEST. Oct 14–15. Dungannon County, Tyrone, Northern Ireland. 55th contest. Ploughing competition for tractors, vintage ploughs and horses. Est attendance: 7,000. For info: Northern Ireland Ploughing Assn, 475 Antrim Road, Northern Ireland BT15 3DA. Phone: (1232) 34-0222. Fax: (1232) 37-0739.

PEACE CORPS PROPOSED: ANNIVERSARY. Oct 14, 1960. At the improbable hour of 2 AM, on Oct 14, 1960, then presidential candidate John F. Kennedy spoke impromptu to several thousand students from the steps of the University of Michigan Union building. He asked: "How many of you who are going to be doctors are willing to spend your days in Ghana? How many of you (technicians and engineers) are willing to work in the Foreign Service?" The response was favorable, and 19 days later in San Francisco, Kennedy formally proposed the Peace Corps, which was created by Executive Order Mar 1, 1961. More than 150,000 volunteers served during the next three and one-half decades.

PENN, WILLIAM: BIRTH ANNIVERSARY. Oct 14, 1644. Founder of Pennsylvania, born at London, England. Penn died on July 30, 1718. "Men are generally more careful," Penn wrote, "of the breed of their horses and dogs than of their children." Presidential Proclamation 5284 of Nov 28, 1984, conferred honorary citizenship of the USA upon William Penn and his second wife, Hannah Callowhill Penn. They were the third and fourth persons to receive honorary US citizenship (following Winston Churchill and Raoul Wallenberg).

"THE RED BUTTONS SHOW" TV PREMIERE: ANNIVERSARY. Oct 14, 1952. This comedy-variety show starred the well-known burlesque comedian Red Buttons. Regulars included Dorothy Joliffe, Joe Silver, Jeanne Carson, Sara Seegar, Jimmy Little, Ralph Stanley, Sammy Birch and the Elliot Lawrence Orchestra. It later switched networks under a new format in 1953, as a sitcom with Phyllis Kirk and Paul Lynde.

SPACE MILESTONE: *SOYUZ 23* (USSR). Oct 14, 1976. Launched this date. Cosmonauts V. Zudov and V. Rozhdestvensky were unable to dock at *Salyut 5* space station as planned. Return landing on Earth, Oct 16.

BIRTHDAYS TODAY

Harry Anderson, 46, actor ("Night Court," "Dave's World"), born Newport, RI, Oct 14, 1952.
John Dean, 60, lawyer (White House counsel during Watergate), born Akron, OH, Oct 14, 1938.
Greg Evigan, 45, actor ("B.J. and the Bear," "Masquerade"), born South Amboy, NJ, Oct 14, 1953.
Gary Graffman, 70, pianist, director of the Curtis Institute of Music (Philadelphia), born New York, NY, Oct 14, 1928.
Charles Everett Koop, 82, former US Surgeon General, born Brooklyn, NY, Oct 14, 1916.
Ralph Lauren, 59, designer, born The Bronx, NY, Oct 14, 1939.
Roger Moore, 70, actor (James Bond movies; "The Saint"), born London, England, Oct 14, 1928.

OCTOBER 15 — THURSDAY

Day 288 — 77 Remaining

ARIZONA STATE FAIR. Oct 15–Nov 1. Phoenix, AZ. Festival, concerts, flea markets, entertainment and food. For info: Martin Dickey, Arizona State Fair, PO Box 6728, Phoenix, AZ 85005. Phone: (602) 252-6771. Fax: (602) 495-1302.

BLACK POETRY DAY. Oct 15. To recognize the contribution of black poets to American life and culture and to honor Jupiter Hammon, first black in America to publish his own verse. Jupiter Hammon of Huntington, Long Island, NY, was born Oct 17, 1711. Est attendance: 200. For info: Alexis Levitin, Black Poetry Day Committee, Dept of English, SUNY-Plattsburgh, Plattsburgh, NY 12901-2681. Phone: (518) 564-2426. Fax: (518) 564-2140. Email: levitia@splava.cc.plattsburgh.edu.

CANADA: SNOW GOOSE FESTIVAL. Oct 15–25. Montmagny, Quebec. Come and join in the family fun which includes a parade, entertainment, food booths, sports events and much more. Est attendance: 160,000. For info: Snow Goose Festival, PO Box 101, Montmagny, Quebec, Canada G5V 3S3. Phone: (418) 248-3954. Fax: (418) 248-3959.

CANADA: TORONTO SKI AND SNOWBOARD SHOW. Oct 15–18. Exhibition Place, Toronto, Ontario. Ski manufacturers (equipment, fashions, accessories), retailers, ski resorts, hotels, travel agencies, tourist bureaus, ski clinics and demonstrations, ski clubs, associations, movies and live entertainment. Catering to all ski disciplines—alpine, cross country and snowboarding. Est attendance: 35,000. For info: Canadian Natl Sportsmen's Shows, 703 Evans Ave, Ste 202, Toronto, Ont, Canada M9C 5E9. Phone: (416) 695-0311. Fax: (416) 695-0381.

CHINA: CANTON AUTUMN TRADE FAIR. Oct 15–Nov 15. The Guangzhou (Canton) Autumn Trade Fair is held during the same dates each year.

CROW RESERVATION OPENED FOR SETTLEMENT: ANNIVERSARY. Oct 15, 1892. By Presidential Proclamation 1.8 million acres of Crow Indian reservation were opened to settlers on Oct 15, 1892. The government had induced the Crow to give up a portion of their land in the mountainous western area in the state of Montana. The Crow received 50 cents per acre for their land.

EAST TEXAS YAMBOREE. Oct 15–17. Gilmer, TX. Est attendance: 100,000. For info: Joan Small, Exec Dir, Upshur County Chamber of Commerce, Box 854, Gilmer, TX 75644. Phone: (903) 843-2413 or (903) 843-3981. Fax: (903) 843-3759.

October 1998

S	M	T	W	T	F	S
				1	2	3
4	5	6	7	8	9	10
11	12	13	14	15	16	17
18	19	20	21	22	23	24
25	26	27	28	29	30	31

ENGLAND: ARMOURY HOUSE ART FAIR. Oct 15–18. Honourable Artillery Company's HQ, London, England. Art of all ages on show in a fine palladian building in the City. Est attendance: 4,000. For info: C. Penman or Barbara Bell, PO Box 114, Haywards Heath, Sussex, England RH16 2YU. Phone: (144) 448-2514. Fax: (144) 448-3412.

FAIR OF 1850. Oct 15–Nov 15. Westville Village, Lumpkin, GA. Special demonstrations of harvest-time activities, cane grinding and syrup making. The last remaining antebellum animal-powered cotton gin will be in operation. Est attendance: 15,000. For info: Patty Cannington, Westville Village, PO Box 1850, Lumpkin, GA 31815. Phone: (912) 838-6310 or (888) 733-1850. WWW: http://www.westville.com

"FURY" TV PREMIERE: ANNIVERSAY. Oct 15, 1955. This popular series starred Bobby Diamond as Joey Newton, an orphan living on the streets. He is relocated to a ranch owned by recent widower Jim Newton (Peter Graves), who eventually adopts Joey. Joey's friend is a black horse given to him by Newton, called Fury. Also featured were William Fawcett, Roger Mobley and Jimmy Baird. In syndication, the series was retitled "Brave Stallion."

GERALD AND BETTY FORD: 50th WEDDING ANNIVERSARY. Oct 15, 1948. Grace Episcopal Church, Grand Rapids, MI. Jerry was 35 and Betty 30. This was Betty's second marriage. The Fords had four children: Michael Gerald Ford in 1950, John "Jack" Gardner Ford in 1952, Steven Meigs Ford in 1956 and Susan Elizabeth Ford in 1957.

"I LOVE LUCY" TV PREMIERE: ANNIVERSARY. Oct 15, 1951. This enormously popular sitcom, TV's first smash hit, starred the real-life husband and wife team of Cuban actor/bandleader Desi Arnaz and talented redheaded actress/comedienne Lucille Ball. They starred as Ricky and Lucy Ricardo, a New York bandleader and his aspiring actress/homemaker wife who was always scheming to get on stage. Costarring were William Frawley and Vivian Vance as Fred and Ethel Mertz, the Ricardos' landlords and good friends who participated in the escapades and dealt with the consequences of Lucy's often harmless or well-intentioned plans. Other famous actors guest-starred on the show in later years, including Harpo Marx, Rock Hudson, William Holden, Hedda Hopper and John Wayne. This was the first sitcom to be filmed live before a studio audience, which turned out to be advantageous for the show, which did extremely well in the ratings both the first time around and in reruns.

"I MARRIED JOAN" TV PREMIERE: ANNIVERSARY. Oct 15, 1952. This sitcom about domestic life featured Joan Davis and Jim Backus as the married couple Joan and Judge Bradley Stevens. Appearing as friends and neighbors were Hal Smith, Geraldine Carr, Dan Tobin, Sheila Bromley, Wally Brown, Sally Kelly and Sandra Gould. Guest stars included Bing Crosby and Hoot Gibson.

IACOCCA, LEE A.: BIRTHDAY. Oct 15, 1924. Lido Anthony Iacocca, son of Italian immigrant parents, was born at Allentown, PA. In the 1980s, he was called "America's first corporate folk hero." His best-selling autobiography, *Iacocca*, sold more than 5 million copies. The mechanical engineer-turned-automobile-executive (former president of Ford Motor Co, and later chairman of Chrysler Corp) served as chairman of the centennial rehabilitation Statue of Liberty–Ellis Island foundation.

MANN, MARTY: BIRTH ANNIVERSARY. Oct 15. American social activist and author was born at Chicago, IL, on Oct 15, 1904. She was founder in 1944 of the National Committee for Education on Alcoholism and author of *A New Primer on Alcoholism*. She died at Bridgeport, CT, on July 22, 1980.

MOUNTAIN STATE APPLE HARVEST FESTIVAL. Oct 15–18. Martinsburg, WV. Total family entertainment including apple pie baking contest and auction, coronation of Queen Pomona, 5K run, pancake breakfast, arts and crafts festival, tours of agricultural facilities, antique car show and the grand feature parade. Annually, the third full weekend in October. Est attendance: 75,000. For info: Mountain State Apple Harvest Festival, PO Box 1362, Martinsburg, WV 25402. Phone: (304) 262-2500. Email: msahf@berkeleycounty.com.

MY MOM IS A STUDENT DAY. Oct 15. On this day kids can show their support to their moms by treating them with new pens, paper clips and other little school supplies. They can also fix mom a school lunch with a supportive note inside. Annually, Oct 15. For info: Patti Veld, c/o Davenport College Library, 8200 Georgia St, Merrillville, IN 46410.

NATIONAL GROUCH DAY. Oct 15. Honor a grouch; all grouches deserve a day to be recognized. Annually, Oct 15. For info: Alan R. Miller, Carter Middle School, 300 Upland Dr, Room 207, Clio, MI 48420. Phone: (810) 686-0503.

NIETZSCHE, FRIEDRICH WILHELM: BIRTH ANNIVERSARY. Oct 15. Influential German philosopher born at Rocken on Oct 15, 1844. Especially remembered among his philosophical beliefs are contempt for the weak and expected ultimate triumph of a superman. Nietzsche died at Weimar on Aug 25, 1900, a decade after becoming insane.

SENATE CONFIRMS THOMAS TO SUPREME COURT: ANNIVERSARY. Oct 15, 1991. After three days of Senate Judiciary Committee hearings on charges of sexual harassment made against Judge Clarence Thomas by a former aide, Anita F. Hill, the Senate confirmed Thomas as the 106th US Supreme Court Justice with a 52–48 vote on Oct 15, 1991. The vote was the closest for a 20th-century justice and made Thomas, who would replace retired Justice Thurgood Marshall, the only other African American to sit on the Supreme Court besides Marshall.

TAMPA BOAT SHOW. Oct 15–18. Tampa Convention Center and adjacent marina, Tampa, FL. 31st annual show is Gulf Coast's premier nautical event, showcasing hundreds of new boats and accessories, plus informative boating and fishing seminars. Est attendance: 22,000. For info: NMMA, 600 Third Ave, 23rd Fl, New York, NY 10016. Phone: (305) 531-8410. Fax: (305) 534-3139.

WAR EAGLE FAIR. Oct 15–18. War Eagle Mills Farm, War Eagle, AR. 45th annual fair with more than 350 booths of baskets, quilts, woodwork, pottery, furniture, wood carving, toys, leather, books, candles, weaving, jams and jellies and food under circus-style tents on the historic farm grounds. "One of the most highly respected shows in the country." Est attendance: 135,000. For info: Shirley Sutton, War Eagle Fair, 11036 High Sky Inn Rd, Hindsville, AR 72738. Phone: (501) 789-5398. Fax: (501) 789-2215.

★**WHITE CANE SAFETY DAY.** Oct 15. Presidential Proclamation always issued for Oct 15 since 1964 (PL88–628 of Oct 6, 1964).

WILSON, EDITH BOLLING GALT: BIRTH ANNIVERSARY. Oct 15, 1872. Second wife of Woodrow Wilson, 28th president of the US, born at Wytheville, VA, Oct 15, 1872. Died Dec 28, 1961.

WODEHOUSE, PELHAM GRENVILLE: BIRTH ANNIVERSARY. Oct 15, 1881. English author, humorist, creator of Jeeves, born at Guildford, Surrey, England, died at Southampton, Long Island, NY, Feb 14, 1975.

WORLD'S LARGEST HALLOWEEN PARTY. Oct 15–18. (Also Oct 22–25.) Louisville, KY. Est attendance: 50,000. For info: Joyce Compton, Coord Spec Events, PO Box 37250, Louisville, KY 40233. Phone: (502) 459-2181. Fax: (502) 459-2196.

BIRTHDAYS TODAY

Victor Banerjee, 52, actor (*A Passage to India, The Home and the World*), born Calcutta, India, Oct 15, 1946.
John Kenneth Galbraith, 90, economist, diplomat, author, born Iona Station, Ontario, Canada, Oct 15, 1908.
Lee Iacocca, 74, former automobile executive (Ford and Chrysler), born Allentown, PA, Oct 15, 1924.
Tito Jackson (Toriano Adaryll Jackson), 45, singer, musician (Jackson 5), born Gary, IN, Oct 15, 1953.
Linda Lavin, 59, actress (Tony for *Broadway Bound*; "Alice"), born Portland, ME, Oct 15, 1939.
Penny Marshall, 56, director (*Big, A League of Their Own*), actress, born New York, NY, Oct 15, 1942.
Ned Ray McWherter, 68, former Governor of Tennessee (D), born Palmersville, TN, Oct 15, 1930.
James Alvin (Jim) Palmer, 53, sportscaster, Baseball Hall of Fame pitcher, born New York, NY, Oct 15, 1945.
Mario Puzo, 78, author (*The Godfather, Fourth K.*), born New York, NY, Oct 15, 1920.
Sarah (Ferguson), 39, Duchess of York (former wife of Prince Andrew), born London, England, Oct 15, 1959.
Arthur Meier Schlesinger, Jr, 81, historian, author, born Columbus, OH, Oct 15, 1917.

OCTOBER 16 — FRIDAY

Day 289 — 76 Remaining

AMERICA'S FIRST DEPARTMENT STORE. Oct 16, 1868. Salt Lake City, UT. America's first department store, "ZCMI" (Zion's Co-Operative Mercantile Institution), is still operating in Salt Lake City. It was founded under the direction of Brigham Young. For info: Museum of Church History and Art, 45 North West Temple, Salt Lake City, UT 84150. Phone: (801) 240-4604.

APPLE BUTTER STIRRIN'. Oct 16–18. Coshocton, OH. Kettles of apple butter simmer over open fires; arts, crafts, contests, in Roscoe Village, a restored canal town. Also, live musical entertainment. Est attendance: 33,000. For info: Roscoe Village Fdtn, 381 Hill St, Coshocton, OH 43812. Phone: (800) 877-1830 or (614) 622-9310. Fax: (614) 623-6555.

BEN-GURION, DAVID: BIRTH ANNIVERSARY. Oct 16, 1886. First prime minister of the state of Israel. Born at Plonsk, Poland, died at Tel Aviv, Israel, on Dec 1, 1973.

BIRTH CONTROL CLINIC OPENED: ANNIVERSARY. Oct 16, 1916. Margaret Sanger, Fania Mindell and Ethel Burne opened the first birth control clinic in the US at 46 Amboy St, Brooklyn, NY. Sanger believed that the poor should be able to control the size of their families.

BLAKEY, ART: DEATH ANNIVERSARY. Oct 16, 1990. American jazz drummer and bandleader Art Blakey (also known as Abdullah Ibn Buhaina) was born at Pittsburgh, PA. He formed his own band, the *Jazz Messengers*, in the 1940s. He was noted for his long solos of tremendous textual control and exclamatory releases. He died at New York, NY.

BOOTH, SHIRLEY: DEATH ANNIVERSARY. Oct 16, 1992. American actress Shirley Booth was born Thelma Booth Ford at New York, NY. She won an Oscar and a Tony Award for her roles in the film (1952) and stage (1950) productions of *Come Back, Little Sheba*, but she is best known for her title role in the television program "Hazel" (1961–66). She died at Chatham, MS.

CRANBERRY HARVEST WEEKEND. Oct 16–18. Nantucket Island, MA. Guided tours of bogs, cookery contest, marketplace, craft exhibitions at this 9th annual festival. Est attendance: 10,000. For info: Nantucket Island Chamber of Commerce, 48 Main St, Nantucket, MA 02554-3595. Phone: (508) 228-1700.

CRIMEAN WAR BEGAN: ANNIVERSARY. Oct 16, 1853. The Ottoman Empire declared war on Russia to stem Russian expansionist policies in the Empire. Britain, France and parts of Italy allied themselves with the Turks against Russia. A battle in this war was immortalized in Tennyson's poem, "The Charge of the Light Brigade." Health conditions for soldiers were scandalous, leading Florence Nightingale to work in the British hospital at Istanbul. This was the first war to be observed firsthand by newspaper reporters and photographers.

DICTIONARY DAY. Oct 16. The birthday of Noah Webster, American teacher and lexicographer, is occasion to encourage every person to acquire at least one dictionary—and to use it regularly.

DODGE PRAIRIE CIRCUIT FINALS RODEO. Oct 16–17. Lazy E Arena, Guthrie, OK. The top 12 cowboys in each event from Oklahoma, Kansas and Nebraska compete for $60,000 and Circuit Championship Titles. Est attendance: 15,000. For info: Lazy E Arena, Route 5 Box 393, Guthrie, OK 73044. Phone: (405) 282-RIDE or (800) 595-RIDE. Fax: (405) 282-3785. Email: arena@lazye.com. WWW: http://www.lazye.com

DOUGLAS, WILLIAM ORVILLE: 100th BIRTH ANNIVERSARY. Oct 16, 1898. American jurist, world traveler, conservationist, outdoorsman and author. Born at Maine, MN, Oct 16, 1898. Served as justice of the US Supreme Court longer than any other (36 years). Died at Washington, DC, Jan 19, 1980.

FALL FESTIVAL OF LEAVES. Oct 16–18. Bainbridge, Ross County, OH. Celebrating the beauty of the season and region. Folk arts, crafts, music, antique car show, log sawing contest, flea markets and parades. To obtain a map of self-guided scenic tours send SASE to sponsor. For info: Fall Festival of Leaves, Box 571, Bainbridge, Ross County, OH 45612. Phone: (614) 634-2085.

FOOTHILLS ART FESTIVAL. Oct 16–18. Jackson, OH. Visual arts exhibits with more than 600 works by 150 artists from the tri-state area. Also live music and arts activities for the entire family. Est attendance: 4,000. For info: Barbara Summers, Southern Hills Arts Council, PO Box 149, Jackson, OH 45640. Phone: (614) 286-6355. Fax: (614) 384-3063.

GRANT PUT IN CHARGE OF THE MISSISSIPPI REGION: ANNIVERSARY. Oct 16, 1863. After his impressive success taking Vicksburg, MS, Ulysses S. Grant, a brigadier general of the militia, was appointed a general in the regular army and, with the subsequent reorganization of the departments of war in Ohio, Cumberland and Tennessee, was placed in charge of the newly formed Military Division of the Mississippi on this date. Grant's first priority was to save the besieged and starving Union troops in Chattanooga, TN.

HARVEST FESTIVAL. Oct 16. Roanoke, VA. This heritage celebration features country music, square dancers, line dancers, demonstrations of spinning, weaving, lace making, etc, as well as pumpkin decorating. Carriage rides around downtown Roanoke and pony rides for children. Est attendance: 4,000. For info: Gayle Williams, Program Mgr, Downtown Roanoke Inc, 310 First St SW, Roanoke, VA 24011. Phone: (540) 342-2028. Fax: (540) 344-1452. Email: dai@roanoke.org.
WWW: http://downtown.roanoke.org

JOHN BROWN'S RAID: ANNIVERSARY. Oct 16. On Oct 16, 1859, fanatical abolitionist John Brown, with a band of about 20 men, seized the US Arsenal at Harpers Ferry, WV. Brown was captured and the insurrection put down by Oct 19. Brown was hanged at Charles Town, WV, Dec 2, 1859.

October 1998

S	M	T	W	T	F	S
				1	2	3
4	5	6	7	8	9	10
11	12	13	14	15	16	17
18	19	20	21	22	23	24
25	26	27	28	29	30	31

LEE COUNTY COTTON FESTIVAL. Oct 16–19. Bishopville, SC. Join the festivities with amusement rides, fireworks, parades, arts and crafts displays, entertainment, rodeos, sports events, food booths and much more. Annually, the third weekend in October. Est attendance: 18,000. For info: Lee County Chamber of Commerce, Lee County Cotton Fest, PO Box 187, Bishopville, SC 29010. Phone: (803) 484-5145. Fax: (803) 484-4270.

MAPLE LEAF FESTIVAL. Oct 16–18. Carthage, MO. Brilliant fall foliage gives this Victorian city the perfect backdrop. A 150+ unit parade, four-state marching band competition, statewide car show, historic homes tour, arts and craft show plus entertainment and much more. Annually, the third weekend in October. Est attendance: 70,000. For info: Chamber of Commerce, 107 E 3rd St, Carthage, MO 64836. Phone: (417) 358-2373. Fax: (417) 358-7479.

MARIE ANTOINETTE: EXECUTION ANNIVERSARY. Oct 16, 1793. Queen Marie Antoinette, whose extravagance and "let them eat cake" attitude toward the starving French underclass made her a symbol and target of the French Revolution, was beheaded on Oct 16, 1793.

MISSOURI DAY FESTIVAL. Oct 16–18. North Central Missouri Fairgrounds, Trenton, MO. 14th annual festival features a parade, car show, quilt show, crafts, a talent show, marching band competition and entertainment of all kinds. Est attendance: 10,000. For info: Missouri Day Festival, Linda Kennebeck, 617 Main, Trenton, MO 64683. Phone: (816) 359-4324. Fax: (816) 359-4325.

NATIONAL BOSS DAY. Oct 16. For all employees to honor their bosses. Annually, Oct 16. For info: Mrs Patricia Bays Haroski, Originator, 2871-F-Walnut View Ct, Winston-Salem, NC 27103.

NORTH CAROLINA STATE FAIR. Oct 16–25. State Fairgrounds, Raleigh, NC. Agricultural fair with livestock, arts and crafts, home arts, entertainment and carnival. Est attendance: 750,000. For info: Sam Rand, Mgr, North Carolina State Fair, 1025 Blue Ridge Blvd, Raleigh, NC 27607. Phone: (919) 821-7400. Fax: (919) 733-5079.
Email: rayfrost@ncdamail.agr.state.nc.us.
WWW: http://www.agr.state.nc.us/fair/index.html

O'NEILL, EUGENE GLADSTONE: BIRTH ANNIVERSARY. Oct 16, 1888. American playwright, recipient of Pulitzer and Nobel Prize. Born at New York, NY, Oct 16, 1888. Died at Boston, MA, Nov 27, 1953.

VIRGINIA CHRISTMAS SHOW. Oct 16–18. Prince William County Fairgrounds, Manassas, VA. 250 artisans, crafters (displaying and selling), specialty Christmas food shops, legendary "Sgt Santa." Craft demonstrations, entertainment and more. 9th annual show. Est attendance: 20,000. For info: Virginia Show Productions, PO Box 305, Chase City, VA 23924. Phone: (804) 372-3996. Fax: (804) 372-3996.

WEBSTER, NOAH: BIRTH ANNIVERSARY. Oct 16, 1758. American teacher and journalist whose name became synonymous with the word "dictionary" after his compilations of the earliest American dictionaries of the English language. Born at West Hartford, CT, on Oct 16, 1758. Died at New Haven, CT, on May 28, 1843.

WILDE, OSCAR: BIRTH ANNIVERSARY. Oct 16. Irish poet and playwright Oscar (Fingal O'Flahertie Wills) Wilde was born at Dublin, Ireland, on Oct 16, 1854. At the height of his career he was imprisoned for two years on a morals offense, during which time he wrote "A Ballad of Reading Gaol." Best known of his plays is *The Importance of Being Earnest.* "There is only one thing in the world worse than being talked about," he wrote in his *Picture of Dorian Gray*, "and that is not being talked about." Wilde died, self-exiled, at Paris, France, on Nov 30, 1900. His dying words are said to have been: "This wallpaper is killing me; one of us has got to go."

WORLD FOOD DAY. Oct 16. To increase awareness, understanding and informed action on hunger. Annually, on the founding date of the UN Food and Agriculture Organization. For info: Patricia Young, US National Committee for World Food Day, 1001 22nd St NW, Washington, DC 20437. Phone: (202) 653-2404.

YALE UNIVERSITY FOUNDED: ANNIVERSARY. Oct 16, 1701. The Collegiate School was founded in Killingworth, CT, started by Congregationalists dissatisfied with the growing liberalism at Harvard. In 1745, the school was moved to New Haven, CT, where it became Yale College, named after Elihu Yale, son of one of the founders of New Haven and a governor of India for the East India Company. Yale became a university in 1887. The first degrees were awarded in 1716.

ZOO BOO. Oct 16–31. Metro Washington Park Zoo, Portland, OR. A special Halloween event featuring the zoo train and other activities. Est attendance: 38,000. For info: Metro Washington Park Zoo, 4001 SW Canyon Rd, Portland, OR 97221-2799. Phone: (503) 226-1561. Fax: (503) 226-6836.

BIRTHDAYS TODAY

Melissa Louise Belote, 42, Olympic gold medal swimmer, born Washington, DC, Oct 16, 1956.

Manute Bol, 36, basketball player, born Gogrial, Sudan, Oct 16, 1962.

Barry Corbin, 58, actor ("Northern Exposure," *Stir Crazy, Any Which Way You Can*), born Dawson County, TX, Oct 16, 1940.

Gunter Grass, 71, author (*The Tin Drum, Dog Years*), born Danzig, Germany, Oct 16, 1927.

Paul Kariya, 24, hockey player, born Vancouver, British Columbia, Canada, Oct 16, 1974.

Angela Lansbury, 73, actress (*National Velvet*; Tony for *Sweeny Todd*; "Murder She Wrote"), born London, England, Oct 16, 1925.

Kellie Martin, 23, actress ("Life Goes On"), born Riverside, CA, Oct 16, 1975.

Tim Robbins, 40, actor (*Top Gun, Shawshank Redemption*), born West Covina, CA, Oct 16, 1958.

Suzanne Somers, 52, actress ("Three's Company," *American Graffiti*), born San Bruno, CA, Oct 16, 1946.

Kordell Stewart, 26, football player, born New Orleans, LA, Oct 16, 1972.

OCTOBER 17 — SATURDAY

Day 290 — 75 Remaining

ARTHUR, JEAN: BIRTH ANNIVERSARY. Oct 17, 1900. American actress Jean Arthur was born Gladys Georgianna Greene at Plattsburg, NY. Her films included *Mr Deeds Goes to Town* (1936), *Mr Smith Goes to Washington* (1939) and *Shane* (1953). She died on June 19, 1991, at Carmel, CA.

ATLANTIQUE CITY ANTIQUES AND COLLECTIBLES HOLIDAY FAIR. Oct 17–18. Atlantic City Convention Center, Atlantic City, NJ. "World's largest" antiques and collectibles show. More than 1,000 dealers with an array of memorabilia. Much weird and wonderful stuff such as Jack Benny's violin, first Superman comic book, etc. Est attendance: 100,000. For info: Mark Soifer, Press Relations, 1803 Clover Ave, Vineland, NJ 08360. Phone: (609) 691-7535. Fax: (609) 691-9458.

AUTUMN HISTORIC FOLKLIFE FESTIVAL. Oct 17–18. Downtown Historic District, Hannibal, MO. The Hannibal Arts Council sponsors its 22nd annual festival celebrating heritage and tradition of the 1800s. Artisans demonstrate the folk arts of the mid-1800s, vendors prepare food and drink over wood fires and street performers play traditional tunes. Also living history and children's areas with many activities. Est attendance: 25,000. For info: Hannibal Arts Council, PO Box 1202, Hannibal, MO 63401. Phone: (573) 221-6545.

COUNTRY AFFAIR. Oct 17–18. Ben Franklin School, Menomonee Falls, WI. Community League's 16th annual fair features antiques, folk art and country collectibles. More than 90 exhibitors from five states; a Country Luncheon of homemade food and desserts; a Quilt Raffle; and a "Country Pantry" and silent auction. Admission charged. Est attendance: 6,500. For info: Jeanne Verbsky, Community League, Inc, Publicity— ACA, PO Box 101, Menomonee Falls, WI 53052. Phone: (414) 297-9446.

DINO-AUCTION. Oct 17. Thermopolis, WY. 2nd annual. International auction (silent, mail, on line and on site) of dino related art and artifacts to benefit Friends of the Dinosaurs and Big Horn Basin Foundation. Sponsored by: The Wyoming Dinosaur Center. For info: Ellen Sue Blakey, The Wyoming Dinosaur Center, PO Box 868, Thermopolis, WY 82443. Phone: (307) 864-2997. Fax: (307) 864-5762. WWW: http://www.wyoming.com/dino

DOLLHOUSE & MINIATURE SHOW. Oct 17–18. Mountain View Inn, Greensburg, PA. A show devoted to beautiful dollhouses and all the miniatures to go with them. For info: Mountain View Inn, Rte 30 East, Greensburg, PA 15601. Phone: (412) 834-5300 or (800) 537-8709. Fax: (412) 834-5304.

DOZENAL SOCIETY OF AMERICA: ANNUAL MEETING. Oct 17. Garden City, Long Island, NY. Est attendance: 24. For info: Prof. Rafael Marino, Nassau Community College, Garden City, Long Island, NY 11530-6793. Phone: (516) 572-7383. Email: marinor@amanda.dorsai.org.

EIGHTEENTH-CENTURY AUTUMN MARKET FAIR. Oct 17–18. McLean, VA. Crafts, games, music and dancing. Period food and wares. Est attendance: 4,200. For info: Publicist, Claude Moore Colonial Farm at Turkey Run, 6310 Georgetown Pike, McLean, VA 22101. Phone: (703) 442-7557. Fax: (703) 442-0714.

FALL FIESTA OF THE ARTS. Oct 17–18. Swan Lake Gardens, Sumter, SC. Features visual and performing arts, concerts and choral groups. Annually, the third weekend in October. Est attendance: 6,000. For info: Sumter County Cultural Commission, 135 Haynsworth St, Sumter, SC 29150. Phone: (803) 436-2260.

FINE ARTS AND CRAFTS FESTIVAL. Oct 17–18. Roseland Cottage, Bowen House, Woodstock, CT. 16th annual festival features 175 juried artists and craftsmen, food court and entertainment for children and adults. Rain or shine. Admission is $4 per person with proceeds to benefit museum. Annually, the weekend after Columbus Day. Est attendance: 10,000. For info: Roseland Cottage, Bowen House, PO Box 186, Woodstock, CT 06281. Phone: (860) 928-4074. Fax: (860) 963-2208.

GRAND MILITIA MUSTER. Oct 17–18. St. Mary's City, MD. The largest gathering of 17th-century military reenactment groups in the US. Tacticals, contests of skill and camp life demonstrations. Annually, the third weekend in October. Est attendance: 1,000. For info: Public Affairs Office, Historic St. Mary's City, PO Box 39, St. Mary's City, MD 20686. Phone: (301) 862-0990 or (800) SMC-1634. Fax: (301) 862-0968.

GREAT TEDDY BEAR JAMBOREE SHOW AND SALE. Oct 17–18. Bristol, CT. To bring together teddy bear lovers, collectors and others to view thousands of bears, old and new. Hungry bear snack bar, teddy bear hospital and other teddy bear activities. Annually, the third weekend in October. Est attendance: 10,000. For info: Cheryl Yetke, Office Mgr, Friends of Bristol Senior Ctr, 240 Stafford Ave, Bristol, CT 06010. Phone: (860) 583-2562. Fax: (860) 584-5063.

HALLOWEEN HAPPENING. Oct 17–18. Cincinnati Zoo and Botanical Garden, Cincinnati, OH. Children can trick-or-treat at the zoo from 14 different treat stations. Other activities include hayrides, pumpkin giveaways, a pumpkin carving contest and the city's largest costume contest. Est attendance: 23,000. For info: Events and Promo Dept, Cincinnati Zoo and Botanical Garden, 3400 Vine St, Cincinnati, OH 45220. Phone: (513) 281-4701 ext 8316. Fax: (513) 559-7790. WWW: http://www.cincyzoo.org.

HAMMON, JUPITER: BIRTH ANNIVERSARY. Oct 17, 1711. America's first published black poet, whose birth anniversary is celebrated annually as Black Poetry Day (Oct 15 this year), was born into slavery, probably at Long Island, NY. He was taught to read, however, and as a trusted servant was allowed to use his master's library. "With the publication on Christmas Day, 1760, of the 88-line broadside poem 'An Evening Thought,' Jupiter Hammon, then 49, became the first black in America to publish poetry." Hammon died in 1790. The exact date and place of his death and burial are as yet unknown.

HERITAGE DAYS. Oct 17–18. Depot Street, Marthasville, MO. Celebration of pioneer founders Daniel Boone and Lewis and Clark. Food, crafts, antiques, wine and a parade on Sunday. Annually, the third weekend in October. Est attendance: 5,000. For info: Marthasville Chamber of Commerce, PO Box 95, Marthasville, MO 63357. Phone: (816) 438-5922.

"THE HOLLYWOOD SQUARES" TV PREMIERE: ANNIVERSARY. Oct 17, 1966. On this game show, nine celebrities sat in a giant grid. Two contestants played tic-tac-toe by determining if an answer given by a celebrity was correct. Peter Marshall hosted the show for many years with panelists Paul Lynde, Rose Marie, Cliff Arquette, Wally Cox, John Davidson and George Gobel among others. John Davidson took over as host in 1986 for a new version of the game show with Joan Rivers and, later, Shadoe Stevens at center square.

October 1998

S	M	T	W	T	F	S
				1	2	3
4	5	6	7	8	9	10
11	12	13	14	15	16	17
18	19	20	21	22	23	24
25	26	27	28	29	30	31

HONG KONG: BIRTHDAY OF CONFUCIUS. Oct 17. Religious observances are held by the Confucian Society at Confucius Temple in Causeway Bay. Observed on 27th day of 8th lunar month.

INTERNATIONAL GOLD CUP. Oct 17. Great Meadow, The Plains, VA. A day of steeplechasing in the heart of Virginia's hunt country. Gates open at 10 AM for special events and activities. Corporate and chalet entertainment packages available. Conducted by the Virginia Gold Cup Association for benefit of free year-round use of Great Meadow for nonprofit community activities. Est attendance: 45,000. For info: Virginia Gold Cup Assn, PO Box 840, Warrenton, VA 22186. Phone: (540) 347-2612. Fax: (540) 349-1829.

INTERNATIONAL SPACE HALL OF FAME INDUCTION. Oct 17. Space Center, Alamogordo, NM. International recognition and induction of space pioneers and explorers into the International Space Hall of Fame. Annually, the third Saturday in October. Sponsor: International Space Hall of Fame Foundation. Est attendance: 500. For info: Jack Moore, Marketing Dir, Space Center, PO Box 533, Alamogordo, NM 88311. Phone: (800) 545-4021. Fax: (505) 437-7722.
Email: space-plan@nmsua.nmsu.edu.
WWW: http://abcc.nmsu.edu/~bwood/

JOHNSON, RICHARD MENTOR: BIRTH ANNIVERSARY. Oct 17. Ninth vice president of the US (1837–1841). Born at Floyd's Station, KY, Oct 17, 1780. Died at Frankfort, KY, Nov 19, 1850.

LENEXA CHILI CHALLENGE. Oct 17. Lenexa Community Center, Lenexa, KS. Free samples give you the chance to vote for your favorite chili, then enjoy a live band and games for all ages including a jalapeño pepper eating contest. Est attendance: 5,000. For info: Bill Nicrs, Lenexa Parks & Rec, 13240 Oak St, Lenexa, KS 66215. Phone: (913) 541-8592. Fax: (913) 492-8118.

MISSISSINEWA 1812. Oct 17–18. Marion, IN. Largest War of 1812 living history event in US includes reenactment of battle. Military, trappers and woodland Indians living as they did 185 years ago. Est attendance: 32,000. For info: Mississinewa Battlefield Society, PO Box 1812, 402 S Washington, Ste 509, Marion, IN 46952. Phone: (800) 662-1809. Fax: (705) 662-1809. Email: war1812@aol.com.

OKTOBERFEST. Oct 17–18. Traders Village, Grand Prairie, TX. Bavarian biergarten setting featuring polka bands, German, Polish, Norwegian and Czech folk dancing and plenty of German food and beer. Est attendance: 60,000. For info: Traders Village, 2602 Mayfield Rd, Grand Prairie, TX 75052-7246. Phone: (972) 647-2331.

POPE JOHN PAUL I: BIRTH ANNIVERSARY. Oct 17, 1912. Albino Luciani, 263rd pope of the Roman Catholic Church. Born at Forno di Canale, Italy, Oct 17, 1912. Elected pope Aug 26, 1978. Died at Rome, 34 days after his election, on Sept 28, 1978. Shortest papacy since Pope Leo XI (Apr 1–27, 1605).

QUINCY PRESERVES FALL ARCHITECTURAL TOUR. Oct 17. Quincy, IL. 10 AM–4 PM. Tour historic homes decked out in their finest. Homes range in size from Quincy's grandest mansions to quaint cottages. Inside each home, ticket holders are awed by the architectural splendors. Annually, the third Saturday in October. Est attendance: 10,000. For info: Fran Cook, Quincy Preserves, 310 S 16th St, Quincy, IL 62301. Phone: (217) 224-2587.

SAINT MARY'S COUNTY OYSTER FESTIVAL. Oct 17–18. Fairgrounds, Leonardtown, MD. Oysters served every style, national oyster shucking contest and national oyster cookoff. Est attendance: 25,000. For info: David L. Taylor, Admin, Oyster Fest Office, Box 766, California, MD 20619-0766. Phone: (301) 863-5015. Fax: (301) 863-7788.

SAN FRANCISCO EARTHQUAKE OF 1989: ANNIVERSARY. Oct 17, 1989. The San Francisco Bay area was rocked by an earthquake registering 7.1 on the Richter scale at 5:04 PM, EDT, just as the nation's baseball fans settled in to watch the 1989 World Series. The quake caused damage estimated at $10 billion and killed 67 people, many of whom were caught in the collapse of the double-decked Interstate 80, in Oakland, CA. A large World Series audience was tuned in to the pregame coverage when the quake hit and knocked the broadcast off the air.

SOUTHERN WILDLIFE FESTIVAL. Oct 17–18 (tentative). Calhoun College, Decatur, AL. Event features original paintings, photography and competition in color and black and white. Vendors specialize in wildlife items and wildlife carvings. Est attendance: 5,000. For info: Jacklyn Bailey, Decatur Conv and Visitors Bureau, 719 6th Ave SE, PO Box 2349, Decatur, AL 35602. Phone: (205) 350-2028 or (800) 524-6181. Email: dcvb@hiwaay.net.

SWEETEST DAY. Oct 17. Observed annually on the third Saturday in October. For info: John M. Sanders, Chair, Detroit Sweetest Day Committee, 901 Wilshire Dr, Ste 360, Troy, MI 48084. Phone: (810) 362-3223. Fax: (810) 362-0878.

TAMARACK TIME! Oct 17 (tentative). Bigfork, MT. Old-fashioned village celebration of harvest and autumn. Local chefs prepare their specialties for a taste treat. Est attendance: 600. For info: Elna Darrow, Box 400, Bigfork, MT 59911-0400. Phone: (406) 837-4848. Email: crossbow@cyberpont.net.

TOWN POINT VIRGINIA WINE FESTIVAL. Oct 17–18. Norfolk, VA. Join us along the Elizabth River for one of the state's largest outdoor wine festivals. More than 25 Virginia wineries provide a sample of wines available for purchase by the glass or bottle. Specialty crafts, wine seminars and more are available for you and your friends. Call for ticket information. For info: Marketing Director, Norfolk Festevents Ltd, 120 W Main St, Norfolk, VA 23510. Phone: (757) 441-2345. Fax: (757) 441-5198.

UNITED NATIONS: INTERNATIONAL DAY FOR THE ERADICATION OF POVERTY. Oct 17. The General Assembly proclaimed this observance (Res 47/196) to promote public awareness of the need to eradicate poverty and destitution in all countries, particularly the developing nations.

WOOLLY WORM FESTIVAL. Oct 17–18. Banner Elk, NC. 21st annual woolly worm races, mountain entertainment, crafts and food. Est attendance: 15,000. For info: Judy Donaghy, Exec Dir, Chamber of Commerce, PO Box 335, Banner Elk, NC 28604. Phone: (704) 898-5605. Fax: (704) 898-8287. Email: beacc@skybest.com. WWW: http://www.banner-elk.com/

☆ ☆ ☆

WORLD RAINFOREST WEEK. Oct 17–25. Rainforest activists from 140 worldwide action groups will sponsor events to increase public awareness of rainforest destruction and motivate people to protect the Earth's rainforest and support the rights of their inhabitants. The global rate of destruction of rainforests is 2.4 acres per second—equivalent to two US football fields. For info: M. Holmgren, Grassroots Coord, Rainforest Action Network, 221 Pine St, 5th Floor, San Francisco, CA 94104. Phone: (415) 398-4404. Email: rags@ran.org. WWW: http://www.ran.org

WYATT EARP O.K. CORRAL ANNIVERSARY. Oct 17. Monmouth, IL. Open House with Wyatt Earp birthplace and Pioneer Cemetery tours 1 PM to 4 PM, and O.K. Corral reenactments. Annually, third Saturday in October. Est attendance: 100. For info: Wyatt Earp Birthplace, Historic House Museum, Office: 1020 E Detroit Ave, Monmouth, IL 61462. Phone: (309) 734-6419 or Chamber of Commerce (309) 734-3181. Fax: (309) 734-6419.

YORKTOWN VICTORY CELEBRATION. Oct 17–18. Yorktown Victory Center, Yorktown, VA. An encampment of Revolutionary War reenactors features military demonstrations, music, games and contests to salute the anniversary of Washington's victory at Yorktown in October 1781. Est attendance: 1,500. For info: Jamestown-Yorktown Fdtn, Media Relations, PO Box 1607, Williamsburg, VA 23187. Phone: (757) 253-4838. Fax: (757) 253-5299. WWW: http://www.historyisfun.org

BIRTHDAYS TODAY

Beverly Garland, 72, actress ("My Three Sons," "Scarecrow and Mrs King"), born Santa Cruz, CA, Oct 17, 1926.

Mae Jemison, 42, scientist, astronaut, host ("Susan B. Anthony Slept Here"), born Decatur, AL, Oct 17, 1956.

Margot Kidder, 50, actress (Lois Lane in *Superman* movies), born Yellowknife, Northwest Territories, Canada, Oct 17, 1948.

Robert Craig ("Evel") Knievel, 60, motorcycle stunt performer, born Butte, MT, Oct 17, 1938.

Michael McKean, 51, actor ("Laverne & Shirley," *This Is Spinal Tap*), born New York, NY, Oct 17, 1947.

Steve Douglas McMichael, 41, former football player, born Houston, TX, Oct 17, 1957.

Arthur Miller, 83, dramatist (*Death of a Salesman, A View from the Bridge, All My Sons*), born New York, NY, Oct 17, 1915.

Tom Poston, 71, actor ("Grace Under Fire," "The Steve Allen Show" [Emmy Award, 1959], *Soldier in the Rain*), born Columbus, OH, Oct 17, 1927.

George Wendt, 50, actor (Norm Peterson on "Cheers"), born Chicago, IL, Oct 17, 1948.

OCTOBER 18 — SUNDAY

Day 291 — 74 Remaining

ALASKA DAY: ANNIVERSARY. Oct 18, 1867. Alaska. Anniversary of transfer of Alaska from Russia to the US. Became official on Sitka's Castle Hill, Oct 18, 1867.

ANDREE, SALOMON AUGUSTE: BIRTH ANNIVERSARY. Oct 18. Swedish explorer and balloonist was born at Grenna, Sweden, on Oct 18, 1854. His North Pole expedition of 1897 attracted world attention but ended tragically. With two companions, Andree left Spitzbergen on July 11, 1897, in a balloon, hoping to place the Swedish flag at the North Pole. The last message from Andree, borne by carrier pigeons, was dated noon, July 13, 1897. The frozen bodies of the explorers were found 33 years later by another polar expedition in the summer of 1930. Diaries, maps and exposed photographic negatives also were found. The photos were developed successfully, providing a pictorial record of the ill-fated expedition.

BERGSON, HENRI: BIRTH ANNIVERSARY. Oct 18. French philosopher, Nobel Prize winner and author of *Creative Evolution*, born Oct 18, 1859. Died Jan 4, 1941.

BROOKS, JAMES DAVID: BIRTH ANNIVERSARY. Oct 18, 1906. James Brooks was born at St. Louis, MO. During the Depression Brooks worked as a muralist in the Federal Art Project of the Works Progress Administration. His best known work of that period was "Flight," a 235-ft mural on the rotunda of the Marine Air Terminal at La Guardia National Airport in New York. It was painted over during the 1950s but restored in 1980. After leaving the WPA he worked as an art correspondent with the US Army from 1942 to 1945. When Brooks returned to New York, his interest shifted to abstraction. He came to be considered one of the greatest abstract expressionists. His paintings were exhibited in the historic "Ninth Street Exhibition" as a part of the Museum of Modern Art's exhibits "Twelve Americans" and "New American Painting," among others. He died on Mar 8, 1992, at Brookhaven, NY.

CANADA: PERSONS DAY. Oct 18. A day to commemorate the anniversary of the 1929 ruling that declared women to be persons in Canada. Prior to this ruling English common law prevailed ("Women are persons in matters of pains and penalties, but are not persons in matters of rights and privileges"). The celebrated cause, popularly known as the "Persons Case," was brought by five women of Alberta, Canada; leader of the courageous "Famous Five" was Emily Murphy (1868–1933). This ruling by the Judicial Committee of England's Privy Council, Oct 18, 1929, overturned a 1928 decision of the Supreme Court of Canada. Fifty years after the Persons Case decision, in 1979, the Governor General's Awards in Commemoration of the Persons Case were established to recognize deserving persons who have made outstanding contributions to the quality of life of women in Canada.

CANALETTO, GIOVANNI ANTONIO: BIRTH ANNIVERSARY. Oct 18, 1697. Italian painter Giovanni Antonio Canaletto (born Canale), who is best known for his detailed landscapes of Venice and London, was born at Venice and died there at age 70 on Apr 20, 1768. He was known for his accurate use of perspective and shadow and light. He went to England in 1746 and expanded his range of subjects to include English landscapes and country homes. Returning to Italy, Canaletto was as popular as ever. He earned election to the Venetian Academy in 1763; that same year he was appointed prior of the Collegio di Pittori.

"COLT .45" TV PREMIERE: ANNIVERSARY. Oct 18, 1957. Spaghetti-western actor Wayde Preston starred in this ABC western as Christopher Colt, son of the inventor of the Colt revolver, and a government agent. Character actor Donald May replaced Preston and played the role of Sam Colt, Jr, Christopher's cousin, until early 1960 when Preston returned to the show.

GERMANY: WAR CRIMES TRIAL: ANNIVERSARY. Oct 18, 1945. The first session of the German war crimes trials started at Berlin with indictments against 24 former Nazi leaders. Later sessions were held at Nuremberg, starting Nov 20, 1945. One defendant committed suicide during the trial, and another was excused because of his physical and mental condition. The trial lasted more than 10 months, and delivery of the judgment was completed on Oct 1, 1946. Twelve were sentenced to death by hanging, three to life imprisonment, four to lesser prison terms, and three were acquitted. It was hoped that the war crimes trials would serve as a deterrent to future world leaders who might consider crimes against humanity.

GETTING THE WORLD TO BEAT A PATH TO YOUR DOOR WEEK. Oct 18–24. To focus attention on improving "public relationships" in order to create success for companies, products and individuals. Free self-evaluation available. Annually, the third full week in October. For info: Barbara Gaughen, Pres, Gaughen Global Public Relations, 7456 Evergreen Dr, Santa Barbara, CA 93117. Phone: (805) 968-8567. Fax: (805) 968-5747. Email: barbara@rain.org.

HARVEST FARM AUCTION. Oct 18. Smith Valley, NV. Family entertainment and some great buys on antiques. Sponsored by the Smith Valley Catholic and Methodist Churches. For info: Mason Valley, Chamber of Commerce, 227 S Main St, Yerington, NV 89447. Phone: (702) 463-2245. Fax: (702) 463-3369.

"JANE FROMAN'S U.S.A. CANTEEN" TV PREMIERE: ANNIVERSARY. Oct 18, 1952. Froman, "the Sweetheart of the Armed Forces," appeared in this series with talented members of the armed services.

October 1998

S	M	T	W	T	F	S
				1	2	3
4	5	6	7	8	9	10
11	12	13	14	15	16	17
18	19	20	21	22	23	24
25	26	27	28	29	30	31

LIEBLING, A.J.: BIRTH ANNIVERSARY. Oct 18, 1904. American journalist and author who said "Freedom of the press belongs to those who own one." Abbott Joseph Liebling was born at New York, NY, on Oct 18, 1904. Died there Dec 28, 1963.

MERCOURI, MELINA: BIRTH ANNIVERSARY. Oct 18, 1922. Greek actress and politician Melina Mercouri was born Maria Amalia Mercouri at Athens, Greece, on Oct 18 of 1922 or 1925 (both reported). Of her more than 70 films and plays she is most known for her role in *Never on Sunday* (1960). In 1977 she was elected to Greece's parliament and became the first woman in Greece's senior cabinet when appointed by Premier Andreas Papandreou to the position of minister of culture in 1981. She died on Mar 6, 1994, at New York, NY.

★**NATIONAL FOREST PRODUCTS WEEK.** Oct 18–24. Presidential Proclamation always issued for the week beginning with the third Sunday in October since 1960 (PL86–753 of Sept 13, 1960).

NATIONAL HEALTH EDUCATION WEEK. Oct 18–24. Annually, the third week in October. For info: Lynne Whitt, National Center for Health Education, 72 Spring St, Ste 208, New York, NY 10012. Phone: (212) 334-9470.

NATIONAL INFECTION CONTROL WEEK. Oct 18–24. To promote awareness of prevention and treatment of infection. For info: Assn for Professionals in Infection Control and Epidemiology, 1016 16th St NW, 6th Floor, Washington, DC 20036. Phone: (202) 296-2742.

NATIONAL SCHOOL BUS SAFETY WEEK. Oct 18–24. This week is set aside to focus attention on school bus safety—from the standpoint of the bus drivers, students and the motoring public. Annually, the third full week of October, starting on Sunday. For info: Natl School Bus Safety Week Committee, PO Box 2639, Springfield, VA 22152.

NATIONAL SUNDAY SCHOOL TEACHER APPRECIATION DAY. Oct 18. Established in 1993, this is a day set aside for churches to honor the 15 million men and women who faithfully serve as Sunday School teachers—one of the largest volunteer forces in America. For info: Natl Sunday School Teacher Appreciation Campaign, Gospel Light, PO Box 3875, Ventura, CA 93006-3875. Phone: (800) 235-3415 ext 165. Fax: (805) 650-8713. Email: glmediarel@aol.com.

ROMP IN THE SWAMP FUN WALK. Oct 18. Gordon Bubolz Nature Preserve, Appleton, WI. Choose to hike 1/4-, 1 1/2-, 2 1/2- or 4-mile distances on the Preserve's beautiful trail system. Music, prizes and gourmet food at rest stops along the way. Prizes for the most money raised. Est attendance: 800. For info: Elaine Meyer, Naturalist, 4815 N Lynndale Dr, Appleton, WI 54915. Phone: (414) 731-6041. Fax: (414) 731-9593.
Email: bubolz@dataex.com.
WWW: http://www.geocities.com/rainforest/4579

SAINT LUKE: FEAST DAY. Oct 18. Patron saint of doctors and artists, himself a physician and painter, author of the third Gospel and Acts of the Apostles. Died about AD 68. Legend says that he painted portraits of Mary and Jesus.

WATER POLLUTION CONTROL ACT: ANNIVERSARY. Oct 18. Overriding President Nixon's veto, on Oct 18, 1972, Congress passed a $25 billion Water Pollution Control Act.

WSBA/WARM 103 HOLIDAY CRAFT SHOW. Oct 18. York Fairgrounds, York, PA. More than 300 crafts, from country to contemporary, Victorian and southwestern, handcrafted furniture, wood carvings, dolls, jewelry, pottery, collectibles, quilts, baskets and much more. Admission fee. Est attendance: 7,000. For info: Gina M. Koch, Special Events Dir, PO Box 910, York, PA 17402-0619. Phone: (717) 764-1155. Fax: (717) 252-4807.

BIRTHDAYS TODAY

Chuck Berry (Charles Edward Anderson), 72, singer, songwriter ("Johnny B. Goode," "Roll Over Beethoven"), musician (famous guitar riff), born St. Louis, MO, Oct 18, 1926.

Peter Boyle, 65, actor (*Medium Cool, Joe, Taxi Driver, The Dream Team*), born Philadelphia, PA, Oct 18, 1933.

Pam Dawber, 47, actress (Mindy on "Mork & Mindy"; Samantha on "My Sister Sam"), born Farmington, MI, Oct 18, 1951.

Mike Ditka, 59, sportscaster, Pro Football Hall of Fame tight end for Chicago Bears and Dallas Cowboys; assistant coach for Dallas; head coach for Chicago Bears; head coach for New Orleans Saints; born Carnegie, PA, Oct 18, 1939.

Jesse Helms, 77, US Senator (R, North Carolina), born Monroe, NC, Oct 18, 1921.

Wynton Marsalis, 37, jazz musician, born New Orleans, LA, Oct 18, 1961.

Erin Moran, 37, actress (Joanie Cunningham on "Happy Days" and "Joanie Loves Chachi"), born Burbank, CA, Oct 18, 1961.

Joe Morton, 51, actor (*The Brother from Another Planet, Trouble in Mind, City of Hope*), born New York, NY, Oct 18, 1947.

Martina Navratilova (born Martina Subertova), 42, tennis player, born Prague, Czechoslovakia, Oct 18, 1956.

George C. Scott, 71, actor (Oscar for *Patton* [which he refused]; "East Side/West Side"), born Wise, VA, Oct 18, 1927.

Ntozake Shange (Paulette L. Williams), 50, dramatist, poet, born Trenton, NJ, Oct 18, 1948.

Vincent Spano, 36, actor (*Baby, It's You, Rumblefish*), born New York, NY, Oct 18, 1962.

Pierre Elliott Trudeau, 79, Former Prime Minister of Canada, 1968–79, 1980–84, born Montreal, Quebec, Canada, Oct 18, 1919.

Jean-Claude Van Damme, 38, actor (*Kickboxer*), born Brussels, Belgium, Oct 10, 1960.

Wendy Wasserstein, 48, playwright (*The Heidi Chronicles, The Sisters Rosenzweig*), born Brooklyn, NY, Oct 18, 1950.

OCTOBER 19 — MONDAY

Day 292 — 73 Remaining

"THE ADVENTURES OF ELLERY QUEEN" TV PREMIERE: ANNIVERSARY. Oct 19, 1950. The first of many series to portray fictional detective Ellery Queen, it began on the DuMont network and later moved to ABC. Queen was played by Richard Hart. In the next four series, he would also be played by Lee Bowman, Hugh Marlowe, George Nadar, Lee Philips, Peter Lawford and Jim Hutton. In each series Queen talked to the home audience at the show's climax to see if they were able to identify the killer. Future series were titled "Ellery Queen" and "The Further Adventures of Ellery Queen."

AMERICAN DIETETIC ASSOCIATION ANNUAL MEETING. Oct 19–22. Bartle Hall Convention Center, Kansas City, MO. Est attendance: 10,000. For info: Gerri Salvatore, American Dietetic Assn, 216 W. Jackson Blvd, Ste 800, Chicago, IL 60606-6995. Phone: (312) 899-0040 or (800) 877-1600. Fax: (312) 899-0008. Email: gsalvat@eatright.org. WWW: http://www.eatright.org

ANNIVERSARY DAY. Oct 19, 1899. So named and observed by Robert Hutchings Goddard, rocket pioneer, as anniversary of day (Oct 19, 1899) when he first began to speculate about a spaceship that could travel to Mars.

BROWNE, THOMAS: BIRTH ANNIVERSARY. Oct 19. Physician, scholar and author, Thomas Browne was born at London, England, on Oct 19, 1605. He wrote: "I could never divide myself from any man upon the difference of opinion, or be angry with his judgment for not agreeing with me in that from which perhaps within a few days I should dissent myself." At age 55 he wrote: "The long habit of living indisposeth us for dying." His most famous work, *Religio Medici*, was published in 1642. Browne died at Norwich, England, on his 77th birthday, Oct 19, 1682.

EVALUATE YOUR LIFE DAY. Oct 19. To encourage everyone to check and see if they're really headed where they want to be. [© 1997 by WPL] For info: Tom and Ruth Roy, Wellness Permission League, PO Box 662, Mt Gretna, PA 17064-0662. Phone: (500) 437-5104 or (717) 964-1308. Fax: (717) 964-1335.

JAMAICA: NATIONAL HEROES DAY. Oct 19. National holiday established in 1969. Always observed on third Monday of October.

JEFFERSON, MARTHA WAYLES SKELTON: 250th BIRTH ANNIVERSARY. Oct 19, 1748. Wife of Thomas Jefferson, third president of the US. Born at Charles City County, VA, on Oct 19, 1748. Died on Sept 6, 1782.

NATIONAL BUSINESS WOMEN'S WEEK. Oct 19–23. National Business Women's Week recognizes the role of the working woman in American society, in the economy and in the family. It is commemorated nationwide by special activities. Annually, starting the third Monday in October. Sponsor: Business and Professional Women/USA. For info: Issues Research Mgr, BPW/USA, 2012 Massachusetts Ave NW, Washington, DC 20036. Phone: (202) 293-1100.

NATIONAL RADON WEEK. Oct 19–25. To increase the public's awareness of the effects of radon. For info: American Lung Association, 1740 Broadway, New York, NY 10019-4374. Phone: (800) LUNG-USA.

PECK, ANNIE S.: BIRTH ANNIVERSARY. Oct 19, 1850. World-renowned mountain climber Annie S. Peck was born in 1850. She won an international following in 1895 when she climbed the Matterhorn in the Swiss Alps. Peck climbed the Peruvian peak Huascaran (21,812 ft), giving her the record for the highest peak climbed in the Western Hemisphere by an American man or woman, and at age 61 she climbed Mt Coropuna in Peru (21,250 ft) and placed a "Votes for Women" banner at its pinnacle. Annie Peck died July 18, 1935, at New York City.

VIRGIN ISLANDS: HURRICANE THANKSGIVING DAY. Oct 19. Third Monday of October is a legal holiday celebrating the end of hurricane season.

YORKTOWN DAY: "AMERICA'S REAL INDEPENDENCE DAY." Oct 19. Yorktown, VA. Representatives of the US, France and other nations involved in the American Revolution gather to celebrate the anniversary of the victory (Oct 19, 1781) that assured American independence. Parade and commemorative ceremonies. Annually, Oct 19. Est attendance: 2,000. For info: Activities Coord, Colonial National Historical Park, Box 210, Yorktown, VA 23690. Phone: (757) 898-3400. WWW: http://www.nps.gov/colo/

YORKTOWN DAY: ANNIVERSARY. Oct 19, 1781. More than 7,000 English and Hessian troops, led by British General Lord Cornwallis, surrendered to General George Washington at Yorktown, VA, effectively ending the war between Britain and her American colonies. There were no more major battles, but the provisional treaty of peace was not signed until Nov 30, 1782, and the final Treaty of Paris, on Sept 3, 1783.

BIRTHDAYS TODAY

Jack Anderson, 76, journalist, columnist, author (*Japan Conspiracy, Stormin' Norman*), born Long Beach, CA, Oct 19, 1922.

Bradley Lee (Brad) Daugherty, 33, basketball player, born Black Mountain, NC, Oct 19, 1965.

Michael Gambon, 58, actor ("The Singing Detective," *The Cook, the Thief, His Wife & Her Lover*), born Dublin, Ireland, Oct 19, 1940.

Evander Holyfield, 36, boxer, born Atlanta, GA, Oct 19, 1962.

Patricia Ireland, 53, feminist, social activist, president of National Organization for Women, born Oak Park, IL, Oct 19, 1945.

John LeCarre (David John Moore Cornwell), 67, author (*The Russia House, A Small Town in Germany*), born Poole, England, Oct 19, 1931.

John Lithgow, 53, actor (*Twilight Zone—The Movie, I'm Dancing As Fast As I Can*, "3rd Rock from the Sun"), born Rochester, NY, Oct 19, 1945.

Peter Max, 61, artist, designer, born Berlin, Germany, Oct 19, 1937.

LaWanda Page, 78, actress (Aunt Esther on "Sanford and Son"), born Cleveland, OH, Oct 19, 1920.

Simon Ward, 57, actor (*The Three Musketeers, The Four Musketeers*), born London, England, Oct 19, 1941.

OCTOBER 20 — TUESDAY

Day 293 — 72 Remaining

AMERICAN THEATRICAL PRODUCTIONS SUSPENDED: ANNIVERSARY. Oct 20. American theatrical productions were brought to an abrupt halt on Oct 20, 1774, along with other entertainments when the Continental Congress passed an order proclaiming that the colonies "discountenance and discourage all horse racing and all kinds of gaming, cock fighting, exhibitions of shows, plays, and other expensive diversions and entertainments."

BIRTH OF THE BAB: ANNIVERSARY. Oct 20, 1819. Baha'i observance of anniversary of the birth in Shiraz, Persia, of Siyyid Ali Muhammad, who later took the title "the Bab"; the Bab was the prophet-herald of the Baha'i Faith. One of the nine days of the year when Baha'is suspend work. For info: Pamela Zivari, Dir, Baha'is of the US, Office of Public Information, 866 UN Plaza, Ste 120, New York, NY 10017-1822. Phone: (212) 803-2500. Fax: (212) 803-2573. Email: usopi-ny@bic.org.

DEWEY, JOHN: BIRTH ANNIVERSARY. Oct 20. American psychologist, philosopher and educational reformer was born at Burlington, VT, on Oct 20, 1859. His philosophical views of education have been termed pragmatism, instrumentalism and experimentalism. Died at New York, NY, on June 1, 1952.

GUATEMALA: REVOLUTION DAY. Oct 20. Public holiday in Guatemala.

KENYA: KENYATTA DAY. Oct 20. Kenya observes this day as a public holiday.

KLAN MEMBERS CONVICTED OF CONSPIRACY: ANNIVERSARY. Oct 20. A federal jury convicted seven members of the Ku Klux Klan of conspiracy in the 1964 murders of three civil rights workers, James Chaney, Andrew Goodman and Michael Schwerner, in Mississippi. Eight others were acquitted and no verdict was reached on three others.

LUGOSI, BELA: BIRTH ANNIVERSARY. Oct 20, 1882. Born Bela Ferenc Denzso Blasko at Lugos, Hungary. Known best for his role as Count Dracula in *Dracula*. Lugosi died of a heart attack at Los Angeles, CA, Aug 16, 1956.

October 1998	S	M	T	W	T	F	S
					1	2	3
	4	5	6	7	8	9	10
	11	12	13	14	15	16	17
	18	19	20	21	22	23	24
	25	26	27	28	29	30	31

MacARTHUR RETURNS: US LANDINGS ON LEYTE, PHILIPPINES: ANNIVERSARY. Oct 20, 1944. In mid-September of 1944 American military leaders made the decision to begin the invasion of the Philippines on Leyte, the small island north of the Surigao Strait. With General Douglas MacArthur in overall command, US aircraft dropped hundreds of tons of bombs in the area of Dulag. On this date four divisions were landed on the east coast, and after a few hours General MacArthur set foot on Philippine soil for the first time since he was ordered to Australia Mar 11, 1942, thus fulfilling his promise, "I shall return." The American forces captured Tacloban airfield, the Cataisan peninsula and the northern approaches to the Leyte Valley, San José and Dulag, meeting only isolated resistance from the Japanese.

MANN, JAMES ROBERT: BIRTH ANNIVERSARY. Oct 20, 1856. American lawyer and legislator, born near Bloomington, IL, Republican member of Congress from Illinois from 1896 until his death, Nov 30, 1922. Mann was the author and sponsor of the "White Slave Traffic Act," also known as the "Mann Act," passed by Congress on June 25, 1910. The act prohibited, under heavy penalties, the interstate transportation of women for immoral purposes.

MANTLE, MICKEY: BIRTH ANNIVERSARY. Oct 20, 1931. Baseball Hall of Famer, born Spavinaw, OK. Died Aug 13, 1995, at Dallas, TX.

MOON PHASE: NEW MOON. Oct 20. Moon enters New Moon phase at 6:09 AM, EDT.

MOSCOW SOCCER TRAGEDY: ANNIVERSARY. Oct 20, 1982. The world's worst soccer disaster occurred at Moscow on Oct 20, 1982, when 340 sports fans were killed during a game between Soviet and Dutch players. Details of the event, blaming police for the tragedy in which spectators were crushed to death in an open staircase, were not published until nearly seven years later (July 1989) in *Sovietsky Sport*. In 1985, three soccer game disasters in England and Belgium took 93 lives and injured nearly 800 persons. In April 1989, 95 persons perished in a crush at a soccer match in Sheffield, England.

SATURDAY NIGHT MASSACRE: 25th ANNIVERSARY. Oct 20, 1973. Anniversary of dramatic turning point in the Watergate affair. The swiftly moving events of Oct 20, 1973: White House announcement (8:24 PM, EDT), that President Richard M. Nixon had discharged Archibald Cox (Special Watergate Prosecutor) and William B. Ruckelshaus (Deputy Attorney

General). The Attorney General, Elliot L. Richardson, resigned. Immediate and widespread demands for impeachment of the president ensued and were not stilled until President Nixon resigned, on Aug 9, 1974.

"THE SIX MILLION DOLLAR MAN" TV PREMIERE: 25th ANNIVERSARY. Oct 20, 1973. This action-adventure series based on the Novel "Cyborg" was a monthly feature on "The ABC Suspense Movie" before becoming a regular series. Lee Majors starred as astronaut Steve Austin, who, after an accident, was "rebuilt" with bionic legs, arms and an eye. He worked for the Office of Strategic Information (O.S.I.) carrying out sensitive missions. Also in the cast were Richard Anderson, Alan Oppenheimer and Martin E. Brooks. "The Bionic Woman," starring Lindsay Wagner, was spun off from this show, and the two main characters were paired for several made-for-TV sequels.

WREN, CHRISTOPHER: BIRTH ANNIVERSARY. Oct 20, 1632. Sir Christopher Wren, English architect, astronomer and mathematician, was born on Oct 20, 1632. Died on Feb 25, 1723. His epitaph, written by his son, is inscribed over the interior of the north door in St. Paul's Cathedral, London: "Si monumentum requiris, circumspice." (If you would see his monument, look about you.)

BIRTHDAYS TODAY

Joyce Brothers, 70, psychologist, author, born New York, NY, Oct 20, 1928.

Art Buchwald, 73, columnist, author (*While Reagan Slept*), born Mount Vernon, NY, Oct 20, 1925.

William Christopher, 66, actor ("M*A*S*H," *With Six You Get Eggroll*), born Evanston, IL, Oct 20, 1932.

Arlene Francis (Arlene Kazanjian), 90, actress, game-show panelist ("What's My Line?"), born Boston, MA, Oct 20, 1908.

Keith Hernandez, 45, former baseball player, born San Francisco, CA, Oct 20, 1953.

Melanie Mayron, 46, actress ("thirtysomething" [Emmy, 1989], *Car Wash, My Blue Heaven*), born Philadelphia, PA, Oct 20, 1952.

Jerry Orbach, 63, actor ("Law & Order," *Crimes and Misdemeanors, Dirty Dancing*; stage: *The Fantasticks* [original cast, 1960], *Promises Promises* [Tony Award, 1969]), born The Bronx, NY, Oct 20, 1935.

Tom Petty, 45, musician, singer ("Stop Draggin' My Heart Around"), born Gainesville, FL, Oct 20, 1953.

OCTOBER 21 — WEDNESDAY

Day 294 — 71 Remaining

BATTLE OF TRAFALGAR: ANNIVERSARY. Oct 21. "This famous naval action, on Oct 21, 1805, between the British Royal Navy and the combined French and Spanish fleets, removed forever the threat of Napoleon's invasion of England. The British victory, off Trafalgar, set the seal of eternal fame on Viscount Horatio Nelson who died in the moment of victory." Inscription under copy of painting in Main Post Office, near Charing Cross, London.

CARLETON, WILL: BIRTH ANNIVERSARY. Oct 21. Anniversary of the birth of poet Will Carleton, Oct 21, 1845, observed (by 1919 statute) in Michigan schools where poems of Carleton must be read on this day. Best known of his poems: "Over the Hill to the Poorhouse." Carleton died in 1912.

CARVEL, TOM: DEATH ANNIVERSARY. Oct 21, 1990. American inventor and businessman Tom Carvel was born Thomas Andreas Carvelas at Greece in 1906. He invented the machine that makes soft-serve ice cream (or frozen custard). His chain of ice cream stores began with a $15 loan and grew into the third-largest ice cream chain in America. He died at Pine Plains, NY.

CIRCLEVILLE PUMPKIN SHOW. Oct 21–24. Circleville, OH. More than 100,000 pounds of pumpkins, squash and gourds. Est attendance: 350,000. For info: Hugh Dresbach, Secy, Pumpkin Show Inc, 159 E Franklin St, Circleville, OH 43113. Phone: (614) 474-7000. Fax: (614) 474-6611.

COLERIDGE, SAMUEL TAYLOR: BIRTH ANNIVERSARY. Oct 21, 1772. English poet and essayist born Oct 21, 1772. Died July 25, 1834. In *Table Talk*, he wrote: "I wish our clever young poets would remember my homely definitions of prose and poetry; that is, prose = words in their best order; poetry = the *best* words in the best order."

DOW-JONES TOPS 6,000: ANNIVERSARY. Oct 21, 1996. The Dow-Jones Index of 30 major industrial stocks topped the 6,000 mark for the first time.

FILLMORE, CAROLINE CARMICHAEL McINTOSH: BIRTH ANNIVERSARY. Oct 21, 1813. Second wife of Millard Fillmore, 13th president of the US, born at Morristown, NJ, Oct 21, 1813. Died Aug 11, 1881.

GILLESPIE, JOHN BIRKS "DIZZY": BIRTH ANNIVERSARY. Oct 21, 1917. Dizzy Gillespie, trumpet player, composer, band leader and one of the founding fathers of modern jazz, was born at Cheraw, SC. In the early 1940s Gillespie and alto saxophonist Charlie (Yardbird) Parker created be-bop. In the late '40s he created a second music revolution by incorporating Afro-Cuban music into jazz. In 1953 someone fell on Gillespie's trumpet and bent it. Finding he could hear the sound better, he kept it that way; his puffed cheeks and bent trumpet became his trademarks. He won a Grammy in 1975 for *Oscar Peterson and Dizzy Gillespie* and again in 1991 for *Live at the Royal Festival Hall*. His autobiography, *To Be or Not to Bop*, was published in 1979. He died Jan 6, 1993, at Englewood, NJ.

INCANDESCENT LAMP DEMONSTRATED: ANNIVERSARY. Oct 21, 1879. On this date Thomas A. Edison demonstrated the first incandescent lamp that could be used economically for domestic purposes. This prototype, developed at his Menlo Park, NJ, laboratory, could burn for 13½ hours.

LOS ANGELES GARDEN SHOW. Oct 21–25. Arboretum of Los Angeles County, Arcadia, CA. The theme of the five-day show held on more than nine acres of the 127 acre Arborteum explores Gardens of Our World. In addition to Style Gardens, the show features The Marketplace, the PlanetMarket, lectures and demonstrations. Est attendance: 45,000. For info: Joan Murphine, McEfee, Murphine & Peters, 333 E 17th St, Ste 7C, Costa Mesa, CA 92627. Phone: (714) 650-4846. Fax: (714) 650-3859. Email: callcafarb@aol.com.

LOUISIANA YAMBILEE. Oct 21–25. Opelousas, LA. Sweet potato, corn, rice and soybean shows, cooked foods contest, yam auction, "yum-yum contest," costume contest, carnival, diaper derby, grand parade and the crowning of King Will Yam and Queen Marigold and the 1998 Louisiana Yambilee Queen. Est attendance: 80,000. For info: Sheryl Badeaux, Louisiana Yambilee, Inc, Box 444, Opelousas, LA 70570. Phone: (800) 210-5298.

MISSOURI DAY. Oct 21. The third Wednesday of October each year. Observed by teachers and pupils of schools with appropriate exercises throughout state of Missouri.

NATIONAL YOUTH HEALTH AWARENESS DAY. Oct 21. To promote healthy children by getting annual check-ups and vaccinations. For info: Natl Federation of State High Schools Assn, PO Box 20626, Kansas City, MO 64195. Phone: (816) 464-5400.

PIONEER DAYS. Oct 21–22. Washington, MS. Through talks and demonstrations, youngsters learn how children lived 200 years ago. Annually, mid-October. Est attendance: 1,500. For info: Anne L. Gray, Historian, Historic Jefferson College, PO Box 700, Washington, MS 39190. Phone: (601) 442-2901.

RELICS AND RODS RUN TO THE SUN. Oct 21–25. London Bridge Resort, Lake Havasu City, AZ. Pre-1960 car show. For info: Tourism Bureau, 314 London Bridge Rd, Lake Havasu City, AZ 86403. Phone: (800) 242-8278.

SHAWN, TED: BIRTH ANNIVERSARY. Oct 21, 1891. Named Edwin Myers Shawn at birth, Ted Shawn was born at Kansas City, MO. Partially paralyzed by diphtheria, Shawn was introduced to ballet for therapeutic purposes and became a professional dancer by the age of 21. The Denishawn School of Dancing was established with the help of his wife, Ruth St. Denis, and became the epicenter of much innovation in 20th century dance and choreography. Among his many achievements is Jacob's Pillow Dance Fesitval, which he inaugurated and directed for the remainder of his years, and such modern ballets as *Invocation to the Thunderbird*, *Osage-Pawnee*, *Labor Symphony* and *John Brown*. He died Jan 9, 1972.

SOMALIA DEMOCRATIC REPUBLIC: NATIONAL DAY. Oct 21. National holiday.

"THE STU ERWIN SHOW" TV PREMIERE: ANNIVERSARY. Oct 21, 1950. This often-imitated sitcom was one of the first of its kind. Stu Erwin starred as himself, a bumbling high school principal; June Collyer (his real-life wife) as his level-headed wife, June; Ann Todd and Merry Anders as their daughter, Joyce; Sheila James as younger daughter, Jackie; Martin Milner as Joyce's boyfriend, and later husband, Jimmy Clark; and Willie Best as Willie, the handyman. The show was also called "Life with the Erwins," "The New Stu Erwin Show" and "The Trouble with Father."

TACOMA HOLIDAY FOOD AND GIFT FESTIVAL. Oct 21–25. Tacoma Dome, Tacoma, WA. Gifts, crafts, gourmet foods and more amidst this glittering extravaganza which transforms the Tacoma Dome into a fairyland of twinkling lights, trees and Christmas cheer. Est attendance: 50,000. For info: Showcase Productions, Inc, PO Box 2815, Kirkland, WA 98083. Phone: (425) 889-9494 or (800) 521-7469. Fax: (425) 889-8165.

October 1998

S	M	T	W	T	F	S
				1	2	3
4	5	6	7	8	9	10
11	12	13	14	15	16	17
18	19	20	21	22	23	24
25	26	27	28	29	30	31

TAIWAN: OVERSEAS CHINESE DAY. Oct 21. Thousands of overseas Chinese come to Taiwan for this and other occasions that make October a particularly memorable month.

VIETNAM WAR PROTESTORS STORM PENTAGON: ANNIVERSARY. Oct 21, 1967. Some 250 protestors were arrested when thousands of the 50,000 participants in a rally against the Vietnam War in Washington, DC, crossed the Potomac River and stormed the Pentagon. No shots were fired, but many demonstrators were struck with nightsticks and rifle butts.

BIRTHDAYS TODAY

Sir Malcolm Arnold, 77, composer, born Northampton, England, Oct 21, 1921.

George Antonio Bell, 39, former baseball player, born San Pedro de Macoris, Dominican Republic, Oct 21, 1959.

Elvin Bishop, 56, musician, born Tulsa, OK, Oct 21, 1942.

Carrie Fisher, 42, actress (*Star Wars, Shampoo*), novelist (*Postcards from the Edge*), born Beverly Hills, CA, Oct 21, 1956.

Frances Fitzgerald, 58, journalist, author, born New York, NY, Oct 21, 1940.

Edward Charles ("Whitey") Ford, 70, Baseball Hall of Fame pitcher, born New York, NY, Oct 21, 1928.

Ursula K. LeGuin, 69, author (*The Wind's Twelve Quarters, A Wizard of Earthsea*), born Berkeley, CA, Oct 21, 1929.

Benjamin Netanyahu, 49, Israeli prime minister, born Tel Aviv, Israel, Oct 21, 1949.

Sir Georg Solti, 86, conductor (formerly of Chicago Symphony Orchestra), born Budapest, Hungary, Oct 21, 1912.

OCTOBER 22 — THURSDAY

Day 295 — 70 Remaining

BEADLE, GEORGE: BIRTH ANNIVERSARY. Oct 22, 1903. George Beadle was born on a farm near Wahoo, NE, on Oct 22, 1903. He began his professional career as a professor of genetics at Harvard, eventually becoming president of the University of Chicago. Dr. Beadle won many international prizes, including the Nobel Prize for Medicine in 1958 for his work in genetic research, as well as the National Award of the American Cancer Society in 1959 and the Kimber Genetica Award of the National Academy of Science in 1960. Beadle demonstrated how the genes control the basic chemistry of the living cell. Because of his work, he has been termed "the man who did most to put modern genetics on its chemical basis." Beadle died June 9, 1989, at Pomona, CA.

BIKETOBERFEST. Oct 22–25 (tentative). Daytona Beach, FL. Bikers return to Daytona Beach for that last chance to ride before winter. Parades, concerts and expos highlight the weekend. Est attendance: 50,000. For info: Daytona Beach Area CVB, 126 E Orange, Daytona Beach, FL 32114. Phone: (904) 255-0415. Fax: (904) 255-5478. Email: daytonabea@aol.com. WWW: http://www.biketoberfest.com

BOO AT THE ZOO. Oct 22–31. Good Zoo, Oglebay, Wheeling, WV. Safe trick-or-treating, Halloween cartoons and train ride. Est attendance: 17,000. For info: Penny Miller, Zoo Dir, Good Zoo Office, Oglebay, Wheeling, WV 26003. Phone: (304) 243-4027. Fax: (304) 243-4110. WWW: http://wvweb.com/oglebay

"BREAK THE BANK" TV PREMIERE: 50th ANNIVERSARY. Oct 22, 1948. As with many shows of the late '40s and '50s, this game show began on radio. Contestants had to answer up to eight questions in their area of expertise (with one wrong answer permitted) in order to answer a ninth question to "break the bank." Winners were paid on the spot. Berk Parks was the first host, followed by Bud Collyer. Parks returned as host to a revised show renamed "Break the $250,000 Bank." Family members were involved this time. After 20 years, "BTB" resurfaced with a panel of celebrities who gave different answers to the same question, while the contestants had to choose which answer was correct. Tom Kennedy hosted the network version, and Jack Barry, the syndicated version.

CUBAN MISSILE CRISIS: ANNIVERSARY. Oct 22, 1962. President John F. Kennedy, in a nationwide television address on Oct 22, 1962, demanded the removal from Cuba of Soviet missiles, launching equipment and bombers, and imposed a naval "quarantine" to prevent further weaponry from reaching Cuba. On Oct 28, the USSR announced it would remove the weapons in question. In return, the US removed missiles from Turkey that were aimed at the USSR.

GREAT PUMPKIN CARVE. Oct 22. Chadds Ford, PA. Local artists carve huge pumpkins on the grounds of the Chadds Ford Historical Society, 5–9 PM. Attractions include judging and food. Annually, the last Thursday before Halloween. Est attendance: 1,500. For info: Chadds Ford Historical Soc, Box 27, Chadds Ford, PA 19317. Phone: (610) 388-7376. Fax: (610) 388-7480.

GROLIER, JEAN: DEATH ANNIVERSARY. Oct 22. The celebrated French bibliophile, Jean Grolier de Servieres, whose exact birthday at Lyon, France, in 1479 is unknown, died at Paris, Oct 22, 1565. A government official, Grolier's consuming interest was books, and he assembled one of the world's finest collections—a library of more than 3,000 elegantly bound volumes. The Grolier Club of New York City is named for him.

HOLY SEE: NATIONAL HOLIDAY. Oct 22. The state of Vatican City and the Holy See observe Oct 22 as a national holiday.

LEARY, TIMOTHY: BIRTH ANNIVERSARY. Oct 22, 1920. Timothy Francis Leary was born at Springfield, MA. Prominent psychologist and professor at Harvard, Leary became an icon of the countercultural movement in the 1960s. He lost his professorship after giving a hallucinogenic drug, psilocybin, to roughly 400 students. Leary was arrested and imprisoned numerous times, and on one occasion, while being held at a California prison, he was forced to submit to a personality test that he had, in fact, designed himself several years earlier. He continued to advocate the use of LSD in the pursuit of spiritual and political freedom, and simply for the fun of it, until his death, of prostate cancer, in June, 1996, at Beverly Hills, CA.

LISZT, FRANZ: BIRTH ANNIVERSARY. Oct 22. Hungarian composer. Oct 22, 1811–July 31, 1886.

METROPOLITAN OPERA HOUSE: OPENING ANNIVERSARY. Oct 22, 1883. Grand opening of the original New York Metropolitan Opera House, on Oct 22, 1883, was celebrated with a performance of Gounod's *Faust*.

RANDOLPH, PEYTON: DEATH ANNIVERSARY. Oct 22. First president of the Continental Congress, died Oct 22, 1775. Born about 1721 (exact date unknown), probably at Williamsburg, VA.

WORLD'S END DAY: ANNIVERSARY. Oct 22. Anniversary of the day, Oct 22, 1844, set as the day on which the world would end, by followers of William Miller, religious leader and creator of a movement known as Millerism. Stories about followers disposing of all earthly possessions and climbing to high places on that date are believed to be apocryphal. (Miller was born at Pittsfield, MA, Feb 15, 1782. Died at Low Hampton, NY, Dec 20, 1849.)

BIRTHDAYS TODAY

Brian Anthony Boitano, 35, Olympic gold medal figure skater, born Mountain View, CA, Oct 22, 1963.

John Hubbard Chafee, 76, US Senator (R, Rhode Island), born Providence, RI, Oct 22, 1922.

Catherine Deneuve (Dorleac), 55, actress (*Repulsion, Indochine*), born Paris, France, Oct 22, 1943.

Annette Funicello, 56, singer, actress ("Mickey Mouse Club"; Beach Party movies), born Utica, NY, Oct 22, 1942.

Jeff Goldblum, 46, actor (*The Big Chill, The Fly, Jurassic Park*), born Pittsburgh, PA, Oct 22, 1952.

Valeria Golino, 32, actress (*Big Top Pee-wee, Hot Shots!, Hot Shots! Part Deux*), born Naples, Italy, Oct 22, 1966.

Derek Jacobi, 60, actor ("I Claudius," *The Day of the Jackal*), born London, England, Oct 22, 1938.

Christopher Lloyd, 60, actor ("Taxi," *Back to the Future, Star Trek III, Who Framed Roger Rabbit?*), born Stamford, CT, Oct 22, 1938.

Robert Rauschenberg, 73, artist (*Monogram*), born Port Arthur, TX, Oct 22, 1925.

Tony Roberts, 59, actor (*Victor, Victoria*; *Annie Hall*), born New York, NY, Oct 22, 1939.

OCTOBER 23 — FRIDAY

Day 296 — 69 Remaining

ALBERMARLE CRAFTSMAN'S FAIR. Oct 23–25. Knobbs Creek Recreation Center, NC. 40th annual Albermarle Craftsman's Fair, one of the oldest demonstrating craft shows in the nation and one of the most unique and prestigious shows of its kind. Features woodworkers, carvers, potters, quilters, weavers, sterling silver jewelry makers and other talented artisans. Annually, the last Friday–Sunday of October. Est attendance: 6,000. For info: President, Albermarle Craftman's Fair, PO Box 1301, Elizabeth City, NC 27906-1301. Phone: (919) 338-3954.

APPERT, NICOLAS: BIRTH ANNIVERSARY. Oct 23. Also known as "Canning Day," this is the anniversary of the birth of French chef, chemist, confectioner, inventor and author Nicolas Appert, at Chalons-Sur-Marne, on Oct 23, 1752. Appert, who also invented the bouillon tablet, is best remembered for devising a system of heating foods and sealing them in airtight containers. Known as the "father of canning," Appert won a prize of 12,000 francs from the French government in 1809, and the title "Benefactor of Humanity" in 1812, for his inventions which revolutionized our previously seasonal diet. Appert died at Massy, France, June 3, 1841, but the methods he developed for preserving food continue in use.

BATTLE OF LEYTE GULF: ANNIVERSARY. Oct 23–26, 1944. In response to the Allied invasion of the Philippines at Leyte, the Japanese initiated their "Sho-Go" (*Operation Victory*), an attempt to counter the Allies' next invasion by heavy air attacks. Four carriers were sent south from Japanese waters to lure the US aircraft carriers away from Leyte Gulf. At the same time Japanese naval forces from Singapore were sent to Brunei Bay, split up into two groups and converged on Leyte Gulf from the north and southwest. The group in the north, under Vice Admiral Kurita Takeo, was to enter the Pacific through the San Bernardino Strait between the Philippine islands of Samar and Luzon. On Oct 23 Kurita lost two of his heavy cruisers to US submarine attack, and one of Japan's greatest battleships, the *Musashi*, was sunk in an aerial attack the next day, but Kurita made his way unopposed through the San Bernardino Strait on Oct 25. The southern group commanded by Vice Admiral Nishimura Teiji was detected on its way to the Surigao Strait and was practically annihilated by the US 7th Fleet as it entered the Leyte Gulf on Oct 25. Kurita, as a result, was forced to turn back from his planned rendezvous with Nishimura. Japan's "Sho-Go," rather than inflicting damage on the Americans, resulted in serious losses for the Japanese.

BEIRUT TERRORIST ATTACK: 15th ANNIVERSARY. Oct 23, 1983. A suicidal terrorist attack on American forces in Beirut, Lebanon, killed 240 US personnel on Oct 23, 1983, when a truck loaded with TNT was driven into and exploded at US Headquarters there. At the same time a similar attack on French forces killed scores more.

EDERLE, GERTRUDE: BIRTH ANNIVERSARY. Oct 23, 1906. American swimming champion, born at New York City, Gertrude Caroline Ederle was the first woman to swim the English Channel (from Cape Gris-nez, France, to Dover, England). At age 19 she broke the previous world record by swimming the 35-mile distance in 14 hours, 31 minutes, on Aug 6, 1926. During her swimming career she broke many other records and was a gold medal winner at the 1924 summer Olympic Games.

FANTASY FEST. Oct 23–Nov 1. Key West, FL. Weeklong adult costume festival with street parties, masked balls and nighttime grand parade. Est attendance: 55,000. For info: Fantasy Fest, Ann Dickinson, Box 230, Key West, FL 33041. Phone: (305) 296-1817. Fax: (305) 294-3335.

HUNGARY: ANNIVERSARY OF 1956 REVOLUTION. Oct 23, 1956. National holiday.

HUNGARY DECLARED INDEPENDENT: ANNIVERSARY. Oct 23. On Oct 23, 1989, Hungary declared itself an independent republic, 33 years after Russian troops crushed a popular revolt against Soviet rule. The announcement followed a week-long purge by Parliament of the Stalinist elements from Hungary's 1949 constitution, which defined the country as a socialist people's republic. Acting head of state Matyas Szuros made the declaration in front of tens of thousands of Hungarians in Parliament Square, speaking from the same balcony from which Imre Nagy addressed rebels 33 years earlier. Nagy was hanged for treason after Soviet intervention. Free elections held in March 1990 placed the Alliance of Free Democrats in control of a coalition government, removing the Communist party to the ranks of the opposition for the first time in four decades.

LONGHORN WORLD CHAMPIONSHIP RODEO. Oct 23–24. Joel Coliseum, Winston-Salem, NC. More than 200 of the best cowboys and cowgirls compete in six professional contests ranging from bronc riding to bull riding for top prize money and world championship points. Featuring colorful opening pageantry and Big, Bad BONUS Bulls. 29th annual. Est attendance: 14,000. For info: W. Bruce Lehrke, Pres, Longhorn World Chmpshp Rodeo, Inc, PO Box 70159, Nashville, TN 37207. Phone: (615) 876-1016. Fax: (615) 876-4685.
Email: lhrodeo@idt.net. WWW: http://www.longhornrodeo.com

MARRIAGE ENRICHMENT WEEKEND. Oct 23–25. Belleville, IL. Join other couples as they gather to discuss, reflect, pray, relax and share their marriage journey. The weekend includes lodging at the Shrine Motel, meals, program materials and refreshments. Registration is limited. Est attendance: 60. For info: Shrine of Our Lady of the Snows, 442 S DeMazenod Dr, Belleville, IL 62223-1094. Phone: (618) 397-6700. Fax: (618) 398-6549. WWW: http://www.apci.net/~oblates/

NATIONAL MOLE DAY. Oct 23. Celebrated on Oct 23 each year from 6:02 AM to 6:02 PM in observance of the "mole." The "mole" is a way of counting the Avogadro number, 6.02 × 10 to the 23rd power of anything (just like a "dozen" is a way of counting 12 of anything). Mole Day owes its existence to an early-19th-century Italian physics professor named Amedeo Avogadro. He discovered that the number of molecules in a mole is the same for all substances. Because of this, chemists are able to precisely measure quantities of chemicals in the laboratory. Mole Day is celebrated to help all persons, especially chemistry students, become enthused about chemistry, which is the central science. Individual teachers develop their own ways of observing Mole Day. For 1998 the Mole Day theme is "Ride the Mole-er Coaster." For info: Maurice Oehler, Exec Dir, Natl Mole Day Fdtn, 1220 S 5th St, Prairie du Chien, WI 53821. Fax: (608) 326-6036.
Email: mole@icsbbs.com.
WWW: http://gamstcweb.gisd.k12.mi.us/~nmdf

NEEWOLLAH. Oct 23–31. Independence, KS. Halloween spelled backwards means a broadway musical presentation (local talent); Queen Neelah talent and coronation ceremonies, carnival, wide range of concessions, street acts, kiddie parade, grand parade, nationally known country western stars and concerts. Annually, the last full week in October. Est attendance: 80,000. For info: Cheryl Betts, CVB Dir, PO Box 386, Independence, KS 67301. Phone: (800) 882-3606. Fax: (316) 331-1890.

RICHMOND HIGHLAND GAMES AND CELTIC FESTIVAL. Oct 23–25 (tentative). Fairgrounds, Strawberry Hill, Richmond, VA. Celebration of Scottish and Celtic heritage featuring athletic competition, clan tents, pipe bands, sheepdog demonstrations; dogs, livestock and horses of the British Isles; fiddle, harp and Highland dance competitions; food, pubs and whisky tasting; kilted and clan miles; storytelling and more. Est attendance: 15,000. For info: Sue Mullins, Strawberry Hill Scot. and Celtic Society, PO Box 26805, Richmond, VA 23261. Phone: (804) 228-3238. Fax: (804) 228-3252.

SAINT JOHN OF CAPISTRANO: DEATH ANNIVERSARY. Oct 23, 1456. Giovanni da Capistrano, Franciscan lawyer, educator and preacher, was born at Capistrano, Italy, in 1386, and died of plague on Oct 23, 1456. Feast Day is Mar 28.

SCORPIO, THE SCORPION. Oct 23–Nov 22. In the astronomical/astrological zodiac that divides the sun's apparent orbit into 12 segments, the period Oct 23–Nov 22 is identified, traditionally, as the sun sign of Scorpio, the Scorpion. The ruling planet is Pluto or Mars.

STATE FAIR OF LOUISIANA. Oct 23–Nov 2. Fairgrounds, Shreveport, LA. Educational, agricultural, commercial exhibits, entertainment. Est attendance: 300,000. For info: Sam Giordano, Pres/Genl Mgr, Louisiana State Fairgrounds, PO Box 38327, Shreveport, LA 71133. Phone: (318) 635-1361. Fax: (318) 631-4909.

STEVENSON, ADLAI EWING: BIRTH ANNIVERSARY. Oct 23. Twenty-third vice president of the US (1893–97) born at Christian County, KY, Oct 23, 1835. Died at Chicago, IL, June 14, 1914. He was grandfather of Adlai E. Stevenson, Democratic candidate for president in 1952 and 1956. See also: "Stevenson, Adlai Ewing: Birth Anniversary" (Feb 5).

SUGARLOAF'S FALL NOVI ART FAIR. Oct 23–25. Novi Expo Center, Novi, MI. This show, now in its 4th year, features 300 nationally recognized craft designers and fine artists displaying and selling their original creations. Craft demonstration, children's entertainment, hourly gift certificate drawings and more. Est attendance: 23,000. For info: Sugarloaf Mountain Works, Inc, 200 Orchard Ridge Dr, #215, Gaithersburg, MD 20878. Phone: (800) 210-9900.

SWALLOWS DEPART FROM SAN JUAN CAPISTRANO. Oct 23. Traditional date for swallows to depart for the winter from old mission of San Juan Capistrano, CA. See also: "Swallows Return to San Juan Capistrano" (Mar 19).

THAILAND: CHULALONGKORN DAY. Oct 23. Annual commemoration of the death of King Chulalongkorn the Great, who died Oct 23, 1910, after a 42-year reign. Special ceremonies with floral tributes and incense at the foot of his equestrian statue in front of Bangkok's National Assembly Hall. It was King Chulalongkorn who abolished slavery in Thailand.

October 1998

S	M	T	W	T	F	S
				1	2	3
4	5	6	7	8	9	10
11	12	13	14	15	16	17
18	19	20	21	22	23	24
25	26	27	28	29	30	31

TV TALK SHOW HOST DAY. Oct 23. To celebrate the many TV talk show hosts whose personalities and intellects enable them to bring out the best in their guests. For info: Glenn Rothenberger, Blue Collar Show, 541 Clinton St, Ste 2B, Brooklyn, NY 11231. Phone: (718) 802-1689.

BIRTHDAYS TODAY

James Paul David (Jim) Bunning, 67, US Congressman, Baseball Hall of Fame pitcher, born Southgate, KY, Oct 23, 1931.

Johnny Carson, 73, former TV talk-show host ("The Tonight Show"), born Corning, IA, Oct 23, 1925.

Michael Crichton, 56, writer (*Jurassic Park, Rising Sun*), born Chicago, IL, Oct 23, 1942.

Douglas Richard (Doug) Flutie, 36, football player, born Manchester, MD, Oct 23, 1962.

Pele (born Edson Arantes do Nascimento), 58, former soccer player, born Tres Coracoes, Brazil, Oct 23, 1940.

Juan ("Chi-Chi") Rodriguez, 64, golfer, born Rio Piedras, Puerto Rico, Oct 23, 1934.

Michael John (Mike) Tomczak, 36, football player, born Calumet City, IL, Oct 23, 1962.

Alfred Matthew "Weird Al" Yankovic, 39, singer, satirist, born Lynwood, CA, Oct 23, 1959.

☆ ☆ ☆

OCTOBER 24 — SATURDAY

Day 297 — 68 Remaining

ALABAMA RENAISSANCE FAIRE. Oct 24–25. Florence, AL. Celebration in grand 16th-century style with music, arts and crafts, costumes, theater and dance. Listen to minstrels, dulcimers and autoharps, watch as knights in shining armor transform Wilson Park into "Fountain-on-the-Green." Annually, the fourth weekend in October. Est attendance: 30,000. For info: Debbie Wilson, Dir, Florence/Lauderdale Tourism, One Hightower Pl, Florence, AL 35630. Phone: (205) 740-4141 or (800) 888-FLO-TOUR. Fax: (205) 740-4142. WWW: http://www.flo-tour.org

AMERICAN DENTAL ASSOCIATION ANNUAL MEETING. Oct 24–28. Convention Center, San Francisco, CA. Est attendance: 26,000. For info: Dorsay Dujon, American Dental Assn, 211 E Chicago Ave, Chicago, IL 60611-2678. Phone: (312) 440-2581. Fax: (312) 440-2707.

ANN ARBOR WINTER ART FAIR. Oct 24–25. Ann Arbor, MI. Fine art and selected craft show. Some of the best artists and craftspersons in the country. 25th annual fair. Est attendance: 15,000. For info: Audree Levy, 10629 Park Preston, Dallas, TX 75230. Phone: (214) 369-4345. Fax: (214) 369-3236. WWW: http://www.annarbor.org

BLUE RIDGE FOLKLIFE FESTIVAL. Oct 24. Ferrum College/Blue Ridge Institute and Museum, Ferrum, VA. The largest celebration of authentic folkways in Virginia featuring food, crafts, music and exhibits. Annually, the fourth Saturday in October. Est attendance: 20,000. For info: Roddy Moore, BRI Dir, Ferrum College/BRI, Rte 40 West, Ferrum, VA 24088. Phone: (540) 365-4415 or (540) 365-4416. Fax: (540) 365-4419.

CARE-ACTER DAY. Oct 24. Today we show the backbone of our care-acter through acts of caring. For info: Adrienne Sioux Koopersmith, 1437 W Rosemont, #1W, Chicago, IL 60660-1319. Phone: (773) 743-5341. Fax: (773) 743-5395. Email: kooper@interaccess.com.

CRAFT FAIR USA: INDOOR SHOW. Oct 24–25. Wisconsin State Fair Park, Milwaukee, WI. Sale of handcrafted items including jewelry, pottery, weaving, leather, wood, glass and sculpture. Est attendance: 19,000. For info: Dir, Craft Fair USA, 9312 W National Ave, West Allis, WI 53227. Phone: (414) 321-2100.

FINGER LAKES CRAFTSMEN CHRISTMAS IN OCTOBER ARTS AND CRAFTS SHOW. Oct 24–25. Monroe County Fairgrounds Dome Arena, Rochester, NY. All media, all categories including photography and prints. Est attendance: 10,000. For info: Ronald L. Johnson, Finger Lakes Craftsmen Shows, 1 Freshour Dr, Shortsville, NY 14548. Phone: (716) 289-9439. Fax: (716) 289-9440.

LOCKWOOD, BELVA A. BENNETT: BIRTH ANNIVERSARY. Oct 24. Belva Lockwood, an educator, lawyer and advocate for women's rights, was born in 1830 at Royalton, NY. In 1879 she was admitted to practice before the US Supreme Court—the first woman to do so. While practicing law in Washington, DC, she secured equal property rights for women. In 1884 she was the first woman formally nominated for the US presidency. Belva Lockwood died May 19, 1917, at Washington, DC.

LONGWOOD GARDENS CHRYSANTHEMUM FESTIVAL. Oct 24–Nov 22. Kennett Square, PA. 15,000 chrysanthemums and amazing topiaries are featured in indoor displays accompanied by performances and activities throughout this late autumn festival. Est attendance: 50,000. For info: Longwood Gardens, PO Box 501, Kennett Square, PA 19348-0501. Phone: (610) 388-1000. WWW: http://www.longwoodgardens.org

MAKE A DIFFERENCE DAY. Oct 24. This national day of community service is sponsored by USA Weekend (a Sunday supplement delivered in more than 400 newspapers). Volunteer projects completed on the day are judged by well-known celebrities, and 60 winning projects receive $2,000 each to donate to their charity of choice. Key projects are honored in April during National Volunteer Week at a special Make A Difference Day awards luncheon and at the White House. The Points of Light Foundation is a partner. For info: Pam Brown, Assoc Editor, USA Weekend, 1000 Wilson Blvd, Arlington, VA 22229-0012. Phone: (800) 416-3824.

MORMON PONY EXPRESS TRAIL RIDE. Oct 24. Cajon Pass, San Bernardino, CA. In 1852, a former Mormon Battalion soldier, Capt Jefferson Hunt, received a federal contract to carry the US Mail by horseback between the Mormon colony of San Bernardino, CA, and Mormon headquarters in Salt Lake City, UT. This 700-mile route continued with monthly service until 1858. The Second US Mormon Battalion Assn sponsors reenactments of this historic service with an annual equestrian trail ride on the original trail. Annually, the fourth Saturday of October. Est attendance: 100. For info: Col John A. Bascom, USMB Historian, 15669 Stoddard Wells Rd, Victorville, CA 92392. Phone: (619) 245-9840.

OKTOBERFEST. Oct 24. Monett, MO. Downtown street festival featuring entertainment, pancake breakfast, pork steak barbeque, car show, beauty pageant, food and craft booths, kiddie carnival, bicycle rodeo, tot fingerpainting, talent contest, cloggers, live dancers and more. Annually, on the fourth Saturday of October. For info: Monett Chamber of Commerce, PO Box 47, Monett, MO 65708. Phone: (417) 235-7919.

PENNSYLVANIA ARTS & CRAFTS CHRISTMAS FESTIVAL. Oct 24–Nov 1. Washington County Fairgrounds, Irwin, PA. More than 165 booths of children's toys, dolls, dried floral arrangements and clothing. Holiday food and entertainment. For info: Debbie Stoner, Family Festivals Assn, Inc, PO Box 166, Irwin, PA 15642. Phone: (412) 863-4577. Fax: (412) 863-4577.

PIONEER AND INDIAN FESTIVAL. Oct 24. Mississippi Crafts Center, Natchez Trace Parkway, Ridgeland, MS. Arts and crafts of the pioneer era (basket weaving, pottery, spinning), Indian stickball, dances, falconry, music and food. Annually, the fourth Saturday in October. Sponsor: Craftsmen's Guild of Mississippi, Inc. Est attendance: 5,000. For info: Martha Garrott, Mississippi Crafts Center, PO Box 69, Ridgeland, MS 39158. Phone: (601) 856-7546. Fax: (601) 981-0488.

SEA WITCH HALLOWEEN FESTIVAL. Oct 24–25. Rehoboth Beach/Dewey Beach, DE. Sea Witch Hunt, broom tossing contest on beach, best costumed pet contest, scarecrow making, haunted house, costume parade, laser show, horse-drawn hayrides and entertainment. Annually, the last weekend in October. Est attendance: 30,000. For info: Carol Everhart, Festival Dir, PO Box 216, Rehoboth Beach, DE 19971. Phone: (800) 441-1329. Fax: (302) 227-8351. Email: rehoboth@dmv.com. WWW: http://www.dmv.com/business/rehoboth

SHERMAN, JAMES SCHOOLCRAFT: BIRTH ANNIVERSARY. Oct 24. Twenty-seventh vice president of the US (1909–12), born at Utica, NY, Oct 24, 1855. Died there Oct 30, 1912.

SORGHUM DAY FESTIVAL. Oct 24. Wewoka, OK. The autumn air fills with the sweet-smelling aroma of sorghum during this old-time festival and fall tradition. Visitors can witness sorghum-making, a quilt show, antique car show and pioneer demonstrations and visit more than 100 craft booths. Annually, the fourth Saturday in October. Est attendance: 30,000. For info: Wewoka Chamber of Commerce, PO Box 719, Wewoka, OK 74884. Phone: (405) 257-5485. Fax: (405) 257-7020.

STOCK MARKET PANIC: ANNIVERSARY. Oct 24. After several weeks of a downward trend in stock prices, investors began panic selling on Black Thursday, Oct 24, 1929. More than 13 million shares were dumped. Desperate attempts to support the market brought a brief rally. See also: "Stock Market Crash Anniversary" (Oct 29).

A TASTE OF PUMPKIN IN CHADDS FORD. Oct 24. The John Chads House, Chadds Ford, PA. The Chadds Ford Historical Society invites visitors to come find out more about pumpkin or "pompion," a staple of the early American diet. Guides in colonial garb will offer tours of the circa 1725 house and springhouse, as well as samples of pumpkin bread. Pumpkins carved by local artists will be on display across the road. Est attendance: 250. For info: Director, Chadds Ford Historical Soc, Box 27, Chadds Ford, PA 19317. Phone: (610) 388-7376. Fax: (610) 388-7480.

★**UNITED NATIONS DAY.** Oct 24. Presidential Proclamation. Always issued for Oct 24 since 1948. (By unanimous request of the UN General Assembly.)

UNITED NATIONS DAY: ANNIVERSARY OF FOUNDING. Oct 24. Official United Nations holiday commemorates founding of the United Nations and effective date of the United Nations Charter, Oct 24, 1945. In 1971 the General Assembly recommended this day be observed as a public holiday by UN Member States (Res 2782/xxvi). For info: United Nations, Dept of Public Info, Public Inquiries Unit, Rm GA-57, New York, NY 10017. Phone: (212) 963-4475. Fax: (212) 963-0071. Email: inquiries@un.org.

October 1998

S	M	T	W	T	F	S
				1	2	3
4	5	6	7	8	9	10
11	12	13	14	15	16	17
18	19	20	21	22	23	24
25	26	27	28	29	30	31

UNITED NATIONS: DISARMAMENT WEEK. Oct 24–30. In 1978, the General Assembly called on member states to highlight the danger of the arms race, propogate the need for its cessation and increase public understanding of the urgent task of disarmament. Observed annually, beginning on the anniversary of the founding of the UN.

WORLD WAR I: THE BATTLE OF VITTORIO VENETO: 80th ANNIVERSARY. Oct 24–Nov 3, 1918. Italian forces, commanded by General Armando Diaz, began the last offensive against Austrian troops in upper Italy on this date. The battle began north of the Piave River, and on Oct 30 the Austrian headquarters in Vittorio Veneto was taken. By Nov 1 Austrian troops were breaking up into deserting mobs. A truce was signed at Villa Giusti on Nov 3, which provided for fighting to end the next day. This Allied victory led to the collapse of the Austro-Hungarian Empire.

ZAMBIA: INDEPENDENCE DAY. Oct 24. Zambia. National holiday commemorates the Instruments of Independence signed on this day in 1964. Celebrations in all cities, but main parades of military, labor and youth organizations are at capital, Lusaka.

BIRTHDAYS TODAY

F. Murray Abraham, 58, actor (Oscar for *Amadeus*), born El Paso, TX, Oct 24, 1940.
Kevin Kline, 51, actor (Oscar for *A Fish Called Wanda; Silverado*), born St. Louis, MO, Oct 24, 1947.
Denise Levertov, 75, poet, born Ilford, England, Oct 24, 1923.
David Nelson, 62, actor ("The Adventures of Ozzie and Harriet"), born New York, NY, Oct 24, 1936.
Yelberton Abraham (Y.A.)Tittle, Jr, 72, Pro Football Hall of Fame quarterback, born Marshall, TX, Oct 24, 1926.
Bill Wyman, 57, musician, born London, England, Oct 24, 1941.

OCTOBER 25 — SUNDAY

Day 298 — 67 Remaining

ARAB-AMERICAN DAY. Oct 25. To highlight the contributions of citizens of Arab descent to American society. For info: Intl Channel, 12401 W Olympic Blvd, Los Angeles, CA 90064. Phone: (310) 442-2721. Fax: (310) 479-8118.

CARTOONISTS AGAINST CRIME DAY™. Oct 25. A day in honor of all those cartoonists, graphic designers and illustrators who join together to promote the prevention of crime through the art and medium of cartooning. Motto: "Cartoonists Against Crime: We Draw Cartoons—Not Guns!" CAC's slogan is to "Toon Out Crime" by employing comic art as an educational tool for implanting seeds of safety prevention into the minds of viewers/readers. For info: Adrienne Sioux Koopersmith, Cartoonists Against Crime, 1437 W Rosemont, #1W, Chicago, IL 60660-1319. Phone: (773) 743-5341. Fax: (773) 743-5395. Email: kooper@interaccess.com.

CHAUCER, GEOFFREY: DEATH ANNIVERSARY. Oct 25. English poet and the best-known English writer of the Middle Ages, was born at London, England, probably about 1340. His greatest work, *Canterbury Tales*, consists of some 17,000 poetic lines. Unfinished at his death, it tells the stories of 23 pilgrims. Among his lesser-known prose writings was a treatise on the Astrolabe entitled *Brede and Milke for Children* (1387), written for "little Lewis, my son." Chaucer died at London on Oct 25, 1400, and is buried at Westminster Abbey.

FIRST FEMALE FBI AGENTS: ANNIVERSARY. Oct 25, 1972. The first women to become FBI agents completed training at Quantico, VA, Oct 25, 1972. The new agents, Susan Lynn Roley and Joanne E. Pierce, graduated from the 14-week course with a group of 45 men.

GRENADA INVADED BY US: 15th ANNIVERSARY. Oct 25, 1983. Some 2,000 US Marines and Army Rangers invaded the Caribbean island of Grenada, taking control after a political coup the previous week had made the island a "Soviet-Cuban colony," according to President Reagan.

HALLOWEEN FESTIVAL AND HAUNTED WALK. Oct 25. Prospect Park, Brooklyn, NY. Carnival games, musicians, storytellers and a haunted walk through the woods with many scary surprises. Est attendance: 15,000. For info: Public Info Office, Prospect Park, 95 Prospect Park W, Brooklyn, NY 11215. Phone: (718) 965-8954. Fax: (718) 965-8972.
Email: prospect1@juno.com.
WWW: http://www.prospectpark.org

KAZAKSTAN, REPUBLIC OF: REPUBLIC DAY. Oct 25. National Day.

LAKESIDE HISTORICAL SOCIETY HOMETOWN REUNION. Oct 25. Lakeside, CA. 20th hometown reunion. Est attendance: 450. For info: Shirley Anderson, Lakeside Historical Society, Box 1423, Lakeside, CA 92040. Phone: (619) 561-1886.

MACAULAY, THOMAS BABINGTON: BIRTH ANNIVERSARY. Oct 25. English essayist and historian, born Oct 25, 1800. Died Dec 28, 1859. "Nothing," he wrote, "is so useless as a general maxim."

MOTHER-IN-LAW DAY. Oct 25. Traditionally, the fourth Sunday in October is occasion to honor mothers-in-law for their contribution to the success of families and for their good humor in enduring bad jokes.

NATIONAL MASSAGE THERAPY AWARENESS WEEK. Oct 25–31. Instituted by the American Massage Therapy Association™ (AMTA) to increase public awareness of the value of massage therapy in wellness and health. Particular attention is given to the benefits of massage therapy as a complement to traditional medicine for illness, injury and pain and in relieving stress. AMTA chapters across the country offer sample massage; provide information about how to locate and choose a qualified massage therapist; and emphasize the importance of legislation in states that do not yet regulate the profession. Annually, the last full week of October. For info: American Massage Therapy Assn (AMTA), 820 Davis St, Ste 100, Evanston, IL 60201. Phone: (847) 864-0123. Fax: (847) 864-1178.
Email: amtainfo@inet.amtamassage.org.

NATIONAL SAVE YOUR BACK WEEK. Oct 25–31. To educate the population on proper back care. For info: Daniel S. Romm, MD, c/o VAMC (117), Rehab Medicine Dept, 400 Veteran's Ave, Biloxi, MS 39531. Phone: (601) 388-5541 ext 5815. Fax: (601) 385-4517.

"NEWHART" TV PREMIERE: ANNIVERSARY. Oct 25, 1982. Bob Newhart starred in this sitcom as Dick Loudon, an author of "how-to" books who moved with his wife, Joanna (Mary Frann), to Vermont to take over the Stratford Inn. Regulars included Tom Poston as George Utley, caretaker of the inn; Steven Kampmann as Kirk Devane, the owner of the Minute Man Cafe; Jennifer Holmes as the maid, Leslie Vanderkellen; and Julia Duffy as princess Stephanie Vanderkellen, who, through bad luck, had to take on the maid's job. Changes in the third season introduced the characters of Michael Harris (Peter Scolari), producer of Dick's talk show and Stephanie's squeeze; and the new owners of the cafe, Larry (William Sanderson) and his silent brothers, both named Darryl (Tony Papenfuss and John Volstad).

PEACE, FRIENDSHIP AND GOOD WILL WEEK. Oct 25–31. To encourage and foster international understanding, good human relations, friendship, good will and peace throughout the world. For complete info, send $3 to cover expense of printing, handling and postage. Annually, the last seven days in October. For info: Dr. Stanley Drake, Pres, Intl Soc of Friendship and Good Will, 412 Cherry Hills Dr, Bakersfield, CA 93309-2866.

PEARL, MINNIE: BIRTH ANNIVERSARY. Oct 25, 1912. Comedian, Grand Ole Opry star born at Centerville, TN. Pearl died at Nashville, TN, Mar 4, 1996.

PICASSO, PABLO RUIZ: BIRTH ANNIVERSARY. Oct 25, 1881. Called by many the greatest artist of the 20th century, Pablo Picasso excelled as a painter, sculptor and engraver. He is said to have commented once: "I am only a public entertainer who has understood his time." Born at Malaga, Spain; died Apr 8, 1973.

REFORMATION SUNDAY. Oct 25. Many Protestant churches commemorate Reformation Day (Oct 31—anniversary of the day on which Martin Luther nailed his 95 theses to the door of Wittenberg's Palace church, protesting the sale of papal indulgences, in 1517), on the Sunday preceding Oct 31, each year.

SOUREST DAY. Oct 25. To emphasize the balance of things in nature. A day for sour (Sauer) people. For info: Richard Ankli, The Fifth Wheel Tavern, 639 Fifth St, Ann Arbor, MI 48103.

SOUTHERN CALIFORNIA FIRESTORMS: 5th ANNIVERSARY. Oct 25, 1993. The Southern California fire season began viciously when fires swept from the celebrity-studded beachfront homes of Malibu to the Mexican border. Blown out of the desert by the fierce Santa Anna winds, the fires destroyed suburban enclaves south of Los Angeles in Laguna Beach and northeast of LA in Altadena. As winds died down, firefighters appeared to gain control as the flames reached the Santa Monica Mountains, but the winds roared again, spreading the fire into Malibu—often jumping the Pacific Coast Highway to destroy the beachfront homes of the wealthy celebrities who lived there. Damage from the fires was estimated at more than $1 billion.

TAIWAN: RETROCESSION DAY. Oct 25. Commemorates restoration of Taiwan to Chinese rule, on Oct 25, 1945, after half a century of Japanese occupation.

US: DAYLIGHT SAVING TIME ENDS; STANDARD TIME RESUMES. Oct 25–Apr 4, 1999. Standard Time resumes at 2 AM on the last Sunday in October in each time zone, as provided by the Uniform Time Act of 1966 (as amended in 1986 by Public Law 99–359). Many use the popular rule: "Spring forward, Fall back" to remember which way to turn their clocks. See also: "US: Daylight Saving Time"(Apr 5).

BIRTHDAYS TODAY

Anthony Franciosa (Anthony Papaleo), 70, actor ("The Name of the Game," "Wheels"), born New York, NY, Oct 25, 1928.
Hanna Gray, 68, educator (former president of University of Chicago), born Heidelberg, Germany, Oct 25, 1930.
Brian Kerwin, 49, actor ("Lobo," "The Blue and the Gray"), born Chicago, IL, Oct 25, 1949.
Robert Montgomery (Bobby) Knight, 58, college basketball coach and former player, born Orrville, OH, Oct 25, 1940.
Helen Reddy, 56, singer, songwriter ("I Am Woman"), born Melbourne, Australia, Oct 25, 1942.
Marion Ross, 62, actress (Marion Cunningham on "Happy Days"), born Albert Lea, MN, Oct 25, 1936.
Anne Tyler, 57, author (*The Accidental Tourist, Searching for Caleb*), born Minneapolis, MN, Oct 25, 1941.

OCTOBER 26 — MONDAY

Day 299 — 66 Remaining

AUSTRIA: NATIONAL DAY. Oct 26. National holiday observed.

CLINTON, HILLARY RODHAM: BIRTHDAY. Oct 26, 1947. First Lady, attorney, born Park Ridge, IL.

ERIE CANAL: ANNIVERSARY. Oct 26. The Erie Canal, first US major man-made waterway, was opened on Oct 26, 1825, providing a water route from Lake Erie to the Hudson River. Started on July 4, 1817, the canal cost $7,602,000. Cannons fired and celebrations held all along the route for the opening.

HANSOM, JOSEPH: BIRTH ANNIVERSARY. Oct 26, 1803. English architect and inventor Joseph Aloysius Hansom registered his "Patent Safety Cab" in 1834. The two-wheeled, one-horse, enclosed cab, with driver seated above and behind the passengers, quickly became a familiar and favorite vehicle for public transportation. Hansom was born at York, England, on Oct 26, 1803, and died at London, on June 29, 1882.

HORSELESS CARRIAGE DAY. Oct 26. From James Boswell's *Life of Samuel Johnson*: Oct 26, 1769. ". . . we dined together at the Mitre tavern. . . . We went home to his house to tea. . . . There was a pretty large circle this evening. Dr. Johnson was in very good humour, lively, and ready to talk upon all subjects. Mr Ferguson, the self-taught philosopher, told him of a new-invented machine which went without horses: a man who sat in it turned a handle, which worked a spring that drove it forward. 'Then, Sir (said Johnson), what is gained is, the man has his choice whether he will move himself alone, or himself and the machine too.' . . . ."

MULE DAY. Oct 26. Anniversary of the first importation of Spanish jacks to the US, a gift from King Charles III of Spain. Mules are said to have been bred first in this country by George Washington from a pair delivered in Boston on Oct 26, 1785.

ROCKEFELLER, ABBY GREENE ALDRICH: BIRTH ANNIVERSARY. Oct 26, 1874. A philanthropist and art patron, Abby Rockefeller was one of the three founders of the New York Museum of Modern Art in 1929. Born at Providence, RI, she died Apr 5, 1948, at New York City.

"ST. ELSEWHERE" TV PREMIERE: ANNIVERSARY. Oct 26, 1982. A popular one-hour medical drama set in St. Eligius Hospital in Boston. Among its extremely large and changing cast were Ed Flanders, William Daniels, Ed Begley, Jr, David Morse, Howie Mandel, Christina Pickles, Denzel Washington, Norman Lloyd, David Birney, G.W. Bailey, Kavi Raz, Stephen Furst, Mark Harmon and Alfre Woodard. In 1987, St. Eligius was sold to a private health care corporation. The last episode of the series was presented in order to cast doubt on the reality of the whole series, suggesting that a child's imagination had dreamed it up.

October 1998

S	M	T	W	T	F	S
				1	2	3
4	5	6	7	8	9	10
11	12	13	14	15	16	17
18	19	20	21	22	23	24
25	26	27	28	29	30	31

SCARLATTI, DOMENICO: BIRTH ANNIVERSARY. Oct 26. Italian composer, born Oct 26, 1685. Died July 23, 1757.

SPACE MILESTONE: *SOYUZ 3* (USSR): 30th ANNIVERSARY. Oct 26, 1968. Launched this date with Colonel Georgi Beregovoy. Orbited Earth 64 times, rendezvousing with unmanned *Soyuz 2*, which had been launched the day before. Both vehicles returned to Earth under ground control.

"VICTORY AT SEA" TV PREMIERE: ANNIVERSARY. Oct 26, 1952. This half-hour series was a documentary of naval warfare during World War II. It was narrated by Leonard Graves, produced by Henry Salomon, with a score composed by Richard Rodgers.

BIRTHDAYS TODAY

Pat Conroy, 53, writer (*The Prince of Tides, The Lords of Discipline*), born Atlanta, GA, Oct 26, 1945.

Cary Elwes, 36, actor (*The Princess Bride, Glory, Bram Stoker's Dracula*), born London, England, Oct 26, 1962.

Bob Hoskins, 56, actor (*Mona Lisa, Who Framed Roger Rabbit?*), born Bury St. Edmonds, Suffolk, England, Oct 26, 1942.

Ivan Reitman, 52, filmmaker (*Ghostbusters* movies), born Komarno, Czechoslovakia, Oct 26, 1946.

Pat Sajak, 52, TV personality ("Wheel of Fortune"), born Chicago, IL, Oct 26, 1946.

Jaclyn Smith, 51, actress (Kelly Garrett on "Charlie's Angels"; former Breck Girl), born Houston, TX, Oct 26, 1947.

OCTOBER 27 — TUESDAY

Day 300 — 65 Remaining

COOK, JAMES: BIRTH ANNIVERSARY. Oct 27, 1728. English sea captain and explorer born Oct 27, 1728. Died Feb 14, 1779.

THE CRACKER LINE: ANNIVERSARY. Oct 27, 1863. In an attempt to reinforce and resupply the besieged Union troops in Chattanooga, TN, General Ulysses S. Grant ordered that a river route to Bridgeport, AL, be opened. In the early morning of Oct 27 Federal troops drifted down the Tennessee River on pontoons to Brown's Ferry. The troops reached their destination, and reinforcements and supplies crossed the bridge formed by the pontoons, opening "The Cracker Line," into Chattanooga, negating some of the Southern army's advantage in the siege.

CRANKY CO-WORKERS DAY. Oct 27. Because all of us have bad days (some more than others), here's a day when crankiness at work is actually encouraged. For info: Candace Smith, PA Renaissance Faire, PO Box 685, Cornwall, PA 17106. Phone: (717) 665-7021.

FEDERALIST PAPERS: ANNIVERSARY. Oct 27, 1787. The first of the 85 "Federalist" papers appeared in print in a New York City newspaper, Oct 27, 1787. These essays, written by Alexander Hamilton, James Madison and John Jay, argued in favor of adoption of the new Constitution and the new form of federal government. The last of the essays was completed Apr 4, 1788.

NAVY DAY. Oct 27. Observed on this date since 1922.

NEW YORK CITY SUBWAY: ANNIVERSARY. Oct 27. Running from City Hall to West 145th St, the New York City subway began operation on Oct 27, 1904. It was the first underground and underwater rail system in the world.

PAGANINI, NICOLO: BIRTH ANNIVERSARY. Oct 27, 1782. Hailed as the greatest violin virtuoso of all time, Paganini was born at Genoa, Italy, Oct 27, 1782. Unusually long arms contributed to his legendary Mephistophelian appearance—and probably to his unique skills as a performer. His immensely popular concerts brought him great wealth, but his compulsive gambling repeatedly humbled the genius. Paganini died at Nice, France, May 27, 1840.

ROOSEVELT, THEODORE: BIRTH ANNIVERSARY. Oct 27, 1858. Theodore Roosevelt, 26th president of the US, succeeded to the presidency on the death of William McKinley. His term of office: Sept 14, 1901–Mar 3, 1909. Roosevelt was the first president to ride in an automobile (1902), to submerge in a submarine (1905) and to fly in an airplane (1910). Although his best-remembered quote was perhaps "Speak softly and carry a big stick," he also said: "The first requisite of a good citizen in this Republic of ours is that he shall be able and willing to pull his weight." Born at New York, NY, Oct 27, 1858, Roosevelt died at Oyster Bay, NY, Jan 6, 1919. His last words: "Put out the light."

SAINT VINCENT AND THE GRENADINES: INDEPENDENCE DAY. Oct 27. National Day.

SERVETUS, MICHAEL: EXECUTION ANNIVERSARY. Oct 27, 1553. Spanish theologian and physician. Servetus was condemned to death on Oct 26, 1553, for blasphemy and burned at the stake at Geneva, Switzerland, on Oct 27, 1553. Servetus was born at Tudela, Navarre, Spain, in 1511 (exact date unknown).

TAMBO, OLIVER REGINALD: BIRTH ANNIVERSARY. Oct 27, 1917. Former president of South Africa's antiapartheid African National Congress, Tambo was born at Transkei, South Africa, and died Apr 24, 1993, at Johannesburg.

THOMAS, DYLAN MARLAIS: BIRTH ANNIVERSARY. Oct 27, 1914. Welsh poet and playwright, born at Swansea, Wales. Died at New York, NY, Nov 9, 1953.

TURKMENISTAN: INDEPENDENCE DAY. Oct 27. National holiday.

"WALT DISNEY" TV PREMIERE: ANNIVERSARY. Oct 27, 1954. This highly successful and long-running show appeared on different networks under different names but was essentially the same show. It was the first ABC series to break the Nielsen's Top Twenty and the first prime-time anthology series for kids. "Walt Disney" was created by Walter Elias Disney and was originally titled "Disneyland" to promote the park and upcoming Disney releases. Later the title was changed to "Walt Disney Presents"; when it switched networks, it was called "Walt Disney's Wonderful World of Color" to highlight its being broadcast in color. Future titles included "The Wonderful World of Disney," "Disney's Wonderful World," "The Disney Sunday Movie" and "The Magical World of Disney." Presentations included edited versions of previously relased Disney films and original productions (including natural history documentaries, behind-the-scenes at Disney shows and dramatic shows, including the popular Davy Crockett segments that were the first TV miniseries).

BIRTHDAYS TODAY

Warren Christopher, 73, US Secretary of State in first Clinton administration, born Scranton, ND, Oct 27, 1925.

John Cleese, 59, actor, writer ("Monty Python's Flying Circus," *A Fish Called Wanda*), born Weston-Super-Mare, England, Oct 27, 1939.

Floyd Cramer, 65, musician, singer, songwriter ("Last Date," "On the Rebound"), born Shreveport, LA, Oct 27, 1933.

Frederick DeCordova, 88, producer (third for "Tonight Show"), director, born New York, NY, Oct 27, 1910.

Ruby Dee, 74, actress ("Ossie and Rubie," *Zora Is My Name, Do the Right Thing*), born Cleveland, OH, Oct 27, 1924.

Nanette Fabray, 78, actress (Emmy "Caesar's Hour"; "One Day at a Time"; *Our Gang* comedies), born San Diego, CA, Oct 27, 1920.

Simon LeBon, 40, singer, born Bushey, England, Oct 27, 1958.

Fran Lebowitz, 48, magazine columnist famous for essays on urban life (*Social Studies*), born Morristown, NJ, Oct 27, 1950.

Roy Lichtenstein, 75, artist, born New York, NY, Oct 27, 1923.

Carrie Snodgrass, 52, actress (*Diary of a Mad Housewife*), born Chicago, IL, Oct 27, 1946.

OCTOBER 28 — WEDNESDAY

Day 301 — 64 Remaining

ARKALALAH FESTIVAL. Oct 28–31. Arkansas City, KS. Ark City's largest celebration features three parades (lighted evening, children's and giant Arkalalah Parade), crowning of Queen Alalah, high school band contest, street events, two-mile-run, food concessions, arts and crafts show, dances and reunions. For info: Christie Rogers, Chamber of Commerce, PO Box 795, Arkansas City, KS 67005. Phone: (316) 442-0230 or (316) 442-6077. Fax: (316) 442-6077. Email: crogers3@aol.com.

CZECH REPUBLIC: FOUNDATION OF THE REPUBLIC: ANNIVERSARY. Oct 28, 1918. National Day, anniversary of the bloodless revolution in Prague on Oct 28, 1918 (after which the Czechs and Slovaks united to form Czechoslovakia, a union they dissolved bloodlessly in 1993).

☆ ☆ ☆

DICKINSON, ANNA ELIZABETH: BIRTH ANNIVERSARY. Oct 28, 1842. Influential American orator and author of the Civil War era was born at Philadelphia, PA, on Oct 28, 1842. As an advocate of abstinence, abolition and woman suffrage, she earned the nickname "American Joan of Arc." She died on Oct 22, 1932.

DONNER PARTY FAMINE: ANNIVERSARY. Oct 28, 1846–Apr 21, 1847. The pioneering Donner Party, a group of 90 people consisting of immigrants, families and businessmen led by George and Jacob Donner and James F. Reed, headed towards California in 1846 from Springfield, IL, with hopes of a new life, sunny weather, lots of land and riches galore. They experienced the normal travails of caravan travel until their trip took several sensational twists. Indian attacks, winter weather, murder, madness, greed, famine and outright cannibalism took its toll on members of the party whose numbers dwindled to 48 by journey's end.

ERASMUS, DESIDERIUS: BIRTH ANNIVERSARY. Oct 28, 1467. Dutch author and scholar Desiderius Erasmus was born at Rotterdam, probably on Oct 28, 1467. Best known of his writings is *Encomium Moriae* (In Praise of Folly). Erasmus died at Basel, Switzerland, on July 12, 1536.

ESCOFFIER, GEORGES AUGUSTE: BIRTH ANNIVERSARY. Oct 28, 1846. Celebrated French chef and author, inventor of the peche Melba (honoring the operatic singer Dame Nellie Melba), Escoffier became known as the "king of chefs and the chef of kings." He was awarded the Legion d'Honneur in recognition of his contribution to the international reputation of French cuisine, and his service at the Savoy and Carlton hotels in London, England, brought him world fame. He died at Monte Carlo, Monaco, on Feb 12, 1935.

FIRST WOMAN US AMBASSADOR APPOINTED: ANNIVERSARY. Oct 28. Helen Eugenie Moore Anderson became the first woman to hold the post of US ambassador when she was sworn in by President Harry S. Truman on Oct 28, 1949. She served as Ambassador to Denmark.

GERMAN REVOLUTION OF 1918: 80th ANNIVERSARY. Oct 28, 1918. On this date in the final days of World War I, crews of six German battleships protested a series of planned cruiser raids. A mutiny broke out in the fleet at Kiel. All but one of the ships remaining in port ran up the red flag of revolution. 600 sailors were arrested and imprisoned on shore. The uprising spread to Hamburg, Bremen and Lubeck. On Nov 9 a general strike in Berlin brought the administration to a halt. The abdication of Kaiser Wilhelm began to be seen as the only way to avoid a full-scale revolution.

GREECE: "OHI DAY." Oct 28. National holiday commemorating Greek resistance and refusal to open her borders when Mussolini's Italian troops attacked Greece on Oct 28, 1940. "Ohi" means no! Celebrated with military parades, especially in Athens and Thessaloniki.

HANSON, HOWARD: BIRTH ANNIVERSARY. Oct 28, 1896. Born at Wahoo, NE, where he began his study of music, Howard Hanson in 1921 became the first American to win the Priz de Rome. In 1924 he became head of the Eastman School of Music at the University of Rochester, NY, where he served for 40 years. Best known for the music he composed, Hanson was awarded the Pulitzer Prize as outstanding contemporary composer in 1944 for his composition *Symphony No. 4*, the George Foster Peabody Award in 1946, the Laurel Leaf of the American Composers Alliance in 1957 and the Huntington Hartford Foundation Award in 1959. He died at Rochester on Feb 26, 1981.

HARVARD UNIVERSITY FOUNDED: ANNIVERSARY. Oct 28, 1636. Harvard University founded at Cambridge, MA, when the Massachusetts General Court voted to provide 400 pounds for a "schoale or colledge."

HONG KONG: CHUNG YEUNG FESTIVAL. Oct 28. This festival relates to the old story of the Han Dynasty, when a soothsayer advised a man to take his family to a high place on the ninth day of the ninth moon for 24 hours in order to avoid disaster. The man obeyed and found, on returning home, that all living things had died a sudden death in his absence. Part of the celebration is climbing to high places.

"THE JACK BENNY PROGRAM" TV PREMIERE: ANNIVERSARY. Oct 28, 1950. One of radio's favorite comedians, Jack Benny made the transition to favorite TV personality with this situation comedy–variety show in 1950. Regulars included Eddie Anderson, Don Wilson, Dennis Day, Mel Blanc, Mary Livingstone (Benny's real-life wife) and Frank Nelson. Benny also had guest stars, including Ken Murray, Frank Sinatra, Claudette Colbert, Basil Rathbone and TV newcomers Johnny Carson, Marilyn Monroe and Humphrey Bogart. Famous for his cheapness, Benny had a guard for his vaults (played by Burt Mustin) which created many laughs.

MOON PHASE: FIRST QUARTER. Oct 28. Moon enters First Quarter phase at 6:46 AM, EST.

"PABST BLUE RIBBON BOUTS" TV PREMIERE: 50th ANNIVERSARY. Oct 28, 1948. Pabst Breweries sponsored this weekly boxing series on CBS for the majority of its run. The announcer was Russ Hodges, and the commercial spokesman was Bill Nimmo.

SAINT JUDE'S DAY. Oct 28. St. Jude, the saint of hopeless causes, was martyred along with St. Simon in Persia, and their feast is celebrated jointly. St. Jude was supposedly the brother of Jesus, and, like his brother, a carpenter by trade. He is most popular with those who attempt the impossible and with students, who often ask for his help on exams.

SALK, JONAS: BIRTH ANNIVERSARY. Oct 28, 1914. Dr. Jonas Salk, developer of the Salk Polio Vaccine, was born at New York, NY, Oct 28, 1914. Salk announced his development of a successful vaccine in 1953, the year after a polio epidemic claimed some 3,300 lives in the US. Polio deaths were reduced by 95% after the introduction of the vaccine. Salk spent the last 10 years of his life doing AIDS research. He died June 23, 1995, of heart failure at LaJolla, CA.

SPACE MILESTONE: INTERNATIONAL SPACE RESCUE AGREEMENT. Oct 28, 1970. US and USSR officials agreed upon space rescue cooperation, Oct 28, 1970.

STATUE OF LIBERTY: DEDICATION ANNIVERSARY. Oct 28, 1886. Frederic Auguste Bartholdi's famous sculpture, the statue of *Liberty Enlightening the World*, on Bedloe's Island in New York Harbor, was dedicated on Oct 28, 1886. Ground breaking for the structure was in April 1883. A sonnet by Emma Lazarus, inside the pedestal of the statue, contains the words: "Give me your tired, your poor, your huddled masses yearning to breathe free, the wretched refuse of your teeming shore. Send these, the homeless, tempest-tost to me, I lift my lamp beside the golden door!"

October 1998

S	M	T	W	T	F	S
				1	2	3
4	5	6	7	8	9	10
11	12	13	14	15	16	17
18	19	20	21	22	23	24
25	26	27	28	29	30	31

BIRTHDAYS TODAY

Jane Alexander (Jane Quigley), 59, actress (*The Great White Hope, Kramer vs. Kramer*), chair of the Natl Endowment for the Arts, born Boston, MA, Oct 28, 1939.

Charlie Daniels, 62, musician, singer, songwriter ("Devil Went Down to Georgia"), born Wilmington, NC, Oct 28, 1936.

Dennis Franz, 54, actor ("Hill Street Blues," "NYPD Blue"), born Maywood, IL, Oct 28, 1944.

Bill Gates, 43, computer software executive (Microsoft), born Seattle, WA, Oct 28, 1955.

Jami Gertz, 33, actress (Muffy on "Square Pegs"), born Chicago, IL, Oct 28, 1965.

Telma Hopkins, 50, singer, actress, born Louisville, KY, Oct 28, 1948.

William Bruce Jenner, 49, sportscaster, Olympic gold medal decathlete, born Mount Kisco, NY, Oct 28, 1949.

Bowie Kent Kuhn, 72, former commissioner of baseball, born Tacoma Park, MD, Oct 28, 1926.

Annie Potts, 46, actress ("Designing Women," *Ghostbusters, Pretty in Pink*), born Nashville, TN, Oct 28, 1952.

Julia Roberts, 31, actress (*Steel Magnolias, Pretty Woman, Mystic Pizza*), born Smyrna, GA, Oct 28, 1967.

OCTOBER 29 — THURSDAY

Day 302 — 63 Remaining

BOSWELL, JAMES: BIRTH ANNIVERSARY. Oct 29. Scottish biographer, born at Edinburgh, Scotland, Oct 29, 1740. Died, London, England, May 19, 1795. "I think," he wrote in his monumental biography, the *Life of Samuel Johnson*, "no innocent species of wit or pleasantry should be suppressed: and that a good pun may be admitted among the smaller excellencies of lively conversation."

EMMETT, DANIEL DECATUR: BIRTH ANNIVERSARY. Oct 29. Creator of words and music for the song "Dixie," which became a fighting song for Confederate troops and unofficial "national anthem" of the South. Emmett was born on Oct 29, 1815, at Mount Vernon, OH, where he died on June 28, 1904.

FORT LAUDERDALE INTERNATIONAL BOAT SHOW. Oct 29–Nov 2. Greater Ft Lauderdale/Broward Co Conv Center. Everything from small boats to mega-yachts to boating equipment. Visitors attend from all over the world. For info: Greater Ft Lauderdale Conv/Visitors Bureau, 1850 Eller Dr, Ste 303, Ft Lauderdale, FL 33316. Phone: (954) 765-4466.

GHOSTWRITERS' TIME©. Oct 29-31. Honoring that group of creative writers who participate in the art of writing from an anonymous vantage point. Recognizing the outstanding contribution these professionals make to the literary world in what is often a thankless profession. For info: Adrienne Sioux Koopersmith, 1437 W Rosemont, #1W, Chicago, IL 60660-1319. Phone: (773) 743-5341. Fax: (773) 743-5395. Email: kooper@interaccess.com.

"GIMME A BREAK!" TV PREMIERE: ANNIVERSARY. Oct 29, 1981. Half-hour sitcom starring singer Nell Carter as Nell Harper, housekeeper, surrogate parent and confidante to a gruff cop, Carl Kanisky (Dolph Sweet) and his three daughters: Katie (Kari Michaelsen), Julie (Lauri Hendler) and Samantha (Lara Jill Miller). Also featured were Alvernette Jiminez, Howard Morton, John Hoyt, Jane Dulo, Pete Schrum, Jonathan Silverman, Joey Lawrence and Telma Hopkins. Sweet's death in 1985 was incorporated into the storyline. Other changes included the marriage of Julie, Samantha going off to college and moving the setting to New York.

GOEBBELS, PAUL JOSEF: BIRTH ANNIVERSARY. Oct 29, 1897. German Nazi leader who became Hitler's minister of propaganda had earlier been rejected by the military because of a limp caused by infantile paralysis. Killed himself and his wife and children on May 1, 1945, in Hitler's bunker in Berlin as Russian forces advanced into the city.

LIMOUSINE SCAVENGER HUNT. Oct 29. Tacoma, WA. Costumed adults form teams and test their endurance, creativity and willpower in a crazy scavenger hunt, traveling around town in limousines in pursuit of items. Annually, the Thursday before Halloween. Est attendance: 230. For info: Metro Parks Tacoma, Rec Dept, Jana Brown, 4702 S 19th St, Tacoma, WA 98405. Phone: (253) 305-1036. Fax: (253) 305-1014.

STOCK MARKET CRASH: ANNIVERSARY. Oct 29, 1929. New York, NY. Prices on the Stock Exchange plummeted and virtually collapsed four days after President Herbert Hoover had declared "The fundamental business of the country . . . is on a sound and prosperous basis." More than 16 million shares were dumped and billions of dollars were lost on Oct 29, 1929. The boom was over and the nation faced nearly a decade of depression. Some analysts had warned that the buying spree, with prices 15 to 150 times above earnings, had to stop at some point. Frightened investors ordered their brokers to sell at whatever price. The resulting Great Depression, which lasted till about 1939, involved North America, Europe and other industrialized countries. In 1932 one out of four US workers was unemployed.

TURKEY: REPUBLIC DAY: 75th ANNIVERSARY. Oct 29. Anniversary of the founding of the republic in 1923.

BIRTHDAYS TODAY

Richard Dreyfuss, 51, actor (*American Graffiti, Jaws*; Oscar for *The Goodbye Girl*), born Brooklyn, NY, Oct 29, 1947.
Kate Jackson, 50, actress ("The Rookies," "Charlie's Angels," "Scarecrow and Mrs King"), born Birmingham, AL, Oct 29, 1948.
Randy Jackson (Steven Randall Jackson), 37, singer, born Gary, IN, Oct 29, 1961.
Dirk Kempthorne, 47, US Senator (R, Idaho), born San Diego, CA, Oct 29, 1951.
Connie Mack III, 58, US Senator (R, Florida), born Philadelphia, PA, Oct 29, 1940.
Bill Mauldin, 77, political cartoonist, born Mountain Park, NM, Oct 29, 1921.
Melba Moore, 53, singer ("You Stepped into My Life"), actress ("Melba"), born New York, NY, Oct 29, 1945.
Winona Ryder, 27, actress (*Beetlejuice, Edward Scissorhands, Little Women*), born Winona, MN, Oct 29, 1971.
John Haley "Zoot" Sims, 73, musician, born Inglewood, CA, Oct 29, 1925.

OCTOBER 30 — FRIDAY

Day 303 — 62 Remaining

ADAMS, JOHN: BIRTH ANNIVERSARY. Oct 30. Second president of the US (term of office: Mar 4, 1797–Mar 3, 1801), had been George Washington's vice president, and was the father of John Quincy Adams (6th president of the US). Born at Braintree, MA, Oct 30, 1735, he once wrote in a letter to Thomas Jefferson: "You and I ought not to die before we have explained ourselves to each other." John Adams and Thomas Jefferson died on the same day, July 4, 1826, the 50th anniversary of adoption of the Declaration of Independence. Adams's last words: "Thomas Jefferson still survives." Jefferson's last words: "Is it the fourth?"

ATLAS, CHARLES: BIRTH ANNIVERSARY. Oct 30, 1893. Charles Atlas (ex-97-lb weakling), whose original name was Angelo Siciliano, was born at Acri, Calbria, Italy. A bodybuilder and physical culturist, he created a popular mail-order bodybuilding course. The legendary sand-kicking episode used later in advertising for his course occurred at Coney Island when a lifeguard kicked sand in Atlas's face and stole his girlfriend. Three generations of comic book fans read his advertisements. He died on Dec 24, 1972, at Long Beach, NY.

CASSIUS CLAY NAMED HEAVYWEIGHT CHAMP: ANNIVERSARY. Oct 30, 1964. Twenty-two-year-old Cassius Clay, who later changed his name to Muhammad Ali, became world heavyweight boxing champion by defeating Sonny Liston. Ali was well known for both his fighting ability and his personal style. His most famous saying was "I am the greatest!" Convicted of violating the Selective Service Act in 1967, he was stripped of his title; the Supreme Court reversed the decision, though, in 1971. Ali is the only fighter to win the heavyweight boxing title three separate times, and he defended that title nine times.

CLOSING OF COLUMBIAN EXPOSITION: ANNIVERSARY. Oct 30, 1893. After a rousing success, the Columbian Exposition held "American Cities Day" Oct 28, and Chicago Mayor Carter Harrison gave a speech before the visiting mayors. He announced during the speech that he'd asked a young woman to marry him (this would be his third wife). A great crowd stayed into the night after the speech. After he arrived home, Harrison's doorbell rang. When the mayor answered the door he was shot by Patrick Eugene Pendergast, who had been disappointed when his request for a position with the city as corporation counsel was turned down. Instead of the elaborate ceremony that had been planned to close the exposition on Oct 30, a single speech was given and the flags lowered to half-mast.

DAYTONA FALL MOTORCYCLE RACES. Oct 30–Nov 2. Daytona International Speedway, Daytona Beach, FL. For info: Daytona Intl Speedway, John Story, PR, Box 2801, Daytona Beach, FL 32120-2801. Phone: (904) 254-6782 or for tickets (904) 253-RACE (7223). Fax: (904) 947-6791.
WWW: http://www.daytonausa.com

DEVIL'S NIGHT. Oct 30. Formerly a "Mischief Night" on the evening before Halloween and an occasion for harmless pranks, chiefly observed by children. However, in some areas of the US, the destruction of property and endangering of lives has led to the imposition of dusk-to-dawn curfews during the last two or three days of October. Not to be confused with "Trick or Treat," or "Beggar's Night," usually observed on Halloween. See also: "Hallowe'en" (Oct 31).

EDGAR ALLAN POE FESTIVAL. Oct 30–Nov 15 (Friday–Sunday only). Mount Hope Estate, Manheim, PA. An evening of suspense featuring the spine-chilling short stories of Edgar Allan Poe. Professionals from the Pennsylvania Renaissance Faire Actors Conservatory perform, wine served. Est attendance: 10,000. For info: Michelle Cunningham, Mgr of PR, Mount Hope Estate and Winery, PO Box 685, Cornwall, PA 17016. Phone: (717) 665-7021. Fax: (717) 664-3466.
Email: prfscrib@postoffice.net.
WWW: http://www.parenaissanceFaire.com/

FAIRY TALE TRAIL. Oct 30–Nov 1. Cedar Rapids, IA. An alternative Halloween event with 12 different theme rooms, hands-on activities and treats. A magical experience for the whole family. Annually, the weekend of or prior to Halloween. Est attendance: 4,000. For info: Shari Damaso, YWCA, 318 Fifth S SE, Cedar Rapids, IA 52401-1675. Phone: (319) 365-1458. Fax: (319) 365-2263.

FRANKENSTEIN FRIDAY. Oct 30. This holiday has been designed to honor and celebrate the "mother" and "father" of Frankenstein, Mary Shelley and Boris Karloff. Every year a different venue will be used to celebrate this occasion. Annually, the last Friday in October. For info: Ron MacCloskey.
Email: sunny@excaliber.com.
WWW: http://www.excaliber.com/frankstn

GHOST TALES AROUND THE CAMPFIRE. Oct 30. Jefferson College, Washington, MS. Storytellers weave their spells of mystery, surprise and suspense as they tell tales around a bonfire. Est attendance: 300. For info: Anne L. Gray, Historian, Historic Jefferson College, PO Box 700, Washington, MS 39190. Phone: (601) 442-2901.

GHOST WALK. Oct 30. Fort Frederick State Park, Big Pool, MD. Join us for a walk through the haunted forest and barracks. Guided groups. Refreshments. 7-8:30 PM. Admission fee charged. Est attendance: 1,800. For info: Fort Frederick State Park, 11100 Fort Frederick Rd, Big Pool, MD 21711. Phone: (301) 842-2155. Fax: (301) 842-0028.

HALSEY, WILLIAM "BULL" FREDERICK: BIRTH ANNIVERSARY. Oct 30, 1882. American admiral and fleet commander who played a leading role in the defeat of the Japanese in the Pacific naval battles of WWII, William Halsey was born at Elizabeth, NJ. In April 1942, aircraft carriers under his command ferried Jimmy Doolittle's B-25s to within several hundred miles of Japan's coast. From that location the aircraft were launched from the decks of the carriers for a raid on Tokyo. In October 1942, as commander of all the South Pacific area, Halsey led naval forces in the defeat of Japan at Guadalcanal, and in November 1943, he directed the capture of Bougainville. He supported the landings in the Philippines in June 1944. In the great naval battle of Leyte (Oct 23–25, 1944) he assisted in an overwhelming defeat of the Japanese. On Sept 2, 1945, Japan's final instrument of surrender was signed in Tokyo Bay aboard Halsey's flagship, the *USS Missouri*. Halsey died at Fishers Island, NY, on Aug 16, 1959, at age 76.

MALLE, LOUIS: BIRTH ANNIVERSARY. Oct 30, 1932. Born in Thumeries, France, film director Louis Malle was known for his experimental approach to filmmaking and his investigation of controversial topics. *Le Souffle Au Coeur* (1971), *Lancombe, Lucien* (1974) and *Pretty Baby* (1978), for instance, dealt with the issues of incest, the collaboration of France with its Nazi occupiers and child prostitution, respectively. Of all his films, Malle wished most to be remebered for *Au Revoir Les Enfants* (1987). Louis Malle died on Nov 23, 1995, at Beverly Hills, CA.

NATIONAL BASKETBALL COACHES DAY. Oct 30. As the new season starts, this day is dedicated to the thousands of basketball coaches at every level who mold tomorrow's adults by teaching teamwork to millions of basketball players around the world. For info: Frank Lessiter, Winning Hoops, PO Box 624, Brookfield, WI 53008-0624. Phone: (414) 782-4480. Fax: (414) 782-1252. Email: Lesspub@aol.com.

POST, EMILY: BIRTH ANNIVERSARY. Oct 30, 1872. Emily Post was born at Baltimore, MD. Published in 1922, her book *Etiquette: The Blue Book of Social Usage* instantly became the American bible of manners and social behavior and established Post as the household name in matters of etiquette. It was in its 10th edition at the time of her death at 87 on Sept 25, 1960, at New York City. *Etiquette* inspired a great many letters asking Post for advice on manners in specific situations. She used these letters as the basis for her syndicated newspaper column, which eventually appeared in more than 200 papers, and for her radio show.

POUND, EZRA LOOMIS: BIRTH ANNIVERSARY. Oct 30, 1885. American poet born at Hailey, ID, Oct 30, 1885. As result of his pro-Fascist radio broadcasts from Italy, Pound was indicted for treason July 26, 1943, and arrested near Genoa, by the US Army, May 5, 1945. Confined to St. Elizabeth's Hospital, Washington, DC, from 1946 to 1958 as being mentally unable to stand trial, he was never tried for treason. Died in Italy, Nov 1, 1972.

SHERIDAN, RICHARD BRINSLEY: BIRTH ANNIVERSARY. Oct 30. Dramatist, born at Dublin, Ireland, Oct 30, 1751. Died, London, England, July 7, 1816. Sheridan is said to have extended the following invitation to a young lady: "Won't you come into the garden? I would like my roses to see you."

SISLEY, ALFRED: BIRTH ANNIVERSARY. Oct 30. French impressionist painter, born at Paris, France, Oct 30, 1839. One of the most influential artists of his time, he died near Fontainbleau, Jan 29, 1899.

SUGARLOAF'S FALL FORT WASHINGTON CRAFT FESTIVAL. Oct 30–Nov 1. Fort Washington Expo Center, Fort Washington, PA. This show, now in its 4th year, features 300 nationally recognized craft designers and fine artists displaying and selling their original creations. Craft demonstrations, children's entertainment, hourly gift certificate drawings and more. Est attendance: 17,000. For info: Sugarloaf Mountain Works, Inc, 200 Orchard Ridge Dr, #215, Gaithersburg, MD 20878. Phone: (800) 210-9900.

UGLY PICKUP PARADE AND CONTEST. Oct 30. Chadron, NE. Honors beat-up old pickups, US manufacturing prowess and ingenuity, and selects the ugliest pickup in all the land. Ugly pickup queen contest held prior to the parade. Est attendance: 2,500. For info: *Chadron Record*, PO Box 1141, Chadron, NE 69337. Phone: (308) 432-5511. Fax: (308) 432-2385.

"WAR OF THE WORLDS": 60th BROADCAST ANNIVERSARY. Oct 30, 1938. As part of a series of radio dramas based on famous novels, Orson Welles (born Kenosha, WI, May 6, 1915) with the Mercury Players produced H.G. Wells's *War of the Worlds*. Near panic resulted when listeners believed the simulated news bulletins, which described a Martian invasion of New Jersey, to be real.

"WURSTFEST." Oct 30–Nov 8. Landa Park, New Braunfels, TX. To honor and celebrate German heritage. Music, dancing, food, arts and crafts, historical exhibits, sporting events and special demonstrations. Est attendance: 100,000. For info: Wurstfest Assn, PO Box 310309, New Braunfels, TX 78131. Phone: (210) 625-9167. Fax: (210) 620-1318.
Email: wurstfest@newbraunfels.com.
WWW: http://www.newbraunfels.com/wurstfest

October 1998

S	M	T	W	T	F	S
				1	2	3
4	5	6	7	8	9	10
11	12	13	14	15	16	17
18	19	20	21	22	23	24
25	26	27	28	29	30	31

BIRTHDAYS TODAY

Nestor Almendros, 68, cinematographer, film director, born Barcelona, Spain, Oct 30, 1930.

Fred Friendly, 83, broadcast journalist, born New York, NY, Oct 30, 1915.

Dick Gautier, 61, actor (Conrad Birdie in *Bye Bye Birdie*; "Here We Go Again"), born Los Angeles, CA, Oct 30, 1937.

Harry Hamlin, 47, actor ("LA Law," "Studs Lonigan"), born Pasadena, CA, Oct 30, 1951.

Ed Lauter, 58, actor (*The Longest Yard, Fat Man and Little Boy*), born Long Beach, NY, Oct 30, 1940.

Diego Armando Maradona, 38, former soccer player, born Lanus, Argentina, Oct 30, 1960.

Gordon Parks, 86, photographer, author, born Fort Scott, KS, Oct 30, 1912.

Grace Slick, 59, singer (with Jefferson Airplane; "White Rabbit"), born Evanston, IL, Oct 30, 1939.

Charles Martin Smith, 45, actor, director, (*American Graffiti, The Buddy Holly Story, The Untouchables*), born Los Angeles, CA, Oct 30, 1953.

Henry Winkler, 53, actor (the Fonz on "Happy Days"; "Henry Winkler Meets William Shakespeare," "An American Christmas Carol"), coproducer ("MacGyver"), born New York, NY, Oct 30, 1945.

OCTOBER 31 — SATURDAY

Day 304 — 61 Remaining

BANKS COUNTY HALLOWEEN FESTIVAL. Oct 31. Banks County Recreation Complex, Homer, GA. 3rd annual event features children's amusements, scavenger hunt, costume contest, concessions, candy and a hayride. Festivities begin at 6 PM. No admission fee. Sponsor: Banks County Fraternal Order of Police. Annually, the Saturday of or just before Halloween. Est attendance: 5,000. For info: Robbin Chitwood, Banks County Chamber of Commerce, PO Box 57, Homer, GA 30547. Phone: (706) 677-2108 or (800) 638-5004.

CANDY, JOHN FRANKLIN: BIRTH ANNIVERSARY. Oct 31, 1950. Comedic actor who got his start in Second City improvisation at Toronto and graduated to film stardom. Born at Toronto, Ontario, Canada, and died Mar 4, 1994, while on location for a film at Chupederos, Mexico.

CHIANG KAI-SHEK: BIRTH ANNIVERSARY. Oct 31, 1887. Chinese soldier and statesman, born at Chekiang on Oct 31, 1887. Educated at the Wampoa Military Academy, Chiang led the KMT (nationalist) forces in the struggle against the Communist army led by Mao Ze Dong. He died at Taipei, Taiwan, on Apr 5, 1975.

FALL FLING. Oct 31–Nov 1. Somerset, PA. Have a fall fling with Glades Pike Winery. See our new juices in their early fermentation stage. Wine, food tasting and entertainment. For info: Glades Pike Winery, 2706 Glades Pike, Somerset, PA 15501. Phone: (814) 445-3753.

FIRST BLACK PLAYS IN NBA GAME: ANNIVERSARY. Oct 31, 1950. Earl Lloyd became the first black ever to play in an NBA game when he took the floor for the Washington Capitols in Rochester, NY. Lloyd was actually one of three blacks to become NBA players in the 1950 season, the others being Nat "Sweetwater" Clifton, who was signed by the New York Knicks, and Chuck Cooper, who was drafted by the Boston Celtics (and debuted the night after Lloyd).

GUAVAWEEN CELEBRATION. Oct 31. Ybor City, Tampa, FL. A Halloween celebration based on Tampa's nickname, "The Big Guava." Each year the zany celebration features the mythical Mama Guava, who has sworn to take the "bore" out of Ybor City, and a parade of her devoted followers. Events include the "Mama Guava Stumble" (a satirical parade), street parties, music, live entertainment, dancing and food. Annually, the last Saturday in October. Est attendance: 75,000. For info: Ybor City Chamber of Commerce, 1800 E 9th Ave, Tampa, FL 33605. Phone: (813) 248-3712.

HALLOWE'EN or ALL HALLOW'S EVE. Oct 31. An ancient celebration combining Druid autumn festival and Christian customs. Hallowe'en (All Hallow's Eve) is the beginning of Hallowtide, a season that embraces the Feast of All Saints (Nov 1) and the Feast of All Souls (Nov 2). The observance, dating from the sixth or seventh centuries, has long been associated with thoughts of the dead, spirits, witches, ghosts and devils. In fact, the ancient Celtic Feast of Samhain, the festival that marked the beginning of winter and of the New Year, was observed on Nov 1. See also: "Trick or Treat or Beggar's Night" (Oct 31).

HALLOWEEN. Oct 31. Arapahoe, NE. Merchants and business personnel dress in Halloween costume, free soup and sandwiches at noon in Ella Missina Community Building, children's parade and prizes, haunted house, chili cook-off and auction. Est attendance: 500. For info: Secretary, Chamber of Commerce, PO Box 624, Arapahoe, NE 68922.

HALLOWEEN FROLIC. Oct 31. Hiawatha, KS. 84th annual celebration for townspeople and schoolchildren at Halloween to promote Hiawatha and surrounding area. Est attendance: 12,000. For info: Hiawatha Chamber of Commerce, 602 Oregon, Hiawatha, KS 66434. Phone: (913) 742-7136.

HALLOWEEN PARADE. Oct 31 (if postponed Nov 2). Toms River, NJ. Reported as the largest Halloween Parade in the nation with 7,000 participants, 118 prizes and 80,000 spectators. Parade covers a one-mile route. For info: Ray Sackmann, c/o Tom Rivers Fire Co, PO Box 1035, Toms River, NJ 08754. Phone: (723) 286-4640 or (723) 349-0144 the day of the parade.

THE HALLOWEEN TRAIL. Oct 31. Pioneer Village, Worthington, MN. Open to all children, 3rd grade and under, accompanied by their parents or a responsible adult. Treats are provided at stations located in various parts of Pioneer Village. Refreshments are available for all in the Fire Hall at the end of the trail. For info: Nobles County Historical Society, 407 12th St, Ste 2, Worthington, MN 56187. Phone: (507) 376-4011 or (507) 376-4431.

KEATS, JOHN: BIRTH ANNIVERSARY. Oct 31. One of England's greatest poets, born at London, England, on Oct 31, 1795, and died (of consumption) at the age of 25, at Rome, Italy, on Feb 23, 1821. Keats wrote to Fanny Brawne (in 1820): "If I should die . . . I have left no immortal work behind me—nothing to make my friends proud of my memory—but I have loved the principle of beauty in all things, and if I had had time I would have made myself remembered."

LANDON, MICHAEL: BIRTH ANNIVERSARY. Oct 31, 1936. American actor Michael Landon was born Eugene Maurice Orowitz at Queens, NY. He is best known for his roles in the television series "Bonanza" (1959–73), "Little House on the Prairie" (1974–83) and "Highway to Heaven" (1984–89). He died on July 1, 1991, at Malibu, CA.

LOW, JULIETTE GORDON: BIRTH ANNIVERSARY. Oct 31. Founded Girl Scouts of the USA Mar 12, 1912, in Savannah, GA. Oct 31, 1860–Jan 17, 1927.

MILL AVENUE MASQUERADE ADVENTURE. Oct 31. Tempe, AZ. A hauntingly fun time for the entire family, the Masquerade features a costume parade through the streets of downtown Tempe. Live entertainment and a costume contest. Annually, Oct 31. Est attendance: 7,500. For info: Doris Walker, Exec Dir, Mill Avenue Merchants Assn, 520 S Mill Ave, Ste 201, Tempe, AZ 85281. Phone: (602) 967-4877. Fax: (602) 967-6638.

MOUNT RUSHMORE COMPLETION: ANNIVERSARY. Oct 31. The Mount Rushmore National Memorial was completed on Oct 31, 1941, after 14 years of work. First suggested by Jonah Robinson of the South Dakota State Historical Society, the memorial was dedicated in 1925, and work began in 1927. The memorial contains sculptures of the heads of Presidents George Washington, Thomas Jefferson, Abraham Lincoln and Theodore Roosevelt. The 60-foot-tall sculptures represent, respectively, the nation's founding, political philosophy, preservation and expansion and conservation.

NATIONAL MAGIC DAY. Oct 31. Traditionally observed on anniversary of death of Harry Houdini in 1926.

NATIONAL PARK OF AMERICAN SAMOA AUTHORIZED: 10th ANNIVERSARY. Oct 31, 1988. An area of American Samoa was authorized to be developed as a national park. For further park info: Natl Park of American Samoa, c/o Pacific Area Office, PO Box 50165, Honolulu, HI 96850.

★**NATIONAL UNICEF DAY.** Oct 31. Presidential Proclamation 3817, of Oct 27, 1967, covers all succeeding years. Always Oct 31.

NEVADA: ADMISSION DAY. Oct 31. Became 36th state on this day in 1864. Observed as a holiday in Nevada.

REFORMATION DAY: ANNIVERSARY. Oct 31, 1517. Anniversary of the day on which Martin Luther nailed his 95 theses to the door of Wittenberg's Palace church, denouncing the selling of papal indulgences, on Oct 31, 1517—the beginning of the Reformation in Germany. Observed by many Protestant churches on Reformation Sunday, the Sunday before Oct 31, each year (Oct 25 in 1998).

SAMHAIN. Oct 31. (Also called November Eve, Hallowmas, Hallowe'en, All Hallow's Eve, Feast of Souls, Feast of the Dead, Feast of Apples and Calan Gaeaf.) One of the "Greater Sabbats" during the Wiccan year, Samhain marks the death of the Sun-God, who then awaits his rebirth from the Mother Goddess at Yule (Dec 21 in 1998). In the Celtic tradition, the feast of Samhain was also celebrated as New Year's Eve, as their new year began on Nov 1. Annually, Oct 31.

SLEIDANUS, JOHANNES: DEATH ANNIVERSARY. Oct 31. German historian, born at Schleiden in 1506, died at Strasbourg, Oct 31, 1556. His *Famous Chronicle of Oure Time*, called *Sleidanes Comentaires*, was first translated into English in 1560. The translator spoke thus to the book: "Go forth my painful Boke, Thou art no longer mine. Eche man may on thee loke, The Shame or praise is thine."

SWAN, JOSEPH WILSON: BIRTH ANNIVERSARY. Oct 31, 1828. English scientist and inventor born at Sunderland, Durham, England, Oct 31, 1828. Pioneer in photographic chemistry, incandescent electric lamp and synthetic fibers. Died at Warlingham, Surrey, England, May 27, 1914.

SWEDEN: ALL SAINTS' DAY. Oct 31. Honors the memory of deceased friends and relatives. Annually, the Saturday following Oct 30.

TAIWAN: CHIANG KAI-SHEK DAY: ANNIVERSARY. Oct 31. National holiday to honor memory of Generalissimo Chiang Kai-Shek, born Oct 31, 1887, the first constitutional president of the Republic of China.

TRICK OR TREAT or BEGGAR'S NIGHT. Oct 31. A popular custom on Hallowe'en, in which children wearing costumes visit neighbors' homes, calling out "Trick or Treat," and "begging" for candies or gifts to place in their beggars' bags. In recent years there has been increased participation by adults, often parading in elaborate or outrageous costumes and also requesting candy.

WATERS, ETHEL: BIRTH ANNIVERSARY. Oct 31. Married when she was 13, Ethel Waters began her singing career at the urging of friends. At age 17 she was singing at Baltimore's Lincoln Center, billing herself as Sweet Mama Stringbean. Her career took her to New York, where she divided her work between the stage, nightclubs and films. She made her Broadway debut in 1927 in the revue *Africana*, and her other stage credits included *Blackbirds, Rhapsody in Black, Thousands Cheer, At Home Abroad* and *Mamba's Daughters*. Her memorable stage roles in *Cabin in the Sky* and *A Member of the Wedding* (for which she won the Drama Critics' Award) were recreated for film. Born Oct 31, 1896, at Chester, PA, she died on Sept 9, 1977, at Chatsworth, GA.

WILD FOODS DAY. Oct 31. Fall Creek Falls State Park, Pikeville, TN. Field trips demonstrating edible wild plants; and workshop on preparing wild meats. Est attendance: 100. For info: Nature Center, Fall Creek Falls State Park, Pikeville, TN 37367. Phone: (423) 881-5162. Fax: (423) 881-5103.

WMAS 94.7 FM ANNUAL HALLOWEEN BALL. Oct 31. Springfield Sheraton Hotel, Springfield, MA. Our annual listener appreciation ball, where listeners come dressed in their wildest and most creative costumes. Lots of prize categories in which people can win trips, VCRs, TVs, jewelry and more. Est attendance: 3,500. For info: Dina Cox, PO Box 9500, Springfield, MA 01102. Phone: (413) 737-1414. Fax: (413) 737-1488.

YOUTH HONOR DAY. Oct 31. Iowa and Massachusetts.

BIRTHDAYS TODAY

Michael Collins, 67, astronaut, born Rome, Italy, Oct 31, 1931.

Dale Evans, 86, actress, evangelist ("The Roy Rogers Show"), born Uvalde, TX, Oct 31, 1912.

Deidre Hall, 50, actress ("Our House," "Days of Our Lives"), born Lake Worth, FL, Oct 31, 1948.

Frederick Stanley (Fred) McGriff, 35, baseball player, born Tampa, FL, Oct 31, 1963.

Larry Mullen, 37, musician (drummer with U2; Grammy for album *The Joshua Tree*), born Dublin, Ireland, Oct 31, 1961.

Dermot Mulroney, 35, actor (*Young Guns, Longtime Companion*), born Alexandria, VA, Oct 31, 1963.

Jane Pauley, 48, TV personality, born Indianapolis, IN, Oct 31, 1950.

Dan Rather, 67, journalist (coanchor "CBS Evening News"), born Wharton, TX, Oct 31, 1931.

Roy Romer, 70, Governor of Colorado (D), born Garden City, KS, Oct 31, 1928.

David Ogden Stiers, 56, actor (Charles on "M*A*S*H"; *North and South*), born Peoria, IL, Oct 31, 1942.

Nouember.

NOVEMBER 1 — SUNDAY

Day 305 — 60 Remaining

ALGERIA: REVOLUTION ANNIVERSARY. Nov 1. National holiday.

ALL HALLOWS or ALL SAINTS' DAY. Nov 1. Roman Catholic Holy Day of Obligation. Commemorates the blessed, especially those who have no special feast days. Observed on Nov 1 since Pope Gregory IV set the date of recognition in 835. All Saints' Day is a legal holiday in Louisiana.

ALPHA PHI OMEGA NATIONAL SERVICE WEEK. Nov 1–7. Each year, all chapters of Alpha Phi Omega national coed service fraternity conduct service projects related to a specific area of concern. The area for emphasis is determined at the national convention in December for the following year. 1997 projects focused on "Hunger and Homelessness." 1998 projects will focus on "Domestic Violence and Domestic Abuse." Annually, the first full week of November. For info: Patrick Burke, Exec Dir, Alpha Phi Omega, 14901 E 42nd St, Independence, MO 64055. Phone: (816) 373-8667.

ANTIGUA AND BARBUDA: NATIONAL HOLIDAY. Nov 1.

AVIATION HISTORY MONTH. Nov 1–30. Anniversary of aeronautical experiments in November 1782 (exact dates unknown), by Joseph Michel Montgolfier and Jacques Etienne Montgolfier, brothers living at Annonay, France. Inspired by Joseph Priestley's book *Experiments Relating to the Different Kinds of Air*, the brothers experimented with filling paper and fabric bags with smoke and hot air, leading to the invention of the hot-air balloon, man's first flight and the entire science of aviation and flight.

BALD EAGLE MIGRATION. Nov 1–Dec 15 (dates approximate). Below Canyon Ferry Dam, 15 miles east of Helena, MT. Approximately 400 Bald Eagles come to feed on spawning salmon during this six-week period every year. For info: Helena Area Chamber of Commerce, 225 Cruse Ave, Helena, MT 59601. Phone: (406) 442-4120 or (800) 743-5362. Fax: (406) 447-1532.

BIG 10 MEN'S/WOMEN'S CROSS COUNTRY. Nov 1. Ohio State University, Columbus, OH. For info: Dennis LaBissoniere, Big 10 Conference, 1500 W Higgins Rd, Park Ridge, IL 60068-6300. Phone: (847) 696-1010. Fax: (847) 696-1110. WWW: http://www.bigten.org

CHILD SAFETY AND PROTECTION MONTH. Nov 1–30. For info: National PTA, 330 N Wabash, Ste 210, Chicago, IL 60611. Phone: (312) 670-6782.

November 1998

S	M	T	W	T	F	S
1	2	3	4	5	6	7
8	9	10	11	12	13	14
15	16	17	18	19	20	21
22	23	24	25	26	27	28
29	30					

DIABETIC EYE DISEASE MONTH. Nov 1–30. Can people with diabetes prevent the onset of diabetic eye disease? During this observance Prevent Blindness America® tells how control of diabetes can affect diabetic retinopathy, cataracts and glaucoma. For info: Prevent Blindness America®, 500 Remington Rd, Schaumburg, IL 60173. Phone: (800) 331-2020. Fax: (847) 843-8458. WWW: http://www.prevent-blindness.org

DRUG FREE BABIES WEEK. Nov 1–7. Participation in programs directly or indirectly concerned with public awareness of the dangers of maternal drinking and other drug use to fetal development. Youngsters damaged from prenatal exposure to drugs or alcohol bring to the tasks of learning and behavior deficits that can impede success. Of most significance to performance are hypersensitivity to stimulation, disorders of alertness, poor organizational abilities, a diminished ability to concentrate and cognitive deficits. Public concern is the fuel to stop this preventable tragedy. For info: Jeanette Soby, Coord, Academic Exchange, 2208 NE 11th, Portland, OR 97212. Phone: (503) 284-2303.

DUMMIES FOR TUMMIES. Nov 1–30. Ventriloquist's dummies mouth off where it really counts. The Ventriloquists' Association of New England raises funds and awareness for hungry people in New England. This month we work with sponsors to provide vaudeville-style shows in different locations in New England. They serve to help fill the mouths and stomachs of those less fortunate and tickle the funny bone of those who sit in the audience. For info: Debbie Jones, The Ventriloquist Assn of New England, 46 Barbara Rd, Tolland, CT 06084. Phone: (860) 871-8392 or (860) 871-8786. Fax: (860) 870-9246.

ENGLAND: RAC LONDON TO BRIGHTON VETERAN CAR RUN. Nov 1. London. A 57-mile run for a maximum of 400 veteran cars, along the A23 road from Serpentine Row, Hyde Park, London, to Madiera Drive, Brighton. Celebrates emancipation—the abolition in 1896 of English law requiring that a man walk in front of motor vehicles carrying a red flag. Annually, the first Sunday in November. Est attendance: 10,000,000. For info: RAC Motor Sports Assn Ltd, Events Dept, Riverside Park, Colnbrook, Slough, England SL3 OHG. Phone: (44) (1753) 681736. Fax: (44) (1753) 682938.
Email: racmsa@compuserve.com.

GUATEMALA: KITE FESTIVAL OF SANTIAGO SACATEPEQUEZ. Nov 1. Long ago, when evil spirits disturbed the good spirits in the local cemetery, a magician told the townspeople a secret way to get rid of the evil spirits—by flying kites (because the evil spirits were frightened by the noise of wind against paper). Since then, the kite festival has been held at the cemetery each year on Nov 1 or Nov 2, and it is said that "to this day no one knows of bad spirits roaming the streets or the cemetery of Santiago Sacatepequez," a village about 20 miles from Guatemala City. Nowadays, the youth of the village work for many weeks to make the elaborate and giant kites to fly on All Saints' Day (Nov 1) or All Souls' Day (Nov 2).

HOCKEY MASK INVENTED: ANNIVERSARY. Nov 1, 1959. Tired of stopping hockey pucks with his face, Montreal Canadiens goalie Jacques Plante, having received another wound, reemerged from the locker room with seven new stitches—and a plastic face mask he had made from fiberglass and resin. Although Cliff Benedict had tried a leather mask back in the '20s and the idea didn't catch on then, after Plante wore his, goalies throughout the NHL began wearing protective plastic face shields.

INTERNATIONAL CREATIVE CHILD AND ADULT MONTH. Nov 1–30. Promote creativity in your life and work. This event is to encourage people to realize ordinary, everyday creativity as well as the high-order creativity present in gifted-talented populations. Creativity can be improved and developed, reducing stress, increasing well-being and benefiting individuals personally and all peoples collectively. For info: send a SASE plus $1 to Ann F. Isaacs, Natl Assn for Creative Children and Adults, 8080 Springvalley Dr, Cincinnati, OH 45236-1395. Phone: (513) 631-1777.

INTERNATIONAL DRUM MONTH. Nov 1–30. To celebrate the worldwide popularity of all types of drums. Annually, the month of November. For info: David Levine, Full Circle Management, Percussion Marketing Council, 12665 Kling St, Studio City, CA 91604. Phone: (818) 753-1310. Fax: (818) 753-1313. Email: DLEVINE360@aol.com.

McDONALD'S ENDS FOAM PACKAGING: ANNIVERSARY. Nov 1, 1990. McDonald's Corporation announced that it would phase out its use of polystyrene plastic-foam containers, and begin using paper containers.

MEDICAL SCHOOL FOR WOMEN OPENED IN BOSTON: 150th ANNIVERSARY. Nov 1, 1848. Founded by Samuel Gregory, a pioneer in medical education for women, the Boston Female Medical School opened on Nov 1, 1848, as the first medical school exclusively for women. The original enrollment was 12 students. In 1874, the school merged with the Boston University School of Medicine and formed one of the first co-ed medical schools in the world.

MEXICO: DAY OF THE DEAD. Nov 1–2. Observance begins during last days of October when "Dead Men's Bread" is sold in bakeries—round loaves, decorated with sugar skulls. Departed souls are remembered not with mourning but with a spirit of friendliness and good humor. Cemeteries are visited and graves decorated.

MISSION SAN JUAN CAPISTRANO FOUNDING: ANNIVERSARY. Nov 1. California mission founded Nov 1, 1776, collapsed during 1812 earthquake. The swallows of Capistrano nest in ruins of the old mission church, departing each year on Oct 23, and returning the following year on or near St. Joseph's Day (Mar 19).

NATIONAL ALZHEIMER'S DISEASE MONTH. Nov 1–30. To increase awareness of Alzheimer's disease and what the Alzheimer's Association is doing to advance research and help patients, their families and their caregivers. For info: Alzheimer's Assn, Joi Mecks, 919 N Michigan, Ste 1000, Chicago, IL 60611. Phone: (800) 272-3900 or (312) 335-5786. Fax: (312) 335-1110. Email: joilette.mecks@alz.org.

NATIONAL AUTHORS' DAY. Nov 1. This observance was adopted by the General Federation of Women's Clubs in 1929 and in 1949 was given a place on the list of special days, weeks and months prepared by the US Dept of Commerce. The resolution states: "by celebrating an Authors' Day as a nation, we would not only show patriotism, loyalty, and appreciation of the men and women who have made American literature possible, but would also encourage and inspire others to give of themselves in making a better America. . . ." It was also resolved "that we commemorate an Authors' Day to be observed on November First each year; . . . [and] that we salute these heroes with waving flags, the emblem of the National existence they have striven to perfect." Originated and first resolution submitted by Mrs Nellie Verne Burt McPherson, Pres, Bement (Illinois) Woman's Club on Oct 30, 1928.

NATIONAL CHEMISTRY WEEK. Nov 1–7. To celebrate the contributions of chemistry to modern life, and to help the public understand that chemistry affects every part of our lives. Activities include an array of outreach programs such as open houses, contests, workshops, exhibits and classroom visits. 10 million participants nationwide. For info: Michael J. Kenney, American Chemical Society, 1155 16th St NW, Washington, DC 20036. Phone: (202) 872-6078. Fax: (202) 833-7722.
Email: ncw@acs.org. WWW: http://www.acs.org/ncw

November 1998

S	M	T	W	T	F	S
1	2	3	4	5	6	7
8	9	10	11	12	13	14
15	16	17	18	19	20	21
22	23	24	25	26	27	28
29	30					

NATIONAL DIABETES MONTH. Nov 1–30. National Diabetes Month is designed to communicate the seriousness of diabetes and the importance of proper diabetes control and treatment to those diagnosed with the disease and their families. Throughout the month, Association affiliates hold special events and programs on a variety of topics related to diabetes care and treatment. For more information, call 1-800-232-3472.

NATIONAL EPILEPSY AWARENESS MONTH. Nov 1–30. To increase public awareness that despite dramatic gains in treatment, epilepsy is a serious and chronic health condition for which there is no cure. Annually, the month of November. For info: Epilepsy Foundation of America, 4351 Garden City Dr, Landover, MD 20785. Phone: (301) 459-3700 or (800) EFA-1000. Fax: (301) 577-2684. Email: vanhpeter@efa.org.

NATIONAL FIG WEEK. Nov 1–7. To celebrate the completion of the California fig harvest and encourage consumers to use California figs as part of their diet for the taste, high fiber and nutritional value. For info: California Fig Advisory Board, PO Box 709, Fresno, CA 93712. Phone: (800) 588-2344. Fax: (209) 224-3449. WWW: http://www.californiafigs.com

NATIONAL HOSPICE MONTH. Nov 1–30. To promote greater awareness of hospice care and the advantages it offers; to educate physicians and other health care professionals about the concept of hospice; to honor patients and family members, as well as the thousands of dedicated professionals and volunteers who devote their time, love and support to the terminally ill and their families; and to educate public officials to ensure hospice care remains a key component in the health care delivery system. For info: Suzanne Kieffer, PR Dir, Hospice Assn of Amer, 228 Seventh St SE, Washington, DC 20003. Phone: (202) 546-4759. Fax: (202) 547-9312. Email: sjk@nahc.org. WWW: http://www.nahc.org/

NATIONAL OSTEOPATHIC MEDICINE WEEK. Nov 1–7. To salute osteopathic physicians, osteopathic medical students and the healthcare professionals who work in osteopathic hospitals. Sponsors: American Osteopathic Association, Auxiliary to the American Osteopathic Association, American Osteopathic Hospital Association and Association of Osteopathic State Executive Directors. For info: Tim McNary, Internal Communications Mgr, American Osteopathic Assn, 142 E Ontario, Chicago, IL 60611. Phone: (800) 621-1773 ext 7401. Fax: (312) 280-3860.

NEW YORK CITY MARATHON. Nov 1. New York, NY. 29,000 runners from all over the world gather to compete with more than 2 million spectators watching from the sidelines. For info: NY Road Runners Club, 9 E 89th St, New York, NY 10128. Phone: (212) 860-4455. Fax: (212) 860-9754.
Email: membership@nyrrc.org. WWW: http://www.nyrrc.org

OZARK MOUNTAIN CHRISTMAS. Nov 1–Dec 31. Branson, MO. Branson theatres are alive with sounds of spectacular holiday music shows and the hills are aglow with the soft twinkling illumination of millions of holiday lights. Annually, November and December. For info: Branson Lakes Area Chamber of Commerce, PO Box 1897, Branson, MO 65615. Phone: (417) 862-5567.

PEANUT BUTTER LOVERS' MONTH. Nov 1–30. Celebration of America's favorite food and #1 sandwich. For info: Peanut Advisory Board, 500 Sugar Mill Rd, Ste 105A, Atlanta, GA 30350.

TREASURES BY THE SEA. Nov 1–Feb 15. Myrtle Beach, SC. Longest continuous display of thematic lights in the US, featuring special events and affordable accommodations, shopping. Est attendance: 100,000. For info: Marilyn Chewning, Festival Dir, Myrtle Beach Area Chamber of Commerce, PO Box 2115, Myrtle Beach, SC 29578. Phone: (803) 626-7444. Fax: (803) 626-0009. WWW: http://www.myrtlebeachlive.com

VIRGIN ISLANDS: LIBERTY DAY. Nov 1. Officially "D. Hamilton Jackson Memorial Day," commemorating establishment of the first press in Virgin Islands, in 1915.

VIRGINIA THANKSGIVING FESTIVAL. Nov 1. Berkeley Plantation, Charles City County, VA. Promotes awareness of the historical significance of Thanksgiving Day by re-creation of the original Thanksgiving celebration, which took place near Richmond, VA, at Berkeley Plantation in 1619. Est attendance: 4,000. For info: Virginia Thanksgiving Festival, PO Box 5132, Richmond, VA 23220. Phone: (804) 272-3226.

WORLD COMMUNICATION WEEK. Nov 1–7. To stress the importance of communication among the more than five billion human beings in the world who speak more than 3,000 languages and to promote communication by means of the international language Esperanto. For complete info, send $3 to cover expense of printing, handling and postage. Annually, the first seven days of November. For info: Dr. Stanley Drake, Pres, Intl Society of Friendship and Goodwill, 412 Cherry Hills Dr, Bakersfield, CA 93309-2866.

BIRTHDAYS TODAY

Larry Claxton Flynt, 56, publisher, born Magoffin County, KY, Nov 1, 1942.

James Jackson Kilpatrick, 78, journalist (conservative side of "60 Minutes" Point-Counterpoint segment), born Oklahoma City, OK, Nov 1, 1920.

Lyle Lovett, 41, country western singer ("Cowboy Man"), born Klein, TX, Nov 1, 1957.

Betsy Palmer (Patricia Bromek), 72, actress (panelist on "I've Got a Secret"; "Knots Landing," "Today"), born East Chicago, IN, Nov 1, 1926.

Gary Jim Player, 63, golfer, born Johannesburg, South Africa, Nov 1, 1935.

Rachel Ticotin, 40, actress (*Total Recall, Natural Born Killers*), born The Bronx, NY, Nov 1, 1958.

Fernando Anguamea Valenzuela, 38, baseball player, born Navojoa, Sonora, Mexico, Nov 1, 1960.

NOVEMBER 2 — MONDAY

Day 306 — 59 Remaining

ALL SOULS' DAY. Nov 2. Commemorates the faithful departed. Catholic observance.

AUSTRALIA: RECREATION DAY. Nov 2. The first Monday in November is observed as Recreation Day in Northern Tasmania, Australia.

BLACK SOLIDARITY DAY. Nov 2. Yale University, New Haven, CT. Students participate in a speak-out, share a common meal, relate important events regarding their heritage and enjoy music and other expressions of talent. Annually, the first Monday in November. Est attendance: 250. For info: Black Solidarity Day, Afro-American Cultural Ctr, Yale University, PO Box 3439, New Haven, CT 06520. Phone: (203) 432-4131.

BOONE, DANIEL: BIRTH ANNIVERSARY. Nov 2. American frontiersman, explorer and militia officer, born in Berks County, near Reading, PA, on Nov 2, 1734 (New Style). In February 1778, he was captured at Blue Licks, KY, by Shawnee Indians, under Chief Blackfish, who adopted Boone when he was inducted into the tribe as "Big Turtle." Boone escaped after five months, and in 1781 was captured briefly by the British. He experienced a series of personal and financial disasters during his life, but continued a rugged existence, hunting until his 80s. Boone died at St. Charles County, MO, Sept 26, 1820. The bodies of Daniel Boone and his wife, Rebecca, were moved to Frankfort, KY, in 1845.

LANCASTER, BURT(ON) STEPHEN: 85th BIRTH ANNIVERSARY. Nov 2, 1913. Distinguished American actor Burt Lancaster began his career in show business as a circus acrobat. He acted and danced in soldier shows during World War II. In a career spanning 45 years he appeared in nearly 80 films. The first was *The Killers* (1945), in which he portrayed a tough guy, a film persona he maintained for most of his early professional life. Some of his more memorable roles are in *From Here to Eternity* (1953), *The Bird Man of Alcatraz* (1962) and *The Leopard* (1963); he received an Academy Award for his performance in the title role of *Elmer Gantry* (1961). Some of his later popular movies include *Atlantic City* (1981), *Local Hero* (1983) and *Field of Dreams* (1989). Lancaster was born at New York City. He died Oct 20, 1994, at Los Angeles.

LONDON BRIDGE DAYS. Nov 2–8. Lake Havasu City, AZ. 27th annual. Celebration of the dedication of London Bridge in Lake Havasu City. Est attendance: 10,000. For info: Tourism Bureau, 314 London Bridge Rd, Lake Havasu City, AZ 86403. Phone: (800) 242-8278.

NEW YORK SUBWAY ACCIDENT: 80th ANNIVERSARY. Nov 2, 1918. The Brighton Beach Express, exceeding its speed limit five times over (going 30 mph) while approaching the station near Malbone Street tunnel in Brooklyn, jumped the tracks Nov 2, 1918, killing 97 people and injuring 100. The supervisor-engineer, taking the place of a striking motorman of the Brotherhood of Locomotive Engineers, was tried and acquitted of charges of negligence.

NORTH DAKOTA: ADMISSION DAY: ANNIVERSARY. Nov 2. Became 39th state on this day in 1889.

PLAN YOUR EPITAPH DAY. Nov 2 (also Apr 6). Dedicated to the proposition that a forgettable gravestone is a fate worse than death, and that everyone can be in the same league with William Shakespeare and W.C. Fields. Semiannually, coincides with Ching Ming Festival and the Day of the Dead. For info: Lance Hardie, Dead or Alive, PO Box 4595, Arcata, CA 95518. Phone: (707) 822-6924. Email: sunrise@hardiehouse.org. WWW: http://www.hardiehouse.org/epitaph

POLK, JAMES KNOX: BIRTH ANNIVERSARY. Nov 2. The 11th president of the US was born at Mecklenburg County, NC, Nov 2, 1795. His term of office: Mar 4, 1845–Mar 3, 1849. A compromise candidate at the 1844 Democratic Party convention, Polk was awarded the nomination on the ninth ballot. He declined to be a candidate for a second term and declared himself to be "exceedingly relieved" at the completion of his presidency. He died shortly thereafter at Nashville, TN, June 15, 1849.

SENECA FALLS CONVENTION SURVIVOR VOTES: ANNIVERSARY. Nov 2, 1920. The only woman who attended the historic Seneca Falls Women's Rights Convention in 1848 who lived long enough to exercise her right to vote under the 19th Amendment, Charlotte Woodward voted in Philadelphia in the general election Nov 2, 1920.

SOUTH DAKOTA: ADMISSION DAY: ANNIVERSARY. Nov 2. Became 40th state on this day in 1889.

SPRUCE GOOSE FLIGHT: ANNIVERSARY. Nov 2, 1947. The mammoth flying boat *Hercules*, then the world's largest airplane, was designed, built and flown (once) by Howard Hughes. Its first and only flight—about one mile and at an altitude of 70 feet—over Long Beach Harbor, CA, was made on Nov 2, 1947. The $25 million, 200-ton plywood craft was nicknamed the "Spruce Goose." It is now displayed near the *Queen Mary* at Long Beach, CA.

BIRTHDAYS TODAY

Shere Hite, 56, author (*The Hite Report, Women and Love*), born St. Joseph, MO, Nov 2, 1942.

William D. Schaefer, 77, former Governor of Maryland (D), born Baltimore, MD, Nov 2, 1921.

David Knapp (Dave) Stockton, 57, golfer, born San Bernardino, CA, Nov 2, 1941.

Ray Walston, 80, actor ("Picket Fences," "My Favorite Martian," *South Pacific, The Sting, The Player*), born New Orleans, LA, Nov 2, 1918.

Alfre Woodard, 45, actress (*Cross Creek, Miss Firecracker, Grand Canyon*), born Tulsa, OK, Nov 2, 1953.

NOVEMBER 3 — TUESDAY

Day 307 — 58 Remaining

AUSTIN, STEPHEN FULLER: BIRTH ANNIVERSARY. Nov 3, 1793. A principal founder of Texas, for whom its capital city was named, Stephen Fuller Austin was born at Wythe County, VA, on Nov 3, 1793. He first visited Texas in 1821 and established a settlement there the following year, continuing a colonization project started by his father, Moses Austin. Thrown in prison when he advocated formation of a separate state (Texas still belonged to Mexico), he was freed in 1835, lost a campaign for the presidency (of the Republic of Texas) to Sam Houston (q.v.) in 1836, and died (while serving as Texas secretary of state), on Dec 27, 1836.

AUSTRIA: TRADITIONAL AMERICAN MUSIC IN VIENNA. Nov 3–8. Oberlaa Center, Vienna, Austria. This is the first world-wide presentation utilizing performers and musicians from the US who play traditional acoustic old-time country and bluegrass, folk and mountain music; teamed up with the Vienna symphony. Concerts of internationally known performers, workshops and city-wide cafe presentations, as well as European bluegrass competition, and a traditional country music lifetime achievement award will be made. Est attendance: 3,000. For info: Bob Everhart, Dir, World Music Events, PO Box 438, Walnut, IA 51557. Phone: (712) 762-4363.
Email: anitapl@nwidt.com.

BRYANT, WILLIAM CULLEN: BIRTH ANNIVERSARY. Nov 3, 1794. American poet born at Cummington, MA, Nov 3, 1794. Died at New York, NY, June 12, 1878.

***DEWEY DEFEATS TRUMAN* HEADLINE: 50th ANNIVERSARY.** Nov 3, 1948. This headline in the *Chicago Tribune* notwithstanding, Harry Truman defeated Republican candidate Thomas E. Dewey for the US presidency.

DOMINICA: NATIONAL DAY. Nov 3. National holiday.

GENERAL ELECTION DAY. Nov 3. Always the first Tuesday after the first Monday in November. Many state and local government elections on this day, as well as presidential and congressional elections in the appropriate years. All US Congressional seats and one-third of US senatorial seats are up for election in even-numbered years. Presidential elections are held in even-numbered years that can be divided equally by 4.

"GOOD MORNING AMERICA" TV PREMIERE: ANNIVERSARY. Nov 3, 1975. This ABC morning program, set in a living room, is a mixture of news reports, fascinating features and interviews with newsmakers and people of interest. It was the first program to compete with NBC's "Today" show. Current hosts are Joan Lunden and Charles Gibson. Previous hosts have included David Hartman (until 1987), Nancy Dussault, and Sandy Hill.

November 1998

S	M	T	W	T	F	S
1	2	3	4	5	6	7
8	9	10	11	12	13	14
15	16	17	18	19	20	21
22	23	24	25	26	27	28
29	30					

JAPAN: CULTURE DAY. Nov 3. National holiday.

MICRONESIA, FEDERATED STATES OF: INDEPENDENCE DAY. Nov 3. National holiday.

NAGURSKI, BRONKO: BIRTH ANNIVERSARY. Nov 3, 1908. Bronislau ("Bronko") Nagurski, College Football Hall of Fame and charter member of the Pro Football Hall of Fame. Born at Rainy River, Ontario, Canada, he played football at the University of Minnesota, earning All-American honors at both tackle and fullback, and for the Chicago Bears. After retiring from football, Nagurski wrestled professionally and operated a gas station. He died at International Falls, MN, Jan 7, 1990.

NATIONAL NOTARY PUBLIC WEEK. Nov 3–7. To recognize the fundamental contributions made by notaries to the law and the people of the US. Annually, the week containing Nov 7. For info: Lisa Fisher, American Society of Notaries, PO Box 5707, Tallahassee, FL 32314-5707. Phone: (904) 671-5164. Fax: (904) 671-5165. Email: amnotary@polaris.net.
WWW: http://www.notaries.com

NEW INUIT TERRITORY APPROVED: ANNIVERSARY. Nov 3, 1992. Canada's Inuit people voted to accept a federal land-claim package granting them control over a new territory, Nunavut, to be carved out of the existing Northwest Territories by 1999. The voting on Nov 3–5, 1992, indicated that 69% of the 9,648 eligible Inuit voters accepted the settlement. In exchange for the new territory, approximately 135,000 square miles, the Inuits will have to give up their current rights to a territory of 775,000 square miles.

PANAMA: INDEPENDENCE DAY. Nov 3, 1903. Independence Day. Panama declared itself independent of Colombia.

PERIGEAN SPRING TIDES. Nov 3–4. Spring tides, the highest possible tides, which occur when New Moon or Full Moon takes place within 24 hours of the moment the Moon is nearest Earth (perigee) in its monthly orbit, on Nov 3, at 7 PM, EST.

RESTON, JAMES: BIRTH ANNIVERSARY. Nov 3, 1909. New York Times journalist, born Clydebank, Scotland. Died Dec 3, 1995, at Washington, DC.

SANDWICH DAY: BIRTH ANNIVERSARY OF JOHN MONTAGUE. Nov 3, 1718. A day to recognize the inventor of the sandwich, John Montague, Fourth Earl of Sandwich, who was born on Nov 3, 1718. England's first lord of the admiralty, secretary of state for the northern department, postmaster general, the man after whom Capt Cook named the Sandwich Islands in 1778. A rake and a gambler, he is said to have invented the sandwich as a time-saving nourishment while engaged in a 24-hour-long gambling session in 1762. He died at London, England, on Apr 30, 1792.

SPACE MILESTONE: *SPUTNIK 2* (USSR). Nov 3, 1957. A dog named Laika became the first animal projected by man into space. Radiation measurements were made. Total weight of craft and dog was 1,121 lbs. Nicknamed "Muttnik" by the American press.

WHITE, EDWARD DOUGLASS: BIRTH ANNIVERSARY. Nov 3. Ninth Chief Justice of the Supreme Court. Born at La Fourche Parish, LA, on Nov 3, 1845. During the Civil War, he served in the Confederate Army after which he returned to New Orleans to practice law. Elected to the US Senate in 1891, he was appointed to the Supreme Court by Grover Cleveland in 1894. He became Chief Justice under President William Taft in 1910 and served until 1921. He died at Washington, DC, on May 19, 1921.

BIRTHDAYS TODAY

Adam Ant (Stewart Goddard), 44, singer ("Goody Two Shoes"), born London, England, Nov 3, 1954.

Ken Berry, 65, actor ("F Troop," "Mayberry RFD," "Mama's Family"), singer, dancer, born Moline, IL, Nov 3, 1933.

Charles Bronson (Charles Buchinsky), 76, actor (*The Dirty Dozen, The Valachi Papers*), born Ehrenfeld, PA, Nov 3, 1922.
Kate Capshaw, 45, actress ("Duke of Groove," *How to Make an American Quilt, Indiana Jones and the Temple of Doom*), born Fort Worth, TX, Nov 3, 1953.
Michael S. Dukakis, 65, former Governor of Massachusetts (D), 1988 presidential candidate, born Brookline, MA, Nov 3, 1933.
Robert William Andrew (Bob) Feller, 80, Baseball Hall of Fame pitcher, born Van Meter, IA, Nov 3, 1918.
Steve Landesberg, 53, actor ("Barney Miller," "Friends and Lovers"), born The Bronx, NY, Nov 3, 1945.
Dolph Lundgren, 39, actor (*A View to a Kill, Rocky IV*), born Stockholm, Sweden, Nov 3, 1959.
Dennis Miller, 45, comedian, actor ("Saturday Night Live," "The Dennis Miller Show"), born Pittsburgh, PA, Nov 3, 1953.
Roseanne, 45, comedienne, actress ("Roseanne," *She Devil*), born Salt Lake City, UT, Nov 3, about 1953.
Philip (Phil) Simms, 42, sportscaster, former football player, born Lebanon, KY, Nov 3, 1956.
Louis Wade Sullivan, 65, former US Secretary of Health and Human Services in Bush administration, born Blakely, GA, Nov 3, 1933.
Monica Vitti (Monica Luisa Ceciarelli), 65, actress (*The Red Desert*), born Rome, Italy, Nov 3, 1933.

NOVEMBER 4 — WEDNESDAY

Day 308 — 57 Remaining

AMERICAN ROYAL LIVESTOCK, HORSE SHOW AND RODEO. Nov 4–22. Kansas City, MO. Since 1899 the American Royal has attracted competitors from across the nation to take part in one of Kansas City's most famous traditions. The world's largest combined show also features a grand parade and western art show. For info: American Royal, 1701 American Royal Ct, Kansas City, MO 64102. Phone: (816) 221-9800.

BALSAM, MARTIN: BIRTH ANNIVERSARY. Nov 4, 1919. Actor ("Archie Bunker's Place," *Twelve Angry Men*), born New York, NY. Died Feb 13, 1996.

CANADA: BANFF MOUNTAIN BOOK FESTIVAL. Nov 4–8. Banff, Alberta. An international mountain book competition that features guest speakers, readings, seminars, book signings, book launches and a mountain book fair. Est attendance: 2,000. For info: Banff Mountain Book Festival, Banff Centre, Box 1020, STN 38, Banff, Alta, Canada T0L 0C0. Phone: (403) 762-6406. Fax: (403) 762-6277. Email: CMC@banffcentre.ab.ca. WWW: http://www.banffcentre.ab.ca/CMC/

"THE FALL GUY" TV PREMIERE: ANNIVERSARY. Nov 4, 1981. An hour adventure series, the story centered around a Hollywood stuntman, Colt Seavers (Lee Majors) who also moonlighted as a bounty-hunter, catching bail-jumpers. It also starred Douglas Barr, Heather Thomas, Jo Ann Pflug, Markie Post and Nedra Volz. Lee Majors also sang the theme song to the show.

KING TUT TOMB DISCOVERY: ANNIVERSARY. Nov 4, 1922. On this day in 1922, one of the most important archaeological discoveries of modern times occurred at Luxor, Egypt. It was the tomb of Egypt's child-king, Tutankhamen, who became pharaoh at the age of nine and died, probably in the year 1352 BC, when he was 19. Perhaps the only ancient Egyptian royal tomb to have escaped plundering by grave robbers, it was discovered more than 3,000 years after Tutankhamen's death by English archaeologist Howard Carter, leader of an expedition financed by Lord Carnarvon. The priceless relics yielded by King Tut's tomb were placed in Egypt's National Museum at Cairo.

MAPPLETHORPE, ROBERT: BIRTH ANNIVERSARY. Nov 4, 1946. Born at Floral Park, NY, Mapplethorpe became one of photography's most controversial artists, known initially for his photographs of sadomasochistic rituals and later famous for his still lifes, nudes and portraits. Mapplethorpe's work can be seen in numerous public collections, including the Art Institute of Chicago, the Metropolitan Museum and the Museum of Modern Art in New York, the Pompidou Center in Paris and the Victoria and Albert Museum in London. Mapplethorpe died at Boston on Mar 9, 1989. Exhibits of his work sparked controversy in 1989 and 1990, leading to intense political debate about the funding practices of the National Endowment for the Arts when its charter was up for renewal by Congress. An exhibition of his work in Cincinnati led to the arrest of the museum's curator, causing an additional uproar over First Amendment freedoms and obscenity issues.

MISCHIEF NIGHT. Nov 4. Observed in England, Australia and New Zealand. Nov 4, the eve of Guy Fawkes Day, is occasion for bonfires and firecrackers to commemorate failure of the plot to blow up the Houses of Parliament on Nov 5, 1605. See also: "England: Guy Fawkes Day" (Nov 5).

MOON PHASE: FULL MOON. Nov 4. Moon enters Full Moon phase at 12:18 AM, EST.

NATIONAL CHILDREN'S GOAL-SETTING DAY. Nov 4. Encourage parents to foster goal-setting habits in their children's lives so that their children can make their dreams come true. For info: Gary Ryan Blair, Blair Leadership Group, 1201 E Fayette St, Syracuse, NY 13210. Phone: (315) 474-5628 or (800) 731-GOAL. Fax: (315) 474-6954. Email: GoalsGuy@aol.com.

"ONE MAN'S FAMILY" TV PREMIERE: ANNIVERSARY. Nov 4, 1949. This short-lived series occured at the same time as the popular radio continuing drama (in fact, the TV show was behind the radio show: the TV show in 1949 started where the radio program had in 1932). In the first season, the cast was Bert Lytell as Henry Barbour, a wealthy San Francisco stockbroker; Marjorie Gateson as his wife Frances (Fanny); Russell Thorsen as their son Paul, a writer and aviator; Patricia Robbins and Lillian Schaaf as daughter Hazel; Nancy Franklin and Eva Marie Saint as daughter Claudia; Billy Idelson and James Lee as Claudia's twin Clifford. Also included were Arthur Casell and Robert Wigginton as son Jack; Walter Brooke, Susan Shaw, Madeline Belgard, Tony Randall and Jim Boles. The second time the show came to TV it was a 15-minute serial and starred an entirely new cast.

PANAMA: FLAG DAY. Nov 4. Public holiday.

PHILLPOTTS, EDEN: BIRTH ANNIVERSARY. Nov 4, 1862. English novelist, poet and playwright, born in India on Nov 4, 1862. A friend of Arnold Bennett, Phillpotts wrote more than a hundred novels. He died near Exeter, England, on Dec 29, 1960.

RE-IMAGING CONFERENCE CONTROVERSY: 5th ANNIVERSARY. Nov 4–7, 1993. In Minneapolis, MN, an interfaith conference was held to begin a "re-imaging" of many basic tenets of Christian theology as related to women. Controversy arose following the conference when it was learned that parts of the conference featured participation in rituals that deviated from church doctrine and included references to God as "Sofia," a biblical reference to the feminine aspects of God. About 200 Presbyterian church women participated in the event which drew the ire of many in the Presbyterian Church when it was learned that church funds had been used to support the event.

ROGERS, WILL: BIRTH ANNIVERSARY. Nov 4. William Penn Adair Rogers, American writer, actor, humorist and grassroots philosopher, born at Oologah, Indian Territory (now Oklahoma), Nov 4, 1879. With aviator Wiley Post, he was killed in an airplane crash near Point Barrow, AK, Aug 15, 1935. "My forefathers," he said, "didn't come over on the *Mayflower*, but they met the boat."

SEIZURE OF US EMBASSY IN TEHERAN: ANNIVERSARY. Nov 4. On Nov 4, 1979, about 500 Iranian "students" seized the US Embassy in Teheran, taking some 90 hostages, of whom about 60 were Americans. They vowed to hold the hostages until the former Shah, Mohammed Reza Pahlavi (in the US for medical treatments), was returned to Iran for trial. The Shah died July 27, 1980, in an Egyptian military hospital near Cairo. The remaining 52 American hostages were released and left Teheran on Jan 20, 1981, after 444 days of captivity. The release occurred on America's Presidential Inauguration Day, during the hour in which the American Presidency was transferred from Jimmy Carter to Ronald Reagan.

WILL ROGERS' BIRTHDAY. Nov 4. Claremore, OK. Traditional ceremony by the Pocohontas Cherokee Indian Women's Club. Oologah school children's birthday party in the Amish-style, 1879 barn at the birthplace of Will Rogers on the shores of Lake Oologah. Texas Longhorn cattle show at Dog Iron Ranch and events at the Claremore Museum. Will Rogers Birthplace Dog Iron Ranch, Debbie and Jim Williams, two miles east of Oologah, OK, (918) 275-4201. Est attendance: 50,000. For info: Will Rogers, Joseph Carter, Greg Malak or Michelle Lefebvre, 1700 W Will Rogers Blvd, Claremore, OK 74018-0159. Phone: (800) 828-9643 or (918) 341-0719. Fax: (918) 343-8119. WWW: http://www.willrogers.org

WILL ROGERS DAY. Nov 4. Oklahoma.

BIRTHDAYS TODAY

Art Carney, 80, actor (Oscar for *Harry and Tonto*; six Emmys for "The Honeymooners"), born Mt Vernon, NY, Nov 4, 1918.

November 1998

S	M	T	W	T	F	S
1	2	3	4	5	6	7
8	9	10	11	12	13	14
15	16	17	18	19	20	21
22	23	24	25	26	27	28
29	30					

Walter Leland Cronkite, Jr, 82, journalist (former anchorman for "CBS Evening News"), born St. Joseph, MO, Nov 4, 1916.

Ralph Macchio, 36, actor ("Eight Is Enough," *The Karate Kid*), born Huntington, NY, Nov 4, 1962.

Andrea McArdle, 35, singer, actress (Broadway's *Annie*), born Philadelphia, PA, Nov 4, 1963.

Markie Post, 48, actress ("Night Court," "Hearts Afire"), born Palo Alto, CA, Nov 4, 1950.

Loretta Swit, 61, actress ("M*A*S*H"), born Passaic, NJ, Nov 4, 1937.

NOVEMBER 5 — THURSDAY

Day 309 — 56 Remaining

AMERICAN MASSAGE THERAPY ASSOCIATION™ NATIONAL CONVENTION. Nov 5–9. Salt Palace Convention Center, Salt Lake City, UT. American Massage Therapy Association (established 1943), the largest association of professional massage therapists, representing more than 27,000 members from all states and 20 other countries. Conventions emphasize continuing education, association governance and current research on therapeutic massage as a complement to traditional medicine. And, practical/innovative products and services pertinent to the profession are exhibited. For info: American Massage Therapy Assn, 820 Davis St, Ste 100, Evanston, IL 60201. Phone: (847) 864-0123. Fax: (847) 864-1178. Email: amtainfo@inet.amtamassage.org.

DEBS, EUGENE VICTOR: BIRTH ANNIVERSARY. Nov 5. American politician, first president of the American Railway Union, founder of the Social Democratic Party of America, and Socialist Party candidate for president of the US in 1904, 1908, 1912 and 1920, sentenced to 10-year prison term in 1918 (for sedition) and pardoned by President Harding in 1921. Debs was born at Terre Haute, IN, Nov 5, 1855, and died at Elmhurst, IL, Oct 20, 1926.

DURANT, WILL: BIRTH ANNIVERSARY. Nov 5, 1885. American author and popularizer of history and philosophy. Among his books: *The Story of Philosophy* and *The Story of Civilization* (a 10-volume series of which the last four were coauthored by his wife, Ariel). Born at North Adams, MA, on Nov 5, 1885, and died Nov 7, 1981 at Los Angeles, CA.

ENGLAND: GUY FAWKES DAY. Nov 5. United Kingdom. Anniversary of the "Gunpowder Plot." Conspirators planned to blow up the Houses of Parliament and King James I, on Nov 5, 1605. Twenty barrels of gunpowder, which they had secreted in a cellar under Parliament, were discovered on the night of Nov 4, the very eve of the intended explosion, and the conspirators were arrested. They were tried and convicted, and on Jan 31, 1606, eight survivors (including Guy Fawkes) were beheaded and their heads displayed on pikes at London Bridge. Though there were at least 11 conspirators, Guy Fawkes is most remembered. In 1606, the Parliament, which was to have been annihilated, enacted a law establishing Nov 5 as a day of public thanksgiving. It is still observed, and on the night of Nov 5, "the whole country lights up with bonfires and celebration." "Guys" are burned in effigy and the old verses repeated: "Remember, remember the fifth of November,/Gunpowder treason and plot;/I see no reason why Gunpowder Treason/Should ever be forgot."

LOEWY, RAYMOND: BIRTH ANNIVERSARY. Nov 5, 1893. Raymond Fernand Loewy, the "father of streamlining," an inventor, engineer and industrial designer whose ideas changed the look of 20th-century life, was born at Paris, France, Nov 5, 1893. His designs are evident in almost every area of modern life—the US Postal Service logo, the president's airplane, *Air Force One*, in streamlined automobiles, trains, refrigerators and pens. Loewy was, he once said, "amazed at the chasm between the excellent quality of much of American production and its gross appearance, clumsiness and noise." "Between two products equal in price, function and quality," he said, "the better looking will outsell the other." Loewy died at Monte Carlo on July 14, 1986.

MAXWELL, ROBERT: DEATH ANNIVERSARY. Nov 5, 1991. Media mogul Robert Maxwell's mysterious death added more controversy to his already controversial and intriguing larger-than-life story. Born Jan Ludwig Hoch to a poor farm family in the Carpathian mountains of Czechoslovakia, he ended his life a billionaire with a media empire that included TV stations in France, Macmillan Publishing Co in the US, newspapers in Hungary and the former East Germany, MTV Europe, the only official English language newspaper in China and two of the biggest tabloids in the English-speaking world: New York's *Daily News* and London's *Daily Mirror*. He earned his first million publishing scientific books. After a brief career as a member of Parliament, he purchased the *Daily Mirror* and began his rise as a media baron. Maxwell died after falling overboard from his yacht, the *Lady Ghislaine*, near the Canary Islands. Since his death, his empire was found to be in significant financial disrepair.

McCREA, JOEL: BIRTH ANNIVERSARY. Nov 5, 1905. American actor Joel McCrea was born at South Pasadena, CA. His more than 80 films include *Wells Fargo* (1937), *Union Pacific* (1939), *Sullivan's Travels* (1941) and *Foreign Correspondent* (1940). He died on Oct 20, 1990 at Los Angeles, CA.

MERLIN'S SNUG HUGS FOR KIDS. Nov 5–Dec 17. Nationwide. Each community is encouraged to provide new winter outerwear for foster and needy children. Event runs for six weeks, and on the final day (Dec 17) Merlin's caravan collects the new winter clothes and delivers them to Children's Home & Aid Society. Sponsor: Merlin's Muffler & Brake. Annually, the first week of November through the second week of December. For info: Kathleen Quinn, ProQuest Communications, 626 Carriage Hill Dr, Glenview, IL 60025-5401. Phone: (847) 998-9950. Fax: (847) 998-9945. Email: proquestpr@aol.com.
WWW: http://www.proquestpr.com

"THE NAT KING COLE SHOW" TV PREMIERE: ANNIVERSARY. Nov 5, 1956. A popular African-American pianist and singer, Cole hosted his own variety show for NBC. The Nelson Riddle Orchestra and the Randy Van Horne Singers also appeared as regulars on the show. It began as a fifteen-minute show which was expanded to half an hour. The show was dropped as a result of lack of sponsorship and because many affiliates declined to carry it.

***NEW YORK WEEKLY JOURNAL*: FIRST ISSUE ANNIVERSARY.** Nov 5, 1733. John Peter Zenger, colonial American printer and journalist, published the first issue of the *New York Weekly Journal* newspaper. He was arrested and imprisoned on Nov 17, 1734, for libel. The trial remains an important landmark in the history of the struggle for freedom of the press. See also: "Zenger, John P: Arrest Anniversary" (Nov 17).

NORSEFEST. Nov 5–7. Madison, MN. Lutefisk supper, Potato (Dumpling) Klub Luncheon and lutefisk eating contest (current record: eight pounds—we're looking for competitors from out of the area). Scandinavian Arts and Crafts Show and outhouse race, variety show and more. Est attendance: 2,500. For info: Donna Ventrella, Chamber of Commerce, 404 Sixth Ave, Madison, MN 56256. Phone: (320) 598-7373 ext 14. Fax: (320) 598-7376.

PAPERWORKS. Nov 5–28. St. Simons Island, GA. A juried exhibit designed to showcase and explore the various artistic expressions utilizing paper as the primary medium. Also includes Photo/National exhibit which is a juried exhibit created to demonstrate the wide dimensions of of the photographic world today. For info: Coastal Center for the Arts, 2012 Demere Rd, St. Simons Island, GA 31522. Phone: (912) 634-0404.

RETURN DAY. Nov 5. Georgetown, DE. The day when officially tabulated election returns are read from the balcony of Georgetown's red brick, Greek Revival courthouse to the throngs of voters assembled below. Always the second day after a general election. An official "half-holiday" in Sussex County. Reportedly Return Day has become so popular "that it is for all intents and purposes a state holiday as well."

SULLY, THOMAS: DEATH ANNIVERSARY. Nov 5, 1872. Artist Thomas Sully, born in June 1783, died at Philadelphia, PA. He is best known as a painter of nearly 2,000 portraits; he also created more than 500 depictions of historical subjects, including the famous *Washington Crossing the Delaware*, rendered around 1818. Sully was born in England but moved with his parents to the US as a child. He studied art first with his brother, a miniaturist, and then with Gilbert Stuart, Benjamin West and others. Among the people Sully painted were Queen Victoria, the Marquis de Lafayette and presidents Thomas Jefferson, James Madison and Andrew Jackson.

TARBELL, IDA M.: BIRTH ANNIVERSARY. Nov 5, 1857. American writer, editor and historian, born at Erie County, PA, Nov 5, 1857. Died at Bethel, CT, Jan 6, 1944.

VIRGINIA CHRISTMAS SHOW. Nov 5–8. Showplace Exhibition Center, Richmond, VA. Featuring 450 artisans and crafters, Christmas food shops and Christmas Holiday Theatre, entertainment, legendary "Sgt Santa." 13th annual show. Est attendance: 40,000. For info: Virginia Show Productions, PO Box 305, Chase City, VA 23924. Phone: (804) 372-3996. Fax: (804) 372-3996.

BIRTHDAYS TODAY

Bryan Adams, 39, singer ("Heaven," "Summer of '69"), songwriter ("Everything I Do"), born Vancouver, British Columbia, Canada, Nov 5, 1959.

Arthur (Art) Garfunkel, 57, singer (formerly of Simon and Garfunkel), actor (*Carnal Knowledge*), born Forest Hills, NY, Nov 5, 1941.

Corin Nemec, 27, actor ("Parker Lewis Can't Lose," *Tucker: The Man and His Dream*), born Little Rock, AR, Nov 5, 1971.

Tatum O'Neal, 35, actress (Oscar for *Paper Moon*; *Bad News Bears*), born Los Angeles, CA, Nov 5, 1963.

Roy Rogers (Leonard Slye), 86, singer, actor (called "King of the Cowboys"; "The Roy Rogers Show"), born Cincinnati, OH, Nov 5, 1912.

Sam Shepard (Samuel Shepard Rogers), 55, dramatist, actor (*A Lie of the Mind, Buried Child*; *Resurrection, The Right Stuff*), born Ft Sheridan, IL, Nov 5, 1943.

Elke Sommer (Elke Schletze), 57, actress (*A Shot in the Dark, The Prize*), born Berlin, Germany, Nov 5, 1941.

Jerry Stackhouse, 24, basketball player, born Kinston, NC, Nov 5, 1974.

Ike Turner, 67, singer (Ike and Tina Turner Revue), born Clarksdale, MS, Nov 5, 1931.

Cecil H. Underwood, 76, Governor of West Virginia (R), born Joseph Mills, WV, Nov 5, 1922.

Geoffrey Woolf, 61, author (*The Duke of Deception, The Age of Consent*), born Los Angeles, CA, Nov 5, 1937.

☆ ☆ ☆

NOVEMBER 6 — FRIDAY

Day 310 — 55 Remaining

CANADA: BANFF FESTIVAL OF MOUNTAIN FILMS. Nov 6–8. Banff, Alberta. Mountain and adventure films from around the world will be entered for this award competition at The Banff Centre. A weekend of film, seminars and exhibits. Est attendance: 6,000. For info: Deb Smythe, Fest Coord, Banff Festival of Mountain Film, Banff Centre, PO Box 1020, Station 38, Banff, Alta, Canada T0L 0C0. Phone: (403) 762-6125. Fax: (403) 762-6277. Email: CMC@banffcentre.ab.ca.
WWW: http://www.banffcentre.ab.ca/CMC/

FRIENDS OF PLANNED PARENTHOOD BOOK FAIR. Nov 6–8 (tentative). Montgomery County Fairgrounds Coliseum, Dayton, OH. More than 250,000 used books, magazines and records on display. Excellent collectibles and antiques. For info: Dvmt Dir, Friends of Planned Parenthood, 224 N Wilkinson St, Dayton, OH 45402. Phone: (513) 226-0780.

GREAT AMERICAN WARM-UP©. Nov 6–8. Just as the weather outside begins to get frightful, this weekend is set aside to clean out those closets and take your warm, wearable coats and jackets that you no longer use and donate them to a homeless shelter or agency for distribution. Do it now, before it gets even colder outside. Annually, the first full weekend in November. For info: Adrienne Sioux Koopersmith, 1437 W Rosemont, #1W, Chicago, IL 60660-1319. Phone: (773) 743-5341. Fax: (773) 743-5395. Email: kooper@interaccess.com.

GREAT LAKES INVITATIONAL BARBERSHOP SHOW. Nov 6–7. Grand Rapids, MI. Presented by Grand Rapids Chapter of Society for the Preservation and Encouragement of Barber Shop Quartet Singing in America. Est attendance: 3,000. For info: Mr J. Schneider, 1311 Northlawn NE, Grand Rapids, MI 49505. Phone: (616) 361-6820. Email: jschnei472@aol.com.

GREAT NY STATE SNOW & TRAVEL EXPO. Nov 6–8. Empire State Plaza, Albany, NY. One of the longest continuous-running snow expos in the country, the 37th annual show features ski deck shows, seminars, videos, auction and fashion shows. Annually, the first full weekend in November. Sponsor: Albany Times Union Newspapers. Est attendance: 20,000. For info: Heather Mabee, Show Promoter, Ed Lewi Assn, 6 Chelsea Pl, Clifton Park, NY 12065. Phone: (518) 383-6183. Fax: (518) 383-6755.

HALFWAY POINT OF AUTUMN. Nov 6. At 10:16 PM, EST, on Nov 6, 1998, 44 days, 21 hours and 39 minutes of autumn will have elapsed and the equivalent will remain before 8:56 PM, EST, on Dec 21 which is the winter solstice and the beginning of winter.

HOLIDAY MARKET. Nov 6–8. Greensboro Coliseum, Greensboro, NC. Holiday gift show with performances by local choral groups and bands and demonstrations of holiday cooking, decoration-making and holiday fashions. More than 250 exhibits—and Santa Claus! Est attendance: 20,000. For info: Gilmore Enterprises Inc, 1240 Oakland Ave, Greensboro, NC 27403. Phone: (910) 274-5550. Fax: (910) 274-1084.

"MEET THE PRESS" TV PREMIERE: ANNIVERSARY. Nov 6, 1947. "Meet the Press" holds the distinction of being the oldest program on TV. The show has changed its format little since it began: a well-known guest (usually a politician) is questioned on current, relevant issues by a panel of journalists. The moderators throughout the years have included Martha Rountree, Lawrence E. Spivak, Ned Brooks, Bill Monroe, Marvin Kalb, Chris Wallace and Garrick Utley. The current host is Tim Russert.

NAISMITH, JAMES: BIRTH ANNIVERSARY. Nov 6. Inventor of the game of basketball was born at Almonte, Ont, Canada, Nov 6, 1861. Died at Lawrence, KS, Nov 28, 1939. Basketball became an Olympic sport in 1936.

NATIONAL FARM TOY SHOW. Nov 6–8. Beckman HS and National Farm Toy Museum, Dyersville, IA. Features tours of the Ertl, Spec Cast, The Toy Factory and Scale Models toy companies, collector social, auction and the Mercy Hospital Bazaar held at St. Francis Xavier Auditorium. Annually, the first weekend in November. Est attendance: 15,000. For info: Dyersville Area Chamber of Commerce, PO Box 187, Dyersville, IA 52040. Phone: (319) 875-2311. Fax: (319) 875-8391.
Email: dacc@juno.com.
WWW: http://www.rcww.com/dyersville/

PADEREWSKI, IGNACE JAN: BIRTH ANNIVERSARY. Nov 6. Polish composer, pianist, patriot born at Kurylowka, Podolia, Poland, Nov 6, 1860. He died at New York, NY, June 29, 1941. When Poland fell into the hands of the Soviets after WW II, his family decided he would remain buried in Arlington National Cemetery. In May 1963, President John F. Kennedy dedicated a plaque to Paderewski's memory and declared that the pianist would rest in Arlington until Poland was free. Paderewski's remains were returned to his native country on June 29, 1992, the 51st anniversary of his death, after Poland held its first parliamentary election following its independence from the Soviet Union.

November 1998

S	M	T	W	T	F	S
1	2	3	4	5	6	7
8	9	10	11	12	13	14
15	16	17	18	19	20	21
22	23	24	25	26	27	28
29	30					

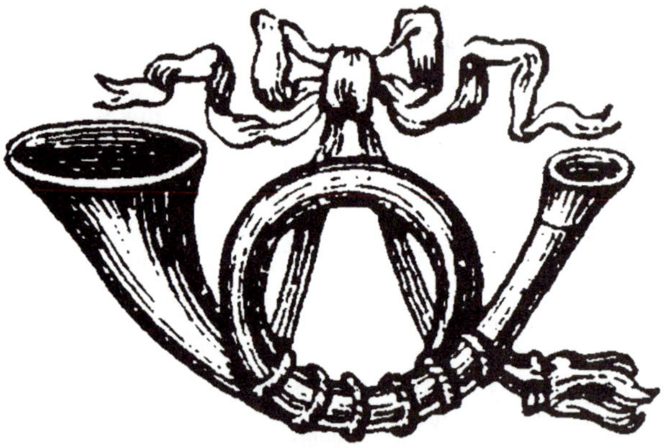

SAXOPHONE DAY (ADOLPHE SAX BIRTH ANNIVERSARY). Nov 6. A day to recognize the birth anniversary of Adolphe Sax, Belgian musician and inventor of the saxophone and the saxotromba. Born at Dinant, Belgium, on Nov 6, 1814, Antoine Joseph Sax, later known as Adolphe, was the eldest of 11 children of a musical instrument builder. Sax contributed an entire family of brass wind instruments for band and orchestra use. He was accorded fame and great wealth, but business misfortunes led to bankruptcy. Sax died in poverty at Paris on Feb 7, 1894.

SOUSA, JOHN PHILIP: BIRTH ANNIVERSARY. Nov 6. American composer and band conductor, remembered for many stirring marches such as "The Stars and Stripes Forever," "Semper Fidelis," "El Capitan," born at Washington, DC, Nov 6, 1854. Died at Reading, PA, Mar 6, 1932. See also: "The Stars and Stripes Forever" (May 14).

STAMP EXPO. Nov 6–8. Elks Lodge, Pasadena, CA. Annual expo. Est attendance: 4,000. For info: Intl Stamp Collectors Society, Box 854, Van Nuys, CA 91408. Phone: (818) 997-6496. Fax: (818) 988-4337.
Email: iibick@aol.com. WWW: http://www.4free.com/bick

STAMP EXPO: FALL. Nov 6–8. Wilshire Ebell Convention Complex, Los Angeles, CA. Est attendance: 4,000. For info: Intl Stamp Collectors Society, PO Box 854, Van Nuys, CA 91408. Phone: (818) 997-6496. Fax: (818) 988-4337. Email: iibick@aol.com. WWW: http://www.4free.dom/bick

STORIES AND SONGS ON THE BECKY THATCHER SHOWBOAT. Nov 6. Becky Thatcher Showboat, Marietta, OH. Presentation of river or historic stories and songs. Est attendance: 400. For info: Donna Foster, Creative Arts Institute, 8021 Kennedy Rd, Blacklick, OH 43004. Phone: (614) 759-9407. Fax: (614) 759-8480.

SWEDEN: GUSTAVUS ADOLPHUS DAY. Nov 6. Honors Sweden's King and military leader killed in 1632.

TCHAIKOVSKY, PETER ILICH: DEATH ANNIVERSARY. Nov 6, 1893. Ranked among the outstanding composers of all time, Peter Ilich Tchaikovsky was born at Vatkinsk, Russia, May 7, 1840. His musical talent was not encouraged and he embarked upon a career in jurisprudence, not studying music seriously until 1861. Among his famous works are the three-act ballet *Sleeping Beauty*, two-act ballet *The Nutcracker* and the symphony *Pathetique*. Mystery surrounds Tchaikovsky's death. It was believed he'd caught cholera from contaminated water, but 20th-century scholars believe he probably committed suicide to avoid his homosexuality being revealed. He died at St. Petersburg.

TIERNEY, GENE: DEATH ANNIVERSARY. Nov 6, 1991. American actress Gene Tierney was born Nov 20, 1920, at Brooklyn, NY. Her films include *Laura* (1944) and *Leave Her to Heaven* (1945), for which she was nominated for an Oscar. She died on Nov 6, 1991 at Houston, TX.

VICTORIAN HOLMES WEEKEND. Nov 6–8. Cape May, NJ. A weekend of mystery and intrigue awaits amateur sleuths when Cape May celebrates the works of Sir Arthur Conan Doyle, creator of Sherlock Holmes. Annually, the first weekend in November. Est attendance: 200. For info: Mid-Atlantic Center for the Arts, PO Box 340, Cape May, NJ 08204. Phone: (609) 884-5404 or (800) 275-4278 (tickets). Fax: (609) 884-2006. Email: mac4arts@algoirthms.com.
WWW: http://www.beachcomber.com/capemay/mac.html

VIRGINIA-CAROLINA CRAFTSMEN'S CHRISTMAS CLASSIC. Nov 6–8. State Fairgrounds on Strawberry Hill, Richmond, VA. Arts and crafts. Est attendance: 35,000. For info: The Carolina Craftsmen, 1240 Oakland Ave, Greensboro, NC 27403. Phone: (910) 274-5550. Fax: (910) 274-1084.

WESTERN SAMOA: ARBOR DAY. Nov 6. The first Friday in November is observed as Arbor Day in Western Samoa.

BIRTHDAYS TODAY

Ray Conniff, 82, bandleader, born Attleboro, MA, Nov 6, 1916.
Sally Field, 52, actress (Oscars for *Norma Rae, Places in the Heart*; Emmy for *Sybil*), born Pasadena, CA, Nov 6, 1946.
Glen Frey, 50, musician, songwriter, singer ("The Heat Is On"), born Detroit, MI, Nov 6, 1948.
Nigel Havers, 49, actor (*Chariots of Fire, Empire of the Sun*), born London, England, Nov 6, 1949.
Ethan Hawke, 28, actor (*Dead Poets Society, Reality Bites*), born Austin, TX, Nov 6, 1970.
Lance Kerwin, 38, actor ("James at 15," "The Family Holvak"), born Newport Beach, CA, Nov 6, 1960.
Mike Nichols (Michael Igor Peschkowsky), 67, comedian, actor, theater producer/director, filmmaker (Oscar for *The Graduate; Working Girl*), born Berlin, Germany, Nov 6, 1931.
Maria Owings Shriver, 43, broadcast journalist ("Today"), born Chicago, IL, Nov 6, 1955.

NOVEMBER 7 — SATURDAY

Day 311 — 54 Remaining

ANTIQUING WEEKEND IN THE QUIET CORNER. Nov 7–8. Northeastern Connecticut. More than 40 antique shops offer special displays, discounts and demonstrations throughout the region. Annually, the first weekend in November. Est attendance: 1,000. For info: Northeast Connecticut Visitors District, PO Box 598, Putnam, CT 06260. Phone: (860) 928-1228. Fax: (860) 928-4720. Email: quietcorner@snet.net.
WWW: http://www.webtravels.com/quietcorner

THE ART OF STORYTELLING CONFERENCE. Nov 7. Marietta, OH. Sharing the art of storytelling with a new generation. Est attendance: 150. For info: Donna Foster, Program Dir, Creative Arts Institute, Inc, 8021 Kennedy Rd, Blacklick, OH 43004. Phone: (614) 759-9407. Fax: (614) 759-8480.

BIG 10 FIELD HOCKEY TOURNAMENT. Nov 7–9. University of Iowa, Iowa City, IA. Est attendance: 1,000. For info: Dennis LaBissoniere, Big 10 Conference, 1500 W Higgins Rd, Park Ridge, IL 60068-6300. Phone: (847) 696-1010. Fax: (847) 696-1110. WWW: http://www.bigten.org

BIG 10 WOMEN'S SOCCER CHAMPIONSHIP. Nov 7–9. University of Minnesota, Minneapolis, MN. Est attendance: 1,000. For info: Dennis LaBissoniere, Big 10 Conference, 1500 W Higgins Rd, Park Ridge, IL 60068-6300. Phone: (847) 696-1010. Fax: (847) 696-1110. WWW: http://www.bigten.org

CAMUS, ALBERT: 85th BIRTH ANNIVERSARY. Nov 7, 1913. French writer and philosopher, winner of the Nobel Prize for Literature in 1957, was born at Mondavi, Algeria, Nov 7, 1913. "The struggle to reach the top is itself enough to fulfill the heart of man. One must believe that Sisyphus is happy," he wrote, in *Le Mythe de Sisyphe*. Camus was killed in an automobile accident in France, Jan 4, 1960.

CANADA: FARMFAIR INTERNATIONAL. Nov 7–15. Edmonton, Alberta. International Purebred Livestock Show and sale. Features traditional western-style family entertainment, best-of-breed shows, purebreed cattle sales, draft horse pulling and team cattle penning competitions and Alberta's only western-themed trade and gift show. Est attendance: 40,000. For info: Roxanne Carr, Northlands Park, Box 1480, Edmonton, Alta, Canada T5J 2N5. Phone: (403) 471-7300 or (888) 800-PARK. Fax: (403) 477-9536. Email: npmarket@planet.eon.net. WWW: http://www.northlands.com

CANADIAN PACIFIC RAILWAY: TRANSCONTINENTAL COMPLETION ANNIVERSARY. Nov 7. At 9:30 AM, on Nov 7, 1885, the last spike was driven at Craigellachie, British Columbia, completing the Canadian Pacific Railway's 2,980-mile transcontinental railroad track between Montreal, Quebec, in the east and Port Moody, British Columbia, in the west.

CONTINENT-SIZED WINDSTORMS DISCOVERED: ANNIVERSARY. Nov 7, 1991. A satellite that had been launched from the space shuttle *Discovery* on Sept 15, 1991, discovered large windstorms in Earth's upper atmosphere. The satellite's 10 instruments became functional on Nov 7 and detected the continent-sized windstorms, which measured up to 200 mile-per-hour velocities in areas that are 600 to 6,000 miles wide in the mesosphere. The largest storm was discovered in the Southern hemisphere and reached from western Australia eastward to points halfway across the Atlantic Ocean.

CURIE, MARIE SKLODOWSKA: BIRTH ANNIVERSARY. Nov 7, 1867. Polish chemist and physicist, born at Warsaw, Poland, Nov 7, 1867. In 1903 she was awarded, with her husband, the Nobel Prize for physics for their discovery of the element radium. Died July 4, 1934.

EVENING OF ASTRONOMY. Nov 7. Florence Marina State Park, Omaha, GA. An evening spent under the stars with an astronomer describing the different heavenly bodies. Guests also get to view the stars and other constellations through a telescope. Est attendance: 75. For info: James Wooten, Interpretive Ranger, Florence Marina State Park, Rte 1, Box 36, Omaha, GA 31821. Phone: (912) 838-4706. Fax: (912) 838-6113.
Email: florence.marina@internetmci.com.

"FACE THE NATION" TV PREMIERE: ANNIVERSARY. Nov 7, 1954. The CBS counterpart to NBC's "Meet the Press," this show employed a similar format: panelists interviewed a well-known guest. In 1983 the panel was changed to include experts in addition to journalists when Lesley Stahl succeeded George Herman as moderator. Though usually produced in Washington, DC, the show occasionally interviewed people elsewhere (such as Khrushchev in Moscow in 1957).

FIRST BLACK GOVERNOR ELECTED: ANNIVERSARY. Nov 7. On Nov 7, 1989, L. Douglas Wilder was elected governor of Virginia, becoming the first elected black governor in US history. Wilder had previously served as lieutenant governor of Virginia.

GAINESVILLE DOWNTOWN FESTIVAL AND ART SHOW. Nov 7–8 (tentative). 17th annual festival, downtown, Gainesville, FL. 240 artists and crafters display work for purchase. Two full days of live music on three stages, children's activity area, food vendors, hands-on art opportunities. Est attendance: 100,000. For info: Linda Piper, City of Gainesville, Division of Cultural Affairs, PO Box 490–Station 30, Gainesville, FL 32602. Phone: (352) 334-2197. Fax: (352) 334-2146.

GREAT OCTOBER SOCIALIST REVOLUTION: ANNIVERSARY. Nov 7, 1917. This holiday in the old Soviet Union was observed for two days with parades, military displays and appearances by Soviet leaders. According to the old Russian calendar, the revolution took place on Oct 25, 1917. Soviet calendar reform causes observance to fall on Nov 7 (Gregorian). The Bolshevik Revolution began in Petrograd, Russia, on the evening of Nov 6 (Gregorian), 1917. A new government headed by Nikolai Lenin took office the following day under the name Council of People's Commissars. Leon Trotsky was commissar for foreign affairs and Josef Stalin became commissar of national minorities.

JAGGER, DEAN: 95th BIRTH ANNIVERSARY. Nov 7, 1903. American actor Dean Jagger was born at Columbus Grove, OH. Predominantly a character actor, he appeared in more than 120 films, including *Twelve O'Clock High* (1950), for which he won an Oscar for best supporting actor. He died on Feb 5, 1991, at Santa Monica, CA.

KECHI'S HOLIDAY FESTIVAL. Nov 7. Kechi, KS. The public is invited to start their 1998 holiday shopping early in Kechi, "The Antique Capital of Kansas," in a small quaint community of 20 different shops which include antique, craft and specialty shops (quilts, electronics, Karg Art Glass & Gallery and two unique restaurants). Est attendance: 500. For info: Kechi Area Chamber of Commerce, PO Box 578, Kechi, KS 67067-0578. Phone: (316) 744-9403. Fax: (316) 744-1337. Email: kechirick@feist.com.

LOVINGTON ARTS AND CRAFTS FESTIVAL. Nov 7–8. Lea County Fairgrounds, Lovington, NM. Displays from more than 100 local and regional crafters. No commercially manufactured items allowed. 21st annual festival. Annually, the first weekend in November. Est attendance: 10,000. For info: Lovington Chamber of Commerce, PO Box 1347, Lovington, NM 88260. Phone: (505) 396-5311. Fax: (505) 396-2823.

NATIONAL NOTARY PUBLIC DAY. Nov 7. To recognize the fundamental contributions made by notaries to the law and the people of the US. Annually, Nov 7. For info: Lisa Fisher, Exec Dir, American Society of Notaries, PO Box 5707, Tallahassee, FL 32314-5707. Phone: (904) 671-5164. Fax: (904) 671-5165. Email: amnotary@polaris.net. WWW: http://www.notaries.com

OLD STOUGHTON MUSICAL SOCIETY: ANNIVERSARY. Nov 7, 1786. Founded at Stoughton, MA, the Stoughton Musical Society is the oldest choral society in the US. Originally consisting of 25 men, it now includes both men and women. The society performed at the Chicago World's Columbian Exposition in 1893.

REPUBLICAN SYMBOL: ANNIVERSARY. Nov 7. Thomas Nast used an elephant to represent the Republican Party in a satirical cartoon in *Harper's Weekly* Nov 7, 1874, and today the elephant is still a well-recognized symbol for the Republican Party in political cartoons.

RICHARD NIXON'S "LAST" PRESS CONFERENCE: ANNIVERSARY. Nov 7, 1962. Richard M. Nixon, having been narrowly defeated in his bid for the presidency by John F. Kennedy in the 1960 election, returned to politics two years later as a candidate for governor of California in the election of Nov 6, 1962. Defeated again (this time by incumbent governor Edmund G. Brown), Nixon held his "last" press conference with assembled reporters in Los Angeles at mid-morning the next day at which he said: ". . . just think how much you're going to be missing. You won't have Nixon to kick around any more, because, gentlemen, this is my last press conference."

November 1998

S	M	T	W	T	F	S
1	2	3	4	5	6	7
8	9	10	11	12	13	14
15	16	17	18	19	20	21
22	23	24	25	26	27	28
29	30					

ROOSEVELT ELECTED TO FOURTH TERM: ANNIVERSARY. Nov 7. Defeating Thomas Dewey on Nov 7, 1944, Franklin D. Roosevelt became the first, and only, person elected to four terms as President of the US. Roosevelt was inaugurated the following Jan 20 but died in office Apr 12, 1945, serving only 53 days of the fourth term.

RUSSIA: OCTOBER REVOLUTION. Nov 7. National holiday.

SADIE HAWKINS DAY. Nov 7. Widely observed in US, usually on the first Saturday in November. Tradition established in "Li'l Abner" comic strip in 1930s by cartoonist Al Capp. A popular occasion when women and girls are encouraged to take the initiative in inviting the man or boy of their choice for a date. A similar tradition is associated with Feb 29 in leap years.

SIEGE OF FORT MIFFLIN. Nov 7–8. Historic Fort Mifflin, Philadelphia, PA. A Revolutionary War reenactment and encampment with battle reenactment, black powder demonstration, living history, blacksmith demonstrations and musical presentation. Est attendance: 500. For info: Historic Fort Mifflin on the Delaware, Fort Mifflin Rd, Philadelphia, PA 19104. Phone: (215) 685-4192. Fax: (215) 492-1608.

STEEPLECHASE AT CALLAWAY GARDENS. Nov 7. Pine Mountain, GA. A seven-race steeplechase "meet" where riders match their horses for speed and split-second timing over brush jumps. Box seating and infield tailgating spaces available. Est attendance: 12,000. For info: The Steeplechase at Callaway Gardens, PO Box 2311, Columbus, GA 31902. Phone: (706) 324-6252. Fax: (706) 324-3651.

VERBOORT SAUSAGE AND KRAUT DINNER. Nov 7. Visitation Parish, Forest Grove, OR. 64th annual event features crafts, Bingo, raffles, beer garden, local produce, homebaked goods and, of course, famous Verboort sausage and kraut. Est attendance: 6,000. For info: Melvin Finegan, Visitation Parish, 4285 NW Visitation Rd, Forest Grove, OR 97116. Phone: (503) 357-3613.

VETERANS DAY WEEKEND CELEBRATION. Nov 7–9. Amargosa Valley, NV. 5th annual parade, chili cook-off, swap meet, pig roast, pancake breakfast and auction. Est attendance: 450. For local info: (702) 372-5459.

☆ ☆ ☆

BIRTHDAYS TODAY

Billy (William Franklin) Graham, 80, evangelist, born Charlotte, NC, Nov 7, 1918.

Al Hirt, 76, jazz musician, born New Orleans, LA, Nov 7, 1922.

Joni Mitchell (Roberta Joan Anderson), 55, singer, songwriter ("Both Sides Now," "Big Yellow Taxi," "Woodstock"), born McLeod, Alberta, Canada, Nov 7, 1943.

Barry Newman, 60, actor ("Petrocelli," *Vanishing Point*), born Boston, MA, Nov 7, 1938.

Dana Plato, 34, actress (Kimberly Drummond on "Diff'rent Strokes"), born Maywood, CA, Nov 7, 1964.

Joan Sutherland, 72, opera singer, born Sydney, Australia, Nov 7, 1926.

Mary Travers, 61, composer, singer (Peter, Paul and Mary; "Blowin' in the Wind"), born Louisville, KY, Nov 7, 1937.

NOVEMBER 8 — SUNDAY

Day 312 — 53 Remaining

ABET AND AID PUNSTERS DAY. Nov 8. Laugh instead of groan at incredibly dreadful puns. All-time greatest triple pun: "Though he's not very humble, there's no police like Holmes." From the register of worst puns of Punsters Unlimited. (Originated by Earl Harris, retired, and the late William Rabe.)

AMERICAN HEART ASSOCIATION SCIENTIFIC SESSIONS: ANNUAL MEETING. Nov 8–11. Convention Center, Dallas, TX. Est attendance: 48,000. For info: Mary Burnett, American Heart Assn, 7272 Greenville Ave, Dallas, TX 75231-4596. Phone: (214) 706-1425. Fax: (214) 373-3406.

CORTÉS CONQUERS MEXICO: ANNIVERSARY. Nov 8, 1519. After landing on the Yucatan peninsula in April, Spaniard Hernau Cortés and his troops marched into the interior of Mexico to the Aztec capital and took the Aztec emperor Montezuma hostage.

"DAYS OF OUR LIVES" TV PREMIERE: ANNIVERSARY. Nov 8, 1965. This popular daytime serial, like many others, has gone through many changes throughout its run. It expanded from 30 minutes to an hour; it went to number one in the ratings and slipped to 9 out of 12 in the 1980s; and it dropped or deemphasized older characters, which angered its audience. The soap is set in Salem and centers around the Horton family. Notable cast members included Mary Frann, Joan Van Ark, Susan Oliver, Mike Farrell, Kristian Alfonso, Garry Marshall, John Aniston, Josh Taylor, Wayne Northrup, John DeLancie, Andrea Barber, Deidre Hall, Thaao Penghlis, Jason Bernard, Marilyn McCoo, Charles Shaughnessy and Genie Francis.

HALLEY, EDMUND: BIRTH ANNIVERSARY. Nov 8, 1656. Astronomer and mathematician born at London, England. Astronomer Royal, 1721–42. Died at Greenwich, England, Jan 14, 1742. He observed the great comet of 1682 (now named for him), first conceived its periodicity and wrote in his *Synopsis of Comet Astronomy*: ". . . I may venture to foretell that this Comet will return again in the year 1758." It did, and Edmund Halley's memory is kept alive by the once-every-generation appearance of Halley's Comet. There have been 28 recorded appearances of this comet since 240 BC. Average time between appearances is 76 years. Often regarded as a harbinger of disaster, Halley's Comet is next expected to be visible in 2061.

MERCHANT SAILING SHIP PRESERVATION DAY. Nov 8. On this day in 1941, the whaler *Charles W. Morgan* arrived in Mystic, CT, to be restored. This was the beginning of the modern era of preservation of merchant sailing ships.

MITCHELL, MARGARET: BIRTH ANNIVERSARY. Nov 8, 1900. American novelist who won a Pulitzer Prize (1937) for her only book, *Gone with the Wind*, a romantic novel about the Civil War and Reconstruction. *Gone with the Wind* sold about 10,000,000 copies and was translated into 30 languages. Born at Atlanta, GA, Mitchell died there after being struck by an automobile on Aug 16, 1949.

MONTANA: ADMISSION DAY: ANNIVERSARY. Nov 8. Became 41st state on this day in 1889.

NATIONAL HIGHER EDUCATION CONFERENCE ON BLACK STUDENT RETENTION. Nov 8–14. Philadelphia, PA. A forum for college and university faculty, administrators and other educators to critically review issues that influence student retention in higher education. Est attendance: 800. For info: Dr. Clinita A. Ford, Dir, Retention Conference, PO Box 10121, Tallahassee, FL 32302-2121. Phone: (800) USA-GRAD. Fax: (904) 599-3913.

NATIONAL RADIOLOGIC TECHNOLOGY WEEK. Nov 8–14. Increases public awareness of the health professionals who utilize medical radiation and diagnostic imaging techniques to aid in the diagnosis and treatment of disease. For info: American Soc of Radiologic Technologists, 15000 Central Ave SE, Albuquerque, NM 87123-3917. Phone: (505) 298-4500 or (800) 444-2778. Fax: (505) 298-5063. WWW: http://www.asrt.org

NATIONAL SPLIT PEA SOUP WEEK. Nov 8–14. To promote the use of split peas in split pea soup. For info: Randy Duckworth, Dir of Mktg, USA Dry Pea and Lentil Council, 5071 Highway 8 W, Moscow, ID 83843. Phone: (208) 882-3023. Fax: (208) 882-6406. Email: pulse@pea-lentil.com.

OPERATING ROOM NURSE WEEK. Nov 8–14. To inform health care consumers that the nurse in the operating room cares for patients before, during and after surgery. Annually, the week including Nov 14. For info: Public Info Coord, Assn of Operating Room Nurses, 2170 S Parker Rd, Ste 300, Denver, CO 80231-5711. Phone: (303) 755-6300. Fax: (303) 752-2044. Email: jpaulson@aorn.org. WWW: http://www.aorn.org

PURSUIT OF HAPPINESS WEEK. Nov 8–14. The purpose of this week is to remind everyone, as stated in the Declaration of Independence, that all men and women are "endowed by their Creator with certain unalienable rights, that among them are life, liberty and the pursuit of happiness." For complete info and quotations about happiness by famous people, send $3 to cover expense of printing, handling and postage. For info: Dr. Stanley Drake, Pres, Intl Society of Friendship and Goodwill, 412 Cherry Hills Dr, Bakersfield, CA 93309.

TUNISIA: TREE FESTIVAL. Nov 8. National agricultural festival. Annually, the second Sunday in November.

X-RAY DISCOVERY DAY: ANNIVERSARY. Nov 8, 1895. Physicist Wilhelm Conrad Roentgen (q.v.) discovered X-rays on this date, beginning a new era in physics and medicine. Although X-rays had been observed previously, it was Roentgen, a professor at the University of Wurzburg (Germany), who successfully repeated X-ray experimentation and who is credited with the discovery.

BIRTHDAYS TODAY

Christiaan Barnard, 76, South African surgeon who performed the first human heart transplant in 1967, born at Beaufort West, South Africa, Nov 8, 1922.

Mary Hart, 47, TV host, born Madison, SD, Nov 8, 1951.

June Havoc, 82, actress (*Brewster's Millions*, "Willy"), born Seattle, WA, Nov 8, 1916.

Christie Hefner, 46, business executive (head of *Playboy*), daughter of Hugh Hefner, born Chicago, IL, Nov 8, 1952.

Ricki Lee Jones, 44, singer, musician ("Chuck E.'s In Love"), born Chicago, IL, Nov 8, 1954.

Virna Lisi, 61, actress (*How to Murder Your Wife, The Secret of Santa Vittoria*), born Ancona, Italy, Nov 8, 1937.

Patti Page (Clara Ann Fowler), 71, singer ("Let Me Go Lover," "Allegheny Moon"), born Clarence, OK, Nov 8, 1927.

Bonnie Raitt, 49, singer ("Sweet Forgiveness"), actress, daughter of John Raitt, born Los Angeles, CA, Nov 8, 1949.

Morley Safer, 67, journalist ("60 Minutes"), born Toronto, Ontario, Canada, Nov 8, 1931.

NOVEMBER 9 — MONDAY

Day 313 — 52 Remaining

AGNEW, SPIRO THEODORE: 80th BIRTH ANNIVERSARY. Nov 9, 1918. Thirty-ninth vice president of the US, born at Baltimore, MD, Nov 9, 1918. Twice elected vice president (1968 and 1972), Agnew, on Oct 10, 1973, became the second person to resign that office. Agnew entered a plea of no contest to a charge of income tax evasion (on contract kickbacks received while he was governor of Maryland and after he became vice president), and was sentenced to pay a $10,000 fine and serve three years probation. On Apr 27, 1981, following a class-action suit, a Maryland circuit court ruled that Agnew must pay the state $248,735 ($147,500 in kickbacks plus $101,235 in interest) for violating the public trust. Agnew did not testify at the trial. He died Sept 17, 1996, at Berlin, MD. See also: "Vice Presidential Resignation: Anniversary" (Dec 28) and "Calhoun, John Caldwell: Birth Anniversary" (Mar 18).

BERLIN WALL OPENED: ANNIVERSARY. Nov 9, 1989. After 28 years as a symbol of the Cold War, the Berlin Wall was opened on this evening, and citizens of both sides walked freely through the barrier as others danced atop the structure to celebrate the end of an historic era. Coming amidst the celebration of East Germany's 40-year anniversary, pro-democracy demonstrations led to the resignation of Erich Honecker, East Germany's head of state and party chief. It was Honecker who had supervised the construction of the 27.9-mile wall across the city during the night of Aug 13, 1961, because US President John Kennedy had ordered a troop build-up in response to the blockade of West Berlin by the Soviets.

BOSTON FIRE: ANNIVERSARY. Nov 9, 1872. Though Boston had experienced several damaging fires, the worst one started on this Saturday evening in a dry-goods warehouse. Spreading rapidly in windy weather, it devastated several blocks of the business district, destroying nearly 800 buildings. Damage was estimated at more than $75 million. It was said that the fire caused a bright red glare in the sky that could be seen from nearly 100 miles away. The Boston fire came one year, one month and one day after the Great Chicago Fire of Oct 8, 1871.

CAMBODIA: INDEPENDENCE DAY. Nov 9. National Day.

DANDRIDGE, DOROTHY: BIRTH ANNIVERSARY. Nov 9, 1922. Actress and singer Dandridge was a child star who toured with her sisters, Vivian, and Etta Jones, as The Dandridge Sisters. They played at the Cotton Club, sharing the stage with artists such as Cab Calloway and W. C. Handy. Dandridge went solo in 1941 to perform in Hollywood movies and on stage with the Desi Arnaz Band. Her big break came with the lead role in Otto Preminger's musical, *Carmen Jones*. Dandridge received an Oscar nomination for her performance. Unfortunately, Dandridge could not overcome Hollywood's racism and tendency to typecast and her career foundered. She died at West Hollywood, CA, on Sept 8, 1965, of an anti-depressant drug overdose.

EAST COAST BLACKOUT: ANNIVERSARY. Nov 9, 1965. Massive electric power failure starting in western New York state at 5:16 PM, Nov 9, 1965, cut electric power to much of northeastern US and Ontario and Quebec in Canada. More than 30 million persons in an area of 80,000 square miles were affected. The experience provoked studies of the vulnerability of 20th-century technology.

GRIMES, LEONARD ANDREW: BIRTH ANNIVERSARY. Nov 9, 1815. Reverend Leonard Grimes was born at Leesburg, VA, on Nov 9, 1815, to parents who were free. A free black man living in Washington, DC, he despised slavery and became active in assisting fugitive slaves to escape. He was caught and imprisoned in Richmond, VA. After his release he founded and became the first minister of the Twelfth Street Baptist Church in Boston, MA, where he served until his death on Mar 14, 1874.

November 1998

S	M	T	W	T	F	S
1	2	3	4	5	6	7
8	9	10	11	12	13	14
15	16	17	18	19	20	21
22	23	24	25	26	27	28
29	30					

KRISTALLNACHT (CRYSTAL NIGHT): 60th ANNIVERSARY. Nov 9–10, 1938. During the evening of Nov 9 and into the morning of Nov 10, 1938, mobs in Germany destroyed thousands of shops and homes carrying out a pogrom against Jews. Synagogues were burned down or demolished. There were bonfires in every Jewish neighborhood, fueled by Jewish prayer books, Torah scrolls and volumes of philosophy, history and poetry. More than 30,000 Jews were arrested and 91 killed. The night got its name from the smashing of glass store windows.

THE LINKS, INC: ANNIVERSARY. Nov 9, 1946. Thousands of African-Americans fought in WW II, but after the war the same old injustices and hatred prevailed. In Philadelphia Margaret Roselle Hawkins and Sarah Strickland Scott founded a nonpartisan, volunteer organization called The Links, "linking" their friendship and resources in an effort to better the lives of disadvantaged African-Americans. From the first group of nine, The Links has grown to an incorporated organization of 8,000 women in 240 local chapters in 40 states plus the District of Columbia and two foreign countries. The Links promotes educational, cultural and community activities through a variety of projects here and in Africa. In May of 1985 The Links became an official Non-Governmental Organization of the UN.

LOVEJOY, ELIJAH P.: BIRTH ANNIVERSARY. Nov 9, 1802. American newspaper publisher and abolitionist born Nov 9, 1802. Died Nov 7, 1837 at Alton, IL in a fire started by a mob angry about his anti-slavery views.

NATIONAL CHILD SAFETY COUNCIL: FOUNDING ANNIVERSARY. Nov 9, 1955. National Child Safety Council (NCSC) at Jackson, MI. NCSC is the oldest and largest nonprofit organization in the US dedicated solely to the personal safety and well-being of young children. For info: Barbara Handley Huggett, Dir Research and Dvmt, NCSC, Box 1368, Jackson, MI 49204-1368. Phone: (517) 764-6070.

NATIONAL FRAGRANCE WEEK. Nov 9–13. Participating cities across the country. Opening day ceremonies to kick off the week. Mayoral Proclamation presented in each city. Special fragrance events at participating retail and other noted locations. Annually, the second week in November. For info: The Fragrance Fdtn, 145 E 32nd St, New York, NY 10016-6002. Phone: (212) 725-2755. Fax: (212) 779-9058. Email: info@fragrance.org. WWW: http://www.fragrance.org

"OMNIBUS" TV PREMIERE: ANNIVERSARY. Nov 9, 1952. This eclectic series deserved its name, offering a variety of presentations, including dramas, documentaries and musicals. Alistair Cooke hosted the program, which was the first major TV project to be underwritten by the Ford Foundation. Notable presentations included: James Agee's "Mr Lincoln"; "Die Fledermaus," with Eugene Ormandy conducting the Metropolitan Opera Orchestra; Agnes DeMille's ballet "Three Virgins and the Devil" (presented as "Three Maidens and the Devil"); and documentaries from underwater explorer Jacques Cousteau.

RELEASE YOUR BEAUTY FOR THE HOLIDAYS WEEK. Nov 9–15. This is the week to concentrate on releasing your natural beauty, just in time for the holidays. Annually, the second full week in November. For info: Susan Jeske, Sharkbait Press, PO Box 11300, Costa Mesa, CA 92627. Phone: (714) 645-0139 or (714) 754-7777.

SAGAN, CARL: BIRTH ANNIVERSARY. Nov 9, 1934. Astronomer, biologist, author (*Broca's Brain, Cosmos*), born New York, NY. Died at Seattle, WA, Dec 20, 1996.

VIETNAM VETERANS MEMORIAL STATUE UNVEILING: ANNIVERSARY. Nov 9, 1984. The Vietnam Veterans Memorial was completed by the addition of a statue, "Three Servicemen" (sculpted by Frederick Hart), which was unveiled on

Nov 9, 1984. The statue faces the black granite wall on which are inscribed the names of more than 58,000 Americans who were killed or missing in action in the Vietnam War.

WHITE, STANFORD: BIRTH ANNIVERSARY. Nov 9, 1853. American architect who designed the old Madison Square Garden, the Washington Arch, and the Players, Century and Metropolitan Clubs in New York City, Stanford White was born there on Nov 9, 1853. White was shot to death on the roof of the Madison Square Garden by Harry Thaw on June 25, 1906.

WILHELM II ABDICATES: 80th ANNIVERSARY. Nov 9, 1918. As World War I was coming to a close and it became clear their cause was lost, a revolt broke out in Germany. The Kaiser was advised by his military staff that the loyalty of the army could not be guaranteed. On Nov 9, 1918, it was announced in Berlin that Kaiser Wilhelm II had abdicated his throne. The former leader then fled to Holland. Philip Scheidemann, a Socialist leader, proclaimed a German Republic and became its first Chancellor.

BIRTHDAYS TODAY

Lou Ferrigno, 47, actor (*Pumping Iron*, "The Incredible Hulk"), former bodybuilder, born Brooklyn, NY, Nov 9, 1951.

Robert (Bob) Gibson, 63, Baseball Hall of Fame pitcher, born Omaha, NE, Nov 9, 1935.

Bob Graham, 62, US Senator (D, Florida), born Coral Gables, FL, Nov 9, 1936.

Thomas Daniel (Tom) Weiskopf, 56, golfer, born Massillon, OH, Nov 9, 1942.

NOVEMBER 10 — TUESDAY

Day 314 — 51 Remaining

BURTON, RICHARD: BIRTH ANNIVERSARY. Nov 10. Welsh-born stage and film actor. Richard Burton was never knighted and never an Oscar winner, but he was generally regarded as one of the great acting talents of his time. Born Richard Jenkins at Pontrhydyfen, South Wales, on Nov 10, 1925, the son of a coal miner later took the name of his guardian, schoolmaster Philip Burton. An intense and tempestuous personal life and career suggested a self-destructive bent. Burton died at Geneva, Switzerland, of a cerebral hemorrhage, at age 58, on Aug 5, 1984.

CHRISTMAS AT BILTMORE. Nov 10–Jan 3. Biltmore Estate, Asheville, NC. Christmas is celebrated in much the same fashion as it was in 1895 when George Vanderbilt formally opened Biltmore House. The celebration includes spectacular Victorian Christmas decorations, holiday music performed daily and more than 30 Christmas trees throughout the house. Closed Nov 26 and Dec 25. Est attendance: 150,000. For info: The Biltmore Estate, 1 N Pack Square, Asheville, NC 28801. Phone: (800) 543-2961. Email: www.marketing@biltmore.com. WWW: http://www.biltmore.com

***EDMUND FITZGERALD* MEMORIAL BEACON LIGHTING.** Nov 10. 3 PM–6 PM, Two Harbors, MN. Slide presentation on *Edmund Fitzgerald* and other shipwrecks on Lake Superior; beacon lighting; lighthouse tour held at Split Rock Lighthouse. Est attendance: 1,000. For info: Lee Radzak, Split Rock Lighthouse, 2010 Hwy 61 E, Two Harbors, MN 55616. Phone: (218) 226-6372.

***EDMUND FITZGERALD* SINKING: ANNIVERSARY.** Nov 10. The ore carrier *Edmund Fitzgerald* broke in two during a heavy storm in Lake Superior (near Whitefish Point) Nov 10, 1975. There were no survivors of this, the worst Great Lakes ship disaster of the decade, that took the lives of 29 crew members.

GOLDSMITH, OLIVER: BIRTH ANNIVERSARY. Nov 10, 1728. Irish writer, author of the play *She Stoops to Conquer*. Born Nov 10, 1728, and died Apr 4, 1774. "A book may be amusing with numerous errors," he wrote (Advertisement to *The Vicar of Wakefield*), "or it may be very dull without a single absurdity."

HOGARTH, WILLIAM: BIRTH ANNIVERSARY. Nov 10, 1697. English painter and engraver, famed for his satiric series of engravings (*A Harlot's Progress, A Rake's Progress, Four Stages of Cruelty*, etc), born at London, England, Nov 10, 1697, and died there on Oct 26, 1764.

HUNTER'S MOON. Nov 4. The full moon following Harvest Moon. So called because the moon's light in evening extends day's length for hunters. Moon enters Full Moon phase at 12:18 AM, EST.

KIRTLAND, JARED: BIRTH ANNIVERSARY. Nov 10, 1793. American physician and naturalist, Dr. Jared Potter Kirtland (for whom Kirtland's Warbler is named) was born at Wallingford, CT, on Nov 10, 1793. The first of the now rare Kirtland's Warblers to be identified and studied was found on his farm near Cleveland, OH, in 1851. Dr. Kirtland died at Rockport, near Cleveland, on Dec 10, 1877.

LUTHER, MARTIN: BIRTH ANNIVERSARY. Nov 10, 1483. Augustinian monk who was a founder and leader of the Reformation and of Protestantism was born at Eisleben, Saxony, Nov 10, 1483. Luther tacked his 95 Theses "On the Power of Indulgences" on the door of Wittenberg's castle church, on Oct 31, 1517, the eve of All Saints' Day. Luther asserted that the Bible was the sole authority of the church, called for reformation of abuses by the Roman Catholic Church and denied the supremacy of the Pope. Tried for heresy by the Roman Church, threatened with excommunication and finally banned by a papal bull (Jan 2, 1521), he responded by burning the bull. In 1525 he married Katherine von Bora, one of nine nuns who had left the convent due to his teaching. Luther died near his birthplace, at Eisleben, Feb 18, 1546.

MARINE CORPS BIRTHDAY. Nov 10. Commemorates the Marine Corps' establishment in 1775. Originally part of the navy, it became a separate unit on July 11, 1789.

MOON PHASE: LAST QUARTER. Nov 10. Moon enters Last Quarter phase at 7:28 PM, EST.

"SESAME STREET" TV PREMIERE: ANNIVERSARY. Nov 10, 1969. An important, successful and long-running children's show, "Sesame Street" educates children while they have fun. It takes place along a city street, targeting inner-city kids and featuring a diverse cast of humans and puppets. Through singing, puppetry, film clips and skits, kids are taught letters, numbers, concepts and lessons. Shows are "sponsored" by letters and numbers. Human cast members have included: Loretta Long, Matt Robinson, Roscoe Orman, Bob McGrath, Linda Bove, Buffy St. Marie, Ruth Buzzi, Will Lee, Northern J. Calloway, Emilio Delgado and Sonia Manzano. Favorite Jim Henson muppets include Ernie, Bert, Grover, Oscar the Grouch, Kermit the Frog, the Cookie Monster, life-sized Big Bird and Mr Snuffleupagus.

SPACE MILESTONE: *LUNA 17* (USSR). Nov 10, 1970. Launched this date, this unmanned spacecraft landed and released *Lunakhod 1* (8-wheel, radio-controlled vehicle) on Moon's Sea of Rains on Nov 17, which explored lunar surface, sending data back to Earth.

STANLEY FINDS LIVINGSTONE: ANNIVERSARY. Nov 10, 1871. Having begun his search the previous March for the then two-years-missing explorer-missionary David Livingstone, explorer Henry M. Stanley found him on this day at Ujiji (Africa) and uttered those now immortal words, "Dr. Livingstone, I presume?"

BIRTHDAYS TODAY

Donna Fargo (Yvonne Vaughan), 49, singer ("Funny Face"), songwriter, born Mt Airy, NC, Nov 10, 1949.

Russell Charles Means, 58, Native American rights activist, born Pine Ridge, SD, Nov 10, 1940.

MacKenzie Phillips, 39, actress (Julie on "One Day at a Time"; *American Graffiti*), daughter of John Phillips of the Mamas and Papas (sang with his later group the New Mamas and Papas), born Alexandria, VA, Nov 10, 1959.

Ann Reinking, 49, dancer, actress (*Pippin*), born Seattle, WA, Nov 10, 1949.

Tim Rice, 54, lyricist (*Evita*), born Amersham, England, Nov 10, 1944.

NOVEMBER 11 — WEDNESDAY

Day 315 — 50 Remaining

ADAMS, ABIGAIL SMITH: BIRTH ANNIVERSARY. Nov 11. Wife of John Adams, 2nd president of the US, born at Weymouth, MA, Nov 11, 1744. Died Oct 28, 1818.

ALDRICH, THOMAS BAILEY: BIRTH ANNIVERSARY. Nov 11. American author and editor. Best known for his book *The Story of a Bad Boy* (1870), an autobiographical work. Aldrich was born at Portsmouth, NH, on Nov 11, 1836, and died at Boston, MA, on Mar 19, 1907.

ANGOLA: INDEPENDENCE DAY. Nov 11. National holiday observed.

ARMISTICE DAY. Nov 11. Anniversary of Armistice between Allied and Central Powers, signed at 5 AM, Nov 11, 1918, in Marshal Foch's railway car in the Forest of Compiegne, France. Hostilities ceased at 11 AM. Also recognized in some places as Remembrance Day, Veterans Day, Victory Day and World War I Memorial Day. Many places observe silent memorial at the 11th hour of the 11th day of the 11th month each year. See also: "Veterans Day" (Nov 11).

BONZA BOTTLER DAY™. Nov 11. To celebrate when the number of the day is the same as the number of the month. Bonza Bottler Day™ is an excuse to have a party at least once a month. For more information, see Jan 1. For info: Gail M. Berger, 109 Matthew Ave, Poca, WV 25159. Phone: (304) 776-7746. Email: gberger5@aol.com.

CANADA: CANADIAN FINALS RODEO. Nov 11–15. Edmonton, Alberta. The 25th annual Canadian Finals Rodeo—the largest annual indoor sporting event in Western Canada—will be held in Edmonton Coliseum. The top ten season money winners in each of rodeo's six premier events will compete for national titles and a share of the richest purse in Canadian rodeo. CFR '98 will feature record prize money, glittering western pageantry, dynamic entertainers and the same classic rodeo action that attracted 83,458 rodeo fans to CFR '96. CFR '98 will also be accompanied by dozens of western-related events during Be Seen in Jeans Week, an annual civic celebration that entertains an estimated 100,000 Albertans each November. Est attendance: 81,000. For info: Cheryl Herchen, PR Mgr, Northlands Park, PO Box 1480, Edmonton, Alta, Canada T5J 2N5. Phone: (403) 471-7295. Fax: (403) 471-8176.
Email: npmarket@planet.eon.net.
WWW: http://www.northlands.com

CANADA: REMEMBRANCE DAY. Nov 11. Public holiday.

CHRISTMAS GIFT AND HOBBY SHOW. Nov 11–15. West Pavilion, Indiana State Fairgrounds, Indianapolis, IN. 49th annual event. Selling show of arts, crafts, collectibles and other gift items. Est attendance: 60,000. For info: Patrick Buchen, Pres, HSI Show Productions, Box 502797, Indianapolis, IN 46250. Phone: (317) 576-9933.

November 1998

S	M	T	W	T	F	S
1	2	3	4	5	6	7
8	9	10	11	12	13	14
15	16	17	18	19	20	21
22	23	24	25	26	27	28
29	30					

CHURCH OF ENGLAND VOTES TO ALLOW WOMEN PRIESTS: ANNIVERSARY. Nov 11, 1992. The Church of England, one of 28 national churches within the international Anglican Communion, voted on Nov 11, 1992, to allow women to become priests.

DEATH/DUTY DAY. Nov 11. Honoring soldiers on both sides who died on Nov 11, 1918, the armistice or Waffenstillstand day that ended the fighting in the First World War of 1914–18. The order was to stop fighting at 11 AM, rather than on receipt of the order. For info: Bob Birch, Punscorpion, The Puns Corps, PO Box 2364, Falls Church, VA 22042-0364. Phone: (703) 533-3668.

DOSTOYEVSKY, FYODOR MIKHAILOVICH: BIRTH ANNIVERSARY. Nov 11, 1821. Russian novelist, author of *The Brothers Karamazov, Crime and Punishment* and *The Idiot*, was born at Moscow, Nov 11, 1821 (New Style), and died at St. Petersburg, Feb 9, 1881 (New Style). A political revolutionary, he was arrested, tried, convicted and sentenced to death, but instead of execution he served a sentence in a Siberian prison and later served in the army there.

"GOD BLESS AMERICA" FIRST PERFORMED: 60th ANNIVERSARY. Nov 11, 1938. Irving Berlin wrote this song especially for Kate Smith. She first sang it during her regular radio broadcast on Nov 11, 1938. It quickly became a great patriotic favorite of the nation and one of Smith's most requested songs.

MARTINMAS. Nov 11. The Feast Day of St. Martin of Tours, who lived about AD 316–397. A bishop, he became one of the most popular saints of the Middle Ages. The period of warm weather often occurring about the time of his feast day is sometimes called St. Martin's Summer (especially in England).

NATIONAL ASSOCIATION FOR GIFTED CHILDREN CONVENTION. Nov 11–15. Louisville. KY. Educational sessions for administrators, counselors, coordinators, teachers and parents. Est attendance: 2,700. For info: Natl Assn for Gifted Children, 1707 L St NW, Ste 550, Washington, DC 20036. Phone: (202) 785-4268.

NATIONAL YOUNG READER'S DAY. Nov 11. Pizza Hut and the Center for the Book in the Library of Congress established National Young Reader's Day to remind Americans of the joys and importance of reading for young people. Schools, libraries, families and communities nationwide use this day to celebrate youth reading in a variety of creative and educational ways. Ideas on ways you can celebrate this special day available. For info: Shelley Morehead, The BOOK IT! Program, PO Box 2999, Wichita, KS 67201. Phone: (800) 426-6548. Fax: (316) 687-8937. Email: read@bookitprogram.com.

PATTON, GEORGE S., JR: BIRTH ANNIVERSARY. Nov 11, 1885. American military officer, graduate of West Point (1909), George Smith Patton, Jr, was born at San Gabriel, CA. Ambitious and flamboyant, he lived for combat. He served in the punitive expedition into Mexico (1916), in Europe in World War I, and in North Africa and Europe in World War II. He received world attention and official censure in 1943 for slapping a hospitalized shell-shocked soldier. While a full general, owing to his critical public statements, he was relieved of his command in 1945. He died at Heidelberg, Germany, on Dec 21, 1945, of injuries received in an automobile accident.

SPACE MILESTONE: *COLUMBIA* STS-5 (US). Nov 11, 1982. Shuttle *Columbia* launched from Kennedy Space Center, FL, with four astronauts: Vance Brand, Robert Overmyer, William Lenoir and Joseph Allen. "First operational mission" delivered two satellites into orbit for commercial customers. *Columbia* landed at Edwards Air Force Base, CA, Nov 16, 1982.

SPACE MILESTONE: *GEMINI 12* (US). Nov 11, 1966. Last Project Gemini manned Earth orbit launched.

SWEDEN: SAINT MARTIN'S DAY. Nov 11. Originally in memory of St. Martin of Tours; also associated with Martin Luther, who is celebrated the day before. Marks the end of the autumn's work and the beginning of winter activities.

SWITZERLAND: MARTINMAS GOOSE (MARTINIGIANS). Nov 11. Sursee, Canton Lucerne. At 3 PM on Martinmas (the day on which interest is due), the "Gansabhauet" is staged in front of Town Hall. Blindfolded participants try to bring down, with a single sword stroke, a dead goose suspended on a wire.

"TOO CLOSE FOR COMFORT" TV PREMIERE: ANNIVERSARY. Nov 11, 1980. "Too Close for Comfort," based on the British series "Keep It in the Family," starred Ted Knight as San Francisco cartoonist Henry Rush, living with his wife Muriel (Nancy Dussault) in the upstairs apartment while their grown daughters, Jackie (Deborah Van Valkenburgh) and Sarah (Lydia Cornell), move in downstairs. This half-hour sitcom also featured Audrey Meadows as Muriel's mother, Iris, and JM J. Bullock as disaster-prone Munroe Ficus, Sarah's friend. In the 1982–83 season, Muriel had baby Andrew (played by twins Jason and Eric Willis; William and Michael Cannon). When "TCFC" was cancelled by ABC in 1983, new episodes were produced in order to assure success in syndication. The main cast members stayed on for most of the episodes; when Van Valkenburgh and Cornell left, the show was renamed "The Ted Knight Show" until his death in 1986.

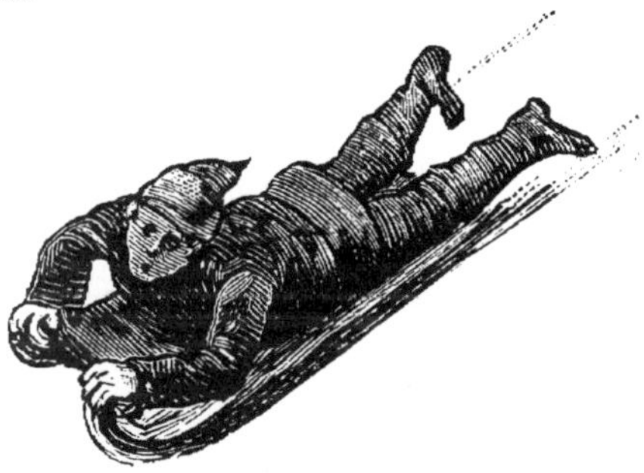

TRIPLE CROWN OF SURFING. Nov 11–Dec 20. Oahu, HI. The 16th annual Triple Crown includes three professional big wave surf meets on Oahu's North shore that mark the conclusion of the year-long Association of Surfing Professionals (ASP) world tour. Following the Triple Crown the ASP Men's and Women's Champions are crowned. Est attendance: 10,000. For info: Randy Rarick, 59-063-A Hoalua St, Haleiwa, HI 96712. Phone: (808) 638-7266 or Ocean Promotion (808) 325 7400. Fax: (808) 638-7764.

VETERANS DAY. Nov 11. Veterans Day was observed on Nov 11 from 1919 through 1970. Public Law 90–363, the "Monday Holiday Law," provided that, beginning in 1971, Veterans Day would be observed on "the fourth Monday in October." This movable observance date, which separated Veterans Day from the Nov 11 anniversary of World War I Armistice, proved unpopular. State after state moved its observance back to the traditional Nov 11 date, and finally Public Law 94–97 of Sept 18, 1975, required that, effective Jan 1, 1978, the observance of Veterans Day revert to Nov 11. See also: "Armistice Day" (Nov 11).

★**VETERANS DAY.** Nov 11. Presidential Proclamation. Formerly called "Armistice Day" and proclaimed each year since 1926 for Nov 11. PL83–380 of June 1, 1954, changed the name to "Veterans Day." PL90–363 of June 28, 1968, required that beginning in 1971 it would be observed the fourth Monday in October. PL 94–97 of Sept 18, 1975, required that effective Jan 1, 1978, the observance would revert to Nov 11.

VETERANS DAY CELEBRATION. Nov 11. Mamou, LA. Memorial services, a parade, live Cajun music and a dance that evening. Annually, on Veterans Day. Sponsor: American Legion Post 123. Est attendance: 1,000. For info: Frank Gervs Bihm, Jr, 520 5th St, Mamou, LA 70554. Phone: (318) 468-5059.

VIETNAM WOMEN'S MEMORIAL DEDICATION: ANNIVERSARY. Nov 11, 1993. In recognition of the 11,500 women who served in the Vietnam war, the bronze sculpture erected in Washington, DC, on Nov 1, was dedicated this day.

VOX POPULI DAY. Nov 11. Vox Populi is the Latin term for "People's Voice." Today is the day to make your voice count. Put your voice to your ideas, dreams and opinions. For info: Adrienne Sioux Koopersmith, 1437 W Rosemont, #1W, Chicago, IL 60660-1319. Phone: (773) 743-5341. Fax: (773) 743-5395. Email: kooper@interaccess.com.

WASHINGTON: ADMISSION DAY: ANNIVERSARY. Nov 11. Became 42nd state on this day in 1889.

☆ ☆ ☆

BIRTHDAYS TODAY

Bibi Andersson (Birgitta Anderson), 63, actress (*Story of a Woman*), born Stockholm, Sweden, Nov 11, 1935.

Barbara Boxer, 58, US Senator (D, California), born Brooklyn, NY, Nov 11, 1940.

Leonardo DiCaprio, 23, actor (*Parenthood, The Outsiders*), born Ridgewood, NJ, Nov 11, 1975.

Philip McKeon, 34, actor (Tommy on "Alice"), older brother of Nancy McKeon, born Westbury, NY, Nov 11, 1964.

Demi Moore, 36, actress ("General Hospital," *Ghost, Indecent Proposal*), born Roswell, NM, Nov 11, 1962.

Daniel Ortega Saavedra, 53, former president of Nicaragua, born La Libertad, Chontales, Nicaragua, Nov 11, 1945.

Kurt Vonnegut, Jr, 76, novelist (*Slaughterhouse Five, Cat's Cradle*), born Indianapolis, IN, Nov 11, 1922.

Jonathan Winters, 73, comedian, actor ("The Jonathan Winters Show," "Mork & Mindy"), born Dayton, OH, Nov 11, 1925.

Frank Urban ("Fuzzy") Zoeller, 47, golfer, born New Albany, IN, Nov 11, 1951.

NOVEMBER 12 — THURSDAY

Day 316 — 49 Remaining

ARCHES NATIONAL PARK ESTABLISHED: ANNIVERSARY. Nov 12, 1971. Area of natural wind-eroded formations in eastern Utah, originally proclaimed a national monument Apr 12, 1929, was established a national park. For further park info: Arches Natl Park, PO Box 907, Moab, UT 84532.

BIRTH OF BAHA'U'LLAH. Nov 12. Baha'i observance of anniversary of the birth of Baha'u'llah (born Mirza Husayn Ali) on Nov 12, 1817, in Nur, Persia. Baha'u'llah was prophet-founder of the Baha'i Faith. One of the nine days of the year when Baha'is suspend work. For info: Pamela Zivari, Dir, Bahais of the US, Office of Public Information, 866 UN Plaza, Ste 120, New York, NY 10017-1811. Phone: (212) 803-2500. Fax: (212) 803-2573. Email: usopi-ny@bic.org.

BLACKMUN, HARRY A.: 90th BIRTHDAY. Nov 12, 1908. Associate justice of the Supreme Court of the United States, nominated by President Nixon on Apr 14, 1970. (Qualified, June 9, 1970.) Justice Blackmun was born at Nashville, IL, on Nov 12, 1908.

CANADA: ROYAL AGRICULTURAL WINTER FAIR. Nov 12–21. Toronto, Ontario. Provides country entertainment, agricultural and equestrian competition and free grandstand show. Est attendance: 325,000. For info: Royal Agricultural Winter Fair, The Coliseum, Exhibition Place, Toronto, Ontario, Canada M6K 3C3. Phone: (416) 393-6400. Fax: (416) 393-6488. Email: rwfair@io.org.

INTERNATIONAL GIFT FESTIVAL. Nov 12–14. Fairfield, PA. Traditional handcrafts from more than 30 countries. Est attendance: 4,500. For info: Gettysburg Conv and Visitors Bureau, 35 Carlisle St, Gettysburg, PA 17325-1899. Phone: (717) 334-6274. Fax: (717) 334-1166. WWW: http://www.gettysburg.com

KELLY, GRACE PATRICIA: BIRTH ANNIVERSARY. Nov 12. American award-winning actress who became Princess Grace of Monaco when she married that country's ruler, Prince Rainier III, in 1956. Born at Philadelphia, PA, Nov 12, 1929. She died of injuries sustained in an automobile accident, Sept 12, 1982.

NATIONAL FFA CONVENTION. Nov 12–14. Municipal Auditorium and H. Roe Bartle Hall, Kansas City, MO. This 71st annual convention is an opportunity for recognition, business, elections and celebration. Delegates from each state discuss topics affecting the national agriculture education organization and elect a new team of national officers. Students compete in final rounds of leadership and career events and learn about education and career opportunities in a 300-exhibitor career show. Est attendance: 45,000. For info: Natl FFA Organization, 5632 Mt Vernon Memorial Hwy, Alexandria, VA 22309-0160. Phone: (703) 360-3600. Fax: (703) 360-5524. WWW: http://www.ffa.org

RODIN, AUGUSTE: BIRTH ANNIVERSARY. Nov 12. French sculptor born at Paris, France, Nov 12, 1840. Died Nov 17, 1917.

SMOKY MOUNTAIN LIGHTS AND WINTERFEST. Nov 12–Feb 28. Gatlinburg, TN. A magical celebration of more than two million twinkling lights in animated motion. The entire city of Gatlinburg is lit up with exciting displays featuring up to 60-ft animated displays, for the entire family to enjoy. More than 100 contemporary and traditional events such as yule log burnings, living Christmas tree and festival of trees. Drive-thru and walk-thru tours available. Annually, mid-November–end of February. Est attendance: 1,000,000. For info: Deana D. Ivey, Dir Communications, Gatlinburg Chamber of Commerce, 234 Airport Rd, Gatlinburg, TN 37738. Phone: (800) 568-4748 or (423) 430-4148. WWW: http://www.gatlinburg.com

SOUTHERN CHRISTMAS SHOW. Nov 12–22. Charlotte, NC. Show filled with exquisite art and crafts from nationally known artisans. Ideas for decorating trees, mantels, doors and wreaths; festive foods for holiday celebrations from fresh hot strudel to plum pudding. Gifts for everyone on your holiday list. Plus cooking demonstrations, Christmas Tree Lane, Santa Claus, Olde Towne Craft demonstrations and musical performances. Est attendance: 140,000. For info: Christine Swan, Asst Show Mgr, Southern Shows, Inc, PO Box 36859, Charlotte, NC 28236. Phone: (704) 376-6594. Fax: (704) 376-6345.

SPACE MILESTONE: *COLUMBIA STS-2* (US). Nov 12, 1981. Shuttle *Columbia*, launched from Kennedy Space Center, FL, with Joe Engle and Richard Truly on board, became first spacecraft launched from Earth for a second orbiting mission. Landed at Edwards Air Force Base, CA, Nov 14, 1981.

November 1998

S	M	T	W	T	F	S
1	2	3	4	5	6	7
8	9	10	11	12	13	14
15	16	17	18	19	20	21
22	23	24	25	26	27	28
29	30					

STANTON, ELIZABETH CADY: BIRTH ANNIVERSARY. Nov 12, 1815. American woman suffragist and reformer, Elizabeth Cady Stanton was born at Johnstown, NY, on Nov 12, 1815. "We hold these truths to be self-evident," she said at the first Women's Rights Convention, in 1848, "that all men and women are created equal." She died at New York, NY, on Oct 26, 1902.

SUN YAT-SEN: BIRTH ANNIVERSARY (TRADITIONAL). Nov 12. Although his actual birth date in 1866 is not known, Dr. Sun Yat-Sen's traditional birthday commemoration is held on Nov 12. Heroic leader of China's 1911 revolution, he died at Peking on Mar 12, 1925. The death anniversary is also widely observed. See also: "Sun Yat-Sen: Death Anniversary" (Mar 12).

TYLER, LETITIA CHRISTIAN: BIRTH ANNIVERSARY. Nov 12. First wife of John Tyler, 10th president of the US, born at New Kent County, VA, Nov 12, 1790. Died Sept 10, 1842.

BIRTHDAYS TODAY

Harry A. Blackmun, 90, Associate Justice of the US Supreme Court (retired), born Nashville, IL, Nov 12, 1908.

Nadia Comaneci, 37, Olympic gold medal gymnast, born Onesti, Romania, Nov 12, 1961.

Kim Hunter (Janet Cole), 76, actress (Nola on "The Edge of Night"; *Planet of the Apes*), born Detroit, MI, Nov 12, 1922.

Stefanie Powers, 56, actress (Jennifer Hart on "Hart to Hart"), born Hollywood, CA, Nov 12, 1942.

Jack Reed, 49, US Senator (D, Rhode Island), born Providence, RI, Nov 12, 1949.

Sammy Sosa, 30, baseball player, born San Pedro de Macoris, Dominican Republic, Nov 12, 1968.

Neil Young, 53, singer (with Buffalo Springfield ["For What It's Worth"] and Crosby, Stills, Nash & Young [*Deja Vu*]), songwriter, born Toronto, Ontario, Canada, Nov 12, 1945.

NOVEMBER 13 — FRIDAY

Day 317 — 48 Remaining

BOOTH, EDWIN (THOMAS): BIRTH ANNIVERSARY. Nov 13, 1833. Famed American actor and founder of the Players Club, born near Bel Air, MD, Nov 13, 1833. His brother, John Wilkes Booth, assassinated President Lincoln. Died at New York, NY, June 7, 1893.

BRANDEIS, LOUIS DEMBITZ: BIRTH ANNIVERSARY. Nov 13, 1856. American jurist, associate justice of US Supreme Court (1916–39), born at Louisville, KY. Died at Washington, DC, Oct 5, 1941.

CAROLINA CRAFTSMEN'S CHRISTMAS CLASSIC. Nov 13–15. State Fairgrounds, Columbia, SC. Arts and crafts. Est attendance: 35,000. For info: The Carolina Craftsmen, 1240 Oakland Ave, Greensboro, NC 27403. Phone: (910) 274-5550. Fax: (910) 274-1084.

FOUR CORNER STATES BLUEGRASS FESTIVAL. Nov 13–15. Wickenburg, AZ. Old-time fiddle, banjo, mandolin, flat-pick guitar championships. Clogging and gospel music. Special entertainment by nationally known bands as well as 14 competitive events. Annually, the second weekend in November. Est attendance: 5,000. For info: J Brooks, Exec Dir, Chamber of Commerce, 216 N Frontier St, Wickenburg, AZ 85390. Phone: (520) 684-5479 or (520) 684-0977. Fax: (520) 684-5470. Email: wburgcoc@primenet.com.

HOLIDAY HIGHLIGHTS. Nov 13–14. Ella Missing Community Center, Arapahoe, NE. Display of craft items hand-made and hand-crafted by the hobbyist. (No commercial crafts accepted.) To insure space, get entries in early. Sponsor: Arapahoe Chamber of Commerce. Est attendance: 600. For info: Arapahoe Chamber of Commerce, PO Box 624, Arapahoe, NE 68922. Phone: (308) 962-5359.

HOLLAND TUNNEL: ANNIVERSARY. Nov 13, 1927. On Nov 13, 1927, the Holland Tunnel, running under the Hudson River between New York, NY, and Jersey City, NJ, was opened to traffic. The tunnel was built and operated by the New York–New Jersey Bridge and Tunnel Commission. Comprised of two tubes, each large enough for two lanes of traffic, the Holland was the first underwater tunnel built in the US.

LONGHORN WORLD CHAMPIONSHIP FINALS RODEO. Nov 13–14. Nashville Arena, Nashville, TN. Features top 96 contestants from more than 1,200 competing in 11 different preceding 1998 Longhorn rodeos across the country for 1998 championships in seven different world class contests. Also colorful opening pageantry and Big, Bad BONUS Bulls. 33rd annual. Est attendance: 30,000. For info: W. Bruce Lehrke, Pres, Longhorn World Championship Rodeo, Inc, PO Box 70159, Nashville, TN 37207. Phone: (615) 876-1016. Fax: (615) 876-4685. Email: lhrodeo@idt.net.
WWW: http://www.longhornrodeo.com

MAXWELL, JAMES CLERK: BIRTH ANNIVERSARY. Nov 13. British physicist noted for his work in the field of electricity and magnetism. Born at Edinburgh, Scotland, on Nov 13, 1831, he died of cancer on Nov 5, 1879, at Cambridge, England.

NORTHERN IRELAND: BELFAST FESTIVAL AT QUEEN'S. Nov 13–29 (tentative). Queen's University, Belfast, County Antrim. International festival of the arts which includes cinema, drama, opera and all types of music from folk to classical. Est attendance: 80,000. For info: Mr Robert Agnew, Festival House, 25 College Gardens, Belfast, Northern Ireland BT9 6BS. Phone: (44) (1232) 667687. Fax: (44) (1232) 663733.

OVERLY'S COUNTRY CHRISTMAS. Nov 13–Jan 3. Westmoreland Fairgrounds, Greensburg, PA. "One of America's Best Outdoor Light Displays" with more than one million lights and animated displays. Enjoy a giant bonfire, photo with Santa, gift shop, barbeques and other foods. Proceeds benefit area children's programs. For info: Stephanie Tomasic, Overly's Country Christmas, RD 2, Box 626, Greensburg, PA 15601. Phone: (412) 925-3539. Fax: (412) 925-6258.

STEVENSON, ROBERT LOUIS: BIRTH ANNIVERSARY. Nov 13. Scottish author, born at Edinburgh, Scotland, Nov 13, 1850. Died at Samoa, Dec 3, 1894.

STOKES BECOMES FIRST BLACK MAYOR IN US: ANNIVERSARY. Nov 13. Carl Burton Stokes became the first black in the US elected mayor when he won the Cleveland, OH, mayoral election on Nov 13, 1967. Died April 3, 1996.

TEXAS PTA CONVENTION. Nov 13–15. Bayfront Plaza, Corpus Christi, TX. The 89th annual business meeting of the Texas PTA. Election of officers, adoption of legislative positions and resolutions are part of the general business. More than 40 workshops are presented on issues such as legislation, reading initiative, HIV/AIDS education, parent involvement and site-based decision making. Est attendance: 2,500. For info: Linda Y. Jackson, Texas PTA, 408 W 11th St, Austin, TX 78701-2199. Phone: (512) 476-6769 or (800) TALK-PTA. Fax: (512) 476-8152. Email: txpta@onr.com. WWW: http://www.onr.com/tpta

TRELAWNEY, EDWARD JOHN: BIRTH ANNIVERSARY. Nov 13, 1792. English traveler and author, friend of Shelley and Byron, born at London, Nov 13, 1792. He died at Sompting, Sussex, Aug 13, 1881, and was buried at Rome, next to Shelley.

WATERFOWL FESTIVAL (WITH GOOSE-CALLING CONTEST). Nov 13–15. Easton, MD. Three-day festival of wildlife art. Five hundred of the country's most prestigious wildlife exhibitors present the finest in wildlife art, carvings, sculpture, decoys, photography, books, gifts and antique guns. Retriever Demonstrations, World Championship Goose and Regional Duck Calling Contests, a Decoy Auction, Sporting Clays Tournament and seminars are also featured. Annually, the second full weekend in November. Proceeds contributed to conservation. Est attendance: 20,000. For info: Waterfowl Festival, PO Box 929, Easton, MD 21601. Phone: (410) 822-4567. Fax: (410) 820-9286. WWW: http://www.waterfowlfest.org

BIRTHDAYS TODAY

Sheila E. Frazier, 50, actress (*Super Fly, I'm Gonna Git You Sucker*), born The Bronx, NY, Nov 13, 1948.

Whoopi Goldberg, 49, comedienne, actress (*Ghost, Sister Act, The Color Purple*), born New York, NY, Nov 13, 1949.

Joe Mantegna, 51, actor (stage: *Glengarry Glen Ross* [Tony Award]; *House of Games, Things Change*), born Chicago, IL, Nov 13, 1947.

Garry Marshall, 64, producer, director (*Beaches, Pretty Woman*), actor ("Murphy Brown"), born New York, NY, Nov 13, 1934.

Richard Mulligan, 66, actor ("Empty Nest," *S.O.B*), born New York, NY, Nov 13, 1932.

Chris Noth, 41, actor ("Law and Order," *Burnzy's Last Call*), born Madison, WI, Nov 13, 1957.

Dack Rambo, 57, actor ("All My Children," "The Guns of Will Sonnett"), born Delano, CA, Nov 13, 1941.

Tracy Scoggins, 39, actress ("The Colbys," *Some Kind of Hero*), born Galveston, TX, Nov 13, 1959.

Madeline Sherwood, 76, actress ("The Flying Nun"), born Montreal, Quebec, Canada, Nov 13, 1922.

Vincent Frank (Vinny) Testaverde, 35, football player, born New York, NY, Nov 13, 1963.

NOVEMBER 14 — SATURDAY

Day 318 — 47 Remaining

AROUND THE WORLD IN 72 DAYS: ANNIVERSARY. Nov 14. Newspaper reporter Nellie Bly (pen name used by Elizabeth Cochrane Seaman) set off on Nov 14, 1889, to attempt to break Jules Verne's imaginary hero Phileas Fogg's record of voyaging around the world in 80 days. She did beat Fogg's record, taking 72 days, 6 hours, 11 minutes and 14 seconds to make the trip.

BEAVER CREEK AT IVEY STATION ARTS AND CRAFTS FESTIVAL. Nov 14–15. Ivey Station near Gordon, GA. 17th annual festival helps raise funds for preservation and restoration of historic site where festival is held. Charles Ivey settled here in 1816 and grew the first watermelons in Georgia (the Ivey Grey, named for him) and Ivey Station became the shipping center for watermelons. The area has significant Indian and Civil War history as well. Festival features arts and crafts, delicious specialty foods and entertainment. Annually, the second full weekend in November. Est attendance: 4,000. For info: Mrs Lee Korwin, Dir, Beaver Creek/Ivey Station Arts & Crafts Fest, PO Box 351, Gordon, GA 31031. Phone: (912) 628-2912.

BIG 10 MEN'S SOCCER CHAMPIONSHIP. Nov 14–16. Indiana University, Bloomington, IN. Est attendance: 1,000. For info: Dennis LaBissoniere, Big 10 Conference, 1500 W Higgins Rd, Park Ridge, IL 60068-6300. Phone: (847) 696-1010. Fax: (847) 696-1110. WWW: http://www.bigten.org

BLOOD TRANSFUSION: ANNIVERSARY. Nov 14. Samuel Pepys, diarist and Fellow of the Royal Society, wrote in his diary for Nov 14, 1666: "Dr. Croone told me . . . there was a pretty experiment of the blood of one dog let out, till he died, into the body of another on one side, while all his own run out on the other side. The first died upon the place, and the other very well and likely to do well. This did give occasion to many pretty wishes, as of the blood of a Quaker to be let into an Archbishop, and such like; but, as Dr. Croone says, may, if it takes, be of mighty use to man's health, for the amending of bad blood by borrowing from a better body." Two days later, Nov 16, Pepys noted: "This noon I met with Mr Hooke, and he tells me the dog which was filled with another dog's blood, at the College the other day, is very well, and like to be so as ever, and doubts not its being found of great use to men. . . ."

A CHRISTMAS WEDDING AT BELLE MEADE PLANTATION. Nov 14–Jan 6. Belle Meade Plantation, Nashville, TN. Antebellum mansion decorated for the holiday wedding of Selene Harding and Billy Jackson in December 1868. Tours led by guides in period costume. For info: Belle Meade Plantation, 5025 Harding Rd, Nashville, TN 37205. Phone: (615) 356-0501 or (800) 270-3991. Fax: (615) 356-2336.

COPLAND, AARON: BIRTH ANNIVERSARY. Nov 14, 1900. American composer Aaron Copland was born at Brooklyn, NY. Incorporating American folk music and, later, the 12-tone system, he strove to create an American music style that was both popular and high-minded. He composed ballets, film scores and orchestral works including *Fanfare for the Common Man* (1942), *Appalachian Spring* (1944) (for which he won the Pulitzer Prize) and the score for *The Heiress* (1948) (for which he won an Oscar). He died on Dec 2, 1990, at North Tarrytown, NY.

CRAFT FESTIVAL AND CANE GRINDING. Nov 14. Oatland Island Education Center, Savannah, GA. 18th annual event. Cane grinding and syrup making just the way it was 150 years ago at two authentic log cabins. More than 70 artists from around the southeast will be at the Heritage farm site selling handmade baskets, pottery, stained glass and much more. Annually, the second Saturday in November. Est attendance: 8,000. For info: Dr. Harris Lentini, Oatland Island Education Center, 711 Sand Town Road, Savannah, GA 31410. Phone: (912) 897-3773.

DOW-JONES TOPS 1,000: ANNIVERSARY. Nov 14, 1972. On Nov 14, 1972, the Dow-Jones Index of 30 major industrial stocks closed at 1,003.16—topping the 1,000 mark for the first time.

EISENHOWER, MAMIE DOUD: BIRTH ANNIVERSARY. Nov 14. Wife of Dwight David Eisenhower, 34th president of the US, born at Boone, IA, Nov 14, 1896. Died Nov 1, 1979, at Washington, DC.

November 1998

S	M	T	W	T	F	S
1	2	3	4	5	6	7
8	9	10	11	12	13	14
15	16	17	18	19	20	21
22	23	24	25	26	27	28
29	30					

FULTON, ROBERT: BIRTH ANNIVERSARY. Nov 14. Inventor of the steamboat, born Nov 14, 1765. Died Feb 24, 1815.

GUINEA-BISSAU: RE-ADJUSTMENT MOVEMENT'S DAY. Nov 14. National holiday.

INDIA: CHILDREN'S DAY. Nov 14. Holiday observed throughout India.

JORDAN: KING HUSSEIN'S BIRTHDAY. Nov 14. H.M. King Hussein's birthday is nationally honored each year on the anniversary of his birth, Nov 14, 1935.

☆ ☆ ☆

KALAMAZOO HOLIDAY PARADE. Nov 14. Kalamazoo, MI. With more than 3,000 participants, the Kalamazoo Holiday Parade is the largest in west Michigan and will be remembered for its giant helium balloons, colorful floats, spirited marching bands and delightful fantasy characters, clowns, musicians and multi-talented performers. Annually, the second Saturday in November. Est attendance: 80,000. For info: Kenna Bridges, Downtown Kalamazoo Inc, 157 S Kalamazoo Mall, Kalamazoo, MI 49007. Phone: (616) 344-0795.

MONET, CLAUDE: BIRTH ANNIVERSARY. Nov 14. French painter born Nov 14, 1840. Died, Dec 5, 1926.

"MURPHY BROWN" TV PREMIERE: 10th ANNIVERSARY. Nov 14, 1988. This intelligent, timely and often acerbic sitcom set in Washington, DC, stars Candice Bergen in the title role, as an egotistical, seasoned journalist working for the fictitious newsmagazine show "F.Y.I." Also featured are Grant Shaud as the show's high-strung producer, Miles Silverberg (later replaced by Lily Tomlin); Faith Ford as the rural-raised, former Miss America, Corky Sherwood (and later Miles's bride); Joe Regalbuto as Murphy's neurotic friend, reporter Frank Fontana; Charles Kimbrough as "F.Y.I.'s" uptight anchorman, Jim Dial; and Pat Corley as Phil, owner of the local watering hole. Colleen Dewhurst appeared as Murphy's mother and Robert Pastorelli appeared as Eldin Bernecky, perfectionist house painter and aspiring artist (he left the series for his own show). The show often blurred the lines between reality and fiction by dealing with topical issues and by including real-life journalists as guest stars playing themselves.

NEHRU, JAWAHARLAL: BIRTH ANNIVERSARY. Nov 14. Indian leader and first prime minister after independence. Born Nov 14, 1889. Died May 27, 1964.

SALISBURY, HARRISON: 90th BIRTH ANNIVERSARY. Nov 14, 1908. American journalist Harrison Evans Salisbury was born at Minneapolis, MN. The *New York Times* Moscow correspondent from 1949 to 1954 Salisbury won the Pulitzer Prize in 1955 for a series of articles on the Soviet Union. He died on July 5, 1993, at Providence, RI.

SPACE MILESTONE: *APOLLO 12* (US). Nov 14, 1969. Launched this date. This was the second manned lunar landing—in Ocean of Storms. Astronauts Conrad, Bean and Gordon. First pinpoint landing. Astronauts visited *Surveyor 3* and took samples. Earth splashdown Nov 24.

STEVENSON, McLEAN: BIRTH ANNIVERSARY. Nov 14, 1929. Actor, born at Bloomington, IL, Stevenson is perhaps best known for his role as the bumbling and womanizing Lt Col Henry Blake in the long-running TV series "M*A*S*H." Other performances include "Hello, Larry." Stevenson died after a heart attack, on Feb 15, 1996, in Los Angeles, CA.

BIRTHDAYS TODAY

Boutros Boutros-Ghali, 76, former Secretary-General of the UN, born Cairo, Egypt, Nov 14, 1922.

Prince Charles, 50, Prince of Wales, heir to the British throne, born London, England, Nov 14, 1948.

Don Stewart, 63, actor, singer (Michael Bauer on "Guiding Light"), born Staten Island, NY, Nov 14, 1935.

NOVEMBER 15 — SUNDAY

Day 319 — 46 Remaining

★**AMERICAN EDUCATION WEEK.** Nov 15–21. Presidential Proclamation 5403, of Oct 30, 1985, covers all succeeding years. Always the first full week preceding the fourth Thursday in November. Issued from 1921–25 and in 1936, sometimes for a week in December and sometimes as National Education Week. After an absence of a number of years, this proclamation was issued each year from 1955–82 (issued in 1955 as a prelude to the White House Conference on Education). Previously, Proclamation 4967, of Sept 13, 1982, covered all succeeding years as the second week in November.

AMERICAN EDUCATION WEEK. Nov 15–21. Focuses attention on the importance of education and all that it stands for. Annually, the week preceding the week of Thanksgiving. For info: Connie Morris, Natl Education Assn (NEA), 1201 16th St NW, Washington, DC 20036. Phone: (202) 822-7262. Fax: (202) 822-7292. WWW: http://www.nea.org

BELGIUM: DYNASTY DAY. Nov 15. National holiday in honor of Belgian monarchy.

BRAZIL: REPUBLIC DAY. Nov 15. Commemorates the Proclamation of the Republic on Nov 15, 1889.

CHRISTMAS AT THE BENJAMIN HARRISON HOME. Nov 15–Dec 31. Indianapolis, IN. (Closed Thanksgiving, Christmas Eve and Christmas Day.) Daily guided tours of the 23rd President's home decorated in seasonal, Victorian style. Est attendance: 4,500. For info: PR Dept, President Benjamin Harrison Home, 1230 N Delaware St, Indianapolis, IN 46202-2598. Phone: (317) 631-1898. Fax: (317) 236-1688.

EIGHTEENTH-CENTURY THRESHING DAY. Nov 15. McLean, VA. Help the farm family thresh wheat, make yeast cakes and celebrate the end of the season with light refreshment. Est attendance: 750. For info: Gretchen Brodtman, Claude Moore Colonial Farm at Turkey Run, 6310 Georgetown Pike, McLean, VA 22101. Phone: (703) 442-7557. Fax: (703) 442-0714.

FIRST BLACK PROFESSIONAL HOCKEY PLAYER: ANNIVERSARY. Nov 15, 1950. When Arthur Dorrington signed a contract to play hockey with the Atlantic City Seagulls of the Eastern Amateur League on Nov 15, 1950, he became the first black man to play organized hockey in the US. He played for the Seagulls during the 1950 and 1951 seasons.

GEORGE SPELVIN DAY. Nov 15. Believed to be the anniversary of George Spelvin's theatrical birth—in Charles A. Gardiner's play *Karl the Peddler* on Nov 15, 1886, in a production at New York, NY. Spelvin, a fictitious creation, is said to have appeared in more than 10,000 Broadway performances. The name (or equivalent Georgina, Georgetta, etc) is used in play programs to conceal the fact that an actor is performing in more than one role. See also: "England: Walter Plinge Day" (Dec 2) for British equivalent.

GERMANY: VOLKSTRAUERTAG. Nov 15. Memorial Day and national day of mourning in all German states. Observed on the Sunday before Totensonntag. See also: "Germany: Totensonntag" (Nov 23).

GYPSY CONDEMNATION ORDER: 55th ANNIVERSARY. Nov 15, 1943. An order was issued by Heinrich Himmler for nomadic Gypsies and part-Gypsies to be placed in concentration camps. In cases of doubt, it was up to local heads of police to determine who was a gypsy. Some estimates put the number of Gypsies killed in the Holocaust as high as half a million.

JAPAN: SHICHI-GO-SAN. Nov 15. Annual children's festival. The *Shichi-Go-San* (Seven-Five-Three) rite, observed on Nov 15, is "the most picturesque event in the autumn season." On this day, parents take their three-year-old children of either sex, five-year-old boys and seven-year-old girls to the parish shrines dressed in their best clothes. There the guardian spirits are thanked for the healthy growth of the children and prayers are offered for their further development.

NATIONAL GEOGRAPHY AWARENESS WEEK. Nov 15–21. Focus public awareness on the importance of the knowledge of geography. To be on the mailing list for information on obtaining a Geography Awareness Week packet of teaching materials, send your name and mailing address to Geography Education Program, Natl Geographic Society, PO Box 98190, Washington, DC 20090-8190. More than 225,000 packets mailed out last year. For additional information, visit the Society's website at WWW: http://www.nationalgeographic.com

NAVRATILOVA RETIRES: ANNIVERSARY. Nov 15, 1994. Ending her professional tennis career, Martina Navratilova played a losing first round match against Gabriela Sabatini in the 1994 season-ending Virginia Slims tournament. Hardly a ripple was made in one of the most impressive records in tennis history. During 21 years of play Navratilova chalked up a career tally of 1,443–211 singles match record and 167 titles (the most ever for anyone, male or female). She recorded 18 Grand Slam singles titles, 31 Grand Slam women's doubles championships and six career Grand Slam mixed doubles championships.

O'KEEFFE, GEORGIA: BIRTH ANNIVERSARY. Nov 15, 1887. Described as one of the greatest American artists of the 20th century, Georgia O'Keeffe was born at Sun Prairie, WI, Nov 15, 1887. In 1924, she married the famous photographer Alfred Stieglitz. His more than 500 photographs of her have been called "the greatest love poem in the history of photography." She painted desert landscapes and flower studies. She died at Santa Fe, NM, on Mar 6, 1986, at age 98.

ROMMEL, ERWIN: BIRTH ANNIVERSARY. Nov 15, 1891. Field marshal and commander of the German Afrika Korps in WW II, Erwin Rommel was born at Heidenheim, in Wurttemberg, Germany. Rommel commanded the 7th Panzer Division in the Battle of France. Considered an excellent commander, Rommel's early success in Africa made him a legend as the "Desert Fox," but in early 1943 he was outmaneuvered by Field Marshal Bernard Montgomery and Germany surrendered Tunis in May of that year. Implicated in July 1944 in an attempted assassination of Hitler, he was given the choice of suicide or a trial and chose the former. Rommel died by his own hand at age 52 on Oct 14, 1944, near Ulm, Germany.

SPACE MILESTONE: *BURAN* (USSR): 10th ANNIVERSARY. Nov 15, 1988. The Soviet Union's first reusable space plane, *Buran*, landed on this date, completing a smooth, unmanned mission at approximately 1:25 AM, EST, after orbiting the Earth twice in 3 hours, 25 minutes. Launched at Baikonur, Soviet central Asia, the importance of this mission was in its computer-controlled lift-off and return.

BIRTHDAYS TODAY

Ed Asner, 69, actor ("The Mary Tyler Moore Show," "Lou Grant"; *Roots*), born Kansas City, MO, Nov 15, 1929.

Daniel Barenboim, 56, musician, conductor, born Buenos Aires, Argentina, Nov 15, 1942.

Joanna Barnes, 64, actress (Katie in "The Trials of O'Brien"), born Boston, MA, Nov 15, 1934.

Petula Clark, 66, singer ("Downtown," "I Know a Place," "This Is My Song"), actress, born Ewell, Surrey, England, Nov 15, 1932.

John Coleman, 63, TV meteorologist, born Champaign, IL, Nov 15, 1935.

Beverly D'Angelo, 44, actress (*Hair, Coal Miner's Daughter, National Lampoon's Christmas Vacation*), born Columbus, OH, Nov 15, 1954.

Yaphet Kotto, 61, actor ("Homicide," *Nothing But a Man, Blue Collar, Midnight Run*), born New York, NY, Nov 15, 1937.

Joseph Wapner, 79, television personality ("People's Court"), retired judge, born Los Angeles, CA, Nov 15, 1919.

Sam Waterston, 58, actor (*Friendly Fire, The Great Gatbsy*; "I'll Fly Away," "Law and Order"), born Cambridge, MA, Nov 15, 1940.

NOVEMBER 16 — MONDAY

Day 320 — 45 Remaining

FINLAND: INTERNATIONAL CHILDREN'S FILM FESTIVAL. Nov 16–22. Oulu. This one-week event gives festival visitors an opportunity to view several dozen feature-length films. Est attendance: 10,000. For info: Finnish Tourist Board, 655 Third Ave, New York, NY 10017. Phone: (212) 949-2333 or (358) (8) 881-1293. Fax: (358) (8) 881-1290.
Email: raimokinisjarvi@oufilmcenter.inst.fl.

HANDY, WILLIAM CHRISTOPHER: 125th BIRTH ANNIVERSARY. Nov 16, 1873. American composer, bandleader, "Father of the Blues," W.C. Handy was born at Florence, AL, Nov 16, 1873. He died at New York, NY, Mar 28, 1958.

HINDEMITH, PAUL: BIRTH ANNIVERSARY. Nov 16, 1895. Prolific composer and teacher, born at Hanau, Germany, Nov 16, 1895. Became a resident and citizen of the US during World War II. Died at Frankfurt, Germany, Dec 28, 1963.

ISRA AL MI'RAJ: ASCENT OF THE PROPHET MUHAMMAD. Nov 16. Islamic calendar date: Rajab 27, 1419. Commemorates the journey of the Prophet Muhammad from Mecca to Jerusalem, his ascension into the Seven Heavens and his return on the same night. Muslims believe that on that night Muhammad prayed together with Abraham, Moses and Jesus in the area of the Al-Aqsa Mosque in Jerusalem. The rock from which he is believed to have ascended to heaven to speak with God is the one inside The Dome of the Rock. Different methods for "anticipating" the visibility of the new moon crescent at Mecca are used by different Muslim groups. *Chase's* uses anticipated dates furnished by the American Muslim Council. US EST date may vary.

NATIONAL CHILDREN'S BOOK WEEK. Nov 16–22. To encourage the enjoyment of reading for children. For info: The Children's Book Council, Inc, 568 Broadway, Ste 404, New York, NY 10012. Phone: (212) 966-1990. Fax: (212) 966-2073. Email: staff@cbcbooks.org. WWW: http://www.cbcbooks.org

OKLAHOMA: ADMISSION DAY: ANNIVERSARY. Nov 16, 1907. Became 46th state on this day in 1907.

RIEL, LOUIS: HANGING ANNIVERSARY. Nov 16. Born at St. Boniface, Manitoba, Canada, on Oct 23, 1844, Louis Riel, leader of the Metis (French/Indian mixed ancestry), was elected to Canada's House of Commons in 1873 and 1874, but never seated. Confined to asylums for madness (feigned or falsely charged, some said), Riel became a US citizen in 1883. In 1885 he returned to western Canada to lead the North West Rebellion. Defeated, he surrendered and was tried for treason, convicted and hanged, at Regina, NWT, Canada, on Nov 16, 1885. Seen as a true patriot and protector of French culture in Canada, Riel's life and death became a legend and a symbol of the problems between French and English Canadians.

ROMAN CATHOLICS ISSUE NEW CATECHISM: ANNIVERSARY. Nov 16, 1992. For the first time since 1563, the Roman Catholic Church issued a new universal catechism, which addressed modern-day issues, on Nov 16, 1992.

November 1998

S	M	T	W	T	F	S
1	2	3	4	5	6	7
8	9	10	11	12	13	14
15	16	17	18	19	20	21
22	23	24	25	26	27	28
29	30					

SAINT EUSTATIUS, WEST INDIES: STATIA AND AMERICA DAY: ANNIVERSARY. Nov 16. St. Eustatius, Leeward Islands. To commemorate the first salute to an American flag by a foreign government, from Fort Oranje in 1776. Festivities include sports events and dancing. During the American Revolution St. Eustatius was an important trading center and a supply base for the colonies.

SPACE MILESTONE: *SKYLAB 4* (US): 25th ANNIVERSARY. Nov 16, 1973. Thirtieth manned US space flight launched with three astronauts, G.P. Carr, W.R. Page and E.G. Gibson. Space walks. Returned to Earth after 84 days, on Feb 8, 1974.

SPACE MILESTONE: *VENERA 3* (USSR). Nov 16, 1965. Launched this date, it crashed into Venus, Mar 1, 1966. First manmade object on another planet.

UNITED NATIONS: INTERNATIONAL DAY FOR TOLERANCE. Nov 16. On Dec 12, 1996, the General Assembly established the International Day for Tolerance, to commemorate the adoption by UNESCO member states of the Declaration of Principles on Tolerance on Nov 16, 1995. Info from: United Nations, Dept of Public Info, New York, NY 10017.

UNIVERSITY OF CHICAGO'S FIRST FOOTBALL VICTORY: ANNIVERSARY. Nov 16, 1892. The University of Chicago, which played to a 0–0 tie with Northwestern in its first-ever football game on the preceding Oct 22, won its first game for Coach Amos Alonzo Stagg 10–4 against Illinois in Chicago on Nov 16, 1892. Formerly a founding member of the Big Ten, Chicago eliminated its football program for many years, but now competes in the University Athletic Assn against the likes of New York University, Emory and Washington University in St. Louis.

BIRTHDAYS TODAY

Lisa Bonet, 31, actress ("The Cosby Show," "A Different World," *Angel Heart*), born San Francisco, CA, Nov 16, 1967.

Elizabeth Drew, 63, journalist, born Cincinnati, OH, Nov 16, 1935.

Bob Gibson, 67, singer (folk music), musician, born New York, NY, Nov 16, 1931.

Dwight Eugene Gooden, 34, baseball player, born Tampa, FL, Nov 16, 1964.

Burgess Meredith, 89, actor (*Rocky*, "Gloria"; Emmy for *Tail Gunner Joe*), born Cleveland, OH, Nov 16, 1909.

Joseph Henry ("Jo Jo") White, 52, former basketball player, born St. Louis, MO, Nov 16, 1946.

NOVEMBER 17 — TUESDAY

Day 321 — 44 Remaining

HOMEMADE BREAD DAY. Nov 17. A day for the family to remember and enjoy the making, baking and eating of nutritious homemade bread. For info: Homemade Bread Day Committee, PO Box 3, Montague, MI 49437-0003.

MOBIUS, AUGUST: BIRTH ANNIVERSARY. Nov 17, 1790. German astronomer, mathematician, teacher and author, August Ferdinand Mobius was born at Schulpforte, Germany, on Nov 17, 1790. Mobius was a pioneer in the field of topology, and first described the Mobius net and the Mobius strip. He died at Leipzig, on Sept 26, 1868.

MONTGOMERY, BERNARD LAW: BIRTH ANNIVERSARY. Nov 17. Bernard Law Montgomery, who commanded the British Eighth Army to victory at El Alamein in north Africa in 1943, was born Nov 17, 1887, at St. Mark's Vicarage, Kennington Oval, London, England. He also led the Eighth Army in the Sicilian and Italian campaigns and commanded all ground forces in the 1944 Normandy landing. Montgomery died Mar 24, 1976, at Alton, Hampshire, England.

NATIONAL COMMUNITY EDUCATION DAY. Nov 17. To recognize and promote strong relationships between public schools and the communities they serve and to help schools develop new relationships with parents, community members, local organizations and agencies. Annually, the Tuesday of American Education Week. For info: Natl Community Education Assn, 3929 Old Lee Hway, Ste 91-A, Fairfax, VA 22030-2401. Phone: (703) 359-8973. Fax: (703) 359-0972.
Email: ncea@ids2.idsonline.com.

NORTH AMERICAN FREE TRADE AGREEMENT PASSES US HOUSE: ANNIVERSARY. Nov 17, 1993. The US House of Representatives approved NAFTA by a 234 to 200 vote on Nov 17, 1993.

PEALE, TITIAN RAMSEY: BIRTH ANNIVERSARY. Nov 17. American artist, naturalist, son of Charles Willson Peale, born at Philadelphia, PA, on Nov 17, 1799. Died there on Mar 13, 1885.

QUEEN ELIZABETH I: ASCENSION ANNIVERSARY. Nov 17. Anniversary of ascension of Elizabeth I to English throne, Nov 17, 1558; celebrated as a holiday in England for more than a century after her death in 1603.

SUEZ CANAL: ANNIVERSARY. Nov 17. Formal opening of the Suez Canal, on Nov 17, 1869.

WORLD PEACE DAY. Nov 17. World Peace Day was created to give the common person a way to demonstrate their desire for peace. To do this, people pray for peace all day, drive on Nov 17 with their headlights on, wear a white ribbon for peace (everyday) and sign our petition for peace (available on our web page) or print our petition for peace and have 20 people sign it. Annually, Nov 17. For info: World Peace Day, Inc, PO Box 561944, Miami, FL 33256-1944. Email: peaceguy@peaceday.org. WWW: http://www.peaceday.org

ZENGER, JOHN PETER: ARREST ANNIVERSARY. Nov 17. Colonial printer and journalist who established the *New York Weekly Journal* (first issue, Nov 5, 1733). Zenger was arrested on Nov 17, 1734, for libels against the colonial governor, but continued to edit his newspaper from jail. Trial was held during August 1735. Zenger's acquittal was an important early step toward freedom of the press in America. Zenger was born in Germany in 1697, came to the US in 1710 and died July 28, 1746, at New York City.

BIRTHDAYS TODAY

Terry E. Branstad, 52, Governor of Iowa (R), born Leland, IA, Nov 17, 1946.

Howard Dean, 50, Governor of Vermont (D), born East Hampton, NY, Nov 17, 1948.

Danny Devito, 54, actor ("Taxi," *Twins, Batman Returns*), director (*Throw Mama From the Train*), born Neptune, NJ, Nov 17, 1944.

Shelby Foote, 82, writer, historian (*Civil War*), born Greenville, MS, Nov 17, 1916.

Lauren Hutton, 54, model, actress (*American Gigolo*), born Charleston, SC, Nov 17, 1944.

Gordon Lightfoot, 60, singer ("Sundown"), songwriter ("Early Morning Rain"), born Orilla, Ontario, Canada, Nov 17, 1938.

Mary Elizabeth Mastrantonio, 40, actress (*The Color of Money, Thieves*), born Oak Park, IL, Nov 17, 1958.

Robert Bruce (Bob) Mathias, 68, former congressman, Olympic gold medal decathlete, born Tulare, CA, Nov 17, 1930.

Martin Scorsese, 56, director (*Mean Streets, The Color of Money, Raging Bull, Goodfellas*), born Flushing, NY, Nov 17, 1942.

George Thomas (Tom) Seaver, 54, Baseball Hall of Fame pitcher, born Fresno, CA, Nov 17, 1944.

NOVEMBER 18 — WEDNESDAY

Day 322 — 43 Remaining

CANADA: SASKATOON FALL FAIR AND MEXABITION. Nov 18–21. Prairieland Exhibition Center, Saskatoon, Saskatchewan. Major livestock show features 11 breeds of beef cattle, commercial cattle show and sale, Cinderella Classic show and sale, prospect calf show and sale, Saskatchewan Jr Classic, 4-H grooming competition. Agricultural trade show features new farm equipment and advances in agricultural practices plus western art displays. Est attendance: 16,000. For info: (306) 931-7149, or Tourism Saskatchewan, 500-1900 Albert St, Regina, Sask, Canada S4P 4L9. Phone: (800) 667-7191.
Email: travel.info@sasktourism.sk.ca.
WWW: http://www.sasktourism.com

DAGUERRE, LOUIS JACQUES MANDE: BIRTH ANNIVERSARY. Nov 18. French tax collector, theatre scene-painter, physicist and inventor, was born at Cormeilles-en-Parisis, France, on Nov 18, 1789. He is remembered for his invention of the daguerreotype photographic process—one of the earliest to permit a photographic image to be chemically fixed to provide a permanent picture. The process was presented to the French Academy of Science on Jan 7, 1839. Daguerre died near Paris, France, on July 10, 1851.

GALLI-CURCI, AMELITA: BIRTH ANNIVERSARY. Nov 18, 1889. Italian-born operatic soprano, made US debut Nov 18, 1916, in Chicago, IL. Born at Milan, Italy, Nov 18, 1889. She died at La Jolla, CA, Nov 26, 1963.

GERMANY: BUSS UND BETTAG. Nov 18. Buss und Bettag (Repentance Day) is observed on the Wednesday before the last Sunday of the church year. A legal public holiday in all German states except Bavaria (where it is observed only in communities with predominantly Protestant populations).

GILBERT, SIR WILLIAM SCHWENCK: BIRTH ANNIVERSARY. Nov 18, 1836. English author of librettos for the famed Gilbert and Sullivan comic operas, born at London, England, Nov 18, 1836. Died May 29, 1911, as a result of a heart attack experienced while saving a woman from drowning.

GINGERBREAD HOUSE COMPETITION & DISPLAY. Nov 18–Jan 2. Lahaska, PA. More than 50 gingerbread house entries compete for over $5,700 in cash prizes in such categories as: Victorian Christmas, Authentic Reproduction of a Significant Building, Amateur, Incredibly Unusual 3-Dimensional and childrens (12 and under; 13–18). The creative masterpieces are displayed throughout the holiday season in the Village Gazebo. Free admission. Est attendance: 75,000. For info: Peddler's Village, Routes 202 & 263, Lahaska, PA 18931. Phone: (215) 794-4000. Fax: (215) 794-4001. WWW: http://www.peddlersvillage.com

GRAY, ASA: BIRTH ANNIVERSARY. Nov 18, 1810. Botanist and natural history professor at Harvard, born at Paris, NY. Gray was known as a pioneer in the field of plant geography and a chief advocate of Darwin. Died at Cambridge, MA, Jan 30, 1888.

HAITI: ARMY DAY. Nov 18, 1803. Commemorates the Battle of Vertieres, Nov 18, 1803, in which Haitians defeated the French.

LATVIA: INDEPENDENCE DAY. Nov 18. National holiday.

LOMBROSO, CESARE: BIRTH ANNIVERSARY. Nov 18. Italian founder of criminology, born at Verona, Italy, Nov 18, 1836. A professor of psychiatry, Lombroso believed that criminality could be identified with certain physical types of people. He died at Turin on Oct 19, 1909.

MERCER, JOHN HERNDON (JOHNNY): BIRTH ANNIVERSARY. Nov 18. American songwriter, singer, radio performer and actor, born Nov 18, 1909, at Savannah, GA. Johnny Mercer wrote lyrics (and often the music) for some of the great American popular music from the 1930s through the 1960s, including "Moon River," "Autumn Leaves," "One for My Baby," "Charade," "Satin Doll," "On the Achison, Topeka, and the Santa Fe," "You Must Have Been a Beautiful Baby," "Come Rain or Come Shine," "Hooray for Hollywood," "Jeepers Creepers" and countless more. Mercer died on June 25, 1976, and was buried at Savannah.

MICKEY MOUSE'S BIRTHDAY. Nov 18. The comical activities of squeaky-voiced Mickey Mouse first appeared Nov 18, 1928, on the screen of the Colony Theatre in New York City. The film, Walt Disney's "Steamboat Willie," was the first animated cartoon talking picture.

MITCHELL, CAMERON: 80th BIRTH ANNIVERSARY. Nov 18, 1918. American actor Cameron Mitchell was born at Dallastown, PA. He is best-known for his role as Willy Loman's son in *Death of a Salesman* on stage and film. He died on July 6, 1994, at Pacific Palisades, CA.

MOON PHASE: NEW MOON. Nov 18. Moon enters New Moon phase at 11:27 PM, EST.

NATIONAL EDUCATIONAL SUPPORT PERSONNEL DAY. Nov 18. A mandate of the delegates to the 1987 National Education Association Representative Assembly called for a special day during American Education Week to honor the contributions of school support employees. Local associations and school districts salute support staff on this 12th annual observance, the Wednesday of American Education Week. For info: Connie Morris, Natl Education Assn (NEA), 1201 16th St NW, Washington, DC 20036. Phone: (202) 822-7262. Fax: (202) 822-7292. WWW: http://www.nea.org

NATIONAL FARM JOKE DAY. Nov 18. An opportunity for the farmers and ranchers who provide consumers with abundant supplies of reasonably priced food to put a smile on everyone's face with the best humor you'll find anywhere. This is a day when farmers try not to take themselves seriously and step back for a few healthy belly laughs aimed at themselves. For info: Frank Lessiter, Lessiter Publications, PO Box 624, Brookfield, WI 53008-0624. Phone: (414) 782-4480. Fax: (414) 782-1252. Email: Lesspub@aol.com.

OMAN: NATIONAL HOLIDAY. Nov 18. Sultanate of Oman celebrates its national day.

PINCHBECK, CHRISTOPHER: DEATH ANNIVERSARY. Nov 18, 1732. English inventor, jeweler and clockmaker. Inventor of the copper and zinc alloy which looked like gold but became synonymous with cheapness. Noted manufacturer of automated musical clocks and instruments. Born at Clerkenwell, London, England, about 1670 (exact date unknown). Died at London, England, Nov 18, 1732.

November 1998

S	M	T	W	T	F	S
1	2	3	4	5	6	7
8	9	10	11	12	13	14
15	16	17	18	19	20	21
22	23	24	25	26	27	28
29	30					

SCOTLAND: SCOTTISH OPEN BADMINTON CHAMPIONSHIP. Nov 18–22. Kelvin Hall International Sports Arena, Glasgow. A European Badminton Union Grand Prix Tournament. Est attendance: 7,000. For info: Scottish Badminton Union, Cockburn Centre, 40 Bogmoor Pl, Glasgow, Scotland G51 4TQ. Phone: (44) (141) 445-1218. Fax: (44) (141) 425-1218.

"SEE IT NOW" TV PREMIERE: ANNIVERSARY. Nov 18, 1951. "See It Now" was a high quality and significant public affairs show of the 1950s. Known for using its own film footage, unrehearsed interviews and no dubbing, "See It Now" covered many relevant and newsworthy stories of its time, including desegregation, lung cancer and anti-Communist fervor. One of the most notable shows focused on Senator Joseph McCarthy, leading to McCarthy's appearance on the show which damaged his credibility. The show was hosted by Edward R. Murrow, who also produced it jointly with Fred W. Friendly. Its premiere was the first live commercial coast-to-coast broadcast.

SOUTH AFRICA ADOPTS NEW CONSTITUTION: ANNIVERSARY. Nov 18, 1993. After more than 300 years of white majority rule, basic civil rights have finally been granted to blacks in South Africa. The constitution providing such rights was approved by representatives of the ruling party, as well as members of 20 other political parties.

UNITED STATES UNIFORM TIME ZONE PLAN: ANNIVERSARY. Nov 18, 1883. Charles Ferdinand Dowd, a Connecticut school teacher and one of the early advocates of uniform time, proposed a time zone plan of the US (four zones of 15 degrees), which he and others persuaded the railroads to adopt and place in operation, on Nov 18, 1883. Info from Natl Bureau of Standards Monograph 155. See also: "US Standard Time Act: Anniversary" (Mar 19).

WEBER, CARL MARIA VON: BIRTH ANNIVERSARY. Nov 18, 1786. Composer, "founder of German romantic school," was born at Eutin, Germany. Member of a musical family, he is remembered mainly for his operas, especially the immensely popular *Der Freischutz* (1821). He died at London, England, on June 5, 1826, at age 39.

☆ ☆ ☆

BIRTHDAYS TODAY

Margaret Eleanor Atwood, 59, author (*Cat's Eye, Dancing Girls & Other Stories, The Handmaid's Tale*), born Ottawa, Ontario, Canada, Nov 18, 1939.

Dante Bichette, 35, baseball player, born West Palm Beach, FL, Nov 18, 1963.

Linda Evans, 56, actress (Crystal Carrington on "Dynasty"; "Bachelor Father"), born Hartford, CT, Nov 18, 1942.

Wilma Mankiller, 53, Chief of the Cherokee Nation from 1985 to 1995. Born at Tahlequah, OK, Nov 18, 1945.

Andrea Marcovicci, 50, actress ("Trapper John, MD"), singer, born New York, NY, Nov 18, 1948.

Harold Warren Moon, 42, football player, born Los Angeles, CA, Nov 18, 1956.

Kevin Nealon, 45, comedic actor ("Champs," "Saturday Night Live"), born St. Louis, MO, Nov 18, 1953.

Jameson Parker, 51, actor ("Simon and Simon," *A Small Circle of Friends*), born Baltimore, MD, Nov 18, 1947.

Elizabeth Perkins, 37, actress (*About Last Night . . ., Big, The Flintstones*), born Queens, NY, Nov 18, 1961.

Katey Sagal, 42, actress ("Married . . . with Children"), born Los Angeles, CA, Nov 18, 1956.

Alan Shepard, 75, former astronaut, first American in space, born East Derry, NH, Nov 18, 1923.

Ted Stevens, 75, US Senator (R, Alaska), born Indianapolis, IN, Nov 18, 1923.

Susan Sullivan, 54, actress ("It's a Living," "Falcon Crest"), born New York, NY, Nov 18, 1944.

Brenda Vaccaro, 59, actress (*Cactus Flower, How Now Dow Jones, The Goodbye People*), born Brooklyn, NY, Nov 18, 1939.

NOVEMBER 19 — THURSDAY

Day 323 — 42 Remaining

BELIZE: GARIFUNA DAY. Nov 19. Public holiday celebrating the first arrival of Black Caribs from St. Vincent and Rotan to Southern Belize.

CAMPANELLA, ROY: BIRTH ANNIVERSARY. Nov 19, 1921. Roy Campanella, one of the first black major leaguers and a star of one of baseball's greatest teams, the Brooklyn Dodgers' "Boys of Summer," was born at Philadelphia, PA. Campy, as he was often called, was named the National League MVP three times in his 10 years of play, in 1951, 1953 and 1955. Campanella had his highest batting average in 1951 (.325) and in 1953 he established three single-season records for a catcher—most putouts (807), most home runs (41) and most runs batted in (142)—as well as having a batting average of .312. His career was cut short on Jan 28, 1958, when an automobile accident left him paralyzed. Campy gained even more fame after his accident as an inspiration and spokesman for the handicapped. He was named to the Baseball Hall of Fame in 1969. Roy Campanella died June 26, 1993, at Woodland Hills, CA.

CLARK, GEORGE ROGERS: BIRTH ANNIVERSARY. Nov 19, 1752. American soldier and frontiersman, born in Albemarle County, VA, on Nov 19, 1752. Died at Louisville, KY, on Feb 13, 1818.

COLD WAR FORMALLY ENDED: ANNIVERSARY. Nov 19–21, 1990. A summit was held at Paris with the leaders of the Conference on Security and Cooperation in Europe (CSCE) on Nov 19–21, 1990. The highlight of the summit was the signing of a treaty to dramatically reduce conventional weapons in Europe, thereby ending the Cold War.

FIRST PRESIDENTIAL LIBRARY: ANNIVERSARY. Nov 19. On Nov 19, 1939, President Franklin D. Roosevelt laid the cornerstone for his presidential library at Hyde Park, NY. He donated the land, but public donations provided funds for the building which was dedicated on June 30, 1941.

GARFIELD, JAMES ABRAM: BIRTH ANNIVERSARY. Nov 19. The 20th president of the US (and the first left-handed president) was born at Orange, OH, Nov 19, 1831. Term of office: Mar 4–Sept 19, 1881. While walking into the Washington, DC, railway station on the morning of July 2, 1881, Garfield was shot by disappointed office seeker Charles J. Guiteau. He survived, in very weak condition, until Sept 19, 1881, when he succumbed to blood poisoning at Elberon, NJ (where he had been taken for recuperation). Guiteau was tried, convicted and, on June 30, 1882, hanged at the jail in Washington.

GETTYSBURG ADDRESS MEMORIAL CEREMONY. Nov 19. Gettysburg, PA. 135th anniversary of Lincoln's Gettysburg Address is celebrated with brief memorial services at the Soldiers' National Monument in Gettysburg National Cemetery at 10 AM. Est attendance: 3,000. For info: Gettysburg Conv and Visitors Bureau, 35 Carlisle St, Gettysburg, PA 17325-1899. Phone: (717) 334-6274. Fax: (717) 334-1166. WWW: http://www.gettysburg.com

GREAT AMERICAN SMOKEOUT. Nov 19. A day observed annually to celebrate smoke-free environments. Annually, the third Thursday in November. For info: PR Dept, American Cancer Society, 1599 Clifton Rd NE, Atlanta, GA 30329. Phone: (404) 329-5735. WWW: http://www.cancer.org

HAVE A BAD DAY DAY. Nov 19. For those who are filled with revulsion at being told endlessly to "have a nice day," this day is a brief respite. Store and business owners are to ask workers to tell customers to "have a bad day." Annually, Nov 19. [© 1997 by WPL] For info: Thomas or Ruth Roy, Wellness Permission League, PO Box 662, Mt Gretna, PA 17064-0662. Phone: (500) 437-5104 or (717) 964-1308. Fax: (717) 964-1335.

HEALTH AND HUMAN SERVICES FUNDS VETOED OVER ABORTION: ANNIVERSARY. Nov 19, 1991. President George Bush vetoed a bill to appropriate $205 billion for the Departments of Health and Human Services, Labor and Education, claiming it would abrogate a rule prohibiting doctors and others who work at clinics that receive federal funding, from dispensing advice about abortion.

JONESTOWN MASSACRE: 20th ANNIVERSARY. Nov 19, 1978. Jonestown, Guyana. On Nov 19, 1978, Indiana-born, 47-year-old Reverend Jim Jones, leader of the "Peoples Temple," was reported to have directed the killing of more than 900 persons. US Representative Leo J. Ryan, of California, and four members of his party were killed in ambush at Port Kaituma airstrip on Nov 18, 1978, when they attempted to leave after an investigative visit to the remote jungle location of the religious cult. On the following day, Jones and his mistress killed themselves after watching the administration of Kool-Aid laced with the deadly poison cyanide to members of the cult. At least 911 persons died in the biggest murder-suicide in history.

LINCOLN'S GETTYSBURG ADDRESS: ANNIVERSARY. Nov 19, 1863. On this day in 1863, 17 acres of the battlefield at Gettysburg, PA, were dedicated as a national cemetery. Noted orator Edward Everett spoke for two hours; the address that Lincoln delivered in less than two minutes was later recognized as one of the most eloquent of the English language. Five manuscript copies in Lincoln's hand survive, including the rough draft begun in ink at the executive Mansion in Washington and concluded in pencil at Gettysburg on the morning of the dedication (kept at the Library of Congress).

MEXICO CITY EXPLOSION: ANNIVERSARY. Nov 19, 1984. More than 300 people were killed when a gas truck explosion set off a series of explosions at a butane and liquefied gas storage facility in the Mexico City suburb Tlalnepantla. An area of approximately 60 acres was razed by the blasts and resulting fires. The four storage tanks involved held more than three million gallons of liquified gas.

MONACO: NATIONAL HOLIDAY. Nov 19.

NATIONAL SCHOOL SUPPLY & EQUIPMENT ASSOCIATION: FALL SHOW. Nov 19–22. Ernest Morial Convention Center, New Orleans, LA. Est attendance: 2,700. For info: Elizabeth Bradley, Natl School Supply & Equipment Assn, 8300 Colesville Rd, Ste 250, Silver Spring, MD 20910. Phone: (301) 495-0240 or (800) 395-5550. Fax: (301) 495-3330.

NEW STAR RISING BLUEGRASS FESTIVAL. Nov 19–22. Live Oak, FL. A great mixture of up-and-coming new artists and well-known bluegrass performers. Est attendance: 3,000. For info: Spirit of the Suwanee Music Park, 3076 95th Dr, Live Oak, FL 32060. Phone: (904) 364-1683. Fax: (904) 364-2998. Email: spirit@musicliveshere.com. WWW: http://www.musicliveshere.com

PUERTO RICO: DISCOVERY DAY: ANNIVERSARY. Nov 19, 1493. Public holiday. Columbus discovered Puerto Rico in 1493 on his second voyage to the New World.

"ROCKY AND HIS FRIENDS" TV PREMIERE: ANNIVERSARY. Nov 19, 1959. This popular cartoon featured the adventures of a talking squirrel, Rocky (Rocket J. Squirrel), and his friend Bullwinkle, a flaky moose. The tongue-in-cheek dialogue contrasted with the simple plots in which Rocky and Bullwinkle tangled with Russian bad guys Boris Badenov and Natasha (who worked for Mr Big). Other popular segments on the show included "Fractured Fairy Tales," "Bullwinkle's Corner" and the adventures of Sherman and Mr Peabody (an intelligent talking dog).

SUFFRAGISTS' VOTING ATTEMPT: ANNIVERSARY. Nov 19, 1868. Testing the wording of the 14th Amendment that says "no State shall make or enforce any law which shall abridge the privileges or immunities of citizens of the United States," 172 New Jersey suffragists, including four black women, attempted to vote in the presidential election. Denied, they cast their votes instead into a women's ballot box overseen by 84-year-old Quaker Margaret Pryer.

SUGARLOAF'S FALL GAITHERSBURG CRAFT FESTIVAL. Nov 19–22. Montgomery County Fairgrounds, Gaithersburg, MD. This show, now in its 23rd year, features 500 nationally recognized craft designers and fine artists displaying and selling their original creations. Craft demonstrations, children's entertainment, live music, food, hourly gift certificate drawings and more. Est attendance: 54,000. For info: Sugarloaf Mountain Works, Inc, 200 Orchard Ridge Dr, #215, Gaithersburg, MD 20878. Phone: (800) 210-9900.

WOMEN'S CHRISTIAN TEMPERANCE UNION ORGANIZED: ANNIVERSARY. Nov 19, 1874. Developed out of the Women's Temperance Crusade of 1873, the Women's Christian Temperance Union was organized in Cleveland, OH. The Crusade had swept through 23 states with women going into saloons to sing hymns, pray and ask saloonkeepers to stop selling liquor. Today the temperance group includes more than a million members with chapters in 72 countries and continues to be concerned with educating people on the potential dangers of the use of alcohol, narcotics and tobacco.

BIRTHDAYS TODAY

Dick Cavett, 62, entertainer ("The Dick Cavett Show"), born Gibbon, NE, Nov 19, 1936.

Jodie Foster, 36, actress (Oscars for *The Accused, The Silence of the Lambs; Taxi Driver*), director (*Home for the Holidays*), born Los Angeles, CA, Nov 19, 1962.

Thomas R. Harkin, 59, US Senator (D, Iowa), born Cumming, IA, Nov 19, 1939.

Scott Jacoby, 42, actor (*The Little Girl Who Lives Down the Lane, Return to Horror High*), born Chicago, IL, Nov 19, 1956.

Larry King, 65, talk show host ("Larry King Live"), born Brooklyn, NY, Nov 19, 1933.

Jeane Kirkpatrick, 72, political scientist, former US ambassador to the UN, born Duncan, OK, Nov 19, 1926.

Calvin Klein, 56, fashion designer (popularized designer jeans), born New York, NY, Nov 19, 1942.

Glynnis O'Connor, 43, actress (*Ode to Billy Joe, Johnny Dangerously*), born New York, NY, Nov 19, 1955.

Kathleen Quinlan, 44, actress (*Twilight Zone—The Movie, The Doors*), born Pasadena, CA, Nov 19, 1954.

Ahmad Rashad (born Bobby Moore), 49, sportscaster, former football player, born Portland, OR, Nov 19, 1949.

Meg Ryan, 37, actress (*When Harry Met Sally . . . , Sleepless in Seattle*), born Fairfield, CT, Nov 19, 1961.

November 1998

S	M	T	W	T	F	S
1	2	3	4	5	6	7
8	9	10	11	12	13	14
15	16	17	18	19	20	21
22	23	24	25	26	27	28
29	30					

Tommy G. Thompson, 57, Governor of Wisconsin (R), born Elroy, WI, Nov 19, 1941.

Ted Turner, 60, baseball, basketball and cable TV executive, born Cincinnati, OH, Nov 19, 1938.

Garrick Utley, 59, journalist, born Chicago, IL, Nov 19, 1939.

John Francis Welch, Jr, 63, chairman and chief executive officer of General Electric Co, born Salem, MA, Nov 19, 1935.

NOVEMBER 20 — FRIDAY

Day 324 — 41 Remaining

BELLO, ANDRES: BIRTH ANNIVERSARY. Nov 20. Venezuelan diplomat, author and humanist, was born at Caracas, Venezuela, Nov 20, 1781. Bello died at Santiago, Chile, Oct 15, 1865.

BILL OF RIGHTS: ANNIVERSARY OF FIRST STATE RATIFICATION. Nov 20. New Jersey on Nov 20, 1789, became the first state to ratify 10 of the 12 amendments to the US Constitution proposed by Congress on Sept 25. These 10 amendments came to be known as the Bill of Rights. See also: "First Proposed Amendments to the US Constitution: Anniversary" (Sept 25).

CANADA: MUSKOKA ARTS AND CRAFTS CHRISTMAS SHOW. Nov 20–22. Bracebridge, Ont, Canada. For info: Muskoka Arts and Crafts, Chapel Gallery, 15 King St, Bracebridge, Ont, Canada P1L 1P7. Phone: (705) 645-5501.

CHATTERTON, THOMAS: BIRTH ANNIVERSARY. Nov 20, 1752. English poet Thomas Chatterton was born at Bristol, England, on Nov 20, 1752, and killed himself at age 17 by taking arsenic in his London garret on the night of Aug 24, 1770. A gifted but lonely child, before he reached his teens Chatterton had created a fantasy poet-priest, Thomas Rowley, who lived in the 16th century. With his own pen, Chatterton created enough verses "by" Rowley to fill more than 600 printed pages. Chatterton's fantasy-forgery poems attracted little attention during his short life, but in spite of their youthful deficiencies they were later admired by Wordsworth, Coleridge, Shelley, Keats, Byron and many others. In addition, he became the subject of at least one play, an opera and a novel.

CHRISTMAS IN ROSELAND. Nov 20–Dec 31. American Rose Center, Shreveport, LA. Holiday magic transforms the American Rose Center with lights, holiday scenes, music and light sculptures. Est attendance: 40,000. For info: American Rose Center, 8877 Jefferson-Paige Rd, Shreveport, LA 71119. Phone: (318) 938-5402. Fax: (318) 938-5405. Email: ars@ars-hq.org. WWW: http://www.ars.org

COLORADO RIVER CROSSING BALLOON FESTIVAL. Nov 20–22. Cibola High School, Yuma, AZ. 8th annual. 55 balloons. Sunrise balloon liftoffs, sunset balloon glow and fireworks. Entertainment, food, vendors. Free admission. Est attendance: 17,000. For info: Caballeros de Yuma, Inc, PO Box 5987, Yuma, AZ 85366. Phone: (520) 343-1715. Fax: (520) 783-1609.

DOW-JONES TOPS 5,000: ANNIVERSARY. Nov 20, 1995. The Dow-Jones Index of 30 major industrial stocks topped the 5,000 mark for the first time.

FANTASY OF LIGHT PARADE. Nov 20. Wheeling, WV. Night parade with more than 100 lighted floats and musical units. Est attendance: 80,000. For info: Wheeling Conv and Visitors Bureau, 1310 Market St, Wheeling, WV 26003. Phone: (800) 828-3097 or (304) 233-7709. Fax: (304) 233-1320.
Email: cuhcvb-wv@worldnet.att.net.
WWW: http://www.com/www/wheeling.html

FESTIVAL OF TREES. Nov 20–29. RiverCenter, Davenport, IA. Outdoors, the lights of the season are spectacular and can be enjoyed from horse-drawn carriages. Indoors, hundreds of spectacular holiday creations for the home are on display, including hundreds of designer trees, wreaths, room vignettes and a spectacular holiday gift shop at the River Center. Additional events include a holiday pops concert by the Quad City Symphony, Fes-

tival luncheons, a Holiday Hoedown and many more. On Nov 21, The Festival of Trees Holiday Parade, the largest helium character balloon parade in the midwest. Est attendance: 71,000. For info: Kate Sweigle, Festival of Trees Administrator, Quad City Arts, 1715 Second Ave, Rock Island, IL 61201. Phone: (309) 793-1213. Fax: (309) 793-1265.
Email: Festoftrees@qconline.com.
WWW: http://www.qconline.com/festoftrees

GOULD, CHESTER: BIRTH ANNIVERSARY. Nov 20, 1900. In 1931, Chester Gould created comic strip character Dick Tracy, the clean-cut, square-jawed, plainclothed detective who represented the code that "crime doesn't pay." The strip first appeared Oct 4, 1931, in the *Detroit Daily Mirror* and later was syndicated in nearly 1,000 newspapers worldwide. *Dick Tracy* (originally called *Plainclothes Tracy*) featured Tess Trueheart (later Mrs Tracy) and a host of bad guys with ugly names and faces to match their ugly ways—Mole, Pruneface, Flat Top, B-B Eyes, Mumbles and others. Closely following actual police methods of crime prevention, it included a "Crimestopper Notebook" with tips on self-protection. More violent than most comic strips, *Dick Tracy* was a combination of realism and science fiction. Chester Gould was born at Pawnee, OK, and died May 11, 1985, at Woodstock, IL.

GRAND ILLUMINATION. Nov 20. Lahaska, PA. At dusk, the Village's brilliant outdoor holiday lights display and sidewalk luminarias debut. Community sing-along, Yule log lighting, free cider and toasted marshmallows. Preview of new gift ideas in shops. Free admission. Est attendance: 4,000. For info: Peddler's Village, Routes 202 & 263, Lahaska, PA 18931. Phone: (215) 794-4000. Fax: (215) 794-4001.
WWW: http://www.peddlersvillage.com

HOLIDAY FOLK FAIR INTERNATIONAL. Nov 20–22. Wisconsin Center, Milwaukee, WI. International festival featuring costumes, dancing, entertainment, exhibits, workshops, folk wares and cuisine. Also children's activities. Annually, the weekend before Thanksgiving. Est attendance: 65,000. For info: Holiday Folk Fair International, Intl Institute of Wisconsin, 1110 N Old World Third St, Ste 420, Milwaukee, WI 53203. Phone: (414) 225-6220. Fax: (414) 225-6235. Email: iiw@execpc.com.

HUBBLE, EDWIN POWELL: BIRTH ANNIVERSARY. Nov 20, 1889. American astronomer Edwin Hubble was born at Marshfield, MO, on Nov 20, 1889. His discovery and development of the concept of an expanding universe has been described as the "most spectacular astronomical discovery" of the twentieth century. As a tribute, the Hubble Space Telescope, deployed Apr 25, 1990, from US Space Shuttle *Discovery*, was named for him. The Hubble Space Telescope, with a 240-centimeter mirror, was to allow astronomers to see farther into space than they had ever seen from telescopes on Earth. Hubble died at San Marino, CA, on Sept 28, 1953.

KENNEDY, ROBERT FRANCIS: BIRTH ANNIVERSARY. Nov 20, 1925. US Senator and brother of John F. Kennedy (35th president), was born at Brookline, MA, Nov 20, 1925. An assassin shot him in Los Angeles, CA, June 5, 1968, while he was campaigning for the presidential nomination. He died on June 6, 1968. Sirhan Sirhan was convicted of his murder.

☆ ☆ ☆

LAGERLOF, SELMA: BIRTH ANNIVERSARY. Nov 20, 1858. Swedish author, member of the Swedish Academy and the first woman to receive the Nobel Prize for literature (1909) was born in Sweden's Varmland Province on Nov 20, 1858. She died there Mar 16, 1940.

LAKE LIGHTS FESTIVAL. Nov 20–Jan 1. Lake Ozark and Osage Beach, MO. 10th annual. Holiday lights and scenic displays adorn Business 54 and Highway 54 from Bagnell Dam to "Y" road. Est attendance: 10,000. For info: Lake Area Chamber of Commerce, PO Box 1570, Lake Ozark, MO 65049. Phone: (573) 365-3002 or (800) 451-4117.

LAND OF MARK TWAIN BLUEGRASS MUSIC FESTIVAL. Nov 20–22. Ramada Inn, Hannibal, MO. Annually, the third weekend in November. Est attendance: 1,500. For info: Delbert Spray, Tri-State Bluegrass Association, RR 1, Kahoka, MO 63445. Phone: (573) 853-4344.

LANDIS, KENESAW MOUNTAIN: BIRTH ANNIVERSARY. Nov 20, 1866. Baseball Hall of Fame executive born at Milville, OH. Landis, a federal judge, was named the first Commissioner of Baseball in 1920. He ruled with an absolutely firm hand and imposed his view of how baseball should operate upon owners and players alike. Inducted into the Hall of Fame in 1944. Died at Chicago, IL, Nov 25, 1944.

LAURIER, SIR WILFRED: BIRTH ANNIVERSARY. Nov 20. Canadian statesman (premier, 1896–1911) born Nov 20, 1841. Died Feb 17, 1919.

LIGHT-UP WEEKEND. Nov 20–21. Downtown Pittsburgh, PA. A perfect spot to watch this spectacular light show would be on top of Mount Washington. Every downtown building lights up to begin the holiday season. For info: Greater Pittsburgh Conv & Visitors Bureau, Four Gateway Center, Pittsburgh, PA 15222-1259. Phone: (412) 566-4190 or (800) 359-0758. Fax: (412) 644-5512.

MARRIAGE OF ELIZABETH AND PHILIP: ANNIVERSARY. Nov 20, 1947. The Princess Elizabeth Alexandra Mary was wed to Philip Mountbatten on Nov 20, 1947. Elizabeth was the first child of the Duke and Duchess of York who became King George VI and Queen Elizabeth in 1936 upon the abdication of Edward VIII. Philip, the former Prince Philip of Greece, had become a British subject nine months earlier and the title Duke of Edinburgh was bestowed on him. The bride later became Elizabeth II, Queen of the United Kingdom of Great Britain and Northern Ireland and Head of the Commonwealth, upon the death of her father on Feb 6, 1952, her coronation taking place at Westminster Abbey on June 2, 1953.

MEXICO: REVOLUTION ANNIVERSARY. Nov 20. Anniversary of the social revolution launched by Francisco I. Madero in 1910. National holiday.

NATIONAL BIBLE WEEK INAUGURAL LUNCHEON. Nov 20. New York, NY. Armed Service Chaplain honored with Witherspoon Chaplains Award. Information upon request. Annually, the Friday before Natl Bible Week. Est attendance: 500. For info: Thomas R. May, Exec Dir, Laymen's Natl Bible Assn, Inc, 1865 Broadway, 12th Fl, New York, NY 10023. Phone: (212) 408-1390. Fax: (212) 408-1448.

★**NATIONAL FARM-CITY WEEK.** Nov 20–26. Presidential Proclamation issued for a week in November since 1956, customarily for the week ending with Thanksgiving Day. Requested by congressional resolutions from 1956–1958; since 1959 issued annually without request.

NEWBERRY LIBRARY VERY MERRY HOLIDAY BAZAAR. Nov 20–22. Chicago, IL. Easy one-stop holiday shopping at booths with gifts from 40 Chicago-area cultural institutions, such as the Museum of Science and Industry and the Frank Lloyd Wright House in Oak Park. For info: Newberry Library, 60 W Walton, Chicago, IL 60610-3380. Phone: (312) 943-9090.

ROCK CITY'S ENCHANTED GARDEN OF LIGHTS: A HOLIDAY SPECTACULAR. Nov 20–Jan 3. Rock City Gardens, Chattanooga, TN. A new spectacular walk-thru outdoor lighting program with more than 25 holiday scenes set to music with Santa, carolers, hot cocoa, gingerbread cookies and more. Annually, the Friday before Thanksgiving through the first weekend in January. Est attendance: 45,000. For info: Shelda Spencer Rees, PR Dept, See Rock City, Inc, PO Box 2315, Chattanooga, TN 37409. Phone: (706) 820-2531. Fax: (706) 820-9623.

SILVER BELLS IN THE CITY. Nov 20–21. Lansing, MI. Michigan's capital city sparkles with hospitality on the streets of downtown Lansing's business district for this celebration of lights, music and holiday cheer including the lighting of the State of Michigan Holiday Tree. Annually, the Friday and Saturday before Thankgiving. Coordinated by Arts Council of Greater Lansing, Inc. Est attendance: 35,000. For info: Arts Council of Greater Lansing, Inc, Center for the Arts, 425 S Grand Ave, Lansing, MI 48933. Phone: (517) 372-4636. Fax: (517) 484-2564.

STAMP EXPO: AMERICA. Nov 20–22. Quality Hotel, Anaheim, CA. Est attendance: 4,000. For info: Intl Stamp Collectors Society, PO Box 854, Van Nuys, CA 91408. Phone: (818) 997-6496. Fax: (818) 988-4337. Email: iibick@aol.com. WWW: http://www.4free.com/bick

TECHNOLOGY AND YOU EXPO. Nov 20–22. Empire State Plaza, Albany, NY. 3rd annual. Showing the public the latest trends in technology, including computers, hardware, software, finances, education and internet village. Est attendance: 10,000. For info: Heather Mabee, Ed Lewi Associates, 6 Chelsea Place, Clifton Park, NY 12065. Phone: (518) 383-6183. Fax: (518) 383-6755.

TIERNEY, GENE: BIRTH ANNIVERSARY. Nov 20, 1920. Known best for the title role in the film *Laura*, actress Gene Tierney was born on Nov 20, 1920, at Brooklyn, NY. Her other films include *Leave Her to Heaven, Belle Starr, Heaven Can Wait, A Bell for Adano, Dragonwyck, Advise and Consent* and her last film, *The Pleasure Seekers*. She died on Nov 6, 1991.

UNITED NATIONS: UNIVERSAL CHILDREN'S DAY. Nov 20. Designated by the United Nations General Assembly as Universal Children's Day. First observance was in 1953. A time to honor children with special ceremonies and festivals and to make children's needs known to governments. Observed on different days and in different ways in more than 120 nations.

WAY OF LIGHTS. Nov 20–Jan 3. Belleville, IL. Remember the birth of Christ while journeying along a path illuminated with 375,000 white lights to the traditional crib. Indoor activities include children's show, choirs and an International Christmas Tree display, all expressing the message of Christ's peace. Est attendance: 350,000. For info: Shrine of Our Lady of the Snows, 442 S De Mazenod Dr, Belleville, IL 62223-1094. Phone: (618) 397-6700. Fax: (618) 398-6549.
WWW: http://www.apci.net/~oblates/

WOLCOTT, OLIVER: BIRTH ANNIVERSARY. Nov 20, 1726. Signer of the Declaration of Independence, Governor of Connecticut, born at Windsor, CT. Died on Dec 1, 1797.

WORLD WAR II: THE BATTLE OF TARAWA-MAKIN: 55th ANNIVERSARY. Nov 20, 1943. The US began its offensive against Japan in the Central Pacific (Operation Galvanic) during the night by attacking the Gilbert Islands, particularly the islets of Betio and Makin. The Japanese had heavily fortified the Tarawa chain of atolls, especially Tarawa, with pillboxes, blockhouses and ferroconcrete bombproofs. In the eight days it took the 5th Amphibious Corps, 2nd Marine Division and the 27th Infantry Division to take the Tarawa and Makin Islands, 1,000 US soldiers were killed and 2,311 wounded. The Japanese loss was tallied at 4,700 men killed, 17 wounded captured and 129 Koreans surrendered. The US public, who through censorship previously had been kept in the dark about the human cost of the war, was appalled by casualty figures and photographs from this battle.

YORK INTERNATIONAL POSTCARD FAIR. Nov 20–21. York Fairgrounds, York, PA. Est attendance: 1,000. For info: Mary Martin Ltd, 4899 Pulaski Hwy, Rt 40, Perryville, MD 21903. Phone: (410) 575-7768. Fax: (410) 642-2053.

BIRTHDAYS TODAY

Joseph Robinette Biden, Jr, 56, US Senator (D, Delaware), born Scranton, PA, Nov 20, 1942.

Robert C. Byrd, 81, US Senator (D, West Virginia), born North Wilkesboro, NC, Nov 20, 1917.

Steve Dahl, 44, Chicago radio personality, born La Canada, CA, Nov 20, 1954.

Richard Dawson, 66, actor, TV game-show host ("Laugh-In"; Emmy for "Family Feud"), born Gosport, England, Nov 20, 1932.

Bo Derek (Cathleen Collins), 42, actress (*"10," Bolero, Tarzan, A Change of Seasons*), born Long Beach, CA, Nov 20, 1956.

Marcus D. (Mark) Gastineau, 42, former football player, born Ardmore, OK, Nov 20, 1956.

Nadine Gordimer, 75, writer (*July's People, Lifetimes Under Apartheid*), born Springs, the Transvaal, South Africa, Nov 20, 1923.

Veronica Hamel, 55, actress (Joyce on "Hill Street Blues"), born Philadelphia, PA, Nov 20, 1943.

Ruth Laredo, 61, concert pianist, born Detroit, MI, Nov 20, 1937.

Richard Masur, 50, actor ("One Day at a Time," *Who'll Stop the Rain, Under Fire, Heartburn*), born New York, NY, Nov 20, 1948.

Estelle Parsons, 71, actress ("Roseanne," *Bonnie and Clyde, Dick Tracy*; stage: *Mrs Dally Has a Lover* [Theater World Award], *Next Time I'll Sing to You* [Obie Award], *In the Summer House* [Obie Award]), born Marblehead, MA, Nov 20, 1927.

Dick Smothers, 60, comedian, folk singer (social commentary in variety show with his brother Tommy led to being fired by CBS), born New York, NY, Nov 20, 1938.

David Walters, 47, former Governor of Oklahoma (D), born Canute, OK, Nov 20, 1951.

Judy Woodruff, 52, journalist, author, born Tulsa, OK, Nov 20, 1946.

Sean Young, 39, actress (*Blade Runner, No Way Out*), born Louisville, KY, Nov 20, 1959.

November 1998

S	M	T	W	T	F	S
1	2	3	4	5	6	7
8	9	10	11	12	13	14
15	16	17	18	19	20	21
22	23	24	25	26	27	28
29	30					

NOVEMBER 21 — SATURDAY

Day 325 — 40 Remaining

ANGLICAN CHURCH OF AUSTRALIA VOTES TO ALLOW WOMEN PRIESTS: ANNIVERSARY. Nov 21, 1992. The ordination of women preists, previously prohibited, was authorized by the General Synod of Australia's Anglican Church. Although the largest of the dioceses voted against the bill, it still received the requisite two-thirds approval.

BEAUMONT, WILLIAM: BIRTH ANNIVERSARY. Nov 21, 1785. US Army surgeon whose contribution to classic medical literature and world fame resulted from another man's shotgun wound. When Canadian fur trapper Alexis St. Martin received an apparently mortal wound on June 6, 1822—a nearly point blank blast to the abdomen—Dr. Beaumont began observing his stomach and digestive processes through an opening in his abdominal wall. His findings were published in 1833 in *Experiments and Observations on the Gastric Juice and the Physiology of Digestion*. St. Martin returned to Canada in 1834 and resisted Beaumont's efforts to have him return for further study. He outlived his doctor by 20 years and was buried at a depth of eight feet to discourage any attempt at posthumous examination. Beaumont, born at Lebanon, CT, on Nov 21, 1785, died Apr 25, 1853, at St. Louis, MO.

CHRISTMAS GALLERY. Nov 21–Jan 2. Firehouse Art Center, Norman, OK. Shoppers find gifts for friends, children and family, from stocking stuffers to "executive" gifts! Original works and limited production pieces by juried and invited artists and craftspeople. Est attendance: 3,500. For info: Asst Dir, Firehouse Art Ctr, 444 S Flood, Norman, OK 73069. Phone: (405) 329-4523.

CUSTER STATE PARK BUFFALO AUCTION. Nov 21. Custer, SD. A live sale at 10 AM, MST, of 300–400 surplus buffalo (calves, yearlings, mature cows and two-year-old bulls). Est attendance: 600. For info: Ron Walker, Custer State Park, HC 83, Box 70, Custer, SD 57730. Phone: (605) 255-4515 or (605) 255-4814. Fax: (605) 255-4460. Email: ronw@gfp-cu.state.sd.us.

FESTIVAL OF LIGHTS AT CINCINNATI ZOO. Nov 21–Jan 3. Cincinnati Zoo and Botanical Garden, Cincinnati, OH. More than a million lights transform the Zoo as new light displays are added each year. Ice skating at the Victorian Wonderland. Also, wagon rides, Enchanted Village, visits with Santa Claus, holiday shopping, hot chocolate and more. Est attendance: 225,000. For info: Events and Promotions Dept, Cincinnati Zoo and Botanical Garden, 3400 Vine St, Cincinnati, OH 45220. Phone: (513) 281-4701 ext 8316. Fax: (513) 559-7790. WWW: http://www.cincyzoo.org

FRENCHMAN ROWS ACROSS PACIFIC: ANNIVERSARY. Nov 21. Gerard d'Aboville completed a four-month solo journey across the Pacific Ocean on Nov 21, 1991. D'Aboville began rowing across the Pacific on July 11 when he left Choshi, Japan. His journey ended at Ilwaco, WA.

GINGERBREAD VILLAGE. Nov 21–Dec 22. Mormon Trail Center at Historic Winter Quarters Visitors Center, Omaha, NE. View approximately 200 gingerbread houses of every shape and size delightfully decorated for the holidays. Gingerbread houses given to charities before Christmas. Est attendance: 15,500. For info: Eldon L. Fletcher, Gingerbread Village, 3250 State St, Omaha, NE 68112. Phone: (402) 453-9372.

GREEN, HETTY: BIRTH ANNIVERSARY. Nov 21. Henrietta Howland Robinson Green, better known as Hetty Green, reported to have been the richest woman in America, was born at New Bedford, MA, Nov 21, 1835. She was an able financier who managed her own wealth, which was estimated to have been in excess of 100 million dollars. Died at New York, NY, July 3, 1916.

HANDEL'S *MESSIAH*. Nov 21. RLDS Auditorium, Independence, MO. 82nd annual performance of Handel's *Messiah* by the Independence Messiah Choir, Messiah Festival Orchestra and renowned soloists, conducted by Jack R. Ergo. Est attendance: 6,000. For info: Public Relations, RLDS Auditorium, PO Box 1059, 111 E Maple, Independence, MO 64051. Phone: (816) 521-3051 or (816) 521-3045. Fax: (816) 521-3043. Email: sflory@rlds.org. WWW: http://www.rlds.org

HOLIDAYS IN THE CITY GRAND ILLUMINATION PARADE. Nov 21. Norfolk, VA. All of Norfolk's downtown skyscrapers and many of its smaller buildings outline their profiles in lights for Holidays in the City. On the first evening of the illumination a downtown lighted street parade kicks off the celebration of the season. All of the floats, bands and entries in this nighttime parade are lighted. Annually, the Saturday before Thanksgiving. Est attendance: 100,000. For info: Parade Manager, Downtown Norfolk Council, 201 Granby St, Ste 101, Norfolk, VA 23510. Phone: (757) 623-1757. Fax: (757) 623-1756. Email: dnc@norfolk.infi.net.

MAN'S FIRST FREE FLIGHT (BALLOON): ANNIVERSARY. Nov 21, 1783. Jean Francois Pilatre de Rozier and the Marquis Francois Laurent d'Arlandes became the first men to fly when they ascended in a Montgolfier hot-air balloon at Paris, France, on Nov 21, 1783, less than six months after the first public balloon flight demonstration (June 5, 1783), and only a year after the first experiments with small paper and fabric balloons by the Montgolfier brothers, Joseph and Jacques, at Annonay, France, in November 1782. The first manned free flight lasted about 25 minutes and carried the passengers nearly six miles at a height of about 300 feet, over the city of Paris. Benjamin Franklin was one of the spectators at the flight.

MARX, HARPO: BIRTH ANNIVERSARY. Nov 21, 1893. Harpo (Adolph Arthur) Marx was born at New York, NY, on Nov 21, 1893. He was the second born of the famed Marx brothers who became a popular comedy team of stage, screen and radio for 30 years. Harpo wore a blond curly wig and pretended to be a mute who communicated by honking a horn. He was an expert player of the harp, though the comedy he brought to his playing tended to distract the viewer from noticing the quality of his musicianship. He died on Sept 28, 1964, at Hollywood, CA. Other family members who participated in the comedy team were Groucho (Julius), Chico (Leonard) and, briefly, Zeppo (Herbert) and Gummo (Milton).

MESSINA HOF'S WINE PREMIERE. Nov 21. Bryan, TX. Traditional celebration of the new vintages. Wine aficionados' palates are treated to the premiere of all the new wines which accompany each free winery tour. Additionally, there are several wine-related activities like Chardonnay Blending Seminars, national and international Cabernet Shoot-Outs and wine and food pairing seminars. In the evening, a new vintage reception will be followed by an elegant gourmet wine premiere dinner. Est attendance: 2,500. For info: Messina Hof Wine Cellars, 4545 Old Reliance Rd, Bryan, TX 77808. Phone: (409) 778-9463. Fax: (409) 778-1729.

NAIA MEN'S AND WOMEN'S CROSS COUNTRY NATIONAL CHAMPIONSHIP. Nov 21. Men compete on an 8K course and women compete on a 5K course with the top 25 individual finishers in each championship receiving All-America honors. 43rd annual men's, 19th annual women's. For info: Kevin Henry, Natl Assn of Intercollegiate Athletics, 6120 S Yale Ave, Ste 1450, Tulsa, OK 74136-4223. Phone: (918) 494-8828. Fax: (918) 494-8841. Email: khenry@naia.org. WWW: http://www.naia.org

NORDIC YULE FEST. Nov 21–22. Nordic Heritage Museum, Seattle, WA. Annual Christmas fair featuring crafts, holiday foods, music and dance and children's activities. Est attendance: 5,000. For info: Nordic Heritage Museum, 3014 NW 67th St, Seattle, WA 98117. Phone: (206) 789-5707. Fax: (206) 789-3271.

NORTH CAROLINA: RATIFICATION DAY. Nov 21. Twelfth state to ratify Constitution, on this day in 1789.

PIER 39'S HOLIDAY TREE LIGHTING FESTIVITIES. Nov 21. Entrance Park, San Francisco, CA. Start the Bay Area holiday season at Pier 39 with a day and evening filled with a great line-up of entertainment for the whole family. The day's festivities lead to the ceremonial countdown to light the 65-ft tree with 2,500 shimmering lights. It's all free and open to the public. Annually, the Saturday before Thanksgiving. Est attendance: 10,000. For info: Alicia Vargas, PR Dir, Pier 39, PO Box 193730, San Francisco, CA 94119. Phone: (415) 705-5500. Fax: (415) 981-8808.

POPE BENEDICT XV: BIRTH ANNIVERSARY. Nov 21. Giacomo dela Chiesa, 258th pope of the Roman Catholic Church, born at Pegli, Italy, Nov 21, 1854, elected pope Sept 3, 1914. Died Jan 22, 1922.

PURCELL, HENRY: DEATH ANNIVERSARY. Nov 21, 1695. English composer of the early Baroque period was born at London circa 1659. Purcell's work includes more than 100 songs, the opera *Dido and Aeneas* and *The Fairy Queen*, incidental music for a version of Shakespeare's *A Midsummer Night's Dream*. Purcell died at London.

RANCH HAND BREAKFAST. Nov 21. King Ranch, Kingsville, TX. A chuck wagon breakfast cooked and served outdoors at the world-famous King Ranch. See Longhorn cattle and real cowboys on horseback. Annually, the Saturday before Thanksgiving. Est attendance: 7,000. For info: Kingsville Conv and Visitors Bureau, Box 1562, Kingsville, TX 78364-1562. Phone: (800) 333-5032. Fax: (512) 592-3227. Email: kcvb@kingsville.org. WWW: http://www.kingsville.org

REMEMBRANCE DAY. Nov 21. Gettysburg, PA. An annual event held in conjunction with the Lincoln Observance, with a parade of Civil War troops to the Albert Woolson Monument for a wreath laying ceremony. Sponsored by the Sons of Union Veterans. For info: Gettysburg Conv & Visitors Bureau, 35 Carlisle St, Gettysburg, PA 17325. Phone: (717) 334-6274. Fax: (717) 334-1166. WWW: http://www.gettysburg.com

"SUPER DAVE" TV PREMIERE: ANNIVERSARY. Nov 21, 1987. Bob Einstein starred in this half-hour comedy as stuntman Super Dave Osborne. This show was a spin-off from "Bizarre" and aired on the cable channel Showtime.

TELLEBRATION! AN EVENING OF ADULT STORYTELLING. Nov 21. As a part of world-wide storytelling, the Storytelling Troupe of Charleston provides an evening of delightful fun and excitement. Folk tales, personal adventures, old favorites and even some music. Annually, the Saturday before Thanksgiving. Est attendance: 300. For info: Storytelling Troupe of Charleston, PO Box 1135, Charleston, SC 29402. Phone: (803) 571-4378 or (803) 571-2178. Fax: (860) 439-5431.

TELLABRATION! AN EVENING OF STORYTELLING FOR GROWN-UPS. Nov 21. Many sites throughout Connecticut. Simultaneous storytelling concerts for adults. Annually, the Saturday before Thanksgiving. Est attendance: 300. For info: Christine Tagg, Adm, Connecticut Storytelling Center, Connecticut College, Box 5295, 270 Mohegan Ave, New London, CT 06320. Phone: (860) 439-2764. Fax: (860) 439-5431. Email: cltag@conncoll.edu.

THAILAND: ELEPHANT ROUND-UP AT SURIN. Nov 21. Elephant demonstrations in morning, elephant races and tug-of-war between 100 men and one elephant. Observed since 1961 on third Saturday in November. Special trains from Bangkok on previous day.

November 1998

S	M	T	W	T	F	S
1	2	3	4	5	6	7
8	9	10	11	12	13	14
15	16	17	18	19	20	21
22	23	24	25	26	27	28
29	30					

UNITED NATIONS: WORLD TELEVISION DAY. Nov 21. On Dec 17, 1996, the General Assembly proclaimed this day as World Television Day, commemorating the date in 1996 on which the first World Television Forum was held at the UN. Info from: United Nations, Dept of Public Info, New York, NY 10017.

VOLTAIRE, JEAN FRANÇOIS MARIE: BIRTH ANNIVERSARY. Nov 21, 1694. French author and philosopher to whom is attributed (perhaps erroneously) the statement: "I disapprove of what you say, but I will defend to the death your right to say it." Born Nov 21, 1694. Died May 30, 1778.

WORLD HELLO DAY. Nov 21. Everyone who participates greets 10 people. People in 179 countries have participated in this annual activity for advancing peace through personal communication. Heads of state of 114 countries have expressed approval of the event. 26th annual observance. For info: Michael McCormack, The McCormack Brothers, Box 993, Omaha, NE 68101.

BIRTHDAYS TODAY

Troy Aikman, 32, quarterback, born West Covina, CA, Nov 21, 1966.

Marcy Carsey, 54, television producer, born South Weymouth, MA, Nov 21, 1944.

James (Anderson) DePreist, 62, conductor, Oregon Symphony, born Philadelphia, PA, Nov 21, 1936.

Richard J. Durbin, 54, US Senator (D, Illinois), born East St. Louis, IL, Nov 21, 1944.

George Kenneth (Ken) Griffey, Jr, 29, baseball player, born Donora, PA, Nov 21, 1969.

Goldie Hawn, 53, actress ("Laugh-In"; Oscar for *Cactus Flower; Private Benjamin, Swing Shift*), born Washington, DC, Nov 21, 1945.

David Hemmings, 57, actor (*Blow-Up, The Charge of the Light Brigade*), born Guildford, England, Nov 21, 1941.

Laurence Luckinbill, 64, actor ("The Delphi Bureau," *The Boyz in the Band, Star Trek V: The Final Frontier*), born Fort Smith, AR, Nov 21, 1934.

Lorna Luft, 46, actress ("Trapper John, MD"), daughter of Judy Garland, born Los Angeles, CA, Nov 21, 1952.

Natalia Makarova, 58, dancer, born Leningrad, USSR, Nov 21, 1940.

Juliet Mills, 57, (father is actor John Mills, sister is actress Hayley Mills), actress ("Nanny and the Professor," *So Well Remembered, Carry on Jack*), born London, England, Nov 21, 1941.

Stanley Frank ("Stan the Man") Musial, 78, Baseball Hall of Fame outfielder/first baseman, born Donora, PA, Nov 21, 1920.

Cynthia Rhodes, 42, actress, dancer (*Flashdance, Dirty Dancing*), born Nashville, TN, Nov 21, 1956.

Nicollette Sheridan, 35, actress ("Knots Landing," *The Sure Thing*), born Worthing, Sussex, England, Nov 21, 1963.

Marlo Thomas, 60, actress ("That Girl"), author (*Free to Be . . . You and Me*), born Detroit, MI, Nov 21, 1938.

NOVEMBER 22 — SUNDAY

Day 326 — 39 Remaining

ALASCATTALO DAY. Nov 22. Anchorage, AK. To honor humor in general and Alaskan humor in particular. Event is named after "alascattalo," said to be the genetic cross between a moose and a walrus. For info: Steven C. Levi, Parsnackle Press, PO Box 241467, Anchorage, AK 99524. Phone: (907) 337-2021. Fax: (907) 337-4485. Email: afscl@alaska.edu.

BIBLE SUNDAY. Nov 22. An ecumenical observance by churches across the country in celebration of the Bible. Annually, the Sunday before Thanksgiving. For info: Arthur Caccese, Office of Development, American Bible Society, 1865 Broadway, New York, NY 10023. Phone: (212) 408-1474. Fax: (212) 408-1360.

BIG D 103 CARAVAN OF CARRIAGES. Nov 22. Windsor, CT. 5th annual. Morning personality Jerry Kristafer's "Big D Big Drive for Foodshare" consists of listeners soliciting monetary donations, purchasing a shopping cart full of food and walking a five-mile route in the "Caravan of Carriages" led by Kristafer, from a local grocery store to Foodshare in Windsor, who collects food for 200 shelters and kitchens across Connecticut. Annually, the last Sunday before Thanksgiving. Est attendance: 1,000. For info: WDRC-FM, Big D 103, 869 Blue Hills Ave, Bloomfield, CT 06002. Phone: (860) 243-1115. Fax: (860) 286-8257. WWW: http://www.wdrc.com

BRITTEN, (EDWARD) BENJAMIN: 85th BIRTH ANNIVERSARY. Nov 22, 1913. English composer born, Lowestoft, Suffolk, England, Nov 22, 1913. Lord Britten, Baron Britten of Aldeburgh, died at Aldeburgh, Dec 4, 1976.

CANADA: CANADIAN WESTERN AGRIBITION. Nov 22–29. Regina, Saskatchewan. Canada's premiere agricultural event is the world's largest indoor livestock show and marketplace. More than 4,000 cattle, sheep, swine and horses are brought to Agribition, plus pedigreed seed show and agricultural trade and technology show. Livestock producers from around the world come to compare breeding stocks and programs, perhaps importing new bloodlines based on what they discover. Winning at Agribition brings recognition as a producer of quality breeding stock. Also, a variety of entertainment, including the province's biggest indoor professional rodeo. Est attendance: 150,000. For info: (306) 565-0565 or Tourism Saskatchewan, 500-1900 Albert St, Regina, Sask, Canada S4P 4L9. Phone: (800) 667-7191. Email: travel.info@sasktourism.sk.ca. WWW: http://www.sasktourism.com

CARMICHAEL, HOAGIE: BIRTH ANNIVERSARY. Nov 22. Hoagland Howard Carmichael, attorney who gave up the practice of law to become an actor and songwriter, was born at Bloomington, IN, Nov 22, 1899. Among his many popular songs: "Stardust," "Lazybones," "Two Sleepy People" and "Skylark." Carmichael died at Rancho Mirage, CA, Dec 27, 1981.

CHINA CLIPPER ANNIVERSARY. Nov 22. A Pan American Martin 130 "flying boat" called the *China Clipper* began regular trans-Pacific mail service on Nov 22, 1935. The plane, powered by four Pratt and Whitney Twin Wasp engines and piloted by Captain Edwin Musick, took off from San Francisco. It reached Manila, Philippines, 59 hours and 48 minutes later. About 20,000 persons watched the historic take-off. Commercial passenger service was established the following year (Oct 21, 1936).

De GAULLE, CHARLES ANDRE MARIE: BIRTH ANNIVERSARY. Nov 22, 1890. President of France from December 1958 until his resignation in April 1969, Charles de Gaulle was born at Lille, France, Nov 22, 1890. A military leader, he wrote *The Army of the Future* (1934) in which he predicted just the type of armored warfare that was used against his country by Nazi Germany in WW II. After France's defeat at the hands of the Germans, he declared the existence of "Free France" and made himself head of that organization. When the French Vichy government began to collaborate openly with the Germans, the French citizenry looked to De Gaulle for leadership. His greatest moment of triumph was when he entered liberated Paris on Aug 26, 1944. De Gaulle died at Colombey-les-Deux-Eglises, France, Nov 19, 1970.

ELIOT, GEORGE: BIRTH ANNIVERSARY. Nov 22. English novelist George Eliot, whose real name was Mary Ann Evans, was born at Chilvers Coton, Warwickshire, England, on Nov 22, 1819. She died at Chelsea, Dec 22, 1880.

GARNER, JOHN NANCE: BIRTH ANNIVERSARY. Nov 22, 1868. Thirty-second vice president of US (1933–41) born at Red River County, TX, Nov 22, 1868. Died at Uvalde, TX, Nov 7, 1967.

GERMANY: TOTENSONNTAG. Nov 22. In Germany, Totensonntag is the Protestant population's day for remembrance of the dead. It is celebrated on the last Sunday of the church year (the Sunday before Advent).

GIFT SHOWCASE. Nov 22. Woodbury, CT. This 7th annual showcase includes more than 50 traditional craftsmen and artisans creating and demonstrating their talents. For info: Merry Go Round, 319 Main St S, Woodbury, CT 06798. Phone: (203) 263-2920.

KENNEDY, JOHN F.: 35th ASSASSINATION ANNIVERSARY. Nov 22, 1963. President John F. Kennedy was slain by a sniper while riding in an open automobile at Dallas, TX, Nov 22, 1963. Accused Lee Harvey Oswald was killed in police custody awaiting trial as assassin.

LEBANON: INDEPENDENCE DAY. Nov 22. National Day.

"LIFE WITH FATHER" TV PREMIERE: 45th ANNIVERSARY. Nov 22, 1953. This less successful comedy followed a very successful book, Broadway play and movie based on Clarence Day, Jr's essays in *Harper's Magazine* and *The New Yorker.* The cast included Leon Ames as Clarence Day, Sr; Lurene Tuttle as his wife Vinnie; Ralph Reed and Steven Terrell as Clarence, Jr, the eldest son; Freddie Leiston and Malcolm Cassell as second son, John; Ronald Keith, B.G. Norman and Freddy Ridgeway as third son, Whitney; Harvey Grant as youngest son, Harlan; and Dorothy Bernard as the maid, Margaret.

MOTHER GOOSE PARADE. Nov 22. El Cajon, CA. "A celebration of children." Floats depict Mother Goose rhymes and fairy tales. Bands, equestrians and clowns. Traditionally, the Sunday before Thanksgiving. Est attendance: 450,000. For info: Mother Goose Parade Assn, 480 N Magnolia Ave, Ste 106, El Cajon, CA 92020. Phone: (619) 444-8712. Fax: (619) 444-3971.

NATIONAL ADOPTION WEEK. Nov 22–28. To commemorate the success of three kinds of adoption—infant, special needs and intercountry—through a variety of special events. Annually, the week of Thanksgiving. Est attendance: 15,000. For info: Natl Council for Adoption, 1930 17th St NW, Washington, DC 20009-6207. Phone: (202) 328-1200. Fax: (202) 332-0935.

NATIONAL BIBLE WEEK. Nov 22–29. An interfaith campaign to promote reading and study of the Bible. Resource packets available. Governors and mayors across the country proclaim National Bible Week observance in their constituencies. Annually, from the Sunday preceding Thanksgiving to the following Sunday. For info: Thomas R. May, Exec Dir, Laymen's Natl Bible Assn, Inc, 1865 Broadway, 12th Fl, New York, NY 10023. Phone: (212) 408-1390.

NATIONAL GAME AND PUZZLE WEEK. Nov 22–28. To increase appreciation of games and puzzles while conserving the tradition of investing time with family and friends. Annually, the last week in November. For info: Dana Heideman, Patch Products, PO Box 268, Beloit, WI 53512-0268. Phone: (608) 362-6896. Fax: (608) 362-8178.
Email: patch@patchproducts.com.
WWW: http://www.patchproducts.com

POST, WILEY: 100th BIRTH ANNIVERSARY. Nov 22, 1898. Barnstorming aviator, stunt parachutist and adventurer, Wiley Post was born at Grand Plain, TX, on Nov 22, 1898. Post, who taught himself to fly, and his plane, the *Winnie Mae*, were the center of world attention in the 1930s. He was co-author (with his navigator, Harold Gatty) of *Around the World in Eight Days*. In 1935, Post and friend Will Rogers started on a flight to the Orient. Plane crashed near Point Barrow, AK, on Aug 15, 1935; both were killed.

TWO CENTURIES OF CHRISTMAS IN AMERICA. Nov 22–Jan 4. Herbert Hoover Presidential Museum, West Branch, IA. The museum's annual holiday display features Christmas trees decorated in the tradition of American customs. Est attendance: 10,000. For info: Herbert Hoover Presidential Museum, PO Box 488, West Branch, IA 52358. Phone: (319) 643-5301. Fax: (319) 643-5825. WWW: http://www.nara.gov/nara/president/hoover

PRIME MINISTER THATCHER RESIGNS: ANNIVERSARY. Nov 22, 1990. Margaret Thatcher announced that she would resign from her position as England's prime minister. No other prime minister in the 20th century has served the post as long as she.

SAINT CECILIA: FEAST DAY. Nov 22. Roman virgin, Christian martyr and patron of music and musicians lived during third century. Survived sentences of burning and beheading. Subject of poetry and musical compositions and her feast day is still an occasion for musical events.

STAR OF WONDER PLANETARIUM SHOW. Nov 22–Jan 4, 1998. Newport News, VA.

BIRTHDAYS TODAY

Boris Franz Becker, 31, tennis player, born Leimen, Germany, Nov 22, 1967.
Tom Conti, 57, actor, born Paisley, Scotland, Nov 22, 1941.
Jamie Lee Curtis, 40, actress (Hannah on "Anything But Love"; *Love Letters, A Fish Called Wanda*), born Los Angeles, CA, Nov 22, 1958.
Rodney Dangerfield (Jacob Cohen), 77, comedian, actor (*Easy Money, Caddyshack, Back to School*, "The Dean Martin Show"), born Babylon, NY, Nov 22, 1921.
Harry Edwards, 56, sports sociologist, born St. Louis, MO, Nov 22, 1942.
Allen Garfield, 59, actor (*Bananas, The Conversation, Dick Tracy*), born Newark, NJ, Nov 22, 1939.
Stephen Geoffreys, 39, actor (*Heaven Help Us, 976-EVIL*), born Cincinnati, OH, Nov 22, 1959.
Terry Gilliam, 58, actor, writer ("Monty Python's Flying Circus," *Life of Brian*), director (*Brazil*), born Minneapolis, MN, Nov 22, 1940.
Mariel Hemingway, 37, actress (*Manhattan, Personal Best, Superman IV*), born Ketchum, ID, Nov 22, 1961.
Billie Jean King, 55, former tennis player who beat Bobby Riggs in the "Battle of the Sexes" match, born Long Beach, CA, Nov 22, 1943.

November 1998

S	M	T	W	T	F	S
1	2	3	4	5	6	7
8	9	10	11	12	13	14
15	16	17	18	19	20	21
22	23	24	25	26	27	28
29	30					

Claiborne Pell, 80, former US Senator (D, Rhode Island), born New York, NY, Nov 22, 1918.
Robert Vaughn, 66, actor ("The Man From U.N.C.L.E.," *The Magnificent Seven*), born New York, NY, Nov 22, 1932.

NOVEMBER 23 — MONDAY

Day 327 — 38 Remaining

ASHFORD, EMMETT LITTLETON: BIRTH ANNIVERSARY. Nov 23, 1914. Emmett Littleton Ashford, born at Los Angeles, CA, was the first black to officiate at a major league baseball game. Ashford began his pro career calling games in the minors in 1951 and went to the majors in 1966. He was noted for his flamboyant style when calling strikes and outs as well as for his dapper dress which included cufflinks with his uniform. He died Mar 1, 1980, at Marina del Rey, CA.

BILLY THE KID: BIRTH ANNIVERSARY. Nov 23, 1859. Legendary outlaw of western US. Probably named Henry McCarty at birth (New York, NY), he was better known as William H. Bonney. Ruthless killer, a failure at everything legal, he escaped from jail at age 21 while under sentence of hanging. Recaptured at Stinking Springs, NM, and returned to jail, he again escaped, only to be shot through the heart by pursuing Lincoln County Sheriff Pat Garrett at Fort Sumner, NM, during the night of July 14, 1881. His last words, answered by two shots, reportedly were "Who is there?"

"DR. WHO" PREMIERE: 35th ANNIVERSARY. Nov 23, 1963. First episode of "Dr. Who" premiered on British TV with William Hartnell as the first doctor. Traveling through time and space in the TARDIS (an acronym for Time and Relative Dimensions in Space), the doctor and his companions found themselves in mortal combat with creatures such as the Daleks. "Dr. Who" didn't air in the US until almost 10 years later.

FIRST PLAY-BY-PLAY FOOTBALL GAME BROADCAST: ANNIVERSARY. Nov 23. The first play-by-play football game broadcast in the United States took place on this day in 1919. Texas A&M blanked the University of Texas 7–0.

GILBERT ISLANDS TAKEN: 55th ANNIVERSARY. Nov 23, 1943. The US Second Marine Division took control of the Gilbert Islands after fierce fighting on the heavily fortified Tarawa Atoll. In the 76-hour battle the Marines beat back a "death charge" in which the Japanese ran directly at the American guns. American troops sustained 3,500 killed and wounded. The Japanese suffered 5,000 killed and 17 wounded and captured. (The Gilbert Islands are the westernmost of the Polynesians, midway between Australia and Hawaii.)

JAPAN: LABOR THANKSGIVING DAY. Nov 23. National holiday.

KARLOFF, BORIS: BIRTH ANNIVERSARY. Nov 23, 1887. Born William Henry Pratt at London, England. An actor known for his portrayl of ghoulish figures. His movies included *Frankenstein, The Body Snatcher* and *The Bride of Frankenstein*. Karloff died Feb 2, 1969.

NAIA MEN'S SOCCER NATIONAL CHAMPIONSHIP. Nov 23–28. 12-team field competes for national championship. 40th annual. For info: Kevin Henry, Natl Assn of Intercollegiate Athletics, 6120 S Yale Ave, Ste 1450, Tulsa, OK 74136-4223. Phone: (918) 494-8828. Fax: (918) 494-8841.
Email: khenry@naia.org. WWW: http://www.naia.org

NAIA WOMEN'S SOCCER NATIONAL CHAMPIONSHIP. Nov 23–28. Site to be determined. Eight-team field competes for national championship. 15th annual. Est attendance: 3,000. For info: Kevin Henry, Natl Assn of Intercollegiate Athletics, 6120 S Yale Ave, Ste 1450, Ste 1450, Tulsa, OK 74136-4223. Phone: (918) 494-8828. Fax: (918) 494-8841. Email: khenry@naia.org. WWW: http://www.naia.org

NATIONAL FAMILY CAREGIVERS WEEK. Nov 23–29. A nationwide week of recognition for the millions of family caregivers. For info: Suzanne Geffen Mintz, Pres, Natl Family Caregivers Assn, 9621 E Bexhill Dr, Kensington, MD 20895-3104. Phone: (800) 896-3650. Fax: (301) 942-2302. Email: info@nfcacares.org. WWW: http://www.nfcacares.org

PIERCE, FRANKLIN: BIRTH ANNIVERSARY. Nov 23. The 14th president of the US was born at Hillsboro, NH, Nov 23, 1804. Term of office: Mar 4, 1853–Mar 3, 1857. Not nominated until the 49th ballot at the Democratic party convention in 1852, he was refused his party's nomination in 1856 for a second term. Pierce died at Concord, NH, Oct 8, 1869.

RUTLEDGE, EDWARD: BIRTH ANNIVERSARY. Nov 23. Signer of the Declaration of Independence, governor of South Carolina, born at Charleston, SC, Nov 23, 1749. Died there Jan 23, 1800.

SAGITTARIUS, THE ARCHER. Nov 23–Dec 21. In the astronomical/astrological zodiac that divides the sun's apparent orbit into 12 segments, the period Nov 22–Dec 21 is identified, traditionally, as the sun-sign of Sagittarius, the Archer. The ruling planet is Jupiter.

SWITZERLAND: ONION MARKET (ZIBELEMARIT). Nov 23. Berne. Best known and most popular of Switzerland's many autumn markets. Great heaps of onions in front of Federal Palace. Fourth Monday in November commemorates granting of market right to people after great fire of Berne in 1405.

BIRTHDAYS TODAY

Susan Anspach, 53, actress (*Five Easy Pieces, Play It Again Sam, Montenegro*), born New York, NY, Nov 23, 1945.

Jerry Bock, 70, composer ("Fiddler on the Roof," "Fiorello"), born New Haven, CT, Nov 23, 1928.

Mary L. Landrieu, 43, US Senator (D, Louisiana), born Arlington, VA, Nov 23, 1955.

Krzysztof Penderecki, 65, composer, born Debica, Poland, Nov 23, 1933.

Maurice Zolotow, 85, author (*Billy Wilder in Hollywood*), born New York, NY, Nov 23, 1913.

NOVEMBER 24 — TUESDAY

Day 328 — 37 Remaining

BARKLEY, ALBEN WILLIAM: BIRTH ANNIVERSARY. Nov 24, 1877. Thirty-fifth vice president of the US (1949–53), born at Graves County, KY, Nov 24, 1877. Died at Lexington, VA, Apr 30, 1956.

BATTLE OF CHATTANOOGA: ANNIVERSARY. Nov 24, 1863. After reinforcing the besieged Union army at Chattanooga, TN, General Ulysses S. Grant launched the Battle of Chattanooga on Nov 24, 1863. Falsely secure in the knowledge that his troops were in an impregnable position on Lookout Mountain, Confederate General Braxton Bragg and his army were overrun by the Union forces, Bragg himself barely escaping capture. The battle is famous for the Union Army's spectacular advance up a heavily fortified slope into the teeth of the enemy guns.

CARNEGIE, DALE: BIRTH ANNIVERSARY. Nov 24, 1888. American inspirational lecturer and author, Dale Carnegie was born at Maryville, MO, Nov 24, 1888. His best known book, *How to Win Friends and Influence People*, published in 1936, sold nearly five million copies and was translated into 29 languages. Carnegie died at New York, NY, Nov 1, 1955.

"D.B. COOPER" HIJACKING: ANNIVERSARY. Nov 24–25. A middle-aged man whose plane ticket was made out to "D.B. Cooper" parachuted from a Northwest Airlines 727 jetliner on Nov 25, 1971, carrying $200,000 which he had collected from the airline as ransom for the plane and passengers as a result of threats he made during his Nov 24th flight from Portland, OR, to Seattle, WA. He jumped from the plane over an area of wilderness south of Seattle and was never apprehended. Several thousand dollars of the marked ransom money turned up in February 1980, along the Columbia River, near Vancouver, WA.

JOPLIN, SCOTT: BIRTH ANNIVERSARY. Nov 24, 1868. American musician and composer famed for his piano rags, born at Texarkana, TX, Nov 24, 1868. Died at New York, NY, Apr 1, 1917.

MANSTEIN, ERICH von: BIRTH ANNIVERSARY. Nov 24, 1887. Considered by many to be the greatest strategist of World War II, Erich von Manstein was born at Berlin, Germany. His plan for the invasion of France in 1940 was a complete success. He was dismissed by Hitler in March 1944. Manstein died at Irschenhausen, Germany, on June 10, 1973.

ROCKWOOD CHRISTMAS. Nov 24–Jan 3. Rockwood Museum, Wilmington, DE. Celebrate Christmas with the Bringhurst family at the turn of the century. Victorian manor house decorated festively. Evening dramas with actors portraying family members on Dec 10, 11, 12; matinees Dec 13. Annually, the Tuesday before Thanksgiving to the Sunday after New Year. Est attendance: 2,300. For info: Rockwood Museum, 610 Shipley Rd, Wilmington, DE 19809. Phone: (302) 761-4340. Fax: (302) 764-4570. Email: info@rockwood.org. WWW: http://www.rockwood.org

"SIMON & SIMON" TV PREMIERE: ANNIVERSARY. Nov 24, 1981. This popular crime show about private eye brothers starred Jameson Parker as smooth, educated A.J. Simon and Gerald McRaney as brother Rick, a Vietnam vet. Other featured actors included Mary Carver as Cecilia Simon, their mother; Eddie Barth as rival detective Myron Fowler; Jeannie Wilson as Myron's daughter Janet, a district attorney; Tim Reid as undercover policeman Downtown Brown; and Joan McMurtrey as Lt Abby Marsh. The series was based on a 1980 made-for-TV movie called "Pirate's Key," with the series locale shifted from Florida to San Diego. Though originally not a hit, its popularity increased after some changes and a time slot following "Magnum, PI."

SPINOZA, BARUCH: BIRTH ANNIVERSARY. Nov 24, 1632. Dutch philosopher, born at Amsterdam, Nov 24, 1632. Died Feb 21, 1677. "Peace is not an absence of war," wrote Spinoza, in 1670, "it is a virtue, a state of mind, a disposition for benevolence, confidence, justice."

☆ ☆ ☆

STERNE, LAURENCE: BIRTH ANNIVERSARY. Nov 24, 1713. Novelist, author, born Nov 24, 1713. Died at London, England, Mar 18, 1768. In his dedication to *Tristram Shandy*, Sterne wrote: "I live in a constant endeavour to fence against the infirmities of ill health, and other evils of life, by mirth; being firmly persuaded that every time a man smiles,—but much more so, when he laughs, that it adds something to this Fragment of Life."

TAYLOR, ZACHARY: BIRTH ANNIVERSARY. Nov 24. The soldier who became 12th president of the US was born at Orange County, VA, Nov 24, 1784. Term of office: Mar 4, 1849–July 9, 1850. He was nominated at the Whig party convention in 1848, but, the story goes, he did not accept the letter notifying him of his nomination because it had postage due. He cast his first vote in 1846, when he was 62 years old. Becoming ill on July 4, 1850, he died at the White House, July 9. His last words: "I am sorry that I am about to leave my friends."

US MILITARY LEAVES PHILIPPINES: ANNIVERSARY. Nov 24. The Philippines became a US colony at the turn of the century when it was taken over from Spain after the Spanish American War. Though President Franklin D. Roosevelt signed a bill Mar 24, 1934, granting the Philippines independence to be effective July 4, 1946, before that date Manila and Washington signed a treaty allowing the US to lease military bases on the island. In 1991 the Philippine Senate voted to reject a renewal of that lease, and Nov 24, 1992, after almost 100 years of military presence on the island, the last contingent of US marines left Subic Base.

BIRTHDAYS TODAY

William Frank Buckley, 73, editor (*The National Review*), author (*God and Man at Yale*), born New York, NY, Nov 24, 1925.

Dan Glickman, 54, US Secretary of Agriculture in Clinton administration, born Wichita, KS, Nov 24, 1944.

Garson Kanin, 86, author (*A Gift of Time, Tracy & Hepburn, Born Yesterday*), director (*Adam's Rib, Pat & Mike*), born Rochester, NY, Nov 24, 1912.

Alfredo Kraus, 71, opera singer, born Las Palmas, Canary Islands, Nov 24, 1927.

Stanley Livingston, 48, actor ("My Three Sons"), born Los Angeles, CA, Nov 24, 1950.

Oscar Palmer Robertson, 60, Basketball Hall of Fame guard, born Charlotte, TN, Nov 24, 1938.

Dwight Schultz, 51, actor ("Star Trek: The Next Generation," *Fat Man and Little Boy*), born Baltimore, MD, Nov 24, 1947.

NOVEMBER 25 — WEDNESDAY

Day 329 — 36 Remaining

AUTOMOBILE SPEED REDUCTION: 25th ANNIVERSARY. Nov 25, 1973. Anniversary of the presidential order, Nov 25, 1973, requiring a cutback from the 70 mile-per-hour speed limit. The 55 mile-per-hour National Maximum Speed Limit (NMSL) was established by the Congress in January 1974 (PL 93–643). The National Highway Traffic Administration reported that "analysis of available data shows that the 55 mph NMSL forestalled 48,310 fatalities through 1980. There were also reductions in crash-related injuries and property damage." Motor fuel savings were estimated at 2.4 billion gallons per year. Notwithstanding, in 1987 the Congress permitted states to increase speed limits on rural interstate highways to 65 miles per hour.

CARNEGIE, ANDREW: BIRTH ANNIVERSARY. Nov 25. American financier, philanthropist and benefactor of more than 2,500 libraries, was born at Dunfermline, Scotland, Nov 25, 1835. Carnegie Hall, Carnegie Foundation and the Carnegie Endowment for International Peace are among his gifts. Carnegie wrote in 1889, "Surplus wealth is a sacred trust which its possessor is bound to administer in his lifetime for the good of the community. . . . The man who dies . . . rich dies disgraced." Carnegie died at his summer estate, "Shadowbrook," MA, on Aug 11, 1919.

CARRS GREAT ALASKA SHOOTOUT. Nov 25–28. Sullivan Area, Anchorage, AK. Top NCAA basketball action as eight men's division I teams from around the country compete. Est attendance: 48,000. For info: Univ of Alaska-Anchorage, Athletic Dept, 3211 Providence Dr, Anchorage, AK 99508. Phone: (907) 786-1230. Fax: (907) 563-4565. Email: antlm@uaa.alaska.edu.

CHRISTMAS LIGHTS (CITY OF LIGHTS). Nov 25–Jan 3. Natchitoches, LA. A fairyland of multi-colored lights, created by 170,000 Christmas bulbs strung along city streets and incorporated into 72 unique set pieces along Cane River Lake. The lights reflect in the waters below and stretch along the historic downtown area, while the set pieces create a panoramic view on the east bank of the river. Est attendance: 100,000. For info: Natchitoches Parish Tourist Commission, Calendar of Events, 781 Front St, Natchitoches, LA 71457. Phone: (318) 352-8072. Fax: (318) 352-2415.

GERMANY: FRANKFURT CHRISTMAS MARKET. Nov 25–Dec 23. "Weinachtsmarkt auf dem Romerberg," the Christmas market in Frankfurt, is one of Germany's best. Bells are rung simultaneously from nine downtown churches. Glockenspiels are sounded by hand and trumpets blown from the old St. Nicolas Church.

NATION, CARRY AMELIA MOORE: BIRTH ANNIVERSARY. Nov 25. American temperance leader, famed as hatchet-wielding smasher of saloons, born at Garrard County, KY, Nov 25, 1846. Died at Leavenworth, KS, June 9, 1911.

POPE JOHN XXIII: BIRTH ANNIVERSARY. Nov 25, 1881. Angelo Roncalli, 261st pope of the Roman Catholic Church, born at Sotte il Monte, Italy, on Nov 25, 1881. Elected pope, Oct 28, 1958. Died June 3, 1963.

SAINT CATHERINE'S DAY. Nov 25. Patron saint of maidens, mechanics and philosophers, as well as of all who work with wheels.

SHOPPING REMINDER DAY. Nov 25. One month before Christmas, a reminder to shoppers that there are only 23 more shopping days (excluding Sundays, Thanksgiving and Christmas Eve) after today until Christmas, and that one month from today a new countdown will begin for Christmas 1999.

SURINAME: INDEPENDENCE DAY. Nov 25. Holiday.

WONDERLAND OF LIGHTS. Nov 25–Dec 30. Marshall, TX. More than seven million tiny white lights cover the city. Features the living Christmas tree, JC's lighted Christmas parade, candlelight home tours. Outdoor ice skating on the square and live entertainment on the square Tuesdays, Thursdays, Fridays and Saturdays. Second Saturday (Dec 12th), Cowboy Christmas Celebration with breakfast, entertainment, stick-horse races, mule rides, carriage rides, bus tours and Santa Claus. Est attendance: 750,000. For info: Pam Whisenant, Dir of Conv & Visitors Dvmt, Greater Marshall Chamber of Commerce, PO Box 520, Marshall, TX 75671. Phone: (903) 935-7868 or cvd@internetwork.net. Fax: (903) 935-9982.

BIRTHDAYS TODAY

Christina Applegate, 27, actress ("Married . . . with Children"), born Hollywood, CA, Nov 25, 1971.

Kathryn Crosby, 65, actress, born Houston, TX, Nov 25, 1933.

Russell Earl ("Bucky") Dent (born Russell Earl O'Dey), 47, former baseball player and manager, born Savannah, GA, Nov 25, 1951.

Joseph Paul (Joe) DiMaggio, 84, Baseball Hall of Fame outfielder, born Martinez, CA, Nov 25, 1914.

Joe Jackson Gibbs, 58, sportscaster, Pro Football Hall of Fame coach, born Mocksville, NC, Nov 25, 1940.

Amy Grant, 38, singer ("Baby, Baby"), born Augusta, GA, Nov 25, 1960.

John F. Kennedy Jr, 38, lawyer, editor (*George*), born Washington, DC, Nov 25, 1960.

Bernie Joseph Kosar, Jr, 35, football player, born Boardman, OH, Nov 25, 1963.

John Larroquette, 51, actor (Emmy for "Night Court"; *Richie Rich*, "The John Larroquette Show"), born New Orleans, LA, Nov 25, 1947.

November 1998

S	M	T	W	T	F	S
1	2	3	4	5	6	7
8	9	10	11	12	13	14
15	16	17	18	19	20	21
22	23	24	25	26	27	28
29	30					

Lenny Moore, 65, Pro Football Hall of Fame halfback, born Reading, PA, Nov 25, 1933.

NOVEMBER 26 — THURSDAY

Day 330 — 35 Remaining

AMERICAN BICYCLE ASSOCIATION GRAND NATIONALS. Nov 26–29. Myriad Convention Center, Oklahoma City, OK. This World Championship BMX (bike motocross) competition draws more than 10,000 contestants and out-of-state spectators from at least 15 countries, making it the largest out-of-state visitor attraction in the nation to be held during the Thanksgiving holidays. Est attendance: 25,000. For info: OK City All Sports Assn, 100 W Main, Ste 285, Oklahoma City, OK 73102. Phone: (405) 236-5000. Fax: (405) 236-5008.

AMERICA'S THANKSGIVING PARADE. Nov 26. Woodward Ave, Detroit, MI. The 72nd annual parade kicks off the holiday season with nearly 100 units marching. Annually, on Thanksgiving morning. Est attendance: 1,300,000. For info: Dennis Carnovale, The Parade Co, 9600 Mt Elliott, Detroit, MI 48211. Phone: (313) 923-7400. Fax: (313) 923-2920.

ATLANTA MARATHON AND ATLANTA HALF MARATHON. Nov 26. Atlanta, GA. 26.2-mile and 13.1-mile races. Advance registration only; entry forms available in July. Send SASE. Est attendance: 8,000. For info: Atlanta Track Club, Calendar Dept, 3097 E Shadowlawn Ave, Atlanta, GA 30305. Phone: (404) 231-9064. Race Hotline (Atlanta area) (404) 262-RACE.

CASABLANCA PREMIERE: ANNIVERSARY. Nov 26, 1942. Due to the landing of the Allies in North Africa on Nov 8, the premiere and release of the film were moved up from June 1943 to Nov 26, 1942, when it premiered in New York City on Thanksgiving Day. The general nationwide release followed on Jan 23, 1943, during the Roosevelt-Churchill conferences in Casablanca.

CHANNEL 6 THANKSGIVING DAY PARADE. Nov 26. Philadelphia, PA. Est attendance: 300,000. For info: Valerie Lagauskas, Parade Dir, WPVI-TV, 4100 City Line Ave, Philadelphia, PA 19131. Phone: (215) 581-4529.

CUSACK, CYRIL: BIRTH ANNIVERSARY. Nov 26, 1910. Irish actor Cyril Cusack was born at Durban, South Africa. He began his acting career in 1932 with the Abbey Theater at Dublin. His films include *The Spy Who Came in from the Cold* (1965), *The Taming of the Shrew* (1967) and *My Left Foot* (1989). He died on Oct 7, 1993, at London, England.

CUSTER BATTLEFIELD BECOMES LITTLE BIGHORN BATTLEFIELD: ANNIVERSARY. Nov 26. The US Congress approved a bill on Nov 26, 1991, renaming Custer Battlefield National Monument as Little Bighorn Battlefield National Monument. The bill also authorized the construction of a memorial to the Native Americans who fought and died at the battle known as Custer's Last Stand. Introduced by then Representative Ben Nighthorse Campbell, the only Native American in Congress, the bill was signed into law by President George Bush.

FIRST US HOLIDAY BY PRESIDENTIAL PROCLAMATION: ANNIVERSARY. Nov 26. President George Washington proclaimed Nov 26, 1789, to be Thanksgiving Day. Both Houses of Congress, by their joint committee, had requested him to recommend a day of public thanksgiving and prayer, to be observed by acknowledging with grateful hearts the many and signal favors of Almighty God, especially by affording them an opportunity to peaceably establish a form of government for their safety and happiness. Proclamation issued Oct 3, 1789.

FOODS AND FEASTS OF COLONIAL VIRGINIA. Nov 26–28. Jamestown Settlement, Williamsburg, VA. Daily activities devoted to the foodways of the 17th-century Jamestown colonists and Powhatan Indians at Jamestown Settlement and 18th-century Revolutionary War soldiers and Virginia farmers at Yorktown Victory Center. Est attendance: 5,000. For info: Media Relations, Jamestown-Yorktown Fdtn, PO Box 1607, Williamsburg, VA 23187. Phone: (757) 253-4838.
WWW: http://www.historyisfun.org

GATLINBURG CHRISTMAS MARKET. Nov 26–28. Gatlinburg Convention Center, Gatlinburg, TN. A Christmas extravaganza with festive shopping, daily entertainment, prizes and holiday fun for the entire family. Thursday-Saturday 10 AM until 6 PM. Est attendance: 14,000. For info: Cindy Crabtree, Esau, Inc, PO Box 50096, Knoxville, TN 37950. Phone: (423) 588-1233 or (800) 588-ESAU. Fax: (423) 588-6938.

GRIMKE, SARAH MOORE: BIRTH ANNIVERSARY. Nov 26, 1792. American antislavery and women's rights advocate along with her sister Angelina. Born on Nov 26, 1792 at Charleston, SC, and died on Dec 23, 1873, at Hyde Park, MA.

JAPAN AGREES TO END USE OF DRIFT NETS: ANNIVERSARY. Nov 26. On Nov 26, 1991, Japan agreed to comply with a 1989 United Nations moratorium on the use of huge fishing nets in the Northern Pacific Ocean. The large nets extend up to 40 miles and have been criticized as "walls of death," causing wide-spread destruction of marine life, including whales, turtles, birds and many varieties of fish. Japan agreed to end half of its driftnet fishing by the June 30, 1992, deadline, and the remainder by the end of 1992.

JOHN HARVARD DAY: BIRTH ANNIVERSARY. Nov 26. English clergyman and scholar, founder of Harvard College. Born Nov 26, 1607 and died Sept 24, 1638.

LONGWOOD GARDENS CHRISTMAS DISPLAY. Nov 26–Jan 3. Kennett Square, PA. Indoor Conservatory display of thousands of poinsettias, decorated trees, daily concerts. Outdoors, 400,000 lights and holiday fountain displays. Est attendance: 150,000. For info: Longwood Gardens, PO Box 501, Kennett Square, PA 19348-0501. Phone: (610) 388-1000. WWW: http://www.longwoodgardens.org

MACY'S THANKSGIVING DAY PARADE. Nov 26. New York, NY. Starts at 9 AM, EST, in Central Park West. A part of everyone's Thanksgiving, the parade grows bigger and better each year. Featuring floats, giant balloons, marching bands and famous stars, the parade is televised for the whole country. 70th annual parade. For info: New York Conv/Visitors Bureau, Macy's Thanksgiving Day Parade, 2 Columbus Circle, New York, NY 10019. Phone: 800-NYC-VISIT. WWW: http://www.nycvisit.com

MOON PHASE: FIRST QUARTER. Nov 26. Moon enters First Quarter phase at 7:23 PM, EST.

NIGHTS OF LIGHTS CELEBRATION. Nov 26–Jan 31, 1999. St. Augustine, FL. The Oldest City presents more than one million lights in a spectacular Christmas holiday backdrop for themed historical events including British Night Watch, The Grand Illumination and the St. Augustine Parade, all on Saturday Dec 5. For info: Gilbert & Manjura Marketing, 346 Freeman St, Longwood, FL 33780-4171. Phone: (407) 261-5700. Fax: (407) 261-5710.

OLD TYME FARM DAYS. Nov 26–29. Live Oak, FL. Festivities include cane grinding, syrup soppin', wagon trail ride, antique farm equipment, bluegrass music and other fun-filled activities. Est attendance: 12,000. For info: James Cornett, Spirit of the Suwannee Music Park, 3076 95th Dr, Live Oak, FL 32060. Phone: (904) 364-1683. Fax: (904) 364-2998.
Email: spirit@musicliveshere.com.
WWW: http://www.musicliveshere.com

PLAZA LIGHTS. Nov 26–Jan 11. Country Club Plaza, Kansas City, MO. Annual lighting ceremony heralds the beginning of the holiday season. Over 200,000 jewel-colored lights, spanning 75 miles, illuminate the outline of every tower, balcony and courtyard of a 14-square block area. Christmas shopping against a backdrop of the Plaza Lights is a Kansas City tradition that began with a single strand of lights over a store entrance in 1925. Est attendance: 250,000. For info: Plaza Merchants Assn, 450 Ward Pkwy, Kansas City, MO 64112. Phone: (816) 753-0100. Fax: (816) 753-4625.

"THE PRICE IS RIGHT" TV PREMIERE: ANNIVERSARY. Nov 26, 1956. This popular show is also TV's longest-running daily game show, surviving changes in format, networks, time slots and hosts. It began in 1956 with Bill Cullen as host, Don Pardo as announcer and a fairly rigid format: four contestants had to bid on an item and the one who bid closest to the manufacturer's suggested price without going over won the item. In 1972, after a seven-year hiatus, "The Price Is Right" came back in two versions. Bob Barker was the host of the network version, which expanded to an hour and which he hosts to this day. Johnny Olsen was the announcer until his death in 1985. Rod Roddy took his place and continues to announce. Also on the show are attractive women who model the prizes to be won and give Bob Barker minimal assistance in setting up the price-guessing games. The number of contestants has expanded to a rotating number, as a contestant wins a chance to play a game and then a new contestant takes his or her place in "Contestant Row." There is also a final round called the "Showcase Showdown," in which two contestants try to come closest to the price of a themed selection of prizes in order to win them. "Price" contestants are drawn from the studio audience and are known for their enthusiasm and love of the show and its sometimes scandal-ridden host.

QUEEN ELIZABETH AGREES TO PAY TAXES: ANNIVERSARY. Nov 26, 1992. Prime Minister John Major announced on Nov 26, 1992, that Britain's monarch, Queen Elizabeth, had decided to begin paying taxes on her personal income.

SEVAREID, ERIC: BIRTH ANNIVERSARY. Nov 26, 1912. American journalist Eric (Arnold) Sevareid was born at Velva, ND. He worked for CBS News as a radio reporter during World War II; appeared regularly on "The CBS News with Walter Cronkite" from 1964 to 1977; won the Peabody Award for news interpretations (1950, 1964 and 1967) and earned two Emmys in 1973. He died on July 9, 1992 at Washington, DC.

SOUTH CAROLINA STATE BLUEGRASS FESTIVAL. Nov 26–28. Convention Center, Myrtle Beach, SC. 29th annual. Family entertainment. For info: Norman Adams, Box 98, Dahlonega, GA 30533. Phone: (706) 864-7203. Fax: (706) 863-1037.

STOCK EXCHANGE HOLIDAY (THANKSGIVING DAY). Nov 26. The holiday schedules for the various exchanges are subject to change if relevant rules, regulations or exchange policies are revised. If you have questions, phone: American Stock Exchange (212) 306-1000; Chicago Board of Trade (312) 435-3500; Chicago Board of Options Exchange (312) 786-5600; New York Stock Exchange (212) 656-2065; Pacific Stock Exchange (415) 393-4000; Philadelphia Stock Exchange (215) 496-5000.

★**THANKSGIVING DAY.** Nov 26. Presidential Proclamation. Always issued for the fourth Thursday in November. See also: "Anniversary of First US Holiday by Presidential Proclamation" (Nov 26).

November 1998

S	M	T	W	T	F	S
1	2	3	4	5	6	7
8	9	10	11	12	13	14
15	16	17	18	19	20	21
22	23	24	25	26	27	28
29	30					

THANKSGIVING DAY. Nov 26. Legal public holiday. (Public Law 90–363 sets Thanksgiving Day on the fourth Thursday in November). Observed on this day in all states.

TRUTH, SOJOURNER: DEATH ANNIVERSARY. Nov 26, 1883. A former slave who had been sold four different times, Sojourner Truth became an evangelist who argued for abolition and women's rights. After a troubled early life, she began her evangelical career in 1843, traveling through New England until she discovered the utopian colony called the Northampton Association of Education and Industry. It was there she was exposed to, and became an advocate for, the cause of abolition, working with Frederick Douglass, Wendall Phillips, William Lloyd Garrison and others. In 1850, she befriended Lucretia Mott, Elizabeth Cady Stanton and other feminist leaders and actively began supporting calls for women's rights. In 1870 she attempted to petition Congress to create a "Negro State" on public lands in the west. Born in Ulster County, NY, about 1790, she died on Nov 26, 1883, at Battle Creek, MI.

TURKEY TROT. Nov 26. Parkersburg City Park Pavilion, Parkersburg, WV. Three-mile fun run/walk on Thanksgiving morning. Drawings held for frozen turkeys and each participant receives a long-sleeved T-shirt. Est attendance: 650. For info: St. Joseph's Hospital, Rehab Services Dept, PO Box 327, Parkersburg, WV 26102. Phone: (304) 424-4393. Fax: (304) 424-4430.

"TWENTY QUESTIONS" TV PREMIERE: ANNIVERSARY. Nov 26, 1949. This game show was based on the old guessing game. A celebrity panel had to guess the identity of an object (at the start they were told only if it was animal, vegetable or mineral) by asking up to twenty questions. Bill Slater hosted two network versions of the show on NBC and DuMont. Jay Jackson took over when it switched from NBC to ABC. "Twenty Questions" first began on radio. Regular panelists included Fred Van Deventer, Florence Rinard, Herb Polesie and Johnny McPhee.

WALKER, MARY EDWARDS: BIRTH ANNIVERSARY. Nov 26, 1832. American physician and women's rights leader, born at Oswego, NY, Nov 26, 1832. First female surgeon in US Army (Civil War). Spent four months in Confederate prison. First and only woman ever to receive Medal of Honor (Nov 11, 1865). Two years before her death, on June 3, 1916, a government review board asked that her award be revoked. She continued to wear it, in spite of official revocation, until her death, Feb 21, 1919. On June 11, 1977, the secretary of the army posthumously restored the Medal of Honor to Dr. Walker.

"WHAT DO YOU LOVE ABOUT AMERICA" DAY. Nov 26. One day to talk about what's great about our country and its people. In the midst of cynicism, let's talk to each other about what we love. For info: Chuck Sutherland, 16 Linden, Wichita, KS 67206. Phone: (316) 688-0115. Fax: (316) 265-6902. Email: suther@swbell.net.

BIRTHDAYS TODAY

Richard (Rich) Caruthers Little, 60, impressionist, born Ottawa, Ontario, Canada, Nov 26, 1938.

Charles Monroe Schulz, 76, cartoonist ("Peanuts"), born Minneapolis, MN, Nov 26, 1922.

Tina Turner, 60, singer (with Ike: "A Fool in Love"; solo: "What's Love Got to Do With It"), born Nutbush, TN, Nov 26, 1938.

NOVEMBER 27 — FRIDAY

Day 331 — 34 Remaining

AGEE, JAMES: BIRTH ANNIVERSARY. Nov 27, 1909. Poet, novelist (*Let Us Now Praise Famous Men*), scriptwriter (*A Death in the Family*), born at Knoxville, TN. Died at New York, NY, May 16, 1955.

BANK BAILOUT BILL: ANNIVERSARY. Nov 27, 1991. Both houses of Congress approved legislation authorizing $70 billion in additional borrowing authority for the Federal Deposit Insurance Corporation (FDIC) on Nov 27, 1991.

BEARD, CHARLES A.: BIRTH ANNIVERSARY. Nov 27, 1874. American historian Charles Austin Beard who wrote many books in collaboration with his wife, Mary R. Beard, was born near Knightstown, IN, on Nov 27, 1874. He died at New Haven, CT, Sept 1, 1948.

BELSNICKEL CRAFT SHOW. Nov 27–28. Boyertown, PA. Sale of quality crafts with folk art emphasis. Annually, the first Friday and Saturday after Thanksgiving. Est attendance: 4,100. For info: Holly K. Green, Museum Dir, Boyertown Area Historical Society, 43 S Chestnut St, Boyertown, PA 19512. Phone: (610) 367-9843.

BENEDICT, JULIUS: BIRTH ANNIVERSARY. Nov 27. The German-born musician and composer Sir Julius Benedict was born at Stuttgart, Germany, on Nov 27, 1804. Knighted in 1871, Benedict died at London, England, June 5, 1885.

BLACK FRIDAY. Nov 27. The traditional beginning of the Christmas shopping season on the Friday after Thanksgiving.

CANADA: WINTERGREEN. Nov 27–29. Regina Sportsplex, Regina, Sask. Craft market features the finest in Saskatchewan crafts. Juried craft exhibition, children's pavilion, craft market and demonstrations. Est attendance: 7,000. For info: (306) 653-3616 or Tourism Saskatchewan, 500-1900 Albert St, Regina, Sask, Canada S4P 4L9. Phone: (800) 667-7191.
Email: travel.info@sasktourism.sk.ca.
WWW: http://www.sasktourism.com

CAPITAL HOLIDAY. Nov 27–Dec 31. Capital-Saratoga Region, NY. More than 100 events throughout the Capital-Saratoga Region. Activities include family events at historic homes, Victorian strolls and festive holiday performances. For info: Albany Conv and Visitors Bureau, 52 S Pearl St, Albany, NY 12207. Phone: (800) 258-3582. Fax: (518) 434-0887.
Email: accvb@albany.org. WWW: http://albany.org

CAROLINA CRAFTSMEN'S CHRISTMAS CLASSIC. Nov 27–29. Coliseum Special Events Center, Greensboro, NC. Arts and crafts. Est attendance: 35,000. For info: The Carolina Craftsmen, 1240 Oakland Ave, Greensboro, NC 27403. Phone: (910) 274-5550. Fax: (910) 274-1084.

A CHARLES DICKENS VICTORIAN CHRISTMAS. Nov 27–Dec 27. Mount Hope Estate and Winery, Manheim, PA. An open house in colorfully decorated Mount Hope Mansion, wine sampling in the billiards room, actors portraying such Dickens favorites as Tiny Tim, Oliver Twist and Ebeneezer Scrooge. Est attendance: 7,000. For info: Michelle Cunningham, Mgr of PR, Mount Hope Estate and Winery, PO Box 685, Cornwall, PA 17016. Phone: (717) 665-7021. Fax: (717) 664-3466.
Email: prfscrib@postoffice.net
WWW: http://www.parenaissancefaire.com/

CHRISTMAS AT THE CAPITOL. Nov 27–Dec 28. State Capitol Rotunda, Pierre, SD. More than 50 evergreens are decorated with handcrafted ornaments, each with its own theme. Est attendance: 50,000. For info: Kris Graham, Project Coord, 500 E Captiol Ave, Pierre, SD 57501. Phone: (605) 773-3661.

CHRISTMAS CANDLELIGHT TOUR. Nov 27–Dec 12. My Old Kentucky Home State Park, Bardstown, KY. Christmas in the style and flavor of the 1800s. Starts the day after Thanksgiving and runs 16 consecutive days. Est attendance: 10,000. For info: My Old Kentucky Home State Pk, PO Box 323, Hwy 150, Bardstown, KY 40004. Phone: (800) 323-7803 or (502) 348-3502. Fax: (502) 349-0054.

CHRISTMAS CANDLELIGHT TOURS. Nov 27–Dec 6. Nemacolin Castle, Brownsville, PA. Tour candlelit rooms adorned with fresh evergreen trees, flowers and holiday decorations. Hot wassail and cookies are served. For info: Tour Coord, Candlelight Tours at Nemacolin Castle, PO Box 24, Brownsville, PA 15417. Phone: (412) 785-6882.

CHRISTMAS CRAFT AND GIFT FESTIVAL. Nov 27–29. Cocoanut Grove, Santa Cruz, CA. A Victorian-themed festival, featuring hundreds of handmade gifts, foods and live entertainment also adorn this Santa Cruz tradition. Est attendance: 7,000. For info: Jan Bollwinkel-Smith, Pub Coord, 400 Beach St, Santa Cruz, CA 95060-5491. Phone: (408) 423-5590.
Email: publicity@scseaside.com.
WWW: http://www.beachboardwalk.com

CHRISTMAS IN OLD DODGE CITY. Nov 27–Dec 24. Citywide, Dodge City, KS. Home tours, bazaar, musical productions, 19th-century Christmas decorations in Old Dodge City and Dodge City Trolley City Christmas light tours. Annually, after Thanksgiving through Christmas. Est attendance: 5,000. For info: Dodge City Conv & Visitors Bureau, PO Box 1474, Dodge City, KS 67801. Phone: (316) 225-8186. Fax: (316) 225-8144. Email: dcvb@pld.com. WWW: http://trails.net/dgcity//

☆ ☆ ☆

DAYTONA TURKEY RUN. Nov 27–29. Daytona International Speedway, Daytona Beach, FL. 25th annual car show of all makes of 1972 and older collector vehicles. Show includes display of classics, sportscars, muscle cars, race cars, custom and special interest vehicles on the speedway infield all three days with a large swap meet of auto parts and accessories and car sales corral. Also crafts sale. Annually, Thanksgiving weekend. Est attendance: 50,000. For info: Rick D'Louhy, Exec Dir, Daytona Beach Racing and Recreational Facilities District, PO Box 1958, Daytona Beach, FL 32115-1958. Phone: (904) 255-7355.

DICKENS OLDE-FASHIONED CHRISTMAS FESTIVAL. Nov 27–30 (also Dec 5–6, 12–13 and 19–20). Holly, MI. Circa 1850 comes to life in downtown Holly. Bah humbug with Scrooge, encourage Tiny Tim, sing with the carolers, banter with the street vendors. Enjoy delicacies such as roasted chestnuts, open-flame baked potatoes and plum pudding. Entertainment on the hour. Annually, Thanksgiving weekend and each Saturday and Sunday until Christmas. Est attendance: 15,000. For info: Holly Area Chamber of Commerce, PO Box 214, Holly, MI 48442. Phone: (810) 634-1900. Fax: (810) 634-1049. WWW: http://www.hollymi.com

"THE DINAH SHORE SHOW" TV PREMIERE: ANNIVERSARY. Nov 27, 1951. Dinah Shore hosted a successful 15-minute musical show until 1957 and then an hour variety show from 1957 to 1962, one of the few females to have done so. The music show was sponsored by Chevrolet (and was officially known as "The Dinah Shore Chevy Show") and featured a back-up group called the Skylarks (George Becker, Earl Brown, Joe Hamilton, Lee Lombard, Gilda Maiken). Shore also starred in specials and hosted a variety series with a guest host filling in for her every fourth week. She later moved on to hosting a talk show.

DRESDEN'S HOLIDAY CELEBRATION. Nov 27–Dec 31. Dresden, OH. There will be many seasonal events such as our holiday parade as well as other entertainment opportunities taking place throughout Dresden and The Longaberger® Company properties. There will be shopping fun for all at The Longaberger Specialty Shops™ and great food at all of our restaurants. Look for fabulous entertainment and fun for the whole family. Est attendance: 15,000. For info: Salle Schlesselman, The Longaberger® Company, 1360 Main St, Dresden, OH 43821. Phone: (614) 754-5778. Fax: (614) 754-5720.

DUBCEK, ALEXANDER: BIRTH ANNIVERSARY. Nov 27, 1921. The man who attempted to give his country "socialism with a human face," Alexander Dubcek was born at Uhrocev, a village in western Slovakia. As first secretary of the Czechoslovak Communist Party during the "Prague Spring" of 1968, he moved to achieve the "widest possible democratization" and to loosen the dominant influence of the Soviet Union. As a result, Czechoslovakia was invaded by armed forces of the Warsaw Pact on Aug 21, 1968. Dubcek died Nov 7, 1992, at Prague.

FAMILY DAY IN NEVADA. Nov 27. Observed annually on the Friday following the fourth Thursday in Nov.

FESTIVAL OF CAROLS. Nov 27. Kansas Capitol Grounds, Topeka, KS. The ringing in of the Christmas season. Musical program, arrival of Santa Claus, lighting of Christmas decorations, hayrides, dance and music. Annually, the Friday after Thanksgiving beginning at 4 PM. Est attendance: 4,250. For info: Marsha J. Sheahan, VP PR, Greater Topeka Chamber of Commerce, 120 SE 6th Ave, Ste 110, Topeka, KS 66603-3515. Phone: (913) 234-2644. Fax: (913) 234-2644.
Email: topekainfo@topekachamber.org.

FINGER LAKES CRAFTSMEN THANKSGIVING WEEKEND CHRISTMAS ARTS AND CRAFTS SHOW. Nov 27–29. Monroe County Fairgrounds Dome Arena, Rochester, NY. All media, all categories including photography and prints. Est attendance: 14,000. For info: Ronald L. Johnson, Finger Lakes Craftsmen Show, 1 Freshour Dr, Shortsville, NY 14548. Phone: (716) 289-9439. Fax: (716) 289-9440.

FISH HOUSE PARADE. Nov 27. Aitkin, MN. 8th annual special parade of uniquely decorated fish houses used for ice fishing during the winter. Annually, the Friday after Thanksgiving. Est attendance: 3,000. For info: Carroll Kukowski, Exec Dir, Aitkin Area Chamber of Commerce, PO Box 127, Aitkin, MN 56431. Phone: (800) 526-8342. Fax: (218) 927-4494.
Email: upnorth@aitkin.com. WWW: http://www.aitkin.com

FUR FREE FRIDAY. Nov 27. Various animal rights organizations, including OCPA (Orange County People for Animals) and PETA (People for Ethical Treatment of Animals) stage demonstrations at shopping malls and furriers to protest the killing of animals for fur use in coats and clothing. Annually, the day after Thanksgiving. For info: Orange County People for Animals (OCPA), PO Box 14187, Irvine, CA 92713-4187. Phone: (714) 751-OCPA.

GARDEN OF LIGHTS. Nov 27–Jan 1. Honor Heights Park, Muskogee, OK. Park sparkles and shimmers with more than one million lights. Three graceful doves with 12-ft wingspans; four lighted nature exhibits; lighted waterfall with sound effects is 200 ft long with a family of deer resting nearby. Lights all over! Est attendance: 300,000. For info: Ervalene Jenkins, Muskogee Convention & Tourism, 425 Boston, Muskogee, OK 74402-0797. Phone: (918) 682-2401. Fax: (918) 682-2403.

GIVING THANKS: HEARTH AND HOME IN EARLY MARYLAND. Nov 27–28. St. Mary's City, MD. Living history event focusing on hearthcooking and food preservation in colonial Maryland. Est attendance: 800. For info: Public Affairs Office, Historic St. Mary's City, PO Box 39, St. Mary's City, MD 20686. Phone: (301) 862-0990 or (800) SMC-1634. Fax: (301) 862-0968.

GROSSE POINTE SANTA CLAUS PARADE. Nov 27. Grosse Pointe, MI. 22nd annual Santa Claus parade includes more than 100 units with 1,500 participants. Annually, the day after Thanksgiving. Est attendance: 15,000. For info: Joan Coyle, Parade Coord, 285 Touraine, Grosse Pointe Farms, MI 48236. Phone: (313) 885-3984.

HENDRIX, JIMI: BIRTH ANNIVERSARY. Nov 27, 1942. American musician and songwriter Jimi Hendrix was born at Seattle, WA. One of the greatest rock guitarists in history, he revolutionized the guitar sound with heavy use of feedback and incredible fretwork. His success first came in England, then in the US after his appearance at the Monterey Pop Festival (1967). His albums included *Are You Experienced?*, *Electric Ladyland*, *Axis: Bold as Love* (all 1968) and *Band of Gypsys* (1970). He died on Sept 18, 1970, at London, England.

November 1998

S	M	T	W	T	F	S
1	2	3	4	5	6	7
8	9	10	11	12	13	14
15	16	17	18	19	20	21
22	23	24	25	26	27	28
29	30					

HOLIDAY CRAFT AND GIFT SHOW: INDOOR SHOW. Nov 27–29. Wisconsin State Fair Park, Milwaukee, WI. Combined show with 200 commercial gift exhibitors and 400 crafters. Est attendance: 48,000. For info: Dir, Holiday Craft and Gift Show, 9312 W National Ave, West Allis, WI 53227. Phone: (414) 321-2100.

HOLIDAY FOLKWAYS. Nov 27–Dec 20, also Dec 26–28. Shakopee, MN. Focuses on the ethnic holiday traditions of the Minnesota River Valley from 1840 to 1890. Music, dance, food and folk arts from a variety of immigrant groups, including Scandinavian, German, French, Slavic and Jewish. For info: Historic Murphy's Landing, 2187 E Highway 101, Shakopee, MN 55379. Phone: (612) 445-6901.

IDAHO FESTIVAL OF LIGHTS. Nov 27–Dec 31. Preston, ID. 14th annual festival featuring a lighted parade, fireworks in the evenings, kids parade and international bed race. Est attendance: 18,000. For info: Travel Rep, City of Preston, PO Box 472, Preston, ID 83263. Fax: (208) 852-0158.

JULE FEST. Nov 27–29. Elk Horn, IA. Danish Christmas festival. Est attendance: 3,000. For info: Lisa Riggs, Danish Windmill, PO Box 245, Elk Horn, IA 51531. Phone: (712) 764-7472 or (800) 451-7960. Fax: (712) 764-7475.

KEMBLE, FANNY: BIRTH ANNIVERSARY. Nov 27, 1809. Frances Anne Kemble, English actress, born at London, England, Nov 27, 1809. Died Jan 15, 1893.

LIVINGSTON, ROBERT R.: BIRTH ANNIVERSARY. Nov 27, 1746. Member of the Continental Congress, farmer, diplomat and jurist, was born at New York City. It was Livingston who administered the oath of office to President George Washington in 1789. He died at Clermont, NY, Feb 26, 1813.

MASTERSON, BAT: BIRTH ANNIVERSARY. Nov 27, 1853. Old American West gambler, saloonkeeper, lawman and news writer/editor. Born at Henryville, Quebec, Canada; died Oct 25, 1921, in New York City.

MYSTIC SEAPORT FIELD DAYS. Nov 27–28. Mystic Seaport, Mystic, CT. Families enjoy special Thanksgiving weekend activities including wagon rides, food, entertainment and outdoor games on the green. Est attendance: 3,000. For info: Mystic Seaport Museum, 75 Greenmanville Ave, PO Box 6000, Mystic, CT 06355-0990. Phone: (203) 572-5315.

REVEREND FRANCIS GASTRELL'S EJECTMENT: ANNIVERSARY. Nov 27. On Nov 27, 1759, the Stratford-upon-Avon town corporation gave orders to bring an "action of Ejectment" against the Rev Francis Gastrell, Vicar of Frodsham, who lived in William Shakespeare's home. Gastrell, it is said, had cut down the 150-year-old mulberry tree that had been planted by William Shakespeare. Gastrell maliciously felled the tree because he was annoyed by the many Shakespeare enthusiasts who came to look at it. He sold the tree for firewood, but it was recovered by a jeweler-woodcarver, Thomas Sharp, who fashioned hundreds of relics from it. Gastrell was ejected from Stratford "amid the ragings and cursings of its people, a citizen well lost"—for one of "the meanest petty infamies in our annals." The Rev Gastrell's wife, Jane, is said to have been an accomplice in this celebrated arboricide.

SANTALAND USA. Nov 27–Dec 23. Downtown, Madison, MN. Santaland USA is a group of child-sized buildings and figures, including a church, schoolhouse, barn, bakery, ice castle, toy shop, Santa and Mrs Claus's house, Santa's Workshop, Santa's sleigh and reindeer, a mouse house, camels and a manger scene. All are built, furnished and decorated by volunteers and along with other scenes, such as a railroad train and pond, take up most of the mezzanine area of a large retail store. Santaland is sponsored by the Madison Chamber; free admission. We also have a holiday parade the first Saturday in December. Est attendance: 2,000. For info: Donna C. Ventrella, 404 6th Ave, Madison, MN 56256. Phone: (320) 598-7373. Fax: (320) 598-7376.

SINKIE DAY. Nov 27. SINKIES (people who occasionally dine over the kitchen sink) are encouraged to celebrate this time-honored, casual-yet-tasteful cuisine culture. This is a particularly appropriate day to become acquainted with the SINKIE style of dining. Christmas shopping and Thanksgiving leftovers provide the perfect reasons to enjoy a quick meal. Annually, the day after Thanksgiving. For info: Norm Hankoff, Founder, Intl Assn of People Who Dine Over the Kitchen Sink, 1579 Farmers Lane, #252, Santa Rosa, CA 95405. Email: normh@sinkie.com. WWW: http://www.sinkie.com

SPACE MILESTONE: *SOYUZ T-3* (USSR). Nov 27, 1980. Launched this date with three cosmonauts, O. Makarov, L. Kizim and G. Strekalov, docked at *Salyut 6* space station on Nov 28. Returned to Earth, Dec 10, 1980.

SUGARLOAF'S FALL ATLANTA CRAFT FESTIVAL. Nov 27–29. Cobb Galleria Centre, Atlanta, GA. This show, now in its 2nd year, features 300 nationally recognized craft designers and fine artists displaying and selling their original creations. Craft demonstrations, hourly gift certificate drawings and more. Est attendance: 15,000. For info or application: Sugarloaf Mountain Works, Inc, 200 Orchard Ridge Dr, Ste 215, Gaithersburg, MD 20878. Phone: (800) 210-9900.

TREE LIGHTING CEREMONY. Nov 27. Town Square, Anchorage, AK. All of Anchorage turns out for this traditional start of the holiday season. For info: Anchorage Conv and Visitors Bureau, 524 W Fourth Ave, Anchorage, AK 99501. Phone: (907) 276-4118. Fax: (907) 278-5559. Email: acvb@alaska.net. WWW: http://www.alaska.net/~acvb

WASHBOURNE, MONA: BIRTH ANNIVERSARY. Nov 27, 1903. British actress Mona Washbourne was born at Birmingham, England. Her only leading role was on stage in *The Anniversary* (1966). She died on Nov 15, 1988 at England.

WEIZMANN, CHAIM: BIRTH ANNIVERSARY. Nov 27. Israeli statesman born near Pinsk, Byelorussia, on Nov 27, 1874. He played an important role in bringing about the British government's Balfour Declaration, calling for the establishment of a national home for Jews in Palestine. He died at Tel Aviv, Israel, on Nov 9, 1952.

WINTERFEST. Nov 27–Jan 1. Larimer Square, Denver, CO. The season brings skating, roasting chestnuts, Santa's Workshop, toy train, gingerbread replica and more to historic Larimer Square. The festivities kick off with the tree-lighting ceremony on Nov 27. Est attendance: 100,000. For info: Events, Larimer Square, 1400 Larimer St, Ste 300, Denver, CO 80202. Phone: (303) 534-2367. Fax: (303) 893-0518. WWW: http://www.larimersquare.com

WORLD'S CHAMPIONSHIP DUCK CALLING CONTEST AND WINGS OVER THE PRAIRIE FESTIVAL. Nov 27–28. Stuttgart, AR. Annually, Thanksgiving weekend. Duck calling contests, duck gumbo cookoff, carnival, 10K race, arts and crafts, beauty pageant, concessions, sporting collectibles, Sportsman's Dinner and Dance, commercial exhibitors, fun shoot. Est attendance: 65,000. For info: Stuttgart Chamber of Commerce, 507 S Main, Stuttgart, AR 72160. Phone: (870) 673-1602. Fax: (870) 673-1604.

YOU'RE WELCOMEGIVING DAY. Nov 27. The day after Thanksgiving, to create a four-day weekend. For info: Richard Ankli, The Fifth Wheel Tavern, 639 Fifth St, Ann Arbor, MI 48103-4840.

BIRTHDAYS TODAY

Buffalo Bob (Bob Smith), 81, TV personality ("The Howdy Doody Show"), born Buffalo, NY, Nov 27, 1917.

Robin Givens, 34, actress ("Head of the Class," *A Rage in Harlem*), born New York, NY, Nov 27, 1964.

David Merrick, 86, producer (*Hello, Dolly!; Beckett*), born St. Louis, MO, Nov 27, 1912.

Eddie Rabbitt, 54, singer ("I Love a Rainy Night"), songwriter ("Kentucky Rain"), born Brooklyn, NY, Nov 27, 1944.

Gail Henion Sheehy, 61, author, journalist (*The Silent Passage: Menopause; Pathfinders*), born Mamaroneck, NY, Nov 27, 1937.

Fisher Stevens, 35, actor (*The Brother from Another Planet, Bob Roberts*), born Chicago, IL, Nov 27, 1963.

Jaleel White, 22, actor ("Family Matters"), born Los Angeles, CA, Nov 27, 1976.

NOVEMBER 28 — SATURDAY

Day 332 — 33 Remaining

ALBANIA: INDEPENDENCE DAY. Nov 28.

ALSTON, CHARLES H.: BIRTH ANNIVERSARY. Nov 28, 1907. African-American painter and sculptor born at Charlotte, NC, and died at New York, NY, Apr 27, 1977. Charles Alston was celebrated in his lifetime for seminal paintings and sculptures that defy categorization. Throughout his career, Alston experimented with styles ranging from realism to total abstraction. His realistic WPA murals at Harlem Hospital depict a narrative in the style of Diego Rivera. The Cubist painting of *The Family* (1955), is an excellent example of Alston's early work, influenced by Italian artist Amedeo Modigliani. *Black Man, Black Woman USA* has a decidedly Egyptian style of portraiture. *Walking* (1958), which depicts a silent crowd, almost prophecies the turmoil and social agitation of the Civil Rights Movement.

BLAKE, WILLIAM: BIRTH ANNIVERSARY. Nov 28, 1757. English poet and artist, born at London, England. Died there Aug 12, 1827.

BRACH'S HOLIDAY CHRISTMAS PARADE. Nov 28. Michigan Ave, Chicago, IL. Syndicated across the country with floats, bands and balloons sponsored by more than 30 corporations. Title Sponsor: Brach's Candy. Est attendance: 750,000. For info: Amy Groff, Production Contractors, Inc, 1711 W Fullerton Ave, Chicago, IL 60614. Phone: (312) 935-8747. Fax: (312) 477-1800.

BUNYAN, JOHN: BIRTH ANNIVERSARY. Nov 28, 1628. English cleric and author of *A Pilgrim's Progress*, born at Elstow, Bedfordshire. Died at London, Aug 31, 1688.

A COLONIAL THANKSGIVING. Nov 28. The Hempsted Houses, New London, CT. Costumed role-players demonstrate how the Hempsted family celebrated Thanksgiving. What did they prepare, and what did they do with the left-overs without refrigerators, freezers or microwaves? Stop by any time between noon and 4. A great alternative to shopping and football! Admission: $4 adults; $1 children. Est attendance: 50. For info: The Hempsted Houses, 11 Hempstead Rd, New London, CT 06320. Phone: (860) 443-7949 or The Antiquarian & Landmarks Society. Phone: (860) 247-8996.

CUT YOUR OWN CHRISTMAS TREE. Nov 28–29 (also Dec 5–6, 12–13, and 19–24). Charlottesville, VA. Est attendance: 100. For info: Ash Lawn–Highland, James Monroe Parkway, Charlottesville, VA 22902. Phone: (804) 293-9539. Fax: (804) 293-8000. Email: ashlawn@comet.net. WWW: http://avenue.org/ashlawn

DESERT STORM: UN DEADLINE RESOLUTION: ANNIVERSARY. Nov 28, 1990. The United Nations passed the twelfth in a series of resolutions concerning the Iraqi invasion of Kuwait. Resolution 678 authorized states "to use all necessary means" against Iraq unless it withdrew its forces from Kuwait by Jan 15, 1991. Iraq did not comply, and the Allied Forces began their attack within hours of the expiration of the deadline.

ELECTRIC LIGHT PARADE. Nov 28. Downtown Lovington, NM. Christmas shines in Lovington with more than 60 entries including floats, motorhomes, cars and motorcycles decorated with Christmas lights. Annually, the first Saturday following Thanksgiving at 8 PM. Est attendance: 7,000. For info: Lovington Chamber of Commerce, PO Box 1347, Lovington, NM 88260. Phone: (505) 396-5311.

FRENCH WEST INDIES: SEMI-MARATHON. Nov 28. Martinique. For info: Ms Muriel Wiltord, Martinique Promo Bureau, 444 Madison Ave, 16th Floor, New York, NY 10022. Phone: (800) 391-4909. Fax: (212) 838-7855. Email: martinique@nyo.com. WWW: http://www.martinique.org

HANGING OF THE GREENS. Nov 28. Main Street, Arrow Rock, MO. The village puts on its winter greenery as the historic boardwalk is decorated with traditional living greenery. Event includes caroling, a visit from Santa and Mrs Claus via fire truck, storytelling and merchants open house is included. Est attendance: 200. For info: HARC, PO Box M, Arrow Rock, MO 65320. Email: tmcglaughlin@vaxl.rain.gen.mo.us.

"THE LIGHT OF THE WORLD" CHRISTMAS PAGEANT. Nov 28 (also Dec 6 and 13). Courthouse square, Minden, NE. Pageant presented on three sides of the courthouse square with around 115 local citizens performing with beautiful costumes. At the climax some 10,000 Christmas lights are turned on the courthouse. 7 PM; free admission. Annually, the first Saturday after Thanksgiving and the first two Sundays in December. Est attendance: 10,000. For info: Marjorie Madsen, Mgr, Minden Chamber of Commerce, PO Box 375, Minden, NE 68959. Phone: (308) 832-1811.

LULLY, JEAN BAPTISTE: BIRTH ANNIVERSARY. Nov 28, 1632. Versatile musician and composer, born at Florence, Italy, on Nov 28, 1632, who chose France for his homeland. Noted for his quick temper, it is said that he struck his own foot with a baton while in a rage. The resulting wound led to blood poisoning, from which he died, at Paris, Mar 22, 1687.

MAURITANIA: INDEPENDENCE DAY. Nov 28. National holiday. Attained sovereignty Nov 28, 1960.

MEXICO: GUADALAJARA INTERNATIONAL BOOK FAIR. Nov 28–Dec 6. Mexico's largest book fair with exhibitors from all over the Spanish-speaking world. Est attendance: 275,000. For info: David Unger, Guadalajara Book Fair–US Office, Div of Hum, NAC 6293, City College, New York, NY 10031. Phone: (212) 650-7925. Fax: (212) 650-7912. Email: daucc@cunyvm.cuny.edu.

PANAMA: INDEPENDENCE FROM SPAIN. Nov 28. Public holiday in Panama.

SPACE MILESTONE: *COLUMBIA STS-9* (US): 15th ANNIVERSARY. Nov 28, 1983. Shuttle *Columbia* launched from Kennedy Space Center, FL, with five astronauts (John Young, Brewster Shaw, Jr, Owen Garriot, Robert Parker, Byron Lichtenberg) and German physicist Ulf Merbold. Landed Edwards Air Force Base, CA, on Dec 8.

November 1998

S	M	T	W	T	F	S
1	2	3	4	5	6	7
8	9	10	11	12	13	14
15	16	17	18	19	20	21
22	23	24	25	26	27	28
29	30					

SPACE MILESTONE: *MARINER 4* (US). Nov 28, 1964. Launched toward Mars. After 228 days, approached within 6,118 miles of Mars on July 14, 1965. Took photographs.

SWINE TIME. Nov 28. Climax, GA. This homecoming for past residents promotes swine and raises funds for the Climax Community Club. A day of special events for people of all ages, including a parade, Best Dressed Pig Contest, Greasy Pig Chase, old time crafts, clogging, music of all kinds and a variety of food. Est attendance: 25,000. For info: Clifford Wells, Publicity, Climax Community Club, PO Box 131, Climax, GA 31734. Phone: (912) 246-0910.

TEHERAN CONFERENCE: 55th ANNIVERSARY. Nov 28–Dec 1, 1943. President Franklin D. Roosevelt, British Prime Minister Winston Churchill and Soviet Premier Joseph Stalin met at Teheran, Iran, to formulate a plan for an Allied assault, a second front, in western Europe. The resulting plan was "Operation Overlord," which commenced with the landing on Normandy's beaches on June 6, 1944 ("D-Day").

TERRITORIAL CHRISTMAS CELEBRATION. Nov 28–Dec 24. Guthrie, OK. Take a step back in time and celebrate Christmas in grand Victorian style. You won't believe your eyes as you walk around Guthrie and take in many sights and sounds of Christmas past. Enjoy the Pollard's production of "A Territorial Christmas Carol," the Victorian Walk, Territorial Homes Tour, Lion's Club Christmas Parade, Christmas Light tour on the trolley, street carolers, peanut vendors, Christmas Tree Auction and Reception and Election of the Territorial Governor. Est attendance: 13,000. For info: Guthrie Conv & Visitors Bureau, PO Box 995, Guthrie, OK 73044-0995. Phone: (800) 299-1889 or (405) 282-1947. Fax: (405) 282-0061.

VICTORIAN CHRISTMAS CELEBRATION. Nov 28–Jan 10. History House, Cumberland, MD. Victorian Christmas tea and candlelight tours with musical entertainment. Various workshops and children's programs. Theme decorating in an 1867 Victorian mansion museum. Est attendance: 600. For info: Sharon Nealis, Admin, History House, 218 Washington St, Cumberland, MD 21502. Phone: (301) 777-8678.

BIRTHDAYS TODAY

Berry Gordy, Jr, 69, record and motion picture executive (founder of Motown), born Detroit, MI, Nov 28, 1929.

Ed Harris, 48, actor (*The Right Stuff*), born Englewood, NJ, Nov 28, 1950.

Gary Hart (Gary Hartpence), 60, former senator, presidential candidate, born Ottawa, KS, Nov 28, 1938.

Hope Lange, 65, actress ("The Ghost and Mrs Muir," *Bus Stop*), born Reading Ridge, CT, Nov 28, 1933.

Judd Nelson, 39, actor (*The Breakfast Club, St. Elmo's Fire*), born Portland, ME, Nov 28, 1959.

Randy Newman, 55, singer/songwriter ("Love Story," "Short People"), composer (film scores *Ragtime, The Natural*), born LA, Nov 28, 1943.

Paul Shaffer, 49, band leader (David Letterman's music man), comedian, born Thunder Bay, Ont, Canada, Nov 28, 1949.

☆ ☆ ☆

NOVEMBER 29 — SUNDAY

Day 333 — 32 Remaining

ADVENT, FIRST SUNDAY. Nov 29. Advent includes the four Sundays before Christmas, Nov 29, Dec 6, Dec 13 and Dec 20 in 1998.

ALCOTT, LOUISA MAY: BIRTH ANNIVERSARY. Nov 29, 1832. American author, born at Philadelphia, PA, Nov 29, 1832. Died at Boston, MA, Mar 6, 1888. Her most famous novel was *Little Women*, the classic story of Meg, Jo, Beth and Amy.

BERKELEY, BUSBY: BIRTH ANNIVERSARY. Nov 29. William Berkeley Enos was born Nov 29, 1895, at Los Angeles,

CA. After serving in World War I as an entertainment officer, he changed his name to Busby Berkeley and began a career in show business as an actor. He turned to directing in 1921, and his lavish Broadway and Hollywood creations include *Forty-Second Street, Gold Diggers of 1933, Footlight Parade, Hollywood Hotel, Stage Struck, Gold Diggers in Paris, Babes in Arms, Strike Up the Band, Girl Crazy* and *Take Me Out to the Ball Game*, among many others. He retired in 1962 and returned to Broadway in 1970 to supervise a revival of *No, No, Nanette*. He died Mar 14, 1976, at Palm Springs, CA.

CHRISTMAS AT UNION STATION. Nov 29–Dec 31. Omaha, NE. Celebration of the Christmas holiday around a giant 45-ft Christmas tree in the splendor of Omaha's old Union Station. Est attendance: 30,000. For info: Liz Cajka, Western Heritage Museum, 801 S 10th St, Omaha, NE 68108-3299. Fax: (402) 444-5397.

CZECHOSLOVAKIA ENDS COMMUNIST RULE: ANNIVERSARY. Nov 29. On Nov 29, 1989, Czechoslovakia ended 41 years of one-party communist rule when the Czechoslovak parliament voted unanimously to repeal the constitutional clauses giving the Communist Party a guaranteed leading role in the country and promoting Marxism-Leninism as the state ideology. The vote came at the end of a 12-day revolution sparked by the beating of protestors on Nov 17. Although the Communist party remained in power, the tide of reform led to its ouster by the Civic Forum, headed by playwright Vaclav Havel. The Civic Forum demanded free elections with equal rights for all parties, a mixed economy and support for foreign investment. In the first free elections in Czechoslovakia since World War II, Vaclav Havel was elected president.

ENGLAND: ROYAL SMITHFIELD SHOW AND AGRICULTURAL MACHINERY EXHIBITION. Nov 29–Dec 2. Earls Court Exhibition Centre, Warwick Road, London. Major farming exhibition with livestock and agricultural equipment on display. Est attendance: 50,000. For info: Sue Silsby, Earls Court Exhibition Centre, Warwick Rd, London, England SW5 9TA. Phone: (44) (171) 370-8226. Fax: (44) (171) 370-8230.

JOHN F. KENNEDY DAY IN MASSACHUSETTS. Nov 29. Annually, the last Sunday in November.

"KUKLA, FRAN AND OLLIE" TV PREMIERE: 50th ANNIVERSARY. Nov 29, 1948. This popular children's show featured puppets created and handled by Burr Tillstrom and was equally popular with adults. Fran Allison, the only human on the show, was also featured. Tillstrom's lively and eclectic cast of characters, called the "Kuklapolitans," included the bald, high-voiced Kukla; the big-toothed Oliver J. Dragon (Ollie); Fletcher Rabbit; Cecil Bill; Beulah the Witch; Colonel Crackie; Madame Ooglepuss; and Dolores Dragon. Most shows were performed without scripts.

LEWIS, C. S. (CLIVE STAPLES): 100th BIRTH ANNIVERSARY. Nov 29, 1898. British scholar, novelist and author (*The Screwtape Letters, Chronicles of Narnia*), born at Belfast, Ireland, died at Oxford, England, Nov 22, 1963.

NETHERLANDS: MIDWINTER HORN BLOWING. Nov 29–Jan 6, 1999. Twente and several other areas in the Netherlands. Midwinter horn blowing, folklore custom of announcing the birth of Christ, begins with Advent and continues until Epiphany (Jan 6) of the following year.

PASADENA DOO DAH PARADE. Nov 29. Pasadena, CA. No theme, no judging, no prizes, no order of march, no motorized vehicles and no animals. Annually, the Sunday following Thanksgiving Day.

PHILLIPS, WENDELL: BIRTH ANNIVERSARY. Nov 29. American women's suffrage, anti-slavery, prison reform leader, born Nov 29, 1811. Died Feb 2, 1884.

RADIOLOGICAL SOCIETY OF NORTH AMERICA SCIENTIFIC ASSEMBLY AND ANNUAL MEETING. Nov 29–Dec 4. McCormick Place, Chicago, IL. 84th annual. Est attendance: 61,000. For info: Michael O'Connell, Radiological Society of North America, 2021 Spring Rd, Ste 600, Oak Brook, IL 60521-1860. Phone: (630) 571-2670. Fax: (630) 571-7837. Email: kuta@rsna.org.

ROSS, NELLIE TAYLOE: BIRTH ANNIVERSARY. Nov 29, 1876. Nellie Tayloe Ross became the first female governor in the US when she was chosen to serve out the last month and two days of her husband's term as governor of Wyoming after he died in office. She was elected in her own right in the Nov 4, 1924, election but lost the 1927 race. Ross was appointed vice chairman of the Democratic National Committee in 1926 and named director of the US Mint by President Franklin D. Roosevelt in 1933. She served in that capacity for 20 years. She died Dec 20, 1977, at Washington, DC.

THOMSON, CHARLES: BIRTH ANNIVERSARY. Nov 29. America's first official record keeper. Chosen secretary of the First Continental Congress on Sept 5, 1774, Thomson recorded proceedings for 15 years and delivered his journals together with tens of thousands of records to the federal government in 1789. Born in Ireland, Nov 29, 1729. Died on Aug 16, 1824. It was Thomson who notified George Washington of his election as president.

WAITE, MORRISON R.: BIRTH ANNIVERSARY. Nov 29, 1816. Seventh Chief Justice of the Supreme Court. Born Nov 29, 1816, at Lyme, CT. Appointed Chief Justice by President Ulysses S. Grant on Jan 19, 1874. The Waite Court is remembered for its controversial rulings that did much to rehabilitate the idea of states' rights after the Civil War and early Reconstruction years. Waite died at Washington, DC, on Mar 23, 1888.

BIRTHDAYS TODAY

Jacques Rene Chirac, 66, French President, born Paris, France, Nov 29, 1932.

Diane Ladd (Rose Diane Ladner), 66, actress (*Alice Doesn't Live Here Anymore, Ramblin' Rose, The Cemetery Club*), born Meridian, MS, Nov 29, 1932.

Madeleine L'Engle, 80, writer (*A Wrinkle in Time, Summer of the Great-Grandmother*), born New York, NY, Nov 29, 1918.

Howie Mandel, 43, comedic actor ("Howie Mandel's Sunny Skies," "Bobby's World"), born Toronto, Ontario, Canada, Nov 29, 1959.

Chuck Mangione, 58, musician, composer (Grammy for "Bellavia"), born Rochester, NY, Nov 29, 1940.

John Mayall, 65, musician, band leader (The Bluesbreakers), born Manchester, England, Nov 29, 1933.

Andrew McCarthy, 36, actor (*Pretty in Pink, Mrs Parker & the Vicious Circle*), born Westfield, NJ, Nov 29, 1962.

Cathy Moriarty, 38, actress (*Raging Bull, The Mambo Kings*), born The Bronx, NY, Nov 29, 1960.

Vincent Edward (Vin) Scully, 71, sportscaster, Ford Frick award winner, born New York, NY, Nov 29, 1927.

Garry Shandling, 49, comedian ("The Larry Sanders Show"), born Chicago, IL, Nov 29, 1949.

Paul Simon, 70, Former US Senator (D, Illinois), born Eugene, OR, Nov 29, 1928.

NOVEMBER 30 — MONDAY

Day 334 — 31 Remaining

ARTICLES OF PEACE BETWEEN GREAT BRITAIN AND THE UNITED STATES: ANNIVERSARY. Nov 30, 1782. These provisional articles of peace, which were to end America's War of Independence, were signed at Paris, France, Nov 30, 1782. The refined and definitive treaty of peace between Great Britain and the US was signed at Paris, on Sept 3, 1783. In it "His Britannic Majesty acknowledges the said United States . . . to be free, sovereign and independent states; that he treats them as such; and for himself, his heirs and successors, relinquishes all claims to the government, propriety and territorial rights of the same, and every part thereof. . . ."

BARBADOS: INDEPENDENCE DAY. Nov 30. National holiday.

CHURCHILL, WINSTON: BIRTH ANNIVERSARY. Nov 30, 1874. Winston Leonard Spencer Churchill, British statesman and the first man to be made an honorary citizen of the US (by an act of Congress, Apr 9, 1963), born (prematurely) Nov 30, 1874, at Blenheim Palace, Oxfordshire, England. Died Jan 24, 1965, at London, England. Dedicated to Britain and total victory over Germany, Churchill as minister of defense and prime minister was considered a strong leader during WW II.

CLEMENS, SAMUEL LANGHORNE (MARK TWAIN): BIRTH ANNIVERSARY. Nov 30. Celebrated American author, whose books include: *The Adventures of Tom Sawyer, The Adventures of Huckleberry Finn* and *The Prince and the Pauper*. Born at Florida, MO, Nov 30, 1835, Twain is quoted as saying "I came in with Halley's Comet in 1835. It is coming again next year, and I expect to go out with it." He did. Twain died at Redding, CT, on Apr 21, 1910 (just one day after Halley's Comet perihelion).

HOFFMAN, ABBOT (ABBIE): BIRTH ANNIVERSARY. Nov 30, 1936. Political activist, born at Worcester, MA, Abbie Hoffman rose to prominence during the 1968 Democratic National Convention in Chicago and at his subsequent trial as a member of the Chicago Seven, a group of radicals accused of conspiring to disrupt the convention. Combining politics and street theatre was a Hoffman trait. During the 1967 march on the Pentagon, he sought a permit to allow 1,200 demonstrators to encircle and levitate the military headquarters in an attempt to end the war in Vietnam. He, Jerry Rubin and Paul Krassner conceived the Yippie movement as a youth festival of life to run concurrently with the Convention. Hoffman fled underground in 1974 to avoid trial on cocaine-possession charges and remained a fugitive for nearly seven years. Surrendering to authorities in 1980, he resumed his political work in 1982 after serving his sentence in a work-release program. Hoffman died on Apr 12, 1989, at New Hope, PA.

PHILIPPINES: BONIFACIO DAY. Nov 30. Also known as National Heroes' Day. Commemorates birth of Andres Bonifacio, leader of the 1896 revolt against Spain. Bonifacio was born Nov 30, 1863.

SAINT ANDREW'S DAY. Nov 30. Feast day of the apostle and martyr, Andrew, who died about 60 AD. Patron saint of Scotland.

SIDNEY, PHILIP: BIRTH ANNIVERSARY. Nov 30. English poet, statesman and soldier was born at Penshurst, Kent, England, on Nov 30, 1554. Best known of his poems is *Arcadia* (1580). Mortally wounded as he led an English detachment aiding the Dutch near Zutphen, on Sept 22, 1586, Sidney gave his water bottle to another dying soldier with the words "Thy necessity is yet greater than mine." He died at Arnheim on Oct 17, 1586, and all of England mourned the death of this man who had given new meaning to English patriotism.

STATUE OF RAMSES II UNEARTzHED: ANNIVERSARY. Nov 30. Egyptian construction workers in the ancient provincial town of Akhimim, 300 miles south of Cairo, unearthed a statue of Ramses II on Nov 30, 1991. Akhimim was an important provincial district that included the city of Ipu, a mecca for worshippers of the fertility god Min. The statue was uncovered during an excavation to prepare a foundation for a post office. An additional statue was uncovered 33 feet away, but the identity of its subject was still unknown.

STAY HOME BECAUSE YOU'RE WELL DAY. Nov 30. So we can call in "well," instead of faking illness and stay home from work. [© 1997 by WPL] For info: Thomas or Ruth Roy, Wellness Permission League, PO Box 662, Mt Gretna, PA 17064-0662. Phone: (500) 437-5104 or (717) 964-1308. Fax: (717) 964-1335.

SWIFT, JONATHAN: BIRTH ANNIVERSARY. Nov 30, 1667. Clergyman and satirist born at Dublin, Ireland, Nov 30, 1667. Died there Oct 19, 1745. Author of *Gulliver's Travels*. "I never saw, heard, nor read," Swift wrote in *Thoughts on Religion* "that the clergy were beloved in any nation where Christianity was the religion of the country. Nothing can render them popular but some degree of persecution."

TANNEHILL VILLAGE CHRISTMAS. Nov 30–Dec 4 (also Dec 7–11). Tannehill Historical State Park, McCalla, AL. 1800s village with cabins decorated in old-fashioned Christmas style and staffed by volunteers wearing period costumes. Est attendance: 6,000. For info: Vicki Gentry, Dir, Iron and Steel Museum, Tannehill Historical State Park, 12632 Confederate Pkwy, McCalla, AL 35111. Phone: (205) 477-5711. Fax: (205) 477-9400.

UKRAINIAN FAMINE FILM BROADCAST: ANNIVERSARY. Nov 30, 1991. In the rapidly changing former Soviet Union, the film *Famine 33* produced by Oles Yanchuk, was broadcast on republic-wide TV. The film chronicled the forced collectivization of the agriculture industry in 1933 and the resulting famine which led to the death of more than seven million Ukrainians. The famine was not officially recognized until 1990, when the Central Committee of the Ukrainian Communist Party first acknowledged that the millions of deaths were caused by the seizure of crops. The airing of the film heralded a significant departure from prior Soviet handling of history.

BIRTHDAYS TODAY

Shirley Chisholm, 74, author, former congresswoman, born Brooklyn, NY, Nov 30, 1924.

Dick Clark, 69, long-time host of "American Bandstand," entertainer, producer, born Mount Vernon, NY, Nov 30, 1929.

Richard Crenna, 71, actor (*Wait Until Dark, Hot Shots! Part Deux*), born Los Angeles, CA, Nov 30, 1927.

Des'ree, 28, singer (*I Ain't Movin'*), born London, England, Nov 30, 1970.

Robert Guillaume, 71, actor ("Soap," "Benson"), born St. Louis, MO, Nov 30, 1927.

Billy Idol, 43, singer ("Mony Mony," "Eyes Without a Face"), songwriter, born Surrey, England, Nov 30, 1955.

Vincent Edward ("Bo") Jackson, 36, former baseball player, former football player, born Bessemer, AL, Nov 30, 1962.

G. Gordon Liddy, 68, Watergate participant, born New York, NY, Nov 30, 1930.

David Mamet, 51, dramatist, director (*American Buffalo, Oleanna, House of Games, Things Change*), born Chicago, IL, Nov 30, 1947.

Virginia Mayo, 76, actress (*The Best Years of Our Lives*), born St. Louis, MO, Nov 30, 1922.

Mandy Patinkin, 46, actor (Tony for *Evita; Sunday in the Park with George*, "Chicago Hope"), born Chicago, IL, Nov 30, 1952.

Paul Stookey, 61, singer, songwriter (Paul of Peter, Paul and Mary), born Baltimore, MD, Nov 30, 1937.

Efrem Zimbalist, Jr, 75, actor ("The F.B.I.," *Airport*), born New York, NY, Nov 30, 1923.

December.

DECEMBER 1 — TUESDAY

Day 335 — 30 Remaining

BINGO'S BIRTHDAY MONTH. Dec 1–31. To celebrate the innovation and manufacture of the game of Bingo in 1929 by Edwin S. Lowe. Bingo has grown into a five-billion-dollar-a-year charitable fund-raiser. For info: Roger Snowden, Pres, Bingo Bugle, Inc, Box 527, Vashon, WA 98070. Phone: (800) 327-6437.

CANADA: YUKON ORDER OF PIONEERS: ANNIVERSARY. Dec 1. The Yukon Order of Pioneers held its founding meeting on Dec 1, 1894, at Fortymile, Yukon. It began as a vigilante police force to deter claim jumping and later inaugurated Discovery Day (Aug 17), a statutory Yukon holiday commemorating the discovery of gold on Bonanza Creek in 1896.

CHRISTMAS IN ROSWELL. Dec 1–31. Roswell, GA. Candlelight tours and antebellum homes decorated for the holidays. Historical re-enactments. Est attendance: 15,000. For info: Historic Roswell Convention and Visitors Bureau, 617 Atlanta St, Roswell, GA 30075. Phone: (770) 640-3253 or (800) 776-7935.

CIVIL AIR PATROL FOUNDED: ANNIVERSARY. Dec 1, 1941. The Director of Civilian Defense, former New York Mayor Fiorello H. LaGuardia, signed a formal order creating the Civil Air Patrol, a US Air Force Auxiliary. The CAP has a three-part mission: to provide an aerospace education program, a CAP cadet program and an emergency services program. For info: Civil Air Patrol, 105 S Hansell St, Maxwell AFB, AL 36112-6332. Phone: (205) 953-5463.

COLORECTAL CANCER EDUCATION AND AWARENESS MONTH. Dec 1–31. To educate consumers, patients and professionals regarding the need for early diagnosis and treatment of colorectal cancer. For info: Frederick S. Mayer, Pres, Pharmacists Planning Service, Inc, PO Box 1336, Sausalito, CA 94966. Phone: (415) 332-4066. Email: ppsi@aol.com.

FLOSSIE BEADLE WEEK. Dec 1–7. Lakeside, CA. Honoring the first historian of Lakeside. Est attendance: 100. For info: Lakeside Historical Society, PO Box 1423, Lakeside, CA 92040. Phone: (619) 561-1886.

GIANT CHRISTMAS TREE AT ROCKEFELLER CENTER. Dec 1. (Date approximate.) New York, NY. Lighting of the huge Christmas Tree in Rockefeller Plaza signals the opening of the holiday season in New York City. Date is usually a weekday during the first week of December.

HOLIDAYS AT THE NATIONALITY CLASSROOMS. Dec 1–31. Univ of Pittsburgh, Oakland, PA. Twenty-four rooms depict the city's diverse ethnic culture through authentic examples of architecture and decor from eastern and Western Europe, Scandinavia, the Middle East, Asia and Africa. For info: Greater Pittsburgh Conv & Visitors Bureau, Four Gateway Center, Pittsburgh, PA 15222-1259. Phone: (412) 624-6000 or (800) 359-0758. Fax: (412) 644-5512.

HUG-A-WEEK FOR THE HEARING IMPAIRED. Dec 1–31. Give a hug to someone who doesn't hear so well, each week until the end of the year. As we approach the holiday season, start with a weekly hug and find out how you might proactively include people with hearing loss in the season's festivities. A little extra time and a few special moments may help someone who can't hear so well be included and more able to share throughout the season. Annually, the month of December. For info: Carol MacKenzie, Communicate with Care, 10 Westwood Rd, Lexington, MA 02173. Phone: (617) 863-8436. Email: commwcare@aol.com.

ICELAND: UNIVERSITY STUDENTS' CELEBRATION: 80th ANNIVERSARY. Dec 1, 1918. Marks the day in 1918 when Iceland became an independent state from Denmark (but still remained under the king of Denmark).

INTERNATIONAL CALENDAR AWARENESS MONTH. Dec 1–31. Celebrate the vital role of the calendar in today's society. Only event of its kind to promote the calendar and its rich history, both past and present. Special events throughout month include exhibit of hundreds of 1999 calendars submitted from around the world, the 9th annual World and National Calendar Awards Program and special theme-related presentations and activities focusing on the calendar. For info: Maria Tuthill, Exec Dir, Calendar Marketing Assn, 621 E Park Ave, Libertyville, IL 60048. Phone: (800) 828-8225 or (847) 816-8660. Fax: (847) 816-8662. Email: calendars@aol.com. WWW: http://www.acpinc.com/calendars.html

MACAU: RESTORATION OF INDEPENDENCE DAY. Dec 1. Macau is Chinese territory under Portuguese administration. Portugal is due to return Macau to China in December 1999. First colonized by Portugal in 1557.

MARTIN, MARY VIRGINIA: 85th BIRTH ANNIVERSARY. Dec 1, 1913. American stage star Mary Martin was born at Weatherford, TX. She is best known for her title role in the Broadway and television productions of *Peter Pan*. She won Tony awards for her starring roles in *South Pacific* and *Peter Pan*. She died on Nov 3, 1990, at Rancho Mirage, CA, at age 76.

MOORE, JULIA A. DAVIS: BIRTH ANNIVERSARY. Dec 1, 1847. Julia Moore, known as the "Sweet Singer of Michigan," was born in a log cabin in Kent County, MI, on Dec 1, 1847. A writer of homely verse and ballads, Moore enjoyed remarkable popularity and gave many public readings before realizing that her public appearances were occasions for laughter and ridicule. One newspaper account of her recitation of a tragic ballad declared: "A wild ovation startled the poet. Pandemonium broke loose in the galleries. The crowd shouted and stamped its feet." Her poems were said to be "so bad, her subjects so morbid and her naivete so genuine" that they were actually gems of humorous genius. At her final public appearance she told her audience: "You people paid 50 cents to see a fool, but I got $50 to look at a house full of fools." Moore died in 1920.

NATIONAL DRUNK AND DRUGGED DRIVING (3D) PREVENTION MONTH. Dec 1–31. For info: 3D Prevention Month Coalition, 1900 L St NW, Ste 705, Washington, DC 20036. Phone: (202) 452-6004.

NATIONAL STRESS-FREE FAMILY HOLIDAYS MONTH. Dec 1–31. The holidays are so fraught with busy schedules that families often miss out on quality time together because outside demands have left them virtually drained. This observance is a reminder for parents to strive for more stress-free holidays for their families. Annually, the month of December. For info send SASE to: Teresa Langston, Dir, Parenting Without Pressure, 1330 Boyer St, Longwood, FL 32750-6311. Phone: (407) 767-2524.

December 1998

S	M	T	W	T	F	S
		1	2	3	4	5
6	7	8	9	10	11	12
13	14	15	16	17	18	19
20	21	22	23	24	25	26
27	28	29	30	31		

NEW ORLEANS CHRISTMAS. Dec 1–31. New Orleans, LA. Nostalgic caroling in Jackson Square, candlelight tours of 19th-century houses in holiday dress, holiday concerts, ice carving competition, cooking demonstrations, Celtic Christmas program, gingerbread house exhibits, tours to celebration in the Oaks, levee bonfire excursions and other family activities. For info: Amy Hymel, Event Coord, 100 Conti St, New Orleans, LA 70130. Phone: (800) 673-5725 or (504) 522-5730. Fax: (504) 522-5711. Email: info@fqfestivals.org. WWW: http://www.FQFestivals.org

***PLAYBOY* FIRST PUBLISHED: 45th ANNIVERSARY.** Dec 1, 1953. *Playboy* magazine was launched in Chicago by publisher Hugh Hefner.

PORTUGAL: INDEPENDENCE DAY. Dec 1. Public holiday.

ROMANIA: NATIONAL DAY. Dec 1. National holiday.

ROSA PARKS DAY: ANNIVERSARY OF ARREST. Dec 1, 1955. Anniversary of the arrest of Rosa Parks, in Montgomery, AL, for refusing to give up her seat and move to the back of a municipal bus. Her arrest triggered a yearlong boycott of the city bus system and led to legal actions which ended racial segregation on municipal buses throughout the southern US. The event has been called the birth of the modern civil rights movement. Rosa McCauley Parks was born at Tuskegee, AL, on Feb 4, 1913.

SAFE TOYS AND GIFTS MONTH. Dec 1–31. What are the top 10 dangerous toys to children's eyesight? Prevent Blindness America® issues a list of toys hazardous to eyesight. Tips on how to choose age-appropriate toys will be distributed. For info: Prevent Blindness America®, 500 E Remington Rd, Schaumburg, IL 60173. Phone: (800) 331-2020. Fax: (847) 843-8458. WWW: http://www.prevent-blindness.org

SPACE MILESTONE: *ATLANTIS* (US): 10th ANNIVERSARY. Dec 1, 1988. Launched this date. Mission deployed a new-generation spy satellite able to peer down on the Soviet Union in darkness and through clouds. All-military crew: Navy Commander Robert Gibson, Air Force Colonel Guy Gardner, Air Force Colonel Richard Mullane, Air Force Lieutenant Colonel Jerry Ross and Navy Commander William Shepherd. Landed Dec 6, 1988.

UNITED NATIONS: WORLD AIDS DAY. Dec 1. In 1988 the World Health Organization of the United Nations declared Dec 1 as World AIDS Day, an international day of awareness and education about AIDS. The WHO is the leader in global direction and coordination of AIDS prevention, control, research and education. More than 18 million adults and 1.5 million children have been diagnosed since AIDS was identified. A program called UN-AIDS was created to bring together the skills and expertise of the World Bank, UNDP, UNESCO, UNICEF, UNFPA and the WHO to strengthen and expand national capacities to respond to the pandemic. Also see the World AIDS Day entry (Dec 1) for information address in US.

UNIVERSAL HUMAN RIGHTS MONTH. Dec 1–31. To disseminate throughout the world information about human rights and distribute copies of the Universal Declaration of Human Rights in English and other languages. Please send $3 to cover expense of printing, handling and postage. Annually, the month of December. For info: Dr. Stanley Drake, Pres, Intl Society of Friendship & Good Will, 412 Cherry Hills Dr, Bakersfield, CA 93309-2866.

US CONGRESS PASSES GATT TREATY: ANNIVERSARY. Dec 1, 1994. Following the lead of the House of Representatives, the US Senate voted 76–24 to approve the Uruguay Round provisions of the General Agreement on Tariffs and Trade (GATT). The worldwide trade pact is intended to reduce tariffs by a third, eliminate trade quotas and protect intellectual property. The GATT agreement is expected to add $300–500 billion to the global economy through the year 2005.

December 1998

S	M	T	W	T	F	S
		1	2	3	4	5
6	7	8	9	10	11	12
13	14	15	16	17	18	19
20	21	22	23	24	25	26
27	28	29	30	31		

WOLCOTT, OLIVER: DEATH ANNIVERSARY. Dec 1, 1797. Signer of the Declaration of Independence, Governor of Connecticut, born Nov 20, 1726, at Windsor, CT.

WORLD AIDS DAY. Dec 1. US observance of UN day to focus world attention on the fight against HIV/AIDS. For info: American Assn for World Health, World AIDS Day, 1825 K St NW, Ste 1208, Washington, DC 20006. Phone: (202) 466-5883. Fax: (202) 466-5896. Email: aawhstaff@aol.com. WWW: http://www.aawhworldhealth.org

YULETIDE TRADITIONS. Dec 1–31. Charlottesville, VA. Special events at Ash Lawn–Highland, Monticello and Historic Michie Tavern. For info: Charlottesville/Albemarle Visitors Bureau, Box 161 Dept YT, Charlottesville, VA 22902. Phone: (804) 977-1783.

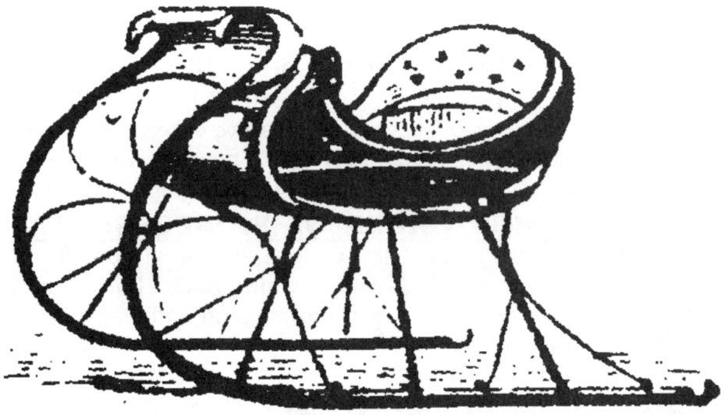

BIRTHDAYS TODAY

Woody Allen (Allen Stewart Konigsberg), 63, actor, writer, producer (Oscar for *Annie Hall; Sleeper, Manhattan, Bullets over Broadway*), born Brooklyn, NY, Dec 1, 1935.
Carol Alt, 38, model, born New York, NY, Dec 1, 1960.
Bette Midler, 53, singer ("You Are the Wind Beneath My Wings"), actress (*Beaches, For the Boys, The Rose, Down and Out in Beverly Hills, Scenes from a Mall*), born Honolulu, HI, Dec 1, 1945.
Richard Pryor, 58, actor, comedian (*Blue Collar, Stir Crazy*, "The Richard Pryor Show"), born Peoria, IL, Dec 1, 1940.
Lou Rawls, 63, blues singer ("A Natural Man," "You've Made Me So Very Happy"), actor, born Chicago, IL, Dec 1, 1935.
Lee Buck Trevino, 59, golfer, born Dallas, TX, Dec 1, 1939.
Treat Williams, 46, actor (*Hair, Smooth Talk*), born Rowayton, CT, Dec 1, 1952.

DECEMBER 2 — WEDNESDAY

Day 336 — 29 Remaining

ARTIFICIAL HEART TRANSPLANT: ANNIVERSARY. Dec 2, 1982. Barney C. Clark, 61, became the first recipient of a permanent artificial heart. The operation was performed at the University of Utah Medical Center in Salt Lake City. Near death at the time of the operation, Clark survived almost 112 days after the implantation. He died on Mar 23, 1983.

BROWN, JOHN: EXECUTION ANNIVERSARY. Dec 2. Abolitionist leader who is remembered for his raid on the US Arsenal at Harper's Ferry was hanged for treason at Charles Town, WV, Dec 2, 1859.

CALLAS, MARIA: 75th BIRTH ANNIVERSARY. Dec 2, 1923. American opera singer born at New York City. Died at Paris, Sept 16, 1977.

DENALI NATIONAL PARK AND PRESERVE ESTABLISHED: ANNIVERSARY. Dec 2, 1980. Alaska's Mount McKinley National Park, which was established Feb 26, 1917, and

Denali National Monument, which was proclaimed Dec 1, 1978, were combined and established as Denali National Park and Preserve. For info about park facilities: Denali Natl Park and Preserve, PO Box 9, McKinley Park, AK 99755.

ENGLAND: WALTER PLINGE DAY. Dec 2. A day to recognize Walter Plinge, said to have been a London pub landlord in 1900. His generosity to actors led to the use of his name as an actor, in play programs, usually to conceal the fact that an actor was playing more than one role. See also: "George Spelvin Day" (Nov 15) for US equivalent.

ESCOBAR, PABLO: 5th DEATH ANNIVERSARY. Dec 2, 1993. Colombian drug trafficker Pablo Emilio Escobar Gaviria was shot dead by police and soldiers at Medellin, Colombia.

FIRST SELF-SUSTAINING NUCLEAR CHAIN REACTION: ANNIVERSARY. Dec 2, 1942. Physicist Enrico Fermi led a team of scientists at the University of Chicago in producing the first controlled, self-sustaining nuclear chain reaction. Their first, simple nuclear reactor was built under the stands of the University's football stadium.

GATES OF THE ARCTIC NATIONAL PARK AND PRESERVE ESTABLISHED: ANNIVERSARY. Dec 2, 1980. Alaska's Gates of the Arctic National Monument, proclaimed Dec 1, 1978, was established as a national park and preserve. For further park info: Gates of the Arctic Natl Park and Preserve, PO Box 74680, Fairbanks, AK 99707.

GLACIER BAY NATIONAL PARK AND PRESERVE ESTABLISHED: ANNIVERSARY. Dec 2, 1980. Alaska's Glacier Bay National Monument, proclaimed Feb 25, 1925, was established as a national park and preserve. For further park info: Glacier Bay Natl Park and Preserve, Bartlett Cove, Gustavus, AK 99826.

KATMAI NATIONAL PARK AND PRESERVE ESTABLISHED: ANNIVERSARY. Dec 2, 1980. Alaska's Katmai National Monument, proclaimed Sept 24, 1918, was established as a national park and preserve. For further park info: Katmai Natl Park and Preserve, PO Box 7, King Salmon, AK 99613.

KENAI FJORDS NATIONAL PARK ESTABLISHED: ANNIVERSARY. Dec 2, 1980. Alaska's Kenai Fjords National Monument, proclaimed Dec 1, 1978, was established as a national park. For further park info: Kenai Fjords Natl Park, PO Box 1727, Seward, AK 99664.

KOBUK VALLEY NATIONAL PARK ESTABLISHED: ANNIVERSARY. Dec 2, 1980. Alaska's Kobuk Valley National Monument, proclaimed Dec 1, 1978, was established as a national park. For further park info: Chief of Education and Interpretation, Kobuk Valley Natl Park, PO Box 1029, Kotzebue, AK 99752. Phone: (907) 442-3890. Fax: (907) 442-8316.
WWW: http://www.nps.gov/kova

LAKE CLARK NATIONAL PARK AND PRESERVE ESTABLISHED: ANNIVERSARY. Dec 2, 1980. Alaska's Lake Clark National Monument, proclaimed Dec 1, 1978, was established as a national park and preserve. For further park info: Lake Clark Natl Park and Preserve, 1011 E Tudor Rd, Anchorage, AK 99503.

LAO PEOPLE'S DEMOCRATIC REPUBLIC: NATIONAL DAY. Dec 2. National holiday.

MONROE DOCTRINE: 175th ANNIVERSARY. Dec 2, 1823. President James Monroe, in his annual message to the Congress, Dec 2, 1823, enunciated the doctrine that bears his name and that was long hailed as a statement of US policy. ". . . In the wars of the European powers in matters relating to themselves we have never taken any part . . . we should consider any attempt on their part to extend their system to any portion of this hemi-sphere as dangerous to our peace and safety. . . ."

NAIA WOMEN'S NATIONAL VOLLEYBALL CHAMPIONSHIP. Dec 2–5. Olivet Nazarene University, Kankakee, IL. 20 teams compete in a pool play tournament to determine the national champion. 19th annual championship. For info: Kevin Henry, Natl Assn of Intercollegiate Athletics, 6120 S Yale Ave, Ste 1450, Tulsa, OK 74136-4223. Phone: (918) 494-8828. Fax: (918) 494-8841. Email: khenry@naia.org.
WWW: http://www.naia.org

NATIONAL COMMUNITY EDUCATION ASSOCIATION CONFERENCE. Dec 2–5. Town & Country Hotel, San Diego, CA. 33rd annual. Largest national gathering for community educators and others interested in promoting parent-community involvement in education, forming community partnerships to address community needs and expanding lifelong learning opportunities for all community residents. Est attendance: 700. For info: Ursula Ellis, Dir of Communications, Natl Community Education Assn, 3929 Old Lee Hwy, Ste 91-A, Fairfax, VA 22030-2401. Phone: (703) 359-8973. Fax: (703) 359-0972. Email: ncea@ids2.idsonline.com.

AN OLD-FASHIONED COUNTRY CHRISTMAS. Dec 2. Mountain View Inn, Greensburg, PA. Includes decorating outside trees, lighting hundreds of luminaries, a yule-log burning, cookies, hot cocoa and a visit by Saint Nick. For info: Ann Nemanic, Mountain View Inn, Rte 30 East, Greensburg, PA 15601. Phone: (412) 834-5300 or (800) 537-8709. Fax: (412) 834-5304.

★**PAN AMERICAN HEALTH DAY.** Dec 2. Presidential Proclamation 2447, of Nov 23, 1940, covers all succeeding years. Always Dec 2. The 1940 Pan American Conference of National Directors of Health adopted a resolution recommending that a "Health Day" be held annually in the countries of the Pan American Union.

SEURAT, GEORGES PIERRE: BIRTH ANNIVERSARY. Dec 2. French painter born at Paris, France, Dec 2, 1859. Died there Mar 29, 1891.

SPACE MILESTONE: *SOYUZ 16* (USSR). Dec 2, 1974. Six-day mission began this date with cosmonauts A.V. Flipchenko and N.N. Rukavishnikov. Rehearsal for US-USSR linkup in July 1975.

SYMS, SYLVIA: BIRTH ANNIVERSARY. Dec 2, 1917. American singer Sylvia Syms was born at New York, NY. She was called the "world's greatest saloon singer" by Frank Sinatra and recorded 15 albums. Died May 10, 1992, at New York, NY.

UNITED ARAB EMIRATES: NATIONAL DAY: ANNIVERSARY OF INDEPENDENCE. Dec 2. Anniversary of the day when a federation of seven sheikdoms declared independence (Dec 2, 1971) and became known as the United Arab Emirates.

UNITED NATIONS: INTERNATIONAL DAY FOR THE ABOLITION OF SLAVERY. Dec 2. Recalls the date of adoption by the General Assembly in 1949 of the Convention for the Suppression of the Traffic in Persons and the Exploitation of Others.

WRANGELL–SAINT ELIAS NATIONAL PARK AND PRESERVE ESTABLISHED: ANNIVERSARY. Dec 2, 1980. Alaska's Wrangell–St. Elias National Monument, proclaimed Dec 1, 1978, was established as a national park and preserve. For further park info: Wrangell-St. Elias Natl Park and Preserve, PO Box 439, Copper Center, AK 99573. Phone: (907) 822-5234.

BIRTHDAYS TODAY

Wayne Allard, 55, US Senator (R, Colorado), born Fort Collins, CO, Dec 2, 1943.

Dennis Christopher, 43, actor (*Sweet Dreams*), born Philadelphia, PA, Dec 2, 1955.

Randy Gardner, 40, figure skater, born Marina del Rey, CA, Dec 2, 1958.

Adolph Green, 83, actor, composer with Betty Green, born New York, NY, Dec 2, 1915.

Alexander Meigs Haig, Jr, 74, general, former secretary of state in Reagan administration ("I am in control"), born Philadelphia, PA, Dec 2, 1924.

Julie Harris, 73, actress ("Knots Landing," *I Am a Camera, The Member of the Wedding*), born Grosse Pointe, MI, Dec 2, 1925.

Edwin Meese III, 67, former US attorney general, born Oakland, CA, Dec 2, 1931.

Garry Meier, 49, Chicago radio personality, born Chicago, IL, Dec 2, 1949.

Harry Reid, 59, US Senator (D, Nevada), born Searchlight, NV, Dec 2, 1939.

Charlie Ventura, 82, musician, born Philadelphia, PA, Dec 2, 1916.

William Wegman, 55, artist/photographer (of dogs), born Holyoke, MA, Dec 2, 1943.

DECEMBER 3 — THURSDAY

Day 337 — 28 Remaining

BELGIUM: LOVER'S FAIR. Dec 3. Arlon, Belgium. Traditional cultural observance. First Thursday in December.

BHOPAL POISON GAS DISASTER: ANNIVERSARY. Dec 3. At Bhopal, India, on the night of Dec 3, 1984, a leak of deadly gas (methyl isocyanate) at a Union Carbide Corp plant killed more than 2,000 persons and injured more than 200,000 in the world's worst industrial accident.

CHRISTMAS AT PIONEER VILLAGE. Dec 3–4. Worthington, MN. Many different activities are held including: Christmas carolers, sleigh rides, Santa and Mrs Claus, their elves, refreshments and the beautiful decorations. Free admission. For info: Nobles County Historical Society, 407 12th St, Ste 2, Worthington, MN 56187. Phone: (507) 376-4431 or (507) 376-4431.

CONRAD, JOSEPH: BIRTH ANNIVERSARY. Dec 3, 1857. Polish novelist, born Dec 3, 1857; died Aug 3, 1924. Author of *Lord Jim* and *Heart of Darkness*, among others.

FESTIVAL OF TREES. Dec 3–6. Kansas Expocentre, Topeka, KS. The sentiments of the holiday season are illustrated in the array of brilliantly decorated Christmas trees which are the focal point of the annual Festival of Trees Celebration. Trees showcased are donated by community groups, businesses and individuals. Victorian facades enhance the setting which also features a Sweet Shoppe serving homemade delicacies, a boutique stocked with unique handcrafted gifts, live entertainment and a special activity center for children. Proceeds benefit Sheltered Living, Inc, a nonprofit agency whose mission is to support individuals with developmental disabilities in achieving their desired lifestyle based upon self-determination, education, information and opportunity. Free admission. Annually, the first weekend in December. Est attendance: 15,000. For info: Merilee Larson, Sheltered Living Dir, 2044 SW Fillmore, Topeka, KS 66604-3093. Phone: (785) 233-2566. Fax: (785) 233-2566.

December 1998

S	M	T	W	T	F	S
		1	2	3	4	5
6	7	8	9	10	11	12
13	14	15	16	17	18	19
20	21	22	23	24	25	26
27	28	29	30	31		

FIRST HEART TRANSPLANT: ANNIVERSARY. Dec 3, 1967. Dr. Christiaan Barnard, a South African surgeon, performed the world's first successful heart transplantation on Dec 3, 1967, at Cape Town, South Africa. See also: "Barnard, Christiaan Neethling: Birthday" (Nov 8).

ILLINOIS ADMISSION DAY: ANNIVERSARY. Dec 3, 1818. Became 21st state on this day in 1818.

LIBERACE MUSEUM CHRISTMAS TREE LIGHTING CEREMONY. Dec 3. The Liberace Museum, Las Vegas, NV. Santa wearing Liberace's gold lamé Santa suit will pull the switch to light the tree. Free admission to all who donate a new toy or nonperishable food item, which will be given to the Salvation Army for distribution to the needy. For info: Jamie G. James, The James Agency, 3630 Coldwater Canyon Ave, Studio City, CA 91604. Phone: (818) 508-4902. Fax: (818) 508-0562. Email: JamesAgy@aol.com.

MITTEN TREE KICK-OFF CEREMONY. Dec 3. Abel Wolman Municipal Building, Baltimore, MD. To collect mittens and gloves for needy families. Kickoff ceremony includes holiday musical entertainment and a visit from Santa Claus and his elves. Public is invited to hang their donations on a 10-foot live fir tree. Donations will be collected throughout the month of December. For info: Dept of Rec and Parks, Office of Adventures in Fun, Patterson Park Recreation Complex, 2601 E Baltimore St, Baltimore, MD 21224. Phone: (410) 396-9177. Fax: (410) 327-4120.

MONTOYA, CARLOS: 95th BIRTH ANNIVERSARY. Dec 3, 1903. Guitarist and composer renowned for popularizing flamenco guitar music. His solo performances of the Spanish folk form lifted flamenco from its traditional accompaniment role. Montoya never learned to read music and relied on the traditional improvisational nature of flamenco rooted in the Andalusian Gypsy form of music that stressed rhythms and harmonic patterns. He was born Dec 3, 1903, at Madrid, Spain, and died on March 3, 1993, at Wainscott, NY.

MOON PHASE: FULL MOON. Dec 3. Moon enters Full Moon phase at 10:19 PM, EST.

SAINT OLAF CHRISTMAS FESTIVAL. Dec 3–6. St. Olaf College, Northfield, MN. This celebration of the Christmas season brings together 500 student musicians (a 90-piece symphony orchestra and 450 singers) to perform sacred and folk songs from around the world. Annually, the first full weekend in December. Est attendance: 16,000. For info: Dan Jorgensen, Dir PR, St. Olaf College, 1520 St. Olaf Ave, Northfield, MN 55057-1098. Phone: (507) 646-3002. WWW: http://www.stolaf.edu

SPANTAX AIRLINES CRASH: ANNIVERSARY. Dec 3, 1972. Soon after takeoff from Santa Cruz, Tenerife, one of the Canary Islands, a Spantax Convair 990-A Coronado plane carrying mostly German nationals crashed. Of the 155 passengers and crew aboard, only one woman survived the impact of the crash, but she died of her injuries later that day.

STUART, GILBERT CHARLES: BIRTH ANNIVERSARY. Dec 3, 1755. American portrait painter whose most famous painting is that of George Washington. He also painted portraits of Madison, Monroe, Jefferson and other important Americans. Stuart was born near Narragansett, RI, and died at age 72 on July 9, 1828, at Boston, MA.

UNITED NATIONS: INTERNATIONAL DAY OF DISABLED PERSONS. Dec 3. With Resolution 47/3 on Oct 14, 1992, at the end of the Decade of Disabled Persons, the General Assembly proclaimed Dec 3 to be an annual observance to promote the continuation of integrating the disabled into general society.

BIRTHDAYS TODAY

Jean Luc Godard, 68, filmmaker (*Breathless, Weekend*), born Paris, France, Dec 3, 1930.

Daryl Hannah, 37, actress (*Splash*), born Chicago, IL, Dec 3, 1961.

Ferlin Husky, 71, singer ("Gone," "On the Wings of a Dove"), born Flat River, MO, Dec 3, 1927.

Rick Ravon Mears, 47, auto racer, born Wichita, KS, Dec 3, 1951.

Jaye P. Morgan, 66, singer ("That's All I Want From You," "The Longest Walk"), born New York, NY, Dec 3, 1932.

Sven Vilhem Nykvist, 76, Swedish cinematographer, born Moheda, Sweden, Dec 3, 1922.

Ozzy Osbourne, 50, singer, songwriter (originally lead singer for Black Sabbath), born Birmingham, England, Dec 3, 1948.

Andy Williams, 68, singer (platinum album *Love Story*, 13 gold albums), born Wall Lake, IA, Dec 3, 1930.

DECEMBER 4 — FRIDAY

Day 338 — 27 Remaining

ARKANSAS CRAFT GUILD CHRISTMAS SHOWCASE AND SALE. Dec 4–6. Statehouse Convention Center, Little Rock, AR. 20th annual. 100 exhibitors of original handcrafted gifts including woodworks, pottery, stained glass, metalworks, musical instruments, jewelry, baskets and quilts. Admission charged. Est attendance: 5,000. For info: Arkansas Craft Guild, PO Box 800, Mountain View, AR 72560. Phone: (870) 269-3897.

BAY MINETTE CHRISTMAS FEST. Dec 4–5. Courthouse Square, Bay Minette, AL. Family-oriented arts and crafts festival featuring local entertainment, parade, city tree lighting ceremony and Santa's arrival. Annually, the first full weekend in December. For info: Bay Minette Area Chamber of Commerce, PO Box 310, 301 McMeans Ave, Bay Minette, AL 36507. Phone: (334) 937-5665. Fax: (334) 937-5670.

BRITISH NIGHT WEEKEND WATCH. Dec 4–6. St. Augustine, FL. Weekend event that includes eighteenth-century living history reenactments, period song, dance and storytelling. For info: Patti Rang (904) 824-9550 or Gilbert & Manjura Marketing, 346 Freeman St, Longwood, FL 33780-4171.

BUTLER, SAMUEL: BIRTH ANNIVERSARY. Dec 4. English author, born Dec 4, 1835. Died London, June 18, 1902.

CANADA: SUNDOG HANDCRAFT FAIRE. Dec 4–6. Saskatchewan Place, Saskatoon, Sask. More than 150 artisans, artists and specialty food producers display their work at this, the largest event of its kind in western Canada. Entertainment, craft demonstrations, free children's activity center and a multicultural food court. Est attendance: 15,000. For info: (306) 384-7364 or Tourism Saskatchewan, 500-1900 Albert St, Regina, Sask, Canada S4P 4L9. Phone: (800) 667-7191.
Email: travel.info@sasktourism.sk.ca.
WWW: http://www.sasktourism.com

CANDLELIGHT TOURS. Dec 4–5. The Atheneum, New Harmony, IN. Evening tours of historic homes decorated for the holidays with a lantern-bearing escort. Coincides with the Christmas in New Harmony festival. Annually, the first weekend in December. Est attendance: 600. For info: Historic New Harmony, PO Box 579, New Harmony, IN 47631. Phone: (812) 682-4488. Fax: (812) 682-4313. Email: cknudson.ucs@smtp.usi.edu.

CARLYLE, THOMAS: BIRTH ANNIVERSARY. Dec 4. Scottish essayist and historian, born Dec 4, 1795. Died at London, Feb 4, 1881. "A well-written Life is almost as rare as a well-spent one," Carlyle wrote in his *Critical and Miscellaneous Essays*.

CHIMNEYVILLE CRAFTS FESTIVAL. Dec 4–6. Jackson, MS. The finest crafts for sale by more than 100 crafters: woodcarving, blown glass, weavings, baskets, stained glass. Est attendance: 6,500. For info: V.A. Patterson, Exec Dir, The Craftsmen's Guild of Mississippi, Inc, 1150 Lakeland Dr, Jackson, MS 39216. Phone: (601) 981-0019.

CHRISTMAS GREENS SHOW. Dec 4–6. Jackman-Long Building, State Fairgrounds, Salem, OR. Half the building houses decorated trees, large Christmas displays, hundreds of floral arrangements, wreaths and wall hangings. The other half houses 106 handcrafters and their wares. Food available. Proceeds benefit community projects. Annually, the second Friday, Saturday and Sunday after Thanksgiving. Est attendance: 15,000. For info: Linda Nelson, Willamette Christmas Assn, 1856 Dearborn Ave, NE, Salem, OR 97303. Phone: (503) 393-4439.

CHRISTMAS ON THE PRAIRIE. Dec 4–6. Saunders County Museum, Wahoo, NE. Old-fashioned Christmas featuring entertainment by local groups, lots of period costumes, special postal cancellation, children's activities common to the 1800s and demonstrations in the historical village decorated in the 1800s style. Annually, the first weekend after Thanksgiving weekend (one full week after Thanksgiving). Sponsor: Christmas on the Prairie Steering Committee. Est attendance: 4,000. For info: Curator, Saunders County Museum, 240 N Walnut, Wahoo, NE 68066-1858. Phone: (402) 443-3090.

CHRISTMAS PAST AT AUDUBON ACRES. Dec 4–5. Audubon Acres, Chattanooga, TN. Enjoy the sights, tastes, smells and excitement of Christmas long ago; see demonstrations and reenactments of early skills; stroll to the swinging bridge to observe signs of nature in the winter. Sponsor: Chattanooga Audubon Society. Annually, first weekend in December. Est attendance: 1,500. For info: Jeanette Eigelsbach, Audubon Acres, 900 N Sanctuary Rd, Chattanooga, TN 37421. Phone: (423) 892-1499.

CHRISTMAS STROLL. Dec 4. Lewistown, MT. Christmas parade, tree decorating contest, Santa comes to Lewistown, food booths, horse and wagon (sled) rides and Christmas button for a chance on prizes. Annually, the first Friday after Thanksgiving weekend. Est attendance: 1,500. For info: Lewistown Chamber of Commerce, PO Box 818, Lewistown, MT 59457. Phone: (406) 538-5436. Fax: (406) 538-5437. Email: lewchamb@lewistown.net. WWW: http://www.lewistown.net/~lewchamb

CHRISTMAS WALK AND OPEN HOUSE. Dec 4. Bay Head, NJ. 17th annual. Santa arrives at the Bay Head Fire House. Many activities in this historic village by the sea. Annually, the first full weekend in December. Est attendance: 500. For info: Evalyn Shippee, Christmas Walk, Bay Head Business Assn, PO Box 135, Bay Head, NJ 08742-5346. Phone: (732) 892-0223 or (800) 4-BAYHED.

COWBOY CHRISTMAS. Dec 4–6. Wickenburg, AZ. Gathering of cowboy poets and singers who carry on the workings of ranch life and traditional cowboy life in verse and song. Annually, the first weekend in December. Est attendance: 1,500. For info: Wickenburg Chamber of Commerce, 216 N Frontier, Wickenburg, AZ 85390. Phone: (520) 684-5479 or (520) 684-0977. Fax: (520) 684-5470. Email: wburgcoc@primenet.com.

DAY OF THE ARTISANS. Dec 4. Honors the nation's workers.

ENGLAND: WINMAU WORLD DARTS CHAMPIONSHIPS. Dec 4–5. London. Major event in the darts calendar with top players from all over the world competing. Est attendance: 1,500. For info: Mr Olly Croft, Dir, British Darts Organisation, 2 Pages Lane, London, England N10 1PS.

"FALCON CREST" TV PREMIERE: ANNIVERSARY. Dec 4, 1981. This nighttime serial was set in California wine country and originally focused on Angela Channing's determined efforts to gain control of the Falcon Crest vineyard and winery; later the emphasis turned to crime. Famous actors who were a part of the cast at one time or another include: Jane Wyman, Lorenzo Lamas, Billy R. Moses, Cliff Robertson, Lana Turner, Gina Lollobrigida, Parker Stevenson, Anne Archer, Apollonia, Cesar Romero, Morgan Fairchild, Ken Olin and Mary Ann Mobley. In the season finale, Angela received Falcon Crest.

FANTASY OF LIGHTS. Dec 4–Jan 4. Wichita Falls, TX. A spectacular light and toyland display on the Midwestern State University campus delights more than 500,000 holiday spectators. A

Wichita Falls Christmas tradition! For info: Wichita Falls Conv & Visitors Bureau, 1000 Fifth St, Wichita Falls, TX 76301. Phone: (817) 716-5500. Fax: (817) 716-5509.

FRENCH WEST INDIES: INTERNATIONAL JAZZ FESTIVAL. Dec 4–12. Martinique. World renowned performers, concerts and study classes. For info: Muriel Wiltord, Martinique Promo Bureau, 444 Madison Ave, 16th fl, New York, NY 10022. Phone: (800) 391-4909. Fax: (212) 838-7855. Email: martinique@nyo.com. WWW: http://www.martinique.org

GENEVA'S CHRISTMAS WALK. Dec 4–5. Geneva, IL. Spend the day touring charming homes aglow with holiday decorations. In the evening, Santa Lucia, the Swedish symbol of the season, arrives and Santa Claus opens his house for children's visits. Merchants graciously serve traditional holiday refreshments, including roasted chestnuts, as carolers fill the air with the sounds of the season. Annually, the first Friday and Saturday in December. For info: Geneva Chamber of Commerce, 8 S Third St, PO Box 481, Geneva, IL 60134. Phone: (630) 232-6060. Fax: (630) 232-6083.

LAST AMERICAN HOSTAGE RELEASED IN LEBANON: ANNIVERSARY. Dec 4, 1991. A sad chapter of US history came to a close when Terry Anderson, an Associated Press correspondent, became the final American hostage held in Lebanon to be freed. Anderson had been held since Mar 16, 1985, one of 15 Americans who were held hostage for from two months to as long as six years and eight months. Three of the hostages, William Buckley, Peter Kilburn and Lieutenant Colonel William Higgins, were killed during their captivity. The other hostages, released previously one or two at a time, were Jeremy Levin, Benjamin Weir, the Reverend Lawrence Martin Jenco, David Jacobsen, Thomas Sutherland, Frank Herbert Reed, Joseph Cicippio, Edward Austin Tracy, Alan Steen, Jesse Turner and Robert Polhill.

LEMOYNE HOUSE CANDLELIGHT CHRISTMAS TOURS. Dec 4–6. (Also Dec 12–13.) Washington, PA. Evening candlelight tours of the beautifully decorated LeMoyne House. Costumed actors portray the LeMoyne family and interact with visitors. For info: Kara Bradstock, Washington County Historical Society, 49 East Maiden St, Washington, PA 15301. Phone: (412) 225-6740. Fax: (412) 225-8495.

MISSION SANTA BARBARA: FOUNDING ANNIVERSARY. Dec 4, 1786. Franciscan Mission to the Indians founded in Santa Barbara, CA. Present structure is the fourth to stand on same site. Last one destroyed by 1812 earthquake.

NATIONAL GRANGE FOUNDING. Dec 4, 1786. The anniversary of the National Grange, the first organized agricultural movement in the US.

NATIONWIDE INSURANCE ZOOLIGHTS FESTIVAL. Dec 4–31. Metro Washington Park Zoo, Portland, OR. Thousands of lights and animal displays, decorated zoo train, gingerbread village, puppet shows and much more. Est attendance: 50,000. For info: Events Coord, Metro Washington Park Zoo, 4001 SW Canyon Rd, Portland, OR 97221-2799. Fax: (503) 220-5754.

PARADE OF LIGHTS. Dec 4–5. Denver, CO. This 24th annual evening holiday parade features dazzling theme floats, giant helium-filled holiday balloons, magical costumed characters, the area's best marching bands, high-stepping equestrian units and much more. Friday at 8 PM, Saturday at 6 PM. Est attendance: 350,000. For info: Susan Rogers Kark, Sr Dir, Mktg & Events, Downtown Denver Partnership, Inc, Parade of Lights, 511 16th St, Ste 200, Denver, CO 80202-4250. Phone: (303) 534-6161. Fax: (303) 534-2803.

December 1998

S	M	T	W	T	F	S
		1	2	3	4	5
6	7	8	9	10	11	12
13	14	15	16	17	18	19
20	21	22	23	24	25	26
27	28	29	30	31		

RUSSELL, LILLIAN: BIRTH ANNIVERSARY. Dec 4. American singer and actress who in 1881 gained fame in the comic opera *The Great Mogul.* Born Helen Louise Leonard on Dec 4, 1861, at Clinton, IA. Married four times, and died on June 6, 1922, at Pittsburgh, PA.

SAINT BARBARA'S DAY. Dec 4. On this day, traditionally the feast day of St. Barbara, a young girl places a twig from a cherry tree in a glass of water. If it blooms by Christmas Eve, she is certain to marry the following year. Because the narratives of her life and martyrdom are legendary, St. Barbara was dropped from the Roman Catholic Calendar of Saints in 1970.

TEMPE FALL FESTIVAL OF THE ARTS. Dec 4–6. Tempe, AZ. Featuring more than 500 artists and craftspeople, traditional and ethnic foods, continuous entertainment and a children's activity area. Annually, the first weekend in December. Est attendance: 225,000. For info: Britt Kimball, Events Coordinator, Mill Avenue Merchants Assn, 520 S Mill Ave, Ste 201, Tempe, AZ 85281. Phone: (602) 967-4877. Fax: (602) 967-6638.

VICTORIAN CHRISTMAS SLEIGHBELL PARADE. Dec 4–6. Manistee, MI. Re-creation of Manistee history. No motorized vehicles, no amplification. Horse-drawn entries, walking entries, singers, animals and St. Nick in historic garb. Est attendance: 5,000. For info: Manistee Area Chamber of Commerce, 11 Cypress St, Manistee, MI 49660. Phone: (616) 723-2575 or (800) 288-2286. Email: chamber@manistee.com. WWW: http://www.manistee.com:80/~edo/chamber/

WICHITA WINTERFEST. Dec 4–5. Wichita, KS. 7th annual festival for all ages to kick off the winter in holiday style. Carnival rides, games and horse-drawn carriage rides. 5K race for running, rolling or walking on Friday evening. Holiday food court, street carolers. Fireworks to Christmas music over the river, accompanied by the official holiday lighting ceremony. Annually, the first Friday and Saturday of December. Est attendance: 35,000. For info: Mark Chamberlin, KAKE TV-10, 1500 N West St, Wichita, KS 67203. Phone: (316) 946-1323 or (316) 946-1323. Fax: (316) 945-2802. Email: kake@kake.com. WWW: http://www.kake.com

WINTER ALE FESTIVAL. Dec 4–6. Pioneer Courthouse Square, Portland, OR. Unique event celebrates the northwest's microbreweries and their seasonal ales by featuring "The Twelve Ales of Christmas." Held in "Portland's living room" under heated tents. Food, crafts and entertainment featured as well. Est attendance: 7,500. For info: The Winter Ale Festival, 1000 SW Broadway #910, Portland, OR 97205. Phone: (503) 223-2168 or (503) 274-0019. Fax: (503) 223-1819. Email: craigo@koopmanostbo.com.

WINTERFEST. Dec 4–6. Luverne, MN. Christmas Light Parade, hockey tournaments, craft show snow sculpture, poker run, historical tours, live nativity pageant. For info: Norma De Jongh, Exec Dir, Luverne Area Chamber of Commerce, 102 E Main, Luverne, MN 56156. Phone: (507) 283-4061. Fax: (507) 283-4061.

WOLF POINT'S ANNUAL CHRISTMAS PARADE. Dec 4. Wolf Point, MT. The city comes alive with the Christmas spirit in this magical and enchanting evening which features a parade in which all the floats are illuminated with lights, Santa is the master of ceremony and awards for floats are given in three catagories. This event will make you remember what Christmas looks like through the eyes of a child. Est attendance: 1,000. For info: Sally Paulson, Wolf Point Chamber of Commerce, PO Box 237, Wolf Point, MT 59201. Phone: (406) 653-2012. Fax: (406) 653-3240. Email: 2sallyp@3rivers.net.

BIRTHDAYS TODAY

Max Baer, Jr, 61, actor, producer ("The Beverly Hillbillies"; produced *Ode to Billy Joe*), born Oakland, CA, Dec 4, 1937.

Tyra Banks, 25, model, actress ("Soul Train Lady of Soul Awards"), born Los Angeles, CA, Dec 4, 1973.

Jeff Blake, 28, football player, born Sanford, FL, Dec 4, 1970.

Jeff Bridges, 49, actor (*The Fisher King, The Last Picture Show*), born Los Angeles, CA, Dec 4, 1949.

Helen M. Chase, 74, retired chronicler of contemporary civilization as coeditor of *Chase's Annual Events*, born Whitehall, MI, Dec 4, 1924.

Deanna Durbin, 77, actress (*It Started with Eve, Can't Help Singing*), born Winnipeg, Manitoba, Canada, Dec 4, 1921.

Chris Hillman, 56, musician, born Los Angeles, CA, Dec 4, 1942.

Stewart Rawlings Mott, 61, philanthropist, born Flint, MI, Dec 4, 1937.

Marisa Tomei, 34, actress (*The Flamingo Kid, My Cousin Vinny*), born Brooklyn, NY, Dec 4, 1964.

Patricia Wettig, 47, actress ("St. Elsewhere," "thirtysomething" [2 Emmy Awards], *City Slickers*), born Cincinnati, OH, Dec 4, 1951.

DECEMBER 5 — SATURDAY

Day 339 — 26 Remaining

ADELPHIAN CLUB CHRISTMAS BAZAAR. Dec 5. American Legion Building, Kennett, MO. Huge sale of arts and crafts with more than 100 exhibitors, plus a bake sale. Free admission. Annually, the first Saturday in December. For info: Adelphian Civic Club, 301 S Everett, Kennett, MO 63857. Phone: (573) 888-9472.

AFL-CIO FOUNDED: ANNIVERSARY. Dec 5, 1955. The American Federation of Labor and the Congress of Industrial Organizations joined together on this day in 1955, following 20 years of rivalry, to become the nation's leading advocate for trade unions.

ANTIETAM NATIONAL BATTLEFIELD MEMORIAL ILLUMINATION. Dec 5. Antietam National Battlefield, Sharpsburg, MD. 10th annual memorial illumination to the 23,110 casualties at the Battle of Antietam. Nearly 600 volunteers light 23,110 luminaries (candles in bags) that are placed along a 4.5-mile route through the Battlefield. Annually, the first Saturday in December; rain/snow date the following Saturday (Dec 12). 6 PM–midnight. Free admission; donations accepted. Sponsor: Little Heiskell Charter Chapter of American Business Women's Association (ABWA). Est attendance: 14,000. For info: Georgene Charles, Chair, ABWA, PO Box 188, 11850 National Pike, Clear Spring, MD 21722-0188. Phone: (301) 733-7373 or (800) 228-STAY. Fax: (301) 733-7385. Email: charassoc@aol.com.

APPALACHIAN POTTERS MARKET. Dec 5. McDowell High School commons area, Marion, NC. One-day display and sale of clay work only. Annually, the first Saturday in December. Sponsor: McDowell Arts and Crafts Assn. Est attendance: 1,500. For info: Appalachian Potters Market, c/o MACA, PO Box 1387, Marion, NC 28752. Phone: (704) 652-8610.

BATHTUB PARTY DAY. Dec 5. Almost everyone nowadays takes showers, so here's a day to recall some of the luxury of days gone by. Immerse yourself in a long, hot bath. Invite a few friends and take turns. [© 1997 by WPL] For info: Tom and Ruth Roy, Wellness Permission League, PO Box 662, Mt Gretna, PA 17064-0662. Phone: (500) 437-5104 or (717) 964-1308. Fax: (717) 964-1335.

CANDLELIGHT CHRISTMAS IN CHADDS FORD. Dec 5. Chadds Ford, PA. Tours of historic private homes and historic house museums. Annually, the first Saturday in December. Sponsored by Chadds Ford Historical Society and the Brandywine Battlefield Park Associates. Est attendance: 1,000. For info: Chadds Ford Historical Society, PO Box 27, Chadds Ford, PA 19317. Phone: (610) 388-7376. Fax: (610) 388-7480.

CHEEKWOOD'S "TREES OF CHRISTMAS." Dec 5–27. Nashville, TN. A display at the Cheekwood Gardens and Museum of Art of 15 larger-than-life trees lavishly trimmed from head-to-toe in their own unique and individual style, transporting you into a world that is sparkling and bright. For info: Cheekwood Tennessee Botanical Gardens and Museum of Art, 1200 Forest Park Dr, Nashville, TN 37205-4242. Phone: (615) 356-8000.

CHESTER GREENWOOD DAY PARADE. Dec 5. Farmington, ME. Celebration of Farmington's famous inventor of the *earmuff*. An earmuff-themed parade with flag raising. Annually, the first Saturday in December. Est attendance: 500. For info: Greater Farmington Chamber of Commerce, PO Box 108, Farmington, ME 04938. Phone: (207) 778-4215.

CHILDREN'S DAY AND PARADE OF LIGHTS. Dec 5. Kingsville, TX. Breakfast with Santa kicks off a fun-filled day of holiday activities for children ending with an illuminated night-time parade for children of all ages in historic downtown Kingsville. Est attendance: 3,000. For info: Kingsville Conv & Visitors Bureau, PO Box 1562, Kingsville, TX 78364-1562. Phone: (800) 333-5032. Fax: (512) 592-3227. Email: kcvb@kingsville.org. WWW: http://www.kingsville.org

CHRISTMAS CANDLELIGHT TOUR. Dec 5–6. Fredericksburg, VA. To instill the spirit of Christmases past by opening historic homes to the public. Eighteenth-century music, street dancers, carriage rides throughout the tour. Est attendance: 10,000. For info: Visitor Center, 706 Caroline St, Fredericksburg, VA 22401. Phone: (800) 678-4748. Fax: (540) 372-6587. Email: fburg@illuminet.net.

CHRISTMAS CANDLELIGHTINGS. Dec 5–31 (except Dec 25). Coshocton, OH. Nineteenth-century holiday atmosphere, 51-room country inn, hot-mulled cider in visitor center, occasional cooking demonstrations in doctor's house, candlelighting ceremony (Dec 5, 12, 19), special weekend activities including Christmas wagon rides first three weekends in December. Est attendance: 5,000. For info: Roscoe Village Fdtn, 381 Hill St, Coshocton, OH 43812. Phone: (800) 877-1830 or (614) 622-9310. Fax: (614) 623-6555.

CHRISTMAS CRAFT SHOW. Dec 5–6. H.O. Weeks Recreation Center, Aiken, SC. This show consists of more than 200 Christmas exhibits and other items from the Southeast's top craftsmen. The displays range from woodwork to fine porcelain sculpture. 28th annual show. Est attendance: 14,000. For info: Anne Hagelston, PO Box 1177, Aiken, SC 29802. Phone: (803) 642-7630. Fax: (803) 642-7739. Email: gparker@scescape.net.

CHRISTMAS CRAFTS FESTIVAL. Dec 5–6. St. Simons Island, GA. 7th annual festival features 100 fine arts and crafts artists exhibiting holiday decorations and gifts. Annually, the first weekend in December. Est attendance: 10,000. For info: The Glynn Art Assn, 319 Mallory St, PO Box 20673, St. Simons Island, GA 31522. Phone: (912) 368-8770. Fax: (312) 638-8770.

CHRISTMAS FESTIVAL OF LIGHTS. Dec 5. Natchitoches, LA. Known as Festival of Lights, featuring two parades, fireworks, food, entertainment, a fun run/walk and Christmas lighting. Listed as one of the "Top 100 Events in North America" by the American Bus Association. Annually, the first Saturday in December. Est attendance: 150,000. For info: Natchitoches Parish Tourist Commission, 781 Front St, Natchitoches, LA 71457. Phone: (318) 352-8072. Fax: (318) 352-2415.

CHRISTMAS IN THE VILLAGES. Dec 5–6. Van Buren County, IA. Event features tour of homes, English High Tea, cookie walk, Festival of Trees, horse-drawn carriage rides, bake sales, lighting contests and displays, soup suppers and the natural beauty of the season that is found throughout the county. Est attendance: 1,200. For info: Mary E. Muir, Exec Dir, Villages of Van Buren, Inc, PO Box 9, Keosauqua, IA 52565. Phone: (800) 868-7822. Email: villages@netins.net. WWW: http://www.net/showcase/villages

CHRISTMAS ON THE RIVER. Dec 5. Demopolis, AL. Fun with arts and crafts, children's parade, AL BBQ Cook-off, and a river boat parade. Est attendance: 40,000. For info: Jane Gross, Exec Dir, Demopolis Area Chamber of Commerce, Box 667, Demopolis, AL 36732. Phone: (334) 289-0270. Fax: (334) 289-1382.

CHRISTMAS STROLL. Dec 5. Nantucket Island, MA. Christmas trees, costumed carolers, theatrical performances. Santa arrives via Coast Guard boat and is driven up Main St in a horse-drawn carriage. Annually, the first weekend in December. Est attendance: 20,000. For info: Nantucket Island Chamber of Commerce, 48 Main St, Nantucket, MA 02554-3595. Phone: (508) 228-1700.

COOSA RIVER CHRISTMAS. Dec 5. Rome, GA. Parade of pontoon boats decorated with Christmas scenes in lights. The night is topped off with a spectacular fireworks display. Annually, the first Saturday in December. Est attendance: 45,000. For info: Diana Shadday, Coosa River Christmas, PO Box 5823, Rome, GA 30162-5823. Phone: (706) 295-5576. Fax: (706) 236-5029. Email: 90romega@romega.com.

COUNTRY CHRISTMAS. Dec 5 (also Dec 12 and 19). Roscoe Village, Coshocton, OH. Nineteenth-century holiday atmosphere, 51-room country inn, hot mulled cider in Visitor Center. Candlelighting ceremony on the first three Saturdays in December. Special weekend activities including Christmas wagon rides, strolling carolers, visits from Mr & Mrs Santa Claus. Est attendance: 6,500. For info: Cheryl Oswald, Roscoe Village Fdtn, 381 Hill St, Coshocton, OH 43812. Phone: (614) 622-9310 or (800) 877-1830. Fax: (614) 623-6555.

DICKENS ON THE STRAND. Dec 5–6. Galveston, TX. Victorian Christmas celebration focuses on the 19th-century architecture of Galveston's Strand and ties to Charles Dickens's 19th-century London. Annually, the first Saturday–Sunday in December. Est attendance: 50,000. For info: Galveston Historical Foundation, 2016 Strand, Galveston, TX 77550. Phone: (409) 765-7834. Fax: (409) 765-7851. Email: ghf@phoenix.net. WWW: http://www.galvestonhistory.org

December 1998	S	M	T	W	T	F	S
			1	2	3	4	5
	6	7	8	9	10	11	12
	13	14	15	16	17	18	19
	20	21	22	23	24	25	26
	27	28	29	30	31		

DISNEY, WALT: BIRTH ANNIVERSARY. Dec 5, 1901. Animator, filmmaker, born at Chicago, IL. He became famous in 1928 with the presentation of Mickey Mouse in *Steamboat Willie*. Disney treatments of classic children's stories include *Peter Pan*, *Cinderella* and *Alice in Wonderland*. Disney died at Los Angeles, CA, Dec 15, 1966.

GETTYSBURG YULETIDE FESTIVAL. Dec 5–6 (also Dec 12–13). Gettysburg, PA. Tours of decorated historic homes, live nativity scene, caroling and handbell choirs, Christmas parade, community concerts, holiday dessert tasting and candlelight walking tour. Annually, the first and second weekends in December. Est attendance: 4,000. For info: Gettysburg Conv & Visitors Bureau, 35 Carlisle St, Gettysburg, PA 17325-1899. Phone: (717) 334-6274. Fax: (717) 334-1166. WWW: http://www.gettysburg.com

GRANT'S SPEECH OF APOLOGY: ANNIVERSARY. Dec 5. On this day in 1876, President Ulysses S. Grant delivered his speech of apology to Congress claiming mistakes he made while he was president were due to his inexperience. His errors, he said, were "errors of judgment, not intent." While Grant's personal integrity was never formally questioned, he was closely associated with many government scandals which became public during his presidency. He unwittingly aided Jay Gould in an attempt to corner the gold market during his first term. During the second, the Credit Mobilier affair involving many of the president's friends aired, while significant fraud was discovered in the Treasury Department and Indian Service.

HAITI: DISCOVERY DAY: ANNIVERSARY. Dec 5. Commemorates the discovery of Haiti by Christopher Columbus in 1492. Public holiday.

HERITAGE CHRISTMAS. Dec 5 (also Dec 12). Old Mill Museum Complex, Lindsborg, KS. A celebration of Christmas past with the music, drama and costumes of a traditional pioneer Christmas on the Kansas prairie. Annually, the first two Saturday evenings in December. Est attendance: 1,200. For info: McPherson County Old Mill Museum, PO Box 94, Lindsborg, KS 67456. Phone: (913) 227-3595. WWW: http://www.lindsborg.org

HOLIDAY CELEBRATION. Dec 5–6. Chimney Rock Park, Chimney Rock, NC. Holiday music, ornament making, Santa and more. Est attendance: 1,500. For info: Mary Ritter, PR, Chimney Rock Park, PO Box 39, Chimney Rock, NC 28720. Phone: (800) 277-9611. Fax: (704) 625-9610. Email: visit@chimneyrockpark.com. WWW: http://www.chimneyrockpark.com

KECHI'S ANTIQUE COUNTRY CHRISTMAS. Dec 5. Kechi, KS. Spend the day in "The Antique Capital of Kansas" strolling through our small quaint community of 20 antique, craft and speciality shops. Enjoy fine dining in local restaurants, Christmas caroling in the downtown area, tour Karg Art Glass & Gallery and an old-fashioned surrey ride. Est attendance: 650. For info: Kechi Area Chamber of Commerce, PO Box 578, Kechi, KS 67067-0578. Phone: (316) 744-9403. Fax: (316) 744-1337. Email: kechirick@feist.com.

KRISTKINDL MARKT. Dec 5–6. Stone Hill Winery Pavilion, Hermann, MO. German Christmas market featuring imported German gifts and decorations plus many handcrafted items. Homemade German specialty soups and cookies and costumed entertainers. Annually, the first weekend in December. Est attendance: 3,000. For info: Visitor Info Center, Hermann Tourism Group, 306 Market St, PO Box 104, Hermann, MO 65041. Phone: (800) 932-8687. Fax: (573) 486-5363.

LIGHTED BOAT PARADE ON THE TENN-TOM WATERWAY. Dec 5. Columbus, MS. Boat owners from throughout the area decorate their boats in holiday themes and parade at Lock and Dam area in Columbus. Grand finale fireworks show lights up the sky and is reflected in the water. Est attendance: 20,000. For info: Columbus Conv and Visitors Bureau, PO Box 789, Columbus, MS 39703. Phone: (800) 327-2686. Fax: (601) 329-8969. Email: ccvb@tilc.com. WWW: http://friendship.columbus.ms.us

MADRIGAL DINNER AND CONCERT. Dec 5–6. Mount Mary College, Milwaukee, WI. Saturday dinner concert and silent auction. Sunday dessert concert and silent auction. Est attendance: 400. For info: Mary Cain, PR Office, Mount Mary College, 2900 N Menomonee River Pkwy, Milwaukee, WI 53222-4545. Phone: (414) 256-1210. Fax: (414) 256-1205. Email: mktg@mtmary.edu. WWW: http://www.mtmary.edu

MONTGOMERY BUS BOYCOTT BEGINS: ANNIVERSARY. Dec 5, 1955. On Dec 1, 1955, Rosa Parks was arrested in Montgomery, AL, for refusing to give up her seat on a bus to a white man. In support of Parks, and to protest the arrest, the black community of Montgomery organized a boycott of the bus system. The boycott lasted from Dec 5, 1955, to Dec 20, 1956, when a US Supreme Court ruling was implemented in Montgomery, integrating the public transportation system.

MOZART, WOLFGANG AMADEUS: DEATH ANNIVERSARY. Dec 5, 1791. Born on Jan 27, 1756, at Salzburg, Austria, Johann Chrysostom Wolfgang Amadeus Mozart is regarded as one of the greatest musical geniuses of all time. As he gained proficiency at the harpsichord and the violin, he began composing at the age of five. He later concentrated his efforts on the pianoforte and under the direction of his father, Mozart and his sister, Maria Anna, began touring Europe in 1762. Throughout the tours, Mozart continued composing and in 1775 began service under the Archbishop in Salzburg. While in Salzburg he composed *Idomeneo*, the first of his mature operas. Mozart broke with the Archbishop in 1781 and settled in Vienna, risking his existence without official patronage. After years of waiting, he was engaged in the service of the emperor, Joseph II, as a chamber composer, but at far less wages than his predecessor. Although he enjoyed artistic and popular success, Mozart's finances were never secure. An ardent Freemason, he borrowed extensively from his Masonic brothers, despite the successes of his operas *The Marriage of Figaro, Don Giovanni, Cosi fan tutti* and *The Magic Flute* and his extensive work for the piano. Mozart became seriously ill in the fall of 1791, and his rapid decline led to speculation that he had been poisoned, although this later was proved false. Mozart died a pauper on Dec 5, 1791, at Vienna, Austria.

NORSKEDALEN'S OLD-FASHIONED CHRISTMAS. Dec 5–6. Coon Valley, WI. Celebrate an old-fashioned Christmas with decorated pioneer log homes to view, entertainment, a la carte ethnic foods, raffle, horse-drawn wagon/sleigh rides and outdoor activities. Fun for all ages. 10 AM–4 PM. Est attendance: 500. For info: Norskedalen's Nature and Heritage Center, PO Box 225, Coon Valley, WI 54623. Phone: (608) 452-3424. Fax: (608) 452-3157.

☆ ☆ ☆

NORWEGIAN CHRISTMAS. Dec 5–6. Brooklyn Park, MN. Old-fashioned farm Christmas with turn-of-the-century decorations, carolers, making of traditional gifts, lefse and other Norwegian delicacies, visit by St. Nicholas and sleigh rides. Est attendance: 3,500. For info: Kay Grotenhuis, Site Mgr, Brooklyn Park Historical Farm, 4345 101st Ave N, Brooklyn Park, MN 55443.

PALM HARBOR ART, CRAFT AND MUSIC FESTIVAL. Dec 5–6. Palm Harbor, FL. Juried arts and craft show with exhibitors from all over the US. Artists cash awards: $13,000. Est attendance: 40,000. For info: Connie Davis, Exec Dir, Palm Harbor Chamber of Commerce, 32845 US 19N, Ste 210, Palm Harbor, FL 34684-3123. Phone: (813) 784-4287. Fax: (813) 786-2336.

PICKETT, BILL: BIRTH ANNIVERSARY. Dec 5, 1870. American rodeo cowboy, born at Williamson County, TX; died Apr 21, 1932, at Tulsa, OK. Inventor of bulldogging, the modern rodeo event that involves wrestling a running steer to the ground.

PROHIBITION REPEAL: 65th ANNIVERSARY. Dec 5, 1933. Congress proposed repeal of Amendment XVIII (". . . the manufacture, sale, or transportation of intoxicating liquors, within, the importation thereof into, or the exportation thereof from the United States and all territory subject to the jurisdiction thereof, for beverage purposes is hereby prohibited. . . .") on Feb 20, 1933. By Dec 5, 1933, the repeal amendment had been ratified by the required 36 states and went into effect immediately as Amendment XXI to the US Constitution.

SANTA BY STAGE COACH PARADE. Dec 5. El Centro, CA. Annually, the first Saturday in December. Est attendance: 25,000. For info: El Centro Chamber of Commerce, Box 3006, El Centro, CA 92244. Phone: (760) 352-3681. Fax: (760) 352-3246. WWW: http://www.elcentro.com

SNOWFLAKE FESTIVAL. Dec 5–13. Klamath Falls, OR. Celebration of winter season in the community. Est attendance: 25,000. For info: City of Klamath Falls, Snowflake Festival, 226 S 5th St, Klamath Falls, OR 97601. Phone: (541) 883-5368. Fax: (541) 883-5395.

THAILAND: KING'S BIRTHDAY AND NATIONAL DAY. Dec 5. Celebrated throughout the kingdom with colorful pageantry. Stores and houses decorated with spectacular illuminations at night. Public holiday.

TWELVE VILLAGES OF CHRISTMAS. Dec 5–6 (also Dec 12–13 and 19–20). Each of 12 cities in Washington County, KS, organizes events including special lighting of entire county, craft festivals, drawings, special musical programs, home tour, retail open houses, youth Christmas card contest; some towns have a Christmas tree in every yard; large Christmas stocking give-aways; and much more. Annually, the three weekends before Christmas. Est attendance: 7,000. For info: Washington County Economic Development, Kansas, Billie Jo Smart, Dir, Court House, Washington, KS 66968. Phone: (913) 325-2116. Fax: (913) 325-2830.

TWENTY-FIRST AMENDMENT TO THE US CONSTITUTION RATIFIED: 65th ANNIVERSARY. Dec 5, 1933. Prohibition ended with the repeal of the Eighteenth Amendment, as the Twenty-First Amendment was ratified on Dec 5, 1933.

UNITED NATIONS: INTERNATIONAL VOLUNTEER DAY FOR ECONOMIC AND SOCIAL DEVELOPMENT. Dec 5. In a resolution of Dec 17, 1985, the United Nations General Assembly recognized the desirability of encouraging the work of all volunteers. It invited governments to observe, annually on Dec 5, the "International Volunteer Day for Economic and Social Development, urging them to take measures to heighten awareness of the important contribution of volunteer service." A day commemorating the establishment in December 1970 of the UN Volunteers program and inviting world recognition of volunteerism in the international development movement. For info: United Nations, Dept of Public Info, Public Inquiries Unit, Rm GA-57, New York, NY 10017. Phone: (212) 963-4475. Fax: (212) 963-0071. Email: inquiries@un.org.

VAN BUREN, MARTIN: BIRTH ANNIVERSARY. Dec 5, 1782. The eighth president of the US (term of office: Mar 4, 1837–Mar 3, 1841) was the first to have been born a citizen of the US. He was a widower for nearly two decades before he entered the White House. His daughter-in-law, Angelica, served as White House hostess during an administration troubled by bank and business failures, depression and unemployment. Van Buren was born at Kinderhook, NY, Dec 5, 1782, and died there July 24, 1862, leaving an estate of about $250,000.

VICTORIAN CHRISTMAS HOME TOUR, BRUNCH AND DINNER. Dec 5 (tentative). Leadville, CO. Highlight of the holiday season—annual showing off of Leadville's historic homes and buildings bedecked in Christmas trimmings. Locals and guests alike dress in period fashions. Est attendance: 425. For info: Gloria Cheshier, Exec Dir, Chamber of Commerce, Box 861, Leadville, CO 80461. Phone: (719) 486-3900 or (800) 933-3901. Email: leadville@sni.net.
WWW: http://www.colorado.com/leadville

WHEATLEY, PHILLIS: DEATH ANNIVERSARY. Dec 5, 1784. Born in Africa in about 1753, Phillis Wheatley was brought to the US in 1761 and purchased as a slave by a Boston tailor named John Wheatley. She was allotted unusual privileges for a slave, including being allowed to learn to read and write. She wrote her first poetry at age 14, and her first work was published in 1770. Wheatley's fame as a poet spread throughout Europe as well as the US after her *Poems on Various Subjects, Religious and Moral* was published in England in 1773. She was invited to visit George Washington's army headquarters after he read a poem she'd written about him in 1776. Phillis Wheatley died at about age 30 on Dec 5, 1784, at Boston, MA.

WILDLIFE ART EXHIBITION. Dec 5–6. New Hope, PA. Meet 50 regionally and nationally known wildlife artists. Find out how artists work in the wild. See art celebrating nature from marine mammals, fish and birds of prey, to wildflowers, insects and songbirds. Est attendance: 2,000. For info: Donna Oliver, Event Coord, Bucks County Audubon Society, 6324 Upper York Rd, New Hope, PA 18938. Phone: (215) 297-5880.

YULETIDE SEASON. Dec 5 (also Dec 12, 19 and 26). Westville, Lumpkin, GA. A time of spirited Christmas cheer, with period decorations and festivities. Special activities include a yule log ceremony, Christmas tree lighting and the Burning of the Greens. Est attendance: 2,000. For info: Westville, PO Box 1850, Lumpkin, GA 31815. Phone: (912) 838-6310 or (888) 733-1850.
WWW: http://www.westville.org

Happy Holiday

BIRTHDAYS TODAY

Morgan Brittany (Suzanne Cupito), 48, actress (Katherine Wentworth on "Dallas," Vivien Leigh in "Moviola"; *The Birds, Marnie*), born Hollywood, CA, Dec 5, 1950.
José Carreras, 52, opera singer, one of the "Three Tenors," born at Barcelona, Spain, Dec 5, 1946.
Margaret Cho, 30, actress ("All American Girl"), born San Francisco, CA, Dec 5, 1968.
Joan Didion, 64, author, journalist (*After Henry, Run River, The White Album*), born Sacramento, CA, Dec 5, 1934.
Carrie Hamilton, 35, actress (Reggie in "Fame"; *Tokyo Pop*), daughter of Carol Burnett, born New York, NY, Dec 5, 1963.
Jeroen Krabbe, 54, actor (*A World Apart, King of the Hill, The Fugitive*), born Amsterdam, The Netherlands, Dec 5, 1944.
Jim Messina, 51, singer (with Loggins and Messina; "Your Mama Won't Dance"), songwriter, born Maywood, CA, Dec 5, 1947.
Chad Mitchell, 62, singer (leader of the Chad Mitchell trio; "Lizzie Borden"), born Portland, OR, Dec 5, 1936.
Art Monk, 41, football player, born White Plains, NY, Dec 5, 1957.
Strom Thurmond, 96, US Senator (R, South Carolina), born Edgefield, SC, Dec 5, 1902.
Calvin Trillin, 63, author (*American Stories, Remembering Denny*), born Kansas City, MO, Dec 5, 1935.

December 1998

S	M	T	W	T	F	S
		1	2	3	4	5
6	7	8	9	10	11	12
13	14	15	16	17	18	19
20	21	22	23	24	25	26
27	28	29	30	31		

DECEMBER 6 — SUNDAY

Day 340 — 25 Remaining

ALTAMONT CONCERT: ANNIVERSARY. Dec 6. A free concert featuring performances by the Rolling Stones; Jefferson Airplane; Santana; Crosby, Stills, Nash and Young; and the Flying Burrito Brothers turned into tragedy on this day in 1969. The "thank-you" concert for 300,000 fans was marred by overcrowding, drug overdoses and the fatal stabbing of a spectator by a member of the Hell's Angels motorcycle gang, who had been hired as security guards for the event. The concert was held at the Altamont Speedway, Livermore, CA.

CHRISTMAS TO REMEMBER. Dec 6. Laurel, MT. To officially open the Christmas season in Laurel, this daylong celebration includes the arrival of Santa, a community bazaar, wagon, children's craft activities, musical entertainment, lighting ceremony, parade of lights and fireworks. Annually, the first Sunday of December. Est attendance: 10,000. For info: Christmas to Remember Committee, Jean Carol Thompson, 616 Sixth Ave, Laurel, MT 59044. Phone: (406) 628-4508.

CHRISTMAS TOUR OF THE INNS. Dec 6. Bay Head, NJ. Annual tour of the Inns; public rooms decorated for Christmas. Refreshments served. Est attendance: 300. For info: Bay Head Business Assn, Attn: Christmas Tour of the Inns, PO Box 135, Bay Head, NJ 08742. Phone: (732) 892-0223 or (800) 4-BAY-HED.

CLERC-GALLAUDET WEEK. Dec 6–12. Martin Luther King Memorial Library, Washington, DC. Week in which to celebrate the birth anniversaries of Laurent Clerc (Dec 26, 1785) and Thomas Hopkins Gallaudet (Dec 10, 1787). Clerc and Gallaudet pioneered education for the deaf in the US while serving as role models to both deaf and hearing people and together they helped to promote literacy and lifelong learning for all people. Activities will include a lecture on Clerc and Gallaudet, storytelling for all ages and a library display of books, videotapes, magazines, newspapers and posters. For info: Janice Rosen, Librarian for the Deaf Community, DC Library, Room 215, 901 G St, NW, Washington, DC 20001. Phone: (301) 572-5168 TTY. Fax: (301) 572-4134. Email: JanRosen@aol.com.

ECUADOR: DAY OF QUITO. Dec 6. Commemorates founding of city of Quito by Spaniards in 1534.

EISENSTAEDT, ALFRED: 100th BIRTH ANNIVERSARY. Dec 6, 1898. American photojournalist Alfred Eisenstaedt was born at Dirschau, Prussia. One of the greatest photojournalists in US history he is best known for his 86 photos that were used on covers of *Life* magazine, including the photo of the sailor kissing a nurse in New York's Time Square at the end of World War II. He died on Aug 23, 1995, at Martha's Vineyard, MA.

ENTOMOLOGICAL SOCIETY OF AMERICA ANNUAL MEETING AND EXHIBITION. Dec 6–10. Nashville, TN. Est attendance: 2,500. For info: ESA, 9301 Annapolis Rd, Lanham, MD 20706-3115. Phone: (301) 731-4535. Fax: (301) 731-4538. Email: meet@entsoc.org.
WWW: http://www@entsoc.org

FINLAND: INDEPENDENCE DAY. Dec 6, 1917. National holiday. Declaration of independence from Russia on this day, 1917.

GERALD FORD SWEARING-IN AS VICE PRESIDENT: 25th ANNIVERSARY. Dec 6, 1973. On this day in 1973, Gerald Ford was sworn in as vice president under Richard Nixon, following the resignation of Spiro Agnew after pleading no contest to a charge of income tax evasion. See also "Agnew, Spiro Theodore: Birthday" (Nov 9) and "Ford, Gerald Rudolph: Birthday" (July 14).

GERSHWIN, IRA: BIRTH ANNIVERSARY. Dec 6, 1896. Pulitzer Prize–winning American lyricist and author who collaborated with his brother, George, and with many other composers. Among his Broadway successes: *Lady Be Good, Funny Face, Strike Up the Band* and such songs as: "The Man I Love," "Someone to Watch Over Me," "I Got Rhythm" and hundreds of others. Born at New York City, Dec 6, 1896; died at Beverly Hills, CA, Aug 17, 1983.

GINGERBREAD VILLAGE AND BAZAAR. Dec 6–12. St. George's Church, Middlebury, CT. Fairy land of newly baked gingerbread houses—all edible and all for sale. Bazaar, food, handicrafts and gingerbread cookie men. Groups by reservation. Handicapped access available. Est attendance: 2,000. For info: St. George's Church, Gingerbread Village and Bazaar, Tuckerhill Rd at Rte 188, 591 3 Mile Hill Rd, Middlebury, CT 06762.

HALIFAX, NOVA SCOTIA, DESTROYED: ANNIVERSARY. Dec 6, 1917. 1,654 people were killed in Halifax when the Norwegian ship *Imo* plowed into the French munitions ship *Mont Blanc. Imo* was loaded with supplies for war-torn Europe, and *Mont Blanc* was loaded with 4,000 tons of TNT, 2,300 tons of picric acid, 61 tons of other explosives and a deck of highly flammable benzene, which ignited and touched off an explosion. In addition to those killed, 1,028 were injured. A tidal wave caused by the explosion washed much of the city's remains out to sea.

KILMER, JOYCE (ALFRED): BIRTH ANNIVERSARY. Dec 6, 1886. American poet most famous for his poem "Trees," which was published in 1913, was born Dec 6, 1886. Kilmer was killed in action near Ourcy, France, in World War I, on July 30, 1918. Camp Kilmer was named for him.

LEVINE, CHARLES A.: DEATH ANNIVERSARY. Dec 6. Charles A. Levine, whose efforts to beat Charles Lindbergh across the Atlantic by plane were stymied by a lawsuit, nevertheless became the first air passenger to cross the Atlantic Ocean. Levine's 225-horsepower plane, *The Columbia*, was grounded when one of his copilots filed a suit hours after Lindbergh took off from Roosevelt Field. Not to be overshadowed by Lindbergh's success, Levine announced that his flight, leaving June 4, 1927, would fly beyond Paris and to Berlin, with himself as a passenger. Piloted by Clarence Chamberlin, the plane exhausted its fuel and landed in Eisleben, Germany, on June 6, 100 miles short of his goal. The flight set a new record of 3,911 miles in 43 hours of nonstop flight, besting Lindbergh by approximately 300 miles. Levine was born at North Adams, MA, in 1897 and died at Washington, DC, on Dec 6, 1991.

MISSOURI EARTHQUAKES: ANNIVERSARY. Dec 6, 1811. New Madrid, MO. Most violent and prolonged series of earthquakes in US history occured not in California, but in the quiet Midwest. Lasted until Feb 12, 1812. There were few deaths because of the sparse population.

NATIONAL PAWNBROKERS DAY. Dec 6. Celebrated on St. Nicholas Day, the patron saint of pawnbroking. Designed to acknowledge the valuable lending and retail services the pawnbroker provides his or her clientele. For info: Nancy Michaels, Impression Impact, 369 Lindsay Pond Rd, Concord, MA 01742. Phone: (508) 287-0718. Fax: (508) 287-0410.

POLISH-AMERICAN CHRISTMAS GALA. Dec 6. Cicero, IL. Traditional and new Polish-American carols, narrated in English; spirited Polish and American folk songs; Polish folk and court dances; Polish holiday customs; colorful folk costumes. Annually, the first Sunday in December. The Gala also takes place in other midwest states—please call for dates and locations. Est attendance: 1,500. For info: Susan Smentek, Asst Mgr, The Lira Ensemble, 6525 N Sheridan Rd, #Sky 905, Chicago, IL 60626. Phone: (800) 547-5472.

RENOIR, CLAUDE: BIRTH ANNIVERSARY. Dec 6, 1914. French film cameraman Claude Renoir was born at Paris, France, a grandson of painter Pierre Renoir. His films include *The River* (1951) and *The Spy Who Loved Me* (1977). He died on Sept 5, 1993, at Troyes, France.

SAINT NICHOLAS DAY. Dec 6. One of the most venerated saints of both eastern and western Christian churches, of whose life little is known, except that he was Bishop Myra in the fourth century, and that from early times he has been one of the most often pictured saints, especially noted for his charity. Santa Claus and the presentation of gifts is said to derive from St. Nicholas.

"TALENT SCOUTS" TV PREMIERE: 50th ANNIVERSARY. Dec 6, 1948. Host Arthur Godfrey took his radio show to TV in 1948. On this talent show, celebrity guests introduced amateur and young professional acts. It was a weekly show until 1958. For several years beginning in 1960 it was a summer replacement series called "Celebrity Talent Scouts" and "Hollywood Talent Scouts." Hosts included Sam Levenson, Jim Backus, Merv Griffin and Art Linkletter. Pat Boone, Shari Lewis and the McGuire Sisters got their start here.

THIRTEENTH AMENDMENT TO THE US CONSTITUTION RATIFIED: ANNIVERSARY. Dec 6, 1865. The Thirteenth Amendment to the Constitution was ratified, abolishing slavery in the United States. The Thirteenth, Fourteenth and Fifteenth amendments are considered the Civil War Amendments.

WSBA/WARM 103 CHRISTMAS CRAFT SHOW. Dec 6. York Fairgrounds, York, PA. More than 300 crafts, from country to contemporary, Victorian and southwestern, handcrafted furniture, wood carvings, dolls, jewelry, pottery, collectibles, quilts, baskets and much more. Admission fee. Est attendance: 7,000. For info: Gina M. Koch, Special Events Dir, PO Box 910, York, PA 17402-0619. Phone: (717) 764-1155. Fax: (717) 252-4807.

BIRTHDAYS TODAY

Stephen Wayne (Steve) Bedrosian, 41, former baseball player, born Methuen, MA, Dec 6, 1957.
Dave Brubeck, 78, jazz musician, born Concord, CA, Dec 6, 1920.
Andrew Cuomo, 41, US Secretary of Housing and Urban Development (Clinton administration), born Queens, NY, Dec 6, 1957.
Otto Graham, 77, former football coach and Pro Football Hall of Fame quarterback, born Waukegan, IL, Dec 6, 1921.
Thomas Hulce, 45, actor (*Amadeus, The Inner Circle*), born Plymouth, MI, Dec 6, 1953.
James Naughton, 53, actor (*The Paper Chase, The Good Mother*; stage: *Long Day's Journey into Night*), born Middletown, CT, Dec 6, 1945.
Don Nickles, 50, US Senator (R, Oklahoma), born Ponca City, OK, Dec 6, 1948.
Walter Ray Perkins, 57, former football coach, born Mount Olive, MS, Dec 6, 1941.
Janine Turner, 36, actress ("Northern Exposure," *Cliffhanger*), born Lincoln, NE, Dec 6, 1962.
JoBeth Williams, 45, actress (*The Big Chill, Murder Ordained*), born Houston, TX, Dec 6, 1953.

DECEMBER 7 — MONDAY

Day 341 — 24 Remaining

ARMENIAN EARTHQUAKE OF 1988: 10th ANNIVERSARY. Dec 7, 1988. An earthquake measuring 6.9 on the Richter scale rocked the Soviet province of Armenia killing upwards of 60,000 people. The devastated area was described as similiar to a war zone, and many of the deaths were blamed on poor construction practices as many homes had been made of adobe, mud, stones, had unreinforced masonry or were prefabricated structures made of loosely connected concrete slabs. In the quake's aftermath, Soviet President Mikhail Gorbachev cut short his trip to the US to fly home and head the massive worldwide relief efforts.

CATHER, WILLA SIBERT: 125th BIRTH ANNIVERSARY. Dec 7, 1873. American author born at Winchester, VA. Died at New York, NY, Apr 24, 1947. Best known for her novels about the development of early 20th-century modern American life, such as *O Pioneers!* and *My Antonia*. She won a Pulitzer Prize in 1922 for her book *One of Ours*.

CENTRAL AFRICAN REPUBLIC: NATIONAL DAY OBSERVED. Dec 7. Commemorates Proclamation of the Republic on Dec 1, 1958. Usually observed on the first Monday in December.

CHAPIN, HARRY: BIRTH ANNIVERSARY. Dec 7, 1942. Anniversary of the birth of folk singer/songwriter Harry Chapin. One of only five songwriters to receive the Special Congressional Gold Medal for his devotion to the issue of hunger throughout the world. Born Dec 7, 1942, at Greenwich Village, NY, and was killed in a car accident in July of 1981 at Long Island, NY. For info: Mike Lizonitz. Phone: (717) 655-1330. Email: magicmik@darklands.microserve.com.

DELAWARE RATIFIES CONSTITUTION: ANNIVERSARY. Dec 7, 1787. Delaware became the first state to ratify the proposed Constitution on Dec 7, 1787. It did so by unanimous vote.

MOST BORING CELEBRITIES OF THE YEAR. Dec 7. 15th annual list of celebrities chosen because of "massive media over-exposure" during the year. For info: The Boring Institute, Alan Caruba, Founder, Box 40, Maplewood, NJ 07040. Phone: (973) 763-6392. Fax: (973) 763-4287.

NATIONAL FIRE SAFETY COUNCIL: FOUNDING ANNIVERSARY. Dec 7, 1979. Founded to promote fire prevention awareness. For info: Barbara Handley Huggett, Dir Research and Development, Natl Fire Safety Council Inc, PO Box 378, Michigan Center, MI 49254-0378. Phone: (517) 764-2811.

PEARL HARBOR DAY: ANNIVERSARY. Dec 7. At 7:55 AM (local time) on Dec 7, 1941, "a date that will live in infamy," nearly 200 Japanese aircraft attacked Pearl Harbor, Hawaii, long considered the US "Gibraltar of the Pacific." The raid, which lasted little more than one hour, left nearly 3,000 dead. Nearly the entire US Pacific Fleet was at anchor there, and few ships escaped damage. Several were sunk or disabled, while 200 US aircraft on the ground were destroyed. The attack on Pearl Harbor brought about immediate US entry into World War II, a Declaration of War being requested by President Franklin D. Roosevelt, and approved by the Congress on Dec 8, 1941.

RECIPE GREETINGS FOR THE HOLIDAYS. Dec 7–13. A week in which to send recipes as great greetings. Create your own or send a large SASE for ideas. Annually, the second week in December. For info: Recipe Greetings, PO Box 416, Denver, CO 80201. Phone: (303) 575-5676.

SPACE MILESTONE: *APOLLO 17* (US). Dec 7, 1972. Launched this date with three-man crew: Eugene A. Cernan, Harrison H. Schmidt, Ronald E. Evans, explored moon, Dec 11–14. Lunar landing module named *Challenger*. Pacific splashdown, Dec 19.

TUSSAUD, MARIE GROSHOLTZ: BIRTH ANNIVERSARY. Dec 7. Creator of Madame Tussaud's waxwork museum born at Strasbourg, France, Dec 7, 1761. Many of the wax figures she created are still on view at Madame Tussaud's in London. She died at London, Apr 15, 1850.

UNITED NATIONS: INTERNATIONAL CIVIL AVIATION DAY. Dec 7. On Dec 6, 1996, the General Assembly proclaimed Dec 7 as International Civil Aviation Day. On Dec 7, 1944, the convention on International Civil Aviation, which established the International Civil Aviation Organization, was signed. Info from: United Nations, Dept of Public Info, New York, NY 10017.

BIRTHDAYS TODAY

Johnny Lee Bench, 51, Baseball Hall of Fame catcher, born Oklahoma City, OK, Dec 7, 1947.

Larry Joe Bird, 42, former basketball player, born West Baden, IN, Dec 7, 1956.

Ellen Burstyn (Edna Rae Gilhooley), 66, actress (Catherine in "Twin Peaks"; *The Hustler, The Exorcist, The Cemetery Club*), born Detroit, MI, Dec 7, 1932.

Thad Cochran, 61, US Senator (R, Mississippi), born Pontotoc, MS, Dec 7, 1937.

Susan M. Collins, 46, US Senator (R, Maine), born Caribou, ME, Dec 7, 1952.

C. Thomas Howell, 32, actor ("Two Marriages," *Soul Man, Tank*), born Los Angeles, CA, Dec 7, 1966.

Tom Waits, 49, singer (album *Foreign Affairs*), songwriter ("I Never Talk to Strangers"), actor (*Down by Law, Short Cuts*), born New York, NY, Dec 7, 1949.

Eli Wallach, 83, actor (*The Tiger Makes Out*; Emmy for "The Poppy Is Also a Flower"), born New York, NY, Dec 7, 1915.

DECEMBER 8 — TUESDAY

Day 342 — 23 Remaining

AMERICAN FEDERATION OF LABOR (AFL) FOUNDED: ANNIVERSARY. Dec 8, 1886. Originally founded at Pittsburgh, PA, as the Federation of Organized Trades and Labor Unions of the United States and Canada in 1881, the union was reorganized in 1886 under the name American Federation of Labor (AFL). The AFL was dissolved as a separate

December 1998

S	M	T	W	T	F	S
		1	2	3	4	5
6	7	8	9	10	11	12
13	14	15	16	17	18	19
20	21	22	23	24	25	26
27	28	29	30	31		

entity in 1955 when it merged with the Congress of Industrial Organizations to form the AFL-CIO. See also: "AFL-CIO Founding: Anniversary (Dec 5)."

BERGALIS, KIMBERLY: DEATH ANNIVERSARY. Dec 8. Kimberly Bergalis, the first patient believed to have contracted the AIDS virus from a health care professional, died on Dec 8, 1991, at Fort Pierce, FL. Her case sparked controversy over how the disease is transmitted and incited calls to ban infected health care professionals from the workplace.

CHINESE NATIONALISTS MOVE TO FORMOSA: ANNIVERSARY. Dec 8, 1949. The government of Chiang Kai-Shek moves to Formosa (Taiwan) after being driven out of Mainland China by the Communists.

CLUTE'S CHRISTMAS IN THE PARK. Dec 8–11. Clute Municipal Park, Clute, TX. A Christmas event with nightly entertainment, Santa's Land, a beautifully decorated Christmas tree forest and a marshmallow roasting pit. Great family fun for all ages. Food and crafts. Annually, the second Tuesday through Friday in December. Est attendance: 4,500. For info: Clute Parks and Recreation, PO Box 997, Clute, TX 77531. Phone: (800) 371-2971.

DAVIS, SAMMY, JR: BIRTH ANNIVERSARY. Dec 8, 1925. Born at New York, NY, Sammy Davis, Jr, was the son of vaudevillians and first appeared on the stage at the age of four. He made his first film appearance in *Rufus Jones for President* in 1931. He then joined the Will Mastin Trio. The popular song-and-dance team featured his father and his adopted uncle, but as Davis matured, his singing, dancing and impersonations soon became the center of the act. After military service in World War II, the trio became popular on the night club circuit. Davis began performing on his own in the 1950s, headlining club engagements, appearing on television variety shows and making numerous popular records. His Broadway debut came in 1956 in the hit musical *Mr Wonderful*, and in the late '50s and early '60s he starred in a number of films, including a series with Frank Sinatra and the Rat Pack. Davis continued to perform in clubs, concerts and on TV until he was stricken with throat cancer in 1987. He died at Los Angeles, CA, on May 16, 1990.

DURANT, WILLIAM CRAPO: BIRTH ANNIVERSARY. Dec 8, 1861. "Billy" Durant, a leading producer of carriages in Flint, MI, promoter of the Buick car, cofounder of Chevrolet, was founder, in 1908, of General Motors. He lost, regained and again lost control of GM, after which he founded Durant Motors, went bankrupt in the Depression and operated a Flint bowling alley in his last working years. Durant was born at Boston, MA, on Dec 8, 1861, and died at New York, NY, Mar 18, 1947.

FEAST OF THE IMMACULATE CONCEPTION. Dec 8. Roman Catholic Holy Day of Obligation.

FIRST STEP TOWARD A NUCLEAR-FREE WORLD: ANNIVERSARY. Dec 8, 1987. The former Soviet Union and the US signed a treaty in Washington eliminating medium-range and shorter-range missiles. This was the first treaty completely doing away with two entire classes of nuclear arms. These missiles, with a range of 500 to 5,500 kilometers, were to be scrapped under strict supervision within three years of the signing.

GUAM: LADY OF CAMARIN DAY HOLIDAY: ANNIVERSARY. Dec 8. Declared a legal holiday by Guam legislature on Mar 2, 1971.

HOBAN, JAMES: DEATH ANNIVERSARY. Dec 8. Irish-born architect who designed the US President's Executive Mansion, later known as The White House. He was born in 1762 (exact date unknown) and died Dec 8, 1831. The cornerstone for the White House, Washington's oldest public building, was laid in 1792.

MORRISON, JIM: 55th BIRTH ANNIVERSARY. Dec 8, 1943. Singer, songwriter, known as "The Lizard King," lead singer of The Doors, Jim Morrison is considered to be one of the fathers of contemporary rock. Born Dec 8, 1943, at Melbourne, FL, and died at Paris, France, July 3, 1971.

NORMAN ROCKWELL'S 1923 CHRISTMAS COVER FOR *THE SATURDAY EVENING POST*: 75th ANNIVERSARY. Dec 8, 1923. One of his earliest covers for the *Post* when they were still in black and red, Norman Rockwell's Dec 8, 1923, Christmas cover for the magazine depicted a trio performing Christmas carols. In Rockwell's biography he reveals that not one of his three models had an iota of musical talent.

RIVERA, DIEGO: BIRTH ANNIVERSARY. Dec 8. Mexican painter whose murals became center of political controversy and demands for banishment, born at Guanajuato, Mexico, Dec 8, 1886. Died in his studio at San Angel, near Mexico City, Nov 25, 1957.

SEGAR, ELZIE CRISLER: BIRTH ANNIVERSARY. Dec 8, 1894. Originally called *Thimble Theater*, the comic strip that came to be known as *Popeye* had the unusual format of a one-act play in cartoon form. Centered on the Oyl family, especially daughter Olive, the strip introduced a new central character in 1929. A one-eyed sailor with bulging muscles, Popeye became the strip's star attraction almost immediately. Popeye made it to the silver screen in animated form, is still a popular addition to Saturday morning TV and in 1980 became a movie with Robin Williams playing the lead. Popeye creator Elzie Crisler Segar was born at Chester, IL. He died Oct 13, 1938, at Santa Monica, CA.

SOVIET UNION DISSOLVED: ANNIVERSARY. Dec 8. On Dec 8, 1991, the Union of Soviet Socialist Republics ceased to exist, as the republics of Russia, Byelorussia and Ukraine signed an agreement in Minsk, Byelorussia, creating the Commonwealth of Independent States. The remaining republics, with the exception of Georgia, joined in the new Commonwealth as it began the slow and arduous process of creating a new confederation while removing the yoke of Communism and dealing with strong separatist and nationalistic movements within the various republics.

THURBER, JAMES: BIRTH ANNIVERSARY. Dec 8. James Grover Thurber, American humorist and artist, born at Columbus, OH, Dec 8, 1894. Died at New York, NY, Nov 2, 1961.

WHITNEY, ELI: BIRTH ANNIVERSARY. Dec 8, 1765. Inventor of the cotton gin, born at Westboro, MA. Died at New Haven, CT, Jan 8, 1825.

BIRTHDAYS TODAY

Gregg Allman, 51, singer ("Ramblin' Man"), actor (*Rush*), born Nashville, TN, Dec 8, 1947.

Kim Basinger, 45, actress (*The Natural, The Getaway, My Stepmother Is an Alien*), born Athens, GA, Dec 8, 1953.

Gordon Arthur ("Red") Berenson, 57, former hockey player and coach, born Regina, Saskatchewan, Canada, Dec 8, 1941.

James Galway, 59, musician, born Belfast, Northern Ireland, Dec 8, 1939.

Teri Hatcher, 34, actress ("Lois & Clark"), born Sunnyvale, CA, Dec 8, 1964.

James MacArthur, 61, actor ("Hawaii Five-O"), born Los Angeles, CA, Dec 8, 1937.

Sinead O'Connor, 32, singer, songwriter, born Dublin, Ireland, Dec 8, 1966.

Maximilian Schell, 68, actor (*Judgment at Nuremberg, The Odessa File*), producer, born Vienna, Austria, Dec 8, 1930.

Flip Wilson, 65, actor, comedian (*Uptown Saturday Night*, "The Flip Wilson Show"), born Jersey City, NJ, Dec 8, 1933.

Mary Woronov, 52, actress (*Rock 'n' Roll High School, Eating Raoul*), born Brooklyn, NY, Dec 8, 1946.

DECEMBER 9 — WEDNESDAY

Day 343 — 22 Remaining

AMERICA'S FIRST FORMAL CREMATION: ANNIVERSARY. Dec 9, 1792. The first formal cremation of a human body in America took place near Charleston, SC. Henry Laurens, colonial statesman and signer of the Treaty of Paris, ending the Revolutionary War, in his will provided: "I do solemnly enjoin it on my son, as an indispensable duty, that as soon as he conveniently can, after my decease, he cause my body to be wrapped in twelve yards of tow cloth and burned until it be entirely consumed, and then, collecting my bones, deposit them wherever he may think proper." Laurens died Dec 8, 1792, at his plantation, and was cremated there.

BIRDSEYE, CLARENCE: BIRTH ANNIVERSARY. Dec 9. American industrialist who developed a way of deep-freezing foods. He was marketing frozen fish by 1925 and was one of the founders of General Foods Corp. Born on Dec 9, 1886, at Brooklyn, NY. Died at New York City, Oct 7, 1956.

FOXX, REDD: BIRTH ANNIVERSARY. Dec 9, 1922. Born John Elroy Sanford on Dec 9, 1922, in St. Louis, MO, Redd Foxx plied his comedic trade on vaudeville stages, in nightclubs, on television, in films and on record albums. His talents reached a national audience with the TV sitcom "Sanford and Son." He died after collapsing during a rehearsal for a new TV sitcom, "The Royal Family," on Oct 11, 1992.

GENOCIDE CONVENTION: 50th ANNIVERSARY. Dec 9, 1948. The United Nations General Assembly unanimously approved the Convention on Prevention and Punishment of the Crime of Genocide on Dec 9, 1948. It took effect Jan 12, 1951, when ratification by 20 nations had been completed. President Truman sent it to the US Senate for approval on June 16, 1949; it was supported by Presidents Kennedy, Johnson, Nixon, Ford, Carter and Reagan. Thirty-seven years after its submission, and after approval by more than 90 nations, the Senate approved it, Feb 19, 1986, by a vote of 83–11.

HARRIS, JOEL CHANDLER: 150th BIRTH ANNIVERSARY. Dec 9, 1848. American author, creator of the "Uncle Remus" stories, born Dec 9, 1848. Died July 3, 1908.

HOPPER, GRACE: BIRTH ANNIVERSARY. Dec 9, 1906. Grace Hopper was born Dec 9, 1906, at New York City. When she retired from the US Navy at the age of 79, she was the oldest naval officer ever on active duty. She attained the rank of Rear Admiral and was a leader in the computer revolution, having developed the computer language COBOL. Grace Hopper died Jan 1, 1992, at Arlington, WV.

MILTON, JOHN: BIRTH ANNIVERSARY. Dec 9, 1608. English poet and defender of freedom of the press born in Bread Street, Cheapside, London, on Dec 9, 1608. Died from gout, Nov 8, 1674. "No man who knows aught," he wrote, "can be so stupid to deny that all men naturally were born free."

O'NEILL, THOMAS PHILIP, II (TIP): BIRTH ANNIVERSARY. Dec 9, 1912. Democratic congressman from Massachusetts 1953–87, Speaker of the House of Representatives 1977–87, Tip O'Neill was born at Cambridge, MA, and died Jan 5, 1994, at Boston, MA.

"ROOTIE KAZOOTIE" TV PREMIERE: ANNIVERSARY. Dec 9, 1950. This half-hour children's show was hosted by Todd Russell and featured John Vee and puppets (Rootie Kazootie, Gala Poochie, Polka Dottie, El Squeako and Poison Zoomack). Also featured were games and prizes for the audience. The puppets were handled by Paul Ashley and Frank Milano. "Rootie Kazootie" switched networks from NBC to ABC and also switched time slots from Saturday mornings to weekday evenings.

December 1998

S	M	T	W	T	F	S
		1	2	3	4	5
6	7	8	9	10	11	12
13	14	15	16	17	18	19
20	21	22	23	24	25	26
27	28	29	30	31		

SANDYS, EDWIN: BIRTH ANNIVERSARY. Dec 9. Sir Edwin Sandys, English statesman and one of the founders of the Virginia Colony (treasurer, the Virginia Company, 1619–20), born at Worcestershire, Dec 9, 1561. Died in October 1629 (exact date unknown).

TANZANIA: INDEPENDENCE AND REPUBLIC DAY: ANNIVERSARY. Dec 9, 1961. Tanganyika became independent of Britain and on Dec 9, 1962, it became a republic within the commonwealth. The republics of Tanganyika and Zanzibar joined to become one state (Apr 27, 1964) renamed (Oct 29, 1964) the United Republic of Tanzania.

BIRTHDAYS TODAY

Joan Armatrading, 48, singer, songwriter (*Me, Myself, I*), born Saint Kitts, West Indies, Dec 9, 1950.

Otis Lee Birdsong, 43, former basketball player, born Winter Haven, FL, Dec 9, 1955.

Beau Bridges, 57, actor ("James Brady Story," *The Fabulous Baker Boys*), born Los Angeles, CA, Dec 9, 1941.

Richard Marvin (Dick) Butkus, 56, sportscaster, actor, Pro Football Hall of Fame linebacker, born Chicago, IL, Dec 9, 1942.

Thomas Andrew Daschle, 51, US Senator (D, South Dakota), born Aberdeen, SD, Dec 9, 1947.

Kirk Douglas (Issur Danielovitch Demsky), 82, actor (*Lonely Are the Brave, Lust for Life*), author, born Amsterdam, NY, Dec 9, 1916.

Douglas Fairbanks, Jr, 89, actor (*The Prisoner of Zenda, State Secret*), a founder of United Artists, born NY, Dec 9, 1909.

Thomas O. (Tom) Kite, Jr, 49, golfer, born Austin, TX, Dec 9, 1949.

John Malkovich, 45, actor (*The Killing Fields, The Sheltering Sky*), filmmaker, born Christopher, IL, Dec 9, 1953.

Michael Nouri, 53, actor ("Search for Tomorrow," "Love and War," *Goodbye Columbus, Flashdance*), born Washington, DC, Dec 9, 1945.

Donny Osmond, 41, actor, singer ("Donny and Marie"; stage: *Joseph and the Amazing Technicolor Dreamcoat*), born Ogden, UT, Dec 9, 1957.

Dick Van Patten, 70, actor ("Eight Is Enough," "Mama"), born Richmond Hill, NY, Dec 9, 1928.

DECEMBER 10 — THURSDAY

Day 344 — 21 Remaining

DEWEY, MELVIL: BIRTH ANNIVERSARY. Dec 10, 1851. American librarian and inventor of the Dewey decimal book classification system was born at Adams Center, NY. Born Melville Louis Kossuth Dewey, he was an advocate of spelling reform, urged use of the metric system and was interested in many other education reforms. Dewey died at Highlands County, FL, on Dec 26, 1931.

DICKINSON, EMILY: BIRTH ANNIVERSARY. Dec 10. One of America's greatest poets, Emily Dickinson was born at Amherst, MA, on Dec 10, 1830. She was reclusive, mysterious and frail in health. Neither she nor her poems were known to more than a few persons. Seven of her poems were published during her life, but after her death her sister, Lavinia, discovered almost 2,000 more poems written on the backs of envelopes and other scraps of paper—locked in her bureau. They were published gradually, over 50 years, beginning in 1890. She died at 6 PM, on May 15, 1886, at Amherst, MA. The little-known Emily Dickinson who was born, lived and died at Amherst now is recognized as one of the most original poets of the English-speaking world.

FIRST GRAND OLE OPRY BROADCAST. Dec 10, 1927. Grand Ole Opry makes its first radio broadcast from Nashville (Tennessee).

FIRST US HEAVYWEIGHT CHAMP DEFEATED IN ENGLAND: ANNIVERSARY. Dec 10. Tom Molineaux, the first unofficial heavyweight champion of the US, was a freed slave from Virginia. He was beaten in the 40th round by Tom Cribb, the English champion, in a boxing match at Copthall Common in London on Dec 10, 1810.

FIRST US SCIENTIST RECEIVES NOBEL PRIZE: ANNIVERSARY. Dec 10, 1907. University of Chicago professor Albert Michelson, eminent physicist known for his research on the speed of light and optics, on Dec 10, 1907, became the first US scientist to receive the Nobel Prize.

GALLAUDET: THOMAS HOPKINS: BIRTH ANNIVERSARY. Dec 10, 1787. A hearing educator who with Laurent Clerc founded the first public school for deaf people, Connecticut Asylum for the Education and Instruction of Deaf and Dumb Persons (now the American School for the Deaf), at Hartford, CT, Apr 15, 1817. Gallaudet was born at Philadelphia, PA, and died Sept 9, 1851, at Hartford, CT.

★**HUMAN RIGHTS DAY.** Dec 10. Presidential Proclamation 2866, of Dec 6, 1949, covers all succeeding years. Customarily issued as "Bill of Rights Day, Human Rights Day and Week."

★**HUMAN RIGHTS WEEK.** Dec 10–16. Presidential Proclamation issued since 1958 for the week of Dec 10–16, except in 1986. See also: "Human Rights Day" (Dec 10) and "Bill of Rights Day" (Dec 15).

LAMOUR, DOROTHY: BIRTH ANNIVERSARY. Dec 10, 1914. Singer, actress (*The Hurricane, Road to Singapore*), born New Orleans, LA. Died Sept 22, 1996.

"THE MIGHTY MOUSE PLAYHOUSE" TV PREMIERE: ANNIVERSARY. Dec 10, 1955. An all-time favorite of the Saturday-morning crowd (including adults). CBS had a hit with their pint-sized cartoon character Mighty Mouse, who was a tongue-in-cheek version of Superman. The show had other feature cartoons such as "The Adventures of Gandy Goose," but most people remember and enjoyed the adventures of Mighty Mouse the best.

MISSISSIPPI: ADMISSION DAY: ANNIVERSARY. Dec 10, 1817. Became 20th state on this day in 1817.

MOON PHASE: LAST QUARTER. Dec 10. Moon enters Last Quarter phase at 12:53 PM, EST.

NOBEL, ALFRED BERNHARD: DEATH ANNIVERSARY. Dec 10, 1896. Swedish chemist and engineer who invented dynamite was born at Stockholm, Sweden, Oct 21, 1833, and died at San Remo, Italy, Dec 10, 1896. His will established the Nobel Prize.

NOBEL PRIZE AWARDS CEREMONIES. Dec 10. Oslo, Norway, and Stockholm, Sweden. Alfred Nobel, Swedish chemist and inventor of dynamite who died in 1896, provided in his will that income from his $9 million estate should be used for annual prizes—to be awarded to people who are judged to have made the most valuable contributions to the good of humanity. The Nobel Peace Prize is awarded by a committee of the Norwegian parliament, and the presentation is made at the Oslo City Hall. Five other prizes, for physics, chemistry, medicine, literature and economics, are presented in a ceremony at Stockholm, Sweden. Both ceremonies traditionally are held on the anniversary of the death of Alfred Nobel. The current value of each prize is about $1,000,000. See also "Nobel, Alfred Bernhard: Death Anniversary" (Dec 10).

NORTON, MARY: 95th BIRTH ANNIVERSARY. Dec 10, 1903. British author Mary Norton was born at London, England. An author of extraordinary children's books, she is best known for *Bedknob and Broomstick* (1957). She died on Aug 29, 1992, at Hartland, England.

RALPH BUNCHE AWARDED NOBEL PEACE PRIZE: ANNIVERSARY. Dec 10, 1950. Dr. Ralph Johnson Bunche became the first black man awarded the Nobel Peace Prize. Bunche was awarded the prize for his efforts in mediation between Israel and neighboring Arab states in 1949.

RED CLOUD: DEATH ANNIVERSARY. Dec 10. Sioux Indian chief Red Cloud was born in 1822 (exact date unknown), near North Platte, NE. A courageous leader and defender of Indian rights, Red Cloud was the son of Lone Man and Walks as She Thinks. His unrelenting determination caused US abandonment of the Bozeman trail and of three forts that interfered with Indian hunting grounds. Red Cloud died at Pine Ridge, SD, on Dec 10, 1909. The US Postal Service issued a postage stamp honoring him in its Great Americans Series in 1987.

SPACE MILESTONE: *SOYUZ 26* (USSR). Dec 10, 1977. Launched this date with Cosmonauts Yuri Romanenko and Georgi Grechko who linked it with *Salyut 6* space station on Dec 11. Returned to Earth in *Soyuz 27*, Mar 16, 1978, after record-setting 96 days in space.

THAILAND: CONSTITUTION DAY. Dec 10. A public holiday throughout Thailand.

THOMASVILLE'S VICTORIAN CHRISTMAS. Dec 10–11. Downtown Thomasville relives Christmas past as it celebrates the Victorian era of the late 1800s. Costumed strollers and carolers, horse-drawn carriages, bell-ringers and colorful characters from the past fill the streets of downtown. Victorian-clad merchants welcome shoppers with hot cider and confections and street vendors offer Christmas delicacies. Free—wonderful family event. Est attendance: 25,000. For info: Sharlene Celaya, Thomasville Victorian Christmas, Thomasville Main Street, 135 N Broad St, Thomasville, GA 31792. Phone: (912) 225 3920.

TREATY OF PARIS SIGNED: 100th ANNIVERSARY. Dec 10, 1898. Following the conclusion of the Spanish-American War in 1898, American and Spanish ambassadors met in Paris, France, to negotiate a treaty. Under the terms of this treaty, Spain granted the US the Philippine Islands and the islands of Guam and Puerto Rico, and agreed to withdraw from Cuba. Senatorial debate over the treaty centered on the US's move toward imperialism by acquiring the Philippines. A vote was taken on Feb 6, 1899 and the treaty passed by a one-vote margin. President William McKinley signed the treaty on Feb 10, 1899.

UNITED NATIONS: HUMAN RIGHTS DAY: 50th ANNIVERSARY. Dec 10. Official United Nations observance day. Date is the anniversary of adoption of the "Universal Declaration of Human Rights" in 1948. The Declaration sets forth basic rights and fundamental freedoms to which all men and women everywhere in the world are entitled. For info: United Nations, Dept of Public Info, New York, NY 10017. Email: inquiries@un.org.

UNITED NATIONS: THIRD DECADE TO COMBAT RACISM AND RACIAL DISCRIMINATION: YEAR FOUR. Dec 10. In 1973 the United Nations General Assembly proclaimed the years 1973–1983, beginning on Dec 10, UN Human Rights Day, as the Decade to Combat Racism and Racial Discrimination. Renewing its efforts, the UN designated the years 1983–1993 as the Second Decade to Combat Racism and Racial Discrimination. The adopted Program of Action states the decade's goals and outlines the measures to be taken at the regional, national and international levels to achieve them. Due to a lack of resources, activities planned for the last year of the second decade were not implemented, and in Res 47/77 of Dec 16, 1992, the Assembly called upon the international community to provide resources for the program to be carried out during a third decade (1993–2003), particularly for the monitoring of the transition from apartheid scheduled to take place in South Africa. Info from: United Nations, Dept of Public Info, New York, NY 10017.

WORLD'S LARGEST OUTLET SALE. Dec 10–20. Pigeon Forge, TN. Pre-holiday savings on famous brands provided by the four outlet malls with almost 200 stores. For info: Pigeon Forge Dept of Tourism, 2450 Parkway, PO Box 1390, Pigeon Forge, TN 37868. Phone: (800) 251-9100.

BIRTHDAYS TODAY

Mark Anthony Aguirre, 39, former basketball player, born Chicago, IL, Dec 10, 1959.

Kenneth Branagh, 38, actor, director (*High Season, Henry V*), born Belfast, Northern Ireland, Dec 10, 1960.

Susan Dey, 46, model, actress ("The Partridge Family," "LA Law," "Love and War"), born Pekin, IL, Dec 10, 1952.

Harold Gould, 75, actor ("Rhoda," "Under One Roof"), born Schenectady, NY, Dec 10, 1923.

Gloria Loring, 52, singer, actress (Lix Chandler DiMera in "Days of Our Lives"), born New York, NY, Dec 10, 1946.

Sinbad, 42, actor (*Unnecessary Roughness*, "A Different World"), born Benton Harbor, MI, Dec 10, 1956.

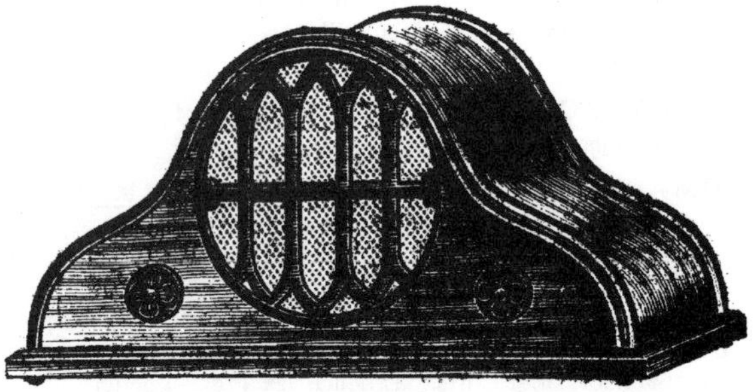

DECEMBER 11 — FRIDAY

Day 345 — 20 Remaining

ALASKA'S FIRST BROADCAST TELEVISION STATION: 45th ANNIVERSARY. Dec 11, 1953. At 6 PM, on Dec 11, 1953, KTVA, Channel 11, at Anchorage, AK, signed on the air, becoming Alaska's first broadcast station.

BATTLE OF THE BULLS. Dec 11, 1846. Sandy, UT. In one of the most unusal battles in military history, US soldiers of the Mormon Battalion were attacked by a herd of wild longhorn bulls while camped on the San Pedro River in Arizona just 10 miles from present-day Tombstone. Men and mules were injured and wagons damaged. Several of the bulls were shot and killed. Lieutenant George Stoneman, one of the injured soldiers, later became Lieutenant Governor of California 1883–87. For info: Second US Mormon Battalion, 1609 E Pepplewood Cir, Sandy, UT 84092. Phone: (801) 572-3129.

BUELL, MARJORIE H.: BIRTH ANNIVERSARY. Dec 11, 1904. Cartoonist, creator of comic strip character Little Lulu, Marjorie Buell was considered a pioneer for creating a female character that outsmarted the neighborhood boys. She was born at Philadelphia, PA, and died May 30, 1993, at Elyria, OH.

BURKINA FASO: NATIONAL DAY. Dec 11.

CANNON, ANNIE JUMP: BIRTH ANNIVERSARY. Dec 11, 1863. American astronomer and discoverer of five stars, was born at Dover, DE, on Dec 11, 1863. Author and winner of the National Academy of Science Draper Medal, she died at Cambridge, MA, Apr 13, 1941.

EDWARD VIII ABDICATION: ANNIVERSARY. Dec 11. Christened Edward Albert Christian George Andrew Patrick David, King Edward VIII was born at Richmond Park, England, on June 12, 1894, and became Prince of Wales in July 1911. He ascended to the English throne upon the death of his father, George V, on Jan 20, 1936, but coronation never took place. He abdicated on Dec 11, 1936, in order to marry "the woman I love," twice-divorced American Wallis Warfield Simpson. They were married in France, June 3, 1937. Edward was created Duke of Windsor by his brother-successor, George VI. The Duke died at Paris, May 28, 1972, but was buried in England, near Windsor Castle.

"THE GABBY HAYES SHOW" TV PREMIERE: ANNIVERSARY. Dec 11, 1950. George "Gabby" Hayes, veteran of western movies, hosted two series: the first was a 15-minute weekday show; the second, a half-hour Saturday morning show. On both shows, Hayes showed clips from old westerns.

GINGERBREAD AND LACE: A CHRISTMAS CELEBRATION. Dec 11. Ash Lawn–Highland, Charlottesville, VA. Customs of 1870s: caroling, ornament making, tree trimming and refreshments. Est attendance: 100. For info: Ash Lawn–Highland, James Monroe Parkway, Charlottesville, VA 22902. Phone: (804) 293-9539. Fax: (804) 293-8000. Email: ashlawn@comet.net. WWW: http://avenue.org/ashlawn

INDIANA: ADMISSION DAY: ANNIVERSARY. Dec 11. Became 19th state on this day in 1816.

LA GUARDIA, FIORELLO HENRY: BIRTH ANNIVERSARY. Dec 11, 1882. Popularly known as the "Little Flower," Fiorello H. LaGuardia was not too busy as mayor of New York City to read the "funnies" to radio listeners during the New York newspaper strike. He said of himself: "When I make a mistake it's a beaut!" LaGuardia was born at New York City, and died there on Sept 20, 1947.

"MAGNUM, PI" TV PREMIERE: ANNIVERSARY. Dec 11. The television series premiered on CBS starring Tom Selleck in the title role of Thomas Magnum, private investigator in Hawaii. Other cast regulars are John Hillerman as Jonathan Quayle Higgins, Roger E. Mosley, Theodore Calvin and Larry Manetti as Orville "Rick" Wright. Orson Welles supplied a voice from 1980 to 1985 for the unseen Robin Masters. Final episode aired May 1, 1988. "Magnum" fans enjoy an open house at "Magnum Memorabilia" (the nonprofit research/production foundation and full-service fan information clearinghouse) in celebration of this day every year. Episode viewings and costume/prop exhibits are featured. For info: David Romas, Dir, 4417 Second Ave, #110, Detroit, MI 48201. Phone: (313) 831-3646. Email: fromas@cms.cc.wayne.edu.

PEGGY V. HELMERICH DISTINGUISHED AUTHOR AWARD PRESENTATION. Dec 11–12. Central Library, Tulsa, OK. The award is given annually by the Tulsa Library Trust to a nationally acclaimed author who has written a distinguished body of work and made a major contribution to the field of literature and letters. The award consists of a $20,000 cash prize and an engraved crystal book. The winning author will be the keynote speaker at this black-tie dinner in his or her honor. Past recipients include Neil Simon (1996), David McCullough (1995), Ray Bradbury (1994), Peter Matthiessen (1993), Norman Mailer (1992), Eudora Welty (1991) and John le Carre (1990). Est attendance: 1,000. For info: Cathy Audley, Mgr, Tulsa Library Trust Dvmt, 400 Civic Center, Tulsa, OK 74103. Phone: (918) 596-7896. Fax: (918) 596-7990.

SUGARLOAF'S WINTER GAITHERSBURG CRAFT FESTIVAL. Dec 11–13. Montgomery County Fairgrounds, Gaithersburg, MD. This show, now in its 21st year, features 300 nationally recognized craft designers and fine artists displaying and selling their original creations. Craft demonstrations, hourly gift certificate drawings, food and more. Est attendance: 18,000. For info: Sugarloaf Mountain Works, Inc, 200 Orchard Ridge Dr, #215, Gaithersburg, MD 20878. Phone: (800) 210-9900.

BIRTHDAYS TODAY

Max Baucus, 57, US Senator (D, Montana), born Helena, MT, Dec 11, 1941.

December 1998

S	M	T	W	T	F	S
		1	2	3	4	5
6	7	8	9	10	11	12
13	14	15	16	17	18	19
20	21	22	23	24	25	26
27	28	29	30	31		

Teri Garr, 49, actress (*Young Frankenstein, Tootsie, The Black Stallion*), born Lakewood, OH, Dec 11, 1949.
David Gates, 58, singer, songwriter, born Tulsa, OK, Dec 11, 1940.
Tom Hayden, 58, journalist, activist, politician (ex-husband of Jane Fonda), born Royal Oak, MI, Dec 11, 1940.
Jermaine Jackson, 44, singer, musician (Jackson 5; "Daddy's Home," "Let's Get Serious"), born Gary, IN, Dec 11, 1954.
John F. Kerry, 55, US Senator (D, Massachusetts), born Denver, CO, Dec 11, 1943.
Brenda Lee (Brenda Mae Tarpley), 54, singer ("I'm Sorry," "All Alone Am I"), born Atlanta, GA, Dec 11, 1944.
Donna Mills, 55, actress (Abby on "Knots Landing"), born Chicago, IL, Dec 11, 1943.
Rita Moreno, 67, singer, actress (Oscar for *West Side Story*; Tony for *The Ritz*), born Hunacao, Puerto Rico, Dec 11, 1931.
Carlo Ponti, 85, producer, born Milan, Italy, Dec 11, 1913.
Susan Seidelman, 46, filmmaker (*Desperately Seeking Susan, Making Mr Right*), born Philadelphia, PA, Dec 11, 1952.
Aleksandr Isayevich Solzhenitsyn, 80, author (*Cancer Ward, One Day in the Life of Ivan Denisovich, The Gulag Archipelago*), born Kislovodsk, USSR, Dec 11, 1918.
Curtis Williams, 36, musician, singer (with the Penguins; "Earth Angel"), born Buffalo, NY, Dec 11, 1962.

DECEMBER 12 — SATURDAY

Day 346 — 19 Remaining

ARMY AND NAVY UNION DAY IN MASSACHUSETTS. Dec 12. Second Saturday in December.

BONZA BOTTLER DAY™. Dec 12. To celebrate when the number of the day is the same as the number of the month. Bonza Bottler Day™ is an excuse to have a party at least once a month. For more information, see Jan 1. For info: Gail M. Berger, 109 Matthew Ave, Poca, WV 25159. Phone: (304) 776-7746. Email: gberger5@aol.com.

CHILDREN'S VICTORIAN CHRISTMAS CELEBRATION. Dec 12–30. Washington, MS. Display of 14 or more Christmas trees decorated by fifth-grade students. Closed Christmas Eve, Christmas and day after Christmas. Est attendance: 2,000. For info: Anne L. Gray, Historian, Historic Jefferson College, PO Box 700, Washington, MS 39190. Phone: (601) 442-2901.

CHRISTMAS BOAT PARADE ON CLEAR LAKE. Dec 12. Clear Lake, TX. Witness more than a hundred decorated boats travel across Clear Lake out to the Galveston Bay. Sponsored by the Clear Lake Area Chamber of Commerce. For info: Shari Liebman, Clear Lake Area Chamber of Commerce, 1201 Nasa Rd One, Houston, TX 77058. Phone: (281) 488-7676. Fax: (281) 488-8981.

CHRISTMAS CRAFT FAIR USA: INDOOR SHOW. Dec 12–13. Wisconsin State Fair Park, Milwaukee, WI. Sale of handcrafted items—jewelry, pottery, weaving, leather, wood, glass and sculpture. Est attendance: 12,000. For info: Dir, Christmas Craft Fair USA, 9312 W National Ave, West Allis, WI 53227. Phone: (414) 321-2100.

CHRISTMAS IN HOPELANDS. Dec 12–26 (closed Dec 24). Aiken, SC. The pathways of Hopeland Gardens in historic Aiken are lined with thousands of sparkling lights. Visitors to the gardens can stroll along the pathways and view lighted displays throughout the gardens. Historic buildings such as the Thoroughbred Racing Hall of Fame, the Dollhouse and Rye Patch are open for the tour. Annually, the second Saturday in December through the fourth Saturday in December. Est attendance: 17,000. For info: City of Aiken Parks and Recreation Dept, PO Box 1177, Aiken, SC 29802. Phone: (803) 642-7630. Fax: (803) 642-7639.

CHRISTMAS ON THE RIVER. Dec 12. Ross's Landing, Chattanooga, TN. The Tennessee River comes alive with the splendid colors of decorated boats as they cruise past Ross's Landing. Area groups perform Christmas carols. Evening commences with the Holiday Nightlight Parade down Market St and concludes with a spectacular fireworks show. Hours: 5–9 PM. Est attendance: 20,000. For info: Carla Watson, Program Mgr, Chattanooga Downtown Partnership, Christmas on the River, 850 Market St, 2nd Fl, Miller Pl, Chattanooga, TN 37402. Phone: (423) 265-0771. Fax: (423) 265-6952.

DAY OF OUR LADY OF GUADALUPE. Dec 12. The legend of Guadalupe tells how in December 1533, an Indian, Juan Diego, saw the Virgin Mother on a hill near Mexico City, who instructed him to go to the bishop and have him build a shrine to her on the site of the vision. Initially rebuffed, the Virgin Mother appeared to Juan Diego three days later. She instructed him to pick roses growing on a stony and barren hillside nearby and take them to the bishop as proof. Although flowers do not normally bloom in December, Juan Diego found the roses and took them to the bishop. As he opened his mantle to drop the roses on the floor, an image of the Virgin Mary appeared among them. The bishop built the sanctuary as instructed. Our Lady of Guadalupe became the patroness of Mexico City and by 1746 was the patron saint of all New Spain and by 1910 of all Latin America.

FIRST BLACK SERVES IN US HOUSE OF REPRESENTATIVES: ANNIVERSARY. Dec 12. Joseph Hayne Rainey of Georgetown, SC, was sworn in on Dec 12, 1870, as the first black to serve in the US House of Representatives. Rainey filled the seat of Benjamin Franklin Whittemore, which had been declared vacant by the House. He served until Mar 3, 1879.

FLAUBERT, GUSTAVE: BIRTH ANNIVERSARY. Dec 12. French author whose works include one of the greatest French novels, *Madame Bovary*, was born at Rouen on Dec 12, 1821. Flaubert died at Croisset, France, on May 8, 1880.

GARRISON, WILLIAM LLOYD: BIRTH ANNIVERSARY. Dec 12. American antislavery leader, poet and journalist, was born at Newburyport, MA, on Dec 12, 1805. Garrison died at New York, NY, on May 24, 1879.

JAY, JOHN: BIRTH ANNIVERSARY. Dec 12. American statesman, diplomat and first chief justice of the US Supreme Court (1789–95), coauthor (with Alexander Hamilton and James Madison) of the influential *Federalist* papers, was born at New York, NY, on Dec 12, 1745. Jay died at Bedford, NY, on May 17, 1829.

KENYA: JAMHURI DAY. Dec 12. Jamhuri Day (Independence Day) is Kenya's official National Day, commemorating proclamation of the republic on Dec 12, 1963.

MEXICO: GUADALUPE DAY. Dec 12. One of Mexico's major celebrations. Honors the "Dark Virgin of Guadalupe," the republic's patron saint. Parties and pilgrimages, with special ceremonies at the Shrine of Our Lady of Guadalupe, in Mexico City.

OLD-FASHIONED DANISH CHRISTMAS. Dec 12–13. Dannebrog, NE. Days filled with Christmas Tree Fantasy, living nativity scene, crafters/working artists expo, Danish buffet luncheon, Danish pastry, Danish tree ornament cutouts demonstration, home tours and spectacular displays of holiday lights. Annually, the second weekend in December. Est attendance: 1,200. For info: Shirley Johnson, Festival Coord, Dannebrog Area Booster Club, 522 E Roger Welsch Ave, Dannebrog, NE 68831. Phone: (308) 226-2237.

PENNSYLVANIA RATIFIES CONSTITUTION: ANNIVERSARY. Dec 12, 1787. Pennsylvania became the second state to ratify the US Constitution, by a vote of 46 to 23, on Dec 12, 1787.

POINSETTIA DAY (JOEL ROBERTS POINSETT: DEATH ANNIVERSARY). Dec 12. A day to enjoy poinsettias and to honor Dr. Joel Roberts Poinsett, the American diplomat who introduced the Central American plant which is named for him into the US. Poinsett was born at Charleston, SC, Mar 2, 1799. He also served as a member of Congress and as secretary of war. He died near Statesburg, SC, Dec 12, 1851. The poinsettia has become a favorite Christmas season plant.

RUSSIA: CONSTITUTION DAY. Dec 12. National holiday.

RUSSIAN ELECTION SURPRISE: 5th ANNIVERSARY. Dec 12, 1993. In a shocking rebuke to Boris Yeltsin's attempts to stabilize the country, Russian voters gave Vladimir Zhironovsky and his misnamed Liberal Democratic Party 28% of the vote, granting them a large block of power in the new Russian Parliament and the world's imagination. Zhironovsky's platform, which has been called racist and fascist, tapped into a groundswell of nationalist fervor with calls to return Russia to the glory days of its empire and emphasizing harsh treatment for minorities and those who would stand in his way.

34th STREET EXPRESS. Dec 12. Chartered Amtrak train leaves from Boston, MA. Christmas shopping special to New York City also takes in the Radio City Christmas Spectacular. Annually, the second Saturday in December. Est attendance: 500. For info: Mystic Valley Railway Society, Inc, PO Box 365486, Hyde Park, MA 02136-0486. Phone: (617) 361-4445. Fax: (617) 361-4445*51 (dial all as one number).

A VICTORIAN YULETIDE. Dec 12–14. Clinton, MD. Candlelight tours with holiday greenery, antique toys, cards, ornaments, music and Father Christmas. Est attendance: 800. For info: Surratt House and Tavern, PO Box 427, Clinton, MD 20735. Phone: (301) 868-1121. Fax: (301) 868-8177.
WWW: http://www.engr.umd.edu/clwspoon/surratt.htm/

WASSAIL CELEBRATION. Dec 12–13. Woodstock, VT. Activities include a horse rider and carriage parade, Santa comes to town, Wassail Dance, concert by Revere Handbell Choir, caroling and burning the Yule Log on the Village Green. Est attendance: 5,000. For info: Joan Sterner, Exec Coord, Woodstock Area Chamber of Commerce, 18 Central St, PO Box 486, Woodstock, VT 05091. Phone: (802) 457-3555.

WATIE, STAND: BIRTH ANNIVERSARY. Dec 12, 1806. Born in Rome, GA, and died Sept 9, 1871. Cherokee chief who, by signing the treaty of New Echota, surrendered his people's land in Georgia, forcing relocation to Oklahoma. Though the three other signers were murdered, Watie escaped and went on to initiate the first volunteer Cherokee regiment for the Confederates in the Civil War. Promoted to brigadier general, he was most active in destroying the property of other Native Americans who supported the Union.

WINTERFEST BOAT PARADE. Dec 12. More than 100 decorated yachts sail up Fort Lauderdale's Intracoastal Waterway starting at Port Everglades. Est attendance: 750,000. For info: Winterfest, 512 NE 3rd Ave, Ft Lauderdale, FL 33301. Phone: (954) 767-0686.

BIRTHDAYS TODAY

Tracy Ann Austin, 36, tennis player, born Rolling Hills Estates, CA, Dec 12, 1962.
Bob Barker, 75, TV personality, game-show host (Emmy for "The Price Is Right"), born Darrington, WA, Dec 12, 1923.
Mayim Bialik, 23, actress ("Blossom"), born San Diego, CA, Dec 12, 1975.
Sheila E (Sheila Escoveda), 39, singer, musician ("The Glamorous Life"), born San Francisco, CA, Dec 12, 1959.
Connie Francis (Constance Franconero), 60, singer ("My Happiness," "Where the Boys Are"), born Newark, NJ, Dec 12, 1938.
Edward Irwin Koch, 74, former mayor of New York City, born New York, NY, Dec 12, 1924.
Rush Limbaugh, 47, talk show host ("The Rush Limbaugh Show"), born Cape Girardeau, MO, Dec 12, 1951.

December 1998

S	M	T	W	T	F	S
		1	2	3	4	5
6	7	8	9	10	11	12
13	14	15	16	17	18	19
20	21	22	23	24	25	26
27	28	29	30	31		

Robert Lindsay, 49, actor (*Me and My Girl* [Olivier, Tony, Theatre World and Drama Desk Awards]), born Derbyshire, England, Dec 12, 1949.
Robert Lee (Bob) Pettit, Jr, 66, Basketball Hall of Fame forward and center, born Baton Rouge, LA, Dec 12, 1932.
Cathy Rigby, 46, former Olympic gymnast, born Long Beach, CA, Dec 12, 1952.
Frank Sinatra (Francis Albert), 83, singer ("All the Way," "Strangers in the Night"), actor (*From Here to Eternity*), born Hoboken, NJ, Dec 12, 1915.
Dionne Warwick, 57, singer ("I Say a Little Prayer for You," "This Girl's in Love With You"), born East Orange, NJ, Dec 12, 1941.
Grover Washington, 55, musician, born Buffalo, NY, Dec 12, 1943.

DECEMBER 13 — SUNDAY

Day 347 — 18 Remaining

BROOKS, PHILLIPS: BIRTH ANNIVERSARY. Dec 13, 1835. American clergyman and composer born at Boston, MA, Dec 13, 1835. Perhaps best remembered for his lyrics for the Christmas carol "O Little Town of Bethlehem." Brooks died at Boston, Jan 23, 1893.

HEINE, HEINRICH: BIRTH ANNIVERSARY. Dec 13, 1797. German author, born at Dusseldorf, Dec 13, 1797. Died at Paris, France, Feb 17, 1856.

HISTORICAL SOCIETY'S CHRISTMAS CANDLELIGHT TOUR. Dec 13. Crawfordsville, IN. A walking tour of fine Victorian homes in Crawfordsville. Horse sleigh rides, hot cider, cookies and musical entertainment: dulcimer players, choral groups and brass quartets. Sponsor: Montgomery County Historical Society. Est attendance: 1,500. For info: Montgomery County Visitors & Conv Bureau, Inc, 412 E Main St, Crawfordsville, IN 47933. Phone: (800) 866-3973. Fax: (317) 362-5215. Email: mcvcb@tctc.com.
WWW: http://tctc.com/~mcvcb/

INTERNATIONAL SHAREWARE DAY. Dec 13. A day to take the time to reward the efforts of thousands of computer programmers who trust that if we try their programs and like them, we will pay for them. Unfortunately, very few payments are received, thus stifling the programmers' efforts. This observance is meant to prompt each of us to inventory our PCs and Macs, see if we are using any shareware, and then take the time in the holiday spirit to write payment checks to the authors. Hopefully this will keep shareware coming. Annually, the second Sunday in December. For info: David Lawrence, Host, Online Today, c/o Noblestar, 3141 Fairview Park Dr, Ste 400, Falls Church, VA 22042. Email: david@online-today.com.
WWW: http://online-today.com

LINCOLN, MARY TODD: BIRTH ANNIVERSARY. Dec 13, 1818. Wife of Abraham Lincoln, 16th president of the US, born at Lexington, KY, Dec 13, 1818. Died July 16, 1882.

MALTA: REPUBLIC DAY. Dec 13. National holiday. Malta became a republic on Dec 13, 1974.

NEW ZEALAND FIRST SIGHTED BY EUROPEANS: ANNIVERSARY. Dec 13, 1642. Captain Abel Tasman of the Dutch East India Company first sighted New Zealand but was kept from landing by Maori warriors. In 1769 Captain James Cook landed and claimed formal possession for Great Britain.

NORTH AND SOUTH KOREA END WAR: ANNIVERSARY. Dec 13, 1991. North and South Korea signed a treaty of reconciliation and nonaggression, formally ending the Korean War—38 years after fighting ceased in 1953. This agreement was not hailed as a peace treaty, and the armistice that was signed on July 27, 1953, between the United Nations and North Korea, was to remain in effect until it could be transformed into a formal peace.

QUINCY PRESERVES CHRISTMAS CANDLELIGHT TOUR. Dec 13. Quincy, IL. Tour historic homes decked out in their Christmas finest. Each year this walking tour features a different neighborhood. Homes range in size from grand mansions to quaint cottages. Annually, the second Sunday in December. Est attendance: 10,000. For info: Fran Cook, Quincy Preserves, 310 S 16th St, Quincy, IL 62301. Phone: (217) 224-2587.

REENACTMENT OF THE BOSTON TEA PARTY. Dec 13. Congress Street Bridge, Boston, MA. Reenactment of "Boston's most notorious protest, the single most important event leading to the American Revolution." Annually, the Sunday closest to Dec 16. Starts at Old South Meeting House 5:30 PM. Est attendance: 1,000. For info: Boston Tea Party Ship, Congress St Bridge, Boston, MA 02210. Phone: (617) 338-1773. Fax: (617) 338-1974.

SWEDEN: SANTA LUCIA DAY. Dec 13. Nationwide celebration of festival of light, honoring St. Lucia. Many hotels have their own Lucia, a young girl attired in a long, flowing white gown, who serves guests coffee and lussekatter (saffron buns) in the early morning.

TELL SOMEONE THEY'RE DOING A GOOD JOB WEEK. Dec 13–19. Every day this week tell someone "you're doing a good job." For info: Joe Hoppel, Radio Station WCMS, 900 Commonwealth Place, Virginia Beach, VA 23464. Phone: (757) 424-1050. Email: WCMS@Norfolk.Inf.net.
WWW: http://www.infi.net/wcms

BIRTHDAYS TODAY

Tim Conway, 65, actor, comedian ("McHale's Navy," "The Carol Burnett Show"), born Willoughby, OH, Dec 13, 1933.

John Davidson, 57, singer, actor, born Pittsburgh, PA, Dec 13, 1941.

Ted Nugent, 49, singer (with Amboy Dukes: "Journey to the Center of the Mind"; solo: "Cat Scratch Fever"), born Detroit, MI, 1949.

Christopher Plummer, 69, actor (Emmy for *The Moneychangers; The Sound of Music, Dolores Claiborne*), born Toronto, Ontario, Canada, Dec 13, 1929.

Dick Van Dyke, 73, actor, comedian (*Mary Poppins*, "The Dick Van Dyke Show"), born West Plains, MO, Dec 13, 1925.

DECEMBER 14 — MONDAY

Day 348 — 17 Remaining

ALABAMA: ADMISSION DAY: ANNIVERSARY. Dec 14. Became 22nd state on this day in 1819.

CHANUKAH. Dec 14–21. Feast of Lights, or Feast of Dedication. Festival lasting eight days commemorates victory of Maccabees over Syrians (165 BC) and rededication of Temple of Jerusalem. Begins on Hebrew calendar date Kislev 25, 5759.

DOOLITTLE, JAMES HAROLD: BIRTH ANNIVERSARY. Dec 14, 1896. American aviator and World War II hero General James Doolittle was born at Alameda, CA. A Lieutenant General in the US Army Air Force, he was the first person to fly across North America in less than a day. On Apr 18, 1942, Doolittle led a squadron of 16 B-25 bombers, launched from aircraft carriers, on the first US aerial raid on Japan of WW II. Bombs were dropped on the Japanese cities of Tokyo, Yokohama, Osaka, Kobe and Nagoya. He was awarded the Congressional Medal of Honor for this accomplishment. Doolittle also headed the Eighth Air Force during the Normandy invasion. He died Sept 27, 1993, at Pebble Beach, CA.

EGYPT: MARITIME DISASTER: ANNIVERSARY. Dec 14. The ferry *Salem Express* sank off the port city of Safaga, Egypt, on Dec 14, 1991, claiming the lives of 462 passengers and crew members. 180 people survived the disaster, the worst in modern Egypt's maritime history.

HALCYON DAYS. Dec 14–28. Traditionally, the seven days before and the seven days after the winter solstice. To the ancients a time when fabled bird (called the halcyon) calmed the wind and waves—a time of calm and tranquility.

MARIS, ROGER: DEATH ANNIVERSARY. Dec 14, 1985. Roger Eugene Maris, baseball player born Roger Eugene Maras at Hibbing, MN, Sept 10, 1934. In 1961, Maris broke one of baseball's sacred records, hitting 61 home runs to surpass the mark set by Babe Ruth in 1927. He won the American League MVP award in 1960 and 1961 and finished his career with the St. Louis Cardinals. Died at Houston, TX.

NATCHEZ CHRISTMAS PILGRIMAGE. Dec 14–31. Natchez, MS. Tours of antebellum mansions furnished with period antiques and decorated for the holidays. Also, carriage and bus sightseeing tours daily. Est attendance: 12,000. For info: Natchez Pilgrimage Tours, PO Box 347, Corner of Canal and State, Natchez, MS 39121. Phone: (800) 647-6742 or (601) 446-6631. Fax: (601) 446-8687.

NOSTRADAMUS: BIRTH ANNIVERSARY. Dec 14, 1503. French physician, best remembered for his astrological predictions (written in rhymed quatrains), was born Michel de Notredame, at St. Remy, Provence, France, Dec 14, 1503. Many believed that his book of prophecies actually foretold the future. Nostradamus died at Salon, France, July 2, 1566.

REMICK, LEE: BIRTH ANNIVERSARY. Dec 14, 1935. American actress Lee Remick was born at MA. Her films include *A Face in the Crowd* (1957), *Anatomy of a Murder* (1959) and *Days of Wine and Roses* (1963). She died on July 2, 1991, at Los Angeles, CA.

SMITH, MARGARET CHASE: BIRTH ANNIVERSARY. Dec 14, 1897. American politician Margaret Madeline Chase Smith was born at Skowhegan, ME. As the first woman to be elected to both houses of Congress (1941 to the House and 1949 to the Senate), she was also one of seven Republican senators to issue a "declaration of conscience" to denounce Senator Joseph R. McCarthy's communist witch-hunt. She died on May 29, 1995, at Skowhegan, ME.

SOUTH POLE DISCOVERY: ANNIVERSARY. Dec 14, 1911. The elusive object of many expeditions dating from the 7th century, the South Pole was located and visited by Roald Amundsen with four companions and 52 sled dogs. All five men and 12 of the dogs returned to base camp safely. Next to visit the South Pole, on Jan 17, 1912, was a party of five led by Captain Robert F. Scott, all of whom perished during the return trip. A search party found their frozen bodies 11 months later. See also: "Amundsen, Roald: Birth Anniversary" (July 16).

WASHINGTON, GEORGE: DEATH ANNIVERSARY. Dec 14. The first President of the United States of America died at Mount Vernon, VA, on Dec 14, 1799.

BIRTHDAYS TODAY

Craig Biggio, 33, baseball player, born Smithtown, NY, Dec 14, 1965.

Jane Birkin, 52, actress (*Blowup, Death on the Nile, Evil Under the Sun*), born London, England, Dec 14, 1946.

Leonardo Boff, 60, Brazilian Catholic theologian, born Concordia, Brazil, Dec 14, 1938.

William Joseph (Bill) Buckner, 49, former baseball player, born Vallejo, CA, Dec 14, 1949.

Patty Duke, 52, actress (Oscar for *The Miracle Worker*; Emmy for *My Sweet Charlie*), born New York, NY, Dec 14, 1946.

Don Hewitt, 76, TV news producer, born New York, NY, Dec 14, 1922.

Dee Wallace Stone, 50, actress (*"10," E.T. the Extra-Terrestrial*), born Kansas City, MO, Dec 14, 1948.

DECEMBER 15 — TUESDAY

Day 349 — 16 Remaining

BATTLE OF SAN PIETRO: 55th ANNIVERSARY. Dec 15, 1943. A German panzer battalion inflicted heavy casualties on American forces trying to take the 700-year-old Italian village of San Pietro, before withdrawing from the town. San Pietro was reduced almost entirely to rubble. The American movie director John Huston, serving as an Army lieutenant, filmed the battle for the military. So graphic was the film that it was described as anti-war by the military brass at the War Department. The film was cut from five to three reels before censors allowed it to be released in 1944. It was later re-edited for the television series "The Big Picture."

★**BILL OF RIGHTS DAY.** Dec 15. Presidential Proclamation. Has been proclaimed each year since 1962, but was omitted in 1967 and 1968. (Issued in 1941 and 1946 at Congressional request and in 1947 without request.) Since 1968 has been included in Human Rights Day and Week Proclamation.

BILL OF RIGHTS: ANNIVERSARY. Dec 15. The first 10 amendments to the US Constitution, known as the Bill of Rights, became effective following ratification by Virginia on Dec 15, 1791. The anniversary of ratification and of effect is observed as Bill of Rights Day.

CURACAO: KINGDOM DAY AND ANTILLEAN FLAG DAY. Dec 15. This day commemorates the Dec 15, 1954, Charter of Kingdom, signed in the Knight's Hall in The Hague, granting the Netherlands Antilles complete autonomy. Solemn meeting of the "Staten," the Parliament of the Netherlands Antilles. The Antillean Flag was hoisted for the first time on this day in 1959.

"DAVY CROCKETT" TV PREMIERE: ANNIVERSARY. Dec 15, 1954. This show, a series of five segments, can be considered TV's first miniseries. Shown on Walt Disney's "Disneyland" show, it starred Fess Parker as American western hero Davy Crockett and was immensely popular. The show spawned Crockett paraphernalia, including the famous trendy coonskin cap (even after we found out that historically, Boone never wore a coonskin hat).

EIFFEL, ALEXANDRE GUSTAVE: BIRTH ANNIVERSARY. Dec 15, 1832. Eiffel, the French engineer who designed the thousand-foot-high, million-dollar, open-lattice wrought iron Eiffel Tower, and who participated in designing the Statue of Liberty, was born at Dijon, France, on Dec 15, 1832. The Eiffel Tower, weighing more than 7,000 tons, was built for the Paris International Exposition of 1889. Eiffel died at Paris on Dec 23, 1923.

INTERNATIONAL LANGUAGE WEEK. Dec 15–21. To disseminate information about mankind's quest for an international language to solve the communication problem of humans, and to supply information about the international language Esperanto. Esperanto was created in 1887 by Dr. L.L. Zamenhof as a solution to the world's language problem. For complete info, send $3 to cover expense of printing, handling and postage. Annually, Dec 15–21. For info: Dr. Stanley Drake, Pres, Intl Society of Friendship and Good Will, 412 Cherry Hills Dr, Bakersfield, CA 93309-2866.

MILITARY DICTATORSHIP ENDED IN CHILE: ANNIVERSARY. Dec 15. In an election on Dec 15, 1989, Patricio Aylwin defeated General Augusto Pinochet's former finance minister, Hernan Buchi, bringing the military dictatorship of Pinochet to an end. Fourteen months previously, Pinochet suffered defeat in a national plebiscite on eight more years of his rule. This defeat prompted democratic elections and crippled the Pinochet regime. Pinochet came to power when the military overthrew a democratically elected government and killed Marxist president Salvador Allende in a 1973 coup. Patricio Aylwin avoided a two-candidate runoff by achieving 55.2% of the vote. He was inaugurated on Mar 11, 1990.

ONE DAY. Dec 15. San Francisco, CA. Celebrating a new "melting pot" tradition of inclusiveness, Men of All Colors Together's One Day holiday echoes Martin Luther King, Jr's vision of global harmony by combining the December celebrations of Christmas, Hanukkah, Kwanzaa and Winter Solstice, as well as other individual personal traditions, into One Day that celebrates diversity and embraces love among us all, as one. For info: Men of All Colors Together, San Francisco Bay Area, 973 Market St, Ste 600, San Francisco, CA 94103. Phone: (415) 675-0201.
Email: mactsfba@aol.com.
WWW: http://users.aol.com/mactsfba/home/page.html

PUERTO RICO: NAVIDADES. Dec 15–Jan 6. Traditional Christmas season begins mid-December and ends on Three Kings Day. Elaborate nativity scenes, carolers, special Christmas foods. Trees from Canada and US. Gifts on Christmas Day and on Three Kings Day.

SITTING BULL: DEATH ANNIVERSARY. Dec 15. (c. 1834–1890) Famous Sioux Indian leader, medicine man and warrior of the Hunkpapa Teton band. Known also by his native name, Tatanka-yatanka, Sitting Bull was born on the Grand River, SD. He first accompanied his father on the warpath at the age of 14 against the Crow and thereafter rapidly gained influence within his tribe. He became known in 1886 when he led a raid on Fort Buford. His steadfast refusal to go to a reservation led General Phillip Sheridan to initiate a campaign against him which led to the massacre of Lieutenant Colonel George Custer's men at the Little Bighorn, after which he fled to Canada, remaining there until 1881. Although many in his tribe surrendered on their return, Sitting Bull remained hostile until his death in a skirmish with the US soldiers along the Grand River on Dec 15, 1890.

SPACE MILESTONE: *VEGA 1* (USSR). Dec 15, 1984. Craft launched this date to rendezvous with Halley's Comet in March 1986. *Vega 2*, launched Dec 21, 1984, was part of same mission which, in cooperation with the US, carried US-built "comet-dust" detection equipment.

WAYNE, "MAD ANTHONY": DEATH ANNIVERSARY. Dec 15, 1796. American Revolutionary War general whose daring, sometimes reckless, conduct earned him the nickname "Mad Anthony" Wayne. His courage and shrewdness as a soldier made him a key figure in the capture of Stony Point, NY (1779), preventing Benedict Arnold's "delivery" of West Point to the British (1780), and in subduing hostile Indians of the Northwest Territory (1794). He was born at Waynesboro, PA, Jan 1, 1745, and died at Presque Isle, PA, at age 51. Wayne was buried at Erie, PA, but in 1809 his body was exhumed and a portion of his remains reburied at Erie and the other portion at Radnor, PA.

ZAMENHOF, DR. L.L.: BIRTH ANNIVERSARY. Dec 15, 1859. Lazarus Ludovic Zamenhof was born Dec 15, 1859, in Bia-

December 1998

S	M	T	W	T	F	S
		1	2	3	4	5
6	7	8	9	10	11	12
13	14	15	16	17	18	19
20	21	22	23	24	25	26
27	28	29	30	31		

lystok, near the borders of Lithuania, Poland and Byelorussia, where many different languages were spoken. Zamenhof realized the need for a common tongue while a child and later developed the International Language, Esperanto, which means "he who hopes." Died Apr 14, 1917 in Warsaw. For complete information about Esperanto and this worldwide organization, please send $3 to cover expense of printing, handling and postage. For info: Dr. Stanley Drake, Pres, Intl Society of Friendship and Good Will (ISFGW), 412 Cherry Hills Dr, Bakersfield, CA 93309-2866.

BIRTHDAYS TODAY

Nicholas (Nick) Buoniconti, 58, former football player, born Springfield, MA, Dec 15, 1940.

Dave Clark, 56, musician (leader of the Dave Clark Five; "I Like It Like That"), born London, England, Dec 15, 1942.

Friedrich Hundertwasser, 70, artist, born Vienna, Austria, Dec 15, 1928.

Don Johnson (Donald Wayne), 49, actor ("Miami Vice," *A Boy and His Dog*), born Flatt Creek, MO, Dec 15, 1949.

Edna O'Brien, 67, author (*Country Girls Trilogy, Time and Tide*), born Tuamgraney, Ireland, Dec 15, 1931.

Daryl Turner, 37, former football player, born Wadley, GA, Dec 15, 1961.

DECEMBER 16 — WEDNESDAY

Day 350 — 15 Remaining

AUSTEN, JANE: BIRTH ANNIVERSARY. Dec 16. English novelist born Dec 16, 1775. Died July 18, 1817.

BAHRAIN: INDEPENDENCE DAY. Dec 16. National holiday.

BANGLADESH: VICTORY DAY. Dec 16. National holiday in the People's Republic of Bangladesh.

BARBIE AND BARNEY BACKLASH DAY. Dec 16. If we have to explain this to you, you don't have kids. It's one day each year when Mom and Dad can tell the kids that Barbie and Barney don't exist. [© 1997 by WPL] For info: Tom and Ruth Roy, Wellness Permission League, PO Box 662, Mt Gretna, PA 17064-0662. Phone: (500) 437-5104 or (717) 964-1308. Fax: (717) 964-1335.

BATTLE OF THE BULGE: ANNIVERSARY. Dec 16, 1944. A German offensive was launched in the French Ardennes Forest on this date. The Nazi commanders, hoping to minimize any aerial counterattack by the Allies, chose a time when foggy, rainy weather prevailed, and the initial attack by eight armored divisions along a 75-mile front took the Allies by surprise, the 5th Panzer Army penetrating to within 20 miles of crossings on the Meuse River. US troops were able to hold fast at bottlenecks in the Ardennes, but by the end of December the German push had penetrated 65 miles into the Allied lines (though their line had narrowed from the initial 75 miles to 20 miles). By that time the Allies began to respond, and the Germans were stopped by Montgomery on the Meuse and by Patton at Bastogne. The weather then cleared, and Allied aircraft began to bomb the German forces and supply lines by Dec 26.

BEETHOVEN, LUDWIG VAN: BIRTH ANNIVERSARY. Dec 16, 1770. Regarded by many as the greatest orchestral composer of all time, Ludwig van Beethoven was born at Bonn, Germany. Impairment of his hearing began before he was 30, but even total deafness did not halt his composing and conducting. His last appearance on the concert stage was to conduct the premiere of his Ninth Symphony, at Vienna, on May 7, 1824. He was unable to hear either the orchestra or the applause. Often in love, he never married. Of a stormy temperament, he is said to have died during a violent thunderstorm on Mar 26, 1827, at Vienna. ". . . I have spent no less than the whole morning and the whole of yesterday afternoon," he wrote to Carl Holz in 1825, "over the correction of the two pieces, and am quite hoarse with swearing and stamping."

BOSTON TEA PARTY: 225th ANNIVERSARY. Dec 16, 1773. Anniversary of Dec 16, 1773, Boston patriots' boarding of British vessel at anchor in Boston Harbor. Contents of nearly 350 chests of tea were dumped into the harbor.

CALABRIA EARTHQUAKE: ANNIVERSARY. Dec 16, 1857. Calabria—an especially quake-prone region near Naples, Italy—experienced "a big one" that left more than 10,000 people dead and entire villages devastated. Between 1783 (the last big quake) and 1857, about 111,000 people lost their lives in the unstable region.

"DRAGNET" TV PREMIERE: ANNIVERSARY. Dec 16, 1951. This famous crime show stressed authenticity, and episodes were supposedly based on real cases. It starred Jack Webb as stoic and determined Sergeant Joe Friday, a man whose life was his investigative police work and who was recognized by his recurring line, "Just the facts, ma'am." Friday had many partners: Barton Yarborough played Sergeant Ben Romero for three episodes; for the rest of the season Barney Phillips played Sergeant Ed Jacobs and Ben Alexander played his comedic sidekick, Officer Frank Smith. Dorothy Abbott and Marjie Millar played Friday's romantic interests. A new version appeared in 1967 with Webb and his new partner, Officer Bill Gannon (Harry Morgan). "Dragnet" is also known for its theme music and its narrative epilogue describing the fate of the bad guys.

MAN WILL NEVER FLY SOCIETY MEETING. Dec 16. Kitty Hawk, NC. Group meets to prove that man will never fly. Society motto: "Birds fly, men drink." Annually on Dec 16, the night before the anniversary of the Wright Brothers' first flight. Est attendance: 300. For info: Ed North, Box 1903, Kill Devil Hill, NC 27948. Phone: (919) 261-6475.

MEAD, MARGARET: BIRTH ANNIVERSARY. Dec 16, 1901. American anthropologist and author, especially known for her studies of primitive peoples of southwest Pacific Ocean area, and for her forthright manner in speaking and writing. Born at Philadelphia, PA, Mead died at New York City, Nov 15, 1978.

MEXICO: POSADAS. Dec 16–24. A nine-day annual celebration throughout Mexico. Processions of "pilgrims" knock at doors asking for posada (shelter), commemorating the search by Joseph and Mary for a shelter in which the infant Jesus might be born. Pilgrims are invited inside, and fun and merrymaking ensue with blindfolded guests trying to break a "piñata" (papier mache decorated earthenware utensil filled with gifts and goodies) suspended from the ceiling. Once the piñata is broken, the gifts are distributed and celebration continues.

NEW WORLD SYMPHONY PREMIERE: ANNIVERSARY. Dec 16, 1893. Anton Dvorak's *New World Symphony* premiered at the newly erected Carnegie Hall with the New York Philharmonic playing. The composer attended and enjoyed enthusiastic applause from the audience. The symphony contains snatches from black spirituals and American folk music. Dvorak, a Bohemian, had been in the US only a year when he composed it as a greeting to his friends in Europe.

"ONE DAY AT A TIME" TV PREMIERE: ANNIVERSARY. Dec 16, 1975. This sitcom about a divorced mother raising two girls in Indianapolis starred Bonnie Franklin as Ann Romano and Mackenzie Phillips and Valerie Bertinelli as daughters Julie and Barbara Cooper. Other regulars included: Pat Harrington as tool-belt wearing, funny maintenance man Dwayne Schneider; Richard Masur as David Kane, Ann's boyfriend; Mary Louise Wilson as neighbor Ginny Wrobliki; John Hillerman and Charles Siebert as Claude Connors and Jerry Davenport, Ann's bosses; John Putch as Bob Morton, Barbara's boyfriend; and Nanette Fabray as Ann's mother Katherine. During the course of the series, all three female leads got married, and Ann opened her own ad agency. Mackenzie Phillips was written out of the show twice, the first time because of her cocaine addiction.

PHILIPPINES: PHILIPPINE CHRISTMAS OBSERVANCE. Dec 16–Jan 6. Philippine Islands. Said to be world's longest Christmas celebration.

PHILIPPINES: SIMBANG GABI. Dec 16–25. Nationwide. A nine-day novena of predawn masses, also called "Misa de Gallo." One of the traditional Filipino celebrations of the holiday season.

SANTAYANA, GEORGE: BIRTH ANNIVERSARY. Dec 16, 1863. Philosopher and author born at Madrid, Spain. At the age of nine he emigrated to the US where he attended and later taught at Harvard University. In 1912 he returned to Europe and traveled extensively. It was Santayana who said, "Those who cannot remember the past are condemned to repeat it." He died at Rome, Italy, on Sept 26, 1952.

UNITED NATIONS REVOKES RESOLUTION ON ZIONISM: ANNIVERSARY. Dec 16. On Dec 16, 1991, the United Nations voted 111 to 25 to revoke Resolution 3379, which equated Zionism with racism. Resolution 3379 was approved Nov 10, 1975, with 72 countries voting in favor, 35 against and 32 abstentions. The largest block of changed votes came from the former Soviet Union and Eastern Europe.

BIRTHDAYS TODAY

Bruce N. Ames, 70, biochemist, cancer researcher, born New York, NY, Dec 16, 1928.

Steven Bochco, 55, TV writer, producer, creator ("Hill Street Blues," "NYPD Blue"), born New York, NY, Dec 16, 1943.

Arthur Charles Clarke, 81, author, scientist (*2001: A Space Odyssey, Islands in the Sky*), born Minehead, England, Dec 16, 1917.

Alison La Placa, 39, actress ("The John Laroquette Show"), raised Lincolnshire, IL, born Dec 16, 1959.

Clifford Ralph Robinson, 32, basketball player, born Buffalo, NY, Dec 16, 1966.

Lesley Stahl, 57, journalist ("60 Minutes," former White House correspondent), born Lynn, MA, Dec 16, 1941.

Liv Johanne Ullmann, 59, actress (*The Immigrants, Scenes from a Marriage*), born Tokyo, Japan, Dec 16, 1939.

DECEMBER 17 — THURSDAY

Day 351 — 14 Remaining

AZTEC CALENDAR STONE DISCOVERY: ANNIVERSARY. Dec 17. On Dec 17, 1790, one of the wonders of the western hemisphere—the Aztec Calendar, or Solar, Stone—was found beneath the ground by workmen repairing Mexico City's Central Plaza. The centuries-old, intricately carved stone, 11 ft, 8 inches in diameter and weighing nearly 25 tons, proved to be a highly developed calendar monument to the sun. Believed to have been carved in the year 1479, this extraordinary time-counting basalt tablet stood originally in the Great Temple of the Aztecs. Buried, along with other Aztec idols, soon after the Spanish conquest in 1521, it remained hidden until 1790. Its 52-year cycle had regulated many Aztec ceremonies, including grisly human sacrifices to save the world from destruction by the gods.

BHUTAN: NATIONAL DAY. Dec 17. National holiday observed.

December 1998

S	M	T	W	T	F	S
		1	2	3	4	5
6	7	8	9	10	11	12
13	14	15	16	17	18	19
20	21	22	23	24	25	26
27	28	29	30	31		

FIRST FLIGHT TRADITIONAL ANNIVERSARY CELEBRATION. Dec 17, 1903. Kill Devil Hills, NC. Each year since 1928, on the anniversary of the Wright Brothers' first successful heavier-than-air flight at Kitty Hawk, NC, Dec 17, 1903, a celebration has been held at the Wright Brothers National Memorial, with wreaths, flyover and other observances—regardless of weather.

FLOYD, WILLIAM: BIRTH ANNIVERSARY. Dec 17. Signer of the Declaration of Independence, member of Congress, born at Brookhaven, Long Island, Dec 17, 1734. Died at Westernville, NY, Aug 4, 1821.

HENRY, JOSEPH: BIRTH ANNIVERSARY. Dec 17, 1797. Scientist Joseph Henry was born at Albany, NY. One of his great scientific discoveries was the principle of self-induction; the unit used in the measure of electrical inductance was named the henry in his honor. In 1831 Henry constructed the first model of an electric telegraph with an audible signal. This formed the basis of nearly all later work on commercial wire telegraphy. In 1832 Henry was named professor of natural philosophy at the College of New Jersey, now Princeton University. Henry was involved in the planning of the Smithsonian Institution and became its first secretary in 1846. President Lincoln named Henry as one of the original 50 scientists to make up the National Academy of Sciences in 1863. He served as that organization's president from 1868 until his death May 13, 1878, at Washington, DC.

"HOUSE CALLS" TV PREMIERE: ANNIVERSARY. Dec 17, 1979. This half-hour sitcom set in Kensington General Hospital starred Wayne Rogers as Dr. Charley Michaels and Lynn Redgrave as Ann Anderson, assistant administrator and Michaels's love interest. Also featured were: David Wayne as flaky chief of surgery Dr. Amos Weatherby; Ray Buktenica as Dr. Norman Solomon; Aneta Corsaut as Head Nurse Bradley; Deedy Peters as Mrs Phipps, elderly volunteer; and Mark L. Taylor as serious administrator Conrad Peckler. After a dispute with the producers, Redgrave was dropped in 1982 and replaced by Sharon Gless (as assistant Jane Jeffreys) for the rest of the series.

KING, W.L. MACKENZIE: BIRTH ANNIVERSARY. Dec 17, 1874. Former Canadian prime minister, born at Berlin, Ontario. Served 21 years, the longest term of any prime minister in the English-speaking world. Died at Kingsmere, July 22, 1950.

LIBBY, WILLARD FRANK: 90th BIRTH ANNIVERSARY. Dec 17, 1908. American educator, chemist, atomic scientist and Nobel Prize winner was born at Grand Valley, CO, Dec 17, 1908. He was the inventor of the Carbon-14 "atomic clock" method for dating ancient and prehistoric plant and animal remains and minerals. Died at Los Angeles, CA, Sept 8, 1980.

★ **PAN AMERICAN AVIATION DAY.** Dec 17. Presidential Proclamation 2446, of Nov 18, 1940, covers all succeeding years (Pub Res No. 105 of Oct 10, 1940).

SAMPSON, DEBORAH: BIRTH ANNIVERSARY. Dec 17, 1760. Born at Plympton, MA, Deborah Sampson spent her childhood as an indentured servant. In 1782, wishing to participate in the Revolutionary War, Sampson disguised herself as a man and enlisted in the Continental Army's 4th Massachusetts Regiment under the name Robert Shurtleff. She received both musket and sword wounds, but it was an attack of fever that unmasked her identity and led to her dismissal from the army in 1783. In 1802 Sampson became perhaps the first woman to lecture professionally in the US when she began giving public speeches on her experiences. Full military pension was provided for her heirs by act of Congress in 1838. Deborah Sampson died Apr 29, 1827, at Sharon, MA.

SATURNALIA. Dec 17–23. Anniversary of ancient Roman festival honoring Saturn, the planter god. Approximates the winter solstice. Most festive period of the year in Rome, and immensely popular. Gifts, lights and the closing of businesses mark the period. Some say that the date for the observance of the nativity of Jesus was selected by the early Christian church leaders to fall on Dec 25 partly to counteract the popular but disapproved of pre-Christian Roman festival of Saturnalia.

WHITTIER, JOHN GREENLEAF: BIRTH ANNIVERSARY. Dec 17, 1807. Poet and abolitionist, born at Haverhill, Essex County, MA. Whittier wrote books of poetry including *Legends of New England* and *Snowbound*. Died at Hampton Falls, NH, Sept 7, 1892.

★**WRIGHT BROTHERS DAY.** Dec 17. Presidential Proclamation always issued for Dec 17 since 1963 (PL88–209 of Dec 17, 1963). Issued twice earlier at Congressional request in 1959 and 1961.

WRIGHT BROTHERS FIRST POWERED FLIGHT: 95th ANNIVERSARY. Dec 17, 1903. Orville and Wilbur Wright, brothers, bicycle shop operators, inventors and aviation pioneers, after three years of experimentation with kites and gliders, achieved the first documented successful powered and controlled flights of an airplane. The flights, near Kitty Hawk, NC, piloted first by Orville then by Wilbur Wright, were sustained for less than one minute but represented man's first powered airplane flight and the beginning of a new form of transportation. Orville Wright was born at Dayton, OH, Aug 19, 1871, and died there Jan 30, 1948. Wilbur Wright was born at Millville, IN, Apr 16, 1867, and died at Dayton, OH, May 30, 1912.

BIRTHDAYS TODAY

Christopher Cazenove, 53, actor (*Zulu Dawn, Eye of the Needle*), born Winchester, England, Dec 17, 1945.
Bob Guccione, 68, publisher, born Brooklyn, NY, Dec 17, 1930.
Bernard Hill, 54, actor (*Gandhi, Shirley Valentine*), born Manchester, England, Dec 17, 1944.
Ernie Hudson, 53, actor (*Ghostbusters, Ghostbusters II, The Hand That Rocks the Cradle*), born Benton Harbor, MI, Dec 17, 1945.
Eugene Levy, 52, comedian, writer ("Second City TV," "SCTV Network 90"), born Hamilton, Ontario, Canada, Dec 17, 1946.
Sy Oliver, 88, music arranger, composer, born Battle Creek, MI, Dec 17, 1910.
Gene Rayburn, 81, former TV game-show host ("Match Game"), comic ("The Steve Allen Show"), born Christopher, IL, Dec 17, 1917.
William Safire, 69, author, journalist (*Coming to Terms, Words of Wisdom*), born New York, NY, Dec 17, 1929.
Tommy Steele, 62, actor (*The Happiest Millionaire, Half a Sixpence*), born London, England, Dec 17, 1936.

DECEMBER 18 — FRIDAY

Day 352 — 13 Remaining

BRANDT, WILLY: 85th BIRTH ANNIVERSARY. Dec 18, 1913. Former West German chancellor Willy Brandt was born Herbert Ernst Karl Frahm at Lubeck, Germany. An anti-Nazi exile during World War II, he won the Nobel Peace Prize in 1971 for seeking better East-West relations. He died on Oct 8, 1992, at Unkel, Germany.

CAPITOL REEF NATIONAL PARK ESTABLISHED: ANNIVERSARY. Dec 18, 1971. Area of outstanding geological features, colorful canyons, prehistoric Fremont petroglyphs and Mormon historic fruit orchards and buildings in south central Utah, originally proclaimed a national monument Aug 2, 1937, was established as a national park. For further park info: Capitol Reef Natl Park, Box 15, Torrey, UT 84775.
Email: care-interpretation@nps.gov.
WWW: http://www.nps.gov/care

COBB, TYRUS RAYMOND "TY": BIRTH ANNIVERSARY. Dec 18, 1886. Famed American baseball player born at Narrows, GA. Died at Atlanta, GA, July 17, 1961. Lifetime batting average of .367 compiled over 24 years during which he played in more than 3,000 games.

GRIMALDI, JOSEPH: BIRTH ANNIVERSARY. Dec 18, 1778. Known as the "greatest clown in history" and the "king of pantomime," Joseph Grimaldi began his stage career at age two. He was an accomplished singer, dancer and acrobat. Born at London, England, on Dec 18, 1778, he is best remembered as the original "Joey the Clown" and for the innovative humor he brought to the clown's role in theater. Illness forced his early retirement in 1823, and he died at London on May 31, 1837.

MacDOWELL, EDWARD ALEXANDER: BIRTH ANNIVERSARY. Dec 18, 1861. Composer of orchestral and piano compositions and songs, born at New York, NY. He was awarded a music professorship at Columbia University. He died at New York, NY, Jan 23, 1908.

MEXICO: FEAST OF OUR LADY OF SOLITUDE. Dec 18. Oaxaca. Pilgrims venerate the patron of the lonely.

MOON PHASE: NEW MOON. Dec 18. Moon enters New Moon phase at 5:42 PM, EST.

NEW JERSEY RATIFICATION DAY: ANNIVERSARY. Dec 18, 1787. New Jersey, on Dec 18, 1787, became the third state to ratify the Constitution (following Delaware and Pennsylvania). It did so unanimously.

NIGER: REPUBLIC DAY. Dec 18. National holiday.

SPACE MILESTONE: *SOYUZ 13* (USSR): 25th ANNIVERSARY. Dec 18, 1973. Two Soviet cosmonauts (P.I. Klimuk and V.V. Lebedev) began eight-day orbit of Earth, returning on Dec 26.

STRADIVARI, ANTONIO: DEATH ANNIVERSARY. Dec 18, 1737. Celebrated Italian violin maker was born probably in the year 1644, and died at Cremona, at about age 93.

THIRTEENTH AMENDMENT TO THE US CONSTITUTION: ANNIVERSARY. Dec 18. On Dec 18, 1865, ratification of the 13th Amendment was proclaimed, abolishing slavery in the nation. "Neither slavery nor involuntary servitude, save as a punishment for crime whereof the party shall have been duly convicted, shall exist within the United States, or any place subject to their jurisdiction." See also: "Emancipation Proclamation Anniversary" (Jan 1) for Abraham Lincoln's proclamation freeing slaves in the rebelling states.

"TO TELL THE TRUTH" TV PREMIERE: ANNIVERSARY. Dec 18, 1956. This long-running popular game show was another production of the Mark Goodson-Bill Todman team. A celebrity panel (and the home audience) tried to guess which of three guests claiming to be the same person was telling the truth. The real person had to tell the truth while the others could lie. Panelists took turns questioning the guests, and, at the conclusion, the identity of the person was revealed. Guests split a cash award. Hosts have included Bud Collyer, Garry Moore, Joe Garagiola, Robin Ward, Gordon Elliott and Alex Trebek. Celebrity panelists included Dick Van Dyke, Tom Poston, Peggy Cass, Kitty Carlisle and Bill Cullen.

UNDERDOG DAY. Dec 18. To salute, before the year's end, all of the underdogs and unsung heroes—the Number Two people who contribute so much to the Number One people we read about. (Sherlock Holmes's Dr. Watson and Robinson Crusoe's Friday are examples.) Annually, the third Friday in December. For info: P. Moeller, Chief Underdog, Box 71, Clio, MI 48420-1042.

BIRTHDAYS TODAY

(William) Ramsey Clark, 71, former US attorney general, born Dallas, TX, Dec 18, 1927.
Ossie Davis, 81, actor (*A Raisin in the Sun, Grumpy Old Men*, "Evening Shade"), born Cogdell, GA, Dec 18, 1917.
Ray Liotta, 43, actor (*Unforgettable, Goodfellas, Field of Dreams, Something Wild*), born Newark, NJ, Dec 18, 1955.
Leonard Maltin, 48, movie critic, author (*Maltin's Guide*), born New York, NY, Dec 18, 1950.
Charles Oakley, 35, basketball player, born Cleveland, OH, Dec 18, 1963.
Brad Pitt, 34, actor (*Interview with a Vampire, A River Runs Through It*), born Shawnee, OK, Dec 18, 1964.

Keith Richards, 55, musician, singer (with the Rolling Stones; "Happy"), born Dartford, England, Dec 18, 1943.

Steven Spielberg, 51, producer, director (*E.T. The Extra-Terrestrial, Indiana Jones* movies, *Close Encounters of the Third Kind, Jurassic Park, The Color Purple*; Oscar for *Schindler's List*), born Cincinnati, OH, Dec 18, 1947.

Kiefer Sutherland, 32, actor (*Flatliners, A Few Good Men*), born Los Angeles, CA, Dec 18, 1966.

DECEMBER 19 — SATURDAY

Day 353 — 12 Remaining

CHRISTMAS GREETINGS FROM SPACE: 40th ANNIVERSARY. Dec 19, 1958. At 3:15 PM, EST, Dec 19, 1958, the US Earth satellite *Atlas* transmitted the first radio voice broadcast from space, a 58-word recorded Christmas greeting from President Dwight D. Eisenhower: "to all mankind America's wish for peace on earth and good will toward men everywhere." Satellite had been launched from Cape Canaveral Dec 18.

A COLONIAL CHRISTMAS. Dec 19–Jan 3. Jamestown Settlement, Williamsburg, VA and Yorktown Victory Center, Yorktown, VA. Recalls traditional English Christmas celebrations with decorations, holiday food preparation and seasonal stories. Est attendance: 12,000. For info: Media Relations, Jamestown-Yorktown Fdtn, PO Box 1607, Williamsburg, VA 23187. Phone: (757) 253-4838. Fax: (757) 253-5299.
WWW: http://www.historyisfun.org

FISKE, MINNIE MADDERN: BIRTH ANNIVERSARY. Dec 19. American theater actress with a long, distinguished career. First stage appearance at the age of three as "Little Minnie Maddern." Born on Dec 19, 1865, at New Orleans, LA, and died on Feb 15, 1932.

LIVERMORE, MARY ASHTON: BIRTH ANNIVERSARY. Dec 19. American reformer and women's suffrage leader, born Dec 19, 1821. Died May 23, 1905.

NAIA FOOTBALL NATIONAL CHAMPIONSHIP GAME. Dec 19. Savannah, TN. 16-team field competes, ending with the final two teams vying for the national championship. 43rd annual. For info: Natl Assn of Intercollegiate Athletics, 6120 S Yale Ave, Suite 1450, Tulsa, OK 74136-4223. Phone: (918) 494-8828. Fax: (918) 494-8841. Email: khenry@naia.org. WWW: http://www.naia.org

PARRY, WILLIAM: BIRTH ANNIVERSARY. Dec 19. British explorer Sir William Edward Parry was born at Bath, England, on Dec 19, 1790. Remembered for his Arctic expeditions and for his search for a Northwest Passage, Parry died at Ems, Germany, July 8, 1855.

POLISH CHRISTMAS OPEN HOUSE. Dec 19. Polish American Cultural Center Museum, Philadelphia, PA. Sw. Mikolaj (Polish St. Nicholas) will greet everyone with gifts for the children. Polish Christmas Tree and entertainment. Free admission. For info: Polish American Cultural Center Museum, 308 Walnut St, Philadelphia, PA 19106. Phone: (215) 922-1700. Fax: (215) 922-1518.

SPACE MILESTONE: *COSMOS 1614* (USSR). Dec 19, 1984. Unmanned space shuttle made one orbit before splashdown in Black Sea.

SPACE MILESTONE: *INTELSAT 4 F-3* (US). Dec 19, 1971. Communications satellite launched by NASA on contract with COMSAT. Mission involved intercontinental relay phone and TV communications.

December 1998

S	M	T	W	T	F	S
		1	2	3	4	5
6	7	8	9	10	11	12
13	14	15	16	17	18	19
20	21	22	23	24	25	26
27	28	29	30	31		

SUSSKIND, DAVID: BIRTH ANNIVERSARY. Dec 19, 1920. American television producer David (Howard) Susskind was born at New York, NY. In 1952 he started his own television production company and soon was producing more live programs than the three networks combined. He began to host talk shows in 1958 and was widely respected for focusing on serious matters. He died on Feb 22, 1987, at New York, NY.

WOODSON, CARTER GODWIN: BIRTH ANNIVERSARY. Dec 19, 1875. Historian who introduced black studies to colleges and universities, born at New Canton, VA. His scholarly works included *The Negro in Our History, The Education of the Negro Prior to 1861*. Woodson was working on a six-volume *Encyclopaedia Africana* when he died at Washington, DC, Apr 3, 1950.

BIRTHDAYS TODAY

Jennifer Beals, 35, actress (*Flashdance, The Bride, Into the Soup*), born Chicago, IL, Dec 19, 1963.

Janie Frickie, 46, singer (Country Music Assn Female Vocalist of Year '82, '83; "It Ain't Easy"), born Whitney, IN, Dec 19, 1952.

Richard E. Leakey, 54, anthropologist, born Nairobi, Kenya, Dec 19, 1944.

Kevin Edward McHale, 41, former basketball player, born Hibbing, MN, Dec 19, 1957.

Alyssa Milano, 26, actress (Samantha Micelli on "Who's the Boss"), born Brooklyn, NY, Dec 19, 1972.

Tim Reid, 54, actor ("Frank's Place," "WKRP in Cincinnati"), born Norfolk, VA, Dec 19, 1944.

Helen Slater, 35, actress (*Supergirl, Ruthless People*), born New York, NY, Dec 19, 1963.

Cicely Tyson, 59, actress (Emmy for *The Autobiography of Miss Jane Pittman*; *Sounder*), born New York, NY, Dec 19, 1939.

Robert Urich, 53, actor ("Marcus Welby, MD," "Spenser: For Hire"), born Toronto, Ontario, Canada, Dec 19, 1945.

DECEMBER 20 — SUNDAY

Day 354 — 11 Remaining

AMERICAN POET LAUREATE ESTABLISHMENT: ANNIVERSARY. Dec 20. A bill empowering the Librarian of Congress to name, annually, a Poet Laureate/Consultant in Poetry was signed into law by President Ronald Reagan on Dec 20, 1985. In return for a $10,000 stipend as Poet Laureate and a salary (about $35,000) as the Consultant in Poetry, the person named will present at least one major work of poetry and will appear at selected national ceremonies. The first Poet Laureate of the US was Robert Penn Warren, appointed to that position by the Librarian of Congress on Feb 26, 1986. See also: "Warren, Robert Penn: Birthday" (Apr 24).

"THE DATING GAME" TV PREMIERE: ANNIVERSARY. Dec 20, 1965. Another game show developed by Chuck Barris, it typically featured a "bachelorette" who questioned three men who were hidden from her view and decided, based on their answers, which guy appealed to her the most. The couple was then sent on a date, courtesy of the show. Occasionally, a bachelor would question three women. Jim Lange was the host of the network series and two syndicated ones. Elaine Joyce and Jeff MacGregor hosted one season each on the retitled "All-New Dating Game."

EIGHTEENTH-CENTURY CHRISTMAS WASSAIL. Dec 20. McLean, VA. Greet the winter solstice and Christmas season with a toast to the apple trees. Caroling and warm refreshments. Bring pots or other noisemakers to frighten off evil spirits threatening next year's apple crop. Est attendance: 800. For info: Gretchen Brodtman, Publicist, Claude Moore Colonial Farm at Turkey Run, 6310 Georgetown Pike, McLean, VA 22101. Phone: (703) 442-7557. Fax: (703) 442-0714.

FIRESTONE, HARVEY S.: BIRTH ANNIVERSARY. Dec 20, 1868. American industrialist, businessman and founder of the Firestone Tire and Rubber Co. Harvey Samuel Firestone was born at Columbiana County, OH, Dec 20, 1868. A close friend of Henry Ford, Thomas Edison and John Burroughs, Firestone was also author of two books about rubber. He died at Miami Beach, FL, Feb 7, 1938.

FIRST JOINT SIBERIAN-AMERICAN MUSICAL THEATRE PRODUCTION: ANNIVERSARY. Dec 20. On Dec 20, 1990, the first joint Siberian-American production of an American musical premiered in the Siberian city of Omsk, Russia. The musical was *Charlie Bar* by Americans Jane Boyd and Gregg Opelka. It was staged by an American production team using a Russian cast performing the play in Russian. The production was a joint effort between the Musical Comedy Theatre of Omsk and New Tuners Theatre of Chicago.

HAWAIIAN CHRISTMAS LOOONG DISTANCE INVITATIONAL ROUGH-H2O SWIM. Dec 20. Waikiki Beach, Honolulu, HI. 7K (4.33 mile) swim across Waikiki Bay and return. Preregistration is required. Hawaii's longest open ocean race. Annually, the week following Honolulu Marathon. Est attendance: 90. For info: Jim Anderson, One Keahole Place #1607, Honolulu, HI 96825-3414. Fax: (808) 396-8868.
Email: waikikijim@aol.com.

INTERNATIONAL LIPSTICK WEEK. Dec 20–26. Celebrating the creation of lipstick and all its beautifying powers. For info: Robin Gorman Newman, 58 Grace Ave, #2J, Great Neck, NY 11021. Phone: (516) 773-0911. Email: rgnewman@aol.com.

LANGER, SUSANNE K.: BIRTH ANNIVERSARY. Dec 20. Susanne Langer, a leading American philosopher, author of *Philosophy in a New Key: A Study in the Symbolism of Reason, Rite, and Art*, was born at New York, NY, on Dec 20, 1895. Her studies of esthetics and art exerted a profound influence on thinking in the fields of psychology, philosophy and the social sciences. She died at Old Lyme, CT, on July 17, 1985.

LOUISIANA PURCHASE DAY. Dec 20, 1803. One of the greatest real estate deals in history was completed on Dec 20, 1803, when more than a million square miles of the Louisiana Territory were turned over to the US by France, for a price of about $20 per square mile.

LUDENDORFF, ERICK: DEATH ANNIVERSARY. Dec 20, 1937. German general who, during the last years of World War I, was chiefly responsible for military policy and strategy. Born Apr 9, 1865, near Pozen, Prussia, and died at Tutzing at age 72.

MENZIES, ROBERT GORDON: BIRTH ANNIVERSARY. Dec 20, 1894. Australian statesman and conservative leader, born at Jeparit, Victoria, Australia, Sir Robert died at Melbourne, Australia, May 14, 1978, at age 83.

MONTGOMERY BUS BOYCOTT ENDS: ANNIVERSARY. Dec 20, 1956. The US Supreme Court ruling of Nov 13, 1956, calling for integration of the Montgomery, AL, public bus system was implemented. Since Dec 5, 1955, the black community of Montgomery had refused to ride on the segregated buses. The boycott was in reaction to the Dec 1, 1955, arrest of Rosa Parks for refusing to relinquish her seat on a Montgomery bus to a white man.

MUDD DAY. Dec 20, 1833. A day to remember Dr. Samuel A. Mudd (born near Bryantown, MD, Dec 20, 1833), sentenced to life imprisonment for giving medical aid to disguised John Wilkes Booth, fleeing assassin of Abraham Lincoln. Imprisoned four years before being pardoned by President Andrew Johnson. Died on Jan 10, 1883.

RAMADAN: THE ISLAMIC MONTH OF FASTING. Dec 20, 1998–Jan 17, 1999. Begins on Islamic lunar calendar date Ramadan 1, 1419. Ramadan, the ninth month of the Islamic calendar, is holy because it was during this month that the Holy Qur'an [Koran] was revealed. All adults of sound body and mind fast from dawn (before sunrise) until sunset to achieve spiritual and physical purification and self-discipline, abstaining from food, drink and intimate relations. It is a time for feeling a common bond with the poor and needy, a time of piety and prayer. Different methods for "anticipating" the visibility of the new moon crescent at Mecca are used by different Muslim groups. *Chase's* uses anticipated dates furnished by the American Muslim Council. US EST date may vary. See also: "Ramadan" (Jan 1).

RICKEY, BRANCH: BIRTH ANNIVERSARY. Dec 20, 1881. Wesley Branch Rickey, Baseball Hall of Fame player, manager and executive born at Lucasville, OH. Rickey was baseball's most innovative general manager. He invented the farm system, instituted unique training and teaching methods and, most prominently, signed Jackie Robinson to play major league baseball with the Brooklyn Dodgers. Inducted into the Hall of Fame in 1967. Died at Columbia, MO, Dec 9, 1965.

SACAGAWEA: DEATH ANNIVERSARY. Dec 20, 1812. As a young Shoshone Indian woman, Sacagawea in 1805 (with her two-month-old boy strapped to her back) traveled with the Lewis and Clark Expedition, serving as an interpreter. It is said that the expedition could not have succeeded without her aid. She was born about 1787 and died at Fort Manuel on the Missouri River, Dec 20, 1812. Few other women have been so often honored. There are statues, fountains and memorials of her, and her name has been given to a mountain peak. Few facts about her life are firmly established and some legends have her living to nearly a hundred years of age.

SOUTH CAROLINA: SECESSION ANNIVERSARY. Dec 20. South Carolina's legislature voted, Dec 20, 1860, to secede from the United States of America, the first state to do so.

UNITED STATES INVASION OF PANAMA: ANNIVERSARY. Dec 20, 1989. The US launched operation "Just Cause," invading Panama in an attempt to seize Manuel Noriega and bring him to justice for narcotics trafficking. Seven months after Noriega had ruled unfavorable election results null and void, the US toppled the Noriega government and oversaw the installation of Guillermo Endara as president. Although the initial military action was declared a success, Noriega eluded capture. He surrendered to US troops on Jan 4, 1990, and was tried, convicted and imprisoned in the US.

VIRGINIA COMPANY EXPEDITION TO AMERICA: ANNIVERSARY. Dec 20. Three small ships, the *Susan Constant*, the *Godspeed* and the *Discovery*, commanded by Captain Christopher Newport, departed London, England, on Dec 20, 1606, bound for America, where the royally chartered Virginia Company's approximately 120 persons established the first permanent English settlement in what is now the United States at Jamestown, VA, on May 14, 1607.

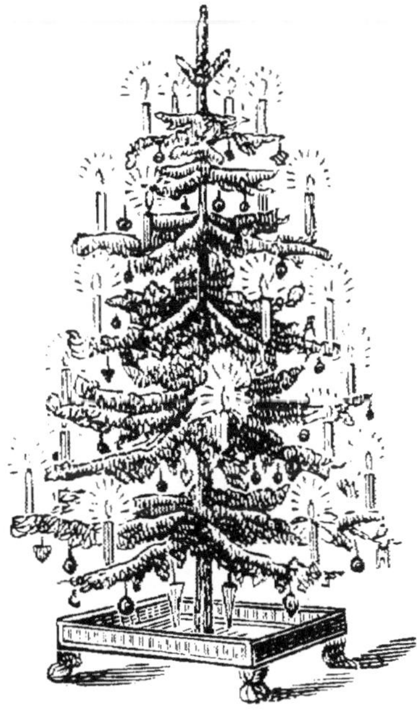

BIRTHDAYS TODAY

Jenny Agutter, 46, actress (Emmy for "The Snow Goose"), born London, England, Dec 20, 1952.

Uri Geller, 52, psychic, clairvoyant, born Tel Aviv, Israel, Dec 20, 1946.

George Roy Hill, 76, filmmaker (*Butch Cassidy and the Sundance Kid*), born Minneapolis, MN, Dec 20, 1922.

John Hillerman, 66, actor ("The Betty White Show," "Magnum, PI"), born Denison, TX, Dec 20, 1932.

Sidney Hook, 96, philosopher, educator, born New York, NY, Dec 20, 1902.

Mark Keyloun, 38, actor (*Sudden Impact, Mike's Murder*), born Dec 20, 1960.

David Levine, 72, artist, caricaturist (for the *New York Review of Books*), born Brooklyn, NY, Dec 20, 1926.

William Julius Wilson, 63, sociologist, educator, writer (*When Work Disappears*), born Derry Township, PA, Dec 20, 1935.

DECEMBER 21 — MONDAY

Day 355 — 10 Remaining

BELGIUM: NUTS FAIR. Dec 21. Bastogne. Traditional cultural observance. Third Monday in December.

BOLL, HEINRICH: BIRTH ANNIVERSARY. Dec 21, 1917. German novelist, winner of the 1972 Nobel Prize for Literature, author of some 20 books including *Billiards at Half-Past Nine, The Clown* and *Group Portrait with Lady*, was born Dec 21, 1917, at Cologne, Germany. He died near Bonn, Germany, on July 16, 1985.

DISRAELI, BENJAMIN: BIRTH ANNIVERSARY. Dec 21. British novelist and statesman, born Dec 21, 1804. Died Apr 19, 1881. "No government," he wrote, "can be long secure without a formidable opposition."

FOLDES, ANDOR: 85th BIRTH ANNIVERSARY. Dec 21, 1913. Pianist Andor Foldes was born at Budapest, Hungary, on Dec 21, 1913. A child prodigy born to a musical family, he played a Mozart piano concerto with the Budapest Philharmonic when he was eight. He moved to the US in 1939 and is renowned for introducing the work of composer Bela Bartok to the US. He died on Feb 9, 1992, at Zurich, Switzerland.

FOREFATHERS' DAY. Dec 21. Observed mainly in New England in commemoration of landing at Plymouth Rock on this day in 1620.

HUMBUG DAY. Dec 21. Allows all those preparing for Christmas to vent their frustrations. 12 "humbugs" allowed. [© 1997 by WPL] For info: Tom or Ruth Roy, Wellness Permission League, PO Box 662, Mt Gretna, PA 17064-0662. Phone: (500) 437-5104 or (717) 964-1308. Fax: (717) 964-1335.

December 1998

S	M	T	W	T	F	S
		1	2	3	4	5
6	7	8	9	10	11	12
13	14	15	16	17	18	19
20	21	22	23	24	25	26
27	28	29	30	31		

PAN AMERICAN FLIGHT 103 EXPLOSION: 10th ANNIVERSARY. Dec 21, 1988. Pan Am World Airways Flight 103 exploded in midair and crashed into the heart of Lockerbie, Scotland, on Dec 21, 1988, the result of a terrorist bombing. The 258 passengers and crew members and a number of persons on the ground were killed in the disaster. The tragedy raised questions about security and the notification of passengers in the event of threatened flights. In the resultant investigation it was revealed that government agencies and the airline had known that the flight was possibly the target of a terrorist attack.

PARKINSON, JAMES: DEATH ANNIVERSARY. Dec 21. The remarkable English physician and paleontologist who first described the "shaking palsy" later had it named for him—Parkinson's disease. He was the author of numerous books and articles on a variety of subjects. His *Organic Remains of a Former World* is called the first attempt to give a scientific account of fossils—"a memorable event in the history of British paleontology." Under oath, Parkinson declared that he was a member of the group that hatched the "Pop-gun Plot" to assassinate King George III in a theater, using a poisoned dart for the deed. His birthplace and date (about 1755) are unknown, but Dr. Parkinson died at London on Dec 21, 1824.

PHILEAS FOGG WINS A WAGER DAY. Dec 21. Anniversary, from Jules Verne's *Around the World in Eighty Days*, of the winning of Phileas Fogg's wager, on Dec 21, 1872, when Fogg walked into the saloon of the Reform Club in London, announcing "Here I am, gentlemen!" exactly 79 days, 23 hours, 59 minutes and 59 seconds after starting his trip "around the world in 80 days," to win his £20,000 wager. See also: "Phileas Fogg's Wager Day" (Oct 2).

PILGRIM LANDING: ANNIVERSARY. Dec 21, 1620. According to Governor William Bradford's *History of Plymouth Plantation*, "On Munday," [Dec 21, 1620, New Style] the Pilgrims, aboard the *Mayflower*, reached Plymouth, MA, "sounded ye harbor, and founde it fitt for shipping; and marched into ye land, & founde diverse cornfields, and ye best they could find, and ye season & their presente necessitie made them glad to accepte of it. . . . And after wards tooke better view of ye place, and resolved wher to pitch their dwelling; and them and their goods." Plymouth Rock, the legendary place of landing since it first was "identified" in 1769, nearly 150 years after the landing, has been a historic shrine since. The landing anniversary is observed in much of New England as Forefathers' Day. See also: "Forefathers' Day" (Dec 21).

SPACE MILESTONE: *APOLLO 8* (US): 30th ANNIVERSARY. Dec 21, 1968. First moon voyage launched, manned by Colonel Frank Borman, Captain James A. Lovell, Jr, and Major William A. Anders. Orbited moon on Dec 24, returned to Earth on Dec 27. First men to see the side of the moon away from Earth.

STALIN, JOSEPH VISSARIONOVICH: BIRTH ANNIVERSARY. Dec 21, 1879. Russian dictator whose family name was Dzhugashvili, was born at Gori, Georgia, Dec 21, 1879. One of the most powerful and most feared men of the 20th century, Stalin died (of a stroke) at the Kremlin, in Moscow, Mar 5, 1953.

SZOLD, HENRIETTA: BIRTH ANNIVERSARY. Dec 21, 1860. Teacher, writer, scholar, social worker, organizer and pioneer Zionist, Henrietta Szold is best remembered as founder and first president of Hadassah, the Women's Zionist Organization of America. Born at Baltimore, MD, she was influenced by her father Rabbi Benjamin Szold, an active and vocal abolitionist. She established the first "Night School" in Baltimore, one of the first to focus on teaching English and job skills to immigrants. Her trip to Palestine in 1910 sparked the genesis of Hadassah. While there, Szold was alarmed by the lack of social, medical and educational services and returned with the idea that a national women's Zionist organization must be formed to carry out practical projects. As the "Mother of Social Service in Palestine," Szold viewed volunteerism as one of the greatest human endeavors. See also: "Hadassah: Anniversary" (Feb 24).

WINTER. Dec 21–Mar 20. In the Northern Hemisphere winter begins today with the winter solstice, at 8:56 PM, EST. Note that in the Southern Hemisphere today is the beginning of summer. Between Equator and Arctic Circle the sunrise and sunset points on the horizon are farthest south for the year, and daylight length is minimum (ranging from 12 hours, 8 minutes, at the equator to zero at the Arctic Circle).

YALDA. Dec 21. Yalda, the longest night of the year, is celebrated by Iranians. The ceremony has an Indo-Iranian origin, where Light and Good were considered to struggle against Darkness and Evil. With fires burning and lights lit, family and friends gather to stay up through the night helping the sun in its battle against darkness. They recite poetry, tell stories and eat special fruits and nuts until the sun, triumphant, reappears in the morning. For info: Yassaman Djalali, Librarian, West Valley Branch Library, 1243 San Tomas Aquino Rd, San Jose, CA 95117. Phone: (408) 244-4766.

YULE. Dec 21. (Also called Alban Arthan.) One of the "Lesser Sabbats" during the Wiccan year, Yule marks the death of the Sun-God and his rebirth from the Earth Goddess. Annually, on the winter solstice.

ZAPPA, FRANK: BIRTH ANNIVERSARY. Dec 21, 1940. Rock musician and composer, Zappa was noted for his satire and as a leading advocate against censorship of contemporary music. He formed the group Mothers of Invention. Born at Baltimore, MD, he died Dec 4, 1993, at Los Angeles, CA, at age 52.

BIRTHDAYS TODAY

Phil Donahue, 63, former TV talk show host ("Donahue"), born Cleveland, OH, Dec 21, 1935.

Christine Marie (Chris) Evert, 44, sportscaster, former tennis player, born Fort Lauderdale, FL, Dec 21, 1954.

Jane Fonda, 61, actress (Oscars for *Klute* and *Coming Home*; *Barbarella, The China Syndrome, Julia, On Golden Pond*), born New York, NY, Dec 21, 1937.

Samuel L. Jackson, 50, actor (*Pulp Fiction, Jurassic Park*), born Washington, DC, Dec 21, 1948.

Delorez Florence Griffith-Joyner, 39, Olympic gold medal track athlete, born Los Angeles, CA, Dec 21, 1959.

Joe Paterno, 72, Penn State football coach, born Brooklyn, NY, Dec 21, 1926.

Barbara Roberts, 62, former Governor of Oregon (D), born Corvallis, OR, Dec 21, 1936.

Michael Tilson Thomas, 54, conductor, pianist, organist, born Hollywood, CA, Dec 21, 1944.

Andrew James (Andy) Van Slyke, 38, former baseball player, born Utica, NY, Dec 21, 1960.

Kurt Waldheim, 80, former President of Austria, former UN Secretary-General, born Woerdern, Austria, Dec 21, 1918.

Paul Winchell, 76, ventriloquist, actor, born New York, NY, Dec 21, 1922.

DECEMBER 22 — TUESDAY

Day 356 9 Remaining

ASHCROFT, PEGGY: BIRTH ANNIVERSARY. Dec 22, 1907. British actress Dame Edith Margaret Emily Ashcroft was born at Croyden, England. In addition to her many accolades on the British stage she won an Oscar for her supporting role in *Passage to India* (1985) and a special British Olivier Award for lifetime achievement in 1991. She died on June 14, 1991, at London, England.

CAPRICORN, THE GOAT. Dec 22–Jan 19. In the astronomical and astrological zodiac that divides the sun's apparent orbit into 12 segments, the period Dec 22–Jan 19 is identified, traditionally, as the sun-sign of Capricorn, the Goat. The ruling planet is Saturn.

DeFORE, DON: 5th DEATH ANNIVERSARY. Dec 22, 1993. American actor Don DeFore was born at Cedar Rapids, IA. He is best known for his roles on "The Adventures of Ozzie and Harriet" (1952–58) and "Hazel" (1961–65). He was president of the National Academy of Television Arts and Sciences in 1954. He died at Santa Monica, CA.

"DING DONG SCHOOL" TV PREMIERE: ANNIVERSARY. Dec 22, 1952. Named by a three-year-old after watching a test broadcast of the opening sequence (a hand ringing a bell), "Ding Dong School" was one of the first children's educational series. Miss Frances (Dr. Frances Horwich, head of Roosevelt College's education department in Chicago) was the host of this weekday show.

ELLERY, WILLIAM: BIRTH ANNIVERSARY. Dec 22, 1727. Signer of the Declaration of Independence. Died Feb 15, 1820.

FIRST GORILLA BORN IN CAPTIVITY: BIRTH ANNIVERSARY. Dec 22, 1956. On this date, "Colo" was born at the Columbus, OH, zoo, weighing in at 3¼ pounds, the first gorilla born in captivity.

JOHNSON, CLAUDIA ALTA "LADY BIRD" TAYLOR: BIRTHDAY. Dec 22, 1912. Widow of Lyndon Baines Johnson, 36th president of the US, born at Karnack, TX, Dec 22, 1912.

OGLETHORPE, JAMES EDWARD: BIRTH ANNIVERSARY. Dec 22. English general, author and colonizer of Georgia. Founder of the city of Savannah. Oglethorpe was born at London on Dec 22, 1696. He died June 30, 1785.

PUCCINI, GIACOMO: BIRTH ANNIVERSARY. Dec 22, 1858. Italian composer, born Dec 22, 1858. Died Nov 29, 1924.

ROBINSON, EDWIN ARLINGTON: BIRTH ANNIVERSARY. Dec 22. Three-time Pulitzer Prize winner best known for his short dramatic poems, including "Richard Cory" and "Miniver Cheevy." Born Dec 22, 1869, at Head Tide, ME, and died at Los Angeles, CA, on Apr 6, 1935.

BIRTHDAYS TODAY

Barbara Billingsley, 76, actress (June Cleaver on "Leave It to Beaver," *Airplane*), born Los Angeles, CA, Dec 22, 1922.

Steven Norman (Steve) Carlton, 54, Baseball Hall of Fame pitcher, born Miami, FL, Dec 22, 1944.

Hector Elizondo, 62, actor (*The Taking of Pelham One Two Three, Pretty Woman, Frankie and Johnny*, "Chicago Hope"), born New York, NY, Dec 22, 1936.

Ralph Fiennes, 36, actor (*Schindler's List, Wuthering Heights*), born Suffolk, England, Dec 22, 1962.

Steve Garvey, 50, former baseball player, born Tampa, FL, Dec 22, 1948.

Claudia Alta "Lady Bird" Johnson, 86, former First Lady, born Karnack, TX, Dec 22, 1912.

Diane K. Sawyer, 52, journalist (former staff assistant to President Nixon; "60 Minutes," "Prime Time Live"), born Glasgow, KY, Dec 22, 1946.

Jan Stephenson, 47, golfer, born Sydney, Australia, Dec 22, 1951.

DECEMBER 23 — WEDNESDAY

Day 357 — 8 Remaining

FEDERAL RESERVE SYSTEM: 85th ANNIVERSARY. Dec 23, 1913. Established pursuant to authority contained in the Federal Reserve Act of Dec 23, 1913, the system serves as the nation's central bank, has responsibility for execution of monetary policy. It is called on to contribute to the strength and vitality of the US economy, in part by influencing the lending and investing activities of commercial banks and the cost and availability of money and credit.

FIRST NONSTOP FLIGHT AROUND THE WORLD WITHOUT REFUELING: ANNIVERSARY. Dec 23, 1987. In 1987 Dick Rutan and Jeana Yeager set a new world record of 216 hours of continuous flight, breaking their own record of 111 hours set on July 15, 1986. The aircraft *Voyager* departed from Edwards Air Force Base in California on Dec 14, 1987, and landed on Dec 23, 1987. The journey covered 24,986 miles at an official speed of 115 miles per hour.

JAPAN: BIRTHDAY OF THE EMPEROR. Dec 23. National Day. Holiday honoring the Emperor, currently Akihito, born Dec 23, 1933.

METRIC CONVERSION ACT: ANNIVERSARY. Dec 23. The Congress of the United States, on Dec 23, 1975, passed Public Law 94–168, known as the Metric Conversion Act of 1975. This act declares that the SI (International System of Units) will be this country's basic system of measurement and establishes the United States Metric Board which is responsible for the planning, coordination and implementation of the nation's voluntary conversion to SI. (Congress had authorized the metric system as a legal system of measurement in the US by an act passed on July 28, 1866. In 1875, the US became one of the original signers of the Treaty of the Metre, which established an international metric system.)

MEXICO: FEAST OF THE RADISHES. Dec 23. Oaxaca. Figurines of people and animals cleverly carved out of radishes are sold during festivities.

MONROE, HARRIET: BIRTH ANNIVERSARY. Dec 23. American poet, editor and founder of *Poetry* magazine. Born Dec 23, 1860, at Chicago, IL. Died on Sept 26, 1936, at Arequipa, Peru.

SMILES, SAMUEL: BIRTH ANNIVERSARY. Dec 23. Scottish writer, born Dec 23, 1812. Died at London, England, Apr 17, 1904. "A place for everything," he wrote in *Thrift*, "and everything in its place."

SMITH, JOSEPH: BIRTH ANNIVERSARY. Dec 23. Mormon prophet born at Sharon, VT, Dec 23, 1805. Killed by a mob while in Carthage, IL, jail, June 27, 1844.

TOJO HIDEKI EXECUTION: 50th ANNIVERSARY. Dec 23, 1948. Tojo Hideki, prime minister of Japan from Oct 16, 1941, until his resignation on July 19, 1944. After Japan's surrender in August 1945, Tojo was arrested as a war criminal, tried by a military tribunal and sentenced to death on Nov 12, 1948. Born at Tokyo on Dec 30, 1884, Tojo was hanged (with six other Japanese wartime military leaders) at Sugamo Prison in Tokyo on Dec 23, 1948, the sentence being carried out by the US 8th Army.

TRANSISTOR INVENTED: ANNIVERSARY. Dec 23, 1947. John Bardeen, Walter Brattain and William Shockley of Bell Laboratories shared the Nobel Prize for their invention of the transistor, which led to a revolution in communications and electronics.

December 1998

S	M	T	W	T	F	S
		1	2	3	4	5
6	7	8	9	10	11	12
13	14	15	16	17	18	19
20	21	22	23	24	25	26
27	28	29	30	31		

BIRTHDAYS TODAY

Akihito, 65, Emperor of Japan, born Tokyo, Japan, Dec 23, 1933.
Robert Bly, 72, author (*Iron John: A Book About Men; What Have I Ever Lost by Dying?*), born Madison, MN, Dec 23, 1926.
Jose Greco, 80, dancer, born Abruzzi, Italy, Dec 23, 1918.
James Gregory, 87, actor ("Barney Miller"; *The Manchurian Candidate*), born New York, NY, Dec 23, 1911.
Corey Haim, 26, actor (*Murphy's Romance, The Lost Boys*), born Toronto, Ontario, Canada, Dec 23, 1972.
James Joseph (Jim) Harbaugh, 35, football player, born Toledo, OH, Dec 23, 1963.
Susan Lucci, 49, actress (Erica Kane on "All My Children"; *Mafia Princess*), born Westchester, NY, Dec 23, 1949.
Gerald O'Loughlin, 77, actor ("The Rookies," "Our House"), born New York, NY, Dec 23, 1921.
Ruth Roman, 75, actress (*The Long Hot Summer*, "Knots Landing"), born Boston, MA, Dec 23, 1923.

DECEMBER 24 — THURSDAY

Day 358 — 7 Remaining

***AIDA* PREMIERE: ANNIVERSARY.** Dec 24, 1871. Guiseppe Verdi's opera *Aida* premiered in Cairo. It was commissioned by the Khedive of Egypt to celebrate the opening of the Suez Canal.

ARNOLD, MATTHEW: BIRTH ANNIVERSARY. Dec 24, 1822. English poet and essayist, born Dec 24, 1822. Died Apr 15, 1888. "One has often wondered," he wrote in *Culture and Anarchy*, "whether upon the whole earth there is anything so unintelligent, so unapt to perceive how the world is really going, as an ordinary young Englishman of our upper class."

AUSTRIA: "SILENT NIGHT, HOLY NIGHT" CELEBRATIONS. Dec 24. Oberndorf, Hallein and Wagrain, Salzburg, Austria. Commemorating the creation of the Christmas carol here in 1818.

CARSON, CHRISTOPHER "KIT": BIRTH ANNIVERSARY. Dec 24, 1809. American frontiersman, soldier, trapper, guide and Indian agent best known as Kit Carson. Born on Dec 24, 1809, in Madison County, KY, he died at Fort Lyon, CO, on May 23, 1868.

CHRISTMAS BELLS RING AGAIN IN ST. BASIL'S: ANNIVERSARY. Dec 24. For the first time since the death of Lenin, the bells of St. Basil's Cathedral, on Red Square in Moscow, rang to celebrate Christmas on Dec 24, 1990.

CHRISTMAS EVE. Dec 24. Family gift-giving occasion in many Christian countries.

FIRST SURFACE-TO-SURFACE GUIDED MISSILE: ANNIVERSARY. Dec 24, 1942. German rocket engineer Wernher von Braun launched the first surface-to-surface guided missile. Buzz bombs, a form of guided missile, were used by Germany against Great Britain starting Sept 8, 1944. On Feb 24, 1949, the first rocket to reach outer space (an altitude of 25 miles) was fired. The two-stage rocket, a Wac Corporal set in the nose of a German V-2, was launched from the White Sands Proving Grounds, NM, by a team of scientists headed by Dr. Wernher von Braun.

GARDNER, AVA: BIRTH ANNIVERSARY. Dec 24, 1922. Actress and leading sex symbol of the 1940s and '50s Ava Lavinnia Gardner was born at Smithfield, NC. Among Gardner's numerous movies are *The Barefoot Contessa, Bhowani Junction, The Sun Also Rises* and *The Life and Times of Judge Roy Bean*. Gardner was married to Mickey Rooney (1942–43), Artie Shaw (1945–46) and Frank Sinatra (1951–57).

HUGHES, HOWARD ROBARD: BIRTH ANNIVERSARY. Dec 24. Wealthy American recluse born Dec 24, 1905.

Died in airplane en route from Acapulco, Mexico, to Houston, TX, on Apr 5, 1976.

JOULE, JAMES PRESCOTT: BIRTH ANNIVERSARY. Dec 24, 1818. English physicist and inventor after whom Joule's Law was named, was born at Salford, Lancashire, England. Joule died at Cheshire on Oct 11, 1889.

LIBYA: INDEPENDENCE DAY. Dec 24, 1951. On this day, Libya gained its independence from Italy.

"THE PERRY COMO SHOW" TV PREMIERE: 50th ANNIVERSARY. Dec 24, 1948. Singer Perry Como hosted "The Chesterfield Supper Club" when it came to TV from radio. Also featured were the Mitchell Ayres Orchestra and the Fontane Sisters. When the show moved from NBC to CBS in 1950, announcer Frank Gallop was added. In 1955, Como moved back to NBC, and the show was retitled "The Perry Como Show" during 1955–59 and then "The Kraft Music Hall" during 1959–63. The Ray Charles Singers and the Louis DaPron Dancers were featured. Como's theme song was "Dream Along with Me."

RUSH, BENJAMIN: BIRTH ANNIVERSARY. Dec 24, 1745. Physician, patriot and humanitarian of the American Revolution, born on a plantation at Byberry, PA, Dec 24, 1745. While Rush was a signer of the Declaration of Independence, his writings on mental illness earned him the title "Father of Psychiatry." His tract *Inquiry* attacked the common wisdom of the time that alcohol was a positive good. He was the first American to call alcoholism a chronic disease. Benjamin Rush died at Philadelphia, PA, Apr 19, 1813.

BIRTHDAYS TODAY

Jill Bennett, 67, actress (*Lust for Life, The Nanny*), born Penang, Federated Malay States, Dec 24, 1931.

Mary Higgins Clark, 67, author (*Where Are the Children?, Silent Night*), born New York, NY, Dec 24, 1931.

A.P. Lutali, 79, Governor of American Samoa (D), born Aunu'u, American Samoa, Dec 24, 1919.

Jeff Sessions, 52, US Senator (R, Alabama), born Hybart, AL, Dec 24, 1946.

DECEMBER 25 — FRIDAY

Day 359 — 6 Remaining

A'PHABET DAY. Dec 25. Also known as "No-L" Day, this celebration is for people who do not want to send Christmas cards but who want to greet their friends; so they send out cards listing the letters of the alphabet in order, but with a gap where L would be. For info: Bob Birch, The Puns Corps, PO Box 2364, Falls Church, VA 22042-0364. Phone: (703) 533-3668.

BARTON, CLARA: BIRTH ANNIVERSARY. Dec 25. Clarissa Harlowe Barton, American nurse and philanthropist, founder of the American Red Cross, was born at Oxford, MA, Dec 25, 1821. In 1881, she became first president of the American Red Cross (founded May 21, 1881). She died at Glen Echo, MD, Apr 12, 1912.

BOGART, HUMPHREY: BIRTH ANNIVERSARY. Dec 25. American stage and screen actor, Humphrey DeForest Bogart was born at New York, NY, on Dec 25, 1899. Among his best remembered films are: *The African Queen*, *The Maltese Falcon*, *Casablanca* and *To Have and Have Not*. Bogart died Jan 14, 1957. A US postage stamp bearing his picture was issued in 1997.

BOOTH, EVANGELINE CORY: BIRTH ANNIVERSARY. Dec 25. Salvation Army general, active in England, Canada and the US. Author and composer of songs, Booth was born at London, England, on Dec 25, 1865. She died at Hartsdale, NY, on July 17, 1950.

CALLOWAY, CAB: BIRTH ANNIVERSARY. Dec 25, 1907. American singer and bandleader Cabell Calloway was born at Rochester, NY. George Gershwin modeled the part of Sportin' Life in *Porgy and Bess* (1953) after this jazz singer who also played the role across the US until 1956. He is best known for his song "Minnie the Moocher" (1931). He died on Nov 18, 1994, at Hosckessin, DE.

CEAUSESCU, NICOLAE: DEATH ANNIVERSARY. Dec 25. On Christmas evening, 1989, a broadcast of a Christmas symphony on state-run television was interrupted with the report that Romanian president Nicolae Ceausescu and his wife had been executed, bringing to an end the last hard-line regime in the Soviet bloc. In a brutally fast uprising, the Romanian people ousted the Ceausescu regime, and the National Salvation Front, an ad hoc pro-democracy coalition, took charge of the country. Ceausescu's downfall began when he ordered members of his black-shirted state police, the Securitate, to use force to quell a disturbance in the town of Timisorara. The brutal crackdown led to estimates of as many as 4,500 killed. Ceausescu's rule was marked by corruption, deprivation and terror.

CHRISTMAS. Dec 25. Christian festival commemorating the birth of Jesus of Nazareth. Most popular of Christian observances, Christmas as a Feast of the Nativity dates from the 4th century. Although Jesus's birth date is not known, the Western church selected Dec 25 for the feast, possibly to counteract the non-Christian festivals of that approximate date. Many customs from non-Christian festivals (Roman Saturnalia, Mithraic sun's birthday, Teutonic yule, Druidic and other winter solstice rites) have been adopted as part of the Christmas celebration (lights, mistletoe, holly and ivy, holiday tree, wassailing and gift giving, for example). Some Orthodox Churches celebrate Christmas on Jan 7 based on the "old calendar" (Julian). Theophany (recognition of the divinity of Jesus) is observed on this date and also on Jan 6, especially by the Eastern Orthodox Church.

CHRISTMAS FIRESIDE CHAT WARNING: 55th ANNIVERSARY. Dec 25. In his Dec 25, 1943, Christmas message to the American people, Franklin D. Roosevelt warned, "The war is now reaching the stage when we shall have to look forward to large casualty lists—dead, wounded and missing. War entails just that. There is no easy road to victory. And the end is not yet in sight."

FARLEY, CAL: BIRTH ANNIVERSARY. Dec 25, 1895. Cal Farley, known as "America's Greatest Foster Father," started Cal Farley's Boys Ranch in 1939 with nine boys. The Ranch has grown into a modern community of 441 boys (and girls since 1992), which has housed and educated more than 4,000 boys and girls over the years. In 1996 the US Postal System issued a stamp in Farley's name. Cal Farley was born at Saxton, IA; he died Feb 19, 1967, at Boys Ranch, TX.

JINNAH, MOHAMMED ALI: BIRTH ANNIVERSARY. Dec 25. The founder of the Islamic Republic of Pakistan, Mohammed Ali Jinnah, was born at Karachi, Dec 25, 1876. When Pakistan became an independent political entity (Aug 15, 1947), Jinnah became its first governor general. He died at Karachi, Sept 11, 1948.

KELLY TIRES BLUE-GRAY ALL STAR FOOTBALL CLASSIC. Dec 25. Cramton Bowl, Montgomery, AL. College seniors from northern schools compete against their southern counterparts. Sponsors: Montgomery Lion's Club and Kelly Tires.

Est attendance: 22,000. For info: Charles W. Jones, Exec Dir, Box 94, Montgomery, AL 36101-0094. Phone: (334) 265-1266. Fax: (334) 265-5944.

NEWTON, ISAAC: BIRTH ANNIVERSARY. Dec 25, 1642. Sir Isaac Newton, mathematician, scientist and author, was born at Woolsthorpe, Lincolnshire, England, on Dec 25, 1642. Best known of his works is the *Philosophiae Naturalis Principia Mathematica* (1687) in which he enunciated the famed three laws of motion. Newton died at London, England, on Mar 20, 1727, and was buried at Westminster Abbey.

"THE STEVE ALLEN SHOW" TV PREMIERE: ANNIVERSARY. Dec 25, 1950. Talented actor, comedian, singer and musician Steve Allen hosted a number of variety shows from 1950 to 1969 (with a few breaks in between to host specials and "The Tonight Show"). For two years, his television show was similar to his radio show and featured singer Peggy Lee, announcer Bern Bennett and Llemuel the llama. His next show competed with Ed Sullivan's show, though Allen's stressed comedy. Some of his "funny men" were Don Knotts, Tom Poston, Louis Nye, Gabe Dell, Pat Harrington, Jr, Dayton Allen, Cal Howard and Bill Dana. His other shows included a talk show, a game show, a comedy show, an educational music show and a flashback-comedy show.

STOCK EXCHANGE HOLIDAY (CHRISTMAS DAY). Dec 25. The holiday schedules for the various exchanges are subject to change if relevant rules, regulations or exchange policies are revised. If you have questions, phone: American Stock Exchange (212) 306-1000; Chicago Board of Options Exchange (312) 786-5600; Chicago Board of Trade (312) 435-3500; New York Stock Exchange (212) 656-2065; Pacific Stock Exchange (415) 393-4000; Philadelphia Stock Exchange (215) 496-5000.

UNITED KINGDOM: CHRISTMAS HOLIDAY. Dec 25. Bank and public holiday in England, Wales, Scotland and Northern Ireland.

WEST, REBECCA: BIRTH ANNIVERSARY. Dec 25, 1892. English author, literary critic, prize-winning journalist and noted feminist, Dame Rebecca West was born Cicely Isabel Fairfield at London, England, on Dec 25, 1892. She died there Mar 15, 1983.

☆ ☆ ☆

BIRTHDAYS TODAY

Jimmy Buffett, 52, singer ("Margaritaville"), songwriter, born Pascagoula, MS, Dec 25, 1946.

Lawrence Richard (Larry) Csonka, 52, Pro Football Hall of Fame running back, born Stow, OH, Dec 25, 1946.

Rickey Henley Henderson, 40, baseball player, born Chicago, IL, Dec 25, 1958.

Annie Lennox, 44, singer (with the Eurythmics, "Sweet Dreams Are Made of This"), born Aberdeen, Scotland, Dec 25, 1954.

Barbara Ann Mandrell, 50, singer ("I Was Country When Country Wasn't Cool"), born Houston, TX, Dec 25, 1948.

Little Richard (Penniman), 63, singer ("Tutti Frutti," "Long Tall Sally"), songwriter, born Macon, GA, Dec 25, 1935.

Gary Sandy, 53, actor ("All That Glitters"; Andy Travis on "WKRP in Cincinnati"), born Dayton, OH, Dec 25, 1945.

Hanna Schygulla, 55, actress (*The Marriage of Maria Braun, Berlin Alexanderplatz*), born Kattowitz, Germany, Dec 25, 1943.

Sissy Spacek (Mary Elizabeth), 49, actress (Oscar for *Coal Miner's Daughter; Missing, The River*), born Quitman, TX, Dec 25, 1949.

December 1998

S	M	T	W	T	F	S
		1	2	3	4	5
6	7	8	9	10	11	12
13	14	15	16	17	18	19
20	21	22	23	24	25	26
27	28	29	30	31		

DECEMBER 26 — SATURDAY

Day 360 — 5 Remaining

BABBAGE, CHARLES: BIRTH ANNIVERSARY. Dec 26, 1792. English mathematician, born at Teignmouth, England. He developed the principles on which modern computers are designed. Babbage died at London, England, Oct 18, 1871.

BAHAMAS: JUNKANOO. Dec 26. Kaleidoscope of sound and spectacle combining a bit of Mardi Gras, mummer's parade and ancient African tribal rituals. Revelers in colorful costumes parade through the streets to sounds of cowbells, goat skin drums and many other homemade instruments. Always on Boxing Day.

BOXING DAY. Dec 26. Ordinarily observed on the first day after Christmas. Now a legal holiday in Canada, the United Kingdom and many other countries. Formerly (according to Robert Chambers) a day when Christmas gift boxes were "regularly expected by a postman, the lamplighter, the dustman, and generally by all those functionaries who render services to the public at large, without receiving payment therefore from any individual." When Boxing Day falls on a Saturday or Sunday, the Monday or Tuesday immediately following may be proclaimed or observed as a bank or public holiday.

BOXING DAY ANNUAL CELEBRATION. Dec 26. North Star Pub, New York, NY. Annual observation of Boxing Day at an authentic British pub featuring free Bangers and Mash (sausages and mashed potatoes), Christmas crackers, games and prizes. Collection of food and clothing for homeless people. Est attendance: 500. For info: Deven Black, Genl Mgr, North Star Pub, 93 South St, New York, NY 10038. Phone: (212) 509-6757. WWW: http://goodeating.com/northstar

CLERC, LAURENT: BIRTH ANNIVERSARY. Dec 26, 1785. The first deaf teacher in America, Laurent Clerc assisted Thomas Hopkins Gallaudet in establishing the first public school for the deaf, Connecticut Asylum for the Education and Instruction of Deaf and Dumb Persons (now the American School for the Deaf), at Hartford, CT, in 1817. For 41 years Clerc trained new teachers in the use of sign language and in methods of teaching the deaf. Clerc was born at LaBalme, France, and died July 18, 1869.

IRELAND: DAY OF THE WREN. Dec 26. Dingle Peninsula. Masked revelers and musicians go from door to door asking for money. Traditional day and night of public merrymaking.

KWANZAA. Dec 26–Jan 1, 1999. American black family observance (since 1966) in recognition of traditional African harvest festivals. Stresses unity of the black family, with communitywide harvest feast (karamu) on seventh day. Kwanzaa means "first fruit" in Swahili. An optional observance to avoid commercialization of Christmas traditions.

LOVERA, JUAN: BIRTH ANNIVERSARY. Dec 26, 1778. Venezuelan "Artist of Independence," whose best-known canvases commemorate the independence dates of Apr 19, 1810, and July 5, 1811, and who is known as the founder of historical painting in Venezuela, was born Dec 26, 1778. Died in 1841 (exact date unknown).

LUXEMBOURG: BLESSING OF THE WINE. Dec 26. Greiveldange, Luxembourg. Winemakers parade to the church, where a barrel of wine is blessed.

MAO TSE-TUNG: BIRTH ANNIVERSARY. Dec 26, 1893. Chinese librarian, teacher, communist revolutionist and "founding father" of the People's Republic of China, born in Hunan Province, China, on Dec 26, 1893. Died at Peking, Sept 9, 1976.

MILLER, HENRY (VALENTINE): BIRTH ANNIVERSARY. Dec 26. Controversial American novelist born at New York, NY, on Dec 26, 1891. Died at Pacific Palisades, CA, on June 7, 1980.

MOON PHASE: FIRST QUARTER. Dec 26. Moon enters First Quarter phase at 5:46 AM, EST.

NATIONAL WHINER'S DAY™. Dec 26. A day dedicated to whiners, especially those who return Christmas gifts and need lots of attention on this day. The most famous whiner(s) of the year will be announced. Nominations accepted through Dec 20. For more info, please send SASE to: Rev. Kevin C. Zaborney, 1900 Campau Dr, Midland, MI 48640. Phone: (517) 631-5740. Email: kzaborney@aol.com.

NELSON, THOMAS: BIRTH ANNIVERSARY. Dec 26, 1738. Merchant and signer of the Declaration of Independence, born at Yorktown, VA, Dec 26, 1738. Died at Hanover County, VA, Jan 4, 1789.

RADIUM DISCOVERED: 100th ANNIVERSARY. Dec 26, 1898. French scientists Pierre and Marie Curie discovered the element radium, for which they later won the Nobel Prize for Physics.

SAINT STEPHEN'S DAY. Dec 26. One of the seven deacons named by the apostles to distribute alms died during 1st century. Feast Day is Dec 26 and is observed as a public holiday in Austria.

SECOND DAY OF CHRISTMAS. Dec 26. Observed as holiday in many countries.

WKA DAYTONA CLASSIC DIRT KARTING RACES. Dec 26–30. Daytona Beach Municipal Stadium, Daytona Beach, FL. For info: Daytona Intl Speedway, John Story, PR, Box 2801, Daytona Beach, FL 32120-2801. Phone: (904) 254-6782 or for tickets (904) 253-RACE (7223). Fax: (904) 947-6791. WWW: http://www.daytonausa.com

WORLD ENDURO CHAMPIONSHIP KART RACES. Dec 26–30. Daytona International Speedway, Daytona Beach, FL. For info: Daytona Intl Speedway, John Story, PR, Box 2801, Daytona Beach, FL 32120-2801. Phone: (904) 253-6782 or for tickets (904) 253-RACE (7223). Fax: (904) 947-6791. WWW: http://www.daytonausa.com

BIRTHDAYS TODAY

Steve Allen, 77, entertainer, TV pioneer (the first "Tonight" show), composer, author, born New York, NY, Dec 26, 1921.

Susan Butcher, 44, sled dog racer, born Cambridge, MA, Dec 26, 1954.

Carlton Ernest Fisk, 51, former baseball player, born Bellows Falls, VT, Dec 26, 1947.

Alan King (Irwin Kniberg), 71, comedian, author ("Seventh Avenue," *Help! I'm a Prisoner in a Chinese Bakery*), born New York, NY, Dec 26, 1927.

Lynn Martin, 59, former US Secretary of Labor in Bush administration, born Evanston, IL, Dec 26, 1939.

Osborne Earl (Ozzie) Smith, 44, former baseball player, born Mobile, AL, Dec 26, 1954.

Phil Spector, 58, music producer, born New York, NY, Dec 26, 1940.

Richard Widmark, 84, actor (*Kiss of Death, Madigan*), born Sunrise, MN, Dec 26, 1914.

☆ ☆ ☆

DECEMBER 27 — SUNDAY

Day 361 — 4 Remaining

CAYLEY, GEORGE: 225th BIRTH ANNIVERSARY. Dec 27, 1773. Aviation pioneer Sir George Cayley, English scientist and inventor, was a theoretician who designed airplanes, helicopters and gliders. He is credited as the father of aerodynamics and he was the pilot of the world's first manned glider flight. Born at Scarborough, Yorkshire, England, Dec 27, 1773. Died at Brompton Hall, Yorkshire, Dec 15, 1857.

DIETRICH, MARLENE: BIRTH ANNIVERSARY. Dec 27, 1901. Marlene Dietrich was born at Berlin, Germany. A wrist injury destroyed her dream of becoming a concert violinist, and she enrolled in Max Reinhardt's drama school. Her first big break on the way to becoming a screen legend was in 1930 when Josef Von Sternberg cast her in *The Blue Angel*, the first talkie made in Germany. A year later, she and Sternberg moved to Hollywood and began a string of six films together with *Morocco*, the only film for which she received an Academy Award nomination. Some of her other films were *Destry Rides Again, Kismet, Around the World in 80 Days, Touch of Evil, Judgment at Nuremberg* and *Witness for the Prosecution*. During the 1950s she was a cabaret singer in a stage revue that toured the globe. Dietrich died May 6, 1992.

"HOWDY DOODY" TV PREMIERE: ANNIVERSARY. Dec 27, 1947. The first popular children's show was brought to TV by Bob Smith and was one of the first regular NBC shows to be shown in color. The original Howdy Doody puppet was created by Frank Paris, who left the show after a few weeks because of contract problems. A new Howdy was created and explained as having undergone "plastic" surgery. The show was set in the circus town of Doodyville, populated by people and puppets. Children sat in the bleachers' "Peanut Gallery" and watched and participated in activities such as songs, stories and films. Human characters were Buffalo Bob (Bob Smith), the assistant and silent clown Clarabell (Bob Keeshan, Bobby Nicholson and Lew Anderson), storekeeper Cornelius Cobb (Nicholson), Chief Thunderthud (Bill LeCornec), Princess Summerfall Winterspring (Judy Tyler and Linda Marsh), Bison Bill (Ted Brown) and wrestler Ugly Sam (Dayton Allen). Puppet costars included Howdy Doody, Phineas T. Bluster, Dilly Dally, Flub-a-Dub, Captain Scuttlebutt, Double Doody and Heidi Doody. The filmed adventures of Gumby were also featured. In the final episode, Clarabell broke his long silence to say, "Goodbye, kids."

KEPLER, JOHANNES: BIRTH ANNIVERSARY. Dec 27, 1571. One of the world's greatest astronomers, called "the father of modern astronomy," German mathematician Johannes Kepler was born at Wurttemberg, Germany; he died at Regensburg, Germany, Nov 15, 1630.

PASTEUR, LOUIS: BIRTH ANNIVERSARY. Dec 27. French chemist-bacteriologist born at Dole, Jura, France, Dec 27, 1822. Died at Villeneuve l'Etang, France, Sept 28, 1895. Discoverer of prophylactic inoculation against rabies. Pasteurization process named for him.

RADIO CITY MUSIC HALL: ANNIVERSARY. Dec 27. Radio City Music Hall, in New York City, opened Dec 27, 1932.

SAINT JOHN, APOSTLE-EVANGELIST: FEAST DAY. Dec 27. Son of Zebedee, Galilean fisherman, and Salome. Died about AD 100. Roman Rite Feast Day is Dec 27. (Observed on May 8 by Byzantine Rite.)

SALK, LEE: BIRTH ANNIVERSARY. Dec 27, 1926. American child psychologist Lee Salk was born at New York, NY. He became well known for proving the calming effect of a mother's heartbeat on a newborn infant. Salk's warning during the 1970s that women should not abandon full-time child rearing was met with wide opposition, especially from working mothers. He died on May 2, 1992, at New York, NY.

SOUNDS OF THE SEASON: A HOLIDAY CONCERT. Dec 27–29. Ash Lawn–Highland, Charlottesville, VA. Madrigal singers, yule log and cider. Annually, Dec 27–29. Est attendance: 150. For info: Ash Lawn–Highland, James Monroe Parkway, Charlottesville, VA 22902. Phone: (804) 293-9539. Fax: (804) 293-8000. Email: ashlawn@comet.net.
WWW: http://avenue.org/ashlawn

BIRTHDAYS TODAY

Gerard Depardieu, 50, actor (*The Return of Martin Guerre, Jean De Florette, Cyrano de Bergerac*), born Chateauroux, France, Dec 27, 1948.

Tovah Feldshuh, 46, actress (*Holocaust*), born New York, NY, Dec 27, 1952.

Bernard Lanvin, 63, fashion designer, born Neuilly, France, Dec 27, 1935.

William Howell Masters, 83, physician, born Cleveland, OH, Dec 27, 1915.

Anna Russell, 87, comedienne, born London, England, Dec 27, 1911.

Ernesto Zedillo Ponce de Leon, 47, president of Mexico, born Mexico City, Mexico, Dec 27, 1951.

DECEMBER 28 — MONDAY

Day 362 — 3 Remaining

AUSTRALIA: PROCLAMATION DAY. Dec 28. Observed in South Australia.

HOLIDAY BOWL PARADE AND GAME. Dec 28 (tentative; confirm after Apr 1). Along Harbor Drive, San Diego, CA. The morning of the Plymouth Holiday Bowl football game (teams picked from Pac 10, Big 12 and Western Athletic conferences). This televised parade features floats, marching bands, giant balloons and unique specialty units. Parade at 10 AM, game in evening. Est attendance: 100,000. For info: Mark Neville, Holiday Bowl, PO Box 601400, San Diego, CA 92160-1400. Phone: (619) 283-5808. Fax: (619) 281-7947.
WWW: http://holidaybowl.com

HOLY INNOCENTS DAY (CHILDERMAS). Dec 28. Commemoration of the massacre of children in Bethlehem, ordered by King Herod who wanted to destroy, among them, the infant Savior. Early and medieval accounts claimed as many as 144,000 victims, but more recent writers, noting that Bethlehem was a very small town, have revised the estimates of the number of children killed to between 6 and 20.

December 1998

S	M	T	W	T	F	S
		1	2	3	4	5
6	7	8	9	10	11	12
13	14	15	16	17	18	19
20	21	22	23	24	25	26
27	28	29	30	31		

IOWA: ADMISSION DAY. Dec 28. Became 29th state on this day in 1846.

MESSINA EARTHQUAKE: 90th ANNIVERSARY. Dec 28, 1908. Messina, Sicily. The ancient town of Messina was struck by an earthquake on Dec 28, 1908. Nearly 80,000 persons died in the disaster, and half of the town's buildings were destroyed.

MOLSON, JOHN: BIRTH ANNIVERSARY. Dec 28, 1763. John Molson, an orphan, left his home at Lincolnshire, England, to settle in Montreal in 1782. He soon acquired a brewery and became patriarch of the Molson brewery family. Born at Lincolnshire, Dec 28, 1763. Died at Montreal, Que, Canada, Jan 11, 1836.

MOST DUBIOUS NEWS STORIES OF THE YEAR. Dec 28. An annual review of news stories based on bogus scientific and other claims, reported during the year by the nation's media. The Center monitors the media for "scare campaigns." For info: Alan Caruba, Founder, Natl Anxiety Center, Box 40, Maplewood, NJ 07040. Phone: (973) 763-6392. Fax: (973) 763-4287.

NEPAL: BIRTHDAY OF HIS MAJESTY THE KING. Dec 28. National holiday of Nepal. Three-day celebration with huge public rally at Tundikkel, gay pageantry, musical bands and illumination in the towns at night.

***POOR RICHARD'S ALMANACK:* ANNIVERSARY.** Dec 28. The *Pennsylvania Gazette* on Dec 28, 1732, carried the first known advertisement for the first issue of *Poor Richard's Almanack* by Richard Saunders (Benjamin Franklin) for the year 1733. The advertisement promised "many pleasant and witty verses, jests and sayings . . . new fashions, games for kisses . . . men and melons . . . breakfast in bed, &c." America's most famous almanac, *Poor Richard's* was published through the year 1758 and has been imitated many times since. From *The Autobiography of Benjamin Franklin*: "In 1732 I first publish'd my Almanack, under the name of *Richard Saunders*; it was continu'd by me about twenty-five years, commonly call'd *Poor Richard's Almanack*. I endeavor'd to make it both entertaining and useful, and it accordingly came to be in such demand, that I reap'd considerable profit from it, vending annually near ten thousand. And observing that it was generally read, scarce any neighborhood in the province being without it, I consider'd it as a proper vehicle for conveying instruction among the common people, who bought scarcely any other books; I therefore filled all the little spaces that occurr'd between the remarkable days in the calendar with proverbial sentences, chiefly such as inculcated industry and frugality, as the means of procuring wealth, and thereby securing virtue; it being more difficult for a man in want, to act always honestly, as, to use here one of those proverbs, *it is hard for an empty sack to stand upright.*"

UNITED KINGDOM: BOXING DAY BANK HOLIDAY. Dec 28. Bank and public holiday in England, Wales, Scotland and Northern Ireland.

VICE PRESIDENTIAL RESIGNATION: ANNIVERSARY. Dec 28, 1832. John C. Calhoun, who had served as vice president of the US under two presidents (John Quincy Adams and Andrew Jackson), Mar 4, 1825–Dec 28, 1832, finding himself in growing disagreement with President Jackson, resigned the office of vice president, the first to do so. He spent most of his subsequent political life as a US senator from South Carolina.

VICTOR EMMANUEL III: DEATH ANNIVERSARY. Dec 28, 1947. Last king of Italy Victor Emmanuel III died in exile at Alexandria, Egypt. He was born at Naples, Italy, Nov 11, 1869, and became king upon the assassination of his father in July of 1900. For the first 20 years of his reign, Victor Emmanuel followed Italy's constitutional custom of selecting a prime minister based on the parliamentary majority, but with parliament in disarray after World War I, he named Benito Mussolini to form a cabinet and then failed to prevent Mussolini and the Fascists from seizing power. The king then became little more than a figurehead. In 1946 Victor Emmanuel abdicated the throne, and both Victor Emmanuel and the Crown Prince went into exile.

WILSON, WOODROW: BIRTH ANNIVERSARY. Dec 28, 1856. The 28th president of the US was born Thomas Woodrow Wilson at Staunton, VA. Twice elected president (1912 and 1916), it was Wilson who said "The world must be made safe for democracy," as he asked the Congress to declare war on Germany, Apr 2, 1917. His first wife, Ellen, died Aug 6, 1914, and he married Edith Bolling Galt on Dec 18, 1915. He suffered a paralytic stroke Sept 16, 1919, never regaining his health. There were many dark speculations about who (possibly Mrs Wilson?) was running the government during his illness. His second term of office ended Mar 3, 1921, and he died at Washington, DC, Feb 3, 1924.

BIRTHDAYS TODAY

Hubert Myatt (Hubie) Green III, 52, golfer, born Birmingham, AL, Dec 28, 1946.

Lou Jacobi, 85, actor (*Irma La Douce*), born Toronto, Ontario, Canada, Dec 28, 1913.

Tim Johnson, 52, US Senator (D, South Dakota), born Canton, SD, Dec 28, 1946.

David Peterson, 55, Canadian political leader, born Toronto, Ontario, Canada, Dec 28, 1943.

Maggie Smith, 64, actress (*The Prime of Miss Jean Brodie*; Tony for *Lettice & Lovage*), born Ilford, England, Dec 28, 1934.

Denzel Washington, 44, actor ("St. Elsewhere," *Glory, Malcolm X*), born Mt Vernon, NY, Dec 28, 1954.

Edgar Winter, 52, singer, musician (*Edgar Winter's White Trash, They Only Come Out at Night*), born Beaumont, TX, Dec 28, 1946.

DECEMBER 29 — TUESDAY

Day 363 — 2 Remaining

ALL-COLLEGE BASKETBALL TOURNAMENT. Dec 29–30. Myriad Convention Center, Oklahoma City, OK. The oldest college basketball tournament in the world, outdating the NCAA, NAIA and the NIT. Host school is Oklahoma University. Rest of field to be announced; 156 universities have competed. Annually, between Christmas and New Year's. Est attendance: 25,000. For info: Stanley Draper, Jr, OK City All Sports Assn, 100 W Main, Ste 285, Oklahoma City, OK 73102. Phone: (405) 236-5000. Fax: (405) 236-5008.

ASARAH B'TEVET. Dec 29. Hebrew calendar date: Tevet 10, 5759. (Also Jan 8, Hebrew calendar date: Tevet 10, 5758.) The Fast of the 10th of Tevet begins at first morning light and commemorates the beginning of the Babylonian siege of Jerusalem in the 6th century BC.

CASALS, PABLO: BIRTH ANNIVERSARY. Dec 29, 1876. Famed cellist Pablo Carlos Salvador Defillio de Casals was born at Venrell, Spain, and died at Rio Pedros, Puerto Rico, Oct 22, 1973.

ESP DAYS. Dec 29–31. There isn't much to do at the end of the year. Many businesses slow down and people take vacation. Folks are still in a festive mood from Hanukkah, Christmas and Kwanzaa. So (E)at, (S)leep and (P)arty! For info: Adrienne Sioux Koopersmith, 1437 W Rosemont, #1W, Chicago, IL 60660-1319. Phone: (773) 743-5341. Fax: (773) 743-5395. Email: kooper@interaccess.com.

GLADSTONE, WILLIAM EWART: BIRTH ANNIVERSARY. Dec 29, 1809. English statesman and author for whom the Gladstone (luggage) bag was named. Inspiring orator, eccentric individual, intensely loved or hated by all who knew him (cheered from the streets and jeered from the balconies), Gladstone is said to have left more writings (letters, diaries, journals, books) than any other major English politician. However, his preoccupation with the charitable rehabilitation of prostitutes was perhaps easily misunderstood. Born at Liverpool, England, on Dec 29, 1809, he was four times Britain's prime minister. Gladstone died at Hawarden, Wales, on May 19, 1898.

JOHNSON, ANDREW: BIRTH ANNIVERSARY. Dec 29, 1808. Seventeenth president of the US, Andrew Johnson, proprietor of a tailor shop in Laurens, SC, before he entered politics, was born Dec 29, 1808, at Raleigh, NC. Upon Abraham Lincoln's assassination Johnson became president. He was the only US president to be impeached, and he was acquitted Mar 26, 1868. After his term of office as president (Apr 15, 1865–Mar 3, 1869) he made several unsuccessful attempts to win public office. Finally he was elected to the US Senate from Tennessee and served in the Senate from Mar 4, 1875, until his death, at Carter's Station, TN, on July 31, 1875.

RASPUTIN, GRIGORI EFIMOVICH: ASSASSINATION ANNIVERSARY. Dec 29, 1916. Russian monk and mystic, born Grigori Efimovich Novjkh, about 1871, in Siberia. Rasputin gained great influence with Russian emperor Nicholas II and the empress Alexandra, urging severe measures in dealing with the peasant masses, virtually dictating government policy. Notoriously dissolute and corrupt, Rasputin was said to have possessed hypnotic powers. He claimed divine inspiration and the ability to perform miracles. His name became synonymous with corruption and evil, and he was called the "plague pot" of Russia. In fact, Rasputin was a nickname from the Russian word *rasputny*, meaning debauched, profligate, licentious. When an attempt to poison him failed, he was shot to death and his body dropped through a hole in the ice into the Neva River. It was recovered three days later and buried in a silver casket at Tsarkoe Selo. The imperial government was crushed by the 1917 Revolution within a year of his death.

SAINT THOMAS OF CANTERBURY: FEAST DAY. Dec 29. Thomas, Archbishop of Canterbury, was born at London in 1118 and was murdered at the Canterbury Cathedral on this date in 1170.

TEXAS: ADMISSION DAY: ANNIVERSARY. Dec 29. Became 28th state on this day in 1845.

WOUNDED KNEE MASSACRE: ANNIVERSARY. Dec 29. Anniversary of the massacre of more than 200 Native American men, women and children by the US 7th Cavalry on Dec 29, 1890, at Wounded Knee Creek, SD. Government efforts to suppress a ceremonial religious practice, the Ghost Dance (which called for a messiah who would restore the bison to the plains, make the white men disappear and bring back the old Native American way of life), had resulted in the death of Sitting Bull on Dec 15, 1890, which further inflamed the disgruntled Native Americans and culminated in the slaughter at Wounded Knee on Dec 29.

"YOU ASKED FOR IT" TV PREMIERE: ANNIVERSARY. Dec 29, 1950. Skippy Peanut Butter sponsored this half-hour human-interest show which was hosted by Art Baker until 1958 and then Jack Smith. The show answered viewers' letters requesting various types of unusual acts, heroic people and talented animals. The format of the network versions involved reading the viewer's letter prior to the feature, with the viewer's picture superimposed onto a jar of Skippy Peanut Butter.

"YOUNG DR. MALONE" TV PREMIERE: 40th ANNIVERSARY. Dec 29, 1958. This daytime serial was first a radio show (1939–60). It was set in the town of Three Oaks at Valley Hospital. Six characters from a serial it replaced, "Today Is Ours," joined the cast. Cast members included: William Prince, Virginia Dwyer, Augusta Dabney, John Connell, Kathleen Widdoes, Freda Holloway, Sarah Hardy, Emily McLaughlin, Peter Brandon, Lesley Woods, Martin Blaine, Zina Bethune, Michele Tuttle, Susan Hallaran, Patty McCormack and Diana Hyland.

☆ ☆ ☆

BIRTHDAYS TODAY

Tom Bradley, 81, former mayor of Los Angeles, born Calvert, TX, Dec 29, 1917.

Ted Danson, 51, actor (Sam on "Cheers"; *Three Men and a Baby*), born San Diego, CA, Dec 29, 1947.

Marianne Faithfull, 52, singer ("As Tears Go By," "Summer Nights"), actress, born London, England, Dec 29, 1946.

Thomas Edwin Jarriel, 64, broadcast journalist, born LaGrange, GA, Dec 29, 1934.

Dina Merrill, 70, actress (*Desk Set, Operation Petticoat*), born New York, NY, Dec 29, 1928.

Mary Tyler Moore, 62, actress (two Emmys for "The Dick Van Dyke Show"; three Emmys for "The Mary Tyler Moore Show"; *Ordinary People, Thoroughly Modern Millie*), born Brooklyn, NY, Dec 29, 1936.

Jon Voight, 60, actor (*Midnight Cowboy, Deliverance*), born Yonkers, NY, Dec 29, 1938.

DECEMBER 30 — WEDNESDAY

Day 364 — 1 Remaining

"CRAZY LIKE A FOX" TV PREMIERE: ANNIVERSARY. Dec 30, 1984. Jack Warden starred as private eye Harry Fox and John Rubinstein as his son and reluctant partner in crime solving, attorney Harrison Fox, in this comedy detective series. Also featured were Penny Peyser as Harrison's wife, Cindy; Robby Kiger as their son, Josh; Lydia Lei and Patricia Ayame Thomson as Harrison's secretary; and Robert Hanley as Lieutenant Walker of the San Francisco Police Department.

GUGGENHEIM, SIMON: BIRTH ANNIVERSARY. Dec 30. American capitalist and philanthropist, born at Philadelphia, PA, Dec 30, 1867. He established, in memory of his son, the John Simon Guggenheim Memorial Foundation, in 1925. Died on Nov 2, 1941.

KIPLING, RUDYARD: BIRTH ANNIVERSARY. Dec 30, 1865. English poet, novelist and short story writer, Nobel prize laureate, Kipling was born at Bombay, India. After working as a journalist in India, he traveled around the world. He married an American and lived in Vermont for several years. Kipling is best known for his children's stories, such as the *Jungle Book* and *Just So Stories* and poems such as "The Ballad of East and West" and "If." He died at London, England, on Jan 18, 1936.

LEACOCK, STEPHEN: BIRTH ANNIVERSARY. Dec 30. Canadian economist and humorist, born Dec 30, 1869. Died Mar 28, 1944. "Lord Ronald . . . ," he wrote in *Nonsense Novels*, "flung himself upon his horse and rode madly off in all directions."

"LET'S MAKE A DEAL" TV PREMIERE: 35th ANNIVERSARY. Dec 30, 1963. Monty Hall hosted this outrageous and no-skill-required game show. Audience members, many of whom wore costumes, were selected to sit in the trading area, and some were picked to "make a deal" with Hall by trading something of their own for something they were offered. Sometimes prizes were worthless ("zonks"). At the end of the show, the two people who had won the most were given the option to trade their winnings for a chance at the "Big Deal," hidden behind one of three doors. Jay Stewart was the announcer and Carol Merrill the assistant. The most recent revival (1990–91) was hosted by Bob Hilton.

MADAGASCAR: NATIONAL HOLIDAY. Dec 30. Anniversary of the Democratic Republic of Madagascar.

***MONITOR* SINKS: ANNIVERSARY.** Dec 30. The Union ironclad ship USS *Monitor* (which achieved fame after the Battle of the *Monitor* and the *Merrimac*) sank on Dec 30, 1862, off Cape Hatteras during a storm. Sixteen of her crew were lost.

PARKS, BERT: BIRTH ANNIVERSARY. Dec 30. Bert Parks was born at Atlanta, GA, on Dec 30, 1914. An actor whose career spanned radio, film, television and Broadway, his name became synonymous with the Miss America pageant which he emceed for 25 years. He was fired from the Miss America post in 1980 when pageant officials wanted to acquire a younger look. Parks made a special return appearance for the 1990 pageant, once again singing his signature song "There She Is." He got his big break in show business in 1945 as the emcee for the radio quiz show "Break the Bank" and later as the host of "Stop the Music." When both shows moved to television they did so with Parks at the microphone, launching a television career that included hosting a variety of quiz shows and guest appearances on dramatic series. He died on Feb 2, 1992, at La Jolla, CA.

PHILIPPINES: RIZAL DAY: ANNIVERSARY. Dec 30. Commemorates martyrdom of Dr. Jose Rizal on this day in 1896.

"THE ROY ROGERS SHOW" TV PREMIERE: ANNIVERSARY. Dec 30, 1951. This very popular TV western starred Roy Rogers and his wife, Dale Evans, as themselves. It also featured Pat Brady as Rogers's sidekick who rode a jeep named Nellybelle; the singing group Sons of the Pioneers; Rogers's horse Trigger; Evans's horse Buttermilk; and a German shepherd named Bullet. This half-hour show was especially popular with young viewers.

TOJO HIDEKI: BIRTH ANNIVERSARY. Dec 30, 1884. Japanese prime minister during World War II. Born on Dec 30, 1884, at Tokyo. Arrested in August 1945 as a war criminal and hanged on Dec 23, 1948. See also: "Tojo Hideki: Execution Anniversary" (Dec 23).

VAN FLEET, JO: BIRTH ANNIVERSARY. Dec 30, 1922. Actress (Oscar for *East of Eden*; "Cinderella"), born at Oakland, CA. Died June 10, 1996.

BIRTHDAYS TODAY

Joseph Bologna, 60, actor, writer (*The Big Bus, My Favorite Year, Blame It on Rio*), born Brooklyn, NY, Dec 30, 1938.

Bo Diddley, 70, singer, songwriter ("Who Do You Love," "Say Man," "I'm a Man"), musician, born McCombs, MS, Dec 30, 1928.

Davy Jones, 52, actor, singer (with the Monkees; "Daydream Believer"), born Manchester, England, Dec 30, 1946.

Sanford (Sandy) Koufax, 63, former sportscaster, Baseball Hall of Fame pitcher, born Brooklyn, NY, Dec 30, 1935.

Matt Lauer, 41, news anchor on "Today," born New York, NY, Dec 30, 1957.

Jack Lord, 68, actor ("Hawaii Five-O," *God's Little Acre*), born New York, NY, Dec 30, 1930.

Michael Nesmith, 56, singer, songwriter, director (member of the Monkees), born Houston, TX, Dec 30, 1942.

Russ Tamblyn, 63, actor ("Twin Peaks," *Peyton Place, West Side Story*), born Los Angeles, CA, Dec 30, 1935.

Tracey Ullman, 39, actress, singer ("The Tracey Ullman Show," *I Love You to Death*), born Buckinghamshire, England, Dec 30, 1959.

Tiger (Eldrick) Woods, 23, golfer, winner of the 1997 Masters tournament, born Long Beach, CA, Dec 30, 1975.

December 1998

S	M	T	W	T	F	S
		1	2	3	4	5
6	7	8	9	10	11	12
13	14	15	16	17	18	19
20	21	22	23	24	25	26
27	28	29	30	31		

DECEMBER 31 — THURSDAY

Day 365 — 0 Remaining

AT&T NEW YEAR'S AT THE NEEDLE. Dec 31. Space Needle, Seattle, WA. A spectacular New Year's Eve tradition on the West Coast. More than 50,000 people enjoy the festivities of a massive outdoor gala and midnight fireworks at the Space Needle. For info: Space Needle, 219 Fourth Ave N, Seattle, WA 98109. Phone: (800) 937-9582.
WWW: http://www.spaceneedle.com

CANADA: FIRST NIGHTS. Dec 31. These Canadian cities have First Night celebrations: Banff, Camrose, Edmonton, and Red Deer, Alberta; Gabriola, Kamloops, New Westminister, Qualicum Beach, Victoria and Whistler, British Columbia; St. John, New Brunswick; and Chatham, Hamilton, Peterborough and Toronto, Ontario.

FIRST BANK OPENS IN US: ANNIVERSARY. Dec 31, 1781. The first modern bank in the US, the Bank of North America, was organized by Robert Morris and received its charter from the Confederation Congress, Dec 31, 1781. It began operations Jan 7, 1782, at Philadelphia.

FIRST NIGHT ALBANY. Dec 31. Downtown Albany, NY. A New Year's Eve celebration of the arts in multiple locations downtown with music, dancing, children's events, fireworks, food and beverages. Annually, on New Year's Eve. For info: Laurie Tenerowicz, 52 S Pearl St, Albany, NY 12207. Phone: (518) 434-5132.
WWW: http://www.albany.org

FIRST NIGHT AUGUSTA. Dec 31. Staunton, VA. An alcohol/drug-free community celebration of performing and visual arts for the whole family with more than 30 performances and/or exhibits at more than 15 sites in the Downtown District. Kicked off with a Grand Processional. Special activities for children. Performances followed by a Grand Finale at midnight. Entry to any and all events and exhibits via entry button ($6 per person; children under five free). Activities run from around 3 PM until midnight. Est attendance: 2,500. For info: President, First Night Augusta, PO Box 716, Waynesboro, VA 22980. Phone: (540) 943-2988.

FIRST NIGHT BOSTON. Dec 31. Boston, MA. A New Year's Eve Arts Festival that magically transforms the streets of Boston from an everyday workplace into a once-a-year, one-of-a-kind community of festivity and awe. More than 250 presentations of the visual and performing arts provide a community experience and energetic environment by 1,000 artists using the streets and buildings of Boston as their theater. Highlights include afternoon Family & Children's Festival, a Grand Procession at 5:30 and fireworks at midnight. Est attendance: 1,500,000. For info: First Night, Inc, 20 Park Plaza, Ste 927, Boston, MA 02116. Phone: (617) 542-1399.

FIRST NIGHT HARTFORD. Dec 31. Hartford, CT. Day-long celebration beginning at 2 PM and ending at midnight. Visual and performing arts, procession, theater, music, activities for children, and fireworks to welcome the New Year. Est attendance: 30,000. For info: Pamela Amodio, Dir, Events Mgmt, Hartford Downtown Council, 250 Constitution Plaza, Hartford, CT 06103. Phone: (860) 728-3089. Fax: (860) 527-9696.

FIRST NIGHT KINGSPORT. Dec 31. Kingsport, TN. A community-wide celebration of New Year's Eve which promotes the arts in a drug- and alcohol-free setting. The wholesome festivities transform downtown into 30 indoor and outdoor stages where singers, instrumentalists, dancers, actors, magicians, comedians, storytellers and artists provide six hours of fun and excitement. Opening parade, children's events, midnight fireworks. Est attendance: 15,000. For info: Barbara Gerwe, First Night Kingsport, PO Box 980, Kingsport, TN 37662. Phone: (423) 246-2017. Fax: (423) 224-2360.

FIRST NIGHT® NORFOLK. Dec 31. Norfolk, VA. Ring in the New Year during this community celebration of family and the arts. Visual and performing arts are featured in every form from the classical to the avant-garde. The festivities come to a brilliant conclusion as 1999 is ushered in with a spectacular fireworks display. Est attendance: 50,000. For info: Robin Evans, Mktg Dir, Norfolk Festevents, 120 W Main St, Norfolk, VA 23510. Phone: (757) 441-2345. Fax: (757) 441-5198.
WWW: http://www.festevents.com

FIRST NIGHT ROANOKE. Dec 31. Downtown, Roanoke, VA. An alcohol-free New Year's Eve Celebration of the Lively Arts. First-rate entertainment and hands-on activities for the entire community, also includes fireworks, dragon processional, carriage rides. 15 site locations. Held annually on New Year's Eve. Est attendance: 10,000. For info: Wendi Schultz, CFE Exec Dir, Roanoke Festival in the Park, PO Box 8276, Roanoke, VA 24014. Phone: (540) 342-2640.

FIRST NIGHT LIMA. Dec 31. Lima Town Square, Lima, OH. Outdoor family-oriented, alcohol-free New Year's Eve performing arts celebration. Est attendance: 30,000. For info: Martin Porter, Exec Dir, Council for the Arts of Greater Lima, PO Box 1124, Lima, OH 45802. Phone: (419) 222-1096. Fax: (419) 222-3871. Email: limaarts@bright.net.
WWW: http://www.bright.net/~limaarts

FIRST NIGHT® STATE COLLEGE. Dec 31. State College, PA. An alcohol-free family celebration of the visual and performing arts. Founding sponsor PNC Bank. Est attendance: 16,500. For info: Central Pennsylvania Festival of the Arts, Box 1023, State College, PA 16804. Phone: (814) 237-3682. Fax: (814) 237-0708.

FIRST NIGHTS. Dec 31. The following US cities have First Night celebrations: Mobile, AL; Escondido, Fullerton, Monterey, San Diego, Santa Cruz, Santa Rosa and Stockton, CA; Colorado Springs, Denver and Fort Collins, CO; Danbury, Mystic, Norwalk, Torrington and Westport/Weston, CT; Dover and Wilmington, DE; Atlantic Beach, Pensacola, St. Petersburg and Tampa, FL; Americus, Athens, Atlanta, Brunswick and Macon, GA; Honolulu and Maui, HI; Boise, ID; Aurora, Bloomington/Normal, Evanston, Godfrey, Joliet, Pontiac, Rockford and Springfield, IL; Bowling Green and Owensboro, KY; Annapolis, Easton and Silver Spring, MD; Beverly, Brockton, Chatham, Fall River, Fitchburg/Leominster, Lowell, Martha's Vineyard, New Bedford, Newburyport, Northampton, Pittsfield, Quincy, Sharon, Sturbridge and Worcester, MA; Birmingham and Wayne, MI; St. Paul, MN; Columbia, St. Louis and Springfield, MO; Missoula, MT; Claremont, Concord/Manchester, Keene, Mount Washington Valley, Portsmouth and Wolfeboro, NH; Bridgewater/Raritan/Somerville, Flemington, Manasquan, Maplewood/South Orange, Montclair, Morristown, Oakland, Ocean City, Red Bank, Ridgewood, Summit, Toms River and Westfield, NJ; Alamagordo, NM; Binghamton, Buffalo, Dunkirk, New York City, Nyack and Saratoga Springs, NY; Asheville, Charlotte, Piedmont, Raleigh and Sanford, NC; Grand Forks and Minot, ND; Akron, Columbus, North Ridgeville and Toledo, OH; Eugene, OR; Bethlehem, Bristol, Erie, Pittsburgh and York, PA; Providence and Westerly, RI; Aiken, Columbia and Greenville, SC; Salt Lake City, UT; Burlington, Montpelier, Rutland and St. Johnsbury, VT; Alexandria, Charlottesville, Fredericksburg, Harrisonburg, Leesburg, Williamsburg and Winchester, VA; Kennewick, WA; and Morgantown, WV.

GHANA: REVOLUTION DAY. Dec 31. National holiday.

JAPAN: NAMAHAGE. Dec 31. In evening, groups of "Namahage" men disguised as devils make door-to-door visits, growling, "Any good-for-nothing fellow hereabout?" The object of this annual event is to give sluggards an opportunity to change their minds and become diligent. Otherwise, according to legend, they will be punished by devils. Oga Peninsula, Akita Prefecture, Japan.

LEAP SECOND ADJUSTMENT TIME. Dec 31. One of the times that have been favored for the addition or subtraction of a second from clock time (to coordinate atomic and astronomical time). The determination to adjust is made by the Central Bureau of the International Earth Rotation Service in Paris. See also: "Leap Seconds" (see Contents).

MAKE UP YOUR MIND DAY. Dec 31. A day for all those people who have a hard time making up their minds. Make a decision today and follow through with it! Annually, Dec 31. For info: A.C. Moeller and M.A. Dufour, Box 71, Clio, MI 48420-1042.

MARSHALL, GEORGE CATLETT: BIRTH ANNIVERSARY. Dec 31. Chairman of the newly formed Joint Chiefs of Staff Committee throughout the US's involvement in WW II, General George Marshall was born Dec 31, 1880, in Uniontown, PA. He accompanied Roosevelt or represented the US at most Allied war conferences. He served as secretary of state and was designer of the Marshall Plan after the war. George Marshall died Oct 16, 1959, at Washington, DC.

"THE MATCH GAME" TV PREMIERE: ANNIVERSARY. Dec 31, 1962. This game show has appeared on all the major networks and in syndication, with most seasons hosted by Gene Rayburn. On the NBC version, two teams of three members each (two contestants and one celebrity) competed to try to match their answers to a fill-in-the-blank with their teammates' answers. On the CBS and syndicated versions, two contestants and a celebrity panel played; contestants won points for every celebrity's answer that matched theirs. Ross Shafer hosted the ABC revival.

NEW YEAR'S EVE. Dec 31. The last evening of the Gregorian calendar year, traditionally a night for merrymaking to welcome in the new year.

NEW YEAR'S EVE CELEBRATION. Dec 31. New York, NY. Fireworks and midnight run in Central Park; lighted "Big Apple" in Times Square; fireworks at Prospect Park in Brooklyn and in South Street Seaport. For info: New York Conv and Visitors Bureau, Special Events, 2 Columbus Circle, New York, NY 10019. Phone: (212) 484-1244. Fax: (212) 397-1938. South Street Seaport (212) 669-9400. Prospect Park, Brooklyn (718) 965-8999.

NEW YEAR'S FEST. Dec 31. Kalamazoo, MI. Kalamazoo comes alive as families, teens and seniors come downtown to welcome the New Year. Featuring more than 27 different artists, performances are hosted in 16 different indoor sites throughout downtown Kalamazoo. The cultural celebration offers music, theatre, puppetry, dance, mime and storytelling. Artists come from throughout the Midwest to join in this non-alcoholic celebration. Est attendance: 7,000. For info: Deborah Droppers, New Year's Fest, Inc, 128 N Kalamazoo Mall, Kalamazoo, MI 49007. Phone: (616) 388-2830. Email: EventKzoo@aol.com.

NIXON, JOHN: DEATH ANNIVERSARY. Dec 31, 1808. Commander of the Philadelphia City Guard, born 1733 (exact date unknown). Died at Philadelphia, PA, Dec 31, 1808. Appointed to conduct the first public reading of the Declaration of Independence, July 8, 1776. Nixon, a revolutionary patriot and businessman, was the son of Richard and Sarah Nixon.

ST. SYLVESTER'S DAY. Dec 31. Observed in Belgium, Germany, France, Switzerland. Commemorates death of Pope Sylvester I in 1335. Feasting, particularly upon "St. Sylvester's Carp."

WESTERN SAMOA: SAMOAN FIRE DANCE. Dec 31. New Year's Eve is occasion for Samoan bamboo fireworks, singing and traditional performances such as the Samoan Fire Dance.

WORLD PEACE MEDITATION. Dec 31. An opportunity for people around the world to focus their thoughts and energy on peace. The event is observed internationally, beginning at noon Greenwich Mean Time (GMT) and lasting one hour (7 AM–8 AM, EST). For info: Quaruts Foundation, PO Box 1768, Boerne, TX 78006. Phone: (210) 249-3985. Fax: (210) 249-3318.

BIRTHDAYS TODAY

Rex Allen, 74, the "Arizona Cowboy," singer ("Don't Go Near the Indians"), actor, narrator, born Willcox, AZ, Dec 31, 1924.

John Denver (Henry John Deutschendorf), 55, singer, songwriter ("Sunshine on My Shoulder," "Annie's Song"), actor (*Oh God*), born Roswell, NM, Dec 31, 1943.

Sir Anthony Hopkins, 61, actor (*Silence of the Lambs, Legends of the Fall*), born Port Talbot, South Wales, UK, Dec 31, 1937.

Val Kilmer, 39, actor (*Batman Forever, Top Secret, The Doors, Heat*), born Los Angeles, CA, Dec 31, 1959.

Ben Kingsley (Krishna Bhanji), 55, actor (Oscar for *Gandhi; Bugsy, Schindler's List*), born Yorkshire, England, Dec 31, 1943.

Tim Matheson, 50, actor (*Animal House*, "The Virginian," "Bonanza"), born Los Angeles, CA, Dec 31, 1948.

Sarah Miles, 57, actress (*The Servant, Blow-Up, Hope and Glory*), born Ingatestone, England, Dec 31, 1941.

Odetta (Odetta Homes Felious Gordon), 68, folksinger, musician, born Birmingham, AL, Dec 31, 1930.

James Remar, 45, actor (*48HRS, Drugstore Cowboy*), born Boston, MA, Dec 31, 1953.

Patti Smith, 52, singer ("Because the Night"), born Chicago, IL, Dec 31, 1946.

Donna Summer (LaDonna Andrea Gaines), 50, singer ("Bad Girls"), born Boston, MA, Dec 31, 1948.

Diane Halfin von Furstenberg, 53, fashion designer, author, born Brussels, Belgium, Dec 31, 1945.

PRESIDENTIAL PROCLAMATIONS ISSUED, JANUARY 1, 1996–JUNE 15, 1997

No. Title, Observance Dates, (Date of signing).

1996

6860 Death of Admiral Arleigh A. Burke (Jan 2, 1996)
6861 Martin Luther King, Jr., Federal Holiday, 1996: Jan 15, 1996 (Jan 12, 1996)
6862 Religious Freedom Day, 1996: Jan 16, 1996 (Jan 12, 1996)
6863 National African American History Month, 1996: February (Jan 30, 1996)
6864 American Heart Month, 1996: February (Feb 1, 1996)
6865 150th Anniversary of the Smithsonian Institution, Aug 10, 1996 (Feb 7, 1996)
6866 American Red Cross Month, 1996: March (Feb 26, 1996)
6867 Declaration of a National Emergency and Invocation of Emergency Authority Relating to the Regulation of the Anchorage and Movement of Vessels (Mar 1, 1996)
6868 Irish-American Heritage Month, 1996: March (Mar 1, 1996)
6869 Save Your Vision Week, 1996: Mar 3–9, 1996 (Mar 1, 1996)
6870 National Park Week, 1996: Apr 22–28, 1996 (Mar 8, 1996)
6871 National Poison Prevention Week, 1996: Mar 17–23, 1996 (Mar 11, 1996)
6872 Women's History Month, 1996: March (Mar 19, 1996)
6873 Greek Independence Day: A National Day of Celebration of Greek and American Democracy, 1996: Mar 25, 1996 (Mar 22, 1996)
6874 Death of Edmund Sixtus Muskie: Mar 30, 1996 (Mar 27, 1996)
6875 Cancer Control Month, 1996: April (Mar 29, 1996)
6876 Education and Sharing Day, USA, 1996: Mar 31, 1996 (Mar 29, 1996)
6877 National Day of Prayer, 1996: May 2, 1996 (Apr 2, 1996)
6878 Death of Those Aboard US Air Force Aircraft in Croatia (Apr 4, 1996)
6879 National Former Prisoner of War Recognition Day, 1996: Apr 9, 1996 (Apr 5, 1996)
6880 National Day of Remembrance of the Oklahoma City Bombing: Apr 19, 1996 (Apr 5, 1996)
6881 National Child Abuse Prevention Month, 1996: April (Apr 8, 1996)
6882 National D.A.R.E. Day, 1996: Apr 10, 1996 (Apr 11, 1996)
6883 National Pay Inequity Awareness Day, 1996: Apr 11, 1996 (Apr 11, 1996)
6884 Pan American Day and Pan American Week, 1996: Apr 14, 1996, Apr 14–20, 1996 (Apr 11, 1996)
6885 National Volunteer Week, 1996: Apr 21–27, 1996 (Apr 17, 1996)

No. Title, Observance Dates, (Date of signing).

6886 National Organ and Tissue Donor Awareness Week, 1996: Apr 21–27, 1996 (Apr 19, 1996)
6887 Jewish Heritage Week, 1996: Apr 21–28, 1996 (Apr 19, 1996)
6888 National Crime Victims' Rights Week, 1996: Apr 21–27, 1996 (Apr 19, 1996)
6889 Loyalty Day, 1996: May 1, 1996 (Apr 30, 1996)
6890 Law Day, USA, 1996: May 1, 1996 (Apr 30, 1996)
6891 Labor History Month, 1996: May (May 3, 1996)
6892 Asian/Pacific American Heritage Month, 1996: May (May 6, 1996)
6893 Mother's Day, 1996: May 12, 1996 (May 7, 1996)
6894 Older Americans Month, 1996: May (May 13, 1996)
6895 Peace Officers Memorial Day and Police Week, 1996: May 15, 1996, May 12–18, 1996 (May 13, 1996)
6896 National Defense Transportation Day and National Transportation Week, 1996: May 17, 1996, May 12–18, 1996 (May 15, 1996)
6897 National Safe Boating Week, 1996: May 18–24, 1996 (May 17, 1996)
6898 Death of Admiral Jeremy M. Boorda (May 17, 1996)
6899 World Trade Week, 1996: May 19–25, 1996 (May 20, 1996)
6900 National Maritime Day, 1996: May 22, 1996 (May 21, 1996)
6901 Prayer for Peace, Memorial Day, 1996: May 27, 1996 (May 24, 1996)
6902 Small Business Week, 1996: June 2–8, 1996 (May 31, 1996)
6903 Flag Day and National Flag Week, 1996: June 14, 1996, June 9–16 1996 (June 7, 1996)
6904 Father's Day, 1996: June 16, 1996 (June 13, 1996)
6905 Centers for Disease Control and Prevention Day, 1996: June 24, 1996 (June 24, 1996)
6906 Victims of the Bombing of Saudi Arabia, 1996: June 26, 1996 (June 26, 1996)
6907 Declaration of a State of Emergency and Release of Feed Grain from the Disaster Reserve (July 1, 1996)
6908 A National Month of Unity, 1996: July (July 1, 1996)
6909 Captive Nations Week, 1996: July 21–27, 1996 (July 18, 1996)
6910 National Korean War Veterans Armistice Day, 1996: July 27, 1996 (July 25, 1996)
6911 Parents' Day, 1996: July 28, 1996 (July 25, 1996)
6912 Women's Equality Day, 1996: Aug 26, 1996 (Aug 21, 1996)
6913 Minority Enterprise Development Week, 1996: Sept 22–28, 1996 (Aug 23, 1996)
6914 To Modify the Allocation of Tariff-Rate Quotas for Certain Cheeses (Aug 26, 1996)
6915 America Goes Back to School, 1996: Sept 8–14, 1996 (Sept 9, 1996)
6916 National Farm Safety and Health Week, 1996: Sept 15–21, 1996 (Sept 13, 1996)

PRESIDENTIAL PROCLAMATIONS (cont'd) ISSUED, JANUARY 1, 1996–JUNE 15, 1997

No. Title, Observance Dates, (Date of signing).

6917 Citizenship Day and Constitution Week, 1996: Sept 17, 1996, Sept 17–23, 1996 (Sept 17, 1996)
6918 National POW/MIA Recognition Day, 1996: Sept 20, 1996 (Sept 18, 1996)
6919 National Hispanic Heritage Month, 1996: Sept 15–Oct 15, 1996 (Sept 18, 1996)
6920 Establishment of the Grand Staircase-Escalante National Monument (Sept 18, 1996)
6921 National Historically Black Colleges and Universities Week, 1996: Sept 22–28, 1996 (Sept 20, 1996)
6922 To Extend Nondiscriminatory Treatment (Most-Favored-Nation Treatment) to the Products of Bulgaria (Sept 27, 1996)
6923 Gold Star Mother's Day, 1996: Sept 29, 1996 (Sept 27, 1996)
6924 National Student Voter Education Day, 1996: Oct 2, 1996 (Oct 2, 1996)
6925 Suspension of Entry as Immigrants and Nonimmigrants of Persons Who Formulate or Implement Policies That Are Impeding the Transition to Democracy in Burma or Who Benefit from Such Policies (Oct 3, 1996)
6926 National Breast Cancer Awareness Month, 1996: October (Oct 3, 1996)
6927 National Domestic Violence Awareness Month, 1996: October (Oct 3, 1996)
6928 Roosevelt History Month, 1996: October (Oct 4, 1996)
6929 National Disability Employment Awareness Month, 1996: October (Oct 4, 1996)
6930 Fire Prevention Week, 1996: Oct 6–12, 1996 (Oct 5, 1996)
6931 German-American Day, 1996: Oct 6, 1996 (Oct 5, 1996)
6932 National Wildlife Refuge Week, 1996: Oct 6–12, 1996 (Oct 7, 1996)
6933 Child Health Day, 1996: Oct 7, 1996 (Oct 7, 1996)
6934 Leif Erikson Day, 1996: Oct 9, 1996 (Oct 9, 1996)
6935 National Day of Concern About Young People and Gun Violence, 1996: Oct 10, 1996 (Oct 10, 1996)
6936 General Pulaski Memorial Day, 1996: Oct 11, 1996 (Oct 10, 1996)
6937 National Character Counts Week, 1996: Oct 13–19, 1996 (Oct 11, 1996)
6938 National School Lunch Week, 1996: Oct 13–20, 1996 (Oct 11, 1996)
6939 National Children's Day, 1996: Oct 13, 1996 (Oct 11, 1996)
6940 Columbus Day, 1996: Oct 14, 1996 (Oct 11, 1996)
6941 White Cane Safety Day, 1996: Oct 15, 1996 (Oct 14, 1996)
6942 To Amend the Generalized System of Preferences (Oct 17, 1996)
6943 Honoring the Filipino Veterans of World War II, 1996: Oct 20, 1996 (Oct 17, 1996)

No. Title, Observance Dates, (Date of signing).

6944 National Forest Products Week, 1996: Oct 20–26, 1996 (Oct 21, 1996)
6945 National Consumers Week, 1996: Oct 20–26, 1996 (Oct 21, 1996)
6946 United Nations Day, 1996: Oct 24, 1996 (Oct 24, 1996)
6947 National Adoption Month, 1996: November (Oct 29, 1996)
6948 To Modify Provisions on Upland Cotton and for Other Purposes (Oct 29, 1996)
6949 National American Indian Heritage Month, 1996: November (Oct 29, 1996)
6950 Veterans Day, 1996: Nov 11, 1996 (Oct 31, 1996)
6951 To Extend Nondiscriminatory Treatment (Most-Favored-Nation Treatment) to the Products of Romania (Nov 7, 1996)
6952 National Farm-City Week, 1996: Nov 22–28, 1996 (Nov 8, 1996)
6953 National Family Caregivers Week, 1996: Nov 24–30, 1996 (Nov 11, 1996)
6954 Thanksgiving Day, 1996: Nov 28, 1996 (Nov 11, 1996)
6955 To Provide Duty-Free Treatment to Products of the West Bank and the Gaza Strip and Qualifying Industrial Zones (Nov 13, 1996)
6956 National Family Week, 1996: Nov 24–30, 1996 (Nov 19, 1996)
6957 National Great American Smokeout Day, 1996: Nov 21, 1996 (Nov 21, 1996)
6958 Suspension of Entry as Immigrants and Nonimmigrants of Persons Who Are Members or Officials of the Sudanese Government or Armed Forces (Nov 22, 1996)
6959 World AIDS Day, 1996: Dec 1, 1996 (Nov 26, 1996)
6960 National Drunk and Drugged Driving Prevention Month, 1996: December (Nov 27, 1996)
6961 To Facilitate Positive Adjustment to Competition from Imports of Broom Corn Brooms (Nov 28, 1996)
6962 To Implement the United States-Israel Agreement on Trade in Agricultural Products (Dec 2, 1996)
6963 National Pearl Harbor Remembrance Day, 1996: Dec 7, 1996 (Dec 5, 1996)
6964 Human Rights Day, Bill of Rights Day, and Human Rights Week, 1996: Dec 10, 1996, Dec 15, 1996, Dec 10–17, 1996 (Dec 10, 1996)
6965 Wright Brothers Day, 1996: Dec 17, 1996 (Dec 13, 1996)

1997

6966 Religious Freedom Day, 1997: Jan 16, 1997 (Jan 16, 1997)
6967 Martin Luther King, Jr., Federal Holiday, 1997: Jan 20, 1997 (Jan 17, 1997)
6968 National Day of Hope and Renewal, 1997: Jan 20, 1997 (Jan 20, 1997)

PRESIDENTIAL PROCLAMATIONS (cont'd) ISSUED, JANUARY 1, 1996–JUNE 15, 1997

No. Title, Observance Dates, (Date of signing).

6969 To Modify Application of Duty-Free Treatment of Certain Articles Under the Generalized System of Preferences, and for Other Purposes (Jan 27, 1997)
6970 National African American History Month, 1997: February (Jan 30, 1997)
6971 American Heart Month, 1997: February (Feb 1, 1997)
6972 National Child Passenger Safety Week, 1997: Feb 9–15, 1997 (Feb 8, 1997)
6973 American Red Cross Month, 1997: March (Feb 25, 1997)
6974 Irish-American Heritage Month, 1997: March (Feb 27, 1997)
6975 Women's History Month, 1997: March (Mar 3, 1997)
6976 Save Your Vision Week, 1997: Mar 2–8, 1997 (Mar 3, 1997)
6977 National Poison Prevention Week, 1997: Mar 16–22, 1997 (Mar 5, 1997)
6978 National Older Workers Employment Week, 1997: Mar 9–15, 1997 (Mar 7, 1997)
6979 Greek Independence Day: A National Day of Celebration of Greek and American Democracy, 1997: Mar 25, 1997 (Mar 25, 1997)
6980 Cancer Control Month, 1997: April (Apr 1, 1997)
6981 National Child Abuse Prevention Month, 1997: April (Apr 1, 1997)
6982 To Implement an Agreement to Eliminate Tariffs on Certain Pharmaceuticals and Chemical Intermediates (Apr 1, 1997)
6983 National Former Prisoner of War Recognition Day, 1997: Apr 9, 1997 (Apr 8, 1997)
6984 National D.A.R.E. Day, 1997: Apr 10, 1997 (Apr 9, 1997)
6985 National Pay Inequity Awareness Day, 1997: Apr 11, 1997 (Apr 10, 1997)
6986 National Service and Volunteer Week, 1997: Apr 13–19, 1997 (Apr 11, 1997)
6987 Pan American Day and Pan American Week, 1997: Apr 14, 1997, Apr 13–19, 1997 (Apr 11, 1997)
6988 To Modify Application of Duty-Free Treatment under the Generalized System of Preferences (Apr 11, 1997)

No. Title, Observance Dates, (Date of signing).

6989 National Crime Victims' Rights Week, 1997: Apr 13–19, 1997 (Apr 15, 1997)
6990 Education and Sharing Day, USA, 1997: Apr 18, 1997 (Apr 17, 1997)
6991 National Day of Prayer, 1997: May 1, 1997 (Apr 18, 1997)
6992 National Organ and Tissue Donor Awareness Week, 1997: Apr 20–26, 1997 (Apr 19, 1997)
6993 National Wildlife Week, 1997: Apr 20–26, 1997 (Apr 19, 1997)
6994 National Park Week, 1997: Apr 21–27, 1997 (Apr 19, 1997)
6995 Law Day, USA, 1997: May 1, 1997 (Apr 22, 1997)
6996 Older Americans Month, 1997: May (May 1, 1997)
6997 Loyalty Day, 1997: May 1, 1997 (May 1, 1997)
6998 Asian/Pacific Heritage Month, 1997: May (May 5, 1997)
6999 Mother's Day, 1997: May 11, 1997 (May 7, 1997)
7000 Peace Officers Memorial Day and Police Week, 1997: May 15, 1997, May 11–17, 1997 (May 9, 1997)
7001 Jewish Heritage Week, 1997: May 11–18, 1997 (May 8, 1997)
7002 National Defense Transportation Day and National Transportation Week, 1997: May 16, 1997, May 11–17, 1997 (May 9, 1997)
7003 National Safe Boating Week, 1997: May 17–23, 1997 (May 14, 1997)
7004 World Trade Week, 1997: May 18–24, 1997 (May 19, 1997)
7005 National Maritime Day, 1997: May 22, 1997 (May 21, 1997)
7006 Prayer for Peace, Memorial Day, 1997: May 26, 1997 (May 22, 1997)
7007 To Modify Duty-Free Treatment Under the Generalized System of Preferences (May 30, 1997)
7008 Small Business Week, 1997: June 1–7, 1997 (May 30, 1997)
7009 Flag Day and National Flag Week, 1997: June 14, 1997, June 8–14, 1997 (June 6, 1997)
7010 Father's Day, 1997: June 15, 1997 (June 12, 1997)

THE NATIONAL EDUCATION GOALS

1. By the year 2000, all children in America will start school ready to learn.
2. By the year 2000, the high school graduation rate will increase to at least 90 percent.
3. By the year 2000, American students will leave grades four, eight, and twelve having demonstrated competency in challenging subject matter including English, mathematics, science, foreign languages, civics and government, economics, art, history, and geography; and every school in America will insure that all students learn to use their minds well, so they may be prepared for responsible citizenship, further learning, and productive employment in our nations modern economy.
4. By the year 2000, the nation's teaching force will have access to programs for the continued improvement of their professional skills and the opportunity to acquire the knowledge and skills needed to instruct and prepare all American students for the next century.
5. By the year 2000, U.S. students will be first in the world in science and mathematics achievement.
6. By the year 2000, every adult American will be literate and will possess the knowledge and skills necessary to compete in a global economy and exercise the rights and responsibilities of citizenship.
7. By the year 2000, every school in America will be free of drugs, violence, and the unauthorized presence of firearms and alcohol and will offer a disciplined environment conducive to learning.

8. By the year 2000, every school will promote partnerships that will increase parental involvement and participation in promoting the social, emotional, and academic growth of children.

Established in 1990 by the nation's governors and endorsed by Presidents George Bush and William Clinton, the National Education Goals provide a focal point for reform and renewal in education. The goals set a series of targets that America's elected leaders hold as a vision for the nation to achieve by the year 2000.

☆ ☆ ☆

DECADE OF THE BRAIN PROCLAMATION

Proclamation 6158 of July 17, 1990

Decade of the Brain, 1990–1999

By the President of the United States of America

A Proclamation

The human brain, a 3-pound mass of interwoven nerve cells that controls our activity, is one of the most magnificent—and mysterious—wonders of creation. The seat of human intelligence, interpreter of senses, and controller of movement, this incredible organ continues to intrigue scientist and layman alike.

Over the years, our understanding of the brain—how it works, what goes wrong when it is injured or diseased—has increased dramatically. However, we still have much more to learn. The need for continued study of the brain is compelling: millions of Americans are affected each year by disorders of the brain ranging from neurogenetic diseases to degenerative disorders such as Alzheimer's, as well as stroke, schizophrenia, autism, and impairments of speech, language, and hearing.

Today, these individuals and their families are justifiably hopeful, for a new era of discovery is dawning in brain research. Powerful microscopes, major strides in the study of genetics, and advanced brain imaging devices are giving physicians and scientists ever greater insight into the brain. Neuroscientists are mapping the brain's biochemical circuitry, which may help produce more effective drugs for alleviating the suffering of those who have Alzheimer's or Parkinson's disease. By studying how the brain's cells and chemicals develop, interact, and communicate with the rest of the body, investigators are also developing improved treatments for people incapacitated by spinal cord injuries, depressive disorders, and epileptic seizures. Breakthroughs in molecular genetics show great promise of yielding methods to treat and prevent Huntington's disease, the muscular dystrophies, and other life-threatening disorders.

Research may also prove valuable in our war on drugs, as studies provide greater insight into how people become addicted to drugs and how drugs affect the brain. These studies may also help produce effective treatments for chemical dependency and help us to understand and prevent the harm done to the preborn children of pregnant women who abuse drugs and alcohol. Because there is a connection between the body's nervous and immune systems, studies of the brain may also help enhance our understanding of Acquired Immune Deficiency Syndrome.

Many studies regarding the human brain have been planned and conducted by scientists at the National Institutes of Health, the National Institute of Mental Health, and other Federal research agencies. Augmenting Federal efforts are programs supported by private foundations and industry. The cooperation between these agencies and the multidisciplinary efforts of thousands of scientists and health care professionals provide powerful evidence of our Nation's determination to conquer brain disease.

To enhance public awareness of the benefits to be derived from brain research, the Congress by House Joint Resolution 174 has designated the decade beginning January 1, 1990, as the "Decade of the Brain" and has authorized and requested the President to issue a proclamation in observance of this occasion.

NOW, THEREFORE, I, GEORGE BUSH, President of the United States of America, do hereby proclaim the decade beginning January 1, 1990, as the Decade of the Brain. I call upon all public officials and the people of the United States to observe that decade with appropriate programs, ceremonies, and activities.

IN WITNESS WHEREOF, I have hereunto set my hand this seventeenth day of July, in the year of our Lord nineteen hundred and ninety, and of the Independence of the United States of America the two hundred and fifteenth.

George Bush

From *The Federal Register*, 55 F.R. 29555

SOME FACTS ABOUT CANADA

Province/Territory	Capital	Population*	Flower	Land/Fresh Water (sq. mi.)	Total Area
Alberta	Edmonton	2,774,512	Wild rose	400,423/10,437	410,860
British Columbia	Victoria	3,835,748	Pacific dogwood	578,230/11,227	589,458
Manitoba	Winnipeg	1,141,727	Prairie crocus	340,834/63,129	403,964
New Brunswick	Fredericton	761,873	Purple violet	44,797/835	45,633
Newfoundland	St. John's	571,192	Pitcher plant	230,219/21,147	251,367
Northwest Territories	Yellowknife	66,164	Mountain avens	2,017,306/82,829	2,100,136
Nova Scotia	Halifax	941,235	Mayflower	32,835/1,647	34,482
Ontario	Toronto	11,209,474	White trillium	553,788/110,229	664,012
Prince Edward Island	Charlottetown	137,316	Lady's-slipper	3,515/0	3,515
Quebec	Quebec City	7,366,883	White garden lily	843,109/114,269	957,379
Saskatchewan	Regina	1,020,138	Red lily	354,365/51,347	405,712
Yukon Territory	Whitehorse	31,107	Fireweed	297,050/2,784	299,835

*1996

STATE & TERRITORY ABBREVIATIONS: UNITED STATES

Alabama . . . . . AL
Alaska . . . . . AK
Arizona . . . . . AZ
Arkansas . . . . . AR
American Samoa . . . . . AS
California . . . . . CA
Canal Zone . . . . . CZ
Colorado . . . . . CO
Connecticut . . . . . CT
Delaware . . . . . DE
District of Columbia . . . . . DC
Florida . . . . . FL
Georgia . . . . . GA
Guam . . . . . GU
Hawaii . . . . . HI
Idaho . . . . . ID
Illinois IL
Indiana . . . . . IN
Iowa . . . . . IA
Kansas . . . . . KS
Kentucky . . . . . KY
Louisiana . . . . . LA
Maine . . . . . ME
Maryland . . . . . MD
Massachusetts . . . . . MA
Michigan . . . . . MI
Minnesota . . . . . MN
Mississippi . . . . . MS
Missouri . . . . . MO
Montana . . . . . MT
Nebraska . . . . . NE
Nevada . . . . . NV
New Hampshire . . . . . NH
New Jersey . . . . . NJ
New Mexico . . . . . NM
New York . . . . . NY
North Carolina . . . . . NC
North Dakota . . . . . ND
Ohio . . . . . OH
Oklahoma . . . . . OK
Oregon . . . . . OR
Pennsylvania . . . . . PA
Puerto Rico . . . . . PR
Rhode Island . . . . . RI
South Carolina . . . . . SC
South Dakota . . . . . SD
Tennessee . . . . . TN
Trust Territories . . . . . TT
Texas . . . . . TX
Utah . . . . . UT
Vermont . . . . . VT
Virginia . . . . . VA
Virgin Islands VI
Washington . . . . . WA
West Virginia . . . . . WV
Wisconsin . . . . . WI
Wyoming . . . . . WY

PROVINCE & TERRITORY ABBREVIATIONS: CANADA

Alberta . . . . . AB
British Columbia . . . . . BC
Manitoba . . . . . MB
New Brunswick . . . . . NB
Newfoundland . . . . . NFLD
Nova Scotia . . . . . NS
Ontario . . . . . ON
Prince Edward Island . . . . . PEI
Quebec . . . . . QC
Saskatchewan . . . . . SK
Yukon Territory . . . . . YK
Northwest Territories . . . . . NWT

CALENDAR INFORMATION FOR THE YEAR 1998

Time shown is Eastern Standard Time. All dates are given in terms of the Gregorian calendar.

(Based in part on information prepared by the Nautical Almanac Office, US Naval Observatory.)

ERAS	YEAR	BEGINS
Byzantine	7507	Sept 14
Jewish*	5759	Sept 20
Chinese (Year of the Tiger)	4696	Jan 28
Roman (AUC)	2751	Jan 14
Nabonassar	2747	Apr 24
Japanese (Heisei)	10	Jan 1
Grecian (Seleucidae)	2310	Sept 14 (or Oct 14)
Indian (Saka)	1920	Mar 22
Diocletian	1715	Sept 11
Islamic (Hegira)**	1419	Apr 27

*Year begins at sunset. **Year begins at moon crescent.

RELIGIOUS CALENDARS

Epiphany	Jan 6
Shrove Tuesday	Feb 24
Ash Wednesday	Feb 25
Lent	Feb 25–Apr 11
Palm Sunday	Apr 5
Good Friday	Apr 10
Easter Day	Apr 12
Ascension Day	May 21
Whit Sunday (Pentecost)	May 31
Trinity Sunday	June 7
First Sunday in Advent	Nov 29
Christmas Day (Wednesday)	Dec 25

Eastern Orthodox Church Observances

Christmas	Jan 7
Great Lent begins	Mar 2
Pascha (Easter)	Apr 19
Ascension	May 28
Pentecost	June 7

Jewish Holy Days

Purim	Mar 12
Passover (1st day)	Apr 11
Shavuot	May 31
Tisha B'av	Aug 2
Rosh Hashanah (New Year)	Sept 21–22
Yom Kippur	Sept 30
Succoth	Oct 5–13
Chanukah	Dec 14–21

Islamic Holy Days

First Day of Ramadan	Dec 20
Islamic New Year (1419)	Apr 27

CIVIL CALENDAR—USA—1998

New Year's Day	Jan 1
Martin Luther King's Birthday (obsvd)	Jan 19
Lincoln's Birthday	Feb 12
Washington's Birthday (obsvd)/Presidents' Day	Feb 16
Memorial Day (obsvd)	May 25
Independence Day	July 4
Labor Day	Sept 7
Columbus Day (obsvd)	Oct 12
General Election Day	Nov 3
Veterans Day	Nov 11
Thanksgiving Day	Nov 26

Other Days Widely Observed in US—1998

Groundhog Day (Candlemas)	Feb 2
St. Valentine's Day	Feb 14
Mother's Day	May 10
Children's Day	June 14
Flag Day	June 14
Father's Day	June 21
Hallowe'en	Oct 31
National Grandparents Day	Sept 13

CIVIL CALENDAR—CANADA—1998

Commonwealth Day	Mar 9
Victoria Day	May 18
Canada Day	July 1
Labor Day	Sept 7
Thanksgiving Day	Oct 12
Remembrance Day	Nov 11
Boxing Day	Dec 26

CIVIL CALENDAR—MEXICO—1998

New Year's Day	Jan 1
Constitution Day	Feb 5
Benito Juarez Birthday	Mar 21
Labor Day	May 1
Battle of Puebla Day (Cinco de Mayo)	May 5
Independence Day*	Sept 16
Dia de La Raza	Oct 12
Mexican Revolution Day	Nov 20
Guadalupe Day	Dec 12

*Celebration begins Sept 15 at 11:00 P.M.

CIVIL CALENDAR—UNITED KINGDOM—1998

Accession of Queen Elizabeth II	Feb 6
St. David (Wales)	Mar 1
Commonwealth Day	Mar 9
St. Patrick (Ireland)	Mar 17
Birthday of Queen Elizabeth II	Apr 21
St. George (England)	Apr 23
Coronation Day	June 2
The Queen's Official Birthday (tentative)	June 13
Birthday of Prince Philip, Duke of Edinburgh	June 10
Remembrance Sunday	Nov 8
Birthday of the Prince of Wales	Nov 14
St. Andrew (Scotland)	Nov 30

BANK AND PUBLIC HOLIDAYS—UNITED KINGDOM—1998

(Observed during 1998 in England and Wales, Scotland and Northern Ireland unless otherwise indicated)

New Year	Jan 1
Bank Holiday (Scotland)	Jan 2
St Patrick's Day (Northern Ireland)	Mar 17
Good Friday	Apr 10
Easter Monday (except Scotland)	Apr 13
May Day Bank Holiday	May 4
Spring Bank Holiday	May 25
Orangeman's Day (Battle of the Boyne) (Northern Ireland)	July 13
Bank Holiday (Scotland)	Aug 3
Summer Bank Holiday (except Scotland)	Aug 31
Christmas Day Holiday	Dec 25
Boxing Day Holiday	Dec 28

SEASONS

Spring (Vernal Equinox)	Mar 20, 2:55 PM, EST
Summer (Summer Solstice)	June 21, 10:03 AM, EDT
Autumn (Autumnal Equinox)	Sept 23, 1:37 AM, EDT
Winter (Winter Solstice)	Dec 21, 8:56 PM, EST

DAYLIGHT SAVING TIME SCHEDULE—1998

Sunday, Apr 5, 2:00 AM–Sunday, Oct 25, 2:00 AM—in all time zones.

CHRONOLOGICAL CYCLES

Dominical Letter	D
Epact	2
Golden Number (Lunar Cycle)	IV
Julian Period (year of)	6711
Roman Indiction	6
Solar Cycle	19

CALENDAR INFORMATION FOR THE YEAR 1999

Time shown is Eastern Standard Time. All dates are given in terms of the Gregorian calendar.

(Based in part on information prepared by the Nautical Almanac Office, US Naval Observatory.)

ERAS	YEAR	BEGINS
Byzantine	7508	Sept 14
Jewish*	5760	Sept 10
Chinese (Year of the Hare)	4697	Feb 16
Roman (AUC)	2752	Jan 14
Nabonassar	2748	Apr 24
Japanese (Heisei)	11	Jan 1
Grecian (Seleucidae)	2311	Sept 14 (or Oct 14)
Indian (Saka)	1921	Mar 22
Diocletian	1716	Sept 12
Islamic (Hegira)**	1420	Apr 16

*Year begins at sunset. **Year begins at moon crescent.

RELIGIOUS CALENDARS

Epiphany	Jan 6
Shrove Tuesday	Feb 16
Ash Wednesday	Feb 17
Lent	Feb 17–Apr 3
Palm Sunday	Mar 28
Good Friday	Apr 2
Easter Day	Apr 4
Ascension Day	May 13
Whit Sunday (Pentecost)	May 23
Trinity Sunday	May 30
First Sunday in Advent	Nov 28
Christmas Day (Wednesday)	Dec 25

Eastern Orthodox Church Observances

Christmas	Jan 7
Great Lent begins	Feb 22
Pascha (Easter)	Apr 11
Ascension	May 20
Pentecost	May 30

Jewish Holy Days

Purim	Mar 2
Passover (1st day)	Apr 1
Shavuot	May 21
Tisha B'av	July 22
Rosh Hashanah (New Year)	Sept 11–12
Yom Kippur	Sept 20
Succoth	Sept 25
Chanukah	Dec 4–11

Islamic Holy Days

First Day of Ramadan	Dec 9
Islamic New Year (1420)	Apr 17

CIVIL CALENDAR—USA—1999

New Year's Day	Jan 1
Martin Luther King's Birthday (obsvd)	Jan 18
Lincoln's Birthday	Feb 12
Washington's Birthday (obsvd)/Presidents' Day	Feb 15
Memorial Day (obsvd)	May 31
Independence Day	July 4
Labor Day	Sept 6
Columbus Day (obsvd)	Oct 11
General Election Day	Nov 2
Veterans Day	Nov 11
Thanksgiving Day	Nov 25

Other Days Widely Observed in US—1999

Groundhog Day (Candlemas)	Feb 2
St. Valentine's Day	Feb 14
Mother's Day	May 9
Children's Day	June 13
Flag Day	June 14
Father's Day	June 20
Hallowe'en	Oct 31
National Grandparents Day	Sept 12

CIVIL CALENDAR—CANADA—1999

Commonwealth Day	Mar 8
Victoria Day	May 24
Canada Day	July 1
Labor Day	Sept 6
Thanksgiving Day	Oct 11
Remembrance Day	Nov 11
Boxing Day	Dec 27

CIVIL CALENDAR—MEXICO—1999

New Year's Day	Jan 1
Constitution Day	Feb 5
Benito Juarez Birthday	Mar 21
Labor Day	May 1
Battle of Puebla Day (Cinco de Mayo)	May 5
Independence Day*	Sept 16
Dia de La Raza	Oct 12
Mexican Revolution Day	Nov 20
Guadalupe Day	Dec 12

*Celebration begins Sept 15 at 11:00 P.M.

CIVIL CALENDAR—UNITED KINGDOM—1999

Accession of Queen Elizabeth II	Feb 6
St. David (Wales)	Mar 1
Commonwealth Day	Mar 8
St. Patrick (Ireland)	Mar 17
Birthday of Queen Elizabeth II	Apr 21
St. George (England)	Apr 23
Coronation Day	June 2
The Queen's Official Birthday (tentative)	June 12
Birthday of Prince Philip, Duke of Edinburgh	June 10
Remembrance Sunday	Nov 14
Birthday of the Prince of Wales	Nov 14
St. Andrew (Scotland)	Nov 30

BANK AND PUBLIC HOLIDAYS—UNITED KINGDOM—1999

(Observed during 1999 in England and Wales, Scotland and Northern Ireland unless otherwise indicated)

New Year	Jan 1
Bank Holiday (Scotland)	Jan 2
St Patrick's Day (Northern Ireland)	Mar 17
Good Friday	Apr 2
Easter Monday (except Scotland)	Apr 5
May Day Bank Holiday	May 3
Spring Bank Holiday	May 24
Orangeman's Day (Battle of the Boyne) (Northern Ireland)	July 12
Bank Holiday (Scotland)	Aug 2
Summer Bank Holiday (except Scotland)	Aug 30
Christmas Day Holiday	Dec 25
Boxing Day Holiday	Dec 27

SEASONS

Spring (Vernal Equinox)	Mar 20, 8:46 PM, EST
Summer (Summer Solstice)	June 21, 3:49 PM, EDT
Autumn (Autumnal Equinox)	Sept 23, 7:31 AM, EDT
Winter (Winter Solstice)	Dec 22, 2:44 AM, EST

DAYLIGHT SAVING TIME SCHEDULE—1999

Sunday, Apr 4, 2:00 AM–Sunday, Oct 24, 2:00 AM—in all time zones.

CHRONOLOGICAL CYCLES

Dominical Letter	C
Epact	13
Golden Number (Lunar Cycle)	V
Julian Period (year of)	6712
Roman Indiction	7
Solar Cycle	20

ASTRONOMICAL PHENOMENA FOR THE YEARS 1998–2000

All dates are given in terms of Eastern Standard or Daylight Time and the Gregorian calendar.

(Based in part on information prepared by the Nautical Almanac Office, US Naval Observatory.)

1998

PRINCIPAL PHENOMENA, 1998
EARTH

Perihelion . . . . Jan 4
Aphelion . . . . July 3
Equinoxes . . . . Mar 20, Sept 23
Solstices . . . . June 21, Dec 21

PHASES OF THE MOON

New Moon	First Quarter	Full Moon	Last Quarter
	Jan 5	Jan 12	Jan 20
Jan 28	Feb 3	Feb 11	Feb 19
Feb 26	Mar 5	Mar 12	Mar 21
Mar 27	Apr 3	Apr 11	Apr 19
Apr 26	May 3	May 11	May 19
May 25	June 1	June 10	June 17
June 23	July 1	July 9	July 16
July 23	July 31	Aug 7	Aug 14
Aug 21	Aug 30	Sept 6	Sept 12
Sept 20	Sept 28	Oct 5	Oct 12
Oct 20	Oct 28	Nov 4	Nov 10
Nov 18	Nov 26	Dec 3	Dec 10
Dec 18	Dec 26		

ECLIPSES

Total eclipse of the Sun . . . . Feb 26
Penumbral eclipse of the Moon . . . . Mar 12
Penumbral eclipse of the Moon . . . . Aug 7
Annular eclipse of the Sun . . . . Aug 21
Penumbral eclipse of the Moon . . . . Sept 6

VISIBILITY OF PLANETS IN MORNING AND EVENING TWILIGHT

	Morning	Evening
Venus	Jan 22–Sept 22	Jan 1–Jan 10 Dec 10–Dec 31
Mars	July 10–Dec 31	Jan 1–Mar 9
Jupiter	Mar 9–Sept 16	Jan 1–Feb 10 Sept 16–Dec 31
Saturn	May 1–Oct 23	Jan 1–Mar 27 Oct 23–Dec 31

1999

PRINCIPAL PHENOMENA, 1999
EARTH

Perihelion . . . . Jan 3
Aphelion . . . . July 6
Equinoxes . . . . Mar 20, Sept 23
Solstices . . . . June 21, Dec 22

PHASES OF THE MOON

New Moon	First Quarter	Full Moon	Last Quarter
		Jan 1	Jan 9
Jan 17	Jan 24	Jan 31	Feb 8
Feb 16	Feb 22	Mar 2	Mar 10
Mar 17	Mar 24	Mar 31	Apr 8
Apr 16	Apr 22	Apr 30	May 8
May 15	May 22	May 30	June 7
June 13	June 20	June 28	July 6
July 12	July 20	July 28	Aug 4
Aug 11	Aug 18	Aug 26	Sept 2
Sept 9	Sept 17	Sept 25	Oct 2
Oct 9	Oct 17	Oct 24	Oct 31
Nov 7	Nov 16	Nov 23	Nov 29
Dec 7	Dec 15	Dec 22	Dec 29

ECLIPSES

Penumbral eclipse of the Moon . . . . Jan 31
Annular eclipse of the Sun . . . . Feb 16
Partial eclipse of the Moon . . . . July 28
Total eclipse of the Sun . . . . Aug 11

2000

PRINCIPAL PHENOMENA, 2000
EARTH

Perihelion . . . . Jan 3
Aphelion . . . . July 3
Equinoxes . . . . Mar 20, Sept 22
Solstices . . . . June 20, Dec 21

PHASES OF THE MOON

New Moon	First Quarter	Full Moon	Last Quarter
Jan 6	Jan 14	Jan 20	Jan 28
Feb 5	Feb 12	Feb 19	Feb 26
Mar 6	Mar 13	Mar 19	Mar 27
Apr 4	Apr 11	Apr 18	Apr 26
May 3	May 10	May 18	May 26
June 2	June 8	June 16	June 24
July 1	July 8	July 16	July 24
July 30	Aug 6	Aug 15	Aug 22
Aug 29	Sept 5	Sept 13	Sept 20
Sept 27	Oct 5	Oct 13	Oct 20
Oct 27	Nov 4	Nov 11	Nov 18
Nov 25	Dec 3	Dec 11	Dec 17
Dec 25			

ECLIPSES

Total eclipse of the Moon . . . . Jan 21
Partial eclipse of the Sun . . . . Feb 5
Partial eclipse of the Sun . . . . July 1
Total eclipse of the Moon . . . . July 16
Partial eclipse of the Sun . . . . July 31
Partial eclipse of the Sun . . . . Dec 25

LOOKING FORWARD

1999 • George Washington death, 200th anniversary
- International Year of Older Persons
- Control of Panama Canal reverts to Panama

2000 • Leap Year
- UN Second World Conference on Natural Disaster Reduction
- US presidential election
- Holy Year for Roman Catholic Church—Great Jubilee. For more info: http://www.vatican.va/
- Summer Olympics (Sydney, Australia)
- Expo 2000—world's fair in Hannover, Germany, with theme "Mankind, Nature and Technology"
- US population projected to be 275,000,000

2001 • 21st Century and Third Millennium of the Christian Era
- James Madison's birth, 250th anniversary

2002 • Winter Olympics (Salt Lake City)

2003 • Ohio Statehood Bicentennial
- Wright Brothers' first flight, 100th anniversary

2004 • First successful newspaper in America, 300th anniversary
- US presidential election

2006 • Benjamin Franklin's birth, 300th anniversary
- Woodrow Wilson's birth, 150th anniversary

2007 • Oklahoma Statehood Centennial
- Jamestown Colony, 400th anniversary
- Sputnik launched by USSR, 50th anniversary
- William H. Taft's birth, 150th anniversary

2008 • James Monroe's birth, 250th anniversary
- Andrew Johnson's birth, 200th anniversary
- Theodore Roosevelt's birth, 150th anniversary
- Lyndon Johnson's birth, 100th anniversary
- US presidential election

2009 • Abraham Lincoln's birth, 200th anniversary

2010 • US population projected to be 298,000,000

2011 • Ronald Reagan's birth, 100th anniversary

2012 • Arizona Statehood Centennial
- Louisiana Statehood Bicentennial
- New Mexico Statehood Centennial
- US presidential election

2013 • Richard Nixon's birth, 100th anniversary
- Gerald Ford's birth, 100th anniversary

2015 • US population projected to be 310,000,000

2016 • Indiana Statehood Bicentennial
- US presidential election

2017 • Mississippi Statehood Bicentennial
- John Q. Adams's birth, 250th anniversary
- Andrew Jackson's birth, 250th anniversary
- John F. Kennedy's birth, 100th anniversary

2018 • Illinois Statehood Bicentennial

2019 • Alabama Statehood Bicentennial
- Apollo 11 astronauts walk on moon, 50th anniversary

2020 • US population projected to be 323,000,000
- Maine State Bicentennial
- US presidential election

2050 • US population projected to be 383,000,000
- World population of 10 billion predicted

2061 • Halley's comet returns

SPACE OBJECTS BOX SCORE

The Space Objects Box Score, furnished by the NASA/Goddard Space Flight Center, reflects the numbers of objects now in orbit by type—payload or debris—and by owning nation or organization. It is based on data computed at Goddard Space Flight Center, or NORAD, or provided by satellite owners. The debris includes pieces launched into space along with the functioning payloads, as well as fragments produced by in-space breakups. More current information can be found on the Web at http://www.spacecom.af.mil/usspace/boxscore.htm

CURRENT AND HISTORIC STATUS (as of 1997)

	OBJECTS IN ORBIT			
COUNTRY	**SATELLITE**	**SPACE PROBES**	**DEBRIS**	**TOTAL**
ARGENTINA	5	0	0	5
ARAB SAT. COMM. ORG.	7	0	0	7
ASIASAT CORP	3	0	0	3
AUSTRALIA	6	0	2	8
BRAZIL	6	0	0	6
CANADA	15	0	0	15
CIS	1322	35	2525	3882
CZECH REPUBLIC	4	0	0	4
ESA	19	2	187	208
ETSO	10	0	0	10
FRANCE/GERMANY	2	0	0	2
FRANCE	29	0	16	45
GERMANY	12	2	1	15
IMSO	7	0	0	7
INDIA	14	0	3	17
INDONESIA	8	0	0	8
ISRAEL	2	0	0	2
ITALY	7	0	3	10
ITSO	51	0	0	51
JAPAN	57	4	58	119
LUXEMBOURG	6	0	0	6
MALAYSIA	2	0	0	2
MEXICO	5	0	0	5
NATO	8	0	0	8
NORWAY	2	0	0	2
PORTUGAL	1	0	0	1
PRC	17	0	97	114
SAUDI ARABIA	3	0	0	3
SOUTH KOREA	4	0	0	4
SPAIN	5	0	0	5
SWEDEN	5	0	0	5
THAILAND	3	0	0	3
TURKEY	2	0	0	2
UK	15	0	1	16
USA	667	38	3326	4031
TOTAL	2331	81	6219	8631

CIS: Russia/USSR
ESA: European Space Agency
ETRO: European Telecom Satellite Organization
IMSO: International Maritime Satellite Organization
ITSO: International Telecommunications Satellite Organization
PRC: People's Republic of China
UK: United Kingdom

Note: The change in the format of this information reflects a change in what information is released to the public.

UNIVERSAL, STANDARD AND DAYLIGHT TIMES

Universal Time (UT) is also known as Greenwich Mean Time (GMT) and is the standard time of the Greenwich meridian (0° of longitude). A time given in UT may be converted to local mean time by the addition of east longitude (or the subtraction of west longitude), where the longitude of the place is expressed in time-measure at the rate of one hour for every 15°. Local clock times may differ from standard times, especially in summer when clocks are often advanced by one hour ("daylight saving" or "summer" time).

The time used in this book is Eastern Standard Time. The following table provides conversion between Universal Time and all Time Zones in the United States. An asterisk denotes that the time is on the preceding day.

Universal Time	Eastern Daylight Time	Eastern Standard Time and Central Daylight Time	Central Standard Time and Mountain Daylight Time	Mountain Standard Time and Pacific Daylight Time	Pacific Standard Time
0^h	* 8 P. M.	* 7 P. M.	* 6 P. M.	* 5 P. M.	* 4 P. M.
1	* 9	* 8	* 7	* 6	* 5
2	*10	* 9	* 8	* 7	* 6
3	*11 P. M.	*10	* 9	* 8	* 7
4	0 Midnight	*11 P. M.	*10	* 9	* 8
5	1 A. M.	0 Midnight	*11 P. M.	*10	* 9
6	2	1 A. M.	0 Midnight	*11 P. M.	*10
7	3	2	1 A. M.	0 Midnight	*11 P. M.
8	4	3	2	1 A. M.	0 Midnight
9	5	4	3	2	1 A. M.
10	6	5	4	3	2
11	7	6	5	4	3
12	8	7	6	5	4
13	9	8	7	6	5
14	10	9	8	7	6
15	11 A. M.	10	9	8	7
16	12 Noon	11 A. M.	10	9	8
17	1 P. M.	12 Noon	11 A. M.	10	9
18	2	1 P. M.	12 Noon	11 A. M.	10
19	3	2	1 P. M.	12 Noon	11 A. M.
20	4	3	2	1 P. M.	12 Noon
21	5	4	3	2	1 P. M.
22	6	5	4	3	2
23	7 P. M.	6 P. M.	5 P. M.	4 P. M.	3 P. M.

The longitudes of the standard meridians for the standard time zones are:

Eastern . . . . . 75° West   Central . . . . . 90° West   Mountain . . . . . 105° West   Pacific . . . . . 120° West

LEAP SECONDS

The information below is developed by the editors from data supplied by the International Earth Rotation Service.

Because of Earth's slightly erratic rotation and the need for greater precision in time measurement it has become necessary to add a "leap second" from time to time to man's clocks to coordinate them with astronomical time. Rotation of the Earth has been slowing since 1900, making an astronomical second longer than an atomic second. Since 1972, by international agreement, adjustments have been made to keep astronomical and atomic clocks within 0.9 second of each other. The determination to add (or subtract) seconds is made by the Central Bureau of the International Earth Rotation Service, in Paris. Preferred times for adjustment have been June 30 and December 31, but any time may be designated by the International Earth Rotation Service. The first such adjustment was made in 1972, and as of June 30, 1997, a total of 21 leap seconds had been added. The additions have been made at 23:59:60 UTC (Coordinated Universal Time) = 6:59:60 EST (Eastern Standard Time). Leap seconds have been inserted into the UTC time scale on the following dates:

June 30, 1972	Dec 31, 1976	June 30, 1982	Dec 31, 1990
Dec 31, 1972	Dec 31, 1977	June 30, 1983	June 30, 1992
Dec 31, 1973	Dec 31, 1978	June 30, 1985	June 30, 1993
Dec 31, 1974	Dec 31, 1979	Dec 31, 1987	June 30, 1994
Dec 31, 1975	June 30, 1981	Dec 31, 1989	Dec 31, 1995
			June 30, 1997

WORLD MAP OF TIME ZONES

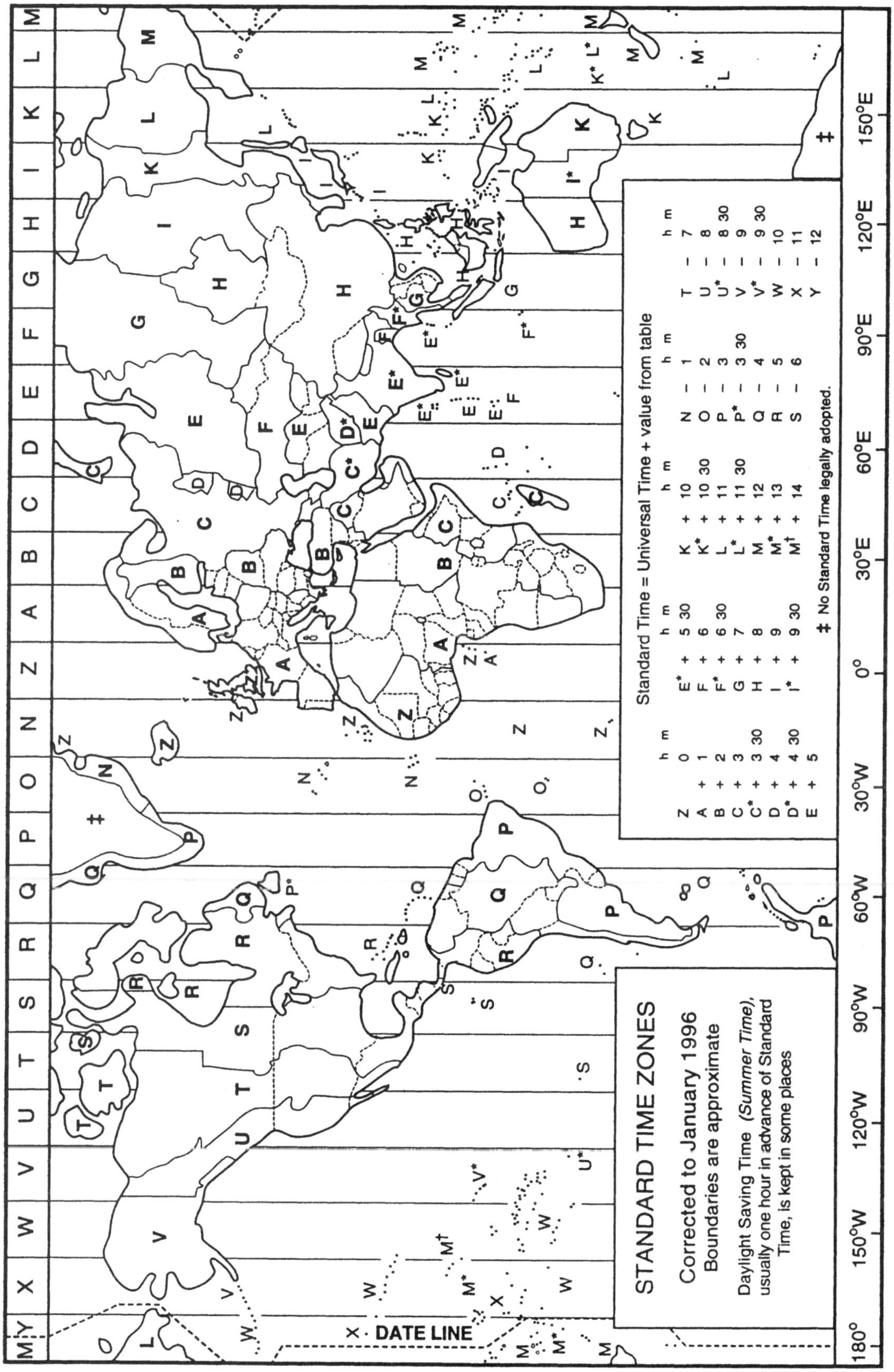

Reprinted from *Astronomical Phenomena for the Year 1992*, prepared jointly by the Nautical Almanac Office of the US Naval Observatory and Her Majesty's Nautical Almanac Office of the Royal Greenwich Observatory.

STATE GOVERNORS/US SENATORS/US SUPREME COURT

GOVERNORS
Name (Party, State)

Fob James, Jr (R, AL)
Tony Knowles (D, AK)
Fife Symington (R, AZ)
Mike Huckabee (R, AR)
Pete Wilson (R, CA)
Roy Romer (D, CO)
John Rowland (R, CT)
Tom Carper (D, DE)
Lawton Chiles (D, FL)
Zell Miller (D, GA)
Ben Cayetano (D, HI)
Phil Batt (R, ID)
Jim Edgar (R, IL)
Frank O'Bannon (D, IN)
Terry E. Branstad (R, IA)
Bill Graves (R, KS)
Paul E. Patton (D, KY)
Mike Foster (R, LA)
Angus King, Jr (I, ME)
Parris Glendening (D, MD)
William F. Weld (R, MA)
John Engler (R, MI)
Arne H. Carlson (R, MN)
Kirk Fordice (R, MS)
Mel Carnahan (D, MO)
Marc Racicot (R, MT)
E. Benjamin Nelson (D, NE)
Bob Miller (D, NV)
Jeanne Shaheen (D, NH)
Christine T. Whitman (R, NJ)*
Gary Johnson (R, NM)
George Pataki (R, NY)
James B. Hunt, Jr (D, NC)
Edward T. Schafer (R, ND)
George V. Voinovich (R, OH)
Frank Keating (R, OK)
John Kitzhaber (D, OR)
Thomas J. Ridge (R, PA)
Lincoln Almond (R, RI)
David Beasley (R, SC)
William Janklow (R, SD)
Don Sundquist (R, TN)
George W. Bush (R, TX)
Mike Leavitt (R, UT)
Howard Dean (D, VT)
George F. Allen (R, VA)*
Gary Locke (D, WA)
Cecil H. Underwood (R, WV)
Tommy G. Thompson (R, WI)
Jim Geringer (R, WY)

*Denotes governorship or senate seat up for reelection at press time.

SENATORS
Name (Party, State)

Jeff Sessions (R, AL)
Richard C. Shelby (R, AL)
Ted Stevens (R, AK)
Frank H. Murkowski (R, AK)
Jon Kyl (R, AZ)
John McCain (R, AZ)
Dale L. Bumpers (D, AR)
Tim Hutchinson (R, AR)
Dianne Feinstein (D, CA)
Barbara Boxer (D, CA)
Wayne Allard (R, CO)
Ben Nighthorse Campbell (R, CO)
Christopher J. Dodd (D, CT)
Joseph I. Lieberman (D, CT)
William V. Roth, Jr (R, DE)
Joseph R. Biden, Jr (D, DE)
Robert Graham (D, FL)
Connie Mack III (R, FL)
Max Cleland (D, GA)
Paul D. Coverdell (R, GA)
Daniel K. Inouye (D, HI)
Daniel K. Akaka (D, HI)
Larry E. Craig (R, ID)
Dirk Kempthorne (R, ID)
Richard J. Durbin (D, IL)
Carol Mosely-Braun (D, IL)
Richard G. Lugar (R, IN)
Dan Coats (R, IN)
Charles E. Grassley (R, IA)
Tom Harkin (D, IA)
Sam Brownback (R, KS)
Pat Roberts (R, KS)
Wendell H. Ford (D, KY)
Mitch McConnell (R, KY)
Mary L. Landrieu (D, LA)
John B. Breaux (D, LA)
Susan M. Collins (R, ME)
Olympia J. Snowe (R, ME)
Paul S. Sarbanes (D, MD)
Barbara A. Mikulski (D, MD)
Edward M. Kennedy (D, MA)
John F. Kerry (D, MA)
Spencer Abraham (R, MI)
Carl Levin (D, MI)
Rod Grams (R, MN)
Paul D. Wellstone (D, MN)
Thad Cochran (R, MS)
Trent Lott (R, MS)
John Ashcroft (R, MO)
Christopher S. Bond (R, MO)
Max S. Baucus (D, MT)
Conrad Burns (R, MT)
Chuck Hagel (R, NE)
J. Robert Kerrey (D, NE)
Harry M. Reid (D, NV)
Richard H. Bryan (D, NV)
Robert C. Smith (R, NH)
Judd Gregg (R, NH)
Robert G. Torricelli (D, NJ)
Frank R. Lautenberg (D, NJ)
Pete V. Domenici (R, NM)
Jeff Bingaman (D, NM)
Daniel Patrick Moynihan (D, NY)
Alfonse M. D'Amato (R, NY)
Jesse A. Helms (R, NC)
Lauch Faircloth (R, NC)
Kent Conrad (D, ND)
Byron L. Dorgan (D, ND)
John Glenn (D, OH)
Mike DeWine (R, OH)
James M. Inhofe (R, OK)
Don Nickles (R, OK)
Gordon Smith (R, OR)
Ron Wyden (D, OR)
Arlen Specter (R, PA)
Rick Santorum (R, PA)
Jack Reed (D, RI)
John H. Chafee (R, RI)
Strom Thurmond (R, SC)
Ernest F. Hollings (D, SC)
Tim Johnson (D, SD)
Thomas A. Daschle (D, SD)
William Frist (R, TN)
Fred D. Thompson (R, TN)
Phil Gramm (R, TX)
Kay Bailey Hutchison (R, TX)
Orrin G. Hatch (R, UT)
Robert F. Bennett (R, UT)
Patrick J. Leahy (D, VT)
James M. Jeffords (R, VT)
John W. Warner (R, VA)
Charles S. Robb (D, VA)
Slade Gorton (R, WA)
Patty Murray (D, WA)
Robert C. Byrd (D, WV)
John D. Rockefeller IV (D, WV)
Herbert H. Kohl (D, WI)
Russell D. Feingold (D, WI)
Michael B. Enzi (R, WY)
Craig Thomas (R, WY)

SUPREME COURT JUSTICES
Name (Appointed by, Year)

William H. Rehnquist, Chief Justice (Reagan, 1986)
John P. Stevens (Ford, 1975)
Sandra Day O'Connor (Reagan, 1981)
Antonin Scalia (Reagan, 1986)
Anthony M. Kennedy (Reagan, 1988)
David H. Souter (Bush, 1990)
Clarence Thomas (Bush, 1991)
Ruth Bader Ginsburg (Clinton, 1993)
Stephen G. Breyer (Clinton, 1994)

THE NAMING OF HURRICANES

(Compiled from information issued by the US Department of Commerce, National Oceanic and Atmospheric Administration.)

Why are hurricanes named? Experience shows that the use of short, distinctive names greatly reduces confusion when two or more tropical storms occur at the same time. The use of easily remembered names in written and spoken communication is quicker and less subject to error than the older, more cumbersome latitude-longitude identification methods, advantages which are especially important in exchanging detailed storm information between hundreds of widely scattered stations, airports, coastal bases and ships at sea.

The practice of naming hurricanes began hundreds of years ago, but only relatively recently did they begin to be named solely for women. During World War II forecasters and meteorologists began using female names for storms in weather map discussions, and in 1953 the US weather services adopted the practice, creating a new international phonetic alphabet of women's names from A–W to name hurricanes. In 1978 men's names were also introduced into the storm lists.

Because hurricanes affect other nations and are tracked by their weather services, the lists have an international flavor. Names are agreed upon during international meetings of the World Meteorological Organization by the nations involved, and can be retired and replaced with new names in the event of particularly severe storms.

The National Hurricane Center near Miami, FL, keeps a constant watch on oceanic storm-breeding areas for tropical disturbances that may herald the formation of a hurricane. If a disturbance intensifies into a tropical storm—with rotary circulation and wind speeds above 39 miles per hour—the Center will give the storm a name from one of six lists. The Atlantic and Eastern Pacific lists are rotated year by year so that the 1998 set, for example, will be used again to name storms in 2004.

The four lists of names for Central Pacific and Western Pacific hurricanes (tropical cyclones) are not rotated on a yearly basis. Meteorologists follow each list until all those names have been used, then go on to the next list. The name of a particularly severe storm is retired and replaced. For example, Iniki—the name of the hurricane that devastated Hawaii—has been replaced with Iolona on List 2.

ATLANTIC HURRICANE NAMES

1998	1999	2000
ALEX	ARLENE	ALBERTO
BONNIE	BRET	BERYL
CHARLEY	CINDY	CHRIS
DANIELLE	DENNIS	DEBBY
EARL	EMILY	ERNESTO
FRANCES	FLOYD	FLORENCE
GEORGES	GERT	GORDON
HERMINE	HARVEY	HELENE
IVAN	IRENE	ISAAC
JEANNE	JOSE	JOYCE
KARL	KATRINA	KEITH
LISA	LENNY	LESLIE
MITCH	MARIA	MICHAEL
NICOLE	NATE	NADINE
OTTO	OPHELIA	OSCAR
PAULA	PHILIPPE	PATTY
RICHARD	RITA	RAFAEL
SHARY	STAN	SANDY
TOMAS	TAMMY	TONY
VIRGINIE	VINCE	VALERIE
WALTER	WILMA	WILLIAM

EASTERN PACIFIC HURRICANE NAMES

1998	1999	2000
AGATHA	ADRIAN	ALETTA
BLAS	BEATRIZ	BUD
CELIA	CALVIN	CARLOTTA
DARBY	DORA	DANIEL
ESTELLE	EUGENE	EMILIA
FRANK	FERNANDA	FABIO
GEORGETTE	GREG	GILMA
HOWARD	HILARY	HECTOR
ISIS	IRWIN	ILEANA
JAVIER	JOVA	JOHN
KAY	KENNETH	KRISTY
LESTER	LIDIA	LANE
MADELINE	MAX	MIRIAM
NEWTON	NORMA	NORMAN
ORLENE	OTIS	OLICIA
PAINE	PILAR	PAUL
ROSLYN	RAMON	ROSA
SEYMOUR	SELMA	SERGIO
TINA	TODD	TARA
VIRGIL	VERONICA	VICENTE
WINIFRED	WILEY	WILLA
XAVIER	XINA	XAVIER
YOLANDA	YORK	YOLANDA
ZEKE	ZELDA	ZEKE

If over 24 tropical cyclones occur in a year, then the Greek alphabet will be used following Zeke or Zelda.

CENTRAL PACIFIC TROPICAL CYCLONE NAMES

LIST1		LIST 2	
AKONI	ah-KOH-nee	AKA	AH-kah
EMA	EH-ma	EKEKA	eh-KEH-kah
HANA	HAH-nah	HALI	HAH-lee
IO	EE-oo	IOLANA	ee-OH-lah-nah
KELI	KEH-lee	KEONI	keh-OH-nee
LALA	LAH-lah	LI	LEE
MOKE	MOH-keh	MELE	MEH-leh
NELE	NEH-leh	NONA	NOH-nah
OKA	OH-kah	OLIWA	oh-LEE-vah
PEKE	PEH-keh	PAKA	PAH-kah
ULEKI	oo-LEH-kee	UPANA	oo-PAH-nah
WILA	VEE-lah	WENE	WEH-neh
LIST 3		**LIST 4**	
ALIKA	ah-LEE-kah	ANA	AH-nah
ELE	EH-leh	ELA	EH-lah
HUKO	HOO-koh	HALOLA	hah-LOH-lah
IOKE	ee-OH-keh	IUNE	ee-OO-neh
KIKA	KEE-kah	KIMO	KEE-moh
LANA	LAH-nah	LOKE	LOH-keh
MAKA	MAH-kah	MALIA	mah-LEE-ah
NEKI	NEH-kee	NIALA	nee-AH-lah
OLEKA	oh-LEH-kah	OKO	OH-koh
PENI	PEH-nee	PALI	PAH-lee
ULIA	oo-LEE-ah	ULIKA	oo-LEE-kah
WALI	WAH-lee	WALAKA	wah-LAH-kah

In Hawaiian, all letters are pronounced, including double or triple vowels.

WESTERN PACIFIC TROPICAL CYCLONE NAMES

LIST 1	LIST 2	LIST 3	LIST 4
ANN	ABEL	AMBER	ALEX
BART	BETH	BING	BABS
CAM	CARLO	CASS	CHIP
DAN	DALE	DAVID	DAWN
EVE	ERNIE	ELLA	ELVIS
FRANKIE	FERN	FRITZ	FAITH
GLORIA	GREG	GINGER	GIL
HERB	HANNAH	HANK	HILDA
IAN	ISA	IVAN	IRIS
JOY	JIMMY	JOAN	JACOB
KIRK	KELLY	KEITH	KATE
LISA	LEVI	LINDA	LEO
MARTY	MARIE	MORT	MAGGIE
NIKI	NESTOR	NICHOLE	NEIL
ORSON	OPAL	OTTO	OLGA
PIPER	PETER	PENNY	PAUL
RICK	ROSIE	REX	RACHEL
SALLY	SCOTT	STELLA	SAM
TOM	TINA	TODD	TANYA
VIOLET	VICTOR	VICKI	VIRGIL
WILLIE	WINNIE	WALDO	WENDY
YATES	YULE	YANNI	YORK
ZANE	ZITA	ZEB	ZIA

BROADCASTING HALL OF FAME

1977
William S. Paley, entrepreneur
Jack Benny, comedian
Fred Allen, comedian
Lowell Thomas, news reporter and commentator
Edward R. Murrow, news reporter and commentator
Milton Cross, music commentator
David Sarnoff, entrepreneur
Ted Husing, sportscaster
Edwin H. Armstrong, inventor
Herbert Hoover, president of the United States
Gene Autry, singer, entertainer
Freeman F. Gosden (Amos) and Charles J. Correll (Andy), comedians
Bob Hope, comedian
Gordon McNamee, announcer

1978
Jim Jordan and Marian Jordan (Fibber McGee and Molly), comedians
Walter Winchell, commentator
Guglielmo Marconi, inventor
Arthur Godfrey, personality
Orson Welles, producer, actor, director of radio, motion pictures and theatre

1979
Paul Harvey, commentator

1980
George Burns, comedian
Bing Crosby, singer/entertainer

1981
Ronald Reagan (Dutch Reagan), president of the United States
Kate Smith, singer, entertainer

1982
Don McNeill, entertainer
Edgar Bergen, comedian

1983
Charles Lauk (Lum) and Norris Goff (Abner), comedians
Benny Goodman, entertainer

1984
Red Skelton, comedian
Bob Elliot and Ray Goulding, entertainers

1985
Fred Palmer, broadcaster, consultant
Casey Kasem, personality, announcer

1986
Mel Allen, sportscaster
Earl Nightingale, commentator

1987
Robert Trout, political journalist
Gordon B. McLendon, innovator
Robert Todd Storz, industry leader

1988
William B. Williams, personality
Roy Acuff, singer
Milton Berle, comedian
Lucille Ball, comedienne

1989
Ernie Kovacs, comedian
Sid Caesar, comedian
Red Barber, sportscaster
Nathan Safir, Spanish broadcasting pioneer

1990
Hal Jackson, entrepreneur
Charles Osgood, correspondent
"The Honeymooners" and Its Original Cast (Art Carney, Audrey Meadows, Joyce Randolph, Jackie Gleason), entertainers
Sylvester L. (Pat) Weaver, TV programming pioneer

1991
Jerry Lewis, comedian
Douglas Edwards, radio correspondent

1992
Larry King, radio personality
"Star Trek," TV series

1993
"60 Minutes," TV program
"Grand Ole Opry," radio program

1994
Harry Caray, radio program
Roone Arledge, network news president

1995
Carol Burnett, TV entertainer
Gary Owens, radio personality

1996
Don Imus, radio personality
"M*A*S*H," cast of TV series

1997
"Today," cast of TV's "Today" show
Wally Phillips, radio personality

THE ACADEMY OF TELEVISION ARTS AND SCIENCES (ATAS) TELEVISION HALL OF FAME

The Academy of Television Arts & Sciences Television Academy Hall of Fame was established in 1984 to recognize the lifelong accomplishments of television's greatest contributors, including, in addition to those who appear before the camera, those who contribute to the industry as writers, executives and producers.

Bronze sculptures and bas reliefs of some of the Hall of Fame's inductees have been erected in the Hall of Fame Plaza. Located in the forecourt of the Television Academy's North Hollywood international headquarters, the plaza's centerpiece is a 27-foot Emmy statue, a replica of the internationally famous Emmy statuette, symbol of television excellence.

1984
Lucille Ball
Milton Berle
Paddy Chayefsky
Norman Lear
Edward R. Murrow
Edward S. Paley
General David Sarnoff

1985
Carol Burnett
Sid Caesar
Walter Cronkite
Joyce C. Hall
Rod Serling
Ed Sullivan
Sylvester "Pat" Weaver

1986
Steve Allen
Fred Coe
Walt Disney
Jackie Gleason
Mary Tyler Moore
Frank Stanton
Burr Tillstrom

1987
Johnny Carson
Jaques-Yves Cousteau
Leonard Goldenson
Jim Henson
Bob Hope
Ernie Kovacs

1988
Jack Benny
George Burns
Gracie Allen
Chet Huntley
David Brinkley
Red Skelton
David Susskind
David Wolper

1989
Roone Arledge
Fred Astaire
Perry Como
Joan Ganz Cooney
Don Hewitt
Carroll O'Connor
Barbara Walters

1990
Desi Arnaz
Leonard Bernstein
James Garner
"I Love Lucy"
Danny Thomas
Mike Wallace

1991
Bill Cosby
Andy Griffith
Ted Koppel
Sheldon Leonard
Dinah Shore
Ted Turner

1992
Dick Clark
John Chancellor
Phil Donahue
Mark Goodson
Bob Newhart
Agnes Nixon
Jack Webb

1993
Alan Alda
Howard Cosell
Barry Diller
Fred Friendly
William Hanna/Joseph Barbera
Oprah Winfrey

1994
Michael Landon
Richard Levinson and William Link
Jim McKay
Bill Moyers
Dick Van Dyke
Betty White

1995
Edward Asner
Steven Bochco
Marcy Carsey/Tom Werner
Charles Kuralt
Angela Lansbury
Aaron Spelling
Lew R. Wasserman

MAJOR AWARDS

1996–97 SEASON TONY AWARDS

ANNUAL
Play: *The Last Night of Ballyhoo*
Musical: *Titanic*
Play Revival: *A Doll's House*, Producer: Bill Kenwright, Thelma Holt
Musical Revival: *Chicago*, Producer: Barry Weissler, Fran Weissler, Kardana Productions Inc.
Leading Actor in a Play: Christopher Plummer, *Barrymore*
Leading Actress in a Play: Janet McTeer, *A Doll's House*
Leading Actor in a Musical: James Naughton, *Chicago*
Leading Actress in a Musical: Bebe Neuwirth, *Chicago*
Book of a Musical: Peter Stone, *Titanic*
Original Musical Score: Maury Yeston, *Titanic*
Director of a Play: Anthony Page, *A Doll's House*
Director of a Musical: Walter Bobbie, *Chicago*
Featured Actor in a Play: Owen Teale, *A Doll's House*
Featured Actress in a Play: Lynne Thigpen, *An American Daughter*
Featured Actor in a Musical: Chuck Cooper, *The Life*
Featured Actress in a Musical: Lillias White, *The Life*
Scenic Design: Stewart Laing, *Titanic*
Costume Design: Judith Dolan, *Candide*
Lighting Design: Ken Billington, *Chicago*
Choreography: Ann Reinking, *Chicago*
Orchestration: Jonathan Tunick, *Titanic*
Special Award for Regional Theater: Berkeley Repertory Theatre, Berkeley, CA

1996 ACADEMY AWARDS (OSCARS)

Picture: *The English Patient*
Actor: Geoffrey Rush, *Shine*
Actress: Frances McDormand, *Fargo*
Director: Anthony Minghella, *The English Patient*
Supporting Actor: Cuba Gooding, Jr, *Jerry Maguire*
Supporting Actress: Juliette Binoche, *The English Patient*
Original Screenplay: Joel Coen, *Fargo*
Adapted Screenplay: Billy Bob Thornton, *Sling Blade*
Cinematography: *The English Patient*
Art Direction: *The English Patient*
Film Editing: Walter Murch, *The English Patient*
Foreign Language Film: *Kolya*
Animated Short Film: *Quest*
Documentary Feature: Leon Gast, Taylor Hackford, *When We Were Kings*
Documentary Short Subject: Jessica Yu, *Breathing Lessons: The Life and Work of Mark O'Brien*
Costume Design: Ann Roth, *The English Patient*
Sound Design: *The English Patient*
Visual Effects: *Independence Day*
Makeup: *The Nutty Professor*
Sound Effects Editing: *The Ghost and the Darkness*
Live Action Short Film: *Dear Diary*
Original Score (Musical or Comedy): *Emma*
Original Score (Drama): *The English Patient*
Original Song: "Evita" from *Evita*

1996 AMERICAN MUSIC AWARDS (Awarded January 27, 1997) 23rd Annual Awards

POP/ROCK
Male Vocalist: Eric Clapton
Female Vocalist: Alanis Morissette
Band, Duo or Group: Hootie & the Blowfish
Album: *Jagged Little Pill,* Alanis Morissette
New Artist: Jewel

SOUL/RHYTHM & BLUES
Male Vocalist: Keith Sweat
Female Vocalist: Toni Braxton
Band, Duo or Group: New Edition
Album: *Secrets,* Toni Braxton
New Artist: D'Angelo

COUNTRY
Male Vocalist: Garth Brooks
Female Vocalist: Shania Twain
Band, Duo or Group: Brooks & Dunn
Album: *Blue Clear Sky,* George Strait
New Artist: LeAnn Rimes

HEAVY METAL/HARD ROCK
Artist: Metallica

RAP/HIP HOP
Artist: 2PAC

ADULT CONTEMPORARY
Artist: Whitney Houston

ALTERNATIVE MUSIC
Artist: The Smashing Pumpkins

SOUNDTRACK
Waiting to Exhale

INTERNATIONAL ARTIST OF THE YEAR
Bee Gees

AWARD OF MERIT
Little Richard

1997 GRAMMY AWARDS

Record of the Year: "Change the World," Eric Clapton
Album of the Year: *Falling Into You*, Celine Dion
Song of the Year: "Change the World," Gordon Kennedy, Wayne Kirkpatrick, Tommy Sims, songwriter
Best New Artist: LeAnn Rimes
Best Female Pop Vocal Performance: "Unbreak My Heart," Toni Braxton
Best Male Pop Vocal Performance: "Change the World," Eric Clapton
Best Pop Performance by a Duo or Group with Vocal: "Free as a Bird," Beatles
Best Pop Collaboration with Vocals: "When I Fall in Love," Natalie Cole and Nat King Cole
Best Pop Instrumental Performance: "The Sinister Minister," Bela Fleck and the Flecktones
Best Pop Album: *Falling Into You*, Celine Dion
Best Traditional Pop Vocal Performance: "Here's to the Ladies," Tony Bennett
Best Female Rock Vocal Performance: "If It Makes You Happy," Sheryl Crow
Best Male Rock Vocal Performance: "Where It's At," Beck
Best Rock Performance by a Duo or Group with Vocal: "So Much to Say," Dave Matthews Band
Best Hard Rock Performance: "Bullet with Butterfly Wings," Smashing Pumpkins
Best Metal Performance: "Tire Me," Rage Against the Machine
Best Rock Instrumental Performance: "SRV Shuffle," Jimmie Vaughan, Eric Clapton, Bonnie Raitt, Robert Cray, B.B. King, Buddy Guy, Dr. John and Art Neville
Best Rock Song: "Give Me One Reason," Tracy Chapman
Best Rock Album: *Sheryl Crow*, Sheryl Crow
Best Alternative Music Performance: "Odelay," Beck
Best Female R&B Vocal Performance: "You're Makin' Me High," Toni Braxton
Best Male R&B Vocal Performance: "Your Secret Love," Luther Vandross
Best R&B Performance by a Duo or Group with Vocal: "Killing Me Softly with His Song," Fugees
Best R&B Song: "Exhale (Shoop Shoop)," Babyface
Best R&B Album: *Words*, Tony Rich Project
Best Rap Solo Performance: "Hey Lover," LL Cool J
Best Rap Performance by a Duo or Group: "Tha Crossroads," Bone Thugs-n-Harmony
Best Rap Album: *The Score*, Fugees
Best Female Country Vocal Performance: "Blue," LeAnn Rimes
Best Male Country Vocal Performance: "Worlds Apart," Vince Gill
Best Country Performance by a Duo or Group with Vocal: "My Maria," Brooks and Dunn
Best Country Collaboration with Vocals: "High Lonesome Sound," Vince Gill featuring Alison Krauss and Union Station
Best Country Instrumental Performance: "Jam Man," Chet Atkins
Best Country Song: "Blue," Bill Mack
Best Country Album: *The Road to Ensenada*, Lyle Lovett
Best Bluegrass Album: *True Life Blues: The Songs of Bill Monroe*, various artists
Best New Age Album: *The Memory of Trees*, Enya
Best Contemporary Jazz Performance: "High Life," Wayne Shorter
Best Jazz Vocal Performance: "New Moon Daughter," Cassandra Wilson
Best Jazz Instrumental Solo: "Cabin Fever," Michael Brecker
Best Jazz Instrumental Performance, Individual or Group: "Tales from the Hudson," Michael Brecker
Best Large Jazz Ensemble Performance: Live at Manchester Craftsmen's Guild, Count Basie Orchestra
Best Latin Jazz Performance: "Portraits of Cuba," Paquito D'Rivera
Best Rock Gospel Album: *Jesus Freak*, DC Talk

Best Pop/Contemporary Gospel Album: *Tribute: The Songs of Andrae Crouch*, various artists
Best Southern Gospel, Country Gospel or Bluegrass Gospel Album: *I Love to Tell the Story: 25 Timeless Hymns*, Andy Griffith
Best Traditional Soul Gospel Album: *Face to Face*, Cissy Houston
Best Contemporary Soul Gospel Album: *Whatcha Lookin' 4*, Kirk Franklin and the Family
Best Gospel Album by a Choir or Chorus: *Just A Word*, Shirley Caesar's Outreach Convention Choir
Best Latin Pop Album: *Enrique Iglesias*, Enrique Iglesias
Best Tropical Latin Performance: *La Rosa de los Vientos*, Ruben Blades
Best Mexican-American Performance: *Un Millon de Rosas*, La Mafia
Best Traditional Blues Performance: *Deep in the Blues*, James Cotton
Best Contemporary Blues Album: *Just Like You*, Keb' Mo'
Best Traditional Folk Album: *Pete*, Pete Seeger
Best Contemporary Folk Album: *The Ghost of Tom Joad*, Bruce Springsteen
Best Reggae Album: *Hall of Fame: A Tribute to Bob Marley's 50th Anniversary*, Bunny Wailer
Best World Music Album: *Santiago*, the Chieftains
Best Polka Album: *Polka! All Night Long*, Jimmy Sturr
Best Musical Album for Children: *Dedicated to the One I Love*, Linda Ronstadt
Best Spoken Word Album for Children: *Stellaluna*, Virginia Callaway, Steven Heller, and David Holt, producers
Best Spoken Word or Non-Musical Album: *It Takes a Village*, Hillary Rodham Clinton
Best Spoken Comedy Album: *Rush Limbaugh Is a Big Fat Idiot*, Al Franken
Best Musical Show Album: *Riverdance*
Best Instrumental Composition: "Manhattan (Island of Lights and Love)," Herbie Hancock and Jean Hancock
Best Instrumental Composition Written for a Motion Picture or for Television: "Independence Day," David Arnold
Best Song Written Specifically for a Motion Picture or for Television: "Because You Loved Me" (from *Up Close and Personal*), Diane Warren
Best Instrumental Arrangement: "An American Symphony," Michael Kamen
Best Instrumental Arrangement with Accompanying Vocal(s): "When I Fall in Love," Alan Broadbent, David Foster and Gordon Jenkins
Best Recording Package: *Ultra-Lounge* (Leopard Skin Sampler), Andy Engel and Tommy Steele
Best Recording Package-Boxed: *The Complete Columbia Studio Recordings* (Miles Davis and Gil Evans), Chika Azuma and Arnold Levine
Best Album Notes: *The Complete Columbia Studio Recordings*, (Miles Davis and Gil Evans), George Avakian, Bob Belden, Bill Kirchner and Phil Schaap

Best Historical Album: *The Complete Columbia Studio Recordings*, (Miles Davis and Gil Evans)
Best Engineered Album, Non-Classical: *Q's Jook Joint*, Francis Buckley, Al Schmitt, Bruce Swedien and Tommy Vicari
Producer of the Year: Babyface
Best Classical Engineered Recording: *Copland: Dance Symphony, Short Symphony, Organ Symphony*, etc., William Hoekstra and Lawrence Rock
Classical Producer of the Year: Joanna Nickrenz
Best Classical Album: *Corigliano: Of Rage and Remembrance (Symphony No. 1, etc.)*, Leonard Slatkin, conductor
Best Orchestral Performance: *Prokofiev: Romeo and Juliet* (scenes from the ballet), Michael Tilson Thomas, conducting the San Francisco Symphony
Best Opera Recording: *Britten: Peter Grimes*, Richard Hickox, conductor; Philip Langridge, Alan Opie and Janice Watson, principal soloists
Best Choral Performance: *Walton: Belshazzar's Feast*, Andrew Litton, conductor, Bournemouth Symphony Chorus; L'Inviti; Waynflete Singers and Bournemouth Symphony Orchestra
Best Instrumental Soloist(s) Performance (With Orchestra): *Bartok: The Three Piano Concertos*, Yefim Bronfman
Best Instrumental Soloist Performance (Without Orchestra): *The Romantic Master*, Earl Wild
Best Chamber Music Performance: *Corigliano: String Quartet*, Cleveland Quartet
Best Small Ensemble Album: *Boulez: . . . Explosante-Fixe . . .*, Pierre Boulez, conductor
Best Classical Vocal Performance: *Opera Arias* (works of Mozart, Wagner, Borodin, etc.), Bryn Terfel
Best Classical Contemporary Composition: *John Corigliano, String Quartet*
Best Music Video, Short Form: *Free as a Bird*, Beatles
Best Music Video, Long Form: *The Beatles Anthology*, Beatles

---

27TH ANNUAL DOVE AWARDS GOSPEL MUSIC ASSOCIATION

Song of the Year: "Butterfly Kisses," Bob Carlisle and Randy Thomas
Songwriter of the Year: Steven Curtis Chapman
Male Vocalist of the Year: Steven Curtis Chapman
Female Vocalist of the Year: CeCe Winans
Group of the Year: Jars of Clay
Artist of the Year: Steven Curtis Chapman
New Artist of the Year: Jaci Valasquez
Alternative/Modern Rock Album: *Free Flying Soul*, The Choir
Rock Album: *Jesus Freak*, dc Talk
Pop/Contemporary Album: *Signs of Life*, Steven Curtis Chapman
Inspirational Album: *Quiet Prayers (My Utmost for His Highest)*, Bryan Duncan
Southern Gospel Album: *Wherever You Are*, The Martins
Country Album: *Little Bit of Faith*, Jeff Silvey
Traditional Gospel Album: *Just A Word*, Shirley Caesar's Outreach Convention Choir
Contemporary Gospel Album of the Year: *Whatcha Lookn' 4*, Kirk Franklin & The Family
Special Event Album: *Tribute: The Songs of Andrae Crouch*, various artists
Instrumental Album: *The Players*, Michael Omartian, Dann Huff, Tommy Sims, Tom Hemby, Terry McMillan, Chris Rodriguez, Shane Keister, Mark Douthit and Eric Darken
Praise and Worship Album: *Welcome Home*, Ron Kenoly
Children's Music Album: *A Very Veggie Christmas (Veggie Tales)*, Phil Vischer, Kurt Heinecke and Mike Nawrocki
Rap/Hip Hop Recorded Song: "R.I.O.T. (Righteous Invasion of Truth)," R.I.O.T.
Alternative/Modern Rock Recorded Song: "Epidermis Girl," Bleach
Rock Recorded Song: "Like It, Love It, Need It," dc Talk
Pop/Contemporary Recorded Song: "Between You and Me," dc Talk
Inspirational Recorded Song: "Butterfly Kisses," Bob Carlisle
Southern Gospel Recorded Song: "Only God Knows," The Martins
Country Recorded Song: "Somebody Was Prayin' for Me," Charlie Daniels
Urban Recorded Song: "Under the Influence," Anointed

Traditional Gospel Recorded Song: "Stop By the Church," Babbie Mason
Contemporary Gospel Recorded Song: "Take Me Back," CeCe Winans
Producer: Charlie Peacock
Musical: "Make Us One," Babbie Mason, Kenny Mann and David T. Clydesdale (creators)
Youth/Children's Musical: "Candy Cane Lane," Celeste Clydesdale (creator)
Choral Collections: "My Tribute: Celebrating the Songs of Andrae Crouch," Dale Matthews (creator)
Recorded Music Packaging: *Take Me To Your Leader*
Short Form Video: *Jesus Freak*, dc Talk
Long Form Video: *Roadwork*, Geoff Moore & The Distance

1996 ACE AWARDS

Dramatic Series: "The Outer Limits," Showtime
Comedy Series: "The Larry Sanders Show," HBO
Comedy Special: "Tracey Takes On," HBO
Actor in a Comedy Series: Garry Shandling, "The Larry Sanders Show," HBO
Actress in a Comedy Series: Tracey Ullman, "Tracey Takes On," HBO
Writing a Comedy Series: Judd Apatow, Jeff Cesario, Garry Shandling, "The Larry Sanders Show," HBO
Directing a Comedy Series: Todd Holland, "The Larry Sanders Show," HBO
Actor in a Dramatic Special or Series: Danny Glover, "America's Dream: 'Long Black Song,'" HBO
Actress in a Dramatic Special or Series: Donna Murphy, "Someone Had to Be Benny," HBO
Writing a Dramatic Special or Series: Ron Stacker Thompson, Ashley Tyler, "America's Dream: 'The Boy Who Painted Christ Black,'" HBO
Directing a Dramatic Special or Series: Bill Duke, "America's Dream: 'The Boy Who Painted Christ Black,'" HBO
Actor in a Movie or Miniseries: Gary Sinise, *Truman*, HBO
Actress in a Movie or Miniseries: Sela Ward, *Almost Golden: The Jessica Savitch Story*, Lifetime
Supporting Actor in a Movie or Miniseries: Tom Hulce, *The Heidi Chronicles*, TNT
Supporting Actress in a Movie or Miniseries: Amanda Plummer, *The Right to Remain Silent*, Showtime
Writing a Movie or Miniseries: John Kane, *Daisies in December*, Showtime
Directing a Movie or Miniseries: Robert Markowitz, *The Tuskegee Airmen*, HBO
Performance in a Comedy Special: Julia Sweeney, "Lifetime Applauds: The Fight Against Breast Cancer," Lifetime
Directing a Comedy Special: Denis Leary, "National Lampoon's Favorite Deadly Sins: Lust," Showtime
Informational or Documentary Host: David Attenborough, "The Private Life of Plants," TBS Superstation
Writing an Entertainment Special: Dennis Miller, "HBO Comedy Hour: Dennis Miller: 'Citizen Arcane,'" HBO
Entertainment/Cultural Documentary Special: "The Typewriter, The Rifle and The Movie Camera," Independent Film Channel
Talk Show Series: "Politically Incorrect with Bill Maher," Comedy Central
Educational or Instructional Special or Series: "Blacklist: Hollywood on Trial," American Movie Classics
Magazine Host: Ian Wright, "Lonely Planet: Central Asia," The Travel Channel
Sports Events Coverage Special: "Baltimore Orioles Baseball: 'Ripken's 2131st Game,'" Home Team Sports
Animation Special or Series: "Duckman," USA Network

PEN/FAULKNER AWARD FOR FICTION (1996)

(An award given by an organization of writers to honor their peers)

Gina Berriault, *Women in Their Beds*

1996 GOLDEN GLOBE AWARDS—54RD ANNUAL For 1996 Achievement

MOVIES

Drama: *The English Patient*
Musical or Comedy: *Evita*
Director: Milos Forman, *The People vs. Larry Flynt*
Actor, Drama: Geoffrey Rush, *Shine*
Actress, Drama: Brenda Blethyn, *Secrets and Lies*
Actor, Musical or Comedy: Tom Cruise, *Jerry Maguire*
Actress, Musical or Comedy: Madonna, *Evita*
Supporting Actor: Edward Norton, *Primal Fear*
Supporting Actress: Lauren Bacall, *The Mirror Has Two Faces*
Screenplay: *The People vs. Larry Flynt*
Foreign Film: Czech Republic, *Kolya*
Original Score: Gabriel Yared, *The English Patient*
Original Song: "You Must Love Me," *Evita*
Cecil B. De Mille Award 1997: Dustin Hoffman

TELEVISION

Series, Musical or Comedy: "3rd Rock from the Sun"
Actor, Series, Musical or Comedy: John Lithgow, "3rd Rock from the Sun"
Actress, Series, Musical or Comedy: Helen Hunt, "Mad About You"
Series, Drama: "The X-Files"
Actor, Series, Drama: David Duchovny, "The X-Files"
Actress, Series, Drama: Gillian Anderson, "The X-Files"
Miniseries or TV Movie: *Rasputin*
Actor, Miniseries or TV Movie: Alan Rickman, *Rasputin*
Actress, Miniseries or TV Movie: Helen Mirren, *Losing Chase*
Actor, Supporting Role: Ian McKellan, *Rasputin*
Actress, Supporting Role: Kathy Bates, *The Late Shift*

1996 GEORGE POLK AWARDS

(Awarded for special achievement in journalism)

Magazine Reporting: Anne-Marie Cusac, *The Progressive*
Cultural Reporting: Chuck Philips, *The Los Angeles Times*
Economics Reporting: *The New York Times*
Criticism: Blair Kamin, *Chicago Tribune*
Political Reporting: *The Los Angeles Times*
Transportation Reporting: Byron Acohido, *The Seattle Times*
Local Reporting: Kevin Collison, *The Buffalo News*
National Reporting: Elizabeth A. Marchak, *The Plain Dealer*
Foreign Reporting: John Burns, *The New York Times*
Network Television Reporting: Matt Meagher and Tim Peek, Inside Edition
Foreign Television Reporting: Christiane Amanpour and Anita Pratap, CNN

1997 AMERICAN LIBRARY ASSOCIATION AWARDS FOR CHILDREN'S BOOKS

NEWBERY MEDAL

For most distinguished contribution to American literature for children published in 1996:
Elaine Konigsburg, author, *The View from Saturday*

Honor Books

Nancy Farmer, author, *A Girl Named Disaster*
Eloise McGraw, author, *Moorchild*
Megan Whalen Turner, author, *The Thief*
Ruth White, author, *Belle Prater's Boy*

CALDECOTT MEDAL

For most distinguished American picture book for children published in 1996:
David Wisniewski, illustrator, *Golem*

Honor Books

Holly Meade, illustrator, *Hush! A Thai Lullaby*
David Pelletier, illustrator, *The Graphic Alphabet*
Dav Pilkey, illustrator, *The Paperboy*
Peter Sis, illustrator, *Starry Messenger*

CORETTA SCOTT KING AWARD

For outstanding books by African-American authors and illustrators:
Walter Dean Myers, author, *Slam!*
Jerry Pinkney, illustrator, *Minty: A Story of Young Harriet Tubman*

Honor Books-Authors

Patricia C. McKissack and Frederick L. McKissack, *Rebels Against Slavery: American Slave Revolts*

Honor Books-Illustrators

Gregory Christie, *The Palm of My Heart: Poetry by African American Children*
Reynold Ruffins, *Running the Road to ABC*
Synthia Saint James, *Neeny Coming, Neeny Going*

MARGARET A. EDWARDS AWARD

For lifetime achievement in writing books for young adults:
Gary Paulsen, recipient

ANDREW CARNEGIE MEDAL FOR EXCELLENCE IN CHILDREN'S VIDEO

Tacy Mangan, *Notes Alive! On the Day You Were Born*

1996/97 NATIONAL ENDOWMENT FOR THE HUMANITIES AWARDS

1996 National Medal of Arts:
Edward Albee, playwright
Sarah Caldwell, opera conductor
Harry Callahan, photographer
Zelda Fichandler, theater director
Eduardo "Lalo" Guerrero, composer, musician
Lionel Hampton, musician, bandleader
Bella Lewitzky, dancer, choreographer, teacher
Vera List, patron of the arts
Robert Redford, actor, director, producer
Maurice Sendak, author, illustrator, designer
Stephen Sondheim, composer, lyricist
Boys Choir of Harlem, arts organization

1996 Charles Frankel Prize:
Rita Dove, Doris Kearns Goodwin, Daniel Kemmis, Arturo Madrid, Bill Moyers.
(This award honors the outstanding achievements of Americans who have helped expand the public's understanding of history, literature, philosophy or other subjects in the humanities.)

1997 Jefferson Lecturer in the Humanities: Dr. Stephen Toulmin, philosopher, physicist and historian. (This award is the highest honor bestowed by the federal government for distinguished intellectual achievement in the humanities.)

1997 PULITZER PRIZES

THE ARTS

Fiction: *Martin Dressler: The Tale of an American Dreamer*, Steven Millhauser
History: *Original Meanings: Politics and Ideas in the Making of the Constitution*, Jack N. Rakove
Biography: *Angela's Ashes*, Frank McCourt
Poetry: *Alive Together: New and Selected Poems*, Lisel Mueller
General Nonfiction: *Ashes to Ashes: America's Hundred-Year Cigarette War, the Public Health, and the Unbashed Triumph of Philip Morris*, Richard Kluger

JOURNALISM

Public Service: *The Times-Picayune*, New Orleans, LA
Spot News Reporting: Staff, *Newsday*, Long Island, NY
Investigative Reporting: Eric Nadler, Deborah Nelson, Alex Tizon, *The Seattle Times*
Explanatory Journalism: Michael Vitez, April Saul, Ron Cortes, *The Philadelphia Inquirer*
Beat Reporting: Byron Acohido, *The Seattle Times*
National Reporting: Staff, *The Wall Street Journal*
International Reporting: John F. Burns, *The New York Times*
Feature Writing: Lisa Pollak, *The Baltimore Sun*
Commentary: Eileen McNamara, *The Boston Globe*
Criticism: Tim Page, *The Washington Post*
Editorial Writing: Michael G. Gartner, *The Daily Tribune*, Ames, IA
Editorial Cartooning: Walt Handelsman, *The Times-Picayune*, New Orleans, LA
Spot News Photography: Annie Wells, *The Press Democrat*, Santa Rosa, CA
Feature Photography: Alexander Zemlianichenko, The Associated Press

MUSIC

Music: *Blood on the Fields*, Wynton Marsalis

1996 PEABODY AWARDS

"Black Radio: Telling It Like It Was," Radio Smithsonian, Washington, for Public Radio International
"Remorse: The 14 Stories of Eric Morse," Sound Portrait Productions for National Public Radio
"This American Life," WBEZ-FM, Chicago
"Kinetic City Super Crew," American Association for the Advancement of Science
Peter Gzowski, CBC Radio
"Who's Guarding the Guardians?" WCVB, Boston
"Newsnight: Afghanistan," BBC News, London
"Passport to Kill," WNBC, New York
"Vote for Me: Politics in America," Center for New American Media, Midnight Films and WETA, Washington
"The Celluloid Closet," Telling pictures, HBO, Channel 4 in London and ZDF-Arte (Germany/France)
"Frontline: The Gate of Heavenly Peace," Long Bow Group Inc. and Independent Television Service for Frontline/WGBH, Boston
"Paradise Lost: The Child Murders at Robin Hood Hills," HBO, Creative Thinking International Ltd
KOMO, Seattle, for excellence in local programming
"Frontline: The Choice '96," Frontline/WGBH, Boston, and Helen Whitney Productions
"Nova: Odyssey of Life," Nova/WGBH, Boston; Agaton Film and Television; Swedish Television, SVTI; ZDF-Arte (Germany/France), and Channel 4 in London
"People Century," BBC, London, and WGBH, Boston
"The American Experience: The Battle Over Citizen Kane," American Experience and Lennon Documentary Group/WGBH, Boston
"The Great War and the Shaping of the 20th Century," KCET, Los Angeles, and BBC, London
"Survivors of the Holocaust," Turner Entertainment Group, Atlanta, and Steven Spielberg in association with Survivors of the Shoah Visual History Foundation
"The X-Files," Fox, Ten Thirteen Productions in association with 20th Television
"Journey of the African-American Athlete," Home Box Office Sports
"Law and Order," NBC, Wolf Films in association with Universal Television
"Pride and Prejudice," A&E and BBC, London
"The Simpsons," Fox, Gracie Films, in association with 20th Television
"N.Y.P.D. Blue," ABC, Steven Bochco Productions
"Mobil Masterpiece Theater" for "House of Cards," "To Play the King" and "The Final Cut," BBC, London and WGBH, Boston
"How Do You Spell God?," Home Box Office
"Wise Up!" Carlton Television for Channel 4 in London
"Edith Ann's Christmas," ABC, Tomlin & Wagner Theatricalz, Kurtz & Friends
"One to One: Mentoring," WCCO, Minneapolis
Bud Greenspan, for sports documentary film making

1997 DAYTIME EMMY AWARDS
24th Annual

Drama: "General Hospital"
Children's Series: "Reading Rainbow"
Children's Special: "Elmo Saves Christmas"
Children's Animated Program: "Animaniacs"
Talk Show: "The Oprah Winfrey Show"
Lead Actress in a Drama Series: Jess Walton, "The Young and the Restless," CBS
Lead Actor in a Drama Series: Justin Deas, "Guiding Light," CBS
Supporting Actress in a Drama Series: Michelle Stafford, "The Young and the Restless," CBS
Supporting Actor in a Drama Series: Ian Buchanan, "The Bold & the Beautiful," CBS
Younger Actress in a Drama Series: Sarah Brown, "General Hospital," ABC
Younger Actor in a Drama Series: Kevin Mambo, "Guiding Light," CBS
Performer in an Animated Program: Louie Anderson, "Life With Louie," Fox
Game Show Host: Pat Sajak, "Wheel of Fortune"
Talk Show Host: Rosie O'Donnell, "The Rosie O'Donnell Show"
Drama Series Directing Team: "The Young and the Restless," Heather Hill, Frank Pacelli, Mike Denney, Kathryn Foster, directors, CBS
Drama Series Writing Team: "All My Children," ABC and "The Young and the Restless," CBS

NATIONAL FILM REGISTRY 1989–1996

The National Film Preservation Board, established by the National Film Preservation Act of 1992 (2 U.S.C. 179b), serves as a public advisory group to the Librarian of Congress. The Board consists of 36 members and alternates representing the film industry, archives, scholars, filmmakers and others who make up the diverse American motion picture industry. As its primary mission, the Board works to ensure the survival, conservation and increased public availability of America's film heritage, including advising the Librarian on the annual selection of films to be added to the National Film Registry, and counseling the Librarian on development and implementation of the national film preservation plan. Films are selected on the basis of historical, cultural and aesthetic significance. A film must be at least 10 years old to be considered. One copy in "archival quality" of each film selected is added to the National Film Registry Collection at the Library of Congress.

FILMS SELECTED FOR THE NATIONAL FILM REGISTRY, 1989–1996

(Titles listed alphabetically)

Adam's Rib (1949)
The Adventures of Robin Hood (1938)
The African Queen (1951)
All About Eve (1950)
All Quiet on the Western Front (1930)
All That Heaven Allows (1955)
American Graffiti (1973)
An American in Paris (1951)
Annie Hall (1977)
The Apartment (1960)
The Awful Truth (1937)
Badlands (1973)
The Band Wagon (1953)
The Bank Dick (1940)
The Battle of San Pietro (1945)
The Best Years of Our Lives (1946)
Big Business (1929)
The Big Parade (1925)
The Birth of a Nation (1915)
The Black Pirate (1926)
Blacksmith Scene (1893)
Blade Runner (1982)
The Blood of Jesus (1941)
Bonnie and Clyde (1967)
Bringing Up Baby (1938)
Broken Blossoms (1919)
Cabaret (1972)
Carmen Jones (1954)
Casablanca (1942)
Castro Street (1966)
Cat People (1942)
Chan Is Missing (1982)
The Cheat (1915)
Chinatown (1974)
Chulas Fronteras (1976)
Citizen Kane (1941)
City Lights (1931)
The Conversation (1974)
The Cool World (1963)
A Corner in Wheat (1909)
The Crowd (1928)
David Holzman's Diary (1968)
The Day the Earth Stood Still (1951)
The Deer Hunter (1978)
Destry Rides Again (1939)
Detour (1946)
Dodsworth (1936)
Dog Star Man (1964)
Double Indemnity (1944)
Dr. Strangelove or: How I Learned to Stop Worrying and Love the Bomb (1964)
Duck Soup (1933)
Eaux d'Artifice (1953)
E.T. The Extra-Terrestrial (1982)
El Norte (1983)
The Exploits of Elaine (1914)
Fantasia (1940)
Fatty's Tintype Tangle (1915)
Flash Gordon Serial (1936)
Footlight Parade (1933)
Force of Evil (1948)
The Forgotten Frontier (1931)
The Four Horsemen of the Apocalypse (1921)
Frank Film (1973)
Frankenstein (1931)
Freaks (1932)
The Freshman (1925)
Fury (1936)
The General (1927)
Gerald McBoing Boing (1951)
Gertie the Dinosaur (1914)
Gigi (1958)
The Godfather (1972)
The Godfather, Part II (1974)
The Gold Rush (1925)
Gone with the Wind (1939)
The Graduate (1967)
The Grapes of Wrath (1940)
The Great Train Robbery (1903)
Greed (1924)
Harlan County, U.S.A. (1976)
The Heiress (1949)
Hell's Hinges (1916)
High Noon (1952)
High School (1968)
His Girl Friday (1940)
Hospital (1970)
The Hospital (1971)
How Green Was My Valley (1941)
I Am a Fugitive from a Chain Gang (1932)
Intolerance (1916)
Invasion of the Body Snatchers (1956)
It Happened One Night (1934)
The Italian (1915)
It's a Wonderful Life (1946)
Jammin' the Blues (1944)
The Jazz Singer (1927)
Killer of Sheep (1977)
King Kong (1933)
The Lady Eve (1941)
Lassie Come Home (1943)
The Last of the Mohicans (1920)
Lawrence of Arabia (1962)
The Learning Tree (1969)
Letter from an Unknown Woman (1948)
Life and Times of Rosie the Riveter (1980)
Louisiana Story (1948)
Love Me Tonight (1932)
Magical Maestro (1952)
The Magnificent Ambersons (1942)
The Maltese Falcon (1941)
The Manchurian Candidate (1962)
Manhatta (1921)
March of Time: Inside Nazi Germany—1938 (1938)
Marty (1955)
*M*A*S*H* (1970)
Meet Me in St. Louis (1944)
Meshes of the Afternoon (1943)
Midnight Cowboy (1969)
Mildred Pierce (1945)
Modern Times (1936)
Morocco (1930)
A Movie (1958)
Mr. Smith Goes to Washington (1939)
My Darling Clementine (1946)
Nanook of the North (1922)
Nashville (1975)
The Night of the Hunter (1955)
A Night at the Opera (1935)
Ninotchka (1939)
North by Northwest (1959)
Nothing But a Man (1964)
On the Waterfront (1954)
One Flew Over the Cuckoo's Nest (1975)
Out of the Past (1947)
The Outlaw Josey Wales (1976)
Paths of Glory (1957)
The Philadelphia Story (1940)
Pinocchio (1940)
A Place in the Sun (1951)
Point of Order (1964)
The Poor Little Rich Girl (1917)
Primary (1960)
The Prisoner of Zenda (1937)
The Producers (1968)
Psycho (1960)
Pull My Daisy (1959)
Raging Bull (1980)
Rebel Without a Cause (1955)
Red River (1948)
Ride the High Country (1962)
Rip Van Winkle (1896)
The River (1937)
Road to Morocco (1942)
Safety Last (1923)
Salesman (1969)
Salt of the Earth (1954)
Scarface (1932)
The Searchers (1956)
Seventh Heaven (1927)
Shadow of a Doubt (1943)
Shadows (1959)
Shane (1953)
She Done Him Wrong (1933)
Sherlock, Jr. (1924)
Shock Corridor (1963)
Show Boat (1936)
Singin' in the Rain (1952)
Snow White (1933)
Snow White and the Seven Dwarfs (1937)
Some Like It Hot (1959)
Stagecoach (1939)
Star Wars (1977)
Sullivan's Travels (1941)
Sunrise (1927)
Sunset Boulevard (1950)
Sweet Smell of Success (1957)
Tabu (1931)
Taxi Driver (1976)
Tevya (1939)
The Thief of Bagdad (1924)
To Be or Not to Be (1942)
To Fly (1976)
To Kill a Mockingbird (1962)
Top Hat (1935)
Topaz (1943–45)
Touch of Evil (1958)
The Treasure of the Sierra Madre (1948)
Trouble in Paradise (1932)
2001: A Space Odyssey (1968)
Verbena Tragica (1939)
Vertigo (1958)
What's Opera, Doc? (1957)
Where Are My Children? (1916)
The Wind (1928)
Within Our Gates (1920)
The Wizard of Oz (1939)
A Woman Under the Influence (1974)
Woodstock (1977)
Yankee Doodle Dandy (1942)
Zapruder film (1963)

ALPHABETICAL INDEX

Events are generally listed under key words; many broad categories have been created, including African-American, Agriculture, Air Shows, Animals, Antiques, Art—Fine and Performing, Arts and Crafts, Auto Shows and Races, Aviation, Balloon (Hot-air), Bicycle, Birds, Boats, Books, Children, Christmas, Cowboys/Old West, Dance, Disabled, Education, Employment/Occupations/Professions, Environment, Ethnic, Family, Film, Fishing, Flowers, Food and Beverages, Gardens/Gardening, Health and Welfare, Home Shows and Tours, Horses, Human Relations, Humor, Journalism, Kites, Labor, Library/Librarians, Literature, Music, Native American, Nature, Parades, Peace, Photography, Poets/Poetry, Prayer, Radio, Railroad/Trains, Renaissance Fairs, Rodeos, Safety, Science/Technology, Senior Citizens, Space, Space Milestones, Storytelling, Television, Theater, Weather, Women, names of sports, types of music, types of animals, etc. Events that can be attended are also listed under the states or countries where they are to be held. Index indicates only initial date for each event. See chronology for inclusive dates of events lasting more than one day.

Yes! Please send me additional copies of *Chase's 1998 Calendar of Events* and *1998 Chase's Sports Calendar of Events*.

Ship to ______________________________

Address ______________________________

____

City, State, Zip ______________________________

Phone (   ) ______________________________

Please send me _____ copies of the 1998 edition of CHASE'S CALENDAR OF EVENTS at $59.95 each $________

and _____ copies of the 1998 edition of CHASE'S SPORTS CALENDAR OF EVENTS at $29.95 each $________

Add applicable sales tax in AL, CA, FL, IL, NC, NJ, NY, OH, PA, TX, WA $________

Shipping & Handling: Add $5.00 for the first copy, $3.50 for each additional copy $________

Total $________

☐ Check or money order enclosed payable to: NTC/Contemporary Publishing Co.

Charge my ☐ Visa ☐ MasterCard ☐ American Express ☐ Discover Card

Acct. # ______________________________ Exp. Date ___/___

X ______________________________

Signature (if charging to bankcard)

Name (please print) ______________________________

STANDING ORDER AUTHORIZATION

To make sure that I receive each year's new edition, please accept this Standing Order Authorization to ship me _____ copies of *Chase's Calendar of Events* and _____ copies of *Chase's Sports Calendar of Events*, beginning with the 1999 edition. Bill me at the address shown at the top of this order form. I understand that I may cancel my Standing Order at any time.

X ______________________________

Signature Date

______________________________ (   )

Name (please print) Phone

GUARANTEE: Any book you order is unconditionally guaranteed and may be returned within 10 days of receipt for full refund.

Prices subject to change without notice. BB98

Mail to: **NTC/Contemporary Publishing Co.**
4255 W Touhy Ave
Lincolnwood, IL 60646-1975

HOW TO SUBMIT AN ENTRY

There is no charge for being listed in ***Chase's***. Use the form below to submit new entries for forthcoming editions of ***Chase's Calendar of Events***. Background information about your entry is also appreciated. Please be sure your dates are confirmed for 1999, or clearly indicate if dates are tentative. Use a separate sheet for each entry submitted. Information selected by the editors may be used and publicized through their books, electronic formats, syndicated services and/or other related products and services. The editors reserve the right to select and edit information received. Please mail all information to: Calendar Editor, Chase's Calendar of Events, NTC/Contemporary Publishing Co, 4255 W Touhy Ave, Lincolnwood, IL 60646-1975.

☞DEADLINE FOR 1999 EDITION: MAY 8, 1998. PLEASE TYPE OR PRINT VERY CLEARLY.

1. Exact name of entry:
2. Exact INCLUSIVE DATES for 1999:
3. If applicable, estimated attendance (one figure—grand total all days):
4. Location (site [not address], city and state):
5. Brief description:

6. Formula—ONLY if used to set date(s) each year (Example: Annually, the third Monday in May):

7. For public use, complete contact info to be printed in book—name, address, phone, fax, e-mail, web.

8. For Chase's staff use, complete address info we can use to mail our update form to you next year—name, title or department, organization name, address:

9. For Chase's staff use, name, dept and phone and fax numbers of person we can call with questions about your entry:

10. Person furnishing information: (print) ______________________ (sign) ______________________
11. PLEASE CIRCLE THE EXACT INCLUSIVE DATES FOR YOUR 1999 EVENT ON THE CALENDAR BELOW.

1999
Key dates

M. L. King Birthday Jan 18	Passover Apr 1–8	Summer June 21	Columbus Day Oct 11
Chinese New Year Jan 16	Easter Apr 4 (Apr 11EO)	Labor Day Sept 6	Thanksgiving Nov 25
Presidents' Day Feb 15	Mother's Day May 9	Rosh Hashanah Sept 11–12	Chanukah Dec 4–11
Lent begins Feb 17 (Feb 22EO)	Memorial Day May 31	Autumn Sept 23	Ramadan Dec 9
Spring Mar 20	Father's Day June 20	Yom Kippur Sept 20	Winter Dec 22

1999

JAN

S	M	T	W	T	F	S
					1	2
3	4	5	6	7	8	9
10	11	12	13	14	15	16
17	18	19	20	21	22	23
24	25	26	27	28	29	30
31						

APR

S	M	T	W	T	F	S
				1	2	3
4	5	6	7	8	9	10
11	12	13	14	15	16	17
18	19	20	21	22	23	24
25	26	27	28	29	30	

JULY

S	M	T	W	T	F	S
				1	2	3
4	5	6	7	8	9	10
11	12	13	14	15	16	17
18	19	20	21	22	23	24
25	26	27	28	29	30	31

OCT

S	M	T	W	T	F	S
					1	2
3	4	5	6	7	8	9
10	11	12	13	14	15	16
17	18	19	20	21	22	23
24	25	26	27	28	29	30
31						

FEB

S	M	T	W	T	F	S
	1	2	3	4	5	6
7	8	9	10	11	12	13
14	15	16	17	18	19	20
21	22	23	24	25	26	27
28						

MAY

S	M	T	W	T	F	S
						1
2	3	4	5	6	7	8
9	10	11	12	13	14	15
16	17	18	19	20	21	22
23	24	25	26	27	28	29
30	31					

AUG

S	M	T	W	T	F	S
1	2	3	4	5	6	7
8	9	10	11	12	13	14
15	16	17	18	19	20	21
22	23	24	25	26	27	28
29	30	31				

NOV

S	M	T	W	T	F	S
	1	2	3	4	5	6
7	8	9	10	11	12	13
14	15	16	17	18	19	20
21	22	23	24	25	26	27
28	29	30				

MAR

S	M	T	W	T	F	S
	1	2	3	4	5	6
7	8	9	10	11	12	13
14	15	16	17	18	19	20
21	22	23	24	25	26	27
28	29	30	31			

JUNE

S	M	T	W	T	F	S
		1	2	3	4	5
6	7	8	9	10	11	12
13	14	15	16	17	18	19
20	21	22	23	24	25	26
27	28	29	30			

SEPT

S	M	T	W	T	F	S
			1	2	3	4
5	6	7	8	9	10	11
12	13	14	15	16	17	18
19	20	21	22	23	24	25
26	27	28	29	30		

DEC

S	M	T	W	T	F	S
			1	2	3	4
5	6	7	8	9	10	11
12	13	14	15	16	17	18
19	20	21	22	23	24	25
26	27	28	29	30	31	

Note: This page may be photocopied in order to submit additional event entries to ***Chase's 1999 Calendar of Events***

4255 W Touhy Ave, Lincolnwood, IL 60646-1975 • Phone (847) 679-5500 • Fax (847) 679-6388